Debra J. DeWitte • Ralph M. Larmann • M. Kathryn Shields

University of Texas at Arlington, TX

University of Evansville, IN

Guilford College, NC

D0002631

GATEWAYS TO ART

Understanding the Visual Arts

THIRD EDITION

With 1,833 illustrations

Thames & Hudson

Gateways to Art © 2012, 2015, and 2018 Thames & Hudson

Text © 2012, 2015, and 2018 Debra J. DeWitte, Ralph M. Larmann, and M. Kathryn Shields

Original design by Geoff Penna, updated for the third edition by Aman Phull

All Rights Reserved. No part of this publication may be reproduced or transmitted in any form or by any means, electronic or mechanical, including photocopy, recording or any other information storage and retrieval system, without prior permission in writing from the publisher.

First published in 2012 in paperback in the United States of America as *Gateways to Art* by Thames & Hudson Inc., 500 Fifth Avenue, New York, New York 10110

www.thamesandhudsonusa.com

Second edition 2015, this third edition 2018

Library of Congress Control Number 2015932504

Paperback: ISBN 978-0-500-841150
Instructor's Copy, Not for Sale: ISBN 978-0-500-841143
Looseleaf/3-Hole-Punch: ISBN 978-0-500-841341

Printed and bound in Slovenia by DZS-Grafik d.o.o.

FRONT COVER

Yayoi Kusama, *All the Eternal Love I Have for the Pumpkins*, 2016.
Wood, mirror, plastic, acrylic, and LED, 9'7⅛" × 13'7⅜" × 13'7⅜".
Photo Noriko Takasugi. Courtesy Ota Fine Arts, Tokyo/Singapore/Shanghai and Victoria Miro, London/Venice. © Yayoi Kusama

Contents

Preface
14

Organization and How to Use this Book . . . 14
New in this Edition . . . 15
Resources for Instructors . . . 15
Resources for Students . . . 16
The Authors . . . 17
Acknowledgments . . . 17
How to Use Gateway to Art and Other Features . . . 18

Introduction
20

What Is Art? . . . 20
Fine Art, Craft, and the Commercial Arts . . . 22
The Visual World . . . 24
Where Is Art? . . . 24
Art and Creativity . . . 26
Who Makes Art? . . . 27
The Power and Value of Art . . . 30
Protest and Censorship of Art . . . 34
Studying Art . . . 35

FEATURES:
Gertrude Stein as an Art Patron . . . 29
Loongkoonan: The Value of Art to Keep Alive Knowledge and Culture . . . 31
Tracy Chevalier: Art Inspires a Novel and a Movie . . . 33

Part 1 Fundamentals 40

Chapter 1.1
Line, Shape, and the Principle of Contrast
42

Line . . . 42
Shape . . . 54
Contrast . . . 55

FEATURES:
Gateway to Art: Kahlo, *The Two Fridas* **Using Line to Guide and Direct a Viewer's Attention** . . . 50
Gateway to Art: Weems, *Kitchen Table* Series **The Principle of Contrast and Dramatic Effect** . . . 56

Chapter 1.2
Form, Volume, Mass, and Texture
61

Form . . . 61
Form in Relief and in the Round . . . 64
Volume . . . 67
Mass . . . 69

FEATURES:
The Guggenheim Museum, Bilbao . . . 70
Brancusi and Rodin: Using Mass to Describe Love . . . 72

Texture . . . 73

Chapter 1.3
Implied Depth: Value and Space
76

Value **77**
Space **81**
FEATURE:
Gateway to Art: Raphael, *The School of Athens* **Perspective and the Illusion of Depth** **90**

Chapter 1.4
Color
95

Color and Light **95**
Color and Pigment **96**
Additive and Subtractive Color **96**
Color Wheels **97**
Key Characteristics of Color **101**
The Sensation of Color **106**
Interpreting Color Symbolism **108**
The Psychology of Color **108**

Chapter 1.5
Motion and Time
113

Motion **113**
Time **120**
FEATURE:
Gateway to Art: Ai Weiwei, *Dropping a Han Dynasty Urn*
Motion and Reproduction as a Metaphor for Time **121**

Chapter 1.6
Unity, Variety, and Balance
125

Unity **125**
Variety **131**
Balance **134**
FEATURES:
Gateway to Art: Hokusai, "The Great Wave off Shore at Kanagawa"
A Masterpiece of Unity and Harmony **126**
Gateway to Art: The Taj Mahal **Love and Perfection** **136**

Chapter 1.7
Scale and Proportion
140

Scale **140**
Proportion **144**
FEATURE:
Gateway to Art: Raphael, *The School of Athens*
Scale and Proportion in a Renaissance Masterpiece **146**

Chapter 1.8
Focal Point and Emphasis
150

Focal Point **150**
Emphasis **153**
Subordination **155**
Focal Point and Emphasis in Action **156**
FEATURE:
Gateway to Art: Gentileschi, *Judith Decapitating Holofernes*
Using Focal Point for Dramatic Emphasis **152**

Chapter 1.9
Pattern and Rhythm
159

Pattern **159**
Rhythm **163**
FEATURE:
Gateway to Art: Maya Lintel Showing Shield Jaguar and Lady Xoc
Pattern Used to Emphasize Royal Power and Hierarchy **162**

Chapter 1.10
Engaging with Form and Content
170

Formal Analysis **170**
Stylistic Analysis **172**
Iconographic Analysis **174**
Contextual Analysis **175**
Analysis, Critique, and Interpretation **179**
Combined Analysis in Historical and Contemporary Art **183**
FEATURES:
Types of Analysis and Critique **176**
Research and Interpretation **180**

Part 2 Media And Processes **190**

Chapter 2.1
Drawing
192

Functions of Drawing **192**
The Materials of Drawing: Dry Media **195**
The Materials of Drawing: Wet Media **202**
Paper **205**
Life Drawing **206**
FEATURES:
Gateway to Art: Raphael, *The School of Athens* **Drawing in the Design Process** **194**
Gateway to Art: Kahlo, *The Two Fridas* **Artist Sketchbooks** **204**

Chapter 2.2
Painting
209

The First Paintings **210**
Encaustic **210**
Fresco **212**
Tempera **214**
Oil **216**
Ink Painting **220**
Watercolor and Gouache **220**
Acrylic **221**
Mixed-Media Painting **222**
Mural Art and Spray Paint **223**
FEATURES:
José Clemente Orozco: Fresco Painting Inspired by the Mexican Revolution **213**
Gateway to Art: Gentileschi, *Judith Decapitating Holofernes* **The Artist in the Act of Painting** . . **219**

Chapter 2.3
Printmaking
226

Context of Printmaking **227**
Relief Printmaking **227**
Intaglio Printmaking **230**
Collagraphy **233**
Lithography **234**
Serigraphy (Silkscreen Printing) **235**
Editions **236**
Monotypes and Monoprints **237**
Print Shops and Digital Reproduction Services **238**
Contemporary Directions in Printmaking **238**
FEATURE:
Gateway to Art: Hokusai, "The Great Wave off Shore at Kanagawa"
Using the Woodblock Printing Method **229**

Chapter 2.4
Sculpture
242

Approaches to Three Dimensions in Sculpture **242**
Bas-Relief and High Relief **244**
Methods of Sculpture **247**
Pushing beyond Traditional Methods **252**
FEATURES:
Gateway to Art: Maya Lintel Showing Shield Jaguar and Lady Xoc
Varying Degrees of Relief for Emphasis **245**
Michelangelo **246**
Antony Gormley: *Asian Field*. **256**

Chapter 2.5
Architecture
259

Structure, Function, and Form **259**
Ancient Construction **262**
Classical Architectural Styles **271**
The Emergence of the Methods and Materials of the Modern World **274**
The Postmodern Reaction to Modernism **281**
Currents in Architecture **283**
FEATURES:
Abbot Suger and the Dynamics of Gothic Architecture **268**
Gateway to Art: The Taj Mahal **Engineering Eternity** **272**
Contrasting Ideas in Modern Architecture: Le Corbusier's Villa Savoye and Frank Lloyd Wright's Fallingwater **278**
Zaha Hadid: A Building for Exciting Events **282**

Chapter 2.6
The Tradition of Craft
285

Ceramics **287**
Glass **290**
Metalwork **292**
Fiber **294**
Wood **297**
FEATURES:
Hyo-In Kim: Art or Craft: What's the Difference? **286**
San Ildefonso-Style Pottery **289**
Faith Ringgold, *Tar Beach*. **295**

Chapter 2.7
Visual Communication Design
300

The Visual Character of Text **300**
The Communicative Image **303**
Layout Design **307**
Web Design **311**
FEATURES:
Influence of the Bauhaus on Visual Design **304**
April Greiman: *Does It Make Sense?* Greiman's *Design Quarterly* #133, 1986 . . . . . **308**
Color in Visual Communication Design **312**

Chapter 2.8
Photography
315

Recording the Image: Film to Digital **315**
The Dawn of Photography **316**
Negative/Positive Process in Black and White **318**
In Living Color **322**
Photojournalism **323**
Photocollage and Photomontage **325**
Postmodern Return to Historic Processes **327**
The Art of Photography **330**

FEATURES:
Traditional and Alternative Darkroom Methods . . . 319
Steve McCurry . . . 324
Gateway to Art: Weems, *Kitchen Table* Series **Story Telling and Sto-re-telling** . . . 329

Chapter 2.9
Film/Video and Digital Art
334

Moving Images before Film . . . 335
Silent and Black-and-White Film . . . 336
Sound and Color . . . 337
Animation and Special Effects . . . 339
Film Genres . . . 342
Film as Art . . . 343
FEATURE:
Bill Viola: How Did Video Become Art? . . . 346

Chapter 2.10
Alternative Media and Processes
350

Context of Alternative Media . . . 350
Conceptual Art . . . 351
Performance Art . . . 353
Installation and Environments . . . 356
Out of the Shadows and into the Light: Enlivened Gallery Space . . . 358
FEATURES:
Gateway to Art: Ai Weiwei, *Dropping a Han Dynasty Urn* and *Colored Vases*
Art that Resists Categories: Interactions with the Individual . . . 357
Molly Gochman: Bringing Light to the Scars . . . 360

Part 3 History And Context 362

Timeline . . . 364

Chapter 3.1
The Prehistoric and Ancient Mediterranean
366

Prehistoric Art in Europe and the Mediterranean . . . 367
Mesopotamia: The Cradle of Civilization . . . 370
Ancient Egypt . . . 374
Art of Ancient Greece . . . 379
Etruscan Art . . . 385
Roman Art . . . 386
FEATURES:
Hieroglyphs . . . 376
Zahi Hawass: The Golden Mask of Tutankhamun . . . 378
Classical Architectural Orders . . . 380
Controversy about the Parthenon Marbles . . . 382
Stylistic Changes in the Sculpture of Ancient Greece . . . 384

Chapter 3.2
Art of the Middle Ages
390

Art of Late Antiquity and Early Christianity . . . 391
Byzantine Art . . . 394
Manuscripts and the Middle Ages . . . 398
Pilgrimage in the Middle Ages . . . 400
The Rise of the Gothic . . . 406
From the Gothic to Early Renaissance in Italy . . . 408
FEATURES:
Three Religions of the Middle Ages . . . 394
Iconoclasm: Destruction of Religious Images . . . 396

Chapter 3.3
Art of India, China, Japan, Korea, and Southeast Asia
410

India ... 411
China ... 416
Japan ... 421
Korea ... 424
Southeast Asia ... 426
FEATURES:
Philosophical and Religious Traditions in Asia ... 411
Gateway to Art: The Taj Mahal **The Gardens of Paradise in the Taj Mahal** ... 412
The Spread of the Image of Buddha along the Silk Road ... 414
Gateway to Art: Ai Weiwei, *Dropping a Han Dynasty Urn*
The Value of Art: Questions of History and Authenticity ... 419
The Three Perfections: Calligraphy, Painting, Poetry ... 420
Sonoko Sasaki: Arts and Tradition in Japan ... 422
Gateway to Art: Hokusai, "The Great Wave off Shore at Kanagawa"
Mount Fuji: The Sacred Mountain of Japan ... 425

Chapter 3.4
Art of the Americas
429

When's the Beginning? ... 429
South America ... 430
Mesoamerica ... 433
North America ... 440
FEATURES:
Gateway to Art: Maya Lintel Showing Shield Jaguar and Lady Xoc
Invoking Ancestors through Bloodletting ... 436
"We Are the Mirrors": Legislation and Activism to Protect Native Rights and Land ... 444

Chapter 3.5
Art of Africa and the Pacific Islands
446

Art of Africa ... 447
African Architecture ... 450
Art of the Pacific Islands ... 453
FEATURE:
Paul Tacon: Australian Rock Art ... 455

Chapter 3.6
Art of Renaissance and Baroque Europe (1400–1750)
460

The Early Renaissance in Italy ... 461
The Renaissance in Northern Europe ... 464
The High Renaissance in Italy ... 468
Late Renaissance and Mannerism ... 471
Italian Baroque ... 477
Northern Baroque ... 481
FEATURES:
Van Eyck, Panofsky, and Iconographic Analysis ... 466
Gateway to Art: Raphael, *The School of Athens* **Past and Present in the Painting** ... 470
Protestant Reformation and Catholic Counter-Reformation:
A Comparison through Last Suppers ... 474
Gateway to Art: Gentileschi, *Judith Decapitating Holofernes* **The Influence of Caravaggio** ... 478
Depictions of David ... 480

Chapter 3.7
Art of Europe and America (1700–1865): Rococo to Romanticism
486

Rococo ... 487
Rejecting the Rococo: Sentimentality in Painting ... 489
Neoclassicism ... 491
Romanticism ... 497
FEATURES:
The French Academy of Painting and Sculpture: Making a Living as an Artist ... 492
Slavery and Colonialism in Eighteenth-Century Art ... 496

Chapter 3.8
The Modern Aesthetic: Realism to Expressionism
501

Art Academies and Modernism **501**
Realism **504**
A Revolutionary Invention: Photography and Art in the Nineteenth Century **506**
Impressionism **508**
Post-Impressionism **514**
Symbolism **517**
***Fin de Siècle* and Art Nouveau** **520**
Expressionism **521**
FEATURES:
Influences on the Impressionists: Japanese Woodcuts and Photography **510**
Gateway to Art: Gentileschi, *Judith Decapitating Holofernes* **Variations on a Theme** **519**

Chapter 3.9
Late Modern and Early Contemporary Art in the Twentieth Century
524

The Revolution of Color and Form **524**
Dada **528**
Surrealism **530**
The Influence of Cubism **533**
Early Twentieth-Century Art in America **536**
Abstract Expressionism **538**
Pop Art **540**
Minimalism **542**
FEATURES:
Gateway to Art: Kahlo, *The Two Fridas* **Was She a Surrealist?** **532**
Modern and Postmodern Architecture **543**

Chapter 3.10
The Late Twentieth Century and Art of the Present Day
546

Conceptual Art **546**
Performance and Body Art **548**
Earthworks **549**
Postmodernism, Identity, and Multiculturalism **549**
Narratives of Fact and Fiction **555**
Installation **557**
Socially Engaged Art **559**
FEATURES:
Borrowing an Image **547**
Gateway to Art: Weems, *Kitchen Table* Series **Personal and Cultural Narrative** **551**
Inside, Outside, Upside Down: Ideas Recontextualized **554**
Gabriel Dawe: Materializing Light, Inverting Constructs **558**

Part 4 Themes **562**

Chapter 4.1
Art and Community
564

Places to Gather **564**
Art by and for the Community **567**
Man-Made Mountains **568**
Rituals and Art of Healing and Community Solidarity **572**
Art in the Public Sphere **573**
FEATURES:
Art, Super-Sized **570**
Richard Serra: A Sculptor Defends His Work **574**

Chapter 4.2
Spirituality and Art
578

Gods, Deities, and Enlightened Beings 578
Spirits and Ancestors 580
Connecting with the Gods 582
Sacred Places 586
Personal Paths to Spirituality 589
FEATURE:
Judgment and the Afterlife 584

Chapter 4.3
Art and the Cycle of Life
591

Life's Beginnings and Endings 591
Marking Time 595
Lineage and Ancestors 597
Mortality and Immortality 599
FEATURES:
Gateway to Art: The Taj Mahal **Mumtaz Mahal: A Life Remembered** 594
Christian Marclay, *The Clock*: "Glue" by Darian Leader 596
Vanitas: Reminders of Transience 600

Chapter 4.4
Art and Science
603

Art Celebrating Science 603
Astronomy and Space Exploration in Art 605
Using Science and Mathematics to Create Art 607
Perception, Senses, and Psychology 608
Science as a Tool to Understand and Care for Art 611

Chapter 4.5
Art, Illusion, and Transformation
615

Art as an Illusionistic Window 615
Illusionism as Trickery 620
Illusion and the Transformation of Ideas 623
FEATURES:
Gateway to Art: Raphael, *The School of Athens* **Architectural Illusion** 617
Satirizing Illusionism: Hogarth's *False Perspective* 619
Art and Spiritual Transformation 624

Chapter 4.6
Art of Political Leaders and Rulers
628

Iconic Portraiture of Leaders 628
Female Rulers 631
Art Used by Rulers to Regulate Society 634
FEATURE:
Gateway to Art: Maya Lintel Showing Shield Jaguar and Lady Xoc
Queens in Support of Their Husbands 632

Chapter 4.7
Art, War, and Revolution
638

Documenting the Tragedies of War 638
Warriors and Battle Scenes 640
The Artist's Response to War 644
Remembrance and Memorials 649
FEATURE:
Wafaa Bilal: *Domestic Tension*: An Artist's Protest against War 648

Chapter 4.8
Art of Protest and Social Conscience
652

Art as Protest and Activism **652**
Art as the Victim of Protest: Censorship and Destruction **655**
Art that Raises Social Awareness **658**
FEATURES:
Gateway to Art: Ai Weiwei, *Dropping a Han Dynasty Urn* and *Colored Vases*
The Art of Activism: Speaking out at all Costs **654**
Censorship of Art: The Nazi Campaign against Modern Art **657**
Gateway to Art: Hokusai, "The Great Wave off Shore at Kanagawa"
Using Famous Art to Make a Social Difference **661**

Chapter 4.9
The Body in Art
663

Archetypal Images of the Body **663**
Ideal Proportion **664**
Notions of Beauty **666**
Performance Art: The Body Becomes the Artwork **670**
The Body in Pieces **673**
The Body Reframed **677**
FEATURES:
Reclining Nudes **668**
Spencer Tunick: Human Bodies as Installations **672**
Henri Matisse: *The Blue Nude*: Cutouts and the Essence of Form **675**
Gateway to Art: Kahlo, *The Two Fridas* **A Body in Pain** **676**

Chapter 4.10
Identity, Race, and Gender in Art
680

Self-Portraits **680**
Challenging the Status Quo **684**
Culture on Display **686**
Identity and Ambiguity **689**
FEATURES:
Gateway to Art: Gentileschi, *Judith Decapitating Holofernes*
Self-Expression in the Judith Paintings **681**
Cindy Sherman: The Artist and Her Identity **683**
Gateway to Art: Weems, *Kitchen Table* Series **Cultural Diplomacy** **687**

Glossary **692**
Further Reading **697**
Sources of Quotations **699**
Illustration Credits **701**
Index **706**

Preface to *Gateways to Art: Understanding the Visual Arts*

Organization and How to Use this Book

Gateways to Art is an introduction to the visual arts, divided into four parts: Part 1, Fundamentals, the essential elements and principles of art that constitute the "language" of artworks; Part 2, Media and Processes, the many materials and processes that artists use to make art; Part 3, History and Context, the forces and influences that have shaped art throughout human history; and Part 4, Themes, the major cultural and historical themes that have motivated artists to create. Each of these parts is color coded to help you move easily from one section to the next.

Gateways to Art gives you complete flexibility in finding your own pathway to understanding and appreciating art. Once you have read the Introduction, which outlines the core knowledge and skills you will need to analyse and understand art, you can read the chapters of our book in any order. Each chapter is entirely modular, giving you just the information you need when you need it. Concepts are clearly explained and definitions of terminology in the margins ensure that you are never at a loss to understand a term; and new Portal features use thumbnail images to make direct links to related artworks throughout the book (see p. 19 for how to identify and use marginal glossaries and Portals).

This means that you can learn about art in the order that works best for you. You can, of course, read the chapters in the order that they are printed in the book. This will tell you all you need to know to appreciate art. But you can also choose your own path. For example, the Introduction discusses how we define art and what it contributes to our lives. Next you might read chapter 2.6, "The Tradition of Craft," which deals with media that artists have used for centuries to create artworks, but which our Western culture sometimes considers less important than "fine art." Then the discussion of Japanese art in chapter 3.3, "Art of India, China, Japan, Korea, and Southeast Asia," reveals how an expertly made kimono (an item of traditional clothing) is appreciated as much as a painting that in our culture is usually considered more prestigious.

In *Gateways to Art* you will discover the pleasure of looking at great artworks many times and always finding something new because there are many ways of seeing and analysing art. That is why our book takes its title from its unique feature, the "Gateways to Art" (introduced on p. 18). Through eight iconic works of world art—four of which are new to this edition—we invite you to come back to these Gateways to discover something different: about the design characteristics of the work; the materials used to make it; how history and culture influenced its creation; or how the work expressed something personal. Sometimes we compare the Gateway image with another artwork, or consider what it tells us about the great mysteries of our existence, such as spirituality or life and death. We hope to encourage you to revisit not only our Gateways, but also other works, as sources of enjoyment for years to come.

Our Gateways to Art boxes are just one of numerous features we provide to help you in your studies. In many chapters you will find Perspectives on Art boxes, in which artists, art historians, critics, and others involved in the world of art explain how diverse people engaged in art think and work. Other boxes will, for example, help you to focus in depth on a single artwork, or alternately to compare and contrast artworks that deal with a similar subject or theme. "Related Images" pages at the end of every chapter perform a similar function to the new marginal Portals: they bring together, in chronological order, relevant artworks from throughout the book, expanding on the works you have encountered in any individual chapter and allowing you to make interesting connections across time periods, themes, and media.

New in this Edition

- More than 150 new artworks, including works by Julie Mehretu, Yinka Shonibare, Jaune Quick-to-See Smith, and Mickalene Thomas.
- The eight "Gateway to Art" features have been refreshed with the substitution of four new works: an eighth-century Maya lintel, Frida Kahlo's *The Two Fridas*, Carrie Mae Weems's *Kitchen Table* series, and Ai Weiwei's *Dropping a Han Dynasty Urn* and *Colored Vases*. See p. 18 for details.
- Portals are new in-chapter features that make connections with related artworks in other chapters, for easy cross-referencing: see p. 19.
- A Global Timeline opens Part 3: History and Context, showing students how art developed over time and across global regions.
- The final chapter of Part 3 has been split into two—now chapters 3.9 and 3.10—to include more contemporary art, featuring new works in innovative media with strong messages, by artists including Wadsworth Jarrell, Jiha Moon, Gabriel Dawe, and Theaster Gates.
- Our e-media package has been expanded with new features and improvements for both instructors and students: see following sections for more information.

Resources for Instructors

Our instructor resources are designed to help you teach in the way that you know best; and for this new edition we have enhanced and added new resources in response to user feedback. For full details of all instructors' resources go to thamesandhudsonusa.com/college; if you require any assistance contact your W. W. Norton representative.

- The Instructor's Manual is now available in digital form; fully revised by the authors, this online manual also now contains the Active Learning Exercises (previously at the end of chapters in Parts 1 and 2) and the Discussion Questions (in Parts 3 and 4). It is available to download from our instructors' website.
- The author-written Test Bank is also in digital form only: more than 1,600 questions are available on disk in ExamView or as a download from our instructors' website.
- A new Interactive Instructor's Guide makes lecture development easy with an array of teaching resources that can be searched and browsed according to a number of criteria. Resources include chapter outlines, active learning exercises, suggested readings, lecture ideas, and discussion questions.
- Author Ralph Larmann has provided ten new videos, including a discussion of such key elements and principles as line and form.
- The interactive e-book links to art videos, activities, and exercises, and links directly to the InQuizitive quizzing platform.

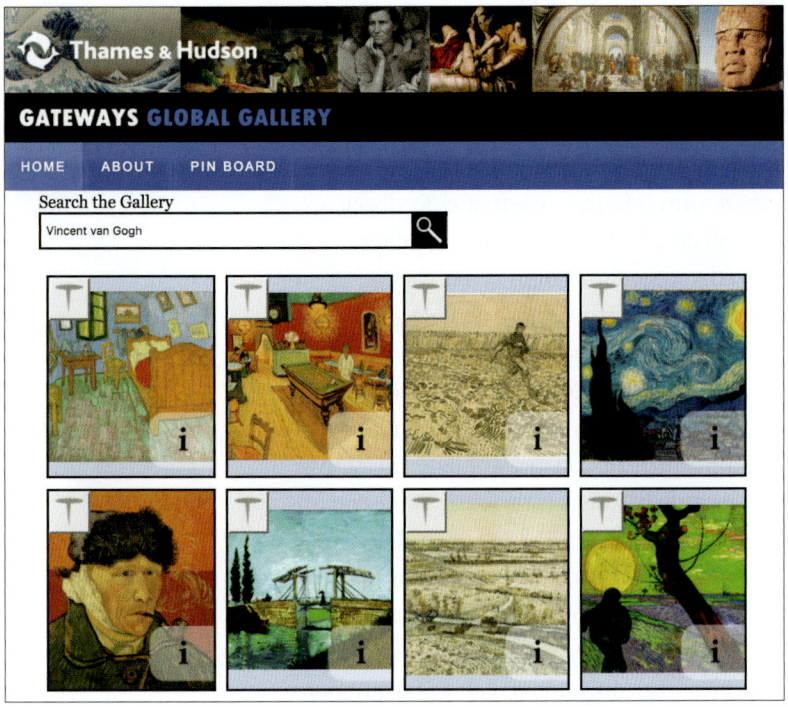

A sample search result in the Gateways Global Gallery shows how you can create your own image collections to download and use in your teaching.

Videos, Animation, and Images

- Fifteen in-the-studio videos demonstrate how art is made; twenty videos present key works of world art; ten new author-created videos discuss various aspects of art; and author-written video quizzes provide another valuable means of assessment.
- An exclusive arrangement with the Museum of Modern Art offers you seventeen additional videos (and quizzes) that feature MoMA curators discussing works in the collection, for example Vincent van Gogh's *Starry Night*, in which the camera zooms in on the canvas, bringing students face to face with the artist's distinctive thick layers of oil paint.
- Fifty multimedia animations demonstrate the elements and principles of art.
- Images from the book are available as JPEGs and PowerPoint slides, and also as PowerPoint lectures, with supporting text written by the authors.
- The Gateways Global Gallery continues to provide more than 6,500 additional artworks for your teaching, all searchable as well as indexed to the chapters of the third edition.

Resources for Students

Our student website (https://digital.wwnorton.com/gateways3) offers a wide range of review materials designed to improve your understanding and your grades.

- The *Gateways to Art Journal for Museum and Gallery Projects* has been revised and restructured, with new activity assignments to make museum visits more valuable.
- InQuizitive provides summative assessment quizzes in a game-like environment, hot-linked directly to the e-book.
- We have retained and revised our other resources: self-test quizzes; terminology and image flashcards; chapter summaries; a full glossary and an audio glossary to aid pronunciation of foreign-language terms and artists' names; interactive exercises demonstrating key concepts; and videos that explain how art is made.

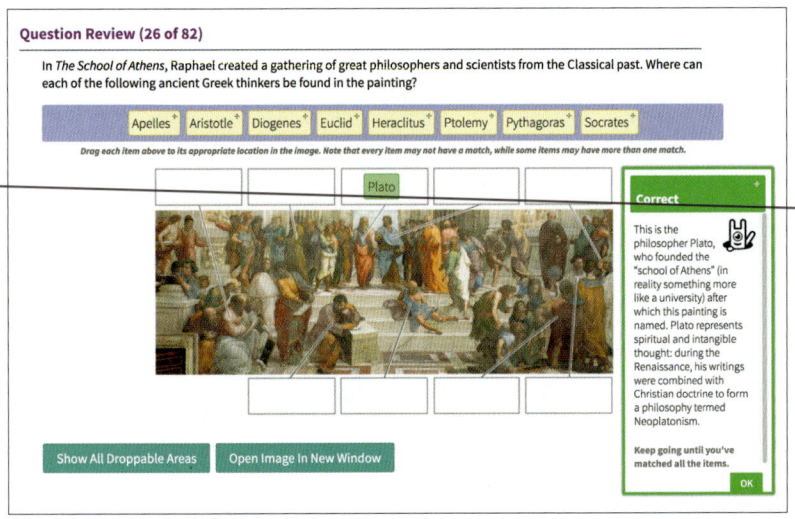

A sample InQuizitive question shows answer feedback for the student.

The Authors

Debra J. DeWitte has a PhD in aesthetics from the University of Texas at Dallas. She now teaches at the University of Texas at Arlington, where she has devised an award-winning online art appreciation course.

Ralph M. Larmann has a BFA from the University of Cincinnati and an MFA from James Madison University. He currently teaches at the University of Evansville and is a past President of Foundations in Art: Theory and Education.

M. Kathryn Shields has a PhD in art history from Virginia Commonwealth University. She is Associate Professor of Art History at Guilford College, where she also serves as Chair of the Art Department and Associate Academic Dean.

Acknowledgments

The publisher would like to thank the following for their generous advice and feedback during the preparation of this new edition:

Naomi Slipp, Auburn University; Cynthia Mills, Auburn University at Montgomery; Ronnie Wrest, Bakersfield College; Jennifer Rush, Central New Mexico Community College; Carolyn Jacobs and Mary Kilburn, Central Piedmont Community College; Laura Stewart, Daytona State College; Brenda Hanegan, Delgado Community College; Barbara Armstrong, El Centro College; Susan Dodge, Frostburg State University; David Cook, Georgia Gwinnett College; Megan Levacy, Georgia Perimeter College; Marion de Koning and Malia Molina, Grossmont College; Melanie Atkinson, Hinds Community College; Jenny Ramirez, James Madison University; Anita Rogers and Eric Sims, Lone Star College System; Buffy Walters, Marion Military Institute; Terrell Taylor, Meridian Community College; Errol Alger, Midlands Technical College; David Hamlow, Minnesota State University–Mankato; Mano Sotelo, Hirotsune Tashima, and Michael Nolan, Pima Community College; Karene Barrow, Pitt Community College; Debra Schafter, San Antonio College; Patricia Ballinger, South Texas College; Christian deLeon, Kristina Elizondo, and Sharon Covington, Tarrant County College; Alice Ottewill Jackson, University of Alabama at Birmingham; Patti Shanks, University of Missouri; Kurt Rahmlow, University of North Texas; Marta Slaughter, University of South Florida; Perry Kirk, University of West Georgia.

The publisher also gratefully acknowledges the following contributors: Wafaa Bilal, Tracy Chevalier, Mel Chin, Gabriel Dawe, Molly Gochman, Antony Gormley, April Greiman, Zaha Hadid, Zahi Hawass, Hyo-In Kim, Darian Leader, Loongkoonan, Steve McCurry, Howard Risatti, Sonoko Sasaki, Richard Serra, Cindy Sherman, Paul Tacon, Spencer Tunick, and Bill Viola.

Debra J. DeWitte would like to thank the following for their scholarly assistance: Richard Brettell, University of Texas at Dallas; Annemarie Carr, Southern Methodist University; Jenny Ramirez, James Madison University; Beth Wright, University of Texas at Arlington (Museum Guide); and for their patience and support she would like to thank her family: Bill Gibney, Jaclyn Jean Gibney, and Connie DeWitte.

Ralph M. Larmann would like to thank the following for their scholarly assistance and support: Ella Combs-Larmann, independent scholar and artist; Dr. Heidi Strobel, University of Evansville; University of Evansville, Office of Academic Affairs, Office of Alumni Relations, University Library, Department of Art; and for their patience and understanding: Ella, Allison, and Tip.

M. Kathryn Shields would like to thank the following: Laura M. Amrhein, independent scholar; Damon Akins, Guilford College; Scott Betz, Winston-Salem State University; Maria Bobroff, Guilford College; Jenny Ramirez; Eric Steginsky, independent artist; and to express love and gratitude to her family: Barry Bell, Gillian Denise Shields Bell, Alden Emmerich Shields Bell; and honor the memory of her mother, Nancy Shields.

How to Use Gateway to Art and Other Features

Four Gateway Works are NEW for the Third Edition

Maya Lintel Showing Shield Jaguar and Lady Xoc (eighth century)
1.9, p. 162; 2.4, p. 245; 3.4, p. 436; 4.6, p.632

Frida Kahlo, *The Two Fridas* (1939)
1.1, p. 50; 2.1, p. 204; 3.9, p. 532; 4.9, p.676

Carrie Mae Weems, *Kitchen Table* series (1990)
1.1, p. 56; 2.8, p. 329; 3.10, p.551; 4.10, p. 687

Ai Weiwei, *Dropping a Han Dynasty Urn* (1995) and *Colored Vases* (2008)
1.5, p. 121; 2.10, p. 357; 3.3, p.419; 4.8, p. 654

Four Gateway Works Return from the Second Edition

Raphael, *School of Athens* (1510–1511)
1.3, p. 90; 1.7 p. 146; 2.1, p. 194; 3.6, p. 470; 4.5, p. 617

Artemisia Gentileschi, *Judith Decapitating Holofernes* (c.1620)
1.8, p. 152; 2.2, p. 219; 3.6, p. 478; 3.8, p.519; 4.10, p. 681

The Taj Mahal (1632–53)
1.6, p. 136; 2.5, p. 272; 3.3, p. 412; 4.3, p.594

Katsushika Hokusai, "The Great Wave..." (1831)
1.6, p. 126; 2.3, p. 229; 3.3, p. 425; 4.8, p.661

The Gateway Artworks

There are many approaches to art, and to help you develop the important skills of looking at, analysing, and interpreting works of art, we have selected eight iconic works—the "Gateways to Art"—that you will encounter repeatedly as you read this book.

Recurrences

Every time you look at a great work of art, it will have something new to say to you—and this is explored through the eight Gateway artworks, which each recur at least once in all four Parts of this book: Fundamentals; Media and Processes; History and Context; and Themes.

If you consider, for example, in Part 1, the way an artist designed the work, you may notice something about the use of color or contrast that had not struck you before. When in Part 2 you study the medium the artist chose (such as the particular choice of paint selected), you will appreciate how it contributed to the impact of the work. In Part 3 we take a historical point of view: how does this work reflect the circumstances and the society in which it was created? Does it express the values of those who held political and economic power, or could it tell us something about the status of women at the time? In Part 4, we will ask whether the work addresses issues that have absorbed the attention of artists ever since humans began to paint, draw, and make sculpture. Does it touch on very big questions, such as the nature of the universe, or life and death? Or is it engaged with more personal concerns, such as gender, sexuality, race, and our own identities?

Gateway to Art: Kahlo, *The Two Fridas*

A Body in Pain

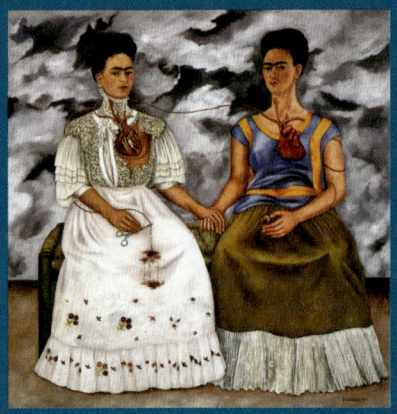

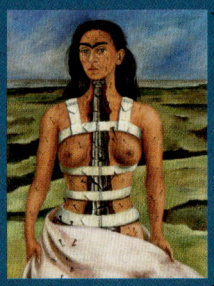

4.9.18a (above) Frida Kahlo, *The Two Fridas*, 1939. Oil on canvas, 5'8" × 5'8". Museo de Arte Moderno, Mexico City, Mexico.

4.9.18b (above right) Frida Kahlo, *The Broken Column*, 1944. Museo Dolores Olmedo Patino Mexico (Mexico City, Mexico) © Banco de México and INBAL Mexico, 2004

A terrible accident brought art into Frida Kahlo's life (1907–1954) in a new way. Around the age of eighteen she was riding in a bus with a friend when it collided with a trolley car. Her right leg and foot were crushed; her ribs, collarbone, and spine were broken; and her abdomen and uterus were pierced with an iron handrail. After the devastating accident she could not leave her bed for three months. Afterward, she endured as many as thirty-five surgeries and she experienced pain for the rest of her life.

While she was recuperating in a full body cast, her father brought her art supplies and she began painting. She created very personal portrayals of the psychological and physical suffering that plagued her throughout her life (even before the accident she had suffered polio as a child, compromising her right foot). Such paintings include *The Two Fridas* (**4.9.18A NEW**) and *The Broken Column* (**4.9.18B NEW**). Kahlo's self-portraits, which comprise up to a third of her artistic output, combine depictions of her outward appearance with metaphorical references to her feelings and graphic depictions of the physical agony she suffered.

In *The Two Fridas*, for example, the presentation of the hearts--one of which is radically torn open--on the outside of the bodies emphasizes the sensitive emotional content of the painting. A few years later, around the time she painted *The Broken Column*, Kahlo said, "I am disintegration." In this painting, nails pierce her skin all over, the front of her body is cracked open, and her spine is exposed. The nails recall depictions of the Catholic martyr St. Sebastian, and her spine takes the form of a Greek temple column. The Ionic column, considered the feminine architectural order, is ancient, ideal, and crumbling. No longer suited to support the body, the spinal column is reinforced by a metal corset.

We see subtle signs of Kahlo's constant anguish in the tears on her cheeks, but not in the expression on her face. It has the iconic, serene appearance seen in the numerous photographs taken of her and the many other self-portraits she made, including both faces in *The Two Fridas*. Like the column, Frida is fractured but whole, showing evidence of disintegration but still somehow surviving, even appearing almost ideal.

676 PART 4 THEMES

Portals

A new feature for this edition, Portals help you make direct connections and encounter new works.

The authors have selected Portals that create interesting comparisons or contrasts: each one shows a thumbnail image of a related artwork, along with a short explanation of its relevance to the current chapter. Each Portal artwork's page and figure number indicate its main position in the book, so you can turn to that chapter to see the work in full and find out more.

Marginal Glossaries

Terminology is defined in the margin of the spread on which the term first appears (also emboldened in the text), so you can build your artistic vocabulary as you read—without having to navigate to the complete glossary at the back of the book.

Compare and Contrast

You can learn more about one work by studying another and comparing the two. For example, consider how an artist might portray herself in different ways at different moments in her life, to express various elements of her identity. An artist might also choose to return to certain aspects, formal or iconographical, that become a running theme: for example, Frida Kahlo worked in the genre of self-portraiture for more than a third of her paintings, a number of which, including the two shown here, depict bodily harm, a repeated reference to the physical pain and multiple surgeries she suffered for much of her life.

Related Images

Now at the end of every chapter, galleries of thumbnail images assemble additional works from throughout the book to help you expand your visual knowledge. In chronological order, these works show you how to get the most out of your textbook—and display interesting connections across time periods, media, and themes.

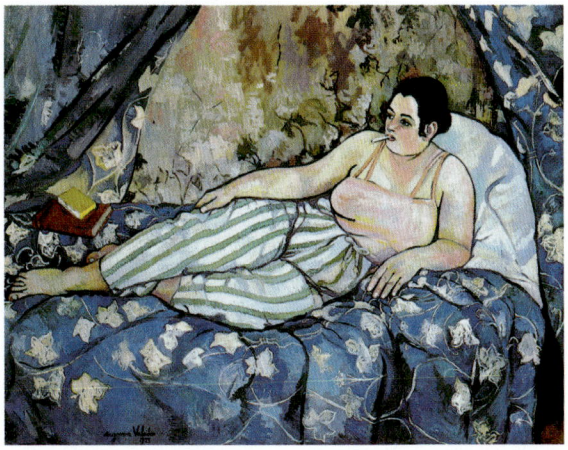

1.9.2 Suzanne Valadon, *The Blue Room*, 1923. Oil on canvas, 35½ × 45¾". Musée National d'Art Moderne, Centre Georges Pompidou, Paris, France

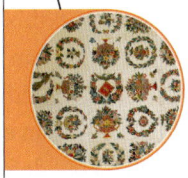

The artist has used pattern and rhythm to structure the floral forms in *Album Quilt*: see 1.6.12, **p.139**

includes three **contrasting** patterns (**1.9.2**). In the blue bed covering, in the lower portion of the painting, Valadon has used an organic pattern of leaves and stems. The green-and-white striped pattern in the woman's pajama bottoms dominates in direct contrast to the blue bed covering. Above the figure is a mottled pattern that again contrasts with the other two. The differences in these patterns energize the work.

Motif

A design repeated as a unit in a pattern is called a motif. Motifs can represent ideas, images, and themes that can be brought together through the use of pattern. An artist can create a strong unified design by repeating a motif.

A single motif can be interlaced with others to create complex designs. Many Islamic works use complex interlaced motifs, as this work created in seventeenth-century India demonstrates. The huqqa base (a huqqa is a water pipe used for smoking) in **1.9.3** may at first glance appear to use little repetition. Nevertheless, as we study the overall design we discover that elements, such as the flowers and leaves of the plants, recur at intervals. As this work shows, Islamic artists delight in the detail of pattern.

Motif is a common occurrence in traditional quilting. By unifying a series of simple patterns into a repeatable motif, a quilter could connect

Contrast: a drastic difference between such elements as color or value (lightness/darkness) when they are presented together
Abstract: art imagery that departs from recognizable images from the natural world

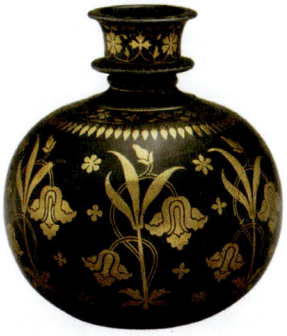

1.9.3 Huqqa base, India, Deccan, last quarter of 17th century. Bidri ware (zinc alloy inlaid with brass), 6⅞ × 6½". Metropolitan Museum of Art, New York

Images Related to 3.4 Art of the Americas

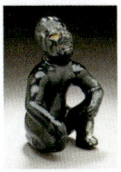

4.5.X Olmec Figure in Combat Stance, c. 900–300 BCE, p. 624

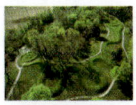

2.6.4 *Zapotec Seated Figure*, 300 BCE–700 CE, p. 295

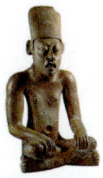

2.4.15 Great Serpent Mound, c. 800 BCE–100 CE, p. 252

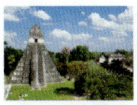

2.5.5 Maya Temple I, Tikal, Guatemala, c. 300–900 CE, p. 26

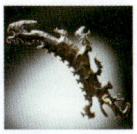

4.4.4 Maya Culture, Flint depicting crocodile canoe, 600–900, p. 601

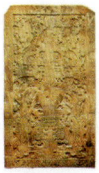

4.3.10 Maya Sarcophagus Lid, tomb of Lord Pacal, c. 680, p. 594

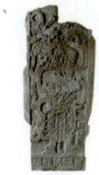

1.2.7 Maya Stela with Supernatural Scene, 761, p. 71

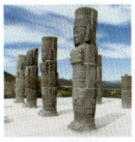

4.7.9 Tula Warrior Columns, 900–1000, p. 642

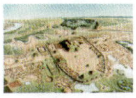

4.4.5 Aztec Calendar Stone, 900–1521, p. 602

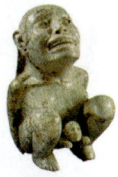

4.1.8 Monk's Mound, Cahokia, Illinois, c. 1150, p. 568

Introduction

Subject, subject matter: the person, object, or space depicted in a work of art
Style: a characteristic way in which an artist or group of artists uses visual language to give a work an identifiable form of visual expression

What Is Art?

The Japanese artist Katsushika Hokusai (1760–1849) is said to have created a painting titled *Maple Leaves on a River* by dipping the feet of a chicken in red paint and letting the bird run freely on a sheet of paper he had just covered in blue paint. Although we know that Hokusai was an unconventional character, this painting has not been found today, and we cannot be certain that the story is true. If we think about this curious anecdote for a while, however, we can begin to understand the most basic question addressed in this book: What is art? This is not an easy question to answer, because people define art in many ways. In Hokusai's case, he captured the peaceful sensations of a fall day by a river, without showing what an actual river and real leaves look like. In this instance, art primarily communicates a sensation.

In nineteenth-century Japan, art could be a means to encourage the quiet contemplation of nature, but to an Egyptian artist almost 3,000 years earlier, art would have meant something very different. The Egyptian who in the tenth century BCE painted the wooden coffin of Nespawershefi had a quite different idea of rivers in mind from the one Hokusai conceived. For ancient Egyptians, rivers were important for survival, because they depended on the flooding of the River Nile to grow their crops. Rivers also had religious significance. Egyptians believed that during the daytime the sun god Re sailed across a great celestial ocean in his day boat. By night, he traveled in his evening boat along a river in the underworld, but before he could rise again he had to defeat his enemy, the serpent Apophis, which in **0.0.1** can be seen swimming in the river. Here the river is again suggested rather than being realistically portrayed. It is a place of danger, not of contemplation, and if Re does not

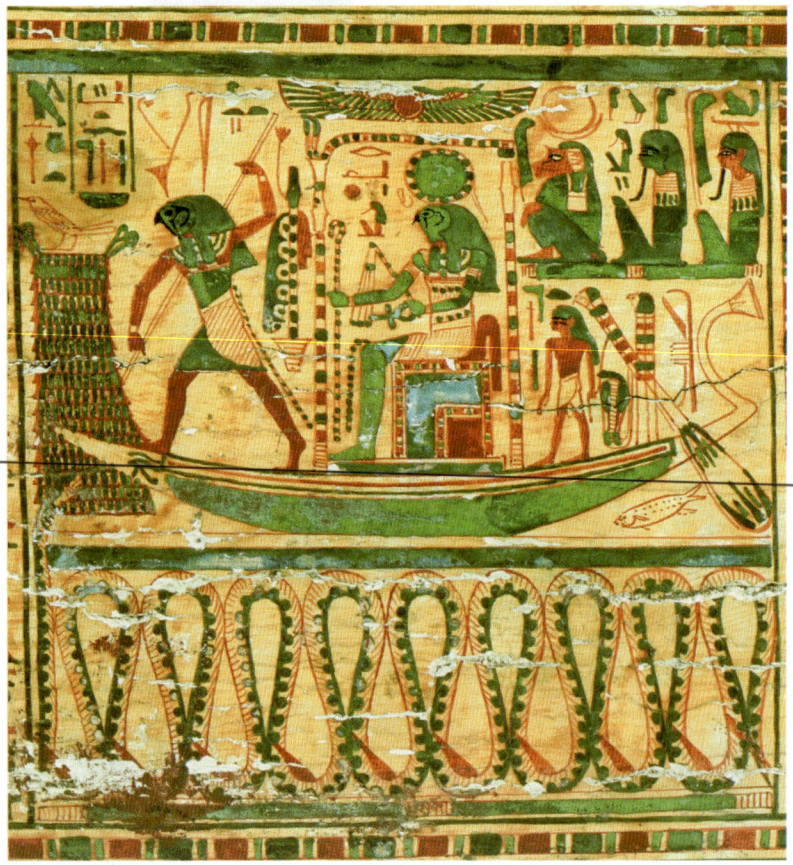

0.0.1 *The Journey of the Sun God Re*, detail from the inner coffin of Nespawershefi, Third Intermediate Period, 990–969 BCE. Plastered and painted wood. Fitzwilliam Museum, Cambridge, England

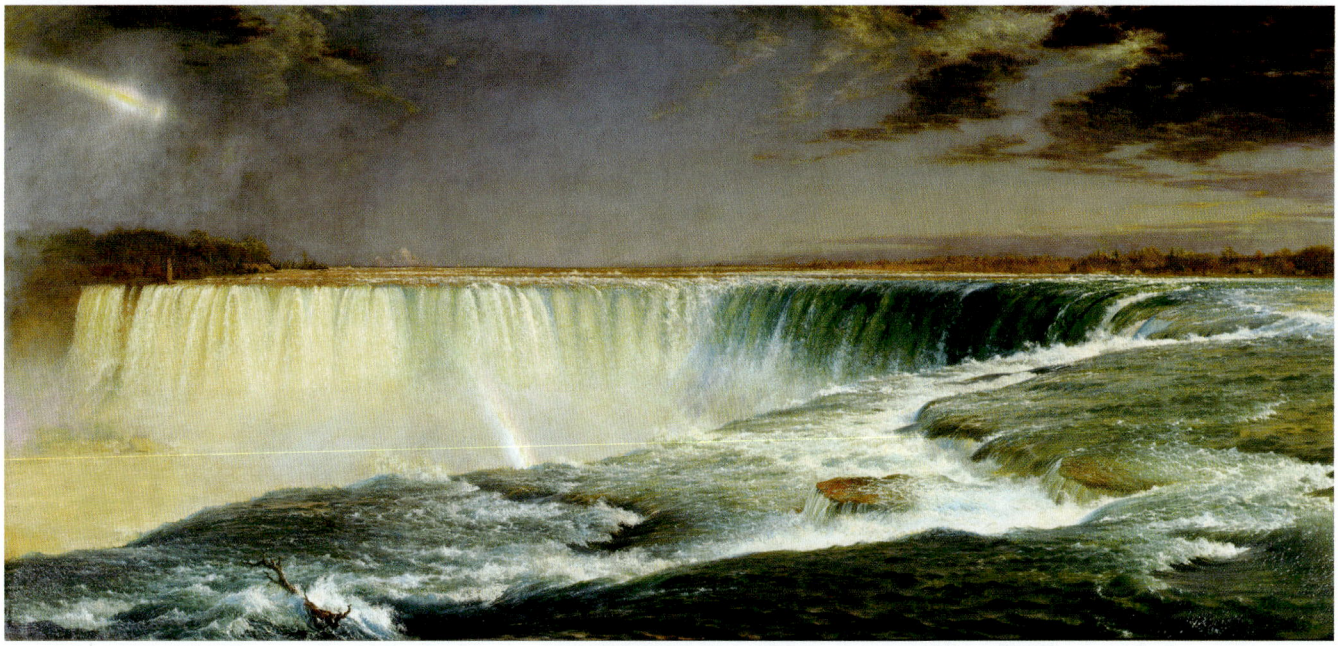

0.0.2 Frederic Edwin Church, *Niagara*, 1857. Oil on canvas, 3'6¼" × 7'6½". Corcoran Gallery of Art, Washington, D.C.

emerge victorious, the world will be deprived of the life-giving light of the sun. Re, who in the image is seated, is protected by another god carrying a spear. The choice of this **subject** was appropriate for a coffin: no doubt Nespawershefi hoped to emerge from the underworld to live a happy afterlife, just as Re rose again every morning. For the painter of this coffin, art was a way to express profound religious ideas and to invoke beliefs in a happy life after death.

The American Frederic Edwin Church (1826–1900) created a very dramatic painting of a river (or, to be more precise, a waterfall) for a different purpose than that of the Egyptian artist who decorated the coffin. Church painted several views of the Niagara river and falls for exhibition to a public eager to learn about the landscape of the still-young American Republic. Niagara was a popular subject for artists in the second half of the nineteenth century, both because of its grandeur and because it symbolized America's territorial expansion and ambitions: it marks the northern border of the United States. Church's *Niagara* of 1857 (**0.0.2**) is more than 7 ft. wide. It positions the viewer as if on the very edge of, or even in, the falls. The miraculous vantage point inspired one critic to remark, "This is Niagara, with the roar left out!" Landscape painters in Church's time also used the beauty and power of the landscape to symbolize the presence of God in nature, and this painting came to represent America, and, for many, God's support for the country. It is a magnificent statement of religion, an expression of national pride, and a spectacular form of public education and entertainment.

Finally, consider a work by the American artist Louise Nevelson (1899–1988) that also features a waterfall (**0.0.3**, p. 22). Nevelson made twenty-five painted rectangular and square wooden sections inside a rectangular frame, measuring 18 × 9 ft. Inside some of the rectangles we can see undulating curved forms that suggest a cascading waterfall or the froth of white water. Other forms in the upper right of the square resemble squirming fish. Clearly, Nevelson's purpose is not to show an instantly recognizable likeness of a waterfall full of fish. Instead we are invited to examine her carefully constructed work closely and to feel the sensations of watching water cascade and fish swimming.

If we go back to our original question, what is art?, can our consideration of these four very different works help us to find a quick and simple definition that will tell us whether we are looking at something called art? Although they have the same **subject matter**, these four works certainly do not have much in common in terms of their appearance or **style**. The definition of art also must include a range of materials (in

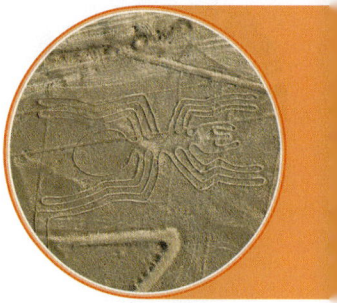

The first Part of this book explains formal analysis, or the language used to read and discuss art: see **1.1.1, p.43**

0.0.3 Louise Nevelson, *White Vertical Water*, 1972. Painted wood, 18 × 9'. Solomon R. Guggenheim Museum, New York

Geometric: predictable and mathematical
Composition: the overall design or organization of a work
Renaissance: a period of cultural and artistic change in Europe from the fourteenth to the seventeenth century
Ceramic: fire-hardened clay, often painted, and normally sealed with a shiny protective coating
Calligraphy: the art of emotive or carefully descriptive hand lettering or handwriting

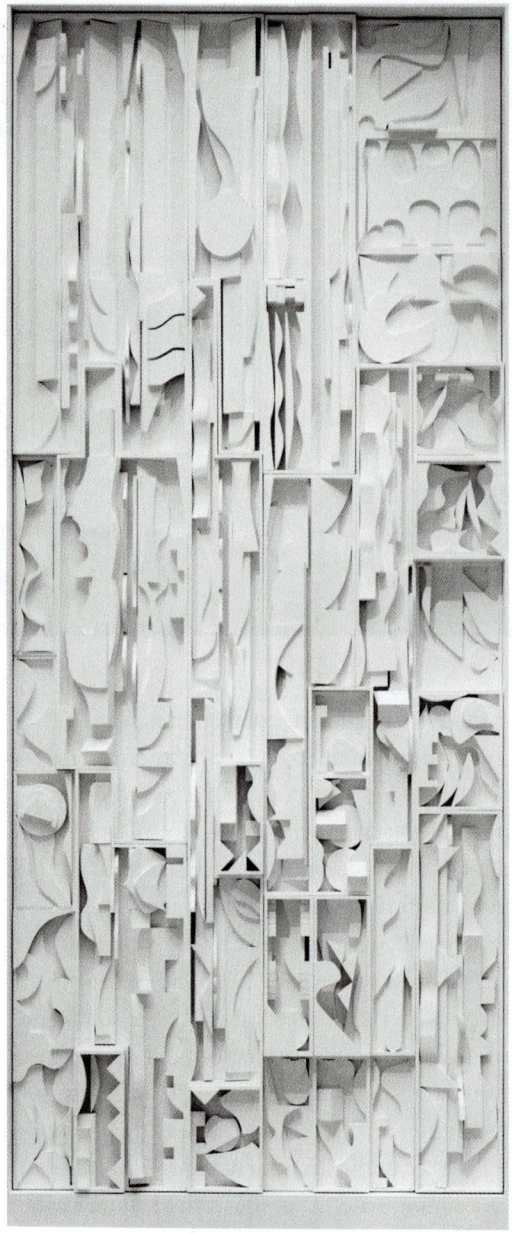

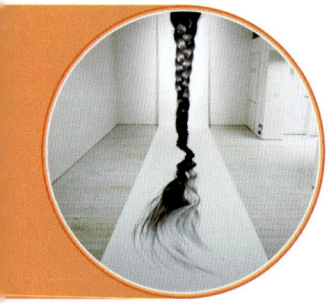

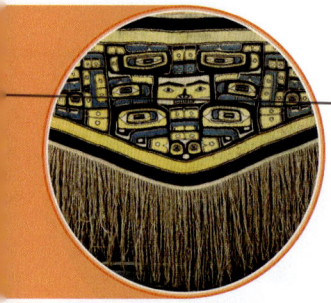

The materials used to make art and how these materials are used are the subjects of Part 2: Media and Processes: see **2.1.12, p. 199** and **2.6.18, p. 296**

fact, art can be made from almost anything). Nor do these works have a common purpose. The Egyptian coffin painting has a clear religious message. Church's painting portrays a dramatic landscape but also carries a powerful message of nationalism and patriotic pride. Hokusai's painting uses very simple means to convey restful sensations. Nevelson's work also focuses on communicating the sensations of being by a river, but in her case with a meticulously constructed **geometric** suggestion of one.

All of these artists arranged their **compositions** to communicate ideas and emotions (religious feelings, national pride, or the sensation of watching fish swim down a waterfall, for example). Art communicates ideas by visual means that can help us see the world in new and exciting ways and strengthen our understanding. In other words, art is a form of language.

Fine Art, Craft, and the Commercial Arts

The terms we choose to label things often tell us more about our own attitudes and stereotypes than about the object under consideration. For example, art from cultures outside the Western tradition (such as the traditional arts of Africa or the Pacific Islands) was once termed "Primitive Art," implying that it was of lesser quality than the "fine" or "high" arts of Europe. But while—as in this case—such labels can be misused, they can nonetheless reflect cultural judgments and sometimes lead to ways of identifying, categorizing, and understanding art.

There is no simple definition to enable us to tell who is an artist and who is not. If we take a global view, we certainly cannot define an artist by what he or she made. In Western culture during some eras of history, particularly since the **Renaissance**, painting and sculpture have been considered to be the most important categories of art ("high art"), while others, such as **ceramics** and furniture, were once considered less important. The term craft was usually applied to such works, and their makers were considered less skilled or of lower status than painters and sculptors. This distinction arose partly because the cost of producing a fine painting or a beautifully carved marble statue was high. Therefore, those things became status symbols of the rich and powerful. In other cultures, the relative importance of various forms of art was quite different. The people of ancient Peru placed special value on wool, and those who made fine woolen textiles were likely considered as skillful as a painter would be in our society. In China the art of **calligraphy** (elegantly painted lettering) was considered one of the highest forms of art.

Fine art usually refers to a work of art (traditionally a painting, drawing, carved sculpture, and sometimes a print) made with skill and creative imagination to be pleasing or beautiful to look at. When the Italian artist Agnolo Bronzino (1503–1572) painted a portrait of Eleonora of Toledo and her son Giovanni (**0.0.4**), he was clearly determined to demonstrate great skill in his lavish portrait of this wife of the powerful Duke of Florence, Cosimo de' Medici, who was a great **patron** of the arts. Eleonora's dress, which was so sumptuous that it would have cost more than the painting itself, is depicted with such great care that one can almost feel the texture of the embroidery. Eleonora, her complexion perfect and her beauty flawless, is composed and icily aloof, her hand resting on the shoulder of her young son to draw our attention to him. The young boy, destined to become a powerful duke like his father, is equally serious and composed, as befits a person of high status. Looking at this painting we can see that Bronzino intended us to marvel at his skill in producing a supreme example of fine art that conveys a vivid sense of wealth and power.

Historically, the graphic arts (those made by a method that enables reproduction of many copies of the same image) have been considered less important, and perhaps less accomplished, than the fine arts. While Bronzino's portrait is unique, made for a single, powerful patron, and probably to be viewed by a select audience, works of graphic art are made to be available to many people and are in that sense much more democratic, which is considered an advantage by many artists and viewers. Graphic art includes a wide range of **media**: books, magazines, posters, advertising, signage, television, computer screens, and social media.

Graphic design is a commercial art, the essence of which is communication. The simplicity of a **logo** created in 1994 to identify the global brand of the logistics company FedEx (**0.0.5**) contrasts with the elaborate luxury of Bronzino's *Eleonora*. The designer, Lindon Leader, discovered that the company's name at the time, Federal Express, gave customers the impression that it operated only in the United States, rather than internationally. In addition, everybody called the company simply FedEx. Leader's task was to design a logo that could be used on package labels, advertisements, trucks, and planes to identify FedEx as a dynamic, global organization. The solution was a design that retained the colors (slightly modified) of the existing logo, but shortened the company name to FedEx. The type was arranged so that the white space between the E and x formed a white arrow that suggested speed and precision.

The design is very simple but we should be careful not to assume that it required much less skill and effort than Bronzino's portrait. The logo did not involve the same kind of

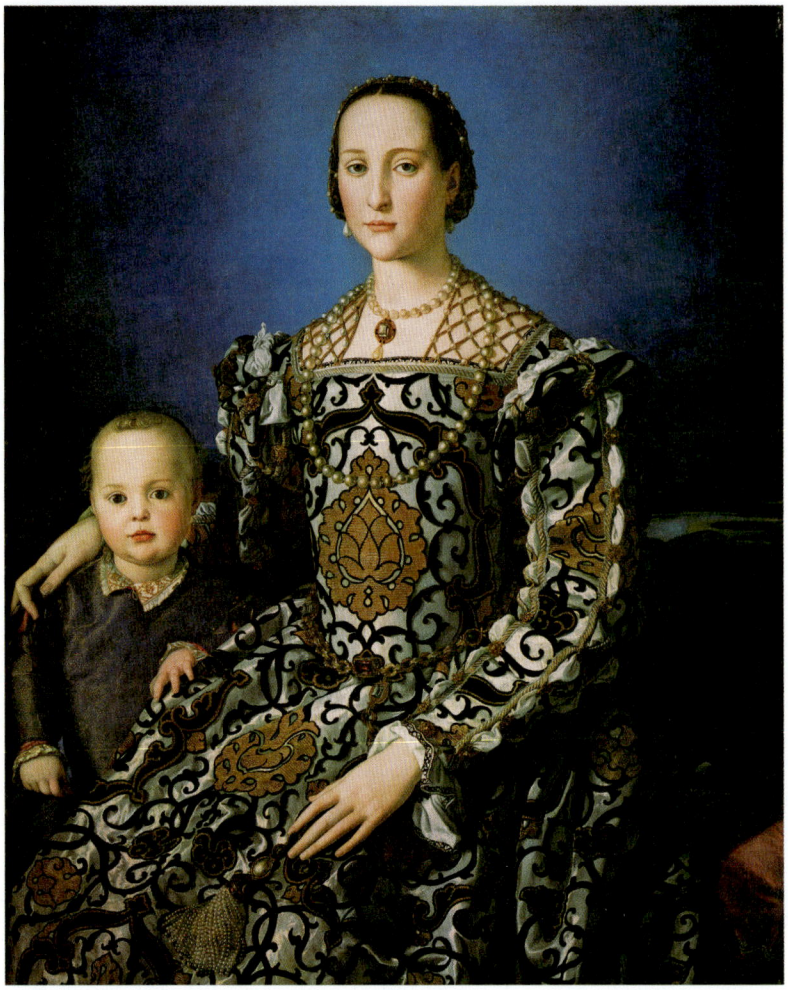

0.0.4 Agnolo Bronzino, *Eleonora of Toledo and Her Son, Giovanni*, c. 1545. Oil on panel, 45¼ × 37¾". Uffizi Gallery, Florence, Italy

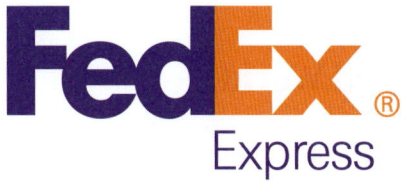

0.0.5 FedEx Express logo

Patron: an organization or individual who sponsors the creation of works of art
Medium (plural **media**): the material on or from which an artist chooses to make a work of art
Graphic design: the use of images, typography, and technology to communicate ideas for a client or to a particular audience
Logo: a graphic image used to identify an idea or entity

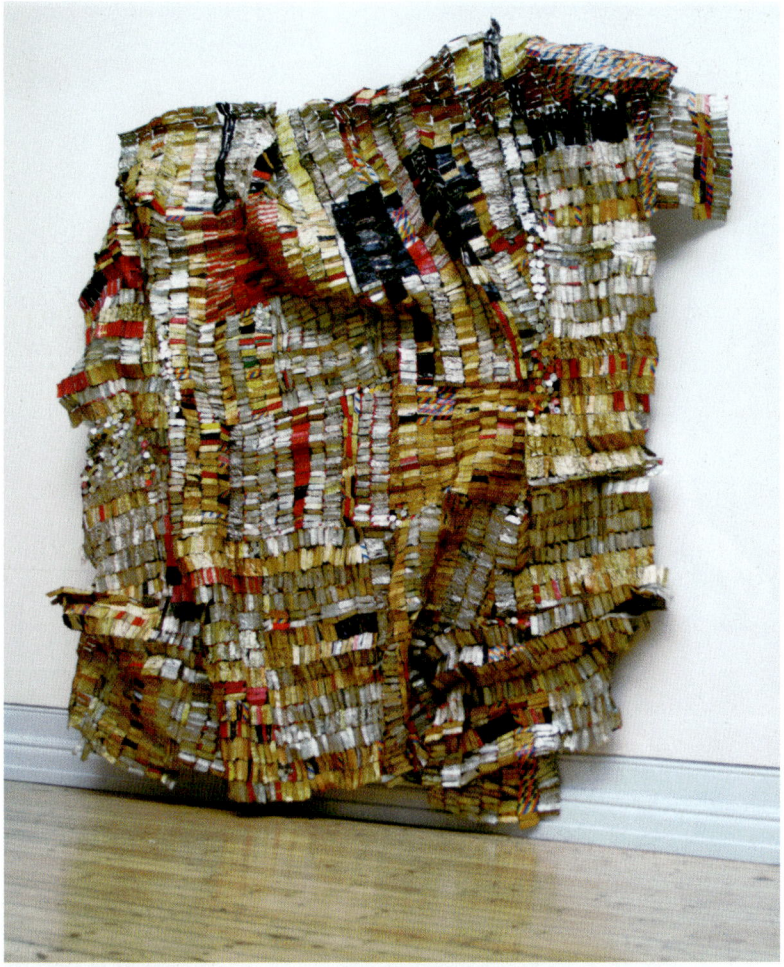

0.0.6 El Anatsui, *Old Man's Cloth*, 2002. Aluminum and copper wire, 15'9" × 17'¾"

technical finesse as the detailed realism of the **oil painting**, or Bronzino's ability to communicate the human character. But Leader and his colleagues held focus groups to research the public's impressions of the company and developed about 200 concepts before they settled on their chosen design. Then they made protoypes of planes, vans, and trucks to test it. Leader's logo has won more than forty design awards. There is one crucial difference between the two works, however. The purpose of the logo is to identify a company and sell its services. Bronzino's portrait was made to please an individual patron, while the FedEx logo is intended to communicate with a worldwide audience.

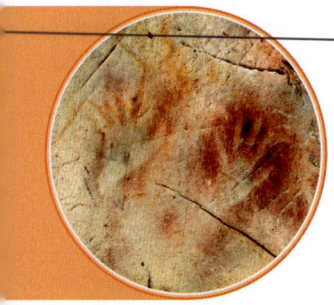

Part 3 considers the history and context in which works of art were made: see **3.1.2, p.367**

The Visual World

When we look at an artwork made by a single artist, we often assume that it was created entirely from the artist's own ideas and inspirations. But art is part of a wider **context** of things we experience: the visual culture in which we live, which includes all of the images that we encounter in our lives. Think about how many images you saw on your way to class today. They will have included traffic signs, roadside billboards, and the logos of businesses along the highway. Once you arrived on campus, you will have seen posters informing you of an upcoming event, the logo of the coffee shop, and maps directing you to where your class takes place. Then a glance at your smartphone or e-mail revealed more ads, all clamoring for your attention. We live in, and respond to, a world of images, and so have artists, whether in ancient Egypt, sixteenth-century Italy, or twenty-first-century America. In other words, art reflects the culture in which it was created, not just the creative achievement of its maker.

The contemporary artist El Anatsui (b. 1944) makes artworks that reference both the colonial history of Africa and the impact of modern consumerism on cultural values. *Old Man's Cloth* (**0.0.6**) is made from discarded liquor-bottle tops. El Anatsui chose bottle tops as his material because European traders bartered alcohol for African goods. Slaves were shipped from Ghana to the sugar plantations of the Caribbean; then in turn, rum was shipped from there back to Africa. El Anatsui's bottle tops thus remind us of the slave trade, as well as highlighting the way in which modern consumerism discards waste. At the same time, the artist's use of traditional designs suggests both the enduring power and the fragility of Ghanaian culture.

Where Is Art?

You almost certainly have some art in your home: perhaps a painting in the living room, a poster in your bedroom, or a beautifully made flower vase; and there are sculptures and memorials in parks or other public spaces in most cities. You have probably also figured out by now that art can be found in many places: in the form of a coffin, in a book, in any number of contemporary media, and, of course, in an art museum.

Our word "museum" comes from the ancient Greek *mouseion*, meaning a temple dedicated to the arts and sciences. The mouseion of Alexandria in Egypt, founded about 2,400 years ago, collected and preserved important objects, still a key function of museums today. Many of the great European art museums began as private collections. The famous Louvre Museum in Paris, France, was originally a fortress and then a royal palace where the king kept his personal art collection. When King Louis XIV moved to his new palace at Versailles, the Louvre became a residence for the artists he employed. After the French Revolution (1789–99), the king's collection was opened to the public in the Louvre.

Museums in America had a different history. The oldest is the Pennsylvania Academy of the Fine Arts, founded in 1805 as a museum and an art school. It continues to serve both functions, as do many other American museums. During the nineteenth century, prominent business figures amassed large private collections of European art. These collectors founded museums modeled on those of Europe. The Brooklyn Museum was founded in 1823, and in the 1870s alone, great museums opened in Boston, New York, Philadelphia (**0.0.7**), and Chicago. Many public buildings, including museums, in the United States were built in the Neoclassical style, which involves symmetrical forms that represent democratic ideals derived from ancient Greece and Rome, where the Classical architectural style was first developed.

Most art museums hold permanent collections of artworks that are regularly displayed, although some can show only a portion of the works in their large collections. Museums also organize exhibitions of works on loan from other institutions. They often have conservation departments to care for and restore the artworks.

If we consider only works that are displayed in museums and galleries, however, we will ignore many works that are placed in communal or religious spaces. Perhaps the most enduring example of such a work is the painting of the Virgin of Guadalupe (**0.0.8**). According to Catholic tradition, in December 1531 the Virgin appeared several times, first on Tepeyac hill, then outside Mexico City, to an indigenous peasant, Juan Diego, when she miraculously imprinted her own image on his cloak made of cactus fiber. (Historical evidence, however, suggests that

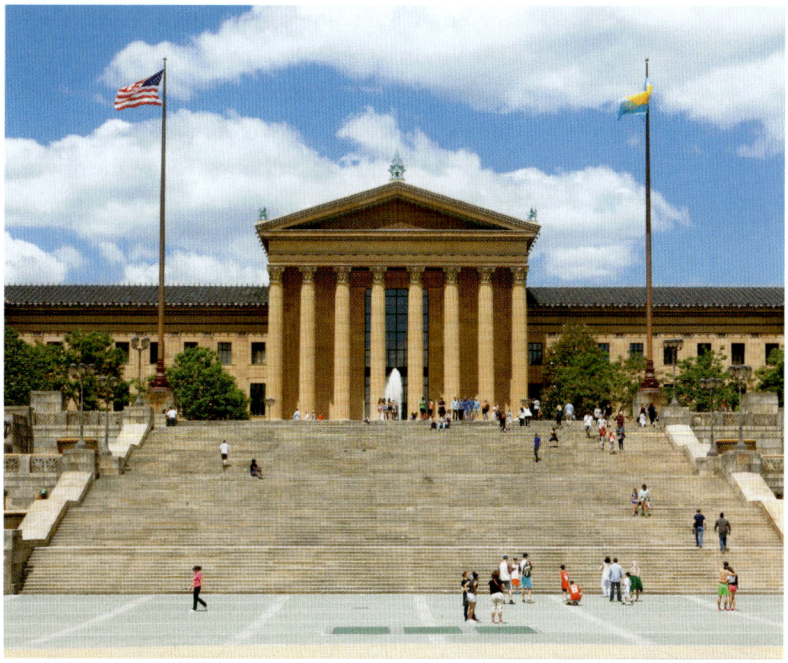

0.0.7 Philadelphia Museum of Art, Pennsylvania

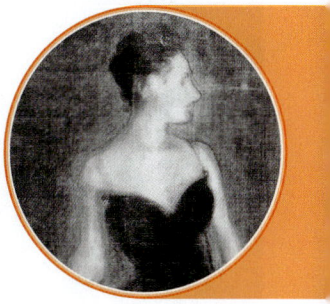

Using such scientific tools as X-ray, museums not only care for artworks, but can also discover clues about how they were made: see **4.4.15b, p. 612**

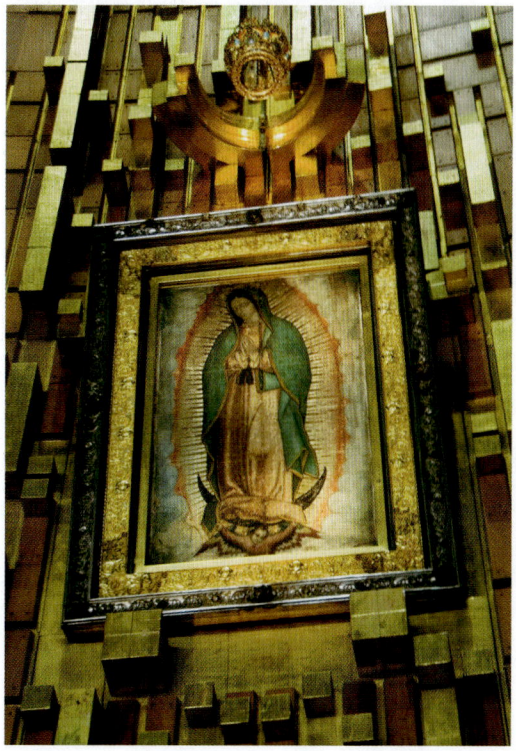

Oil paint(ing): paint made of pigment suspended in oil
Context: circumstances surrounding the creation of a work of art, including historical events, social conditions, biographical facts about the artist, and his or her intentions

0.0.8 *The Virgin of Guadalupe*, 1531. Tempera on linen. Basilica of St. Mary of Guadalupe, Mexico City, Mexico the Virgin was painted in **tempera** on linen.) The Virgin became the symbol of the Mexican nation, not just for Mexicans of Indian descent but also for all the citizens of the country—and not only for devout Catholics. Today, the original painting of the Virgin is housed in the National Basilica of St. Mary of Guadalupe at the base of Tepeyac hill, which receives hundreds of thousands of pilgrims annually.

Some works of art are still ***in situ***, in their original locations. For example, from 1921 to 1954 Simon Rodia (1879–1965) built seventeen interconnected structures on a residential lot in a neighborhood of Los Angeles (**0.0.9**). Rodia's work is now known as the Watts Towers, although he named it *Nuestro Pueblo* (Spanish for "our town"). Rodia, a construction worker, made his structures out of materials he found or that local people brought to him. The towers are made of steel rods and pipes, wire mesh, and mortar, and decorated with bits of broken glass and pottery. Rodia's neighbors and the City of Los Angeles did not approve of his work, and unsuccessful efforts were made to destroy it, but the tide eventually turned in his favor. In 1990 Watts Towers was named a National Historic Landmark, and today it is recognized internationally and protected as an important work of public art.

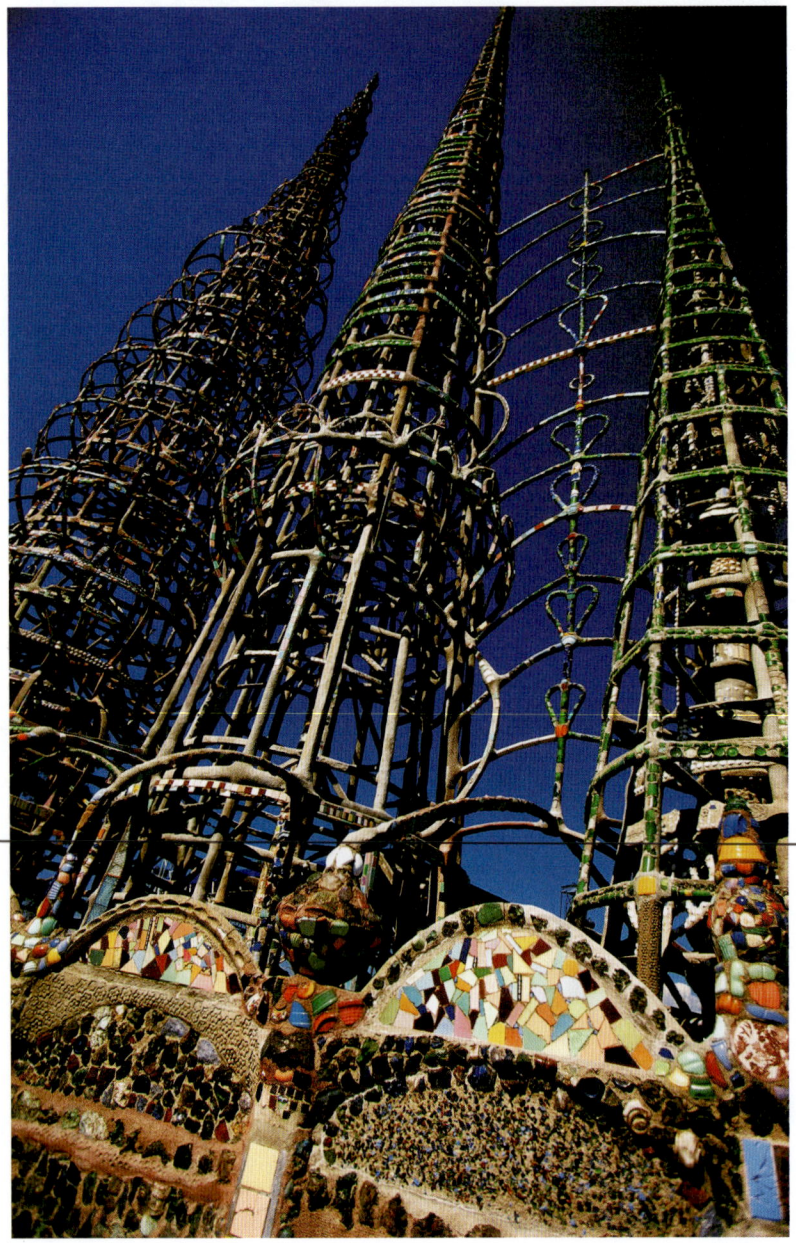

0.0.9 Simon Rodia, Watts Towers, 1921–54. Seventeen mortar-covered steel sculptures with mosaic, height 99' 6" at tallest point. 1761–1765 East 107th Street, Los Angeles, California

Art and Creativity

Simon Rodia's work demonstrates that art can be found in one's own neighborhood, and that many—perhaps most—people possess the creative impulse to make art, and express it in numerous, and often surprising, ways. Rodia devoted many years of his life to creating a single artwork. He had never trained to be an artist but he shared with professional artists a creative impulse that dominated his life. If we consider the role of creativity in our own lives, we see that images are ever present in our world: we make our own photos and videos, and share them through social-networking services or using our cell phones. These activities, so common now, show how people naturally respond to images and seek to express themselves visually—just as they did 3,000 years ago in ancient Egypt. In other words, most of us instinctively relate to human creativity.

The American painter James McNeil Whistler (1834–1903) believed in "art for art's sake," or the idea that art had intrinsic value regardless of its subject matter or message. Whistler often titled his paintings *Nocturne*, *Symphony*, or *Arrangement* to convey the idea that he wished his art to trigger emotions and sensations in the same way music did. Whistler's painting *Nocturne in Black and Gold: The Falling Rocket* (**0.0.10**) was exhibited in 1877 in London. The British critic John Ruskin described the painting as lacking in subject

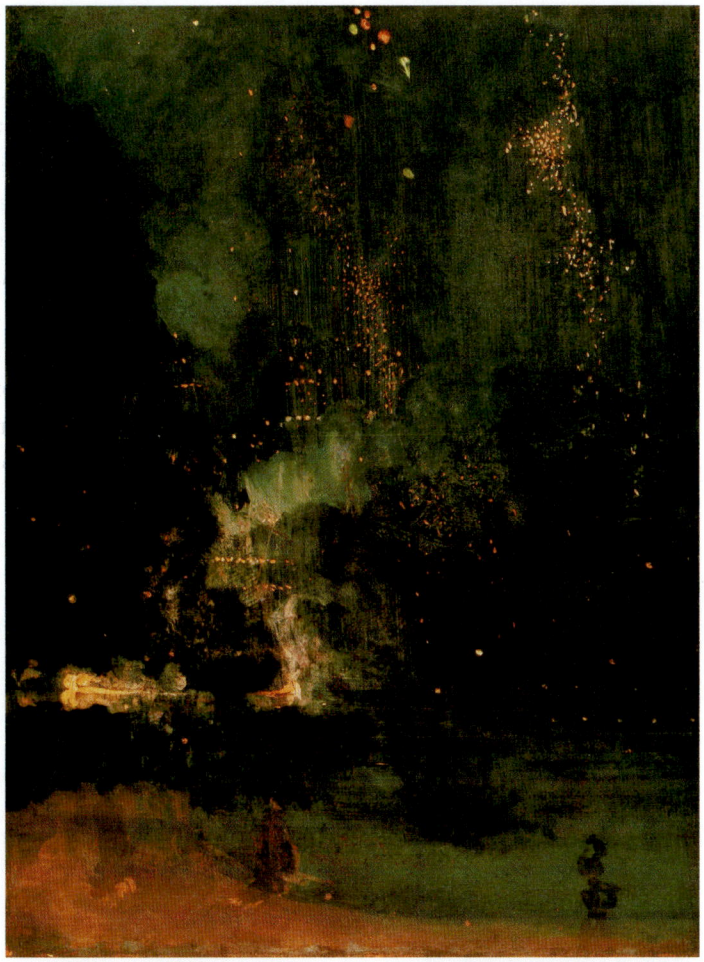

0.0.10 James Abbott McNeil Whistler, *Nocturne in Black and Gold: The Falling Rocket*, 1875. Oil on canvas, 23¾ × 18⅜". Detroit Institute of Arts, Michigan

matter and quality and shamed the artist for asking "two hundred guineas for flinging a pot of paint in the public's face." Whistler sued the famous critic for these comments, and the trial became a public discussion about the definition of art and creativity. Ruskin's lawyer argued that the painting could not have taken much time to make, that its subject matter was not clear, and that it therefore did not have much value. Whistler defended himself by saying that it was an artistic arrangement that represented fireworks. He believed its value lay not just in the time it took to make the work, but also in the knowledge he had gained over a lifetime, which he shared with the public through this work. Although the jury found in favor of Whistler, he was awarded an amount equal to pennies today, and the trial led him to bankruptcy. Despite his difficulties, however, the outcome of the trial became a catalyst or inspiration for future artists to create works that were not always readily understood or appreciated by all viewers.

Tempera: fast-drying painting medium made from pigment mixed with water-soluble binder, such as egg yolk
In situ: in the location for which it was originally made
Medieval: relating to the Middle Ages; roughly, between the fall of the Roman empire and the start of the Renaissance

Who Makes Art?

Who decides what an artwork looks like? The simple answer might seem to be the artist who makes it. We know that art has been made for thousands of years: at least since humans first painted images on the walls of caves, and probably long before then. In general, art from earlier cultures was a communal effort in which spirituality and notions of the cycle of life were common themes. As time progressed, artists addressed social issues (war and social conscience) and created more individual expressions of their identity (gender and race).

The great temples of ancient Egypt, Greece, and Rome were certainly not the work of one person, and in some cases, we cannot tell if their overall design was the idea of a single individual. Archaeologists have discovered near the Valley of the Kings in Egypt an entire village, Deir el-Medina, which was occupied by artisans who made the tombs that we admire today. The cathedrals of **medieval** Europe were the result of the skills of many different artists and

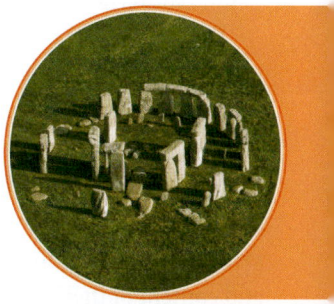

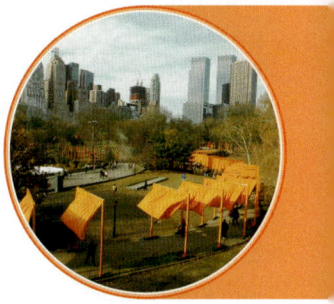

Part 4 compares works with common themes, such as the community artworks Stonehenge and *The Gates* by Christo and Jeanne-Claude: see **4.1.8** and **4.1.9, pp. 570–71**

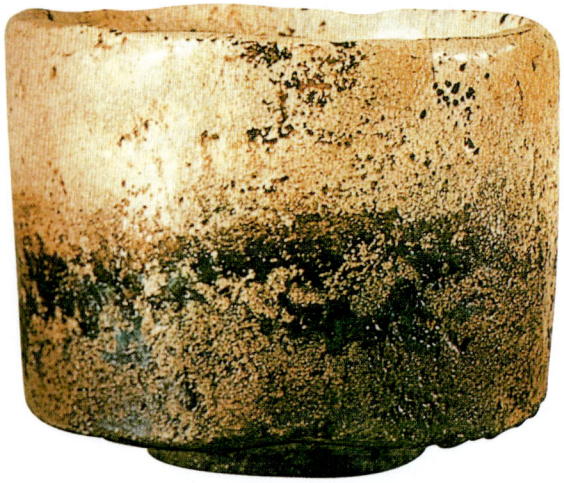

0.0.11 Hon'ami Koetsu, Tea bowl (called Mount Fuji), Edo period, early 17th century. Raku ware, height 3⅜". Sakai Collection, Tokyo, Japan

For centuries, in Japan, tea bowls have been highly esteemed for their beauty. The bowl seen in **0.0.11** would have been prized for its subtle variations of color, the pleasant tactile sensations of its slightly irregular surface, and its shape. It was designed to be appreciated slowly as the user sipped tea. The Italian Renaissance artist Leonardo da Vinci (1452–1519) lived approximately 200 years earlier than the artist who made this tea bowl, but the two had different ideas of what it meant to be an artist. The Japanese maker of the tea bowl worked in a society that valued tradition. Japanese artists followed with supreme skill the established methods of working and making. Leonardo, however, became famous in an era

Manuscripts: handwritten texts

0.0.12 Leonardo da Vinci, *Mona Lisa*, c.1503–6. Oil on wood, 30⅜ × 20⅞". Musée du Louvre, Paris, France

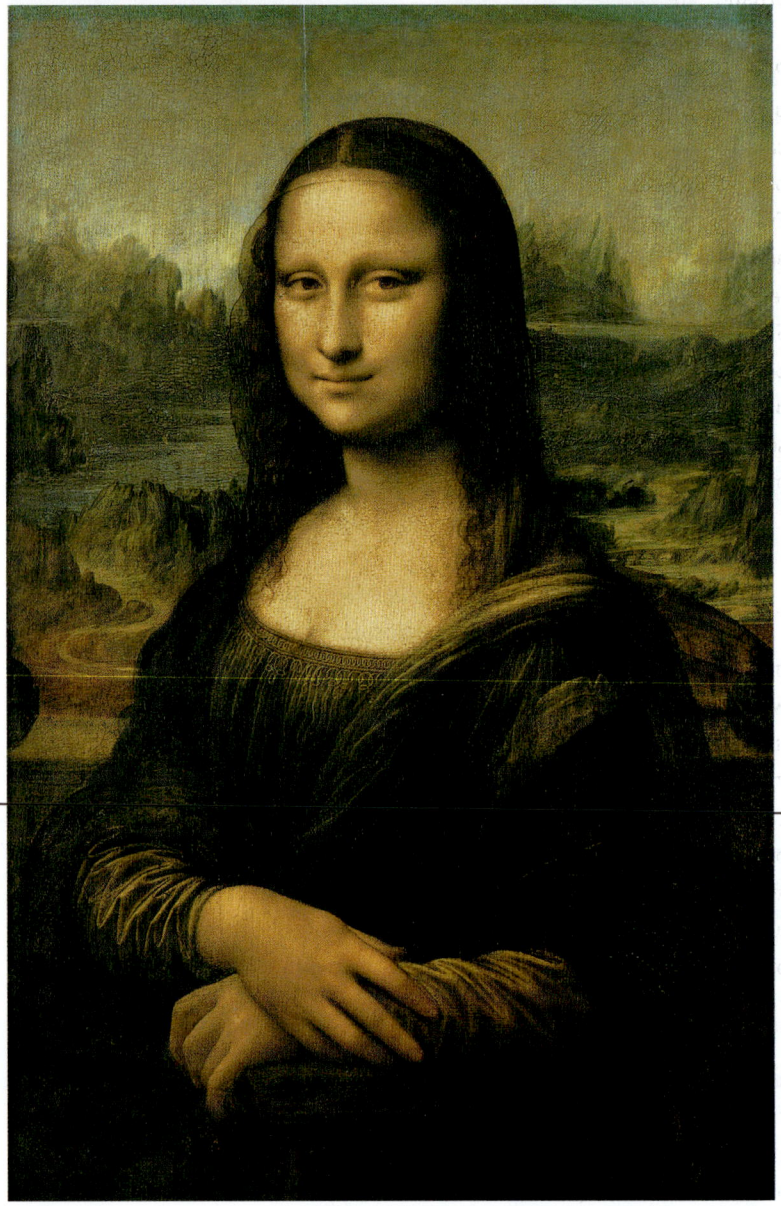

artisans: stone carvers, the makers of stained-glass windows, and carpenters who made the furniture. These skilled workers remain mostly anonymous, except for a very few whose names have been found in **manuscripts** or carved on works of art. But though we may never identify most of these early artists, it is clear that humans have always wanted to create art. This urge is part of our nature, just like our need to eat and sleep.

Due to the efforts of Renaissance artists to elevate their profession as a liberal art, the Western world has popularized the idea of a lone individual creating his or her own art to express something very personal. In the nineteenth and twentieth centuries it became more common for artists to determine individually the appearance and content of their own work, and, in their search for new forms of self-expression, to make art that was often very controversial. This remains true today. But for many centuries before this, very few artists worked alone. Even Renaissance artists who promoted the idea of creative genius operated workshops staffed by artist assistants who carried out most of the work involved in turning their master's design into a work of art. In nineteenth-century Japan, the eccentric Katsushika Hokusai was famous around the world for his prints, but he could not have made them alone. A wood carver cut his designs into blocks from which a printer manufactured copies. Even today, artists often employ a workshop of assistants to help them.

Gertrude Stein as an Art Patron

Much of the art that survives today would not have been made without patrons, who financially supported artists or commissioned specific works of art. The American writer Gertrude Stein (1874–1946) and her brother Leo (1872–1947) built an outstanding collection of modern art, which decorated their home in Paris. The weekly gatherings Gertrude held in her studio apartment provided a meeting place for both artists and writers. In fact, the Steins introduced Pablo Picasso (1881–1973) and Henri Matisse (1869–1954) to each other, sparking their friendship and artistic rivalry.

In 1905, Gertrude Stein commissioned Picasso to paint her portrait (seen in Man Ray's photograph of her, **0.0.13**). She wrote that she sat for Picasso ninety times: he worked on the painting for months but was never satisfied. Eventually he abandoned the naturalistic approach and painted out the details of her facial features after seeing ancient Iberian sculptures in Spain and at the Louvre museum in Paris. When comparing Stein's actual appearance with her painted likeness, we see that Picasso replaced the soft contours of her cheeks, eyes, and mouth with mask-like forms. The painting is now famous, not only because it represents their interaction, but also because it inspired a new phase of Picasso's work that relied on his personal vision rather than on what he observed, starting him on the path toward Cubism. When someone remarked that Gertrude Stein did not look like her portrait, Picasso responded, "She will."

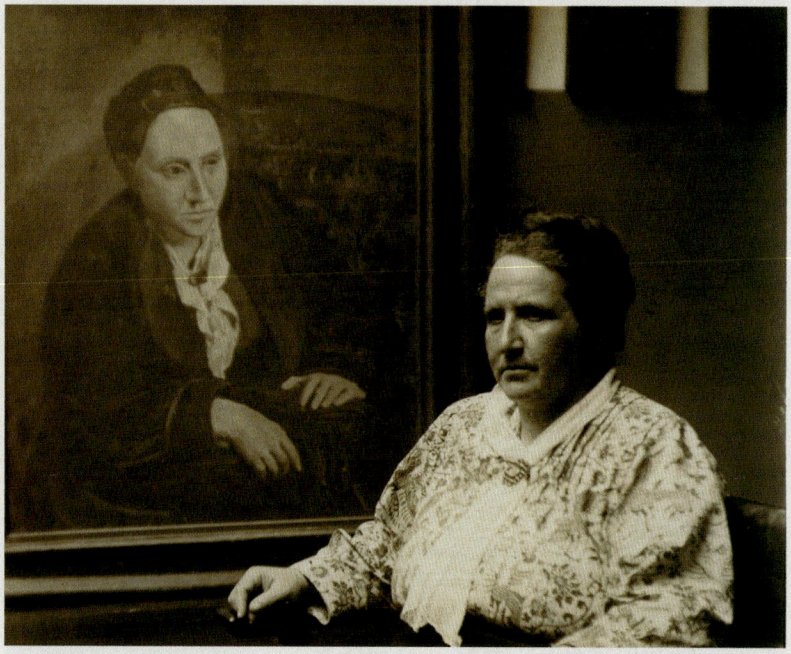

0.0.13 Man Ray, *Gertrude Stein with Portrait by Picasso*, 1922. Vintage gelatin silver print, 3¾ × 4¾". The Richard and Ellen Sandor Art Foundation

in Europe that valued individual ingenuity. He was a supremely talented artist whose visionary interests and inventions extended far beyond the visual arts, to engineering and science. Between 1503 and 1506 he created a portrait that is now probably the most famous painting in the world, although in his own time the work was virtually unknown because it was not commissioned by an important patron. Leonardo was not content to create a likeness of the subject (Lisa Gherardini, wife of a silk merchant in Florence). The *Mona Lisa* smiles and looks out at the viewer, inviting us to seek in her face, her pose, and the surrounding landscape a meditation on the human soul (**0.0.12**). Both the tea bowl and the portrait are great works of art, but they display very different ideas of what it means to be an artist.

We must also consider that artworks are not only the result of the work of those who made them, but are also influenced by the input of others: the patrons who employ an artist to make a work (see Box: Gertrude Stein as an Art Patron); the collectors who buy it; and the dealers and gallery owners who sell it. In contemporary times, both the publicist who presents artworks and the critic who reviews them in a newspaper, on TV, or on the Internet help to make an artist's work well known and desirable. All of these people, not just the artist,

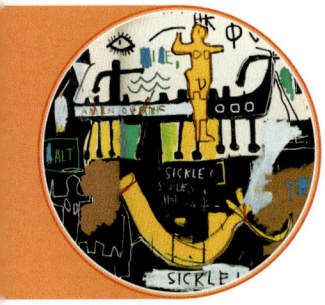

Jean-Michel Basquiat became famous for his graffiti; he later made canvas paintings critiquing racism, class injustices, and other social issues: see **3.10.14, p. 555**

Guilds: medieval associations of artists, craftsmen, or tradesmen
Academies: institutions training artists in both the theory of art and practical techniques

0.0.14 Jean-Michel Basquiat, *Untitled*, 1982. Acrylic, spray paint, and oilstick on canvas, 72 ⅛ × 68⅛". Collection Yusaku Maezawa

help to determine what art we see, and to some extent they can influence what we consider to be art. By controlling access to those who buy art, the places where art is displayed, and the media that inform the public about art and artists, they also often influence what kind of art an artist actually produces.

Fame and success do not always come in an artist's lifetime. Perhaps the most famous example of this is the Dutch painter Vincent van Gogh (1853–1890). In his ten years as an active artist, Van Gogh produced about 1,000 drawings, sketches, and watercolors, as well as around 1,250 other paintings. Very few people saw his work in his lifetime, however; he received only one favorable notice in a newspaper; his work was shown in only one exhibition; and he sold only one painting. Yet today his work is extraordinarily famous, it sells for millions of dollars, and in his native Netherlands an entire museum is devoted to his work.

The training of artists also helps to determine who makes art and what art is shown in galleries and museums. For example, traditional training for painters in China focused on the passing of artistic skill from a master to his students, who learned by copying his works and those of other famous artists. Only scholars and government officials could become professional painters. Other painters were considered to be just craftspeople whose work was of lower status. Similarly, in medieval Europe, only those trained in associations of craftsmen called **guilds** were allowed to make works of art. For example, there were guilds of carpenters, glassmakers, and goldsmiths. The system in Europe changed in the sixteenth century. Schools called **academies** were organized (first in Italy) to train artists in a very strict curriculum devised by specialized teachers. It was very difficult to succeed as an artist without being trained in an Academy. In modern Europe and North America, most practicing artists are trained in art schools, which are sometimes independent schools, but often part of a university or college that teaches many different subjects. It would be a mistake, however, to assume that artists must be formally trained: as we have seen in the case of Simon Rodia, non-professional, self-taught artists (often referred to as "naïve" or "outsider" artists) have always produced art that is just as admired.

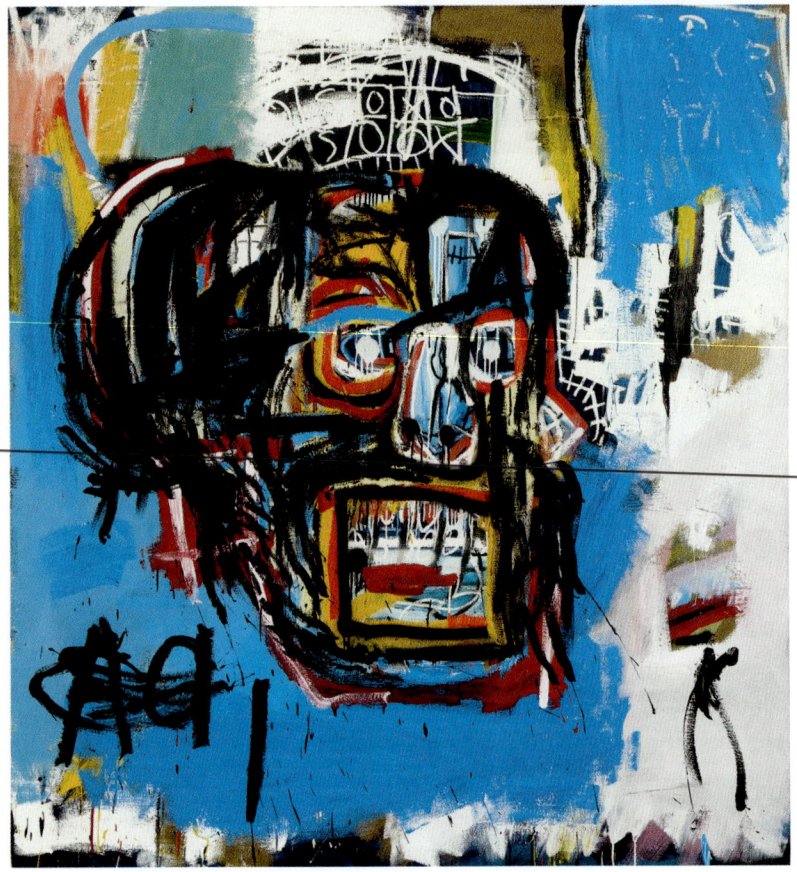

The Power and Value of Art

The American artist Jean-Michel Basquiat (1960–1988) set a record in May 2017 when his painting *Untitled* (**0.0.14**) sold for $110.5 million. What determines the value of an artwork? And why would someone pay so much money for a painting?

Yusaku Maezawa, the man who purchased *Untitled*, stated that he felt a strong connection to the artist and the painting: "Generationally, I relate to Basquiat's culture and the essence of his life story. Rather than monetary or investment value, I felt I had a personal responsibility to take care of this masterpiece and preserve it for the next generation."

In our modern society, art is often valued by its sale price, but there are many other ways of valuing it (see Perspectives on Art: The Value of Art to Keep Alive Knowledge and Culture, opposite). When we visit art museums and see

Perspectives on Art: Loongkoonan
The Value of Art to Keep Alive Knowledge and Culture

Loongkoonan (born c. 1910) is an Aboriginal from Western Australia who started painting in her nineties, depicting with complexity and beauty the land she lives in. Her paintings have won several prestigious awards in Australia, and exhibitions of her work have been shown as far away as the United States.

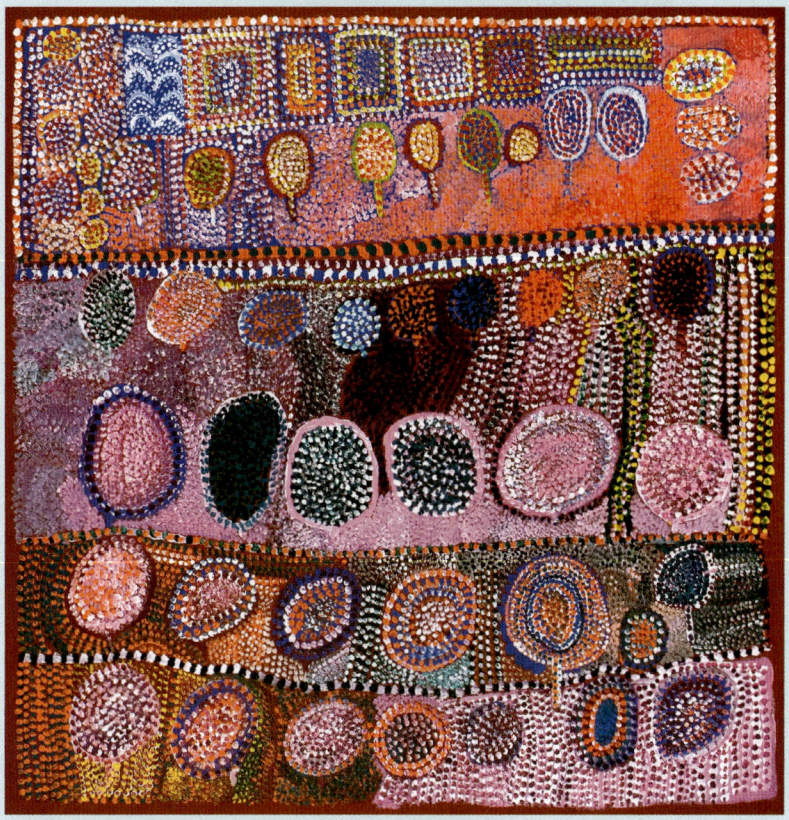

I am Loongkoonan and I am an elder of the Nyikina people. I am a proper Nyikina, one of the Yimadoowarra or riverside people. I am only Nyikina, not mixed up with anything else. My grandfather was proper Nyikina too. He died at Udialla. I was born at Mount Anderson Station near the Fitzroy River. When I was born, no one worried much about recording the births and deaths of Indigenous people, or teaching us to read or write. Research by my niece Margaret suggests that I am aged in my late nineties, but I am still very lively.

My parents worked on stations, and I was a good-sized girl when I started work mustering *kookanja* [sheep] and cooking in stock camps. Later on, I rode horses and mustered cattle too. Wet season was our holiday time for footwalking Nyikina Country with my grandparents....I have been a busy person all my life, no drinking, no smoking, just bush medicine....I had a good life on the stations, and three husbands.

Footwalking is the only proper way to learn about the Country, and remember it. That is how I got to know all of the bush tucker [wild food] and medicine. Nowadays I show young people how to live off the Country, and how to gather spinifex wax, which is our traditional glue for fixing stone points to spear shafts, patching *coolamons* [shallow vessels with curved sides], and making all kinds of things. Nyikina spinifex wax is really strong. It was so well known in the olden days that it was traded all over the Kimberley and desert....I still enjoy footwalking my country, showing the young people how to chase *barni* [goannas] and how to catch fish.

I was always used to working hard, and the chance came up for me to start painting with my friends, so I thought that I would give it a try....In my paintings I show all types of bush tucker—good tucker that we lived off in the bush....I paint Nyikina Country the same way eagles see Country when they are high up in the sky. I paint the bush foods and fruits and rivers of Nyikina Country.

I am happy that people like my paintings and that they get to understand more about Nyinkina Country and my life. I am happy to be an example for my community and people.

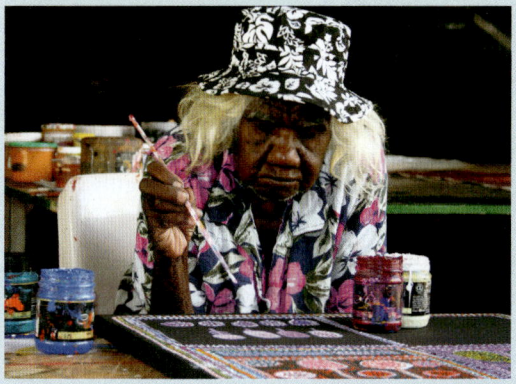

0.0.15a (above) Loongkoonan, *Bush Tucker Nyikina Country*, 2006. Acrylic on canvas. Collection of Diane and Dan Mossenson, Perth, Western Australia

0.0.15b (left) Loongkoonan at work in her studio in Derby, Western Australia, 2007

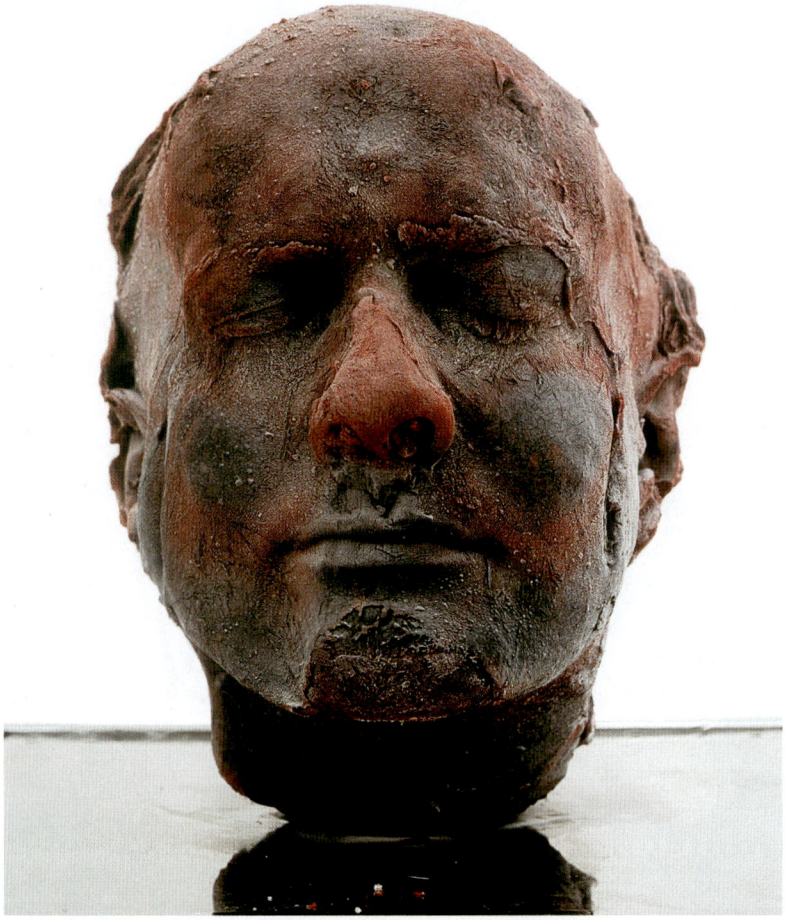

0.0.16 Marc Quinn, *Self*, 1991. Blood (artist's), stainless steel, Perspex, and refrigeration equipment, 81⅞ × 24 × 24¾". Private collection

Form: an object that can be defined in three dimensions (height, width, and depth)
Cast: a sculpture or artwork made by pouring a liquid (for example molten metal or plaster) into a mold
Monumental: having massive or impressive scale

artworks displayed inside glass cases or at a distance from the viewer, who must not touch, the care to preserve them in perfect condition is an indication that these works are highly valued. Sometimes a work is valued because it is very old or rare, or indeed unique.

In many societies, however, artworks were not made to be sold or displayed where they cannot be touched. As we have seen, the Japanese made fine tea bowls. These bowls were to be used as part of a ceremony, involving other fine objects, good conversation, and, of course, excellent tea. The tea bowl was valued because it formed part of a ritual that had social and spiritual significance. Similarly, in the African art section of many museums we can see masks displayed that were originally made to form part of a costume that, in turn, was used in a ceremony involving other costumed figures, music, and dancing. In other words, the mask often had some kind of spiritual or magic significance for its original creators: but they would have regarded it as holding this value only when used as intended, not when displayed in isolation in a museum.

An essential reason why we value art is because it has the power to tell us something important about ourselves, to confront us with ideas and feelings about the human condition that we recognize as true, but may otherwise struggle to understand fully. Art is a powerful means of self-expression because it enables us to give physical shape or **form** to thoughts and sensations and to see them for what they are. Marc Quinn (b. 1964) is a British artist whose art often not only focuses on the body but also deliberately uses his actual body as a basis for making the work. Since 1991, Quinn has been making a lifesize self-portrait of his head every five years, each time using between eight and ten pints of his blood, **cast** and then frozen by means of a refrigerating device (**0.0.16**). These works have an immediate impact, partly because they are made of blood, a substance we recognize as viscerally related to the life force and that we all depend on for survival: looking at *Self*, we naturally contemplate our own mortality and our fear of it. The effect is underscored by our knowledge that if the refrigerator should fail, the sculpture would dissolve.

Self is powerful too because when we look at such a raw portrait we instinctively compare its effect on us with how we appear to other people, which makes us think about self-image: who we really are, physically, and who we think ourselves to be. The use of the head and face, which are so intimately connected to our sense of identity, also make the image dramatically arresting, in a way that is similar to sculptures from ancient cultures, such as Africa and Oceania, where people have created carved heads, often on a **monumental** scale, that still resonate with compelling power. Despite its title, which could be interpreted as if it were only a portrait of the artist, this is a work that strikes a universal human chord as we view and recognize in it our own physical vulnerability.

So we see that price is, of course, not the only, or the most important, measure of the

Perspectives on Art: Tracy Chevalier
Art Inspires a Novel and a Movie

Art can have value as a source of inspiration. Tracy Chevalier is the author of the bestselling novel Girl with a Pearl Earring *(1999), which in turn inspired a movie (2003) starring Scarlett Johansson and Colin Firth. Tracy tells how her novel was inspired by a poster of the famous painting by the Dutch painter Johannes Vermeer.*

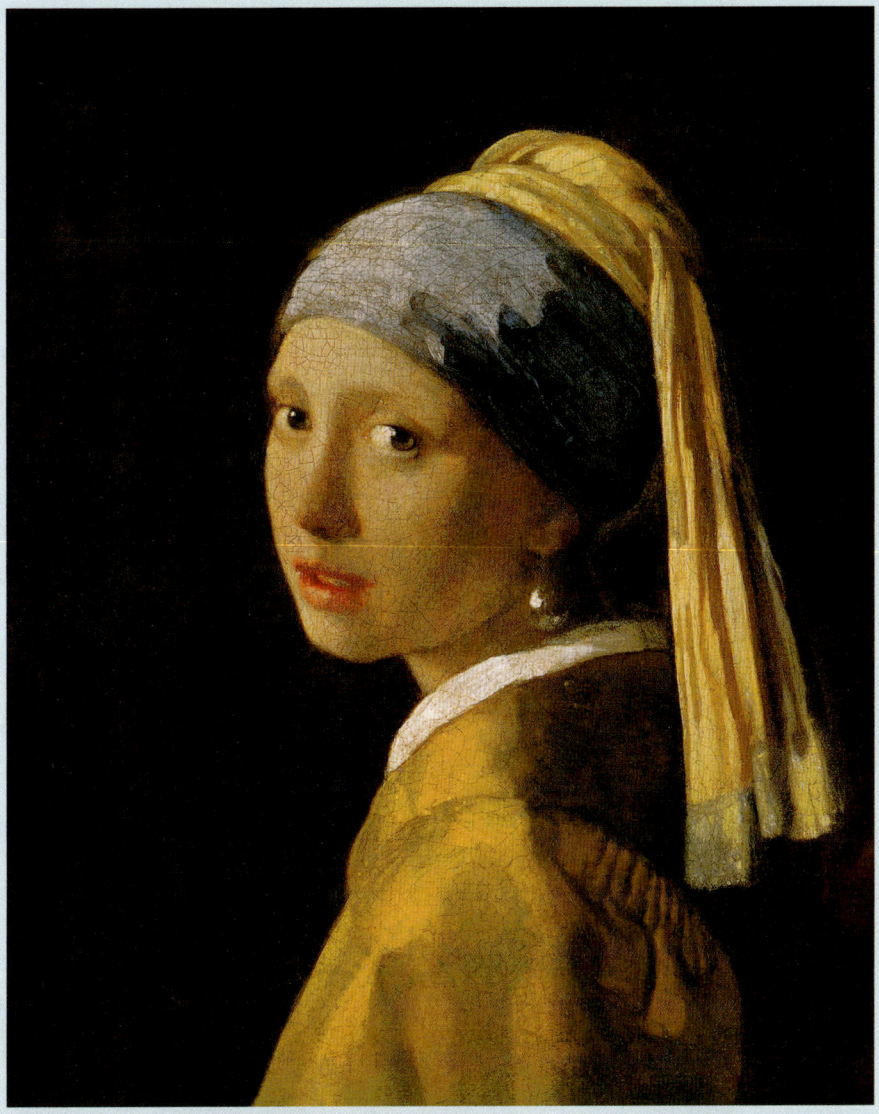

0.0.17 Johannes Vermeer, *Girl with a Pearl Earring*, c. 1665. Oil on canvas, 17½ × 15⅜". Mauritshuis, The Hague, The Netherlands

I first saw the painting *Girl with a Pearl Earring* (**0.0.17**) when I was nineteen and visiting my sister in Boston for spring break. She'd hung a poster of it in her apartment. I was so struck by it—the color! the light! the girl's look!—that the next day I bought a poster of it myself. That same poster has accompanied me for twenty-nine years, hanging in my bedroom or—as it does now—in my study.

Over the years I've hung many other paintings on my walls. But most art, even great art, loses its punch after a while. It becomes part of the space designated for it; it becomes decorative rather than challenging. It turns into wallpaper. Occasionally someone will ask a question about one of the paintings in my house, or I'll notice one's crooked and straighten it, and I'll look at it again and think, "Oh yeah, nice painting. I forgot about you."

Girl with a Pearl Earring is not like that. She has never become wallpaper. I have never grown tired or bored of her. I notice her all the time, even after twenty-nine years. Indeed, you'd think I'd have nothing left to say about the painting. But even after writing a whole novel about her, I still can't answer the most basic question about the girl: Is she happy or sad?

That is the painting's power. *Girl with a Pearl Earring* is unresolved, like a piece of music that stops on the penultimate chord. Vermeer draws us in with his technique—his remarkable handling of light and color—but he holds us with her. He has somehow managed the impossible, capturing a flickering moment in a permanent medium. You would think that, with the paint static, the girl would be too. But no, her mood is always changing, for we ourselves are different each time we look at her. She reflects us, and life, in all its variations. Few paintings do that so well, which is why *Girl with a Pearl Earring* is a rare masterpiece.

value of an artwork. We might place a high value on a work because it is aesthetically pleasing or because its creation involved great skill. This can be true even if there is no possibility of our owning it. Many museums organize large exhibitions of the work of famous artists because they know that great numbers of people will pay to see the work. Enthusiasts will travel long distances, even to other continents, to visit such exhibitions. In 2012, for example, 758,000 people visited an exhibition of the work of various Old Master artists, including Vermeer's famous *Girl with a Pearl Earring* (see Perspectives on Art: Art Inspires a Novel and a Movie, p. 33), as well as paintings by Rembrandt, Frans Hals, and Anthony van Dyck at the Tokyo National Museum, Japan.

Protest and Censorship of Art

Art can be a form of expression and communication so powerful that those who are challenged or offended by it wish to censor it. If we examine the history of the censorship of art, we see that people have found many reasons to attack, destroy, or prevent the display of artworks. Art may be censored because it challenges the politically or economically powerful; because some consider it pornographic; because it offends religious beliefs; or because it represents values that somebody considers offensive or improper.

Probably the most famous contemporary artist who has suffered for his work and his opinions is Chinese artist Ai Weiwei (b. 1957). Ai's father was a revered Chinese poet and a member of the ruling Communist Party, and Ai was involved in the design of the stadium for the Beijing Olympics in 2008. He was therefore, in some ways, an establishment figure in China. But 2008 was also the year of a devastating earthquake during which several schools collapsed, killing many children. Their parents complained that poor construction, because of official corruption, was responsible for their children's deaths. Ai made a memorial to the dead out of children's backpacks and exhibited it in Münich, Germany. In January 2011 Chinese government officials ordered the demolition of his studio and in April Ai was arrested for "economic crimes."

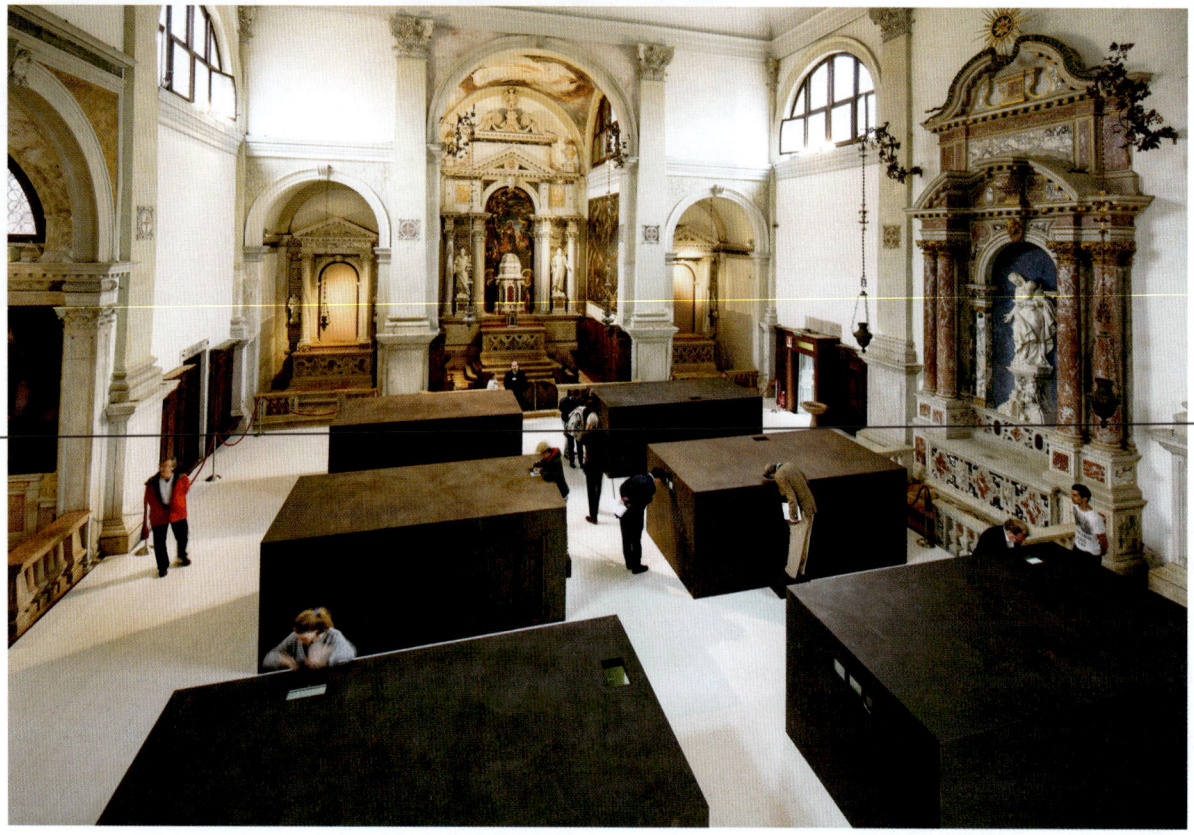

0.0.18a Ai Weiwei, *S.A.C.R.E.D.*, a six-part work composed of (i) *S upper*, (ii) *A ccusers*, (iii) *C leansing*, (iv) *R itual*, (v) *E ntropy*, (vi) *D oubt*, 2011–13. Six dioramas in fiberglass and iron, 148½ × 77½ × 58½". Installed in the Church of Sant'Antonin, Venice, Italy for the Venice Biennale 2013

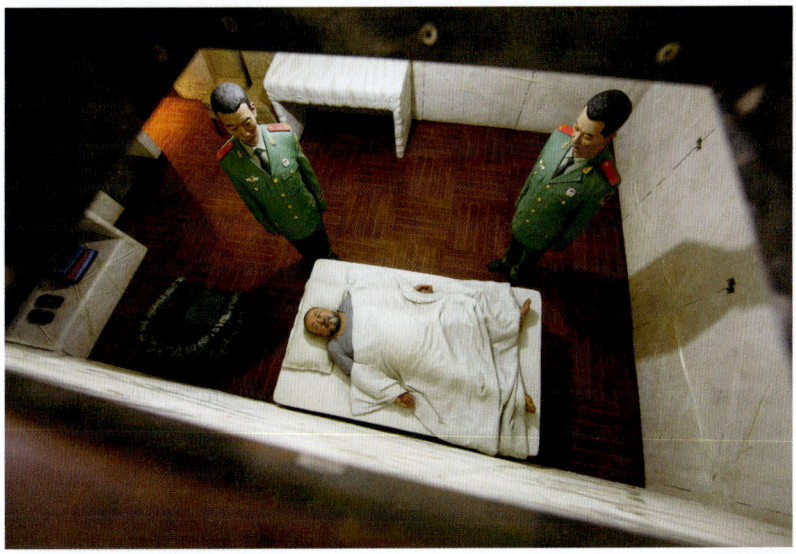

0.0.18b Ai Weiwei, *E ntropy* (detail), from *S.A.C.R.E.D.*, 2011–13

Ai used his imprisonment as inspiration for an artwork. Ai told a reporter that for the eighty-one days of his imprisonment, "I memorized every crack in the ceiling, every mark on the wall. I'm an artist and architect, so I have a good memory for these things." After his release Ai had six iron boxes, roughly half-scale models of his cell, installed in a disused **Baroque** church in Venice, Italy, at the Biennale exhibition (**0.0.18a**). He named each box (*S upper, A ccusers, C leansing, R itual, E ntropy, D oubt*) and titled the work *S.A.C.R.E.D.*, from the initial letters of the box titles. Viewers could step onto a block to look through a small slit in the wall to view a scene from Ai's captivity as if they were themselves guards checking on him. In *E ntropy* (**0.0.18b**), viewers see detailed figures of Ai asleep and two guards who stand by his bed.

Other scenes show him eating, being interrogated, taking a shower, walking the length of his cell, and using the toilet, all under guard in extremely cramped quarters. Ai is considered by many people around the world to be a hero, yet his artwork is highly skeptical, even irreverent. At the same time it is informed by Chinese history and is of great integrity. In addition to sculptures, photographs, and videos, Ai has also made a music video and inspired a play. The power of art pervades Ai's work and he willingly uses it to share his personal message, even though his work cannot be shown in China and he is forbidden from leaving the country.

Baroque: European artistic and architectural style of the late sixteenth to early eighteenth century, characterized by extravagance and emotional intensity
Content: the meaning, message, or feeling expressed in a work of art
Representation(al): art that depicts figures and objects so that we recognize what is represented

Studying Art

Why take a course that teaches you how to look at art? Surely we all have eyes and we all see the same thing when we look at a work of art, so we can decide what we like or dislike about it? In fact, it is not quite that simple. Our interpretations of works of art may differ from other people's according to our perceptions, beliefs, and ideas. Art is also a form of language; one that can communicate with us even more powerfully than written language. Art communicates so directly with our senses (of sight, touch, even smell and sound) that it helps us to understand our own experiences. By learning to see, we experience new sensations and ideas that expand our horizons beyond our daily lives.

Content

Art, as we have already seen, is a form of communication using visual language. All communication has a purpose, a message—in other words, **content**. In art, content is rarely just about subject matter, but instead about underlying meanings expressed in the way the subject is shown. To understand the content of a work of art, one must first identify its subject, consider the context in which the artwork was made, and then perform a formal analysis (study the work's arrangement of the visual elements and principles.)

Subject Matter

The subject matter of a work offers preliminary information about its content. As we have seen, although the four works of art at the beginning of this chapter all had a river as their subject, the content and purpose of each work was different. Of course, there are many artworks in which the subject matter itself is not clear, and many have no title (indeed, there are artworks that the artist specifically designates as "Untitled")—but such artworks still have content. This point will be clearer if we understand the concepts of representation, non-objectivity, and abstraction. Works of art may be **representational** (depicting objects or people so that we can

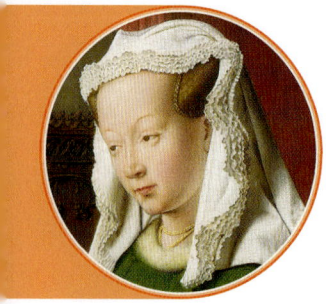

This detail from the famous *Arnolfini Portrait* is representational, with its attention to realistic texture and details: see **3.6.8a, p. 466**

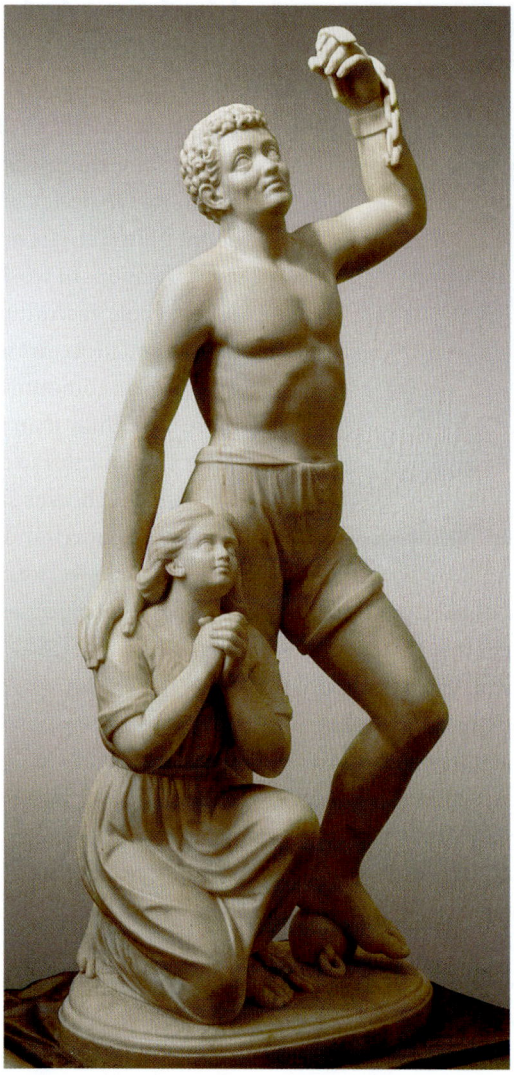

0.0.19 Edmonia Lewis, *Forever Free*, 1867. Marble, 41¼ × 22 × 17". Howard University Art Gallery, Washington, D.C.

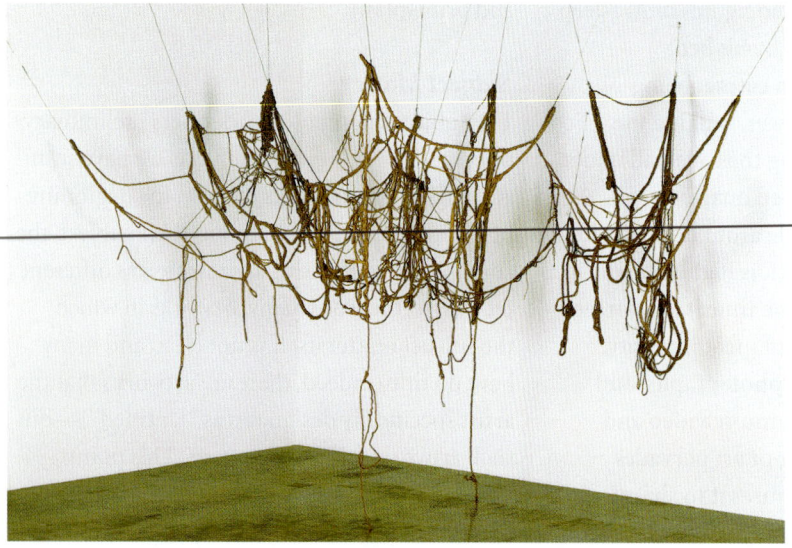

0.0.20 Eva Hesse, *Untitled (Rope Piece)*, 1969–70. Latex, rope, string, and wire, dimensions variable. Whitney Museum of American Art, New York

recognize them), or **non-objective** (depicting subject matter that is unrecognizable). Most, however, lie somewhere in between, depending on their degree of **abstraction**. These concepts help us to analyse what the artist had in mind or wished to communicate to us when creating the work.

For example, the marble sculpture made by Edmonia Lewis (**0.0.19**) is a representational artwork because anyone looking at it would agree that there is a man standing with a chain around his wrist and a woman kneeling beside him with her hands held together. The proportions of the figures, and the details of their expressions and clothing, are all made by the artist to represent reality as closely as possible. Representational artworks are also called objective, meaning that everyone agrees on the subject matter.

Non-objective works of art are deliberately not recognizable as something we might see in the world around us. Eva Hesse's *Untitled (Rope Piece)* (**0.0.20**) is an example of non-objective art. The materials used to make the artwork, especially the rope, may be identifiable, but the subject matter is not. Non-objective art is, by definition, subjective: without contextual information about the artist's intentions or experiences (see p. 37), we each determine our own interpretations of what the artwork means or communicates—or whether it means anything at all.

The concepts of representational and non-objective may be thought of as two endpoints in a continuum of abstraction. "To abstract" means to extract something or to emphasize it. Abstraction in art refers to the ways artists can emphasize, distort, simplify, or arrange the formal (visual) elements of an artwork. A representational work, such as the sculpture by Edmonia Lewis, contains very little abstraction, while Eva Hesse's work is highly abstract.

Allan Houser's *Reverie* is representational because we can recognize two faces, one larger and one smaller (**0.0.21**). We also interpret the swoop of the form downward from the larger face to be a back, and that the smaller face probably represents a baby being held in its mother's arms. The mother's entire body (her back, arms, and knees) is, however, abstracted to be one smooth form in which to cradle the baby. The baby's body is just a bump on the lap of the mother, as if it is swaddled tightly. We can interpret the subject and form of the sculpture because the detailed representation of the figures' faces enables us to see a mother holding her baby. *Reverie* is a representational work with a considerable degree of abstraction.

Context

How can we interpret a work that is several centuries old and comes from a completely different culture than our own? Some research will help us to learn more about such an artwork by understanding its context. Context includes, for example, information about the society in which it was created: how was the society organized and ruled, and who ruled it? Context also includes information about the economics and religion of the people who created it; specific details about the person who ordered it made; and the status of the artist who created it.

If we know more about the context in which a work of art was made, we can learn more about it than we probably expected at first glance. For example, the title of Edmonia Lewis's sculpture is *Forever Free* (opposite), and we learn from context that it was made in 1867, four years after Abraham Lincoln's Emancipation Proclamation, which freed slaves. We then better understand that the work expresses the sense of extraordinary relief felt by two recently freed slaves , as well as a sense of hope for the future. Context often helps to enrich even more our understanding of non-objective works, which may not be easy to decipher otherwise. When Hesse was creating *Untitled (Rope Piece)* (opposite), she had recently been diagnosed with a brain tumor, from which she died later that year. Elements of her works were often seen as relating to parts of the human body, and *Untitled (Rope Piece)* does look like the intestines, veins, or other inner elements. As in this piece, she frequently used latex, which feels like human skin. Latex deteriorates, just as the human body does. Hesse described this work as representing the chaos of life and death.

Caspar David Friedrich's (1774–1840) painting *Abbey Among Oak Trees* (**0.0.22**) appears to represent precisely what the title describes. The artist has painted what initially seems simply to be the ruins of a Gothic church flanked by two large oaks where the church's towers would have been. The content of the work becomes clearer, however, when we consider the context of Friedrich's world. He was a German **Romantic** painter. Romantic painters often infused scenes of nature with spiritual meaning. Friedrich was also a Lutheran who believed that one's connection with God

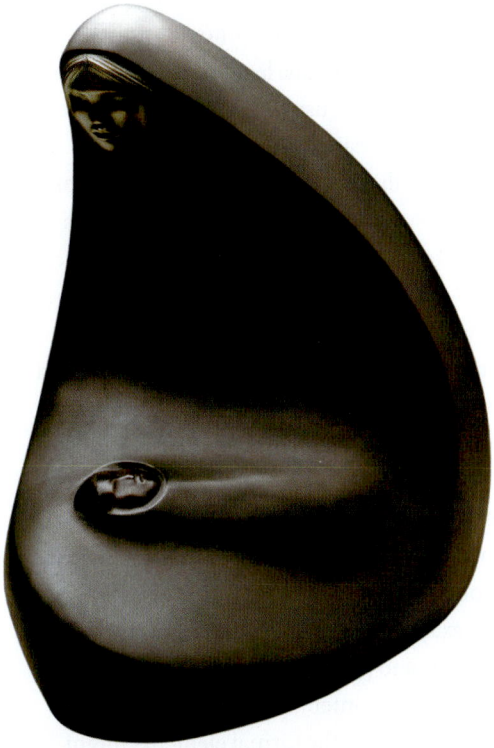

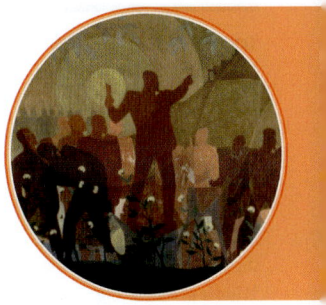

Aaron Douglas's painting *Aspects of Negro Life...* is representational, but also involves a considerable degree of abstraction: see **3.9.23, p. 537**

0.0.21 (left) Allan Houser, *Reverie*, 1981. Bronze, 25 × 23 × 13", edition of 10. Allan Houser Archives

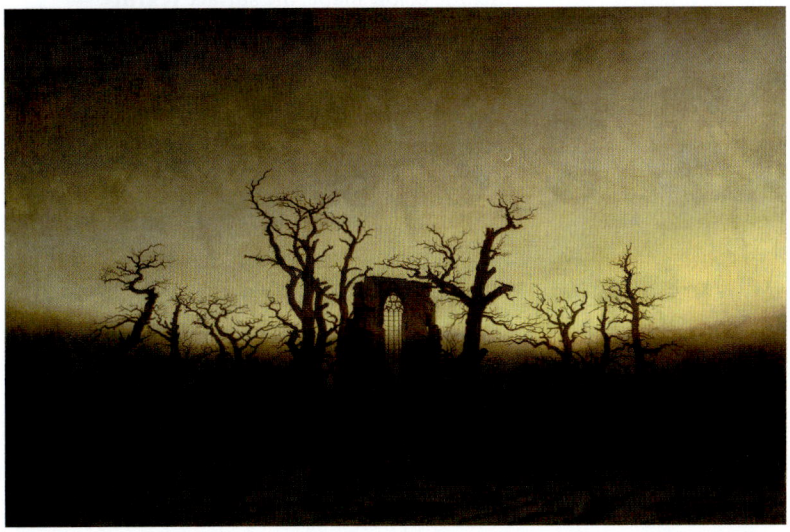

0.0.22 Caspar David Friedrich, *Abbey Among Oak Trees*, 1809–10. Oil on canvas, 43½ × 67⅜". Alte Nationalgalerie, Berlin, Germany

Non-objective, non-objectivity: art that does not depict a recognizable subject
Abstraction: the degree to which an image is altered from an easily recognizable subject
Romantic, Romanticism: movement in nineteenth-century European culture, concerned with the power of the imagination and greatly valuing intense feeling

Texture: the surface quality of a work, for example fine/coarse, detailed/lacking in detail
Contrast: a drastic difference between such elements as color or value (lightness/darkness) when they are presented together
Middle ground: the part of a work between the foreground and the background
Atmospheric perspective: use of shades of color and clarity to create the illusion of depth. Closer objects have warmer tones and clear outlines, while objects set further away are cooler and become hazy
Space: the distance between identifiable points or planes
Value: the lightness or darkness of a plane or area
Organic: having irregular forms and shapes, as though derived from living organisms
Two-dimensional: having height and width
Emphasis: the principle of drawing attention to a particular content within a work
Foreground: the part of a work depicted as nearest to the viewer

survives even without the intervention of churches and religious leaders. Knowing that Friedrich's works usually contained religious meaning, one can see the spiritual quality created by the lighting in the painting. Upon closer inspection, it is clear that the landscape is covered with crosses marking burial sites, and a procession of people can be seen in the snow. Even though the religious structure is gone, people still come to worship. Because of his beliefs, Friedrich has infused the cold wintry scene with spiritual light.

Formal Analysis

Finally, since art communicates with the viewer through vision, we should introduce briefly how examining the arrangement of the visual elements and principles of an artwork helps us to analyse its content.

For example, the formal elements might include color, shape, the surface **texture** (perhaps rough or smooth), and so on. It is worth pointing out that form has another meaning in art: it describes an artwork that can be defined in three dimensions (height, width, and depth). For the purposes of understanding formal analysis, however, we are concerned here with form in the sense of understanding the use of the formal elements in an artwork.

When we communicate in writing or speech, our communication consists of a vocabulary of individual words that are structured by rules of grammar that enable us to determine meaning. Similarly, in art, the elements (like vocabulary) are organized by the principles (the visual equivalent of grammar). In Part 1 of this book we will examine in depth the elements and principles of art: color; form; line; mass; motion and time; shape; space; texture; value; volume. In addition, we will discuss the principles: balance; contrast; emphasis; focal point; pattern; proportion; rhythm; scale; unity; variety.

Artists can utilize the elements and principles in many ways to communicate ideas, emotions, beliefs, social or political convictions, and sensations, visually: in fact there is almost no limit to what an artist can achieve by combining creative imagination with the elements and principles of art.

A brief formal analysis of a painting by British artist David Hockney (b. 1937) will show us how he used the visual language of the elements and principles to create an apparently simple artwork that in fact reflects on and expresses important events and complex emotions that were unresolved in his life at the time (**0.0.23**).

Hockney had visited Los Angeles for the first time in 1964, where he lived in the Hollywood Hills. He was fascinated by the colors, the sun, and the landscape of the city, so different from his native Yorkshire in the north of England. Color plays an important part in this painting, as it did in all of Hockney's Los Angeles works. The light, sunny gold of the tiles around the pool **contrasts** both with the dazzling bright blue of the part of the pool in the **middle ground** and with the lush greens and sparkling aquamarine of the hills immediately behind. The hills furthest from us are painted in lighter, hazier colors, using **atmospheric perspective** to convey a sense of distance. Together with the white, wavy lines suggesting the motion of rippling water, in which we can sense the movement of the swimmer below, the artist thus creates what appears initially to be a calm and beautiful scene, a kind of untroubled paradise.

The portrait also conveys a sense of **space**. The pool and the standing figure on the right occupy more than half the surface, overlapping the hills, behind. The light **value** of the tiles around the pool contrasts with the much darker greens of the nearby hills, emphasizing how close the viewer is to the pool. Hockney intensifies this sense of being on the edge through his use of shape. The sharp, geometric angles and shapes formed by the pool contrast with the softer, **organic** shapes of the hills. The further the hills stretch away toward the horizon, the more they lack contrast, detail, and definition. Even on the **two-dimensional** surface of the canvas, this gives us a powerful sense of distance: and this, as we look more closely at the work, is a clue to the emotional predicament it seeks to express.

The first figure in the painting that the artist **emphasizes** is the man on the right, in reality the artist's ex-lover, Peter Schlesinger. Our eyes

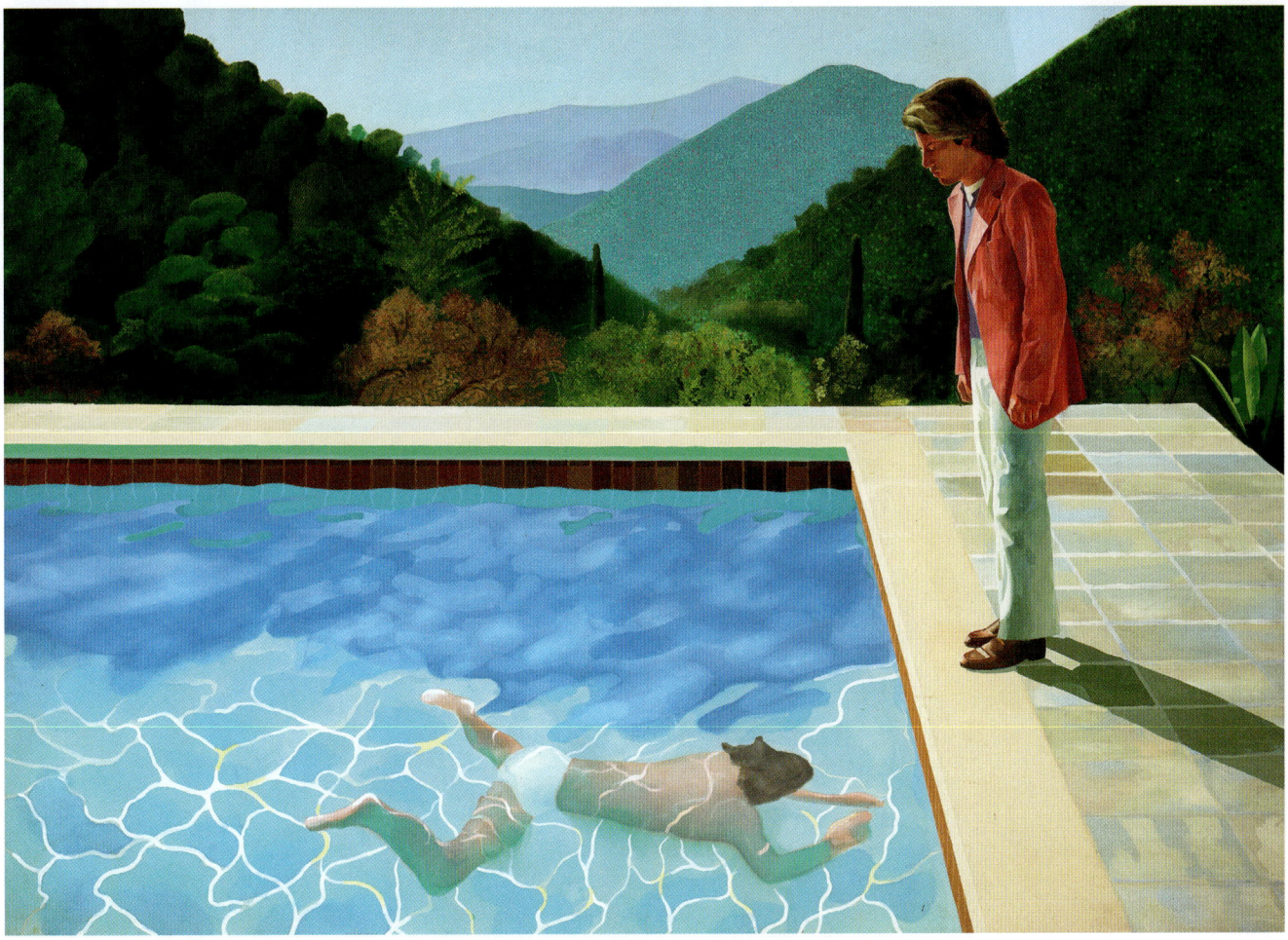

0.0.23 David Hockney, *Portrait of an Artist (Pool with two figures)*, 1972. Acrylic on canvas, 7 × 10'. Art Gallery of New South Wales, Sydney, Australia

are drawn to him by the red of his jacket and also because he is the largest figure in the work. Because he is in the **foreground**, Peter appears to be taller than the hills in the **background**: the artist uses **scale** to focus our attention on him and to bring him close to the viewer. Line also plays a part in making him the **focal point** of the painting: the lines of the far edge of the pool seem to point to Peter's figure, as do those of the tiles he stands on. In turn, Peter's gaze toward the water forms a kind of invisible line (artists call this an **implied line**) down to the swimmer in the pool, John St. Clair, a friend of Hockney, whose face is concealed underwater, and who forms the second area of emphasis in the painting.

Once we combine the formal aspects of this painting with the context of the artist's life, we arrive at the content, or meaning, of the work.

Painted in the aftermath of the ending of his relationship with Peter Schlesinger, Hockney was creating a portrait of a lost love. Peter stands still and reserved by the edge of the pool in the bright sun, gazing down at the swimmer. As we perceive him from the same viewpoint as the artist, his figure conveys a certain detachment, an absence or loss of emotion, which suggests the end of their connection. At the same time, the fractured surface of the pool, in its watery dissolve, communicates a sense of things breaking up, and of deep sadness and loss beneath the brightly colored surface of this deceptively tranquil scene. Finally, the pale, enigmatic figure of the swimmer, heading toward Peter, who looks at him rather than at us, intimates that he may already have his eyes on the future—from which the artist is excluded.

As such examples show, if we learn how to look at art, and appreciate the skill involved in its making, we will discover how fascinating and even exciting it can be. This book aims to help you not just to get a good grade in your course, but also to begin a lifetime of enjoying and being inspired by art.

Background: the part of a work depicted furthest from the viewer's space, often behind the main subject matter
Scale: the size of an object or artwork relative to another object or artwork, or to a system of measurement
Focal point: the center of interest or activity in a work of art, often drawing the viewer's attention to the most important element
Implied line: a line not actually drawn but suggested by elements in the work

Art is a form of visual language, and much as we use vocabulary and grammar to communicate verbally, artists use a visual vocabulary (the elements of art) and rules similar to grammar (the principles of art). When we study an artwork, we can use the same elements and principles to analyse the work: a process called visual analysis. In this part you will learn about the elements and principles and will be shown how to apply them in a visual analysis. You will also learn how to use two other concepts when you analyse a work of art: style and content.

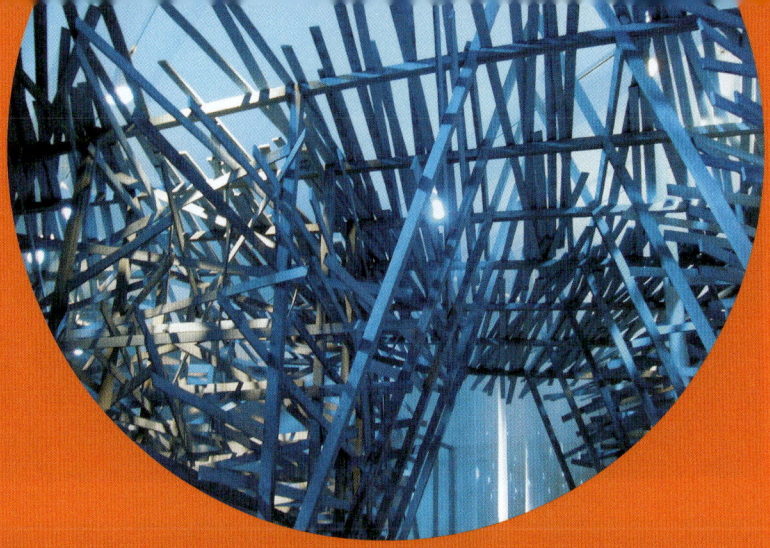

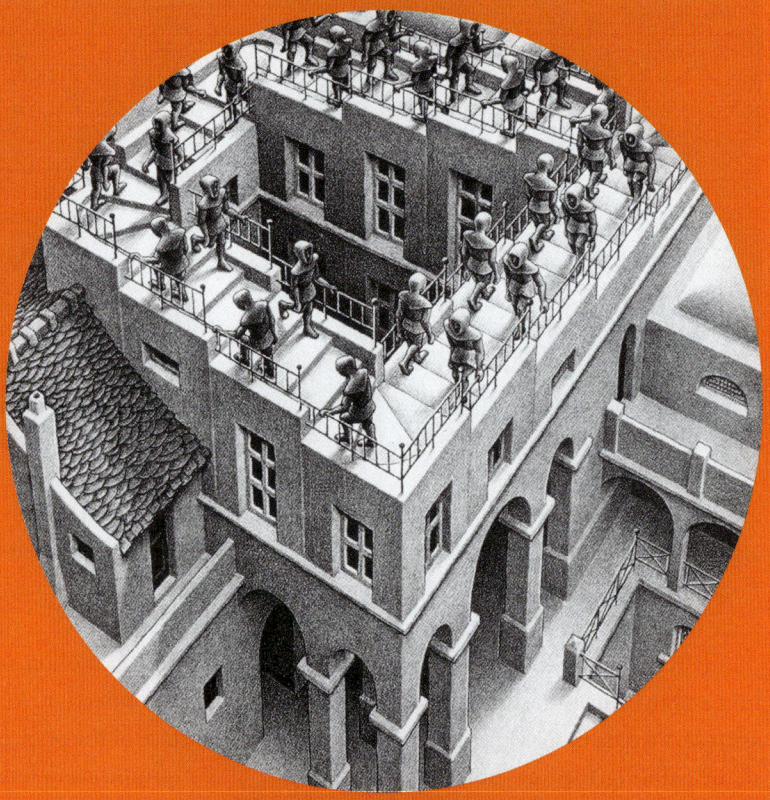

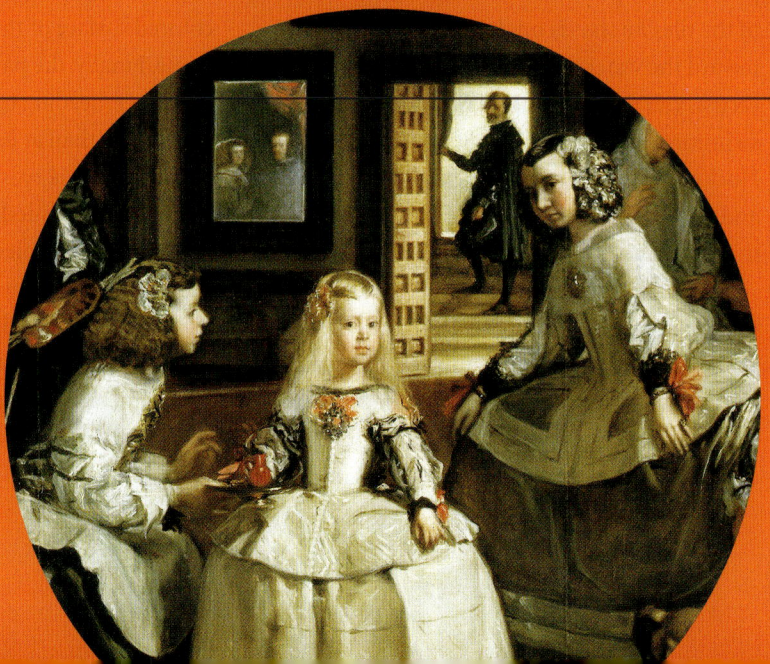

Part 1

Fundamentals

The ten elements of art are:

Color
Form
Line
Mass
Motion and Time
Shape
Space
Texture
Value
Volume

The ten principles of art are:

Balance
Contrast
Emphasis
Focal Point
Pattern
Proportion
Rhythm
Scale
Unity
Variety

1.1 Line, Shape, and the Principle of Contrast

Elements of art: the basic vocabulary of art—line, shape, form, volume, mass, texture, value (lightness/darkness), space, color, and motion and time
Principles: the principles, or "grammar" of art—contrast, unity, variety, balance, scale, proportion, focal point, emphasis, pattern, and rhythm—describe the ways the elements of art are arranged in an artwork
Line: a mark, or implied mark, between two endpoints
Shape: a two-dimensional area, the boundaries of which are defined by lines or suggested by changes in color or value
Two-dimensional: having height and width
Three-dimensional: having height, width, and depth
Contrast: a drastic difference between such elements as color or value (lightness/darkness) when they are presented together
Engraving: a printmaking technique where the artist gouges or scratches the image into the surface of the printing plate
Outline: the outermost line or implied line of an object or figure, by which it is defined or bounded
Plane: a flat, two-dimensional surface on which an artist can create a drawing or painting. Planes can also be implied in a composition by areas that face toward, parallel to, or away from a light source

Just as we use the principles of grammar to turn vocabulary into sentences, so the language of art consists of **elements** (the basic vocabulary of art) and **principles** (the grammar that artists apply to turn the elements into art). The principles of design are a set of rules that explain how the elements of a work of art are organized.

In this chapter we will look at **line** and **shape**, basic elements of any kind of artwork, and we will principally consider how they function in examples of **two-dimensional** art. (In chapter 1.2, we will focus more on **three-dimensional** art.) We will then see how to apply them to the understanding of works of art by using the principle of **contrast**.

Two-dimensional art is a remarkably elegant way to express ideas and share our mental pictures of the world. Two-dimensional art can be measured only by height and width, and is most often associated with a flat surface—for example, a drawing of a triangle. It can be made very simply, with a pencil on paper. The first plans for the grandest of designs can be drawn up on a napkin with a few squiggles of a pen. As well as drawing and painting, two-dimensional arts include the graphic arts: printmaking, graphic design, and photography.

In contrast to two-dimensional art, three-dimensional art can be measured by height, width, and *depth*, and it exists in real space. Because two-dimensional art has only height and width, any depth that we see when we look at a flat artwork—for example, a drawing of a pyramid—is an illusion: it exists solely in our imagination.

Line

Lines are the most fundamental element that artists use. They exist in almost every work of art or design. Lines organize the visible world. Without line, an artist hardly knows where to begin.

The ancient designs known as the Nazca Lines, on the high desert plains of Peru, include some of the most unusual drawings in the world. They show us much about line and shape.

In the spider "drawing," lines define the shape onto the landscape at such an enormous scale that it can be seen only from the sky (**1.1.1**). (In fact, the Nazca Lines were first discovered in modern times by overflying commercial aircraft.) Unlike most drawings, the Nazca Lines cannot be rolled up in a tube or carried off in a portfolio. First of all, they are too huge: the spider shown here is 150 ft. long; side by side, two such spiders would nearly fill up a football field. Second, they are hardly "drawings" at all. Instead, they were made by scraping off the layer of dark gravel that covers the flat Nazca plain, to expose the white gypsum that lies just beneath the surface. In this sense, they are a sort of incision or **engraving**.

The lines are mysterious. Why would such huge designs, so huge they can hardly be understood at ground level, be made? What was their purpose? The designs resemble symbolic decorations found on local pottery made at least 1,300 years ago. We do not know what they were used for, but their size suggests they played an important part in the lives of the

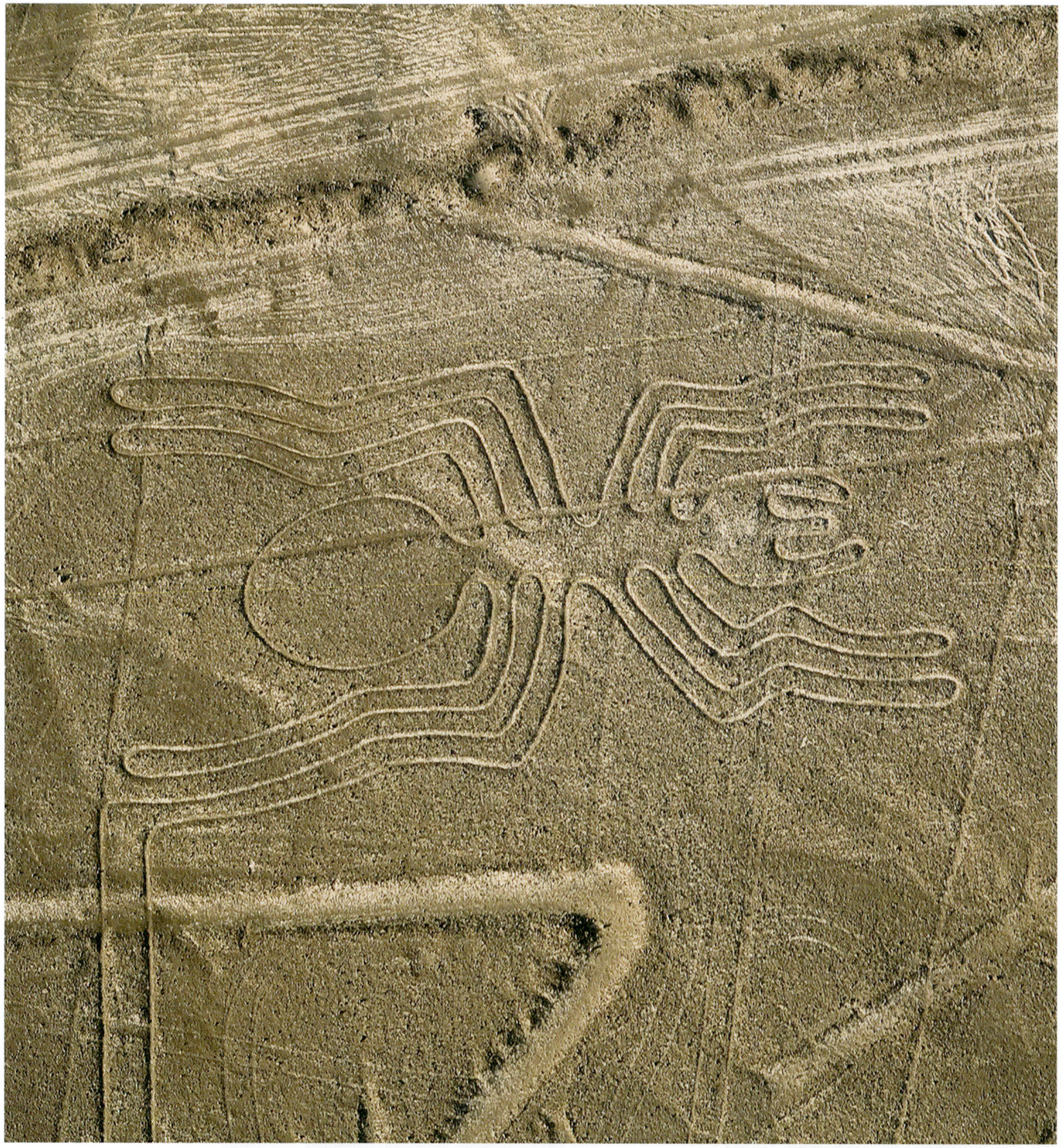

1.1.1 Spider, *c.* 500 BCE–500 CE. Width 150'. Nazca, Peru

people who made them. How were they made? There are postholes found at intervals along their edges—perhaps strings from post to post formed guidelines for the scraping of the pathway. Notably, the Nazca Lines do not cross over themselves—in the photograph, the parallel tracks intersecting with the spider were made by off-road vehicles. The lines define the **outline** of the shape.

Definition of Line

The variety of different types of line is virtually infinite. A line can be a mark that connects two points, like the strings that must have run from post to post at Nazca. Artists can use lines to define the boundaries between **planes** in a two-dimensional work of art: notice how the lines at Nazca divide one area of the gravel surface of the land from another. In two-dimensional art, line

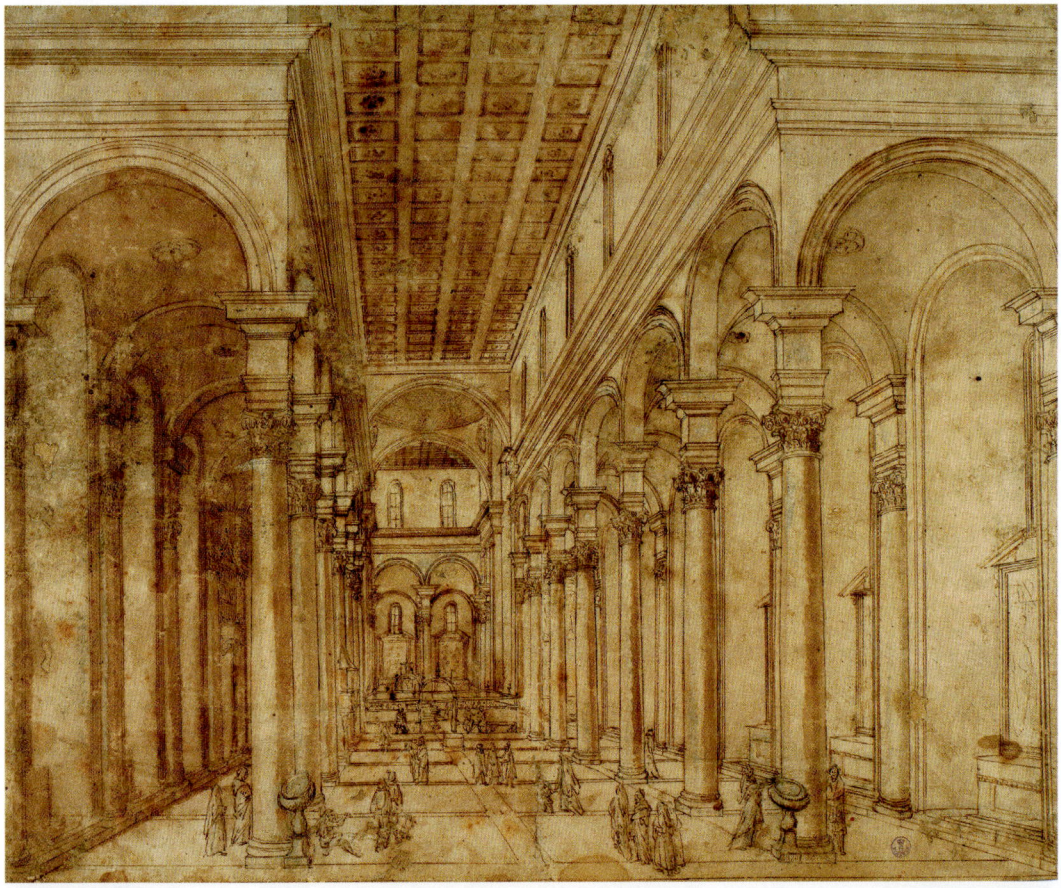

1.1.2a Giovanni Antonio Dosio, *Church of Santo Spirito at Florence* (n. 6746 Ar), *c.* 1576–90. Pen and watercolor on yellowish paper, traces of black chalk, 14⅜ × 18". Department of Prints and Drawings, Uffizi Gallery, Florence, Italy

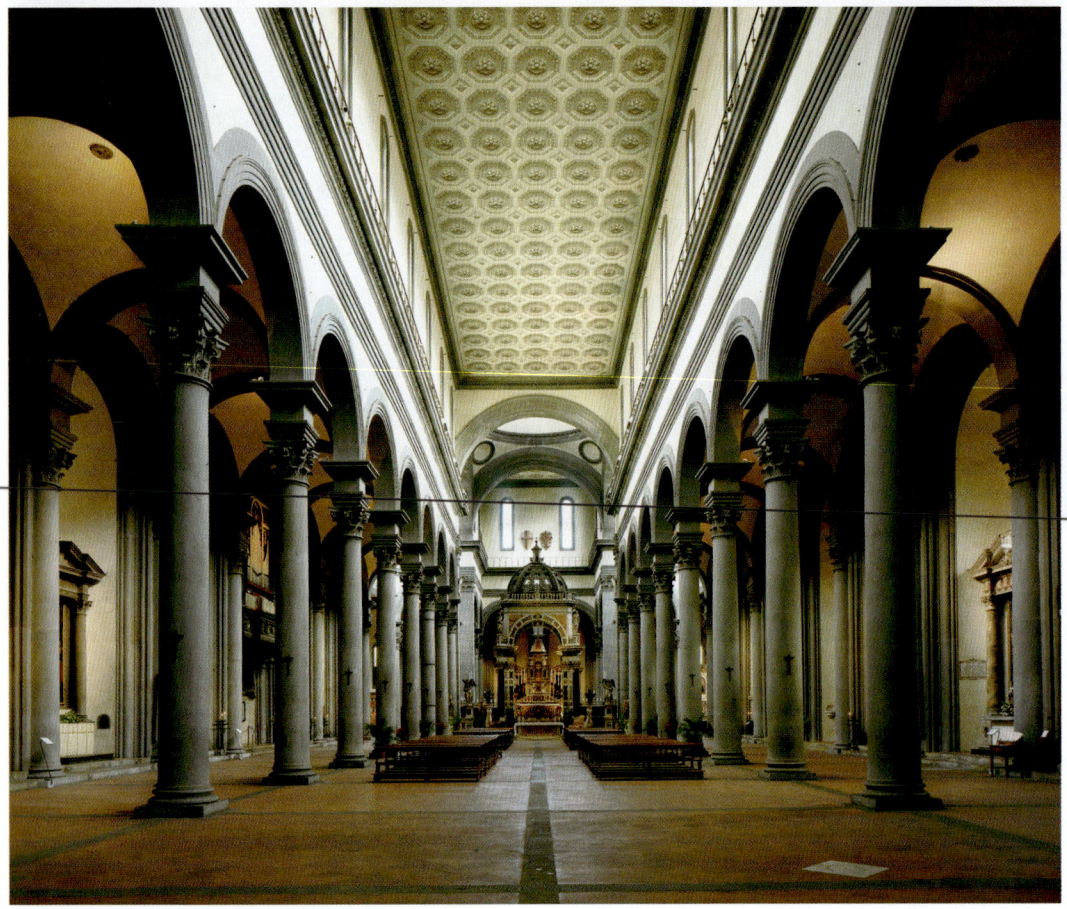

1.1.2b Filippo Brunelleschi, Santo Spirito, 1436–82, inside view toward the apse. Florence, Italy

Texture: the surface quality of a work, for example fine/coarse, detailed/lacking in detail
Space: the distance between identifiable points or planes
Volume: the space filled or enclosed by a three-dimensional figure or object

can also define shapes (in this case, the shape of a giant spider). A line may direct our eyes to look at something the artist particularly wants us to notice. Finally, line can convey a sense of movement and energy, even the movement of a giant spider.

In Figures **1.1.2a** and **1.1.2b** we see a drawing, the *Church of Santo Spirito at Florence*, and a modern photograph of the Church of Santo Spirito in Florence, Italy. The drawing is by the architect and antiquarian Giovanni Antonio Dosio (1533–1609) and shows a church designed by the Italian artist and architect Filippo Brunelleschi (1377–1446). In the drawing, Dosio uses line to differentiate one part of the building from another and to give an illusory sense of depth. Although line is two-dimensional, by using it the artist points out where one plane meets another, and creates an illusion of three dimensions. Line is thus a tool for describing, in a simple way and in two dimensions, the boundaries and edges of three-dimensional surfaces. For example, Dosio's drawing uses line (rather than lightness, darkness, and **texture**) to define where the flat ceiling at the top of the building ends and the walls begin. The artist was thus creating a visual record so that others interested in historic buildings could see in detail how the church was designed.

In the photo of the church, we see the dividing line between the ceiling and the vertical walls because of the changes in lightness, darkness, and texture. The lines in the drawing therefore represent the places where, in the real building, the different planes meet.

Some of Dosio's lines also create a sense of surface and depth. The artist accentuates the patterned surface of the ceiling using lines that increase in frequency to define and differentiate the ceiling from the walls. Dosio also uses converging lines to help the viewer visualize the architectural **space**. If you compare the drawing with the photo, you can see how accurately the artist was able to communicate, with line, how the building actually looks.

The following sections of this chapter will show us some of the different types, functions, and expressions of line:

Types of line:
- contour line
- implied line

Functions of line:
- directing the viewer's gaze
- communicating an idea

Different feelings or ideas that can be expressed by line:
- lines can regulate and control
- lines can express freedom and passion
- lines can be regular or irregular

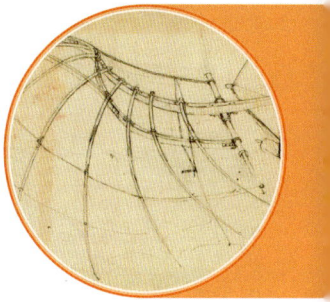

Leonardo da Vinci's *Drawing for a wing of a flying machine* is an example of lines that organize and illustrate an idea: see **2.1.1, p. 192**

Types and Functions of Line

Contour Line

A contour is an edge or profile of an object, but is not necessarily the complete outline of a shape. Contour lines can suggest a **volume** in space by giving us clues about the changing character of a surface.

Woman Seated in an Armchair by the French artist Henri Matisse (1869–1954) is drawn almost entirely using contour lines (**1.1.3**). The confident line that sets the boundary between

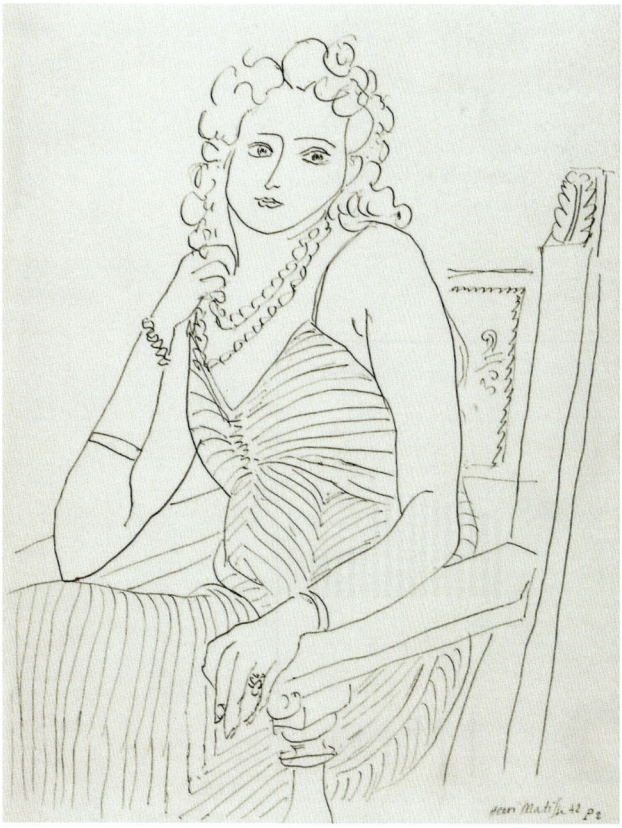

1.1.3 Henri Matisse, *Themes and Variations*, series P, *Woman Seated in an Armchair*, pl. 2, 1942. Pen and ink, 19¾ × 15¾". Musée des Beaux-Arts, Lyons, France

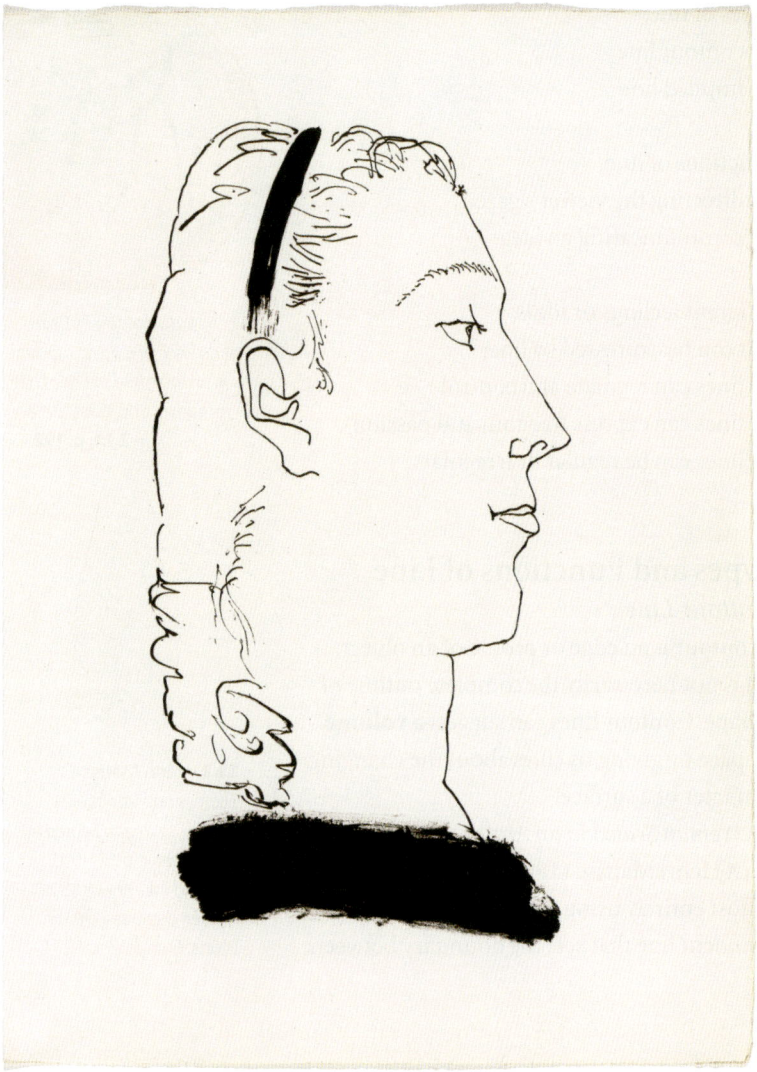

1.1.4 Pablo Picasso, *Blonde Woman in Profile*, plate, folio 16 from the illustrated book *Vingt poëmes*, 1947. Lift ground aquatint, 11⅞ × 6½". MoMA, New York

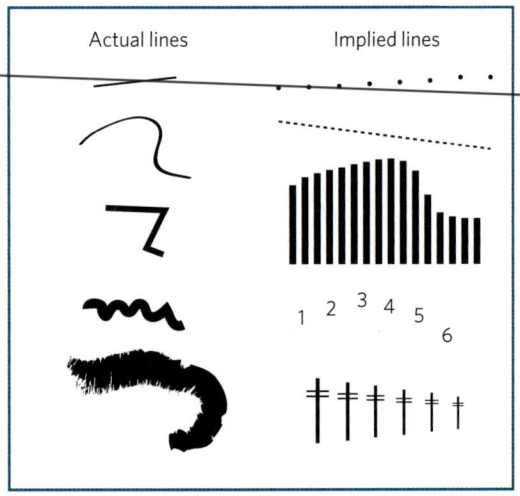

1.1.5 Actual and implied lines

the figure and the **background** represents one kind of contour line, marking the edge of the figure's overall shape. Although contour drawing is a methodical and measured process, here Matisse manages to create an impression of spontaneity that gives the work a fresh, relaxed feeling. He has nonetheless paid close attention to the lines that define the woman's face. Contour lines are also used in her dress to describe its surface as it falls across her figure. Matisse, a master of artistic simplicity and directness, uses solid continuous lines to reveal complex three-dimensional shapes and surfaces. He loved bold, simple lines and shapes and used them deliberately to put the viewer at ease, as if he or she, too, like the subject of this drawing, were sitting in a comfortable armchair.

Contour drawing is a process that requires an artist's focused attention on a surface edge. Imagine focusing your stare on a single point, perhaps on the top of a forehead in profile, then moving your eye painstakingly slowly around the tip of the nose and on along the roundness of the lips and around the chin until it meets the neckline. If you carefully follow that edge and move your pencil along a sheet of paper, recording your progress across the page in a long continuous line, then you are engaging in contour drawing. This type of drawing helps to develop eye–hand coordination and reveal subtle changes in a subject.

The Spanish artist Pablo Picasso (1881–1973), was famous for his ability to describe the shapes and planes that make up an object. In his line drawing *Blonde Woman in Profile*, the artist uses a continuous line that follows the contours of the profile (**1.1.4**). The pencil line wraps around the outer edge of the subject, a woman's head, describing the undulating texture of the hair. By giving the viewer clues resembling the kind of curves found in real life, these contour lines communicate shape and indicate some depth using just directional changes. Picasso is often associated with the **Cubist style**, a way of representing simultaneously all aspects of a three-dimensional object on a flat, two-dimensional surface.

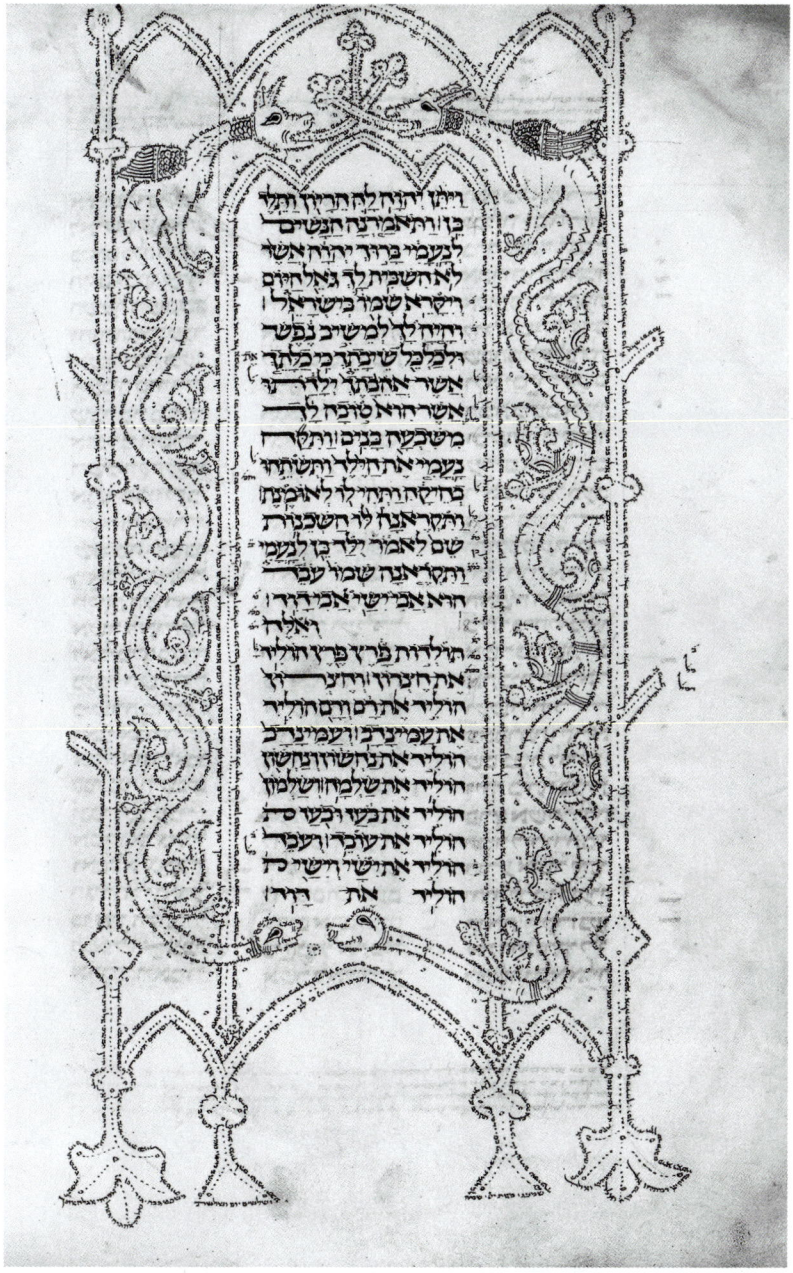

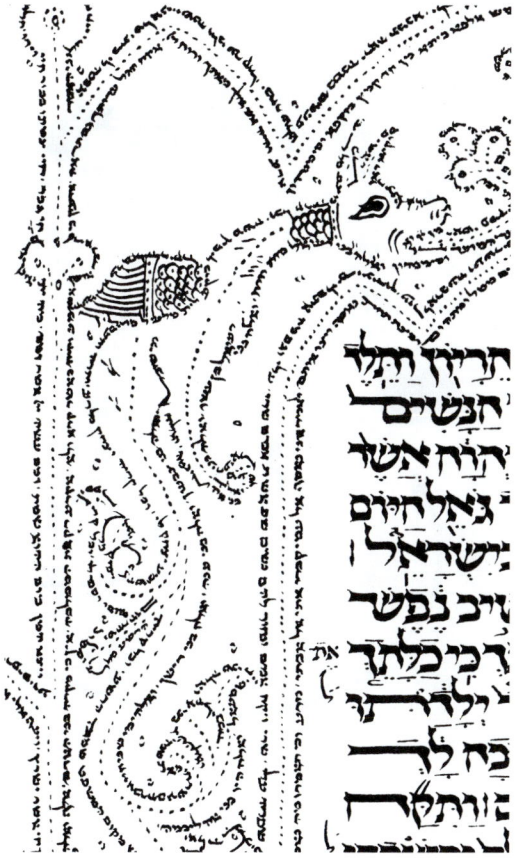

1.1.6b (above) Detail of *Pentateuch with Prophetical Readings and the Five Scrolls*

1.1.6a (left) Franco-German hand, *Pentateuch with Prophetical Readings and the Five Scrolls*, 13th–14th century. Illustrated manuscript. British Library, London, England

Background: the part of a work depicted furthest from the viewer's space, often behind the main subject matter
Cubism, Cubist: twentieth-century movement and style in art, especially painting, in which perspective with a single viewpoint was abandoned and use was made of simple geometric shapes, interlocking planes, and, later, collage; the Cubists were artists who formed part of the movement. "Cubist" is also used to describe their style of painting
Style: a characteristic way in which an artist or group of artists uses visual language to give a work an identifiable form of visual expression
Actual line: a continuous, uninterrupted line
Implied line: a line not actually drawn but suggested by the positions of elements in the work, for example, an aligned series of dots

Implied Line

The lines we have discussed so far can be clearly seen as continuous marks. We can call these lines **actual lines**. But line can also be implied by a series of marks. An **implied line** is an illusion: it gives us the impression we are seeing a line where there is no continuous mark (**1.1.5**).

Implied line is important in the Jewish art of micrography, the creation of designs using very small writing. At first glance, the text border in **1.1.6a** appears to be an ornate line drawing that has been used to help embellish the text. In fact, the ornate frame is made from tiny Hebrew letters and words. If we look at the detail in **1.1.6b**, it becomes more obvious there is no line at all, but an implied line created by the skillful arrangement of the lettering. The "microscopic" text has been added as a guide (called a *masorah*) that provides advice about pronunciation and intonation.

Implied line is used in a more freeform way in the work by Sauerkids, the Dutch graphic

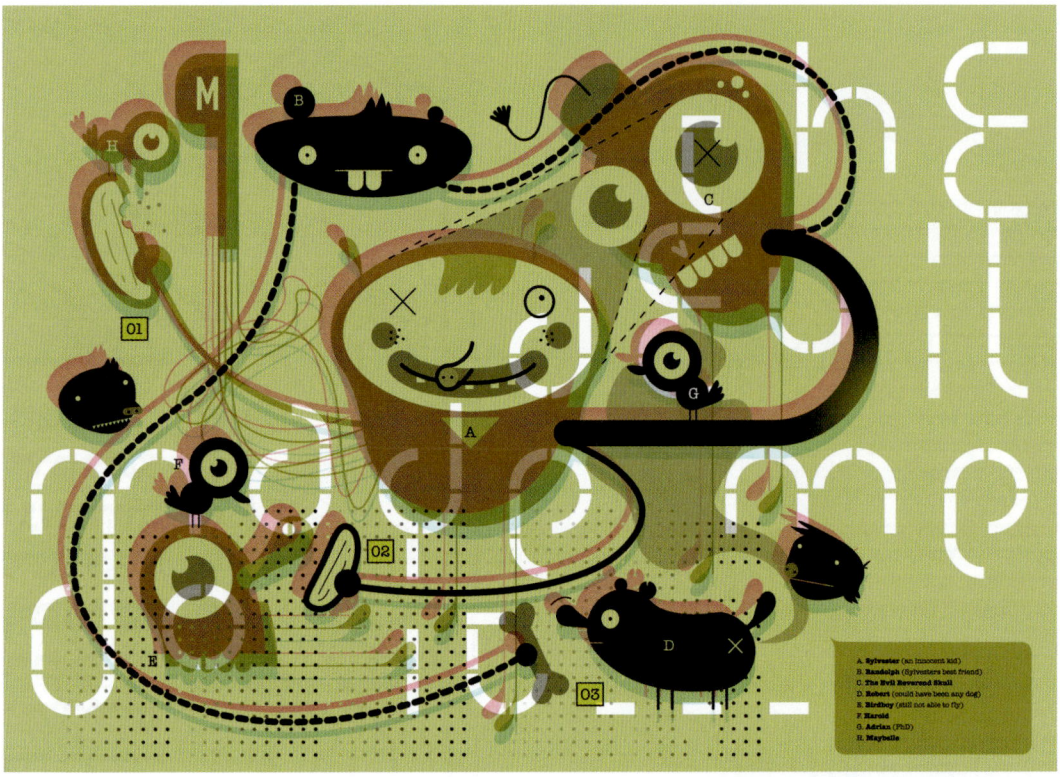

Rhythm: the regular or ordered repetition of elements in the work
Etching: an intaglio printmaking process that uses acid to bite (or etch) the engraved design into the printing surface
Logo: a graphic image used to identify an idea or entity

1.1.7 (left) Sauerkids, *The Devil Made Me Do It*, 2006. Digital image, 16½ × 8¼"

1.1.8 (below) James Allen, *The Connectors*, 1934. Etching, 12⅞ × 9⅞". British Museum, London, England

designers Mark Moget (b. 1970) and Taco Sipma (b. 1966). *The Devil Made Me Do It* uses implied line to influence visual **rhythms** that add to the excitement of the design (**1.1.7**). The many dashes and the grid of dots at the bottom of the work imply vertical and horizontal lines. Even the title of the work is spelled out using implied line.

Directional Line

Besides demarcating boundaries, indicating depth, and noting surface changes, line can also communicate direction and movement. An artist can use line to direct our attention to something he or she wants us to notice. An example of directional line occurs in the American artist James Allen's (1894–1964) **etching** of Depression-era construction workers. They are depicted working in New York City on the Empire State Building, which was to become the tallest building in the world at the time.

In *The Connectors*, the steel girders appear to be slightly closer together at the bottom of the picture than at the top. As a result of this, the girders direct the viewer's eye downward in order to accentuate great height (**1.1.8**). The narrowing lines showing the buildings in

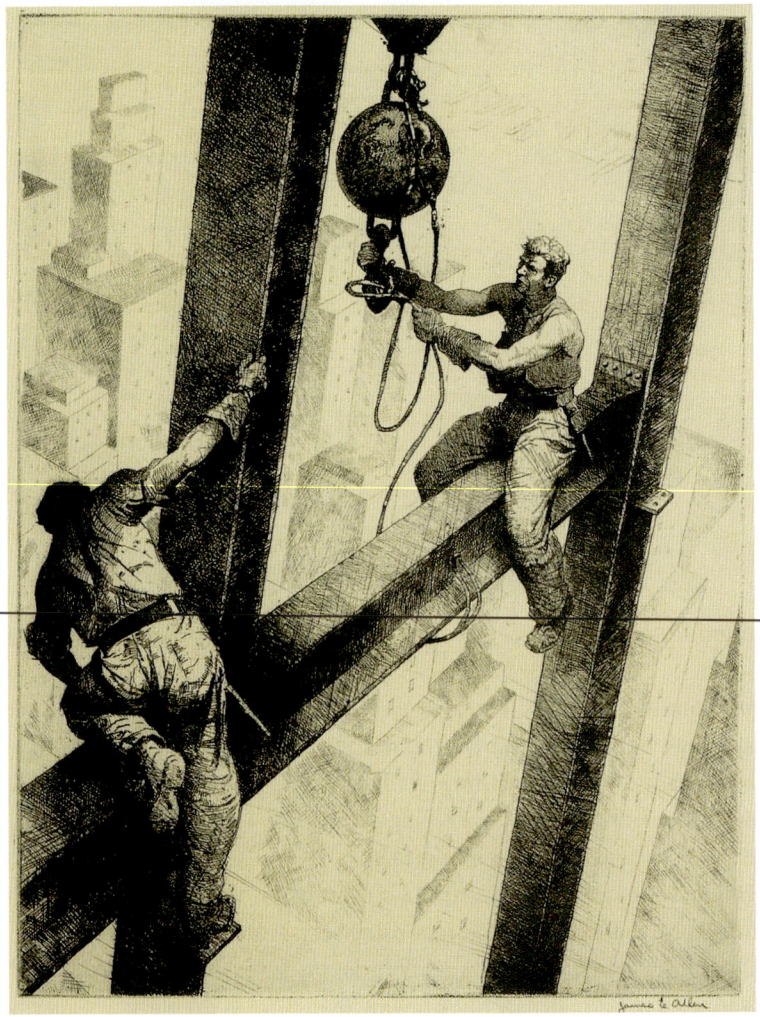

the background of the print help reinforce the same effect.

When an artist uses line to direct the viewer's eye to more than one area in a composition, the feeling of movement is communicated as the eye darts from place to place. The page from the manga (Japanese comic/cartoon book) *Tsubasa RESERVoir CHRoNiCLE* (**1.1.9**) is divided into two major sections. A close-up view of a character is compressed into the bottom, and a larger action scene occupies the upper two-thirds of the page. In this section, directional lines converge on a light area in the upper right of the page, then our attention is redirected to the left, where a figure is being blasted away by an explosion. The mangaka (group of manga artists) CLAMP has cleverly used the strong diagonals to add an intense feeling of movement to the page.

Communicative Line

The directions of lines (whether they go up, across, or diagonally) both guide our attention and suggest particular feelings. Vertical lines tend to communicate strength and energy; horizontal lines can suggest calmness and passivity; diagonal lines are associated with action, motion, and change (**1.1.10**).

Graphic designers use the communicative qualities of directional line when creating **logos**. To convey the strength of government or the stability of a financial institution, they

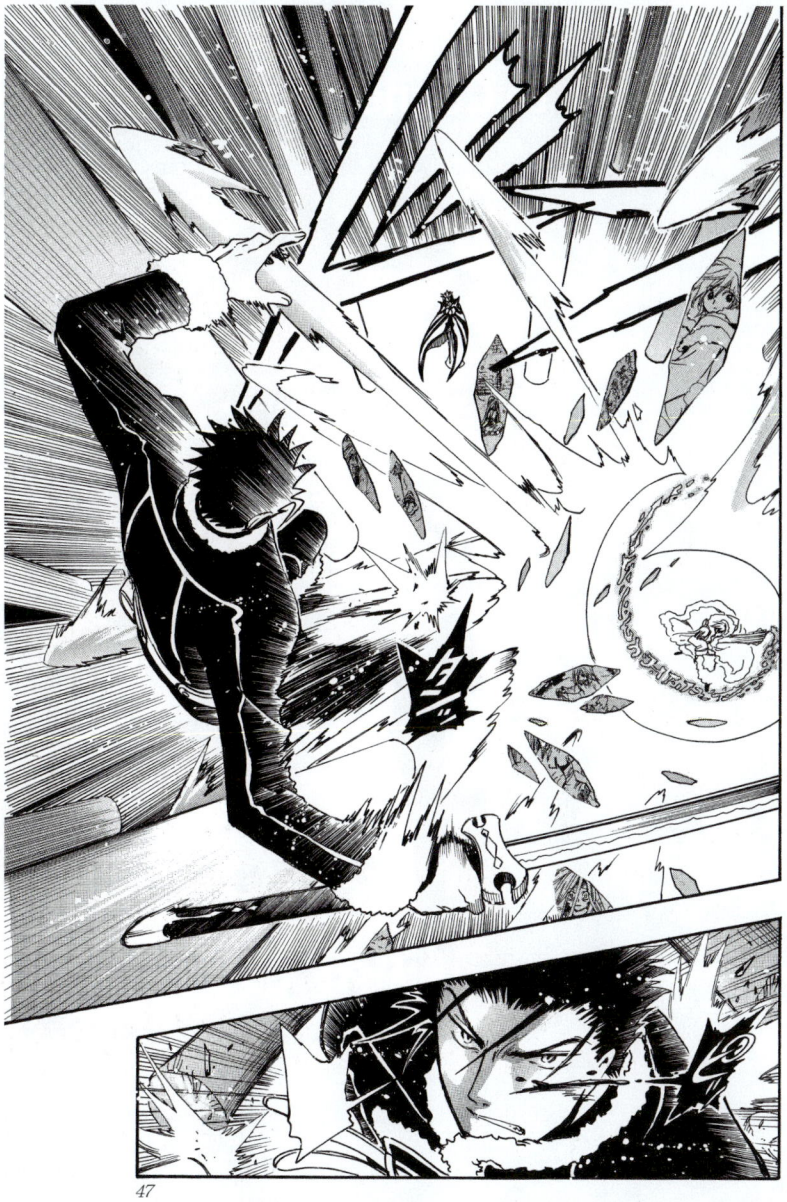

1.1.9 CLAMP, page from the *Tsubasa RESERVoir CHRoNiCLE*, volume 21, page 47, 2007

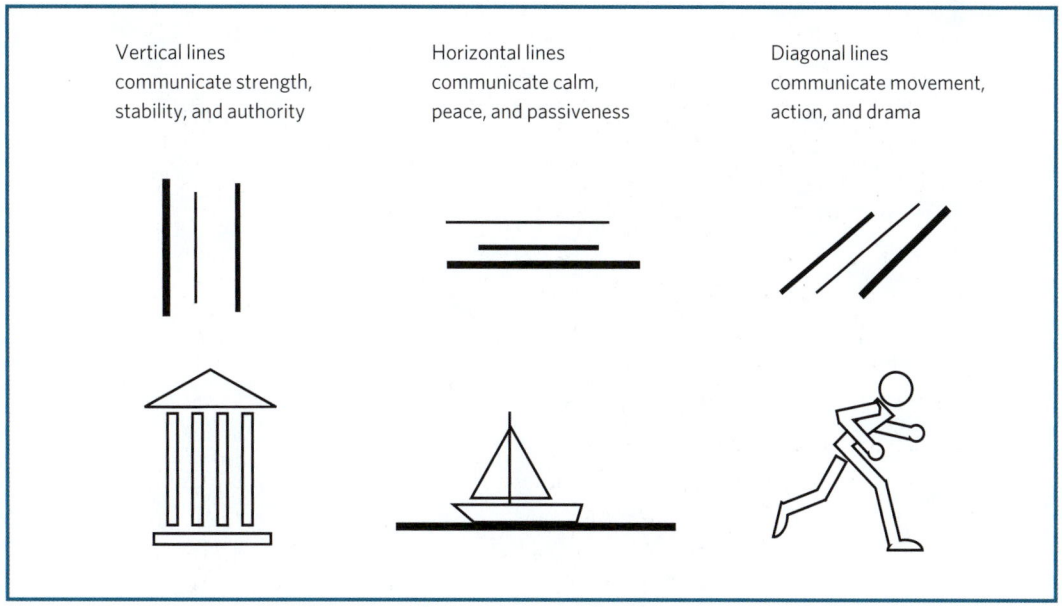

1.1.10 Communicative qualities of line

Gateway to Art: Kahlo, *The Two Fridas*
Using Line to Connect and Direct a Viewer's Attention

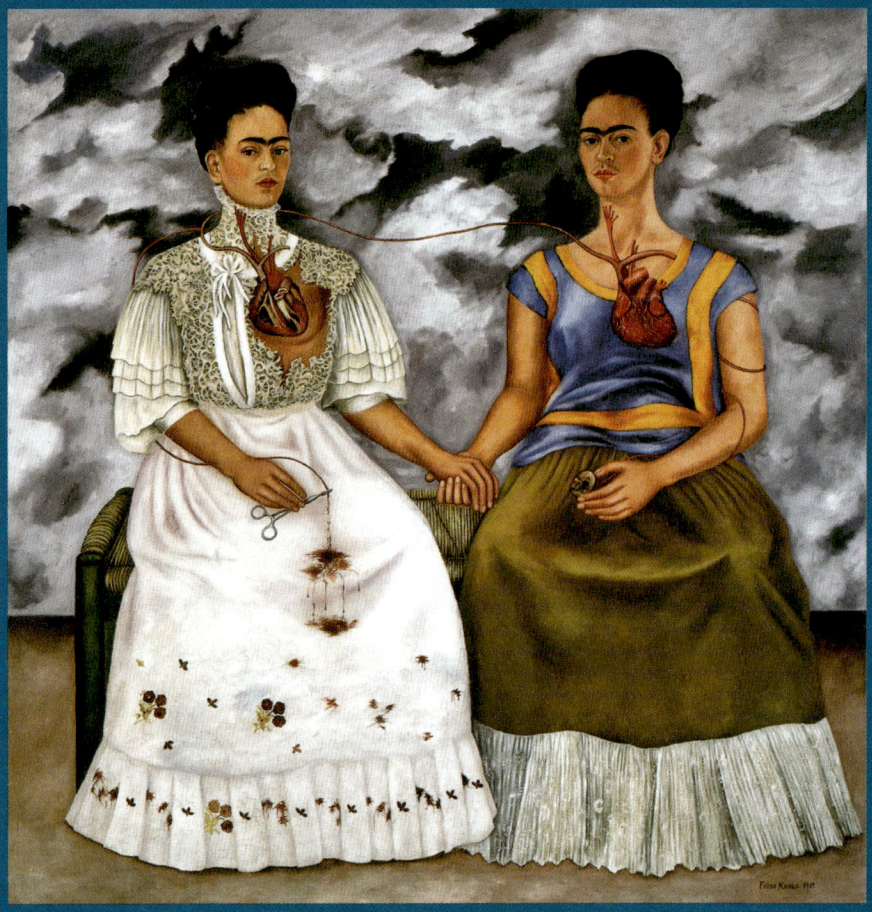

1.1.11 Frida Kahlo, *The Two Fridas*, 1939. Oil on canvas, 5'8" × 5'8". Museo de Arte Moderno, Mexico City, Mexico

In *The Two Fridas* line plays an important role in connecting areas of the painting and directing the viewer's attention. Connections were important in the life of the Mexican artist Frida Kahlo (1907–1954). The artist's connections to her family lineage, to her husband, and to her history of physical suffering are all encapsulated in this work.

The line created by the vein that connects the two images of Frida (**1.1.11**) makes reference to her lineage (or bloodline) as it winds from the Frida on the right, in traditional Tehuana (from Tehuantapec, Mexico) clothing, to the Frida on the left, in white European dress. It refers to her Spanish-Native Mexican and European parents and links the two. The vein sometimes disappears behind or inside the clothing, implying a continuous but hidden line. On the European figure, the vein alludes to Frida's recent divorce from her husband, fellow Mexican artist Diego Rivera (1886–1957), because it directs us to her broken heart. The Mexican Frida holds in her hand a small picture of Rivera.

The vein continues to wrap around and meander throughout the figures. It also tells us about the lifelong pain that Frida endured after being badly injured in a traffic accident when she was eighteen years old. She had many surgeries, as symbolized here by the scissor-like surgical clamp on the left, which almost stops the blood flow—though drips of her life essence still stain the white dress. This red line becomes the main element in expressing the story of Frida's life. Other lines that contribute to the overall composition are the strong crisp outlines of the figures and the soft irregular lines of the clouds. Each gives character to this story of strength in the face of hardship.

For the other Kahlo Gateway boxes, see p. 204, p. 532, and p. 676

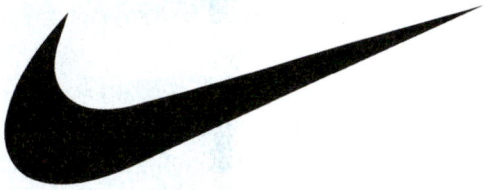

1.1.12 Carolyn Davidson, Nike Company logo, 1971

may choose verticals. Logos for vacation resorts often feature horizontal lines to communicate peaceful repose. Diagonals can express the excitement and energy of athletic activity. For example, Carolyn Davidson's (b. *c.* 1943) distinctive Nike "swoosh" conveys action with a shape comprising a stylized, diagonal line (**1.1.12**).

Line gives an unsettling energy to a painting of the bedroom (**1.1.13**) of the Dutch artist Vincent van Gogh (1853–1890). Most of the lines that make up the room are strong verticals. This suggests that Van Gogh's bedroom was not a calm place of rest, as horizontal lines might imply. The floor also nervously changes **color** and **value**. The varying width of the vertical lines communicates the anxiety Van Gogh may have felt in the months leading up to his suicide in 1890.

The strength of the verticals combined with the agitation of the emphatic diagonals makes for a powerful sense of unease. Yet Van Gogh may also have been trying to ground himself in the here and now by painting the simple room in which he slept.

Lines to Regulate and Control

Whether straight or curved, a line can be regular and carefully measured. Regular lines express control and planning, and impart a sense of cool-headed deliberation and accuracy. Such lines are effective for communicating ideas that must be shared objectively by groups of people, such as the plans an architect provides to guide builders.

Color: the optical effect caused when reflected white light of the spectrum is divided into separate wavelengths
Value: the lightness or darkness of a plane or area

1.1.13 Vincent van Gogh, *The Bedroom*, 1889. Oil on canvas, 28¾ × 36¼". Art Institute of Chicago, Illinois

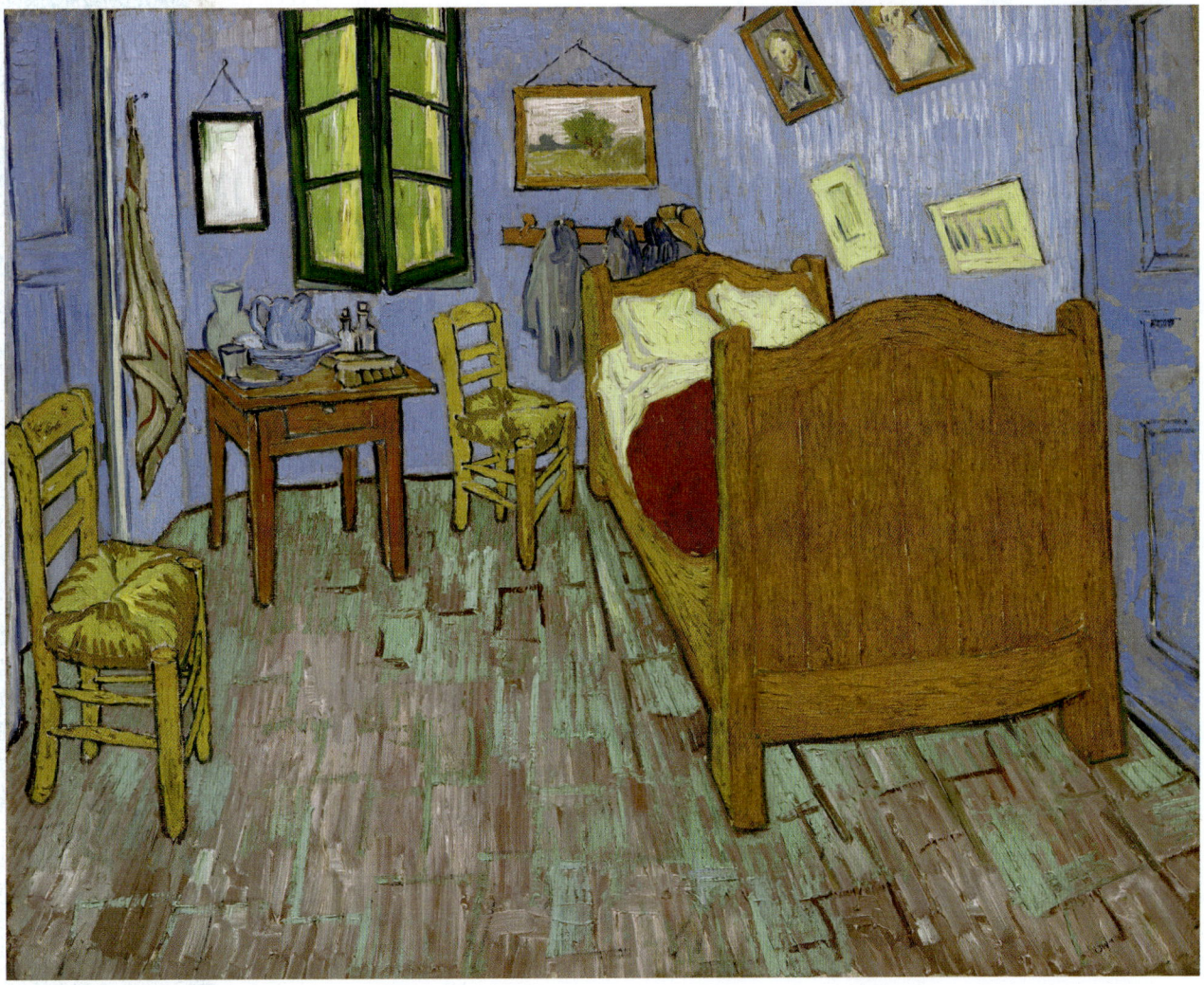

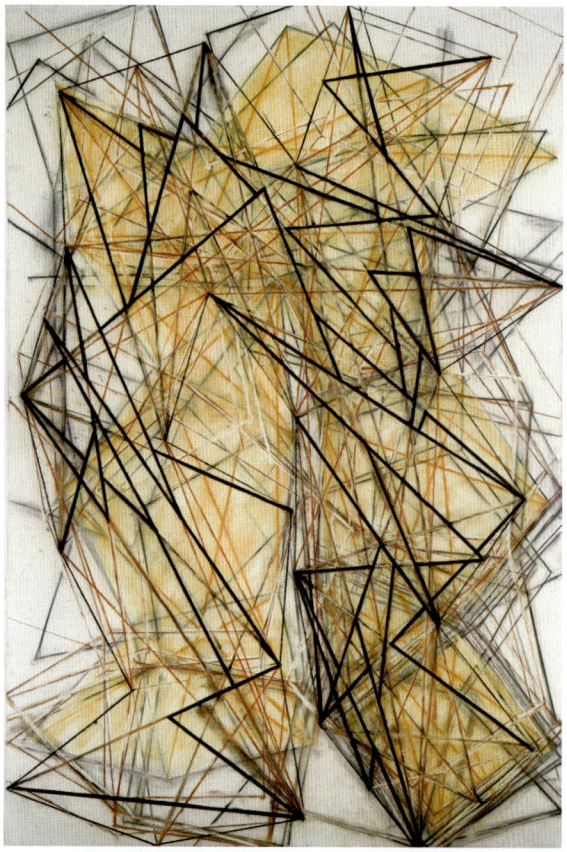

1.1.14 (above) Mel Bochner, *Vertigo*, 1982. Charcoal, Conté crayon, and pastel on canvas, 9' × 6'2". Albright-Knox Art Gallery, Buffalo, New York

The American **conceptual artist** Mel Bochner (b. 1940) uses ruled line in his work *Vertigo* (**1.1.14**). By using a regular line drawn with the aid of a straightedge, Bochner speaks in the language of mechanical planning. He seems to contradict the use of regular line to convey a sense of control, however. The repetitious diagonal movement and hectic crossing and overlapping of his lines impart a sense of motion in disarray, as if his machine has somehow gone out of whack.

The British sculptor Barbara Hepworth (1903–1975) utilized regulated line in the preliminary drawings she made for her sculptures. The lines she uses are crisp and clear. They combine to represent feelings or sensations that Hepworth wants to make visible in her sculpture. Hepworth said, "I rarely draw what I see. I draw what I feel in my body."

In **1.1.15**, the artist has projected four views of a future sculpture. As she rotates this imaginary work in her mind's eye, the precision of her line helps her comprehend the complexity of her sensations. Like a dancer who responds to the rhythm of music, Hepworth has revealed the kind of lines that she feels, rather than sees, and has translated them into a visual "dance." Like an architect preparing the blueprints of a real building, Hepworth uses regulated line to translate her feelings into drawing and then, finally, into a real sculpture.

Lines to Express Freedom and Passion

Lines can also be irregular, reflecting the wildness of nature, chaos, and accident. Such lines—free and unrestrained—seem passionate and full of feelings otherwise hard to express. Some artists decide to use irregular lines to reflect their drawing and thinking process. French artist André Masson (1899–1987)

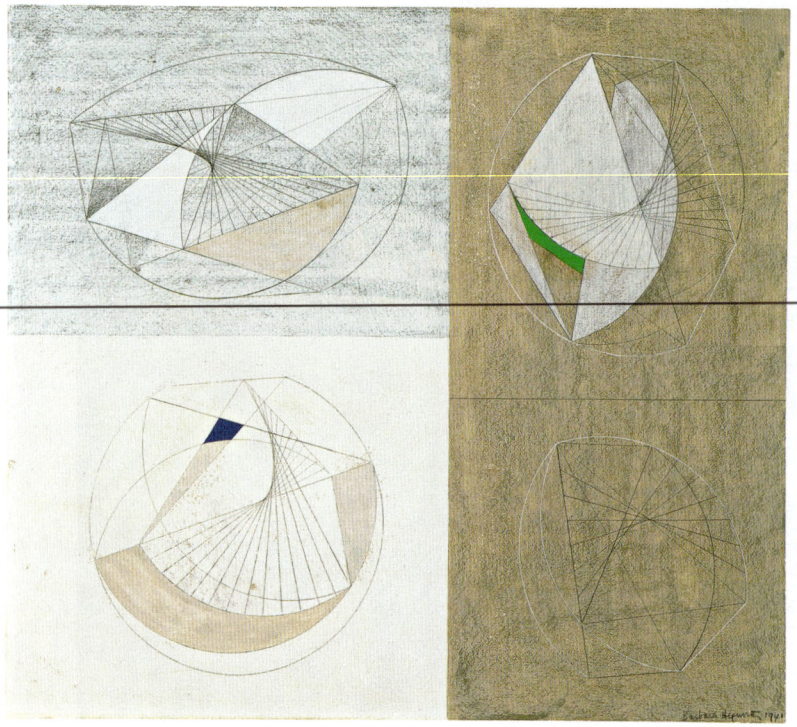

1.1.15 (left) Barbara Hepworth, *Drawing for Sculpture (with color)*, 1941. Pencil and gouache on paper mounted on board, 14 × 16". Private collection

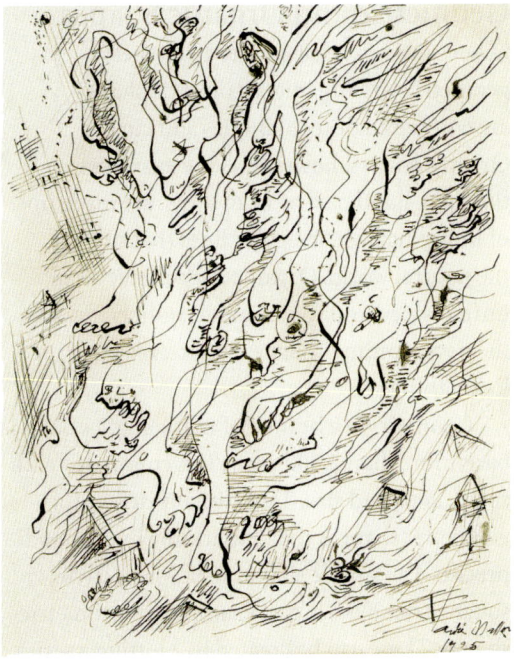

1.1.16 (above) André Masson, *Automatic Drawing*, 1925–26. Ink on paper, 12 × 9½". Musée National d'Art Moderne, Centre Georges Pompidou, Paris, France

wanted to create images that expressed the depths of his subconscious. Sometimes he would go for days without food or sleep in an attempt to force himself to explore deeper-rooted sources of creativity and truth. His **automatic** drawings look spontaneous and free, and also perhaps unstructured and rambling (**1.1.16**).

The drawings of British nineteenth-century artist and spiritualist Georgiana Houghton (1814–1884) share André Masson's uninhibited style. The lines appear irregular and loose, yet repetitious. At first sight, *Glory be to God* may seem chaotic and unpredictable, but, according to the artist, the overall composition is systematically organized by spiritual forces (**1.1.17**). Houghton was one of the first artists to derive her ideas and images from non-visual sources and depict them in a non-representational way. She chose to interpret her spiritual experiences and create visual representations of them, introducing viewers to a unique world that they would never otherwise have been able to encounter.

Conceptual art: a work in which the communication of an idea or group of ideas is most important to the work
Automatic: suppressing conscious control to access subconscious sources of creativity and truth

Regular and Irregular Lines

Although line can be either regular or irregular, most art exhibits a combination of both. The

1.1.17 (below) Georgiana Houghton, *Glory be to God*, 1864. Pencil, watercolor, and ink on paper, 9⅜ × 12⅞". Victorian Spiritualists Union, Melbourne

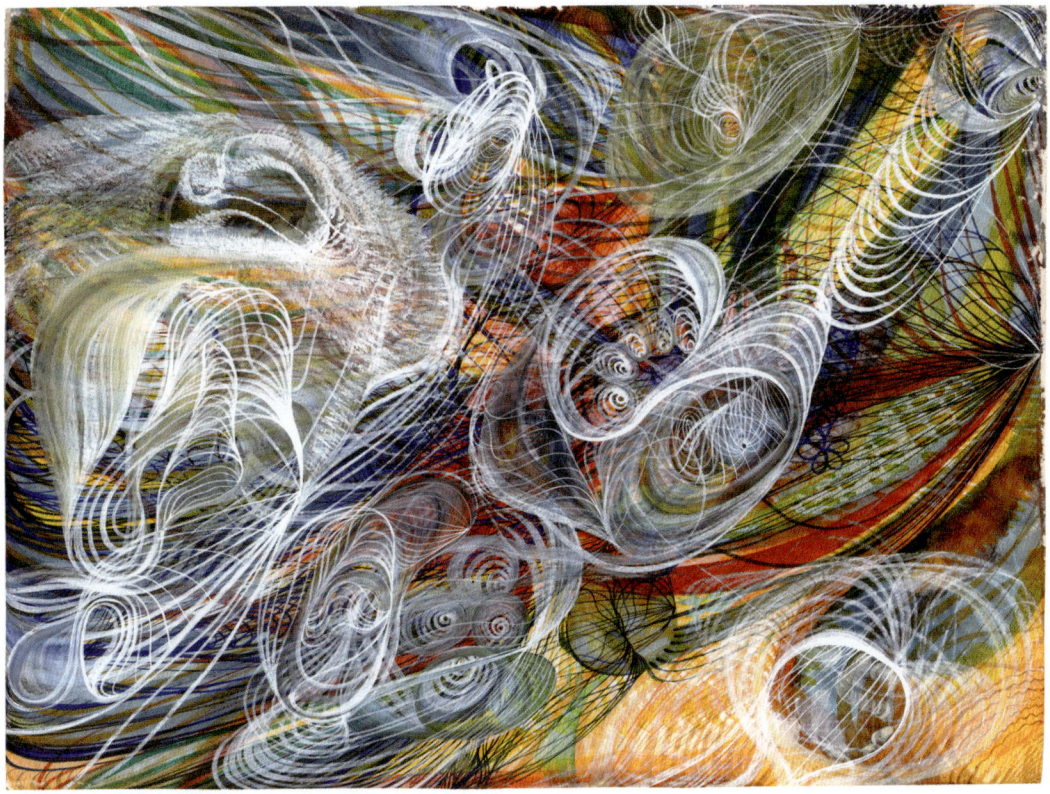

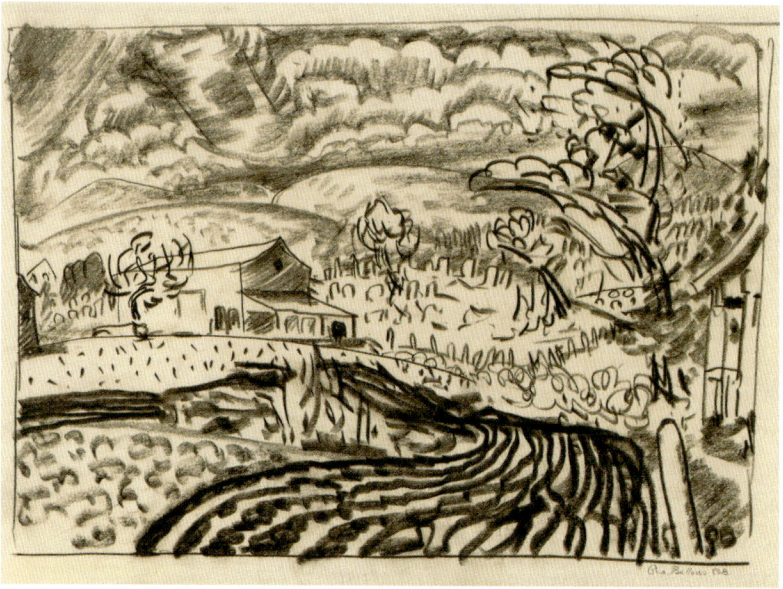

1.1.18 George Bellows, *Woodstock Road, Woodstock, New York, 1924*, 1924. Black crayon on wove paper, image 6⅛ × 8⅞", sheet 9¼ × 12⅜". National Gallery of Art, Washington, D.C.

American artist George Bellows (1882–1925) uses both varieties of line in his work *Woodstock Road, Woodstock, New York, 1924* (**1.1.18**). He contrasts the natural and organic lines of landscape and sky with the restrained and regular line of the man-made and architectural features. It seems that Bellows made this drawing as a preliminary sketch for another work. In the center at the bottom is the inscription, "all lights as high as possible/get color out of shadows." He wrote this to remind himself later of ideas he had while sketching the scene.

Shape

A shape is a two-dimensional area the boundaries of which are defined by lines or suggested by changes in color or value. In **1.1.19** we can see the central circular shape because its edges are defined by the sudden transition from white to medium gray. Two-dimensional figures can be defined only by their height and width: they have no depth. As a result, they can function as a simple concept (for example, circles, squares, triangles) that can be used to organize what we see. So a three-dimensional object, such as a sphere, can be drawn using a circle shape, then an artistic device, such as shading, can be used to suggest depth. In art, shape is a basic, two-dimensional element that can be used to define space.

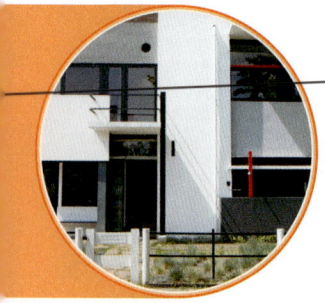

Another example of geometric shape can be found in Gerrit Rietveld's Schröder House, which is made up of rectangles: see **3.9.31, p. 543**

Geometric and Organic Shapes

Shapes can be classified into two types: geometric and organic. Geometric shapes are composed of regular lines and curves. Organic shapes, however, as the examples in the right-hand part of **1.1.20** show, are made up of unpredictable, irregular lines that suggest the natural world. Organic shapes may seem unrestrained and sometimes chaotic, reflecting the never-ending change characteristic of living things.

Geometry is a branch of mathematics dating back more than 2,000 years. It is concerned with space, area, and size. Traditionally defined, a geometric shape is mathematically regular and precise. The simple shapes we know—circle, square, triangle—are all examples of geometric shapes. These can be created by plotting a series of points and connecting them with lines, or simply enclosing a space using regulated and controlled line. Although artists can draw by hand something similar to a geometric shape, they often use tools to control and regulate the precision of the line. For example, an artist may use a ruler to create perfectly straight lines, or alternatively, a computer graphics application can be used to generate a clean, sharp edge. In both cases the artist adds a layer of control that gives the shape greater predictability.

While line may be the most fundamental element of art, often shape is the element we see most clearly. The **collage** by Canadian-born feminist artist Miriam Schapiro (1923–2015)

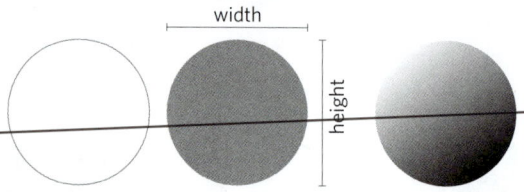

1.1.19 Two-dimensional circular shapes

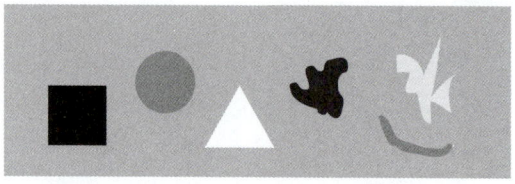

1.1.20 Geometric and organic shapes

Collage: a work of art assembled by gluing materials, often paper, onto a surface. From the French *coller*, to glue
Pattern: an arrangement of predictably repeated elements
Highlight: an area of lightest value in a work

illustrates differences between geometric and organic shapes (**1.1.21**). In *Baby Blocks*—also the name of a traditional quilting pattern—images of flowers and children's clothes overlap a tiling of orange, blue, and black diamond shapes. The work's title suggests a **pattern** of diamond shapes creating an illusion of cubes. The organic shapes of the flowers are clearly distinct from the hard geometric shapes of the "blocks" and the red frame; they overflow the boundaries of both.

The stylized floral designs, derived from old-fashioned wallpaper and upholstery patterns, are simplified representations of real flowers. Even so, the shapes have an irregularity that reflects the kind of shapes we find in living things. By contrast, the interlocked blue and yellow blocks are so predictable and regular that we can even envision the pattern where it disappears behind the flowers. This geometric regularity acts as a foil to the organic shapes casually arranged "on" it, introducing contrast between the geometric and organic elements.

By incorporating doll clothes, home decorations, and sewing materials into her "femmages" (homages to the work of women), Schapiro opens our eyes both to the remarkable artistry of much traditional "women's work," and to the cultural forces that undervalue it.

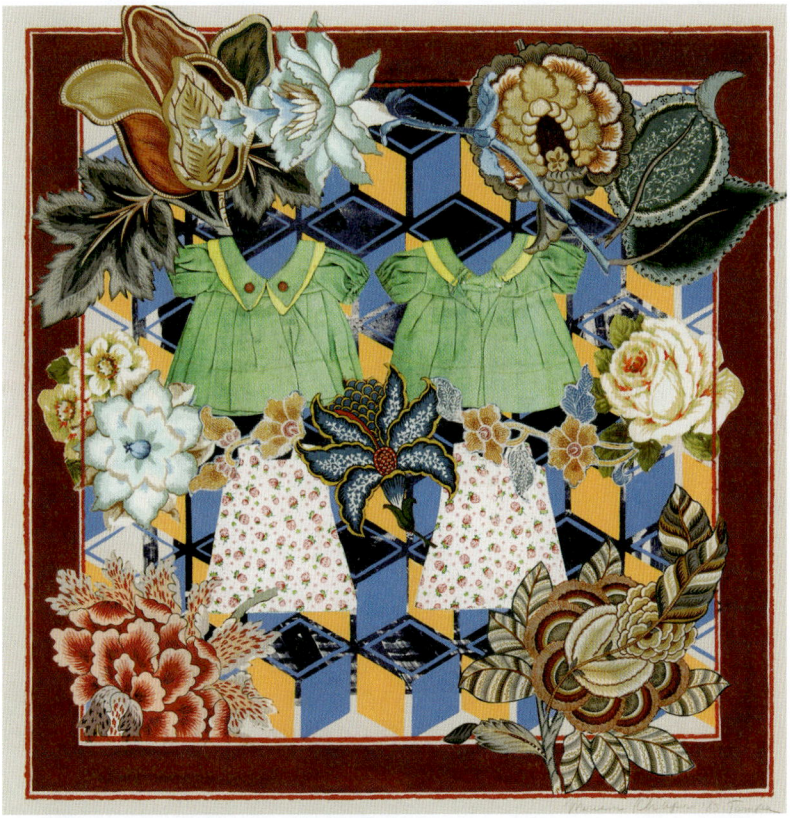

1.1.21 Miriam Schapiro, *Baby Blocks*, 1983. Collage on paper, 29⅞ × 30". University of South Florida Collection, Tampa

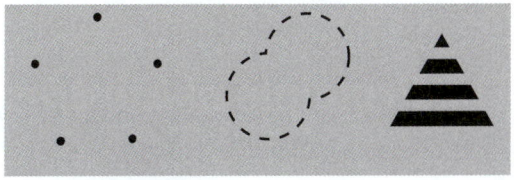

1.1.22 Implied shapes

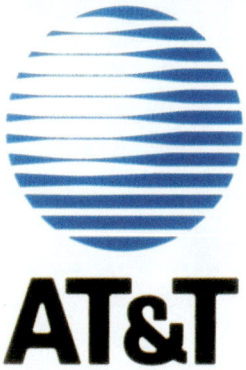

1.1.23 Saul Bass, Bass & Yager, AT&T logo, 1984

Implied Shape

Most shapes are defined by a visible boundary, but we can also see a shape where no continuous boundary exists. Just as line can be implied, so too can shape (**1.1.22**).

The AT&T logo, created in the 1980s by American graphic designer Saul Bass (1920–1996), uses horizontal lines to imply a sphere or globe (**1.1.23**). Twelve horizontal lines are trimmed to form a circle. By constricting the width of nine of these lines, a **highlight** appears on the circular shape, implying the swell of a globe. This logo communicates the idea of an expansive telecommunication network operating all over the world. The image is simple, creating an appropriately meaningful and readily recognizable symbol for a global company.

Contrast

When an artist uses two noticeably different states of an element, he or she is applying the principle of contrast. For example, lines can be both regular and irregular, or shapes can be both geometric and organic. Strong differences in the state of an element can be a very useful effect for an artist; it is especially effective to use opposites.

Gateway to Art: Weems, *Kitchen Table* Series

The Principle of Contrast and Dramatic Effect

The African American artist Carrie Mae Weems (b. 1953) concentrates on personal, cultural, and racial identity in her work. In her photograph **series** *Kitchen Table*, she poses an invented family in real-life situations that highlight interpersonal relationships.

As she focuses on these subjects, Weems uses the principle of contrast as an important device in her photography. Weems exploits contrast in the image "Untitled (Woman and Daughter with Makeup)" (**1.1.24**) by balancing opposite shapes and values. Black and white are opposite values, and the **monochromatic** palette, along with the spotlight above the table, adds a level of drama to the seemingly everyday scene of a normal domestic routine. Weems arranges the organic shapes of the two figures to contrast against the geometry of the rectangular table and door, circular mirrors, and triangular light fixture. Strong differences in dark and light values are evident in the bright overhead light and the shadows. The dark clothing of the woman also contrasts with the girl's white dress. These contrasts bring clarity to the intimate scene, which may imply that life can sometimes be tough but it contains both positive and negative experiences.

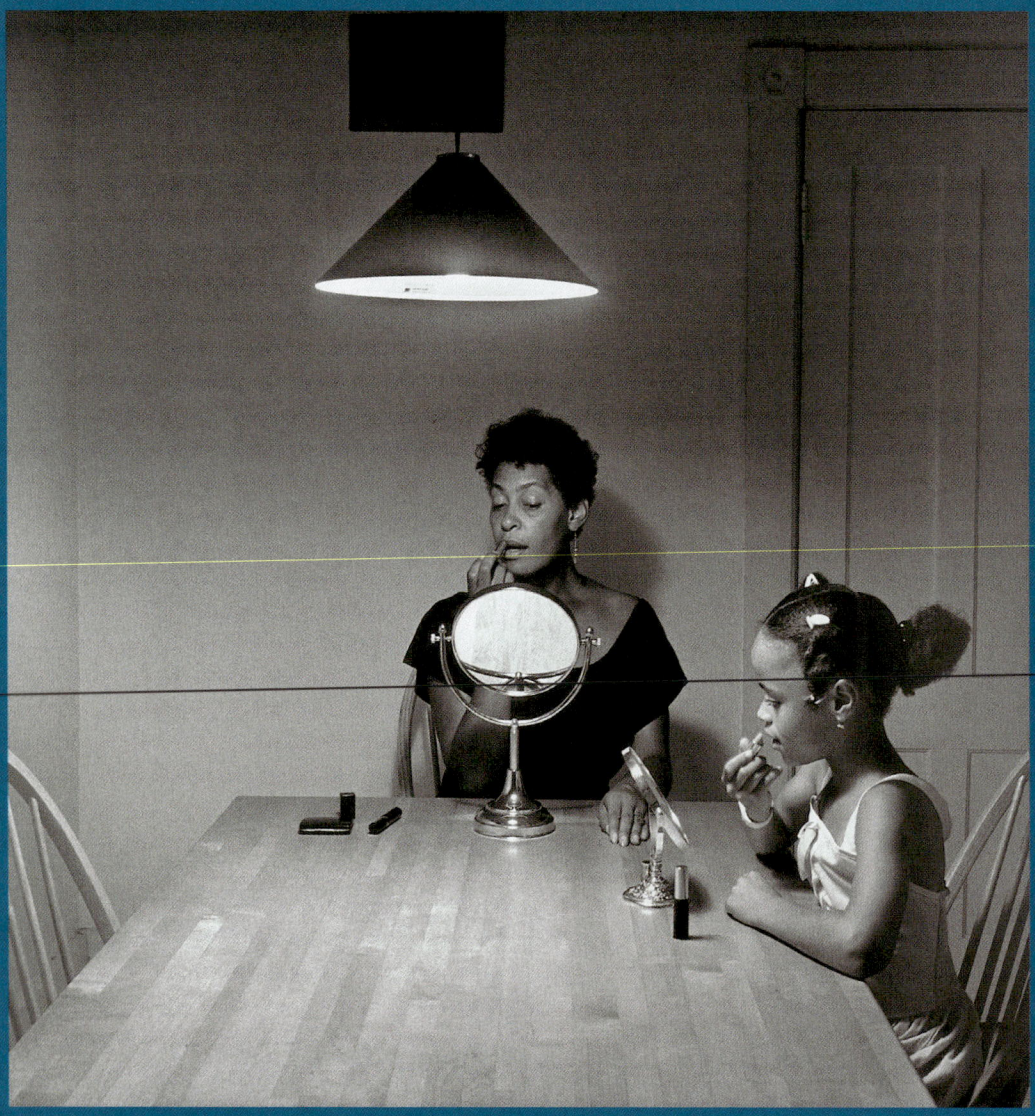

1.1.24 Carrie Mae Weems, "Untitled (Woman and Daughter with Makeup)," 1990, from *Kitchen Table* series, 1989–90. Inkjet print, 41¼ × 41¼ × 2¼" (framed)

For the other Weems Gateway boxes, see p. 329, p. 551, and p. 687

Positive and Negative Shapes

In everyday life, positive and negative are opposites: one needs the other for contrast and comparison. Without positives, negatives would not exist, and vice versa. When we speak of positive and negative in visual form, they are most often represented by black and white. The words on this page, for example, are **positive shapes** of printed black ink that we can see on the **negative space** of the white paper. The space, which is the ground area where such shapes are present, supports the solidity of the placement of the words or shapes. Although black and white are common examples of positive and negative, any color combination can work the same way. Sometimes, too, the lighter color becomes the positive shape.

We can see the interlock of positive and negative shape in the work of American Shepard Fairey (b. 1970). The black features and the blank white space contrast with and complement each other, intensifying the design of this poster (**1.1.25a** and **1.1.25b**). Fairey wants a strong impact because, as a street artist, he needs to catch his audience's attention quickly as they pass by. In this case, the image is of the professional wrestler Andre the Giant (Fessick in the movie *The Princess Bride*), captioned with the word "Obey." Without seeking prior permission, Fairey posts these images in public places as an expression of guerrilla marketing and street theater. The tension between contrasting positive and negative shapes draws our attention, while the cryptic slogan makes us wonder what it is all about.

The works of the American artist Georgia O'Keeffe (1887–1986) often play upon the

Series: a group of related artworks that are created as a set
Monochromatic: having one or more values of one color
Positive shape: a shape defined by its surrounding empty space
Negative space: an unoccupied or empty space that is created after positive shapes are positioned in a work of art

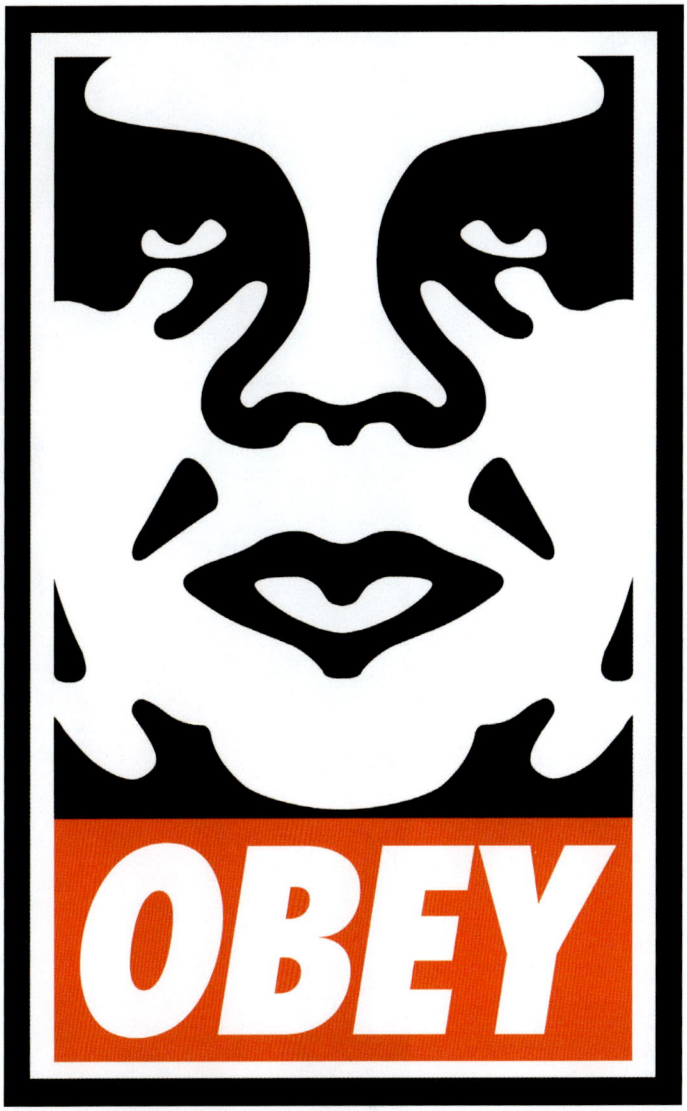

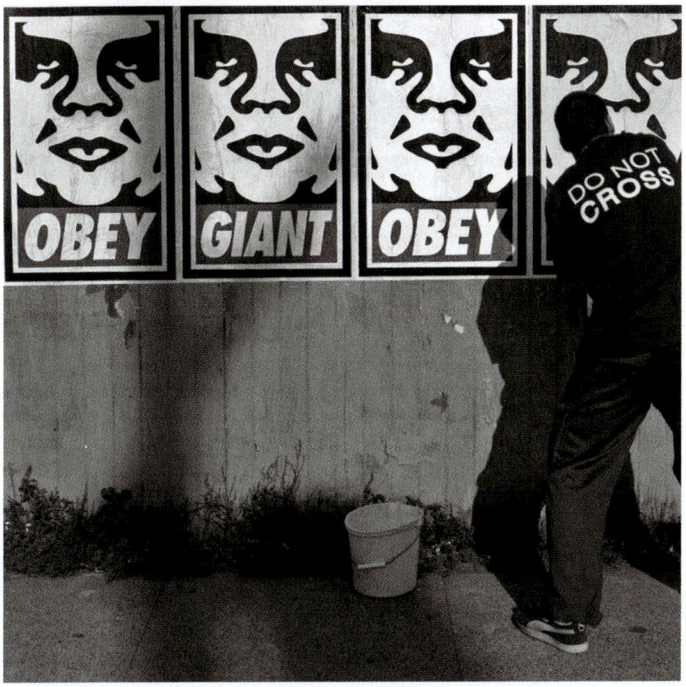

1.1.25a and **1.1.25b**
Shepard Fairey, *Obey*, 1996. Campaign poster and a view of the posters as they were installed in public

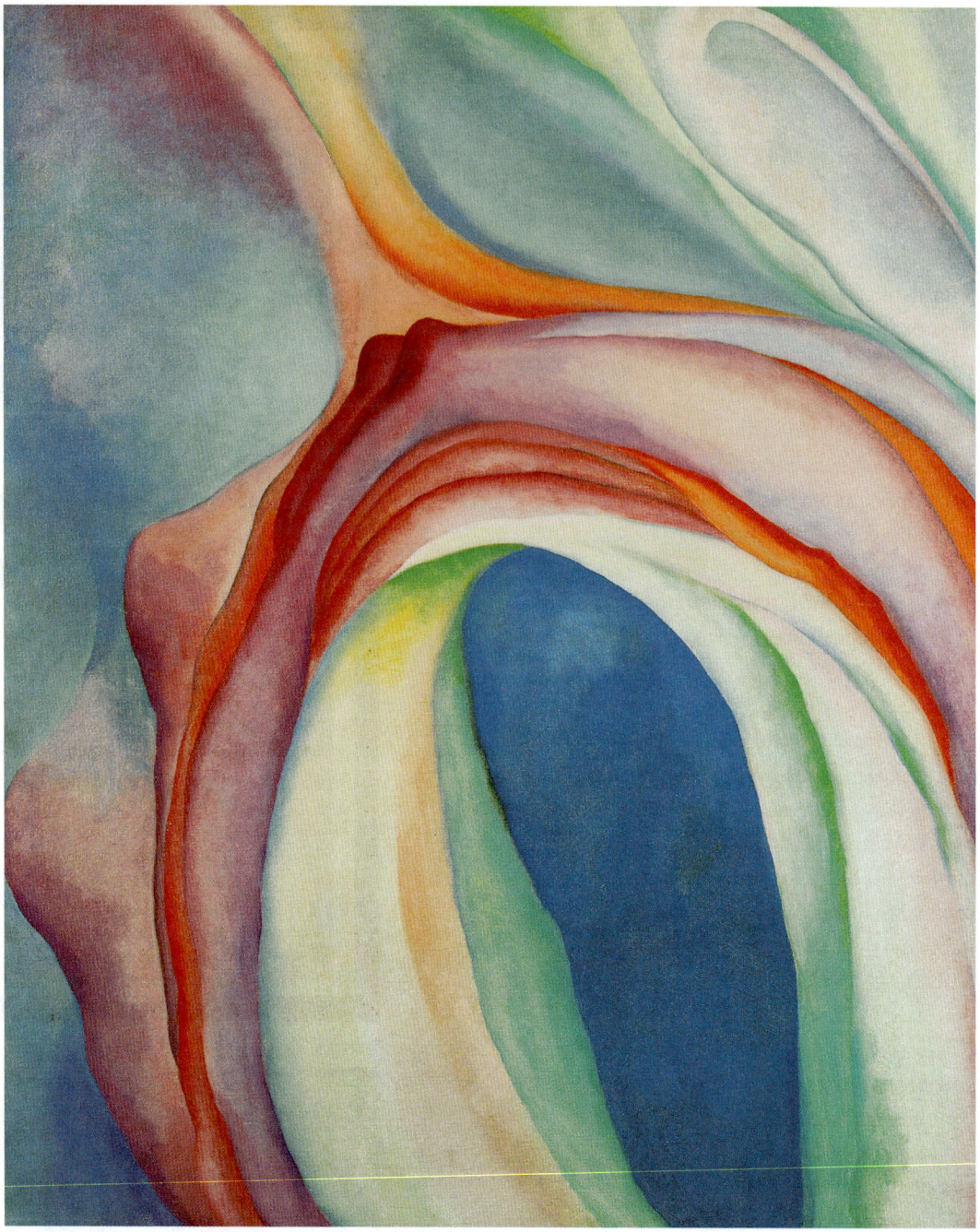

1.1.26 Georgia O'Keeffe, *Music—Pink and Blue II*, 1919. Oil on canvas, 35 × 29⅛". Whitney Museum of American Art, New York

Abstract: art imagery that departs from recognizable images of the natural world
Silhouette: a solidly colored-in shape represented in outline, which contains no detail inside its border
Woodcut: a relief print made from a design cut into a block of wood
Figure–ground reversal: the reversal of the relationship between one shape (the figure) and its background (the ground), so that the figure becomes background and the ground becomes the figure

relationship between positive and negative shape. Her **abstract** shapes derive from a close observation of organic objects. In the painting *Music—Pink and Blue II*, O'Keeffe puts emphasis on the negative blue shape in the bottom right of the picture (**1.1.26**). That negative shape initially draws our attention into a deep interior, so that the positive shape of the pink arc above it carries us back to the surface through a maze of tender folds. O'Keeffe's paintings are inspired by landscape and flower shapes to make associations to objects that live and grow. The interplay of positive and negative space becomes symbolic of the natural ebb and flow of life.

Sometimes illustrators use negative shape to convey information subtly. For example, the Israel-born illustrator and designer Noma Bar (b. 1973) cleverly combined complementary symbols to superimpose two connected ideas. In his illustration *Gun Crime* (**1.1.27**), Bar uses a **silhouette** of a handgun to create the positive, or black, shape on the lighter tan background. But in the area where the trigger has been drawn, we see a small crescent shape and a vertical swatch

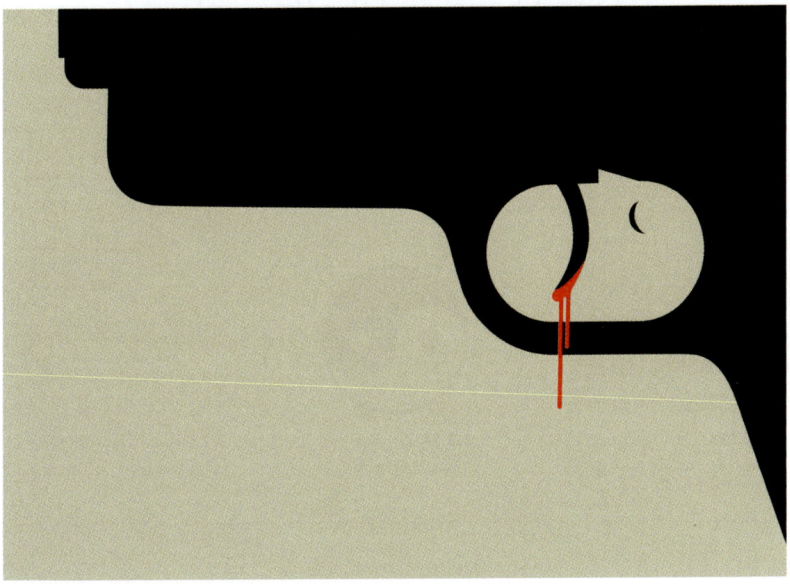

1.1.27 Noma Bar, *Gun Crime*, 2009. Digital, dimensions variable

of red. When we consider the image by looking at the negative tan space in this area, we see a simple image of a head with blood running from its mouth. The alternation of positive and negative shape communicates the act of gun crime and the terrible result in a single image.

In the **woodcut** *Sky and Water I*, the Dutch artist M. C. Escher (1898–1972) applies many of the concepts we have been exploring in this chapter (**1.1.28**). The negative shape changes from white in the upper part of the picture to black in the lower. The most refined version of each animal occurs at the top and bottom extremes of the image. As we follow each transition upward or downward, each animal becomes more simplified until it forms part of the background negative shape. Strong geometric patterns change into the organic shapes of animals. The woodcut, where removed material prints white and preserved material prints black, is conducive to exploring **figure–ground reversal**, which is the very essence of Escher's technique here.

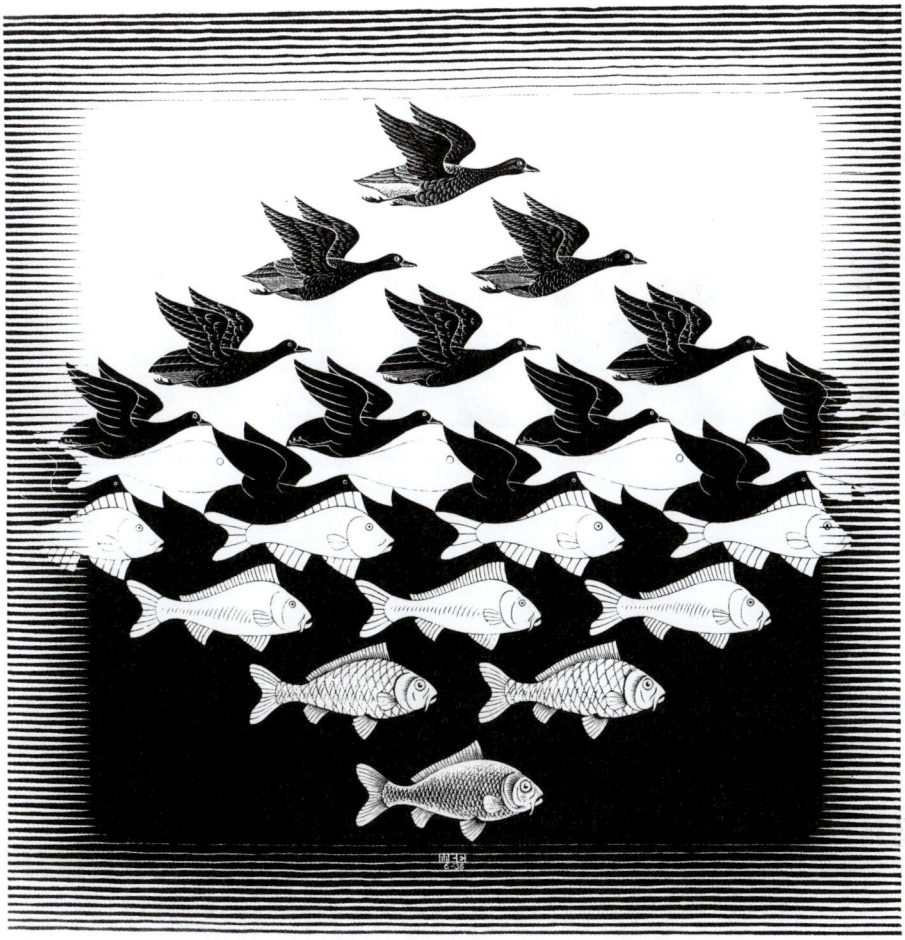

1.1.28 M. C. Escher, *Sky and Water I*, 1938. Woodcut, 17⅛ × 17⅜". The M. C. Escher Company, The Netherlands

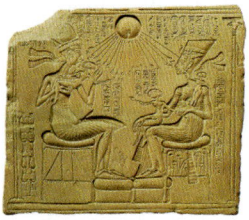

4.6.6 Relief of Akhenaten, Egypt, c. 1353–1335 BCE, p. 632

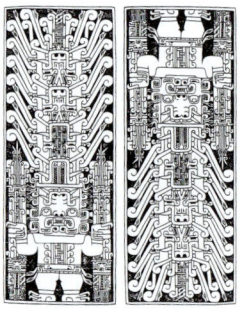

3.4.2b and **c** Drawings of Raimondi Stela, Peru, 460–300 BCE, p. 430

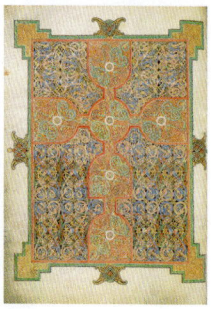

3.2.12a Cross-and-carpet page, Lindisfarne Gospels, 710–721 CE, p. 399

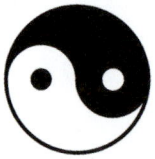

3.3.24 Yin and yang symbol, p. 425

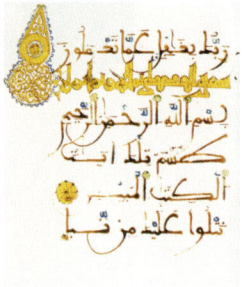

3.2.11 Page from the Koran, probably late 13th century, p. 398

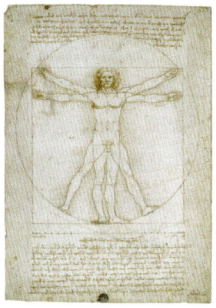

4.4.1 Leonardo da Vinci, *Vitruvian Man*, c. 1490, p. 603

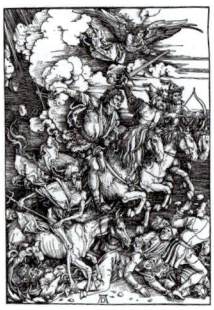

2.3.2 Albrecht Dürer, "The Four Horsemen," 1498, p. 227

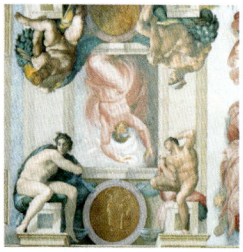

2.4.7 Michelangelo, *Separation of Light and Darkness*, 1508–10, p. 246

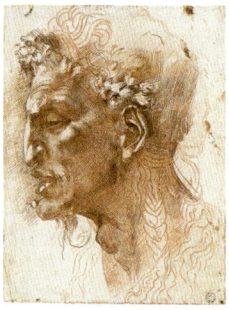

1.3.8 Michelangelo, *Head of a Satyr*, c. 1520–30, p. 80

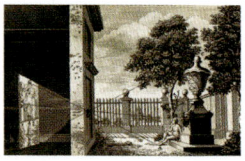

2.8.1 *Optics: the principle of the camera obscura*, 1752, p. 316

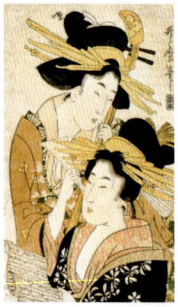

3.8.10 Kitagawa Utamaro, *Two Courtesans*, second half of 18th century, p. 510

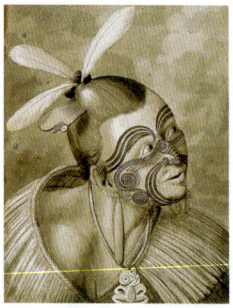

3.5.13 Sydney Parkinson, Drawing of a Maori tattoo, 1784, p. 454

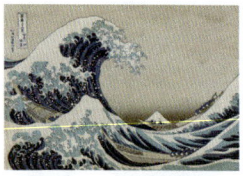

2.3.5 Katsushika Hokusai, "The Great Wave off Shore at Kanagawa," 1826–33, p. 229

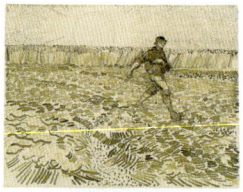

2.1.20 Vincent van Gogh, *Sower with Setting Sun*, 1888, p. 205

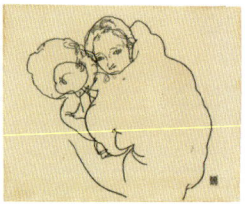

2.1.25 Egon Schiele, *Mother and Child*, 1918, p. 207

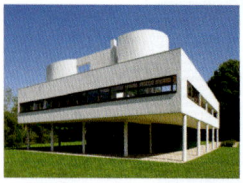

2.5.32 Le Corbusier, Villa Savoye, 1928–31, p. 278

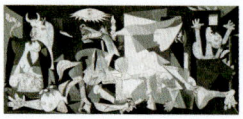

4.7.10 Pablo Picasso, *Guernica*, 1937, p. 646

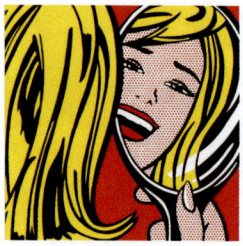

3.9.30 Roy Lichtenstein, *Girl in Mirror*, 1964, p. 541

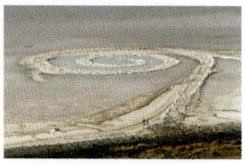

2.4.16 Robert Smithson, *Spiral Jetty*, 1969–70, p. 252

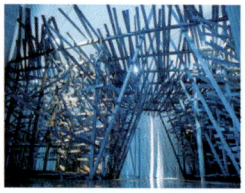

1.2.12 Carol Mickett and Robert Stackhouse, *In the Blue (Crest)*, 2008, p. 68

1.2 Form, Volume, Mass, and Texture

In 1802 a French artist and archaeologist described his impression of the great pyramids of Egypt:

> On approaching these colossal monuments, their angular and inclined form diminishes the appearance of their height and deceives the eye…but as soon as I begin to measure… these gigantic productions of art, they recover all their immensity…
>
> (Vivant Denon, *Travels in Upper and Lower Egypt*)

The massive structures that so impressed Denon have, like every object in our world, three dimensions, which can be expressed as their height, width, and depth (**1.2.1**). Because the pyramids can be measured in these three dimensions they are classified as **three-dimensional** works of art, and like all the art discussed in this chapter they possess four of the visual **elements**: form, volume, mass, and texture. We need to understand these terms in sequence so that we can analyse and understand three-dimensional art.

Three-dimensional: having height, width, and depth
Elements of art: the basic vocabulary of art—line, shape, form, volume, mass, texture, value (lightness/darkness), space, color, and motion and time
Two-dimensional: having height and width
Shape: a two-dimensional area, the boundaries of which are defined by lines or suggested by changes in color or value
3-D modeling: a computer-generated illusion that emulates an object in three dimensions; it can be modified to show visual movement
Form: an object that can be defined in three dimensions (height, width, and depth)
Scale: the size of an object or artwork relative to another object or artwork, or to a system of measurement

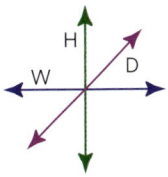

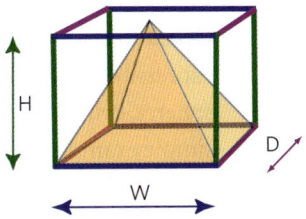

1.2.1 Three dimensions: height, width, and depth

Form

A **two-dimensional** object, such as a drawing of a triangle, is called a **shape**. Shapes are flat and do not have depth, mass, or volume, although they can be made to give an illusion of actual depth.

Shapes that have the illusion of three dimensions are an integral part of **3-D modeling** and animation: a computer-generated image is made using mathematical calculations that enable it to emulate the appearance of an object in real space. The digital environment makes it easier to visualize what something might look like in real life (modeling), and users are even able to give their creations the illusion of movement (animation).

An actual three-dimensional object, such as a pyramid, is called a **form**. A form occupies three-dimensional space and exists in a real and solid way. Forms are tactile; we can feel them with our hands because they are actual objects that exist in real space. Some forms are so tiny they cannot be seen with the naked eye, while others are as large as a galaxy. When artists and designers create forms, they consider how we will experience them in three dimensions. Architects usually make buildings that accord with our physical size, in proportions that are convenient and easy to live in, but sometimes they might build to a larger **scale** in order to leave us in awe. A jeweler makes objects at a small scale that few people can experience at once: we are drawn closer to examine the work more intimately.

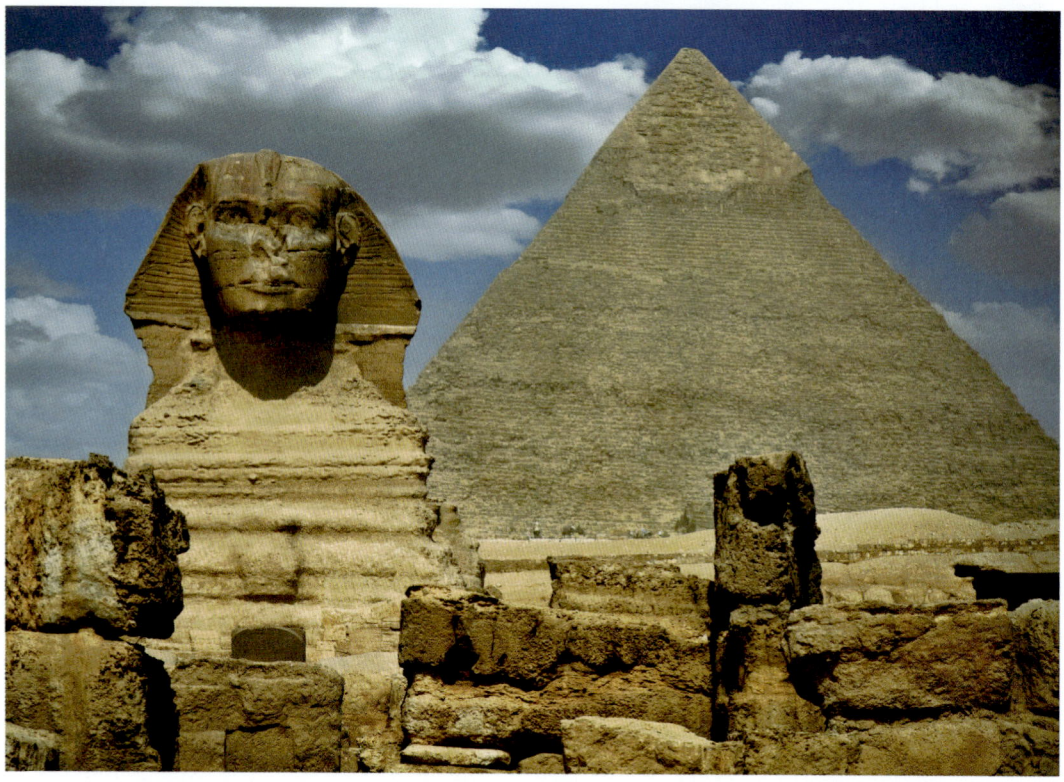

1.2.2 Great Sphinx of Giza (front), c. 2500 BCE, and Pyramid of Khafre, c. 2500 BCE, Giza, Egypt

Forms have two fundamental attributes: **volume** and **mass**. Volume is the amount of actual **space** a form occupies. Mass describes the concept that volume is solid and occupies space, whether it is enormous, such as a pyramid, or relatively small, such as a piece of jewelry.

The surface of a form can be cool and slick, rough and jagged, soft and warm. Such sensations arise from the **texture** of the form. Texture can be experienced directly, but we can also imagine how the surface of a form may feel simply by looking at it. Some hand-made objects, such as ceramics or basketry, attract our touch naturally. They were touched by the hands that formed them, and they fit in our hands just as they used to fit in the hands of the artist. Some machine-made forms reflect the crisp precision of mechanical perfection; their smooth, shiny forms seduce our senses. Artists and designers create forms with full knowledge that they can evoke our memories of other three-dimensional objects in the world and allow us to experience our own world in a richer way.

The forms created by artists in the ancient world reflected the everyday experiences of people of that time. For example, stone was a common material in ancient Egypt, easily accessible and so durable that artists must have thought it would last for a very long time—a correct assumption, as we can still see.

The Great Sphinx guards the tombs of the Egyptian kings at Giza, near Cairo (**1.2.2**). It is the largest carving in the world made from a single stone. The sculpture stands as a symbol of the power to change our surroundings. The Egyptians who created this work changed the very earth by sculpting the living rock. We do not know what the Egyptians called this half-man, half-lion, but we now call it a "sphinx" after the creature from Greek mythology with the body of a lion, the wings of an eagle, and the head of a man. The Great Sphinx's face is believed to be a likeness of the Egyptian king Khafre.

There are two types of form: geometric and organic.

Volume: the space filled or enclosed by a three-dimensional figure or object
Mass: a volume that has, or gives the illusion of having, weight, density, and bulk
Space: the distance between identifiable points or planes
Texture: the surface quality of a work, for example fine/coarse, detailed/lacking in detail
Geometric form: three-dimensional form composed of predictable and mathematically derived planes and curves

Geometric Form

Geometric forms are regular and are readily expressible in words or mathematics: cubes, spheres, cylinders, cones, and pyramids are simple examples. The Pyramid of Khafre, which is guarded by the Great Sphinx of Giza in **1.2.2**, is a stunning example of geometric form in

Plane: a flat, two-dimensional surface on which an artist can create a drawing or painting. Planes can also be implied in a composition by areas that face toward, parallel to, or away from a light source

Organic form: three-dimensional form made up of unpredictable, irregular planes that suggest the natural world

architectural design because of the straight, controlled **planes** that articulate the four sides. The crisp regularity of the pyramids derives from attention to detail. For example, the base of another of the pyramids, Khufu's, is level to within less than an inch, and the greatest difference in the length of its sides is 1¾ in. The emphasis on precise mathematical proportion reflects an ordered culture in which artists were governed by a canon, or set of rules, that imposed strict controls on how an artist worked and the images that he or she created.

The American sculptor David Smith (1906–1965) also relied on geometric forms to create his compositions. In *Cubi XIX*, made of stainless steel, Smith uses cubes, cuboids, and a thick disk (**1.2.3**). Smith learned welding in an automobile factory and became expert while fabricating tanks of thick armor plate during World War II. The late works of his *Cubi* series combine geometric forms in angular relationships. The diagonal angles imply movement, giving these basic geometric forms a visual energy. Smith burnished their surfaces to create a counterpoint between industrial and natural form.

Organic Form

The form of most things in the natural world is organic: it is irregular and unpredictable. Living things, such as plants and animals, change constantly, and their forms change too. Artists accentuate the irregular character of **organic form** for expressive effect.

The human figure gives an artist a subject that can communicate the rich experience of humanity and organic form in a way we can all understand. The human body, like other organic forms, constantly changes in concert with its surroundings. Forms representing the human figure can provide the artist with a subject conveying symmetry and balance. But by visually contradicting such order, an artist can make a work seem uncomfortable or uneasy to look at. The unknown artist who carved the *Roettgen Pietà* in the fourteenth century expresses the agony of death and grief by making the bodies of Jesus and Mary irregular, awkward, and distorted (**1.2.4**).

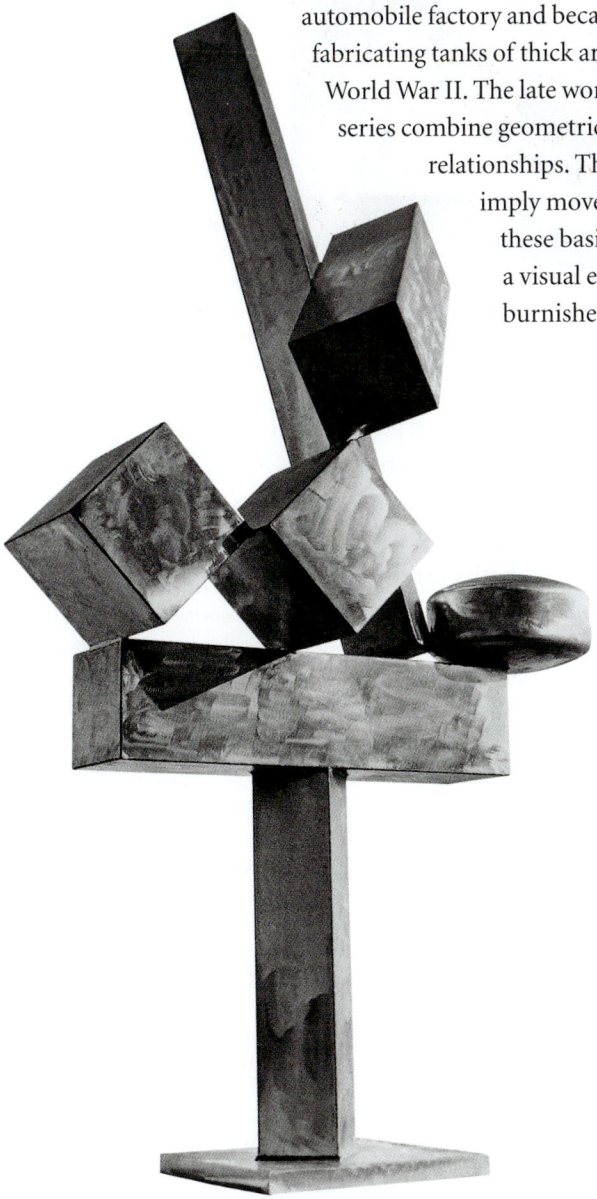

1.2.3 David Smith, *Cubi XIX*, 1964. Stainless steel, 113¼ × 21⅝ × 20⅝". Tate Gallery, London, England

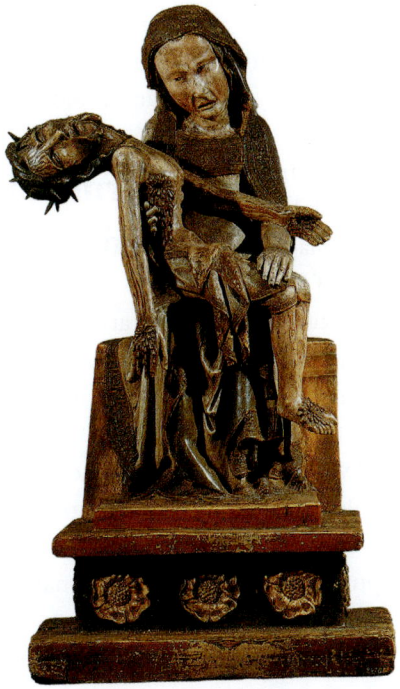

1.2.4 *Roettgen Pietà* (*Vesperbild*), Middle Rhine region, c. 1330. Wood, height 34½". Rheinisches Landesmuseum, Bonn, Germany

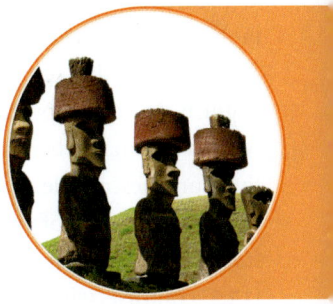

The Easter Island *moai* ancestor figures are examples of artistically accentuated organic forms: see **3.5.16, p. 457**

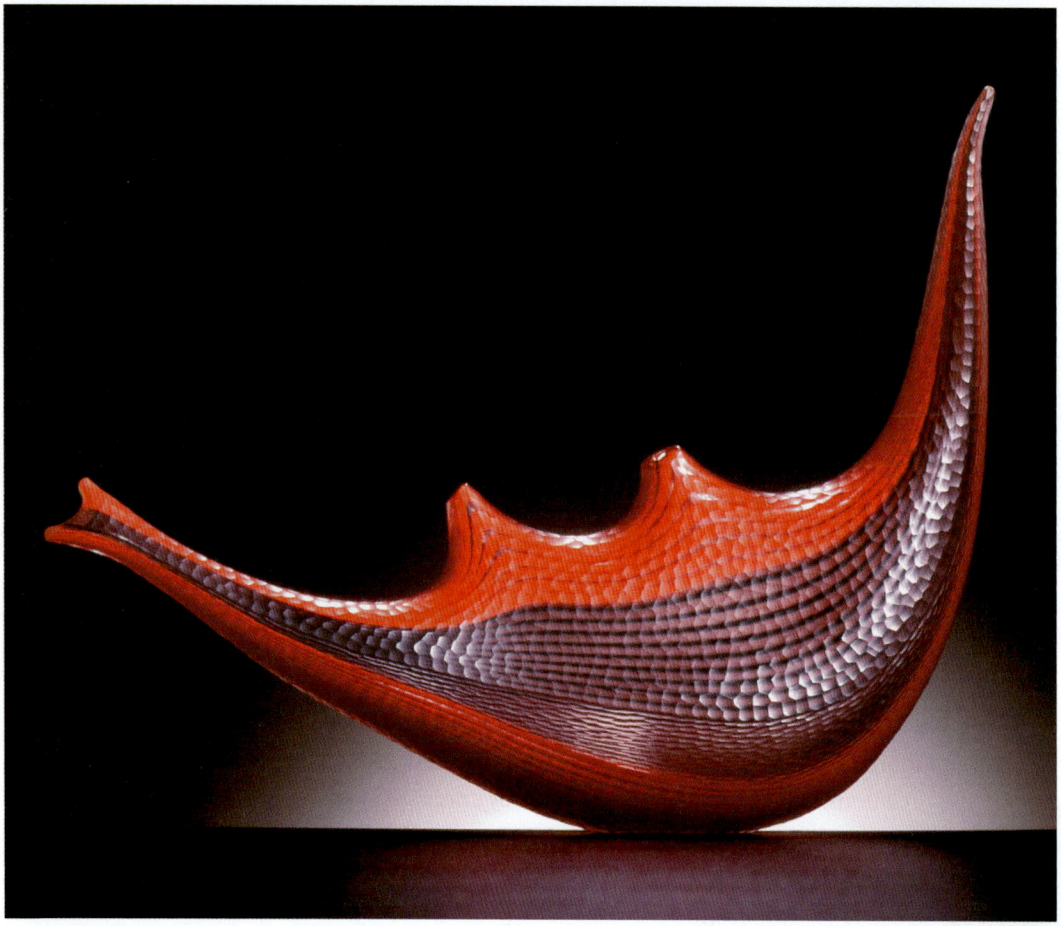

1.2.5 Lino Tagliapietra, *Batman*, 1998. Glass, 11½ × 15½ × 3½"

The suffering of torture is made shocking by the disjointedness of the lifeless Jesus. Stiffly angular, he is stretched across the lap of his mother Mary. Prickly thorns, gushing wounds, and crumpled drapery give texture to pain and anguish. The disproportionate size of Mary's twisted face makes her unbearable sorrow all the more inescapable.

The expression of vigor and uplift in Italian glass artist Lino Tagliapietra's *Batman* (**1.2.5**) contrasts with the expression of death and despair in the *Roettgen Pietà*. Tagliapietra (b. 1934) wanted to convey the idea of "a creature who emerges from his dark cave to share goodness and light." He has enhanced the positive emotion of this **abstract** image by using bright **color** and stretching the extreme edges upward as if this were a growing, living object. Rather than producing hard, angular distortions, the artist uses a form that is lively and organic. The natural energy of light is captured in the glowing transparency of the glass. Tagliapietra, a master of glassblowing technique, wants the form to allude, without making a literal reference, to the idea behind the character Batman. Thus we are free to revel in the life, energy, and power of the superhero through an expressive form, rather than a carefully depicted, lifelike representation. Tagliapietra says of the work, "I imaged pieces that allow the viewer to see both the reality and fantasy of Batman's world."

Form in Relief and in the Round

An artist who works with three-dimensional form can choose to create a work in **relief** or **in the round**. A relief is a work in which forms project from a flat surface. It is designed to be viewed from one side only. A form in the round can be seen from all sides.

Forms in relief combine aspects of two-dimensional and three-dimensional works of art. Like a two-dimensional work, a relief can be mounted on a wall or other surface. Although

Abstract: art imagery that departs from recognizable images of the natural world
Color: the optical effect caused when reflected white light of the spectrum is divided into separate wavelengths
Relief: a raised form on a largely flat background. For example, the design on a coin is "in relief"
In the round: a freestanding sculpted work that can be viewed from all sides
Facade: any side of a building, usually the front or entrance
Foreground: the part of a work depicted as nearest to the viewer
High relief: a carved panel where the figures project with a great deal of depth from the background
Bas-relief (low relief): a sculpture carved with very little depth: the carved subjects rise only slightly above the surface of the work
Stela (plural **stelae**): upright stone slab decorated with inscriptions or pictorial relief carvings
Composition: the overall design or organization of a work
Freestanding: any sculpture that stands separate from walls or other surfaces so that it can be viewed from a 360-degree radius

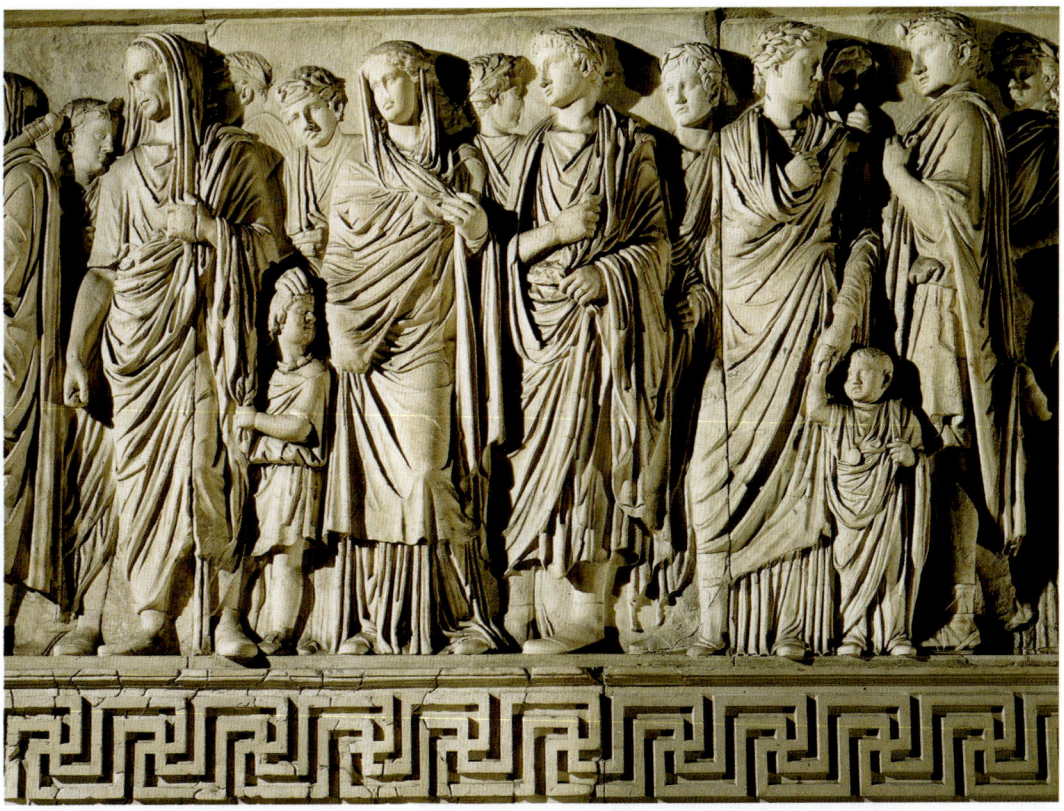

1.2.6 Imperial Procession from the Ara Pacis Augustae, 13 BCE. Marble altar, Museo dell'Ara Pacis, Rome, Italy

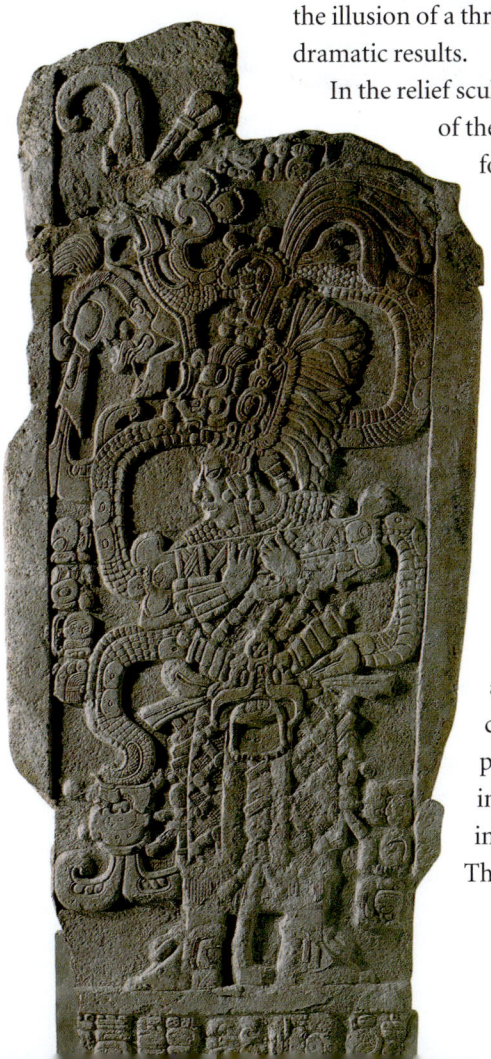

1.2.7 (below) Stela with supernatural scene, Mexico or Guatemala, 761 CE. Limestone, 92 × 42 × 3". Fine Arts Museums of San Francisco

relief may appear to limit the work's potential visual impact, in fact the sculptor can create the illusion of a three-dimensional space, with dramatic results.

In the relief sculptures on the south **facade** of the Ara Pacis Augustae (Latin for Altar of Peace of Augustus) in Rome, Italy, a sculptor chose to fit many figures into a limited space (**1.2.6**). The unknown artist uses the depth of the carvings to suggest that some areas of the composition are further away from us than others. The figures in the **foreground** are deeply carved (in **high relief**) so that the folds in their togas are strongly delineated by shadows. But the artist wanted to imply a large crowd rather than just a line of people. The figures behind those in the foreground are also carved in relief, but not quite so deeply. They appear to be further away because there is less shadow defining their shape. The artist suggests greater depth by using a third group of figures who are carved in shallow relief, so that there is no shadow at all to make them stand out. This effect is clear in the upper left-hand corner, where the carving overlaps and diminishes in height.

The Maya artist who carved **1.2.7** in **bas-relief** worked in a tradition quite different from that of the Roman sculptor of the Ara Pacis, with its deeply incised figures. On the Maya **stela** all the carving is carefully arranged on the same plane. The sculptor has created a large figure of a Maya ruler, shown wearing a highly detailed and elaborate costume. The Maya writing to the left of the figure seems to be of equal visual weight; the sculptor intended the viewer to read every element of the **composition**.

A sculpture is no longer a relief when the work can be viewed from all sides: this kind of form is known as in the round. Such **freestanding** works of art occupy space in the same way that other real-life objects do. When an artist composes a work that is designed in the round, he or she considers how the viewer will interact with the work. In the ancient Roman

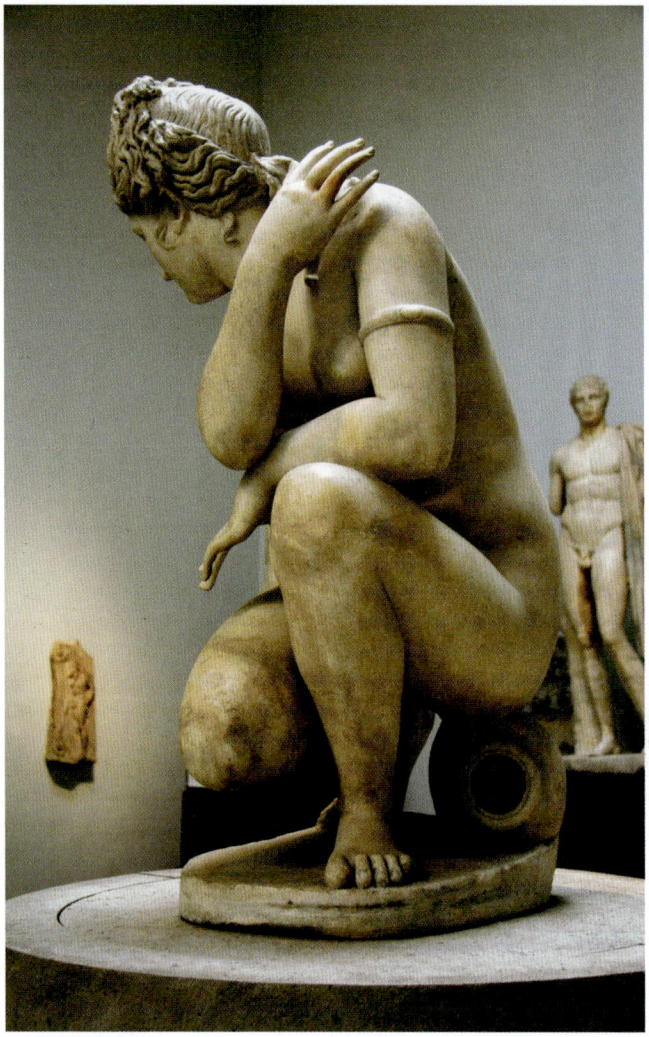

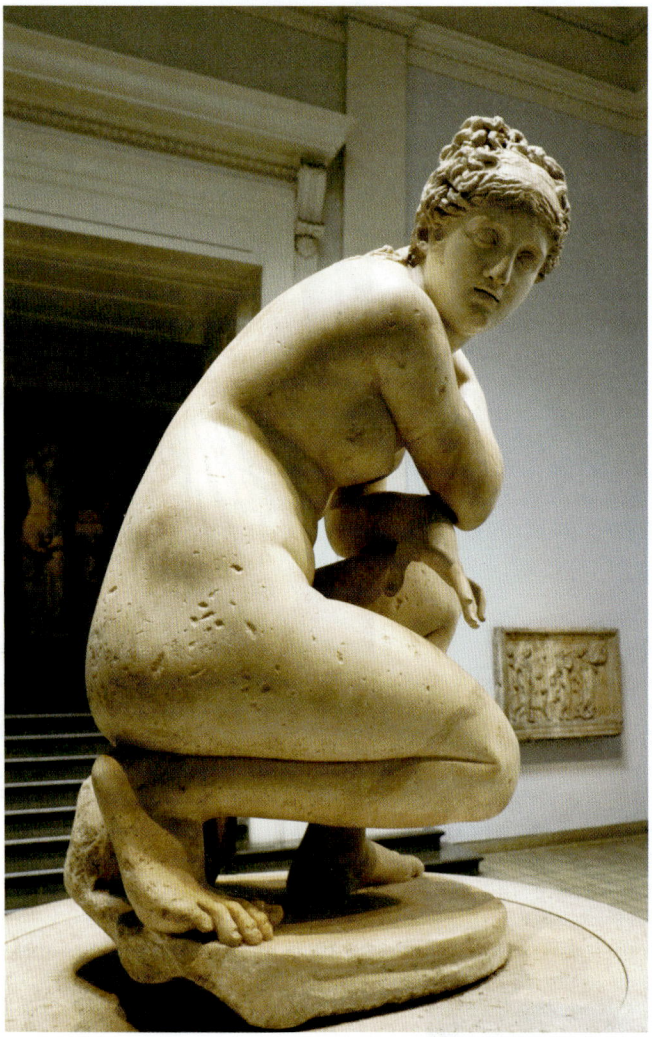

1.2.8a and **1.2.8b** *Naked Aphrodite Crouching at Her Bath (Lely's Venus)*. Marble, Roman, 2nd century CE; copy of lost Greek original of the late 3rd/2nd century BCE, height 44⅛". British Museum, London, England (on loan from Her Majesty the Queen)

statue *Naked Aphrodite Crouching at Her Bath*, also known as *Lely's Venus*, the artist rewards the viewer who walks around the work, by constantly changing the elements of the design (**1.2.8a** and **1.2.8b**). You can see that the figure's face is turned away from a forward-looking position, and the body is slightly twisted. So, if a viewer moves from one side to another, there will be new surface changes and interesting angles from which to look, enlivening the experience and holding the viewer's attention. Each time he or she moves, the design of the work reveals a different aspect, and the viewer's perception of it changes. From the view in **1.2.8a**, you are encouraged to move to the opposite side to view Aphrodite's face (**1.2.8b**). The artist has effectively designed the work so that you feel compelled to look further and experience it more fully, while the sculpture's form remains satisfying from every viewpoint. This is one important attribute of good three-dimensional design.

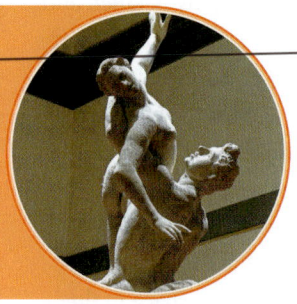

Giambologna's freestanding *Rape of a Sabine* has been sculpted for the viewer to experience in the round: see **2.4.2a, p. 243**

Focal point: the center of interest or activity in a work of art, often drawing the viewer's attention to the most important element
Axis: an imaginary line showing the center of a shape, volume, or composition

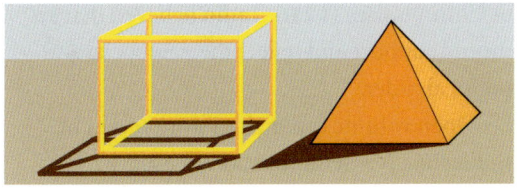

1.2.9 Volume (left) and mass (right)

Volume

Three-dimensional objects necessarily have volume. Volume is the amount of space occupied by an object. Solid objects have volume; so do objects that enclose an empty space. Mass, by contrast, suggests that something is solid and occupies space (**1.2.9**). Architectural forms usually enclose a volume of interior space to be used for living or working. For example, some hotel interiors feature a large, open atrium that becomes the **focal point** of the lobby. Some sculptures accentuate weight and solidity rather than openness. Such works have very few open spaces that we can see. The presence of mass suggests weight, gravity, and a connection to the Earth. The absence of mass suggests lightness, airiness, flight. Asymmetrical masses—or masses that cannot be equally divided on a central **axis**—can suggest dynamism, movement, change.

Open Volume

When artists enclose a space with materials that are not completely solid, they create an open volume. In *Ghostwriter*, Ralph Helmick (b. 1952) and Stuart Schechter (b. 1958) use carefully suspended pieces of metal to make an open volume that, when looked at as a whole, creates the image of a large human head (**1.2.10a** and **1.2.10b**). The small metal pieces, which represent letters of the alphabet, little heads, and other objects, are organized so that they delineate the shape of the head but do not enclose the space. In the stairwell where the piece hangs, the empty space and the "head" are not distinct or separate, but the shape is nonetheless implied.

The Russian artist Vladimir Tatlin's (1885–1953) *Monument to the Third International* was intended to be a huge tower housing the offices

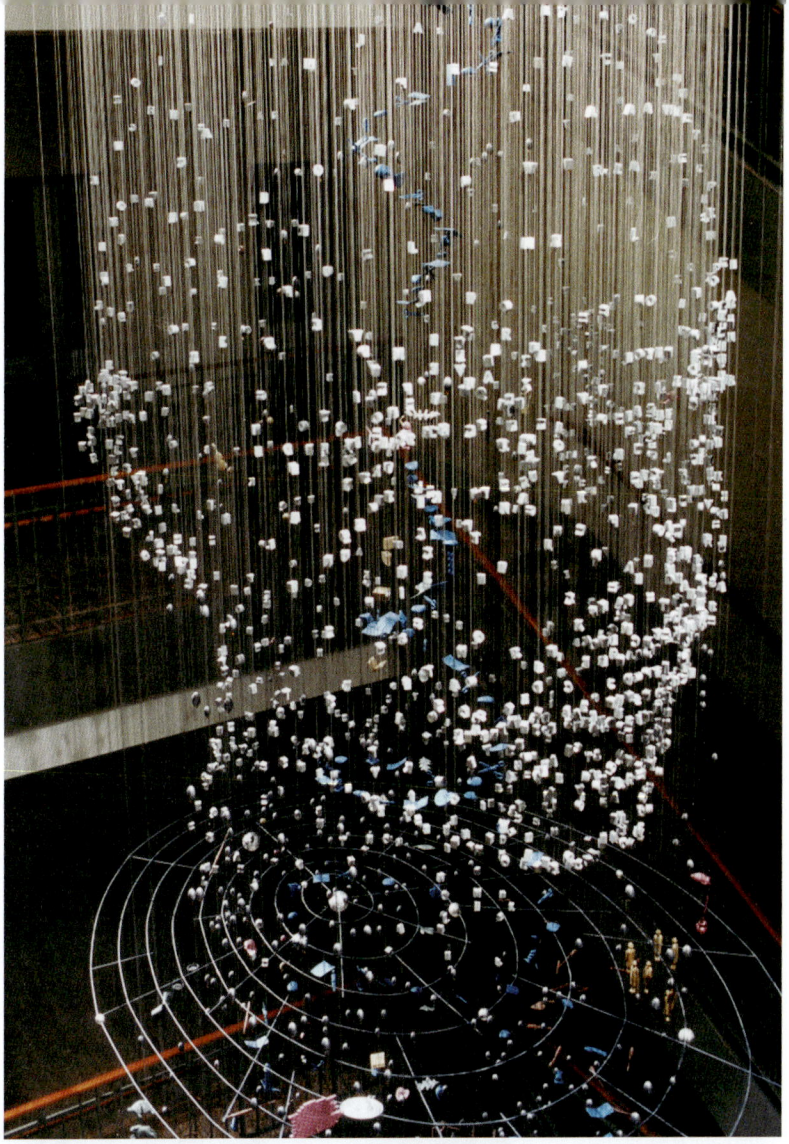

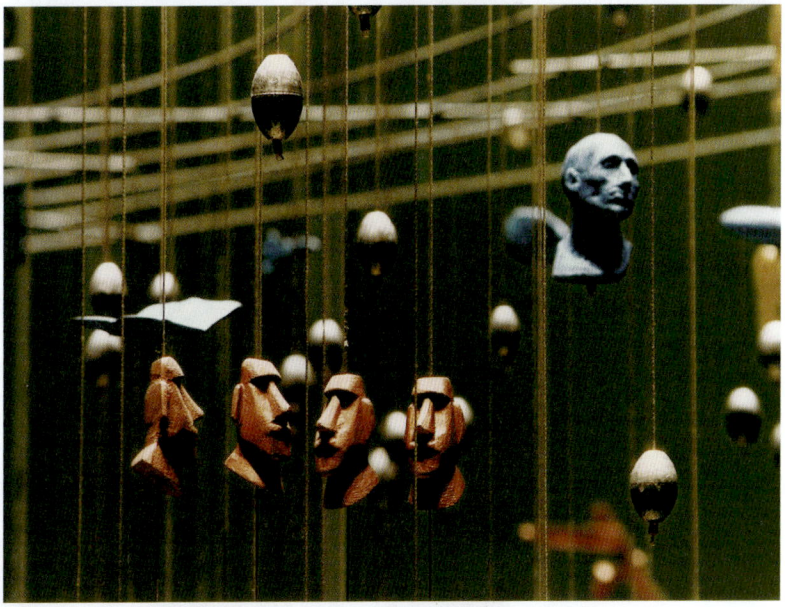

1.2.10a (top) Ralph Helmick and Stuart Schechter, *Ghostwriter*, 1994. Cast metal/stainless cable, 36 × 8 × 10'. Evanston Public Library, Illinois

1.2.10b (above) Detail of *Ghostwriter*

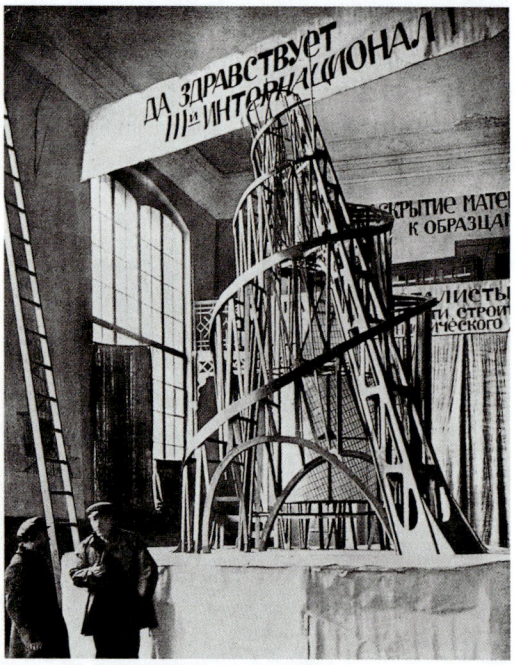

1.2.11 Vladimir Tatlin, Model for *Monument to the Third International*, 1919

and chamber of delegates of the Communist International. It was going to commemorate the triumph of Russia's Bolshevik Revolution. Never built, it would have been much higher than the Eiffel Tower in Paris, France. In its planned form, the spiraling open volume of the interior, and its proposed novel use of such materials as steel and glass, symbolize the modernism and dynamism of Communism (**1.2.11**). Tatlin believed that art should support and reflect the new social and political order.

Open volume can make a work feel light. *In the Blue (Crest)*, a collaborative work by American sculptors Carol Mickett (b. 1952) and Robert Stackhouse (b. 1942), was created to imply the presence of water (**1.2.12**). By creating **negative space** (the openings between the wooden slats) with crowds of horizontal struts, the artists make the work seem to float. Mickett and Stackhouse also curve the pieces and place them at irregular intervals to create many subtle changes in direction. This arrangement gives a feeling of motion, like the gentle ripples of flowing water. The artists hope that viewers will experience a sensation of being surrounded by water as they walk through the passage.

Negative space, like that used in *In the Blue (Crest)*, illustrates the importance of leaving areas of a work "visually empty." These openings allow light to become a more active part of the work by adding light and dark **contrasts**. Negative space is also common in two-dimensional work, but instead of allowing light to play a more active role, the emptiness contrasts with the positive shapes and lines.

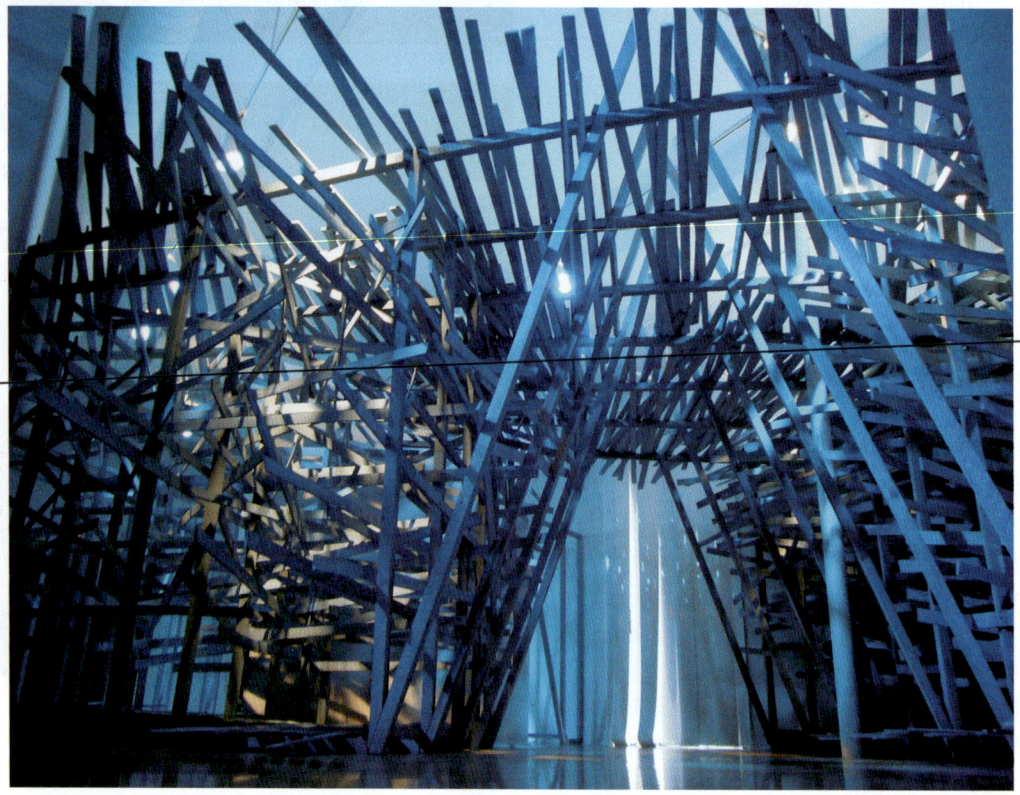

1.2.12 Carol Mickett and Robert Stackhouse, *In the Blue (Crest)*, 2008. Painted cypress, 24 × 108 × 11'. Installation at St. Petersburg Art Center, Florida

Negative space: an unoccupied or empty space that is created after positive shapes are positioned in a work of art
Contrast: a drastic difference between such elements as color or value (lightness/darkness) when they are presented together

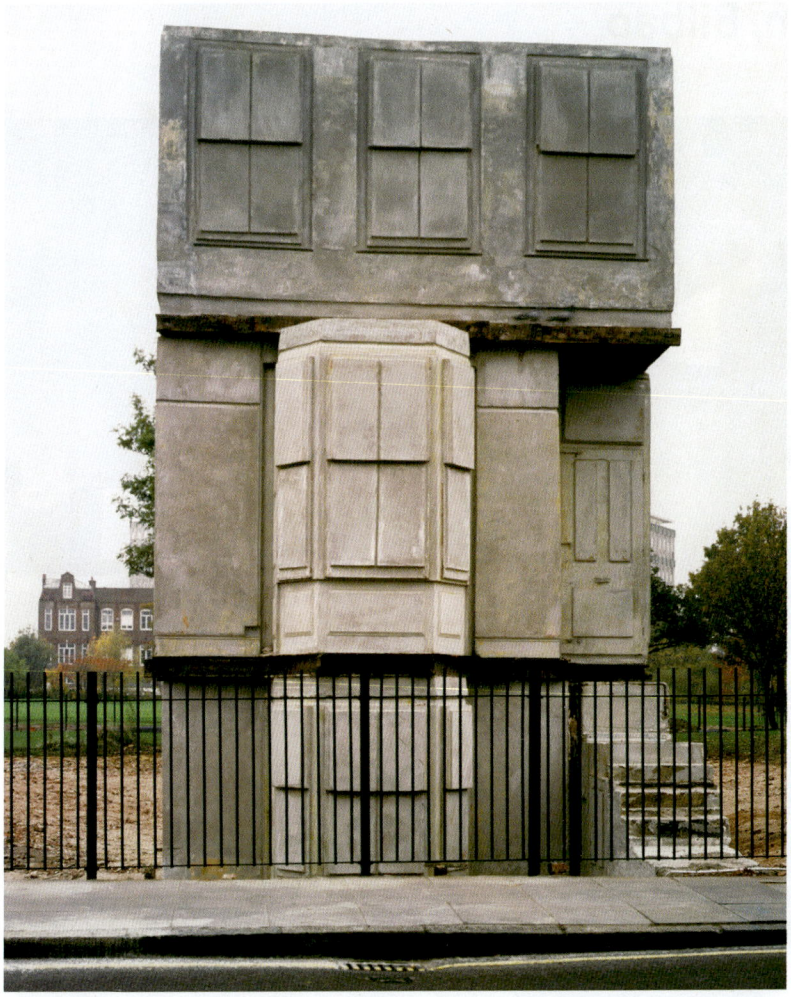

Mass

Mass suggests that a volume is solid and occupies space. Every substance has mass. Our perception of mass influences how we react to and what we feel about that substance. We can feel the weight of a pebble in the palm of our hand, or the heaviness of a chair as we pull it away from a table. Our perception of mass in large objects is derived from our imagination, our previous experience with smaller objects, and our understanding of the forces of nature. Artists tap into these various intuitions when they create a work of art.

Mass can suggest weight in a three-dimensional object. Some artists imply mass (without it necessarily being there) to give us the impression that the object we are looking at is very heavy. In movies, special-effect artists play on the use of illusion to create the impression of great weight; for instance, boulders that look crushingly heavy (and real) are actually made of foam. Mass does not necessarily imply heaviness, only that a volume is solid and occupies space.

The mass of British sculptor Rachel Whiteread's *House* suggests great weight and solidity (**1.2.13**). To create this work, Whiteread (b. 1963) filled the interior space of a house with tons of concrete before demolishing the exterior. The empty volume that was once filled with the happy and sad moments of ordinary domestic life was thus turned into a commemoration of its former self. Whiteread took the volume of this building's interior and transformed it into a memorial of the lives of the people who used to live in it, and in other houses just like it. We comprehend not only the weight of the concrete, but also the related associations of life and death, memory and change.

The sculpture of Father Damien by the American artist Marisol (b. Maria Sol Escobar, 1930) stands as an immovable object against an irresistible force (**1.2.14**). It depicts the courage of a humanitarian hero. Father Damien was

1.2.13 (above) Rachel Whiteread, *House*, 1993. Concrete. Bow, London, England (demolished 1994)

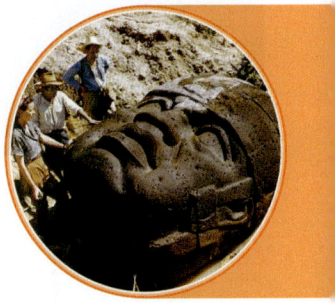

Another example of mass can be found in the colossal Olmec head from Veracruz, Mexico: see **3.4.8, p. 434**

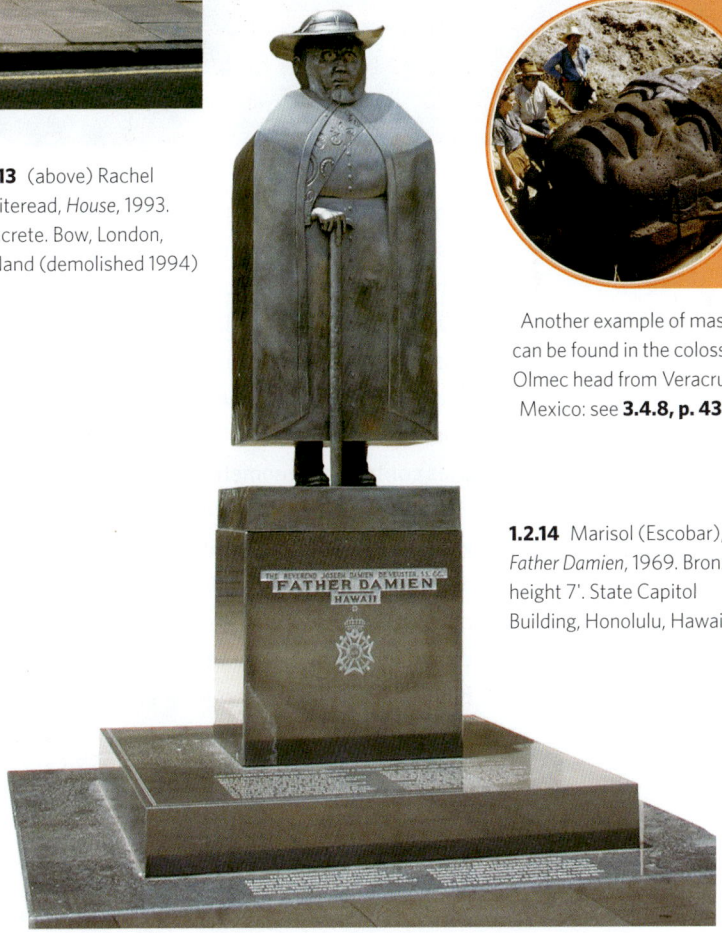

1.2.14 Marisol (Escobar), *Father Damien*, 1969. Bronze, height 7'. State Capitol Building, Honolulu, Hawaii

The Guggenheim Museum, Bilbao

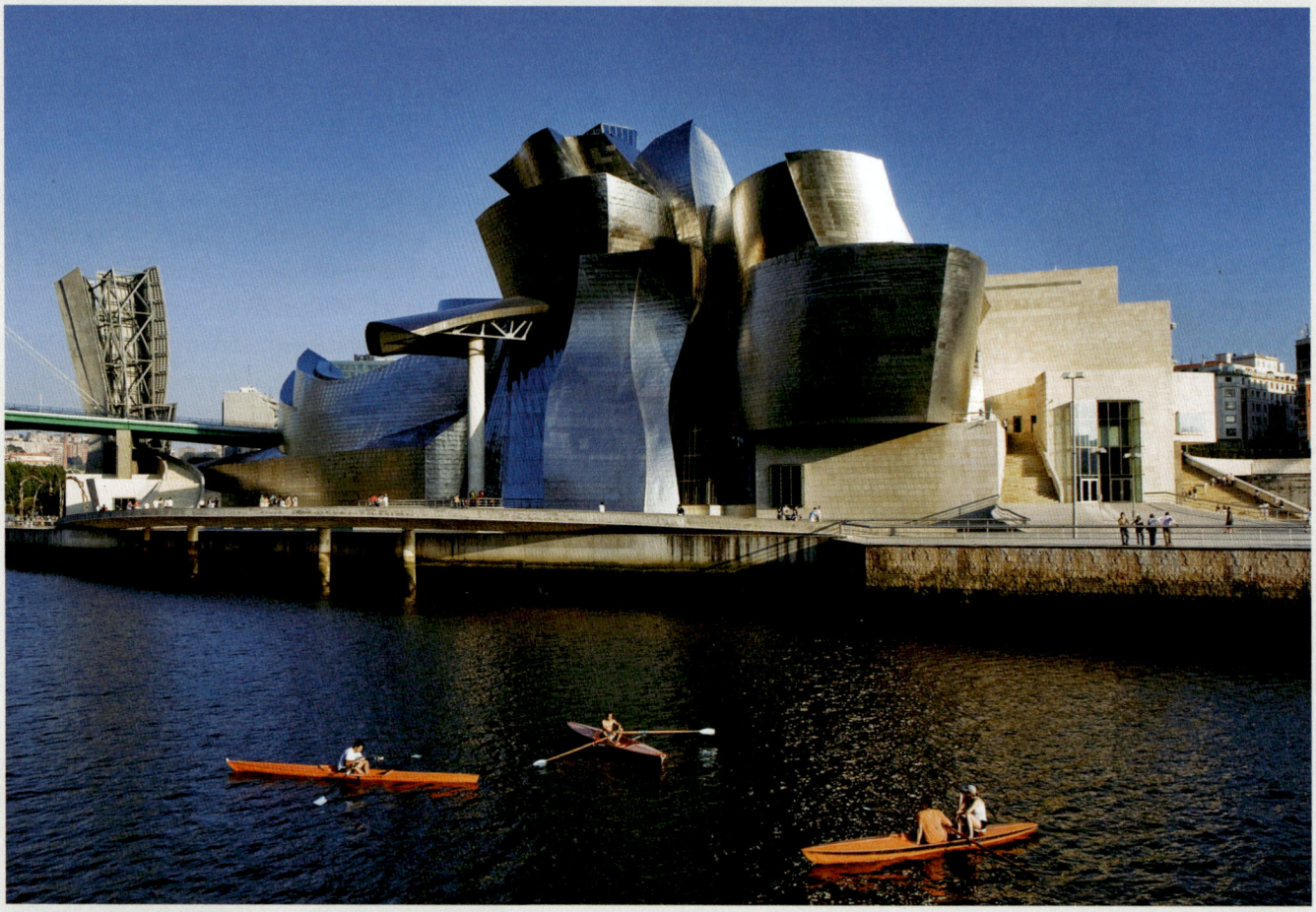

1.2.15 Frank Gehry, Guggenheim Museum, 1997, Bilbao, Spain

The American architect Frank Gehry (b. 1929) designed the Guggenheim Museum, located between a river and a motorway, in Bilbao, Spain; it was completed in 1997 (**1.2.15**). Bilbao was once a center for shipbuilding, and the undulating surfaces of Gehry's creation suggest ships and ship construction. Gehry's design uses contrasts in geometric and organic form. Historically, architectural design has relied on geometric form. Organic forms, by comparison, are more difficult to visualize and plan in advance; curved and irregular structures are difficult to survey, measure, plumb, and level. But Gehry used computer programs originally invented for aerospace design to plan buildings that contradict our preconceived ideas about architecture as geometric form. Most of the walls of the Guggenheim Museum consist of irregular, curving, organic forms that rise and fall unpredictably. The undulating surfaces give a sense of movement and life to the structure. This could make some visitors feel disoriented, but Gehry counters this at critical junctures by using strongly geometric form. At the entrance, for instance, the reassurance of geometric form encourages even the most apprehensive visitor to enter the building.

Gehry employs both sculptural relief and in-the-round forms. The surfaces of the organic portion of the building are covered with titanium tiles. The subtle changes to the surfaces of this material resemble an abstract bas-relief. But the entire building is also like a sculpture in the round that the viewer can stroll around to appreciate its unexpected juts and curves.

Gehry's museum has reshaped its location. The interior space, designed to meet the changing needs of art and artists in the future, can also be extended or reduced, creating interesting exhibition opportunities. The complex shapes

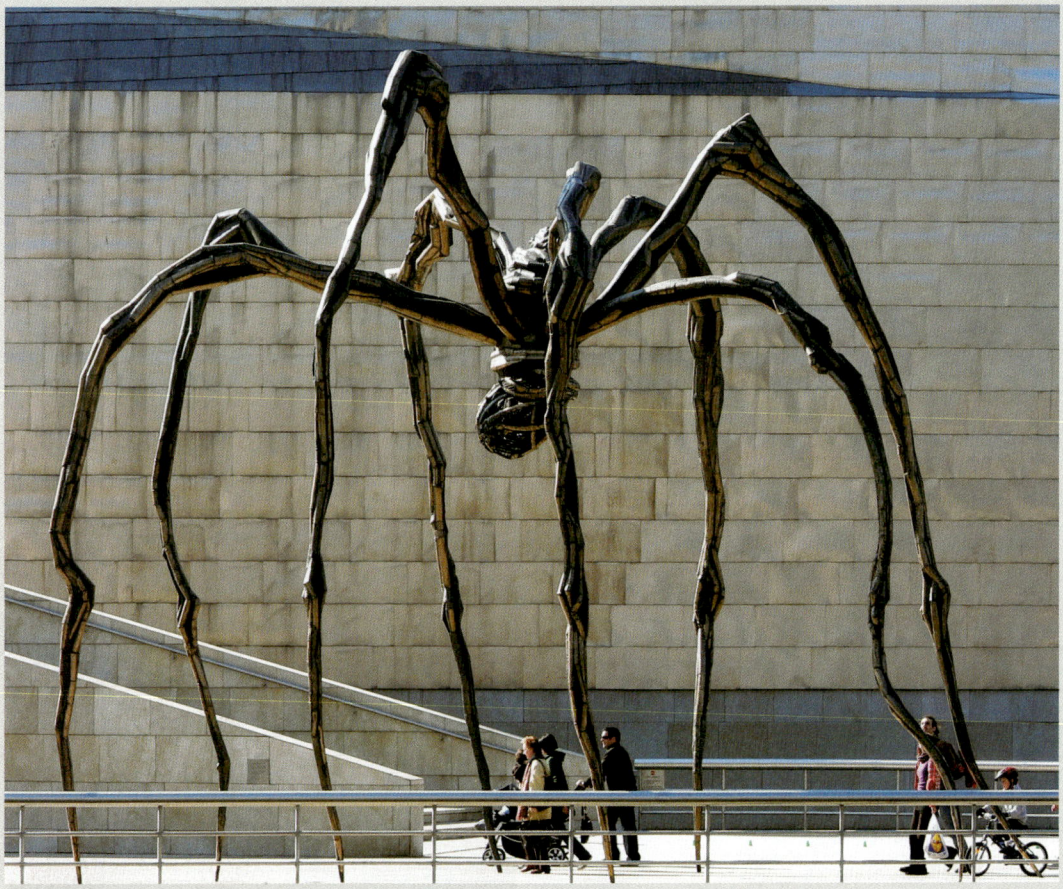

1.2.16 Louise Bourgeois, *Maman*, 1999 (cast 2001). Bronze, stainless steel, and marble, 29'4⅜" × 32'9⅛" × 38'1". Guggenheim Museum, Bilbao, Spain

of the building extend out into space like a huge boat, emphasizing its relationship to the nearby River Nervión. When it was first constructed, the building stood in stark contrast to the surrounding urban landscape. It was designed to offer an optimistic vision in what was at that time a deteriorating industrial district, and has done so in the most extraordinary way: inspired by Gehry's creation, this part of the city has been transformed into the vibrant cultural and commercial area it is today.

The shimmering titanium tiles of Gehry's building are complemented by a sculpture that stands beside the museum, *Maman* (**1.2.16**; meaning "Momma" in French), by French artist Louise Bourgeois (1911–2010). The Guggenheim's apparently solid mass is contrasted with the spindly form and open volume of *Maman*. The negative space surrounding its legs and body imparts lightness. The subtle variations of angle in the legs imply movement. The wobbly vulnerability of the spider contrasts with the massive solidity of the building. Even though this spider is made of bronze, the effect is one of lightness. And by suspending below the central body a container of marble spheres like an egg sac, Bourgeois wants to suggest both the tenderness and fierce protectiveness of motherhood.

Brancusi and Rodin
Using Mass to Describe Love

Mass is an element of art that deals with solidity in three-dimensional objects. We can see how two artists can work in the same medium—carved stone—and manipulate its mass to create two very different interpretations of the idea of romantic love.

The Romanian-born French sculptor Constantin Brancusi (1876–1957) used the element of mass to support his idea about the nature of love and its permanence. In his work *The Kiss* (**1.2.17a**) Brancusi carves directly into a block of limestone to express the idea of two lovers unified in their relationship with each other. Stone is a material that implies a heavy mass, and it is associated with some of the oldest man-made monuments in human history. By fusing the separate figures into one solid stone mass, Brancusi communicates a transcendent and timeless love that is not bound by the human body and its limited time on Earth, but becomes symbolic of something ancient and lasting.

In comparison to Brancusi's *The Kiss* is a work of the same name by the French sculptor Auguste Rodin (1840–1917). Considered a true example of a modern sculptor, Rodin dismissed Classical sculpture and traditional poses. Instead, he used live models and depicted energetic and passionate figures. Rodin's *The Kiss* (**1.2.17b**) also depicts two lovers, but in a more literal and realistic way than that of Brancusi's work. The figures closely resemble real human bodies, and the artist portrays the "inner feelings" of the couple by emphasizing their muscles and anatomy. The couple was originally conceived to be part of Rodin's *Gates of Hell*, two large bronze doors depicting scenes from a masterpiece of medieval Italian literature, Dante's *Divine Comedy*. *The Kiss* is based upon the story of Paolo and Francesca (wife of Paolo's brother). Rodin did not include the figures in the final composition, and instead made several copies of *The Kiss*, one of which was a marble commissioned by the French government.

Although both artists chose to work in the same medium, Rodin decided to carve a naturalistic image of two figures embracing, with much less remaining of the original block of stone than in Brancusi's work. Rodin downplays the role of the material, instead creating a lighter expression of mass and revealing the form and texture of the human body to communicate the power of real, physical love.

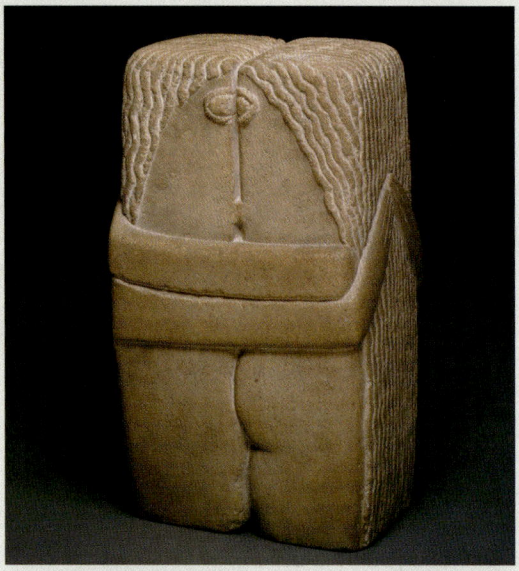

1.2.17a Constantin Brancusi, *The Kiss*, 1916. Limestone, 23 × 13¼ × 10". Philadelphia Museum of Art

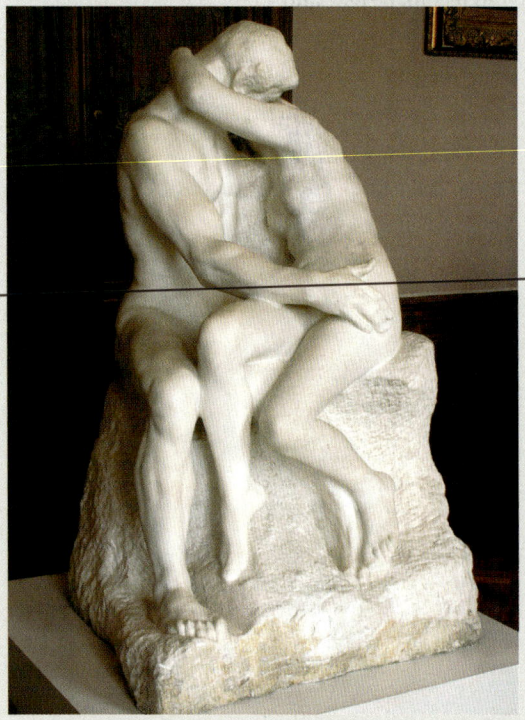

1.2.17b Auguste Rodin, *The Kiss*, c. 1882. Marble, 71½ × 44¼ × 46". Musée Rodin, Paris

a Catholic missionary who supervised a leper colony on the Hawaiian island of Molokai during the nineteenth century. His steadfast compassion is suggested by the four-square mass of Marisol's work, while his upright correctness is reflected in its vertical lines—in the cane, in the cape, and in the straight row of buttons. The stout form communicates stability and determination. Father Damien, who himself died of leprosy while serving its victims, exemplified such heroism that the Hawaiian legislature voted to place this memorial to him in front of the State Capitol Building in Honolulu.

Texture

Any three-dimensional object that can be touched and felt has actual texture, the tactile sensation we experience when we physically encounter a three-dimensional form (two-dimensional images have *implied* texture, which means the artist creates an effect that reminds us of our tactile memory of an actual texture). Textures vary, from the slick, cold surface of a finely finished metal object, to the rough-hewn splintery character of a broken branch, to the pebbly surface of a rocky beach.

When you hold this book in your hands, you feel its weight and the surface of its pages. We mostly rely on the impressions we receive from our hands when we think of texture, and these tactile experiences influence the way we look at art.

Viewers of Indian-born British artist Anish Kapoor's (b. 1954) sculpture *Cloud Gate* experience actual texture when they see and touch the work (**1.2.18**). We understand the tactile sensation of touching a smooth, stainless-steel surface. Kapoor presents us with a highly polished, organic (bean-like) form that literally reflects the city of Chicago and the surrounding activity as it takes place. By providing such an invitingly slick surface, he wants the viewer to interact with the sculpture in visual and tactile ways. A viewer feels welcome to touch the work, knowing that it will feel cool and slippery: the invitation would not be as clear, or as appealing, if a rougher surface had been presented. The sleek actual texture of this work influences the actions of those viewers who encounter it.

Even if we do not touch three-dimensional works of art, we can still think of them as having actual texture. This is an association we can make based on our previous experience of touching objects that have similar surfaces. We know what polished stone feels like (cool and smooth), so when we look at a highly polished marble sculpture we can imagine how its texture feels, based on our past experience.

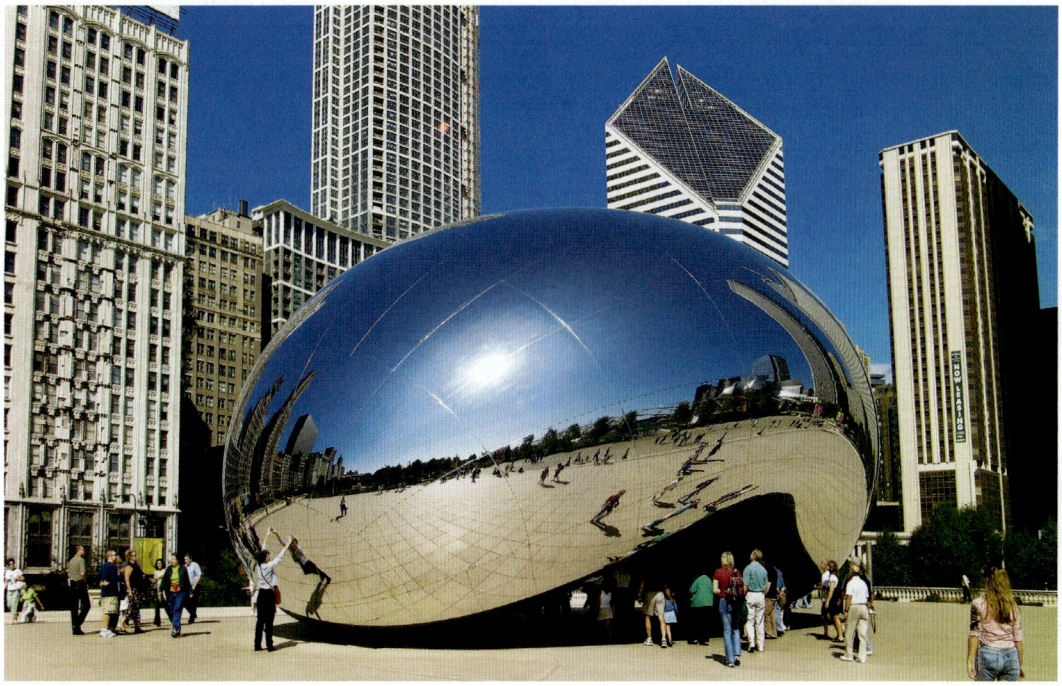

1.2.18 Anish Kapoor, *Cloud Gate*, 2004. Stainless steel, 32'9" × 65'7" × 41'12". Millennium Park, Chicago, Illinois

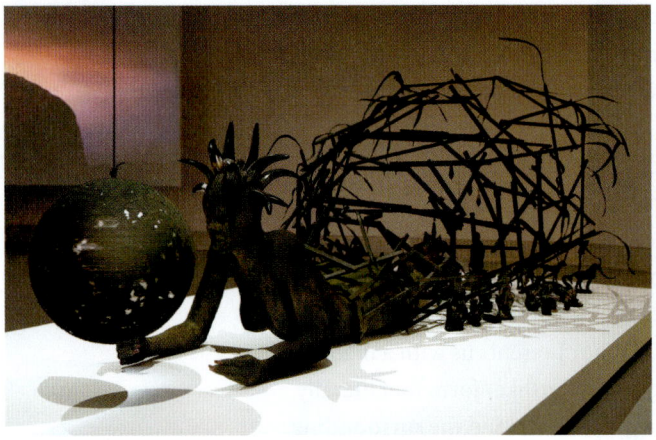

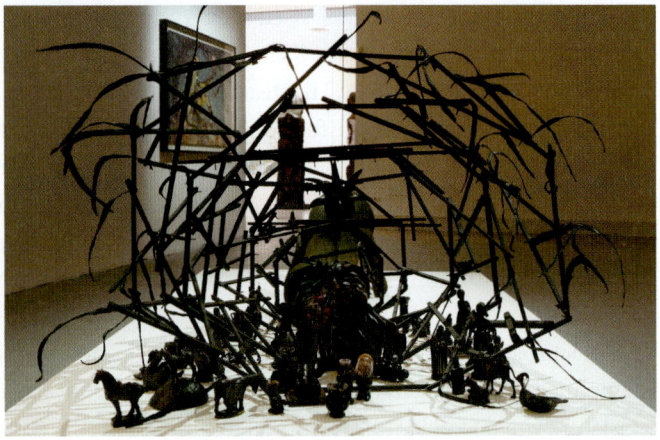

1.2.19a and b Wangechi Mutu, *She's Got the Whole World in Her*, 2015. Mannequin, paper, wax, and lights, 9' × 5' × 3'5"

Although viewers are not encouraged to handle the works of contemporary African-born artist Wangechi Mutu (b. 1972), texture is still an effective element. The artist employs a wide variety of organic textures derived from such transient materials as paper and wax to symbolize issues of gender, colonialism, and other concerns unique to people in Africa or of African descent. In the sculpture *She's Got the Whole World in Her* (**1.2.19a** and **1.2.19b**) Mutu uses textured objects to express the changing role of African women, from traditional agrarian responsibilities to careers in business and government, as well as modern society in general. This work features a female figure surrounded by natural textures—wood, animal horns, and rough papier mâché—gazing at a lighted globe. Feathers protrude from the rear of the body, which is encased in a basket-like space where small models of animals and figures are placed. The light of the globe and the soft texture of the feathers allude to the elegant and dignified nature of the feminine figure contrasted with the hardness of the horns and the rough construction of the basket-like skirt that imprisons the body.

Surrealism, Surrealist: an artistic movement in the 1920s and later; its works were inspired by dreams and the subconscious

Subversive Texture

A subversive texture contradicts our previous tactile experience. Some types of cactus appear to have a soft, furry covering, but touching them will be painful. Artists and designers use the contradictions and contrasts of subversive texture to invite viewers to reconsider their preconceptions about the world around them.

In the early twentieth century, artists calling themselves **Surrealists** created work that drew on ideas and images from dreams and the unconscious mind. The Swiss Surrealist Méret Oppenheim (1913–1985) used texture to contradict the conscious logical experiences of viewers. In her sculpture *Object*, Oppenheim takes a cup, saucer, and spoon, normally hard and cool to the touch, and instead makes them soft and furry (**1.2.20**). The idea of sipping tea from this object conjures up an unexpected sensation of fur tickling our lips. The artist is counting on our tactile memory to conflict with the actual experience of sipping tea from a shiny teacup. In this case, the form is recognizable, but the associated experience is not.

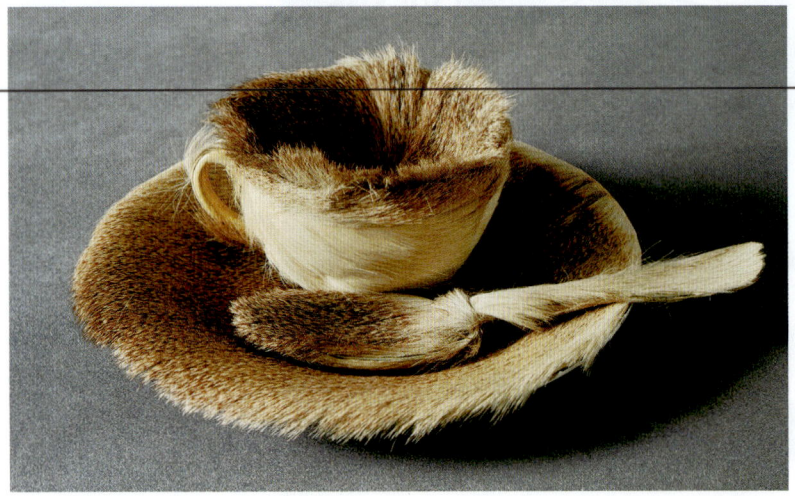

1.2.20 Méret Oppenheim, *Object*, 1936. Fur-covered cup, saucer, and spoon, height 2⅞". MoMA, New York

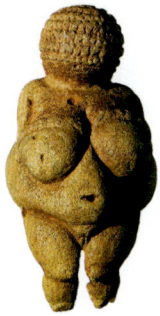

4.9.1 Woman from Willendorf, c. 24,000–22,000 BCE, p. 663

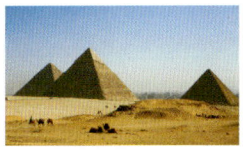

3.1.14 Pyramids at Giza, Egypt, c. 2500 BCE, p. 374

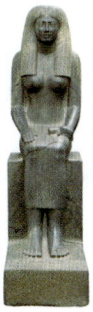

2.4.1 Sculpture of the Lady Sennuwy, Egypt, 1971–1926 BCE, p. 243

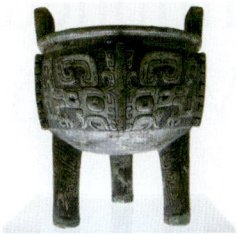

1.6.13 Liu Ding (ritual container), China, c. 1600–c. 1050 BCE, p. 134

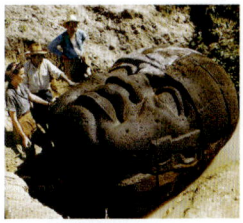

3.4.8 Colossal Olmec head, 1500–400 BCE, p. 434

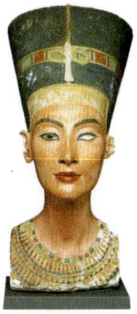

1.10.1a Bust of Queen Nefertiti, Egypt, c. 1340 BCE, p. 171

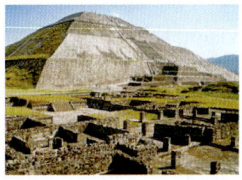

3.4.10 Pyramid of the Sun, Teotihuacan, Mexico, c. 225 CE, p. 435

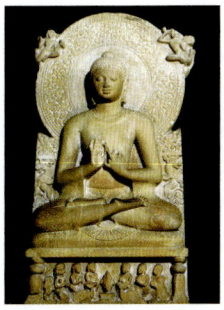

3.3.6 Seated Buddha from the Gupta period, (5th century CE), India, p. 414

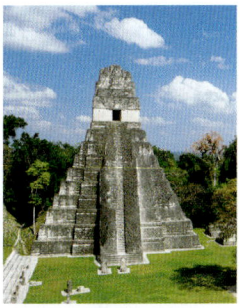

2.5.5 Maya Temple, Tikal, Guatemala, c. 300–900, p. 262

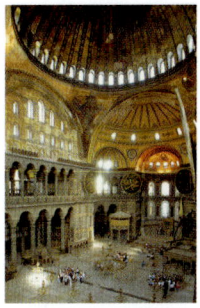

2.5.19 Hagia Sophia, Istanbul, Turkey, 532–35, p. 270

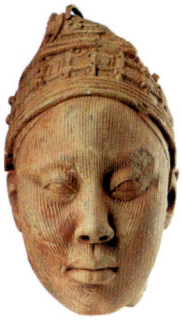

4.9.6 Head, possibly an Ife king from West Africa, 12th–14th century, p. 667

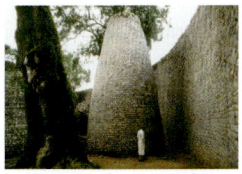

3.5.9 Conical Tower, Great Zimbabwe c. 1350–1450, p. 452

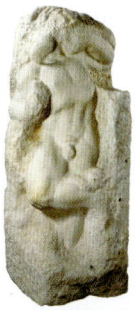

2.4.6 Michelangelo, *Awakening Slave*, 1519–20, p. 246

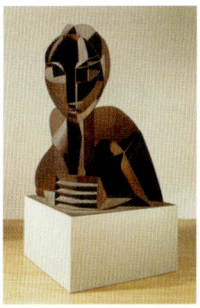

2.4.17 Naum Gabo, *Constructed Head No. 2*, 1916, p. 253

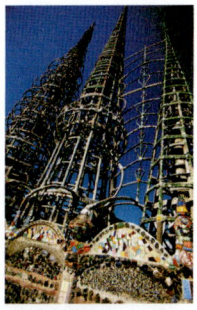

0.0.9 Simon Rodia, Watts Towers, 1921–54, p. 26

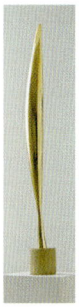

3.9.19 Constantin Brancusi, *Bird in Space*, c. 1928, p. 535

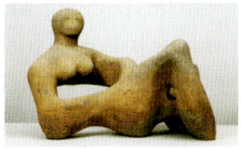

4.9.15 Henry Moore, *Recumbent Figure*, 1938, p. 674

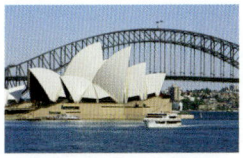

2.5.34 Jørn Utzon, Sydney Opera House, Australia, 1973, p. 280

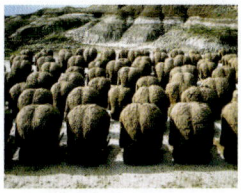

1.10.7 Magdalena Abakanowicz, *80 Backs*, 1976–80, p. 178

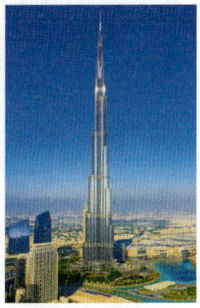

2.5.31 Adrian Smith and Bill Baker, Burj Khalifa, Dubai, 2010, p. 277

1.3 Implied Depth: Value and Space

Three-dimensional: having height, width, and depth
Two-dimensional: having height and width
Value: the lightness or darkness of a plane or area
Space: the distance between identifiable points or planes
Perspective: the creation of the illusion of depth in a two-dimensional image by using mathematical principles

> Reality is merely an illusion, albeit a very persistent one.
>
> (Albert Einstein, physicist and Nobel Prize winner)

When Albert Einstein suggested that not everything we see is real, he probably did not have art in mind. But artists readily understand his remark, because when they create a picture of real space on a flat surface they know they are creating an illusion. When we watch a magician perform a trick, we instinctively wonder how the magic was achieved. In this chapter we will reveal some of the secrets that artists rely upon to create the appearance of **three-dimensional** depth in a **two-dimensional** work of art.

The techniques artists use to imply depth—**value**, **space**, and **perspective**—evoke our past visual experiences and the way we see. Value, the lightness or darkness of a surface, emulates the effects of light and shadow, and can be used to suggest solidity. Artists have a variety of techniques based on the optics of vision that enable them to create the illusion of pictorial space. One of these is called atmospheric perspective, a method that mimics our visual perceptions of color, clarity, and form at a distance (see p. 83). Isometric and linear perspective (also explained on pp. 84–88) are drawing methods that can express the idea of three-dimensional space on a two-dimensional surface. In this chapter we will introduce these methods of creating the illusion of space and discuss why some artists choose to use them.

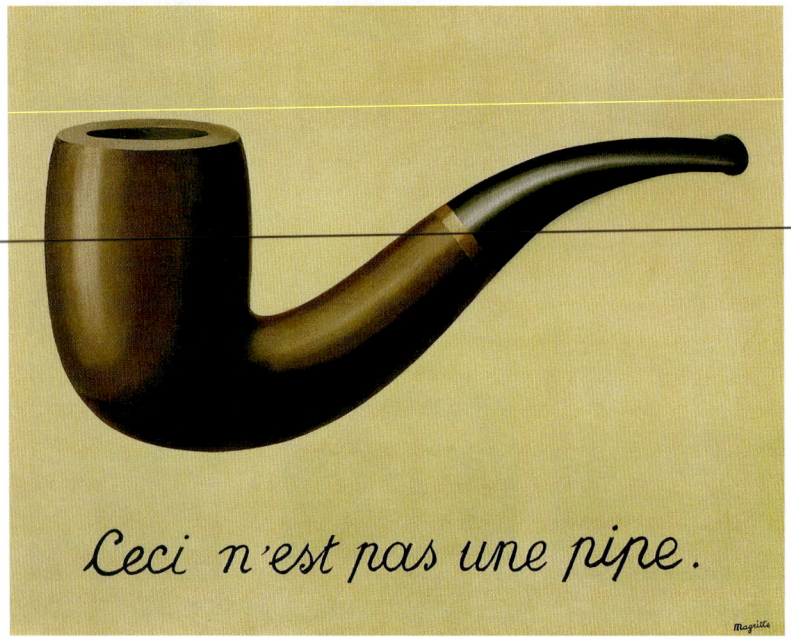

1.3.1 René Magritte, *The Treachery of Images ("This Is not a Pipe")*, 1929. Oil on canvas, 23¾ × 32". Los Angeles County Museum of Art (LACMA), California

In *The Treachery of Images*, Belgian **Surrealist** artist René Magritte (1898–1967) uses value and perspective to imply depth (**1.3.1**). The pipe is painted in varying values (light and dark tones), which create the appearance of shadows that suggest depth. The top of the pipe bowl is composed of two concentric ellipses, which is how circles appear in perspective. We know what a real pipe looks like in real space, and Magritte understands our habits of visual perception. He paints a picture of a pipe that "feels" solid, but then playfully invites us to re-examine our habits of mind.

In this painting, Magritte tells us that painting is a visual trick. By writing *"Ceci n'est pas une pipe"* ("This is not a pipe"), Magritte wants us to recognize that what appears to be a pipe is not really a pipe: it is an illusion, nothing more than paint on a flat surface. Magritte

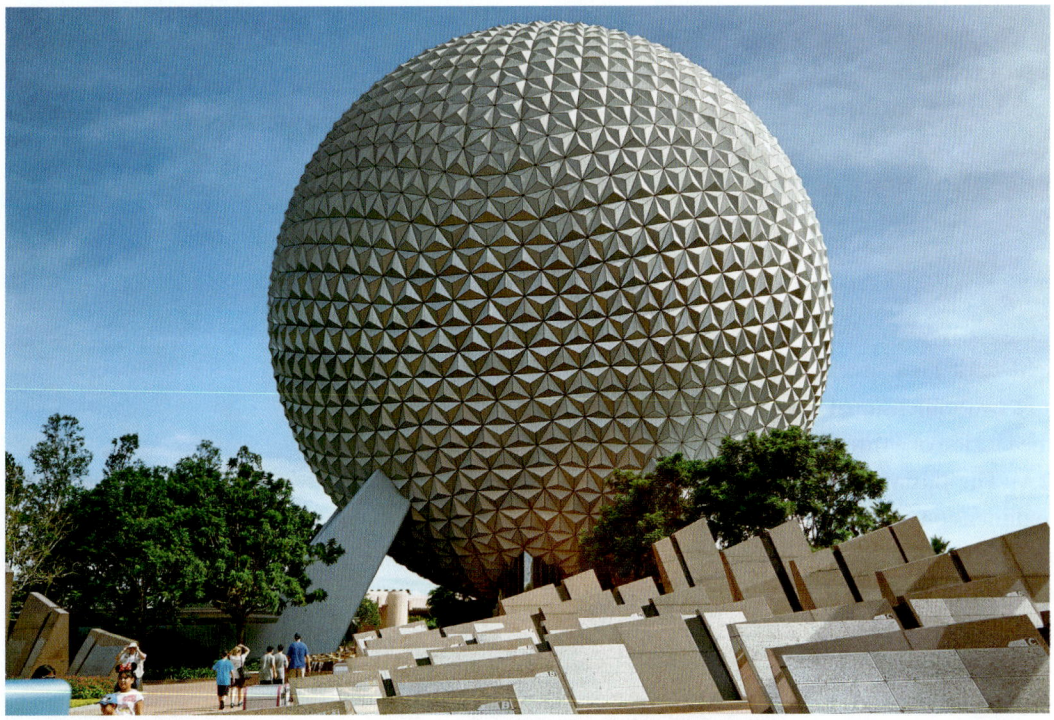

1.3.2 Spaceship Earth, Future World, Walt Disney World Resort, Orlando, Florida

confirmed this when someone asked him about the painting once. He replied that it obviously was not a real pipe, as anyone who tried to fill it with tobacco would discover.

Value

Value refers to lightness and darkness. An artist's use of value can produce a sense of solidity and can influence our mood. For example, detective movies of the 1940s were filmed in such dark tones that they had their own **style** called *film noir*, French for "black film." The serious mood of these mysteries was enhanced by the filmmaker's choice of dark values. Artists use dark and light values as tools for creating depth.

Artists learn to mimic the appearance of things by observing the effects of light as it illuminates a surface. Spaceship Earth—a large sphere, inside which is an educational ride, located in the Future World area of Walt Disney World Resort—demonstrates the effect of light on **planes** in varying locations (**1.3.2**). Many triangular planes make up the sphere's surface. Each of these planes has a different value, the relative degree of lightness or darkness of the plane depending upon the amount of light shining on it. The light source (high and to the right of the sphere here) hits some of the triangular planes of Spaceship Earth more directly than others. The planes that have a lighter value are facing the light source; the darker ones are facing away.

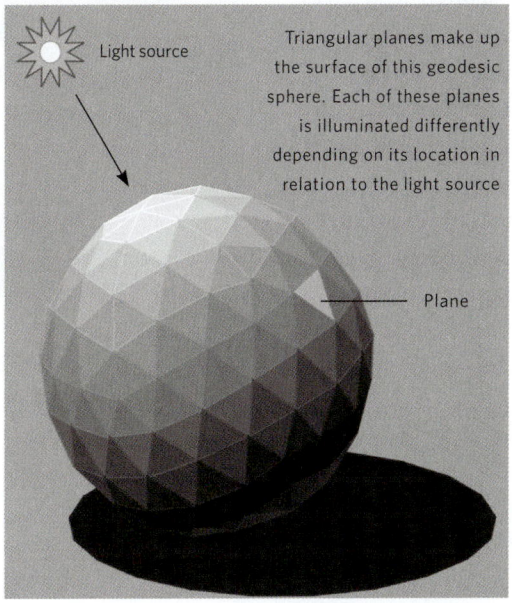

1.3.3 Values and planes of a geodesic sphere

Value changes often occur gradually. If you look at Spaceship Earth, you will notice that the relative dark values increase as the planes get further away and face away from the light (**1.3.3**).

Surrealism, Surrealist: an artistic movement in the 1920s and later; its works were inspired by dreams and the subconscious
Style: a characteristic way in which an artist or group of artists uses visual language to give a work an identifiable form of visual expression
Plane: a flat, two-dimensional surface on which an artist can create a drawing or painting. Planes can also be implied in a composition by areas that face toward, parallel to, or away from a light source

These changes occur on any object. There are subtle value changes even in a white object.

A value range refers to a series of different values. In the image of the geodesic sphere there is a value range of black, white, and eight values of gray. Black and white are the values at the extreme ends of this range.

Chiaroscuro

Chiaroscuro (Italian for "light-dark") is a method of applying value to a two-dimensional piece of artwork to create the illusion of a three-dimensional solid form (**1.3.4**). The illusion of solidity and depth in two dimensions can be achieved by using an approach devised by artists of the Italian **Renaissance**. Using a sphere as their model, Renaissance artists identified five distinct areas of light and shadow. A **highlight** marks the point where the object is most directly lit. This is most often depicted as bright white. From the highlight, moving toward the shadow, progressively less light is cast on the object until the point is reached where the surface faces away from the light. Here there is a more sudden transition to darker values, or core shadow. At the bottom of the sphere a lighter value is produced by shadow mixed with light reflected from the surrounding environment.

1.3.4 Diagram of chiaroscuro

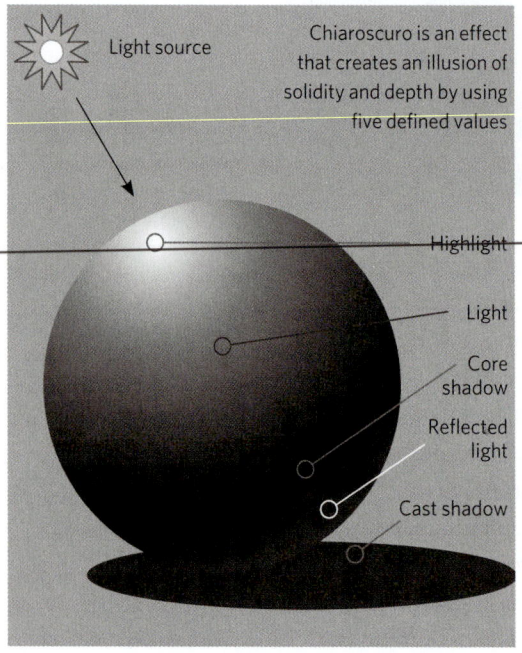

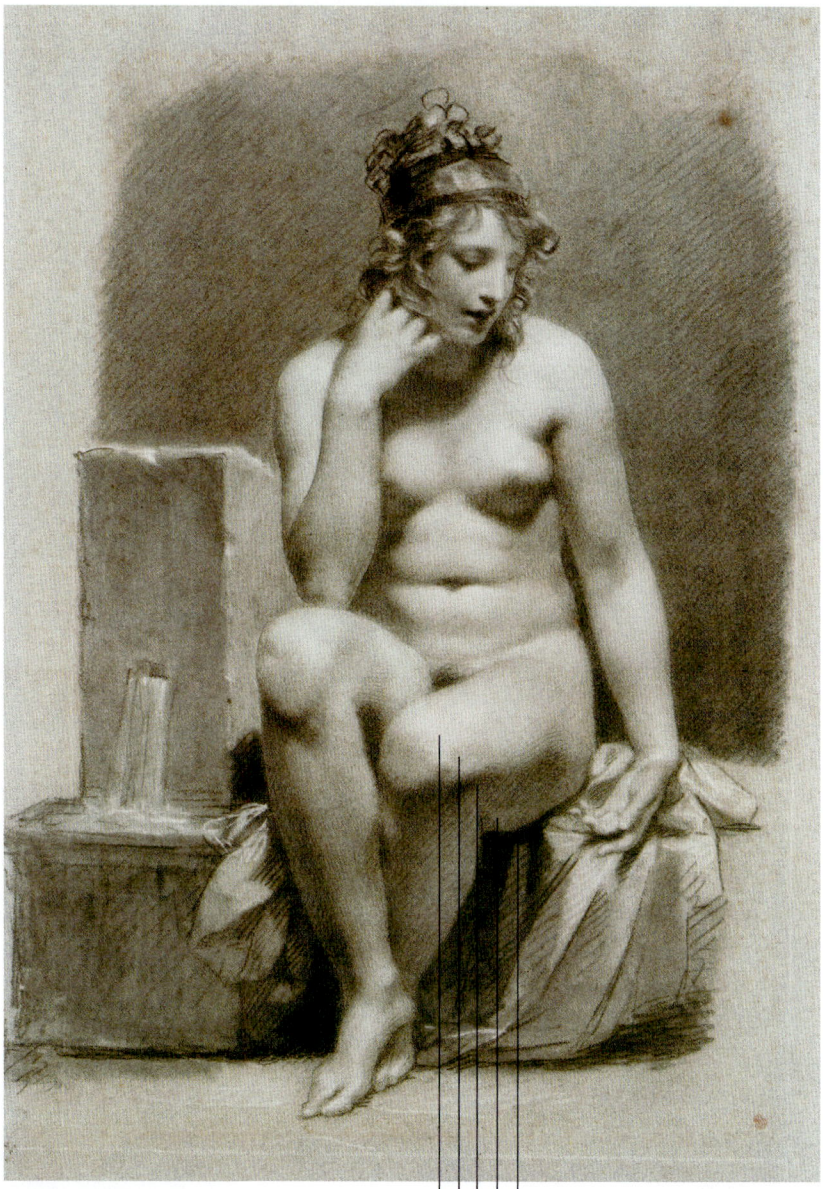

1.3.5 Chiaroscuro graphic applied to Pierre-Paul Prud'hon, *La Source*, c. 1800–10. Black and white chalk, stumped, on light blue paper, 21⅛ × 15⅜". Sterling and Francine Clark Art Institute, Williamstown, Massachusetts

This lighter value defines the bottom edge of the sphere. In contrast, the sphere casts a shadow away from the direction of the light source. Near the edge of the cast shadow, as light from the surrounding environment increases, the shadow becomes lighter.

In *La Source*, the French artist Pierre-Paul Prud'hon (1758–1823) uses chiaroscuro to draw a female figure (**1.3.5**). If you look carefully at

Renaissance: a period of cultural and artistic change in Europe from the fourteenth to the seventeenth century
Highlight: an area of lightest value in a work

the figure's upper left leg (the leg on the viewer's right), you can see that the chiaroscuro is used just as it is in **1.3.4**. There is an area of highlight on the knee transitioning to the lighted thigh. Under the knee and thigh there is a strong core shadow: reflected light can be seen on the calf and the underside of the thigh. This light is accentuated by the dark cast shadow behind the calf. Prud'hon's use of black and white chalk on a light blue paper allows him to accentuate the lightest and darkest areas, the chiaroscuro.

Dramatic and beautiful effects can be achieved through the use of chiaroscuro, especially if it is exaggerated. *The Calling of St. Matthew* by the Italian artist Caravaggio (1571–1610) uses strongly contrasting values to convert a quiet gathering into a pivotal and powerful event (**1.3.6**). This extreme type of chiaroscuro, often referred to as **tenebrism**, relies on a single light source and broad areas of darkness or shadow. The intense difference between lights and darks places extra **emphasis** on Christ's hand as he singles out Matthew, who points to himself in response. The light also frames Matthew and highlights the surprised looks of the others in the room as he is called to become one of Christ's disciples.

Tenebrism: dramatic use of intense darkness and light to heighten the impact of a painting
Emphasis: the principle of drawing attention to particular content in a work

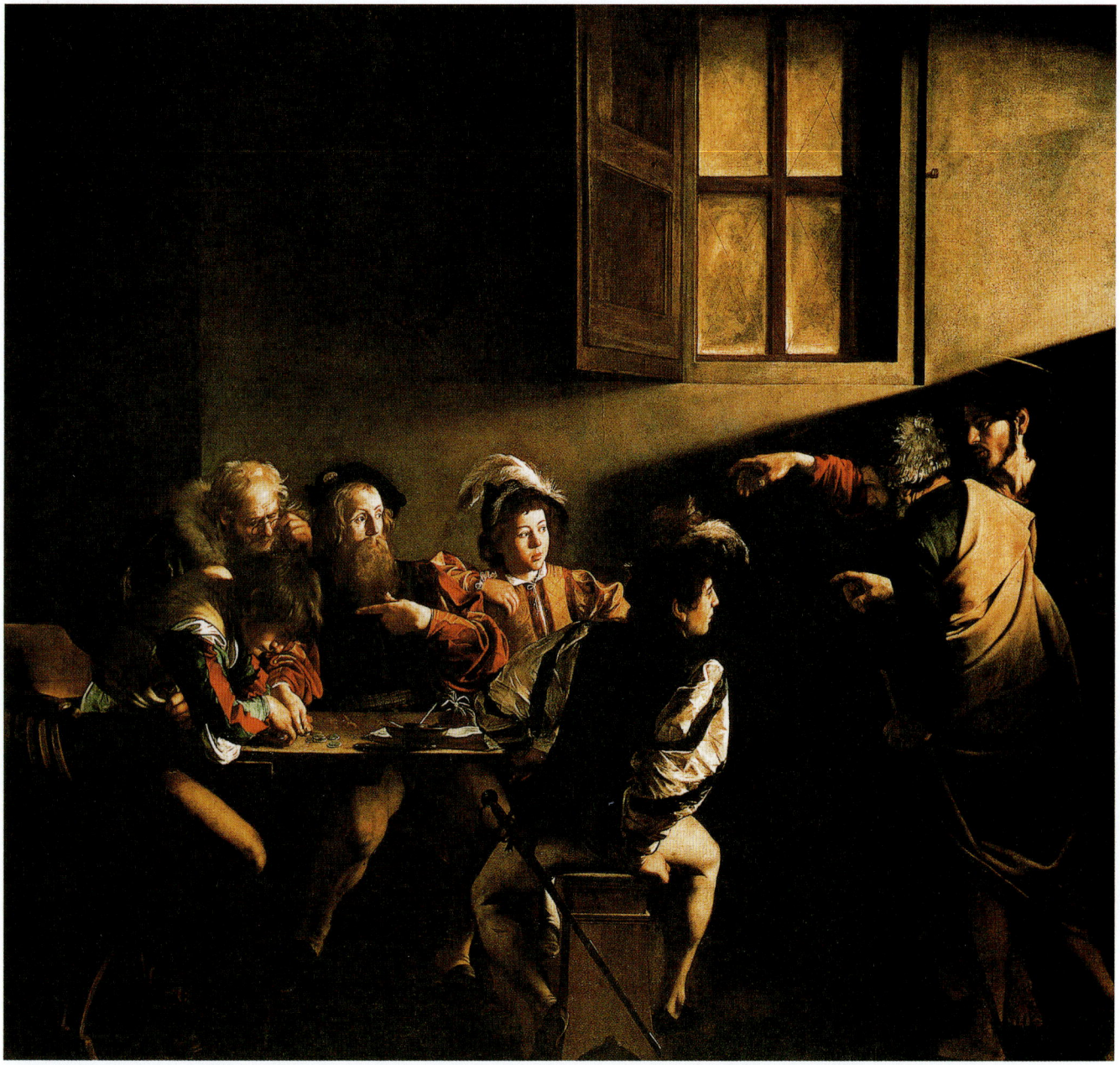

1.3.6 Caravaggio, *The Calling of St. Matthew*, c.1599–1600. Oil on canvas, 11'1" × 11'5". Contarelli Chapel, San Luigi dei Francesi, Rome, Italy

Hatching and Cross-Hatching

Artists also use a method called **hatching** to express value (**1.3.7**). Hatching consists of a series of lines, close to and parallel to each other. **Media** that demand a thin line, for example engraving or pen-and-ink drawing, do not allow much variation in the width of the line. Here an artist may choose hatching or **cross-hatching** (a variant of hatching in which the lines overlap) to suggest values that create a greater sense of form and depth.

The Italian artist Michelangelo Buonarroti (1475–1564) uses cross-hatching in his pen and ink drawing *Head of a Satyr* (**1.3.8**). Cross-hatching gives the face of the satyr solidity and depth. By building up layers of brown ink, Michelangelo overcomes the restrictions created by the thin line of the pen. For example, if we look carefully at the cheekbone of the satyr it appears to be jutting out toward us. This effect is created by hatching and cross-hatching. The bright white highlight uses no lines; the surrounding hatch lines define the transition from bright light to a darker value.

As we move our gaze downward and to the right of the highlight, we notice that a second layer of overlapping hatching lines intersects the diagonals bordering the highlight. Then, as we continue to scan downward and to the right, we see more layers of hatching lines crossing

Hatching: the use of non-overlapping parallel lines to convey darkness or lightness
Medium (plural **media**): the material on or from which an artist chooses to make a work of art, for example canvas and oil paint, marble, engraving, video, or architecture
Cross-hatching: the use of overlapping parallel lines to convey darkness or lightness
Shape: a two-dimensional area, the boundaries of which are defined by lines or suggested by changes in color or value

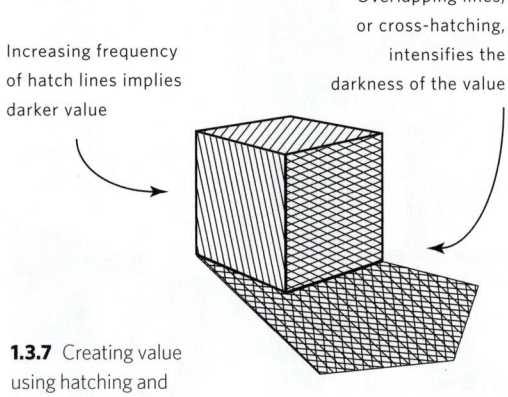

1.3.7 Creating value using hatching and cross-hatching

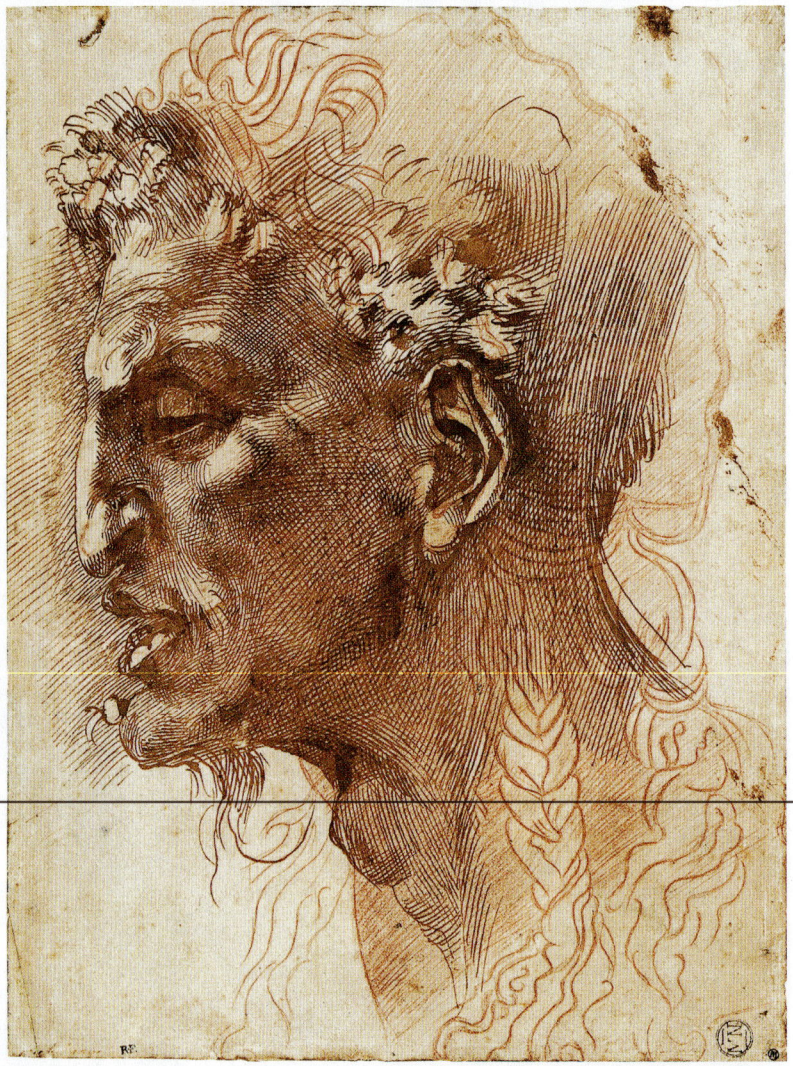

1.3.8 Michelangelo, *Head of a Satyr*, c. 1520–30. Pen and ink on paper, 10⅝ × 7⅞". Musée du Louvre, Paris, France

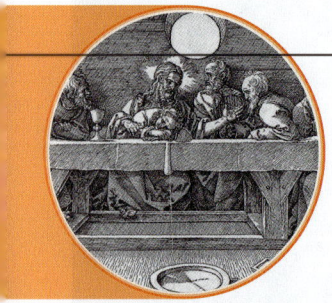

The techniques of hatching and cross-hatching can be found in Albrecht Dürer's version of the Last Supper: see **3.6.16, p. 475**

over the previous ones. As the hatching lines cross over and over, the value appears to get darker. Michelangelo communicates three-dimensional depth by using narrow and two-dimensional lines.

Space

Value is just one of a variety of techniques artists use to create a sense of depth and the illusion of space in a work of art. We will now explain some other methods.

Size, Overlapping, and Position

In a work of art, the size of one **shape** compared to another often suggests that the larger object is closer to us. Another way to create the illusion of depth is to overlap shapes. If one shape appears to overlap another, the shape in front seems closer than the shape that is partially covered. Position in the **picture plane** is also an effective device for implying depth. A shape lower in the picture plane appears to be closer.

The Finnish artist Beda Stjernschantz (1865–1910) uses all of these devices—relative size, overlapping, and strategic positioning of shapes in the picture plane—to create an illusion of depth in her work *Pastoral (Primavera)* (**1.3.9**). The passive, idyllic scene draws us into a landscape that does not exist, but we feel a sense of depth because the artist makes it possible for us to be imaginatively transported there. In the painting there are two pairs of figures; one is larger than the other, which informs the viewer's understanding of space. The two figures in the center left of the image, who are positioned near a river, are notably smaller than those that dominate the lower right corner of the work. We see the larger figures as closer because of this difference in size.

Stjernschantz also implies depth by positioning the larger figure with the flute in a way that conceals the foot of one of the smaller figures. Similarly, we interpret the woman in the white dress as being closest to us because she partly obscures the left foot of the flute player. The artist further enhances the illusion of depth by placing the figure in white against the bottom of the work and setting the smaller pair of figures higher in the composition.

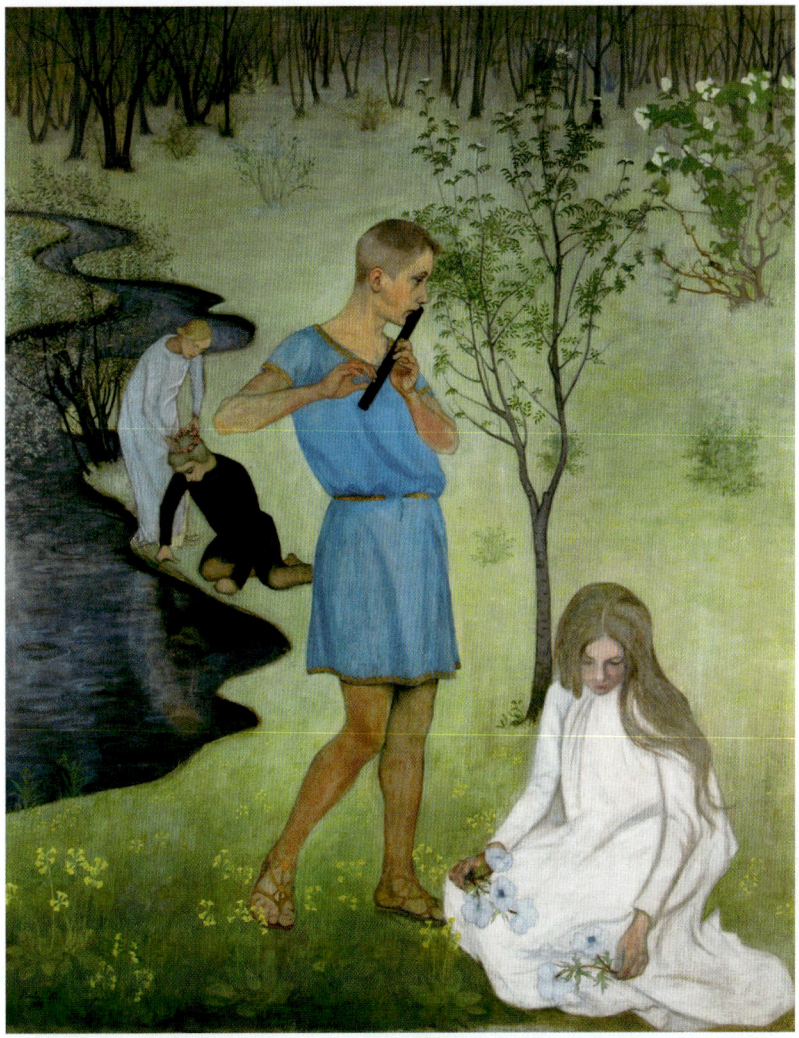

1.3.9 Beda Stjernschantz, *Pastoral (Primavera)*, 1897. Oil on canvas, 49⅝ × 41¾". K. H. Renlund Museum, Kokkola, Finland

In using such **relative placement**, the artist invites us to saunter visually from the **foreground** (where the two largest figures are placed) to the middle ground (where the smaller group of figures is set), and continue on our visual journey along the softly curving river and into the beckoning woods in the **background** (the uppermost area of the work). Even though there are no noticeable value differences between the groups, Stjernschantz uses enough placement strategy and size change to imply depth to a viewer.

Beda Stjernschantz was one of a group of artists known as the Finnish **Symbolists**, who

Picture plane: the surface of a painting or drawing
Relative placement: the arrangement of shapes or lines to form a visual relationship to one another in a design
Foreground: the part of a work depicted as nearest to the viewer
Background: the part of a work depicted furthest from the viewer's space, often behind the main subject matter
Symbolist: artist or artistic style belonging to the movement in European art and literature, c. 1885–1910, that conveyed meaning by the use of powerful yet ambiguous symbols

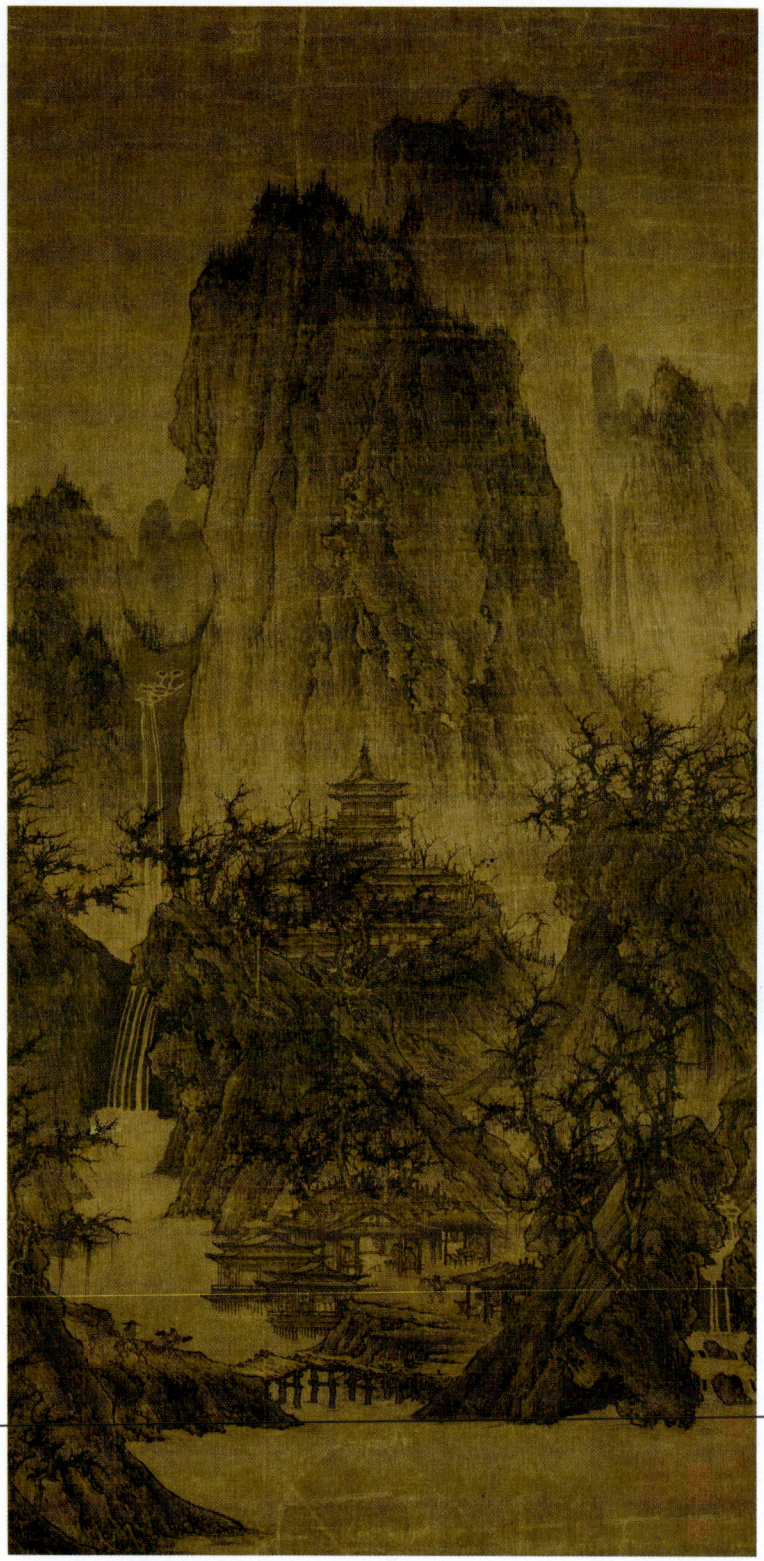

1.3.10 Li Cheng (attributed), *A Solitary Temple Amid Clearing Peaks*, Northern Song Dynasty, c. 960–1127. Hanging scroll, ink, and slight color on silk, 44 × 22". Nelson-Atkins Museum, Kansas City, Missouri

were influential at the turn of the twentieth century. They were especially interested in landscape and the relationship between the arts, including music and what is known as **synesthesia**, where one of the body's senses experiences something that triggers an experience in another sense—hence the inclusion of the flute player in this painting.

Alternating Value and Texture

The illusion of depth in two dimensions is often influenced by the arrangement of value and **texture**. Artists intersperse value and visual texture to create a sense of **rhythm**. Look at *A Solitary Temple Amid Clearing Peaks* (**1.3.10**), attributed to Chinese painter Li Cheng (*c.* 919–967). From the bottom up, we first confront a section of water, perhaps the shoreline of a lake, followed by a small bridge and then some architectural structures set amongst a rocky, tree-filled landscape. Moving upward we see a light area—immediately behind and above the solitary temple that gives this work its name—after which the values gradually darken as our view climbs the face of the mountain. Finally, as we reach above the peaks, the sky is again lighter, completing the alternating rhythm from bottom to top. Each area of light and dark occupies different amounts of space, making the design more interesting. We can also note the change in visual texture from bottom to top. The texture appears to be extremely rough and detailed near the bottom, with craggy rocks and gnarled trees dominating the foreground. From this point it progressively becomes less precise: as Li's landscape rises, it also appears to recede behind the soft mist, then reappear with great vertical strength. The trees at the top of the scroll have lost the gnarled texture and now look soft and fuzzy as they crown the mountain crest. These visual layers create a sense of depth as they accentuate differences in both value and texture.

Brightness and Color

Brightness and color can both be used to suggest depth in a work of art. Lighter areas seem to be closer as dark areas appear to recede. This is especially true of color. For example, we are more likely to think that a green that is very pure and intense is closer to us than a darker green. The American painter Thomas Hart Benton (1889–1975) used brightness and color to create and manipulate our sense of distance in his painting *The Wreck of the Ole '97* (**1.3.11**). Benton wanted the viewer to be a witness to one of the most notorious train disasters in American history, in which several people died. In the green areas we see the bright, pure greens come forward as the darker, less intense greens fall away. The greens in the lower central portion of the work are more intense than the greens on the far left. Because we perceive color that is more intense as being closer, this difference in color **intensity** helps us to feel that we are *just* at enough distance to witness the terrible train wreck without becoming another of its casualties. Yet by painting the engine steaming ahead, at an angle that suggests it is about to hit the broken rail in the foreground and head straight out of the picture, hurtling inevitably toward us, Benton simultaneously manages to convey a fearful sense of danger.

Perspective

Artists, architects, and designers who wish to suggest the illusion of depth on a two-dimensional surface use perspective. They have the choice of several ways to do this, of which three are the most common. **Atmospheric perspective** modifies value, color, and texture to create the sense that some parts of an image are situated further away than others. **Isometric perspective** uses diagonal parallels to communicate depth, while **linear perspective** relies on a system where lines appear to converge at points in space. All these forms of perspective tap into some of the ways we see the world and think about space.

Atmospheric Perspective

Some artists use atmospheric perspective to create the illusion of depth. Distant objects lack contrast, detail, and sharpness of focus, because the air that surrounds us is not completely transparent. The effect makes objects with strong color take on a blue-gray middle value as they get further away: the atmosphere progressively veils a scene as the distance increases.

Synesthesia: when one of the five senses perceives something that was stimulated by a trigger from one of the other senses
Texture: the surface quality of a work, for example fine/coarse, detailed/lacking in detail
Rhythm: the regular or ordered repetition of elements in the work
Intensity: the relative clarity of color in its purest raw form, demonstrated through luminous or muted variations
Atmospheric perspective (aerial perspective): use of shades of color and clarity to create the illusion of depth. Closer objects have warmer tones and clear outlines, while objects set further away are cooler and become hazy
Isometric perspective: a system using diagonal parallel lines to communicate depth
Linear perspective: a system using converging imaginary sight lines to create the illusion of depth

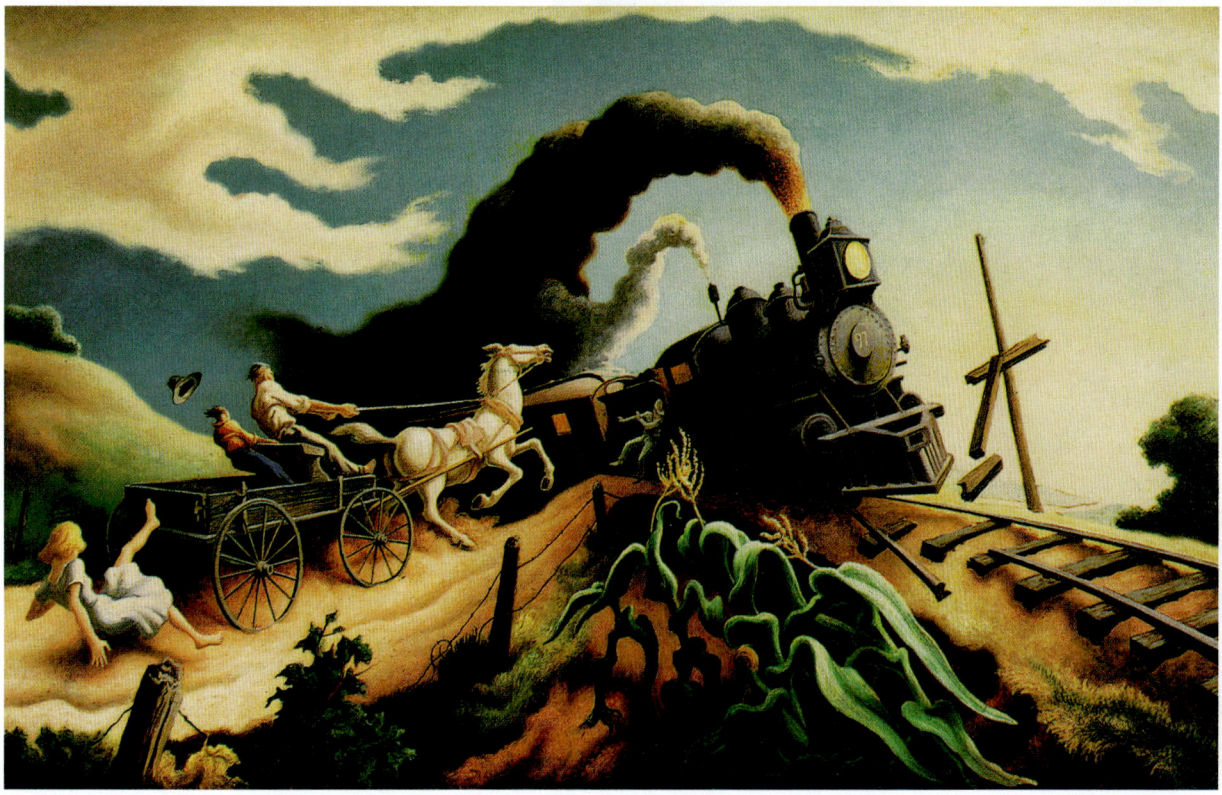

1.3.11 Thomas Hart Benton, *The Wreck of the Ole '97*, 1943. Egg tempera on gessoed masonite, 28½ × 44½". Hunter Museum of Art, Chattanooga, Tennessee

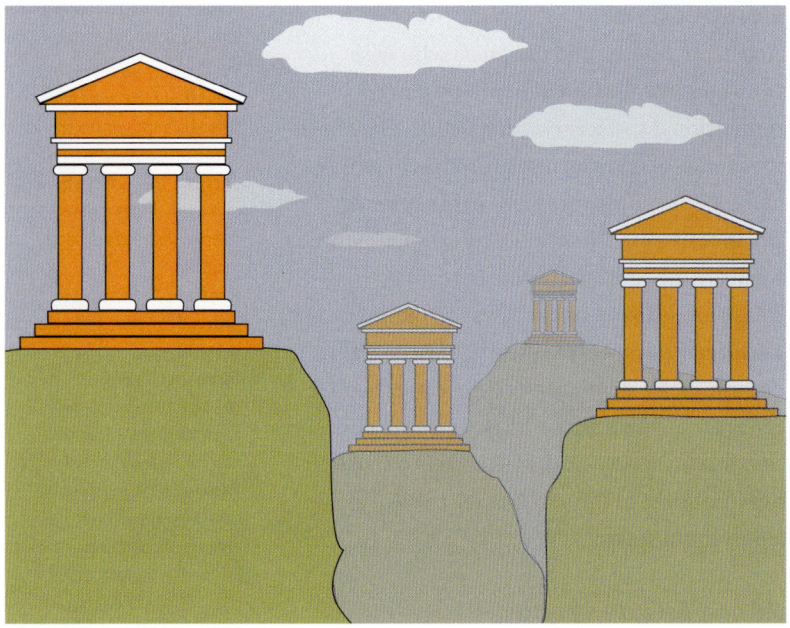

1.3.12 (above) The effects of atmospheric perspective

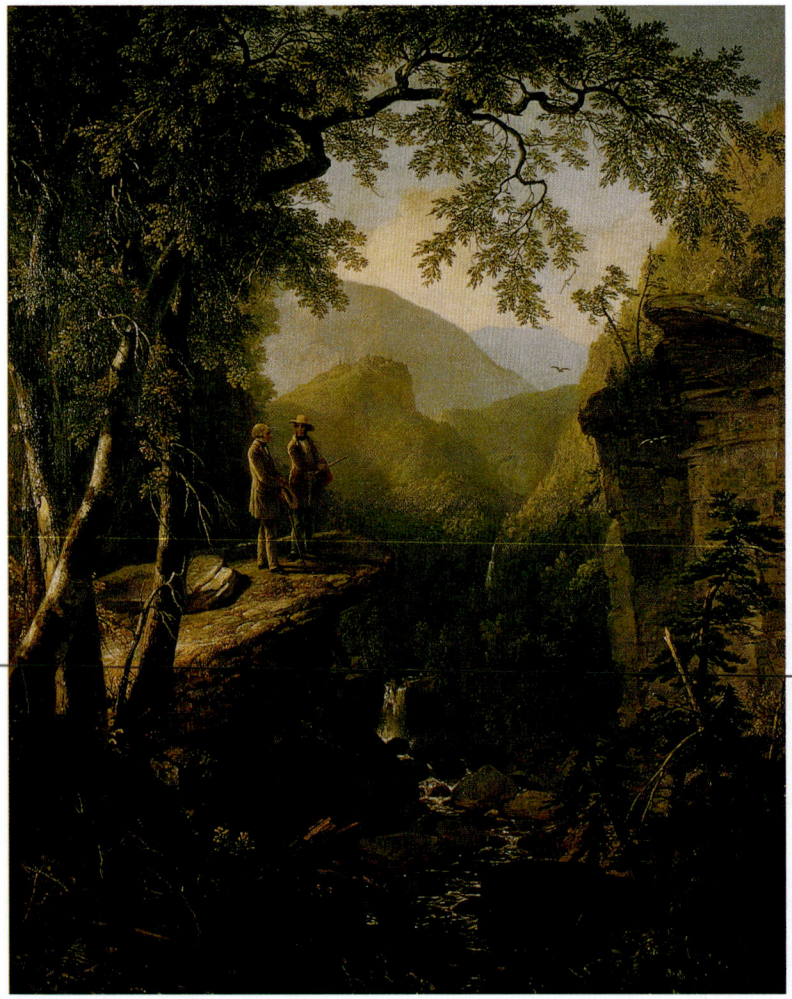

1.3.13 Asher Brown Durand, *Kindred Spirits*, 1849. Oil on canvas, 44 × 36". Crystal Bridges Museum of American Art, Bentonville, Arkansas

Contemporary filmmakers use this atmospheric effect to give the illusion of great depth, just as traditional artists have always done.

In **1.3.12** the Greek temple to the left appears to be closer to the viewer than the other temples because its colors are brighter and its shape is more sharply defined. The smallest temple lacks detail and is tinged blue-gray, making it seem the furthest away. The American Asher Brown Durand (1796–1886) used comparable effects in his painting *Kindred Spirits* (**1.3.13**). The trees in the foreground are detailed and bright green, but as the trees recede into the landscape behind the two figures, they become a lighter gray and increasingly out of focus. Lines and shapes also become less distinct as the illusion of distance increases. By using atmospheric perspective, Durand conveys an impression of the vastness of the American landscape.

Isometric Perspective

Isometric perspective arranges parallel lines diagonally in a work to give a sense of depth. The word isometric derives from the Greek meaning "equal measure." The system has been used by artists in China for more than a thousand years. It was particularly suitable for painting on scrolls, which can be examined only in sections. Since Chinese landscape painters were never really interested in portraying space from a single viewpoint—they preferred to convey multiple viewpoints simultaneously—isometric perspective was their chosen technique to convey the illusion of space in the structural lines of architecture and other rectilinear objects.

A section from the painting *The Qianlong Emperor's Southern Inspection Tour, Scroll Six: Entering Suzhou and the Grand Canal* by Xu Yang shows this system in action (**1.3.14**). The parallel diagonal lines that define the small L-shaped building in the center right of the work suggest a three-dimensional object (**1.3.15**). Xu Yang, a Chinese artist working in the 1770s, uses this method to give the architecture along the Grand Canal the illusion of depth. This method of implying depth is not "realistic" according to the Western tradition, but the artist makes use of other spatial devices to help us understand how the space is structured. For example, the

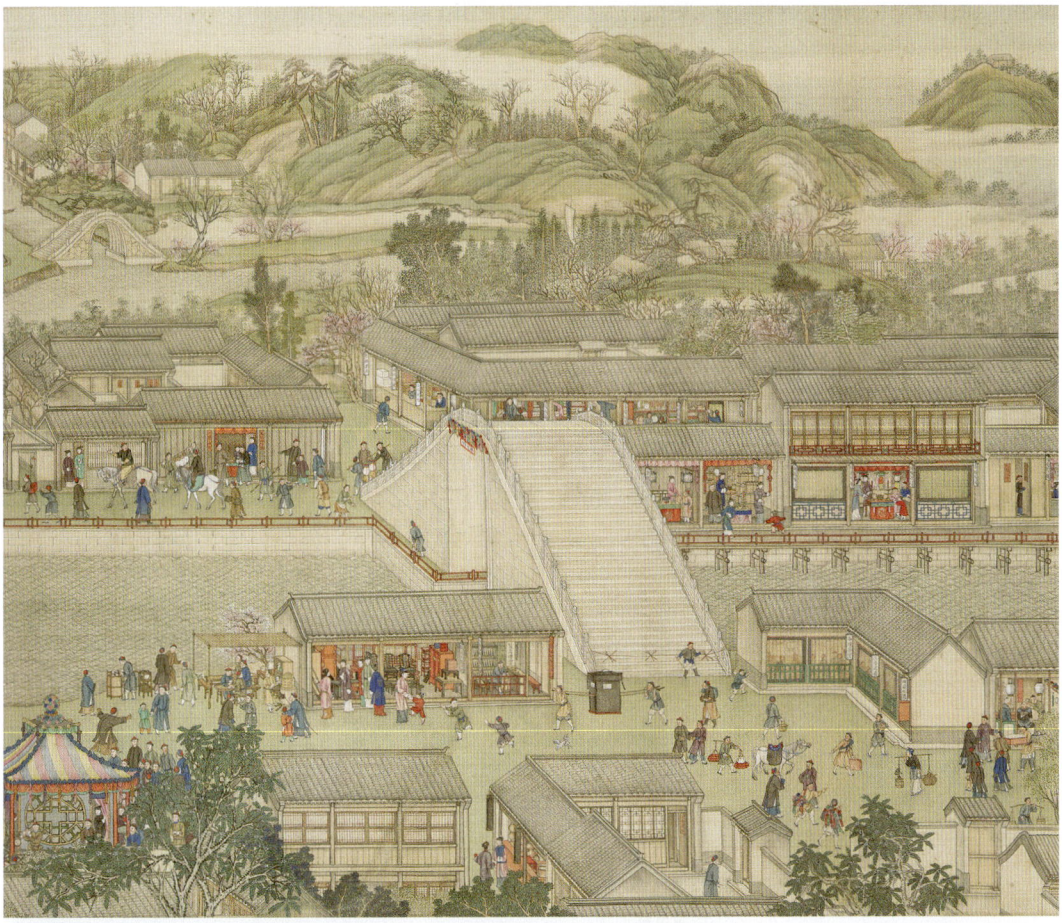

1.3.14 (left) Xu Yang, *The Qianlong Emperor's Southern Inspection Tour, Scroll Six: Entering Suzhou and the Grand Canal*, Qing Dynasty, 1770 (detail). Hand scroll, ink and color on silk, 2'3⅛" × 65'4½". Metropolitan Museum of Art, New York

Lines are drawn parallel and diagonal to create depth in isometric perspective

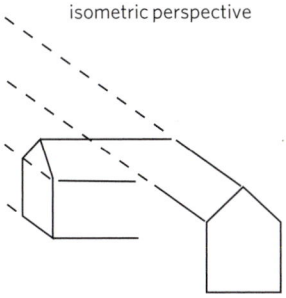

1.3.15 (above) Graphic detailing isometric perspective in scroll image

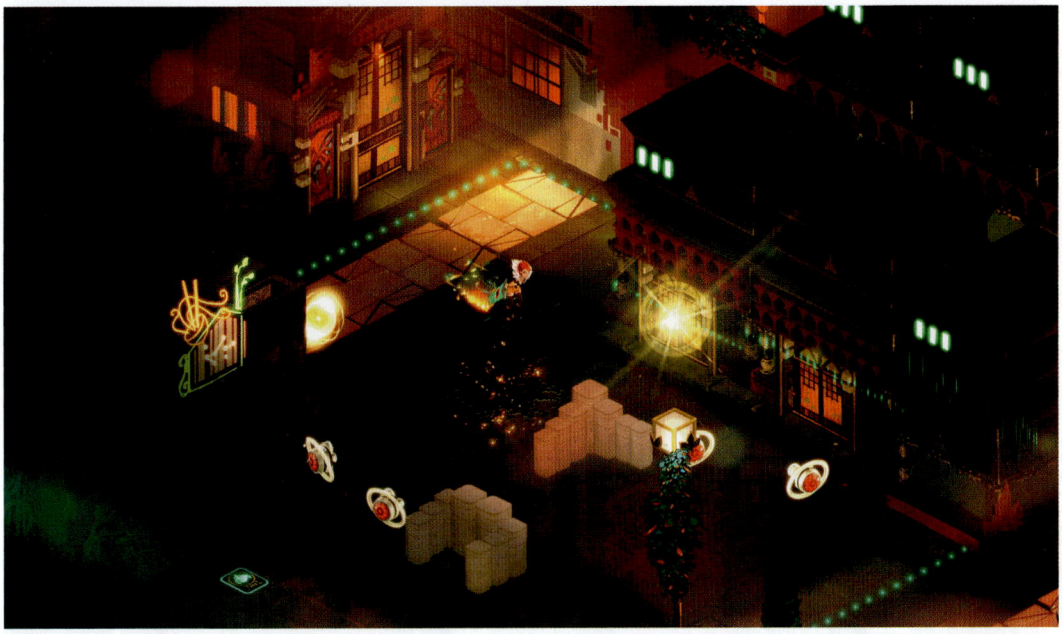

1.3.16 Supergiant Games, screenshot from *Transistor*, 2014. Art Director, Jen Zee

diminishing size of the trees as they recede into the distance reinforces the sense of depth.

Isometric perspective is now common in contemporary computer graphics as well. The computer and video console game *Transistor* (**1.3.16**) is designed to express depth using a perspective method similar to the one Xu Yang used in 1770. The designers have created the architecture of the game with parallel diagonal lines so that the playing area consists of small

Actual line: a continuous, uninterrupted line
Implied line: a line not actually drawn but suggested by the positions of elements in the work, for example, an aligned series of dots

rectangular graphic images that are known as tiles. The tiles allow uniform objects to remain the same size, yet as the objects are moved around the game environment, they still imply depth. The game designers' choice of isometric perspective allows players to move from level to level and space to space without distortion because the individual tiles remain the same size.

Linear Perspective

Linear perspective is a mathematical system that uses lines to create the illusion of depth in a two-dimensional artwork. (The "lines" can be **actual lines**, for example of buildings, or **implied lines** of figures or shapes.) The linear perspective systems used by artists are based on observation of space in the world we see around us. For example, the two sides of a straight railway line or road appear to converge as they recede into the distance, even though in reality they are parallel. This system, created through the use of line, emulates the observed effect of diminishing size that naturally occurs where distant identical objects appear smaller than those nearby.

ORIGINS AND HISTORY

Like many ideas in human history, linear perspective was developed with knowledge acquired over centuries. Mozi, a Chinese philosopher working in the fifth century BCE; Alhazen, an Arab mathematician from around the year 1000; and Leon Battista Alberti (1404–1472), an Italian Renaissance architect, each contributed ideas that helped artists to understand light and its properties more fully. Knowledge of light's properties led other Renaissance artists to use a projection device called a camera obscura (Latin for "dark room")

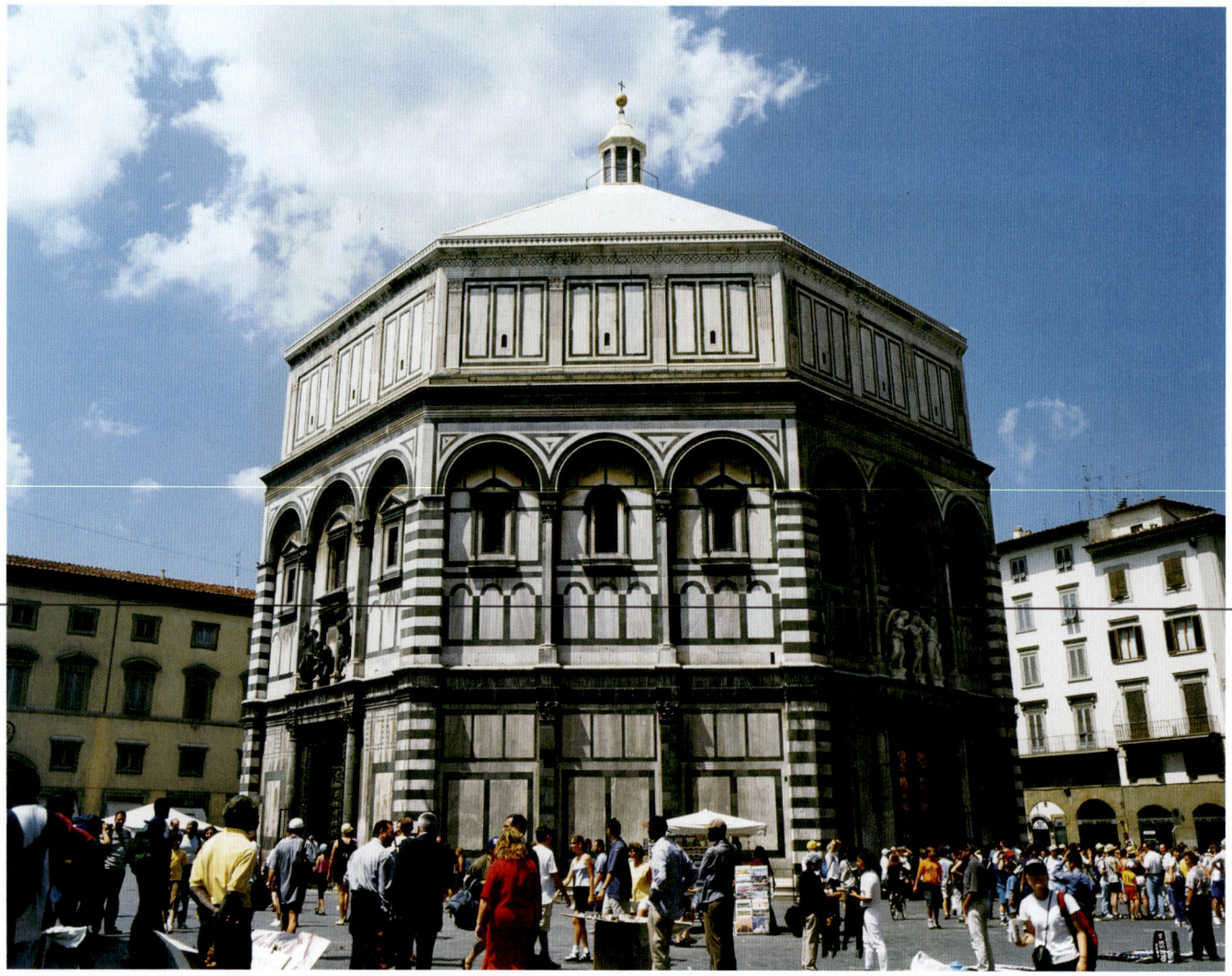

1.3.17a The Baptistery, Florence, Italy

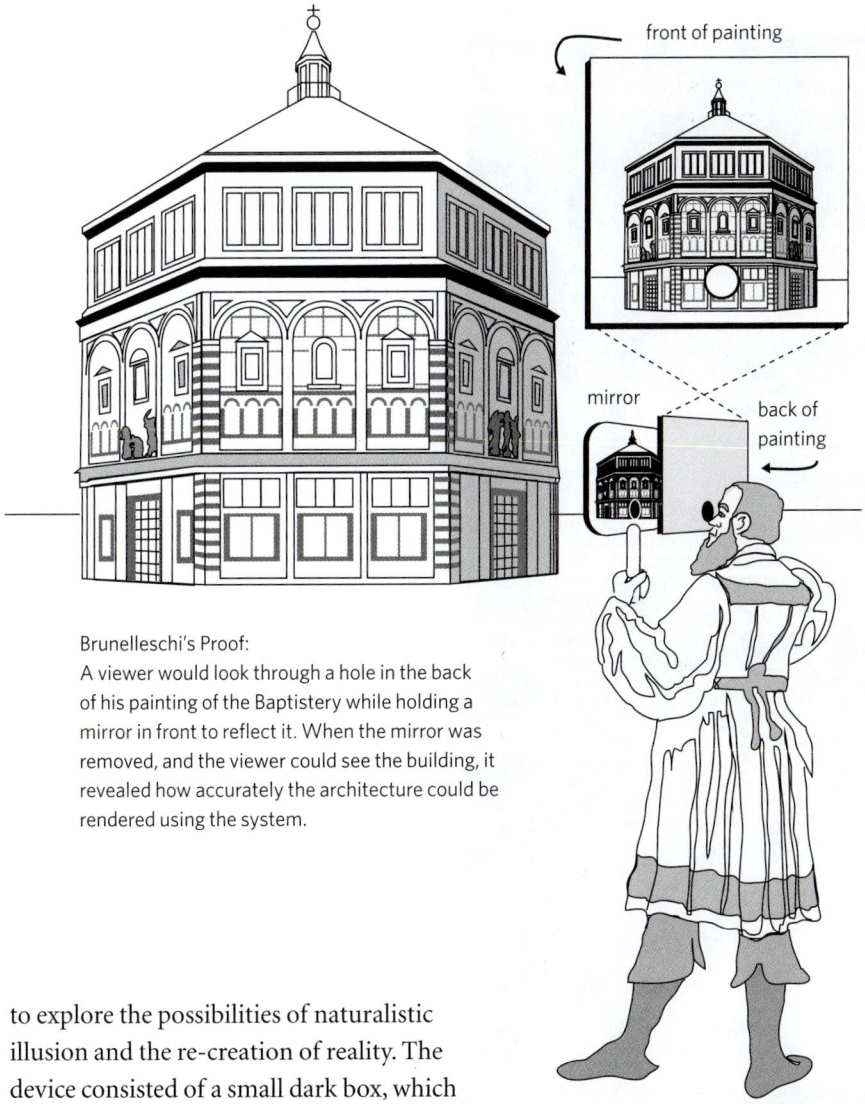

1.3.17b Brunelleschi's proof of the accuracy of linear perspective

Brunelleschi's Proof:
A viewer would look through a hole in the back of his painting of the Baptistery while holding a mirror in front to reflect it. When the mirror was removed, and the viewer could see the building, it revealed how accurately the architecture could be rendered using the system.

to explore the possibilities of naturalistic illusion and the re-creation of reality. The device consisted of a small dark box, which by means of a little pinhole would conduct sunlight through the hole and allow a real, full-color, upside-down image of the objects outside the device to be projected with light onto a surface. The artist could then draw the projected image, or trace it directly onto paper or canvas. Images created using this device revealed recurring ways in which lines could be arranged, and this influenced the artist and architect Filippo Brunelleschi (1377–1446) to create a practical way of expressing the theories of depth using linear perspective.

Because Brunelleschi, as an architect, was interested in the realistic representation of buildings, he began to work with ideas about perspective and the idea that light enters the eye. He combined this with use of the camera obscura to prove that reality could be re-created in art using a system of lines. It had been demonstrated that an image projected onto a surface in a camera obscura could be traced to produce a convincing illusion of depth, but this did not explain exactly how the illusion of depth was created. Brunelleschi took this discovery one step further by formulating rules of linear perspective to allow an artist to depict realistically something observed without the aid of a camera obscura. To prove his point, Brunelleschi painted an image of the Florence Baptistery (**1.3.17a**), applying his rules, on a polished piece of silver. He then drilled a small hole in the silver plate so that a viewer could look through the back of it and, holding a mirror up in front of it, could see the painted image of the Baptistery reflected in the mirror (**1.3.17b**). The viewer could then compare the degree of realism of the painting with the real Baptistery itself to confirm that Brunelleschi's rules worked. Although many artists had

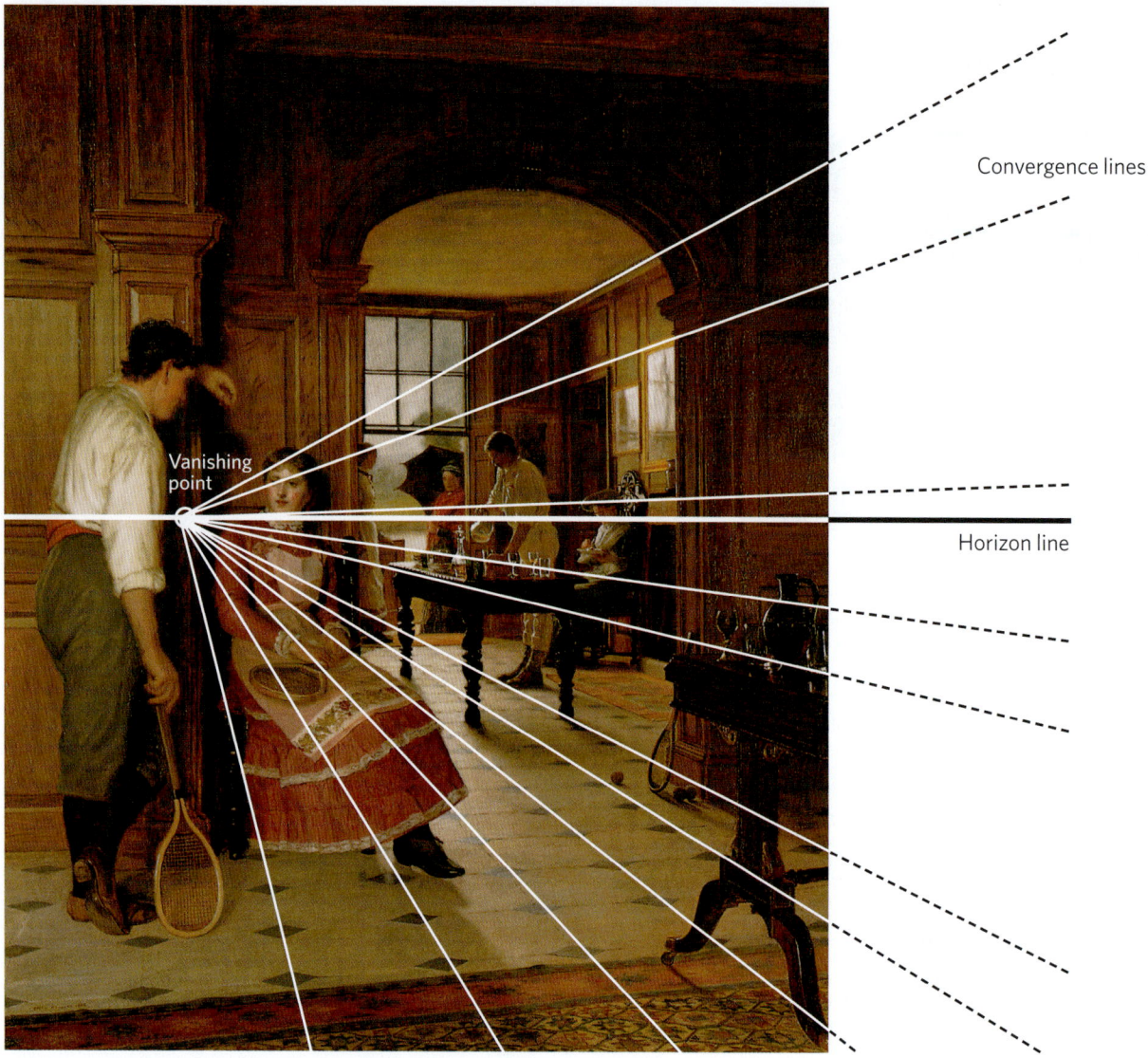

1.3.18 The effect of convergences: Edith Hayllar, *A Summer Shower*, 1883. Oil on panel, 21 × 17⅜". Private collection

effectively approximated linear perspective, Brunelleschi was the first to define it formally as a practical system.

Brunelleschi's discovery became for hundreds of years a standard systematic process for creating an impression of realistic depth. The British artist Edith Hayllar (1860–1948) exhibited many works at the Royal Academy (a rare honor for a woman artist at the time) between 1882 and 1897. The enhanced photograph of her painting *A Summer Shower* shows the basis for linear perspective (**1.3.18**). The converging lines represent planes that are parallel to each other in reality. Notice how, if we were to draw lines from the right side of the image and continue them until they intersect, these parallel lines would appear to converge on one single point in front of the male tennis player on the left of the painting. This is the **vanishing point**. These converging parallel lines are also known as **orthogonals**; the artist uses them here to create a composition that reflects the orderly life of upper-middle-class Victorian England.

There are a number of variations of linear perspective—one-point, two-point, and multiple-point—depending on the effect the artist wants to achieve. These formal approaches to conveying a sense of depth are important tools, so we will now look at each one in some detail to see how they function and the different kinds of effects they produce.

Vanishing point(s): the point or points in a work of art at which imaginary sight lines appear to converge, suggesting depth

Orthogonals: in perspective systems, imaginary sight lines extending from forms to the vanishing point

One-point perspective: a perspective system with a single vanishing point on the horizon

Fresco: a technique where the artist paints onto freshly applied plaster. From the Italian *fresco*, "fresh"

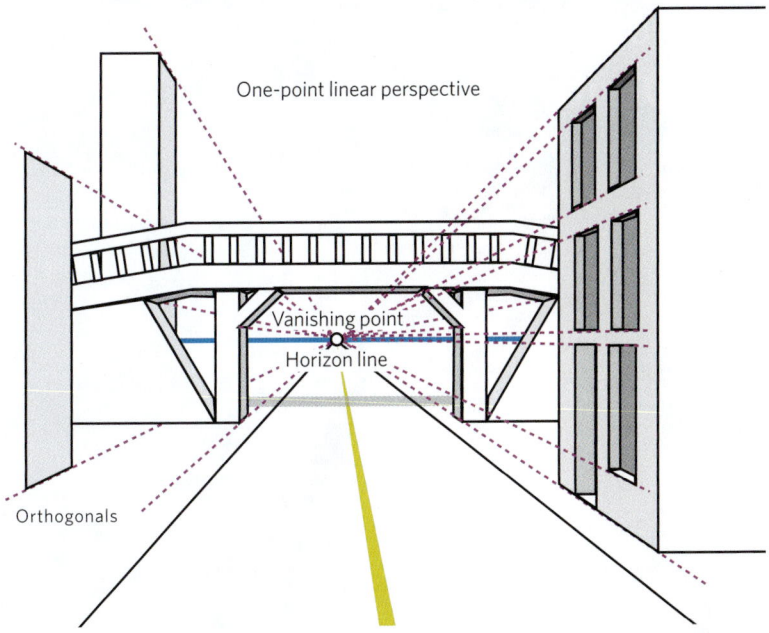

1.3.19 Applying one-point perspective technique

One-Point Perspective

Brunelleschi created his painting of the Florence Baptistery using one-point perspective, but the **one-point perspective** system has some limitations. Although the system makes it possible to represent "real" space, certain rules have to be followed. Since one-point perspective relies on a single vanishing point, the scene must be directly in front of the artist and receding. The effect is something like standing on an empty highway facing an underpass (**1.3.19**). The sides of the road and the inside of the underpass appear to follow converging paths to a single point on the horizon. But if you redirect your gaze to the right or left of the underpass, the edges of the roadway and underpass are out of direct sight and it is not as easy to see the recession of space.

One of the first artists to use one-point perspective was the Italian painter Masaccio (1401–1428). In his **fresco** of the Trinity, Masaccio places the horizon line, an imaginary line that mimics the horizon, at the viewer's eye level (note the figure) and centers the vanishing point in the middle of that line (**1.3.20**). The horizon line represents our eye level and is the basis for the setting-out of a perspective drawing. The orthogonals create an illusion that the background is an architectural setting. The end result is an effective illusion of depth on a two-dimensional surface that must have amazed visitors at the church of Santa Maria Novella in Florence, Italy. Masaccio's work was innovative for its time and influenced other significant artists of the Renaissance, including Michelangelo.

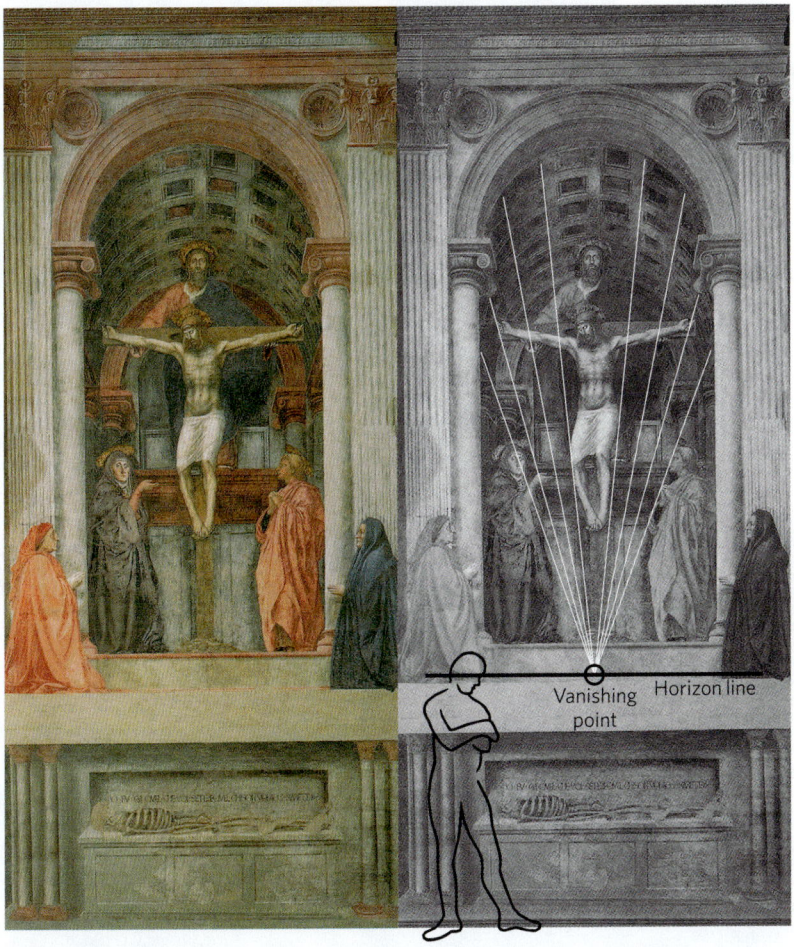

1.3.20 Use of one-point perspective: Masaccio, *Trinity*, c. 1425–26. Fresco, 21'10½" × 10'4⅞". Santa Maria Novella, Florence, Italy

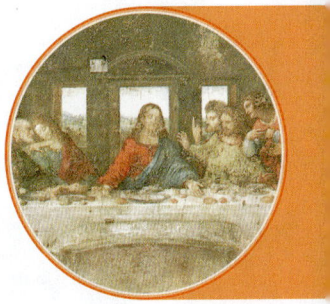

Another famous example of one-point linear perspective is Leonardo da Vinci's *The Last Supper*: see **3.6.15, p. 474**

Gateway to Art: Raphael, *The School of Athens*
Perspective and the Illusion of Depth

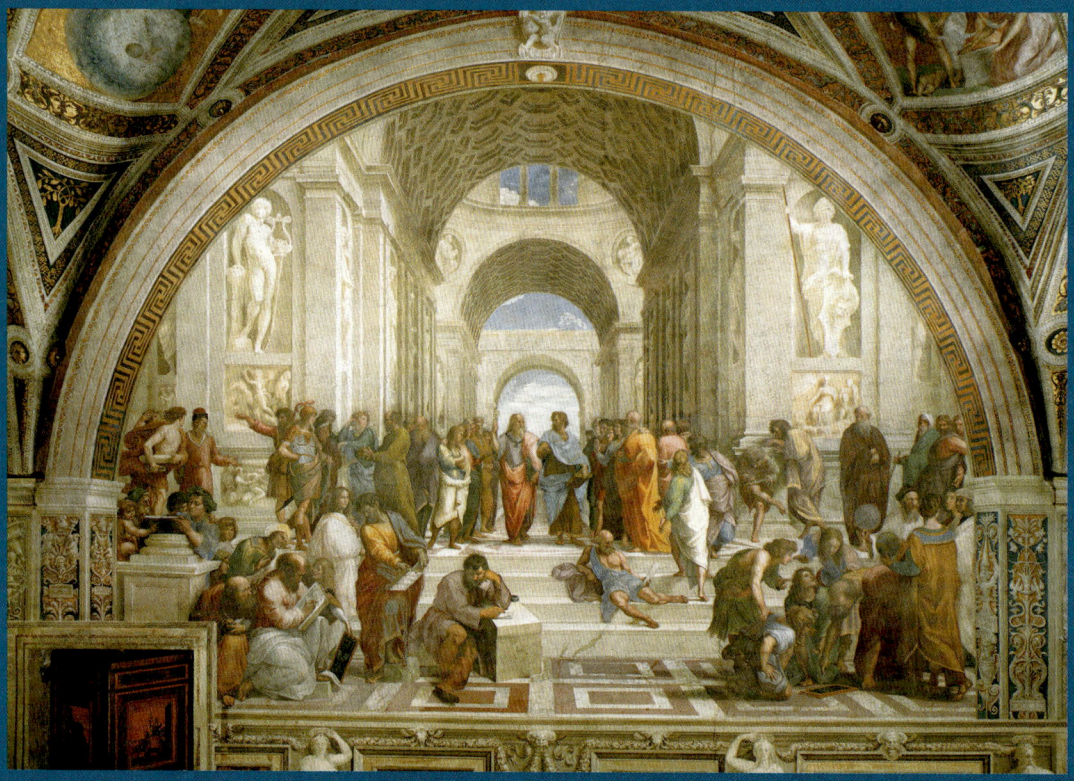

1.3.21a Raphael, *The School of Athens*, 1510–11. Fresco, 16'8" × 25'. Stanza della Segnatura, Vatican City, Italy

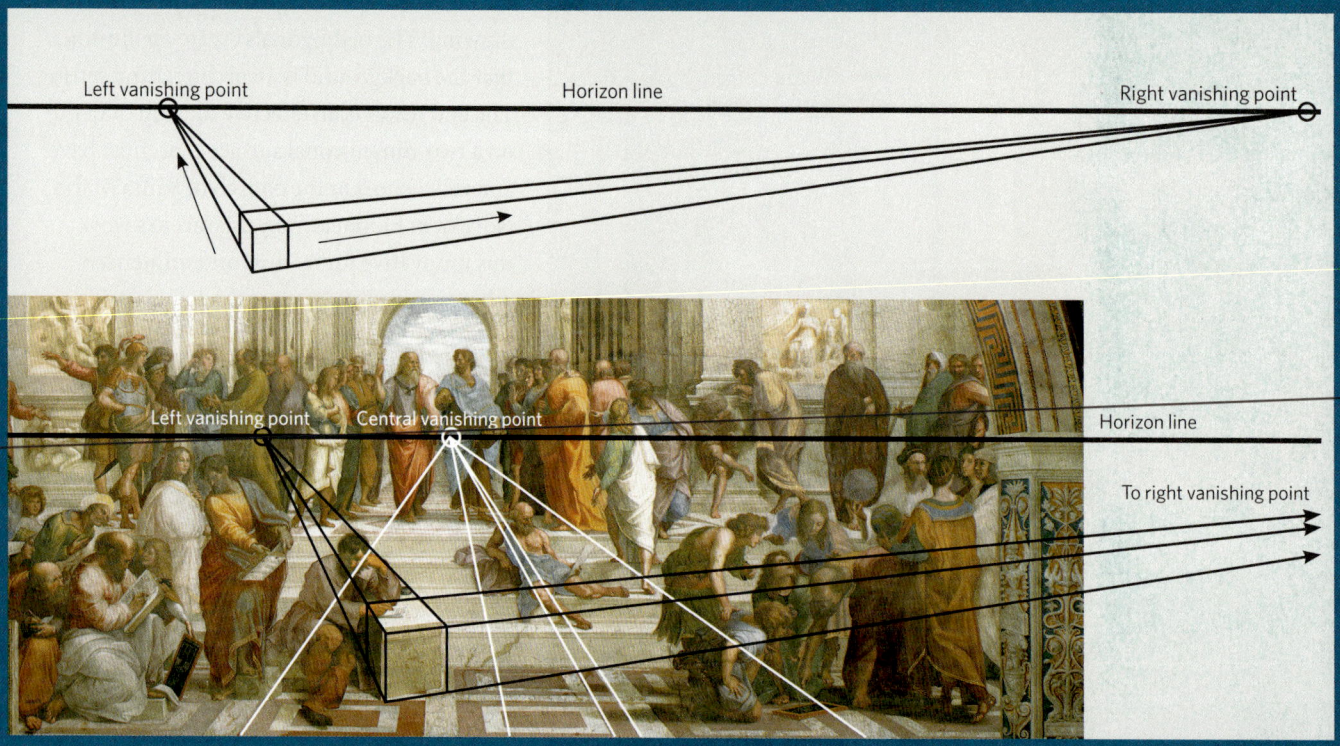

1.3.21b Applying two-point perspective: detail from Raphael, *The School of Athens*

In *The School of Athens* Raphael combines one-point perspective and two-point perspective in one composition (**1.3.21a** and **1.3.21b**). The figure in the foreground is leaning against an object set at an angle that is not perpendicular and parallel to the rest of the architectural setting. Consequently, it cannot depend on the central vanishing point that has been determined following the rules of one-point perspective, or it will be distorted. Raphael deals with this situation by introducing two additional vanishing points. Notice that both of these fall on the horizon line, following the established rules of perspective (vanishing points must fall on the horizon line). One vanishing point is positioned to the left of the central vanishing point that anchors the architecture, and the right vanishing point is outside of the picture. The block in the center is the only object in the composition that uses these two vanishing points, because the viewer is not perpendicular or parallel to it. Since it is turned at an angle, Raphael had to integrate another level of perspective into the work. All of the objects and architectural spaces depicted in this painting rely on one of these two perspective points.

For the other Raphael Gateway boxes, see p. 146, p. 194, p. 470, and p. 617

Two-Point Perspective

The one-point perspective system worked for Masaccio because his composition relied on the viewer standing directly in front of the vanishing point. But if the vanishing point is not directly (or near directly) in front of a viewer, or if the objects in the work are not all parallel, one-point perspective does not create a believable illusion of depth. The Italian artist Raphael (1483–1520) dealt with this problem in his famous painting *The School of Athens* (**1.3.21a** and **1.3.21b**).

Multiple-Point Perspective

As artists discovered that linear perspective afforded them many new possibilities for creating illusions of space, they began to expand on the idea of multiple-point perspective systems. Any object that exists in our cone of vision—the area we can see without moving our head or eyes—can usually be depicted using vanishing points on the horizon line (**1.3.22**). But if we are looking at an object from a position other than ground level, then we will need points *away* from the horizon line and other variations on perspective.

Objects and spaces that have right angles make it easy to work out where vanishing points should be: we can use one-point perspective. Unfortunately, many objects are made up of multiple angles that need even more vanishing points. As more of these are incorporated into a design, the artist can more readily reflect the complexities of the real world.

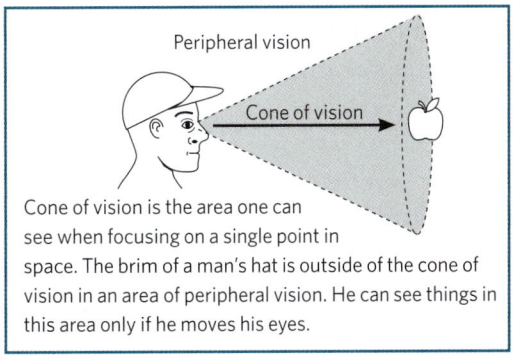

Cone of vision is the area one can see when focusing on a single point in space. The brim of a man's hat is outside of the cone of vision in an area of peripheral vision. He can see things in this area only if he moves his eyes.

1.3.22 Cone of vision

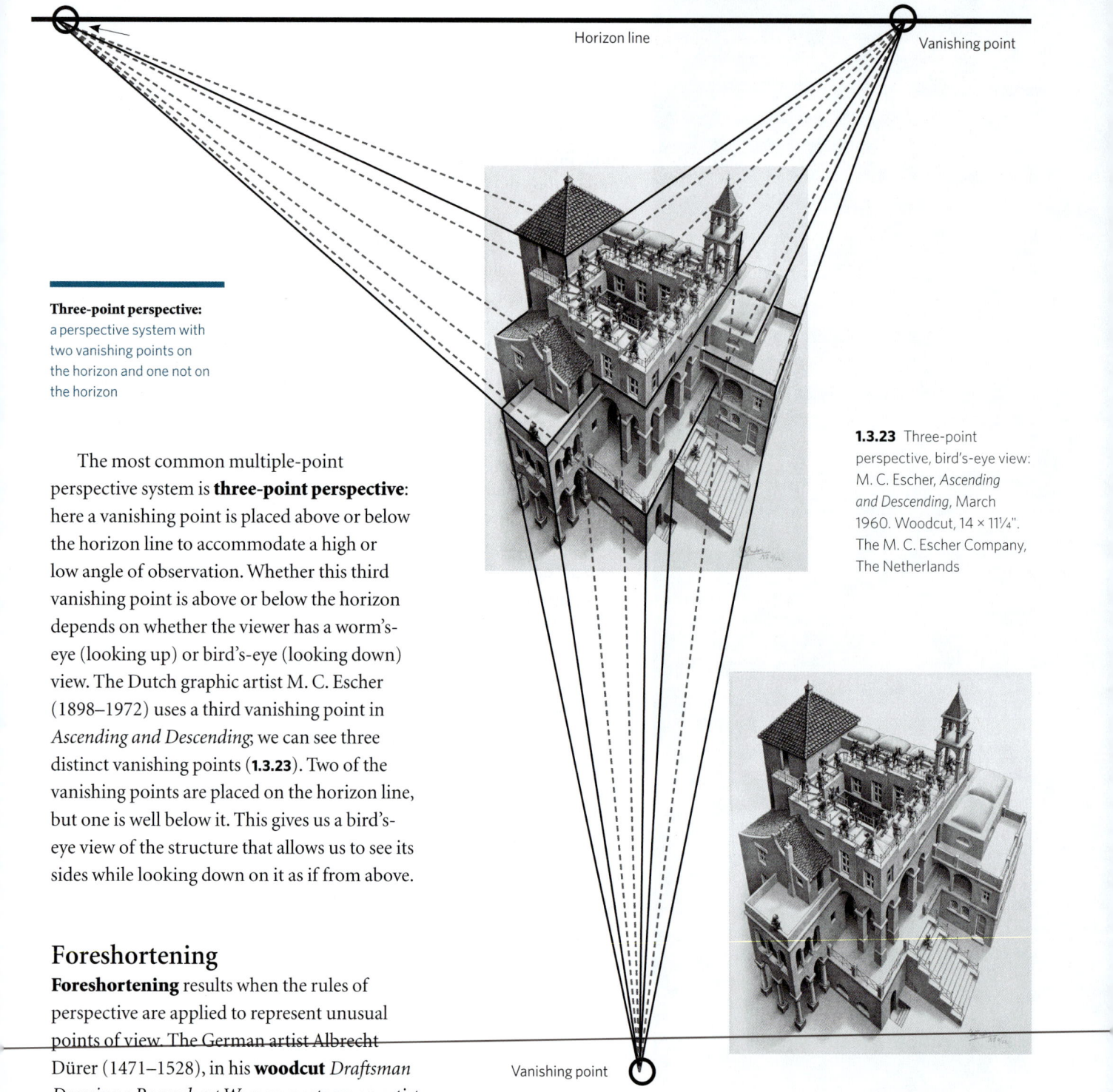

Three-point perspective: a perspective system with two vanishing points on the horizon and one not on the horizon

1.3.23 Three-point perspective, bird's-eye view: M. C. Escher, *Ascending and Descending*, March 1960. Woodcut, 14 × 11¼". The M. C. Escher Company, The Netherlands

The most common multiple-point perspective system is **three-point perspective**: here a vanishing point is placed above or below the horizon line to accommodate a high or low angle of observation. Whether this third vanishing point is above or below the horizon depends on whether the viewer has a worm's-eye (looking up) or bird's-eye (looking down) view. The Dutch graphic artist M. C. Escher (1898–1972) uses a third vanishing point in *Ascending and Descending*; we can see three distinct vanishing points (**1.3.23**). Two of the vanishing points are placed on the horizon line, but one is well below it. This gives us a bird's-eye view of the structure that allows us to see its sides while looking down on it as if from above.

Foreshortening

Foreshortening results when the rules of perspective are applied to represent unusual points of view. The German artist Albrecht Dürer (1471–1528), in his **woodcut** *Draftsman Drawing a Recumbent Woman*, portrays an artist at work drawing a figure (**1.3.24**). At this oblique angle, the usual proportions of different parts of the body do not apply. The artist has a fixed lens or aperture in front of him to make sure he always views from the same point. As he looks through the gridded window, he can see the coordinates, in relation to the grid, of the different parts of the model's body. He can then transfer those coordinates onto the similar grid

Foreshortening: a perspective technique that depicts a form—often distorting or reducing it—at an angle that is not parallel to the picture plane, in order to convey the illusion of depth
Woodcut: a relief print made from a design cut into a block of wood

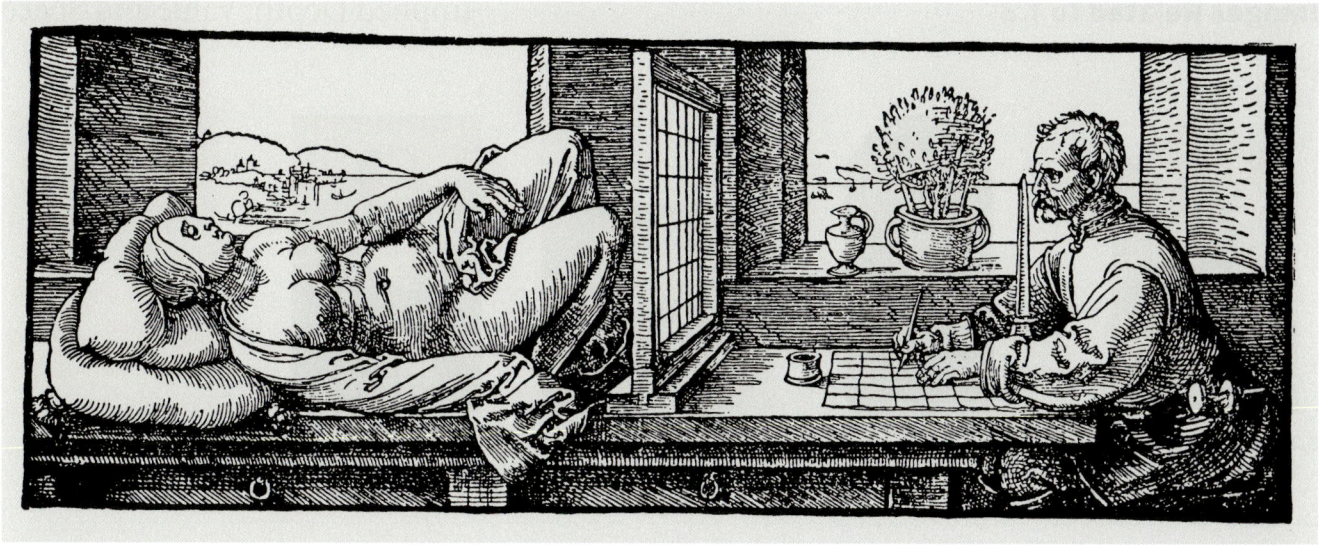

marked on the piece of paper in front of him. The gridded screen in the illustration helps the artist to translate a three-dimensional form into a foreshortened two-dimensional composition.

An illustration of Superman for DC Comics also illustrates foreshortening (**1.3.25**). The figure of Superman is oriented so that his fist is placed in the extreme foreground, with the rest of the body receding away from the reader back into space. The artist makes the fist on the right side larger than Superman's head, exaggerating the depth. The entire figure is vertically shortened, compared to a frontal standing position, because of the oblique angle from which we are viewing the character. Like the linear perspective in the city below, foreshortening has the effect of grabbing our interest. In this work we feel as though Superman is blasting toward us through the air over downtown Metropolis, on his way to save the day.

1.3.24 Albrecht Dürer, *Draftsman Drawing a Recumbent Woman*, 1525. Woodcut, 3 × 8¾". Graphische Sammlung Albertina, Vienna, Austria

1.3.25 Wonder Woman, Superman, and Batman, pages from *Trinity: Volume 1*™ and © DC Comics

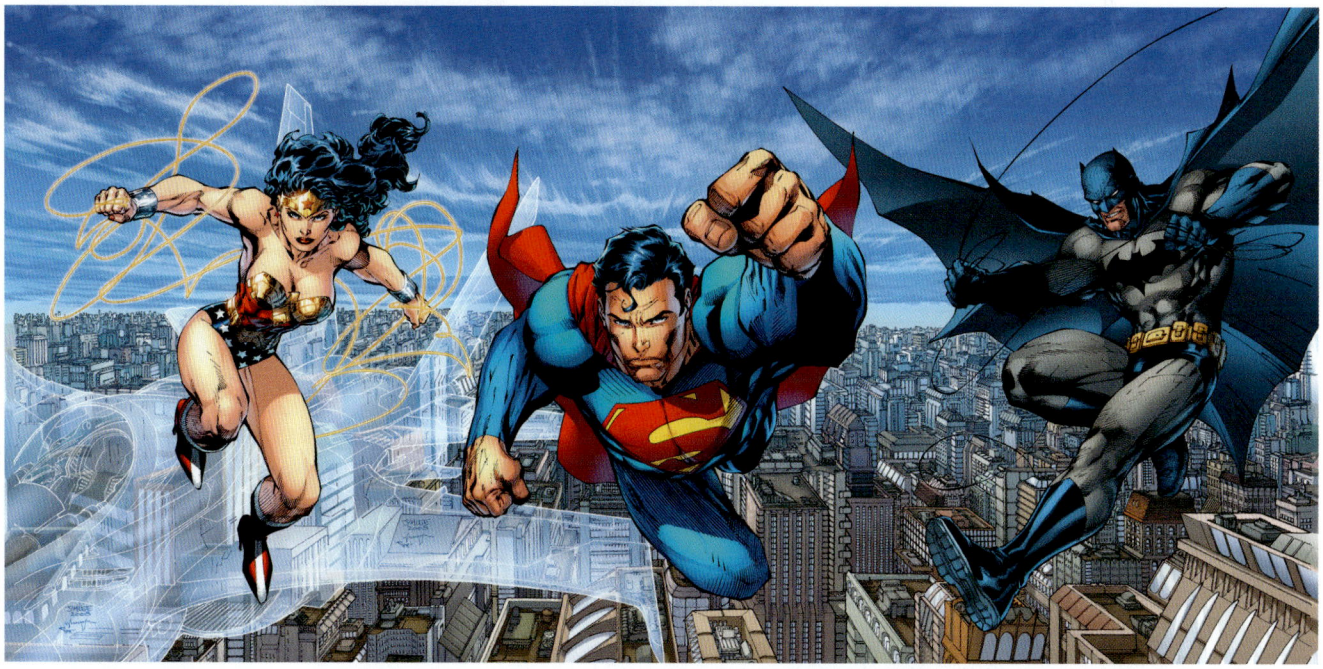

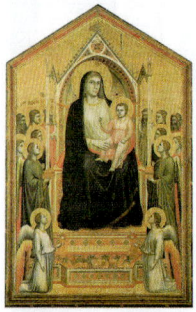

3.2.28 Giotto, *Virgin and Child Enthroned*, c. 1310, p. 408

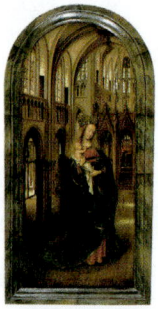

1.7.5 Jan van Eyck, *Madonna in a Church*, 1437–38, p. 143

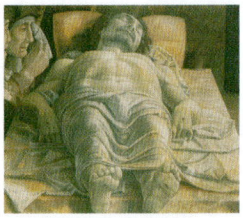

4.3.3 Andrea Mantegna, *Dead Christ*, c. 1480, p. 593

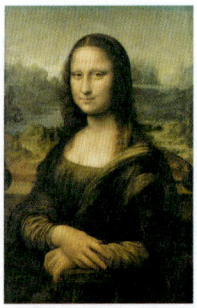

0.0.12 Leonardo da Vinci, *Mona Lisa*, 1503–6, p. 28

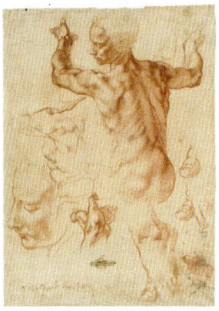

2.1.13 Michelangelo, *Studies for the Libyan Sibyl*, 1510–11, p. 200

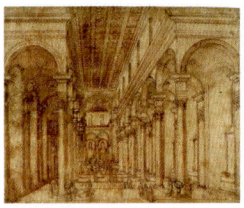

1.1.2a Giovanni Dosio, *Church of Santo Spirito at Florence*, c. 1576–90, p. 44

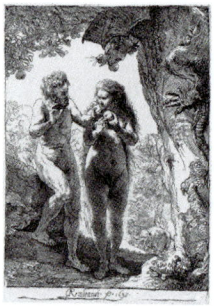

2.3.10 Rembrandt van Rijn, *Adam and Eve*, 1638, p. 232

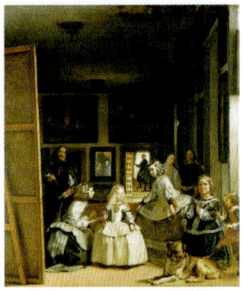

1.10.12a Diego de Silva y Velázquez, *Las Meninas*, c. 1656, p. 183

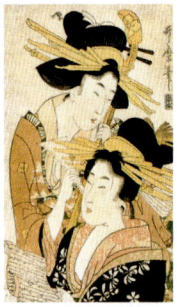

3.8.10 Kitagawa Utamaro, *Two Courtesans*, second half of 18th century, p. 510

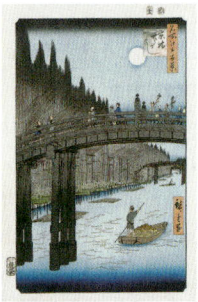

1.8.10 Ando Hiroshige, "Riverside Bamboo Market, Kyo-bashi," 1857, p. 157

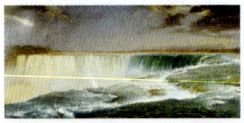

0.0.2 Frederic Edwin Church, *Niagara*, 1857, p. 21

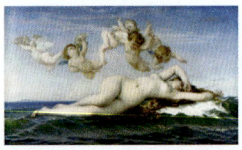

3.8.1 Alexandre Cabanel, *Birth of Venus*, 1863, p. 502

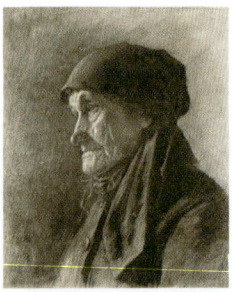

2.1.11 Léon Augustin Lhermitte, *An Elderly Peasant Woman*, c. 1878, p. 198

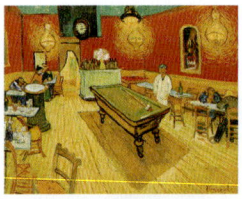

1.4.29 Vincent van Gogh, *The Night Café*, 1888, p. 109

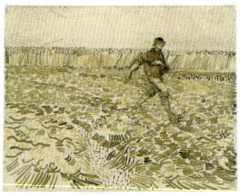

2.1.20 Vincent van Gogh, *Sower with Setting Sun*, 1888, p. 205

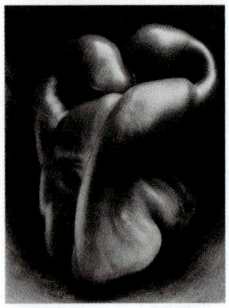

2.8.12 Edward Weston, *Pepper No. 30*, 1930, p. 321

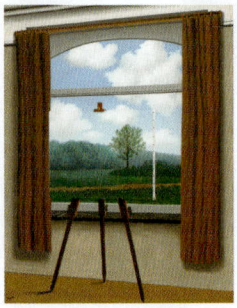

4.5.15 René Magritte, *The Human Condition*, 1933, p. 626

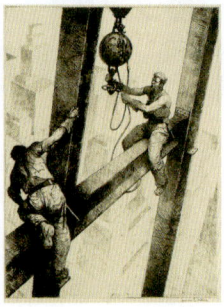

1.1.8 James Allen, *The Connectors*, 1934, p. 48

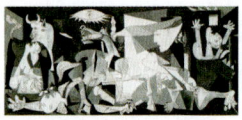

4.7.10 Pablo Picasso, *Guernica*, 1937, p. 646

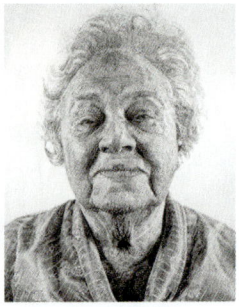

4.5.10 Chuck Close, *Fanny/Fingerpainting*, 1985, p. 622

1.4 Color

Color: the optical effect caused when reflected white light of the spectrum is divided into separate wavelengths
Wavelength: a term from physics that measures light as the distance between two corresponding points on a wave of energy, e.g. between two high points of a wave
Prism: a transparent material with flat, polished surfaces—a form with at least three sides—that can be used to disperse light to reveal the range of color present in the visible spectrum
Pigment: the colored material used in paints. Often made from finely ground minerals

> The first colors that made a strong impression on me were bright, juicy green, white, carmine red, black and yellow ochre. These memories go back to the third year of my life. I saw these colors on various objects which are no longer as clear in my mind as the colors themselves.
>
> (Vasily Kandinsky, Russian painter)

Color is the most vivid element of art and design. By its very essence, color attracts our attention and excites our emotion. Just as personality and mood vary from one person to the next, our perceptions of color are personal and subjective. Few other phenomena touch our innermost feelings as deeply and directly. Due to the complex nature of color, it is useful to approach the subject by focusing first on the science of color and second on the psychological effects it has on us. It is important to note the difference between these two aspects: color as a scientific phenomenon and the idea of color.

Color and Light

Scientists understand a great deal about how we perceive color, although, because it is a complicated element, there are dimensions of color that are not yet fully explained. But the science of color is the best place to begin to understand the role of color in art.

Science tells us that we cannot perceive color without light. Light consists of energy that travels in waves, much as water forms waves. The distance between the peak of each wave of this energy is its **wavelength**. If white or normal daylight passes through a **prism** we see that it is composed of constituent colors of light, which have different wavelengths (**1.4.1**). Therefore, the colors of light make up the spectrum of potential visible colors. But if we need light in order to perceive color, and daylight is white, how is it that we can see individual colors (blue, red, and so on) when we look at particular objects? Our perception of the color of objects is the result of the interaction between light and something in the surface of an object that we call **pigment**.

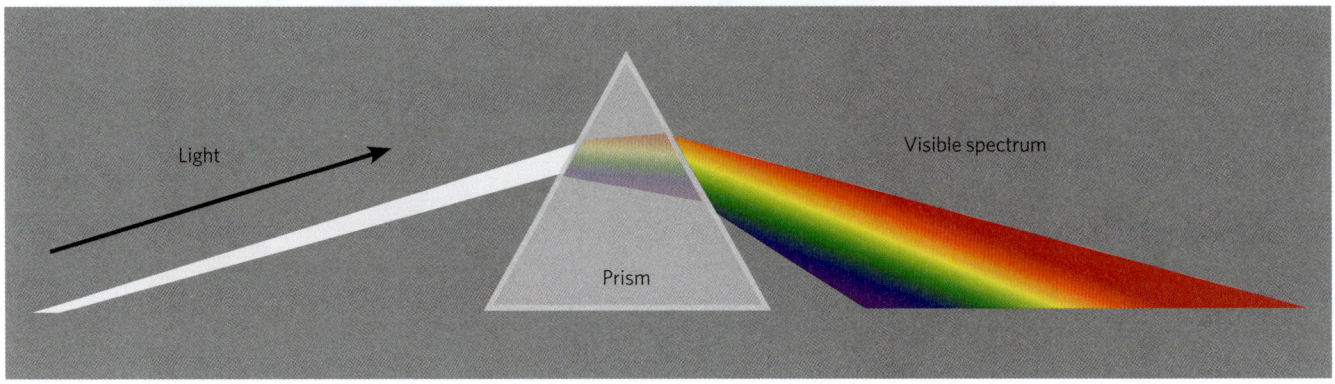

1.4.1 White light can be separated into the visible spectrum using a prism

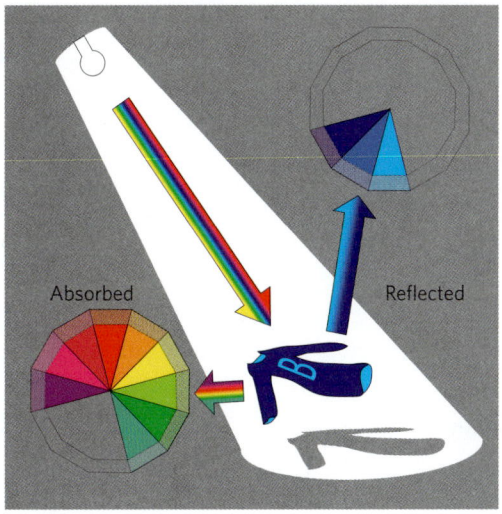

1.4.2 White light reaches a blue object and blue light is reflected

Light is necessary to activate the color of an object, but light alone does not determine the color that we perceive. This depends on light and pigment.

Color and Pigment

We see a blue sweater as blue only when light strikes. If light consists of all the colors of the spectrum, not just blue, how is it that we perceive only the blue portion of the spectrum when we look at the sweater? This occurs because the colors we see in objects are those portions of the light spectrum that a surface fails to absorb, and reflects instead. So, if the surface of the sweater contains blue pigment, when white light reaches that surface, all the other colors in the spectrum are absorbed by the pigment, and only the blue is reflected back. Physiologists explain that our visual perception of reflected colors begins when the reflected color excites the nerve cells that line the back of our eyes. These nerve signals are processed and interpreted as color in the brain. Thus, when we see someone wearing a blue sweater, the blue we see is the portion of the spectrum that is reflected back to our eyes; the rest of the light is absorbed by the sweater (**1.4.2**).

Additive and Subtractive Color

Although light and pigment are both essential for the perception of color, when colors of light are mixed together, the result is not the same as when we mix colors of pigment. This is because pigment is a solid material and light is made from transient waves of energy. When white light strikes a particular pigment, a color is reflected back to the eye. Spectral light is created when naturally occurring white light is divided, for example by a prism. Like white

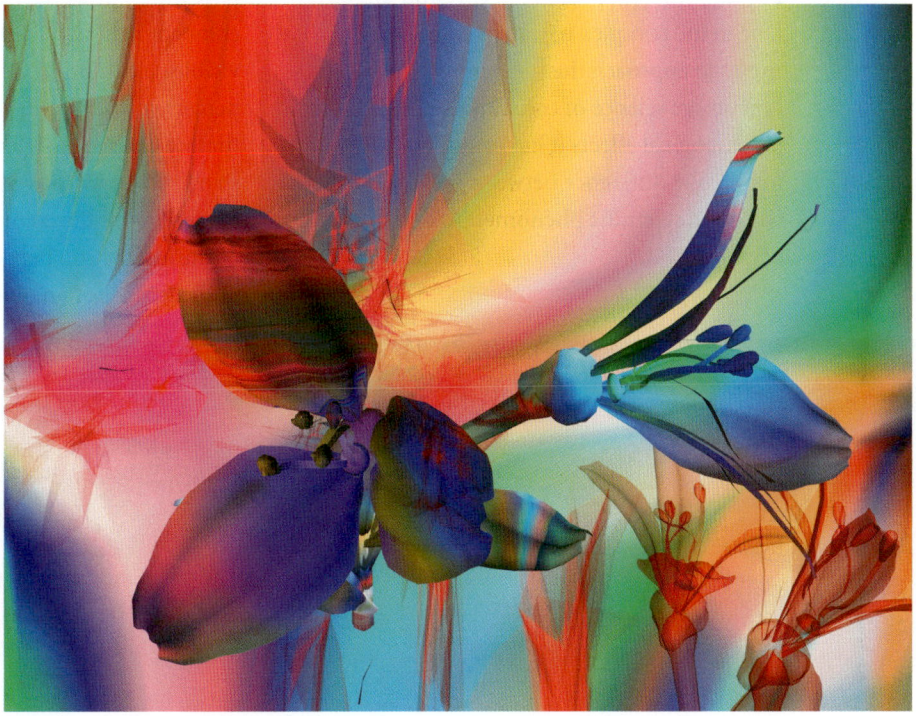

1.4.3 Charles Csuri, *Wondrous Spring*, 1992. Computer image, 4' × 5'5"

light, spectral light can be perceived only when it strikes a surface. Imagine that we take two flashlights with different colored lenses. If we shine the two colored beams of light onto the same spot on a white surface, the resulting color appears brighter than the original two. Because combining the two colors *increases* the brightness of the color, this mixture is termed **additive** (and adding more and more color will eventually lead to white light).

The brilliant illuminated color of a video display is a seductive **medium** for computer artists. The digital artist Charles Csuri (b. 1922) has been creating imagery on computers since 1963. A pioneer in the merging of art with scientific innovations in computer technology, Csuri has explored and helped develop the digital realm as a viable art medium. In *Wondrous Spring*, only red, green, and blue phosphors, or tiny light emitters in the monitor, are used to create a dazzling illuminated array of colors reminiscent of a modern-day stained-glass window (**1.4.3**). The entire spectrum of color that makes the work so lustrous was made visible by numerous additive combinations of red, green, and blue light. The computer creates an almost infinite range of color by systematically turning off and on the phosphors to create the various additive color mixtures present in the work.

Although our perception of the colors of pigment depends on the reflection of the colors of light to our eyes, when we mix pigments together, they do not behave in the same way as when we mix colors of light. Since paint is made of pigment mixed with a **binder**, if two different-colored paints, containing different-colored pigments, are mixed, the result is not brighter but tends to be duller. This is called **subtractive color** because in such a pigment mixture, more of the spectrum is absorbed (or subtracted) from the light that hits the pigmented surface.

Color Wheels

As we have seen, different results occur when artists mix colors of light—for example in televisions and computer monitors, or beams of different-colored light from flashlights—and when artists mix colors of pigment (such as paint). Artists are faced with many ways of mixing color to achieve different effects. In addition, our eyes can perceive a total of 360 colors. These two factors, taken together, mean that predicting and managing the effects of color mixing is often an important aspect of an artist's work—and it is at this stage that a tool called a color wheel can be of assistance.

A color wheel displays important information about **hue** relationships. Hue is a way we identify a color group, such as reds, rather than a specific color, for example blood red. A color wheel acts as a kind of color "map" that allows us to assess the attributes of hues as they relate to each other. There are many color wheels that chart color combinations, but three basic wheels are most commonly used. The first two that we will study show the fundamental hues of pigment-based color, that is, the color that we associate with colored objects. These two wheels are maps or models of subtractive color combinations. The third color wheel maps out the ways that colors of light combine with one another. There are different color wheels for the hues of light and the hues of pigment because the two types of hues react and are perceived independently of each other. As we have seen, when pigments are mixed, the result is referred to as subtractive color, as the blended hues tend to be less intense than in their original, unmixed state. When color in spectral light is blended, the resulting hues tend to be lighter, and this is referred to as additive color. We will start by discussing color wheels used to manage the mixing of hues of pigment as they occur in white light.

Since the eighteenth century, scientists and color theorists have produced color wheels that artists have used (and continue to use today) to manage the mixing of paint and any other pigment-based medium. The hues of this color wheel are the building blocks of most color combinations (**1.4.4**). "Artist's colors"

Additive color: the colors produced from light
Medium (plural **media**): the material on or from which an artist chooses to make a work of art, for example canvas and oil paint, marble, engraving, video, or architecture
Binder: a substance that makes pigments adhere to a surface
Subtractive color: the colors produced from pigment
Hue: general classification of a color; the distinctive characteristics of a color as seen in the visible spectrum, such as green or red

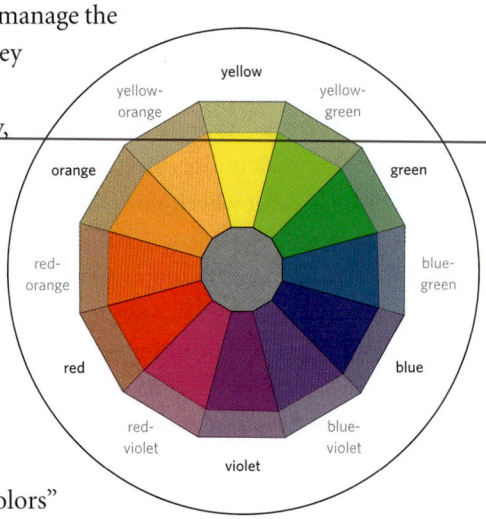

1.4.4 Traditional twelve-step color wheel using "artist's colors"

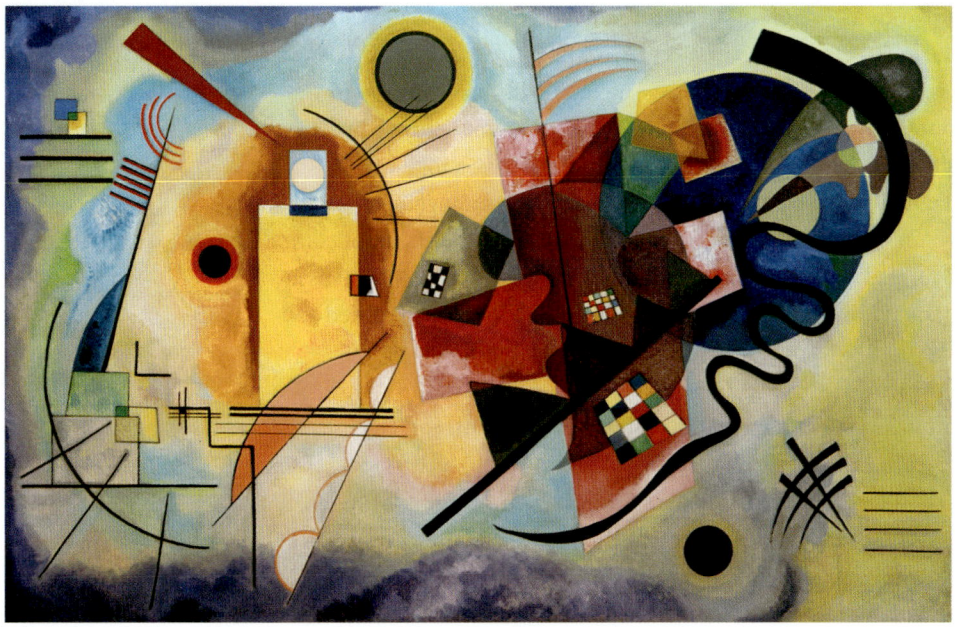

1.4.5 Vasily Kandinsky, *Yellow-Red-Blue*, 1925. Oil on canvas, 50⅜ × 79¼". Musée National d'Art Moderne, Centre Georges Pompidou, Paris, France

Primary colors: three basic colors from which all others are derived
Secondary colors: colors mixed from two primary colors
Tertiary colors: colors that can be mixed from a secondary and a primary color

are the traditional **primary colors**—red, yellow, blue. They are called primary because they cannot be created by mixing any other two colors. The **secondary colors** can be produced by mixing two primary colors. They are the hues orange (that can be created by blending red and yellow), green (a blend of yellow and blue), and violet (a blend of red and blue). In this color wheel, the secondary colors are located between the primary ones because they naturally fall between them in the visible spectrum. The remaining hues in the wheel are called **tertiary colors** and can be created by blending a primary and a secondary color: for example, red-violet is (as its name suggests) a blend of red and violet.

One work that uses the traditional combination of primary red, yellow, and blue is a painting by the Russian artist Vasily Kandinsky (1866–1944) (**1.4.5**). Appropriately titled *Yellow-Red-Blue*, this work utilizes the basic colors of the traditional color wheel, along with black and white. Kandinsky advocated the use of these fundamental elements to simplify and celebrate art and design in their purest sense. Since no primary can be mixed from any other two colors in this wheel, the three he chose exemplified the purest and simplest color available.

If you look again at the color wheel in figure **1.4.4** (p. 97), you will notice the gray in the center. In theory, a perfect subtractive mix of the primary colors of red, yellow, and blue should result in a perfect black, which absorbs all the colors of the spectrum. In practice, however, if an artist mixes the primaries as they are arranged on this color wheel, the result is not black but a brownish gray. This is not a problem for artists who are accustomed to working with this color wheel; their past experience with color and their knowledge of their own personal preferences enable them to create the colors they need. But for graphic designers working on materials that need to be printed using layers of transparent printing inks in a very exact way, it is necessary to be able to create more accurate color mixtures that conform to universal rules. Modern research has therefore provided a new set of primary colors that are better suited to producing specific blended colors when these are printed.

Although the colors red, yellow, and blue have traditionally been accepted as the basic hues of pigment, scientific discoveries in physics have provided a new set of primaries that can be combined into a subtractive mix that enables

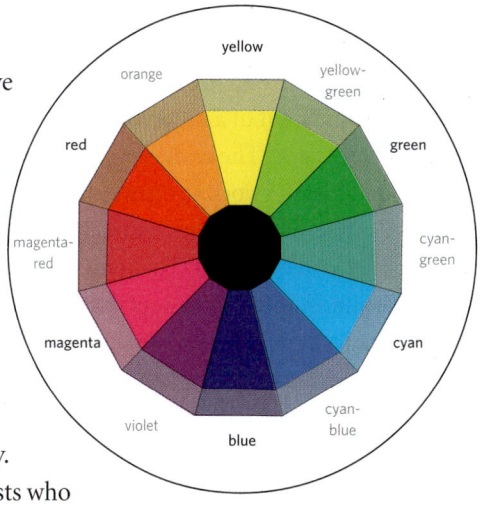

1.4.6 (above) Cyan, Magenta, Yellow (CMY) pigment twelve-color wheel with black center

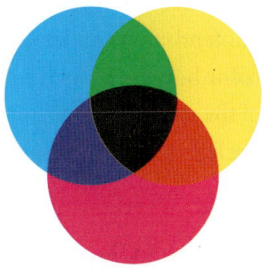

1.4.7 Subtractive color mixtures using CMY primaries. When the three colors are perfectly layered together, the result is black

designers to produce a real ("true") black for printing purposes. If we mix these primaries—cyan (a slightly greenish light blue), magenta (a pinkish light violet), and yellow—their color combination results in black (**1.4.6** and **1.4.7**). The entire spectrum of white light is absorbed (subtracted) in the combination of cyan, magenta, and yellow pigments, so not a single segment of the spectrum is reflected.

Like Kandinsky, the contemporary Argentine-born artist Analia Saban (b. 1980) also works with primary colors to distill art and design to their purest state. But in her work *Layer Painting (CMY): Flowers* (**1.4.8**), Saban wants to "debunk the mysteries of contemporary art." To do this she has adopted the scientifically proven primary combination of cyan, magenta, and yellow to paint a still life of flowers. In so doing, Saban challenges traditional beliefs about color. Red, considered a primary color since the eighteenth century, can now be mixed from the two colors magenta and yellow. Although Saban is questioning ideas about color in painting, the CMY primaries are already the accepted colors used in most visual communication design and commercial printing (**1.4.7**).

These two subtractive color wheels are used to manage the mixing of pigments and to help artists predict the results (**1.4.6** and **1.4.7**). They are useful for painters who mix paints, graphic designers who design for the mixing of printing inks, and for anyone making color combinations of any pigment-based medium. But subtractive color wheels are not useful for artists who work with spectral color. For this, an additive color wheel is required.

Additive color is not generated from pigment, like the traditional or subtractive hue combinations, but from light. For example, an artist who creates an installation consisting of different spectral lights in a room painted white needs to understand how the colors of the different lights combine. Digital artists use the color combinations of red, green, and blue that make up the matrix for color in computer monitors (see, for example, Charles Csuri, *Wondrous Spring*, **1.4.3**, p. 96). Although white light contains the entire spectrum, it is useful to divide light into individual colors so that we can manage combinations as simply as possible (**1.4.9**). The primary hues of light are red, green, and blue. When colors of light are mixed, we call the mixture additive color, because each time a color is added, the blended mix gets lighter, until eventually it results in white (**1.4.9**). The secondary colors of light are cyan, yellow, and magenta and are created by mixing two primaries (**1.4.10**). As in the pigment color wheels, tertiary colors in light are derived from combinations of a primary and a secondary color.

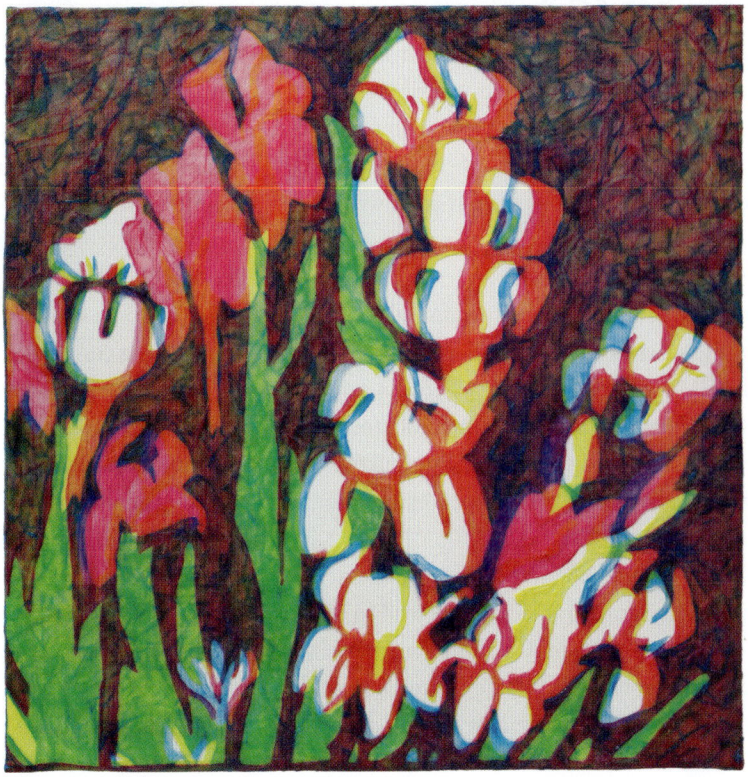

1.4.8 (above) Analia Saban, *Layer Painting (CMY): Flowers*, 2008. Acrylic and screen printing ink on canvas, 36 × 36 × 1½". Thomas Solomon Gallery

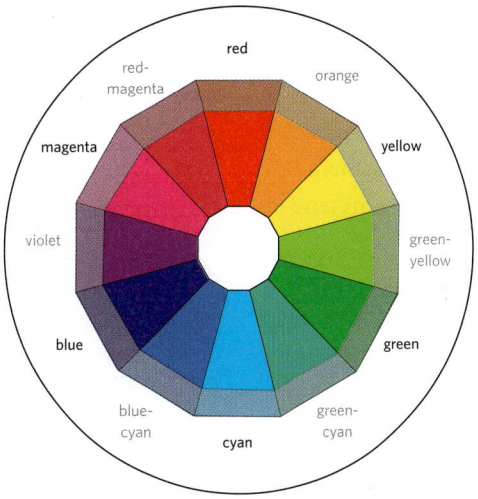

1.4.9 (left) Red, green, blue (RGB) light twelve-color wheel with white center (primary mixture)

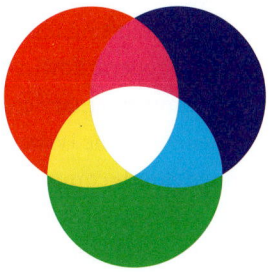

1.4.10 Additive color mixtures using red, green, and blue (RGB) primaries

Dynamics of Color

Color wheels place hues in a visual arrangement that can be a guide to the many attributes of color and how to use them. We will now consider two other important aspects of color that can be clearly understood by looking at color wheels.

Complementary Color

Complementary colors can be found on opposite sides of a color wheel. For example, in the CMY subtractive color wheel (**1.4.6**, p. 98), magenta is the complement of green. For an artist or designer, understanding the juxtaposition of these two colors on the color wheel can be very helpful.

When complementary colors are mixed, they produce gray (or black); they tend to dull one another. But when two complementary colors are painted side by side, these "opposite" colors create visual anomalies: they intensify one another. This happens because complementary colors have markedly different wavelengths, creating an illusion (in the photoreceptors of the eye) of vibrating movement where their edges meet (**1.4.11**). When the eye tries to compensate for the different wavelengths of two complementary colors, we tend to see each color more intensely than when we see them separately. So when red is present, greens tend to appear more vibrantly green.

Practical applications of complementary colors mimic the system that is observed on the color wheel. For example, makeup artists, whose work involves making their clients' eyes show to maximum effect, will apply an eyeshadow with red undertones to green eyes (**1.4.12**). Even though the combination is not exactly the same as that of the strong hues of the color wheel, it uses the same principle.

More traditionally, American landscape painter Frederic Edwin Church (1826–1900) used complementary colors for dramatic effect. In *Twilight in the Wilderness*, the intense red-orange clouds complement swathes of the blue-green evening sky, creating magnificence within a quiet landscape (**1.4.13**). The powerful color of the sky and its reflection in the water below reveal Church's awe and respect for the American landscape.

Analogous Color

Analogous colors fall adjacent to each other on a color wheel and are similar in wavelength, so they do not create optical illusions or visual vibrations the way complementary colors do. Painters use analogous color to create color unity and harmonies that steer viewers toward a particular attitude or emotion. By keeping the color within a similar range, artists avoid jarring, contrasting combinations of colors and moods.

In *The Boating Party* by Mary Cassatt (1844–1926), her color palette creates a harmonious effect (**1.4.14**). This is the result of using analogous colors that are next to one another on the color wheel. In this painting, yellows, greens, and blues predominate. These colors have relatively similar wavelengths and do not intensify one another when placed in close proximity. Cassatt's color seems relaxed, reinforcing her theme. Cassatt was one of the few female members of the **Impressionists**, a group of artists who shared an interest in the effects of light and color on the natural world, which they depicted in their paintings of everyday life.

We will now examine some other important aspects of color.

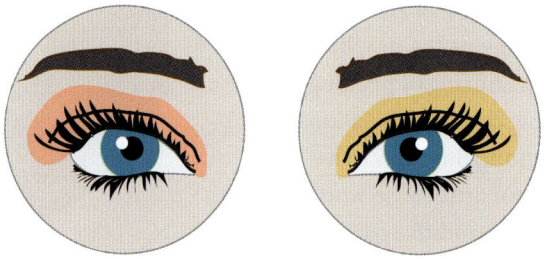

Color complements for blue eyes

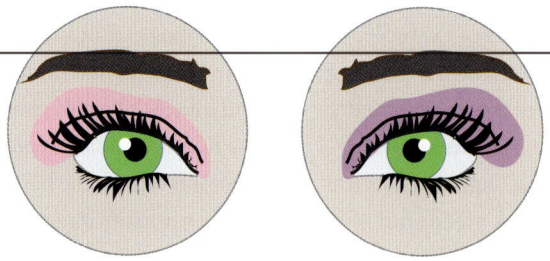

Color complements for green eyes

1.4.12 Makeup artists' guide to complementary colors

primary/secondary analogous combinations

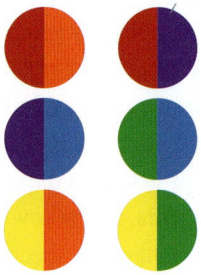

primary/secondary and tertiary complements

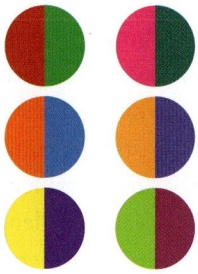

1.4.11 Color combinations and color complements in pigment

Complementary colors: colors opposite one another on the color wheel
Analogous colors: colors adjacent to each other on the color wheel
Impressionist, Impressionism: In the visual arts, a late nineteenth-century style conveying the fleeting impression of the effects of light; Impressionists were artists working in this style

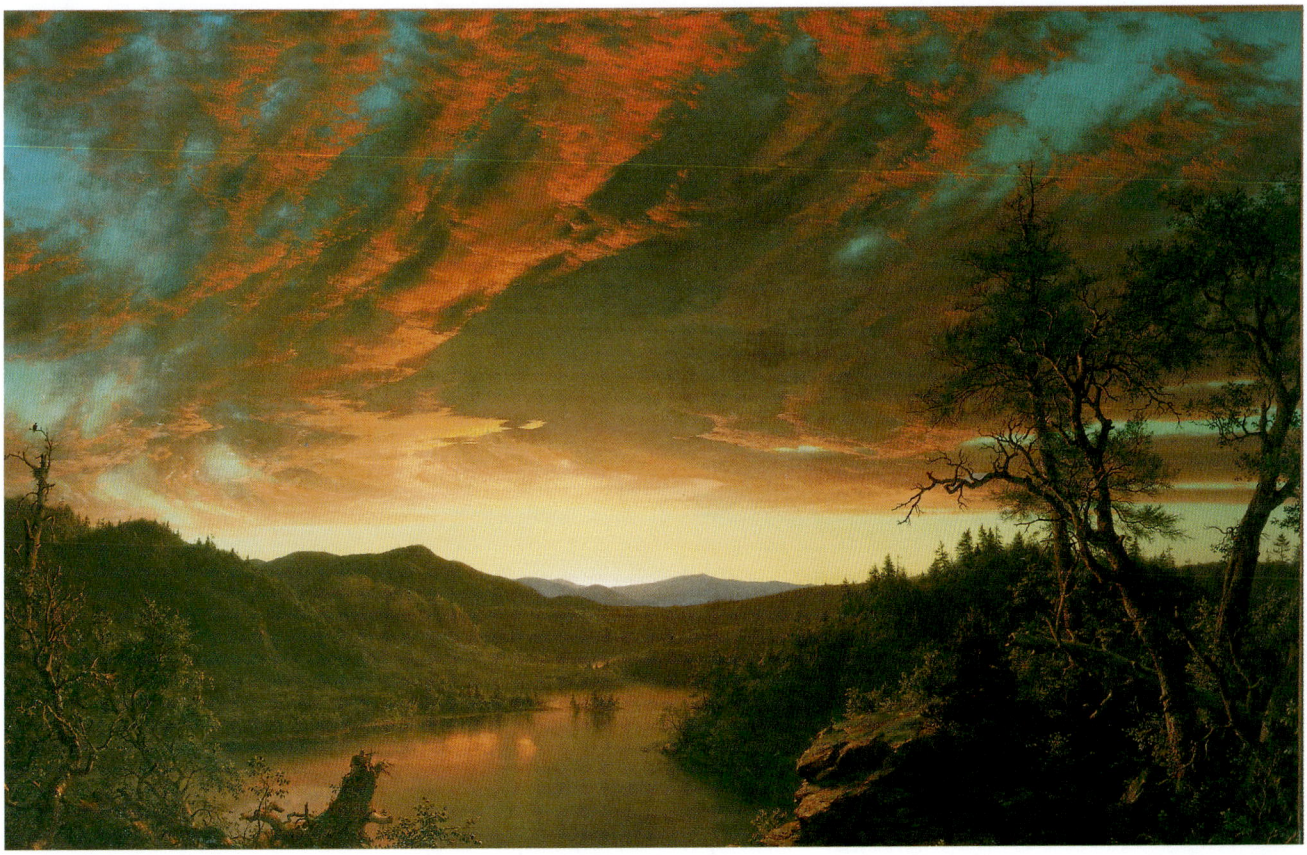

Key Characteristics of Color

Because of the wide range of attributes associated with color, artists and designers use specific terms to be more descriptive. We will now identify these terms as we examine the main properties of color.

Properties of Color

All colors have four basic properties: hue, value, chroma, and tone. By manipulating these four properties, artists and designers can achieve an endless range of visual effects.

Hue

When many of us refer to "the color orange", we are really referring to the hue orange. Hues represent the individual color ranges of the spectrum, that is, red, yellow, blue, green, orange, and violet. Orange is therefore a hue that describes a broad color range, while cocoa-pod orange (**1.4.15**, p. 102) refers to a specific single point in the spectrum of that overall hue family.

For the sake of reference, we associate a hue with an ideal version of a given color. For example, the hue orange is usually associated with a bright, warm, intense orange color of the kind we might see in sports jerseys and industrial surfaces, such as farm equipment. So, when we use the term "hue," we most often are

1.4.13 (above) Frederic Edwin Church, *Twilight in the Wilderness*, 1860. Oil on canvas, 40 × 64". Cleveland Museum of Art, Ohio

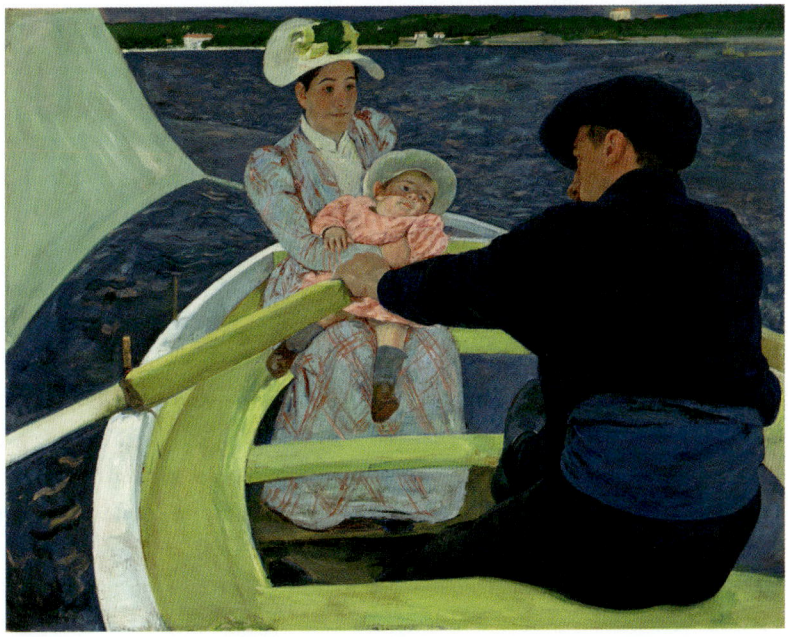

1.4.14 Mary Cassatt, *The Boating Party*, 1893–94. Oil on canvas, 35⅜ × 46⅛". National Gallery of Art, Washington, D.C.

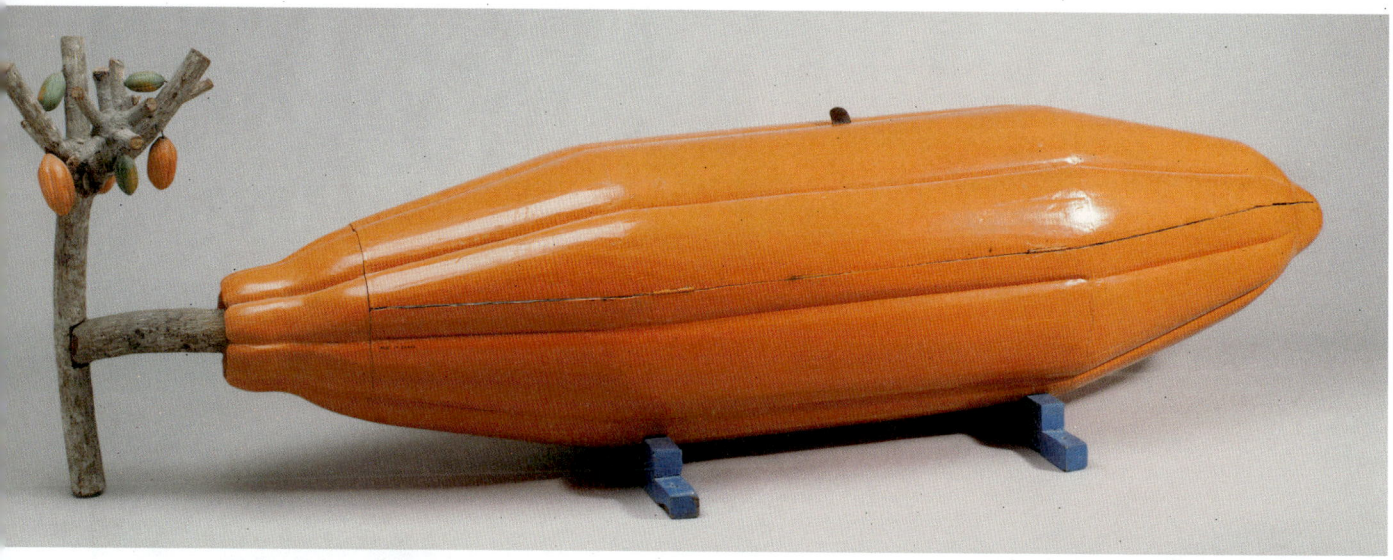

1.4.15 Kane Kwei, *Coffin in the Shape of a Cocoa Pod (Coffin Orange)*, c. 1970. Polychrome wood, 2'10" × 8'6" × 2'5". Fine Arts Museums of San Francisco

making associations to a brilliant color, or at least one as strong as it can be.

Color is such an important aspect of a coffin created by the African sculptor Kane Kwei (1922–1992) that the work is sometimes nicknamed *Coffin Orange* (**1.4.15**). Kwei's coffin is painted with a brilliant mid-hue orange color, that of a half-ripened cocoa pod. Although ripening cocoa pods generally turn some sort of orange hue, the specific color chosen by the artist for this coffin is intentionally bright and exaggerated.

In Ghana, Kwei's native country, funerals are celebratory, loud affairs where bright color adds to the festive mood. Ghanaians believe that having lots of happy people at a funeral gives solace to the family of the deceased, reminding them that they still have many friends. Kwei got started in his career when his dying uncle asked the artist to build him a boat-shaped coffin. It was such a hit in the community that others began to ask for coffins made in interesting shapes. *Coffin in the Shape of a Cocoa Pod* was commissioned by a cocoa farmer who wanted to tell everybody about his lifelong passion at his last party on Earth.

Value

Each hue has a **value**, meaning its relative lightness or darkness compared to another hue. For example, a pure yellow has a light value, and a pure blue has a dark value. Similarly, different colors of the same hue vary in terms of their value: there are light reds and dark reds. **Tints** are colors that are lighter than their basic hue, implying that they have been mixed with white; **shades** are colors that are darker and imply that they have been mixed with black. Figure **1.4.16** shows relative values of red, blue, and yellow. The purest values, compared with those visible in the spectrum, are indicated by the black outline. Figure **1.4.16** also shows the grayscale values; these are described as **neutral**, meaning there is an absence of color.

A work that uses only one hue is called **monochromatic**. An artist can give variety to such a work by using a range of values. Creating dramatic differences in the values of a color allows for ordered transitions from one value to another. Many of American Mark Tansey's (b. 1949) large paintings are monochromatic. In *Picasso and Braque*, Tansey depicts two figures, whom he calls "Orville and Wilbur," a reference to aviators the Wright Brothers (**1.4.17**). He is also referring wryly to Pablo Picasso's (1881–1973) and Georges Braque's (1882–1963) habit of calling each other Orville and Wilbur during the pioneering days of **Cubism**. The two figures here have created a flying machine that resembles an early Cubist **collage**. The monochromatic **palette** is reminiscent of the black-and-white photos of the Wright Brothers' experiments with flight, and the blue tone refers to an early **style** of Picasso's known as his Blue Period.

Picasso's *Old Guitarist* (**1.4.18**) was painted during this period (1901–4); it was a time of poverty and personal depression after the suicide

Value: the lightness or darkness of a plane or area
Tint: a color lighter in value than its purest state
Shade: a color darker in value than its purest state
Neutral: colors (such as blacks, whites, grays, and dull gray-browns) made by mixing complementary hues
Monochromatic: having one or more values of one color
Cubism, Cubist: twentieth-century movement and style in art, especially painting, in which perspective with a single viewpoint was abandoned and use was made of simple geometric shapes, interlocking planes, and, later, collage; the Cubists were artists who formed part of the movement. "Cubist" is also used to describe their style of painting

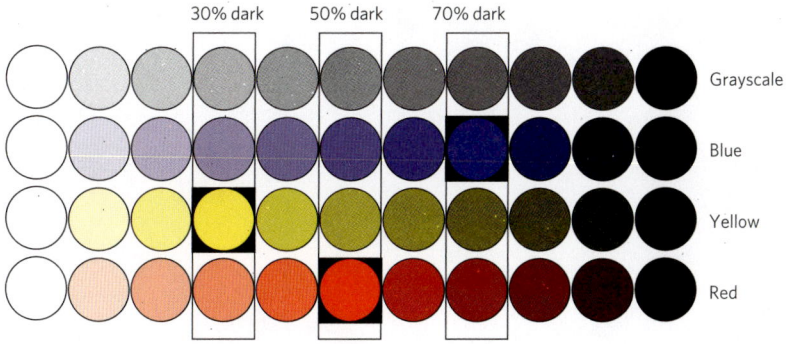

1.4.16 Color-value relationships

Collage: a work of art assembled by gluing materials, often paper, onto a surface. From the French *coller*, to glue
Palette: the range of colors used by an artist
Style: a characteristic way in which an artist or group of artists uses visual language to give a work an identifiable form of visual expression

of a good friend. This artwork is characteristic of the color palette of blues, browns, and grays that Picasso was using during this time. Limiting himself to only a few colors, he relies heavily on value to suggest depth and the solidity of the guitar, figure, and its surroundings. The colors chosen by the artist create a sad and somber mood (see also p. 108 for more about the psychology of color) and the use of different values to create a realistically modeled figure increases the viewer's empathy for the hunched old man—we feel a part of his sorrowful song.

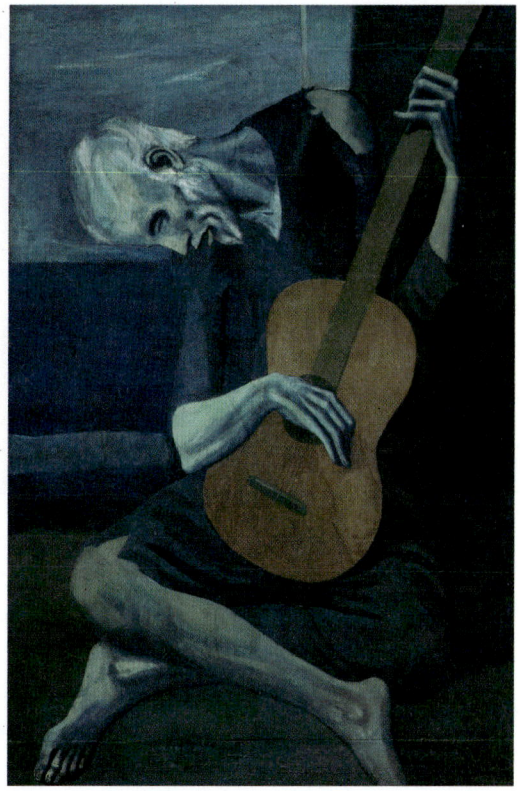

1.4.18 (above) Pablo Picasso, *The Old Guitarist*, 1903–4. Oil on panel, 48⅖ × 32½", Art Institute of Chicago, Illinois

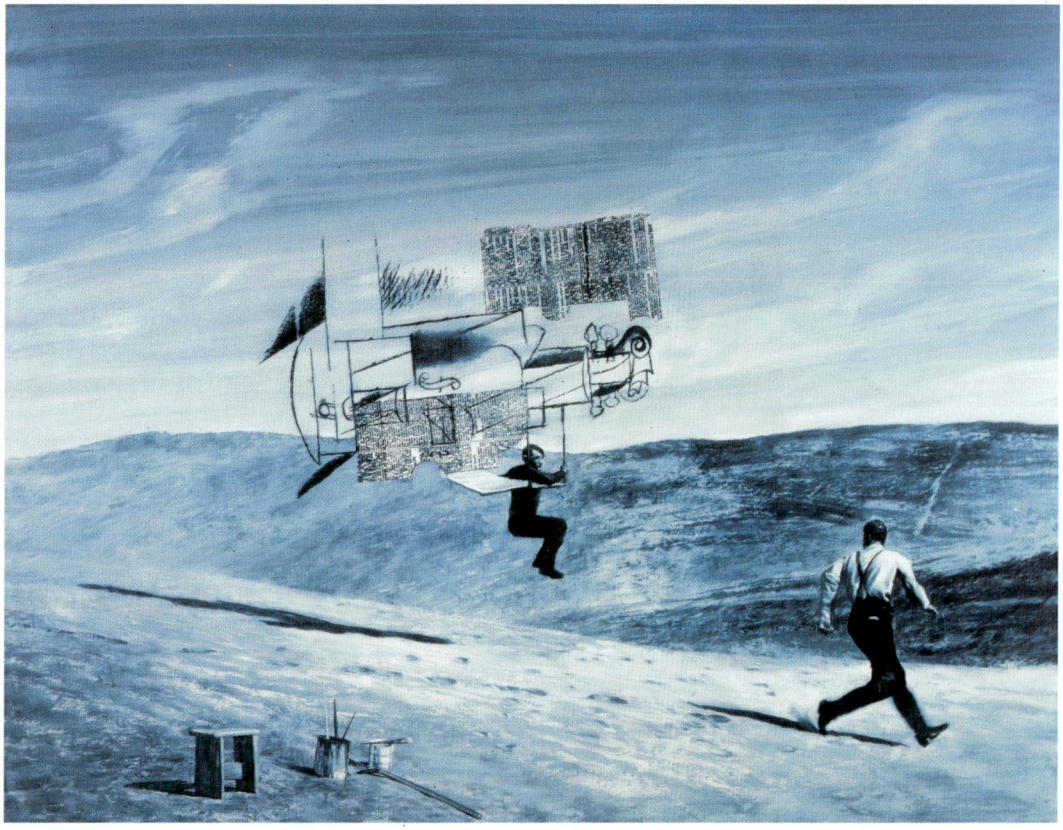

1.4.17 Mark Tansey, *Picasso and Braque*, 1992. Oil on canvas, 5'4" × 7'

1.4.19 Barnett Newman, *Vir Heroicus Sublimis,* 1950, 1951. Oil on canvas, 7'11⅜" × 17'8¼". MoMA, New York

Chroma

When we think of the color yellow, we often imagine something strong, bright, and intense. Many shades of yellow exist, but we tend to associate a color with its purest state, or its highest level of **chroma**. The color mustard yellow, which has a brownish tone, has a weaker chroma, because the intensity of the color is less than the purest hue. Chroma is sometimes described as **saturation**, chromaticness, or intensity, but these terms all generally refer to the strength of color.

Such works as *Vir Heroicus Sublimis* (Latin for "heroic sublime man") by the American painter Barnett Newman (1905–1970) rely, for their visual impact, on value and strong chroma (**1.4.19**). The differing colors of the vertical lines (which Newman calls "zips") break up a broad red **plane**. The white zip makes a gap, while the maroon zip seems to meld into the red field. Subtle variations in the red hues create the sensation that parts of the work are separately lit.

Newman wants viewers to stand close to the canvas, engulfed by color, meeting the artwork as one might another person. The square area in the center of this painting suggests Newman's idealistic vision of the perfectibility of humankind.

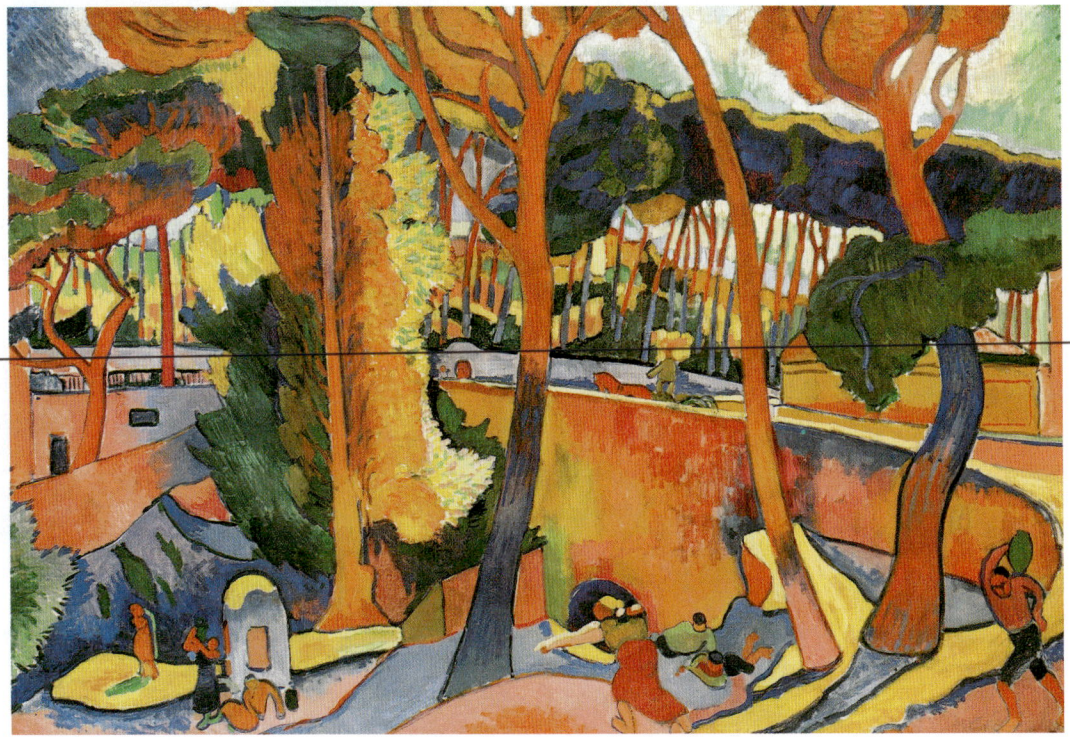

1.4.20 André Derain, *The Turning Road, L'Estaque,* 1906. Oil on canvas, 4'3" × 6'4¾". Museum of Fine Arts, Houston, Texas

Chroma: the degree of purity of a color
Saturation (also known as **chroma**)**:** the degree of purity of a color
Plane: a flat, two-dimensional surface on which an artist can create a drawing or painting. Planes can also be implied in a composition by areas that face toward, parallel to, or away from a light source

The French painter André Derain (1880–1954) was a great advocate of strong chroma. In his work *The Turning Road, L'Estaque*, his use of vivid, bright color makes the entire scene glow with energy and vitality (**1.4.20**). Derain was a member of an artistic movement known as the **Fauves** (French for "wild beasts"). The Fauves delighted in using the new and brighter-colored pigments made available by advances in industrial manufacturing. They used colors in their purest and strongest states as an act of defiance against the Academy, a state-sponsored school of art that set rigid rules for acceptable standards for art and artists at the turn of the twentieth century. Although today it might seem as though the Fauves' subjects and colors are tame by comparison with those of contemporary artists, in their day they were perceived as revolutionary and fierce, challenging the Academy and Western artistic conventions generally and earning the artists their nickname. Derain's painting is energized by high chroma and color complements that intensify adjacent colors when seen close together.

Tone

Chroma is a term that also describes the purity of a hue derived from the spectrum of pure white light. A green at its highest chroma is closest to its pure state in the spectrum of light (**1.4.21**), and when a color is in its strongest chromatic state, it has no tints or shades. Yet green, for example, can also be a very muted hue. The weaker chromatic states of any hue are known as **tones**. Tone is a property of any color that is not at its highest chroma within its value range. A hue that is almost gray is a tone because it has been dulled from its most intense chromatic state, even though it may be similar in *value* to the hue at its highest chroma. Therefore a muted tone, whatever its hue, is less intense as it gets further from the purity of its spectral origin. A pastel-green tone and a dark-green tone would each have a restricted value of green, but a grayed-green hue that is just as dark as the original green would also have a low chroma.

Many artists have used the tonal qualities of color and associated them with sound. In the painting *Ancient Sound* (**1.4.22**) by the Swiss artist Paul Klee (1879–1940), varying tones of green and orange are organized so that a viewer might make associations to sounds, for example seeing the yellows as similar to bright, high-pitched noises, and the darks as similar to deep, low sounds. Klee, who excelled as both artist and accomplished violinist, organized a grid full of colors that varied from an extremely light tone of

Fauves: a group of early twentieth-century French artists whose paintings used vivid colors. From the French *fauve*, "wild beast"
Tone: a color that is weaker than its brightest, or most pure, state

1.4.21 Sampling of chroma, tone, shades, and tints in green hue

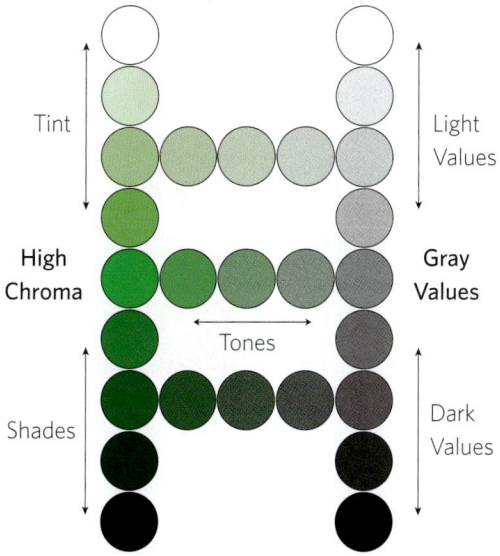

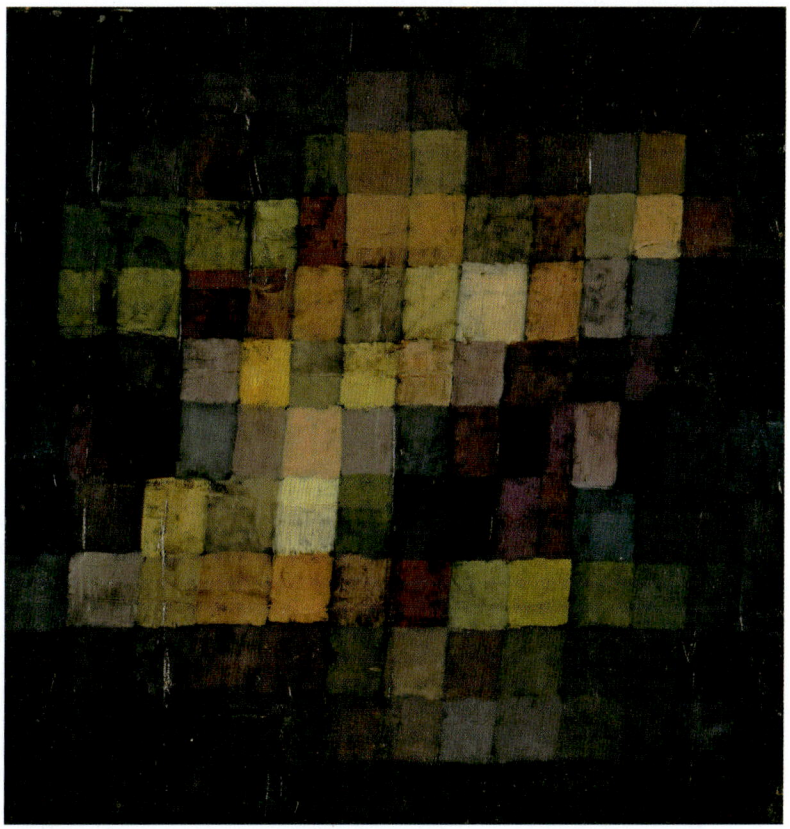

1.4.22 Paul Klee, *Ancient Sound*, 1925. Oil on cardboard, 15 × 15". Kunstmuseum Basel, Switzerland

yellow-orange to greens and browns that nearly become black in value. The tones are carefully darkened and lightened to take full advantage of the adjacent colors to increase or decrease the **contrast**. Like the changing notes in a piece of music, the chroma of these colors rises and falls as if they are notes that have been unleashed through a voice or musical instrument.

The Sensation of Color

Our sensations of color are both evocative and physical. Some colors are associated with emotional states: if we say we are feeling "blue," we are describing a psychological state of mind. Blue is also associated with cold, and red with hot: an association that can be referred to as color **temperature**. Color temperature is relative to other surrounding colors, and interpretation is highly subjective.

Color can also affect the way we see. Because of the difference in color wavelengths, our eyes cannot fully comprehend all the colors at the same time, so our brain translates (or distorts) the incoming information. This is the basis of an illusion known as optical color. Our interpretation of color can also be completely inaccurate because of the limitations of our optical senses.

Color Temperature

We associate color with temperature because of our previous experiences. We may have been burned by something red-hot, or chilled by cool blue water. Our perception of the temperature of a color can be altered if it is placed next to an analogous, or similar, color. For example, green, a color we might associate with coolness, can be warm if we see it next to a cooler color, such as blue. A yellow-green would be warmer than a blue-green. Color temperature is relative to the other colors nearby. Artists use such associations to communicate physical and emotional states.

The colors chosen for the underglaze-painted lamp from the Islamic shrine the Dome of the Rock, in Jerusalem, are blue and green, on a white **ground** for contrast (**1.4.23**). They reflect the kind of color influence valued in the meditative atmosphere of a holy place. The choice of colors is cool and peaceful. Many people associate green and blue with water, plant life, or a clear sky. Our life experiences with blue and green things can easily be associated with passive environments. The color green has positive associations in Islamic art and supports the peacefulness of prayer.

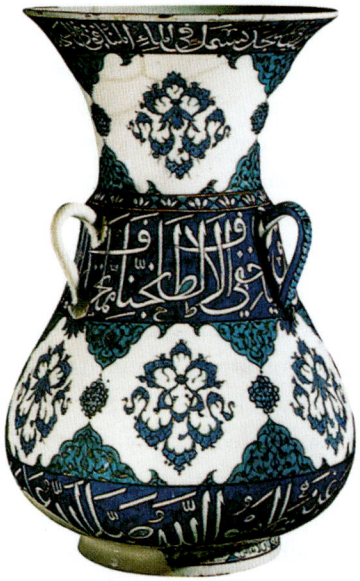

1.4.23 Mosque lamp from the Dome of the Rock in Jerusalem, 1549. Iznik pottery, height 15". British Museum, London, England

Contrast: a drastic difference between such elements as color or value (lightness/darkness) when they are presented together
Temperature: a description of color based on our associations with warmth or coolness
Ground: the surface or background onto which an artist paints or draws
Pointillism: a late nineteenth-century painting style using short strokes or points of differing colors that optically combine to form new perceived colors
Modernist, Modernism: a radically new twentieth-century art and architectural movement that embraced modern industrial materials and a machine aesthetic

Optical Color

Sometimes our brains receive so much information that they simplify it. Optical colors are colors our minds create based on the information we can perceive. In **1.4.24**, the square above contains so many red and blue dots that our brain interprets them as a violet color. In the square below, red and yellow dots are interpreted as an orange tone.

The French painter Georges Seurat (1859–1891) used the optical qualities of color to create a new style of painting, called **pointillism** because it relied on small dots (or points) of color. In *The Circus* Seurat paints a scene of lively entertainment, imbued with bright color and texture through the use of small dots (**1.4.25a** and **b**). Because these dots are so close together, the colors we see are different from the actual colors of the dots.

This optical mixing makes the colors more intense because they have retained their individual intensity, whereas if they were mixed

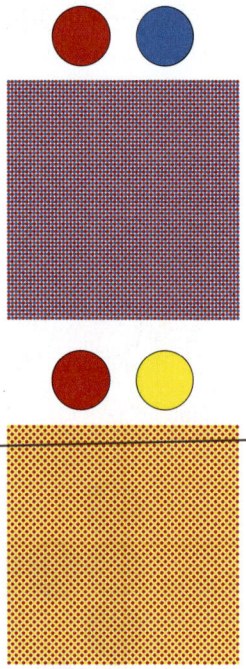

1.4.24 Two squares, one filled with red and blue dots and the other with red and yellow dots to create optical color mixing effect

on the palette they would appear more subdued. *The Circus*'s jewel-like diffusion of light and the illusion of visual vibrations between the colors make it visually exciting.

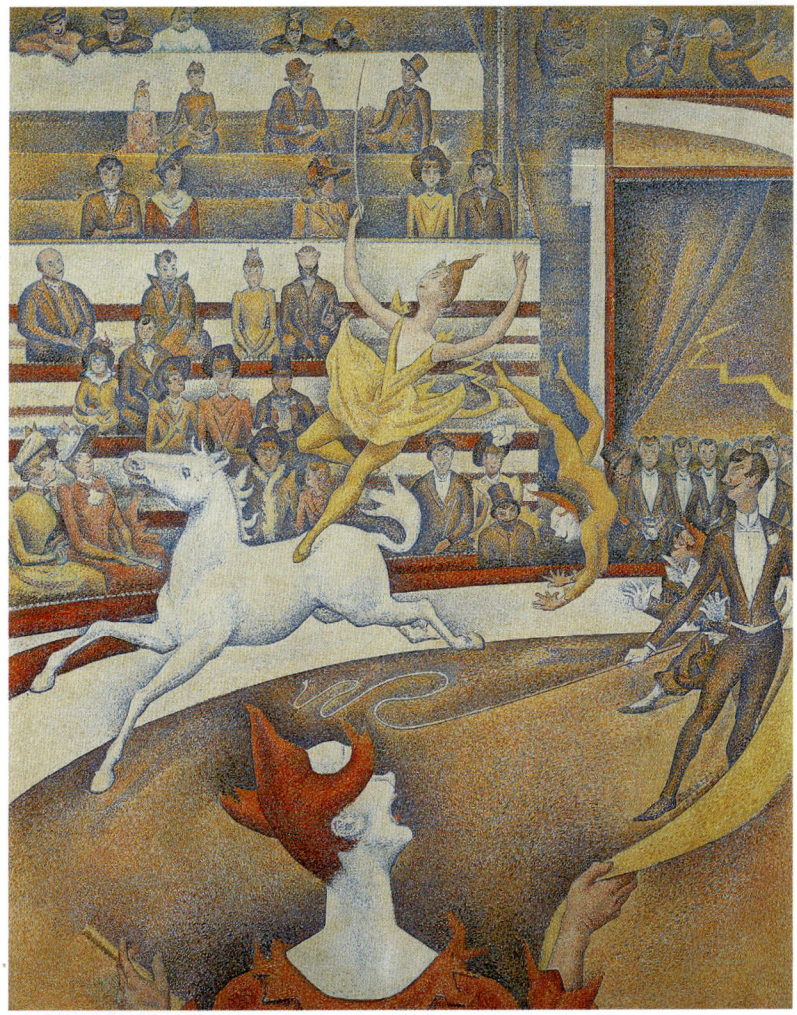

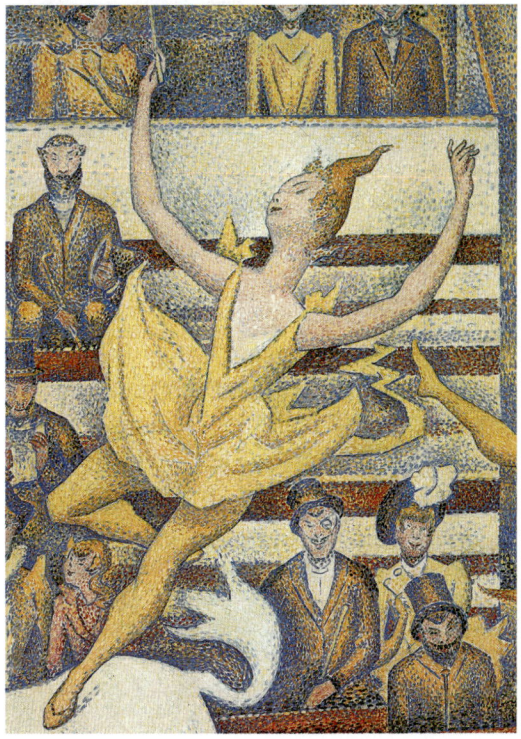

1.4.25a (above) Georges Seurat, *The Circus*, 1890–91. Oil on canvas, 6'⅞" × 4'11⅞". Musée d'Orsay, Paris, France

1.4.25b (left) Detail of Georges Seurat, *The Circus*

Color Theory and Deception

Researchers called color theorists experimented and observed the many attributes of perception and interaction. Two significant theorists were Johannes Itten (1888–1967) and Josef Albers (1888–1976). Itten was a painter, designer, and teacher who worked on finding ideal color combinations while at the Bauhaus, a school of art in twentieth-century Germany that focused on **Modernist** ideas. Some theorists found that we can be deceived by a color because of the influences of color next, or adjacent, to it. As we see from optical color mixtures that can imply colors that are not actually present, color can trick our perception. Itten's contemporary, Albers, described some color deceptions in his experiments. In Figures **1.4.26 a** and **b** Albers, a teacher of color theory and design at the Bauhaus, Black Mountain College, and Yale, has created an illustration of how one color can look like two. If you look at state A, the brown squares on either side of the horizontal center stripes look distinctly different, but when the blue and yellow center stripes are removed, we see that the different browns are actually exactly the same. Albers realized that color is relative to its surroundings and that by changing the adjacent colors, he could change how a color is perceived.

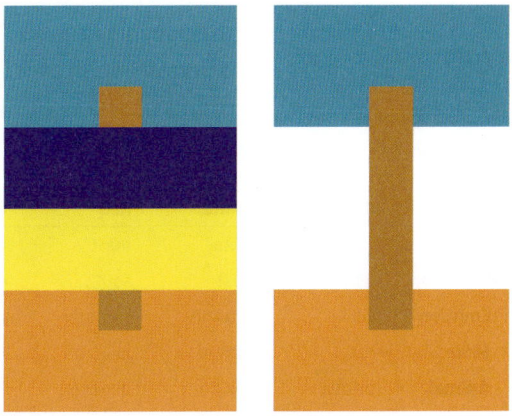

1.4.26a (right) Josef Albers, *Two Colors Look Like One, State A. From Interaction of Color*, Ch. IV, plate 1

1.4.26b (far right) Josef Albers, *Two Colors Look Like One, State B. From Interaction of Color*, Ch. IV, plate 2

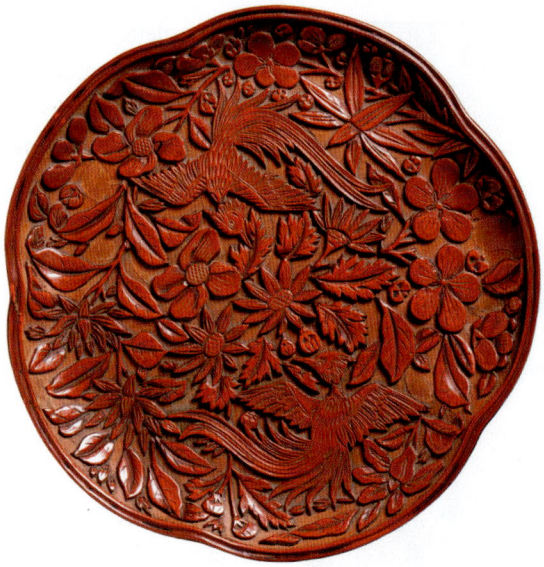

1.4.27 Tray in the form of a plum blossom with birds and flowers, China, Late Southern Song Dynasty, c. 1200–1279. Carved red lacquer on wood core, 7⅜" diameter. Los Angeles County Museum of Art (LACMA), California

Interpreting Color Symbolism

Color can affect how we think and feel. Studies by Faber Birren (1900–1988), a color psychologist, indicate that when people are constantly exposed to red light they can often become loud, grow argumentative, and eat voraciously: it appears that red can influence aggression in our behavior.

Colors also have traditional symbolic values. As we have seen, green, traditionally, has positive associations for Muslims; Buddha wore yellow or gold; Jews and Christians associate the color blue with God (the Virgin Mary is most frequently depicted wearing blue). Our cultural beliefs about color also affect the way we think and feel.

In China there are five particular colors that stand out in traditional history, derived from Wu Xing, the Theory of Five Elements or Five Virtues. Wu Xing was a philosophy that sought to explain how change affects the cosmos through five elements: water, metal, fire, earth, and wood. Black, white, red, yellow, and green-blue (sometimes called "qing") were established as the basic colors representing these five elements. Each color also stood as a symbol that had multiple associations (see **1.4.28**). For example, black represented water, the direction north, winter, and more. Hence, particular colors communicate particular ideas to others who share the same cultural understanding and history. For instance, black was chosen by the founder of the Qin empire as a color that represented the north, and all who lived during that period passed this cultural knowledge on to future generations. The color red represents fire and the direction south; it is also symbolic of warmth, good luck, and happiness. Because of this, red would never be worn to a funeral in China, but it is a popular color for brides because of its associations with joy and life-giving.

The color red is used for the lacquer tray from China dating to the Song Dynasty (**1.4.27**). Lacquer is made from tree sap, and it is a very laborious substance both to produce and to apply. Several colored pigments can be added to lacquer, but red and black are by far the most common. During the Song Dynasty (from 960 to 1279 CE) the ideas of Wu Xing were well established, and this tray features some of the traditional symbols associated with red. The two long-tailed birds could be phoenixes; they may also remind us of the "Vermillion Bird," one of four symbols of the constellations in the night sky. The Vermillion Bird is linked with summer and the south, as is the color red.

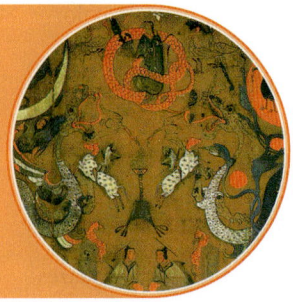

An example of the elemental colors of ancient China can be found in the painted banner from the tomb of Lady Dai: see **3.3.12, p. 417**

1.4.28 Chart of the colors, or "qing," representative of the Five Virtues and other associated symbols

	Black	White	Red	Green-Blue	Yellow
Element	water	metal	fire	wood	earth
Direction	north	west	south	east	center
Emotion	winter	autumn	summer	spring	"fifth season"
State	fear	sorrow	joy	anger	desire
Animal	tortoise	unicorn	phoenix	dragon	human

The Psychology of Color

Although science explains how light can be separated or refracted so that we can experience it, and books and treatises can tell us of the symbolic color associations practiced in different cultures, color is also experienced in ways that are non-objective—that is, dependent on our individual character, background, and nature. Ancient Greek philosophers speculated that color might be a state of mind and that the color we see is a unique experience for every person, because our interpretations of color are deeply associated with the psychological and social aspects of our lives.

Color affects us because it can alter the way we feel and react. In Western cultures, we associate love and danger with red, and sadness with blue. The potential impact of color on our sense of well-being is such that some ancient cultures, such as the Egyptians and Chinese, used colors for healing. The ancient Persian philosopher Avicenna created a chart that associated color with medical symptoms and their treatment. For example, it was believed that a bleeding open wound would be aggravated by the presence of red, but if the patient was exposed to blue (by simply looking at it), the effect would be beneficial.

Artists understand that color affects the way we think and react to the world. Some of these reactions are culturally biased: in the United States blue is paired with masculinity, but in China it is associated with the feminine. As we have seen, red (which we can easily associate with blood) can arouse feelings not only of anxiety, aggression, and anger, but also of passion, eroticism, and vitality. Green, a color we associate with growing plant life, encourages restfulness, but it also suggests decay and illness.

The Dutch painter Vincent van Gogh (1853–1890) was enormously affected by color, and studied its psychological effects. Van Gogh was plagued by periods of deep depression and was hospitalized on many occasions; through his treatment he learned a great deal about psychology. The colors in his painting *The Night Café* are not taken from life, but were carefully chosen to elicit emotional responses from viewers (**1.4.29**). In a letter to his brother Theo, Van Gogh writes about the work, "I have tried to express with red and green the terrible passions of human nature." Like any skilled artist, Van Gogh interpreted the color of the Café de la Gare (as it was called) as he painted it, in order to express something more about the place. The color intensifies the psychological implications of the scene, in a seedy nightspot in Arles, France, as we wander visually into this menacing place as outsiders. By choosing fierce and oppressive red, a feverish yellow, and the rather bilious or sickly green, Van Gogh expresses his sense that this nightspot had a detrimental psychological influence on its patrons. The almost lurid hues convey a strong feeling of unease and sorrow, and the strange, lurching perspective in the room opens up irregular spaces that intensify the painting's lonely atmosphere.

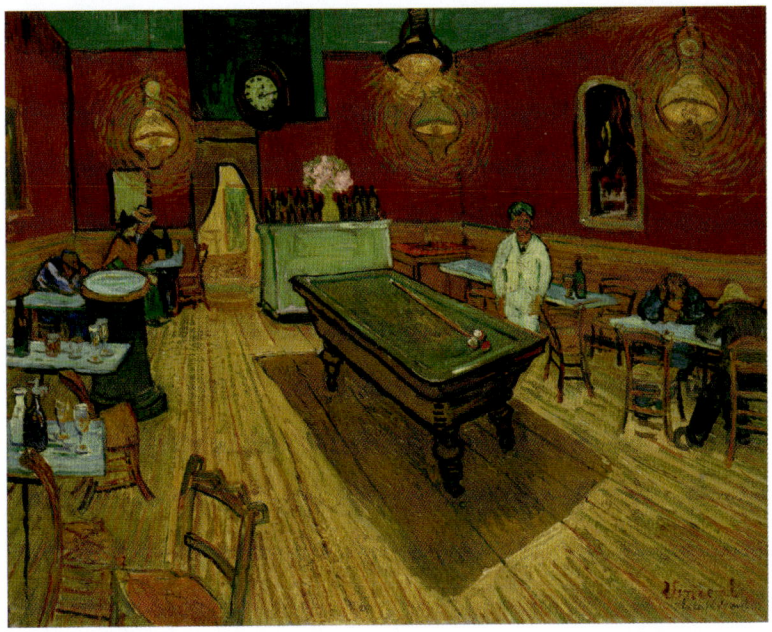

1.4.29 Vincent van Gogh, *The Night Café*, 1888. Oil on canvas, 28½ × 36¼". Yale University Art Gallery, New Haven, Connecticut

The color green has different associations for the Puerto Rican artist Chemi Rosado-Seijo (b. 1973) and the people of Naranjito, Puerto Rico. The term "green" often refers to things that are environmentally friendly, and this is the idea reflected in Rosado-Seiji's *El Cerro* (**1.4.30**),which is a collaboration between the artist and the local community. An entire neighborhood began painting houses and other buildings in the El Cerro district of Naranjito in 2002. The residents

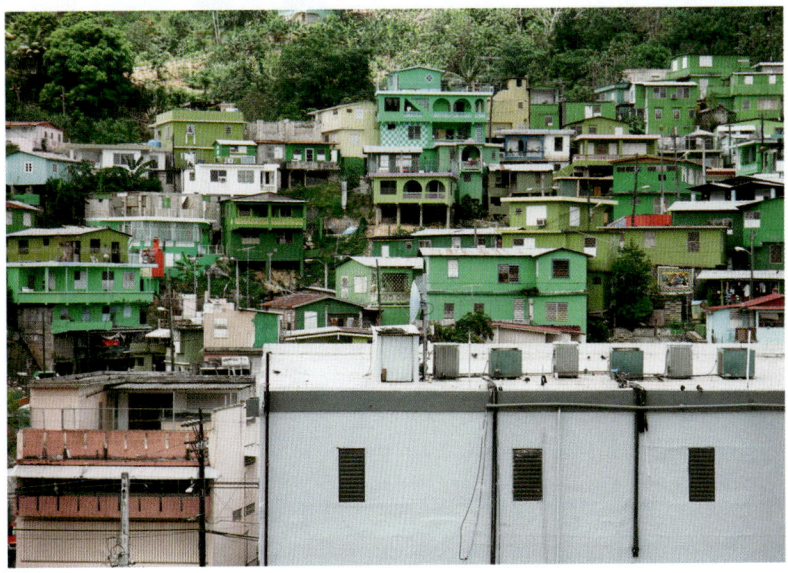

1.4.30 Chemi Rosado-Seijo, *El Cerro*, 2003 (started 2002). Collaboration, Naranjito, Puerto Rico

decided to paint their homes different shades of green, showing respect for the surrounding mountainous environment. The work helped to unify the community and promote programs that support positive changes, such as the creation of a space that is both a museum and classroom, as well as the establishment of a community center.

Expressive Aspects of Color

Such artists as Van Gogh wanted viewers to "feel" artworks, rather than merely to understand them. Color in particular can express a wide range of emotions—for example, the bright yellow of a happy-face symbol attracts our attention and lifts our spirits. Artists and designers can use color to engage the viewer, whether by using blue around the image of a political candidate to suggest traditional values, or green to imply environmental awareness.

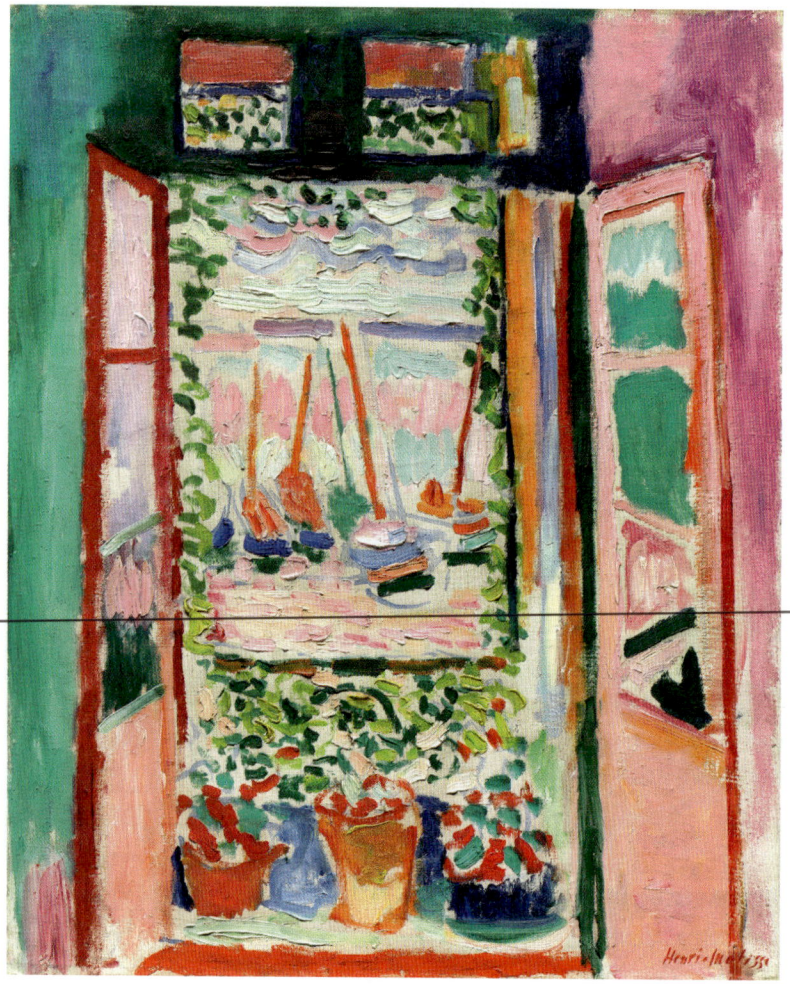

1.4.31 Henri Matisse, *Open Window, Collioure*, 1905. Oil on canvas, 21¾" × 18⅛". National Gallery of Art, Washington, D.C.

Henri Matisse (1869–1954) was a French artist who was a great and influential practitioner of the expressive use of color. He and the artists of the Fauve movement focused especially on using color as intensely as they could to reveal the rich character of painting. For example, in Matisse's *Open Window, Collioure* (**1.4.31**), the artist uses pairs of complementary colors to enhance the painting. In this scene we see such combinations as the orange and blue boats, through the window, and the red-pink wall on the right paired with the greenish-blue one on the left. Since complementary colors influence each other, the resulting experience is a brilliant expression of vibrant color.

The French painter Paul Gauguin (1848–1903) used yellow for its uplifting associations when he painted *The Yellow Christ* (**1.4.32**). Gauguin painted this scene—a deliberately populist portrayal of folk spirituality—while in Brittany, France. In it, three women in traditional Breton dress appear to attend the crucifixion. Although Gauguin is known to have been inspired by a woodcarving in a local chapel, his choice of color is primarily symbolic. Through color he connects the crucifixion of Christ to the seasons of Earth and the cycle of life. Here, yellows and browns correspond to the colors of the surrounding autumnal countryside, harvested fields, and turning leaves. Gauguin's color palette relates the background natural world to the body on the cross, so that our gaze too is drawn in and upward. By using bright color, Gauguin creates a simple and direct emotional connection with the viewer. While depicting death, Gauguin chose colors that nonetheless express the optimism of rebirth.

While some expressions of color can be experienced in the same way by entire groups of people or societies, others are intensely personal, and can hold meanings that are known fully only to the individual concerned. Swedish artist Hilma af Klint (1862–1944) used color to create her own visual vocabulary. She was a prolific artist, and created many hundreds of paintings inspired by her spiritual experiences. According to af Klint, the designs

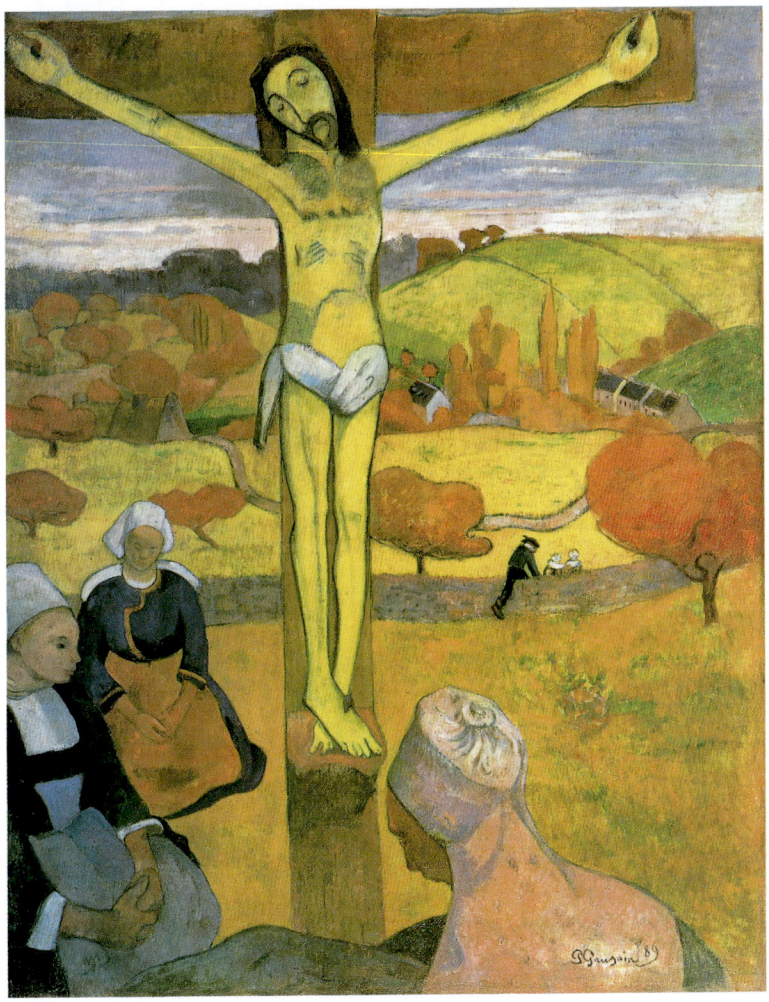

1.4.32 Paul Gauguin, *The Yellow Christ*, 1889. Oil on canvas, 36¼ × 27⅞". Albright-Knox Art Gallery, Buffalo, New York

and colors in a number of her works were directed by a spirit guide whom she contacted during séances. Many of her works are painted in an **abstract** style: the subject matter is not immediately recognizable. The artist also felt that certain colors symbolized particular meanings, for example yellow was "the splendid color of light, of the foundation of knowledge." The strong yellow in her work *Group IV, No. 7, Adulthood* (**1.4.33**) represents light and the knowledge that one achieves with adulthood. Af Klint may not have intended for viewers to understand completely her paintings and their symbolism—in fact, she requested that her spiritual works not be shown publicly until twenty years after her death.

Color has always been used expressively by artists and designers, sometimes to change the way that a viewer feels about his or her surroundings. Take for example a project by the Polish-born New York artist Adrian Kondratowicz (b. 1984), where the artist has asked his Harlem neighbors to look at trash a bit differently (**1.4.34**). Adrian, as he is known locally, distributed bright pink, rodent-repellent, biodegradable trash bags to his community. When these pink polka-dotted bags were used, they subverted the standard black and elicited a positive emotion from the community.

Abstract: art imagery that departs from recognizable images of the natural world

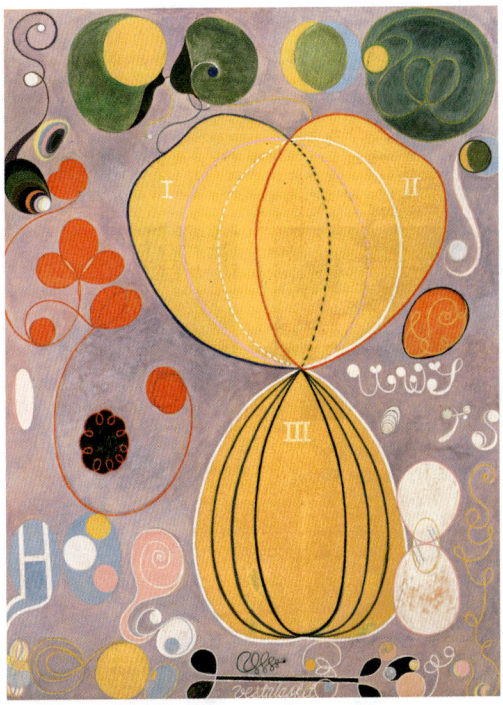

1.4.33 Hilma af Klint, *Group IV, No. 7, Adulthood*, 1907. Tempera on paper mounted on canvas, 10'4½" × 7'8½". Moderna Museet, Stockholm, Sweden

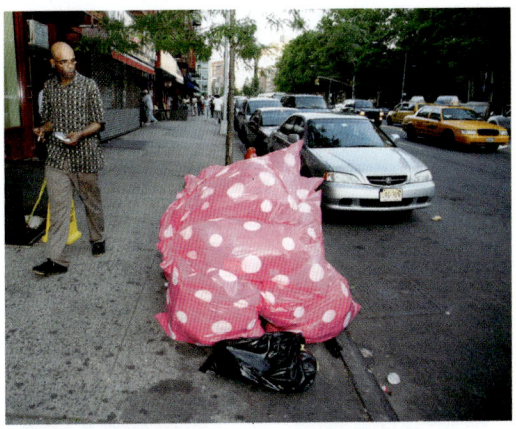

1.4.34 Adrian Kondratowicz, *TRASH maximalism NYC (Harlem), TRASH project*, 2008–

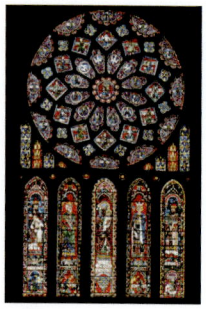

2.6.11 Rose window and lancets, Chartres Cathedral, France, 13th century, p. 291

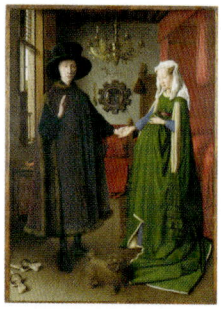

3.6.8a Jan van Eyck, *The Arnolfini Portrait*, 1434, p. 466

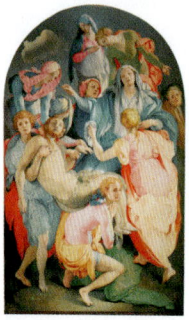

3.6.11 Jacopo da Pontormo, *Deposition*, 1525–28, p. 471

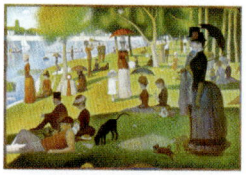

4.4.10 Georges Seurat, *Sunday on La Grande Jatte*, 1884–86, p. 609

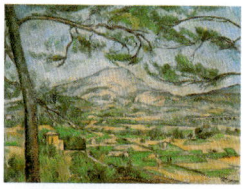

3.8.16 Paul Cézanne, *Mont Sainte-Victoire*, c. 1886–88, p. 514

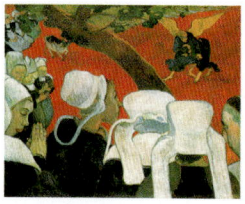

3.8.17 Paul Gauguin, *The Vision after the Sermon*, 1888, p. 515

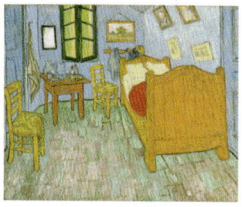

1.1.13 Vincent van Gogh, *The Bedroom*, 1889, p. 51

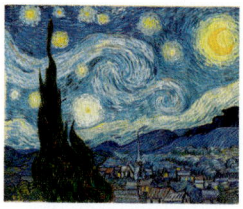

3.8.18 Vincent van Gogh, *Starry Night*, 1889, p. 515

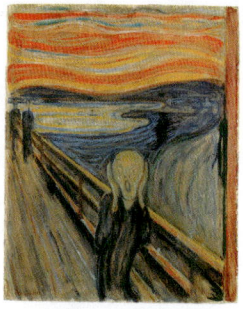

1.10.11 Edvard Munch, *The Scream*, 1893, p. 182

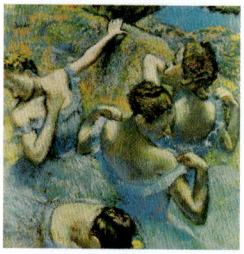

3.8.12 Edgar Degas, *The Blue Dancers*, c. 1898, p. 511

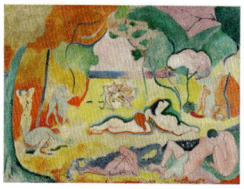

3.9.1 Henri Matisse, *Joy of Life*, 1905–6, p. 525

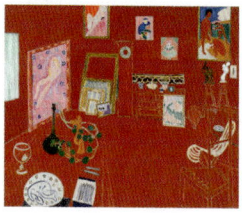

3.9.2 Henri Matisse, *The Red Studio*, 1911, p. 526

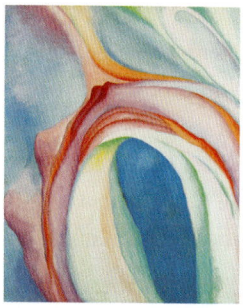

1.1.26 Georgia O'Keeffe, *Music—Pink and Blue II*, 1919, p. 58

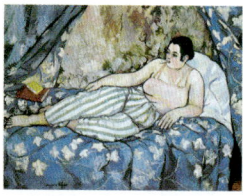

1.9.2 Suzanne Valadon, *The Blue Room*, 1923, p. 160

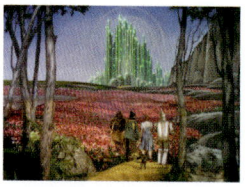

2.9.7 Victor Fleming, *The Wizard of Oz* (scene), 1939, p. 338

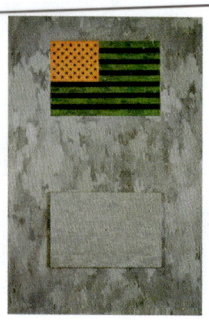

4.4.11 Jasper Johns, *Flag*, 1965, p. 609

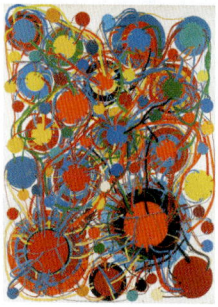

1.6.6 Atsuko Tanaka, *Untitled*, 1968, p. 128

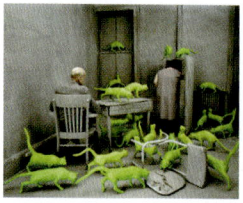

2.8.14 Sandy Skoglund, *Radioactive Cats*, © 1980, p. 323

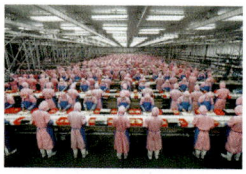

2.8.27 Edward Burtynsky, *Manufacturing #17...*, 2005, p. 332

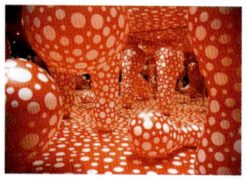

4.4.14 Yayoi Kusama, *Dots Obsession*, 2009, p. 611

1.5 Motion and Time

Motion: the effect of changing placement in time
Medium (plural **media**): the material on or from which an artist chooses to make a work of art, for example canvas and oil paint, marble, engraving, video, or architecture

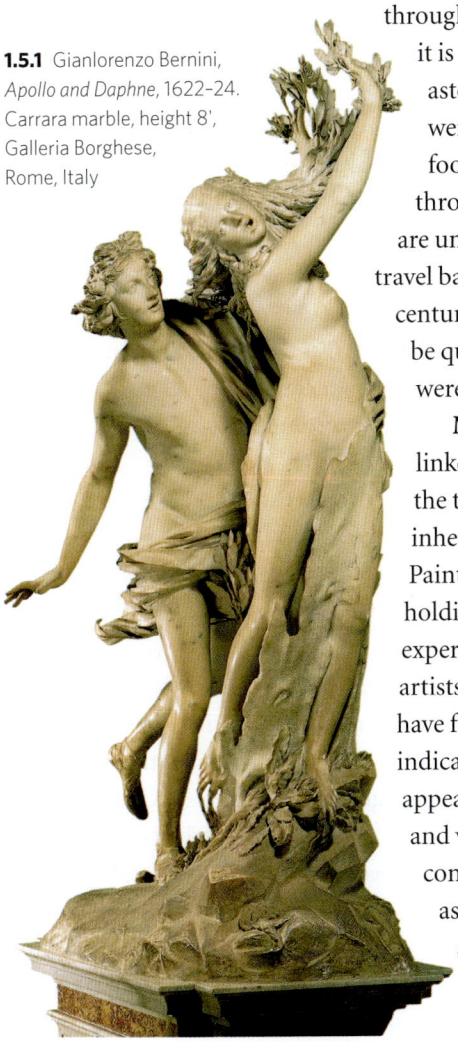

1.5.1 Gianlorenzo Bernini, *Apollo and Daphne*, 1622–24. Carrara marble, height 8', Galleria Borghese, Rome, Italy

Moving images are part of our daily experience of life in the twenty-first century. We see them on our TV and computer screens, on displays in stores, and on the street. In an age where we can see hugely sophisticated and dynamic movies in 3-D, and we know that what we are seeing are brilliant illusions and special effects created through technological wizardry, it is difficult to imagine how astonished, even afraid, audiences were when they first watched footage of objects hurtling through space. But such reactions are understandable. If we could travel back in time little more than a century, our visual experience would be quite different: all art images were still.

Motion and time are closely linked elements of art. Most of the traditional art **media** are inherently motionless and timeless. Paintings, for example, are static, holding a moment so that it can be experienced through the ages. But artists who work in static media have found imaginative ways to indicate the passage of time and the appearance of motion. And film and video have overturned the conventions of traditional art, as new technology and media allow artists to capture motion and time.

Motion

> The aim of every artist is to arrest motion, which is life, by artificial means and hold it fixed so that a hundred years later, when a stranger looks at it, it moves again since it is life.
>
> (William Faulkner, American novelist)

Faulkner tells us that an artist can make even a still image move and come to life. Motion occurs when an object changes location or position. Because this process occurs as time passes, motion is directly linked to time. To communicate motion without actually making anything move, artists can choose to imply time or, alternatively, create the illusion of it.

Implied Motion

When artists imply motion, they give us clues that a static work of art portrays a scene in which motion is occurring or has just occurred. In the case of implied motion, we do not actually see the motion happening, but visual clues tell us that it is a key aspect of the work.

The seventeenth-century Italian sculptor Gianlorenzo Bernini (1598–1680) emphasizes implied motion in many of his marble sculptures. *Apollo and Daphne* illustrates a story from ancient Greek mythology in which the sun god Apollo falls madly in love with the wood nymph Daphne (**1.5.1**). Terrified, she runs from him and begs her father, the river god Peneius, to save her. As Apollo reaches Daphne, Peneius

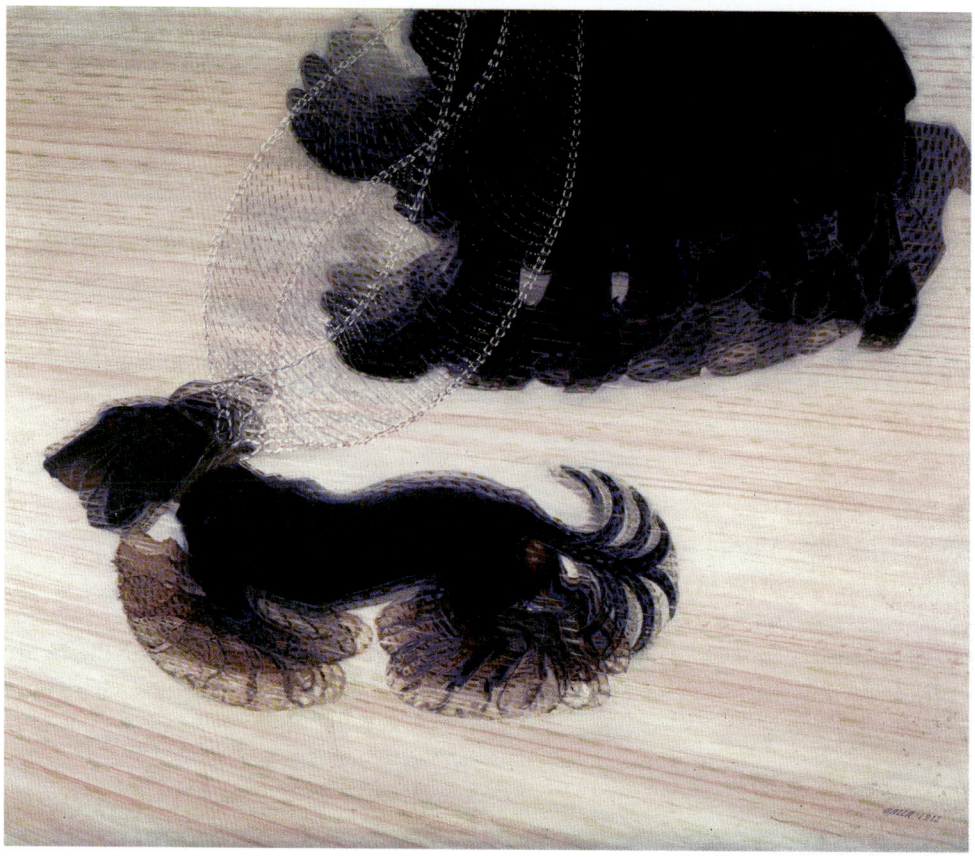

1.5.2 Giacomo Balla, *Dynamism of a Dog on a Leash*, 1912. Oil on canvas, 35⅜ × 43¼". Albright-Knox Art Gallery, Buffalo, New York

Futurism, Futurist: an artistic movement originating in Italy in 1909 that violently rejected traditional forms in favor of celebrating and incorporating into art the energy and dynamism of modern technology; Futurists were artists working in this style

Implied line: a line not actually drawn but suggested by the positions of elements in the work, for example, an aligned series of dots

Composition: the overall design or organization of a work

Installation: originally referring to the hanging of pictures and arrangement of objects in an exhibition, installation may also refer to an intentional environment created as a completed artwork

transforms his daughter into a bay laurel tree. To convey the action, Bernini uses diagonal lines in the flowing drapery, limbs, and hair. Daphne's fingers sprout leaves as bark encases her legs. At the pivotal moment in the story, the scene is suddenly frozen in time. Thereafter, since she could not be Apollo's wife, Daphne became his tree, and Apollo made the laurel wreath his crown.

The Italian **Futurist** Giacomo Balla (1871–1958) uses a different method of implying motion in his painting *Dynamism of a Dog on a Leash* (**1.5.2**). Balla paints a series of repeating marks to give the impression that we are seeing motion as it happens, as if we are viewing several separate moments at once. He paints the dog's tail in eight or nine different positions to communicate movement. Its feet are merely indicated by a series of strokes that give a sense of very rapid motion. The leash, a white **implied line** created by the artist using small dotted brush strokes in close proximity, is also repeated in four different positions. The **composition** gives viewers a sense of ongoing forward motion even though the paint on the canvas is perfectly still.

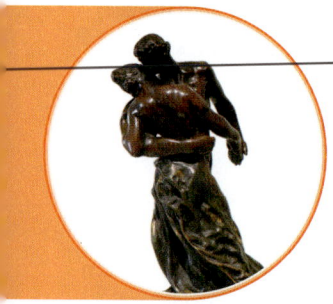

Another great example of implied motion is *The Waltz* by Camille Claudel: see **3.8.19, p. 516**

The Illusion of Motion

In the works by Bernini and Balla, the artists *imply* motion: we do not actually see it occurring, but visual clues tell us that the works, although static, portray motion. Artists can also communicate the idea of motion by creating an illusion of it. Artists create this illusion through visual tricks that deceive our eyes into believing there is motion as time passes, even though no actual motion occurs.

The American artist Jenny Holzer (b. 1950) uses the illusion of motion to enhance her text-based presentations. Her untitled **installation** of 1989 (in the Guggenheim Museum, New York, which was designed by Frank Lloyd Wright) displays messages as text (**1.5.3**). Although the text does not actually move, it appears to spiral up the ramped circular atrium of the museum as the tiny light-emitting diodes (LEDs) are illuminated and then switched off in an automated sequence. Thus the impression is created that the text is moving as time elapses. The intermittent flashing of lights creates a scrolling series of letters and words, like the flashing lights of the casinos on the Las Vegas

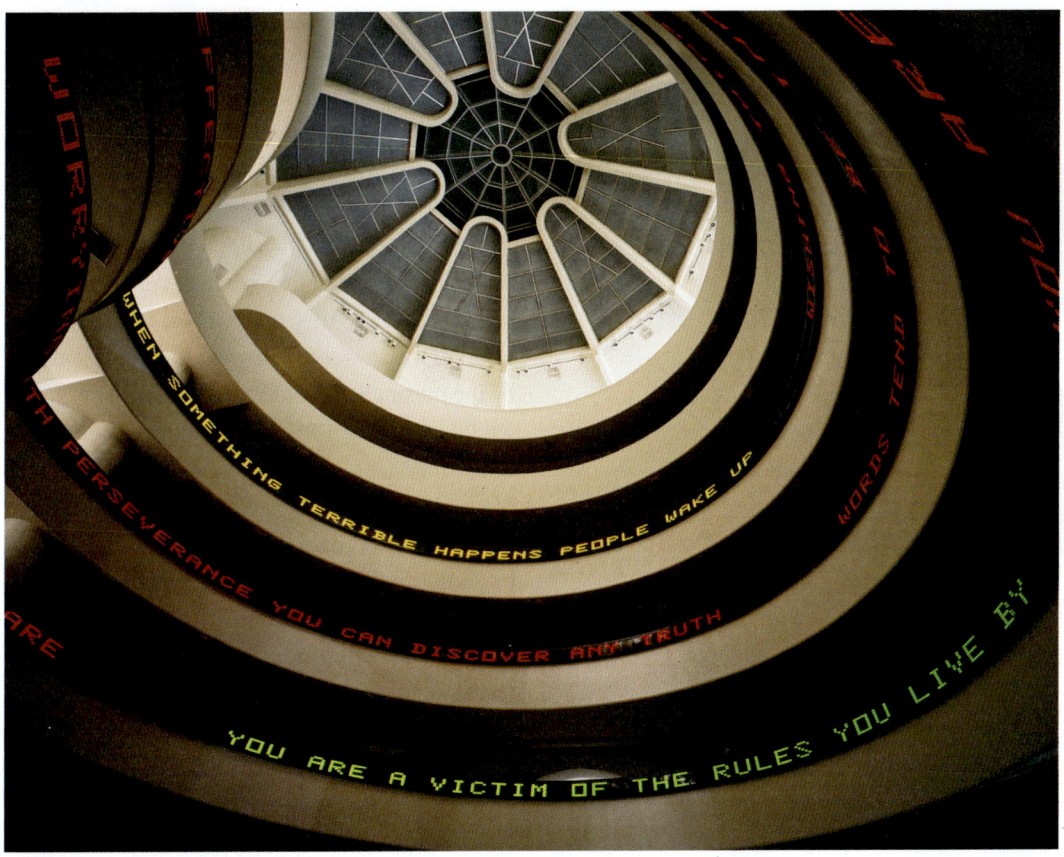

1.5.3 Jenny Holzer, *Untitled* (Selections from *Truisms*, *Inflammatory Essays*, *The Living Series*, *The Survival Series*, *Under a Rock*, *Laments*, and *Child Text*), 1989. Extended helical tricolor LED, electronic display signboard, site-specific dimensions. Solomon R. Guggenheim Museum, New York

Op art: a style of art that exploits the physiology of seeing in order to create illusory optical effects
Positive–negative: the relationship between contrasting opposites

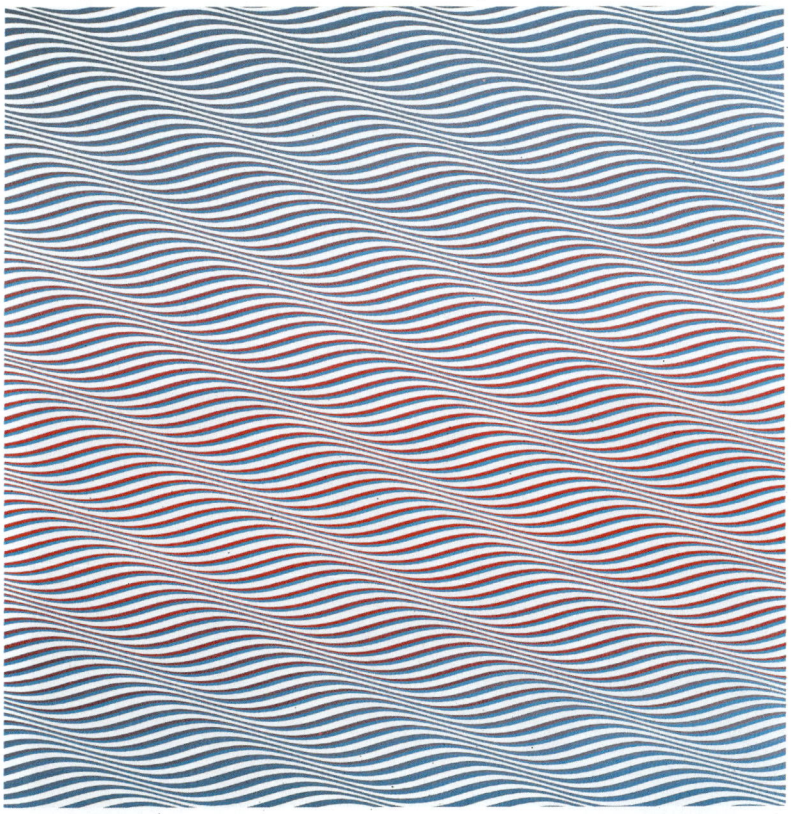

1.5.4 Bridget Riley, *Cataract 3*, 1967. PVA on canvas, 7'3¾" × 7'3¾". British Council Collection

Strip. Holzer uses this illusion to invigorate her messages and critiques of society.

Another illusion of motion that deceives the eye forms the basis for **Op art** (short for Optical art). During the 1960s, Op art painters experimented with discordant **positive–negative** relationships. There is a noticeable sense of movement when we look at *Cataract 3* (**1.5.4**), by the British artist Bridget Riley (b. 1931). If we focus on a single point in the center of the work, it appears there is an overall vibrating motion. This optical illusion grows out of the natural physiological movement of the human eye; we can see it because the artist uses sharp contrast and hard-edged graphics set close enough together that the eye cannot compensate for its own movement. Riley understands that the natural oscillation of the eye combined with the passage of time makes us feel a sense of motion.

Stroboscopic Motion

When we see two or more repeated images in quick succession, they tend visually to fuse together. Many early attempts to show

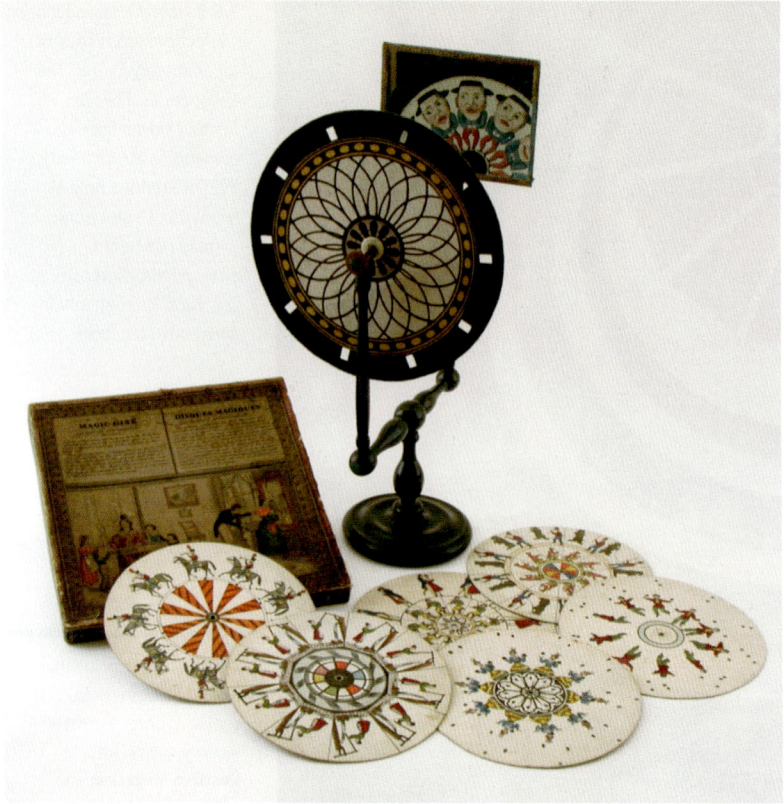

1.5.5 Phenakistoscope, or "Magic Disk," c. 1840. Wood and glass with 8 paper disks. Made in France

moving images were based on this effect, known as stroboscopic motion. One was the phenakistoscope, meaning "spindle viewer," a device invented in 1832 that featured a series of drawings placed on one side of a disc (**1.5.5**). A viewer who looked through another slotted disc while the illustrated disc was spinning (or looked through the back in front of a mirror) could see the images appear to move and repeat, even though the drawings that made up the series were, of course, static. Such inventions as the phenakistoscope were early forms of animation.

The image of motion created when viewing a phenakistoscope is attributed to the theory of persistence of vision, which explains how visual sensations persist even after they are no longer in sight. For example, when a lightstick or sparkler is waved about, there is a visible trail of light that remains. Artists today still use this theory to make amazing impressions of motion. The American sculptor Gregory Barsamian (b. 1953) creates spinning sculptures that are intended to be viewed in an environment with strobe (intermittently flashing) lighting. The resulting effect is much like that of the phenakistoscope, as the visual interruptions created by the flashing lights make a series of sculptural forms appear to move. Barsamian's work *Drum 52* (**1.5.6**) is a **kinetic**, or moving, sculpture and also an installation that depends on the surrounding lighting to complete the viewer's experience. When the work is spinning, the viewer sees an illusion that consists of green liquid spheres rising out of a vat until caught by a series of hands that turn upward and then disappear as the cycle starts again. If the viewer's vision was not interrupted by the pulsing effect of the strobe, the image would disappear into a blur of motion and the individual steps would be lost. Hence, persistence of vision is here aided by the flickering light.

Cartoon animation grew out of early stroboscopic experiments, and today's computer animation follows the same principle. Disney's *Finding Nemo* is compiled from individual frames that were computer-generated using **3-D modeling** software (**1.5.7**). The animator can make changes to the images and then produce all the individual frames in a sequence that the computer plays in rapid succession. This succession of images is combined with other scenes and eventually committed to film—or, increasingly, digital media—for distribution to movie theaters.

"Movie" is an abbreviation of "moving picture," and during the twentieth century movies became the dominant mode of artistic expression in motion. Film relies on individual frames played in quick succession. Similar advanced forms of stroboscopic motion have been developed to stream digital video for the

1.5.6 Gregory Barsamian, *Drum 52*, 2013. Kinetic sculpture/installation: steel, ureathane foam, sculpy, strobe light, motor. Artist's collection

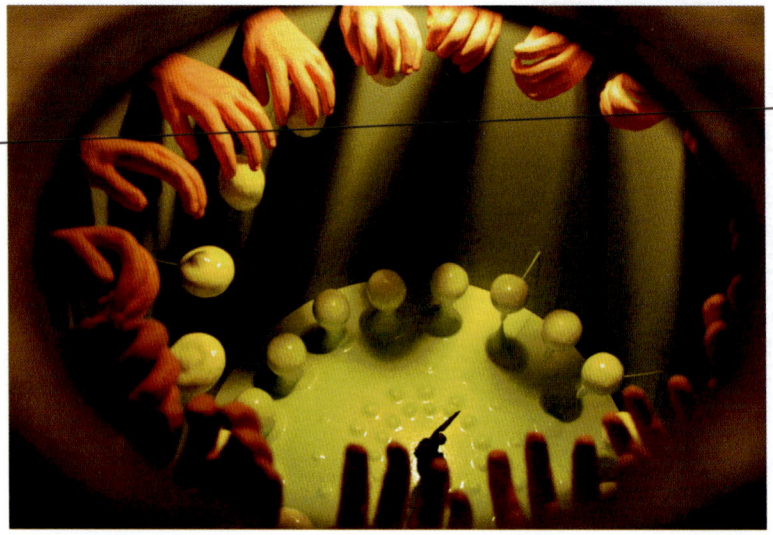

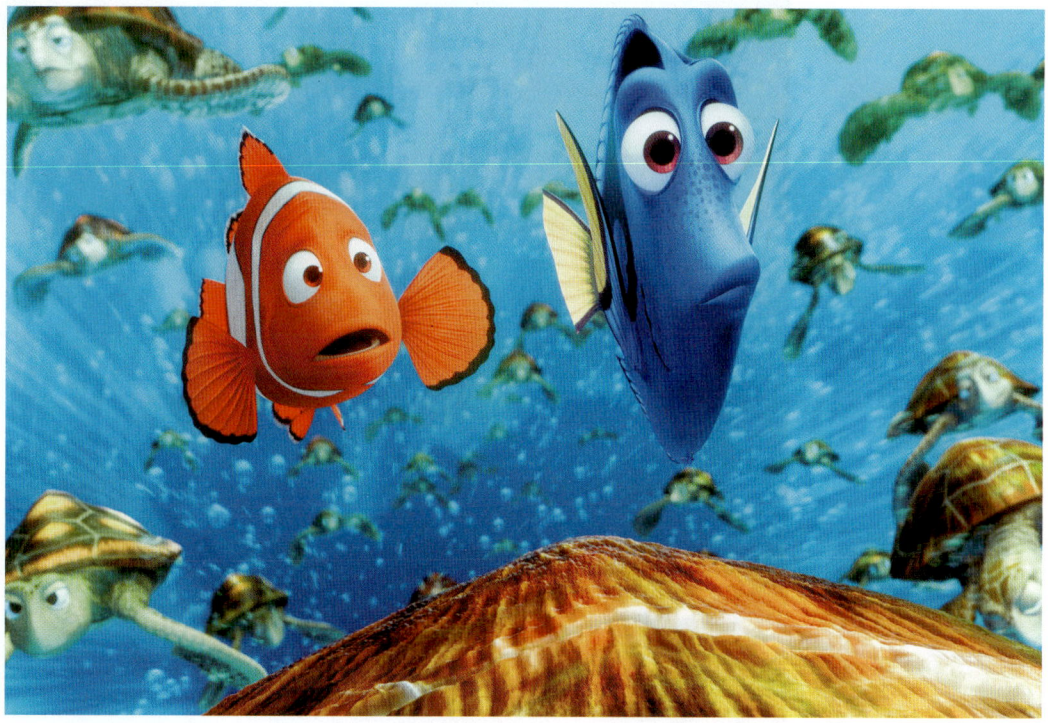

1.5.7 Frame from *Finding Nemo*, 2003. Duration 100 minutes. Director Andrew Stanton, Walt Disney Pictures

Kinetic art/sculpture: three-dimensional art that moves, impelled by air currents, motors, or people
3-D modeling: a computer-generated illusion that emulates an object in three dimensions; it can be modified to show visual movement

Web. Files with a series of multiple images (and sound files) are electronically transferred to a computer where they are played in rapid succession, much like a film movie. Internet users experience this when they view Flash animations posted on YouTube.

Such films as Tom Tykwer's (b. 1965) *Run Lola Run* (**1.5.8**) experiment with the notion of story and time. Set in Berlin, the story revolves around a young woman, Lola, who receives a panicked call from her boyfriend, Manni. If she does not get him 100,000 Deutschmarks (approximately $70,000) within 20 minutes, he will be forced to rob a grocery store in order to escape being killed by the mobster who is threatening him. Lola, desperate to save his life, does everything in her power to obtain the money, but only gets shot herself.

We discover, however, that the scope of the storyline extends beyond the everyday passage of time. Lola refuses to die, and so the story reboots and begins again, this time with a new set of circumstances, some of which Lola is now prepared for from the first version of events. In all, she does three runs: in each, the time allowed for the run is the same, but the action takes a different course.

The film's reinterpretation of time engages the viewer and helps to explore the characters in greater depth with each reset. The director thus uses stroboscopic motion as a tool to question the nature of time, and to demonstrate the impact that a few seconds' difference can make.

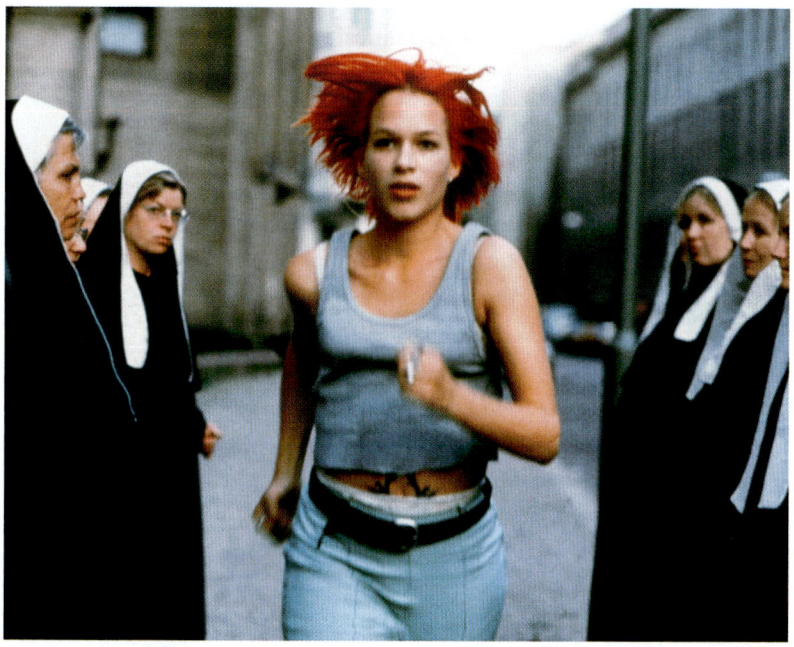

1.5.8 Scene from *Run Lola Run*, 1998. Duration 81 minutes. Director Tom Tykwer, X-Filme Creative Pool/WDR/Arte

1.5.9 Cirque du Soleil performing *Totem* in Montreal, Quebec, July, 2010

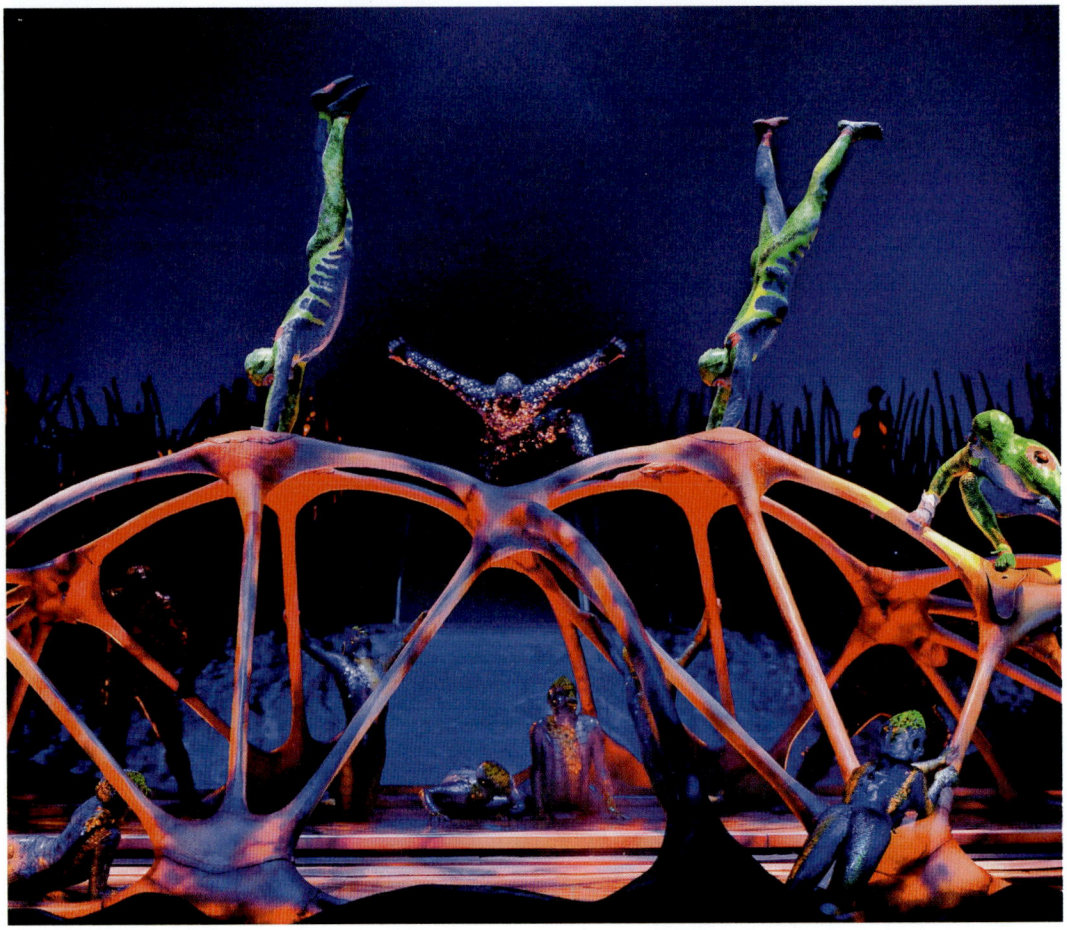

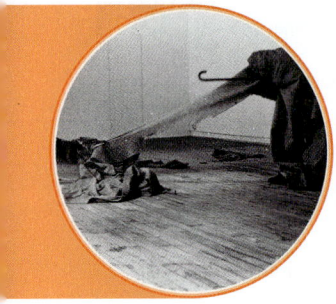

Joseph Beuys was a pioneer in the creation of performance art: see **2.10.5, p. 354**

Actual Motion

We perceive actual motion when something really changes over time. We see it in **performance art** and in kinetic art, when objects physically move and change in real **space** and time. Performance art is theatrical; the artist's intention is to create not an art object, but an experience that can exist only in one place and time in history. Kinetic art plays out the passage of time through an art object, usually a sculpture, that moves.

Performance art emerged as a specific form of visual art during the twentieth century when such artists as the German Joseph Beuys (1921–1986) began performing his works, which he called actions. Following his traumatic experiences in the German Air Force in World War II, Beuys incorporated a range of elements—fat, machinery, sticks, even live animals—into his actions, a series of self-performed situations in which the artist would interact with these things in a defined space and time. By putting common items in new situations, Beuys conjured up different ways of thinking about our world so that we might question past practices. For example, Beuys once played a piano filled with animal fat that changed the sound and mechanics.

Performance artists need not focus on a social or political issue. For example, since 1984 the touring entertainment act Cirque du Soleil (French for "Circus of the Sun") has performed in ways that integrate music and acrobatics, enacted before a live audience (**1.5.9**). In order to keep the show continuous and seamless, transitions between different acts are choreographed into the show and set changes are done by the performers.

In performance art, the motion we see is made by a person, or people, whereas kinetic sculpture can appear to move of its own accord, unaided by human action. The earliest kinetic artwork is credited to French artist Marcel Duchamp (1887–1968), who mounted a bicycle wheel on a barstool so that the wheel could be spun. Later, the American sculptor

Performance art: a work involving the human body, usually including the artist, in front of an audience
Space: the distance between identifiable points or planes
Mobile: suspended moving sculptures, usually impelled by natural air currents
Form: an object that can be defined in three dimensions (height, width, and depth)

Alexander Calder (1898–1976) invented the **mobile**, taking the name from a suggestion by Duchamp. The mobile relies on air currents to power its movement, and Calder's kinetic sculptures were so finely balanced that even the smallest breeze would set them in motion. His final sculpture is the huge aluminum-and-steel mobile suspended in the National Gallery of Art in Washington, D.C. (**1.5.10**). It resembles its predecessors in being made up of counterbalanced organic shapes that move independently of each other. This is made possible by balancing the parts on points of equilibrium so that they can easily move. The result is a constantly changing visual **form**.

Sculptures by the Dutch artist Theodorus Gerardus Jozef "Theo" Jansen (b. 1948) have been carefully designed to appear to move by themselves, as if they were living beings. Jansen builds moving sculptures that he calls "Strandbeests," or beach animals (**1.5.11**). These sculptures, made primarily out of plastic pipe, are engineered so that they appear to "walk" as the wind catches their outstretched sails. Jansen incorporates bicycle pumps that compress air into plastic bottles using the wind power supplied by sails on the Strandbeests. The compressed air then pushes back, supplying a countermovement that allows the system to reset. The result gives the object the remarkable appearance of continuous movement that looks like an animal walking. Both Calder and Jansen use kinetic sculpture to enliven the environments in which these works are displayed. Calder's work energizes the Atrium of the National Gallery and Jansen's "beasts" are free to roam the beaches.

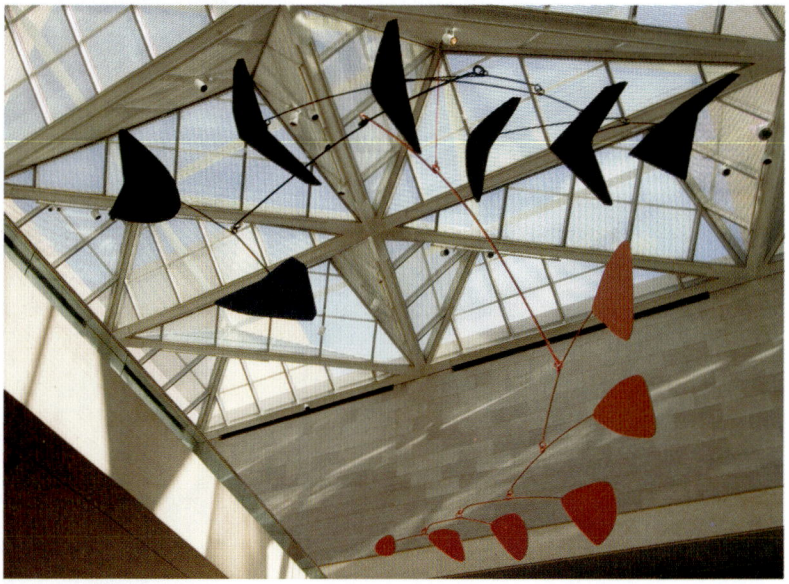

1.5.10 Alexander Calder, *Untitled*, 1976. Aluminum and steel, 29'10⅜" × 75'11¾". National Gallery of Art, Washington, D.C.

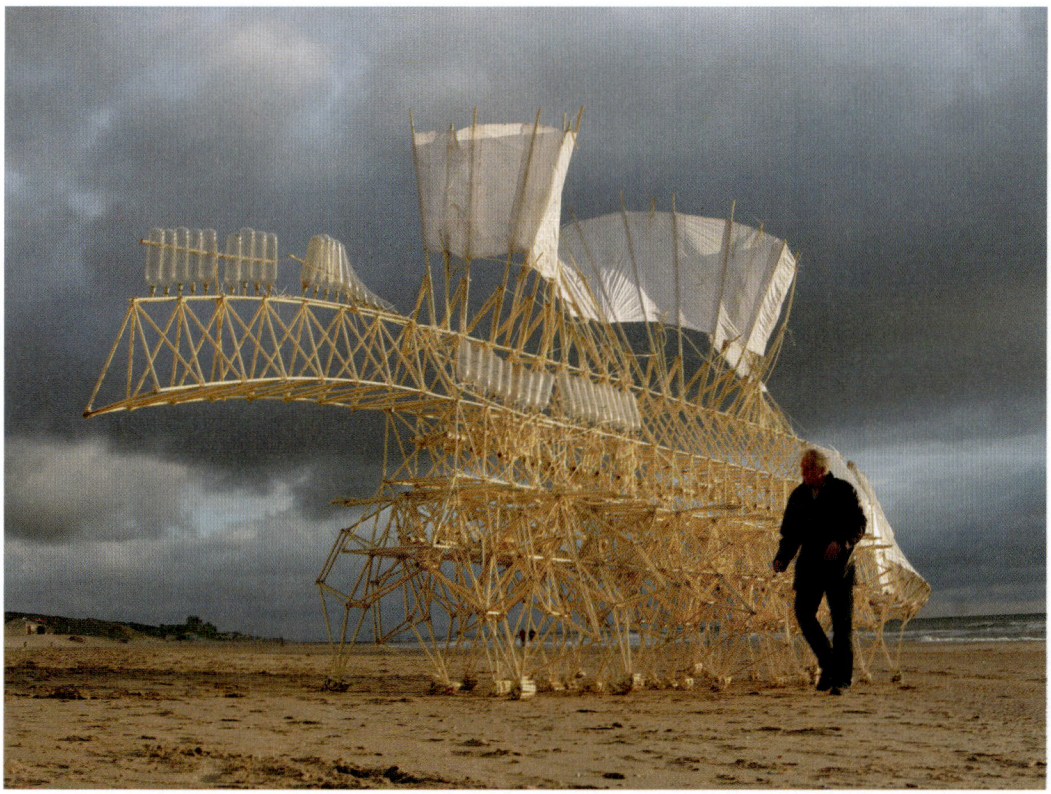

1.5.11 Theodorus Gerardus Jozef "Theo" Jansen, *Animaris Umeris (Strandbeest #48)*, 2009. Recycled plastic bottles, plastic tubing, PVC pipe, wood, and fabric. Scheveningen Beach, The Netherlands

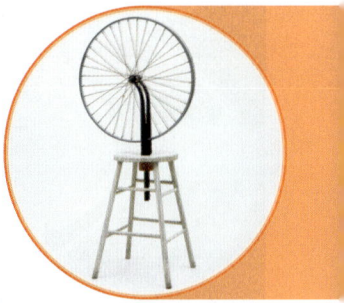

Marcel Duchamp was one of the first artists to create kinetic sculptures: see **3.9.8, p. 529**

Time

Since events necessarily take place over time, any artwork that deals with events must show how time goes by. Writers use chapters and other tools to give us a sense of how stories unfold. Artists also find ways to communicate the passage of time and to remind us of its influence on our lives. Motion can exist only because connected images, actions, and the ideas that they conjure in the mind of the viewer cannot be conceived of without time as a measure.

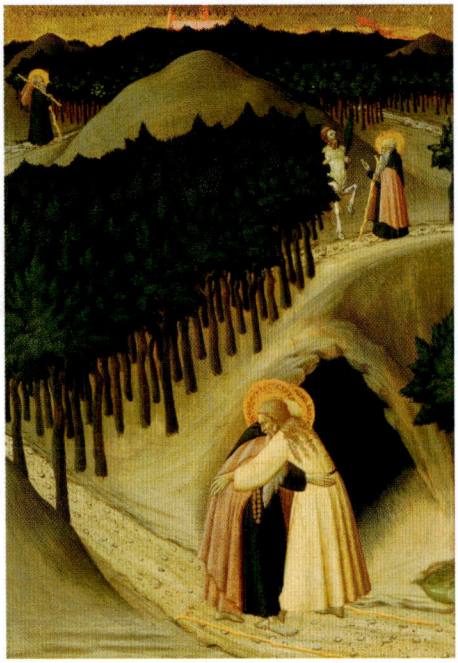

1.5.12 Workshop of the Master of Osservanza (Sano di Pietro?), *The Meeting of St. Anthony and St. Paul*, c. 1430–35. Tempera on panel, 18½ × 13¼". National Gallery of Art, Washington, D.C.

The Passage of Time

In **1.5.12**, *The Meeting of St. Anthony and St. Paul*, painters in the workshop of the fifteenth-century artist known as the Master of Osservanza solved the problem of how to tell a story in a single painting by merging a series of episodes into one picture. The story begins in the upper left-hand corner, where St. Anthony sets out across the desert to seek the hermit St. Paul. In the upper right, St. Anthony encounters a mythical creature called a centaur: half-man, half-horse, it was associated with the Greek god of wine, Bacchus. This symbol of earthly temptation does not deter St. Anthony. He continues on his lone journey through thick forest until he finally meets and embraces St. Paul: their meeting is the culminating incident in the foreground. The entire painting signifies a pilgrimage on the long and winding road of time, rather than merely a single moment. This linear method is still used by artists, comic-book writers, and designers as a story-telling device and a way of expressing the passing of time.

The American artist Nancy Holt (1938–2014) examines cycles of time in her works. Many of Holt's sculptures intertwine the passage of time with the motion of the sun. Her *Solar Rotary*, at the University of South Florida, Tampa, is designed to express meaning from shadows cast by the sun throughout the year (**1.5.13**). The work features an aluminum

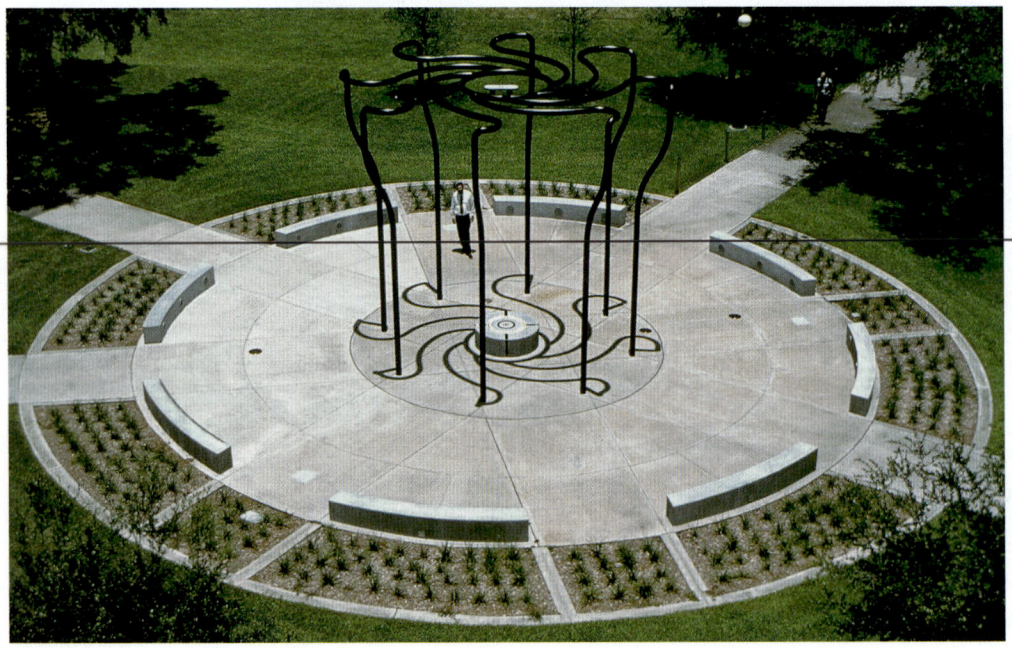

1.5.13 Nancy Holt, *Solar Rotary*, 1995. Aluminum, concrete, and meteorite, approx. height 20', approx. diameter 24'. University of South Florida

Gateway to Art: Ai Weiwei, *Dropping a Han Dynasty Urn*
Motion and Reproduction as a Metaphor for Time

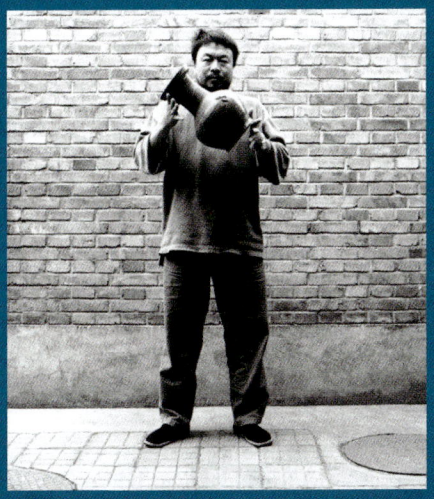
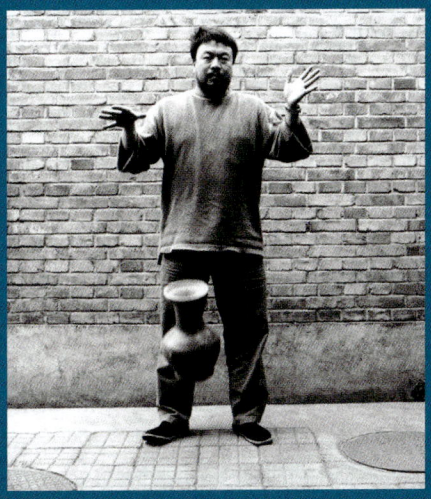
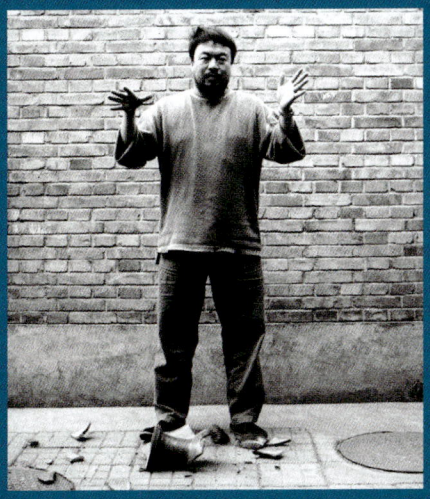

1.5.14 Ai Weiwei, *Dropping a Han Dynasty Urn*, 1995. Three black-and-white photographs, each 53½ × 42⅞"

> The act of changing the understanding and perspective of an object, or reworking an established concept, disrupts its stability and makes it questionable.
>
> Ai Weiwei

In 1995 Chinese artist Ai Weiwei (b. 1957) created a time-based work that sparked great controversy: he was photographed dropping a 2,000-year-old Chinese urn (**1.5.14**). The act of destruction, and its photographic record, raised a furor not only because he had smashed an ancient artifact, but also for his seeming lack of concern. Yet, through the use of the elements of time and motion, the artist was actually acknowledging both the antiquity and importance of the object.

The three large-scale photographic panels are documentation of the passage of time as the artist committed the irreversible act of destruction. The left panel shows the artist holding the vase somewhat carelessly. The second shows the vase falling to the ground and the artist's hands boldly (or shamelessly) in the air. The third photo captures the vase smashing on the ground without any reaction on his part.

The images link the old and the new in Chinese art and culture. Chinese ceramics are symbols of centuries-long innovation and ingenuity. Ai himself emphasizes a Chinese "look," with his traditional slippers and a beard that recalls the appearance of an ancient emperor. As an artist, he also symbolizes modern Chinese ingenuity with this action, which both challenges and draws attention to the prominence of Chinese tradition.

Important artifacts, such as the one that Ai is here seen, shockingly, smashing on the ground, and the ones he painted over, were—and still are—frequently damaged by government-run demolition and construction projects. Ai's seemingly emotionless expression, as he withdraws any responsibility for preserving this urn and lets it fall to the ground, references the Chinese government's similar lack of care and preservation of ancient objects. Through the elements of time and motion, *Dropping A Han Dynasty Urn* sparked a renewed interest in ancient objects that were being taken for granted by the Chinese government and society as a whole.

For the other Ai Weiwei Gateway boxes, see p. 357, p. 419, and p. 654

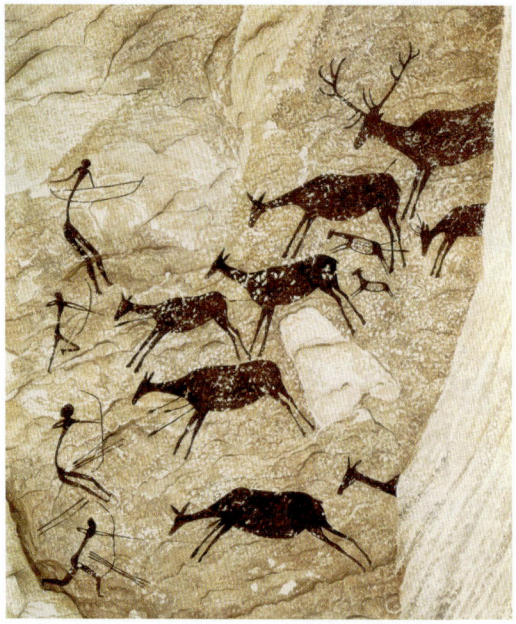

1.5.15 Hunting scene, painting from Cova dels Cavalls (Horses' Cave), Mesolithic period. Valltorta, Valencia, Spain

sculptural "shadow caster" perched on eight poles high above the center of a circular concrete plaza. The shadow caster—a ring with eight serpentine arms—is oriented so that shadows cast by its central ring encircle notable dates set into the surrounding concrete. The different angles of the sun at different times of the year make shadows at different locations in the sculpture. For example, on March 27 a circle shadow surrounds a marker that recounts the day in 1513 when the Spanish explorer Juan Ponce de León first sighted Florida. In the center, a concrete circular bench, into which a meteorite has been set, is encircled by the shadow at noon on the summer solstice, the longest day of the year (in the northern hemisphere), when the sun reaches its northernmost point. The meteorite symbolizes the connection between our world and the larger universe.

Depicting time in art is not a concept that exists only in the modern world. The most ancient pieces of art that we know, cave paintings, show the passage of time. Cave paintings at Valltorta Gorge, Spain, show, variously, bow hunters as the bow is aimed; the arrows in flight; and arrows piercing deer (**1.5.15**).

The Attributes of Time

Time is the fourth measurable dimension of a work of art after width, height, and depth. Time-based arts, such as film, embody six basic attributes of time: duration, tempo, intensity, scope, setting, and chronology. All these attributes exist in one of the first American movies, *Fred Ott's Sneeze*, made by Thomas Edison and W. K. Dickson in 1894 (**1.5.16**). Since we measure time in seconds, minutes, hours, and days, the duration, or length, of this film is 5 seconds. Duration provides a standard measurement that can be shared by others to insure uniformity in the editing process. The tempo, or speed, is 16 frames per second. Contemporary filmmakers set tempo at 24 frames per second (or faster) for a smoother effect. The intensity, or level of energy, is high because the activity is sudden and strong. Since a viewer has to perceive and then process the perception of movement, moments with less change in the image are regarded as having less intensity. This film has a limited scope, or range of action, because it is confined to a simple activity. If the film were presented from multiple viewing angles it would have a broader scope. The setting, or context, is Thomas Edison's studio. The chronology, or order of events, can be seen in the still frames as Fred Ott appears to be placing some snuff in his nose, recoiling, then jerking forward as he sneezes. Art that uses motion is sometimes called **temporal art** because it exists only within the passage of time.

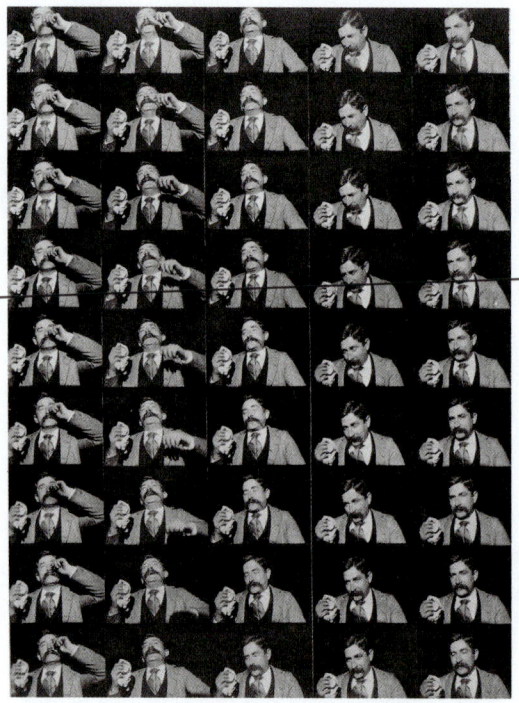

1.5.16 Thomas Edison and W. K. Dickson, *Fred Ott's Sneeze*, 1894. Still frames from kinetoscope film. Library of Congress, Washington, D.C.

Temporal art: an artist's image or action that is transitory, existing in a passage of time
Bioart: art that is created with living, changing organisms

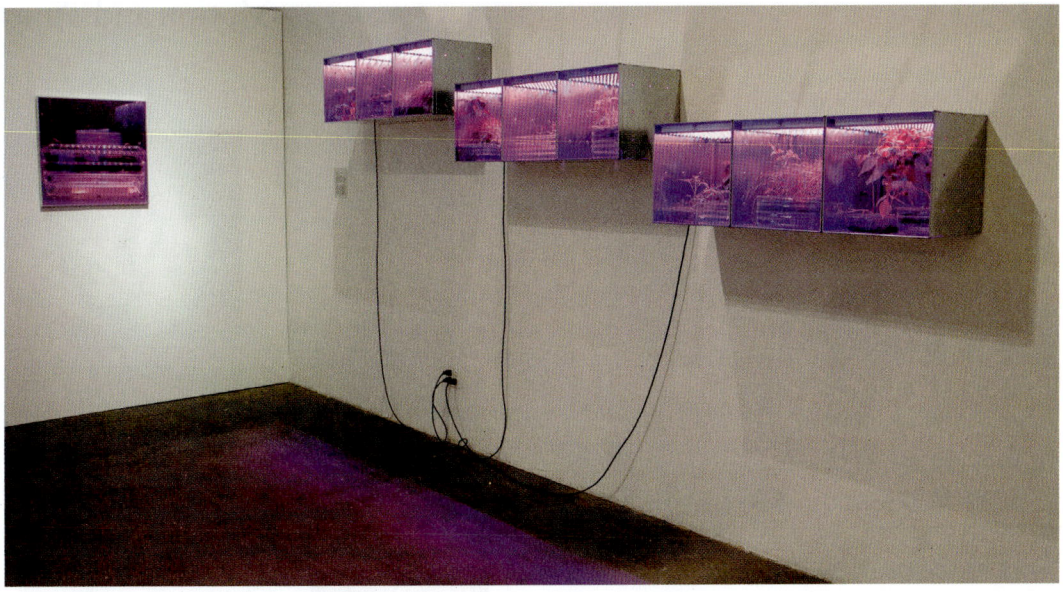

1.5.17 Suzanne Anker, *Astroculture (Shelf Life)*, 2009. Aluminum, plastic, red and blue LED lights, plants, water, soil, and no pesticides. Dimensions variable. Vegetable-producing plants grown from seed using LED lights. Installation view at Corpus Extremus (LIFE+), Exit Art, New York

Natural Processes and the Passage of Time

Some artistic media—such as aluminum or stone—will last for centuries, or even millennia, whereas others change states or begin to degrade almost immediately, for example artworks that are made from organic or biological materials. **Bioart** is art that reflects the passage of time through the natural processes of growth and decay that organic materials undergo. Thus, work by bioartists is always changing. In her work *Astroculture (Shelf Life)* (**1.5.17**), the American bioartist Suzanne Anker (b. 1946) has created a piece of bioart that experiments with how plants might react in such artificial conditions as those necessary to sustain life in outer space. In this case, the artist has used red and blue LED lights to provide the equivalent of the nourishing rays of sunlight, reducing the amount of light and energy required. Even though the leaves would appear green if under normal light, in this environment they appear to be a strong magenta color. The artificial conditions eliminate the need for insecticide and result in lower carbon emissions, and are therefore a better option for such rarefied environments as outer space. Anker's work blurs the lines between science and art, contributing to our understanding of the universe while delivering interesting and colorful visual forms.

Natural processes also dominate the work of American sculptor Ron Lambert (b. 1975), for whom the water cycle illustrates the passage of time. For *Sublimate (Cloud Cover)* he created a large transparent plastic environment in which water endlessly evaporates and condenses (**1.5.18**). Lambert draws attention to our immediate environment as he shows how the rhythms of nature become a measure of natural time that we gauge by how long we have to wait for the next rain.

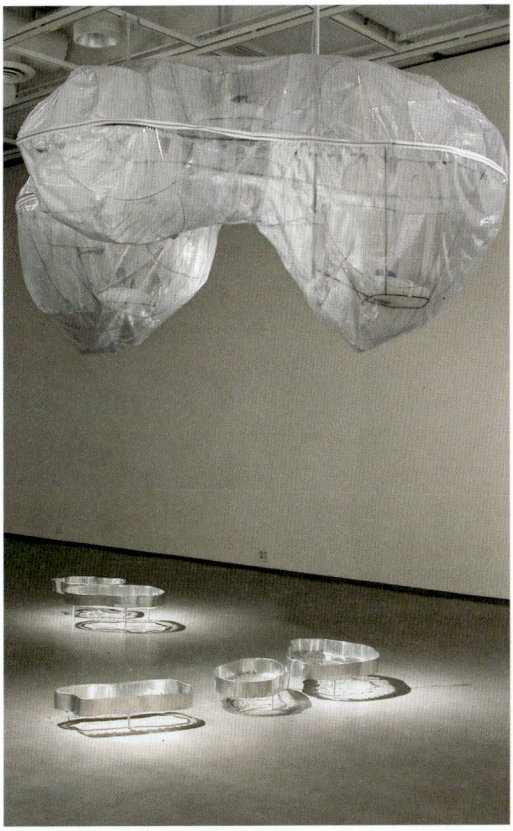

1.5.18 Ron Lambert, *Sublimate (Cloud Cover)*, 2004. Water, vinyl, humidifiers, steel, aluminum, and acrylic, dimensions variable

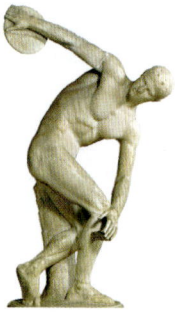

4.9.4 Myron, *Discus Thrower (Discobolos)*, c. 450 BCE, p. 666

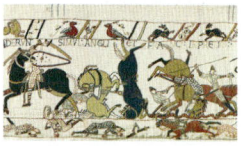

4.7.5 Detail of the Battle of Hastings, *Bayeux Tapestry*, c. 1066–82, p. 642

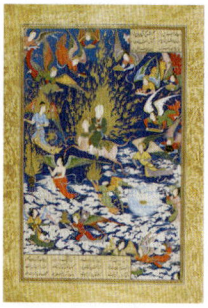

3.2.14 *The Ascent of the Prophet Muhammad*, from Nizami's *Khamsa*, 1539–43, p. 400

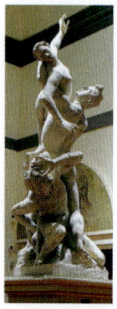

2.4.2a Giambologna, *Rape of a Sabine* (model), 1582, p. 243

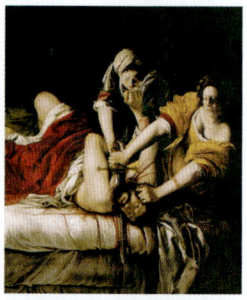

1.8.3 Artemisia Gentileschi, *Judith Decapitating Holofernes*, c. 1620, p. 152

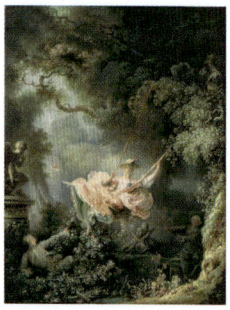

3.7.1 Jean-Honoré Fragonard, *The Swing*, 1766, p. 487

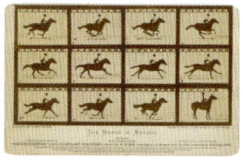

2.9.3 Eadweard Muybridge, *The Horse in Motion*, 1878, p. 336

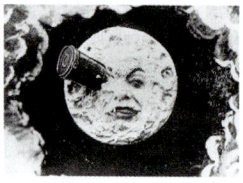

2.9.4 Georges Méliès, *A Trip to the Moon* (scene), 1902, p. 336

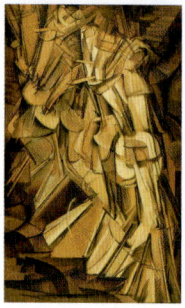

3.9.16 Marcel Duchamp, *Nude Descending a Staircase, No. 2*, 1912, p. 533

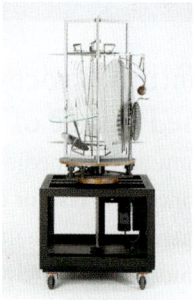

2.4.22 László Moholy-Nagy, *Light Prop for an Electric Stage*, 1929–30, p. 255

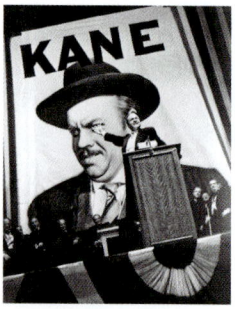

2.9.6 Orson Welles, *Citizen Kane* (scene), 1941, p. 337

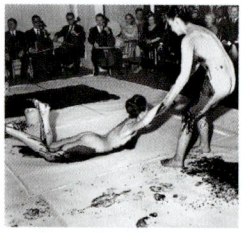

4.9.11a Yves Klein, *Anthropométries de l'époque bleue*, 1960, p. 670

1.1.12 Carolyn Davidson, Nike Company logo, 1971, p. 51

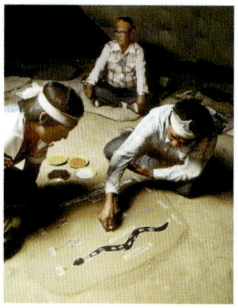

4.2.5 Navajo medicine man in healing ceremony, photo 20th century, p. 581

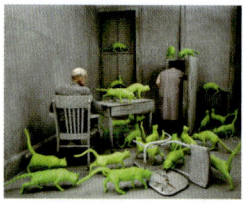

2.8.14 Sandy Skoglund, *Radioactive Cats*, © 1980, p. 323

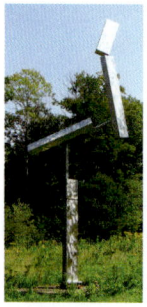

2.4.21 George Rickey, *Breaking Column*, 1986 (completed 2009), p. 255

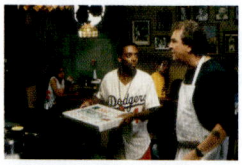

4.10.11 Spike Lee, *Do the Right Thing*, 1989, p. 687

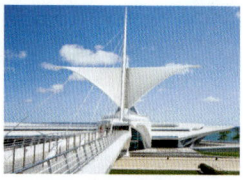

2.5.36 Santiago Calatrava, Quadracci Pavilion, Milwaukee Art Museum, 2001, p. 281

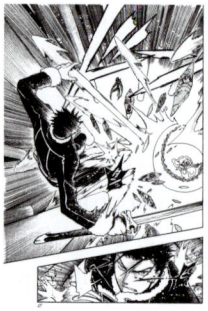

1.1.9 CLAMP, page from the *Tsubasa RESERVoir CHRoNiCLE*, 2007, p. 49

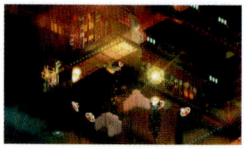

1.3.16 Supergiant Games, screenshot from *Transistor*, 2014, p. 85

1.6 Unity, Variety, and Balance

Unity: the appearance of oneness or harmony in a work of art: all of the elements appearing to be part of a cohesive whole
Elements of art: the basic vocabulary of art—line, shape, form, volume, mass, texture, value (lightness/darkness), space, color, and motion and time
Principles: the principles, or "grammar" of art—contrast, unity, variety, balance, scale, proportion, focal point, emphasis, pattern, and rhythm—describe the ways the elements of art are arranged in an artwork
Composition: the overall design or organization of a work
Variety: the diversity of different ideas, media, and elements in a work
Medium (plural **media**): the material on or from which an artist chooses to make a work of art, for example canvas and oil paint, marble, engraving, video, or architecture
Grid: a network of horizontal and vertical lines; in an artwork's composition, the lines are implied
Gestalt: complete order and indivisible unity of all aspects of an artwork's design

Unity, variety, and balance are central principles that artists use to create visual impact. **Unity**—creating order or wholeness, the opposite of disorder—is central in the creation of a work of art or design. Unity refers to the imposition of order and harmony on a design. It is the sense of visual harmony that separates the work of art from the relative chaos of the surrounding world. Unity refers to the "oneness" or organization of similarities between **elements** that make up a work of art. Artists use the **principle** of unity to make choices that link visual elements to each other in a **composition**.

By comparison, **variety** is a kind of visual diversity that brings many different ideas, **media**, and elements together in one composition. It is expressed in contrast and difference, which create visual interest and excitement. Sometimes artists will use the discordance of variety to create uneasy relationships between visual elements. Sometimes, too, this lack of similarity between elements can actively create a sense of unity when an artist imposes on the work a **grid** or other visual structure.

Balance refers to the distribution of elements, whether unified or varied, within a work. The number and distribution of different elements influence the composition. Balance in visual art is much like the balance we experience in real life. If we carry a large heavy bucket in one hand it pulls us to one side and we orient our body to offset its weight. In art, the visual elements in one half of a work are offset by the elements on the opposite side. By making sure that the elements are distributed in an organized way, artists create balance.

It is possible for an artist to depict an unbalanced design. Such a design is usually created to carry a message or create an unsettled feeling in the viewer. To create an unbalanced composition the artist or designer will intentionally violate the guidelines for good design for a specified effect.

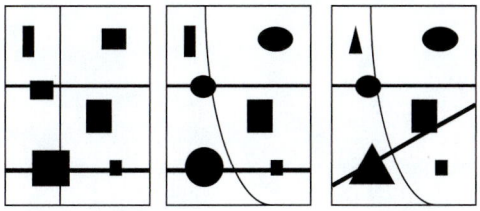

1.6.1 Three diagrams of compositional unity

Unity

Unity provides an artwork with its cohesiveness and helps to communicate the visual idea it embodies. Artists face a communication challenge: to find a structure within the chaos of nature and to select and organize materials into a harmonious composition. An artist will identify specific elements in a scene and use them to create unity. Artists are concerned with three kinds of unity: compositional, conceptual, and **gestalt**.

Compositional Unity

An artist creates compositional unity by organizing all the visual aspects of a work. This kind of harmony is not easy to achieve. The three similar diagrams in **1.6.1** illustrate

Gateway to Art: Hokusai, "The Great Wave off Shore at Kanagawa"
A Masterpiece of Unity and Harmony

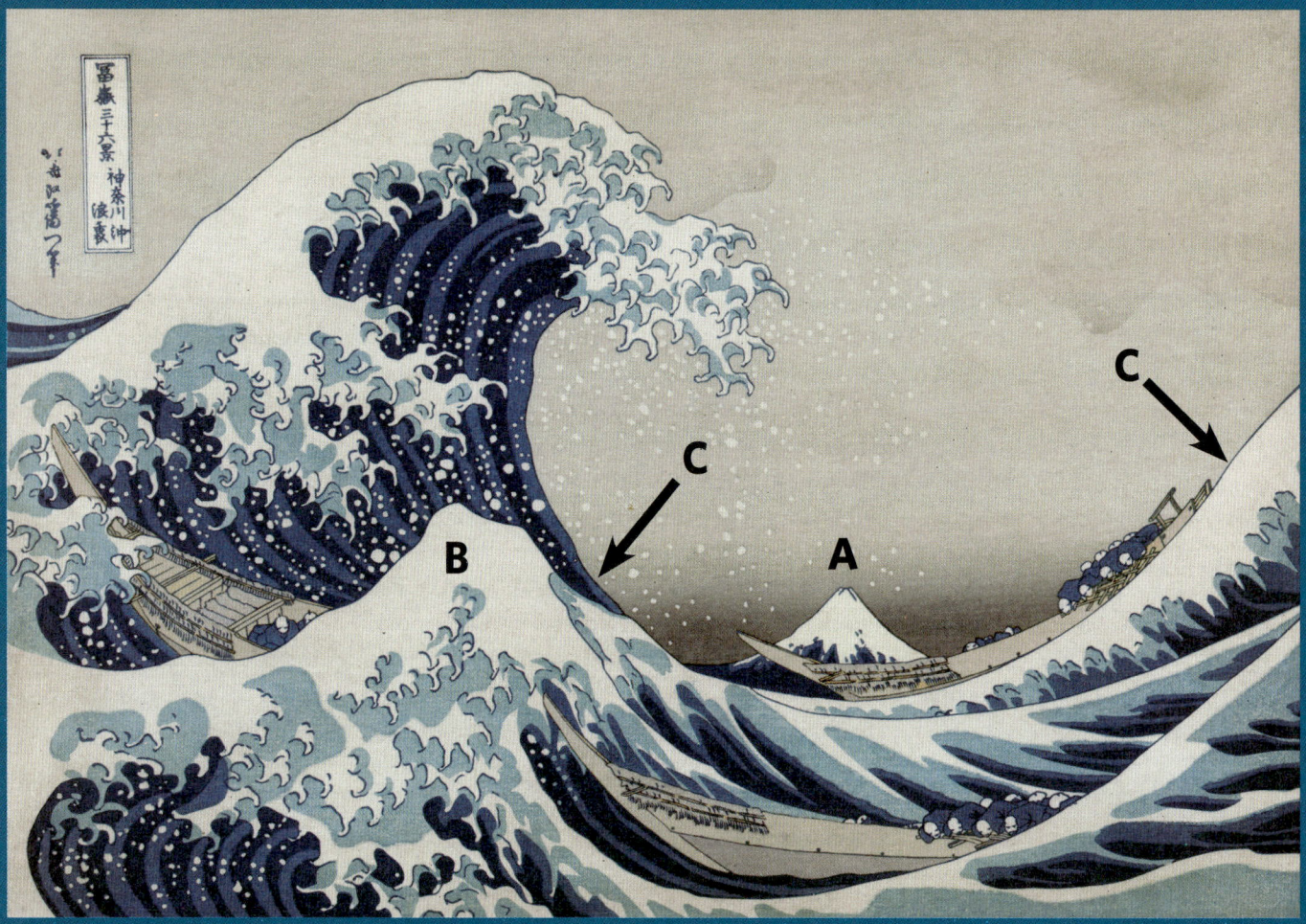

1.6.2 Katsushika Hokusai, "The Great Wave off Shore at Kanagawa," from *Thirty-Six Views of Mount Fuji*, 1826–33 (printed later). Print, color woodcut. Library of Congress, Washington, D.C.

In his print "The Great Wave off Shore at Kanagawa," Japanese artist Katsushika Hokusai (1760–1849) created a unified composition by organizing repetitions of shapes, colors, textures, and patterns to create a visual harmony even though the scene is chaotic (**1.6.2**). These repetitions visually link different parts of the picture. Even Mount Fuji (A), in the middle of the bottom third of the work, almost blends into the ocean: because whitecaps on the waves (B) mimic the snow atop Mount Fuji, the mountain's presence is felt and reiterated throughout the composition. The shape and placement of the boats also create a pattern amongst the waves. Because the great wave on the left is not repeated, it has a singular strength that dominates the scene. Hokusai has also carefully selected the solids and voids in his composition to create opposing but balancing areas of interest. As the solid shape of the great wave curves around the deep trough below it (C), the two areas compete for attention, neither one possible without the other.

The words unity and harmony suggest peaceful, positive coexistence in a chaotic world. A skillful artist can depict unity and harmony even in a work portraying a scene that in reality would be chaotic and threatening. Here, Hokusai has organized a group of visual elements into a structure that makes sense because it has been simplified and ordered.

For the other Hokusai Gateway boxes, see p. 229, p. 425, and p. 661

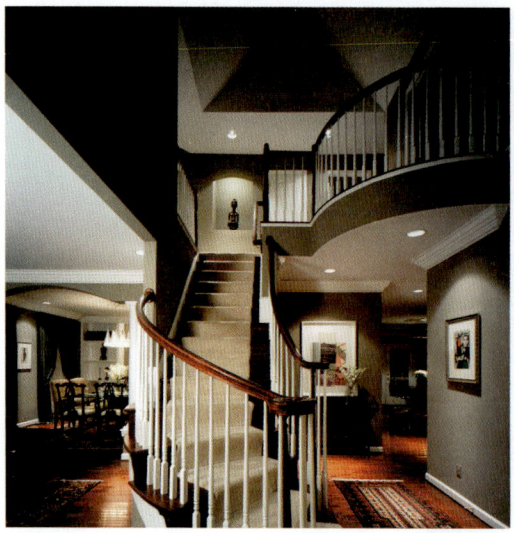

1.6.3a Interior design, I. Michael Interior Design, Bethesda, Maryland

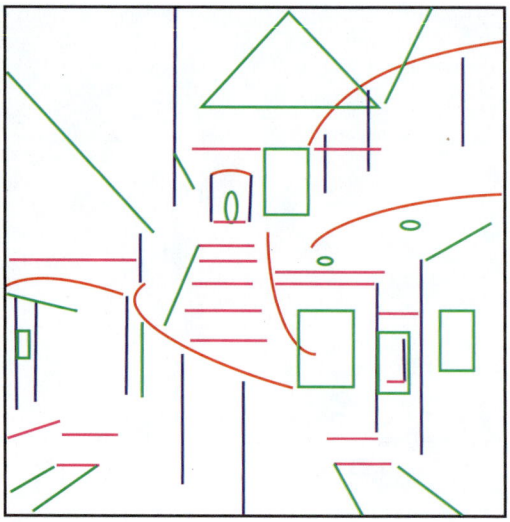

1.6.3b Linear evaluation of elements in interior design by I. Michael

the idea of compositional unity. Although A is unified, it lacks the visual interest of B. While C is a unified work, its visual variety feels incoherent and chaotic. These diagrams show how too much similarity of shape, color, line, or any single element or principle of art can be monotonous and make us lose interest. Too much variety can lead to a lack of structure and the absence of a central idea. Experienced artists learn to restrict the range of elements: working within limitations can be liberating.

The interior designed by I. Michael Winegrad (**1.6.3a**) closely reflects the design in **1.6.3b**. The interior has a balance of curved and straight lines that complement each other. The linear patterns of curved lines repeat (red), as do the other directional lines. Shapes are distributed throughout the scene (green). The composition appears harmonious without being boring.

In the work of Russian artist Marie Marevna (1892–1984), the unifying features are the angular lines and flat areas of color or pattern (**1.6.4**). Marevna was one of the first female members of the **Cubist** movement; here her Cubist **style** breaks apart a scene and re-creates it from a variety of different angles. In this

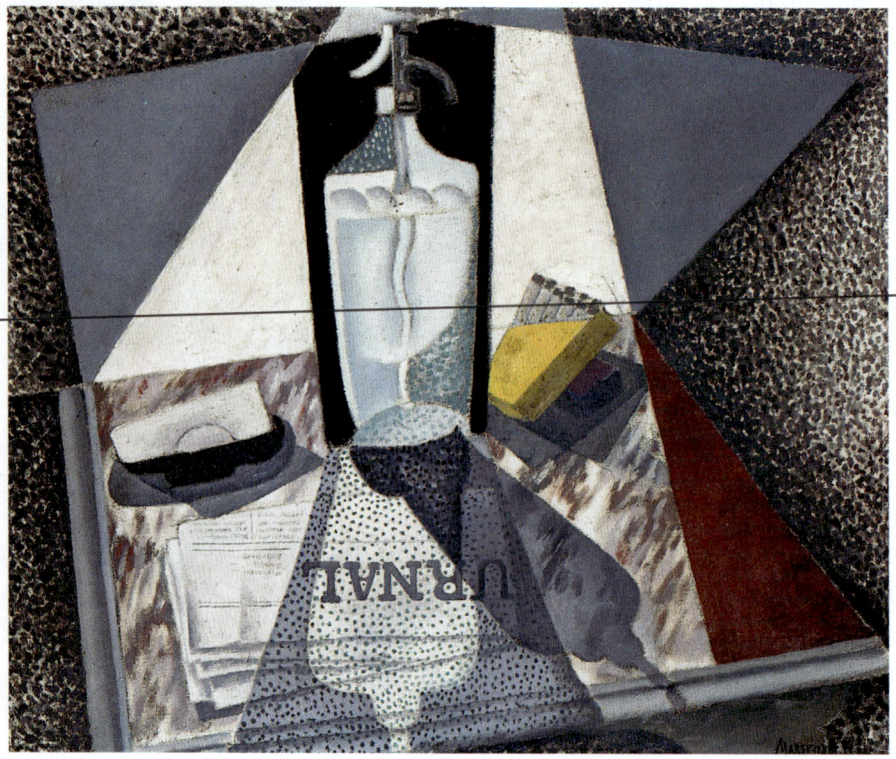

1.6.4 Marie Marevna (Marie Vorobieff-Stebelska), *Nature morte à la bouteille*, 1917. Oil on canvas with plaster, 19¾ × 24"

Cubism, Cubist: twentieth-century movement and style in art, especially painting, in which perspective with a single viewpoint was abandoned and use was made of simple geometric shapes, interlocking planes, and, later, collage; the Cubists were artists who formed part of the movement. "Cubist" is also used to describe their style of painting

Style: a characteristic way in which an artist or group of artists uses visual language to give a work an identifiable form of visual expression

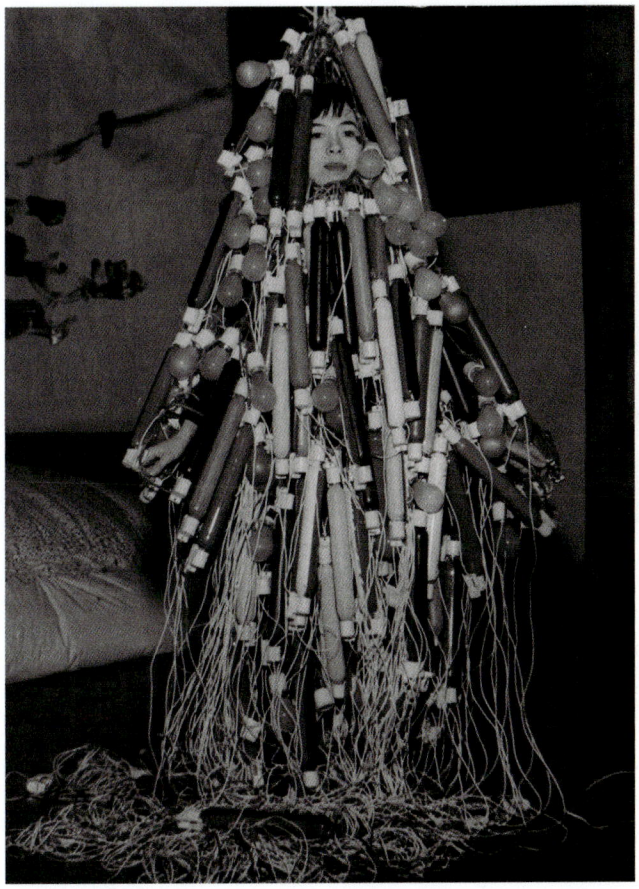

1.6.5 Atsuko Tanaka wearing *Electric Dress*, c. 1956.

Still life: a scene of inanimate objects, such as fruits, flowers, or dead animals
Performance art: a work involving the human body, usually including the artist, in front of an audience
Abstract: art imagery that departs from recognizable images of the natural world
Collage: a work of art assembled by gluing materials, often paper, onto a surface. From the French *coller*, to glue

image, she shows us the seltzer bottle from the side, while we look down at the tabletop from above. The entire work becomes unified, however, because the artist paints a variety of different viewing angles using flat areas of color and pattern throughout, rather than relying on a more realistic representation. Even though we view the **still life** from many different angles, the artist was able to unify the composition by using similar elements. The texture of the paint, the hard diagonal angular lines, and the dominant gray-brown color all work together to counteract the potentially excessive variety that could have come from the many points of view presented.

As demonstrated above (see p. 127), artists add unity to a design by matching visual similarities, but connected ideas can help support that principle as well. The Gutai group was a collection of Japanese artists working in the 1950s and 1960s that experimented with different kinds of artistic expression. The term Gutai is formed of the words "gu," which translates as "tool," and "tai," meaning body—and this represents the physical methods of

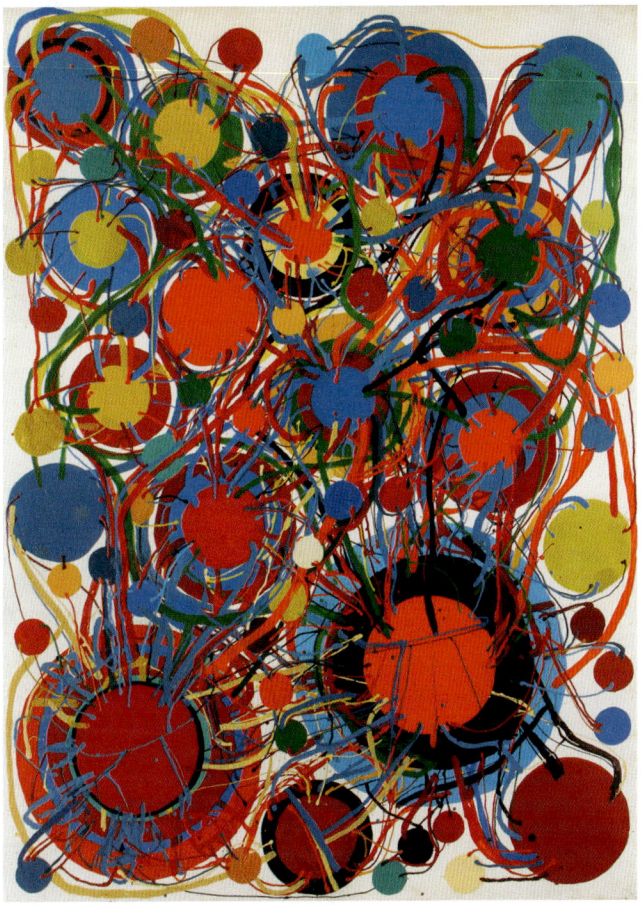

1.6.6 Atsuko Tanaka, *Untitled*, 1968. Enamel on canvas, 51¼ × 38¼". Lito and Kim Camacho Collection, Manila, Philippines

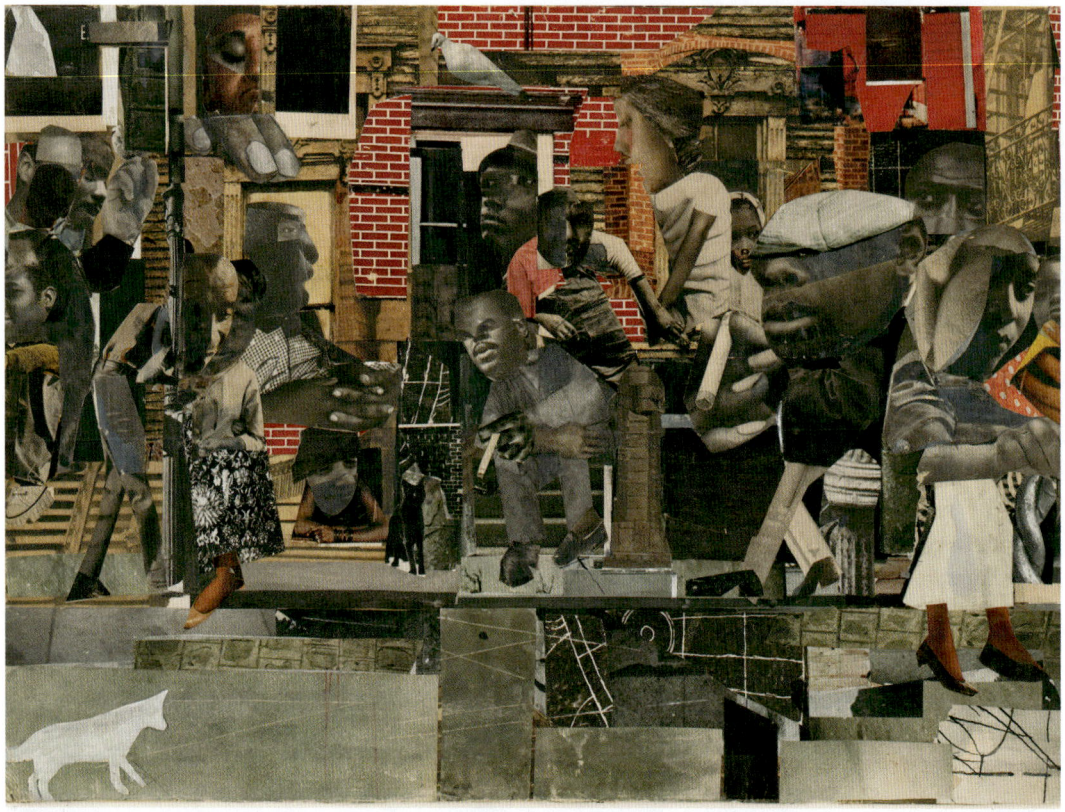

1.6.7 Romare Bearden, *The Dove*, 1964. Cut-and-pasted printed papers, gouache, pencil, and colored pencil on board, 13⅜ × 18¾". MoMA, New York

many of the group's artists, who used their own bodies in their works in ways that anticipated **performance art** of the 1960s and 1970s in the US and Europe. One of the notable members of the Gutai Group was Atsuko Tanaka (1932–2005). Tanaka had traditional training as an artist, but she found new creative outlets when she joined the group in 1965. She is best remembered for *Electric Dress* (**1.6.5**), which she wore to exhibition openings. She derived her idea from a neon pharmaceutical sign that would turn off and on sporadically. Tanaka's painting *Untitled* (**1.6.6**) reflects the sensibilities of *Electric Dress*. Both the dress and her painting are **abstract** works that together find unification in the repeated motifs of lines and circular shapes presented in a variety of bold colors.

Some artists create compositional unity while gathering together bits and pieces of visual information. The African American artist Romare Bearden (1911–1988) captures the unity of New York in the fragments that make up his **collage** *The Dove* (**1.6.7**). In this work we see snippets of faces and hands, city textures of brick walls and fire escapes, and other associated images assembled into a scene that, at first glance, seems frenetic and chaotic. We may feel this pace of life when we visit a big city, but if we look beyond our first impressions, we often notice the orderly grid of streets and the organization that underpin city life.

Bearden reflects this order in an underlying grid of verticals and horizontals in the street below, and in the vertical streetposts and buildings in the upper section of the work.

The hectic composition is subtly coordinated by an implied triangular shape that runs from the cat in the lower left and the woman's feet in the lower right to the dove (hence the title) at the top center. These three points create a sense of depth while stabilizing the lively image of a bustling street scene.

Conceptual Unity

Conceptual unity refers to the cohesive expression of ideas within a work of art. Ideas can come to us in haphazard and unpredictable ways. Sometimes the expression of these ideas may not look organized, but an artist can still communicate them effectively by selecting images that conjure up a single notion. For

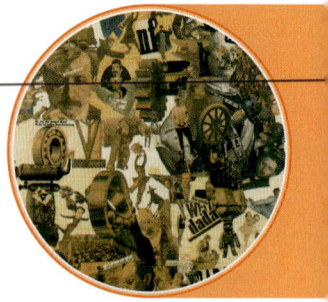

Another great example of compositional unity and collage is *Cut with the Kitchen Knife through the Last Weimar Beer-Belly Cultural Epoch of Germany*, by Hannah Höch: see **2.8.20, p. 327**

example, an artist wishing to communicate the feeling of flight can use such symbols as feathers, kites, or balloons. Each of these has different visual attributes, but they all have an idea in common. That common idea is emphasized when they are placed together in the same work. The artist links images that, although different—perhaps even drastically different—in their appearance, have an idea, symbol, aspect, or association in common. Sometimes, on the other hand, an artist may deliberately break or contradict linkages between ideas to freshen up our tendency to find conventional—even boring—connections between them.

Artists bring their own intentions, experiences, and reactions to their work. These ideas—conscious and unconscious—can also contribute to the conceptual unity of a work and are understood through the artist's style, attitude, and intent. In addition, the conceptual links that artists make between symbols and ideas derive from the collective experiences of their culture: this too influences both the means that artists use to create unity and the viewer's interpretation of the work.

American **Surrealist** sculptor Joseph Cornell (1903–1972) created boxes that contain compositions of **found objects**. His works seem to suggest mysterious ideas and elusive feelings. The diverse shapes, colors, and other characteristics of everyday things come together to form distinctive images. Cornell's works are like a complex game with the viewer, a game that reveals and conceals—just as in a dream or psychoanalysis—the artist's personality. In *Untitled (The Hotel Eden)*, Cornell has collected objects from life and sealed them in a box (**1.6.8**). Although the interior of the box is a

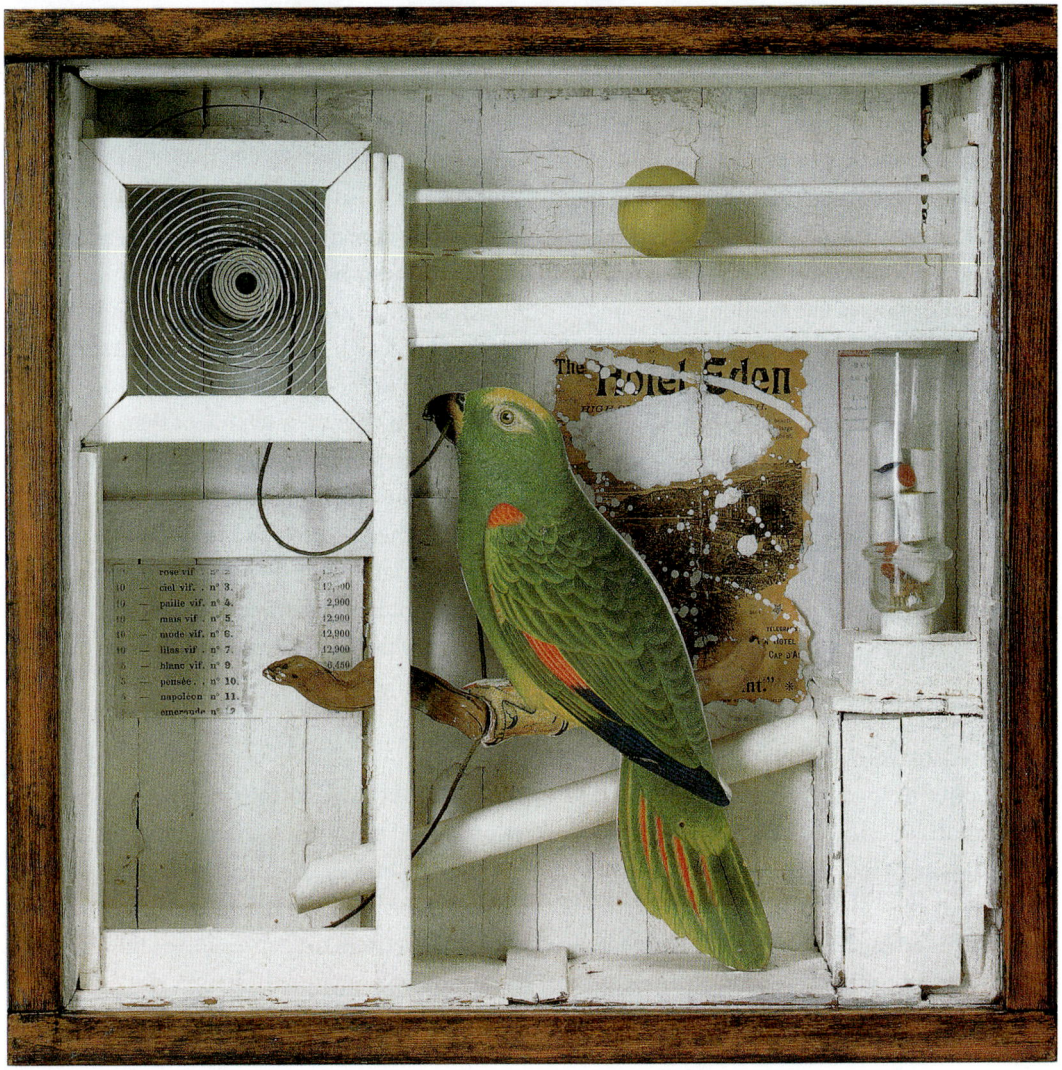

1.6.8 Joseph Cornell, *Untitled (The Hotel Eden)*, 1945. Assemblage with music box, 15⅛ × 15⅛ × 4¾". National Gallery of Canada, Ottawa

Surrealism, Surrealist: an artistic movement in the 1920s and later; its works were inspired by dreams and the subconscious

Found image or **object:** an image or object found by an artist and presented, with little or no alteration, as part of a work or as a finished work of art in itself

protected place, the bird is caged and unable to get out. A yellow ball sits trapped on two rails that limit its freedom of movement to roll back and forth. Neither the bird nor the ball is free. Placed together, all the different objects in the box make an idea greater than any one of them could create on its own. The artist has fused (and deliberately confused) his memories, dreams, and visualizations; the resulting artwork is a rich and complex visual expression of Cornell's personality and methods.

Gestalt Unity

Gestalt, a German word for form or shape, refers to something (here a work of art) in which the whole seems greater than the sum of its parts. The composition and ideas that go to make a work of art—as well as our experience of it—combine to create a gestalt. We get a sense of gestalt when we comprehend how compositional unity and conceptual unity work together.

We can discover the many faces of gestalt by examining the ancient Hindu relief *Vishnu Dreaming the Universe* (**1.6.9**). In this stone carving, an abundance of human figures surrounds a much larger reclining figure; this is the god Vishnu dreaming. The repetition of the human shapes that attend Vishnu creates compositional unity: these similar shapes link to each other visually.

According to some texts written in the ancient Indian language known as Sanskrit, the existence of the universe, and its creation, are directly dependent on the god Vishnu, who is sheltered by the great serpent Ananta and sleeps on the Cosmic Sea. Through his sleep, the universe is reborn over and over into eternity. Hindu pantheism (the unity of many gods as one) is elegantly illustrated in this work. Brahma is the upper figure seated on a lotus that had sprouted from Vishnu's navel. Here he becomes the active agent of creation. The god Shiva, riding a bull (Nandi), is at Brahma's left. Lakshmi, Vishnu's wife, attends her sleeping husband. Their unity of male and female creates a partnership that results in the birth of a new universe and many other universes into eternity. The dualities of male/female, life/death, good/evil are illustrated in the complex stories of the gods. Shiva, for example, is both creator and destroyer, destruction being necessary for creation—yet another unifying duality.

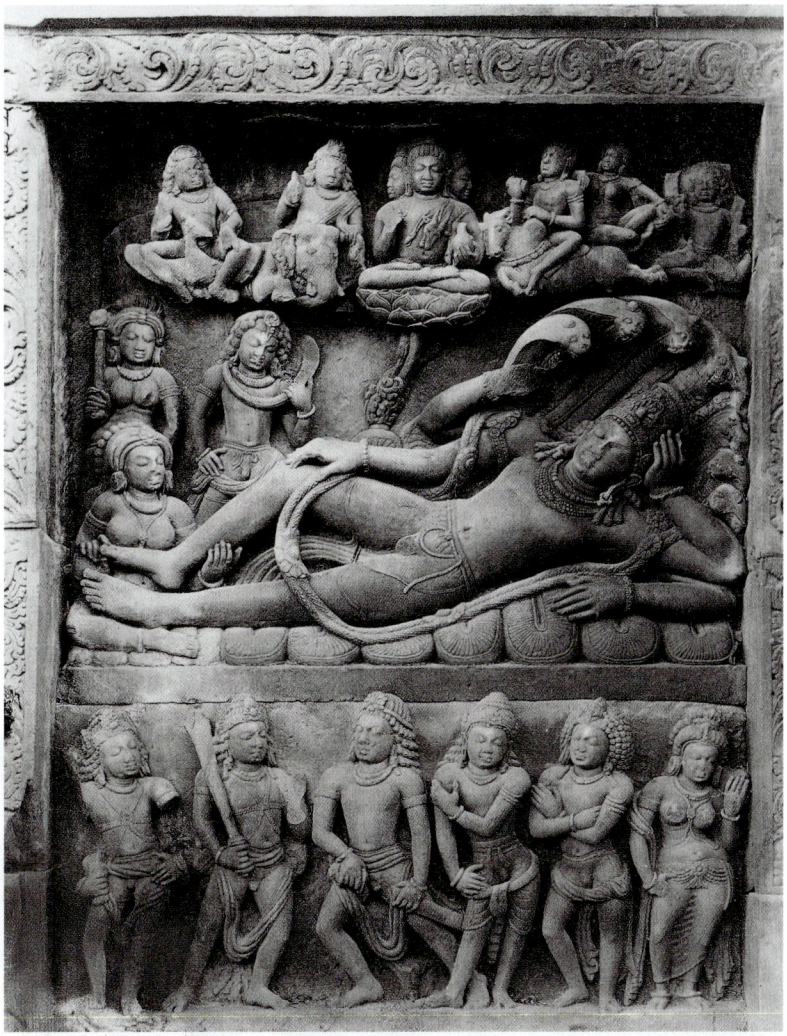

1.6.9 *Vishnu Dreaming the Universe*, c. 450–500 CE. Relief panel. Temple of Vishnu, Deogarh, Uttar Pradesh, India

As is often the case, a religious idea provides profound conceptual unity. The image, the religious idea that the image illustrates, and the fervent belief of the artist who created the work interconnect through a symbolic representation in carved stone. As we come to appreciate how these aspects combine so completely in an artwork, we experience a sense of gestalt, an awakened understanding of the whole. This is a goal in any artwork.

Variety

If "variety is the spice of life," it is also the spice of the visual world. In art, variety is a collection of ideas, elements, or materials that are fused together into one design. Inasmuch as unity is about repetition and similarity, variety is about uniqueness and diversity. Artists use a multiplicity of values, textures, colors, and so on to intensify the impact of a work. It is unusual to see a good composition that has just one type of **value**, shape, or color. Variety can invigorate a design. The example in **1.6.10** shows a composition of shapes set into a rectangle on a grid. Even though the grid structure is predictable, the variety of shapes and values counteracts the rigid structure. Many artists use this kind of variety to express an energy that would be lost if there were too much unity. Variety is the artist's way of giving a work of art a jolt.

The American Robert Rauschenberg (1925–2008) used variety to energize his artwork and challenge his viewers. In the work *Monogram*, Rauschenberg has used all kinds of different things to form his composition (**1.6.11**). The work features a stuffed goat with a tire around its middle standing on a painting. By combining these objects, Rauschenberg creates an outlandish symbol of himself as a rebel and outcast. The goat, an ancient symbol of male lust and a Christian symbol of souls cast out from

Value: the lightness or darkness of a plane or area

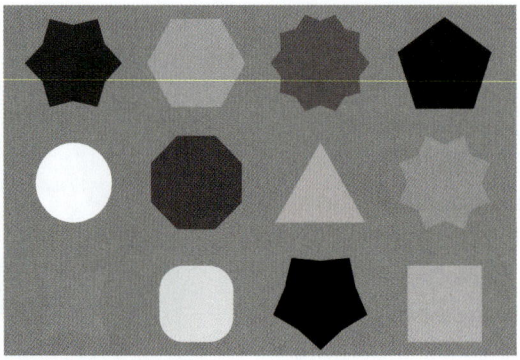

1.6.10 Variety of shapes and values set into a grid

1.6.11 Robert Rauschenberg, *Monogram*, 1955–59. Mixed media with taxidermy goat, rubber tire, and tennis ball, 42 × 63¼ × 64½". Moderna Museet, Stockholm, Sweden

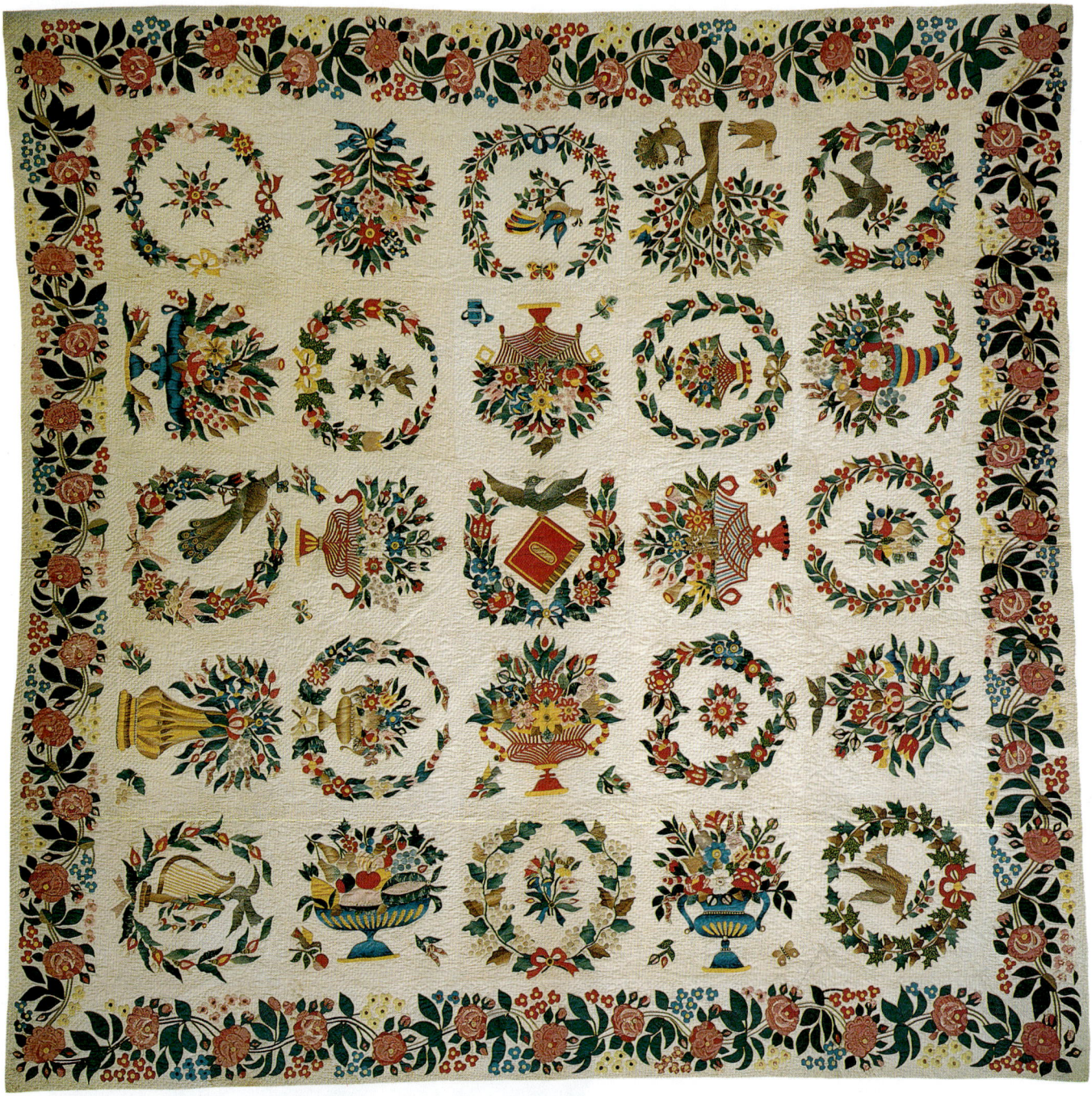

1.6.12 Album quilt, probably by Mary Evans, Baltimore, Maryland, 1848. Appliquéd cottons with ink work, 9 × 9'. Private collection

salvation, becomes the totem of Rauschenberg's own provocative behaviors and his violation of art-world conventions. The stuffed goat penetrates the tire and stands atop a symbol of the established art world (painting) while defecating a dirty tennis ball on it. For the first time in modern art, too, Rauschenberg breached the divide between painting and sculpture and took painting "off the wall." By using a variety of non-traditional art materials and techniques, the work becomes a transgression against traditional art and morals.

Using Variety to Unify

Although it might seem contradictory, variety can be unifying. Even while using a variety of different shapes, colors, values, or other elements, an artist can create visual harmony. This can be seen in Baltimore album quilts, created by such Maryland artists as Mary Evans in the nineteenth century (**1.6.12**). These carefully sewn quilts are named after the scrapbooks kept by Baltimore girls, although rather than being constructed from scraps of leftover material, as many quilts are, these fiber works were made from new pieces of fabric, a reflection of the wealth of this port city. Like a scrapbook, however, these quilts use a variety of images and fuse them together into a finished work. Because a strong structure is imposed on the many different shapes through the use of a grid, the work holds together as a unified whole. The quilted surface is an arrangement of shapes that form a unified composition.

Balance

Just as real objects have physical weight, parts of a work of art can have visual weight, or impact; these need to be balanced to achieve a sort of visual equilibrium. We can identify visual balance in a form or composition, the same as we can with weighted objects, by noting differences between the two halves we are looking at. If the amount of visual weight does not have a reasonable counterweight on the opposite side, the work may appear to be unsuccessful or unfinished. If there are reasonable visual counterweights the work seems complete, and balance has been achieved. Even placing a visual weight in the center of a composition can impose a strong balance on a design.

Finding visual weight and counterweight is a challenge for the artist; balance in a work is not always easy to define. But there are some situations that often arise. For example, dark and light, although opposites, can act as counterbalances. Large shapes or forms can be countered by groups of smaller shapes or forms. For many artists this process is intuitive; they make decisions about the work based on what looks right, rather than on a rigid set of rules.

Symmetrical Balance

If a work can be cut in half and each side looks exactly (or nearly exactly) the same, then it is symmetrically balanced. Near-perfect symmetry exists in the human body. For example, each side of our face has half a nose, half a mouth, half a chin, and so on. The same is true for most animals and a number of geometric shapes, such as circles and squares. Because it is a part of our physical body, symmetry can seem very natural and we can make natural connections to it.

Artists of ancient China designed a creature born of symmetry called the *t'ao t'ieh*. The image of the creature in an artwork is not immediately apparent, because its form is "hidden" amongst many separate symmetrical shapes and forms. It is as if a symmetrical collection of elements coalesces to reveal a monster mask. The image of the t'ao t'ieh has been used widely in Chinese art since the Shang Dynasty (*c.* 1600–*c.* 1050 BCE), when it appeared on ceremonial bronze objects. The meaning of this **motif** is mysterious, but it may symbolize communication with the gods. According to some accounts, the t'ao t'ieh mask represents a monster that, through its own gluttony, is devouring itself: a warning against overindulgence.

The t'ao t'ieh can be found on the bronze ritual container in **1.6.13** by identifying a pair of perfectly round "eyes" on either side of the

Motif: a design or color repeated as a unit in a pattern

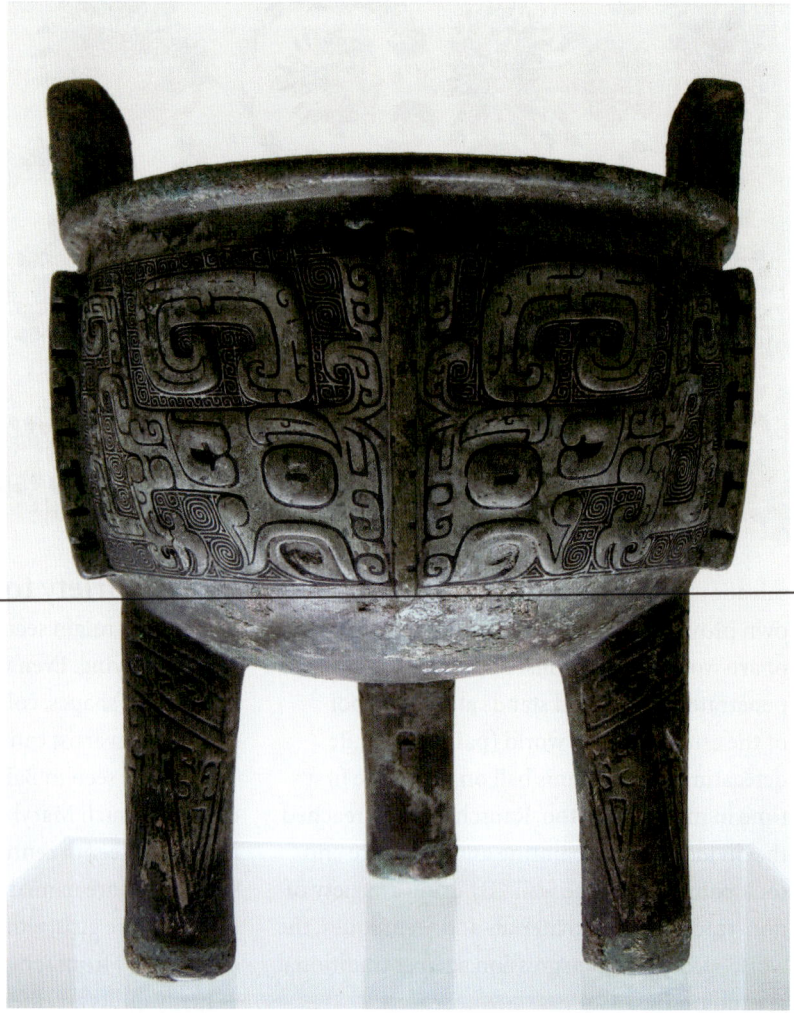

1.6.13 *Liu Ding* (ritual container), China, late Shang Dynasty, c.1600–c.1050 BCE. Bronze. Shanghai Museum, China

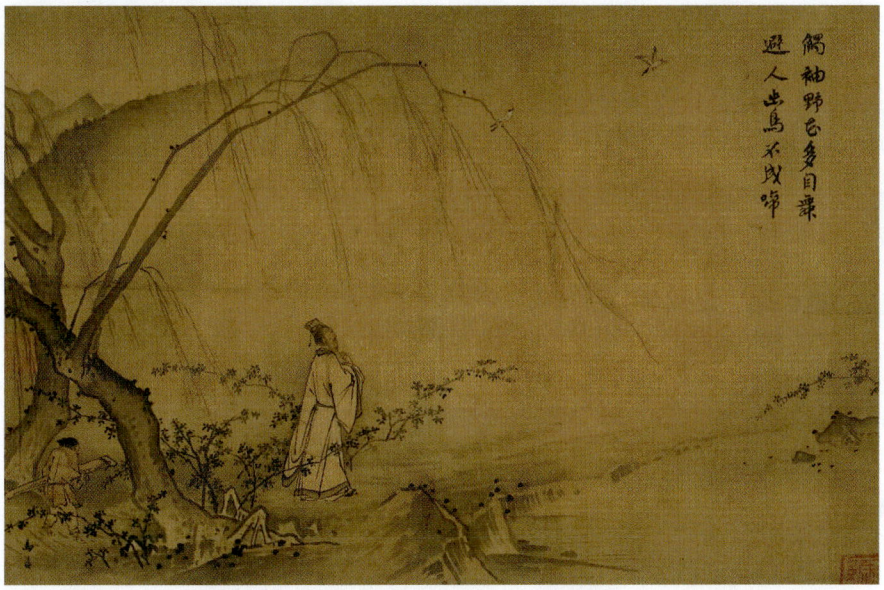

1.6.14 Ma Yuan, *Walking on a Mountain Path in Spring*, Song Dynasty (960–1279). Album leaf, ink and color on silk, 10¾ × 17". National Palace Museum, Taipei, Taiwan

central vertical ridge. On each side of this central ridge are patterns that mirror each other. Some of these signify horns, claws, fangs, ears, and even smaller images of animals. If you look carefully you may see two rams' heads in profile as they butt heads along the vertical central **axis**. The "monster" of symmetry lurks amongst the many parts of the image and waits for us to discover its hiding place.

Asymmetrical Balance

On an old-fashioned scale, the kind with a long arm centered on top of a vertical support, a single heavy object on one side can be balanced by several lighter objects on the other side as long as the weight on both sides is the same. Similarly, when artists organize a composition they often use different visual "weights" on each side of the composition. This is asymmetrical balance, also called dynamic balance; it applies when the elements on the left and right sides are not the same, but the combination of elements counter one another.

Chinese artists have long used asymmetrical balance to reflect on life and the landscape. The twelfth/thirteenth-century academic painter Ma Yuan (1160–1225) expresses balanced asymmetry in his work *Walking on a Mountain Path in Spring* (**1.6.14**). In this painting, dark, light, and the placement of elements in the composition are not distributed evenly between the left and right sides. Ma Yuan is intentional in the way he positions shapes and figures on each side of the central axis. On the left are the large, dark shapes of trees, two figures, and distant mountains, which place a heavy visual weight on that side. On the right there are few shapes and a great deal of light, open space. Ma Yuan brilliantly counteracts the visual "heaviness" of the left side by placing the poetic inscription at the top right as a counterweight that leads the viewer's eye down to a small branch and some little rocks. For many Chinese artists, the use of brush and ink was a form of meditation, through simple, thoughtful actions, in search of higher knowledge. Yuan's asymmetrical design, with mostly empty space on the right, reminds the viewer of the expansive unknown that eludes discovery.

Radial Balance

Radial balance (or symmetry) is achieved when all elements in a work are equidistant from a central point and repeat in a symmetrical way from side to side and top to bottom. Radial symmetry can imply circular and repeating elements. Although the term "radial" suggests a round shape, in fact any geometric shape can be used to create radial symmetry. Artists can employ this kind of balance when it is necessary to depict an element more than twice. It is sometimes used in religious symbols and

Axis: an imaginary line showing the center of a shape, volume, or composition

Gateway to Art: The Taj Mahal
Love and Perfection

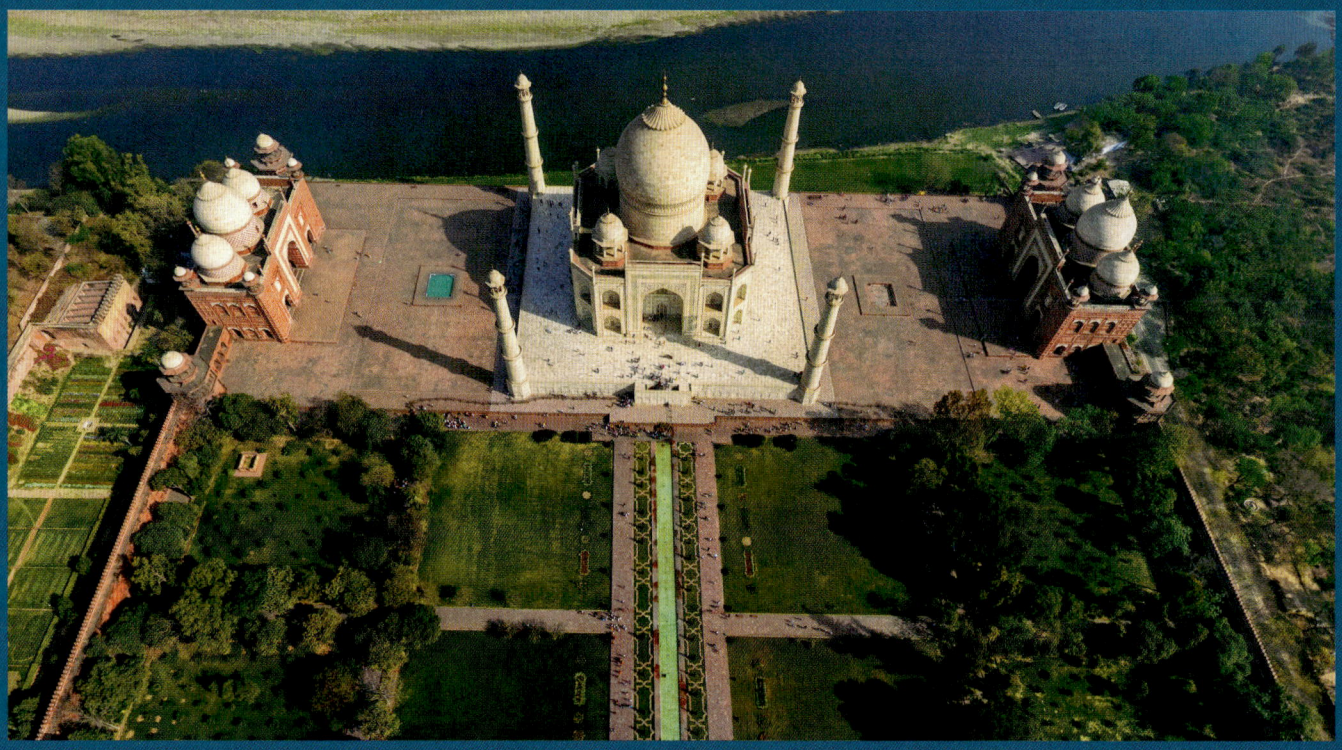

1.6.15a The Taj Mahal, designed by Ustad Ahmad Lahauri, Abd al-Karim Ma'mur Khan, and Makramat Khan; commissioned by Shah Jahan, 1632–43. Marble architecture. Agra, India

The building that we know as the Taj Mahal is an exemplary and enduring study in pure symmetry (**1.6.15a**). It was commissioned by the grieving Shah Jahan (1592–1666), the fifth Mughal Emperor of India, as a memorial to his third and beloved wife, Mumtaz Mahal (1593–1631). She and Shah Jahan were devoted to each other, and in recognition of their love and as an expression of his admiration for her, he sought after her death to create a building that would, through its visual perfection, honor her memory and stand as a testament to the transcendent power of timeless love.

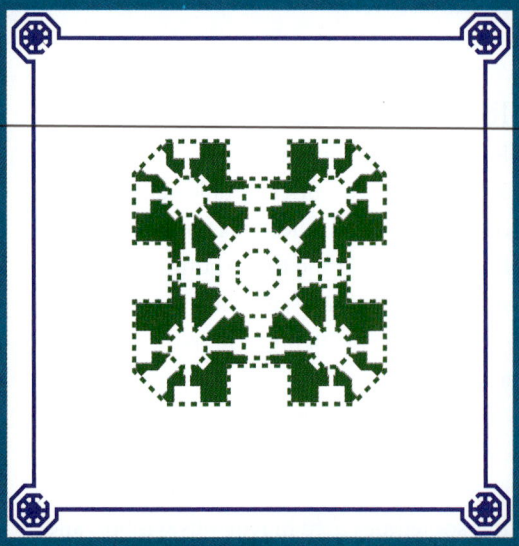

1.6.15b Plan of the tomb of Mumtaz Mahal

In art, symmetrical balance is created when harmony unites all the elements, just as Shah Jahan and Mumtaz felt united in their relationship based on requited love. A stable visual form is achieved when opposite sides of a design mirror each other exactly, creating this perfect balance. In most cases symmetry suggests pleasing tranquility, order, and numerical perfection to the viewer, so its use in the proportions and design of the Taj Mahal carries associations of beauty and stability.

The Taj Mahal uses both bilateral and radial symmetry in the design of the central tomb building (**1.6.15b**) and the surrounding complex in which it stands. The entire complex includes the central mausoleum and four minarets, a meeting house, a mosque, two pavilions, a gatehouse, two plaza areas, and a grand garden (**1.6.16a**), all of which can be bisected to reveal identical components on the opposite side. There are even some additional areas adjacent

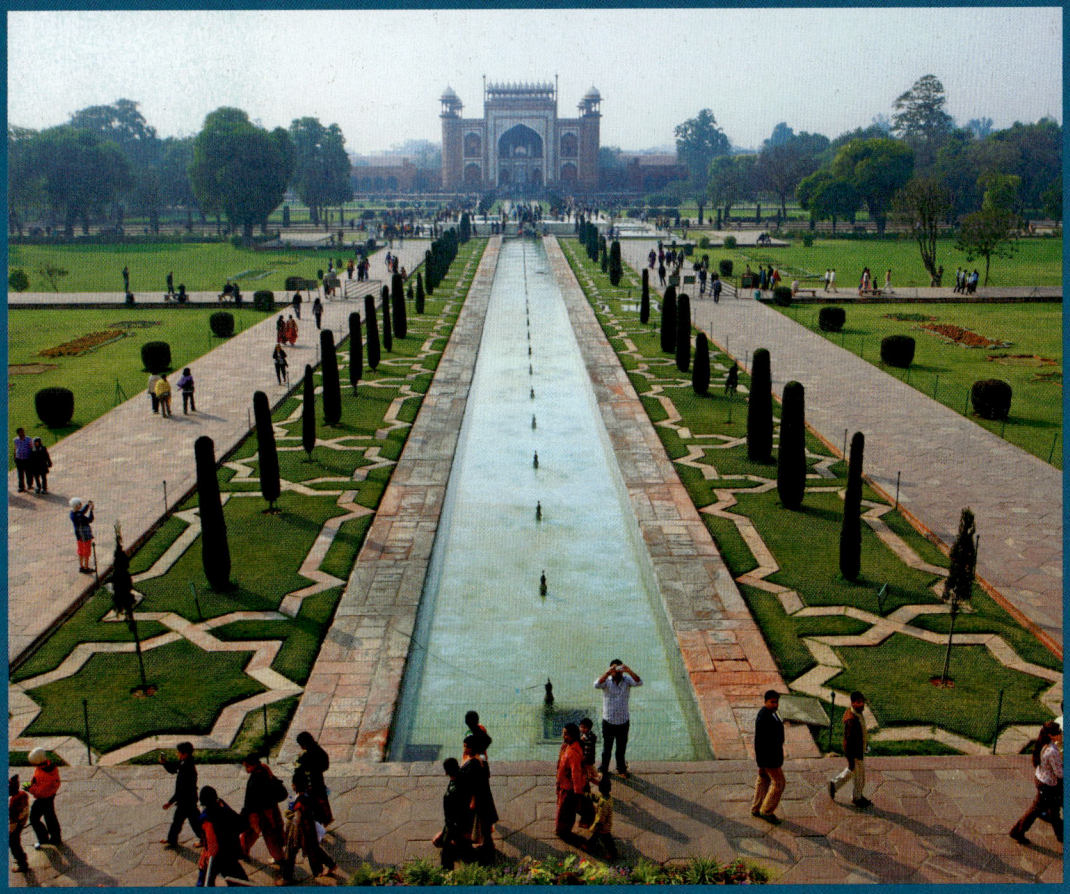

For the other Taj Mahal Gateway boxes, see p. 272, p. 412, and p. 594

1.6.16a (left) Mughal gardens and the South Gate of the Taj Mahal, Agra, India

1.6.16b (below) Plan of the charbagh (Mughal garden)

and across the Yamuna River that also share the same characteristics. The entire plan, if bisected parallel to its longest axis, would find an exact replication in its opposite side. The carefully apportioned symmetrical balance in this plan expresses a sense of perfection.

Radial balance exists in both the main building and the adjacent *charbagh* (Mughal garden) (**1.6.16b**). Both are planned in such a way that each design element is repeated equidistant to a central point. So the symmetry exists along not only the bilateral axis, but also the principal intersecting axis. The multiple repetition of this balance in the design is a deliberate affirmation, in its sustained artistry, of the depth of Shah Jahan's love. Similarly, the complete design itself reflects his overarching commitment to perfection, shared by his architects Ustad Ahmad Lahauri, Abd al-Karim Ma'mur Khan, and Makramat Khan, as an expression, and indeed a proof, of the timelessness of true love.

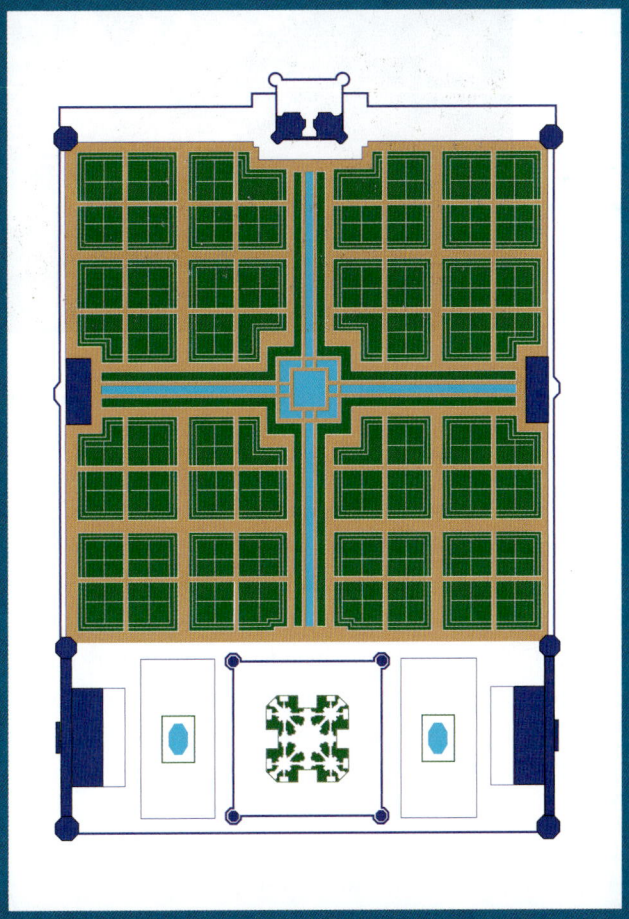

1.6.17 Amitayus Mandala created by the monks of Drepung Loseling Monastery, Tibet

Mandala: a sacred diagram of the universe, often involving a square and a circle

architecture where repetition plays an important role in the design.

The Tibetan sand painting shown in **1.6.17** is a diagram of the universe (also known as a **mandala**) from a human perspective. The Tibetan Buddhist monks who created this work have placed a series of symbols equidistant from the center. In this mandala the colors vary but the shapes pointing in four different directions from the center are symmetrical. The square area in the center of the work symbolizes Amitayus, or the Buddha of long life, and surrounds a central lotus blossom. The creation of one of these sand paintings is an act of meditation that takes many days, after which the work is destroyed. The careful deconstruction of the work after it has been completed symbolizes the impermanence of the world.

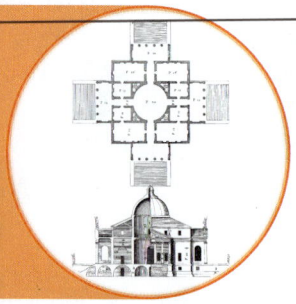

Another example of radial balance is the Villa Rotonda by Andrea Palladio: see **3.6.14b, p. 473**

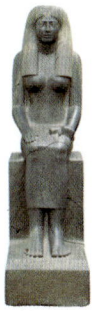

2.4.1 Sculpture of the Lady Sennuwy, Egypt, 1971–1926 BCE, p. 243

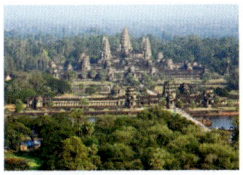

3.3.26 Angkor Wat, Siem Reap, Cambodia, 12th century, p. 426

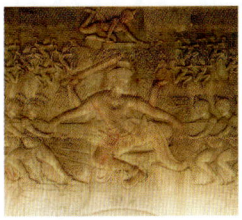

3.3.27 *Vishnu Churning the Ocean of Milk*, Angkor Wat, p. 427

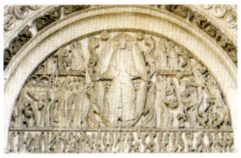

4.2.11 Gislebertus, *The Last Judgment*, c. 1120–35, p. 585

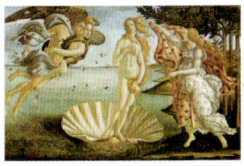

4.9.5 Sandro Botticelli, *The Birth of Venus*, c. 1482–86, p. 666

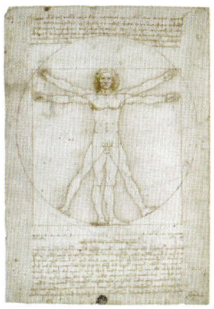

4.4.1 Leonardo da Vinci, *Vitruvian Man*, c. 1490, p. 603

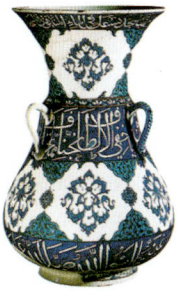

1.4.23 Mosque lamp from the Dome of the Rock, Jerusalem, 1549, p. 106

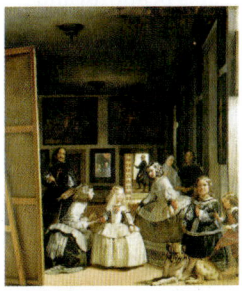

1.10.12a Diego de Silva y Velázquez, *Las Meninas*, c. 1656, p. 183

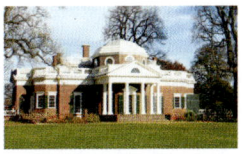

3.7.10 Thomas Jefferson, Monticello, Virginia, 1769–1809, p. 495

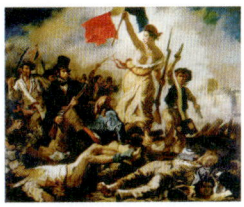

3.7.13 Eugène Delacroix, *Liberty Leading the People*, 1830, p. 497

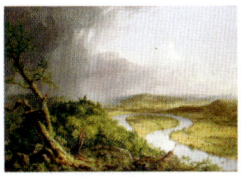

3.7.16 Thomas Cole, *The Oxbow*, 1836, p. 499

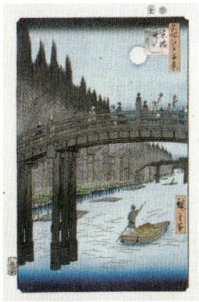

1.8.10 Ando Hiroshige, "Riverside Bamboo Market, Kyo-bashi," 1857, p. 157

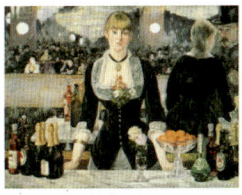

4.5.11 Édouard Manet, *A Bar at the Folies-Bergère*, 1882, p. 623

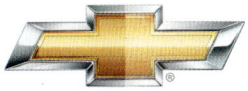

2.7.7 Chevrolet logo, first used in 1913, p. 303

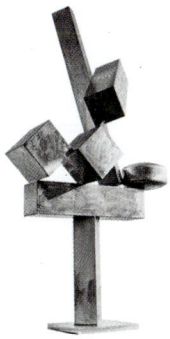

1.2.3 David Smith, *Cubi XIX*, 1964, p. 63

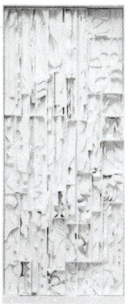

0.0.3 Louise Nevelson, *White Vertical Water*, 1972, p. 22

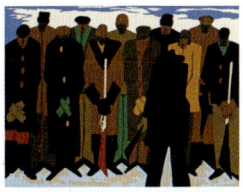

1.8.6 Jacob Lawrence, "John Brown Remained a Full Winter...," 1977, p. 154

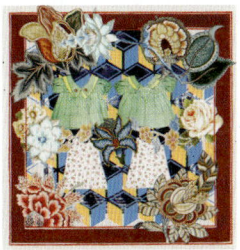

1.1.21 Miriam Shapiro, *Baby Blocks*, 1983, p. 55

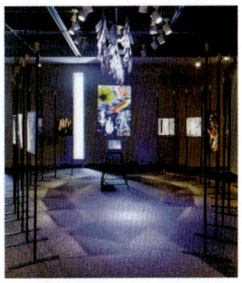

3.10.10 Jolene Rickard, *Corn Blue Room*, 1998, p. 552

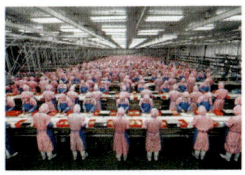

2.8.27 Edward Burtynsky, *Manufacturing #17...*, 2005, p. 332

1.7 Scale and Proportion

The nineteenth-century French poet Charles Baudelaire wrote that "All that is beautiful and noble is the result of reason and calculation." Baudelaire was speaking of cosmetics and makeup, and not referring specifically to works of art, but his statement neatly summarizes the care with which artists determine **scale** and **proportion**. Artists use these key **principles** of design to control how they implement the basic **elements of art**, just as grammar controls how words work in a sentence.

We perceive scale in relation to our own size. Art objects created on a **monumental** scale appear larger than they would be in normal life. This monumentality imposes itself on us. In a work created on a human scale, its size corresponds to the size of things as they actually exist. Work at this scale often surprises us. Small-scale objects appear smaller than our usual experience of them in the real world. Often, scale is used to indicate importance, yet this is not always the case: sometimes the smallest thing is the most significant.

Proportion is a core principle in the **unity** of any art object. Usually, an artist ensures that all the parts of an object are in proportion to one another. Alternatively, an artist can create a contradiction by portraying objects or figures out of proportion. For example, a cartoonist may portray a figure with disproportionately large nose or ears to exaggerate the prominent facial features distinctive to a famous personality. Careful proportion is a sign of technical mastery; discordant proportions can express a wide range of meanings.

Scale: the size of an object or artwork relative to another object or artwork, or to a system of measurement
Proportion: the relationship in size between a work's individual parts and the whole
Principles: the principles, or "grammar" of art—contrast, unity, variety, balance, scale, proportion, focal point, emphasis, pattern, and rhythm—describe the ways the elements of art are arranged in an artwork
Elements of art: the basic vocabulary of art—line, shape, form, volume, mass, texture, value (lightness/darkness), space, color, and motion and time
Monumental: having massive or impressive scale
Unity: the appearance of oneness or harmony in a work of art: all of the elements appearing to be part of a cohesive whole

Scale

The scale of a work of art communicates ideas. A small work communicates something very different than a larger one does. Small-scale pieces force viewers to come in close to experience the artwork. A small-scale work implies intimacy, like whispering in someone's ear or admiring a ring on his or her finger. Large-scale works can be experienced by groups of viewers, and usually communicate big ideas directed at a large audience. Artists and designers make conscious choices about the scale of a work when they consider the message they want to convey.

Artists may also consider scale as they make more practical choices about a work. Considerations of cost, the time it will take to execute the piece, and the demands that a specific location may place on the work: all come into play in decisions about scale.

Scale and Meaning

Usually a monumental scale indicates heroism or other epic virtues. War monuments, for example, often feature figures much larger than lifesize in order to convey the bravery of the warriors. The Swedish-born artist Claes Oldenburg (b. 1929), however, uses monumental scale to poke fun while expressing admiration for the little things of everyday life. Oldenburg believes that the items of mass culture, no matter how insignificant they might seem, express a truth about modern life. So he restyles small, often overlooked objects on a monumental

1.7.1 Claes Oldenburg and Coosje van Bruggen, *Mistos (Match Cover)*, 1992. Steel, aluminum, and fiber-reinforced plastic, painted with polyurethane enamel, 68' × 33' × 43'4". Collection La Vall d'Hebron, Barcelona, Spain

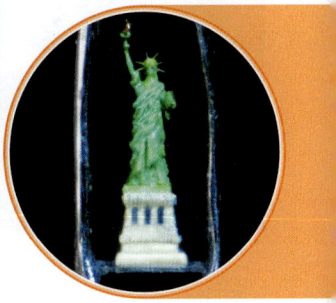

Scale is an important attribute in Willard Wigan's miniature *Statue of Liberty*: see **4.4.8, p. 607**

scale, giving clothes pins and ice-cream cones a grandeur and significance they do not usually have. In the process, Oldenburg transforms the essence of these everyday things as he magnifies their sculptural form. Look at, for example, the enormous book of matches in **1.7.1**, a collaboration between Oldenburg and his wife, the Dutch-born sculptor Coosje van Bruggen (1942–2009).

The American Robert Lostutter (b. 1939) uses small scale to enhance the character of his work. Lostutter likes to create his works on the scale not of a human but of a bird. He paints the plumage of exotic birds in great detail onto human faces, while the tiny size evokes the bird from which the plumage was copied (**1.7.2**). The small scale of Lostutter's work—only one person at a time can see it properly—forces us to come closer; looking at it becomes an intimate experience.

1.7.2 Robert Lostutter, *The Hummingbirds*, 1981. Watercolor on paper, 1¾ × 5⅝". Collection of Anne and Warren Weisberg

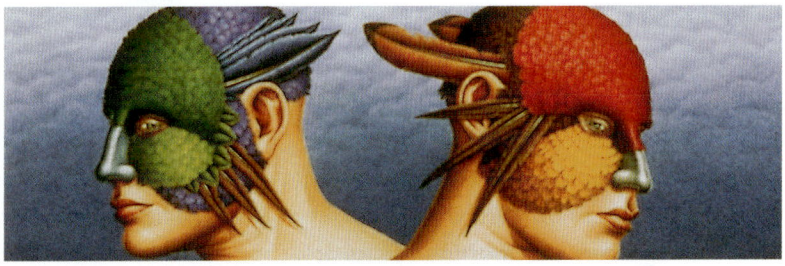

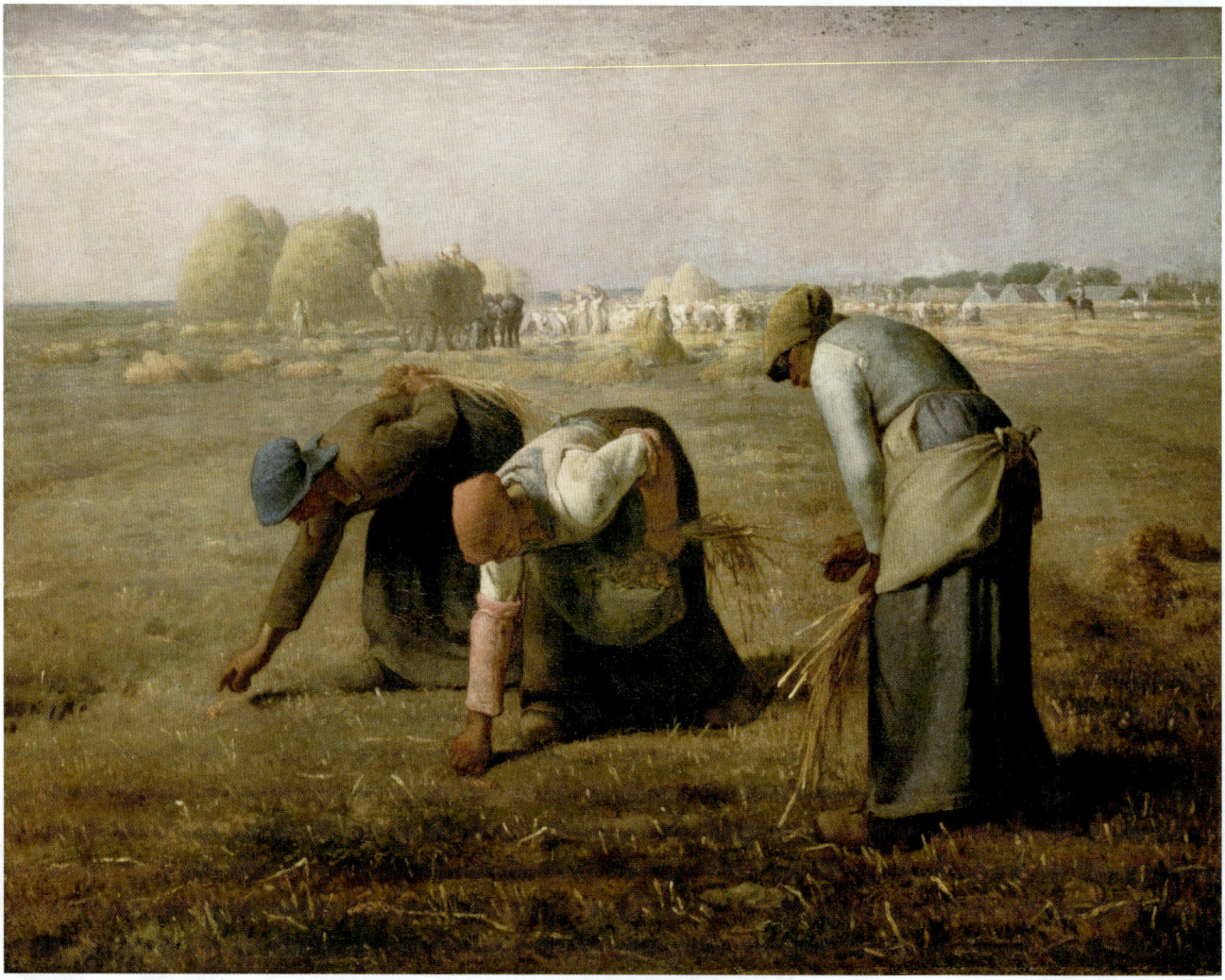

1.7.3 Jean-François Millet, *The Gleaners*, 1857. Oil on canvas, 2' 9" × 3' 8". Musée d'Orsay, Paris

The scale of a work can add meaning in profound ways. In the French artist Jean-François Millet's (1814–1875) first major work, *The Gleaners* (**1.7.3**), the artist uses scale to comment on the class system in nineteenth-century France. In the foreground Millet shows three poor women who are pulling the last stubble from a recently harvested wheat field, while in the background members of the middle class harvest straw. In the upper right, a man on horseback—probably a representative of the wealthy landowner—supervises the activities in the field. In other artworks of the time, and in previous artistic periods, large-scale paintings were typically reserved for depicting religious subjects, royalty, and other figures of political or cultural importance. In this work, however, the artist chooses as his main focus three lower-class subjects. The suggestion that the poor, and their backbreaking labors, were worthy of pictorial honor ignited hostile responses from Millet's contemporaries. Simply by depicting this scene on a heroic scale Millet adds a deeper meaning to the painting, commenting on the divides in the society in which he lives.

Hierarchical Scale

Artists can use size to indicate the relative importance of figures or objects in a composition: almost always, larger means more important, and smaller means less important. Hierarchical scale refers to the deliberate use of relative size in a work in order to communicate differences in importance. In **1.7.4a** and **b** we can see the use of hierarchical scale in a **relief** sculpture from ancient Egypt. In the art of that culture, the king, or pharaoh, was usually the largest figure depicted because he had the highest status in the social order. This is exemplified here,

Relief: a raised form on a largely flat background. For example, the design on a coin is "in relief"

Gothic: Western European architectural style of the twelfth to sixteenth century, characterized by the use of pointed arches and ornate decoration where figure (A) represents the pharaoh; he is visually more dominant than the others (B and C). This scene depicts the military campaign of Seti I against the Hittites and Libyans.

The Flemish artist Jan van Eyck (*c.* 1395–1441) uses hierarchical scale to communicate spiritual importance. In his painting *Madonna in a Church*, Van Eyck enlarges the scale so that the enormous mother and child fill the massive space of a **Gothic** church (**1.7.5**). In his effort to glorify the spiritual importance of Mary and the Christ child, Van Eyck also separates them from normal human existence. Their gigantic appearance, relative to the interior, makes these figures appear to be larger than normal human beings. Van Eyck has scaled them to symbolize their central importance in the Christian religion.

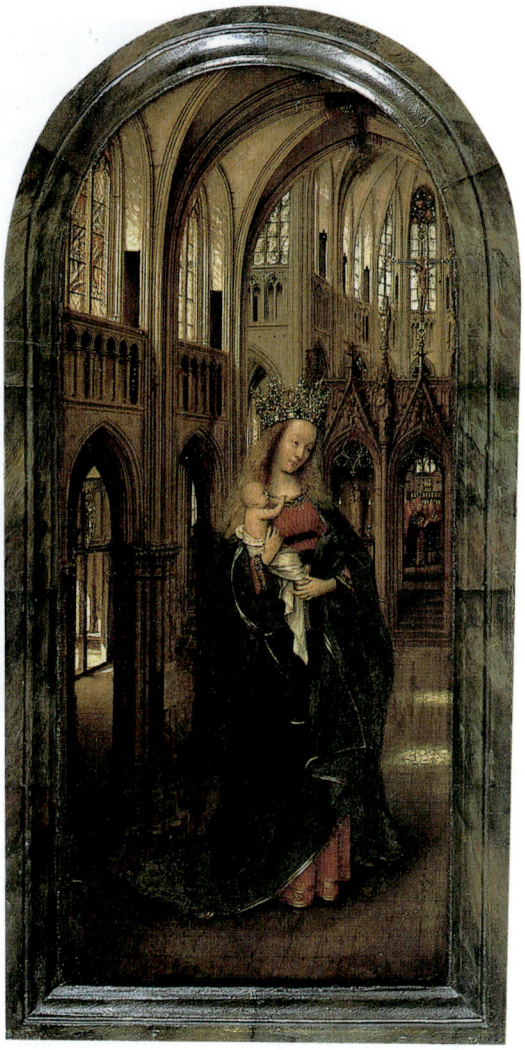

1.7.5 Jan van Eyck, *Madonna in a Church*, 1437–38. Oil on wood panel, 12⅝ × 5½". Gemäldegalerie, Staatliche Museen, Berlin, Germany

1.7.4a and **b** (below) Hierarchical scale: relief from the northern wall of the great temple of Amun-Re, 19th Dynasty, c. 1295–1186 BCE. Karnak, Egypt

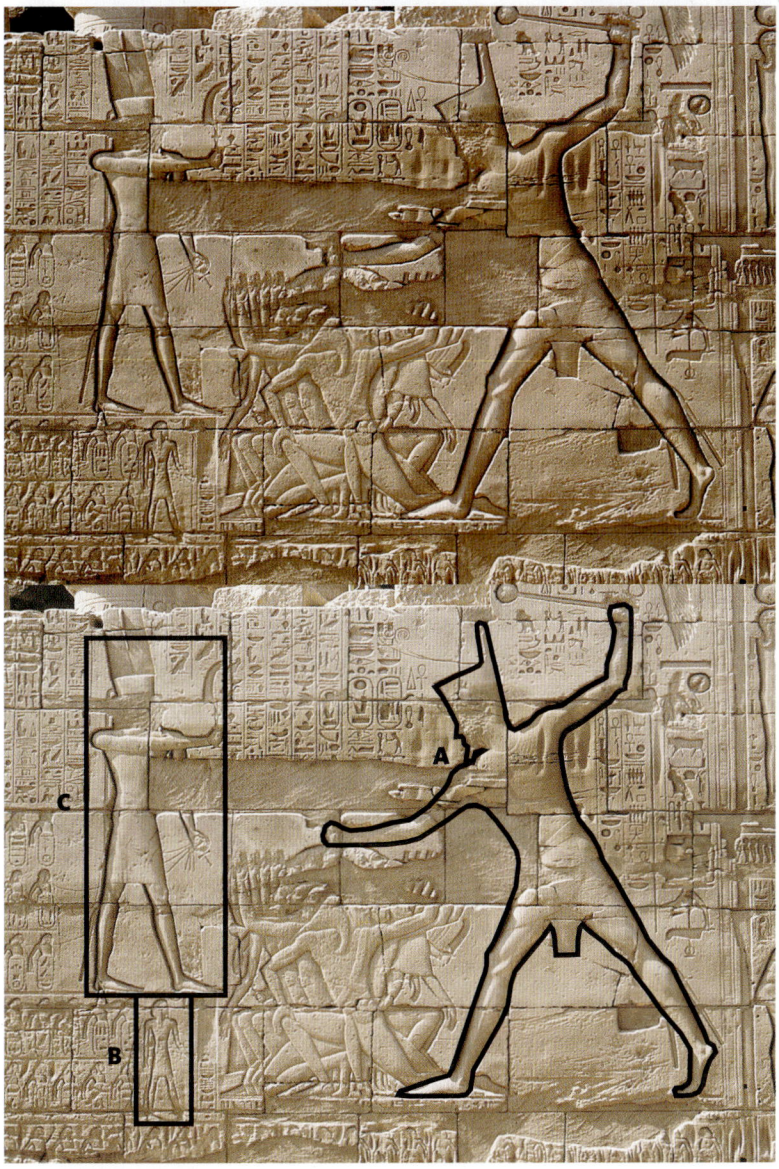

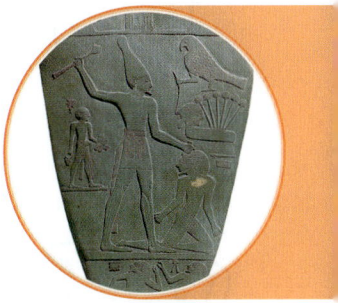

Hierarchical scale can also be seen in another Egyptian relief, the Palette of Narmer: see **4.7.4b, p. 641**

1.7.6 Dorothea Tanning, *Eine Kleine Nachtmusik*, 1943. Oil on canvas, 16⅛ × 24". Tate, London, England

Surrealism, Surrealist: an artistic movement in the 1920s and later; its works were inspired by dreams and the subconscious
Format: the shape of the area an artist uses for making a two-dimensional artwork

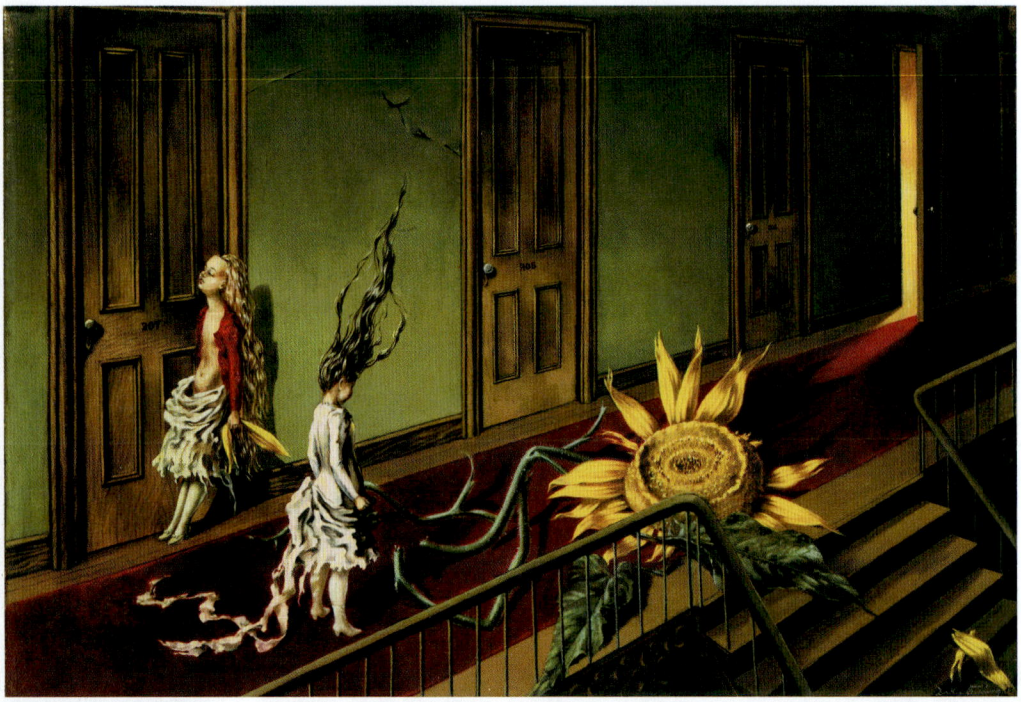

Distorted Scale

An artist may deliberately distort scale to create a supernatural effect. In the twentieth century, artists known as **Surrealists** created works that use dreamlike images to subvert our conscious experiences. The American Surrealist artist Dorothea Tanning (1910–2012), in *Eine Kleine Nachtmusik*, paints a sunflower at a scale that contradicts its surroundings (**1.7.6**). The flower seems huge in relation to the interior architecture and the two female figures standing on the left. By altering our ordinary experience of scale, Tanning invites us into a world unlike the one we know: a realm of childhood dreams and nightmares where odd things happen, such as the strangely "alive" sunflower and the unexplained wind that lifts the hair of one figure. The title, *Eine Kleine Nachtmusik* ("A Little Night Music"), derives from a lighthearted piece of music by the eighteenth-century Austrian composer Wolfgang Amadeus Mozart, but ironically Tanning's scene exhibits a strange sense of dread.

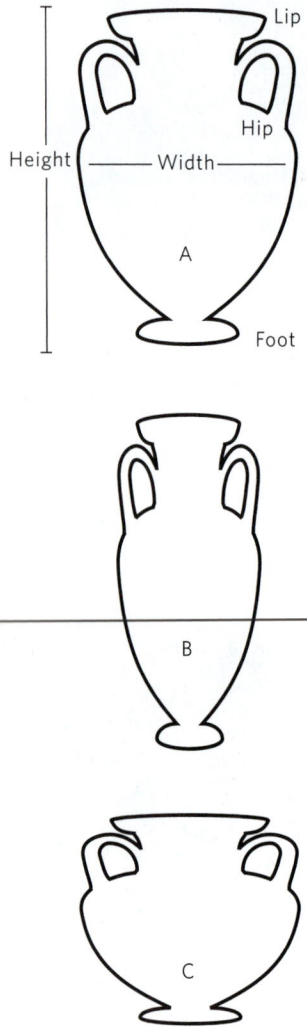

1.7.7 Examples of how proportion changes on vertical and horizontal axes

Proportion

The relationships between the sizes of different parts of a work make up its proportions. By controlling these size relationships an artist can enhance the expressive and descriptive characteristics of the work.

As size relationships change, proportions change. For example, **1.7.7** (A) shows the profile of a Greek vase. If we change the width (B) or the height (C), the overall proportions change. Each of these vase profiles communicates a different feeling simply because the ratio of height to width is different. When the width is reduced, the vase seems elegant and light. Reducing the height produces the opposite effect: the vase seems clumsier and weightier than the original profile (A).

For a two-dimensional work, the artist chooses an area, or **format**, on which to make a drawing, painting, print, or design. The format's dimensions—its height and width—dictate a great deal about what kind of image can be created. For example, a format that is only 2 in. tall and 10 in. across will require that the artist create an image that is short and wide. Artists must plan ahead and choose the format that best fits their intended image.

Human Proportion

As we saw when discussing **1.7.7**, carefully chosen proportion can make an art object seem pleasing to the eye. As it happens, the parts of a vase are given names based on the human body: the lip, hip, and foot. Just as the body of a vase can have agreeable or disagreeable proportions, the same is true of the human body.

In ancient Egypt, the palm of the hand was a unit of measurement (**1.7.8**). Six palm widths equaled a unit of measurement called a cubit. The height of an average man was estimated at 4 cubits or 24 palms: the proportion of the man's palm to the height of his body was therefore 24:1.

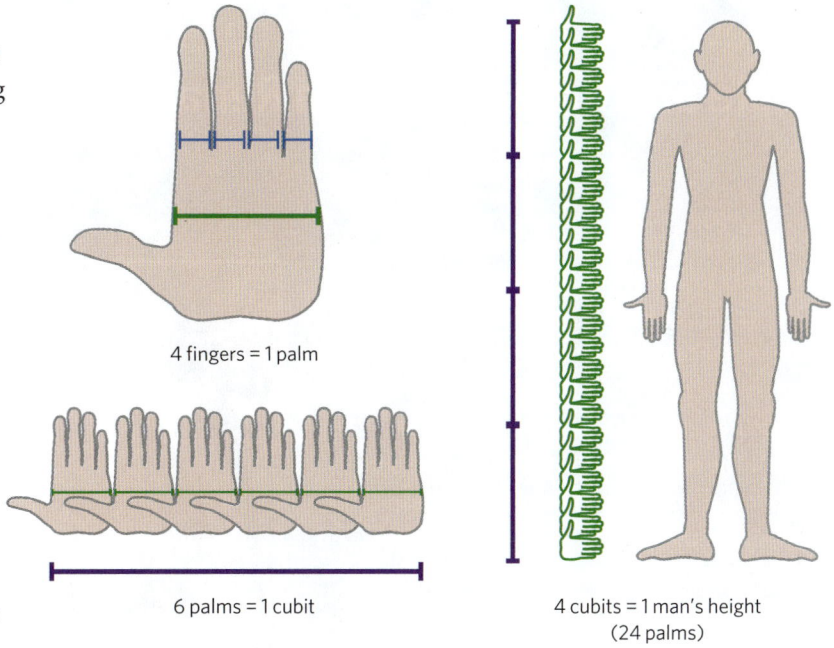

1.7.8 Ancient Egyptian system using the human hand as a standard unit of measurement

The ancient Greeks were especially interested in proportion. Greek mathematicians investigated, in the visual arts and in other art forms, such as music, the mathematical basis of beauty and of ideal proportions. The Greek sculptor Polykleitos wrote a treatise describing how to create a statue of a human being with ideal or perfect proportions. In the first century BCE the Roman writer Vitruvius wrote his book *On Architecture*, in which he claimed to set out the rules that Greeks and Romans applied to the design of architecture.

The Greeks sought an ideal of beauty in the principle of proportion. Figures made during the **Classical period** of Greek sculpture share similar proportions. To the Greeks, these proportions embodied the perfection of the gods. In contrast, fifteenth-century African sculptors preferred to show status and individuality. Pictured in **1.7.9** is a sculpture of the Oni of Ife in **cast** brass. The Oni, or Monarch, of the Ife Dynasty of the Yoruba people is shown standing in full regalia (ceremonial clothing and adornments). The Oni is the most powerful and important figure in this culture, yet his proportions here are neither realistic nor idealized. The head—about a quarter of the entire figure—is large; the Yoruba believe that the head is the seat of a divine power from whence a life source emanates to control personality and destiny. This figure, like Ife kings, represents a direct descendant of Oduduwa, the heroic leader whose children became the great leaders of the Yoruba. The facial features are idealized, suggesting that a personal heritage shapes one's destiny as a great leader. Many African sculptures exaggerate the head and face as a way to communicate status, destiny, and a connection to the spiritual. Both the Yoruba and the Greeks were concerned with creating a connection to the spiritual world, but African artists celebrated the importance of history (inheritance) and one's unique affiliation or office, while the Greeks sought an impersonal, ideal model.

The models used by the Greeks for calculating human proportion were later adopted by artists of ancient Rome and then by the artists of the **Renaissance**. Raphael used them in *The School of Athens* (see Gateway Box: Raphael, p. 146) to ensure that the figures in his composition had the ideal human proportion used in the ancient world.

Classical period: a period in the history of Greek art, c. 480–323 BCE
Cast: a sculpture or artwork made by pouring a liquid (for example molten metal or plaster) into a mold
Renaissance: a period of cultural and artistic change in Europe from the fourteenth to the seventeenth century

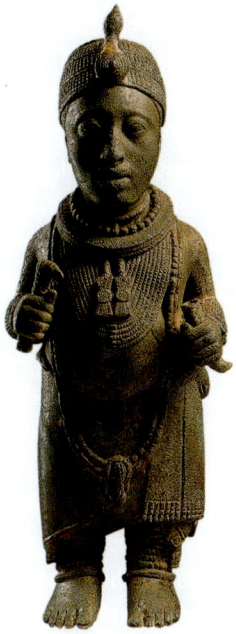

1.7.9 Nigerian Ife artist, Figure of Oni, early 14th–15th century. Brass with lead, height 18⅜". National Museum, Ife, Nigeria

Gateway to Art: Raphael, *The School of Athens*
Scale and Proportion in a Renaissance Masterpiece

The Italian painter Raphael's (1483–1520) sensitivity to proportion reflects his pursuit of perfection, an ideal of Renaissance artists. Raphael indicated the importance of his masterpiece by creating it on a magnificent scale: it measures 200 × 300 in. (16 ft. 8 in. × 25 ft.) (**1.7.10**). The figures inhabit a well-proportioned interior that makes them seem human despite the large size of the work.

An analysis of the dimensions of *The School of Athens* may provide a viewer with some insight into how proportion plays a role in the creation of a design. Because this work measures exactly 200 × 300 in., it can be visually subdivided, horizontally, into three one-hundred-inch increments from left to right (A). When the work is subdivided in this way, we can perceive some recognizable divisions in the composition. For example, the central vertical area that is highlighted by coffered arches in the ceiling falls into the middle third of the work. Another interesting correlation is made when we subdivide the work into thirds vertically (B). When we view the vertical divisions, it appears that the vast majority of figures in the foreground area (in front of the steps) are positioned in the bottom third of the design. Interestingly enough, the figures in the background (in the elevated section) fall just beneath one-third of the second vertical division (C) when we subdivide the central horizontal section.

These clear divisions seem intentional and lead one to assume that Raphael was working with a proportional system when he first designed *The School of Athens*. The format appears to reflect a system that some artists call the Rule of Thirds because it organizes the spatial area of a composition according to regular units of one- or two-thirds. The Rule of Thirds is used by artists, designers, photographers, and architects to provide pleasing proportional associations.

Within this carefully structured composition, Raphael further enhances the impression of Classical harmony and grace in the artwork by using perspective to give the architectural elements of the painting a sense of depth and to draw our eyes to the center of the work, in which he has also placed the two key figures of Greek philosophy, Plato (in the center, left) and Aristotle (center, right). Plato (c. 428–347 BCE) and Aristotle (384–322 BCE), the two greatest philosophers of ancient Greece whose thinking directly influenced the culture of the Renaissance, stand side by side. In Raphael's painting Plato points to the sky. He is the idealist who seeks truth in the world of ideas. Aristotle, who bases his thinking on the study of the material world (and who influenced the scientific method as we know it today) points to the ground. In this way, Raphael brilliantly deploys artistic techniques that perfectly express and complement his subject matter.

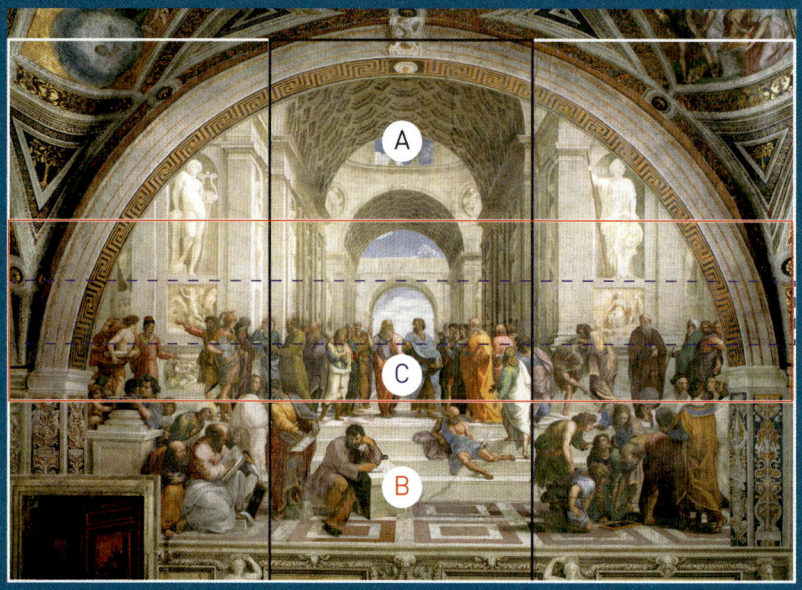

1.7.10 Raphael, *The School of Athens*, with overlaid diagram showing proportional structure

For the other Raphael Gateway boxes, see p. 90, p. 194, p. 470, and p. 617

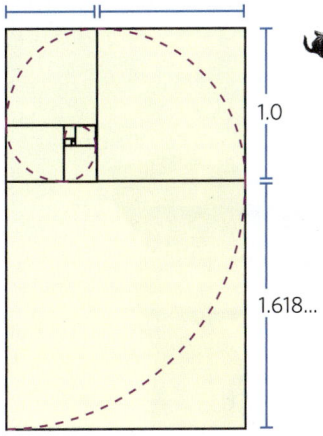

Golden Section
1:1.6180337...

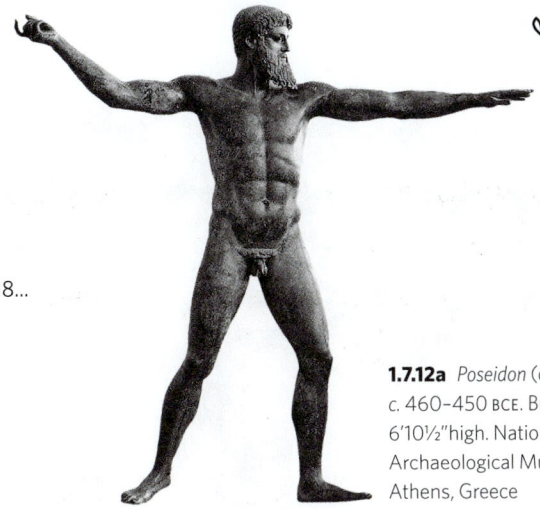

1.7.12a *Poseidon* (or *Zeus*), c. 460–450 BCE. Bronze, 6'10½"high. National Archaeological Museum, Athens, Greece

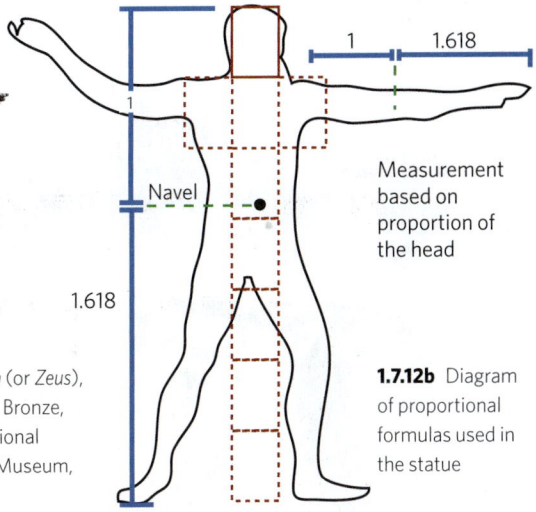

1.7.12b Diagram of proportional formulas used in the statue

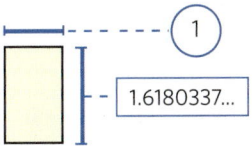

1.7.11 The Golden Section

Golden Section: a unique ratio of a line divided into two segments so that the sum of both segments (a + b) is to the longer segment (a) as the longer segment (a) is to the shorter segment (b). The result is 1:1.618

The Golden Section

The Greeks' interest in the use of mathematical formulas to determine perfect proportions has fascinated artists ever since. One of the best-known formulas is what has become known since the Renaissance as the **Golden Section** (**1.7.11**) (also referred to as the Golden Mean or Golden Ratio), a proportional ratio of 1:1.618, which occurs in many natural objects. It turns out that real human bodies do not have exactly these proportions, but when the ratio 1:1.618 is applied to making statues, it gives naturalistic results. It is likely that Greek sculptors used much simpler methods than the Golden Section to calculate the proportions of their sculptures, but the resulting proportions are often very close to the Golden Section. The sculpture of Poseidon (some art historians say it is Zeus) is a famous example (**1.7.12a**). Poseidon, a Greek god, had to be portrayed with perfect proportions. The Greek sculptor applied a conveniently simple ratio, using the head as a standard measurement. In **1.7.12a** and **1.7.12b** you can see that the body is three heads wide by seven heads high.

Proportional Ratios

Artists have learned other ways to apply proportional formulas to organize their compositions and ensure that their work is visually interesting. One such technique is known as "Golden Rectangles," because it is based on a succession of rectangles, nesting inside each other, based on the 1:1.618 proportions of the Golden Section. The shorter side of the outer rectangle becomes the longer side of the smaller rectangle inside it, and so on. The result is an elegant spiral shape. In 1858 the English photographer Henry Peach Robinson (1830–1901), one of the great innovators of the photographic arts, used this idea to compose a photograph titled *Fading Away* (**1.7.13a** and **1.7.13b**). Robinson was well known for

1.7.13a (below, left) Henry Peach Robinson, *Fading Away*, 1858. Combination albumen print, 9½ × 15½". George Eastman House, Rochester, New York

1.7.13b (below, right) Proportional analysis of the photograph

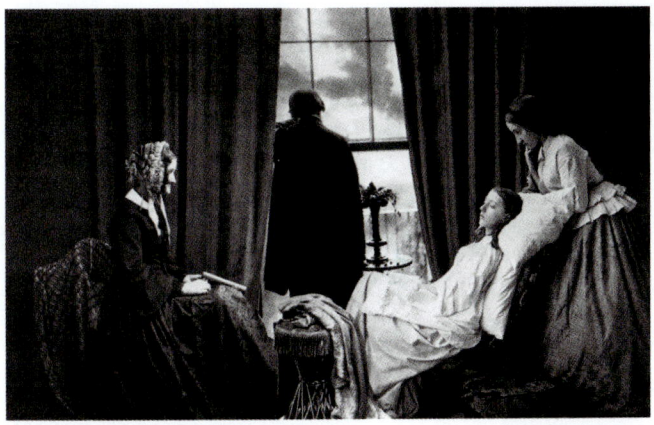

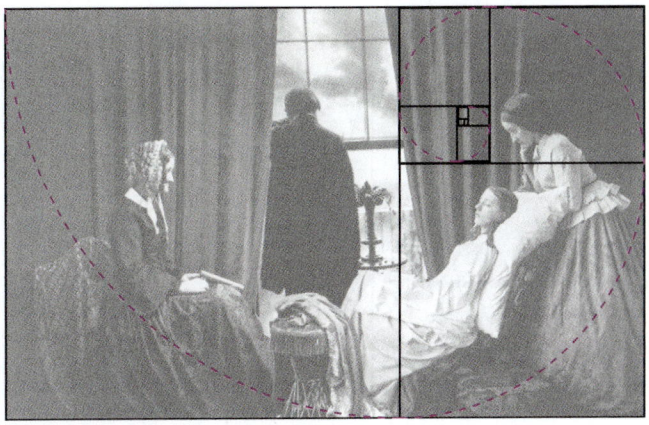

1.7.14a Iktinos and Kallikrates, Parthenon, 447–432 BCE, Athens, Greece

his work in fusing many different **negatives** to create a new image. This image shows his attention to the coordinated ratios in artistic composition. Notice how the right-hand drape divides the photograph into two Golden Rectangles and how the spiral draws our eye to the dying young woman.

The Greeks applied their proportional systems to architecture as well as to sculpture. By applying the idealized rules of proportion for the human body to the design of the Parthenon, a temple of the goddess Athena, the Greeks created a harmonious design. As it happens, the proportions correspond quite closely to the Golden Section (**1.7.14a**). The vertical and horizontal measurements work together to create proportional harmony (**1.7.14b**).

1.7.14b The use of the Golden Section in the design of the Parthenon

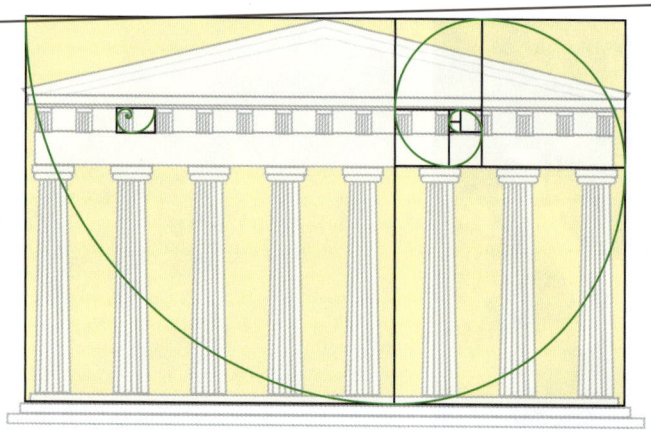

Negative: a reversed image, in which light areas are dark and dark areas are light (opposite of a positive)

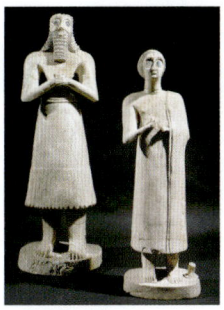

1.10.5 Votive Figures, Temple of Abu (Tell Asmar), Iraq, *c.* 2700 BCE, p. 175

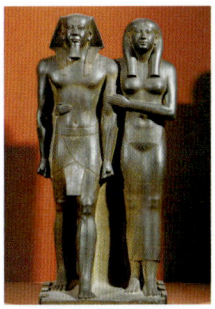

4.9.3b *Menkaure and His Wife, Queen Khamerernebty*, Egypt, *c.* 2520 BCE, p. 665

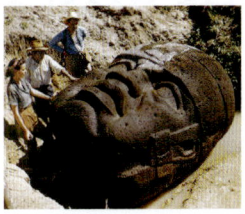

3.4.8 Colossal Olmec head, 1500–400 BCE, p. 434

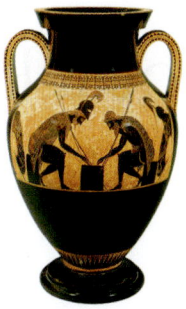

3.1.26 Exekias, amphora with Achilles and Ajax playing dice, *c.* 530 BCE, p. 383

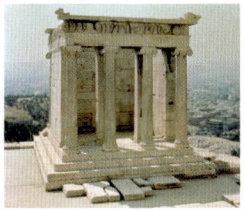

2.5.9 Kallikrates, Temple of Athena Nike, Athens, Greece, *c.* 421–415 BCE, p. 264

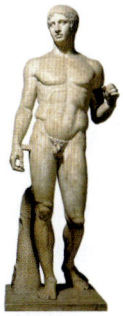

3.1.29 Polykleitos, *Doryphoros* (Roman version), 120–50 BCE, p. 384

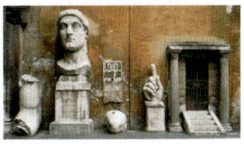

4.6.10 Remnants of colossal statue of Constantine, 325–26 CE, p. 635

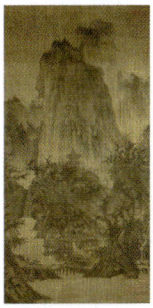

1.3.10 Li Cheng (attrib.), *A Solitary Temple Amid Clearing Peaks*, *c.* 960–1127, p. 82

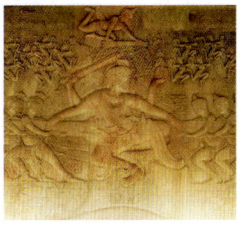

3.3.27 *Vishnu Churning the Ocean of Milk*, Angkor Wat, p. 427

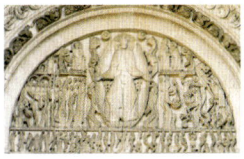

4.2.11 Gislebertus, *The Last Judgment*, *c.* 1120–35, p. 585

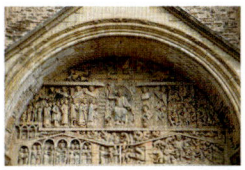

3.2.24 Tympanum of the west portal of Sainte-Foy, Conques, *c.* 1130–46, p. 406

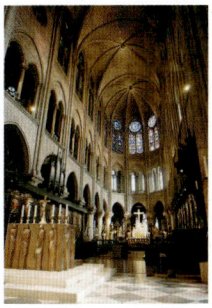

4.1.1 Notre Dame Cathedral, Paris, France, 1163–1250, p. 565

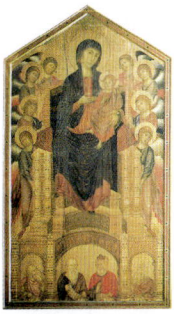

3.2.27 Cimabue, *Virgin and Child Enthroned*, *c.* 1280, p. 408

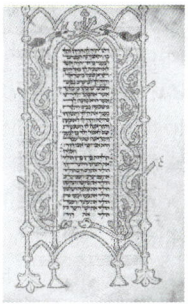

1.1.6a Franco-German hand, *Pentateuch*, 13th–14th century, p. 47

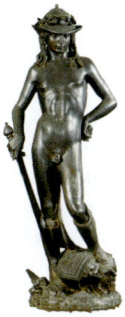

3.6.22 Donatello, *David*, *c.* 1430, p. 480

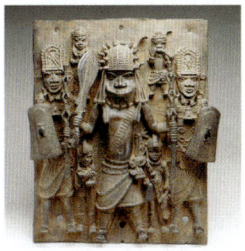

4.7.8 Benin plaque with warrior and attendants, 16th–17th century, p. 644

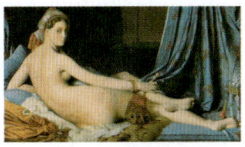

1.10.8 Jean-Auguste-Dominique Ingres, *Grande Odalisque*, 1814, p. 179

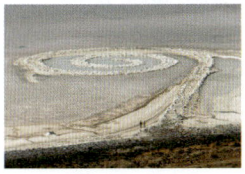

2.4.16 Robert Smithson, *Spiral Jetty*, 1969–70, p. 252

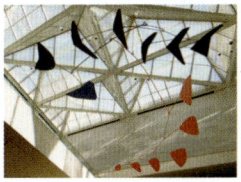

1.5.10 Alexander Calder, *Untitled*, 1976, p. 119

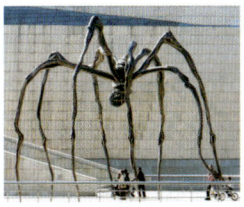

1.2.16 Louise Bourgeois, *Maman*, 1999 (cast 2001), p. 71

1.8 Focal Point and Emphasis

Emphasis: the principle of drawing attention to particular content in a work
Principles: the principles, or "grammar" of art—contrast, unity, variety, balance, scale, proportion, focal point, emphasis, pattern, and rhythm—describe the ways the elements of art are arranged in an artwork
Focal point: the center of interest or activity in a work of art, often drawing the viewer's attention to the most important element
Elements of art: the basic vocabulary of art—line, shape, form, volume, mass, texture, value (lightness/darkness), space, color, and motion and time
Subordination: the opposite of emphasis; it draws our attention away from particular areas of a work
Composition: the overall design or organization of a work
Line: a mark, or implied mark, between two endpoints
Implied line: a line not actually drawn but suggested by elements in the work
Contrast: a drastic difference between such elements as color or value (lightness/darkness) when they are presented together

When we emphasize something, we draw attention to it. This is a valuable part of communication that allows us to set some things apart. In art, **emphasis** is the **principle** by which an artist draws attention to particular content.

An entire work, a broad area within a work of art, multiple areas, and even specific points can be emphasized. The term **focal point** can be used both to describe a particular place of visual emphasis in a work of art or design, and to refer to another of the principles of art which, similarly to emphasis, is a way of highlighting certain locations in a work.

An artist can emphasize focal points through the use of line, implied line, value, color—in fact, any of the **elements of art** can help to focus our interest on specific areas. In a way that is similar to the effect of the bull's-eye on a target, focal points concentrate our attention. Even though our field of vision is fairly wide, at any given moment we can focus our vision only on a small area. The physiology of vision underlies the principle of focal point.

The opposite of emphasis is **subordination**: subordination draws our attention away from certain areas of a work. Artists choose carefully—in both two- and three-dimensional works—which areas to emphasize or subordinate in order to heighten the impact of their artworks.

Focal point and emphasis usually accentuate concepts, themes, or ideas the artist wants to express: they signal what the artwork is about.

Focal Point

Focal point is a tool that artists use to give specific emphasis to an important symbol, event, or distinguishing feature in a work. In any **composition**, a focal point is the place in an area of emphasis to which the artist draws our eye. He or she can do so by using **line**, **implied line**, or **contrast**. These techniques focus our gaze on that point in the work. We can see an intensely dramatic use of focal point in Artemisia Gentileschi's ferocious painting, *Judith Decapitating Holofernes* (**1.8.3**, see Gateway Box: Gentileschi, p. 152).

Directing the viewer's gaze to a specific location in a work of art is especially important when the subject of the painting, and its purpose, involve a hierarchy that must be observed. In the Dutch artist Dieric Bouts's (1415–1475) painting *The Coronation of the Virgin Mary* (**1.8.1**), it is critical that the viewer's gaze is drawn to a particular point in the design. As the artist, it was Bouts's responsibility to highlight the Virgin Mary even when she was in the presence of the Holy Trinity: God the Father, Jesus, and the Holy Spirit (pictured here as a dove). Bouts, who lived at a time when great piety was an essential part of life, is able to render the Holy Trinity with appropriate reverence, but at the same time skillfully focus attention on Mary, who is being crowned in the foreground. The artist does this by orienting the eyes of all in attendance on the Virgin, who is centrally placed with a light oval shape behind her head. Although the composition features many heads,

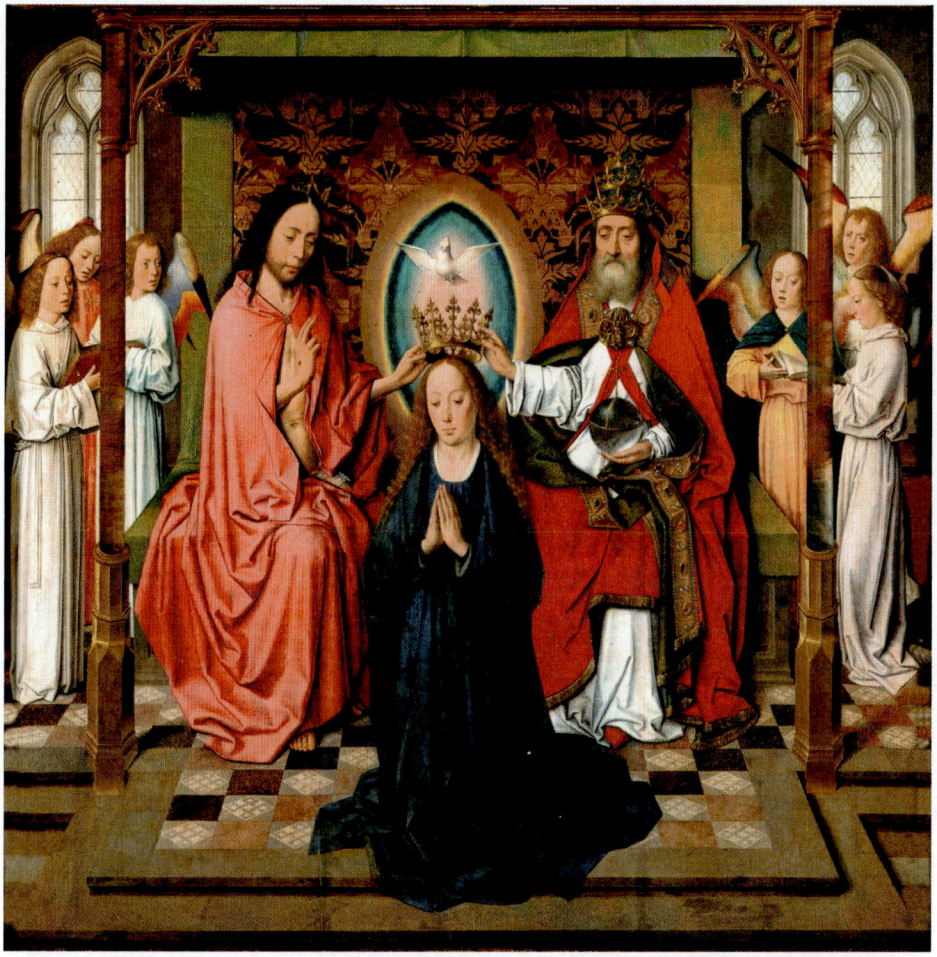

1.8.1 Dieric Bouts (the Elder), *The Coronation of the Virgin Mary*, 1455/60. Tempera on oak panel, approximately 32⅞ × 33½". Akademie der Bildenden Künste, Vienna, Austria

it is clear to where the viewer's attention is being beckoned. Mary's face, with eyes cast downward in humble respect, is framed by the crown above her head and her folded hands below, and the dove hovering over her provides a further visual clue about where we should look. In this way Bouts invites the viewer to share in this majestic, solemn, and otherworldly event.

In his painting *The Fall of Icarus*, Marc Chagall (1887–1985) draws attention to, and illustrates, a critical moment from a haunting story from Greek mythology (**1.8.2**). Icarus and his father Daedalus had been imprisoned on the island of Crete by its ruler, Minos. In order to escape, Daedalus fashioned two sets of wings from feathers and wax. As father and son flew away from their prison, Icarus became overly exuberant. Although his father had warned him not to, Icarus, recklessly enjoying his new wings, flew too high and close to the sun. The wax in his wings melted, and he fell to his death in the sea below. In Chagall's version, Icarus is

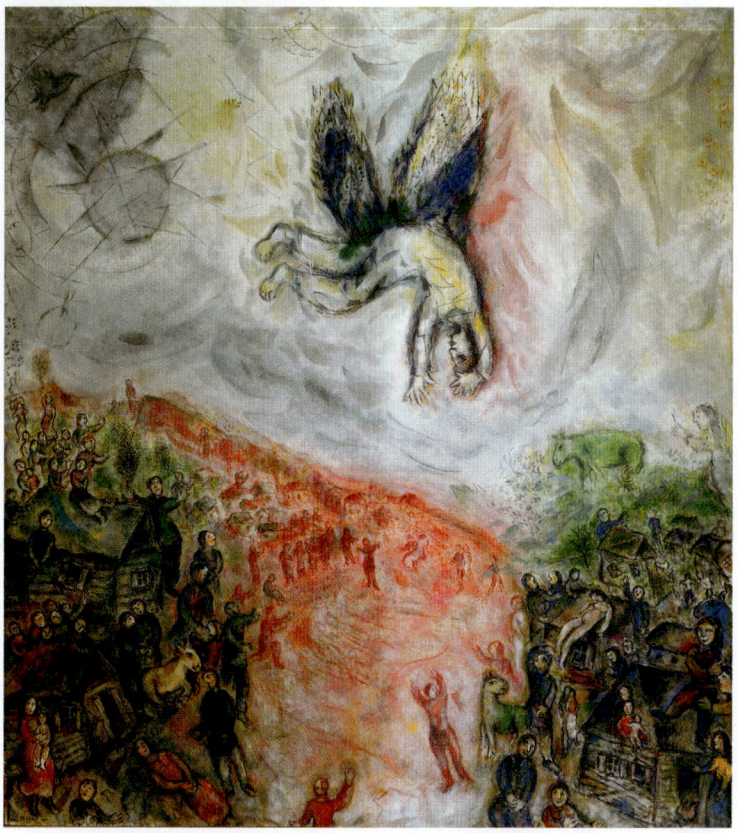

1.8.2 Marc Chagall, *The Fall of Icarus*, 1975. Oil on canvas, 6'11⅞" × 6'6". Musée National d'Art Moderne, Centre Georges Pompidou, Paris, France

Gateway to Art: Gentileschi, *Judith Decapitating Holofernes*

Using Focal Point for Dramatic Emphasis

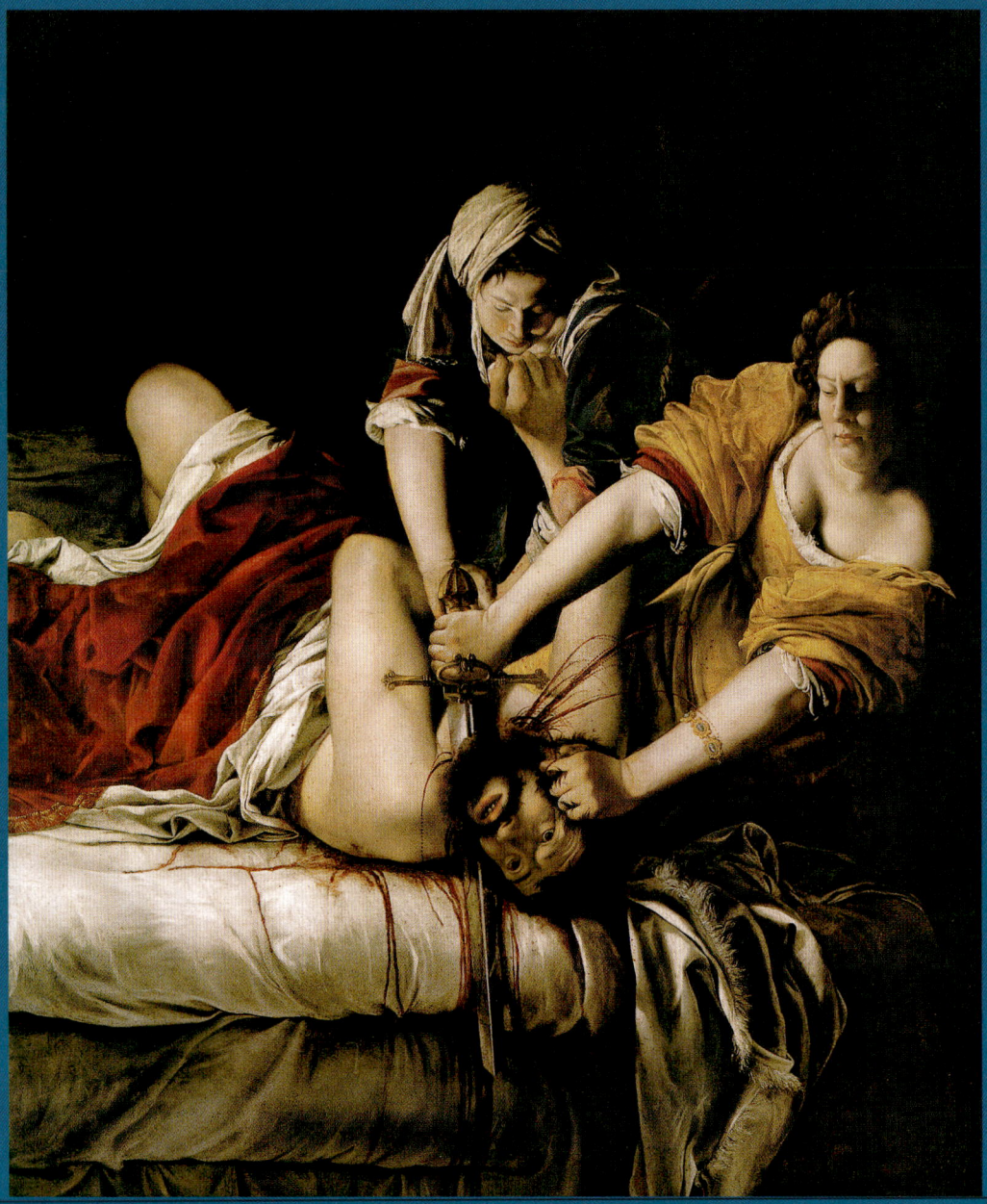

1.8.3 Artemisia Gentileschi, *Judith Decapitating Holofernes*, *c.* 1620. Oil on canvas, 6′6⅜″ × 5′3¾″. Uffizi Gallery, Florence, Italy

Artists often take advantage of the strength of a single focal point to force us to give our attention to the crux or pivot of the work. Although a composition can have more than one focal point, the Italian Baroque painter Artemisia Gentileschi (1593–*c.* 1656) uses just one in her *Judith Decapitating Holofernes* (**1.8.3**). Through Gentileschi's use of directional line and contrasting **values**, we are drawn irresistibly to the point where the climax of the story is unfolding.

Bright light emphasizes Judith's arms and those of her maidservant (visually connected to the sword itself) as they stretch toward the dark values of their victim's head. The light values of the five bare arms create strong directional lines that lead to the focal point where blood spurts from the violent attack on Holofernes' neck. This double emphasis (contrast of values and directional line) freezes our stare upon the fatal blow, even as it obscures it in darkness.

For the other Gentileschi Gateway boxes, see p. 219, p. 478, p. 519, and p. 681

the focal point, distinctly set apart from the light sky not only by his position at the top and center of the work, but also by the use of bold red, yellow, and blue **primary colors** to depict the flailing figure. Using the contrast between the brightly colored wings and the dull, pale-gray sky isolates and draws attention directly to the poor boy, whose futile fluttering is captured in Chagall's energetic brushstrokes. Even though there are many figures in this work, the main emphasis is clearly on the tumbling one in the sky. The Icarus story has proved a compelling one for artists and writers. Four centuries before Chagall created his painting, Pieter Bruegel the Elder (*c.* 1525/30–1569) took a very different approach to depicting Icarus's plunge into the sea (see p. 155).

Emphasis

Sometimes an artist is interested in emphasizing an entire work in its wholeness. When he or she wants to do this, the artist will intentionally create a composition that does not have a dominant area of emphasis. For example, *Untitled (Ocean)* by Latvian-born American artist Vija Celmins (b. 1938) has an overall field of undulating value changes with no singular point that the eye is drawn to (**1.8.4**). Celmins's parents brought her to the United States when she was ten years old, eventually settling in Indianapolis, Indiana. In the work *Untitled (Ocean)*, Celmins creates a photorealistic drawing of the ocean surface, drawing attention to the vast and repetitive

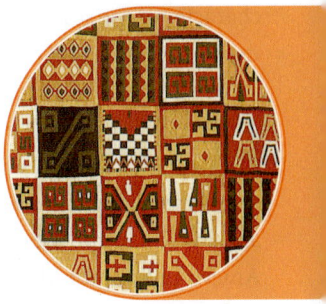

We can also see overall emphasis in the design of this Inca tunic: see **3.4.6, p. 433**

Value: the lightness or darkness of a plane or area
Primary colors: three basic colors from which all others are derived

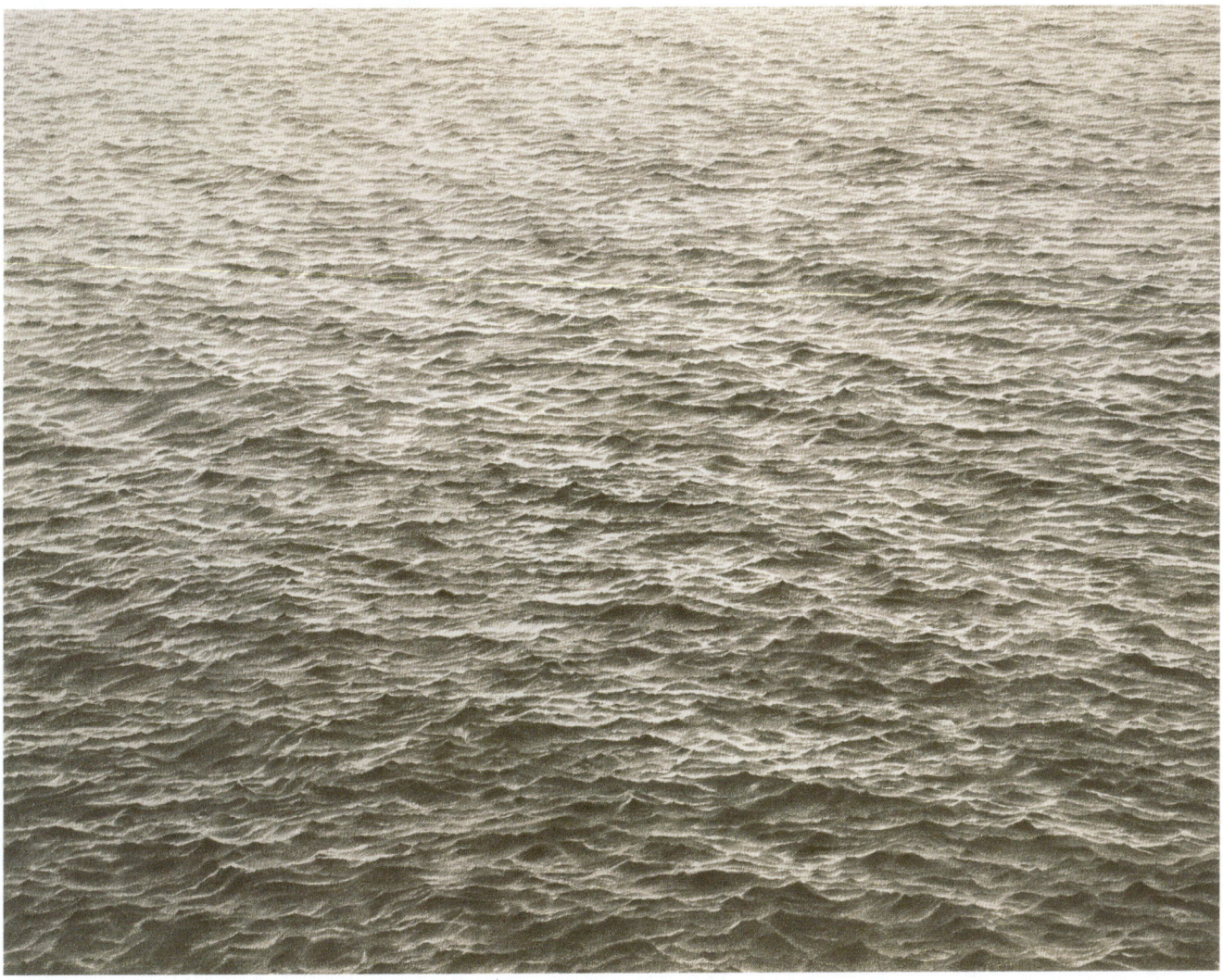

1.8.4 Vija Celmins, *Untitled (Ocean)*, 1977. Graphite on acrylic ground on paper, 10 × 12⅞". San Francisco Museum of Modern Art

character of the sea. The resulting effect allows us to immerse ourselves in the work, as if it were a place for reflective meditation.

Emphasis can also be used to draw attention to a large portion of a work. Sometimes an artist wants the emphasis to encompass a significant area, but not quite the entire surface. The African American sculptor Martin Puryear (b. 1941) makes connections between a nineteenth-century trading company and African masks in his work *C.F.A.O.* (**1.8.5**). The Compagnie Française de L'Afrique Occidentale, or CFAO, was a company that connected Europe to ports in Sierra Leone in Africa, where Puryear also worked as a member of the Peace Corps. Using vertical and horizontal axes made of pine strips that fill the **background**, all supported by a discarded wheelbarrow, Puryear frames our attention on the elongated white shape in the center of the work. The wheelbarrow and the pine structure, by being more neutral and having more geometric lines, both support and highlight by contrast the large area of emphasis—the white, blank, mask-like shape in the center. Puryear created the mask to mimic the designs of the Fang tribe of Gabon, West Africa, and the piece is intended to recall French colonialism in the region by associating it with the CFAO. It invites the viewer to lift the wheelbarrow and peer through the two eye-holes in the mask, encouraging him or her to see things from the point of view of, or assume the role of, the colonized instead of the colonist.

Emphasis can occur broadly over a large section when there are multiple elements within a work but where no one element dominates. For example, in a print from the series *The Life of John Brown* by the African American artist Jacob Lawrence (1917–2000), each of the twelve figures shown (one facing away from the viewer) attracts enough attention so that none stands out as most significant (**1.8.6**). The John Brown to whom Lawrence refers in the title is the Civil War-era abolitionist who believed that slavery could be eradicated only through armed insurrection. Brown is not depicted in the image, but the solemn poses of the figures imply homage to this anti-slavery militant who was hanged for leading a violent revolt

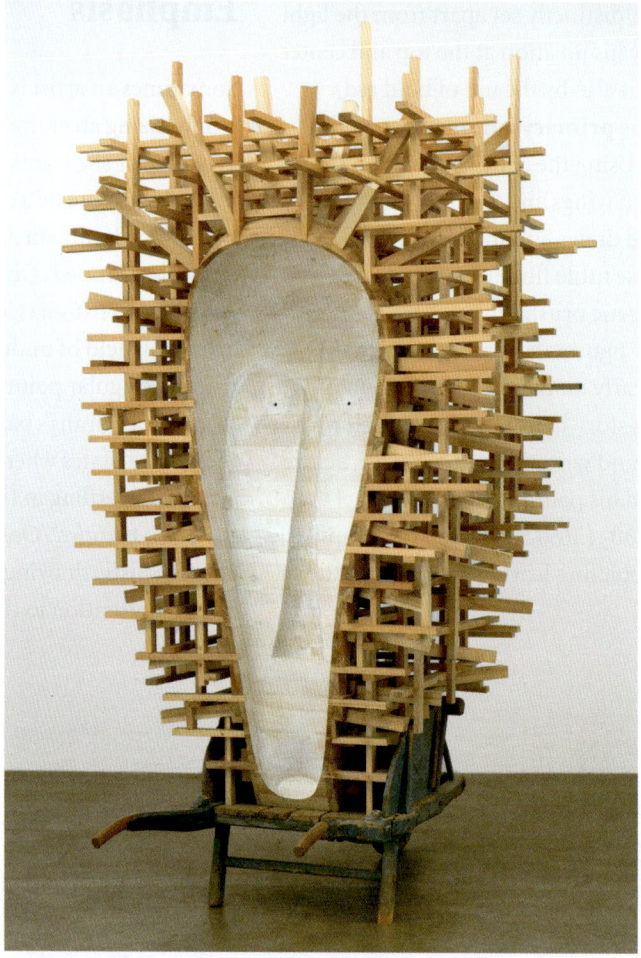

1.8.5 Martin Puryear, *C.F.A.O.*, 2006–7. Painted and unpainted pine and found wheelbarrow, 8'4¾" × 6'5½" × 5'1". MoMA, New York

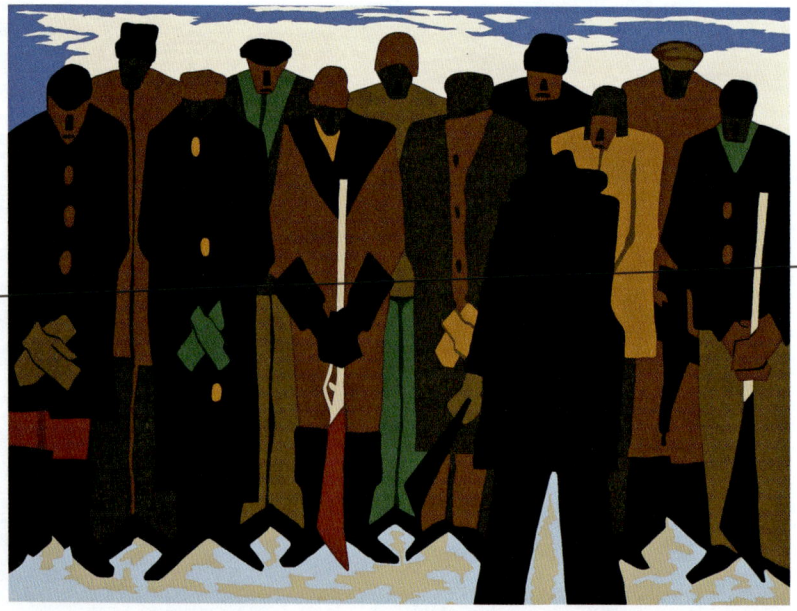

1.8.6 Jacob Lawrence, "John Brown Remained a Full Winter in Canada, Drilling Negroes for His Coming Raid on Harpers Ferry (no. 17)," from *The Life of John Brown* (22 prints), 1977. Gouache and tempera on paper, 20 × 14"

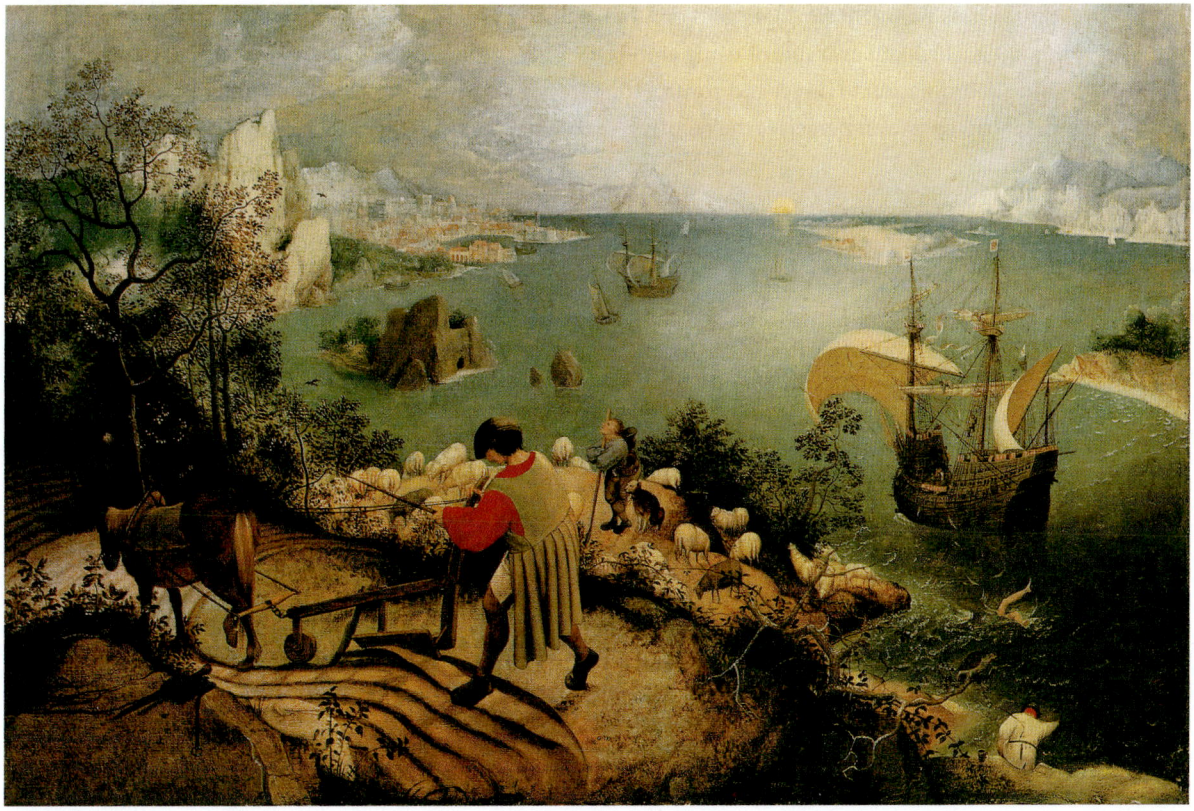

against the US government at Harpers Ferry, West Virginia. In the print, Lawrence's visual balancing of the figures is complemented by his creation of separate areas of emphasis, for example the figure on the right in the yellow coat is immediately emphasized in contrast to the dark figure in the foreground, as is the white rifle held by the figure in brown on the left side of the work. These areas are also evenly balanced by size and contrasting values, unifying all of the parts into a larger whole with no strong single focal point. This methodical counter-balancing is critical to the composition because it implies equality amongst the men, thus subtly supporting the ideals for which John Brown fought and died.

Subordination

Subordination is the use of emphasis to draw the viewer's attention away from a particular part of a composition. We are so attuned to looking for emphasized areas and focal points that some artists can use this technique to redirect our attention cleverly from one area of an artwork to another. Subordination does not emphasize, but involves deliberately reducing the impact of certain details.

In direct contrast to Marc Chagall, who in his painting wanted to place the attention of the viewer on Icarus as he fell to Earth (**1.8.3**, p. 151), in the work *Landscape with the Fall of Icarus*, by Flemish artist Pieter Bruegel the Elder, the painter deliberately diverts our attention so that we scarcely notice Icarus plunging to his doom (**1.8.7**): a fine example of subordination. In Bruegel's version of this story, our attention is drawn first to the figure in the foreground, in his eye-catching scarlet shirt, plowing his field, unaware of the tragedy. As the painting's title suggests, several other areas of emphasis—the tree on the left, the sunset, the fanciful ships—also capture our interest. We hardly notice poor Icarus, whose legs are disappearing into the sea just in front of the large ship on the right, his feet barely distinguishable from the whitecaps and the tiny seabirds circling near the vessel. Because Bruegel has gone to such lengths to draw attention away from the plight of his subject, art historians think he is illustrating the Flemish proverb, "No plough stands still because a man

1.8.7 Pieter Bruegel the Elder, *Landscape with the Fall of Icarus*, c. 1555–58. Oil on canvas, mounted on wood, 29 × 44⅛". Musées Royaux des Beaux-Arts de Belgique, Brussels, Belgium

Background: the part of a work depicted furthest from the viewer's space, often behind the main subject matter

Color: the optical effect caused when reflected white light of the spectrum is divided into separate wavelengths
Rhythm: the regular or ordered repetition of elements in the work
Outline: the outermost line or implied line of an object or figure, by which it is defined or bounded
Woodcut: a relief print made from a design cut into a block of wood

dies." Or, as we might say, "Life goes on." Either way, it is a brilliant example of using emphasis and subordination to direct and control the way in which the viewer perceives the painting.

Focal Point and Emphasis in Action

Artists can use direction, dramatic contrasts, and placement relationships to organize the elements in a work and draw our attention to areas of emphasis and to focal points.

Contrast

Artists look to create effects of contrast by positioning elements next to one another that are very different, for example areas of different value, **color**, or size. Value is an effective and frequently used means of creating emphasis and focal point. It also has the advantage that it can be used in subtle ways. In *The Funeral of St. Bonaventure*, a painting by Spanish artist Francisco de Zurbarán (1598–1664), most of the lightest values are reserved for the clothing adorning the dead body of St. Bonaventure (**1.8.8**). They create a central focal point that stands out in contrast to the surrounding dark values. We are drawn to the whiteness (symbolic of Bonaventure's chaste and spotless reputation) before we look at the surrounding characters. Enough light value is distributed to the other figures to allow our eyes to be drawn away from Bonaventure's body, making the composition more interesting.

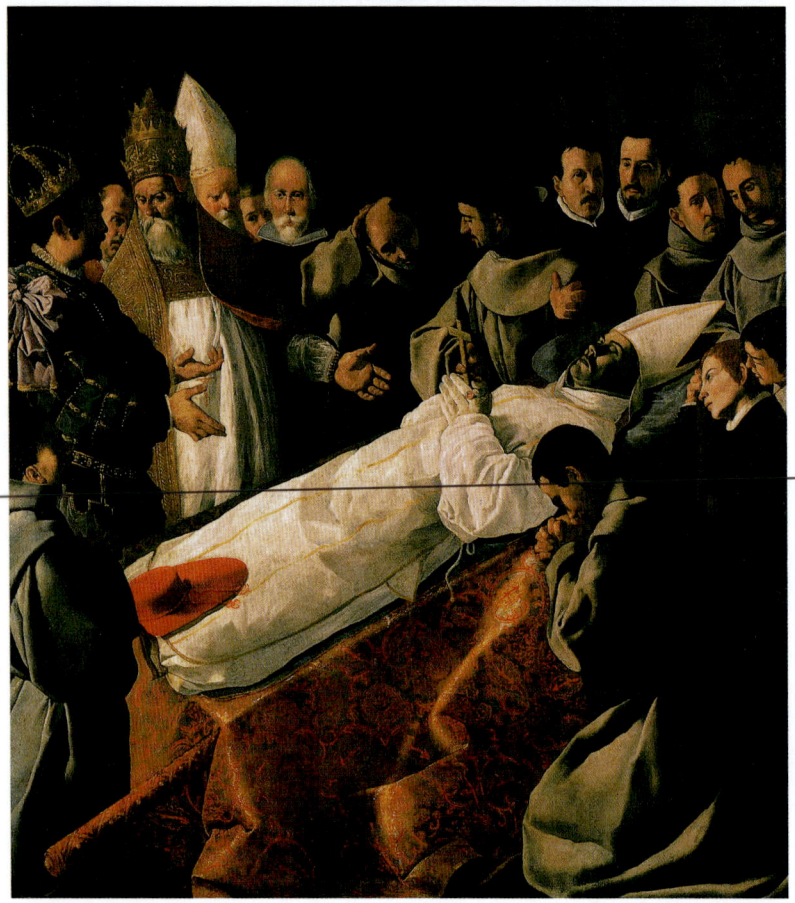

1.8.8 Francisco de Zurbarán, *The Funeral of St. Bonaventure*, 1629. Oil on canvas, 8'2" × 7'4". Musée du Louvre, Paris, France

Line

Line is an effective way to focus our attention in an artwork. In Mughal India (the period from 1526 until the mid-nineteenth century), a garden was considered a work of art, one that symbolized the promise of paradise. Zahir ud-Din Muhammad bin Omar Sheikh, nicknamed Babur, founded the Mughal empire in India when he conquered most of Central Asia and northern India. In **1.8.9**, the gardener/artist Babur is pointing to a feature that channels water in four directions. The life-giving properties of water and the four cardinal directions were important symbols of life and eternity. Because the garden was based on the perfect geometry of a square, it could be expanded an infinite number of times without disturbing the original plantings. In this image of the garden, water is the focal point, both conceptually and visually.

We tend to notice diagonal lines because they appear to be more visually active than either horizontal or vertical lines. The strong diagonal of the channel draws our attention to the water as it runs toward us. The central cross-shaped confluence of the waters in the middle of the garden becomes the focal point of the composition.

Placement

The placement of elements within a composition controls **rhythm** and creates multiple focal points. In the print "Riverside Bamboo Market, Kyo-bashi," the Japanese artist

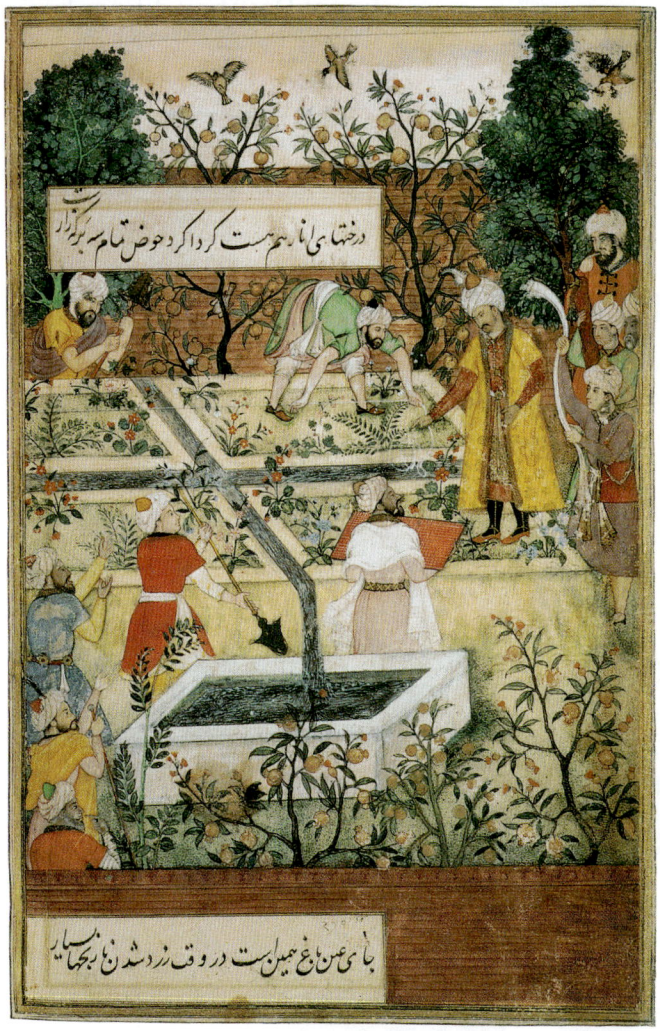

1.8.9 *The Emperor Babur Overseeing His Gardeners*, India, Mughal period, c. 1590. Tempera and gouache on paper, 8¾ × 5⅝". Victoria and Albert Museum, London, England

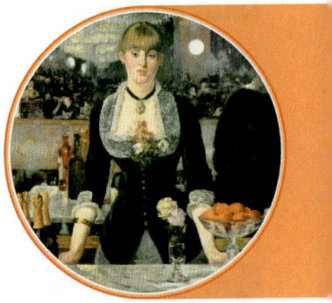

The placement of intriguing elements that surround the main figure creates multiple focal points in Édouard Manet's *A Bar at the Folies-Bergère*: see **4.5.11, p. 623**

Ando Hiroshige (1797–1858) has oriented three shapes; all of them are visually independent of each other (**1.8.10**). The positions of the moon, the bridge, and the figure in a boat form three separate focal points. Each shape commands our attention and draws more of our focus to the right side of the work. Even though the bridge is the largest shape, and so naturally catches our attention, the light value and hard geometry of the moon divert our gaze, and the moon becomes a secondary focal point. We look at the figure under the bridge because of its careful placement under the moon, and because it has a definite **outline** that contrasts strongly with the flat color of the water. The varying distances between the placements of the three focal points also create rhythm, which adds visual interest. Hiroshige, a master of **woodcut** printing, uses placement to emphasize specific points in the work and enliven the composition.

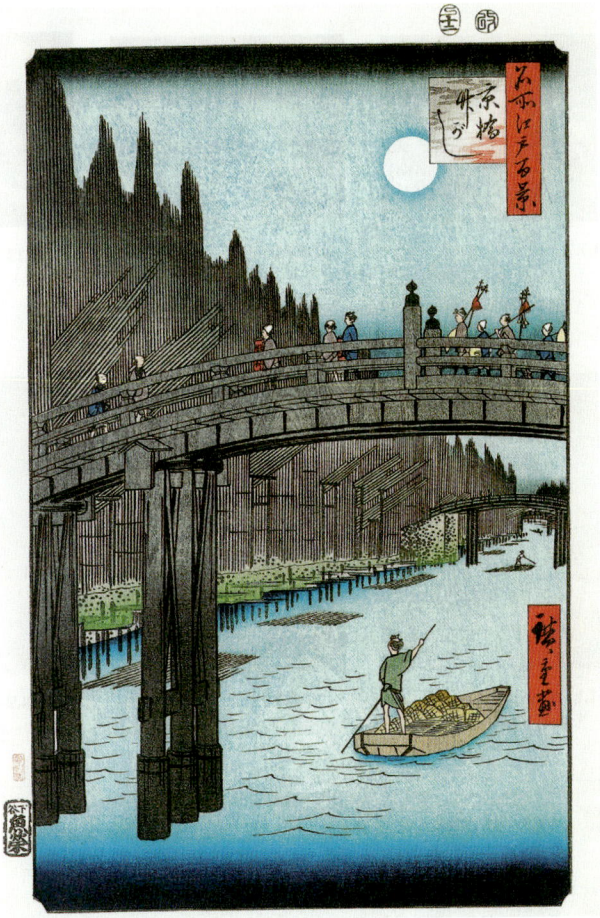

1.8.10 Ando Hiroshige, "Riverside Bamboo Market, Kyo-bashi," from *One Hundred Famous Views of Edo*, 1857. 15 × 10⅜". James A. Michener Collection, Honolulu Academy of Arts, Hawaii

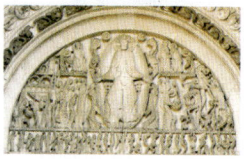

4.2.11 Gislebertus, *The Last Judgment*, c.1120–35, p. 585

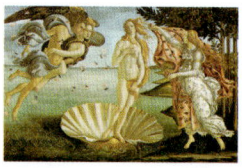

4.9.5 Sandro Botticelli, *The Birth of Venus*, c.1482–86, p. 666

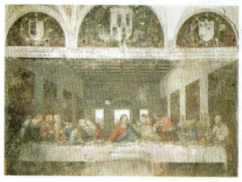

3.6.15 Leonardo da Vinci, *The Last Supper*, c.1497, p. 474

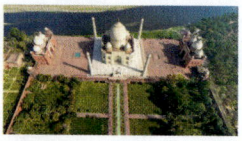

1.6.15a Ustad Ahmad Lahauri *et al.*, Taj Mahal, Agra, India, 1632–43, p. 136

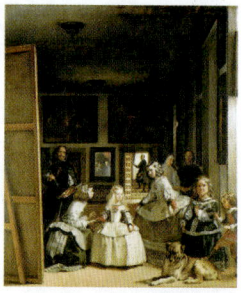

1.10.12a Diego de Silva y Velázquez, *Las Meninas*, c. 1656, p. 183

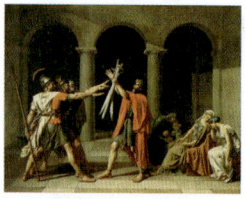

3.7.7 Jacques-Louis David, *The Oath of the Horatii*, 1784, p. 493

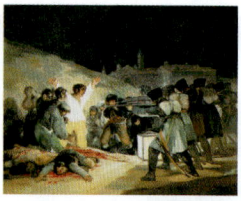

4.7.9 Francisco Goya, *The Third of May, 1808*, 1814, p. 645

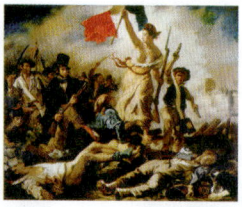

3.7.13 Eugène Delacroix, *Liberty Leading the People*, 1830, p. 497

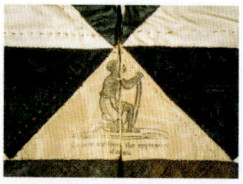

1.9.5b Deborah Coates, detail of quilt, Pennsylvania c. 1840–50, p. 161

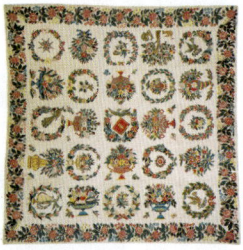

1.6.12 Album quilt, probably by Mary Evans, 1848, p. 133

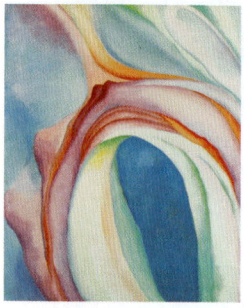

1.1.26 Georgia O'Keeffe, *Music–Pink and Blue II* 1919, p. 58

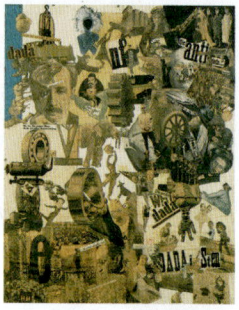

2.8.20 Hannah Höch, *Cut with the Kitchen Knife...*, 1919–20, p. 327

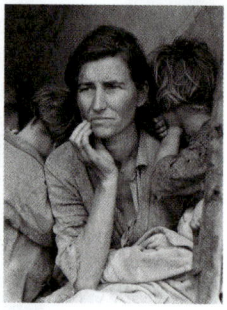

4.8.9 Dorothea Lange, *Migrant Mother*, 1936, p. 659

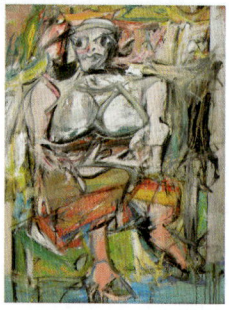

4.9.2 Willem de Kooning, *Woman I*, 1950–52, p. 664

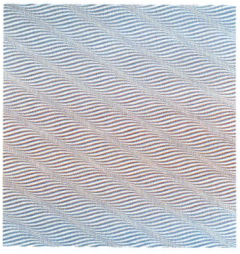

1.5.4 Bridget Riley, *Cataract 3*, 1967, p. 115

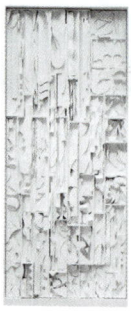

0.0.3 Louise Nevelson, *White Vertical Water*, 1972, p. 22

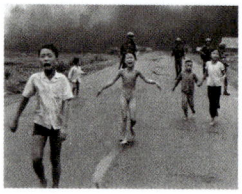

4.7.2 Nick Ut, *Vietnamese Girl Kim Phuc Running after Napalm Attack*, 1972, p. 639

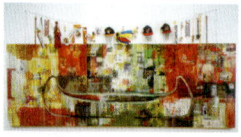

1.9.14 Jaune Quick-to-See Smith, *Trade...*, 1992, p. 168

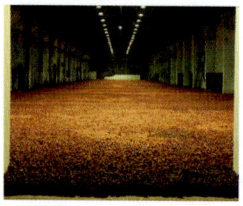

2.4.24b Antony Gormley, *Asian Field*, 2003, p. 257

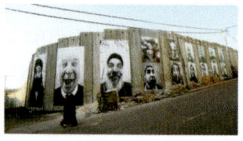

4.8.11 JR and Marco, *28 Millimeters, Face2Face*, 2007, p. 660

1.9 Pattern and Rhythm

Space: the distance between identifiable points or planes
Pattern: an arrangement of predictably repeated elements
Elements of art: the basic vocabulary of art—line, shape, form, volume, mass, texture, value (lightness/darkness), space, color, and motion and time
Unity: the imposition of order and harmony on a design
Rhythm: the regular or ordered repetition of elements in the work
Composition: the overall design or organization of a work
Shape: a two-dimensional area, the boundaries of which are defined by lines or suggested by changes in color or value
Value: the lightness or darkness of a plane or area
Color: the optical effect caused when reflected white light of the spectrum is divided into separate wavelengths
Contrast: a drastic difference between such elements as color or value (lightness/darkness) when they are presented together

Each day the sun rises and sets; we believe it will do so again tomorrow. Patterns and rhythms in nature help us make sense of the world. They express the order and predictability of our lives. Artists use pattern and rhythm to bring order to **space** and to create a dynamic experience of time.

When events recur, this creates a **pattern**. But other patterns are more regular, more predictable. In art, we can see patterns as the recurrence of an art **element**. In a work of art, the repetition of such patterns provides a sense of **unity**.

Rhythm arises through the repetition of pattern. It adds cohesiveness in artistic **composition** because it links elements together. Rhythm affects our vision as we study a work of art. The rhythm of a series of linked elements guides the movement of our eyes across and through a design. The artist can also use rhythm to add variety.

Pattern

The use of repetition in a work of art usually results in the creation of a pattern. These patterns are sometimes based on occurrences in nature, such as the regular repetition of fish scales, or the pattern created by the cracks that open as mud dries in the desert. Other patterns may be derived from the repeated shapes of mass-produced human-made objects, such as stacked tin cans or the warp and weft of woven cloth. Artists often create unity in works of art by repeatedly using a similar **shape**, **value**, or **color**, for example.

An artist can use repetition of a pattern to impose order on a work. But simple repetition can become more complex and make a work even more interesting when the pattern changes (see Gateway box: Maya Lintel, p. 162). Sometimes artists use alternating patterns to make a work more lively. The area covered by pattern is called the field; changes in the field can invigorate visual forms. The pattern in **1.9.1** shows a series of star shapes set on alternating black and white backgrounds on a rectangular field. The drastic difference in value combined with the active shape causes a visual vibration.

A variety of different colors and patterns enlivens work by the French painter Suzanne Valadon (1865–1938). In *The Blue Room*, she includes three **contrasting** patterns (**1.9.2**, p. 160). In the blue bed covering, in the lower portion

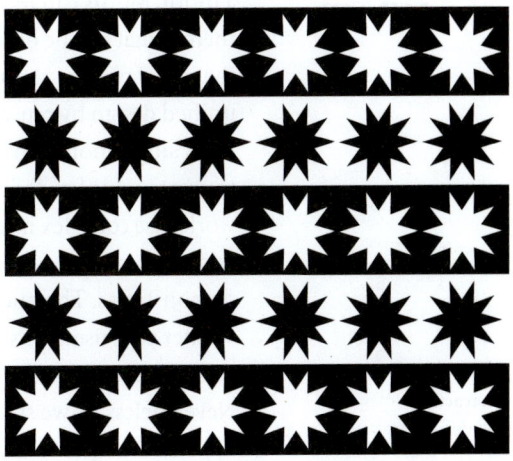

1.9.1 Vertical alternating pattern

1.9.2 Suzanne Valadon, *The Blue Room*, 1923. Oil on canvas, 35½ × 45⅝". Musée National d'Art Moderne, Centre Georges Pompidou, Paris, France

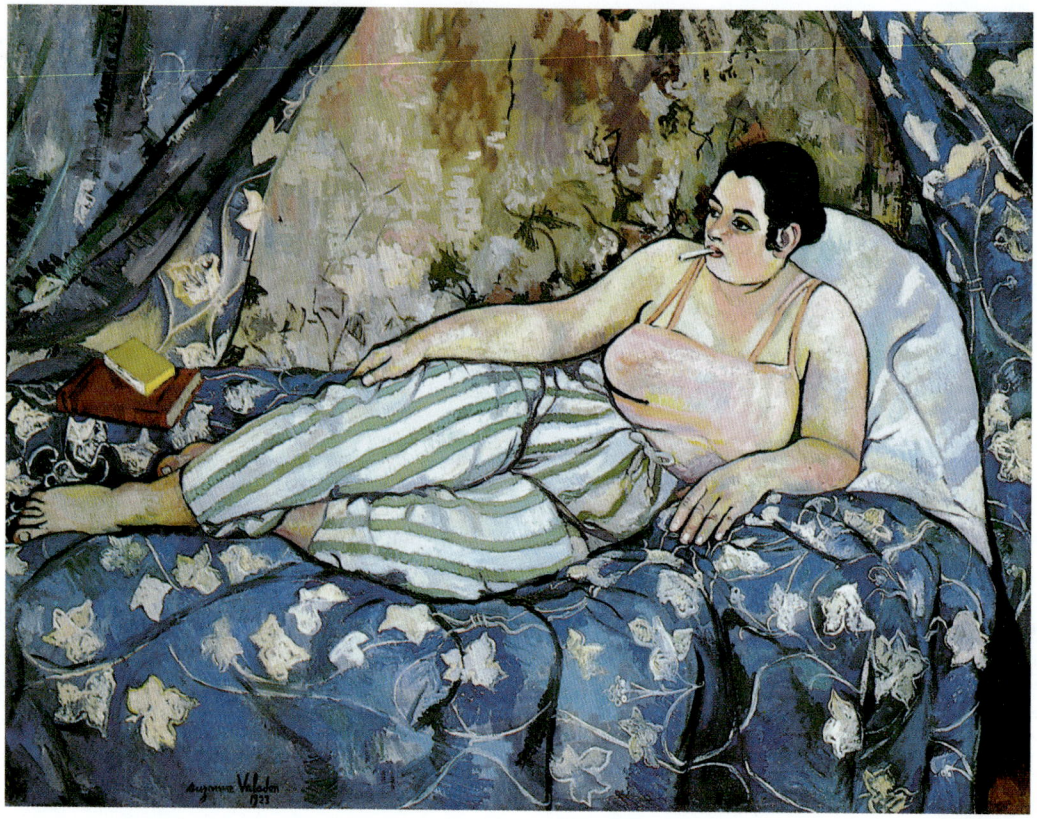

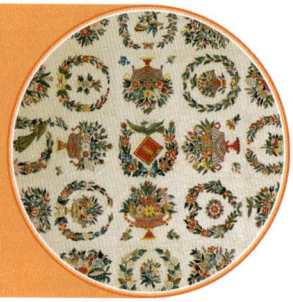

The artist has used pattern and rhythm to structure the floral forms in this nineteenth-century quilt from Baltimore: see **1.6.12, p.133**

of the painting, Valadon has used an organic pattern of leaves and stems. The green-and-white striped pattern in the woman's pajama bottoms dominates in direct contrast to the blue bed covering. Above the figure is a mottled pattern that again contrasts with the other two. The differences in these patterns energize the work.

Motif

A design repeated as a unit in a pattern is called a motif. Motifs can represent ideas, images, and themes that can be brought together through the use of pattern. An artist can create a strong unified design by repeating a motif.

A single motif can be interlaced with others to create complex designs. Many Islamic works use complex interlaced motifs, as this work created in seventeenth-century India demonstrates. The huqqa base (a huqqa is a water pipe used for smoking) in **1.9.3** may at first glance appear to use little repetition. Nevertheless, as we study the overall design we discover that elements, such as the flowers and leaves of the plants, recur at intervals. As this work shows, Islamic artists delight in the detail of pattern.

Motif is a common occurrence in traditional quilting. By unifying a series of simple patterns into a repeatable motif, a quilter could connect

Abstract: art imagery that departs from recognizable images of the natural world

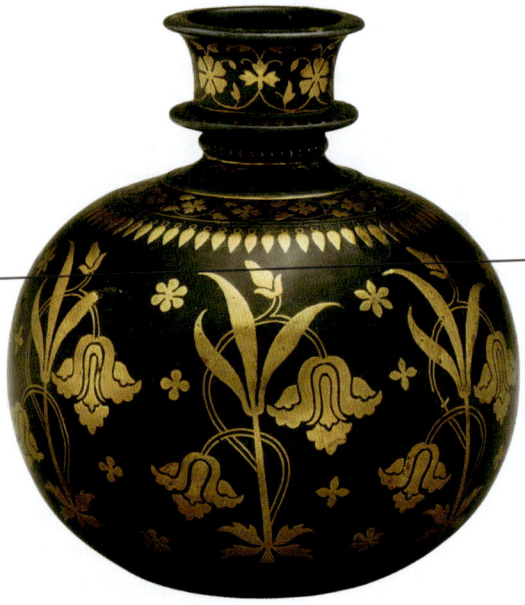

1.9.3 Huqqa base, India, Deccan, last quarter of 17th century. Bidri ware (zinc alloy inlaid with brass), 6⅞ × 6½". Metropolitan Museum of Art, New York

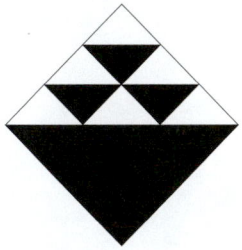

1.9.4 Diagram of block quilt pattern known as "Birds in the Air"

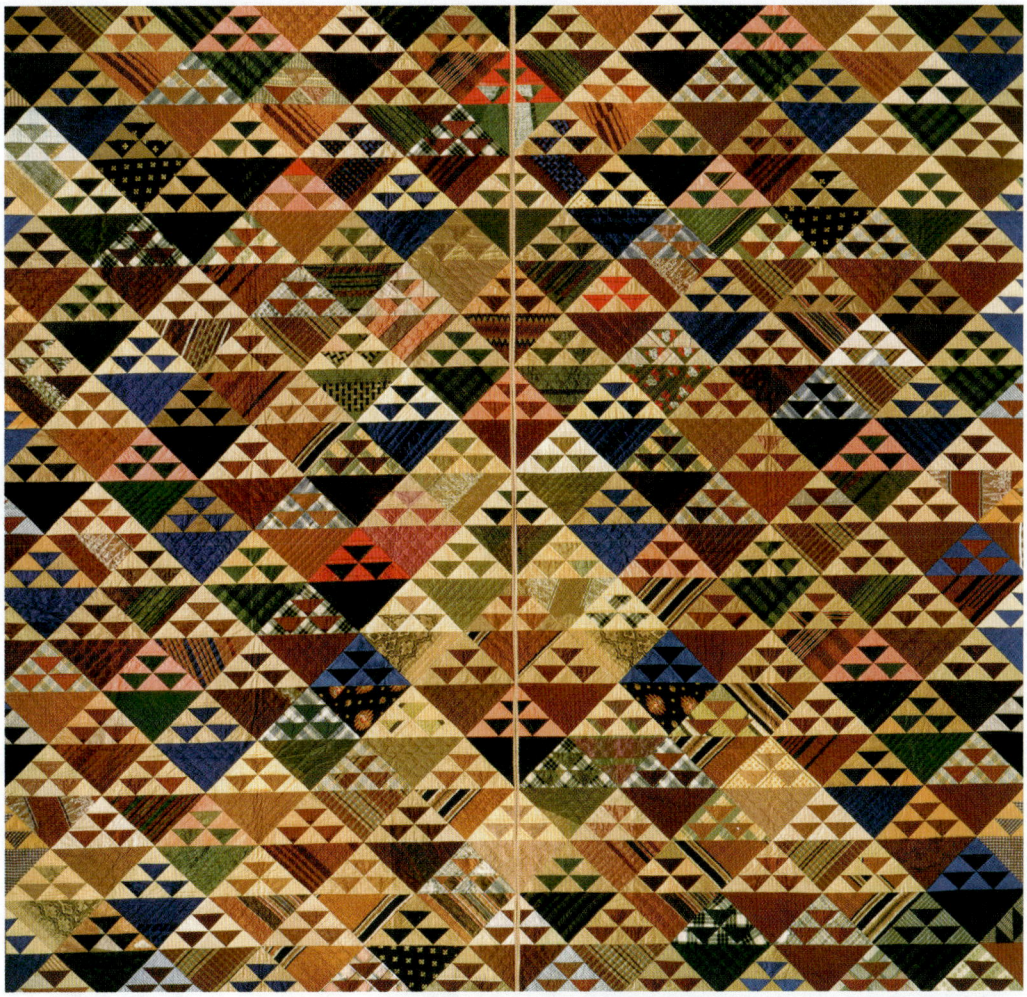

1.9.5a Deborah Coates, quilt, *c.* 1840–50. Pieced silk with stamp work, 96½ × 89". Heritage Center Museum: Lancaster Quilt and Textile Museum, Lancaster, Pennsylvania

a series of blocks into a cohesive design. One such traditional pattern, called "Birds in the Air" (**1.9.4**), was used as the integral component for a quilt design by the early American quilter Deborah Coates (1801–1888). Coates, the wife of the famed abolitionist (anti-slavery campaigner) Linley Coates, created "abolitionist quilts" to raise awareness and funding to free slaves. Such quilts as **1.9.5a** were sold at popular quilting fairs in northern cities, such as Philadelphia, and were often inscribed with messages similar to the one in the detail, "Deliver me from the oppression of man," in **1.9.5b**. The choice of "Birds in the Air" was probably because the design, which implies the freedom of birds to fly away at will, was especially appropriate to the anti-slavery cause.

The American artist Chuck Close (b. 1940) uses motif to unify his paintings. Close uses a repeated pattern of organic concentric rings set into a diamond shape as the basic building blocks for his large compositions. These motifs, which appear as **abstract** patterns when viewed closely, visually solidify into realistic portraits of the model. In his *Self-Portrait*, there is a distinct difference between a close-up view of the painting and the overall effect when we stand

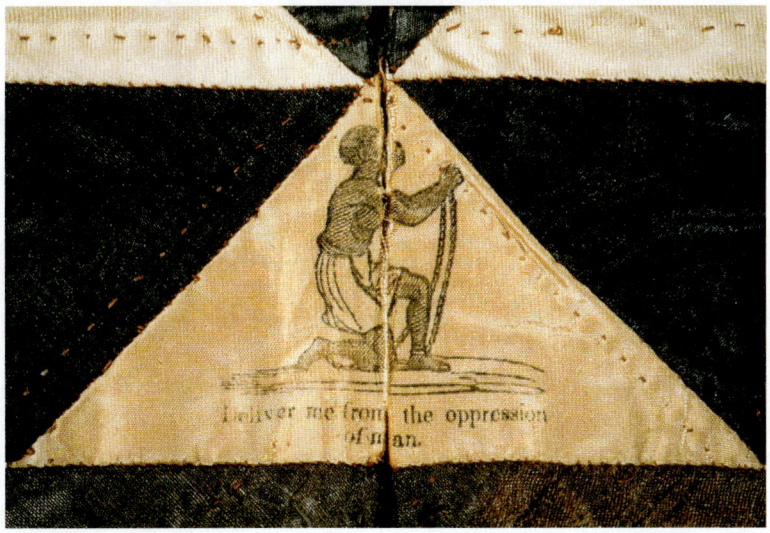

1.9.5b Detail of stamp work by Deborah Coates

Gateway to Art: Maya Lintel Showing Shield Jaguar and Lady Xoc

Pattern Used to Emphasize Royal Power and Hierarchy

An artist who is knowledgeable about the communicative attributes of pattern can add a great deal of information to a work. Strong patterning can reinforce an image by consistently repeating the exact same visual information.

As we look at the Maya lintel showing the ruler Shield Jaguar and his wife Lady Xoc (**1.9.6**) we encounter a composition with one standing figure to the left and one kneeling on the right side. A pattern of small square modules runs across the top of the image and again down the left side; these are glyphs—the system of writing used by the ancient Maya—which identify the characters, explain what they are doing, and provide important historical dates.

The costumes of these two figures also feature jewelry with repetitive patterns, and these patterns guide the viewer's eye toward the figures and focus attention on the wealth of objects worn by this powerful couple. On the right is Lady Xoc; she pulls a rope with a regularly spaced pattern of thorns through her tongue as part of a bloodletting ritual, while her husband looks on. Shield Jaguar's authoritative presence is enhanced by a burning torch, featuring flames that are also regularly spaced and curve in an undulating pattern, amplifying his imposing figure.

The lintel attests to Shield Jaguar's power, and the use of intricate pattern unites the two figures visually: we understand both the ruler and his wife to be individuals of high status.

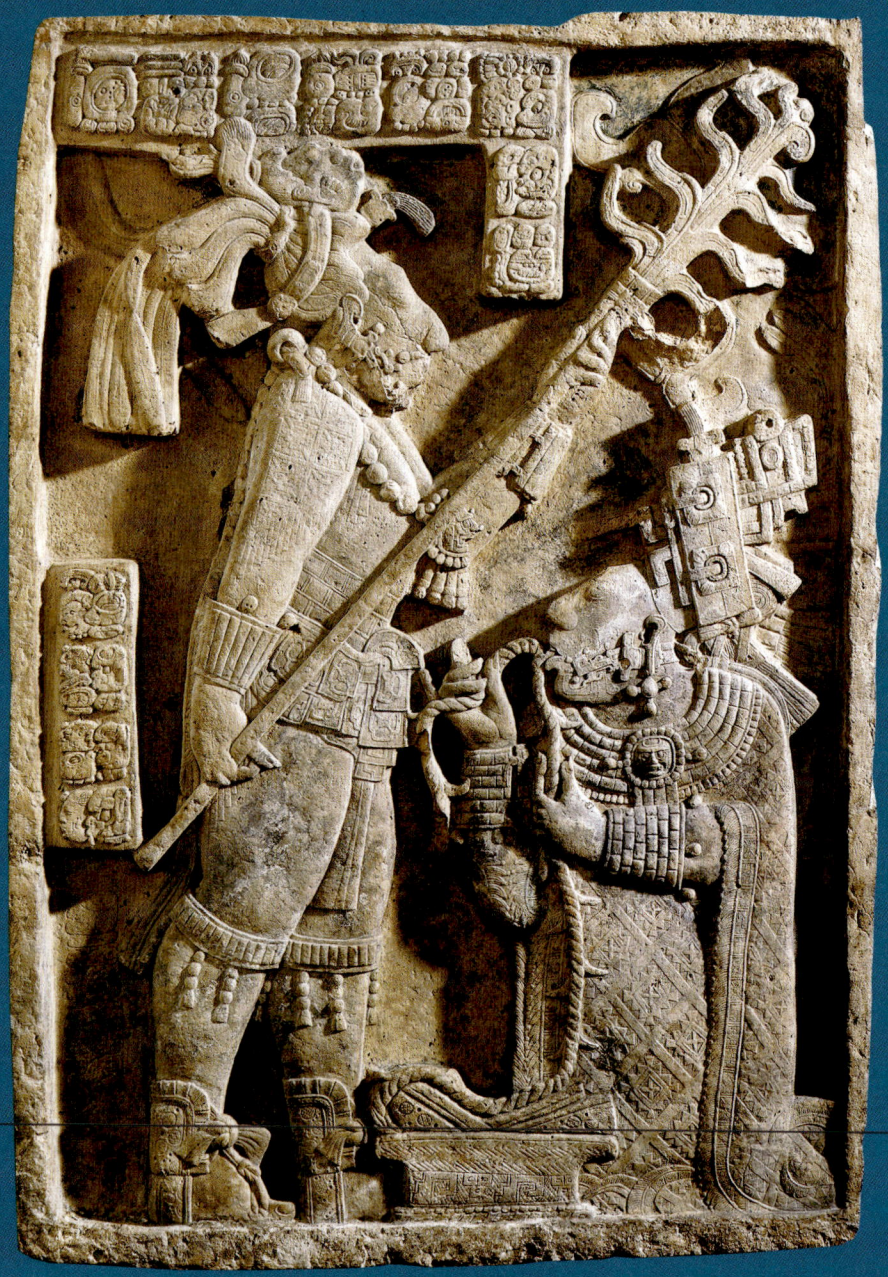

1.9.6 Maya lintel showing Shield Jaguar and Lady Xoc, c. 725 CE. Limestone, 43 × 30¾ × 2⅜". British Museum, London, England

For the other Maya lintel Gateway boxes, see p. 245, p. 436, and p. 632

Texture: the surface quality of a work, for example fine/coarse, detailed/lacking in detail

back from this enormous canvas (**1.9.7a–1.9.7c**). The motif unifies the work and allows Close the freedom to control the color, **texture**, and value. In this case, the motif that Close uses is the result of a technical process. When applied to the larger image, however, it almost disappears because each unit that makes up the whole is so tiny in size. A grid that subdivides the entire image organizes the placement of each cell. In this way Close uses an intricate system of patterns within patterns to achieve a dramatic effect.

Rhythm

> Rhythm is something you either have or don't have, but when you have it, you have it all over.
>
> (Elvis Presley)

Rock-and-roll icon Elvis Presley might as well have been speaking about visual art when he was talking about musical rhythm. Rhythm is something that visual art has "all over." Rhythm gives structure to the experience of looking, just

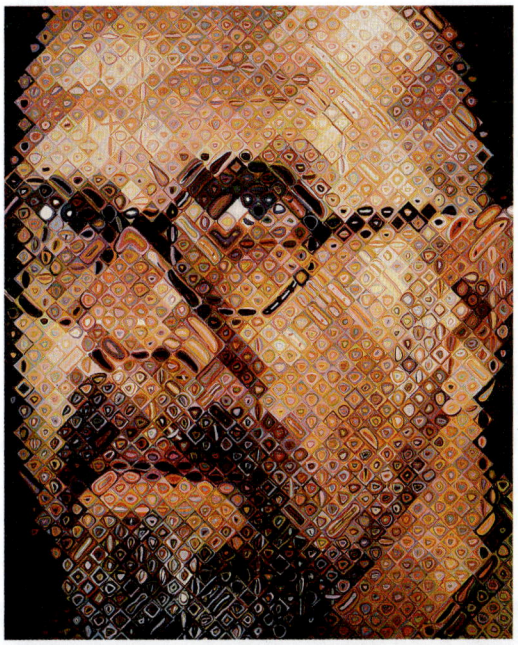

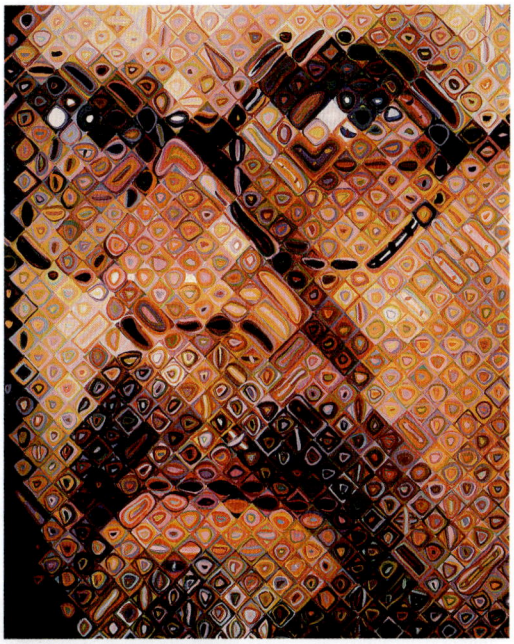

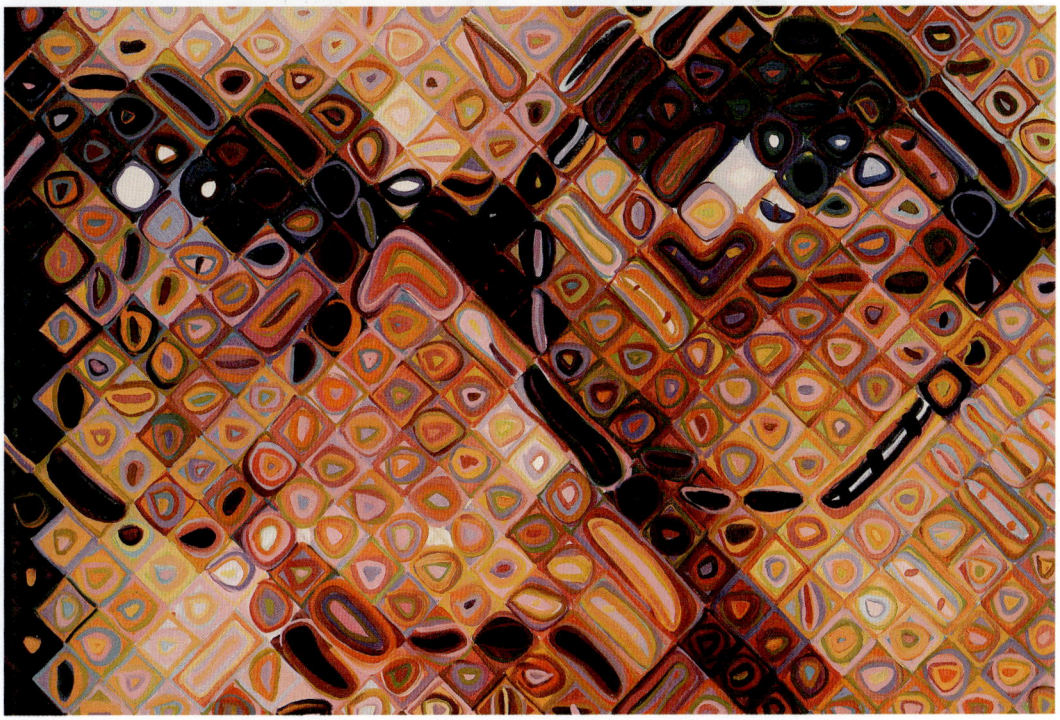

1.9.7a Chuck Close, *Self-Portrait*, 1997. Oil on canvas, 8'6" × 7'. MoMA, New York

1.9.7b Chuck Close, *Self-Portrait*, detail

1.9.7c Chuck Close, *Self-Portrait*, detail

Foreground: the part of a work depicted as nearest to the viewer
Middle ground: the part of a work between the foreground and the background
Background: the part of a work depicted furthest from the viewer's space, often behind the main subject matter
Focal point: the center of interest or activity in a work of art, often drawing the viewer's attention to the most important element

as it guides our eyes from one point to another in a work of art. There is rhythm when there are at least two points of reference in an artwork. For example, the horizontal distance from one side of a canvas to the other is one rhythm, and the vertical distance from top to bottom, another. So, even the simplest works have an implicit rhythm. But most works of art involve shapes, colors, values, lines, and other elements too; the intervals between them provide points of reference for more complex rhythms.

In Flemish painter Pieter Bruegel's work, we see not only large rhythmic progressions that take our eye all around the canvas, but also refined micro-rhythms in the repetition of such details as the trees, houses, birds, and colors (**1.9.8**). All these repetitive elements create a variety of rhythms "all over."

In *Hunters in the Snow*, the party of hunters on the left side first draws our attention into the work. Their dark shapes contrast with the light value of the snow. The group is trudging over the crest of a hill that leads to the right; our attention follows them in the same direction, creating the first part of a rhythmic progression. Our gaze now traverses from the left **foreground** to the **middle ground** on the right, where figures appear to be skating on a large frozen pond. Thereafter, the color of the sky, which is reflected in the skaters' pond, draws our attention deeper into the space, to the horizon. We then look at the **background** of the work, where the recession of the ridgeline pulls the eye to the left and into the far distance. As a result of following this rhythmic progression, our eye has circled round and now returns to re-examine the original **focal point**. We then naturally inspect details, such as the group of figures at the far left making a fire outside a building. As our eye repeats this cycle, we also notice subsidiary rhythms, such as the receding line of trees. Bruegel masterfully orchestrates the winter activities of townspeople in sixteenth-century Flanders (a region now divided between Belgium, The Netherlands, and part of northern France) in a pulsating composition that is both powerful and subtle at the same time.

Simple Repetitive Rhythm

Artists create repetition by using the same shape, color, size, value, line, or texture over and over again. A repeating "pulse" of similar elements sets up a visual rhythm that a viewer can anticipate.

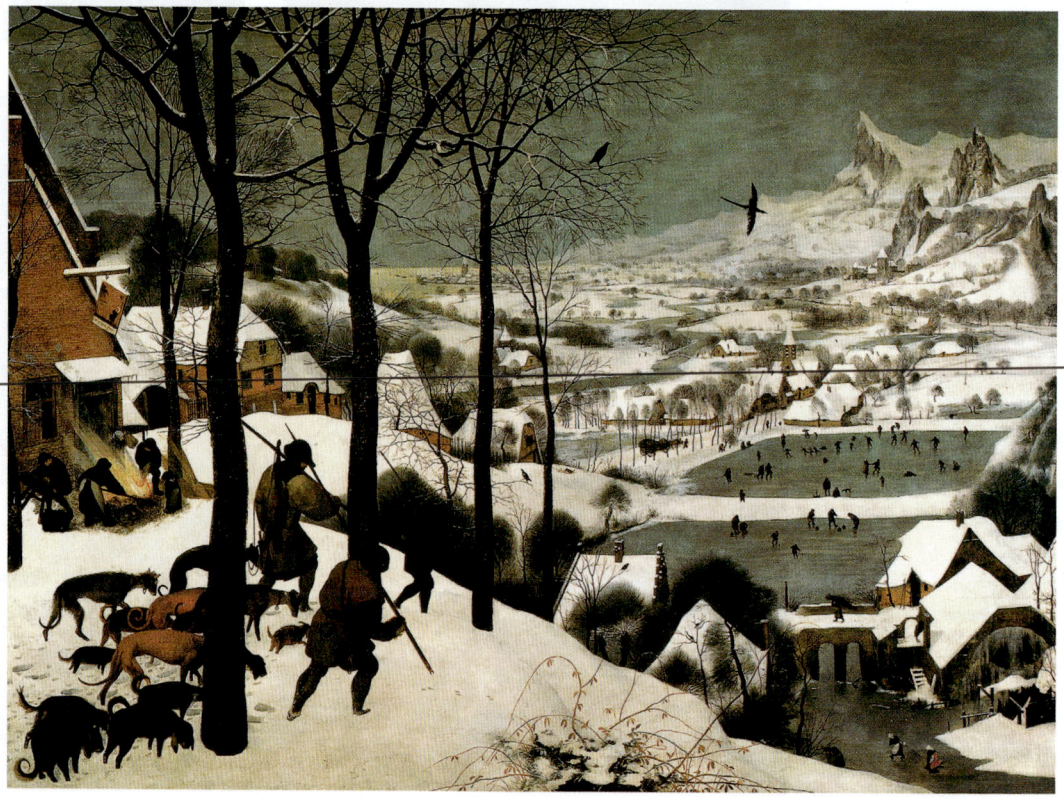

1.9.8 Pieter Bruegel, *Hunters in the Snow*, 1565. Oil on panel, 46 × 63¾". Kunsthistorisches Museum, Vienna, Austria

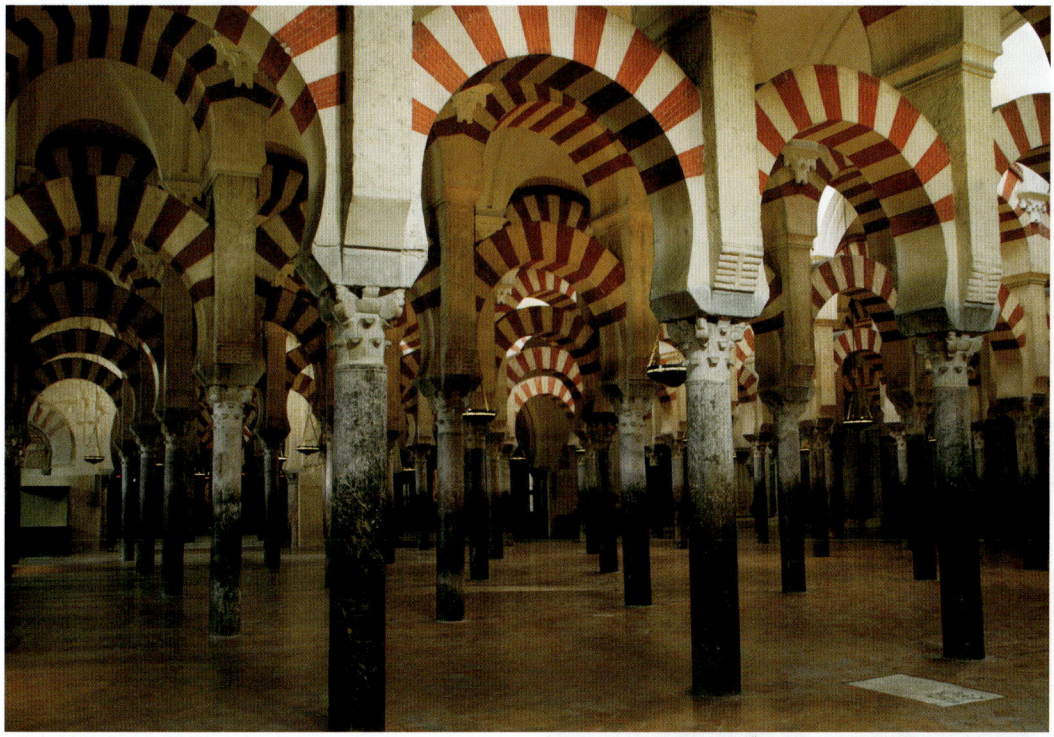

1.9.9 Great Mosque of Córdoba, prayer hall of Abd al-Rahman 1, 784–86, Córdoba, Spain

Such regularity communicates reassurance.

The design of buildings is often intended to reassure us about the stability and durability of the structure. Stability was so important to the ancient Romans that when the builders finally removed the temporary support structures for archways, the architects who had designed them were made to stand underneath. If the arch failed, the architect would be crushed. In common with Roman architects, we also want reassurance that our structures will endure. For this reason, architectural designs often incorporate simple repetition.

The main hall of the Great Mosque of Córdoba in Spain is full of seemingly endless rows of identical columns and arches made from alternating red and white voussoirs (stone wedges that make up the arch) (**1.9.9**). Each of these repeating elements—columns, arches, and voussoirs—creates its own simple rhythm. The accumulation of these simple repetitions also enhances the function of the space and becomes a part of the activity of worship, like prayer beads, reciting the Shahada (profession of faith), or the five-times-a-day call to prayer. Our trust in the permanence of architecture is combined with the timelessness of prayer in the repetitions of the Great Mosque of Córdoba.

Progressive Rhythm

Repetition that regularly increases or decreases in frequency creates a progressive rhythm as the eye moves faster or slower across the surface of the work. In the photograph *Artichoke Halved*, by American Edward Weston (1886–1958), the outer layers (bracts) of the artichoke bud are closer together nearer the center (**1.9.10**).

Then, as they form the triangular center of the bud, a second progressive rhythm begins

1.9.10 Edward Weston, *Artichoke Halved*, 1930. Silver gelatin print, 7⅜ × 9⅜". Collection Center for Creative Photography, University of Arizona, Tucson

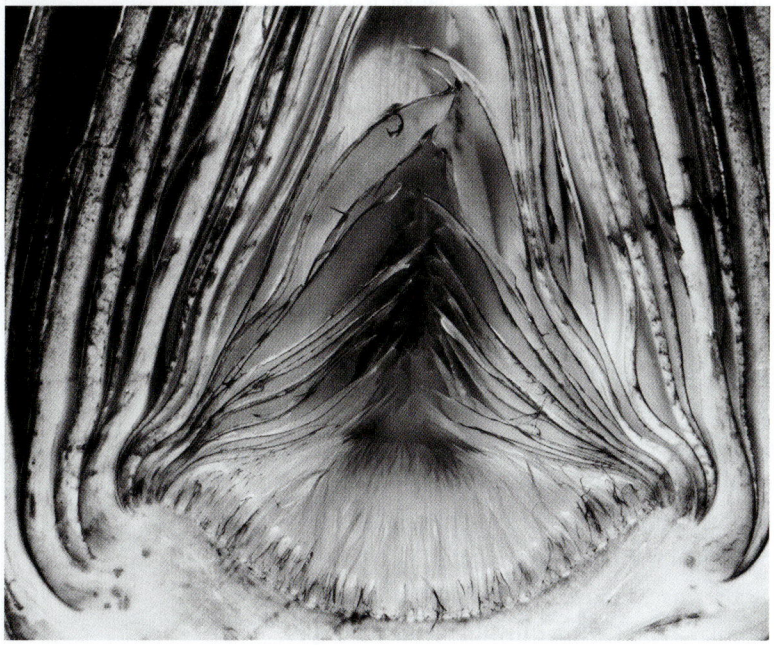

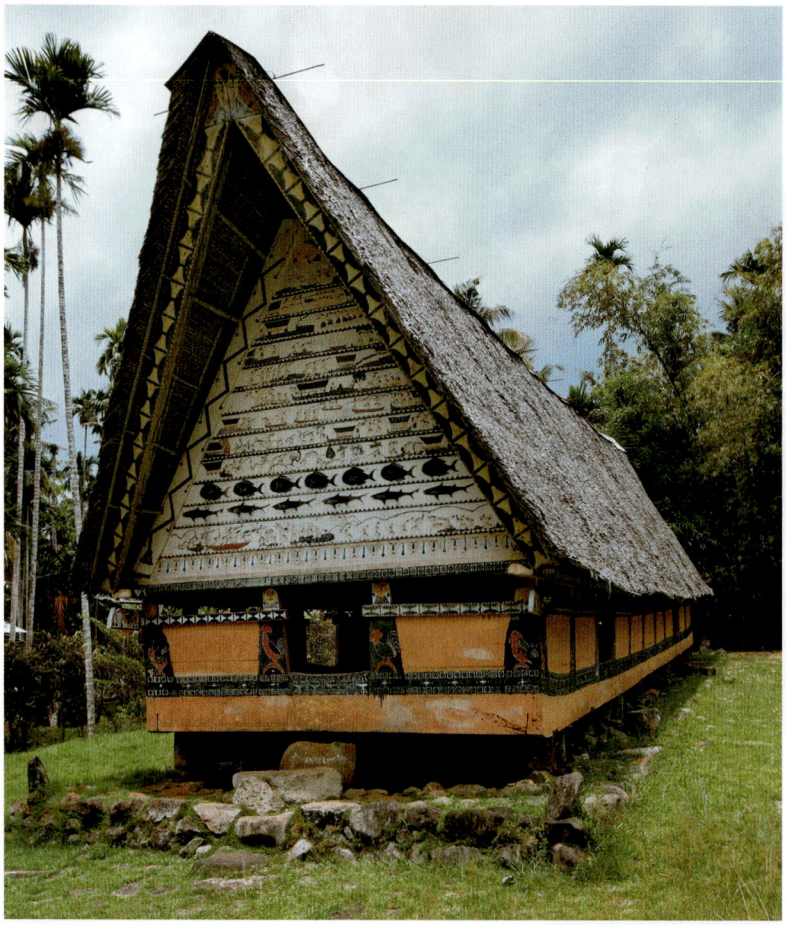

1.9.11 (above) Bai-ra-Irrai, originally built *c.* 1700 and periodically restored, Airai village, Airai State, Republic of Palau

and the small bracts below the triangle form a third rhythm. The highly focused close-up view and strong photographic contrasts of black and white accentuate the sense of speeding up.

Alternating Rhythm

Artists can intertwine multiple rhythms until they become quite complex. The addition and alternation of rhythms can add unpredictability and visual excitement. In Palau, an island group in the western Pacific, a traditional men's long house, called the *bai*, serves as a place for meeting and ritual (**1.9.11**). The imagery above the entry of this bai begins, at the bottom, with the regular rhythms of horizontal lines of fish, but the images above become increasingly irregular as they change to other kinds of shapes.

The edges of the roof display a regular series of symbolic icons that, together with the building's horizontal beams, frame the composition and give the building's **facade** a dynamic feel.

Rhythmic Design Structure

The idea of rhythmic structure helps us understand how artists divide visual space into different kinds of sections to achieve different kinds of effects. In her painting of 1849 *Plowing in the Nivernais: The Dressing of the Vines*, the French artist Rosa Bonheur (1822–1899) creates a horizontal structure that leads our eye in sequence from one group of shapes to the next (**1.9.12a** and **1.9.12b**). Bonheur expertly organizes

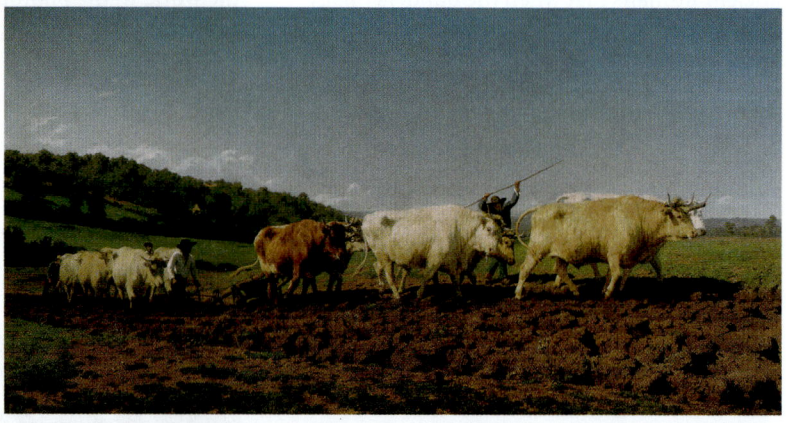

1.9.12a (below) Rosa Bonheur, *Plowing in the Nivernais: The Dressing of the Vines*, 1849. Oil on canvas, 4'4¾" × 8'6⅜". Musée d'Orsay, Paris, France

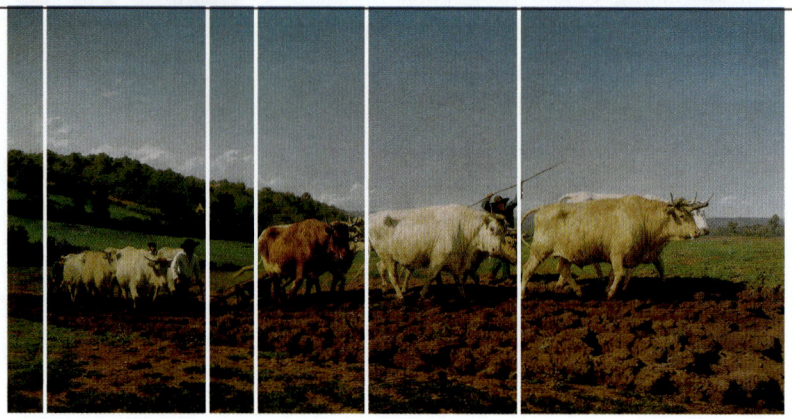

1.9.12b (bottom) Rhythmic structural diagram of **1.9.12a**

the composition, emphasizing the cumulative effect of the rhythm of the groupings as they move from left to right. Because the composition is so horizontal, the design **emphasis** directs our gaze sideways using a linear direction and rhythm. By changing the width of the gaps between the animals, Bonheur suggests their irregular movement as they plod forward, drawing the heavy plow. Each group also has a different relative size and occupies a different amount of space, creating a visual rhythm and energy that pulls our attention from left to right.

The careful composition and rhythmic structure in such paintings give an air of respectability and nobility to laborers of the field and the hard work they had to do. Bonheur may have been sympathetic toward those who worked outside of the stuffy social order of the time, since her gender may have been a disadvantage in a traditionally male profession. Yet her effort to bring respectability to such lives and labor did not seek to glamorize her subject: in this painting she insistently reminds us of the slow physical rhythms created by the brute strength of these beasts and the irregularity of the plowmens' steps as all of them, men and cattle, work together to turn the weighty soil.

The Spanish painter Francisco Goya (1746–1828) uses differing visual rhythms to denote ideas of good and evil in the work *The Sleep of Reason Produces Monsters* (**1.9.13**) from the series "The Caprices" (*Los Caprichos*). Long considered one of the most significant Spanish painters, Goya established an expressive painting style and is well known for chronicling the harsh realities of the Napoleonic occupation of Spain. "The Caprices", however, is a strange, intriguing, and sometimes disturbing series of eighty **etchings** and **aquatints** depicting subjects as various as the clergy, witches, and prostitutes. The use of aquatint, particularly, heightens the contrast between dark and light, creating a shadowy, mysterious quality. The focus of the series is fantasy and invention, or the artist's imaginative powers. In fig. **1.9.13**, particularly, he depicts the artist's dream (this is indicated in the inscription at lower left). But as the title suggests, the image is more than just a fantastical vision: it seems likely that the artist was expressing a belief that without rationality, there was a danger that life would descend into chaos and irrational prejudices and superstition.

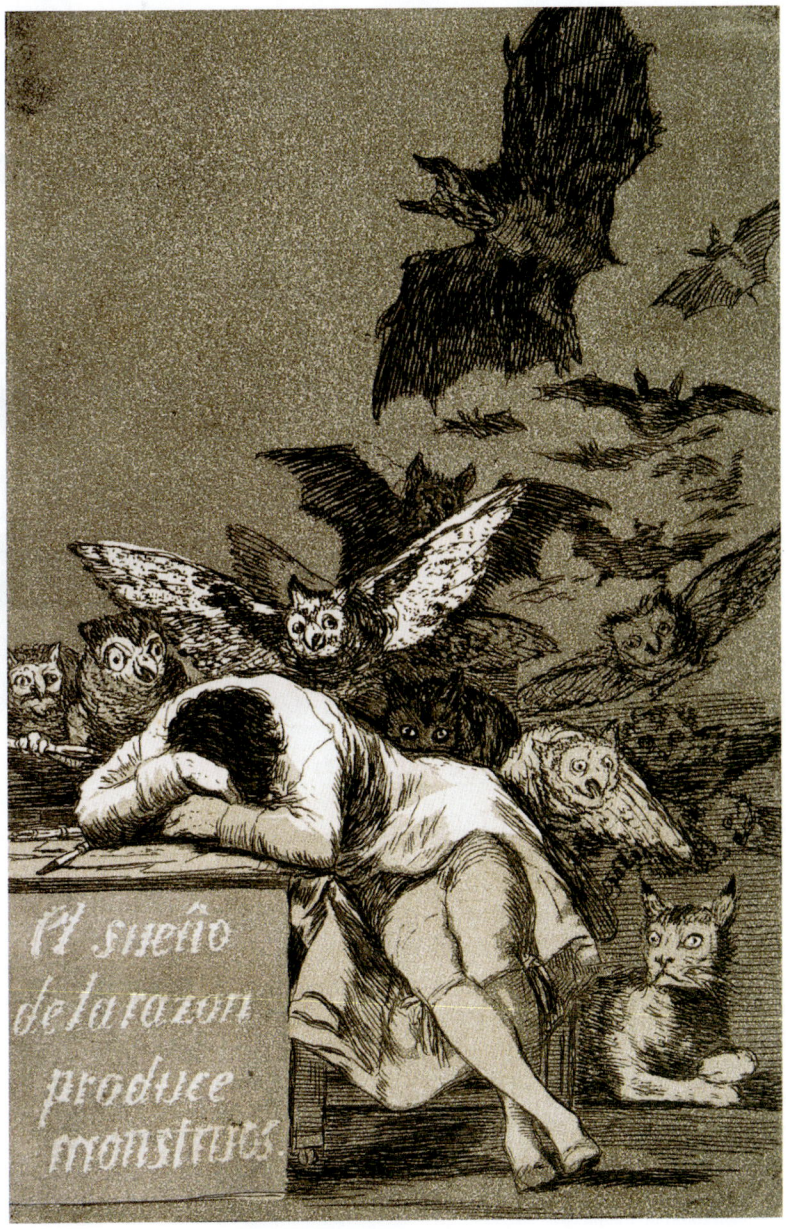

1.9.13 Francisco Goya, *The Sleep of Reason Produces Monsters:* plate 43 from *The Caprices (Los Caprichos)*, 1799. Etching, aquatint, drypoint, and burin, 8⅞ × 5⅞". Metropolitan Museum of Art, New York

The two conflicting forces in the picture are skillfully contrasted: the box in the lower left corner stabilizes and anchors the image by means of the straight and regular lines of a square. The visual rhythm created through the vertical and horizontal lines is predictable and logical, symbolizing reason as a guarantee of safety and goodness. The evil monsters that

Facade: any side of a building, usually the front or entrance
Emphasis: the principle of drawing attention to particular content in a work
Etching: an intaglio printmaking process that uses acid to bite (or etch) the engraved design into the printmaking surface
Aquatint: an intaglio printmaking process that uses melted rosin or spray paint to create an acid-resistant ground

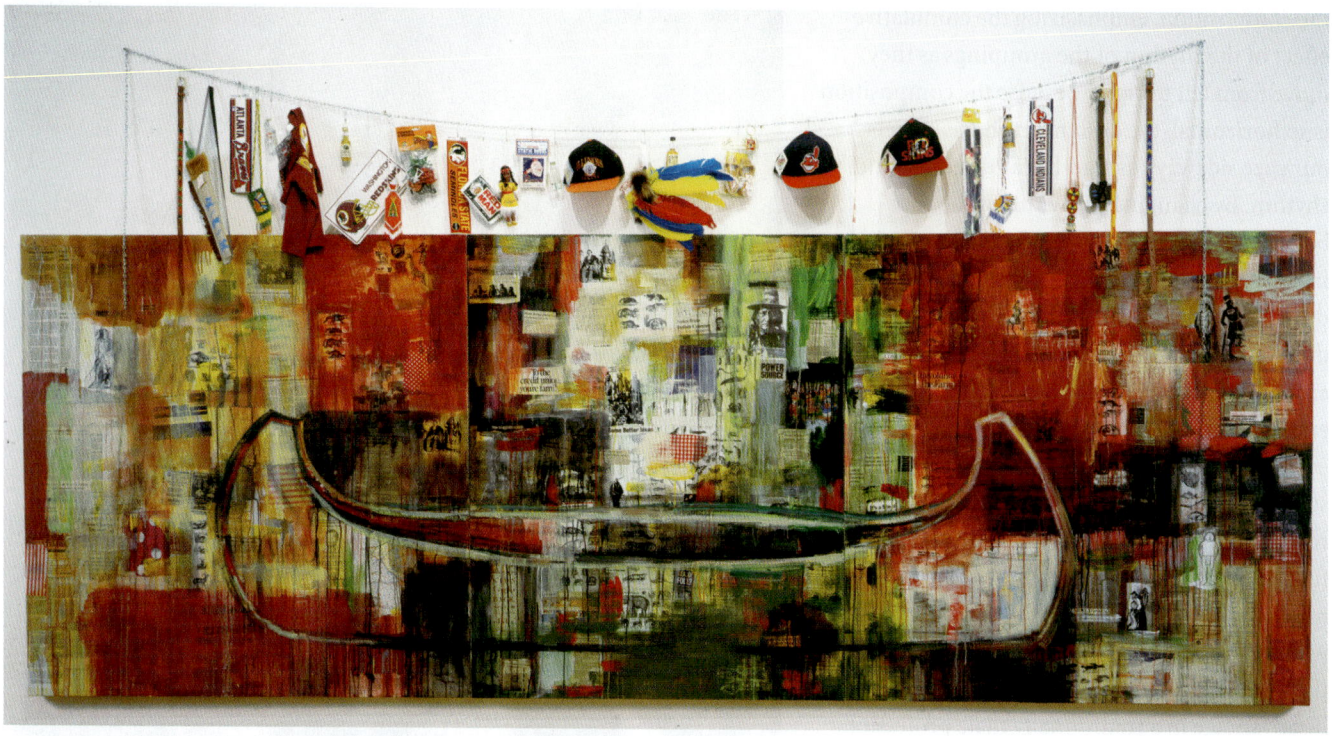

1.9.14 Jaune Quick-to-See Smith, *Trade (Gifts for Trading Land with White People)*, 1992. Oil paint and mixed media, collage, objects, canvas, 5' × 14'1⅝". Chrysler Museum of Art, Norfolk, Virginia

Triptych: an artwork comprising three panels, normally joined together and sharing a common theme

dominate the upper portion of the image are more haphazard, active, and threatening in their placement within the work, rising as if to overwhelm the sleeper below.

The Native American artist Jaune Quick-to-See Smith (b. 1940) also used a rhythmic structure as she created the work *Trade (Gifts for Trading Land with White People)* (**1.9.14**). The work, created in 1992, was a reaction to the celebration of the five-hundredth anniversary of Columbus's landing in the Caribbean. Smith uses multiple rhythmic elements to communicate a reaction against the mistreatment of Native Americans that began with the arrival of Europeans. Two major components interact in this composition: a **triptych**, or three-panel artwork, in this case on canvas, and a hanging collection of objects. The three panels of the canvas are equal and create a simple repetitive rhythm that is unified by a nearly life size painted canoe. The surface of the painting is made up of collaged printed images of the many generalized ways in which Native people have been depicted. The hanging objects, a collection of stereotyped commercial images of Native Americans (mostly sports-team mascots), dangle above and in front of the canvas. The suspended objects, because of their changing size and shape, establish an alternating rhythm in real space. The physical presence of real objects alongside the flat, collaged surface implies a connection between the past and present, and the notion that misconceptions from the past have led to distorted realities that persist today.

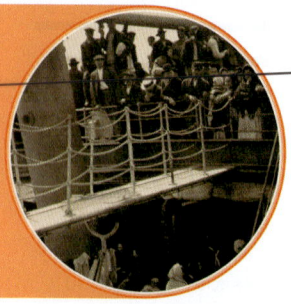

Another example of rhythmic structure can be seen in Alfred Stieglitz's photograph *The Steerage*: see **2.8.25, p. 330**

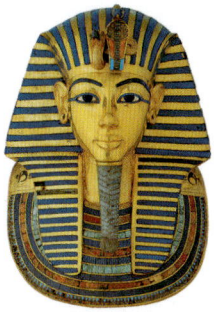

3.1.19 Funerary mask of Tutankhamun, Egypt, 1333–1323 BCE, p. 378

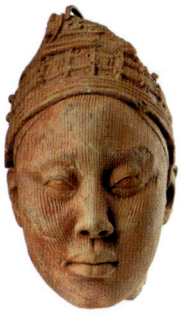

4.9.6 Head, possibly an Ife king, West Africa, 12th–14th century, p. 667

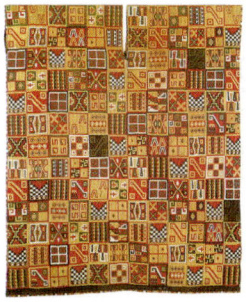

3.4.6 Inca tunic, Andes, c.1500, p. 433

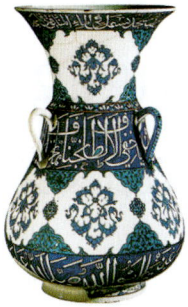

1.4.23 Mosque lamp from the Dome of the Rock, Jerusalem, 1549, p. 106

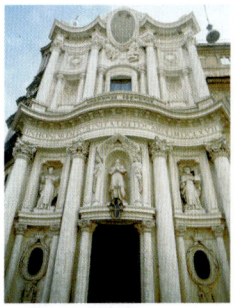

3.6.21a Francesco Borromini, San Carlo alle Quattro Fontane, Rome, p. 479

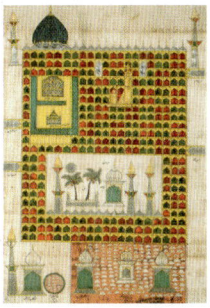

3.2.19 *View of the Sanctuary at Medina*, 17th or 18th century, p. 403

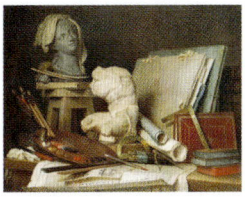

3.7.8 Anne Vallayer-Coster, *Attributes of Painting, Sculpture, and Architecture*, 1769, p. 494

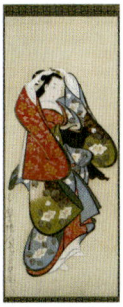

4.9.7 Kaigetsudō Dohan, *Beautiful Woman*, Edo Period, Japan, 18th century, p. 667

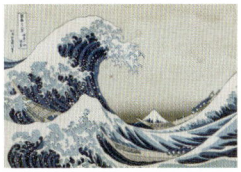

3.3.23 Katsushika Hokusai, "The Great Wave off Shore at Kanagawa," 1826–33, p. 425

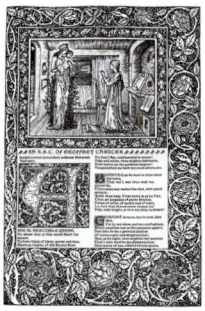

2.7.10 William Morris and Edward Burne-Jones, page from *Chaucer*, 1896, p. 305

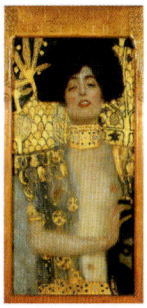

3.8.24 Gustav Klimt, *Judith I*, 1901, p. 519

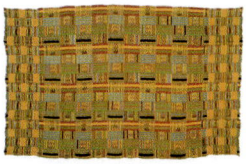

3.5.5 Asante textile wrapper (*kente*), Africa, 20th century, p. 449

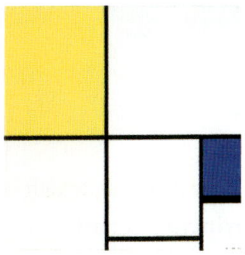

3.9.17 Piet Mondrian, *Composition with Yellow and Blue*, 1932, p. 534

3.9.26 Jackson Pollock, *Number 1A*, 1948, p. 539

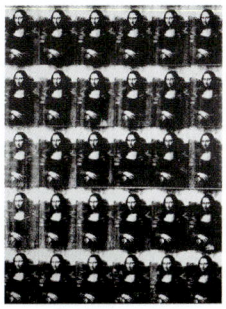

3.9.29 Andy Warhol, *Thirty Are Better than One*, 1963, p. 541

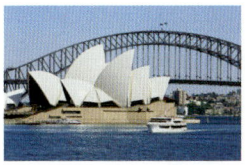

2.5.34 Jørn Utzon, Sydney Opera House, Australia, 1973, p. 280

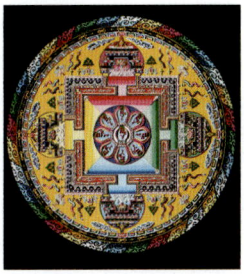

1.6.17 Amitayus Mandala, Drepung Loseling Monastery, Tibet, p. 138

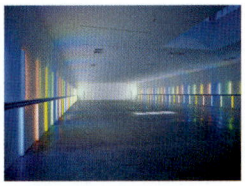

3.9.34 Dan Flavin, *Untitled* (installation), 1996, p. 544

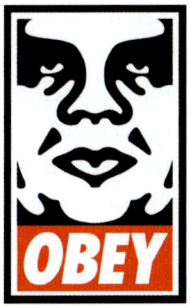

1.1.25a Shepard Fairey, *Obey*, 1996, p. 57

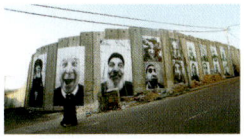

4.8.11 JR and Marco, *28 Millimeters, Face2Face*, 2007, p. 660

1.10 Engaging with Form and Content

Elements of art: the basic vocabulary of art—line, shape, form, volume, mass, texture, value (lightness/darkness), space, color, and motion and time
Principles: the principles, or "grammar" of art—contrast, unity, variety, balance, scale, proportion, focal point, emphasis, pattern, and rhythm—describe the ways the elements of art are arranged in an artwork
Formal Analysis: a visual study that includes careful description of the artwork and its use of elements and principles
Three-dimensional: having height, width, and depth
Texture: the surface quality of a work, for example fine/coarse, detailed/lacking in detail
Color: the optical effect caused when reflected white light of the spectrum is divided into separate wavelengths
Implied line: a line not actually drawn but suggested by elements in the work
Symmetry, symmetrical, symmetrical balance: an image or shape that looks exactly (or nearly exactly) the same on both sides when cut in half

Artworks communicate visual ideas, just as speaking and writing communicate verbal ideas. In order for viewers to engage with art more deeply than through personal response alone (like/dislike), we must interpret the visual language of the artist. We use a combination of various methods, such as description, analysis, and critique, to understand the appearance and meaning—or content—of a work. Careful looking and research contribute to effective analysis. We can also apply our own viewpoints, or critique. In this chapter we look at the interpretive methods that are most frequently used and are most effective (see Box: Types of Analysis and Critique, p. 176).

Formal Analysis

Artists have many tools at their disposal, which we call the **elements** and **principles** of art (discussed throughout Part I of this book). The elements include line, form, shape, volume, mass, color, texture, space, motion and time, and value. Artists use the principles, such as contrast, balance, unity, variety, rhythm, emphasis, pattern, scale, proportion, and focal point, to organize the elements. A work of art is therefore a product of the dynamic interrelationships between the various art elements and principles.

The process of analysing the elements and principles used by the artist is called **formal analysis**. Making a formal analysis—a visual study—of a work of art is one way to understand more clearly the language used by an artist and to grasp how he or she applies elements and principles in a particular artwork.

To analyse a work of art fully, formally, one describes in specific detail how each element and principle is utilized within it. The examples given on pp. 171–72 focus on specific aspects of the chosen works in order to highlight the elements and principles most prominently used by the artists. For a more complete formal analysis, see the discussion of "Chaos Machine" (pp. 187–88) and the "Combined Analysis" of *Las Meninas* later in this chapter (pp. 183–85).

In order to analyse a **three-dimensional** sculpture formally, you need to see the piece from all sides. As the separate photographs of the Bust of Queen Nefertiti (**1.10.1a** and **b**) show, different aspects of the sculpture emerge as we view it from various angles, yet as a whole, it is a vision of an elegant and confident woman. Seen from in front, the face of the Egyptian queen is symmetrically balanced, except for the missing pupil in one eye, and she holds her head high. In addition to the sculpture being three-dimensional, its volume and lifelike quality are further enhanced by the queen's painted skin. The sculpture itself is smooth, but **texture** is implied by the use of **color** in the rich headdress and in the necklace that drapes her graceful neck. Nefertiti's marked cheekbones, full red lips, well-defined eyes, and strongly defined eyebrows portray her as an ideal beauty.

The edges of the tall, flat-topped crown create two sides of a triangle. Two points of the triangle are the upper corners of her crown, and the third point is slightly below her neck.

This triangle of her crown has a central vertical line, originally a complete cobra, which helps to enhance the elongation of her neck. The patterned ribbon that crosses under the broken cobra encircles her head, making one want to circle the sculpture, and on either side, the end of the ribbon is placed right above the ear.

When looking at Nefertiti in profile, one sees that the ribbon tips function like **implied lines** that point to the queen's eyes. From the side, the dramatic height and angle of her crown meet the nape of her neck to create a sideways "v." This "v" functions like a directional arrow and creates an implied line from the right to Nefertiti's chin, highlighting the formal **symmetry** of her beauty. Her long, thin neck lends the queen grace and femininity.

Nighthawks (**1.10.2**, p. 172), by the American artist Edward Hopper (1882–1967), conveys a sense of absence and loneliness. When making a formal analysis of a two-dimensional work, such as this painting, useful aspects you can consider are the locations of objects, the colors used, and the relationships between the parts of the **composition**. In this scene, we see a darkened building in the background, with large shop windows on the bottom floor and five tall windows on the red-brick upper story. Together, these areas form repeated dark gulfs that communicate a sense of hollowness, gloom, and vacancy. We notice that even though the scene takes place in a city, the streets around are devoid of people and activity, creating a slightly eerie sense of stillness and quiet.

In front of this building, the sidewalk wraps around a curved diner on the street corner, cutting off the group of people inside, whom we see through the glass outer walls. The struts

Composition: the overall design or organization of a work

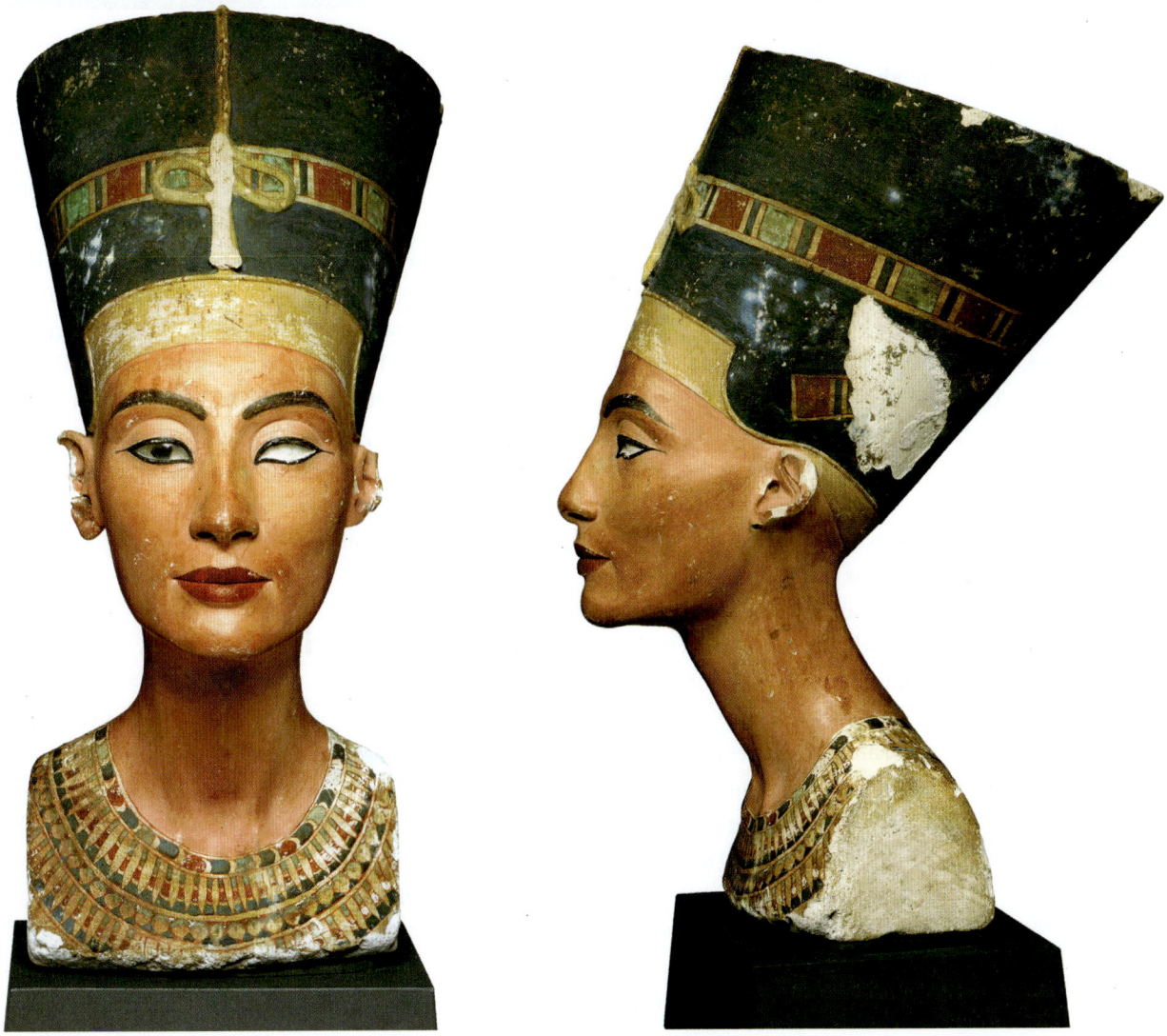

1.10.1a and 1.10.1b
Thutmosis's workshop, Bust of Queen Nefertiti, from Amarna, Egypt, c. 1350 BCE (New Kingdom, 18th Dynasty). Painted limestone, gypsum, crystal, and wax, height 19¾". Aegyptisches Museum, Staatliche Museen zu Berlin, Germany

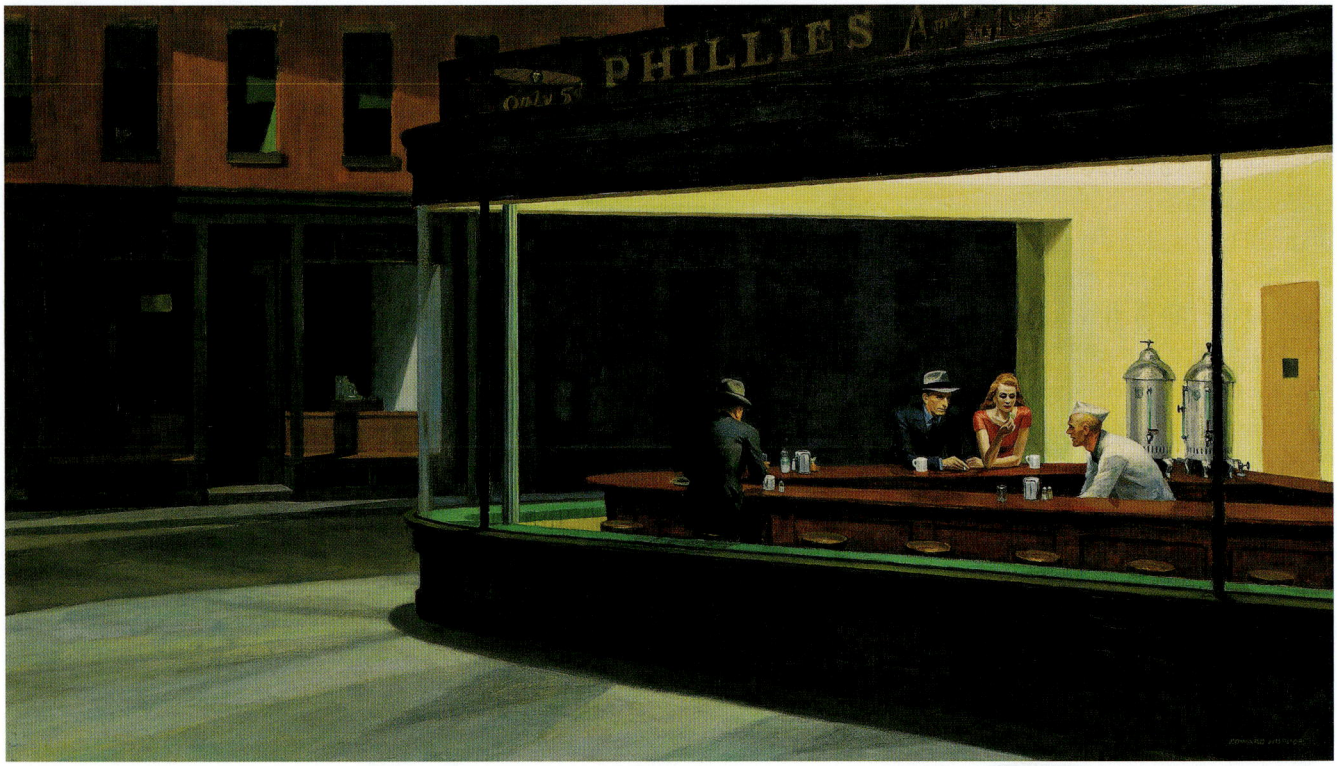

1.10.2 Edward Hopper, *Nighthawks*, 1942. Oil on canvas, 33⅛ × 60". Art Institute of Chicago

Contrast: a drastic difference between such elements as color or value (lightness/darkness) when they are presented together
Emphasis: the principle of drawing attention to particular content in a work
Style: a characteristic way in which an artist or group of artists uses visual language to give a work an identifiable form of visual expression
Triptych: an artwork comprising three panels, normally joined together and sharing a common theme
Realism: nineteenth-century artistic style that aimed to depict nature and everyday subjects in an unidealized manner. "Realism" is also used to describe a historical movement from the same period, which tried to achieve social change and equality by highlighting, in art and literature, the predicament of the poor

dividing the panes, and the solid walls above and below, create a strong framework through which we focus on the four figures. The inside is brightly lit, in **contrast** to the streets outside. This makes the room a particular area of **emphasis** in the picture: it further draws our attention to the people, and, together with the use of brilliant color in the yellow wall behind the counter, exposes them clearly to us, showing how isolated they are. The stark contrasts between the woman's red dress and hair, the black suits and hats of the two male customers, and the white uniform of the waiter make the figures more distinct, both within the scene and from one another.

The artist remarked some time after finishing the work, "Unconsciously, probably, I was painting the loneliness of a large city," and if we look more closely, within this careful use of formal devices we see that he intensifies the painting's effect through his choice of specific details. Despite being gathered together, the figures are not smiling and have very little interaction with one another; these individuals appear to be alone in their own thoughts. One cannot tell whether the man and woman sitting together are actually a couple—they do not look at each other: he stares ahead, while her eyes are downcast. Their hands are close, but do not touch. These figures echo the two drink urns to the right: set very nearly together, but apart. The man and woman are further separated visually by the line of her right arm. The waiter is enclosed on his own within the triangular space of the bar, and the other customer sits with his back to us, surrounded by six empty barstools. Although the waiter is in an active pose, it appears that time has stopped. This stillness only further enhances the sense of quiet, as if these lives are frozen, sealed off in their separate loneliness.

Stylistic Analysis

We recognize style in our own lives: the way we dress and arrange our hair reflects our personal style. Artworks also have **style**, or specific characteristics that make them look the way they do. Style allows us to recognize that an artwork was made by a particular artist. A group of artists might share a style because they all used similar techniques, worked at the same time, or studied in the same place. The

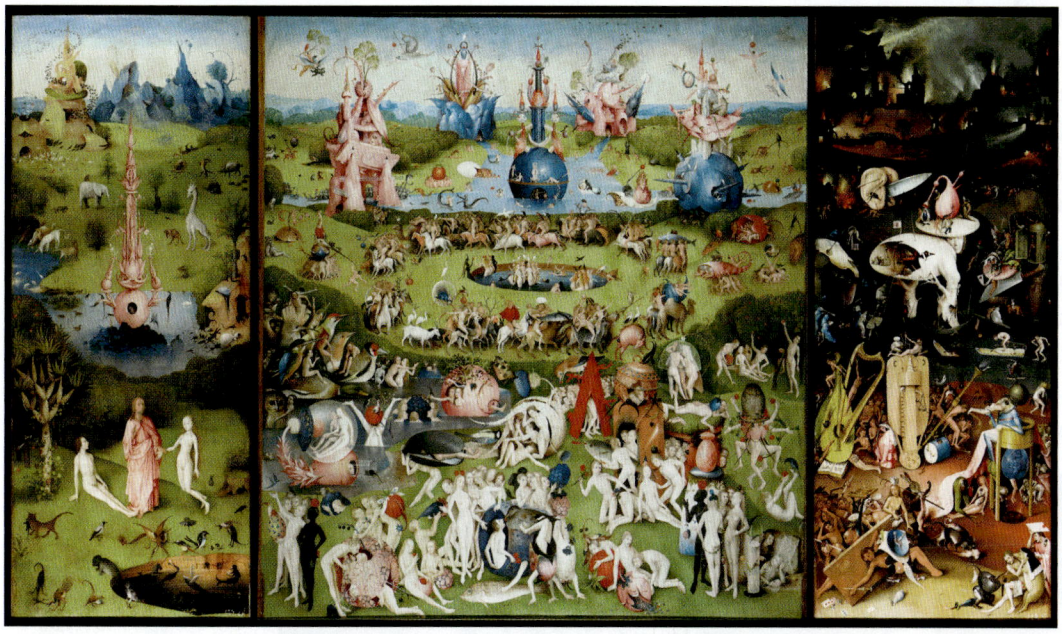

1.10.3 Hieronymus Bosch, *The Garden of Earthly Delights*, 1500–1505. Oil on wooden panel, central panel 7'1⅝" × 6'4¾", wings 7'1⅝"x 38¼". Museo Nacional del Prado, Madrid, Spain

Romanticism: movement in nineteenth-century European culture, concerned with the power of the imagination and greatly valuing intense feeling

characteristics that contribute to style include the use of formal elements (line, shape, color, texture, and so on), the use of design principles (symmetry or asymmetry, for example), and the level of abstraction or representation used. Style can be related to the brushstrokes or marks an artist makes, the way light shines brightly on one part of the picture while the rest is in darkness, or the consistent use of a particular color in a certain way.

Style can be individual or shared by a group, school, time period, or movement. Analysing style allows us to make connections between artworks. We can use style as a way to categorize them or to identify who made a work of art, where it came from, or when it was created.

Known for his unique style, Netherlandish artist Hieronymus Bosch (*c.* 1450–1516) is most famous for his painted **triptych** *The Garden of Earthly Delights* (**1.10.3**). Unlike many other artists working in Europe in the sixteenth century, Bosch was not interested in convincing **realism** or perfect proportion. His works are known for their fantastical quality: humans, fruits, and futuristic-looking objects (all in various distorted sizes) mingle in odd, erotic, and nonsensical ways. The specific meanings of the activities in Bosch's work are uncertain, but on the whole scholars agree that he is expressing a religious condemnation of immorality, particularly in regard to sexual behavior. In this sense his style has something in common with medieval biblical sermons and folkloric sources, which also suggested that sinful actions are reflected in distortions of human anatomy. As a Spanish monk, José de Sigüenza, wrote upon studying the work in 1605, "other artists depicted people as they appear outwardly, but only Bosch had the audacity to paint them as they are on the inside."

The left panel of *The Garden of Earthly Delights* shows God's presentation of Adam and Eve before the Fall; the center panel shows elongated nude figures inhabiting the false paradise of Earth, seduced by the ephemeral pleasures of frolicking and eroticism. The right panel shows the consequences of their behavior, with endless forms of tortured damnation for the sinners. Bosch's distinctive style may look quite modern in some ways, but he was an artist of the late medieval period.

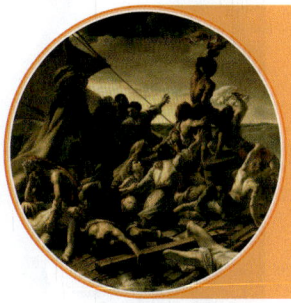

Raft of the Medusa is a work from the **Romanticism** movement; its style combines detailed realism with idealized form, emphasizing imagination and emotional content: see **4.8.1, p. 652**

Iconographic Analysis

When we identify and interpret the symbolic meanings of the objects and elements in artworks, we often find unexpected insights into their content (see Box: Types of Analysis and Critique, p. 176, and "Critical Race Theory," pp. 181–82). *The Ambassadors*, by German artist Hans Holbein the Younger (1497–1543), was painted while the artist was at the court of King Henry VIII of England, and is extraordinarily rich in symbolic significance (**1.10.4a**). We can begin by identifying the broader meanings of what the work includes. It shows Jean de Dinteville and the bishop Georges de Selve, Frenchmen who served as ambassadors to England. In 1533, when the work was made, England was on the brink of breaking with the Catholic Church and becoming a Protestant country, and art historians who have been able to study the painting close up have revealed how its **iconography** reflects this religious predicament: the globe, hymn book, crucifix, and lute all carry specific religious meanings (**1.10.4a–c**).

Most symbolic of all is the large, distorted skull in the foreground, which signifies human

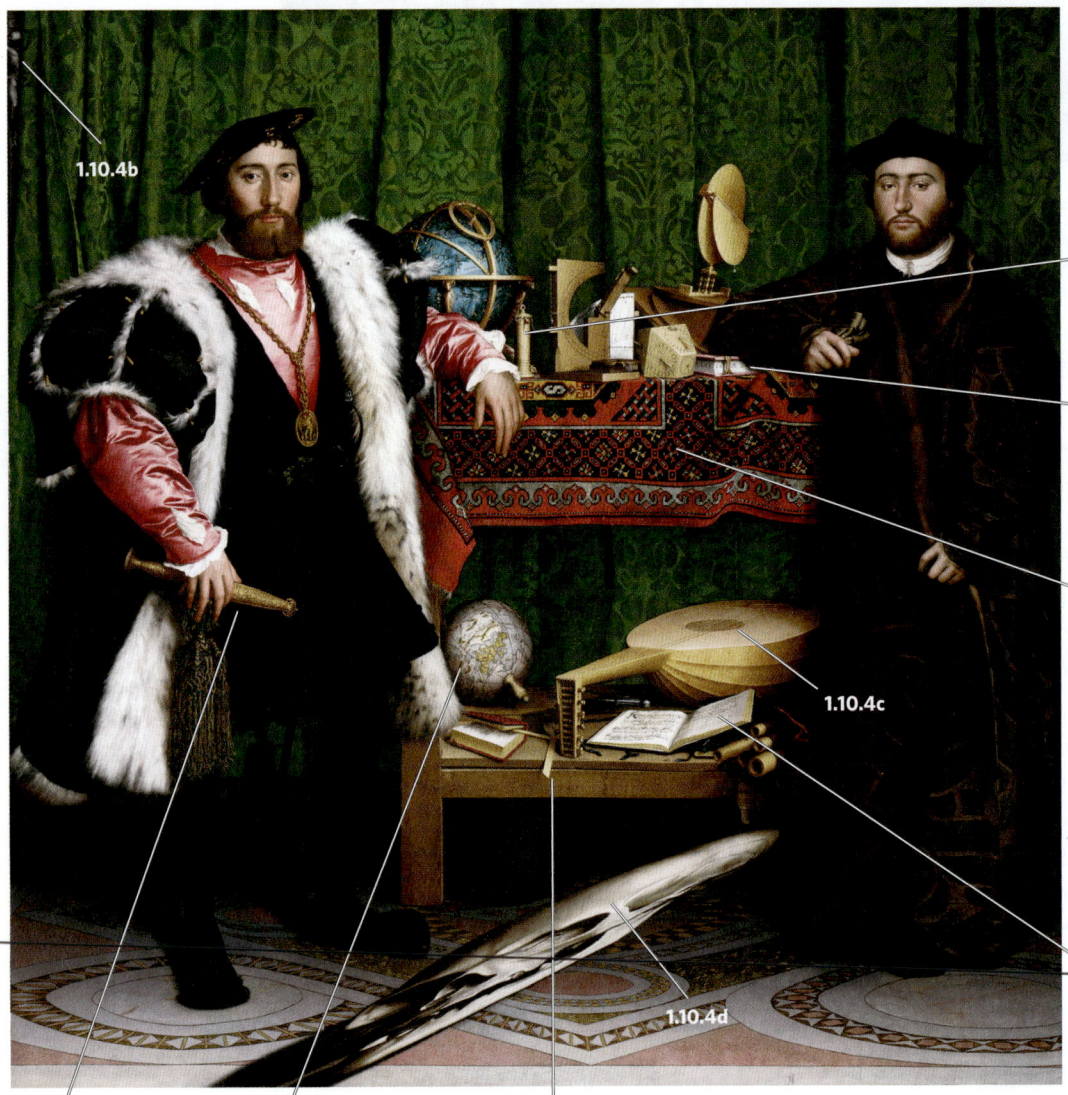

1.10.4a Hans Holbein the Younger, *Jean de Dinteville and Georges de Selve ("The Ambassadors")*, 1533. Oil on oak, 6'9½" × 6'10⅓". National Gallery, London, England

The cylindrical sundial gives the date (April 11, 1533) on which the painting was completed

25, the age of de Selve, is inscribed along the top of the page of the book he is leaning on

The upper shelf, symbolically nearer to Heaven, features devices to understand the heavens and measure time, including a celestial globe, sundial, and compasses. These objects indicate both how learned these men are and that they are well-traveled, as their occupation would demand

The hymn book, which is so exactly painted that it is possible to read the verses by Martin Luther, the German pioneer of Protestantism, inscribed on its pages, may be included to encourage the restoration of religious concord

29, the age of Dinteville, is engraved on his dagger

The center of the globe on the lower shelf shows Rome, hub of the Catholic faith

The lower shelf, which is concerned with more earthly matters, includes—painted in meticulously precise detail—secular and religious objects including musical instruments, a hymn book, a mathematical book, and a terrestrial globe mortality, and the inclusion of which indicates that the painting as a whole is what is known as a ***memento mori***—a symbolic reminder of the inevitability of death (**1.10.4d**). Despite the ambassadors' success, wealth, and youth, they are aware of the fleeting nature of life. The strange, haunting form of the skull, facing away from their worldly possessions and toward the half-hidden crucifix, affirms that the men believe their salvation, and eternal life, depend on God.

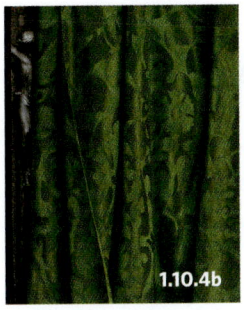

1.10.4b, c, and d Hans Holbein the Younger, *Jean de Dinteville and Georges de Selve ("The Ambassadors")*, 1533 (details)

In the upper left corner, partially concealed by the green curtain, is a crucifix

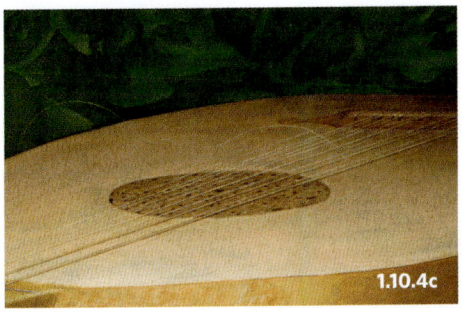

The lute has a broken string: this may be a reference to the religious discord that was occurring at the time—harmony (hence the musical instrument) was a key idea in the sixteenth century

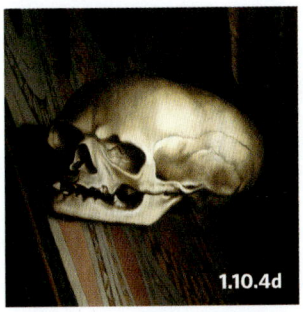

The large, distorted skull in the foreground, painted using **anamorphosis**, a type of optical illusion, signifies human mortality. This skull looks realistic only when the viewer stands in one specific spot, in front and to the right of the canvas

Contextual Analysis

The **content**, or meaning, of a work of art varies greatly between artworks. Both artists and viewers play roles in providing this meaning. An artwork may convey a particular message to those who view it in the context in which it was made, but the same artwork may convey a different meaning to someone living in another time and place. To understand the context of a work of art fully, you will usually have to undertake some research (see Box: Research and Interpretation, p. 180), in addition to looking very closely at the artwork itself. Analysis involves gathering information (sometimes from multiple sources). There are numerous types of contextual analysis that you can use to decipher the meaning of a work of art.

Iconography: study of the symbolic meaning of an artwork or the general study of symbolism
***Memento mori*:** Latin phrase that means "remember that you must die." In artworks, such symbols as skulls, flowers, and clocks are used to represent the transient nature of life on Earth
Anamorphosis: the distorted representation of an object so that it appears correctly proportioned only when viewed from one particular position
Content: the meaning, message, or feeling expressed in a work of art

Analysis of Religious Context

The powerful feelings behind religious beliefs have often been a motivator for creating art. The rituals of the Sumerians (4000–1000 BCE) included bringing to their temples offerings for the gods. A dozen small praying figures were found under a Sumerian temple in modern-day Iraq; the two largest ones are shown here (**1.10.5**). Because the figures were found in a temple, we know they were created and used in a religious context. Their wide-eyed upward glances and clasped hands, together with inscriptions on some of them, tell us that they are in eternal prayer. All the figures have similar conical forms, their faces stoically forward with hands intertwining slightly above the waist. Yet each is unique as well: the sizes, hairstyles, and gender vary. While they are not precise portraits, every figure loosely represents the person who brought it to the temple. Each of these figures holds a goblet for a votive—an offering made in accordance with a vow—to the gods, and would remain in the temple to offer continual prayer when the actual people represented in the statues could not be there.

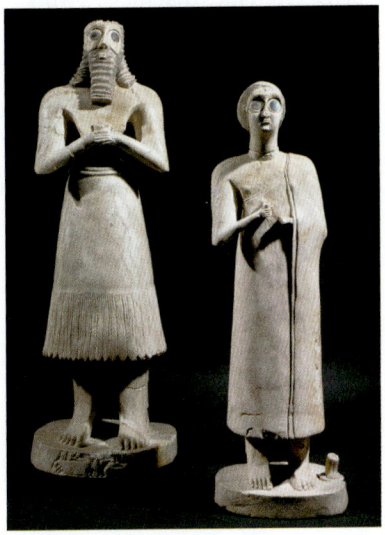

1.10.5 Votive Figures from the Temple of Abu, Eshnunna (Tell Asmar), c. 2700 BCE. Gypsum, male figure height 28⅜", female figure height 23¼". Iraq Museum, Baghdad, Iraq

Types of Analysis and Critique

There is no single right way to examine a work of art, and, as we shall see later on in this chapter, different methods can be combined to develop a more complete interpretation. Here is a summary of some important types of analysis.

Certain kinds of analyses (for example feminist, gender studies, and critical race) may be used when describing and explaining a set of ideas in the work of art itself, ideas related to beliefs held by the artist, or the context of the time period. Critique moves beyond the artist's biography, intentions, and the direct content to include contextual information (such as the historical treatment of women, considerations related to gender, or the way that race impacts a work of art) and highlights beliefs held by the person interpreting an artwork.

Formal analysis
Formal analysis involves looking closely and in detail at the work in order to consider how the formal elements and principles of art are used to create it and to convey meaning, and then carefully to describe them.

Stylistic analysis
Style in art is the particular combination of characteristics that make a work (or works) of art distinctive. Stylistic analysis focuses on these characteristics in a way that clearly identifies how they typify the work of an individual, are shared by a group of artists to create a movement, or are concentrated in a particular place or time period.

Iconographic analysis
Iconography—"image writing" or "writing with images"—examines the visual images and symbols used in a work of art and leads to an interpretation of the work's meaning. Iconographic analysis identifies objects and figures in an artwork as signs or symbols that can reflect religious or historical contexts, and the meaning of which was often more directly understood at a particular time by a specific culture, but may now be less apparent to us.

Contextual analysis
Contextual analysis looks at the making and viewing of the work in its context: it studies the atmosphere and ideas, often from a particular time or culture, which the artwork itself includes and reflects. Various aspects of context can be considered; for example, religious, historical, and biographical analysis are all types of contextual analysis.

Religious analysis considers the artwork in relation to the religious context in which it was made; this method often includes identification of narratives, key symbolism, and important figures.

Historical/social analysis considers historical events, either past or present, and the way they appear in an artwork.

Biographical analysis considers whether the artist's personal experiences and opinions may have affected the making or meaning of the artwork in some way.

Feminist analysis and critique
Inspired—as its name suggests—by feminism, feminist interpretations consider the role of women in an artwork as its subjects, creators, patrons, and viewers. A feminist approach can reflect the intentions of an artist, the perspective of a viewer, the interpretation of a critic, or a combination of two or three of these.

Gender studies analysis and critique
Gender studies analysis expands the considerations raised by feminist analysis to explore ways in which the work reflects experience based on a person's gender. This method of interpretation can also reflect the intentions of an artist, the perspective of a viewer, the interpretation of a critic, or all three.

Critical race analysis and critique
A method of interpretation that critically examines society and culture as it intersects with race, power, and institutional practices. It can also reflect the intentions of an artist, the perspective of a viewer, the interpretation of a critic, or all three.

Psychological analysis
This type of analysis investigates an artwork through consideration of the state of the artist's mind. Sometimes such interpretations make use of important psychological studies, such as those of Sigmund Freud or Carl Jung.

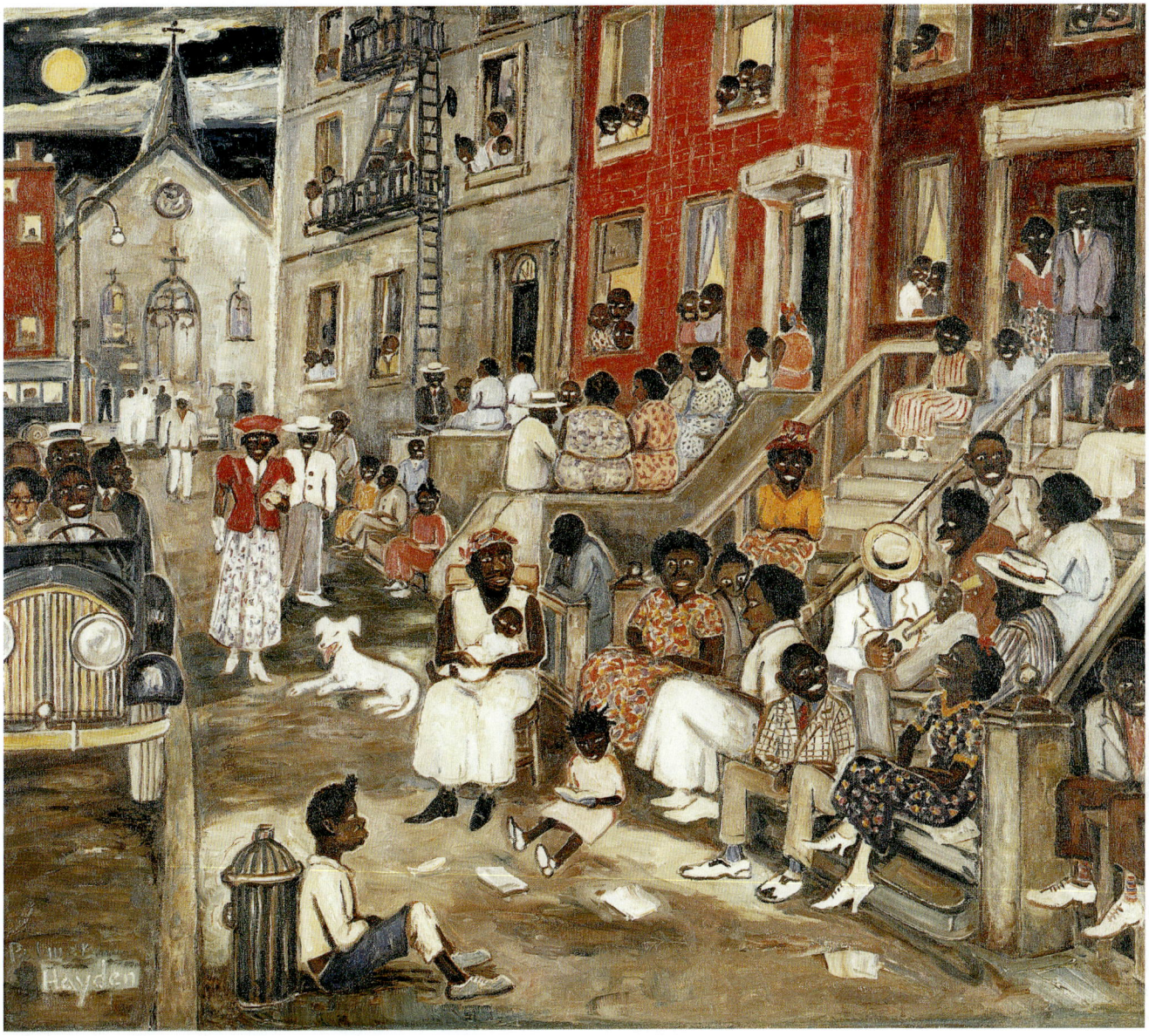

1.10.6 Palmer Hayden, *Midsummer Night in Harlem*, 1936. Oil on canvas, 25 × 30". Museum of African American Art, Los Angeles, California

Analysis of Historical Context

In the 1920s and 1930s African American history, cultural traditions, and ways of life were widely explored in literature, music, and the visual arts. The Harlem Renaissance movement flourished in Northern US cities as many people had moved from the rural south to find better opportunities and escape persecution. Harlem, New York, became an important center for African American cultural growth that American artist Palmer Hayden (1890–1973) wanted to celebrate. In *Midsummer Night in Harlem* (1936), he highlights the strong sense of community in his **subject matter** by showing people in the neighborhood gathering on stoops and sticking their heads out of apartment windows. Most people are shown awake and lively, with large smiles and bright eyes (**1.10.6**). The prominent location of the church at the end of the street to our left, and the dresses and hats people are wearing, indicate that they have just returned from an evening at church. The artist makes this, one of many daily-life scenes he painted, accessible by emphasizing realistic details of the gathering, such as the clothing, the car, the fire hydrant, and the fire escape. Hayden captures the time and place of this New York community by depicting joyful activity and the bonding of the people collectively under the full moon. At the same time, his use of flat, bright **hues** is a deliberate reference to the colors commonly found in traditional African art and

Subject matter: the topic depicted or dealt with in an artwork
Hue: general classification of a color; the distinctive characteristics of a color as seen in the visible spectrum, such as green or red

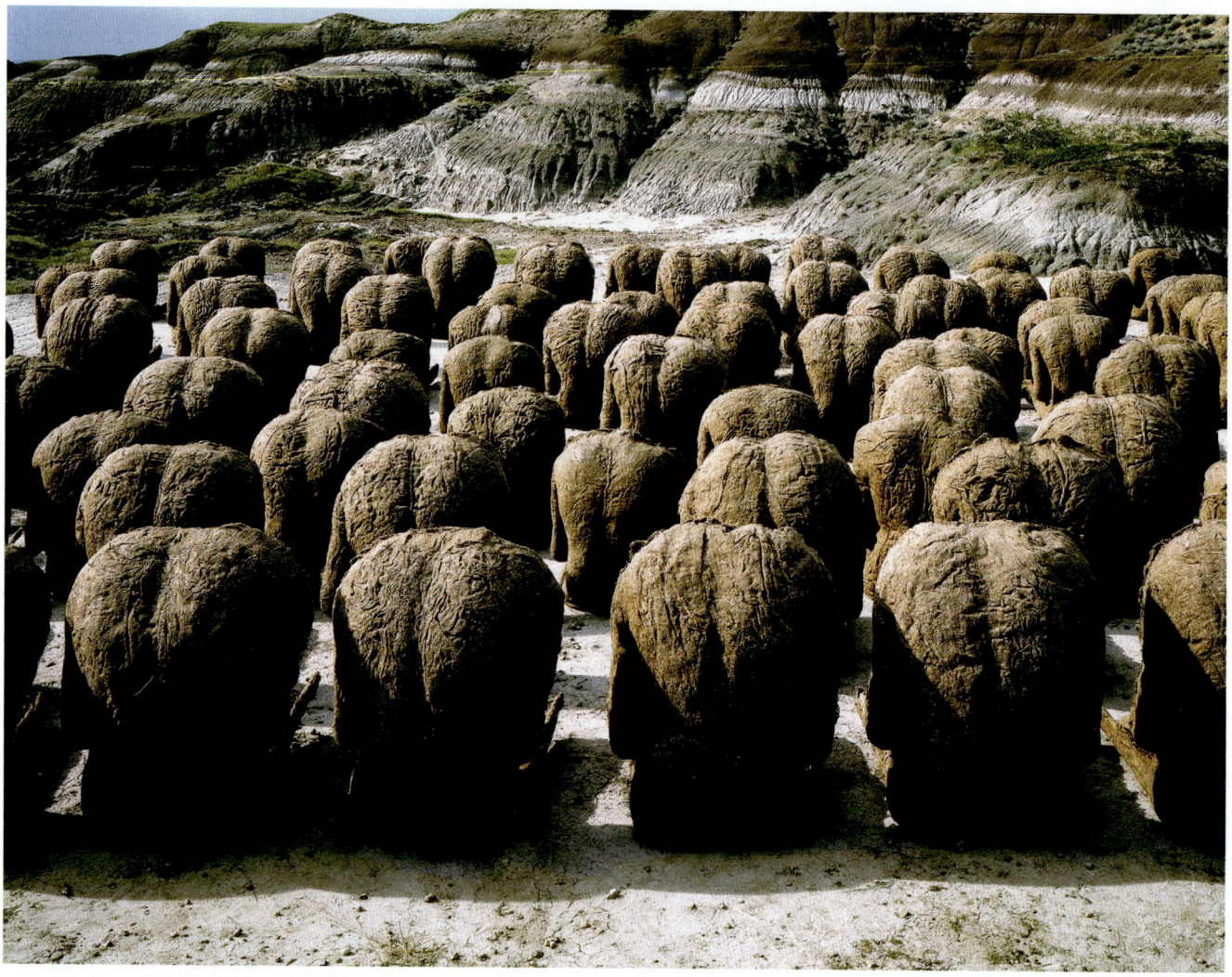

1.10.7 Magdalena Abakanowicz, *80 Backs*, 1976–80. Burlap and resin, height 24–27"; depth 19½–22"; width 21½–26". Museum of Modern Art, Pusan, South Korea

also in the modern artworks that the artist had encountered during his training in Paris in the late 1920s.

Analysis of Biographical Context

The Polish artist Magdalena Abakanowicz (b. 1930) uses as her source material her personal life experiences, Polish heritage, and imagery derived from Poland during World War II. We can understand her work much better if we know about her life. When she was nine years old, at the beginning of World War II, her village was occupied by invading German troops, and she witnessed at first hand the violent consequences of those events. At the end of the war, Poland spent the next forty-five years as a Soviet-Union-dominated Communist state. Abakanowicz chose to become a weaver and, instead of making realistic depictions of heroic workers, the style of art favored and indeed demanded by the ruling Soviet Union, she made abstract sculpture that explores issues of dignity, courage, and a will to survival under a totalitarian government. In *80 Backs* (**1.10.7**), the fragile, perishable fiber materials reflect her keen awareness of the human vulnerability to which she was so exposed during the war and its aftermath, and also the fact that in the early years of her career she had no conventional materials from which to sculpt: burlap sacks were some of the few things available to her. She also had no studio in which to work, and soft, pliable materials were useful in that they could be easily folded and stored.

Abakanowicz has often created works involving multiple, repeated figures. This reflects her experience of the Communist regime's emphasis on the collective over the individual, and its attempts to control personal expression.

In *80 Backs*, the burlap fabric is shaped into recognizable but abstracted human forms without heads or faces. A few years after making *80 Backs*, Abakanowicz said, "A human being turned into a crowd loses his human qualities. A crowd is only a thousand-times duplicated copy, a repetition, a multiplication. Amongst such a great number, one person is extremely close and at the same time terribly distant."

Analysis, Critique, and Interpretation

It could be said that all interpretation involves a balance between fact and opinion. Analysis involves careful consideration and discussion of specific aspects of an artwork while critique offers a theoretical framework for understanding it. Critiques of artworks often highlight the ideas, opinions, and experiences of the viewer. Art criticism, meaning critical review or commentary, includes judgment, but it does not have to result in a negative opinion.

Feminist Analysis and Critique

Biographical analysis usually takes gender, race, and societal position into account. Feminist analysis is a subset of biographical analysis when it studies the life experience of women artists in relation to their work. Feminist analysis has been expanded to include gender studies, and feminist critique additionally considers viewers' perspectives toward gender, the treatment of women as subjects, and the role of women at the time the artwork was made.

Grande Odalisque by the French artist Jean-Auguste-Dominique Ingres (1780–1867) was made in 1814 for a male French audience (**1.10.8**). Feminist analysis might compare this artwork to others made at the time and find that female nudes were often depicted as objects of desire and beauty. The woman is dressed as an odalisque (a woman in a harem), and so a feminist analysis might study the French view of women in Near Eastern society, who were considered fascinating for their exotic sensuality. Feminist analysis could seek an explanation for the interest in harem women in art during this period, and might find that women in France were demanding equal rights, causing men to pine for docile females.

1.10.8 Jean-Auguste-Dominique Ingres, *Grande Odalisque*, 1814. Oil on canvas, 35⅞ × 63¾". Musée du Louvre, Paris, France

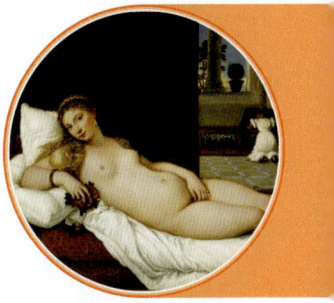

The tradition of "reclining nudes" began during the Renaissance and continued to influence later artists: see **4.9.8, p. 668**

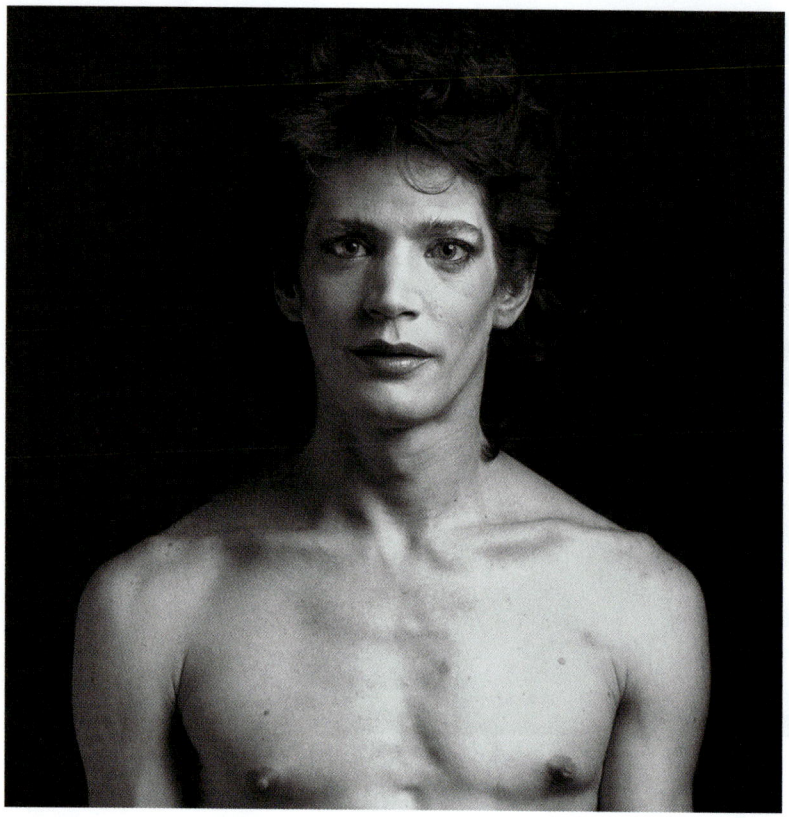

1.10.9 Robert Mapplethorpe, *Self-Portrait (#385)*, 1980. Gelatin silver print, 20 × 16"

A feminist might also study this subject's demure gaze, whereby she accepts her status as an object of beauty. At the time the picture was painted, critics complained that the figure's body parts were disproportionate: her back was too long, and her hips too wide. A feminist analysis would point out that Ingres believed that the back was a very sensual part of a woman's body, and that the painter claimed he could not stop himself, when painting, from adding what appear to be extra vertebrae.

Gender Studies Analysis

The American artist Robert Mapplethorpe (1946–1989) used his own lifestyle as inspiration for his photographs. The issue of gender affects his imagery because he chose subjects that were highly sexualized and often related to his own interests as a gay man. His photographs are carefully composed, elegantly lit, and technically perfect, making subjects that might previously have been seen as deviant appear normal, even beautiful. A national controversy was sparked

Research and Interpretation

The most effective research will include both primary and secondary sources.

Primary sources include:

- Artworks themselves (the most important primary source)
- Artists' statements
- Interviews with the artist
- Manuscripts, correspondence, and reviews written at the time that exhibitions of the artist's work were held
- Artists' own accounts of their life and work: autobiographies, memoirs, and oral histories recorded later
- Even the title of an artwork is verbal information, provided sometimes by the artist and sometimes by someone else.

Secondary sources include interpretations and analyses of primary sources by someone else, such as:

- Reference books (dictionaries of art, encyclopedias)
- Books by scholars
- Scholarly journal articles
- Book reviews
- Museum websites.*

*The Internet is a rich source of information, but you need to be very careful to evaluate the legitimacy of the sites. In general, websites are unreliable if it is unclear who wrote the information or what contributors' qualifications are. Many of the great museums around the world have their own websites, however, which are excellent and trustworthy sources of fascinating information. These websites are generally considered secondary sources, but may include primary source information, too.

Once you have done your research, you need to pull it all together to present a coherent interpretation of the artwork that shows that you understand the content and context. This interpretation should include your own opinion, carefully developed by considering your research findings. The strongest interpretations of an artwork combine the viewer's formal analysis, factual evidence from primary and secondary sources, and support from the work of specialists who know about the topics being covered.

by the exhibition of Mapplethorpe's work that traveled to several museums across the US shortly after the artist died of an AIDS-related illness in the late 1980s. Some museum officials and politicians considered the graphic sexual nature of some of Mapplethorpe's photographs to be problematic because the artist had been awarded a grant from public funds. Mapplethorpe, however, did not see a significant difference between a flower, a Classical sculpture, or a nude male figure.

Mapplethorpe's non-conformist view can be seen in his 1980 *Self-Portrait (#385)* in which his hair is curled and he wears eye shadow, blush, and lipstick (**1.10.9**). If one looks solely at his face, he seems to be a woman. His bare chest, however, tells us that he is a man. Mapplethorpe's appearance raises many questions about the assumptions we make based on the way people look. It also reveals the degree to which gender is a construction and suggests that not all people fit the conventional distinctions between the sexes. Mapplethorpe photographed what he wanted to see, the things that he considered visually interesting but did not find elsewhere in the art world. Interpreting Mapplethorpe's photograph from the perspective of gender studies encourages us to take his intentions into account, and to think about how gender affects our experience.

Critical Race Theory

Critical race theory is a method of interpretation that critically examines society and culture as it intersects with race, power, and institutional practices. Interpreting an artwork in this way takes into account the biography and life experience of the artist, the artist's intended meaning, and contextual cultural practices related to racial identity.

Le Déjeuner sur l'herbe: Les trois femmes noires (**1.10.10**) by the American artist Mickalene Thomas (b. 1971) continues and comments on the long tradition of reclining female nudes in the history of art. As the title indicates, the artist has borrowed the composition from Édouard Manet's famous painting from the mid-nineteenth century (see Portal, right). By changing the identity of the models to three black women instead of two clothed white men and a nude white woman, Thomas is bringing new considerations to a familiar artistic construct. Beyond the bold posture, which was used so often by male artists since Manet's time that it is now recognized as a convention, Thomas radically changes both the traditional form and the content in this painting. Thomas's work reconsiders ideals of beauty by foregrounding black women in leading rather than supporting (or non existent) roles.

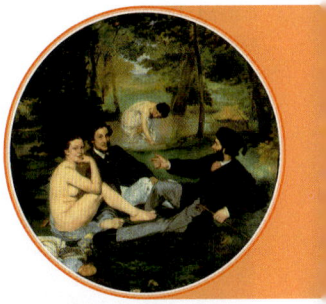

Mickalene Thomas's work directly quotes Manet's *Le Déjeuner sur l'Herbe*: see **3.8.2, p. 503**

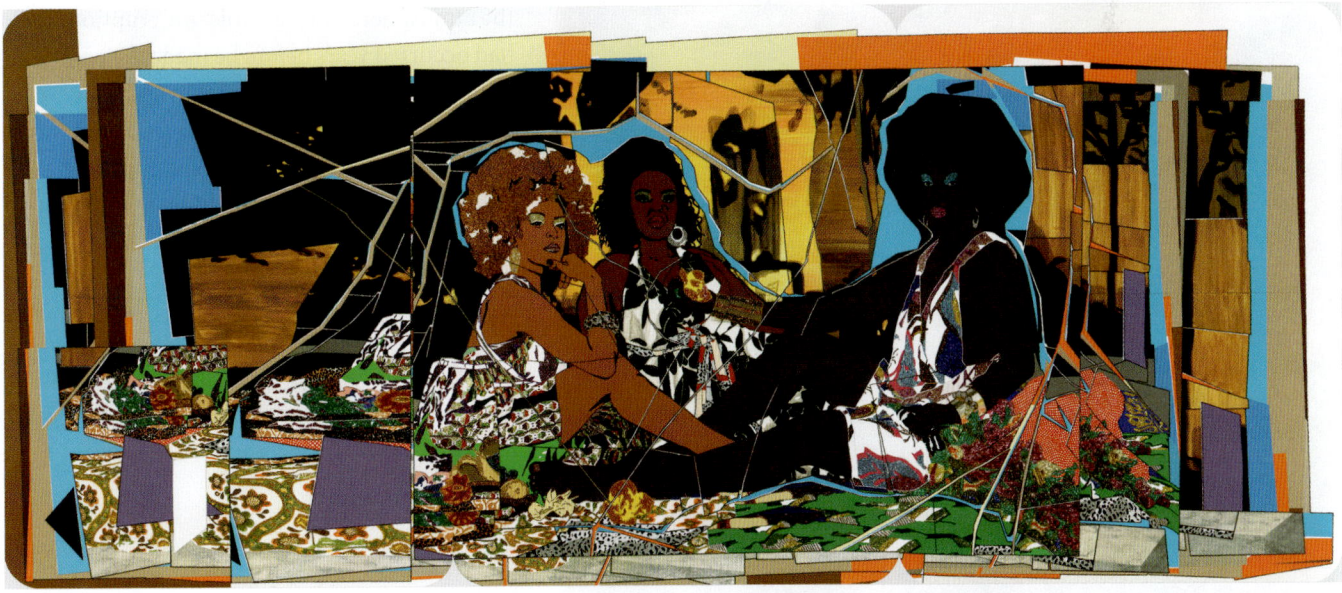

1.10.10 Mickalene Thomas, *Le Déjeuner sur l'herbe: Les trois femmes noires*, 2010. Rhinestones, acrylic, and enamel on wood panel, 10′ × 24′. Private collection

Collage: a work of art assembled by gluing flat materials, often paper, onto a surface. From the French *coller*, to glue
Mixed media: the use of a variety of materials to make a work of art
Pattern: an arrangement of predictably repeated elements
Genre: category of artistic subject matter, often with strongly influential histories and traditions
Expressionism, Expressionist: an artistic style at its height in 1920s Europe, devoted to representing subjective emotions and experiences instead of objective or external reality

In addition to cultural lenses, or the ways people from different cultures see the world, physical layering blends the past and present in the form of **collage** and **mixed media**. These materials are now familiar but were once considered radical in the realm of fine art. *Le Déjeuner sur l'Herbe: Les Trois Femmes Noires* is made of such traditional art materials as acrylic and enamel but it also introduces the less conventional rhinestones as a medium, and craft sensibility as a visual element.

An iconographic examination of the **patterns** and textures Thomas uses leads us back to her childhood. The fashions in New Jersey, where Thomas grew up in the 1970s, featured animal prints, faux fur, Marimekko fabric (brightly colored Finnish designs that had first been produced in the 1960s), and wood grain. Similarly, the style of the big hoop earrings, disco makeup, and Afros recalls 1970s Blaxploitation films (a **genre** that highlighted urban black experience and used anti-establishment plots). Thomas ultimately transforms the complexity of visual culture into a new realm beyond simplistic tradition or stereotypes. She incorporates and celebrates identities and experiences that might previously have been considered marginal.

Psychological Analysis

Psychological analysis considers the artist's state of mind when creating an artwork.

The Norwegian artist Edvard Munch (1863–1944) used the realm of his own mind as inspiration for *The Scream* (**1.10.11**). As a child he endured the death of his mother and sister, and throughout his life the artist suffered from physical illness and depression. These tragic experiences and psychological disturbances motivated his work. Munch reported that he felt psychologically driven to make art. His painting *The Scream* presents a ghoul-like figure on a bridge, with a vibrant red sky in the background. At first glance it appears to be a fictional scene. Entries in Munch's diary, however, indicate that his painting in fact represents his interpretation of an actual event. While walking on an overlook road with two friends (the figures looming in the distance), Munch saw the sky turn red and he froze with anxiety. Some scholars have suggested that Munch witnessed an incredibly intense sunset caused by the dust thrown into the atmosphere during a volcanic eruption that had occurred years before he made the painting. Others believe he experienced an attack of agoraphobia, or fear of open spaces. Like many **Expressionist** artworks, this painting does not depict what Munch actually saw, but what he felt.

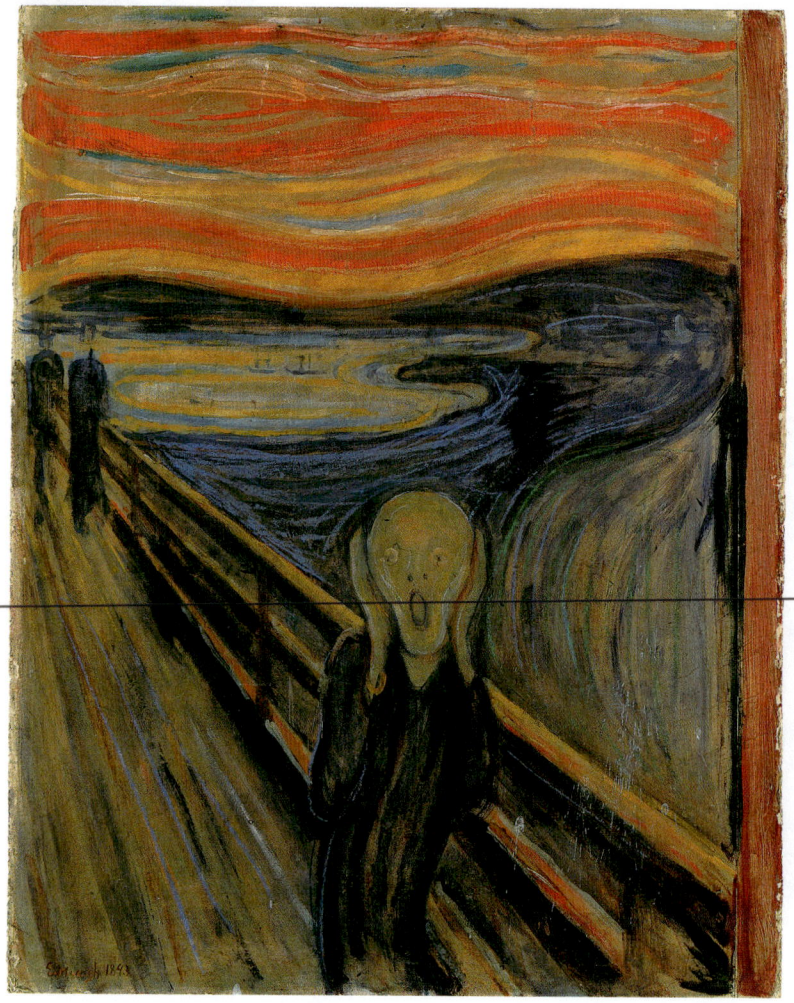

1.10.11 Edvard Munch, *The Scream*, 1893. Casein and tempera on cardboard, 35⅞" × 29⅛". Munch Museum, Oslo, Norway

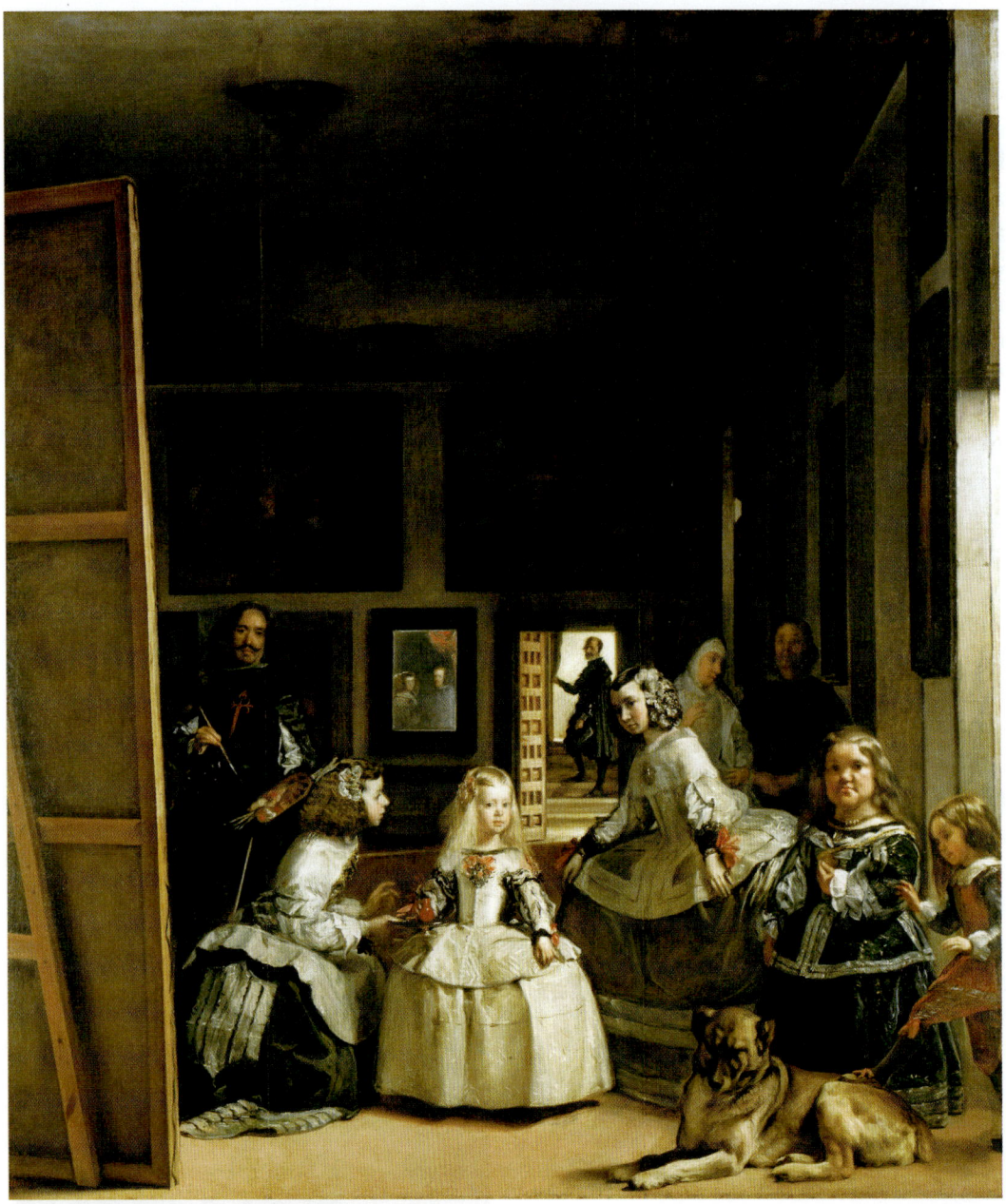

1.10.12a Diego de Silva y Velázquez, *Las Meninas*, c. 1656. Oil on canvas, 10'5¼" × 9'¾". Museo Nacional del Prado, Madrid, Spain

Combined Analysis in Historical and Contemporary Art

While it is rare to be able to use every method discussed in this chapter for every artwork, we can often consider one work in many ways. Using these modes of analysis, we can arrive at a better and more rounded understanding of both famous pieces that have been studied by scholars for a long time and more recent artworks that the artists themselves help us to understand through their statements and explanations.

Form and Content in *Las Meninas*

A *formal* analysis considers what the artist has communicated using a visual language. This kind of detailed description often enhances our awareness of the appearance of a work of art. *Las Meninas* (*The Maids of Honor*) by Diego de Silva y Velázquez (1599–1660) shows members of the court of the Spanish King Philip IV gathering in a room in the Alcázar Palace (**1.10.12a**). The painter depicts himself on the left, painting a large canvas. The Princess Margarita is posed in the center, with her ladies-in-waiting ("las meninas") surrounding her. Court workers, including dwarfs, are present as well.

Vanishing point: the point in a work of art at which imaginary sight lines appear to converge, suggesting depth
Linear perspective: a system using converging imaginary sight lines to create the illusion of depth
Depth: the degree of recession in perspective
Volume: the space filled or enclosed by a three-dimensional figure or object
Neutral: colors (such as blacks, whites, grays, and dull gray-browns) made by mixing complementary hues
Palette: the range of colors used by an artist
Foreground: the part of a work depicted as nearest to the viewer
Background: the part of a work depicted furthest from the viewer's space, often behind the main subject matter
Balance: a principle of art in which elements are used to create a symmetrical or asymmetrical sense of visual weight in an artwork
Focal point: the center of interest or activity in a work of art, often drawing the viewer's attention to the most important element
Rhythm: the regular or ordered repetition of elements in the work

The implied lines suggested by the black frames on the right wall and the ceiling fixtures converge on the chest of the man standing in the doorway. This is the **vanishing point** required in **linear perspective** to create an illusion of **depth**, as if the viewer is looking into a real room. All the figures in the painting have a realistic sense of **volume** and are arranged to emphasize further the illusion of looking into a real space. Notice how they overlap one another, and that those toward the back of the room are smaller than those at the front. The painting is more than 10 ft. tall, which allows Velázquez to make the figures lifesize, further reinforcing the illusion of three-dimensional space. Finally, most of the colors in the painting are **neutral**. The **palette** of brown, gray, beige, and black creates the impression of a dark space the depth of which is emphasized by the light coming in from a window on the right and the door at the back.

Velázquez highlights several areas he wants to emphasize. The young princess is in the central **foreground**, the part of the painting nearest to us, well lit, and shown attended by her maids. In the **background**, the mysterious male figure is emphasized because his black form contrasts with the light coming through the doorway. The painter himself stands proudly at his work. And we notice the mirror on the back wall because of its blurry shiny surface: whom does it reflect? (**1.10.12b**). Touches of red lead our eye around the painting to significant points of interest: from Margarita's flowers, to the cross on Velázquez's chest, to the red curtain in the mirror on the back wall.

The painting is **balanced** in various ways. (**1.10.12c**) All of the figures are placed in the lighter bottom half of the canvas, balanced by the sparseness of the wall and darker ceiling that take up the top half. While the figures at first appear to be arranged chaotically, they are actually placed in several stable pyramidal arrangements. One triangle highlights three of the composition's **focal points**: the mirror, Margarita, and the man in the doorway. The figures are of different heights and arranged so that our eye is led in a rhythmic line from Velázquez on the left through to the right of the painting: if you trace the heads of the figures in the foreground with your finger, you will sense the visual **rhythm**.

A *contextual* analysis gives us a better understanding of the content of the work of art by providing information about the time in which it was made. The young girl is the Spanish princess Margarita Habsburg; the couple in the mirror are her parents, King Philip IV of Spain and Marianna of Austria. The mysterious man in the doorway is Nieto, the queen's chamberlain. Velázquez uses the mirror and this portrayal of an essential aide to the queen subtly to indicate the presence of the royal couple without violating etiquette, which did not permit the showing of the king and queen in a portrait with lesser court members.

A *biographical* analysis suggests why Velázquez placed himself in a painting that obliquely shows the presence of the king. One reason was that he was the king's favorite painter and assistant. It was extremely bold of him to paint himself into a scene with the royal family; by doing so, he wished to show his closeness with the king, and to raise his own status.

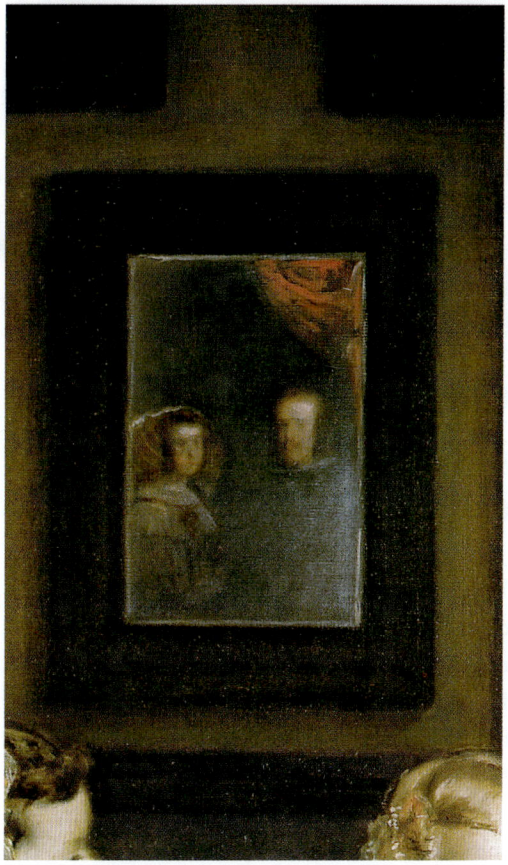

1.10.12b Detail of Diego de Silva y Velázquez, *Las Meninas*

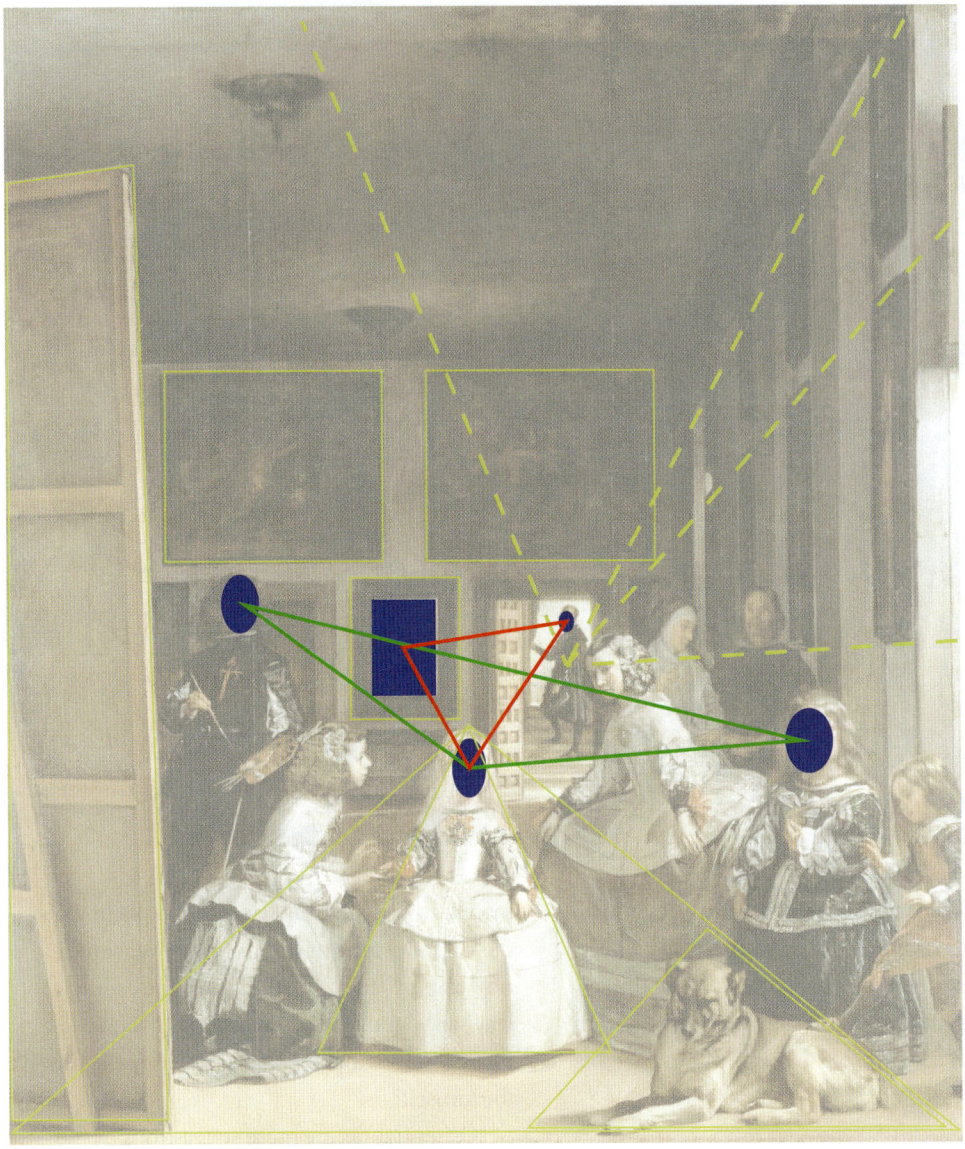

1.10.12c A formal analysis of Las Meninas reveals that the artist carefully organized the objects and people in his painting. Yellow lines show us the balance of shapes in the composition, and the two triangles connect various focal points (picked out in blue)

An *iconographic* analysis focusing only on the cross Velázquez wears, the cross of the Order of Santiago, tells us a lot about the symbol and about the times. Velázquez had a lifelong ambition to become a knight of the order, but the order challenged his membership for decades because he was not a noble, he had some Moorish (Muslim) ancestry, and he was considered a craftsman. The members saw painting as simply a manual craft rather than a liberal (or high-minded) art. In truth, Velázquez did not meet any of the criteria, but after hundreds of supportive interviews, and with the backing of both the king and the pope, the artist was finally knighted in 1659, three years after he painted *Las Meninas*. Historians have found evidence that the king ordered the cross painted on after Velázquez's death to honor the artist for having achieved his lifelong goal.

What Is the Meaning of *Las Meninas*?

After considering the various methods of analysis discussed above, scholars have arrived at a hypothesis as to what Velázquez wanted to say. They suggest that the artist was defending the nobility of painting itself. In order to be accepted as a knight, he needed to prove that his skill was not mere craft, but also an intellectual endeavor. Therefore Velázquez created a brilliant illusion of space through his mastery of atmosphere and perspective. Even more boldly, he included the king in a painting that also featured a

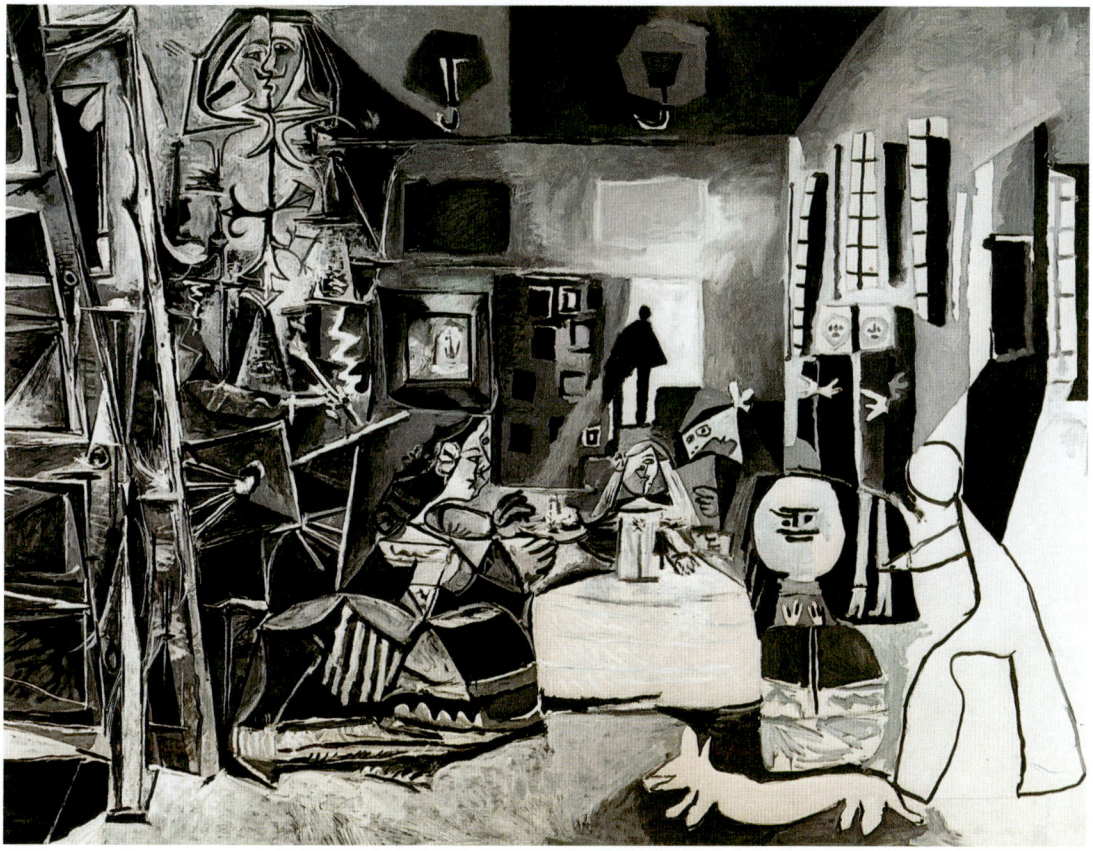

1.10.13 Pablo Picasso, *Las Meninas*, first in a series, 1957. Oil on canvas, 6'4⅜" × 8'6⅜". Museo Picasso, Barcelona, Spain

self-portrait of the artist, demonstrating the king's clear support for the painter. Velázquez's painting is an intentional effort to raise the status of painters, and to raise his own status in Spanish society.

The Influence of *Las Meninas*

Artists often study and copy the work of artists they admire, and may use such studies to create works in their own individual style. The Spanish painter Pablo Picasso (1881–1973) reimagined *Las Meninas* many times.

Pablo Picasso did not come to admire Velázquez until late in his own career, when he began to set his skills against the great artists of the past. At the age of seventy-six, Picasso locked himself in a room with a poster of *Las Meninas* and created forty-five paintings in response to Velázquez's masterpiece. In the first work in the series, Picasso alters the size of the canvas (**1.10.13**). While mimicking Velázquez, he uses the elements and principles differently. For example, although Picasso does not use linear perspective, he creates a sense of depth by making Nieto small in scale and placing his dark figure in the bright doorway. Velázquez now appears to be floating up to the ceiling, leaving his paintbrushes and palette below. Is Picasso removing the old master to make room for himself?

Other figures are mere suggestions of the forms they were in the original painting. Picasso has broken them down into **abstract** parts. Margarita is outlined with no sense of volume, and the heads of the figures on the right are just black lines on white circles. The play of light on the figures is similar to the original, but Picasso's approach is more abstract: on the right, he lines up a row of windows that shine a bright white on the figure there (which correlates to the male dwarf in the original). Margarita, highlighted in Velázquez's painting, is of a much lighter value than the other figures in Picasso's version, emphasizing that she is the most important person in the group. The majority of the rest of the series, in fact, are studies of Margarita specifically. This may relate to Picasso's own life. He first saw *Las Meninas* as a boy, just after his younger sister had died; she had been about the

Abstract: art imagery that departs from recognizable images of the natural world

same age as Margarita here. Picasso has totally reinterpreted this artwork to make it his own; he has even replaced the large mastiff in Velázquez's painting with his own dog.

Form and Content in "Chaos Machine"

The drawing "Chaos Machine," from *The Chaos Series* by the Welsh contemporary artist Clive King (b. 1944) is much more abstract than the **representational** painting *Las Meninas*, but its imagery can similarly be accessed through description and analysis. After examining both artworks more fully we come to a deeper understanding. With *Las Meninas* we initially see imagery we recognize as people in a room, but we do not actually know who those individuals are, the circumstances of their gathering, or the meaning of the symbolism until we have analysed the imagery and conducted research. Similarly, the lines and shapes in "Chaos Machine" may at first seem meaningless to us and it may be hard to make sense of the drawings (**1.10.14**). As we learn more about the piece, though, this imagery opens up to tell a story of the artist's memories from an intense childhood experience.

What do we see when we look at "Chaos Machine"? A formal analysis reveals three panels with a **monochromatic** palette. We will be looking at the triptych as a unified whole, but each part could also be considered a separate work on its own. Each section contains similar curving **lines** in varying densities: smaller and more ribbon-like on the left, larger and more scroll-like in the middle, and smallest and more confetti-like on the right. We also see a repeated ladder-like structure from varying distances: furthest away and more fully included on the left, closer and less complete in the middle, closest and most obscure on the right. The dark structure functions as a kind of focal point in each panel, with the curving lines filling in the foreground and background. All three panels feature a composition based on symmetrical balance, with elements on the left matched by similar elements on the right.

King uses the **medium** of drawing, specifically pen and ink, which has traditionally been considered to play a supporting or secondary role to painting and sculpture. The artist feels that drawing allows him to involve the viewer in an "equal physical and emotional engagement" through scale, depth, and intensity. Because each paper is 6 ft. 6 in. tall, somewhat larger than the artist, he works from inside the picture. As he is making the marks, they surround and overwhelm him, much as they do viewers when they look at the piece. The forms build up over time and create dense areas

Representational: art that depicts figures and objects so that we recognize what is represented
Monochromatic: having one or more values of one color
Line: a mark, or implied mark, between two endpoints
Medium (plural **media**): the material on or from which an artist chooses to make a work of art, for example canvas and oil paint, marble, engraving, video, or architecture

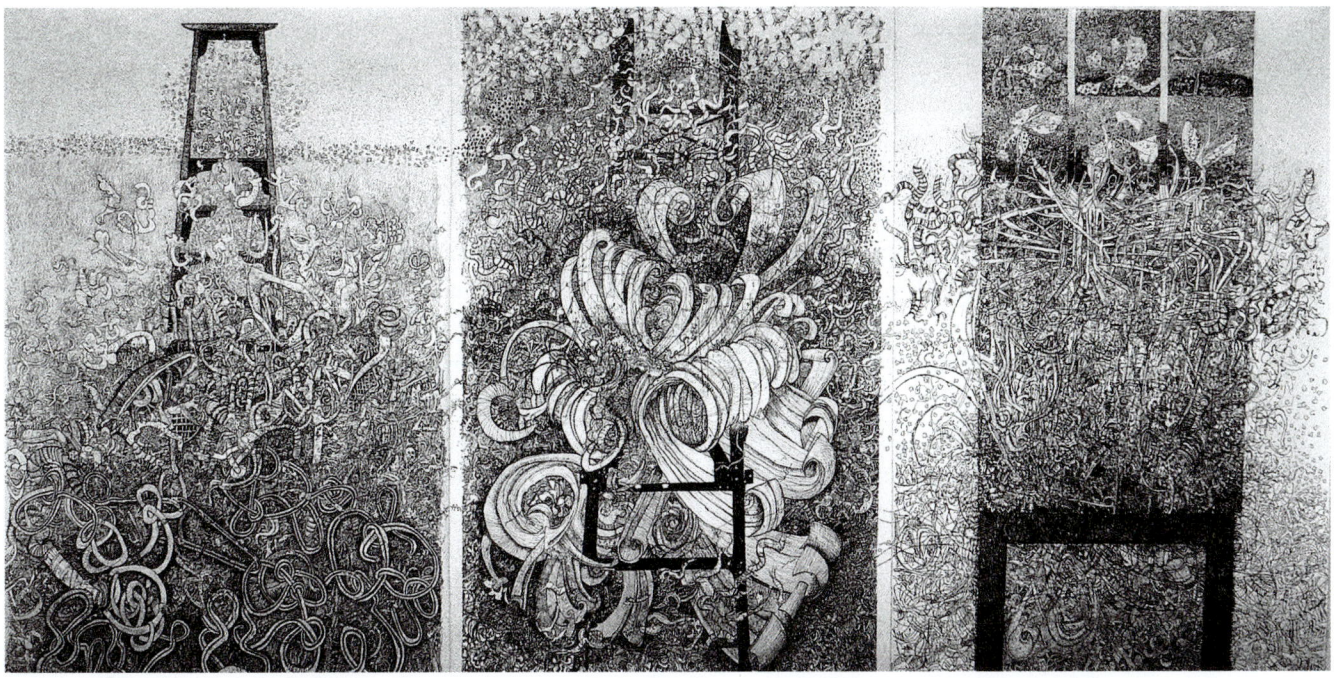

1.10.14 Clive King, "Chaos Machine," 2015–16 (from *The Chaos Series*, an ongoing series of drawings). Black ink on paper, three drawings, each 6' 6" × 4' 8"

Organic: having irregular forms and shapes, as though derived from living organisms

at the bottom of the left panel, throughout the entire middle panel, and down the center of the right panel.

A contextual analysis of "Chaos Machine" would include a historical event the artist experienced when he was twelve years old. King grew up near Aberfan (pronounced "ab-air-van"), a Welsh coal-mining village located on a hillside. As a bi-product of the mining, millions of tons of debris from the Merthyr Valley Colliery were deposited on the side of Mynydd Merthyr (pronounced "munnith murthur"), the ridge directly above Aberfan. These deposits, called spoil heaps or tips, consisted of loose rock and earth. At Mynydd Merthyr the porous sandstone ridge was located over several underground springs. On October 21, 1966 the ground shifted and the tip collapsed, causing a landslide of the cones of waste coal and debris that destroyed everything in its wake. The Pantglas Junior School happened to be in the village below and 116 of its students and 5 teachers were amongst the casualties of the catastrophe. The timing was especially poignant, as minutes before the collapse the students had not been in their classrooms, and had the landslide happened several hours later, they would have already left for the half-term holiday.

Very few people were recovered from the rubble right after the collapse. In total, 144 people died from impact and suffocation, including virtually all the village's children: an entire generation disappeared in the blink of an eye. Residents and school officials had raised complaints and concerns about the dangers associated with the tip for years. The National Coal Board, which operated the mine, was blamed for extreme negligence and paid out compensation to families for loss, trauma, and destruction of property. After the accident, new legislation from Parliament created safety regulations in consultation with mines and quarries.

A *biographical* analysis helps us understand that these drawings represent the artist's memories of the Aberfan disaster. For more than forty years he tried unsuccessfully to interpret his feelings of the experience through figurative approaches. With "Chaos Machine" (and several later artworks), King felt that he had finally come up with a workable solution to express his experience. The ambiguity possible through a more abstract system of dynamic imagery allowed the artist to make better sense of what he had seen, and to convey it more appropriately.

In addition to autobiographical events, King's work explores the uneasy relationship between landscape and industry, cultural erosion and synthesis, through the evocation of a sense of place. An *iconographic analysis* helps us understand the symbolism the artist created. The left panel shows the top of the winding tower, or headframe (the structure above an underground mine), with the debris from the tip rising from below like an explosion. In the center, we are engulfed by the momentum of the coal tip collapsing. On the right, we see wreckage inspired by the crunched-up mess, including windows and doorways, which the artist witnessed during secret visits to the inside of some of the houses and the school after the disaster.

What Is the Meaning of "Chaos Machine"?

By synthesizing the visual and contextual, biographical, and iconographic information we have gathered about "Chaos Machine," we can suggest an explanation of what King was trying to say. The symbolism in "Chaos Machine" combines the horrors of factual information and personal experience into a vision of a tragedy resulting from human error. After decades of attempting to do this subject justice through realism, the artist found that the ephemeral and suggestive nature of abstraction produced a more fitting expression of both the event and his experience. The simultaneous whimsy, visual intrigue, and violence of the **organic** shapes interweaving through the industrial frame of the mine equipment and exploding around the architecture, create a beautiful and powerful memorial to the victims and the historical moment when their lives were lost.

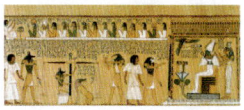

4.2.10 Book of the Dead of Hunefer, Egypt, *c.* 1275 BCE, p. 584

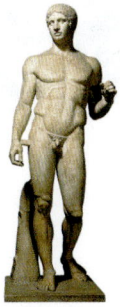

3.1.29 Polykleitos, *Doryphoros* (Roman version), *c.* 120–50 BCE, p. 384

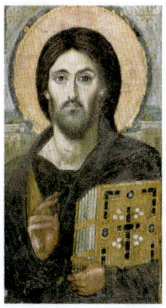

3.2.7 Christ icon, Egypt, 6th century, p. 395

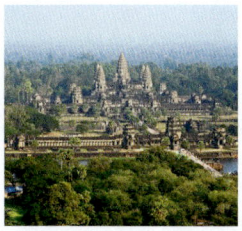

3.3.26 Angkor Wat, Siem Reap, Cambodia, 12th century, p. 426

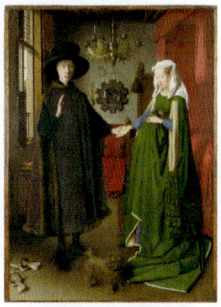

3.6.8a Jan van Eyck, *The Arnolfini Portrait*, 1434, p. 466

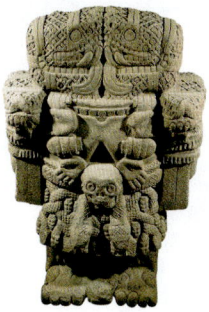

3.4.16 *The Mother Goddess*, Coatlicue, Aztec, *c.* 1487–1520, p. 439

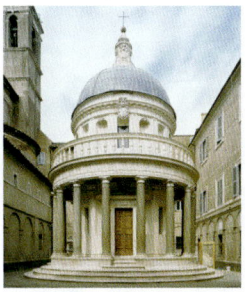

2.5.25 Donato Bramante, Tempietto, San Pietro in Montorio, Italy, *c.* 1502, p. 273

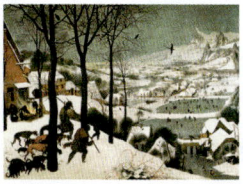

1.9.8 Pieter Bruegel, *Hunters in the Snow*, 1565, p. 164

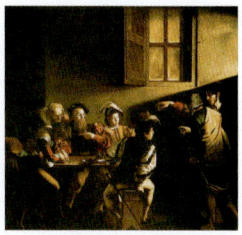

1.3.6 Caravaggio, *The Calling of St. Matthew*, *c.* 1599–1600, p. 79

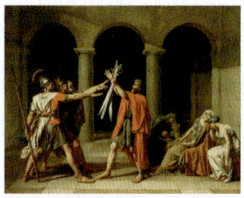

3.7.7 Jacques-Louis David, *The Oath of the Horatii*, 1784, p. 493

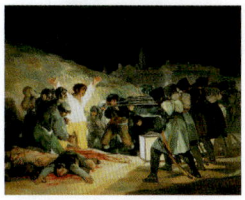

4.7.9 Francisco Goya, *The Third of May, 1808*, 1814, p. 645

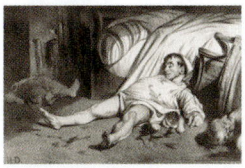

2.3.15 Honoré Daumier, *Rue Transnonain, April 15, 1834*, 1834, p. 234

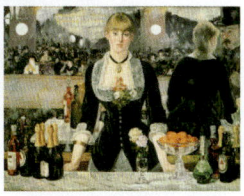

4.5.11 Édouard Manet, *A Bar at the Folies-Bergère*, 1882, p. 623

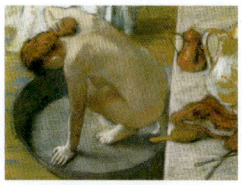

2.1.14 Edgar Degas, *The Tub*, 1886, p. 200

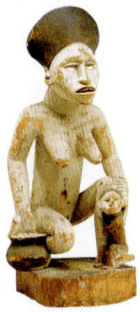

4.3.9 Kneeling female figure, Yombe, late 19th/early 20th century, p. 598

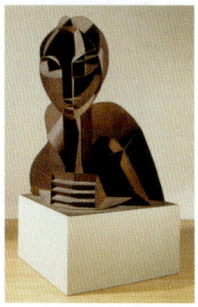

2.4.17 Naum Gabo, *Constructed Head No. 2*, 1916, p. 253

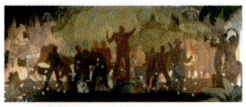

3.9.23 Aaron Douglas, *Aspects of Negro Life...*, 1934, p. 537

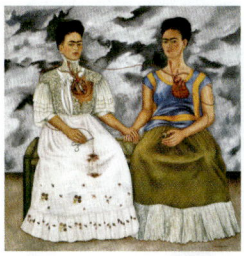

3.9.13 Frida Kahlo, *The Two Fridas*, 1939, p. 532

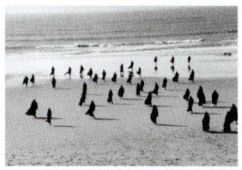

3.10.12b Shirin Neshat, *Rapture* series, 1999, p. 553

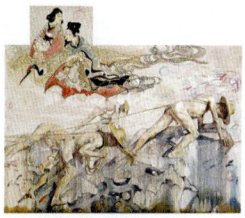

2.2.16 Hung Liu, *Interregnum*, 2002, p. 218

Art is a form of visual communication: artists make art because they want to express something. Just as writers consider carefully the form that best expresses what they want to say (a long novel, a brief poem, a play or film script, for example), artists consider carefully the materials and processes available to communicate their visual ideas. In fact, art can be made from almost anything: one contemporary artist has used elephant dung in his paintings. There are certain media and processes that have been commonly used by artists, some of them for thousands of years, but others that have been developed more recently. In this part you will learn how most of the art that you will encounter has been made.

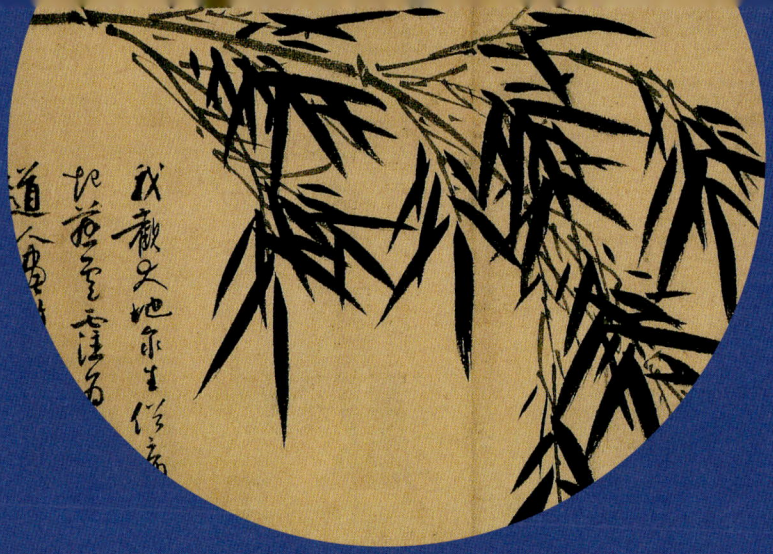

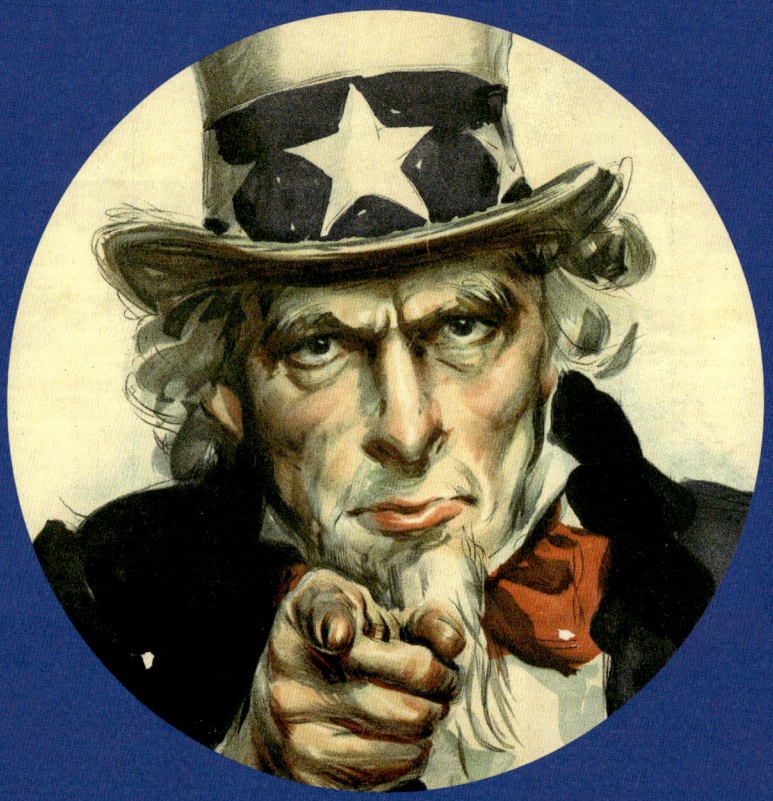

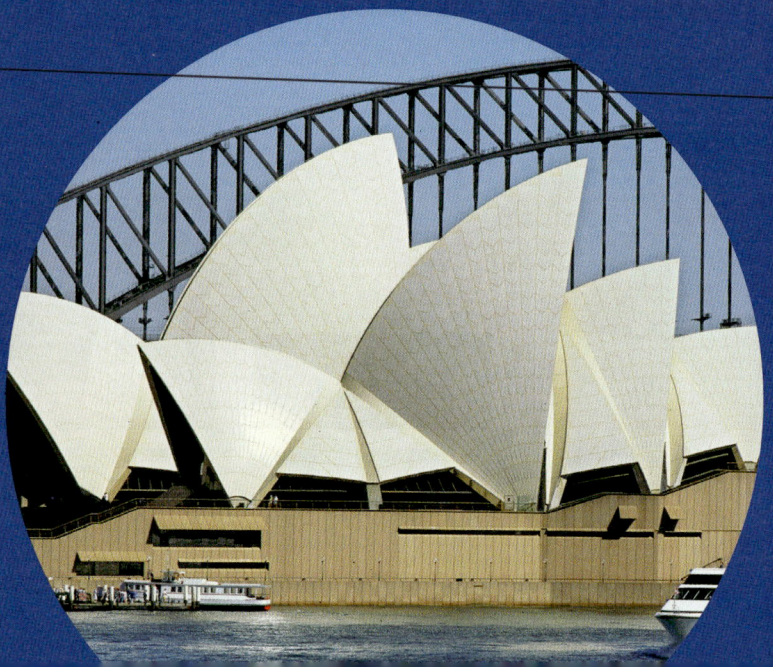

Part 2

Media and Processes

The main media and processes of art are:

Drawing

Painting

Printmaking

Sculpture

Architecture

The Tradition of Craft

Visual Communication Design

Photography

Film/Video and Digital Art

Alternative Media and Processes

2.1 Drawing

Sketch: a rough preliminary version of a work or part of a work

> He who pretends to be either painter or engraver without being a master of drawing is an imposter.
>
> (William Blake, English artist and poet)

As William Blake suggests, drawing—defined as the depiction of shapes and forms on a surface, primarily by means of lines—is a fundamental artistic skill. Even before we learn to write, we learn to draw; we draw the shape of a cat before we can write the word. Drawing is spontaneous, a convenient way for us to "make our mark" on the world. Like the instinctive crayon marks children make as they explore and develop their fine motor skills, drawing provides a primal outlet for artistic energy and ideas.

Artists draw for many reasons: to define their ideas, to plan for larger projects, to resolve design issues in preparatory **sketches**, and to record their visual observations. Of course, drawings can also be finished works of art in their own right.

Drawing is the basis of all visual communication. Most artists and designers continue to develop their drawing skills throughout their lives.

Functions of Drawing

Because drawing is a fundamental skill it is used, to some degree, in every artistic medium. Leonardo da Vinci (1452–1519) used drawing to examine the world. His sketchbooks are full of ideas and images, illustrating both his speculative thought and his careful observations. Amongst his explorations, Leonardo dissected

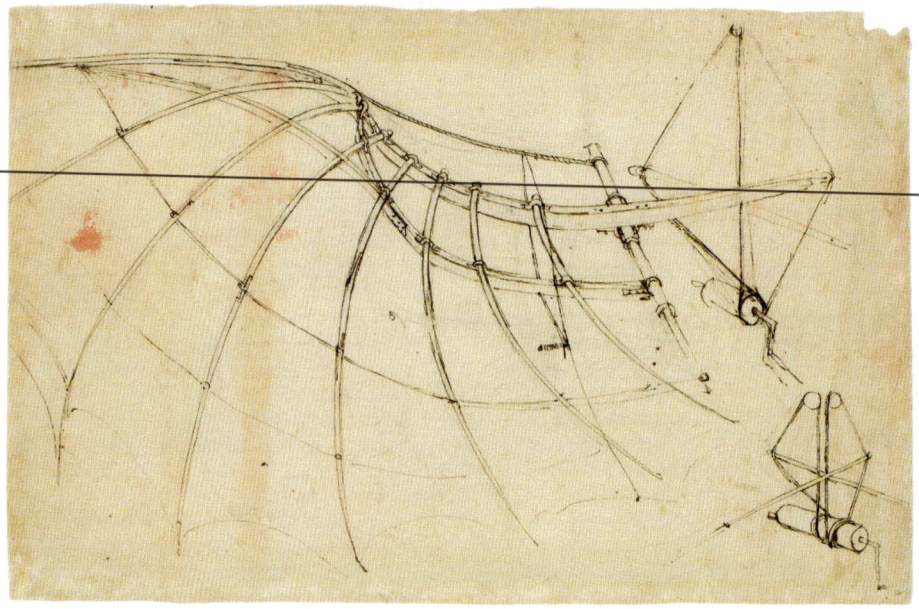

2.1.1 Leonardo da Vinci, *Drawing for a wing of a flying machine*, from the *Codice Atlantico*, fol. 858r. Pen and ink. Biblioteca Ambrosiana, Milan, Italy

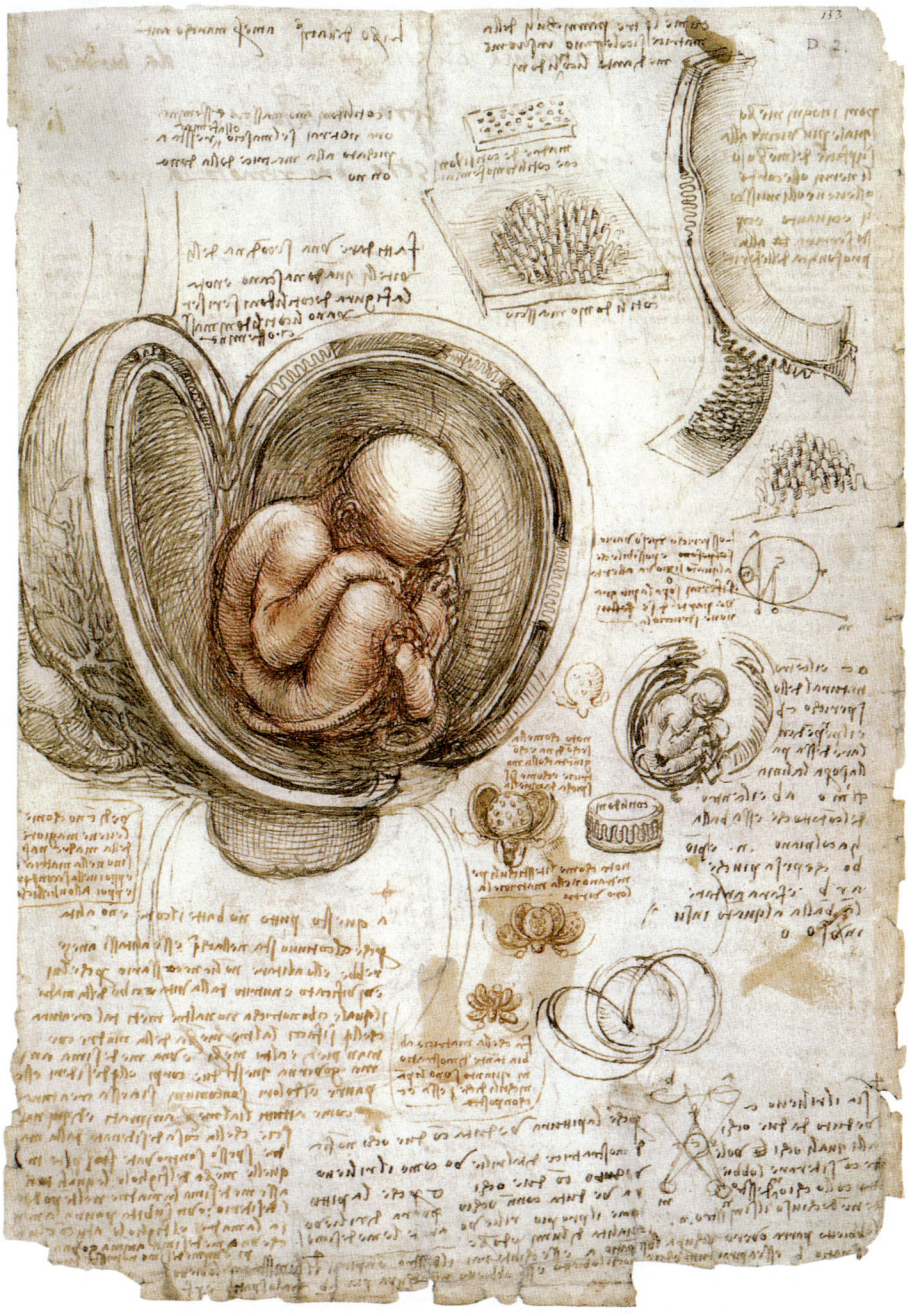

2.1.2 Leonardo da Vinci, *Studies of the fetus in the womb*, c. 1510–13. Pen and ink and wash over red chalk and traces of black chalk, 12 × 8¾". Royal Collection, London, England

human bodies and then drew what he saw. He also studied the works of other artists, and observed the effects of light and shadow on a form. He investigated the mechanics of a bird's wing, and considered whether humans might also be able to fly if such mechanics were re-created on a human scale. His drawing of a flying machine illustrates a concept that had never been considered in this way before (**2.1.1**). Drawing enabled Leonardo to express his ideas beyond what could be said in words.

Some of Leonardo's most revolutionary drawings depict the interior anatomy of the human body (**2.1.2**). These drawings are especially rare because the Church banned all acts that desecrated the body, including dissection. Leonardo may have been allowed to record his observations because he practiced his drawing methodically and with great care. Some speculate that the Church was interested in Leonardo's observations as possible evidence of how the human soul resides in the body.

All artists draw for the same reasons as Leonardo: as an end in itself, to think, and to prepare and plan other works. Drawing played an essential role in Raphael's planning

Gateway to Art: Raphael, *The School of Athens*
Drawing in the Design Process

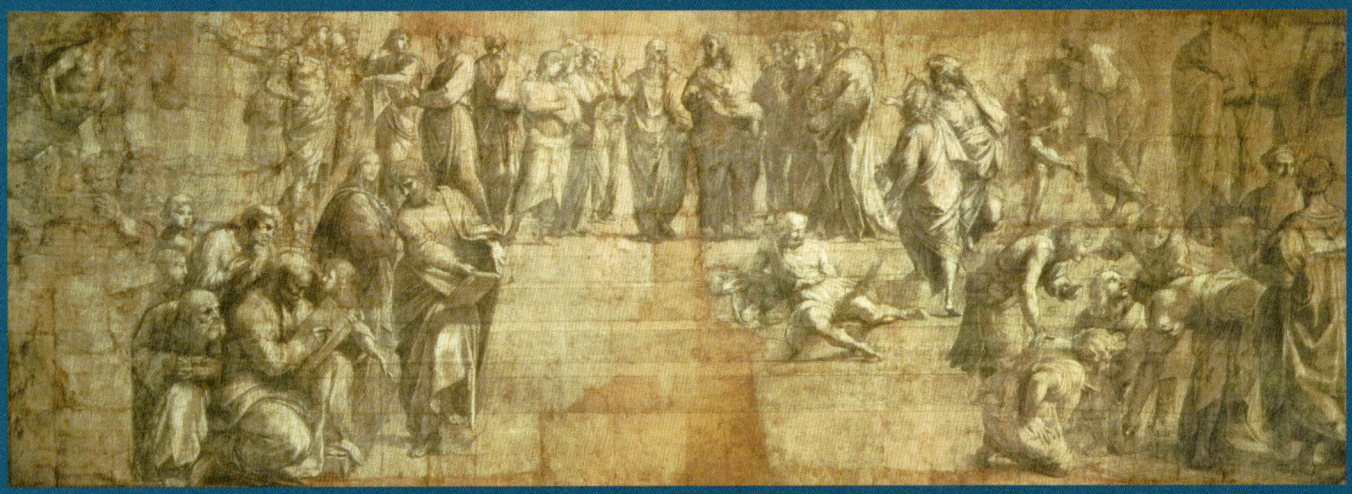

2.1.3a Raphael, Cartoon for *The School of Athens*, c. 1509. Charcoal and chalk, 9'4¼" × 26'4⅝". Biblioteca Ambrosiana, Milan, Italy

When the Italian painter Raphael (1483–1520) prepared to paint *The School of Athens*, he drew the image in advance (**2.1.3a**), practicing before he tackled the larger work (**2.1.3b**).

His preliminary drawings allowed Raphael to refine his ideas and perfect the image at a smaller scale before investing in the more expensive painting materials he used for the final version.

The artist began the painting process by creating a large drawing of the work, almost the same size as the final painting, to use as the design for a mural. This design, called the cartoon, was perforated with small pinholes all along where the lines were drawn. It was then positioned on the wall where Raphael intended to paint the work, and powdered charcoal dust was forced through the small holes in the cartoon's surface, leaving behind an impression of the original drawing. These marks would aid Raphael in drawing the image onto the wall. He applied a thin layer of plaster, re-powdered the charcoal dust through the cartoon if necessary, and then began to paint *The School of Athens*.

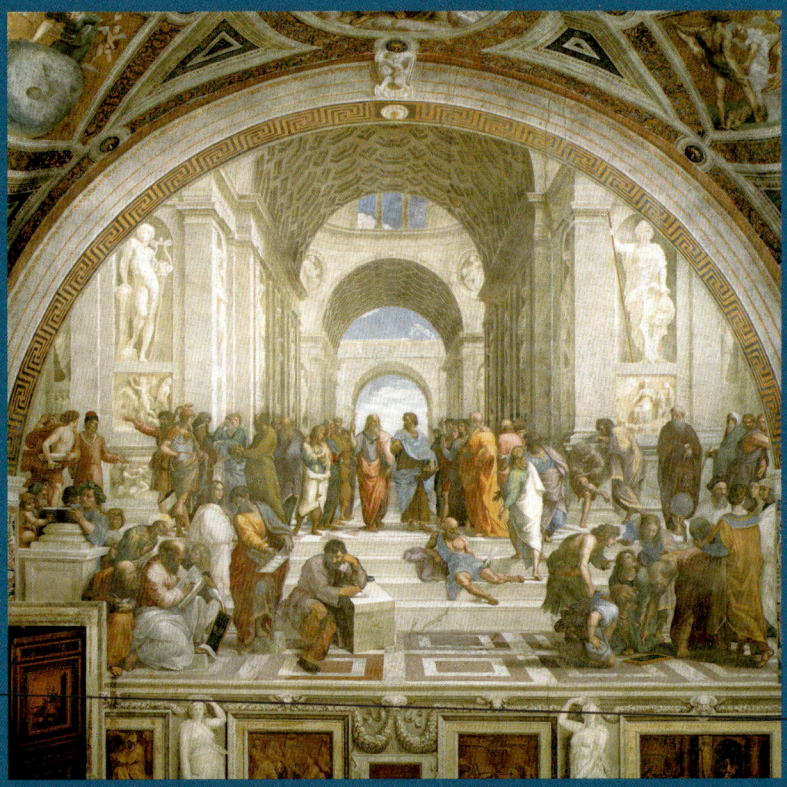

2.1.3b Raphael, *The School of Athens*, 1510–11. Fresco, 16'8" × 25'. Stanza della Segnatura, Vatican City, Italy

For the other Raphael Gateway boxes, see p. 90, p. 146, p. 470, and p. 617

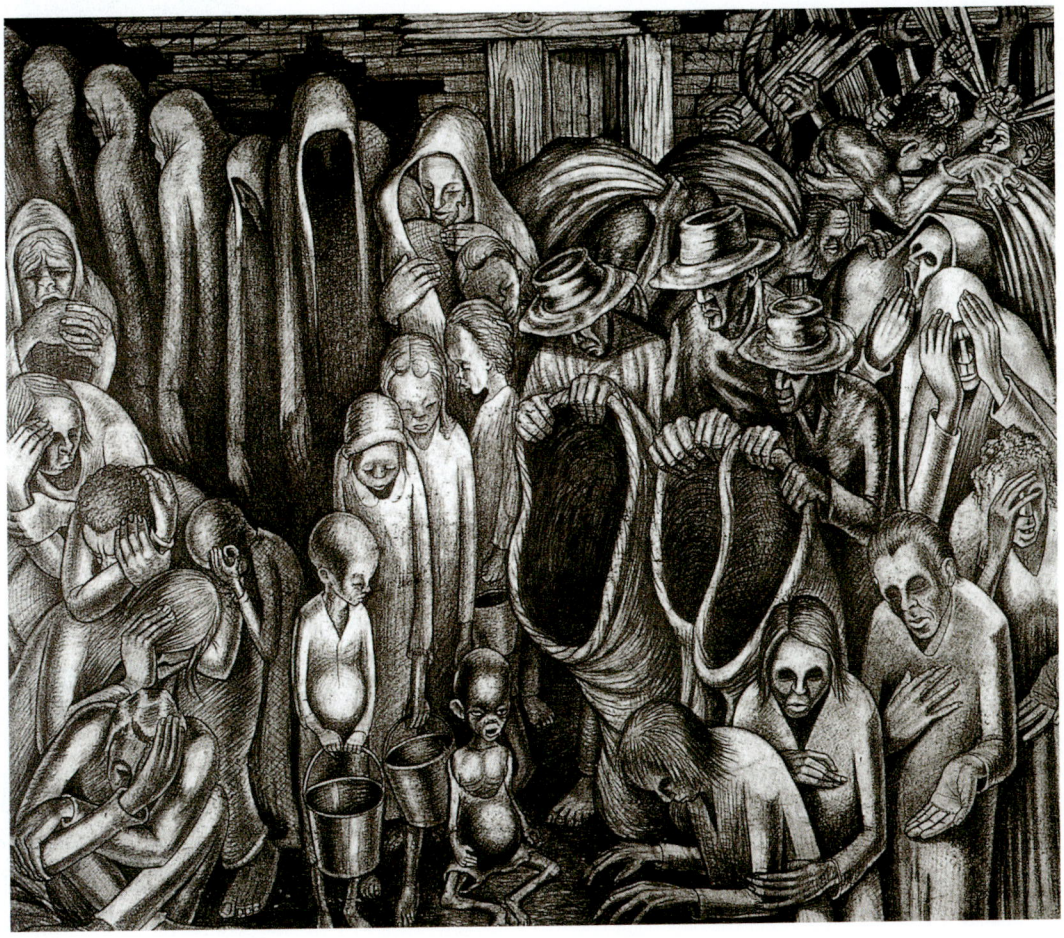

2.1.4 John Biggers, *Night of the Poor*, 1949. Preparatory study for mural, Pennsylvania State University

of his **fresco** *The School of Athens* (see Gateway Box: Raphael, **2.1.3a** and **2.1.3b**).

Like Raphael, contemporary artists still use drawing as a way to prepare for larger, more involved works. African American artist John Biggers (1924–2001) used pencil drawing in his preparation process, leading to large, permanent mural works. Such works as *Night of the Poor* (**2.1.4**) highlight how denial of education to the poor has a chilling effect on their future prospects. The finished painting was installed in Burrowes Hall, where Penn State's School of Education is housed. Even though it is a preparatory drawing, Biggers approaches it with the same energy and resolve that an artist might reserve for a grand painting, so the drawing stands as a great work in its own right.

Although most works that are generally considered drawings are done on paper, some notable exceptions exist. For example, watercolor, because it is executed on a heavy paper, is sometimes classified as a drawing. Pastel, which is sometimes drawn on a rough panel, is occasionally referred to as painting. The surface on which a drawing is executed can affect how it is categorized.

The Materials of Drawing: Dry Media

When creating a drawing, an artist must first choose whether to draw using dry **media** or wet media. Dry media offer the artist some unique and versatile properties.

Silverpoint

Almost every metal will leave a mark on a fibrous surface. Artists during the Italian **Renaissance** used lead, tin, copper, and silver to draw images. The most common of these drawing metals was silverpoint.

Silverpoint is a piece of silver wire set in some type of a holder, usually wood, to make the wire

Fresco: a technique in which the artist paints onto freshly applied plaster. From the Italian *fresco*, "fresh"
Medium (plural **media**): the material on or from which an artist chooses to make a work of art, for example canvas and oil paint, marble, engraving, video, or architecture
Renaissance: a period of cultural and artistic change in Europe from the fourteenth to the seventeenth century

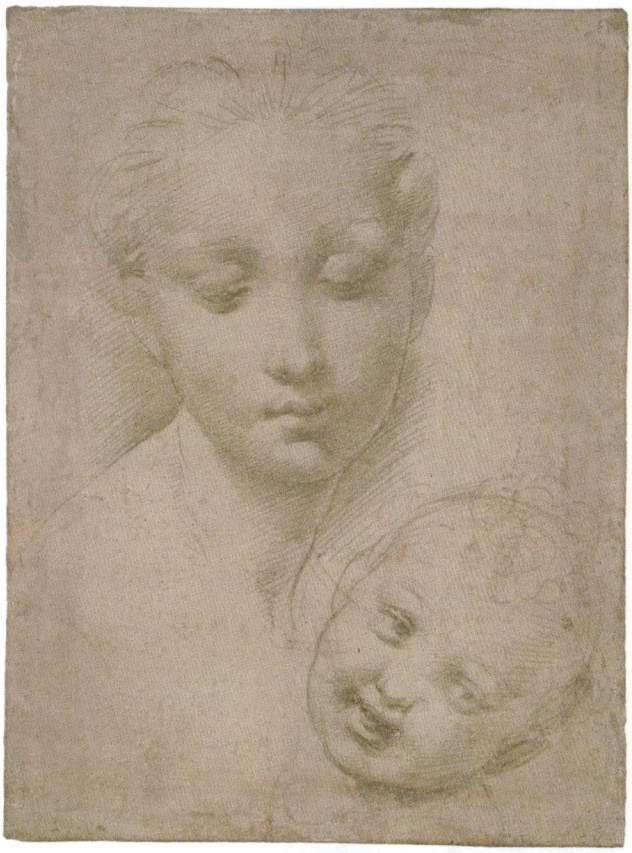

2.1.5 Raphael, *Heads of the Virgin and Child*, c. 1509–11. Silverpoint on pink prepared paper, 5⅝ × 4⅜". British Museum, London, England

easier to grasp and control. The artist hones the end of the wire to a sharp point. Because of the hardness of the silver, artists can create finely detailed drawings. Historically, artists have drawn with silverpoint on wood primed with a thin coating of bone ash. This creates a white **ground** for the light **value** of the silver. Because silver tarnishes, the drawing becomes darker and the image more pronounced over time. Working on colored paper creates distinctive effects and was particularly popular in Renaissance Italy (*c.* 1400–1600).

In *Heads of the Virgin and Child*, a silverpoint drawing by Raphael, the artist uses **hatching** and **cross-hatching** to create a stronger dark value (**2.1.5**). Because silverpoint has such a light value and is usually drawn with very thin lines, much of the pale paper is exposed. By closely overlapping many parallel lines across each other, Raphael covers more of the paper, creating the illusion of a darker value. Many artists use this technique to darken values and create the effect of shading (**2.1.6**).

2.1.6 How hatching and cross-hatching lines are used to create the effect of shading

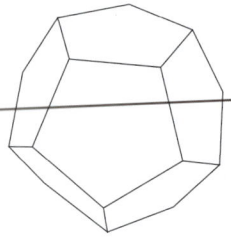

Planar contours

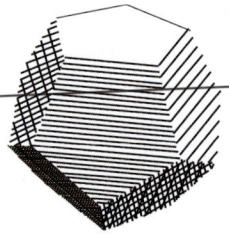

Hatching and cross-hatching

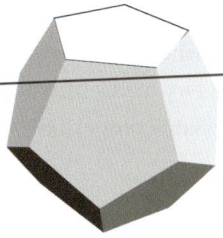

Shaded planes

Pencil

Everyone knows what pencils are. We like them because we can erase and correct errors. This makes the pencil a valuable tool for artists as well. Most artists' pencils differ from those used for writing and are categorized by their relative hardness or softness.

A deposit of solid graphite—which looks and writes like lead, but without its weight—was discovered in the mid-1500s and gave rise to the manufacture of the basic pencil we know today.

Pencils have different degrees of hardness (**2.1.7**). The softer the pencil, the darker the mark, or grade, and the quicker the pencil loses its point. The B or black graphite pencils are softer and darker than the H series. Number 2 (HB to be precise) pencils are the writing tools used by nearly every American elementary-school student. The H or hard graphite pencils create a relatively light mark. This type of pencil is useful when an artist is doing layout work and does not want pencil lines to show in the final product. Artists carefully choose the grade of the pencil lead they use.

The self-portrait by the Hungarian artist Ilka Gedö (1921–1985) shows how an artist can vary the pressure of a pencil line to suggest **texture** and create **emphasis** in a drawing (**2.1.8**). Gedö

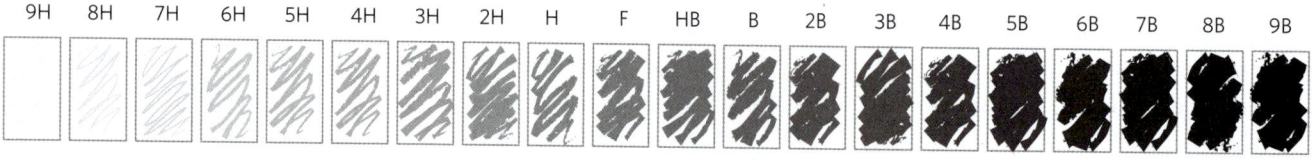

2.1.7 Pencil hardness scale from 9H to 9B

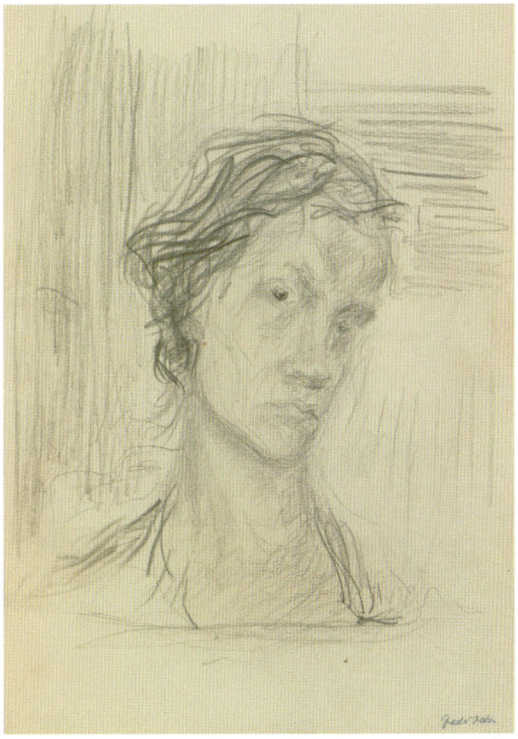

2.1.8 Ilka Gedö, *Self-portrait*, 1944. Graphite on paper, 11⅝ × 8⅜". British Museum, London, England

Ground: the surface or background onto which an artist paints or draws
Value: the lightness or darkness of a plane or area
Hatching: the use of non-overlapping parallel lines to convey darkness or lightness
Cross-hatching: the use of overlapping parallel lines to convey darkness or lightness
Texture: the surface quality of a work, for example fine/coarse, detailed/lacking in detail
Emphasis: the principle of drawing attention to particular content in a work
Background: the part of a work depicted furthest from the viewer's space, often behind the main subject matter
Pigment: the colorant in art materials. Often made from finely ground minerals
Color: the optical effect caused when reflected white light of the spectrum is divided into separate wavelengths

has used thick dark lines to imply darkness and thin light lines to suggest lightness. The dark value of the eye and wavy hair, where the pencil has been pressed hard, concentrates our attention on the artist's face, while the different sets of straight horizontal and vertical lines recede into the **background**. In further contrast, notice how softly the artist handles the graphite in the areas representing the skin compared with the hair or clothing. Gedö was a survivor of the Holocaust; this drawing records her gaunt features shortly after her internment.

Color Pencil

Color pencil is manufactured much like the traditional graphite pencil, but the mixture that makes up the lead contains more wax and **pigment**. Color pencils are used just like graphite pencils, although their marks may be harder to erase or alter. The California artist D. J. Hall (b. 1951) exploits the richness of colored pencil when she creates a work. In *Piece of Cake* (**2.1.9**) the artist pushes the waxy shaft of **color** into the fibers of the paper to achieve maximum richness. By pushing color this aggressively and leaving some strong white areas, Hall implies a sense of the intense light of a California afternoon.

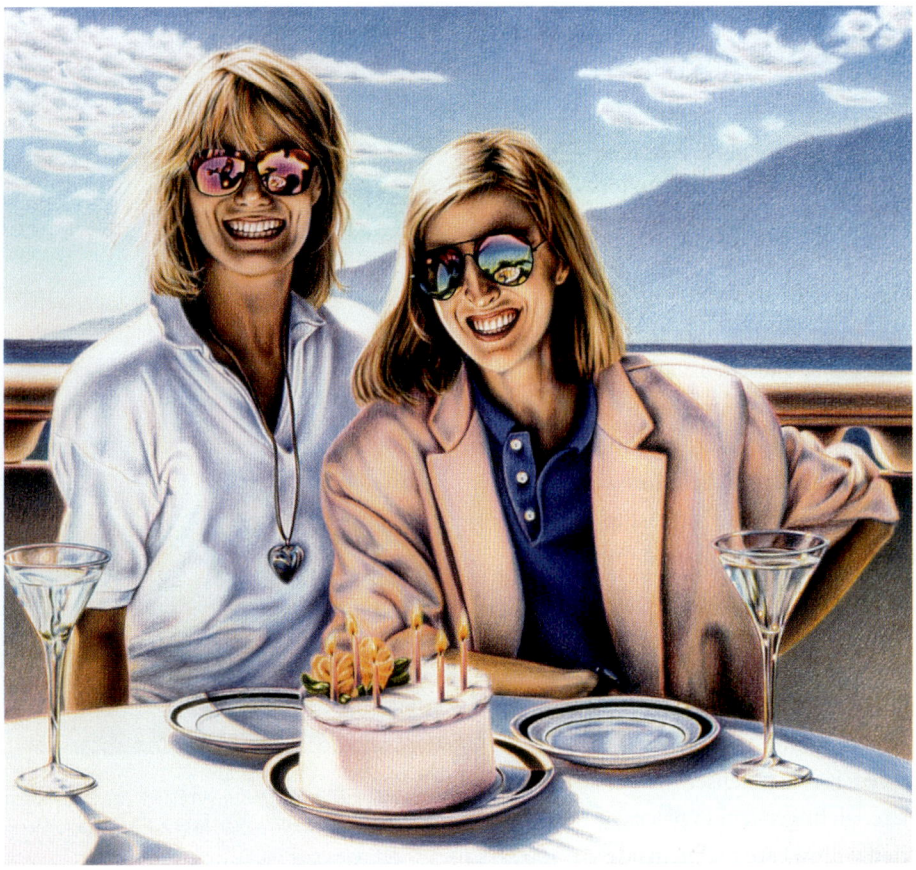

2.1.9 D. J. Hall, *Piece of Cake*, 1987. Colored pencil on paper, 30 × 39½". Metropolitan Museum of Art, New York

2.1.10 Käthe Kollwitz, *Self-portrait in Profile to Left*, 1933. Charcoal on paper, 18¾ × 25". National Gallery of Art, Washington, D.C.

Charcoal

Charcoal has long been an important material in the history of drawing: samples from cave drawings in France have been dated back to 30,000 BCE. Unlike pencils and silverpoint, charcoal smudges easily, creates lines that can be easily shaped and altered, usually has strong dark value, and is soft compared to metal-based drawing materials. Artists choose charcoal as a drawing material when they want to express strong dark tones, add interest to a surface, and make something look solid rather than linear.

Two types of charcoal are common. Vine charcoal is made from thin vine branches and is very soft and easily erased. Compressed charcoal, to which a binding agent, such as wax, is sometimes added, is much denser.

To make charcoal, finger-length pieces of wood (often dried willow) are placed inside

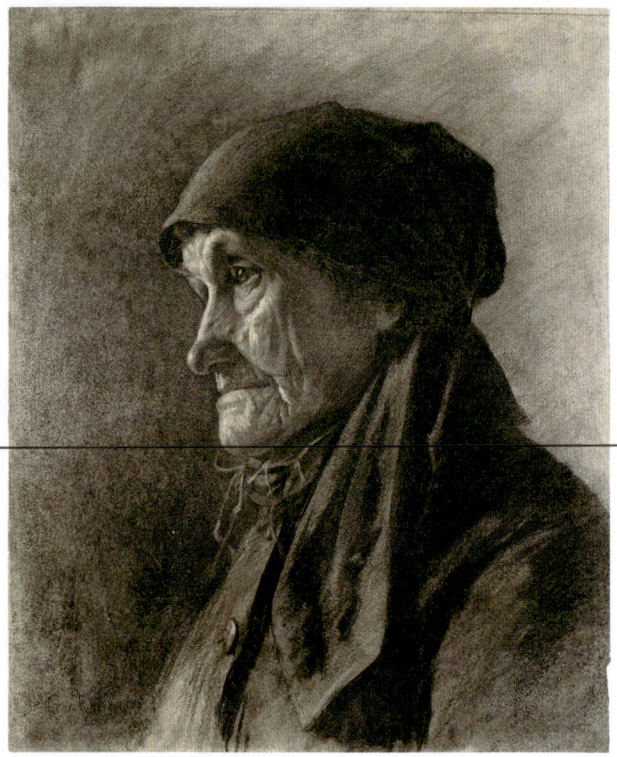

2.1.11 Léon Augustin Lhermitte, *An Elderly Peasant Woman*, c. 1878. Charcoal on wove paper, 18¾ × 15⅝". National Gallery of Art, Washington, D.C.

an airtight container (to prevent the loss of important binding chemicals) and heated in an oven until all the wood has been burned.

To draw with charcoal, an artist drags the stick across a fibrous surface, usually paper, leaving a soft-edged line. By using just the end, an artist can create thin strokes; by using the side, he or she can cover a lot of surface quickly. The amount of pressure an artist exerts while drawing controls the lightness or darkness of the stroke. Sandpaper can be used to sharpen the stick for more detail. An artist can achieve a soft visual effect by rubbing the newly charcoaled drawing surface with a bare finger, some tissue paper, or a rolled-paper cone called a tortillion, made expressly for this purpose.

Charcoal is so soft that the texture of the paper surface—even the drawing board's texture below the paper—profoundly affects the image. Charcoal works best on paper with a fairly rough texture (known as **tooth**), which catches the charcoal better in its fibers.

Charcoal portraits by the German artist Käthe Kollwitz (1867–1945) and the French artist Léon Augustin Lhermitte (1844–1925) show how artists work with the characteristics of the medium (**2.1.10** and **2.1.11**).

In Kollwitz's self-portrait, we feel a sense of energy from the way she applies the charcoal. Although she renders her own face and hand realistically, in the space between we see the nervous energy connecting the eye to the hand. Kollwitz draws with a spontaneous burst of charcoal marks along the arm, in **expressive contrast** to the more considered areas of the head and hand.

In *An Elderly Peasant Woman*, Lhermitte works with the characteristics of charcoal to describe his **subject** carefully. Each line and blemish on this woman's face has been carefully rendered. The charcoal's dark value accentuates the contrast between the **highlights** in the face and the overall darkened tone of the work. It even carefully preserves the light reflected in her eye. Lhermitte has controlled charcoal's inherent smudginess to offer an intimate view of the effects of ageing.

Although there is precise detail in both drawings, each artist allows the "personality" of the charcoal into the softened background through smudges and irregular soft marks.

The Chinese-born artist Zhang Chun Hong (b. 1971) has utilized both charcoal and graphite for dramatic effect in the work *Life Strands* (**2.1.12**). In this work, charcoal provides the deep, dark values that describe a long strand of braided hair. Because charcoal has a rich, dark softness, the tightly interlocked braid can cascade down the page into a scatter of gestural marks where the hair has been unleashed from its binding. The strand metaphorically represents the passage of time from the dark, full hair of childhood to the grayed and thinning hair of old age. In this drawing Zhang masterfully uses drawing on a long Chinese scroll to make parallels between life and art.

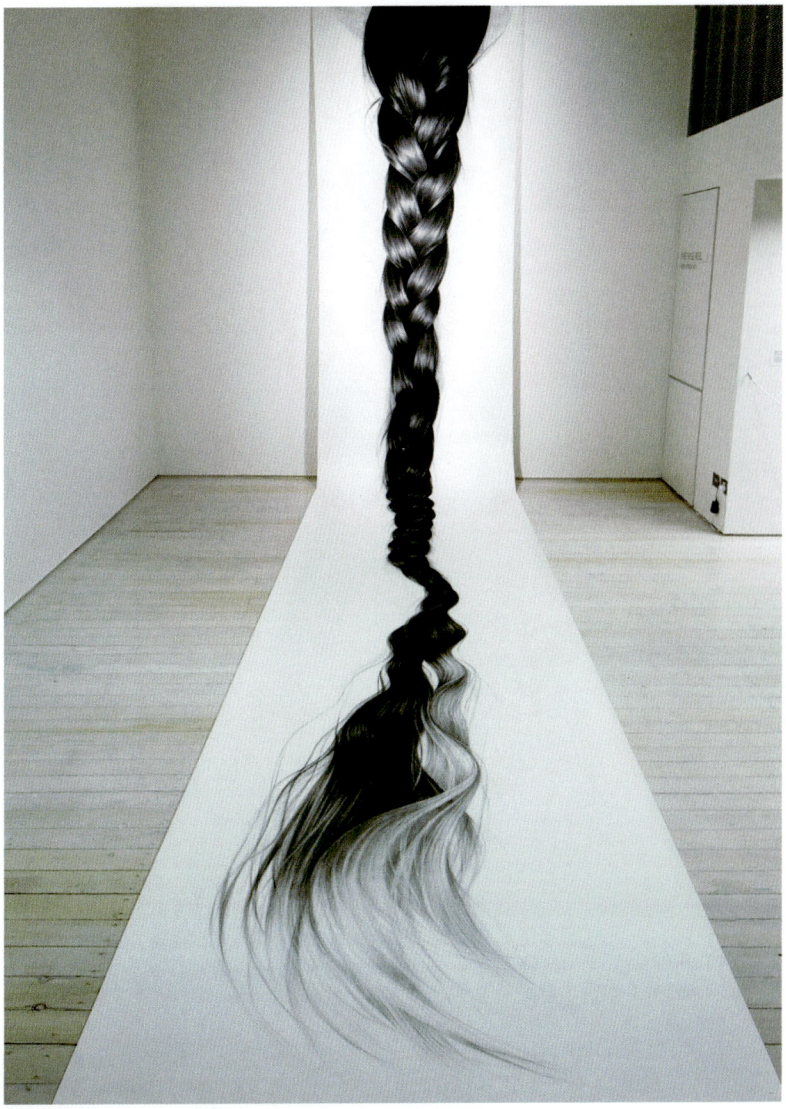

2.1.12 Zhang Chun Hong, *Life Strands*, 2004. Charcoal and graphite on paper, 38' × 4'11". Private collection

Tooth: the textural quality of a paper surface for holding drawing media in place
Expressive: capable of stirring the emotions of the viewer
Contrast: a drastic difference between such elements as color or value (lightness/darkness) when they are presented together
Subject: the person, object, or space depicted in a work of art
Highlight: an area of lightest value in a work

Chalk, Pastel, and Crayon

Sticks of chalk, pastel, and crayon are made by combining pigment and **binder**. Traditional binders include oil, wax, gum arabic, and glues. The type of binder gives each material a unique character. Chalks, pastels, and crayons can be prepared in any color. Chalk is powdered calcium carbonate mixed with a gum arabic (a type of tree sap) binder. Pastel is pigment combined with gum arabic, wax, or oil, while crayon is pigment combined with wax. Conté crayon, a variation invented by Nicolas-Jacques Conté (1755–1805), who was a French painter and army officer, is a heavily pigmented crayon sometimes manufactured with graphite.

For their preparatory sketches, artists of the Renaissance used colored chalks, in particular a red chalk known as sanguine. The Italian artist Michelangelo Buonarroti (1475–1564) used this red chalk for his *Studies for the Libyan Sibyl* (**2.1.13**), which he made in preparation for painting the Sistine Chapel ceiling in Rome. Michelangelo uses hatching and cross-hatching (**2.1.6**, p. 196) to build up the values and give the figure depth. The artist's study concentrates on the muscular definition of the back and on the face, shoulder, and hand, and gives repeated attention to the detail of the

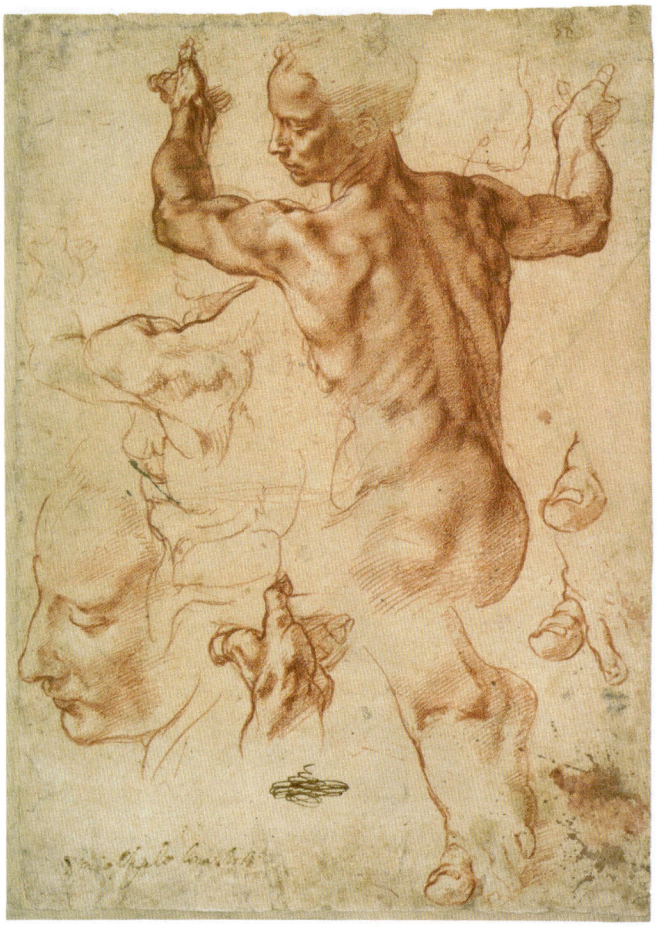

2.1.13 Michelangelo, *Studies for the Libyan Sibyl*, 1510–11. Red chalk, 11⅜ × 8⅜". Metropolitan Museum of Art, New York

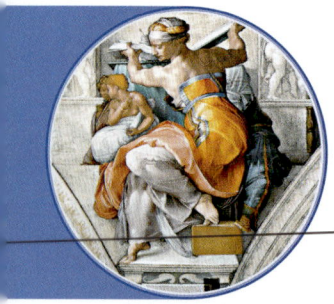

For the final result of Michelangelo's chalk study for *The Libyan Sibyl* in the Sistine Chapel, see **2.2.6, p. 212**

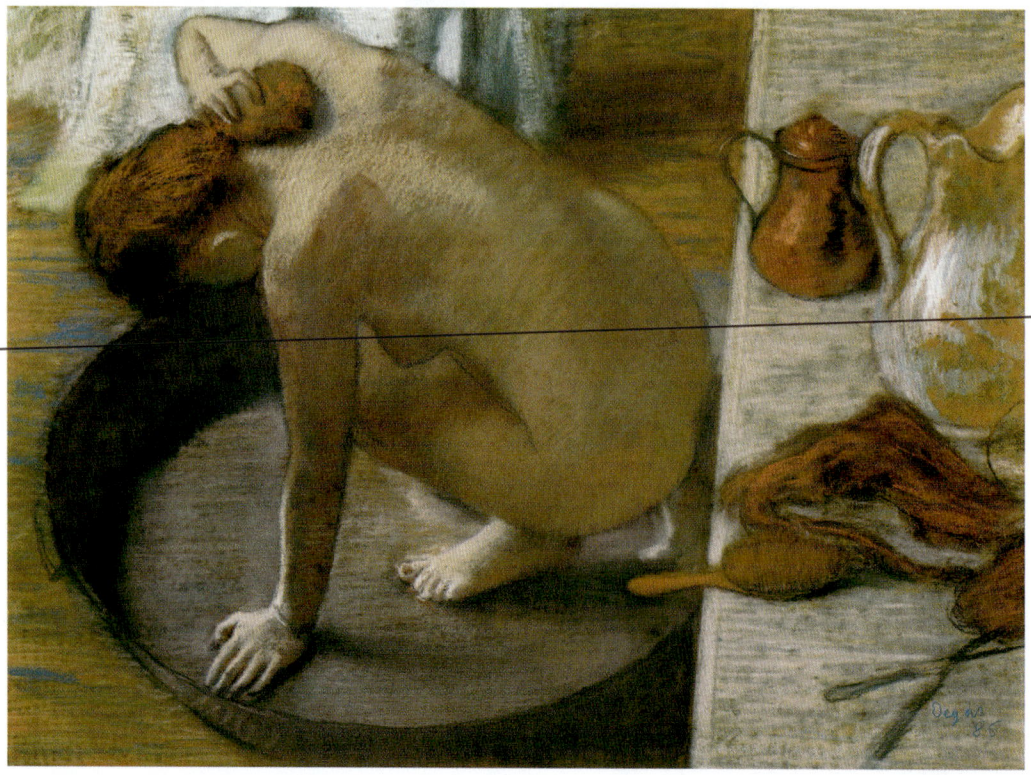

2.1.14 Edgar Degas, *The Tub*, 1886. Pastel, 23⅝ × 32⅝". Musée d'Orsay, Paris, France

big toe. These details are essential to making this twisting pose convincing, and Michelangelo spent extra time refining them.

The French artist Edgar Degas (1834–1917) is noted for pastel studies that stand as finished works of art. In *The Tub*, Degas lays down intermittent strokes of different-color pastel (**2.1.14**). He takes advantage of the charcoal-like softness of the material to blend the colors together, thus giving them a rich complexity and creating a variety of contrasting textures. In pastel as in painting, Degas was a master at re-creating the effects of light and color seen in nature.

In the Conté crayon drawing *The Ploughing*, the French artist Georges Seurat (1859–1891) uses expressive marks to build up value and create depth (**2.1.15**). Seurat designates the **foreground** by using darker values; he allows the lightness of the paper to be more dominant in areas he wants to recede into the distance. The shaded silhouetted figures in this work look as if they are the subjects of a dim nineteenth-century photograph. Seurat exploits the rich blackness available in dark Conté to add depth and dramatic contrast to his design.

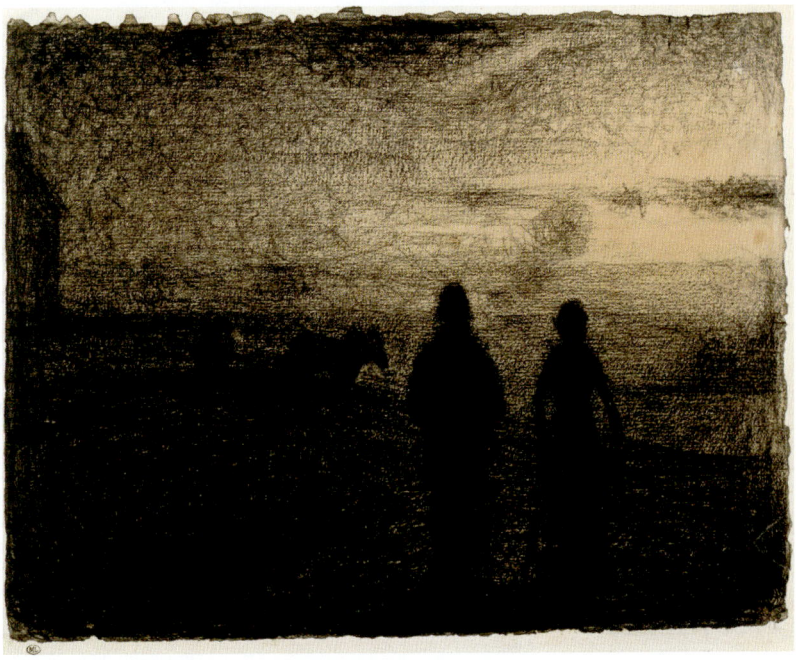

2.1.15 Georges Seurat, *The Ploughing*, 1882–83. Conté crayon, 9⅔ × 12½". Musée D'Orsay, Paris

Erasers and Fixatives

Erasers are not only used for correction but also to create light marks in areas already drawn. In this way the artist can embellish highlights by working from the dark to light.

Erasers can be used to create works of art by destroying the marks made by an artist. In 1953 the artist Robert Rauschenberg (1925–2008) created a new work of art by erasing a drawing by Willem de Kooning (**2.1.16**).

Rauschenberg, a young, unknown artist at that time, approached the famous De Kooning (1904–1997) and asked if he could erase one of his drawings. De Kooning agreed, understanding what the younger artist had in mind. But, in order to make it more difficult, De Kooning gave Rauschenberg a drawing made with charcoal, oil paint, pencil, and crayon. It took Rauschenberg nearly a month to erase it, but he did so, leaving a drawing on the back of the work intact. Some in the art world dubbed him "L'Enfant Terrible," which means a young person who behaves badly, but Rauschenberg's idea was to create a performed work of **conceptual art** and display the result. Conceptual art, like Rauschenberg's modification of a De Kooning drawing, places emphasis on the idea, rather than the visual image. Since the drawing material in the work had been trapped in the fibers of the paper, minute parts of the image survived the erasure. This act created a new, collaborative work resulting from the original additive drawing by De Kooning and the subtractive method used by Rauschenberg.

2.1.16 Robert Rauschenberg, *Erased de Kooning Drawing*, 1953. Traces of ink and crayon on paper, in gold-leaf frame, 25¼ × 21¾ × ½". San Francisco Museum of Modern Art

Binder: a substance that makes pigments adhere to a surface
Foreground: the part of a work depicted as nearest the viewer
Conceptual art: artwork in which the ideas are most important to the work

A fixative is a type of coating that can be applied to a drawing to preserve its appearance by making the dry medium adhere to the surface of the paper. Once an artist has applied a dry medium and manipulated it by smudging, marking, or erasing, he or she can apply a fixative to set the image. Because artists usually need to make changes throughout the drawing process, most use a "workable" fixative that can be removed by erasing the surface of the coating. Most commercial fixatives used today are available in an aerosol can or spray bottle for easy and even application.

The Materials of Drawing: Wet Media

The wet media used in drawings are applied with brushes or pens. Wet media dry or harden as the liquid evaporates.

Ink

Ink is a favorite of artists because of its permanence, precision, and strong dark color. There are many types of ink, each with its own individual character.

Carbon ink, made by mixing soot with water and gum, has been in use in China and India since around 2500 BCE. This type of ink tended to discolor over time and could become smudged in moist or humid environments. A contemporary version of carbon ink, called India (or Indian) ink, is a favorite of comic-book artists.

Most European ink drawings from the Renaissance to the present day are made with iron gall ink. Gall ink is prized for its near-permanence and rich black color. It is manufactured from a mixture of tannin (from oak galls—parasitic growths on oak trees), iron sulfate, gum arabic, and water. Gall ink is not entirely lightfast, however, and tends to lighten to brown after many years.

Other types of fluid media include bister, which is derived from wood soot and usually a yellow-brown color, and sepia, a brown medium that is derived from the secretions of cuttlefish.

Brush Drawing

Because ink is a liquid medium, it can also be applied with a brush. The ancient Chinese used brush and ink for both writing and drawing. Even today, children throughout east Asia who are learning to write must learn to control a brush effectively, in much the same way that students in the West learn to use pens and pencils.

East Asian artists use the same brush for writing and drawing. These brushes are made with a bamboo shaft and either ox, goat, horse, or wolf hair. Traditionally, Asian artists use a stick of solid ink that they hold upright and grind on a special ink stone with a small amount of water. As the ink reaches the desired consistency, it is pushed into a shallow reservoir at the rear of the stone. Artists wet the brush by dipping it into this reservoir, and then adjust the shape and charge of the brush by stroking it on the flat of the grinding stone. They can readily adjust the dilution of the ink with water to create an infinite range of grays. This is called a wash, and it allows the artist to control value and texture.

In **2.1.17** the fourteenth-century Chinese artist Wu Zhen (sometimes spelled Wu Chen) (1280–1354) uses brush, ink, and wash to create a masterpiece of simplicity. This finely planned design contains carefully controlled brushstrokes as well as loose, freer ink applications, thereby bringing together two opposing influences and reflecting the central principle of Daoism, a belief in the importance of balanced opposites. Because the artist uses only a few shapes, the arrangement of the bamboo leaves becomes like a series of letters in a word or sentence. Wu achieves the changing dark and light values by adding water to create a wash and lighten the ink. This work was intended as a model for Wu's son to follow as he learned the art of brushwork from his father.

In his image of the landscape just north of Rome, *The Tiber from Monte Mario Looking South*, the French artist Claude Lorrain's (1604/5–1682) thoughtful brushstrokes give us a feeling of the great expanse of the Italian countryside (**2.1.18**). The wash that Lorrain uses creates a sense of depth by making the values of the foreground areas both the darkest and lightest of the whole drawing.

2.1.17 Wu Zhen, leaf from an album of bamboo drawings, 1350. Ink on paper, 16 × 21". National Palace Museum, Taipei, Taiwan

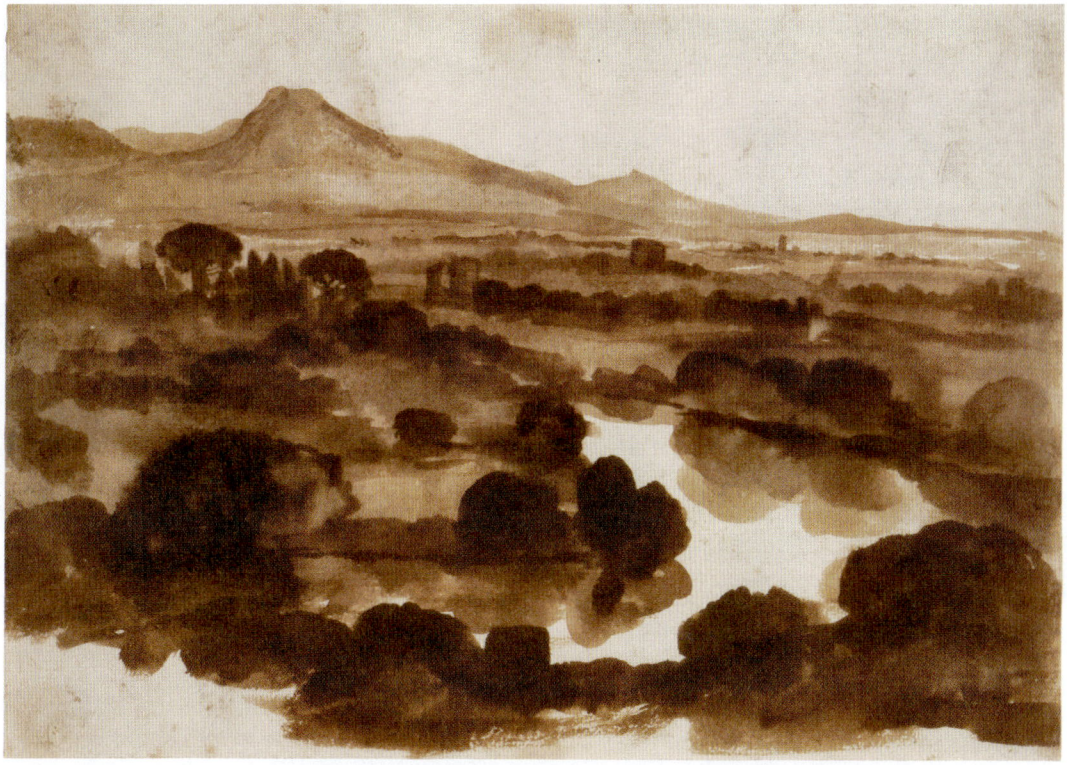

2.1.18 Claude Lorrain, *The Tiber from Monte Mario Looking South*, 1640. Dark-brown wash on white paper, 7⅜ × 10⅝". British Museum, London, England

Gateway to Art: Kahlo, *The Two Fridas*

Artist Sketchbooks

For the other Kahlo Gateway boxes, see p. 50, p. 532, and p. 676

While the Mexican painter Frida Kahlo (1907–1954) was suffering from the effects of childhood polio and a disabling back injury, she spent time reflecting on her life experiences in sketches she drew in a diary (**2.1.19a**). Her diary was like many others in that she wrote about people she had met, relationship struggles, and expressed her opinions on a variety of issues. But Kahlo's diary was different because it was filled with richly colored drawings of the people she knew, influences in her life, and many self-portraits.

Like her double portrait *The Two Fridas* (**2.1.19b**), Kahlo reveals her most intimate experiences through these sketches, which express the pain and happiness that permeated her life. These diary pages are titled "El horrendo 'Ojosauro' primitivo" (horrible, monstrous Eyesaurus) and contain a sketch of an imagined "Eyesaurus" monster with a long pointed snout. The sketched monster visually connects the two pages, much the same way that the veins connect the two images of Frida. The horrible monster stands as a witness to, and a symbol of, the many painful operations and medical procedures that Frida endured during her forty-seven years of life. In *The Two Fridas*, Kahlo pushes the anatomy of the human heart to dominate the double portrait, accentuating the physiological dependence that her conflicting dual ethnic identity—European and Mexican—has had on her declining health. Like the "Eyesaurus" in her diary, the heart is an ominous reminder of the limitations of the flesh.

The "eyesaurus" monster was created with watercolor, a favorite medium of Kahlo in her final decade of life. Because her health was failing, Kahlo's movement was limited, but she could still express her ideas through her diary. The sophisticated design of these pages reflects a mastery of watercolor sketches in combination with text and a vivid imagination that was both delightful and horrible.

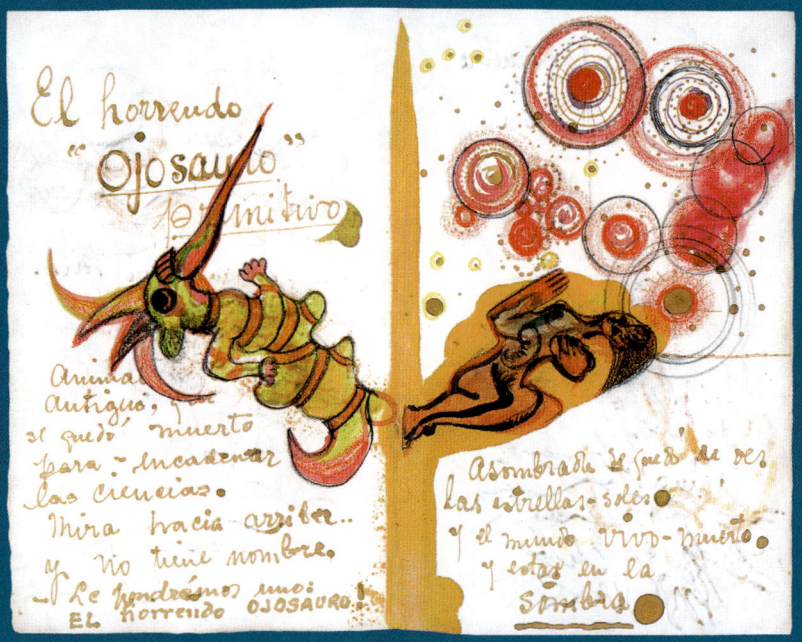

2.1.19a Frida Kahlo, pages from the artist's diary, c. 1944–54

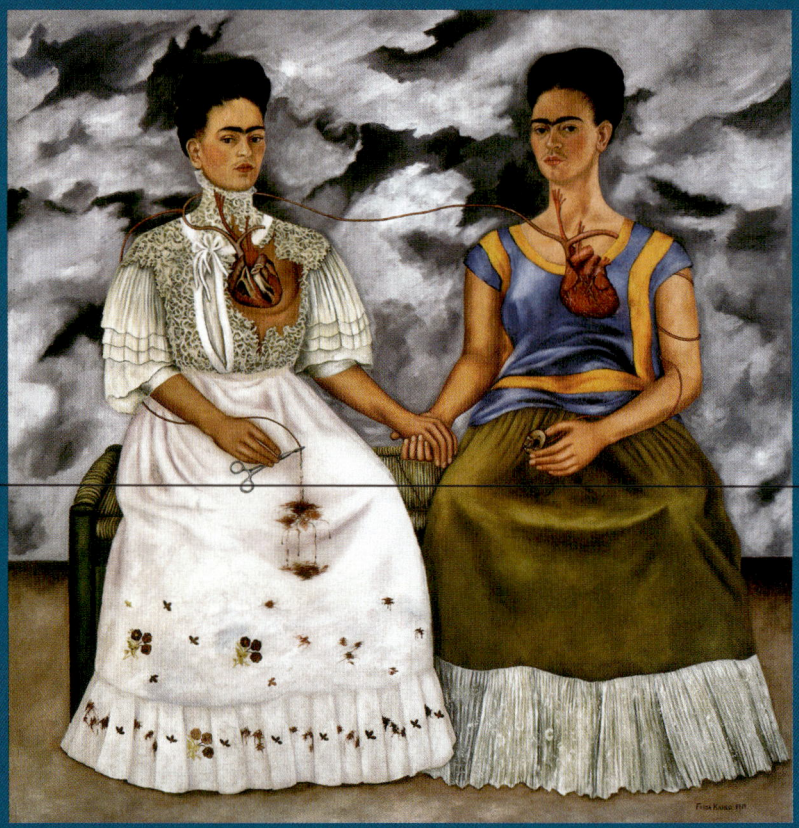

2.1.19b Frida Kahlo, *The Two Fridas*, 1939. Oil on canvas, 5'8" × 5'8". Museo de Arte Moderno, Mexico City, Mexico

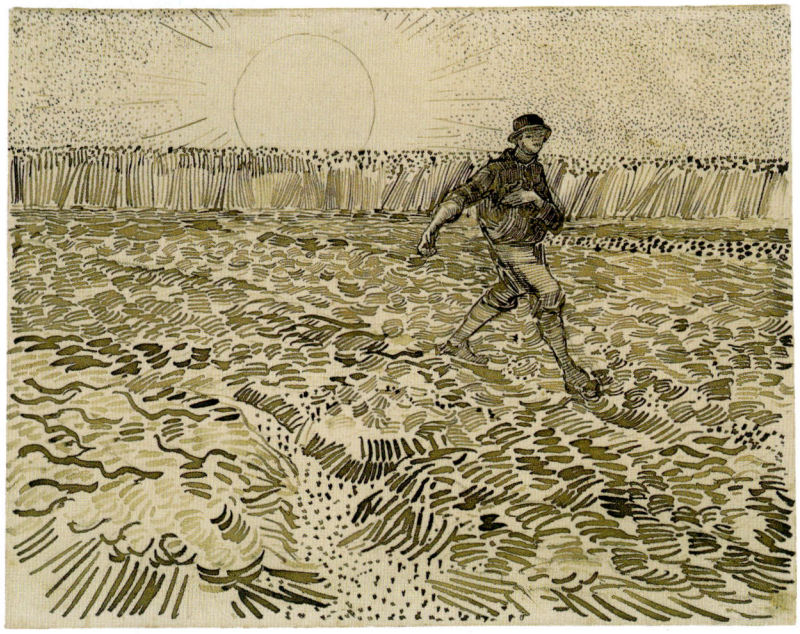

2.1.20 Vincent van Gogh, *Sower with Setting Sun*, 1888. Pen and brown ink, 9⅝ × 12⅝". Van Gogh Museum, Amsterdam, The Netherlands

Quill and Pen

Traditionally a quill—the shaft of a bird's feather, or a similarly hollow reed—is carved to a point to apply the ink. A slit, running parallel to the shaft, helps control its rate of flow. The modern version is a pen with a metal nib. The artist can control the flow of the ink by pressing harder or more softly. Apart from choosing different widths of nib, the artist can further increase or decrease the width of the drawn line by holding the pen at different angles. Often, pen-and-ink drawings employ hatching and cross-hatching to create variations in value (**2.1.6**, p. 196).

The Dutch artist Vincent van Gogh (1853–1890) uses a reed pen and brown ink for his *Sower with Setting Sun* (**2.1.20**). By changing the way he applies his pen strokes and by controlling their width, he creates an undulating, restless design. Van Gogh's emphatic direction of line expresses the characteristic energy of his work.

Paper

Before the invention of paper, drawings were made on papyrus (a plant material), cloth, wood, and animal hide (parchment and vellum). Paper was invented in China by a court official of the Han Dynasty, Cai Lun, who manufactured it from pounded or macerated plant fibers from around the end of the first century CE. The image in **2.1.21**, even though it was made more than 1,500 years later, shows how this was done. The fibers are suspended in water and then scooped up into a flat mold with a screen at the bottom, so that the water can escape. The fibers are now bonded enough to each other to keep their shape when they are taken out. The sheet is then pressed and dried.

Over the centuries, improvements were made to the construction of the mold to speed up times for papermakers to flip out molded sheets of paper and reuse the mold. Hand-made papers are still manufactured this way in many countries, mostly from cotton fiber, although papers are also made of hemp, abaca (a leaf-based fiber derived from a banana-like plant), flax, and other plant fibers.

In addition to their fiber content, papers are classified by their surface texture and weight. Depending on the construction of the mold, the paper usually has a surface texture described as either wove or laid. The laid texture derives from a screen (bottom of the mold) composed of many parallel rods, like a bamboo mat, whereas the wove texture derives from the use of a grid-like mesh of metal wire or cloth (see **2.1.22**, p. 206).

Paper in bulk is normally measured by the ream (a quantity of 500 sheets). The standard measurement for defining the character of

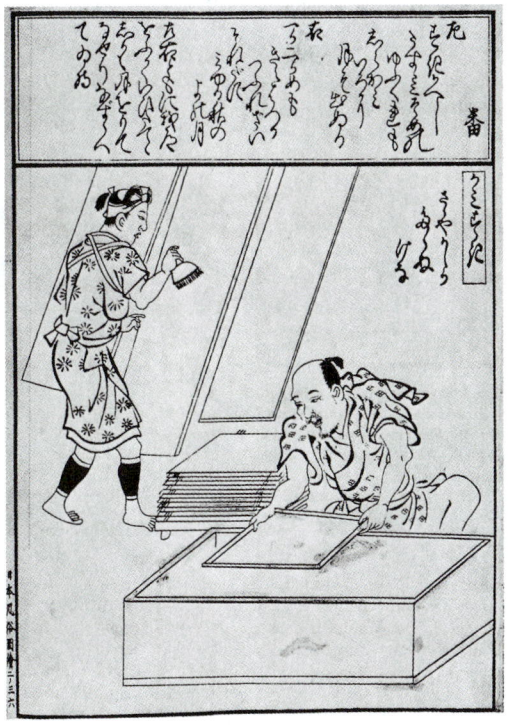

2.1.21 Hishikawa Moronobu, *Papermaking in Japan*, showing the vatman and the paper-drier, 1681. Woodblock print from the four-volume *Wakoku Shōshoku Edzukushi*, 1681

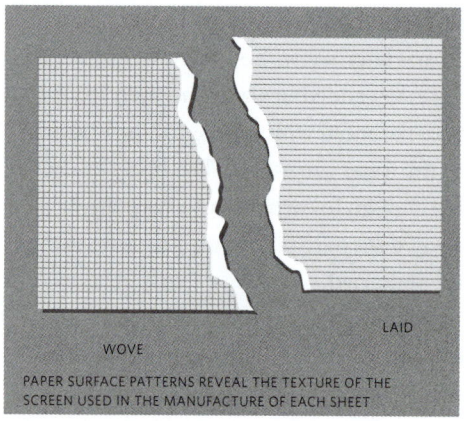

2.1.22 Surface texture of wove and laid paper

paper is its weight per ream in the paper's basic sheet size. (For cotton rag paper, the sheet size is usually 17 × 22 in.) For example, if 500 sheets of 17 × 22-in. paper weigh 20 lbs., the paper is referred to as "20 lb." Heavier papers are stronger and usually better to work with, but cost more.

Life Drawing

Life drawing is the practice of drawing from a live model, as opposed to using photographs, plaster **casts**, or other existing artworks as source material. We associate this process with nude models, but life drawing can also involve animals, plants, and architecture. Life drawing is one of the core skills that art students learn. In addition to the extended study of live models, two types of introductory drawing methods are popular in the teaching of life drawing: gesture and **contour**.

Gesture Drawing

Gesture drawing aims to identify and react to the main visual and expressive characteristics of a form. Since artists often confront changing subjects and situations, capturing the energy and dynamics of the moment is the essential goal of gesture drawing.

The Swiss artist Alberto Giacometti (1901–1966) practiced gesture drawing in a way that exemplifies its function. Giacometti would capture a moment in time by focusing on the energy of the subject in front of him. Such gesture drawings as *The City Square* (**2.1.23**) are a record of a moment trapped in black ballpoint pen. The abrupt marks give indications of architectural features, the surrounding landscape, and figures milling about. This process of looking at a scene as it occurs at a precise moment challenges an artist to work holistically, capturing all related interacting parts of a scene. Giacometti would often execute these drawings in his sketchbook, or on scraps of paper that were to hand.

Cast: a sculpture or artwork made by pouring a liquid (for example molten metal or plaster) into a mold
Contour: an edge or outline that defines a form, but not necessarily the complete outline of a shape
Rhythm: the regular or ordered repetition of elements in the work
Composition: the overall design or organization of a work
Outline: the outermost line or implied line of an object or figure, by which it is defined or bounded
Plane: a flat, two-dimensional surface on which an artist can create a drawing or painting. Planes can also be implied in a composition by areas that face toward, parallel to, or away from a light source

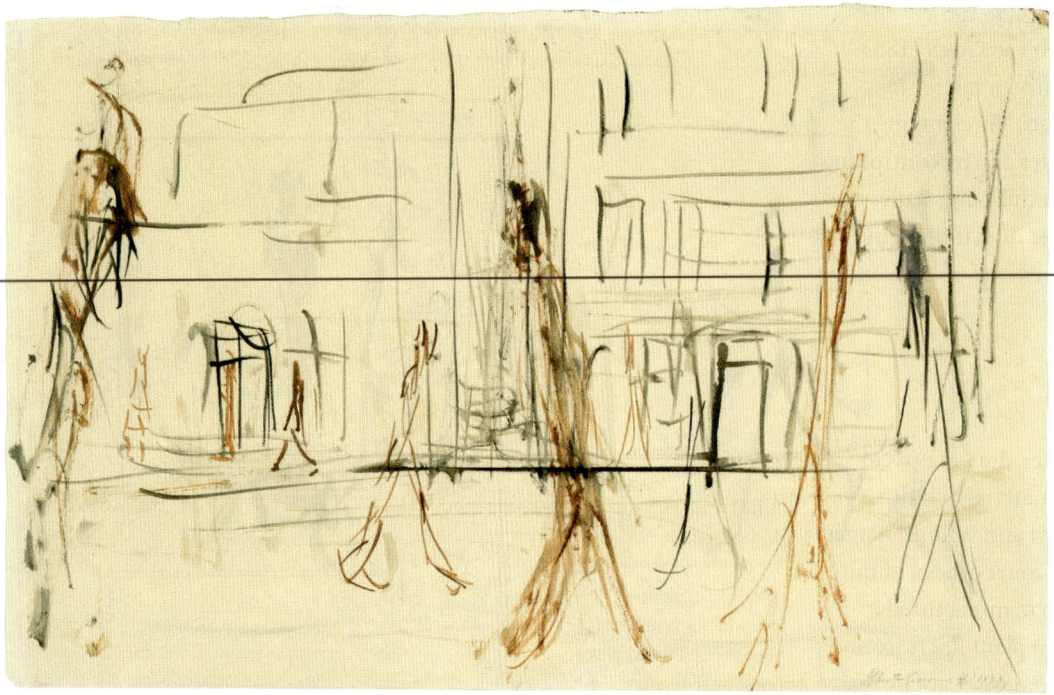

2.1.23 Alberto Giacometti, *The City Square*, 1949. Ink and colored ink on paper, 12⅜ × 20⅛". MoMA, New York

The energy of the human figure is evident in *Muscular Dynamism* (**2.1.24**), by the Italian artist Umberto Boccioni (1882–1916). In this gestural drawing, the movement of the body is implied by the undulating strokes of the chalk and charcoal. The **rhythms** of the **composition** lead our eye through a series of changing curves and values that give us a feeling of the energy of the figure. Like Giacometti, Boccioni is primarily interested in capturing the essence of movement by reacting to the subject and employing gestural movement of the human hand.

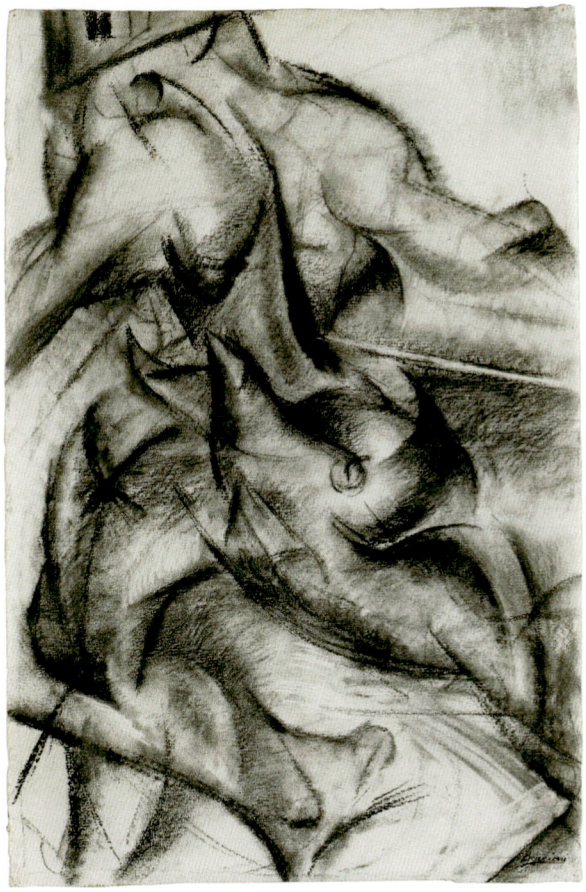

2.1.24 Umberto Boccioni, *Muscular Dynamism*, 1913. Pastel and charcoal on paper, 34 × 23¼". MoMA, New York

Contour Drawing

Contour drawing aims to register the essential qualities of three-dimensional form by rendering an edge, or contour, of an object. An artist uses contour drawing to sharpen hand–eye coordination and gain an intimate understanding of form, increasing his or her sensitivity to essential detail. For example, contour drawing can help an artist copy the shape of a leaf as faithfully as possible by forcing him or her to focus on the subtleties of the object's shape. Because the artist concentrates his or her attention on a single point and incrementally progresses slowly along the visible edge, attributes of the subject may be slightly exaggerated, bringing attention to otherwise-overlooked visual cues. If the artist follows the edge with careful precision until it meets the starting point he or she may create an **outline** of the object, rendering a complete shape. Also, contour drawing can help an artist to identify the changing **planes** that make up the surface of a three-dimensional object.

A wonderful example of contour drawing is illustrated by **2.1.25**, *Mother and Child*, by the Austrian artist Egon Schiele (1890–1918). If you look carefully at the long line that describes the right side of the woman's back, you will see many subtle changes in line direction, indicating stretching muscles that the mother is using as she embraces her child. The economy of this single line carries so much descriptive information that the artist brilliantly opts to allow it to support the entire right side of the composition.

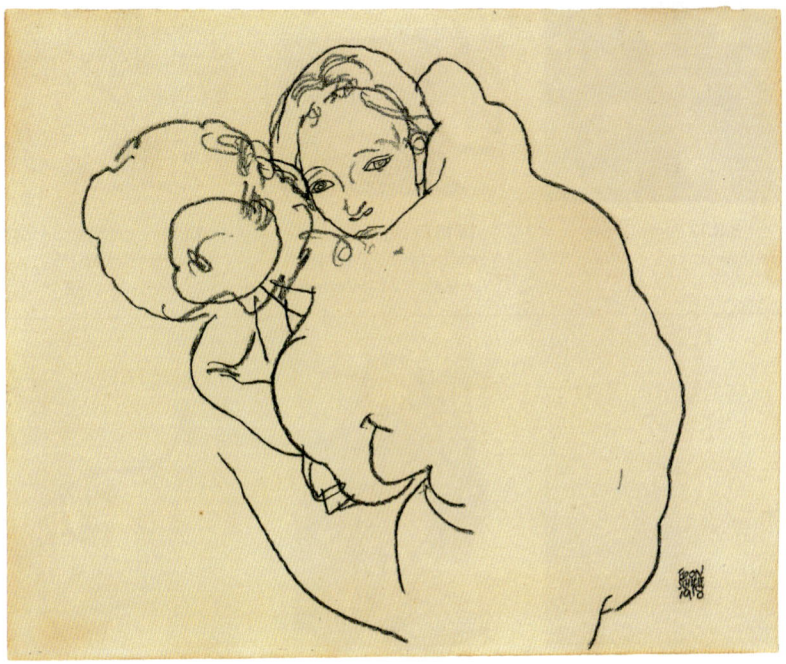

2.1.25 Egon Schiele, *Mother and Child*, 1918. Black Conté crayon on paper, 11¾ × 14⅝"

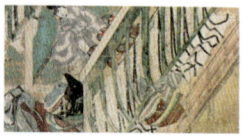

3.3.22 Scene from the *Tale of Genji*, first half of 12th century, p. 424

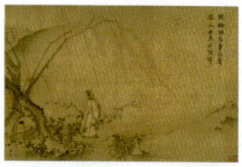

1.6.14 Ma Yuan, *Walking on a Mountain Path in Spring*, Song Dynasty (960–1279), p. 135

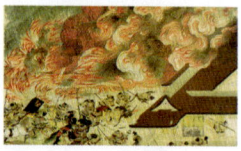

4.7.6 *Night Attack on the Sanjo Palace*, late 13th century, p. 643

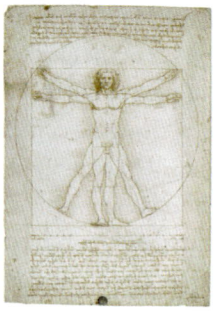

4.4.1 Leonardo da Vinci, *Vitruvian Man*, c. 1490, p. 603

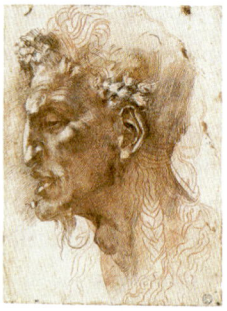

1.3.8 Michelangelo, *Head of a Satyr*, c. 1520–30, p. 80

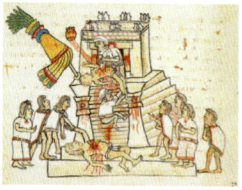

3.4.15 Aztec human sacrifice, from *Codex Magliabechiano*, 16th century, p. 439

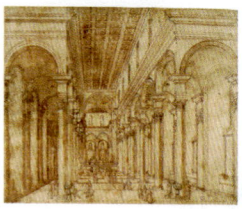

1.1.2a Giovanni Dosio, *Church of Santo Spirito at Florence*, c. 1576–90, p. 44

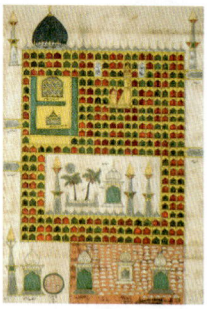

3.2.19 *View of the Sanctuary at Medina*, 17th or 18th century, p. 403

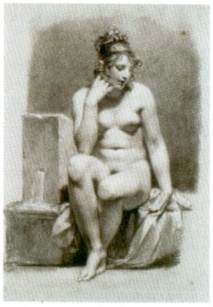

1.3.5 Pierre-Paul Prud'hon, *La Source*, c. 1801, p. 78

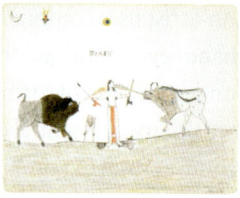

3.4.22 Wo-Haw, *Wo-Haw between Two Worlds*, c. 1875–77, p. 442

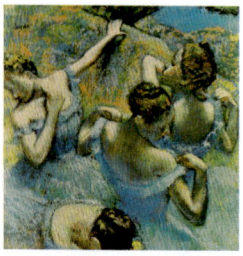

3.8.12 Edgar Degas, *The Blue Dancers*, c. 1898, p. 511

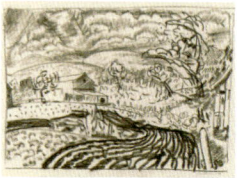

1.1.18 George Bellows, *Woodstock Road, Woodstock, New York, 1924*, 1924, p. 54

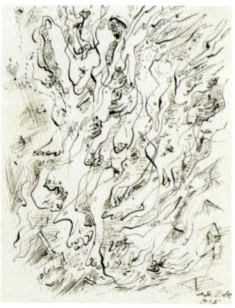

1.1.16 André Masson, *Automatic Drawing*, 1925–26, p. 53

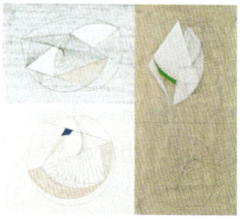

1.1.15 Barbara Hepworth, *Drawing for Sculpture*, 1941, p. 52

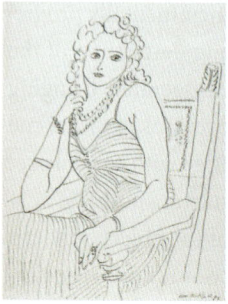

1.1.3 Henri Matisse, *Themes and Variations*, series P, 1942, p. 45

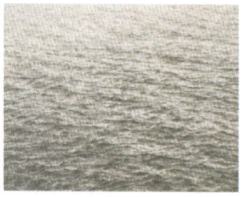

1.8.4 Vija Celmins, *Untitled (Ocean)*, 1977, p. 153

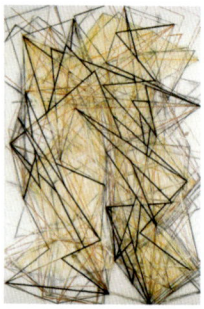

1.1.14 Mel Bochner, *Vertigo*, 1982, p. 52

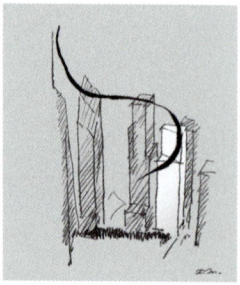

2.5.2 Fumihiko Maki, sketch of Four World Trade Center, 2006, p. 260

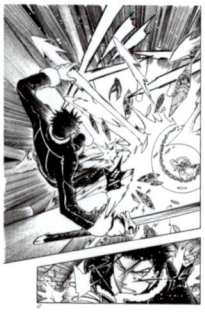

1.1.9 CLAMP, page from the *Tsubasa RESERVoir CHRoNiCLE*, 2007, p. 49

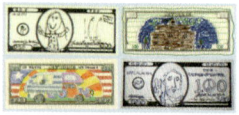

3.10.20b Mel Chin, *Operation Paydirt...* project, 2008, p. 559

2.2 Painting

When most of us think of art, painting is the **medium** that most often comes to mind. Perhaps this is not surprising, since artists have painted surfaces of many kinds for tens of thousands of years. In prehistoric times, artists painted on the walls of caves. The temples of ancient Greece and Mexico were painted in bright **colors**, although what remains now is muted by comparison. About five hundred years ago, artists began painting on linen cloth, a surface that was lighter and easier to handle. Modern muralists and graffiti artists also paint on walls. Of course, artists also paint on a much smaller and more intimate **scale**, on a stretched canvas or a sheet of paper. The artistic possibilities paint offers are almost limitless, and the effects achieved are often amazing.

There are many kinds of paints, suitable for different purposes, but they all share the same components. Paint in its most basic form is composed of **pigment** suspended in a liquid **binder** that dries after it has been applied and holds pigment in place. Pigment gives paint its color. Traditionally, pigments have been extracted from minerals, soils, vegetable matter, and animal by-products. The color umber, for example, originated from the brown clay soil of Umbria in Italy. Ultramarine—from the Latin *ultramarinus*, beyond the sea—is the deep, luxurious blue favored for the sky color in some **Renaissance** painting; it was ground from lapis lazuli, a blue stone found in Afghanistan. In recent times, pigments have been manufactured by chemical processes. The bright cadmium reds and yellows, for instance, are by-products of zinc extraction.

Pigments by themselves do not stick to a surface. They need a liquid binder, a substance that allows the paint to be applied and then dries, leaving the pigment permanently attached. Just as there are many kinds of pigments, there are many binders, traditionally beeswax, egg yolk, vegetable oils and gums, and water; in modern times, art-supply manufacturers have developed such complex chemical substances as **polymers**. Painters also use solvents for different reasons, for example adding turpentine to oil paint to make it thinner.

Artists use many kinds of tools to help them paint. Brushes are the tools most commonly associated with painting. Traditionally made from animal hair like hog bristle or sable fur, it is now common to see brushes made of vinyl and polyester. Although historically brushes have been the most popular tools for paint, some artists have used compressed air to spray paint onto their chosen surface; others have spread it around with a palette knife as if they were buttering toast. Sometimes they have poured it from buckets, or have ridden across the canvas on a bicycle the wheels of which were covered in it; others have dipped their fingers, hands, or entire body in it so they can make their marks.

Paint is an attractive and versatile material with a long and fascinating history; artists have continually experimented with and developed it as a medium. In turn, such developments have reflected the changing pace and values in people's way of life. In the prehistoric era, with little scientific knowledge and no technology

Medium (plural **media**): the material on or from which an artist chooses to make a work of art, for example canvas and oil paint, marble, engraving, video, or architecture
Color: the optical effect caused when reflected white light of the spectrum is divided into separate wavelengths
Scale: the size of an object or artwork relative to another object or artwork, or to a system of measurement
Pigment: the colorant in art materials. Often made from finely ground minerals
Binder: a substance that makes pigments adhere to a surface
Renaissance: a period of cultural and artistic change in Europe from the fourteenth to the seventeenth century
Polymer: a chemical compound commonly referred to as plastic

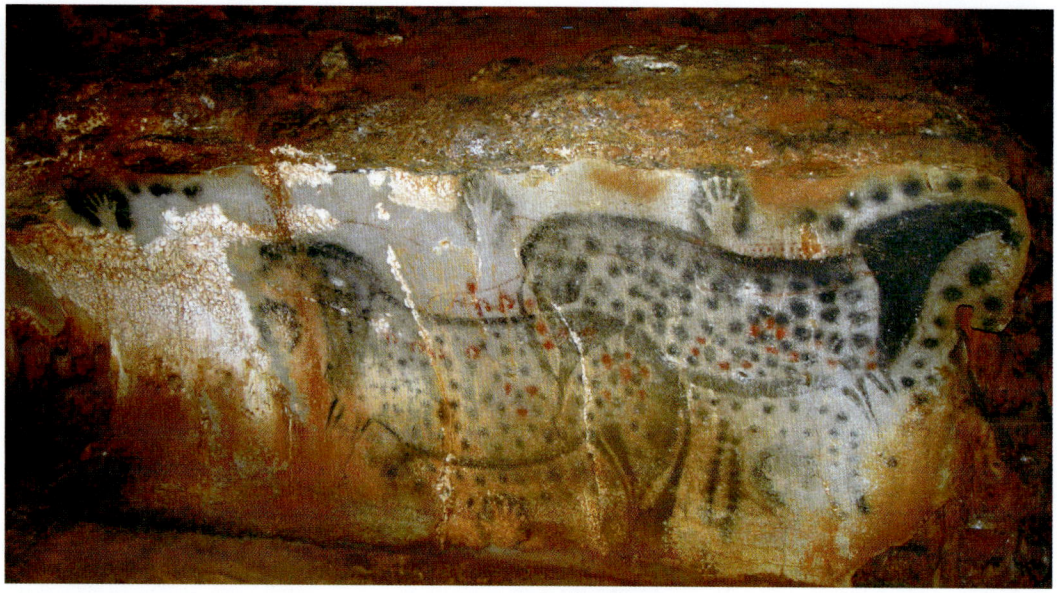

2.2.1 Cave paintings from Pech Merle cave, c. 23,000 BCE. Pigment with saliva. Near Cabrerets, Lot département, France

available to them, artists used saliva or animal fat to fix pigment made from colored mineral soil and ash from fires to mark and decorate their dwellings. As civilizations became more settled, domestic, and sophisticated, artists employed wax (**encaustic**) and egg (**tempera**) as binding agents for mineral pigments; eventually, artists who wanted their work to endure developed **fresco** techniques, using pigment with plaster to embed their paintings permanently in the walls of buildings. In the East, artists painted using the delicate medium of ink to express the complexities of human experience. In the fifteenth and sixteenth centuries travel became more common and widespread due to, in part, the endeavors of the famous explorers of the era. As travel became more accessible, Western artists moved from painting principally on wood panels with tempera, to painting with oil on linen canvases, which could be transported much more easily and could support larger works. Oil was the dominant paint type used by artists until the quickening pace of the modern world, and the industrialization of life, encouraged artists to favor such quick-drying paint types as watercolor and acrylic (a modern, chemical invention), which proved both flexible in application and durable.

This chapter will survey the most common forms of paint, and the many methods and tools used in creating paintings. It will also introduce some notable painters and paintings.

The First Paintings

Researchers have discovered that some images on the cave walls of Pech Merle (**2.2.1**) near Cabrerets, France, were made of a saliva-and-pigment solution that was applied with a small tube. The application of this paint (with saliva as binder) took place 25,000 years ago and the images are mostly of animals, although some human imagery is also present. The two spotted horses in one room at Pech Merle were painted by blowing the solution, which held a pigment that was probably derived from charcoal, through a tube onto the stone cave walls. There have been many discoveries of cave paintings in southern France and Spain, and in each example, the same medium, saliva, has been used as the binding agent.

It seems likely that there were both men and women creating ancient cave art. Recent findings at Pech Merle, involving the finger lengths from handprints that surround the spotted horse paintings, lead researchers to believe that most of the artists involved in this work were female.

Encaustic

Another binding technique that was perfected many centuries ago is encaustic, a relatively semi-transparent paint medium that was used by the ancient Greeks and Romans. Encaustic

Encaustic: a painting medium that primarily uses wax, usually beeswax, as the binding agent
Tempera: fast-drying painting medium made from pigment mixed with water-soluble binder, such as egg yolk
Fresco: a technique in which the artist paints onto freshly applied plaster. From the Italian *fresco*, "fresh"
Support: the material on which painting is done
Naturalism, naturalistic: a very realistic or lifelike style of making images
Translucent: semi-transparent

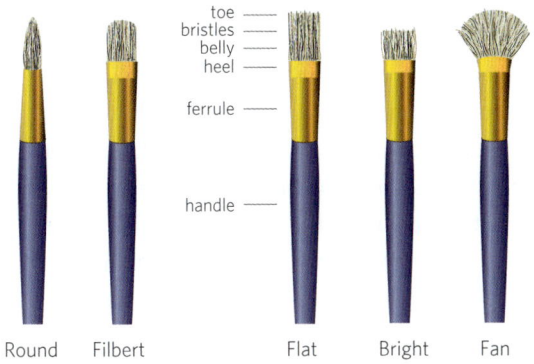

2.2.2 (left) Commonly used brush types, and the parts of an artist's brush: Round: sketching and thinned paint application, can be rolled in hand for special effect; Filbert: for applying color, short bristles for more control and softened edges; Flat: for long, fluid strokes and sharp edges; Bright: for controlled detailing and applying areas of color; Fan: for blending slow-drying paint and softening edges

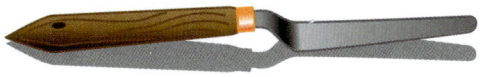

2.2.3 (left) Palette knife, a tool that can be used by the painter for mixing and applying paint

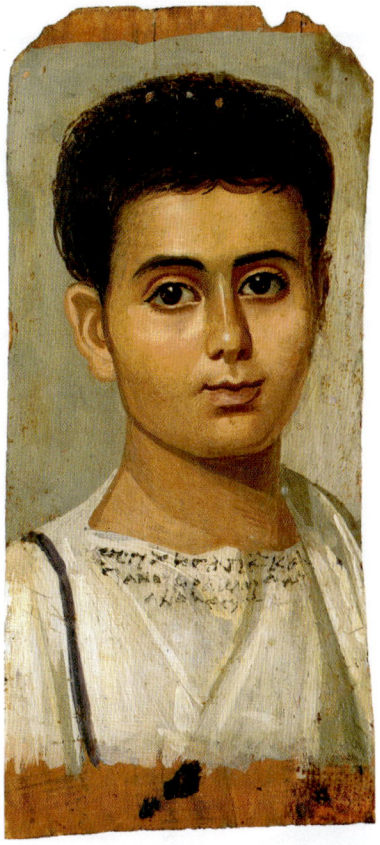

2.2.4 (above) Portrait of a boy, c. 100–150 CE. Encaustic on wood, 15⅜ × 7½". Metropolitan Museum of Art, New York

continues to be chosen by some artists today because of the unique character of beeswax. To use encaustic, an artist must mix pigments with hot wax and then apply the mixture quickly. He or she can use brushes (**2.2.2**), palette knives (**2.2.3**), or rags, or can simply pour it. A stiff-backed **support**, such as a wooden panel or metal plate, is necessary because encaustic, when cool, is not very flexible and may crack. The Greeks and Romans typically painted encaustic on wood panel.

Ancient Roman painters showed great ability in controlling encaustic paint and produced beautiful results. The image of a boy in **2.2.4** was made by an anonymous artist during the second century CE in Roman Egypt. This type of portrait would have been used as a funerary adornment that was placed over the face of the mummified deceased or on the outside of the sarcophagus, above where the head was positioned. The artist took great care to create a lifelike image and probably captured a fairly **naturalistic** likeness of the deceased boy. Encaustic portraits from this era are referred to as Fayum portraits, after the Fayum Oasis in Egypt where many of them were found.

The art of encaustic painting did not end in the ancient world, but has been adapted to contemporary trends in art. One such contemporary encaustic artist is the American Mary Black (b. 1948) who uses the medium exclusively. Black's experimental approach to encaustic painting can be seen in her use of the medium through a process of destruction, then creation, to build up layers of depth with the **translucent** wax and some added material. In her work *Natura 9* (**2.2.5**) the evidence of destruction then creation becomes a visible record of spontaneous reactions that the artist values in her work. The result is a visually rich surface of pocked and dripped paint with a strong physical presence.

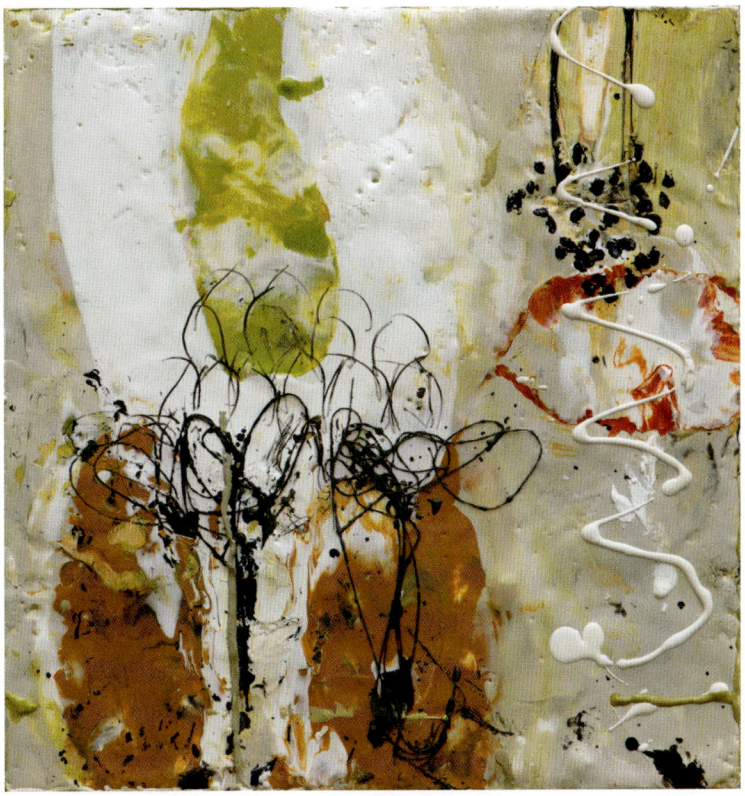

2.2.5 Mary Black, *Natura 9*, 2015. Encaustic, oil stick, graphite, ink, and Sheetrock tape on panel, 10 × 10". Collection of the artist.

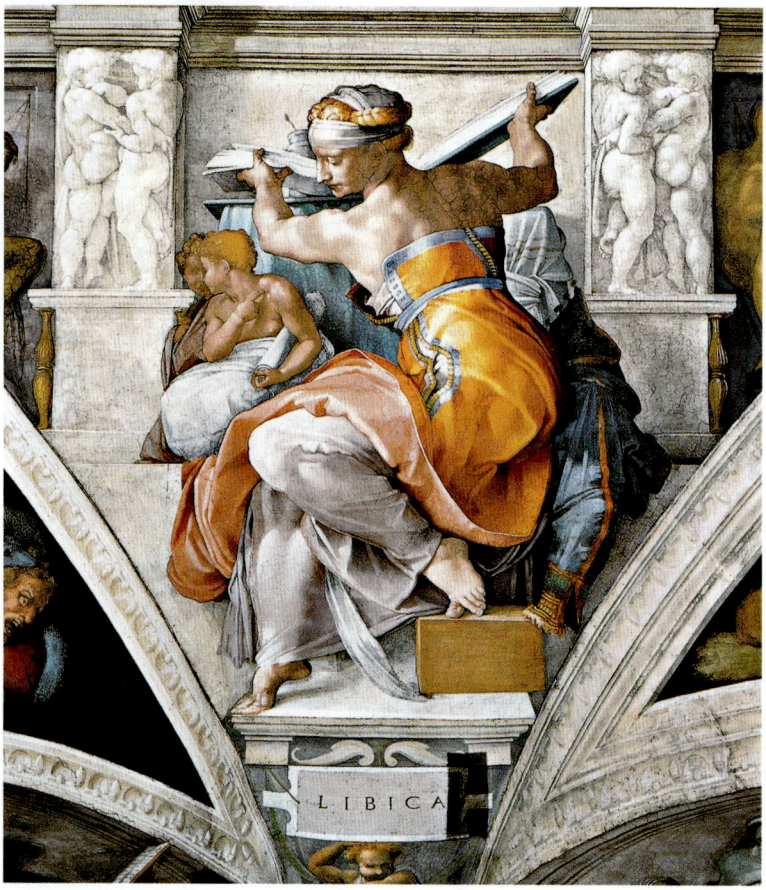

2.2.6 Michelangelo, *The Libyan Sibyl*, 1511–12. Fresco. Detail of the Sistine Chapel ceiling, Vatican City, Italy

Foreground: the part of a work depicted as nearest to the viewer
Value: the lightness or darkness of a plane or area

Fresco

Fresco is a painting technique in which the artist paints onto freshly applied plaster. The earliest examples of the fresco method come from Crete in the Mediterranean (the palace at Knossos and other sites) and date to *c.* 1600–1500 BCE. Frescoes were also used later, to decorate the inside of Egyptian tombs. The technique was used extensively in the Roman world for the decoration of interiors, and its use was revived during the Italian Renaissance. The pigment is not mixed into a binder, as it is in other painting techniques. Instead, pigment mixed with water is applied to a lime-plaster surface. The plaster absorbs the color and the pigment binds to the lime as it sets. Once this chemical reaction is complete, the color is very durable, making fresco a very permanent painting medium.

There are two methods of fresco painting: *buon fresco* (Italian for good fresco) and *fresco secco* (dry fresco). When artists work with buon fresco, they must prepare the wall surface by overlaying undercoats of rough plaster containing sand, gravel, cement, and lime. The artist adds a further (but not final) layer of plaster and allows it to dry for several days; he or she then transfers onto it the design from a full-scale drawing (referred to as a cartoon) in preparation for the final painting. Next, the artist applies the last finishing layer of plaster, re-transferring onto it the required part of the cartoon. Onto this, he or she will paint pigment suspended in water. Because there are just a few hours before the lime plaster sets, only a portion of the wall is freshly plastered each day. If the artist makes a mistake, the plaster must be chiseled away and the procedure repeated. These technical challenges are offset by the brilliance of color for which fresco is renowned.

Many of the Renaissance fresco paintings were made to decorate the interiors of churches. The Italian artist Michelangelo Buonarroti (1475–1564) used the buon fresco method to decorate the ceiling of the Sistine Chapel in Rome (**2.2.6**). For this monumental undertaking, requiring four years to complete, Michelangelo needed to craft a strategic approach in order to disguise the seams between separate days' work. For example, in one section, called *The Libyan Sibyl*, he plastered only the area where the leg in the **foreground** was to be painted (**2.2.6**). This was probably a day's work, and the seam of the plaster could be camouflaged because the surrounding edges (the purple drapery in particular) change color and **value**.

If an artist cannot finish painting a section within a day of plastering, or needs to retouch a damaged fresco, he or she employs the dry fresco method (fresco secco). To encourage absorbency, wet rags moisten the lime plaster that has already set, and the wall is then painted. The once-dry lime surface soaks up some of the pigment. Frescoes painted using the fresco secco method tend to be less durable than buon fresco, because the surface is less absorbent.

Although buon fresco is an ancient and temperamental art medium, many contemporary artists still choose to execute their works using this process. The American artist

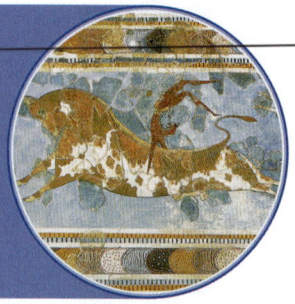

Some of the earliest examples of fresco are from the Minoan civilization (in modern Crete): see **3.1.7, p. 369**

Perspectives on Art: José Clemente Orozco
Fresco Painting Inspired by the Mexican Revolution

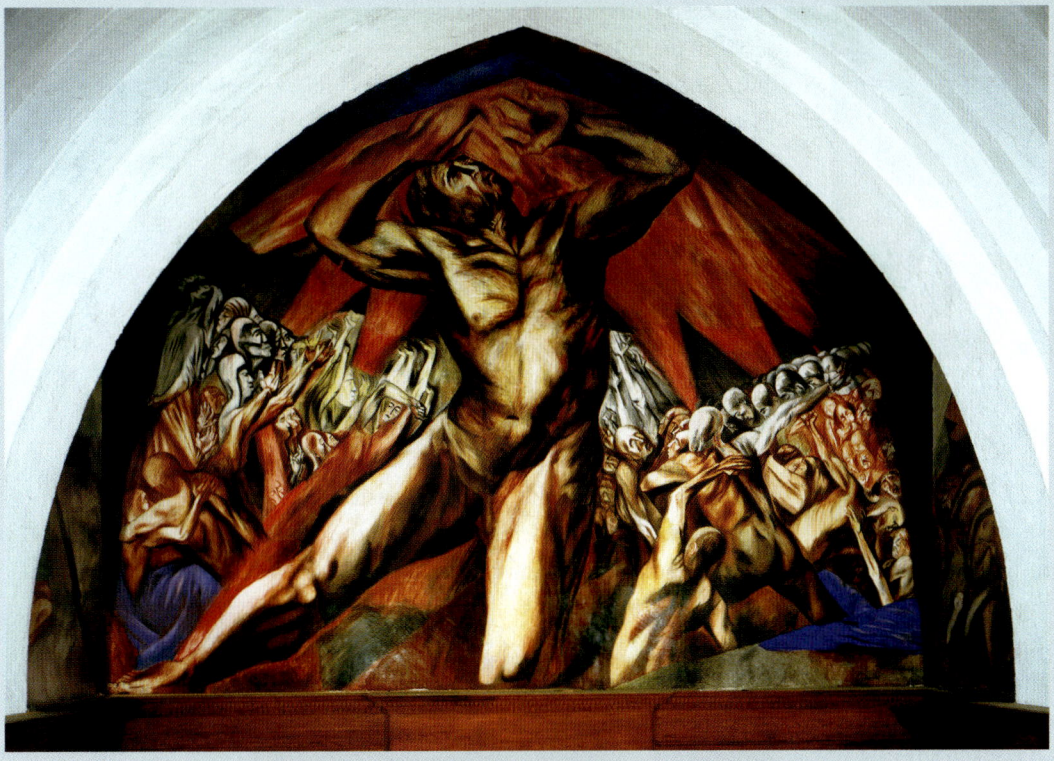

2.2.7 José Clemente Orozco, *Prometheus*, 1930. Fresco mural (central panel), approx. 20 × 28½'. Frary Hall, Pomona College, Claremont, California

For more than thirty years Porfirio Díaz ruled Mexico as a dictator. This was a time of injustice and great divisions between the powerful rich and the poor masses. In 1911, the Mexican people rebelled and forced Díaz to resign. For ten years revolutionary groups led the fight for social justice, and from the 1920s to the mid-1930s, in an outpouring of national creativity, Mexican mural artists painted the walls of public buildings with works that expressed their aspirations for social justice and freedom, and revived the art of fresco painting. Subsequently, scholars termed this period the Mexican Mural Renaissance. One of the most famous mural painters of this time was José Clemente Orozco (1883–1949), who lost his left hand and had his sight and hearing damaged in an explosion during his childhood. Despite these disabilities, he went on to become a significant and radical artist who struggled for the rights of peasants and workers in revolutionary Mexico. His writings about art emphasize his interest in the medium of fresco painting and in its formal aspects: as he wrote, he saw art as visual poetry.

Fresco painting is free from the inconveniences of oils and varnishes, but the wall upon which the painting is done is subjected to many causes of destruction, such as the use of the wrong kind of building materials, poor planning, moisture from the ground or from the air, earthquakes, dive bombing, tanking or battleshipping, excess of magnesia in the lime or the marble dust, lack of care resulting in scratches or peeling off, et cetera. So, fresco must be done only on walls that are as free as possible from all these inconveniences.

There is no rule for painting al fresco. Every artist may do as he pleases provided he paints as thinly as possible and only while the plaster is wet, six to eight hours from the moment it is applied. No retouching of any kind afterwards. Every artist develops his own way of planning his conception and transferring it onto the wet plaster...Or the artist may improvise without any previous sketches.

A painting is a Poem and nothing else. A poem made of relationships between forms...

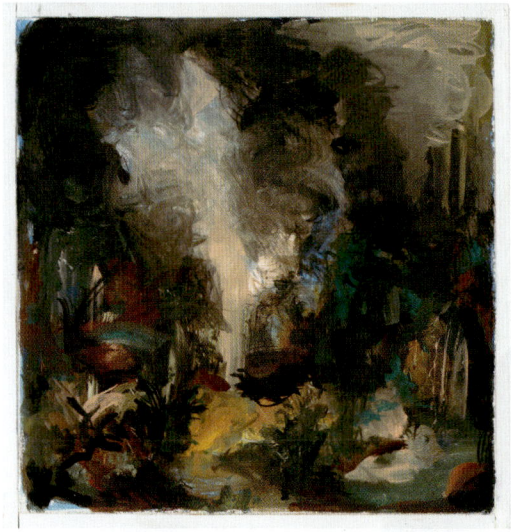

2.2.8 Walter O'Neill, *Untitled*, 2002. Fresco on wire mesh on wood, 24 × 24". Courtesy Walter O'Neill

Walter O'Neill (b. 1951) takes a more **painterly** and abstract approach to the buon fresco process in *Untitled* (**2.2.8**) by working in a loose style that suggests more traditional compositions. Since buon fresco demands that the paint be applied within hours after the lime-plaster surface has been established, the artist has taken advantage of this trait by using energetic gestural strokes that appear to have been executed quickly. O'Neill, a student of Renaissance fresco painting, captures the essence of ancient techniques and fuses them with the expressive character of modern and contemporary painting.

Tempera

If you have ever scrubbed dried egg off a plate while washing dishes, you know how surprisingly durable it can be. Painters who use egg tempera have different ideas about what parts of the egg work best for tempera painting, but many artists have favored the yolk. Despite its rich yellow color, egg yolk does not greatly affect the color of pigment; instead, it gives a transparent soft glow. Tempera is best mixed fresh for each painting session.

Tempera is usually applied with a brush and dries almost immediately. The earliest examples of egg tempera have been found in Egyptian tombs. From the fifth century onward, painters of icons (**stylized** images of Jesus and saints) in what we know today as Greece and Turkey perfected the use of the medium and transmitted the technique to early Renaissance painters in Europe and the Middle East.

As in many Italian paintings of the fourteenth century, the paint of the *Entry into Jerusalem*, from the back of the **altarpiece** called the *Maestà*, consists of pigment and egg yolk (**2.2.9**). For the *Maestà*, Duccio di Buoninsegna (*c.* 1255–1319) created a large, freestanding construction made up of many paintings that can be viewed from both front and back, with the latter comprising a series of images that depict important moments in the life of Christ, of which the *Entry into Jerusalem* is one. Although egg tempera can be challenging because it dries so quickly, Duccio's mastery of the medium, which demanded short, thin strokes, resulted in brilliant detail to enlighten a population of believers.

Painterly: a loosely executed style in which paint and brushstrokes are evident
Stylized: art that represents objects in an exaggerated way to emphasize certain aspects of the object
Altarpiece: an artwork that is placed behind an altar in a church

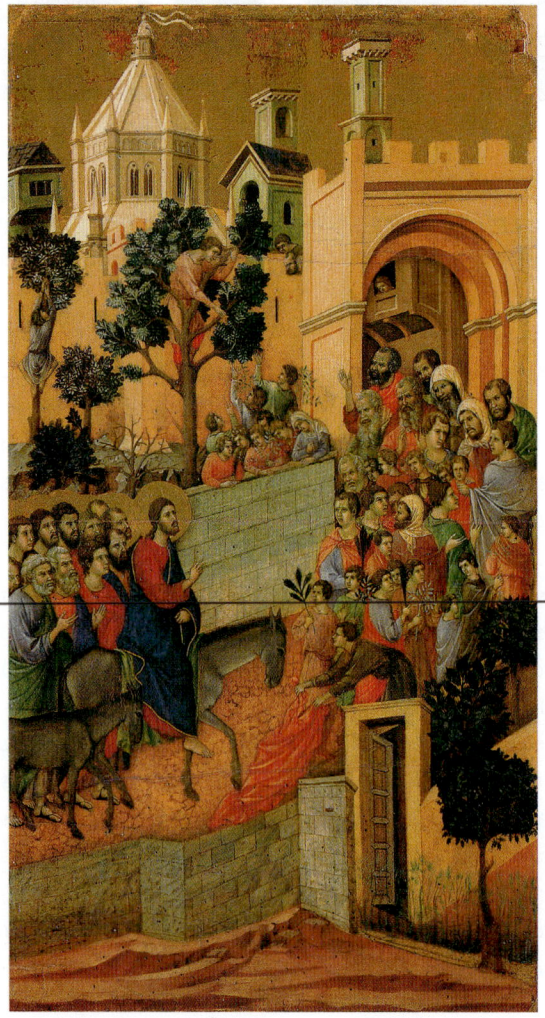

2.2.9 Duccio di Buoninsegna, *Entry into Jerusalem* (from the back of the *Maestà* altarpiece, Siena Cathedral), 1308–11. Tempera and gold leaf on wood, 3'4½" × 1'9⅛". Museo dell'Opera Metropolitana del Duomo, Siena, Italy

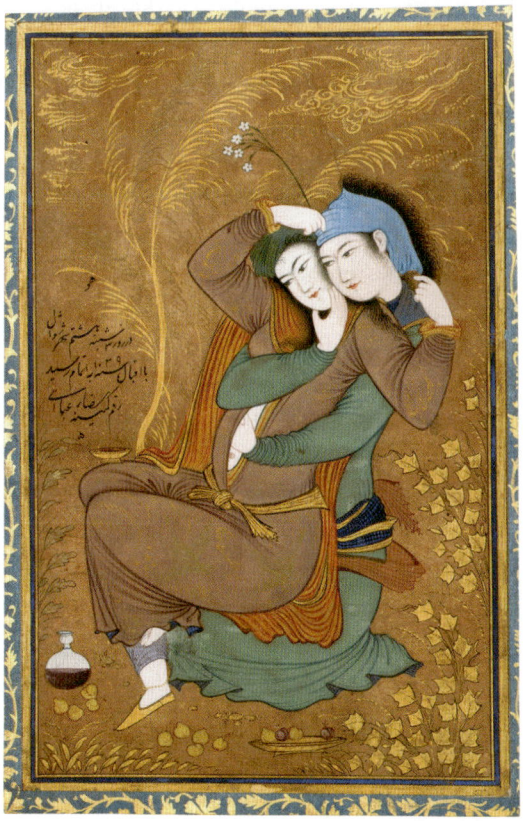

2.2.10 Riza Abbasi, *Two Lovers*, Safavid period, 1629–30. Tempera and gilt paint on paper, 7⅛ × 4¾". Metropolitan Museum of Art, New York

Islamic artists also enjoyed the sensitive detail that can be achieved with tempera, and some used tempera with gold leaf to create rich images for the ruling class. In *Two Lovers* by the Persian miniaturist Riza Abbasi (1565–1635), we see the rich gold-leaf finish combined with the high detail of tempera (**2.2.10**). Riza, who worked for Shah Abbas the Great, has used the transparency of the medium to make the plant life look delicate and wispy. The intertwined lovers stand out proudly from the softness of the plants in the **background**.

The appeal of tempera painting continues today. It has been used to create some of the most recognizable works in American art. Andrew Wyeth (1917–2009), loved by Americans for his sense of realism and high detail, chose tempera to create works that provide a glimpse into American life in the mid-twentieth century. The **subject** of *Christina's World* (**2.2.11**) is a neighbor of Wyeth's in Maine who had suffered from polio and could not walk. Wyeth has chosen to place her in a setting that expresses (in Wyeth's words) her "extraordinary conquest of life." The scene appears placid and bright, reflecting Wyeth's great admiration for her. The high degree of detail creates a sense of mystery that stimulates our imagination.

Background: the part of a work depicted as furthest from the viewer's space, often behind the main subject matter
Subject: the person, object, or space depicted in a work of art

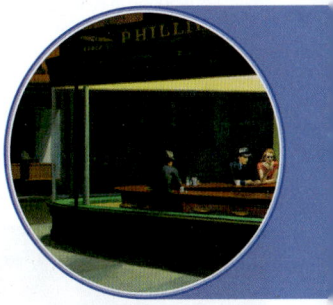

Edward Hopper's *Nighthawks* is a piece of realism that provides a snapshot of American life in the mid-twentieth century: see **1.10.2, p.172**

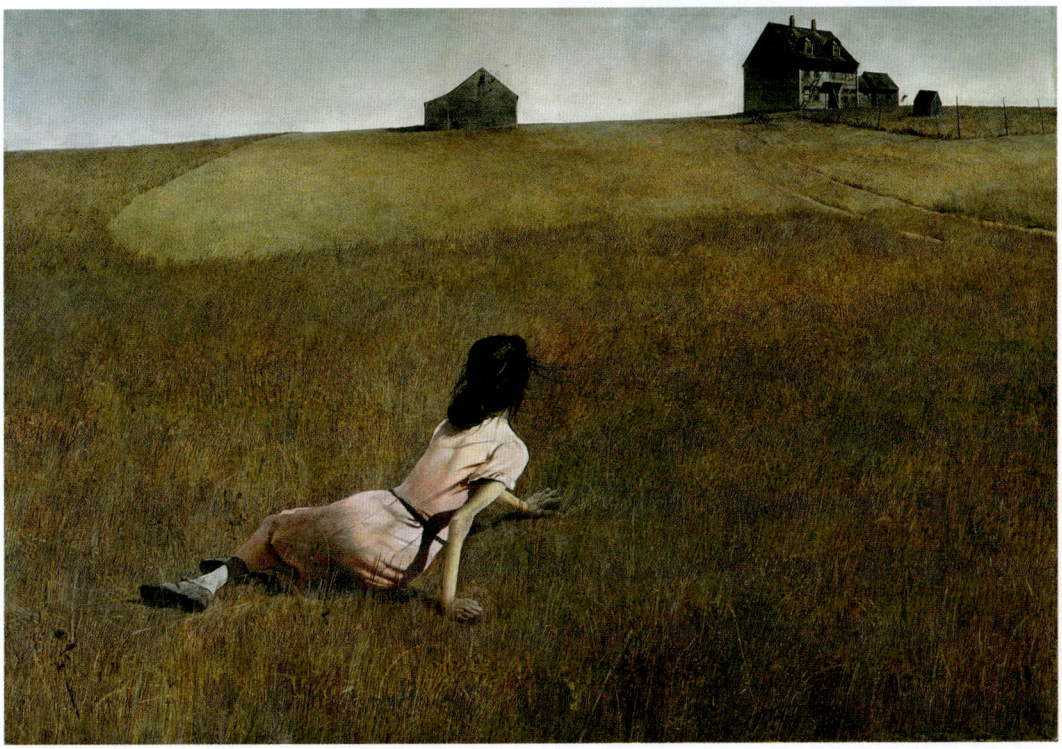

2.2.11 Andrew Wyeth, *Christina's World*, 1948. Tempera on gessoed panel, 32¼ × 47¾". MoMA, New York

Luminosity: a bright, glowing quality
Underpainting: in oil painting, the process of painting the canvas in a base, often monochrome color as a first step in creating the areas of light and dark value
Grisaille: painting in gray or grayish monochrome, either as a base or underpainting for the finished work, or as the final artwork itself
Verdaccio: a mixture of black, white, and yellow pigments resulting in a grayish or yellowish soft greenish brown. It is used in oil painting, and sometimes in frescoes, as a base layer to refine the values in the work
Impressionism: a late nineteenth-century painting style conveying the impression of the effects of light; Impressionists were painters working in this style

Oil

Painting with oil is a relatively recent invention compared to encaustic, tempera, and fresco. Artists used oil paint during the Middle Ages, but have done so regularly only since the fifteenth century, particularly in Flanders (modern-day Belgium, The Netherlands, and northern France). The oil used as a binder there was usually linseed oil, a by-product of the flax plant from which linen cloth is made. Giorgio Vasari, an Italian Renaissance writer and artist, credits the fifteenth-century Flemish painter Jan van Eyck (*c.* 1395–1441) with the invention of oil paint. In fact, Van Eyck did not invent it, but he is its most astonishing early practitioner. His virtuosity with the medium is apparent in his work known as *The Madonna of Chancellor Rolin* (**2.2.12**).

Because it is so flexible, oil paint readily adheres to a cloth support (usually canvas or linen)—unlike encaustic, which is usually painted onto a stiff panel. Painters like oil paint because its transparency allows the use of thin layers of color called glazes. In the hands of such artists as Van Eyck, glazes attain a rich **luminosity**, as though lit from within. This happens because many layers of transparent and semi-transparent color are applied, allowing light to pass through, then reflect light back, creating an impression that light is emanating from behind the glass-like paint. Because oil paint is slow drying, artists can blend it and make changes days after the initial coating has been applied, thereby achieving smooth effects and a high level of detail.

The use of transparent pigment in glaze painting also encouraged the use of **underpainting**. An underpainting is a preliminary layer of paint that is intended to support the final version of the work. It does this by setting up favorable conditions that allow the artist to achieve particular effects. For example, a **grisaille** (from the French term meaning to turn gray) is a black-and-white underpainting (similar to a black-and-white photograph in appearance) that establishes the light and dark values of the work. The French artist Jean-Auguste-Dominque Ingres (1780–1867) created a grisaille and did not add the finishing layers as an example for his students. The work, titled *Odalisque in Grisaille* (**2.2.13**) is made up entirely of gray values, then color was added in the next layer. A **verdaccio** (from the Italian word for green), or green underpainting, creates conditions that, for example, were well suited to realizing the light flesh tones often used in Renaissance portraiture. Although underpainting became more popular for use with oils, painters have used this technique with many other painting media. Grisaille can also be used as a technique to create a finished work of art rather than just for underpainting.

Oil painting gained another surge in popularity when the American artist John G. Rand (1801–1873) invented a new way of storing and transporting paint. In the late nineteenth century, the collapsible tube replaced the use of pig bladders as the favored container for oil paints. Whereas the pig bladder was sealed with string and the artist would poke a hole in to access the paint, a collapsible tube could be reclosed using a screw-on cap, and was less likely to burst at inopportune moments. The French **Impressionist** movement, in particular,

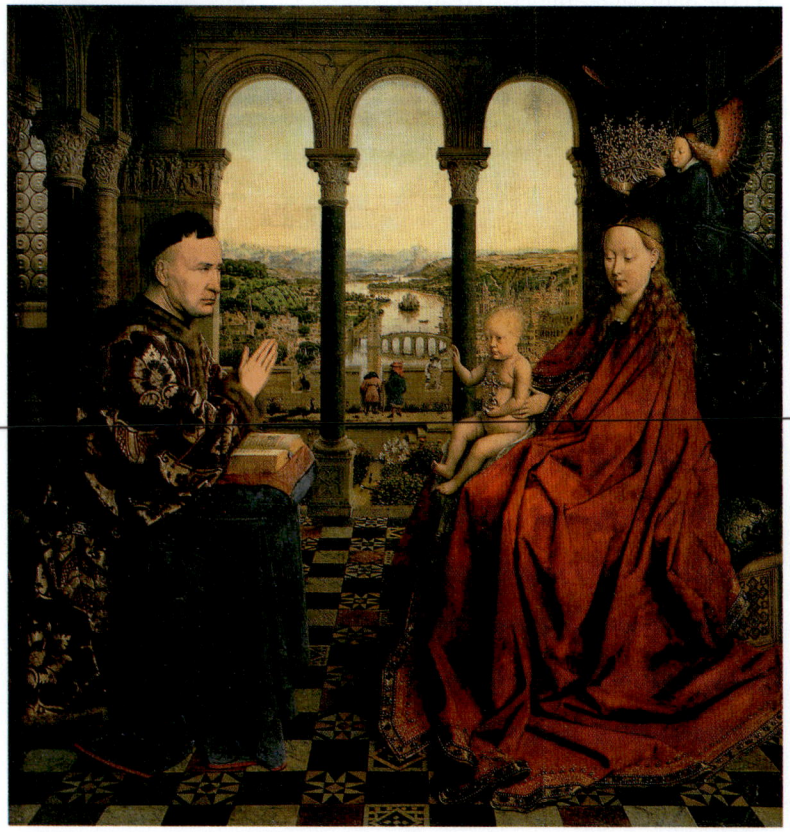

2.2.12 Jan van Eyck, *The Madonna of Chancellor Rolin*, 1430–34. Oil on wood, 26 × 24⅜". Musée du Louvre, Paris, France

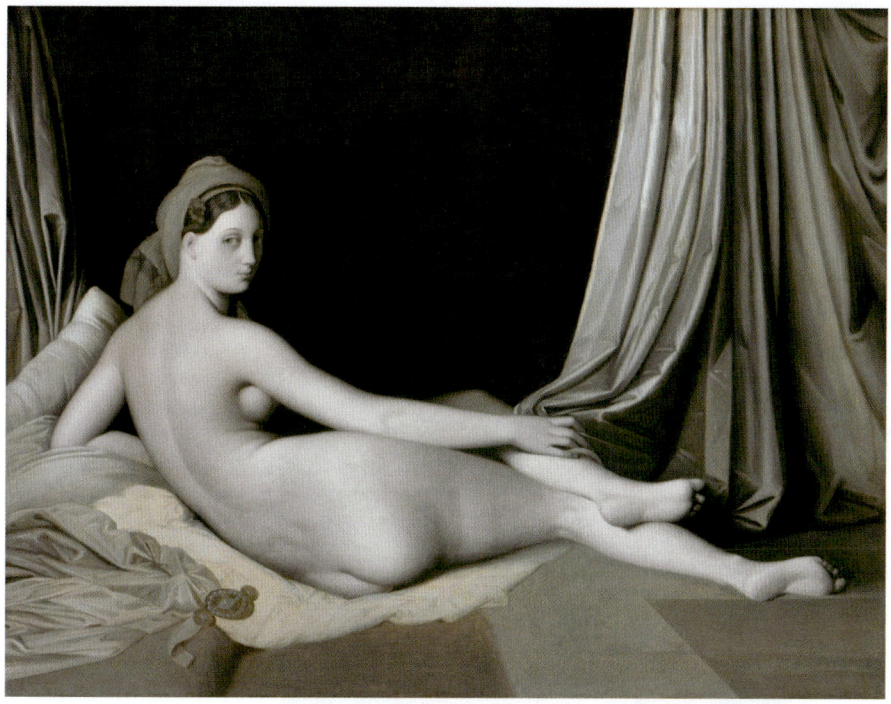

2.2.13 Jean-Auguste-Dominique Ingres, *Odalisque in Grisaille*, c. 1824–34. Oil on canvas, 32¾ × 43". Metropolitan Museum of Art, New York

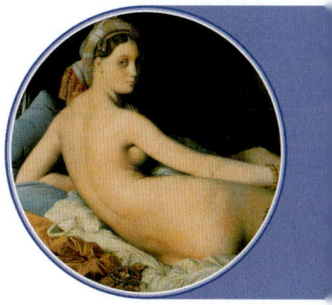

The finished version of Jean-Auguste-Dominique Ingres's *Grande Odalisque* uses verdaccio to great effect: see **1.10.8, p.179**

benefitted greatly from this advance, because it became much easier to transport a large variety of colors when painting outdoors.

Oil paint became a popular medium for expressive applications when used by artists who wanted to depict energetic scenes. One artist who exploited this energetic quality was Rosa Bonheur (1822–1899). Bonheur was the eldest child in a family of French artists. In her early life she was a disruptive student and was moved from one school to another until her father decided to educate her himself. She carried the same enthusiastic disdain for convention into her career as an artist. She was best known in her time because she chose to wear pants and conduct her life as a man—although Bonheur said her dress was a matter of practicality because she was often working with animals, the main subject in most of her paintings. Her most famous work was *The Horse Fair* (**2.2.14**), an image derived from the horse market in Paris. All of her artworks address changing rhythms in

2.2.14 Rosa Bonheur, *The Horse Fair*, 1852–55. Oil on canvas, 8' × 16'7½". Metropolitan Museum of Art, New York

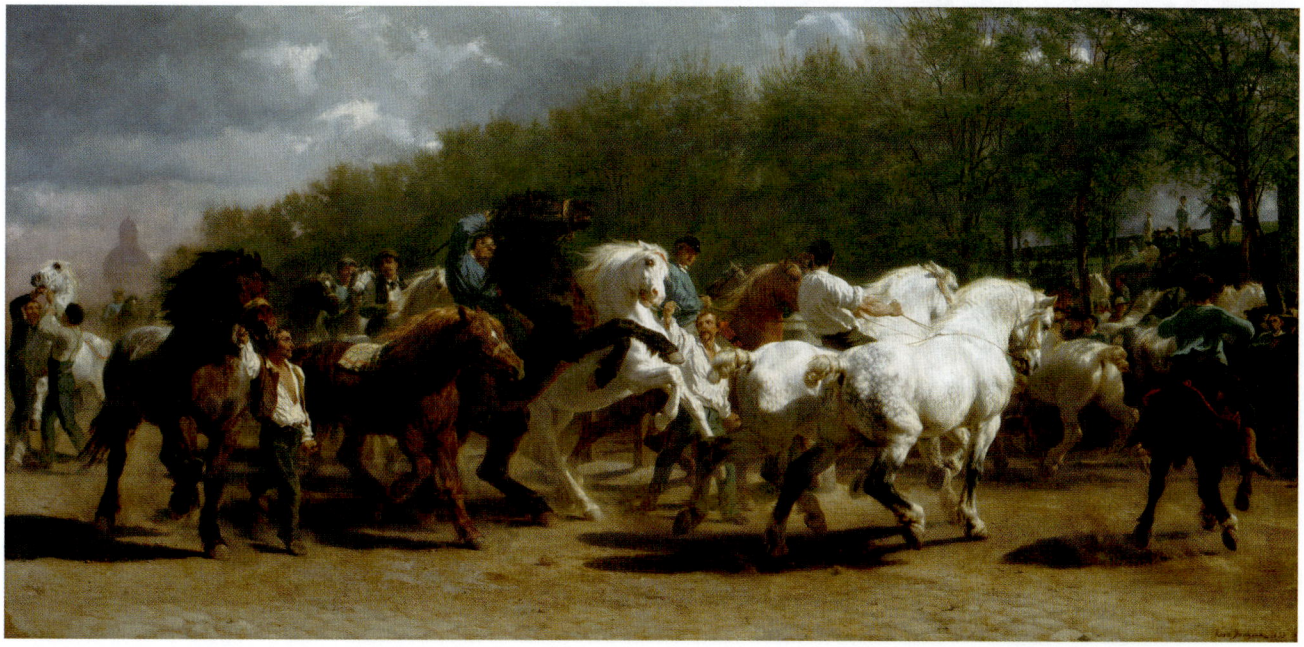

order to communicate the animal biorhythms as they move in concert with their surroundings. The lively scene of horses rearing, trotting, and prancing is amplified by Bonheur's loose and vivacious oil brushwork.

Modern and contemporary artists have used oils to achieve quite different **expressive** effects. The San Francisco artist Joan Brown (1938–1990) used oil in an **impasto** (thickly painted) fashion (**2.2.15**). Because oil paint is normally thick enough to hold its shape when applied to a surface, the paint can pile up, giving Brown's work a **three-dimensional** presence.

The Chinese-born artist Hung Liu (b. 1948), who grew up in Communist China before immigrating to the United States, utilizes the different qualities of oil paint to achieve her own unique **style**. Hung's images express her Chinese roots. Her work *Interregnum* juxtaposes images and styles (**2.2.16**). The traditional Chinese style is reflected in the idyllic figures in the upper part of the work, in contrast with the back-breakingly hard reality of life under the Communist leader Mao Zedong in the lower part. Hung's work shows the discontinuity between reality and the ideal. It also reflects the meaning of the title: an interregnum is a period when normal government is suspended, especially between successive reigns or regimes.

Expressive: capable of stirring the emotions of the viewer
Impasto: paint applied in thick layers
Three-dimensional: having height, width, and depth
Style: a characteristic way in which an artist or group of artists uses visual language to give a work an identifiable form of visual expression
Baroque: European artistic and architectural style of the late sixteenth to early eighteenth century, characterized by extravagance and emotional intensity

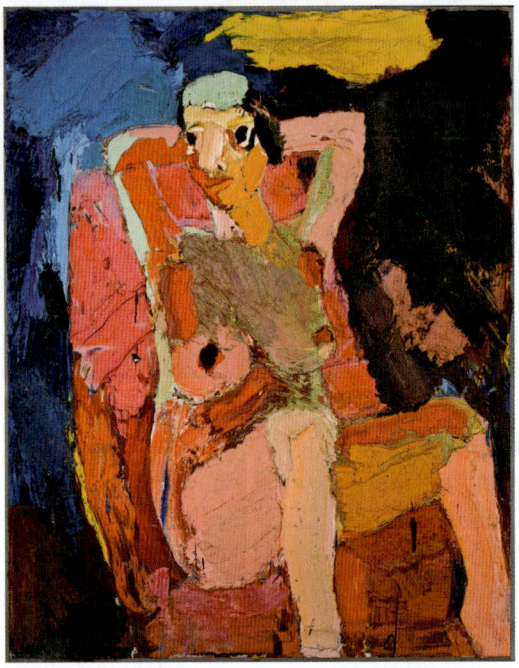

2.2.15 Joan Brown, *Girl in Chair*, 1962. Oil on canvas, 5 × 4'. Los Angeles County Museum of Art (LACMA), California

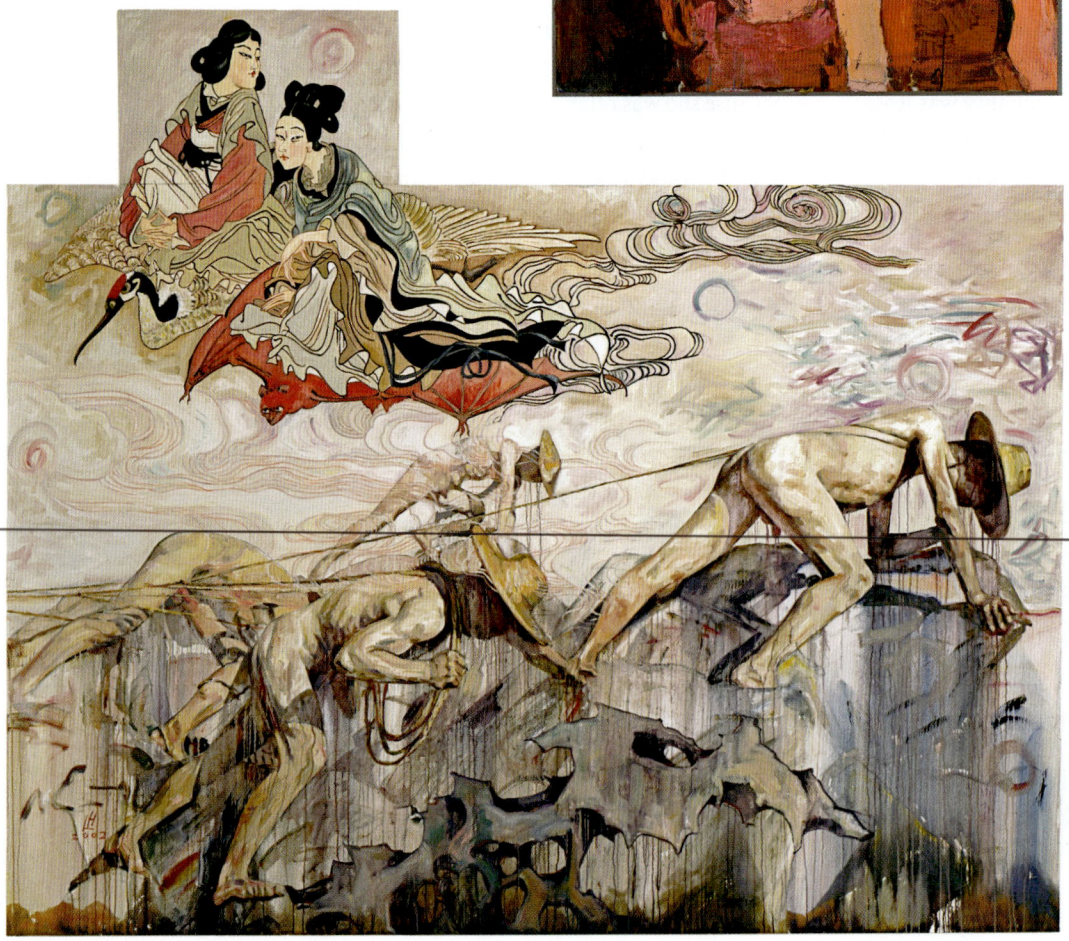

2.2.16 Hung Liu, *Interregnum*, 2002. Oil on canvas, 8' × 9'6". Kemper Museum of Contemporary Art, Kansas City, Missouri

Gateway to Art: Gentileschi, *Judith Decapitating Holofernes*

The Artist in the Act of Painting

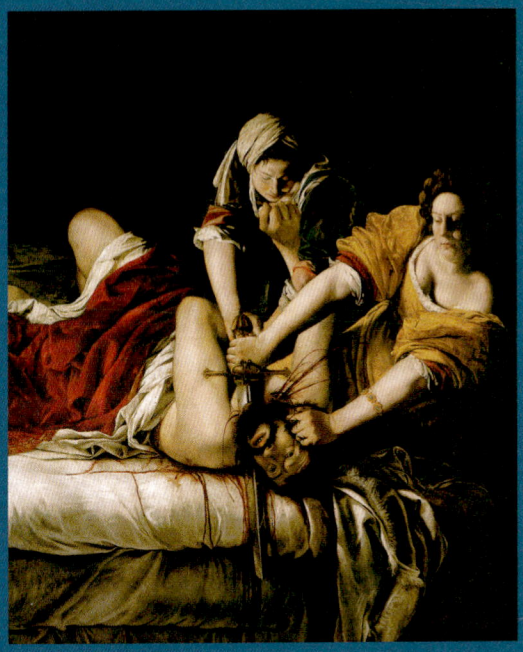

2.2.17 (above) Artemisia Gentileschi, *Judith Decapitating Holofernes*, *c.* 1620. Oil on canvas, 6′6⅜″ × 5′3¾″. Uffizi Gallery, Florence, Italy

At a time when there were very few women working as professional artists, Italian **Baroque** artist Artemisia Gentileschi (1593–*c.*1656) earned a reputation as a talented and accomplished painter. Women were not allowed to follow the traditional avenues of apprenticeship to complete their training as painters, but Gentileschi was the daughter of an artist, and her talent was recognized and fostered by her father.

In the oil painting *Self-portrait as the Allegory of Painting* (**2.2.18**), Gentileschi depicts painting as a physical, energetic act, showing herself holding a brush in one hand and her palette in the other. The mask pendant around her neck signifies that painting is an illusion only an inspired master can produce.

Under her left hand is a block of stone to grind pigments, which she would then blend on her palette. She reaches up towards a large blank canvas that nearly covers the background of the scene. It was common for artists to prepare their canvas with a thinned dark oil, as is shown here. Gentileschi then painted a rough structure of the painting with white oil paint, which was followed by translucent glazes to create luminosity and vibrancy that is striking, for example, in the green sleeve. Just as *Judith Decapitating Holofernes* portrays strong female figures (**2.2.17**), Gentileschi's self-portrait shows her succeeding in the male-dominated world of the professional artist.

For the other Gentileschi Gateway boxes, see p. 152, p. 478, p. 519, and p. 681

2.2.18 (below) Artemisia Gentileschi, *Self-portrait as the Allegory of Painting (La Pittura)*, 1638–39. Oil on canvas, 38 × 29″. Royal Collection, London, England

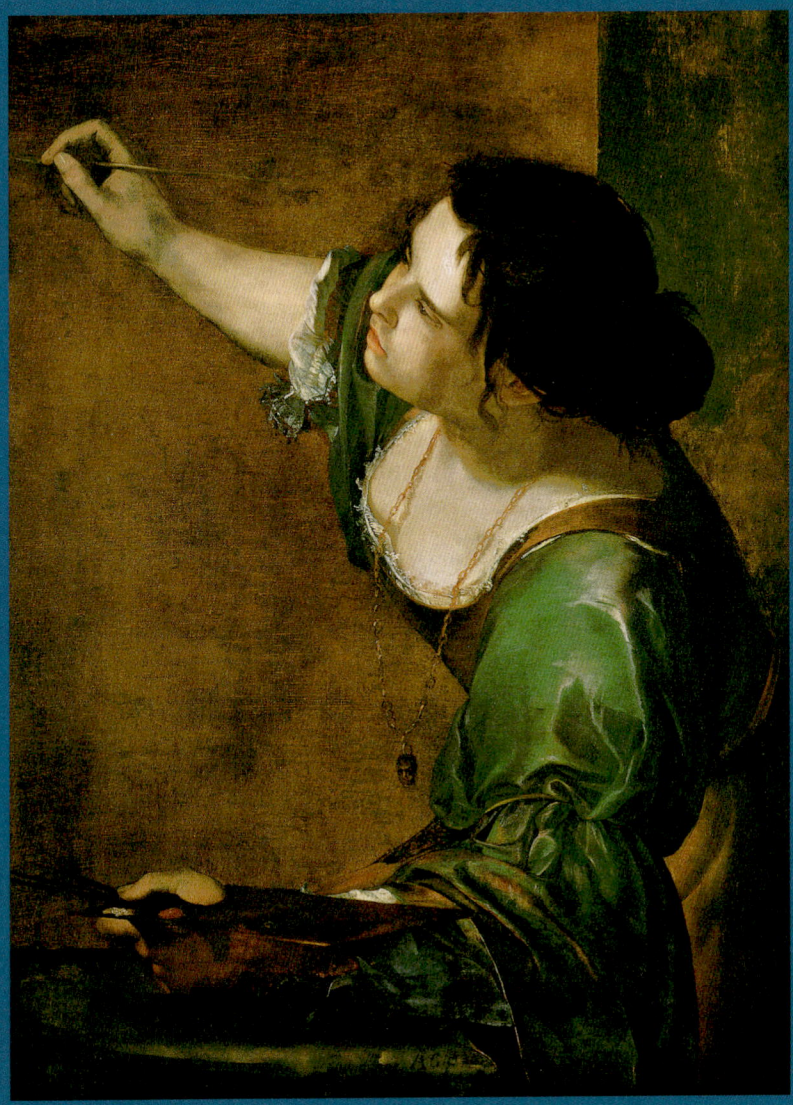

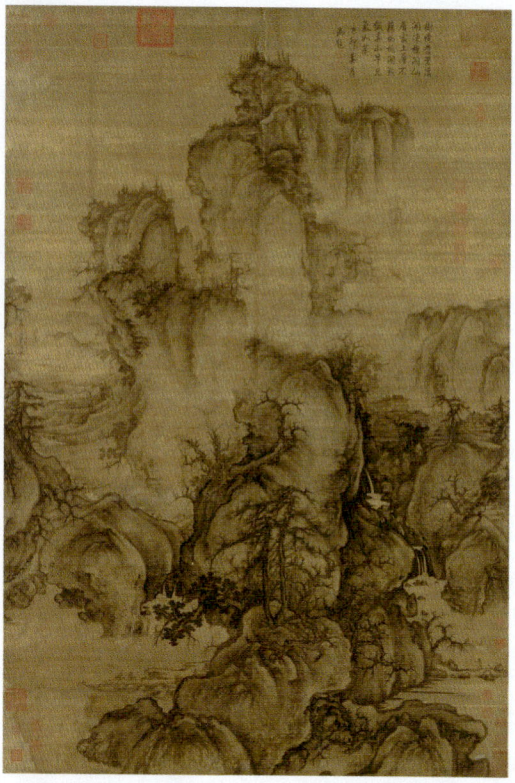

2.2.19 Guo Xi, *Early Spring*, 1072 (Northern Song Dynasty). Ink and color on silk, 62⅜ × 42½". National Palace Museum, Taipei, Taiwan

Gouache: a type of paint medium in which pigments are bound with gum and a white filler added (for example, clay) to produce a paint that is used for opaque watercolor
Opaque: not transparent
***En plein air*:** French for "in the open air"; used to describe painting out of doors from start to finish rather than working in a studio for all or part of the process
Artist's book: a book produced by an artist, usually an expensive limited edition, often using specialized printing processes

Ink Painting

Although artists often use ink with a pen on paper, they also use it for painting. Different surfaces require differences in ink. If you are drawing on a surface that is not fibrous enough, you need to modify the ink. Ink is commonly used on paper because the fibers hold the pigment, but a slicker surface needs an additional binder. Painting inks are slightly different from drawing inks because they have a binder, usually gum arabic, rather than simply being suspended in water.

Chinese literati painting grew out of the rich tradition of Chinese poetry. Any young aspiring government worker in ancient China was expected to be well-versed in the creation of poetry in a calligraphic style. The artistic influences of these two disciplines led artists to go beyond the decorative use of language into the visual form of ink painting. These paintings were first images of people and animals, but by the time of the Song Dynasty (960–1279) an established academic painting style evolved that was distinctively different than the calligraphic style that had been in use for hundreds of years. One of the great practitioners of academic landscape painting was Guo Xi (1020–1090). Guo developed a process that he called "the angle of totality." This system enables artists to present a scene from many vantage points at the same time. The ink painting *Early Spring* (**2.2.19**) displays this kind of perspective, referred to as "floating perspective" because the viewer is not set in a fixed position, but can "move about" the scene to gain a stronger understanding of the landscape.

Watercolor and Gouache

Ink can be painted in much the same way as watercolor; artists sometimes incorporate it into their watercolor paintings to give extra richness and darker values. Watercolor and **gouache** suspend pigment in water with a sticky binder, usually gum arabic (honey is used for French watercolor), which helps the pigment adhere to the surface of the paper when dry. Watercolor is transparent, but an additive (often chalk) in gouache makes the paint **opaque**. Usually watercolor and gouache are painted on paper, because the fibers of the paper help to hold the suspended pigments in place. The portability of watercolor (all the artist needs is brushes, small tubes or cakes of paint, and paper) has made it vastly appealing, especially to artists who paint ***en plein air***, or outdoors, using the landscape as subject matter. The American artist John Singer Sargent (1856–1925) sometimes worked *en plein*

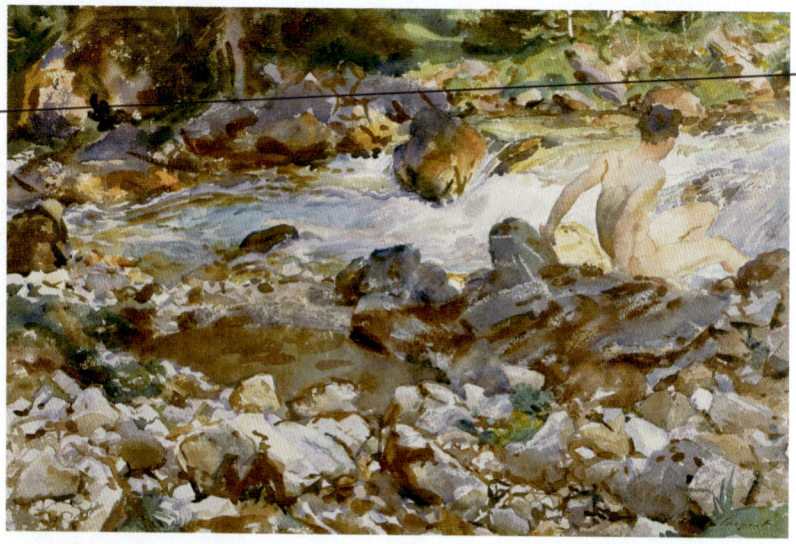

2.2.20 John Singer Sargent, *Mountain Stream*, c. 1912–14. Watercolor and graphite on off-white wove paper, 13¾ × 21". Metropolitan Museum of Art, New York

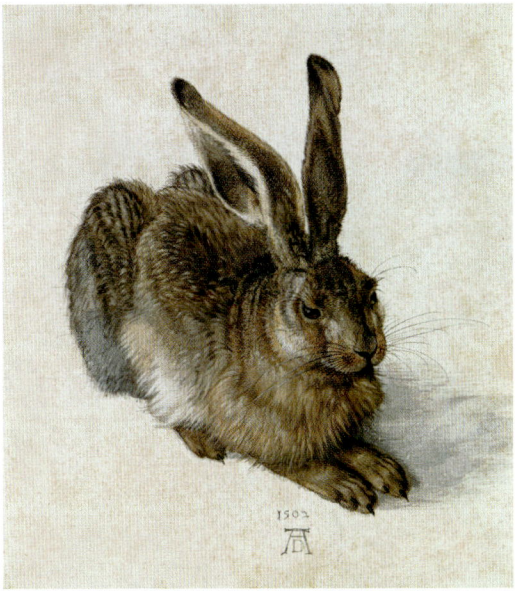

2.2.21 Albrecht Dürer, *A Young Hare*, 1502. Watercolor and gouache on paper, 9⅞ × 8⅞". Graphische Sammlung Albertina, Vienna, Austria

air, and such paintings as *Mountain Stream* (**2.2.20**) were executed outdoors, on location. As with other *plein air* artists, portraying the brilliance of outdoor light is an integral part of Sargent's work. The portability of the medium of watercolor allowed Sargent to work directly from the landscape. Watercolor paint demands that the lightest areas of the work be left untouched, to reveal the white of the paper. Because of this, artists have to be efficient and restrained with each stroke of the brush. This need for discipline is the greatest challenge inherent in mastering watercolor.

The watercolors of the German Albrecht Dürer (1471–1528) are noted for their masterful naturalism. Dürer's works, such as *A Young Hare*, reflect direct observation of a natural subject (**2.2.21**). But unlike *plein air* artists who focused on similar subject matter, Dürer opted to paint in his studio. Regardless of the location in which *A Young Hare* was created, the artist convincingly conveys a sense of the creature's soft, striped fur through a combination of watercolor with opaque white heightening.

The French artist Sonia Delaunay (1885–1979)—the first woman to have her work shown at the Louvre Museum in Paris, France, during her lifetime—mastered the art of watercolor. *Prose of the Trans-Siberian Railway and of Little Jehanne of France* (**2.2.22**), an **artist's book**, was part of a collaboration with the poet Blaise Cendrars (1887–1961). If all 150 copies of the first edition were placed end to end, it was intended that they would stretch the height of the Eiffel Tower. The book was also meant to be folded like a roadmap, and it recounts a trip from Russia to Paris. Delaunay's work is a "simultaneous book" in which her watercolor illustration on the left is set next to the Cendrars poem on the right. She used the bright colors that watercolor affords to create an illustration that progressively changes as the reader advances down the page.

Acrylic

Acrylic paints are composed of pigments suspended in an acrylic polymer resin. They dry quickly and can be cleaned up with relative ease. Latex house paint is made of acrylic polymer. These paints have been in use only since about 1950, but they have become popular with artists because of their versatility and practicality. Unlike oil paints, which dissolve only in turpentine or mineral spirits, acrylics can be cleaned up with water. When dry, however, they have similar characteristics to those of oil paint, although they can also be used in ways that mimic the soft effects of watercolor. They also set easily on a variety of different artistic supports, from paper through to canvas and wood.

Many professional artists, including the contemporary Ethiopian-born American artist Julie Mehretu (b. 1970), prefer acrylics as their primary painting medium. Mehretu uses them to better alternate between layers of the work, changing the traditional convention of drawing the design, then painting over. Mehretu will paint first, then add drawing, then return to painting again, a process that is best achieved in acrylic paint. This combination

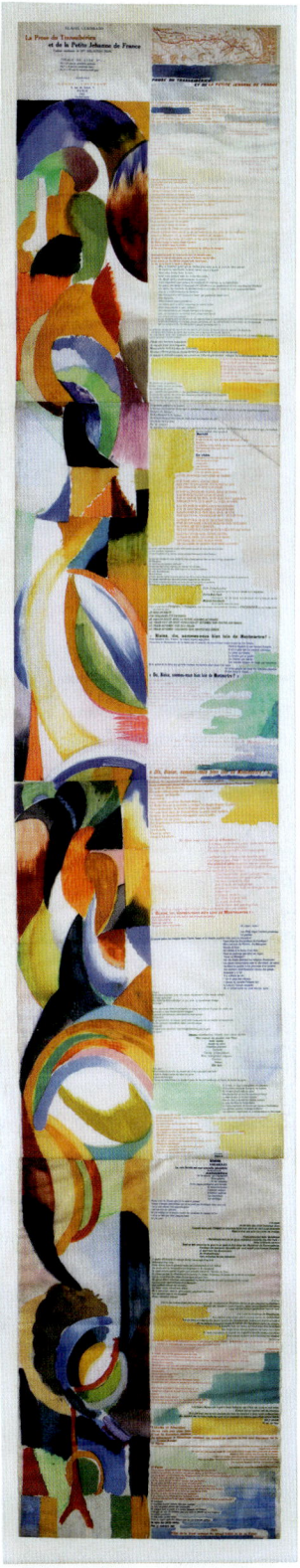

2.2.22 Sonia Delaunay, *Prose of the Trans-Siberian Railway and of Little Jehanne of France*, 1913. Watercolor and relief print on paper, support 77 × 14". Tate, London, England

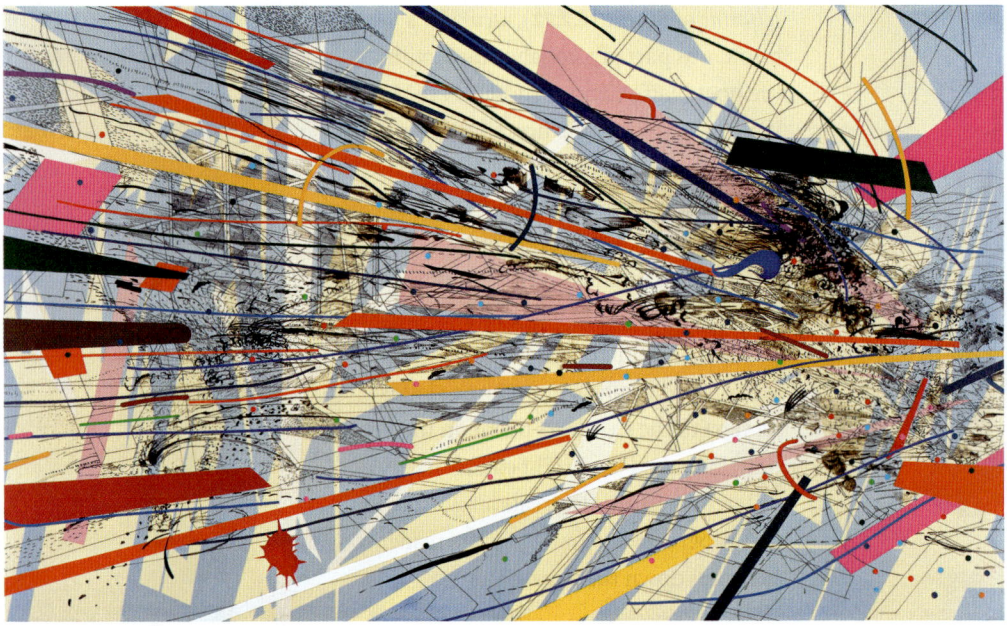

2.2.23 Julie Mehretu, *Excerpt (Suprematist Evasion)*, 2003. Ink and acrylic on canvas, 32 × 54"

Found image or object: an image or object found by an artist and presented, with little or no alteration, as part of a work or as a finished work of art in itself
Graffiti: markings that are scratched, scribbled, or sprayed on a wall without the consent of the owner

of layers was used to create the work *Excerpt (Suprematist Evasion)* (**2.2.23**). Because a shiny finish is easily achieved with acrylic, it is easier to draw on and integrates well with drawing media. Acrylic paint can also offer versatility to an artist because it is compatible with water-based media. This compatibility allows such artists as Mehretu to integrate other media they might need, for example ink or collage, for crisp sharp edges or quick-drying layers.

Artists will sometimes choose a painting medium that helps to support the idea being communicated in the work. Ralph M. Larmann (b. 1959) chose to use acrylic paint for his work, *Coalopolis* (**2.2.24**), because the plastic quality of the polymer reflects and is derived from contemporary manufacturing processes. In Larmann's industrial, menacing landscape, twisting clouds of coal soot rise in dark coils to fill the sky over a fictional town, emphasizing the uncomfortable relationship between economic progress and ecological damage. Even though this message of impending environmental disaster and the acrylic medium are contemporary, Larmann employs an old-fashioned glaze process that is similar to that of such early Dutch painters as Van Eyck, which in this case gives the image a strange glow or luminosity.

2.2.24 Ralph M. Larmann, *Coalopolis*, 2010. Acrylic on canvas, 40 × 60". Collection Indiana State University, Terre Haute, Indiana

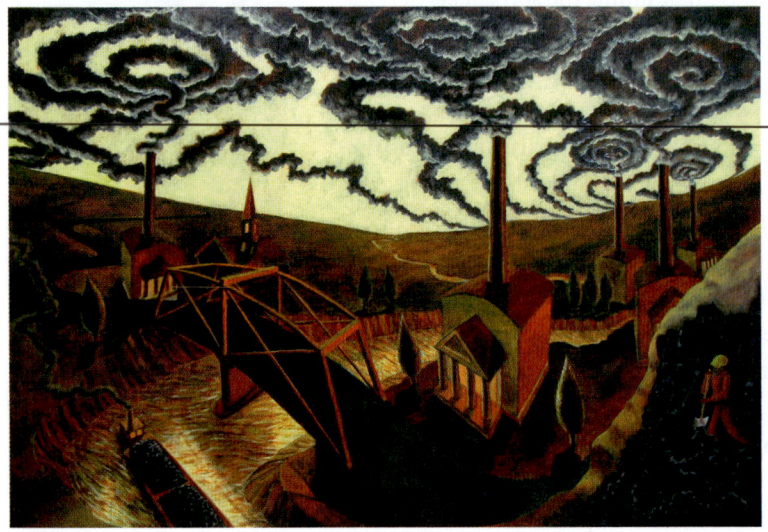

Mixed-Media Painting

The traditional boundaries between art media have been blurred as artists explore new ways to express themselves. Mixed-media and collage work have become popular ways of integrating imagery into a painted artwork. The best known master of mixed-media painting was Robert Rauschenberg (1925–2008). Rauschenberg, an often controversial artist, approached art as if no boundaries existed between the different categories of media. He would often integrate painting, printmaking, drawing, and sculpture into the same work of art. He dubbed his early experiments into mixed media "combines," which are primarily a combination of painting and sculpture. In his iconic combine painting

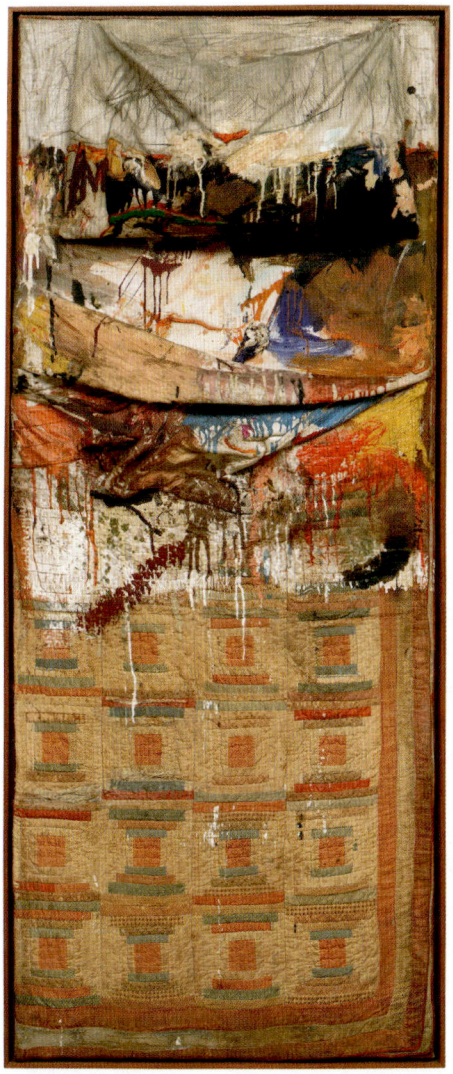

2.2.25 Robert Rauschenberg, *Bed*, 1955. Oil and pencil on pillow, quilt, and sheet on wood supports, 75¼ × 31½ × 8". MoMA, New York

Bed (**2.2.25**), Rauschenberg uses sheets and other bedding material as his "canvas," accentuating the physical nature of the cloth and pillows so that they stick out toward the viewer. The physicality of *Bed* is also emphasized in the manner in which the paint was applied by splattering it on the surface.

One of the first leading female practitioners of mixed-media painting was the American artist Jane Frank (1918–1986). In her work *Frazer's Hog Cay #18* (**2.2.26**) the artist incorporates oil paint and stones together to create an association to a quiet Bahamian island. Even though Frank, who had studied under the abstract artist Hans Hofmann (1880–1966), did not represent a recognizable landscape, she alludes to it through the use of the **found objects**. The added natural sand and stones influence our senses so that we can more easily imagine the island where they may have been discovered.

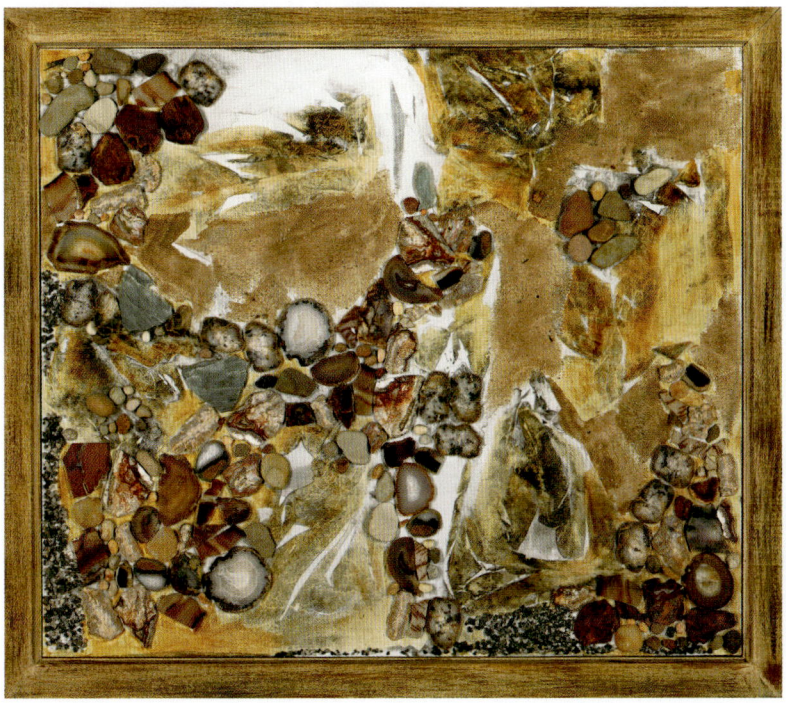

2.2.26 Jane Frank, *Frazer's Hog Cay #18*, 1968. Mixed media: oil paint and stones, 38 × 46". Smithsonian American Art Museum, Washington, D.C.

Mural Art and Spray Paint

The Mexican Muralists, who espoused ideas about social justice and freedom in their works, believed that a painting should belong to all the people of a community, so they often worked outside, usually on a large scale so all could share (see Perspectives on Art Box: Fresco Painting Inspired by the Mexican Revolution, p. 213). This idea of collaborating on a painted work with an entire neighborhood has become an important tool for urban renewal and community. Judith Baca's (b. 1946) *Danza de la Tierra* (**2.2.27**, p. 224), was painted in 2008 for an interior wall in the Dallas Latino Cultural Center. Baca created this work using influences from the surrounding community and local traditions. It is intended to offer the viewer a vibrant and energetic expression of Latino culture. Baca will often employ members of the local area to help create her wall paintings, encouraging strong community involvement.

Spray paint can be applied using a spray gun or spray can, a favorite of tag and **graffiti** artists. Graffiti artists prefer to use spray enamel, a commercially produced paint, packaged in an

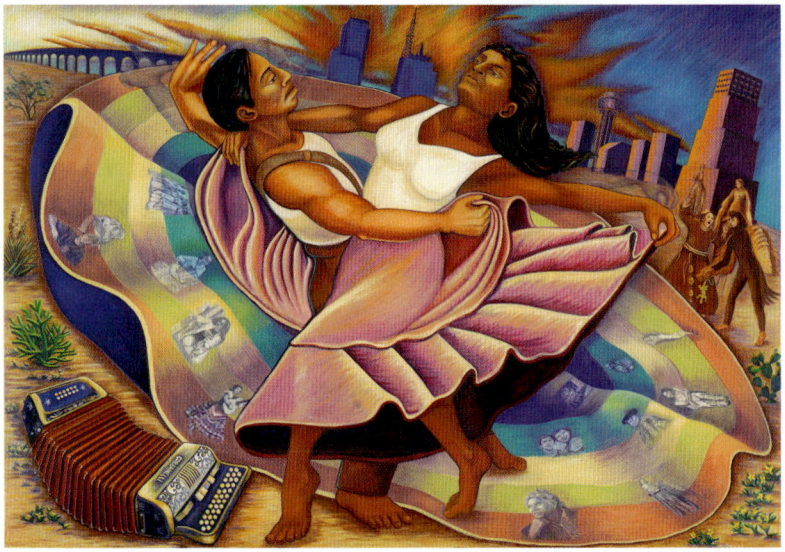

2.2.27 Judith F. Baca, *Danza de la Tierra*, 2008. Acrylic on canvas, 10 × 15'. Dallas Latino Cultural Center, Texas

aerosol can and generally used for applying an even coating on a slick surface. A propellant forces the paint out in a fine mist when the user pushes down on the valve button. Graffiti artists often cut into the spray nozzle with a knife to alter the spray stream, for example to spread a wider mist.

Practitioners of spray-painted graffiti art are considered vandals and criminals by local governments when they paint places without the permission of the property owners. Because of this, many keep their identity secret and sign their work with an alias, called a tag. Even so, many graffiti artists have become known, even celebrated.

The British graffiti artist known as Banksy (b. 1973?) uses **stencils** as a quick way of transferring his designs to surfaces. (Speed of application is important to graffiti artists, who often risk being arrested for defacing private property.) In *Graffiti Removal Hotline*, Banksy, who carefully guards his identity and personal information, skewers and taunts the authorities who seek to curb his street art activities (**2.2.28**). Banksy's street art is full of such lampooning, and he often also points out the absurdity of modern life. In this work the boy pictured on the right has applied pink paint to "deface" a wall that carries a dull and rigid message. Banksy captures the irony of the moment by using pink, traditionally a "passive" color, as a tool of criminal vandalism.

As we have seen, the ancient artists who created the spotted horses at Pech Merle (**2.2.1**, p. 210) did so by blowing a saliva-and-pigment solution through a small tube. Although today's spray paint comes in a can, the technique closely resembles that method, used 25,000 years ago. Because the spray spreads out in a fine mist, the ancient spray-paint artist, like today's spray painters, would **mask** out areas to create hard edges. Ancient artists may even have done this with the edge of their hand, covering the wall where they did not want the paint to fall. The contemporary street artist Banksy and the ancient women and men of Pech Merle may seem worlds apart, but they share a common technique, attesting to the timelessness of painting.

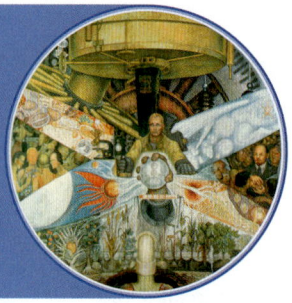

Diego Rivera, a Mexican muralist, was keenly aware of the important role art can play within local communities: see **4.1.13, p. 576**

Stencil: a perforated template allowing ink or paint to pass through to print a design
Mask: in spray painting or silkscreen printing, a barrier the shape of which blocks the paint or ink from passing through

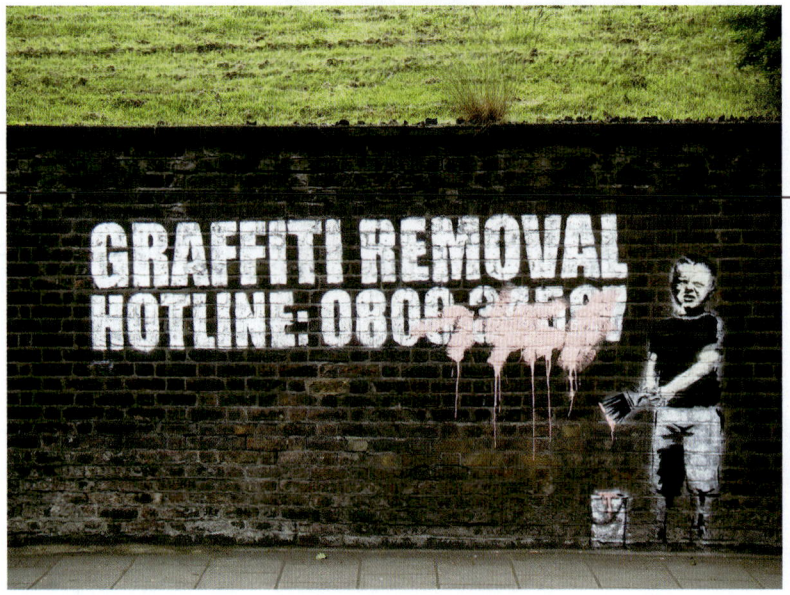

2.2.28 Banksy, *Graffiti Removal Hotline*, 2008. London, England

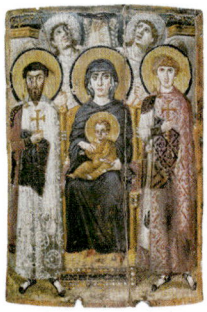

3.2.8 Icon of *Virgin and Child Surrounded by Saints*, 6th century, p. 396

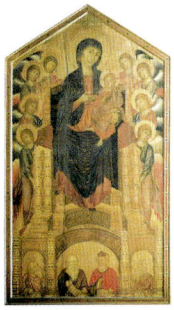

3.2.27 Cimabue, *Virgin and Child Enthroned*, c. 1280, p. 408

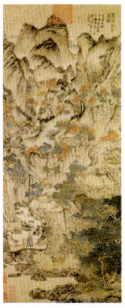

3.3.14 Wang Meng, *Ge Zhichuan Moving His Dwelling*, c. 1360, p. 418

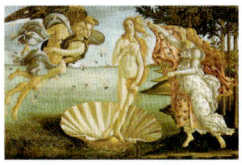

4.9.5 Sandro Botticelli, *The Birth of Venus*, c. 1482–86, p. 666

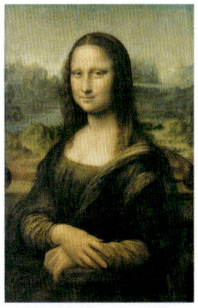

0.0.12 Leonardo da Vinci, *Mona Lisa*, c. 1503–6, p. 28

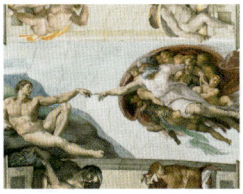

3.6.9b Michelangelo, detail of *Creation of Adam*, 1508–12, p. 468

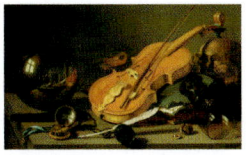

4.3.13 Pieter Claesz (attr.), *Vanitas (Still Life with Glass Globe)*, c. 1628, p. 600

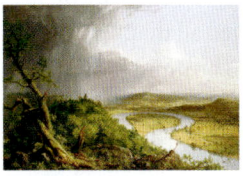

3.7.16 Thomas Cole, *The Oxbow*, 1836, p. 499

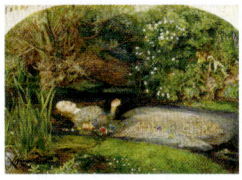

3.8.4 John Everett Millais, *Ophelia*, 1851–52, p. 505

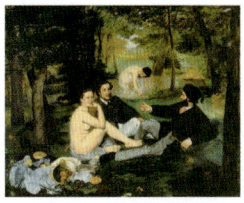

3.8.2 Édouard Manet, *Le Déjeuner sur l'Herbe*, 1863, p. 503

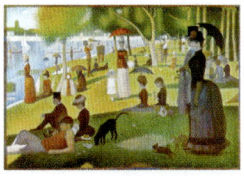

4.4.10 Georges Seurat, *Sunday on La Grande Jatte*, 1884–86, p. 609

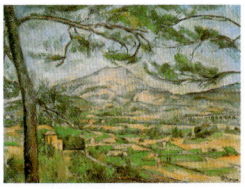

3.8.16 Paul Cézanne, *Mont Sainte-Victoire*, 1886–88, p. 514

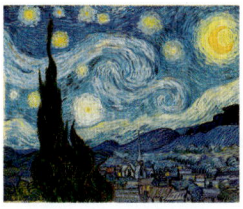

3.8.18 Vincent van Gogh, *Starry Night*, 1889, p. 515

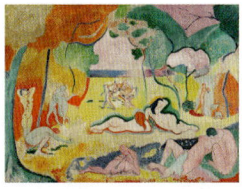

3.9.1 Henri Matisse, *Joy of Life*, 1905–6, p. 525

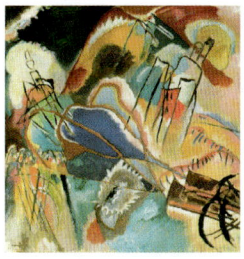

3.8.28 Vasily Kandinsky, *Improvisation #30*, 1913, p. 522

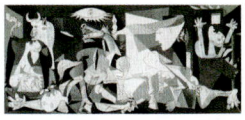

4.7.10 Pablo Picasso, *Guernica*, 1937, p. 646

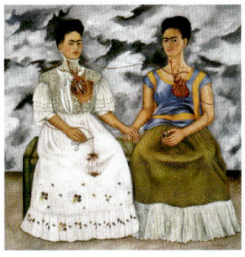

4.9.18a Frida Kahlo, *The Two Fridas*, 1939, p. 676

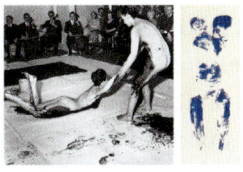

4.9.11a, 4.9.11b Yves Klein, *Anthropométries de l'époque bleue*, 1960, p. 670

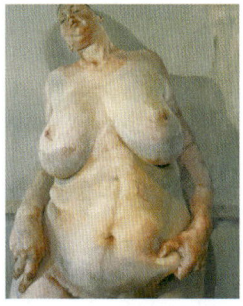

4.9.19 Jenny Saville, *Branded*, 1992, p. 677

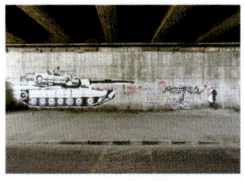

4.7.12 Ganzeer, *Tank vs Bike*, 2011, p. 647

2.3 Printmaking

Edition: all the copies of a print made from a single printing
Relief printing: a print process where the inked image is higher than the non-printing areas
Intaglio: any print process where the inked image is lower than the surface of the printing plate; from the Italian for "cut into"
Lithography, lithographic: a print process done on a flat, unmarred surface, such as a stone, in which the image is created using oil-based ink with resistance to water
Serigraphy: printing that is achieved by creating a solid stencil in a porous screen and forcing ink through the screen onto the printing surface
Matrix: an origination point, such as a woodblock, from which a print is derived
Impression: an individual print, or pull, from a printing press
Incised: cut
Woodblock: a relief print process where the image is carved into a block of wood
Woodcut: a print created from an incised piece of wood

Before the invention of printing, artists who wanted to have multiple copies of their work needed to copy it over by hand, one reproduction at a time. Printing with inks, first used in China to print patterns on fabrics in the third century CE, changed all that. Printing allowed the same designs to be more easily reproduced and distributed to many people. In the world of art, however, printmaking is much more than a way of copying an original. There are many different techniques, and each one gives a unique character to every work it creates. Artists may well choose a particular technique because they think it will suit the kind of effect they want to achieve.

Although artists may not always do the production work themselves, if they create the master image, supervise the process, and sign the artwork, it is considered an original print. This differs from a commercial reproduction of an artwork, where the artist may not be involved in the process. The production of two or more identical images, signed and numbered by the artist, is called an **edition**. When an artist produces only one print, it is called a monoprint. The method used to create a print may dictate the number of works that can be produced. There are four main printing processes: **relief**, **intaglio**, **lithography**, and **serigraphy**. Each process involves a different **matrix**, or point of origination from which the print is derived—for example, the plate used in etching, or the woodblock used to make a woodcut.

In relief printmaking, the artist cuts or carves into a workable surface, such as wood or linoleum, to create the image. The printmaker rolls ink onto the raised surface that remains, and presses a sheet of paper or similar material onto the image to make what is known as an **impression**.

Intaglio printing requires the artist or printmaker to cut or scrape (in many different ways) into what is usually a metal plate. Ink is applied and then wiped off the surface, leaving ink in the lines or marks made by the artist. The pressure of the printing press transfers the image from the plate to the paper.

In the printing process known as lithography, the image is drawn with an oily crayon onto a special kind of limestone. The non-image area of the stone absorbs a little water, but enough so that when the printmaker applies oil-based ink to the whole stone, the ink remains only on the image area. In the printing press the image transfers to the paper.

Serigraphy, more commonly called silk-screen printing, physically blocks out non-image areas so that ink passes through the screen only where required.

Like any manufacturing process, traditional printmaking methods are being replaced by more efficient systems. Artists often rely on group workshops to reproduce images for commercial sale. The digital revolution has also introduced the means to create impressions in virtual environments that can be viewed electronically, printed two-dimensionally, or even three-dimensionally. Printmaking is experiencing resurgence in the contemporary art world.

Context of Printmaking

Ancient civilizations in Egypt and Mesopotamia reproduced images by rolling cylindrical **incised** stones across clay or pressing them into wax. These early relief impressions were used as a tamper-proof seal to show if the contents of a sack had been opened. Elsewhere, in ancient China, Chinese craftspeople used wooden stamps to print patterned designs into textiles.

The earliest existing printed artworks on paper (itself invented in China in the second or first century BCE) were created in China and date back to the eighth century CE. By the ninth century, printed scrolls containing Buddhist *sutras* (scriptures or prayers) were being made across east Asia. Over the ensuing centuries, paper technology spread across the Islamic world as clever entrepreneurs created small prints that were sold as if they were handwritten charms. **Woodblock** printing and papermaking workshops became common throughout Europe by the beginning of the fifteenth century, and paper was no longer an expensive, exotic commodity.

While the woodblock print remained the primary vehicle for the development of the print in Asia (especially Japan), in the West a number of additional techniques developed over time.

Relief Printmaking

Relief prints are made by carving away a certain amount from a block of a suitably workable material, such as wood or linoleum, in order to create a raised image. The artist then applies ink to the raised surface and transfers the image to paper or similar material by applying pressure in a printing press (see **2.3.1**). The areas of the block that remain print the image because the carved areas are recessed and are not inked.

Traditionally, wood has been used for relief prints because it is readily available, familiar to work with, and holds up under the pressure exerted by the printing process; these prints are known as **woodcuts**. Today, for linocuts, printmakers use linoleum, an inexpensive material that cuts easily and can produce a clean, sharp image.

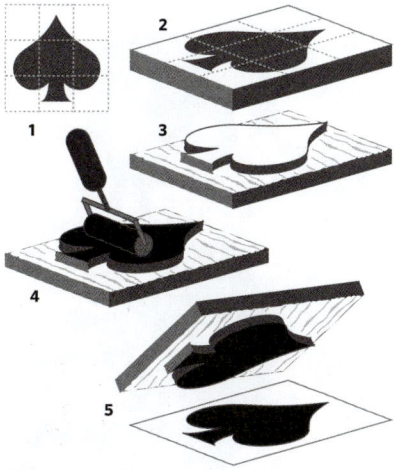

2.3.1 A brief overview of the relief printing process:

1. An image is designed and is prepared for transfer to the block surface.
2. The image is now transferred to the block.
3. The surface area that will not be printed is carved away.
4. The remaining protruding surface is carefully inked.
5. The raised inked area is transferred to the surface to be printed.

Woodblock

The German artist Albrecht Dürer (1471–1528) combined images and the printed word (with text printed on the reverse) when he illustrated *The Apocalypse* with fifteen scenes from the final book of the Bible, the Book of Revelation. "The Four Horsemen" (**2.3.2**) is the most famous image in this series of illustrations and was made from a specially prepared woodblock. In this process, unlike cutting from a solid block of wood, a print craftsman stacks and glues a

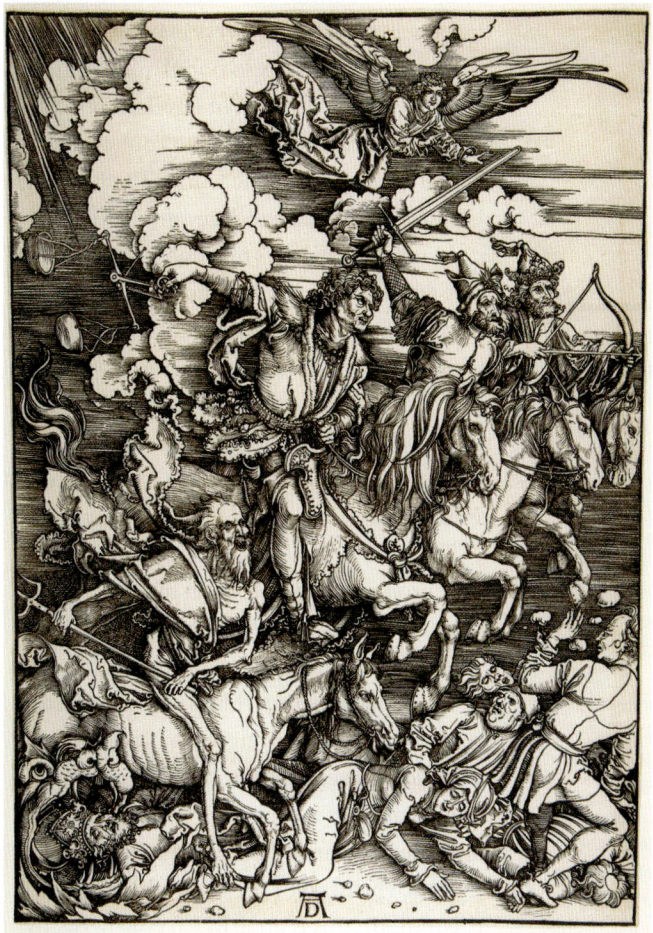

2.3.2 Albrecht Dürer, "The Four Horsemen" from *The Apocalypse*, 1498. Woodcut, 15¼ × 11". Metropolitan Museum of Art, New York

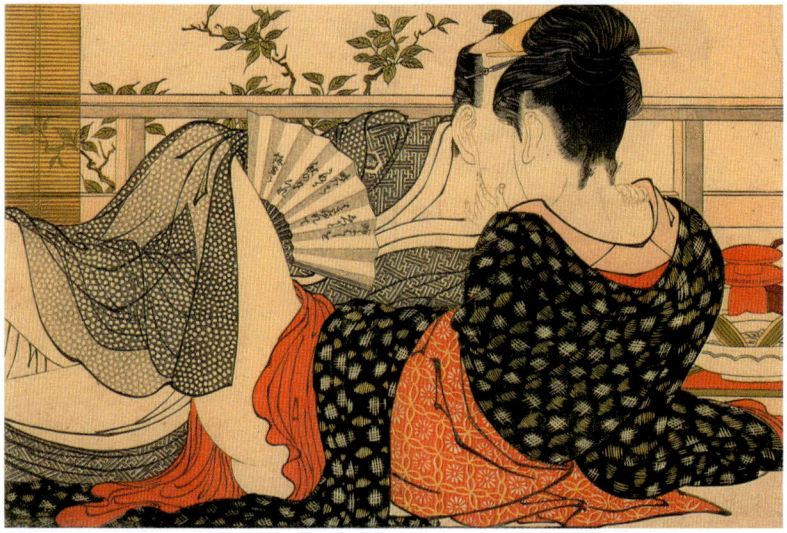

2.3.3 Kitagawa Utamaro, *Lovers in an Upstairs Room*, from *Uta Makura (Poem of the Pillow)*, 1788. Color woodblock print, 10 × 14½". British Museum, London, England

series of thin, sliced layers of wood to create a more stable printing block (similar to plywood) that will be less likely to splinter or crack. Dürer commissioned professional block cutters to perform the layering, and they also cut the highly detailed lines of his original drawing into the block. This technique resulted in thin lines and detail that could withstand the compression of repeated printings. Because it required expert craftsmen, the labor was very expensive. But the series of works was so popular that it made Dürer wealthy. The Book of Revelation is a symbolic piece of writing that prophesies the Apocalypse, or end of the world. The horsemen represent Death, Plague, War, and Famine.

Many great masters of woodblock printing were active in eighteenth- and nineteenth-century Japan. Kitagawa Utamaro's (1753–1806) print, entitled *Lovers in an Upstairs Room*, uses multiple **colors** and shows great graphic skill in controlling the crisp character of the print and the interplay of multiple blocks in different colors (**2.3.3**).

To create a color woodblock print, an artist must produce a separate relief block for every color. Utamaro uses at least three colors to create *Lovers in an Upstairs Room*: red ocher (a shade of red-brown), black, and green. In color woodblock printing, each block must be accurately carved and planned, because each individual color is printed in sequence on the same sheet of paper. Care must be taken to align each print color perfectly (this is called registration); this is done by carving perfectly matching notches along two sides of each block to guide the placement of the paper. Utamaro is regarded as one of the greatest Japanese printmakers. He made images for the Japanese middle and upper classes of figures, theaters, and brothels, in a **style** known as *ukiyo-e* printmaking. Ukiyo-e means "pictures of the floating world," a reference to a young urban cultural class who separated themselves from the agrarian life of traditional Japan by indulging in a fashionable and decadent lifestyle. The people of the "floating world" were the celebrities of their time.

In his woodcut *Prophet*, the German artist Emil Nolde (1867–1956) uses the natural character of the wood to suggest the hardships and austerity of the life of his **subject** (**2.3.4**). The crude carving of the block has produced splintering, and the printing has revealed the grain of the wood. The print's lack of refinement reflects the raw hardness of the **ascetic** life that one might associate with a prophet. This print also demonstrates one of the principal advantages of relief printmaking: it favors dark images that involve strong **contrast**, as illustrated here.

2.3.4 Emil Nolde, *Prophet*, 1912. Woodcut, printed in black, composition 12⅝ × 8¾". MoMA, New York

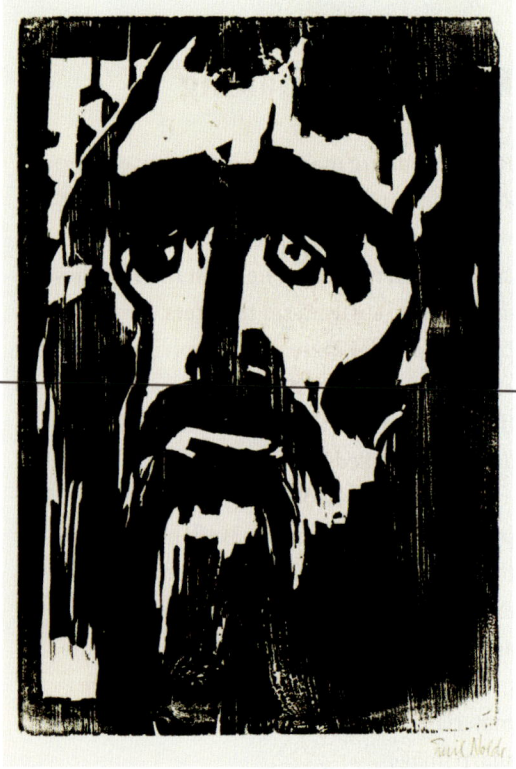

Color: the optical effect caused when reflected white light of the spectrum is divided into separate wavelengths
Style: a characteristic way in which an artist or group of artists uses visual language to give a work an identifiable form of visual expression
Subject: the person, object, or space depicted in a work of art
Ascetic: austerely simple; rigorously abstaining from pleasure or material satisfaction
Contrast: a drastic difference between such elements as color or value (lightness/darkness) when they are presented together

Gateway to Art: Hokusai, "The Great Wave off Shore at Kanagawa"
Using the Woodblock Printing Method

Katsushika Hokusai's woodblock print "The Great Wave off Shore at Kanagawa" (**2.3.5**) uses multiple colors and shows great graphic skill. It is a fine example of the printmaker's art. Hokusai (1760–1849) was not solely responsible for the production of this print: he relied on skilled craftsmen. Hokusai made a drawing of his subject, which a print craftsman then transferred face down onto a block of cherry wood. When the drawing was peeled away, the image remained, and the craftsman then carved the image into the wood. To create a color woodblock print, a printer must produce a new relief block for each separate color. (Incidentally, "The Great Wave" was one of ten prints in the series *Thirty-Six Views of Mount Fuji* to use a new blue color, imported from Europe, known as Prussian blue.) Nine blocks were used to print "The Great Wave." Each block had to be carefully carved, and the printmaker had to carry out the sequence of printing skillfully, because each new color was printed directly on top of the same sheet of paper. If all nine blocks were not printed in exactly the correct position, the print would be discarded because it did not match the others in the edition. The blocks of wood were used so many times that the carving eventually deteriorated. Although it is unknown how many prints were made, it is estimated there were more than 5,000.

For the other Hokusai Gateway boxes, see p. 126, p. 425, and p. 661

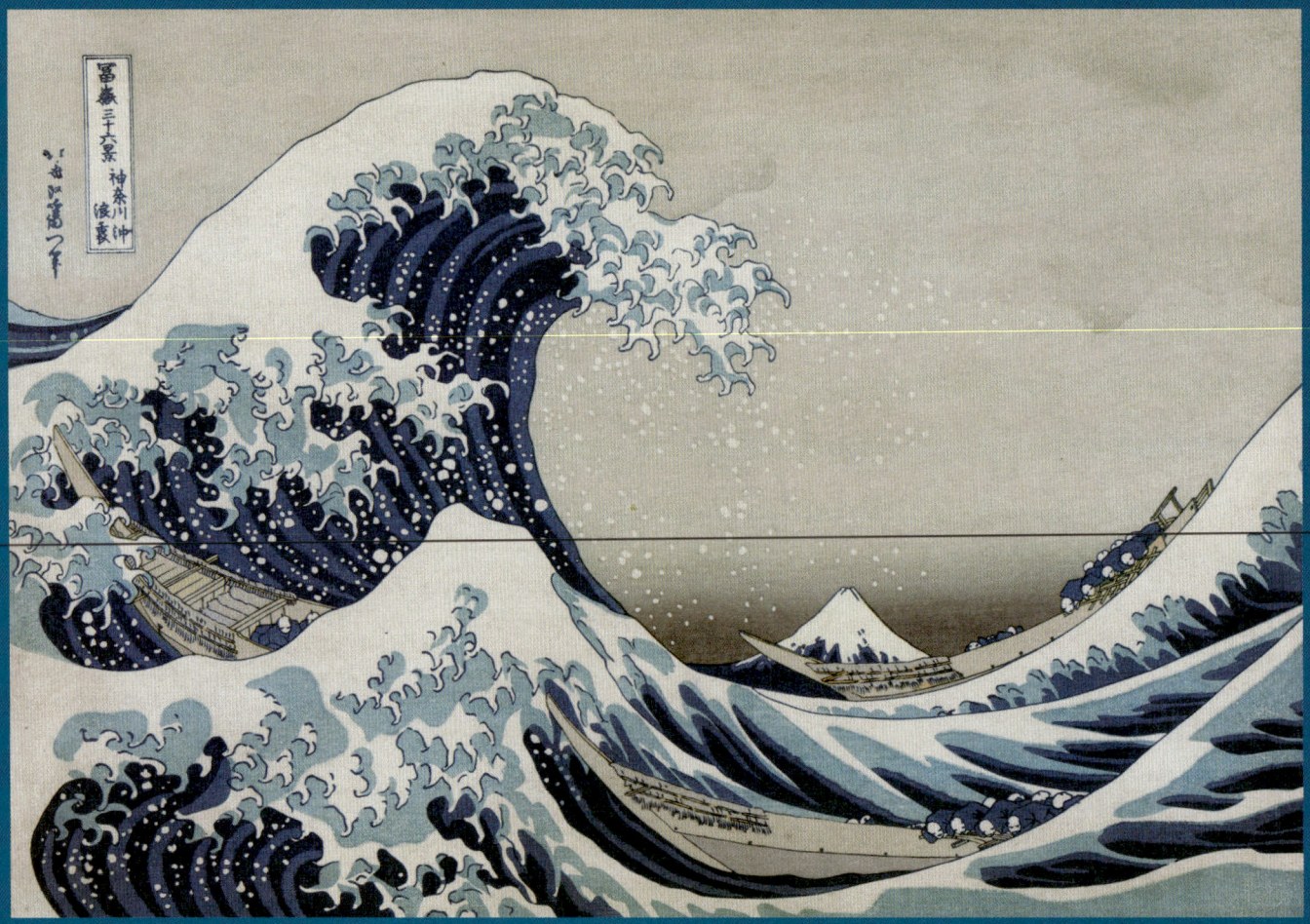

2.3.5 Katsushika Hokusai, "The Great Wave off Shore at Kanagawa," from *Thirty-Six Views of Mount Fuji*, 1826–33 (printed later). Print, color woodcut. Library of Congress, Washington, D.C.

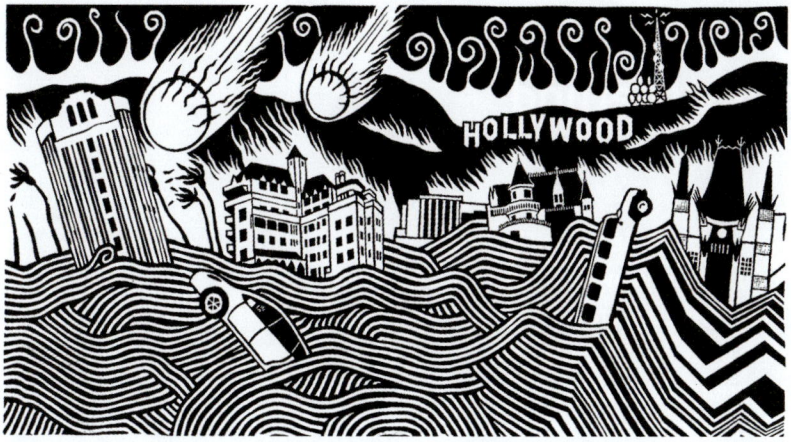

2.3.6 Stanley Donwood, "Hollywood Limousine," from the *Lost Angeles* series, 2012. Black screenprint on a silver foil layer (based on an original linocut), 22 × 35¾"

Linocut

Linoleum ("lino") printmaking, similarly to the woodblock method, is done by carving into the surface of a material, then printing the raised surface left behind. The resulting prints are commonly known as linocuts. Because linoleum is softer than most woodblocks and does not show a wood grain, many contemporary printmakers prefer it for relief printing. One such artist is Stanley Donwood (real name: Dan Rickwood; b. 1968), who is best known for his creation of artwork for the rock band Radiohead. Donwood produced a series, or group of associated works, which depicts the last days of the city of Los Angeles, titled *Lost Angeles* (**2.3.6**). To create these works, he cut into sheets of linoleum to create the image, then printed the results on fine Japanese paper. The soft linoleum allowed Donwood to capture the myriad of fictional events in great detail, with the kind of clarity that a storybook illustration might have.

Intaglio Printmaking

Intaglio is derived from an Italian word that means "cut into" a surface. Usually the artist uses a sharp tool (a burin) to cut or gouge into a plate made of metal (or sometimes acetate or Plexiglas). Intaglio printing differs from relief printmaking because little of the base material is removed. The ink on the raised surface is also wiped away before printing, leaving ink in the scarred surface of the plate. The pressure of the printing press squeezes the plate against the paper, transferring the ink. There are several variations of intaglio printing, all of which give the resulting artwork a different visual character (see **2.3.7**).

Engraving

Albrecht Dürer printed from a woodblock for his depiction of the Four Horsemen of the Apocalypse, but chose a different technique, **engraving**, for *Adam and Eve* (**2.3.8**). The intaglio engraving method is based on the careful scoring of a metal plate so that clean gouges are created in the surface. An engraving can achieve fine detail, making the resulting print more like the artist's original drawing.

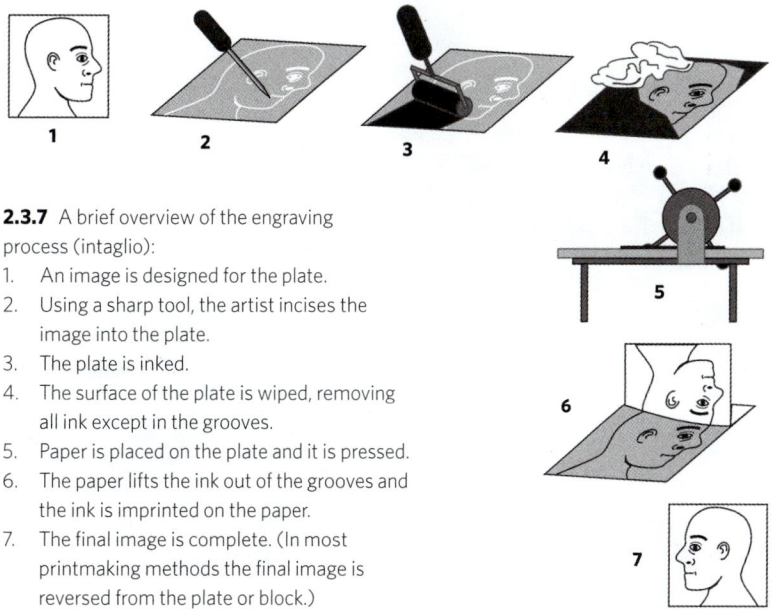

2.3.7 A brief overview of the engraving process (intaglio):

1. An image is designed for the plate.
2. Using a sharp tool, the artist incises the image into the plate.
3. The plate is inked.
4. The surface of the plate is wiped, removing all ink except in the grooves.
5. Paper is placed on the plate and it is pressed.
6. The paper lifts the ink out of the grooves and the ink is imprinted on the paper.
7. The final image is complete. (In most printmaking methods the final image is reversed from the plate or block.)

Engraving: a printmaking technique where the artist gouges or scratches the image into the surface of the printing plate
Drypoint: an intaglio printmaking process where the artist raises a burr when gouging the printing plate
Expressionism, Expressionist: an artistic style, at its height in 1920s Europe, devoted to representing subjective emotions and experiences instead of objective or external reality

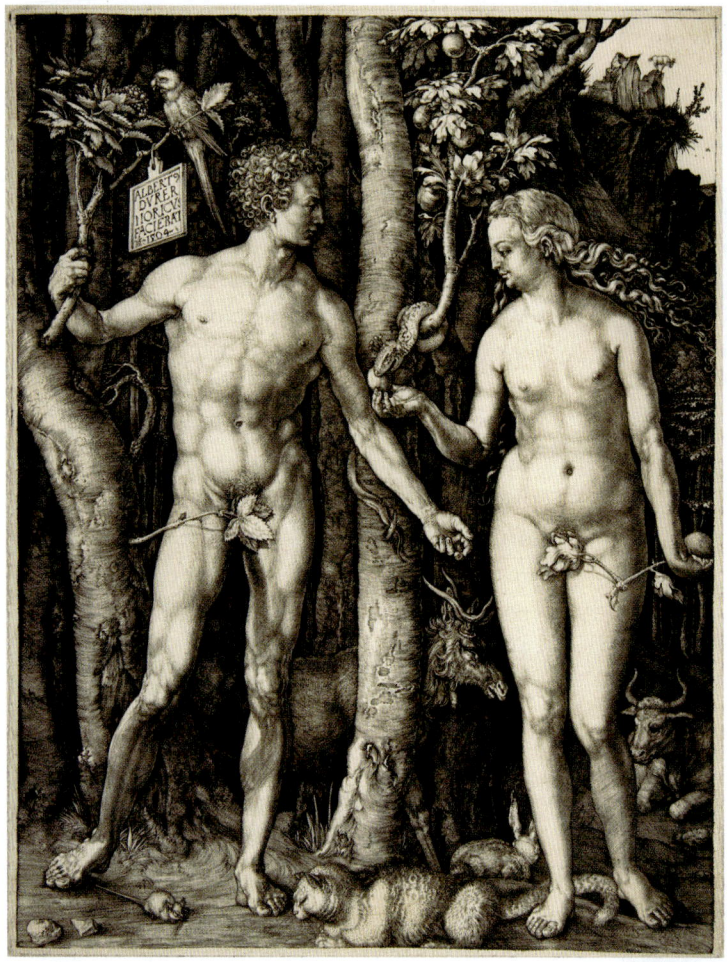

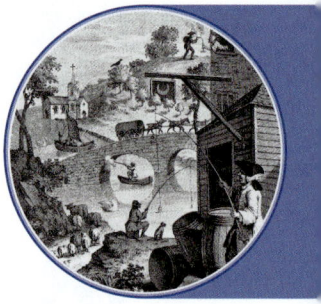

William Hogarth's *False Perspective* is another engraving with fine details: see **4.5.6, p.619**

Dürer also had a business reason for choosing to engrave his work. He had to pay engravers to make his printing plate, and because the metal plate is much more durable than the woodblock, he could make and sell many more copies.

2.3.8 Albrecht Dürer, *Adam and Eve*, 1504. Engraving on paper, 9⅞ × 7⅞". Metropolitan Museum of Art, New York

Drypoint

For his *Adam and Eve*, Max Beckmann (1884–1950) chose the **drypoint** intaglio method rather than engraving (**2.3.9**). In engraving, the burin is pushed across the surface, but in drypoint it is pulled, leaving a rough edge, or burr. When the plate is wiped the ink is caught under the burr. The result is a less precise line that has more irregularities. Artists can use this irregularity to add new dimensions to a work. For example, in Beckmann's *Adam and Eve* the lines appear more irregular than those in Dürer's version of the same subject. Beckmann, a German **Expressionist** artist, probably chose drypoint because its slightly uneven quality of line expresses unpredictability and an organic naturalness—two attributes that suit his choice of subject matter. In this image, Adam and Eve have eaten the apple from the Tree of the Knowledge of Good and Evil. We can tell this because they are beginning to express a sense of shame at being naked (in the Bible, they felt no shame before they had eaten from the tree, as nakedness was their natural state), covering their genitals with their hands. They know that they will be punished, and this uncertainty about their future, together with their growing worldliness, is captured in the rougher, less finished-looking lines created by using drypoint.

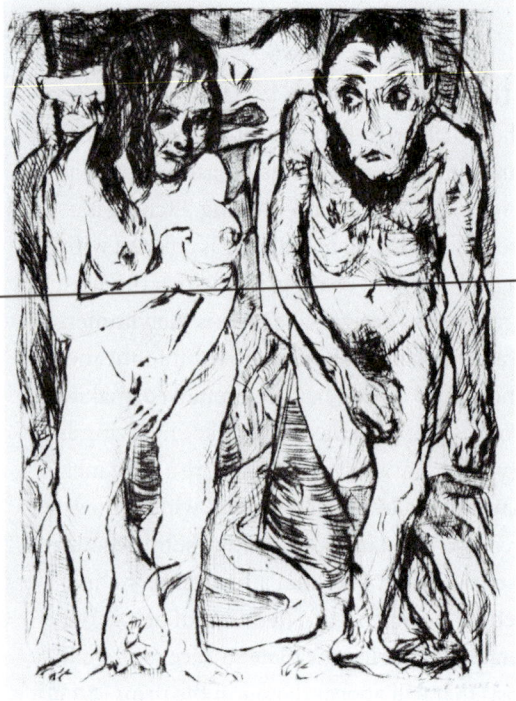

2.3.9 Max Beckmann, *Adam and Eve*, 1917, published 1918. Drypoint, 9⅜ × 7". Private collection, New York

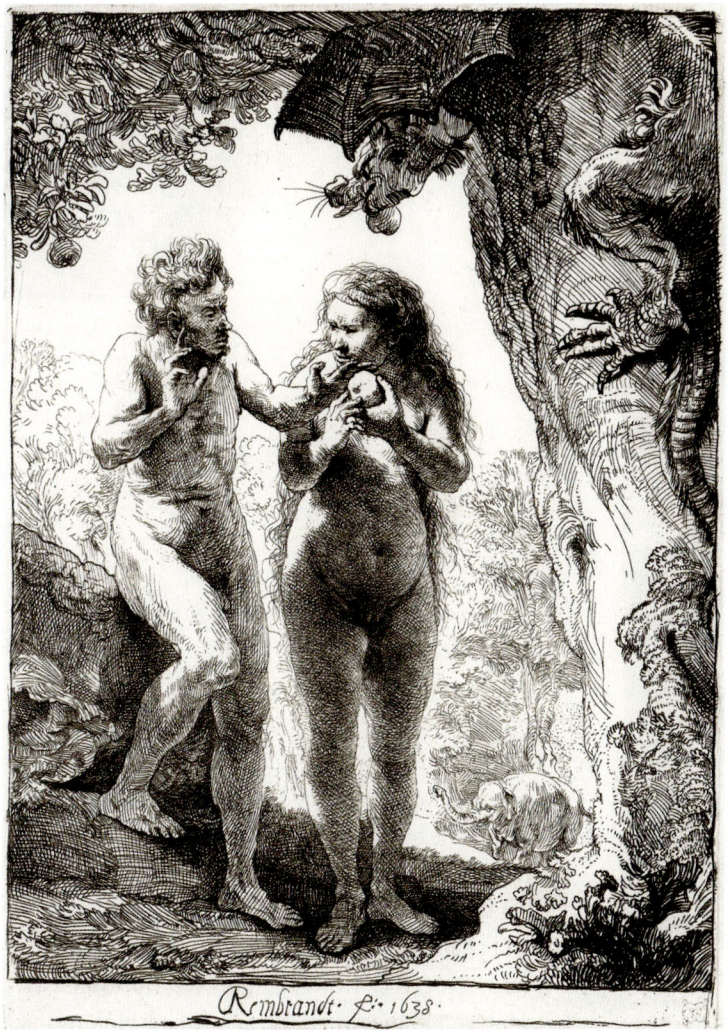

2.3.10 Rembrandt van Rijn, *Adam and Eve*, 1638. Etching, 9¾ × 7". Rijksmuseum, Amsterdam, The Netherlands

Etching

The Dutch artist Rembrandt Harmenszoon van Rijn (1606–1669) was a master of intaglio printmaking, especially **etching**. Etching is a process in which a metal plate is covered with an acid-resistant coating, into which the artist scratches the design. The plate is then immersed in a bath of acid. The acid "bites" into the metal where the covering has been removed, making grooves that hold the ink. Unlike engraving and drypoint, the artist does not score a hard metal plate but makes small incisions, which allows for greater control in incorporating subtle changes of dark or light lines that affect **value**. In his etching *Adam and Eve*, Rembrandt brings out details by marring the plate surface more in the areas that will appear darker in the print (**2.3.10**).

Aquatint

Another process that requires the use of an acid bath to etch the surface of the plate is **aquatint** (from its Italian name *acqua tinta*, meaning "dyed water"). Despite the name, water does not play a role in aquatint printmaking. The image is created in a coating of powdered **rosin** (a tree sap), or spray paint, on the surface of the plate. When heated, the rosin melts onto the surface of the plate, creating a mottled, acid-resistant barrier into which the design is etched. Since the rosin leaves irregular areas of the plate exposed, a soft **organic** texture (similar to that created when one uses brush and ink) dominates the image. The artist can even use a brush to push around the dry rosin (before heating) to draw the original design, adding to the watery effect. Francisco Goya (1746–1828) utilizes the wash-like appearance of aquatint in his print *Giant* (**2.3.11**). Goya probably used a rosin box, a device that allows the artist to control the distribution and amount of powder that falls onto the plate, then he scraped away the heated rosin in the areas where he wanted the dark values of the final printed image to appear. The artist can progressively scrape more and more to get darker values. The **implied texture** of the aquatint print is soft and rich, giving a softness and subtlety to the contours of the giant's body that communicate the sense of its being a fantastical, unreal creature.

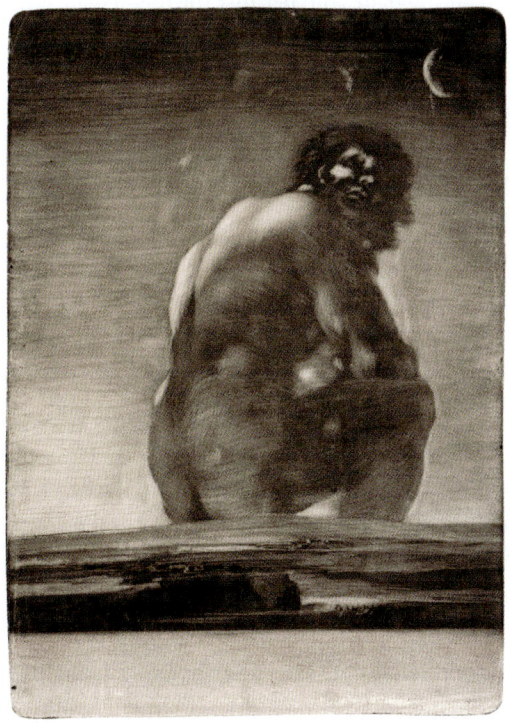

2.3.11 Francisco Goya, *Giant*, c. 1818. Burnished aquatint, first state, sheet size 11¼ × 8¼". Metropolitan Museum of Art, New York

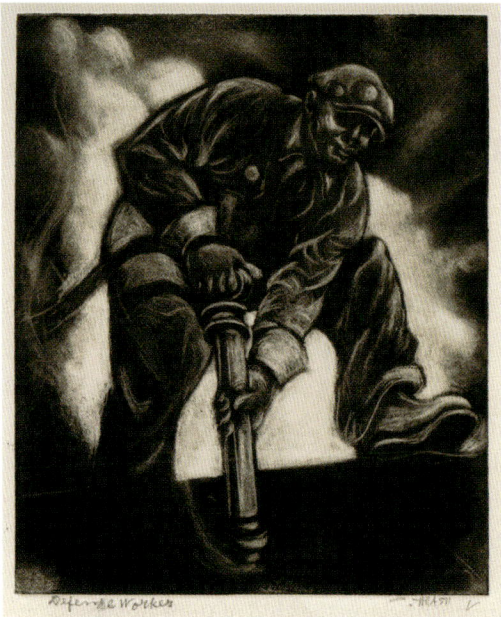

2.3.12 Dox Thrash, *Defense Worker*, c. 1941. Carborundum mezzotint over etched guidelines, 9¾ × 8". Print and Picture Collection, Free Library of Philadelphia

Mezzotint

Because each intaglio method leaves its own unique mark on the plate, many artists have opted to use more than one method when making a print. In his *Defense Worker*, the African American artist Dox Thrash (1893–1965) uses **mezzotint** over etched guidelines (**2.3.12**). Mezzotints often produce dark, rich values because the ink has many places to settle. To make a mezzotint, the entire surface is roughened with a heavy rocking tool, which is a metal object with a spiked, curved bottom. This can be rocked back and forth across the surface of the plate so that it is completely covered in burrs. The burrs are then smoothed in the areas where the printmaker wants the light tones. Ink is removed from the smoothed areas when the plate is wiped: the inked areas create dark tones, and the smoothed areas hold less ink, to create light tones. Thrash wanted to use this dark mood to reflect the drama and seriousness of the war effort at home. This work was sponsored by the Works Projects Administration, a government program originally created during the Great Depression to employ Americans at a time when jobs were hard to find. Artists, writers, musicians, and others contributed to American culture and infrastructure by applying their skills, first in support of rebuilding America and then, during World War II, in support of the war effort. Thrash, like other artists of the time, uses the dark values afforded by the medium to express the spirit and strength of the American worker.

Collagraphy

Relief and intaglio printmaking rely on a compromised surface—in a printmaking context, one that has been cut into in order to fashion an image. The ink is then applied to the surface and transferred to paper. But **collagraphic** prints are created by building up (rather than cutting into) a surface that can be inked for the purpose of transfer to paper. The artist glues materials to a rigid support, such as wood or heavy cardboard; this effectively "**collages**" the image to that surface. The image can then be printed by inking the materials with printing ink, and pressing paper onto them.

The artist most closely associated with the development of the collagraph was Glen Alps (1914–1996), a longtime faculty member at the University of Washington in Seattle. Alps first used the term **collagraph** to describe the process. In his work *Roll-Up #2* (**2.3.13**), pieces of material are glued in a way that allows the printmaker more freedom because the surface

Etching: an intaglio printmaking process that uses acid to bite (or etch) the engraved design into the printing surface
Value: the lightness or darkness of a plane or area
Aquatint: an intaglio printmaking process that uses melted rosin or spray paint to create an acid-resistant ground
Rosin: a dry powdered resin that melts when heated, used in the aquatint process
Organic: having irregular forms and shapes, as though derived from living organisms
Implied texture: a visual illusion expressing texture
Mezzotint: an intaglio printmaking process based on roughening the entire printing plate to accept ink; the artist smoothes non-image areas
Collagraphy, collagraphic, collagraph: a type of relief print that is created by building up or collaging material on or to a stiff surface, inking that surface, then printing
Collage: artwork assembled by gluing materials, often paper, onto a surface. From the French *coller*, to glue

2.3.13 Glen Alps, *Roll-Up #2*, 1956. Collagraph, 26¼ × 32½"

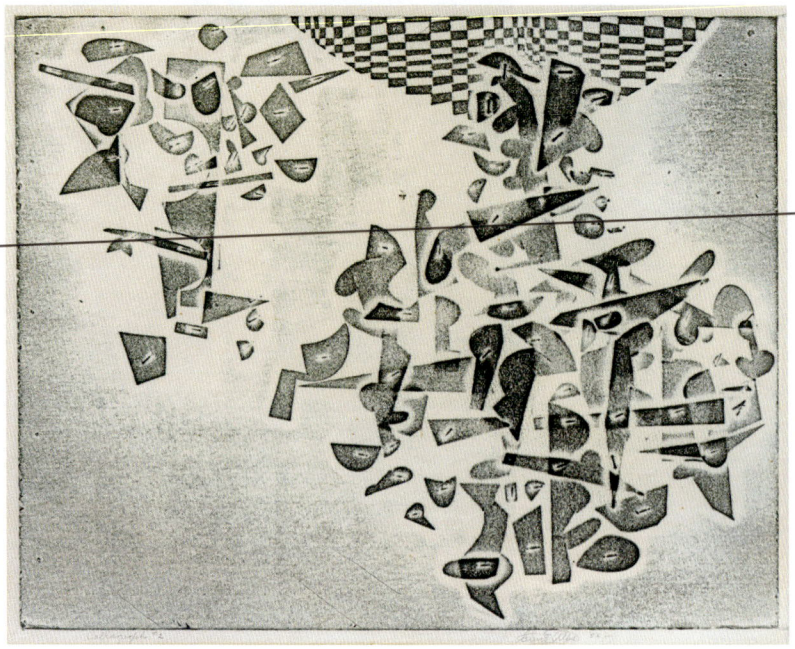

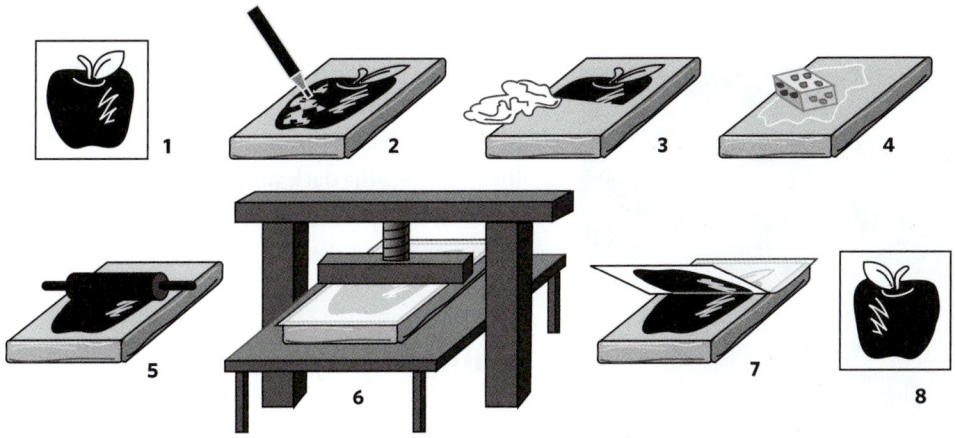

2.3.14 A brief overview of the lithography process:

1. The artist designs the image to be printed.
2. Using a grease pencil, the design is drawn onto the limestone, blocking the pores.
3. The stone is treated with acid and other chemicals that are brushed onto its surface. Then the surface is wiped clean with a solvent, such as kerosene.
4. The stone is sponged so that water can be absorbed into the pores of the stone.
5. Oil-based ink is repelled by the water and sits only on areas where the oil crayon image was drawn.
6. Paper is laid on the surface of the stone and it is drawn through a press.
7. The print is removed from the stone.
8. The completed image appears in reverse compared with the original design.

can be easily manipulated. Although Alps did not invent the collagraphic technique, he was the first printmaker to succeed in mastering and promoting the process.

Lithography

Lithography (from the Greek for stone writing) is traditionally done on stone. It is what is known as a **planographic** printmaking technique; that is, the print is made from an entirely flat surface, rather than one that is carved or otherwise modified. The German author Alois Senefelder (1771–1834), out of money and looking for a cheaper method to print his newest play, devised the lithographic printing process in 1796. The complex presses used nowadays by commercial printers for producing newspapers, magazines, and brochures ("offset lithography") use thin sheets of zinc or aluminum instead of stone, but the basic principles are the same as Senefelder's original discovery.

Contemporary artists' lithographic prints are still made on the kind of stone used by Senefelder. Some artists like lithography because it allows them to draw a design in the same way they do a drawing. Successive stages in the process are illustrated in **2.3.14**. An artist first draws a design, using a grease pencil or other oil-based drawing material, directly onto a piece of specially selected, cleaned, and prepared limestone. Next, the artist applies a number of materials to the stone, including a gum arabic and nitric acid solution that makes the image more durable. Then he or she wipes the surface clean using kerosene. Even though the image appears to have been obliterated by the

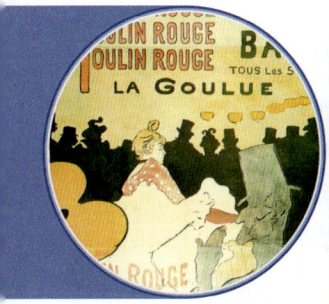

Henri de Toulouse-Lautrec used lithography for a more light-hearted purpose in his poster promoting a famous Parisian destination: see **2.7.16, p. 309**

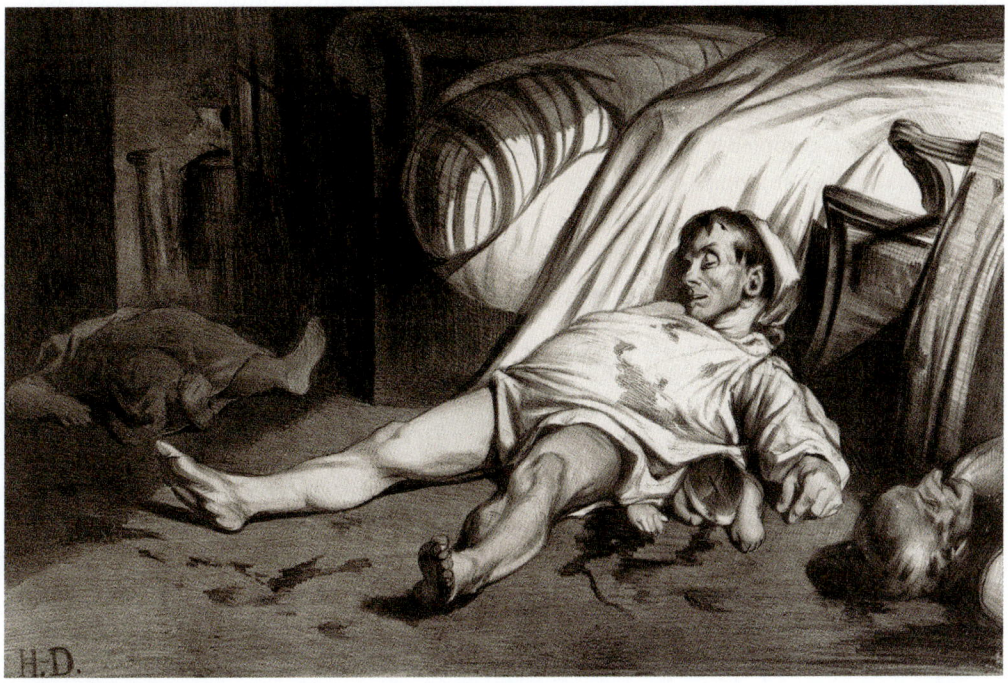

2.3.15 Honoré Daumier, *Rue Transnonain, April 15, 1834*, 1834. Lithograph, 11½ × 17⅝". Metropolitan Museum, New York

kerosene (this is a most unnerving moment for novice printmakers!), the stone is now ready to be printed. The surface is sponged with water, which is repelled by the greasy areas of the drawing, and rolled with oil-based ink. In the ungreased regions the water repels ink, leaving only the image covered with ink. At this point the artist carefully places paper over the stone and lightly presses down, usually by passing it through a printing press.

In 1834, the French artist Honoré Daumier (1808–1879) used his skills combined with the lithographic process to tell the citizens of Paris about an incident of police brutality. Daumier, who worked for the monthly magazine *L'Association Mensuelle*, depicted the aftermath of a horrible incident that took place at Rue Transnonain on April 15, 1834 (**2.3.15**). That night, police responded to a sniper attack they believed had come from that street by entering a property there, no. 12, and ruthlessly killing everyone inside. Daumier, a great critic of the French government's treatment of workers, drew the massacred in gruesome detail, including placing the most shocking—the dead child—in the center, under its father's body.

Serigraphy (Silkscreen Printing)

Serigraphy, also known as silkscreen printing, is another planographic printing process, as well as one of the most versatile, capable of placing a heavy coverage of ink on a wide variety of surfaces, from printed circuit boards to packaging, from solar panels to T-shirts. Artists value, amongst its many other virtues, its potential for printing strong colors.

Unlike all the other printing processes discussed in this chapter, only silkscreen printing produces "right-reading" reproductions of the original artwork. Relief, intaglio, and litho prints all make mirror images, so an artist making such a print needs to think in reverse.

Silkscreen printing was first developed in China during the Song Dynasty (960–1279) and uses a **stencil** process. A stencil **masks** out areas so that ink will take on the shape of the unmasked, open parts. It can be used to create a large number of prints. The silkscreen itself is nowadays a fine mesh, usually made out of nylon. The image area of the screen is open and allows ink to pass through, while the rest of the screen is masked off. As the printmaker moves the squeegee (like a heavy flat windshield wiper) over the screen, the mask prevents ink from passing through in unwanted areas. The mask can be a kind of thick glue painted on with a brush, or it can be a physical barrier, such as tape. Photographic silkscreen prints can be produced using a photosensitive masking material.

The American artist Andy Warhol (1928–1987) utilized photographic silkscreen techniques over aluminum paint to create a distinctive style, seen in his work *Four Marilyns* (**2.3.16**). Warhol reproduces a sultry image of Marilyn Monroe from a photograph taken at

Planography: a print process—lithography and silkscreen printing—where the inked image area and non-inked areas are at the same height
Stencil: a perforated template allowing ink or paint to pass through to print a design
Mask: in spray painting or silkscreen printing, a barrier the shape of which blocks the paint or ink from passing through

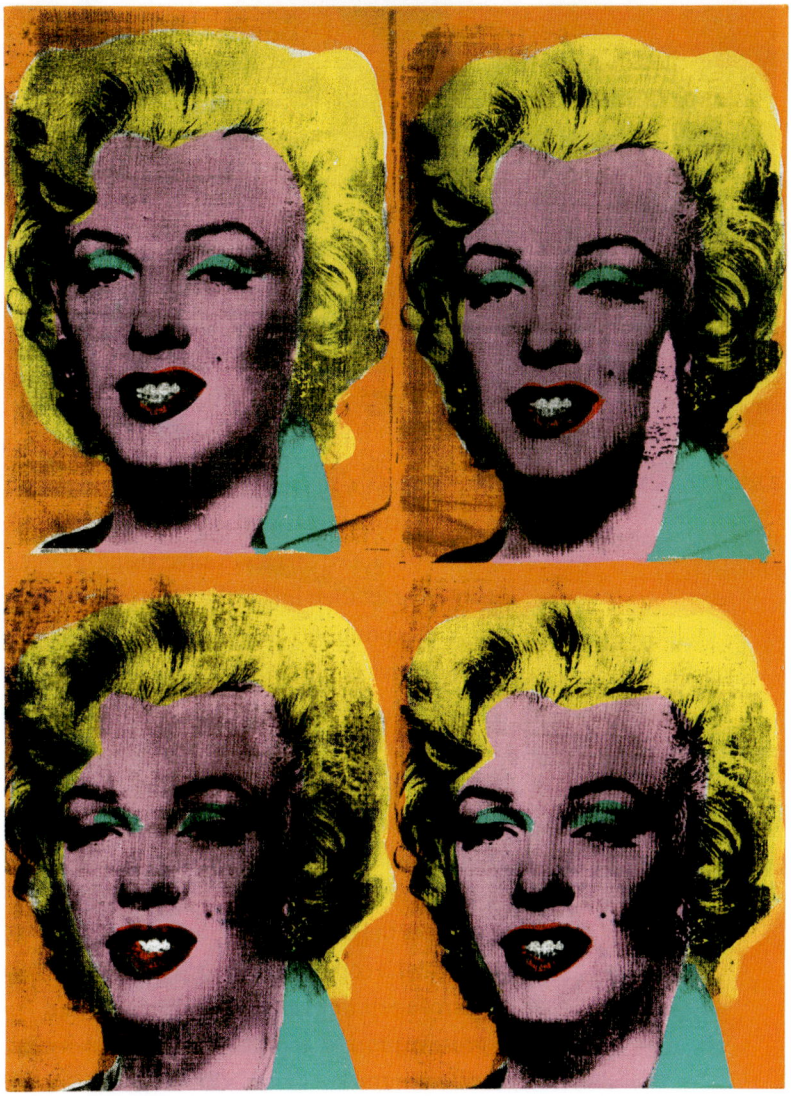

2.3.16 Andy Warhol, *Four Marilyns*, 1962. Acrylic, silkscreen ink, pencil on linen, 29 × 21½". Sold at Phillips, New York 2014

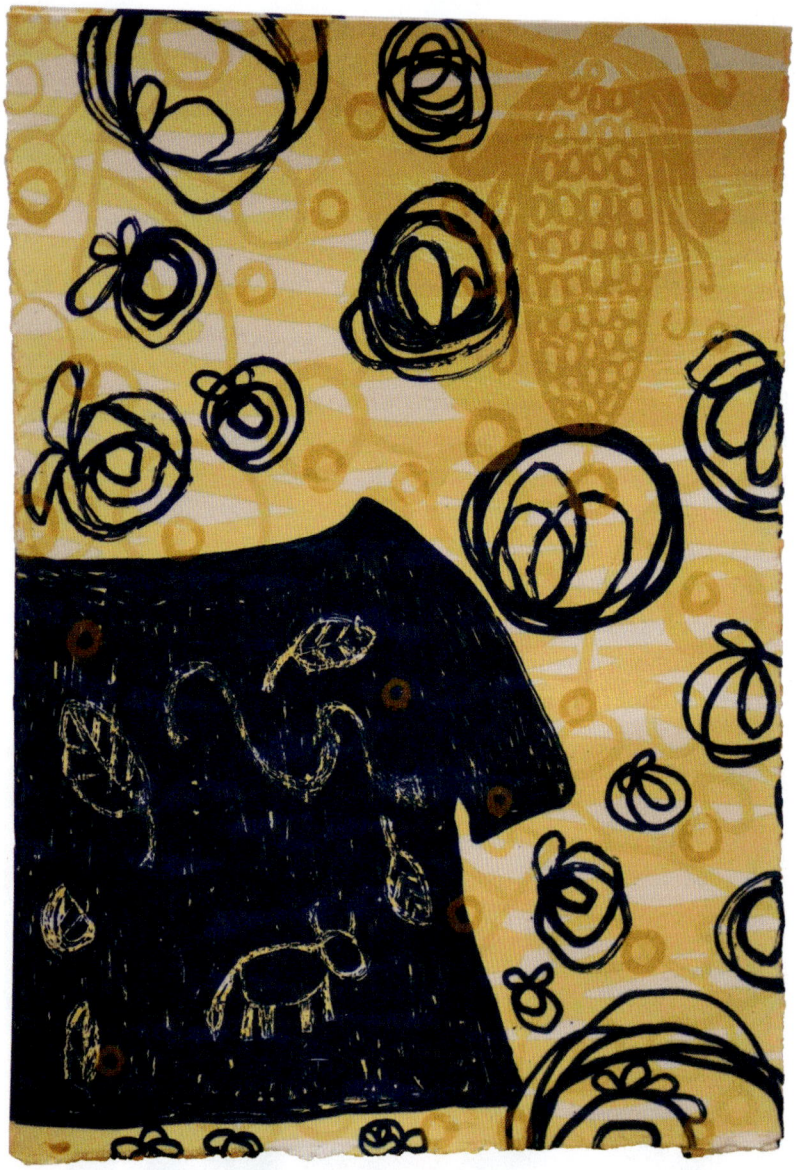

2.3.17 Melanie Yazzie, *Untitled*, 2016. Screen print. Mesa Contemporary Art, Arizona

the height of the actress's career, deliberately repeating her image to comment on the nature of mass-produced images in advertising. Public figures market their image the same way food companies promote cans of soup. Silkscreen printing is particularly suited to printing large areas of flat, heavy color, and by using this technique, Warhol emphasizes the flatness and lack of depth in the image of Marilyn, showing how it has become a commodity rather than a genuine attempt to capture her individuality. The repeating "clones" of Marilyn also accentuate the degeneration that occurs when an original is copied.

Screen printing can be a spontaneous and expressive process, as evidenced in the work of Navajo printmaker Melanie Yazzie (b. 1966). For her *Untitled* (**2.3.17**) screen print, Yazzie created irregular marks, printed the image, then after it had dried, created a new image and superimposed it over the previous layer. This kind of spontaneous imagery contrasts with the well-planned processes that most printmaking demands. Yazzie, who explores her Navajo heritage in her work, uses an impulsive approach to express the human condition combined with an intimate view of her people's history. The energetic character of her work projects an optimistic vision of the future, in contrast to the past hardships imposed on indigenous people.

Editions

Prints are produced in limited numbers of identical impressions, called editions. The printmaker has the ethical responsibility for making sure that each print is similar enough to the others so that each person who buys a print has a high-quality image. When a print is deemed identical to others in the edition, it is assigned a number in the production sequence. For example, a print marked 2/25 is the second print in an edition of twenty-five. Some unnumbered prints bear the letters A/P. These prints, called artist's proofs, are used by the printmaker to check the quality of the process and are not intended to be part of the edition. Some artist's proofs are sold as one-of-a-kind works, rather than as part of an edition, because variations in the process may produce visually engaging results. Even though most artists could create more prints than they do, they usually decide to print a set number: a limited edition. The artist afterward destroys the original plates so it is impossible to make any more copies. Destroying the plates protects the integrity of the edition, because no more can be made. It also limits the number in the edition so that each print is rarer and therefore more valuable.

Abstract: art imagery that departs from recognizable images of the natural world

Monotypes and Monoprints

Nearly all printmaking is done in editions, or multiple impressions, but some artists who like the way a printed image looks will opt to create unique prints. Monotypes and monoprints are print techniques that enable an artist to produce an image that is one of a kind.

A monotype image prints from a polished plate, perhaps glass or metal. The artist puts no permanent marks on it. He or she makes an image on it in ink or another medium, then wipes away the ink in places where the artist wants the paper to show through. The image is then printed. Only one impression is possible.

Hedda Sterne (1910–2011) was the sole woman in a group of **abstract** painters called the Irascibles. Although abstract, Sterne's *Untitled (Machine Series)* monotype makes associations with architectural and mechanical images (**2.3.18**). Sterne probably employed a straightedge to maintain the regularity of line in the print.

Monoprints can be made using any print process. The artist prepares the image for printing as described previously in this chapter, but will ink or modify each impression in a unique way. This includes varying colors, changing the spread of the ink across the image area, and adding features by hand. The individual modifications possible are as infinite as for any hand-made work of art. Artists choose to make monoprints to explore "themes and variations," where some elements of the work remain the same but others are different. If two prints are identical, they are not monoprints.

Kathy Strauss's (b. 1956) monoprint *Kepler Underneath 1* painstakingly depicts the Milky Way Galaxy (**2.3.19**, p. 238). The artist has first incised a series of calculus problems into the metal plate. As with any other intaglio print, the plate was then completely covered with ink and

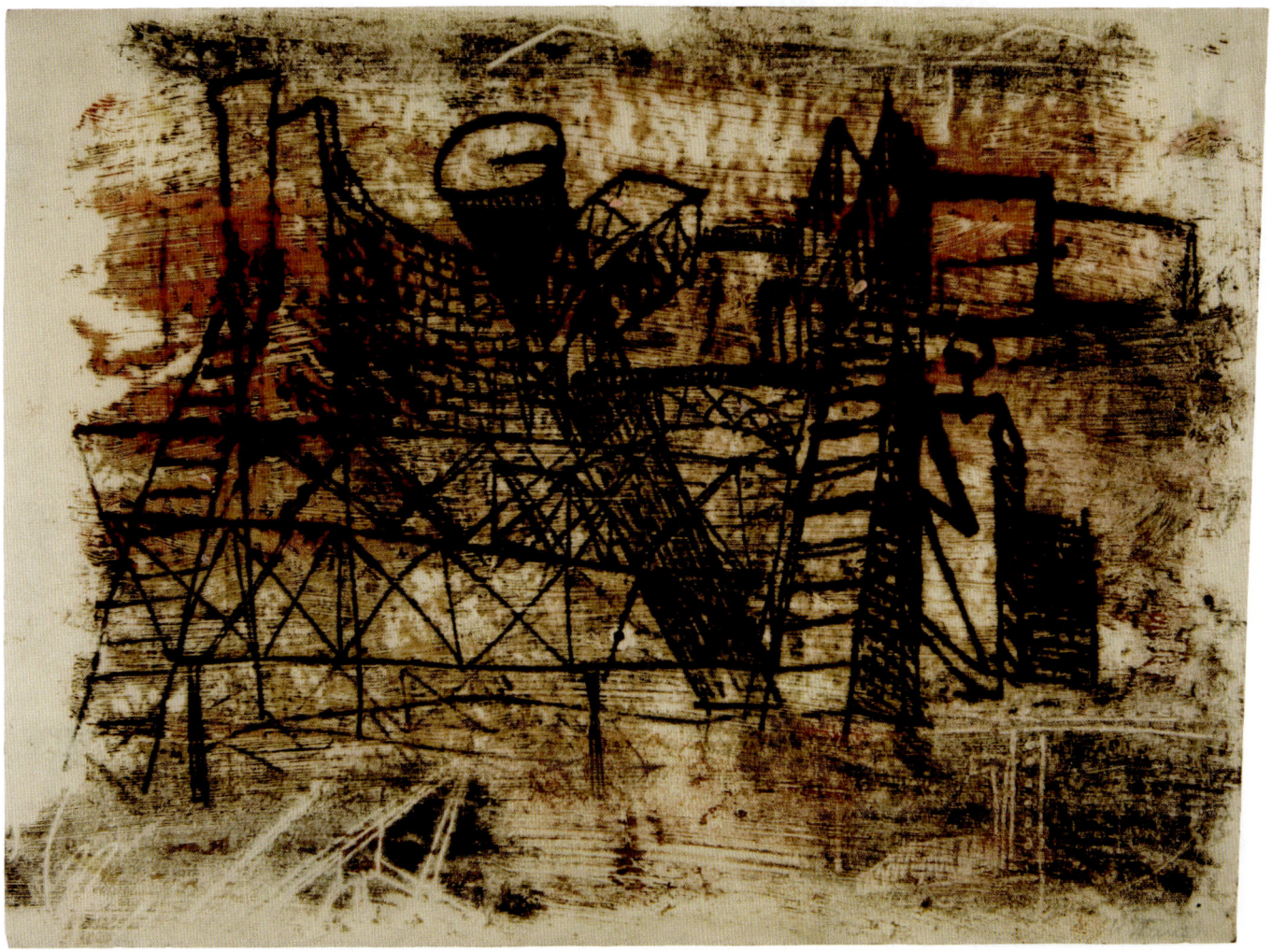

2.3.18 Hedda Sterne, *Untitled (Machine Series)*, 1949. Trace monotype, design 12 × 16⅜". Harvard Art Museums, Fogg Art Museum, Cambridge, Massachusetts

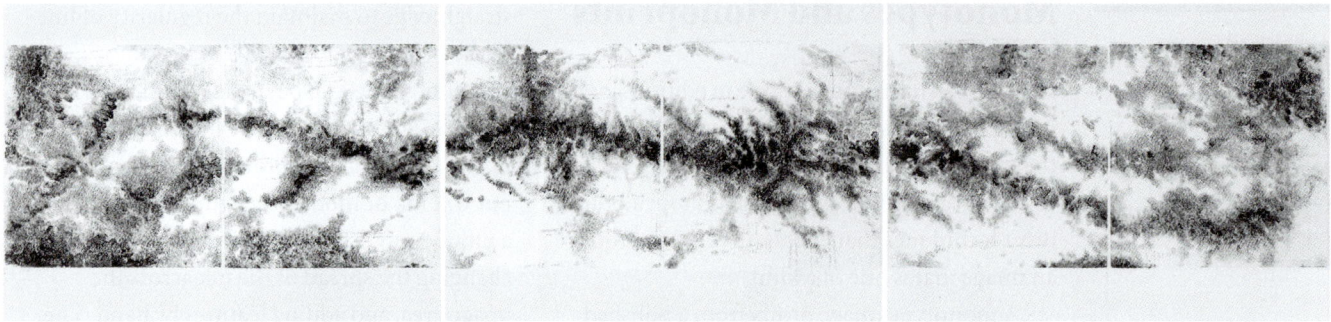

2.3.19 Kathy Strauss, *Kepler Underneath 1*, 2007. Monotype over India-inked calculations, Somerset velvet paper, each panel 30 × 23". Collection of the artist

wiped. Ink stayed in the incised grooves. Strauss has then painted the image of the Milky Way in ink directly onto the same plate; when the inking was complete, she centered the paper over the image and ran it through the press. Because Strauss painted the ink on by hand, she cannot re-create the result exactly in a second print, so it is not part of an edition.

Print Shops and Digital Reproduction Services

Contemporary printmakers sometimes rely on the technical expertise of craftspeople who may not be artists themselves, but have developed the knowledge and expertise to bring creative ideas to a well-crafted artwork. For example, Skyline Art Editions is a commercial printing service, based in Austin and Dallas, that works with artists and other creative professionals to re-create original imagery (**2.3.20**). This studio, like many others, works with the individual artist to find the right paper, surface appearance, and archival qualities that meet his or her high standard. Although some print shops will provide traditional printmaking tools and equipment along with their expertise, Skyline Art Editions provides digital reproductions that replicate the character of the original work, be it a print, painting, or another two-dimensional piece.

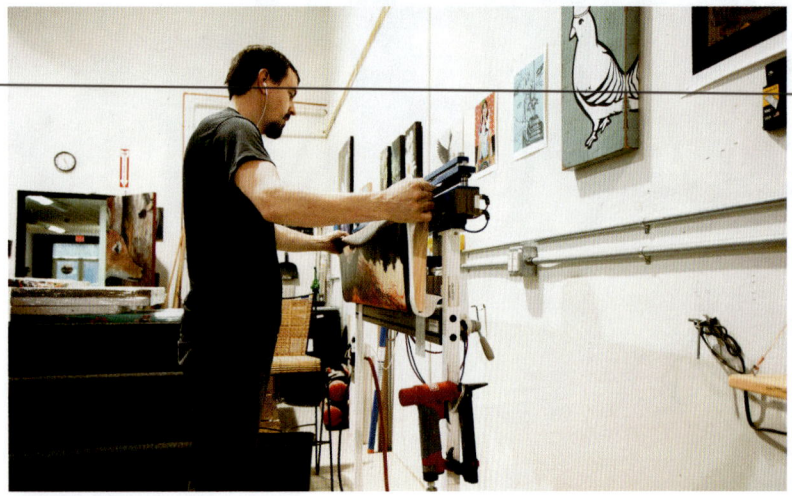

2.3.20 Drying racks at Skyline Art Editions, Austin, Texas

Contemporary Directions in Printmaking

The freedom of expression and changing technologies that artists have experienced over the past fifty years have inspired printmakers to innovate, developing new processes. Printmakers have reimagined the printmaking process so that it can be utilized by artists working in a variety of media, from sculpture to the digital realm. Much of this innovation has happened through collaborative print shops, where many craftspeople and artists have joined forces to redefine the nature of the print.

One of the first innovative print shops of the contemporary era was Mixografia®. Originally founded by Luis Remba (b. 1932) as Taller de Gráfica Mexicana (TGM) in Mexico City, the print shop worked with famous Mexican artists, beginning in the late 1960s, to create editions of their artwork for commercial distribution. While working on a series of lithographs with the Mexican artist Rufino Tamayo (1899–1991), the shop began incorporating paper pulp, creating their own bespoke surfaces to meet Tamayo's request for more texture. The technique was called the Mixografia® printing technique, which eventually lent its name to the current print shop, established in Los Angeles in 1984. One of Tamayo's first prints using this process

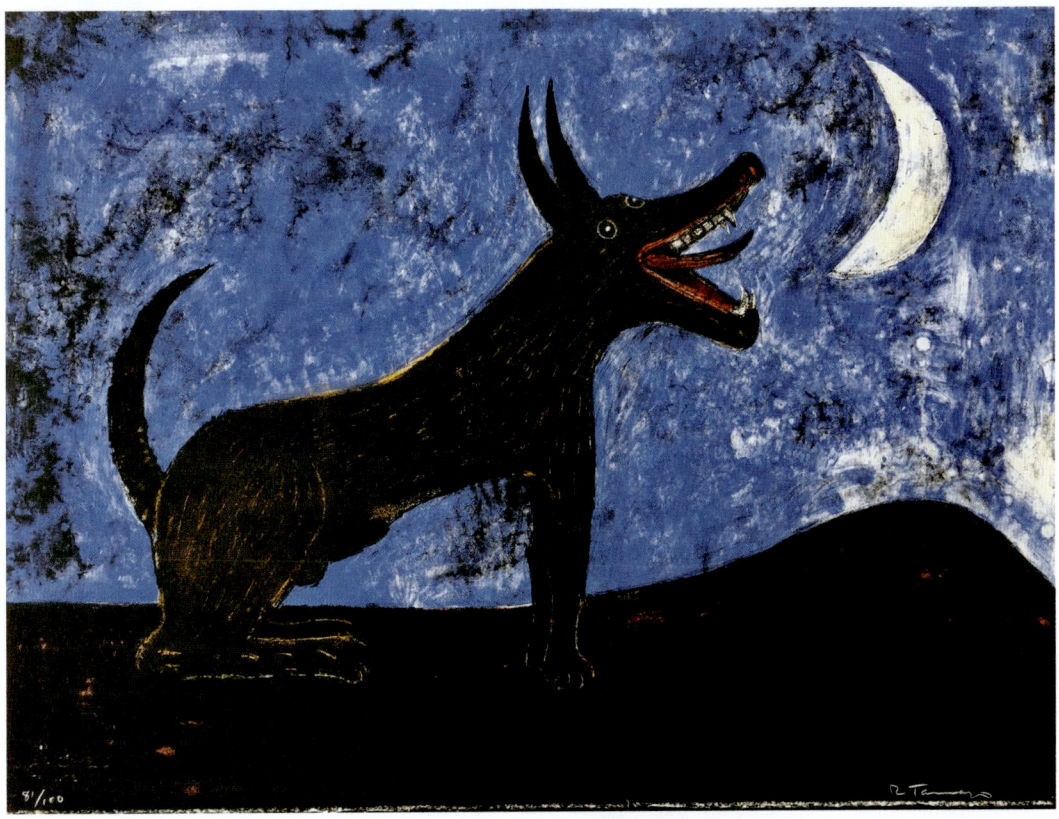

2.3.21 Rufino Tamayo, *Perro de Luna*, 1973. Mixograph, edition of 100, 22¼ × 30¼"

was *Perro de Luna* ("Moon Dog"), which is a lithograph executed in heavily textured handmade paper (**2.3.21**). Tamayo's print pushed the boundaries of printmaking beyond the traditional flat surface to such an extent that the print itself became a relief from which multiple copies could be produced.

In the 1980s the digital age thrust art into a new era with the introduction of computer graphics and other technical innovations that created new opportunities for artists. One of the most notable innovations in print technology was the inkjet printer. It allowed an electronic image to be re-created on a paper surface, but this model had serious weaknesses for use as an art medium because the ink color was not permanent and the paper size was limited. In the early 1990s, however, high-resolution commercial print devices overcame these disadvantages. While working at the digital printing company Nash Editions, the printmaker Jack Duganne (b. 1942) introduced the term *giclée* to identify and separate fine art print methods that used permanent ink color from their commercial counterparts. Duganne now leads his own print shop, Duganne Atelier, where he uses the giclée process to print the work of such significant contemporary artists as Ilana Raviv (b. 1945). Raviv, an Israeli artist, works in a number of different media and has her work reproduced for commercial distribution. A reproduction of one of her paintings, *Doll with Toys* (**2.3.22**) has been replicated using the

2.3.22 Ilana Raviv (Oppenheim), *Doll with Toys*, 2003. Acrylic on canvas, 29 × 37"

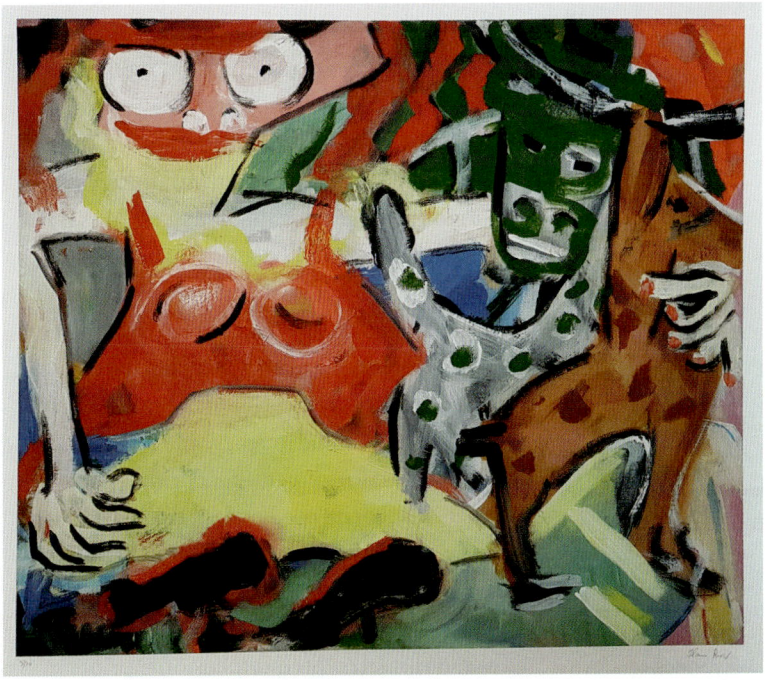

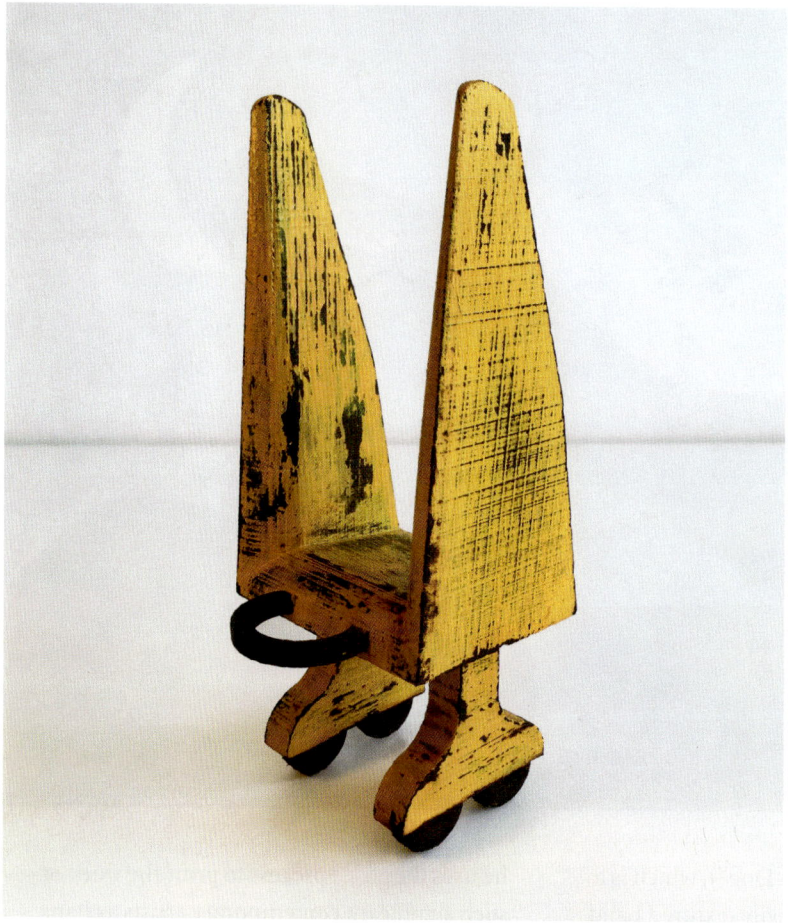

2.3.23 Kurt Dyrhaug, *Unterschieden Tonka*, 2017. Three-dimensional print, metal coating, and acrylic paint, 7 × 3 × 3". Museo de Arte Contemporano Costa da Morte, Corme, Spain

giclée process because the resolution and color permanence insures that an art buyer will have a lasting piece of art that encapsulates Raviv's unique gestural style.

Technical innovations in computer graphics have pushed the boundaries of traditional image-making so that an illusion of three dimensions can be fabricated in real space with the use of **3-D modeling** software. Three-dimensional printing begins with the creation of a computer graphic that is described as if it has height, width, and depth. Of course these dimensions do not exist, but are formulated within a computer application that allows the artist to "draw" the form. Once the object is created, the artist can print the object as a real object, add finishing touches, then exhibit. Like a traditional two-dimensional print, a three-dimensional print can be made many times and can even be considered an edition when all the works are identical.

The American sculptor Kurt Dyrhaug (b. 1966) creates three-dimensional prints of sculptures using 3D-modeling. His work *Unterschieden Tonka* (**2.3.23**) may look like a cast metal object, but in fact it has been printed. The original computer graphic information (designed by the artist) is passed to the printer, which uses a thick, glue-like liquid plastic that is organized into thin layers, each placed on top of the previous until the form takes shape. Dyrhaug, who has extensive training in iron and aluminum sculpting, coats the surface with an iron metal coating and acrylic paint after cleaning up any excess print material left on the object. Although it may seem very different from a traditional woodcut, this process is very much like a multiple-color print where one color must be printed over another.

From woodcuts to three-dimensional prints, printmaking has evolved with new advances in technology and to meet the needs of creative artists. These radical changes in the printed form may signal future trends in art production.

3-D modeling: a computer-generated illusion that emulates an object in three dimensions; it can be modified to show visual movement

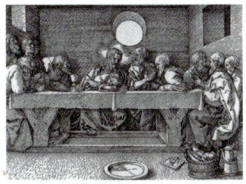

3.6.16 Albrecht Dürer, *The Last Supper*, 1523, p. 475

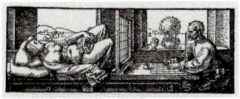

1.3.24 Albrecht Dürer, *Draftsman Drawing a Recumbent Woman*, 1525, p. 93

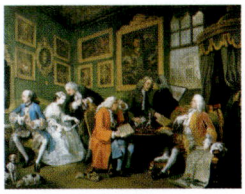

3.7.4 William Hogarth, *The Marriage Settlement*, c. 1743, p. 490

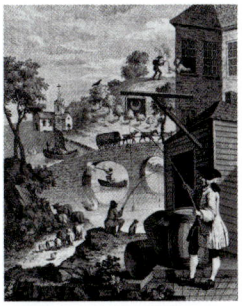

4.5.6 William Hogarth, *False Perspective*, 1754, p. 619

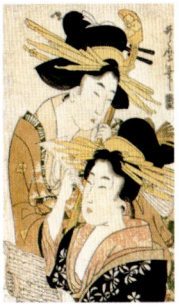

3.8.10 Kitagawa Utamaro, *Two Courtesans*, second half of 18th century, p. 510

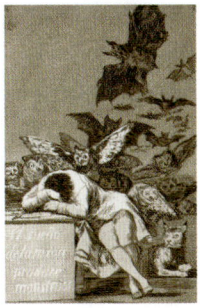

1.9.13 Francisco Goya, *The Sleep of Reason Produces Monsters*, 1799, p. 167

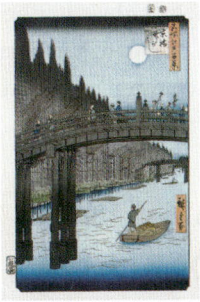

1.8.10 Ando Hiroshige, "Riverside Bamboo Market, Kyo-bashi," 1857, p. 157

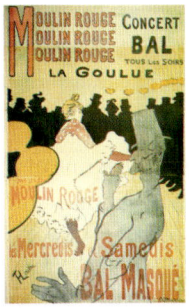

2.7.16 Henri de Toulouse-Lautrec, *La Goulue at the Moulin Rouge*, 1891, p. 309

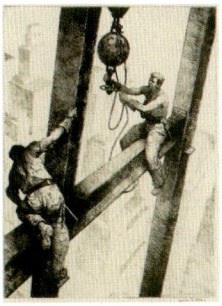

1.1.8 James Allen, *The Connectors*, 1934, p. 48

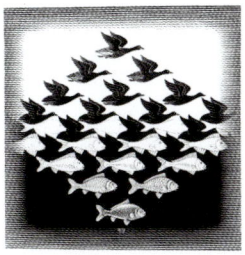

1.1.28 M. C. Escher, *Sky and Water I*, 1938, p. 59

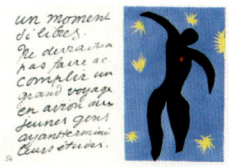

4.9.17b Henri Matisse, *Icarus*, 1943–47, p. 675

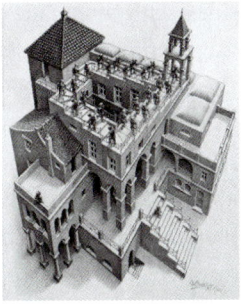

1.3.23 M. C. Escher, *Ascending and Descending*, 1960, p. 92

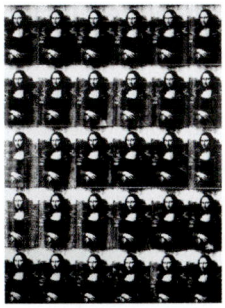

3.9.29 Andy Warhol, *Thirty Are Better than One*, 1963, p. 541

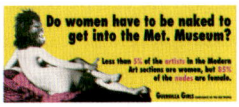

4.10.7 Guerrilla Girls, *Do Women Have to Be Naked...*, 1989, p. 685

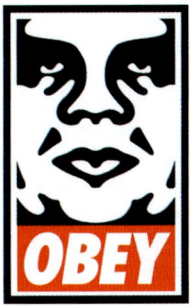

1.1.25a Shepard Fairey, *Obey*, 1996, p. 57

2.4 Sculpture

> A great sculpture can roll down a hill without breaking.
>
> (Michelangelo Buonarroti, Italian sculptor, painter, and architect)

Michelangelo is generally regarded as one of the finest sculptors in the Western tradition—some would say the greatest (see Box: Michelangelo, p. 246). When the **Renaissance** Italian artist made the humorous remark above, he probably had in mind most of his own sculptures: statues chiseled out of durable marble. This might be the first response of most of us when asked to define what we mean by sculpture, although we might broaden our definition to include other materials, such as metal, ceramics, and wood (see table of principal materials for sculpture **2.4.14**, p. 251). But, as we will see in this chapter, sculpture can be made from many materials: for example, glass, wax, ice, plastic, and fiber. In fact, the materials of modern sculpture can include, for example, neon lights and even animals. Sculptors' methods today still include chiseling (as Michelangelo did), carving, molding, assembling, and constructing, but inventive sculptors are finding new ways to create their art, and new materials to make it with.

It is probably because artists are so inventive that it is difficult to define sculpture exactly. Look up the word in a dictionary and then check whether the definition fits all the works in this chapter; it probably will not. But we can agree on a few things that are true of all sculptures. They exist in three dimensions and occupy physical space in our world. And they invite us to interact with them: by looking at them, by walking round them, or by entering them and being immersed in an environment created by the sculptor, including sights, sounds, textures, and other sensory experiences.

Renaissance: a period of cultural and artistic change in Europe from the fourteenth to the seventeenth century
In the round: a freestanding sculpted work that can be viewed from all sides
Three-dimensional: having height, width, and depth
Relief: a raised form on a largely flat background. For example, the design on a coin is "in relief"
Bas-relief (low relief): a sculpture carved with very little depth: the carved subjects rise only slightly above the surface of the work
High relief: a carved panel where the figures project with a great deal of depth from the background
Plane: a flat, two-dimensional surface on which an artist can create a drawing or painting. Planes can also be implied in a composition by areas that face toward, parallel to, or away from a light source

Approaches to Three Dimensions in Sculpture

Sculptors planning new sculptures have two basic options for displaying them. The first approach invites us to examine them on all sides; sculpture made to be enjoyed in this way is known as freestanding, or sculpture **in the round**. Many freestanding sculptures are made so that we can move around them, but sculptures in the round can also be displayed in a way that prevents a viewer seeing every side of them. Sculptures can be made, for example, to be placed in a niche or standing against a wall. In such cases, the location of the statue determines the vantage points from which it can be viewed, and the sculptor will design his or her work with the viewer's position in mind.

The second fundamental approach to the **three-dimensional** nature of sculpture is **relief**, a type of sculpture specifically designed for viewing from one side. The image in a relief either protrudes from or is sunk into a surface. It can have very little depth (**bas-relief**) or a great deal (**high relief**).

Freestanding Sculpture

Some freestanding sculpture is not intended to be experienced from every point of view. The Egyptian sculpture (1971–1926 BCE) of the Lady Sennuwy, wife of the very powerful governor of an Egyptian province, was designed to be seen from the front (**2.4.1**). (Many Egyptian sculptures were made to be displayed with their backs to a wall or a pillar.) In this work we can get a sense of the original block of granite from which the work was chiseled. Egyptian figure sculptures often sit, as this one does, very straight and upright on the stone from which they were carved, with the arms and legs drawn in close to the body.

Giambologna (1529–1608), a Flemish artist working in Florence, Italy, designed the *Rape of a Sabine* at the request of Florence's ruler, Francesco de' Medici (**2.4.2a** and **2.4.2b**). The sculpture forms a kind of spiral that draws the viewer around to view its many changing **planes**. With

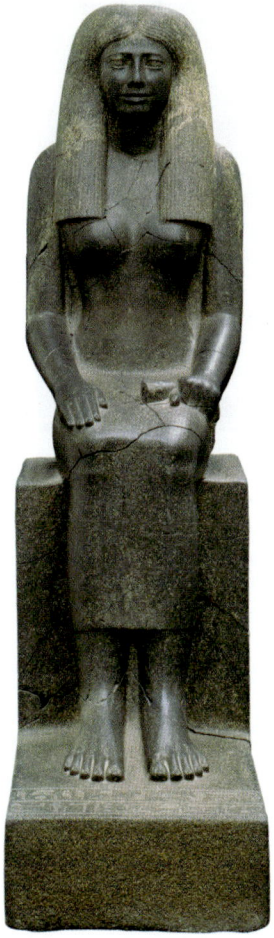

2.4.1 Sculpture of the Lady Sennuwy, 1971–1926 BCE. Granite, 67 × 45¾ × 18". Museum of Fine Arts, Boston, Massachusetts

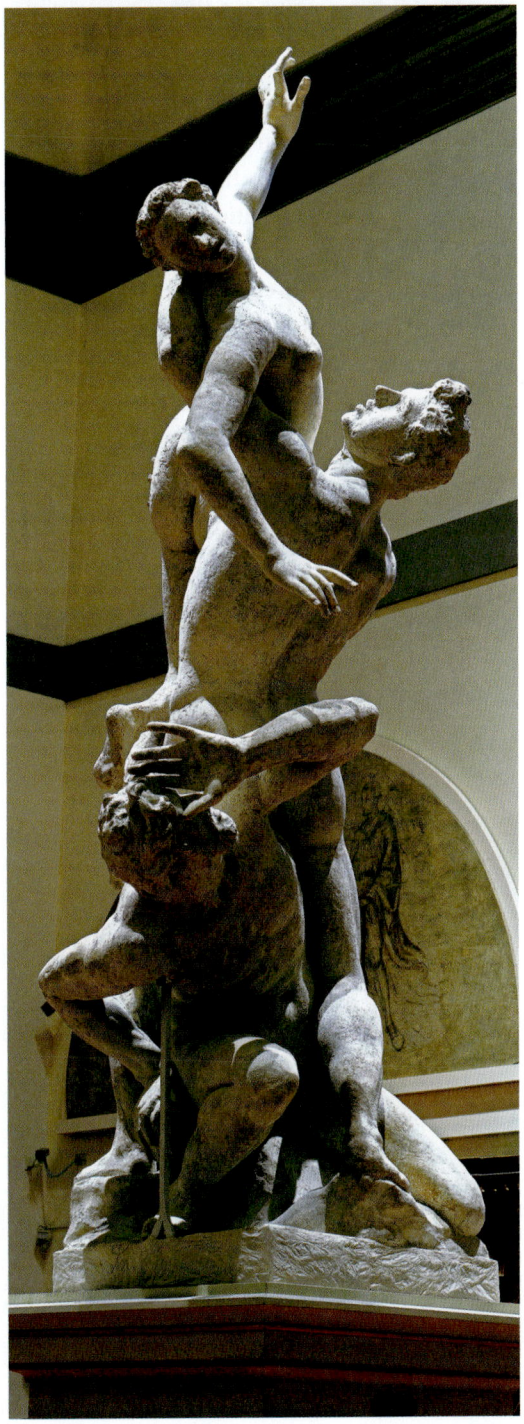

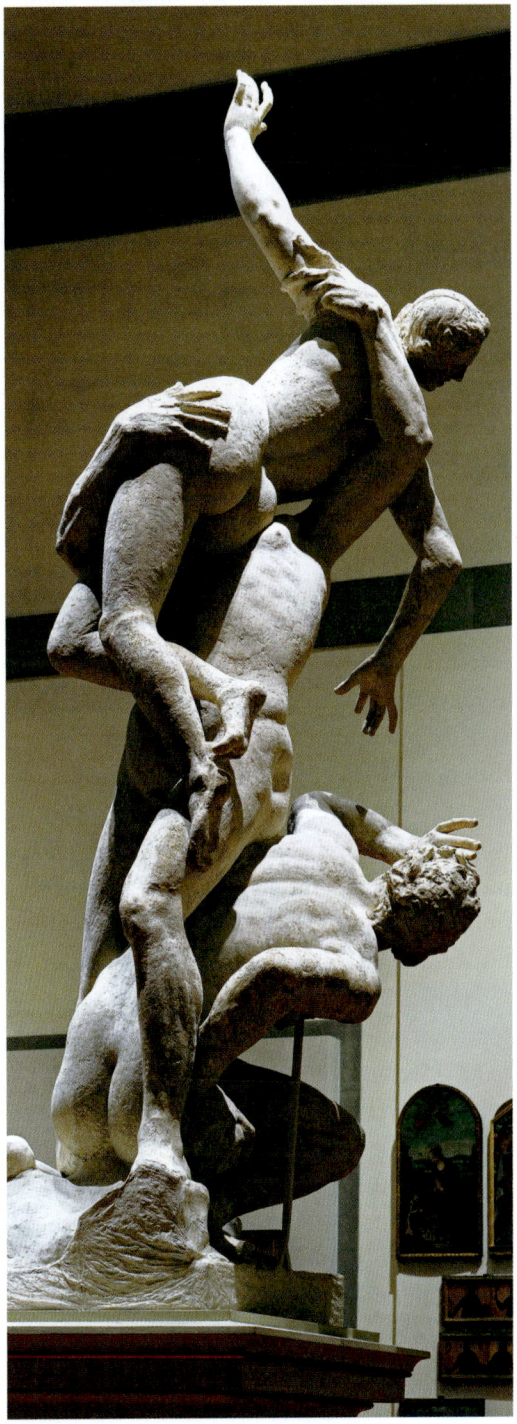

2.4.2a and 2.4.2b Giambologna, *Rape of a Sabine* (model), 1582. Gesso, height 13'8". Galleria dell'Accademia, Florence, Italy

each step, the viewer can discover unexpected details as the surfaces spiral upward. This is a powerful and beautiful work, but Giambologna had more in mind when he created it than just a dramatic design. His statue was a piece of political propaganda. It re-creates an ancient story about the foundation of Rome around 753 BCE. Most of the early founders of Rome were male. For the city to grow, the Romans needed wives. They solved this problem by inviting their neighbors the Sabines to a festival, during which the Romans seized the Sabine women and forced them to marry. This story symbolized the ability of a small community to become the most powerful city in Italy—as Rome was by Giambologna's time—and with this dramatic sculpture Francesco announced to the Florentines and their enemies that, like Rome, Florence had risen to become a force to be reckoned with.

Bas-Relief and High Relief

In bas-relief (the French word *bas* means "low"), the sculptor's marks are shallow. An example of this kind of sculpted surface was found in the North Palace of the Assyrian king Ashurbanipal in the ancient city of Nineveh in Mesopotamia (modern-day Iraq, eastern Syria, and southeastern Turkey). Assyrian kings ruled over a large territory and had powerful armies. They decorated the interior walls of their palaces with images depicting their strength and power. The artist who carved away the stone to create *Dying Lioness* intended to reflect the great strength and bravery of King Ashurbanipal as he hunted the most fearsome beast known to the Assyrians (**2.4.3**).

The symbol of the lion is also used to represent power and bravery in the *Memorial to King Leopold of the Belgians*, created to commemorate the death of Belgium's first king (it declared independence from the Netherlands in 1830) in 1865 (**2.4.4**). The British sculptor Susan Durant (1827–1873) chose to incise the surface more deeply for the figures closer to the viewer; this means that they are in high relief (see Gateway to Art: Maya Lintel). Thus these figures—the lion and the reclining Leopold—protrude from the surface more than the angels in the **background**, which have been carved in low relief. The illusion of depth emphasizes Leopold's bravery in accepting the Belgian National Congress's invitation to become king. Durant was unusual in being a successful sculptor in nineteenth-century England at a time when it was not easy for women to break into such a profession; she was in demand for her portraits, which included a **bust** of Harriet Beecher Stowe, the author of the anti-slavery novel *Uncle Tom's Cabin* (1852). Durant became a favorite sculptor to the British royal family, and her memorial to King Leopold I was originally installed in the chapel of his niece Queen Victoria at Windsor Castle in 1867 but was moved to Christ Church, Esher, in 1879.

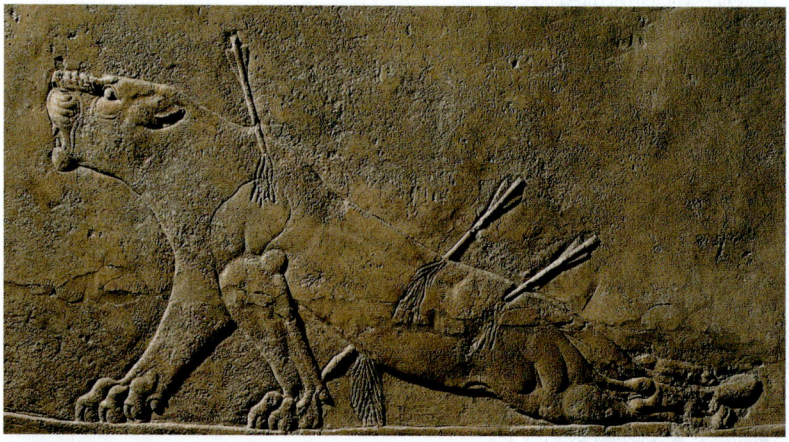

2.4.3 *Dying Lioness*, limestone relief from the North Palace of Ashurbanipal, Nineveh, Assyrian period, c. 650 BCE. British Museum, London, England

Background: the part of a work depicted furthest from the viewer's space, often behind the main subject matter
Bust: a statue of a person depicting only his or her head and shoulders

2.4.4 Susan Durant, *Memorial to King Leopold of the Belgians*, 1867, Christ Church, Esher, England

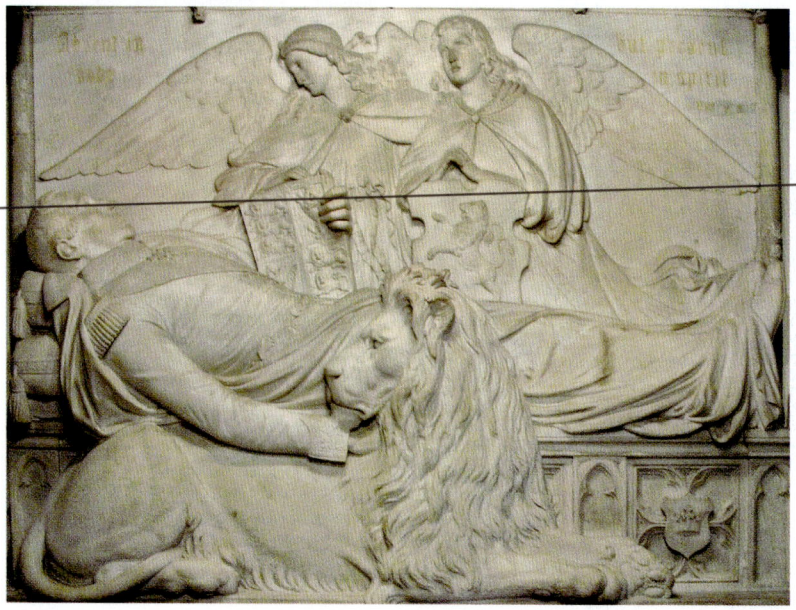

Gateway to Art: Maya Lintel Showing Shield Jaguar and Lady Xoc
Varying Degrees of Relief for Emphasis

The Maya **lintel** showing Shield Jaguar and his wife Lady Xoc (**2.4.5**) is a relief sculpture, or a type of carved surface intended to be seen from one side, like a written document. The flat surface of the limestone was probably chiseled using stone hammers and wooden drills, since Maya craftspeople had no metal tools. Shield Jaguar was a Maya ruler from 681 to 742 CE, and his influence is recorded in such sculptures as these. Various degrees of relief were used to emphasize different areas of the scene.

What we know about the Maya culture comes from a pictorial language that was carefully incised into the stone surfaces of buildings. These images display part of an elaborate written language made up of glyphs, or symbolic pictures, that tell the story of life in ancient Mesoamerica. Artists who were responsible for the creation of these carved messages would enclose a series of stylized symbols in low relief within a square or rectangular block, like those shown in the upper left and left side of the Maya lintel. These blocks as a whole are carved in high relief and protrude to the same measure as the figures, showing their importance.

Sculpting deeper into the stone had the effect of accentuating the major shapes, such as that of Shield Jaguar, the figure on the left, and Lady Xoc, who is positioned in the right bottom corner. Surfaces within those deeply incised areas are more lightly carved, detailing the stately attire of these Maya royals. The use of different degrees of relief contributes to the realism of the image. For example, the texture on Lady Xoc's dress is not as prominent as her necklace. And the rope she holds is in higher relief and therefore is clearly in front of her. Originally the lintel would have been painted, and analysis reveals traces of red and blue pigment.

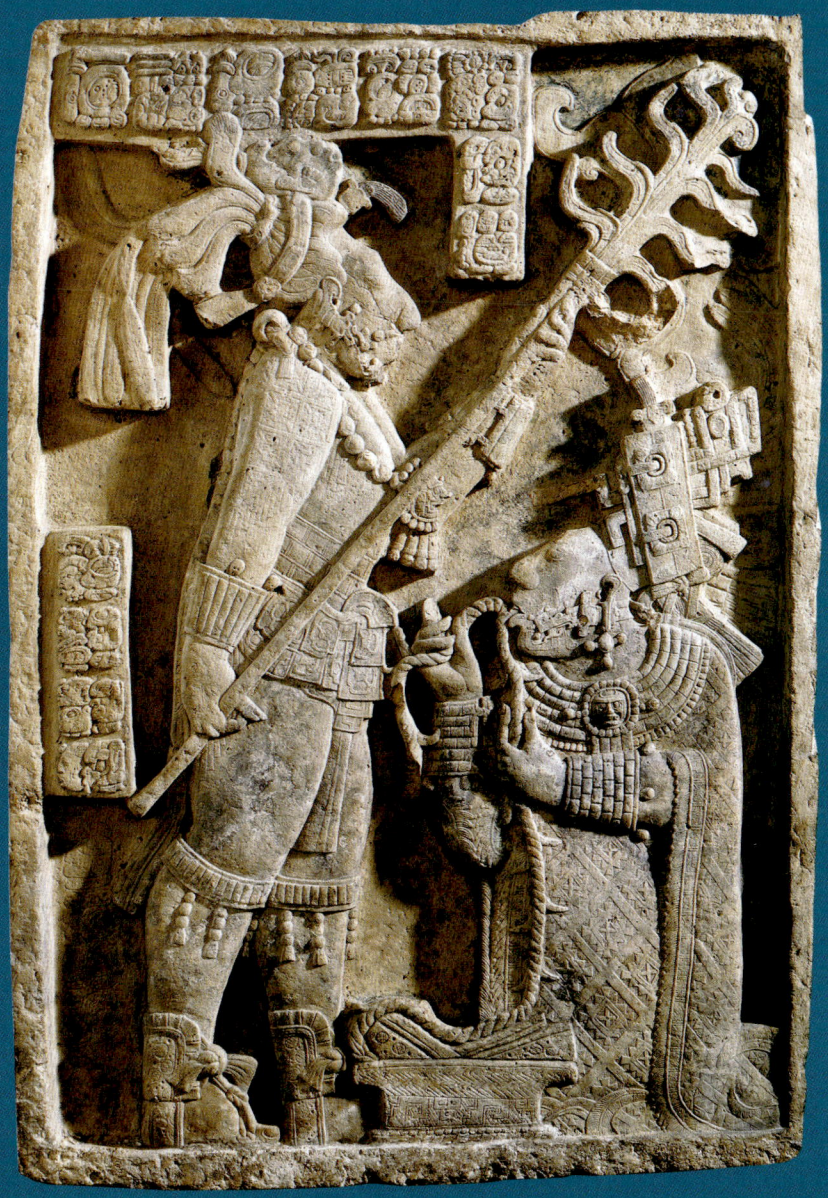

2.4.5 Maya lintel showing Shield Jaguar and Lady Xoc, *c.* 725 CE. Limestone, 43 × 30¾× 2⅜". British Museum, London, England

Lintel: the horizontal beam over the doorway of a portal

For the other Maya lintel Gateway boxes, see p. 162, p. 436, and p. 632

Michelangelo

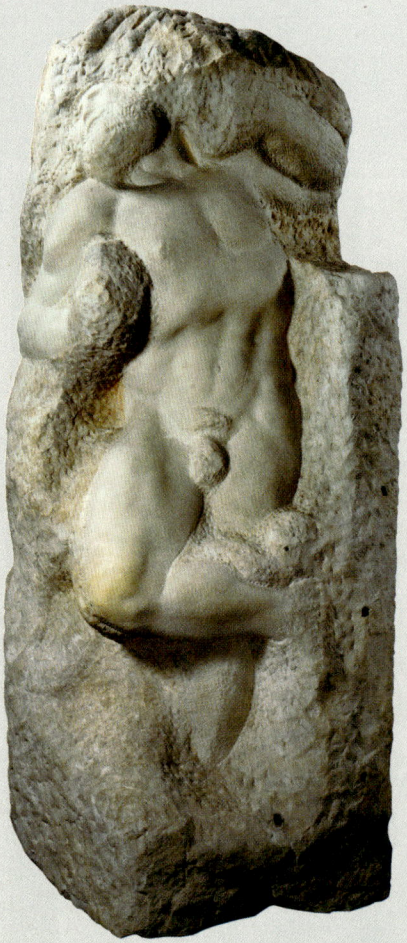

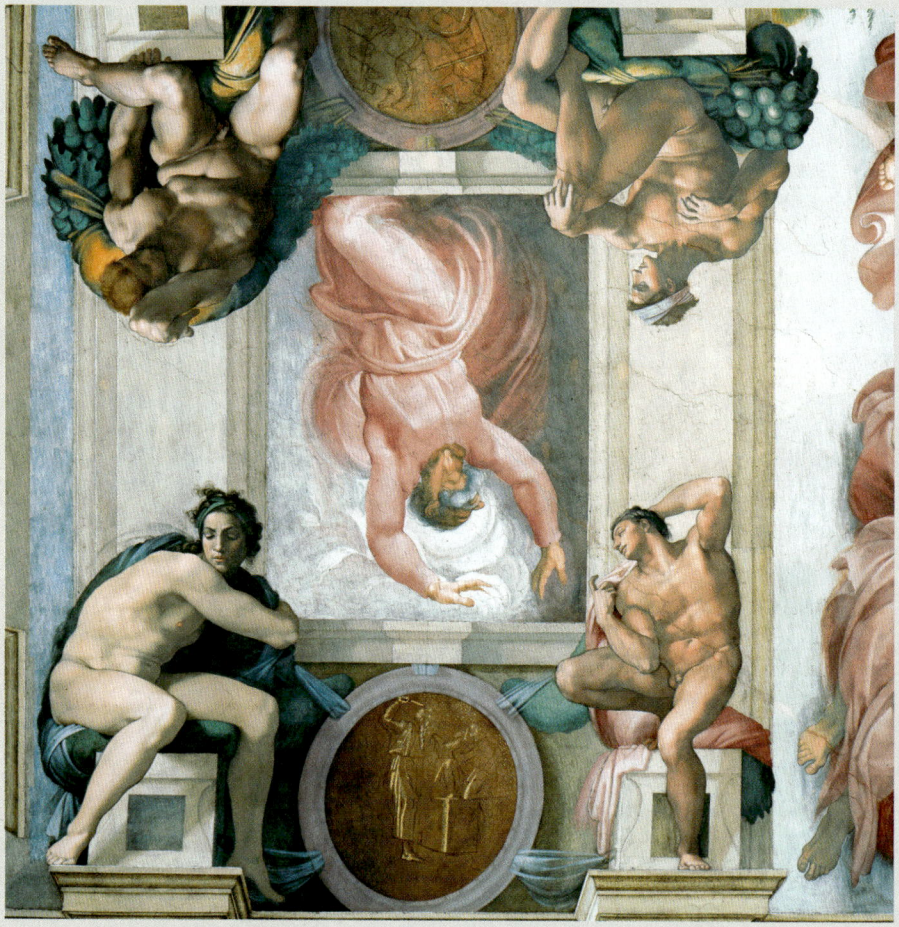

One artist in history stands out because of his unique mastery of the materials and methods of sculpture. Michelangelo (b. Michelangelo Buonarroti, 1475–1564) used an unconventional technique to "release" the figure, as he saw it, from the stone. Rather than remove stone progressively from all sides, as most sculptors do, Michelangelo began on one side of the stone and sculpted through to the other side. He felt that he was freeing the figure from the stone in which it had been trapped. His unfinished sculpture, *Awakening Slave*, gives an insight into the artist's technique (**2.4.6**).

Michelangelo excelled in architecture and painting as well as sculpture. Yet he saw these arts through the eyes of a sculptor; he believed sculpture itself was the finest, the most challenging, and the most beautiful of all the visual arts. While painting the Sistine Chapel ceiling (**2.4.7**), which many see as his grandest work, Michelangelo dreamed of finishing the ceiling quickly so that he could get back to work on several large sculptures intended for the tomb of Pope Julius II. He made many **sketches** of the figures intended for the nude male sculptures (which he called *ignudi*, from the Italian word for nude) that he planned would cover the tomb. Unfortunately, the tomb was never completed in the way that Michelangelo intended, but some sculptures carved for the project survive. Figure **2.4.8**—*Moses*—is one example, and if we compare this polished statue with the *Awakening Slave*, we can see how much refining of his sculptural work the artist did after the initial carving stage.

The muscular figures painted on the Sistine Chapel ceiling have led many viewers to believe they are looking at sculptures. The figures have the appearance of **mass**, particularly the

2.4.6 (above left) Michelangelo, *Prisoner*, known as the *Awakening Slave*, 1519–20. Marble, height 8'9⅛". Galleria dell'Accademia, Florence, Italy

2.4.7 (above right) Michelangelo, *Separation of Light and Darkness*, 1508–12, detail of the vault, Sistine Chapel, Vatican City, Italy nudes, which really seem to be men perched on architectural platforms. The ceiling is smooth, however; the illusion of these three-dimensional forms was created through the use of shading. Michelangelo painted darker shades in the areas that would have been carved more deeply if the figures had been sculptures. Thus, even when he painted, he thought like a sculptor.

2.4.8 Michelangelo, Tomb of Julius II, detail of *Moses*, 1513–16. Marble, height 7'8½". San Pietro in Vincoli, Rome, Italy

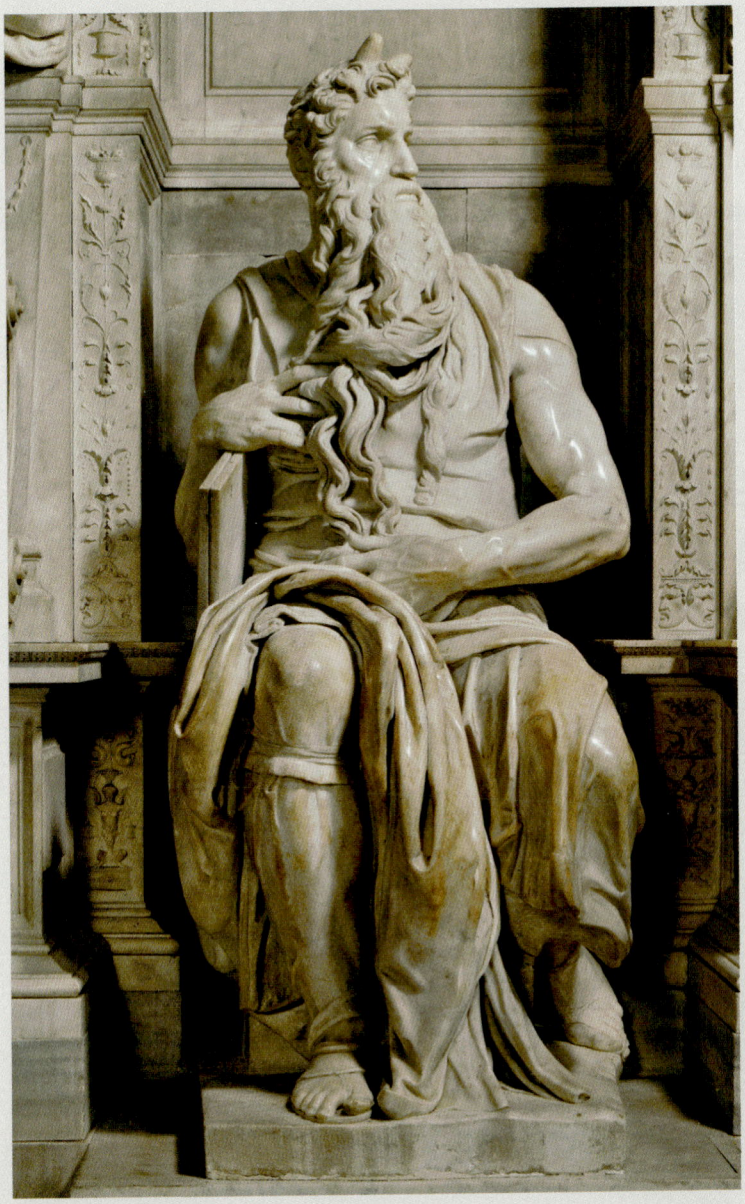

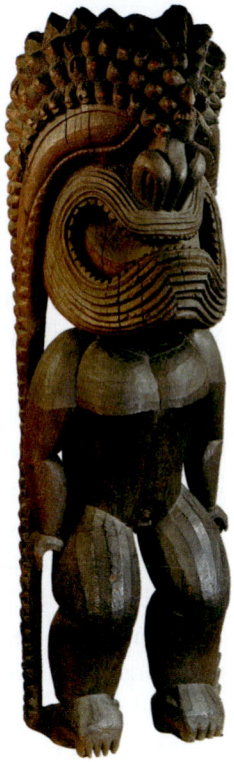

Sketch: a rough preliminary version of a work or part of a work
Mass: a volume that has, or gives the illusion of having, weight, density, and bulk
Subtractive (sculpture): the methodical removal of material to produce a sculptural form
Additive (sculpture): a sculpting process in which the artist builds a form by adding material
Cast: a sculpture or artwork made by pouring a liquid (for example molten metal or plaster) into a mold

2.4.9 Figure of the war god Ku-ka'ili-moku, Hawaii, 18th or 19th century. Wood, height 8'11". British Museum, London, England

Methods of Sculpture

Sculptural methods are either **subtractive** or **additive**. In the subtractive processes, a sculptor uses a tool to carve, drill, chisel, chip, whittle, or saw away unwanted material. In the additive processes of modeling, **casting**, or constructing, sculptors add material to make the final artwork.

Carving

The most ancient works of art that still exist were made using subtractive methods of sculpture. Most of these were made of stone or ivory (because wood eventually decays, we have few ancient wooden sculptures) and were worked by chipping, carving, sanding, and polishing.

The nearly nine-foot-tall figure of the Hawaiian war god Ku-ka'ili-moku was carved (the subtractive method) from large pieces of wood (**2.4.9**). The sculpture represents a god whose name translates from Hawaiian as "Ku, the land-grabber." Originally created for the powerful King Kamehameha I, the image of the god exhibits an open mouth (a disrespectful gesture) and was probably intended to gain divine favor. Another god, Lono (god of prosperity), is also symbolized

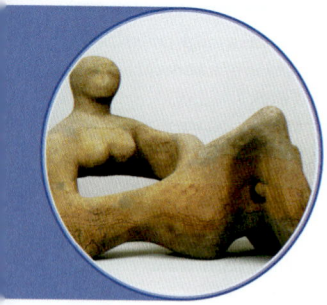

Carving is not limited to the ancient world. Twentieth-century sculptor Henry Moore also carved large stone sculptures, such as *Recumbent Figure*: see **4.9.15, p. 674**

by pigs' heads in Ku's hair. The combination of the two gods may have represented Kamehameha's invasions and conquests of adjacent kingdoms.

One of the largest and most famous sculptural portraits was executed using the subtractive method on a mountainside in South Dakota. The Mount Rushmore National Memorial (**2.4.10**) was executed by John G. de la Mothe Borglum (1867–1941), the son of Danish Mormon immigrants, who grew up in Idaho and Utah. The project was first conceived by Doane Robinson, superintendent of the South Dakota State Historical Society, in 1923, who had envisioned massive images of Chief Red Cloud, Buffalo Bill Cody, Lewis and Clark, and other figures who were directly connected to the area. Borglum was contacted by Robinson in 1924 and agreed to take on the project. Borglum approached the task with great care and drive, changing the original idea of local figures to that of four presidents. He spent two years looking for a mountain with the right stone characteristics to make the work a success. Most of the subtractive sculpting was done by skilled miners using dynamite, placed strategically, to remove large masses of stone. The choice of location and drilling practice were essential because once the stone was removed, it could not be replaced.

Modeling

Modeling in clay and wax (for example) is an additive process; the artist builds up the work by adding material. Clay and wax are pliable enough for sculptors to model them with their hands; sculptors also use specialized tools to manipulate them. Because such materials as clay often cannot support their own weight, sometimes an artist will employ a skeletal structure, called an **armature**, to which the clay will be added; the armature will then later be removed (or burned away) when the work is dry. Permanent

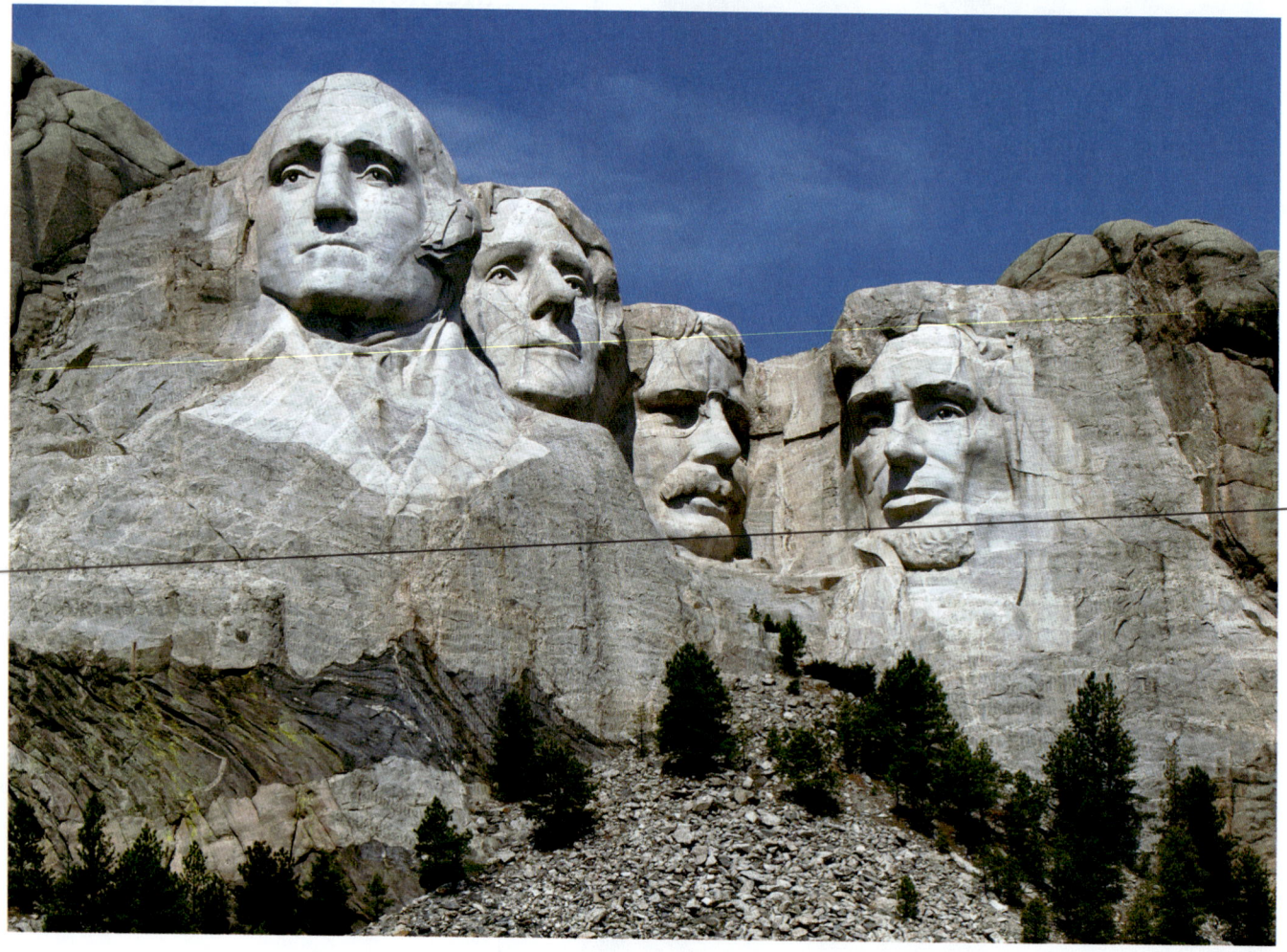

2.4.10 John G. de la Mothe Borglum, Mount Rushmore National Memorial, 1927–41. Keystone, South Dakota

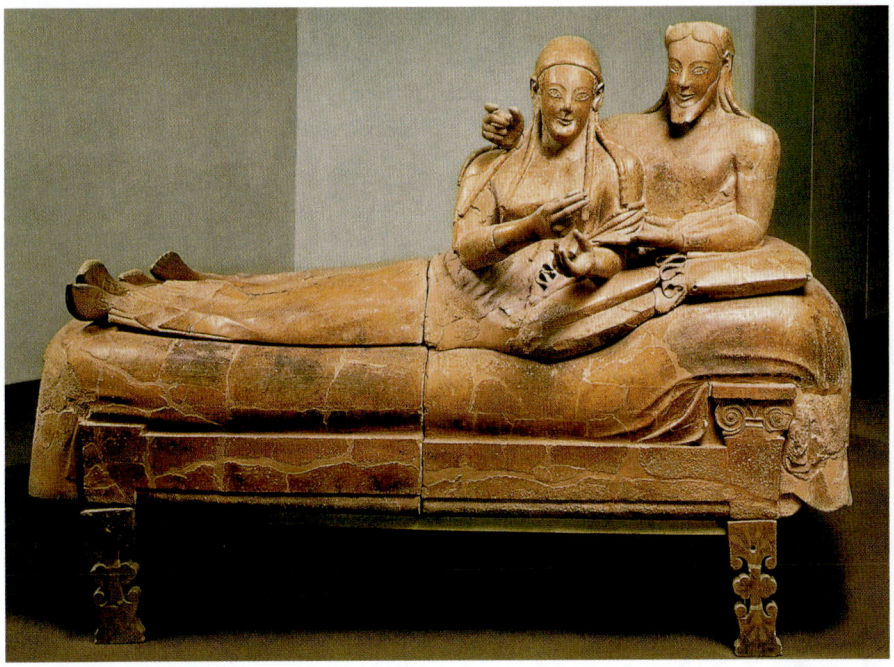

2.4.11 Sarcophagus from Cerveteri, *c.* 520 BCE. Painted terra-cotta, 3'9½" × 6'7". Museo Nazionale di Villa Giulia, Rome, Italy

sculptures created from clay will most often be dried, then fired in a kiln until the chemical structure of the clay changes. Because this process produces a very dry and hard material, many clay works from antiquity still exist.

Large sculptures, such as the Etruscan sarcophagus (a type of coffin) in **2.4.11**, are built from multiple pieces fired individually. Four separate terra-cotta (baked clay) pieces make up this sarcophagus, which contains the ashes of the deceased. The sculptor paid particular attention to the gestures and expressions of the couple, shown relaxed and enjoying themselves at an Etruscan banquet, although the expressions are **stylized** and not a likeness of the deceased. The **plastic** character of clay allowed the artist to make images that are **expressive** and capture the mood of the event.

The way the sculptor interpreted the figures tells us two interesting things about their culture. Women actively participated in social situations; this woman is shown gesturing, and even reclines in front of her husband. And, since this sculpture is part of a tomb, it suggests that celebrations took place upon the death of loved ones, although the figures' joyful expressions may simply indicate the deceased in an eternal state of happiness.

Casting

Casting, another additive process, involves adding a liquid or pliable material to a mold. It is done in order to set a form in a more durable material, or to make it possible to create multiple copies of a work. The first step in casting is to make a model of the final sculpture. This is used to make a mold. A casting liquid (often molten metal, but other materials, such as clay, plaster, acrylic polymers, or glass are also used) is poured into the mold. When it hardens, the result is a detailed replica of the original model.

Plaster casts are often used to create models and finished products. To create a plaster cast, the artist makes a clay original, coats it with a release agent (usually a slick, oily substance), then creates a plaster coating to go over the original. The artist is careful to make divisions so that the plaster mold can be easily separated, in sections, from the clay original. After the plaster has cured—set in a permanent state—the sections are carefully detached, the inside of the parts of the mold coated with release agent, and the mold reassembled. Plaster, or another pliable casting material, can then be poured into the mold, allowed to set, and the cast form removed.

The ancient Greeks cast bronze to produce many of their sculptures. Bronze is an alloy, or mixture, of copper and tin. It melts at a relatively low temperature (an average of 1,750°F

Armature: a framework or skeleton used to support a sculpture
Stylized: art that represents objects in an exaggerated way to emphasize certain aspects of the object
Plastic, plasticity: referring to materials that are soft and can be manipulated, or to such properties in the materials
Expressive: capable of stirring the emotions of the viewer

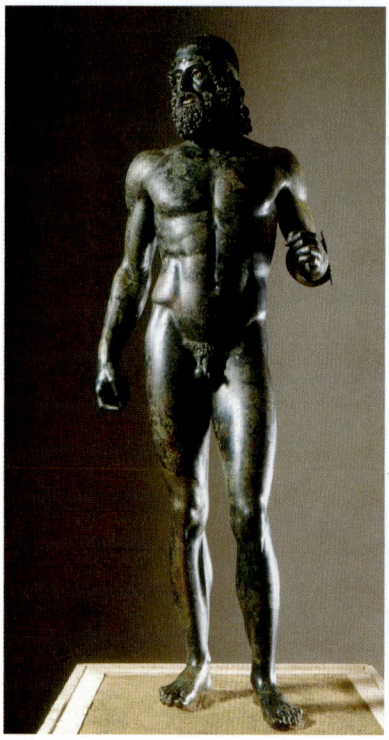

2.4.12 *Riace Warrior A*, c. 460 BCE. Bronze with copper, silver, and ivory, height 6'6". Museo Nazionale della Magna Grecia, Reggio di Calabria, Italy

Contrapposto: a pose in sculpture in which the upper part of the body twists in one direction and the lower part in another

Patina: surface color or texture on a metal caused by ageing

depending on the composition of the alloy) and is comparatively easy to cast. Once formed and cooled it is light (compared to stone) and durable. The so-called *Riace Warrior A* is a fine example of the casting skills of ancient Greek artists (**2.4.12**). It is one of two sculptures found in 1972 by divers off the coast of Riace, Italy. This sculpture reflects great attention to detail and was made at a time when the Greeks emphasized the perfection of the human body. The figure is posed in a **contrapposto** (Italian for "opposite"), which uses the natural curvature of the body to enliven the design. By shifting the weight to the right leg, the hips are set at a slight angle, which is countered by small shifts in the shoulders, with the head fractionally tilted. The work may have been cast to celebrate the victory of the Athenians over the invading Persians, and the relaxed contrapposto reflects strength and confidence.

Riace Warrior A was created using the lost-wax method of casting. (Each numbered stage refers to **2.4.13**.) The artist begins by building an armature (1) and then adds clay to it to create the form (2). A thick layer of wax is added to the form, and any detail the sculptor wishes to see in the final work is carved into the wax (3). Clay, sand, and ground-up pieces of old molds are used to cover the surface of the wax form, preserving all the detail. This hard coating, which needs to be strong enough to bear the heat and weight of the metal until it cools, will be the mold (4). Small holes are drilled in the bottom of the mold, which is then placed in a kiln. In the oven, the wax melts out through the holes in the bottom of the mold, leaving a hollow space inside the mold (5). Immediately after the mold has been removed from the kiln, very hot molten metal—in this case, bronze—is poured into it (6). When the metal has cooled, the mold is removed (usually by breaking it with a hammer) to reveal the work—which is still not finished (7). The artist cuts off any extra metal, then sands and polishes. Over time, exposure to the elements can add surface color, called a **patina**, to bronze sculpture. Such a patina can enhance the beauty of the work. Nowadays it is commonly applied more artificially, by using chemical preparations.

Lost-wax casting is called a substitution process because the molten metal takes the place of the wax. Other materials, such as foam or wood, are occasionally used as substitution materials instead of wax, because they can be burned out of the mold.

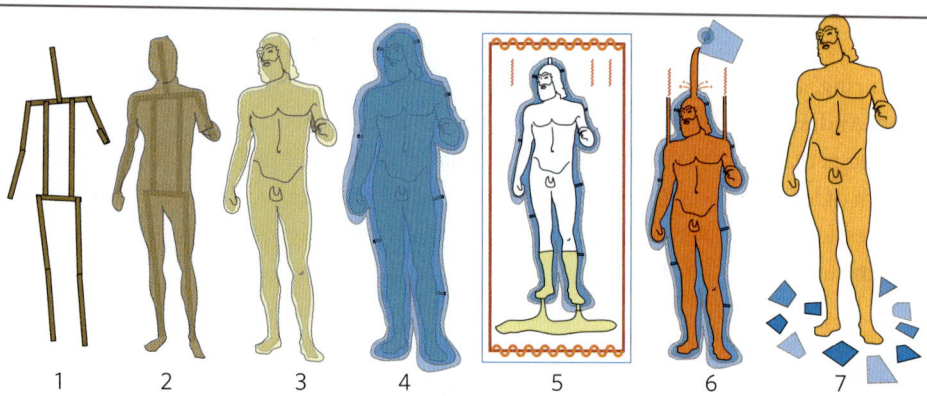

2.4.13 (left) Seven steps in the lost-wax casting process

2.4.14 (right) Principal materials of sculpture

Material	Family	Method	Example		Tools
Marble	Metamorphic stone	The sculptor can subtract material from the block until it has been reduced to the intended final shape. Finishing can be done by sanding and polishing.	Michelangelo, *David*; **3.6.23, p. 480**		Chisels, files, sandpaper, polishing cloths
Hardwood	Wood	The sculptor can subtract through carving and sawing or construct by gluing or nailing. Finishing can be done by sanding, polishing, oiling, and then varnishing.	Andrew Early, turned bowl; **2.6.23, p. 298**		Chisels, wood rasps, sandpaper, penetrating oils, varnish
Plaster	Sulfate of lime	The sculptor can cast the form or carve a cast block. Finishing is done by sanding. Plaster is sometimes used as a preliminary form if casting clay.	John Rogers, *Slave Auction*		Chisels, files, sandpaper
Ceramic	Clay	The sculptor can model this pliable material into any shape, or cast it in a mold. Finishing can be done by drying, heating in a kiln, then adding a clay and chemical compound before re-firing to achieve a glaze.	Aztec vessel with mask of Tlaloc		Wire, smoothing tools (like a thin rounded piece of flexible metal called a rib), kiln
Beeswax	Wax	The sculptor can model this pliable material or make a cast using the material in liquid form. Finishing is achieved by heating the surface and polishing. Wax is sometimes used as the preliminary form for bronze casting.	Patience Lovell Wright, *William Pitt, Earl of Chatham*		Carving tools, heated surface (like a griddle), heat gun
Bronze	Metal	The sculptor can cast molten bronze, weld pieces together using a torch, or hammer, usually with some heat, until it reaches the desired form. Finishing is done by adding a chemical compound to the surface to stabilize oxidation.	Alberto Giacometti, *Man Pointing*; **4.9.16, p. 674**		Hammers, furnace, welding torches, grinders, sandpaper

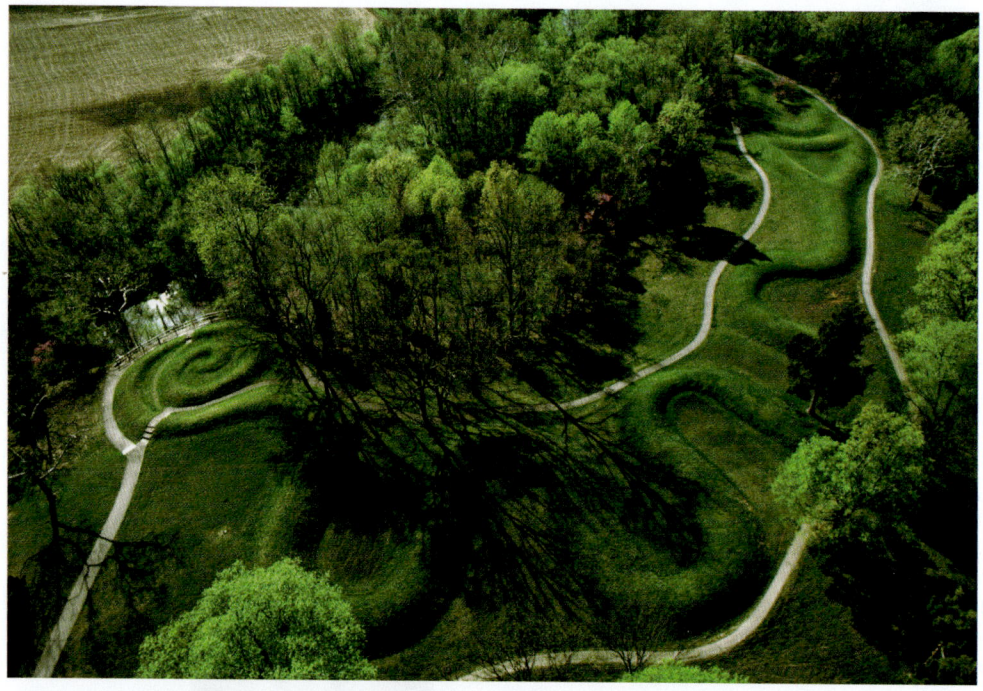

2.4.15 Great Serpent Mound, *c.* 800 BCE–100 CE, 1330 × 3', Locust Grove, Adams County, Ohio

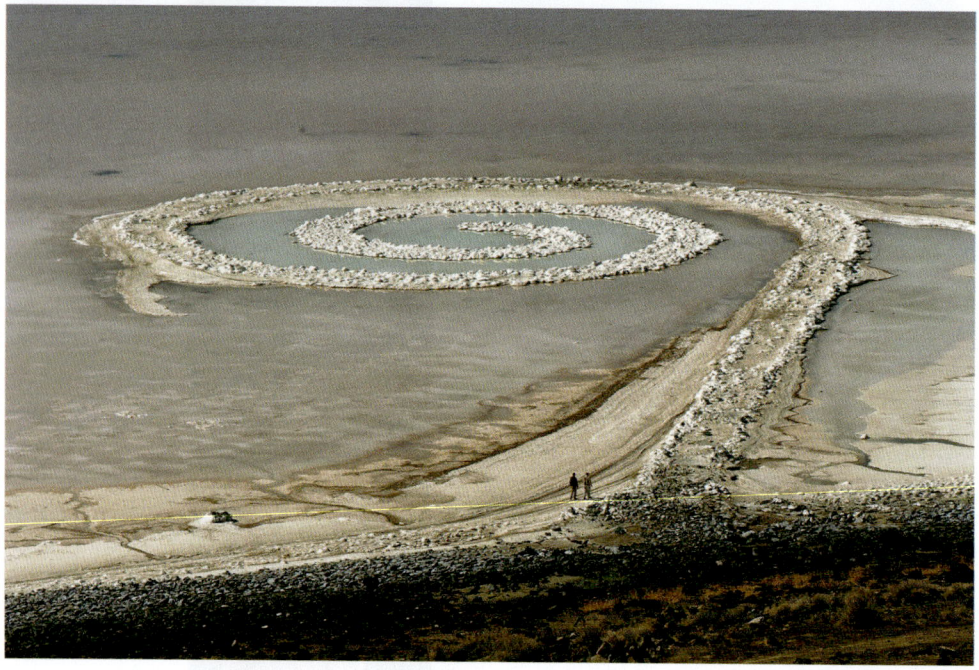

2.4.16 Robert Smithson, *Spiral Jetty*, 1969–70. Black rock, salt crystals, and earth, diameter 160', coil length 1500 × 15'. Great Salt Lake, Utah

Pushing beyond Traditional Methods

Monumental: having massive or impressive scale
Constructivism: an art movement in the Soviet Union in the 1920s, primarily concerned to make art of use to the working class
Space: the distance between identifiable points or planes

The traditional processes used for sculpting were ideal for the creation of static objects, but artists have found other ways to enliven the medium that go beyond conventional additive and subtractive techniques. They have challenged conventional notions of what sculptures can be.

Earthworks

Prehistoric artists of the Americas made **monumental** sculptures that used the surface of the Earth itself as material: this was additive sculpture on a very large scale. The most prominent of these is the Great Serpent Mound near Locust Grove, Ohio. As can be readily seen from the air, it resembles a snake with its mouth open, ingesting an egg (**2.4.15**). The identity of the people who created it is still debated. The head of the serpent and the egg are aligned to the position of the setting sun on the summer solstice (the longest day of the year), suggesting that the Great Serpent Mound was used in making solar observations. The original artists heaped piles of earth to "sculpt" this work onto the Ohio landscape.

In the 1960s artists again became interested in earthworks. The best-known modern earthwork is Robert Smithson's (1938–1973) *Spiral Jetty* in the Great Salt Lake in Utah (**2.4.16**). Smithson chose a spiral, a shape naturally found in shells, crystals, and even galaxies. The coiled artwork was made by dumping 6,550 tons of rock and dirt off dump trucks, gradually paving a spiralling roadbed out into the salt lake. The sculpture is not static in the way it interacts with nature: over the years the lake has repeatedly submerged and then revealed it, so that it is constantly evolving as it drowns and rises with a new encrustation of salt crystals.

Because of their enormous size, earthwork projects need the collaboration of many artists and workers, and equipment. Such works as the Great Serpent Mound required a community effort. Today, earthwork projects are obliged to have permits and community approval, and to involve large groups of workers. Earthwork artists do not earn money from their works, but create them as a service to the community. Many believe their earthworks should represent a harmony between nature and humanity.

Construction

When engineers make a piece of machinery, they use a variety of methods—for example, sawing, grinding, and milling, or molding and casting—to create and put together its components. All the components are then assembled. Some artists construct sculptures in a similar way.

The idea of constructing sculptures is relatively new. Methods for doing so have proliferated with the growth of standardized, engineered materials, such as sheet metals and plastics. In the late nineteenth century, sculptors began to look beyond traditional carved or cast forms to the process of constructing. The **Constructivist** art movement in the Soviet Union created sculptural construction

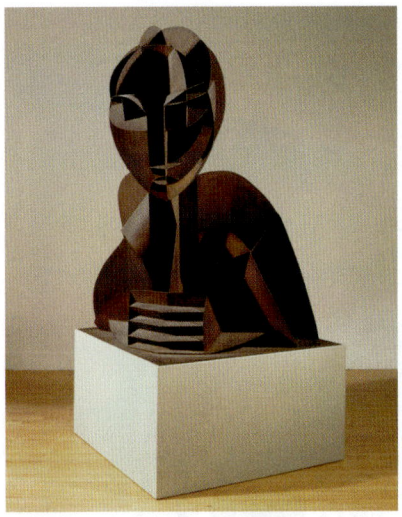

2.4.17 Naum Gabo, *Constructed Head No. 2*, 1916. Cor-ten steel, 69 × 52¾ × 48¼". Tate, London, England

techniques based on practices associated more with a factory than with an art studio. Naum Gabo (b. Naum Neemia Pevsner, 1890–1977) used his *Constructed Head No. 2* (**2.4.17**) to investigate the sense of **space** and form implied by flat planes, in contrast to the solid mass of conventional sculpture. Here Gabo is more interested in showing the interior construction of the work than the exterior surface, and has welded the intersecting planes of metal together.

Contemporary artists have adopted modern-day industrial techniques and unconventional materials to create their sculptures. The British artist Damien Hirst (b. 1965) made his work *The Physical Impossibility of Death in the Mind of Someone Living* out of a large tank full of formaldehyde, in which he suspended a dead shark (**2.4.18**). Of course, not every part of his

2.4.18 Damien Hirst, *The Physical Impossibility of Death in the Mind of Someone Living*, 1991. Glass, painted steel, silicone, monofilament, shark, and formaldehyde solution, 7'1½" × 17'9⅜" × 5'10⅞"

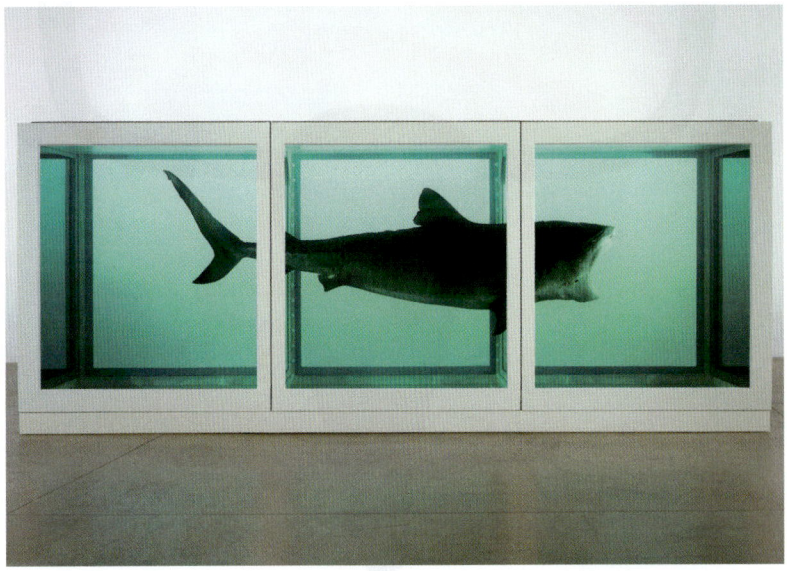

Assemblage: artwork made of three-dimensional materials, including found objects
Found image or **object:** an image or object found by an artist and presented, with little or no alteration, as part of a work or as a finished work of art in itself
Artifact: an object made by a person
Readymade: an everyday object presented as a work of art
Appropriation: the deliberate incorporation in an artwork of material originally created by other artists
Kinetic sculpture: three-dimensional art that moves, impelled by air currents, motors, or people

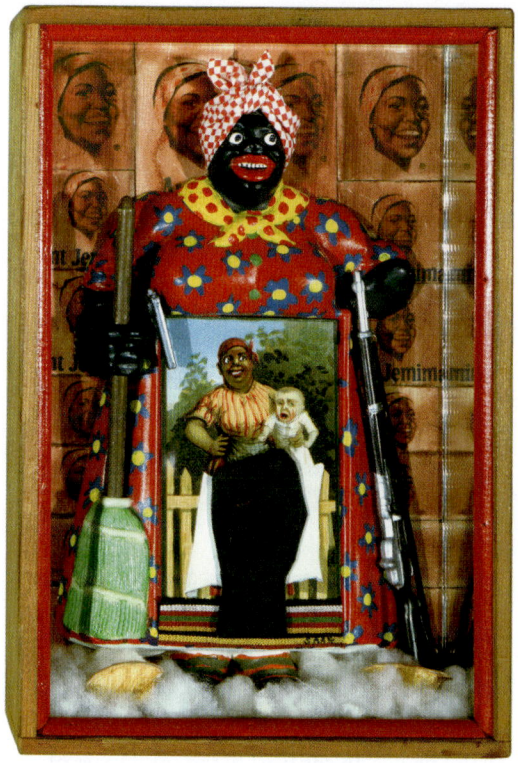

2.4.19 Betye Saar, *The Liberation of Aunt Jemima*, 1972. Mixed media assemblage, 11¾ × 8 × 2¾". Collection University of California, Berkeley Art Museum, California

Assemblage

The practice of gathering objects and fabricating them into a work of art is called **assemblage**. The gathered objects, sometimes called **found objects**, are repurposed so that they support the visual ideas and compositions of the artist. When the contemporary African American artist Betye Saar (b. 1926) created the work *The Liberation of Aunt Jemima* (**2.4.19**), she collected a variety of different found objects, such as cotton, syrup-bottle labels, and a stereotypical "Mammy" doll, and assembled them in a wooden box. The objects symbolize the relics and memorabilia of both personal and societal history as it relates to issues of gender and race; these pieces represent influences that were important to traditional African groups. Saar is interested in exploring themes of personal and communal identity: her art examines the survival of African traditions in black culture and often challenges stereotypes, for example those represented by such figures as "Aunt Jemima."

work was constructed; Hirst had the shark caught by fishermen. The entire work resembles a dissection specimen in a biology class. Hirst is known for creating his sculptures from unusual objects that contrast life and death.

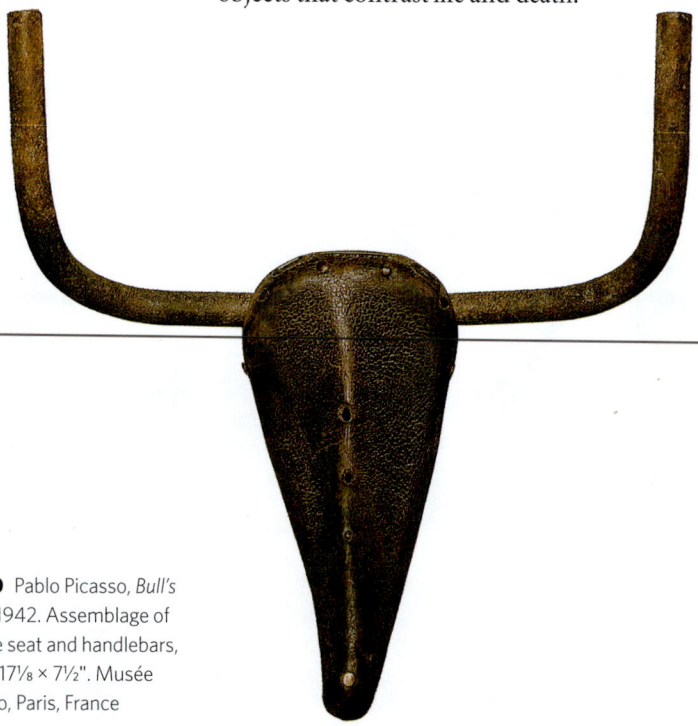

2.4.20 Pablo Picasso, *Bull's Head*, 1942. Assemblage of bicycle seat and handlebars, 13¼ × 17⅛ × 7½". Musée Picasso, Paris, France

Readymades

In the early twentieth century, a few artists began to create works using as raw materials **artifacts** that already existed. Sometimes, they simply decided that found objects were works of art. The Spanish artist Pablo Picasso (1881–1973) once took the handlebars and the seat of a bicycle and combined them to make his *Bull's Head* (**2.4.20**). Such artworks are known as **readymades**. Although Picasso did not make the individual parts, he arranged them in such a way that they resemble a bull's head, yet they are also readily recognizable as parts of a bicycle. The artist's intent was both a serious and a humorous attempt to redefine art.

Picasso was following in the footsteps of the French artist Marcel Duchamp (1887–1968), who pioneered a practice known as **appropriation**, as a way of challenging traditional ideas about art. Duchamp argued that any object, by virtue of being chosen and presented by an artist, can become a work of art. This way of making art is known as appropriation, because the artist appropriates a pre-existing image or object and alters its

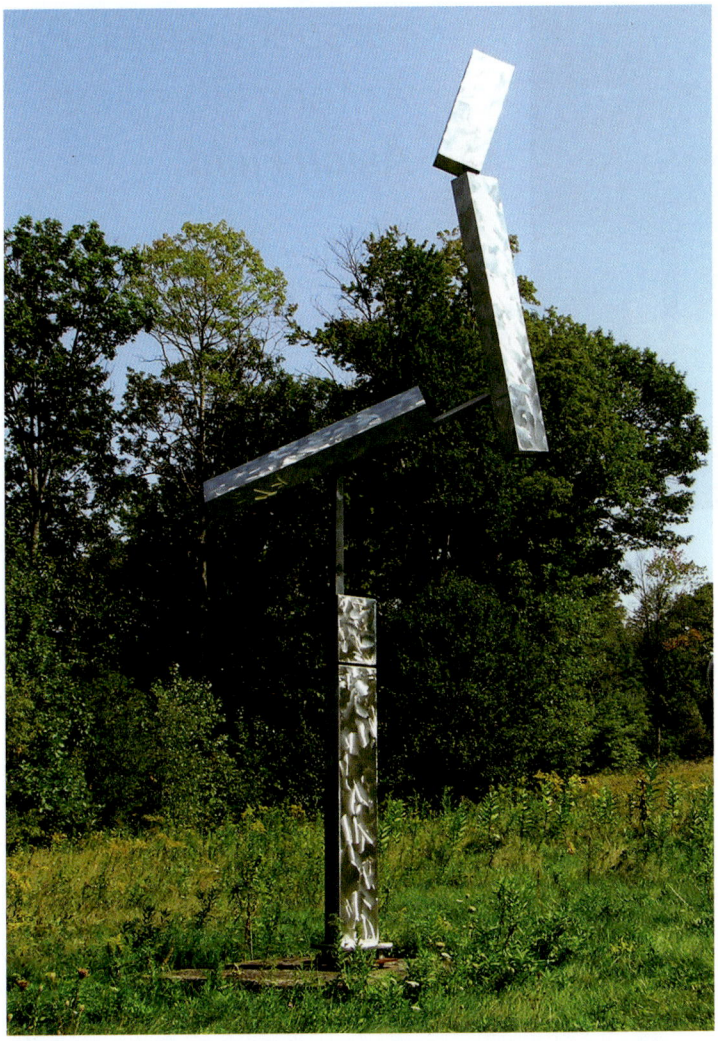

2.4.21 George Rickey, *Breaking Column*, 1986 (completed by the artist's estate, 2009). Stainless steel, 9'11⅜" × 5½". Contemporary Museum, Honolulu, Hawaii

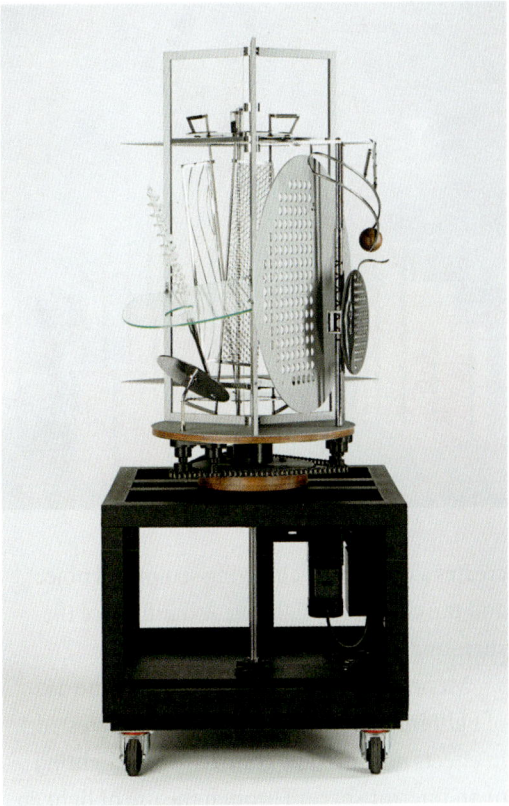

2.4.22 László Moholy-Nagy, *Light Prop for an Electric Stage*, 1929–30. Exhibition replica, constructed 2006, through the courtesy of Hattula Moholy-Nagy. Metal, plastics, glass, paint, and wood, with electric motor, 59½ × 27⅝ × 27⅝". Harvard Art Museums, Busch-Reisinger Museum, Cambridge, Massachusetts

appearance in a way that changes its original meaning or purpose. For Duchamp, the act of discovery (of conceiving the artwork) was the most important part of the artist's process; he believed that the artist's original interpretation of the appropriated object is what makes it art. "I chose it!" Duchamp exclaimed, creating endless possibilities for artists to redefine art as ideas, and to help us see things differently.

Kinetic and Light Sculpture

Technological advances in our society have created more opportunities for creativity. Sculptors who work with movement and light express their ideas in ways that would not have been possible just a century or two before. These moving and lighted sculptural works, similarly to those of the Constructivists, rely on mechanical engineering as well as the creative input of the artist.

Sculpture that moves is called **kinetic sculpture**. The American artist George Rickey (1907–2002) designed works that were carefully balanced so that they could pivot in a variety of directions and provide an infinite number of changing views. His *Breaking Column* is moved by the slightest current of air; it also has a motor, and moves even when there is no wind (**2.4.21**).

One of the first artists to merge movement, lighting, and performance into a single work was the Hungarian artist László Moholy-Nagy (1895–1946). Moholy-Nagy was interested in the work of the Constructivists and wanted to incorporate technology into his art. The sculpture *Light Prop for an Electric Stage* (**2.4.22**), initially created as a stage lighting device, eventually became the main character in a film, also by Moholy-Nagy. The work has a motor that moves a series of perforated discs so that they cross in front of the lighting unit. This

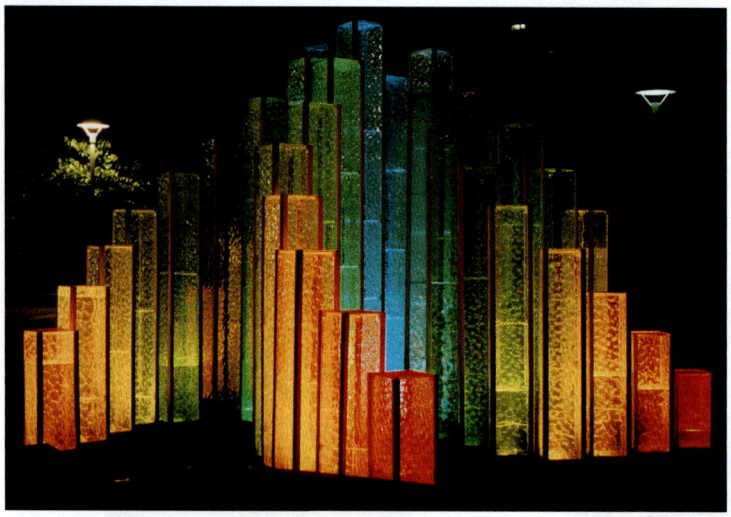

2.4.23 Athena Tacha in collaboration with EDAW of Alexandria, Virginia, *Star Fountain* (night view), 2009. Sandstone, cast stone, granite, brick, glass, animated RGB-LEDs. Muhammad Ali Plaza, Louisville, Kentucky

creates a constantly changing sculptural object, and the changes in lighting also influence the surrounding environment.

Moholy-Nagy's investigations into the use of light influenced artists who were interested in effects produced by controlling the lighting of an interior space. Through the use of light an artist can change how a viewer perceives a three-dimensional space. Carefully organized light projection can create the illusion that a surface exists in three dimensions even if it has only two.

Installations

Modern artists have explored many ways of expanding the range of sculpture as a **medium**. **Installation** sculpture involves the construction of a space or the assembly of objects to create an environment; we are encouraged to experience the work physically using all our senses, perhaps entering the work itself.

An installation work by the Greek-born artist Athena Tacha (b. 1936) deals with action. The movement in Tacha's work implies the action of dance, as the rhythms of her installations flow and repeat in graceful patterns. One gets the fullest impression of these rhythms at night, as her works are infused with constantly changing colored lighting. *Star Fountain* (**2.4.23**) is a series of vertical glass columns organized into a spiraling shape, with color changes over a four-minute time span. The reflecting water and the adjacent *Dancing Steps* enliven the surrounding plaza, enveloping those near by.

Medium (plural **media**): the material on or from which an artist chooses to make a work of art, for example canvas and oil paint, marble, engraving, video, or architecture

Installation: originally referring to the hanging of pictures and arrangement of objects in an exhibition, installation may also refer to an intentional environment created as a completed artwork

Perspectives on Art: Antony Gormley
Asian Field

*Antony Gormley (b. 1950) is a British sculptor whose work is concerned with the human form (**2.4.24a**). He developed the vast installation,* Asian Field *(1991–2003), as an art project beginning in 1983 (**2.4.24b**).*

Traveling to communities around the world, Gormley handed out fist-sized balls of clay and instructed participants to form them into an image of their own bodies, working as quickly as possible. Then participants were told to place the figure in front of them, at arm's length, and give it eyes. Gormley explains his approach to the human form and to Asian Field *in particular.*

The figures in my work are not portraits, they are corpographs: a three-dimensional equivalent of a photograph but which is left as a negative, as a void. They don't do anything, they don't represent anything, they are simply still objects in a moving world. And their meaning, if they have one, comes only when they act as a response to the lived time that surrounds them.

To make a work I have to stand very still and concentrate. One of the most direct ways to re-establish direct first-hand experience is to close your eyes and be in whatever that space is that you find yourself in. I've called this experience lots of things: the space of the body, the space behind appearance, the darkness of the body, the space of embodied consciousness.

My work is at its best when inserted into the stream of everyday life—whether that's in rooms, standing on walls or ceilings, or on the street. They may look at first hand like statues, but in fact they are simply lived moments made into matter. They identify a space that was occupied at a particular time by a particular body, and by implication can be occupied by anyone.

I am working in the most direct way I can to build a bridge between art and life. What the effect of my works is on their environment

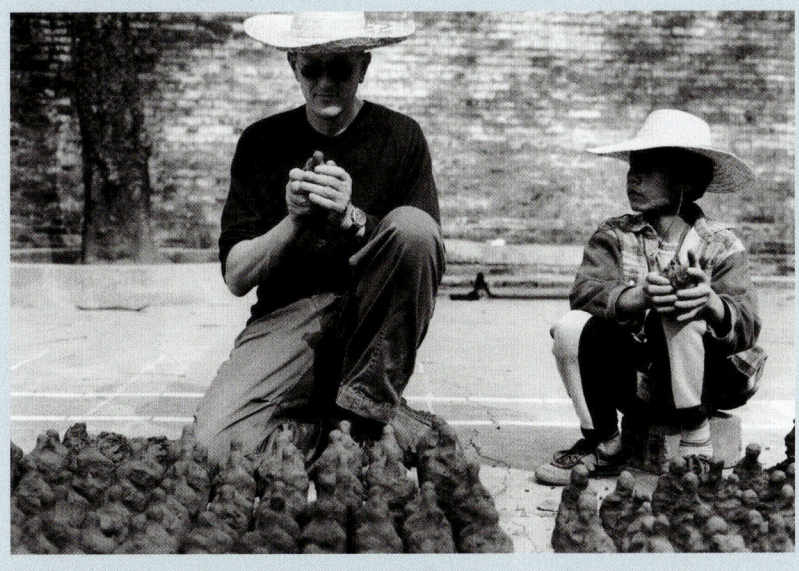

2.4.24a Antony Gormley, *Asian Field*, work in progress, 2003. Clay from Guangdong Province, China. Hand-sized clay elements made in collaboration with people from Xiangshan village. Xiangshan, China

and on the internal condition of others I have no control over. I think of my works as objects that act on the space in which they are placed, allowing it to become a space for imagination and reflection.

The *Field* works were made differently from much of my work, in collaboration with large numbers of people. In each rendition of the installation there are thousands of clay figures, each modeled by an individual hand. The figures have empty voids for eyes. This is because sight is itself a form of blindness. It wraps us in a world of names and forms that are immediately translated into symbols, signs, emblems.

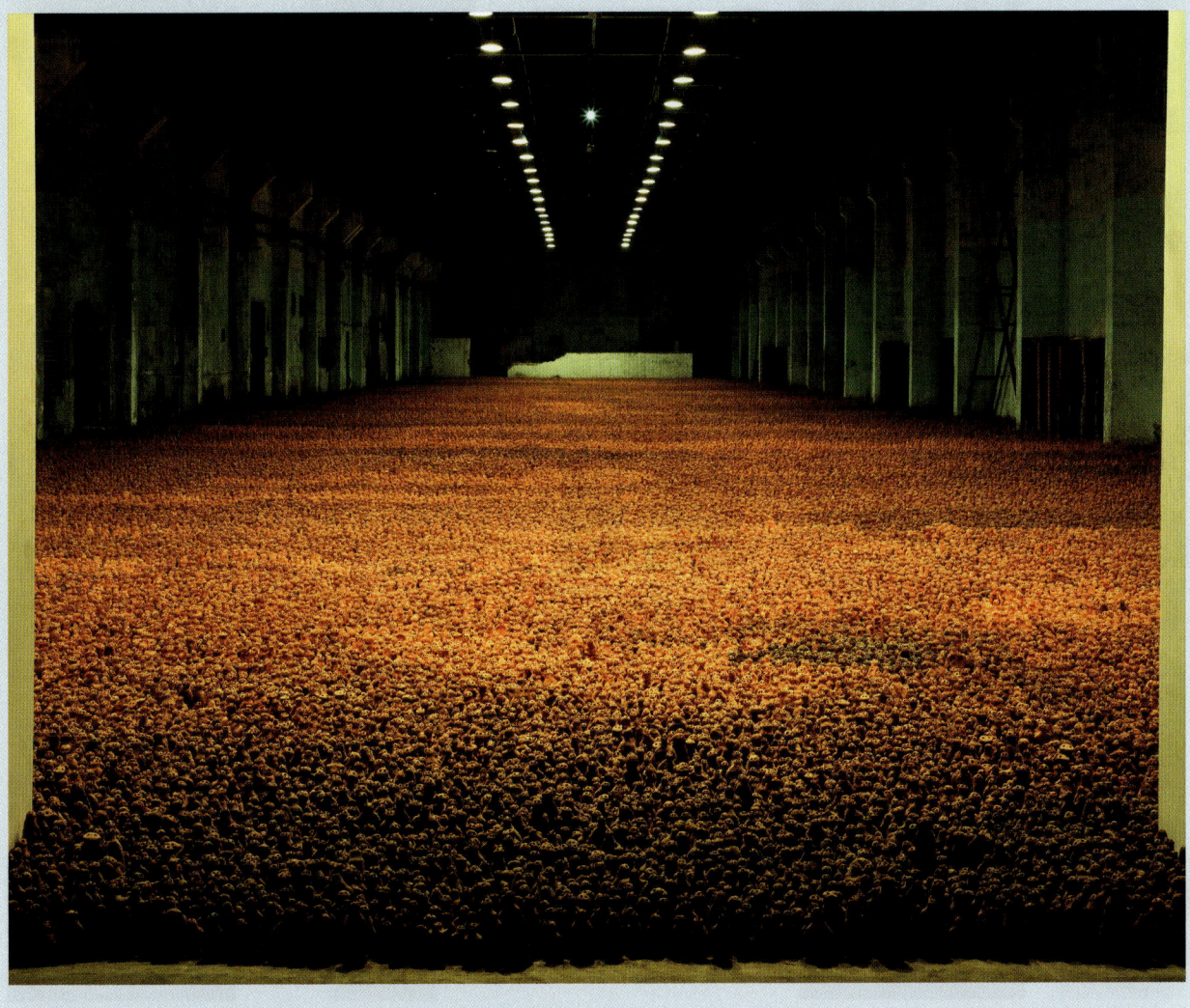

2.4.24b Antony Gormley, *Asian Field*, 2003. 210,000 hand-sized clay elements, installation view, warehouse of former Shanghai No. 10 Steelworks, China

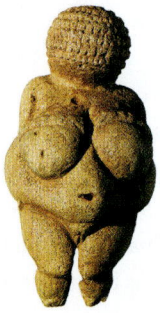

4.9.1 *Woman from Willendorf*, c. 24,000–22,000 BCE, p. 663

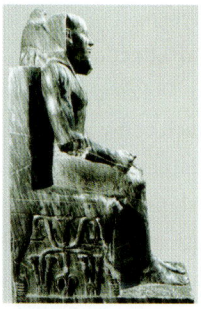

3.1.15 Statue of Khafre with Horus, Egypt, c. 2500 BCE, p. 375

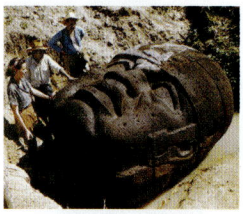

3.4.8 Colossal Olmec head, 1500–400 BCE, p. 434

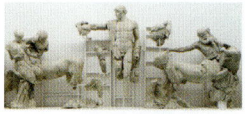

4.2.1 Apollo, Centaur, and Lapith, c. 460 BCE, p. 578

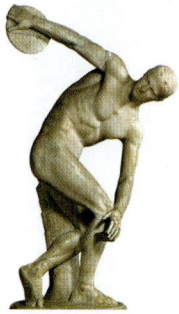

4.9.4 Myron, *Discus Thrower (Discobolos)*, c. 450 BCE, p. 666

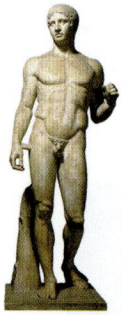

3.1.29 Polykleitos, *Doryphoros*, (Roman version) 120–50 BCE, p. 384

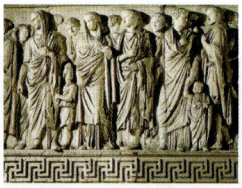

1.2.6 Imperial Procesion from the Ara Pacis Augustae, 13 BCE, p. 65

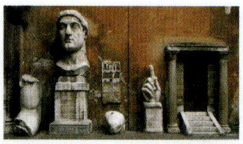

4.6.10 Remnants of colossal statue of Constantine, 325–26 CE, p. 635

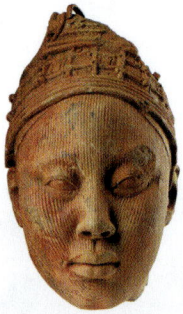

4.9.6 Head, possibly an Ife king, West Africa, 12th–14th century, p. 667

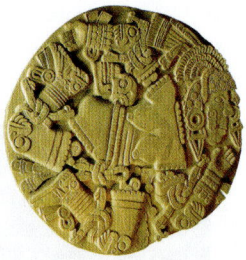

3.4.17 *The Dismemberment of Coyolxauhqui, Goddess of the Moon*, late Postclassic, p. 439

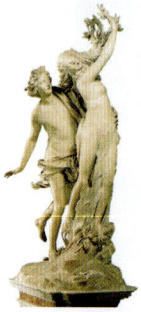

1.5.1 Gianlorenzo Bernini, *Apollo and Daphne*, 1622–24, p. 113

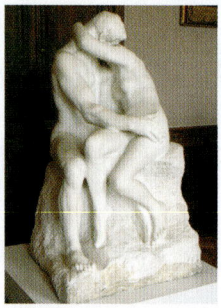

1.2.17b Auguste Rodin, *The Kiss*, c. 1882, p. 72

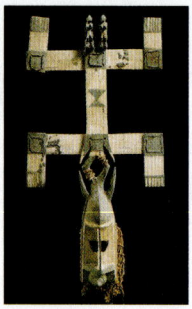

3.5.6a Kanaga mask, Mali, early 20th century, p. 450

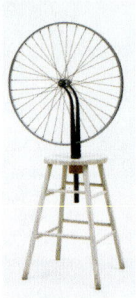

3.9.8 Marcel Duchamp, *Bicycle Wheel*, 1913, p. 529

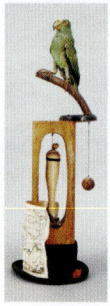

3.9.12 Joan Miró, *Object*, 1936, p. 531

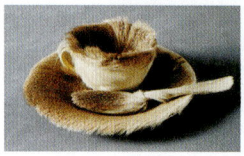

1.2.20 Méret Oppenheim, *Object*, 1936, p. 74

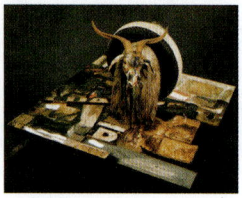

1.6.11 Robert Rauschenberg, *Monogram*, 1955–59, p. 132

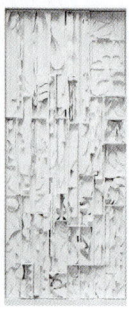

0.0.3 Louise Nevelson, *White Vertical Water*, 1972, p. 22

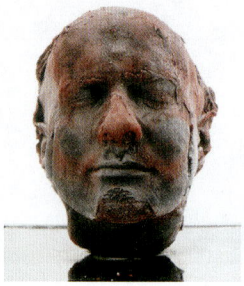

0.0.16 Marc Quinn, *Self*, 1991, p. 32

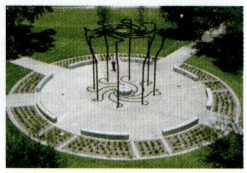

1.5.13 Nancy Holt, *Solar Rotary*, 1995, p. 120

2.5 Architecture

Architecture communicates important ideas; it has a special place in our lives. Architecture—three-dimensional art and design that surrounds and influences us—represents the safety of home, the strength of government, the energy of commercial enterprise, and the power of human innovation. It connects us to our history in a very real way: a historic building shows us how people lived in the past, while a new building adapts design ideas from previous eras to a contemporary context. Architecture suggests feelings of permanence and place. It is no wonder we all have an opinion about a new building, because a building inevitably affects all who see or enter it, whether or not they are aware of this.

Architectural space is the result of thoughtful design by an artist, or by a team of artists working to a common idea. The architect is the master planner who creates a building's overall design. Thoughtful design reflects a building's function and its intended role in the community. For example, an architect designing a college building will consider its users—the instructors and students—and will design classroom spaces that are well lit and flexible. Sometimes an interior designer is responsible for making the space inside appropriate for the building's intended use. In the case of a college classroom, an interior designer will choose colors and furnishings and plan the organization of the space in a way that reflects the needs of students and teachers. A landscape architect may be employed to organize the outdoor spaces around the building. This designer will plan the landscaping, parking, and entry and exit routes to be consistent with the rest of the structure. The architect, interior designer, and landscape architect actively communicate with the building contractors to ensure that the final construction will accord with the design team's intentions. Some good architectural design even acts as a symbol that identifies the function of the space. For example, many college buildings use such features as Greek columns to make reference to the foundations of Western civilization and academic endeavor.

Form: an object that can be defined in three dimensions (height, width, and depth)

Structure, Function, and Form

Architecture is principally concerned with structure, function, and **form**. The engineering and science of architecture strives to understand and control the forces pushing or pulling the structure of the building. These forces, called stresses, are constantly at work. When stresses pull they create tension, which lengthens and stretches the materials of the building. When stresses push they create compression, which can squash and shorten the same materials. Architectural engineers work to create balances between tension and compression so that the amount of push equals pull. Each kind of building material resists the stress of compression or tension differently. Architects measure the strength of the material so that they can anticipate and control the balance of forces at work. If balanced correctly, a building can stand for many thousands of years; if not, it may collapse.

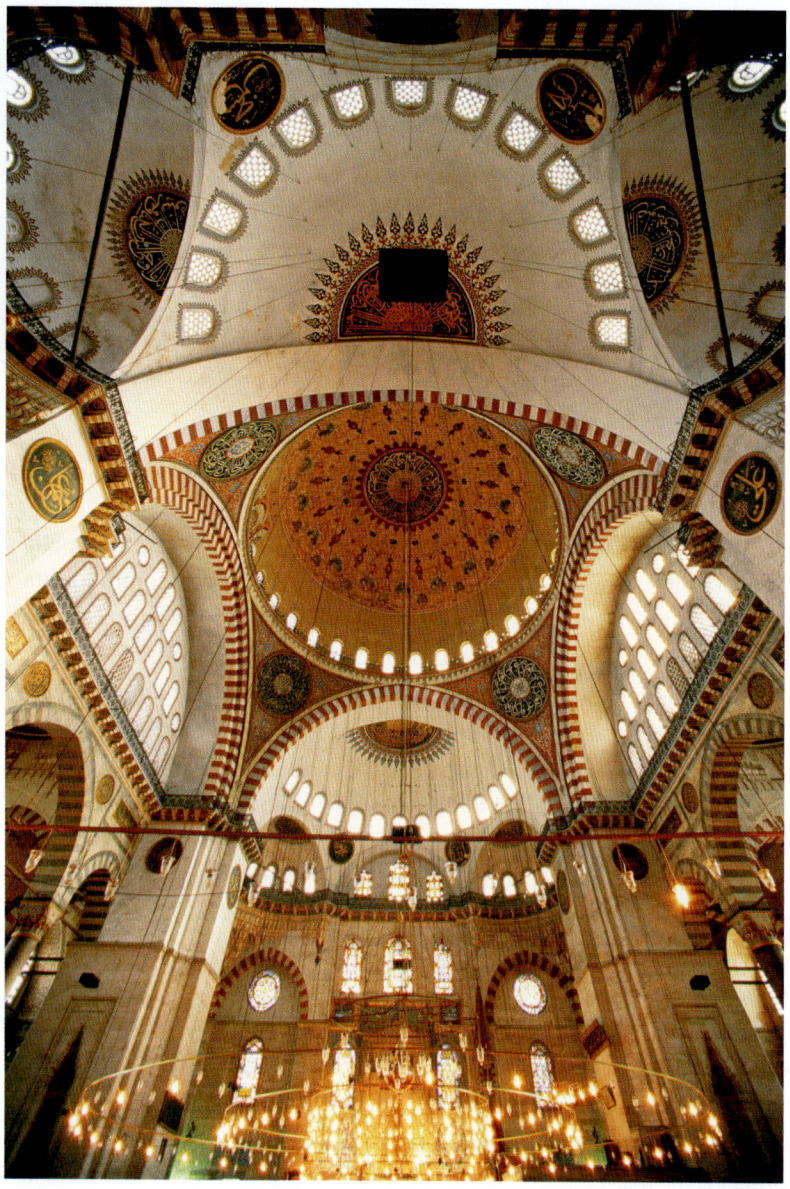

2.5.1 Sinan, Süleymaniye mosque, 1557, Istanbul, Turkey

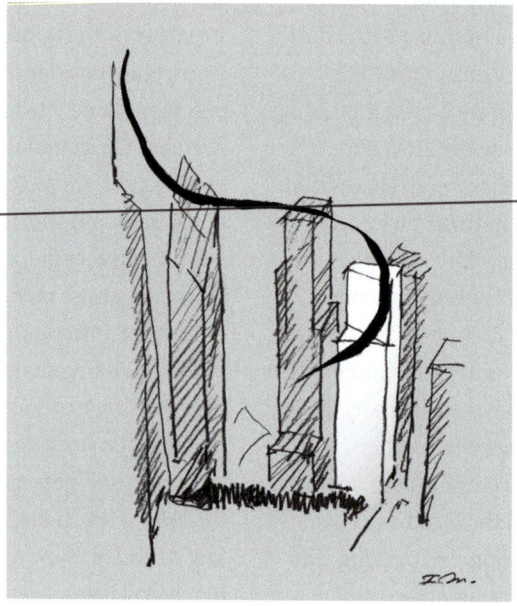

2.5.2 Fumihiko Maki, sketch of Four World Trade Center, 2006

The Turkish architect Sinan (1489–1588) was chief architect to the Ottoman court under Sultan Süleyman, who commissioned him to design the magnificent mosque shown in **2.5.1**. Sinan's visionary ingenuity and grasp of engineering principles enabled him to develop new ways of opening up the architectural space thus creating this extraordinary building, which includes not only the principal dome but also four half-domes around it. The skillful design, perfectly balancing all of the different parts, has enabled this elaborate and complex structure to endure for more than 500 years. The integration of light in this building is striking as the many windows created by the architect illuminate the upper portion of the domes. This draws the worshiper's attention upward, as if to the heavens, symbolically supporting the intended function as a place of worship.

The engineering of a building, or its structural integrity, dictates some of the design decisions. Wood-frame buildings may require waterproof external cladding to protect the timber from damp and rot. Tall office buildings may need to have a strong steel frame (or an alternative) to bear the combined weight of the whole structure (see p. 276).

An architect collects information about the planned location of the building, its place in the community, and its purpose; selects the appropriate building techniques; and decides which materials are needed to construct it.

The location, or site, influences the design. Is the building going to sit on a plain or a mountainside, in a city or a rural community, on a waterfront or in a desert? Each of these sites presents different challenges the design must answer. For example, a building facing the sea might need to be strong and resilient to resist the effects of storms, while one in a desert must be made of materials that can help keep the building cool.

Artists must consider the availability and cost of building materials when they plan their projects. The unique character of these materials—for example their flexibility, strength, **texture**, and appearance—also affects the architect's choices.

Although buildings can be some of the largest and most complicated man-made

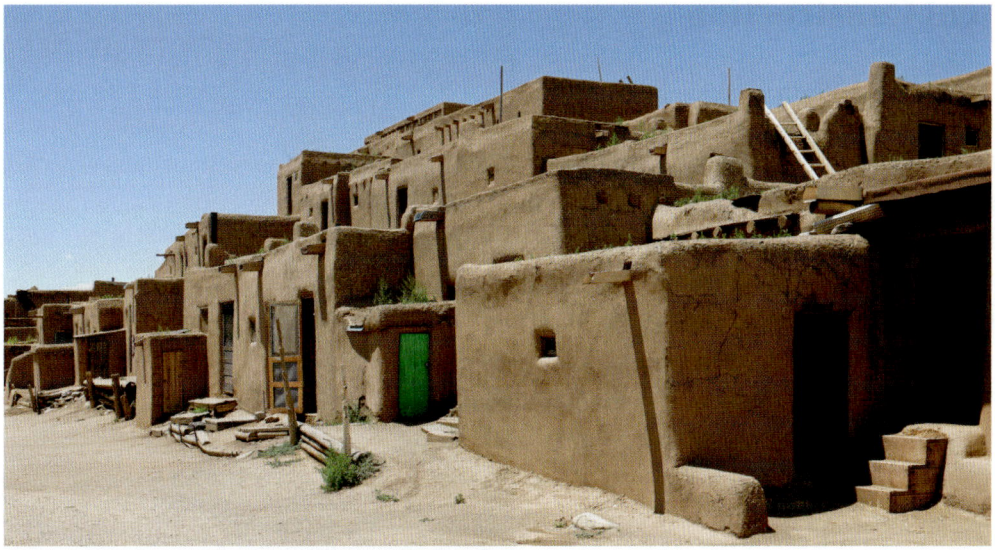

2.5.3 Taos Pueblo, New Mexico, pre-1500

objects, they usually begin from the simplicity of a drawing. Fumihiko Maki (b. 1928) created a simple drawing as he began working on a design for the New World Trade Center in New York City (**2.5.2**). The drawing shows how his building was designed to fit in with other buildings on or around the site by continuing a spiral design.

In a successful architectural work, the final appearance of a building's structure will also reflect—in some way—the community.

In Taos Pueblo, New Mexico, for instance, many buildings are made of adobe brick (**2.5.3**). Their character derives from the available materials, such as the abundance of sand and clay; perhaps the community has traditional standards, such as the building methods and styles of the native Pueblos and Spanish settlers. The architecture of New York City looks very different, but is based on similar principles. Generations of people have admired the coherent **composition** of the forms of the skyscrapers, like a **Cubist** painting, as if the community had somehow combined together as a single artist to make something beautiful (**2.5.4**).

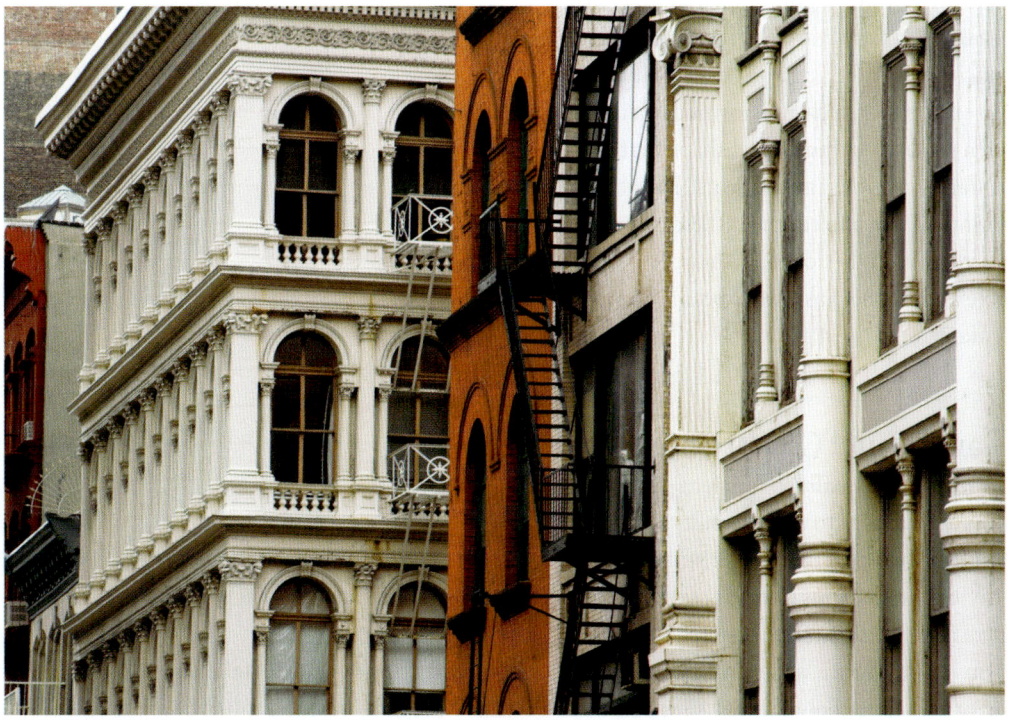

2.5.4 SoHo lofts, New York City

Texture: the surface quality of a work, for example fine/coarse, detailed/lacking in detail
Composition: the overall design or organization of a work
Cubism, Cubist: twentieth-century movement and style in art, especially painting, in which perspective with a single viewpoint was abandoned and use was made of simple geometric shapes, interlocking planes, and, later, collage; the Cubists were artists who formed part of the movement. "Cubist" is also used to describe their style of painting

Ancient Construction

Ancient cultures derived their building materials from the Earth. Stone, wood, and clay are plentiful and easily available, but they must be modified for use in architecture. When shaped and used with great care and skill, these raw materials can result in architecture that transcends time.

Basic Load-Bearing Construction

Probably the most direct way to build something is the apparently simple process of piling one stone or brick on top of another, as for example in a Maya pyramid. Such massive load-bearing works have occurred throughout history. Protruding out of the Guatemalan rain forest at Tikal are hundreds of such pyramids that rise sharply toward the sky, emphasizing their role as gateways to the gods. Maya pyramids primarily served as platforms for temples. The pyramid that makes up the support for Temple I is basically a carefully organized stack of stones (**2.5.5**). The weight of the temple structure at the top, which is a three-room building where Maya priests conducted religious rites, bears down on the stone platform beneath it, which, in turn, bears down on the stone platform beneath *it*, and so on, holding all the stones securely in place (**2.5.6**). Construction on this scale required sophisticated engineering and mathematical skills to ensure that such an enormous structure formed a perfectly symmetrical shape that would stand for thousands of years. The ability of the ancient Maya to engineer these massive structures using only stones, with the few tools available at the time, has always been a cause of wonder.

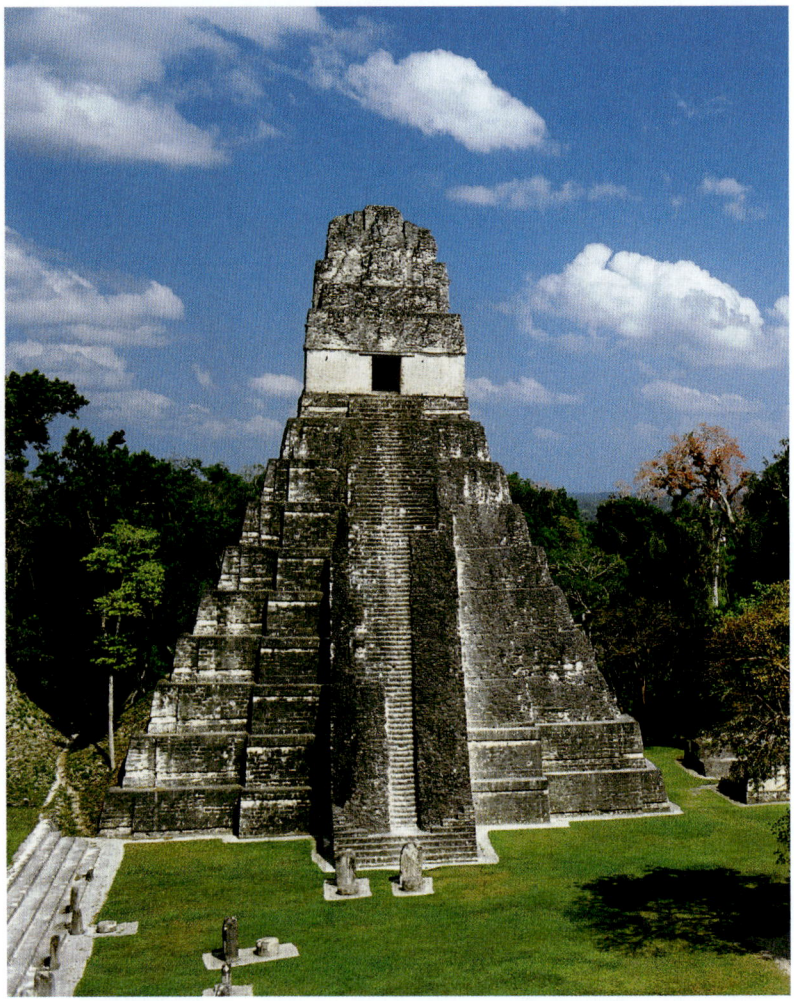

2.5.5 Temple I in the Great Plaza, Maya, c. 300–900 CE, Tikal, Guatemala

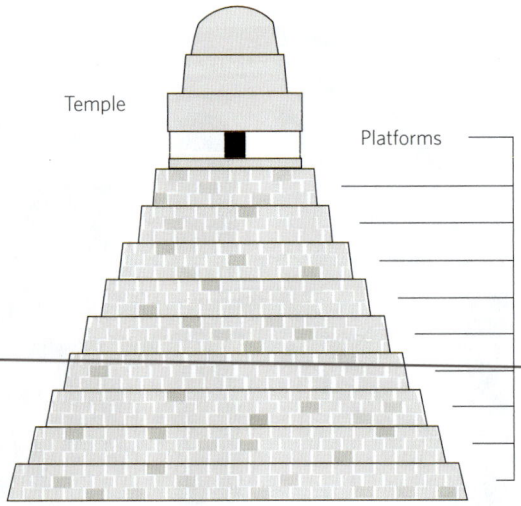

2.5.6 Basic load-bearing architecture: Maya pyramid

Post-and-Lintel Construction

The **monumental** quality of ancient pyramids stands as a testament to the ingenuity and will of humankind. But these impressive structures did not provide the spacious interiors we have come to expect in everyday architecture. In order to create an interior space, an architect must create a **span**, or a distance between two supports in a structure. One of the oldest and most effective ways of doing this is a system called post-and-lintel construction.

In basic **post-and-lintel construction** (**2.5.7**) the lintel rests on top of two posts.

Monumental: having massive or impressive scale
Span: the distance bridged between two supports, such as columns or walls

Post-and-lintel construction: a horizontal beam (the lintel) supported by a post at either end
Column: freestanding pillar, usually circular in section

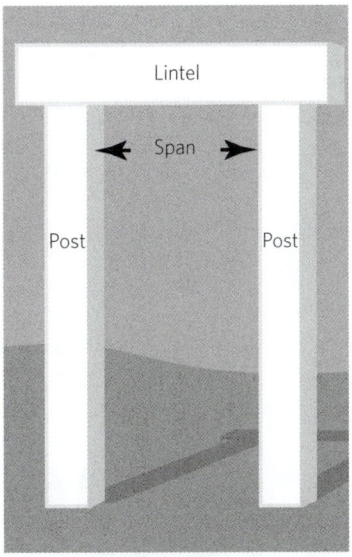

2.5.7 (right) Post-and-lintel construction

2.5.8 (below) Great Court at Temple of Amun-Re, Middle Kingdom, c. 950–730 BCE, Karnak, Egypt

Ancient Egyptian architects built the Temple of Amun-Re at Karnak by placing a series of post-and-lintel spans side by side to create a spacious interior, as seen in the Great Court (**2.5.8**). The temple also includes an architectural space known as a hypostyle hall, a room created by using a series of **columns**, or a colonnade, to support a flat ceiling. The hall was used by Egyptian priests for rituals to worship the god Amun-Re, while ordinary people stood outside in an open courtyard. Amun-Re's temple, still one of the largest religious structures in the world, is just one of many at Karnak. The material used for the posts and lintels, in this instance stone, needs to be strong enough to

2.5.9 (right) Kallikrates, Temple of Athena Nike, c. 421–415 BCE, Acropolis, Athens, Greece

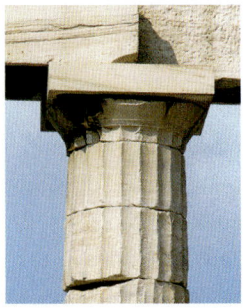

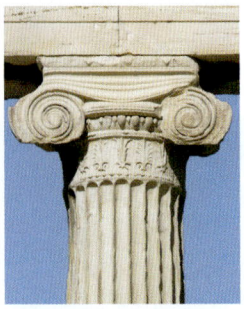

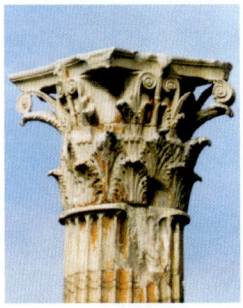

2.5.10 (above, from top) Doric, Ionic, and Corinthian capitals

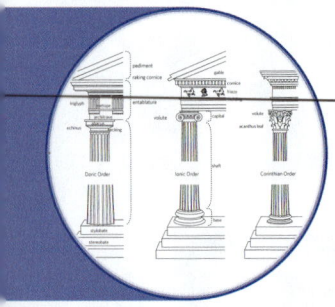

The use of post-and-lintel architecture by the ancient Greeks can be seen in three distinct styles: Doric, Ionic, and Corinthian: see **3.1.21, p. 380**

support the roof of the building to absorb the stresses placed on the columns and lintel.

The architects of ancient Greece must have been aware of the majestic architecture of the Nile Valley, where such monuments as the Temple of Amun-Re can be found. Greek architects of the era adapted the systems invented by the Egyptians and went on to become some of the world's greatest practitioners of post-and-lintel construction. They standardized the basic post, or column, an essential point of compression to support the weight of a building (see **2.5.9**). Classical Greek architecture is dominated by the use of columns, a structural element with three basic parts: **capital**, **shaft**, and **base**. The capital, or uppermost part of the column, supplies the transition point from the lintel to the shaft, or main vertical attribute of the post. The base acts as a stabilizing point where the building's weight is concentrated. Three different column styles help identify architectural orders (or stylistic distinctness). Doric columns have a plain round lozenge-shaped capital, Ionic are distinguished by a scroll-like formation called a volute, and Corinthian columns sport a leafy top modeled after the acanthus plant (**2.5.10**).

The ancient Greeks made a lasting impact on Western traditions in architectural style. The Romans quickly adopted Greek orders while adding their own new stylistic accents. Rome's architectural innovations then influenced the later styles of the **Renaissance** (see p. 271) and the **Baroque**, even being revived again in the eighteenth century to celebrate the rise of democratic government, especially in the US and France. The architectural character of Washington, D.C., with its many columns (the White House is a good example), reflects the ideals of democracy that the ancient Greeks instituted in order to free citizens of Athens to decide their own destiny.

Arches in Ancient Architecture

A limitation of early post-and-lintel architecture is that the lintels could not span large spaces. Stone, while enormously strong in compression, is fairly weak in tension. Since stone cannot stretch, its use risks creating a weakness in the middle of a span that can snap under heavy pressure. Architects who want to design large interior spaces in stone have to be aware of the weight of the building constantly pressing down. The ancient Babylonians in Mesopotamia (modern-day Iraq) and the Mycenaeans of early Greece both employed the **corbeled** arch (**2.5.11**) as a solution to this problem. The stepping inward of successive layers of stonework over the doorway allows for the compression created by the weight of the building to be directed outward through **cantilevered** (secured at only one end) stones, rather than downward. This reduces the pressure on the structure and allows the architect to design and span larger spaces.

Early inhabitants of the Greek coastline experimented with ways to open up interior spaces through the use of corbeled arches. The entrance to the Treasury of Atreus (also called the Tomb of Agamemnon: **2.5.12**), built around 1250 BCE, provides a glimpse into ancient construction using a corbeled arch. Although a lintel interrupts the space between the doorway and the arch above, the progressive cantilevering of stones above the lintel provides an additional opening so that more light can enter the chamber beyond.

The Romans perfected the rounded arch (**2.5.13**, p. 266), which was a more efficient way of distributing compressive stress over the

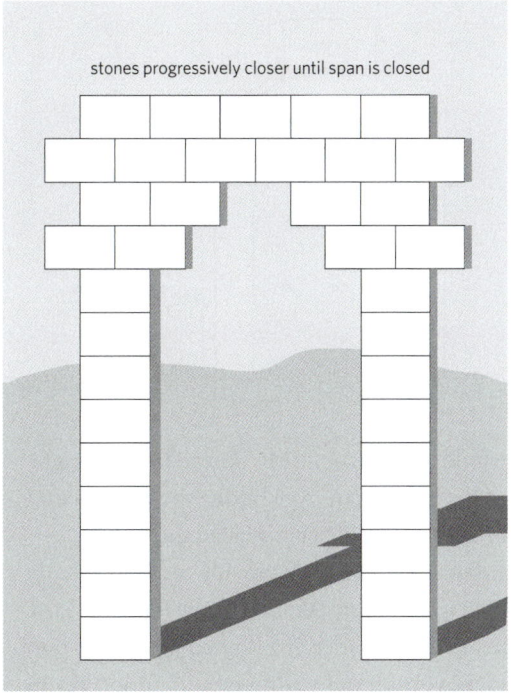

2.5.11 Corbeled arch

Capital: the architectural feature that crowns a column
Shaft: the main vertical part of a column
Base: the projecting series of blocks between the shaft of a column and its plinth
Renaissance: a period of cultural and artistic change in Europe from the fourteenth to the seventeenth century
Baroque: European artistic and architectural style of the late sixteenth to early eighteenth century, characterized by extravagance and emotional intensity
Corbeled: with a series of corbels—architectural feature made of stone, brick, wood, etc.—each projecting beyond the one below
Cantilever: a long beam or lintel that projects out from a structure beyond a support

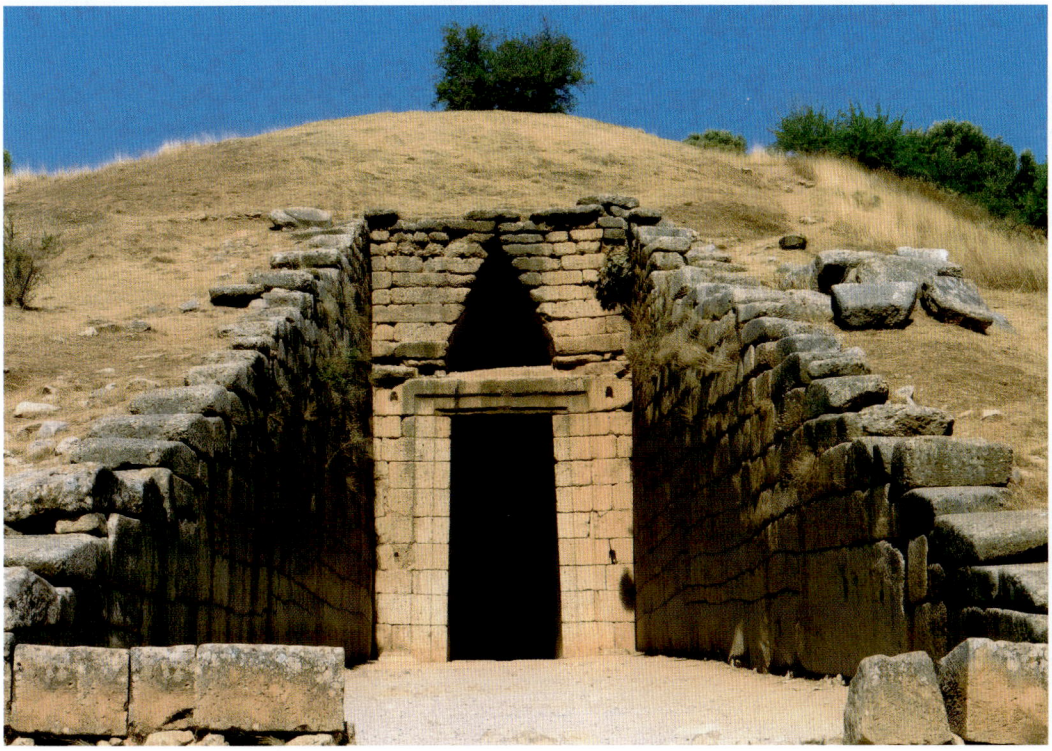

2.5.12 Entrance, Treasury of Atreus, *c.* 1250 BCE, Mycenae, Greece

2.5.13 Arch construction

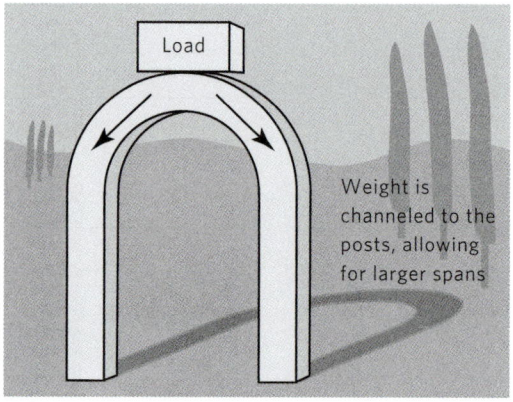

whole of the structure by spreading the weight of the building outward along the entire span of the arc. Its efficiency helped them span wider spaces than any previous architects had managed. The upper level of the Pont du Gard, in southern France, is a Roman **aqueduct**, built to move fresh water from mountain springs 30 miles away to the populated territories recently conquered by Rome (**2.5.14**). The lower level is a bridge across the river. The goal of the aqueduct was to create a consistent downhill path for the water: 1 in. down for every 33 in. along. The Romans made this impressive structure without any mortar holding the stones together, so perfectly were they cut to fit. After conquering an area, the Romans often built aqueducts and roads. These structures benefitted the local community, projected Roman imperial power, and enabled the army to move quickly across its new territory.

Vaults

Roman architects used three important architectural structures: the arch, vault, and dome. A **vault** is an arch that has been extended like a long hallway to create an open space overhead. The structural integrity of arches, vaults, and domes is created when the outward-pushing forces of the building weight are stopped by a heavy support, or buttress. The

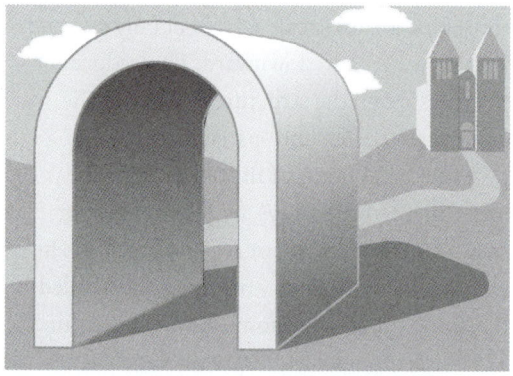

2.5.14 (below) Pont du Gard, first century CE, Nîmes, France

2.5.15 (right) Barrel vault

most common type of vault, the barrel vault, consists of a long, semicircular arch (**2.5.15**). The vault helped to span larger areas of an interior space; this was especially important during the European Middle Ages, as churches became more significant centers of community activities that more people wished to attend.

The Church of Sainte-Madeleine at Vézelay (**2.5.16**) in France was a stop along the Christian pilgrimage route to the holy church Santiago de Compostela in Spain. The builders of the **Romanesque** church at Vézelay needed to create a space that could accommodate thousands of religious pilgrims. Their solution was to use the barrel vault, but they had to deal with an important limitation of vault construction. Because the weight of the vault thrusts outward, the walls supporting it must be massive so as not to collapse. Vaulted **aisles** counteract this outward pressure on the walls and support both

Aqueduct: a structure designed to carry water, often over long distances
Vault: an arch-like structure supporting a ceiling or roof
Romanesque: an early medieval European style of architecture based on Roman-style rounded arches and heavy construction
Aisles: in a basilica or other church, the spaces between the columns of the nave and the side walls

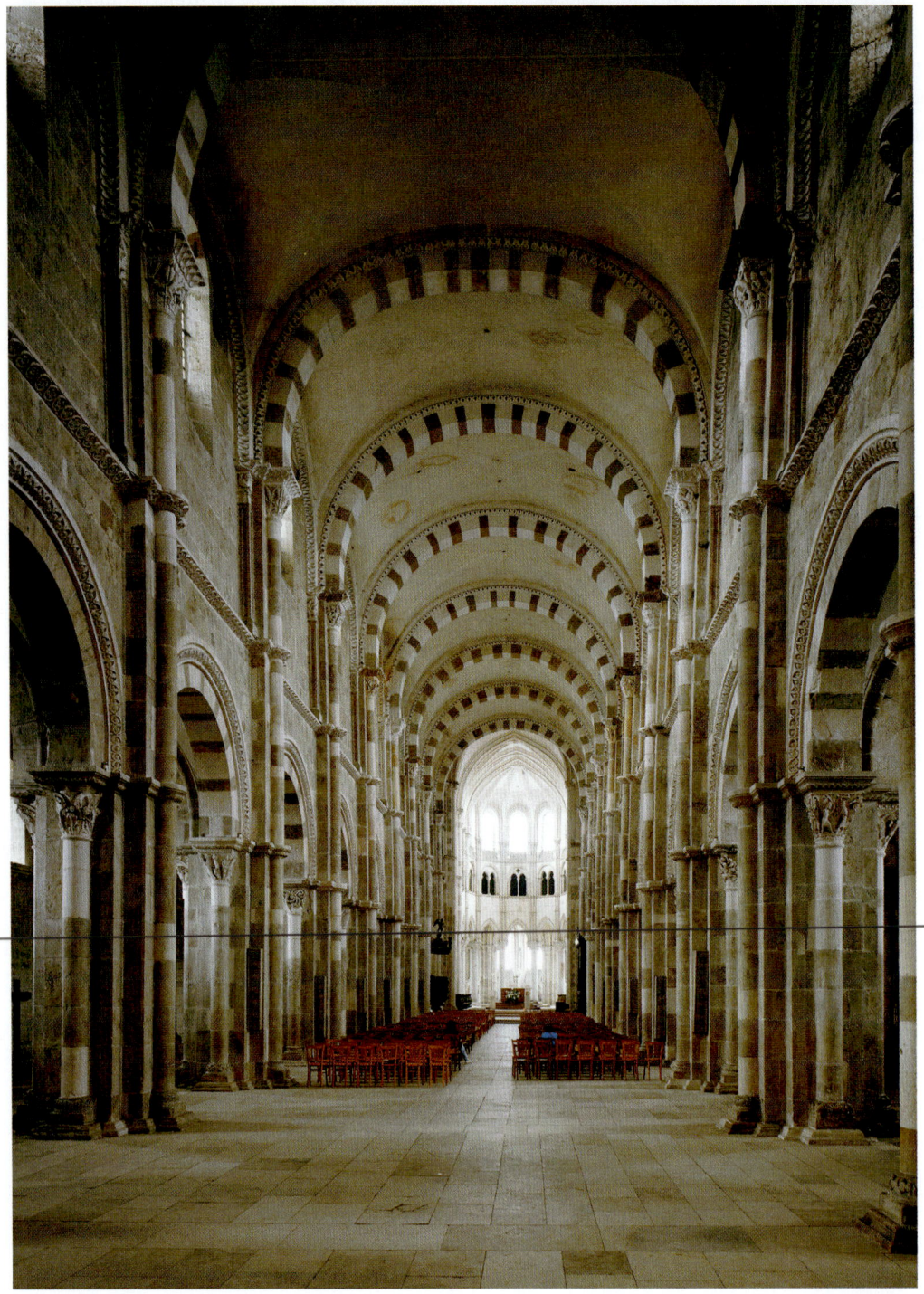

2.5.16 Church of Sainte-Madeleine, 12th century. Vézelay, France

Abbot Suger and the Dynamics of Gothic Architecture

The austere interiors of Romanesque churches led one particular church leader to seek innovations in the prevailing architectural style. Abbot Suger (1081–1151) had the Abbey Church of Saint-Denis, near Paris, France, rebuilt from its original Romanesque style to provide a much grander place for worship. The Abbey was the national church of France; it housed the remains of the country's patron saint, Saint Denis, and many French kings. Suger decided that the existing church was too small and lacked sufficient grandeur. Two ideas were central to Suger's new church: the worshiper should be bathed in divine light, and should feel lifted up toward heaven.

Adding larger windows to the structure could provide more light, but that would weaken the walls and increase the chance of a collapse. The walls of Saint-Denis had to be supported by external structures. Suger's plan incorporated an architectural structure called a **flying buttress** (see **2.5.17a** and **2.5.17b**), designed to transfer the weight of the ceiling outward beyond the walls. This idea worked well: as the walls no longer needed to bear the weight of the building, the windows could be much larger to allow light into the interior. Suger was still not satisfied, however, because the light was not yet "divine."

Suger had seen small colored-glass windows in German churches and decided that the methods used to make these smaller windows could be applied on a larger scale. By dividing up the window spaces into components of a larger

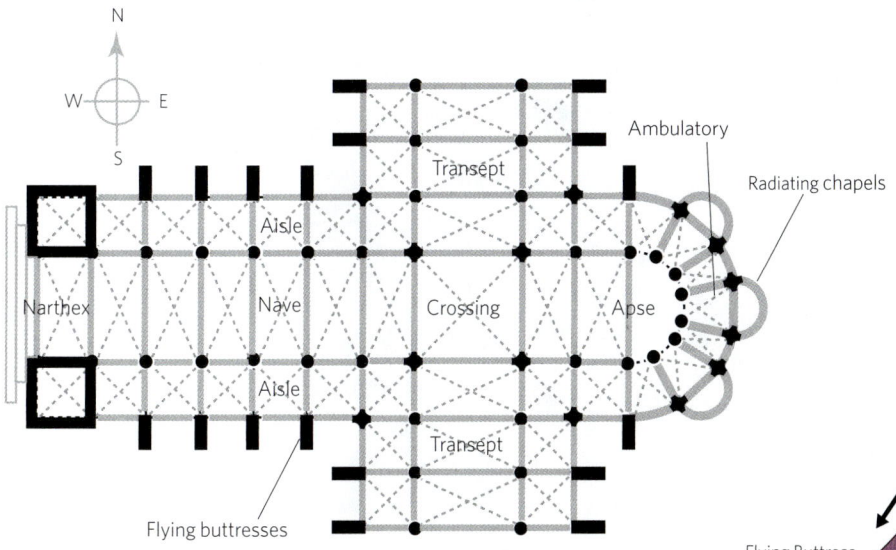

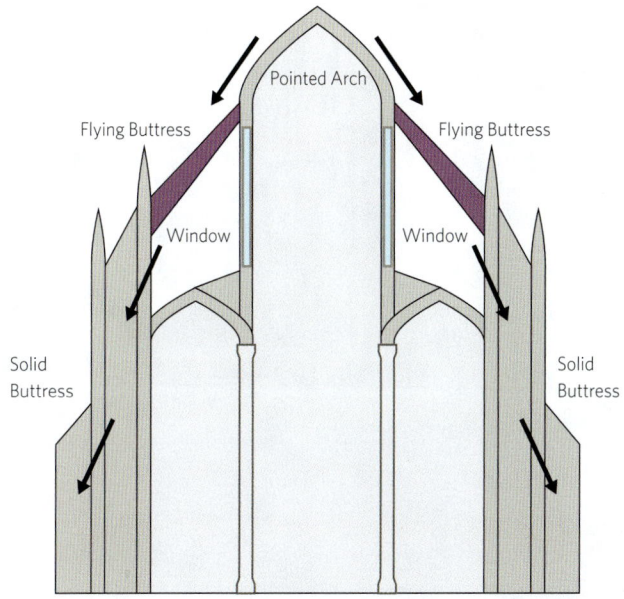

2.5.17a (above) Gothic architectural features

2.5.17b (right) Weight transfer in Gothic cathedral engineering

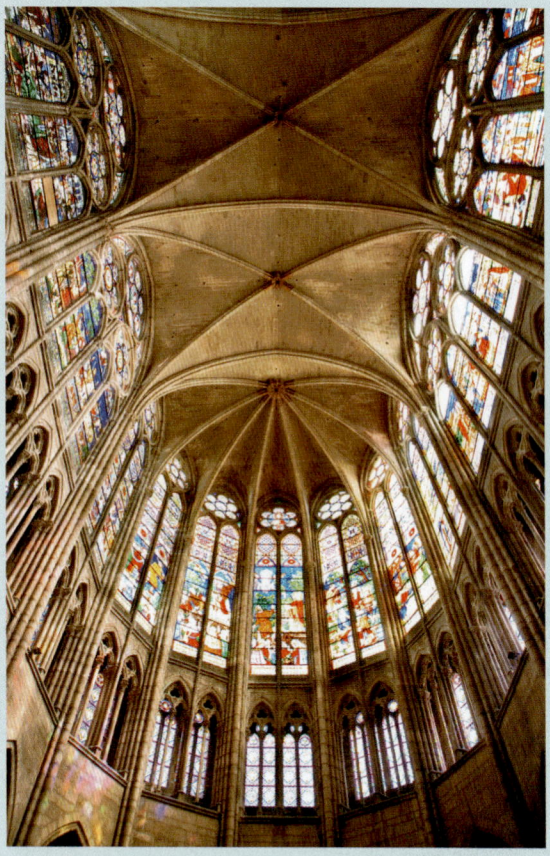

2.5.18 Elongated stained-glass windows and soaring rib vaults, Abbey Church of Saint-Denis, France

design, Suger's glaziers were able to make enormous **stained-glass** windows (**2.5.18**). The light would pass through images based on biblical narratives and be projected onto the worshiper. This was Suger's "divine light."

What about Suger's other requirement, that the worshiper feel lifted up toward heaven? The rounded arch of Romanesque churches tended to appear squat, and Suger wanted an arch that would raise the worshiper's gaze upward. He achieved this by adding a point to the arch. **Pointed arches** are structural features that help conduct the downward thrust of the vault outward, but they also have a strong upward visual **emphasis**. They could be arranged so that two vaults intersected to form **rib vaults**, which could be repeated in rows to open up long areas. Often associated with pointed arches, rib vaults appear in some earlier structures, but they were used throughout Saint-Denis. Suger, through his role in creating this remarkable building, was pivotal in establishing this highly influential architectural style, which came to be known as Gothic.

sides of the **nave**. **Groin vaults** can be seen as intersecting v-shapes in the ceiling between the arches of Vezelay and were an innovation that expanded the space where two vaults intersected, opening up even more architectural space. Even though Romanesque churches are large enough for plenty of pilgrims and worshipers, the thick walls have only small windows, creating dark and gloomy interior spaces. One visionary, named Abbot Suger, was not satisfied with the dreariness of Romanesque architecture and embarked on the formulation of a new, more dynamic style that was to become one of the most important and influential movements in Western architecture (see Box: Abbot Suger and the Dynamics of Gothic Architecture).

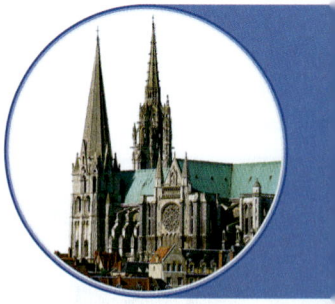

Chartres Cathedral in France is another example of Gothic engineering designed with flying buttresses: see **3.2.25, p. 407**

Flying buttress: an arch built on the exterior of a building that transfers some of the weight of the vault
Stained glass: colored glass used for windows or decorative applications
Pointed arches: arches with two curved sides that meet to form a point at the apex
Emphasis: the principle of drawing attention to particular content in a work
Rib vault: an arch-like structure supporting a ceiling or roof, with a web of protruding stonework
Nave: the central space of a cathedral or basilica
Groin vault: an architectural feature created by the intersection of two vaults

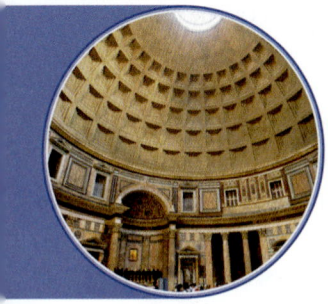

The Pantheon is an iconic Roman domed building that influenced similar structures that came after it: see **3.1.34, p. 387**

Domes

Abbot Suger had said he wanted his church to be more impressive than the Church of Hagia Sophia (Holy Wisdom) in Constantinople (modern Istanbul, Turkey). Hagia Sophia is a magnificent Byzantine (Late Roman, with Eastern influences) structure that had already been standing for more than 500 years by Suger's time. Its most impressive feature is its enormous **dome** roof (**2.5.19**). Structurally, a dome is like an arch rotated 360 degrees on its vertical **axis**. Shaped like an umbrella or a ball cut in half, it is a very strong structure. Domes can span large areas, because, as in other arch structures, the weight of the dome is dispersed outward toward the walls. Most dome constructions require the support of thick walls or some other system for distributing the weight. The dome of Hagia Sophia is so large and high that, for nearly 1,000 years, it was the largest interior space of any cathedral in the world. Prior to that, the Pantheon, a temple to the gods of Rome, had established the standard for all later domed buildings, including the Hagia Sophia.

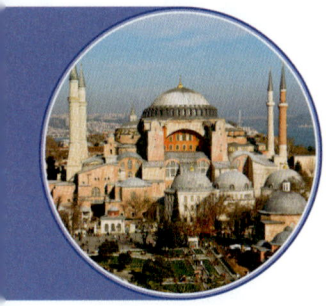

The Hagia Sophia is an architectural marvel that has pendentives to transition from a round dome to a square support: see **3.2.6, p. 395**

Dome: an evenly curved vault forming the ceiling or roof of a building
Axis: an imaginary line showing the center of a shape, volume, or composition
Clerestory windows: a row of windows high up in a church to admit light into the nave
Pendentive: a curving triangular surface that links a dome to a square space below

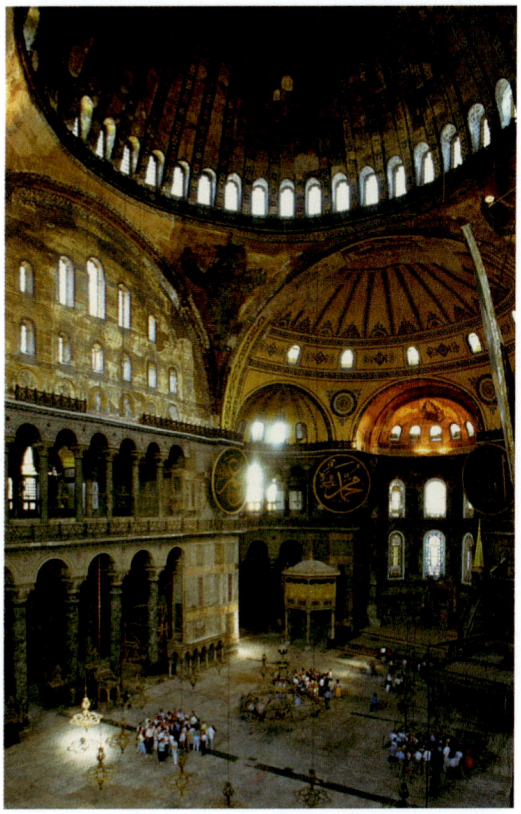

2.5.19 Hagia Sophia, 532–35 CE, Istanbul, Turkey

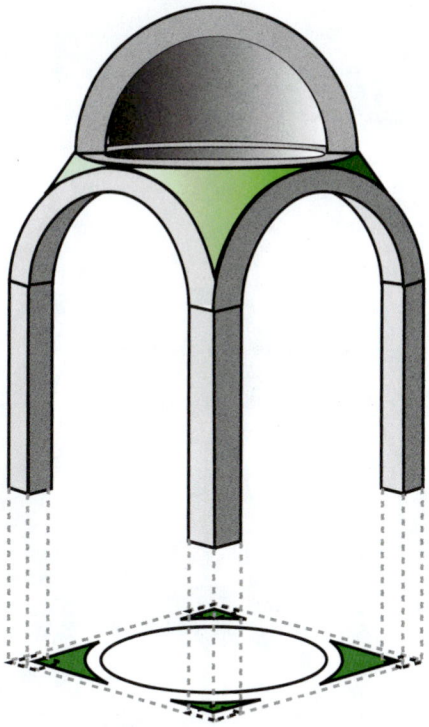

2.5.20 Pendentives

The inside of Hagia Sophia is illuminated by a series of **clerestory windows** in the lower portion of the dome and in the walls just below it. The dome rests on four arches. **Pendentives** (**2.5.20**) elegantly transfer the load of the circular dome to the four massive pillars of the square building beneath it. It is no wonder that Suger admired and revered the architecture of this building.

Post-and-Beam (Wooden) Architecture

The post-and-beam construction technique (**2.5.21**) has been used to build some of the world's finest wooden architecture. Two of the oldest wooden buildings in the world are in the grounds of the Buddhist Horyu-ji (Horyu Temple) in Nara, Japan (**2.5.22**). The construction of the Horyu-ji complex was the idea of the Japanese emperor Yomei, who hoped to gain spiritual favor so he could recover from illness, but he died before work started. In 607 Empress Suiko and Crown Prince Shotoku

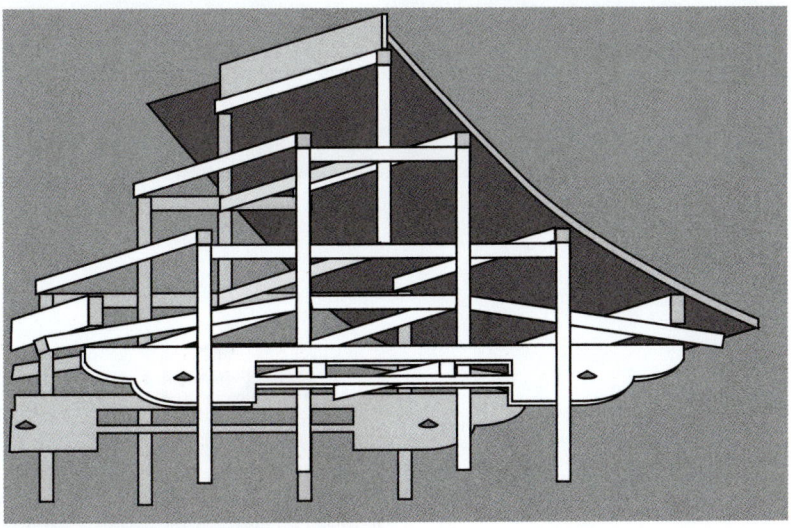

2.5.21 Post-and-beam architecture

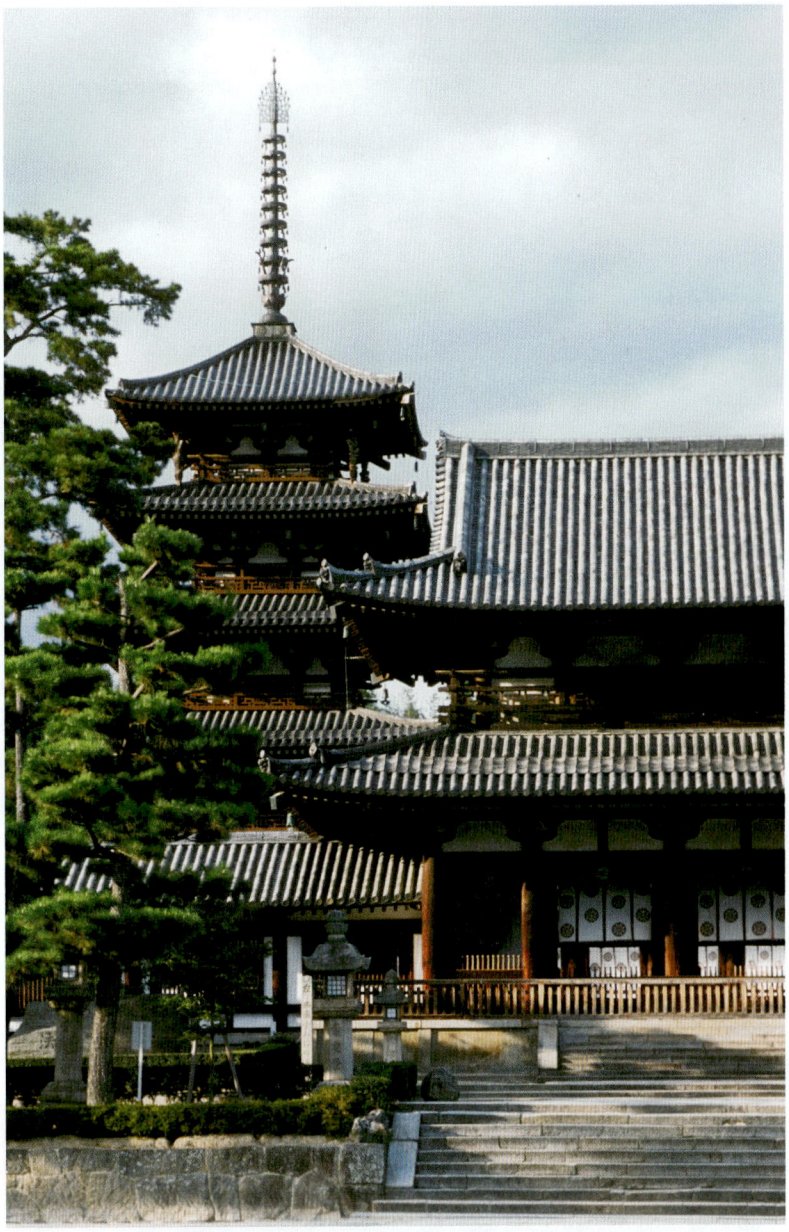

2.5.22 Horyu-ji (Horyu Temple), Kondo and pagoda, *c.* 7th century, Nara, Japan

fulfilled the emperor's dying wish and built the first temple in the complex. Since then it has withstood the ravages of time, and is an example of the durability of well-constructed wooden buildings.

These buildings use a complex post-and-beam design that is both beautiful and structurally sound. Crossbeams and counter-beams create a series of layers supporting the elaborate curved roof. The main building of the complex, the Kondo, is almost 61 ft. long by 50 ft. wide. This same structural design also enabled the architects to construct buildings that were very tall: the Goju-no-To (Five-story Pagoda) is 122 ft. tall. The pagoda's height was designed to impress rather than serve any practical purpose, since it is not possible to enter the top four floors.

Classical Architectural Styles

Since the fall of the Roman empire, architects of Western civilization have sought to revive the majesty displayed in the architectural style of the Greeks and Romans. The Romans had incorporated the unique architectural designs of the Greeks into their own after conquering Greek territory by 46 CE. These buildings endured a millennium of disrepair, surviving the ravages of time to a significant degree and affirming the great architectural engineering of the ancients. As Italian city-states, such as Florence, gained greater economic power in

Gateway to Art: The Taj Mahal
Engineering Eternity

In 1631, the Mughal Emperor Shah Jahan experienced a terrible personal tragedy when his third wife, Mumtaz Mahal, died in childbirth. Mumtaz, a Persian princess, had devoted her life to Shah Jahan, even, while pregnant, accompanying him on multiple military campaigns. The Shah's grief was so profound he dedicated all of his vast resources to the creation of a mausoleum complex in her honor that would endure throughout eternity.

The Shah assembled a team of architects and engineers who, under his supervision, would build a symbol of his love that could defy the instability of this world. The lead architect was probably Ustad Ahmad Lahauri, who borrowed design elements from Persia, India, and Turkey, incorporating them into a masterpiece of Islamic symmetry. The Taj Mahal (**2.5.23**) was built of white marble with a unique crystalline character that absorbs and radiates the light of northern India. When it was first constructed, many artists created lavish decorative work for the buildings on the site, including mosaic inlays, relief carvings, gold details, and inlaid precious stones.

2.5.23 View of the Taj Mahal from the Yamuna River, Agra, India

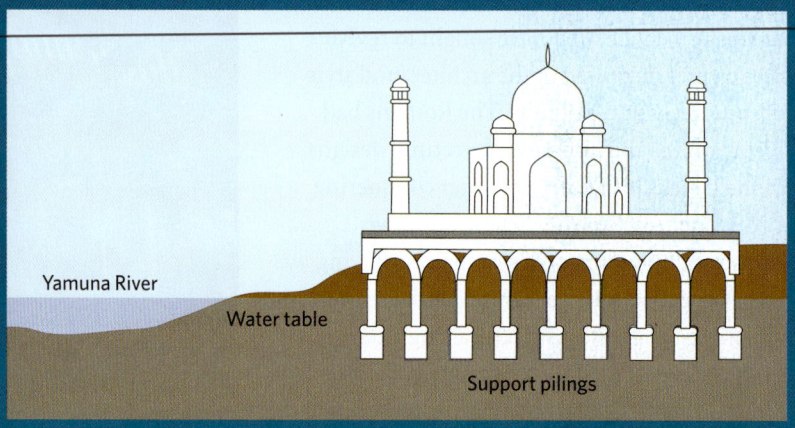

2.5.24 Diagram illustrating the support structure of the Taj Mahal

The central dome is 58 ft. in diameter and 213 ft. tall. The structure is completely symmetrical both when viewed from above and from any of its four sides. Four domed chambers emanate from this central dome, balanced on an octagon-shaped platform. Four towers called minarets, each 162 ft. high, frame the corners of the large structure. The minarets and pointed domes are characteristic of Islamic art.

Because Shah Jahan wished for a pastoral site, the complex was built next to the Yamuna River, away from the hustle and bustle of nearby Agra. Because the building was so close to the river, which would rise and fall with the seasons, a clever combination of stone filler material and wooden supports was constructed to hold the foundation in place.

The promise of a masterwork that would endure throughout eternity has been challenged in recent years, as experts have reported threats to the longevity of the building. Discoloration of the marble has led some to believe that polluted air, produced as India grows into a world economic power, is causing a yellowing of the marble surfaces. That concern is dwarfed by more serious issues regarding the integrity of the structure's foundation-support system as river conditions change. The support structure (**2.5.24**), which incorporates submerged sal (a teak-like timber) and ebony wood, may be in jeopardy as river levels drop, allowing the wood to dry out and contract. Recent water-management projects leave the riverbed nearly dry for months. Cracks have been observed in the Taj Mahal's marble structure and many fear that this building, which has so far transcended time, may not be able to survive the realities of the mortal world for ever.

For the other Taj Mahal Gateway boxes, see p. 136, p. 412, and p. 594

Central-plan church: church design, often in the shape of a cross with all four arms of equal length

Rococo: an eighteenth-century style in France characterized by organic forms, ornate extravagance, and whimsy

the fourteenth century, it became possible to erect large architectural projects in homage to the monumental Classical ruins that dotted the Italian and Greek landscapes. So, it was natural that the architects of the Renaissance looked to the Greeks and Romans for inspiration.

One of the great architects of the High Renaissance who drew inspiration from the ancients was Donato Bramante (1444–1514). Bramante is credited with introducing the architectural style of the High Renaissance when he built a memorial at the place where St. Peter was believed to have been crucified. The Tempietto (Italian for "small temple") is a **central-plan** church with a dome in Rome, Italy (**2.5.25**). The circular plan and dome reflect influences from Roman domed structures, for example the remains of Hadrian's villa at Tivoli, and colonnaded Greek temples. Bramante, like many Renaissance architects, particularly sought to design works that used geometric shapes and forms, such as circles, spheres, and cylinders.

The architectural style of the Greeks and Romans was once again revived during the mid-eighteenth century. This renewed Classical style, appropriately labeled Neoclassicism, was a reaction against such opulent and ornamented styles as **Rococo** (see the palace of Versaille, p. 484), which had dominated the previous century. Rococo was a decorative style characterized by asymmetrical balance,

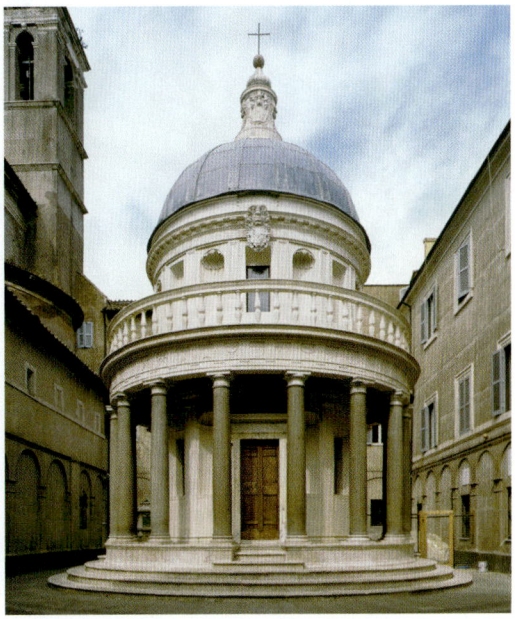

2.5.25 Donato Bramante, Tempietto of San Pietro in Montorio, c. 1502. Rome, Italy

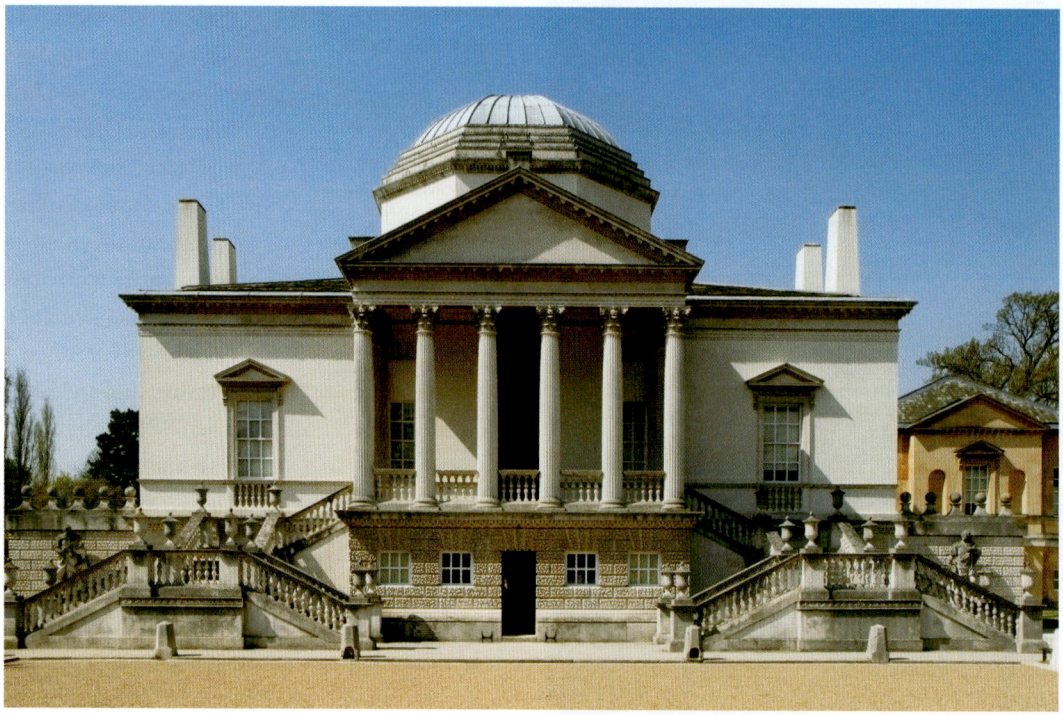

2.5.26 Lord Burlington, Chiswick House, 1729. Chiswick, London, England

abundant curves, and opulent finishes, unlike the more reserved Classical architectural style that dominated the Italian Renaissance. Neoclassicism sprang from the orderly attention to simple geometric shapes and forms that had characterized the architectural styles of the ancients. One of the first expressions of Neoclassical architecture was designed by an English aristocrat named Richard Boyle, better known as Lord Burlington. His design for Chiswick House (**2.5.26**) exemplifies the character of earlier Classical styles, but also integrates more contemporary elements, such as the chimneys that straddle the domed central roof. The design reflects an interest in the historical beginnings of Western architecture combined with the practical concerns of the eighteenth century.

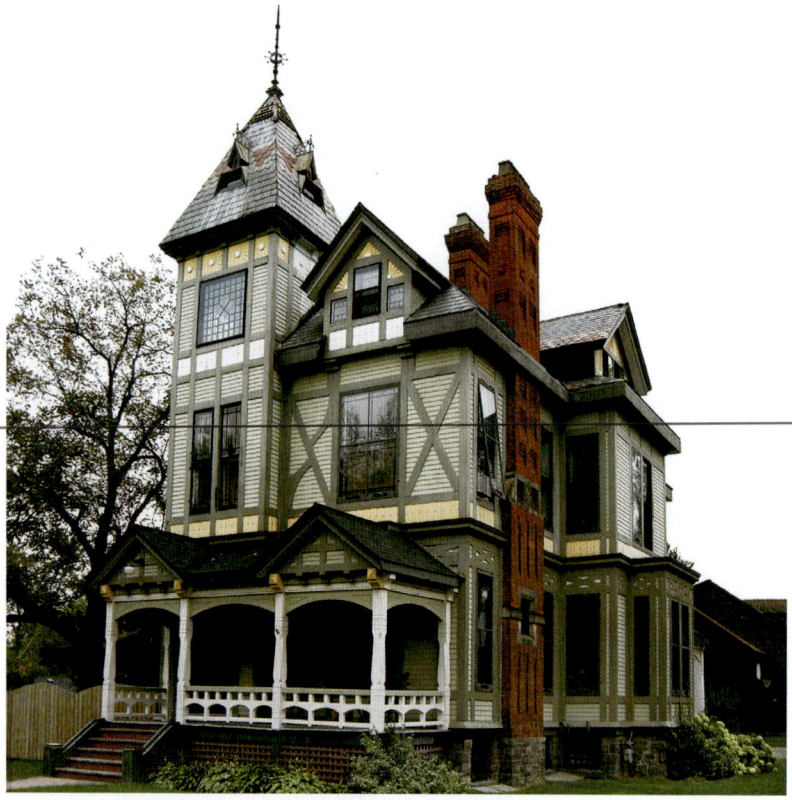

2.5.27 Stick Style house using balloon framing, Brockville, Ontario, Canada

The Emergence of the Methods and Materials of the Modern World

A new and different type of construction, made of wood, was invented in the United States in 1832. Balloon framing (**2.5.27**) involves the fabrication of lightweight wooden frames to support the structure, instead of utilizing heavy timbers. It was introduced when the advent of power sawing could efficiently and economically produce smaller cross-section lumber from saw logs. The Stick Style took advantage of balloon framing to support a decorative design that often used asymmetry with steep roofs to create a dynamic visual statement. Originally balloon framing was a derisive term used by builders who stayed with traditional building methods and felt the new method was too fragile to support a building. Today, however, most houses in America are built using this method.

In the nineteenth century, iron, steel, and concrete became both less costly and more widely available, and so came into common architectural use. New possibilities emerged as architects began to examine innovative ways to control tension and compression. Buildings could be built taller and in different configurations. Architects found exciting new ways to distribute the stress forces in their buildings. New types of building emerged, and the use of previously untried materials made buildings look radically different.

Cast-Iron Architecture

Cast iron has been available to humankind since ancient times. Iron is a more flexible material than stone. Molten iron can be cast in a mold to almost any shape, but it was not until the eighteenth century that it could be smelted in large enough quantities to play a significant role in building. An important example of the use of cast iron during the Industrial Revolution was the Crystal Palace, designed by Sir Joseph Paxton (1803–1865) for the Great Exhibition of 1851 in London (**2.5.28**). This event was intended to promote trade, and to showcase Great Britain's goods, services, horticulture, and technical innovation—for which the building was a very good advertisement. The walls and roof were of glass, supported by the skeletal cast-iron structure. The building was more than a third of a mile long; it was completed in only eight months by 2,000 men; and it used 4,500 tons of cast iron and 990,000 square feet of glass. Paxton's expertise in greenhouse building was applied to the design of this massive temporary space and the use of mass-produced parts heralded the later rise of Modernist architecture.

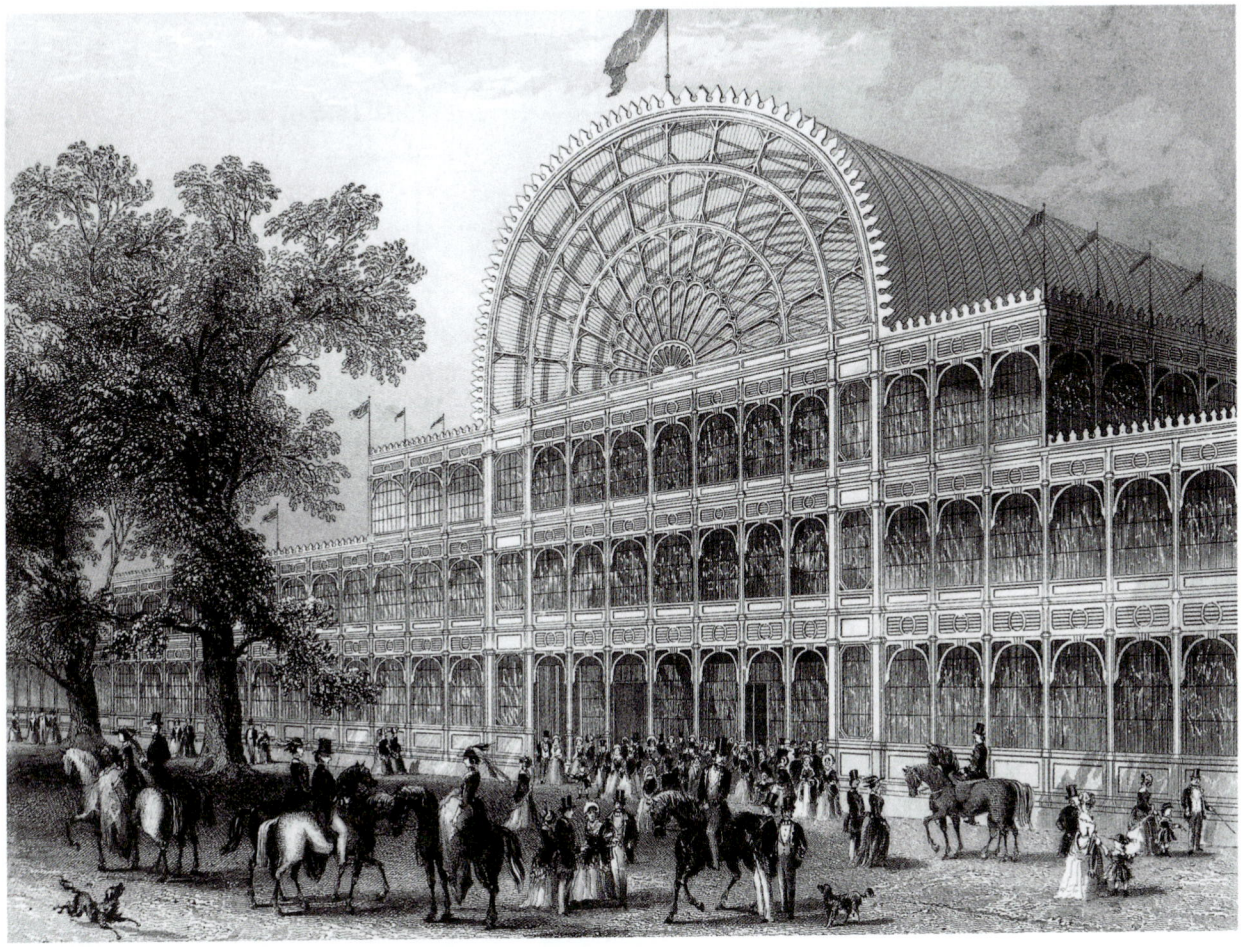

2.5.28 Joseph Paxton, Crystal Palace, 1851, London. 19th-century engraving

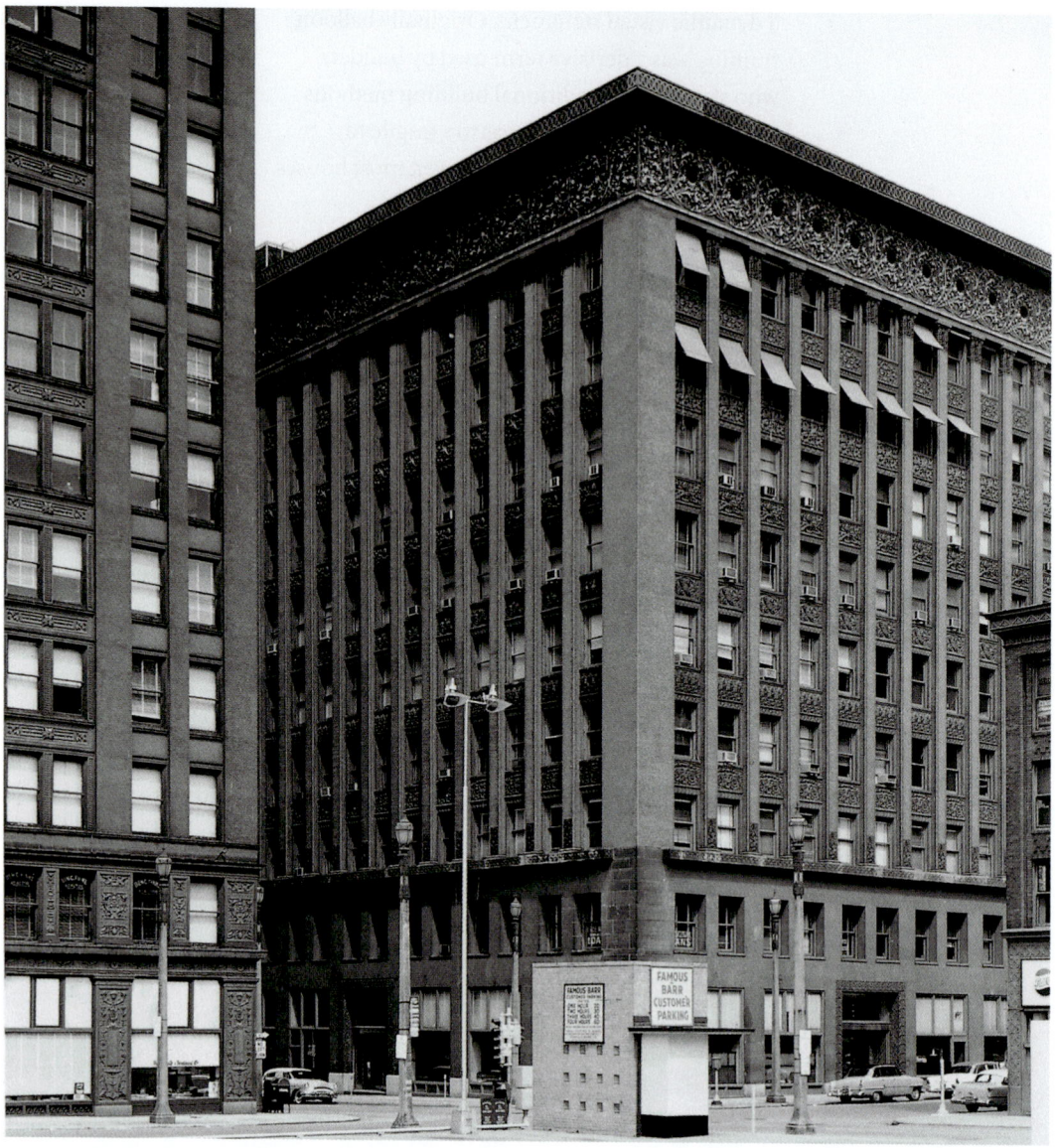

2.5.29 Louis Sullivan, Wainwright Building, 1890–91, St. Louis, Missouri

The Crystal Palace inspired other architects to work with iron, including French engineer Gustave Eiffel. It was eventually dismantled and reassembled in south London, where it became an exhibition center and concert hall. It was destroyed by fire in 1936.

Steel-Frame Construction

The use of cast iron for construction opened up new possibilities for architects. Cast iron was stronger than wood and more flexible than stone. It could be shaped into any form and was cheap, since iron ore was plentiful. Steel, a material made from iron and a small quantity of carbon, was stronger than pure iron and had even greater potential. Paxton and Eiffel's successful use of iron, considered unsightly as a finish material in their own time, invited architects to think about new alternatives to past styles. Architects began to question traditions and create structures that featured simplicity, mass-produced building materials like steel, glass, and concrete, and a lack of historical ornamentation, to usher in a new style called **Modernism**.

Modernism, Modernist: a radically new twentieth-century art and architectural movement that embraced modern industrial materials and a machine aesthetic

One architect who noted the advantages of steel was Louis Sullivan (1856–1924), called the "father of Modernism," who became a pioneer in the creation of the modern skyscraper. Sullivan, who attended Massachusetts Institute of Technology at the age of sixteen and took his first architect job at seventeen, participated in the rebuilding of Chicago after the Great Fire of 1871. Chicago provided fertile ground for creative young architects, and Sullivan pushed the use of steel frame to new heights.

Although Sullivan was based in Chicago, one of his masterpieces is in St. Louis, Missouri. The Wainwright Building, a ten-story office building, is one of the world's oldest skyscrapers (**2.5.29**). In this building Sullivan obeys his famous phrase, "form follows function," by providing versatile interior space. Because the steel frame supports the building, and because it is mostly located at its outer edges, the space of the interior can easily be reconfigured to meet the specific needs of the user.

The skyscraper was a completely new idea, and architects like Sullivan had no precedents on which to base their design. The Wainwright Building reflects the elements of a column (base, shaft, capital; see p. 264) in the organization of the exterior. Representing the capital, at the top of the building, is a **cornice**, or protruding ledge, which is highly ornamented with designs derived from Gothic cathedrals. The middle and tallest area shows strong vertical emphasis, with its projecting rectangular-section shafts and high, narrow windows. The lower section (base) shows little ornamentation and reflects ideas of the time about the frivolous nature of ornament. Later architects would avoid ornament altogether and rely on the **aesthetic** characteristics of the structure to provide excitement and interest in their design.

Because steel frames carry the load of the building, many Modernist architects realized there was no need to use a facing material, such as brick; the entire side of the building could be sheathed in glass. The simplicity of this idea captured the imagination of such remarkable architects as Germany's Ludwig Mies van der Rohe (1886–1969) (**2.5.30**), who proclaimed that "less is more," and the Swiss Le Corbusier (1887–1965), who called a building a "machine for living." (See Box: Contrasting Ideas in Modern Architecture, p. 278.) A building could now reflect its surroundings while also giving people inside it a spectacular view of the landscape.

When it opened on January 4, 2010, the Burj Khalifa (**2.5.31**) became the most impressive piece of steel-frame construction in the world, as well as the tallest man-made structure. Designed and built by the architecture and engineering firm Skidmore, Owings & Merrill under the supervision of American architect Adrian Smith (b. 1944) and engineer Bill Baker (b. 1953), the Burj Khalifa is the tallest building in the world. Its design was derived from the spiraling minarets—towers that surround mosques

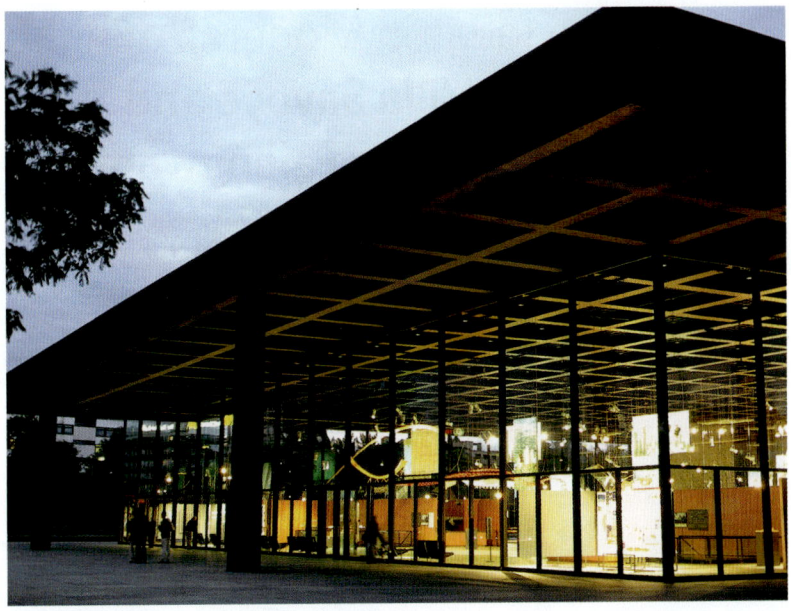

2.5.30 Mies van der Rohe, Neue Nationalgalerie, 1968, Berlin, Germany

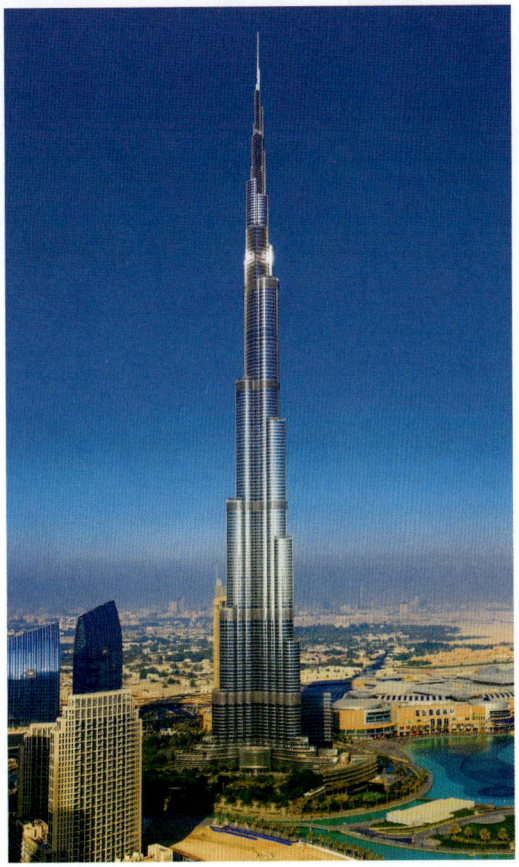

2.5.31 Adrian Smith and Bill Baker (Skidmore, Owings & Merrill), Burj Khalifa, 2010. Dubai, United Arab Emirates

Cornice: horizontally projecting molding round the top of a building
Aesthetic: related to beauty, art, and taste

Contrasting Ideas in Modern Architecture: **Le Corbusier's Villa Savoye and Frank Lloyd Wright's Fallingwater**

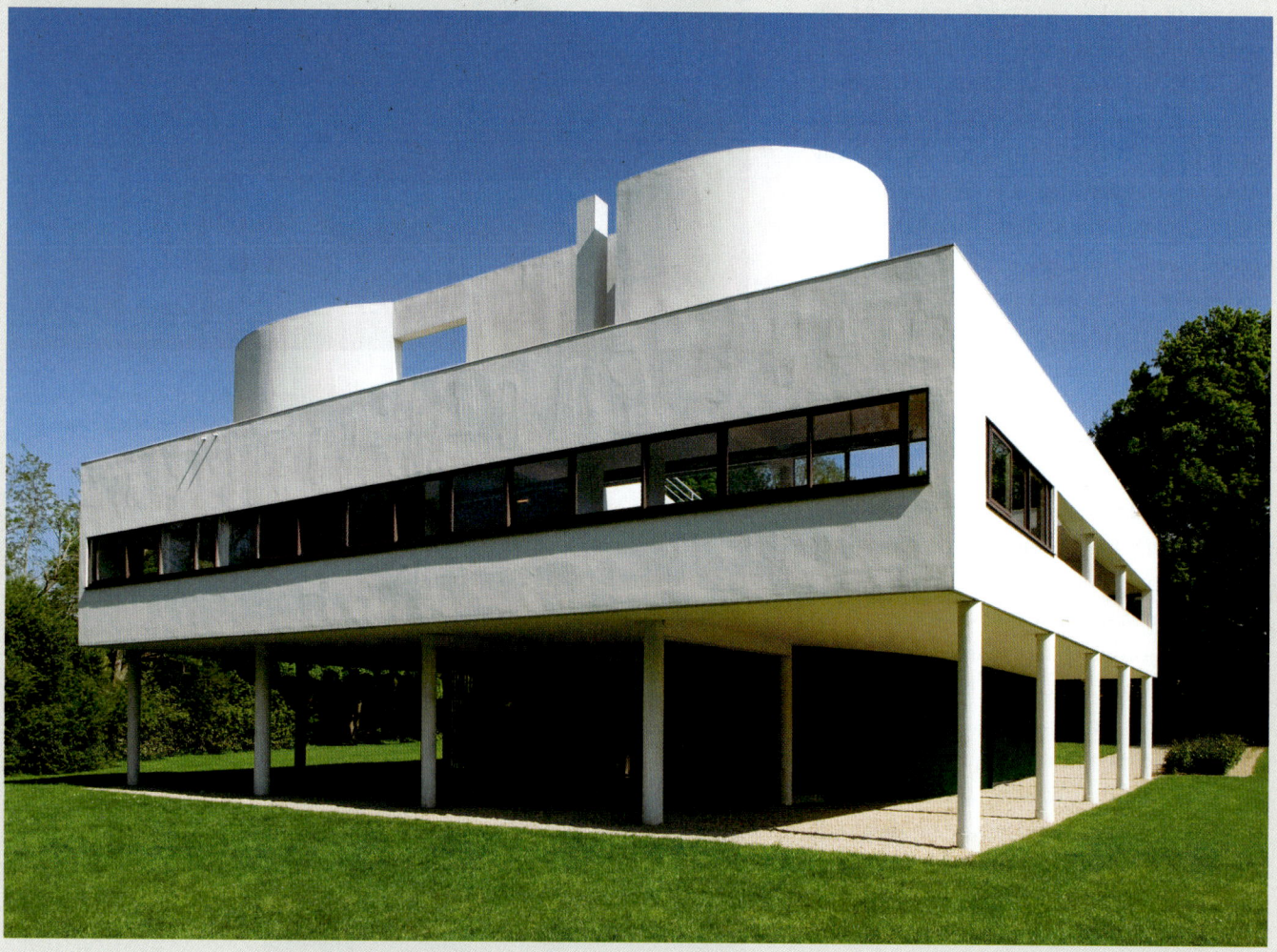

2.5.32 Le Corbusier, Villa Savoye, 1928–31, Poissy, France

Architecture is one of the most visible expressions of the Modernist movement.

A building's appearance can be a visual expression of an idea the architect wants to communicate. Two buildings constructed about the same time, the Villa Savoye and Fallingwater, share certain similarities, but are based on radically different ideas about architecture.

The Villa Savoye in Poissy, France, was completed in 1931 as a weekend residence for a family that lived in Paris during the week. It is one of Le Corbusier's finest expressions of his architectural philosophy (**2.5.32**). Le Corbusier (b. Charles-Edouard Jeanneret, 1887–1965) was a Swiss-French architect (also a designer and painter) who saw architecture as a "machine for living": the architecture of a building should be designed around the lifestyle of the occupants. Le Corbusier's architectural designs were part of the International Style, promoted as a universal aesthetic form that could be built in any geographical or cultural environment relatively inexpensively. This style emphasized industrial and (in theory) cheap materials, such as steel, glass, and concrete. It also favored a strongly geometric visual organization of spaces and elements of the building, including the shapes of the windows, roofline, and walls. With its preferences for unadorned, open interiors, the International Style claimed that its rational approach to design could (and should) be used universally, for rich and poor alike.

Five years later, the American architect Frank Lloyd Wright (1867–1959) was commissioned to build Fallingwater in Bear Run, Pennsylvania, as a weekend getaway for the Kaufmann family (**2.5.33**). It was completed in 1939. The profile of the house features vertical and horizontal elements much like those of the Villa Savoye, but Wright did not think that a house should be a machine. He believed the design of a house should respond **organically** to its location.

Rather than position the house so that the Kaufmanns could view the waterfall from inside, Wright placed the house right on top of it. He made the house so integral to the environment that the bottom step of one of the stairways hovered just above the creek. Wright believed so strongly in the organic relationship between site and building that he had many of the materials collected from the surrounding countryside. The stone was quarried nearby and the wood for the supports between the windows came from the surrounding forest. The design mimics the layers in the rocks around the site, and the reinforced concrete is colored to fit in as well. Sometimes underlying rock juts into the living space of the house so that the occupants may take pleasure in stepping over or around the stone.

Le Corbusier's design was inexpensive compared with Wright's, particularly since Wright's building materials needed to be specially collected from the surrounding countryside. Each design creates a beautiful modern space. In Wright's work, architecture becomes part of the natural surroundings, whereas Le Corbusier wants nature to be viewed from a comfortable vantage point.

Organic: having irregular forms and shapes, as though derived from living organisms

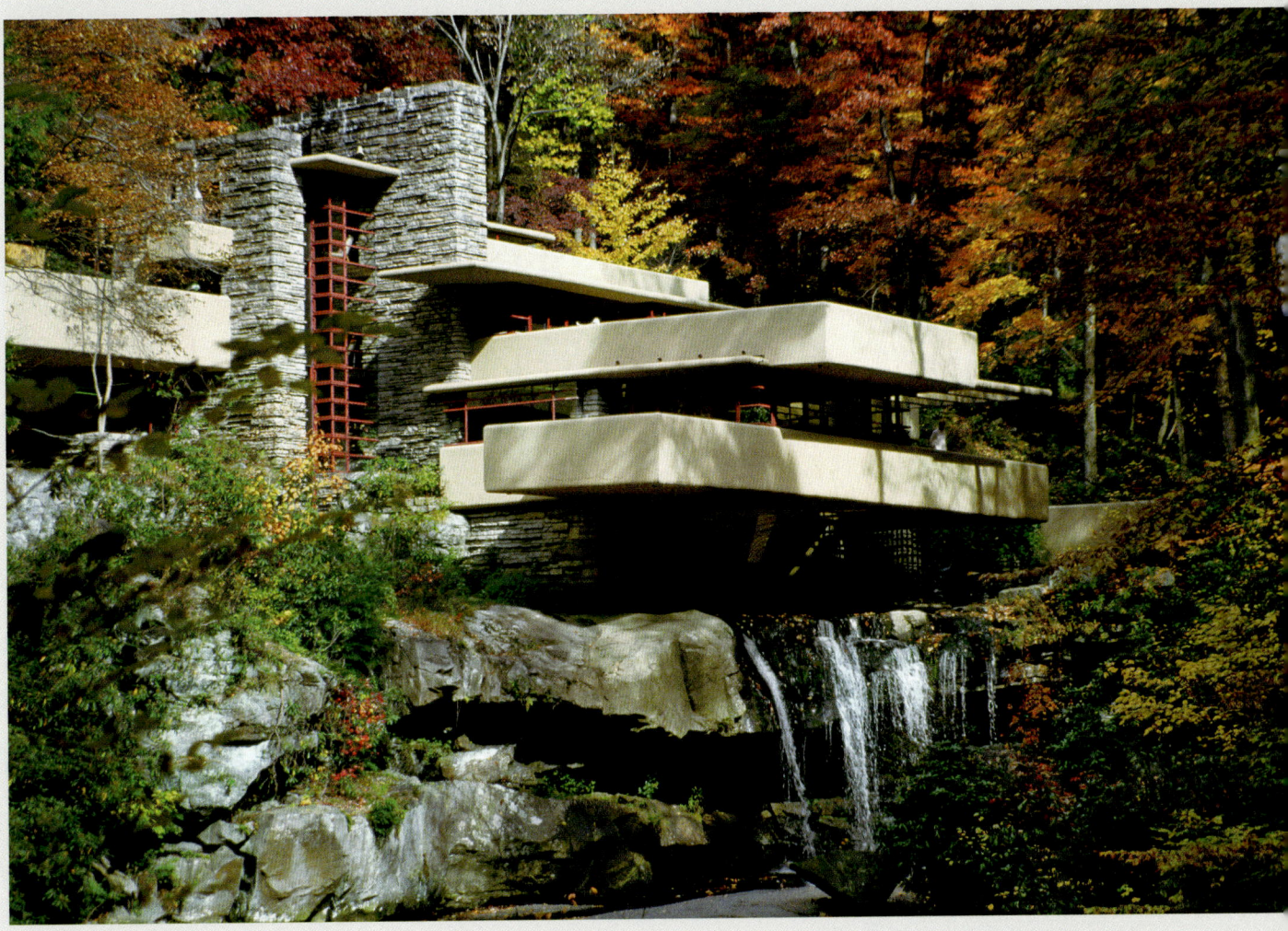

2.5.33 Frank Lloyd Wright, Fallingwater, 1939, Bear Run, Pennsylvania

Expressive: capable of stirring the emotions of the viewer

and are used to call the faithful to prayer—of Islamic architecture. The structural framing that supports the building is created from tubular steel to make the support lighter without compromising the integrity.

Reinforced Concrete

The character of architecture comes from its use of building materials, the sourcing or manufacture of which determines much of modern buildings' visual form. Steel and glass are produced in rectangular shapes that are a vital part of the visual aesthetic prizing the integration of form and function. But what aesthetic form would a material have if its raw manufactured state was liquid?

Architects began to use reinforced concrete as a way of avoiding the hard, right-angled edges of buildings made from blocks or bricks. Beginning with the architecture of the nineteenth century, steel, cast iron, and reinforced concrete came into widespread use. Concrete is a mixture of cement and ground stone. It is reinforced through the use of either a fibrous material (such as fiberglass) or steel rods called rebars. The inclusion of fibrous or metal reinforcing helps the concrete resist cracking. In architecture, steel rebar is shaped to the architect's design specifications; builders make a large wooden mold, and then pour the concrete into the "form." Reinforced concrete gave rise to shell architecture, which is the use of a solid shell that also provides support for the structure.

When the Danish architect Jørn Utzon (1918–2008) designed the Sydney Opera House, overlooking the harbor of Sydney, Australia, he broke away from Modernist rectangular designs (**2.5.34**). The structure is a testament to the **expressive** character of reinforced concrete. The rooflines resemble billowing sails, a reference to the building's harbor location. The "sails" were created over precast ribs and then set into place, allowing the architect more freedom in the creation of the design and (in theory) reducing the cost. In fact, owing to a succession

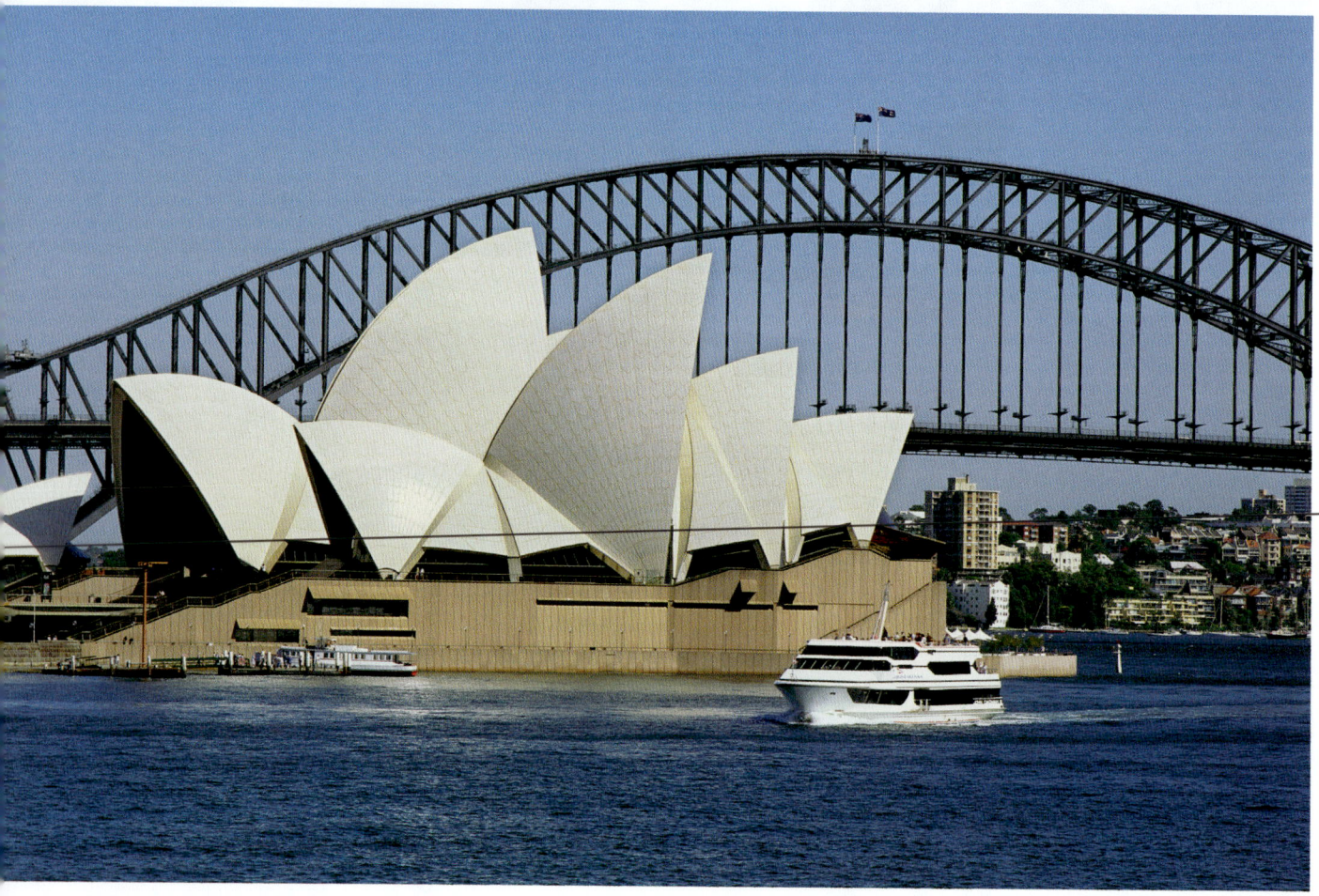

2.5.34 Jørn Utzon, Sydney Opera House, 1973, Sydney, Australia

of technical problems with this innovative building, the project cost fourteen times its intended budget. As controversy surrounding the project escalated, Utzon resigned nine years before its completion.

The Postmodern Reaction to Modernism

Beginning in the 1980s, a new approach to architecture, known as **Postmodernism**, combined the hard, pure rectangles of Modernism with unusual materials and features of styles from the past. Postmodernism took hold as architects sought new ways to reflect a complex and changing world.

The Humana Building in downtown Louisville, Kentucky, designed by the American architect Michael Graves (1934–2015), is an intriguing mix of historical styles and references (**2.5.35**). The **facade** onto the street has a **stylized** Greek **portico**. The **negative space** of large windows and openings implies columns that rise up to support a cornice and triangular glass structure similar to the triangular **pediment** of a Greek temple. The upper portion of the building (set back from the street) suddenly changes from simple right angles to a series of curved surfaces that undulate in a manner similar to the architecture of the Baroque period. Graves also artfully varies the facing material, changing its color and texture at different intervals, seeking to avoid the austere simplicity and purity of Modernism. A piece of Modernist architecture would not include influences from Greek or Baroque architecture because the Modernist idea was to create a new style that was not based on the past.

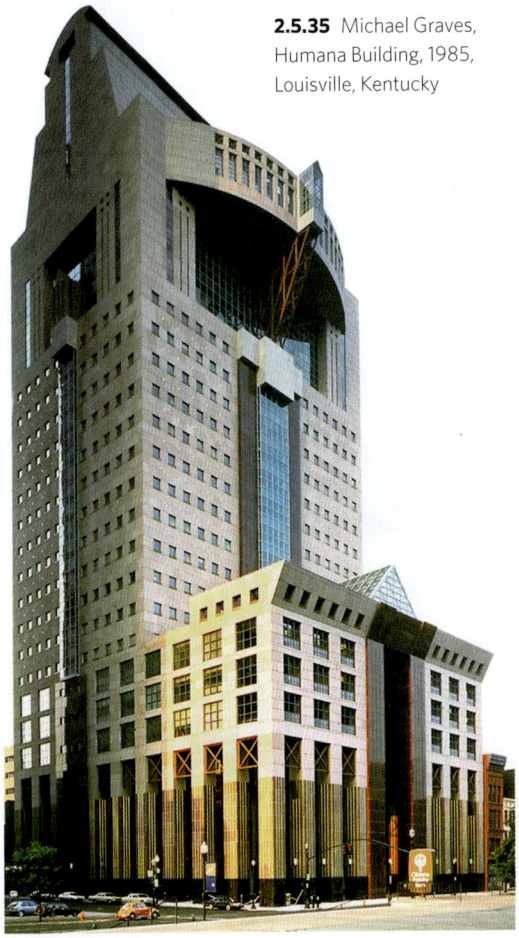

2.5.35 Michael Graves, Humana Building, 1985, Louisville, Kentucky

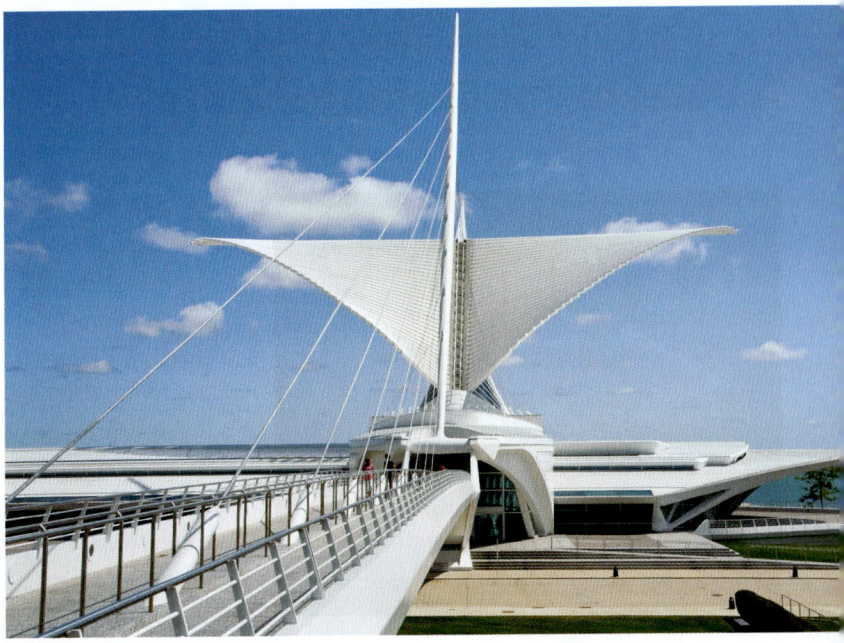

2.5.36 Santiago Calatrava, Quadracci Pavilion, Milwaukee Art Museum, Wisconsin, 2001

In Postmodernist architecture, form no longer follows function with the same dedication as it did during the Modernist period. In fact, sometimes the building seems like a huge toy, a playful exploration of what we expect a building to be. The Quadracci Pavilion at the Milwaukee Art Museum was designed by the Spanish architect Santiago Calatrava (b. 1951) to express the character of the site (**2.5.36**). Built on the shores of Lake Michigan, the pavilion reminds us of ships passing by; a cable-suspended bridge over a beautiful expanse of water also connects the museum to downtown Milwaukee. The building becomes a **kinetic sculpture** when a large moveable sunscreen atop

Postmodernism, Postmodernist: a late twentieth-century style of architecture and art that playfully adopts features of earlier styles
Facade: any side of a building, usually the front or entrance
Stylized: art that represents objects in an exaggerated way to emphasize certain aspects of the object
Portico: a roof supported by columns at the entrance to a building
Negative space: an unoccupied or empty space that is created after positive shapes are positioned in a work of art
Pediment: the triangular space, situated above the row of columns, on the facade of a building in the Classical style
Kinetic sculpture: three-dimensional art that moves, impelled by air currents, motors, or people

Perspectives on Art: Zaha Hadid
A Building for Exciting Events

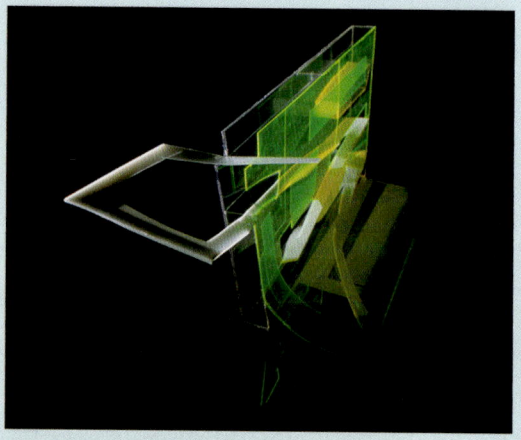

Zaha Hadid (1950–2016) was born in Iraq and trained as an architect in London. She was one of the world's most prominent and successful architects of her generation, and developed and ran her own practice, designing notable buildings in Europe and the United States. Here she describes how an architect thinks about a new building for art exhibitions, performances, and installations in downtown Cincinnati, Ohio.

The new home for the Contemporary Arts Center is located on a small space in downtown Cincinnati (**2.5.37a** and **2.5.37b**). Our challenge was to design for a prominent location an exciting new building that would provide spaces for many different activities: temporary exhibitions, site-specific installations and performances, an education facility, offices, art-preparation areas, a museum store, a café, and public areas.

We designed the gallery spaces as a three-dimensional "jigsaw puzzle" of interlocking solids and voids suspended above the lobby. The unique geometry, scale, and varying heights of the gallery spaces offer organizational flexibility to accommodate and respond to the size and media of the contemporary art that will be displayed.

We wanted to draw visitors into the building from the surrounding areas by creating a dynamic public space. Pedestrians enter the building and move around it through an "urban carpet" of polished undulating surfaces that curves slowly upward. As it rises and turns, the urban carpet leads visitors up a suspended mezzanine ramp through the full length of the lobby, which functions during the day as an open, daylit artificial park. The urban carpet also connects to zigzag ramps that take visitors to the galleries.

Seen from the street, the building appears to be made up of stacked horizontal blocks of glass, metal, and concrete, suspended above the glass at ground level. We wanted to give the building a weightless quality, as if it were a sculpture, not just a building. The public and administrative spaces are glass, so that those outside are invited to look into the building, and those inside to look out at the cityscape. In this way the center's building is connected to the city it serves.

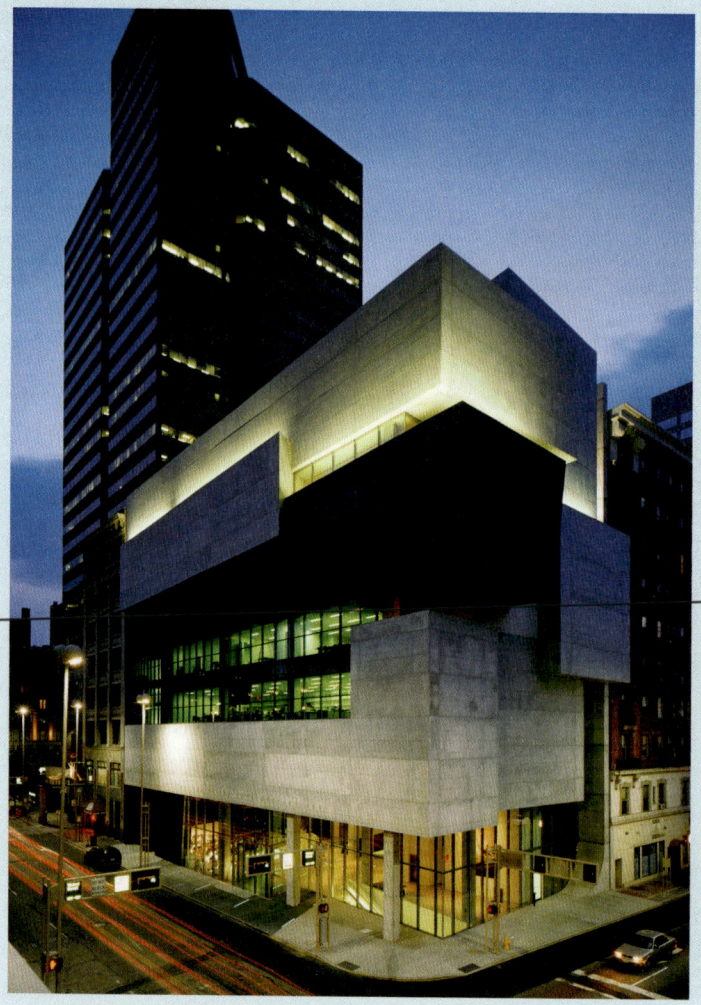

2.5.37a Zaha Hadid, Contemporary Arts Center, Cincinnati, Ohio. Study model by the architects, experimenting with different structural ideas

2.5.37b Zaha Hadid, Contemporary Arts Center, 2003, Cincinnati, Ohio

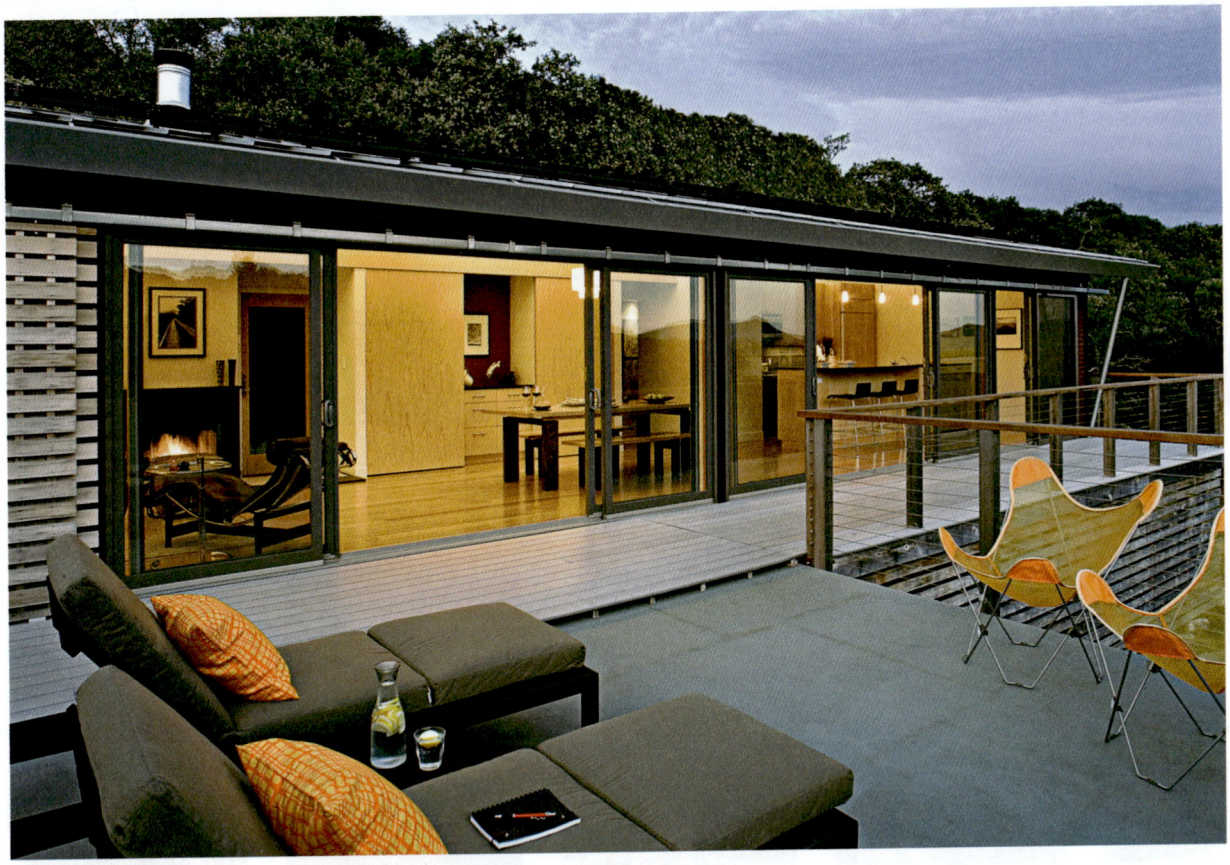

2.5.38 Michelle Kaufmann, Glidehouse, 2004. Marin County, California

the structure slowly rises and lowers throughout the day, like the flapping wings of the many species of birds that flock near the lake. The inside is reminiscent of the curved interior of a sailing ship. The Quadracci Pavilion provides an exciting exhibition space for the display of contemporary art.

Currents in Architecture

Architecture faces both challenges and opportunities as the twenty-first century unfolds. Concerns over limited resources, energy conservation, and sustainability have become important issues. The American architect Michelle Kaufmann (b. 1968) responded to these challenges by introducing the Glidehouse concept in 2004. The Glidehouse (**2.5.38**) was developed because Kaufmann was looking for an inexpensive alternative to the costly California homes in the Bay area. She developed a prefab module made of sustainable wood and finished it with double-pane windows, roof solar cells, and other materials that were reused or recyclable. The resulting plan was oriented to the everyday usage of the occupant so that it made life easier, while also lowering cost. Because the Glidehouse is modular, adding more modules, then modifying them to fit with the intended plan, allows for expansion into a larger living space. Kaufmann's idea has influenced new trends in architecture, such as tiny houses and portable homes. In 2017, Kaufmann was Artist-in-Residence at Google where she worked on new company buildings and innovated ideas through research and development.

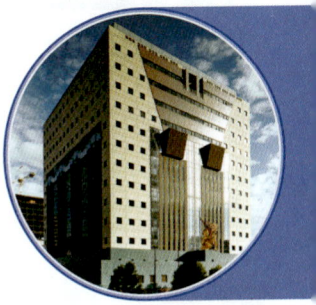

For more information about the roots of contemporary architecture: see **3.9.32, p. 543**

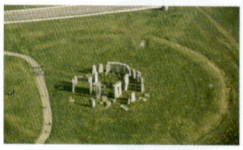

4.1.8 Stonehenge, England, *c.* 3200–1500 BCE, p. 570

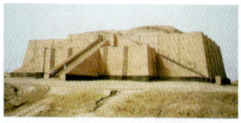

4.1.6 Ziggurat, Ur, Iraq, *c.* 2100 BCE, p. 569

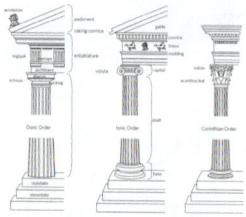

3.1.21 Diagram of Classical architectural orders, p. 380

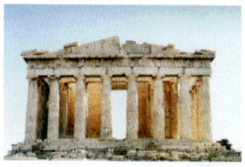

1.7.14a Iktinos and Kallikrates, Parthenon, Athens, 447–432 BCE, p. 148

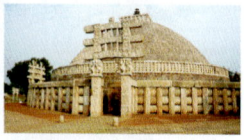

3.3.4 Great Stupa, Sanchi, India, *c.* 150–50 BCE, p. 413

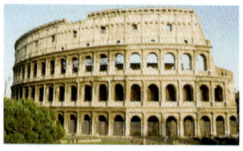

4.1.2 Colosseum, Rome, Italy, 72–80 CE, p. 566

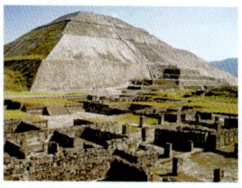

3.4.10 Pyramid of the Sun, Teotihuacan, Mexico, *c.* 225 CE, p. 435

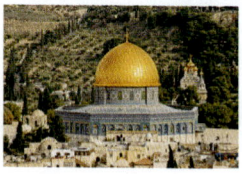

3.2.16 Dome of the Rock, Jerusalem, 688–91, p. 401

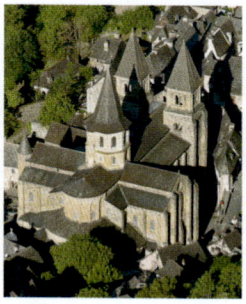

3.2.21 Sainte-Foy, Conques, France, *c.* 1120, p. 404

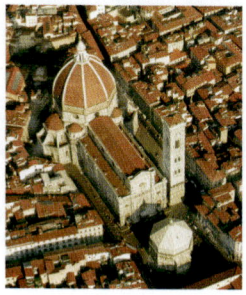

3.6.3 Arnolfo di Cambio and others, Florence Cathedral, begun 1296, p. 462

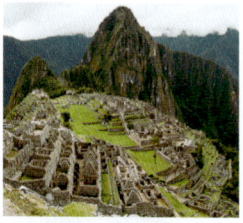

3.4.5 Machu Picchu, Peru, 1450–1530, p. 432

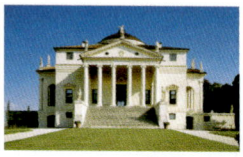

3.6.14a Andrea Palladio, Villa Rotonda, Vicenza, Italy, begun 1565/66, p. 473

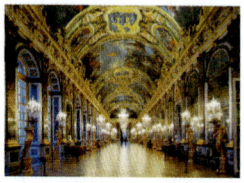

3.6.29 Jules Hardouin-Mansart, Hall of Mirrors, Versailles, 1678–84, p. 484

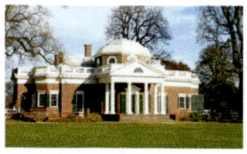

3.7.10 Thomas Jefferson, Monticello, Charlottesville, 1769–1809, p. 495

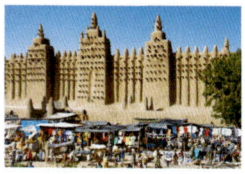

3.5.7 Great Mosque, Djenné, Mali, completed *c.* 1907, p. 451

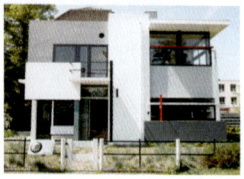

3.9.31 Gerrit Rietveld, Schröder House, Utrecht, 1924–25, p. 543

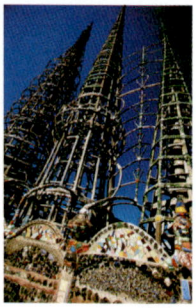

0.0.9 Simon Rodia, Watts Towers, Los Angeles, California, 1921–54, p. 26

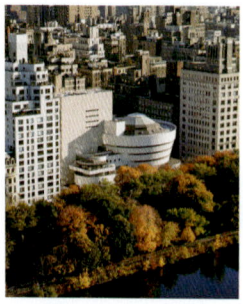

4.1.4 Frank Lloyd Wright, Guggenheim Museum, New York, 1956–59, p. 567

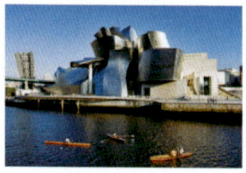

1.2.15 Frank Gehry, Guggenheim Museum, Bilbao, Spain, 1997, p. 70

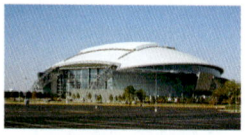

4.1.3 AT&T Stadium, Arlington, Texas, 2009, p. 566

2.6 The Tradition of Craft

Life is so short, the craft so long to learn.

(Geoffrey Chaucer, English poet)

In Geoffrey Chaucer's (*c.* 1340–1400) time, the makers of the fine objects we can see today in the world's great art museums learned their trade in associations called guilds. Fourteenth-century aspiring craftsmen trained with masters, a process that lasted many years, as Chaucer's comment suggests. In medieval Europe, painting (for example) was not considered to be of higher status than the work of either turning ceramics into fine vessels or weaving exquisite tapestries.

Things gradually changed after 1400 during the **Renaissance**, and by the eighteenth century, certain **media**, notably painting and sculpture, came to be considered as art, while ceramics, weaving, and embroidery were termed crafts. Other materials, such as metals, were used to make fine sculpture (which was "art") as well as practical and household objects ("craft"). Crafts came to mean the disciplines that produced hand-made items to be used rather than simply looked at. This view was generally accepted, even though utilitarian objects require technical skill to produce, and craftspeople devote years to mastering their craft. Indeed, some hand-crafted objects, because of their ingenuity and refinement, stand out as artworks that transcend mere utility.

The distinction between art and craft was unique to Western culture, and it has now broken down in the twentieth and twenty-first centuries, as this chapter will show. As for the rest of the world, the maker of a bronze vessel in China during the Shang Dynasty (1300–1045 BCE), the maker of a fine embroidered wool tunic in Paracas, South America (600–175 BCE), and the **ceramist** who made lamps for the Dome of the Rock in Jerusalem (sixteenth century) probably did not consider themselves any less skillful or "artistic" than painters or sculptors. Craftspeople working today still produce works using traditional craft materials and techniques, but have updated their methods and subjects to reflect a changing world; they also sometimes apply traditional skills but use new, contemporary materials to create their work. Examples of contemporary artists working in this way include Hyo-In Kim (p. 286), Sheila Hicks (pp. 296–97), and Toshiko Horiuchi (p. 297). Through the development of their craftsmanship, such artists are able to enhance their understanding of materials involved in a work's creation.

In this chapter we will examine both craft objects and works of art, each made with the same materials. If we try to define precisely the difference between art and craft we will discover it is difficult, perhaps impossible. As you read this chapter, ask yourself whether you think the objects discussed can be considered art or craft. At the same time, think about whether the makers of the objects, and the people they made them for, could tell the difference either. In the hands of skillful designers, great craft objects such as those discussed here possess artistry equal to great works of art.

Renaissance: a period of cultural and artistic change in Europe from the fourteenth to the seventeenth century
Medium (plural **media**): the material on or from which an artist chooses to make a work of art, for example canvas and oil paint, marble, engraving, video, or architecture
Ceramist: a person who makes ceramics

Perspectives on Art: Hyo-In Kim
Art or Craft: What's the Difference?

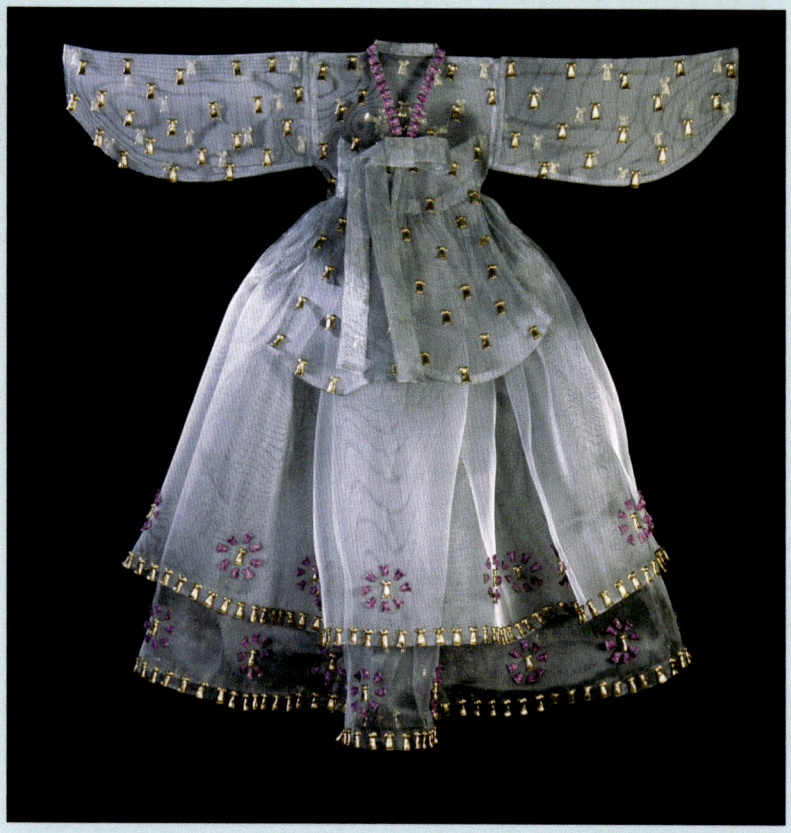

2.6.1 Hyo-In Kim, *To Be Modern #2*, 2004. Metal screen, wire, porcelain, acrylic paint, and found objects, slightly over lifesize

2.6.2 Hyo-In Kim

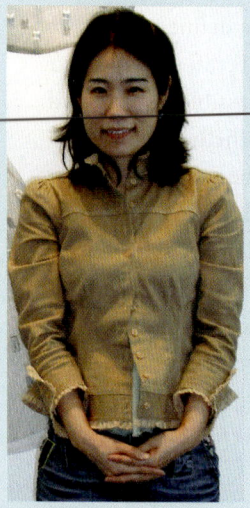

When we look at a fine painting we will almost certainly describe it as being art. But is a fine example of clothing, for example, art or craft? If craft is something that has a useful function, then presumably a dress is craft. Here, however, Professor Howard Risatti, an art historian at Virginia Commonwealth University, examines a work based on a traditional Korean dress that transforms a practical piece of clothing to comment on our modern globalized world (**2.6.1**). *He asks: What makes something a work of art rather than a work of craft?*

Only by understanding something essential about a work of art can we begin to appreciate its richness and complexity as an aesthetic object. So to begin, we must ask, "What is essential to a work of craft?" To my thinking, it is that craft is an object constructed around the idea of function, say the way a container functions to hold water, or a chair to support a person, or clothes to cover someone's body. The work shown here is from a series by the Korean American artist Hyo-In Kim (**2.6.1**). It is a *hanbok*, a traditional Korean dress worn with shoes and a hairpin by women of the upper and royal classes. Its gold-colored decoration indicates its prestige; such expensive materials were costly and well beyond the means of commoners, who mostly wore plain white garments.

The title, *To Be Modern #2*, however, suggests the artist has something more in mind than simply a fondness for traditional Korean clothes. Kim is faithful to the original dress design; she wants it to be correct to tradition. But she also wants it to indicate something important about tradition. That is why she has subtly transformed it by making it out of silver-colored wire mesh (instead of cloth) and by molding the decorative details out of porcelain, which she has then painted gold. And in keeping with the idea of transformation, instead of displaying it on a manikin like a dress in a store window, like something to be bought and sold, she decided to suspend it with its sleeves outstretched so that its transparency and weightlessness would be emphasized.

Kim intends us to see through the material so that the dress, like the hairpin, appears to float like a ghostly, disembodied figure—something almost there and yet not quite. This apparitional effect, enhanced by the glittering gold of the decoration, is then undercut when, upon close-up inspection of the dress, the decoration turns out to be tiny versions of fashionable Western clothing: jeans, skirts, shoes, purses. What Kim wants us to see and appreciate, both literally and figuratively, is that those traditional cultural values that give structure and form to people's lives, including our own, are fading away and disappearing as globalization spreads.

Ceramics

Our word ceramic comes from the Greek word *keramos*, meaning "pottery," which was probably derived from a word in Sanskrit (a language of ancient India) meaning "to burn." The accepted interpretation of the word, burnt earth, aptly describes the ceramic process. The manufacture of a ceramic object requires the shaping of clay, a natural material dug from the earth, which is then baked at high temperatures to make it hard.

We know that the basic techniques used to make ceramics date back thousands of years because archaeologists investigating the earliest known civilizations have found potsherds, small pieces of ancient ceramics.

The first step in making a ceramic object is to choose a clay. Ceramists can choose from a variety of clays, each with unique characteristics; they often select a mixture they have developed themselves that fits their own working methods. Clay used to make earthenware has good **plasticity**, or pliability, but it can be somewhat brittle after firing. Earthenware is often red in color and hardens at a lower temperature than other clays. Stoneware clays are less plastic than earthenware clays. Stoneware (as its name implies) is much harder than earthenware and is fired at a higher temperature. Stoneware is a good clay for the creation of items for everyday use, such as mugs and bowls. Porcelain, a durable, high-temperature ceramic commonly used for fine dinnerware, is made of a mixture of three clays: feldspar, kaolin, and silica. Porcelain is strong but sometimes hard to manipulate. Fine white china, bathroom fixtures, and dental crowns are made of porcelain.

When the ceramist has selected the clay, the next step in the making process is called wedging. This means the clay is kneaded to work out pockets of air (which can destroy a piece of ceramic ware when it is heated) and make the clay easier to work. Next, the ceramist uses one of a number of hand methods to shape the clay into the form of the finished object. For example, the artist can build up an object using slabs or coils of clay, or by modeling a lump of clay into the desired shape by pressing or pinching. Another method is to shape the clay as it turns on a rapidly turning potter's wheel, a process known as **throwing**.

Once it has been shaped, the clay is left to dry. The dried clay, called **greenware**, is very fragile. It is ready to be loaded into an oven called a kiln, and to be fired at a high temperature (between 2,000 and 3,000°F). The firing process takes an entire day of slowly raising the temperature to the appropriate level, then another day to allow for a slow cool-down to prevent cracking. The fired object, called **bisqueware**, is now permanently a hard ceramic and cannot be wetted and returned to a soft-clay state.

To add the finishing touches to a ceramic object, artists apply a glaze, a liquid mixture of clay, water, and chemical compounds that will give the object a glass-like finish and that adds color, **texture**, and protection to the object's surface. (A glaze can also make an object more watertight.) Some ceramists opt for a more matte finish, so they use a thin liquid clay called slip. The artist usually applies the slip or glaze with a brush. The object is again placed in the kiln and fired to melt and harden the glaze or slip, which fuses with the clay body.

Plastic, plasticity: referring to materials that are soft and can be manipulated, or to such properties in the materials
Throwing: the process of making a ceramic object on a potter's wheel
Greenware: a clay form that has been shaped and dried, but not yet fired to become ceramic
Bisqueware: a ceramic form that has been fired but not glazed or that has not received other surface finishing
Texture: the surface quality of a work, for example fine/coarse, detailed/lacking in detail

Pinch Method

One of the most basic ways of working with clay is to squeeze it between the fingers. This process, called the pinch method, has for millennia provided artists with a spontaneous and effective way to create a clay object. To create an object using this method an artist will work the clay with his or her fingers, pushing and pulling it into the desired shape.

During the Majapahit period of Indonesia (1293–1520), artists squeezed and pinched clay into images that honored the manifested gods and goddesses of Hinduism. One such image made using this technique is the terra-cotta work *The Mother Goddess Men Brajut (Hariti)* (**2.6.3**), which was originally created as a pillar ornament for an open

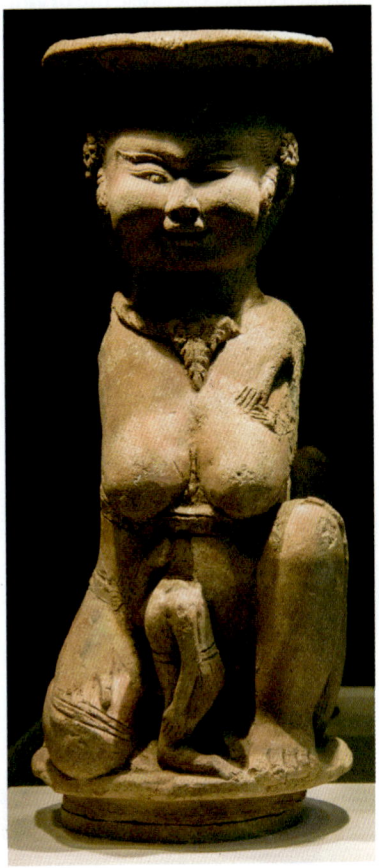

2.6.3 *The Mother Goddess Men Brajut (Hariti)*, Indonesian, c. 14th–15th century. Terra-cotta, 18⅞ × 8½ × 8". Metropolitan Museum of Art, New York

pavilion. The artist would have manipulated the clay carefully to portray Hariti (or *Men Brajut* in Javanese), the protector of children, and to create a hollow to hold a wooden pillar to fulfill the functional element of this piece.

Coil Method

The art of using coils to create a clay object has been a common hand-building method since ancient times. A coil is created by rolling the clay on a flat surface so that it extends into a long, rope-like shape. When making a round vessel, the artist wraps the coil around upon itself and then fuses the sections together by smoothing.

Seated Figure, a work from the Zapotec culture of Mexico, was made using the coil method (**2.6.4**). This figure was made to be buried in the tomb of a Zapotec ruler, and may portray a god or possibly a companion for the deceased. On its headdress and chest the artist has carved two calendar dates in Zapotec writing. Most of the pottery made by Native American cultures was carefully crafted by hand. The coil method was preferred for constructing rounded objects because the **organic** line of the coil could be controlled in a way that would complement the piece's essence or spirit.

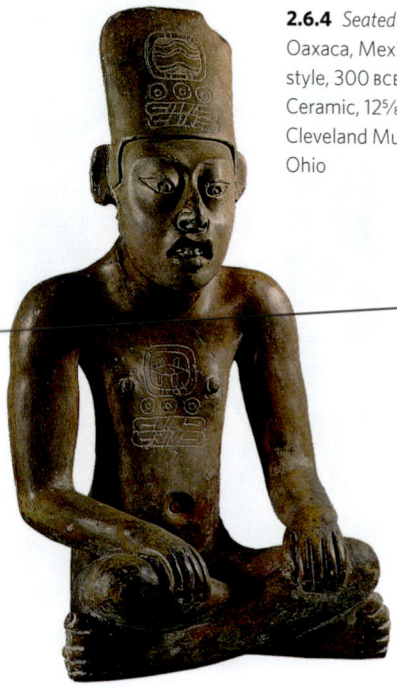

2.6.4 *Seated Figure*, Oaxaca, Mexico, Zapotec style, 300 BCE–700 CE. Ceramic, 12⅝ × 7 × 7⅜". Cleveland Museum of Art, Ohio

Throwing

The use of a potter's wheel probably began when an artist, in order to make the process of coiling more efficient, placed his or her clay object on a round mat and turned it while adding coils of clay to a piece of pottery. A potter's wheel consists of a round disk that revolves while the ceramist shapes the object. No one is sure exactly when such wheels were invented, but by 3000 BCE the Chinese were using them to produce ceramic objects.

The process of making pottery on a wheel is known as throwing. The potter centers a mound of clay on the turning wheel and then shapes a pot by poking a hole in the middle of the mound, and then pushing and pulling the wall of the pot up and out with both hands as it turns. To finish the surface of the pot, the potter can employ sponges and scrapers as it spins, or simply let the natural grooves made by the fingertips remain. Finally, a piece of wire is used to cut the finished piece from the wheel.

The ceramic artists of China invented porcelain and used a greater variety of high-quality glazes than any ceramic tradition in the world, many of which are still in use today. This porcelain flask (**2.6.5**) was produced on a potter's wheel during the Ming Dynasty almost 600 years ago. Chinese ceramists of the Ming Dynasty were known for their use of multiple glaze layers. Their wares were so fine that the users of Ming Dynasty porcelain included the emperor of China himself. In this piece the artist used, first, a blue glaze and then a clear glaze over that to complete the work. The clear glaze gave the flask a luxurious glossy finish.

Organic: having irregular forms and shapes, as though derived from living organisms
Three-dimensional: having height, width, and depth

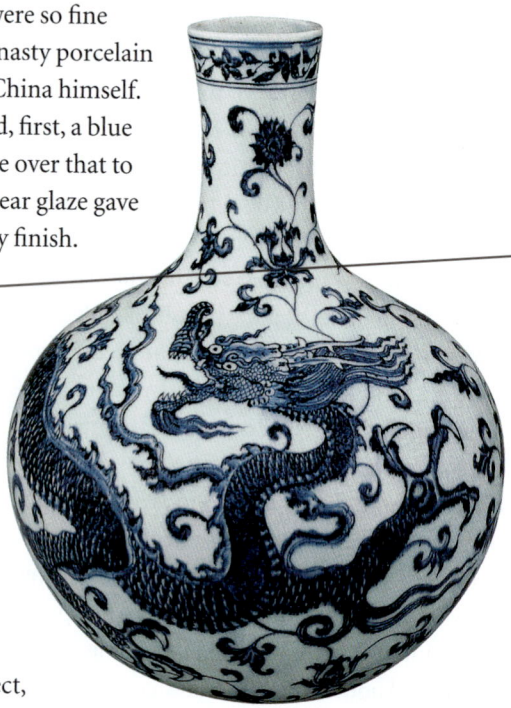

2.6.5 Porcelain flask with decoration in blue underglaze, Ming Dynasty, 1425–35. Palace Museum, Beijing, China

Slab Method

When an artist uses slab construction to make a ceramic object he or she first rolls out a flat sheet of clay. The artist then cuts this clay into the shapes needed to make the object. To make a **three-dimensional** object,

San Ildefonso-Style Pottery

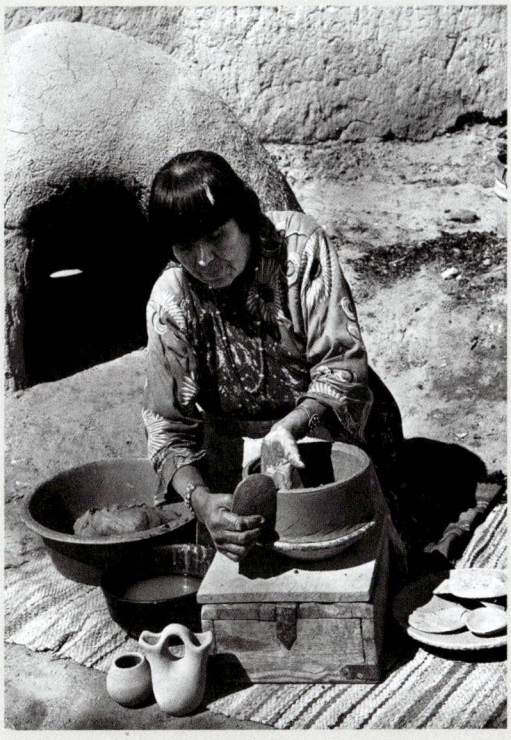

2.6.6 Maria Martinez, San Ildefonso Pueblo, New Mexico, *c.* 1930–40

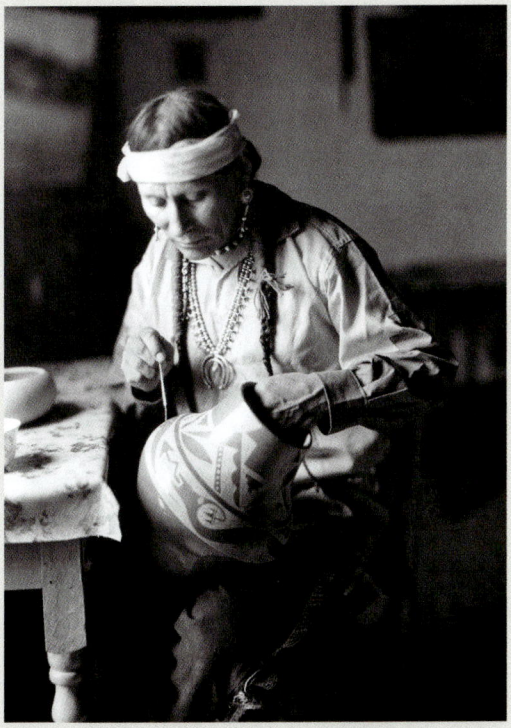

2.6.7 Julian Martinez, San Ildefonso Pueblo, New Mexico, *c.* 1925–45

Native American pottery is regarded as some of the most distinctive in the world. Ceramic objects created in the Americas were constructed using hand-building methods, rather than with a potter's wheel, yet the pottery created possesses great symmetry.

One family of Native American potters revived and perfected the pottery traditions of the Tewa people in Southwestern North America from the early twentieth century. Dr. Edgar Lee Hewett discovered sherds of pottery near San Ildefonso Pueblo in New Mexico and asked a local potter to produce replicas of the originals. That potter, Maria Martinez (1887–1980), whose Tewa name was Po've'ka ("Pond Lily"), and her husband Julian (1879–1943) re-created ceramic objects that their distant ancestors had made. They were asked to demonstrate the process at the Panama California Fair in 1915, and then in other major public venues.

Maria and Julian Martinez went on to develop their own distinctive San Ildefonso style, which became internationally famous. Maria would carefully craft the pottery objects from the volcanic ash-laden clays of the region, then Julian would apply the designs. Matte slip is painted over the stone-burnished surfaces, leaving a shiny finish. Then the pieces are fired in a mound of wood and manure that gives the piece its rich black color.

One of the favorite designs used is that of the *avanyu* (**2.6.8**). An avanyu is a water guardian serpent god of the Tewa peoples. The image is common in the many caves that dot the canyons in this area. It bears a close resemblance to the **Mesoamerican** serpent god Quetzalcoatl. Avanyus are frequently used as decorative motifs in Southwest pottery.

Mesoamerican: an archaeological term referring to people or objects from the area now occupied by Mexico and Central America

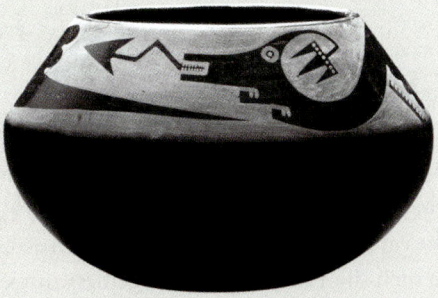

2.6.8 Maria Martinez and Julian Martinez, bowl with plumed serpent, *c.* 1925. Coiled and burnished earthenware, 6" × 9½". Newark Museum, New Jersey

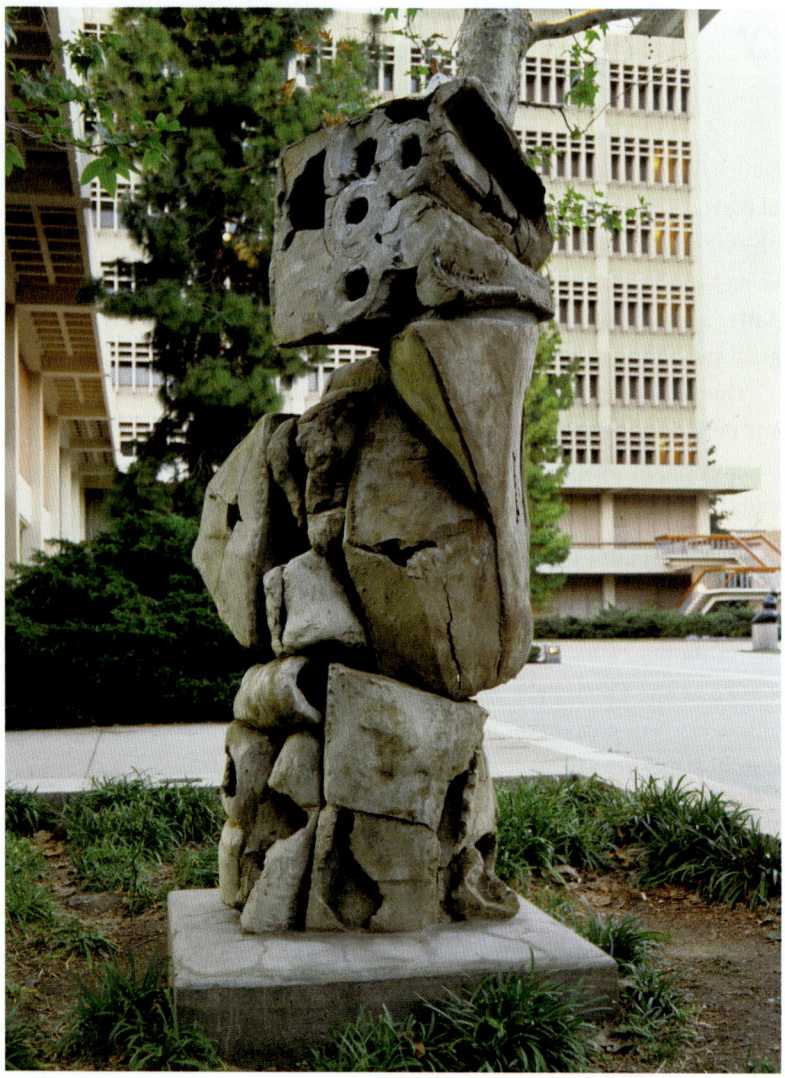

2.6.9 Peter Voulkos, *Gallas Rock*, 1960. Stoneware with slip and glaze, 84 × 37 × 26¾". University of California at Los Angeles, Franklin D. Murphy Sculpture Garden

the ceramist takes care to join the corners. This style of working lends itself to making boxes and other forms that have large flat sides.

In *Gallas Rock*, by the American sculptor Peter Voulkos (1924–2002), we see slab construction (and wheel throwing) used in an organic and **Expressionist** way (**2.6.9**). The slabs are evident in the flat **planes** that dominate this 8-foot-tall sculptural object. Voulkos is known for using clay's naturalness—its tendency to take on organic forms—and plasticity.

Glass

As with ceramics, the manufacture of glass objects relies on heat and materials dug from the earth. The process of applying intense heat to melt silica (usually sand) together with lead (historically used to help the melted silica to flow) is the basis for most glass production. As in the making of ceramics, slow cooling of heated objects is critical to avoid serious cracking.

Glass was probably first used in ancient Mesopotamia (modern-day Iraq) and Egypt around 3500 BCE. At that time, glass was cast in small molds and core formed, that is, molten glass was wrapped around a lump of clay or dung attached to the end of a metal rod. The ancient Egyptians valued glass as highly as gold. Glassblowing—the process of forming a glass vessel by forcing air into molten glass, usually by blowing through a tube—was in use by the first century BCE in Syria and was later adopted and perfected by the Romans.

The Portland Vase (named after one of its owners, Margaret Bentinck, Duchess of Portland), is a stunningly beautiful vessel, created in the Roman empire during the first century CE (**2.6.10**). Modern research has shown that it was made by the dip-overlay method: an elongated bubble of blue glass was partially dipped into a crucible of white glass, before the two were blown together. After cooling, the white layer was cut away to form the design. The cutting was probably performed by a skilled gem-cutter. The blue glass forms the **background** to the figures picked out in white.

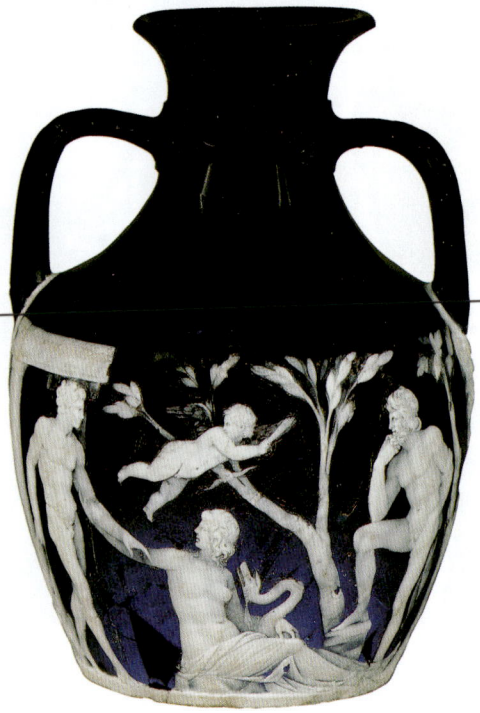

2.6.10 Portland Vase, Roman, *c.* 1–25 CE. British Museum, London, England

The amazing degree of detail attests to the artist's skill, as we can see from the four figures and a tree-like plant.

The designers of the **Gothic** cathedrals of medieval France adopted a type of colored glass, known as **stained glass**, which had been used previously on a smaller scale in northern Europe. But the French did something extraordinary with stained glass by using it to make enormous decorative windows that bathed the cathedral in colored light. The windows of the cathedral in the northern French town of Chartres are magnificent examples of stained glass (**2.6.11**). The large (43 ft. in diameter) circular windows

Expressionism, Expressionist: an artistic style at its height in 1920s Europe, devoted to representing subjective emotions and experiences instead of objective or external reality

Plane: a flat, two-dimensional surface on which an artist can create a drawing or painting. Planes can also be implied in a composition by areas that face toward, parallel to, or away from a light source

Background: the part of a work depicted furthest from the viewer's space, often behind the main subject matter

Gothic: Western European architectural style of the twelfth to sixteenth century, characterized by the use of pointed arches and ornate decoration

Stained glass: colored glass used for windows or decorative applications

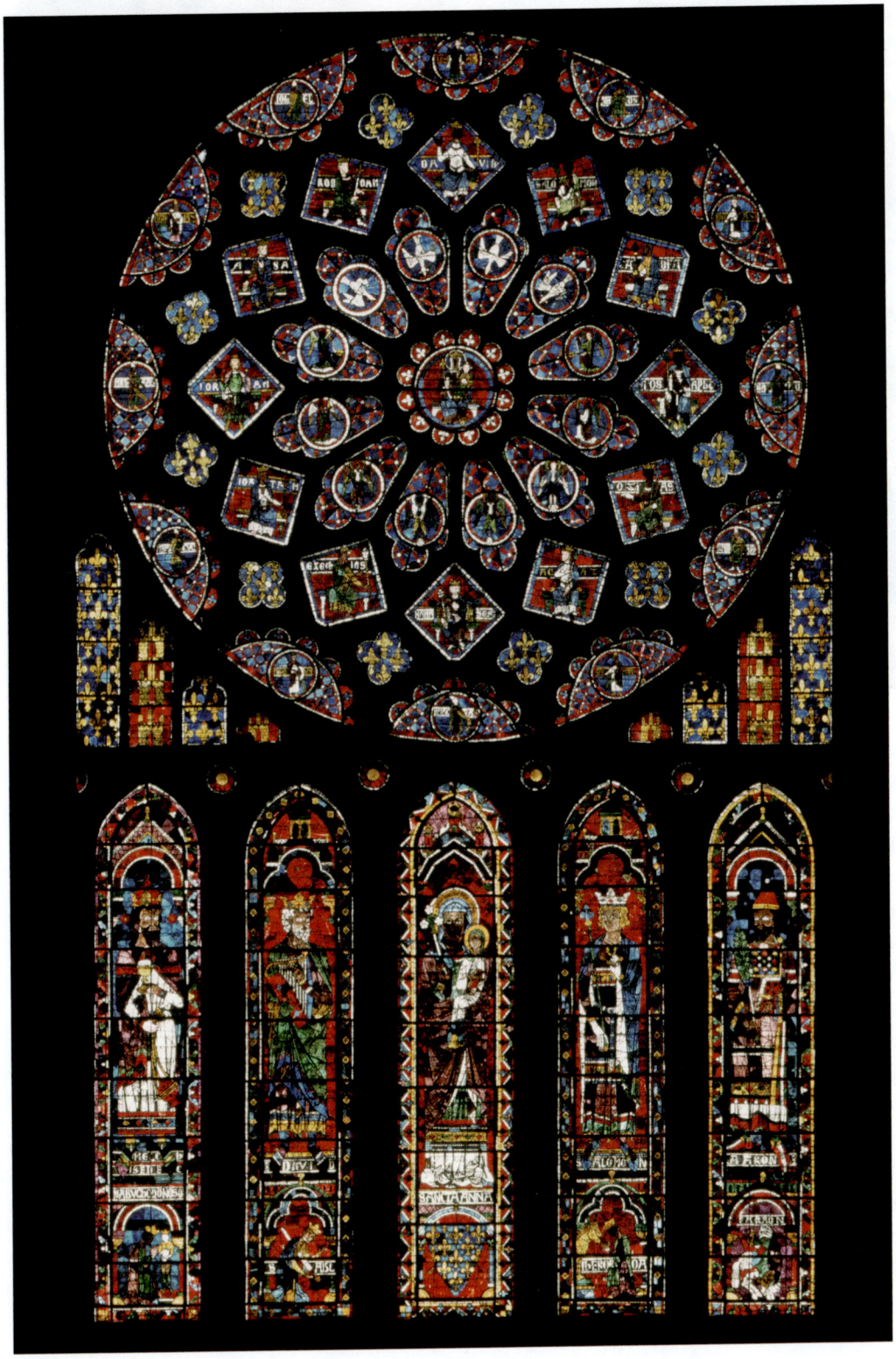

2.6.11 Rose window and lancets, north transept, 13th century. Chartres Cathedral, France

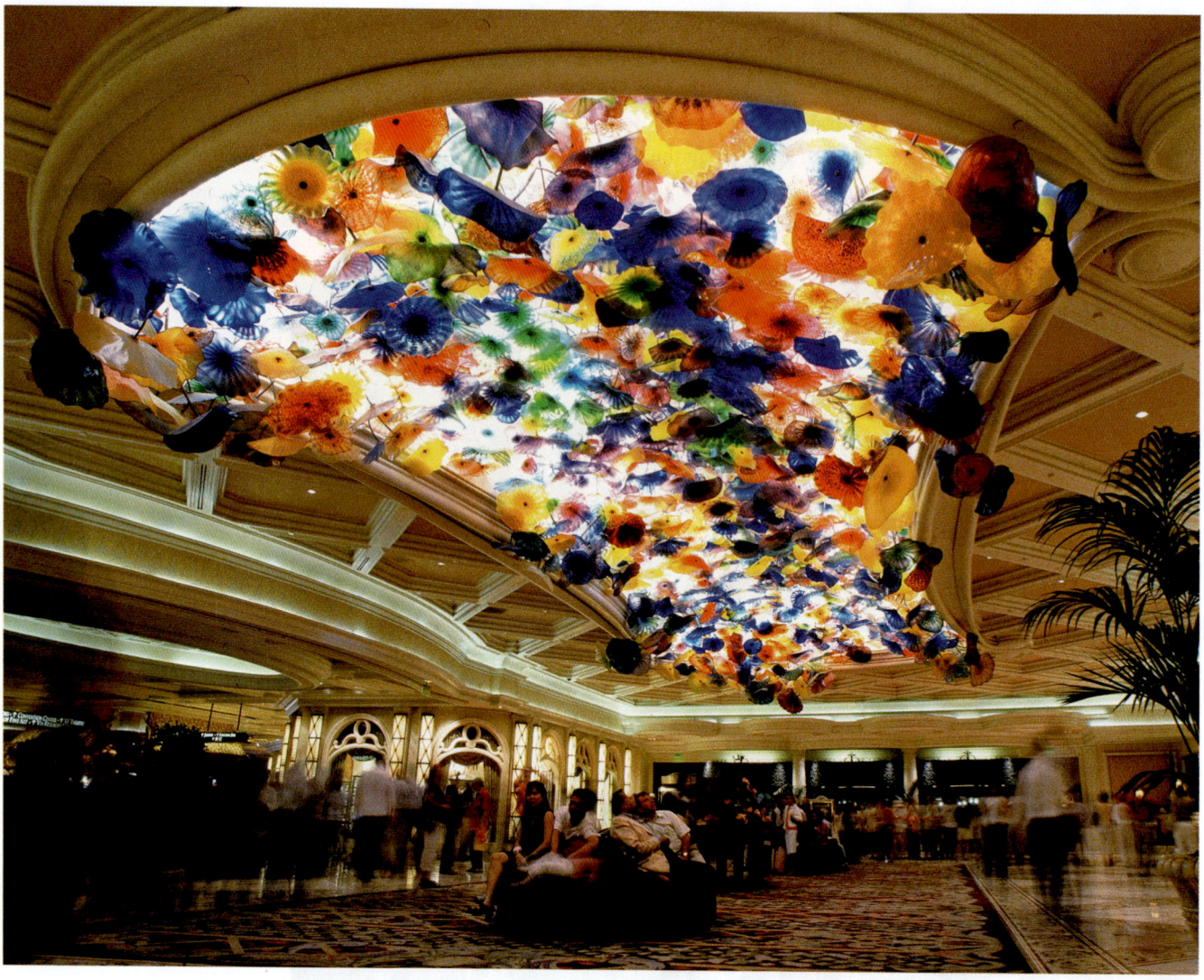

2.6.12 Dale Chihuly, *Fiori di Como*, 1998. Hand-blown glass and steel, 70 × 30 × 12'. Bellagio Hotel, Las Vegas, Nevada

are accented by the **contrast** with smaller, tall thin windows with pointed tops. The brilliant blue color in these windows stands apart as one of the most extraordinary achievements of the early thirteenth century. They are so valued that to prevent them from being damaged during World War II, they were removed and placed in storage until after the war had ended.

The contemporary American glass artist Dale Chihuly (b. 1941) makes comparable use of the kind of visual experience that glass can bring to an interior. To enhance the reception area at the Bellagio Hotel in Las Vegas, Chihuly has created a dazzling ceiling made of 2,000 individually blown glass flowers (**2.6.12**). The strong color, reminiscent of stained glass, enlivens and invigorates the interior and becomes an inviting and memorable symbol of the hotel. The effect is mesmerizing.

Metalwork

As with ceramics, the use of metal in the creation of objects goes back to ancient times. Metal has been so important in human history that some archaeological periods, such as the Bronze Age (more than 5,000 years ago) and Iron Age (more than 3,000 years ago), are named for the metal most commonly used at that time. The working of metal has been a measure of human development and, like most traditional crafts, an important medium for utilitarian purposes.

The properties of a metal object are derived from its basic components. Some metals, such as iron or copper, are natural materials and can be dug from the ground and then refined. Others are **alloys**, or combinations of two or more naturally occurring metals, combined to take advantage of the specific properties of each. For

Contrast: a drastic difference between such elements as color or value (lightness/darkness) when they are presented together
Alloy: a mixture of a metal combined with at least one other element

example, if tin is mixed with copper, it produces bronze. As a result of the addition of tin, the bronze is harder and has a lower melting point than copper, so it is easier to manipulate. Other common alloys include pewter, brass, and steel.

Metal can be heated to a liquid state and poured into molds. It can also be heated and then hammered into shape, or it can be worked (usually, again, by hammering) when it is cold. Most metals are strong but malleable, and can be bent or stretched to fit the needs of the artist. Gold is particularly well suited for decorative metalwork because it is comparatively soft (for a metal) and easy to shape.

The gold mask in **2.6.13** was created by laying a thin piece of metal over an object carved to resemble a human face. The artist then carefully hammered the surface of the thin metal, a process called **chasing**, until the shape and texture of the design were imprinted in the metal. The artist has deftly given us the impression of a human face by placing objects, such as cowrie shells for the eyes, under the surface of the metal and forcing the gold sheet into its final shape. This process would have been repeated with different textures and objects to create the detailed ears, eyebrows, beard, and so on. This type of mask was used as a burial mask to cover the face of the departed.

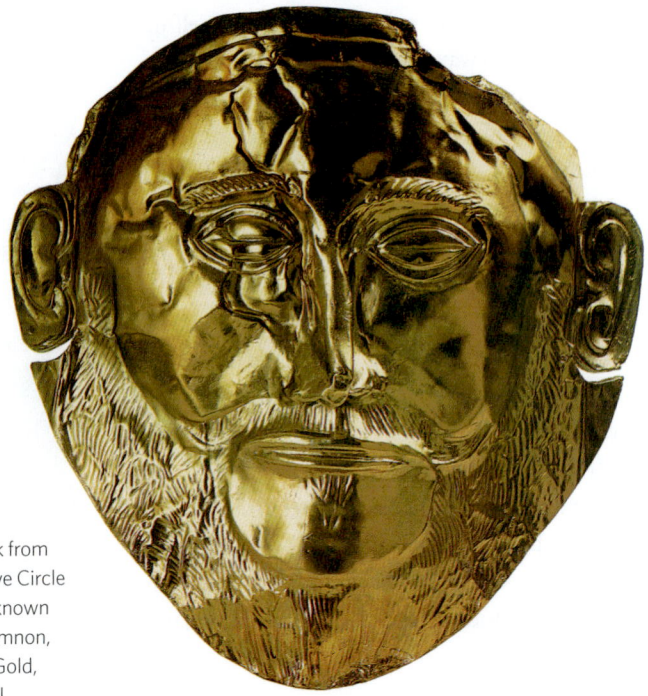

2.6.13 Death mask from Shaft Grave V, Grave Circle A, Mycenae. Also known as Mask of Agamemnon, c. 1550–1500 BCE. Gold, height 12". National Archaeological Museum, Athens, Greece

The process of chasing involves hammering the front of a metal surface that has a form beneath it, in order to create a relief design; but reversing the process can have equal impact. This technique is known as **repoussé**. Take for example the *Chalice with Apostles Venerating the Cross* (**2.6.14**), a silver cup that was created in around 600 CE. In order to create this precious object, the artist hammered a blunt tool against the back of the image. Consequently the opposite side was systematically pushed out to form the images of figures, columns, crosses, and arches. These symbols were used by early Christians to represent elements of their belief system.

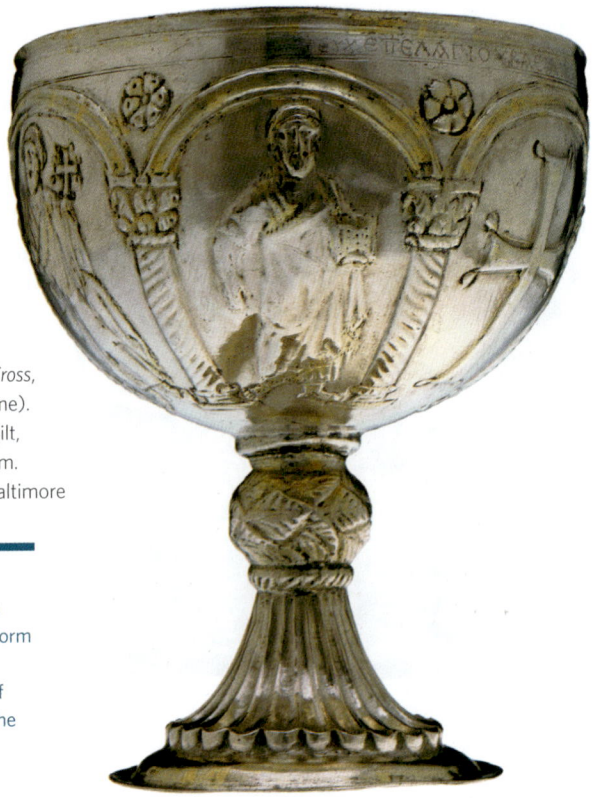

2.6.14 *Chalice with Apostles Venerating the Cross*, c. 600 CE, Syria (Byzantine). Silver repoussé, partial gilt, 6⅝ × 5½" diameter at rim. Walters Art Museum, Baltimore

Chasing: a technique of hammering the front of a metal object to create a form or surface detail
Repoussé: a technique of hammering metal from the back to create a form or surface detail

An artist with good technical skills can control metals to make almost any object he or she can imagine. The Italian goldsmith Benvenuto Cellini (1500–1571) created the *Salt Cellar of Francis I* as an extremely elaborate object to go on the dining-table of the king of

France (**2.6.15**). To make this salt cellar, Cellini first sculpted wax models of Neptune (the Roman god of the salty sea) and Mother Earth (whence table salt was extracted) in harmony and at rest. Cellini then covered the wax model with a strong material, perhaps sand and lime, to make a mold. The mold was then heated so that the wax melted and left the center of the mold empty. Once the metal had reached the required 2,000°F, Cellini poured the molten gold into the mold. When it was cool, the artist could remove the mold and then carefully finish off the piece. The salt was held in a bowl shape next to Neptune, and the pepper inside the small triumphal arch next to the symbolic image of Earth. This magnificent example of Renaissance metalwork took more than two years to make.

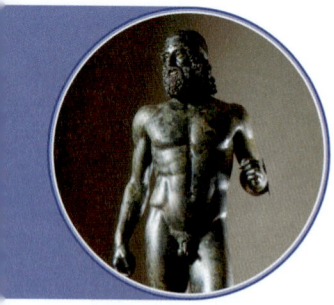

More information about the process of metal casting can be found in chapter 2.4: see **2.4.12, p. 250**

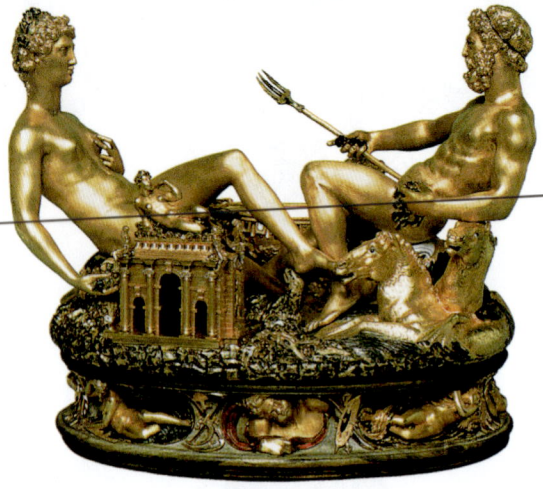

2.6.15 Benvenuto Cellini, *Salt Cellar of Francis I*, 1540–43. Gold, enamel, ebony, ivory, 11¼ × 8½ × 10⅜". Kunsthistorisches Museum, Vienna, Austria

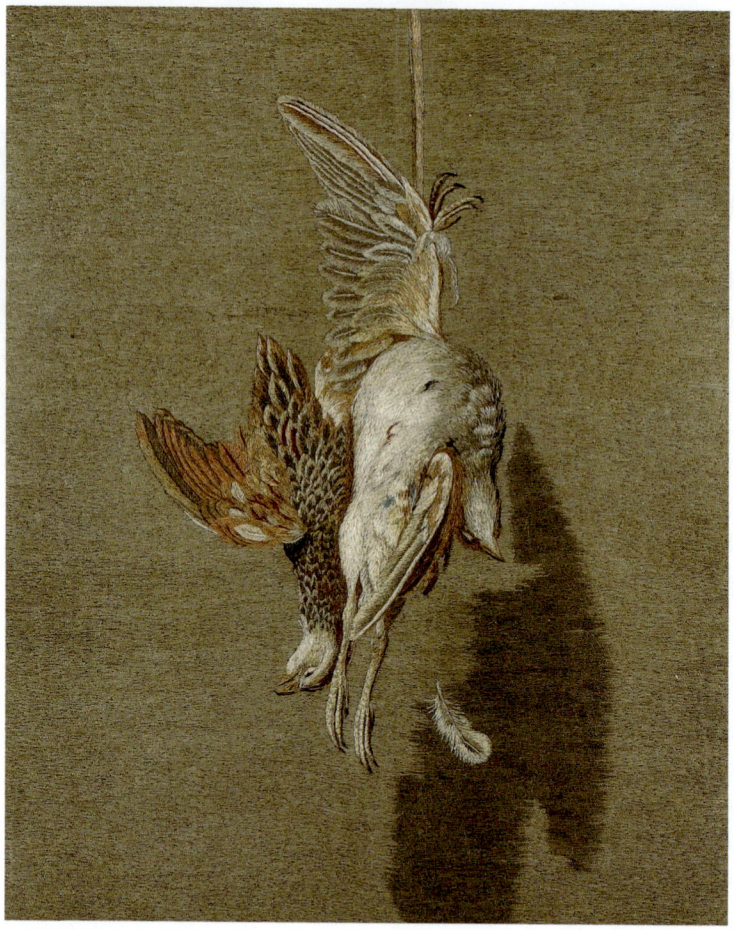

2.6.16 Mary Linwood, detail from *Hanging Partridge*, late 18th century. Crewelwork embroidery, approximately 24½ × 28". Private collection

Fiber

Fibers are threads made from animal or vegetable materials (such as fur, wool, silk, cotton, flax, or linen) or, more recently, synthetic materials (for example nylon or polyester). Fiber art is most often associated with the creation of textiles. The fibers can be spun into yarn, string, or thread, then woven or knitted into lengths of textiles. In the case of embroidery, the thread, string, or yarn is applied using stitching techniques. Relatively stiff fibers, such as grass and rushes, can be woven together to make baskets and similar objects. Processing plant fibers begins with separating the fiber from the plant, then preparing it for use by spinning the fiber into a long thread. In the case of cotton, once the cotton bolls are collected, the fibers are separated and washed; then the individual fibers are spun, or twisted, into thread. Wool is sheared from sheep in the spring, washed and separated, then spun into yarn. Silk fibers are very fine and are the product of silkworms, which spin cocoons. Once the cocoons are complete, they are harvested. They are softened in warm water to loosen the gum that binds the fibers together. The silk can then easily be removed and spun into an exquisite fabric.

Embroidery is the process of stitching an image into a fabric surface using a needle and thread (or yarn). An embroiderer attaches the thread to the fabric by way of a variety of stitches, each with its own function in a design. The British artist Mary Linwood (1755–1845) practiced the art of crewel embroidery, a process that uses freeform, fine wool thread stitching on a drawn design. The detail from *Hanging Partridge* (**2.6.16**) shows that the process is a lot like "painting with thread," as the artist applies the thread colors the way a painter would apply color in a painting. This kind of needlework is intricate and slow (one of Linwood's pieces reportedly took ten years to complete), but it shows exceptional patience and skill. Linwood's work was held in high esteem, and indeed she was popular with royalty in England and Russia.

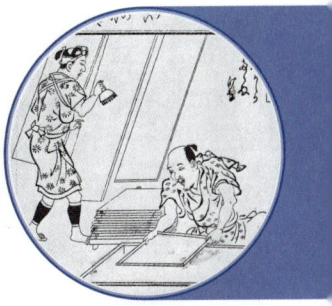

A diverse range of materials can be used in the creation of fiber art, including paper: see **2.1.21, p. 205**

Faith Ringgold, *Tar Beach*

"There once was a little girl named Cassie who lived in an apartment in New York. On warm summer evenings, she and her family would lay out blankets and have picnics under the stars on their tar beach. The roof was a wonderful place to lie back and look at the city and its lights, and dream about wonderful things like flying through the sky. She could dream that her father, who had helped to build the building where she lived, could join the union, even though being half-Black and half-Indian made it impossible. She could dream that her mother owned an ice-cream factory and was able to eat ice cream every night for dessert."

In this artwork, the African American artist Faith Ringgold (b.1930) tells a story of a child called Cassie (**2.6.17**). Ringgold relates the African American experience, her personal history, and her family life by presenting her own childhood memories in a work that combines painting on canvas with the quilting skills of her family and ancestors. Ringgold began to paint on fabrics in the 1970s. As she did, the works evolved into a collaborative effort with her mother, who was a dressmaker and fashion designer. Ringgold would create the painted part of the work, and her mother would stitch the edges and sew patches of cloth and quilted areas together to form a border. Her great-great-great-grandmother had been a slave who made quilts for plantation owners in the South. Ringgold's works thus possess many layers of meaning that relate to this history and these craft skills. Together these layers communicate the richness of human experience.

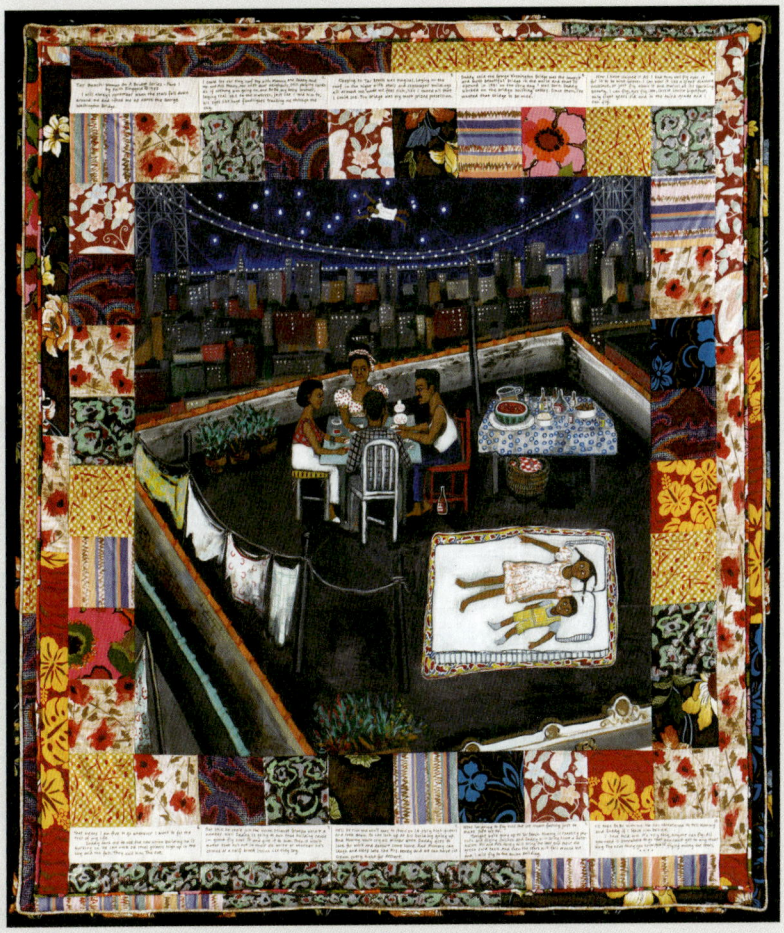

2.6.17 Faith Ringgold, *Tar Beach*, 1988. Acrylic on canvas, bordered with printed, painted, quilted, and pieced cloth, 6'2⅝" × 5'8½". Solomon R. Guggenheim Museum, New York

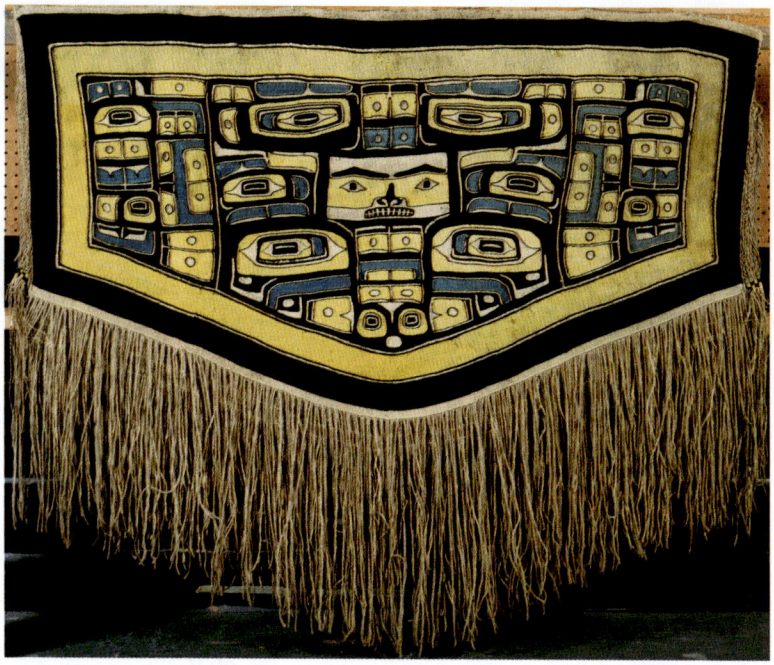

2.6.18 Tlingit Chilkat dancing blanket, 19th century

Chilkat: a traditional form of weaving practiced by Tlingit and other Northwest Coast peoples of Alaska and British Columbia
Abstract: art imagery that departs from recognizable images of the natural world

The Tlingit people, who live on the western coast of Canada and Alaska, combine both animal and plant material in their fiber art. The blanket shown in **2.6.18** has been woven entirely by hand (without a loom) from goat wool and cedar bark in their traditional **Chilkat** style. As Chilkat weaving is intended to be a two-dimensional portrayal of totem carving, the designs for the blankets come from pattern boards developed by wood carvers who use symbols that convey subjects of significance to their tribe or family. In many cases these designs are **abstract** depictions of animals. The central figure here looks like a bear or raccoon. Note the large eyes on either side of the image, which imply the presence of even bigger creatures. Blankets like this are worn on civic and ceremonial occasions by high-ranking tribal members, their long fringe intended to sway against the body in both dances and rituals. They are very expensive, and the prized possessions of anyone fortunate enough to inherit or purchase one.

Contemporary art responds to current culture and trends. While the ancient process of weaving fibers is still used to create modern artworks, contemporary artists have developed interesting new techniques to respond to the culture of their time and locale. A modern master of woven fiber is the American-born Sheila Hicks (b. 1934) who challenges the traditional nature of fiber by using it in more expressive ways on a massive scale. In

2.6.19 Sheila Hicks, *The Silk Rainforest*, c. 1975. Silk, linen, and cotton, 96 × 270 × 3", Smithsonian American Art Museum, Renwick Gallery, Washington, D.C.

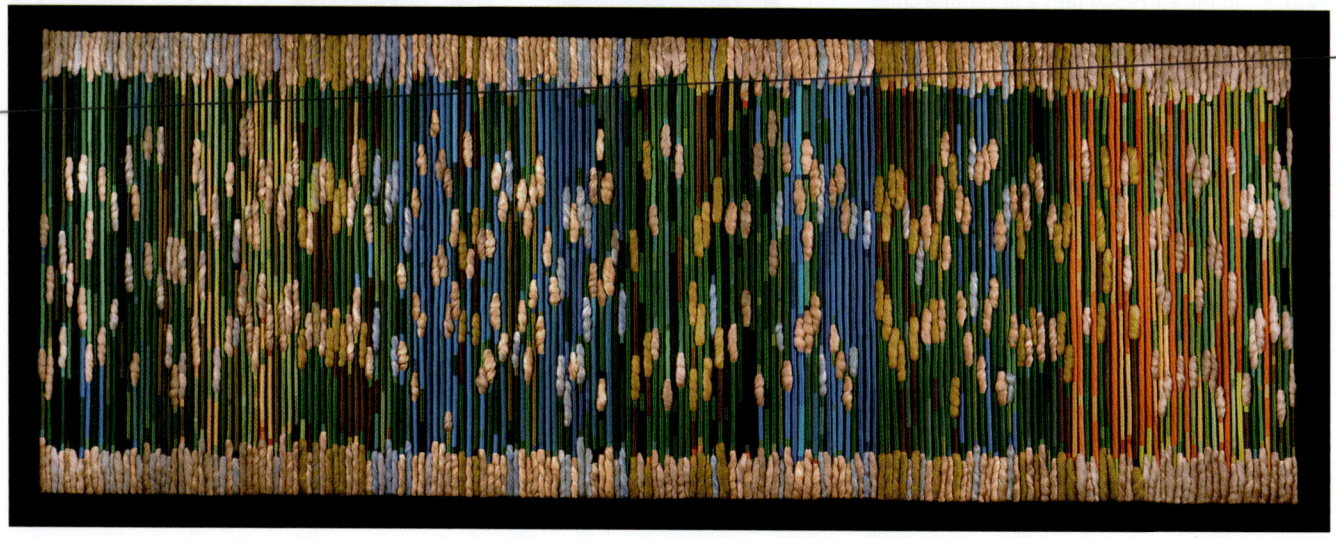

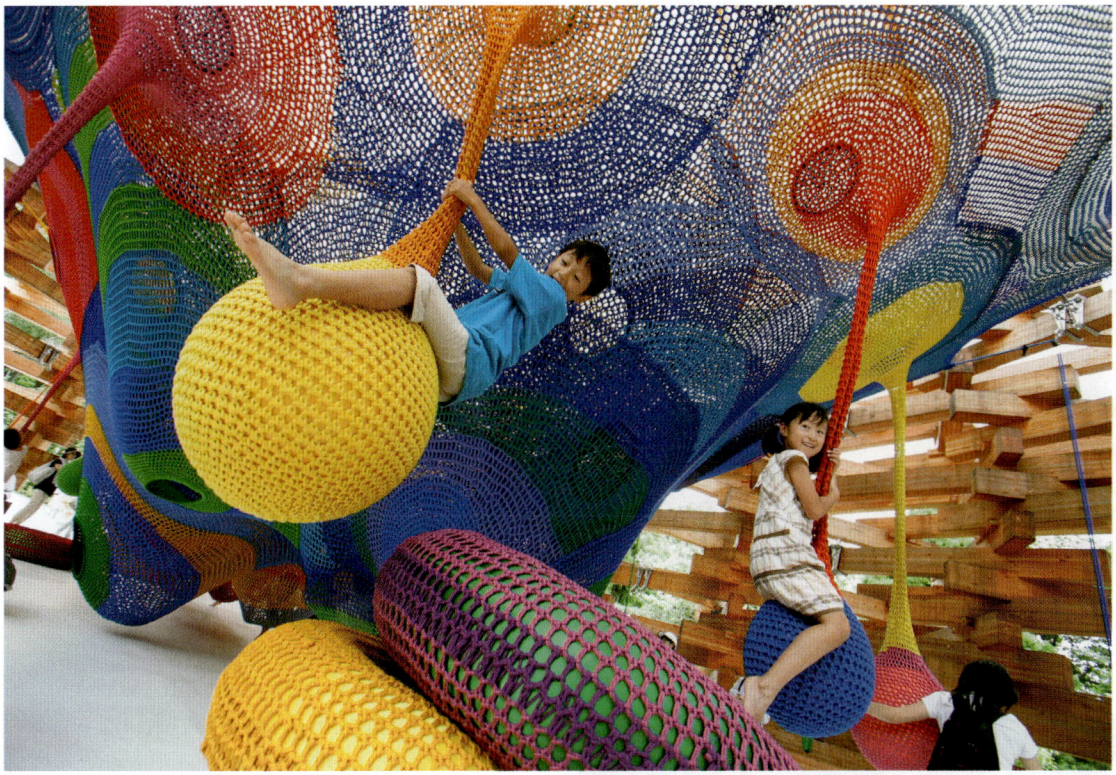

2.6.20 Toshiko Horiuchi MacAdam, *Knitted Wonder Space II*, 2009. Braided nylon 6-6; hand crochet, 49'2" × 29'6" × 21'3". Woods of Net Pavilion, Hakone Open Air Museum, Hakone, Japan

her woven work *The Silk Rainforest* (**2.6.19**) Hicks created a huge work that rivaled the kind of measured and controlled corporate installation being created in other media by leaving the raw irregularity of the frayed fiber. The rich fiber surface and the interplay of color display a unique sensitivity to the tactile characteristics of the silk, linen, and cotton for the viewers at the AT&T Headquarters in Basking Ridge, New Jersey, where it was originally installed. Hicks created a composition that conjured the physical sense of touch and paired it with a rich visual experience, making the viewer's experience more holistic.

Knitting is a process of creating a fabric using loops and stitching. Various materials can be knitted, including wool, cotton, and nylon. The Japanese artist Toshiko Horiuchi MacAdam (b. 1940) knits entire environments where viewers are invited to touch the artwork. Her early work in architectural fabric structures led her to create interactive environments. For example, *Knitted Wonder Space II* (**2.6.20**) is a knitted structure designed to be a children's playground. MacAdam builds these large-scale fiber constructions in her studio in Canada, and installs them as required: her work can be found in many countries worldwide. These works challenge preconceived ideas of what fiber art can be, as do others in which artists have knitted metals and plastics as if they are also fibrous.

Wood

Wood, an organic plant-based material, deteriorates over time, so we have few ancient examples of art objects made from it. But we know that wood has been utilized for objects and architecture throughout history. Trees provide many colors and hardnesses of wood, the innate beauty of which can be brought out by cutting and carving. Sanding and polishing a piece of wood gives its surface a mesmerizing beauty.

Around 1480, the Italian artist Francesco di Giorgio Martini (1439–1501) used a decorative wood technique called **intarsia** in his design for a *studiolo* (a private room, often a library or study) in Gubbio, Italy. Intarsia is a kind of wood mosaic using woods of different colors. Giuliano da Maiano, who executed the work, took very thin, shaped pieces of wood and organized them to create a masterpiece of **illusionistic** depth and **value**

Intarsia: the art of setting pieces of wood into a surface to create a pattern
Illusionism, Illusionistic: the artistic skill or trick of making something look real
Value: the lightness or darkness of a plane or area

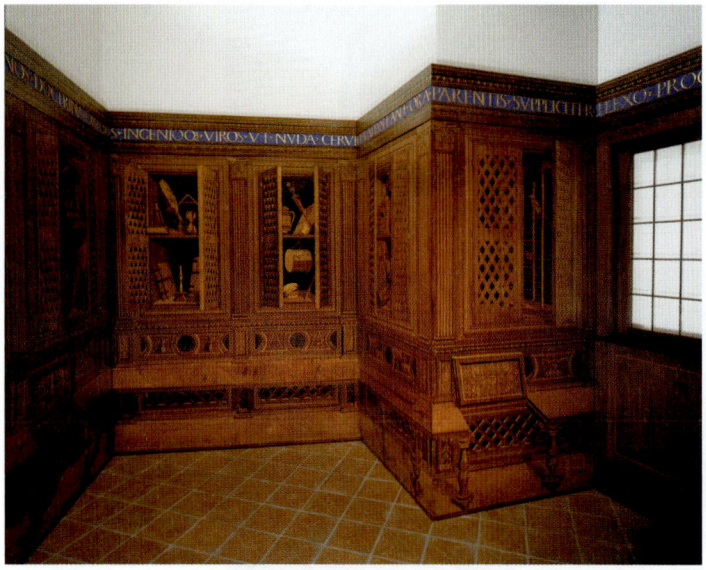

2.6.21 Detail of *studiolo* from the Ducal Palace in Gubbio, Italy, by Giuliano da Maiano, after a design by Francesco di Giorgio Martini, *c.* 1480. Walnut, beech, rosewood, oak, and fruit woods in walnut base, 15'11" × 16'11" × 12'7¼". Metropolitan Museum of Art, New York

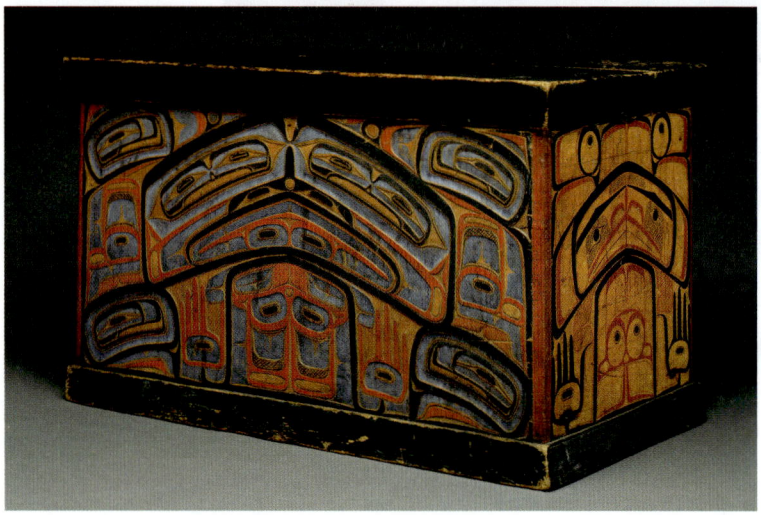

2.6.22 Captain Richard Carpenter, bent-corner chest, c. 1860. Yellow cedar, red cedar, and paint, 21¼ × 35¾ × 20½". Seattle Art Museum, Washington

(**2.6.21**). To the casual viewer, because the artists employed such skill, it is not clear where reality ends and the illusion begins. Federico da Montefeltro, the Duke of Urbino, who commissioned Martini to create this work, wanted the symbols in this magnificent design to reflect his achievements as a ruler, military commander, collector of books, and patron of the arts.

A Native American artist of the Heiltsuk tribe worked with wood to make the bent-corner chest shown in **2.6.22**. To create this vessel, a plank of cedar was smoothed, notches known as kerfs were cut at three corners, and then the wood was made flexible by exposing it to steam created by fire-baked rocks and water. The plank was then bent at the kerfs and joined at the juncture of the last corner. After that, the chest was carved and painted with an elaborate, symmetrical design that fills the whole surface. A separate base and top were then fitted to the whole.

The practice of wood turning, or fashioning a wooden object using a lathe (a power-driven spinning support), continues to grow in popularity. The artist who practices this craft must, naturally, be knowledgeable about wood and its attributes; prepare the wood by seasoning (careful ageing and drying); and control the orientation of the grain of the wood on the turning axis. Andrew Early (b. 1970), a South African wood turner who was taught this craft by his father, John, has become one of today's most collected and exhibited wood turners. Early places emphasis on selecting and preparing the wood to capture its natural organic character, often ageing the wood for many years. He leaves voids and irregularities that naturally occur in the lumber to preserve its rich innate "personality" or quality. Such works as the turned wood bowl in **2.6.23** reflect the sensitivity to the material that most craftspeople and artisans possess after having spent long hours in the study and execution of excellence. Early would probably agree with Chaucer that "life is so short, the craft so long to learn."

2.6.23 Andrew Early, turned bowl, 2010. Indian mahogany, 13¾ × 29½"

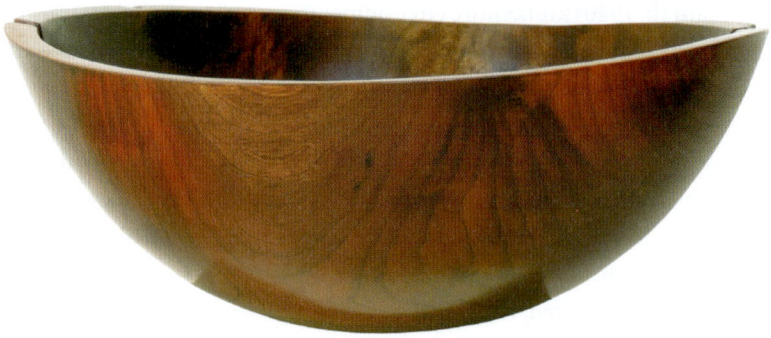

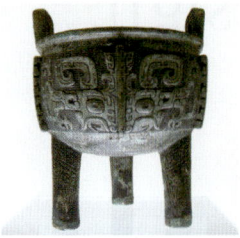

1.6.13 *Liu Ding* (ritual container), China, c. 1600–c. 1050 BCE, p. 134

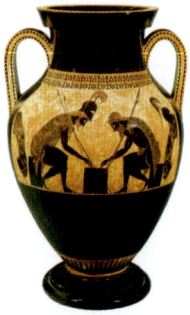

3.1.26 Exekias, amphora with Achilles and Ajax playing dice, 530 BCE, p. 383

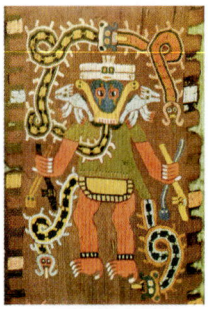

3.4.3 Paracas textile, Peru, 3rd century BCE, p. 431

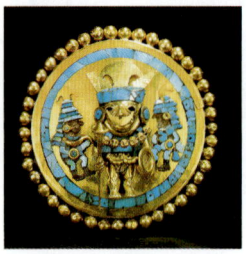

3.4.4 Moche earspool, c. 300 CE, Peru, p. 431

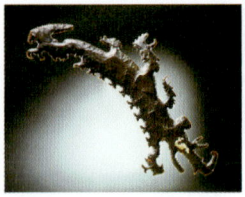

4.4.4 Maya flint depicting a crocodile canoe, 600–900 CE, p. 605

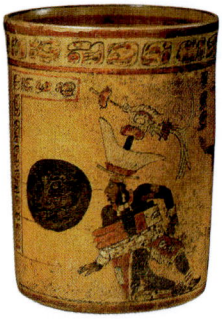

3.4.13 Cylindrical vessel with ritual ball-game scene, c. 700–850, p. 437

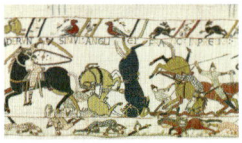

4.7.5 Detail of the Battle of Hastings, *Bayeux Tapestry*, c. 1066–82, p. 642

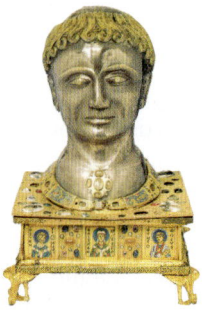

3.2.15 Reliquary of the Head of St. Alexander, 1145, p. 400

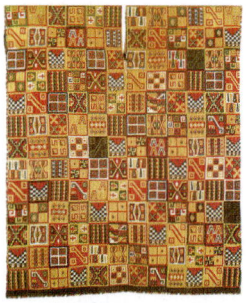

3.4.6 Inca tunic, Andes, c. 1500, p. 433

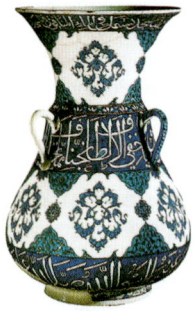

1.4.23 Mosque lamp from the Dome of the Rock, Jerusalem, 1549, p. 106

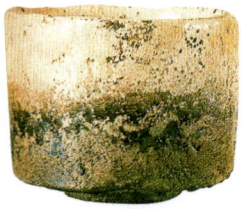

0.0.11 Hon'ami Koetsu, tea bowl, early 17th century, p. 28

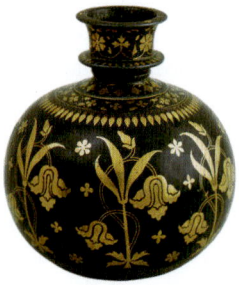

1.9.3 Hugga base, India, last quarter of 17th century, p. 160

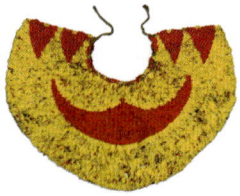

3.5.15a Feather cloak (*ahu'ula*), Hawaii, 18th century (?), p. 456

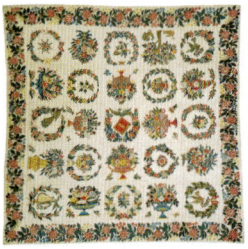

1.6.12 Album quilt, probably by Mary Evans, 1848, p. 133

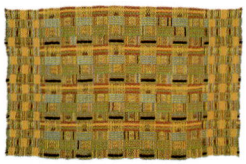

3.5.5 Asante textile wrapper (*kente*), Africa, 20th century, p. 449

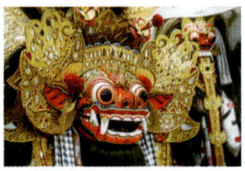

3.3.28 Barong dance mask of a lion, Ubud, Bali, Indonesia, p. 427

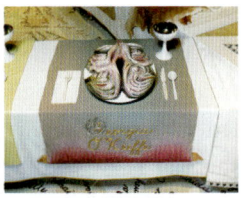

4.10.6 Judy Chicago, *The Dinner Party*, 1974–79, p. 684

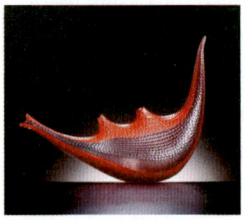

1.2.5 Lino Tagliapietra, *Batman*, 1998, p. 64

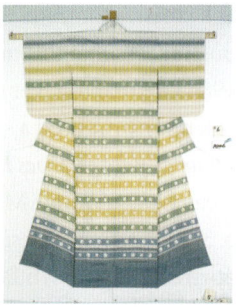

3.3.19 Sonoko Sasaki, *Sea in the Sky*, 2007, p. 422

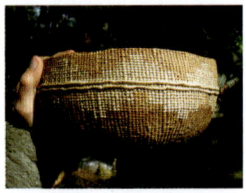

3.4.24 Julia Parker, basket for cooking acorns, c. 2011, p. 443

2.7 Visual Communication Design

Typefaces: The particular unified style of a family of typographical characters
Medium (plural **media**): the material on or from which an artist chooses to make a work of art, for example canvas and oil paint, marble, engraving, video, or architecture
Abstract: art imagery that departs from recognizable images of the natural world

The essence of visual communication design is the use of symbol to communicate information and ideas. Traditional communication design was known as graphic design: the design of books, magazines, posters, advertising, and other printed matter by arranging drawings, photographs, and type. Advances in printing processes, television, the computer, and the growth of the Web have expanded graphic design to include many more design possibilities. A better and more complete term for it now is visual communication design. Furthermore, while graphic design was the responsibility of specialists, the typographical power of the computer—both for print and the Web—means that many more people can, with a little practice, create effective and even innovative design work, provided they understand the principles of visual communication design.

The term visual communication design was first introduced by the designer April Greiman (b. 1948), shortly after she was named chair of the Department of Design at the California Institute of the Arts in 1981. Unlike other designers at that time Greiman embraced the computer as a creative tool, and experimented with the possibilities that this new medium afforded. In 1986 Greiman forever changed the design world when she produced a six-page fold out *Design Quarterly* cover, *Does It Make Sense?*, that was created on an Apple Macintosh computer (**2.7.15**, p. 308). Greiman's design integrated a nude self-portrait, graphic symbols, and creative **typefaces** into one dynamic piece of cover art that dazzled the industry and ushered in the digital age. The computer allowed the integration of elements that did not need to be rigidly set into a grid, reflecting the looseness of 1980s punk culture, a style that came to be called New Wave design.

This chapter will discuss the development of the **media**, systems, and processes used in visual communication design. While based on simple ideas, visual communication design enables us to express visual ideas with increasing clarity, style, and sophistication.

The Visual Character of Text

Early History of Writing

The peoples of ancient Mesopotamia—who inhabited a region that covers modern-day Iraq, southeast Turkey, and northeast Syria—were the first (*c.* 3400 BCE) to employ picture symbols in a consistent language system. The ancient Egyptians later created their own version of picture symbols, known as hieroglyphics, as a written form of communication. In particular, the Egyptians wrote them on scrolls made of a paper-like substance created from the pith of the papyrus plant (see, for example, **2.7.1**). While early Chinese written characters also frequently resembled the subject they identified, later forms of picture writing became increasingly **abstract**. The Western alphabet has followed the same trajectory; while originally (for example) the letter A was supposed to be derived from the shape of a cow's skull, and B from a house, it has now lost any of its earliest connections with the representations of things.

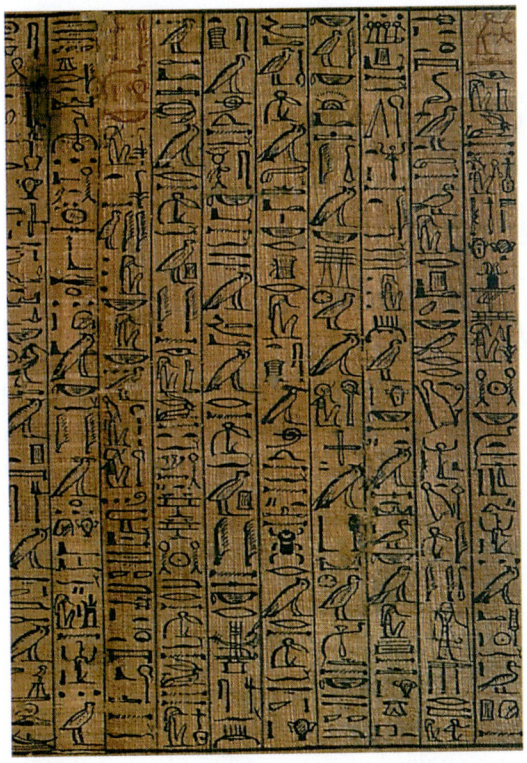

2.7.1 Section of papyrus from Book of the Dead of Ani, *c.* 1250 BCE. British Museum, London, England

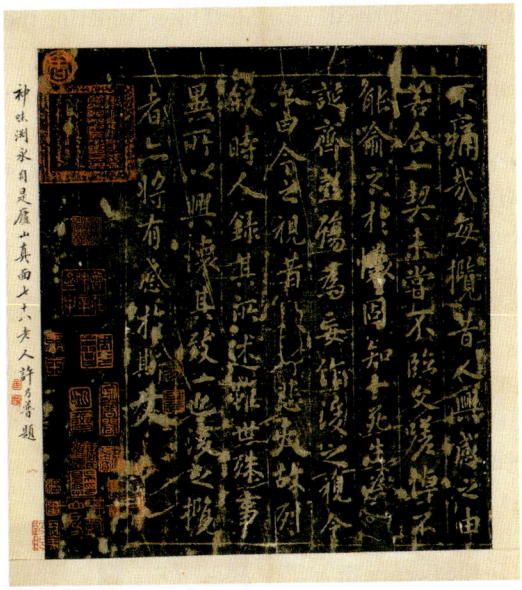

2.7.2 Rubbing of stela inscription, *Preface of the Lanting Gathering*, Ding Wu version (Inukai version), original by Wang Xizhi, Eastern Jin Dynasty, dated 353 CE. Album, ink on paper, 9⅝ × 8⅞". Tokyo National Museum, Japan

Wherever literacy takes hold, **calligraphy** usually develops as a form of art concerned to express layers of meaning and feelings by means of the shape of written letterforms. For example, handwritten wedding invitations are created using calligraphy because the flowing line and distinctive character of the lettering communicate the upcoming event in an elegant and romantic way. In oral communication, changes in tone, volume, facial expression, hand gestures, and body movement work together; in calligraphy, the physical act of writing, the thought expressed, and the visual form of the text become one. Chinese culture particularly exalts calligraphy executed in black ink with a brush. The Chinese calligrapher Wang Xizhi (303–361 CE) defined the art of calligraphy in China during the Jin Dynasty (265–420 CE). Although none of Wang's originals still exists, other calligraphers copied his work through the ages, perpetuating his ideal of perfect form. In ancient China, fine specimens of writing were carved on large standing stone tablets, from which visitors could take copies by making rubbings—a rudimentary printing technique (**2.7.2**).

Calligraphy: the art of emotive or carefully descriptive hand lettering or handwriting
Typography: the art of designing, arranging, and choosing type
Illuminated manuscript: a hand-lettered text with hand-drawn pictures

Typography

The visual form of printed letters, words, and text is called **typography**. Type, a word derived from a Greek word meaning "to strike," first came into existence with Johannes Gutenberg's (*c.* 1398–1468) invention of the printing press in Germany around 1450. Gutenberg also created a technique for producing small cast-metal letter shapes, known as letterforms, that could be set next to each other in a row, inked, and then printed in relief on paper using his press. Gutenberg's letterforms have angled thick and thin strokes that mimic the pen calligraphy used in **illuminated manuscripts** (called Black Letter; see p. 302). Scholars believe his intention was to emulate handwritten texts; his first bibles used the exact same letterforms as those used in manuscripts, and the pages even included illustrations drawn by hand.

The German master printmaker Albrecht Dürer (1471–1528) wrote systematically on the subject of typography in order to teach others. In *Course in the Art of Measurement with Compass and Ruler* (1538), he sought to create a set of rules for the design of letter shapes (**2.7.3**, p. 302). His was the first text to standardize how to create each letter using such geometric elements as squares, circles, and lines. Through these careful instructions, a typographer could create letterforms similar to those used by the ancient Romans.

Dürer's Roman alphabet is notably different from Gutenberg's letterforms. A complete

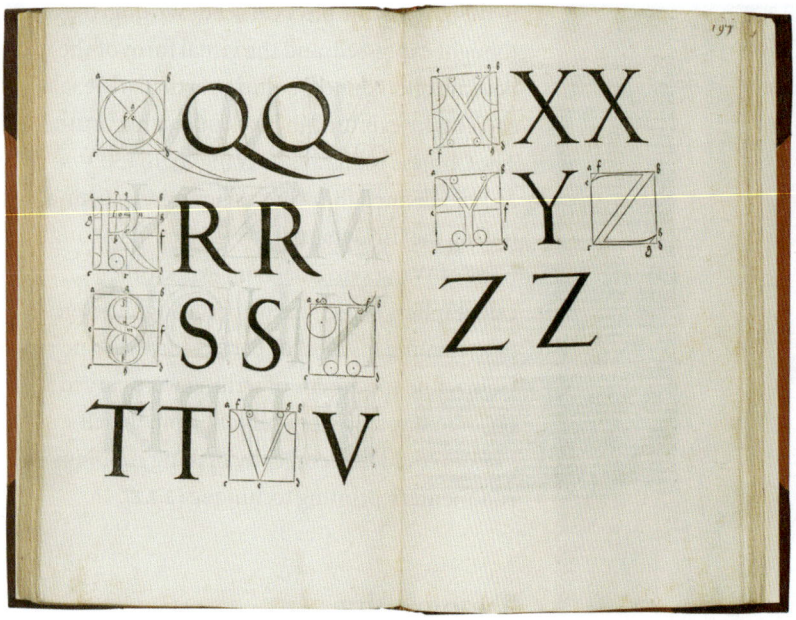

2.7.3 Albrecht Dürer, pages from *Course in the Art of Measurement with Compass and Ruler*, 1538. Victoria and Albert Museum, London, England

alphabet of letterforms and matching punctuation is called a font. A font is a group of letterforms designed to have a unified appearance. Roman-style fonts were derived directly from the letters chiseled into stone on the buildings and monuments of ancient Rome. Those characters had a vertical or horizontal mark at the edges of some letters. These marks, called serifs, were integrated into many early typefaces. The differences between these kinds of fonts are shown in **2.7.4**.

In books and newspapers, serif fonts are traditionally used in the main text because they are considered easier to read. Typographers often use a sans serif font, or a font without serifs, in headings. (Sans serif derives its name from the French word *sans*, meaning "without," and perhaps from the Dutch word *schreef*, meaning a stroke of a pen.) In the twenty-first century, sans serif has become the standard font style in electronic media, as tiny serifs may not fully appear in comparatively low-resolution electronic displays.

Typographers follow some simple rules to make sure a written message is clear. When using multiple fonts, the fonts must be different enough to avoid confusion between the typefaces. The visual weight, or thickness, of the letters can be used for **contrast** and to emphasize a section of the text simply by changing type to bold. The choice of larger or smaller font sizes also adds another level of contrast and **emphasis**. Finally, even more emphasis and contrast can be gained through the choice of **color**. Typographers use these options carefully to "keep it simple" and to create a message that is clear, concise, and easily understood.

Contemporary typographers coax expression from the printed word by carefully balancing message with visual form. The Malaysian-born American typographer Kok Cheow Yeoh (b. 1967) pushes the limits of text by considering the relationship between the message and the visual form. In the poster design *Hegemony* (**2.7.5**) the designer has visually balanced most of the letters and symbols atop a large blue letter "A". In this

Contrast: a drastic difference between such elements as color or value (lightness/darkness) when they are presented together
Emphasis: the principle of drawing attention to particular content in a work
Color: the optical effect caused when reflected white light of the spectrum is divided into separate wavelengths

Gütenberg Bible

Roman Serif Font

Sans Serif Font

2.7.4 Some font styles:
1. Replica of Black Letter style used in Gutenberg's 1454 Bible
2. Times New Roman with some serifs circled
3. Helvetica font with no serifs (sans serif)

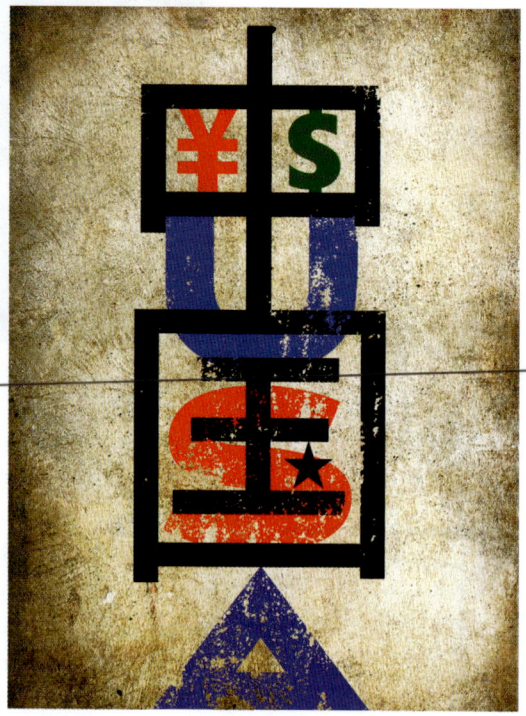

2.7.5 Kok Cheow Yeoh, *Hegemony*, 2016. Poster design for International Art and Design Exhibition (INAD), Selçuk University, Konya, Turkey

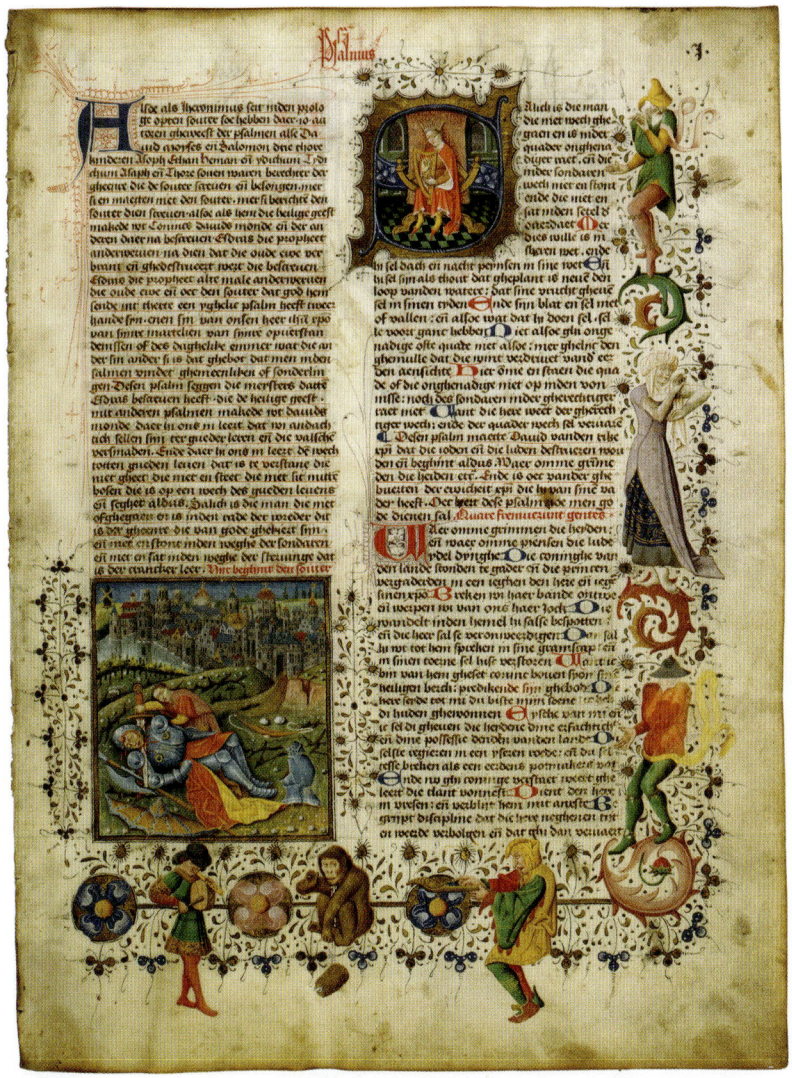

2.7.6 *Dutch History Bible*, copied by Gherard Wessels van Deventer in Utrecht, 1443, fol. 8r. National Library of the Netherlands, The Hague

work the word hegemony, meaning authority or dominance, refers to the world economic leadership of the US and China. Both countries compete economically, but also rely on each other for trade, resulting in a balanced tension that keeps the commercial and financial markets healthy and positive. The designer has interspersed letters and symbols from the dominant language of each competing country to illustrate this relationship.

The Communicative Image

The first communicative graphic was probably created when a prehistoric person spat pigment through a reed to **stencil** a handprint on the wall of a cave. During the Middle Ages, European artists combined calligraphy and illustration to craft illuminated manuscripts (for example **2.7.6**). Illuminated manuscripts were executed in monasteries on prepared animal skins, called parchment. After being painted and lettered by hand, they were bound as books. This kind of design was very time-consuming and produced only one copy of the book. The invention of printing technology simplified the design process and made it possible to print multiple copies. In other words, printing made graphic design possible.

Stencil: a perforated template allowing ink or paint to pass through to print a design

Logos and Icons

Businesses and other organizations use logos as communication tools. A logo (from the Greek *logos*, meaning "word") is often simply a carefully designed piece of type, called a logotype, that is unique and easily identified. Sometimes a designer communicates an idea using a pictorial symbol instead of type. The Chevrolet logo was first used in 1913 and has been an identifying mark for the company ever since. Originally, the name "Chevrolet" was written across the simple stylized cross (called the "bowtie"). Over time, the symbol became associated in people's minds with the name, which was then removed from the design. It now communicates the company name without using one letter of the alphabet (**2.7.7**).

The immediacy and the universal communicative properties of logos have become the basis for a new kind of labeling system that is now used worldwide. Icons, or simple symbolic graphic shapes, are being used in place of written labels because they provide an immediate message that can be understood in any language. For example, on car dashboards, the icon in the shape of two concentric triangles (third row down, sixth icon on the right in

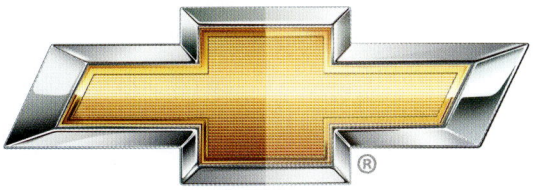

2.7.7 Chevrolet logo, first used in 1913

Influence of the Bauhaus on Visual Design

The Bauhaus was a German school of art and design that operated in the early twentieth century. From about 1919 to 1933, the students at the school were immersed in the creation of art and design relating to every object and idea that could be addressed using **Modernist** theory, or the idea that the design of an object and the material from which it is made should be determined by its purpose ("form follows function"). Although the Bauhaus was initially conceived as a school of architecture by its founder, Walter Gropius (1883–1969), the school worked to establish design ideals that could be applied universally with no constraints on culture or medium. Bauhaus artists designed and redesigned furniture, kitchenware, and household items, and set a new standard for visual communication design.

The mission of the school was to create designs that fit the modern world. Using inexpensive and common materials, the artists of the Bauhaus sought to imagine a style that was universal and did not favor one culture over another. This was evident in the printed materials that were generated by such professors as Herbert Bayer. Bayer created a sans serif typeface that he named "Universal" (**2.7.8a**). Bayer's typeface had its own character that could not be immediately associated with any one culture, but that was easy to read and facilitated visual communication. This same typeface was used to spell out the name of the Bauhaus on the outside of the building (**2.7.8b**).

After the rise of the Nazi Party in Germany and the subsequent closure of the school in 1933, a number of artists and designers relocated outside of Europe, many moving to the United States. Amongst them was Ludwig Mies van der Rohe (1886–1969), who had been Head of the Bauhaus. He re-established the school and continued its ideals by founding the Armour Institute of Technology (later called the Illinois Institute of Technology) in Chicago. Mies van der Rohe is often best remembered for his emphasis on simplicity of design, and his quips, "Less is more" and "God is in the details," expressed two key ideas that inspired an entire generation of architects and designers in the mid-twentieth century, whose influence can still be seen in design practice today.

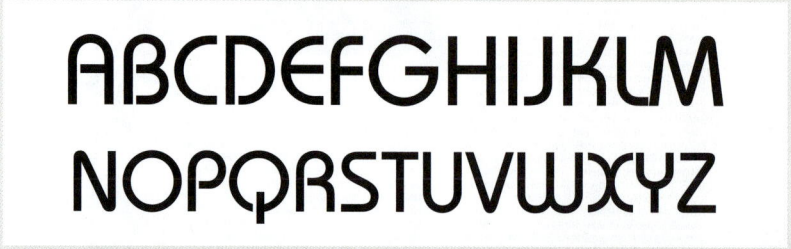

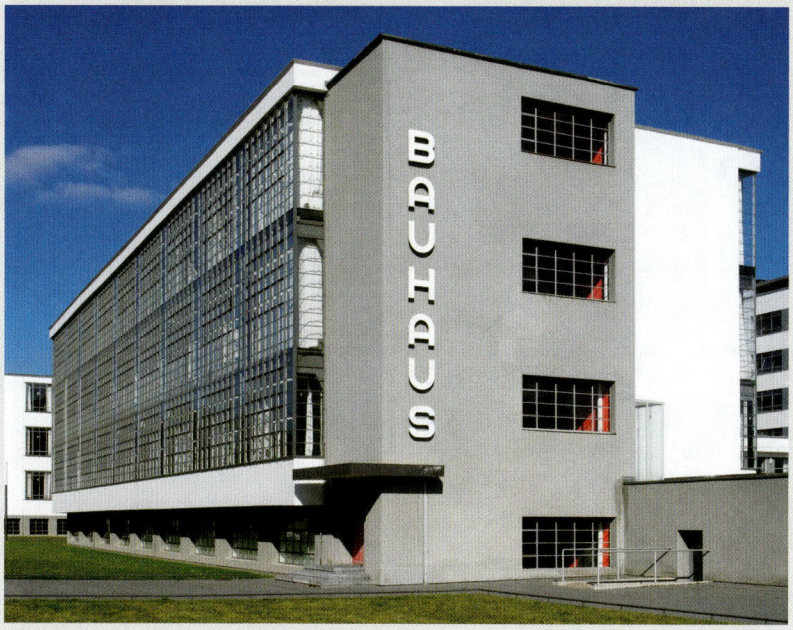

2.7.8a (above, top) Herbert Bayer, *Universal* typeface, 1925

2.7.8b (above) Walter Gropius, Bauhaus building, 1925–26, Dessau, Germany

Modernist, Modernism: a radically new twentieth-century art and architectural movement that embraced modern industrial materials and a machine aesthetic

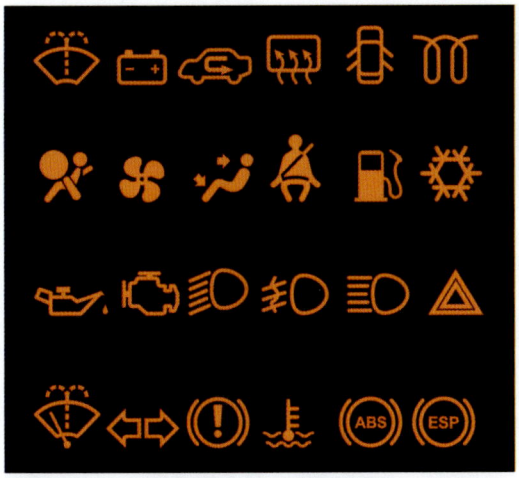

2.7.9 Illuminated car dashboard icon set

Figure **2.7.9**) indicates the control button for the hazard blinkers. The triangular icon has provided an accepted meaning across cultures and has therefore become recognized by drivers everywhere, so that no words need to be printed on the button.

Illustration

Illustrations are images created to inform as well as to embellish the printed page. Good illustration is critical in such fields as medicine and science, where it may communicate essential information more effectively than text or a photograph.

The nineteenth-century English artists and designers William Morris (1834–1896) and Edward Burne-Jones (1833–1898) believed that society should reject rampant industrialization and restore hand-craftsmanship. Their illustrated book of the works of the medieval poet Geoffrey Chaucer was handcrafted so that each page contained illustrations, **illuminated characters**, and patterns (**2.7.10**). The illustrations allow readers to experience and understand the works of Chaucer more richly. They support and enhance the written words.

The American illustrator James Montgomery Flagg (1877–1960) brought a patriotic literary figure to life and created a memorable icon of the United States when he drew the first image of "Uncle Sam." Although Uncle Sam was a fictional character from the early nineteenth century, it was Flagg in his poster of 1917,

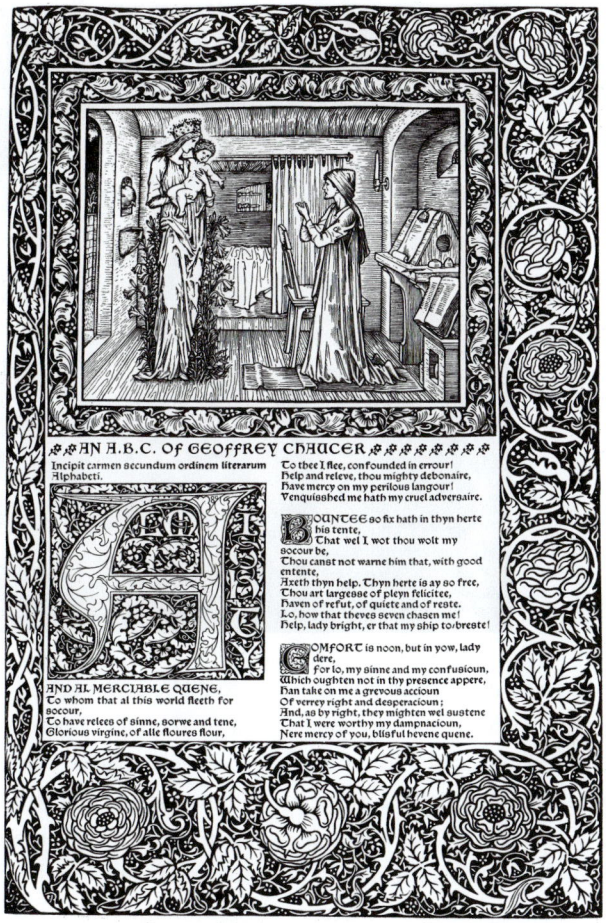

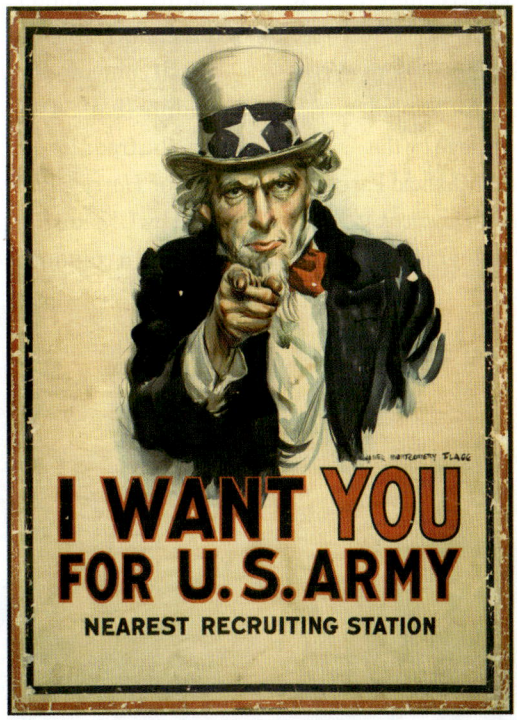

2.7.10 (above) William Morris and Edward Burne-Jones, page from *Works of Geoffrey Chaucer*, Kelmscott Press, 1896. British Museum, London, England

2.7.11 (left) James Montgomery Flagg, *I Want You for U.S. Army*, recruitment poster, c. 1917

"I Want YOU for U.S. Army," who created an image that would become a representation of the US government (**2.7.11**). The poster—

Illuminated characters: highly decorated letters, usually found at the beginning of a page or paragraph

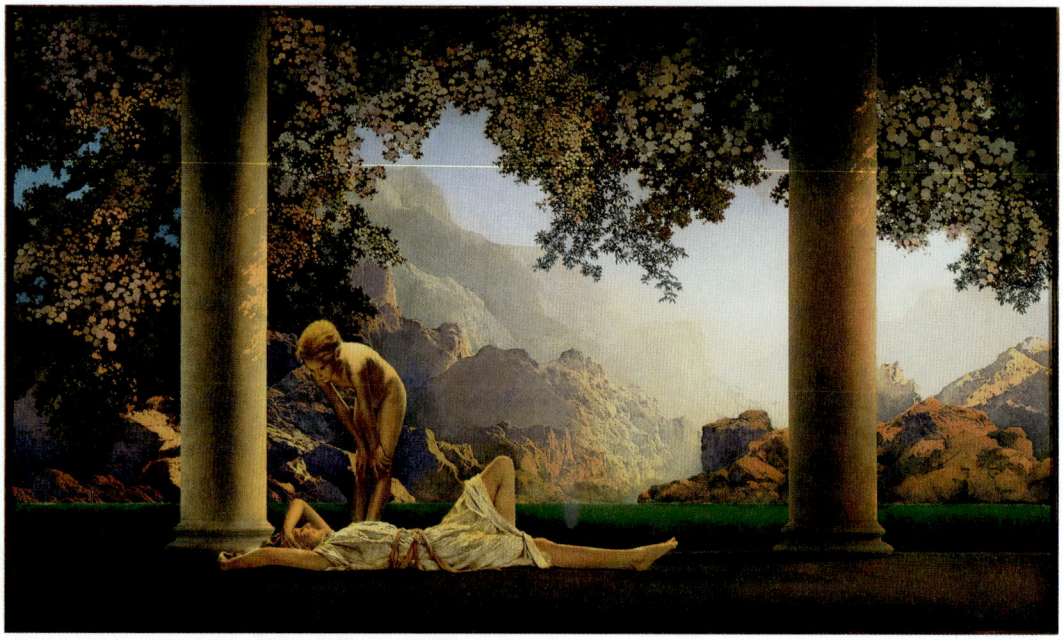

2.7.12 Maxfield Parrish, *Daybreak*, 1922. Oil on board, 26 ½ × 45", Private collection

which was inspired by a similar British poster featuring the former secretary of state for war, Lord Kitchener—helped to recruit soldiers for World Wars I and II. Flagg designed the image of Uncle Sam using his own face, its intimidating authoritarian stare and the outstretched pointing finger intended to confront and single out the viewer and challenge his commitment to the defense of the nation.

One of the most popular illustrations ever created, based on the number of printed copies made, was a striking image by the American painter-illustrator Maxfield Parrish (1870–1966). Parrish painted *Daybreak* (**2.7.12**) for use as a printed lithograph that could be commercially marketed. The work, a vivid image of two figures positioned between a pair of columns in front of a dramatic and colorful landscape, was so popular that experts estimate that 25 percent of American households may have owned a copy in the 1920s. The image continues to influence artists and filmmakers because of its otherworldly visual qualities.

Such contemporary illustrators as Mary Grandpré (b. 1954) have continued, and built upon, the traditions of the past. In her illustrated cover for *Harry Potter and the Sorcerer's Stone*, (**2.7.13**) by J. K. Rowling, Grandpré has also integrated a colonnaded vista through which

2.7.13 Mary Grandpré, cover art for *Harry Potter and the Sorcerer's Stone*, published by Scholastic, 1997

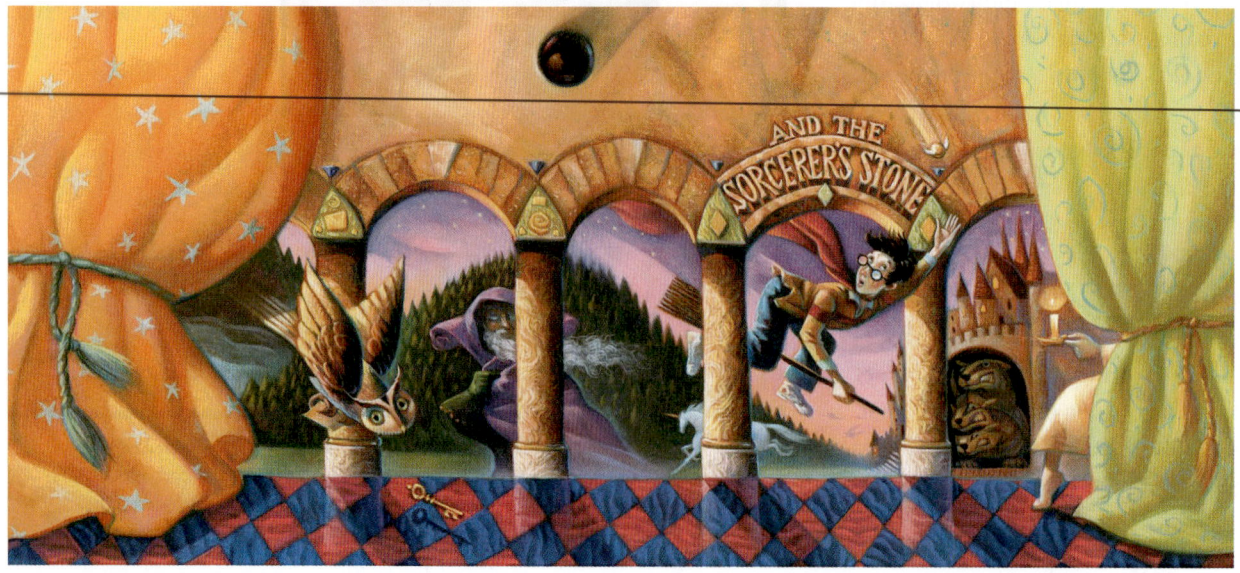

the bespectacled protagonist, Harry Potter, flies toward the viewer while attempting to catch a shiny object called a Golden Snitch. Grandpré introduces the reader to the main character and an exciting scene that will be encountered as the story unfolds. The imagery complements the written text and creates a visual introduction via the clues that are scattered, half-hidden, throughout the artwork.

Digital illustration has become a popular way for designers to incorporate illustrations into a printed design. Digital drawings are produced through the use of computer applications that use mathematical formulas dependent on the relative placement of points. In these math-based applications, the computer generates an image, called a vector graphic, from a series of lines plotted from the relationship between individual points. Since points and lines are the basic units of this system, it bears a resemblance to drawing processes. Most of the line art in this book was created using this type of digital illustration application.

The Portuguese-born illustrator Jorge Colombo (b. 1963) creates drawings digitally, using his iPhone in the streets of New York City. His images have become well known, having graced several covers of *The New Yorker* magazine (**2.7.14**). The artist likes to create his work this way because passersby think that he is just checking his e-mail and do not disturb him as he works. The results are fresh and spontaneous enough to capture the vibrant energy of New York.

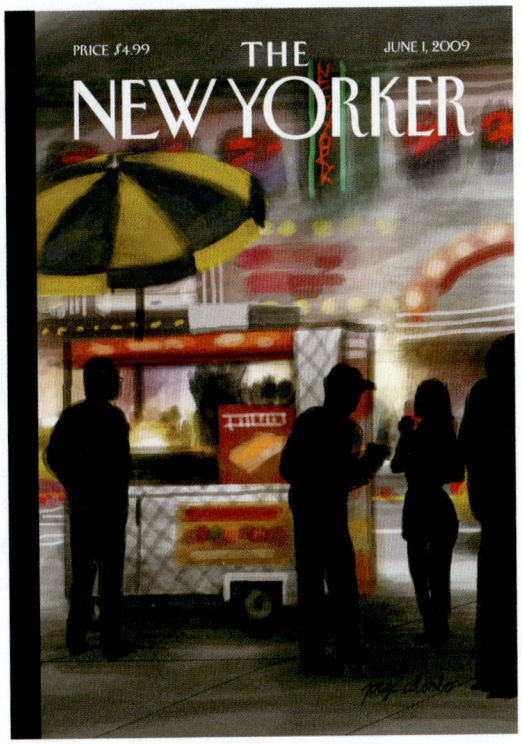

2.7.14 Jorge Colombo, *Finger Painting. The New Yorker* magazine cover, June 1, 2009. Digital sketch using iPhone

Layout Design

Graphic design is the art of improving visual communication. As you read this text, you may have noticed the way the information is organized. Headings, page numbers, illustrations, and the definitions of terms in the margin have all been carefully considered with you in mind. The use of **boldface** type and columns of text helps you read and understand. In other visual arts it may be preferable to invite a viewer to consider and contemplate. But in graphic design, the communication is intended to be instantaneous, clear, and direct.

Layout design is the art of organizing type, logos, and illustrations to optimize communication. Good layout design is essential if information is to be easily understood. One of the main considerations in layout design is spacing. Designers are very aware of **white space**—the **voids** that lie between text areas and images—and are careful in its organization and distribution in their layouts.

If you examine the way this page is designed, you will notice the relationships between columns of text, images, and other features, such as page numbers. The designer responsible for this page has made sure each feature has enough white space around it to be easily identified and understood, but is close enough to related elements, such as the pictures, so that the text and images complement each other.

The French artist Henri de Toulouse-Lautrec (1864–1901) created posters for his favorite Parisian nightspot, the Moulin Rouge. In *La Goulue at the Moulin Rouge*, Toulouse-Lautrec uses a free, rounded writing style that is as casual as the spectators in the nightclub scene, as they watch La Goulue (the nickname, meaning "The Glutton," of the dancer Louise Weber) dance

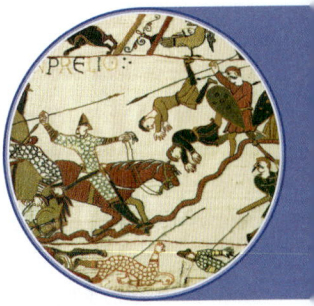

An example of early layout design is the embroidered eleventh-century *Bayeux Tapestry*: see **4.7.5, p. 642**

Boldface: a darker and heavier typeface than its normal instance
White space: in typography, the empty space around type or other features in a layout
Void: an area in an artwork that seems empty

Perspectives on Art: April Greiman

Does It Make Sense? Greiman's *Design Quarterly* #133, 1986

***New Wave design** reflected the alternative counter-culture of the 1980s, exemplified by such movements as Punk, a reaction against the slick commercial style of the time. Here, the visual communication designer April Greiman talks about her issue of the* Design Quarterly *magazine. She turned the entire magazine into a two-sided poster, the self-portrait* Does It Make Sense? *(**2.7.15**). The pixellation of the image shows it to be a product of the digital age, but its subjects, the human mind and body, are some of the oldest in art.*

I like to think of my process as one of jumping into a stream, to see where it takes me. The final product emerges after following questions and guidance from my internal voice, trying a thousand iterations of the work, and having solutions to problems come to me in dreams. I try to go into all my work with a sense of openness and a desire for discovery.

It seems crazy now, but the design community was very reluctant to begin using computers. Back in the 1980s, graphic designers were deeply focused on print and analog technology. As for me, I wouldn't even call myself a graphic designer. The term is too closely tied to print, which wasn't the only medium then and isn't the dominant medium now. So in 1986, when *Design Quarterly* asked me to design an issue of their magazine, I knew I wanted to create something using digital technology.

Back in 1984, I attended the first TED (Technology, Education, and Design) conference, co-founded by my friend Harry Marks. After the conference, Harry dragged me out to see the first Macintosh computer, which had only just been released. I got my hands on it and never looked back. When I was commissioned by *Design Quarterly*, I was using a 512k Mac, which is a minuscule amount of processing power—it probably couldn't handle the full text of this feature. I reimagined *Design Quarterly*, usually a 32-page magazine, as a two-by-six-foot fold-out poster covered in images, text, and symbols. To make it, I used this little add-on device called the MacVision, which could port directly from a video camera to the computer so that the Mac could digitize the photos. There was no one-stop photo-editing tool, such as Photoshop, back then, so I was cutting out images and layering and resizing them across several different programs. The final image is 289kb, smaller than a photo you'd make on a smartphone today, but which at the time was large enough to generate dozens of error messages and take all night to print.

The shift from print to digital is really a shift from working with matter to working with light. When I created *Does It Make Sense?*, the images I was layering and manipulating weren't physical, they were light. Money, art, books—all these things that were once objects can now exist as nothing more than patterns of light on a screen. We can make art that has no real physical existence; the computer, in a way, changed my body to light, then the printer gave it physical form again.

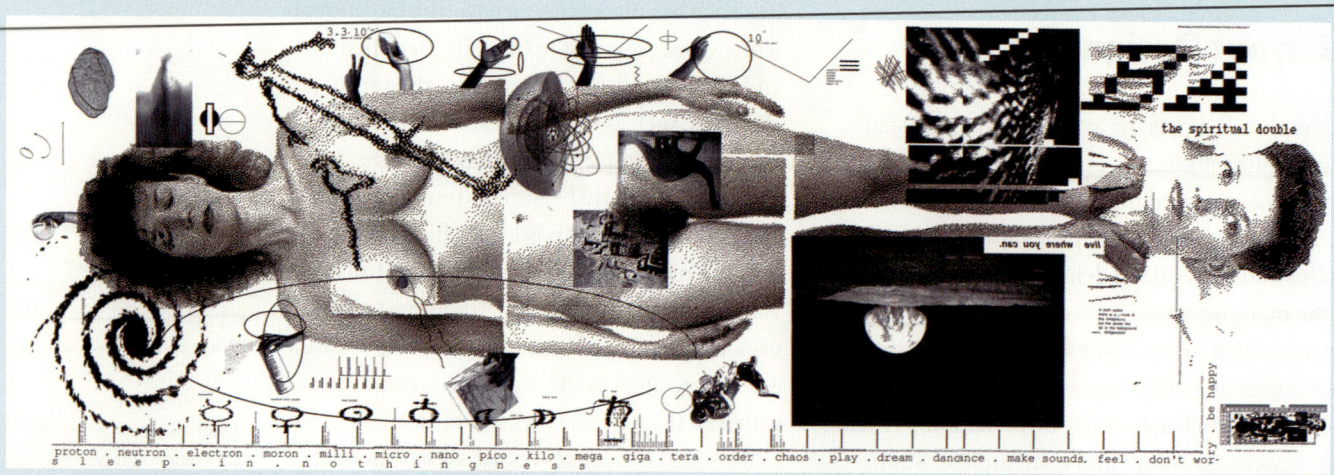

2.7.15 April Greiman, *Does It Make Sense?* from *Design Quarterly* Issue #133, 1986. Magazine cover design the can-can (**2.7.16**). Here, the text is calligraphy rendered by hand directly (in mirror-writing) on the **lithographic** stone from which it is printed. Toulouse-Lautrec's great skill as an illustrator and typographer is apparent in the excellent hand-rendered text and images.

The New York City-born visual communication designer April Greiman is widely considered responsible for bringing the New Wave design style to the US. *Does It Make Sense?* demonstrates the changing relationship between people and their machines; it seems to predict our current era of the Internet and life lived via a computer (see Box: April Greiman, opposite).

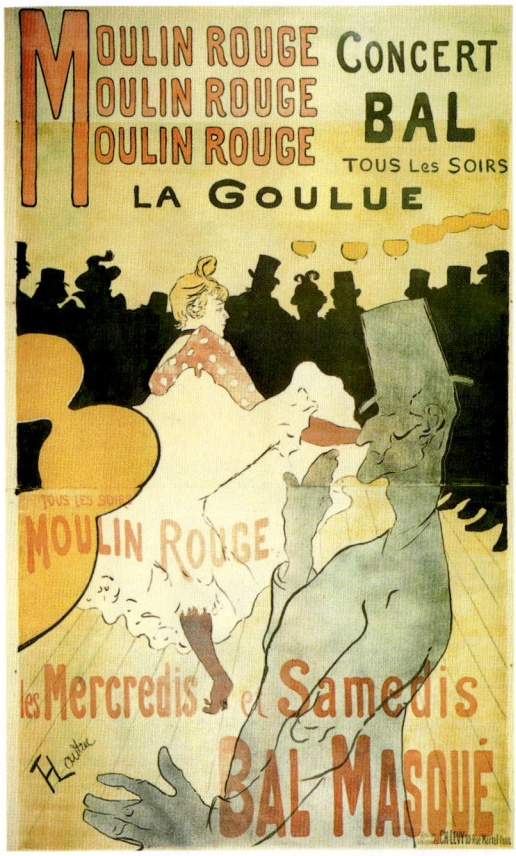

2.7.16 Henri de Toulouse-Lautrec, *La Goulue at the Moulin Rouge*, 1891. Lithograph in black, yellow, red, and blue on three sheets of tan wove paper, 6'2½" × 3'9⅝". Art Institute of Chicago, Illinois

Advertising Design

Design specifically created to sell a product or service has become a common part of contemporary life. The same care that an artist puts into the expressive character of a great work of art is similar to the designer's process when creating an advertisement. In the early twentieth century, the Japanese cosmetic company Shiseido integrated traditional Japanese design with influences from European art movements to create a series of elegant and memorable designs. In the 1920s the company produced a number of eye-catching designs in which type, illustration, symbol, and message come together within the advertising layout to promote cosmopolitan and elegant beauty goods, in this case a teeth whitening product (**2.7.17**). An image of a relaxed and elongated figure dominates a design where both English and Japanese writing are organized along with a stylized camellia, the

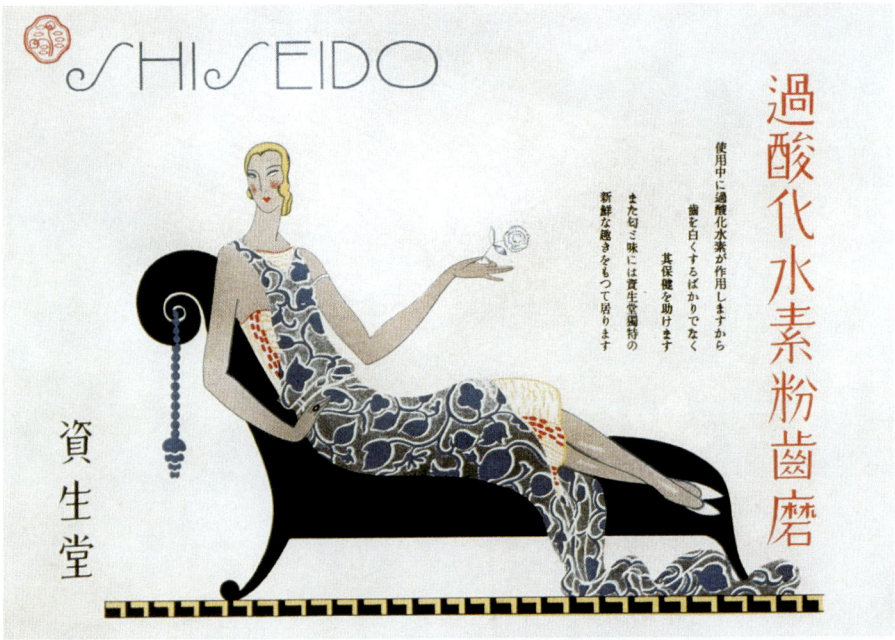

2.7.17 Poster for Hydrogen Peroxide Tooth Powder, *c.* 1927. Shiseido Corporate Museum, Tokyo

New Wave design: A design movement that exemplified the counter cultural currents of the 1980s

Lithography, lithographic: a print process done on a flat, unmarred surface, such as a stone, in which the image is created using oil-based ink with resistance to water

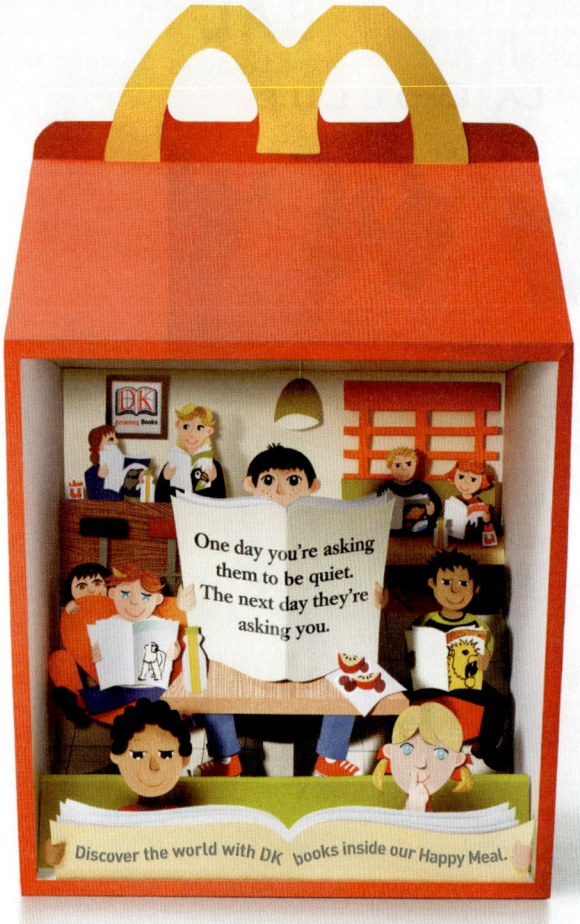

2.7.18 Leo Burnett Company, Inc. and Helen Musselwhite, McDonald's Happy Meal Campaign, 2013

symbolic identity used by the company. Originally founded in 1872, Shiseido still produces beautiful, understated designs to advertise its cosmetics.

The considered placement of textual and visual elements to unify an advertising design conceptually has become common in contemporary practice. In fact, some of the biggest advertising firms have teamed up with illustrators and typographers to produce such designs. The Leo Burnett Company, Inc. is one of the largest advertising firms in Chicago and is an influential player in the commercial design world. Even though the company already had a strong team of designers and creative directors, they chose to team up with a well-known paper artist for an advertising campaign in 2013. Helen Musselwhite (b. 1963) is a British illustrator who uses cut paper to create relief and three-dimensional artwork. She was invited to work with Burnett's team on a campaign for McDonald's Happy Meal (**2.7.18**). For this campaign, Musselwhite designed a Happy Meal box that incorporated text from small books that were to be part of the package. The final advertising design is the result of this collaboration between Burnett's creative designers and Musselwhite's artistic talents.

A skilled and experienced graphic designer can create designs that transcend simple

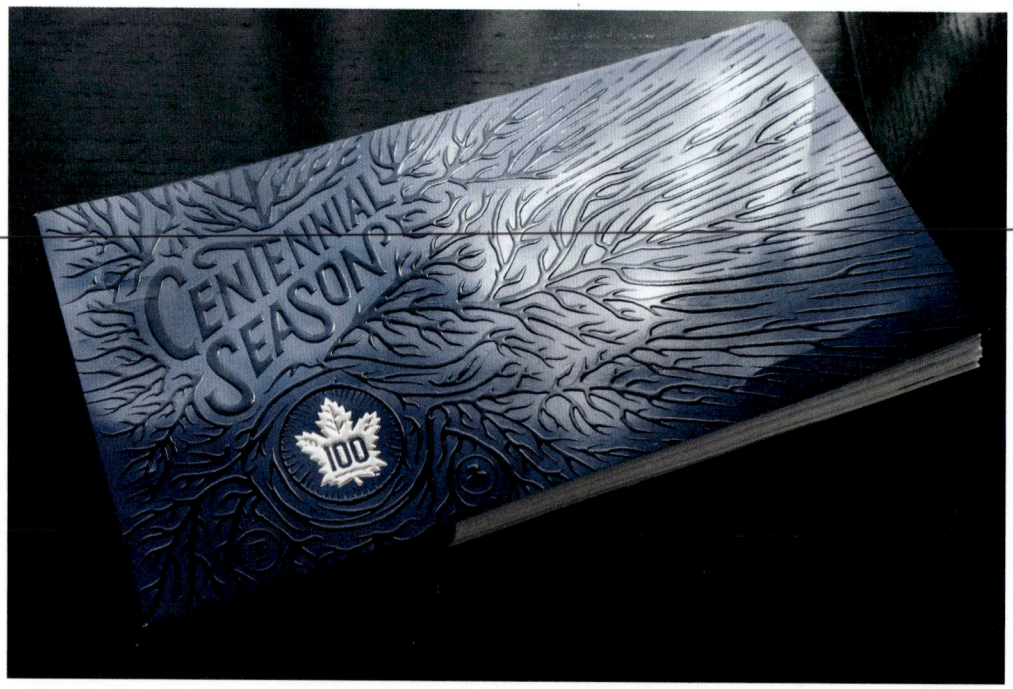

2.7.19a Conrad Garner, Toronto Maple Leafs Centennial Season Ticket Package, 2016.

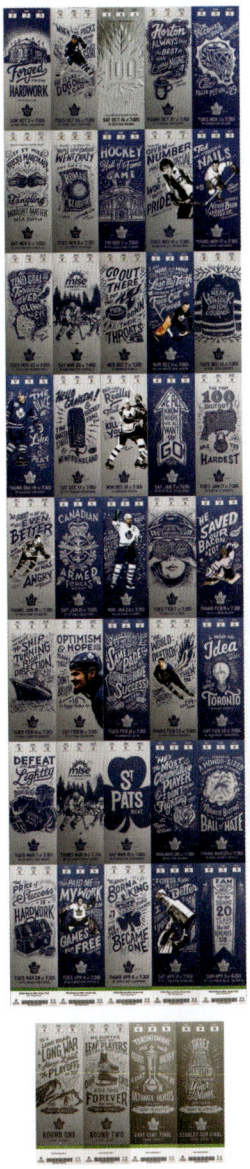

2.7.19b Conrad Garner, Toronto Maple Leafs Centennial Season Tickets, 2016

advertising and become iconic objects. The Canadian-American artist, designer, and illustrator Conrad Garner (b. 1983) did just that when he was hired to create a season-ticket package for the Toronto Maple Leafs hockey team (**2.7.19a**) to commemorate their 100th year. Garner used his ingenuity and a skillful fusion of innovative typography and elegant imagery to create a design that reflects a centennial of great hockey stories and personalities. Garner's historical research inspired the quotations that are featured on each of the tickets in the season-ticket holder's package (**2.7.19b**) . He designed each one so that every game would seem to be a unique and important event. Garner used a design derived from the vein pattern in a maple leaf and developed a font that fits his vision for the piece. The result is a beautiful, unique, and memorable design that honors the history of one of the most famous hockey franchises.

Web Design

In the past twenty-five years, visual communication design has been dramatically influenced by the Internet. The use of text and image in mass communication has evolved from the motionless design of print publications to the interactive designs used on the World Wide Web. The Web allows designers more freedom to add interactivity so that text and image can change as the reader progresses through the information presented.

Web design is strongly connected to layout design because the process of creating a good web design also involves the careful organization of text and image. The idea that design is important is exemplified by the recipient of the Webby Award Winner for Best Visual Design – Aesthetic 2016, the Internet music provider Spotify (**2.7.20**). In this web design by the communication company Razorfish, the emphasis is placed on simplicity and ease of use. This project, called Taste Re-wind, allows a listener to select music from a specific time period, then customize it to his or her own taste. Razorfish, one of the preeminent web communication companies in the world, designed the work so that type, image, and music all integrate into a richer experience for the listener-viewer.

Contemporary website designers try to connect the subject to the design by incorporating interesting features. The web design group Hello Monday did just that when

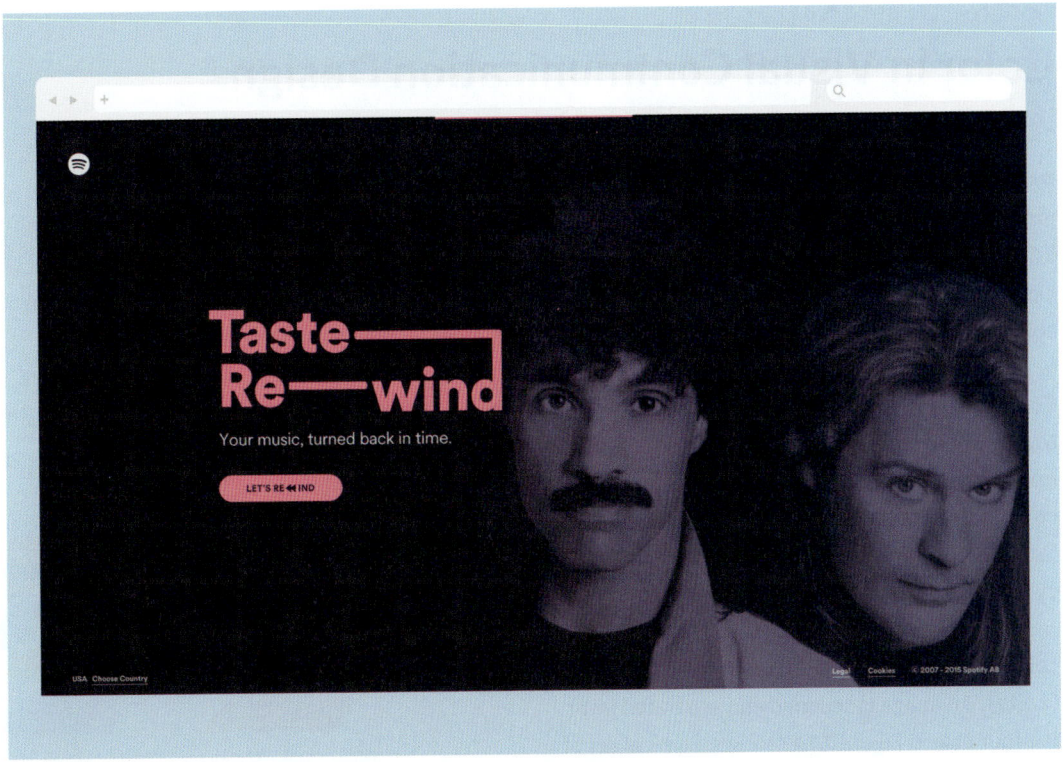

2.7.20 Razorfish, Taste Re-wind, 2016. Web design

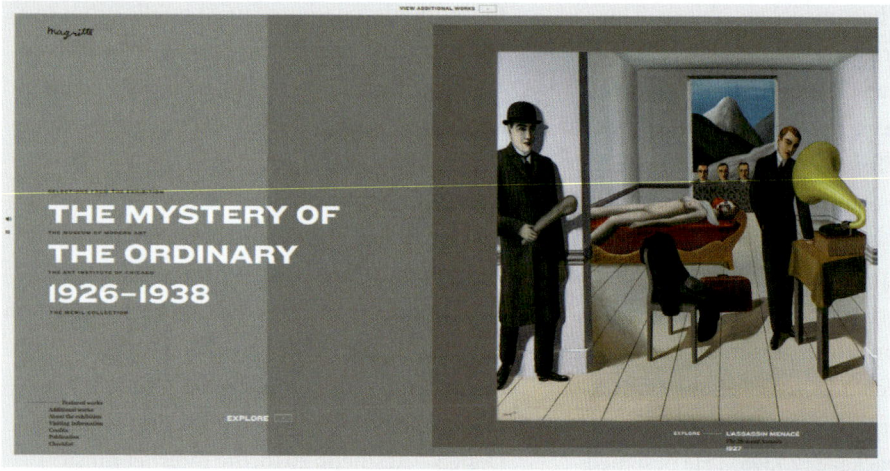

2.7.21a "Magritte: The Mystery of the Ordinary, 1926–1938," MoMA, 2013. Screenshot from exhibition website, design by Hello Monday, 2013. Featuring detail of René Magritte's *The Menaced Assassin*, Brussels, 1927

2.7.21b René Magritte, *The Menaced Assassin*, Brussels, 1927. Oil on canvas, 4' 11"x 6' 4⅞". MoMA, New York. Screenshot from "Magritte: The Mystery of the Ordinary, 1926–1938" exhibition website, MoMA, 2013

it created a website for an exhibition of the Belgian artist René Magritte's (1898–1967) work (**2.7.21a** and **2.7.21b**) at MoMA in New York and the Art Institute of Chicago. In this work the designers have programmed the interactivity so that sounds, movement, and other features are revealed as the viewer enters the site and is invited to discover new aspects of it while being introduced to the artist's work. Magritte's art possesses a mysterious character that the designers have captured in the intriguing ways in which windows open (often from the side and center of the screen) and the media are experienced by the viewer (various sounds are activated as the user selects content).

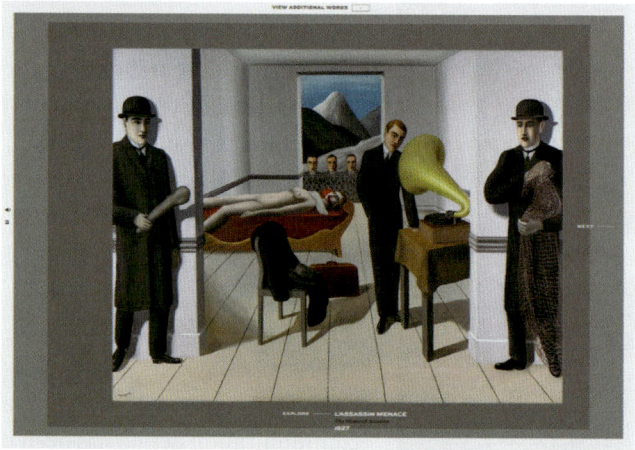

Color in Visual Communication Design

Artists who design images for commercial printing or to display on video screens take a different approach to color than painters or other kinds of artists. In this section we will look at how color is used in print and electronic displays.

Primary colors: three basic colors from which all others are derived

Color in Print

Most printed color images—from posters, to magazines, to this book—rely on four separate colors to create the range of colors that we see. Commercial printers use three **primary colors**—cyan (a kind of light blue-green), magenta (a light red-violet), and yellow—plus black, or key; the color system for printing is referred to as CMYK (**2.7.22**). An image is scanned and separated into the four colors. Figure **2.7.23** shows a typical set of color separations. The image is re-created when the separated colors are printed in sequence, overlapping each other. The four colored inks are printed on paper as dots in a regular pattern ("screen"): the smaller the dot, the less of each color is printed. In the darkest colors the dots are nearly joined together. If you look very closely (using a magnifying lens) at the pictures in this book, you will be able to see the dots. This color

2.7.22 Cyan, Magenta, Yellow, and Black ink overlays, showing the resulting secondary color when they are combined

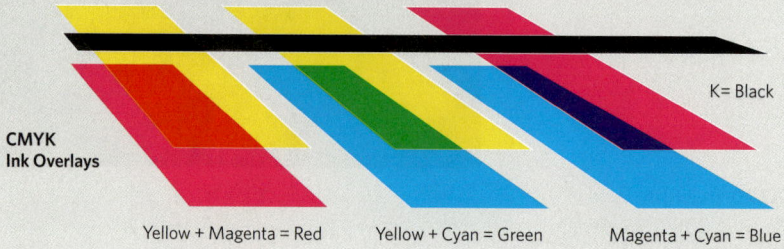

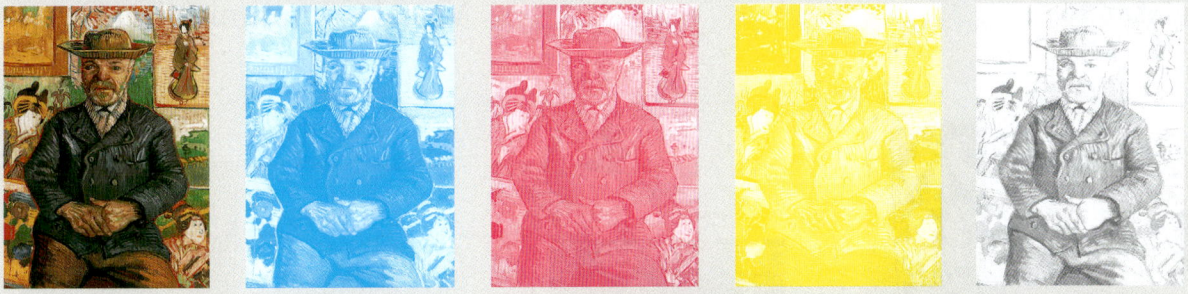

2.7.23 (above) Color separation for a commercially printed reproduction of an artwork by Van Gogh. The image on the extreme left is Van Gogh's original; the other four show how it reproduces in each of the separate, different-colored ink printing screens

2.7.24 (below, top) Combinations of Red, Green, and Blue (RGB) light, overlaid to reveal mixtures

2.7.25 (below, bottom) Dreamhack Gaming Conference, Bucharest, Romania, 2013

printing process, called offset printing, saves time and money, but still provides good color quality for a viewer. Variations in color printing can be expected depending on the paper used. A coated paper will support more rich, lustrous color than an uncoated one. Like other aspects of visual communication, the perception of color is important to support comprehension, because color provides more levels of information by attracting attention and differentiating visual data. Because printed color relies on reflected light and computer monitors are directly lit, a printed color may not have the same appearance as one on an electronic display.

Color in Electronic Displays

A computer-generated image produces color very differently. First, the digital display is illuminated by three different colored light cells, called phosphors, which project the primary colors of red, green, and blue (this color system is referred to as RGB) (**2.7.24**). Then, the electronic monitor turns a combination of phosphors on or off to produce the colors the designer wants. For example, if the red and blue phosphors are on, the color on the display will be magenta. If all three of the primaries are on, the combination will result in white light. Complex combinations of these color lighting cells will result in millions of color possibilities.

The brilliant illuminated color of a video display is a seductive medium for video-game developers. Blizzard Entertainment developed the game *Starcraft* using RGB primaries to create a dazzling illuminated array of colors reminiscent of a modern-day stained-glass window. *Starcraft*'s rich colors are displayed for a large audience each year at the annual Dreamhack (**2.7.25**) computer gaming conference in Bucharest, Romania. Teams of professional game players generate vivid animated scenes for audiences that fuse the experience of an animated movie with that of a sporting event. Digital works have a glow and rich color that bring new sensations to art and design, and they attract a growing number of artists and game developers.

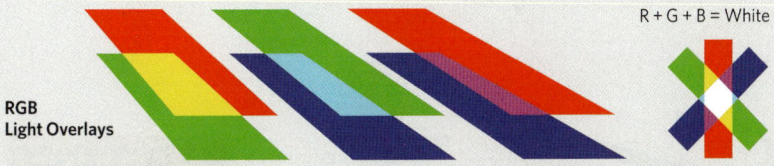

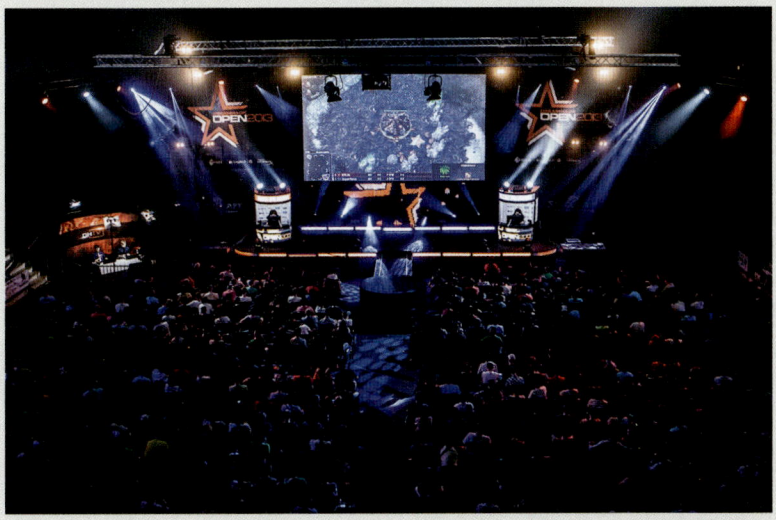

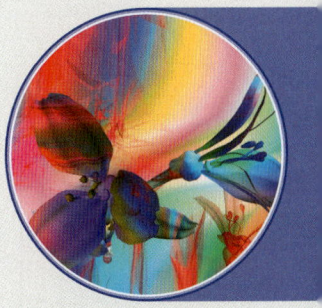

An example of a work that was produced on a computer monitor then printed is Charles Csuri's *Wondrous Spring*: see **1.4.3, p.96**

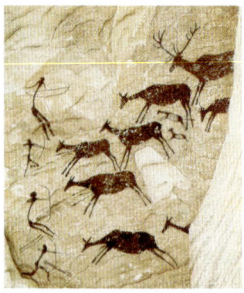

1.5.15 Cave paintings, Valltorta Gorge, Spain, *c.* 20,000 BCE, p. 122

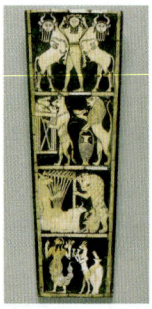

3.1.10 Sumerian lyre panel, 2550–2400 BCE, p. 371

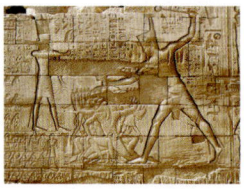

1.7.4a Relief from the temple of Amun, Egypt, *c.* 1295–1186 BCE, p. 143

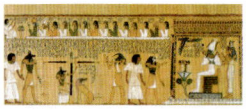

4.2.10 Book of the Dead of Hunefer, Egypt, *c.*1275 BCE, p. 584

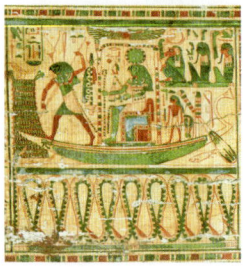

0.0.1 *The Journey of the Sun God Re*, detail from coffin, Egypt, 990–969 BCE, p. 20

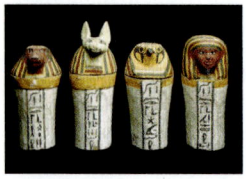

3.1.16 Hieroglyphs on canopic jars, Egypt, 700 BCE, p. 376

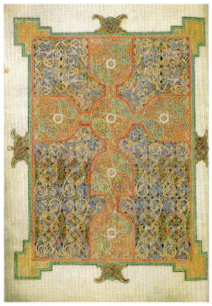

3.2.12a Cross-and-carpet page, Lindisfarne Gospels, 710–721 CE, p. 399

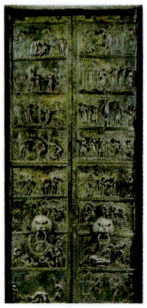

4.2.2b Doors, Church of St Michael's, Hildesheim, Germany, 1015, p. 579

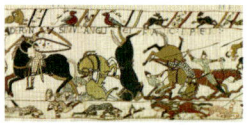

4.7.5 Detail of the Battle of Hastings, *Bayeux Tapestry*, *c.* 1066–82, p. 642

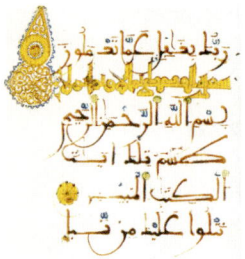

3.2.11 Page from the Koran, probably late 13th century, p. 398

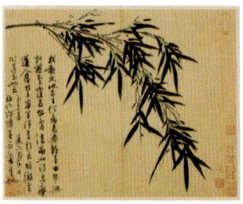

2.1.17 Wu Zhen, leaf from an album of bamboo drawings, 1350, p. 203

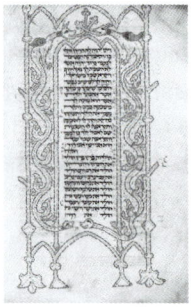

1.1.6a Franco-German hand, *Pentateuch*, 13th–14th century, p. 47

1.1.12 Carolyn Davidson, Nike Company logo, 1971 p. 51

1.1.23 Saul Bass, Bass & Yager, AT&T logo, 1984, p. 55

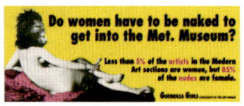

4.10.7 Guerrilla Girls, *Do Women Have to be Naked...*, 1989, p. 685

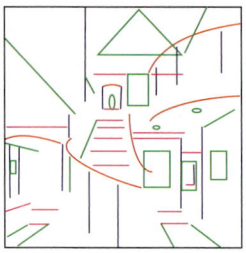

1.6.3b I. Michael Interior Design, linear evaluation of elements, 1990s, p. 127

0.0.5 FedEx Express logo, 1994, p. 23

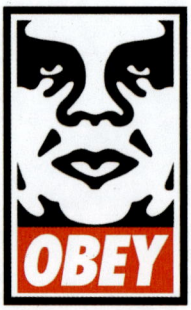

1.1.25a Shepard Fairey, *Obey*, 1996, p. 57

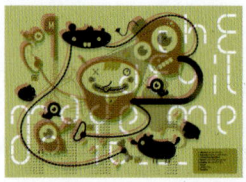

1.1.7 Sauerkids, *The Devil Made Me Do It*, 2006, p. 48

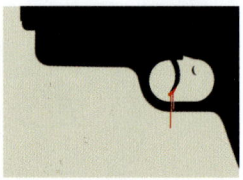

1.1.27 Noma Bar, *Gun Crime*, 2009, p. 59

2.8 Photography

Recording the Image: Film to Digital

The word photography derives from two Greek words, *phos*, meaning "light," and *graphein*, meaning "to draw": or "writing with light." Before the digital era, traditional photographic processes recorded an image onto a light-sensitive material, which darkened when it was exposed to light. Because this produces what is known as a **negative** (a piece of film or paper in which the lights and darks are the opposite of what we see in life, with the tones reversed), the image is repeatable. This negative can be reversed again, with chemicals or by re-exposure to light, to make an infinite number of **positive** prints, called photographs. Until the 1980s, this was how most photographs were created.

With the development of digital cameras in the 1980s, it became possible to record images in the form of pixels, which can then be stored as files on a computer. Today, digital photography is the most common way of creating photographic images. The portability of digital devices, and the fact that they make it easy and quick to capture images directly and instantly review them, whether indoors or out, have made them hugely popular. Additional adjustments, often quite complex and involving a lot of skill, can be made afterward to produce the final image on a monitor or in the form of a print.

While a smartphone, a Polaroid, and an antique camera may look very different to one another, the mechanics of all cameras are very similar to those of the human eye. Light enters the eye through the pupil; similarly, light enters the camera through a small opening, the aperture. In both eye and camera the lens adjusts, or is adjusted, to bring things into focus and give a clear vision of what is being viewed. The image is received by the retina, a piece of film, or an image sensor.

We now encounter photography everywhere. Many of us regularly take photographs and snapshots, and we have also become familiar with photographers producing enduring works of art. But—perhaps surprisingly—when photography was invented in the nineteenth century, its reliance on mechanical and chemical processes led many to refuse to consider it an art form. Photography seemed to be a simple recording of the real world by a machine, not the result of an artist's creative imagination and highly developed skill. Because of the medium's tie to the external world (we take a picture of something), this belief that photographs offer evidence of factual information remains strong. It is important to keep in mind that photographers can also *make* photographs to express ideas in many different ways, for example by deciding the way the **subject** is photographed, by manipulating the image after it has been captured, or by combining the photograph with other images.

The invention of photography had an enormous impact on the development of modern art because of its ability to record reality in a way that seems to replicate the

Negative: a reversed image, in which light areas are dark and dark areas are light (opposite of a positive)
Positive: an image in which light areas are light and dark areas are dark (opposite of a negative)
Subject: the person, object, or space depicted in a work of art

world precisely as we see it, something that had previously only been possible through an artist's rendering. In fact, one of the first books illustrated with photographs was called *The Pencil of Nature* by William Henry Fox Talbot (see **2.8.6**, p. 318). Photography's ability to record directly minute visual details opened up additional possibilities for art. As photography became widely practiced and accepted, artists working in any medium, including photography itself, no longer felt obliged to restrict their work to depicting reality convincingly: many began to experiment with other approaches that would revolutionize art from the late nineteenth century onward.

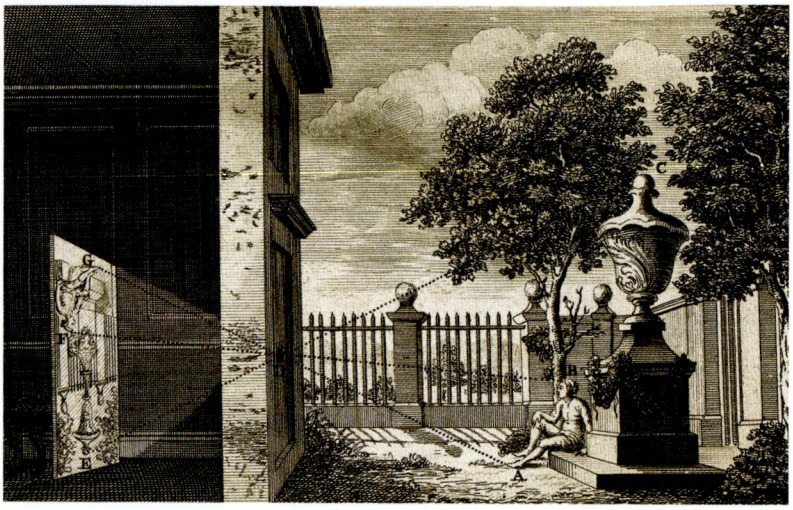

2.8.1 *Optics: the principle of the camera obscura*, 1752. Engraving, 3¾ × 6½"

The Dawn of Photography

The basic principles of photography were known long before modern photographic processes were invented. A simple kind of camera, called the camera obscura (Latin for dark room), had been used by artists for several centuries as an aid to drawing. It was not until the nineteenth century, however, that inventors discovered a number of ways to make permanent camera images that could be reproduced: in other words, photography.

The first cameras were actually room-sized, and the projections they created were used as guides for making drawings. An early illustration of a camera obscura shows the basic principles of all cameras today (**2.8.1**). When a small hole, or aperture, is placed in an exterior wall of a darkened room, light rays project the outside scene onto the opposite wall inside the room. A person could stand inside a camera obscura and trace over the image projected onto the wall. Inside a camera, the image, no matter what size it was, continued to appear in **color**, but upside down and backward. Smaller, portable models used as drawing aids throughout Europe in the eighteenth century were adapted to make the first photographic cameras.

The images projected in a camera obscura are not permanent, but looking at the work of a contemporary artist allows us to see what a camera obscura image looks like. The Cuban-American photographer Abelardo Morell (b. 1948) records camera obscura images using a second camera. He turned an entire hotel room into a camera obscura to project an upside-down image of the dome of the Panthéon, a building in Paris, France (**2.8.2**). The image projected in Morell's hotel room was only temporary until he made a picture of it, showing that the principles of the camera obscura are the same as those in a photographic camera.

The earliest images projected in the camera obscura could be recorded only when traced over by hand. Photography could not exist until the image could be **fixed** (as photographers say). The first photographic image from nature was made using a camera obscura. The inventor

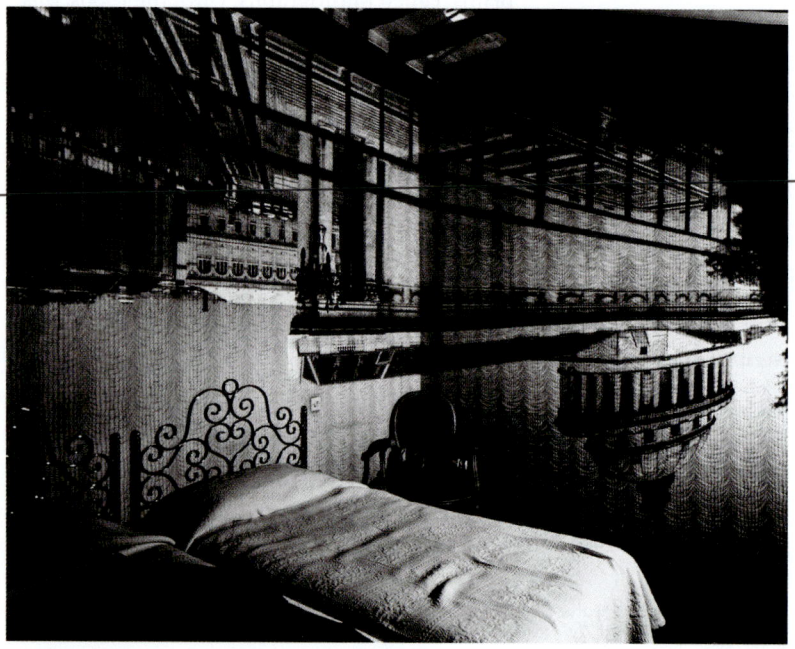

2.8.2 Abelardo Morell, *Camera Obscura Image of the Panthéon in the Hotel des Grands Hommes*, 1999. Gelatin silver print, 20 × 24"

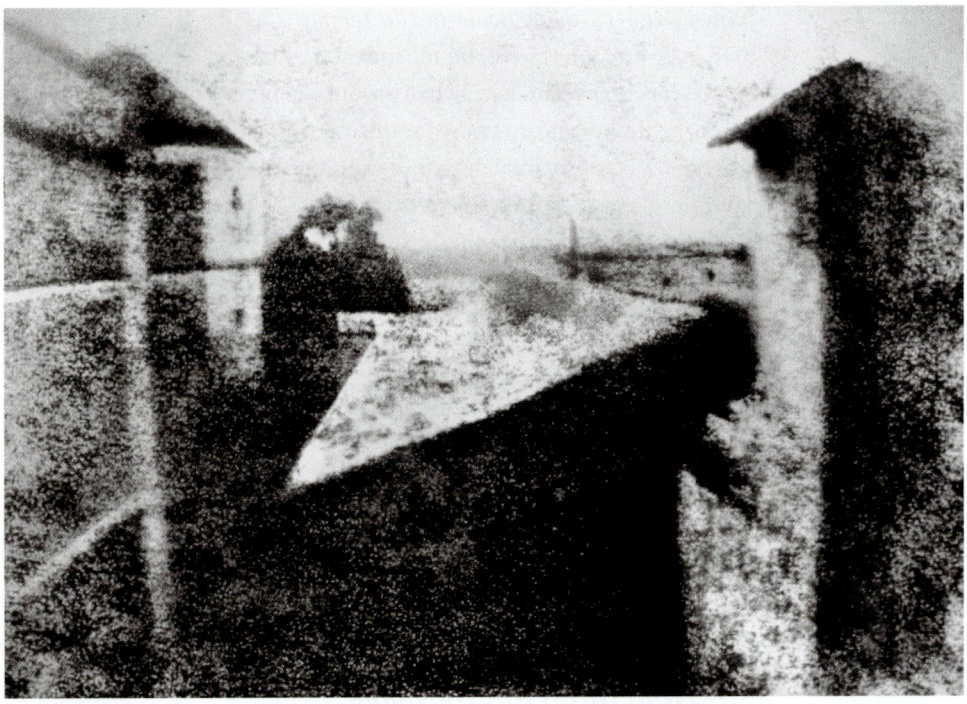

2.8.3 Joseph Nicéphore Niépce, *View from the Window at Le Gras,* c.1826. Gernsheim Collection, Harry Ransom Humanities Research Center, University of Texas at Austin

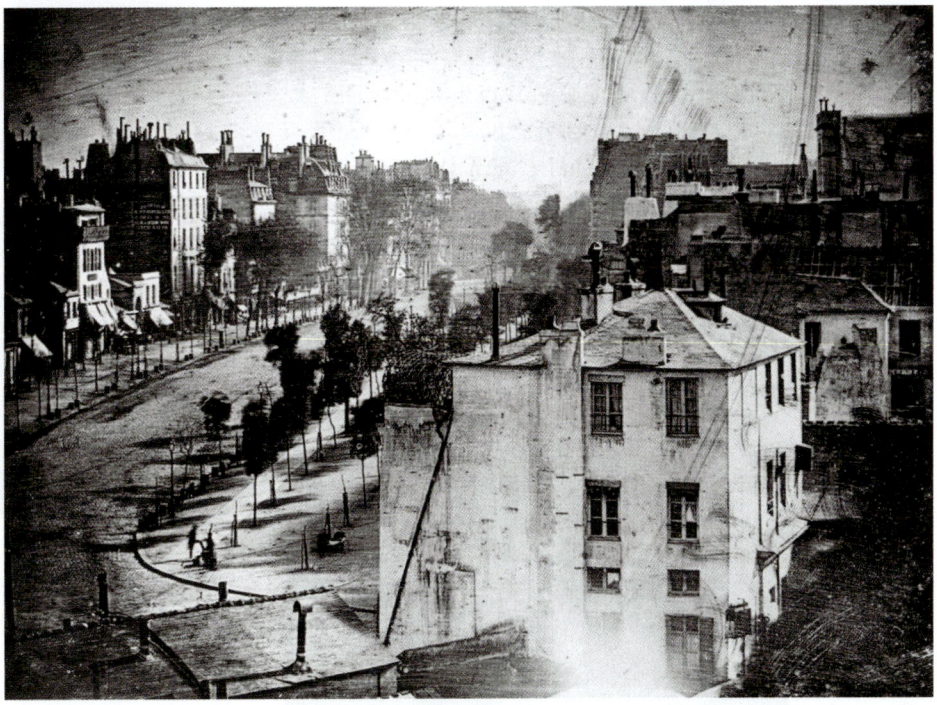

2.8.4 Louis-Jacques-Mandé Daguerre, *Boulevard du Temple, c.* 1838

Color: the optical effect caused when reflected white light of the spectrum is divided into separate wavelengths
Fixing: the chemical process used to ensure a photographic image becomes permanent

Joseph Nicéphore Niépce (1765–1833) made his famous *View from the Window at Le Gras* (**2.8.3**) using a method he kept secret, though he went on to work with fellow Frenchman Louis-Jacques-Mandé Daguerre (1787–1851)—a painter and stage designer—and invent the process known as daguerreotypes (**2.8.4**). The pair worked together during the 1820s and 1830s to develop a method of producing and fixing a camera image. They placed a polished metal plate, made light sensitive by silver iodide, inside the camera. The camera's shutter was somehow opened for 20–30 minutes to expose the plate to sunlight and record an image on its surface. Mercury vapor revealed the image before it was chemically fixed with table salt (later, daguerreotypes would be fixed with sodium thiosulfate, commonly known as hypo).

Cyanotype: photographic process using light-sensitive iron salts that oxidize and produce a brilliant blue color where light penetrates and remain white where light is blocked; a variant of this process was used historically to copy architectural drawings
Developer: after an image has been recorded on light-sensitive film or photographic paper (usually in a camera), immersion in this liquid substance chemically transforms a latent (or invisible) image into a visible one

When Daguerre made *Boulevard du Temple* in 1838, exposure times were still too long to photograph people easily. Even when produced in full daylight, the exposure time for this photograph was approximately 8 to 10 minutes, a great improvement from Niépce's 8 hours. The only person captured on this busy Parisian street was a man who had stopped on the corner to have his shoes shined for the duration of the exposure. After Daguerre publicly presented the process in 1839 advancements were quickly made to reduce exposure time to around one minute in the right lighting conditions. While the daguerreotype process created very detailed images captured through a camera, these single, positive images on metal plates could not be readily reproduced.

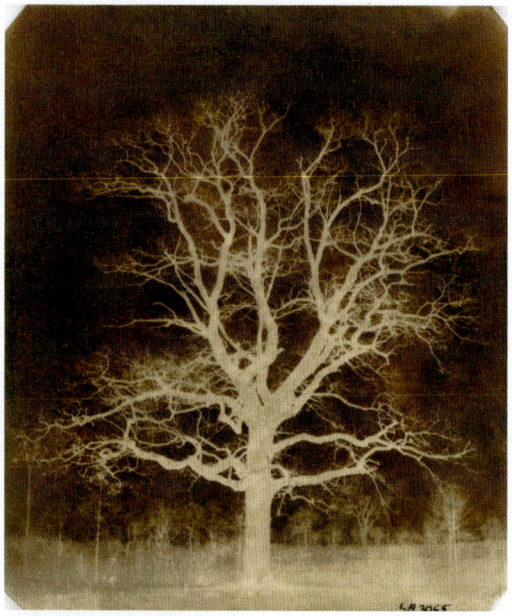

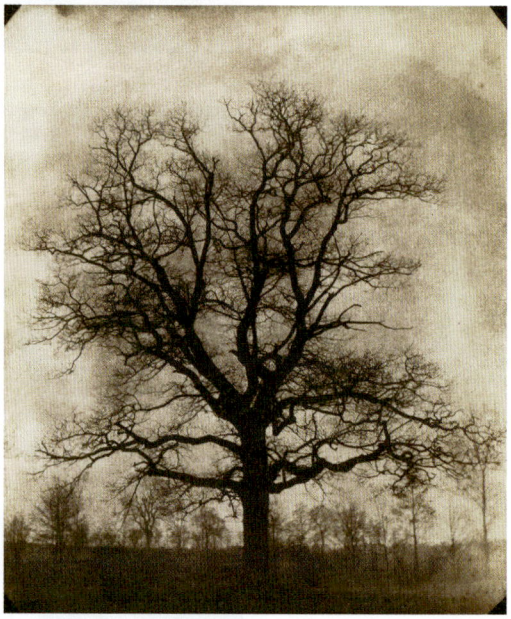

Negative/Positive Process in Black and White

In 1819, the English scientist John Herschel (1792–1871) discovered a chemical compound that could fix, or make permanent, camera obscura images. Using another of Herschel's processes, the English botanist and photographer Anna Atkins (1799–1871) made **cyanotype** images in 1843. She placed pieces of algae directly on paper that had been treated with a special light-sensitive solution, and exposed the sensitized paper to direct sunlight (**2.8.5**). The areas of the paper exposed to the light turned dark, but in the places where the plant's leaves and stems created a shadow, the paper remained white. Although Atkins made this image without a camera, the same principles are at work when a film camera is used, and her images look like film negatives.

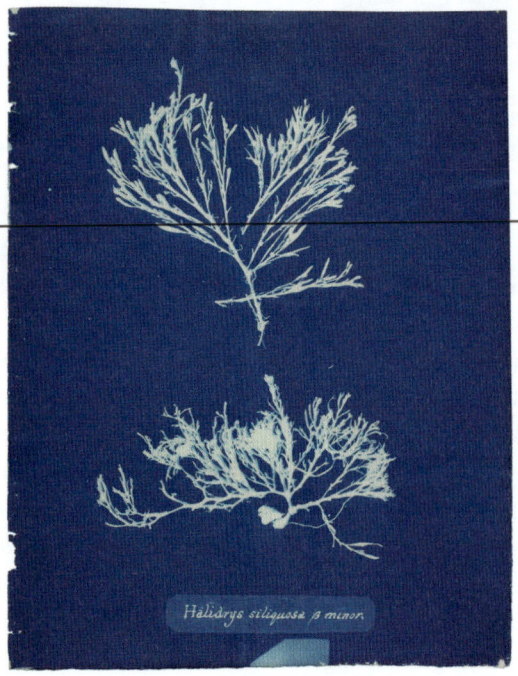

2.8.5 (right) Anna Atkins, *Halydrys siliquosa ß minor*, 1843. Folio 19 from Volume 1 of *Photographs of British Algae*. Cyanotype, 5 × 4". British Library, London, England

2.8.6 (above right) William Henry Fox Talbot, *Oak Tree in Winter*. Top: Calotype, c. 1842–43; and below: salted paper print, c. 1892–93

At about this time, the Englishman William Henry Fox Talbot (1800–1877) captured on light-sensitive paper a negative image of a tree (**2.8.6**, above). This image, known as a calotype, resembled Atkins's botanical specimens. Talbot

Traditional and Alternative Darkroom Methods

Once a photographer captures an image on film inside a camera, he or she must develop the film to produce a negative, and they can then make photographic prints. A darkroom prevents any further light from reaching the light-sensitive materials and damaging the image during the process. Shining a light from an enlarger through the negative reverses the tones and projects a positive image onto light-sensitive paper. At this point the photographer chooses what size to make the image, but it is not yet visible on the paper. The paper then goes through a series of chemical solutions: first, a fluid called the **developer** reveals the image; next, placing the paper in the stop bath halts the development process; then fix, or fixer—a compound that also stops and stabilizes the photographic image—makes it permanent. Finally, the print is washed and dried.

In 1995 Professor of Chemistry and Material Science Scott A. Williams (b. 1962) and his Technical Photography class at Rochester Institute of Technology, New York, discovered that successful negatives and photographic prints could be made using a coffee-based developer. The ingredients are simple: caffeinated instant coffee, washing soda, and vitamin C. The development time is longer but no chemical stop bath is required. While no alternatives for chemical fix exist, using the Caffenol process, as it is now called, greatly reduces the environmental toxicity of traditional darkroom photography. In recent years environmentally conscious photographers, such as Maia Dery (**2.8.8**), have begun to use Caffenol as an alternative to more toxic chemical developer.

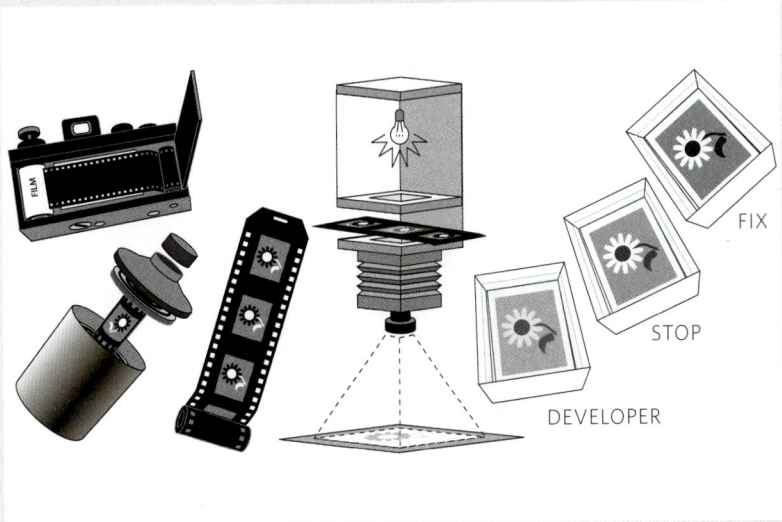

2.8.7 Diagram of film photography darkroom

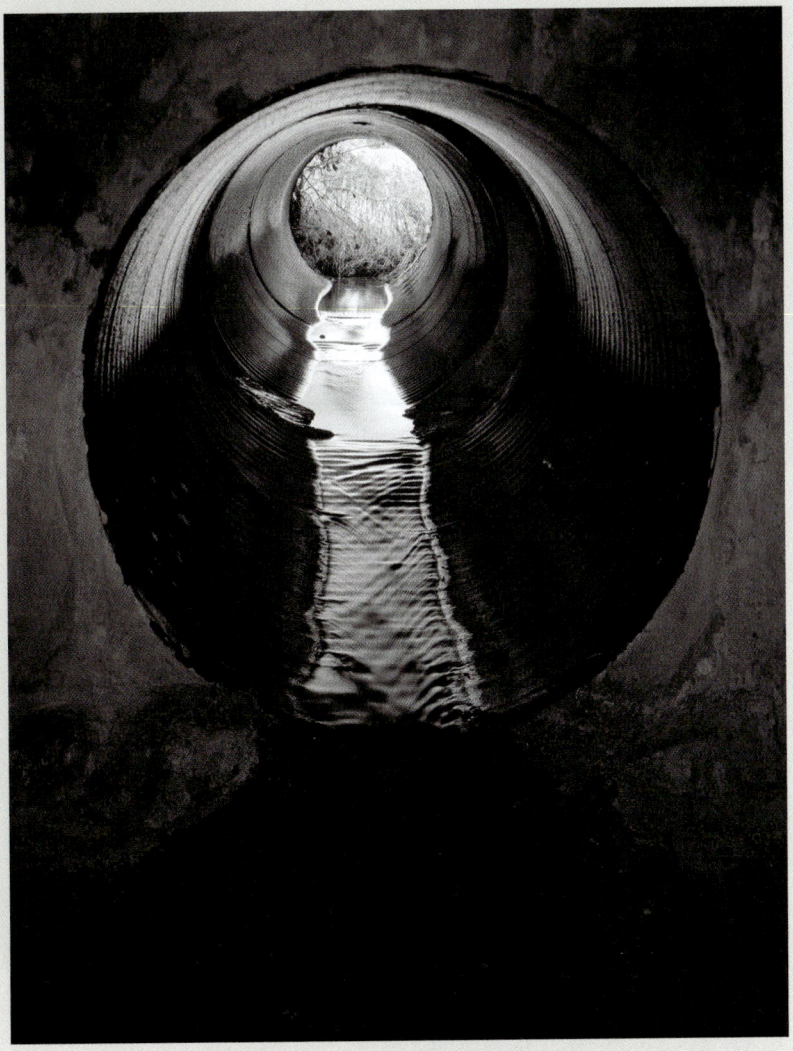

2.8.8 Maia Dery, *Storm Drain–Cape Fear River Basin*, 2013. Caffenol negative/Caffenol silver gelatin print, 9¾ × 7½"

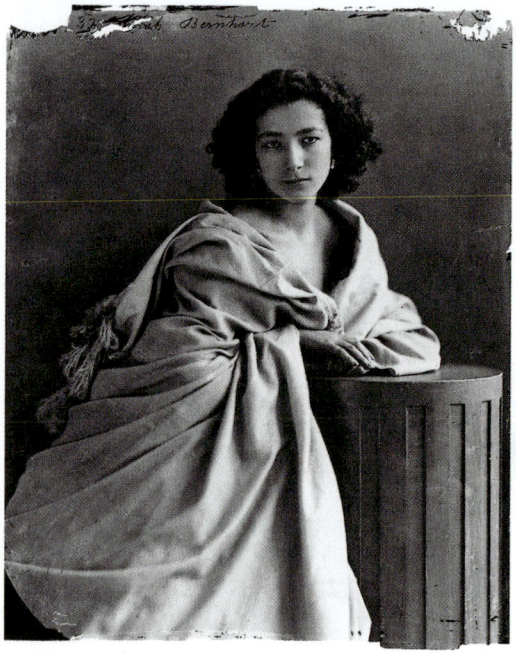

2.8.9 Nadar, *Sarah Bernhardt*, 1865. Albumen print, Bibliothèque Nationale, Paris, France

made collodion negative/albumen print portraits of many well-known artists, writers, and politicians. His photographs of the actress Sarah Bernhardt helped to increase her celebrity (**2.8.9**). Rather than showing the actress posed with elaborate props, which was the norm for portraits at the time, Nadar placed her in the **foreground**, surrounded only by luxurious fabric and leaning on a plain column. Most photographs at this time had to be posed because, while shorter than those for the daguerreotype, exposure times were anywhere from a second to a minute.

Also known for her portraits of celebrities, the British photographer Julia Margaret Cameron (1815–1879) intentionally avoided the sharp focus that many photographers sought

Value: the lightness or darkness of a plane or area
Collodion (wet plate) process: black-and-white darkroom photography process invented by Frederick Scott Archer in 1850–51 and popular until the 1880s
Foreground: the part of a work depicted as nearest to the viewer

also discovered how to reverse the negative, which enabled him to make numerous positive prints: the places that appeared light in the negative, such as the trunk and branches, would be dark in the print, while the dark areas, such as the sky, would change to light. The resulting print (**2.8.6**, p. 318, lower image) contained shades of gray that matched the **values** of the original scene. This negative/positive process is the basis of film photography (see Box: Traditional and Alternative Darkroom Methods).

Many inventors wanted to combine the detail of the daguerreotype with the reproducibility of the calotype. In 1850–51 Frederick Scott Archer (1813–1857) invented the **collodion** or **wet-plate process**. Even though it was very cumbersome, requiring a lot of equipment and chemistry that had to be wet to be light sensitive, this process allowed a crisp image to be recorded on glass. The collodion negative could be used in many ways, one of which was to make prints on paper. Photographers used this popular process until around the 1880s.

Before photography was invented, the only way to get a portrait was to have an artist paint one—an expensive and time-consuming process. Photography changed all that. The French photographer Nadar (1820–1910)

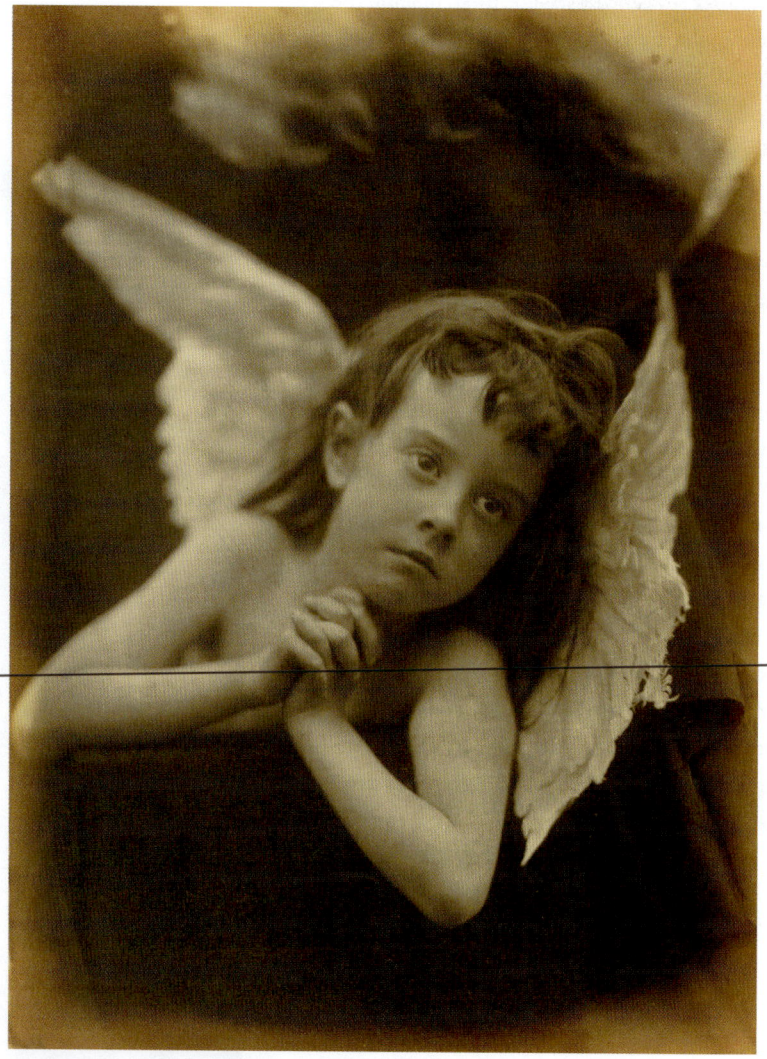

2.8.10 Julia Margaret Cameron, *Angel of the Nativity*, 1872. Albumen print, 12⅞ × 9½". The J. Paul Getty Museum, Los Angeles, California

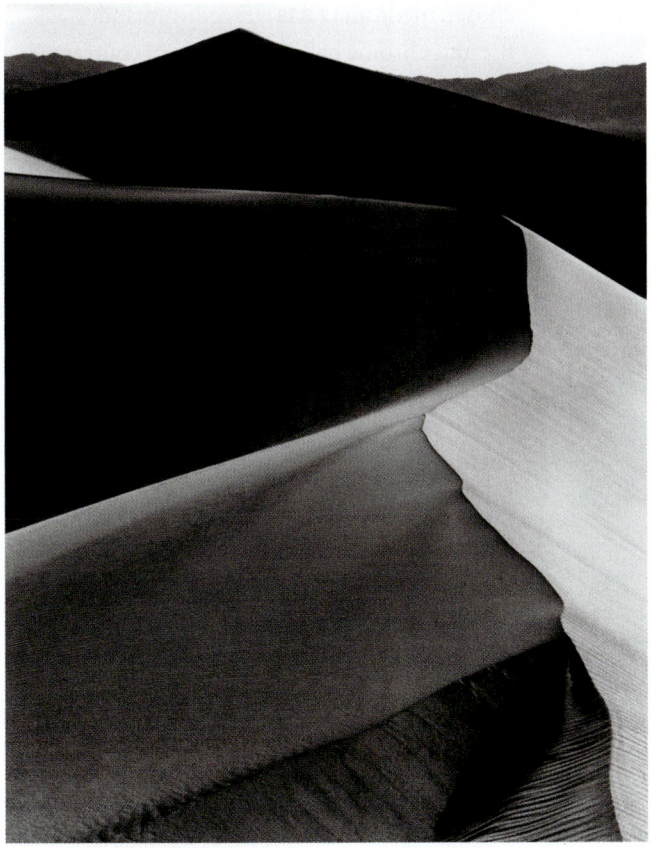

2.8.11 Ansel Adams, *Sand Dunes, Sunrise—Death Valley National Monument, California*, c. 1948. Gelatin silver print, 19½ × 14¾"

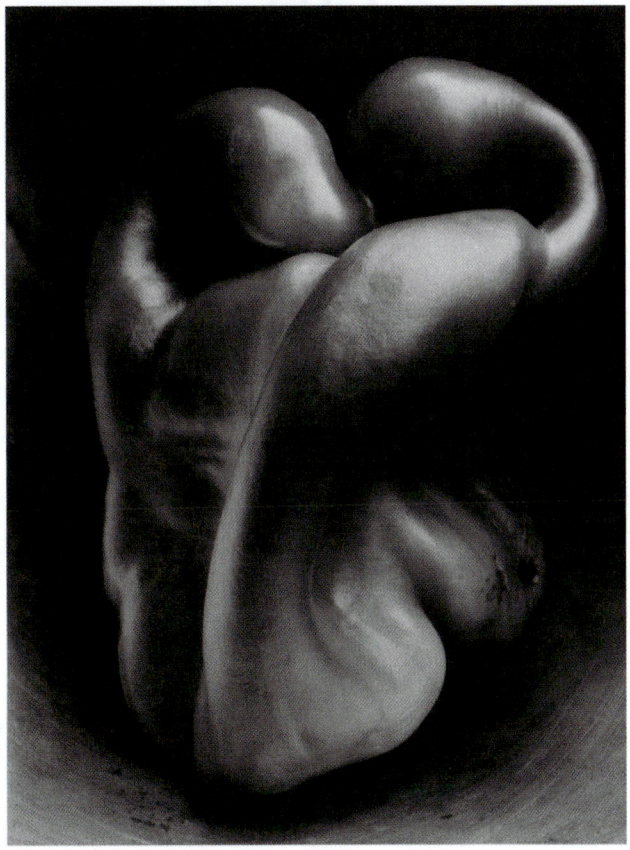

2.8.12 Edward Weston, *Pepper No. 30*, 1930. Gelatin silver print, 9⅜ × 7½". Collection Center for Creative Photography, University of Arizona

from the collodion process. Cameron believed that photography could show — in addition to what was visible — allegorical, poetic, and intuitive aspects of life that we may not readily see in the course of our daily lives. In order to emphasize spiritual and literary aspects, she used specially designed lenses as well as long exposure times to create a **soft-focus** look. In *Angel of the Nativity* (**2.8.10**) her characteristic technique helps transform her niece into a cherub, similar to those commonly featured in Renaissance and **Baroque** paintings.

The film/print process still used in many darkrooms today, **gelatin silver**, was introduced to the public in 1871. Much later , such artists as Ansel Adams (1902–1984) preferred this process because it allowed him to capture the subject the way he wanted to, with everything in the picture clearly in focus. In *Sand Dunes, Sunrise—Death Valley National Monument, California*, Adams captures a full range of black, white, and gray tones that creates a balanced effect (**2.8.11**). He was also deeply involved with the Sierra Club, which is dedicated to preserving America's wilderness. Such landscape photographs as these can raise awareness of nature's grandeur.

Like Adams, fellow American Edward Weston (1886–1958) sought to enhance visual experience through the lens of the camera. By focusing so closely on an object that it became almost **abstract**, Weston believed in photographing a subject as he found it, creating sharply focused gelatin silver prints on glossy paper, and framing images with white mats (cardboard surrounds in which a window for the image was cut) and simple frames. Weston's *Pepper No. 30* concentrates the viewer's attention on the **form** and texture of the vegetable, so it begins to look like something other than itself, taking on qualities similar to those of a human form; at the same time it clearly represents what it is, a pepper (**2.8.12**).

Soft focus: deliberate blurring of the edges or lack of sharp focus in a photograph or movie
Baroque: European artistic and architectural style of the late sixteenth to early eighteenth century, characterized by extravagance and emotional intensity
Gelatin silver print process (or **silver gelatin**): process for making glossy black-and-white photographic prints in the darkroom based on silver halide gelatin emulsions
Abstract: art imagery that departs from recognizable images of the natural world
Form: an object that can be defined in three dimensions (height, width, and depth)

Hand-tint: early process for adding color to monochrome photographic products by adding pigment in a manner very much like painting
Autochrome: early additive color photography process patented by the Lumière brothers in 1904 and primarily used from 1907 to the 1930s
Additive color process: creates colors by mixing RGB colors on a screen to create a direct positive print; same principle used in LED, LCD, plasma, and CRT video screens
RGB: additive system that mixes color based on the primary colors of light: red, green, and blue
Transparency: in film and photography, a positive image on film that visible when light is shone through it
Subtractive color process: colors subtracted from white light by CMY dyes or pigments; in photography light-sensitive film or paper absorbs the opposite colors of cyan, magenta, and yellow dyes to create a negative image, reversed to make a positive print

In Living Color

By the early 1900s, shutter speeds allowed virtually instantaneous photographs of form frozen in time. Photographers still wanted more. Before color photography was made practicable in the 1880s, people would **hand-tint** photographs to make them look more lifelike. Once available, color processes were hard to market (and also hard to convince some artists to use) because they tended to be complicated and the results were not as chemically stable as black and white.

Autochromes, one of the first commercially viable color processes, are made using an **additive color process**. Potato starch grains colored with **RGB** dyes create a filter and transform an exposed glass plate into a **transparency**. The colors captured on the plate resemble a mosaic or a pointillist painting, though optical mixing prevents us from noticing the very tiny dots. Because they can be easily damaged by light, autochromes are best preserved by limited sun exposure.

The Belgian painter and photographer Alfonse van Besten (1865–1926) enjoyed the painterly potential of the autochrome in his landscapes and romantic views of figures in fancy dress, especially in gardens. Flowers are a common element in his autochromes, maximizing the visual potential of his chosen medium (**2.8.13**). *Fragility* includes the autochrome hallmarks of sharp contrast and dreamy atmosphere in the color-pop of the white, violet, and green cuttings against a dark floral wallpaper. Van Besten's title could be a general reference to the fragility of all living things, like a *memento mori*, or a specific invocation of the symbolic language long associated with flowers.

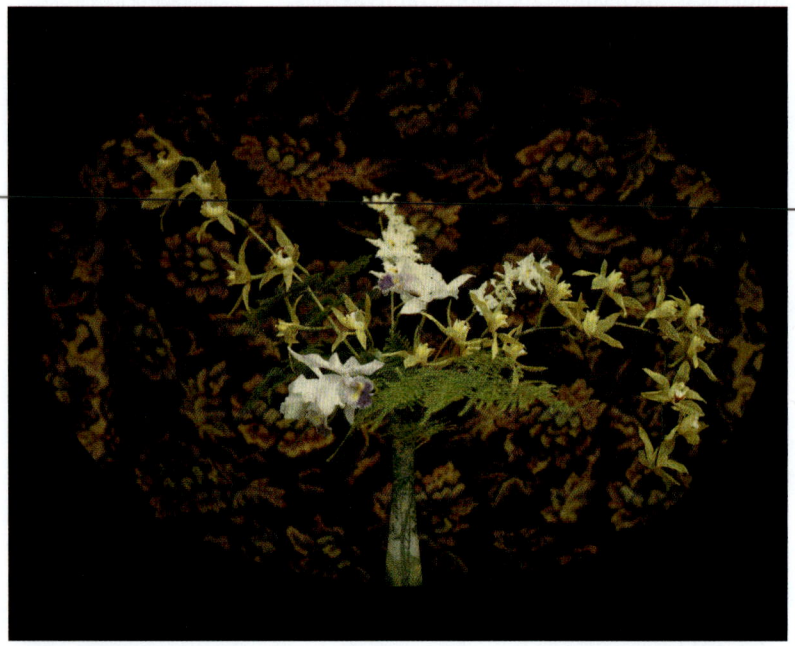

2.8.13 Alfonse van Besten, *Fragility*, c. 1912, autochrome

Unlike the autochrome, the process used to make most color photographs in the twentieth century was a **subtractive process** known as **chromogenic** or **c-prints**. Such products as **Kodachrome** slide film (see **2.8.15**, p. 324) and some photo papers create light-sensitive material by replacing silver with a color emulsion. The emulsion reacts chemically and forms color dyes that absorb the opposite colors in a negative (or reverse them to make a positive print).

A more recent (though now virtually obsolete) process for color prints, is **Cibachrome** (also known as Ilfochrome). This additive method uses layers of **CMY** dyes that are bleached away based on the exposure in order to form a transparent, direct positive image. The Cibachrome photograph *Radioactive Cats* by the American Sandy Skoglund (b. 1946) displays the **tableau**'s vibrant, crisp color profie on a super high-gloss base (**2.8.14**). In *Radioactive Cats*, the outlandish color contributes to a **surreal** combination of factual and fictional elements that make us question whether seeing really should be believing.

In the later part of the twentieth century most color film photography used by the general public was commercially processed. Black-and-white darkroom processes continued to be used by serious amateurs and professional photographers (though black-and-white film could also be processed commercially). Even after color film became commercially viable in the 1930s, some people preferred to use black and white because it makes elements of the composition clearer, specifically the lines, contrast, and overall design. Today, the majority of images we see are in color. As a result, black-and-white photographs can sometimes give the impression of being old-fashioned. But, whether the image is captured in black and

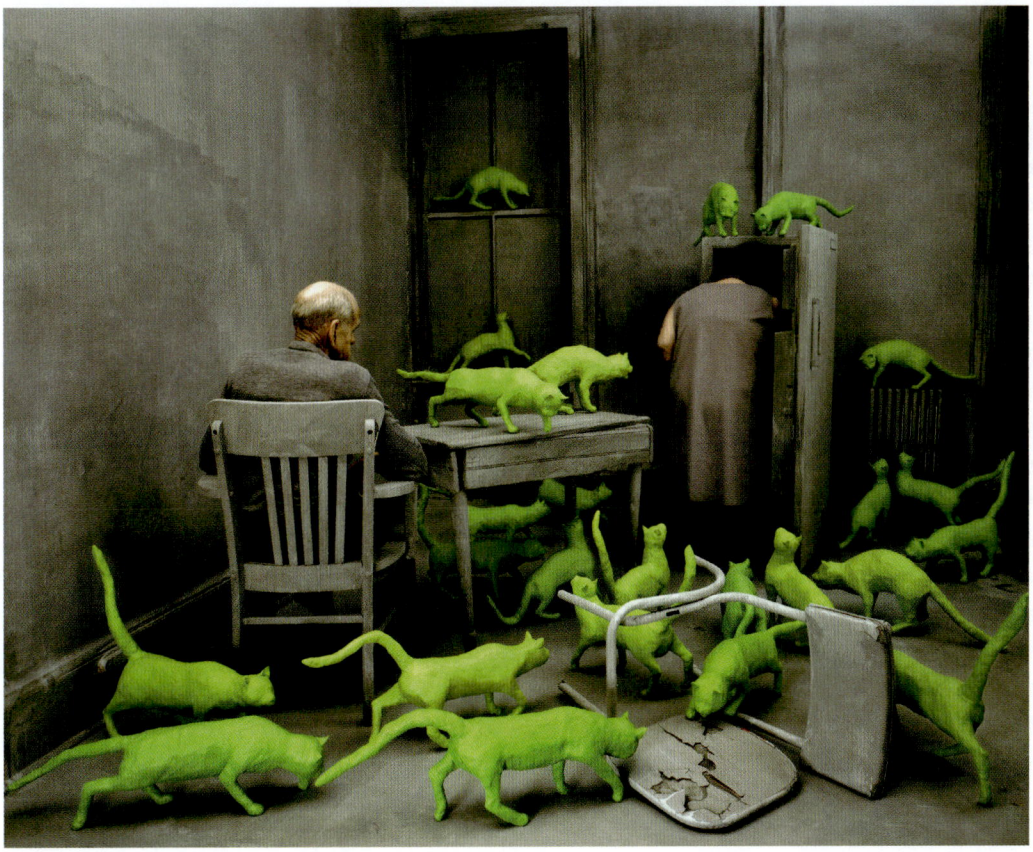

2.8.14 Sandy Skoglund, *Radioactive Cats* © 1980. Cibachrome or pigmented inkjet color photograph, 25⅝ × 35"

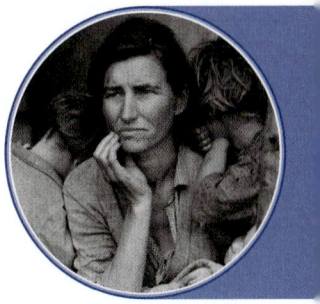

The impact of this famous photograph on its subject, Florence Owens Thompson, has raised issues about ethics in documentary photojournalism: see **4.8.9, p. 659**

Chromogenic (c-prints) prints: most widespread color process until digital prints; dyes couple with developers to create a negative image, reversed to make positive prints
Kodachrome: Created by Kodak Research Laboratories, Kodachrome is a subtractive reversal process for making color photographic film slides
Cibachrome: dye-destruction process for making direct positive photographic images available in the 1960s
CMY: the primary colors used in inkjet printing: cyan, magenta, and blue
Tableau: a stationary scene arranged for artistic impact
Surreal: reminiscent of the Surrealist movement in the 1920s and later, whose art was inspired by dreams and the subconscious

white or color, digital technology now makes it easy to alter the tonality of photographs. Tonal manipulation can be achieved by using a number of digital effects that replicate the results of early photographic processes, including black-and-white and sepia tones.

When digital cameras became available around 1985 they marked a huge shift in the medium of photography. By around 2000, when such cameras started being integrated in cell phones, people could have one at their fingertips. Digital photography records images not on film but in the form of pixels (tiny square dots arranged in a grid). Images recorded as pixels can be stored as digital files and printed on paper or projected on a screen or computer monitor. Some photographers present these images as they were originally taken, but others make alterations to them on a computer. Photographers often use archival inks to improve longevity of digital prints (see **2.8.28**, p. 332).

Photojournalism

Photojournalism is the use of photography to tell a news story. Some of the earliest examples of photojournalism date back to the American Civil War, when collodion photographic equipment was portable enough to be used in the field. Although we now readily accept that photographs can distort, exaggerate, and even lie—because they can be manipulated, altered, cropped in particular ways, and only ever give a partial view—the medium was once believed to be inherently truthful. This credibility, even today, is crucial for news reportage. As a result, the question of what constitutes "truth" in photography impacts its ethical use in photojournalism.

The American Lewis Wickes Hine (1874–1940) used photography to expose the injustice of child labor in the early 1900s (**2.8.16**, p. 325). He went into factories and mines under the guise of a salesman, repairman, or safety investigator, and then took photographs as well as detailed notes about the ages of the children he found there. When he later published his findings,

Perspectives on Art: Steve McCurry

Steve McCurry is a photographer who launched his photojournalism career by entering Afghanistan disguised in native clothing shortly before the Russian invasion in 1978. He estimates that during his career he made more than 800,000 photographs, including the famous Afghan Girl, *on Kodachrome film. For 75 years Kodachrome film was known for its rich, vibrant colors; archival durability; poetic rendition of reality; and being what McCurry called "probably the best film ever made." As a result of the digital revolution in photography, however, Kodak stopped manufacturing the film in 2009. McCurry decided to mark the demise of the film by launching a project to use the last roll of Kodachrome film to come off the assembly line. In a National Public Radio interview with Audie Cornish (July 24, 2010) and a National Geographic documentary about the making of the project, McCurry talked extensively about his process and the challenges he faced.*

Discussing the pressure associated with taking photographs on the last-ever 36 frames of Kodachrome, McCurry wondered, "What do you photograph?... I need to find iconic situations and iconic people that are going to be kind of a great celebration of this last roll of film."

McCurry decided to make a series of portraits because it was the final roll of film and he could not take as many risks as outdoor settings and street scenes would require. He started the project in New York City, where he lived; then traveled to India, "where color is culturally important," as evidenced by its symbolic importance and prominence in religion, politics, festivals, and celebrations; went to Rajasthan because he felt a personal connection with people he had recently photographed there; and ended up in Parsons, Kansas, the location of the last Kodachrome-processing lab in the world.

Along the way McCurry worried about technical mishaps common with film as opposed to digital cameras: "it was really nerve-wracking because...you load [the film] in and, heaven forbid, somebody opens the back by mistake. You know, going through security...I was worried sick that there was going to be X-ray damage..." Opening the camera outside of a darkroom can ruin unprocessed film by exposing it to light, while subjecting it to X-ray screening can cause fogging and discoloration. "[And then...] am I

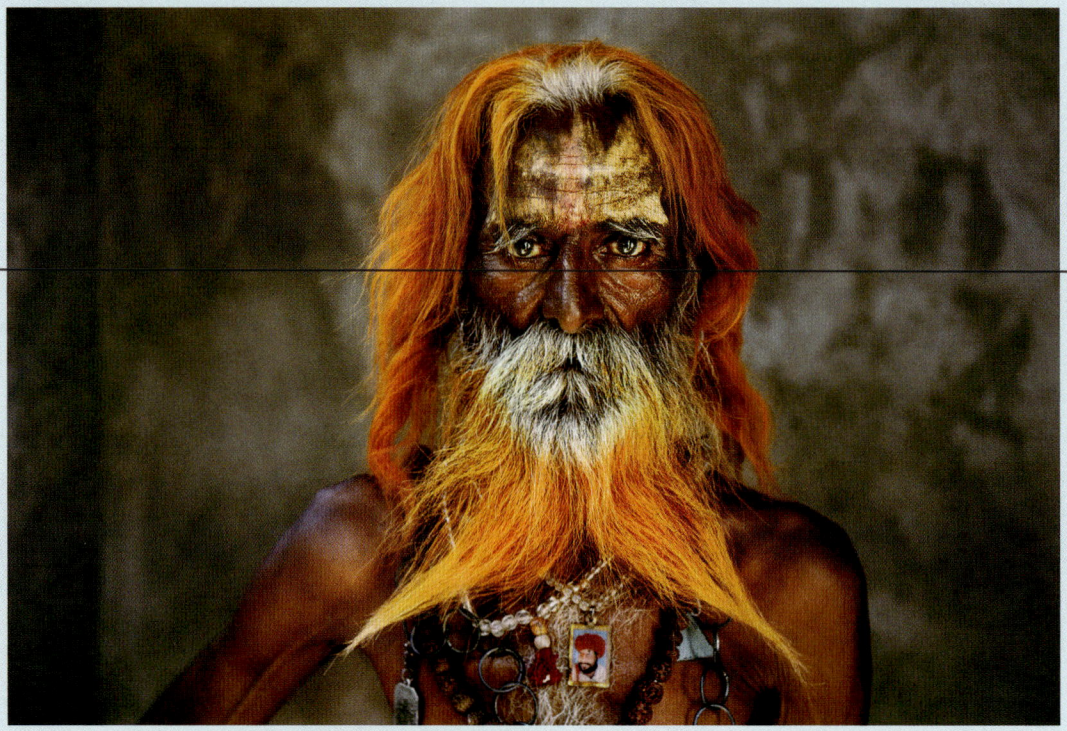

2.8.15 Steve McCurry, *Rabari Tribal Elder, India*, 2010

getting the right moment?...is it in focus, is the exposure right?" While many of these challenges exist when McCurry uses a digital camera, with digital photography, being able to see the results immediately (rather than having to wait until the film is developed) affords the opportunity to take another picture. McCurry used his digital camera to set the lighting, determine the composition and design, and make test photos before shooting any film with his analog (traditional) camera.

During his week in Rajasthan, McCurry photographed an ancient tribe of nomads (**2.8.15**). He felt it was especially fitting to "honor the film... with the memory and history of these Rabari shepherds" whose migratory way of life is coming to a close extremely rapidly due to modernization and land development....Some of the nomads are entertainers. These snake charmers, storytellers, and fortune-tellers will have to find new ways to make a living. McCurry's powerful and compelling portrait demonstrates his belief that it is "the whole face that tells a story, not just the eyes...all the features work together."

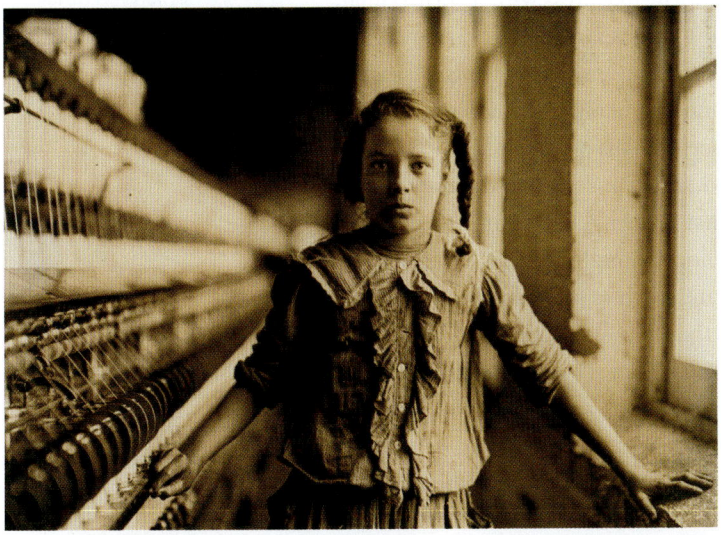

2.8.16 Lewis Wickes Hine, *Ten Year Old Spinner, Whitnel Cotton Mill*, 1908. Photographic print. Library of Congress, Washington, D.C.

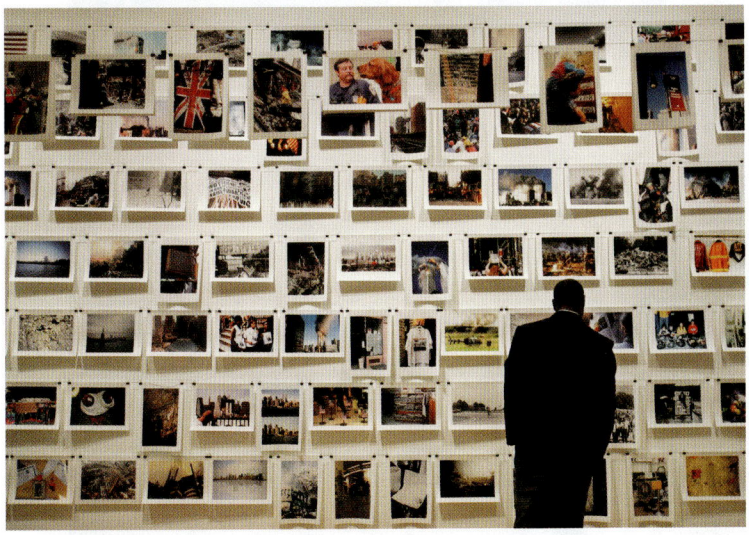

2.8.17 *Here Is New York: A Democracy of Photographs*, exhibition at the New York Historical Society, September 2007

the public was shocked by his photos of these children and their often grueling and dangerous working conditions. His efforts eventually led to the establishment of laws preventing children from working at such young ages.

Contemporary photojournalism communicates events almost immediately on television and the Internet, but those same images can also be used to record events for posterity. Photographs made during the attack on the World Trade Center on September 11, 2001, were published all over the world right after the event. In the days following 9/11, a group of photographers organized an exhibition called *Here Is New York: A Democracy of Photographs on the Streets of SoHo in New York City* (**2.8.17**). The collection of photos gave voice to almost 800 people who had experienced the attack at first hand, whether they were professional photographers or people who just happened to be carrying a camera that day. The exhibition traveled all over the world and was later donated to the New York Historical Society.

Photocollage and Photomontage

Photojournalists generally focus on documenting a real event as accurately as possible, while artists often use photography for a variety of creative purposes. Some make compositions created by gluing together fragments of separate materials to form an image, a technique known as **collage**. The term is also used for the resulting artwork. A photocollage is made from photo-based images and pre-printed materials, or combines photographs and text. A collage is a unique artwork, like a drawing or a painting, that is not generally reproduced. By contrast, a **photomontage** is made to be reproduced. In photomontage, the artist combines smaller photographic images (using prints or negatives), then rephotographs or scans the result. Today, photomontage and photocollage can be made relatively easily by cutting, pasting, and merging image files on a computer.

Although it may not look like it, *Two Ways of Life* was made with thirty separate negatives, which were cut out like puzzle pieces (**2.8.18**). The Swedish photographer Oscar Gustav Rejlander (1813–1875) worked in a labor-intensive, time-consuming way, just as traditional artists do. By emulating the appearance and process of painting, Rejlander hoped his photographs would earn the respect that at that time was reserved for painting. He exposed the negatives one at a time, covering the rest of the print every time he exposed another negative. The resulting image, which took him six weeks to make, looks like one seamless scene.

While Rejlander used manual methods to create his images, the German photographer Loretta Lux (b. 1969) uses digital technology to assemble the elements in her compositions in a very similar way. She takes pictures of her friends' children and then subtly manipulates the colors and **proportions**, making the subjects look as if they just stepped out of a fairy tale. Sometimes she also paints **backgrounds**, which she then photographs and retouches digitally to contribute to the otherworldly effect. She works on each photograph for anywhere from several months to a year. *The Waiting Girl* shows a little girl and a cat on a vintage sofa (**2.8.19**). The girl's severely knotted hair, her uniform-like dress with its prim collar, and the emptiness of the background give the impression she spends her time in a confined environment, likely with people much older than herself. This picture, like the one Rejlander created, shows a scene that did not exist before the artist made it. Lux's subtle use of digital technology, though, allowed her to alter certain attributes, such as **scale** and proportion, to create the effect she wanted.

The German artist Hannah Höch (1889–1978) was one of the first to make photomontages. She used them to protest social conditions, especially during and after World

Collage: artwork assembled by gluing materials, often paper, onto a surface. From the French *coller*, to glue
Photomontage: a single photographic image that combines (digitally or using multiple film exposures) several separate images
Proportion: the relationship in size between a work's individual parts and the whole piece
Background: the part of a work depicted furthest from the viewer's space, often behind the main subject matter
Scale: the size of an object or an artwork relative to another object or artwork, or to a system of measurement

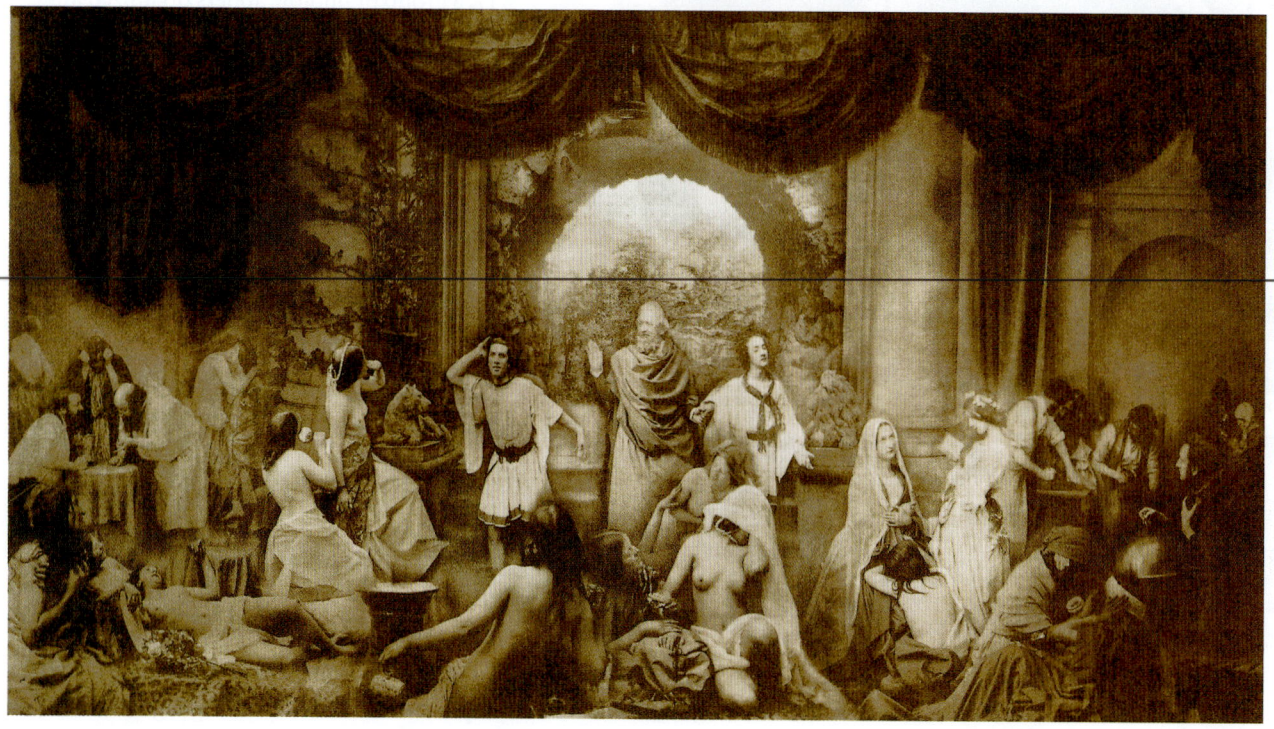

2.8.18 Oscar Gustav Rejlander, *The Two Ways of Life*, 1857. Albumen silver print, 16 × 31". Royal Photographic Society, Bath, England

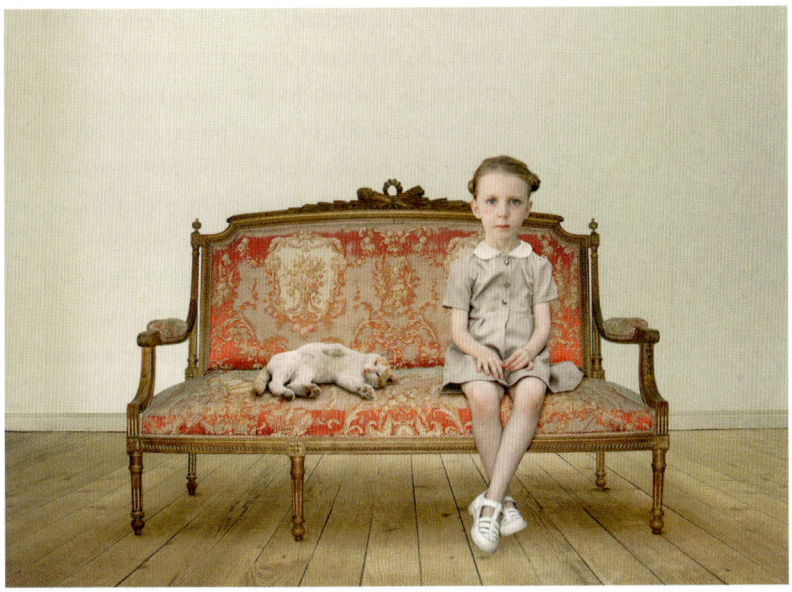

2.8.19 Loretta Lux, *The Waiting Girl*, 2006. Ilfochrome print, 11⅞ × 15⅞"

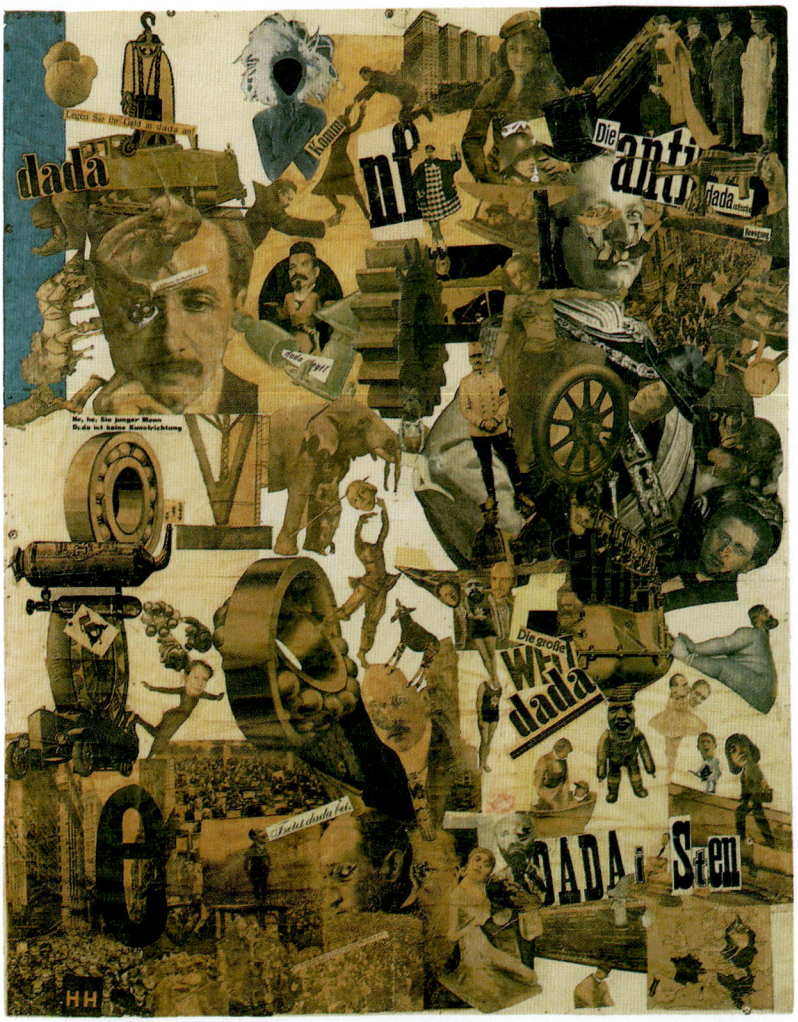

2.8.20 Hannah Höch, *Cut with the Kitchen Knife through the Last Weimar Beer-Belly Cultural Epoch of Germany*, 1919–20. Photomontage and collage with watercolor, 44⅞ × 35½". Nationalgalerie, Staatliche Museen, Berlin, Germany

War I. In *Cut with the Kitchen Knife through the Last Weimar Beer-Belly Cultural Epoch of Germany*, Höch's **Dada** combination of text and images, like the image's title, is at once complex and apparently nonsensical (**2.8.20**). The disorder of the image, which comprises pictures of political figures and modern technology from mass-media publications, reflects the chaos of life at that time. Höch also expresses her concern about women's issues in post-war Germany, highlighting their traditional tool of the kitchen knife and also including, in the lower right corner, a map showing where women had obtained the right to vote. Höch is purposely subverting that picture space (that Rejlander sought to create) by making a flat image with no perspective.

Postmodern Return to Historic Processes

A prominent characteristic of **Postmodernism** is the focus on historical references, including past artworks. In the 1960s photography began to be taught in college art programs and many artists became interested in critically considering the medium, what it could do, and what could be done with it. A large number of photographers looked to alternative and vintage processes to reflect their artistic focus or to create a particular look.

The photographs of the British artist Roger Fenton (1819–1869) illustrate some of the haunting effects made possible through early nineteenth-century processes. Fenton, who photographed the Crimean War, made his salt prints using paper negatives, which gave them a grainy appearance and allowed the landscape to

Dada: anarchic anti-art and anti-war movement, dating back to World War I, that reveled in absurdity and irrationality

Postmodernism, Postmodernist: a late 20th-century style of architecture and art that playfully adopts features of earlier styles and critically focuses on content

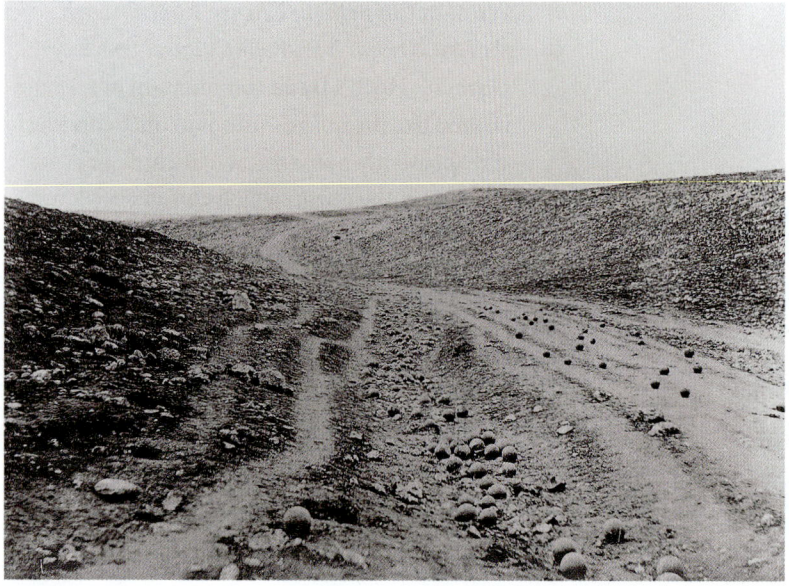

2.8.21 Roger Fenton, *Valley of the Shadow of Death*, 1855. Salted paper print from a paper negative. Gernsheim Collection, Harry Ransom Humanities Research Center, University of Texas at Austin

take on symbolic associations. The title, *Valley of the Shadow of Death*, seems to derive from a passage from Psalm 23 in the Bible, referring to the comfort God offers for life's suffering. In fact, Fenton chose it some time after he had taken the photograph, as a result of the popularity of a now-famous poem by Alfred, Lord Tennyson (1809–1892). "The Charge of the Light Brigade" contains the refrain "Into the Valley of Death/ Rode the six hundred," echoed in Fenton's title (**2.8.21**). In black and white, the cannonballs littering the battlefield take on an eerie quality, like human skulls. Fenton's process captures the emptiness and desolation of the aftermath of combat in a poetic and thought-provoking scene.

In the series *Battlefields* the American photographer Sally Mann (b. 1951) chose to capture present-day views of Civil War battlefields using a vintage process. In a manner similar to her other series, the artist uses black and white to transform ordinary moments into nostalgic and provocative statements (**2.8.22**). The collodion (wet plate) process was in use at the time of the Civil War, and the artist used the silver gelatin method to create prints from her wet-plate negatives. In an interview for the PBS series ART21 in 2000, Mann explained that she chose to work in the way she did because she was "so immersed in that whole glass-plate, nineteenth-century aesthetic, it was natural to want to learn how to do this....I'm surprised it took me this long to get to this process, because I've always admired that aesthetic and find it redolent with [the] past. I just need to inject a little of the present in it."

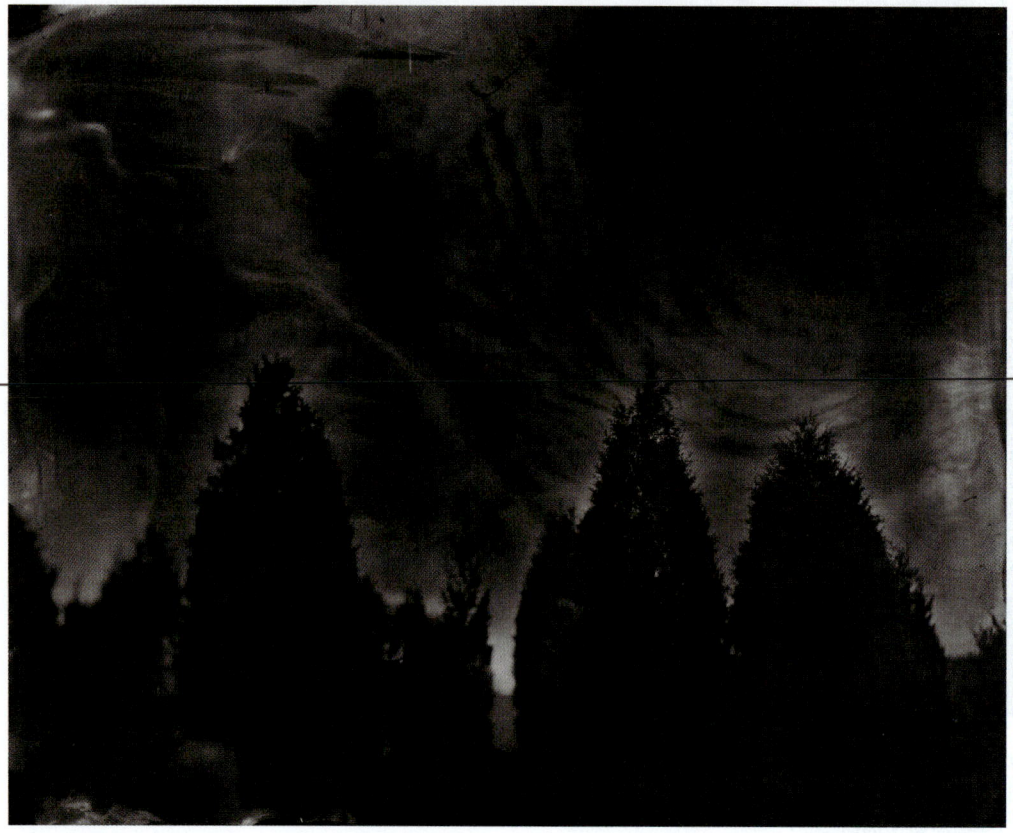

2.8.22 Sally Mann, *Untitled #7, Fredericksburg*, 2000. Silver gelatin print, 38 × 48"

Gateway to Art: Weems, *Kitchen Table* Series

Story Telling and Sto-re-telling

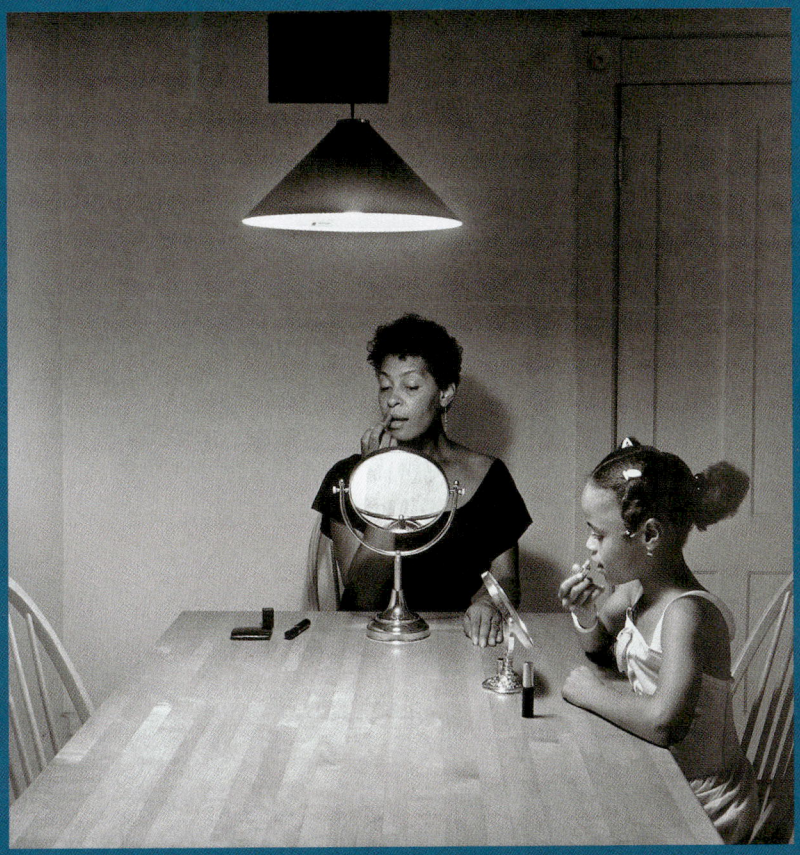

2.8.23 Carrie Mae Weems, "Untitled (Woman and Daughter with Makeup)," 1990, from *Kitchen Table* series, 1989–90. Inkjet print, 41¼ × 41¼ × 2¼" (framed)

The American artist Carrie Mae Weems (b. 1953) used the gelatin silver process for her *Kitchen Table* series. The glossy black-and-white prints yield a great deal of detail and call attention to the subject rather than the process itself. Her work embodies an interest in personal and cultural identity.

In her series *From Here I Saw What Happened and I Cried*, Weems continued to investigate the collective African American experience through photographs (**2.8.24**). In this case, the historical stories are rooted in slavery: Weems reinterprets a series of nineteenth-century daguerreotypes of African slaves in America. In the original photographs the sitters were stripped and exposed to the scrutiny of racist theorists who sought to examine and investigate them in a coldly analytical, supposedly "scientific" way

Weems rephotographed the images, colored them red, and framed them with circular mats to highlight the fact that they were being seen through the camera lens. The text she inscribes on the glass challenges ideas of race, gender, and class that were once taken for granted. Weems points out that these individuals had become "scientific profiles" used as evidence to support anthropological theories; her retelling of these images aims to restore some of the dignity that had been denied to the sitters and motivate viewers to understand and respect their humanity.

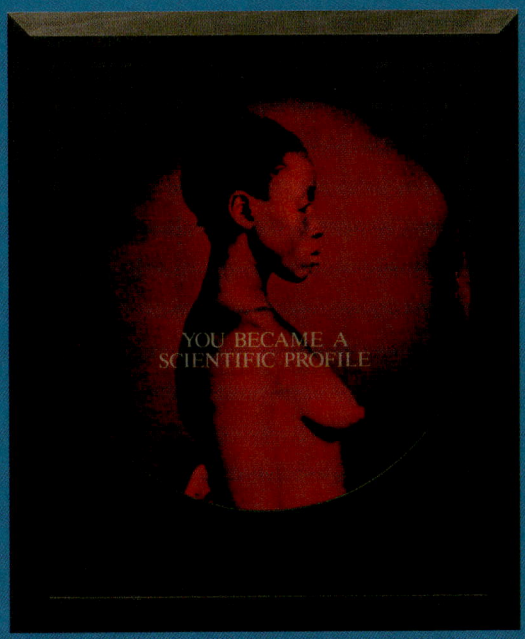

2.8.24 Carrie Mae Weems, "You Became a Scientific Profile," from the series *From Here I Saw What Happened and I Cried*, 1995. Chromogenic color prints with sand-blasted text on glass, 25⅝ × 22¾". MoMA, New York

For the other Weems Gateway boxes, see p. 56, p. 551, and p. 687

The Art of Photography

Soon after it was invented, there were heated debates about whether photography worked best for recording reality or as a way to make works of art. Even though photographs have been collected in major fine art museums since the early twentieth century, the immediacy of the medium still causes some people to have trouble considering photography as "art." A walk through today's galleries in any major city will show that photography is a favored medium of many contemporary artists.

Recording Detail and Stopping Time

At a time when other photographers were trying to imitate traditional painting, the American Alfred Stieglitz (1864–1946) was amongst the first to emphasize what he considered to be the particular strengths of the photographic medium: its clarity and realism. In addition to making artistic photographs, Stieglitz actively promoted photography as a fine art medium in the journal *Camera Work* (first published in 1902) and in his New York galleries. *The Steerage* shows the decks of a passenger ship in the cheapest accommodations, separate from the first-class passengers, including Stieglitz himself (**2.8.25**). Stieglitz was struck by the **composition** of **shapes** and **rhythms** in the photograph, including the straw hat on the upper deck near the center, the crossed suspenders on the man below, the funnel leaning left, the stairway on the right, and the shapes of round machinery, draping chains, and the triangular mast. This composition seemed thoroughly modern and reminiscent of the abstract paintings of that era.

Composition: the overall design or organization of a work
Shape: the two-dimensional area the boundaries of which are defined by lines or suggested by changes in color or value
Rhythm: the regular or ordered repetition of elements in the work

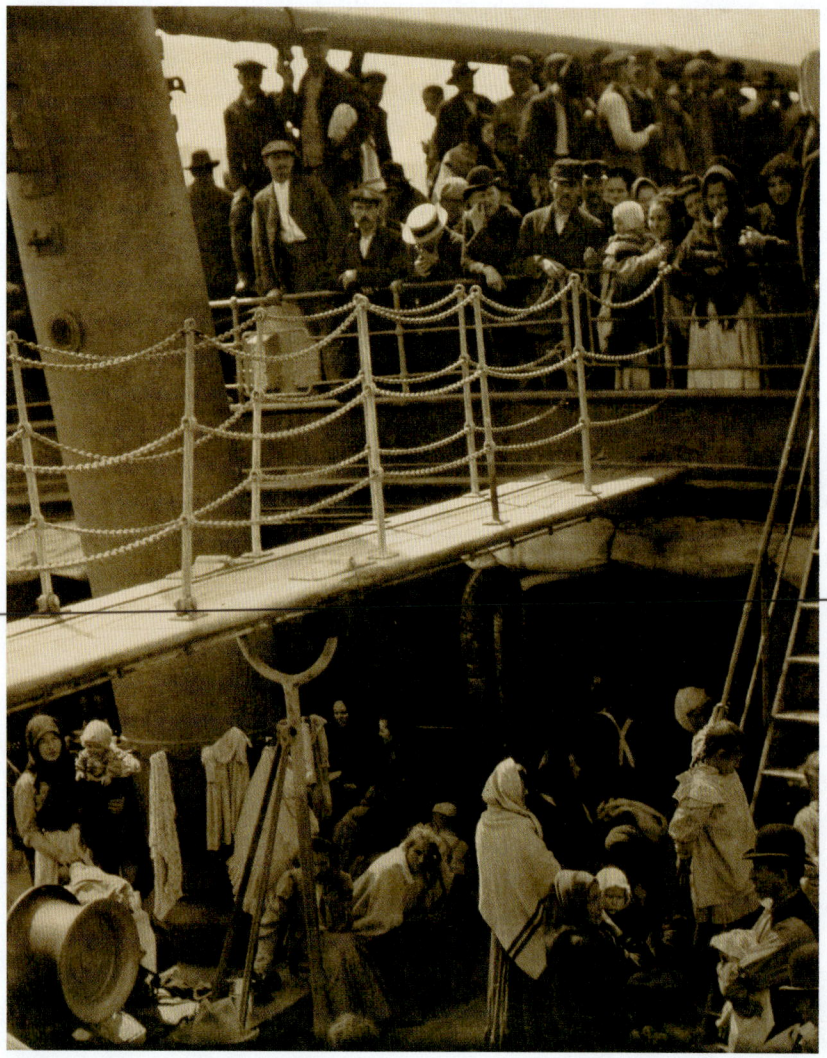

2.8.25 Alfred Stieglitz, *The Steerage*, 1907. Photogravure, 13¼ × 10⅜". J. Paul Getty Museum, Los Angeles, California

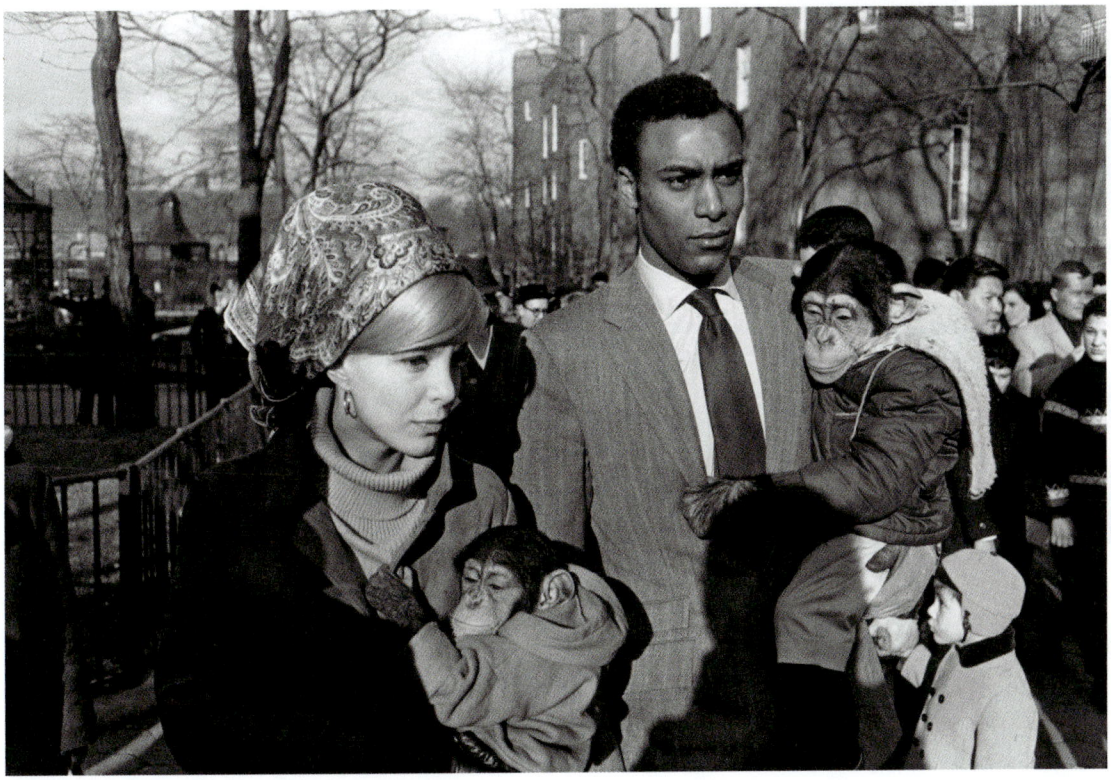

2.8.26 Garry Winogrand, *Central Park Zoo, New York City*, 1967. Gelatin silver print, 11 × 14"

In contrast to Stieglitz's concern with sharp focus and formal composition, the American Garry Winogrand (1928–1984) was more interested in photography's ability to directly capture a fleeting moment in time. Winogrand used a small camera he could easily carry around. He generally did not pose his subjects or set up shots beforehand. Many of his photographs seem spontaneous, as in *Central Park Zoo, New York City*: he walked the city's streets and captured what he found there (**2.8.26**). Winogrand's subjective approach, known as the snapshot aesthetic, seems casual, but he intended his photographs to be serious and artistic with some room for interpretation on the viewer's part.

Reality and Artifice in the Anthropocene

We live during a time known as the Anthropocene because human impact on natural conditions, systems, and processes has become so far-reaching that many scientists consider it geologically significant. For most of its existence photography has presented the nuanced interactions between life, nature, and human intervention through varying degrees of factual depiction and fictional representation. Some contemporary artists prefer to focus on the strangeness of reality while others emphasize its fabricated nature.

The Canadian Edward Burtynsky (b. 1955) prints his powerful color photographs on a large scale, about 3 × 4 ft., so that small details create an impression of the vast scale of urban landscapes and the relative smallness of humankind. His series called *China* focuses on factories driven by mass consumerism, where raw and recycled materials are brought to be turned into commercial products and shipped all over the world. *Manufacturing #17: Deda Chicken Processing Plant* shows a vista of workers in the industrial grimness of a chicken-processing plant (**2.8.27**, p. 332), evidence of the fact that chicken bones are expected to be a defining marker in the geologic profile of the Anthropocene. This prediction is due to the vast human consumption of chicken, the most common bird in the world. Also, the size of chickens has significantly increased through factory farming since the 1950s (making identification from its pre-war relative clear), which aligns with the beginning of the

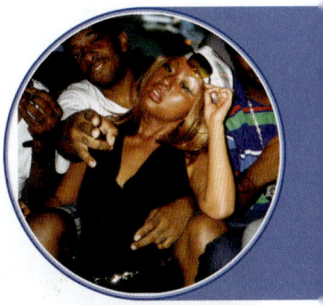

Nikki S. Lee's photographs confront ideas of fact and fiction as the artist takes on different identities: see **4.10.16, p. 690**

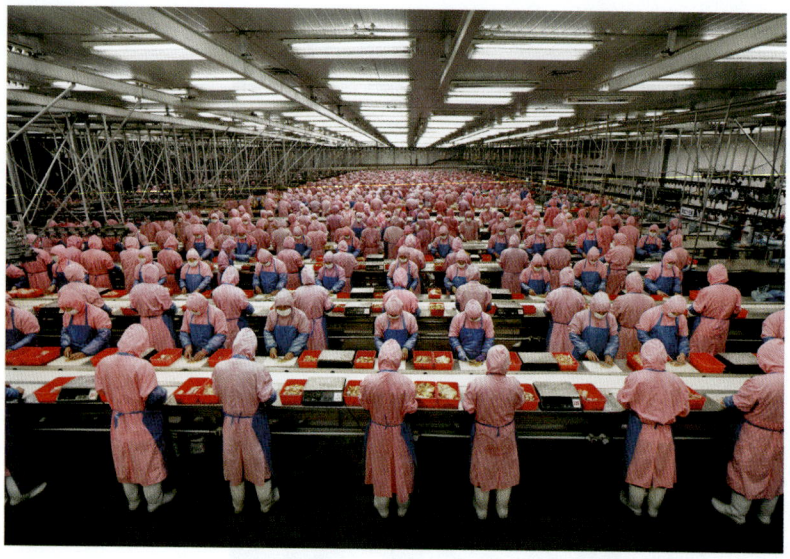

2.8.27 Edward Burtynsky, *Manufacturing #17: Deda Chicken Processing Plant*, Dehui City, Jilin Province, China, 2005

Anthropocene. The vivid pinks, bright-blue aprons, white boots, and the rows upon rows of hooded figures, create a surreal effect, as if this is a scene from an alien world. Without passing judgment, Burtynsky's arresting images call attention to things not usually in our consciousness. Burtynsky has said he wants viewers to come to their own conclusions about civilization's impact on the planet because "it's not a simple right or wrong. It needs a whole new way of thinking."

The American artist Daniela Edburg (b. 1975) lives in Mexico and exhibits her art around the world. She works with elements that "define our human nature, particularly the artificial world we inhabit and the nonsense that it generates." Her fictional scenarios are exaggerated to the point that they become contradictory. Her series *Drop Dead Gorgeous* features outrageous scenarios where women meet their demise in absurd and darkly humorous ways. In "Death by Cotton Candy" (**2.8.28**) a woman in a pink-flowered dress runs through a field of pink flowers carrying a stick of cotton candy. Terrified, she looks behind her as a pink tornado—or, more likely, an atomic blast—billows up into the sky. As in many of the works in this series, Edburg includes references to earlier artworks: in this case the photograph of the iconic mushroom cloud over Nagasaki by Lieutenant Charles Levy (1945) and Nick Ut's famous Vietnam war photo (see **4.7.2**, opposite). The contrasts between nature and culture in the "feminine" pink of the sickly-sweet confection, the fabricated dress, and wild landscape create a witty friction as we confront the chilling realities and looming effects of human civilization.

2.8.28 Daniela Edburg, "Death by Cotton Candy" from the series *Drop Dead Gorgeous*, 2006. Archival Ink Print

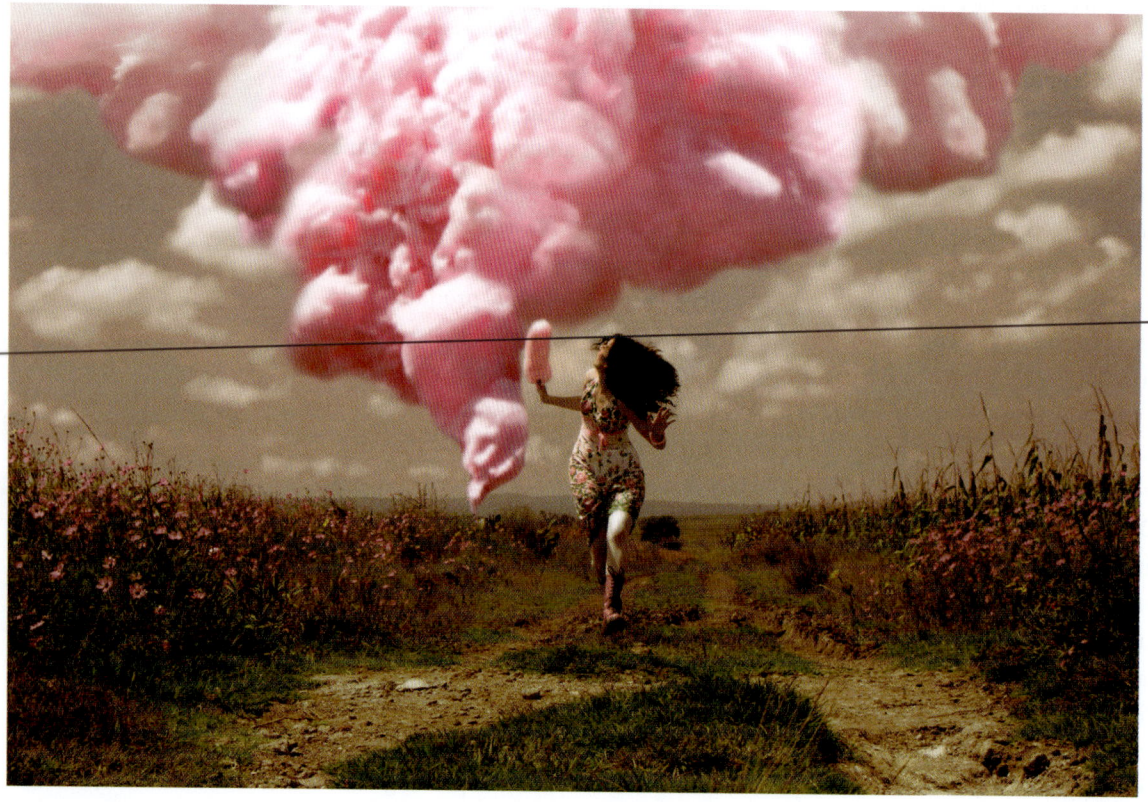

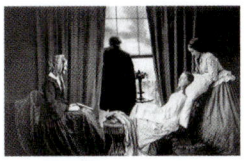

1.7.13a Henry Peach Robinson, *Fading Away*, 1858, p. 147

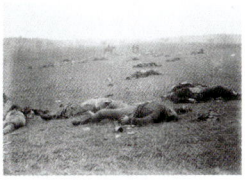

4.7.1 Timothy O'Sullivan, *Harvest of Death, Gettysburg, Pennsylvania*, 1863, p. 638

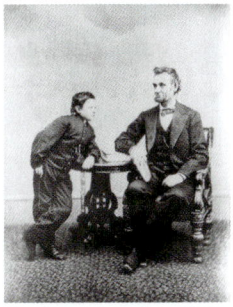

3.8.6 Alexander Gardner, *Abraham Lincoln and His Son Thomas (Tad)*, 1865, p. 506

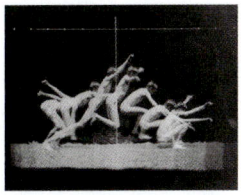

3.8.8 Thomas Eakins, *Motion Study: Male Nude, Standing Jump to Right*, 1884, p. 508

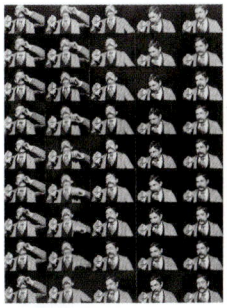

1.5.16 Thomas Edison and W. K. Dickson, *Fred Ott's Sneeze*, 1894, p. 122

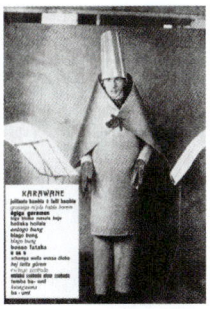

3.9.7 Hugo Ball, Performance of "Karawane" at Cabaret Voltaire, 1916, p. 529

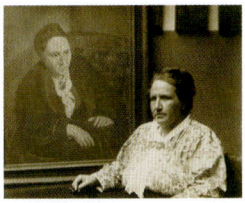

0.0.13 Man Ray, *Gertrude Stein with Portrait by Picasso*, 1922, p. 29

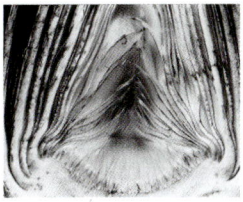

1.9.10 Edward Weston, *Artichoke Halved*, 1930, p. 165

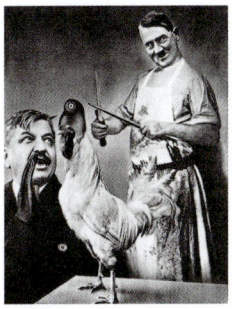

3.9.9 John Heartfield, *Have No Fear, He's a Vegetarian*, 1936, p. 530

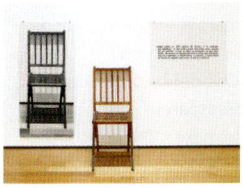

3.10.3 Joseph Kosuth, *One and Three Chairs*, 1965, p. 548

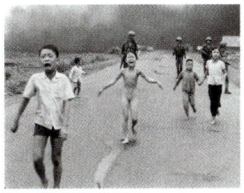

4.7.2 Nick Ut, *Vietnamese Girl Kim Phuc Running after Napalm Attack*, 1972, p. 639

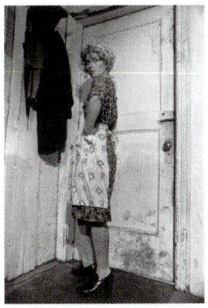

4.10.5 Cindy Sherman, "Untitled Film Still #35," 1979, p. 683

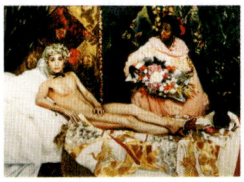

4.9.10 Yasumasa Morimura, *Portrait (Futago)*, 1988–90, p. 669

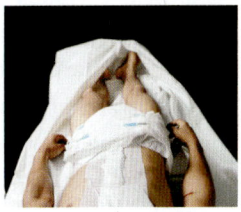

4.3.4 Andres Serrano, *The Morgue (Gun Murder)*, 1992, p. 593

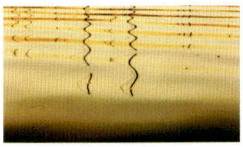

4.4.12 Marcia Smilack, *Cello Music*, 1992, p. 610

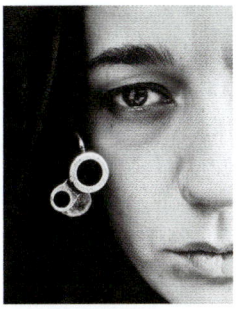

4.8.10 Shirin Neshat, "Speechless," from *Women of Allah*, 1996, p. 659

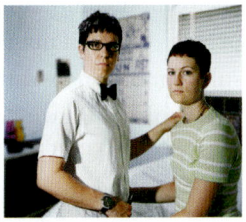

4.10.17 Catherine Opie, "Melissa & Lake, Durham, North Carolina," 1998, p. 690

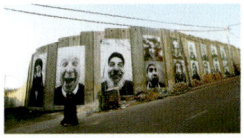

4.8.11 JR and Marco, *28 Millimeters, Face2Face*, 2007, p. 660

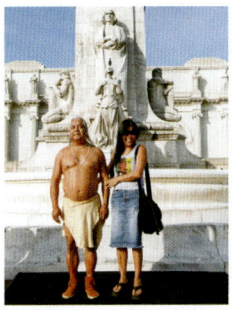

4.10.13 James Luna, *Take a Picture with a Real Indian*, 2010, p. 688

2.9 Film/Video and Digital Art

Medium (plural **media**): the material on or from which an artist chooses to make a work of art, for example canvas and oil paint, marble, engraving, video, or architecture

Celluloid: tough, transparent plastic used to make motion-picture film, photographic film, and X-rays; until relatively recently most movies were filmed on celluloid

Frame: a single image from the sequence that makes up a motion picture; on average, a 90-minute film contains 129,600 separate frames

SLR (single-lens reflex camera): hand-held digital or film camera that uses a mirror and prism system so the focus screen matches the image captured

Analog: photography or movie made using a film camera that chemically records images using a continuous gradation of value ranges from light to dark, so that they directly match the actual appearance of the object or scene

Cloud (the Cloud): can refer to any electronic network; generally refers to shared resources on the Internet rather than local servers or devices for storage and computer applications

Of all the **media** chosen by artists, the moving image is one of the youngest, most widely used, and most rapidly changing. The products of film, video, and digital art include home movies, artworks, independent films, television shows, video games, and major motion pictures. Until relatively recently, the dominant process for making movies has been film: flexible, **celluloid**, and light-sensitive. A movie camera captures movement by taking many separate **frames** per second, all exposed in sequence onto the same strip of film. After being developed and edited, the moving film passes in front of a bright light in a projector that shines the image onto a screen.

Because of the high costs of the medium, making a full-length movie requires serious, usually commercial, investment. Digital cameras have become the dominant process used by both individuals and professional production teams. For a while digital cameras could not match the resolution, or detail, possible with film cameras, due to the number of megapixels required. Now, technological advancements in digital film have outpaced traditional film. Digital film also has the considerable advantages of streamlining workflow for the director and editor; eliminating the costs of film and film processing; giving greater access to footage; and increasing the possibilities for more accessible and affordable manipulation than 35mm film. Nevertheless, even after technological advances made digital the industry standard, a number of talented and high-profile directors have continued to use film both for the way it looks and because they prefer the film process.

While cinematic films are made using a movie camera and viewed with a projector, most movies are now primarily made with digital video cameras (commercially available since 1986), and videos are generally made with small, hand-held cameras. For various reasons (including the look and the process), sometimes moving images are recorded on film and transferred to a digital format for the purposes of editing and presentation, requiring the skills of many different people. More common today, digital single-lens reflex cameras (**SLRs**) record images in the form of pixels as files on a DVD, Blu-ray, or computer hard drive. Digital film editing can be done by single individuals, whereas the traditional film-editing process requires a production team. Video—initially an **analog** technology, like film—has the advantages of being less expensive and highly portable, yet the quality is still generally lower than film and digital SLRs.

Relatively recent technological developments in both film- and video-making processes mean that viewing motion-picture productions no longer requires a dedicated room, projector, and screen. Over time such shows transitioned to broadcasts and recordings seen on televisions and computer monitors in businesses and people's homes. Public viewing on a screen is still common, now with digital rather than film projectors, or via wireless technology. Accessing movies remotely, viewing videos on the Internet, and streaming from the **Cloud** have made viewing increasingly portable. Today, everything from full-length productions to clips can be watched on a variety of devices and screen sizes, almost anywhere at any time: so much so that it is hard now to imagine a time when they did not exist.

Moving Images before Film

How is the illusion of movement created? The principle was understood long before the invention of still or moving film images. Representations of movement adorn ancient examples of pottery from Asia and South America. By the nineteenth century, a child's toy developed in Europe, known as the **zoetrope**, was able to produce a convincing effect of a sequence of movement. The zoetrope contains a rotating cylinder with a series of images on the inside (**2.9.1**). By looking through the outer ring of the cylinder, which has slots cut into it, and spinning the zoetrope, the viewer gets the impression of a single image in continuous **motion**.

More recently, a similar principle is at work in the sequential images on Laboratorio Paravicini's "Play Plates" (**2.9.2**), which create the impression of a single moving image when they are spun in rapid succession. The decorations on these contemporary plates utilize the same concept of implied motion, and consist of still images from stages of an action using animals, acrobats, children, dancers, hunters, and demons in a vintage style. The illusion of movement created in this way, known as **stroboscopic motion,** is the basis of modern film and video technique.

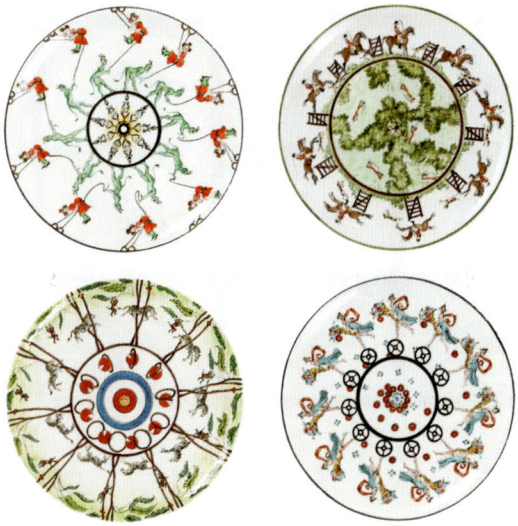

2.9.2 Costanza Paravicini/ Laboratorio Paravicini, "Play Plates," 2016. Ceramic, diameter 9¾"

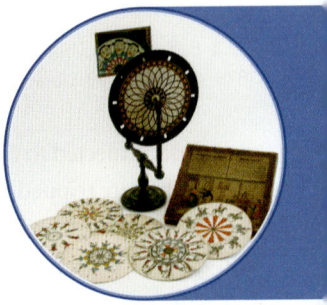

For further discussion of persistence of vision and stroboscopic motion as seen in the optical device called a phenakistoscope, see **1.5.5, p. 116**

A theory known as persistence of vision explains that this illusion results from the presentation to the eye of separate images at regular intervals so that they appear to be a continuous sequence. Because visual sensations persist even after the seen object is no longer there, the mind connects them together. This concept is illustrated in a rudimentary way by a flip book with separate still images in a sequence that, when flipped, become visually connected and appear to move. Images captured in the camera use the same concept: the faster the succession of images, the smoother the impression of movement. In the earliest film projectors there was a visible "blink" between frames. While higher resolutions are available even for personal use, a standard movie will show images at twenty-four frames per second; **IMAX** and other high-definition films can show forty-eight, to provide a heightened sense of reality.

As strange as it may seem, in order to make moving pictures it was first necessary to freeze movement in the form of still images. After many failed attempts, the English photographer Eadweard Muybridge (1830–1904) arranged a line of twelve cameras to take a sequence of twelve pictures of a running horse. The

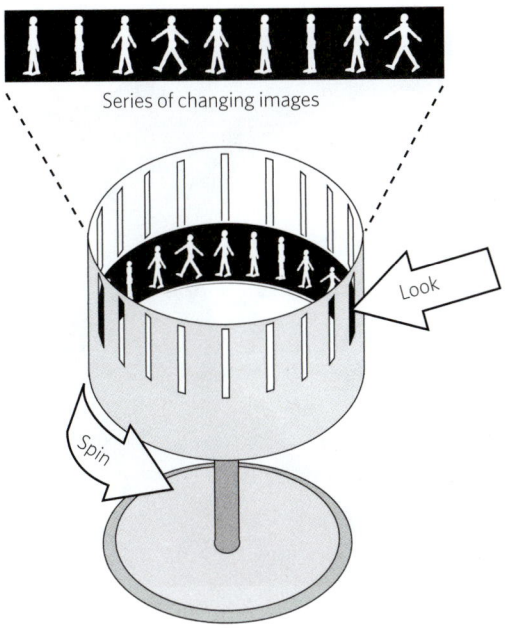

2.9.1 Diagram of a zoetrope

Zoetrope: an antique, European toy; contains a rotating cylinder with a sequence of images on the inside that creates the impression of a single action in continuous motion when spun
Motion: the effect of changing placement in time
Stroboscopic motion: the effect created when we see two or more repeated images in quick succession in such a way that they visually fuse together
IMAX: "Image Maximum," a format for film presentation that allows presentation of films at ten times larger sizes than the conventional one

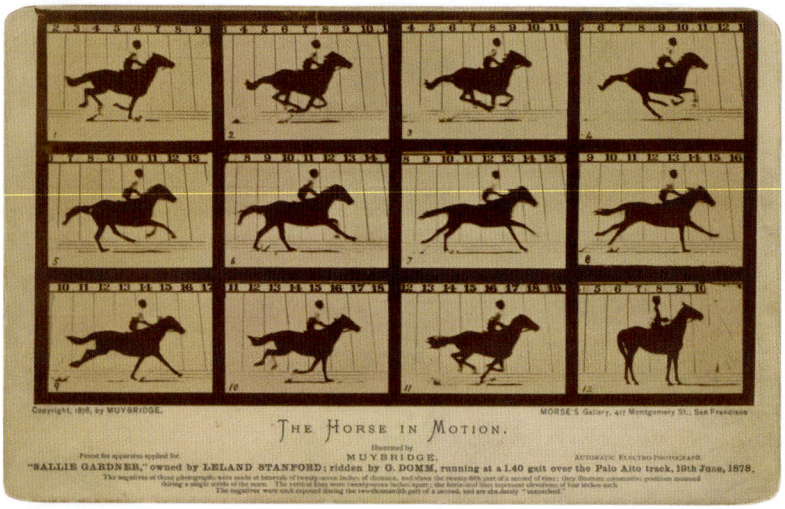

2.9.3 Eadweard Muybridge, *The Horse in Motion*, June 18, 1878. Albumen print. Library of Congress, Washington, D.C.

cameras, connected to cables stretched across the racetrack, were tripped as the horse passed.

Muybridge's experiments cost about $42,000 and resolved a wager that a galloping horse has all four of its legs off the ground at once. The camera proved what the naked eye could not see: the horse does (see the third frame of **2.9.3**). Before then, people thought the legs of the horse were extended, like those of a rocking horse, when off the ground. When prints of Muybridge's photographs were published in *Scientific American* magazine, they were accompanied by instructions to cut them out and place them in a zoetrope.

Silent and Black-and-White Film

The very earliest films were short clips usually documenting single instances of everyday occurrences—feeding the baby, doing a dance, leaving the factory gate at closing time, watching the arrival of a passenger locomotive. The earliest motion pictures were black and white and silent: they had no soundtrack. They were shown in nickelodeons, small storefront movie theaters popular in the early years of the twentieth century. Nickelodeons provided musical accompaniments with live piano and drums, and some provided lecturers to explain the action as the moving pictures, or movies, played. As movies grew into a business, they were shown in huge, ornate movie palaces that might also feature a pipe organ.

Style: a characteristic way in which an artist or group of artists uses visual language to give a work an identifiable form of visual expression
Pace: speed at which something moves; rhythmic flow of dialogue or action related to an overall scene or sequence

By 1896, movies were being shown all over Europe and the United States. Georges Méliès (1861–1938), a French magician and filmmaker, began showing films as part of his theatrical magic show. His silent science-fiction and fantasy films featured special effects and humor. In *A Trip to the Moon* (1902), Méliès's most famous film, a group of astronomers flies to the moon in a spaceship launched from a cannon (**2.9.4**). Their vessel crashes into the man-in-the-moon's right eye, and then the astronomers encounter wondrous sights and moon inhabitants called Selenites. Méliès was one of the first to use multiple settings, repeated scenes, and cuts to establish a sense of time moving forward.

The American filmmaker D. W. Griffith's (1875–1948) silent film *Birth of a Nation* (1915) was Hollywood's first blockbuster and one of the first films to tell an epic , though controversial, story (**2.9.5**). The film introduced a number of new techniques, including original editing **styles** to make transitions between scenes and vary the sense of **pace**. *Birth of a Nation* uses symbolism, gesture, and intertitles (onscreen text), rather than spoken dialogue, to move the story along. The film is now seen as extremely offensive for its reinforcement of racist views and stereotypes

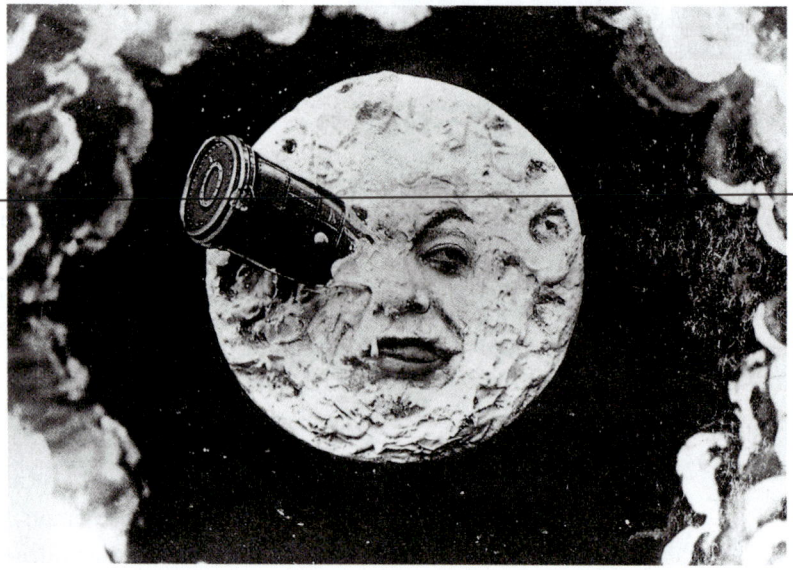

2.9.4 Georges Méliès, scene from *A Trip to the Moon (Le Voyage dans la Lune)*, 1902, 14 minutes, Star Film

Propaganda: art that promotes an ideology or a cause
Flashback: transition to an earlier time in a story that disrupts the chronological order of events

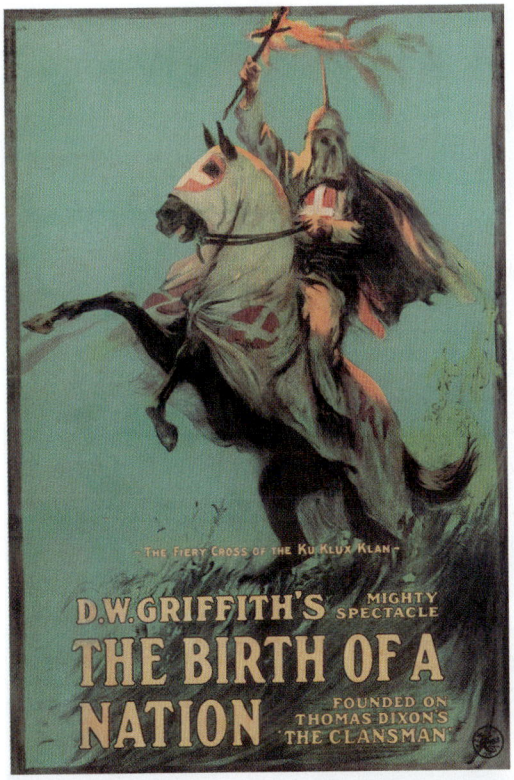

2.9.5 (right) D. W. Griffith, *Birth of a Nation*, 1915, publicity poster

2.9.6 (below) Orson Welles, scene from *Citizen Kane*, 1941, 112 minutes, RKO Pictures

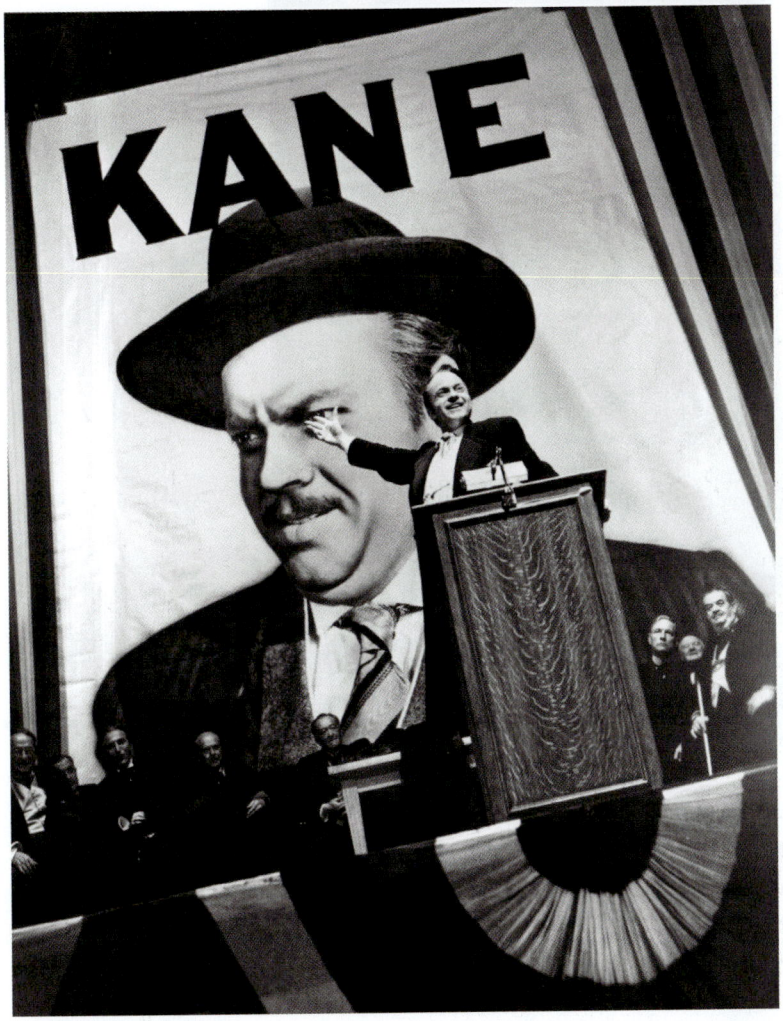

of the Old South; in fact, the Ku Klux Klan used it for recruitment. Despite this unpleasant history, *Birth of a Nation* is important for the epic scale of its production, its stylistic and technical innovations, and its use of the film medium as a **propaganda** tool.

Another American filmmaker, Orson Welles (1915–1985), wrote, directed, and starred in *Citizen Kane* (1941), a film that was a box-office failure but hailed by critics as brilliant (**2.9.6**). It is now widely considered one of the most important films of all time. Welles's film tells the story of Charles Foster Kane, a character modeled on the real-life newspaper tycoon William Randolph Hearst. To tell Kane's story, Welles used what were then highly innovative techniques, including fabricated newspaper headlines and newsreels that give the impression of following a factual story. Other parts of the plot are told using **flashbacks**, which was then a new mode of storytelling; these are now commonplace. *Citizen Kane* also features additional techniques that were revolutionary for the time, such as dramatic lighting, innovative editing, natural sound, elaborate sets, moving camera shots, deep focus, and low camera angles. The movie questions the values of the American Dream and was controversial for its criticism of Hearst, a powerful public figure.

Sound and Color

From the late 1920s, movie studios promoted color as a novelty to attract audiences. One of the first popular films to make use of color combined both the new and old approaches. In *The Wizard of Oz* (1939), Dorothy Gale is transported by a cyclone from Kansas to the Technicolor Land of Oz (**2.9.7**, p. 338). The story's two separate locales are distinguished by the use or absence of color. The film opens with Dorothy in the black-and-white world of her home on a Kansas farm. Later, the brilliant colors of the Land of Oz transport us into a fantasy world clearly far removed from Kansas. Color features prominently throughout the film: Dorothy wears ruby slippers as she travels

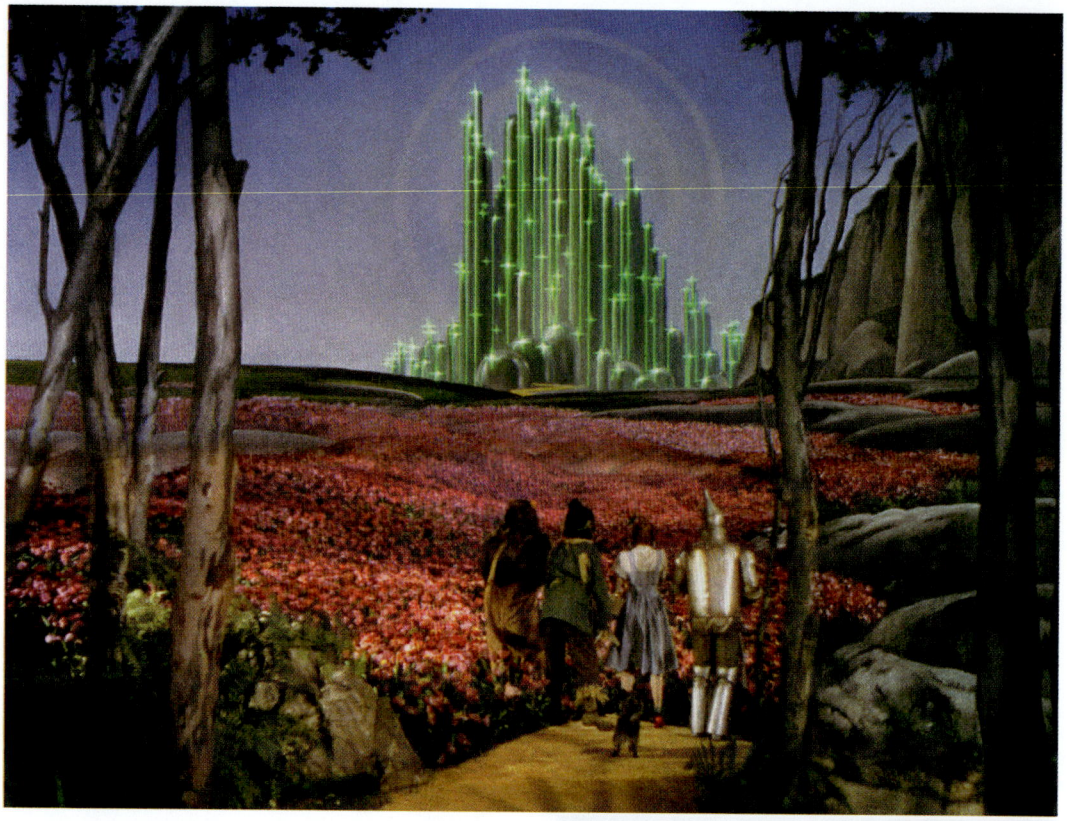

2.9.7 Victor Fleming, scene from *The Wizard of Oz*, 1939, 101 minutes, Metro-Goldwyn-Mayer (MGM)

with her companions—her dog Toto, the Scarecrow, the Tin Man, and the Lion—along the yellow-brick road to the Emerald City to find the wizard.

Before 1927, any sound in a cinema was performed live by musicians in the theater building. After that, integrated sound made it possible to build dialogue, background noise, and music into the film itself. *Singin' in the Rain*, made in 1952, looked back to the silent era by telling the story of a silent-film company making the difficult transition to sound. Synchronizing sound with the actors' lip movements and **dubbing** was one of the great technical challenges of early sound movies, as songs could not be performed on camera by the actors, but had to be recorded separately. *Singin' in the Rain* finds much humor in this situation. In the movie's most famous scene, actor Gene Kelly jubilantly performs the title song in the rainy streets (**2.9.8**). **Musicals** usually tell their story in a combination of dialogue, songs, and dance, with song being their dominant characteristic. Frequently, as in this scene, dialogue stops completely, and song and dance move the story along.

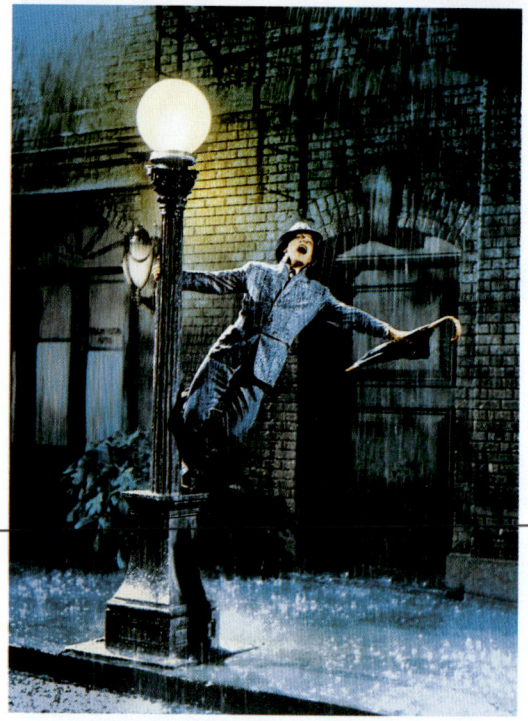

2.9.8 Stanley Donen and Gene Kelly, still from *Singin' in the Rain*, 1952, 103 minutes, produced by Loew's Incorporated, distributed by MGM

In 2011 the French film director Michel Hazanavicius (b. 1967) achieved a huge success with his film, *The Artist*, which harks back to the impact of sound on the silent-film industry (**2.9.9**). In the words of one critic, the film "uses old technology to dazzling effect to illustrate the

Dubbing: post-production addition or mixing of voices (or sounds) that do not belong to the original recording
Musical: genre of film in which the story is told through song, usually combined with dialogue and dancing

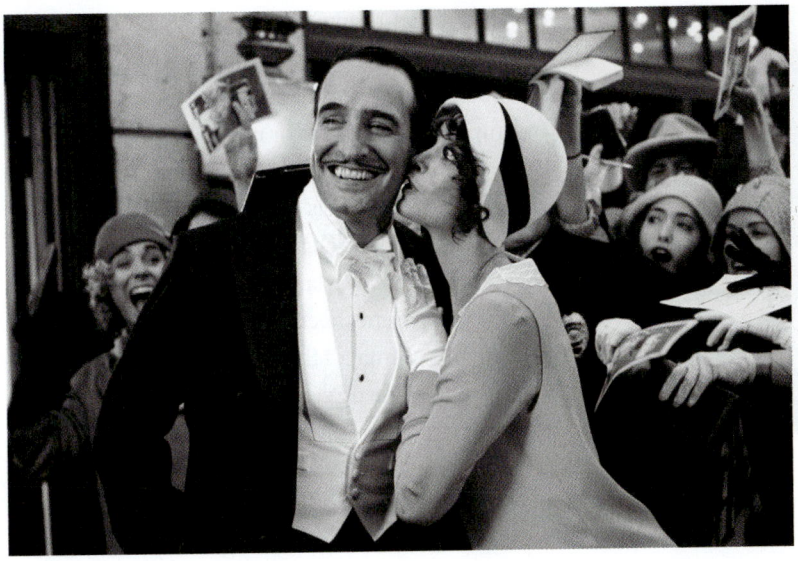

2.9.9 Michel Hazanavicius, still from *The Artist*, 2011, 100 minutes, Studio 37

insistent conquest of a new technology." All of the technical details, including lenses, lighting, and camera moves, were calculated to match the look of original silent films of the 1920s and 1930s as closely as possible. *The Artist* won eighteen major awards, including the Academy Award for Best Picture, for its witty, stylish, and ingenious story, told almost entirely in silence and in black and white. It shows how vividly actors can communicate through gesture, expression, and dance, without relying on a soundtrack. The film's extraordinary success proved that cinema's appeal remains primarily visual, and that, despite all of the technological progress that has been made in the industry in the past century, audiences are still nostalgic for the "good old days" of black-and-white movies.

Animation and Special Effects

Animation creates the illusion of movement in films by taking a still image of an object or drawing, changing it slightly for each new frame, and then presenting all the images in sequence. The many thousands of images in modern animations, such as those from Pixar Studios, are generated and manipulated on computers.

Special effects can be created by using models, props, or makeup during filming, or by the use of digital technology during or post-production.

Some of the earliest film animations were made using puppets or dolls. In **puppet** or **stop-motion animation**, the figures are photographed in a pose, moved very slightly, and then photographed again; the process is repeated until the desired sequence of movements has been acted out. One of the most famous stop-motion animated movies was made by the US animator Tim Burton (b. 1958) in 1993. *The Nightmare Before Christmas* (**2.9.10**), the first

Animation: genre of film made using stop-motion, hand-drawn, or digitally produced still images set into motion by showing them in sequence

Puppet: figure in the form of an animal or person used for entertainment purposes that appears to move on its own but is actually controlled by a person's hand(s), strings, or another mechanism

Stop-motion animation: figures, puppets, or dolls are photographed in a pose, moved very slightly, and then photographed again; the process is repeated until the desired sequence of movements has been acted out

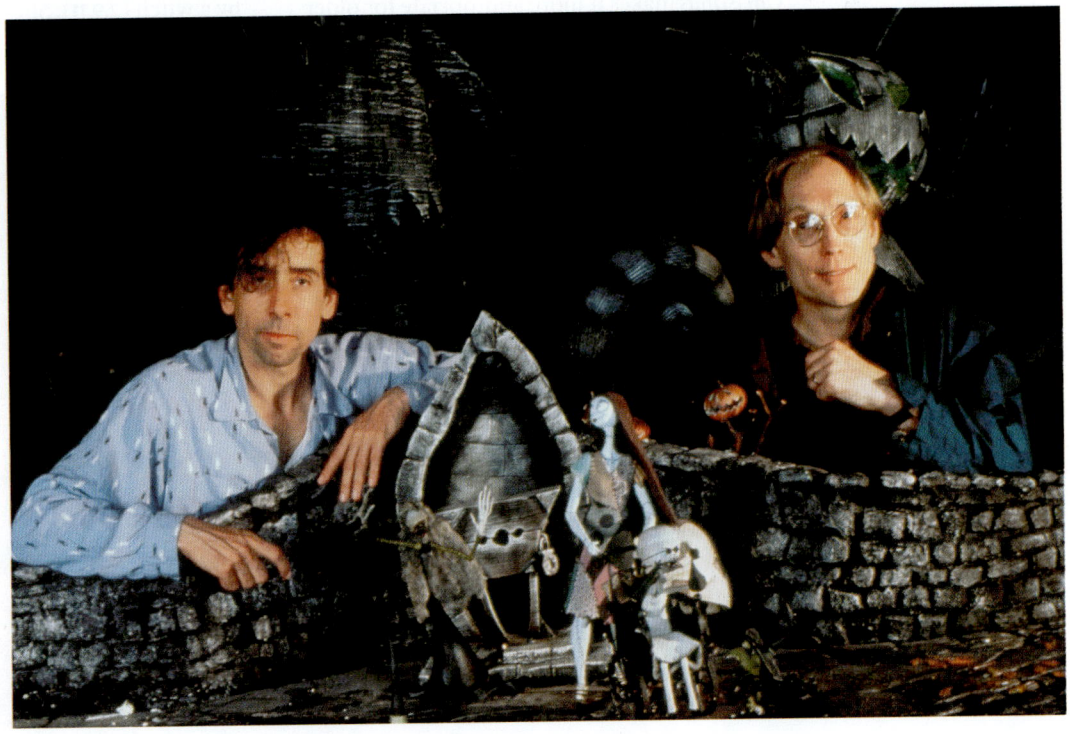

2.9.10 Tim Burton (left) and director Henry Selick, set of *The Nightmare Before Christmas*, 1993

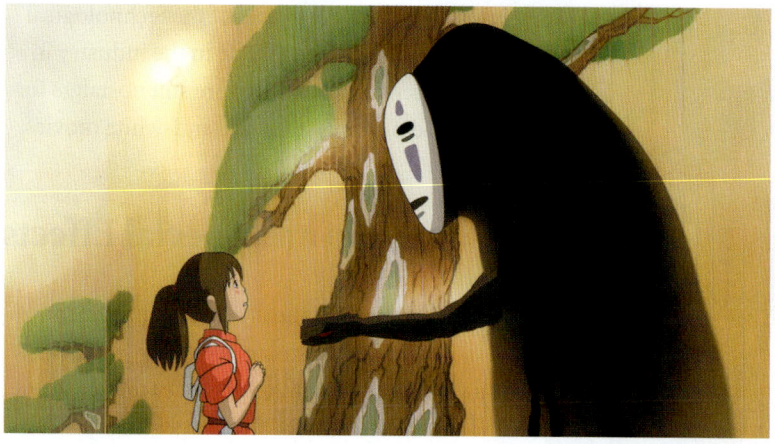

2.9.11 Hayao Miyazaki with Kirk Wise (English version), still from *Spirited Away*, 2001, 125 minutes, Studio Ghibli

stop-motion animated feature to be converted entirely to 3-D (in 2006), was based on a poem Burton wrote ten years prior to its initial release. After accidentally entering the portal to Christmastown, the "Pumpkin King," Jack Skellington, decides that what they do there is far more interesting than his "real" life. He plots to kidnap "Sandy Claws," impersonates him, and tries to lead the ghouls and goblins of Halloweentown to take over the preparations for bringing peace on earth and goodwill to humanity. Somewhat of a misfit himself, Jack and his comrades set out on a series of misadventures that inadvertently almost wreck Christmas. In common with many animated films, the dark nature of *The Nightmare Before Christmas* makes it more appropriate for older kids and adults than for young children.

Background: the part of a work depicted furthest from the viewer's space, often behind the main subject matter

In hand-drawn animation, a separate drawing must be created for each frame. For much of the twentieth century, the most common technique for making animated films was cel animation, which uses a sequence of drawings called cels (originally on celluloid, then acetate). **Backgrounds** and stationary sections were overlaid by the moving parts on transparent sheets, greatly reducing the number of images that had to be generated. Though some directors still use cel animation, for the most part it has been replaced by digital technology. Digital animation more efficiently generates all the individual frames on a computer, but original images may still be made using stop-motion or hand drawings. Digital processes also provide more options for the creation and inclusion of imagery, sound, and narrative components of the sequence or movie, because using digital technology enables these elements to be imported and then manipulated.

The Oscar-winning film *Spirited Away* (2001), written and directed by Hayao Miyazaki (b. 1941), tells the story of a ten-year-old girl named Chihiro who is unhappy about moving to a new town with her family. After she is introduced to a world filled with spirits from Japan's mythology, she discovers that her parents have been transformed into pigs by a witch (**2.9.11**). She must go on a quest to conquer her fears in order to find the strength

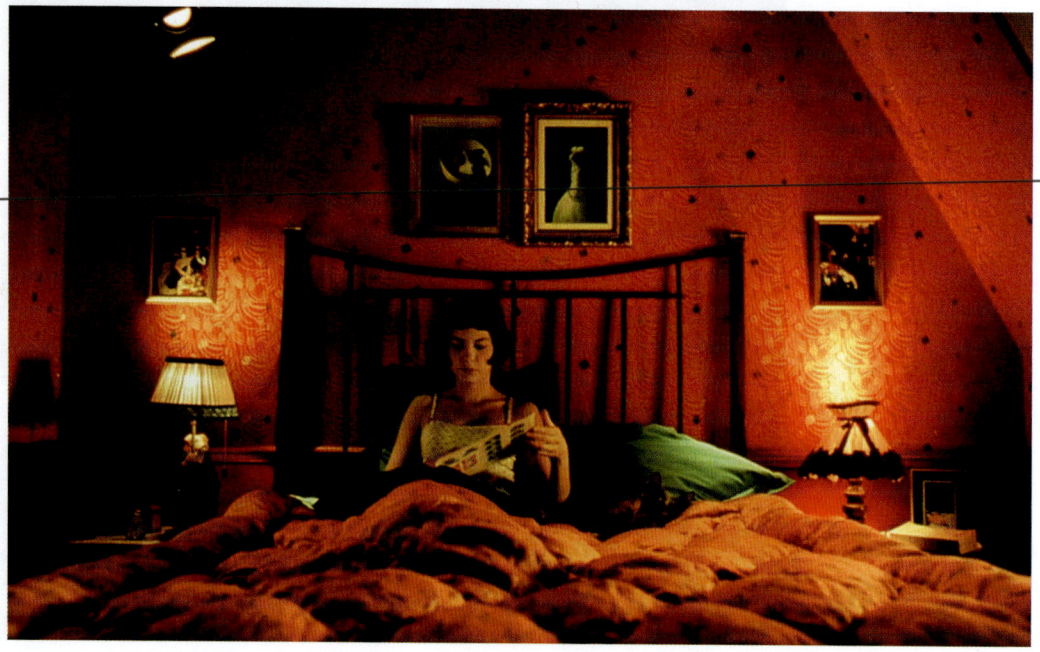

2.9.12 Jean-Pierre Jeunet, still from *Amélie (The Fabulous Destiny of Amélie Poulain)*, 2001, 122 minutes, Claudie Ossard Productions

to bring her family back together. Miyazaki personally created detailed storyboards, or series of drawings, to be used as the basis for the animations, which were then completed by a team of artists, with a separate drawing made for each stage in the movement of any moving object in a scene. At least twelve drawings, and sometimes thirty, were required for every second of *Spirited Away*. Thus a film of this length (125 minutes) requires a minimum of 90,000 drawings, and perhaps as many as 200,000.

The French director Jean-Pierre Jeunet (b. 1953) adds animation and special effects to live-action film in order to tell the story of *Amélie* (2001), a shy twenty-three-year-old waitress (**2.9.12**). Amélie's heart beats out of her chest at one point; in another scene, when her crush Nino walks away, she melts into a puddle on the floor. Inanimate objects, such as the **Impressionist** artist Pierre-Auguste Renoir's painting *Luncheon of the Boating Party* (1881), take on so much significance that they almost function as additional characters. Jeunet creates an environment in which fantasy, reality, and rich color are mixed together to reveal the magical qualities of ordinary life.

Cutting-edge visual effects in the *Lord of the Rings* film trilogy (2001–3, **2.9.13a** and **b**) brought to life the fictional world of J. R. R. Tolkien's (1892–1973) novels by combining live action and **CGI**. Directed by Peter Jackson (b. 1961), these adventure/fantasy films won many Oscars, including Best Picture and Best Visual Effects. One of the most remarkable actors from the series was deemed ineligible for the Best Supporting Actor award, though, because his character was computer generated. Andy Serkis (b. 1964) was responsible for the facial expressions, bodily movements, and distinctive voice of Gollum. Serkis acted out all of the scenes twice: once on set, which allowed him to interact directly with the other actors and greatly assisted the animators; and again on the performance-capture stage. Combining traditional acting, **motion capture** (also known as mo-cap or performance capture), and the skills of animators enabled the transformation of Serkis into a fictional character. The motion-capture process involved putting dots on Serkis's face and body suit to track and record his movements with twenty-five cameras in order to register as much information as possible so the software could replicate the movements digitally. The animators then used **key-frame animation** to edit Gollum into the movie. Because Tolkien wrote that the character was called Gollum for the gurgling sound his voice made, Serkis based the voice on the sounds and motions his cat made coughing up a furball. Serkis's method of intense psychological and emotional character development, and his dedication to realizing the physicality of the character, make Gollum believable and haunting.

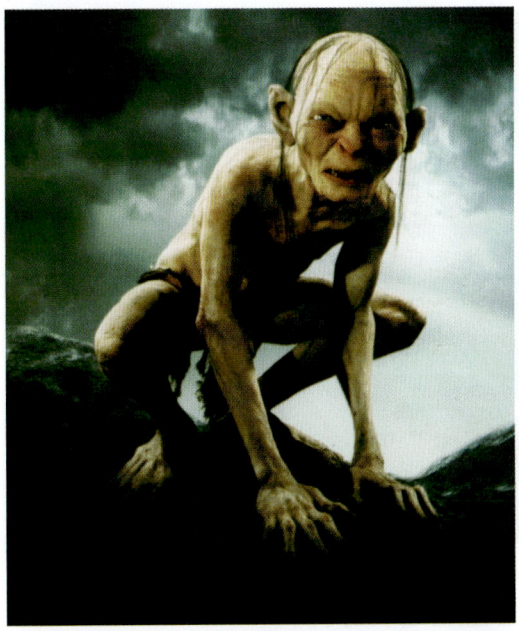

2.9.13a Gollum from Peter Jackson's *The Lord of the Rings: The Return of the King*, 2003. 201 minutes, New Line Cinema

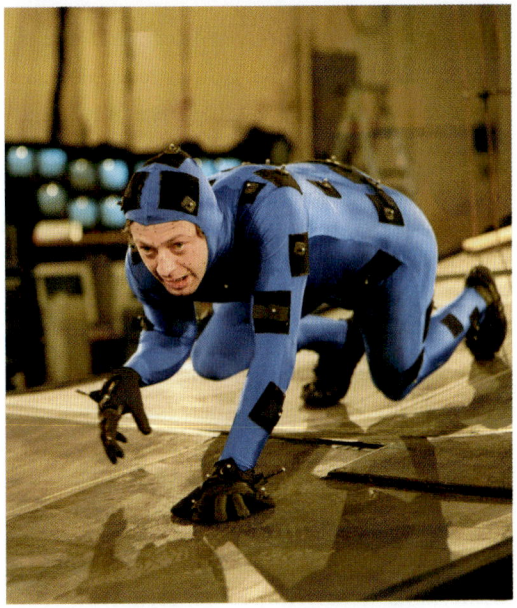

2.9.13b Andy Serkis playing Gollum in *The Lord of the Rings: The Two Towers*, 2002

Impressionist, Impressionism: a late nineteenth-century painting style conveying the impression of the effects of light; Impressionists were artists working in this style
CGI: computer-generated imagery
Motion capture: Also known as mo-cap or performance capture; technology developed to animate CGI characters by translating into a digital performance the live, exact motions of people or objects, using specially designed suits or equipment with sensors
Key-frame animation: technique in which an animator creates important frames in the sequence, and software fills in the gaps

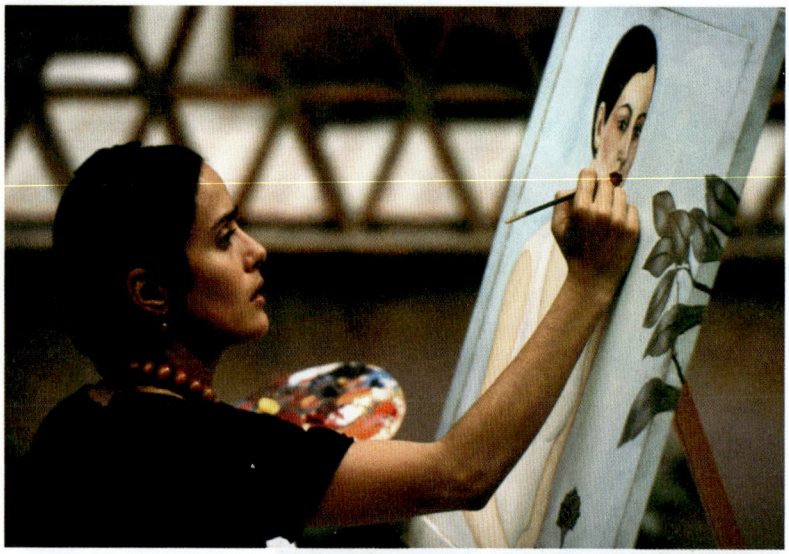

2.9.14 Julie Taymor, still from *Frida*, 2002

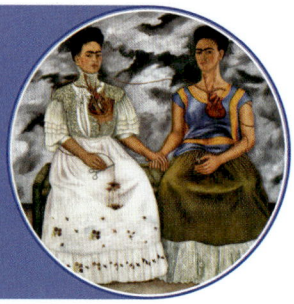

For a further discussion of Frida Kahlo's life and how it influenced her art, see **4.9.18a, p. 676**

Genre: category of artistic subject matter, often with a strongly influential history and tradition
Science-fiction (Sci-fi): genre of film in which fictional stories include advanced science and technology, often in futuristic settings
Biopic: movie that tells the story of a person's life, often filling in facts with narration and plotlines
Historical drama: based on real-life events or time periods; can be factual or fictionalized
Documentary: non-fiction films based on actual people, settings, and events

Film Genres

Over time, certain **genres**, or categories, of film have developed their own conventions, plotlines, and stock characters. As we have seen, musicals interweave singing and (usually) dancing into the narrative flow; animation and **science-fiction** films explore fantasy in a context of space and time beyond the everyday. Some genres reflect cross-cultural influence. For example, the narratives of many Indian films influenced the development of the "coming of age" genre in Western film culture. Also, there is a great deal of crossover between the Japanese films of the 1950s and the American Western. In addition to westerns, the New York Film Academy identified the following film genres: action, animation, crime, fantasy, historical, romance, horror, and science-fiction.

Within the historical genre, **biopics** and **historical dramas** comprise two approaches to movies about individuals and time periods, past or present. A biopic focuses on a person's life, often filling in facts with added narration and plotlines to craft an effective story. Historical drama places more emphasis on portraying real-life events in believable ways, though the stories themselves can be fictionalized or based on facts. Both genres differ from **documentary**, which uses photographs, newsreels, home movies, shots on location, and interviews for the imagery instead of actors and stage sets.

The American director Julie Taymor's biopic *Frida* (2002) focuses on the Mexican painter Frida Kahlo (**2.9.14**). Based on the biography by the art historian Hayden Herrera (b. 1940), the movie effectively brings to life Frida's fearless journey as an artist, activist, and individual while invoking Kahlo's artistic style and subject matter. Taymor selected actors with physical resemblance to the individuals they play, including Salma Hayek (b. 1966) as Frida and Alfred Molina (b. 1953) as the Mexican painter Diego Rivera. The film fleshes out Frida's recovery from a serious accident, her journey as an artist, and the turbulent relationship with her husband, Rivera; it also references her bi-sexuality. Taymor intended *Frida* to transcend the biopic genre and produce an effective story beyond the historical figures who are its focus. In addition to realistic scenes based on photographs and personal accounts, Taymor included dream-like creations based on Frida's experiences. For example, the surgery scene at Calaca Hospital, which takes place after the fateful trolley accident that Kahlo endured when she was eighteen, allowed Taymor to apply her background in puppetry by using shadowy *dia de los muertos* (Day of the Dead) figures to re-enact the procedure.

Hidden Figures (2016) is a historical drama that tells a story it is hard to believe is not already an integral part of established history. The film centers on three women who worked at NASA, Langley as "computers," or mathematicians, in the early 1960s (**2.9.15**). The book of the same name that served as inspiration for the film was written by Margot Lee Shetterly (b. 1969). Shetterly researched for five years and wrote *Hidden Figures* to tell the story of the black scientists and engineers who worked with her father at NASA but were omitted from former stories of the pioneering days of US space exploration. The movie, directed by Theodore Melfi (b. 1971), highlights the impact of Jim Crow segregation on Katherine Goble Johnson, Dorothy Vaughan, and Mary Jackson, as they performed their professional assignments and sought rightful advancement. During the 2017 Oscars ceremony, the ninety-eight-year-old Johnson was recognized for her long-overlooked contributions to the progress of aeronautical and scientific discovery.

2.9.15 Theodore Melfi, still from *Hidden Figures*, 2016. 127 minutes, Fox 2000 Pictures

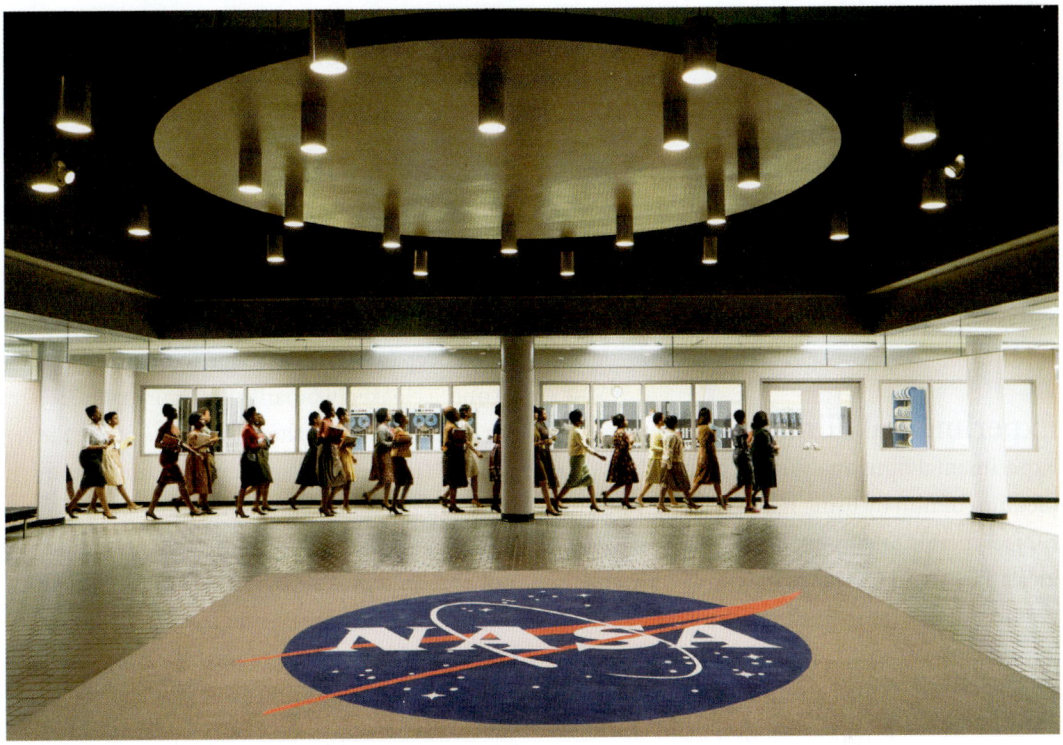

Auteur theory/auteur films: from the French word for "author," refers to films that notably reflect the director's creative vision above other criteria

Film as Art

The category "indie," or independent film, generally refers to feature movies made outside the major production studios and distributed by independent film agencies. Regardless of budget or connections to preexisting genres, independent films tend to champion creative and non-mainstream approaches and content.

2.9.16 Wong Kar-wai, *Chungking Express*, 1994. 102 minutes, Jet Tone Production

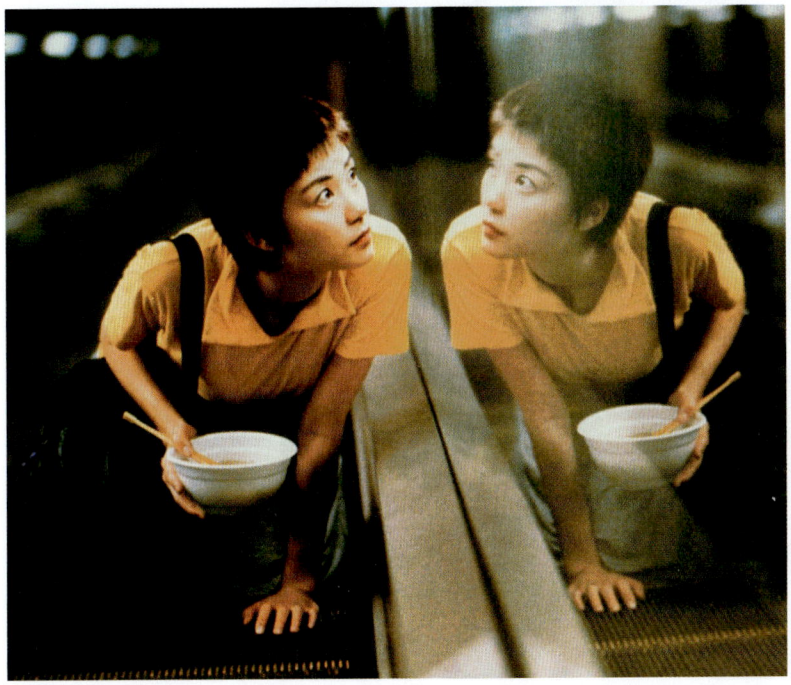

Auteur Films

Auteur theory, from the French word for "author," considers films to be works of art due to the fact that they are the realization of a director's creative vision. This theory, focusing on the director or screenwriter, has been controversial because the nature of movies is collaborative, and auteur theory does not acknowledge the creative contribution of actors, cinematographers, set and costume designers, and the many other people who help to make a film. Proponents of the theory, though, cite the films of François Truffaut, Jean-Luc Godard, Akira Kurosawa, Alfred Hitchcock, Jean Renoir, Woody Allen, Jane Campion, Julie Taymor, and Wes Anderson as especially guided by the artistic vision of their directors.

The distinctive vision of the Chinese director Wong Kar-wai (b. 1958) permeates *Chungking Express* (**2.9.16**). In the crowded urban metropolis of Hong Kong, we follow the stories (one after the other) of two police officers. Two tales overlap, like the strangers who brush past each other in a Hong Kong crowd depicted at the beginning of the film. In both cases the officers are transitioning from one romance to another, but the future of each new romance remains uncertain. The suspenseful story of drug dealing in the first tale in some ways contrasts with the odd comedy of the second; in other ways, however, the two stories resonate poetically, each evoking the other in its depiction of lost love and longing. Wong's work is characterized by complicated narratives in addition to a stylized, color-rich, impressionistic cinematography (by Christopher Doyle) that highlights the fast pace and isolation of contemporary life.

Experimental Films

Experimental films analyse and extend the medium of film by using new technology or subject matter, and by exploring new **aesthetic** ideas. They tend to be visually compelling and poetic, notable for their unusual content and idiosyncrasy. They are often the production of a single person or small group, and experimental filmmakers use inexpensive equipment and low-budget formats to create the desired effects. Such films frequently do not have integrated sound, or typically use it in unnatural ways. Experimental filmmakers tend to adopt innovative approaches, including dream sequences and fantastic imagery created by manipulating the filmstrip. Their films are also often autobiographical.

The American dancer, choreographer, and filmmaker Maya Deren (1917–1961) wrote *Meshes of the Afternoon* (1943) and co-directed it with her husband, cinematographer Alexander Hammid (1907–2004). The short (14-minute) film follows a woman's experience of an afternoon, shuffled together with her dreams after she has drifted off to sleep (**2.9.17**). Two sequences are repeated: in one, a cloaked woman with a mirror over her face walks down the road; in the other, the woman (played by Deren) enters a house and walks up the stairs. These sequences seem to be replaying themselves in the woman's mind rather than representing actual events. Several objects are shown again and again: a flower, a key, a telephone, a knife, a record player, billowy curtains, rumpled sheets. Elements change each time the sequences occur. For instance, one moment the flower is placed on the pillow, the next the knife appears in the same position. Toward the end of the film a man replaces the female figures, in one sequence entering the house and in the next walking on the road.

Aesthetic: related to beauty, art, and taste

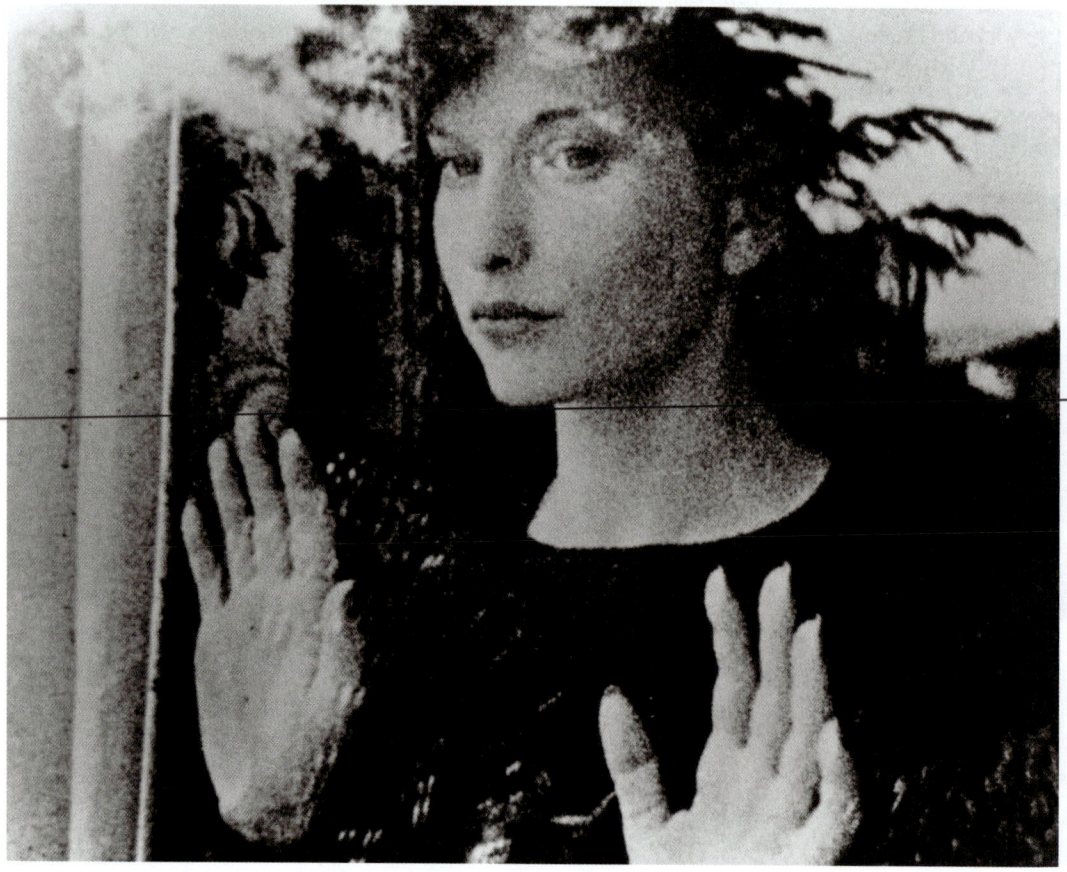

2.9.17 Maya Deren, still from *Meshes of the Afternoon*, 1943, 14 minutes, 16mm black-and-white silent film

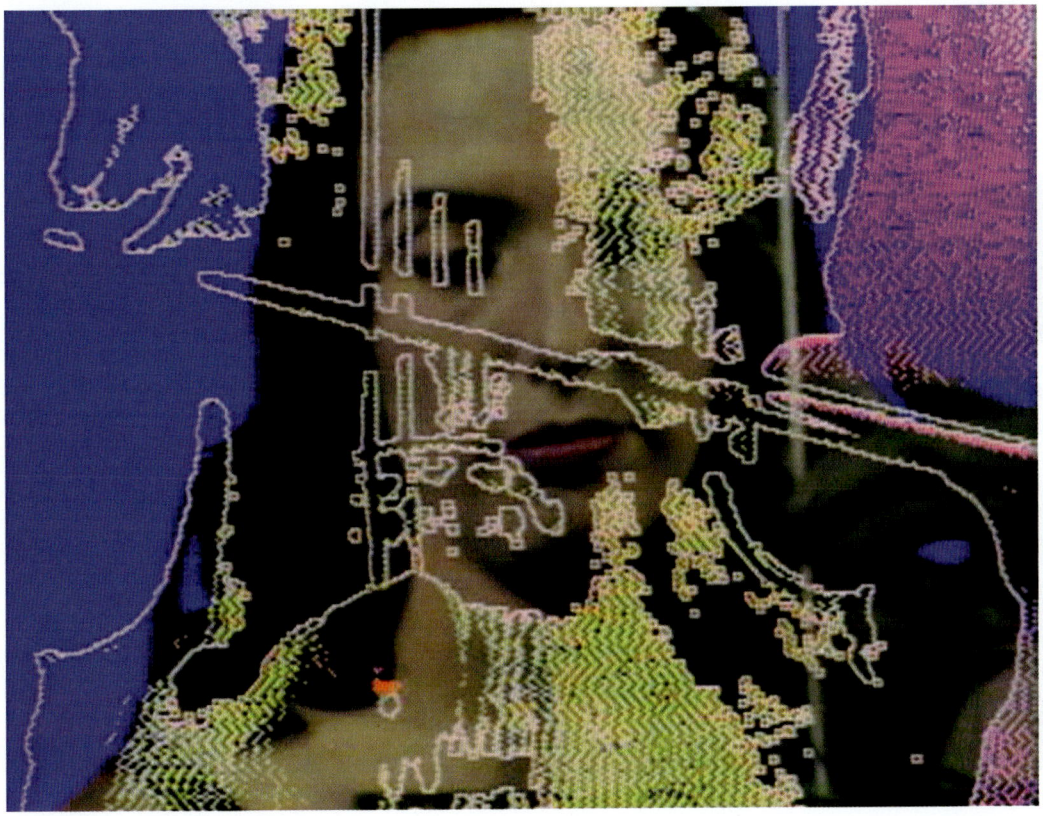

2.9.18 Nam June Paik and John J. Godfrey, still from *Global Groove*, 1973, single-channel videotape, color with sound. Courtesy Electronic Arts Intermix (EAI), New York

Time is circular in this film, and the overall effect mimics a dream in which events that make sense to the dreamer seem illogical to others. Each object seems to have an unnamed symbolic significance, and it is impossible to separate actual occurrences from memories or fiction. Ultimately, the film reflects a state of mind, and can be best understood as visual poetry. This ability to express psychological states is one of film's particular strengths as an artistic medium.

Video

Typically, video artworks are made to be presented in art galleries or at art events. They may be shown on television monitors or projected onto walls. Sometimes artists incorporate video displays (along with other media) in a darkened area in ways that transform the space and create a total environment of sight and sound. Because high-quality video equipment is relatively inexpensive, artistic experimentation with video is widespread.

The Korean American artist Nam June Paik (1932–2006) was a pioneer of video art. In 1969 Paik worked with Shuya Abe, an engineer from Tokyo, to modulate video signals with a device called the Paik-Abe Synthesizer. The results combined both recognizable and distorted pictures that were recorded and could be replayed later. Paik's *Global Groove* (1973), a 30-minute video recording, comments on the increasing role of media and technology in daily life.

Global Groove replicates the variety of things that were available on television at the time the video was made, from Pepsi commercials and news footage to game shows and President Richard Nixon's face. All these scenes are interspersed, like glimpses of changing channels. Most of the clips integrate music and visuals, consisting of either performers or dancers. For example, the performance artist and musician Charlotte Moorman (1933–1991) is shown playing several experimental cellos designed by Paik. The close-up of her face (**2.9.18**) is surrounded by visual noise, static translated into changing designs that correspond to the rhythms of the music she is playing. *Global Groove* draws on contemporary culture, and foreshadows music video by integrating visual and musical inputs.

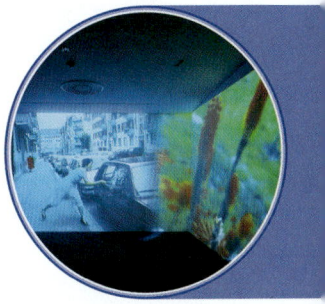

Some videos are projected to create visual connections as well as sensory experiences. The elements of *Ever Is Over All* juxtapose still life and narrative scenes with ambient music: see **3.10.15, p. 556**

Perspectives on Art: Bill Viola
How Did Video Become Art?

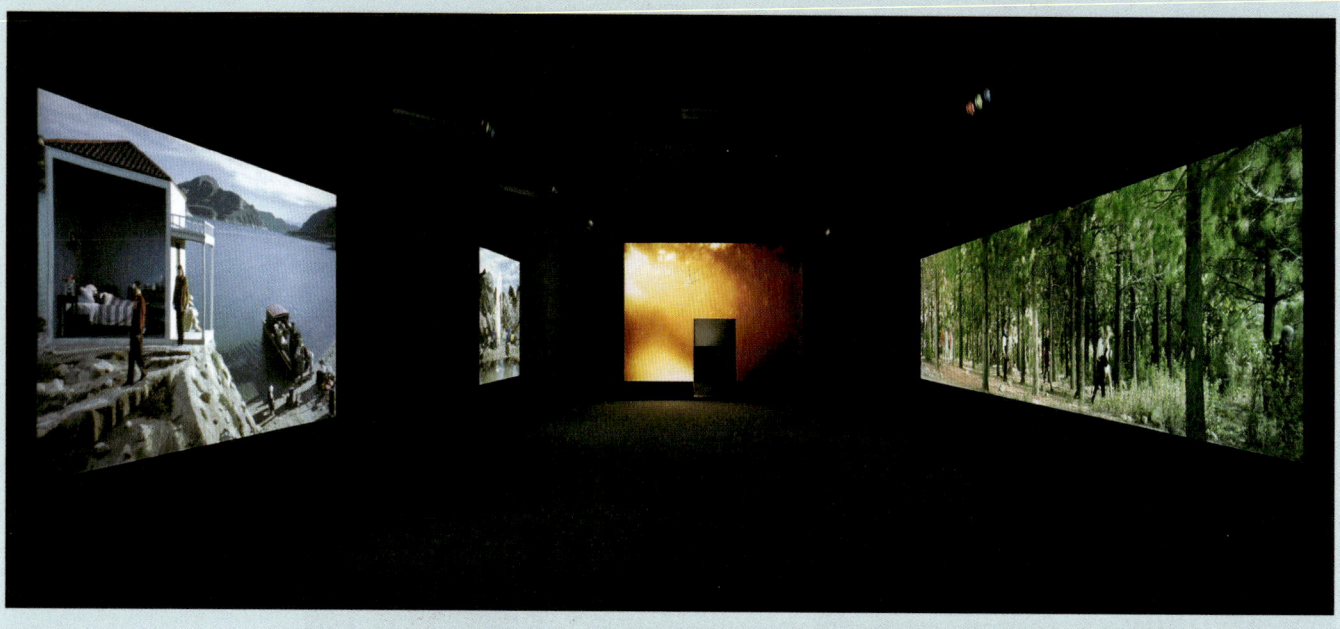

2.9.19a Bill Viola, *Going Forth by Day*, 2002. Installation view, video/sound installation, five-part projected image cycle

Bill Viola, one of the world's leading video artists, has been working in video since the 1970s. In 2005 he gave the following explanation for why many contemporary artists prefer video as an art form.

I first touched a video camera in 1970 as a first-year art student. In those politically charged times, making art took on a renewed urgency, and the new electronic communication technologies played a central role in reimagining not only what a work of art could be but also how it could reach beyond the art world to engage life and society directly and transform the world. By the early 1970s, political and social activists, documentary filmmakers, and artists of all disciplines were using video and showing their work together in art museums, film festivals, community centers, universities, and on television.

Video as art exists somewhere between the permanence of painting and the temporary existence of music. Technically, the video system of camera and recorder mimics the human eye and memory. The so-called video "image" is actually a shimmering energy pattern of moving

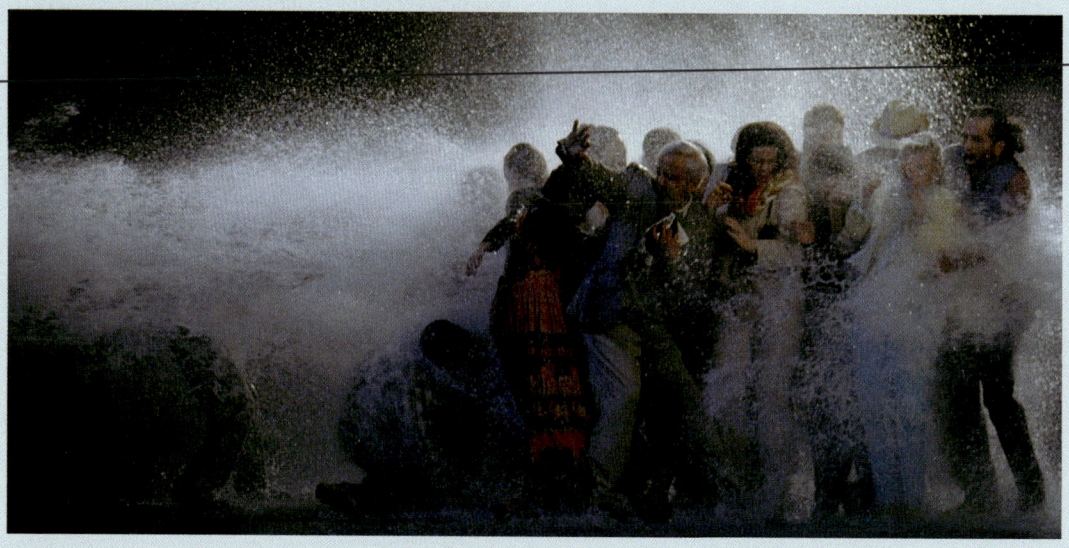

2.9.19b Bill Viola, *The Raft*, May 2004. Video/sound installation, color, high-definition video projection on wall in darkened space, screen size 13' × 7' 3⅜"

electrons vibrating in time. To exist, the fabric of the image needs to be in a constant state of motion. The electronic image is not fixed to any material base, and as digital data it is infinitely reproducible. It can be copied, stored, and transferred onto new formats in a continuous chain of eternal life. As an electronic signal it can travel at the speed of light around the Earth and beyond, and it can appear in multiple places at the same time. As an international technical standard, the image exists in the same form as the dominant mass media, allowing artists the potential to address the global culture. Since the production and distribution of images is now accomplished by the same technological system, today's artists have the freedom to work within existing institutions or become their own producers and distributors.

Technology is the imprint of the human mind onto the material substance of the natural world. Like the Renaissance, today's technological revolution is fueled by a combination of art, science, and technology, and the universal human need to share our individual ideas and experiences in ever-new ways. The medium of video, where images are born and die every instant, has brought a new humanism to contemporary art. The digital image has become the common language of our time, and through it living artists are once again emerging from the margins of the culture to speak directly to the people in the language of their experience.

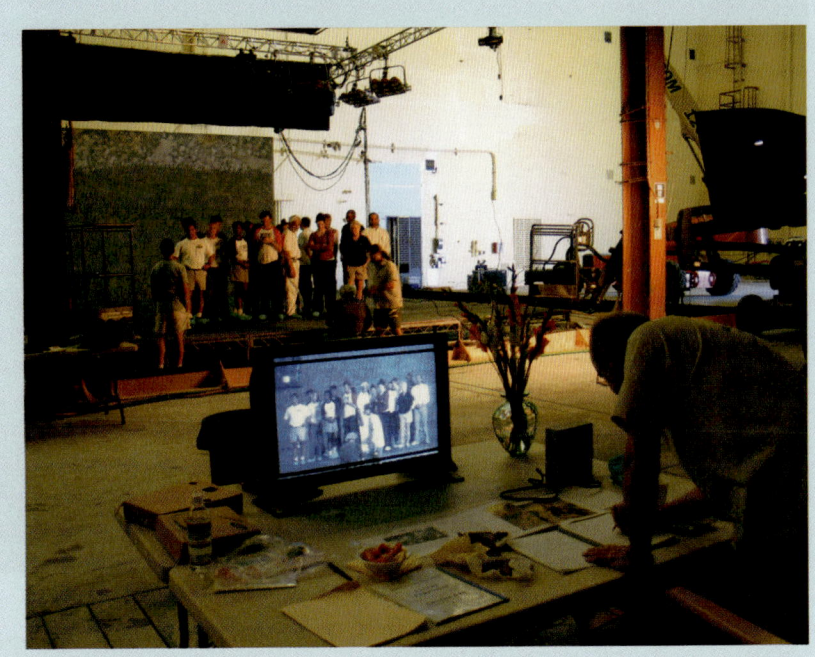

2.9.19c Bill Viola (on the right) in production for *The Raft*, Downey Studios, Downey, California, 2004

Interactive Technology and Television

Artists and designers create artworks, installations, websites, video games, and television shows that provide new possibilities for sharing and accessing creative expressions. Developments in digital technology have allowed artists to involve viewers as active participants in the artwork by, for example, determining the appearance of the work or choosing different paths to follow. **GIFs**, developed in 1987 by the software engineer Steve Wilhite, are used extensively for animated and static images. These image files, compressed to reduce transfer times, are good for simple graphics or logos with solid areas of color. Activated by clicking or opening, GIFs are popular because they enhance communication with quick, isolated, and repeated gestures or motions.

The video-game industry has grown so much that it rivals the film industry in revenue. Many games feature imagery inspired by elements and principles of visual art and even specific artistic traditions. *Limbo* (**2.9.20**, p. 348) by Playdead was released for Xbox Live Arcade

GIF (graphics interchange format): compressed image file type to reduce transfer time

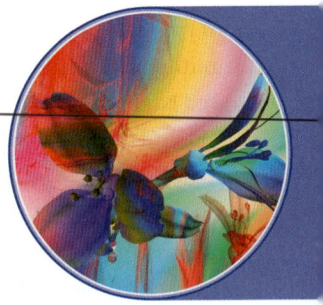

In addition to interactivity, the technology used in computer images allows an unprecedented range of colors and visual effects: see **1.4.3, p. 96**

2.9.20 Playdead, still from *Limbo*, 2010

2-D side scrolling game: gameplay is seen from a side-view camera angle with onscreen characters generally moving left to right and backgrounds made up of scrolling graphics

Atmospheric perspective: use of shades of color and clarity to create the illusion of depth. Closer objects have warmer tones and clear outlines, while objects set further away are cooler and become hazy

Fantasy: fiction genre set in an imaginary universe; often uses magical or supernatural elements in the plots, themes, or settings

Epic: style or genre in film/television that focuses on grand-scale storytelling with dramatic music, elaborate costumes, and high production values; may use historical events or people but does not focus on historical accuracy

in 2010 and expanded to various platforms in 2015. It is a puzzle platform, **2-D side scrolling game** in which a nameless boy uses a few simple motions to face challenges, obstacles, and dangerous environments on a quest to find his sister. The game has received numerous awards for its innovation and striking artistic visuals, which include grayscale, silhouettes and **atmospheric perspective**.

Once seen as an inferior medium to film and cinema, television has created its own set of entertainment criteria. In 2013 Netflix began releasing complete seasons simultaneously, allowing viewers to access shows through the Internet and decide whether to watch all at once or over time. This format has given viewers much more control over the viewing experience and created the phenomenon of binge watching, which approximates the rhythms and time commitment of reading books. This format also allowed Netflix to compete better with industry giants HBO (Home Box Office) and Showtime, which delay releasing digital content long after the filming (HBO a full year later). Since the release of its first season in 2011, *Game of Thrones* (**2.9.21**) has consistently been critically acclaimed and is HBO's most-watched series ever. Initially based on the *A Song of Ice and Fire* novels by George R. R. Martin (b. 1948), the story lines for the last two seasons (seasons 7 and 8) are taken from unpublished, new material.

The medieval **fantasy epic** is largely character driven, with expansive and concurrent plotlines. *Game of Thrones*, noted for graphic violence, sex, and ruthless elimination of even the most central characters, proves compelling in part because it renders good and evil as a mesh of complex, conflicting forces, rather than a simple binary.

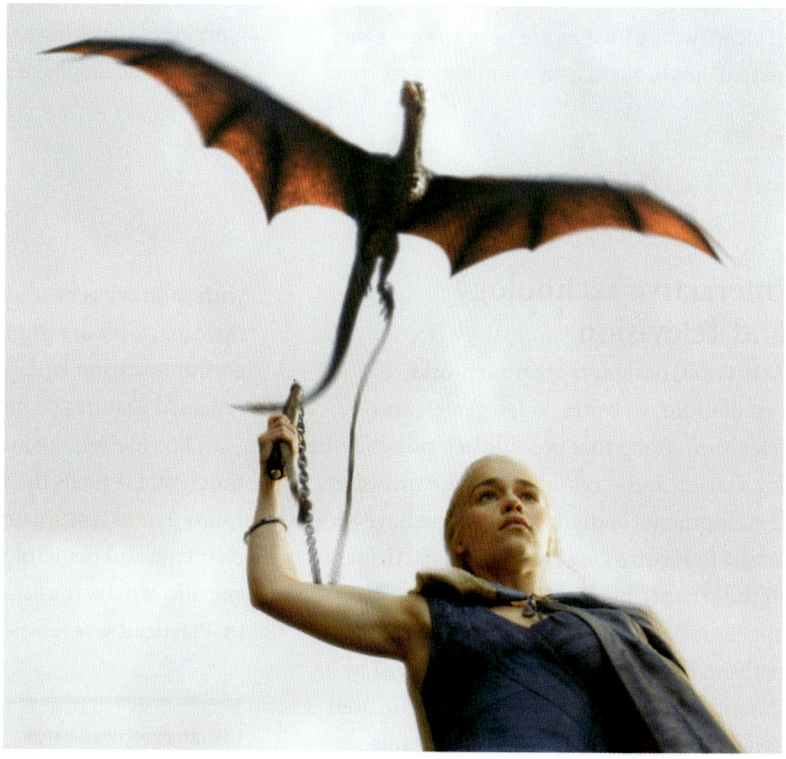

2.9.21 David Benioff and D.B. Weiss, still from *Game of Thrones*, 2011–present, HBO original television series

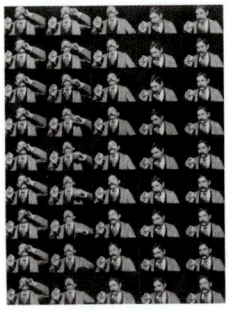

1.5.16 Thomas Edison and W. K. Dickson, *Fred Ott's Sneeze*, 1894, p. 122

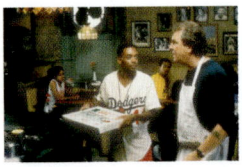

4.10.11 Spike Lee, *Do the Right Thing*, 1989, p. 687

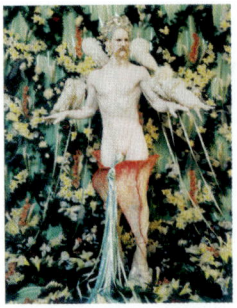

3.10.16 Matthew Barney, *Cremaster 5*, 1997, p. 556

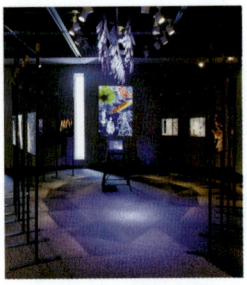

3.10.10 Jolene Rickard, *Corn Blue Room*, 1998, p. 552

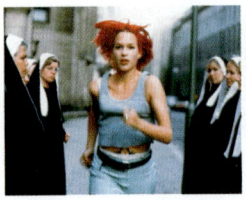

1.5.8 Tom Tykwer, *Run Lola Run* (scene), 1998, p. 117

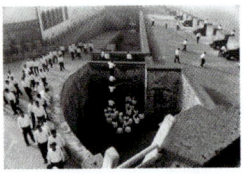

3.10.12a Shirin Neshat, *Rapture*, 1999, p. 553

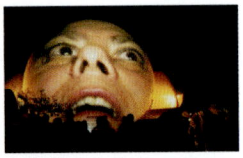

4.1.14 Krzysztof Wodiczko, *Tijuana Projection*, 2001, p. 576

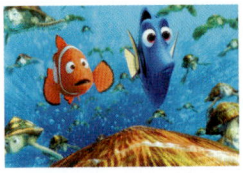

1.5.7 Walt Disney Pictures, frame from *Finding Nemo*, 2003, p. 117

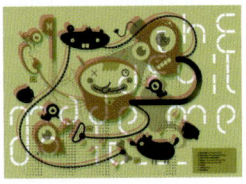

1.1.7 Sauerkids, *The Devil Made Me Do It*, 2006, p. 48

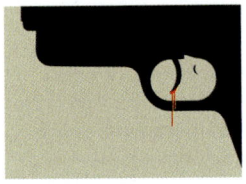

1.1.27 Noma Bar, *Gun Crime*, 2009, p. 59

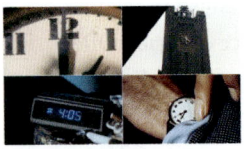

4.3.7 Christian Marclay, stills from *The Clock*, 2010, p. 596

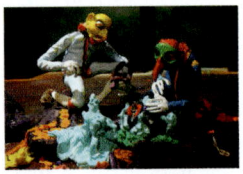

3.10.17 Nathalie Djurberg, *I Wasn't Made to Play the Son* (video still), 2011, p. 557

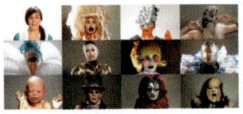

4.3.10 Jillian Mayer, *I Am Your Grandma* (selected video stills), 2011, p. 598

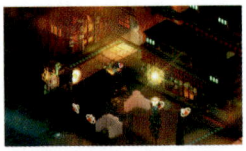

1.3.16 Supergiant Games, screenshot from *Transistor*, 2014, p. 85

2.10 Alternative Media and Processes

Medium (plural **media**): the material on or from which an artist chooses to make a work of art, for example canvas and oil paint, marble, engraving, video, or architecture
Conceptual art: artwork in which the ideas are most important to the work
Performance art: a work involving the human body, usually including the artist, in front of an audience
Installation: originally referring to the hanging of pictures and arrangement of objects in an exhibition, installation may also refer to an intentional environment created as a completed artwork
Action painting: application of paint to canvas by dripping, splashing, or smearing that emphasizes the artist's gestures
Dada: anarchic anti-art and anti-war movement, dating back to World War I, that reveled in absurdity and irrationality
Kinetic art/sculpture: three-dimensional art that moves, impelled by air currents, motors, or people
Readymade: an everyday object presented as a work of art
Assemblage: artwork made of three-dimensional materials, including found objects

Artworks made using alternative **media** and processes break down the traditional boundaries between art and life. They tend to draw our attention to actions or ideas rather than to only a physical product. The creative process produces events, ideas, and experiences as artworks in and of themselves. Many artworks that are interactive or involve the viewer in unusual and significant ways fall into this category. In addition, many alternative processes incorporate more than one medium (often several) and make categorization of artworks much more complicated.

In **conceptual art**, the idea behind an artwork is more important than any visible subject or material product. Artists generally plan the piece and make all of the major decisions beforehand; the execution of the piece itself is secondary. Conceptual art often produces no permanent artwork and very little that can be promoted and sold: sometimes a set of instructions, a documentary photograph, or nothing at all remains as evidence that the piece existed.

For example, if an artist printed a set of instructions for the viewer, the actual, tangible result of the piece would be the actions that person performed. Yoko Ono's *Wish Tree* artworks (**2.10.3**, see p. 352) existed only in a potential state when the artist first made them. Each piece requires the viewer's participation to be realized. In Vito Acconci's *Following Piece* (**2.10.6**, see p. 354), there was no audience at the time, but the artist took pictures of each "following" he made.

Performance art has some similarities to theater because it is (usually) performed in front of a live audience; it includes varying amounts of music, dance, poetry, video, and multimedia technology. Unlike traditional theater, however, there is rarely a conventional story and the performance takes place in consciously artistic venues. The actions of the artist, or individuals chosen by the artist, become the focus. These actions, which occur in a gallery, on a stage, or in a public place, may last from a few minutes to a few days and may not be repeated.

When artists design an entire exhibition space as an artwork, usually in a gallery or museum, it is called an **installation**. Installations might consist of props and sets to transform the space into a room in a house or a place of business; they might incorporate electronic displays or video projections; or they might involve artworks arranged in relation to one another in a sequence or series. Often installations are designed to fit the dimensions or environment of a particular location: these installations are called "site-specific." The artist plans the space, considers how people will move through it, and arranges the elements to create a certain effect. Whether they are designed for an interior or exterior space, installations immerse viewers in the artwork.

Context of Alternative Media

During the twentieth century, a way of making art emerged that focused on modes of creation, such as actions, texts, and environments. These approaches differed from the traditional Western

practices of "fine art," narrowly defined as paintings on canvas and sculptures on pedestals. The American artist Jackson Pollock's (1912–1956) **action paintings** of the 1950s brought the canvas off the easel and onto the floor to become a surface around which the artist moved as he splashed, dripped, and flung his paint. His unusual and exciting painting techniques galvanized public interest in "difficult" modern art. Pollock rocketed to popular fame following an article published on August 8, 1949 in *Life Magazine* that asked, "Is he the greatest living painter in the United States?" Not long after Pollock's early death in a car crash, though, there was a sense that artists had exhausted all they could say with paint on canvas. Artists began to turn to performance, conceptualism, and installations to explore radical new ideas about art.

Because this chapter focuses on the ideas expressed in the making of artworks rather than the finished objects themselves, we shall also look at the documentation about them—instructions used to plan an activity, notes taken by the artist related to a piece, or photographs or video made during a performance. The works themselves tend to last for a relatively short period of time.

Conceptual Art

Conceptual art is a form of art that emphasizes ideas and radically downplays the importance of the work of art as craft object. It has flourished from the 1960s onward. In some ways conceptual art is similar to **Dada** absurdist events in Zürich in 1916, where artists performed nonsense poetry as a release from and savage commentary on the events of World War I. The Dadaist Marcel Duchamp (1887–1968) also made artworks that challenged traditional notions of art. One of his works, *Fountain*, was rejected for an art exhibition in New York in 1917 because it was simply a factory-made white porcelain urinal, signed "R. Mutt." While the group hosting the exhibition was outraged, it missed Duchamp's entire point: the meaning of the artwork transcends its medium. An artist can communicate worthwhile ideas using any sort of material because the message is what matters. As the first artist truly to promote this kind of art, Duchamp was very influential for many artists later in the twentieth century. His approach opened up possibilities of making art from everyday things and materials, imagery from popular culture, or even simply *ideas*.

Duchamp was also one of the first artists to experiment with **kinetic art**, or art with moving pieces, although his works of this kind are less well known than his **readymades**. Similarly, the Swiss artist Jean Tinguely (1925–1991) was interested in exploring impermanence, accident, and uncertainty as legitimate forces within the creation and experience of a work of art. His 1960 *Homage to New York* (**2.10.1**), a mechanized **assemblage** of discarded junk, was designed to mimic the automatic processes and spontaneous painting techniques that had become popular amongst artists (methods such as those used by Jackson Pollock, see p. 538). Once set in motion, in the sculpture garden of the Museum of Modern Art, the piece behaved unpredictably in its one-off "performance." In addition to the crashing, whirring, and smoke that the artist intended it to produce, flames shot out from a piano, where a can of gasoline had been set to overturn on a burning candle; a small carriage also hurtled out, making a shrieking noise and

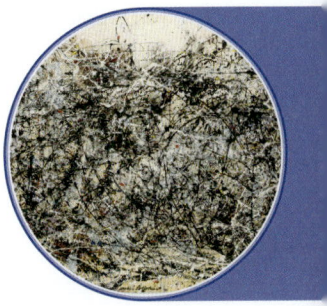

The painting method used by Jackson Pollock brought attention to the physical movement of the artist in the creation of art, in addition to the artwork itself: see **3.9.26, p. 539**

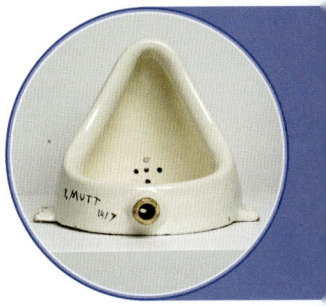

Marcel Duchamp pioneered the readymade: a regular object (e.g. an urinal) that becomes an artwork (here, *Fountain*) by the decision of the artist: see **3.10.1, p. 547**

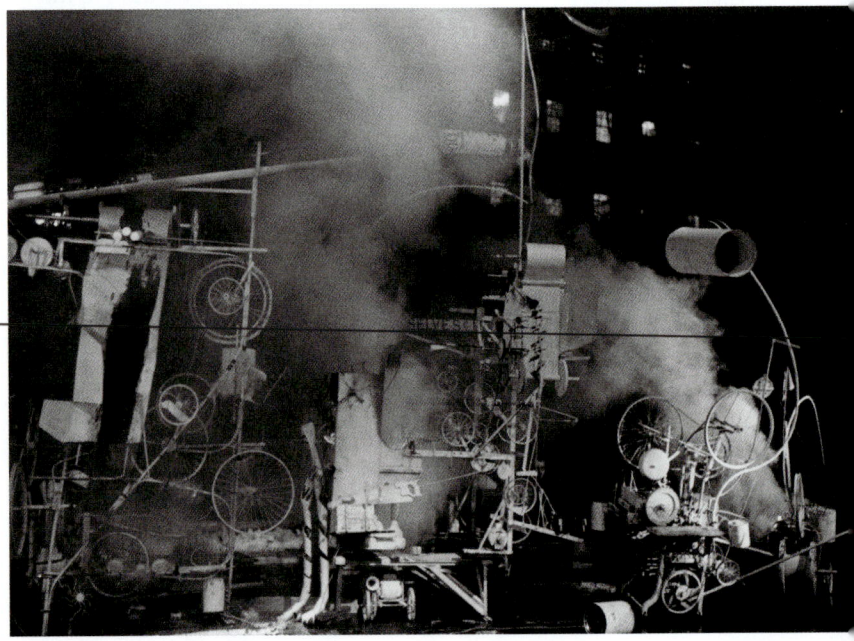

2.10.1 Jean Tinguely, *Homage to New York*, MoMA, New York, March 17, 1960. Photo David Gahr

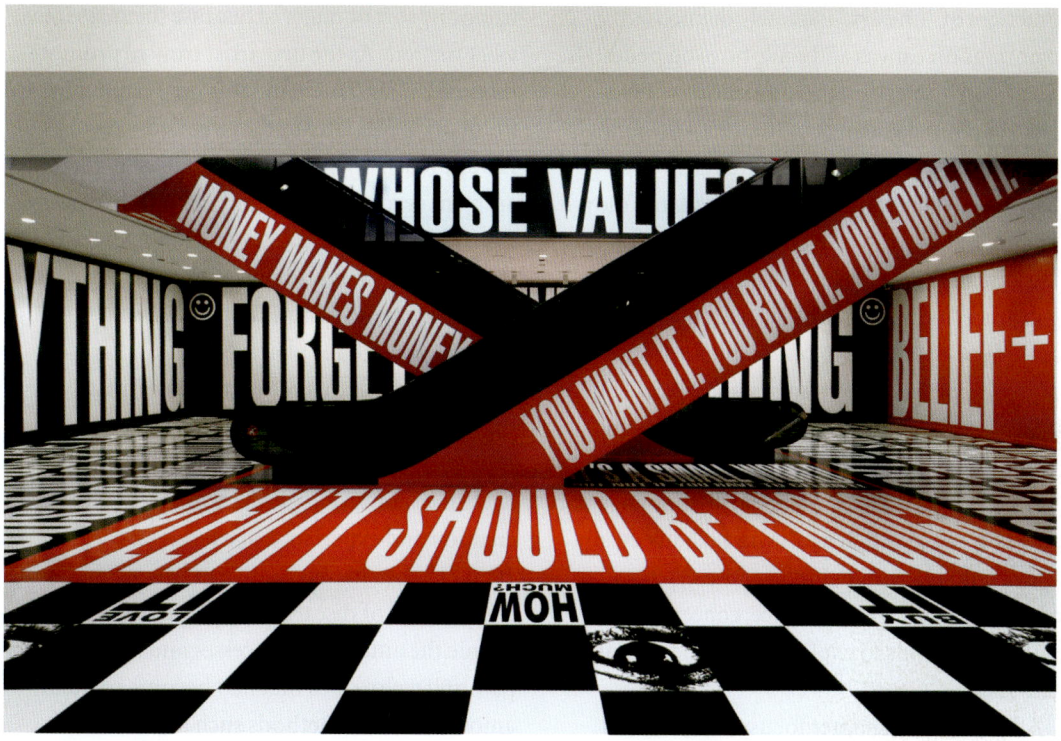

2.10.2 Barbara Kruger, *Belief + Doubt (=Sanity)*, 2012–present, installation view, Hirshhorn Museum

heading straight for the audience (a journalist sent it back in another direction); and eventually a fire fighter put out the flames. This piece revived many of Dada's (and Duchamp's) rebellious and humorous antics, in the form of a huge self-destructing sculpture.

Many examples of conceptual art consist of words on a page or background. These words cut to the chase, directing our attention to the core concept and allowing us to make the words meaningful for ourselves. Since the 1980s the American artist Barbara Kruger (b. 1945) has used her experience as a graphic designer to combine **found images** and words to give them new meanings. Her pieces address the powerful institutions of society and stereotypes that are often seen in visual culture. *Belief + Doubt (=Sanity)* (2012–present), consists of giant wall wraps (up to 12 ft. tall) with the artist's trademark text and image combinations in bold black and white with red accents (**2.10.2**). As the text is written in the first person, it addresses viewers directly and engages them to think about their place in the world, consumerism, and feminist interventions. In an interview in 2012 Kruger said about this piece: "I try to make work about how we are to one another, in this broader sense of what our social relations are."

Found image or **object:** an image or object found by an artist and presented, with little or no alteration, as part of a work or as a finished work of art

Yoko Ono (b. 1933), a Japanese-born American artist and musician, began making conceptual artworks in the early 1960s. Her first pieces were poetic instructions to be performed or just imagined. Sometimes they were typescripts framed and put on the wall. Other times, Ono painted right on the museum or gallery wall (highlighting the transient nature of some of these pieces: when the exhibition ended, those instructions would disappear).

She then started to ask viewers to complete her pieces by, for example, burning or walking on the paintings. Eventually she made "Instruction Paintings," consisting of typed instructions, rather than finished works of art. The instructions are open-ended and serve as a beginning point rather than a final product. They rely heavily on the interaction and participation of the viewer. The instructions for *Wish Tree for Washington D.C.* (2007) state: "Make a wish, Write it down on a piece of paper, Fold it and tie it around the branch of a Wish Tree, Ask your friends to do the same, Keep wishing Until the branches are covered with your wishes." Inspired by the Japanese practice of tying prayers to a tree, Ono has made *Wish Trees* like the one in **2.10.3** all over the world.

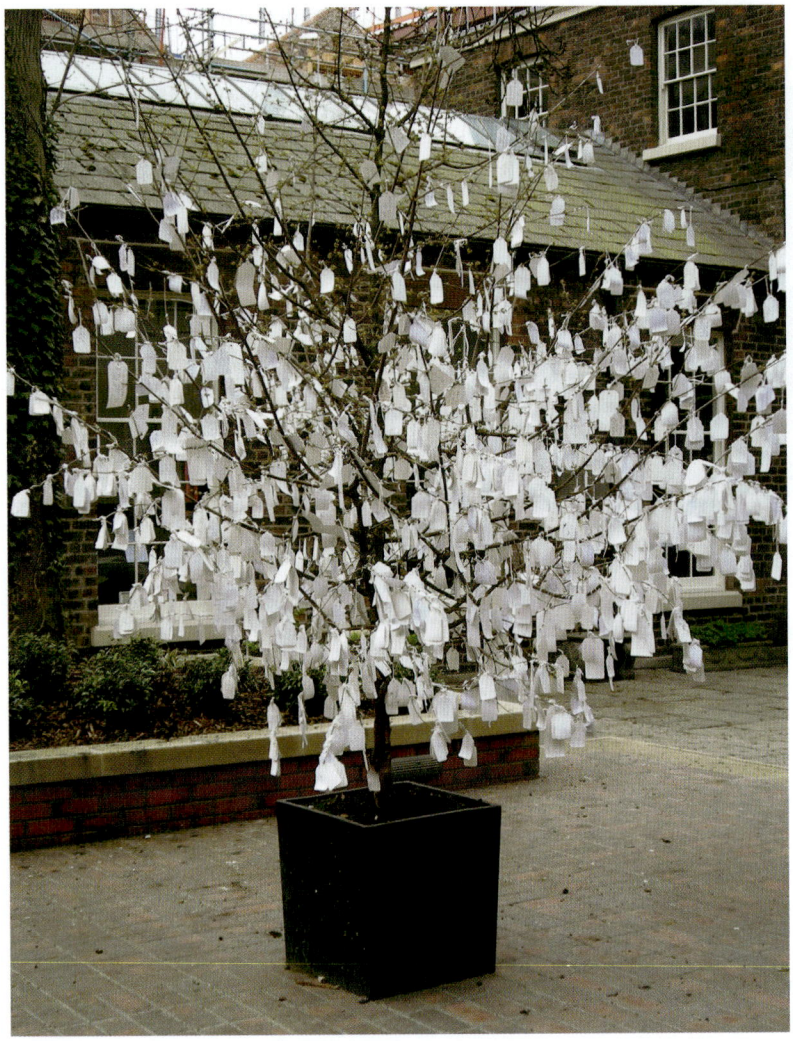

2.10.3 Yoko Ono, *Wish Tree for Liverpool*, 2008. Bluecoat Arts Centre, Liverpool, England

Performance Art

During the 1960s and 1970s, artists all over the world began exploring theatrical actions or performances as a new form of creative activity they termed performance art. American composer John Cage (1912–1992) (**2.10.4**) incorporated into his music chance operations, experimental techniques, and even silence. Heavily influenced by Zen Buddhism, Cage wanted to jolt his audiences into paying attention to the life all around them. He was one of the first artists to conduct **happenings**, or impromptu art actions. *Theater Piece No. 1* (1952) was an unrecorded collaboration in poetry, music, dance, and paintings by the faculty and students at Black Mountain College in North Carolina. The performers mingled with the members of the audience, and the piece relied for its outcome on improvisation and chance rather than a script or musical score. Its lasting influence comes from its emphasis on performance rather than documentation. Happenings expanded the scope of art to include the lived moment—actions as they happen, here and now.

The work of the German artist Joseph Beuys (1921–1986) explores his own German heritage and wider issues of social identity. Beuys's early life under the Nazis, especially his compulsory membership of the Hitler Youth and volunteer

Happening: impromptu art action, initiated and planned by an artist, the outcome of which is not known in advance

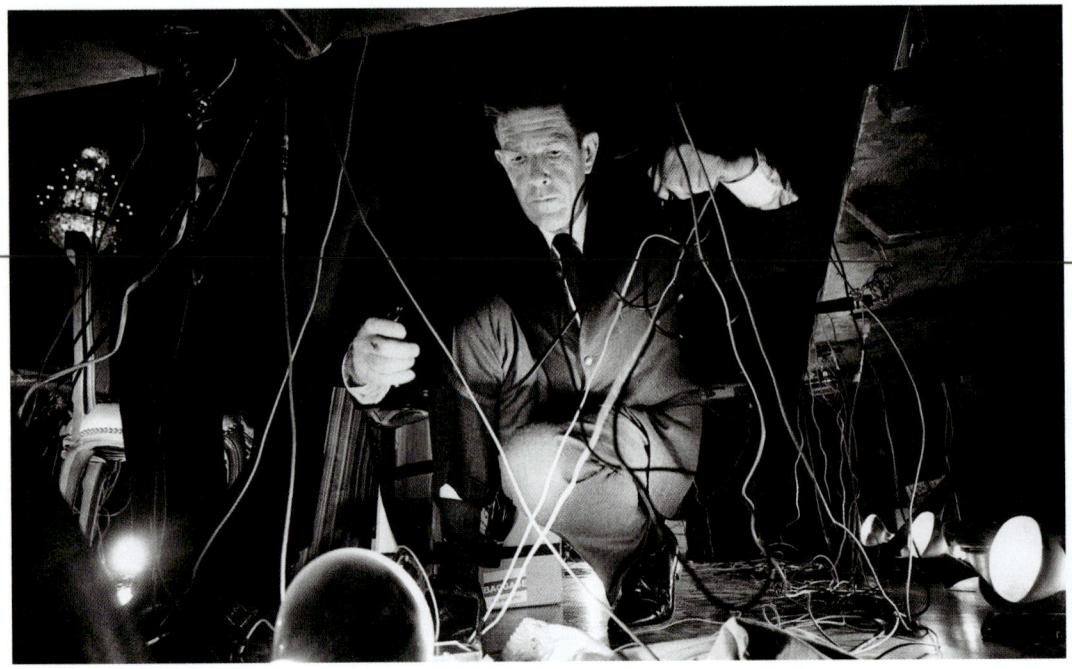

2.10.4 John Cage, during his concert held at the opening of the National Arts Foundation, Washington, D.C., 1966

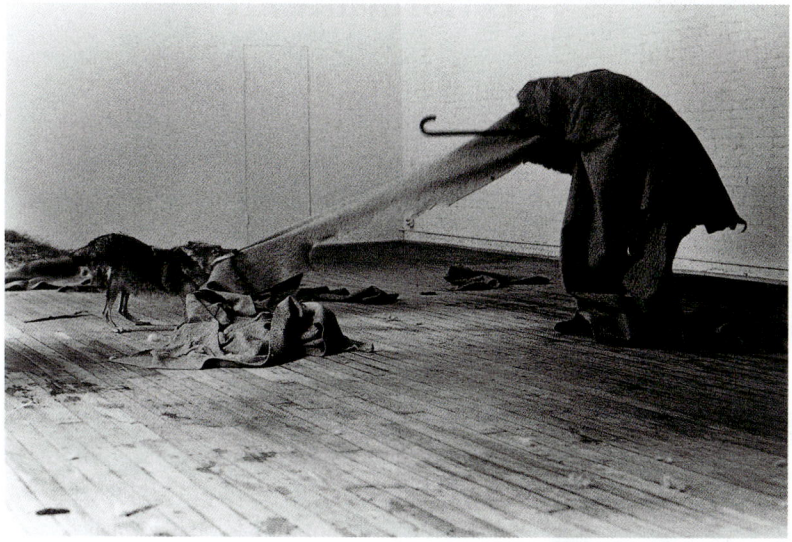

2.10.5 Joseph Beuys, *Coyote, I Like America and America Likes Me*, May 1974. Living sculpture at the René Block Gallery, New York

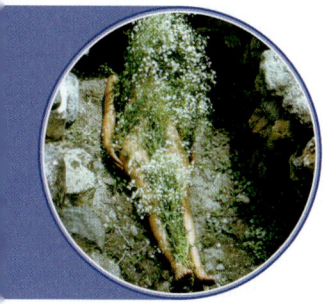

Ana Mendieta's *Silueta* series places the artist's body in various natural scenarios: see **3.10.4, p. 548**

service as a fighter pilot in the German Air Force, strongly influenced his artwork. He claimed that nomads rescued him in North Africa after a plane crash he sustained in World War II, and prevented him from freezing to death by wrapping him in fat and felt. Hence those materials became symbolic elements in many of his sculptures and performances.

A large piece of felt was one of the major props in his piece *Coyote, I Like America and America Likes Me* (**2.10.5**). The piece is mysterious. Because Beuys did not speak or interact with anyone during the five-day performance (which included his travel time), a sense of myth surrounds the events that actually took place. Upon arrival in America, Beuys was transported from the airport to the gallery in an ambulance. He was wrapped in felt, covered in hospital blankets, and carried on a gurney so he could not see his surroundings or touch American soil. For the following three days he was confined in the gallery with a coyote, a trickster or mischievous figure in Native American mythology, and symbolic of the spirit world. Beuys's action (as he called his performances) was intended to activate a process of spiritual healing and reconciliation, to make amends for the desecrations caused by the coming of Europeans to the New World.

When he was finished with his performance, the artist was wrapped up and whisked away by ambulance in the same manner as he had come. Beuys saw his actions as a way to make art more connected to society, incorporating commitments to activism and political reform.

Early in his career, the American artist Vito Acconci (b. 1940) was known for art actions and performances. These works consisted of situations he set up for himself, and records of how he completed them. His stated intentions for *Following Piece* (**2.10.6**) were: "Choosing a person at random, in the street, a new location, each day. Following him wherever he goes, however long or far he travels. (The activity ends when he enters a private place—his home, office, etc.)." Acconci performed this activity for twenty-three days; the longest following lasted nine hours. An exhibition of *Following Piece* includes documents of the events, such as the artist's handwritten note cards, and photographs of Acconci walking behind the person being followed. *Following Piece* examines both the relationship between the artist and the viewer and the way an artist's actions create interactions with another person. In this sense, Acconci's work is a conceptual performance: it is about ideas and a set of actions as much as about the production of a work of art. It is interesting to note how our view of such

2.10.6 (below) Vito Acconci, *Following Piece*, 1969, "Street Works IV," 23-day activity

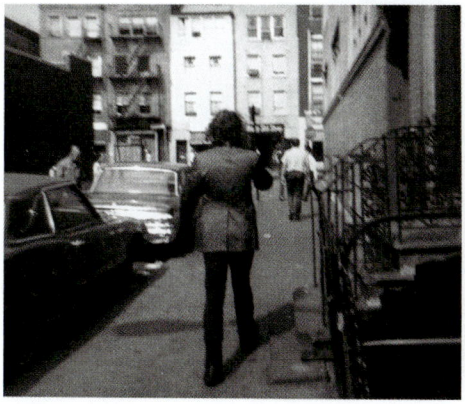

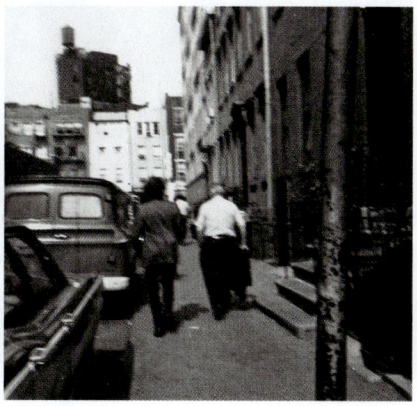

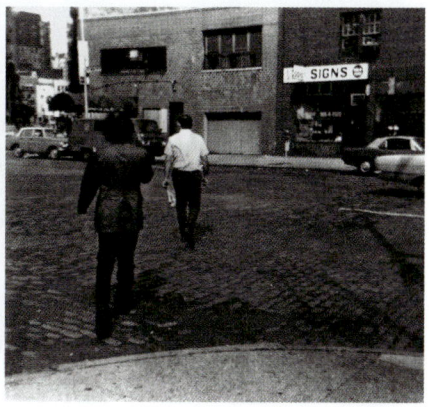

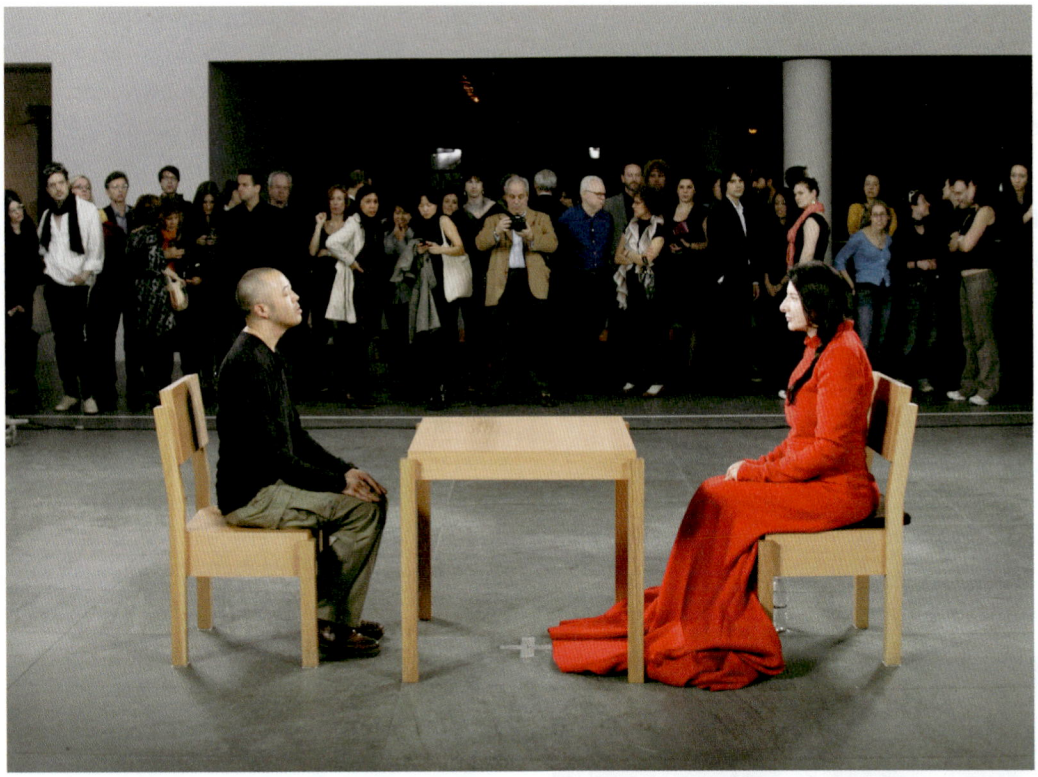

2.10.7 Marina Abramović, *The Artist Is Present*, Performance, 3 months. MoMA, New York, 2010

works can change through time. In 1969, when the piece was first developed, it was regarded as a new idea, but nowadays, we might look on the artist's actions in following and photographing someone without their knowledge as disturbing or even menacing.

Some performances put the body through extremes of endurance, as Serbian artist Marina Abramović (b. 1946) has done in a number of works dating back to the 1970s. In one piece she lay in a ring of fire until she fainted from asphyxiation (and had to be rescued by onlookers). In another, one of her longest pieces (it took almost three months), she and her partner Ulay started at opposite ends of the Great Wall of China and met in the middle after walking more than 1,242 miles.

In 2010, Abramović performed the longest-lasting work of her solo career so far, *The Artist Is Present*, for three months at the Museum of Modern Art, New York (MoMA) (**2.10.7**). Every day during that period she sat quietly at a table in the museum's gallery all day, from before it opened until after it closed. Museum visitors were invited to sit—one at a time, for as long as they wished—in the chair opposite her. The title of the piece poignantly calls attention to its purpose: for the artist to be personally in the space and engage with people, creating what she has called an "energy dialogue," without talking, touching, or otherwise overtly communicating. Through this engagement, Abramović put her mental and physical abilities to the test. At the same time, the audience experienced the intensity of this seemingly simple interaction. Portraits were made of each person who sat in the chair, showing most of them staring intently forward, some of them smiling, and a number of people crying.

This piece was a part of a retrospective exhibition of Abramović's work, which was the first major performance exhibition at MoMA. The show revealed the numerous challenges institutions must deal with when displaying performance art, such as the unpredictability of audience members who have been invited to participate. Crowd control took on epic proportions for this retrospective, with around 1,400 museum visitors per day and an estimate of more than 500,000 over the whole course of the exhibition. In addition to photographs, video documentation, and written accounts of performance pieces made throughout Abramović's career, for the first time, performers

Tableau: a stationary scene arranged for artistic impact

re-enacted her earlier pieces so that visitors could experience them first hand, and visitors shared their perspectives on personal blogs and through social media.

Installation and Environments

The Beanery by American Ed Kienholz (1927–1994) reflects the artist's desire to break down barriers between art and life (**2.10.8a** and **b**). Kienholz meticulously replicated the interior of his local bar, Barney's Beanery, complete with lifesize figures inspired by people he knew. This very specific place has been transformed into an assemblage through the products, interior design, technology, clothing, newspapers, music, and even odors it contains. To keep the experience as true to the artist's intentions as possible, the original soundtrack on tape has recently been converted to CD, and "odor paste" that smells like a bar is replenished by the museum. By placing clocks in place of the faces, Kienholz reiterated the fact that time now stands still in this sculptural **tableau**.

The London-born Nigerian Yinka Shonibare (b. 1962), creates more disembodied and conceptual sculptural groupings that explore issues of race and colonialism. He uses parody and masquerade to suggest that things are not always what they seem. His mannequin figures, headless to reflect the violence of capitalism, wear Victorian-style garments made out of distinctive "African" textiles. These fabrics, widely associated with Africa, in this context represent the multi-layered product of colonial exploitation. Wax-printed cotton, originally made in Indonesia, began to be industrially manufactured by a Dutch company at the end of the nineteenth century. When the material proved unpopular in Indonesia, these cheap fabrics were successfully marketed in West Africa. Shonibare inverts colonialist expectations by using cloth associated with poverty-stricken West Africans to outfit faceless and raceless aristocrats.

In *Mobility* (**2.10.10**, p. 358), Shonibare created a family of three aristocrats riding unicycles with differing degrees of confidence

2.10.8a (below) Edward Kienholz, detail of *The Beanery*

2.10.8b (bottom) Edward Kienholz, *The Beanery*, 1965 (restored 2012). Installation, 8'3½" × 21'11¾" × 6'2¾". Stedelijk Museum, Amsterdam, The Netherlands

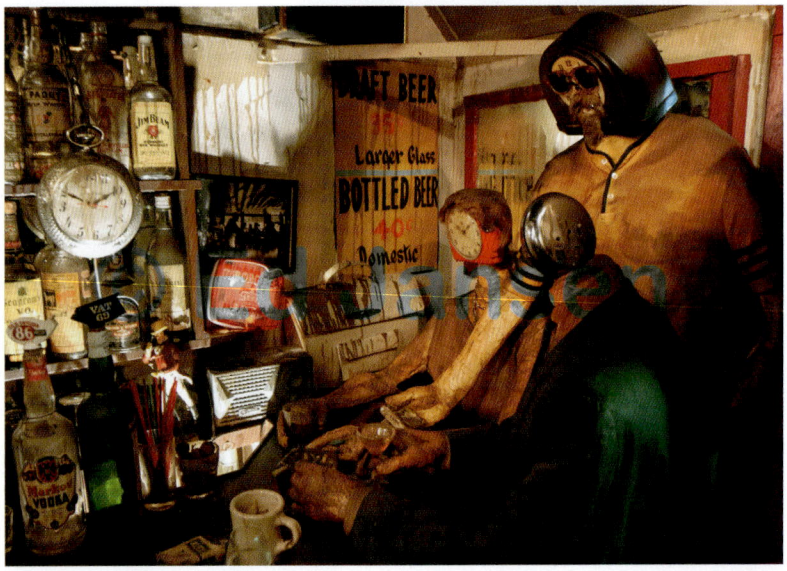

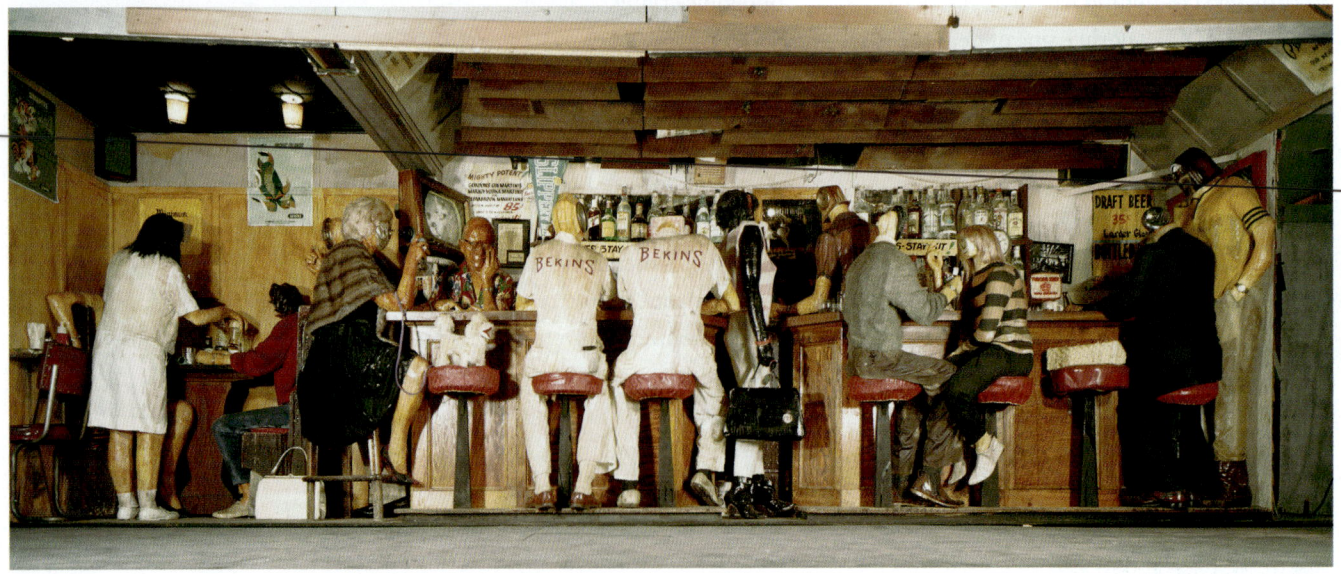

Gateway to Art: Ai Weiwei, *Dropping a Han Dynasty Urn* and *Colored Vases*

Art that Resists Categories: Interactions with the Individual

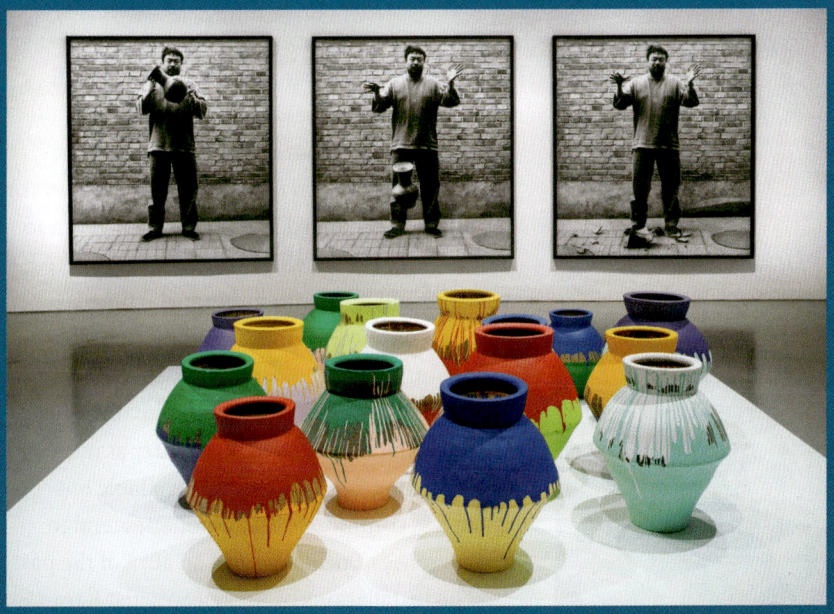

2.10.9 Installation view showing Ai Weiwei's *Colored Vases* in front of his *Dropping a Han Dynasty Urn*, displayed at the "According to What?" exhibition, held at the Hirshhorn Museum and Sculpture Garden, Washington, D.C.

> Art is an action that transforms our thoughts. It is a process that turns nothing into something.
>
> Ai Weiwei

Because of the diversity of materials used and the complexity of the underlying messages he conveys, Ai Weiwei's work cannot be easily defined or categorized. His sculptures, photographs, audio, videos, site-specific installations, performances, and designs do not conform to traditional definitions of how such media should be used, and Ai's emphasis on political commentary and the bold, activist statements contained in his works connect them with conceptual art.

In 2012, the exhibition "According to What?," held at the Hirshhorn Museum and Sculpture Garden in Washington, D.C. (**2.10.9**), the first international survey of Ai Weiwei's career, brought together works from 1995–2010. Installation of *Dropping a Han Dynasty Urn* (1995) and another work, *Colored Vases* (2010) in the same visual space called attention to issues of consumerism and commodification, appreciation and value, preservation and destruction, political commentary and personal responsibility. In the earlier work, a single, valuable urn or vase is shown—contrary to how we might expect it to be treasured—being willfully destroyed by the artist.

In *Colored Vases*, even though they may have functioned as everyday or funerary objects when they were made, these painted vases become altered found objects and take on new significance as they are incorporated into Ai Weiwei's work. The way Ai dripped the paint onto each urn allows us to see still the weathered surface of an ancient vessel underneath and, at the same time, foregrounds the artist's actions. A tension arises in the work from the fact that cultural artifacts have been dipped in cheap, garish, industrial paint. Not only is the past colliding with the present here, but the cultural tradition of the East also meets an artistic individualism that is more typical of the West.

The vases' presentation in a museum announces their status. At the same time, the multiplicity of objects highlights their mass production, which can be traced back to at least 3000 BCE in China, and references the work of the Pop artist Andy Warhol, who greatly influenced Ai Weiwei. Ai's work thus leads us beyond the solitary and unified artwork into the space of the gallery and, further, into the realm of our own ideas and reflections.

For the other Ai Weiwei Gateway boxes, see p. 121, p. 419, and p. 654

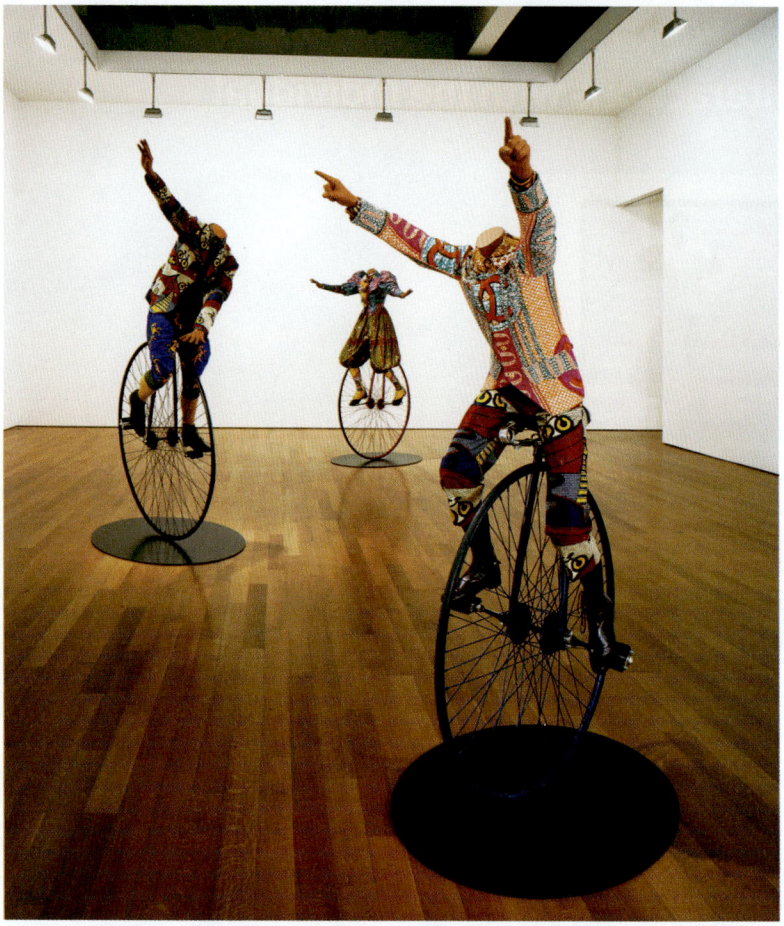

2.10.10 Yinka Shonibare, installation view of *Mobility*, James Cohan, New York, 2005. From left to right: *Man On Unicycle*, 2005. Metal, fabric, resin, and leather, 86 × 53 × 47½"; *Lady On Unicycle*, 2005. Metal, fabric, resin, and leather, 86 × 53 × 47½"; *Child On Unicycle, 2005.* Metal, fabric, resin, and leather, 79 × 46 × 38½"

and implied stability. The title of this piece brings in connotations of wealth (economic mobility), travel (the ability to go places, often for pleasure), and bodily movement (how able one is to get around). The playful and joyous mood of these artworks carries a serious message. In addition to commenting on economic disparities resulting from colonialism and capitalism, he is also referring to assumptions about physical ability. Having suffered complete paralysis after contracting a virus at age nineteen, Shonibare has been recovering ever since. A few years before he made this installation Shonibare began using his art to confront his own mortality and the difficulty of living in his body. Like the unicyclists, for Shonibare the very act of getting around presents distinct challenges. Shonibare's work parallels his life and world views: just as he cannot be easily labeled as Nigerian or British, his figures and the textiles they wear cannot be easily categorized according to class, culture, or physical ability.

Silhouette: a portrait or figure represented in outline and solidly colored in
Subject: the person, object, or space depicted in a work of art

Out of the Shadows and into the Light: Enlivened Gallery Space

Several contemporary artists have used installations and performance as ways to call attention to historical media and ways of thinking while encouraging viewers to take a longer look and attend to the way things have (or should have) changed. From the seventeenth to nineteenth century, **silhouette** cutouts offered a cheaper alternative to individual painted portraits in Europe, America, and colonized countries. Also called "shades" or "likenesses", the process of making silhouettes involves an artist tracing the shadow of the sitter as it is cast from a strong light source. Still available but much less common today, silhouettes tend to carry a sense of nostalgia and an aura of the past.

The installations of American artist Kara Walker (b. 1969) combine silhouettes and projections in the gallery space to address overlooked history from the pre-Civil War South. These silhouettes provide a glimpse of the **subject** in an indirect way, a view of history that once existed but may never have been told. The addition of projectors in her installations enables the artist to cast more shadows on the walls, including those of viewers in the room. As their shadows appear on the wall, the viewers are included and even implicated in the events unfolding there. The combined projections and silhouettes can be seen in *Insurrection! (Our Tools Were Rudimentary, Yet We Pressed On)*, which presents a story that combines fact and fiction (**2.10.11**). Walker explains that this scene is intended to show "a slave revolt in the antebellum South where the house slaves got after their master with their instruments, their utensils of everyday life." Each grouping of figures highlights the bodies of the individuals, the stories they represent, and the scenarios of which they become a part.

Projected silhouettes in the performance *Taualuga: The Last Dance* (2006) bring to light contemporary issues of race and identity within a cultural context of colonialism, (mis)representation, and consumerism

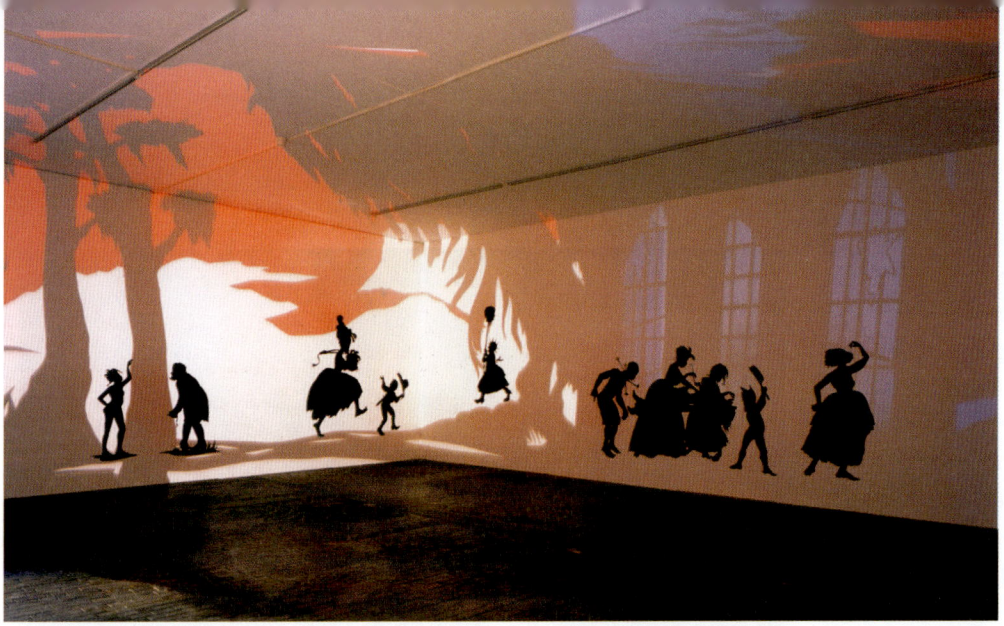

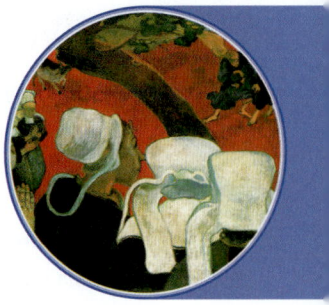

Paul Gauguin sought to leave the trappings of his civilized life and traveled to Brittany to find simpler, more spiritual ways of living; at the end of his life he also lived and painted in Tahiti: see **3.8.17, p. 515**

2.10.11 Kara Walker, *Insurrection! (Our Tools Were Rudimentary, Yet We Pressed On)*, 2000. Cut paper and projection on wall, dimensions variable Installation view: *Why I Like White Boys, an Illustrated Novel by Kara E. Walker Negress*, Centre d'Art Contemporain, Geneva, Switzerland

(**2.10.12**). The Samoan/Japanese artist who lives in New Zealand, Yuki Kihara (b. 1975), created an alter ego named Salomé to embody a nineteenth-century Samoan woman she had seen in ethnographic photographs. Her Victorian mourning dress references the losses and struggles resulting from colonialism, natural disasters, tourism, and life. Traditionally her dance, called *taualuga*, is a carefully choreographed, celebratory method of narrative storytelling. Salomé embodies more than meets the eye, bringing together past and present, suggesting creation and destruction, and representing the artist's identity as a *fa'afafine*, Samoan third gender. The Samoan woman in colonial dress steps out of the mythical paradise of the untouched Pacific wilderness, passes through iconic cultural images (for example, paintings by Paul Gauguin), and dances into the present day by simultaneously embracing and dismantling stereotypes.

Kara Walker brought the silhouette into the contemporary art context through her installations and Yuki Kihara further extended its use in multimedia performances. Both artists train a postcolonial lens on historical subjects through their explorations of the interactions between art and life.

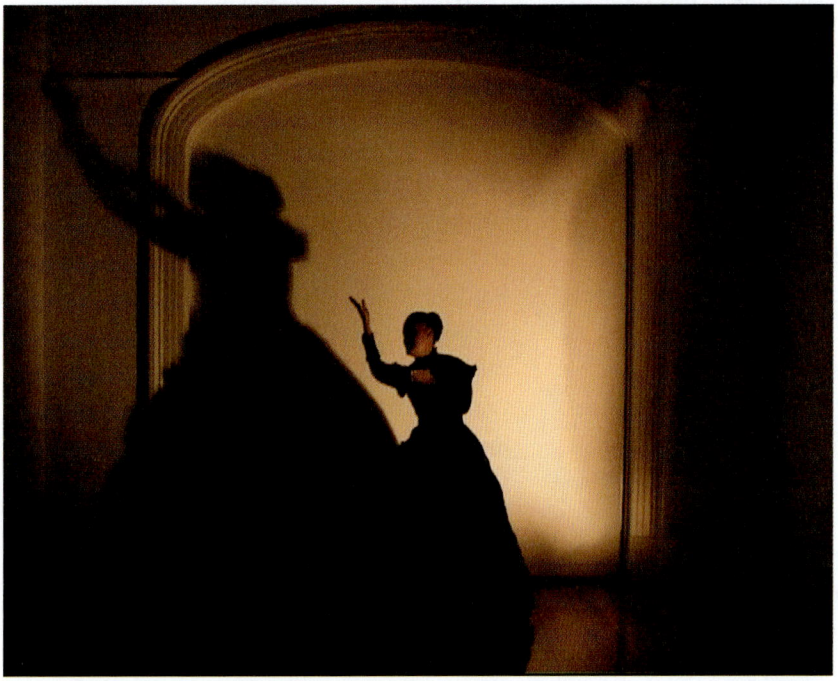

2.10.12 Yuki Kihara, *Taualuga: The Last Dance*, 2006. Performance/digital video. Still courtesy of Milford Galleries, Dunedin and Yuki Kihara. © Yuki Kihara

Perspectives on Art: Molly Gochman
Bringing Light to the Scars

Molly Gochman (b.1978, San Antonio Texas) is an interdisciplinary artist and activist whose work hopes to prompt questioning by providing opportunities to pause and awaken sensations. Based in New York City, her work engages larger social issues and challenges the traditional role of the artist and the expected outcomes of artworks. Here Gochman describes how Red Sand Project, *a collective work of art* **(2.10.13)** *made by participants from across the United States and around the world, raises awareness about modern-day slavery and human trafficking.*

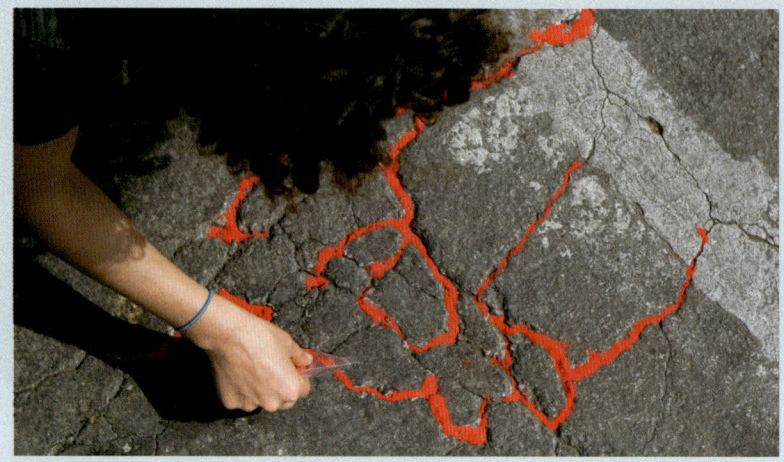

2.10.13 A *Red Sand Project* participant spreads sand in sidewalk cracks in their neighborhood, New York City, October, 2015

As both an artist and activist, I believe all art documents moments in time. In a world where we tend to overlook so much, I think we have the opportunity to look ahead to what can be and to create cultural change through empathy. For me, art has served as my invitation for people to reflect upon and participate in the experience of humanity. Our experiences as humans are vastly different, but we don't often take the time to understand them. I hope to encourage people to stop, soften, and really feel the meaning that exists in the objects and communities that surround us.

That is one of the main reasons why I started *Red Sand Project*, a participatory artwork that uses sidewalk interventions, earthwork installations, and convenings to create opportunities for people to question, to connect, and to take action against vulnerabilities that can lead to human trafficking and exploitation.

Several hundred thousand *Red Sand Project* toolkits have been requested and used by people and groups of diverse backgrounds—from students to educators, businesses to outreach organizations, concerned citizens to celebrities.

Since its inception, installations and events have taken place in all fifty United States and in more than seventy countries around the world. In partnership with organizations, I've sought to create works that invite public participation from people of all different cultures, ethnicities, and backgrounds. With the goal, in so doing, that people will participate in a communal effort to raise awareness of vulnerabilities and social injustices facing people around the world.

The sidewalk interventions remind us that we can't merely walk over the most marginalized people in our communities—those who fall through the metaphoric cracks—and allow anyone anywhere to fill sidewalk cracks with red sand and to then document their images on social media using #*RedSandProject*, thereby expanding the reach of their artistic expression and participation.

While I was nervous, at first, about what this project might mean to some, specifically survivors, I have been so lucky to receive positive feedback. Many survivors of human trafficking have embraced the project and even brought it to their own communities. This project has shown me that while this is an incredibly sensitive issue, art gives space to share images and stories in a way that doesn't exploit the people being affected.

Whether through sidewalk interventions, gallery exhibits, earthworks, or panel discussions, I've used my work to bring new audiences together to find common ground around what's affecting them most deeply. The simple act of placing sand in a crack, posting a photo on social media, chatting with someone as they pass by or finding a brief moment of connection may seem inconsequential, but small actions build upon each other to make transformational change.

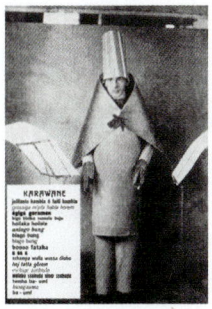

3.9.7 Hugo Ball, Performance of "Karawane" at Cabaret Voltaire, 1916, p. 529

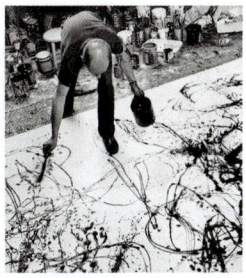

3.9.25 Hans Namuth, photograph of Jackson Pollock painting, 1950, p. 538

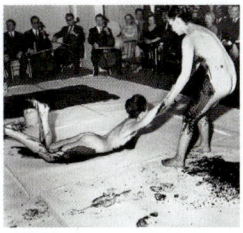

4.9.11a Yves Klein, *Anthropométries de l'époque bleue*, 1960, p. 670

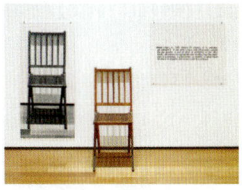

3.10.3 Joseph Kosuth, *One and Three Chairs*, 1965, p. 548

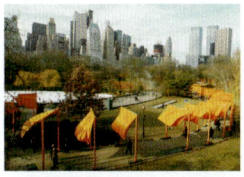

4.1.9 Christo and Jeanne-Claude, *The Gates*, 1979–2005, p. 571

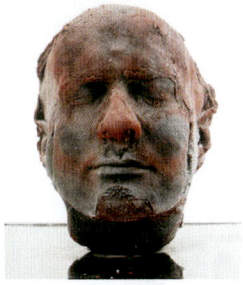

0.0.16 Marc Quinn, *Self*, 1991, p. 32

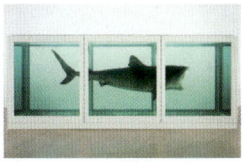

2.4.18 Damien Hirst, *The Physical Impossibility of Death in the Mind of Someone Living*, 1991, p. 253

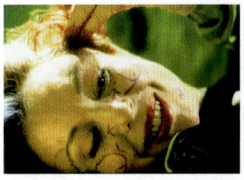

4.9.20b ORLAN, Seventh surgery-performance, entitled *Omnipresence*, 1993, p. 678

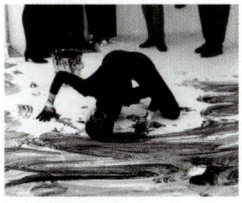

4.9.12 Janine Antoni, *Loving Care*, 1993, p. 671

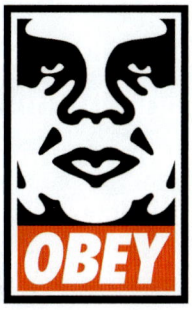

1.1.25a Shepard Fairey, *Obey*, 1996, p. 57

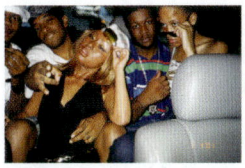

4.10.16 Nikki S. Lee, *Hip Hop Project (25)*, 2001, p. 690

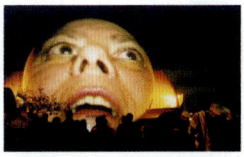

4.1.14 Krzysztof Wodiczko, *Tijuana Projection*, 2001, p. 576

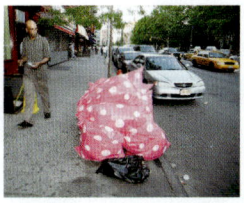

1.4.34 Adrian Kondratowicz, *TRASH project*, 2008–, p. 111

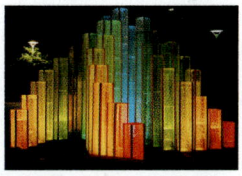

2.4.23 Athena Tacha with EDAW, *Star Fountain*, 2009, p. 256

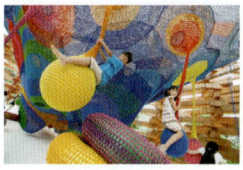

2.6.20 Toshiko Horiuchi McAdam, *Knitted Wonder Space II*, 2009, p. 297

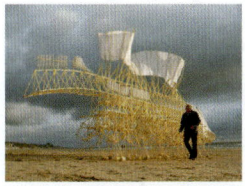

1.5.11 Theo Jansen, *Animaris Umeris (Strandbeest #48)*, 2009, p. 119

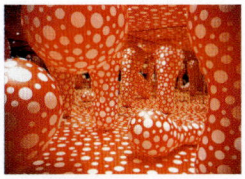

4.4.14 Yayoi Kusama, *Dots Obsession*, 2009, p. 611

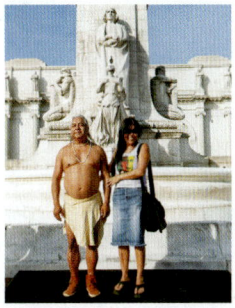

4.10.13 James Luna, *Take a Picture with a Real Indian*, 2010, p. 688

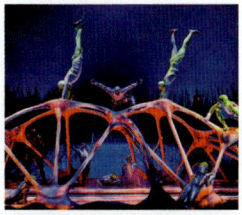

1.5.9 Cirque du Soleil performing *Totem*, 2010, p. 118

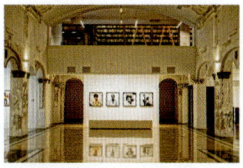

3.10.21b Theaster Gates, Stony Island Arts Bank after restoration, p. 560

The history of art is an important aspect of the many ways in which we can understand a work. Art is not just the skillful application of design concepts and materials to produce an impressive work. Inevitably, an artwork is influenced by the time and place in which it was created. This influence is known as the context in which the art was made. In this part, as well as learning about context, you will discover how history has influenced art and how art, in its turn, reflects history.

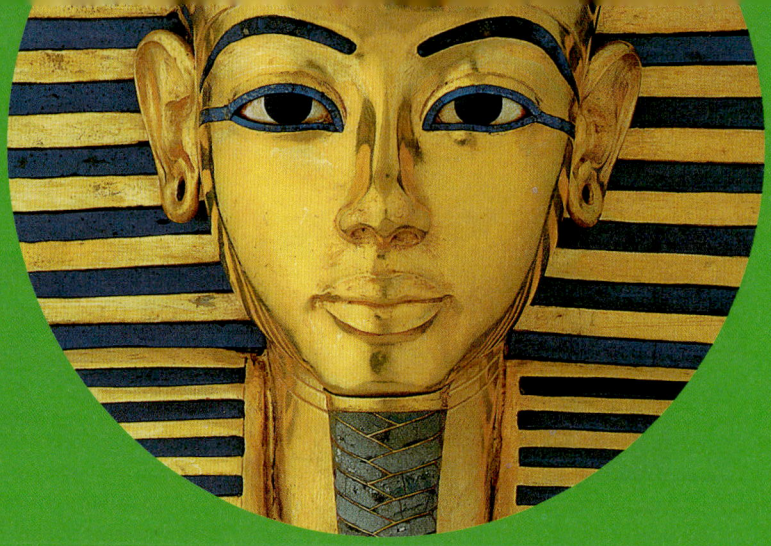

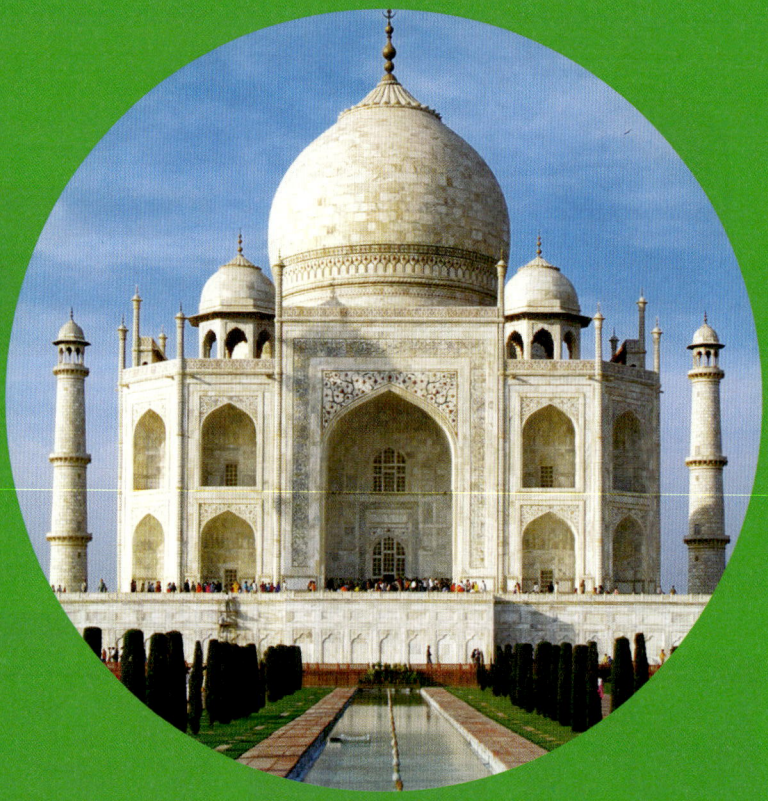

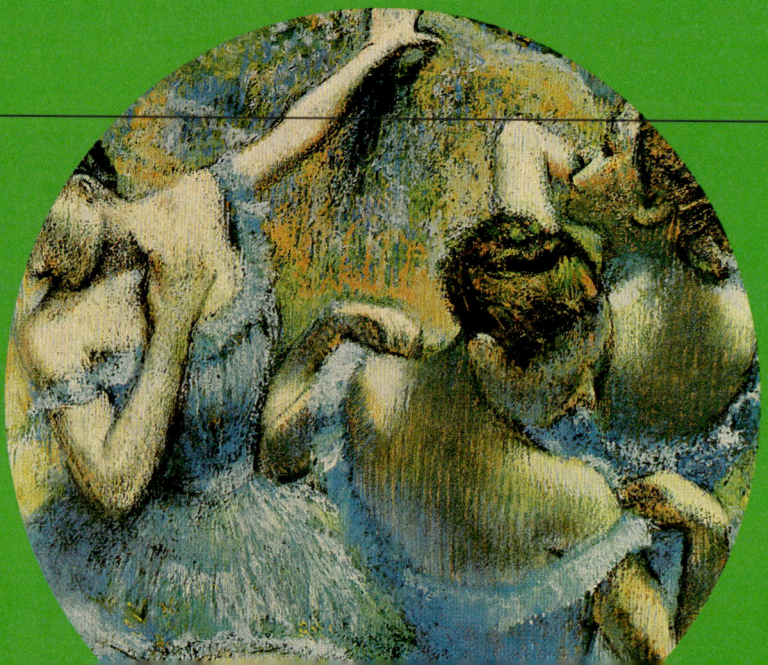

Part 3

History and Context

In this part you will study:

The Prehistoric and Ancient Mediterranean

Art of the Middle Ages

Art of India, China, Japan, Korea, and Southeast Asia

Art of the Americas

Art of Africa and the Pacific Islands

Art of Renaissance and Baroque Europe (1400–1750)

Art of Europe and America (1700–1865): Rococo to Romanticism

The Modern Aesthetic: Realism to Expressionism

Late Modern and Early Contemporary Art in the Twentieth Century

The Late Twentieth Century and Art of the Present Day

Part 3 Timeline

	200,000 BCE	1000 BCE	350 BCE	100 CE
ART AND ARCHITECTURE	**c. 75,000 years ago *Africa*:** Portable art objects, for example made from shell **c. 40,000–25,000 BCE *Africa, Australia, Europe*:** First cave paintings **c. 7000–5700 BCE *Near East*:** Çatalhöyük (modern Turkey) **c. 4000–3000 BCE *Mesopotamia*:** Incised stones rolled across clay or pressed into wax to create relief impressions **c. 3500 BCE *Mesopotamia and Egypt*:** Use of glass begins **c. 3300 BCE *Mesopotamia*:** First written script developed by Sumerians **c. 3300 BCE *New Zealand*:** Earliest known preserved tattooed bodies **c. 2900–2400 BCE *Europe*:** Stonehenge is built in England **c. 2580–2510 BCE *Egypt*:** Great Pyramids at Giza **2500 BCE *China and India*:** Use of carbon ink begins **c. 2100 BCE *Near East*:** Ziggurat of Ur is built (modern Iraq) **c. 1600–1500 BCE *Europe*:** First fresco paintings, Palace of Knossos, Crete	**900 BCE *South America*:** Chavín de Huantar (modern Peru) **800 BCE–100 CE *North America*:** Great Serpent Mound (modern Ohio) **c. 500 BCE–500 CE *South America*:** Nazca lines carved into the ground (modern Peru) **c. 480–323 BCE *Greece*:** In the Classical period, Polykleitos develops canon for ideal human proportions and the three architectural orders are perfected **447–438 BCE *Greece*:** Parthenon built **c. 400 BCE *Egypt*:** Museum of Alexandria founded	**3rd century BCE *India*:** Great Stupa at Sanchi begun **c. 246–210 BCE *China*:** Mausoleum of Qin Shi Huangdi, the first emperor of China **c. 200 BCE *China*:** Printing ink on fabric first used **1st century BCE *Europe*:** In Rome, Vitruvius writes *On Architecture* **72–80 CE *Rome*:** Colosseum: Romans first to exploit concrete's full potential **End of 1st century CE *China*:** Paper invented	**c. 200–300 *Europe*:** Catacombs of Saints Peter and Marcellinus (modern Italy) **c. 225 *Mesoamerica*:** Pyramid of the Sun, Teotihuacan (modern Mexico) **244–45 *Near East*:** Dura Europos synagogue (modern Syria) **c. 300–400 *Japan*:** Ise Jingu shrine first built **532–35 *Near East*:** Hagia Sophia first built (modern Turkey) **7th century *Japan*:** Construction of Horyu Temple, Nara **688–691 *Middle East*:** Dome of the Rock built in Jerusalem **8th century *China*:** Earliest existing printed artworks on paper **8th and 9th centuries *Egypt*:** Emperor Justinian protects icons from iconoclastic destruction **900–1500 *Easter Island*:** *Moai* heads and figures made **960–1279 *China*:** Silkscreen printing develops
POLITICS, SOCIETY, RELIGION, AND PHILOSOPHY	**c. 200,000 years ago *Africa*:** First modern humans **c. 24,000–13,000 years ago *North America*:** First populated by humans **c. 4000 BCE–331 BCE *Mesopotamia*:** Civilizations include Sumerians, Akkadians, Assyrians, and Babylonians **c. 3100–332 BCE *Egypt*:** Ancient Egyptian civilization **c. 2700–1200 BCE *Europe*:** Minoan civilization, Crete **c. 2000 BCE *Middle East*:** Judaism begins **2000 BCE–1500 CE *Mesoamerica*:** Maya civilization **1600–1050 BCE *China*:** Shang Dynasty **1500–400 BCE *Mesoamerica*:** Olmec civilization **c. 1000 BCE *India*:** Hinduism first practiced	**900 BCE *South America*:** Chavín culture flourishes (modern Peru) **604 BCE *China*:** Birth of Lao Zi, founder of Daoism **c. 600 BCE *Hawaii*:** First humans arrive **600–200 BCE *South America*:** Paracas culture **6th century–c. 280 BCE *Europe*:** Etruscan civilization (modern Italy) **563–483 BCE *Nepal*:** Life of Siddhartha Gautama (Buddha), founder of Buddhism **551–479 BCE *China*:** Life of Confucius, founder of Confucianism **c. 480–323 BCE *Greece*:** Classical Greek civilization **5th and 4th centuries BCE *Greece*:** Lives of philosophers Plato (c. 428–347 BCE) and Aristotle (384–322 BCE)	**304–232 BCE *India*:** King Ashoka reigns **221–207 BCE *China*:** Qin Dynasty: the first unified Chinese dynasty **206 BCE–220 CE *China*:** Han Dynasty **200 BCE–600 CE *South America*:** Moche culture **27 BCE–476 CE *Europe*:** Roman empire **c. 7–2 BCE to c. 30–36 CE *Middle East*:** Life of Jesus, the son of God for Christians	**265–420 *China*:** Jin Dynasty **306–337 *Europe*:** Constantine the Great rules the Roman empire as the first Christian Roman emperor **320–550 *India*:** Gupta period **c. 330–1453 *Europe*:** Byzantine empire **500 *Mesoamerica*:** Peak of Teotihuacan civilization **c. 570–632 *Saudi Arabia*:** Life of Muhammad, primary messenger of Allah: beginning of Islam **800–1527 *South America*:** Inca culture **960–1279 *China*:** Song Dynasty

1000 CE	1600 CE	1800 CE	1900 CE	1950 CE
c. 1000–1500s *Europe*: Architectural styles: Romanesque (c. 1000–1150) and Gothic (c. 1150–1500s) **1100–1300 *North America*:** Mesa Verde established by ancient Puebloans **12th century *Cambodia*:** Angkor Wat built as a Hindu monument; Buddhist statues are added in the 14th century **1350–1450 *Africa*:** Great Zimbabwe, center of Shona state in Zimbabwe **1377–1446 *Europe*:** In Florence, Brunelleschi invents linear perspective and technique for building large domes **1400–1600 *Europe*:** Renaissance art and architecture in Italy and Northern Europe **Early 15th century *Europe*:** Woodblock printing and papermaking become common throughout Europe; in 1450 Gutenberg invents the printing press **1450–1700 *Africa*:** Benin bronze artworks **c. 1530–1600 *Europe*:** Mannerist style in art **Late 16th–early 18th century *Europe*:** Baroque style in art and architecture	**1632–53 *India*:** Taj Mahal is built in Agra **1678–84 *France*:** Construction of Versailles **18th century *France*:** Rococo style in art and architecture **1722–1868 *Easter Island*:** Many *moai* figures destroyed **Late 18th century *Europe and US*:** Neoclassical style in art and architecture; Thomas Jefferson designs Monticello **1796 *Europe*:** In Germany, Senefelder invents lithographic printing **1799 *Egypt*:** Discovery of the Rosetta Stone, which leads to the translation of ancient Egyptian hieroglyphs **18th–19th centuries *Japan*:** Ukiyo-e woodblock printing	**19th century *Europe and US*:** In architecture, iron, steel, and concrete more commonly used **Early 19th century *Europe*:** Romanticism in art and literature **1805 *US*:** Pennsylvania Academy of the Fine Arts is the first museum (and arts school) in the US **1820s–1830s *Europe*:** Invention of photography **Mid-19th century *Europe*:** Realism in art **1874–86 *Europe*:** Impressionism **1880s–1905 *Europe*:** Post-Impressionism **1880s–1914 *Europe*:** *Fin de siècle* and Art Nouveau in art and architecture **1890–91 *US*:** Wainwright Building in St. Louis is one of the world's first skyscrapers **1894 *US*:** Edison and Dickson create one of the first American movies **1896 *Europe and US*:** Black-and-white movies are being shown all over Europe and the US	**Early 20th century *Europe*:** Expressionist, Fauvist, and Cubist styles **1907 *Africa*:** World's largest mud-brick structure: latest version of the Great Mosque, Djenné, Mali **1910s–1930s *Europe*:** Art movements include Dada, Surrealism, Futurism, De Stijl, and Suprematism **1911 *Mexico*:** Mexican Revolution; Mural Renaissance in the 1920s–30s **1913 *US*:** Armory Show brings European Modernist art to New York **1919–33 *Europe*:** Bauhaus school in Germany promotes Modernism **1920s–1930s *US*:** Regionalist style and the Harlem Renaissance **1930s–1950s *Europe and US*:** Modernist architecture pioneered by Mies, Le Corbusier, and Lloyd Wright **1937 *Europe*:** Nazis hold Degenerate Art exhibition in Germany; many artworks stolen during World War II **1939 *US*:** *The Wizard of Oz* is one of the first popular color movies; integrated sound in movies also begins	**1950s *US*:** Acrylic paint comes into wide use **1950s *US*:** Abstract Expressionist and Pop art styles pioneered **1960s *Worldwide*:** Contemporary period in art begins: Minimalism and Conceptual art; performance art; earthworks; and Postmodernism in art and architecture **1960s *US*:** Black Arts movement begins **1980s *US and Japan*:** Development of digital camera for photography and video **1990 *US*:** NAGPRA laws legislate the repatriation of artifacts and sacred remains **2010 *United Arab Emirates*:** World's tallest building (to date) completed in Dubai **2011 *China*:** Ai Weiwei arrested by Chinese government and imprisoned for 81 days **2017 *US*:** Basquiat's painting *Untitled* sells for a record $110.5 million: the most expensive work by an American artist to date
c. 1000 *Mesoamerica*: Toltec empire at its peak; Tula is the largest city in Mexico **1054 *Europe*:** Christian Church splits in two: Greek Orthodox in the east and Roman Catholic in the west **1066 *Europe*:** Battle of Hastings **12th century *Japan*:** Zen Buddhism arrives from China **1368–1644 *China*:** Ming Dynasty **15th century *Europe*:** Philosophy of Humanism **1400– c. 1530 *Mesoamerica*:** Aztec culture **1450–1700 *Africa*:** Kingdom of Benin at its height **1453 *Europe*:** Ottomans take control of Constantinople: end of the Byzantine empire **Late 15th century *Americas*:** Arrival of Europeans **1517 *Europe*:** Reformation begins **1526–mid-19th century *India*:** Mughal empire **1527 *Europe*:** Sack of Rome **1545–1648 *Europe*:** Counter-Reformation	**18th century *Europe*:** Age of Enlightenment **1760–c. 1840 *Europe*:** Industrial Revolution **1776 *US*:** Declaration of Independence **1789 *France*:** French Revolution **1789 *US*:** George Washington is first US president	**1828–1910 *US*:** Industrial Revolution **1830, 1848 *France*:** Revolutions in France **1833 *UK*:** Abolition of slavery **1836–1939 *Europe*:** Life of Sigmund Freud, Austrian founder of psychoanalysis **1848 *Europe*:** *The Communist Manifesto* published by Marx and Engels **1861–65 *US*:** American Civil War **1863 *US*:** Abraham Lincoln's Emancipation Proclamation frees slaves **1865 *US*:** Abolition of slavery **1875–1961 *Europe*:** Life of Carl Jung, Swiss founder of analytical psychology	**1914–18 *Worldwide*:** World War I **1918 *UK*:** Women partially gain the right to vote in Britain; and in the US in 1920 **1929 *US*:** Great Depression; Works Progress Administration begins **1937 *Spain*:** General Franco approves aerial attack of small town of Guernica **1939–45 *Worldwide*:** World War II **c. 1947–91 *Worldwide*:** Cold War **1948–91 *South Africa*:** Apartheid **1949 *China*:** Mao Zedong leads Communist Party to power	**1955–75 *Vietnam*:** Vietnam War **1955–68 *US*:** Civil Rights Movement **1960s onward *Worldwide*:** Feminist and LGBT movements promote gender and sexual equality **1966–76 *China*:** Cultural Revolution **1978–79 *Iran*:** Iranian Revolution **1979–2003 *Iraq*:** Saddam Hussein rules Iraq; he is executed in 2006 **1989 *China*:** More than 100,000 people gather in Tiananmen Square to protest government corruption **2001 *US*:** World Trade Center attack, September 11 **2011 *Egypt*:** Egyptian Revolution begins in February

3.1 The Prehistoric and Ancient Mediterranean

Human prehistory is the long period during which humans and their ancestors developed societies for which no written record has been found. We know about the achievements of these early people from the material traces they left behind. In Europe, this takes us back thousands of years—even 2.5 million years, if we include tools. These ancient people survived by gathering wild plants and hunting, and some found time to produce what we admire today as prehistoric art. Prehistoric art has been discovered in this region from as early as *c.* 40,000 BCE.

As humans formed larger communities, the Mediterranean region—the ancient Near East, northern Africa, and southern Europe—flourished as an area of trade. The region thrived because it was surrounded by bodies of water;

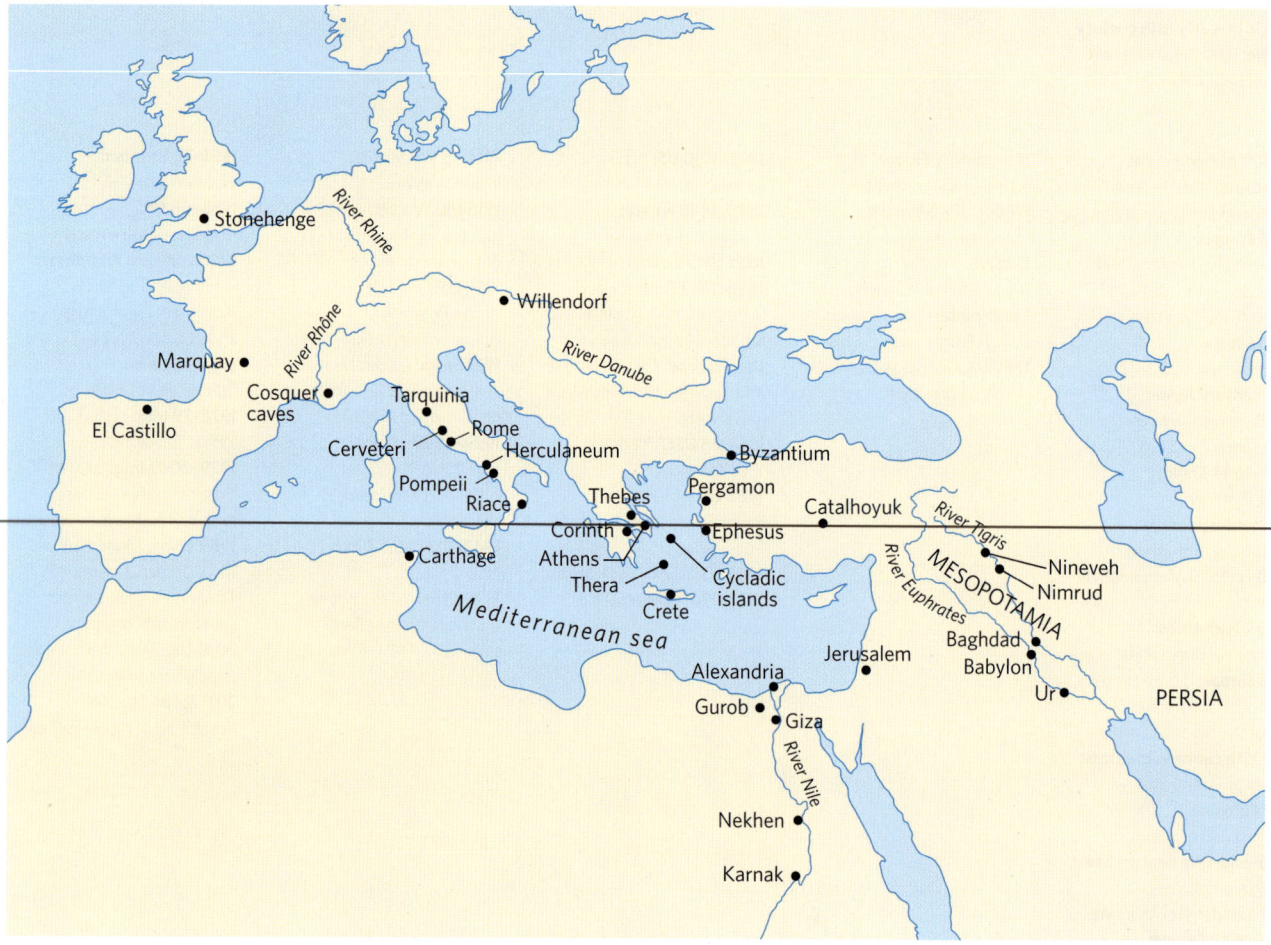

3.1.1 Map of prehistoric Europe and the ancient Mediterranean

frequently, the most powerful were those who controlled access to the seas. Here, a succession of civilizations arose that continue to shape the ways we live, even in the twenty-first century. It was here that humans first invented agriculture, started to live in urban settlements, and eventually planned cities; it was here that people invented writing, and produced works of art we still regard as great wonders of the world. The achievements of these people remain evident in our own lives. We write with an alphabet refined by the ancient Romans of Italy. Farmers who raise wheat crops today can do so because other farmers domesticated wheat and barley nearly 10,000 years ago.

These achievements, which we generally describe as the beginning of civilization, were matched independently elsewhere, for example in Asia and the Americas. The developments in the Mediterranean, however, are also part of the history of the Americas because of the arrival there of Europeans more than 500 years ago. This chapter first tells the story of the sculptures, cave paintings, and palaces made by prehistoric Europeans. Then we will look at the emergence of early civilizations in the ancient Near East and the rise of a great civilization in Egypt. Lastly we will study the powerful societies of ancient Greece and Rome and the beautiful sculptures, paintings, and buildings they produced.

Prehistoric Art in Europe and the Mediterranean

As long as 40,000 years ago, prehistoric people painted the interiors of caves; and sculptures still survive from 5,000 years after that. Not surprisingly, such art is preoccupied with the basics of life: procreation and sources of food. Prehistoric artworks are particularly important records of the lives of our early ancestors, because written records of these cultures do not exist. Often, what we know about their lives is based upon archaeological finds, and our modern interpretations of these discoveries.

The earliest paintings in Europe are found on walls in El Castillo Cave in Spain (**3.1.2**). Dating is possible through scientific study of the calcite

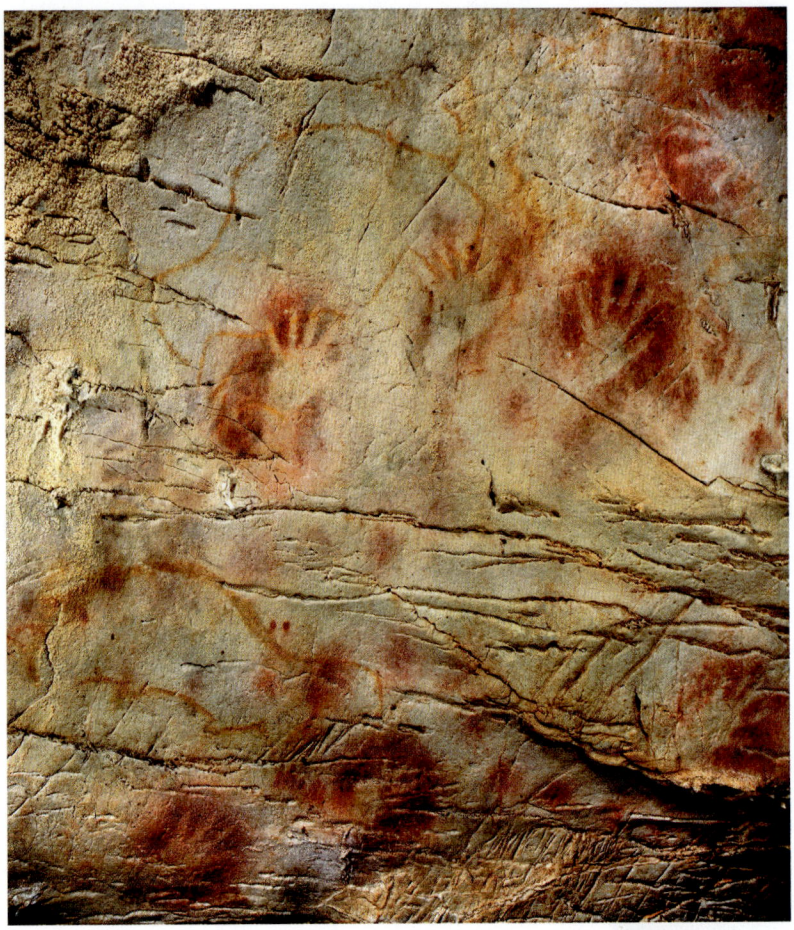

3.1.2 Hand stencils from El Castillo Cave, Cantabria, Spain c. 37,300 BCE

(a carbonate mineral frequently found in caverns) that has formed on top of the paintings. The calcite in El Castillo is at least 40,000 years old, so the paintings underneath may date from much earlier. Prehistoric humans often painted over previous images already on the wall. The very earliest paintings in this cave were red spheres, made by blowing **pigment**, in this case red **ocher**, through a reed. Humans often blew the pigment around their hand, creating an effect similar to a reversed **stencil**. Later, people would use the same method to create images of animals they hunted.

The most common type of prehistoric artworks found throughout the world are small female sculptures that suggest a preoccupation with fertility. Like other such "fertility figures," the Venus of Laussel (**3.1.3**, p. 368) shows a faceless woman with large breasts, belly, and vulva, signifying her fertility. Made approximately 25,000 years ago, the figure was carved into

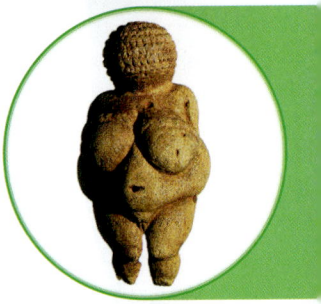

This prehistoric fertility figure can fit in one's hand and may have been carried around as a kind of talisman, or charm against bad luck: see **4.9.1, p. 663**

Pigment: the colored material used in paints. Often made from finely ground minerals
Ocher: a pigment found in nature containing hydrated iron oxide
Stencil: a perforated template allowing ink or paint to pass through to print a design

3.1.3 (right) Venus of Laussel, found in Marquay, Dordogne, France, *c.* 23,000 BCE. Low relief on limestone block, height 18⅛". Musée d'Aquitaine, Bordeaux, France

3.1.4 (below) Attributed to the Steiner Master, Reclining female figure of the Late Spedos variety, Cyclades, 2500–2400 BCE. Island marble, height 23⅜". The J. Paul Getty Museum, Villa Collection, Malibu, California

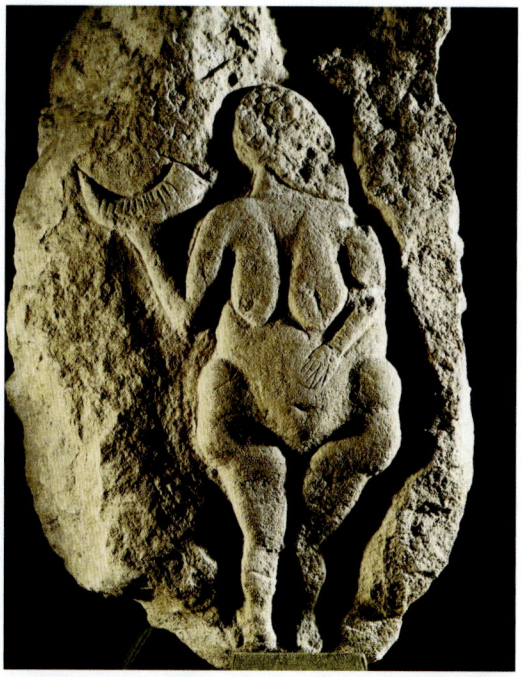

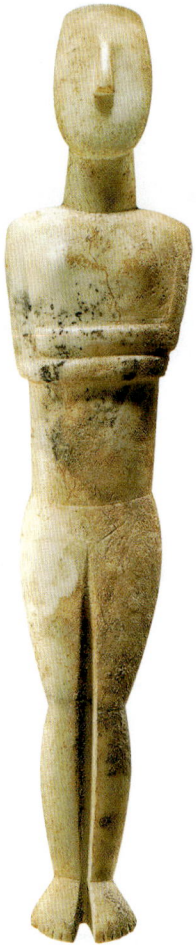

limestone and originally painted with red ocher. The carving is unique in that the woman holds a horn-shaped object that has thirteen short lines carved on it, which have led scholars to develop different opinions about the work. For example, the figure may represent a **shaman** and the horn could have been used for a ritual designed to ensure a successful hunt, or as a musical instrument. Other experts have suggested the horn may be a phallic symbol, emphasizing the woman's role for procreation. Further, as the number thirteen corresponds to the number of menstrual cycles a woman may have in a year, some scholars have speculated that the horn may symbolize a waning crescent moon, which, with the number of stripes, could be intended to represent a woman's monthly cycle.

On the Cycladic Islands, now part of modern-day Greece, a number of human figures, carved out of white marble, have been found, many of them at grave sites (**3.1.4**). Cycladic sculptures of females far outnumber those of males. Curiously, however, the female Cycladic figures look similar to their male counterparts, with barely noticeable breasts and only minimal anatomical detail. The figures usually have a long head and protruding nose; they are generic renderings of females, rather than individual portraits. Originally, these figures were painted in black, red, and blue to show some facial details, body ornamentation, and probably jewelry. Little is known about the Cycladic culture because it did not have a written language, but these expressive, almost geometric figures are some of the most intriguing in the history of art.

Other significant early works of art from the Mediterranean region come from Çatalhöyük, Turkey. Here, fragments of wall paintings remain from a large building complex that stood between *c.* 7000 and 5700 BCE. Inhabitants of the Çatalhöyük settlements lived in mud-brick homes, which they entered from the rooftops; there was no organized street system. The deceased were buried beneath the floors, and sometimes homes were demolished to create a higher base from which to build new ones. More than twelve layers of building have been discovered at the site.

While many paintings from Çatalhöyük depict humans and animals (often in hunting scenes), one intriguing but faint wall painting re-creates the design of the town (reproduced here in a watercolor copy for ease of reading), with rectangular houses closely aligned side by side (**3.1.5**). In the background is the double-peaked volcano, Hasan Da, which in reality is

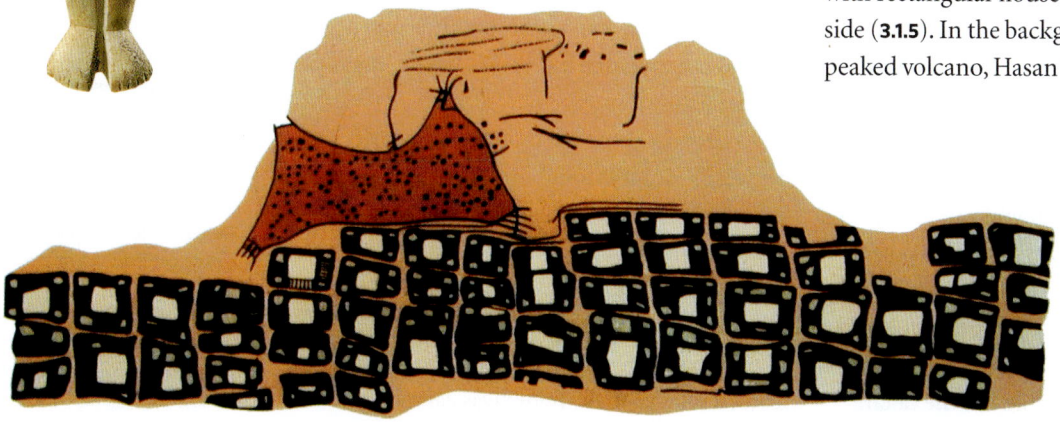

3.1.5 Landscape with erupting volcano, detail of watercolor copy of a wall painting from Level VII, Çatalhöyük, Turkey, *c.* 6150 BCE. Wall painting: Ankara Museum of Anatolian Civilizations, Turkey. Watercolor copy: Private collection

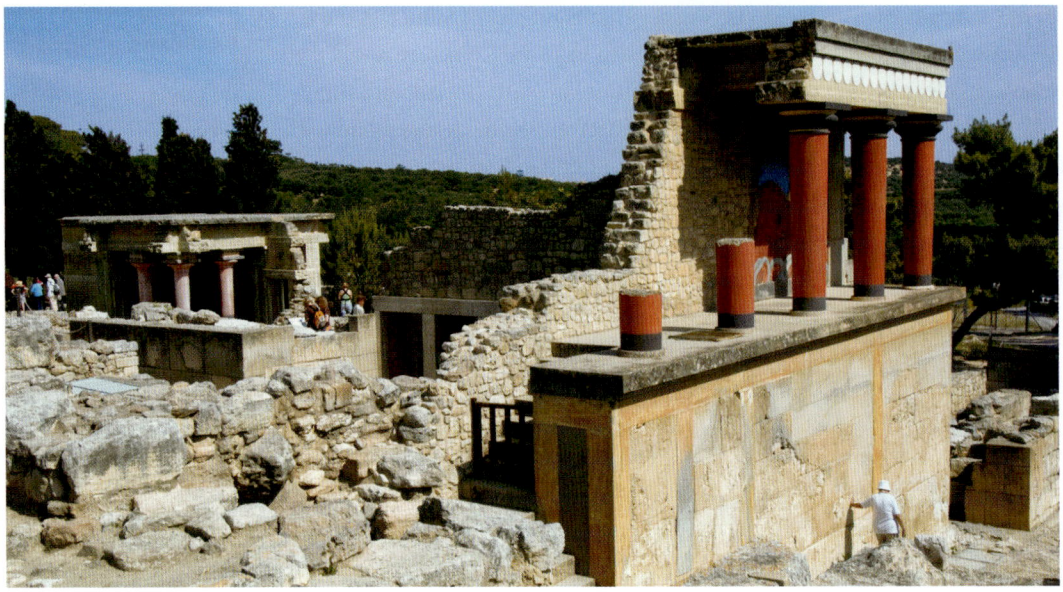

3.1.6 Ruins of Palace of Knossos, Crete, Greece, c. 1700–1400 BCE. From 1900, parts of the palace were reconstructed, as seen here

8 miles away. The volcano appears to be erupting; lava falls in droplets down the mountain, and smoke fills the sky. Scholars have not determined an exact volcanic eruption that could be the one referred to in this image: this makes it possibly the first "pure" landscape (a picture of a setting in its own right, without life and narrative) ever created in the history of mankind.

Just over 100 miles south of the Cyclades and dating from a little later in time, there is ample archaeological evidence of a sophisticated and complex civilization, the Minoan, on the island of Crete from about 2700 to about 1200 BCE. Minoan cities, with their powerful fleets and their location at the hub of the eastern Mediterranean, grew wealthy as centers of trade. Some of our written evidence of Minoan culture comes from the Greeks. According to their legend, King Minos was the stepfather of the Minotaur, half-man, half-bull, a man-eating creature trapped in a labyrinth. The powerful Minos required the Athenians to send seven young men and seven young women as tribute each year to satisfy the Minotaur's appetite.

The Minoans built palaces in the center of their cities, the largest being King Minos's Palace of Knossos (**3.1.6**). This complex—up to five stories high—was a maze of some 1,300 rooms, corridors, and courtyards. These spaces were used for governmental and ceremonial functions, as accommodation for the king's family and their servants, as large storerooms, and even as a theater. The palace complex was so full of twists and turns that it is easy to see how the Greeks developed a myth about the labyrinth.

The importance of bulls in Minoan culture can be seen from their inclusion in the Minotaur myth and in much of Minoan art. Several sculptures and **frescoes** with scenes of bulls were found throughout the Palace of Knossos, including the lively *Bull-Leapers* (**3.1.7**). In this scene, three young acrobats are jumping a spirited bull. The boy flips over the beast as a young woman on the left—lighter-skinned to identify her gender—prepares to take the next leap. The girl on the right has apparently just landed. The creature is depicted with great energy, yet the Cretans seem able to match it. Bull-leaping, boxing, and acrobatic scenes were common **subjects** in Minoan art, evidence of an athletic people; these activities may have been for pleasure, or for more ritualistic ceremonies.

Shaman: a priest or priestess regarded as having the ability to communicate directly with the spiritual world
Fresco: a technique in which the artist paints onto freshly applied plaster. From the Italian *fresco*, "fresh"
Subject: the person, object, or space depicted in a work of art

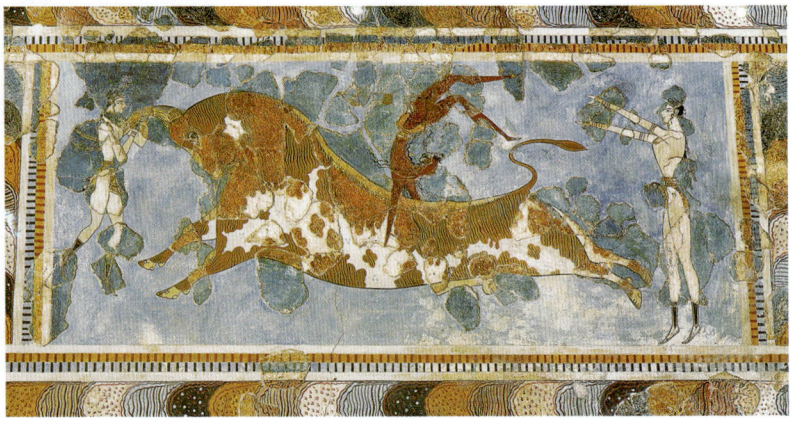

3.1.7 *Bull-Leapers*, from Palace of Knossos, Crete, Greece, c. 1450–1375 BCE. Archaeological Museum, Heraklion, Crete, Greece

Minoan civilization suffered a variety of upheavals, natural and man-made, from around 1500 BCE, when, as some believe, a volcanic eruption on the nearby island of Thera created a huge tidal wave that destroyed the Minoans' cities and fleets. Some decades later, Mycenaean invaders from mainland Greece overran Crete, taking over such palace sites as Knossos.

Mesopotamia: The Cradle of Civilization

Mesopotamia, from the Greek for "the land between the rivers" (a reference to the Tigris and Euphrates rivers), includes the regions of modern Iraq and portions of Syria, Turkey, and Iran. Ancient Mesopotamia is often called the "Cradle of Civilization," for it was here that urban centers first developed as early as 4000 BCE. The earliest forms of writing, using pictograms, also developed in Mesopotamia in the fourth millennium BCE. Here too, in the rich land of the Fertile Crescent, complex irrigation systems enabled people to produce plentiful crops. Mesopotamia was frequently conquered by rulers desiring the wealth of its farmland. Amongst the many cultures that battled for control of the region were the Sumerians, Akkadians, Assyrians, and Babylonians.

Sumerians

The Sumerian civilization was the first great power in Mesopotamia. By the third millennium BCE, under the Sumerians, a writing system evolved from pictograms: it was called cuneiform, and consisted of wedge-shaped symbols drawn with a reed "pen" in soft clay. The Sumerians also seem to have invented the wheel, which was probably first used to help potters make circular pots. The people of Mesopotamia worshiped many gods and goddesses (a practice known as **polytheism**) in temples or shrines located on huge ziggurats—stepped pyramid structures made of baked and unbaked mud bricks—which they constructed in the center of their communities.

Ur was an important city of Sumer, and the treasures found at its Royal Cemetery reveal the wealth of the Sumerian elite. Buried with the bodies were gold jewelry and daggers inlaid with **lapis lazuli**. Whether the dead were royalty or religious leaders is unknown, but the chariots, weapons, and musical instruments buried with them indicate their importance. Servants and soldiers were also interred with their leaders, perhaps to protect and serve them in the afterlife.

The artists of Sumer excelled in the art of inlaying ivory and shell in wood, as seen in the *Standard of Ur* found in the Royal Cemetery of Ur (**3.1.8a** and **b**). When it was first discovered, scholars thought it must have been carried on the end of a pole, like a standard, but there is no real evidence for this. The wooden box is only 8 in. high and decorated with inlaid pieces of shell, lapis lazuli, and red limestone. One side of the box shows war scenes (**3.1.8a**), while the other shows life during times of peace (**3.1.8b**). Each side is divided into three sections, known as **registers**. The bottom register of the war side shows chariots running over the bodies of the enemy. In the middle register, the box shows soldiers (from left to right) marching,

Polytheism: the worship of more than one god or goddess
Lapis lazuli: bright-blue semiprecious stone containing sodium aluminum silicate and sulphur
Register: one of two or more horizontal sections into which a space is divided in order to depict the episodes of a story

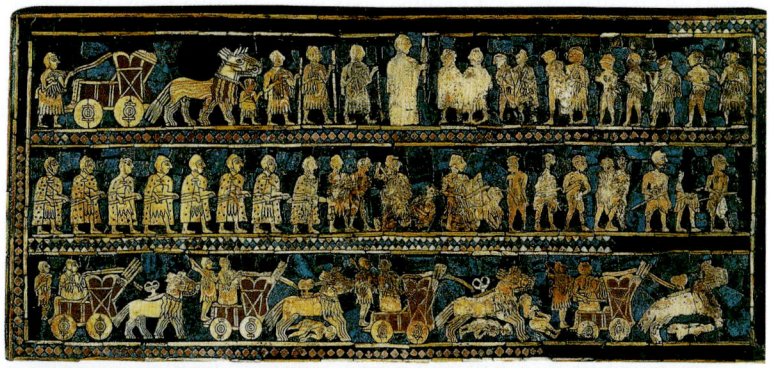

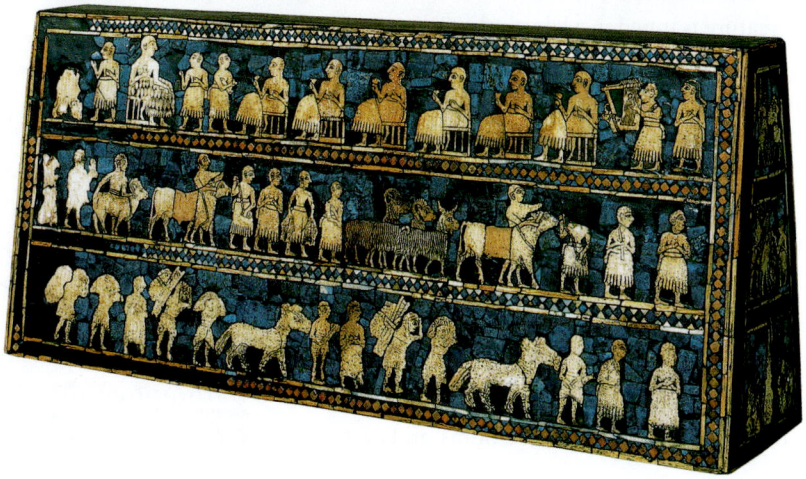

3.1.8a and **3.1.8b**
Standard of Ur, c. 2600–2400 BCE. (a: top) War and (b: bottom) Peace. Wood inlaid with shell, lapis lazuli, and red limestone, 7⅞ × 18½". British Museum, London, England

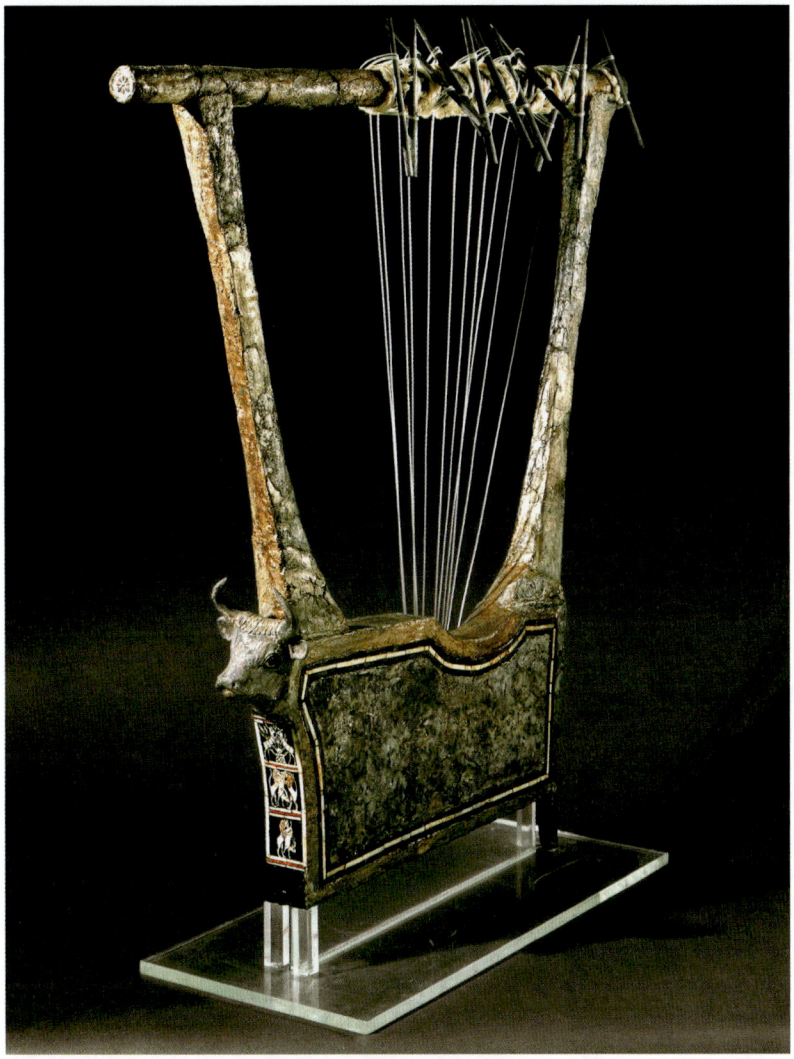

3.1.9 Sumerian bull lyre, c. 2550–2400 BCE. Wood, lapis lazuli, gold, silver, shell, bitumen, in modern wood support, 46 × 55". From the King's Grave, Royal Cemetery, Ur, Iraq. British Museum, London, England

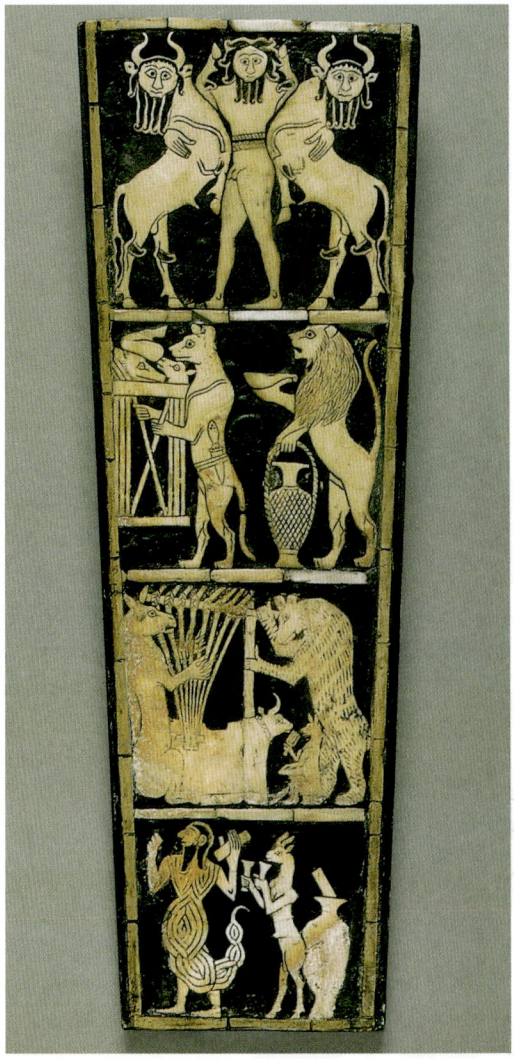

3.1.10 Inlaid panel from a Sumerian lyre's sound box, showing mythological figures, c. 2550–2400 BCE. Gold, silver, lapis lazuli, shell, bitumen, and wood, height 13". From the King's Grave, Royal Cemetery, Ur, Iraq. University of Pennsylvania Museum of Archaeology and Anthropology, Philadelphia

shaming their enemies by stripping them of their clothing, and forcing them to continue walking. In the center of the top register is the ruler. His larger size indicates his importance, a convention known as **hierarchical scale**. His status is reinforced by the fact that all the surrounding people are facing him. He has stepped out of his chariot while prisoners are brought before him. On the peace side, animals, fish, and other foods are brought to a banquet where seated figures drink while a musician playing a lyre entertains them. The standard is a fine example of narrative art and a source of evidence about what food the Sumerians ate, their clothing and weapons, their musical instruments, and their success in war.

Hierarchical scale: the use of size to denote the relative importance of subjects in an artwork

Three lyres, stringed instruments similar to a harp, were found amongst the magnificent objects in the Royal Cemetery of Ur. Lyres were popular musical instruments in ancient Sumer, but the example in Figure **3.1.9** is more elaborate than most. As it was found in a grave, it seems to have been intended as a suitable burial offering for a powerful person. Although the body of the instrument disintegrated long ago, the wooden section of the lyre has been reconstructed to give an idea of its appearance. The original panels on the sound box of another of the lyres, made of lapis lazuli and shell, have survived (**3.1.10**). They reveal that the lyre, which played music we can no longer hear, was also covered in symbols that we now do not entirely understand. The panels

Relief: a sculpture that projects from a flat surface

show animals engaged in such human activities as dancing, walking on two legs, and bringing instruments and drinks to a ceremony, probably much like the ones in which this lyre was used. The fusion of humans and beasts, such as the scorpion man below and the human-headed bulls above, suggests a sacred event, perhaps a marriage or a funeral procession. Some scholars, however, suggest that the scenes decorating the lyre show activities in the supernatural realm of the dead.

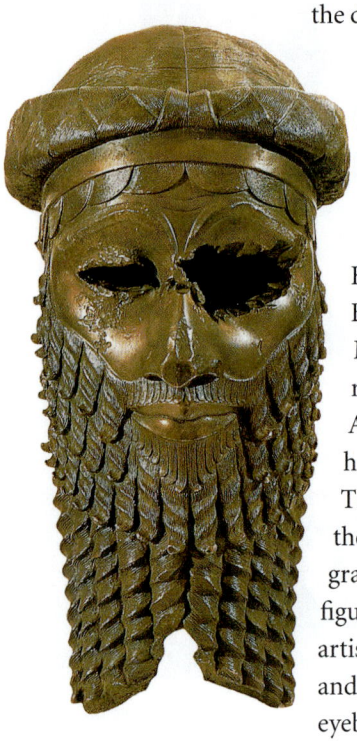

3.1.11 Head of an Akkadian ruler, *c.* 2300–2200 BCE. Bronze, height 15". National Museum of Iraq, Baghdad

Akkadians

The next Mesopotamian empire was founded by the Akkadian king Sargon, who ruled between *c.* 2334 and 2279 BCE. He conquered the Sumerian city-states. Before King Sargon, most rulers of Mesopotamia were believed to be merely representatives of the gods on Earth. The Akkadian rulers who followed Sargon, however, elevated themselves to divine status. The bronze, lifesized Akkadian Head (**3.1.11**) is the portrait of a great king, probably Sargon's grandson Naram-Sin (*c.* 2254–2218 BCE). The figure's expression is one of proud majesty. The artist paid particular attention to the texture and patterning of the hair on the ruler's beard, eyebrows, and head. The eye sockets have been damaged from violent gouging, either to remove the materials (probably shells or lapis lazuli) used to make the eyes, or to make the figure's presence less powerful. The head was originally discovered in Nineveh in northern Iraq, and was one of the many objects missing after the looting of the National Museum of Iraq in Baghdad in 2003 during the US invasion of Iraq. More than 15,000 artifacts were stolen, of which fewer than half have been recovered—this Akkadian head being one of them.

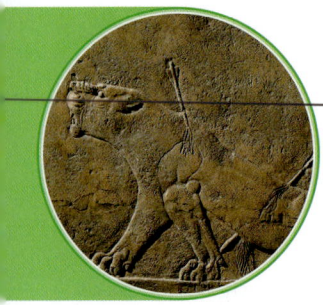

The palace of the Assyrian king Ashurbanipal was decorated with spectacularly skilled relief carvings of lion hunts: see **2.4.3, p. 244**

Assyrians

The Assyrians, who had intermittently enjoyed considerable power in the second millennium BCE, ruled much of Mesopotamia during the Neo-Assyrian period (883–612 BCE). The first great Assyrian king, Ashurnasirpal II (who ruled between 883 and 859 BCE), used slave labor to build the large city of Nimrud (near modern Mosul, Iraq), which became the capital of Assyria.

Ashurnasirpal II's grand palace was covered with **relief** sculptures of battles, hunting scenes, and religious rituals. An accompanying inscription refers to guardian figures (called *lamassu*) at gateways and entrances throughout the palace: "Beasts of the mountains and the seas, which I had fashioned out of white limestone and alabaster, I had set up in its gates. I made it [the palace] fittingly imposing."

These figures were meant to show the fearsome power of the Assyrian ruler and the authority given to him by the gods (**3.1.12**). Almost twice as tall as a human, this lamassu combines the head of a man with the body

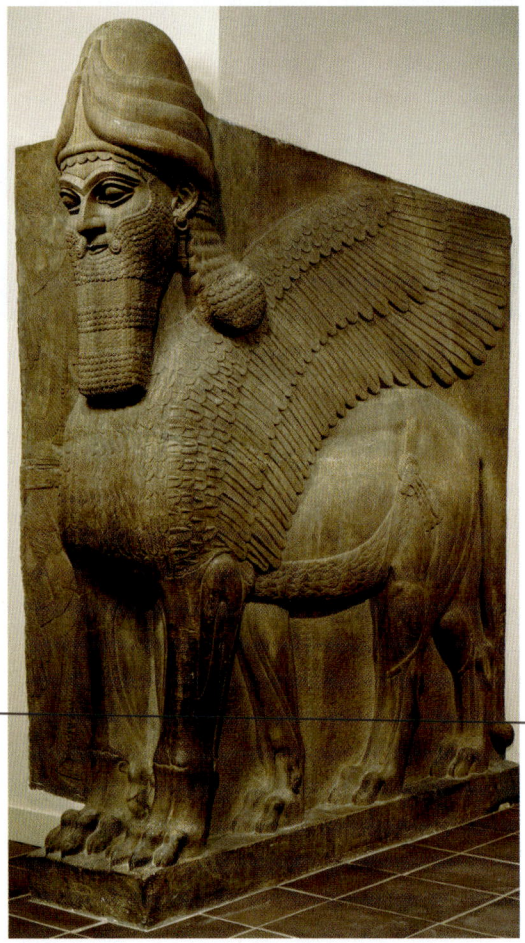

3.1.12 Human-headed winged lion (*lamassu*) from gateway in Ashurnasirpal II's palace in Nimrud, Mesopotamia, Neo-Assyrian, 883–859 BCE. Alabaster (gypsum), height 10'3½". Metropolitan Museum of Art, New York

and strength of a lion and the wings and all-seeing eyes of an eagle. The horned cap signifies divinity, representing the gods' support and protection of the rulers of Assyria. Lamassu often have five legs, so they appear to be standing still when viewed from the front and striding forward when seen from the side. The lion is an animal that is often associated with kingship, and at this time in this civilization, only Assyrian kings were considered powerful enough to protect the people from the lions that roamed the areas outside the cities, and only kings were allowed to hunt the creatures. Some of the reliefs decorating Ashurnasirpal II's palace show the king hunting lions.

Babylonians

In the late seventh century BCE the Babylonians defeated the Assyrians and re-emerged as a powerful force in Mesopotamia. The ruler Nebuchadnezzar II (605–562 BCE) built a grand palace famous for its Hanging Gardens. Around the city, he built fortified walls with eight gateways. The dramatic Ishtar Gate was the main entrance to the streets and temples of Babylon (**3.1.13**). This enormous ceremonial entrance was actually two arched gates, the shorter of which (shown here) stood 47 ft. high. Golden reliefs of animals that symbolize Babylonian gods project out from a background of blue glazed bricks.

A Processional Way ran through the Ishtar Gate, leading to the ziggurat on the south side of the city, which some believe to be the inspiration for the Old Testament story of the Tower of Babel. Walls on either side of the Processional Way were covered with 120 glazed reliefs of lions (60 on each side), symbols of the goddess Ishtar.

The Ishtar Gate was taken to Germany in pieces in the early twentieth century and is now reconstructed at the Pergamon Museum in Berlin. In the same museum, next to the Gate, is a wall from the entrance to Nebuchadnezzar's throne room, which shows **stylized** palm trees above lions that are similar to those that covered the walls of the Processional Way.

Stylized: art that represents objects in an exaggerated way to emphasize certain aspects of the object

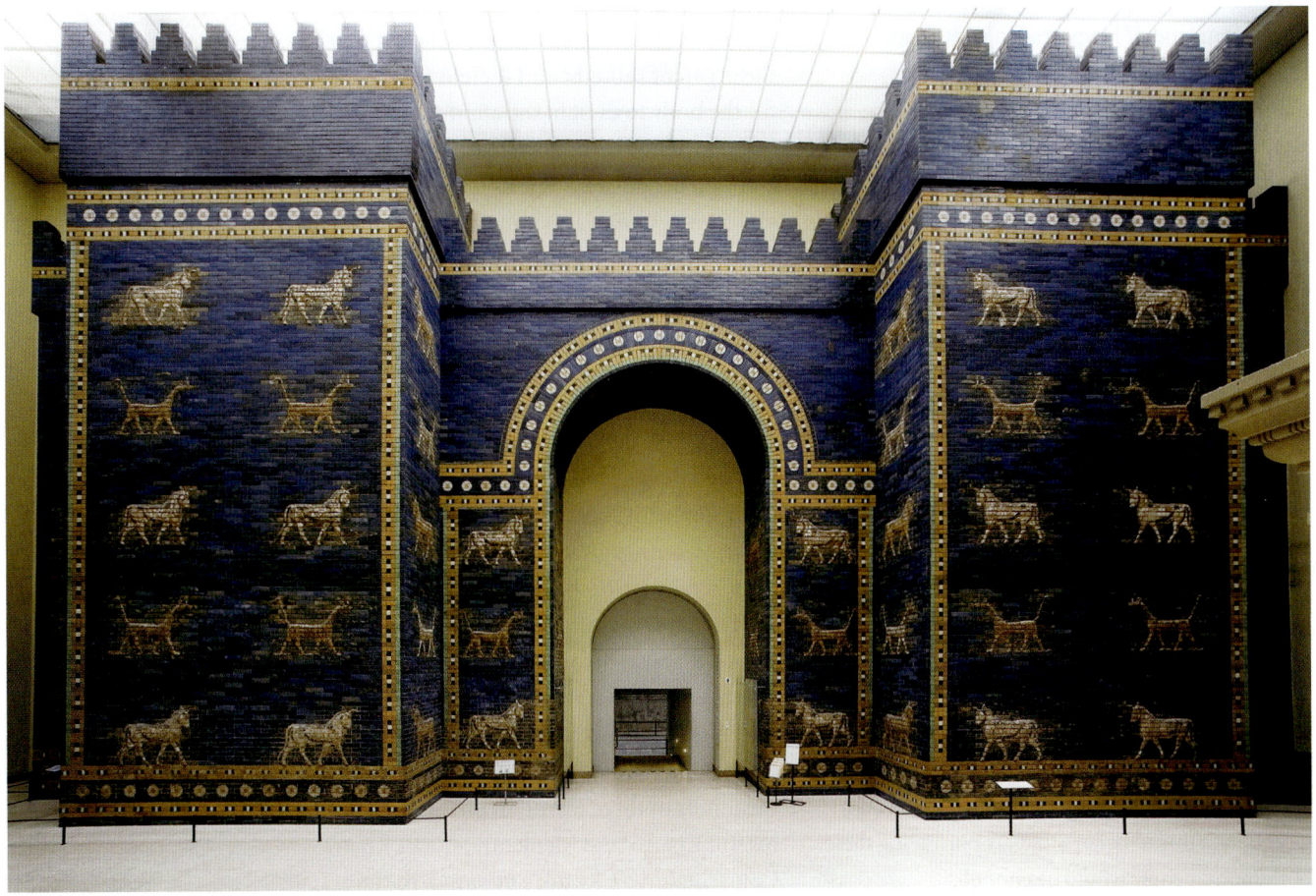

3.1.13 Ishtar Gate from Babylon (Iraq), reign of Nebuchadnezzar II (602–562 BCE). Colored glazed terra-cotta tiles, 48'4" × 51'6" × 14'3¾". Vorderasiatisches Museum, Staatliche Museen, Berlin, Germany

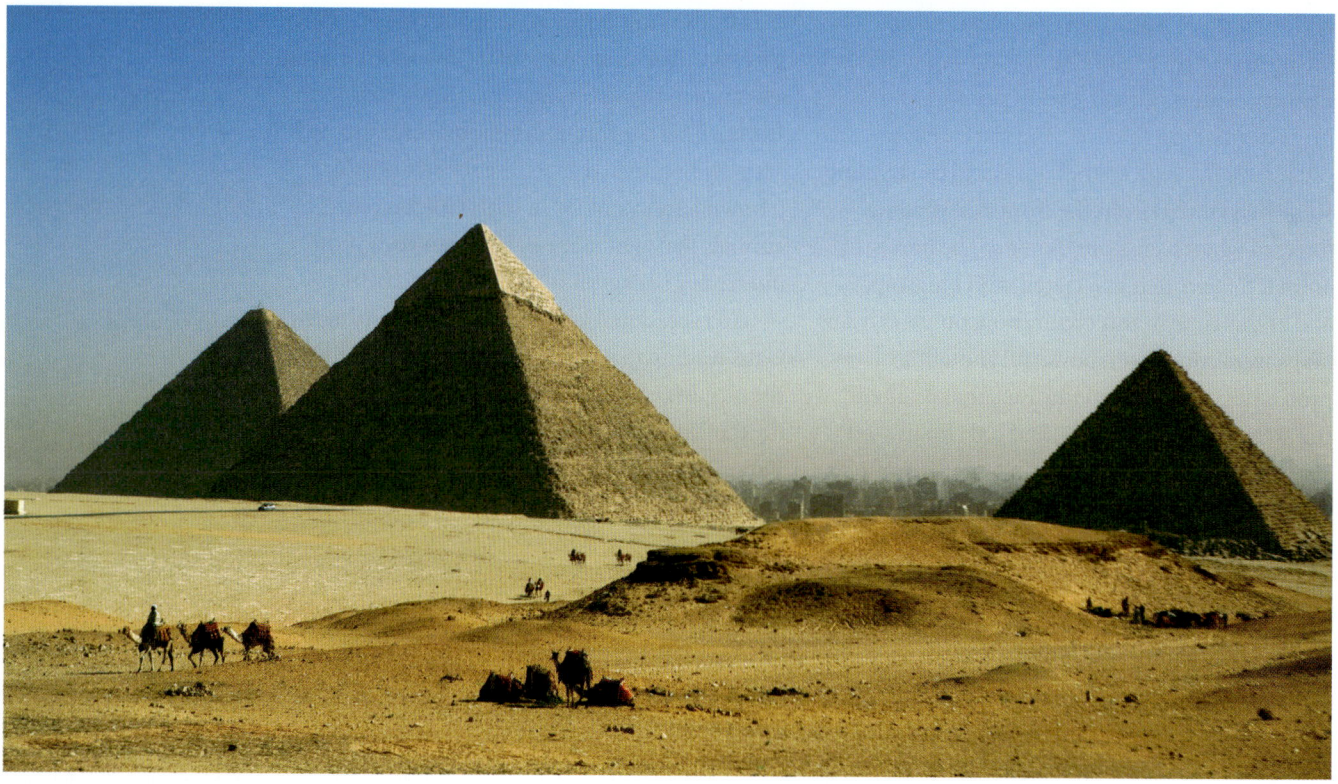

3.1.14 Pyramids at Giza, Egypt: from left to right, the pyramids of Khufu (*c.* 2580–2560 BCE), Khafre (*c.* 2570 BCE), and Menkaure (*c.* 2510 BCE)

Ancient Egypt

At the time of the pharaohs, or Egyptian kings, the African land of Egypt traded with peoples throughout the Mediterranean, and thus many of the ideas and techniques invented by Egyptian artists were taken up by Mediterranean civilizations. Indeed, some thousands of years after they were made, the ancient Egyptians' extraordinary artistic and architectural achievements continue to be a source of wonder and astonishment worldwide.

It is perhaps appropriate that our fascination with Egyptian art should be so long-lasting when so much of early Egyptian culture focused on eternity and the afterlife. The Egyptians believed that their pharaohs ruled with the authority of gods, and as a result, the Egyptian people took great care to ensure that, when a pharaoh died, his needs in the afterlife—where it was believed a person would require everything he or she had needed when living—would be met. So in the pharaohs' tombs were buried furniture, weapons, jewelry, and food. Family and servants were even killed to accompany the dead pharaohs, although as time went on the Egyptians came to believe that art portraying these objects and people would be enough.

When a pharaoh died, in order to preserve his body for its afterlife, it was mummified, a process that took several months. The heart was left inside the body; Egyptians believed it to be the organ of thought and therefore necessary for the body to exist in the afterlife. The brain was deemed to be of no value and was removed through the nostrils. The liver, lungs, intestines, and stomach were also removed, and preserved in containers called canopic jars (**3.1.16**; see Box: Hieroglyphs, p. 376). The body was then soaked in a salt preservative called natron (a hydrated carbonate of sodium, found on some lake borders) for forty days and was finally wrapped in linen. An elaborate funerary mask was placed upon the face of the pharaoh, and he was buried inside layers of **sarcophagi**. These complex burials were meant to protect the treasure and life force, or ***ka***, of the buried.

The great investment of time, labor, and wealth that was involved in creating the pyramids demonstrates further the importance the Egyptians placed on the afterlife. The three pyramids at Giza (**3.1.14**) were built to house the tombs of three Egyptian pharaohs: Khufu, his son Khafre, and Menkaure, son of Khafre. Construction on Khufu's pyramid, the largest

Sarcophagus (plural **sarcophagi**): a coffin (usually made of stone or baked clay)
Ka: in Egyptian belief, the spirit of a person that leaves the body upon death and travels to the afterlife

of the three at 481 ft. high and 750 ft. per side, began about 2551 BCE, and all three were completed over three generations. The sides of each pyramid are precisely the same length and all are placed precisely at the **cardinal points**, revealing the Egyptians' mastery of engineering and mathematics.

The pyramids were built of carefully stacked stones clad in white limestone. The pyramid of Khufu contains about 2,300,000 blocks of stone that have been calculated to weigh on average 2.5 tons. The methods used by the Egyptians to move such massive stones are still debated today, although scholars have suggested that they probably used the Nile for transportation, then either dragged the stones across the sand or rolled them over a series of logs. Once the stones made it to the site, tumbling, systems of levers, and ramps were likely used.

Connected to Khafre's pyramid through an underground walkway is Khafre's temple, next to which is a colossal stone sculpture of a Sphinx, a mythical creature with the body of a lion and the head of a human ruler (see Images Related to 3.1, p. 389). As in Assyrian culture, the image of the lion was in part an expression of royal power, but for the Egyptians it was also a symbol of the sun god, Re, who was believed to carry away the dead in his boat to their afterlife. One theory is that the pyramids themselves may also have been seen to represent Re; for when the sun could be seen at the apex of a pyramid, the pyramid glistened and reflected the light of the sun. According to this theory, the corners of the pyramid extended the rays of the sun, and thus symbolically represented a ladder for the pharaoh to ascend to the afterlife. The funerary temples of these three pharaohs were placed on the east side of the pyramids, to symbolize that, just as the sun rises again in the east, they would be reborn into the afterlife.

The image **3.1.15** shows the statue of the pharaoh Khafre, which was found in the pharaoh's temple. When Khafre died, his body was taken to his temple and mummified (see p. 374) before being taken to his pyramid. In this statue, Khafre and the chair in which he sits have been carved from a single block of hard stone called diorite. He seems to sit stiffly, as if attached to his throne. Egyptian sculptures portrayed people with gracefully proportioned bodies, but they only subtly suggested movement, in this case by showing one hand clenched in a fist. To signify the pharaoh's importance, the powerful sky god Horus, symbolized as a falcon, perches on the throne behind his head. In Egyptian belief, Khafre's statue provides a place for his ka to rest during the afterlife. In fact, in Egyptian writing, "sculptor" translates as "he who keeps alive." The Egyptians invented a system of writing using **hieroglyphs** and often carved or painted them on their artworks. Egyptian hieroglyphs were gradually deciphered after the finding of the Rosetta Stone in 1799 (see Box: Hieroglyphs, p. 376). This single discovery made possible a much greater understanding and appreciation of the art and culture of Egypt.

Cardinal points: North, South, East, and West
Hieroglyph: written language involving sacred characters that may be pictures as well as letters or signifiers of sounds

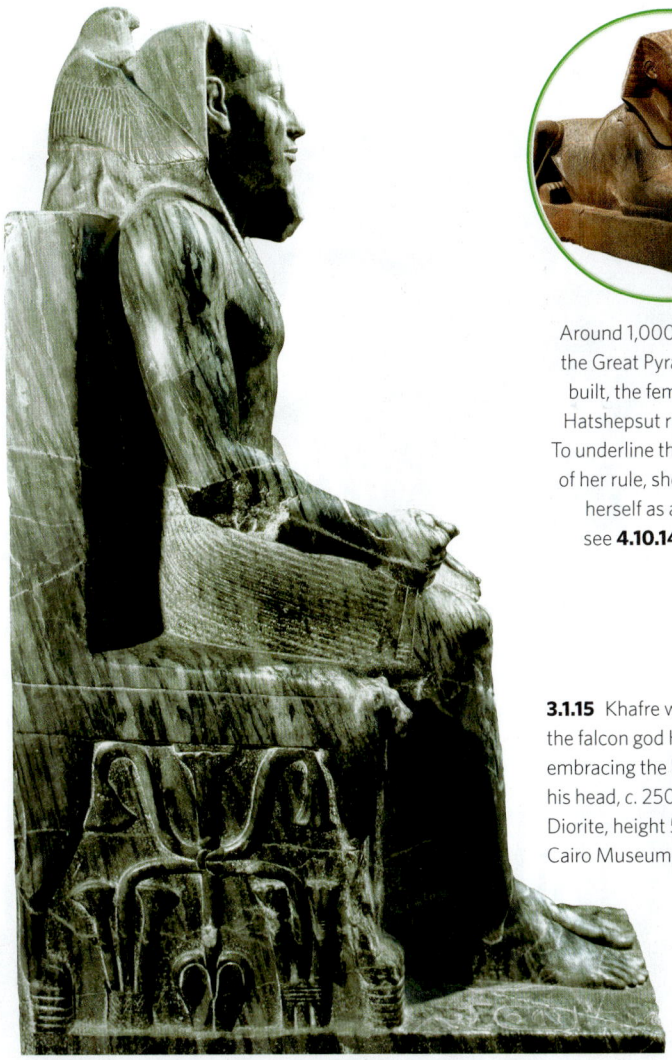

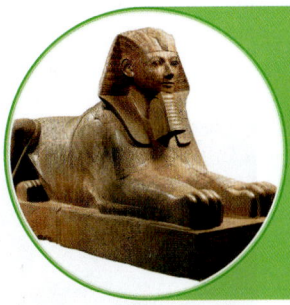

Around 1,000 years after the Great Pyramids were built, the female leader Hatshepsut ruled Egypt. To underline the legitimacy of her rule, she presented herself as a sphinx: see **4.10.14, p. 689**

3.1.15 Khafre with the falcon god Horus embracing the back of his head, *c.* 2500 BCE. Diorite, height 5'6⅛". Cairo Museum, Egypt

Hieroglyphs

We can understand Egyptian art largely because we can translate hieroglyphs, the written language of the ancient Egyptians. This was made possible in 1799 through the discovery of the Rosetta Stone, which was found by the French army led by Napoleon during the course of his invasion of Egypt. The lettering on the stone is dated to 196 BCE and repeats the decrees of Ptolemy V, the Greek ruler of Egypt, in three separate forms of writing. Hieroglyphic and Demotic were different written forms of the Egyptian spoken language; Greek was familiar to many scholars and was the key to deciphering the other two. Hieroglyphs are often images of recognizable objects, but the image can represent the object itself, an idea, or even just a sound associated with that object. In 1822 Frenchman Jean-François Champollion was finally able to claim that, thanks to studying the Rosetta Stone, he understood the meaning of the complex hieroglyphic writing of the ancient Egyptians.

We know quite a bit about the burial practices of the Egyptians from the hieroglyphs written on the objects buried with the dead. Canopic jars like the ones shown here (**3.1.16**), each only 12 in. high, were designed so that each would hold an organ of the deceased. The hieroglyphic inscription painted down the vertical band on the front of each canopic jar identifies the figure it portrays and the organ it was meant to protect. Each jar represents one of the sons of Horus, who protects the organ contained within: the baboon-faced Hapy guards the lungs, the jackal-headed Duamutef guards the stomach, the falcon-headed Qebhsenuef guards the intestines, and the human-looking Imsety guards the liver.

3.1.16 Painted wooden canopic jars, *c.* 700 BCE (25th Dynasty). Painted sycamore fig wood, height 12¼". British Museum, London, England

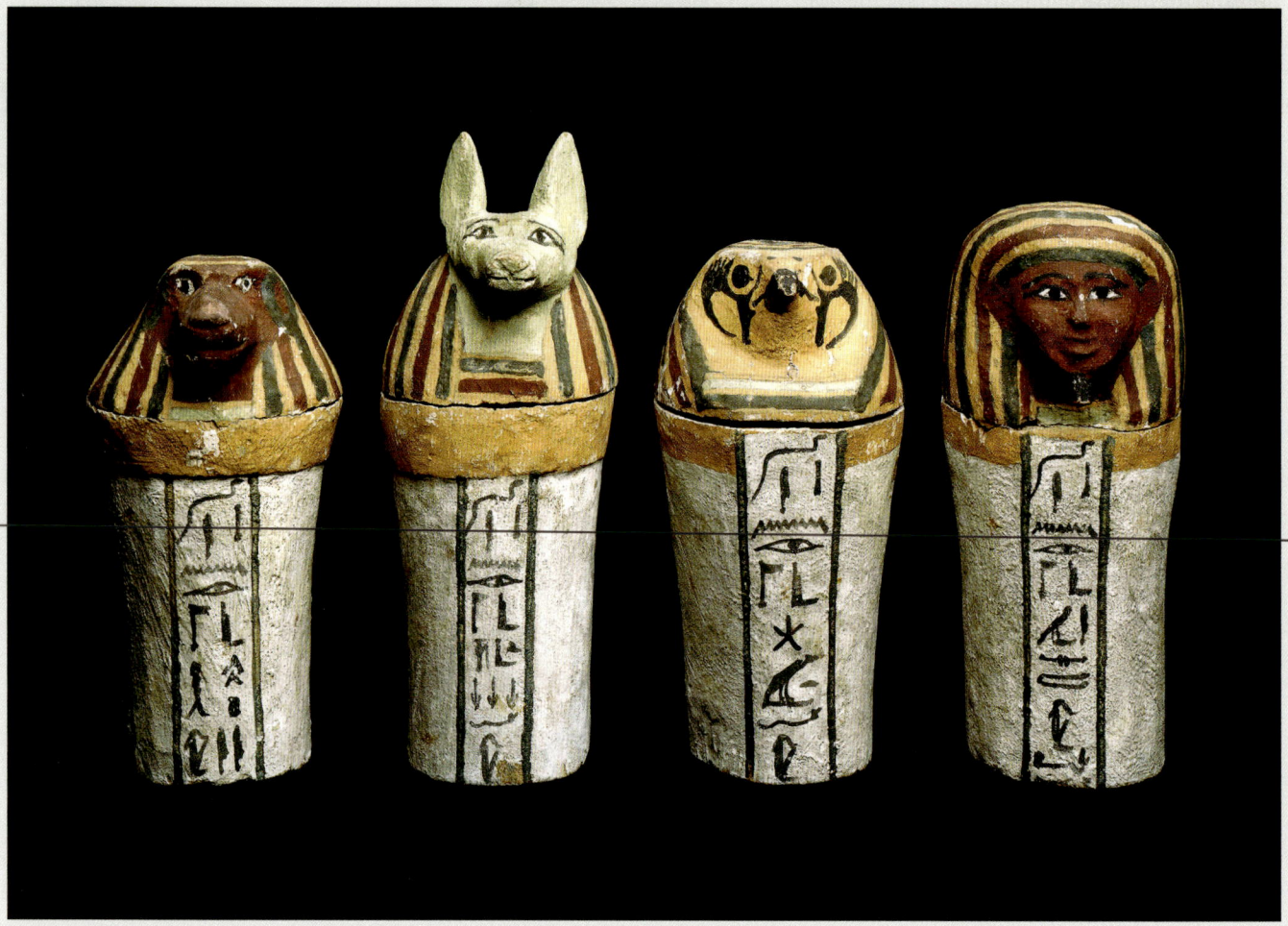

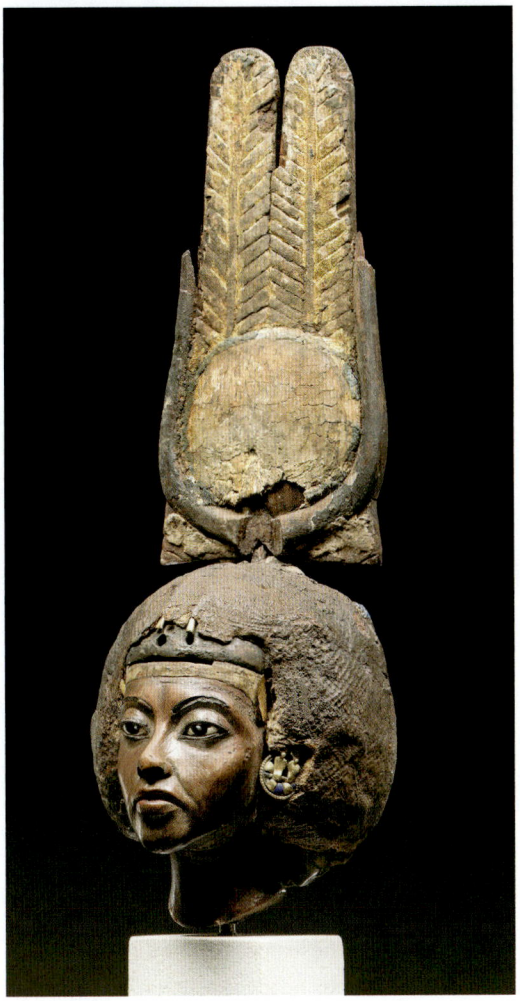

3.1.17 *Queen Tiye of Egypt portrait head, c.* 1355 BCE, (18th Dynasty), from Medinet el-Gurob, Egypt. Yew wood, ebony, gold, silver, lapis lazuli, textiles, faience. Head 4 × 3 × 3¼", base 4 × 4¾ × 4¾". Aegyptisches Museum, Staatliche Museen, Berlin, Germany

Portraits of rulers were common in ancient Egypt, as is exemplified by this portrait of Queen Tiye (**3.1.17**), the grandmother of the now-famous pharaoh King Tutankhamun. The portrait head is extraordinarily well preserved, considering it was made out of wood thousands of years ago. Its preservation is due to the fact that it was found buried underground in Gurob, and protected by the dry Egyptian desert. The portrait was made when Tiye was wife to the pharaoh Amenhotep III; it originally had a gold crown, the remnants of which still cover the queen's forehead. One of her gold-and-blue earrings is visible in her left ear. When her husband died, Tiye's son Akhenaten became pharaoh, and she was one of his main advisors.

Akhenaten's rule was significant in that he introduced worship centered on Aten, the disk of the sun. Akhenaten formally **deified** his mother, and several additions were made to this sculpture. The earlier gold crown was covered with a finely woven linen cap and decorated with blue **faience** beads. The added tall headdress with a gold disk framed by horns, along with two long gold feathers, also signified her new status as a goddess. The inclusion of the disk, a symbol of Re, is significant because Tiye's son had rejected the polytheism of the pharaohs who ruled before him. Akhenaten ruled for 17 years; his son Tutankhamun ruled as a child shortly after his father's death, and polytheism was restored. In 1922, the revelation of the extraordinary riches hidden within the tomb of Tutankhamun fueled renewed interest in the ancient dynastic culture (see Perspectives on Art Box: The Golden Mask of King Tutankhamun, p. 378).

Paintings made during the time of the ancient Egyptians are rich in details that tell us about the way people lived. Wealthy people filled their tombs with paintings showing what they wished to take with them into the afterlife. The image in **3.1.18** is from the tomb-chapel of Nebamun, a "scribe and grain accountant in the granary of divine offerings" in the Temple

Deify: to worship and make into a god or goddess
Faience: quartz or sand ground and heated to create a shiny, glasslike material

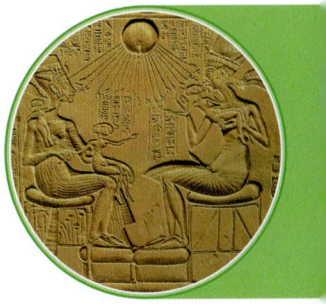

The rays of the sun god Aten shine down on pharaoh Akhenaten and his family, who are shown with very elongated heads and bodies: a style used during the Amarna period (late 18th Dynasty): see **4.6.6, p. 632**

3.1.18 Fowling scene, from the tomb of Nebamun, Thebes, Egypt, 18th Dynasty, *c.* 1350 BCE. Painted plaster, 38⅝ × 8¾". British Museum, London, England

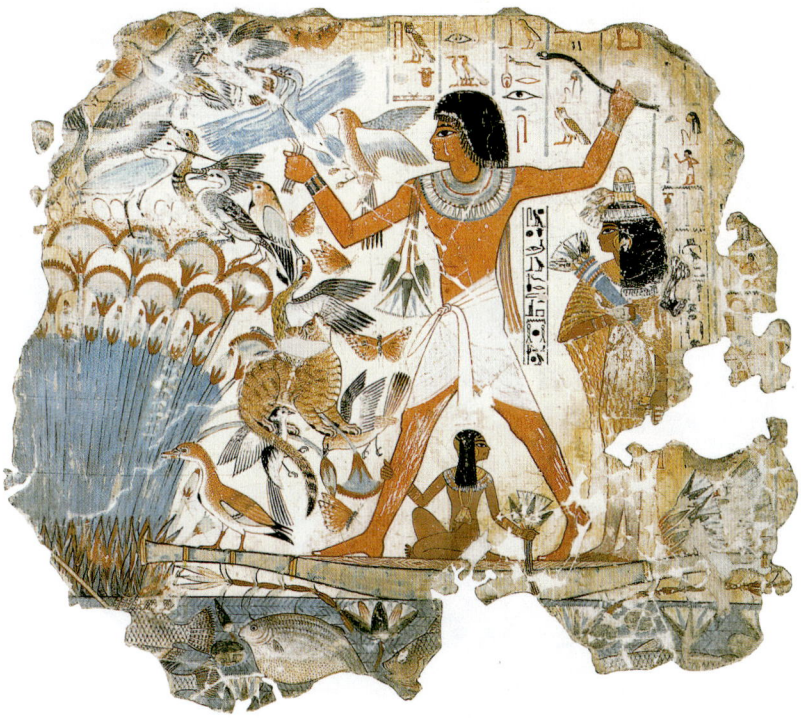

Perspectives On Art: Zahi Hawass
The Golden Mask of King Tutankhamun

3.1.19 Funerary mask of Tutankhamun, reign of Tutankhamun (1333–1323 BCE). Solid gold, semiprecious stones, quartz, and vitreous paste, height 21¼". Cairo Museum, Egypt

Zahi Hawass is an Egyptian archaeologist and was formerly Secretary General of the Supreme Council of Antiquities. Amongst his responsibilities was the care of the fabulous treasures of King Tutankhamun, discovered by the English archaeologist Howard Carter in 1922. Dr. Hawass is one of the few people to have studied the famous mask of the king up close. Here he describes how the mask was made.

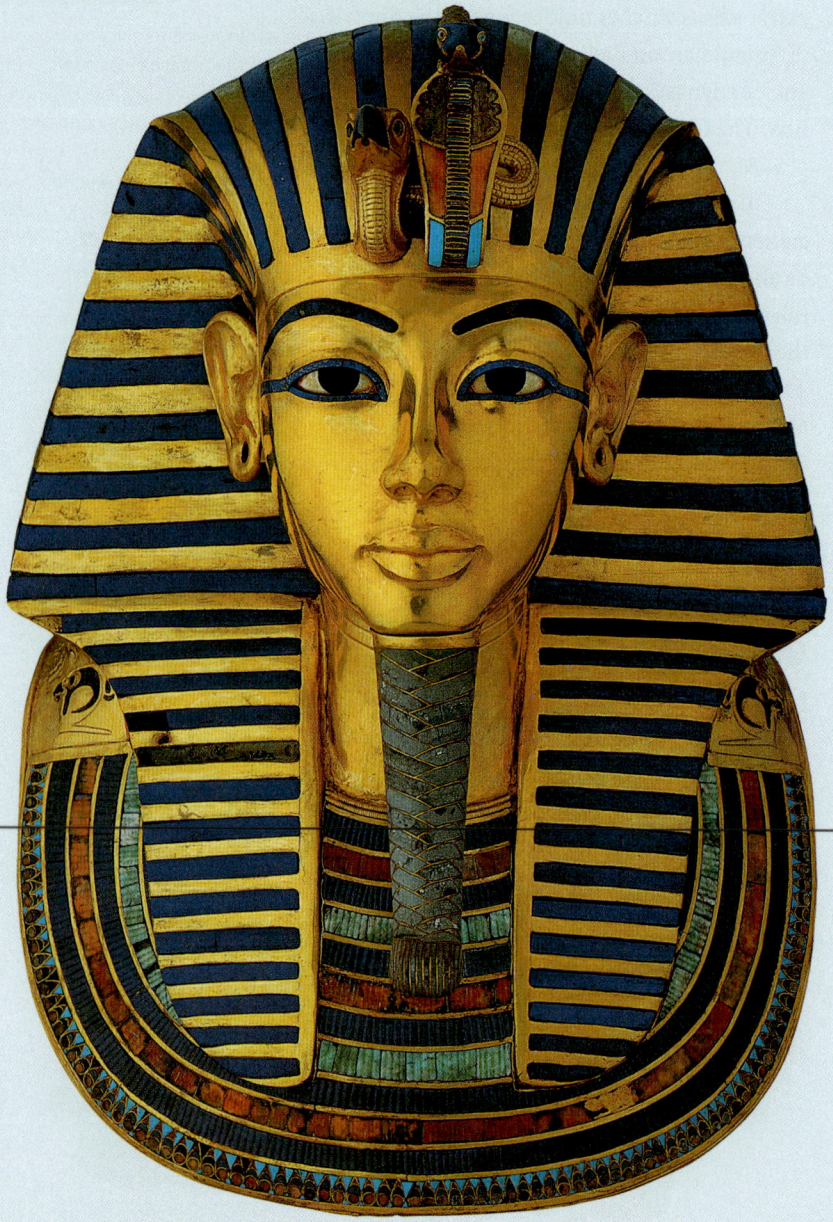

Whenever a television program wants to interview me about the golden king, I go directly to the mask (**3.1.19**). While the film crew is setting up the cameras, I have a chance to look again at the mask and I always discover something new. Each time, its beauty makes my heart tremble.

This spectacular mask represents an idealized portrait of the king. Intrinsically beautiful owing to the precious materials and masterful workmanship that went into its creation, it was also an essential item of the royal burial equipment, serving as an image that the soul could enter and occupy during the afterlife if something happened to the body.

The artisans who crafted this masterpiece began by hammering together two thick sheets of gold, thought by the ancient Egyptians to echo the flesh of the gods. They then shaped this metal into the likeness of the king wearing the striped nemes headcloth, using inlays of semiprecious stones and colored glass to add color and detail. The whites of the eyes were inlaid with quartz, and obsidian was used for the pupils. Red paint was lightly brushed into the corners of the eyes, subtly increasing their realism.

The vulture and cobra adorning the king's brow, images of the protective goddesses of Upper and Lower Egypt respectively, were made of solid gold with inlays of lapis lazuli, carnelian, faience, and glass. The long curled beard on the king's chin, emblematic of divinity, is made of blue glass laid into a golden framework.

On the shoulders and the back of the mask is a magical text that refers to the different parts of the body and mask, and their connection to particular gods or goddesses. This served to protect the king's body and render it functional for the afterlife.

Twisted perspective (also known as **composite view**): a representation of a figure, part in profile and part frontally

of Amun-Re at Karnak. The hieroglyphic writing (see Box: Hieroglyphs, p. 376) on the right identifies him and tells us that he enjoyed hunting. Nebamun is depicted hunting several species of birds; a cat holding birds in its mouth is shown underneath his right elbow. The artist included an Egyptian boat and the rich, lush growth of the reed-like papyrus plant. This scene highlights the importance of the River Nile to the Egyptians, and how the flooding of the Nile symbolized a cycle of regeneration and new life each year, just as Egyptians believed that after death they would be reborn. The artist depicted the figures in hierarchical scale, that is, in proportion to their importance: Nebamun is shown the largest, his wife is smaller, and their daughter is the smallest of all. Nebamun's legs are shown in profile while his torso is shown frontally, and although his face is in profile, his eye looks straight at the viewer. This method of depicting figures is known as **twisted perspective**, also called **composite view**.

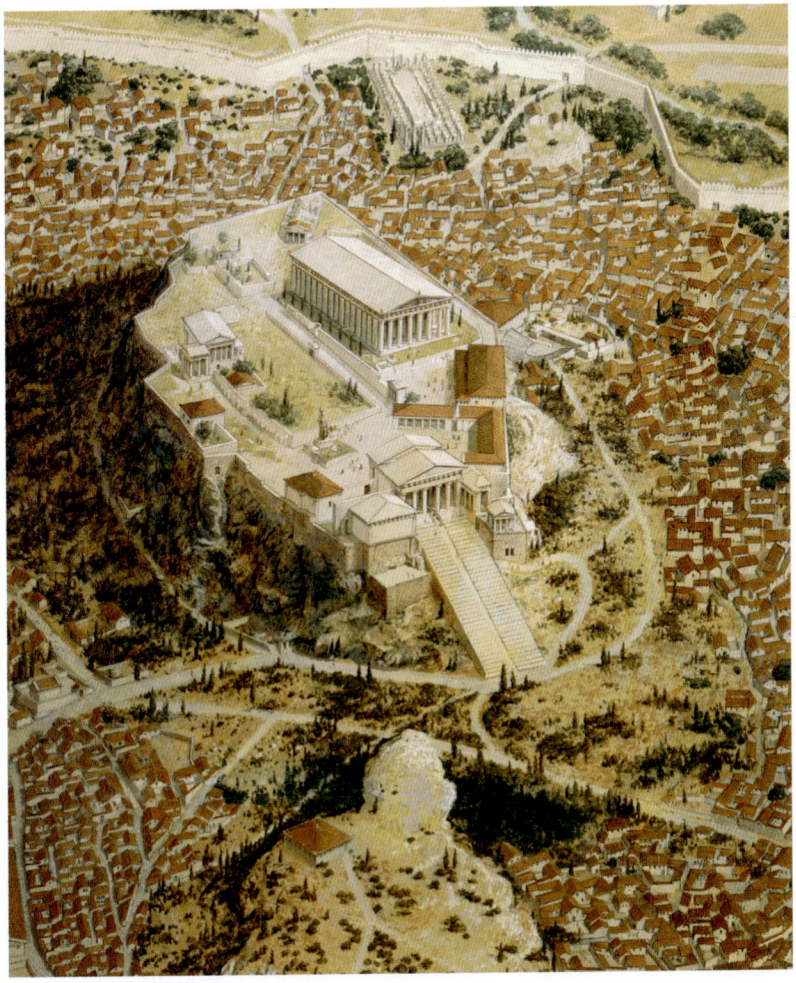

3.1.20 Reconstruction view of the Acropolis, Athens, Greece, at the beginning of the 4th century BCE

Art of Ancient Greece

Man is the measure of all things.

(Protagoras, Greek philosopher)

The Greeks, like the civilizations that came before them, worshiped gods. But, as the quote from Protagoras indicates, they also valued humanity. Although their gods were portrayed as idealized and beautiful beings, they looked like humans and had some human weaknesses. The emphasis on the individual led the Greeks to practice democracy (the word means rule by the *demos*, or people), although their society did not give equal rights to women or slaves. Their great advances in philosophy, mathematics, and the sciences continue to influence our thinking up to the present day.

Athleticism was important in Greek culture and the Greeks held sporting contests, the origins of the modern Olympic Games, at which individuals competed for glory and money. Sculptures of men were predominantly of the nude body, shown with ideal proportions. For the Greeks, the idealized human form represented high intellectual and moral goals. Indeed, Greek architecture was based on mathematical systems of proportion similar to those applied to the human form. Greek pride in their own physical and intellectual achievements is evident in the art they produced.

Every large city in Greece had its own government and was protected by its own god. Each had an acropolis, a complex of buildings on the highest point in the city that was both a fortress and a religious center, dedicated to the city's patron deity. The best-known acropolis is in Athens, and is dedicated to Athena, the goddess of war, wisdom, and the arts (**3.1.20**). According to Greek mythology—stories of the gods—the city was won by the goddess in a competition with Poseidon, god of the sea. Legend says that the goddess grew an olive tree, giving Athenians a source of wealth and defeating Poseidon, who had created a spring by striking the earth with his trident.

The original temple complex to Athena on the acropolis was burned by the Persian army in 480/479 BCE, less than a decade after it

Classical Architectural Orders

The Greeks developed three types of designs, called **architectural orders**, for their temples (**3.1.21**). Elements of Greek temple design have been used in government buildings throughout the United States, particularly in state capitols and in Washington, D.C. See if you can recognize the architectural order used on **3.1.34**, or **2.5.26**, and **3.6.14a**, or on buildings you see in person. The Doric and Ionic orders were first used as early as the sixth century BCE. The Parthenon is unusual in that it combines the two: its exterior columns and **frieze** are Doric, while the inner frieze (as viewed from the outside) is Ionic. The reason for this is debated, but it is likely that the blending of two styles popular in different parts of Greece marked a unity between different Greek cities. The Corinthian order was invented toward the end of the fifth century BCE. It was used for very few Greek buildings, but was widely applied by the Romans. The easiest way to recognize which order was used in a building is to look at the columns, and more specifically the **capitals**. Ionic and Corinthian columns both have a more decorative and slender quality than the bolder, more masculine Doric order. The Doric column has the least amount of ornamental detail. The Ionic column has the most noticeable fluting (vertical grooves) on the **shaft** and a volute (inverted scroll) on the capital. The Corinthian column is the most ornate, with layers of acanthus leaves decorating the capital. The **entablatures** of the three architectural orders are also quite distinct. The Doric frieze is divided by triglyphs (a kind of architectural decoration so named because it always has three grooves) that alternate with **metopes** (panels often containing relief sculpture). The Ionic and Corinthian friezes have relief sculpture along the entire frieze, and do not contain metopes or triglyphs.

Architectural order: a style of designing columns and related parts of a Greek or Roman building
Frieze: the strip that goes around the top of a building, often filled with sculptural ornamentation
Capital: the architectural feature that crowns a column
Shaft: the main vertical part of a column
Entablature: the part of a Greek or Roman building that rests on top of a column
Metope: a square space between triglyphs, often decorated with sculpture

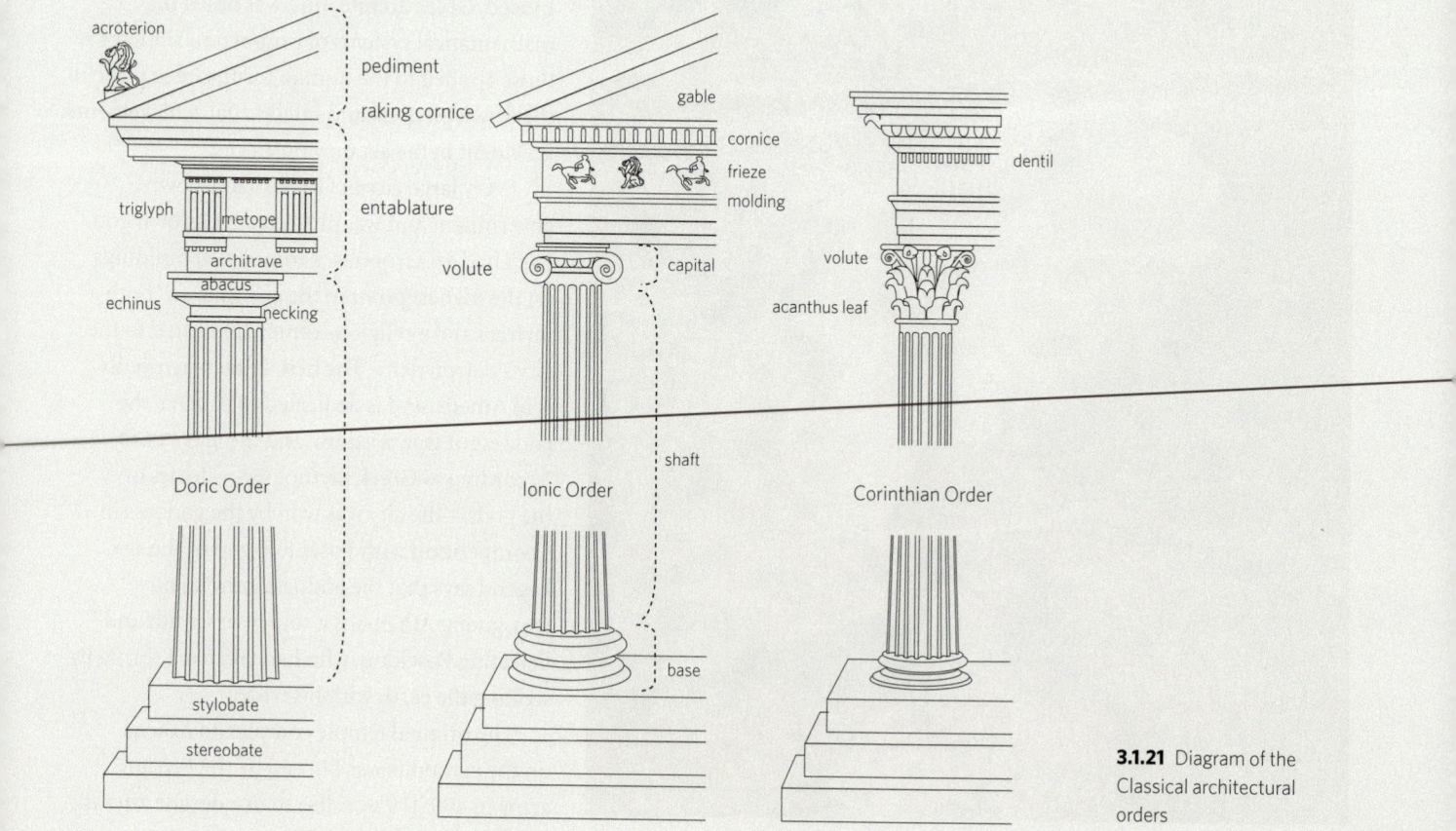

3.1.21 Diagram of the Classical architectural orders

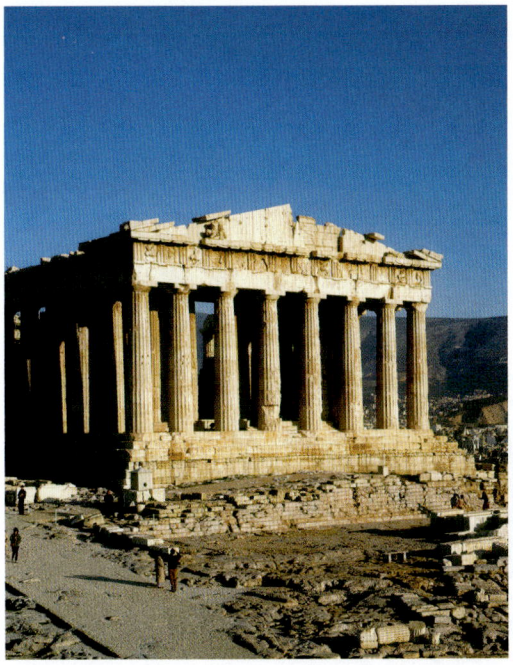

3.1.22 Iktinos and Kallikrates, Parthenon, 447–432 BCE, Acropolis, Athens, Greece

was begun. A new temple was built on the site because, according to legend, a new olive tree grew from the ashes of the old temple. This new temple, the Parthenon, was both the main temple to Athena and a war treasury. After the Persian attack the Athenians formed an alliance with other Greek cities to protect one another from further attacks by the so-called "barbarians." The cities contributed funds to prepare for future wars; these were housed in the Parthenon.

The new Parthenon was so important that it was made of glistening white marble, which was transported several miles to Athens, and then carried up the steep slope to the acropolis. Its design was thought to epitomize ideal proportions, symbolizing for the Athenians their achievements as an enlightened society. For many, the Parthenon is the iconic example of **Classical** architecture (see Box: Classical Architectural Orders). Modern visitors to the Parthenon can see the basic architectural structure of the building, but can gain only a slight impression of its original appearance (**3.1.22**). Originally it had a timber roof covered with marble tiles, but this was destroyed in 1687, when Turkish army munitions stored there exploded. When it was first made, the structure was covered with sculptures. Both building and sculptures were painted in red, yellow, and blue. The bright paint has fallen off or faded over time, giving modern viewers the incorrect impression that Greek architecture and sculpture were intentionally made the natural color of marble. In several places there were statues of Athena to receive offerings and prayer. One enormous statue of the goddess, 38 ft. tall and made of gold and ivory, dominated the interior space.

Placed in the metopes of the frieze in the Parthenon were sculptural reliefs of the battle in which the Lapiths, a legendary people in Greek mythology, tried to prevent the centaurs (creatures that are half-man and half-horse) from kidnapping the Lapith women (**3.1.23**). The scenes are intensely energetic, yet neither side seems to win. This subject was chosen as a metaphor for the Athenians (represented by the civilized Lapiths) who were always at war with the Persians (represented by barbaric centaurs). The sculptural scenes of gods that filled the **pediments**, and the reliefs in the metopes, were taken away between *c.* 1801 and 1805 by the British ambassador Lord Elgin (see Box: Controversy over the Parthenon Marbles, p. 382).

Classical: Greek art of the period *c.* 480–323 BCE
Pediment: the triangular space, situated above the row of columns, on the facade of a building in the Classical style

3.1.23 Metope of a Lapith and centaur in combat, from the south side of the Parthenon, designed by Pheidias, *c.* 445 BCE. Marble, height 52⅝". British Museum, London, England

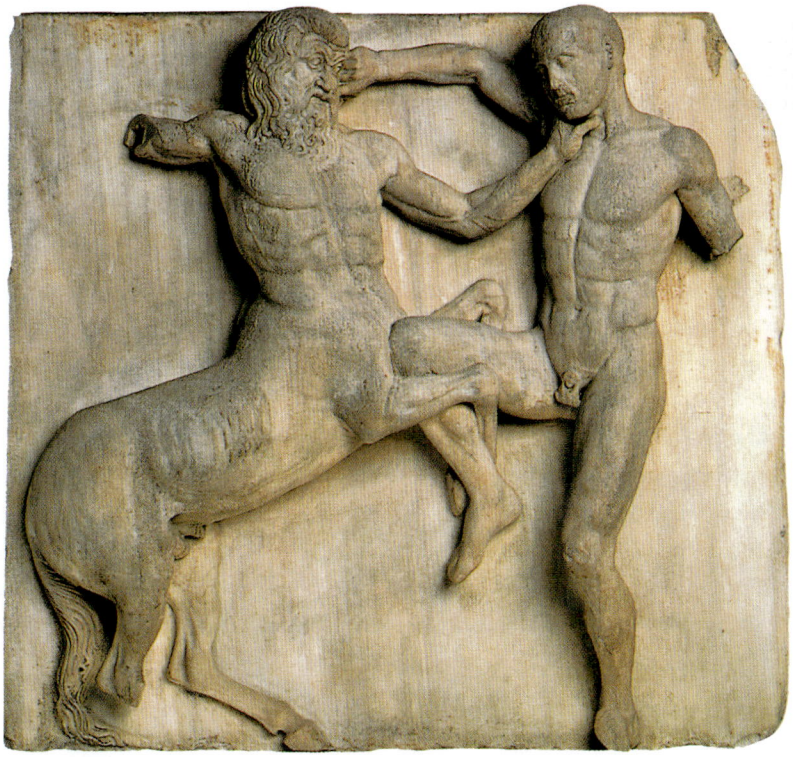

Controversy over the Parthenon Marbles

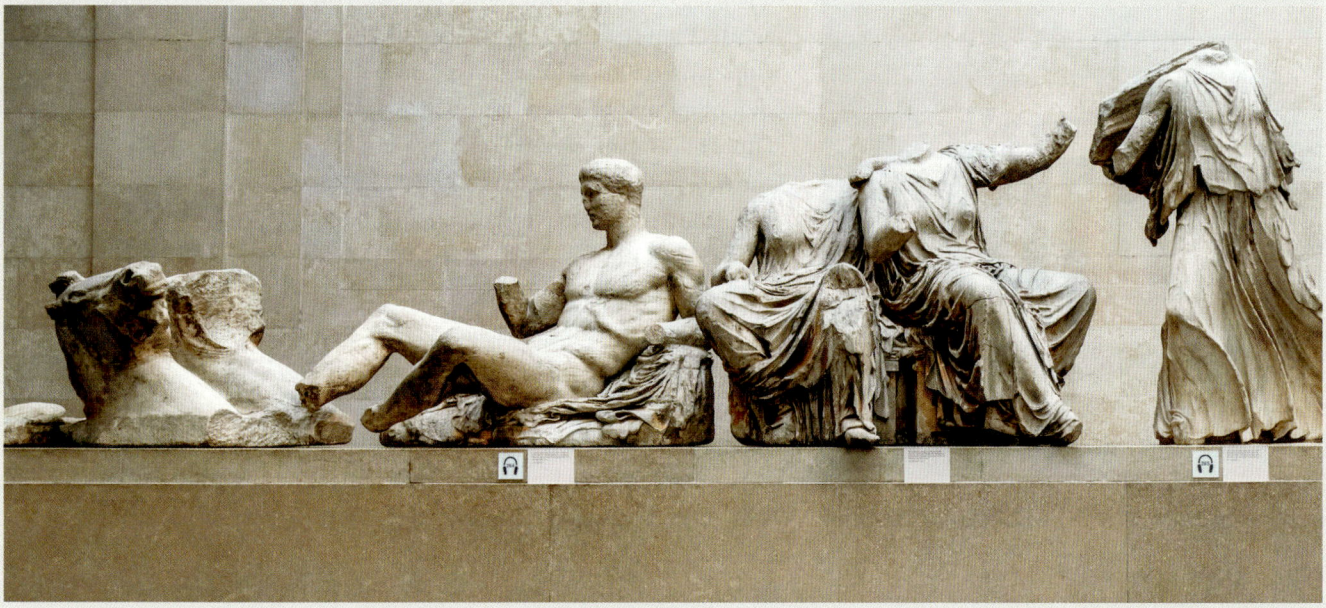

3.1.24 Parthenon Marbles in the British Museum, London, England

The magnificent sculptures that once adorned the Parthenon (**3.1.22**, p. 381) are now widely dispersed. Today, about one-third of the surviving sculptures (taken mostly from the pediments and metopes) form the Elgin marble collection in the British Museum, in London, England; one-third of the sculptures remain in Athens; and one-third are in various other places around the globe. Between 1801 and 1805, the British ambassador Lord Thomas Elgin removed the marbles from the Acropolis after receiving permission from the Ottoman empire, which controlled Athens at the time. The Greek government now wants the British to return the marbles currently in London, but the British have refused.

The Greeks argue that since the Ottoman empire was occupying Greece when the sculptures were taken, the Turks did not have the authority to give Lord Elgin permission to take the artifacts. The British have responded that many objects in museum collections are acquired during times of war, so to return the Parthenon marbles based on the state of Greece at the time the sculptures were acquired would set a precedent in which many museums would be asked to return most of their collections.

The British claim that the sculptures have been preserved because of their removal from the Parthenon and protection in the British Museum (**3.1.24**). When Lord Elgin removed the marbles, the Parthenon was in a dilapidated state. For centuries, the Parthenon had been treated not as a site of Classical antiquity, but as a church, a mosque, and as a storage site for weapons. Therefore, care of the building and the mythological sculpture that covered it was often neglected. At the British Museum, the marbles have been protected from warfare and environmental damage.

The Greek government contends that it has protected the sculptures from the Parthenon that are in its care by building a museum to house them. Additionally, the marbles taken by Lord Elgin were certainly damaged during their removal from the site and their transportation down the steep Acropolis hill and across the sea. Further, the marbles are part of the Greek national heritage and can be better appreciated by people when the sculptures are housed near the Parthenon itself. The British argue, however, that the Parthenon sculptures would not be as well known if they had not been exhibited in a place where they are compared to other works from the ancient world.

Contrapposto: a pose in sculpture in which the upper part of the body twists in one direction and the lower part in another

Three-dimensional: having height, width, and depth

***Amphora*:** a type of pot used to carry and store such goods as wine or olive oil

***Krater*:** a container for mixing wine with water, into which cups can then be dipped to ladle out the diluted wine for drinking

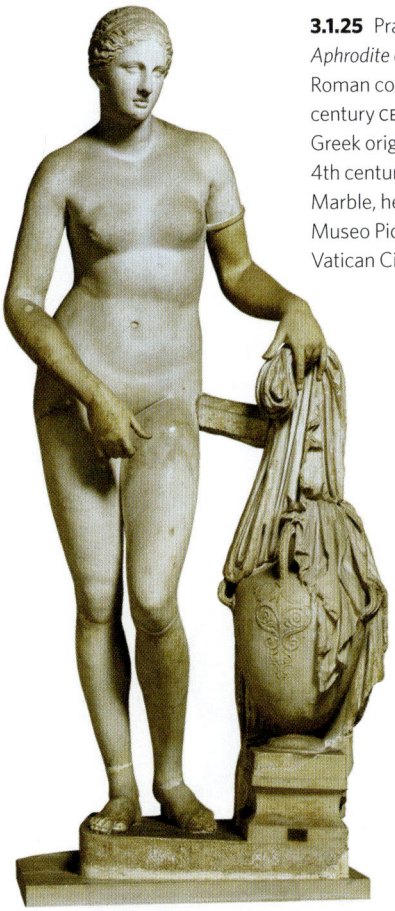

3.1.25 Praxiteles, *Aphrodite of Knidos*, Roman copy, 2nd century CE, after a Greek original of the 4th century BCE. Marble, height 6'8¼". Museo Pio-Clementino, Vatican City, Italy

The *Aphrodite of Knidos* by Praxiteles was the first Greek sculpture to show a completely nude woman; while the original no longer exists, dozens of Roman copies and adaptations still survive (**3.1.25**; and see also Box: Stylistic Changes in Sculpture of Ancient Greece, p. 384). The goddess's **contrapposto** stance shows her in the act of getting ready to take a bath, having just removed her clothing, which is hanging on the water vase beside her. This type of sculpture, in which Venus (the Roman name for Aphrodite) is seen covering her genital area with her right hand, is called "*Venus Pudica*" or "modest Venus." The believable consistency of her flesh, and the curvature of her body, made this sculpture both shocking and erotic to viewers in ancient Greece.

Ancient accounts tell us that Greek paintings were remarkably convincing scenes with **three-dimensional** figures that seemed to come to life. Unfortunately, only incomplete fragments survive. Several Roman mosaics were made as copies of Greek paintings, however. We can also surmise the skill of Greek painters by looking at the scenes painted on pottery.

The vase in **3.1.26** shows the Greek warriors Achilles and Ajax playing a game while waiting to battle with the Trojans. Through the layering of clothing, body parts, and even facial hair, the Athenian artist Exekias was able to represent figures that seem to fill a real space. The shields perched behind the figures also help to create a sense of depth. The long body of the pot and its two handles identify this as an ***amphora***.

Greek pots were made in large workshops headed by both a master potter, who formed the vase, and a master painter. The two worked together closely, as the painting technique was intricately connected with the process of firing the pot. Exekias was particularly talented in that he was both a skilled painter and potter. There were two main types of Greek vase painting: black-figure and red-figure. To make a black-figure vase the painter used slip (watered-down clay) to paint the design on the pot; he then incised the details into the slip. A three-phase firing method then turned the slip-covered areas black, while the rest of the pot remained the original red color.

The red-figure technique was invented around 530 BCE, after the time of Exekias. It used the reverse process to black-figure: the slip was used to outline the figures and paint in the details. This can be seen on a ***krater***, showing Heracles and Antaios in Battle (**3.1.27**). The red-figure method had the advantage of making the

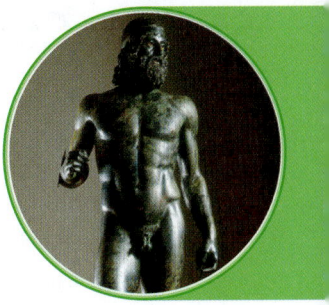

The Greeks often created sculpture out of bronze using lost-wax casting. Many of these sculptures do not survive because they were melted down for their materials: see **2.4.12**, **p. 250**

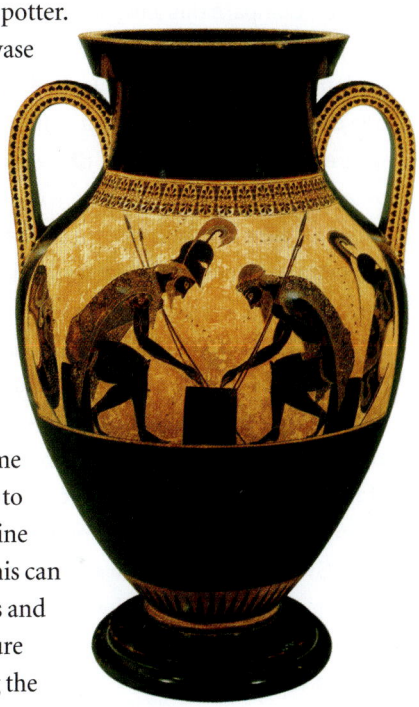

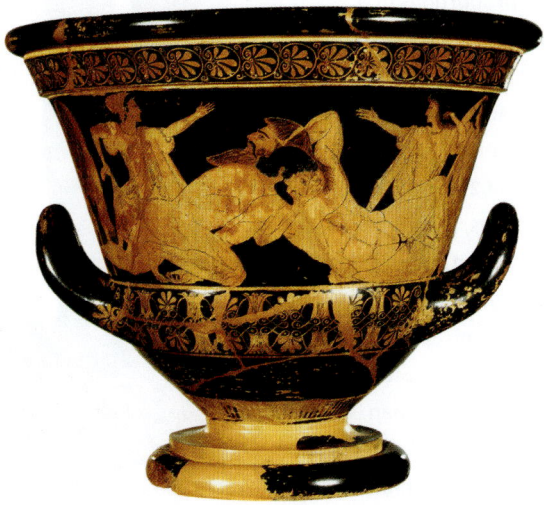

3.1.26 (above) Exekias (potter and painter), black-figure amphora with Achilles and Ajax playing dice, Vulci, c. 530 BCE. Height 24", diameter at mouth 11". Vatican Museums, Vatican City, Italy

3.1.27 (left) Euphronios (painter) and Euxitheos (potter), attic red-figure calyx-krater showing Heracles and Antaios in battle, c. 515–510 BCE. 17⅝ × 21⅝". Musée du Louvre, Paris, France

Stylistic Changes in the Sculpture of Ancient Greece

Greek sculptures are categorized generally in three types, referring to both the date of their making and to their style. **Archaic** works were produced from the late seventh to early fifth century BCE. Art from *c.* 480 to 323 BCE is labeled Classical. Later works are known as **Hellenistic**. A comparison of sculptures from these three periods demonstrates the main differences between them.

The name for one of the earliest Archaic types of Greek statues is *kouros*, or "male youth" (**3.1.28**). Compare this work with the Egyptian sculpture of Khafre (**3.1.15**, p. 375). The Greek sculptor subtly suggests movement by placing one of the statue's feet in front of the other, whereas the seated statue of Khafre seems bound to the block of diorite from which it was carved. Unlike the distant stare of Khafre, which suggests he is in the spiritual world of the dead, the kouros has lively energy and seems to be part of the world of the living. He wears nothing more than an Archaic smile, which conveys innocence and serenity. Statues like this were grave markers and offerings at sanctuaries. Statues of young maidens were called *korai*; interestingly, these were all clothed, as were most Greek statues of females at the time. It was not until the end of the Classical period that women were portrayed in the nude (see **3.1.25**, p. 383).

Sculptors of the Classical period tried to give their work the idealized proportions of a perfect human form. The subjects of most Greek sculptors are heroes or gods. The *Doryphoros* (Spear Bearer) is a famous example of the work of Polykleitos; unfortunately, only a Roman copy of the original survives (**3.1.29**). Polykleitos developed a canon, or set of rules, for creating a harmoniously proportioned human body using a set of mathematical ratios. Polykleitos also gave his statue a new stance, called contrapposto, which imitates the way humans balance their own weight. The *Doryphoros* portrays a man who stands naturally with his left knee bent and whose weight is shifted to his right hip. His raised left arm balances this shift in weight. Such poses made figures appear less stiff than the earlier kouros.

One of the most compelling Hellenistic sculptures is the *Laocoön*, in which the priest Laocoön and his sons are shown struggling in agony as they are attacked by twisting sea serpents, sent by the god Poseidon (**3.1.30**). Hellenistic sculpture shows the same idealized muscular bodies as earlier Greek sculptures.

3.1.28 (below left) Statue of a *kouros* (youth), Naxian, c. 590–580 BCE. Marble, height 6'4⅝". Metropolitan Museum of Art, New York

3.1.29 (below right) Roman version of the *Doryphoros* of Polykleitos, 120–50 BCE, after a bronze original of c. 460 BCE. Marble, height 6'6". Minneapolis Institute of Arts, Minnesota

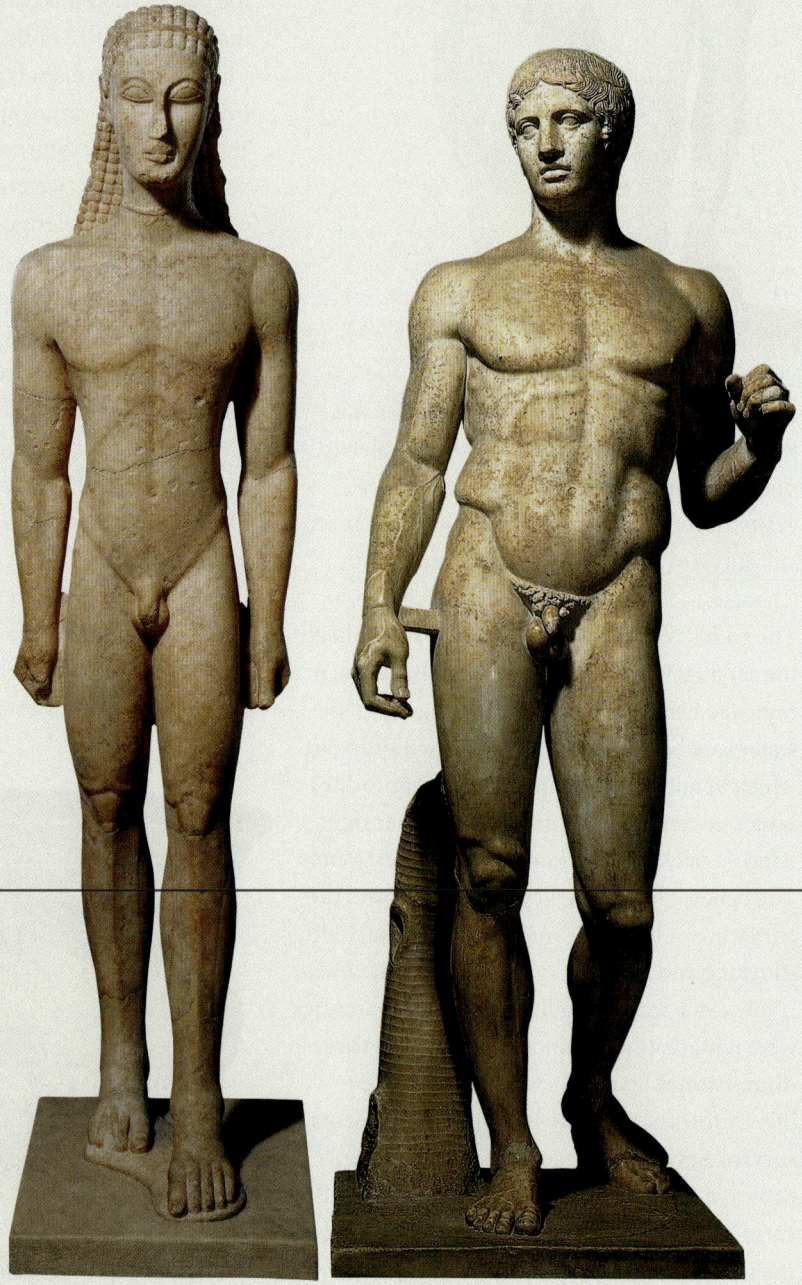

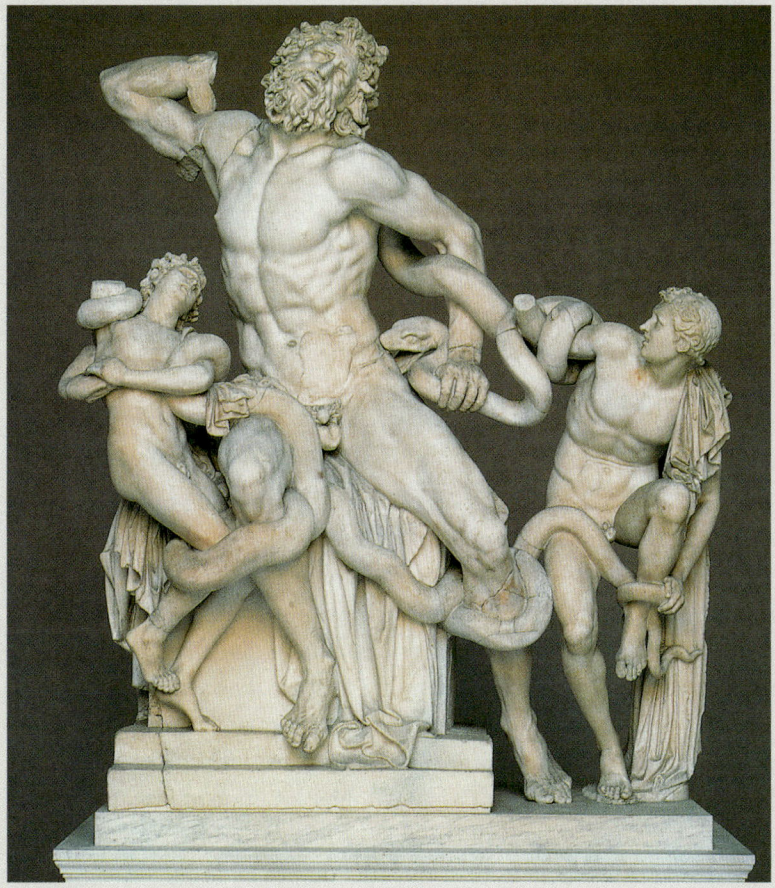

Hellenistic artists, however, chose subjects that involved creating figures in dramatic poses, challenging the artist to convey an even greater sense of movement and heightened emotion. **Renaissance** artists were often impressed by the balanced forms from the Classical period, but this dynamic Hellenistic sculpture, discovered in Rome in 1506, inspired such artists as Michelangelo and Bernini to imbue their art with similar drama and movement.

3.1.30 *Laocoön and His Sons*, copy of bronze original probably made at Pergamon c. 150 BCE. Marble, height 6'½". Vatican Museums, Vatican City

Archaic: Greek art of the period c. 620–480 BCE
Hellenistic: Greek art of the period c. 323–100 BCE
Renaissance: a period of cultural and artistic change in Europe from the fourteenth to the seventeenth century

figures appear slightly more three-dimensional, which is advantageous for showing these two muscular figures actively struggling. Very close attention is also paid to their facial expressions and hair. Depth and space are created by the two smaller female figures in the background, who frame the scene with comparative calmness as they raise their arms. As the Greeks developed a strong trade market through ports throughout the Mediterranean, a variety of Greek vases and pots have survived in great numbers outside of Greece, particularly in Etruscan tombs, where they were collected and buried with their owners.

Etruscan Art

During the sixth century BCE, the Etruscans were successful seafarers and traders who lived in central Italy, and formed the first urban civilization in the northern Mediterranean. Despite their prosperity, the Etruscans were eventually conquered by the Romans around 280 BCE. We understand much about Etruscan funerary customs because they built necropolises, or large cemeteries, containing hundreds of tomb chambers, which were filled with sculptures, or decorated with images of objects. The Etruscans were also very talented metalworkers; many intricate objects for personal use, such as gold jewelry and bronze mirrors, have also been found in the tombs in Italy, and must have been buried with the deceased. These indicate that, like the ancient Egyptians, the Etruscans believed that all of these things would be needed in the afterlife.

Large Etruscan tomb chambers, often containing the remains of generations of one family, were buried within mounds made of raised dirt and limestone. The tomb chambers were designed to mimic Etruscan houses, and portrayed settings in which celebrations could be held in the afterlife. The painting in the Tomb

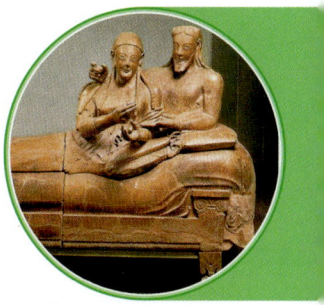

Etruscan husbands and wives were often buried in the same sarcophagus. In this work, a couple is shown celebrating the afterlife together: see **2.4.11, p. 249**

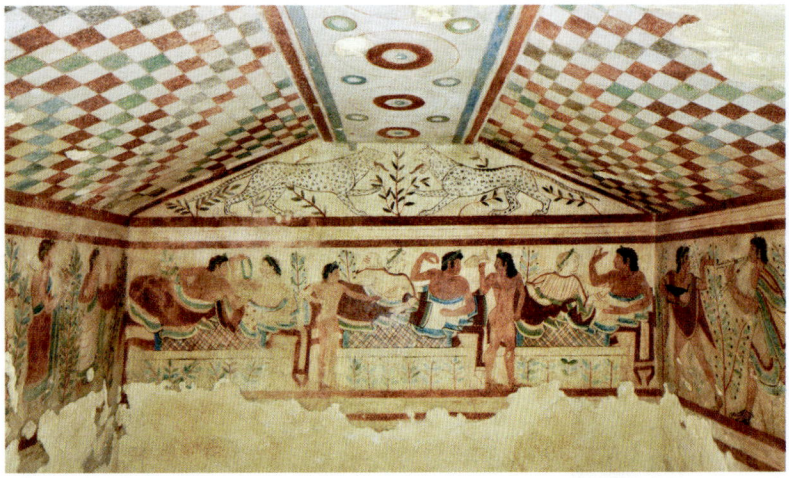

3.1.31 Tomb of the Leopards, *c.* 530–520 BCE. Monterozzi Necropolis, Tarquinia, Italy

of the Leopards (**3.1.31**) shows a banquet in which men (portrayed as dark-skinned) and women (portrayed as light-skinned) are enjoying music, food, and drink. Etruscan women held a higher status within their own culture than other women were afforded in the ancient world. This is reflected here by their placement as equals, lounging with their husbands.

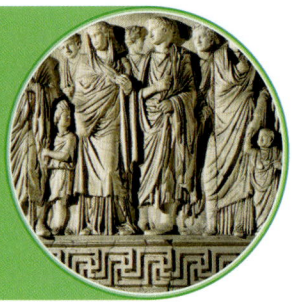

Under the Roman emperor Augustus there was a period of peace, celebrated with the Ara Pacis Augustae (Altar of Peace of Augustus): see **1.2.6**, **p. 65**

Roman Art

The first evidence of a settlement at Rome dates back to about 900 BCE. This small village grew to become the center of an enormous empire that at its zenith covered much of Europe, northern Africa, and large parts of the Middle East. In the process of conquering such extensive territories, the Romans absorbed many cultures, frequently adopting the gods of others but giving them Latin names. In fact, Roman emperors often associated themselves with the qualities of such gods.

The Romans used Greek methods to create ideal proportions in their architecture (see p. 381), and adopted the Corinthian architectural order the Greeks had originally devised (see p.380). The Romans also greatly admired Greek bronze sculptures and often remade them in marble. While the Greeks celebrated the idealized human body and mostly portrayed nude gods and mythological heroes, Roman art focused instead on emperors and civic leaders, who were usually portrayed clothed in togas or wearing armor. Roman sculpture often portrayed the individual character of its subject with recognizable, rather than ideal, facial features.

Bust: statue of a person depicting only his or her head and shoulders

The Roman Republic

During the Roman Republic (509–27 BCE), in which power was held by a group of powerful families, called patricians, aged members of Roman society were portrayed—and viewed—as wise and experienced, particularly in political settings.

Roman artists recognized individuals' accomplishments with naturalistic, lifelike portraits often made from death masks. Family members treasured such portraits as recording their loved one's likeness and character. In **3.1.32** a Roman patrician proudly displays the **busts** of his ancestors in order to reinforce his own social standing. His face shows individuality and believable signs of aging, and he wears clothing appropriate to his status.

The catastrophic eruption of Mount Vesuvius in 79 CE buried the buildings of the Roman cities of Pompeii and Herculaneum in a matter of hours under some 60 ft. of volcanic ash. This unique act of accidental preservation has given us, centuries later, an incomparable opportunity to witness how Romans lived in their homes. Frescoes covered the walls of many rooms in the houses in Pompeii. Some of the paintings offer convincing illusions of landscape scenes. Some of the interiors are covered with what appear to be marble panels, but which in reality are only painted. One such room is decorated with scenes believed

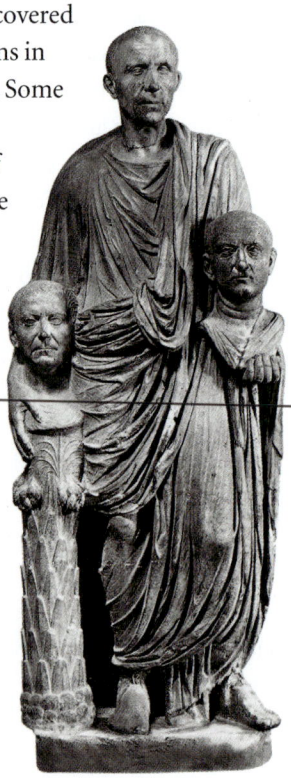

3.1.32 A Roman citizen carrying death masks of his ancestors, *c.* 80 BCE. Marble, lifesize. Barberini Museum, Rome, Italy

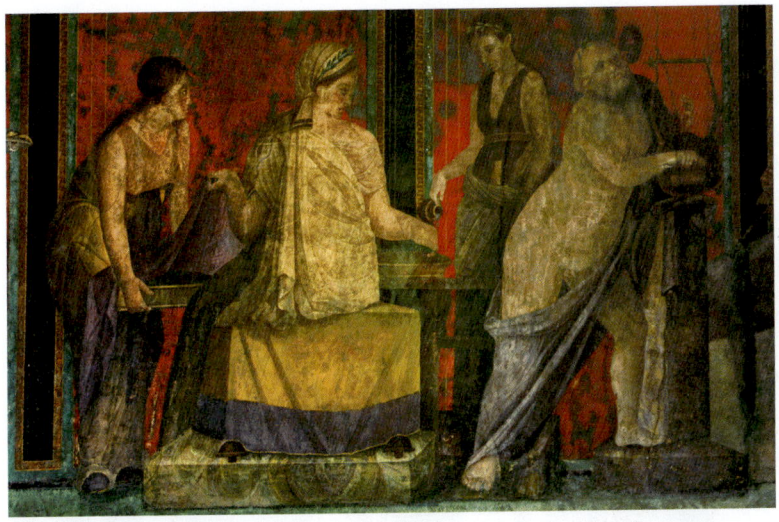

3.1.33 (above) Detail from Dionysiac mystery frieze in Room 5 of the Villa of the Mysteries, Pompeii, Italy, *c.* 60 BCE. Wall painting, height 5'4"

to describe rituals relating to the worship of Dionysus, the god of wine, ecstasy, agriculture, and the theatre (**3.1.33**). Excavation of Pompeii began in the eighteenth century, and the remarkable discoveries there stimulated interest in ancient art throughout Europe.

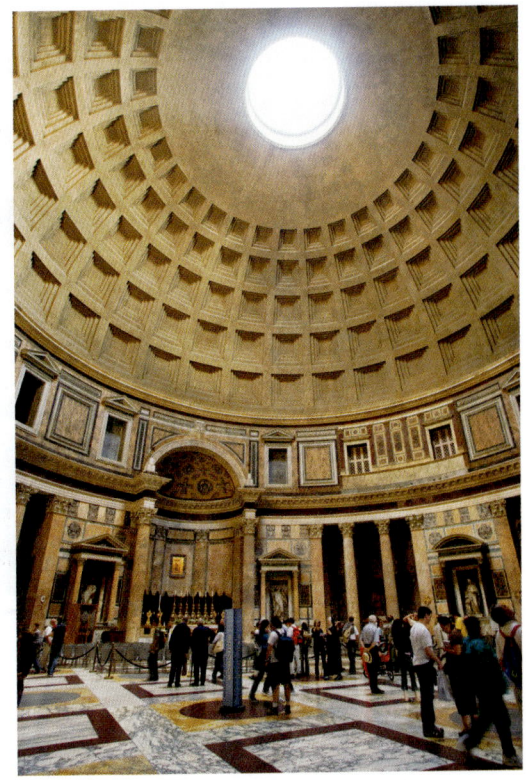

The Roman Empire

Beginning in 27 BCE, Rome became an imperial state under the rule of Augustus. One of the Romans' most impressive works of architecture under the Roman empire (27 BCE–1453) is the Pantheon ("Temple of all the Gods"). It was originally constructed in the first century BCE. Emperor Hadrian had it rebuilt from *c.* 118 to 125 CE in order to enhance his own status. The entrance **facade** is a pediment atop Corinthian columns (**3.1.34**). Once inside, one is standing under a spectacular **coffered** dome 143 ft. in diameter and 143 ft. from the ground (**3.1.35**). The dome was made possible by the Romans' revolutionary use of concrete and their

3.1.35 (above) Pantheon, interior view, *c.* 118–125 CE, Rome, Italy

3.1.34 (below) Pantheon, entrance porch, *c.* 118–125 CE, Rome, Italy

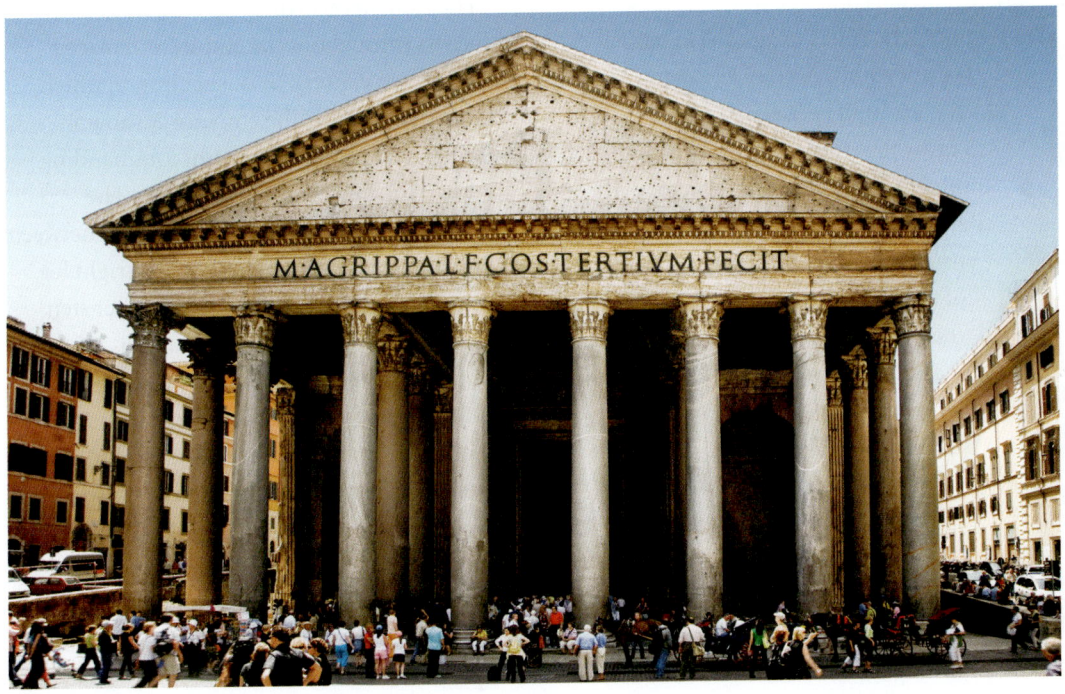

Facade: any side of a building, usually the front or entrance
Coffered: decorated with recessed paneling

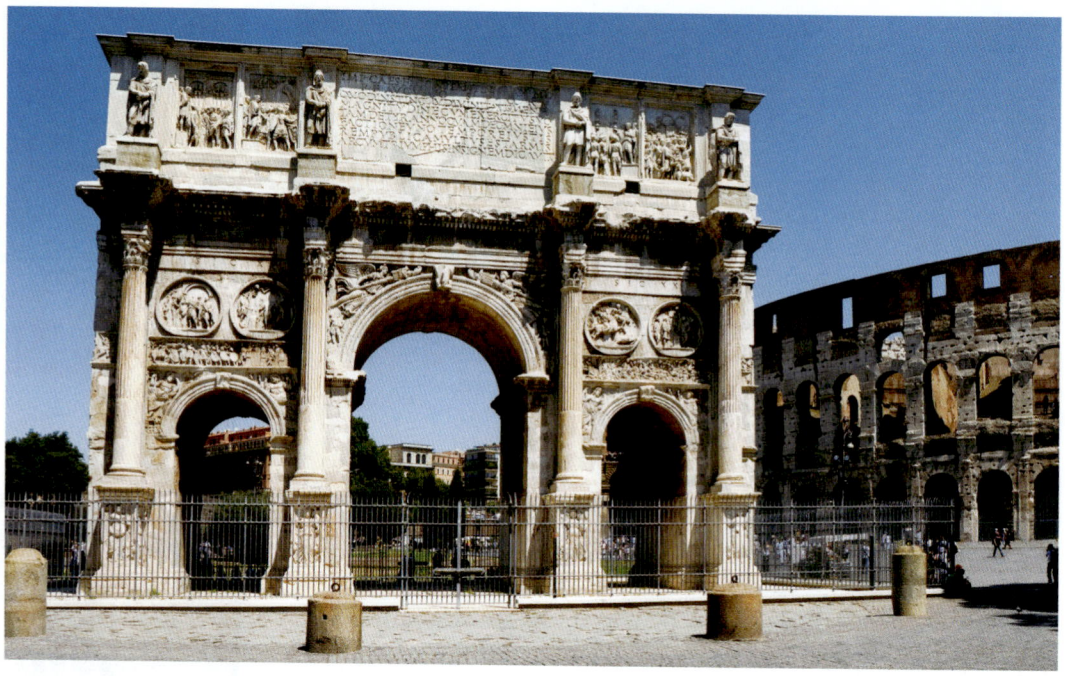

3.1.36 Arch of Constantine, south side, 312–15 CE, Rome, Italy

Oculus: a round opening at the center of a dome

engineering genius. In the center of this dome is an **oculus**, (the Latin word for "eye,") open to the skies. One can tell the season and time of day by where the sunlight hits the interior. Any rain coming in runs quickly away into a central drain because the entire floor slopes gradually.

At the center of each Roman city was a forum, or marketplace, which was surrounded by temples, basilicas, and civic buildings. Emperors made a public show of their power by commissioning architects to create grand arches and tall columns, which usually celebrated the rulers' triumphs in battle.

The enormous Arch of Constantine (**3.1.36**) was built between 312 and 315 CE by the emperor Constantine to commemorate the military victory (the Battle of the Milvian Bridge) that would ensure his future position as sole ruler of the empire. Constantine declared his place in history by placing the arch close to the famed Colosseum, built by an earlier family of powerful emperors (see Images Related to 3.1). Constantine also had sculpture removed from other imperial monuments, often erasing the faces of previous emperors from such statues and replacing them with his own likeness; he then had the sculptures placed upon the triumphal arch. By doing so, he proclaimed both his lineage to previous great emperors and his belief in his superiority over them. Constantine associated himself with Apollo and other pagan gods, as well as with Christianity. He became known as Constantine the Great, and would eventually make it legal to practice all religions, opening the doors for Christianity to grow into the primary religion of the empire. He was baptized as a Christian on his deathbed.

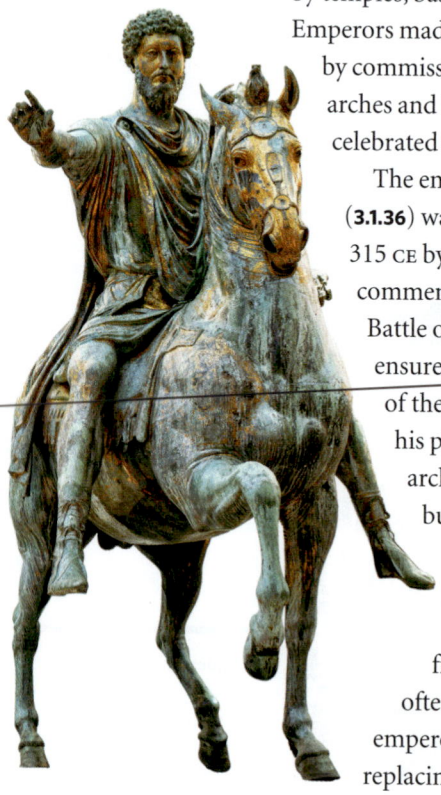

3.1.37 Equestrian statue of Marcus Aurelius, c. 175 CE, Rome, Italy. Height 11'6".

The Romans also distributed statues of their emperors throughout the empire and placed them in town centers. In this sculpture, which is more than lifesize, the emperor is shown exuding great physical strength, commanding his powerful, muscular horse (**3.1.37**). The sculptor has conveyed a sense of tension between action and stillness. The horse's front right leg appears in motion, ready to take another step, while Marcus Aurelius raises his arm as if he is about to orate to an audience.

Although sculptures showing emperors powerfully atop a horse were common in ancient Rome, few have survived because they were melted down for their bronze to make weapons during the Middle Ages. The equestrian statue of Marcus Aurelius escaped destruction because it was thought to represent Emperor Constantine.

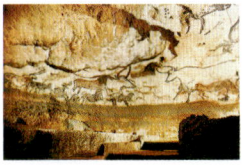

4.2.13b Hall of the Bulls, Lascaux Caves, France, c. 17,000–15,000 BCE, p. 586

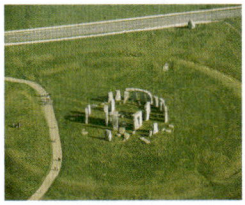

4.1.8 Stonehenge, England, c. 3200–1500 BCE, p. 570

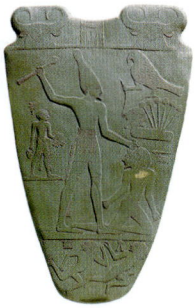

4.7.4b Palette of Narmer (back), Egypt, c. 2950–2775 BCE, p. 641

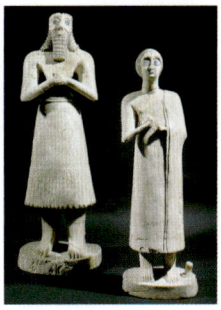

1.10.5 Votive Figures, Temple of Abu (Tell Asmar), Iraq, c. 2700 BCE, p. 175

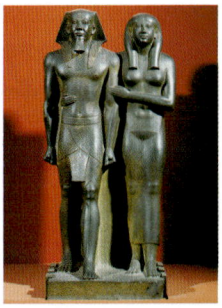

4.9.3b *Menkaure and His Wife, Queen Khamerernebty*, Egypt, c. 2520 BCE, p. 665

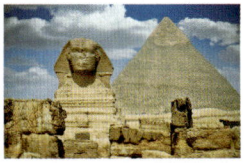

1.2.2 Great Sphinx of Giza, Egypt, c. 2500 BCE, p. 62

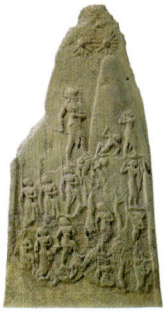

4.2.7 Stela of Naram-Sin, c. 2254–2218 BCE, p. 582

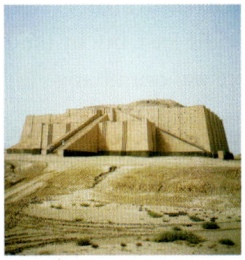

4.1.6 Ziggurat, Ur, Iraq, c. 2100 BCE, p. 569

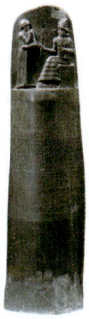

4.6.9 Stela of Hammurabi, c. 1792–1750 BCE, p. 634

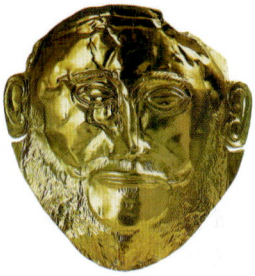

2.6.13 Gold death mask, Mycenae, Greece, c. 1550–1500 BCE, p. 293

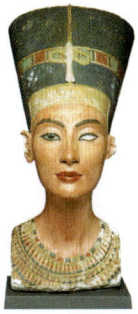

1.10.1a Bust of Queen Nefertiti, Egypt, c. 1340 BCE, p. 171

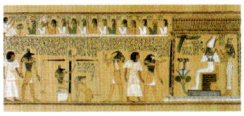

4.2.10 Book of the Dead of Hunefer, Egypt, c. 1275 BCE, p. 584

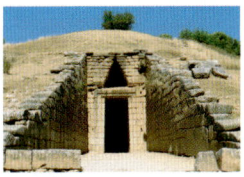

2.5.12 Treasury of Atreus, Mycenae, Greece, c. 1250 BCE, p. 265

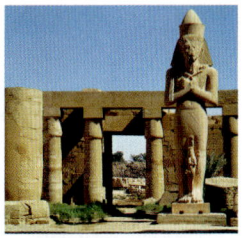

2.5.8 Great Court, Temple of Amun-Re, Egypt, c. 950-730 BCE, p. 263

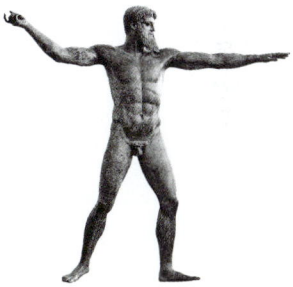

1.7.12a *Poseidon* (or *Zeus*), Greece, c. 460–450 BCE, p. 147

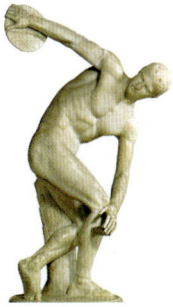

4.9.4 Myron, *Discus Thrower* (*Discobolos*), c. 450 BCE, p. 666

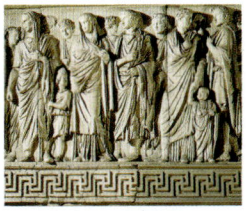

1.2.6 Imperial Procession from the Ara Pacis Augustae, 13 BCE, p. 65

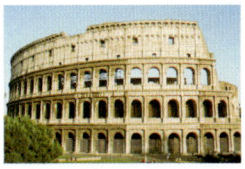

4.1.2 Colosseum, Rome, 72–80 CE, p. 566

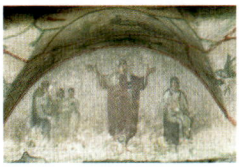

4.2.14b Fresco from the Catacomb of Priscilla, Italy, 2nd–3rd centuries CE, p. 587

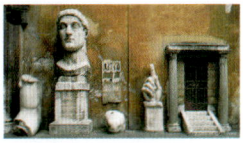

4.6.10 Remnants of colossal statue of Constantine, 325–26 CE, p. 635

3.2 Art of the Middle Ages

The Roman empire dominated the Mediterranean region from the second century BCE, later extending its control of Western Europe and the Middle East, but by the fourth century CE the empire was crumbling in the west. In 330 the Roman emperor Constantine I (272–337 CE) moved the center of the Roman empire from Rome to Byzantium, which he renamed Constantinople (today's Istanbul, Turkey). The eastern part of the empire became known as the Byzantine empire and lasted a millennium, until Constantinople fell to the Turks in 1453. In the west, however, a series of invasions had ended the Roman empire by 476. The period that followed is known as the Middle Ages, or the medieval period, because it comes between the time of the ancient civilizations of the Mediterranean region and the rebirth, or **Renaissance**, of Greek and Roman ideals in the fifteenth century.

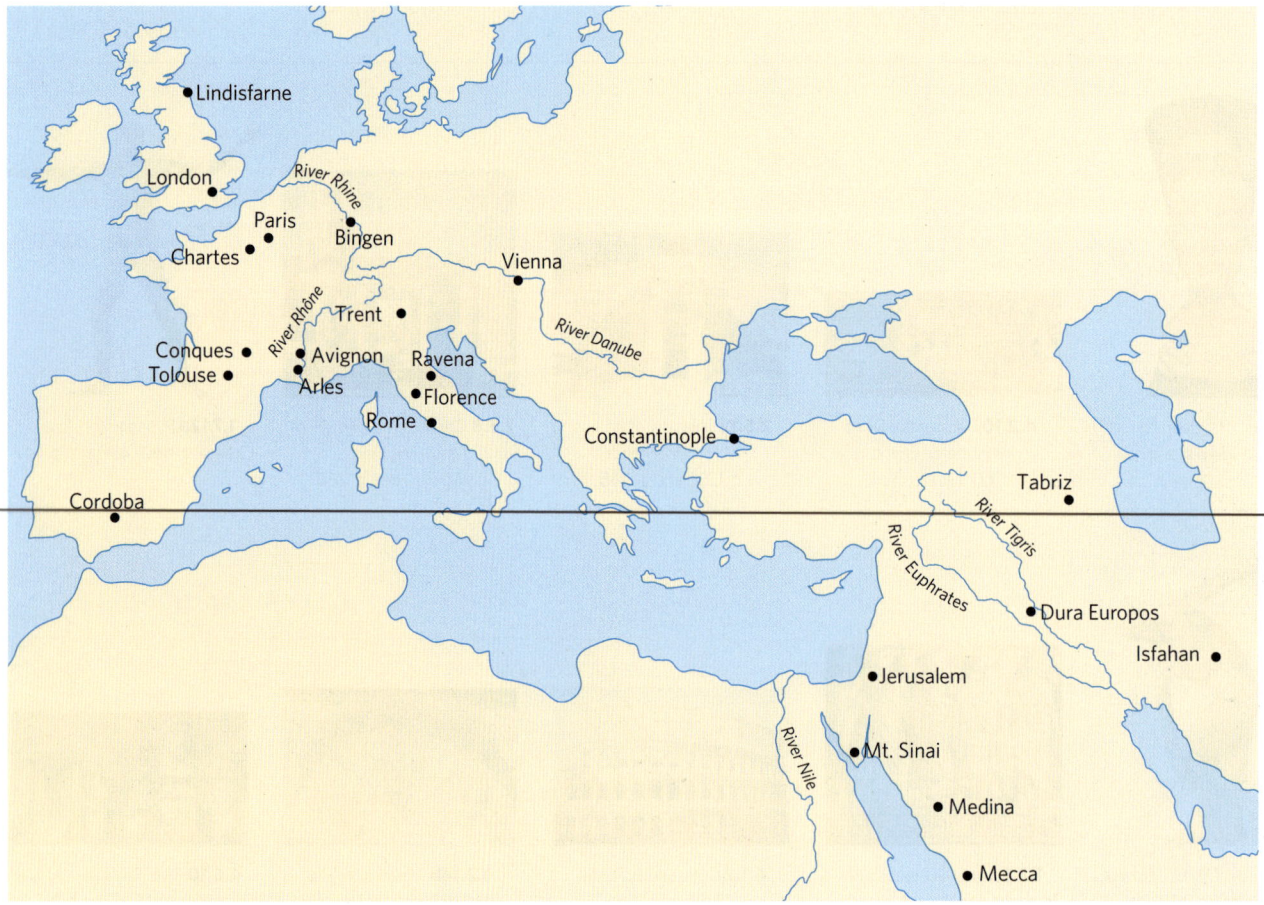

3.2.1 Map of Europe and the Middle East in the Middle Ages

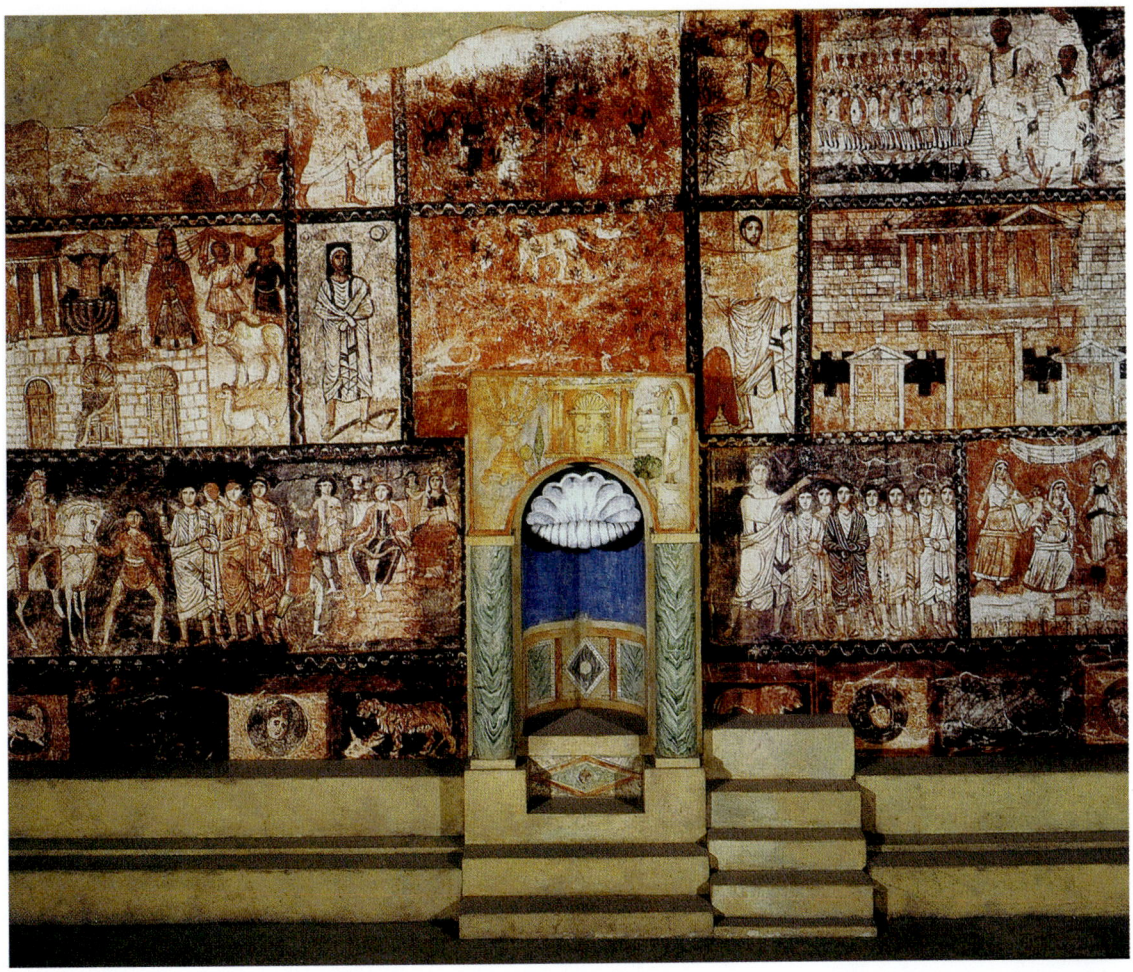

3.2.2 Interior west wall of synagogue at Dura Europos, Syria, 244–245 CE. Reconstruction in National Museum, Damascus, Syria

Renaissance: a period of cultural and artistic change in Europe from the fourteenth to the seventeenth century
Romanesque: an early medieval European style of architecture based on Roman-style rounded arches and heavy construction
Gothic: Western European architectural style of the twelfth to the sixteenth century, characterized by the use of pointed arches and ornate decoration
Fresco: a technique in which the artist paints onto freshly applied plaster. From the Italian *fresco*, "fresh"

In the study of the history of art, the Middle Ages is often broken down further because of the stylistic variations of its art, particularly its architecture. Beginning in the eleventh century, large stone churches, heavily ornamented with sculpture inside and out, were built throughout the Christian world. These churches were later given the name **Romanesque** for their similarity to the heavy, round-arched style of the Romans. This comparison is not obvious, but the term Romanesque was meant as a contrast to the architectural style that followed it, from around 1150, in which great **Gothic** cathedrals, the spires of which reached toward the heavens, were built. Religious belief was integral to the lives of the people—whether Christian, Jew, or Muslim—who lived in Europe and the Middle East during the Middle Ages (see Box: Three Religions of the Middle Ages, p. 394). Much of the art from the period reflects their beliefs.

Art of Late Antiquity and Early Christianity

Jewish culture thrived periodically during the Middle Ages, although this was also a time of persecution. Partially as a result of the constant displacement of many Jews, few examples of Jewish art from the Middle Ages survive. The oldest surviving Jewish artwork (other than coins) can be found in a synagogue in the ancient Roman city of Dura Europos, on the River Euphrates in modern Syria. Here, more than fifty stories are displayed in **fresco** paintings on the wall. The paintings were used to teach the stories upon which Jewish history and belief are based. The didactic (with the aim of teaching) nature of these images explains why figures are shown, a feature that is uncommon in later Jewish art. On the center of the west wall facing Jerusalem is a shrine containing the Torah, the most important part of the Jewish Bible, which contains the commandments given to Moses by God (**3.2.2**).

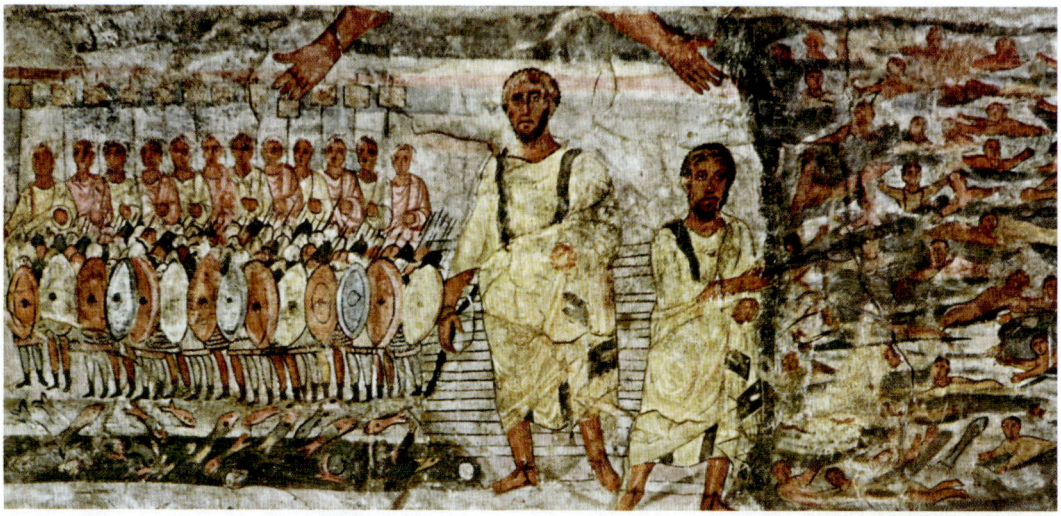

3.2.3 *Exodus and Crossing of the Red Sea*, panel from west wall of synagogue at Dura Europos, Syria, 244–45 CE. Reconstruction in National Museum, Damascus, Syria

The fresco painting of the scene in **3.2.3** does show God, but not his face; only his hands are seen, reaching down from the sky. In the passage from the Book of Exodus in the Torah, God tells Moses to guide the Israelites out of Egypt toward Mount Sinai, where Moses will receive the Ten Commandments. When they arrive at the Red Sea, God tells Moses to place his rod in the water. This action parts the sea, creating a safe crossing for Moses and his people. When they are safely on the other side, Moses again places his rod in the water. The Red Sea floods, drowning the Egyptian soldiers who have been chasing the Israelites. The Exodus painting is a **continuous narrative**, in which different points in time in the story are shown within the same scene. Moses is shown in the center, while the soldiers on the left are lined up to follow him. A second Moses is shown slightly in front and to the side of the first. Behind the second Moses on the right side of the scene, the soldiers have been washed away as the sea has flooded.

3.2.4 Painted ceiling, late 3rd–early 4th century CE. Catacombs of Saints Peter and Marcellinus, Rome, Italy

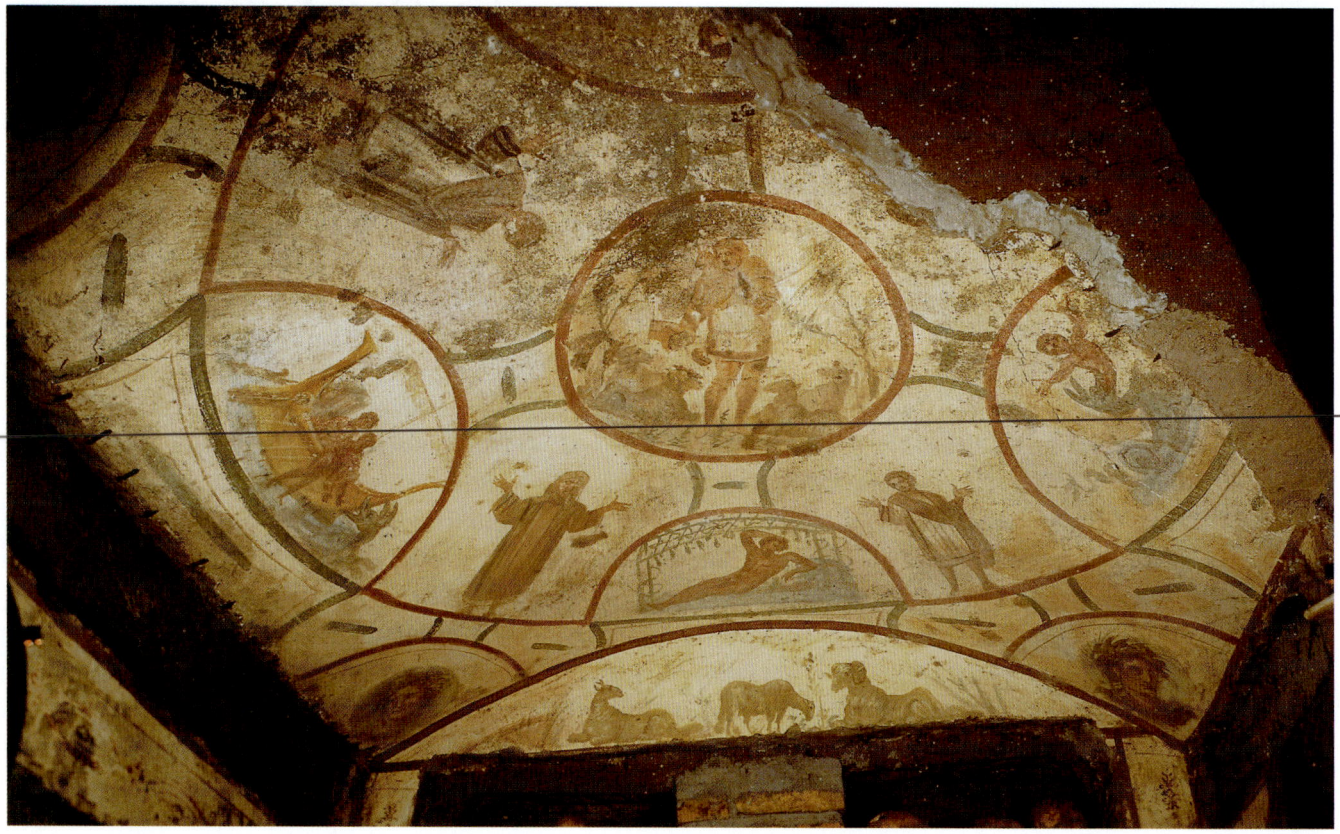

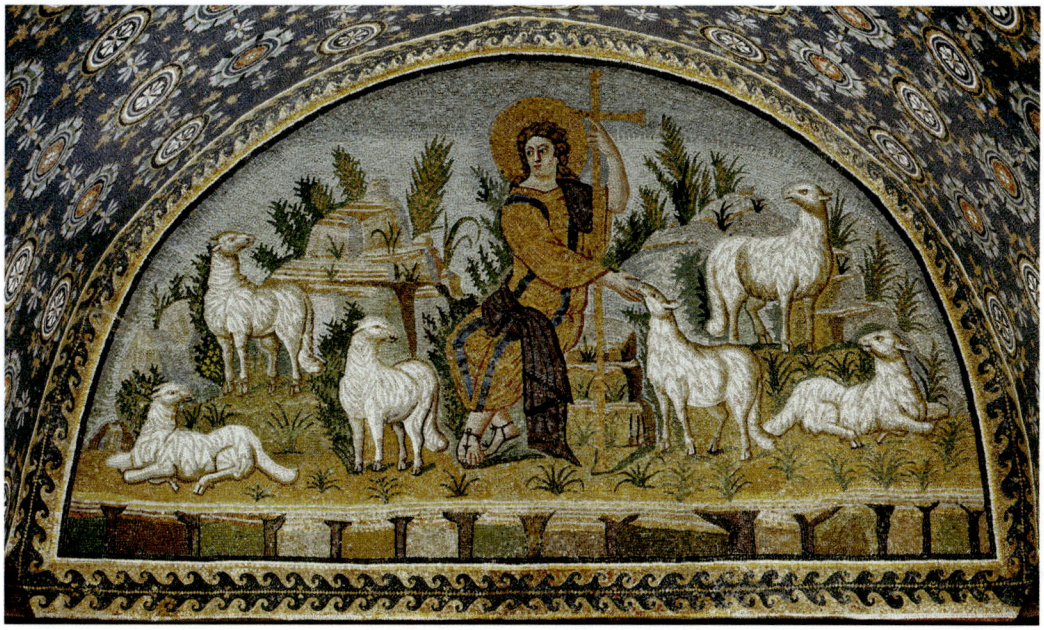

3.2.5 *Good Shepherd*, 425–46 CE. Mosaic in lunette. Mausoleum of Galla Placidia, Ravenna, Italy

The Christian Church, which had been unified under Roman rule, split in 1054. The result was a Greek Orthodox Church in the east and a Roman Catholic Church in the west, each ruled by separate leaders and following different doctrines and practices. The earliest examples of Christian art date from the early third century. From 200 CE to the sixth century, it was common practice amongst Christians, Jews, and others in Italy to bury the dead in underground cemeteries known as catacombs. The catacombs may also have served as sites for Christian worship. Scenes were often painted on burial-room walls and ceilings. One such scene in a catacomb in Rome shows Jesus as the Good Shepherd in the center and tells the Old Testament story of Jonah in the semicircular areas around the central image (**3.2.4**). Christians believe that the story of Jonah, who was swallowed by a whale and then spat out alive three days later, foreshadows the death and resurrection of Jesus.

In their depiction of Christian themes, early Christian artists often used motifs and figures adapted from pagan cultures. Under the Roman empire, religious **syncretism**—the blending of multiple religious or philosophical beliefs—was common; as Christianity spread, rituals, symbols, and even objects were assimilated from the pagans. For example, statues of the Egyptian goddess Isis, mother to the god Horus, were altered and used as models for images of the Virgin Mary. The Good Shepherd in **3.2.4** was adapted from images of several pagan figures, including the Greek hero Orpheus (who could charm animals with his songs) and the Greek god Apollo (god of music, the sun, and healing, who was always shown as a beardless youth).

A century later, the depiction of Christ changed. Christian artists developed a range of symbols that were more varied and elaborate. The **mosaic** in **3.2.5** was made for the building known as the Mausoleum of Galla Placidia, which was the family tomb of the Roman emperor Flavius Honorius. We can see that Christ is still portrayed as a Good Shepherd, here flanked by three lambs on each side, but he is seated and more mature. Compared to the image on the catacomb ceiling, Christ's appearance is regal. He wears a fine gold robe with a purple (the traditional color for royalty) cloth draped over his shoulder; he holds a golden cross. His hair is long, and a prominent gold halo shines behind him; the **tesserae**, small pieces of glass that make up the mosaic, create a beautiful glow that glitters and reflects light. Unlike figures in Roman art, Christ's body is sharply delineated and flat-looking rather than fully **three-dimensional**. These stylistic qualities foreshadow the art of Byzantium, the Christian empire that continued in the east after the fall of the western Roman empire.

Continuous narrative: when different parts of a story are shown within the same visual space
Syncretism: the blending of multiple religious or philosophical beliefs
Mosaic: a picture or pattern created by fixing together small pieces of stone, glass, tile, etc.
Tesserae: small pieces of stone or glass or other materials used to make a mosaic
Three-dimensional: having height, width, and depth

Three Religions of the Middle Ages

> You shall not make for yourself an idol, whether in the form of anything that is in heaven above, or that is on the Earth beneath, or that is in the water under the Earth. You shall not bow down to them or worship them.
>
> (Second Commandment, Exodus 20:4–5)

Judaism, Islam, and Christianity all have their origins in the Middle East. They have some similar beliefs—each religion considers Abraham to be a prophet, for example, and each considers their God to be the one true God. Importantly for the study of art, each also warns against the worship of false idols. Understanding some basic beliefs of followers of these faiths can help us to understand better some of the art produced during the Middle Ages.

- Judaism began with a contract between Abraham and God (Yahweh) in *c.* 2000 BCE. Abraham promised to exalt Yahweh as the one true God, and in exchange Yahweh promised Abraham many descendants, who are the Jewish people of today. The Torah (or "Teaching") was written by Moses under divine inspiration and is the core of Jewish belief and law. Jewish art does not show any more than the hands of Yahweh, and rarely shows human figures. Instead, it usually depicts objects used in acts of worship—scroll holders, candelabra, and the like.
- Christians worship Jesus Christ (a Jew who lived from *c.* 7–2 BCE to *c.* 30–36 CE), who they believe was the son of God. The Bible contains both the writings of the Jewish Bible ("The Old Testament") and what Christians see as their fulfillment in the life of Jesus ("The New Testament"). For Christians, Jesus was a great teacher who demonstrated how to lead a good and pious life, but who also suffered, was sacrificed and then rose again to show that the sins of humanity could be forgiven and that for those who were true believers, eternal life could be achieved after death. Christians have interpreted the Second Commandment in different ways, at times causing great conflict and even the destruction of images (see Box: Iconoclasm, p. 396).
- Muslims (followers of Islam) call their one true God Allah. They believe that Jesus was a prophet but that Muhammad (*c.* 570–632 CE) was the primary messenger of Allah. The Koran is the word of Allah given to Muhammad and is Islam's primary sacred text. Islamic art never depicts the figure of God. Also, human figures are not shown within the holy space of a mosque. The majority of Islamic art is decorative and often makes beautiful use of **calligraphy** to show the word of Allah.

Byzantine Art

Calligraphy: the art of emotive or carefully descriptive hand lettering or handwriting
Patron: an organization or individual who sponsors the creation of works of art
Minaret: a tall slender tower, particularly on a mosque, from which the faithful are called to prayer

The Byzantine emperor Justinian I (483–565) was a devoted **patron** of the arts. He funded hundreds of churches, mosaics, and paintings throughout his empire, including Hagia Sophia in the center of Constantinople (**3.2.6**). Although Hagia Sophia was built as a Christian basilica, it was altered into a mosque when the Ottomans took control of Constantinople in 1453. The four **minarets** were added after that date. At the time it was built, the dome of Hagia Sophia was the largest ever built, at 182 ft. high. At the base of the dome are forty closely aligned windows, making the dome appear to float on a bed of light from the inside. Hagia Sophia is based on a **central-plan** design where the width and length of the building are almost identical. One of Justinian's greatest achievements was his protection of more than 2,000 icons at the monastery of St. Catherine, Mount Sinai, in Egypt (see Box: Iconoclasm, p. 396). **Icons**, paintings of religious figures

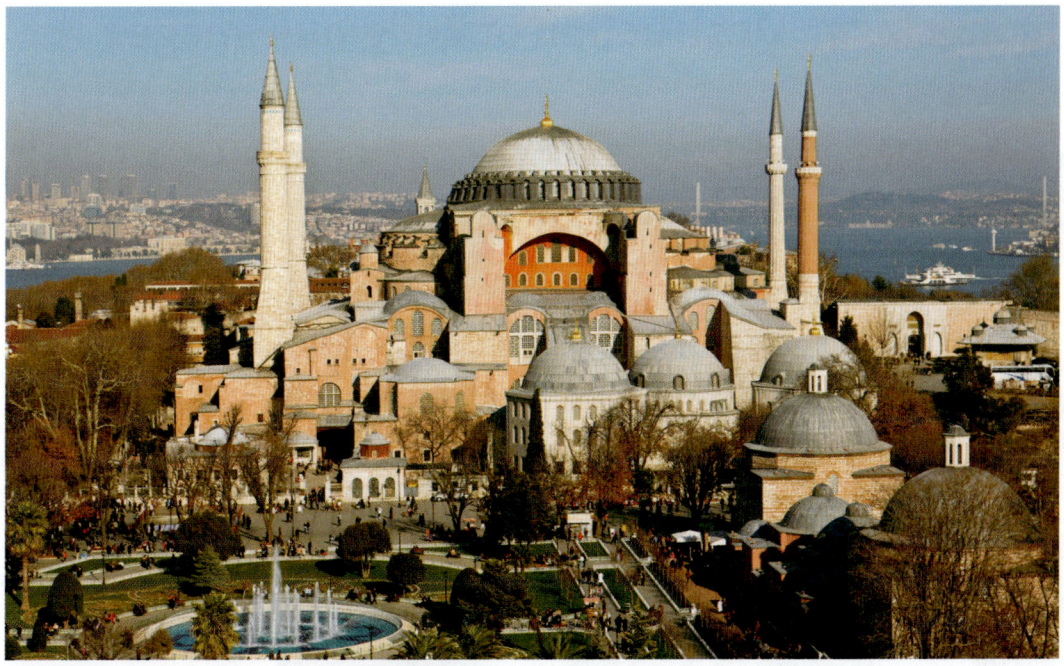

3.2.6 Hagia Sophia (exterior), 532–35 CE, Istanbul, Turkey

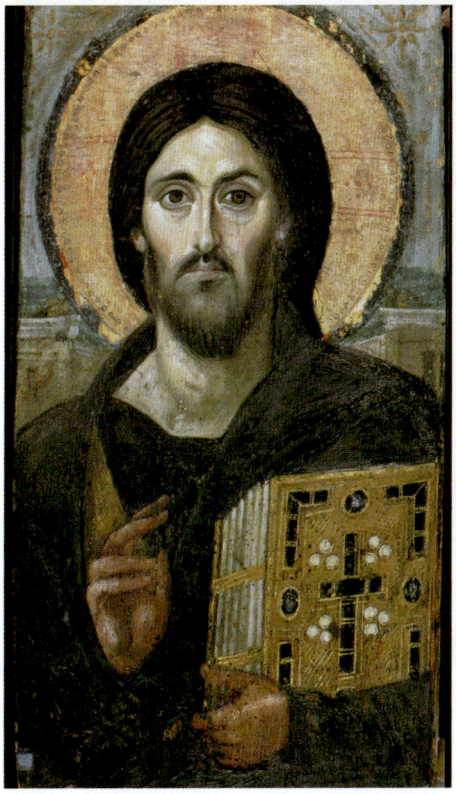

3.2.7 Christ icon, 6th century. Encaustic, 33 × 18". St. Catherine Monastery, Mount Sinai, Egypt

Central plan: Eastern Orthodox church design, often in the shape of a cross with all four arms of equal length
Icon: a small, often portable, religious image venerated by Christian believers; first used by the Eastern Orthodox Church
Nave: the central space of a cathedral or basilica

on wooden panels, are still used in the Eastern Orthodox Church for meditation and prayer. Many early Christians believed icons had special healing powers; therefore, icons that survive are often faded from being kissed and touched by numerous worshipers.

The sixth-century icon of Christ (**3.2.7**) from the St. Catherine Monastery is intended to show the dual nature of Christ as both human and God. As in the Good Shepherd mosaic (**3.2.5**, p. 393), here Christ is shown as a regal figure, wearing a rich purple robe. He is now represented with a beard and long hair, which became the convention in subsequent Christian art. Christ's duality is brilliantly portrayed here by the differences made to each side of his face; his right side (the viewer's left) represents his heavenly half, and his left side his human half. The right side of Christ's face is ideally proportioned, with a healthy glow, and his hair is in place. By comparison, his left side seems to sag slightly, his eyes and mouth have wrinkles, and his hair is somewhat disheveled. His right hand forms into a gesture of holy blessing, while his left hand holds scripture, sacred writings read by those on Earth.

One of the most beautiful Byzantine churches was built in Ravenna, Italy, in the sixth century (**3.2.9**, p. 397). Central-plan churches were a common style in the Eastern Orthodox tradition, as opposed to the Latin-cross design of the West (see **3.2.22**, p. 405). The floor plan of the Church of San Vitale is based on two octagons, one inside the other. The smaller octagon, the **nave**, is a space nearly 100 ft. high, filled with windows, and covered by a dome. Natural light glistens off the glass mosaics that cover the walls. Eight semicircular bays emanate from the

Iconoclasm: Destruction of Religious Images

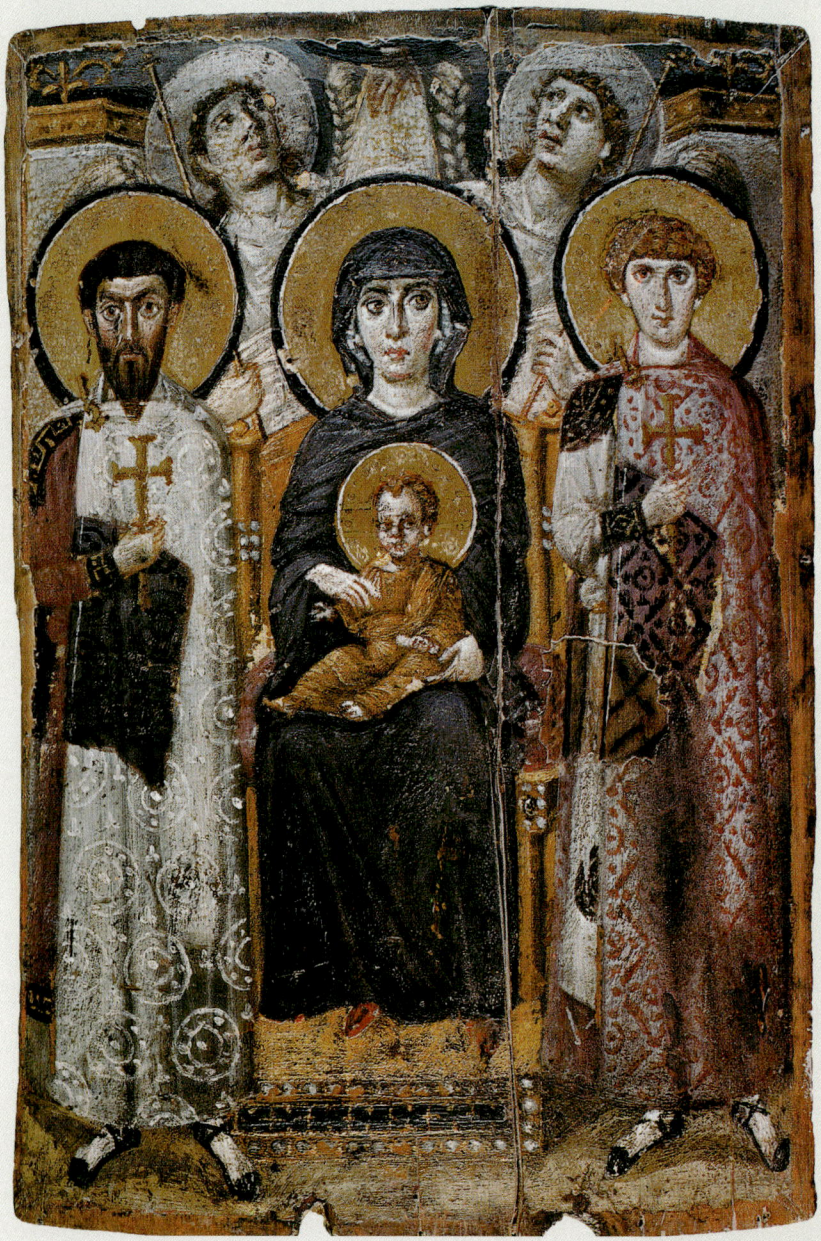

3.2.8 *Virgin and Child Surrounded by Saints*, 6th century. Encaustic, 27 × 19⅝". Monastery of St. Catherine, Sinai, Egypt

Iconoclast: someone who destroys images, often out of religious belief
Intercessor: one who pleads with God on behalf of others

Icons, or religious images, are designed to create a state of meditation, in which the artworks are studied for long periods, inspiring worship. Iconoclasm, or the destruction of religious images, shows the power art can have, and the fear its power can generate.

The Byzantine empire's iconoclastic controversy in the eighth and ninth centuries was provoked by divisions amongst Christians over the interpretation of the Bible's Second Commandment: "You shall not make for yourself an idol, whether in the form of anything in heaven above, or that is on the Earth beneath, or that is in the water under the Earth. You shall not bow down to them or worship them." Some Christians took this commandment to mean that icons, which might inspire too much worship, should be prohibited.

A study of the icon *Virgin and Child Surrounded by Saints* (**3.2.8**) can help us understand why the **iconoclasts** were so concerned that Christians might confuse worship of an image with worship of the holy figures themselves. In the icon, Mary initially attracts our attention because she sits in the center, wearing a dark purple gown (purple being the imperial color), and presents Christ, who sits on her lap. The bearded St. Theodore and the beardless St. George stand slightly in front of the Virgin's throne. The saints are closest to us because they are human and therefore most like us. The two figures behind the enthroned Mary are angels looking up at heaven. Between them and above Mary is the hand of God. A hierarchy is thus created as we "enter" the picture through Mary, who is herself an **intercessor** for believers to pray to Christ and God.

Many of these icons were so well loved, and so frequently touched and kissed, that they have deteriorated significantly. Iconoclasts were concerned that the faithful were worshiping icons of religious figures rather than worshiping Mary and Jesus directly. This fundamental disagreement led to the destruction of thousands of Byzantine icons, including almost all portrayals of Christ and Mary. Most of the surviving icons from before the ninth century are in St. Catherine's Monastery at the foot of Mount Sinai, where they were protected by their location in the Egyptian desert.

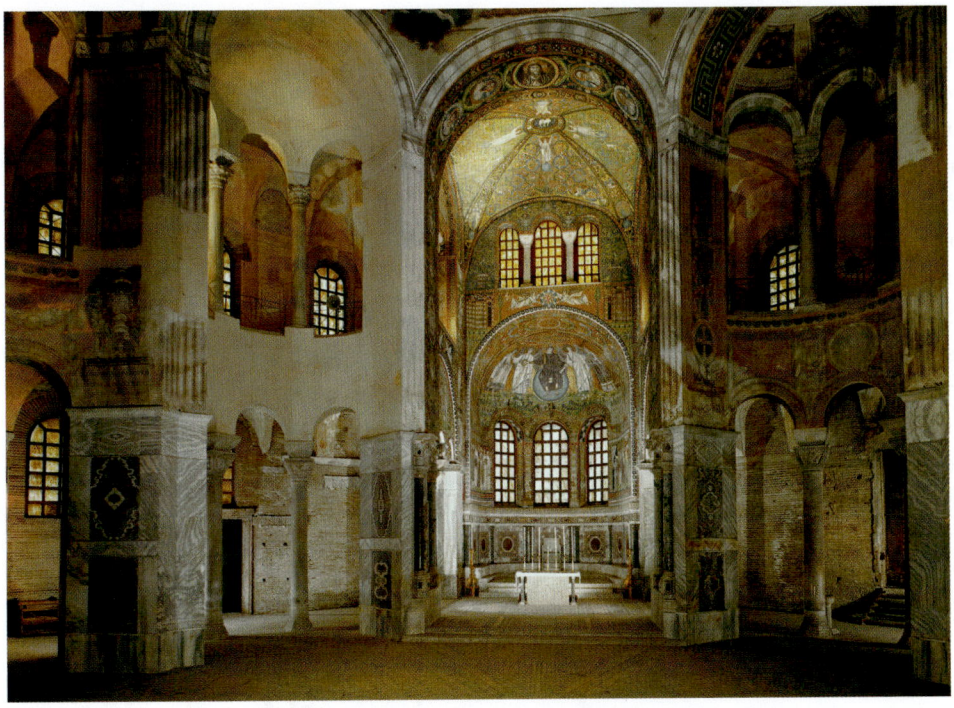

Apse: semicircular vaulted space in a church
Altar: an area where sacrifices or offerings are made
Outline: the outermost line or implied line of an object or figure, by which it is defined or bounded

3.2.9 Church of San Vitale, *c.* 547 CE, Ravenna, Italy

center, with the **apse** that contains the **altar** on the southeast side; above the altar is a mosaic of Christ enthroned on Earth. Flanking either side of the apse are glorious glass mosaics of the emperor Justinian and the empress Theodora.

It is characteristic of Byzantine art that figures and their clothing are often boldly **outlined**. Such delineation creates a flatness to the figures and decreases their three-dimensionality. This lack of volume or mass, along with the way the figures seem to float, gives a timeless, spiritual quality to the image, as if it belongs somewhere between the heavenly and earthly realms. The figures in the image are even layered so that their repetition creates a sense of movement toward the altar.

Justinian stands in the center of his mosaic (**3.2.10**), wearing the imperial color purple. On either side of him are clergy in white robes. To his far right are soldiers, who display a large shield that bears the Greek letters for Christ (*chi-rho*), emphasizing Justinian's role as a Christian military leader. There are other Christian symbols in the mosaic: the men to the left of the emperor hold a cross, a copy of the gospels (the first four books of the New Testament), and a censer used to burn incense in church services. Justinian holds the bread

3.2.10 Emperor Justinian, *c.* 547, glass mosaic, San Vitale, Ravenna, Italy

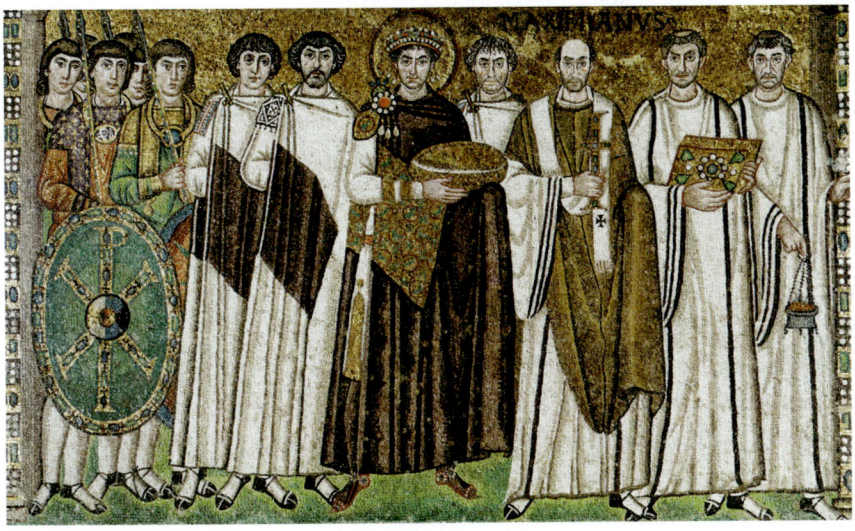

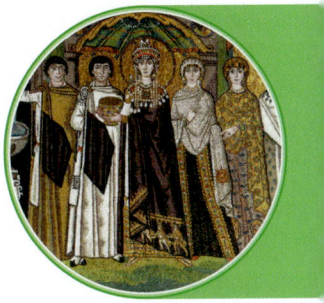

A mosaic featuring Empress Theodora holding a chalice of wine, representing Christ's blood, is placed across the apse from the mosaic of her husband, Emperor Justinian: see **4.6.4, p. 631**

used to represent the body of Christ in the communion service, recalling that the mosaic itself is displayed near the altar where the service would take place. Interestingly, one other figure in this mosaic is given special recognition: the local bishop, Maximianus. It was Maximianus who arranged the commission and organized the composition so that his figure was the only one identified in writing on the image (his name is written above his portrait). The bishop also requested that his feet should be placed slightly in front of the emperor. Justinian himself needed no such label; the imperial robe, in addition to his crown and halo, were enough to identify the ruler.

Manuscripts and the Middle Ages

Manuscripts (books written and decorated by hand) are some of the richest and most detailed artworks made by Muslims and Christians in the Middle Ages. The production of manuscripts was intensely laborious, from making the pages out of animal hides to copying painstakingly in careful handwriting. Manuscripts were the work of many artists (usually monks and sometimes nuns), some specializing in decorative lettering (scribes), and others in painting images (illuminators). Jewelers and workers in fine metals often contributed to decorating the covers. The great effort required to create a manuscript was considered a tribute to God.

Islamic manuscripts rarely show human figures, and never the image of Allah (God). Rather, attention is paid to the word of Allah, recorded in the Koran, and revealed in elegant script. Islamic artworks often have an **arabesque** quality, and this is particularly apparent in manuscripts.

Surah (chapters) from the Koran are written in Arabic, from right to left, but the script varies from region to region. In a beautiful page of the Koran from thirteenth-century Spain (**3.2.11**), the oldest Arabic script, *kufic*, is used for the headings, while the script *maghribi* is used for the rest of the text. This regional script derived its name from its popularity in the region of Maghreb, which in the Middle Ages included northern Africa and Islamic areas of Spain. The areas in the manuscript where the text is thicker and in gold signify the heading for a new chapter. The ornamental circular designs in gold break the reading into appropriate sections.

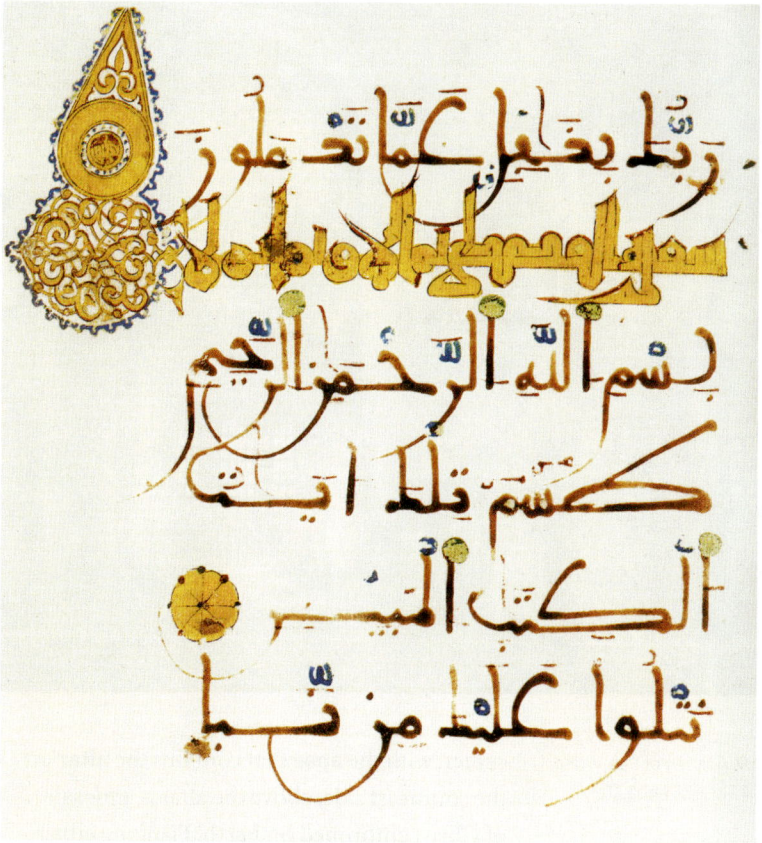

3.2.11 Page from the Koran, probably late 13th century, *maghribi* on vellum, 7½ × 7½". British Library, London, England

The Lindisfarne Gospels are an illuminated manuscript book of the Christian gospels of Matthew, Mark, Luke, and John (known as the Four Evangelists). They were made during the early eighth century. Each gospel is decorated with a "cross-and-carpet" page (named for its similarity to a carpet design). The design in the cross-and-carpet page at the beginning of St. Matthew's gospel appears to be made up of numerous intertwining lines (**3.2.12a**). Upon closer inspection, however, tiny animal heads can be seen twisting throughout (**3.2.12b**). While the specific meaning of these animals is unclear, this decorative element was common in the Middle Ages, particularly in northeast England, where the Lindisfarne Gospels were made.

The Lindisfarne Gospels were scribed fully or in part by a bishop named Eadfrith, who signed his name to the manuscript. The pages, written

Manuscripts: handwritten texts
Arabesque: an abstract pattern derived from geometric and vegetal lines and forms
Illuminations: illustrations and decorations in a manuscript
Stained glass: colored glass used for windows or decorative applications

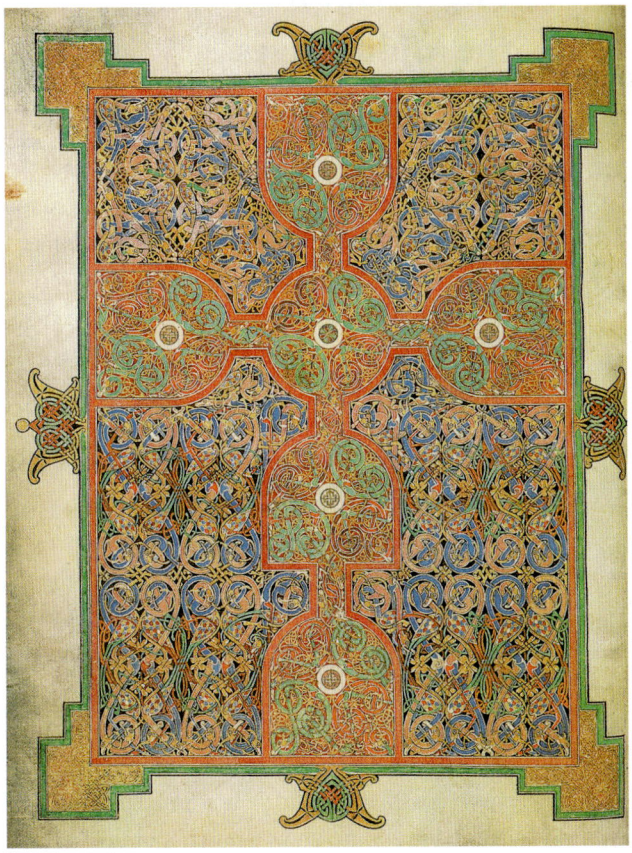

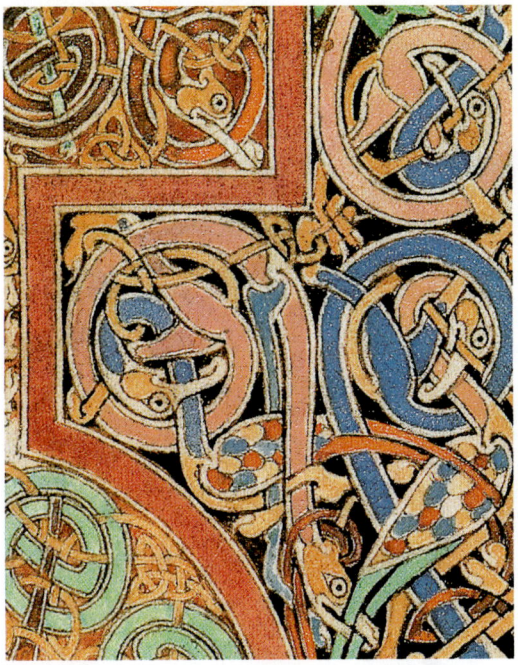

3.2.12a (left) Cross-and-carpet page introducing the Gospel according to St. Matthew. Lindisfarne Gospels, fol. 26b, 710–721. Illuminated manuscript, British Library, London, England

3.2.12b (above) Detail of **3.2.12a**

in Latin, would have taken him at least five years to complete. Such beautiful pages as these are often called **illuminations** because their rich colors recall light shining through **stained glass** in a cathedral. (Similarly, because of their didactic nature, stained-glass windows have been called "books in glass," and the sculpture around cathedrals "books in stone.") Both the Lindisfarne Gospels and the Spanish Koran were made to be studied and enjoyed over long periods of contemplation.

Manuscripts often illustrated religious stories or the visions of spiritual leaders. Hildegard of Bingen was a Christian mystic and visionary; she advised kings and popes, who often traveled long distances to meet with her. Born into an aristocratic family and educated as a nun, she eventually became abbess of a convent in Germany. Her visions included insights into medicine, astronomy, and politics, which she shared in a book called *Scivias* (*Know the Ways*), which was read throughout Europe. The original manuscript was destroyed during World War II; however, from copies of *Scivias* we know that Hildegard was repeatedly portrayed in the act of receiving a vision. Her assistant is also usually shown transcribing her vision (**3.2.13**). This misleadingly suggests that the scribe wrote on the pages after they were bound. In reality, the manuscript took months to make: it was carefully graphed out on pieces of paper before being put together as a book. Hildegard

3.2.13 *The Fifth Vision of Hildegard of Bingen*, frontispiece for *Scivias*, c. 1230, original manuscript lost. Biblioteca Governativa, Lucca, Italy

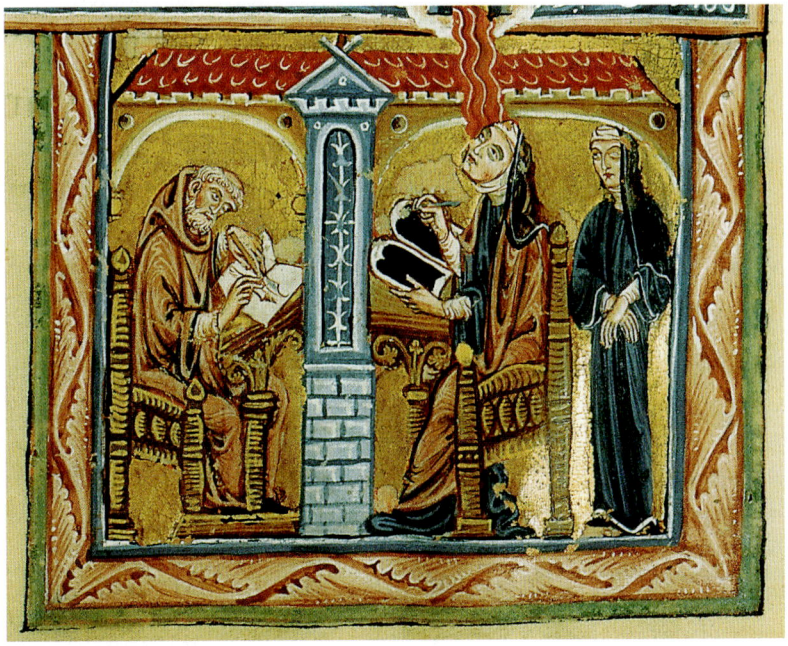

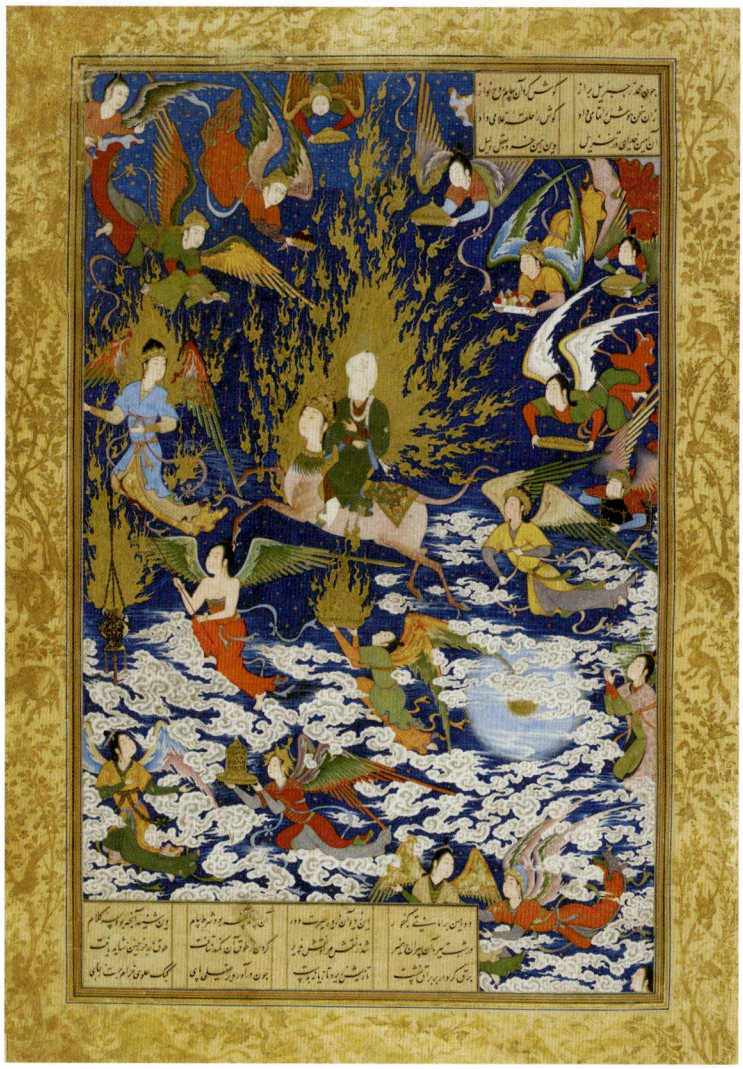

Pilgrimage in the Middle Ages

Pilgrimages were integral to the practice of Christianity, Islam, and Judaism. In medieval Europe, devout Christian pilgrims journeyed to holy sites where significant religious events had occurred or where relics were kept. Relics were holy objects (such as a piece of the wooden cross on which Christ was crucified), or body parts of saints or holy figures. Elaborately decorated containers called reliquaries were made to house individual relics, and they were designed to look like the relic they contained. Thus, the reliquary of the Head of St. Alexander (**3.2.15**) houses a skull. This reliquary was made in 1145 for the Abbot Wibald of Stavelot in Belgium. The face is made of beaten silver (**repoussé**), with the hair made from gilded bronze. The emphasis on the portrait itself recalls the Roman heads of antiquity. The head is placed upon a base covered with gems and pearls. Small plaques painted in enamel show a portrait of the sainted Pope Alexander in the center, flanked by two other saints.

3.2.14 *The Ascent of the Prophet Muhammad on His Steed, Buraq, Guided by Jibra'il and Escorted by Angels*, 1539–43. Miniature painting from a manuscript of Nizami's *Khamsa (Five Poems)*, originally produced in Tabriz, Iran

described the experience of receiving visions as "a fiery light, flashing intensely, which came from the open vault of heaven and poured through my whole brain," an apt description for what is taking place in the manuscript shown here.

Islamic manuscripts often depict events from the life of Muhammad, the main prophet of Allah. The manuscript painting in **3.2.14** shows the ascension of Muhammad, which Muslims believe took place at the Dome of the Rock in Jerusalem (see **3.2.16**). Muhammad's face is not shown, but is covered with a veil. He is surrounded by blinding flames, which signify his holiness, as he rides his half-human horse Buraq toward the heavens. On the left, guiding Muhammad, is the angel Gabriel (Jibra'il), whose head is also encircled with fire. Manuscripts in the Middle Ages are richly detailed objects that reflect the piety of the time.

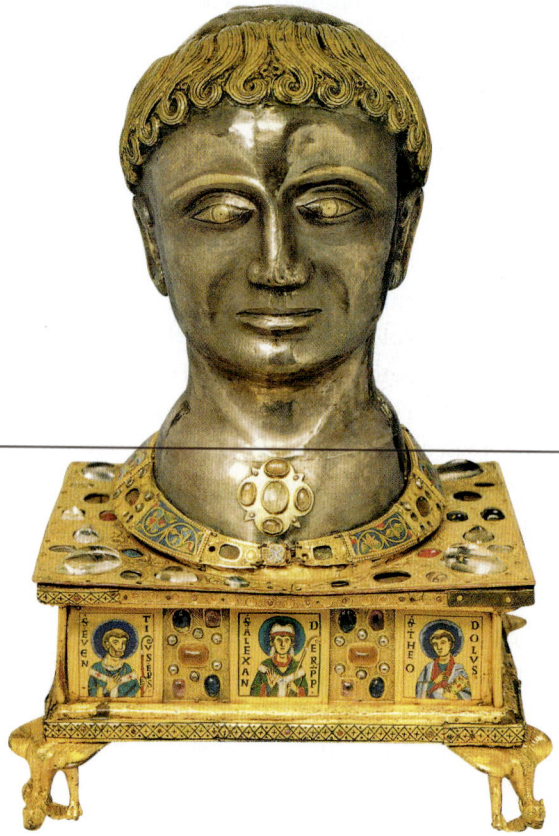

3.2.15 (right) Reliquary of the Head of St. Alexander, 1145. Silver repoussé, gilt bronze, gems, pearls, and enamel, height 7½". Musées Royaux d'Art et d'Histoire, Brussels, Belgium

Repoussé: a technique of hammering metal from the back to create a form or surface detail

Jerusalem

Throughout the Middle Ages, devout people made pilgrimages to the city of Jerusalem; a shining gold dome still marks a site in the city that is sacred to Jews, Christians, and Muslims alike (**3.2.16**). The Dome of the Rock surrounds the sacred Foundation Stone, which Jews believe is the site of the beginning of the world, and Muslims believe is the rock from which Muhammad ascended to heaven. To Jews and Christians, this site is also thought to be the place where Adam was created and where Abraham was asked to sacrifice his son.

The Dome of the Rock was built as a site for pilgrims (not as a mosque) between 688 and 691 under the order of Abd al-Malik, who wanted it to surpass all Christian churches in the Middle East. Although al-Malik was a caliph (an Islamic ruler), the Dome of the Rock was probably built by Christian laborers; its proportions, octagonal shape, dome, and mosaic designs show a clear Byzantine style.

The glorious dome that crowns the shrine was originally solid gold, but was rebuilt in the twentieth century with aluminum. In 1993, King Hussein of Jordan spent more than $8 million of his own money to gild the aluminum with gold. The height and diameter of the dome are approximately 67 ft. each, as is the length of each of the eight walls. The walls of the octagon are covered with verses in Arabic calligraphy from the Koran. Since 2006, although all religions are permitted on the Temple Mount, only Muslims have been allowed within the domed shrine.

Mecca and Mosques

Mecca, Saudi Arabia, is the most important pilgrimage site for Muslims. The prophet Muhammad was born in Mecca around 570.

3.2.16 Dome of the Rock, 688–91, Jerusalem, Israel

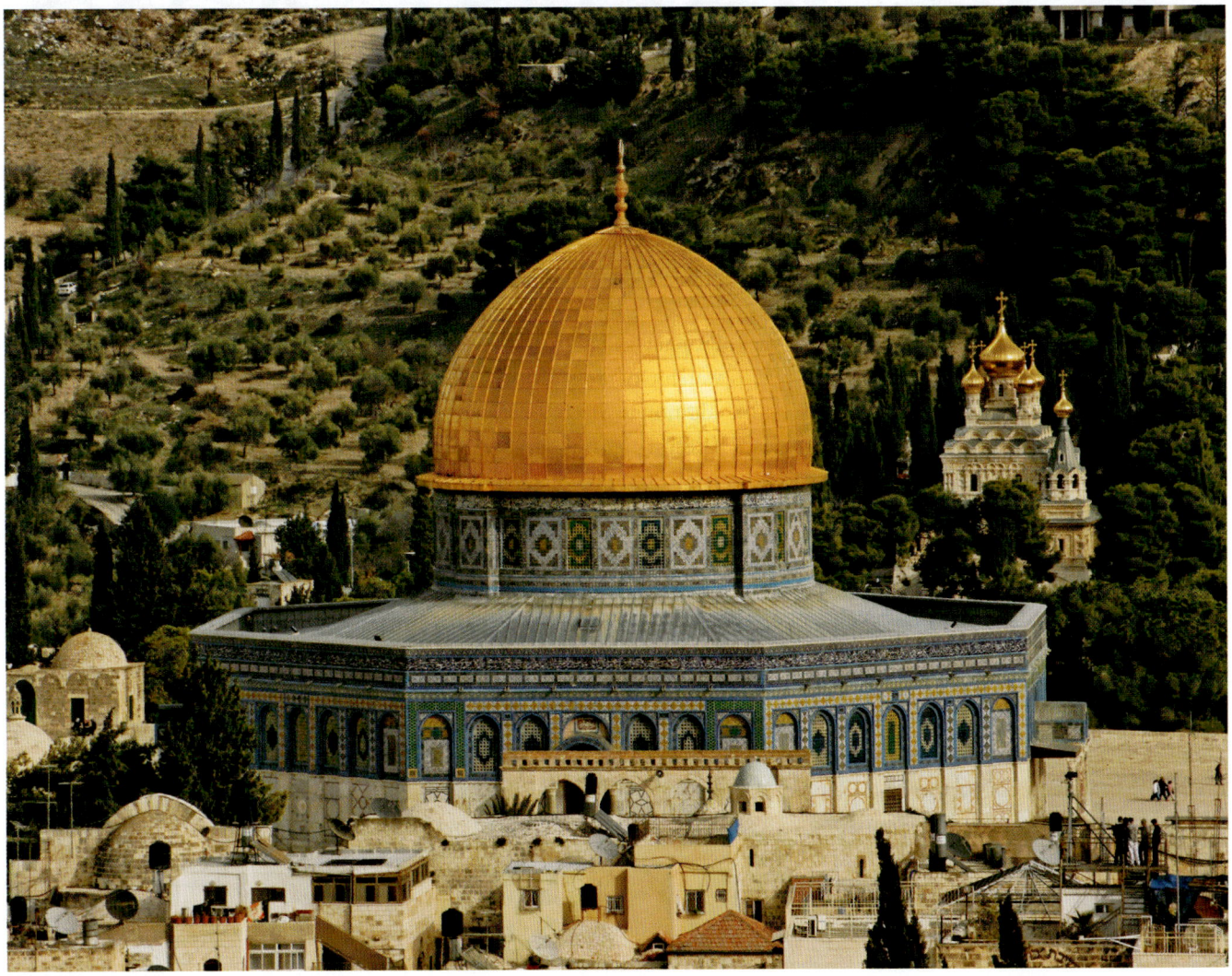

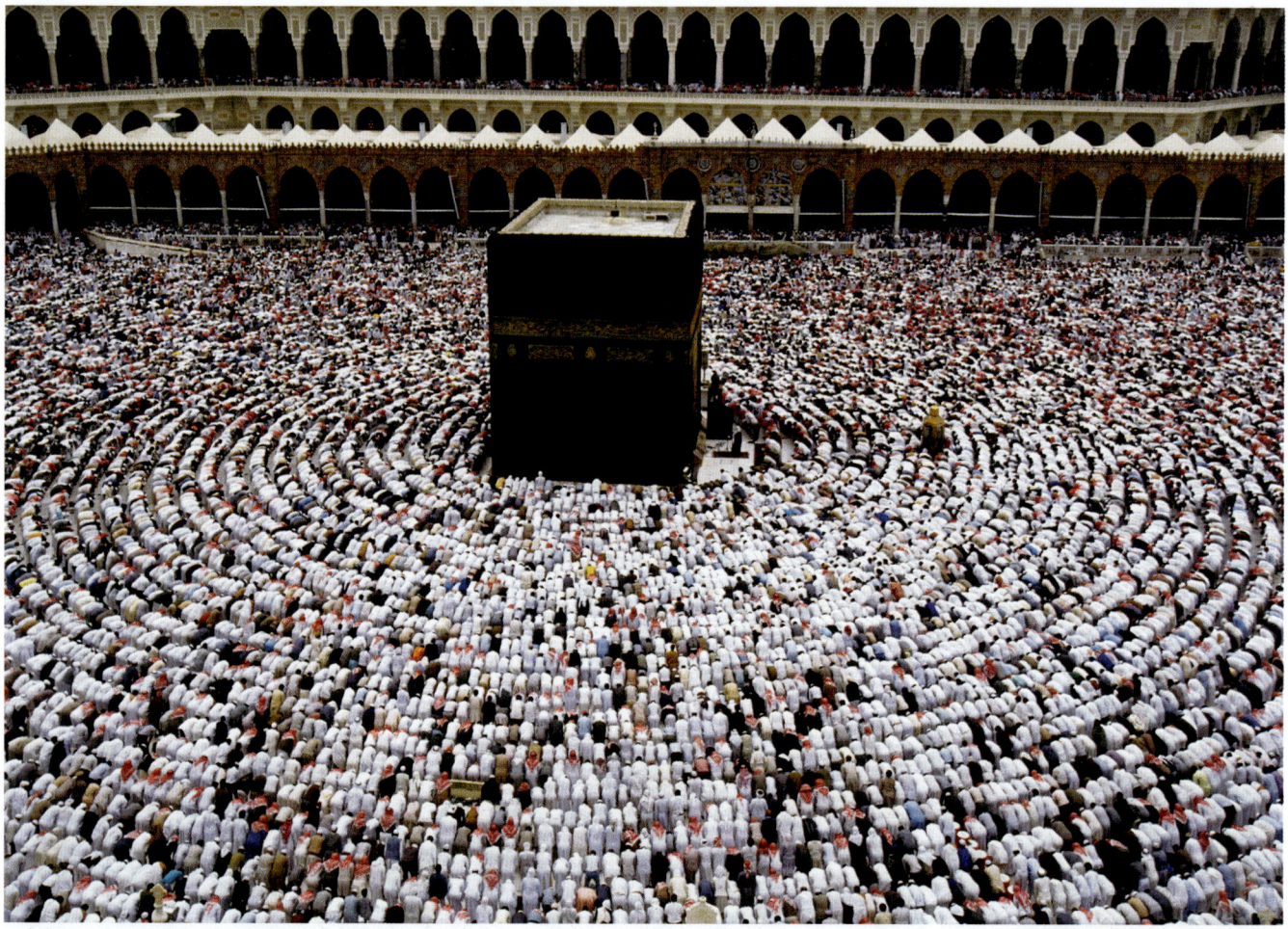

3.2.17 Pilgrims surrounding Kaaba, Al Masjid al-Haram, Mecca, Saudi Arabia

Mecca is also the site of the Kaaba, a large cube-shaped building (today draped in black-and-gold cloth), built by Abraham for God (**3.2.17**), which is surrounded by a large mosque. Like Christian churches, mosques are designed to reflect religious belief and practice. In the center of each mosque complex is usually a large courtyard with a pool where the faithful can cleanse themselves before entering the mosque itself to pray. Muslims must pray five times a day in the direction of Mecca. They are called to prayer from the mosque's large minarets that rise above the city: nine distinctive minarets surround the mosque in Mecca. One of the five important commitments of the Muslim faith (known as the Five Pillars of Islam) is the obligation to visit Mecca once in one's lifetime, unless sickness or some other factor makes this impossible, to honor the house of Allah. Although pilgrimage is important to many Christians, it has never been an obligation as it is in Islam.

Unlike Christians, Muslims do not worship relics of holy figures and saints since for Muslims there is only one God, called Allah, and the Prophet Muhammad specifically forbade the worship of idols. Nevertheless, one holy place in addition to Mecca, Medina, is a destination for Muslim pilgrims because it is the location of the tomb of Muhammad himself. Many pilgrims do visit the mosque (**3.2.18**), often before or after a visit to Mecca, in order to "greet" the Prophet, but limit themselves to a greeting as Islam prohibits worship of any other than Allah.

The original mosque on the site was built by Muhammad himself and was his house as well as a place of worship. The building measured 100 cubits (about 183 ft.) on all sides, and was built of mud-brick, with palm trunks to support a flat roof over the northern part of the building, where worshipers prayed toward Jerusalem. In 624, however, Allah revealed to Muhammad that the direction of prayer (known as the ***qibla***) should be redirected to the south, toward Mecca.

Qibla: the direction to Mecca, toward which Muslims face when praying

***Mihrab*:** a niche in a mosque that is in a wall oriented toward Mecca
Minbar: a platform in a mosque, from which a leader delivers sermons

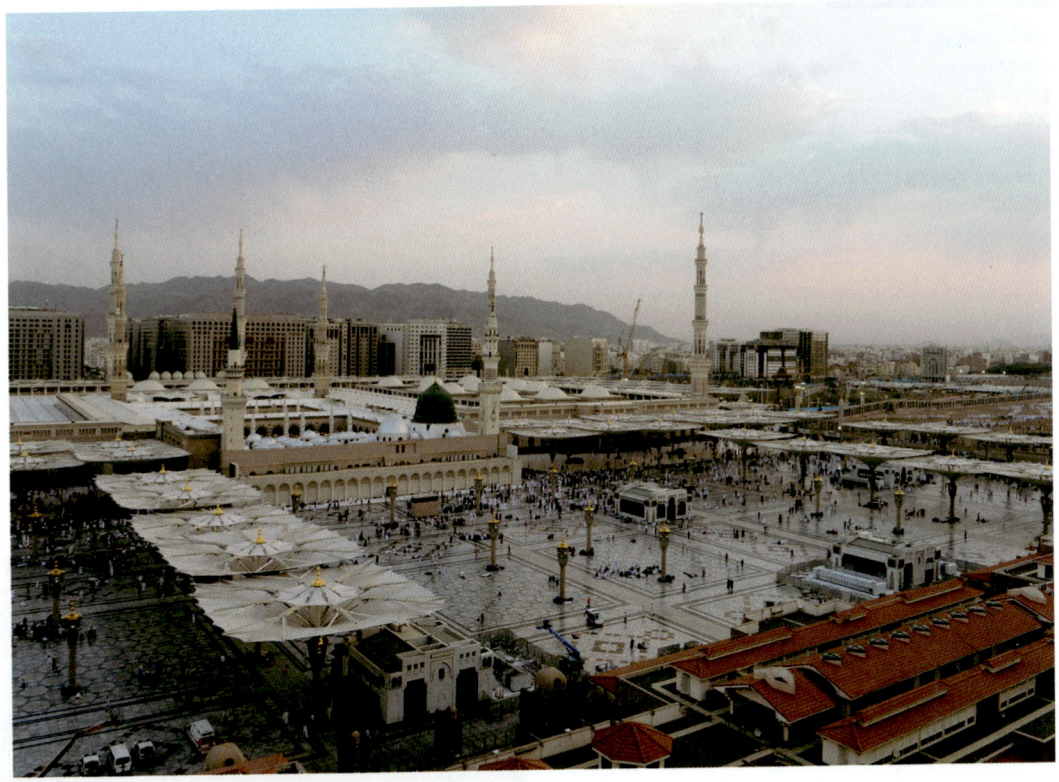

3.2.18 (right) Masjid al-Nabawi (The Prophet's Mosque), Medina, Saudi Arabia

3.2.19 (below) *View of the sanctuary at Medina*, 17th or 18th century. Opaque watercolor, gold, silver, and ink on paper, 25½ × 18¼". Nasser D. Khalili Collection of Islamic Art

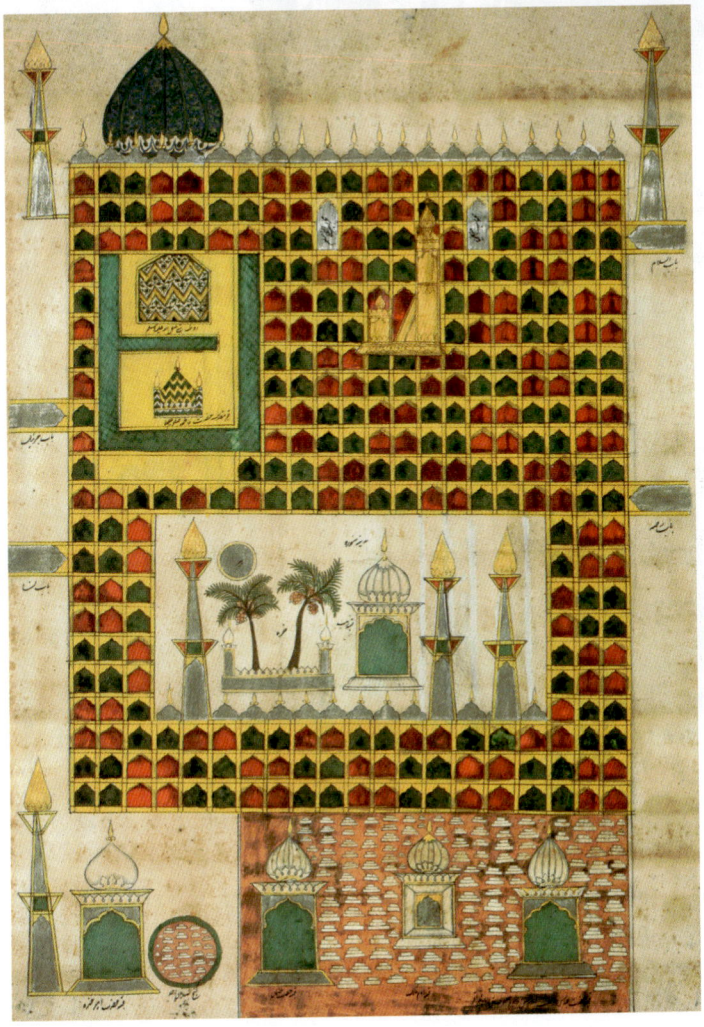

In the eighth century a curved prayer niche, called a ***mihrab***, was built into the southern wall. All mosques include a mihrab within them, placed on the wall facing Mecca (known as the qibla wall). This enables Muslims to pray toward Mecca from any mosque in which they may happen to be.

Subsequent rulers have greatly enlarged the mosque, making it one hundred times bigger than the original. They have added a courtyard, school, resting places for pilgrims, ten minarets, and twenty-four domes. The slightly taller green dome marks the spot of Muhammad's tomb (**3.2.18**). Within the mosque, the most sacred spot is the Riad-ul Jannah. Placed between the prophet's **minbar** (pulpit) and his tomb, it is believed to be a piece of the Garden of Paradise.

A two-dimensional diagram, including labels (**3.2.19**), shows the sanctuary at Medina. Both the sanctuary and Mecca were quite often depicted in this way. This image shows the tomb chamber of the Prophet (identifiable by its green dome) in the upper left-hand corner. A textile covering patterned in green and white chevrons is visible on the grille and tomb within the chamber.

At the center of the image is the garden that Fatima, the daughter of the Prophet, planted

Arcade: a series of connected arches
Arches: structures, usually curved, that span an opening
Vault: an arch-like structure supporting a ceiling or roof
Column: freestanding pillar, usually circular in section

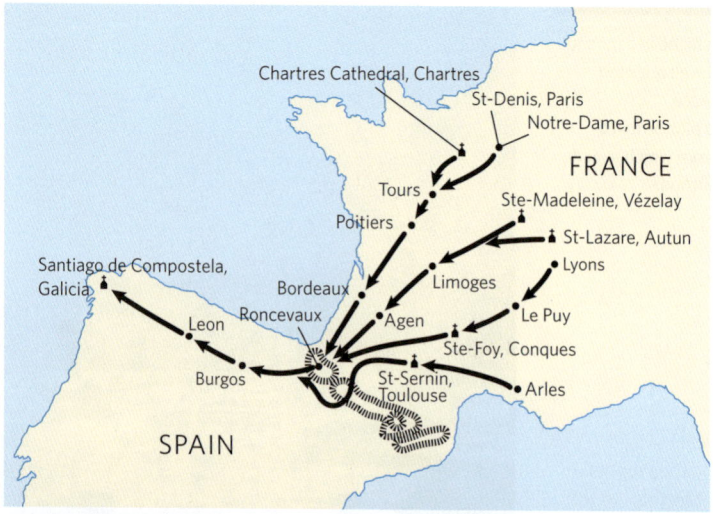

3.2.20 Pilgrimage map showing the routes from France toward Santiago de Compostela, with important churches including Sainte-Foy at Conques

with two palm trees; her tomb is also shown there, while others—belonging to some of the Prophet's companions—can be seen outside the walls of the sanctuary. To the right of the diagram, standing in the **arcades**, we can see the Prophet's minbar, from which he preached.

Romanesque Art and Christian Pilgrimages

One of the most traveled pilgrimage journeys in the Middle Ages was to the burial site of St. James at the Cathedral of Santiago de Compostela in Galicia, Spain. The official paths to the cathedral (The Way of St. James) started at four important sites in France (**3.2.20**), each of which held a religious relic. During the journey, which could take several months, pilgrims would stop at other important sites for rest, food, and spiritual nourishment. Along the way large churches were built, even in small towns that could not otherwise have funded such expansive construction, in order to accommodate the crowds of pilgrims.

One such small town was Conques in France. Conques was a stop along one of the French routes to Santiago de Compostela, but was also a pilgrimage destination in its own right. In the ninth century, a monk from Conques stole the relics of Sainte Foy (Saint Faith) from their original resting place in the much larger town of Agen. According to legend, Sainte Foy was a young woman who lived in Agen in the third century. She was tortured to death with a red-hot brazier during the persecution of Christians in about 290 or 303 CE. A number of miracles attributed to the relics made Conques a famous pilgrimage site, and by the eleventh century the numbers of pilgrims made a new church to house the relics necessary.

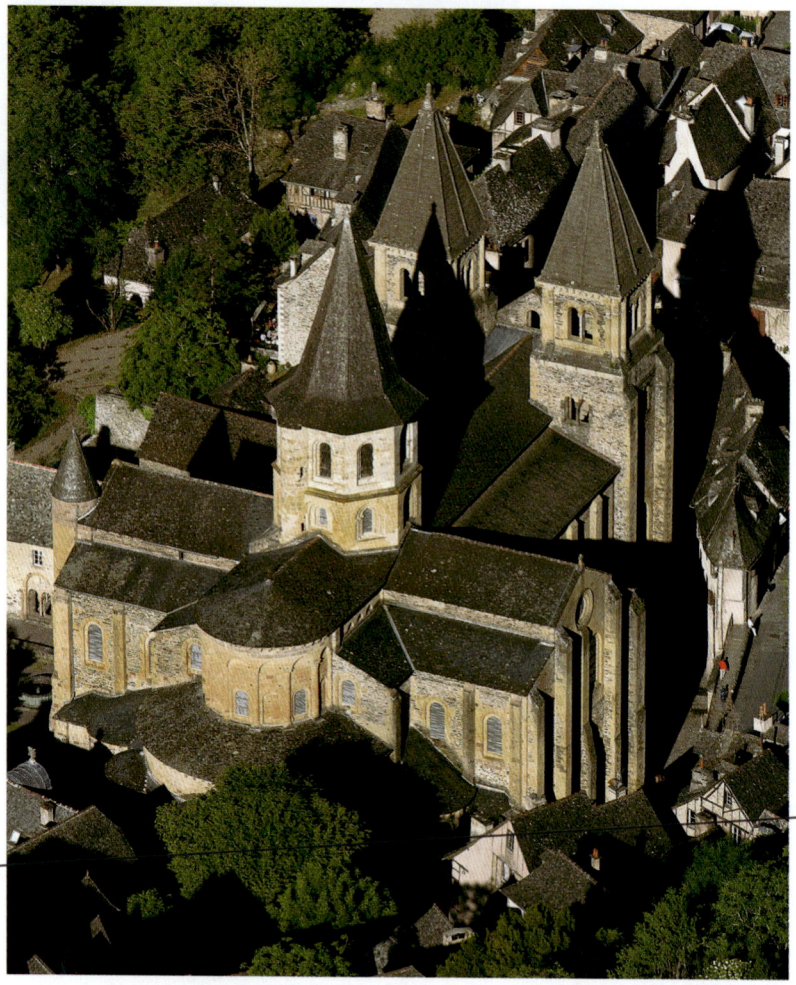

3.2.21 Church of Sainte-Foy, Conques, France

Sainte-Foy is a characteristically Romanesque church (**3.2.21**). Its **arches**, **vaults**, and **columns** recall architectural elements from ancient Rome. For example, the exterior arches are rounded.

Churches in the Middle Ages in the Western tradition were often designed, as Sainte-Foy was, in the shape of a Latin cross (**3.2.22**). In this kind

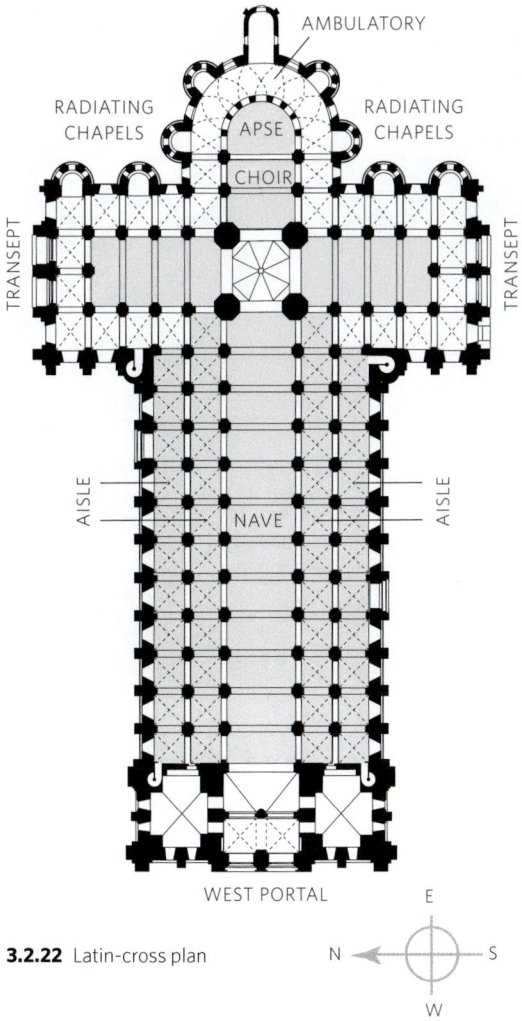

3.2.22 Latin-cross plan

of plan the main and longer **axis** (the nave) usually runs from west to east, with a shorter axis (the **transept**) at right angles across it nearer the east end. Cathedral floor plans were designed to guide the flow of visiting pilgrims and the congregation during services. Worshipers entered at the west end and walked eastward down the nave toward the altar. The **choir** continued the nave on the other side of the crossing. As it was closest to the apse, which contained the altar, it was reserved for the clergy and, as its name suggests, the choir of singers. Pilgrims could also circle around behind the apse through the **ambulatory** and visit individual chapels, most of which held sacred relics.

The west–east orientation of churches, like the shape of the cross, also has symbolic meaning. The crucifixion is often depicted in a painting or sculpture at the east end, while an artwork of the Last Judgment may be displayed at the western **portal**, where parishioners and pilgrims would enter and exit. The orientation of the church also mimics the natural course of the sun: thus to the east, Christ, as "light of the world," rises like the sun in the morning, while to the west, the setting sun reminds worshipers of their own mortality and the impending Judgment Day.

Most people in the Middle Ages were illiterate, so pictures taught religious stories to pilgrims and parishioners alike, and thus reinforced their faith. Portals, or gateways, served as both entrances and exits to the church for the public (see diagram, **3.2.23**). In many Romanesque churches, the **tympanum**, **lintel**, **trumeau**, and **door jambs** were all covered with **relief** sculptures, often of scenes from the Bible, and originally colorfully painted.

The tympanum above the entryway to Sainte-Foy (**3.2.24**, p. 406) shows the Last Judgment, using **hierarchical scale** to highlight the importance of Christ in the center; he is larger than the angels, prophets, and ancestors that surround him. He raises his right hand to show the salvation of those to his right, and lowers his left hand, marking the damnation

Axis: an imaginary line showing the center of a shape, volume, or composition
Transept: structure crossing the main body of a Latin-cross-plan church
Choir: part of a church traditionally reserved for singers and clergy, situated between the nave and the apse
Ambulatory: a covered walkway, particularly around the apse of a church
Portal: an entrance. A royal portal (main entrance) is usually on the west front of a church and features sculpted forms of kings and queens
Tympanum: an arched recess above a doorway, often decorated with carvings
Lintel: the horizontal beam over the doorway of a portal
Trumeau: within a portal, a central column that supports a tympanum
Door jamb: vertical sections, often containing sculpture, that form the sides of a portal
Relief: a sculpture that projects from a flat surface
Hierarchical scale: the use of size to denote the relative importance of subjects in an artwork

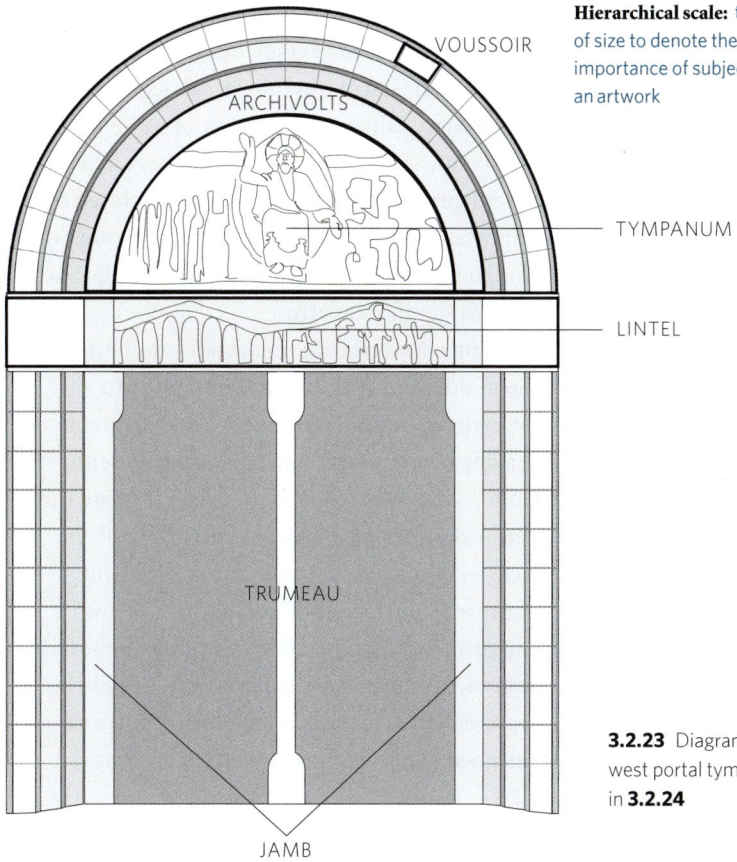

3.2.23 Diagram of the west portal tympanum in **3.2.24**

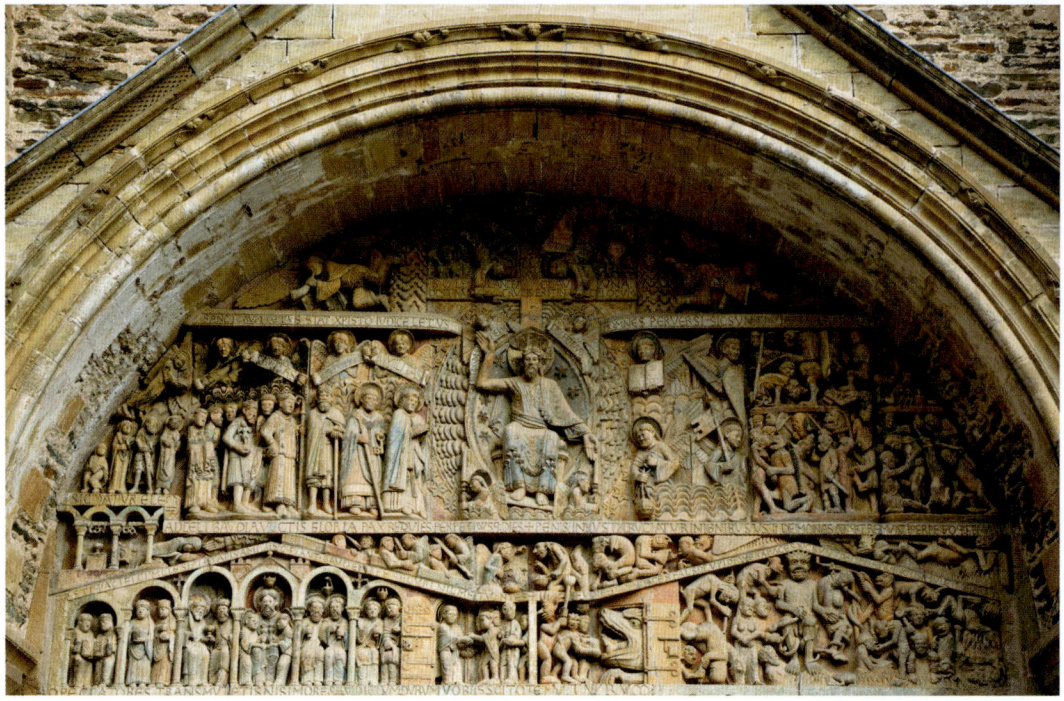

3.2.24 Tympanum of the west portal of Sainte-Foy, Conques, France

Mandorla: in art, an almond-shaped light, resembling a halo, which surrounds a holy person
Register: one of two or more horizontal sections into which a space is divided in order to depict the episodes of a story
Rib vault: an arch-like structure supporting a ceiling or roof, with a web of protruding stonework
Flying buttress: an arch built on the exterior of a building that transfers some of the weight of the vault

of those to his left. He is enclosed within a **mandorla**, an oval, pointed, full-body halo that is a decorative hallmark of the Romanesque style.

The entire scene is divided into three **registers**. The top register contains four angels, two of whom hold the cross and two who herald the Last Judgment with their horns. In the middle register, Christ is surrounded by more angels. To the left of Christ (Christ's right) are the Virgin Mary, with a faint amount of surviving blue paint, and St. Peter holding his keys. The other figures are historical people who played an important role in the history of the monastery of Conques, including King Charlemagne, who was its most significant patron.

Sainte Foy is shown on the left side, between the middle and bottom register, slightly to the right of some arches. She is bowing down, praying before a large hand, which represents God. To the right of Christ (Christ's left) are the damned, suffering a variety of tortures, often based on the kind of sin the damned person performed during his or her lifetime. Below Christ are scenes of souls being guided either to heaven, through an arched doorway, or to hell, represented by the head of a monster and a door designed to bolt in the damned for eternity.

The Rise of the Gothic

Gothic cathedrals have been called books or bibles in stone. Stories from the bible were carved into the stone and captured in the dazzling glass that covers and illuminates these cathedrals. First built in the twelfth century, the structures are distinguished by their immense height that reach toward the heavens, and glorious stained-glass windows, which symbolically fill the space with the light of God. The grand interior of Chartres Cathedral in France (**3.2.26**) combines all of the characteristic elements of Gothic architecture. The vaulted ceiling is 118 ft. above the floor and the nave is more than 50 ft. wide, surrounding receptive visitors with height and light to transport them beyond the cares and concerns of the mundane world.

Rib vaults make the great height of Gothic cathedrals possible: the weight of the structure is spread through the ribs of the ceiling vaults (see **3.2.26**), before further dividing the burden between the walls and **flying buttresses** (see **3.2.25** and **2.5.17b**, p. 268). Flying buttresses function like many long, outstretched fingers to prevent the walls from falling outward. Because these engineering achievements distributed the weight previously carried by very thick walls, it was possible to build with walls that

became progressively thinner. In addition, large stained-glass windows now filled cathedrals with light, as the walls no longer needed to bear all the weight of the structure. The cathedral at Chartres is famous for the beautiful blue cast from its stained-glass windows.

Cathedrals were built by hired mason-workers headed by one main architect. Funding for the cathedral was donated by townspeople and pilgrims, but part of the money came from bishops, the centralized Catholic Church, and wealthy individuals. By offering gifts to the Church, benefactors were not only acknowledged by others, but would also often be pardoned by religious officials for their sins.

Upon entering Chartres, pilgrims walked the labyrinth on the floor, symbolic of their physical and spiritual journey (**3.2.26**). Again, as at Sainte-Foy, the architects created a pathway through the cathedral that guided the pilgrims to the numerous chapels containing relics. The site of Chartres was particularly important for holding the tunic worn by the Virgin Mary at Christ's birth. When the tunic survived a fire in 1194, the townspeople believed this to be a sign that Mary continued to protect them and wished for them to rebuild the cathedral.

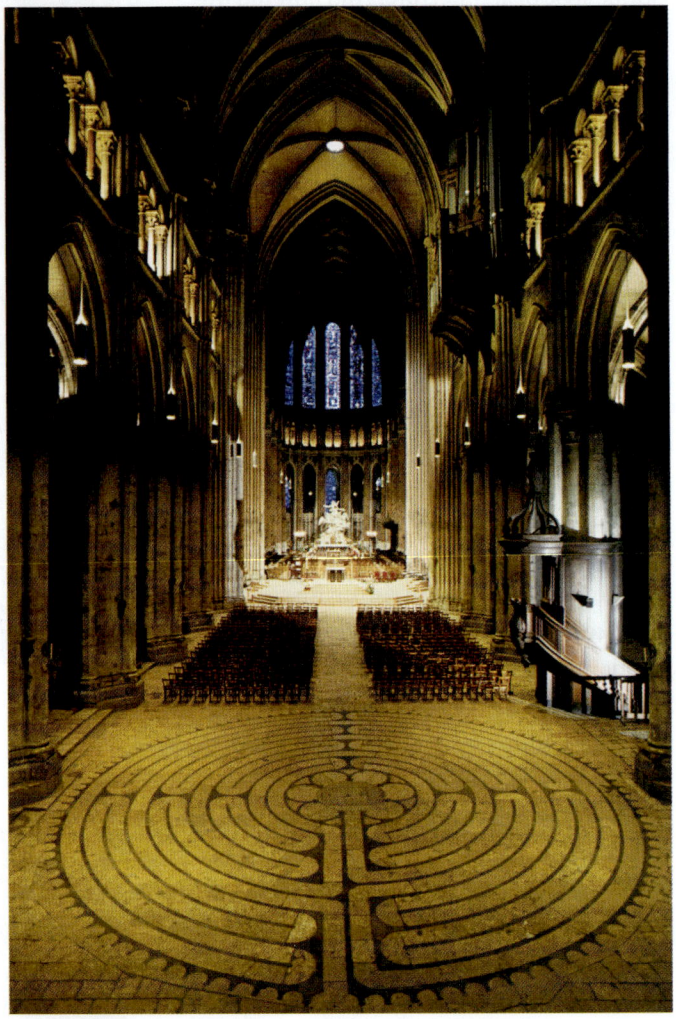

3.2.26 (above) Chartres Cathedral, interior view showing labyrinth

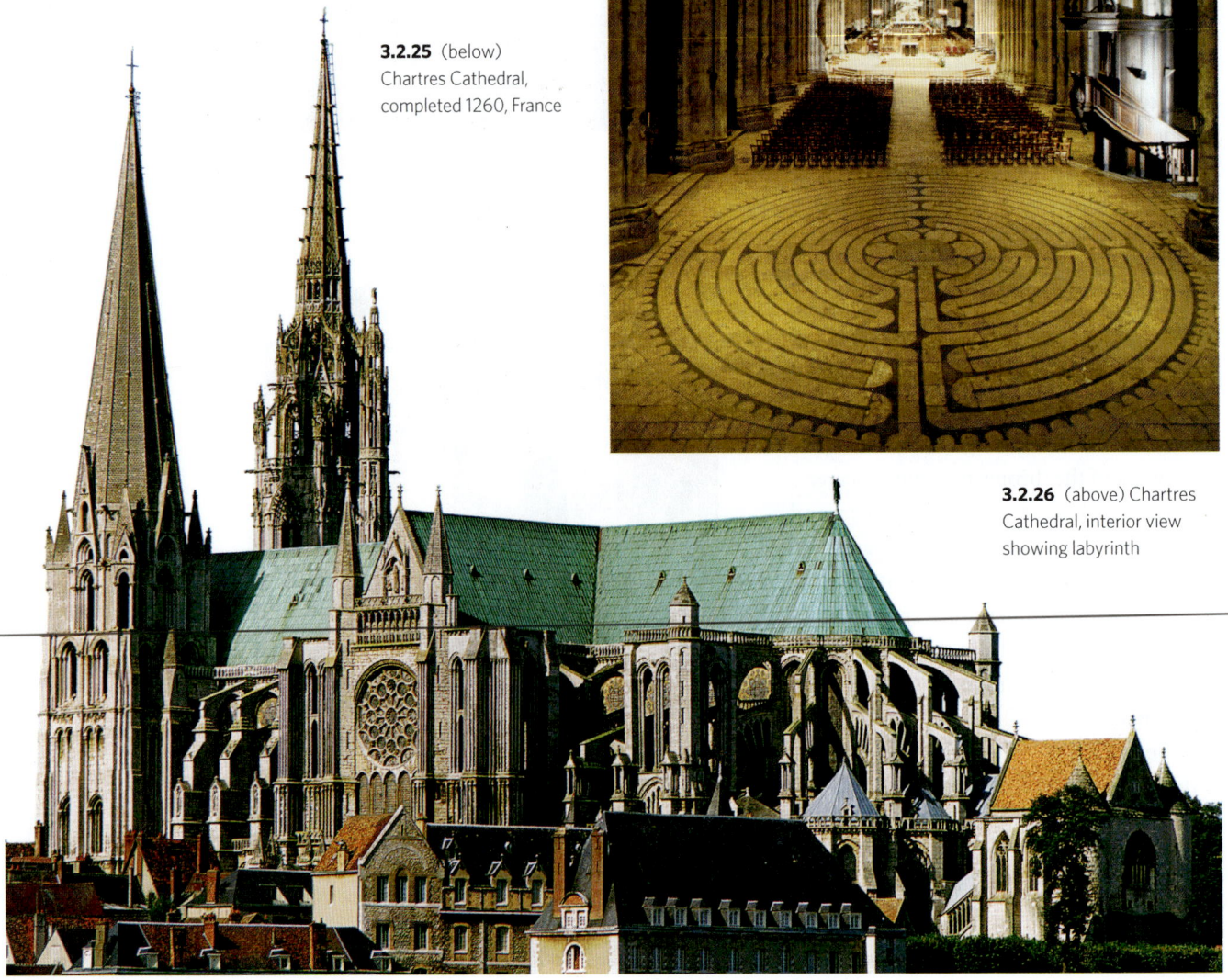

3.2.25 (below) Chartres Cathedral, completed 1260, France

From the Gothic to Early Renaissance in Italy

How did artists represent in two dimensions the equivalent of the soaring spirituality of the Gothic style of architecture? And how did this evolve into a new style of painting that would come to be known as Renaissance art? Two paintings of the Virgin Mary and Christ Child, one by Cimabue (*c.* 1240–1302) and the other made thirty years later by his student Giotto di Bondone (*c.* 1266–1337), illustrate some of the characteristics that mark the transition from the Gothic to the early Renaissance style.

Cimabue's Gothic painting is reminiscent of Byzantine icons, with the rich gold throughout, the **stylized** quality of Mary's robe, the organization of the angels' faces and halos in orderly rows, the elongation of the bodies, and the flatness of the figures appearing somewhat like paper cutouts (**3.2.27**). Cimabue's figures seem to float in space and rise up toward the top of the **composition** in much the same way that Gothic cathedrals emphasized height to inspire worshipers to look up toward the heavens.

While Giotto's *Virgin and Child Enthroned* (**3.2.28**) clearly shows architectural elements that recall Gothic churches (such as the pointed arch on Mary's throne), his painting makes many innovations, such as the three-dimensionality of his **forms** and the emphasis on creating a believable sense of the space in which Mary sits. We can also see through the spaces in the framework of the throne: the figures nearer to us overlap those that are behind them, and light seems to shine in a natural way and cast consistent shadows, helping to create the illusion that this is a three-dimensional space. Mary, Jesus, and the angels all also look more three-dimensional than the more delineated figures in Cimabue's painting. Cimabue's *Virgin and Child Enthroned* seems to focus only on the spirituality of the scene; Giotto seems to wish to create a realistic space, more like the world in which we live. This shift in approach was revolutionary, and Giotto's artistic inventions were at the forefront of the stylistic changes that would take place in the fifteenth and sixteenth century.

Stylized: art that represents objects in an exaggerated way to emphasize certain aspects of the object
Composition: the overall design or organization of a work
Form: an object that can be defined in three dimensions (height, width, and depth)

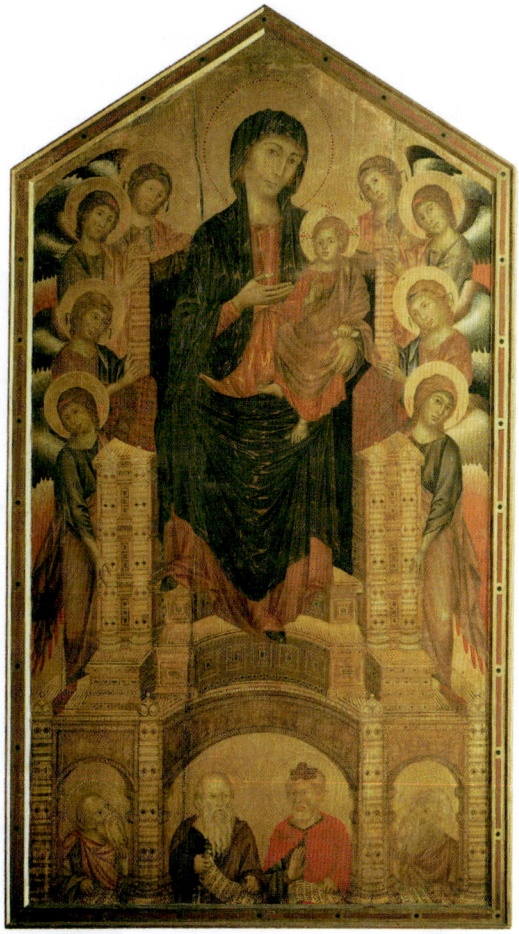

3.2.27 Cimabue, *Virgin and Child Enthroned*, *c.* 1280. Tempera and gold on wood, 12'7½" × 7'4". Uffizi Gallery, Florence, Italy

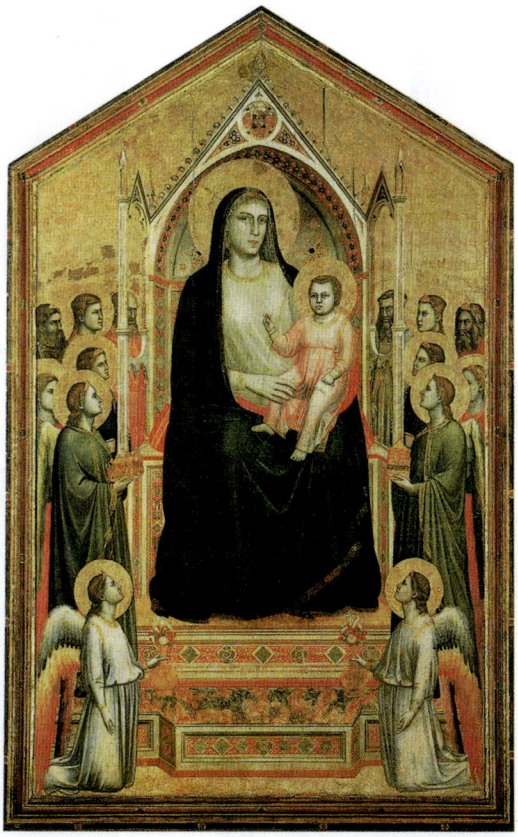

3.2.28 Giotto, *Virgin and Child Enthroned*, *c.* 1310. Tempera on wood, 10'7" × 6'9". Uffizi Gallery, Florence, Italy

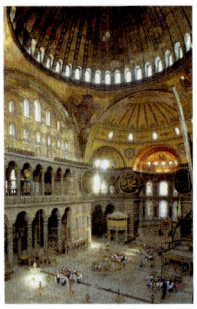

2.5.19 Hagia Sophia, Istanbul, Turkey, 532–35 CE, p. 270

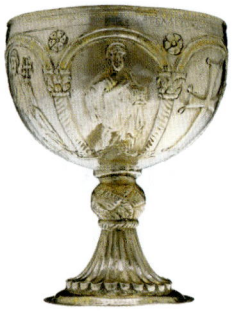

2.6.14 *Chalice with Apostles Venerating the Cross*, Byzantine, c. 600 CE, p. 293

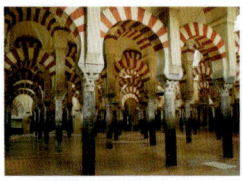

1.9.9 Great Mosque of Córdoba, Spain, 784–86 CE, p. 165

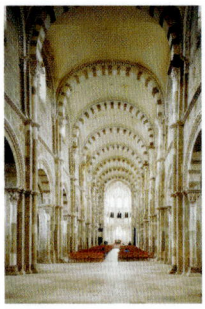

2.5.16 Church of Sainte-Madeleine, Vézelay, France, 9th–13th century, p. 267

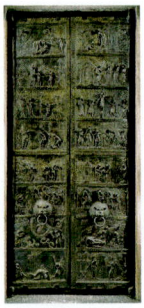

4.2.2b Doors, Church of St. Michael's, Hildesheim, Germany, 1015, p. 579

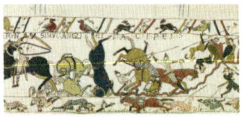

4.7.5 Detail of the Battle of Hastings, *Bayeux Tapestry*, c. 1066–82, p. 642

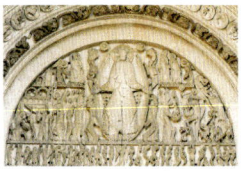

4.2.11 Gislebertus, *The Last Judgment*, c. 1120–35, p. 585

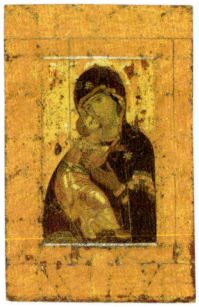

4.2.8 *Virgin of Vladimir*, 12th century (before 1132), p. 582

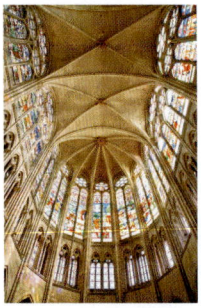

2.5.18 Stained-glass windows, Abbey Church of St. Denis, France, 12th century, p. 269

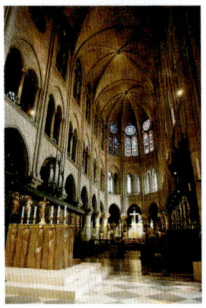

4.1.1 Notre Dame Cathedral, Paris, France, 1163–1250, p. 565

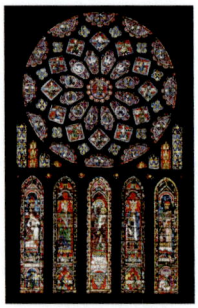

2.6.11 Rose window with lancets, Chartres Cathedral, France, 13th century, p. 291

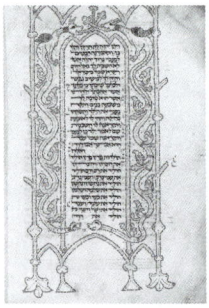

1.1.6a Franco-German hand, *Pentateuch*, 13th–14th century, p. 47

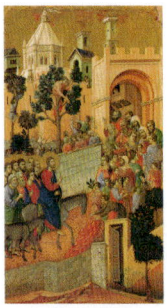

2.2.9 Duccio di Buoninsegna, *Entry into Jerusalem* (from the *Maestà*), Siena, 1308–11, p. 214

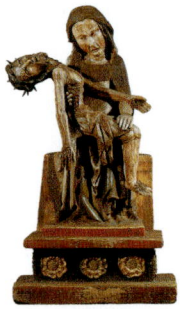

1.2.4 *Roettgen Pietà (Vesperbild)*, Germany, c. 1330, p. 63

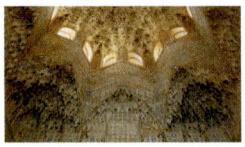

4.4.7 Hall of the Abencerrages, Alhambra, Spain, late 14th century, p. 607

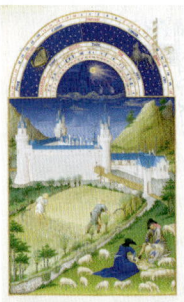

4.3.6 Limbourg Brothers, *Très Riches Heures du Duc de Berry*, 1412, p. 595

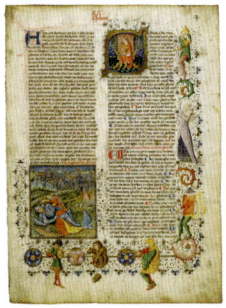

2.7.6 *Dutch History Bible*, Utrecht, The Netherlands, 1443, p. 303

3.3 Art of India, China, Japan, Korea, and Southeast Asia

Asia is home to artistic traditions that date back many thousands of years. India and China are large landmasses, both bordered by land and by great expanses of ocean. Southeast Asia lies east of India and south of China; the arts of the region have been influenced by these large neighbors. Japan, on the other hand, is a country of more than 3,000 islands off the eastern coast of mainland Asia. Trade by sea and along the famed Silk Road—a network of trade routes between Asia and the Mediterranean world—led to the spread of cultural ideas and a sharing of religious and philosophical beliefs.

Religion and philosophy have been integral to the art of the entire region (see Box: Philosophical and Religious Traditions in Asia), yet certain stylistic characteristics make the art of each of these cultures distinctive. In Indian art, there is a noticeable tendency toward elaborate decoration and an emphasis on the human body, frequently showing sensual movement and suggesting fertility. Chinese art combines an interest in religious subject matter with a great respect for Chinese heritage and ancestors. In general, Chinese artworks are also very precise and symmetrically balanced; Chinese artists desire to create uniformity and convey control of their material. In contrast, Japanese artworks tend to be more asymmetrical, organic, individual, and to convey spontaneity. Japanese art is also distinctively contemplative and reveals a great reverence for nature. Korea, in East Asia, was divided into two states (North and South) in 1945 as a consequence of the Allied victory of World War II. In South Korea Christianity, Buddhism, and Korean Shamanism survive, while in North Korea religious practice is minimal and not supported by the government. Southeast Asia is an immensely diverse region; strong influences of Hinduism and Buddhism, from India, often feature in Southeast

3.3.1 Map of Asia

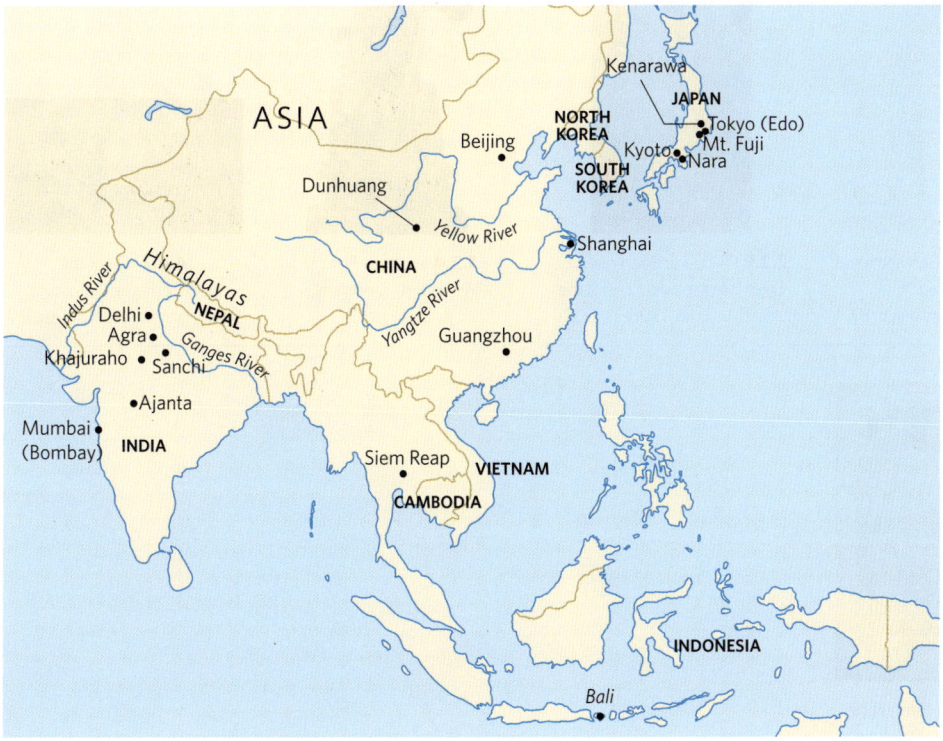

Asian art and architecture. For example, many Hindu temples were built to represent cosmic mountains, homes for Hindu gods who were believed to support local rulers. This chapter highlights both the individuality of these countries and the themes and ideas that unite their artistic traditions.

India

The landmass of India occupies a peninsula in southern Asia that is bordered on the north by the Himalayan Mountains. It is about one-third the size of the United States. Buddhist and

Philosophical and Religious Traditions in Asia

The arts of India, China, Japan, Korea, and Southeast Asia can be fully understood only in relation to each country's religions and philosophies. All have a long tradition of religious pluralism, in other words the acceptance of beliefs from different religions and philosophies. They can also be described as syncretic: meaning that their religions blend two or more belief systems. As one example, it is common in Japan to be a follower of Shinto, and a Buddhist, and to practice Confucianism all at the same time. This is possible partly because of the similar values of the various religions and philosophies. For instance, many of these religions strive for harmony with nature, and have a component of ancestral worship.

Buddhist beliefs are founded on the teachings of Siddhartha Gautama (Buddha) (563–483 BCE). Buddhism emphasizes an acceptance of the difficulties of life and of samsara (the cycle of birth, suffering, death, and rebirth). Once one attains Enlightenment, the ultimate wisdom, one arrives at nirvana, the end of suffering for eternity. Chan Buddhism, influenced by Daoism, originated in China and became Zen Buddhism in Japan; it promotes meditation and introspection, and a focus on individual moments and daily tasks.

Confucianism is based on the philosophy of Chinese Master Kong (Confucius) (551–479 BCE), who promoted the use of ethics to attain social order. His teachings emphasize self-discipline, moral duty, and paying respect both to one's ancestors and (by extension) to the elders of society. Confucianism is common in China and Japan, and is also practiced in Korea.

Daoism (The Way) comes from the teachings of Laozi (b.604 BCE), who explained in *Dao de jing* ("The Book of the Way") how to live in harmony with nature and the universe. Yin and yang is the concept that seemingly opposing forces are interconnected and need each other for balance. Such opposing forces might be male and female, or light and dark. Daoism is found throughout Asia, but most prominently in China.

Hinduism encompasses a number of beliefs, including reincarnation, rebirth of the soul or of the body, and karma, the idea that one's actions will cause a reaction or consequence in the universe. Hindus believe that while on Earth their main goals should be to practice righteous living (*dharma*), acquire wealth, achieve physical and emotional love, and attain spiritual salvation. Hindus believe in the existence of several gods (including Brahma, Shiva, and Vishnu), although individual practice and worship vary greatly amongst adherents. Hinduism originated in India and has been adopted throughout Asia, although India still holds the largest Hindu population.

Islam: Muslims base their beliefs on a sacred text called the Koran that records the will of Allah (God) as revealed to the prophet Muhammad (c.570–632 CE). Islam originated at the birthplace of Muhammad (Mecca, Saudi Arabia) but today is practiced worldwide, with many followers in Asia, including India and China.

Shinto is a native religion of Japan. Its name means "The Way of the Gods." Shinto worships several gods, of whom the most significant is Amaterasu-omikami, the sun goddess, and emphasizes respect for nature and ancestors. Followers believe that non-human entities (animals, plants, and inanimate objects) all possess a spiritual essence. *Kami*, for example, are believed to be forces in nature (such as wind or trees), or spirits of ancestors.

Gateway to Art: The Taj Mahal

The Gardens of Paradise in the Taj Mahal

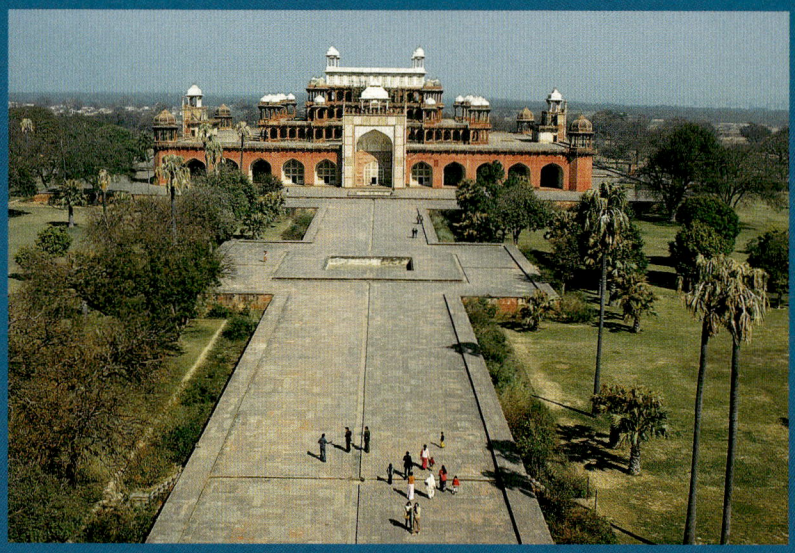

3.3.2 Gardens of the Tomb of Akbar, Sikandra, India

By the mid-sixteenth century, the Mughals (distant Muslim descendants of the historic Mongolian conqueror Genghis Khan) had conquered part of northern India and were based in Delhi. In the Islamic faith, gardens are symbolic of the paradise of heaven, and the Mughal emperor Akbar (1542–1605) created a garden for the site of his own tomb, which was completed by his son Jahangir. Akbar's garden is vast and square, and enclosed by high walls. Red sandstone causeways divide it into quarters, which link the tomb to the gates into the garden (**3.3.2**).

Following in the footsteps of his grandfather, Akbar, in the seventeenth century Shah Jahan created his own vision of heaven for the burial site of his beloved wife, Mumtaz (**3.3.3**). The immense gardens that cover the Taj Mahal complex are designed to represent the paradise of the afterlife for those of Muslim faith. Forty-two acres are divided by four rivers that extend from a raised central pool that contains five fountains. The channels of water represent the promised rivers of paradise, that is, rivers of water, milk, wine, and honey. The pool represents the water from which the deceased will drink upon immediately entering paradise. Each of these sections is then subdivided by walkways into quadrants, creating sixteen sections in all. Trees and flowers are planted in beds raised higher than the river. Cypress trees (representing death or immortality) and roses and fruit trees (representing life) originally filled the grounds, which are placed precisely between the tomb and the gateway entrance (*darwaza*) that separates the worldly atmosphere of the market from the heavenly gardens.

3.3.3 Aerial view of the gardens of the Taj Mahal, Agra, India

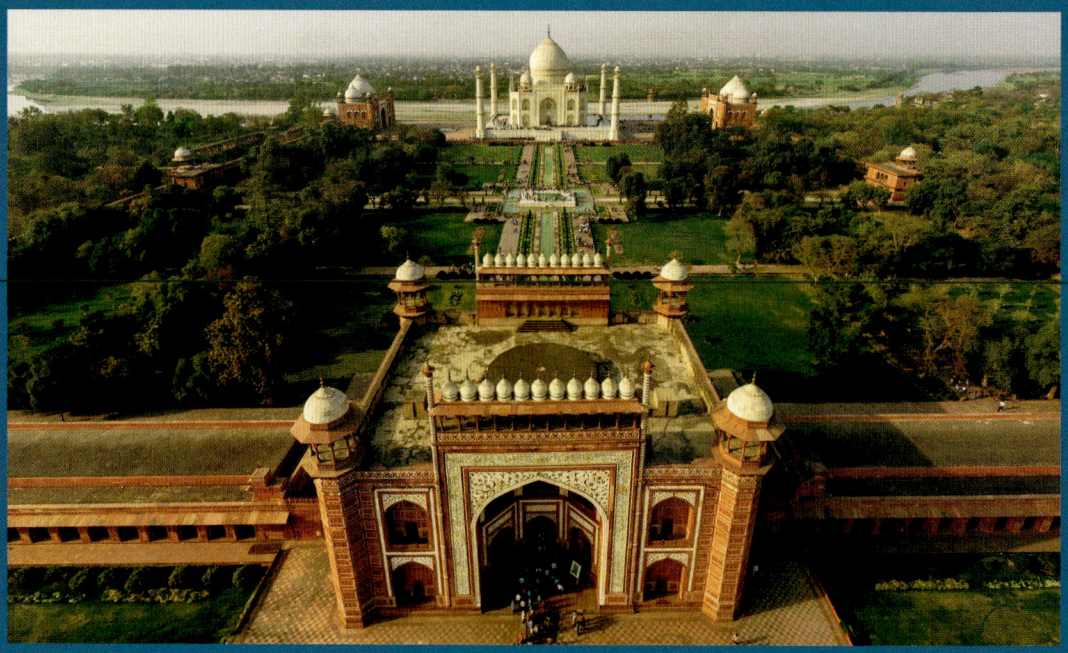

For the other Taj Mahal Gateway boxes, see p. 136, p. 272, and p. 594

Hindu beliefs have been important influences on India's rich visual history. The shrines and temples built for both of these religions are designed to be small replicas, or microcosms, of the universe, places to meditate and worship the gods. In the early twelfth century, Muslim invaders from what is now Afghanistan began centuries of rule in India. These Islamic rulers were responsible for magnificent works of art, including India's best-known landmark, the Taj Mahal (see Gateway Box: The Taj Mahal).

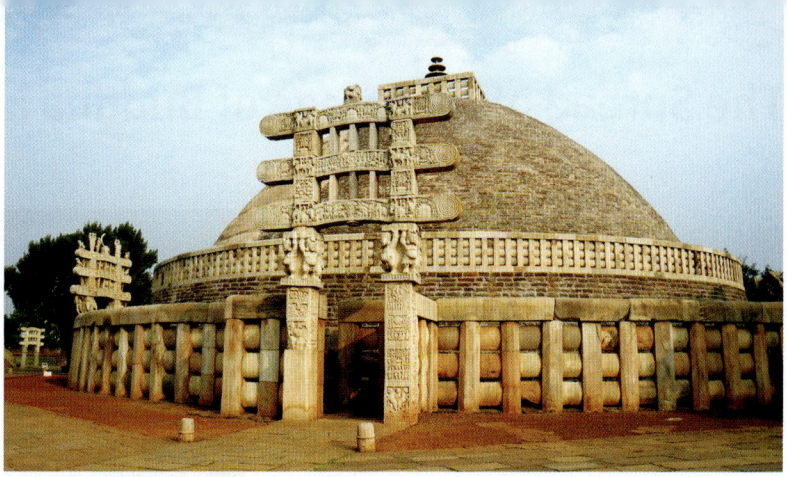

3.3.4 Great Stupa, third century BCE, enlarged *c.* 150–50 BCE. Sanchi, India

Buddhism in Indian Art

Siddhartha Gautama (563–483 BCE), who would become the Buddha or "The Enlightened One," was born a prince in what is now Nepal. Traditions tell how Siddhartha was raised in comfort in the royal palace, but at the age of twenty-nine, he witnessed the lives of the poor and sick and became an ascetic: a person who practices self-discipline and rejects his or her wealth and worldly pleasures. Buddhists believe that he achieved Enlightenment through meditation and self-discipline; he spent the second half of his life teaching others to try to do the same. After his death, his life and teachings were spread by word of mouth throughout India. The Buddha's remains were cremated and buried within eight large dirt mounds, called **stupas**, the locations of which were relevant to important periods in his life.

The Great Stupa in Sanchi, India, was built by King Ashoka as part of a large Buddhist monastery (**3.3.4**). Ashoka (304–232 BCE) was emperor of India in the mid-third century BCE. He was born a Hindu, but it is said that he became a Buddhist after feeling ashamed of the murderous destruction caused by a war in which his army killed more than 100,000 people. He became known as "the pious Ashoka" and gained a reputation as a charitable and peace-loving ruler who built hospitals and schools throughout India. When Ashoka converted to Buddhism, he disinterred the Buddha's remains and distributed them to be reburied within thousands more stupas he built throughout India.

Surrounding the Great Stupa at Sanchi are four gateways, or ***toranas***, placed at the four cardinal points surrounding the large mound. Sensual female figures of tree spirits hang from the brackets on some of the toranas (**3.3.5**). These figures symbolize procreation, abundance, and the source of all life. At a height of 35 ft., the

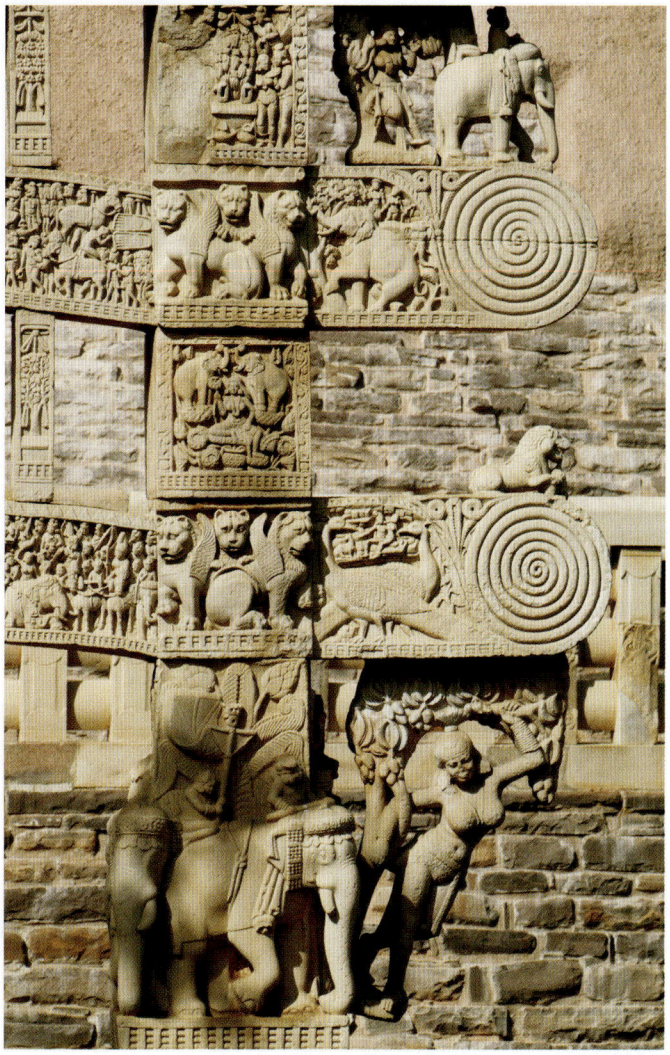

3.3.5 East gate of the Great Stupa, Sanchi, India

Stupa: a burial mound containing Buddha's remains
Torana: a gateway used in Hindu and Buddhist architecture

The Spread of the Image of Buddha along the Silk Road

The Silk Road—an immense system of trade routes used for many centuries across Asia and Europe—was a channel for the spread of Buddhism and also, therefore, for the dispersal and development of the image of Buddha. While certain attributes of the Buddha—knotted bun and stretched earlobes - remain consistent, stylistic changes often reflect the regions in which the depictions were made.

Representations of Buddha first appeared in India during the first few centuries CE. A Buddha sculpture from the Gupta period (320–550 CE) (**3.3.6**) sits in a meditative, serene pose, with his eyes closed, spiritually turning inward to develop inner strength and enlightenment. His body is graceful, with a solid posture and elegantly crossed legs. The soft facial features and overall idealized beauty of the sculpture are typical of the Gupta period. Buddha is presented here as a compassionate teacher, with the orb of the sun—symbolizing the Wheel of Law (Buddha's teaching of the path to nirvana)—behind him.

The meaning of such depictions is often communicated through the figure's hand gestures (mudras). In this case, Buddha is setting the Wheel of Law into motion while teaching the principles of his Eightfold Path of Righteousness; the sculpture also represents his eternal guidance. This statue was found in Sarnath, the site of Buddha's first sermon, and the figures carved below the Buddha are his disciples, giving him their rapt attention.

More than 1,200 miles away, the city of Dunhuang in northwest China marked the crossroads of two branches of the Silk Road. Here, the Mogao Caves (Caves of the Thousand Buddhas) were first carved by Buddhist monks in the fourth century CE and came to be used as places of meditation for weary travelers. Filled with manuscripts, **murals**, and sculptures, the caves became an important pilgrimage site in their own right. The mudra of one painted Buddha (**3.3.7**) informs us that he is preaching. This confident and dignified interpretation of Buddha reflects the power of the Tang Dynasty in China at the time, and his features and facial hair recall depictions of Chinese emperors.

Via the Silk Road, Buddhism also spread as far as Bamiyan, Afghanistan. Between the fifth and ninth centuries, more than 800 caves were

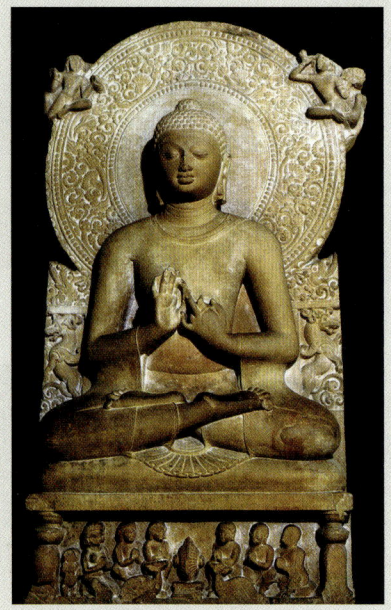

3.3.6 Seated Buddha from the Gupta period (5th century CE), India

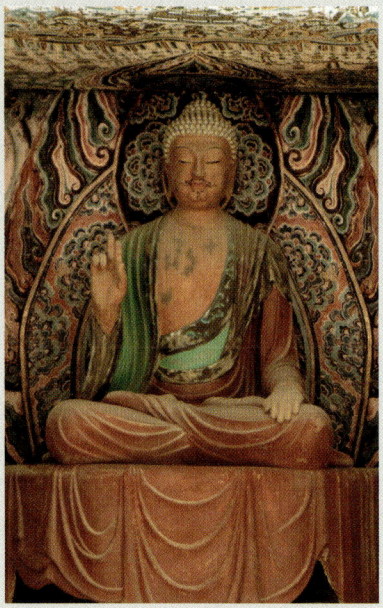

3.3.7 Buddha from the Mogao Caves (replica of cave 45 in Dunhuang Museum), 618–907 CE, Dunhuang, China

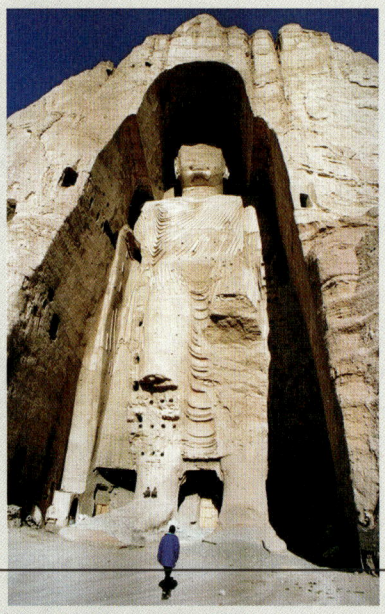

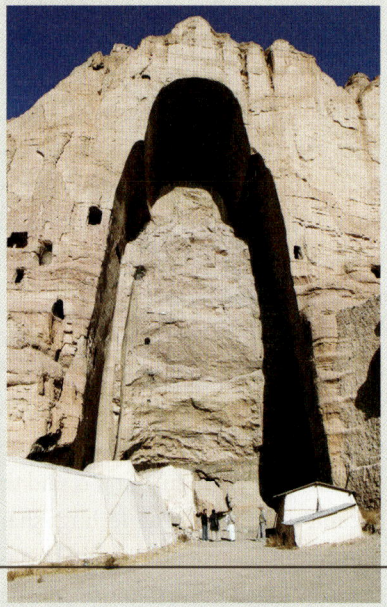

3.3.8a and **3.3.8b** Colossal Buddha from Bamiyan, Afghanistan, 6th or 7th century CE, destroyed by Taliban, 2001. Before and after destruction

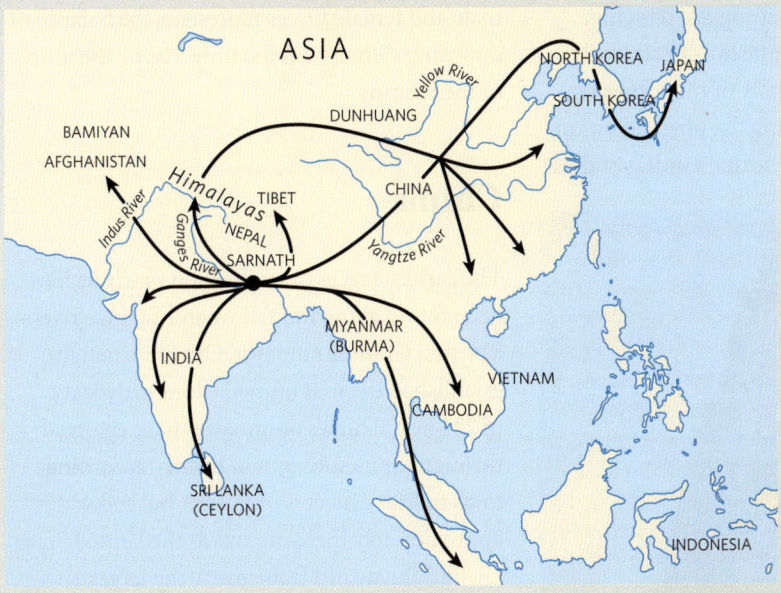

3.3.9 Map showing the spread of Buddhism via the Silk Road

carved into the cliffs, which were used as Buddhist temples and monasteries. Two colossal standing Buddhas, the taller one reaching 175 ft. high (**3.3.8a** and **3.3.8b**), were the largest Buddhas in the world until the Taliban destroyed them with dynamite in 2001, claiming that they lead to the worship of false idols. The elegant folds of the drapery on these Buddhas show the influence of a **Classical** Greek/Roman style that had been passed through India. The feet of these standing Buddhas were carved away from the cliff wall so that pilgrims could circumambulate the sacred figures. The larger statue was the Vairocana Buddha, which embodies emptiness and impermanence—a meaning that now holds a strong sense of irony, since the sculpture was destroyed so violently.

columns and horizontal crossbeams of these toranas are covered with scenes of the Buddha's multiple lives (*jatakas*). The Buddha himself is not shown, but there are signs of his presence, such as an empty throne and his footprints. In this way, Buddhists are invited to **circumambulate** the structure, symbolically following in the footsteps of the Buddha. Pilgrims enter through the east gate and circle the stupa in a clockwise direction, following the path of the sun. Stone railings added after Ashoka's time allow pilgrims to climb higher safely as they encircle the mound in which the Buddha's remains are interred, a ritual that emulates Buddha's path toward Enlightenment. The stupa and its four gateways represent a three-dimensional **mandala**, or a re-creation of the universe.

Hinduism in Indian Art

Hinduism has been practiced at least as far back as 1000 BCE. Today, it is the world's third largest religion, with the majority of its followers living in India. The kinds of personal practices and gods that are worshiped vary greatly amongst Hindus, but they all share the belief that one's spirit is eternal. Just as Buddhism grew because powerful people promoted it, the increase in popularity of Hinduism was largely due to the efforts of rulers to encourage Hindu worship, particularly by building religious temples.

Around 1020 CE, King Vidyadhara built a large complex containing Hindu temples in Khajuraho, in northern India. The largest of these, the Kandariya Mahadeva, is dedicated to Shiva, the Hindu god of creation and destruction (**3.3.10**, p. 416). Hindus see their temples as "cosmic mountains," links between heaven and Earth. The large towers on Hindu temples are called *shikharas* and represent mountain peaks. The vertical towers pull the eye upward to the heavens, suggesting to Hindus a desire for *moksha*, or the release from suffering. Every temple has a central room underneath the shikhara that contains an image of the god to whom the temple is dedicated. A Hindu priest's job is to maintain the sculpture (which embodies the god itself) through prayer, meditation, incense burning, feeding and clothing the sculpture, and pouring milk or honey on it.

The temple is aligned with the rising and setting of the sun, with stairs for entrance on the east. Horizontal decoration encourages the viewer to walk around the temple and view the intricate carving and relief sculpture. The exterior is covered with more than

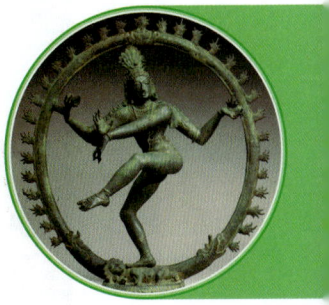

Shiva is often portrayed in the act of balancing opposing forces of the universe: see **4.3.12, p. 599**

Mural: a painting executed directly onto a wall
Classical: Greek art of the period c. 480–323 BCE
Circumambulate: the act of walking around a sacred object
Mandala: a sacred diagram of the universe, often involving a square and a circle

600 sculptures in poses that suggest dancing, which creates a rhythmic pulsing effect over the entire structure (**3.3.11**). Many of the scenes are sensual and erotic, depicting the physical union of males and females. The sexual joining of these male and female forces represents the balance of opposing elements in the universe, or the unity of the cosmos.

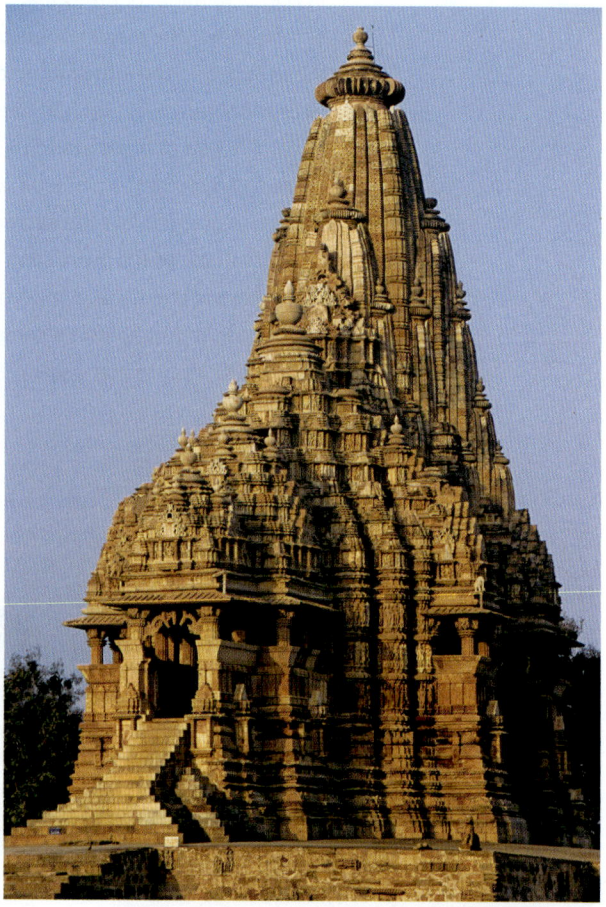

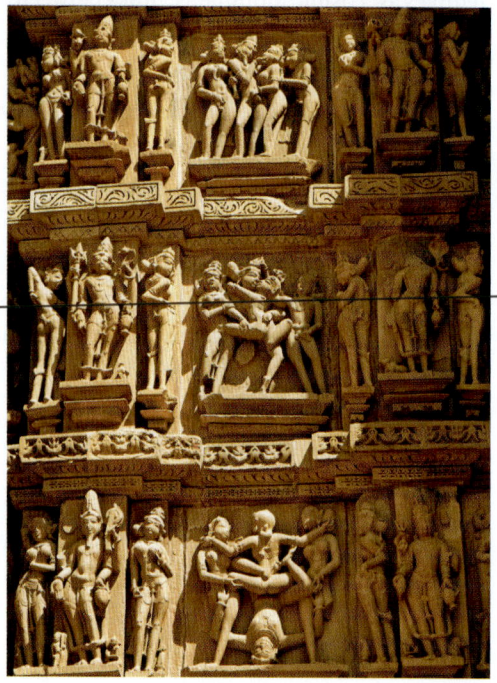

3.3.10 (top) Kandariya Mahadeva temple, c. 1000, Khajuraho, Madhya Pradesh, India

3.3.11 (right) Detail of exterior sculpture, Kandariya Mahadeva temple

China

The earliest traces of civilization in China have been found along the Yellow and Yangtze rivers. The first Chinese emperor, Qin Shi Huangdi, established the first unified Chinese dynasty in 221 BCE. China's boundaries have changed throughout its subsequent history according to its military success or failure, but today it is approximately the same size as the United States.

Buddhism and Daoism are the largest religious and philosophical systems in China. Each faith integrates the beliefs of the other and of Confucianism (see Box: Philosophical and Religious Traditions in Asia, p. 411) as well: the Chinese believe a person may practice more than one belief system. This affects the whole of Chinese culture. In Chinese art, for example, scroll paintings are intended to enhance meditation, and respect for nature and one's elders—virtues that are valued by all three faiths. Many great Chinese artworks have been discovered in tombs, providing evidence both of a widespread reverence for ancestors, and of the importance of the idea of the afterlife.

Death and the Afterlife

For thousands of years, Chinese people have worshiped their ancestors, who they believe are transformed after death into supernatural entities with the power to communicate with the gods and protect the living. To show the ancestors due respect, and so that the deceased would have what they needed in the afterlife, both valuable and everyday items were buried with them in their tombs. Humans and animals were also sacrificed, in the belief that they would serve the dead in the next realm. Today, similar customs persist: the Chinese often burn money, food, and other objects in the hope that these will reach their ancestors in the spirit world.

The tomb of Lady Dai (d. 168 BCE), a noblewoman of the Han Dynasty (206 BCE–220 CE),

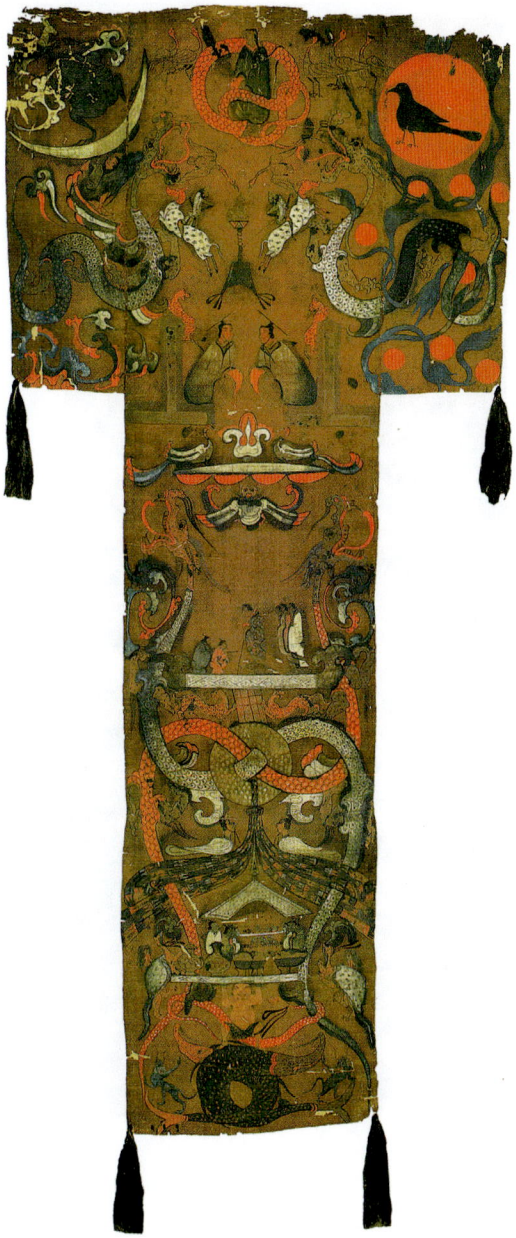

3.3.12 (left) Painted banner from tomb of Lady Dai Hou Fu-ren, Han Dynasty, c. 168 BCE. Silk, length 80½", width at top 36", width at bottom 18¾". Hunan Museum, Changsha, China

3.3.13a (below, top) Building housing pit number 1 of the terra-cotta army, mausoleum of Qin Shi Huangdi, China, c. 210 BCE. Xi'an, Shaanxi Province, China

3.3.13b (below, bottom) Soldiers from the mausoleum of Qin Shi Huangdi, c. 210 BCE. Terra-cotta and pigment, figures approximately lifesize. Xi'an, Shaanxi Province, China

was excavated in 1972, revealing a wealth of objects intended to accompany her into the afterlife. A stunning richly painted silk textile (**3.3.12**) had been placed over Lady Dai's coffin, protected by several additional layers of wooden coffins. The silk banner is in the shape of a T; the wide horizontal section represents heaven, with twisting dragons, a toad on a gold moon, and a crow on a red sun. At the top in the center, surrounded by a red serpent, is probably an imperial ancestor. Lady Dai stands upon a central white platform about halfway down the banner, awaiting her ascent to the heavenly realm. Above her is a bird and, at the cross of the T, two kneeling figures who are thought to be guardians or guides of some kind. A jade circle, crossed by two writhing dragons and known as a *bi*—frequently used as a symbol for heaven—sits below Lady Dai on her platform. Scholars have hypothesized that this banner either shows Lady Dai's funeral and her journey to heaven, or views of the three spiritual realms of heaven, Earth, and the underworld.

The emperors of ancient China sought to take their riches with them to the afterlife. Ancient records described how the first emperor of China, Qin Shi Huangdi, prepared for his death by constructing a burial mound with a vast underground city palace that matched the one he occupied in life. These accounts were believed to be sheer legend until 1974, when, in a spectacular archaeological discovery, excavations of a tomb mound revealed evidence that the ancient stories were true (**3.3.13a** and **b**).

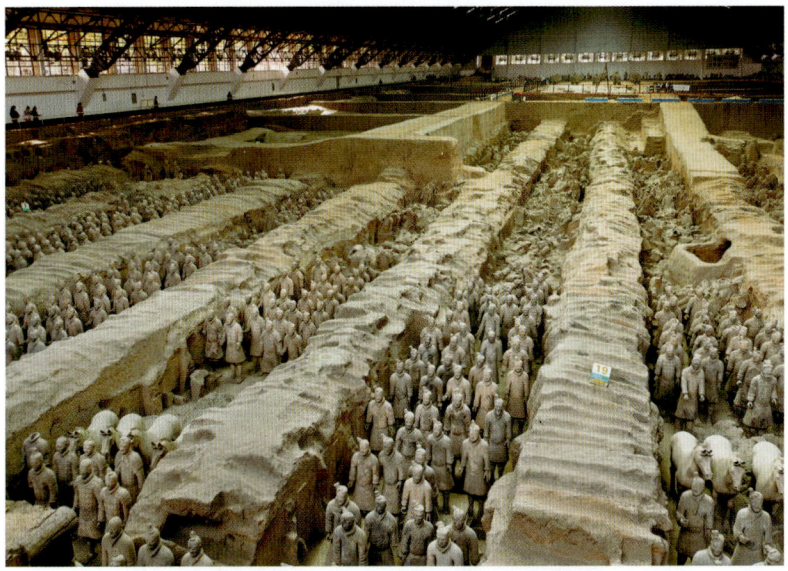

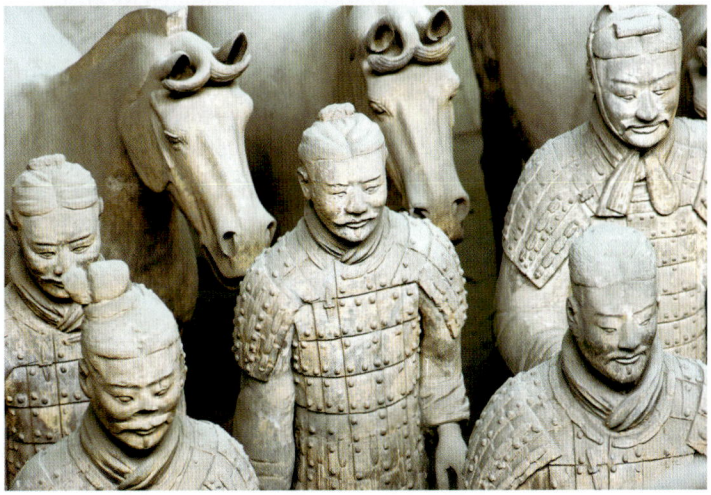

3.3.14 (right) Wang Meng, *Ge Zhichuan Moving His Dwelling*, c. 1360. Hanging scroll, ink and color on paper, 54¾ × 22⅞". Palace Museum, Beijing, China

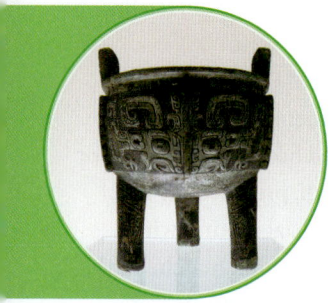

Sophisticated bronze objects have been found in the tombs of Shang Dynasty rulers: see **1.6.13, p. 134**

Terra-cotta: iron-rich clay, fired at a low temperature, which is traditionally brownish-orange in color
Calligraphy: the art of emotive or carefully descriptive hand lettering or handwriting

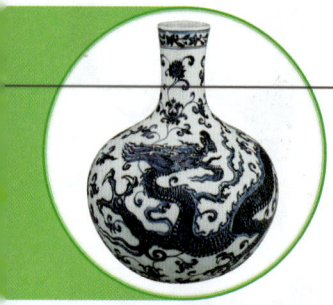

Cobalt imported from Persia was combined in innovative ways with white porcelain during the Ming Dynasty: see **2.6.5, p. 288**

Soon after he came to the throne at the age of thirteen, Qin Shi Huangdi began overseeing the elaborate preparations for his own resting place, which continued for thirty-six years until his death in 210 BCE. Artisans filled the complex surrounding Qin Shi Huangdi's tomb with the treasures he would need in the afterlife, including an army of **terra-cotta** soldiers, chariots, and horses, all of which were originally painted.

The 8,000 lifesize figures found in the largest pit were intended to guard the body of the emperor. They have similar rigid and upright poses because molds were used for the various body parts and then pieced together. The unique portions of each soldier (clothing, weaponry, and facial features) were added on individually, however, with a layer of moist clay.

Chinese Painting

The earliest known painting in China dates back some 10,000 years. Archaeologists have found painted pots, and paint on the walls and floors of caves and huts. From 200 BCE until today, however, many Chinese paintings have been made with ink on silk or paper, the same materials used in the arts of **calligraphy** (fine hand lettering) and poetry. These three arts are inextricably linked for the Chinese (see Box: The Three Perfections: Calligraphy, Painting, Poetry, p. 420). Most Chinese paintings are made as hanging or hand scrolls; their subject matter includes battles, scenes of daily life, landscapes, and animals. Chinese scroll paintings are meant to be experienced as though we are on a slow, contemplative journey. Artists who paint scrolls do not intend their work to be viewed from one position, as is usual in artworks created in the European tradition. Instead, the complexity and (in the case of a hand scroll) length of a painting invite us to view one portion of it at a time.

The calligraphy in the upper right of the hanging scroll shown in **3.3.14** tells us that *Ge Zhichuan Moving His Dwelling* is a historical scene from the life of a well-known Chinese writer. Ge Zhichuan was one of the first alchemists (someone who seeks to make gold or silver from lead or iron). He is also considered

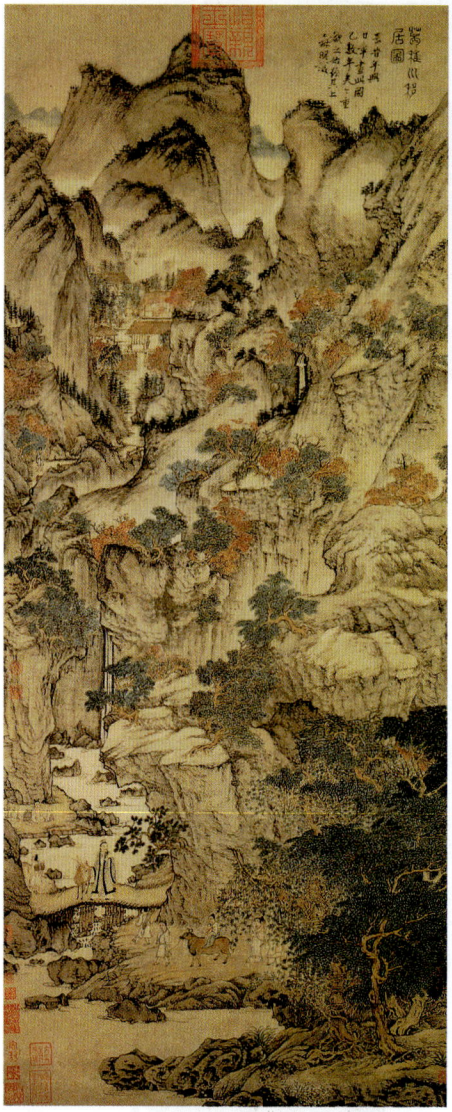

a great teacher of Daoism. In the painting, Ge Zhichuan is traveling to Guangzhou to find the red, mercury-based mineral cinnabar. He is shown in the lower left on a bridge. His family follows in the lower center. The scene shows the power of nature compared to the small scale of man.

The fantastic landscape, full of twisting trees, steep cliffs, and high waterfalls, shows the mystical nature of Ge Zhichuan's journey; it also symbolizes the wondrous path we all take through life. We cannot view the entire scroll at one time, just as we cannot see everything going on around us. This is a metaphor for the Zen-like philosophy in which one can comprehend the universe in its entirety only through the mind, thus achieving Enlightenment. As Ge Zhichuan follows his meandering path, he will

Gateway to Art: Ai Weiwei, *Dropping a Han Dynasty Urn*

The Value of Art: Questions of History and Authenticity

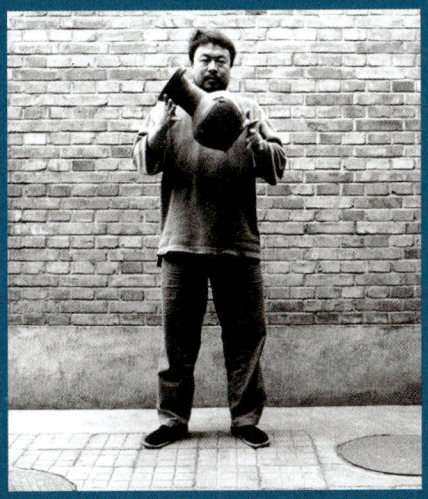

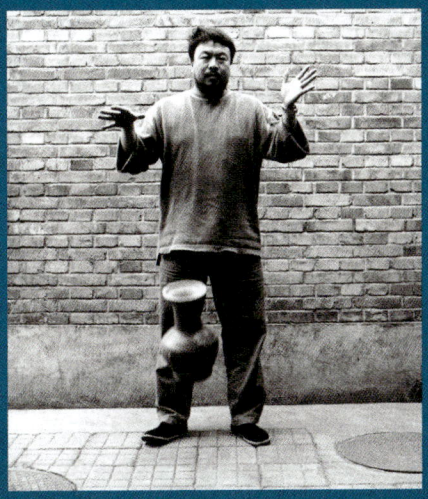

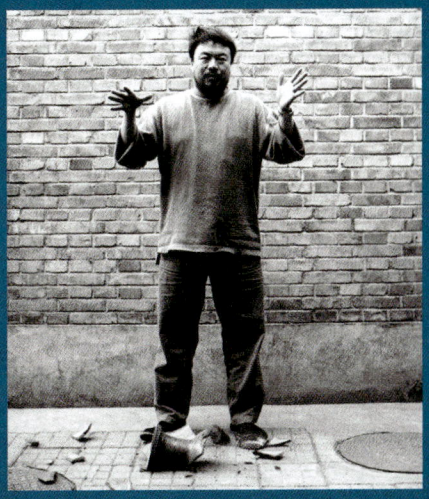

3.3.15 Ai Weiwei, *Dropping a Han Dynasty Urn*, 1995. Three black-and-white photographs, each 53½ × 42⅞"

> The significant value about any act or art really exists in the viewer's mind.
>
> Ai Weiwei

When Chinese artist Ai Weiwei (b.1957) damaged and altered numerous ancient pots, he was highlighting his belief that the value of an object is based on personal perception. In exhibitions, Ai's work is often installed according to the dates of the objects he has appropriated. The vase shown in this group of photos (**3.3.15**), for example, was made during the Han Dynasty (206 BCE–220 CE). Ai began collecting ancient vases in the 1990s, and is thought to have paid around $2000 for the one smashed in the third photograph in the *Dropping a Han Dynasty Urn* **triptych**. Some scholars have questioned whether the vases shown are authentic historical specimens, or fakes. This speculation only furthers Ai's desire to inspire questions about how value is determined and by whom.

The Chinese ceramics appropriated by Ai Weiwei reference long-standing traditions and an impressive history of significant technical innovations. Vases produced in China have traditionally been made for utilitarian purposes or buried with the dead. Pottery from the Neolithic period (*c.*5000–2000 BCE) is notable for its painted decoration. Artists from the Shang Dynasty (1600–1046 BCE) were distinctively skilled in the process of **piece-mold casting**. The Han Dynasty was notable for developing massive numbers of high-quality ceramics covered with a low-fired lead glaze. High-quality Imperial pottery production was a focus of the Ming Dynasty (1368–1644 CE), when artists developed a formula for adding manganese (a chemical element) to cobalt (a blue pigment) to create distinctive blue-and-white porcelain pieces in such a way that the blue does not bleed into the white.

Ceramics artists today still learn and use these once innovative, now traditional, methods. In fact, imitation of past styles is part of the tradition of Chinese ceramics, which has led to the production of countless replicas. Knowing this, Ai Weiwei's art leads us to consider whether such old objects should still be considered important if they can be reproduced almost identically. Further, are copies of ancient pots authentic works in their own right? What if another artist alters the original object? Interestingly, in 2012, a collector purchased a work made by Ai Weiwei—one in which the artist had painted a Coca-Cola logo on a Han vase—and purposely let it fall and shatter to the ground, in an exact mimicry of Ai's photo triptych.

The artist has said, "To have other layers of color and images above the previous ones calls into question both the identity and authenticity of the object. It makes both conditions non-absolute: you cover something so that it is no longer visible but is still there underneath, and what appears on the surface is not supposed to be there but is still there." The questions raised by Ai Weiwei's works are not meant to be definitively answered, but to trigger thoughts about the value of art.

Triptych: three panels, normally joined together and sharing a common theme
Piece-mold casting: A process for casting metal objects in which a mold is broken into several pieces that are then reassembled into a final sculpture

For the other Ai Weiwei Gateway boxes, see p. 121, p. 357, and p. 654

The Three Perfections: Calligraphy, Painting, Poetry

In Chinese society, talented calligraphers are accorded the highest respect. The Chinese script used today goes back to at least the Qin Dynasty (221–207 BCE). Chinese calligraphers can convey a mood through the handling of a brush, the thickness of a line, the quickness of a stroke. Skilled calligraphers can communicate through their script elegance, formality, sadness, or joyful exuberance. Historically, many poets became calligraphers so that they could express most eloquently the moods of their poems. Many painters, too, were calligraphers, because both art forms require great skill in the handling of the brush.

During the Song Dynasty (960–1279), painters called **literati** wrote poems—either their own or the work of other poets—next to their paintings. The tradition continues to this day. Room for calligraphic inscriptions is often left on paintings, not only for the artist's signature but also to describe a scene, dedicate the painting, or add poetry.

The Chinese believe that any inscriptions on a painting become part of the work, whether or not they are written by the painter. Frequently, red seals or stamps are pressed onto part of a work to claim authorship, or to show admiration for that part. Colophons are inscriptions—often poems or historical information about the artwork—usually written in black ink by the artist or admirers of the work. Therefore, a scroll painting with many inscriptions and colophons is one that has been much enjoyed, and this becomes part of the story of the painting.

Literati: Chinese scholar-painters who created expressive paintings rather than formal academic works

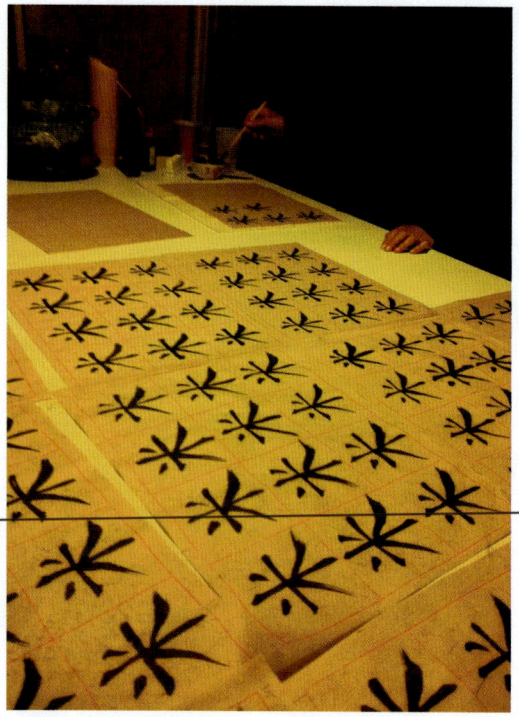

3.3.16 Monika Lin, *TenThousand*, 2012. Durational performance. Performance Art Institute, San Francisco, California

eventually arrive at a new village, seen in the upper left. His destination is higher in the scroll than his present location; this is a device used in Daoist painting to symbolize the growth that the subject will experience on his spiritual path. Just like the people in the painting, the viewer may wander in any direction, exploring new territory and facing challenges; all of this is a metaphor for the journey of life. The mountain ridges high in the distance speak of the journeys yet to come.

The Contemporary American-born Chinese artist Monika Lin (b. 1968) utilizes the tradition of calligraphy to consider the lives of the poorer members of Chinese society, those who did not have the means to spend hours contemplating nature, practicing calligraphy, or painting detailed landscapes. In her **performance artwork** *TenThousand*, the artist repeatedly writes the Chinese symbol for rice: 米 (**3.3.16**). The act of bending down to arrange the papers is designed to re-enact the back-breaking labor of the peasant class who planted the rice. This arduous work made the lives of the literati possible, while at times, according to the artist, the peasants could not afford even to eat the rice they harvested. The number 10,000 is also symbolic in China of the notion of infinity; an infinite amount of sacrifice by many allowed for the lifestyle of the few who created the Chinese landscape paintings we treasure today.

Performance art: a work involving the human body, usually including the artist, in front of an audience

Japan

Japan is a country of many islands off the eastern coast of Asia. In size, it covers about the same area as California. Combining its own cultural and religious traditions with influences from mainland Asia, Japanese art reflects stories of Buddha and of emperors, and (in modern times) the lives of ordinary people as well. Vulnerable to frequent tsunamis, earthquakes, and volcanic eruptions, the Japanese have a great respect for nature. According to the long-established Shinto religion, spirits called kami are present everywhere, including within nature. Many Japanese combine aspects of Shinto with a belief in Buddhism, which came to Japan in the sixth century CE, having developed in India and then spread through China and Korea, changing and adapting to each culture as it went. The other primary religion in Japan is Confucianism (see box: Philosophical and Religious Traditions in Asia, p. 411). The Japanese reverence for nature, their desire for meditation, quiet reflection, and mental discipline, are all seen in the art they create (see Box: Sonoko Sasaki, pp. 422–23).

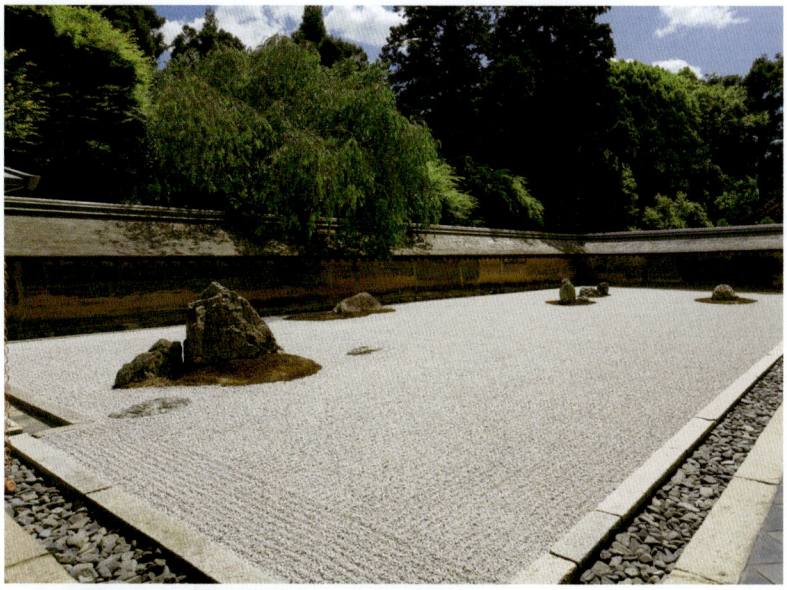

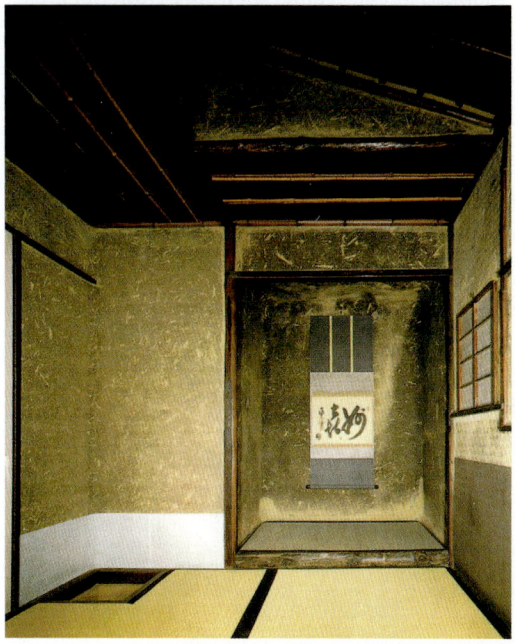

3.3.17 (above) Garden at Ryoan-ji, c. 1480. Stone and gravel. Kyoto, Japan

3.3.18 (left) Sen no Rikyu, Taian teahouse, interior, c. 1582. Myoki-an Temple, Kyoto, Japan

Meditative Spaces

Zen dry gardens, such as the one at Ryoan-ji in Kyoto, Japan (**3.3.17**), have been popular since the fifteenth century CE. A microcosm of the larger earthly landscape, white quartz gravel represents water, and the bigger rocks are surrounded by moss, mimicking islands. The garden is maintained to create a serene space for contemplation. Practitioners of Zen Buddhism cultivate mental calm on the path to enlightenment by emphasizing rigorous discipline and personal responsibility, here achieved by raking the gravel regularly. This practice reinforces the impermanence of earthly existence; any design—however beautiful—that is raked into the garden will soon disappear or be replaced. The garden features fifteen stones of assorted shape and size, but at any one time the viewer can catch sight of only fourteen; only those who have reached enlightenment possess the ability to see all fifteen stones at once. Zen gardens are designed to be places to embrace the present moment and meditate on nature and life.

Chanoyu (Way of the Tea) is the Japanese word for the traditional tea ceremony. Rooted in Zen Buddhism, chanoyu is a set of rituals that helps one find peace and solace from the ordinary world. It is a tenet of Buddhism that disciplined observation of the mundane things in life leads one toward Enlightenment, and chanoyu is designed to facilitate such observation. It also helps create an environment for intense concentration. Tea masters train for many years in the practice of creating a meditative environment through the serving of tea and the preparation of the teahouse (**3.3.18**). In the sixteenth century, the tea master Sen no

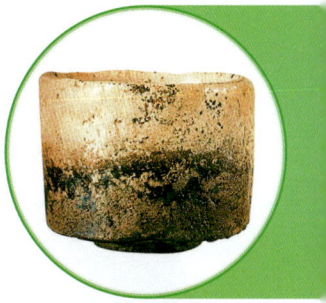

During chanoyu, participants slowly meditate on the design and texture of tea bowls: see **0.0.11, p. 28**

Perspectives on Art: Sonoko Sasaki
Arts and Tradition in Japan

In an effort to protect the skills needed to preserve Japan's traditional art forms, the Japanese government designates outstanding traditional artists "Important Intangible Cultural Property Holder" (popularly known as National Living Treasures). Sonoko Sasaki was named a National Living Treasure for her skills in weaving a traditional textile known as tsumugi-ori. Here she explains her work.

I work with *tsumugi-ori* textiles because the touch and look of the material are very attractive to me. Tsumugi thread is different from cotton thread because it consists of extremely long fibers that are tough, waterproof, and glossy.

Actually, tsumugi-ori was originally quite a rustic textile made by women involved in silk cultivation after their farming work. As a result, tsumugi-ori has always had a strong connection with the Earth and nature, and with the cycle of the four seasons that in Japan shows us the beautiful scenes of the natural world. I always try to sharpen my sense of color with all five of my senses, which helps me give a variety of colors to my work. The colors I use also come from nature. The dyes I use to color my textiles come from roots, flowers, and fruits of plants of every season.

Water, light, and wind are also essential for tsumugi-ori textiles. Water is important for me, and fills me with awe, since the threads must be boiled in a dye and then washed. Sunlight and wind are needed to dry the dyed thread.

I weave my textiles using a hand-loom and then tailor the material to make kimonos, a traditional Japanese dress. In other words, my works have meaning and value only if someone wears them. Here the key is again the four seasons. I delicately change the color of the

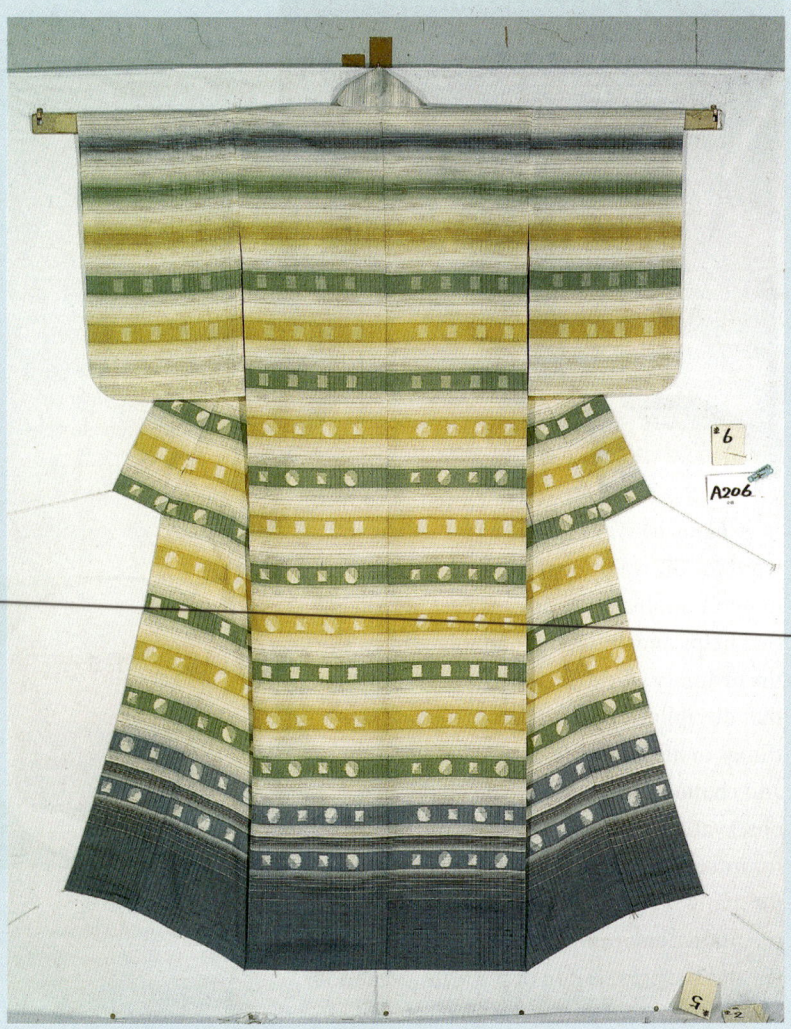

3.3.19 Sonoko Sasaki, *Sea in the Sky*, 2007. Tsumigi-ito silk thread and vegetable dyes, 70⅞ × 51¼". Collection of the artist

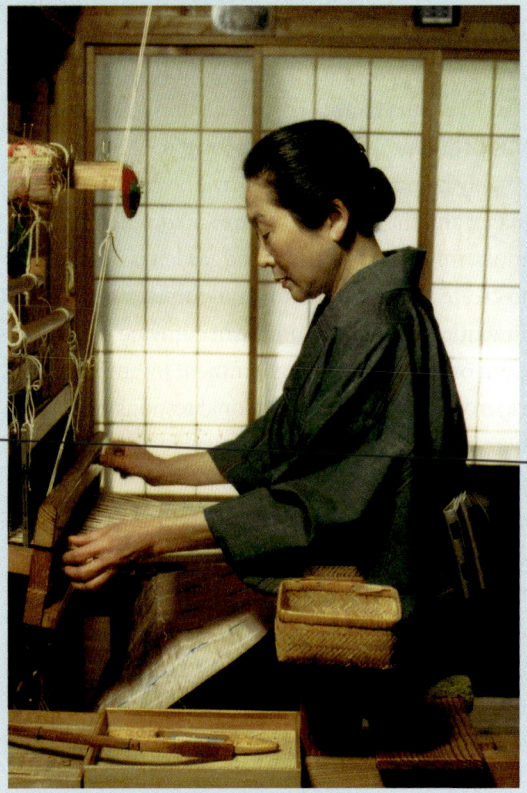

3.3.20 Sonoko Sasaki at work at her loom

textiles according to the seasons. At the same time, people who wear my kimonos place a high value on their sense of the seasons. In this way the artist and the wearer share their consciousness of the seasons, a tradition, inherited by generations of women, that I think is special to Japan.

I do not have any idea why I have been designated as a National Living Treasure, but I understand that I have accepted a responsibility to work on and protect the art and culture of tsumugi-ori for the rest of my life. I am truly happy to pursue my "road of coloration" and "road of weaving" now and forever. Even if I were born again, I would still like to choose tsumugi-ori, as, for me, nothing is more glamorous than dyeing and weaving.

Rikyu developed an influential tea ritual; the Taian tearoom in Kyoto is the only remaining teahouse by this master (**3.3.18**, p. 421). The modest room is made with natural materials, such as mud for the walls, and bamboo and other wood for the trim and ceilings. The windows are made of paper, and the *tatami* (floor mats) are made of straw. The simple room has no decoration except for a scroll or small floral arrangement, placed in a niche called a *tokonoma*.

Chanoyu can take hours. It involves preparing and drinking the tea, and quiet conversation. The ceremony begins as one removes one's shoes and enters the house on hands and knees, showing humility. The contemplative environment invites participants to enjoy conversation, and also to appreciate each object involved in the ceremony.

Storytelling

One of the oldest examples of storytelling in Japanese art appears on a wooden shrine in the Buddhist Horyu-ji Temple in Nara (**3.3.21**). One side of the shrine is painted with a jataka (a story from the life of Buddha) known as *The Hungry Tigress*. The painting is a **continuous narrative**, meaning that it shows multiple scenes of a story in one pictorial **space**. In this story, Buddha sacrificed his own body to save a starving tigress and her cubs. Buddha is shown first at the top of a cliff carefully hanging his clothes from a tree, his slender body reflecting the curves of the natural elements that surround him. He then jumps off the cliff, and is finally devoured by the tigers in the valley below.

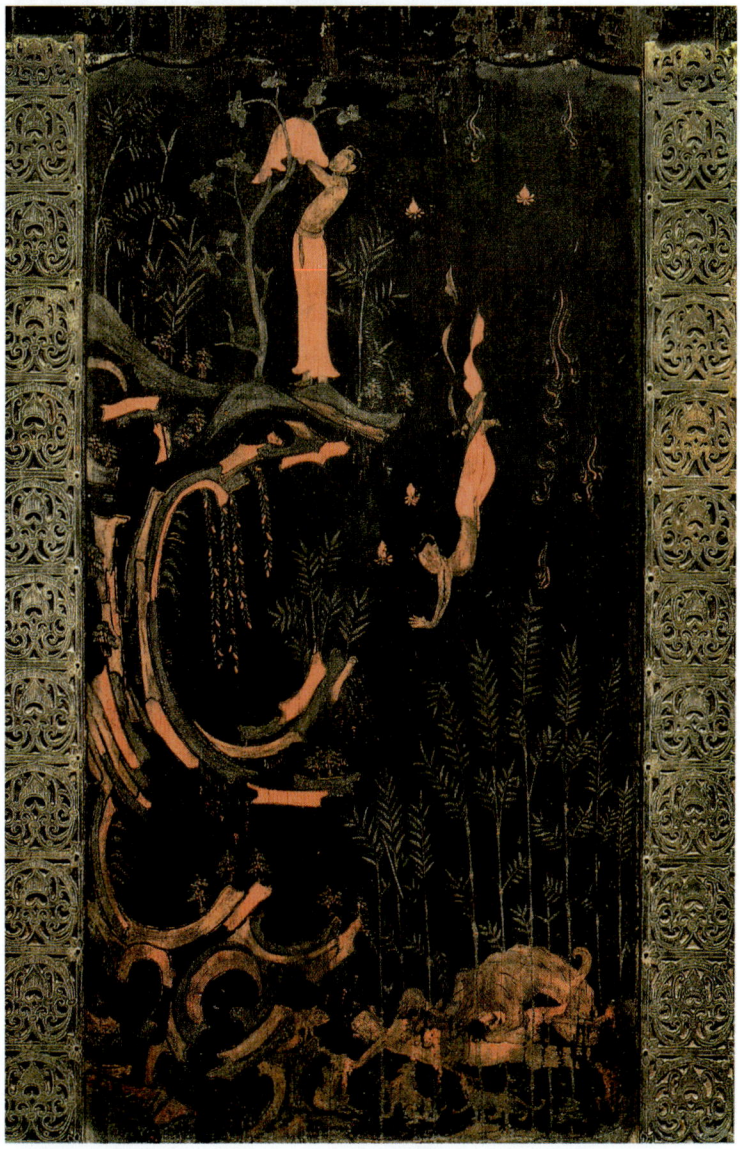

Continuous narrative: when different parts of a story are shown within the same visual space
Space: the space between identifiable points or planes

3.3.21 *The Hungry Tigress*, panel from the Tamamushi Shrine, Horyu-ji Temple, Nara, Asuka period, *c.* 650. Lacquer on wood, shrine height 7'7¾". Horyu-ji Treasure House, Japan

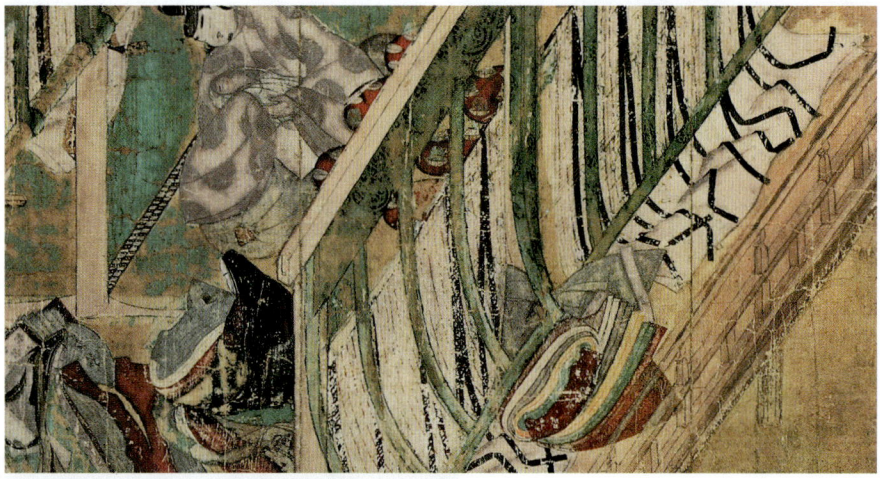

3.3.22 Scene from the *Tale of Genji*. Heian period, first half of 12th century. Hand scroll, ink and color on paper, 8⅝ × 18⅞". Tokugawa Art Museum, Nogoya, Japan

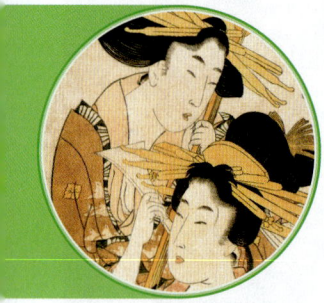

Ukiyo-e prints became extremely popular exports to Europe and America from the 1860s onward, and influenced Western artists, in particular the **Impressionists**: see **3.8.10, p. 510**

Impressionism: in the visual arts, a late nineteenth-century style conveying the fleeting impression of the effects of light; Impressionists were artists working in this style
Diagonal: a line that runs obliquely, rather than horizontally or vertically
Woodblock: a relief print process where the image is carved into a block of wood
Series: a group of related artworks that are created as a set
Abstract: an artwork the form of which is simplified, distorted, or exaggerated in appearance. It may represent a recognizable form that has been slightly altered, or it may be a completely non-representational depiction

The *Tale of Genji* is one of the great works of Japanese literature. Written in the eleventh century by Murasaki Shikibu, a noblewoman at the court of the emperor at Heian-kyo (modern-day Kyoto), it tells of the love affairs of Prince Genji. The chapters are filled with undercurrents of sadness, reflecting the Buddhist view that earthly happiness is fleeting, and that there will always be consequences from our actions. Some of the earliest surviving Japanese painting illustrates the *Tale of Genji*, including the scroll section shown in **3.3.22**.

The scroll is designed so that different portions of the tale are revealed as the scroll is unrolled from right to left. In this scene we see the prince from a so-called "blown-off roof" perspective, in which we as viewers peer, almost voyeuristically, into the private space of the palace. The flat figures and use of strong **diagonal** lines to guide the viewer through the scene are both qualities frequently used in Japanese painting. The strict diagonal and vertical lines not only powerfully divide the space within the scene, but also create a sense of drama and tension.

This scene specifically shows Genji at the naming ceremony for his first son. Unbeknownst to anyone but Genji and his wife, however, the baby he holds is actually his father's son, and Genji is being forced to raise the child as his own. The claustrophobic positioning of Genji, trapped between two rows of curtains and crushed against the top edge of the page, reflects the trapped feeling of the character in the story. In the tale, he is being punished for his past deeds because he had an affair with one of his father's wives.

Ukiyo-e

An important artistic development in Japanese art history was ukiyo-e, or "pictures of the floating world." These were **woodblock** prints that were first produced in the seventeenth century and showed characters and scenes from the entertainment districts of Edo, modern Tokyo. Later, the prints came to include landscapes and images of women from different social classes, such as courtesans. One of the best-known ukiyo-e **series** is Katsushika Hokusai's *Thirty-Six Views of Mount Fuji* (see Gateway Box: Hokusai, **3.3.23**, opposite).

Korea

Korea, located between China and Japan, has been influenced by the arts and culture of both of those countries, but it is unique in its elegantly simplified and organic forms.

The South Korean contemporary artist Do Ho Suh (b. 1962) explores issues of identity, individuality, and collectivism in his immense sculpture *Some/One*. The work recalls traditional armor of the type worn by the successful sixteenth-century military leader Yi Sun-sin, who defeated the Japanese in several naval invasions of Korea. All Korean men are required to serve in the military, and Do Ho Suh's work comments on his experience in the Korean army.

Gateway to Art: Hokusai, "The Great Wave off Shore at Kanagawa"

Mount Fuji: The Sacred Mountain of Japan

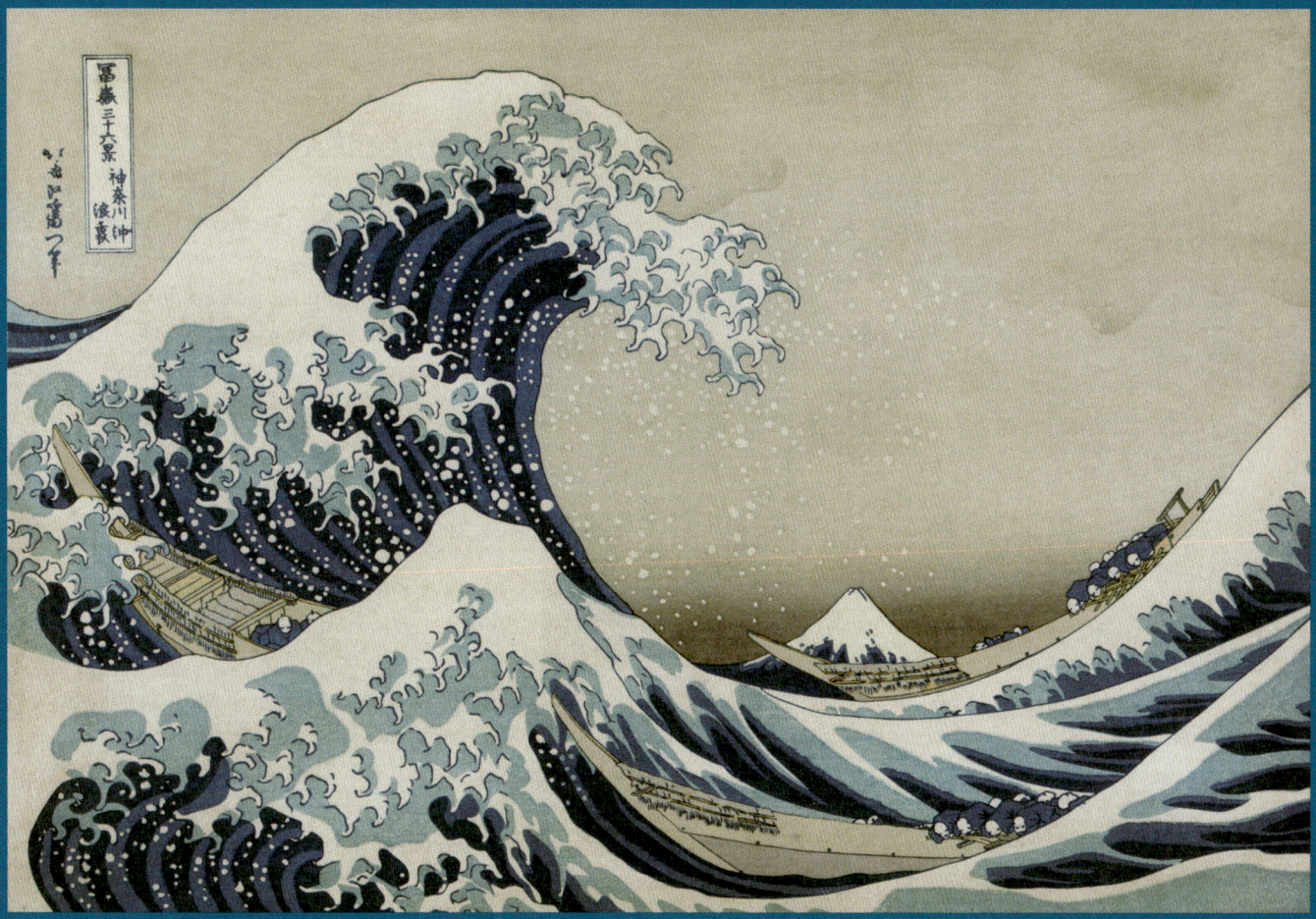

Katsushika Hokusai's series *Thirty-Six Views of Mount Fuji* was so popular in his time that he made thirty-six scenes, to which he later added ten more. Mount Fuji is the largest mountain in Japan (12,388 ft. high), and has become a recognizable symbol of the country. The mountain is sacred to believers of both Buddhism and Shinto. Because it is an active volcano, it is believed to have a particularly powerful kami, or spirit, although it has not erupted since 1708. In one print from Hokusai's series, "The Great Wave off Shore at Kanagawa" (**3.3.23**), the mountain is the only part of the scene that is not in motion; it is therefore a powerful stabilizing force. Indeed, the fierce movement of the wave thrashing the boats around contrasts markedly with the eternal and still form of the mountain. As one looks at the print, an **abstract** yin and yang (**3.3.24**), symbolic of the Daoist belief that the forces may seem opposed, but are dependent on each other (see Box: Philosophical and Religious Traditions in Asia, p. 411), appears in the intertwining of the large wave with the sky. Two smaller focal points then become Mount Fuji, the reduced size of which serves to make the curling wave seem to tower even higher, and the boat on the left.

All of the views in this series contrast the stable form of Mount Fuji with the daily actions (fleeting life) of people. In "The Great Wave," Hokusai shows the hard lifestyle of the fishermen who worked in the area of Edo, and their courage in the face of the power of the sea. The rhythmic composition also highlights the balance and harmony of man and nature.

3.3.23 Katsushika Hokusai, "The Great Wave off Shore at Kanagawa," from *Thirty-Six Views of Mount Fuji*, 1826–33 (printed later). Print, color woodcut. Library of Congress, Washington, D.C.

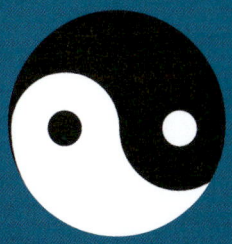

3.3.24 Yin and yang symbol

For the other Hokusai Gateway boxes, see p. 126, p. 229, and p. 661

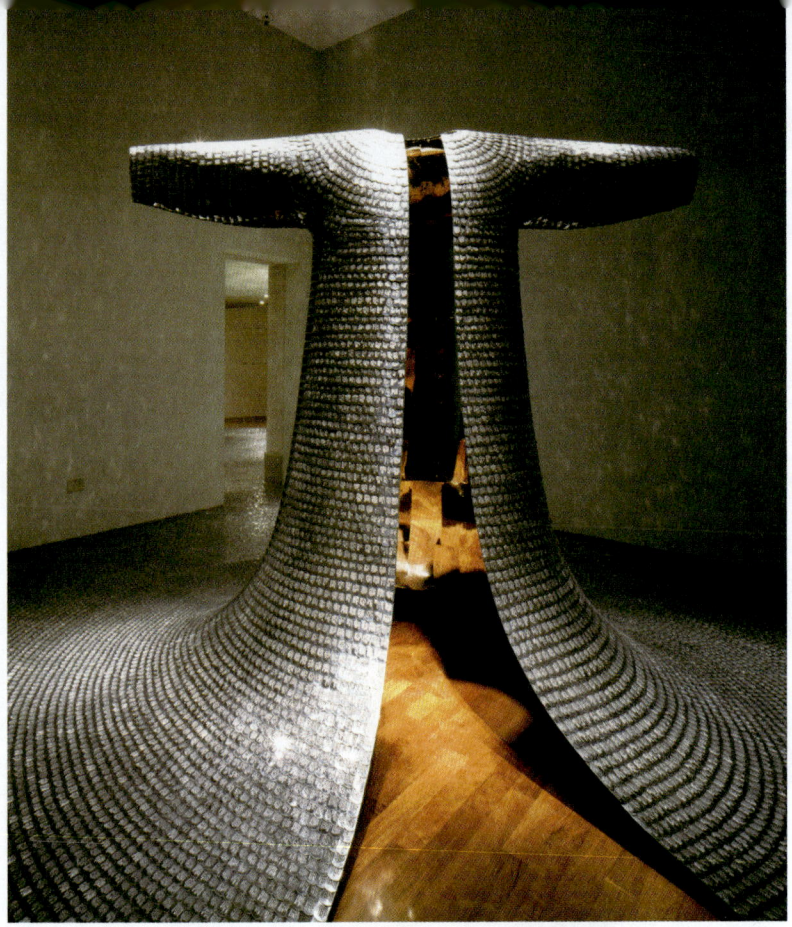

3.3.25 Do Ho Suh, *Some/One*, 2001 (installation at the 49th Venice Biennale, Korean Pavilion). Stainless steel military dog tags, nickel plated copper sheets, steel structure, glass fiber reinforced resin, and rubber sheets, dimensions variable

He describes it as dehumanizing, a feeling that as an individual you are beaten down to become part of a larger collective. At the same time, by pushing himself physically and psychologically to extremes, he felt he was made into something strong and invincible. *Some/One* reflects this in its **medium**: it is made of a huge collection of stainless steel dog tags (**3.3.25**). Each of the tags loses its individuality when it becomes part of the whole; but at the same time, viewers of the artwork are able to reflect on their own identities, as they look inside the opening at the front and see themselves reflected in a smooth, mirrored surface.

Medium: the material on or from which an artist chooses to make a work of art, for example canvas and oil paint, marble, engraving, video, or architecture

Southeast Asia

Covering more than 500 acres (three-quarters of a square mile, or some 380 football fields), the largest religious monument in the world is in Cambodia, Southeast Asia (**3.3.26**). Angkor Wat was created in the twelfth century by Suryavarman II, ruler of the Khmer empire. The temple complex was built to worship the Hindu god Vishnu, believed to be the preserver of the universe who restores the balance of good and evil during difficult times, and as a burial site for the king. Therefore, the temple is oriented toward the west where the sun sets (representing the end of life). Angkor Wat was designed as a re-creation of the heavens on Earth: the site is tiered, with the center being the highest point. In the center is a temple mount, in which five towers represent Mount Meru, in Hindu belief the home of the gods. Each of the towers resembles a lotus flower, a plant often associated with Vishnu. The massive moat that surrounds this complex symbolizes the ocean, encompassing the water-floating lotus

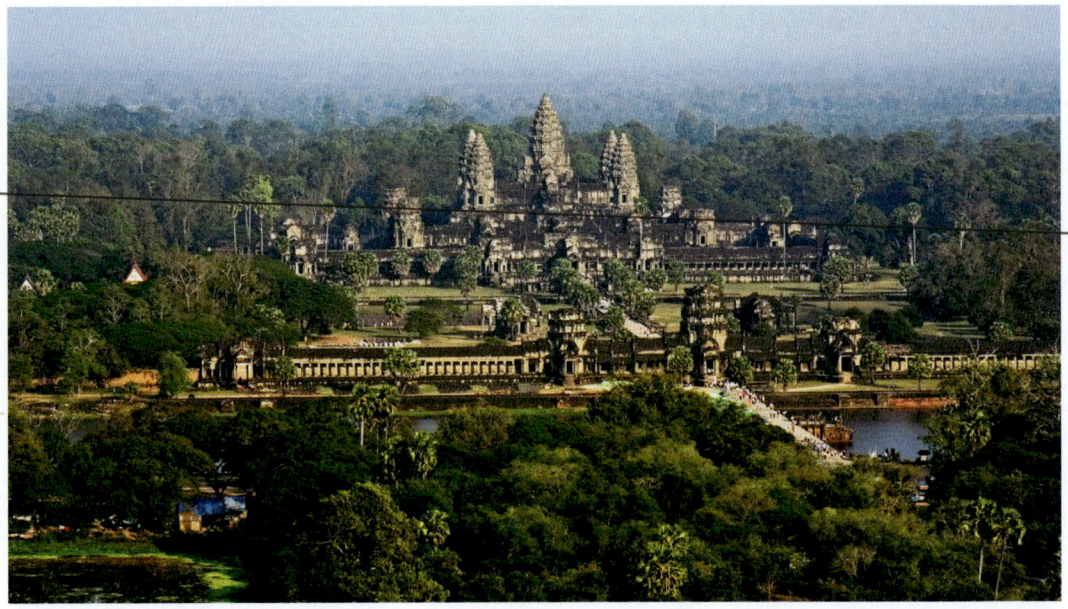

3.3.26 Angkor Wat, 12th century. Siem Reap, Cambodia

flowers. Emanating from the temple mount is a richly modeled complex built of sandstone and covered with **bas-reliefs**.

The bas-reliefs that adorn Angkor Wat show military and religious scenes, all designed to convey Suryavarman's power. *Vishnu Churning the Ocean of Milk*, which is 161 ft. long, depicts the story of the creation of a potion for reinvigorating the life force (**3.3.27**). Vishnu is in the center, with two arms holding weapons (a sword and disk). The gods, on the right, and the demons, on the left, struggle against one another as they each pull on one side of a serpent wrapped around the mountain that is behind Vishnu. Vishnu utilizes the tortoise shell on his back to help hold up the mountain as it churns. The movement of the serpent causes the mountain to move and release Amrita, the magical potion, or elixir, of eternal life, to rise from the depths of the ocean. In the original story that inspired the bas-reliefs, this is how Vishnu and the gods trick the demons into helping them release the powerful elixir, which transforms the ocean into milk. Milk, of course, gives nutrients and life to newborns. In fact the process of churning milk into buttermilk is very similar to the scene shown here.

Angkor Wat is an example of the way in which, commonly throughout Asia, different religions have, over time, been expressed and blended in architectural sites: what is often described as their syncretic nature. Although Angkor Wat was originally built under Hindu rule, Cambodia has been primarily Buddhist since 1200. The lotus-shaped towers hold a different symbolic meaning for Buddhists, for whom the lotus flower represents strength and beauty in the face of adversity, since it must grow through the muck of the earth in order to bloom into a work of beauty. Similarly, Buddhists experience difficulties and struggles in life in order to gain Enlightenment. During the fourteenth century, because of the many Buddhist pilgrims who visited Angkor, statues of Buddha were added to the artworks of Vishnu there.

In Indonesia, a tropical nation of volcanic islands, religious stories are kept alive through mask-making and theatrical dances in village temples. Barong is a protector spirit from the ancient mythology of the people of Bali, Indonesia. He is portrayed in animal masks, often with characteristics similar to a lion (**3.3.28**). Such masks are used in sacred performances in which Barong battles with Rangda, an evil witch. The characters are played by important individuals in the community, and performers or audience members are often placed into a trance as the presence of either Barong or Rangda comes forth. Although today similar masks are sold to tourists, true Barong masks are sacred objects. Each village or region has its own Barong mask to protect its people.

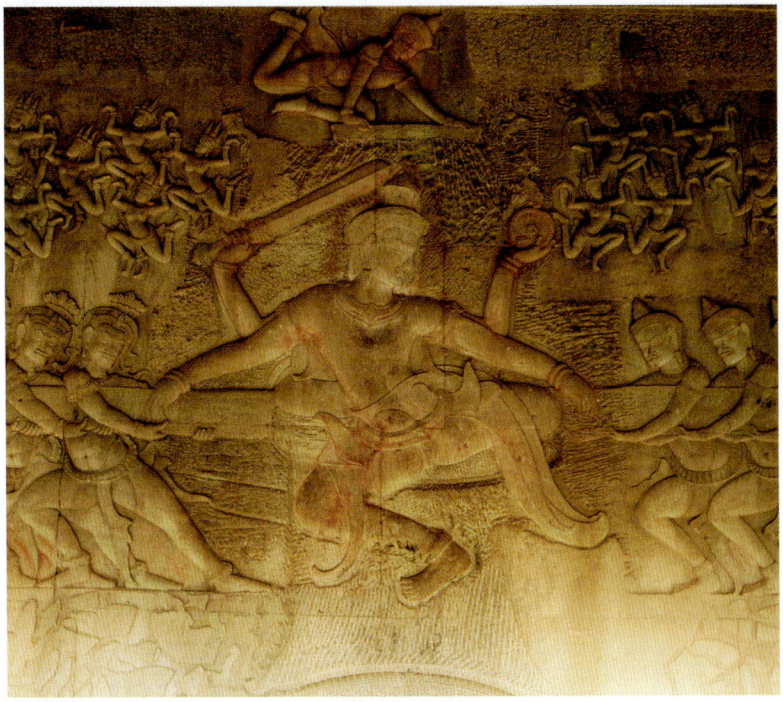

3.3.27 *Vishnu Churning the Ocean of Milk*. Relief sculpture, length 161'. Angkor Wat, Siem Reap, Cambodia

Bas-relief (low relief): a sculpture carved with very little depth: the carved subjects rise only slightly above the surface of the work

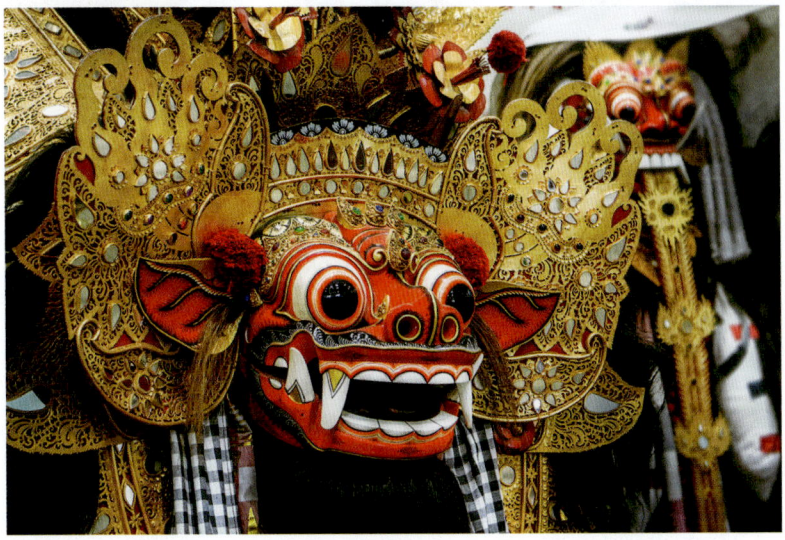

3.3.28 Barong dance mask of a lion, Ubud, Bali, Indonesia

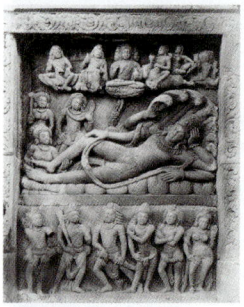

1.6.9 *Vishnu Dreaming the Universe*, India, c. 450–500 CE, p. 131

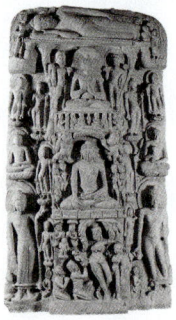

4.2.3 Life of Buddha, stela, Gupta period, India, c. 475 CE, p. 580

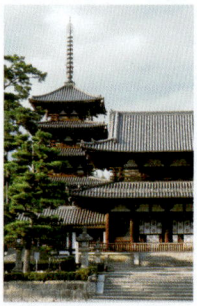

2.5.22 Horyu Temple, Japan, 7th century, p. 271

1.6.14 Ma Yuan, *Walking on a Mountain Path in Spring*, Song Dynasty (960–1279), p. 135

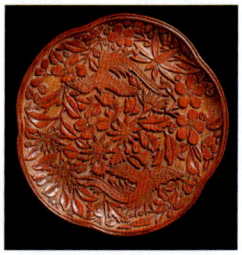

1.4.27 Red lacquer tray, China, Southern Song Dynasty, c. 1200–1279, p. 108

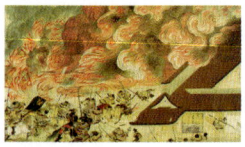

4.7.6 *Night Attack on the Sanjo Palace*, Japan, late 13th century, p. 643

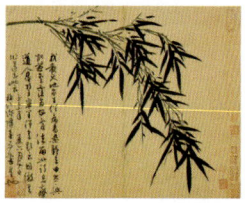

2.1.17 Wu Zhen, leaf from an album of bamboo drawings, 1350, p. 203

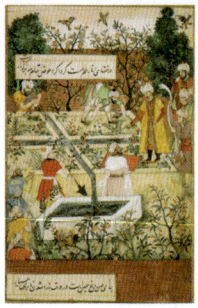

1.8.9 *The Emperor Babur Overseeing His Gardeners*, India, c. 1590, p. 157

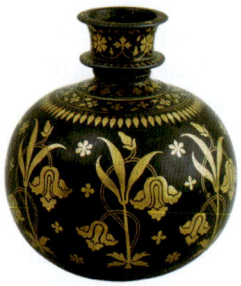

1.9.3 Huqqa base, India, last quarter of 17th century, p. 160

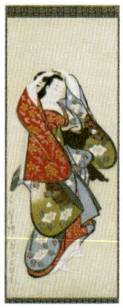

4.9.7 Kaigetsudō Dohan, *Beautiful Woman*, Japan, 18th century, p. 667

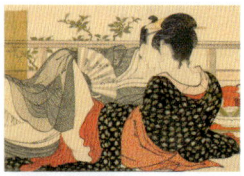

2.3.3 Kitagawa Utamaro, *Lovers in an Upstairs Room*, 1788, p. 228

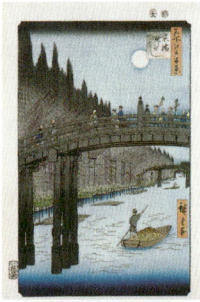

1.8.10 Ando Hiroshige, "Riverside Bamboo Market, Kyo-bashi," 1857, p. 157

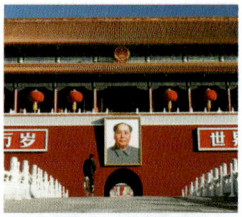

4.6.11 Mao Zedong's portrait, Tiananmen, Beijing, China, p. 635

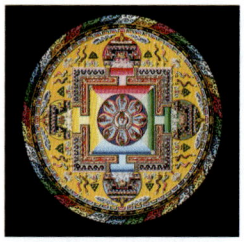

1.6.17 Amitayus Mandala, Drepung Loseling Monastery, Tibet, p. 138

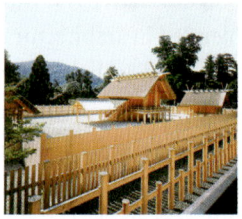

4.2.16 Ise Jingu (shrine), Japan, 4th century, rebuilt 1993, p. 589

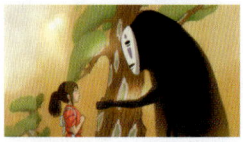

2.9.11 Hayao Miyazaki with Kirk Wise, *Spirited Away* (still), 2001, p. 340

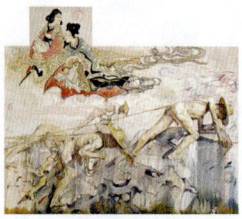

2.2.16 Hung Liu, *Interregnum*, 2002, p. 218

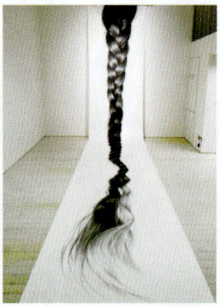

2.1.12 Zhang Chun Hong, *Life Strands*, 2004, p. 199

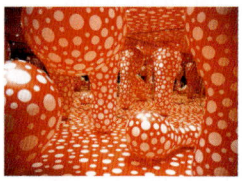

4.4.14 Yayoi Kusama, *Dots Obsession*, 2009, p. 611

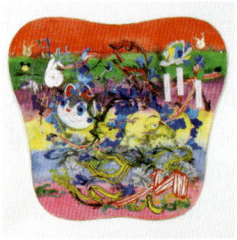

3.10.11 Jiha Moon, *Mystery Myo...*, 2010, p. 552

3.4 Art of the Americas

When's the Beginning?

We may never be sure when the first human arrived in the Americas, but scholars believe that there were no humans there at all until a time spanning anywhere from *c.* 23,000 to 14,600 years ago, when groups of people crossed a land bridge called Beringia that linked Asia to North America. Expertly made spear points, discovered on a farm in Clovis, New Mexico, in 1933, are dated to around 13,400 years ago. Similar Clovis points, as they are called, have been found all over North America, indicating that the continent was populated with people using the same type of hunting technologies and sharing genetic similarities. Ongoing research has convinced many scholars that the Americas were inhabited long before the Clovis spear points were made. Archaeological discoveries and scientific testing have revealed earlier dates of habitation in Oregon, Virginia, and the oldest site known so far in the Americas, Monte Verde in Chile (dating perhaps to 14,600 years ago).

We can trace the early civilizations of South America, ancient Mexico and Central America (Mesoamerica), and North America through their art and architecture. Some descendants of these people still live in the Americas, speaking their own languages, continuing ancient cultural practices, and following artistic traditions hundreds of years old. The arrival of Europeans from the fifteenth century onward drastically altered the ways of life of the native peoples. Direct impacts included widespread disease and forced relocation to reservations, or areas of public land set aside for use by Native Americans. European settlers destroyed many great cities and magnificent works of art, especially those made of gold and silver, which they melted down for their monetary value. Enough remains, however, to tell us much about how people lived in the Americas. Although they were spread over the two continents and their cultures were enormously varied, these people shared some common interests. Their art reflects the ways in which their societies were organized; their cultural and spiritual beliefs; and their connections with nature.

As is the case when looking at all prehistoric and ancient art, understanding the art of the ancient Americas requires the careful interpretation of a variety of clues. In addition

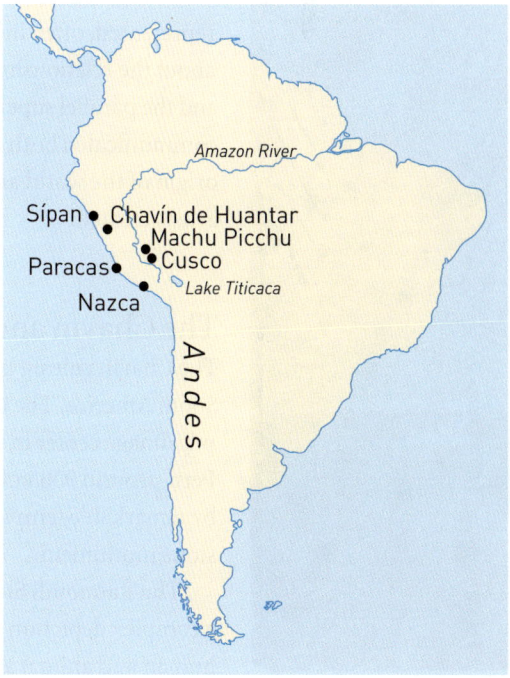

3.4.1 (right) Map showing sites of ancient South America

Stylized: art that represents objects in an exaggerated way to emphasize certain aspects of the object
Stela: upright stone slab decorated with inscriptions or pictorial relief carvings
Contour rivalry: a design in which the lines can be read in more than one way at the same time, depending on the angle from which it is viewed

to the artwork itself, scholars use scientific testing and written accounts to piece together the story of ancient American artifacts. Indigenous narratives include oral histories, handwritten accounts with painted pictures and glyphs in bark books, and inscriptions on stone monuments that have survived for many generations. The intricate writing of the Maya has been deciphered and has provided vast amounts of information about their beliefs and the way they lived their lives. European explorers wrote firsthand descriptions, translated indigenous writing, and continued to interpret the art and culture well after the conquest. The legacy of European conquest persists in the form of language (some find the term "Indian" insensitive or offensive, while others embrace it); legal rights over citizenship and land use; and in striking a balance between celebrating native cultures and exploiting them.

South America

From about 3000 BCE, the region around the Andes Mountains was home to a host of cultures, including the Chavín, Paracas, Nazca, Moche, Tiwanaku, and Inca. The objects created by Andean artists frequently reflected the local environment and resources, with animals, plants, and people represented, often in a **stylized** form. Beliefs about the relationship between humans and the parallel supernatural realm were communicated both in myths about the origin of the world and in the images that artists created.

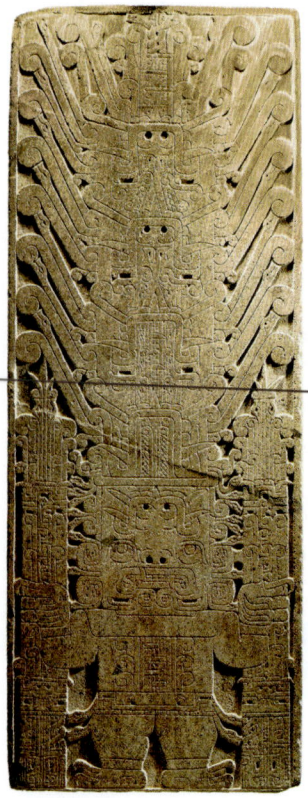

3.4.2a Raimondi Stela, Chavín de Huantar, 7th century BCE. Granite, 6'5 × 2'5". Museo Arqueología, Lima, Peru

The Chavín and the Paracas

The Chavín culture is one of the oldest in South America. The Chavín established a pilgrimage center in Chavín de Huantar, Peru, around 900 BCE. This site is marked by remarkable temples and elaborate stone monuments.

The Raimondi Stela (**3.4.2a**) contains a complex depiction of a deity with both human and animal attributes. (The carving on the stone surface is so delicate that the design is easier to see in drawings; see **3.4.2b** and **3.4.2c**.) At the bottom of the **stela** is a creature with eagle talons for feet. The figure's hands hold two staffs, which have faces, snakes, swirls, and vegetation tangling along their surfaces. A headdress, with scroll-ended projections, takes up more than half of the composition. Its eyes, resembling those of a stalking jaguar, are looking up. When we turn the stela upside down, though, the second creature seems to descend from above; its eyes look down over a crocodile snout with an additional face above it with thin eyes, a scroll nose, and fanged smile. What was formerly the headdress repeats the crocodile face menacingly. Such designs, with lines that describe more than one object at the same time, possess what

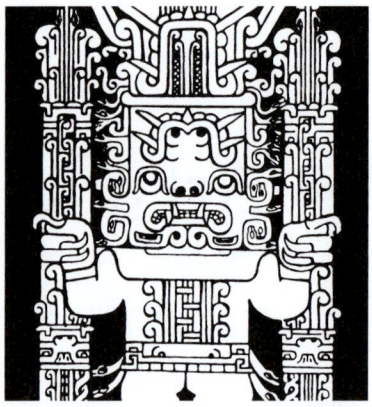

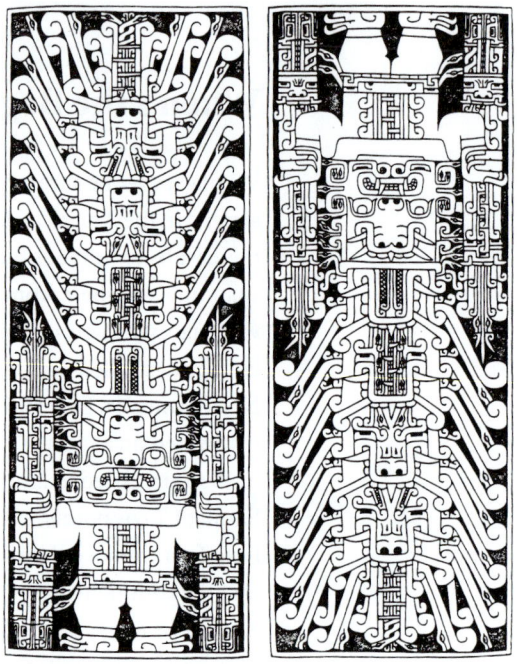

3.4.2b (top) and **3.4.2c** Drawings of details from the Raimondi Stela

is known as **contour rivalry**. They allow marks to serve dual purposes and figures to project multiple readings.

The Chavín culture's principal deity, known as the Staff God, has a close connection to nature, agriculture, and fertility, as does the crocodile. In Chavín culture generally and in this artwork in particular, animals feature prominently and are associated with all three realms of the cosmos: snakes with the earth; crocodiles, or caymans, with the watery underworld; and birds with the celestial realm of the sky.

Andean textile design is closely related to carved stone **relief** sculpture, such as the Raimondi Stela. They both use contour rivalry to create complex patterns that encourage multiple interpretations. Some of the most spectacular textiles were made by the Paracas people, who lived on the coast of Peru from about 600 to 200 BCE. The dry conditions of their necropolis (burial place) have preserved a great number of these textiles. They show a continuation of the style (contour rivalry with single lines describing more than one thing and readable in more than one direction) and content (natural life and mythical beings) developed by the Chavín culture. This Paracas textile (**3.4.3**) is a detail from a mantle, a cape-like garment often made by the Paracas people for burial purposes. Intricately **embroidered** stitches form each figure; their repetition creates a pattern. Outlines merge into body parts, and costumes resemble animals (in **3.4.3**, a kind of mythical being with deer on its shoulders—a shaman with its animal self as a disguise). Plant forms and animals appear frequently in Paracas imagery, and deer shown here represent revered creatures associated with the hunt.

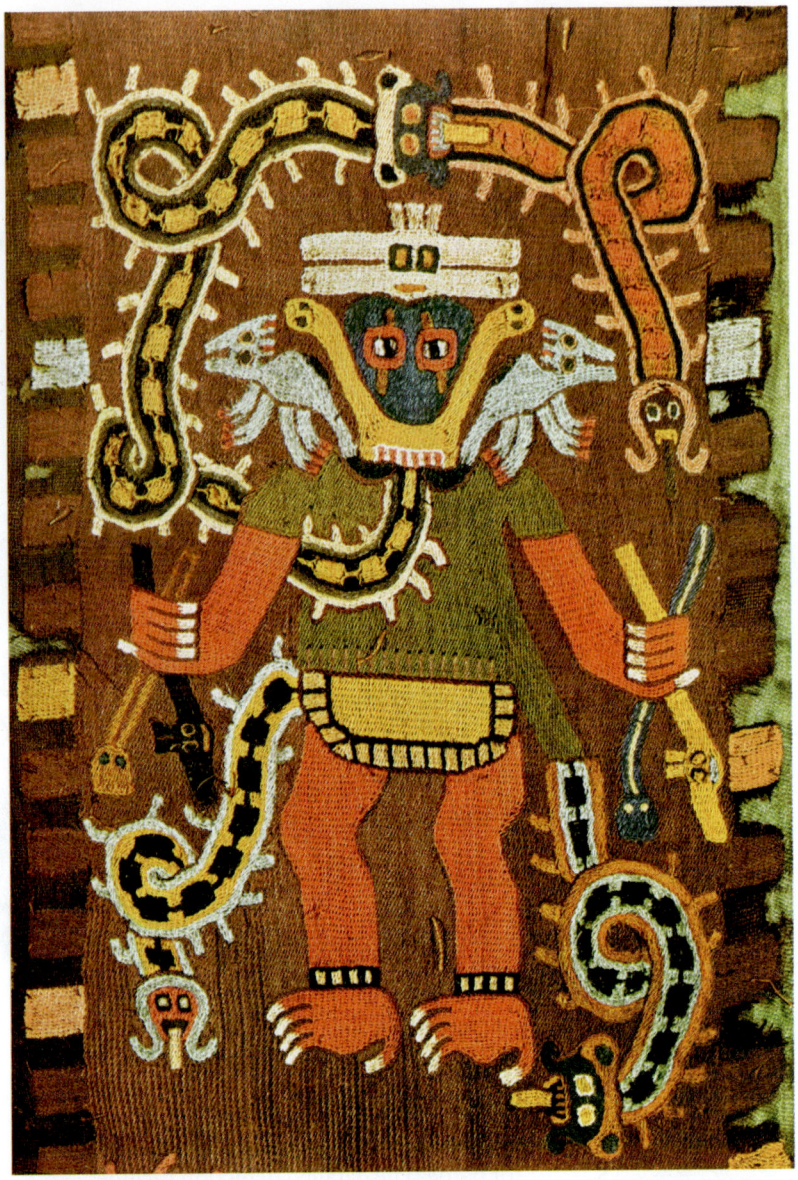

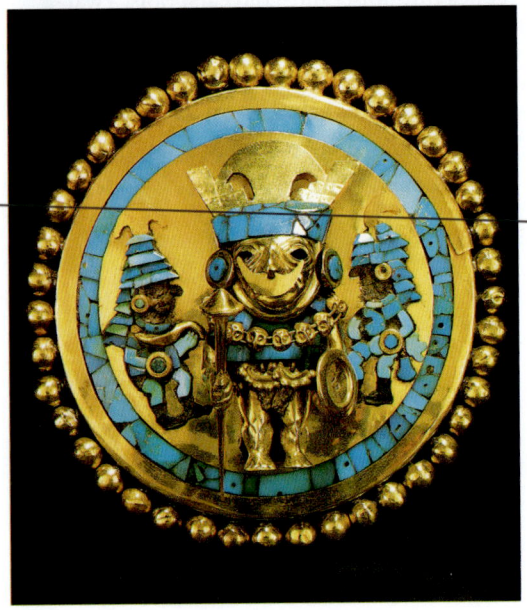

3.4.3 (above) Paracas textile, embroidered with mythological figure, 3rd century BCE. Wool embroidery. Museo Arqueología, Lima, Peru

3.4.4 (left) Earspool, c. 300 CE. Gold, turquoise, quartz, and shell, diameter 5". Royal Tombs of Sipán Museum, Sipán, Peru

Relief: a sculpture that projects from a flat surface
Embroidery: decorative stitching generally made with colored thread applied to the surface of a fabric

The Moche

Visually and conceptually intricate designs were also common for the Moche culture of northern Peru. Moche art, made from about 200 BCE to 600 CE, tells us much about their society. The earspool (a large-gauge ornament worn through the earlobe) in **3.4.4** was found in a royal tomb at Sipán. It shows a figure dressed almost exactly

3.4.5 Machu Picchu, 1450–1530, Peru

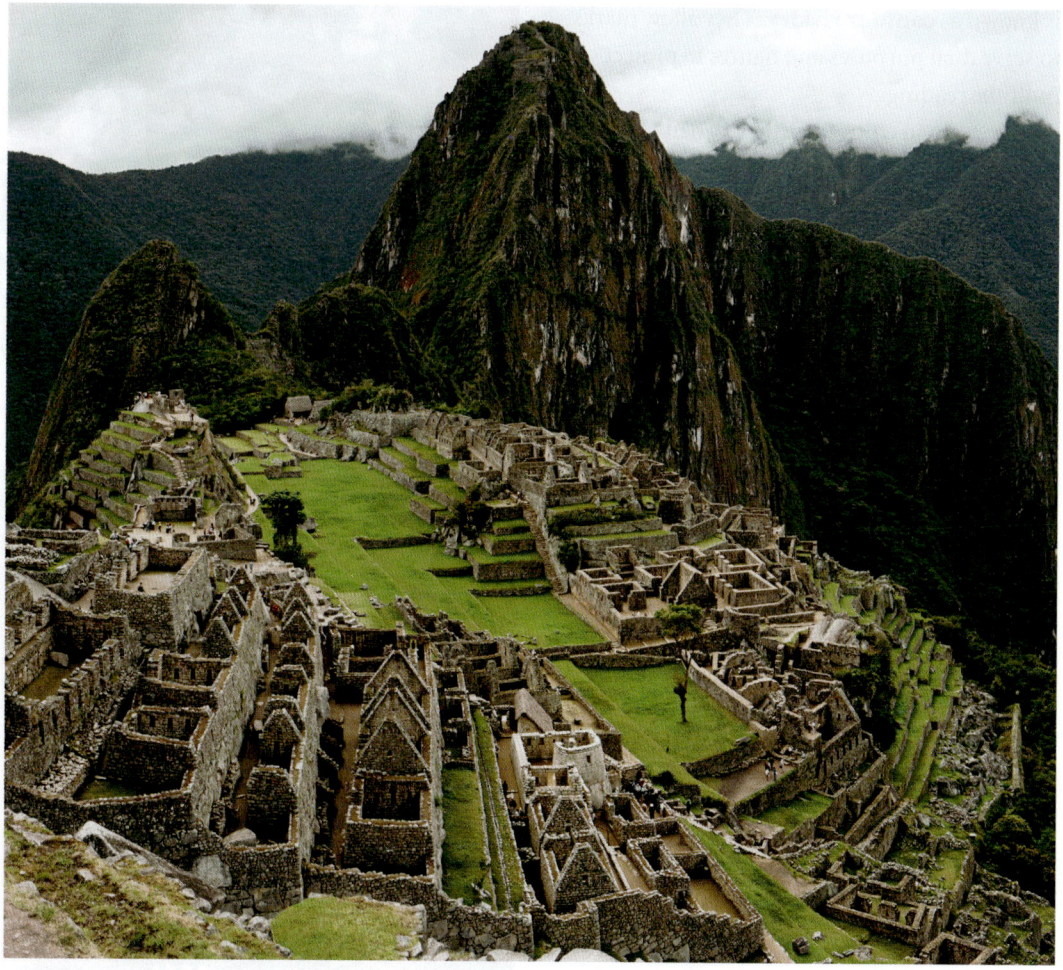

like the man found buried in the tomb, who is believed to be a warrior-priest. Pictured standing next to him on the earspool (and also lying next to him in the tomb) are two attendants dressed for battle. The detailed depiction includes replica turquoise-and-gold earspools, a war-club and shield, a necklace of owls' heads, and a crescent-shaped helmet. Although gold was not considered as valuable as textiles in the ancient Andes, its symbolic associations with the sun's energy and power made it nonetheless very important.

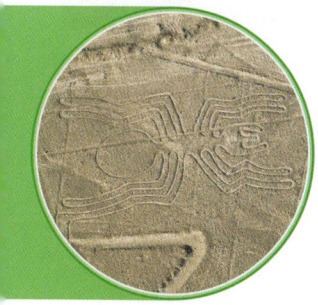

The designs of many Andean art forms, including the giant drawings on the Nazca plain, were inspired by organic forms from the natural world. This 150-ft. spider on the desert floor was also influenced by textile designs: see **1.1.1, p. 43**

The Inca

The Inca, like the Moche metalworkers who integrated into their designs the world they saw around them, were inspired by nature. The Inca culture may have existed as early as 800 CE. It became an empire when the powerful Inca ruler Pachacuti centralized the government. By the early 1500s a series of rulers had increased the area of land under their control until it covered more than 3,000 miles of the western coast of South America, thus becoming the largest empire in pre-Columbian America. Pachacuti selected a ridge high on a mountaintop in Peru for Machu Picchu, his private estate and religious retreat (**3.4.5**).

The location, on what is now known as the Inca trail, offered privacy and protection as well as breathtaking views; the site is now one of the world's most popular tourist destinations. The condor, a majestic bird of prey, is depicted throughout the site, which includes a building known as the Condor Temple, and a stone carved in the shape of a curved beak. The walls, terraces, platforms, and buildings are constructed of huge stones precisely stacked and fitted together without mortar. Machu Picchu was abandoned around 1527, probably after a devastating smallpox epidemic caused by contact with Europeans. Because of its elevated location, the site was not excavated until 1911,

when the Yale archaeologist Hiram Bingham led an expedition to the Inca trail.

After more than 100 years in the collection of Yale University, the artifacts gathered by Bingham and his crew were returned to Peru from 2011 to 2012. When collected artifacts are returned to indigenous cultures (a process known as repatriation), the focus is usually on legal rights. This case is different: with the return of these items, the focus has been on stewardship (careful and responsible management), preservation, research, and exhibition of the materials, rather than ownership. (For further discussion of indigenous rights see Box: "We Are the Mirrors": Legislation and Activism to Protect Native Rights and Lands, p. 444.)

In the Andes, stone architecture was a hallmark of the Inca culture. Similarly, textiles had a cultural significance more valuable than gold or silver. Weaving was such a sacred art that it had its own god, Spider Woman, who featured prominently in the Inca creation story. Textiles were thus considered sacred and made exclusively by women. This scale of values was not shared by the Spaniards who conquered Peru in the sixteenth century: they demanded gold and silver from the Inca and melted down fine works of art to ship the precious metals home to Spain.

The checkerboard tunic in **3.4.6** was worn by an Inca ruler. Its square designs contain a number of patterns that together indicate the high status and importance of the person who wore it. The little checkerboard designs would have decorated tunics worn by warriors serving the ruler; similarly, the diagonal lines and dots indicate the clothing of administrators. The other patterns do not directly represent specific roles or people as such, but through the complexity and variety of designs, they stand for the conquest of all possible ethnicities. The tunic refers to an important Inca creation myth, when the great god Viracocha sent out all the different peoples with their ethnic patterns painted on their bodies.

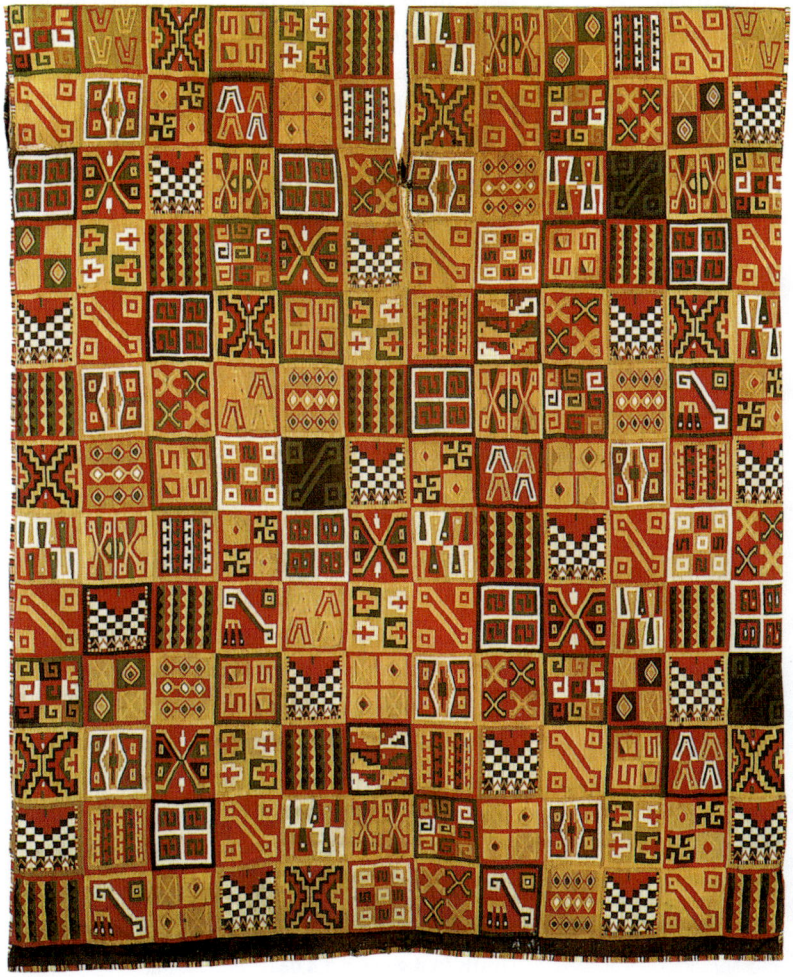

3.4.6 Tunic, *c.* 1500. Interlocked tapestry of cotton and wool, 35⅞ × 30⅛". Dumbarton Oaks Research Library and Collections, Washington, D.C.

Mesoamerica

"Mesoamerica" is the name given by archaeologists to the area occupied by modern-day Mexico and Central America. The many different peoples and cultures that inhabited the region founded powerful city-states and produced diverse artworks. Skilled astronomers and mathematicians, Mesoamericans developed an accurate calendar that they used to calculate the dates of important ceremonies and rituals and to predict astronomical events. They shared similar religious beliefs and many cultural traditions, including a ball game played with a hard rubber ball (see **3.4.13**, p. 437).

The Olmec

The art and architecture of the Olmec, who lived on the fertile lowlands of Mexico's Gulf Coast from *c.* 1500 to 400 BCE, influenced later Mesoamerican people, for example the inhabitants of the city of Teotihuacan, the Maya, and the Aztecs. The Olmec used images to record

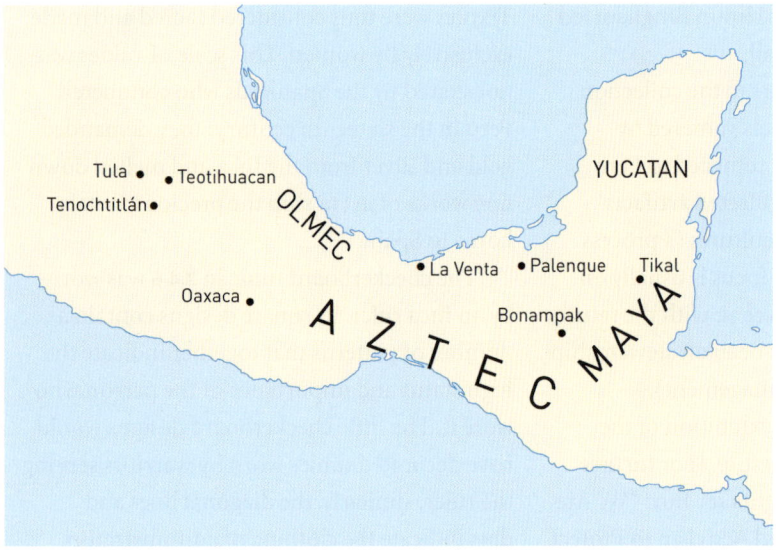

3.4.7 Map of Mesoamerica

information, a tradition also common amongst other people of Mesoamerica. Eventually the Olmecs, and later the Teotihuacanos, used images as a form of writing, although scholars have not yet been able to interpret their scripts. The Maya also developed a system of writing, called **hieroglyphs**, much of which can now be read. Some Aztec **pictographs**, too, can be deciphered.

Amongst the most spectacular and mysterious products of the Olmec creative vision were the colossal sculpted heads (see **3.4.8**). Olmec artists carved these giant heads out of a hard volcanic stone called basalt. Today we often see Olmec art (and replicas of it) in modern museums, but centuries ago these massive monuments were displayed in the ceremonial centers of Olmec cities. They were then forgotten for hundreds of years, as they lay buried in remote locations.

In 1938 the archaeologists Matthew and Marion Stirling "discovered" a colossal Olmec head at Tres Zapotes. A few years later they found several more Olmec heads *in situ*, or in their original positions. After ten days of exploring La Venta, the Stirlings explain that they finally found a colossal head in a densely overgrown area of the forest. Then, a small boy standing nearby took the couple about a half mile to another location, where they found three more heads "positioned about 100 yards north of the pyramid" in an east–west row about thirty yards from one another.

In total, seventeen of these colossal heads have been found at four sites in Mexico. They range in size from 5 to 12 ft. tall and each head weighs approximately 6 to 25 tons; astonishingly, they were carved using only stone hammers and wooden drills. In terms of scale, the eye of one of these sculptures would be the size of a human head. All portray mature males with flat noses, large cheeks, and slightly crossed eyes. Because of their **monumental** scale and individual appearance, many scholars believe that the impressive heads depict mighty Olmec rulers.

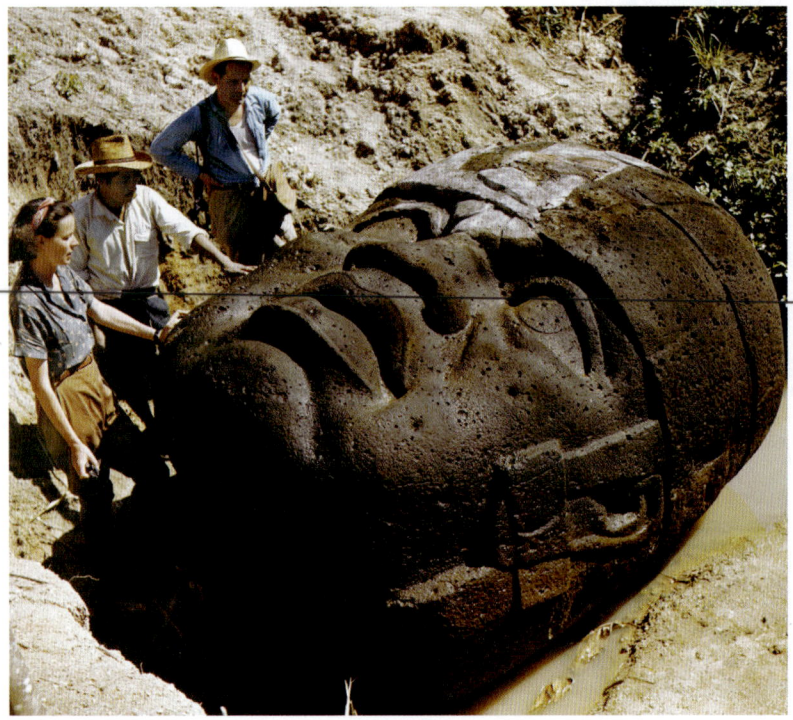

3.4.8 With the help of local villagers, Matthew and Marion Stirling discovered this 8-foot-tall colossal head in San Lorenzo in the state of Veracruz, Mexico, in 1945—a few years after their discoveries at La Venta.

Teotihuacan

The main components of Olmec sites are a pyramid and a plaza, a layout that also features, on a much larger scale, at Teotihuacan, in the Central Highlands of Mexico about 30 miles from modern-day Mexico City. Teotihuacan was one of the largest cities in the world at the time. Around 500 CE, at the peak of its power, it had 600 pyramids and 2,000 apartment compounds. A wide street, the Avenue of the Dead, runs north–south and is about 3 miles long. At its northern end lies the Pyramid of the Moon. The Pyramid of the Sun lies on its east and the Temple of the Feathered Serpent is located to the south (**3.4.9a** and **3.4.9b**).

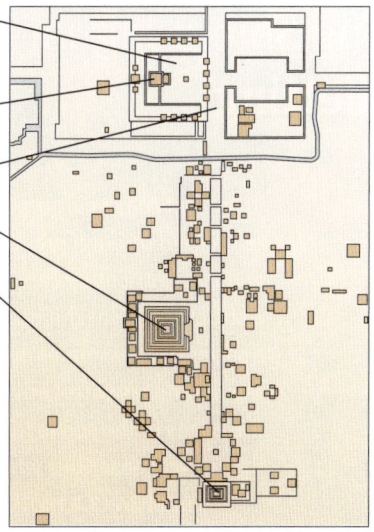

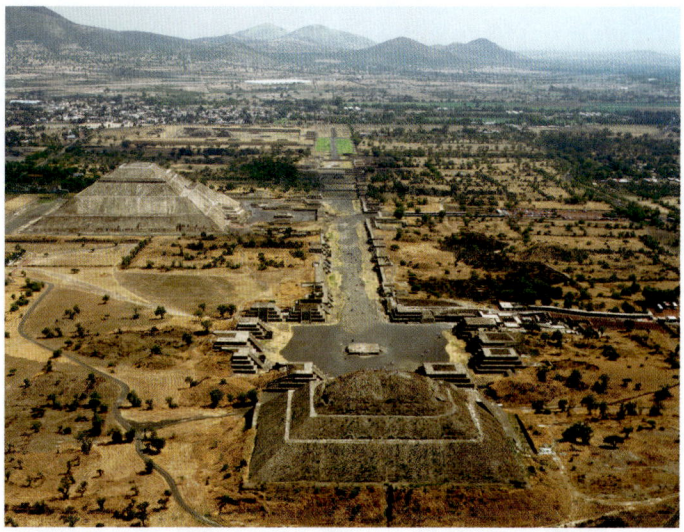

3.4.9a and **3.4.9b** Plan and aerial view of the ceremonial center, Teotihuacan

The Pyramid of the Sun, Teotihuacan's largest structure, is a **stepped pyramid** (**3.4.10**). Covering 13 acres, its base is about 700 ft. across on each side; it is 210 ft. tall. The location of the Pyramid of the Sun was of utmost importance. It faced west—toward the setting sun and the Avenue of the Dead—and was built on top of a cave and a spring. Caves had religious significance throughout Mesoamerica because they were thought to connect the world of humans with the world of the gods. The Aztecs, who established a powerful empire in central Mexico about 800 years after Teotihuacan was abandoned, admired the cultural achievement of the Teotihuacanos. In fact, the name Teotihuacan is Aztec for "The Place of the Gods," and the Pyramid of the Sun was a place of pilgrimage for the Aztecs. The Temple of the Feathered Serpent at Teotihuacan is located in an enclosed compound. The plaza next to it is below ground level, to symbolize the underworld. Sculpted heads on the temple

Hieroglyph: written language involving sacred characters that may be pictures as well as letters
Pictograph: picture used as a symbol in writing
Monumental: having massive or impressive scale
Stepped pyramid: a pyramid consisting of several rectangular structures placed one on top of another

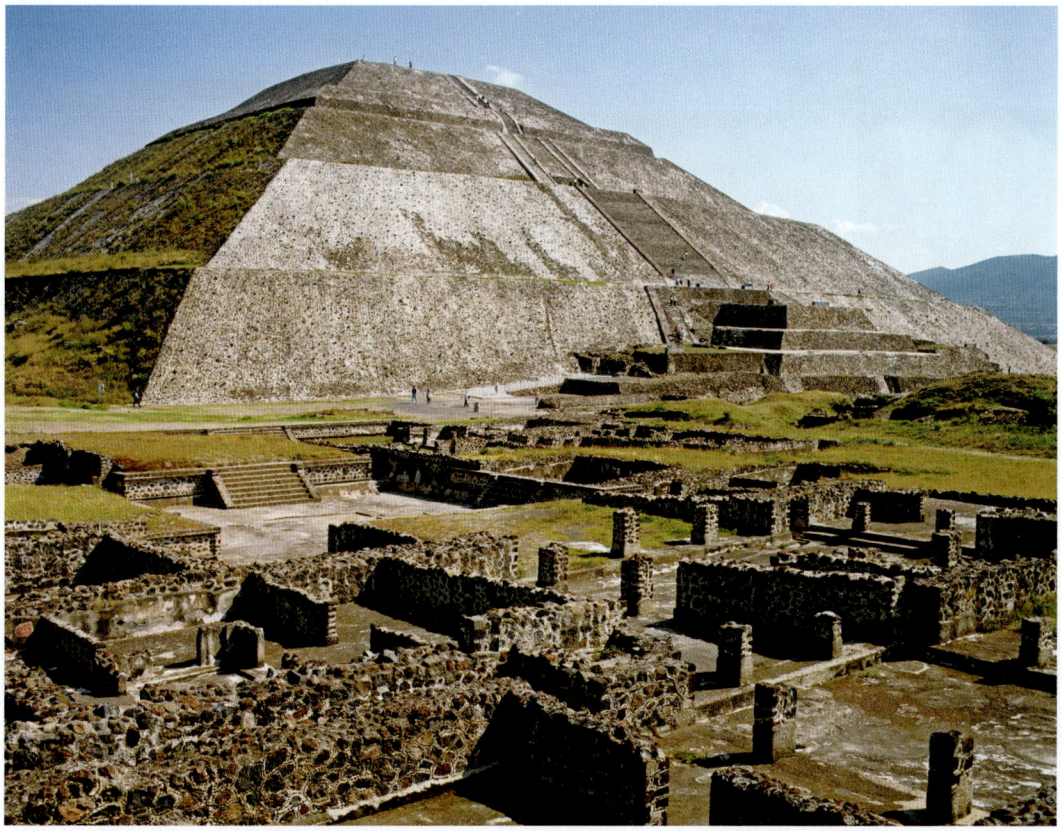

3.4.10 Pyramid of the Sun, c. 225 CE, Teotihuacan, Mexico

Gateway to Art: Maya Lintel Showing Shield Jaguar and Lady Xoc

Invoking Ancestors through Bloodletting

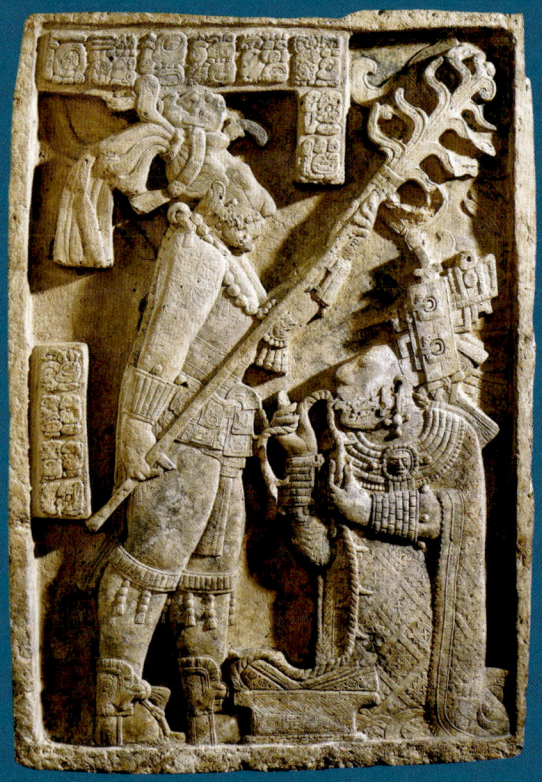

3.4.11a Maya Lintel 24 showing Shield Jaguar and Lady Xoc, *c.* 725 CE. Limestone, 43 × 30¾ × 2⅜". British Museum, London, England

In ancient Maya culture, a ruler's power was reinforced through prayers and sacrifices to the gods. An intricately carved set of three lintels from a structure in Yaxchilán, southern Mexico, depicts a series of ceremonies undertaken by Shield Jaguar and his wife, Lady Xoc. The writing around the edges of the scene tells us the names of the figures and describes what is taking place.

In Lintel 24 (**3.4.11a**), Lady Xoc kneels before Shield Jaguar, who holds a large burning torch to light the evening ritual. Lady Xoc pulls a rope studded with thorns through her tongue; the blood itself is visible in the form of scrolls around her mouth and spots on the paper in the basket in front of her. This bloodletting ritual was considered necessary to win the favor of the gods for important events, in this case the birth of Shield Jaguar's son (by another wife), Bird Jaguar III. According to the symbols above the king's head, this ritual took place on October 28, 709 CE.

In Lintel 25 (**3.4.11b**) we see a vision of a serpent arising from a bowl of burning, blood-soaked

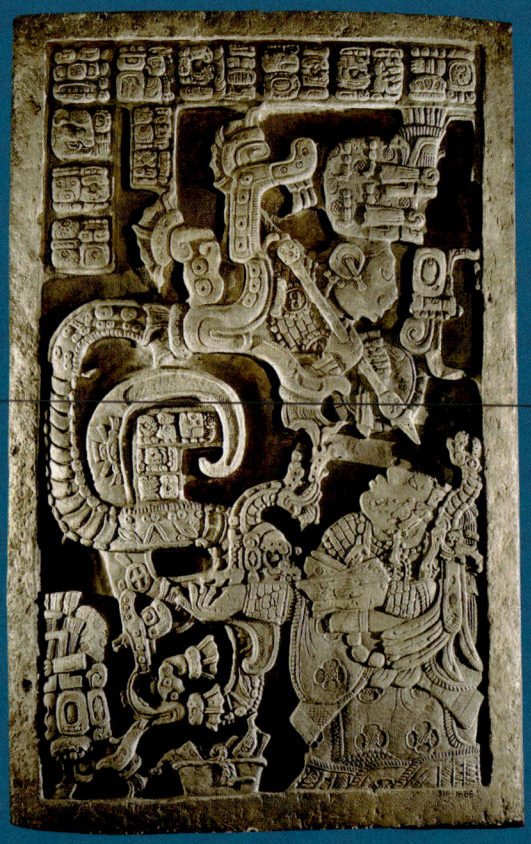

3.4.11b (left) Maya Lintel 25. Limestone, 47⅝ × 33¾ × 5⅜". British Museum, London, England

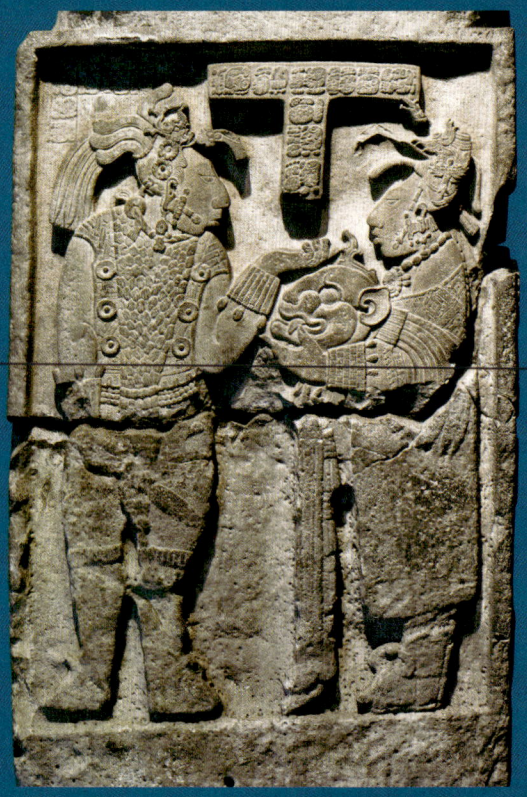

3.4.11c (right) Maya Lintel 26. Limestone, 72½ × 33⅞ × 10⅝". British Museum, London, England

paper. Bloodletting led to a hallucinogenic state in which the participant imagined that he or she was seeing visions. The Maya may have enhanced such states by fasting and taking drugs to induce spiritual and mystical interactions. In this scene we see an armed ancestor—believed to be the founder of the dynasty, or Shield Jaguar, or perhaps both of them—emerging from the mouth of the vision serpent. The date on the inscription, October 20, 681, indicates that this event occurred the year that Shield Jaguar ascended the throne.

The third and final scene, in Lintel 26 (**3.4.11c**), shows Lady Xoc handing her husband a jaguar helmet and shield in preparation for battle. Shield Jaguar, dressed as a warrior, wears an elaborate headdress that includes the shrunken head of a victim sacrificed to the gods. The three panels together show Lady Xoc's role in conjuring the ancestors while telling the story of Shield Jaguar's rule and affirming his place in the lineage of kings.

For the other Maya lintel Gateway boxes, see p. 162, p. 245, and p. 632

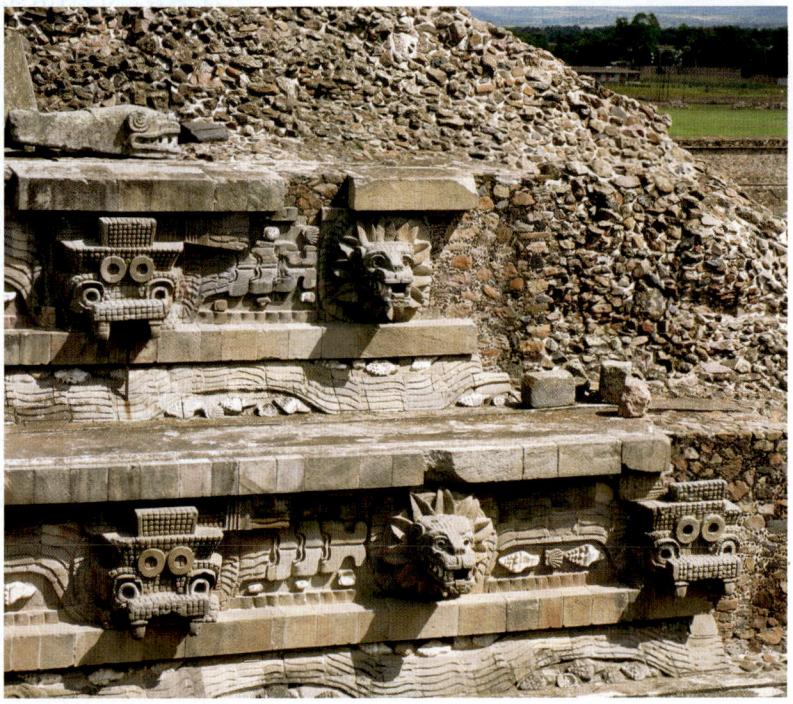

depict serpents with feathers and jaguar features alongside square heads with goggle eyes and fang-like teeth (**3.4.12**). To the Aztecs, these sculptures looked like images of their gods Quetzalcoatl, the feathered serpent, and Tlaloc, the goggle-eyed rain god. These figures symbolized warfare and fertility, or perhaps cycles of wet and dry seasons.

3.4.12 (above) Architectural sculpture with serpent heads and masks on the Temple of Quetzalcoatl at Teotihuacan, Mexico (also known as the Temple of the Feathered Serpent)

The Maya

The dates for Maya civilization are from about 2000 BCE to 1500 CE. At the peak of the Maya empire, from about 300 to 900 CE, there were Maya centers in Mexico, Guatemala, Belize, Honduras, and El Salvador. By 900 most of them had faded away, but the civilization continued to exist in isolated locations. Surviving Spanish colonization, the Maya continue to speak their own language and now number an estimated seven million.

Mythology and cosmology and their associated rituals were important to Maya society (see Gateway Box: Maya Lintels of Shield Jaguar and Lady Xoc, opposite). The ball game was a common ritual event in Mesoamerica and could also be played for sport, gambling, or as a gladiatorial contest to the death (**3.4.13**). The rubber ball, magnified on the cylindrical vessel shown here, was about 8 in. in diameter. The game was played on a court; the objective was to get the ball through a ring or into a goal area without using one's hands. The rings were very high off the ground and virtually impossible to get the ball

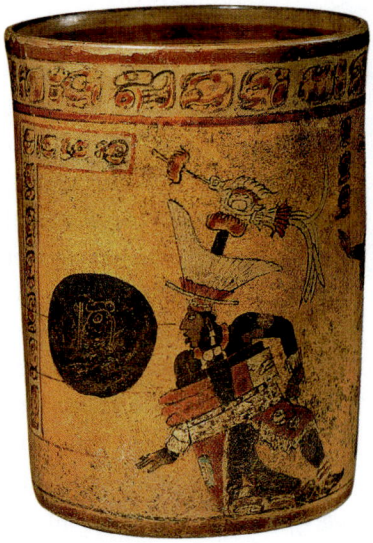

3.4.13 (right) Cylindrical vessel with ritual ball-game scene, c. 700–850. Ceramic, 6¼ × 4". Dallas Museum of Art, Texas

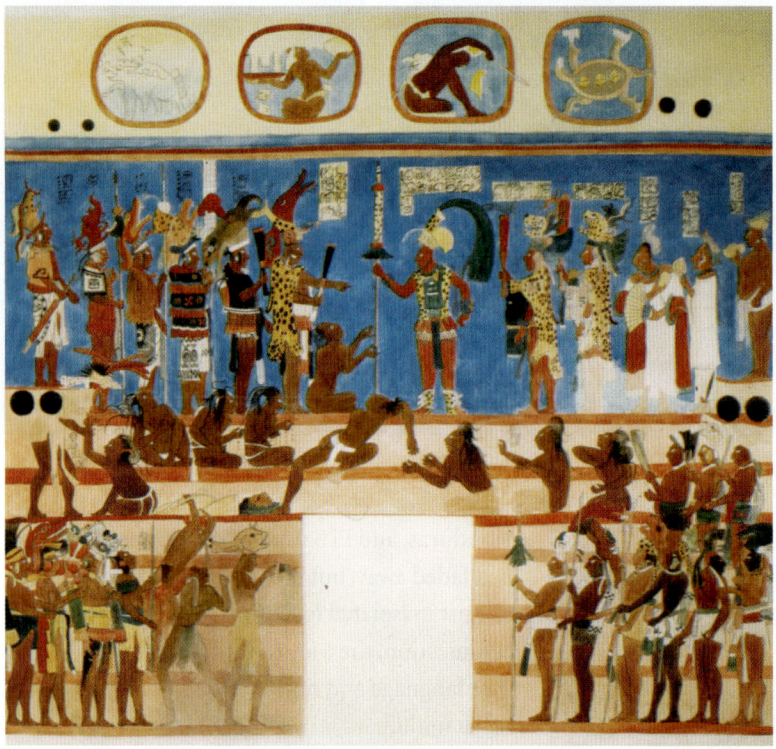

3.4.14 Bonampak mural, copy of fresco from Room 2, original 8th century. Peabody Museum, Harvard University, Cambridge, Massachusetts

through. Players' uniforms offered physical and symbolic fortification: yokes were fitted around the waist to strike the ball and protect the body. *Hachas* (stone objects often shaped like a human head) and *palmas* (thin flat stones) were worn on the yokes to guide and deflect the ball. The elaborate quality of the yokes and helmet-like headdresses of the players on the vessel in **3.4.13** indicate that this was a ceremonial game played for the purposes of ritual.

Mesoamerican ball games often served as the arena for the final stages of warfare in which captured enemies met their fate. The murals at the Maya city of Bonampak in southern Mexico show the victory of the Lord of Bonampak, Chaan Muan, in 790 CE, and the treatment of his defeated opponents. The wall illustrated in **3.4.14** shows the ritual presentation of captives on the steps of a temple. Chaan Muan is shown at the center of the composition, wearing a headdress with long green feathers; his ministers and aides stand beside him, well armed and in full regalia. The prisoners have been stripped of their own clothing and weapons, leaving them naked and vulnerable. They have been tortured, perhaps starved, and likely made to play a fixed and fatal ball game in which the losers are eventually executed. The man sprawled out at the ruler's feet has an incision in his side, indicating that he is already dead. To the left of this figure are several prisoners with blood dripping from their fingers, their fingernails recently ripped out. The Maya considered blood on the steps a sign of their triumph and a sacrifice to please the gods, so they wanted as much of it on the building as could be spilled.

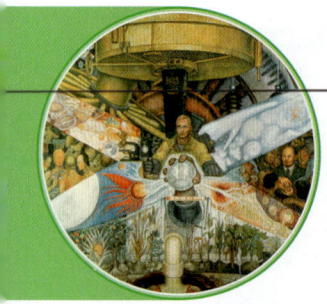

The twentieth-century Mexican artist Diego Rivera was influenced by the style, appearance, symbolism, and narrative techniques of Mesoamerican murals, one of the world's richest painting traditions: see **4.1.13, p. 576**

The Aztecs

The Aztecs formed a powerful empire in Mesoamerica, which they dominated at approximately the same time the Inca were in power in South America (from 1400 until Spanish occupation in the 1520s and 1530s). At its peak, the empire covered central Mexico, Guatemala, El Salvador, and Honduras; the Aztecs were conquered by Cortés in 1524.

In a manner similar to the Olmec, Teotihuacan, and Maya societies before them, the Aztecs placed pyramid structures in the center of their cities, emphasizing their importance as the site of rituals. Amongst the most notorious of these rituals was the practice of sacrificing a person by extracting from the body his or her still-beating heart (**3.4.15**). Sacrifices to the gods were performed at specific times of the year, such as planting season, and at certain points in the ceremonial calendar, for example the end of a 52-year cycle. Important events, such as the dedication of a new temple, might also be the occasion for sacrifices. Capturing victims for this purpose was one of the major goals of warfare, another being to expand the empire. People sometimes sacrificed members of their own community. In some cases it was considered an honor to die by the sacrificial blade; other individuals were selected because they had been born on an "unlucky" day.

The Aztecs based some of their sacrifice rituals on the story of their origins, which they traced to a mythical place called "Aztlan." The Aztecs believed that their ancestors had journeyed from Aztlan to their future capital at Tenochtitlán (modern Mexico City). During their journey they met Coatlicue, or "Serpent Skirt," the guardian at Serpent Mountain. Coatlicue had been impregnated

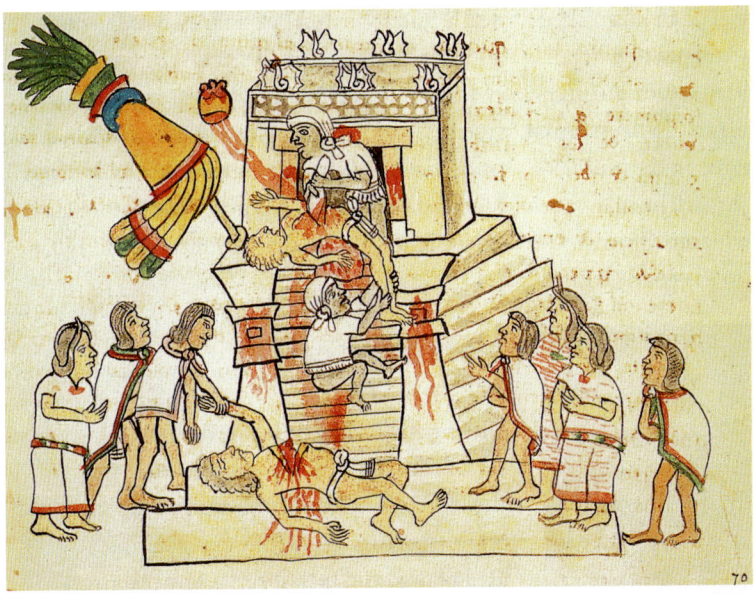

3.4.15 A human sacrifice, fol. 70r of the *Codex Magliabechiano*, 16th century. European paper, 6½ × 8⅞". Biblioteca Nazionale Centrale, Florence, Italy

by a ball of feathers that fell from the sky; her son Huitzilopochtli, the god of war, was miraculously born fully armed. When Coatlicue's other children attempted to murder their dishonored mother, Huitzilopochtli defended her by attacking his sister Coyolxauhqui, or "She of the Golden Bells." Coyolxauhqui's dismembered body was rolled in pieces down Serpent Mountain.

The events of Huitzilopochtli's birth are the source for many Aztec artworks, including a colossal sculpture of Coatlicue (**3.4.16**). A ferocious face, created by the profiles of two facing serpent heads, enhances her imposing presence. She also has a necklace made of human hearts and hands, with a skull pendant. Coatlicue was the Mother Goddess, associated with the Earth, fertility, and transformation, who was seen as both creator and destroyer.

Coyolxauhqui's dismemberment was commemorated on a stone disk (**3.4.17**) placed at the base of an early temple built on the site of Templo Mayor, the Great Temple of the Aztecs, in Tenochtitlán. The goddess is shown in a simplified but realistic way, with parts of her body scattered across the circular surface. Each limb, like her waist, is tied with a rope that has snake heads on the ends. The incorporation of skulls throughout the scene—at her waist, elbows, and knees—evokes her violent murder. The placement of the disk also symbolized the treatment of sacrificial victims: as a sign of their defeat, their bodies were thrown down the steps of the Great Temple to land where the disk of Coyolxauhqui lay.

This story poetically explains astronomical phenomena observed by the Aztecs. Coatlicue (the Earth) gives birth to Huitzilopochtli (the sun), who then slices up his sister (the moon), as their siblings (the stars) stand by. It is a metaphor for the phases of the moon, when the sun—with the help of the Earth's shadow—appears to cut across the moon during an eclipse.

The profound cultural resonance of the Aztec creation myth can be seen in *Coatlicue*

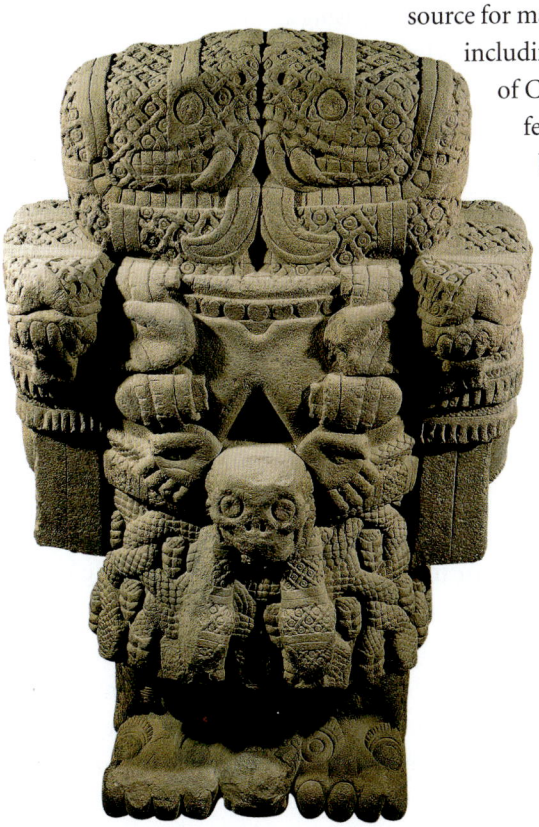

3.4.16 (left) *The Mother Goddess, Coatlicue*, c. 1487–1520. Andesite, 11'6". National Museum of Anthropology, Mexico City

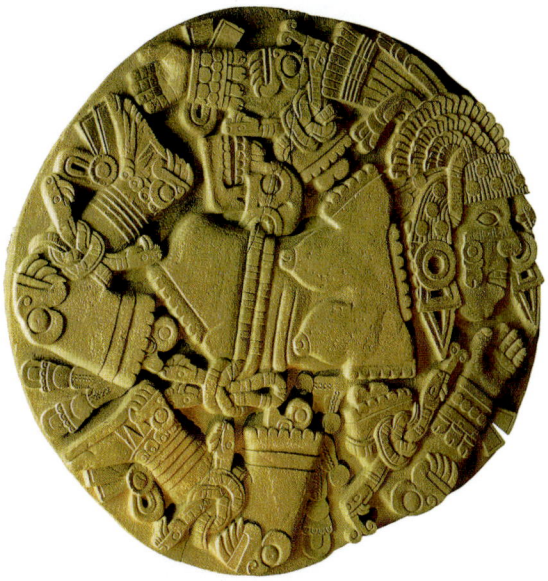

3.4.17 (right) *The Dismemberment of Coyolxauhqui, Goddess of the Moon*, late Postclassic. Stone, diameter 9'10⅛". Museo del Templo Mayor, Mexico City

Triptych: an artwork comprising three panels, normally joined together and sharing a common theme
Expressionism, Expressionistic: an artistic style at its height in 1920s Europe, devoted to representing subjective emotions and experiences instead of objective or external reality

Transformed, the central panel of an unfinished **triptych** (**3.4.18**) by the Mexican painter Saturnino Herrán (1887–1918). Made during the Mexican Revolution, Herrán's **Expressionist** depiction of Coatlicue includes, in the middle, the image of the crucified Christ. The side panels (not shown here) include Aztec and Spanish worshipers paying homage to the goddess of life, death, and rebirth. The combined indigenous and Christian imagery reflects the complex and syncretic (the blending of two or more belief systems) nature of Mexican identity, in which traditional gods persist even while much of the Mexican population has practiced Catholicism since Spain colonized the country in the 1500s.

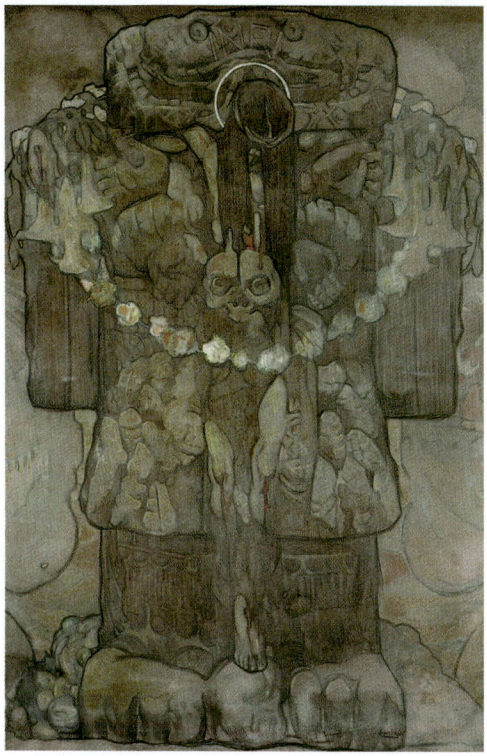

3.4.18 (right) Saturnino Herrán, *Coatlicue Transformed* (central panel of *Our Gods*), 1915. Crayon and watercolor on paper, 34⅞ × 24⅝". Museo de Aguascalientes, Mexico

3.4.19 (below) Map of North America

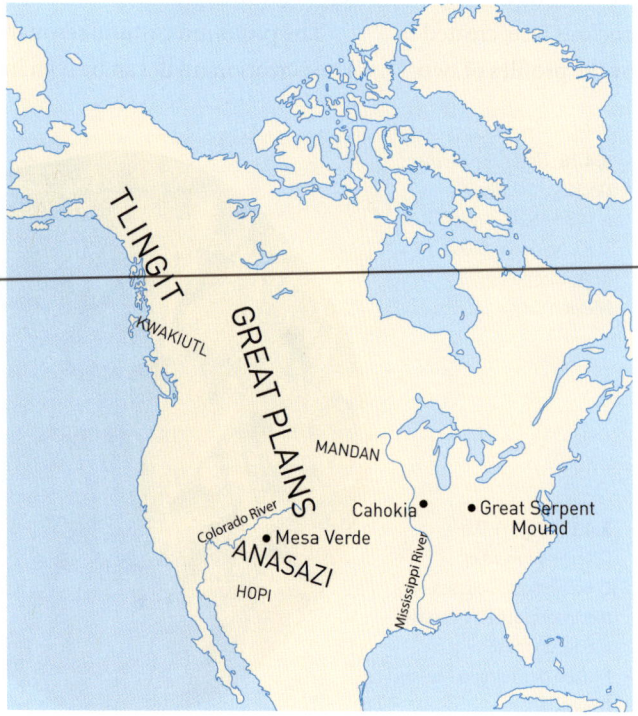

North America

During the thousands of years before Europeans arrived, the people who lived in the North American continent occupied arctic regions, ocean coasts, dry desert lands, semi-arid plains, and lush forests. The resources available to these original Americans were therefore very diverse. Groups who lived east of the Mississippi River utilized the plentiful trees, earth, and water surrounding them. In modern Arizona, New Mexico, and Colorado, some groups lived in permanent dwellings made of adobe. Other people, from the Midwest to modern-day Mississippi and Louisiana, constructed settlements of wood and earth and made large ceremonial mounds. On the northwest coast, fishing communities built villages, using abundant local wood. Still others lived nomadic lives, moving to find their food and other essential materials. Not surprisingly, the people of North America spoke many different languages and developed diverse cultural traditions. Their structures and domestic objects met their practical needs, but many were so beautifully designed that today we call them "art." Although European invaders killed many native people and displaced others, some survived, maintained their cultural traditions, and continued to make fine artworks.

Ancient Puebloans (The Anasazi)

The people of North America used local materials to build practical structures that provided shelter. Late in the twelfth century (*c.* 1150 CE), a drought forced the Ancient Puebloans, also referred to as the Anasazi, to abandon their homes, called pueblos, on the

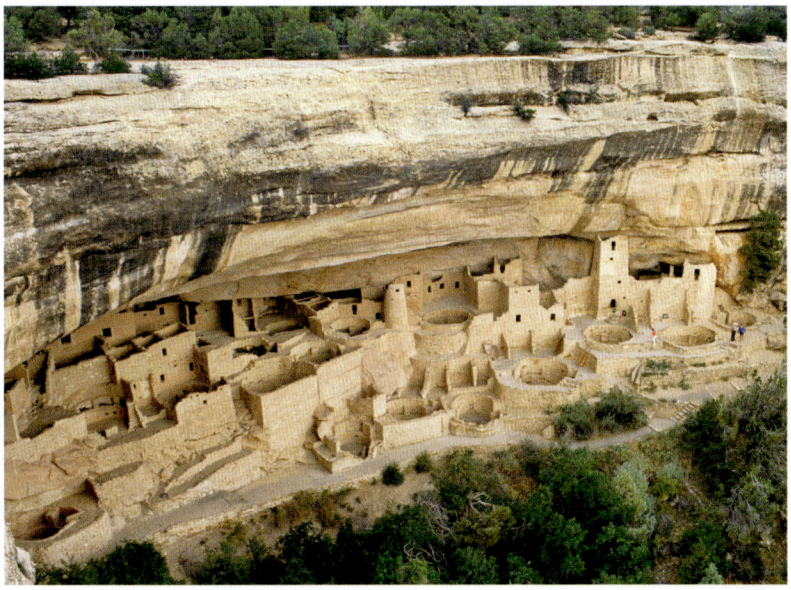

3.4.20 Cliff Palace, 1100–1300, Mesa Verde, Colorado

canyon floors of New Mexico, and move north to what is now southwestern Colorado. When they arrived at Mesa Verde they constructed communal dwellings of stone, timber, and adobe (sun-dried bricks made of clay and straw) in ridges high on cliff faces, often hundreds of feet above the canyon floor (**3.4.20**). These locations took advantage of the sun's orientation to heat the pueblo in the winter and shade it during the hot summer months. Exactly why or even how the cliff dwellings were constructed we do not know. Similarly, we do not know what happened to the Ancient Puebloans after the four-corners area (the place where today Utah, Colorado, New Mexico, and Arizona meet) was abandoned between about 1300 and 1540. Although modern descendants of the Ancient Puebloans—the Hopi, Zuni, Tewa, and Taos Indians—have many cultural and symbolic connections with their ancestors, even they do not know the full story.

Plains Indians

Pushed westward by European expansion, many Native Americans were forced into the Great Plains region. Groups belonging to the Sioux clan, such as the Lakota and Crow, became nomadic, living in portable homes called tipis (also spelled teepees), made of wooden poles covered with bark or deer and buffalo hides. The Mandan had been living on the Plains in what is now North and South Dakota for more than a thousand years. They had established permanent villages, but they used tipis when hunting or traveling. The painted buffalo hide in **3.4.21a** and **3.4.21b** shows a detailed, **naturalistic** representation of a battle in 1797 between the Mandan of North Dakota and the encroaching Sioux. Sixty-four combatants, twenty of them on horseback, are engaged in battle with spears, bows and arrows, tomahawks, and guns. This hide was meant to be draped over the shoulders of its wearer, likely someone who played a key role in the battle it depicted. Hides used for tipis

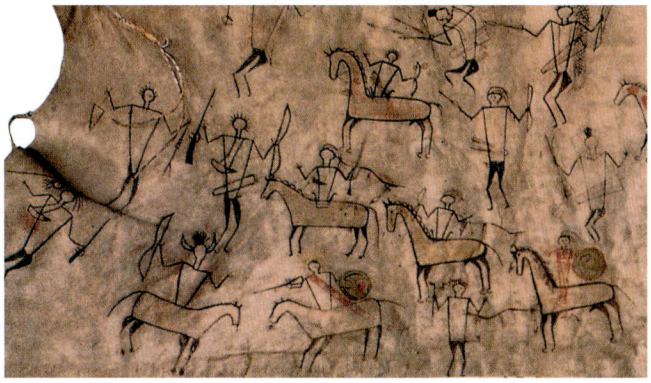

3.4.21a (above) Detail of robe with battle scene

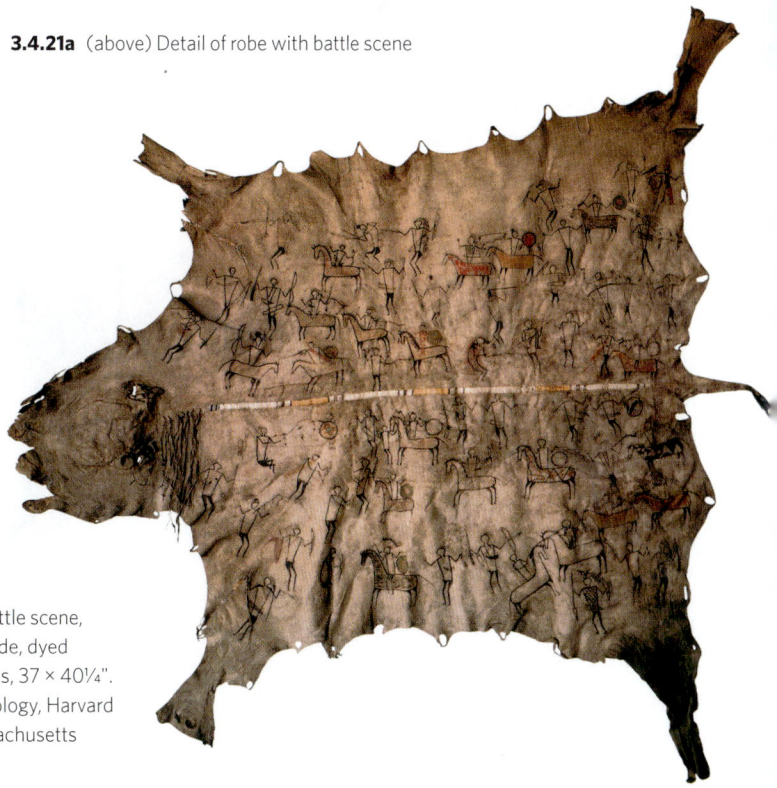

3.4.21b (right) Robe with battle scene, 1797–1800. Tanned buffalo hide, dyed porcupine quills, and pigments, 37 × 40¼". Peabody Museum of Archaeology, Harvard University, Cambridge, Massachusetts

Naturalistic: a very realistic or lifelike style of making images

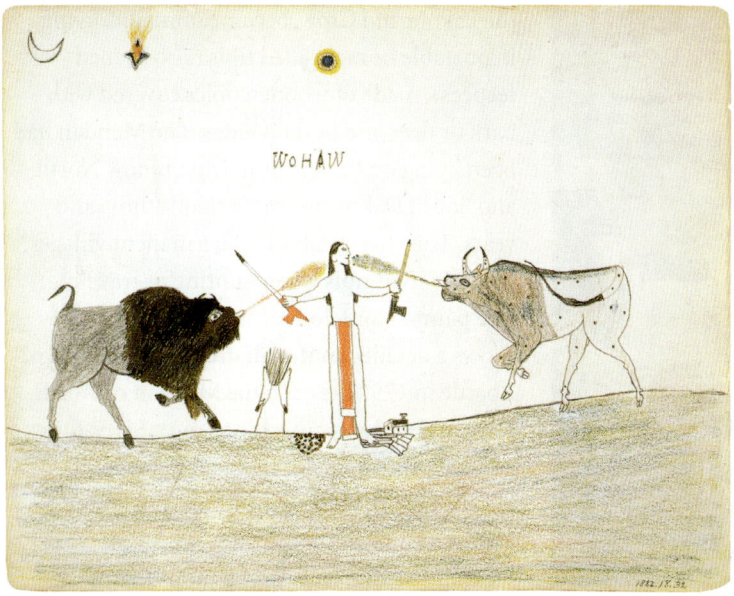

3.4.22 Wo-Haw, *Wo-Haw between Two Worlds*, 1877. Graphite and colored pencil on paper, 8½ × 11". Missouri Historical Society, St. Louis

and as garments were decorated with different **motifs**. This narrative scene would have served a commemorative purpose for the individual wearer, and as an aid to the oral storytelling tradition of the Mandan people.

While the Mandan robe tells us something of a battle between two native North American tribes, *Wo-Haw between Two Worlds* offers a window into the changing existence of one individual as a result of westward European expansion (**3.4.22**). It is a drawing from a sketchbook kept during the artist's imprisonment in Fort Marion, Florida, between 1875 and 1878. Wo-Haw was one of about seventy Kiowa, Cheyenne, and other Plains individuals arrested in Oklahoma for allegedly committing crimes against white settlers. Twenty-six of the men made art while they were in captivity. No traditional materials, such as the buffalo hide and mineral pigments used in the Mandan robe, were available, so they used the pencils and paper provided for them.

Wo-Haw's self-portrait shows him caught between the two worlds referenced in the drawing's title: that of his ancestry on his right side (our left) and the new presence of European settlers on his left. His Kiowa heritage is represented by a buffalo and a tipi underneath a crescent moon and a shooting star. The world of whites is represented by a domesticated bull, cultivated fields, and a European-style frame house. Wo-Haw holds peace pipes toward both the Native American and European worlds, expressing the hope that they can learn to live in peace (see Box: "We Are the Mirrors": Legislation and Activism to Protect Native Rights and Lands, p. 444.) .

Motif: a distinctive visual element, the recurrence of which is often characteristic of an artist's work

The Kwakiutl

The Kwakiutl, Native Americans in southern British Columbia, Canada, continue to practice ceremonies passed down through the generations. They are known for their masks, which they use ceremonially in different ways, depending on the time of year. The late nineteenth-century *Eagle Transformation Mask* (**3.4.23**) was probably used in a public summer performance for a male coming-of-age ceremony. The eagle was likely the spirit guardian revealed during a vision quest undertaken at the onset of puberty. As such, the *Eagle Transformation Mask* showed the deep, inner reality of the wearer, who used the strings to open and close the mask, giving the impression he was transforming into an animal. In flickering firelight the mask's movement created an impressive spectacle as its human aspects, such as the large nose, combined with animal features, in this case a curved beak. The dancer thus transformed himself from

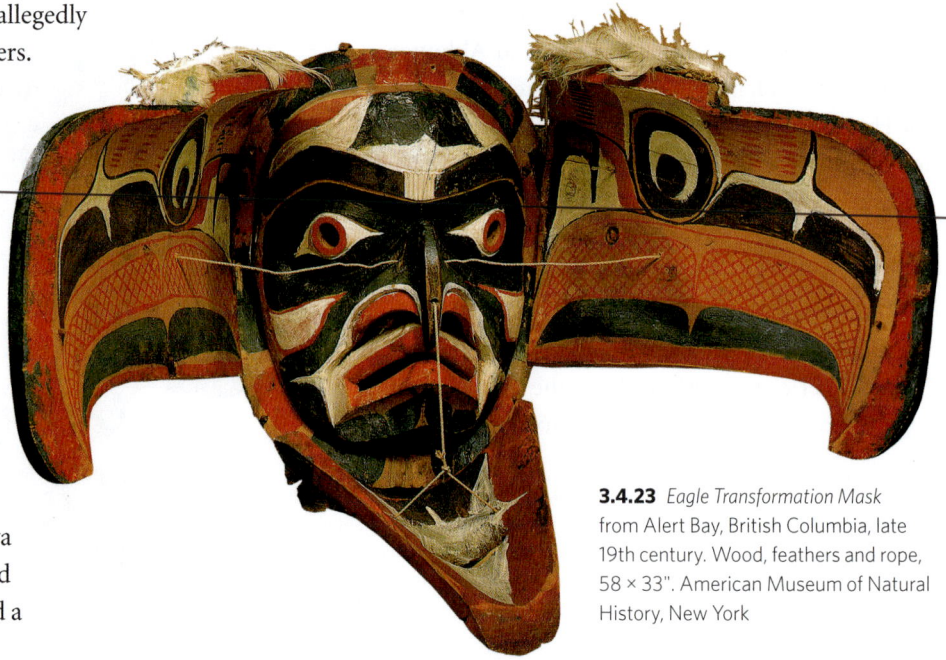

3.4.23 *Eagle Transformation Mask* from Alert Bay, British Columbia, late 19th century. Wood, feathers and rope, 58 × 33". American Museum of Natural History, New York

human to eagle and back again as he danced. This performance served a ritual function, highlighting the powerful nature of the eagle, and transferring that bravery and strength to the human wearer and his community. It also represented the ancestral connections between humans and eagles. The transformation that was enacted during the performance also symbolized the changes the wearer experienced during initiation.

The Great Basin and California Indians

Basket-making, a long-standing tradition for California Indians, served functional, symbolic, and metaphorical purposes for their communities. Although in the past several groups developed unique approaches in isolation, many of today's basket-weavers share their techniques with each other and work to revive the practices used by their ancestors. **Coiling** and **twining** are the two most common methods of construction.

Understanding a basket requires consideration of the materials, construction, form, design, and intended use. Baskets of different shapes were made to be balanced on the head, worn on the back, or carried to help transport items including water, food, supplies, and even babies. Other functions include storage, fishing, and cooking. Baskets woven to contain clothing and building materials provided protection, and some baskets have been used for ceremonial purposes. Native American weavers even made baskets, such as the one shown in **3.4.24**, that were watertight and could be filled with boiling water to cook acorn mush, a staple in the diet of California Indians for centuries.

The plants chosen for a basket's construction were often determined by what grew in the region, but also by the characteristics of the material that made it suitable for its purpose. For example, willow bark was commonly used for storage containers and for baskets for other uses in the home because it contains salicin, a natural insect repellent (which would help protect the contents from the ravages of mites and weevils) and an agent that would prevent the basket from catching fire if placed near a stove or other source of heat.

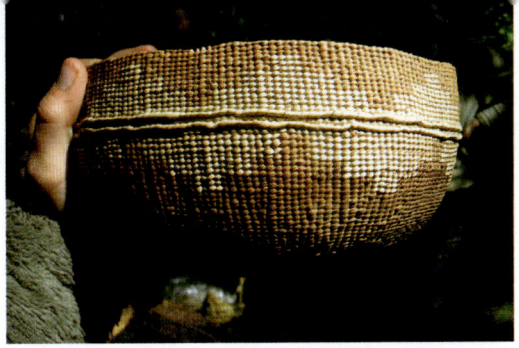

3.4.24 Julia Parker, basket for cooking acorns, c. 2011. Collection Julia Parker

The names of many weavers of the baskets in museum collections are unknown because little information was recorded when they were collected. Julia Parker (b. 1928), a Coast Miwok-Kashaya Pomo weaver, learned from talented elders, including her husband's Paiute grandmother Lucy Telles, how to make such baskets as the one in **3.4.24**. The collective nature of basket-making is reflected in Parker's practice, which she has taught to her family (her granddaughter Ursula Min-ne-ah Jones, great-granddaughter Naomi Kashaya Jones, and daughter Lucy Ann Parker are also basket-weavers, see **3.4.25**) and shared with the public as a cultural specialist at Yosemite Museum, giving basket demonstrations and workshops. Because it is so time-consuming, basket-making has become increasingly rare, though it is now highly valued for its intricacy, craft, and visual appeal.

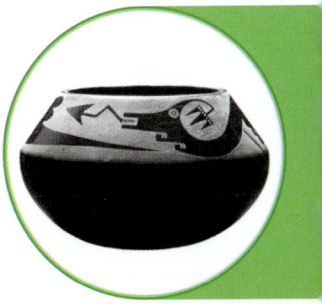

Similarly to Julia Parker, other Native American artists worked to revive traditional methods; for example, earlier in the twentieth century, Maria Martinez and her family made blackware pottery: see **2.6.8, p. 289**

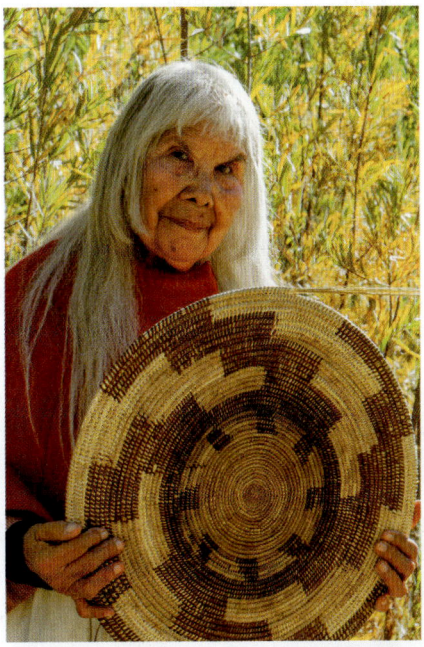

3.4.25 Julia Parker holding one of her baskets

Coiling: basket-weaving technique using a central foundation that is spiraled or coiled, and wrapped with another fiber that is stitched back into the previous row
Twining: basket-weaving technique consisting of twisting two strands of material around a foundation of parallel sticks

"We Are the Mirrors": Legislation and Activism to Protect Native Rights and Land

Repatriation: return of cultural artifacts, often sacred remains, to their country of origin

In North America, a federal law known as NAGPRA (Native American Graves Protection and Repatriation Act) was enacted on November 16, 1990 to legislate the **repatriation** of artifacts and sacred remains, such as those at Machu Picchu (see p. 432). According to the National Park Service, NAGPRA addresses "rights of lineal descendants, Indian tribes, and Native Hawaiian organizations to Native American cultural items, including human remains, funerary objects, sacred objects, and objects of cultural patrimony." Since the time of European contact in the Americas, issues of ownership have extended to include occupation, access, and treatment of the land itself.

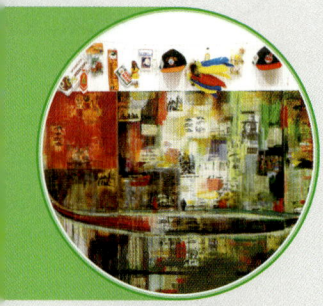

The artist Jaune Quick-to-See Smith also features the (mis)treatment and (mis)representation of Native Americans in her collages: see **1.9.14, p. 168**

In 2016 the construction of an oil pipeline under the Missouri River in North Dakota drew a great deal of media attention. The Standing Rock and Cheyenne River Sioux (and thousands of allied protesters) opposed the Dakota Access Pipeline (DAPL) that the developer, Energy Transfer Partners, was running through indigenous land, because of its potential to harm their access to clean water, necessary for life in both physical and spiritual ways. The situation came to a head on November 20 when police attacked unarmed protestors with rubber bullets, tear gas, and water canons in sub-freezing temperatures.

In response to the situation, artists made posters to raise awareness, sold artwork to donate to the Standing Rock cause, and made narrative videos telling the tale of a mythical beast (oil) devouring the natural world. One artist incited people to create "mirror shields" to be used on the frontlines of the protest (**3.4.26**). Born on the Standing Rock Reservation, the artist Cannupa Hanska Luger is of Mandan, Hidatsa, Arikara, Lakota, Austrian, and Norwegian descent. Luger was inspired by Ukranian activists to use mirrors as a way to draw the oppressors' attention to their own actions. Actual battle regalia using mirrors as spiritual (and physical) protection can be traced back to the Bronze Age and is found in antiquity all over the world, including in parts of Europe, Asia, and the Middle East. Using social media, Luger shared directions for making "Mirror Shields for Water Protectors" using inexpensive materials and asking contributors to mail them to the camps. In an interview in the *LA Times*, Luger explained that artists "live on the periphery. But we are the mirrors. We are the reflective points that break through a barrier." According to the artist's Facebook page, the mirror shields are meant to offer reflection. They are "designed to let them [the people reflected in the mirrors] know that we love them and they stand with water as well. The wall the mirror shields create is not a wall of division, but a wall of unity."

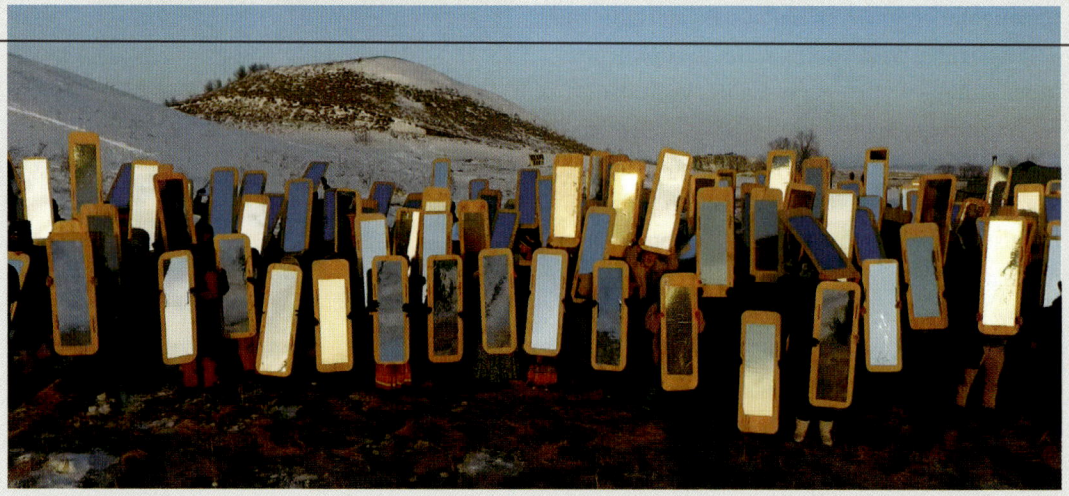

3.4.26 Cannupa Hanska Luger, The Mirror Shield Project, 2016. Oceti Sakowin Camp, Standing Rock, North Dakota

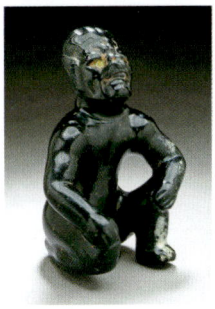

4.5.13 Transformation figurine, Olmec, c. 900–300 BCE, p. 624

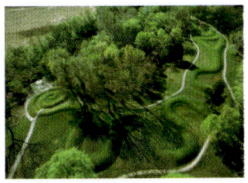

2.4.15 Great Serpent Mound, c. 800 BCE–100 CE, Ohio p. 252

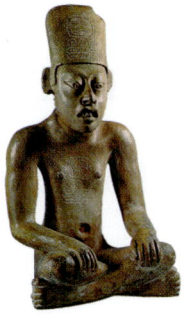

2.6.4 *Seated Figure*, Zapotec, Oaxaca, Mexico, 300 BCE–700 CE, p. 288

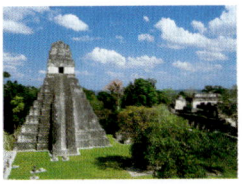

2.5.5 Maya Temple I, Tikal, Guatemala, c. 300–900 CE, p. 262

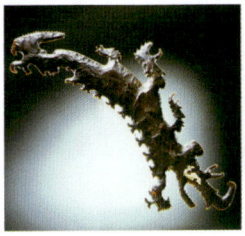

4.4.4 Maya flint depicting crocodile canoe, 600–900 CE, p. 605

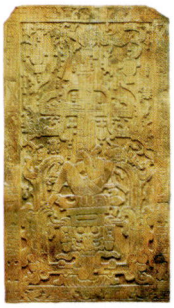

4.3.11 Maya sarcophagus lid, tomb of Lord Pacal, Mexico, c. 680, p. 599

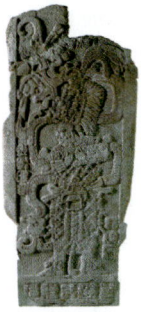

1.2.7 Maya stela with supernatural scene, Mexico or Guatemala, 761 CE, p. 65

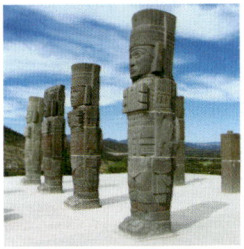

4.7.7 Tula warrior columns, Mexico, 900–1000 CE, p. 643

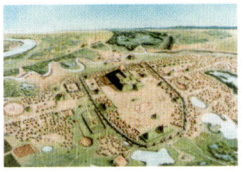

4.1.7 Monks Mound, Cahokia, Illinois, c. 1150, p. 569

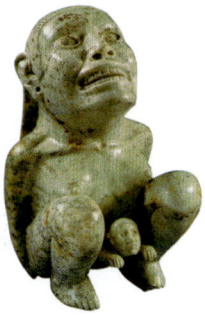

4.3.1 Tlazolteotl giving birth to the maize god, Aztec, c. 1500, p. 591

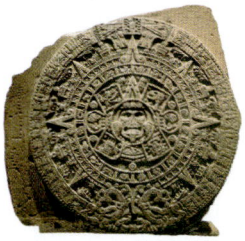

4.4.5 Aztec calendar stone, Mexico, 1502–1521, p. 606

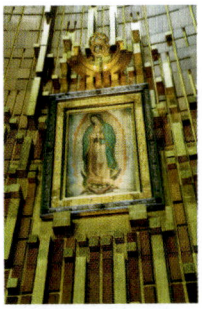

0.0.8 *The Virgin of Guadalupe*, Mexico City, 1531, p. 25

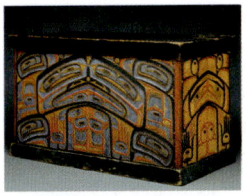

2.6.22 Captain Richard Carpenter, bent-corner chest, c. 1860, p. 298

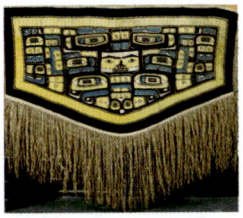

2.6.18 Tlingit Chilkat dancing blanket, 19th century, p. 296

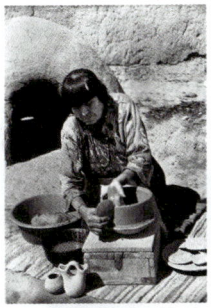

2.6.6 Maria Martinez at work, New Mexico, c. 1930–40, p. 289

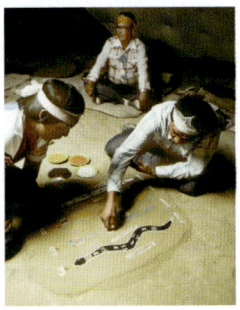

4.2.5 Navajo medicine man in healing ceremony, photo 20th century, p. 581

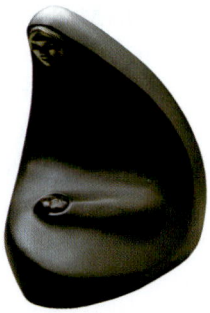

0.0.22 Allan Houser, *Reverie*, 1981, p. 37

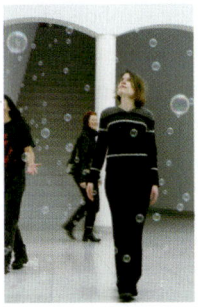

4.8.2 Theresa Margolles, *En el Aire (In the Air)*, 2003, p. 653

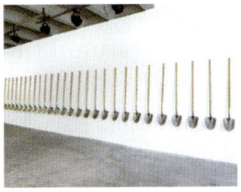

4.8.4 Pedro Reyes, *Palas por Pistolas (Guns for Shovels)*, 2007–present, p. 655

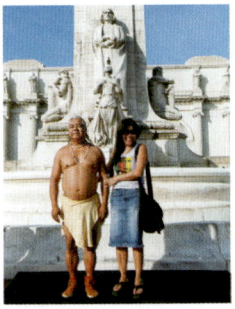

4.10.13 James Luna, *Take a Picture with a Real Indian*, 2010, p. 688

3.5 Art of Africa and the Pacific Islands

As diverse as they may at first seem, the artworks produced on the expansive continent of Africa and in the remote islands of the Pacific Ocean have some intriguing similarities. In both areas traditional art integrates and responds to the environment, incorporates important mythological beliefs, and follows conventional methods of construction and decoration. Perhaps the most striking similarity between art made in Africa and that of the Pacific Islands is the continuity of traditional techniques. Historically, artists have had to undergo apprenticeships lasting several years. In these cultures, learning traditional ways to make objects was more important than building an individual reputation. Although some past artists earned legendary status while alive, the names of most have been forgotten over time.

Both of these regions' artistic traditions have relied on such natural materials as wood, reeds, shells, and earth. For example, cowrie shells feature prominently in the *nkisi nkonde* (see p. 448) from the Democratic Republic of Congo and the decoration of the Abelam cult house in Papua New Guinea (see **3.5.18**, p. 458). In both parts of the world, the shells are symbols of fertility. Natural materials often have symbolic significance, but because they—wood in particular—are usually perishable, few examples of ancient artworks made from such substances remain.

As we find elsewhere in the world, traditional artists in Africa and the Pacific Islands have tended to serve as communicators for and within their communities. They record events and relate important cultural beliefs, such as rules for acceptable behavior, or fables that seek to explain the mysteries of the world. Communication beyond the human realm, enhanced by the ritualistic use of hallucinogens that induce shamanic trances, reflects belief in supernatural powers that infuse the natural world. In both areas, ritual, archetypes, and the collective unconscious are integral to the creation of art. Special objects studied in this chapter were produced for ceremonies to celebrate birth, to mark a child's passage into adulthood, and to remember those who have died.

All around the world contemporary art tends to focus on both personal and communal expression, but artists from Africa and the Pacific Islands often incorporate references to their culture's mythology, religion, and history, along with industrial materials, found objects, and references to popular culture. Many scholars consider that the study of African art extends into the African Diaspora (the regions—including the Americas, the Caribbean, Asia, and Europe—impacted by the mass dispersal of Africans by the slave trade or by choice). During the **Modernist** period (*c.* 1860–1970) art from Africa and the Pacific Islands, as well as the Americas, served as an inspiration for European abstraction. Today, individual African and Pacific Island artists do not exclusively focus on their own communities but, instead, actively participate in the global art world.

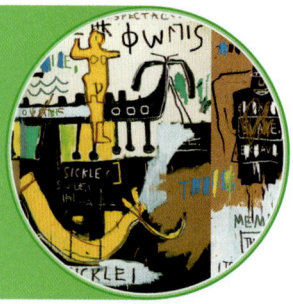

Jean-Michel Basquiat made Africa and the African Diaspora the subject of his painting *The Nile*, also known as *The History of Black People* or *The Grand Spectacle*: see **3.10.14, p. 555**

Modernism, Modernist: a radically new twentieth-century art and architectural movement that embraced modern industrial materials and a machine aesthetic

Art of Africa

Modern Africa includes 54 different countries, more than 1.2 billion inhabitants, and at least 1,500 different languages. Archaeological evidence from about 200,000 years ago suggests that the first modern humans lived on the African continent, before moving to other parts of the world. As regards more recent records of human activity, oral history has been more important for African communities than written documentation; records of specific events do not exist in many areas, especially south of the Sahara. Art has therefore been a particularly important form of communication and cultural expression. Amongst the earliest examples of African art are portable objects, such as beads made from shells that date back 75,000 years ago. Wooden sculpture and architecture also have long traditions, although ancient examples have largely perished.

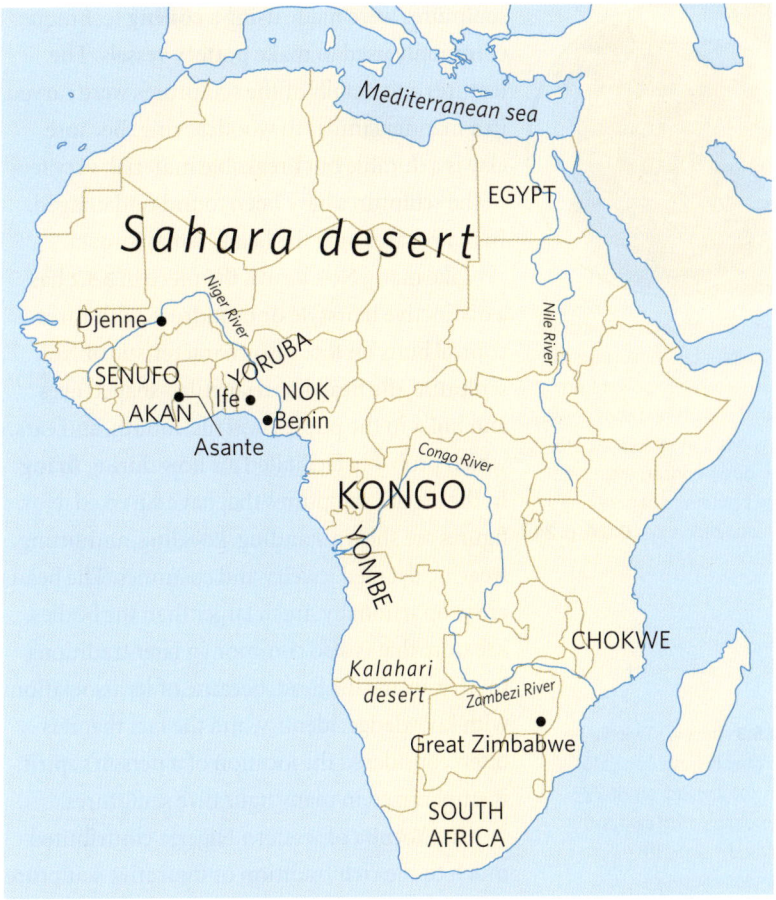

3.5.1 Map of Africa

Portraits and Power Figures

For thousands of years, people have used art to tell stories about and create images of their daily lives. African rulers, like elites everywhere, have used art to assert and reinforce their power, and some of the art they have commissioned has also emphasized their connection with the supernatural realm, thereby encouraging a sense that gods or ancestor spirits have bestowed upon them the authority to rule. It is also believed that artworks can act as conduits to the spirit world, and permit supernatural forces entry into the human world, to bestow good or ill fortune.

The objects themselves are invested with power, and a certain amount of power is also associated with the owner. Often objects or artworks communicate the rules and customs that members of society are expected to follow. These objects can be symbolic, related to a particular position or role; or they can tell a tale, illustrating a proverb or a story with a specific message.

Although we do not know the exact meanings and uses of some of the oldest known **figurative** sculptures in Africa, they have a strong physical presence. The Nok of Nigeria made hollow, lifesize **terra-cotta** figures (see **3.5.2**). These

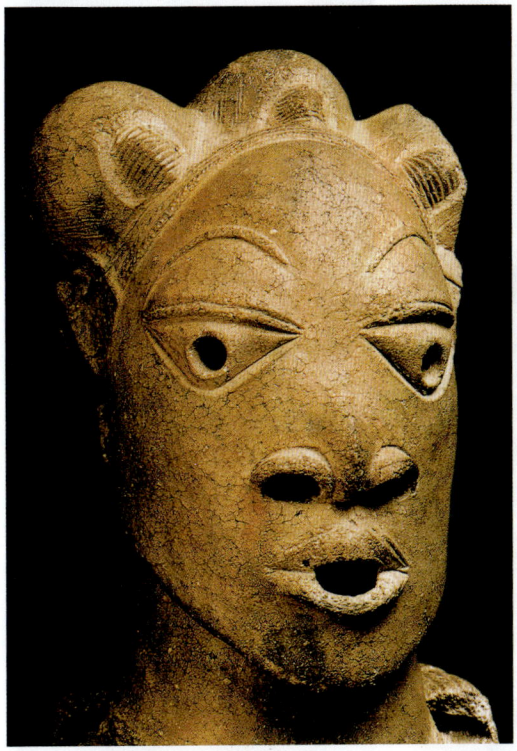

3.5.2 Head from Rafin Kura, c. 500 BCE–200 CE. Terra-cotta, height 14¼". National Museum, Lagos, Nigeria

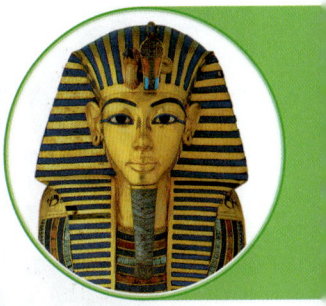

King Tutankhamun ruled Egypt from 1333 to 1323 BCE. Egypt is located on the African continent, but its proximity to the Middle East and Mediterranean Sea also gave it a position of unique influence on Western and European art: see **3.1.19, p. 378**

Figurative: art that portrays items perceived in the visible world, especially human or animal forms

Terra-cotta: iron-rich clay, fired at a low temperature, which is traditionally brownish-orange in color

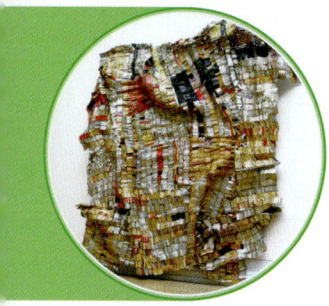

The contemporary Ghanaian sculptor El Anatsui invests his work with power from found objects and commercial goods that reference both modern consumerism and the economics of bartering in colonial Africa: see **0.0.6, p. 24**

sculptures were made using a **coiling** technique commonly used to make pottery vessels. The features and details of the sculptures were carved in a manner similar to woodcarving. Because clay is a durable but breakable material, very few of the sculptures have been found undamaged. In many cases only the heads remain intact.

Like many Nok heads, the piece in **3.5.2** has a distinctive hairstyle or headdress, with three conical buns on top. Also characteristic of Nok sculpture, the head has triangular-shaped eyes and holes in the pupils, nostrils, mouth, and ears, which probably facilitated air flow during **firing**. In the lifesize sculptures that have survived, Nok figures are shown standing, kneeling, and sitting, wearing detailed jewelry and costumes. The heads are proportionally much larger than the bodies, a feature that is also common in later traditions in African art: the head, because of its association with knowledge, identity, and the fact that it is often considered the location of a person's spirit, is emphasized in many figurative sculptures.

The Yoruba of western Nigeria contributed much to the rich tradition of figurative sculpture in Africa. Sculptors working in the Yoruba city of Ile-Ife produced impressive terra-cotta and metal sculpture; and the twin figure in **3.5.3** displays Yoruba skill at woodcarving. Its features, characteristic of the regional style, include small size, large eyes, and elongated breasts. Such figures, known as *ere ibeji*, were sometimes carved when a twin died at birth or in infancy, in order to harness the life force of the deceased and bring prosperity to their families. This twin figure shows how Yoruba hand-made objects are invested with spiritual powers of their own.

Also known for a strong sculptural tradition, the Yombe use power figures as reminders of social obligations and enforcers of proper behavior. Objects called minkisi (the singular *nkisi* means "sacred medicine") could take the form of shells, bags, pots, or wooden statues. Substances, or actual medicines, might be placed inside the minkisi to give them certain properties. In carved figures, these medicines were placed in the head or stomach area. A particular type of nkisi, called a ***nkisi nkondi,*** is a standing figure with its feet spread apart in a poweful, assertive pose (**3.5.4**). Nkondi means "hunter," as in, to hunt down and call to account those who have done wrong in society. White kaolin clay, shells, and other reflective objects on such figures as this symbolized contact with the supernatural. Ritual specialists, with the power to release the spiritual presence of the object, activated all minkisi.

Each figure served a specific function, but generally a nkisi nkondi was responsible for making sure that oaths sworn in its presence were honored. Each time the figure was needed, the ritual specialists would drive nails, blades, and other metal objects into its wooden surface to make it "angry" and "rouse it into action." As a mediator between the ancestral spirit world and the living world of human beings, the nkisi nkondi was able to bring protection and healing to the community. The nkisi nkondi shown here has been activated many times by iron blades that have been thrust into it. The giant cowrie

3.5.3 (below) Twin figure, probably from Ado Odo in Yorubaland, pre-1877 (probably 19th century). Wood, height 10". Linden Museum, Stuttgart, Germany

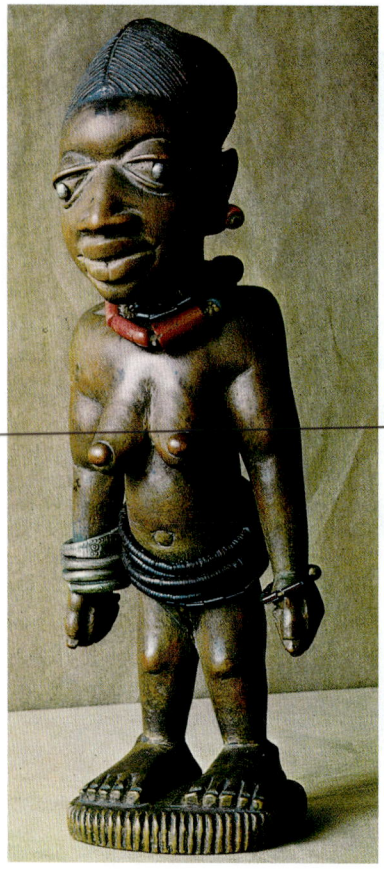

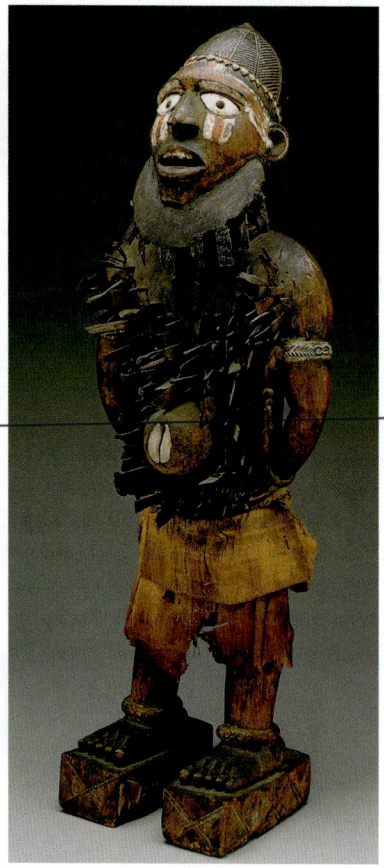

3.5.4 (left) Standing power figure (*nkisi nkondi*), late 19th century. Wood, iron, raffia, ceramic, kaolin pigment, red camwood powder (tukula), resin, dirt, leaves, animal skin, and cowrie shell, 43¾ × 15½ × 11". Dallas Museum of Art, Texas

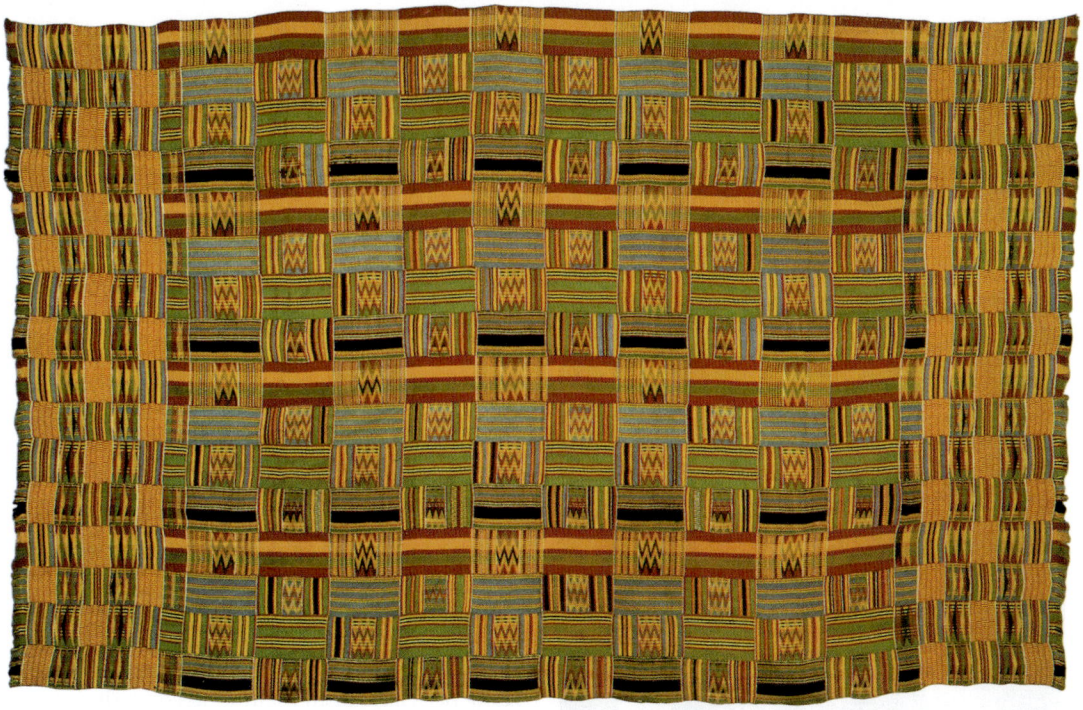

3.5.5 Textile wrapper (*kente*), 20th century. Silk, length 6'10 ½". National Museum of African Art, Smithsonian Institution, Washington, D.C.

Coiling: the use of long coils of clay—rather than a wheel—to build the walls of a pottery vessel
Firing: heating ceramic, glass, or enamel objects in a kiln, to harden them, fuse the components, or fuse a glaze to the surface
Nkisi nkondi (plural ***minkisi minkondi***)**:** combines the words for "sacred medicine" and "to hunt"; figurative sculpture(s) used in rituals by the Yombe of Nigeria
Abstract: an artwork the form of which is simplified, distorted, or exaggerated in appearance. It may represent a recognizable form that has been slightly altered, or it may be a completely non-representational depiction
Representational: art that depicts figures and objects so that we recognize what is represented
***Kente* cloth:** well-known African textile made of silk and cotton fabric and consisting of interwoven strips of cloth; native to the Akan group in Ghana
Geometric: predictable and mathematical

shell on its abdomen is a symbol of fertility and wealth for the Yombe people as well as other cultures; such shells are also widely used as currency. This nkisi nkondi has wide, staring eyes and an imposing stance to help ensure that no other forces will interfere with the fulfillment of its ritual function.

Personal Stories and Symbolism

Because many kinds of information have traditionally been communicated visually rather than verbally in Africa, objects are often made with a specific purpose or even a specific person in mind. Artworks that contain **abstract** designs and patterns can convey information that is just as important, recognizable, and specific as **representational** images. They can also communicate a great deal about the maker or the user of an object. The symbols that decorate utilitarian objects, from clothing and pipes to bowls and chairs, and the care that went into making them, give them significance.

The colors, materials, and designs of textiles can indicate a person's age, station in life, and cultural connections. In the West African kingdom of Asante in Ghana, woven fabrics called ***kente*** were traditionally worn only by royalty and state officials: they were too expensive for ordinary people to afford the cloth. More recently, kente have become accessible to the general public, though they are typically reserved for special and ceremonial occasions.

Making kente requires a loom that allows the weaver to integrate vertical and horizontal designs in a strip ranging from 2 in. to 4 in. wide. The strips are sewn together to make a complete cloth of **geometric** shapes and bright colors. Women wear the cloth in two parts, as a floor-length skirt and a shawl over the shoulder, while men drape it around themselves like a toga. The kente in **3.5.5** contains yellow, representing things that are holy and precious; gold, a symbol of royalty, wealth, and spiritual purity; green, for growth and good health; and red, for strong political and spiritual feelings.

Another highly recognizable and influential African art form, masks appear widely in ceremonies. Similarly to kente cloth, masks emphasize geometric shapes, though, unlike kente, they also reference human features. In museums, masks are often presented as lifeless objects on display, isolated from the vibrant sights, sounds, smells, and movements of the masquerade. For African groups, though, the mask is most meaningful when being worn in

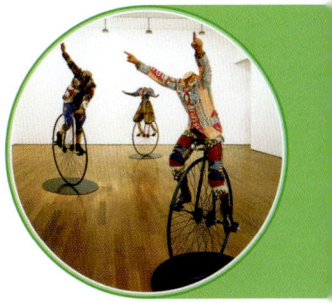

Distinctive fabrics associated with Africa also feature prominently in contemporary British-Nigerian artist Yinka Shonibare's sculptural installations: see **2.10.10, p. 358**

Minaret: a tall slender tower, particularly on a mosque, from which the faithful are called to prayer

live performance. In fact, sometimes masks are created for a particular event and discarded afterward because they are no longer "alive."

The Dogon of Mali in West Africa traditionally used the Kanaga mask in ceremonies designed to assist the deceased in their journey into the spiritual realm (**3.5.6a** and **3.5.6b**).

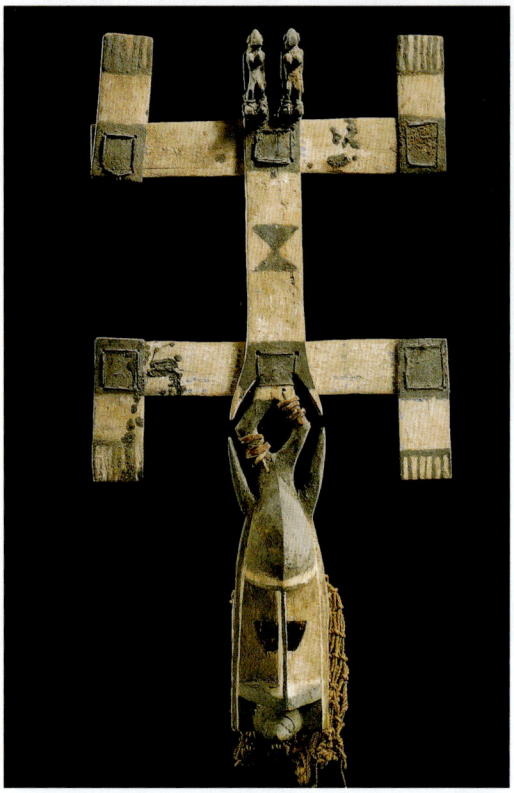

3.5.6a (right) Kanaga mask from Mali, Dogon culture, early 20th century. Polychrome wood, leather cords, and hide, height 45¼". Musée Barbier-Mueller, Geneva, Switzerland

According to one interpretation, the two cross bars on the mask represent the lower earthly realm and the upper cosmic realm of the sky. In performance, dancers swoop down and touch the mask to the ground; loud noises, like the crack of gunfire, scare away any souls that might be lingering in the village. Today such funeral rituals, called *dama*, continue to be performed, though rarely, and still include masks.

African Architecture

The early history of architecture in Africa is difficult to track because so many buildings were made of perishable materials, such as mud-brick and wood. Some ceremonial structures, places of worship, and royal residences have been maintained over time, but others have fallen into ruin, creating a mysterious sense of the past. Contemporary architects in Africa combine traditional approaches and non-local/Western solutions to create innovative, customized buildings. Whether they are designing rural schools, open-access train stations, luxury homes, or high-profile business or government headquarters, sustainability is a key concern in postcolonial Africa as populations grow rapidly.

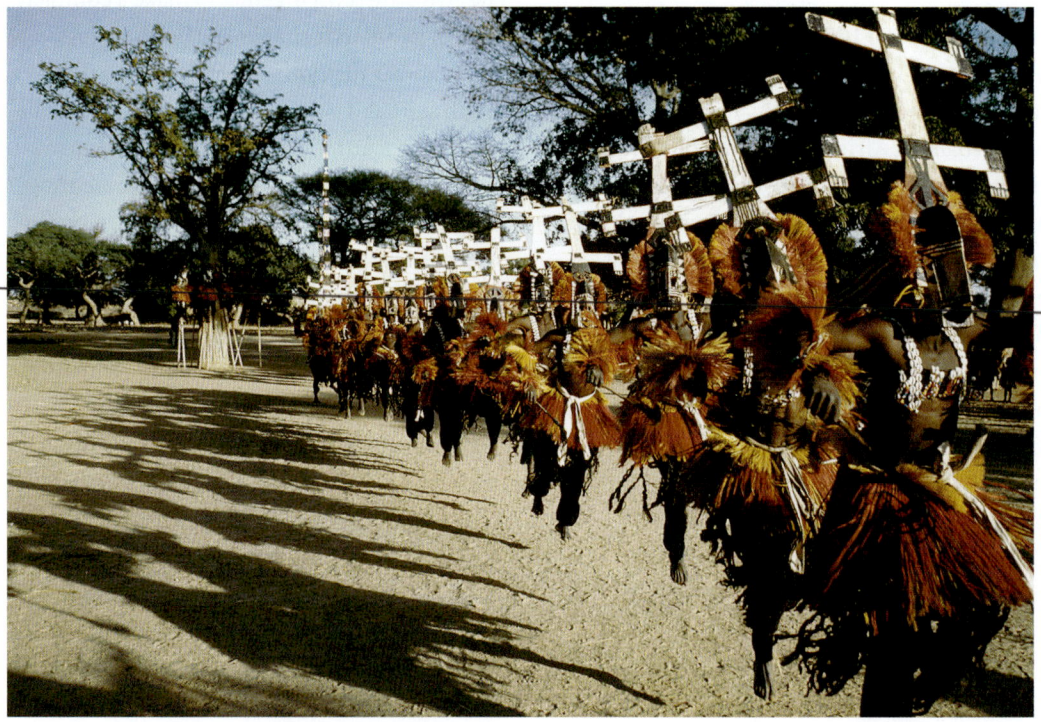

3.5.6b (right) Dogon Kanaga mask ceremony, Bandiagara, Mali, West Africa

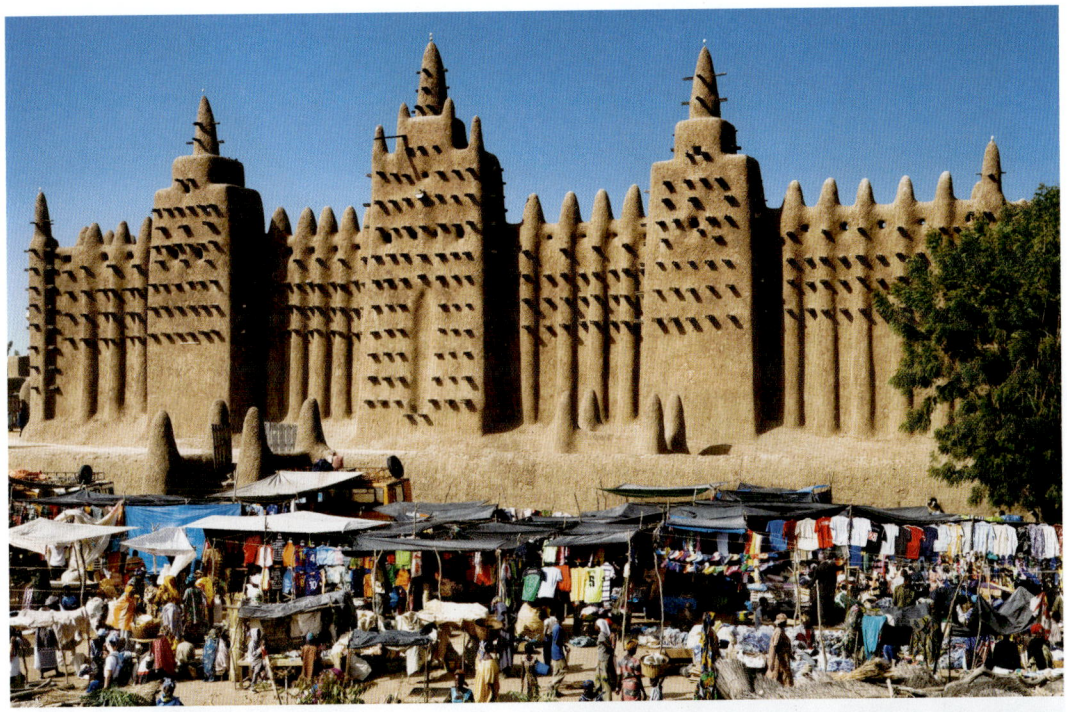

3.5.7 Monday market, Great Mosque, Djenné, Mali, Africa

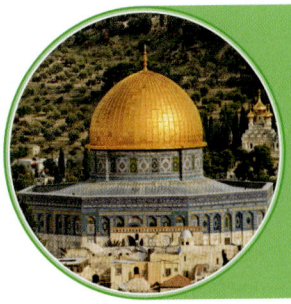

For further discussion of the form and context of mosques as religious architecture, see **3.2.16, p. 401**

The town of Djenné in Mali has long been a trade center and site of Islamic learning and pilgrimage. The town's Great Mosque (**3.5.7**) is located next to Djenné's bustling marketplace. An earlier building on this site was a mosque adapted from the palace of King Koi Konboro when he converted to Islam in 1240. Several centuries later, in 1834, Sheikh Amadou Labbo ordered that the mosque be demolished. He considered the original too lavish, and built a more modest one on the site. The current building, more in keeping with the thirteenth-century version, was finished around 1907 while Mali was under French occupation. It is considered the largest mud-brick structure in the world.

The Great Mosque combines characteristics of Islamic mosques with West African architectural practices. Three **minarets**, or towers, are used to call the faithful to prayer. Spiral staircases inside lead to the roofs, which feature cone-shaped spires topped by ostrich eggs. These ostrich eggs are important symbols of fertility and purity for the people of Djenné.

The clay-mud and palm-wood exterior of the building is similar to the houses of Mali. Numerous wooden beams line the mosque's surface and interior (**3.5.8**), not only to give it a distinctive look, but also to serve functional

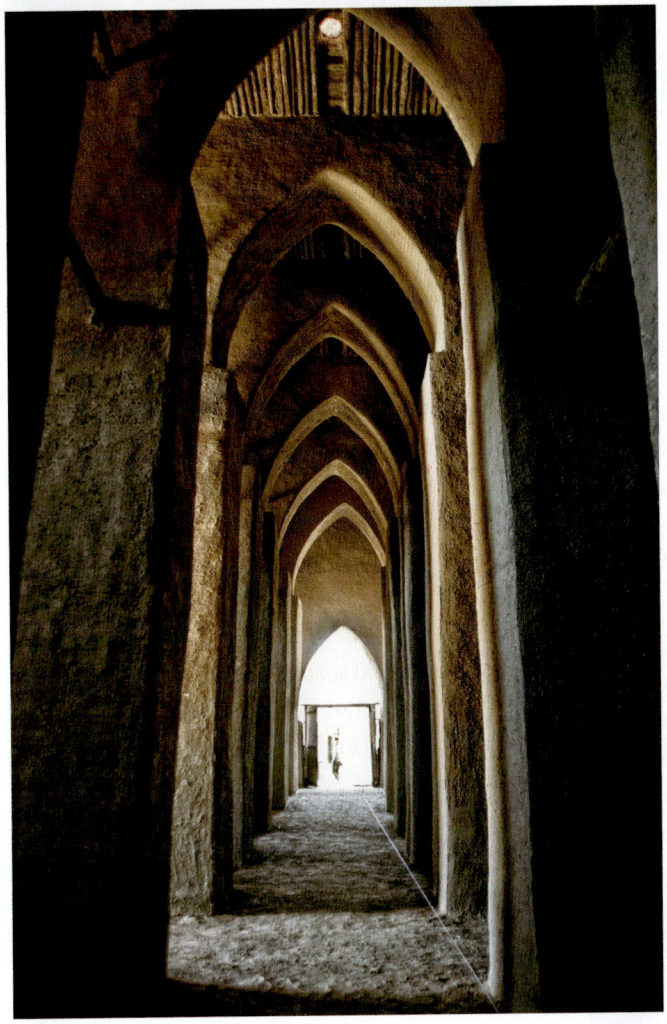

3.5.8 Interior, Monday market, Great Mosque, Djenné, Mali, 1907 (on this site since 1240)

Monolith: a monument or sculpture made from a single piece of stone

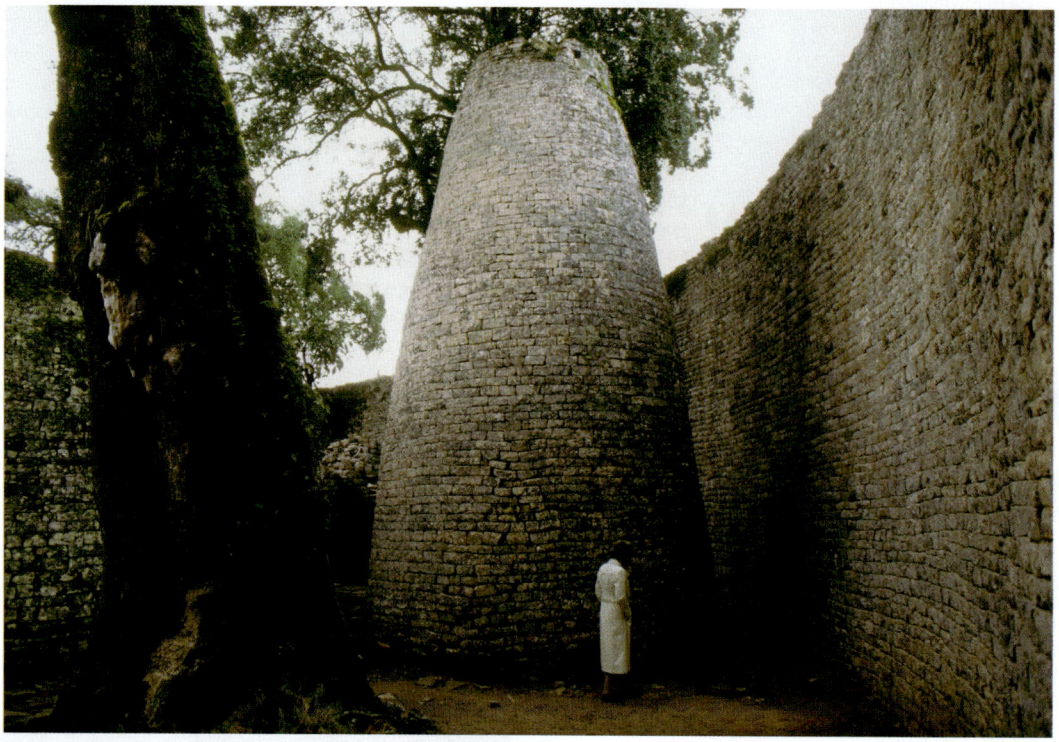

3.5.9 (right) Conical Tower, *c.* 1350–1450, Great Zimbabwe, Zimbabwe

3.5.10 (below) Bird on top of stone monolith, 15th century. Soapstone, height 14½" (bird image). Great Zimbabwe Site Museum, Zimbabwe

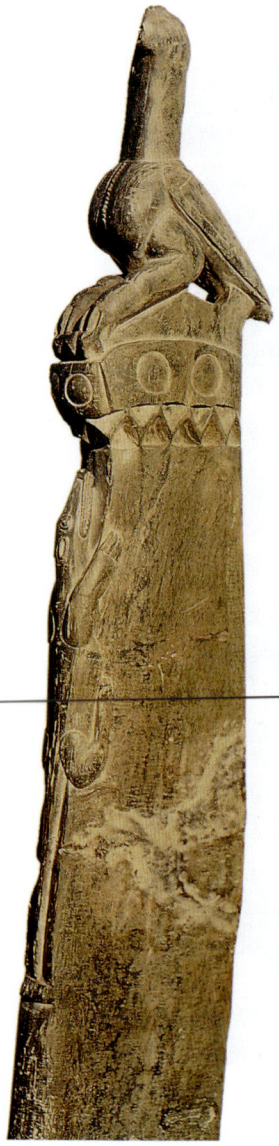

purposes. Some beams structurally support the ceiling, but most are used to access the walls for annual maintenance. The area's hot climate has also affected the building's design, with roof ventilation to cool the building, and mud-brick walls to regulate the temperature. The walls' thickness ranges from 16 to 24 in.; they are thickest where they are tallest. They absorb heat to keep the interior cool during the day, and release it at night to keep it warm.

Amongst the largest and most impressive examples of ancient architecture south of the Sahara Desert are the massive stone walls of Great Zimbabwe, built and expanded from the thirteenth to the fifteenth century in southern Africa (**3.5.9**). The remnants of altars, stone **monoliths**, and soapstone sculptures found at Great Zimbabwe suggest that it served as both a political and religious center for the Shona state. Indeed, the name of the site comes from the Shona phrase for "houses of stone" or "royal court," and we know that it included three main areas: the seat of the king's rule, a royal residence, and a residential area for at least 10,000 goldsmiths, potters, weavers, blacksmiths, and masons. During its prime, from about 1350 to 1450, Great Zimbabwe also functioned as an important cattle farm and international trade center. By the end of the fifteenth century, when centers of trade moved to the north, the site had been abandoned.

Many of the original mud-and-thatch buildings and platforms have long since disintegrated, but the sturdily built stone walls remain. Made from slab-like granite quarried from the nearby hills and stacked without mortar, the stability of the walls is increased by their design; they slope slightly inward at the top. The Conical Tower is an imposing structure, 18 ft. in diameter and 30 ft. tall, it rises above the high wall of the Great Enclosure and is completely solid. Its purpose remains a mystery. Like the walls, the Conical Tower likely served as a symbolic display of authority, a way to distinguish the areas used by royalty from the rest of the village.

Eight carved pieces of soapstone, each about 16 in. tall, were found integrated into buildings on top of columns at Great Zimbabwe. The image of the creature in **3.5.10** combines the features of a human-like bird and crocodile (the crocodile's eyes and zigzag mouth are visible just below the bird's leg and tail feathers). The bird's beak has been replaced with human lips, and its claws look more like feet, suggesting that these figures have supernatural significance. In

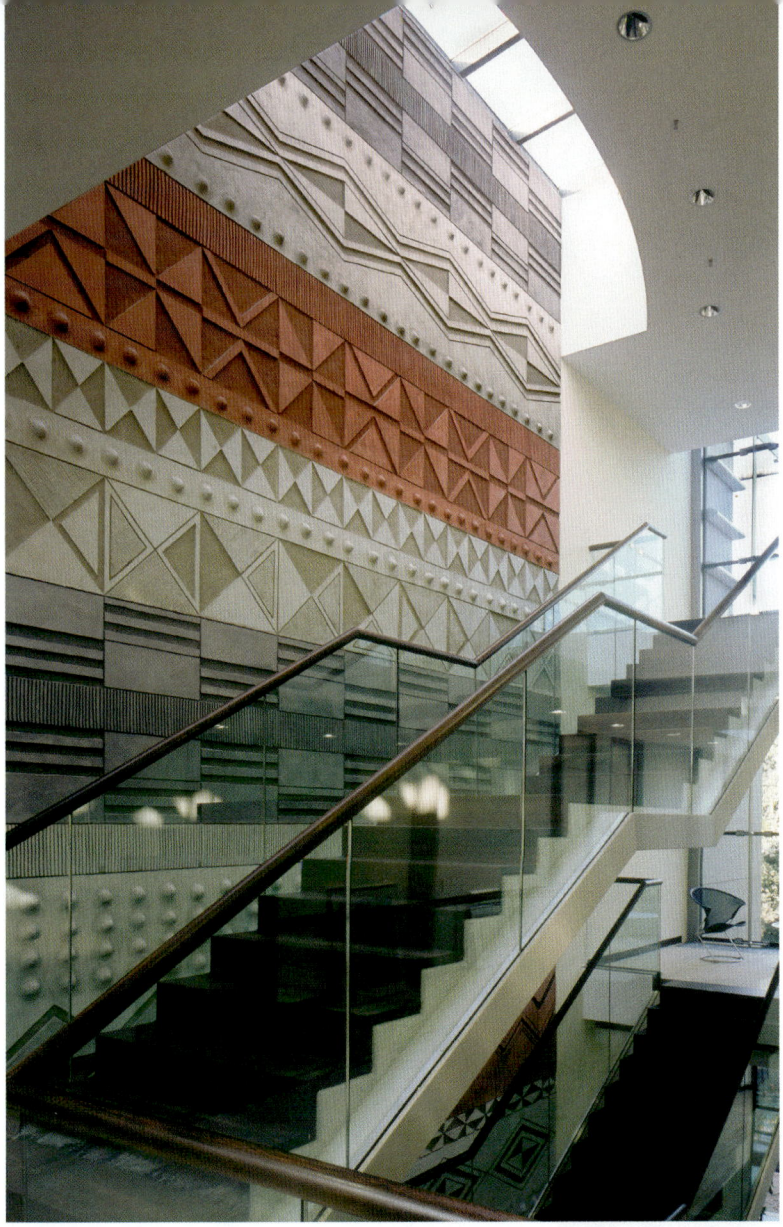

3.5.11 Mphethi Morojele (MMA Architects), South African Embassy, Berlin, Germany, 2003

fact, the Shona believe that royal ancestral spirits visit the living world through birds, especially eagles. Birds are considered messengers from the spirits because they traverse freely between the realms of the sky and the Earth. These sculptures reflect some of the core beliefs in many African cultures: the symbolic use of emblems of royal authority, reminders of familial relationships, and expectations of spiritual reward in the afterlife.

Many contemporary African architects combine features of the past and the present in their designs. In the plan for the South African Embassy in Berlin, Mphethi Morojele (b. Maseru, Lesotho) included a central courtyard as a reference to South African *kraal* (or corral) spaces, like the 820 ft. one seen in the Great Enclosure, Great Zimbabwe complex. The kraal, a roughly circular area within an African village or settlement, was used to hold cattle or other livestock. Within the embassy's largely glass and European Modernist-styled building, traditional African design features include the geometric wall decoration made of red ocher and white chalk (seen in **3.5.11**), fittings, artwork, and furniture.

South Africans lived under apartheid, a political system of racial segregation and discrimination, from 1948 to 1991. When Morojele founded MMA Architects in 1995 he was one of the first black men in the country to own an architectural practice. Focused on building a post-apartheid architectural language, Morojele says he is inspired by the "syncretic" (a word typically used in religious contexts; the blending of ideas from two or more cultures or belief systems) nature of African design and its ability to absorb many influences, yet remain "of Africa, her people, her landscapes."

Medium (plural **media**): the material on or from which an artist chooses to make a work of art, for example canvas and oil paint, marble, engraving, video, or architecture

Art of the Pacific Islands

The geographic area of the Pacific Islands includes Polynesia, Melanesia, Micronesia, and Australia. The islands are separated by enormous expanses of ocean, but since ancient times the people living there have been connected by shared beliefs, languages, and similarities in their cultures, which strongly value customary ways of life and behavior, such as farming, ancestor worship, and the preservation of social and artistic traditions. *Mana*, or pervasive magical power and associated prestige, has been a strong influence in Polynesian, Melanesian, and Maori belief.

The art of the Pacific Islands includes such portable objects as jewelry, furniture, and weapons; body ornamentation; wooden sculpture; paintings on rock; monumental sculptures; masks; and ceremonial architecture. The works often combine practical usefulness with sacred significance, thus linking the everyday world and living people with their ancestors and gods. Contemporary artists work in all types of artistic **media**—from traditional

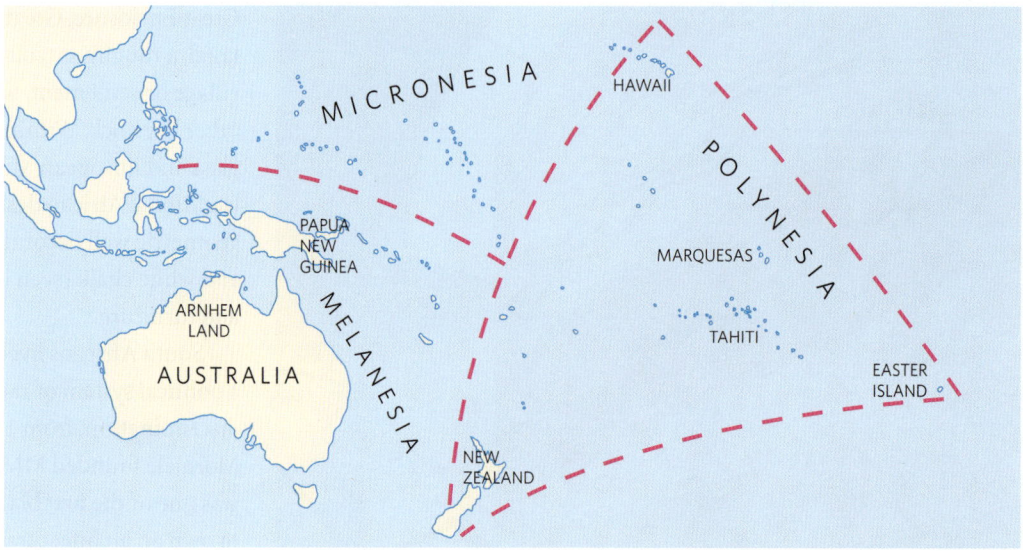

3.5.12 Map of the Pacific Islands

Tattoos: designs marked on the body by injecting dye under the skin

to technological—see for example the Aboriginal artworks described by Paul Tacon in Perspectives on Art: Australian Rock Art, opposite.

New Zealand

The Maori of New Zealand have one of the most elaborate traditions of tattooing in the world. Their words for it are *ta moko*. **Tattoos** (or moko) are made by injecting a pigment or dye under the skin so that a permanent mark is left on the body. It is not known when the first tattoos were made. The earliest known preserved tattooed bodies date back to *c.* 3300 BCE and feature abstract tattoos composed of designs with dots and line patterns; Maori designs are part of this tradition (**3.5.13**).

The designs mark specific events in the wearer's life, such as reaching puberty, becoming a warrior, making a kill, getting married, having a child, and so on. Tattoos covering the entire face and body were originally worn by chiefs and their families, indicating lineage and social status. The patterns may seem to be the same at first: however, upon closer inspection, no two designs are exactly alike. In fact, elaborate facial designs were so distinctive and specific to an individual that at times they were used as a form of legal signature.

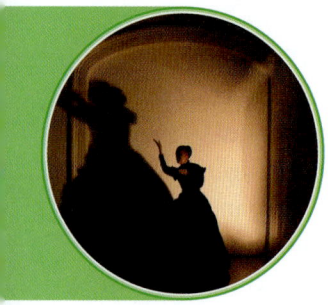

The contemporary New Zealand artist Yuki Kihara examines the challenges to Samoan cultural identity as a result of colonialism, natural disasters, and stereotypes by performing the traditional narrative dance form *taualuga*: see **2.10.12, p. 259**

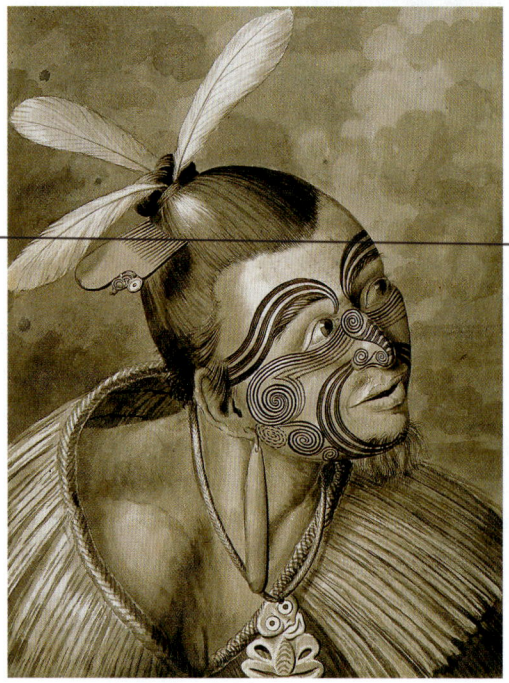

3.5.13 Sydney Parkinson, Drawing of traditional Maori tattoo, from *A Journal of a Voyage to the South Seas* (1784), plate 16

Hawaii

The first inhabitants of Hawaii (*c.* 600 CE) were Polynesians from the Marquesas Islands, more than 2,000 miles away. Five hundred years later, Tahitian settlers introduced a strict social hierarchy based on a system of *kapu* (or taboo) and a new host of gods and demigods. King Kamehameha unified the islands' warring factions during the eighteenth century. In modern times Hawaii became the fiftieth state of the United States in 1959, though it has also kept cultural connections with its Polynesian and Tahitian roots.

The ceremonial and warfare attire for Hawaiian nobility included thickly woven cloaks called *ahu'ula*, made of feathers

Perspectives on Art: Paul Tacon
Australian Rock Art

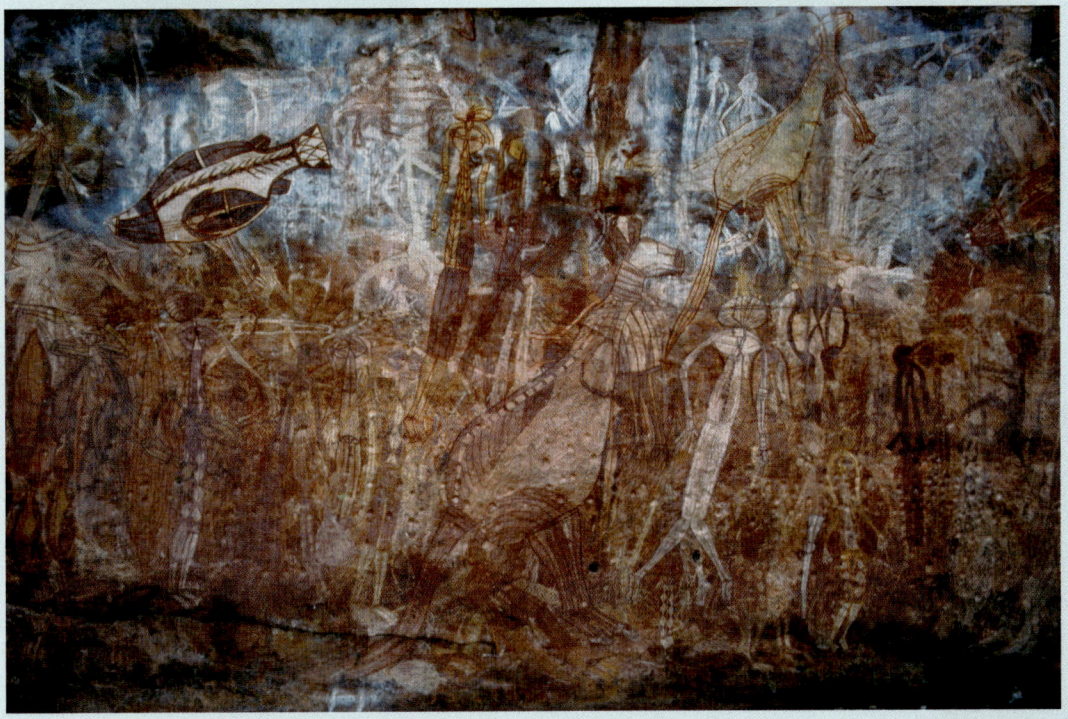

3.5.14 X-ray kangaroo rock painting, *c.* 1900. Ocher and kaolin paint, height 6'9½". Kakadu National Park, Northern Territory, Australia

Paul Tacon is an Australian anthropologist and archaeologist who specializes in the art of the Aboriginal people of Australia. Here he describes how Aboriginal rock paintings thousands of years old served communal purposes. He also connects them to the practice of contemporary Aboriginal artists.

Rock art subject matter in Australia is often derived from the life experience of the Aboriginal people and from nature, but it also has much mythological content. In many cases it is intimately linked to oral history and storytelling, singing, and performance. Hunting kangaroos would have been a familiar activity, but the slender figure, a "Mimi," is one of the spirits who taught humans to hunt and paint during one of the early eras of the "Dreaming," or the creation period. Paintings of this type from Arnhem Land in Australia's north are less than 4,000 years old. They often show figures with aspects of internal or "X-ray" detail, such as an indication of the spine and some internal organs, in addition to the exterior **contour** lines. Although these paintings could be used to teach young people about hunting and food-sharing practices, it seems most paintings were not used as a magical aid to hunting. Rather, both X-ray and solid infill animals were more often painted after they were caught and as part of storytelling.

Aboriginal Australian designs are tremendously variable across the country and over time. Some form of art has been practiced for at least 40,000 years, although most surviving prehistoric art is less than 15,000 years old. It is estimated there are far more than 100,000 surviving rock art sites—places with paintings, drawings, stencils, carvings, and figures made out of beeswax; these artworks have been made on the walls and ceilings of rock shelters, in caves, on boulders, and on rock platforms. Today, Aboriginal artists paint on such surfaces as sheets of bark, paper, canvas, bodies, houses, and cars. They use cameras, make films, and produce multimedia and computer-manipulated works. A concern for the land, people, and other creatures has always been important for all Aboriginal groups.

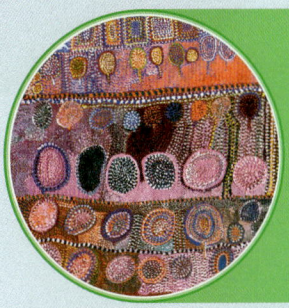

Loongkoonan is one of the oldest practicing artists in Australia. Her lifelong experience with the land led her to paint it from the perspective of an eagle's eye view: see **0.0.15a, p. 31**

Contour: the outline that defines a form

3.5.15a Cloak of red and yellow feathers, Hawaii, 18th century (?). Width 26½ x 12¼". British Museum, London, England

3.5.15b Detail of Hawaiian feather cloak

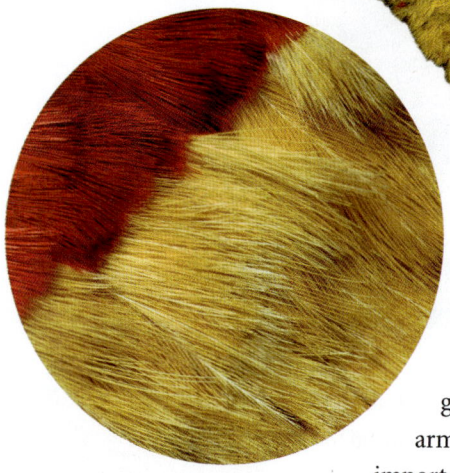

(**3.5.15a** and **3.5.15b**). These garments were used as a kind of armor in hand-to-hand combat; more importantly, however, they were believed to offer the protection of the gods. Ahu'ula cloaks were generally made by men. This was a time-consuming task that required a great degree of skill, and was by and large considered a sacred activity. The feathers were tied to a plant-fiber netting with cording, based on an ancient belief that knots reflected a metaphorical binding between humans and gods.

The cloak in **3.5.15a** is decorated with geometric designs, and identifies the wearer as a high-ranking member of society. The red feathers on ahu'ula came from the 'i'iwi bird, and the yellow feathers from the 'o'o bird. Because the yellow birds were very rare, cloaks with more yellow feathers were considered more valuable, and all-yellow cloaks were the most valuable of all.

These feather cloaks were prized possessions that were passed from generation to generation, unless they had been collected by enemies as war trophies or presented as political gifts. One famous cloak was presented by King Kamehameha III to American naval officer Lawrence Kearny as a gesture of gratitude for his diplomatic service on behalf of Hawaii.

Easter Island

Easter Island is small, measuring 15 miles long and 7½ miles wide. It is also extremely isolated, almost 1,300 miles off the nearest inhabited landmass, the coast of Chile. Easter Island's famous stone sculptures are called *moai* (meaning "seamount," "image," "statue," or "bearers of the gift"). These monolithic heads and torsos are unique but their abstracted and symmetrical features resemble the style of other faces made throughout Polynesia (**3.5.16**). Between 900 and 1500 CE, about a thousand of these huge figures were carved out of volcanic rock and scattered around the island, especially along the coast. They represent deified ancestors who were chiefs. The large quantities and size of the moai also suggest some kind of ritual, ceremonial, or cultural importance. Measuring from 10 to 60 ft. in height and weighing as much as 50 tons, these figures have unique individual features as well as common general characteristics.

While their heights and body shapes vary, they all have deep eye sockets (perhaps originally inlaid), angular noses, pointed chins, elongated earlobes, and an upright posture; their arms are by their sides, and they have no visible legs. Many of the moai (887 documented to date) were originally placed on platforms along the coastline, facing inland; a small number of them wore flat cylindrical hats of red volcanic stone, each weighing more than 10 tons. Scholars believe it likely that the hats on the sculptures represented crowns, identifying them as ancestor chiefs and thus providing a connection between the present and the past, the natural and the cosmic realms. During a period of civil strife from 1722 to 1868, all of the moai on the coastline were torn down by islanders. Thanks to recent archaeological efforts, many of the statues have been put back in their original place, appearing to emerge from the sea.

Papua New Guinea

The Abelam live in the wetland areas of the northern part of Papua New Guinea. One of the principal activities of their society is farming, especially yams, taro, bananas, and sweet potatoes. Yams are the main crop of Abelam society. Symbolically, they are associated with male fertility. The Abelam hold yam festivals each year to display the most impressive yams, with the grower of the largest yam achieving higher social status and helping to secure the prosperity of the village as a whole. In the

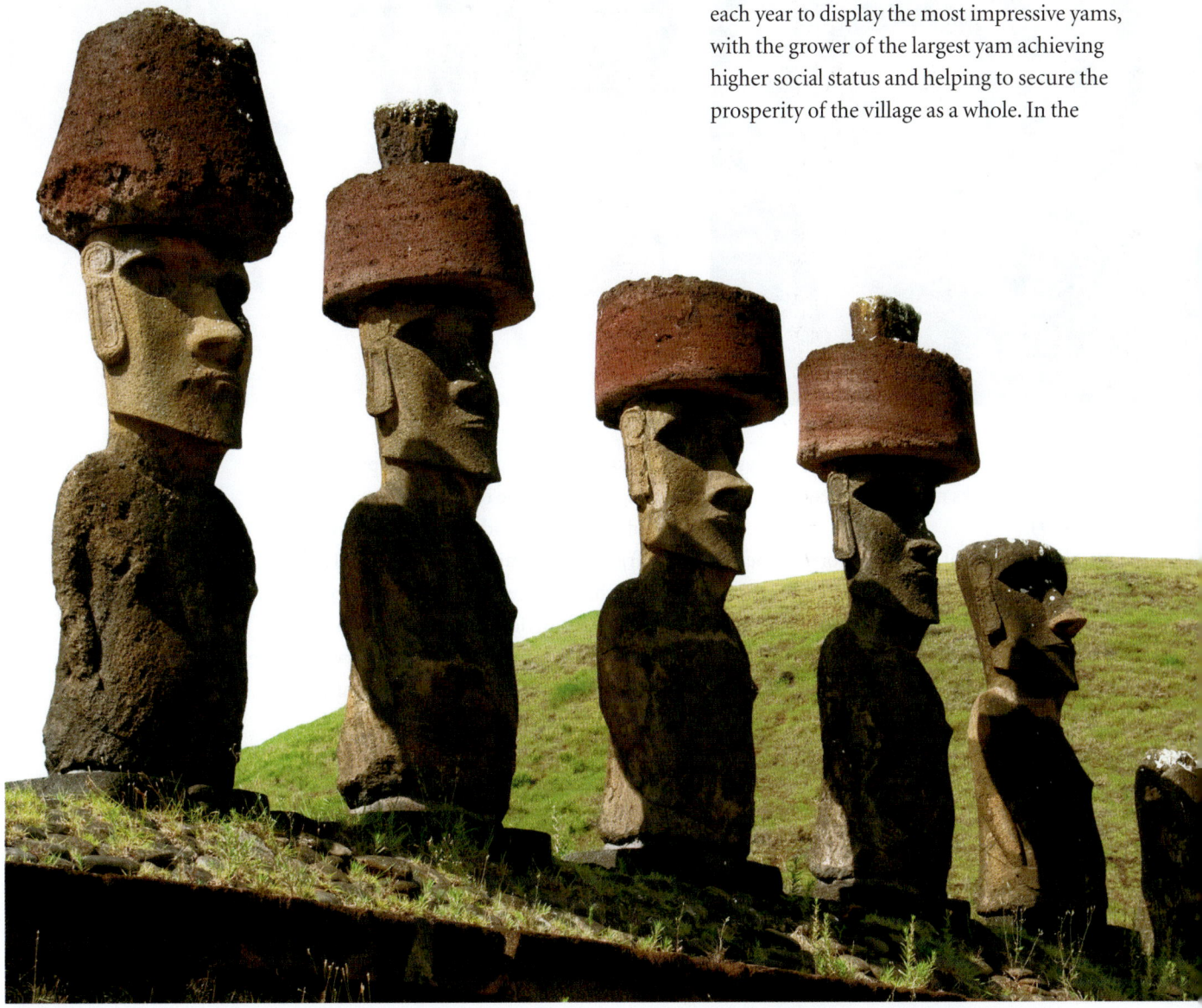

3.5.16 Moai ancestor figures, Ahu Nau Nau, Easter Island (Chile), Polynesia, before the 15th century

3.5.17 (below) Yam mask, Abelam, Maprik district, Papua New Guinea. Painted cane, height 18". Musée Barbier-Mueller, Geneva, Switzerland

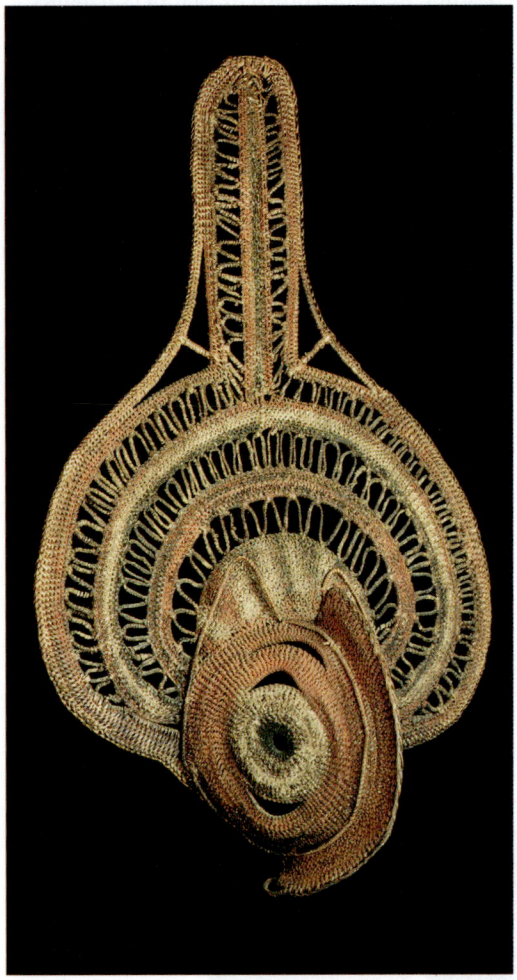

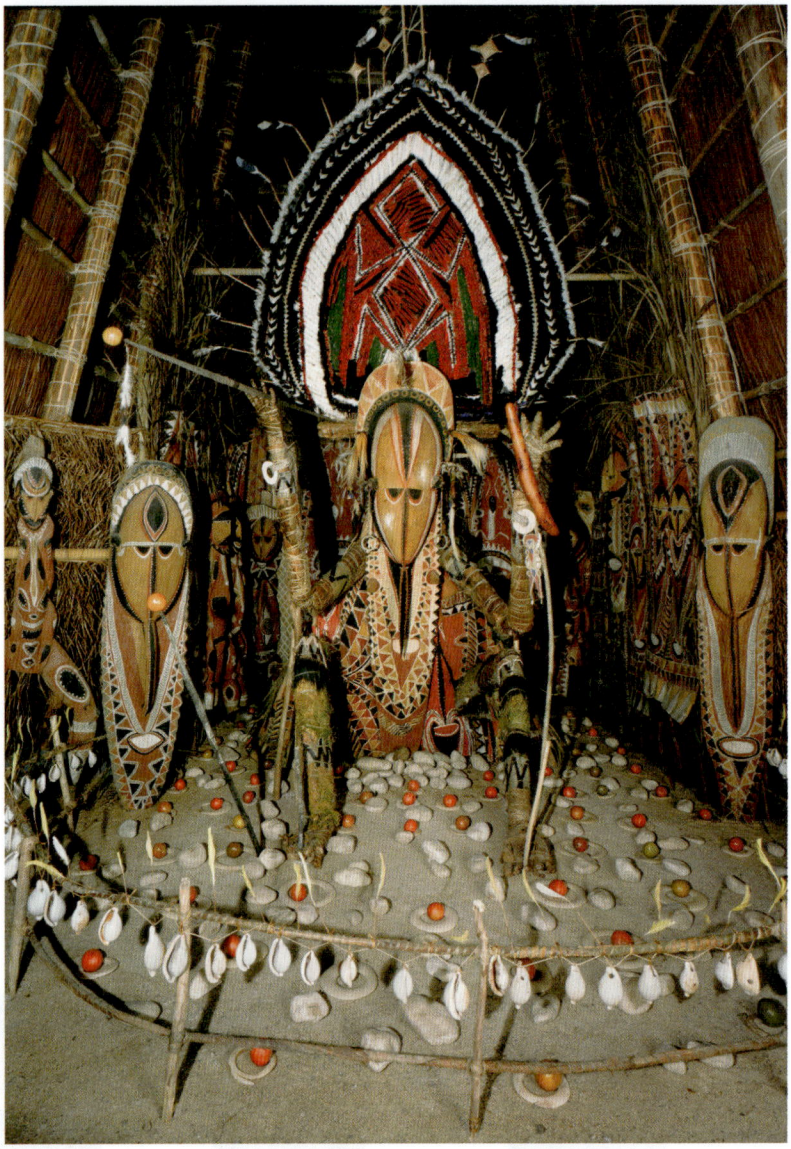

festivals associated with these contests, the yams actually "wear" masks made of baskets and wood (**3.5.17**).

Another important ceremony for the Abelam has traditionally been the initiation cycle for male members of the community. Eight separate rituals take place over the course of twenty or thirty years before a man is fully initiated. The elaborate ceremonial houses where some rites of passage take place are meant to impress the initiate with the power and intrigue of Abelam deities and traditions (**3.5.18**). The interior space is filled with detailed wooden figures representing supernatural beings, and with meaningful objects.

Colors and shapes have symbolic meaning in Abelam art; for example, white is believed to make long yams grow, and the pointed oval shape represents the belly of a woman. The use of yellow, red, and white is common. As in African art, certain objects, such as large cowrie shells, represent fertility and prosperity. Abelam see individual carvings, as well as the entire ceremonial house, as temporary. They are important during use but discarded afterward. Because of the powerful nature of the objects and imagery, they must be taken far away from the village, and are sometimes abandoned in the jungle or sold to collectors or museums.

3.5.18 Interior of Abelam cult house, Bongiora, Maprik, Papua New Guinea, Melanesia. Museum der Kulturen, Basle, Switzerland

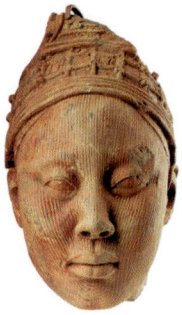

4.9.6 Head, possibly an Ife king, West Africa, 12th–14th century, p. 667

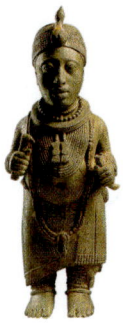

1.7.9 Nigerian Ife artist, Figure of Oni, Ife culture, early 14th–15th century, p. 145

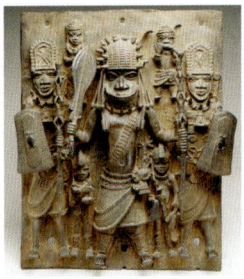

4.7.8 Benin plaque with warrior and attendants, Benin, 16th–17th century, p. 644

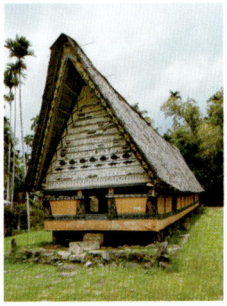

1.9.11 Bai-ra-Irrai, Republic of Palau, c. 1700, p. 166

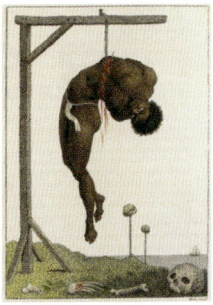

3.7.11 William Blake, *A negro hung alive by the ribs to a gallows*, 1796, p. 496

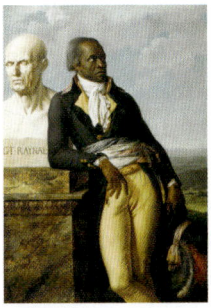

3.7.12 Anne-Louis Girodet, *Jean-Baptiste Belley*, 1797, France, p. 496

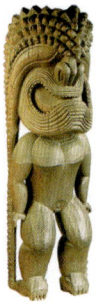

2.4.9 Figure of the war god Ku-ka'ili-moku, Hawaii, 18th or 19th century, p. 247

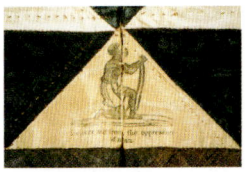

1.9.5b Deborah Coates, detail of quilt, Pennsylvania, c. 1840–50, p. 161

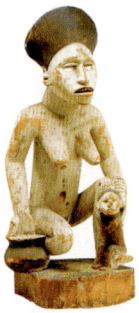

4.3.9 Kneeling female figure, Yombe, late 19th/ early 20th century, p. 598

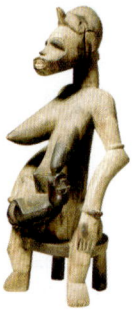

4.2.4 Mother-and-child figure, West Africa, late 19th–mid-20th century, p. 580

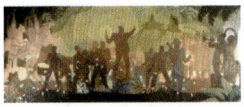

3.9.23 Aaron Douglas, *Aspects of Negro Life...*, 1934, p. 537

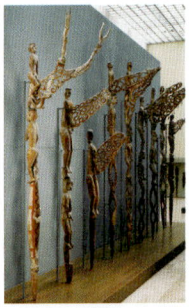

4.3.8 Asmat culture, *Bis* ancestor poles, late 1950s, p. 597

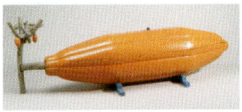

1.4.15 Kane Kwei, *Coffin in the Shape of a Cocoa Pod*, c. 1970, p. 102

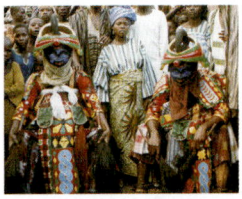

4.1.10 Yoruba culture, Gèlèdé masqueraders in Benin, 1971, p. 572

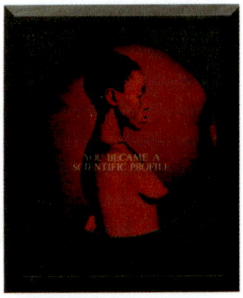

2.8.24 Carrie Mae Weems, "You Became a Scientific Profile," 1995, p. 329

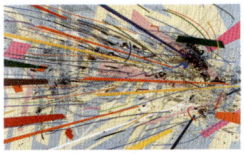

2.2.23 Julie Mehretu, *Excerpt (Suprematist Evasion)*, 2003, p. 222

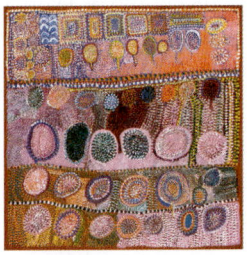

0.0.15a Loongkoonan, *Bush Tucker Nyikina Country*, 2006, p. 31

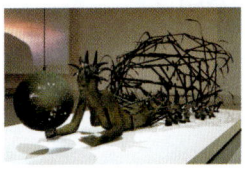

1.2.19a Wangechi Mutu, *She's Got the Whole World in Her*, 2015, p. 74

3.6 Art of Renaissance and Baroque Europe (1400–1750)

Renaissance: a period of cultural and artistic change in Europe from the fourteenth to the seventeenth century
Subject (subject matter): the person, object, or space depicted in a work of art
Oil paint: paint made of pigment floating in oil
Humanism, humanist: the study of such subjects as history, philosophy, languages, and literature, particularly in relation to those of ancient Greece and Rome

The thousand years of European history known as the Middle Ages were followed by the period known as the **Renaissance** (1400–1600). The term means "rebirth," a reference to a renewed interest in the Classical world of Greece and Rome. The influence of Classical **subject matter** is evident in the numbers of nudes and mythological figures in Italian Renaissance art. Yet artworks from the Italian Renaissance, even those with Classical subjects, often have a Christian message. In the Northern Renaissance, which occurred in areas of Europe north of Italy, Christian morality was also depicted, but Northern Renaissance artists preferred to depict clothed religious or everyday figures and focus on both textural details, using primarily **oil paint**, and symbolic meaning to convey moral messages.

The Renaissance was also marked by an interest in education and the natural world. Improved literacy, means of travel, and printed books (made possible by the invention of moveable type in the 1400s) expanded the transmission of ideas and artistic developments throughout Europe. **Humanism** became influential as a philosophical approach to life that stressed study of the Classical world and promoted the success of individuals as a reflection of their gifts from God. The humanist focus on individual achievement and earthly **naturalism**, as opposed to the Middle Ages, in which artists were often unidentified and scenes depicted a spiritual, otherworldly space, created tension between religious leaders and humanists. In general, when looking at art from the Renaissance, one can see that different religious parameters are in play in Italy and in the north of Europe. Northern Renaissance imagery often includes more intimate scenes and intricate details that promote personal interaction with an artwork. Italian artists often depict grand-scale imagery (frequently **frescoes**) that promotes saints or other intermediaries (people who act as interpreters or go-betweens, in this case between "ordinary" people and God) and therefore highlights the role of the Catholic Church as an essential intercessor to God (see Box: Protestant Reformation and Counter-Reformation: A Comparison through Last Suppers, pp. 474–76).

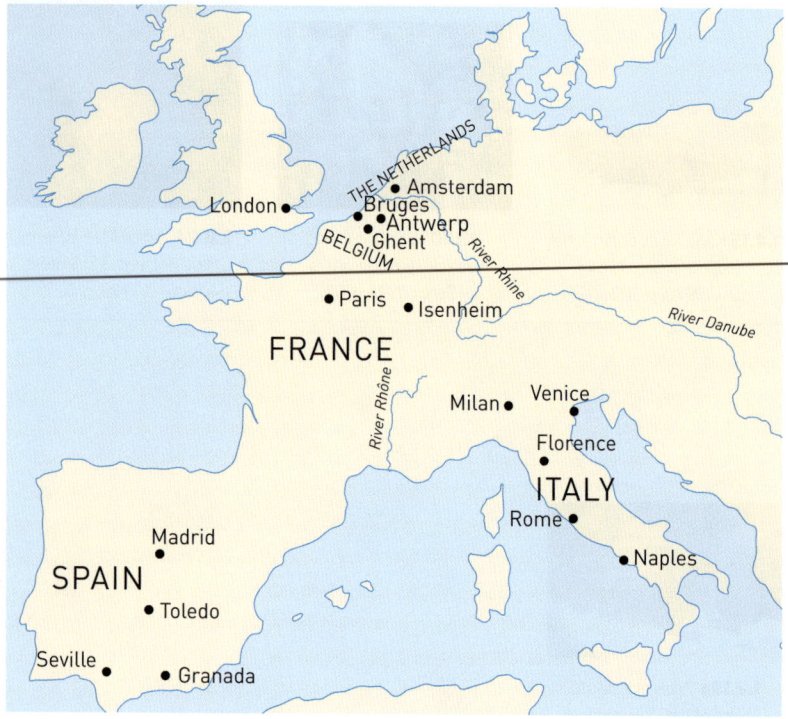

3.6.1 Map of Renaissance and Baroque Europe

Italian artist and historian Giorgio Vasari (1511–1574) used the term Renaissance (*rinascità*) in the first art history book, *The Lives of the Most Excellent Painters, Sculptors, and Architects* (sometimes known as *Lives of the Great Artists*). Published in 1550, it began with a biography of Giotto as the father of the Italian Renaissance and culminated in Vasari's attribution of Michelangelo as the master of the period. Vasari's text emphasized the intellectual ability needed to make paintings, sculptures, and architecture. Around this time, artists began to be seen as creative geniuses, even divinely inspired, rather than manual makers of craft works.

The period that followed the Renaissance is known as the **Baroque** (1600–1750). Like the word Renaissance, Baroque refers to both a historical period and a style of art. The seventeenth century is noted for an increase in trade and advancements in science. Baroque art draws on much of the same subject matter as the Renaissance, but Baroque images tend to include more motion and emotion. The Renaissance and Baroque periods were both marked by constant warfare throughout Europe, and art was often used to memorialize battles or to inspire people to support their rulers. Throughout this time, artworks were commissioned by wealthy **patrons**, often a church or ruling family, who determined such things as the size, subject matter, and even how much of an expensive **pigment**, such as ultramarine blue, the artist could use.

The Early Renaissance in Italy

Following the renewed interest in the Classical past and the influence of humanist thought, Italian artists during the early Renaissance were preoccupied with making pictures that their viewers would find entirely believable. The real, however, was balanced by the **ideal**, especially when the subjects were mythological or religious. Whereas, during the Middle Ages, depictions of the nude body had been avoided except to show the weakness and mortality of such sinners as Adam and Eve, during the Renaissance, artists portrayed the idealized nude figure as the embodiment of spiritual and intellectual perfection.

In art, although religious subjects remained popular, the emphasis switched from a belief in faith as the only factor in attaining immortality after death, to a concentration on how human actions could enhance the quality of life on Earth. Mathematics and science, derived from a renewed study of Classical Greek and Roman works, encouraged the systematic understanding of the world. Renaissance artists used and refined new systems of **perspective** to translate their careful observations more consistently into realistic artistic representations. These influences inspired Renaissance artists to combine existing subject matter and techniques with innovative approaches.

Due to artists' interest in exploration and high individual achievement, competitions between them were common. In 1401, seven artists submitted **relief** panels portraying the Sacrifice of Isaac to compete for the commission to create a large set of bronze panels for the north doors of the Florence Baptistry. The requirements for the submissions were very specific. Each Old Testament scene depicting Abraham, who, at the behest of God, is about to kill his son Isaac, should also include an altar for the boy, a rocky landscape, an angel, a ram, a donkey, and two shepherds, all encased in a so-called **quatrefoil** frame.

Filippo Brunelleschi (1377–1446) and Lorenzo Ghiberti (1378–1455) took very different approaches to the scene. Brunelleschi (**3.6.2a**, p. 462) shows a father terrified to kill his son and a boy who, although he tries to hold his adolescent body up, appears to shrink in fear. The extraordinary emotion conveyed by these two figures shows what a heart-wrenching act God has asked Abraham to commit. Ghiberti's depiction (**3.6.2b**, p. 462) instead shows a very muscular boy and a father who looks like an ancient god himself. They appear proud and willing to accept their fate. In both scenes, an angel swoops down at the last minute to stop Abraham. The committee chose Ghiberti's depiction, likely in part because of the Classical-looking figures and

Naturalism: a very realistic or lifelike style of making images
Fresco: a technique in which the artist paints onto freshly applied plaster. From the Italian *fresco*, "fresh"
Baroque: European artistic and architectural style of the late sixteenth to early eighteenth century, characterized by extravagance and emotional intensity
Patron: an organization or individual who sponsors the creation of works of art
Pigment: the colored material used in paints. Often made from finely ground minerals
Ideal: more beautiful, harmonious, or perfect than reality; or exists as an idea
Perspective: the creation of the illusion of depth in a two-dimensional image by using mathematical principles
Relief: a sculpture that projects from a flat surface
Quatrefoil: a symmetrical framework that has four lobes or leaves
Three-dimensional: having height, width, and depth
Mass: a volume that has, or gives the illusion of having, weight, density, and bulk
Volume: the space filled or enclosed by a three-dimensional figure or object

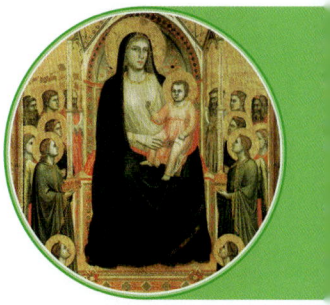

Toward the end of the Middle Ages, the artist Giotto created believable **three-dimensional** space with figures that convey **mass** and **volume**: see **3.2.28, p. 408**

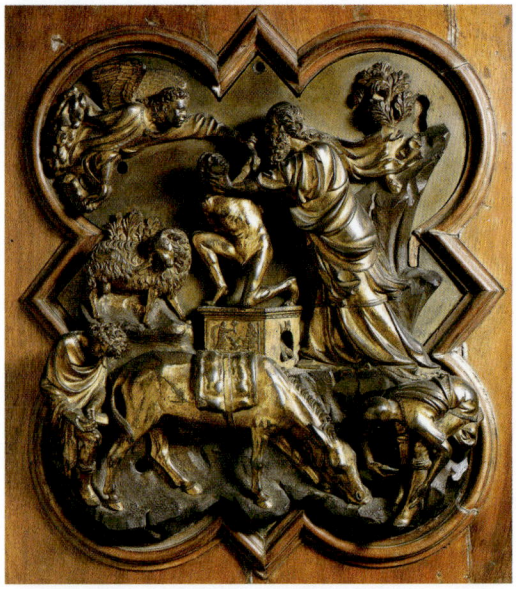

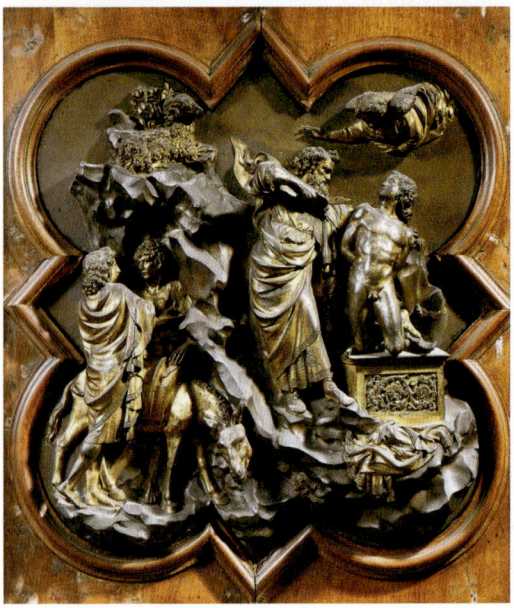

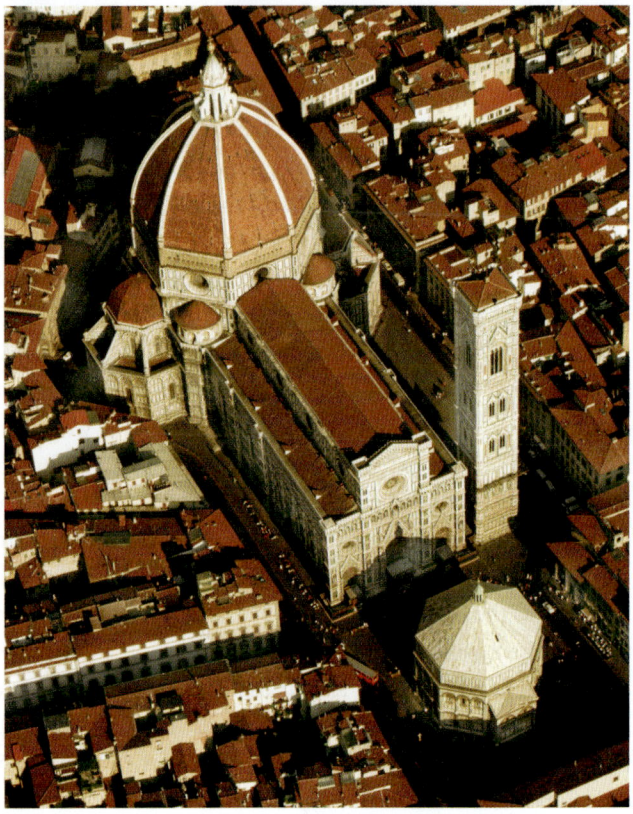

3.6.3 (top right) Arnolfo di Cambio and others, Florence Cathedral (Italy), begun 1296, view from south

3.6.4 (right) Modern diagram showing Filippo Brunelleschi's dome of Florence Cathedral, 1420–36

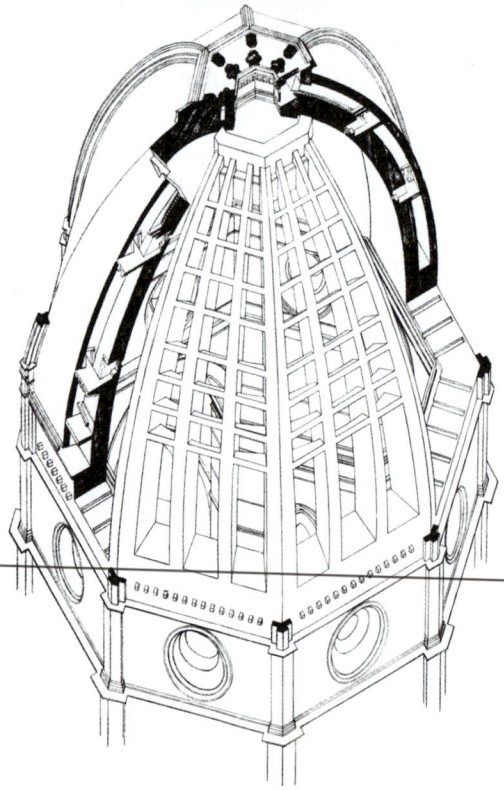

3.6.2a (top) Filippo Brunelleschi, *Sacrifice of Isaac*, 1401. Bronze. Museo Nazionale del Bargello, Florence

3.6.2b (above) Lorenzo Ghiberti, *Sacrifice of Isaac*, 1401, bronze. Museo Nazionale del Bargello, Florence

Dome: an evenly curved vault forming the ceiling or roof of a building
Linear perspective: a system using converging imaginary sight lines to create the illusion of depth

fearlessness of Abraham and Isaac. In addition, Ghiberti utilized one piece of bronze with some small attachments for his panel, requiring less bronze than Brunelleschi's panel, which was made by casting seven separate pieces. Ghiberti created twenty-eight panels for the north doors of the baptistry over the next nineteen years. He was then commissioned to realize ten very intricate scenes for the northern doors of the baptistry, which Michelangelo coined The Gates of Paradise.

It is fortunate that Brunelleschi lost the competition because shortly thereafter he went to Rome and, among other pursuits, studied its Classical architecture. When he returned to Florence, he won a competition in 1419 to complete the 140-ft.-diameter **dome** for Santa Maria del Fiore (Florence Cathedral). The dome was a great technological challenge and Brunelleschi's proposal was radical. He not only designed the dome but also devised the machinery used to build it and oversaw the construction itself, thus earning himself the right to be called the first Renaissance architect (**3.6.3**).

Existing construction techniques required temporary wooden scaffolding to form the dome shape (170 ft. above the ground at its top) until the stonework was finished—which in this case would have been too costly and heavy. The enormous weight of the bricks and stone could not be held up by external stone supports either, because of the existing buildings around the cathedral. Brunelleschi invented equipment to hoist the building materials and came up with an ingenious system that used each stage of the structure to support the next as the dome was built, layer by layer (**3.6.4**). The dome's construction began in 1420 and took sixteen years to complete.

Brunelleschi is also credited with inventing a new method for drawing, known as **linear perspective**, a technique for creating the illusion of three-dimensional space. He shared the process with other Florentine artists, including his close friend, a painter nicknamed Masaccio, or "Big Clumsy Tom" (1401–1428). Leon Battista Alberti (1404–1472) wrote in his treatise *On Painting* (1435) about the theories of perspective that were already being put into practice by Brunelleschi and Masaccio, and the technique spread.

Masaccio applied the rules of linear perspective in several large-scale fresco paintings, including *Tribute Money* (**3.6.5**). This painting depicts the biblical story from the gospel of Matthew, in which, as advised by Jesus, St. Peter has to pay the local tax collector. Here, figures, architecture, and landscape are integrated into a believable scene. The buildings in the foreground appear on the same **scale** as the group of figures standing next to them. As the buildings and people get further away from us, they get smaller, and lead, in a naturalistic way, toward a **vanishing point** on the horizon. The **focal point** converges on Jesus, and the vanishing point lies behind his head, making him the visual and symbolic center of the scene. Masaccio uses **atmospheric perspective** to show the distant landscape, where the mountains fade from greenish to gray.

Innovations in this painting include consistent lighting throughout, a wide range of colors, and the use of **chiaroscuro** (extremes of light and dark) to enhance the illusion of three-dimensional form. *Tribute Money* is one of Masaccio's most original paintings: it also shows three scenes in a sequence within one setting. While the fresco maintains the **medieval** tradition of **narrative** painting, the **composition** deviates from the earlier practice in an important way. Rather than showing each scene on a separate panel, events that take

Scale: the size of an object or artwork relative to another object or artwork, or to a system of measurement
Vanishing point(s): the point or points in a work of art at which imaginary sight lines appear to converge, suggesting depth
Focal point: the area in a composition to which the eye returns most naturally
Atmospheric perspective: use of shades of color to create the illusion of depth. Closer objects have warmer tones and clear outlines, while objects set further away are smaller and become hazy
Chiaroscuro: the use of light and dark in a painting to create the impression of volume
Medieval: relating to the Middle Ages; roughly, between the fall of the Roman empire and the start of the Renaissance
Narrative: an artwork that tells a story
Composition: the overall design or organization of a work

3.6.5 Masaccio, *Tribute Money*, c. 1427. Fresco, 8'1" × 19'7". Brancacci Chapel, Santa Maria del Carmine, Florence, Italy

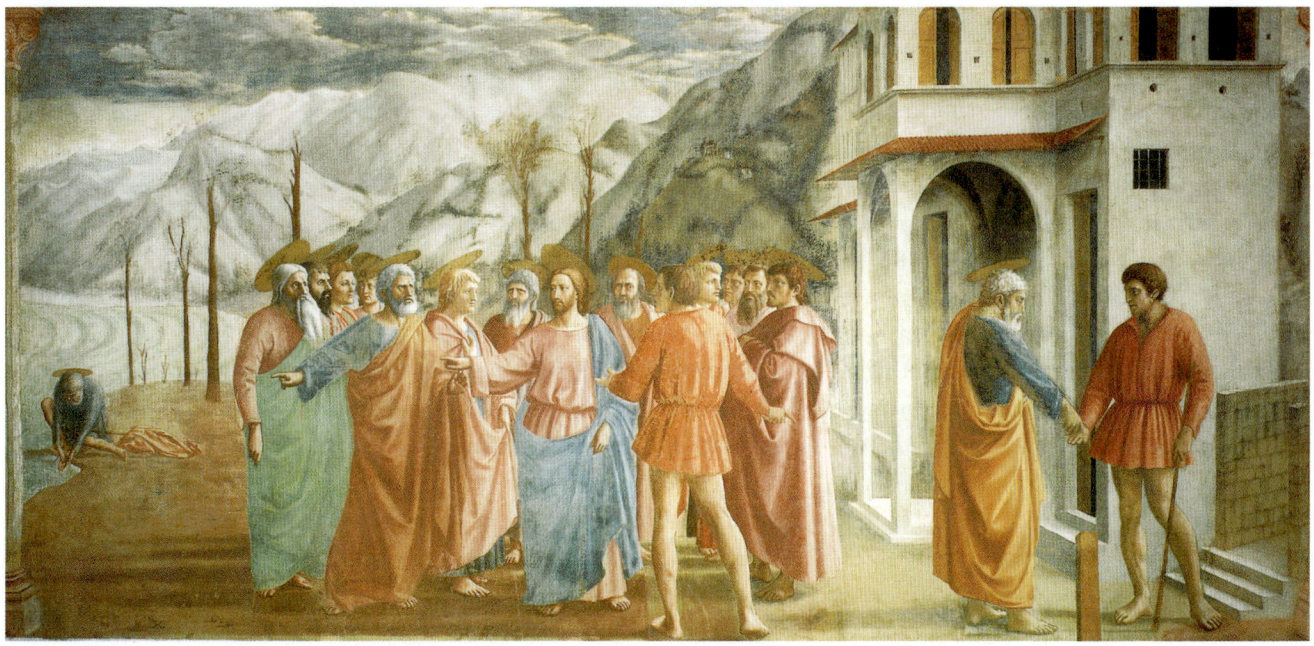

place at different times are shown together in a unified space, or a **continuous narrative**. In the center, the tax collector, with his back to us, demands the Jewish temple tax as the disciples look on. The tax collector is shown in a natural stance called **contrapposto**, which was found in ancient sculpture and imitated by Renaissance artists. On the left of the scene we see Peter following the instructions of Jesus to retrieve the money from the mouth of the first fish he catches. On the right, Peter pays the collector double the amount owed, using the money miraculously obtained from the fish's mouth. This story would have been particularly relevant for contemporary Florentines, who were required to pay a tax for military defense in 1427, the same year the painting was made.

Like other Early Renaissance artists, Masaccio used both linear and atmospheric perspective to convince viewers they were looking at reality rather than a symbolic representation. He incorporated an understanding of the movement of the human bodies beneath the drapery to increase the sense of volume. This series of frescoes, which was displayed in the Brancacci family chapel, was a major influence on later artists, including Michelangelo (**3.6.9a** and **b**, p. 468), who specifically went to the chapel to study Masaccio's paintings.

The Renaissance in Northern Europe

The Renaissance that took place in northern Europe in the countries we now know as the Netherlands, Germany, France, and Belgium differed significantly, visually, from the developments in Italy. Throughout the fifteenth century, the artists of the Netherlands continued using the traditional methods established in medieval manuscript **illumination** painting. At that time they had a reputation for producing much of the best art in Europe, and their work influenced the visual arts elsewhere on the continent.

Unlike early Renaissance works from Italy, Northern Renaissance artworks are less concerned with idealized figures and precise perspective, but often contain messages expressed through **symbolism**. Artists in the northern countries are known for their skilled use of oil paint as opposed to the more common use of fresco and **tempera** painting in Italy. While a fresco painting has to be completed quickly (it dries within a day), the slow drying process of oil paint allowed artists to create fine details and **texture** in their work. The development of oil paint was attributed to Dutch artist Jan van Eyck (*c.* 1395–1441) by Giorgio Vasari, but it was actually used in the Middle Ages to decorate stone, metal, and, occasionally, plaster walls. The technique of **glazing**, which Van Eyck developed with such virtuosity, was widely adopted throughout Europe after 1450 (see Box: Van Eyck, Panofsky, and Iconographic Analysis, pp. 466–67).

In the Northern Renaissance, it was common to infuse works of art with religious meaning. Instead of conveying such meaning through mythological subjects as was often the practice in Italy, however, northern artists frequently depicted people from everyday life. On the surface, Quentin Metsys's *The Moneylender and His Wife* (**3.6.6**) shows a shopkeeper weighing the coins of his trade as his wife looks on. The scene depicts a businessman enjoying

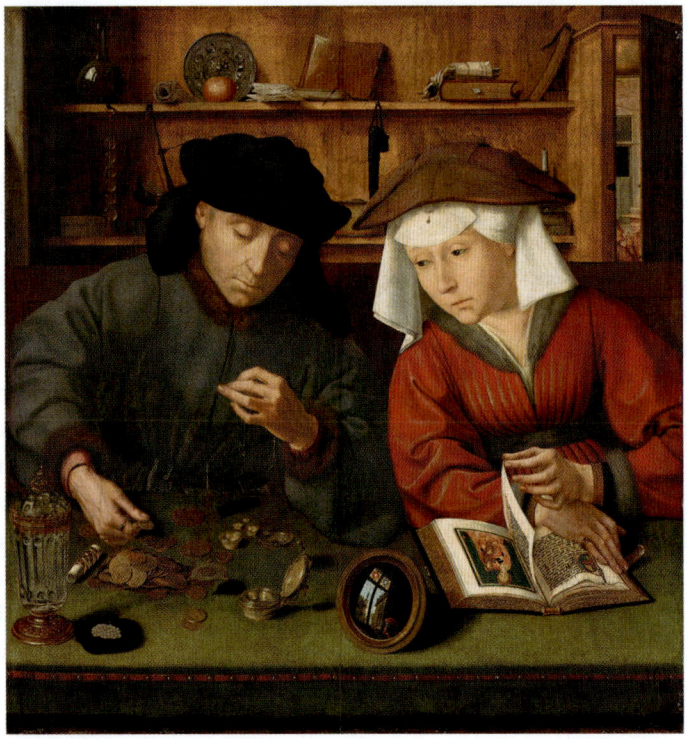

3.6.6 Quentin Metsys, *The Moneylender and His Wife*, 1514. Oil on panel, 27¾ × 26⅜". Musée du Louvre, Paris, France

Continuous narrative: when different parts of a story are shown within the same visual space
Contrapposto: a pose in sculpture in which the upper part of the body twists in one direction and the lower part in another
Illumination: illustration and decoration in a manuscript
Symbolism: using images or symbols in an artwork to convey meaning; often obvious when the work was made but requiring research for modern viewers to understand
Tempera: fast-drying painting medium made from pigment mixed with water-soluble binder, such as egg yolk
Texture: the surface quality of a work, for example fine/coarse, detailed/lacking in detail
Glazing: in oil painting, adding a transparent layer of paint to achieve a richness in texture, volume, and form

his growing wealth thanks to the increasing commerce in their port town of Antwerp (in modern-day Belgium). Furthermore, the artist has created a scene in which the couple's morals are being questioned. The woman, who was in the process of reading her daily devotional, has been distracted by the beautiful material objects featured to her right on the table. The glass pitcher filled with water and the rosary are symbols of the Virgin's purity, and the wife's devotional was turned to a page discussing Mary. But the tempting fruit and the candle above the woman's head are symbols of the presence of the devil. Thus, the scale used to weigh the gold coins, pearls, and jewels is also symbolic of the struggle taking place between morals and greed; in a sense, the couple's spiritual future hangs in the balance.

The artist also created an intricate sense of a larger space, by showing the shelves behind the couple, the front of the tablecloth, the two men outside the door on the right (just visible here), and the extraordinarily illusionistic convex mirror reflecting a figure by a window, which some scholars relate to Van Eyck's self-portrait in *The Arnolfini Portrait* (see Box: Van Eyck, Panofsky, and Iconographic Analysis, pp. 466–67).

But the scene is not as three-dimensionally accurate as those by artists working in Italy. This is not because northern artists did not have the skill. Rather, they were more concerned with creating impressive texture and details, such as those found in the textiles, book, or mirror, and with highlighting the importance of the religious symbolism in their works. The table in this scene is tilted so that, in reality, the objects would slide off, but the artist angled the table in this way so that all the objects would be easy for the viewer to read.

Many Northern Renaissance artists also explored explicitly religious subject matter in the form of painted **altarpieces** with multiple framed panels. The German artist Matthias Grünewald (*c.* 1475/80–1528) painted a complex and explicit altarpiece for the chapel in a hospital that cared for patients with skin diseases, the Abbey of St. Anthony in Isenheim (in what is now northeastern France). The Crucifixion scene, which forms the center panel when the altarpiece is closed, is one of the most graphic images of Christ's crucifixion in the history of art (**3.6.7**). The vivid details offered patients

Altarpiece: an artwork that is placed behind an altar in a church

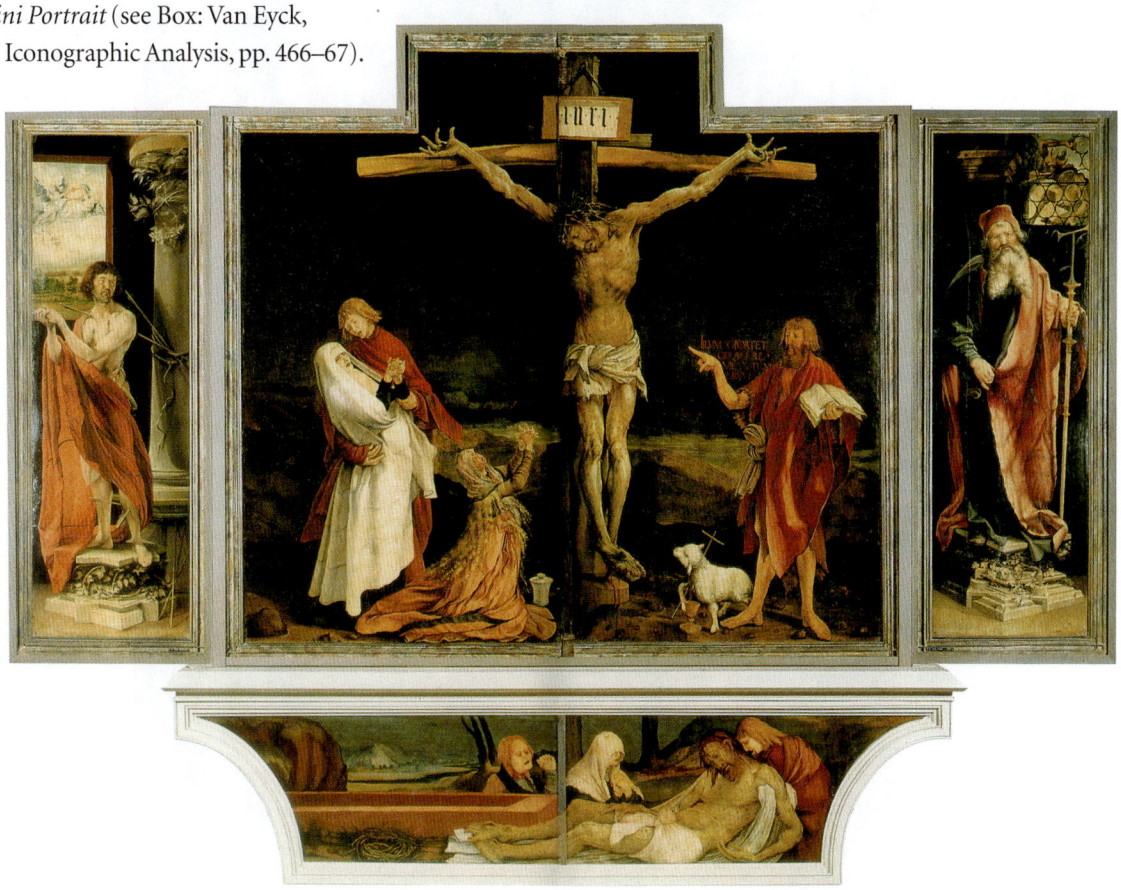

3.6.7 Matthias Grünewald, *Isenheim Altarpiece* (closed), *c.* 1510–15. Oil on panel, center panel: Crucifixion, 8'9½" × 10'; predella: Lamentation, 29¾" × 11'1¾"; side panels: Saints Sebastian and Anthony, 7'6½" × 29½" each. Musée d'Unterlinden, Colmar, France

Van Eyck, Panofsky, and Iconographic Analysis

One of the most important Northern Renaissance paintings, *The Arnolfini Portrait* by Jan van Eyck, has been a source of mystery for scholars for generations (**3.6.8a**). Like many works from this time and region, it depicts an intimate, domestic scene, and the young couple and the room in which they stand are painted in such detail that viewers feel as if they are looking into a real room with real people. Indeed, since the nineteenth century, the portrait was thought to depict Giovanni Arnolfini, a wealthy merchant, and his wife. In 1934, the art historian Erwin Panofsky (1892–1968) suggested it could have been some kind of legal document, perhaps certifying their wedding ceremony. An inscription on the wall above the mirror says "Johannes de eyck fuit hic 1434," or "Jan van Eyck was here 1434," which Panofsky argued announces the painter's presence and suggests he was declaring himself as one of two witnesses, visible in the convex mirror behind the principal figures, at the event (**3.6.8b**). Fifteenth-century viewers would probably have paid careful attention to the mirror, with its circular mini-pictures, or roundels, depicting scenes from the crucifixion of Christ, since such an object would have been very expensive, a truly luxurious possession. The mirror helps extend the illusion of reality by showing in its reflective surface the room in front of the couple, which is otherwise not in the picture.

Through intense study of the culture in which this artwork was made, Panofsky argued that

3.6.8a Jan van Eyck, *The Arnolfini Portrait*, 1434. Oil on panel, 32⅜ × 23⅝". National Gallery, London, England

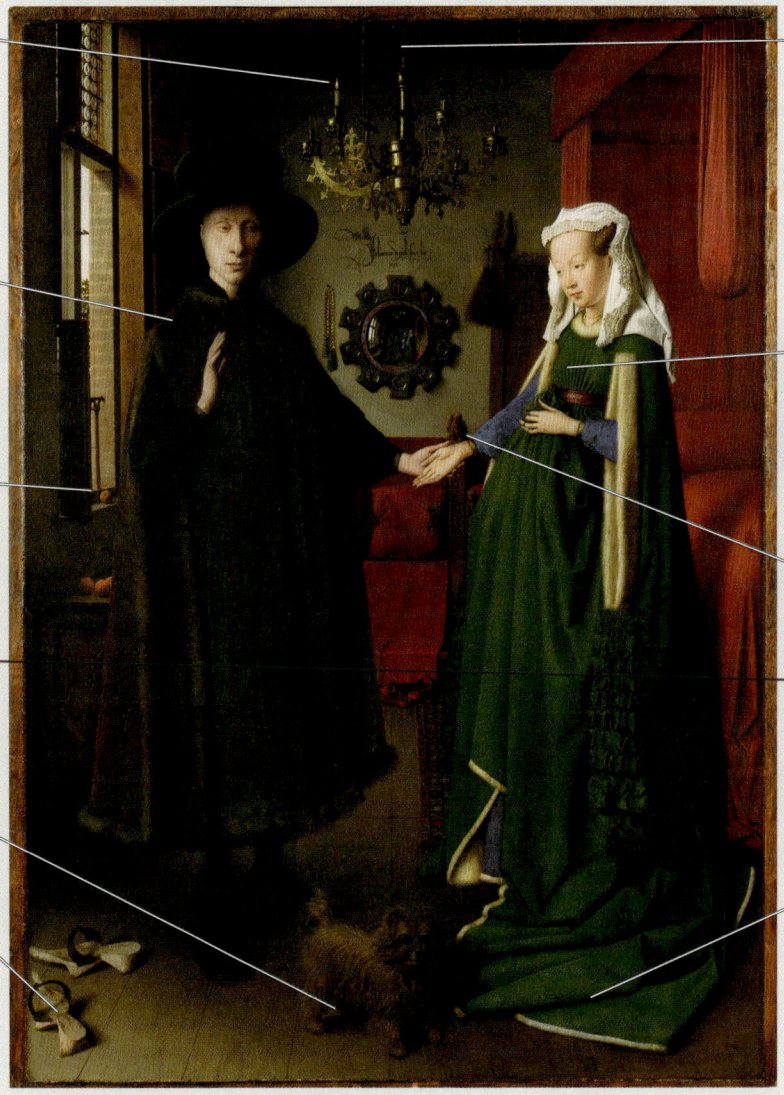

Single candle burning in the chandelier: possibly a symbolic reference to Christ; or a unity candle used in a marriage ceremony; or a sign of a legal event

Chandelier is very ornamental and expensive, a clear sign of wealth

Man stands near the window to show that he is part of the world outside

Woman stands near the elaborate bed to indicate her domestic role and the hope that she will bear children

Fruit on the windowsill: sign of fertility. Indicates wealth (oranges and lemons were expensive because they had to be imported from Spain); also a reference to innocence and purity before humans sinned in the Garden of Eden

Figure carved on the chair: St. Margaret, protector of women in childbirth

Dog: sign of fidelity and wealth

Full-skirted dress: fashion of the day because the current queen was pregnant (despite appearances, we know that the woman in the painting is not pregnant herself, because she never had children)

Shoes/clogs: given to a woman as a wedding gift; symbol of stability; removed to show that the event taking place here is sacred and makes the ground sacred, too

Iconographic analysis: the study of art by interpreting symbols, themes, and subject matter as sources of meaning

numerous objects in this painting had symbolic meanings that are lost to modern viewers, and that the image is about the sacramental nature of marriage. For example, the shoes on the left and in the back behind the couple can be interpreted as having been taken off because the ground is considered sacred for the event; the dog is, traditionally, a sign of fidelity; the single candle lit in the chandelier suggests unity; and the exotic, ripe fruit near the window indicates the hope of fertility.

While Panofsky's **iconographic analysis** has been adopted as a valid approach by many art historians, scholars still debate the meaning of this specific painting. Recent discoveries prove that not all of the above interpretation can be true. In 1997, documents were found that show that the Arnolfini couple were not married until 1447, six years after the death of Van Eyck. The artist, therefore, cannot have painted this portrait as a depiction of their wedding, although some argue that it could be a statement of intent to marry.

3.6.8b Detail of Jan van Eyck, *The Arnolfini Portrait*

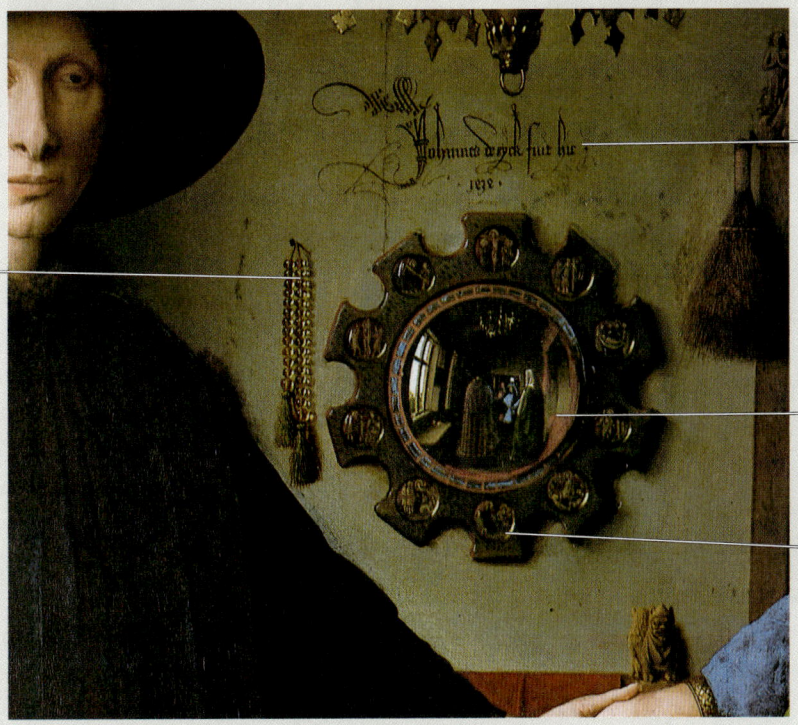

who were suffering from a variety of serious diseases a way to identify with Christ in his human form, as well as comfort that they were not alone in their own suffering. St. Anthony, shown on the right wing of the altarpiece, was the patron saint of sufferers from skin disease. Indeed, a common disease that caused a swollen stomach, convulsions, gangrene, and boils on the skin was named "St. Anthony's Fire." When patients prayed before this altarpiece they saw the green pallor of Christ's skin, the thorns that drew blood from his body, and the deformations of his bones caused by hanging on the cross for so long. The altarpiece can be opened to reveal additional scenes inside that also relate to St. Anthony.

Christ's suffering was further emphasized when the altarpiece was opened on certain occasions, such as Easter Sunday. When the left door was swung open, Christ's arm would appear to separate from the rest of his body. Similarly, opening the left side of the Lamentation scene at the bottom of the altarpiece would make his legs appear to be cut off. As limbs were often amputated to prevent the further spread of disease, many patients could directly identify with Christ's experience.

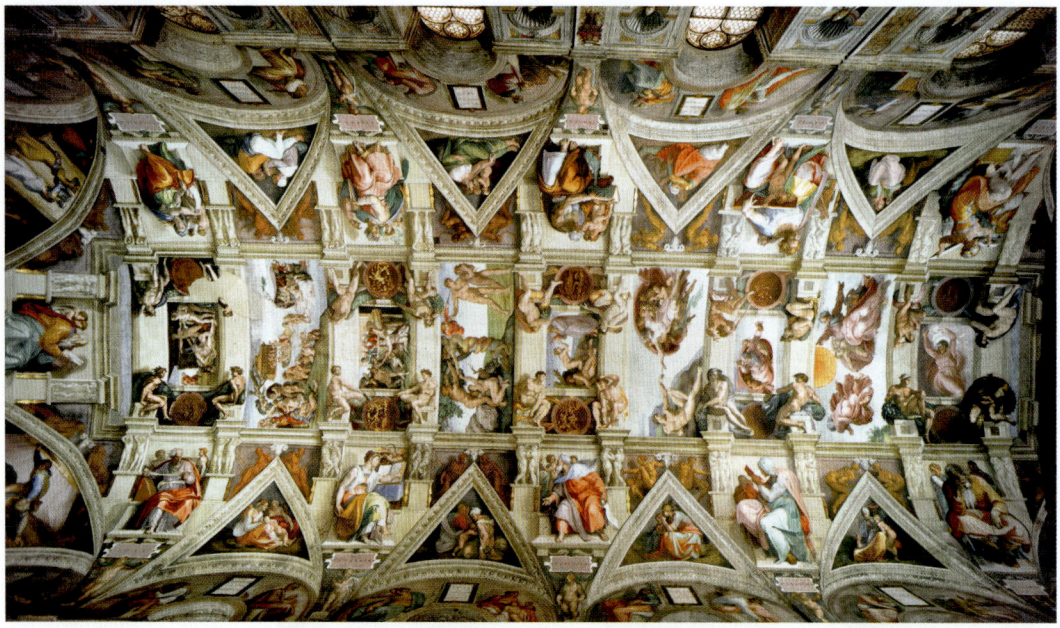

3.6.9a (left) Michelangelo, view of the ceiling frescoes in the Sistine Chapel, 1508–12. Vatican City, Italy

3.6.9b (below) Michelangelo, detail of *Creation of Adam*, Sistine Chapel ceiling

Sfumato: in painting, the application of layers of translucent paint to create a hazy or smoky appearance and unify the composition
Sitter: person who poses, or "sits," for an artist to paint, sculpt, or photograph
Pedestal: a base upon which a statue or column rests

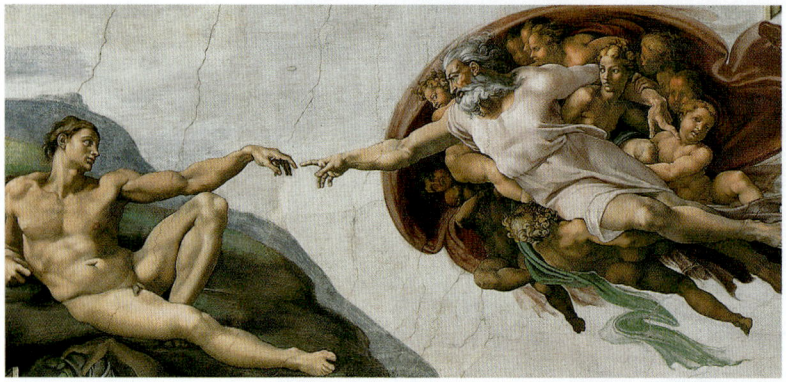

The High Renaissance in Italy

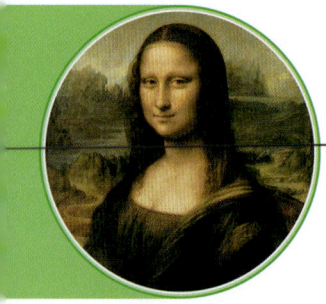

In the *Mona Lisa*, Leonardo da Vinci used a new painting technique he had invented, **sfumato**, as well as a mystical landscape and the gaze of the **sitter** to create a sense of mystery about the woman's mood: see **0.0.12, p. 28**

The Italian artists Leonardo da Vinci (1452–1519), Michelangelo Buonarroti (1475–1564), and Raphael (1483–1520) dominated the art world at the beginning of the sixteenth century. All three of them, like other artists of the high Renaissance, utilized the rules of perspective and illusionism, but willingly departed from exact mechanical precision in order to create desired visual effects. Leonardo was the eldest amongst these three great artists of the period. He was known not only as a great painter but also as a scientist and engineer. He was a great observer of the world around him, as can be seen by the emotional expressions on the faces of the characters in his famous work *The Last Supper* (see Box: Protestant Reformation and Catholic Counter-Reformation: A Comparison through Last Suppers, pp. 474–76).

As part of Pope Julius II's (1443–1513) campaign to restore Rome and the Vatican to its ancient grandeur, he assigned Michelangelo to paint the ceiling of the Vatican's Sistine Chapel while Raphael was working on the *School of Athens* fresco nearby in the Vatican apartments between 1510 and 1511 (see Gateway Box: Raphael, **3.6.10**, p. 470). Michelangelo's enormous painting, which took the artist four years to complete, is so believable that we could be fooled into thinking the beams, **pedestals**, and structural elements are real (**3.6.9a**). Michelangelo preferred stone carving to painting, which perhaps explains why he painted the ceiling with such apparently three-dimensional figures and surrounded them with architectural elements and sculpture. The nine panels at the ceiling's center detail the Old Testament stories of Genesis, from the creation of the heavens and Earth, to the creation and fall of Adam and Eve, and ending with scenes from the Great Flood. The ceiling is covered with detailed figure studies, Michelangelo's specialty. In the *Creation of Adam* panel, for example, human nudity could be associated with the perfection of man (**3.6.9b**).

Michelangelo also painted *The Last Judgment* on the west wall of the Sistine Chapel more

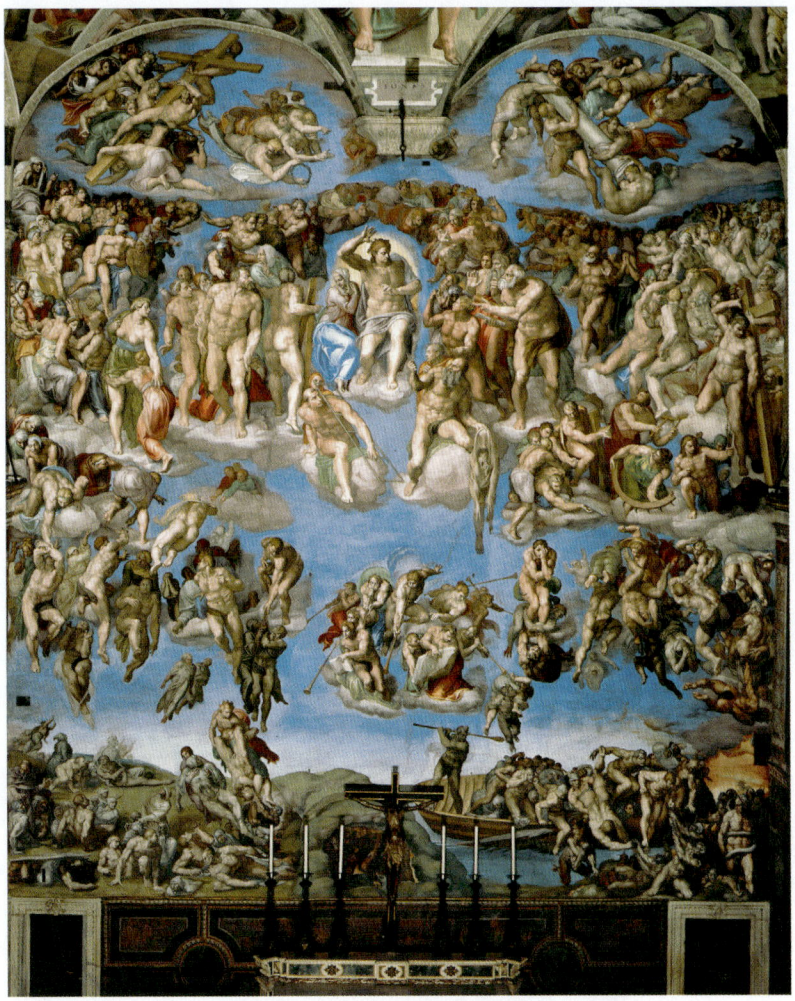

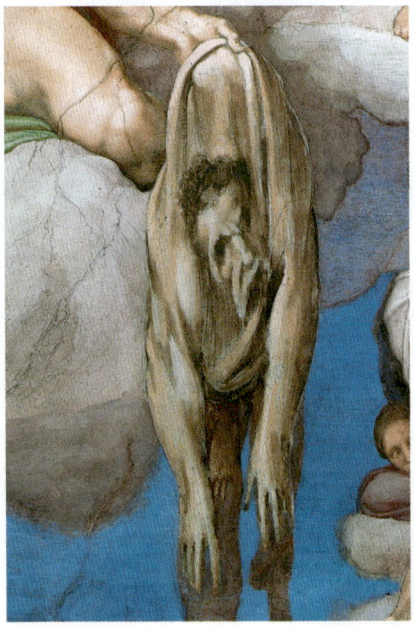

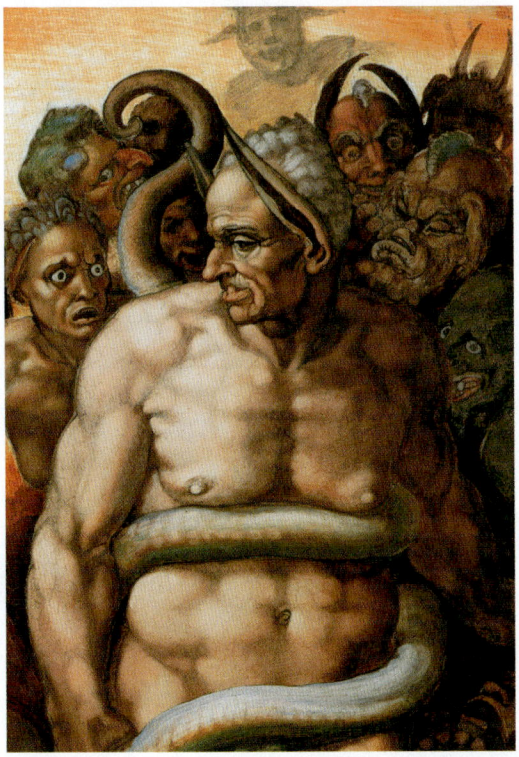

3.6.9c (above) Michelangelo, *Last Judgment*, 1534–41. Sistine Chapel, Vatican City, Italy

3.6.9d (top right) Michelangelo, detail of *Last Judgment* showing self-portrait in St. Bartholomew's skin, 1534–41. Sistine Chapel, Vatican City, Italy

3.6.9e (left) Michelangelo, detail of *Last Judgment* showing Minos, Judge of the Damned, 1534–41. Sistine Chapel, Vatican City, Italy

than twenty years later for Pope Clement VII (**3.6.9c**). The artist's muscular, dynamic figures on both the ceiling and the altar wall highlight Michelangelo's first love of sculpting the nude male body. After years of wishing he could be sculpting rather than painting, and of enduring frequent unsolicited advice regarding his compositions and choice of nude figures, Michelangelo painted the mask on St. Bartholomew's flayed skin within *The Last Judgment* as a self-portrait of the tortured artist who would have preferred his chisel and hammer (**3.6.9d**). Some scholars speculate that the location of Bartholomew (and Michelangelo's self-portrait) on the side of the damned is a cloaked reference to the artist's homosexuality because, at that time, the Catholic Church considered homosexuality a sin. The energetic, whirlpool effect of the judgment scene is much more chaotic and psychologically dark than many other Last Judgment scenes made by previous artists. The multitude of nude figures include saints (surrounding Christ), and the blessed and damned souls as they face their last moments on Earth (**3.6.9e**). The Pope's Master of Ceremonies, Biagio da Cesena, criticized the artist for the prolific nudity. Michelangelo responded by painting the official as King Minos, Judge of the Damned, with donkey ears and with a serpent wrapped and coiling around him.

Gateway to Art: Raphael, *The School of Athens*

Past and Present in the Painting

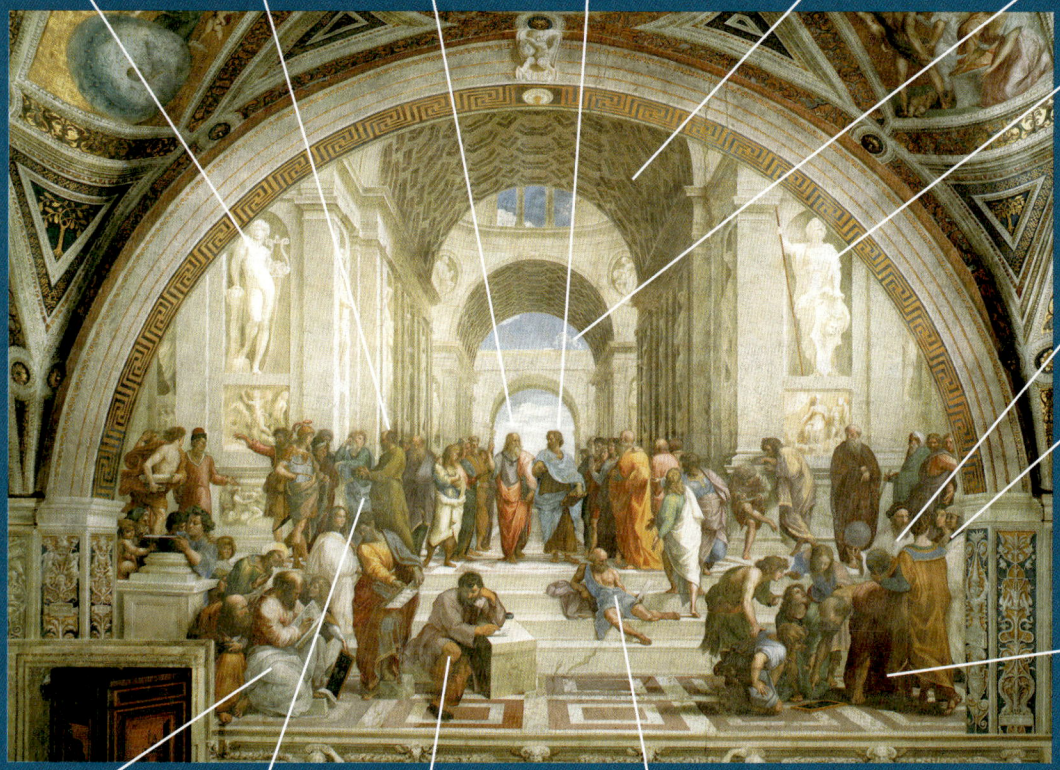

3.6.10 Raphael, *The School of Athens*, 1510–11. Fresco, 16′8″ × 25′. Stanza della Segnatura, Vatican City, Italy

For the other Raphael Gateway boxes, see p. 90, p. 146, p. 194, and p. 617

In *The School of Athens*, Raphael links a gathering of great philosophers and scientists from the Classical past—Plato, Aristotle, and Pythagoras, for example—to sixteenth-century Italy by using people he knew as models for the figures from ancient Greece and Rome. The two figures in the center combine spiritual and intangible thought, represented by Plato pointing toward the heavens, and the study of things observable in nature, represented by Aristotle, whose hand is open toward the ground. During the Renaissance, writings by Plato (*c.* 427–347 BCE) were combined with Christian doctrine to form a philosophy termed Neoplatonism. Renaissance humanists believed that individuals' achievements in the arts and sciences reflected the beauty of God.

By using the Renaissance painter Leonardo da Vinci (see pp. 468) as the model for the Greek philosopher Plato, Raphael expresses admiration for Leonardo's accomplishments. Using the face of Leonardo also allows us to see Plato in the flesh as a believable individual. Raphael pays homage to his contemporary Michelangelo, too, who is shown sitting by himself on the steps, in the guise of the pessimistic philosopher Heraclitus. This is a reflection of Michelangelo's solitary personality. Raphael subtly includes a self-portrait of himself

as the Greek painter Apelles in the group on the right listening to the mathematician and astronomer Ptolemy (holding a globe), showing himself to be a gregarious, intellectual person.

The thinkers on the left represent the Liberal Arts of grammar, arithmetic, and music, while those on the right are involved with the scientific pursuits of geometry and astronomy. The setting for this symposium is a grand Roman building with majestic **arches** and **vaults** that open up to the heavens. The Classical past is further invoked through the sculptures of Apollo (on our left) and Athena (on our right) in the niches behind the crowd. Despite its sixteenth-century references, the scene is utterly convincing, with calm, orderly groups of scholars and thinkers from throughout history gathered according to Raphael's carefully organized plan.

Arch: structure, usually curved, that spans an opening
Vault: an arch-like structure supporting a ceiling or roof

Mannerism: from Italian *di maniera*, meaning charm, grace, playfulness; mid- to late sixteenth-century style of painting, usually with elongated human figures elevating grace as an ideal
Dissonance: a lack of harmony
Deposition: a scene showing the removal of Christ's body from the cross

Late Renaissance and Mannerism

Pope Julius II's building campaign and patronage of the arts had helped make Rome the center of artistic and intellectual activity in Italy. The Sack of Rome by the troops of Charles V of Spain in 1527 happened as the high Renaissance came to a close, and forced many artists to flee the city. When Pope Clement VII, one of Julius's successors, humiliatingly had to crown Charles as Holy Roman Emperor in 1530, it was further evidence of the end of those days of supremacy and assuredness. The disorder of the period was reflected in its art.

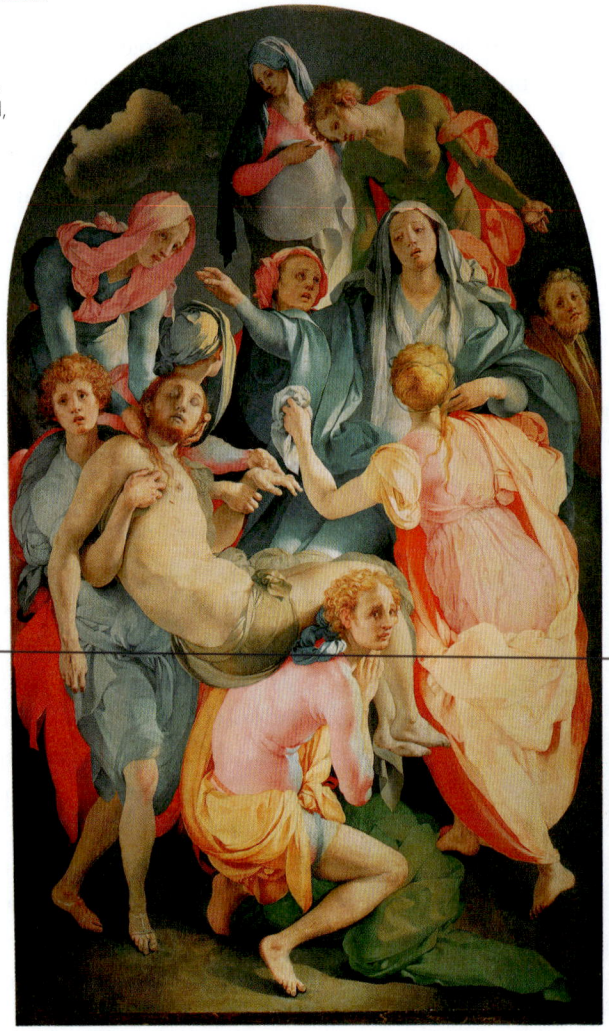

3.6.11 Jacopo da Pontormo, *Deposition*, 1525–28. Oil on wood, 10'3¼" × 6'3½". Capponi Chapel, Santa Felicita, Florence, Italy

Compared to the art that came before it, works in the late phase of the Renaissance are often depicted in a style called **Mannerism** (*c.* 1520–1600), which tends to feature compositions that are more chaotic, emphasize movement, and possess greater emotional intensity. The successes of the high Renaissance could not be rivaled: Leonardo, Raphael, and Michelangelo were thought to have achieved perfection in the arts. Artists were faced with the predicament of where to go from there. In reaction, instead of harmony, many artworks stressed **dissonance**. Distortion and disproportion were intentionally used to emphasize certain anatomical features and themes. Rather than mathematically precise depictions, artists created ambiguous spaces with multiple focal points.

In Jacopo da Pontormo's (1494–1556) Mannerist painting of the Deposition, the arrangement of the group of figures appears to be very unstable (**3.6.11**). Pontormo has stacked the figures vertically and placed them in an oddly swirling pattern, almost as if they are supported by the figure at the bottom of the composition, who is crouching unsteadily on tiptoe. Far from being a realistic depiction of observable reality, the figures are overly muscular and the colors are strikingly unnatural. We would expect to see grief and sorrow in a **deposition** scene,

3.6.12 El Greco, *Laocoön*, *c.* 1610/14. Oil on canvas, 54 × 68". National Gallery of Art, Washington, D.C.

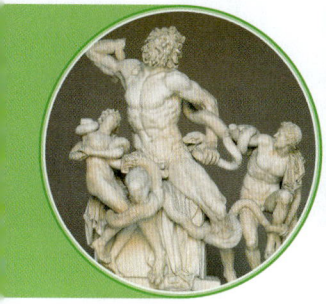

This sculpture of *Laocoön and His Sons* from ancient Greece would have been known to El Greco: see **3.1.30, p. 385**

Expressionistic: devoted to representing subjective emotions and experiences instead of objective or external reality

Outline: the outermost line or implied line of an object or figure, by which it is defined or bounded

but here the faces show expressions of loss and bewilderment. Everything contributes to an unsettling sense of disorder.

Another artist working in the Mannerist style, Domenikos Theotokopoulos (*c.* 1541–1614), called El Greco ("The Greek"), lived in Venice and Rome before moving to Spain. *Laocoön* is a subject from Greek mythology. The Trojan priest Laocoön attempted to warn the inhabitants of Troy that Greek soldiers were trying to infiltrate their fortifications by hiding inside the Trojan Horse, seen in the middle ground at the center of this painting. El Greco shows the priest and his sons being attacked by snakes sent by the god Poseidon (who supported the Greeks) to stop Laocoön's warning (**3.6.12**). The landscape in the background is a view of Toledo, Spain, where El Greco lived and made his best-known works late in his life. El Greco combined Mannerist exaggeration, seen in the elongated forms and distorted figures, with his own **expressionistic** use of color, **outlines**, and **modeling**. Like other Mannerist artworks, this intricate composition combines carefully observed factual information with mythological stories according to the dictates of the artist's imagination.

The Late Renaissance artist Sofonisba Anguissola (*c.* 1532–1625) achieved a level of success rarely enjoyed by women during this time. Known primarily for her portraits, she gained an international reputation that led to an official appointment at the court of the Queen of Spain. Anguissola emphasized emotion and heightened the realism in her artworks. *Portrait of the Artist's Sisters Playing Chess* (**3.6.13**) shows an everyday scene in the outdoors, as indicated

3.6.13 Sofonisba Anguissola, *Portrait of the Artist's Sisters Playing Chess*, 1555. Oil on canvas, 28¼ × 38¼". National Museum, Poznań, Poland

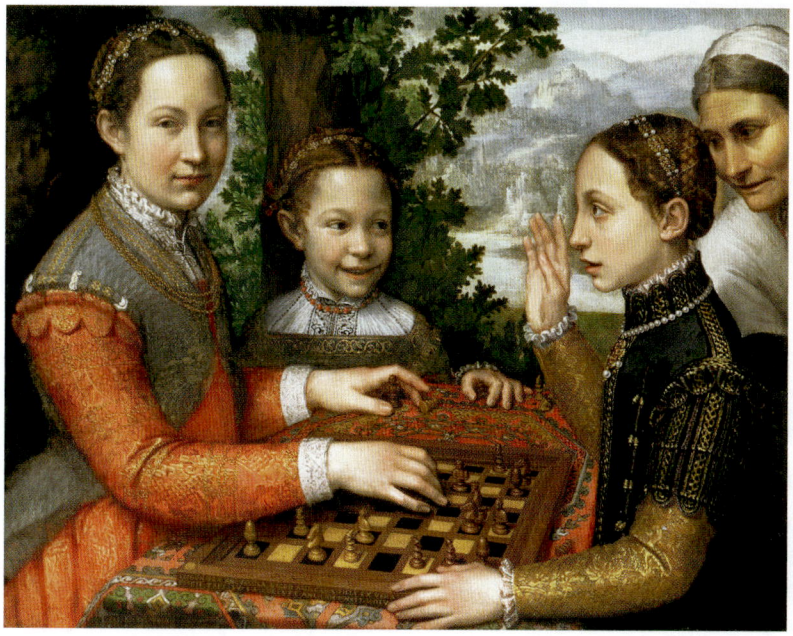

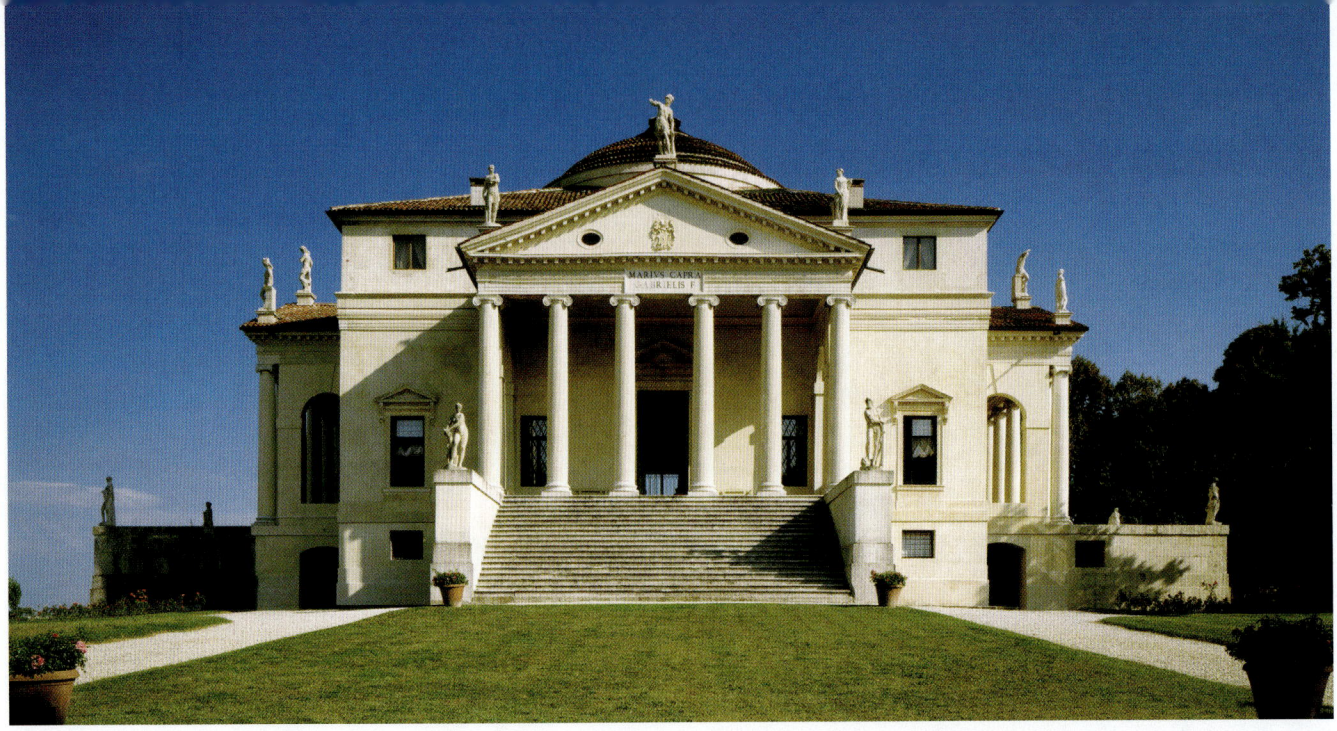

3.6.14a (above) Andrea Palladio, Villa Rotonda, Vicenza, Italy. Completed after 1580 by Vincenzo Scamozzi

3.6.14b (right) Andrea Palladio, plan and part elevation/section of the Villa Rotonda

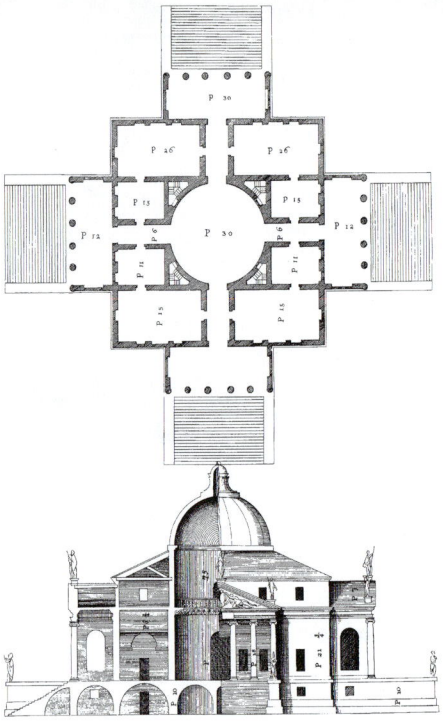

Modeling: the representation of three-dimensional objects in two dimensions so that they appear solid
Column: freestanding pillar, usually circular in section
Pediment: the triangular space, situated above the row of columns, on the facade of a building in the Classical style
Hemispherical: having half the form of a spherical shape divided into identical, symmetrical parts
Facade: any side of a building, usually the front or entrance
Symmetrical balance: an image or shape that looks exactly (or nearly exactly) the same on both sides when cut in half
Proportion: the relationship in size between a work's individual parts and the whole

by the tree behind the girls and the landscape in the distance. Anguissola concentrates on the rich details of the textures of the girls' clothing, jewelry, and hair. Rather than focusing on creating a unified and mechanically precise scene, Anguissola has emphasized the individuality of each one of her sitters, from the expressions on their faces to the elegant placement of their fingers. As the older sisters play their game, the clear sense of joy in the youngest sister's face is balanced by the expression of the maid, who looks on with care and concern.

Like all Renaissance architects, the Italian architect Andrea Palladio (1508–1580) was influenced by Classical architecture and, in particular, the writings of the Roman architect Vitruvius. The Villa Rotonda (**3.6.14a** and **b**) shows Classical architectural features including **columns**, **pediments**, and a **hemispherical** dome. The bishop Paolo Almerico commissioned Palladio to build him this retirement home in the Venetian countryside. The hilltop location with panoramic views of this aristocratic refuge inspired Palladio. The building's plan consists of a square, made up of a number of rectangles and other symmetrical shapes, surrounding a circle in the center (see **3.6.14b**). This configuration creates a clear, balanced design that allows a visitor to look out from a central point in the circular courtyard toward four different views. In addition, people approaching the building would see four identical **facades** (see **3.6.14a**) each with a stately set of stairs topped by six columns that hold up a triangular pediment. The central plan and repeated facades create a building that expresses **symmetrical balance**, **proportion**, and clarity. Palladio's designs were tremendously influential in the design of churches and domestic architecture in sixteenth-century Italy and subsequently.

Protestant Reformation and Catholic Counter-Reformation: A Comparison through Last Suppers

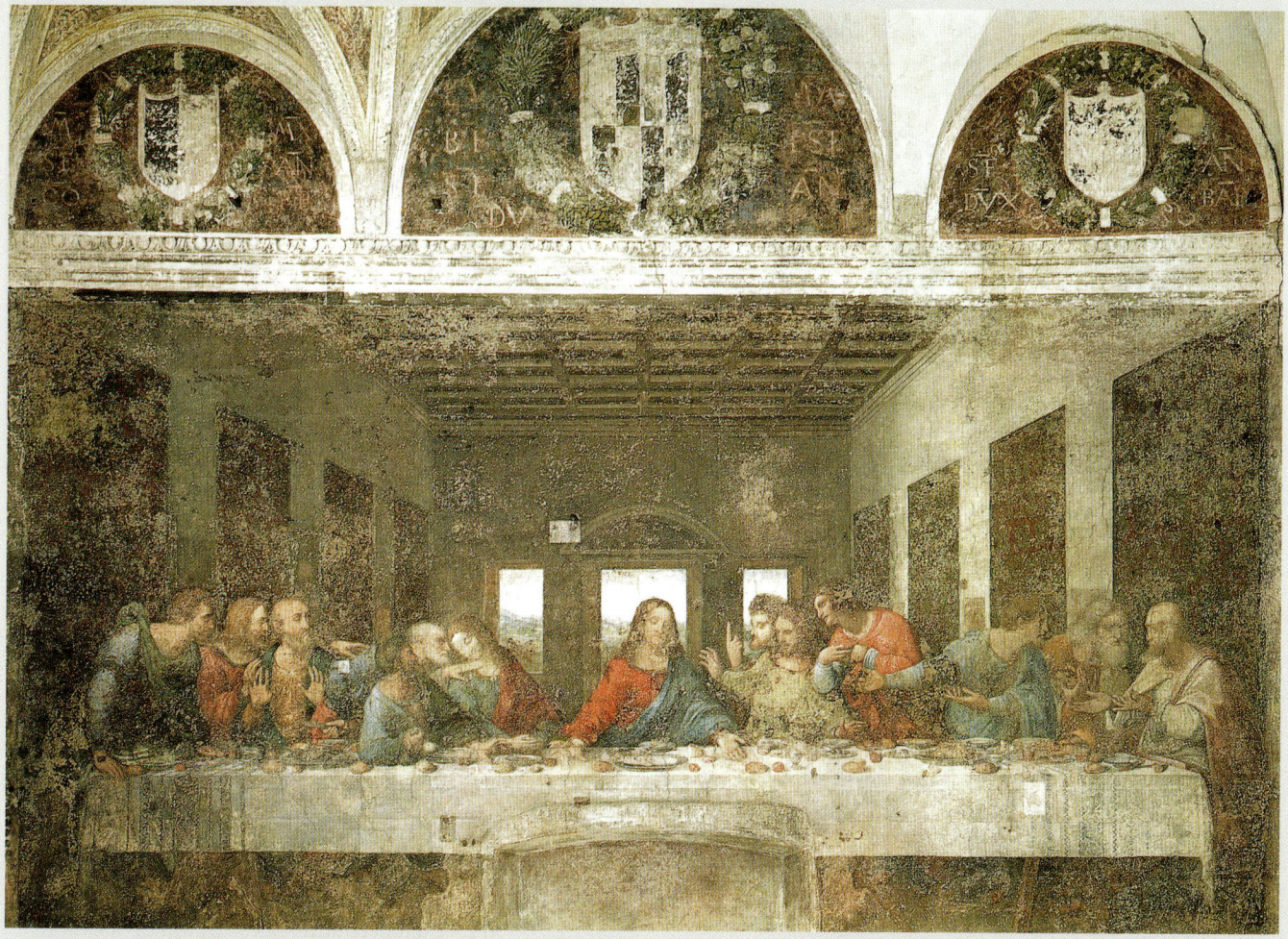

3.6.15 Leonardo da Vinci, *The Last Supper*, c. 1497. Fresco: tempera on plaster, 15'1" x 28'10½", Refectory of Santa Maria delle Grazie, Milan, Italy

Iconoclasm: the destruction of images or artworks, often out of religious belief
Medium (plural **media**): the material on or from which an artist chooses to make a work of art

The differences in beliefs between Catholicism and Protestantism were reflected in the art of the Renaissance and Baroque. Generally, Catholic artwork highlighted the power of intermediaries—such as saints and the Church—between Christians and God. Since the Catholic leadership was based in Rome, much of the artwork of the Italian Renaissance reflects Catholic doctrine. By contrast, in northern Europe, artworks inspired by Protestant beliefs were common. Protestantism was based on a more individual and direct relationship with God rather than one strictly guided by and through the Church.

The Reformation (beginning in 1517) resulted in Protestants breaking away from the Catholic Church and a period of Protestant **iconoclasm**. The Catholic Church's Counter-Reformation (1545–1648) was an attempt to define further the beliefs of Catholics in opposition to Protestants. In particular, the Council of Trent, active between 1545 and 1563, regulated the types of subjects that could be depicted in Catholic art, and the way in which they should be portrayed.

One can see how these differing beliefs played out in art by comparing scenes of the religious subject of the Last Supper, painted across a period of almost one hundred years.

In Leonardo da Vinci's *Last Supper*, the best-known depiction of Christ sharing a last meal with his disciples before his crucifixion, the artist used an experimental mixture of **media** (**3.6.15**), which is why it survives in poor condition today. Leonardo was commissioned by Dominican friars to paint *The Last Supper* for their dining hall in the

monastery of Santa Maria delle Grazie in Milan, Italy. In this masterpiece, Christ is emphasized as the most important figure in four ways. First, he is depicted in the center of the painting. Second, he is shown as a stable, triangular form, in contrast with the agitated activity of the other figures. Third, his head is framed by the natural light of the middle of the three windows behind him. Finally, Leonardo arranged the linear perspective of this painting so that the vanishing point is directly behind Christ's head.

This work is not simply a representation of a meal, however, for Leonardo highlights two important aspects of religious doctrine related to this event: the Eucharist, or communion ceremony, and the betrayal of Judas. Here Leonardo portrays the tradition accepted by Catholics, who believe that the communion bread and wine are the body and blood of Christ. The artist also invites the viewer to locate Judas: by depicting the moment when Christ has just announced, "One of you is about to betray me" (Matthew 26:21), Leonardo shows, through gesture and facial expression, the individual reaction of each of the disciples. Judas has his elbow on the table and is in the group of three to Christ's right (our left). The betrayer clutches a money bag in his right hand and has just knocked down a salt dish, which is a bad omen.

A quarter of a century after Leonardo's famous painting, the **woodblock** print of the same subject made by the German artist Albrecht Dürer (1471–1528) offers a different interpretation of the subject. Dürer was a talented draftsman and one of the first painters to work seriously on woodcuts, etchings, engravings, and printed books. Like Leonardo, Dürer draws attention to Christ in his composition by placing him centrally and surrounding his head with white light (**3.6.16**). Only eleven disciples are there; the absence of Judas tells us that he has already left to betray Jesus to the authorities. Dürer's print reflects the ideas of the Protestant Reformation and, in particular, the doctrine of the Lutheran Church. While Lutherans accepted the communion ceremony, they insisted it was only a re-enactment of the Last Supper, not a literal receiving of Christ's body and blood. To emphasize this important doctrinal point, Dürer displays an empty plate in the foreground, signifying that the meal has already taken place. The still, quiet, and somewhat bare scene reflects the Protestant contemplative practice of direct connection with Jesus. Rather than being created →

Woodblock: a relief print process where the image is carved into a block of wood

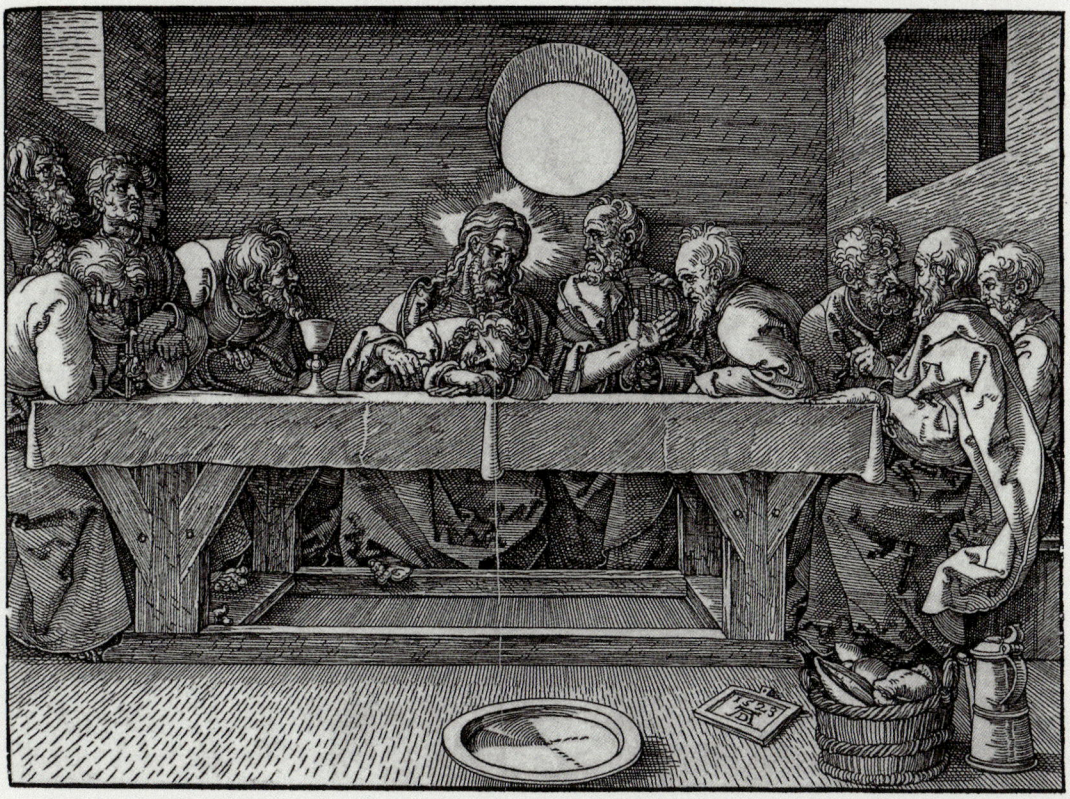

3.6.16 Albrecht Dürer, *The Last Supper*, 1523. Woodcut, 8½ × 11". British Museum, London, England

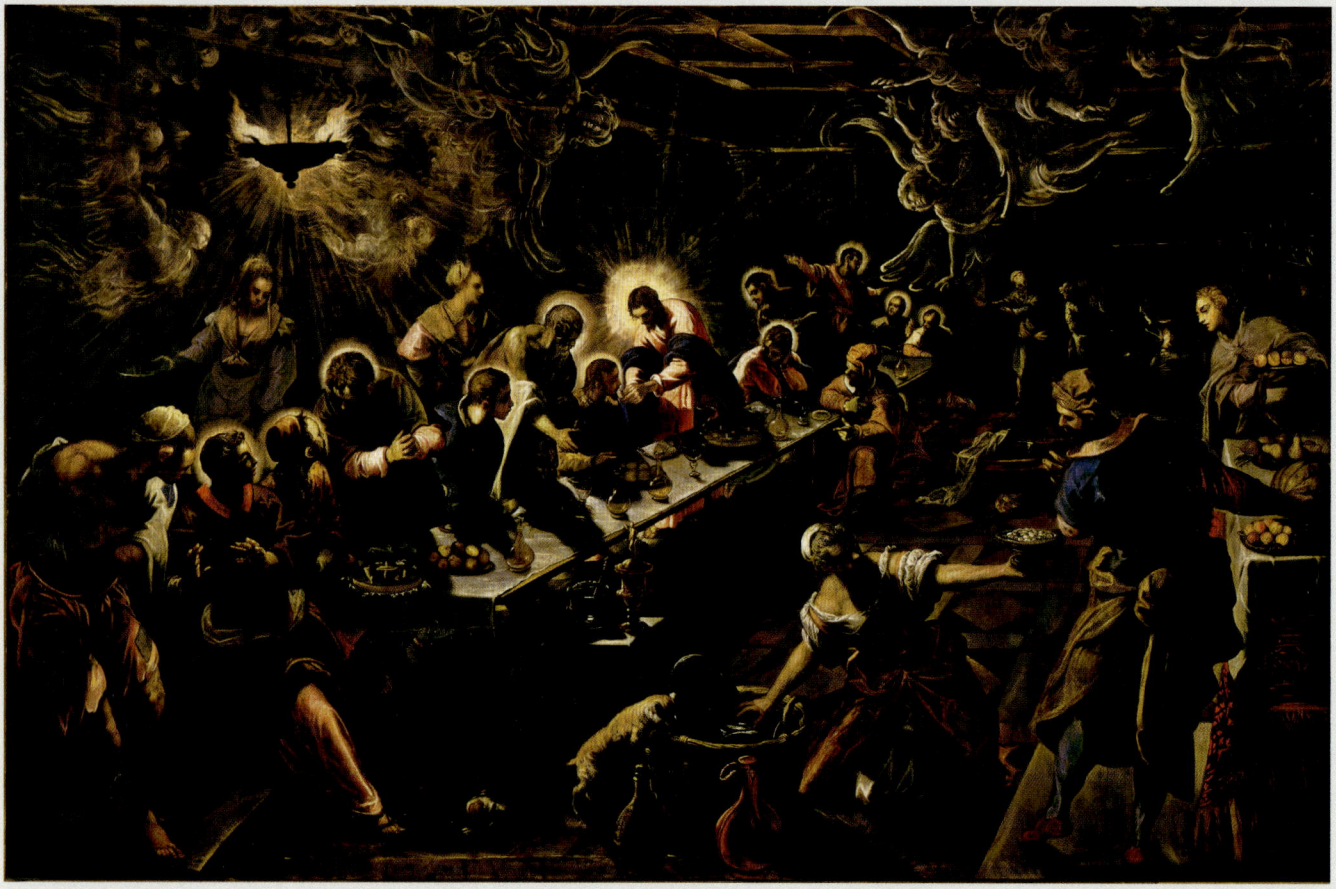

3.6.17 Tintoretto, *The Last Supper*, 1592–94. Oil on canvas, 11'11¾" × 18'½". San Giorgio Maggiore, Venice, Italy

for a religious space, this work is a print that individual believers could carry with them.

The surge of Protestantism at this time led in its turn to the Counter-Reformation, in which the Catholic Church influentials reasserted core Catholic values and enforced them through the Inquisition. Catholicism had long believed that images should be used as powerful teaching tools, and this belief now became more apparent in the art of the time. For example, the intensely dramatic quality of *The Last Supper* by the Venetian artist Tintoretto (1519–1594) highlights the urgency of the Catholic mission to encourage believers to remain in the Church rather than converting to Protestantism (**3.6.17**). Tintoretto depicts the Last Supper as a glorious and spiritual event. There are many ordinary people busy in service and discussion—we can almost hear the buzz of conversation and clatter of dishes. At the same time, the heavens seem to be opening up to send down angels, depicted as otherworldly, turbulent figures, twisting through the darkness overhead, to witness the event.

This scene is a marked change from the **symmetry** and emotional **balance** of both Leonardo's and Dürer's versions. Tintoretto still makes Christ the focal point by placing him in the center with the largest and brightest halo, reaching out with a glass to one of the disciples; Judas is easy to find, too, alone without a halo on the opposite side of the table from Jesus. But Tintoretto's picture conveys a dynamic—even disturbed—sense of motion and drama, with the table placed at an angle pointing off-center deep into space, dramatic contrasts of lighting, and the theatrical gestures of the characters. The combination of the domestic, earthly setting with the hovering, shadowy angels above hints at the imminent spiritual crisis that is about to occur when Judas, tempted by the worldly offer of money, will betray Jesus and cause his death.

Symmetry: the correspondence in size, form, and arrangement of items on opposite sides of a plane, line, or point that creates direct visual balance
Balance: a principle of art in which elements are used to create a symmetrical or asymmetrical sense of visual weight in an artwork

Italian Baroque

The Baroque period was a time of exploration, increased trade, and discovery in the sciences. The Western world now accepted the theory of astronomer Nicolaus Copernicus that the Sun, rather than the Earth, was the center of the universe—a theory the Catholic Church had previously rejected. Light, both heavenly and otherwise, became a prominent feature in many Baroque artworks. The seventeenth century was also a time of battles throughout Europe, largely the result of the divisions in the Catholic Church after the Reformation (see Box: Protestant Reformation and Catholic Counter-Reformation: A Comparison through Last Suppers). Baroque artworks give us a sense of this turmoil: their theatrical, dynamic compositions feature movement and light, and both visually and physically invade the space of the viewer. The painter Caravaggio and the sculptor and architect Gianlorenzo Bernini, who both created intensely emotional and dramatic scenes, are regarded as the masters of the Baroque period (see Gateway Box: Gentileschi, p. 478; and Box: Depictions of David, p. 480;).

Baroque painters selected subjects with high emotional impact. One such is the story of Susannah and the Elders, a biblical story in which the young wife Susannah is spied upon by two lascivious men while she bathes in her garden. The older men threaten to spread a rumor that she is an adulteress if she does not agree to sleep with them. Guido Reni paints this highly dramatic moment in the story (**3.6.18**), in which the vulnerable Susannah is caught off guard by the lecherous men, one of whom is grabbing at her clothing as he gestures for her silence, while the other places his hand on her left shoulder. One can see the influence of Caravaggio in this work in the way that **tenebrism** is used for ultimate dramatic effect. The background is shrouded in darkness, whereas Susannah's pale skin appears

Tenebrism: dramatic use of intense darkness and light to heighten the impact of a painting

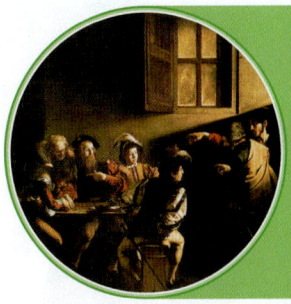

Caravaggio's use of tenebrism was imitated by artists throughout the Baroque period: see **1.3.6, p. 79**

3.6.18 Guido Reni, *Susannah and the Elders*, 1620–25. Oil on canvas, 45 × 59¼". National Gallery, London, England

Gateway to Art: Gentileschi, Judith Decapitating Holofernes

The Influence of Caravaggio

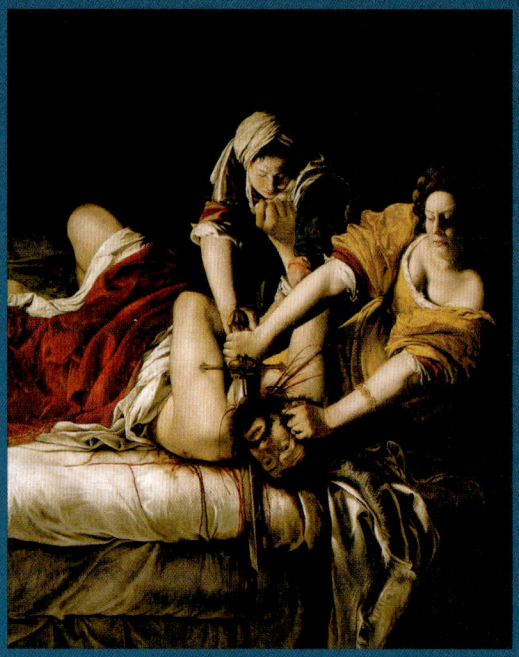

3.6.19 Artemisia Gentileschi, *Judith Decapitating Holofernes*, c. 1620. Oil on canvas, 6'6⅜" × 5'3¾". Uffizi Gallery, Florence, Italy

Along with many other artists in Europe in the seventeenth century, Artemisia Gentileschi (1593–c. 1656) imitated the artistic style of Italian artist Caravaggio (1571–1610). In addition to being an accomplished painter, Caravaggio led a tumultuous existence. By the time he was in his late twenties, his innovative approach to painting had earned him an impressive reputation and he was receiving Church commissions. At the same time, he was involved in brawls; he eventually killed a man in a fight over a tennis match. While on the run from these charges, he died of unknown causes at the age of thirty-nine.

Caravaggio's paintings, although often of religious stories, look like everyday **genre** scenes, filled with people from the lower classes, shown unidealized and wearing unkempt clothes. This naturalistic, down-to-earth approach offended some viewers who believed religious figures in artworks should be presented as idealized individuals to signify their holiness. Caravaggio's talent, however, was also greatly appreciated by many art lovers and patrons. His development of tenebrism was adopted by other painters during his lifetime and by later artists as well.

In Caravaggio's *Judith Decapitating Holofernes* (**3.6.20**), a strong beam of light seems to stop time as Judith's knife slices through the general's neck. The light emphasizes the drama of this moment and shows the main characteristics of Caravaggio's style. The scene seems to emerge into the light from a darkened background with an effect similar to a modern spotlight. Because the background is so dark, the action takes place in a shallow, stage-like space, again reinforcing dramatic effect. The details Caravaggio has focused on, such as the seventeenth-century clothing, emphasize the ordinary aspects of this biblical event.

Artemisia Gentileschi's style was greatly influenced by Caravaggio's detailed realism and dramatic use of tenebrism. In their paintings of Judith decapitating Holofernes, both artists use extreme darks and lights for dramatic effect, emphasize the violence of the scene through spurting blood and blood-stained sheets, and show the female characters with a marked determination that was not typical at the time.

Gentileschi also infuses her Judith image with active physical strength on the part of the women in a way that allows the viewer to sense the sheer effort required to sever the brute's head. By contrast, Caravaggio's Judith, apart from having powerful forearms, appears quite delicate, and shocked at her deadly deed. Similarly, Caravaggio shows Judith's maidservant as an old woman who seems to take no active part in the murder; Gentileschi's servant, however, physically restrains the Assyrian general as Judith severs his head.

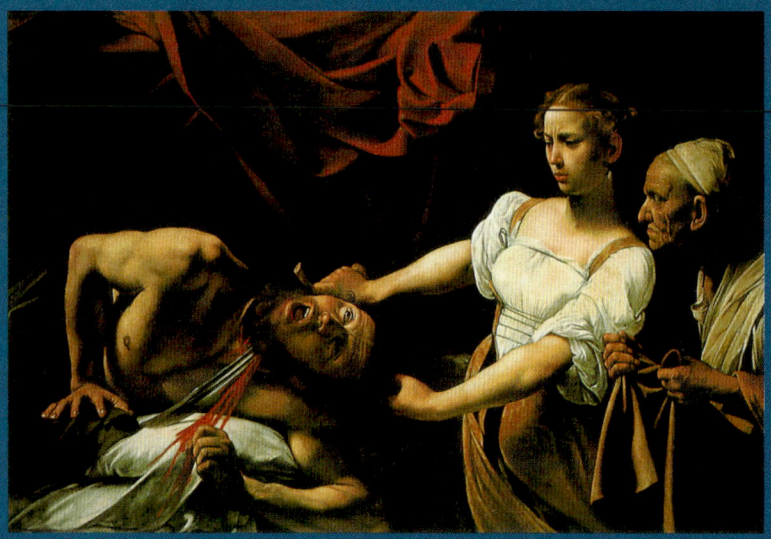

3.6.20 Caravaggio, *Judith Decapitating Holofernes*, 1599. Oil on canvas, 4'9" × 6'4¾". Galleria Nazionale d'Art Antica, Rome, Italy

For the other Gentileschi Gateway boxes, see p. 152, p. 219, p. 519, and p. 681

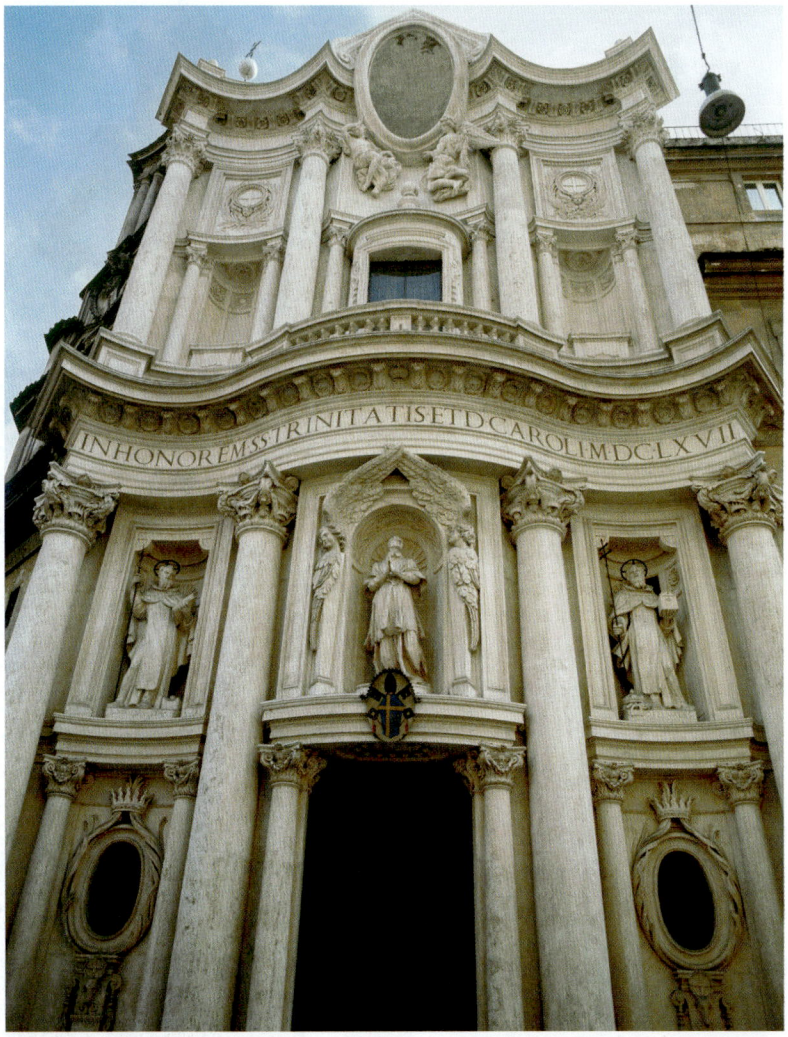

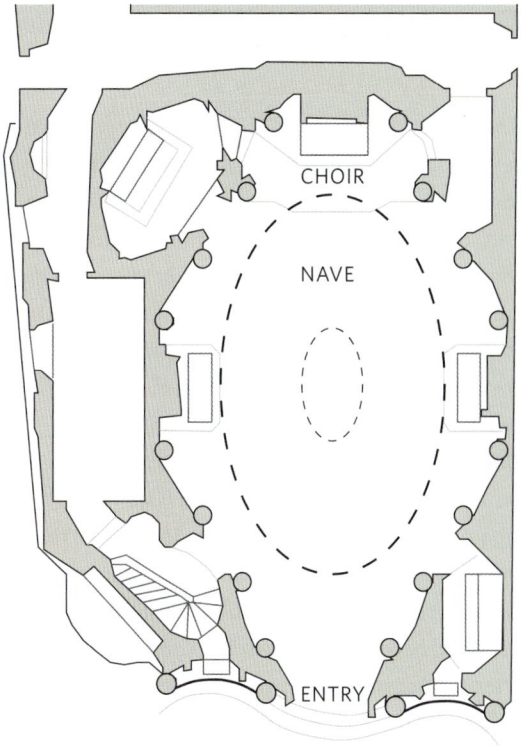

3.6.21b (above) Plan of the Church of San Carlo alle Quattro Fontane

3.6.21a Francesco Borromini, Church of San Carlo alle Quattro Fontane, Rome, Italy, 1638–46. Facade added *c.* 1677

in a spotlight. In the story, the men will try to discredit her reputation when Susannah rejects them, but her innocence will be proven.

During the seventeenth century, popes and powerful royal patrons commissioned numerous important buildings in Italy. Architecture at this time evolved so that, instead of the harmonious proportions and austere simplicity that were common in Renaissance designs, architectural works now incorporated much more ornate decorations and more complex forms. The result was that Baroque buildings became stages for dramatic expressions of the architect's art.

One example is the Baroque church of San Carlo alle Quattro Fontane (**3.6.21a** and **b**), in Rome, designed by Italian architect Francesco Borromini (1599–1677). Borromini, similarly to his Renaissance predecessors, incorporated **geometric** shapes into his design, but he did not aim to achieve the perfectly balanced symmetry of such buildings as Palladio's Villa Rotonda (**3.6.14b**, p. 473). Instead, this church takes on the qualities of a dramatic sculpture. At the center of the plan is an oval (see **3.6.21b**), which is less symmetrical than the flawless equilibrium of a central circle found at the heart of Renaissance designs. In the interior of the building, columns divide the walls into undulating spaces. The irregular shapes of the interior are echoed in the curving, wavelike walls of the facade (see **3.6.21a**). Because the walls are curving instead of flat, they create dramatic shadows. The surfaces and spaces of this church are typically Baroque in that they are very ornamental and spectacular. The complexity of this design influenced later Baroque architects. In addition to the new emphasis on opulence, light was emphasized both through the use of windows and in the imagery of painted frescoes in Baroque church interiors.

Genre: in painting, scenes that depict everyday life
Geometric: predictable and mathematical

Depictions of David

The biblical story of David and Goliath inspired three renowned Renaissance and Baroque sculptors in three centuries. Donatello, Michelangelo, and Bernini each took a different approach to the appearance of the hero, David. Each work displays the characteristic cultural and artistic concerns of their respective eras. In the Bible, David is a young Israelite who battles the giant Goliath. Goliath challenges the Israelites to send a champion to fight in single combat. Only David is brave enough to face him. Armed with just his shepherd's hook, slingshot, and a handful of stones, he fells Goliath with a single slingshot to the forehead and then uses the giant's own sword to cut off his head. David's triumph against a powerful opponent became an emblem for the city of Florence after its forces defeated a much stronger army from Milan in 1428. Our comparison of statues of David considers two sculptures made for Florence and one made in Rome.

Donatello (*c.*1386/87–1466) was a skilled sculptor of both bronze and marble. At the time he made *David*, he was reinvigorating the ancient technique of bronze casting. His *David*, the first nearly full-scale male nude since antiquity, also reflects the sculptor's familiarity with and admiration for the Classical ideal depictions of the human body (**3.6.22**). Rather than emphasizing the mortal and corruptible nature of the body, as was common during the Middle Ages, Donatello follows the idealized nude model used by Greek and Roman sculptors. His statue reveals the artist's careful observation of physical posture. David stands with his weight on his right leg, leaving the left leg relaxed, his left shoulder higher and his right lower as a result—a pose known as contrapposto. Donatello's understanding of human anatomy makes his *David* look mobile and lifelike.

Michelangelo's *David* was carved from a single block of marble (**3.6.23**). It was originally intended to be placed in a high niche of Florence Cathedral as a symbol of the city's power and (temporary) freedom from the tyranny of the Medici. The sculpture was so popular that on its completion in 1504 it was instead placed near the entrance to the main piazza, or plaza, where it could be viewed by masses of people. Its Classical attributes include athletic musculature and essentially ideal proportions. By presenting David as nude, with a scarcely noticeable slingshot over his shoulder—the only reference to his identity—Michelangelo creates a sculpture of a man as well as a hero. David's facial expression is idealized and calm, but his gaze, which is purposefully directed off to the side, reveals a mood of concentration and intensity.

Gianlorenzo Bernini (1598–1680) created his *David* in the Baroque period. It is a dynamic, three-dimensional sculpture that emphasizes movement and action (**3.6.24**). Whereas Donatello's sculpture shows David as triumphant and Michelangelo's sculpture shows him as contemplative, Bernini's shows David at a moment of dramatic, heightened tension, when he is about to launch the stone. The energy of David's entire body is focused on the physical movement he is about to make. Even the muscles

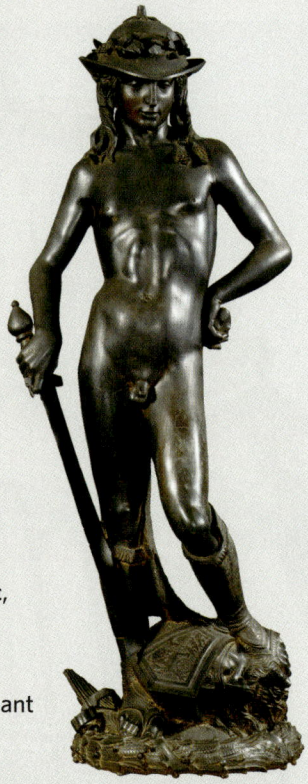

3.6.22 (above) Donatello, *David*, *c.*1430. Bronze, height 5'2¼". Museo Nazionale del Bargello, Florence, Italy

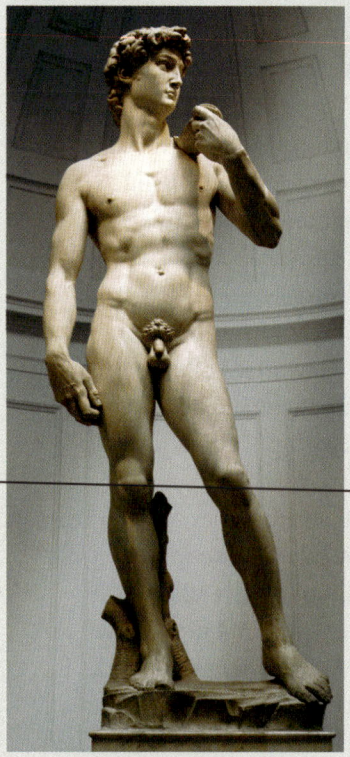

3.6.23 Michelangelo, *David*, 1501–4. Marble, height 14'2". Galleria dell'Accademia, Florence, Italy

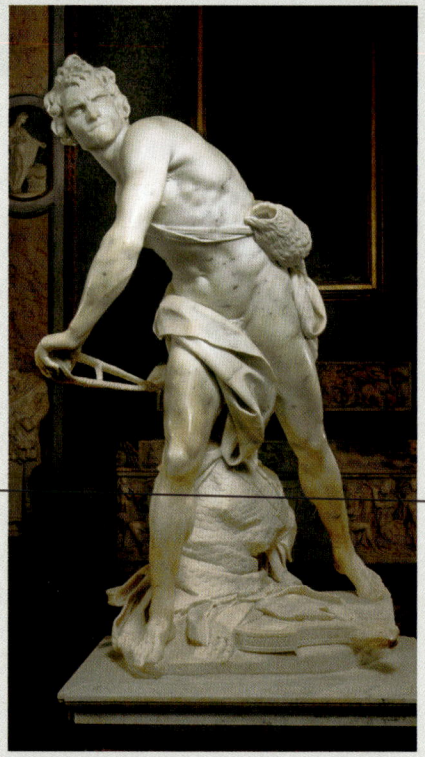

3.6.24 Gianlorenzo Bernini, *David*, 1623. Marble, height 5'7". Galleria Borghese, Rome, Italy

In the round: a freestanding sculpted work that can be viewed from all sides

in his face tighten. Bernini is said to have studied his own reflection to create the perfect facial expression for such an energetic feat. Unlike Michelangelo's and Donatello's sculptures, which are meant to be viewed from the front, Bernini's is intended to be seen and understood **in the round.**

These three sculptures are clearly different in several ways. Michelangelo's sculpture is more than twice the size of the other two, in order to allow viewers to see all of the detail had the sculpture been installed in its originally planned location, high above the ground. Donatello's sculpture is the only one to include weaponry other than a slingshot: his David holds the sword with which he has just beheaded his opponent, whose head lies at his feet. Bernini's sculpture, like Michelangelo's, features the slingshot, but it is in action, and a pile of cast-off armor lies beneath. Such a prop was necessary to allow for the wide stance and gesture of the figure, as marble sculptures are prone to snap if their weight is unsupported.

The moment each artist chose to depict has a strong influence on the resulting appearance and effect of their sculptures. Donatello shows a triumphant, boyish David standing in calm repose after the fight. Michelangelo presents David as an adult: the sheer size and mass of his form are much more man-like than Donatello's slim, youthful figure. Michelangelo's David stands poised at a moment of anticipation and determined contemplation before the battle; a concentrated expression is visible on his face. Bernini's David, more mature, is dynamically focused on casting a lethal strike at the giant Goliath—the time of calculation and reflection has passed; now it is time for action.

Religious stories were common subjects for artworks during the Renaissance and Baroque. These three artists' *David* sculptures show the stylistic characteristics of their time as well as their individual originality.

Northern Baroque

Baroque in northern Europe also included some of the characteristics, such as drama, a sense of grandeur, and use of intense light and darkness (tenebrism), that were common in Italy. Just as their Italian counterparts did, Northern Baroque artists utilized ways to include the viewer in the visual space of works of art. Northern Baroque painters also excelled at depictions of non-religious subject matter, such as landscapes, still lifes, genre scenes, or portrayals of people from their contemporary world.

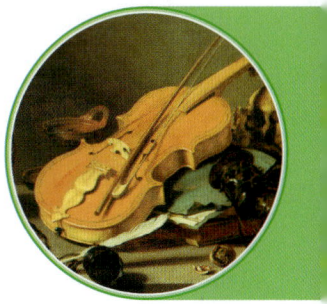

Still lifes during the Northern Baroque were executed with extraordinary attention to detail and symbolized the brevity of life: see **4.3.13, p. 600**

Peter Paul Rubens (1577–1640) produced about 2,000 paintings in his lifetime, an impressive output made possible because he operated a large workshop in Antwerp. His assistants were responsible for producing some of his paintings, but Rubens generally finished works for important clients himself. His *The Raising of the Cross* was one of several paintings commissioned by wealthy merchants to be installed in a church (**3.6.25**).

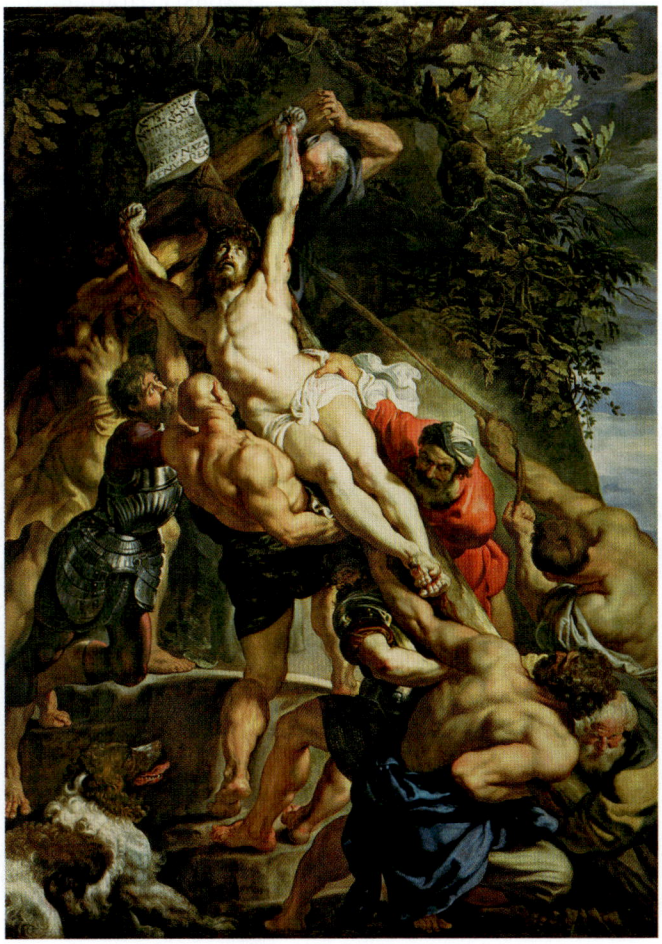

3.6.25 Peter Paul Rubens, center panel from *The Raising of the Cross* triptych, 1610–11. Oil on panel, 15'1" x 11'1½". Onze Lieve Vrouwkerk, Antwerp Cathedral, Belgium

In *The Raising of the Cross*, we can sense the physical exertions of these muscular men as they raise Christ on the cross. A dynamic tension is created along the diagonal line of the cross that visually connects the men at its base as they strain to pull Christ up toward the right side of the painting. The muscular arms and shoulders of the men holding the cross, in fact, project out toward the **picture plane** into the viewer's space. Although, in fact, Christ would have been tortured and close to death at this point, the artist has painted his flesh as almost immaculate, and lighter than that of those around him. In this way, and by bathing him in light, Rubens makes Christ the focal point and emphasizes his holiness.

Rembrandt Harmenszoon van Rijn (1606–1669) was an extremely popular painter who also had a large workshop at one point in his life. Yet, despite his impressive reputation, he filed for bankruptcy in old age. In *The Night Watch*, the gathering of officers and guardsmen likely commemorates a visit by Queen Marie de'Medici to Amsterdam in 1638 (**3.6.26**). The painting was commissioned by the civic militia, and scholars believe that all of those portrayed in this scene contributed financially to the artist's fee. *The Night Watch* is a fine example of Rembrandt's innovative approach to a group portrait. His painting is not only convincing but also full of the vitality and energy typical of a group getting ready for an important occasion. The various members of the company are shown busily organizing themselves. This painting came to be known as *The Night Watch* because its dark atmosphere made it look like a night scene. Rembrandt made skillful use of chiaroscuro, tenebrism, and dramatic lighting to enliven his composition, but the impression of night-time was actually created by years of accumulated dirt and layers of varnish. The painting was revealed to be a daytime scene when it was cleaned after World War II.

French artist Nicolas Poussin (1594–1665) specialized in paintings of subjects from Classical antiquity. Everything in his paintings was carefully constructed and positioned to create a sense of refined balance and order. He would even arrange miniature figures on a small

Picture plane: the transparent division between the space depicted by the artist and the real space in which the viewer is placed

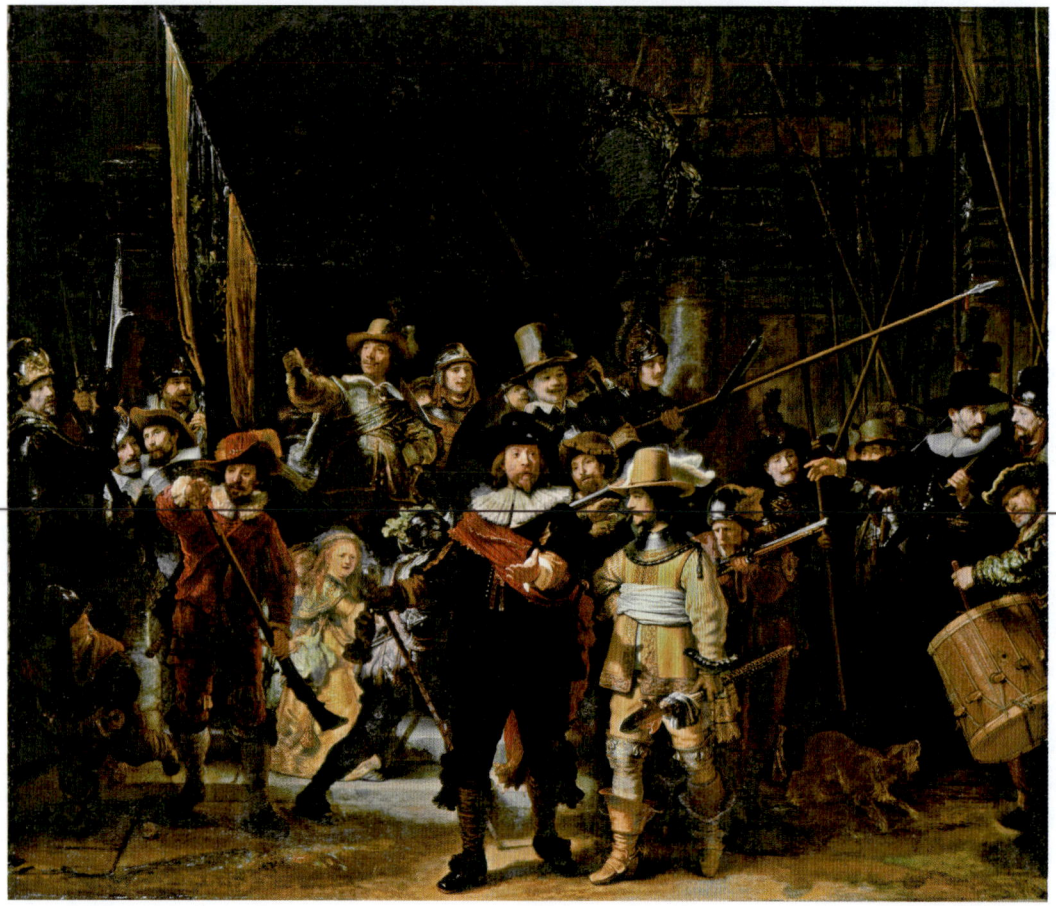

3.6.26 Rembrandt van Rijn, *The Company of Frans Banning Cocq and Willem van Ruytenburch (The Night Watch)*, 1642. Oil on canvas, 11'11" × 14'4". Rijksmuseum, Amsterdam, The Netherlands

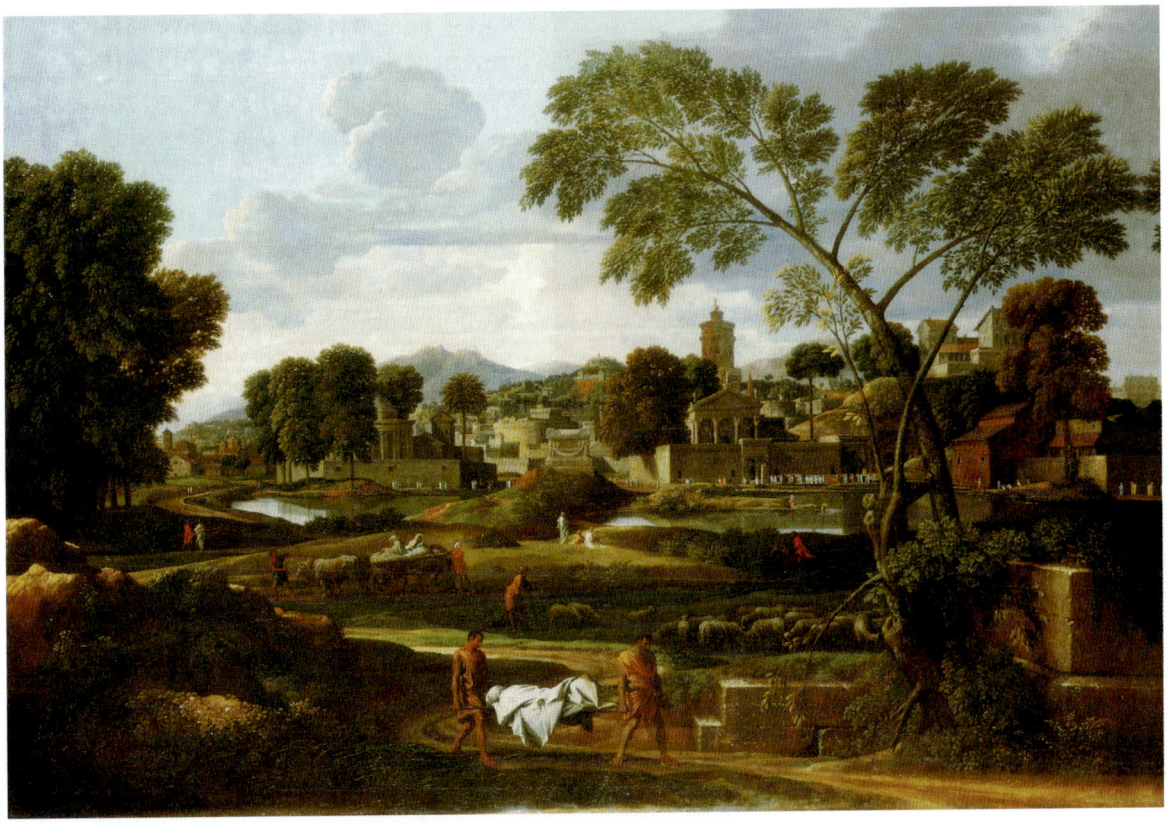

3.6.27 Nicolas Poussin, *The Funeral of Phocion*, 1648. Oil on canvas, 44 × 68". National Museum of Wales, Cardiff

stage when choreographing the scenes for his landscapes. Yet, though these and his Classical buildings look detailed and realistic, their appearance and placement were always invented from his imagination. *The Funeral of Phocion* depicts two men carrying the deceased Phocion, an Athenian general, over a winding road that leads away from the city (**3.6.27**). Phocion had been executed after being falsely accused of treason; because he was considered a traitor, he was buried outside the city.

Poussin's landscapes were designed to create a sense of depth, and often the Classical subject of the scene was secondary to this goal. The two figures carrying Phocion's body, covered with a white sheet, are prominently placed in the **foreground**. The large tree to the right arches over and creates an **implied line** from the pallbearers through the figures, trees, and buildings that gradually become smaller as they recede into space. The winding road both emphasizes the distance of Phocion's burial from the city and creates a sense of deep space, skillfully guiding our gaze into the landscape.

Through much of the seventeenth century, many northern European countries were governed by absolute monarchs—rulers who, it was believed, derived their power and authority from God. Some Baroque artworks of the time are evidence of the extreme wealth and frivolous attitude of these rulers. The extravagance of the monarchy in France was epitomized by King Louis XIV (1638–1715), whose grandiose view of himself and his role in the world demonstrated the power of the absolute monarch. Louis called himself the Sun King to associate himself with the Greek sun god Apollo, and to imply that the activities of France began when—like the sun—Louis arose in the morning, and stopped when he retired at night. The exaggerated self-regard, even pomposity, of the royal circle would eventually prove their downfall and lead to their demise by the end of the eighteenth century.

The regal portrait by Hyacinthe Rigaud (1659–1743) is meant to demonstrate the king's power (**3.6.28**, p. 484), and exudes the luxurious drama of the Baroque style. Louis is dressed in royal attire, with the gold fleur-de-lis (or "lily-flower," the symbol of the French monarchy) embroidered on a rich blue velvet gown, lined in expensive white fur known as ermine. Insisting

Foreground: the part of a work depicted as nearest to the viewer
Implied line: a line not actually drawn but suggested by the positions of elements in the work

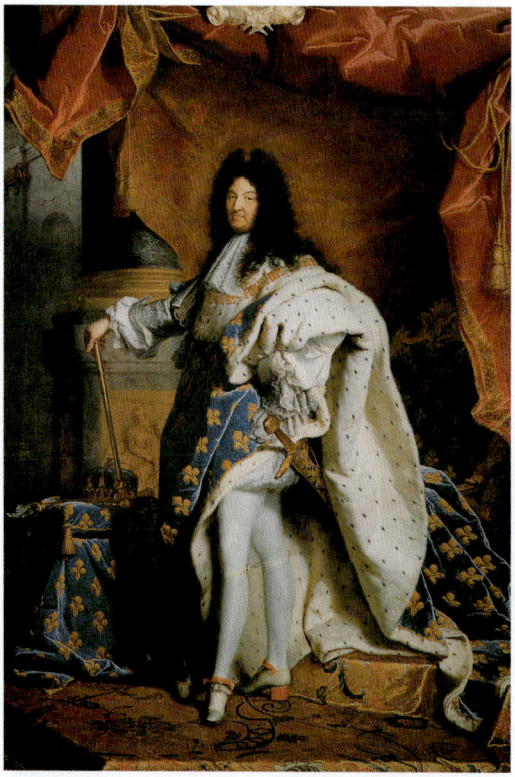

3.6.28 Hyacinthe Rigaud, *Louis XIV*, 1701. Oil on canvas, 9'1" × 6'4¾". Musée du Louvre, Paris, France

on the finest of everything, Louis XIV dressed in the most opulent textiles from around the world. He invented the high heels shown here, which he used to increase his height (5 ft. 4 in.) and to show off his trim legs. This painting was made when the monarch was in fact in his sixties.

It was common practice for painters to depict royal figures in the best light, often portraying them decades younger than they actually were.

In this portrait, the Sun King stands at the entrance to the famed Baroque Hall of Mirrors (**3.6.29**), an opulent chamber filled with mirrors (highly expensive at the time) that reflect the gardens surrounding his grand new palace of Versailles, near Paris. Louis XIV was a great patron of the arts, and had commissioned the finest artists in Europe to construct and decorate Versailles to be the largest and finest palace in the world. The Hall of Mirrors was used for greeting dignitaries, for formal celebrations, and as a ballroom. The 239-foot-long hallway is lavishly decorated with gilding, chandeliers, sculpture, and paintings depicting scenes of Louis XIV's political successes. The bright light that fills the room and is reflected in the numerous mirrors is not only a characteristic of the Baroque period, but also symbolizes Louis's identity and power as the Sun King. One of Louis XIV's greatest contributions to the art world was his development of a French art academy (1648), based on those in Italy, which would define much of the art produced in the following centuries.

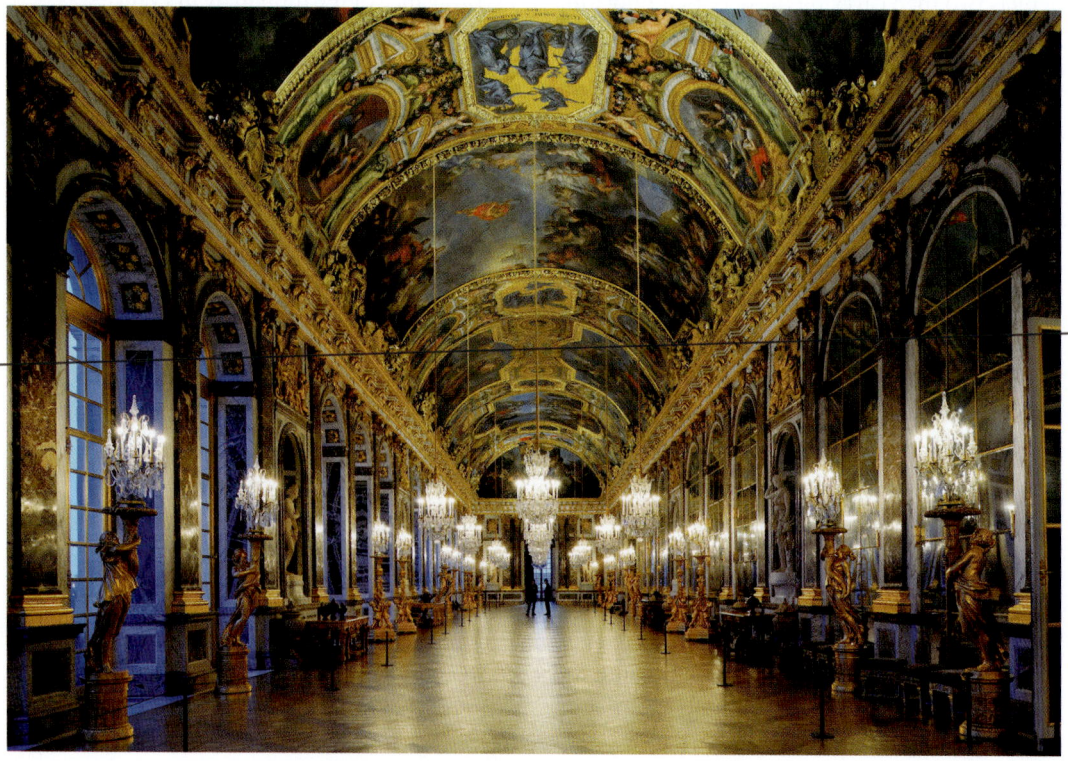

3.6.29 Jules Hardouin-Mansart, Château de Versailles, Hall of Mirrors (Galerie des Glaces) 1678–84, Versailles, France

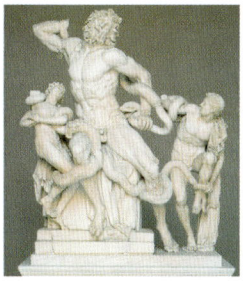

3.1.30 *Laocoön and His Sons*, Hellenistic Greece, 150 BCE, p. 385

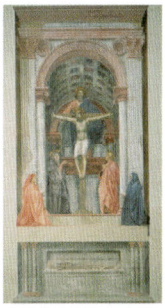

1.3.20 Masaccio, *Trinity*, c. 1425–26 , p. 89

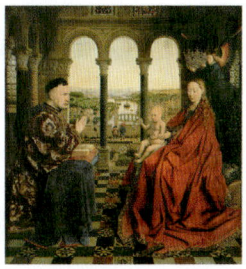

2.2.12 Jan van Eyck, *The Madonna of Chancellor Rolin*, 1430–34, p. 216

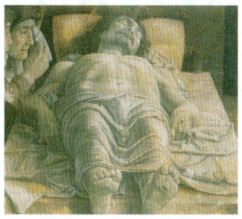

4.3.3 Andrea Mantegna, *Dead Christ*, c. 1480, p. 593

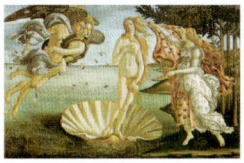

4.9.5 Sandro Botticelli, *The Birth of Venus*, c. 1482–86, p. 666

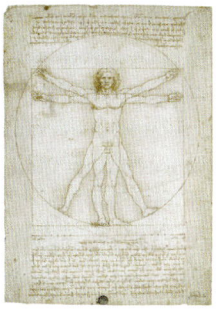

4.4.1 Leonardo da Vinci, *Vitruvian Man*, c. 1490, p. 603

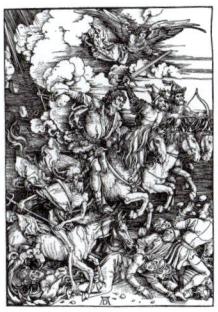

2.3.2 Albrecht Dürer, "The Four Horsemen," 1498, p. 227

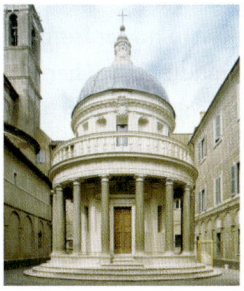

2.5.25 Donato Bramante, Tempietto, San Pietro in Montorio, Italy, c. 1502, p. 273

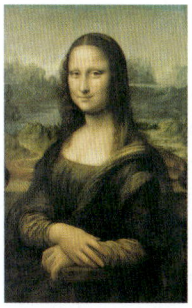

0.0.12 Leonardo da Vinci, *Mona Lisa*, c. 1503–6, p. 28

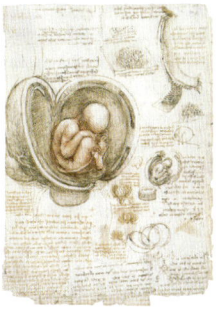

2.1.2 Leonardo da Vinci, *Studies of the fetus in the womb*, c. 1510–13, p. 193

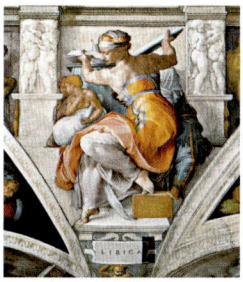

2.2.6 Michelangelo, *The Libyan Sibyl*, 1511–12, p. 212

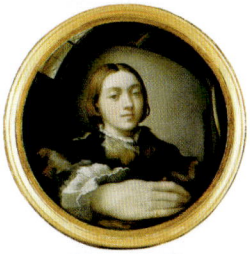

4.5.2 Parmigianino, *Self-Portrait in a Convex Mirror*, c. 1524, p. 616

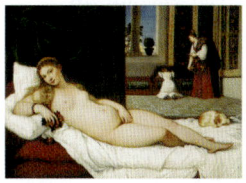

4.9.8 Titian, *Venus of Urbino*, 1538, p. 668

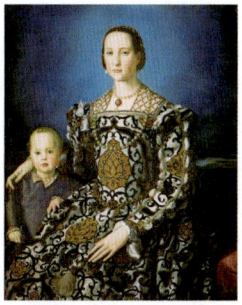

0.0.4 Agnolo Bronzino, *Eleonora of Toledo and Her Son, Giovanni*, c. 1545, p. 23

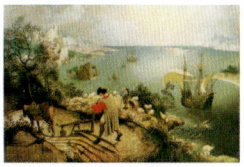

1.8.7 Pieter Bruegel the Elder, *Landscape with the Fall of Icarus*, c. 1555–58, p. 155

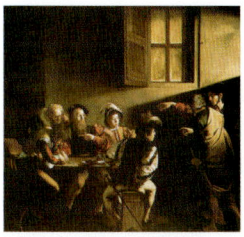

1.3.6 Caravaggio, *The Calling of St. Matthew*, c. 1599–1600, p. 79

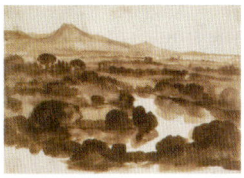

2.1.18 Claude Lorrain, *The Tiber from Monte Mario Looking South*, 1640, p. 203

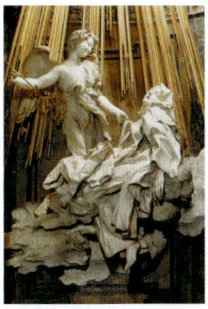

4.2.9 Gianlorenzo Bernini, *The Ecstasy of St. Teresa*, 1647–52, p. 583

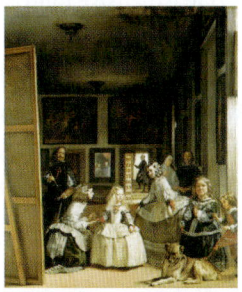

1.10.12a Diego de Silva y Velázquez, *Las Meninas*, c. 1656, p. 183

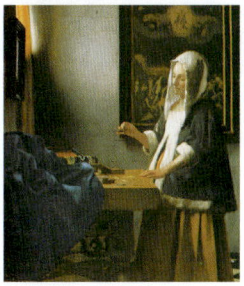

4.2.12 Johannes Vermeer, *Woman Holding a Balance*, c. 1664, p. 585

3.7 Art of Europe and America (1700–1865): Rococo to Romanticism

Enlightenment: historical period, also called the Age of Reason, in which reason was prized above faith, liberty above oppression, and there was a movement to secure equal rights for all men

The eighteenth and nineteenth centuries in Europe are characterized by concerns about social equality, and a transition in power from the wealthy to the growing middle class. There was resentment against the absolute monarchs who believed that they derived their authority from God and inflicted their will on the people of both their own countries and their colonies. Thus this period is often called an Age of Revolutions, beginning with the American Declaration of Independence in 1776. There were three revolutions in France during this period (1789, 1830, and 1848), all of which called for government by and for the people and equality for the lower classes, and all of which inspired revolutions elsewhere in Europe. At the same time, the Industrial Revolution, instigated by advancements in technology, began in Britain and spread throughout Europe, creating a shift from agrarian societies to more urban ones offering new working opportunities for the majority of people. Within Europe, the development of the telegraph in the 1830s allowed for ever-quickening communication, and the invention of the steam engine in 1869 led to expansive railroads, enabling more people to travel greater distances faster. Europe and America therefore became more aware of the world at large. As a result of all of these factors, as well as through colonization and trade, the Western art world was influenced by other cultures.

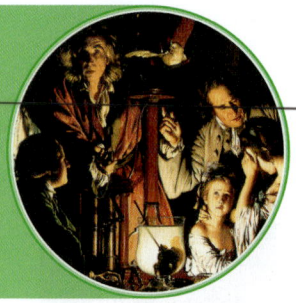

Artists often used light during the Enlightenment to symbolize reason, as in this painting of a scientific experiment: see **4.4.2, p. 604**

This was an age also known as the **Enlightenment**, sometimes called the Age of Reason. Enlightenment thinkers called for reason over faith, liberty over oppressive systems of government, and equal rights for all men. The English philosopher John Locke promoted a theory of empiricism, according to which humans are born with minds (blank slates) that are influenced by their experiences, rather than being innately functioning. This notion had significant ramifications, particularly in regard to education and the impact of social experience on individuals.

In his treatise called *The Social Contract* (1762), the writer and political theorist Jean-Jacques Rousseau (1712–1778) states that, "Man is born free, and everywhere he is in chains." Influenced by the ideas of John Locke, Rousseau believed that society should be governed by the consent and involvement of all the people. For this kind of community to work, Rousseau argues, society must support equal rights and education.

Artworks of this time both reflect and promote contemporary changes in economics, politics, and personal expression. While art historians have determined stylistic tendencies, it is important to note that the various styles in this period often overlapped; that is, each style did not strictly follow another chronologically. At times, artworks possess qualities of more than one style, or will not seem to fit easily into any single category. This complexity reflects the richness of ideas that were being exchanged in the eighteenth century and the first half of the nineteenth century.

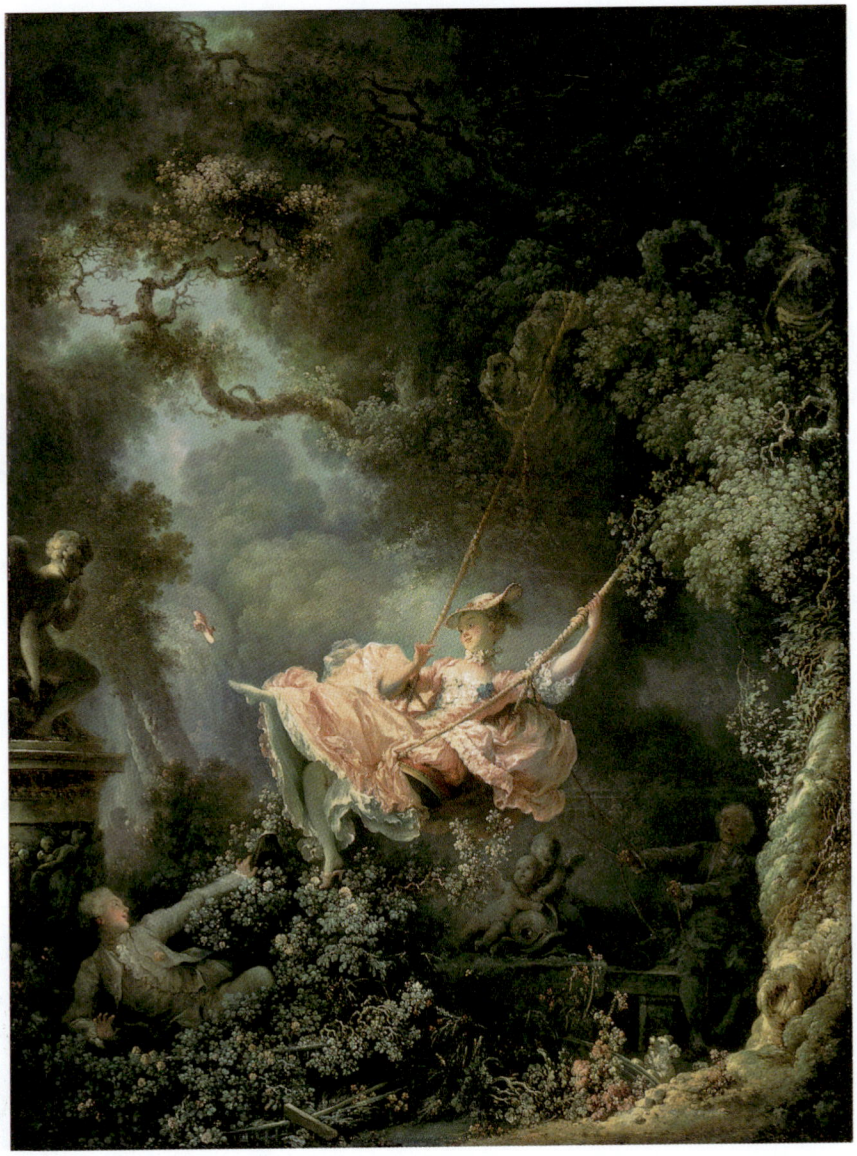

3.7.1 Jean-Honoré Fragonard, *The Swing*, 1766. Oil on canvas, 32 × 25¼". Wallace Collection, London, England

Rococo: an eighteenth-century style in France characterized by organic forms, ornate extravagance, and whimsy
Baroque: European artistic and architectural style of the late sixteenth to the early eighteenth century, characterized by extravagance, movement, and emotional intensity
Subject (subject matter): the person, object, or space depicted in a work of art
Organic: having irregular forms and shapes, as though derived from living organisms
Patron: an organization or individual who sponsors the creation of works of art

Rococo

The undisputed power of the European ruling classes during the seventeenth and much of the eighteenth century inspired a period of extravagance amongst the very wealthy. Desiring the finest in everything, the ruling classes financed endless commissions of artworks in a style known as the **Rococo**. Stylistically, in its abundance of rich decoration, the Rococo is an outgrowth of the **Baroque**, but while the Baroque's **subject matter** was very formal and moralistic, the Rococo's was more whimsical. Rococo artworks tend to be lighthearted, indulgent, and even somewhat superficial, featuring elaborately curved lines and **organic** forms.

Rococo paintings were usually commissioned by the aristocracy and are playful in mood, often with erotic undertones. The delicate brushstrokes and pastel colors create a sense of lightness and ease, and the frequently frivolous subject matter suggests that those who commissioned such artworks had ample time to amuse themselves.

At first sight, *The Swing*, by Jean-Honoré Fragonard (1732–1806), appears to be an innocent scene of a refined young lady enjoying her swinging (**3.7.1**). Upon closer inspection, however, we see that the woman has flirtatiously kicked her shoe into the air, which allows the "gentleman" (thought by some to be the **patron** of this painting) in the bushes below a view up her skirt. In a statue on the left side of the canvas,

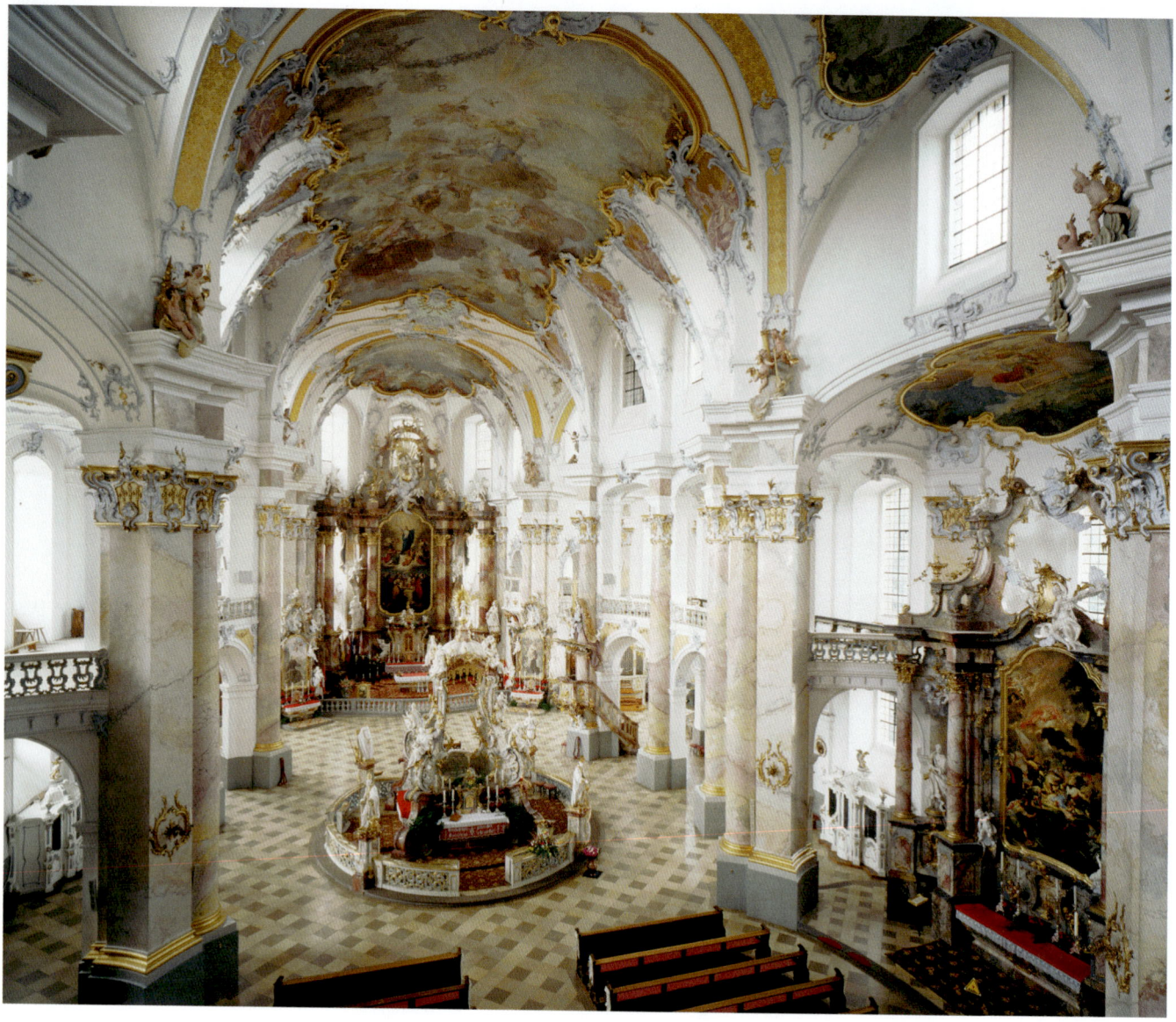

3.7.2 Johann Balthasar Neumann, Basilica of Vierzehnheiligen, 1743–72, near Bamberg, Germany

Cupid puts his finger to his lips, suggesting a secret love tryst between the young couple. The feathery brushstrokes, pastel colors, abundance of delicate greenery, and soft plumes of clouds support the romantic and trivial nature of the subject matter. A bishop, standing in the shadows in the lower right-hand part of the canvas, holds a rope that controls the swing, and he appears to be completely unaware of the couple's mischievous behavior. The artist's inclusion of this figure has been interpreted by some as a comment on the Church's ignorance of immoral behavior, and by others as a chiding of the Catholic Church for not condemning such conduct.

Rococo palaces and churches throughout Europe also convey the desire of the time that art should stimulate the eyes with pleasure. The German architect Johann Balthasar Neumann (1687–1753) built churches with predominantly bright white interiors, as if to reflect Germany's glistening winter snow. The Basilica of Vierzehnheiligen ("Fourteen Holy Ones") near Bamberg, in Bavaria, southern Germany, has fourteen statues around the altar, depicting Catholic saints; believers pray to the saints for protection against sickness. These saints are venerated in this region for the help they are thought to have given during the severe suffering caused by the Black Plague centuries before. Although this is a place of worship, there is constant interest and vivacity in the organic forms and ornate decoration of the church's brightly lit interior. From the subtle pink and yellow in the columns, to the paintings on the recesses in the ceilings, to the gilded touches throughout, rich detail creates a luxurious and fanciful space (**3.7.2**).

Rejecting the Rococo: Sentimentality in Painting

The Rococo's lighthearted subject matter did not appeal to all eighteenth-century artists: some were interested instead in creating art with moral messages that often pulled on the heartstrings of the audience. Jean-Baptiste Greuze (1725–1805) was known for his images that **idealized** the virtue of the simple life of the lower classes. In *The Marriage Contract* a young loving couple, whose arms are intertwined, is about to be married (**3.7.3**). A notary on the right documents the formal agreement. The bride's humble father has just given the young man her dowry, and the members of her family are crying over how much they will miss her. The scene emphasizes the rustic surroundings of the family, highlighting their lack of financial wealth and suggesting that the poor are closer to nature. The family's situation is echoed by the hen feeding her chicks in the lower portion of the canvas. One chick goes off to the right to sit upon a saucer, just as the young bride is about to go off to start her own family. While the family is financially poor, it is rich in love. The simplicity and purity of the setting and the people contrast with the frivolous materialism of the Rococo.

The works of British painter and **engraver** William Hogarth (1697–1764) were also a reaction to the aristocratic classes of the Rococo era. Hogarth's **narratives** criticized the morals of his time. Many of his paintings were reproduced as **prints**, which were released one at a time to spur interest and curiosity; these were the soap operas of the eighteenth century. Hogarth's prints (often engraved by others) made his work affordable for the lower and middle classes, who were a receptive audience for his satirical series. The prints were extremely popular and forged copies were rampant, so much so that Hogarth requested protection from Parliament for his original creations, leading to the Engraving Copyright Act of 1734, also called Hogarth's Act.

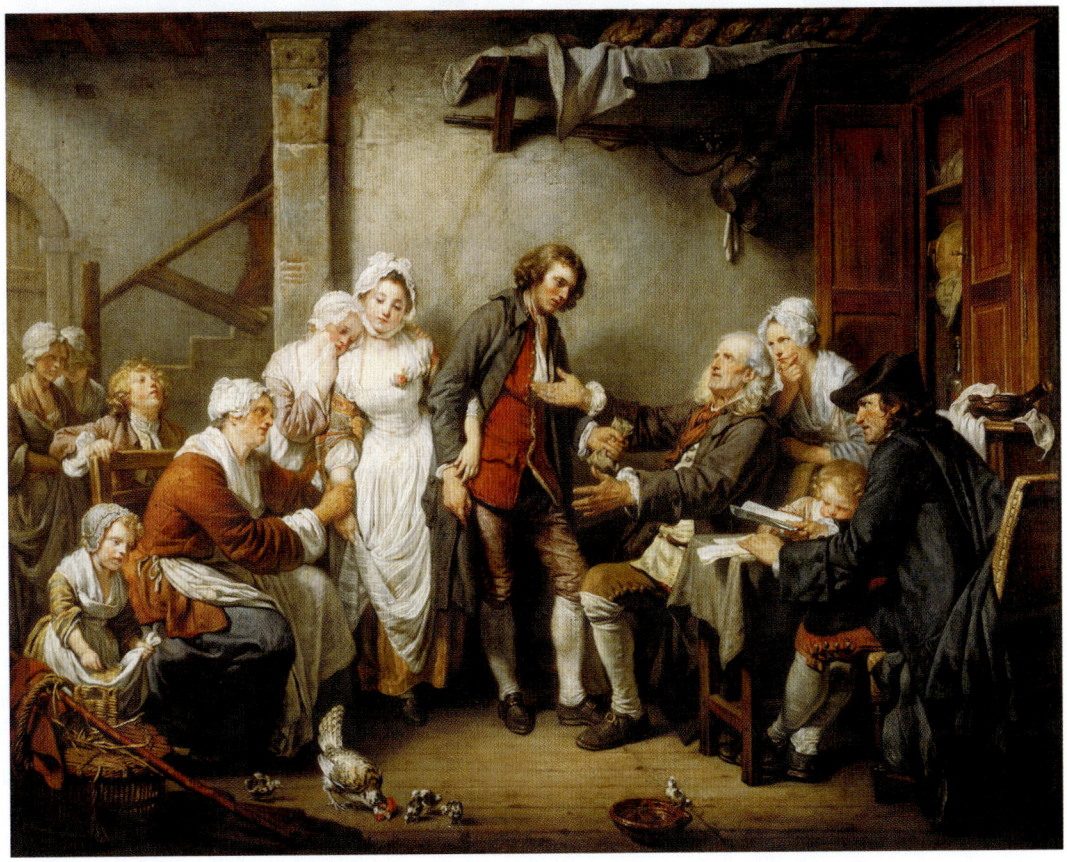

3.7.3 Jean-Baptiste Greuze, *The Marriage Contract*, 1761. Oil on canvas, 25¼ × 31½". Musée du Louvre, Paris, France

Idealized: represented as perfect in form or character, corresponding to an ideal
Engraving: a printmaking technique where the artist (the **engraver**) gouges or scratches the image into the surface of the printing plate
Narrative: an artwork that tells a story
Print: a picture reproduced on paper, often in multiple copies

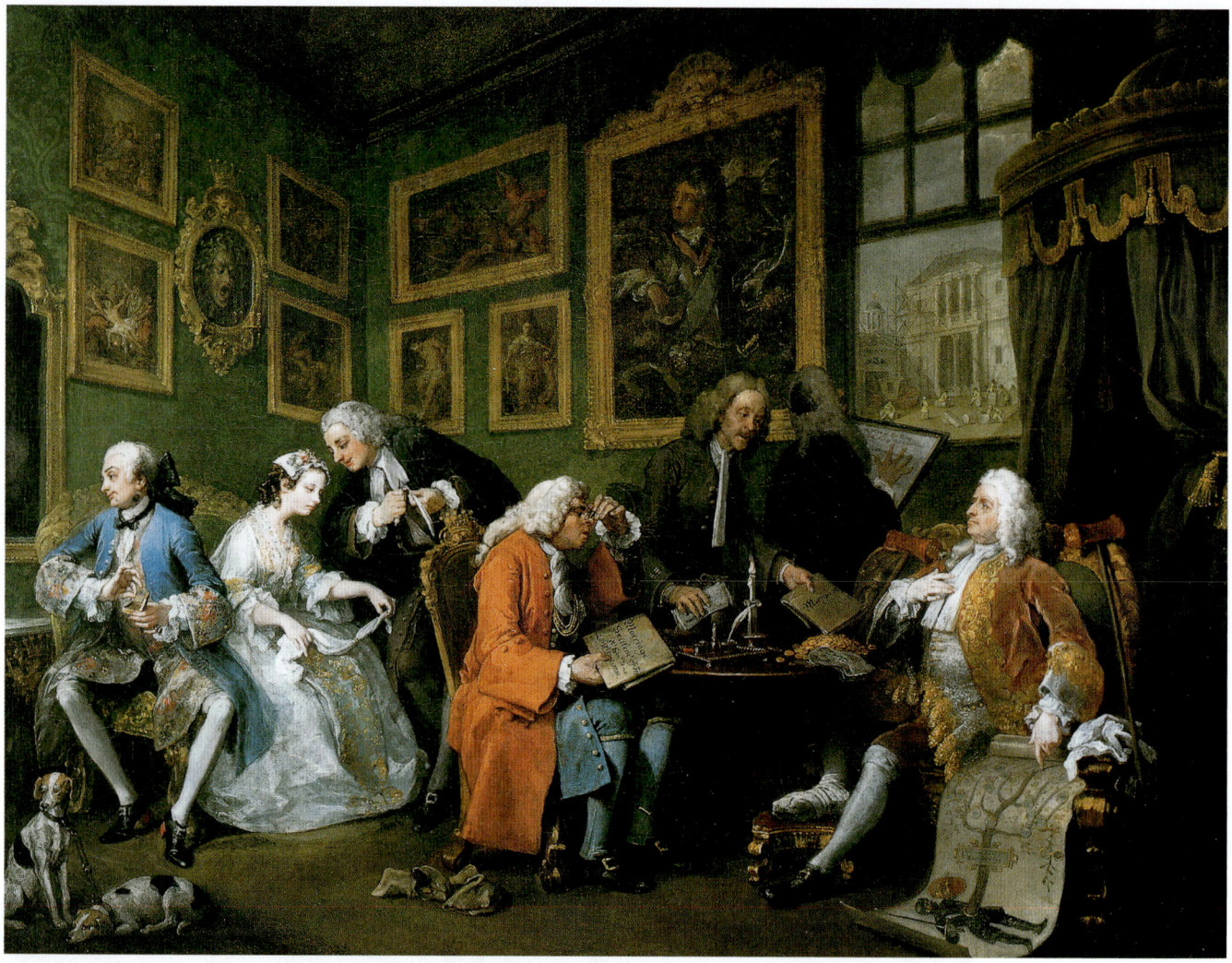

3.7.4 William Hogarth, "The Marriage Settlement" (from the series *Marriage à-la-Mode*), c. 1743. Oil on canvas, 27½ × 35¾". National Gallery, London, England

The series *Marriage à-la-Mode (A Fashionable Marriage)* includes six paintings on which the highly successful engravings were based. "The Marriage Settlement" is the first in the series (**3.7.4**), and shows a quite different marriage arrangement than that in Greuze's depiction (**3.7.3**, p 489). The betrothed couple sits together on the left, completely uninterested in each other. The miserable bride toys with her handkerchief while her father's lawyer, Silvertongue, flirts with her. The bridegroom admires himself in a mirror, too much of a snob even to look at his bride. The two dogs shackled together in the foreground echo the attitudes of the bride and groom. The marriage contract is being arranged by their fathers. The groom's father, on the far right, proudly displays in his family tree his aristocratic lineage as Earl Squander. The bride's father, a successful merchant, offers a fine dowry in the form of a pile of coins placed in front of the earl. Out the window above the earl can be seen his building project, which will be financed by the dowry.

Much of Hogarth's artwork addresses the need for social change, and the *Marriage à-la-Mode* series condemns the devastating effect of immorality on society. In the rest of the series, both husband and wife have affairs and gradually fritter away their fortune; Silvertongue becomes the wife's lover, kills her husband, and is executed for the murder. The final scene of the series, called "The Lady's Death," is shown here as an engraving, the way most of the public would have seen it (**3.7.5**). In this scene, the wife has poisoned herself, devastated by the death of her lover. The bride's father has just removed the ring from his daughter's finger, while the old earl is represented by his completed building project out the window. The disastrous coupling of the pair is recalled by means of the emaciated dog on the table, which

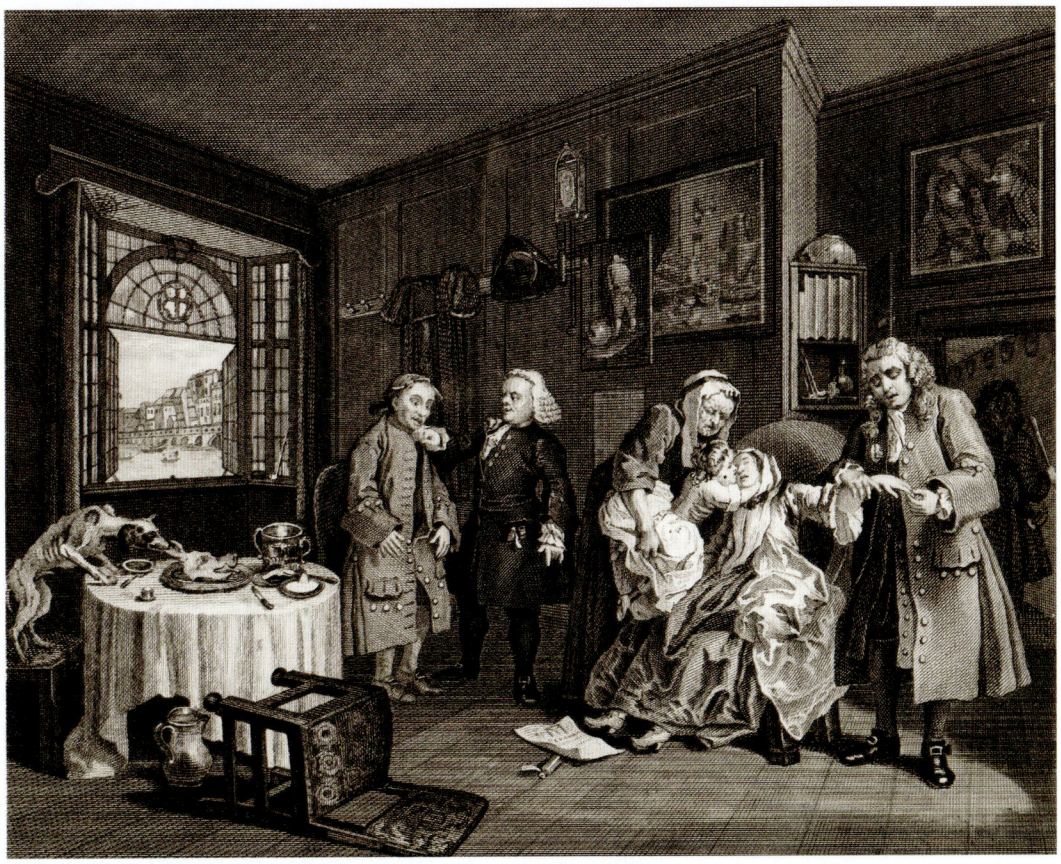

3.7.5 "The Lady's Death" (plate 6 from the series *Marriage à-la-Mode*). Engraving after the original painting by William Hogarth, *c.* 1743

is eating the carcass of a dead dog. Much of Hogarth's work addressed the need for protection of children. In this final scene, it is the child who suffers. Shown kissing her mother goodbye, she bares a sore on her face that indicates she has contracted syphilis, a sexually transmitted disease, from her promiscuous parents.

Neoclassicism

> Those marks of heroism and civic virtue presented to the eyes of the people will electrify the soul, and sow the seeds of glory and loyalty to the fatherland.
>
> (Jacques-Louis David)

This statement by the French painter David summarizes the moral objectives of **Neoclassical** (literally, "new Classical") art. This was a movement that developed during the late eighteenth century as an even bolder reaction against the artificiality of the Rococo. Neoclassical artworks recall, in their imagery and subject matter, the ancient **Classical** cultures of Greece and Rome. This interest in the ancient world was fueled by such archaeological discoveries at about this time as the remains of the Roman city of Pompeii. During this period, many well-to-do Europeans participated in the **Grand Tour**, which was a lengthy excursion to travel and visit ancient ruins, and be exposed to Classical and **Renaissance** culture. Ancient Greece and Rome were thought to embody such virtues as civic responsibility and an emphasis on rational thought. At a time of public unrest, Neoclassical artworks used historical or mythological stories to convey a moral message, and sought to convey rationalism and stability visually through structure and stillness, creating visions of balance and order.

Jacques-Louis David (1748–1825) lived through one of the most tumultuous periods in French history. He made paintings purchased by the monarchy, then supported revolutionary leaders who opposed the king, and later painted numerous portraits of the French emperor, Napoleon. Although David's painting *The Oath of the Horatii* (**3.7.7**, p. 493), because of its promotion of civic duty, or accepting personal

Neoclassicism: European style that flourished during the late eighteenth and early nineteenth centuries, characterized by an extreme interest in the Classical world, strictly ordered scenes, and heroic subjects
Classical: ancient Greek and Roman; art that conforms to Greek and Roman models, or is based on rational construction and emotional equilibrium
Grand Tour: a trip for the cultured and wealthy to study Classical and Renaissance artworks and culture found mostly in Italy
Renaissance: a period of cultural and artistic change in Europe from the fourteenth to the seventeenth century

The French Academy of Painting and Sculpture: Making a Living as an Artist

Throughout the eighteenth century and for much of the nineteenth, in Europe, government-sponsored art academies provided the main outlet for European artists to exhibit their work. France was the artistic center of Europe at this time, and the French Academy of Painting and Sculpture, founded in 1648 (renamed the Academy of Fine Arts in 1816), was vastly influential in determining artistic success. Its strict curriculum required artists to copy ancient works of art before they were allowed to study a living model. Students also studied history, mythology, literature, and anatomy—important subjects of academic art. The Academy thrived on the notion of competition. The winner of the most important competition, the Prix de Rome (Rome Prize), was sent to Rome to study Classical works and the Renaissance masters. Following the French model, Britain's Royal Academy of Arts was founded in 1768. The first Art Academy in America was founded in 1805 in Philadelphia, Pennsylvania.

The French Academy also developed a hierarchy that determined the relative importance of the subject matter of a painting. History paintings (**3.7.7**, **3.7.9**, **3.7.13**), which depicted historical, biblical, or mythological scenes, usually containing large groups of people, were considered to be the finest of the genres. Portraits were the next most valued paintings, then scenes of the lower class (**3.7.3**), landscapes (**3.7.16**), and finally still-life paintings (**3.7.8**). History paintings highlighted an artist's use of their academic training in that they showed subjects, often with idealized nude bodies, that the artists had studied in their readings. Artists who painted other **genres** would often try to increase the importance of their artworks by including elements important to the Academy, such as references to human beings, Classical stories, and messages of morality. While artists who excelled in any of these subjects could belong to the Academy, only those who were considered history painters were allowed to teach there.

During the eighteenth and nineteenth centuries only four women were allowed into the French Academy. It was very difficult for women to become artists because of a lack of training venues and because women were not allowed to study nude models, which was considered a critical skill in the Academy, particularly in the

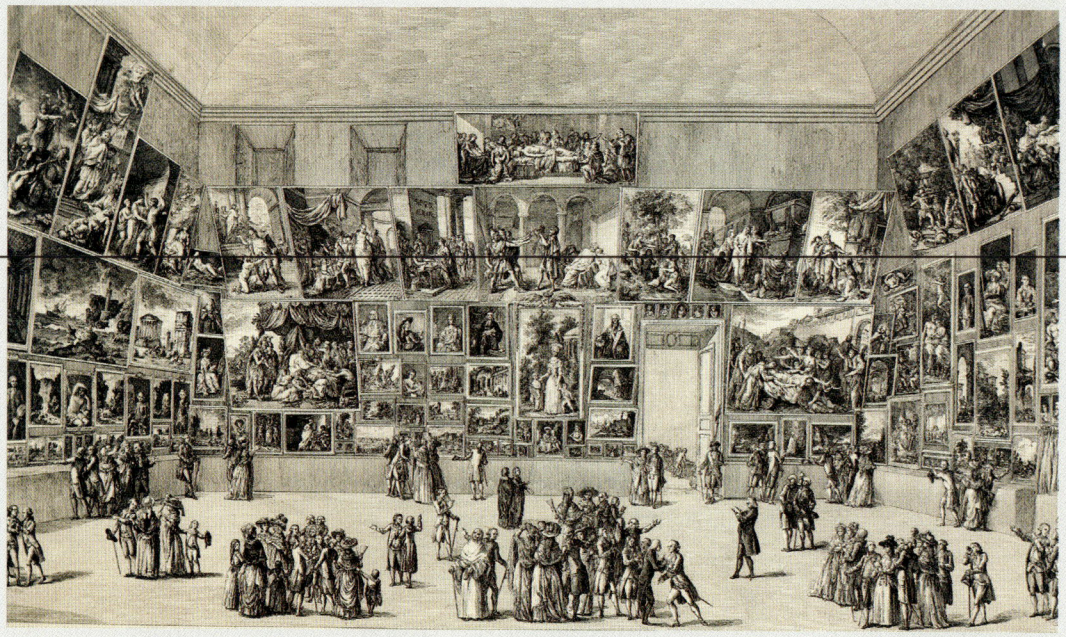

3.7.6 Pietro Antonio Martini, *The Salon*, 1785. Musée du Château de Versailles, France

creation of history paintings. The female artists who did become successful academic painters did so in one of the "lesser" genres, and thanks to extra familial or royal support (**3.7.8**).

The Royal Academy of Painting and Sculpture held an exhibition in Paris called the Salon every one or two years, which was highly competitive and popular. In Pietro Antonio Martini's print of the Salon of 1785, paintings fill the walls from floor to ceiling (**3.7.6**). The history paintings (always much larger in scale) were given prominent places, and the lowest of the genres, the still lifes, were usually hung lower. Martini's print highlights the prominent placement (at the center of the middle wall) of David's history painting The *Oath of the Horatii* (**3.7.7**). Critics from around the world reviewed these exhibitions, making or breaking artists' reputations.

sacrifice in the service of one's nation, is often linked with the ideas that fueled the French Revolution of 1789, in fact the image was made for King Louis XVI, five years before the revolution that removed him from the throne.

The Oath of the Horatii was an exceptionally popular work when it was shown at the 1785 **Salon** and is often credited with pioneering Neoclassicism (see Box: The French Academy of Painting and Sculpture: Making a Living as an Artist). The painting is based on a story from early Roman history that tells of self-sacrifice and civic duty. Three brothers are shown making a vow to their father to fight for Rome. The scene is Neoclassical in its muscular Classical figures, with distinct **linear outlines**, and its stable, balanced composition, created in part by the pyramidal groupings of the figures and the strict vertical columns. David used **linear perspective**, with **orthogonal** lines in the geometric floor that lead to the **vanishing point** at the father's hand as he holds the swords. The three Roman archways separate the empty, dark background from the figures and organize the people into three groups. The brothers on the left are contrasted with the women of the family on the

Genre: categories of artistic subject matter, often with strongly influential histories and traditions
Salon: an official exhibition of French painting, first held in 1667
Linear outline: a line that clearly separates a figure from its surroundings
Linear perspective: a system using converging imaginary sight lines to create the illusion of depth
Orthogonals: in perspective systems, imaginary sightlines extending from forms to the vanishing point
Vanishing point(s): the point or points in a work of art at which imaginary sight lines appear to converge, suggesting depth

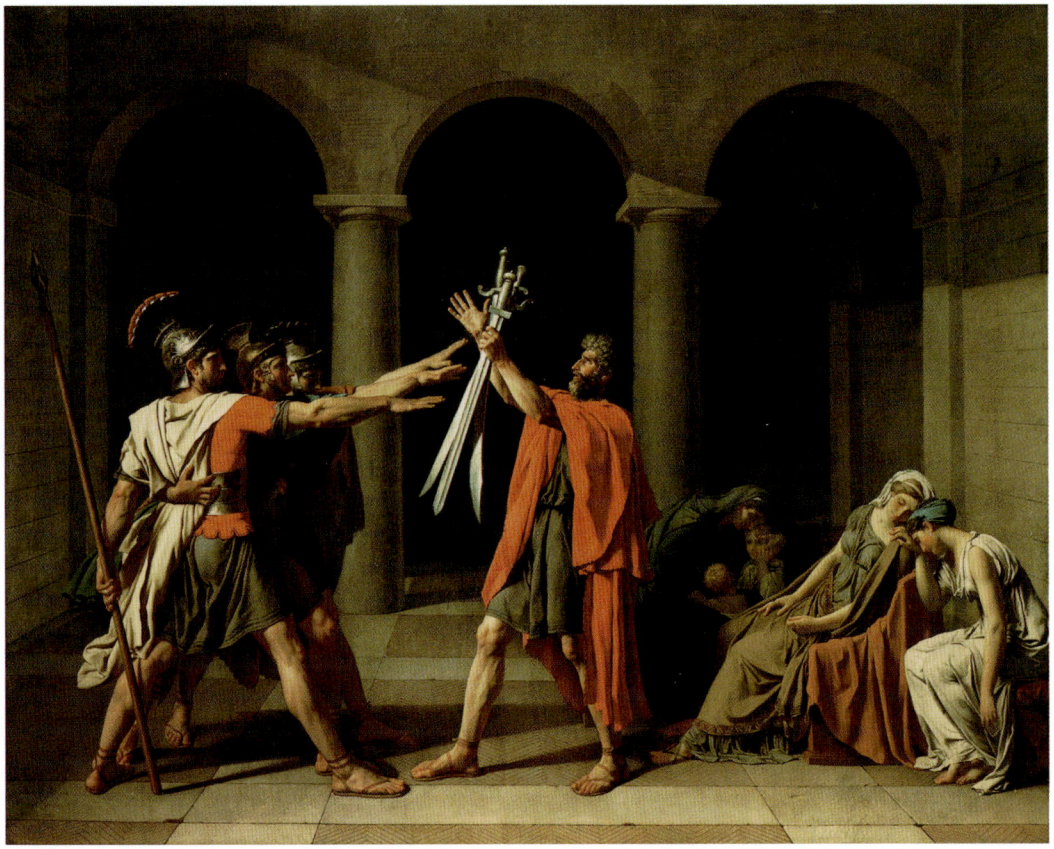

3.7.7 Jacques-Louis David, *The Oath of the Horatii*, 1784. Oil on canvas, 10'10" × 13'11½". Musée du Louvre, Paris, France

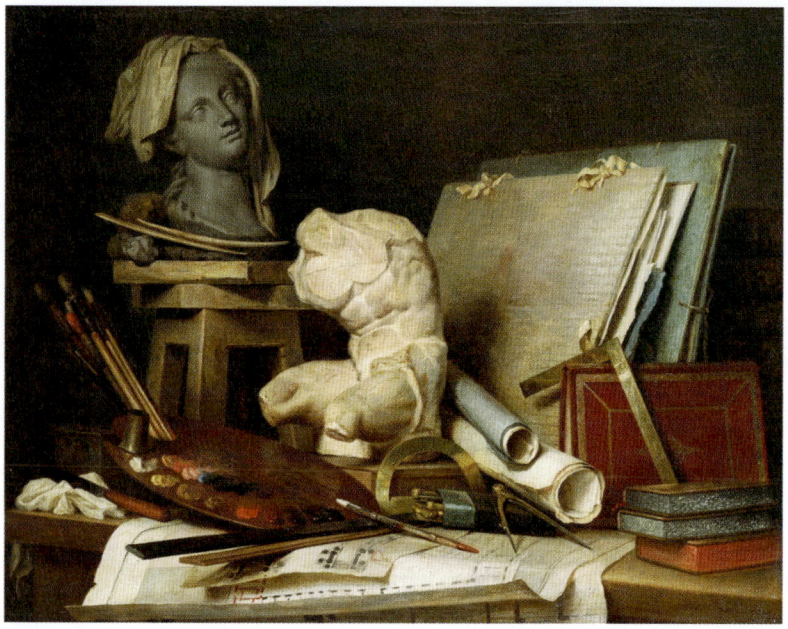

3.7.8 Anne Vallayer-Coster, *Attributes of Painting, Sculpture, and Architecture*, 1769. Oil on canvas, 35½ × 47¾". Musée du Louvre, Paris, France

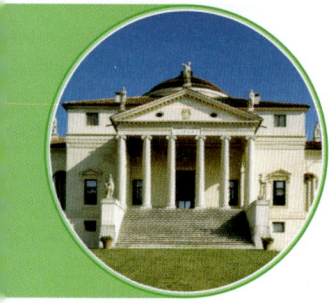

Jefferson was inspired by the Renaissance architect Andrea Palladio's Villa Rotonda, which is placed upon a little hill in Vicenza, Italy: see **3.6.14a, p. 473**

Arch: structure, usually curved, that spans an opening
Dome: an evenly curved vault forming the ceiling or roof of a building
Pediment: the triangular space, situated above the row of columns, on the facade of a building in the Classical style
Oculus: a round opening at the center of a dome

right, and the father is central. While the soldiers stand heroically, the women mourn the losses they know will come.

Anne Vallayer-Coster (1744–1818), trained by her father and other artists, was a brilliant painter of still lifes. Although she often painted fruits or flowers, she chose the subject of *Attributes of Painting, Sculpture, and Architecture* (**3.7.8**) to gain entrance into the French Academy (see Box: The French Academy of Painting and Sculpture: Making a Living as an Artist). The painting, Neoclassical in its powerfully structured composition, was sized to be an "overdoor," meaning that it would have been hung high above a doorway. The dynamism of the composition is enhanced when one stands below the work and feels a sense of anxiety that the precariously arranged objects could fall. Vallayer-Coster chose objects referencing intellectualism in other artistic endeavors, including architectural plans, tools, and a Classically styled sculpture that seems to point its missing head to the upper right. Unlike other paintings of the attributes of the arts, however, the artist includes an unfinished bust. We know it is unfinished because of its darker shade, signifying that the clay is moist, and the temporarily removed cloth that is used to prevent it drying. The bust might be interpreted as a self-portrait, in which the artist is presenting herself as an unfinished work, ready to be molded by the Academy.

The Swiss-Austrian Angelica Kauffmann (1741–1807) used purely Neoclassical elements, such as Classical subject matter, Classical architecture, and stable compositions, in her paintings. Kauffmann was one of only two women amongst the thirty-four original members of the British Royal Academy of the Arts. Kauffmann was trained in painting by her father in her youth, and became a well-respected artist with commissions from international patrons. She was fortunate to travel extensively and her works were appreciated by those who had experienced a Grand Tour. Her best-known works are Neoclassical scenes that portray strong female characters. In *Cornelia Pointing to Her Children as Her Treasures*, a Roman woman is represented as a model of motherhood and morality (**3.7.9**). While the woman on the right displays her fine jewelry, Cornelia gestures to her sons as her source of pride, her own jewels; they will grow up to be the political leaders Tiberius and Gaius Gracchus. Cornelia's daughter, curious, strokes the woman's jewels, but Cornelia holds her hand firmly and models strength of character rather than pride in material wealth.

Neoclassicism represented the ideals of Americans in the late eighteenth century: equality, patriotism, and civic responsibility. The new American cities chose Neoclassicism as their preferred architectural style. Thomas Jefferson (1743–1826), author of the Declaration of Independence and America's third president, designed a Neoclassical home for himself in Charlottesville, Virginia; he named it Monticello, meaning "little hill" in Italian. (**3.7.10**). He was inspired by the Renaissance architect Andrea Palladio's use of Classical elements, such as **arches**, **domes**, and **pediments**, all of which can be seen in the design of Monticello. Its central dome has an **oculus**, like the Roman Pantheon. The house has forty-three rooms, eight fireplaces, and thirteen skylights. It was begun in 1769, but Jefferson continued to make changes and additions to it until his death, more than fifty years later.

3.7.9 (right) Angelica Kauffmann, *Cornelia Pointing to Her Children as Her Treasures*, c. 1785. Oil on canvas, 40 × 50". Virginia Museum of Fine Arts, Richmond

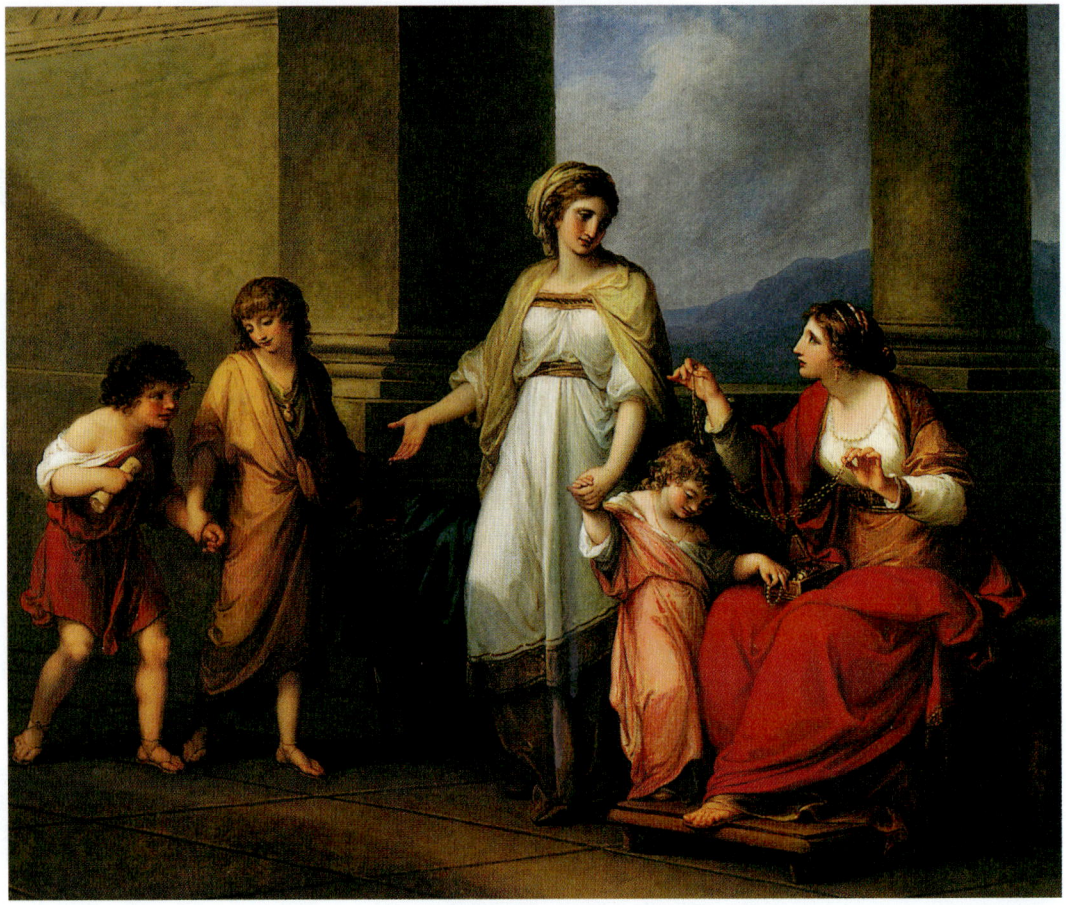

3.7.10 (below) Thomas Jefferson, Monticello , 1769–1809, Charlottesville, Virginia

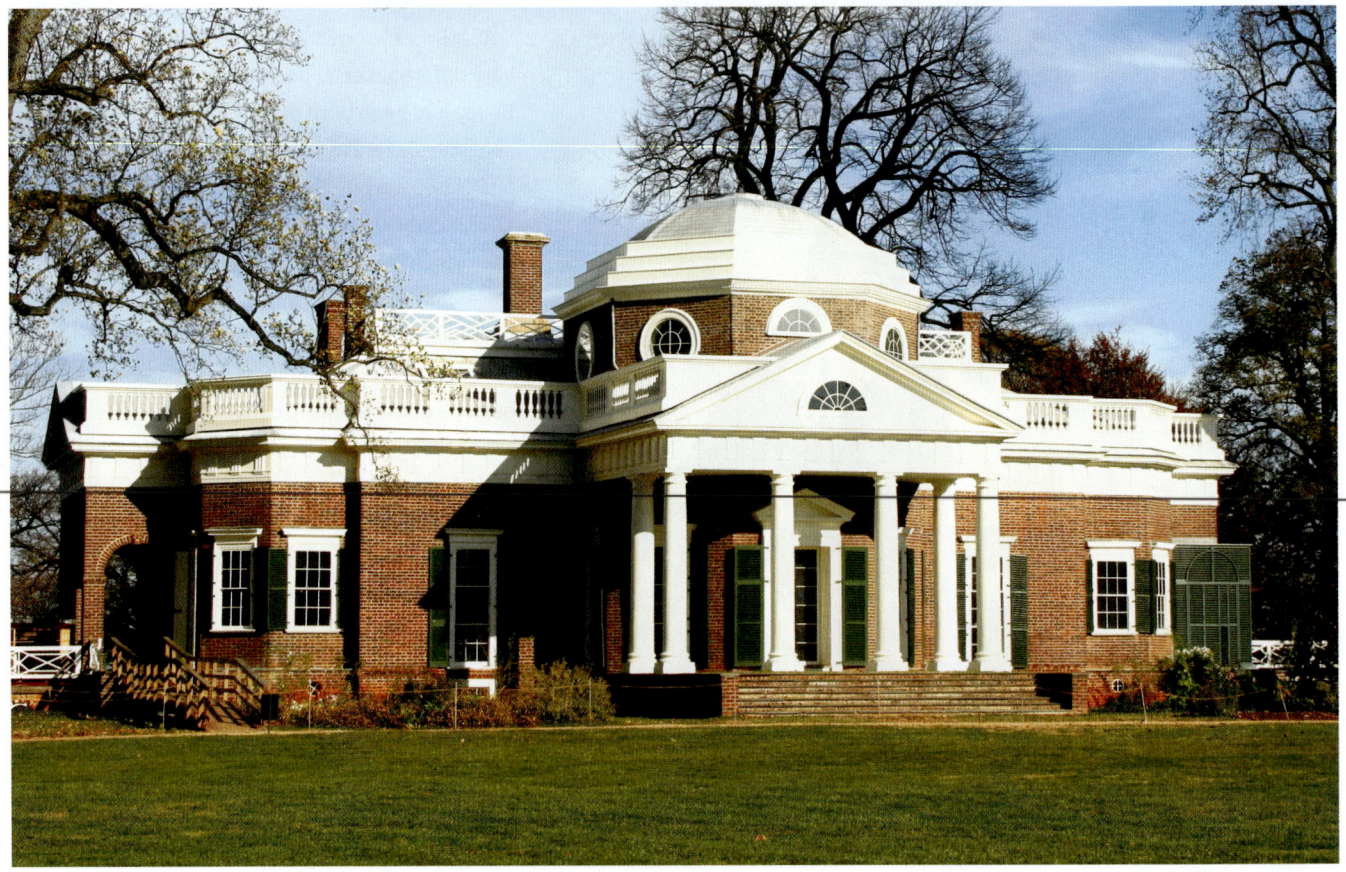

Slavery and Colonialism in Eighteenth-Century Art

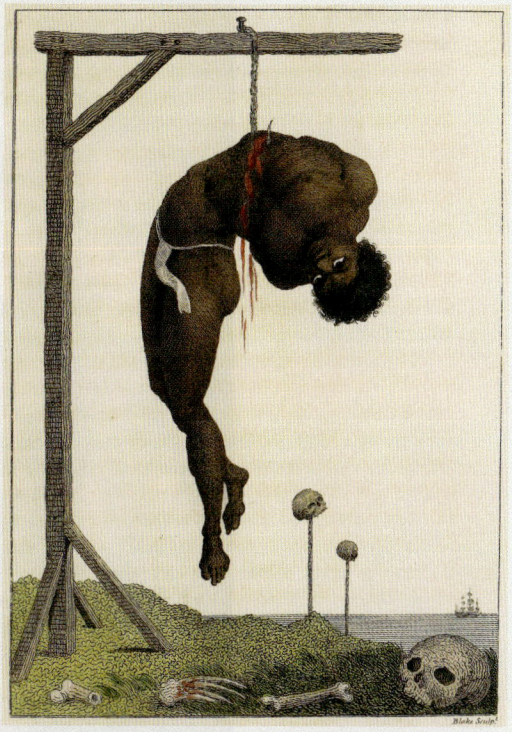

3.7.11 William Blake after J. G. Stedman, *A negro hung alive by the ribs to a gallows*, 1792. Engraving, 17⅛ × 5⅛". From J. G. Stedman, *Narrative of a five years' expedition, against the revolted negroes of Surinam...* (London: 1796). Wellcome Collection, London, England

A negro hung alive by the ribs to a gallows was an illustration made by William Blake for the book *Narrative of a five years' expedition, against the revolted negroes of Surinam...* (1796), written by the Scottish-Dutch soldier John Gabriel Stedman (**3.7.11**). Blake was passionate about the abolition of the British slave trade, speaking out against it in his writings and images. This print shows the shocking brutality of the murder of a black man who was hung by a hook through his ribs. Stedman's narrative states that the slave was left to die slowly and did so without complaint, a comment that reveals Stedman's still wavering opinions on the degree to which such torture would have affected the man. Blake's image shows the man's eyes wide open, highlighting both his humanity and the slow death he underwent. The emotionally charged nature of the scene reveals Blake's tendency toward **Romanticism** (see **3.7.14**, p. 498). Bones and skulls on the ground and on nearby poles suggest the high quantity of slave murders, and the ship in the distance highlights that this is the result of colonialism and the slave trade.

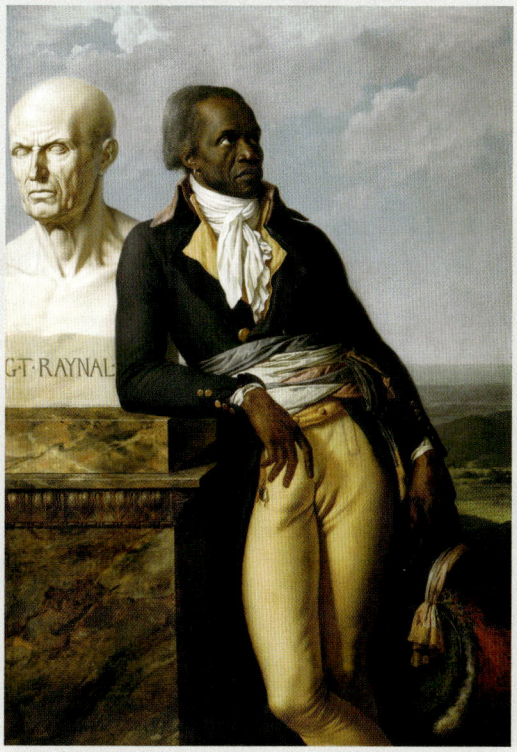

3.7.12 Anne-Louis Girodet, *Jean-Baptiste Belley*, 1797. Oil on canvas, 62⅝ × 44". Châteaux de Versailles et de Trianon, Versailles, France

The painting of Jean-Baptiste Belley by Anne-Louis Girodet shows a dark-skinned man in a very different social position (**3.7.12**). Although Belley had been born in Senegal in *c.* 1747 and sold into slavery in Saint-Dominigue, Haiti, at the age of two, he bought his freedom as an adult. In 1793, Belley was the first black man elected to the French National Convention. He argued for the abolition of slavery, which led to a unanimous vote to end the brutal practice in France and its colonies. The pose, subjects, and compositional balance of the painting convey a Neoclassical rationalism. The dark skin of Belley contrasts with the marble bust of the recently deceased Enlightenment philosopher Guillaume Thomas Raynal, who argued vehemently against slavery in his treatise of 1770. Belley is leaning on the base of the sculpture, thus symbolically leaning on the writings of Raynal. They balance one another further by staring in opposite directions and in the sense that one is living, and is carrying on the ideas of the deceased, who has empty eyes and appears somewhat ghost-like next to the colorful and robust figure of Belley.

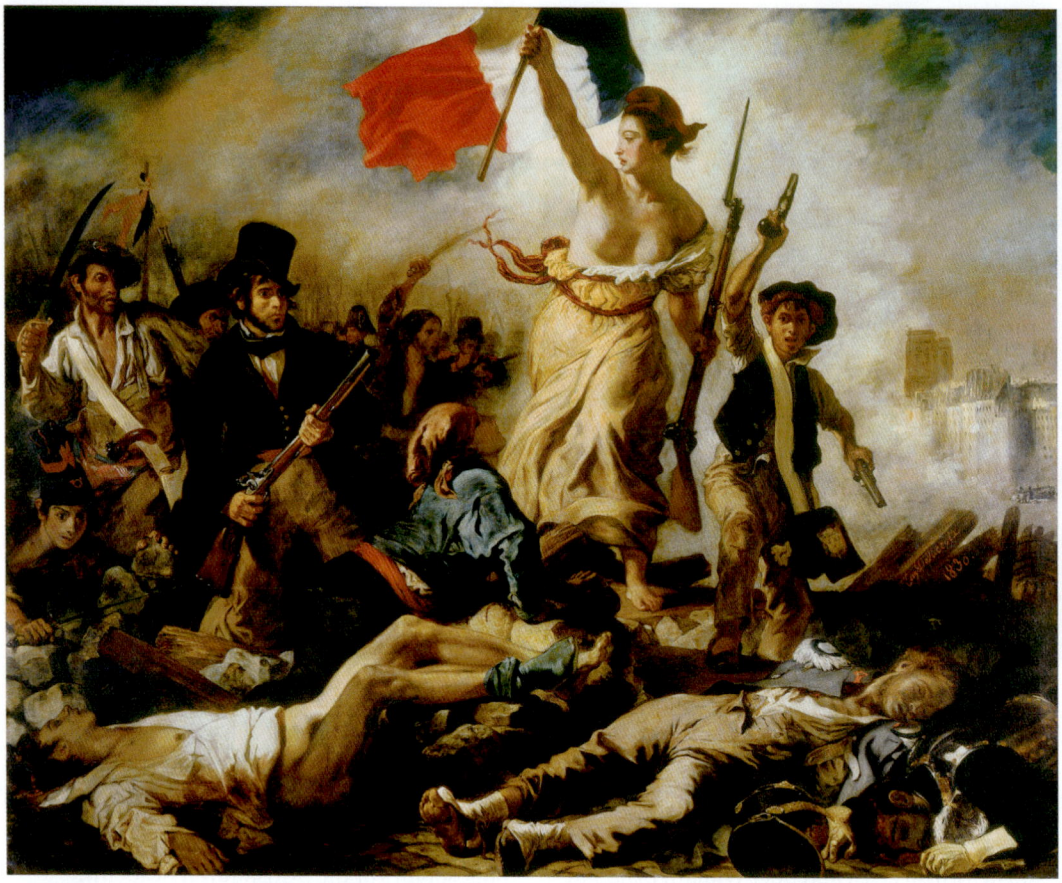

3.7.13 Eugène Delacroix, *Liberty Leading the People*, 1830. Oil on canvas, 8'6¼" × 10'8". Musée du Louvre, Paris, France

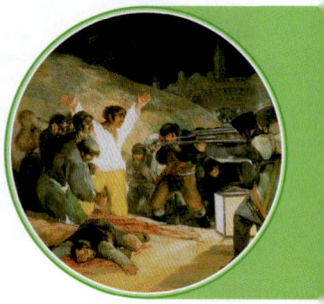

Goya's painting *The Third of May, 1808* commemorates the Spanish resistance to Napoleon's occupation of Madrid: see **4.7.9, p. 645**

Romanticism

While the style and subject matter of Neoclassical art were designed to express rationalism, stability, and traditional notions of duty, Romantic artworks, by contrast, emphasize individuality, and surge with drama, fantasy, and heightened emotion. Additionally, many Romantic images portray the power and beauty of nature and man's relationship with it, both as a rejection of the encroaching industrialization of the period and as a symbol for the natural impulses and creativity of humans. Romantic artists valued emotion over reason, and Romanticism in art, which emerged in the first half of the nineteenth century, reflects the turmoil of the European and American revolutions, when the people rose up against the ruling classes and demanded their freedom.

Romantic art challenged the traditional norms and structures of society and often showed citizens' sacrifices for ideals of liberty, equality, and humanity, in images charged with energy created by the use of **implied lines** in all directions, frequent **asymmetry**, and visual movement and **rhythm**.

Liberty Leading the People, by Eugène Delacroix (1798–1863), depicts the French people bravely rising up against their government in the three-day July Revolution of 1830 (**3.7.13**). In the painting, the bare-breasted symbol of freedom, Liberty, carries the flag of the revolution in one hand and a musket in the other. The depiction of this **personification** of France's symbol of Liberty was shocking at the time for its portrayal of a modern, dirty figure rather than an idealized goddess. Although partly an imagined scene, the painting accurately shows the chaos of the event and the sacrifice of people of all ages and social classes. A little boy fearlessly marches forward carrying two pistols, while an upper-class gentleman in a top hat holds a rifle. Crowds of people with muskets and swords follow Liberty as she climbs over those who have died, signifying that such sacrifice is worth the greater good. In contrast to David's *Oath of the Horatii* (**3.7.7**, p. 493), which glorifies a Roman story for a modern purpose, Delacroix's

Romanticism: movement in nineteenth-century European culture, concerned with the power of the imagination and greatly valuing intense feeling
Implied line: a line not actually drawn but suggested by the positions of elements in the work
Asymmetry: a type of design in which balance is achieved by elements that contrast and complement one another without being the same on either side of an axis
Rhythm: the regular or ordered repetition of elements in the work
Personification: representation of a thing, an idea, or an abstract quality, such as "freedom," as a person or in human form

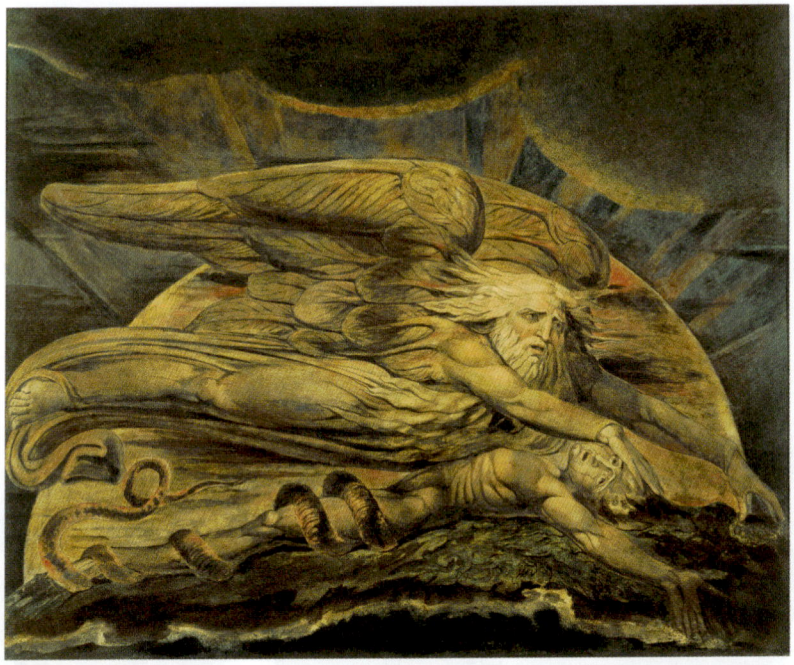

3.7.14 William Blake, *Elohim Creating Adam*, 1795. Color print finished in ink and watercolor on paper, 17 × 21". Tate, London

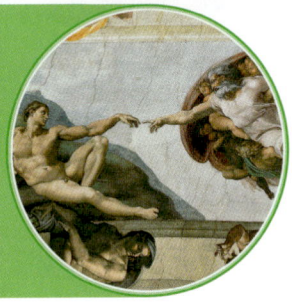

William Blake knew about Michelangelo's frescoes in the Sistine Chapel through engravings; for the paintings, see **3.6.9b, p. 468**

Romantic image highlights the emotion felt by many Parisians about a contemporary event.

The British artist and poet William Blake (1757–1827) conveys in both his visual and literary works emotionally charged messages about his beliefs in personal and creative freedom (see Box: Slavery and Colonialism in Eighteenth-Century Art, p. 496). In *Elohim Creating Adam* (**3.7.14**), Blake transforms Michelangelo's famous *Creation of Adam* (see p. 468) from the Sistine ceiling in Rome into a Romantic image filled with anguish and struggle. In Blake's vision, God ("Elohim" in Hebrew) has enormous wings that seem to grow from the tendons in his shoulders. The process of creation is shown to be painful for both creator and created, rather than a cause for joy and celebration. The sadness evident in Elohim's face may convey his knowledge that the creation of man will inevitably bring about humanity's fall from grace, implied in the image by the presence of a snake. Blake believed that man's spiritual freedom was suppressed on the day of his creation, and his painting shows it: Adam's body is restrained by the serpent, while his mind is restrained by the hand of God. Blake resisted any controls on either his creativity or behavior, rejecting many of the accepted Christian values of the time and rebelling as well against the philosophies of the British Royal Academy.

Some fifty years after Blake's work, another British painter, J. M. W. Turner (1775–1851),

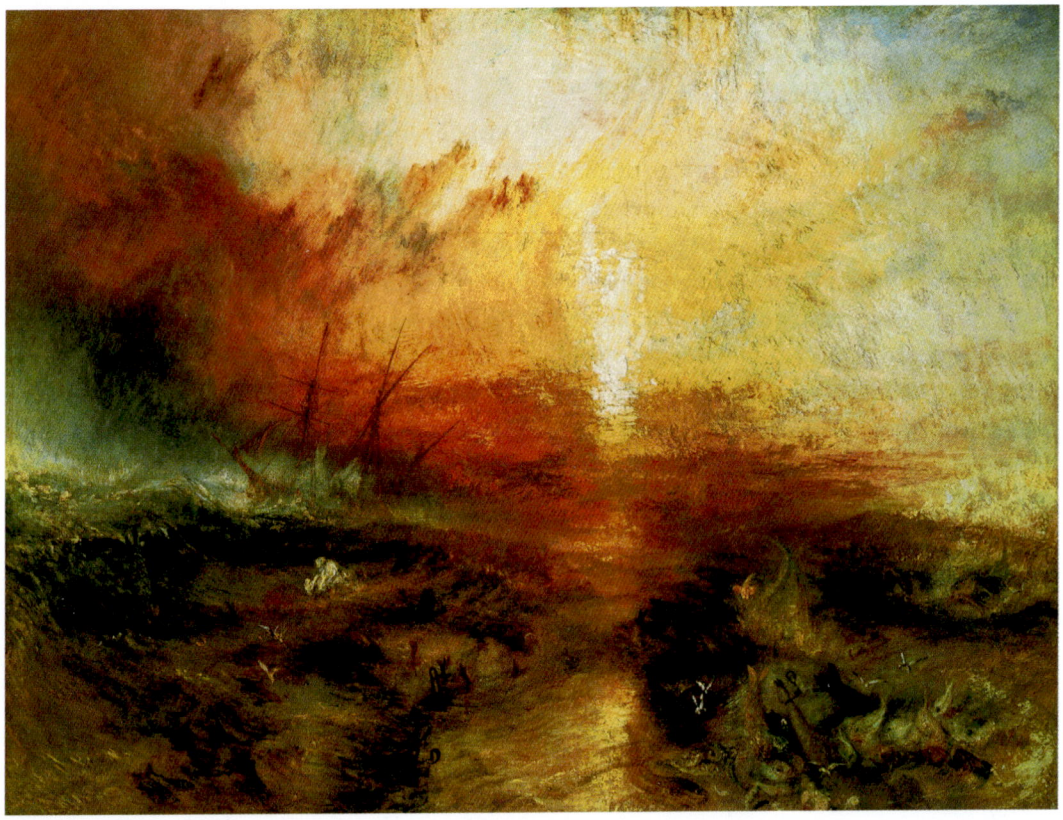

3.7.15 Turner, *Slave Ship (Slavers Throwing Overboard the Dead and Dying, Typhoon Coming On)*, 1840. Oil on canvas, 35¾ × 48¼". Museum of Fine Arts, Boston, Massachusetts

Abstract: an artwork the form of which is simplified, distorted, or exaggerated in appearance. It may represent a recognizable form that has been slightly altered, or it may be a completely non-representational depiction
Sublime: feeling of awe or terror, provoked by the experience of limitless nature and the awareness of the smallness of an individual

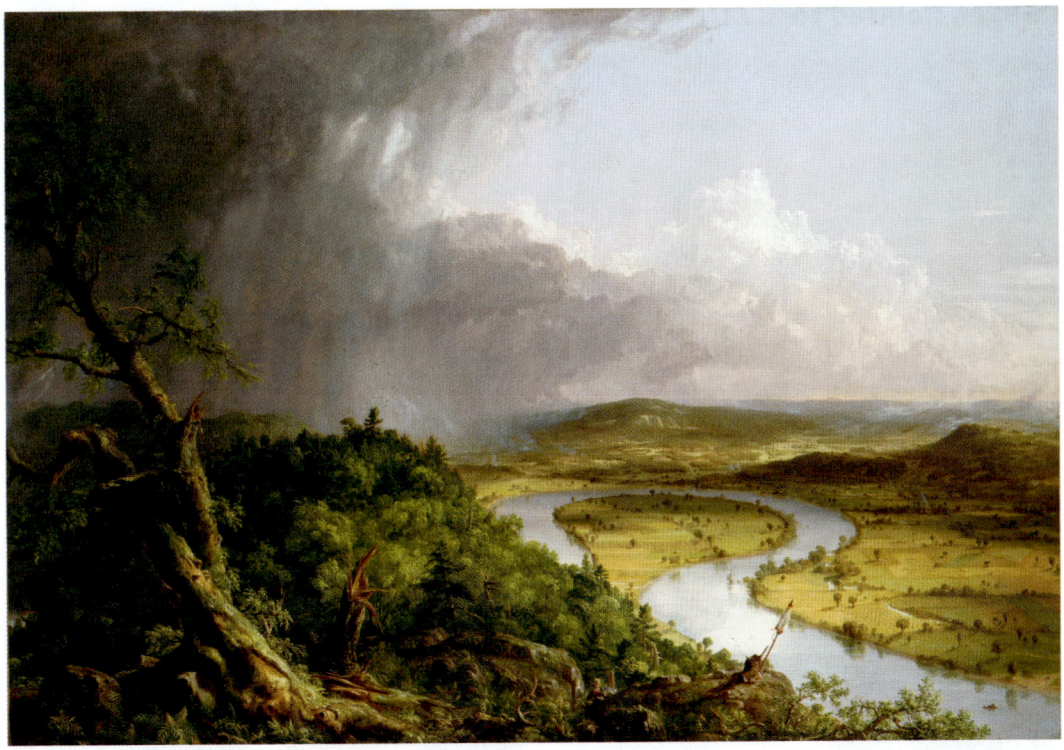

3.7.16 Thomas Cole, *View from Mount Holyoke, Massachusetts, after a Thunderstorm—The Oxbow*, 1836. Oil on canvas, 4'3½" × 6'4". Metropolitan Museum of Art, New York

also used his art to express his views, in the instance shown here as a force for social protest. In his dramatic painting in the Romantic style, *Slave Ship (Slavers Throwing Overboard the Dead and Dying, Typhoon Coming On)* (**3.7.15**), Turner condemns the slave trade. Although slavery was illegal by this time throughout Britain, Turner was highlighting the injustice of the slave trade and protesting against any consideration of its renewal. His powerful canvas portrays an infamous incident aboard the slave ship *Zong* in 1781. It was common practice for slave-ship captains to fill their vessels with more slaves than they would need, knowing that disease might spread amongst them. The captain of the *Zong* knew that he would be paid for any slaves lost at sea, but not for those who were sick when they arrived. He therefore had sick slaves thrown overboard while still far from land.

Turner's chaotic canvas displays several aspects of the Romantic style. Man versus nature was a common theme in Romantic art, and here the immense power of nature, expressed as a fierce storm, overpowers the slaves. Body parts, still shackled and being attacked by sharp-teethed fish, can be seen in the central and right foreground. Turner uses intense colors and turbulent brushstrokes to convey the heightened emotion and fearful horror of the event. His canvas also has an **abstract** quality, making its subject matter difficult to understand. Turner placed beside his painting a quotation from the book that had inspired it, in order to help viewers understand his artwork's meaning.

Born in England, the painter Thomas Cole (1801–1848) emigrated to America at the age of seventeen and went on to found the Hudson River School, a group of Romantic American painters who painted the American landscape as an expression of pride in the expansion of the developing nation and its great natural beauty. This group's paintings embody the idea of the **sublime**, where the awe-inspiring power of nature overwhelms the smallness of man. In his painting, *View from Mount Holyoke, Massachusetts, after a Thunderstorm—The Oxbow*, Cole views the twisting Connecticut River from a dramatic vantage point (**3.7.16**). A tree in the foreground has been battered by weather, while the river is far below in the valley. Above are fierce thunderclouds, but in the distance we can see the sky after the storm has passed. The only trace of man in this scene, hard to pick out against the dense trees, is the artist, wearing a hat. We can just glimpse him, engulfed by the grandeur of the landscape, in the lower center of the canvas.

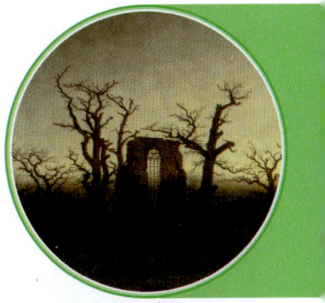

The German Romantic artist Caspar David Friedrich used nature to symbolize spirituality: see **0.0.22, p. 37**

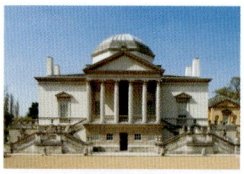

2.5.26 Lord Burlington, Chiswick House, 1729, p. 274

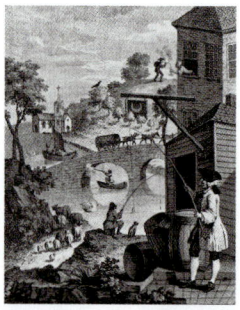

4.5.6 William Hogarth, *False Perspective*, 1754, p. 619

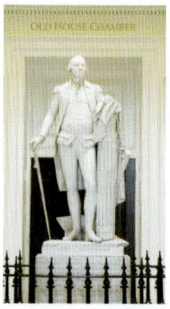

4.6.1 Jean-Antoine Houdon, *George Washington*, 1788–92, p. 629

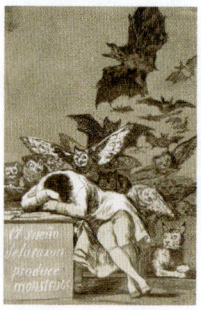

1.9.13 Francisco Goya, *The Sleep of Reason Produces Monsters*, 1799, p. 167

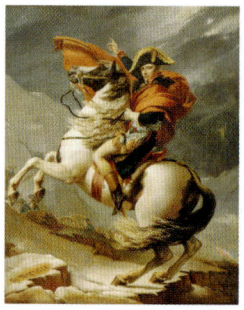

4.6.2 Jacques-Louis David, *Napoleon Crossing the Alps*, 1801, p. 629

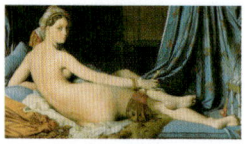

1.10.8 Jean-Auguste-Dominique Ingres, *Grande Odalisque*, 1814, p. 179

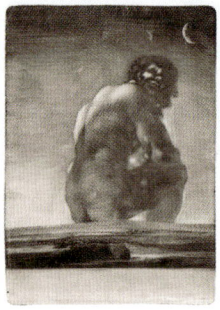

2.3.11 Francisco Goya, *Giant*, c. 1818, p. 232

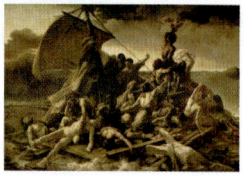

4.8.1 Théodore Géricault, *Raft of the Medusa*, 1819, p. 652

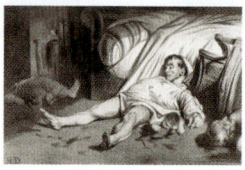

2.3.15 Honoré Daumier, *Rue Transnonain*, 1834, p. 234

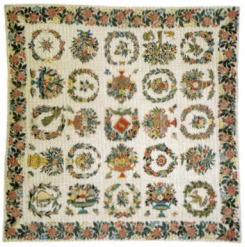

1.6.12 Album quilt, probably by Mary Evans, 1848, p. 133

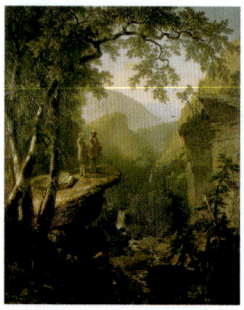

1.3.13 Asher Brown Durand, *Kindred Spirits*, 1849, p. 84

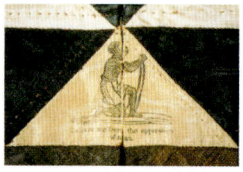

1.9.5b Deborah Coates, detail of quilt, Pennsylvania, c. 1840–50, p. 161

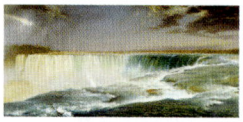

0.0.2 Frederic Edwin Church, *Niagara*, 1857, p. 21

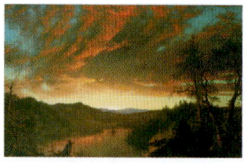

1.4.13 Frederic Edwin Church, *Twilight in the Wilderness*, 1860, p. 101

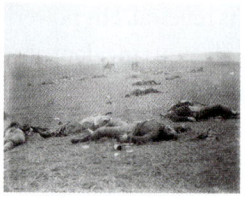

4.7.1 Timothy O'Sullivan, *Harvest of Death, Gettysburg, Pennsylvania*, 1863, p. 638

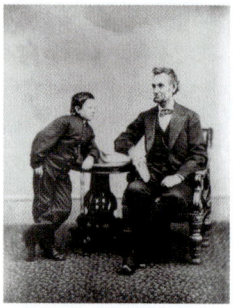

3.8.6 Alexander Gardner, *Abraham Lincoln and His Son, Thomas (Tad)*, 1865, p. 506

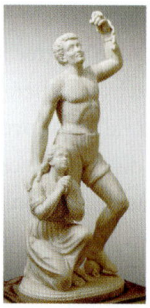

0.0.19 Edmonia Lewis, *Forever Free*, 1867, p. 36

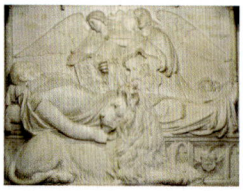

2.4.4 Susan Durant, *Memorial to King Leopold of the Belgians*, 1867, p. 244

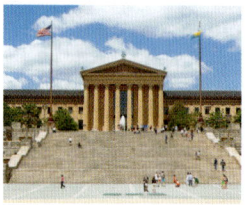

0.0.7 Philadelphia Museum of Art, Pennsylvania, p. 25

3.8 The Modern Aesthetic: Realism to Expressionism

Impressionism: in the visual arts, a late nineteenth-century style conveying the fleeting impression of the effects of light; Impressionists were artists working in this style
Post-Impressionists: artists either from or living in France, *c.* 1885–1905, who moved away from the Impressionist style—notably Cézanne, Gauguin, Seurat, and Van Gogh
Representational: art that depicts figures and objects so that we recognize what is represented
Symbolist: artist or artistic style belonging to the movement in European art and literature, *c.* 1885–1910, that conveyed meaning by the use of powerful yet ambiguous symbols
Expressionism, Expressionistic: an artistic style at its height in 1920s Europe, devoted to representing subjective emotions and experiences instead of objective or external reality
Abstract: art imagery that departs from recognizable images of the natural world
Modernism, Modernist: a radically new twentieth-century art and architectural movement that embraced modern industrial materials and a machine aesthetic
Salon: official annual exhibition of French painting, first held in 1667

In the second half of the nineteenth century, art entered a period of great experimentation. European and North American cultures and lifestyles were changing radically: railways expanded rapidly, steamships crossed the world's oceans, and industrial growth brought the rural poor to cities. Increasingly, the city, which offered modern forms of transport, such as the tram, and new technologies, such as electricity, became the center of economic activity and growth. The expanding economy, in turn, created a prosperous middle class who had the time and money to devote themselves to leisure and cultural pursuits. Those who could not afford hand-painted or -drawn portraits of themselves could purchase mass-produced photographic prints; for the first time in history, the culture people consumed became a central part of their identity, and an indication of their desired status. Economic prosperity also had political consequences: powerful European nations conquered empires worldwide and entered into competition for territory and resources. These tensions culminated in the cataclysm of World War I from 1914 to 1918.

Artists responded to the rapid and continuing pace of change in society with multiple forms of experimentation. Some, such as the **Impressionists** and **Post-Impressionists**, continued to be interested in **representational** art, but chose to explore the impact of the formal qualities of their artwork. They sought to capture the impression of the fleeting moment through quick brushstrokes, dabs of paint, and the use of vibrant color and light. Then there were artists who did the complete opposite. **Symbolists** and **Expressionists** attempted to portray what could be felt but not seen, venturing into the realm of the **abstract**.

Art Academies and Modernism

Much of the art of the late nineteenth and the early twentieth centuries that is most familiar to us today is often from experimental artists, pushing traditional boundaries and fighting against long-held artistic conventions with a view toward conveying the spirit of their time. **Modernism** itself is often defined as a movement that essentially broke with tradition. It is important to remember that much of the art respected today was considered shocking in its time, particularly to those who admired artists using classic conventions established and maintained by the Art Academies. Often, these were government-sponsored institutions set up to train artists to produce work in a particular style and following certain prescribed ideas about what was suitable subject matter for artworks. Indeed, modern artists were often held up for comparison, frequently in a negative manner, with those who were supported and exhibited by the academic system. By the end of the nineteenth century, this division led to artists establishing new avenues for selling and exhibiting their artworks outside of the traditional **Salon**.

Composition: the overall design or organization of a work
Illusionism: the artistic skill or trick of making something look real
Atmospheric perspective: use of shades of color and clarity to create the illusion of depth. Closer objects have warmer tones and clear outlines, while objects set further away are cooler and become hazy
Space: the distance between identifiable points or planes
Volume: the space filled or enclosed by a three-dimensional figure or object

The contrast between art produced within the traditions established by the Academy and the work of artists experimenting with other forms of representation can be understood by comparing two very different French paintings from 1863. Alexandre Cabanel's *Birth of Venus* (**3.8.1**) is an example of the kind of work that was highly appreciated in academic circles. A nude Venus, the mythical Greek goddess of love, lounges invitingly on the ocean, her sensual body on full display, offered submissively to the viewer's gaze, her eyes almost covered by her arm, and barely open. Flying young boys, known as *putti*, accompany her, creating a fluttering decorative "ribbon" above her reclining form.

The French painter Édouard Manet's (1832–1883) *Le Déjeuner sur l'Herbe (Luncheon on the Grass)* (**3.8.2**) also includes a naked woman, but a very different one from Cabanel's Venus. Manet's nude is completely awake, self-possessed, and looks self-confidently and directly at the viewer. She is accompanied, not by naked *putti*, but by fully clothed, middle-class men with whom she appears to be having a picnic. Far from being submissive, Manet's woman sits up, at ease with her nudity—she has casually discarded her clothes—and her businesslike gaze suggests she may be a modern prostitute, or perhaps an artist's model, rather than a mythological goddess. Viewers were shocked to see two men dressed in contemporary clothing casually placed in a local park next to a naked woman who (despite the speculation about her profession) does not seem to be portrayed for the erotic pleasure of the audience—her body is much less fully displayed than the Venus Cabanel depicted.

The artworks of Cabanel and Manet also differ in their painting and **compositional** techniques. Cabanel's artwork has a sense of depth and **illusionism**: for example, **atmospheric perspective** is used to show the land in the far distance. His Venus is fully rounded to give maximum appeal to the viewer. Manet, instead, flattens the visible **space** in his scene. In the small area of distant landscape in the center of the painting, he further destroys the illusion of depth by using thick brushstrokes and obscuring access to the objects in the distance with trees and the figure of an enigmatic woman stooping in the stream.

Manet's figures appear almost as cutouts, much less **volumetric** than Cabanel's erotic and fleshy nude, and whereas Cabanel uses

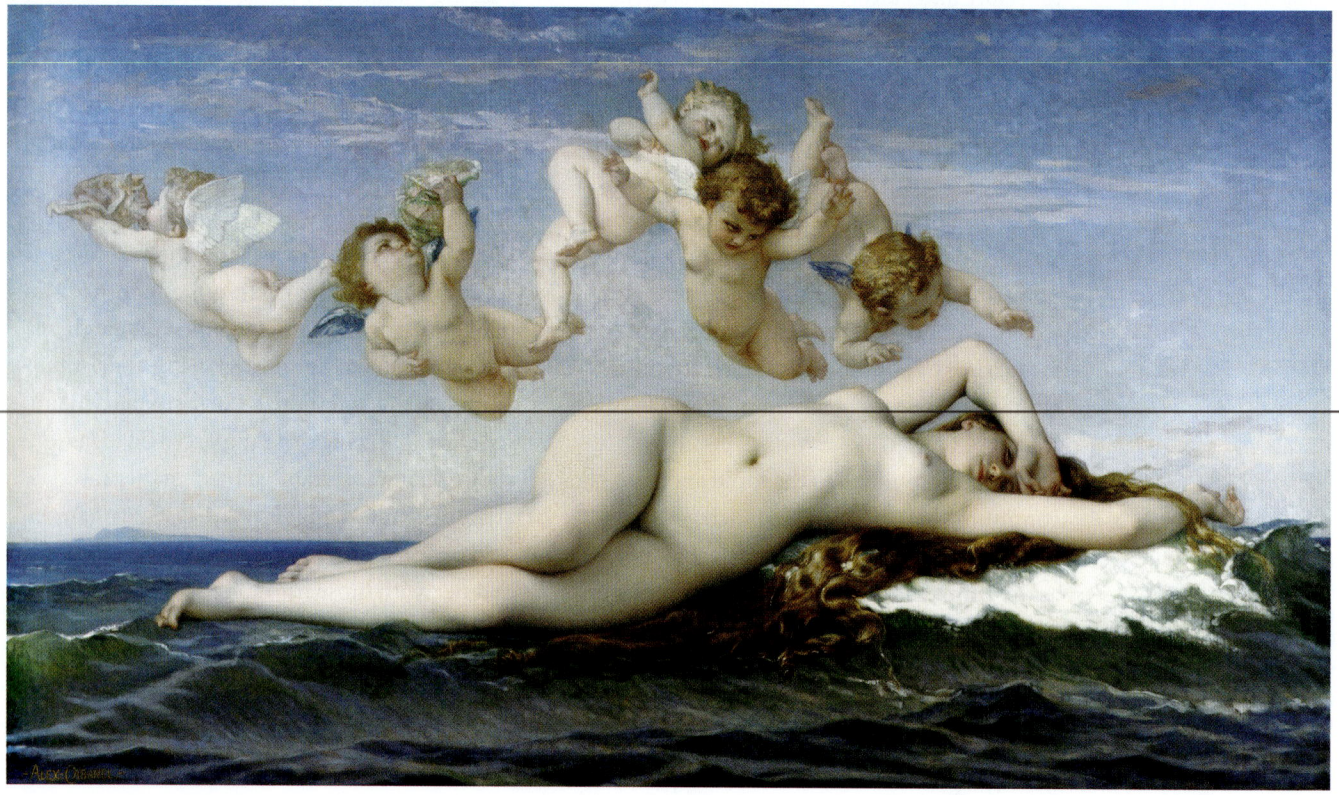

3.8.1 Alexandre Cabanel, *Birth of Venus*, 1863. Oil on canvas, 51⅛× 88½" Musée d'Orsay, Paris, France

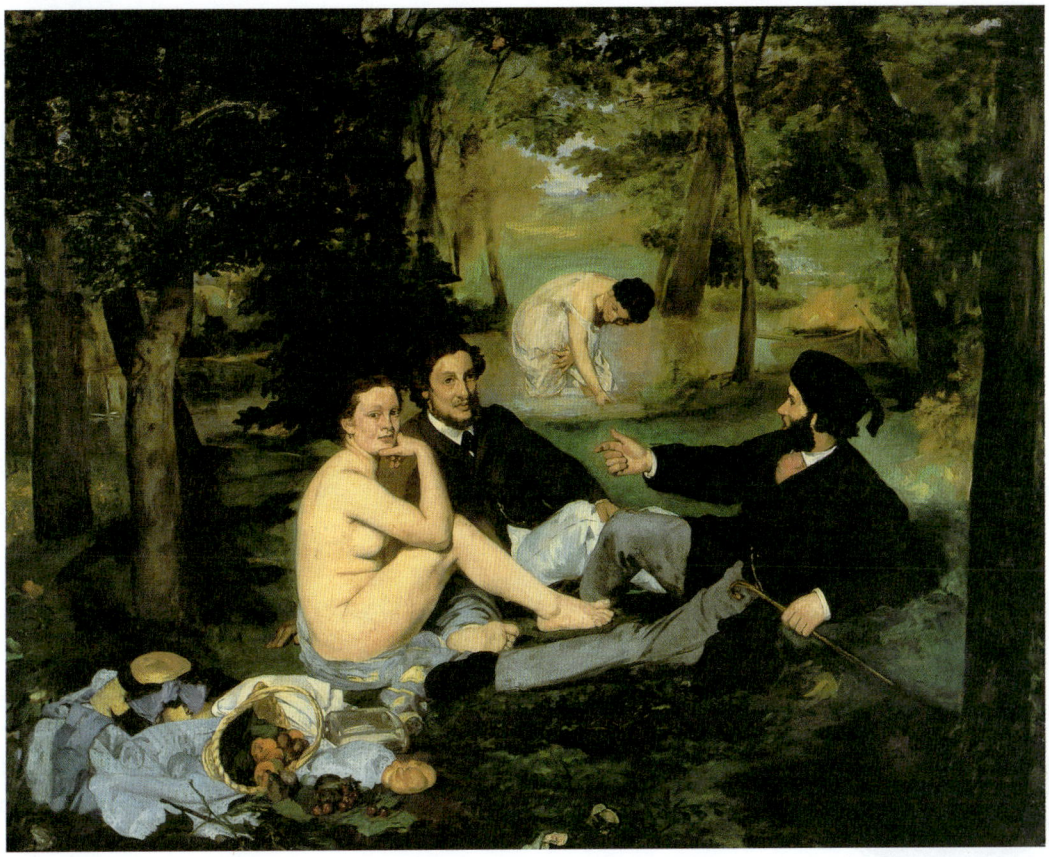

3.8.2 Édouard Manet, *Le Déjeuner sur l'Herbe (Luncheon on the Grass)*, 1863. Oil on canvas, 6'9⅞" × 8'8⅛". Musée d'Orsay, Paris, France

different degrees of **value** to model the flesh of his Venus, Manet's female appears as if sitting in an unnatural spotlight: unlike Cabanel's painting, there is no gradual, soft gradation from light to dark, and the **outline** of her body is harsh. Although shocked by the composition, contemporary viewers would have realized that Manet had based both his arrangement of figures and the fact that some were naked and some were clothed on already esteemed artworks, depicting mythological themes, in the Louvre museum. Manet is not interested in re-creating a mythological subject in an **idealized** way, however, but rather in portraying figures from his own era, and reflecting on the act of painting itself. By thinly disguising his use of **Classical** models to portray a controversial scene of leisure, Manet highlights in *Luncheon on the Grass* how distant the artistic standards of the Academy were from the styles adopted by modern painters.

Alexandre Cabanel had been supported by the Academy throughout his career, having been sent to study in Rome, and winning awards at previous Salons. Inclusion in the Salon was important to a successful artistic career, and could lead to both government and private commissions, but the jury that selected the works for the Salon was very conservative and increasingly out of step with developments in both technique and subject matter. Unhappiness with the traditional Academy and its Salon came to a head in 1863. While Cabanel's *Birth of Venus* was praised in the Salon of that year and purchased by Emperor Napoleon III for his personal collection, more unconventional works by Manet, Gustave Courbet and Camille Pissarro were rejected. Manet's *Luncheon on the Grass* was instead placed in an exhibition called the Salon des Refusés (Salon of the Rejected), which was arranged by Napoleon III to address the many complaints that year about the large number of artworks not accepted in the official Salon. Installed near the Salon, this second exhibition was designed to appease artists who felt unfairly excluded from that show. The Academy also anticipated that visitors to the exhibition would heap ridicule upon the artists and works its jury had rejected, but in this it was not entirely successful. Such paintings as Manet's *Luncheon on the Grass* were indeed mocked by some critics,

Value: the lightness or darkness of a plane or area
Outline: the outermost line or implied line of an object or figure, by which it is defined or bounded
Idealism: elevating depictions of nature to achieve more beautiful, harmonious, and perfect depictions
Classical, Classicism: art that conforms to Greek and Roman models, or is based on rational construction and emotional equilibrium

Realism, Realist: artistic style that aims to represent appearances as accurately as possible
Neoclassicism: European style that flourished during the late eighteenth and early nineteenth centuries, characterized by an extreme interest in the Classical world, strictly ordered scenes, and heroic subjects
Romanticism: movement in nineteenth-century European culture, concerned with the power of the imagination and greatly valuing intense feeling

but the public, thousands of whom flocked to the Salon des Refusés due to the controversy, was now exposed to art that had not been approved by the Academy. Artists were emboldened to exhibit independently in venues throughout Paris, and the power of the Salon was weakened. With this painting Manet proved that it was possible for an artist to create arresting work that did not conform to convention, and to break away from or alter traditional subjects and modes of representation. It is regarded by some as the work that marks the beginning of modern art, and Manet himself came to epitomize the notion of a modern painter.

Realism

> Show me an angel, and I'll paint one!
>
> (Gustave Courbet, French painter, defending Realism)

Beginning around the mid-nineteenth century, a significant shift took place in the objectives of the visual arts and in the way art looked. To varying degrees, a number of artists broke away from the traditions of earlier eighteenth- and nineteenth-century art to create objective representations of the real world. The movement called **Realism** refers specifically to writers and artists in France who were concerned about achieving social change after the Revolution of 1848. They created depictions of individuals in modern society, with underlying political messages about the inequality of the poor. Realism in general, however, can also refer to artists (in France and elsewhere) who observed their modern subjects in great detail yet did not have a social or political agenda. Realist artists also began to allow the process of creating art to show through in their final works, and were less concerned with illusionistic surfaces.

Gustave Courbet (1819–1877) is credited with first using the term "realist" to describe his own work. As a reaction to the **Neoclassical**, moralizing images of historic scenes, or the extremely emotional paintings of the **Romantics**, Courbet argued that it was more meaningful to paint people and things in everyday life.

The painting *Stonebreakers* was shocking for its depiction of working-class people on a large-sized canvas, a scale normally reserved for the heroic subject matter of history paintings (**3.8.3**). Courbet's painting highlights the backbreaking, monotonous work of the poor. The breaking of stones was a job taught by older generations to young men, and it was a job a man would have for a lifetime. The painting shows an older worker and his young assistant as powerful and unrelenting—qualities that alarmed the upper classes: a year before Courbet painted this work, in the Revolution of 1848, workers throughout Europe had rebelled and demanded an end to bad working conditions and to low pay.

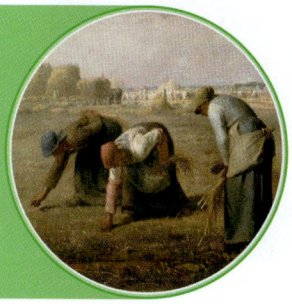

As with Courbet's work, Jean-François Millet's *The Gleaners* highlights respect for the struggling working class: **1.7.3, p. 142**

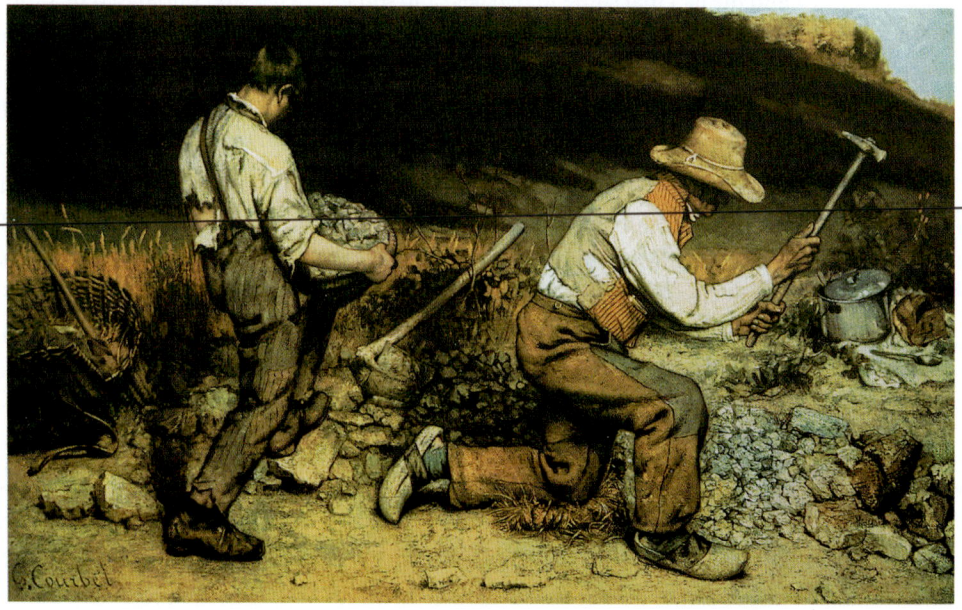

3.8.3 Gustave Courbet, *Stonebreakers*, 1849. Oil on canvas, 5'3" × 6'8". Formerly in the Gemäldegalerie, Dresden, Germany; believed to have been destroyed in 1945

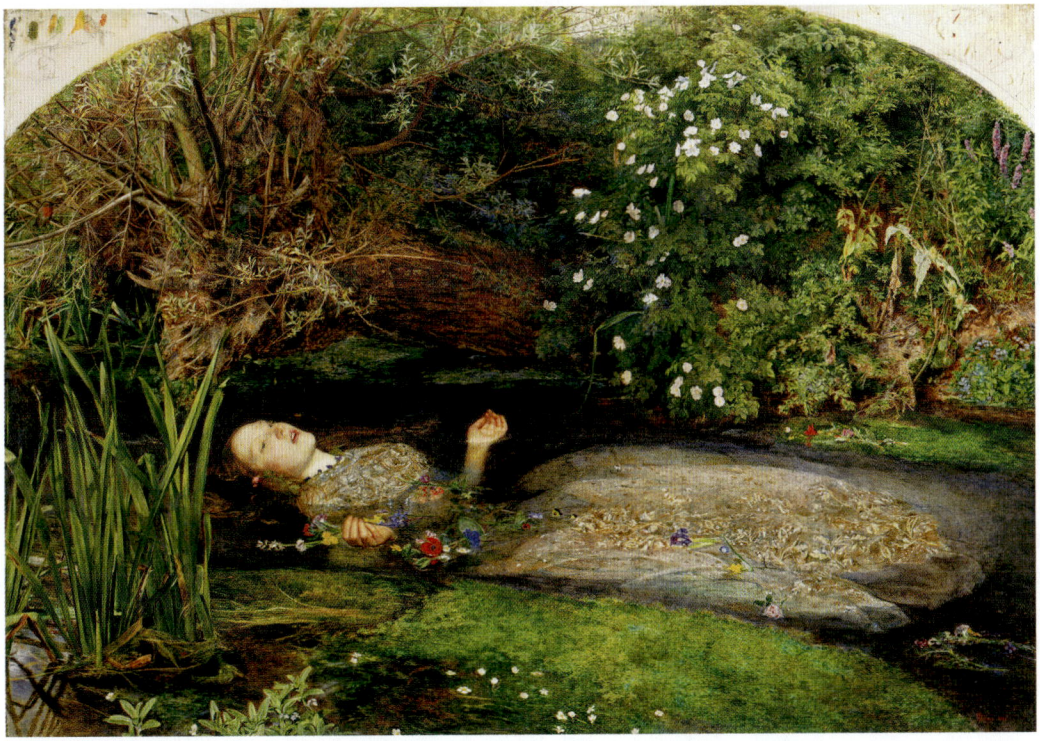

3.8.4 John Everett Millais, *Ophelia*, 1851–52. Oil on canvas, 30 × 44". Tate, London, England

Pre-Raphaelite Brotherhood: English art movement formed in 1848 by painters who rejected the academic rules of art, and often painted medieval subjects in a naïve style
Renaissance: a period of cultural and artistic change in Europe from the fourteenth to the seventeenth century

Realist tendencies took a different form in the case of a group of English painters and writers, formed in 1848, who called themselves the **Pre-Raphaelite Brotherhood**. While many Realist painters in France were rejecting the traditions of their Academy, the Pre-Raphaelites, as they became known, were opposed to the values of the Royal Academy of Arts in Britain, which promoted artwork inspired by artists of ancient Greece and Rome and of the **Renaissance**. Pre-Raphaelite artists were instead inspired by medieval subject matter. They were realist in their intense attention to visual details and their true-to-life depictions of nature and people.

Ophelia (**3.8.4**) by the Pre-Raphaelite John Everett Millais (1829–1896) depicts a scene from Shakespeare's tragedy *Hamlet*, in which the young female character, Ophelia, drowns herself because her lover Prince Hamlet has rejected her and accidentally killed her father. Millais's depiction of nature is painstakingly detailed. To make this painting, he selected a single spot on a nearby river and painted the plants growing there so carefully that botanists can identify every one. He worked at the site almost every day over a five-month period. Millais also included flowers that were not growing by the river but that are mentioned in *Hamlet*. He then took realism to the extreme by having his model pose for the painting in a filled bathtub so that he could study the way her hair and dress floated. Although she often had oil lamps around her to keep her warm, the model caught a severe cold from spending so many hours in the water in the middle of winter.

Emily Mary Osborn (1828–1925) exhibited *Nameless and Friendless* (**3.8.5**) at the Royal Academy of Arts, London, in 1857, the same

3.8.5 Emily Mary Osborn, *Nameless and Friendless*, 1857. Oil on canvas, 32½ × 40⅞". Tate, London, England

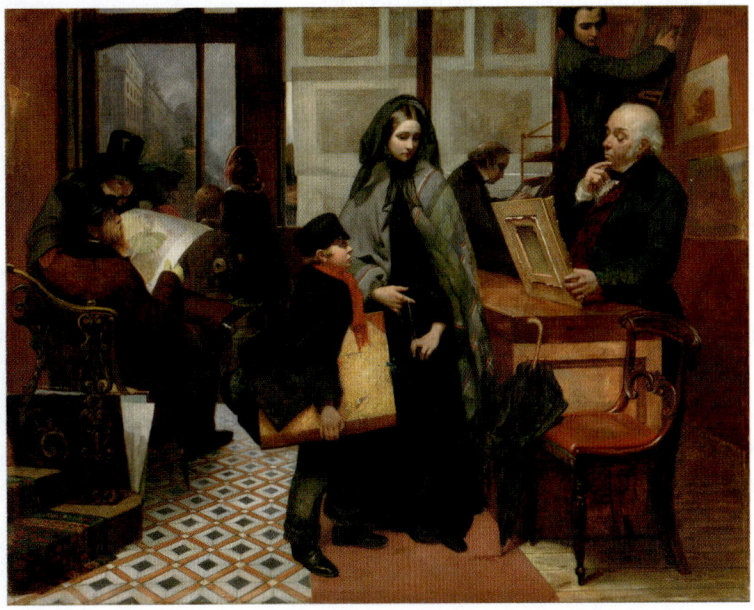

year she became a member of the Society of Female Artists, which was an organization designed to support the unique challenges of being a woman artist. Osborn was actively involved in women's suffrage, and, in 1859, petitioned to allow women to become students at the Academy. *Nameless and Friendless* shows the experience of a female artist, wearing black (so in mourning), trying to sell her work to a local dealer. She is accompanied by a boy who carries her work, also suggesting that she does not have a man in her life to escort her. As she humbly looks down and plays with some string in her hand, she awaits the assessment of the shopkeeper. The two men on the left look up from studying an artwork of a ballet dancer to leer at the woman, suggesting that they are thinking of her unclothed like the dancer. Osborn is making a statement in this work about the roles to which women are restricted in society. A third woman, one of higher status, is exiting the shop with her son; she is barely noticed, as Osborn argued was the case for many women at this time.

A Revolutionary Invention: Photography and Art in the Nineteenth Century

Realism was partly inspired and fueled by the invention of photography in the first decades of the nineteenth century, which led many artists to feel pressured to capture the truth of everyday life the way that photographers could. The advent of photography also affected artists directly in terms of their income. A client who wanted, for example, a portrait, had previously had only one option: to pay a portrait artist to paint a likeness, which was a time-consuming task for both the artist and the **sitter**, expensive for the client, and lucrative for the artist. Photography provided another, much less laborious and less expensive way to record a likeness or an event in a very realistic manner.

By the 1860s, portraits were commonly taken of celebrities, and portraits of families were common. Exposure times, while still taking several seconds, no longer took minutes, so sitters did not have to be still for very long. President Lincoln had more than forty individual photographic portraits taken of himself while in office, and credited these photos, often reproduced in small sizes for the public, with helping Americans feel like they knew him, and with fueling support for his political decisions. Figure **3.8.6** shows Lincoln, donning a rare, slight smile, sitting with a book while one of his sons stands casually nearby.

Since portraits had long been produced by professionally trained painters and sculptors, the ability of the camera to record such scenes as Lincoln's portrait raised some important questions. Could portraits made with a camera be considered art? In other words, were photographers artists, or simply technicians creating reproductions? The notion that photographers could replace the role of painters sparked a debate that raged during the second half of the nineteenth century.

Sitter: person who poses, or "sits," for an artist to paint, sculpt, or photograph

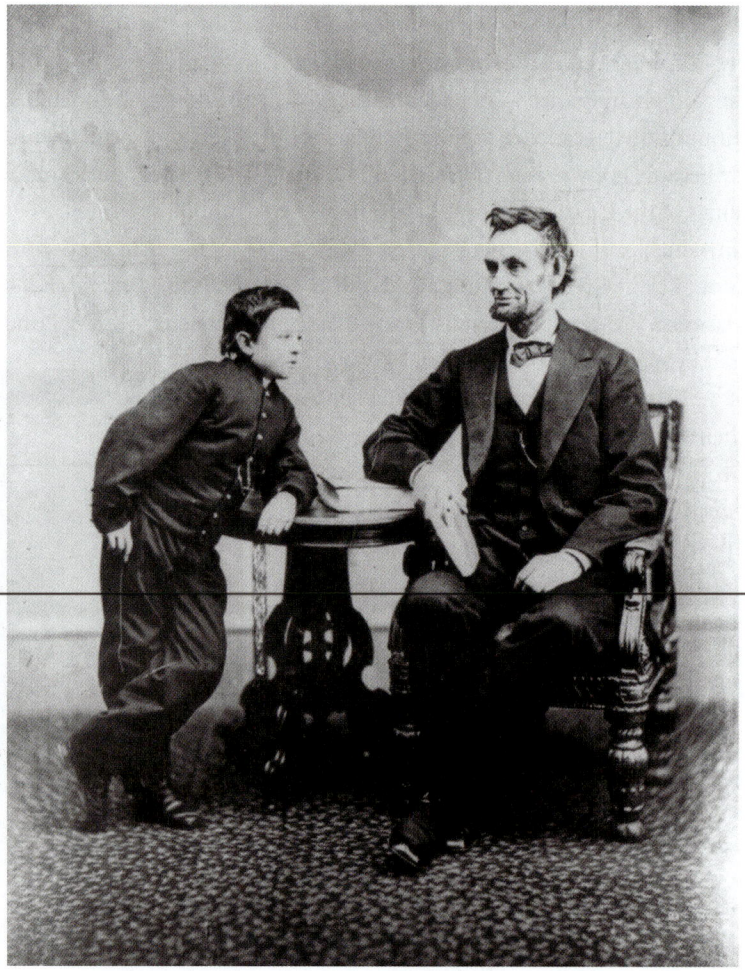

3.8.6 Alexander Gardner, *Abraham Lincoln and His Son Thomas (Tad)*, February 5, 1865. Silver gelatin print, 8 × 10". Library of Congress Prints, Washington, D. C.

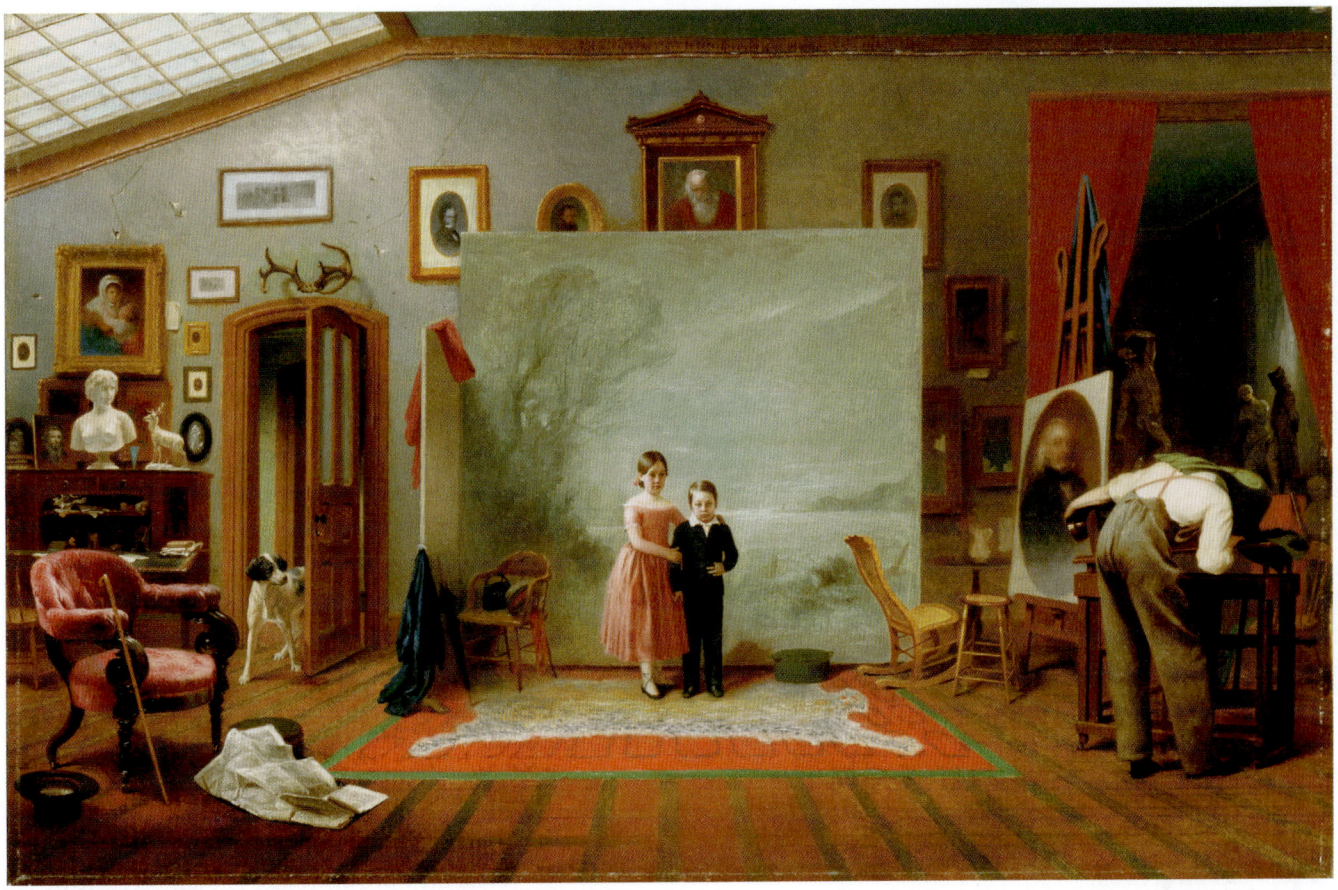

3.8.7 Thomas Le Clear, *Interior with Portraits*, c. 1865. Oil on canvas, 25⅞ x 40½". Smithsonian American Art Museum, Washington, D. C.

Thomas Le Clear's *Interior with Portraits* at first seems to be self-explanatory (**3.8.7**). A young brother and sister are posed before a painted landscape while a photographer on the far right snaps their picture. Le Clear, however, is highlighting the tension between photographers and painters as they competed for **patrons** in this period. While photographs are often thought to be accurate accounts of reality, Le Clear shows that in some ways paintings can be more truthful.

The date of the painting, 1865, marks the year of the death of the young boy shown, James Sidney. Yet Sidney did not die as a child, but as a firefighter at the adult age of twenty-six. His sister, Parnell, however, died years prior, in 1849. Therefore, the children shown in the painting were not this age nor even alive when this canvas was painted. The scene is effectively a memorial to the lost pair, and the painting is able to create an apparent reality and transcend time in a way that the camera, used to capture particular real-life moments, could not. While post-mortem photographs of deceased children, which helped the bereaved remember their loved ones' faces, were common during this period, Le Clear shows that, in this case, a painting could keep these children alive in the memory of their loved ones better than a photograph.

In the decades that followed Le Clear's painting, some artists responded to the advent of photography and the restrictions of their traditional academic training by continuing to question what the purpose of art should be. The French poet Charles Baudelaire declared that "As the photographic industry became the refuge of all failed painters with too little talent, or too lazy to complete their studies. . .the badly applied advances of photography. . .have greatly contributed to the impoverishment of French artistic genius." Others, however, saw positive opportunities, and experimented with the artistic potential of the new medium.

For instance, the American artist Thomas Eakins (1844–1916) was a student at the first American art academy, the Pennsylvania Academy of the Fine Arts. When he started teaching there in 1876, and later became its director in

Patron: an organization or individual who sponsors the creation of works of art

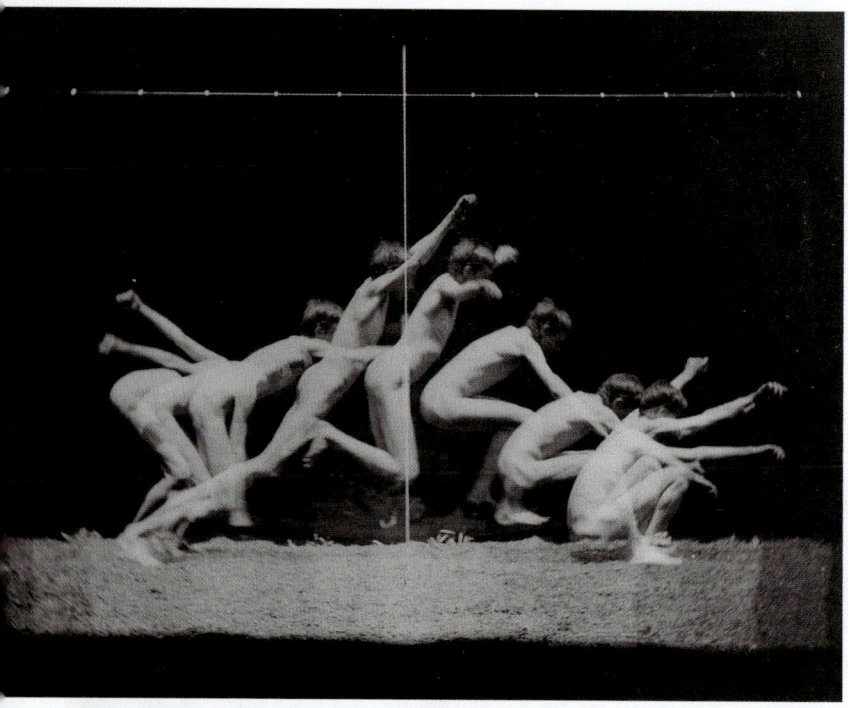

3.8.8 Thomas Eakins, *Motion Study: Male Nude, Standing Jump to Right*, 1884. Dry plate negative, 3⅝ × 4½". Pennsylvania Academy of the Fine Arts, Philadelphia

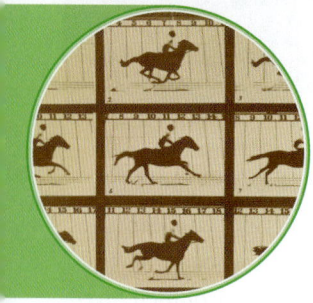

Eadweard Muybridge studied horse movements using photography in 1878: see **2.9.3, p. 336**

1882, his methods were controversial because of their deviation from traditional European approaches. Rather than follow the standard artistic norm—that of the intense study of the nude figure, Classical statuary and the work of earlier artists—Eakins promoted the study of anatomy through photographs and through observation of dissections. Influenced by the photography of Eadweard Muybridge and his study of horses and humans in motion, he, too, observed the human body in motion through photography. Eakins superimposed several exposures of a jumping man onto one negative (**3.8.8**), creating a tool to improve his understanding of anatomy for his paintings. Due to his unconventional teaching methods, including allowing women to study the full male nude, Eakins was forced to resign in 1886.

Impressionism

The artists who came to be called Impressionists worked in individual, sometimes very different styles, but they were united in rejecting the formal approach of the art taught in the Academy in Paris. Their art attempted not so much to portray exactly and realistically such scenes as a landscape or life in a city (although they did depict those subjects), as to capture the light and sensations produced by the scene. The Impressionists formed a group to show their work together outside the official Salon, in eight exhibitions held between 1874 and 1886. Their subject matter was scenes of everyday life: rural landscapes, and life in the modern and growing cities of France—especially scenes of the middle classes engaged in leisure pursuits. The Impressionists were often intent on capturing the essence of moments in time, and many of them painted ***en plein air***, made possible by the advent of tubed containers for oil paint.

Before the Impressionists, artists who followed traditional methods of painting gave their work a smooth surface, often finishing paintings with a topcoat of varnish, so that the application of the paint was not evident. Impressionists, on the other hand, chose to reveal their brushstrokes. The almost sketchy, unfinished appearance of many Impressionist works breaks away from the academic tradition of simply creating an illusion of three-dimensional space on the canvas. Instead, Impressionists flattened space, welcomed texture created by the paint, and often allowed the canvas to be seen beneath the painting. Many Impressionist paintings do indeed have an apparently unfinished quality, because the artists are interested in capturing instantaneous moments rather than creating a highly finished, technically flawless piece of work.

The Impressionists lived during a time in which great strides were made in the studies of optics and color theory, which changed the way these artists painted. They discovered that if they applied individual colors in their purest form on the canvas, rather than mixing them beforehand on the **palette**, the colors remained more intense. Through observation they realized that objects are not one single color, but are made up of many variations of color; to imitate this, Impressionist artists placed brushstrokes of different colors next to one another, knowing that the viewer's eye would blend disparate **hues**,

En plein air: French for "in the open air", used to describe painting out of doors from start to finish rather than working in a studio for all or part of the process

Palette: a smooth slab or board used for mixing paints or cosmetics

Hue: general classification of a color; the distinctive characteristics of a color as seen in the visible spectrum, such as green or red

Optical mixture: when the eye blends two colors that are placed near one another, creating a new color
Woodblock: a relief print process where the image is carved into a block of wood
Cropping: trimming the edges of an image, or composing it so that part of the subject matter is cut off
Asymmetry: a type of design in which balance is achieved by elements that contrast and complement one another without being the same on either side of an axis
Rhythm: the regular or ordered repetition of elements in the work

a process known as **optical mixture**. Often, too, Impressionists reinterpreted the bright natural light of day in their paintings by applying a layer of white paint as a base coat.

The Impressionists were also influenced by photography and Japanese **woodblock** prints (see Box: Influences on the Impressionists: Japanese Woodcuts and Photography, p 510). They adopted unusual vantage points and **cropping** of scenes in ways resembling these media, including arranging space within an image using **asymmetry** and the layering of objects. While photographers could capture a single moment in time, the Impressionists tried to capture the sensations of such moments: the atmosphere, colors, light, and individual impressions.

Whereas many painters in the past, working within their studios, had taken the upper classes as their subject, the Impressionists instead often painted outdoors and chose to capture the urban middle classes in such places as bustling cafés. In a period when people had more leisure time than ever before, the Impressionists depicted Parisians, for example, dancing, drinking, swimming, and attending the opera or the ballet. Such paintings as *Bal du Moulin de la Galette* by Pierre-Auguste Renoir (1841–1919) were intended to transport viewers into a world of beauty and pleasure (**3.8.9**). Renoir shows people at a popular outdoor café in the Montmartre district of Paris. The dappled sunlight falls through the trees onto the scene as if to create a **rhythm** that reflects the joyfulness of the gathering. The absence of strong outlines, the feathery brushstrokes, and his use of dark blues and purples instead of black, are characteristic of Renoir's style.

3.8.9 Pierre-Auguste Renoir, *Bal du Moulin de la Galette*, 1876. Oil on canvas, 51⅝ × 68⅞". Musée d'Orsay, Paris, France

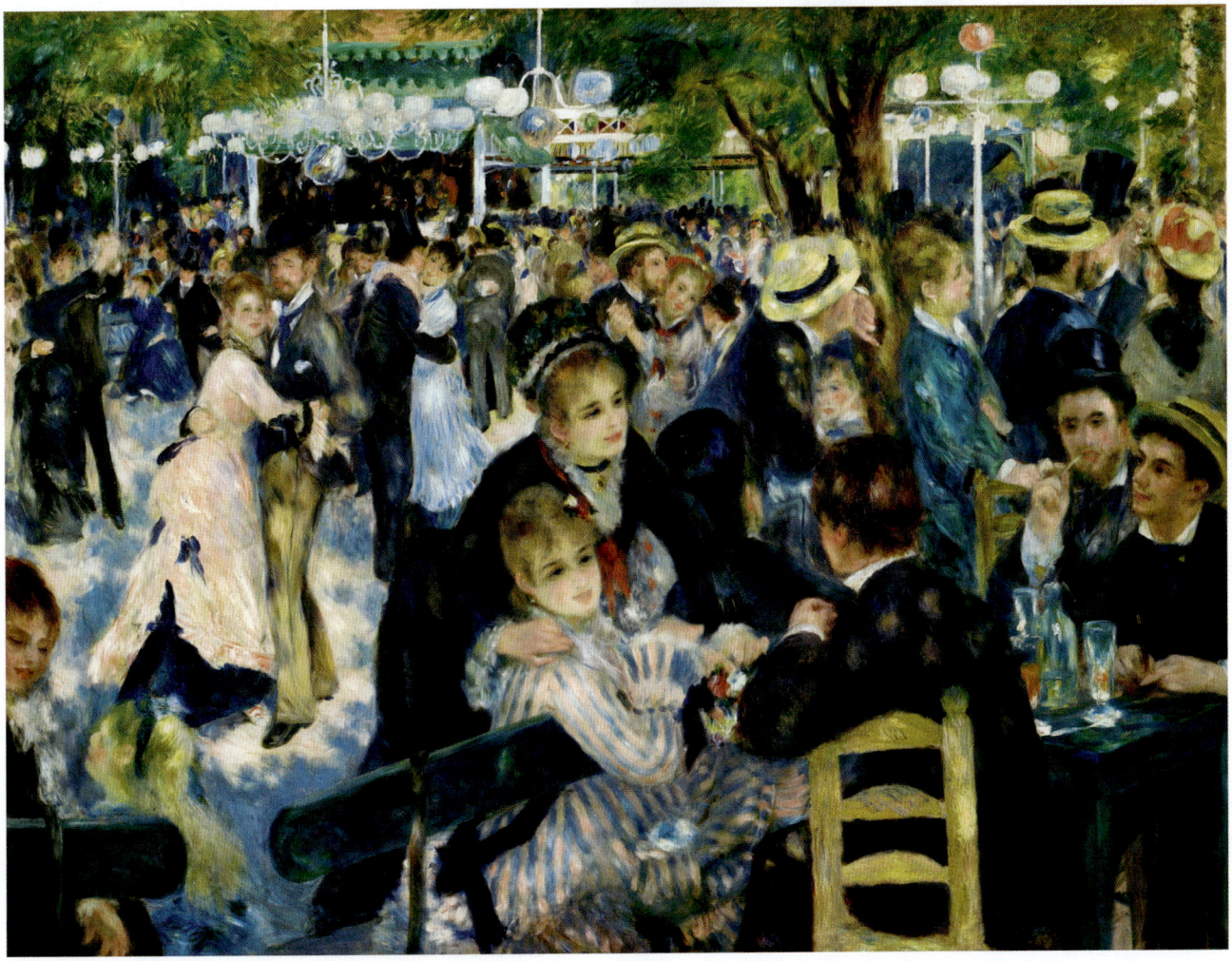

Influences on the Impressionists: Japanese Woodcuts and Photography

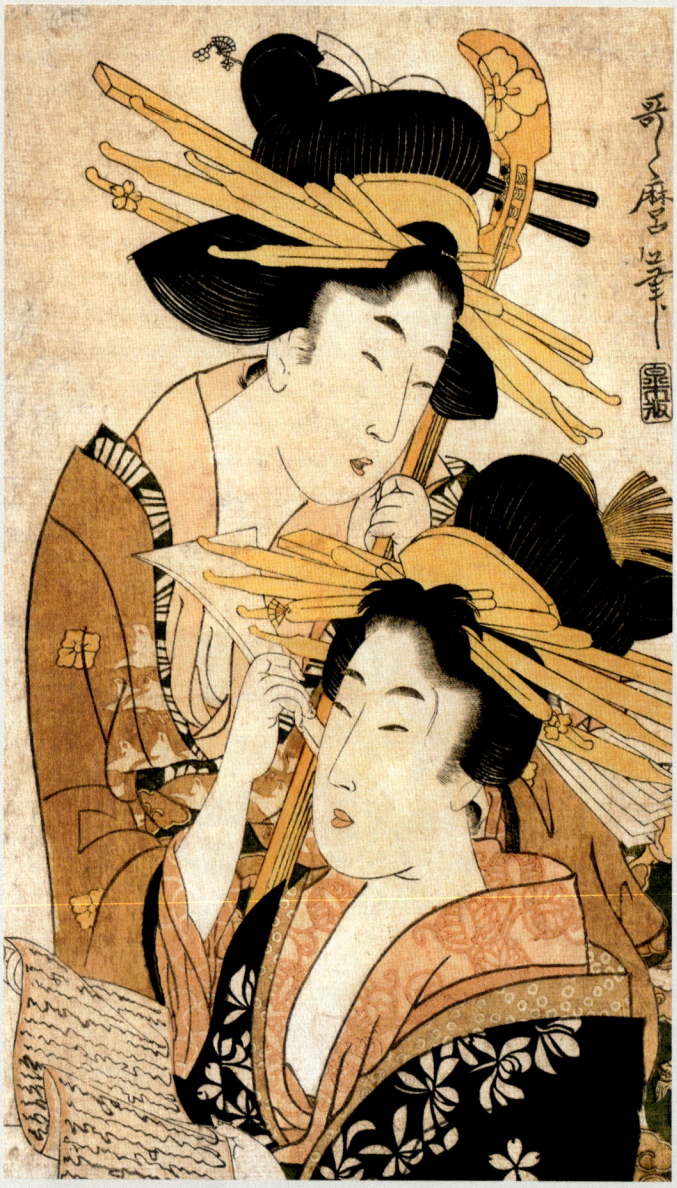

3.8.10 Kitagawa Utamaro, *Two Courtesans*, second half of 18th century. Woodblock print, 12⅝ × 7½". Victoria and Albert Museum, London, England

Japanese prints depicted cropped, asymmetrical scenes, which had a flattened sense of space because objects were emphasized with bold outlines rather than shadows. After studying such prints, the Impressionist painters and other modern artists began to incorporate slanted viewpoints, bright colors, and busy patterns into their work. This influence is known as *Japonisme.*

The American painter Mary Cassatt (1844–1926) lived most of her life in France and exhibited with the Impressionists. After seeing more than one hundred of the Japanese printmaker Kitagawa Utamaro's prints exhibited in Paris in 1890, Cassatt wrote to friends raving about him; later, she began creating prints very much in his style. Cassatt herself had always focused on the daily lives of women in her paintings. A comparison between one of Utamaro's prints (**3.8.10**) and a painting by Cassatt (**3.8.11**), made three years after she had seen the Japanese artist's work in Paris, highlights the techniques Cassatt emulated.

3.8.11 Mary Cassatt, *The Child's Bath*, 1893. Oil on canvas, 39½ × 26". Art Institute of Chicago, Illinois

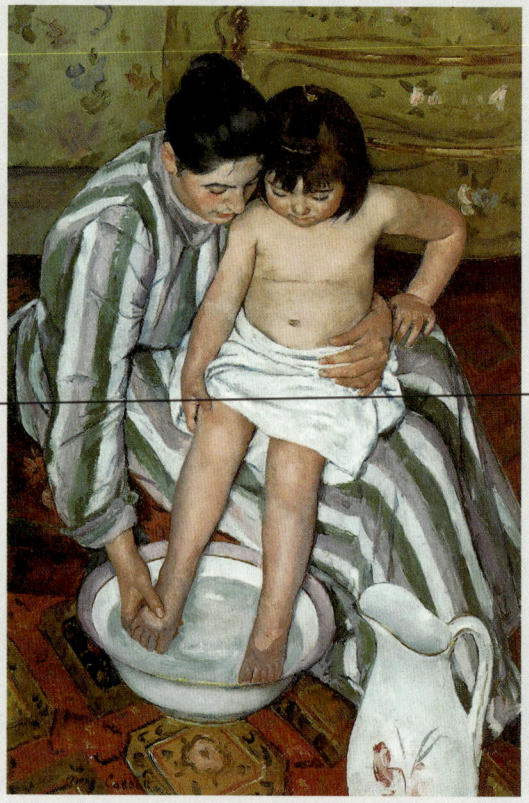

The art of the Impressionists reflected the world they lived in, and they were inspired by other new art forms that surrounded them in Paris. Most importantly, the influx of woodblock prints from Japan, and the advent of photography, changed the way Impressionist artists perceived and composed their own works.

Modeling: the representation of three-dimensional objects in two dimensions so that they appear solid

The composition of the two scenes is very similar. Each creates a strong diagonal line from the upper right to the lower left. The musical instrument is gently being played by the lady in the background of Utamaro's print, while in Cassatt's painting the child's foot is gently stroked by her mother's hand. The mother's right arm and that of the musician are both, in contrast to the objects that they hold, strictly vertical.

Both artists use bold lines to create a flattening of space and absence of **modeling**. In Utamaro's print, lines in the ladies' dresses suggest folds, but also make the women appear as two-dimensional as the writing on the paper one of them holds. Cassatt creates a similar effect with the striped lines on the mother's dress, which lengthen the figure but give her body less volume than the child she holds. The child, in contrast, has softer outlines and a range of values on her skin.

The background of Utamaro's print is mostly empty, creating a space behind the ladies apart from some twisting flowers on one of the robes, and crowded calligraphy on the pages at the left. Cassatt fills her background space, but her busy floral patterns echo the flowers in the Japanese work.

Lastly, Japanese prints often look at their subject from multiple vantage points. Utamaro's ladies are viewed from up close and at the same height, but the bottom of the rearmost lady's dress, the music, and parts of the instrument are seen from above. Similarly, in Cassatt's painting, the viewer looks at the child's torso, the dresser in the background, and at the pitcher in the lower right corner from directly in front at the same height. Yet, simultaneously, the bowl of water and the rug are viewed from above.

The formal qualities of photography, such as sharp framing and the cropping of the world it portrays, its lack of even focus across the **picture plane**, and its tendency to flatten the illusion of depth, were also mimicked by Impressionist and modern artists in their paintings.

Edgar Degas (1834–1917) was a prolific artist who reveled in experimentation in pastel, charcoal, oil, photography, **lithography**, and sculpture. For his artworks he frequently studied female subjects, including prostitutes, singers, and bathers. One of his favorite subjects was ballet dancers, whom he studied both during performances, in practice, and backstage (**3.8.12**). Degas's scenes of dancers evoke the everyday quality of a dancer's life, and his composition gives the impression of immediacy, as if the viewer has caught the dancers off guard, primping before their performance. The artist masterfully drew on the surface by holding the pastel in his hand (rather than using a paintbrush), to create a rich texture in which light bounces off the flesh and dresses of the dancers.

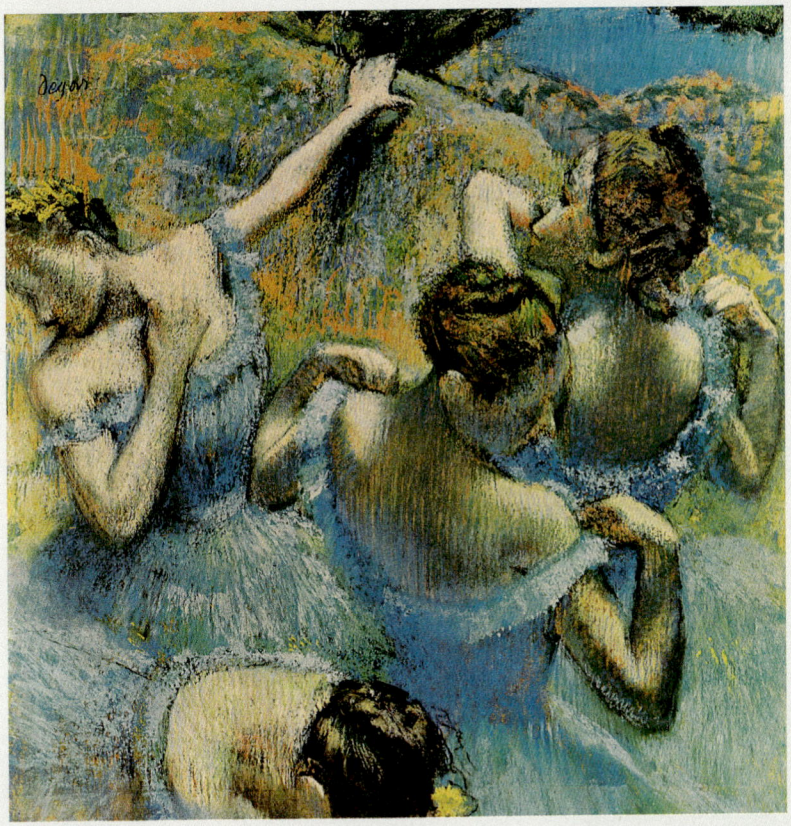

3.8.12 Edgar Degas, *Blue Dancers*, c. 1898. Pastel on paper, 25½ × 25½". The Pushkin State Museum of Fine Arts, Moscow, Russia

Influence from Japanese prints is evident in Degas's dynamic composition, which uses diagonal lines to guide the viewer's eyes around the scene. The head of the girl on the left and the body of the girl at the bottom of the composition are cropped, a device he learned from studying photography as well as Japanese prints. Likewise, the scene is viewed from above (a device known as **bird's-eye view**), a vantage point used by many early photographers when shooting scenes out of their windows.

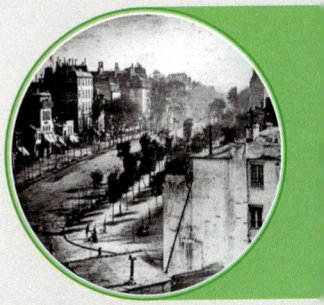

This photograph by Daguerre, looking down on a Paris street, is the first to contain a person: see **2.8.4, p. 317**

Picture plane: the surface of a painting or drawing
Lithography: a print process done on a flat, unmarred surface, like a stone, in which the image is created using oil-based ink with resistance to water
Bird's-eye view: an artistic technique in which a scene or subject is presented from some point above it

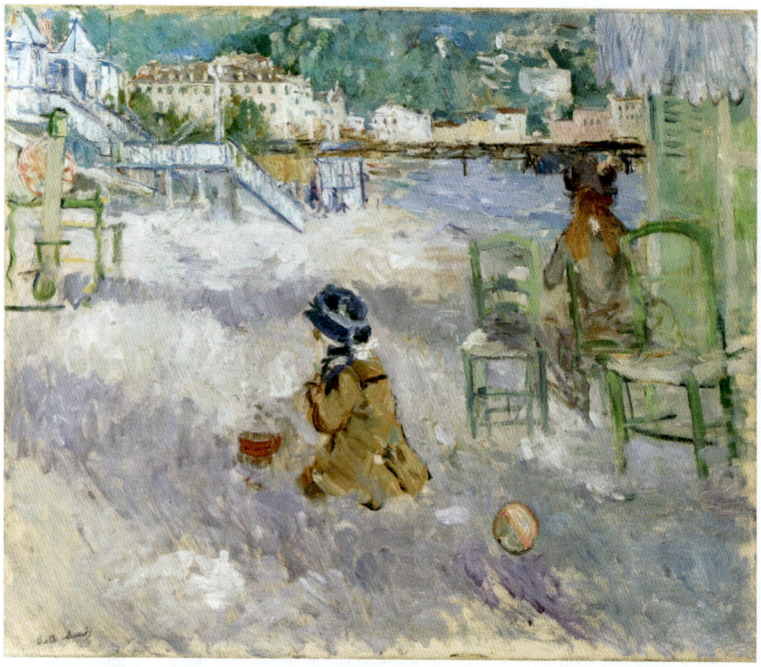

3.8.13 Berthe Morisot, *The Beach at Nice*, 1882. Oil on canvas, 18¼ × 22"

Berthe Morisot (1841–1895) exhibited in all but one of the Impressionist exhibitions and was particularly close friends with Édouard Manet, who became her brother-in-law. As a female of upper-class stature, Morisot did not have access to many of the modern subjects painted by her fellow Impressionists. Therefore, her images are usually of women, children, gardens, or domestic spaces, all subjects she would see in her daily life. As with many of the Impressionists, Morisot portrayed people doing everyday things, who are unaware or uninterested in the fact that they are being watched.

The Beach at Nice (**3.8.13**) shows a young girl playing in the sand at the beach next to a woman reading. Morisot captures the sensations of being at the beach: the bright light, the brisk breeze, and quiet relaxation. Her seemingly quick brushstrokes appear to blur into nothing when one stands close to the painting but transform into objects and shadows when one steps away. The exquisitely painted blue hat in the center of the painting draws the viewer to the little girl, likely Morisot's daughter Julie. Although the painting appears to have been created *en plein air*, Julie writes in her journal of how her mother painted watercolors at the beach and then painted this scene back in their hotel room.

Another perspective on the everyday life of the French middle class can be seen in a painting by Gustave Caillebotte (1848–1894) of the newly renovated busy streets of Paris. The artist was a wealthy lawyer as well as a painter, who supported other Impressionists financially.

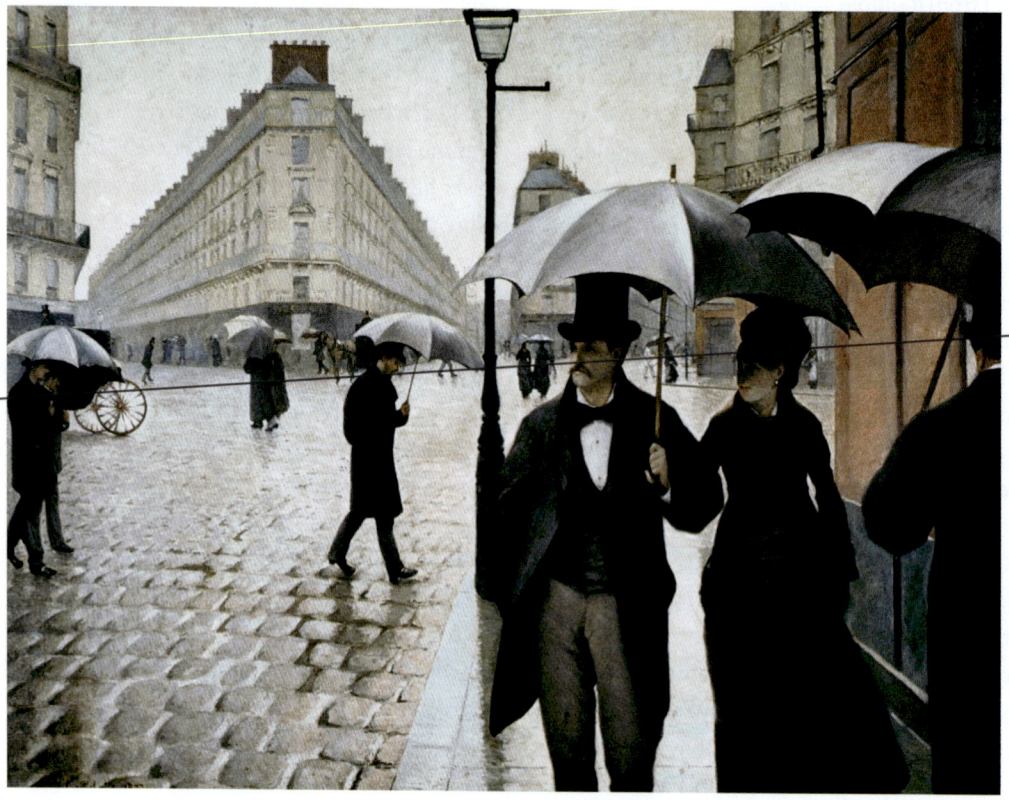

3.8.14 Gustave Caillebotte, *Paris Street, Rainy Day*, 1877. Oil on canvas, 6'11½" × 9'¾". Art Institute of Chicago, Illinois

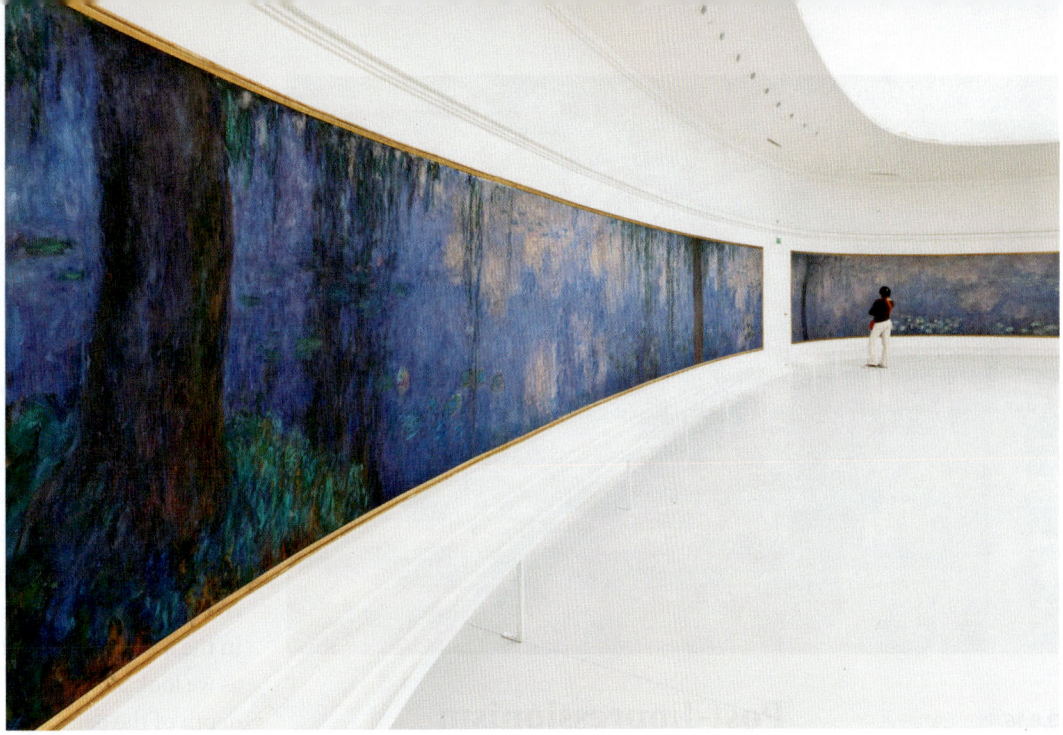

3.8.15 Claude Monet, *Waterlillies*, c. 1914–18. Oil on canvas. Musée de l'Orangerie, Paris, France

Linear perspective: a system using converging imaginary sight lines to create the illusion of depth

Foreshortening: a perspective technique that depicts a form—often distorting or reducing it—at an angle that is not parallel to the picture plane, in order to convey the illusion of depth

Caillebotte's *Paris Street: Rainy Day* (**3.8.14**) shows the results of the massive rebuilding of Paris organized by Baron Haussmann, the prefect or state representative of the region. Under the direction of Napoleon III, Haussmannization involved tearing down much of the medieval city, an action that displaced thousands, and building glorious new boulevards, townhouses, and parks. Caillebotte makes use of **linear perspective** to show how the modern boulevards extend in every direction, like spokes on a wheel. A green lamppost and its shadow extend beyond the height of the canvas, creating a strong vertical line that divides the composition. To the left of the post, very **foreshortened**, is a newly designed apartment building. To the right is a well-dressed couple who, although surrounded by the different classes of people in the city, seem to be alone and in their own world. Caillebotte captures the mood of a rainy day with the cloudy atmosphere and soaked streets and pavement.

The works of Claude Monet (1840–1926) most exemplified the "impressionistic" brushstrokes for which the group of painters was known. At the first Impressionist exhibition in 1874, his painting *Impression, Sunrise* (1872)—which indicated with only a few brushstrokes the sea, the reflection of the sun, and the boats in the background—helped to give the group their famous name. As his work evolved, Monet made series of paintings that focused on individual subjects, such as cathedrals, haystacks, poplars, and train stations. Within these series, rather than altering the subject, each work varied slightly in the way it captured mood, light, color, time of day, and atmosphere. In 1890, Monet purchased a house and land in the French town of Giverny, where he designed his own pond filled with water lilies. He created more than 300 water-lily paintings based on his pond. While at first these paintings might seem similar, they are each unique. Monet would paint both from a distance and up close, both above and beside the flowers, and both single flowers and large groups. To mark the end of World War I, and as a symbol of peace, Monet created his largest water-lily project, which he described as "a bouquet for France" (**3.8.15**). The project consists of eight painted panels, later hung within two white oval rooms at his house at Giverny, now a museum for the public. Rather than looking at the water lilies and the pond, the display places viewers within the pond. From this vantage point, viewers experience changes in weather, light, and atmosphere as the windows of the room affect the space. The elliptical rooms were also designed to create the symbol for infinity, as the space forever changes with and responds to nature.

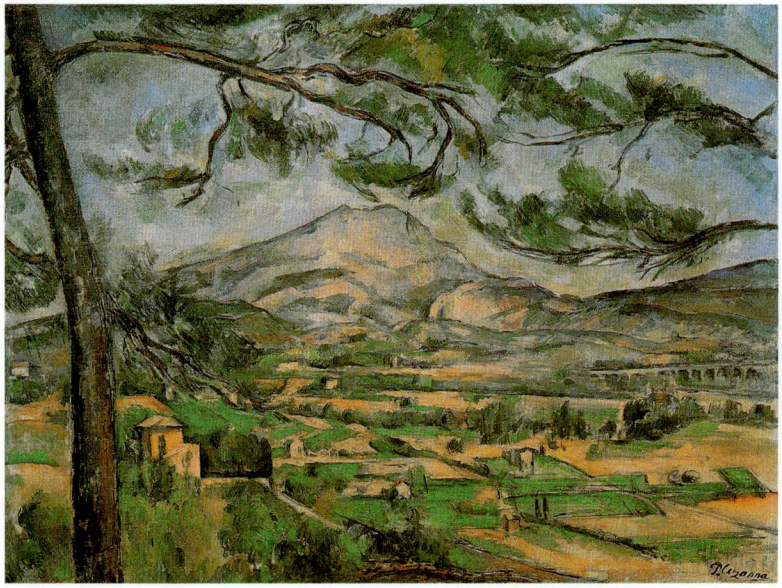

3.8.16 Paul Cézanne, *Mont Sainte-Victoire*, c. 1886–88. Oil on canvas, 26 × 36¼". Courtauld Gallery, London, England

Post-Impressionism

By the 1880s, the once-revolutionary Impressionism had gained great public popularity amongst the newly risen middle class. Yet the Academy critics accused the Impressionists of lacking discipline and training, and of having no intellectual substance other than a shallow preoccupation with the depiction of beauty. Impressionist artists responded to these criticisms in different ways: Monet developed his serial approach, in which he analysed atmosphere rather than subject matter; Renoir returned to Classical models and created a series of bathers. The movement that resulted, that of Post-Impressionism, consisted of artists who had been exposed to, and often participated in, the Impressionist movement, but who wanted to differentiate themselves from what was then perceived to be the simplicity of the Impressionists. They preferred instead to emphasize abstract qualities or subjective content in their artworks.

The French painter Paul Cézanne (1839–1906) developed a new type of landscape painting through intense study of Mont Sainte-Victoire, a mountain he could see from his studio (and childhood home) in Aix-en-Provence, where he worked for much of his adult life. Cézanne made several paintings of this mountain, working on some of them for years. By gradually adding brushstrokes to reflect the mountain's changing atmosphere and weather conditions, Cézanne sought to construct the essence of the mountain as it appeared over time, rather than at a single moment.

Cézanne created the structure of his landscape in a very different way from earlier painters. He conceived a view of nature in which the subject was analysed from multiple views, forms became abstracted, and planes shifted. For example, Cézanne utilized his understanding of atmospheric perspective to blend warm and cool colors within the same structure, as in the mountain (**3.8.16**). This creates a push–pull effect for viewers, as the warm hues of the mountain come toward us, and cool colors recede. The tree in the foreground creates a similar experience as we look at it, a feeling of being pulled into the depth of the painting and then being pushed forward, as if the image has been flattened. The upper branch seems to echo the outline of the distant mountain, bringing it closer to us.

The French painter Paul Gauguin (1848–1903) was a successful stockbroker, but at the age of thirty-five gave up his career to become a painter. Modern civilization was, in Gauguin's view, materialistic and lacking in spirituality. This belief led him to seek to portray people whom he considered pure, untouched by materialistic values. *The Vision after the Sermon* shows the pious people of the small town of Pont-Aven dressed in their Sunday clothes (**3.8.17**). The scene in the upper right depicts the sermon the townspeople have just heard, that of the biblical story of Jacob wrestling with the angel. The spaces are abruptly flattened, the figures lack volume and are closely cropped. Yet rather than just showing a scene from everyday life, Gauguin expresses what is in these people's minds: a vision. The way the tree slices the scene in two (one section for the dreamers and one for the dream) is a device Gauguin observed in Japanese prints. Some scholars believe that Gauguin depicted himself as the figure with closed eyes in the lower right of the canvas, as if he too is experiencing the vision. Gauguin once said, "I shut my eyes in order to see." The bold red charges this image with a vivid power that speaks to the intense spirituality of the women and the drama of their vision, but also suggests

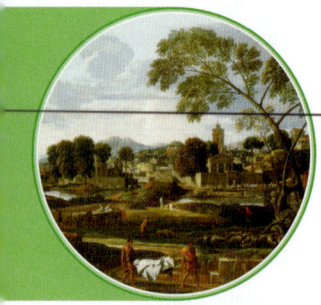

Cézanne greatly admired the earlier French painter Nicolas Poussin. Compare how the two artists created structure in their landscapes: see **3.6.27, p. 483**

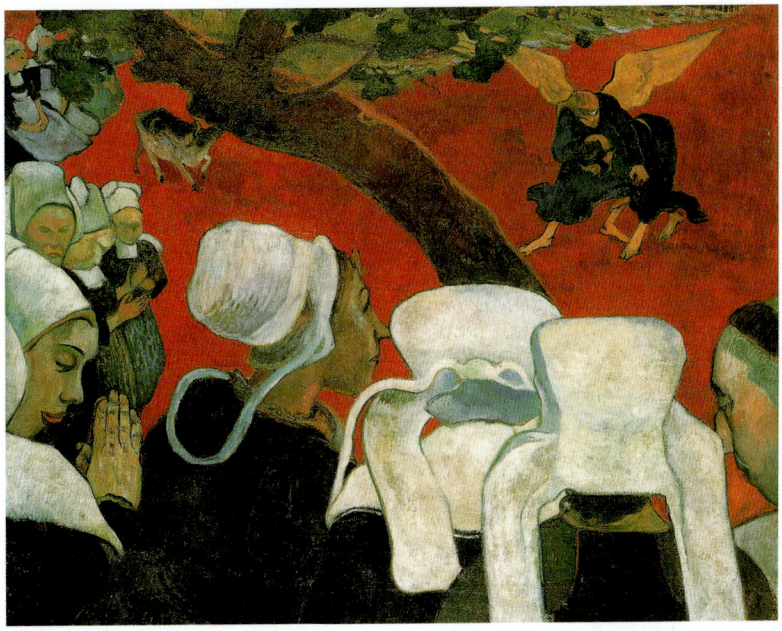

3.8.17 Paul Gauguin, *The Vision after the Sermon (Jacob Wrestling with the Angel)*, 1888. Oil on canvas, 28½ × 35⅞". Scottish National Gallery, Edinburgh, Scotland

Impasto: paint applied in thick layers

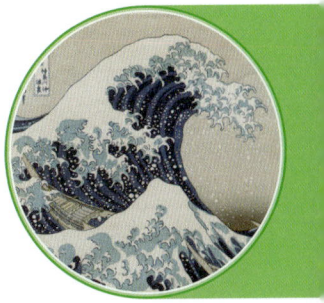

Van Gogh admired Japanese woodblock prints, for example "The Great Wave off Shore at Kanagawa" by Hokusai, see **2.3.5** on **p. 229**. Its form seems echoed in the turbulent night sky of *Starry Night*.

the violence of the struggle they are witnessing between Jacob and the angel. Gauguin's ability to use color as an expressive element would greatly influence later artists, particularly the Symbolists (see pp. 517–20).

After leaving Pont-Aven in 1888, Gauguin shared a house with the Dutch painter Vincent van Gogh (1853–1890) for two months in the southern French town of Arles. The two artists challenged and annoyed one another. While Van Gogh envisioned an artistic exchange, a brotherhood of painters, Gauguin made it clear that he felt his work was superior to the gentler Van Gogh's. Van Gogh's mood fluctuated between pure joy in their working closely alongside each other and frustration at Gauguin's intense bouts of criticism and anger. Shortly before Christmas of the same year, Vincent van Gogh was hospitalized for slicing off his left earlobe and, after this, he and Gauguin never spoke again. Gauguin took his desire to study people of a pure and "primitive" nature to Tahiti, while Van Gogh remained in France.

Famous to us now, yet largely unremarked upon in their time, the paintings of Vincent van Gogh express strong emotions. Yet, unlike Gauguin, Van Gogh claimed he could not invent images, but instead painted emotion into what he saw. He once stated: "I cannot work without a model. I won't say that I don't turn my back on nature to transform a study into a picture, arranging the colors, exaggerating, simplifying, but when it comes to form I'm too fearful of departing from the possible and the true…I exaggerate, sometimes I make changes… but I do not invent the whole picture."

Van Gogh, who struggled with mental illness all his life, painted *Starry Night* during a stay in an asylum; the scene includes elements of the real-life view from his window (**3.8.18**). The artist infused the scene with his own emotions: one can sense the very physical act of applying the thick paint (**impasto**), and Van Gogh's intense energy, in swirls that show movement

3.8.18 Vincent van Gogh, *Starry Night*, 1889. Oil on canvas, 29 × 36½". MoMA, New York

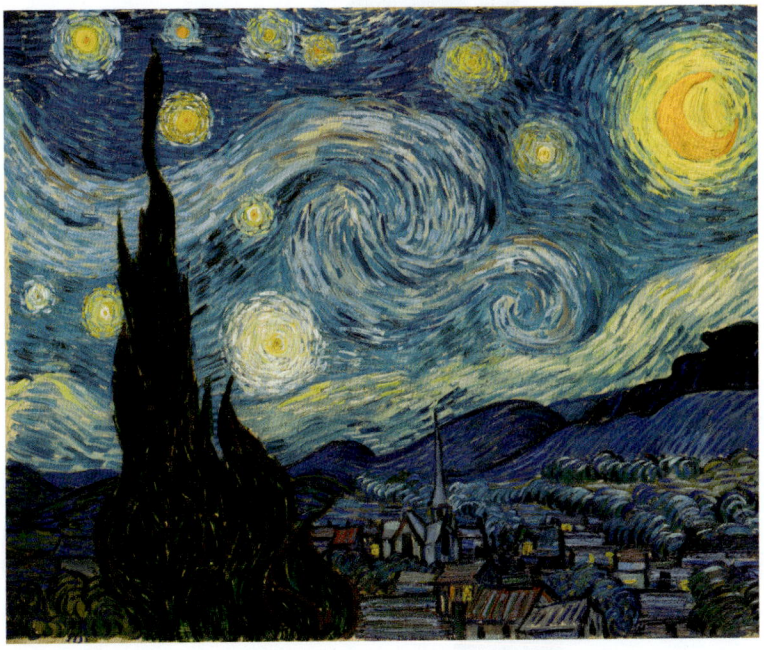

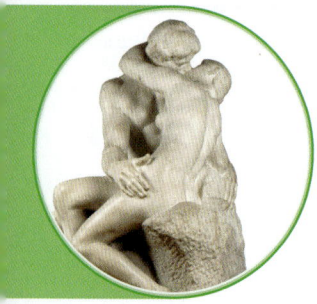

Auguste Rodin epitomizes the modern sculptor because he studied live models rather than copying Classical nudes: see **1.2.17b, p. 72**

in the sky and the light emanating from the stars. A cypress tree, resembling flames reaching up to the sky, fills much of the left side of the canvas. The church in the distance may hint at Van Gogh's personal trials with religion; some believe it relates to his childhood church in the Netherlands.

In a letter to his brother Theo, Van Gogh wrote of how looking at stars put him into a state of dreaming: "Why, I say to myself, should spots of light in the firmament be less accessible to us than the black spots on the map of France? Just as we take the train to go to Tarascon or Rouen [French towns], we take death to go to a star." His use of color, bold texture, and form in this work have been variously interpreted as exuberant and hopeful, but also as expressing his emotional suffering; in 1890, the year after this painting, Van Gogh shot himself in the chest with a revolver and died two days later.

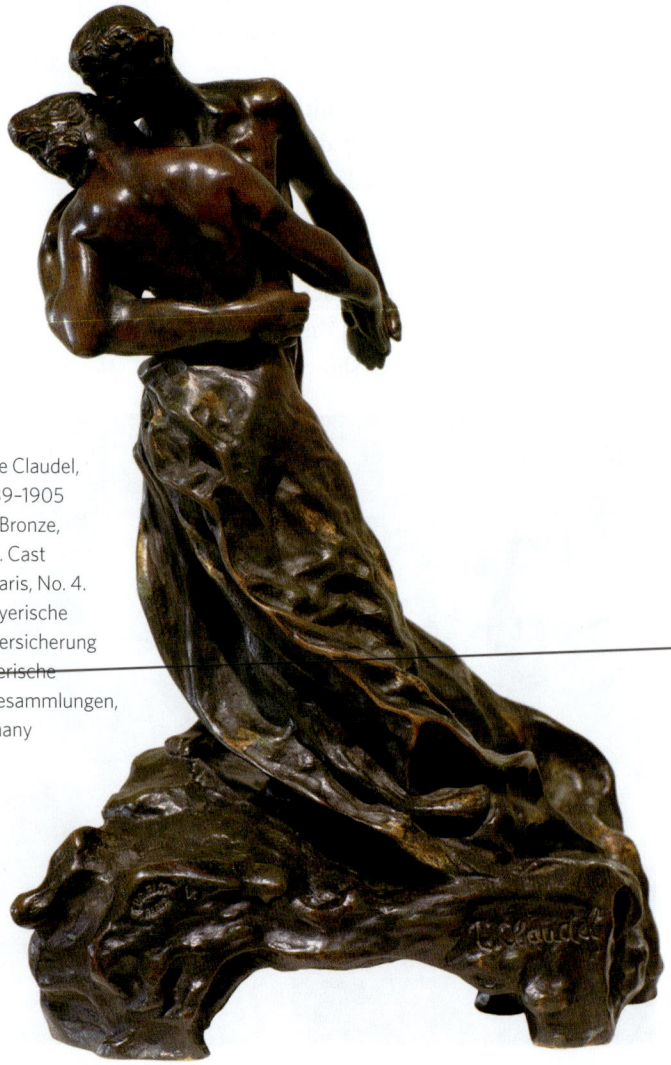

3.8.19 Camille Claudel, *The Waltz*, 1889–1905 (dated 1895). Bronze, 9⅞ × 5¾ × 4". Cast Eugene Blot, Paris, No. 4. Loan of the Bayerische Landesbrandversicherung AG to the Bayerische Staatsgemäldesammlungen, Munich, Germany

Camille Claudel (1864–1943) was one of the most talented sculptors of the late nineteenth and early twentieth centuries. In *The Waltz* (**3.8.19**) one can see her ability to vary texture, as in the smooth skin of the woman's back compared to the folds of the cloth that falls from her waist. In addition to technical acumen, she created incredibly lyrical compositions. In *The Waltz*, the physicality and sensuality of the couple create a rhythmic energy as they seem to glide through their dance.

Claudel trained in the workshop of Auguste Rodin, and quickly became his lover as well. Through Rodin's connections, she met important people, and received commissions she might not otherwise have had. However, there was a clear discrepancy, based on gender, in the way that Rodin and Claudel were treated professionally. Rodin's works were often of nude and sexualized figures, yet his works were judged more on their technical skill than were Claudel's. A government representative who had purchased many of Rodin's erotic nudes remarked that *The Waltz* was too erotic, and suggested that Claudel should put clothes on the figures. One writer proclaimed, "In this group of a waltzing couple, they seem to want to finish the dance so they can go to bed and make love."

Additionally, while there is no evidence that *The Waltz* was made in reference to the love affair between the two sculptors, Claudel's work was often disproportionately seen as an emotional response to her relationship with Rodin, while no one ever thought to view his work in such a light. Unfortunately, Camille Claudel's family forcibly placed her in an insane asylum for the last thirty years of her life. The degree and legitimacy of her mental illness is difficult for scholars to determine, but the fact that she was institutionalized has further clouded all interpretations of her work.

Henry Ossawa Tanner (1859–1937) was born into a middle-class African American family. He was educated at the Pennsylvania Academy of the Fine Arts, where his professor, the painter Thomas Eakins, encouraged him to study anatomy and observe nature closely. Later Tanner moved to Paris, where he was influenced by French painters, including Courbet. Just as

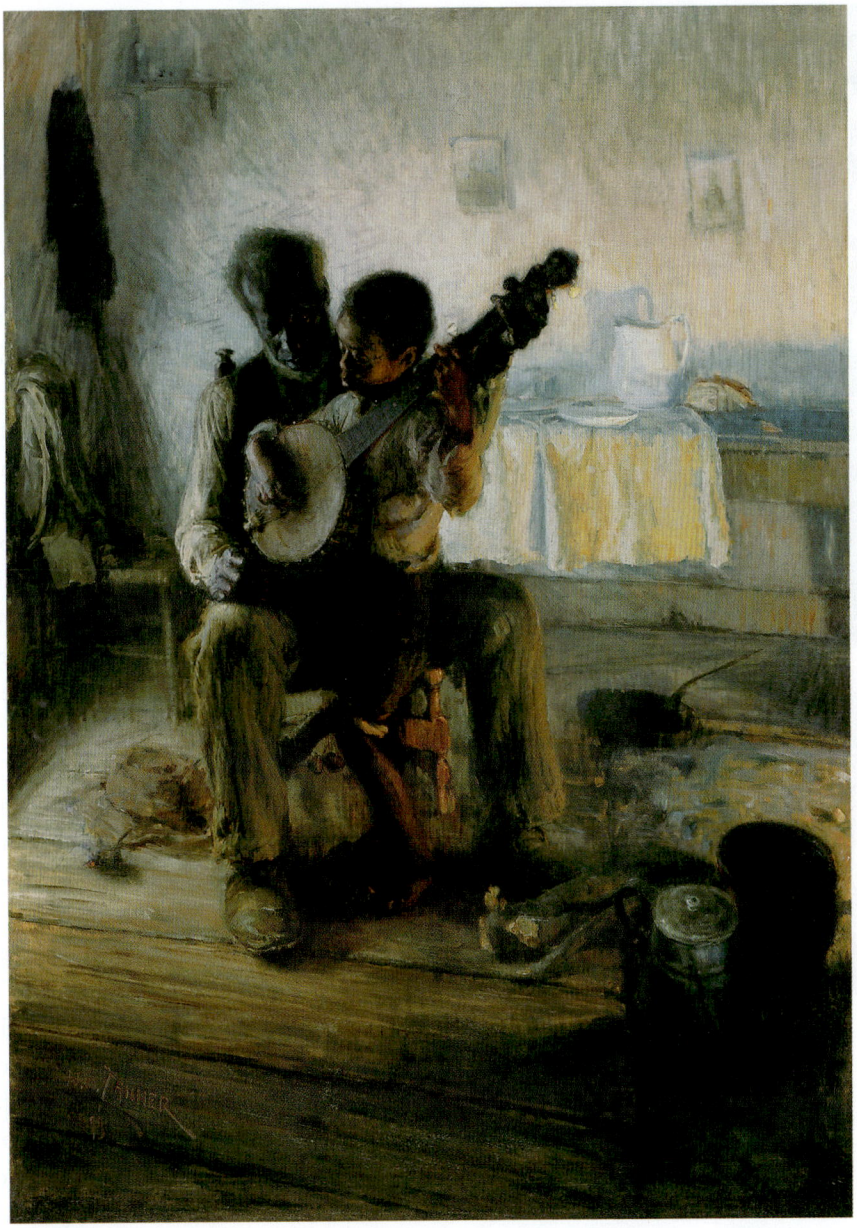

3.8.20 Henry Ossawa Tanner, *Banjo Lesson*, 1893. Oil on canvas, 48 × 35½". Hampton University Museum, Hampton, Virginia

Courbet's *Stonebreakers* showed an older man training a younger worker, Tanner's *Banjo Lesson* shows the passing of knowledge between generations (**3.8.20**). In a humble home, a young African American boy is patiently being taught by his grandfather to play the banjo.

Tanner's painting challenges the stereotype then common in America, of smiling black men as simple-minded entertainers. The artist creates a dignified image of a poor black family by showing a thoughtful black man as a teacher, and an intelligent black child engaged in learning. Tanner sets a calm scene with natural objects and earthy colors, but he symbolizes the boy's spiritual and mental growth with the light coming in through the window, creating a soft rhythm, which can be likened to the act of playing the banjo.

Symbolism

Symbolist painters were inspired by the use of emotionally charged and often dreamlike images. Although they frequently made use of psychologically potent symbols, such as biblical or mythological subjects, and women in the guise of a virgin or seductress (see Gateway Box: Gentileschi, p. 519), they also engaged in individual explorations of otherworldliness.

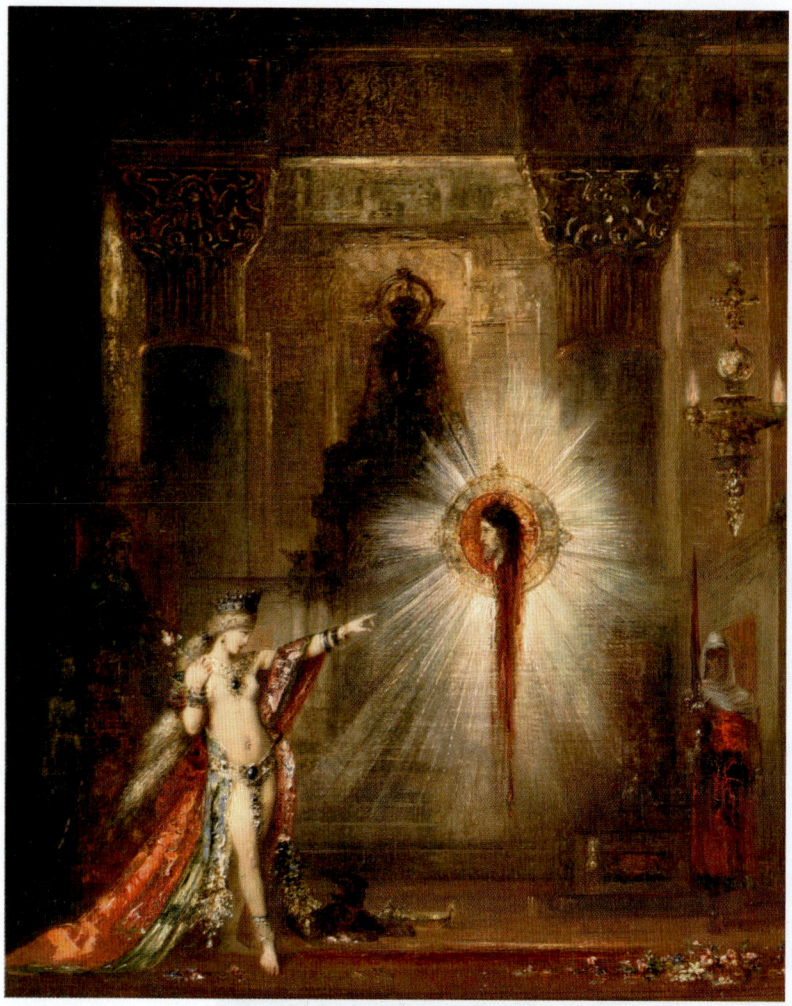

3.8.21 Gustave Moreau, *The Apparition*, c. 1876. Oil on canvas, 22 × 18⅜". Fogg Art Museum, Harvard Art Museums, Cambridge, Massachusetts

They created works that often look like visions and express spiritualism, relying on **abstraction** and the distortion of form and color. Like Paul Gauguin, who greatly inspired the Symbolists, these artists often saw the role of the artist as a guide who reveals universal inner truths.

Gustave Moreau (1826–1898) painted the biblical figure Salome sensually dancing—a true *femme fatale* (a woman whose sexual allure is believed to be dangerous to men)—in front of King Herod (shown on the left, **3.8.21**). She points toward the head of St. John the Baptist, dripping with blood. Light emanates from the floating head suggesting it may be an apparition or a vision of her desire. However, the scene is ambiguous. The soldier on the right holds a bloodied sword suggesting that John the Baptist has just been killed and offered to the temptress. Symbolist writers and painters often influenced one another. This painting was given a lengthy description by Joris-Karl Huysmans (1848–1907) in his famous novel *À rebours* (*About Nature*): "She was no longer the mere performer who wrests a cry of desire and of passion from an old man by a perverted twisting of her loins; who destroys the energy and breaks the will of a king by trembling breasts and quivering belly. She became, in a sense, the symbolic deity of indestructible lust."

The Swiss Ferdinand Hodler (1853–1918) created a heart-stopping painting centered on a man being awakened by a black-cloaked figure climbing on top of him (**3.8.22**). This frightening figure is a symbol of death and the scene reflects Hodler's fear of death. This fear is not surprising given his difficult childhood in which his father, mother, and two brothers died of tuberculosis. The terrorized central figure contrasts with the figures that encircle him, all of whom are sleeping and oblivious of his panicked state. The two women portrayed in the foreground are his current lovers: his mistress (left) and wife (right), with her arm around another man. The painting caused a scandal because of its

3.8.22 Ferdinand Hodler, *The Night*, 1889/90. Oil on canvas, 46" × 9'10". Kunstmuseum, Bern, Switzerland

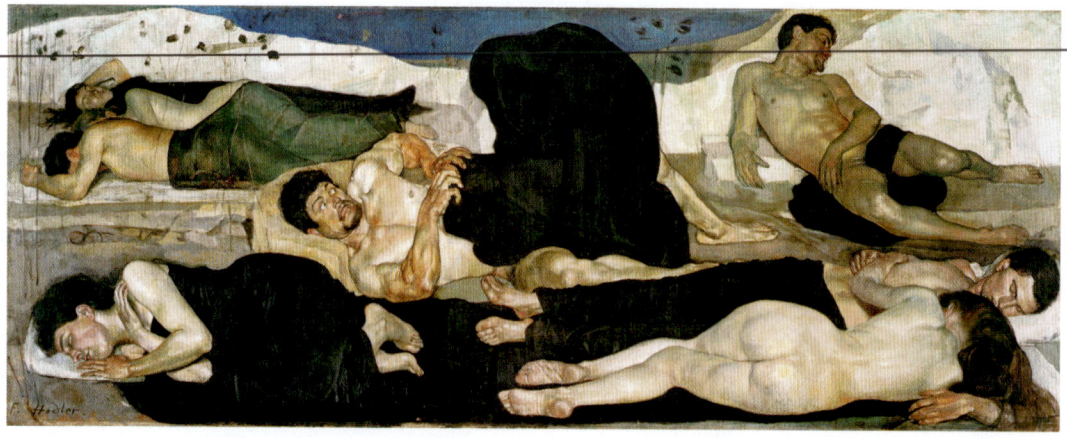

Abstraction: the degree to which an image is altered from an easily recognizable subject

Gateway to Art: Gentileschi, *Judith Decapitating Holofernes*

Variations on a Theme

Artemisia Gentileschi's *Judith Decapitating Holofernes* (**3.8.23**), from the **Baroque** era, and Gustav Klimt's *Judith I* (**3.8.24**) are both paintings based on the biblical story of Judith beheading Holofernes, an Assyrian general who was planning to attack her homeland—but the two images clearly reveal striking differences in style and approach. While Gentileschi's work displays Baroque qualities, the work by Klimt (1862–1918) embodies many qualities of Symbolism.

Gentileschi's scene is staged for maximum dramatic effect, like a theatrical performance, shining a spotlight on the gory beheading of Holofernes, making the portrayal of Judith that of a powerful, surprisingly physical being. She is shown in the act of attacking the general, sword in hand, and with her sleeves rolled up.

In Gustav Klimt's *Judith I*, on the other hand, the artist fills his scene with fantasy and eroticism, qualities favored by the Symbolists. His Judith appears as a glamorous seductress, or *femme fatale*, dripping with gold, her lush black hair piled high, heavy-lidded eyes half shut, body half exposed. The model for Judith in real life was Adele Bloch-Bauer, a wealthy, married patron with whom Klimt was madly in love, and Judith's seductive quality is the focus of his work, which we absorb firstly as the portrait of a beautiful, sensual woman. The artist seems to trap her, visually, with the thick gold choker round her neck, a device that also hints at the beheading that has just occurred.

Contrary to Gentileschi's painting, where the wounded head is in the center, Klimt's version lures us in with Judith's beauty, and then shocks us with the realization that she is clasping the severed head victoriously in her hands. This attitude lends the work its sinister, disturbing power; instead of grappling with her victim, as in Gentileschi's version, Judith here seems almost to be caressing his dead head. The lavish use of gold, both in the frame and the decorative gold leaf that surrounds and nearly engulfs Judith, is characteristic of Klimt's art. Its rich, gleaming appeal, so much at odds with the grim subject matter, intensifies the strange, spellbinding quality of the painting.

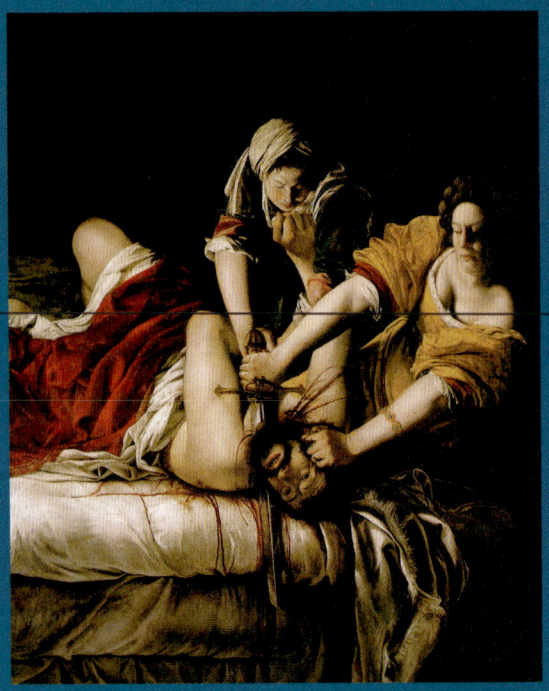

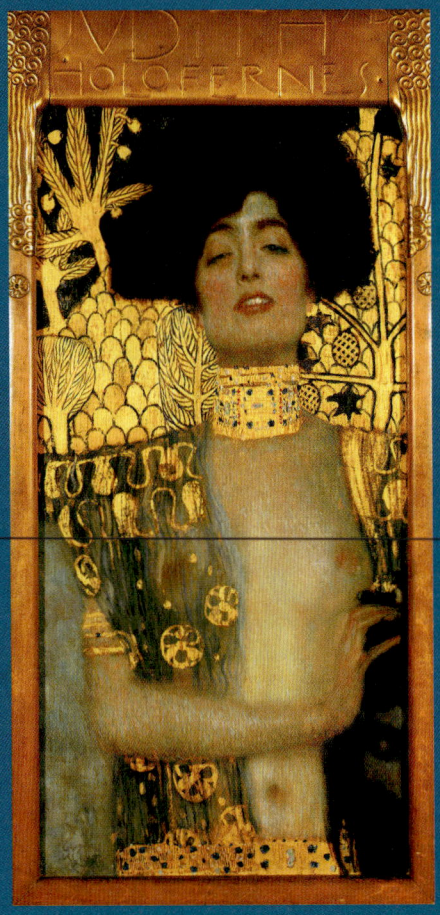

Baroque: European artistic style of the late sixteenth to early eighteenth century, characterized by extravagance and emotional intensity

For the other Gentileschi Gateway boxes, see p. 152, p. 219, p. 478, and p. 681

3.8.23 (far left) Artemisia Gentileschi, *Judith Decapitating Holofernes*, c. 1620. Oil on canvas, 6'6⅜" × 5'3¾". Uffizi Gallery, Florence, Italy

3.8.24 (left) Gustav Klimt, *Judith I*, 1901. Oil and gold painting on canvas, 33 × 16½". Österreichische Galerie Belvedere, Vienna, Austria

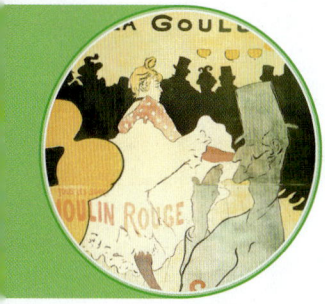

Such artists as Toulouse-Lautrec made a living creating posters to advertise the exciting night-life of the *fin de siècle*: see **2.7.16, p. 309**

blatant nudity and was denied inclusion in the primary fine arts exhibition in Geneva in 1891. In response, Hodler organized an independent exhibition in which he charged visitors, of which there were over a thousand, to view the notorious work.

Fin de Siècle and Art Nouveau

Fin de siècle (from the French, "end of the century") refers to the period from the end of the nineteenth century to the start of World War I in 1914. This was a time of great social change in Europe. A growing middle class had sufficient income to enjoy the pleasures that life had to offer. As they faced the new century, however, some were anxious (and rightly, in view of the war that ensued a decade later), about the changes it would bring. In art and design, the **Art Nouveau** style emphasized decorative pattern and applied it to the traditional "fine arts" (such as painting and sculpture), the decorative arts (such as furniture, glass, and ceramics), and architecture and interior design. Art Nouveau is characterized by **organic** flowing lines, gold decoration, and the simulation of forms in nature.

The Belgian architect Victor Horta (1861–1947) designed a home for Emile Tassel infused with elements that would come to epitomize Art Nouveau (**3.8.25**). Horta utilized new, modern materials, such as cast steel and glass. He created a home in which form and light seem to be in constant motion, even alive like the organic forms that inspired him. The elegant staircase twists like a roller coaster and widens as it spills onto the floor. Further spirals flood the walls and the **mosaic** floor, creating an eternally active space.

Louis Comfort Tiffany brought Art Nouveau to America with works whose designs derived from complex forms found in nature. His "Wisteria" lamp from *c.* 1905 is made with leaded glass (**3.8.26**). This process involved creating a **cartoon** of the design, transferring to a form (made out of wood or plaster) that was

3.8.25 Victor Horta, stairway of Tassel House, Brussels, Belgium, 1892–93

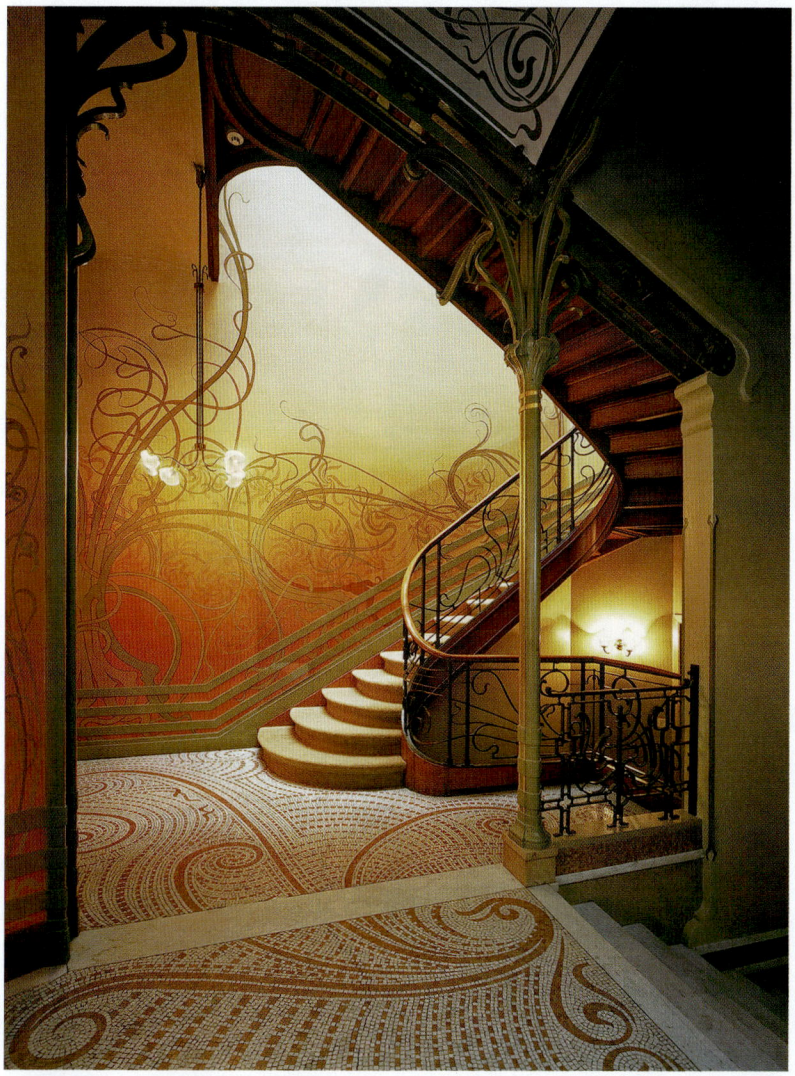

3.8.26 Tiffany Studios, "Wisteria" table lamp, *c.* 1905. Leaded glass and patinated bronze, height 26⅞"

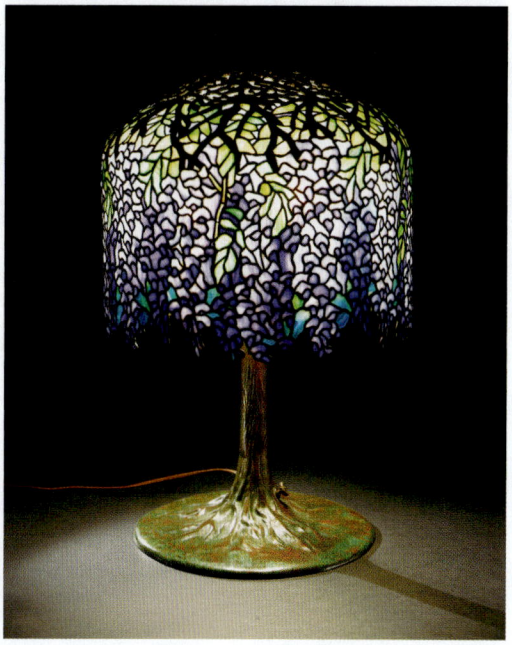

the shape of the shade, cutting the glass pieces, wrapping them in copper foil, and soldering them together. The Wisteria lamp utilized 2,000 separate pieces of glass. The thick bronze vine at the top of the shade highlighted that there was no opening at the top because electrical lighting no longer required venting of a flame. The bronze base mimics a tree trunk from which the glorious colors of the wisteria grow forth. It was not known until the twenty-first century that Clara Driscoll, who had been the head of Tiffany's Women's Glass Cutting Department, was also the designer for many of his lamps, including Wisteria. When they were made, Tiffany lamps sold for about $400. In 2014, two Wisteria lamps sold for more than $1 million each.

Expressionism

From around 1905 to around 1920, other artists evolved a style that came to be known as Expressionism, in which they chose to explore ways of portraying emotions to their fullest intensity by exaggerating and emphasizing the colors and shapes of the objects depicted. Expressionists were concerned with the representation of objects and the world. But as Expressionists depicted their subjects, they emphasized inner states of feeling. Expressionist artists tried to depict what they felt rather than what they saw, with sometimes unconventional results.

The making of self-portraits was central to Expressionism because artists could explore a great variety and intensity of emotions through repeated studies. Self-portraits also allow artists to express both the inner and outer worlds that they know most fully. For instance, when making a portrait of someone else, an artist could only guess at the other person's mood, thoughts, or motivations. While making a self-portrait, however, he or she could decide which moods or motivations to show and how best to do so.

The German Expressionist artist Paula Modersohn-Becker (1876–1907) made several self-portraits (**3.8.27**). She also has the distinction of being one of the first women to make nude self-portraits. Her style reflects the flattened

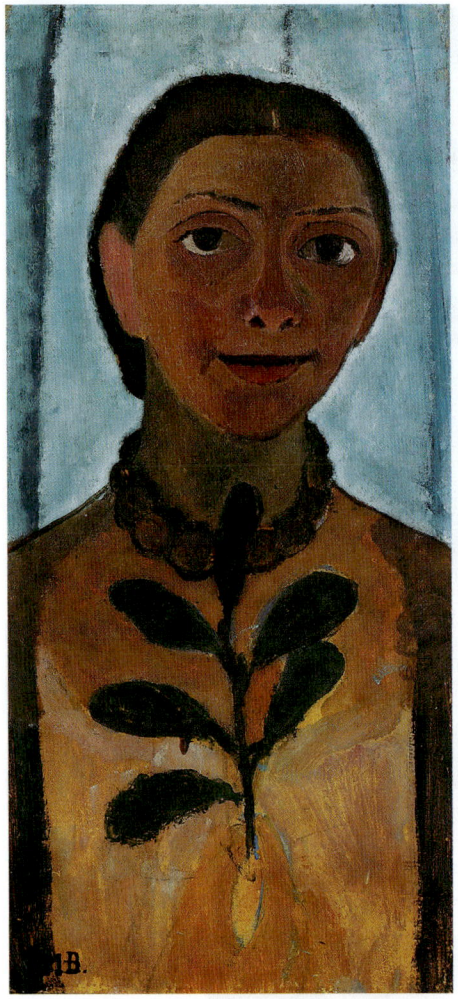

3.8.27 (left) Paula Modersohn-Becker, *Self-Portrait with Camellia*, 1906–7. Oil on canvas, 24¼ × 12". Museum Folkwang, Essen, Germany

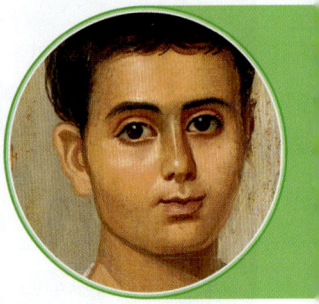

Modersohn-Becker frequently studied Roman portraits from Egypt, which were placed directly over the bodies of the deceased: see **2.2.4, p. 211**

forms, reduced details, heavy outlines, and solid geometry she saw in earlier **avant-garde** styles of such artists as Paul Cézanne and Paul Gauguin in Paris (see p. 514). At the same time, her work balances delicate details in gesture and mood with a portrayal of the physical substance of her body.

Russian Vasily Kandinsky (1866–1944) was one of the first artists to make **non-objective**, or completely abstract, paintings. Inspired from an early age by a love of color, he became part of the German Expressionist group **Der Blaue Reiter**. These artists rejected Classical approaches in favor of radical experimentation. Non-objective art makes no reference to recognizable subjects; there are only abstract shapes, designs, and colors. Kandinsky's abstract paintings can be thought of as a visual equivalent for the non-verbal experience of instrumental music. He frequently used such titles as "improvisation" or "composition" for his paintings, a reference to the

Art Nouveau: French for "new art," a visual style of the late nineteenth and early twentieth century, characterized by organic flowing lines, simulating forms in nature and involving decorative pattern

Organic: having irregular forms and shapes, as though derived from living organisms

Mosaic: a picture or pattern created by fixing together small pieces of stone, glass, tile, etc.

Cartoon: A full-scale preparatory drawing for a painting or tapestry; from the Italian *cartone*, meaning "large sheet of paper."

Avant-garde: early twentieth-century emphasis on artistic innovation, which challenged accepted values, traditions, and techniques

Non-objective: art that does not depict a recognizable subject

Der Blaue Reiter: ("The Blue Rider") German Expressionist movement (1911–14) in Munich; used abstract forms to suggest spiritual content as a contrast to the corruption and materialism of the times

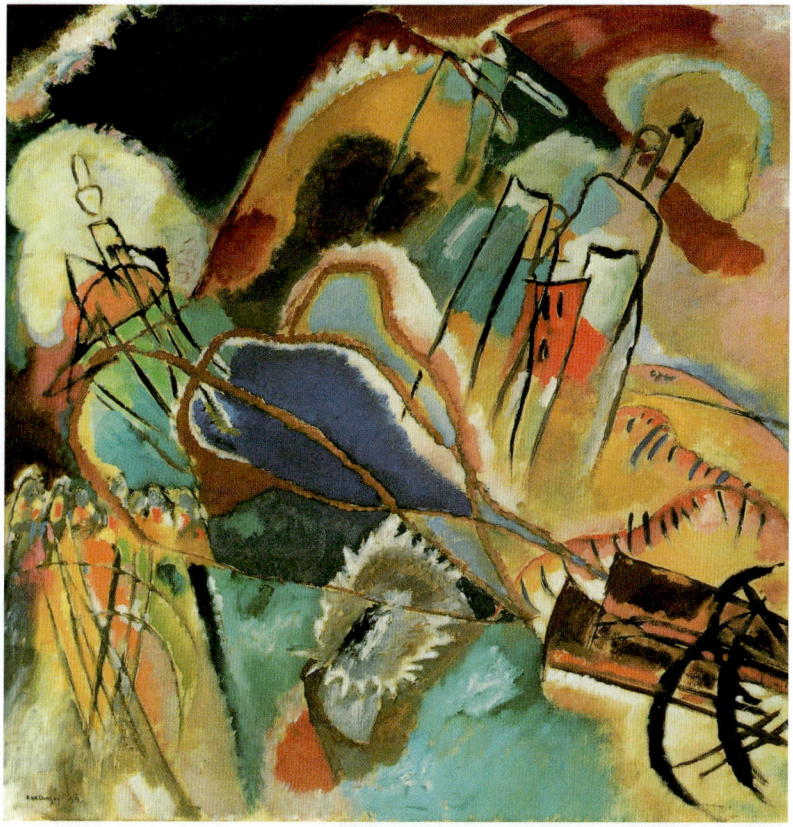

3.8.28 Vasily Kandinsky, *Improvisation #30 (Cannons)*, 1913. Oil on canvas, 43¾ × 43¼". Art Institute of Chicago, Illinois

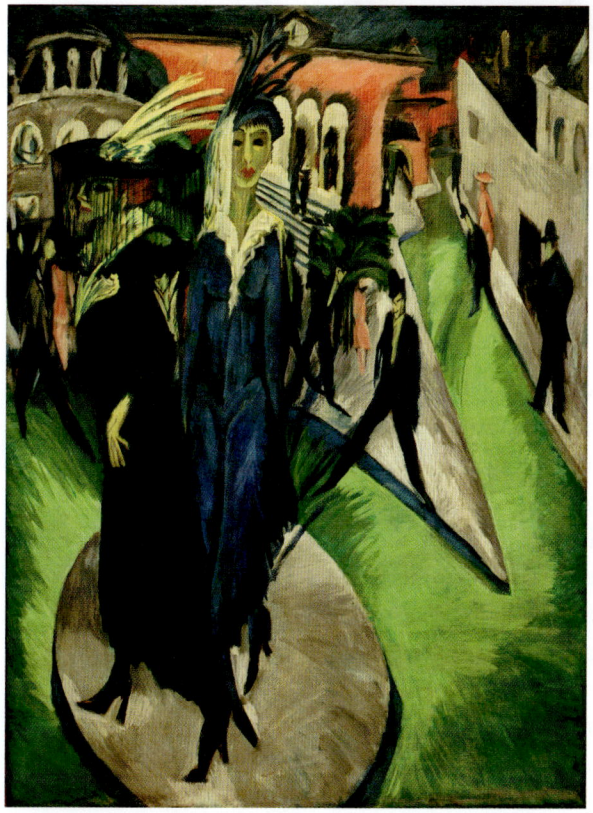

3.8.29 Ernst Ludwig Kirchner, *Potsdamer Platz*, 1914. Oil on canvas, 78¾ × 59". Nationalgalerie, Berlin, Germany

work of contemporary composers whose music he admired. Kandinsky said his *Improvisation #30* was inspired by talk of war in 1913, a year before World War I began (**3.8.28**). The chaotic and energetic forms reflect the turmoil of the time, though they do not illustrate any particular event. While the artist made the painting spontaneously, with no specific scene in mind, as we look at it we can make out some leaning buildings, a crowd of people, and a cannon firing. Many of Kandinsky's later pieces avoid such recognizable objects because, as he famously wrote in his book *Concerning the Spiritual in Art*, instead of expressing any outward and visible content, art should express an inner spiritual necessity. This book has become a major document reflecting art's move away from material reality in the early twentieth century.

German artist Ernst Ludwig Kirchner (1880–1938) used a deliberately raw painting style in his search for meaning beyond surface appearance. Kirchner used flat planes of intense color, simplified forms, and rough, even aggressive, brushwork. Kirchner's painting *Potsdamer Platz* reflects his belief that art should come from direct experience (**3.8.29**). The figures he saw in this street scene appear very civilized and dressed for a night on the town, but their similar clothing and mask-like faces drain them of individuality, almost turning them into clones. In this painting Kirchner seems to ask why these people lack purpose and why they all appear to be the same. He had been part of a group of artists, called **Die Brücke**, who intended their new mode of expression to form a bridge between the past, present, and future. According to these artists, the decadence and dehumanization of society could only be counteracted by the younger generation—such artists as themselves.

Die Brücke: ("The Bridge") German Expressionist movement of painters and printmakers formed in Dresden (1905–13) with the aim of defying anything Classical and using art as a bridge between the past, present, and a utopian future

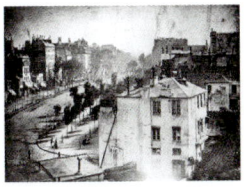

2.8.4 Daguerre, *Boulevard du Temple*, c. 1838, p. 317

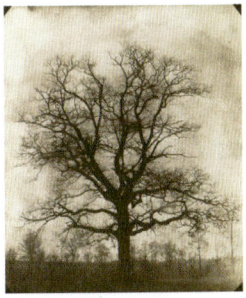

2.8.6 William Henry Fox Talbot, *Oak Tree in Winter*, c. 1842, p. 318

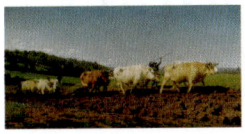

1.9.12a Rosa Bonheur, *Plowing in the Nivernais: The Dressing of the Vines*, 1849, p. 166

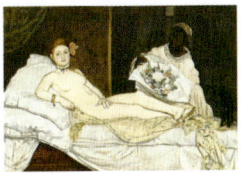

4.9.9 Édouard Manet, *Olympia*, 1863, p. 669

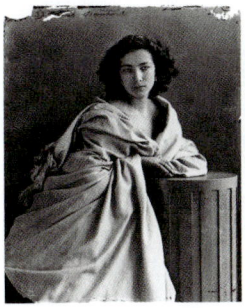

2.8.9 Nadar, *Sarah Bernhardt*, 1865, p. 320

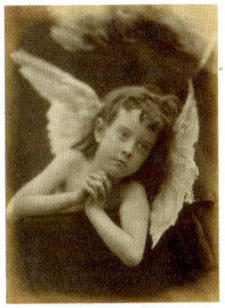

2.8.10 Julia Margaret Cameron, *Angel of the Nativity*, 1872, p. 320

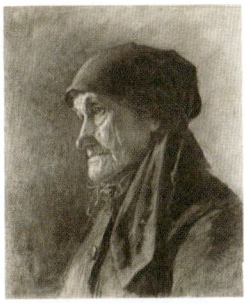

2.1.11 Léon Augustin Lhermitte, *An Elderly Peasant Woman*, c. 1878, p. 198

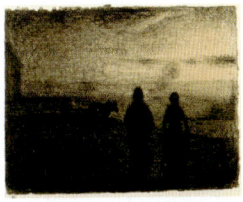

2.1.15 Georges Seurat, *The Ploughing*, 1882–83, p. 201

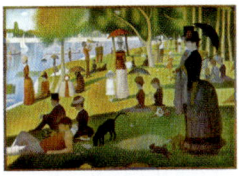

4.4.10 Georges Seurat, *Sunday on La Grande Jatte*, 1884–86, p. 609

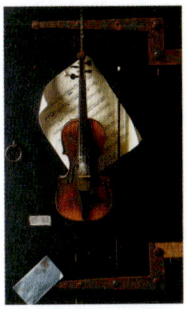

4.5.4 William M. Harnett, *The Old Violin*, 1886, p. 618

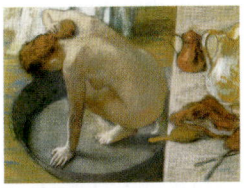

2.1.14 Edgar Degas, *The Tub*, 1886, p. 200

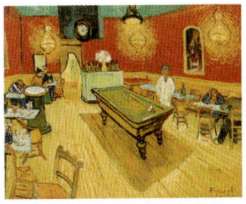

1.4.29 Vincent van Gogh, *The Night Café*, 1888, p. 109

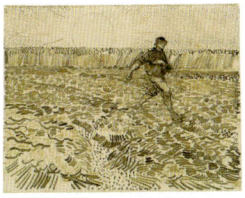

2.1.20 Vincent van Gogh, *Sower with Setting Sun*, 1888, p. 205

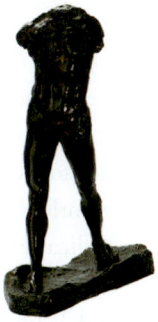

4.9.14 Auguste Rodin, *Walking Man*, c. 1890–95, p. 673

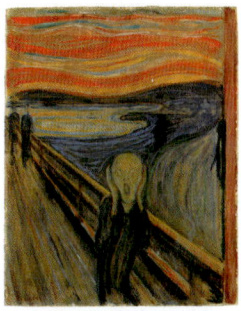

1.10.11 Edvard Munch, *The Scream*, 1893, p. 182

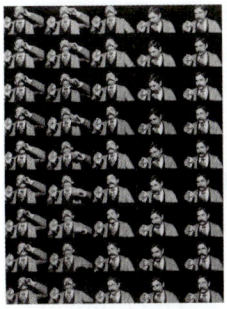

1.5.16 Thomas Edison and W. K. Dickson, *Fred Ott's Sneeze*, 1894, p. 122

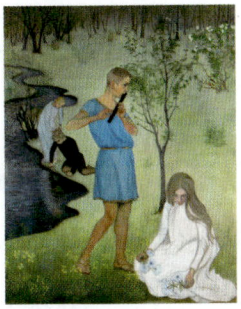

1.3.9 Beda Stjernschantz, *Pastoral (Primavera)*, 1897, p. 81

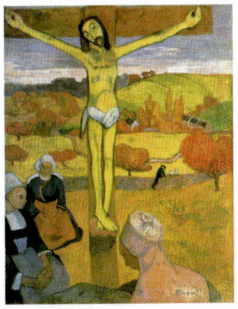

1.4.32 Paul Gauguin, *The Yellow Christ*, 1889, p. 111

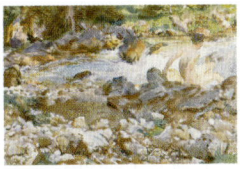

2.2.20 John Singer Sargent, *Mountain Stream*, c. 1912–14, p. 220

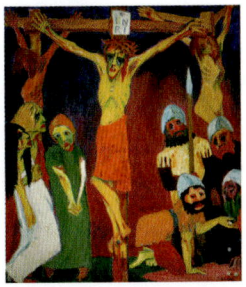

4.8.8 Emil Nolde, *Crucifixion*, 1912, p. 658

3.9 Late Modern and Early Contemporary Art in the Twentieth Century

Modernism, Modernist: a radically new twentieth-century art and architectural movement that embraced modern subjects, industrial materials, a machine aesthetic, and experimental approaches
Dada: art movement formed in Europe and the US in reaction to the horror and folly of World War I
Surrealism: an artistic movement in the 1920s and later; its works were inspired by dreams and the subconscious
American Scene: naturalistic style of painting in the US from the 1920s to 1950s that celebrated American themes, locations, and virtues
Subject (subject matter): the person, object, or space depicted in a work of art
Abstraction: the degree to which an image is altered, simplified or distorted from an easily recognizable subject
Style: a characteristic way in which an artist or group of artists uses visual language to give a work an identifiable form of visual expression

Although experiments in **Modernism** occurred on both sides of the Atlantic in the first decades of the twentieth century, the devastation of World War I spurred the creation of European movements in the 1920s that were very distinct from those inspired by the impact of the Great Depression in America in 1929. The art of the European **Dadaists** and **Surrealists** reacted against the evils of war and what these artists saw as the corruption pervading modern society by making attacks on art itself and by exploring the psyche, while **American Scene** artists chose to respond to the suffering surrounding them through the portrayal of **subjects** and spaces close to their heart. After World War II, the center of the art world shifted to the US, where many of the European Modernists had emigrated to escape persecution.

The world that emerged from World War II was radically changed. Millions of people had been killed and hundreds of thousands displaced. When the war was over, the great powers of Europe—Great Britain, Germany, France, Spain, and Italy—found their societies devastated by the destruction of years of war. Two new super-powers now dominated the world. The United States had become an economic powerhouse based on free enterprise and capitalism. On the other hand, the Soviet Union, which now controlled much of central Europe, adopted a centrally planned system of economic management, Communism, and focused on rivaling the industrial might of America in what came to be called the Cold War.

After World War II, the global expansion in commerce and politics was paralleled by the fact that territories that until then had been colonized by European countries (for example India under Britain) gained political independence to become new nations in their own right. These developing nations promoted their own cultural traditions, including Muslim, Hindu, and Buddhist religions. People emigrated (forcibly or by choice) from Africa, Asia, Latin America, and throughout Europe, bringing their belief systems and customs to countries the populations of which had previously been unfamiliar with them.

In art, the Modern period (*c.* 1860–1960) continued, and was followed by the Contemporary period (1960–present). Artists responded to events occurring in the wider world as well as to developments in the world of art. During this time period, some artists continued the formal experiments, such as **abstraction** and experimental ways of depicting the world or expressing their ideas, which had been pioneered by early Modernist artists. While the latter had largely rejected the use of recognizable imagery in their art, as well as the **styles** and approaches of artists from earlier eras, contemporary artists experimented seemingly without limit and in a variety of ways.

The Revolution of Color and Form

Henri Matisse (1869–1954) and Pablo Picasso (1881–1973) are very important figures now

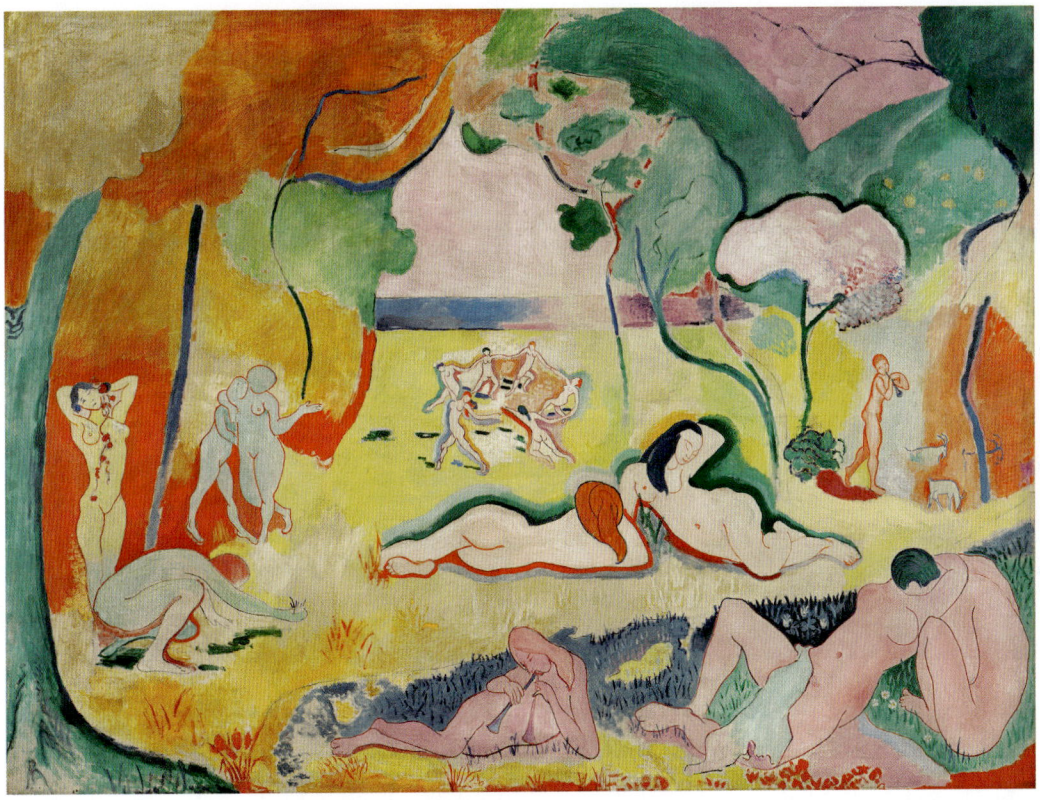

3.9.1 Henri Matisse, *Joy of Life*, 1905–6. Oil on canvas, 5'9⅛" × 7'10⅞". Barnes Foundation, Merion, Pennsylvania

permanently associated with the development of modern art. Matisse, a Frenchman, had earned some professional notoriety by the time Picasso moved from Spain to Paris in 1904. Picasso left behind his academic training in **representational** art to embrace the brave new world of experimental approaches he found there. Meanwhile, Matisse was working in Paris, exploring the expressive potential of **color** and its relation to **form**—as he was to do throughout his career. Matisse and Picasso developed a mutual respect for each other, but they were also rivals because each one wanted to be considered the leader of the progressive art world. As it turns out, both artists enjoyed extremely productive careers and have been extraordinarily influential: Matisse for his expressive forms, **decorative** style, and bold use of color; Picasso for his radical handling of form and shape.

Henri Matisse

The colors in Matisse's *Joy of Life*—orange and green bodies, pink trees, a multicolored sky—are not strictly **naturalistic** (**3.9.1**). These departures from everyday appearances are intentional. An artist's inspired choice of colors varies according to what he or she sees or imagines. For Matisse, color was principally a way to express emotions. In fact, Matisse founded a movement now known as **Fauvism** (from French *fauve*, "wild beast"). The group's name derived from a comment by a critic who found their work a little mad, especially in comparison to **Classical** approaches, because the bold colors the Fauves used did not correspond to natural appearances. Matisse continued to explore the potential of pure color throughout his career. He often emphasized colors and made them vibrant and intense rather than rendering them as subdued or blending them to make a scene look more natural. Matisse was interested in making an artwork, not in imitating nature or copying external appearances. He was not trying, as many artists from earlier times had principally done, to persuade us into believing that we are looking through a window onto a "real" world. In response to a viewer who complained that one of his portraits did not resemble the dimensions of an actual woman, Matisse said, "I did not create a woman. I made a picture."

Representation: the depiction of recognizable figures and objects
Color: the optical effect caused when reflected light of the spectrum is divided into separate wavelengths
Form: an object that can be defined in three dimensions (height, width, and depth)
Decorative: intentionally making an artwork pleasant or attractive
Naturalism, naturalistic: a very realistic or lifelike style of making images
Fauvism: early twentieth-century art movement that emphasized bold, exaggerated colors and simplified forms to favor creative expression over accuracy. From the French fauve, "wild beast"
Classical: ancient Greek and Roman; art that conforms to Greek and Roman models, or is based on rational construction and emotional equilibrium

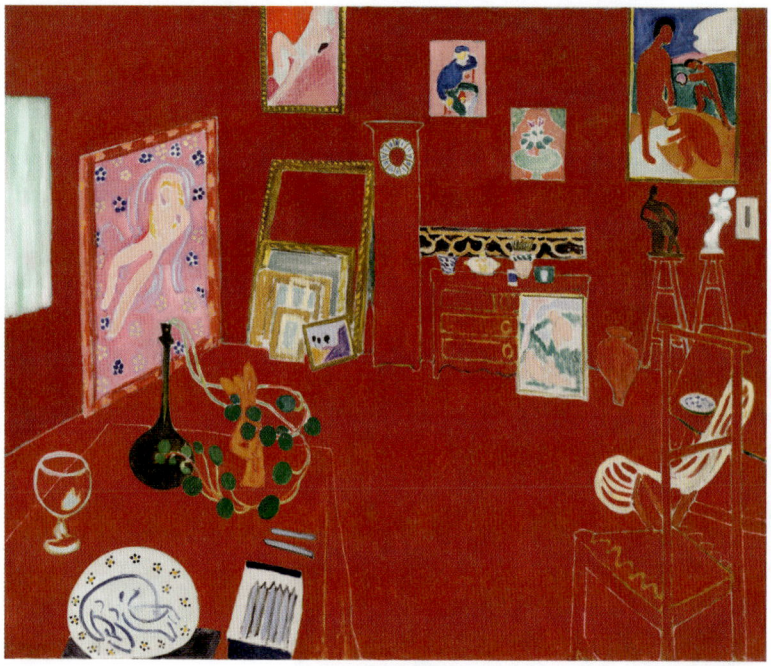

3.9.2 Henri Matisse, *The Red Studio*, 1911. Oil on canvas, 5'11¼" × 7'2¼". MoMA, New York

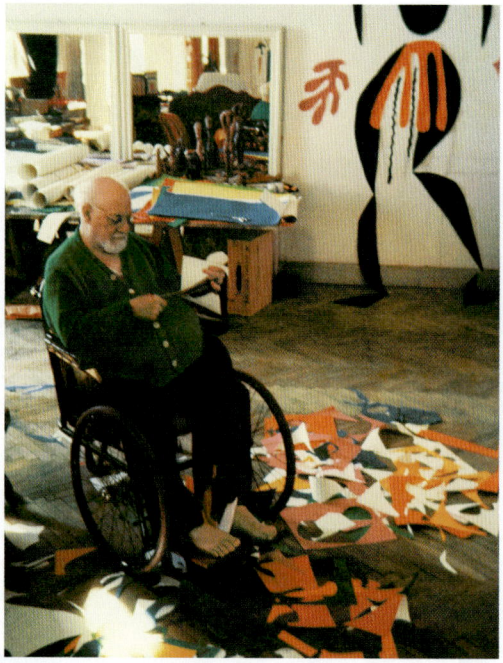

3.9.3 Henri Matisse in his studio, 1953

Plane: a flat, two-dimensional surface on which an artist creates a drawing or painting. Planes can also be implied in a composition by areas that face towards, parallel to, or away from a light source
Outline: the outermost line or implied line of an object or figure, by which it is defined or bounded
Sketch: a rough preliminary version of a work or part of a work
Geometric form: three-dimensional form composed of predictable and mathematically derived planes and curves
Cubism: twentieth-century movement and style in art, especially painting, in which perspective with a single viewpoint was abandoned and use was made of simple geometric shapes, interlocking planes, and, later, collage
Three-dimensional: having height, width, and depth
Renaissace: a period of cultural and artistic change in Europe from the fourteenth to the seventeenth century

In *The Red Studio* Matisse has included a lot of information about his working environment, but he has also left a lot out (**3.9.2**). He accurately shows a number of the paintings, sculptures, and ceramics he had been working on. The space is filled with an intense red; this makes the artworks stand out against the walls and floor, which have been collapsed into a single flat **plane**. The furniture is also red, with subtle gold **outlines** indicating the edges and details. Matisse is keenly concerned with the use of color to convey his experience of place.

When Matisse worked on a painting he generally started with complex **sketches** and, over time, simplified the image by eliminating details and paring down the composition. He also used paper cutouts as preparatory sketches, pinning them on a canvas to help him place the figures in a composition. In early 1941 Matisse was diagnosed with cancer of the intestines. After his treatment, he was permanently confined to a wheelchair (**3.9.3**), making painting any large-scale work impossible. So Matisse began to present the cutouts as the completed works themselves. He created his cutouts from paper his assistants would paint in bright colors; the artist would then use scissors as if "drawing" the elegant lines of the shapes he was making, creating images filled with movement and life.

There seems to have been no limit to the ideas Matisse could fashion in this way. He used cutouts to design tapestries, the interior decoration of buildings, and stained-glass windows. His final cutout compositions were on a large scale, some covering an area of more than 87 square feet. Toward the end of a long career Matisse found that simple scissors and paper offered a way to help him continue, once again, finding new ways to experiment with line and color.

Picasso, Braque, and Cubism

In the early twentieth century, shortly after Matisse was experimenting with new ways of using color in the 1900s, Picasso and the French artist Georges Braque (1882–1963) revolutionized the way artworks were made. They concentrated on their underlying **geometric form** and the construction of pictorial space, and together eventually developed the style known as **Cubism**. Instead of showing conventionally realistic objects in the illusion of **three-dimensional** space in the way that had fascinated Western artists since the **Renaissance**, they enabled us to see what an object might look like if we could see more than

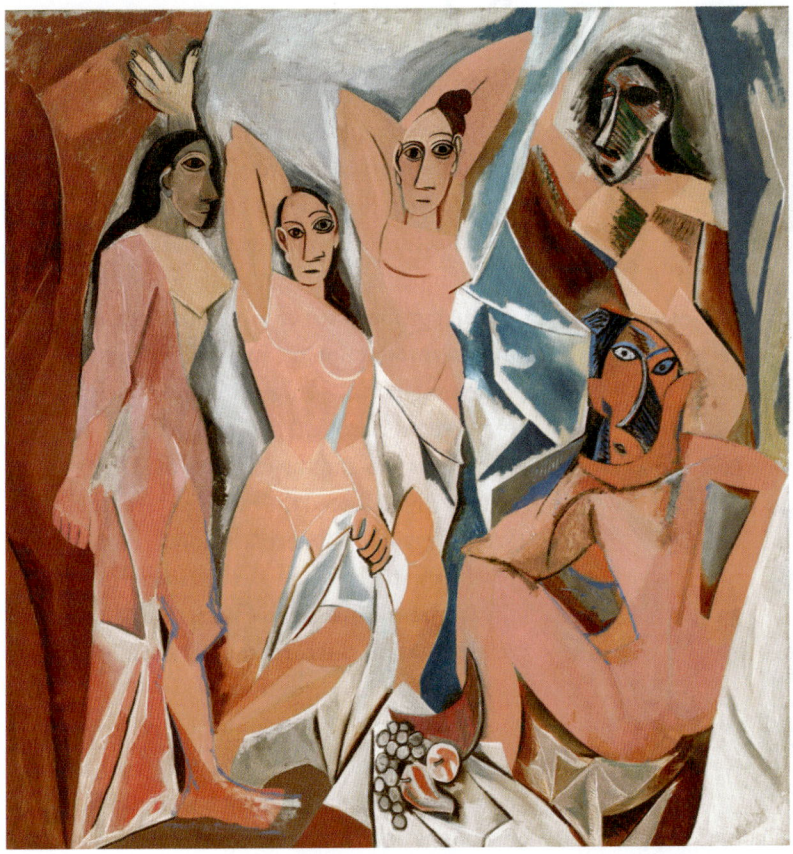

3.9.4 (above) Pablo Picasso, *Les Demoiselles d'Avignon*, 1907. Oil on canvas, 8' × 7'8". MoMA, New York

3.9.5 (right) Georges Braque, *Houses at L'Estaque*, 1908. Oil on canvas, 28⅜ × 23½". Kunstmuseum, Bern, Switzerland

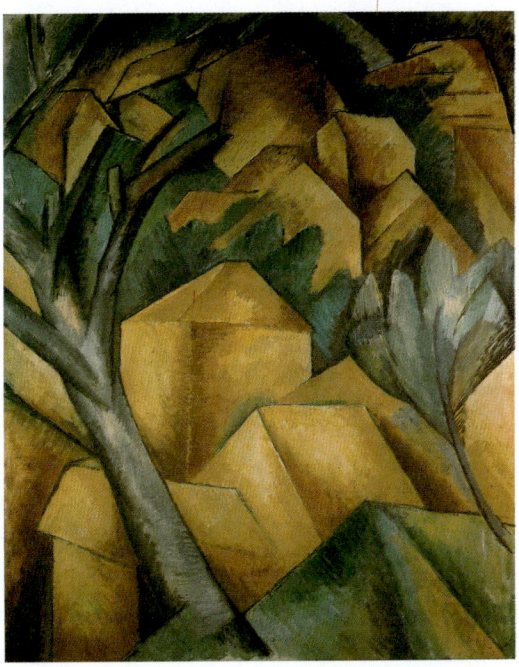

Background: the part of a work depicted furthest from the viewer's space, often behind the main subject matter
Composite view: representation of a subject from multiple viewpoints at one time
Post-Impressionists: artists either from or living in France, c. 1885–1905, who moved away from the Impressionist style—notably Cézanne, Gauguin, Seurat, and Van Gogh

one side of it at the same time. They broke up objects and figures into geometric shapes and changed them according to their own conception of deeper truth.

Picasso explored new methods of depicting the human figure in his painting *Les Demoiselles d'Avignon* (**3.9.4**). Rather than re-creating the way we actually see a room with people standing in it, Picasso has treated the space in the picture, and the figures within it, in a revolutionary way. He simplified the forms into abstract planes, made the figures more angular, and transformed faces and bodies into geometric pieces. The blue and white planes of what would usually be called the **background** clash violently with the angular pink figures of the women, in a complex struggle for dominance.

The three figures on the left are shown in historical, even Classical poses. The forms of the two women near the center of the painting are simplified, with almond-shaped eyes, triangular noses, and outlines for bodies, but they are still recognizable as female figures. The heads of the standing figures on the far left and far right have been dramatically replaced by African masks. Picasso, along with Matisse and other European artists in the early twentieth century, studied and collected art from outside the Western tradition, especially Africa and the Pacific Islands, and this interest is reflected in the masked faces.

The crouching figure at the bottom right has the most abstract features. Her body is splayed out, and the geometric shapes that make up the woman's face do not correspond to the usual orientation. The eye on our left is shown from the front, while the eye on our right can be read as if it is in profile. The nose is also in profile with the mouth off to the side and a crescent shape in place of the jawline. The **composite view** of this figure shows us more parts of her body than we could see from one vantage point. Yet the figures are still fairly recognizable. Picasso's later Cubist pieces become far more abstract, but always intentionally retain a connection to the visible world.

An early Cubist painting, Georges Braque's *Houses at L'Estaque*, emphasized the geometry of the setting (**3.9.5**). In this painting, inspired by the style of the **Post-Impressionist** artist Paul Cézanne (see p. 514), the houses become stacked golden cubes and pyramids surrounded by the slightest suggestion of trees and shrubs. By eliminating the details and making all of the houses the same color, Braque focuses attention on the underlying shapes and overall

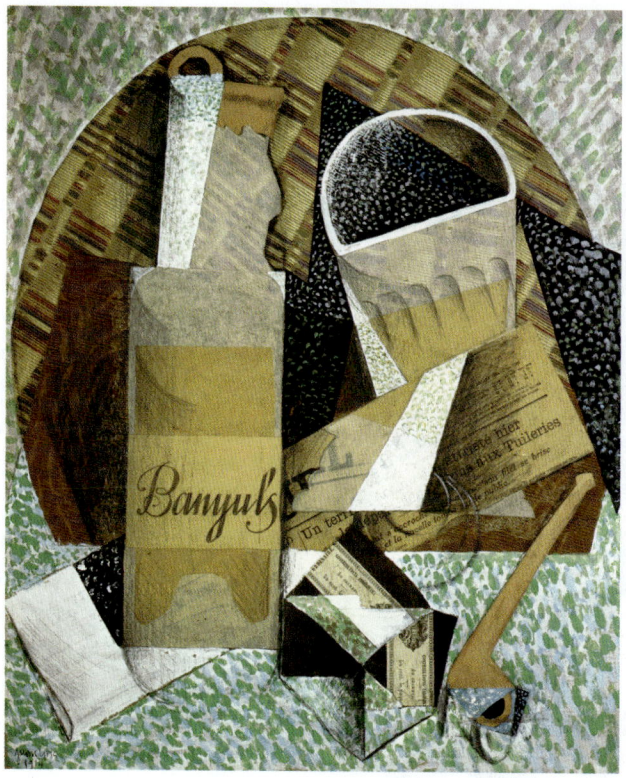

3.9.6 Juan Gris, *Bottle of Banyuls*, 1914. Pasted papers, oil, charcoal, and gouache, and pencil on canvas, 21½ × 18". Kunstmuseum, Bern, Switzerland

Collage: From the French *coller*, to glue; a work of art assembled by gluing materials, often paper, onto a surface
Impressionism: in the visual arts, a late nineteenth-century style conveying the fleeting impression of the effects of light; Impressionists were artists working in this style
Bohemian: derived from the gypsies of the former Czech Kingdom of Bohemia who moved around; a wanderer; an artist or writer who functions outside the bounds of conventional rules and practices
Avant-garde: early twentieth-century emphasis on artistic innovation, which challenged accepted values, traditions, and techniques

pattern of the picture. The shading is applied in a decorative way to give the shapes more definition. The bold treatment of this painting's forms might seem to come solely from the artist's imagination. Photographs taken at this site, however, indicate that, in fact, Braque was surprisingly true to the configuration and placement of the trees and houses. The changes he made to the colors and shapes make the painting an abstraction based on nature.

During the second phase of Cubism, artists used newspaper and wallpaper as well as fine art papers to make paper **collage**. The papers were cut into shapes and glued to a support. This kind of construction is very familiar to us today, but in the early twentieth century it was a completely new technique for making art. *Bottle of Banyuls* (**3.9.6**) by Spanish painter and sculptor Juan Gris (1887–1927) includes some shapes that relate to a table (the patchwork circle around the objects near the center), glass (suggested by the transparent paper he used), and a bottle (the layered rectangular shape on the left). By using an actual bottle label from the southern French wine Banyuls, the artist is able to identify the shapes as a bottle and to bring everyday materials into the picture.

Dada

The devastating effects of World War I had a profound impact on how people thought about the world, "progress," and civilization. Improvements in science and industrial manufacturing may have led to some positive developments in life, but to many people they seemed primarily to have resulted, disastrously, in arms production on an unprecedented scale, and in mass slaughter in the trenches of northern Europe. The war inevitably also affected artists and the way they made art. Artists who adopted the term Dada for their art protested the kinds of "rational" thought processes that had led to war. Dadaism also took the **Impressionists**' and Cubists' questioning of representation still further and radically rejected the notion of art altogether.

The name Dada was notoriously chosen at random from the dictionary. It is both a nonsense word and one that has contradictory meanings in several languages. Dada was anti-art and refused to call itself a movement. It was founded by a group of artists and writers who avoided the draft in World War I by taking refuge in the neutral country of Switzerland. Dada soon spread to the United States and later to Berlin, Cologne, Paris, Russia, Eastern Europe, and Japan. Dada works, performances, and publications were critical and playful. They emphasized individuality, irrationality, chance, and imagination.

In keeping with its activist nature, Dada was inspired by revolutionary thinking and initially took the form of events, posters, and pamphlets. In February 1916 German actor and anarchist Hugo Ball (1886–1927) opened the Cabaret Voltaire in Zürich, Switzerland, with his future wife, Emmy Hennings (1885–1948). The Cabaret was a **bohemian**, **avant-garde** nightclub that provided artists and writers with a place to meet, perform, and be entertained. Ball organized and promoted many of the events. The performances were lively and highly theatrical. At a particularly flamboyant recital of one of his sound poems, "Karawane," Ball wore a costume that made him look like a figure from a Cubist painting (**3.9.7**). His poems were made of nonsense words and

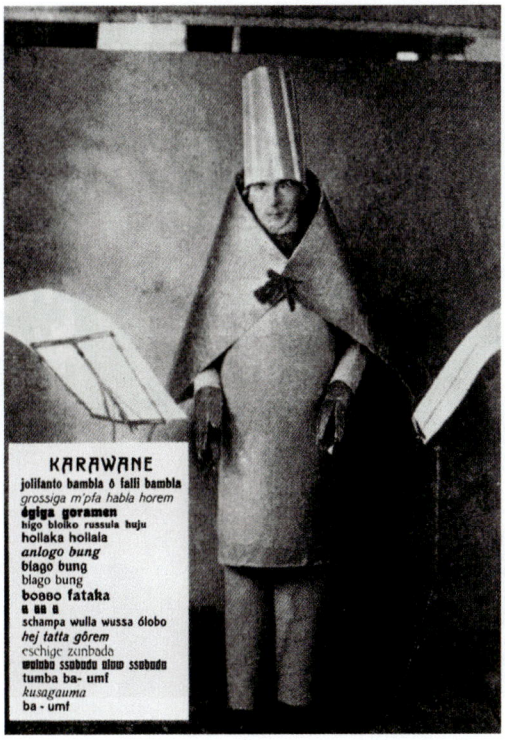

3.9.7 Hugo Ball, performance of "Karawane" at Cabaret Voltaire, Zürich, Switzerland, 1916

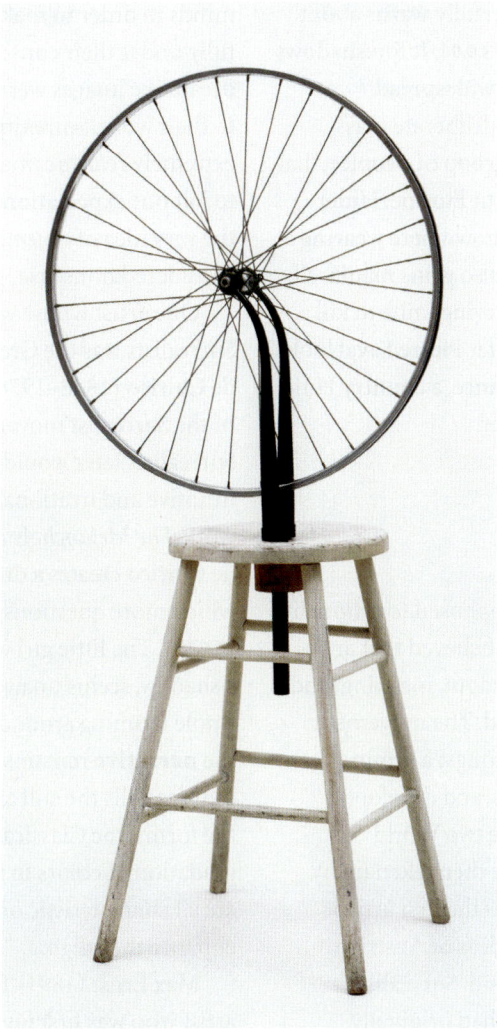

3.9.8 Marcel Duchamp, *Bicycle Wheel*, 1951. Metal wheel mounted on painted wood stool, 50½ × 25½ × 16⅝". MoMA, New York

Assemblage: artwork built up from three-dimensional materials including found objects
Found image or object: an image or object chosen by an artist and presented, with little or no alteration, as part of a work or as a finished work of art in itself
Readymade: an everyday object presented as a work of art
Kinetic art: art, usually three-dimensional, with moving parts activated by wind, personal interaction, or motors
Conceptual art: artwork in which the ideas are most important to the work
Photomontage: a single photographic image that combines (digitally or using multiple film exposures) several separate images

sounds, intended to be chanted, screamed, and howled. Sometimes several poets would recite at the same time while others yapped like dogs.

The French artist Marcel Duchamp (1887–1968) was a key figure in the New York branch of Dada (he became an American citizen in 1955). Following his early career as a painter (see chapter 3.9.16, p. 533), one of his first and most enduring anti-art statements was his *Bicycle Wheel* (**3.9.8**). Its date of production, 1913, shows that the spirit of Dada pre-dates the war. This **assemblage** of **found objects** resembles a sculpture, with a stool serving as the base, and the wheel itself as the main subject. Duchamp first made the piece for his own pleasure, because he "enjoyed looking at it, just as I enjoy looking at the flames dancing in the fireplace."

The original *Bicycle Wheel* was lost when Duchamp moved to the United States in 1915. Usually, an artwork's value partly depends on the existence of "an original" creation that is unique, but Duchamp unflinchingly re-created the piece for an exhibition in 1916. This version, too, was lost. According to the Museum of Modern Art in New York, the *Bicycle Wheel* in its collection is the third remake. Duchamp, in true Dada style, subverts the institution and originality of art.

Duchamp was responsible for three major innovations in art in the twentieth century: **readymades** (ordinary objects turned into artworks simply by the decision of the artist), **kinetic** sculptures (sculptures with moving parts), and what came to be known as **conceptual art** (see chapter 3.10, p. 546). For Duchamp, the making of the work and its appearance were secondary. What mattered were the choices of the artist and art's effects in our mind.

A member of Berlin Dada, the German John Heartfield (born Helmut Herzfeld, 1891–1968) made political statements using the medium of **photomontage**. He boldly published works criticizing the then leader of Nazi Germany, Adolf Hitler. As a result, Heartfield eventually had to flee to Prague (in what is now the Czech Republic) and later to England to escape arrest and persecution. He distributed his work on

3.9.9 (right) John Heartfield, *Have No Fear, He's a Vegetarian*, published in *Regards*, no. 121 (153), Paris, May 7, 1936. Stiftung Archiv der Akademie der Künste, Berlin, Germany

3.9.10 (far right) Giorgio de Chirico, *The Melancholy and Mystery of the Street*, 1914. Oil on canvas, 34¼ × 28⅛". Private collection

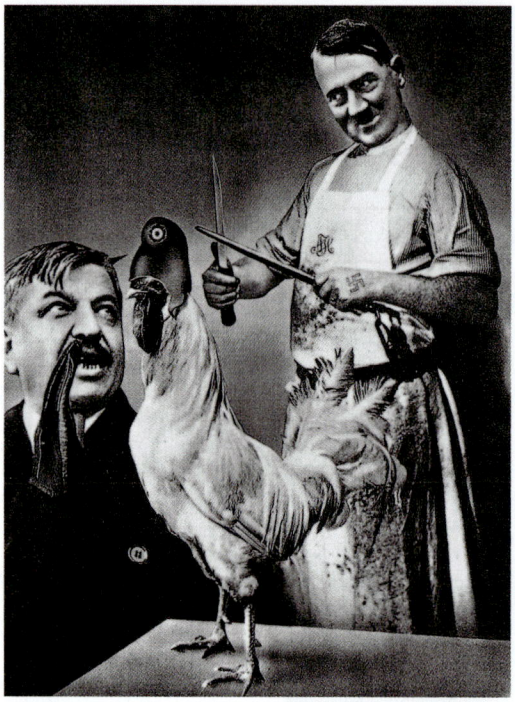

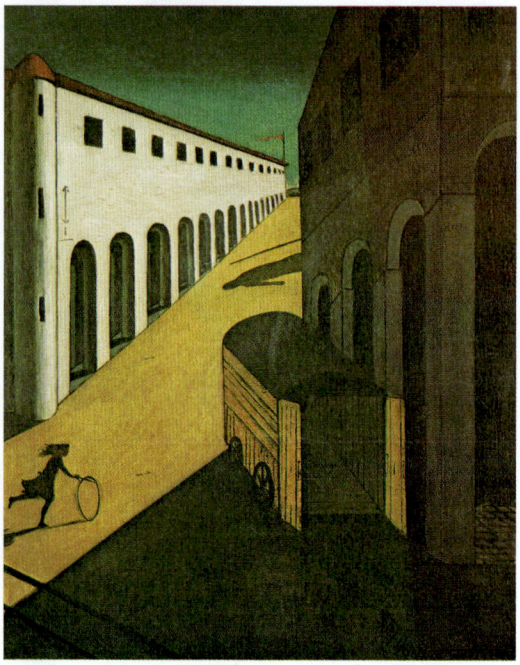

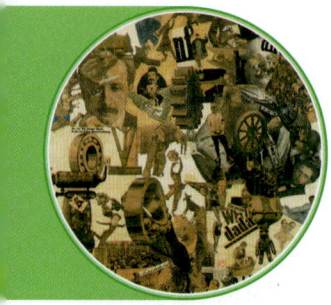

The German artist Hannah Höch used photomontage and collage to create artworks of political protest: see **2.8.20, p. 327**

posters and in magazines. His piece *Have No Fear, He's a Vegetarian* powerfully warns about Hitler's plans for conquest (**3.9.9**). It foreshadows many of the disasters, from widespread starvation to genocide (the deliberate mass killing of a specific race or group of people), that were to take place throughout Europe. Hitler was a vegetarian, but he is shown here wearing a blood-spattered apron. He also grins maniacally while he sharpens a large carving knife to kill a cock as French prime minister Pierre Laval looks on. The cock symbolizes France, a country Hitler would invade four years later.

Surrealism

Like Dada, Surrealism was opposed to rationality and convention. Surrealists believed that art was a model for human freedom, meaning, and creativity in an absurd world. The movement began in the early 1920s amongst a group of writers and poets in Paris, and developed during the time between the two World Wars; the group's ideas were then taken up by visual artists. Surrealism was the first artistic style based directly on the ideas of Austrian psychoanalyst Sigmund Freud. Surrealists used techniques that Freud had originally pioneered to access his patients' unconscious minds in order to make artwork that was not fully under their conscious control: dreams and dreamlike images were therefore very important to their work. Sometimes the Surrealists used extremely realistic images in surprising ways to jolt our expectations. Surrealists challenged the very idea of objective reality, which they considered nonsense.

One artist whose work influenced the Surrealists was the Greek-born Italian Giorgio de Chirico (1888–1978). He was not a member of the Surrealist movement, but, as the Surrealists later would be, he was interested in intuitive and irrational approaches to art. In his work *The Melancholy and Mystery of the Street*, de Chirico creates a dreamlike environment in which more questions are posed than resolved (**3.9.10**). The little girl with the hoop, herself a shadow, seems unaware of the figure with a pole looming around the corner. Although the **narrative** remains unclear, a vague sense of threat fills the still air. The crisp clarity of the forms, the Classical architecture, and the gradation of colors in the otherwise empty sky are all characteristic of de Chirico's work and enhance the enigma.

Max Ernst (1891–1976) was a German-born artist who was first involved with Dada and

Narrative: an artwork that tells a story; the story that the artwork expresses then Surrealism. For him, the process of making art was of utmost importance. Ernst used different techniques—such as collage, rubbing, and scraping—to encourage chance events that would reduce his conscious control over his work. These processes, as he stated, would liberate the human imagination. He deliberately embraced the bizarre, strange, and irrational to express truths that he believed were buried by logic in the conscious mind. In Ernst's *Le Surréalisme et la Peinture (Surrealism and Painting)*, the figure shown painting is not a human being but an amorphous blob (**3.9.11**). This shapeless being can be interpreted in different ways. It may refer to the general difficulty of understanding or explaining creativity. Perhaps it depicts the chance processes Ernst used in making art. The painting on the easel is a representation of the equally uncertain results, here seen as abstractions that seem vaguely cosmic, such as planets and intergalactic matter in the uncharted territory of outer space. Overall, Ernst made a strong statement about how liberating it can be to allow the imagination to wander in the mysterious realm of creativity.

Using the technique of assemblage, Surrealists created the three-dimensional equivalent of collage. These assemblages were principally intended to be playful and nonsensical and to reflect new ways of thinking. Spanish artist Joan Miró (1893–1983) compiled an unexpected assortment of items in his sculpture called *Object* (**3.9.12**). A derby hat, which serves as the sculpture's base, has a map placed on one side of its brim and a red plastic fish on the other. A block of wood sits on the hat with a perch on top of it that supports a stuffed parrot. Miró fashioned a miniature woman's leg by stuffing a silk stocking in a shapely manner, placing a doll's shoe on one end, and wrapping a band for a garter on the other. This leg is hanging in an oval-shaped opening of the wooden block. A cork ball hangs from the parrot's perch beside the leg. The objects have the whimsical quality of toys. When viewed together, as the artist has arranged them, they also have an air of mystery, as if they are clues to an unsolved crime or random items that make sense only to their owner.

3.9.11 (below) Max Ernst, *Le Surréalisme et la Peinture (Surrealism and Painting)*, 1942. Oil on canvas, 6'5" × 7'8". The Menil Collection, Houston, Texas

3.9.12 (right) Joan Miró, *Object*, 1936. Assemblage: stuffed parrot on wood perch, stuffed silk stocking with velvet garter and doll's paper shoe suspended in hollow wood frame, derby hat, hanging cork ball, celluloid fish, and engraved map, 31⅞ × 11⅞ × 10¼". MoMA, New York

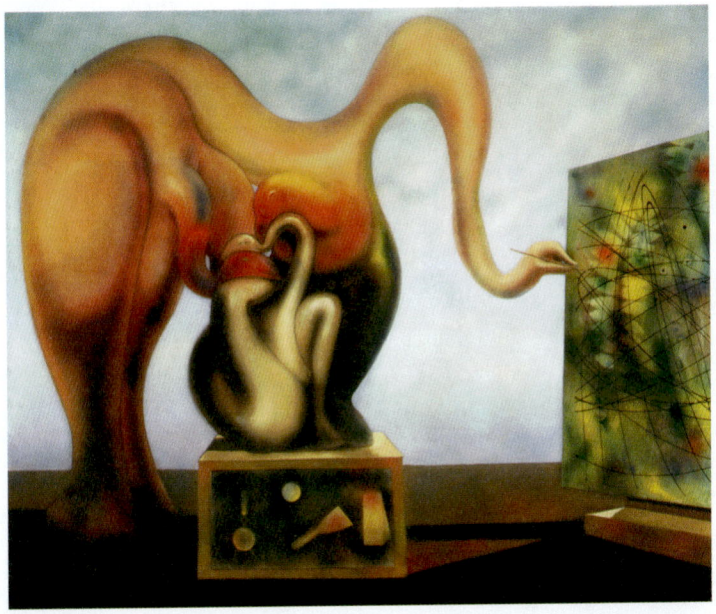

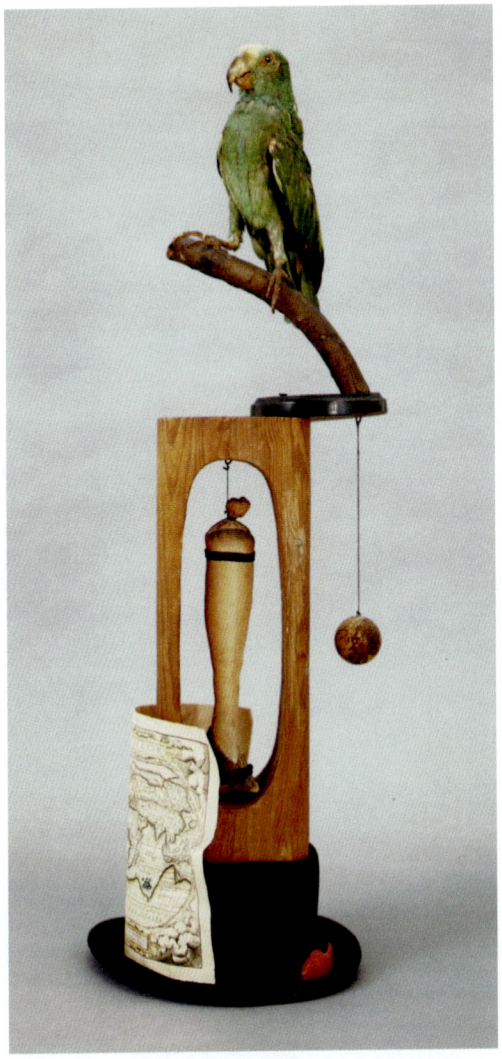

Gateway to Art: Kahlo, *The Two Fridas*
Was She a Surrealist?

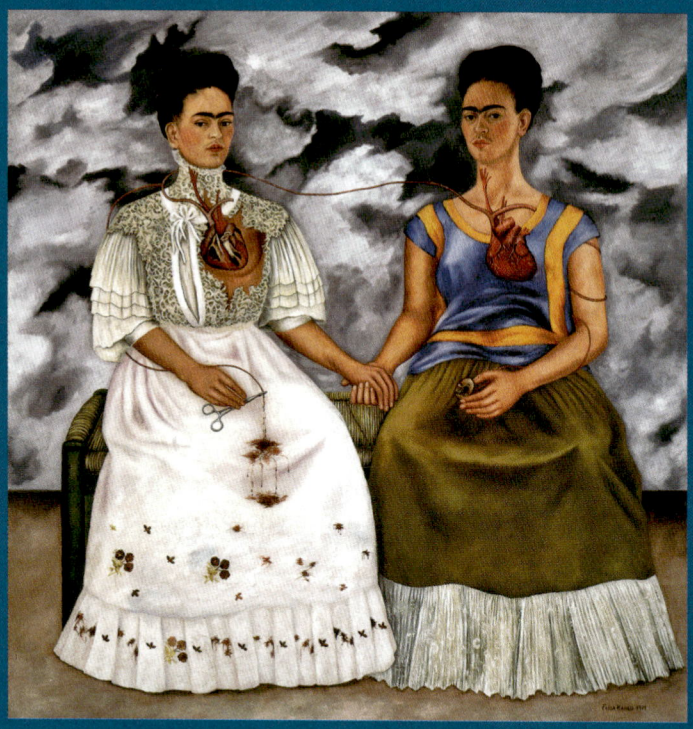

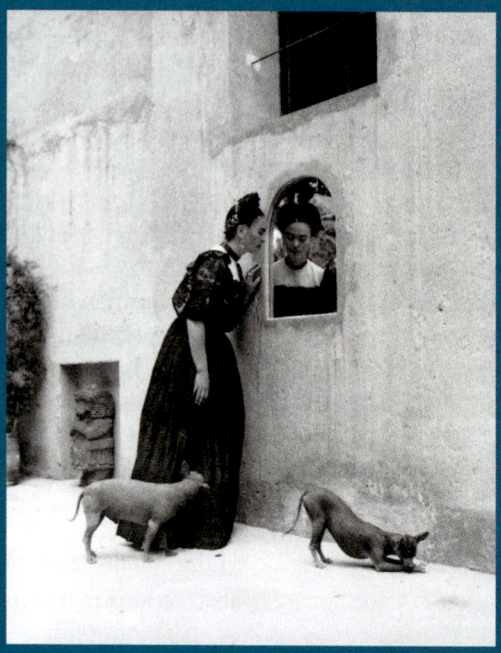

3.9.13 (above) Frida Kahlo, *The Two Fridas*, 1939. Oil on canvas, 5'8" × 5'8". Museo de Arte Moderno, Mexico City, Mexico

3.9.14 (above right) Lola Álvarez Bravo, *Frida Kahlo*, c. 1944. Gelatin silver print

The Modern period in art is especially filled with "-isms," as many artists tried to give a name to their original approaches. The fact is that, unless they consciously associated with a particular group that shared their sensibility, many artists resist being labelled as belonging to a specific artistic movement. Frida Kahlo was such an artist. Like Giorgio de Chirico (**3.9.10**, p. 530), her work is often called Surrealist even though neither of them was part of the movement.

Kahlo said she never knew she was a Surrealist "until André Breton came to Mexico and told me I was one." What is it in Kahlo's work that aligns it with Surrealism? If we use *The Two Fridas* (**3.9.13**) as our example, we notice many unexpected, illogical, and fantastic elements that reflect a logic that makes sense only in dreams. The fact that we can see internal and external anatomy at the same time, in addition to the body doubling, draws our attention to the sense that something is out of the ordinary here. The otherwise blank, cloud-filled sky and sharp, linear contours further evoke the apocalyptic, deserted landscapes of many other Surrealist works.

For the other Kahlo Gateway boxes, see p. 50, p. 204, and p. 676

In response to being called a Surrealist, Kahlo wrote, "Really I do not know whether my paintings are Surrealist or not, but I do know that they are the frankest expression of myself." Perhaps it is more accurate to focus on the personal nature of her vision than to take the shortcut of calling her a Surrealist. Her cultural identity was complex: she was a mestiza (with mixed native Mexican and European ancestry); her revolutionary politics coincided with her deep embrace of Mexican heritage; she was bisexual; she was physically disabled by polio and injury; and yet she had fierce *alegría* (lust for life). The apparently fantastic mirroring of her own body recalls the reality of the mirrors installed around her home at Casa Azul (**3.9.14**) and the mirror installed over her bed so she could paint herself during her recovery from a traffic accident. The use of the "doubling" or mirror-image device in the painting also enables the artist to express distinct aspects of her identity—the Frida on the right wears a Mexican dress (related to her mother's heritage); the Frida on the left, a European gown (reflecting her father's German roots). Ultimately, in the case of Frida's work and life, truth is tragically and fascinatingly stranger than fiction.

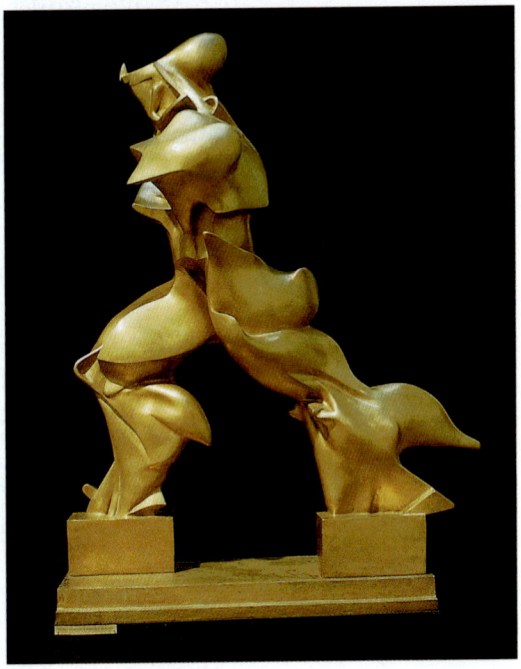

3.9.15 Umberto Boccioni, *Unique Forms of Continuity in Space*, 1913 (cast 1931). Bronze, 49¾ × 35 × 16". Private collection

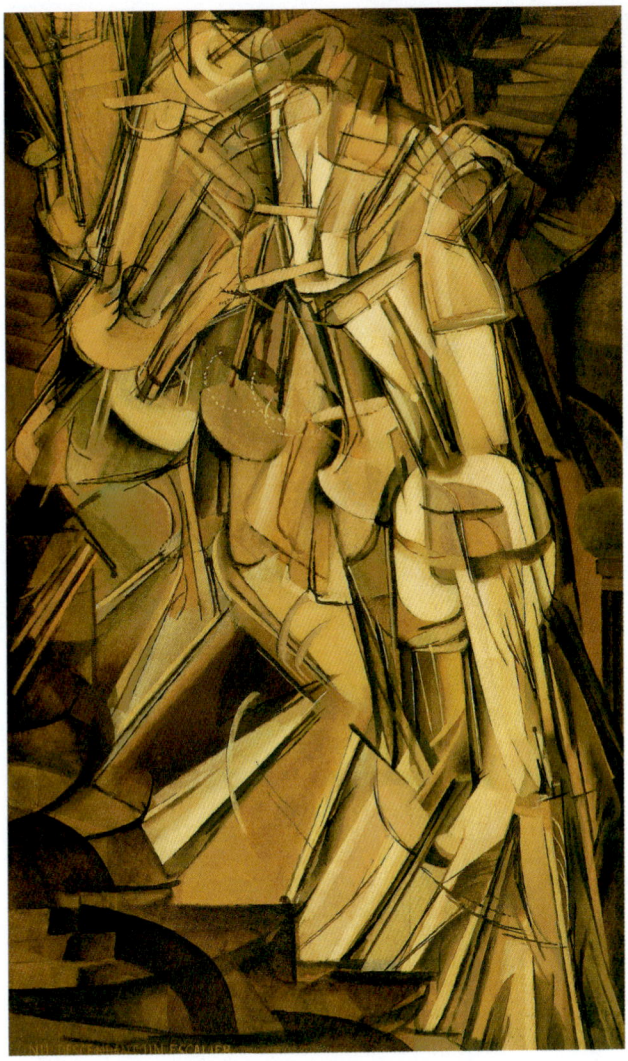

3.9.16 Marcel Duchamp, *Nude Descending a Staircase, No. 2*, 1912. Oil on canvas, 57⅞ × 35⅛". Philadelphia Museum of Art, Pennsylvania

The Influence of Cubism

Cubism's ground-breaking approach to art (see pp. 526–28) had a huge impact throughout Europe. Many artists adopted the Cubist style, while others explored ways of making art and depicting objects that had not been conceived of before Cubism.

Futurism, De Stijl, and Suprematism

In Italy, during the period from 1909 to the late 1920s, some artists were influenced by Cubism's clashing planes and geometry to develop a style known as **Futurism**. Unlike Cubist artworks, though, Futurist works celebrated dynamic movement, progress, modern technology, and political beliefs that were later to be known as Fascist. They also expressed contempt for the past. Italian Umberto Boccioni (1882–1916) explored some of these concepts in his Futurist sculpture *Unique Forms of Continuity in Space* (**3.9.15**). Looking like a flame, the figure forcefully strides through space. Boccioni made the sculpture in plaster; it was not cast in bronze during his lifetime. The shiny, golden appearance of the metal version embodies the words of the founder of Futurism, Filippo Marinetti: "War is beautiful because it inaugurates the long dreamed-of metallization of the human body." At the same time, the figure has heroic **monumentality** as it leaves behind the artistic traditions of the past.

As we have seen, Marcel Duchamp (see pp. 529–30) had a huge impact on the development of modern art. It was his *Nude Descending a Staircase, No. 2* and the scandal it caused at the **Armory Show** in New York in 1913 that earned him an international reputation (**3.9.16**). For this short period in his career Duchamp combined Cubism's figures—broken into geometric planes—with Futurism's emphasis on movement. The mechanization of

Futurism: an artistic movement begun in Italy in 1909 that violently rejected traditional forms in favor of celebrating and incorporating into art the energy and dynamism of modern technology; Futurists were artists working in this style
Monumental: having massive or impressive scale
Armory Show: exhibition in 1913 in New York City that introduced America to Modernist European abstraction; continues as an annual international exhibition

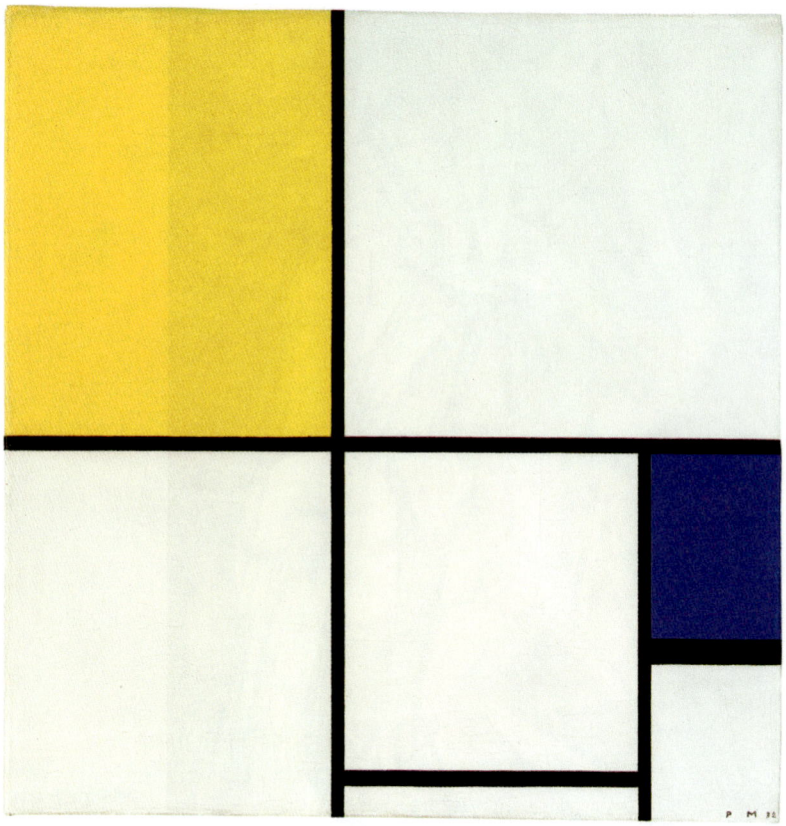

3.9.17 Piet Mondrian, *Composition with Yellow and Blue*, 1932. Oil on canvas, 21⅝ × 21⅝". Bayeler Collection, Bayeler Foundation, Riehen/Basel, Switzerland

De Stijl: a group of artists originating in the Netherlands in the early twentieth century, associated with a utopian style of design that emphasized primary colors and straight lines
Palette: the range of colors used by an artist
Primary colors: three basic colors from which all others are derived
Golden Section: a unique ratio of a line divided into two segments so that the sum of both segments (a + b) is to the longer segment (a) as the longer segment (a) is to the shorter segment (b). The result is 1:1.618
Suprematism: Russian art movement of the early twentieth century focused on geometric shapes and limited colors that emphasized feeling over visual phenomena
Aesthetic: related to beauty, art, and taste
Ground: the surface or background onto which an artist paints or draws

the figure in this painting reflected a widespread contemporary interest in machines, industrial progress, and stop-motion photography. Like many other works at the Armory Show, this painting shocked an audience familiar only with representational imagery, or pictures "of" something.

The Dutch painter Piet Mondrian (1872–1944) was the founder of the movement called **De Stijl** ("The Style") in the Netherlands. He painted in a naturalistic style early in his career and was influenced by avant-garde movements, including Cubism, to move away from directly depicting visible reality. Always interested in the underlying structure in his subjects, Mondrian increasingly began to concentrate on creating non-representational works. In 1914 he began making compositions entirely of intersecting lines, right-angled shapes, and linear planes. In 1921 he restricted his **palette** to the **primary colors**, and black, white, and gray. Using these select formal elements for decades, Mondrian is known for his geometric abstractions (**3.9.17**). The subtle adjustments in the proportions and arrangements in his paintings result from mathematical principles and the ratios of the **Golden Section**. Mondrian believed that the clarity and organization of his compositions reflected rational beauty that is objective and appeals to the mind in a universal way, as opposed to subjective beauty, which appeals to the senses.

Like Mondrian and Kandinsky (p. 521), Russian Kazimir Malevich (1878–1935) was one of the first artists to make completely non-objective paintings. Unlike Kandinsky, Malevich concentrated solely on direct geometric forms. He called his approach **Suprematism** because he considered it morally, spiritually, and **aesthetically** superior to what had been done in the past. Malevich believed that recognizable objects were a burden for the viewer and that geometric abstraction helped to free the mind from the thoughts of politics, religion, and tradition that were so much on people's minds in the early twentieth century, partly as a result of the cataclysmic conflict of World War I. Most of Malevich's Suprematist works consist of rectangular shapes floating on a white **ground**. While they look like Cubist collages, the shapes are actually painted. In *Suprematist Composition: White on White* the palette has been reduced to two shades of white, and the inner square is tilted to suggest movement (**3.9.18**).

3.9.18 Kazimir Malevich, *Suprematist Composition: White on White*, 1918. Oil on canvas, 31¾ × 31¾". MoMA, New York

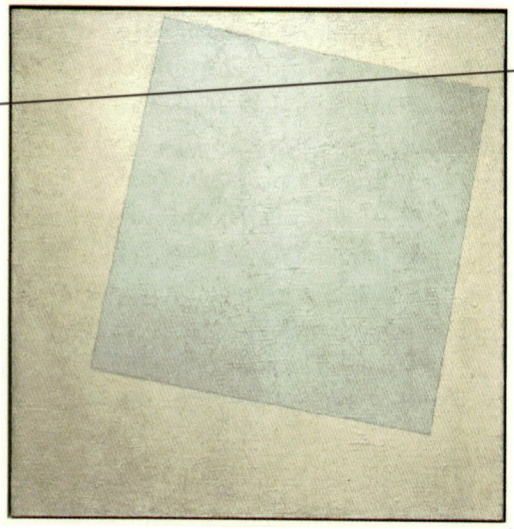

Twentieth-Century Abstraction

The road to abstraction began with the Impressionist emphasis on the immediate effects of color and light instead of details in line work and shading. From there, Post-Impressionists emphasized visual structure and emotion, Matisse and the Fauvists released color from its representational obligations, Expressionists explored non-representational approaches, and the Cubists revolutionized form by showing multiple viewpoints at one time. Twentieth-century abstract artists continued where these avant-garde pioneers left off.

The Romanian-born French sculptor Constantin Brancusi (1876–1957) devoted his working life to finding the very simplest and most elegant way to express the essence of his chosen subject. His *Bird in Space* distills the vital qualities of a bird to what, at first sight, looks like a totally abstract form (**3.9.19**). The shape exquisitely reminds us of a bird's body, a feather, or even the soaring quality of flight.

This sculpture, with the polished bronze form stacked on top of a small stone cylinder with a lighter-colored stone rectangular prism underneath, shows Brancusi's careful consideration of even the *base* of the sculpture. He chose the materials of the base—usually wood, metal, stone, or marble—to contrast in texture with a different material used for the rest of the sculpture. In this case, the solidity and bulk of the stone suggest heaviness and earth, while the contrasting thinness of the smooth and shiny bronze makes it look as if it would slip easily through the air.

Abstraction has continued to be a guiding principle for many artists, such as Canadian-born artist Agnes Martin (1912–2004). Her painting *Starlight* has an overall field of a soft, nebulous blue color with a superimposed grid that is so uniform that no one area of the work dominates (**3.9.20**). Martin, who grew up in Vancouver, became interested in Eastern philosophy, especially Daoism, and for many years lived a life of solitude and simplicity in New Mexico. She explored the idea that art could enable people to experience a profound sense of calm and so "leave themselves behind." In the work *Starlight*, Martin's Daoist ideas about the importance of harmony in the universe are reflected in the emphasis on the work as a whole, held together by the essential simplicity of the grid, the structure of which, with its faint but regular and insistent lines, permeates the entire painting. The resulting effect allows us to immerse ourselves in the work, as if it were a place for reflective meditation.

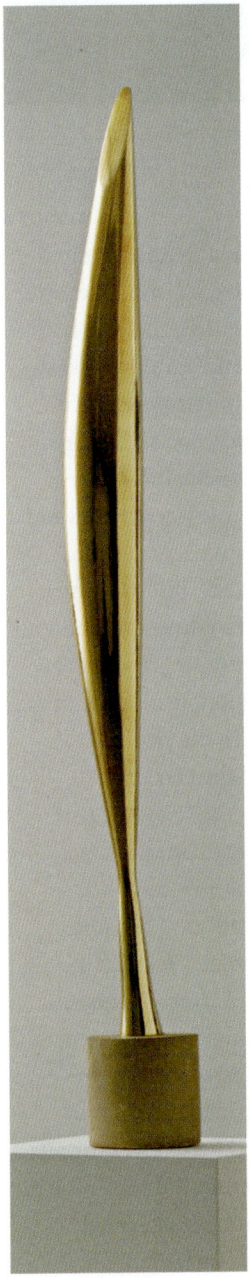

3.9.19 Constantin Brancusi, *Bird in Space (L'Oiseau dans L'Espace)*, 1928. Bronze, 54 × 8½ × 6½". MoMA, New York

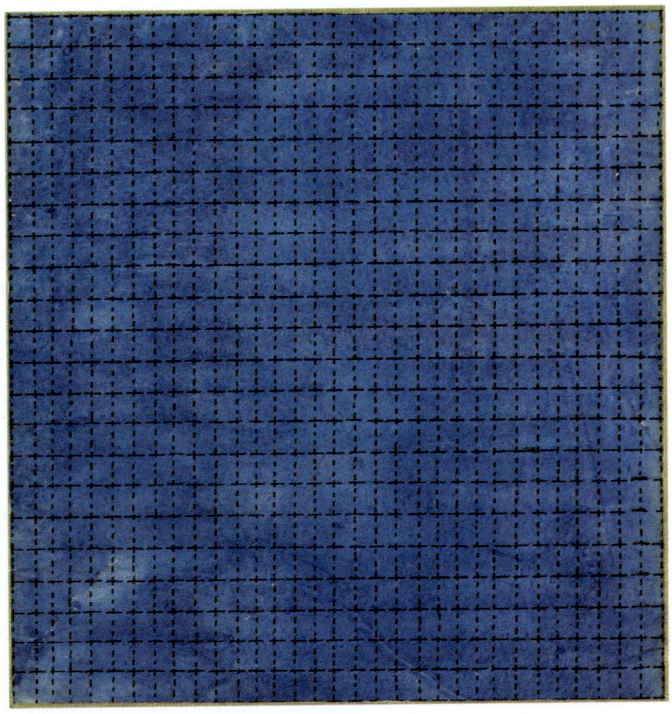

3.9.20 Agnes Martin, *Starlight*, 1963. Watercolor and ink on paper, 11¾ × 10½". Private collection

Early Twentieth-Century Art in America

The move toward abstraction in the US happened after the Armory Show of 1913 in New York City, when the American public was introduced to the work of such artists as Matisse, Picasso, Kandinsky, and Duchamp. While European artists and some Americans continued experiments with abstraction during the 1930s, another group, inspired by the harsh realities presented by the advent of the Great Depression in 1929, chose to focus on distinctly American subjects and representational styles with a shared sense of nationalism. This approach came to be known as the American Scene. The **Regionalists** focused on rural environments and promoted American virtues, such as patriotism and hard work. The **Social Realists** were interested in promoting social justice through their artwork. **Harlem Renaissance** artists specifically focused on the expression of African American experience through music, writing, and visual art.

An American Regionalist, Grant Wood (1891–1942) studied in Europe but realized that his inspiration came from his home in the Midwest and the places he knew best. Wood's sister and his dentist were the models for the farmer and his daughter in Wood's now-famous *American Gothic* (**3.9.21**). They stand in front of an Iowa farmhouse built in a style called Carpenter Gothic, inspiring the painting's title. Their full-frontal posture and the clarity of detail and light come from Flemish Renaissance art (see chapter 3.6) that Wood had studied while in Europe. While this painting has been the subject of many artistic parodies, it was meant to be a serious reflection of hope in spite of the Depression, and an affirmation of the Midwestern American values of individuality, morality, and hard work.

Also focused on distinctively American subjects, Isabel Bishop (1902–1988) was part of a group called the 14th Street School and is associated with the Social Realists due to her scenes of urban life in Union Square. She came to New York at age sixteen to attend the School of Applied Design for Women and entered the Art Students League a few years later. In addition to street scenes, Bishop's most frequently cited subject is women. She created a distinctive style of detailed realistic figures emerging from light-filled background settings and patterned, washy environments using layers of **tempera** and oil glazes on gessoed prestwood panels. Her direct observations capture in-between moments of working women on breaks, often with awkward expressions and unique gestures. As seen in images such as *Waiting* (**3.9.22**), Bishop's quick brushstrokes suggest busy **rhythms** and show an enduring sympathy for the underprivileged at the same time as raising consciousness about the experience of everyday life in the city.

In the 1920s and 1930s the Harlem Renaissance was known as the "New Negro" movement. Interested in art at an early age, American Aaron Douglas (1899–1979) moved to New York City and soon became a leading figure of the movement. As seen in *Aspects of Negro Life: From Slavery Through Reconstruction* (**3.9.23**), Douglas's work depicts African-American life and post-slavery/pre-Civil Rights struggles. Part of a series of four paintings commissioned by the Works Progress Administration (WPA) for the 135th St. branch of the New York Public Library, each panel depicts a different aspect of black life, from

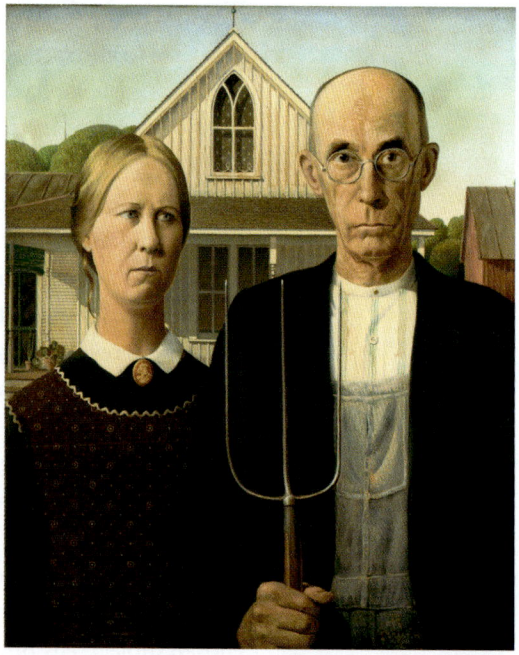

3.9.21 Grant Wood, *American Gothic*, 1930. Oil on beaverboard, 30¾ × 35¾". Art Institute of Chicago, Illinois

Regionalism: branch of American Scene painting that promoted rural, small-town virtues and values, especially related to the Deep South and Midwest US
Social Realism: branch of American Scene painting that focused on Depression-era social issues and hardships of daily life
Harlem Renaissance: movement in literature, music, and the visual arts from the end of WWI into the 1930s celebrating black experience and culture
Tempera: fast-drying painting medium made from pigment mixed with water-soluble binder, such as egg yolk
Rhythm: the regular or ordered repetition of elements in the work

Africa to the migration to northern US cities. The *Slavery to Reconstruction* panel combines the past and the present—jungle plants and animals referencing Africa alongside a trumpet and drum referencing jazz and its importance to society at the time the painting was made. The **silhouettes**, which became a signature aspect of Douglas's work, were created from the combined influences of Egyptian wall paintings, Art Deco (a style similar to **Art Nouveau**) designs, African art, and Modernist abstraction. The lively atmosphere, dancing, and jazz music shown here also represent the intersections of African heritage, African American culture, and nationalistic identity in relation to Black American experience in the 1930s.

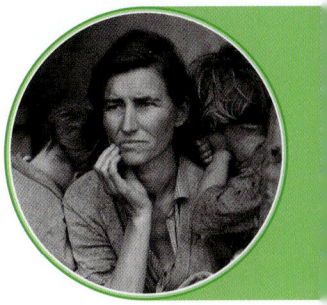

Dorothea Lange made Social Realist work as part of a government-sponsored documentation of the Great Depression. For a discussion of ethical questions surrounding photojournalism and her photograph of migrant workers in California, see **4.8.9, p. 659**

Silhouette: a portrait or figure represented in outline and solidly colored in
Art Nouveau: French for "new art," a visual style of the late nineteenth and early twentieth century, characterized by organic flowing lines, simulating forms in nature and involving decorative pattern

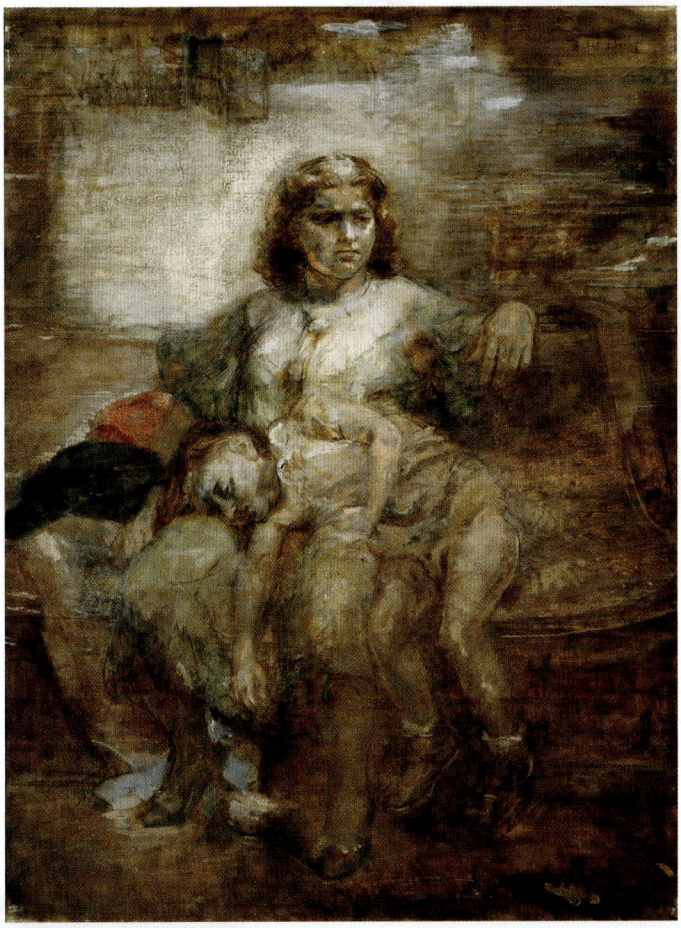

3.9.22 (right) Isabel Bishop, *Waiting*, 1938. Oil and tempera on gesso panel, 29 × 22½". Newark Museum

3.9.23 (below) Aaron Douglas, *Aspects of Negro Life: From Slavery Through Reconstruction*, 1934. Oil on canvas, 57¾ × 108¼". The New York Public Library, Schomburg Center for Research in Black Culture, New York

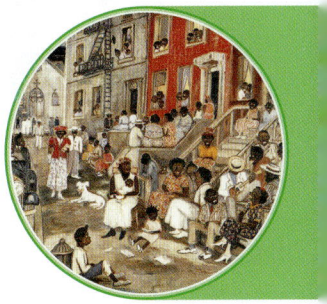

Palmer Hayden's *Midsummer Night in Harlem* is another example of Harlem Renaissance painting that focuses in a more realistic way on daily life: see **1.10.6, p. 177**

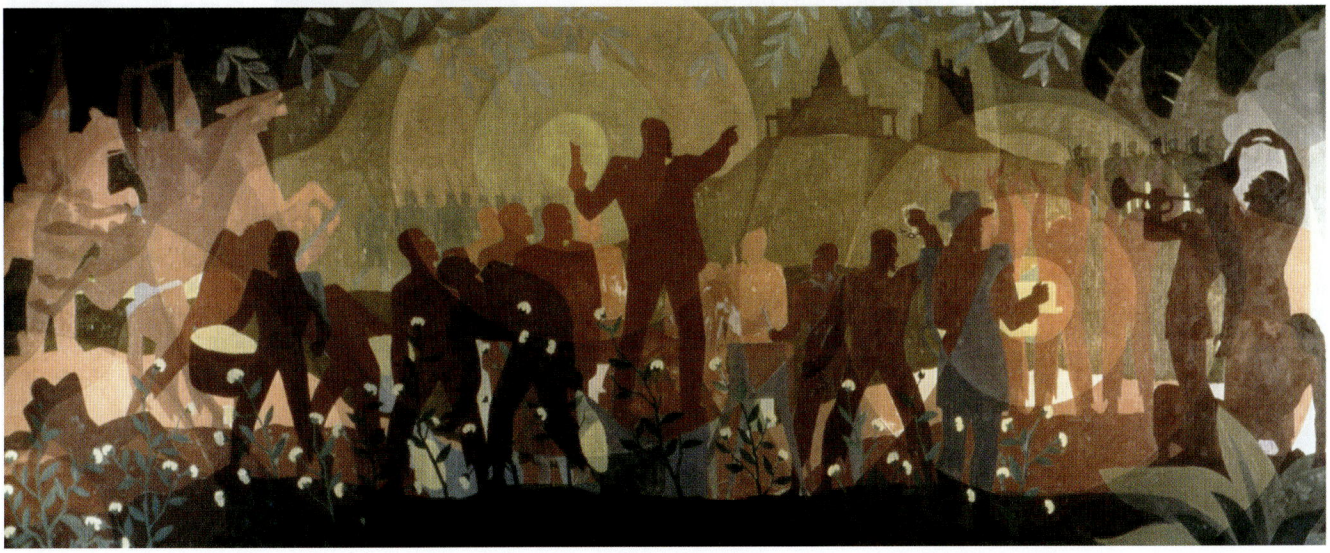

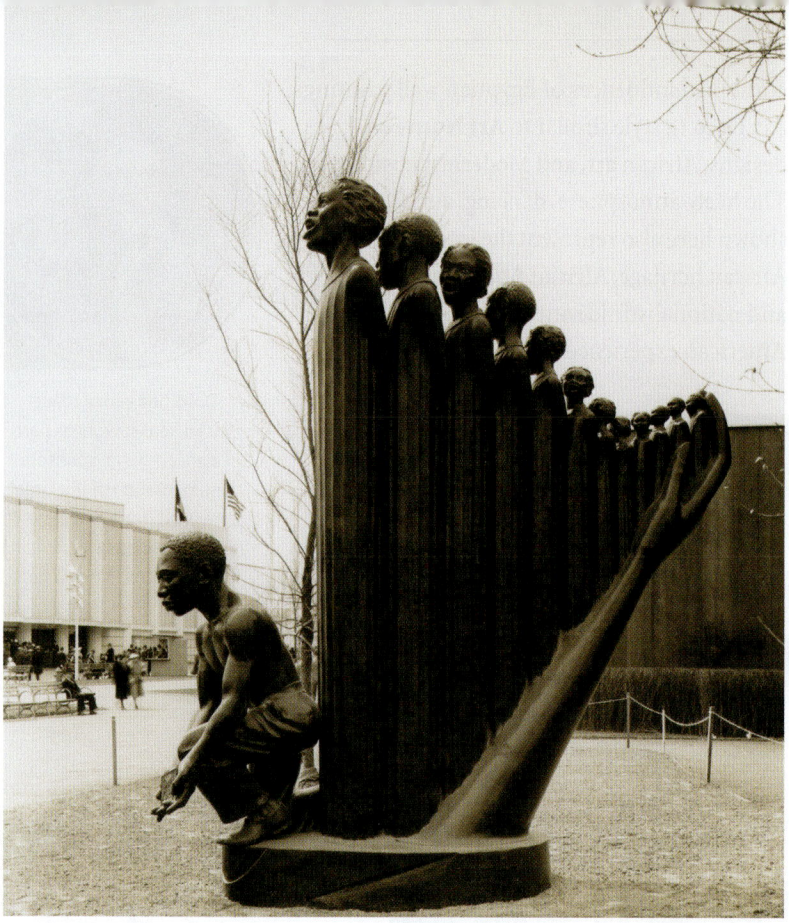

3.9.24 Augusta Savage, *The Harp ("Lift Every Voice and Sing")*, 1939, plaster sculpture for the New York World's Fair (destroyed), photo by Carl Van Vechten

Also an active member of the Harlem arts community, Augusta Savage (1892–1962) came to New York to become an artist. She studied at Cooper Union School of Art and in Paris. In 1939 she was commissioned to make a sculpture celebrating African American contributions to music for the World's Fair in New York (**3.9.24**). She used the 1900 song "Lift Every Voice and Sing" by James Weldon and J. Rosamund Johnson as her inspiration. The figures of the 16-ft. plaster sculpture seem to personify the lyrics,

> Sing a song full of faith that the dark past has taught us,
> Sing a song full of hope that the present has brought us;
> Facing the rising sun of our new day begun,
> Let us march on till victory is won.

Along with dozens of other sculptures made for the fair, the original was destroyed because there was no budget for casting or storage. In addition to being an accomplished practicing artist, Savage was a teacher and mentor, including serving as the first director of the Harlem Community Arts Center. The Center was funded by the WPA and it invited African Americans to learn more about their culture by studying the fine arts.

Abstract Expressionism: a mid-twentieth-century artistic style characterized by its capacity to convey intense emotions using non-representational images

Abstract Expressionism

European refugees including numerous artists, intellectuals, and scientists came to the US during World War II to escape persecution. Many of them settled in New York City, which became a globally important cultural center. Whereas the avant-garde artistic developments described earlier and in chapter 3.8 began in Europe, **Abstract Expressionism** was the first Modernist art movement to originate in the US, a sign of increasing national self-confidence. In this distinctly American movement, Abstract Expressionist artists wanted to create, with energy and emotion, a universal visual experience that anyone could respond to, without needing to refer to their own life experience and religious or political beliefs.

To make his enormous paintings, American artist Jackson Pollock (1912–1956) started by unrolling the canvas onto the floor. Then he could move about freely, almost dancing around and over the piece (**3.9.25**). Pollock also

3.9.25 Jackson Pollock painting in his Long Island studio, 1950. Photo by Hans Namuth

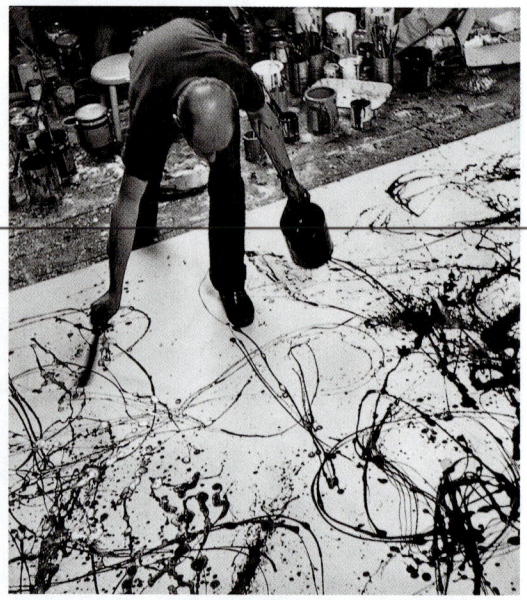

Action painting: application of paint to canvas by dripping, splashing, or smearing that emphasizes the artist's gestures
Organic: having irregular forms and shapes, as though derived from living organisms
Color Field painting: branch of Abstract Expressionism focusing on non-objective abstractions

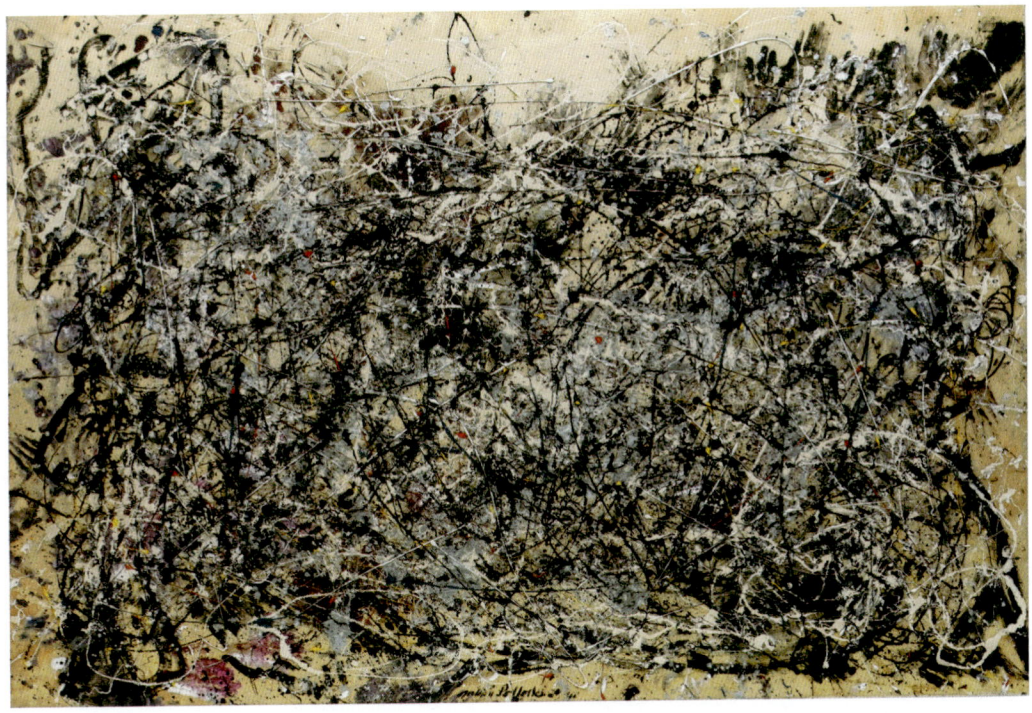

3.9.26 Jackson Pollock, *Number 1A*, 1948. Oil and enamel paint on canvas, 5'8" × 8'8". MoMA, New York

used sticks as well as brushes to drip and pour the paint onto the surface. The absence of any recognizable subject fixes our attention on the actions and gestures of the artist. The process becomes the subject, making the painting about the act of creation itself. The results of Pollock's process, known as **action painting**, are complex abstract paintings so large that when we stand before them they completely dominate our field of vision. Pollock's artworks evolved **organically** and spontaneously rather than from precise pre-planning. The improvisational process and the tension between the rhythms and cross-rhythms of Pollock's paintings also have some similarities to jazz music, which he liked to listen to as he worked (**3.9.26**).

American artist Mark Rothko (1903–1970) emigrated to the US from Russia with his family. He became interested in Surrealist art as a way to move beyond depicting familiar subjects and to explore archetypes (a psychoanalytical term used to describe an original model after which later examples follow) and mythic narratives that might generally appeal to any viewer regardless of his or her background. Eventually, Rothko entirely eliminated representation from his work and what we see in the example shown is a composition consisting solely of form and color, known as **Color Field** painting.

For about twenty years, from *c.* 1950 to 1970, his works consisted of luminous rectangles floating in fields of color, such as *No. 5/No. 22* from 1950 (**3.9.27**). This painting includes subtle color shifts, not only in the oranges and

3.9.27 Mark Rothko, *No. 5/No. 22*, 1950 (dated 1949 on reverse). Oil on canvas, 9'9⅞" × 8'11⅛". MoMA, New York

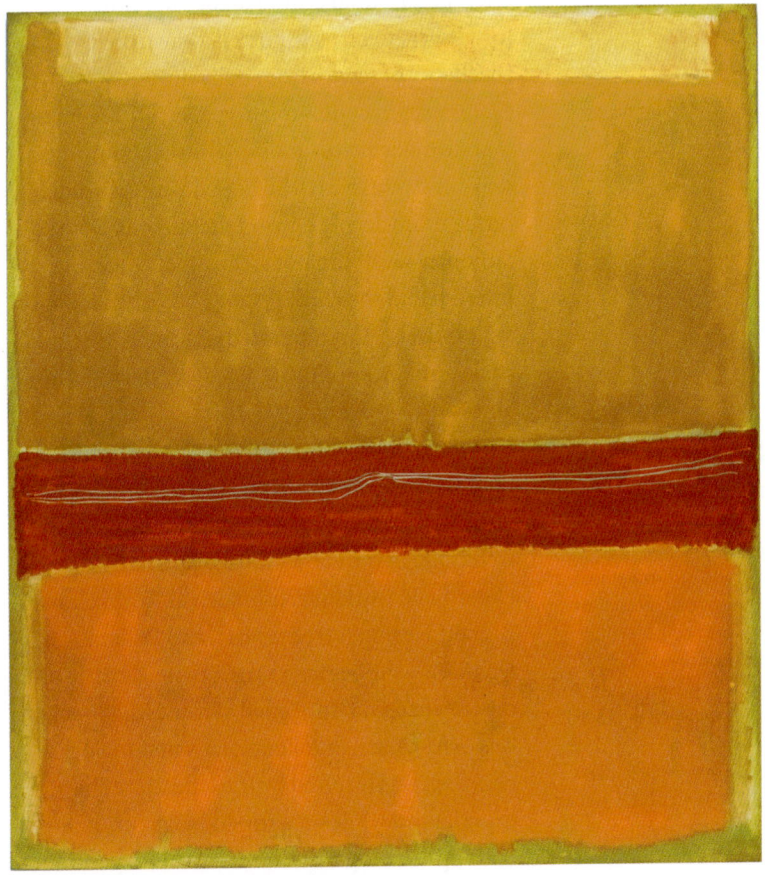

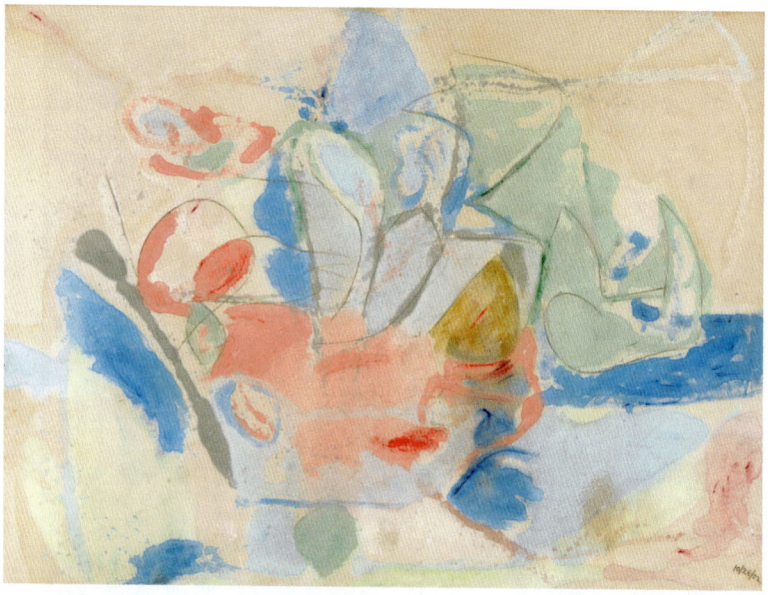

3.9.28 Helen Frankenthaler, *Mountains and Sea*, 1952. Oil and charcoal on canvas, 86⅜ × 117¼". Helen Frankenthaler Foundation, New York on extended loan to the National Gallery of Art, Washington, D.C.

variations of yellows in the large fields, but also within the undertones, with a greenish shade in the golden-yellow background to heighten contrast with the red band. Rothko chose not to give his works narrative titles and to allow us to respond deeply and individually. By reducing the formal elements he used and eliminating representational frames of reference, Rothko creates an opportunity for viewers to be transported away from the specificity of scenes from daily life and lose themselves in contemplation. Despite the fact that he made these kinds of abstract paintings for over twenty years, he hoped viewers would probe more deeply beyond the surface. Rothko famously said, "I'm not an abstractionist. I'm not interested in the relationship of color or form or anything else. I'm interested only in expressing basic human emotions: tragedy, ecstasy, doom, and so on."

One of the few women in the Abstract Expressionism movement, Helen Frankenthaler (1928–2011) pioneered a new and influential technique in the early 1950s. Inspired by the Color Field work of artists such as Rothko and Barnett Newman (see p. 104), and Pollock's drip technique, she began pouring paint directly onto unstretched and unprimed canvas. *Mountains and Sea* (**3.9.28**), Frankenthaler's first major painting, was inspired by the landscape she experienced while on a trip to Nova Scotia. She applied **oil paint** thinned with turpentine for this painting then tilted and lifted the canvas rather than using brushes to move the paint around. Because the canvas was not primed with gesso, the paint soaked into the weave of the fabric. Frankenthaler, like other second-generation Abstract Expressionists, saw abstraction as a way to focus attention on formal elements such as line and color in and of themselves rather than using them to represent other things. Water and geography informed many of her artworks, though she was not focused on context or speculation and, as she said, "sentiment and nuance are being squeezed out."

Oil paint: paint made of pigment floating in oil
Pop art: mid-twentieth-century artistic movement inspired by commercial art forms and popular culture
Silkscreen: method of printmaking using a stencil and paint pushed through a screen
Acrylic: a liquid polymer, or plastic, which is used as a binder for pigment in acrylic paint

Pop Art

Unlike the Abstract Expressionists, the artists who began producing **Pop art** in the late 1950s embraced everyday subject matter in their work. Consumer culture and futuristic high-tech gadgets promised ways for "everyone" to live a life of plenty and leisure. In reality, however, middle-class suburban living was out of reach for people who lived in the inner cities—primarily African Americans at the time—not to mention countries outside the West. In addition, even the latest movie idols and pop music playing on the radio could not fully tune out the threat of atomic war.

Pop art embraced the objects and experiences of daily life in a way that was entirely new to the art world at the time. Jasper Johns (b. 1930) and Robert Rauschenberg (1925–2008), who believed that Abstract Expressionist art was too obscure and personal, served as inspiration for Pop artists by highlighting common objects taken directly from the life they were living. Because Pop artists wanted their subjects to be immediately familiar to their audiences, they borrowed their imagery from popular culture, including famous artworks, comic-books, commercial advertising, car design, television, movies, and the news. At the time there was a division between fine art (a supposedly sophisticated part of "high" culture) and its opposite, popular culture (considered unrefined and ordinary). Pop artists bridged this gap by combining fine art materials with commercial elements, such as pictures from magazines, sometimes printing by **silkscreen** (which is used for printing packaging), and then selling their pieces in fine art galleries.

American Andy Warhol (1928–1987) began his professional career as an illustrator and graphic designer in advertising. Around 1960, using the expressive brushwork and drips of paint that were characteristic of Abstract Expressionism, Warhol made **acrylic** paintings of the comic-book heroes Superman, Batman, and Dick Tracy. He then quickly turned to the imagery of advertising, using as his subjects such familiar products as Campbell's soup and Coca-Cola. He also began using the silkscreen technique. This process allowed him not only to make art more quickly, but also to give it a depersonalized and mass-produced quality very different from some art's emphasis on personal expression or technique. Warhol even borrowed, or appropriated, the famous image of the Italian Renaissance artist Leonardo da Vinci's *Mona Lisa*. The title of this piece, *Thirty Are Better than One*, clearly echoes the language of advertising and consumerism—"more is better" (**3.9.29**). It refers to the multiple reproductions of the painting in Warhol's work while also undermining the "high art" tendency to value an artwork financially and aesthetically only if it is "original" and unique.

The American artist Roy Lichtenstein (1923–1997) also made works based on comics. Lichtenstein challenged traditional notions of the subject matter and appearance of fine art painting by embracing everyday subjects. In his painting *Girl in Mirror* he uses strong black outlines filled with bold primary colors (**3.9.30**). In order to create gradations of a color, Lichtenstein borrowed a technique from older

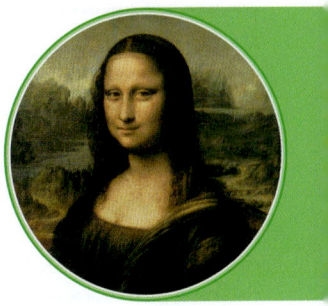

For further discussion of the masterpiece Warhol reproduced in his painting, see **0.0.12, p. 28**

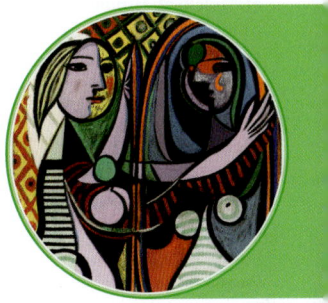

In his version of the subject of a woman peering into a mirror, Pablo Picasso uses abstraction and symbolism to reference his own life and the concept of *vanitas*: see **4.3.14, p. 600**

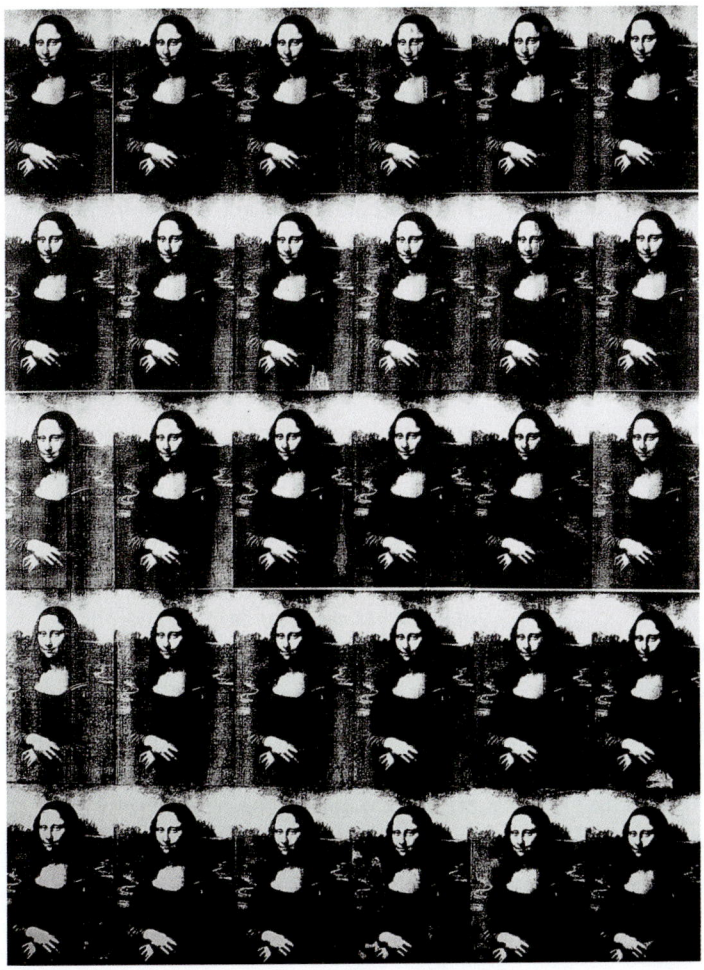

3.9.29 Andy Warhol, *Thirty Are Better than One*, 1963. Silkscreen ink on synthetic polymer paint on canvas, 9'2" × 7'10". Private collection

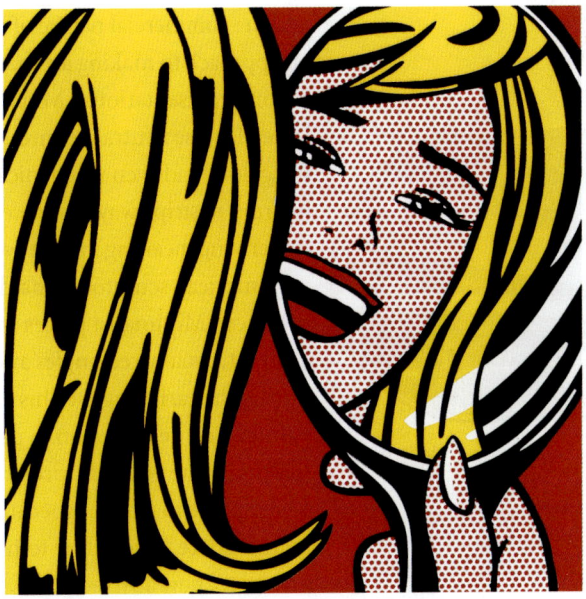

3.9.30 Roy Lichtenstein, *Girl in Mirror*, 1964. Enamel on steel, 42 × 42". Private collection

Ben-Day dots: technique used in printing to create gradations and suggest a range of tones; named for its inventor
Value: the lightness or darkness of a plane or area
Pointillism: a late nineteenth-century painting style using short strokes or points of differing colors that optically combine to form new perceived colors
Graphic design: the use of images, typography, and technology to communicate ideas for a client or to a particular audience
Minimalism, Minimalist: a mid-twentieth-century artistic style that references industrial production modes through materials and seriality, often with unified arrangements of geometric shapes and massive forms that become part of the viewer's space
Postmodern: a late twentieth-century style of architecture and art that playfully adopts features of earlier styles to think "outside the box"
Column: freestanding pillar, usually circular in section

kinds of newspaper printing and comics. The regular pattern of dots, called **Ben-Day dots**, emulates the screen visible on printed pictures, where areas of light **value** have small dots, and those of dark value have large ones nearly joined together. Lichtenstein's dots give a commercial edge to the technique of **pointillism**, while his use of black, white, and primary colors references the color palette of such geometric abstract artists as Piet Mondrian (see 3.9.17, p. 534). It is also interesting to compare and contrast his very different treatment of the subject, the girl with a mirror, with that of Pablo Picasso in his painting *Girl before a Mirror* (p. 600).

Warhol's and Lichtenstein's work used appropriation to bring recognizable and familiar imagery into galleries and museums. By combining the practices of what was then considered "high art" at the time with the "low art" of **graphic design**, these artists were able to bridge the gap between the two and expand the boundaries of acceptable fine art practices to include popular imagery and commercial printing processes.

Minimalism

Minimalist artists in the 1960s reacted against both what they saw as the excessive emphasis on the artist's personality in Abstract Expressionism, and the commercial nature of Pop. Minimalism is an approach to making art that by its very nature is non-representational. Minimalists sought instead to use neutral textures, geometric shapes, flat colors, and even mechanical construction in order to strip away any traces of emotion or underlying meaning in their work.

American sculptor Donald Judd (1928–1994) produced Minimalist pieces that were totally abstract, usually rectangles and cubes. Although during the early stages of his career Judd was a painter, and he did go on to paint some of his sculptures, he generally preferred the medium of sculpture to painting because it existed in "actual space." According to Judd, any painting, no matter how abstract, shows something, whereas a sculpture *is* something, in real space. His sculptures had an industrial appearance

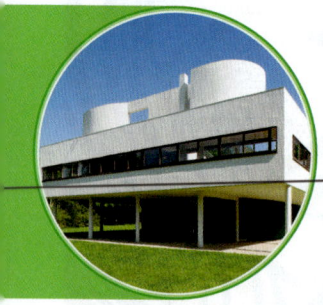

Villa Savoye, a Modernist building, and the Postmodern Guggenheim Museum in Bilbao offer a good comparison of the characteristics of the two movements: see **2.5.32, p. 278** and **1.2.15, p. 70**

Modern and Postmodern Architecture

Around the 1960s, **Postmodernism** began as a form of architecture reacting and responding to Modernism, the predominant architectural style from the late nineteenth century until that time. Modernist architecture was characterized by straight lines and geometric shapes (see, for example, Le Corbusier's [1887–1965] Villa Savoye, p. 278). Its designs were intended to be direct, clean, uncluttered, and progressive. As early as the 1960s, Postmodernist architects reacted against the Modernists' use of angular lines, severe geometry, and subdued colors, considering the aims of Modernists to be too idealistic and inaccessible. As a result, Postmodern designs often combine dynamic forms (see, for example, Frank Gehry's [b. 1929] Guggenheim Museum, Bilbao, p. 70) and incorporate familiar elements from different historical periods, such as **columns** reminiscent of buildings in ancient Greece.

Like his fellow Dutch De Stijl artists, Modernist designer Gerrit Rietveld (1888–1964) emphasized geometric shapes, horizontals and verticals, and a limited color palette of black, white, and primary colors. His Schröder House, created in 1924–25, integrates Modernist design into a building that served the specific needs of Rietveld's client (**3.9.31**). The lower floor consists of traditional kitchen, dining, and living areas, while upstairs Rietveld took an innovative approach to the bedrooms. Modular partition walls separate the areas of the upper floor, providing private quarters for sleeping but allowing a more open space to be used during the day. The balconies, windows, concrete planes, and linear elements on the building's exterior, which resembles a three-dimensional version of an abstract painting, show

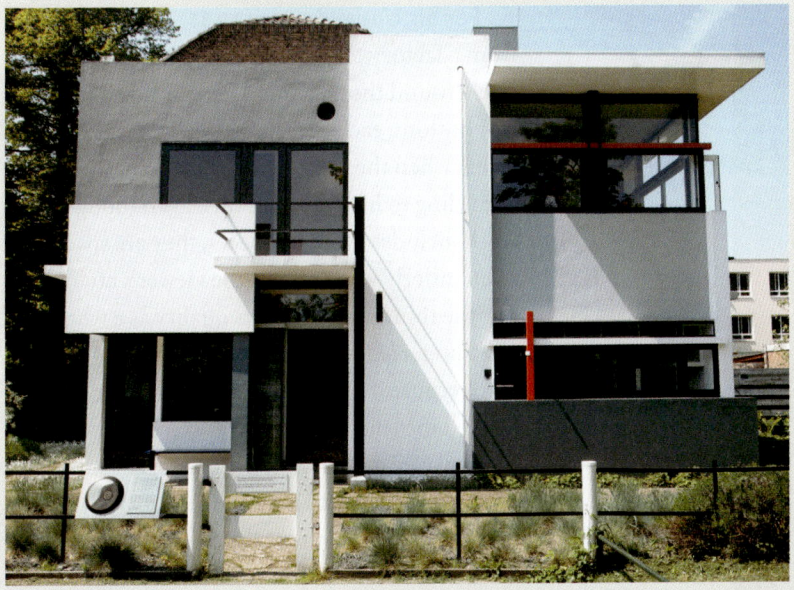

3.9.31 (above) Gerrit Rietveld, Schröder House, 1924–25, Utrecht, Netherlands

how architects achieve balance through **asymmetry**. Rietveld's emphasis on geometry and function influenced the International Style of architecture, developed in the 1920s and 1930s, which stressed logical planning, followed an industrial or machine aesthetic, and eliminated all arbitrary decoration.

Postmodern architects reacted against the severity of International Style Modernism, incorporated references to earlier buildings, and included ornamentation that was not required by the structural design. The Portland Public Services Building, designed by American Michael Graves (1934–2015) in 1980–82, was the first public building to employ the Postmodern approach (**3.9.32**). Its distinctive design includes a brightly colored exterior, small square windows, and Classical architectural forms. Columns have been extended up to ten stories tall on either side of the entrance and on the sides of the building. On the **facade**, the shape of the exaggerated **capitals** has been repeated on the upper floors. While this building has generated some controversy due to the strong negative opinions about its appearance, and claims of shoddy workmanship, it stands as a significant example of Postmodern ingenuity and of Postmodernism's potential to integrate diverse ideas. More recently, Graves has become well known for a line of kitchenware and domestic merchandise widely available in stores and online. The line of household products, which Graves originally designed for Target, features sleek shapes and stylish colors that incorporate many Postmodern design principles and integrate distinctive design into functional items.

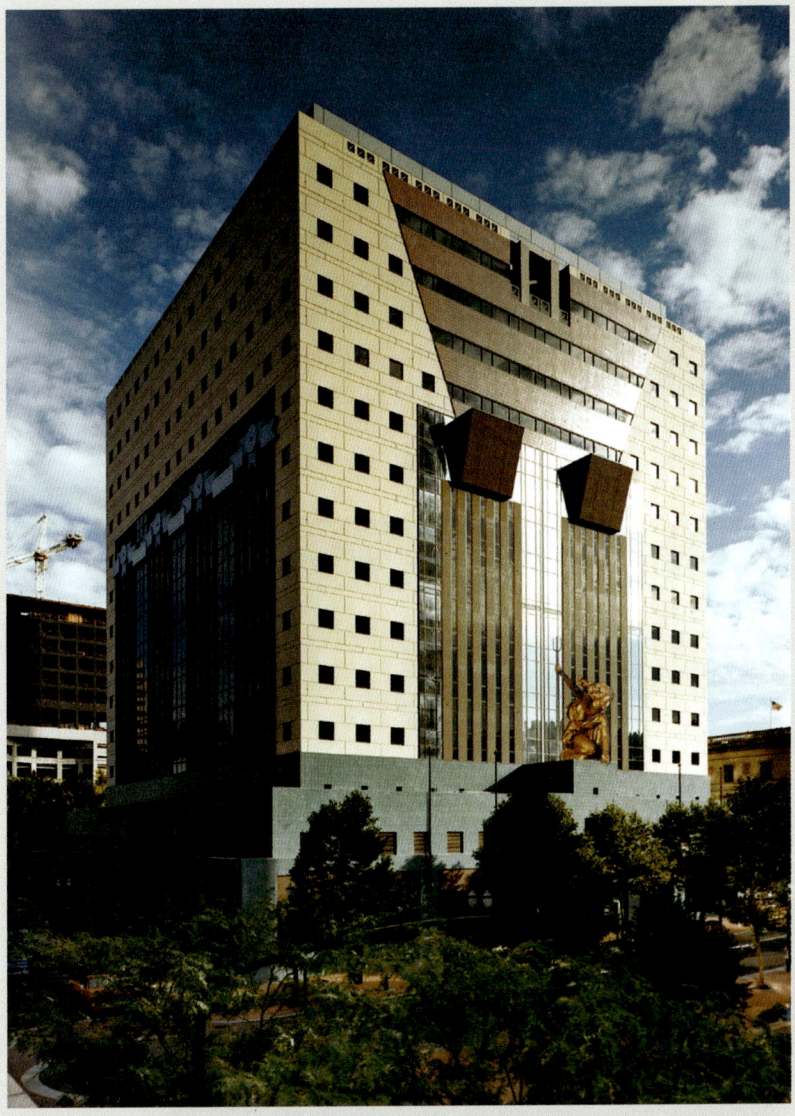

3.9.32 (left) Michael Graves, Portland Public Services Building, 1980–82, Portland, Oregon

Asymmetry: a type of design in which balance is achieved by elements that contrast and complement one another without being the same on either side of an axis

Facade: any side of a building, usually the front or entrance

Capital: the architectural feature that crowns a column

Installation: originally referring to the hanging of pictures and arrangement of objects in an exhibition, installation may also refer to an intentional environment created as a completed artwork

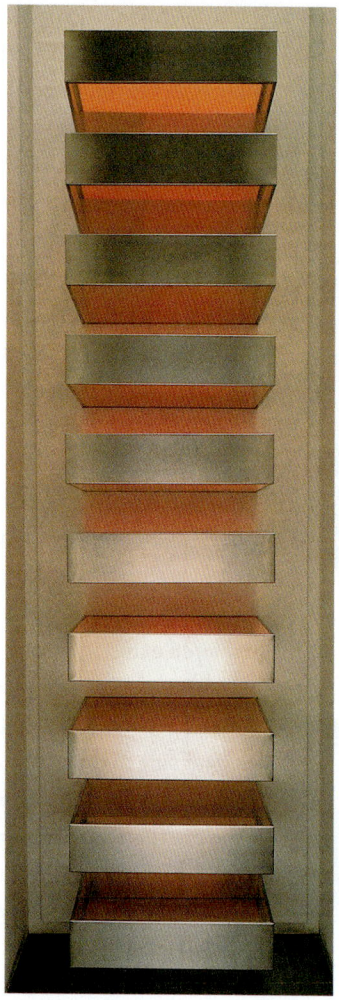

3.9.33 Donald Judd, *Untitled*, 1967. Stainless steel and Plexiglas, 190⅛ × 40 × 31". Modern Art Museum of Fort Worth, Texas

and were commercially manufactured to allow the artist to focus on new materials rather than fine art conventions, which he believed had become limiting.

For his *Untitled* piece (**3.9.33**), Judd ordered from a factory ten boxes made with stainless steel around the edges and Plexiglas on the top and bottom, each measuring 9⅛ × 40 × 31 in. Then, when the piece was installed, it was placed according to his specifications. Even though the work includes multiple pieces, they are spaced in an orderly way to focus the viewer's attention on "the thing as a whole, its quality as a whole." Judd preferred to have his pieces made in this way because it made them stand on their own, limited the role of the artist as creator, and downplayed any underlying message.

American artist Dan Flavin's (1933–1996) work, like that of other Minimalists, is made from industrial materials and has a clean, geometric quality. Flavin created individual artworks and **installations** with fluorescent light tubes. The sculptures have a physical aspect (the fixtures and tubes), but they also focus our attention on the use of light itself as a means to impact the space. The light from the bulbs, which are commonly used in offices, stores, and even homes, takes on a new significance in the form of a sculpture on the walls of an art gallery. When the fluorescent tubes are placed together in an installation (see **3.9.34**), the noticeable glow transforms the space. Flavin's work promotes the idea that a simple object that has been commercially purchased can become a work of art and cause us to look at such familiar objects in new ways.

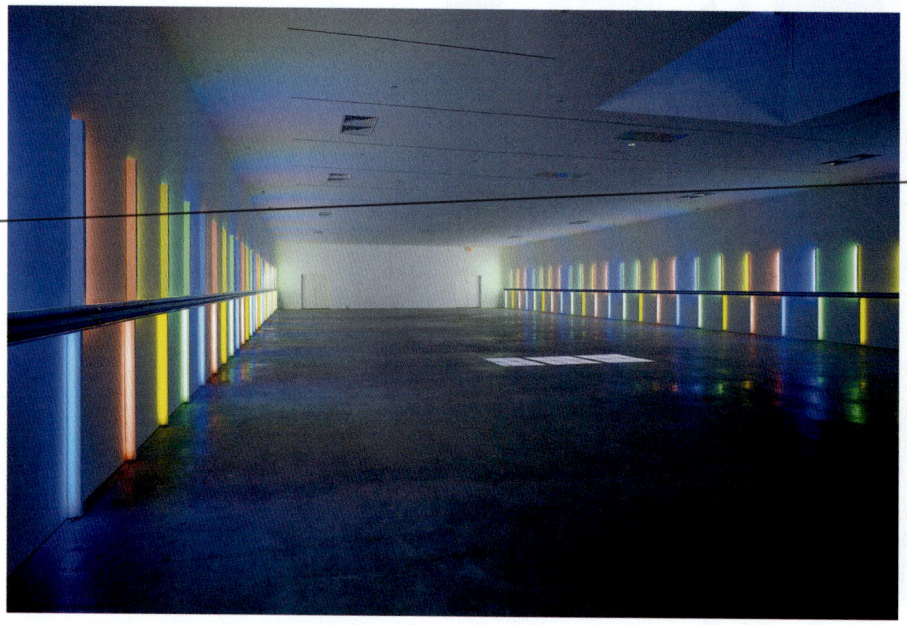

3.9.34 Dan Flavin, *Untitled*, 1996. Installation of 4' fixtures in two opposing banks for the east and west interior walls of Richmond Hall. Pink, yellow, green, blue, and ultraviolet fluorescent tubes and metal fixtures, two sections, each 8' high, approx. 128' wide. Menil Collection, Houston, Texas

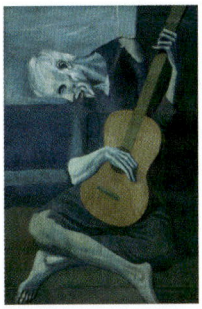

1.4.18 Pablo Picasso, *The Old Guitarist*, 1903–4, p. 103

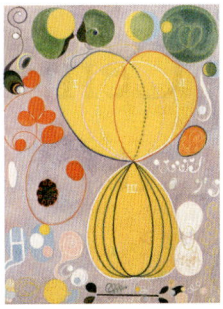

1.4.33 Hilma af Klint, *Group IV, No. 7, Adulthood*, 1907, p. 111

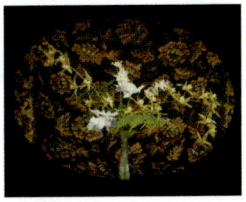

2.8.13 Alfonse van Besten, *Fragility*, c. 1912, p. 322

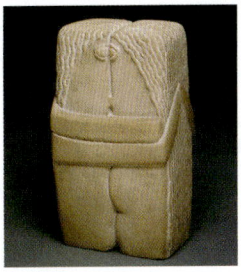

1.2.17a Constantin Brancusi, *The Kiss*, 1916, p. 72

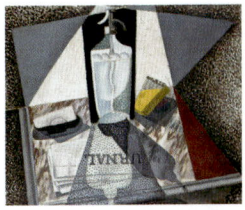

1.6.4 Marie Marevna, *Nature morte à la bouteille*, 1917, p. 127

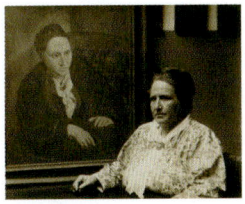

0.0.13 Man Ray, *Gertrude Stein with Portrait by Picasso*, 1922, p. 29

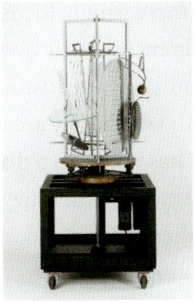

2.4.22 László Moholy-Nagy, *Light Prop for an Electric Stage*, 1929–30, p. 255

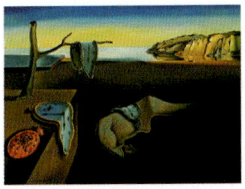

4.4.13 Salvador Dalí, *Persistence of Memory*, 1931, p. 610

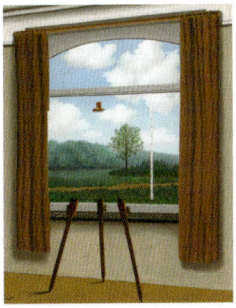

4.5.15 René Magritte, *The Human Condition*, 1933, p. 626

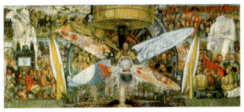

4.1.13 Diego Rivera, *Man, Controller of the Universe...*, 1934, p. 576

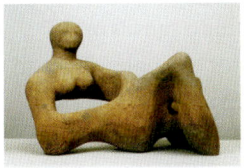

4.9.15 Henry Moore, *Recumbent Figure*, 1938, p. 674

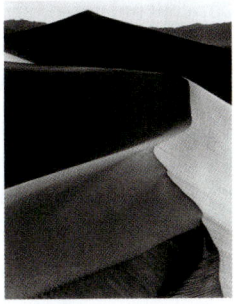

2.8.11 Ansel Adams, *Sand Dunes, Sunrise...*, c. 1948, p. 321

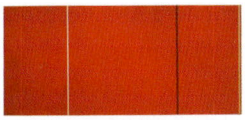

1.4.19 Barnett Newman, *Vir Heroicus Sublimis*, 1950, 1951, p. 104

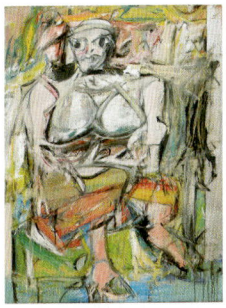

4.9.2 Willem de Kooning, *Woman I*, 1950–52, p. 664

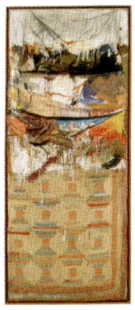

2.2.25 Robert Rauschenberg, *Bed*, 1955, p. 223

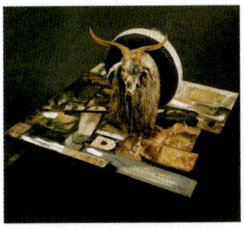

1.6.11 Robert Rauschenberg, *Monogram*, 1955–59, p. 132

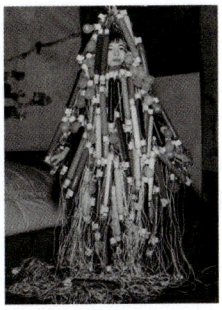

1.6.5 Atsuko Tanaka wearing *Electric Dress*, c. 1956, p. 128

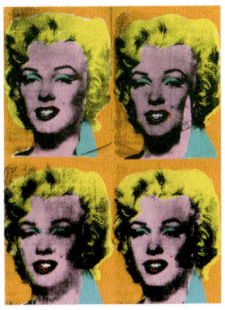

2.3.16 Andy Warhol, *Four Marilyns*, 1962, p. 235

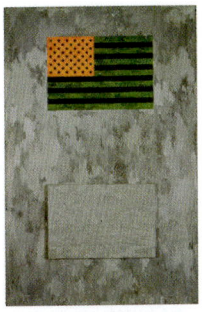

4.4.11 Jasper Johns, *Flag*, 1965, p. 609

3.10 The Late Twentieth Century and Art of the Present Day

Conceptual art: artwork in which the ideas are most important to the work
Sketch: a rough preliminary version of a work or part of a work
Artist's book: a book produced by an artist, usually an expensive limited edition, often using specialized printing processes
Readymade: an everyday object presented as a work of art

During the later part of the twentieth century, far-off places became more accessible to Western and industrialized countries by means of new communication technologies (radio, television, computers) and advancements in air travel (high-speed jets, space exploration). Goods, people, and ideas could now circulate around the globe faster than ever before.

In the Contemporary period (1960–present) ideas, concepts, actions, and experiences sometimes took precedence over the physical objects created by artists. Artists looked to a wide range of influences, from current popular culture to traditional cultural identity, for inspiration. Multiculturalism embraced a wider range of perspectives than the male Eurocentric views that had traditionally dominated the art world.

Postmodernism, which began in the 1960s (see Box: Modern and Postmodern Architecture, see pp. 542–43) and postcolonialism are hallmarks of the history and art of this period. Some artists have continued the formal explorations of Modernist abstraction, but more often postmodern artworks embrace complexity, ambiguity, even contradictions. Indeed, some have reintroduced realistic imagery into their artworks and refer to past artistic styles, earlier artworks or buildings, philosophical ideas, or political issues.

Postcolonial art explores new social structures in addition to diverse perspectives, and in the process inevitably—and often deliberately—challenges or raises questions about existing conventions and preconceptions. Artists have responded to the feminism and Civil Rights movements of the 1960s and 1970s by increasingly focusing on identity politics, referencing their own personal history, or examining the history of the nation or culture with which they are connected. In recent years art has taken on a distinctly international character, with renewed interest in engaging audiences and making an impact on the world around us.

Conceptual Art

Conceptual art, or art centered on ideas above all other things, takes the non-representational tendencies that are apparent in Minimalism even further, often eliminating the art object altogether. Instead of painting a canvas or carving a block of marble, for example, an artist might arrange certain objects together in a way that makes people reconsider each one in a new light. Some conceptual artists focused their efforts on planning, rather than producing, artwork. The results of conceptual art include documentation, **sketches**, **artist's books**, photographs, performances, and mail art (any artwork, often in the form of postcards or small packages, distributed through the mail).

The work of American Conceptual artist Joseph Kosuth (b. 1945) provokes questions in the minds of viewers. His processes, approach, and materials were inspired by Marcel Duchamp's readymades (see Box: Borrowing an Image, opposite) as well as by his interest in art that appeals to the mind rather than

Borrowing an Image

Many artworks are personal statements, and those statements can take many forms. Some artworks are created by borrowing objects, figures, or entire compositions from the work of other artists. This practice, known as appropriation, can be traced to the invention by the French artist Marcel Duchamp (1887–1968) of **readymades** (**3.10.1**), which consist of ordinary objects transformed into artworks simply by a decision taken by the artist. When Duchamp introduced such readymades as *Fountain* into the realm of art, he was challenging existing artistic practice and shifting the focus to the ideas behind the work rather than its physical appearance.

Duchamp appropriated such objects as urinals, bicycle wheels, snow shovels, and even existing artworks as viable material for his art. Over time, other artists followed in his footsteps by continuing to appropriate artworks (including ones by Duchamp). Some also borrowed images from the realms of popular culture, advertising, and even social stereotypes. Thus, an artist can make a personal statement by appropriating the work of another.

The American artist Sherrie Levine (b.1947) is known for her appropriation of famous paintings, sculptures, and photographs from the past. These pieces raise many questions: Who can be an artist? What role does the artist play? How has that role changed over time? What is originality? Who can be original? The pieces Levine appropriates are generally by male artists who worked at a time when there were very few women in the art world, as has been the case throughout most of history. As feminist statements, Levine's work leads us to reconsider the structures of art institutions as they existed in the past and highlights the historic exclusion/absence of women. Her sculpture *Fountain (After Marcel Duchamp: A. P.)* (**3.10.2**) recalls Duchamp's famous porcelain urinal from 1917. Unlike Duchamp, though, who took an existing urinal and declared it to be art, Levine had a urinal cast in bronze, a material traditionally used for fine art sculptures. Levine encourages the viewer not just to interact with her own piece, but also to consider his or her attitude toward Duchamp's urinal; so her quotation of a past artwork makes Levine's sculpture most meaningful for viewers who are familiar with Duchamp's work.

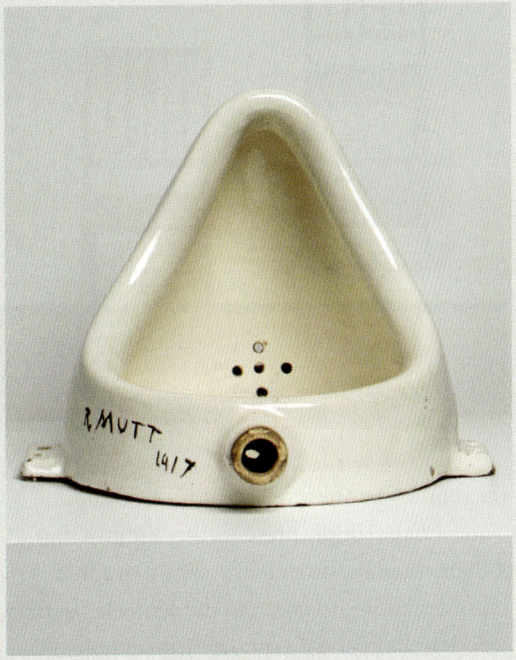

3.10.1 Marcel Duchamp, *Fountain*, 1950 (replica of original from 1917). Porcelain urinal, 12 × 15 × 18". Philadelphia Museum of Art

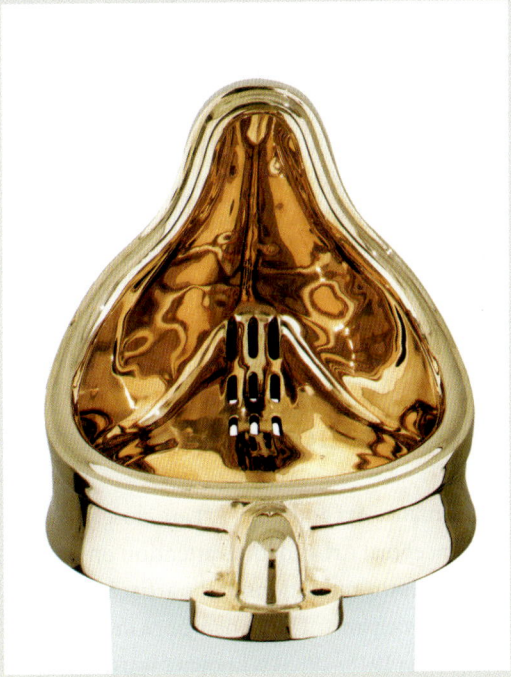

3.10.2 Sherrie Levine, *Fountain (After Marcel Duchamp: A. P.)*, 1991. Bronze, 26 × 14½ × 14"

3.10.3 (right) Joseph Kosuth, *One and Three Chairs*, 1965. Mounted photograph of a chair, wooden folding chair, and photographic enlargement of a dictionary definition of "chair," photographic panel 36 × 24⅛", chair 32⅜ × 14⅞ × 20⅞", text panel 24 × 24⅛". MoMA, New York

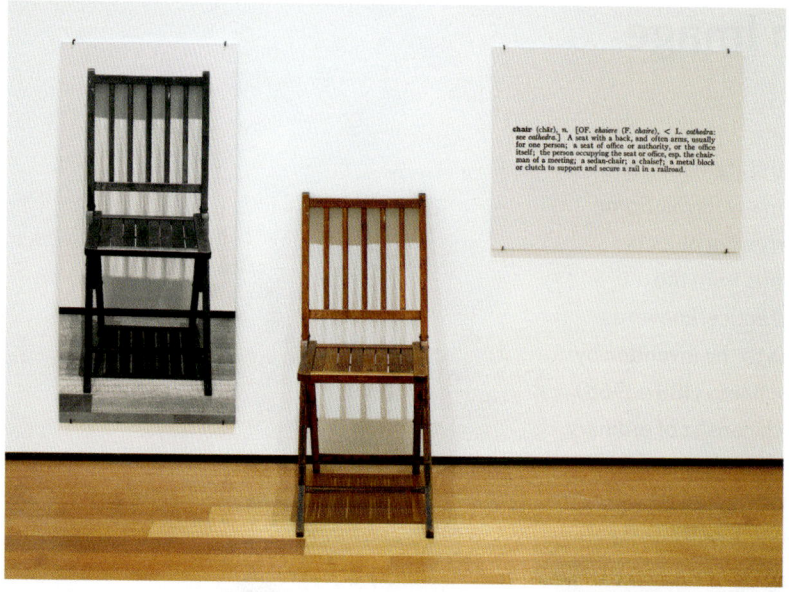

3.10.4 (below) Ana Mendieta, "Untitled" (*Silueta* series, Mexico, 1973–80). Color photograph from 35mm slide, 20 × 16"

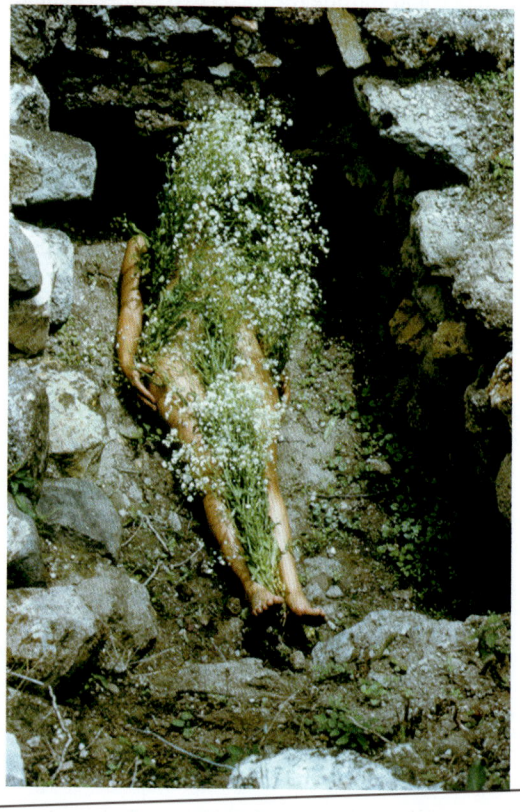

Silhouette: a portrait or figure represented in outline and solidly colored in

the senses. On one level, Kosuth's *One and Three Chairs* simply presents three things that a chair could be: on our left, a photographic representation of a chair; in the center, an actual wooden chair; and on our right, an enlarged dictionary definition of the word "chair" (**3.10.3**). On another level, this piece represents a sophisticated investigation into how we know and understand the world around us. Which of these chairs is more familiar? Which is more "real"? Which one provides us with the most information? Ultimately, our experience of a "chair," its meaning, our awareness of how we communicate ideas, and the way all these things impact art is changed after seeing this piece.

Performance and Body Art

Performance Art and Body Art are closely related to Conceptual Art and focus attention on the physical form and actions of the artist and/or other participants. The Cuban-born artist Ana Mendieta (1948–1985) is known for using her own body as an integral part of her art-making. Her performances and art actions explore personal themes (such as the displacement she experienced by moving away from the country of her birth to the United States). She also incorporates references to natural elements (water, earth, fire, blood) and biological cycles (life, death, spiritual rebirth). For her *Silueta* series of 1973–80 (see **3.10.4**), Mendieta situated her body in various outdoor environments: on the ground, in front of a tree, on a sandy beach. In the example shown here, the artist's body is camouflaged by the flowers and mud that cover it. Whether her body or its **silhouette** is shown in the photograph, the images of this series reinforce the powerful connection between a woman's body and nature, and show them as sources of strength, endurance, and nourishment.

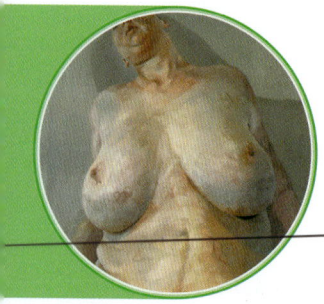

While the human body has been a crucial subject for art throughout its long history, contemporary artists have explored such body issues as sexuality, gender presentation, and perceptions of the ideal: see **1.10.9, p. 180** and **4.9.19, p. 677**

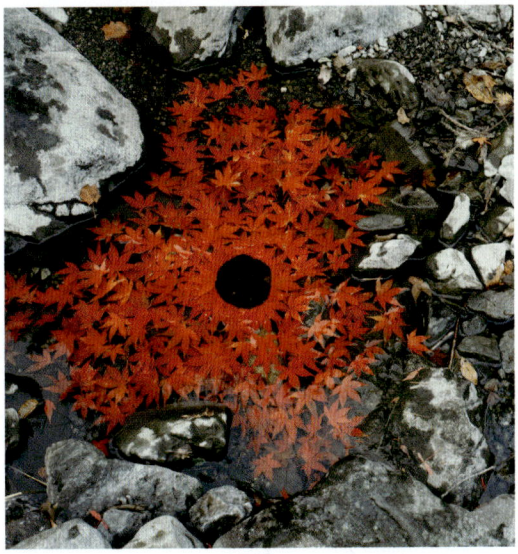

3.10.5 Andy Goldsworthy, *Japanese maple / leaves stitched together to make a floating chain / the next day it became a hole / supported underneath by a woven briar ring / Ouchiyama-Mura / Japan, 21–22 November / 1987.* Print size 24 × 24"

Earthworks

Minimalist and Conceptual art expanded the existing notion of art. Similarly, artists who create earthworks (a term coined by Robert Smithson [1938–1973]) make art using the earth itself, or natural elements of it, on such a large scale that it cannot be displayed in commercial art galleries. Also known as land art, this art was hard (but not quite impossible) to sell and required a great effort to see. These works unite sculpture and nature and blur the boundary between art and life. The media that earthwork artists have used range from collections of natural materials, big and small, to expanses of mesas in Nevada, lakes in Utah, fields in New Mexico, and beyond. Since almost all land art is in a specific location, it cannot be shown in traditional art venues, although photographic documentation and fragments of an earthwork can be displayed in galleries and museums.

Not all earthworks are made on an enormous scale, however. In fact, the British artist Andy Goldsworthy (b. 1956) creates both intimate and larger-scale site-specific structures out of grass, rocks, leaves, flowers, bark, snow, ice, and water. *Japanese maple ...* (**3.10.5**) consists of a ring of leaves invisibly stitched together and placed in a rocky pool supported by a briar ring. This piece draws attention to the splendor of nature in the unrivalled vibrancy of the leaves' red hue, configured to **contrast** with the gray of the stones, almost as if they had arranged themselves. An environmentalist as well as an artist, Goldsworthy meticulously creates his pieces, then photographs them before they disintegrate and return to nature due to the impact of time and weather.

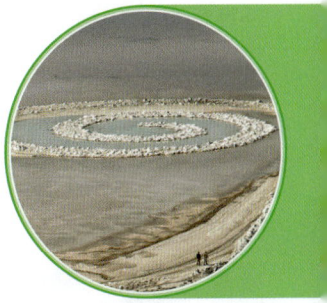

One of the aims of earthwork artists in the 1960s and 1970s was to make large-scale art in remote locations, far outside the walls of a gallery, so that they could not be easily bought or sold: see **2.4.16, p. 252**

Postmodernism, Identity, and Multiculturalism

Art and society in the second half of the twentieth century responded to earlier political and cultural events, including the atrocities resulting from the Nazis' totalitarian regime, the Cold War, and debates over US involvement in Vietnam. Those who in the past had been oppressed or discriminated against began to claim their rights. The Civil Rights movement in the US claimed equality for African Americans, while feminism asserted the right of women to the same treatment, privileges, opportunities, pay, and status as men. Reacting against the principally Eurocentric, "white male" perspective of Modernism, some artists and scholars promoted the idea that meaning is ultimately unreliable and that truth arises from multiple sources.

A disillusionment with big government inspired some **Postmodernist** thinkers to suggest that power does not come from a single leader, but instead from the masses. As a result, art became noticeably concerned with social issues and with addressing the concerns of a multicultural world. By the 1980s, artists and art institutions recognized the need to be more inclusive in their consideration of artists from all cultural backgrounds. Postmodern artists are driven by a desire to have their voices heard so that their artwork reveals the specificity of their cultural backgrounds and identity, rather than a reflection of the old Modernist ideal of shared, universal experience.

Soon after the 1964 race riots in Chicago, Wadsworth Jarrell (American, b. 1929) became part of several seminal Black Arts movement

Contrast: a drastic difference between such elements as color or value (lightness/darkness) when they are presented together
Postmodernism: late twentieth-century movement in art, architecture, and criticism responding to Modernism (*c.* 1860–1960) with a distrust of grand narratives and questioning the very nature of art by acknowledging the constructed nature of reality and experience

3.10.6 (right) Wadsworth Jarrell, *Revolutionary*, 1972, screenprint on paper, 34 × 26½". Brooklyn Museum, New York

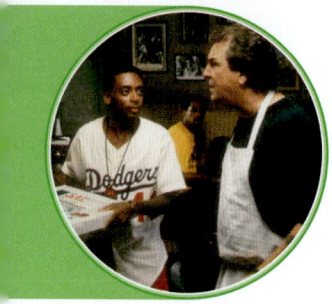

For a discussion of Spike Lee's *Do the Right Thing*, which featured Xenobia Bailey's designs, see **4.10.11, p. 687**

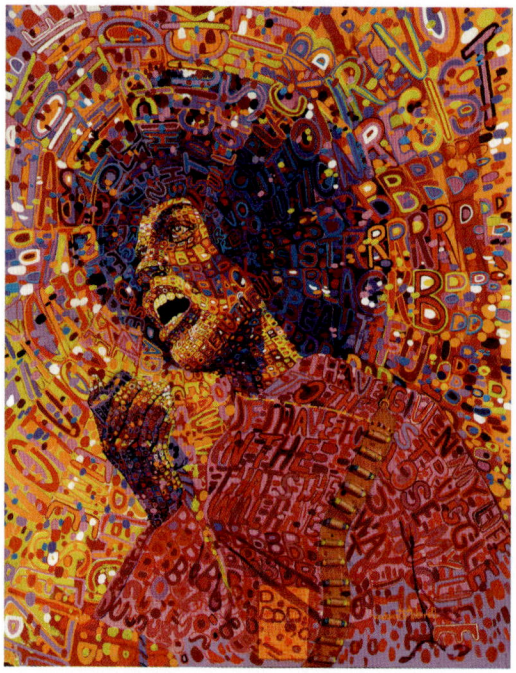

groups, OBAC (Organization of Black American Culture) and AFRICOBRA (African Commune of Bad Relevant Artists), which he co-founded. Their use of art to promote black pride and black empowerment messages gained international acclaim. Jarrell's dynamic 1972 screenprint, *Revolutionary* (**3.10.6**), features high key "coolade" [*sic*] colors, named for the flavored drink mix often known for hue rather than flavor. Such words as "resist," "love," "black," "nation," "revolution," and "beautiful" radiate from the head and body of political activist Angela Davis to signal the intensity and necessity of the message, like a call to activism.

Intrigued by the impact of African art on contemporary culture, the American Xenobia Bailey (b. 1955) established her reputation initially by making crocheted hats. After her designs were featured in *Elle* magazine, they appeared as props in Spike Lee's film *Do the Right Thing* (see **4.10.11**, p. 687) and on the American television series *The Cosby Show*. Over time, Bailey's work has expanded to include costumes, wall hangings, and full-blown museum installations. The forms, shapes, and colors she uses are inspired by African hairdos, architecture, and headdresses; Hindu religious figures; and Chinese opera headpieces. Her work *(Re)Possessed* (**3.10.7**) is a tipi-like structure that, in addition to looking like an enlarged version of one of her hats, references the absence of historical information about enslaved Africans in America. Bailey created Sistah Paradise, a mythological individual, as a reminder of colonization and as a figure to inspire the continued pursuit of justice and equality for African Americans.

Throughout her artistic career, Native American artist Jolene Rickard (b. 1956) has also told complex stories as she examines her heritage through myths, stories, cultural practices, and experiences, both past and present. As a

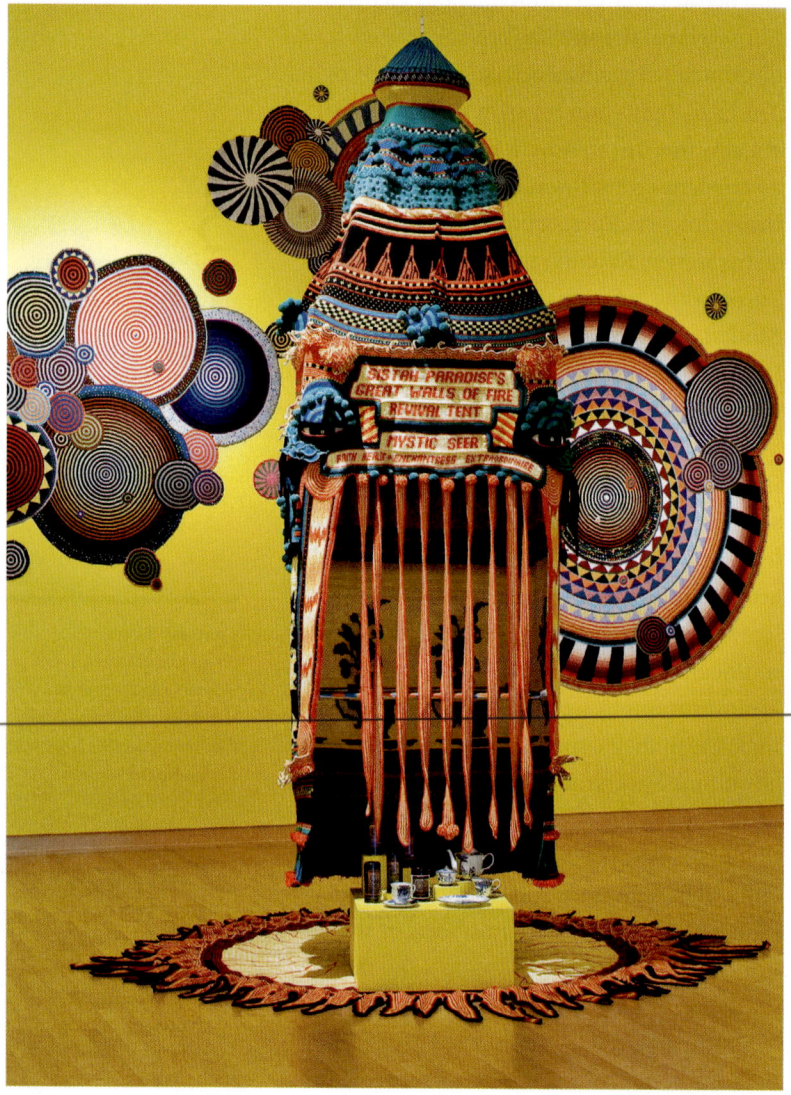

3.10.7 (left) Xenobia Bailey, *(Re)Possessed* (installation view, John Michael Kohler Arts Center), 1999–2009; mixed-media environment; dimensions variable. Photo courtesy of John Michael Kohler Arts Center © the artist and Stefan Stux Gallery, New York. Components include the following: Xenobia Bailey, *Mandalas*, 1999–2009 and *Sistah Paradise's Great Walls of Fire Revival Tent*, 1993; Doughba H. Caranda-Martin, *Teas*, 2008; Barbara Garnes, *Tea Service*, 2006

Gateway to Art: Weems, *Kitchen Table* Series
Personal and Cultural Narrative

The American artist Carrie Mae Weems (b.1953) has always been fascinated by stories. Her *Kitchen Table* series (**3.10.8**), centers around a common piece of household furniture, the kitchen table. It recalls old sayings about everyone congregating in the kitchen and the kitchen table being the site of the most important discoveries, memories, and decisions.

Twenty photographs and seventeen text panels in the series tell a story about a fictional character and the relationships that develop in her home. The photos and text can each function on their own or, when considered together, they form a third thing. Overall, the texts serve to highlight the struggles the woman faces as she tries to balance personal aspirations with domestic and interpersonal obligations. The last photographs of the series show the woman by herself, as her journey of self-discovery ends with empowerment and inner peace.

The photograph featured in **3.10.8** shows the woman seated at the table with a young girl, both of them applying lipstick with a few extra tubes on the table. The girl's age is enhanced by her youthful hairstyle and smaller mirror. We do not see her seeking guidance, though, as they both focus independently on the task at hand, perhaps suggesting a parallel development with a hint of growing up too fast. This moment of generational bonding is also a moment of transition, like a rite of passage into womanhood.

Elements of this fictional story invoke historical events. Because the character is not given a name (and because Weems herself plays the main character), the self-portraits are sometimes interpreted as autobiographical. They do not document moments in the artist's own life, however. Her daughter, for example, was around twenty years old at the time the *Kitchen Table* series was made.

A few years before, though, Weems created *Family Pictures and Stories* (**3.10.9**) with snapshots of her actual family and an accompanying oral-history recording. She was responding to the controversial Moynihan Report of 1965, which attributes crumbling socio-economic conditions for poor blacks and, by extension race-relation challenges, to the single-parent African American family led by mothers. Weems's response was to simultaneously move away from and engage the generalizations. The stories she tells are,often unidealized presentations of complex realities. While the *Family Pictures* series is more documentary and the *Kitchen Table* series is constructed, both of them present love and support triumphing alongside dysfunction, and determination generated by, yet overcoming, struggle.

For the other Weems Gateway boxes, see p. 56, p. 329, and p. 687

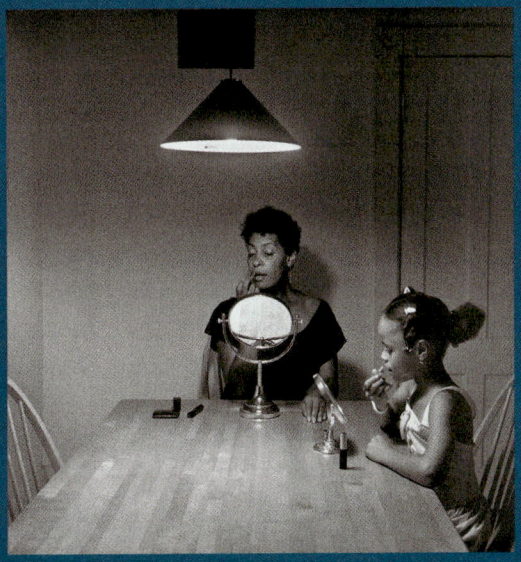

3.10.8 (left) Carrie Mae Weems, "Untitled (Woman and Daughter with Makeup)," 1990, from *Kitchen Table* series, 1989–90. Inkjet print, 41¼ × 41¼ × 2¼" (framed)

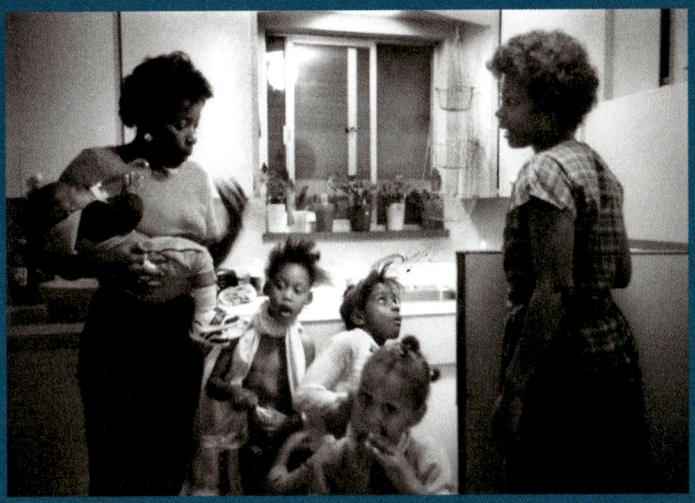

3.10.9 (below) Carrie Mae Weems, "Van and Vera with Kids in the Kitchen" from *Family Pictures and Stories*, 1978–84. Vintage gelatin silver print, 8½ × 12¾"

member of the Tuscarora nation (from the Iroquois language family), Rickard creates work that often combines spiritual experiences and events from daily life, which are familiar to the Tuscarora, but less so to outside audiences. Her installation *Corn Blue Room* (**3.10.10**), part of an exhibition called "Reservation X: The Power of Place," explores the importance of home in the formation of identity, and also the changing nature of the reservation as a community and home. Ears of corn hang from above, saturated with blue light. The photographs and images projected from a CD-ROM in the space relate to nature on one side (corn, the seasons, community) and technology on the other (the towers of a hydroelectric plant owned by the New York Power Authority), both of which

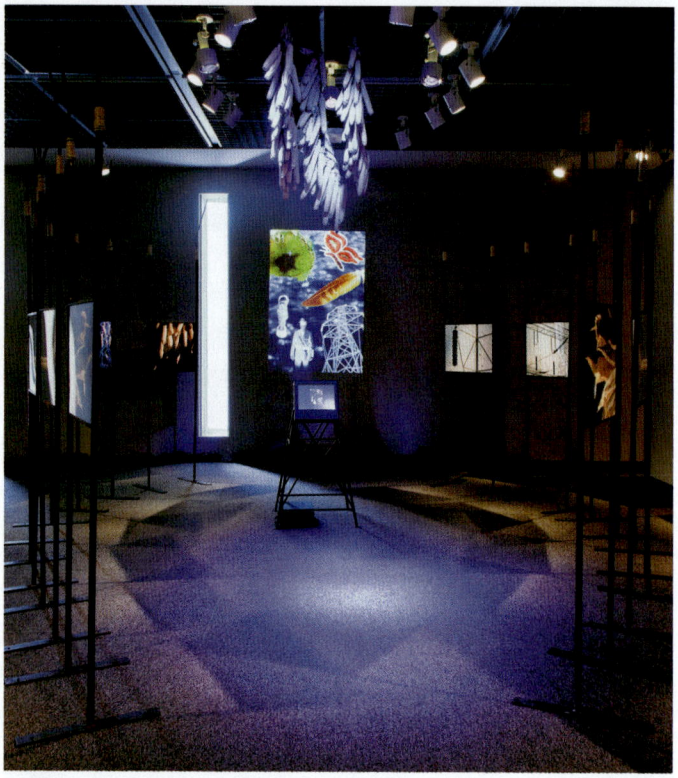

3.10.10 Jolene Rickard, *Corn Blue Room*, 1998. Mixed-media installation, Denver Art Museum, Colorado

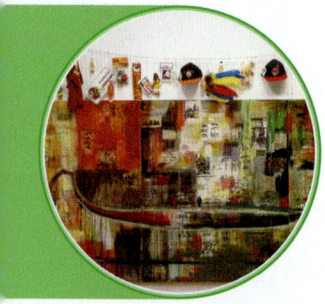

Jaune Quick-to-See Smith also confronts issues related to the Native American community, such as environmental awareness and preservation, racial and gender stereotyping, cultural commodification, and problems of alcoholism: see **1.9.14, p. 168**

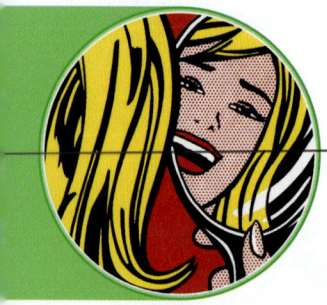

The bold colors and dot patterns of Lichtenstein's Modernist style influenced Jiha Moon and have become so iconic that they are now recognizable even when used in isolation: see **3.9.30, p. 541**

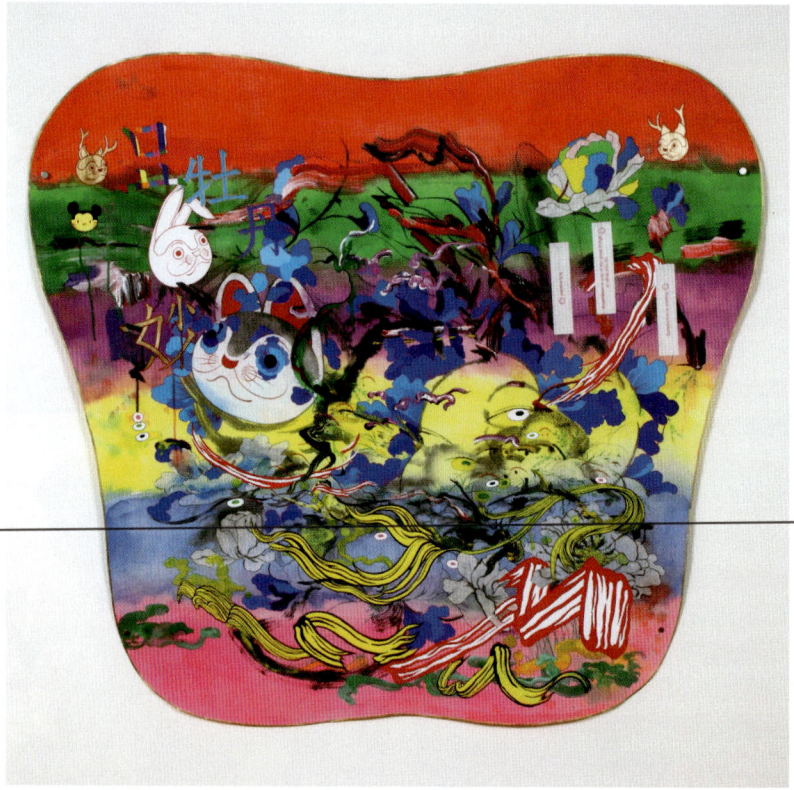

3.10.11 Jiha Moon, *Mystery Myo—frustration is one of the great things in what you do*, 2010. Ink and acrylic on hanji, 51 × 44¾"

have significantly impacted the Tuscarora community's land in upper New York State. The installation invites viewers to walk into the space and interact with it. By looking at the imagery, they can experience the importance of songs and dances as ways of expressing kinship and of passing knowledge from one generation to the next.

In such works as *Mystery Myo—frustration is one of the great things in what you do* (**3.10.11**), Jiha Moon (b. 1973 in Daegu, South Korea, lives in Atlanta, GA) visually communicates the complexity of identity through densely collaged works and wide-ranging symbolism. The mashup of styles ranges from smoky shadows and traditional brush painting to bold colors and graphic outlines of cartoons and Roy Lichtenstein's Pop art-style marks. Moon is interested in the simplifications, stereotypes, and shortcuts people take as they access people outside their own cultural background, sometimes referred to as "the other" or "foreign." While her work has a light and humorous tone, it takes a critical stance toward misunderstandings about identity, refuses simplistic labels, and results in an intriguing and empowering expression.

Iranian-born artist Shirin Neshat (b. 1957) has lived in the United States since 1974, when she was seventeen years old. Her photographs and films explore the experience of a woman caught between the tradition and heritage of her native Iran and her perspective as a woman living outside that culture. When she was allowed to return to Iran in 1990, following the Islamic Revolution, the country had become a conservative, theocratic republic. One of the most striking changes was the requirement for women to wear the *chador*, a loose robe that covers them from head to toe, leaving only their faces and hands exposed. Neshat made art as a way to process her feelings of displacement, exile, and loss. Over time her work has taken a more critical stance against the erosion of individual freedom in the extremist environment she knows the people of her country are enduring.

In such artworks as the film *Rapture* (**3.10.12a** and **b**) Neshat projects two images into the space at the same time. One screen shows men wearing white shirts and black pants in a stone fortress. The motivation behind their collective actions is never explained, but they seem to revolve around the cannons located on the building's rooftop. On the other screen, women wearing black chadors are shown making their way to a beach where they push a small group of women out to sea in a rowboat. Whether the women are being persecuted or liberated, whether they chose to leave or were forced to go, is unclear. This scene in *Rapture* takes on added resonance in relation to the worldwide refugee crisis. Because she deals with social, political, and cultural issues in a very poetic way, Neshat's work has a broad appeal to audiences from diverse communities and backgrounds.

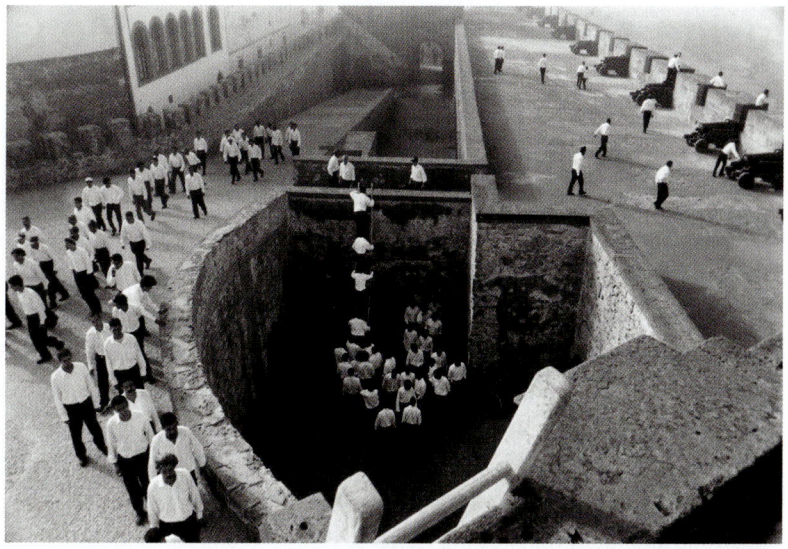

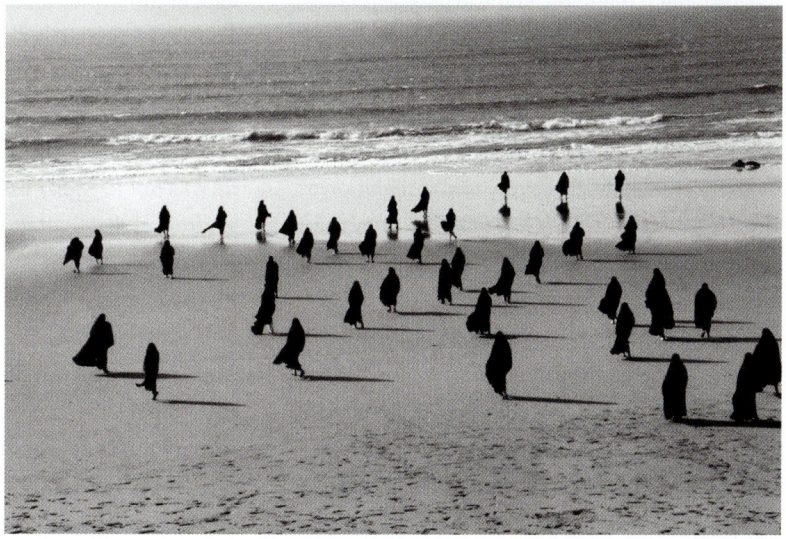

3.10.12a (top) Shirin Neshat, *Rapture*, 1999. Production still

3.10.12b (above) Shirin Neshat, *Rapture* series, 1999. Gelatin silver print, 42½× 67½"

Inside, Outside, Upside Down: Ideas Recontextualized

Contemporary artists often defy expectations by blurring the boundaries between elements that had once seemed very separate, even in opposition to one another. They mix such **genres** as fiction and non-fiction, such categories as craft and fine art, and such media as painting and sculpture. The environment where an artist makes their work and the venues by which people access it often has a big impact. Artists also emphasize the fact that the meaning in their works is open-ended and ultimately requires the viewer to decide what it might be. Some artists, like James Hampton, work entirely outside the institutions of art (schools, museums, and galleries) while others, like Jean-Michel Basquiat, changed positions to be included over the course of their career. Perhaps the discovery and recognition of worthy artists after they have passed away (as was the case with Hampton) may have led to a widened definition of what we consider "art."

The **visionary artist** James Hampton (1909–1964) worked as a janitor in Washington, D.C. and in his spare time secretly made what he called his "life's work," *The Throne of the Third Heaven of the Nations' Millennium General Assembly* (**3.10.13**). Hampton constructed about 180 pieces for *The Throne* with found materials, including furniture, jelly jars, cardboard, construction paper (originally deep purple, now faded to tan), and electrical wire, which he transformed with coverings of gold and silver foil. Hampton arranged the pieces into a large **tableau** suggesting the Kingdom of Heaven at the second coming of Christ on Judgment Day, as described in the Book of Revelation in the Bible. There are what appear to be lecterns at the back, while the wall plaques along the sides represent the Ten Commandments. Crowns (a sign of spiritual kingship), wing shapes (suggesting angels), and light bulbs (symbolic of God as the light of the world) also express Hampton's vision. Though he hoped to open his own church one day, very few people saw this piece during his lifetime.

The American Jean-Michel Basquiat (1960–1988) was also an outsider of sorts, because he was not formally trained, and started as a **graffiti** artist. His style has been called **Neo-Expressionist** because, like earlier Expressionists, it used aggressive lines, rough **textures**, and personal narrative. His painting *The Nile* (**3.10.14**), also known as *The History of Black People* or *The Grand Spectacle*, is an expansive collage of images inspiring us to reconsider many potentially outsider groups with which Basquiat was connected. The scribbled text and intentionally primitive figures acknowledge his beginnings as an untrained artist tagging buildings, or

Genres: categories of artistic subject matter, often with strongly influential histories and traditions
Visionary art (also **Outsider art**): art made by self-taught artists following a personal vision
Tableau: a stationary scene arranged for artistic impact
Graffiti art: markings that are scratched, scribbled, or sprayed on a wall without the consent of the owner
Neo-Expressionist: a broad term, first used in the late 1970s to early 1980s; describes figurative and allegorical, not totally abstract, art with materials used aggressively to give clear evidence of the artist's gestures
Texture: the surface quality of a work, for example fine/coarse, detailed/lacking in detail

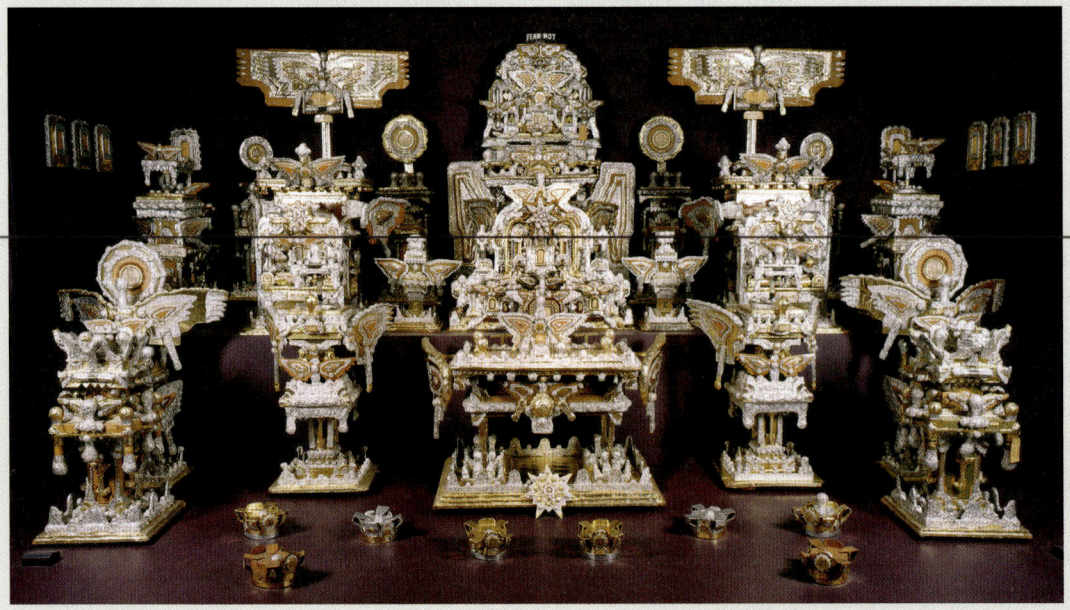

3.10.13 James Hampton, *The Throne of the Third Heaven of the Nations' Millennium General Assembly*, 1950–64. Gold and silver aluminum foil, colored kraft paper, and plastic sheets over wood, paperboard, and glass, 180 pieces, 10½ × 27 × 14½". Smithsonian American Art Museum, Washington, D.C.

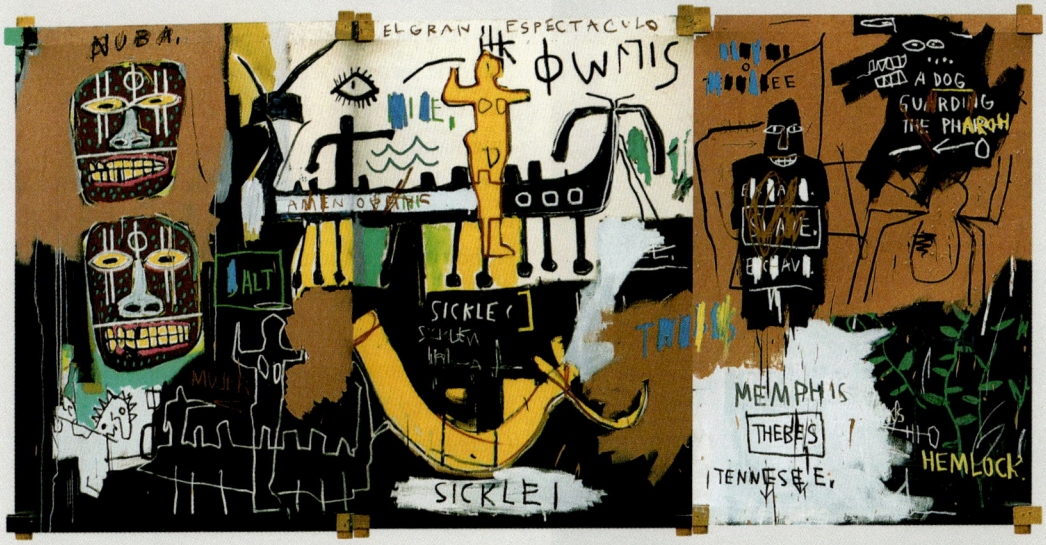

3.10.14 Jean-Michel Basquiat, *The Nile*, 1983. Acrylic and oilstick on canvas mounted on wood supports, triptych, 5'8" × 11'11". Private collection

anonymously signing them with recognizable marks, on the streets of New York. Numerous references to Egypt, including a female figure in the center, the boats, pharaoh, and guard dog to the right, together with the African masks on the left, connect to African heritage. By referring to Memphis both in connection with Thebes (Egypt) and Tennessee, Basquiat reinforces the spread of African culture and traditions into other parts of the world, a development known as the "African Diaspora." Spanish words filtered throughout refer to his immigrant parents, who came from Puerto Rico and Haiti. Notably, the word "slave" written on the figure to the right has been crossed out, suggesting that, while the sufferings of slavery cannot be erased or ignored, new terminology and expectations beyond its history are needed.

Narratives of Fact and Fiction

In the late twentieth and early twenty-first centuries, computers, televisions, and smartphones bombard us with an increasing and overwhelming number of images and ideas twenty-four hours a day, seven days a week. Many contemporary artists acknowledge and embrace the complexity and chaos of the world in which we live. The Internet and increasingly easy international travel make the world seem smaller, and have hugely expanded our awareness of and interest in other cultures. Some artists have brought order to their experiences of this global culture by creating their own systems of symbols and signs. Others incorporate widely ranging styles, techniques, and messages into single artworks. Reflecting the experience of living in the twenty-first century, contemporary artists assimilate approaches from all kinds of sources, past and present, real and imagined. Artworks made in response to the complexity of today's world, not surprisingly, contain many elements that operate on more than one level. The more you learn, the more each individual element makes sense and comes alive. Many artists navigate this complexity by integrating and fusing the once-distinct realms of fact and fiction.

A captivating video installation called *Ever Is Over All* (**3.10.15**, p. 556), by the Swiss artist Pipilotti Rist (b. 1962), creates a multi-sensory experience that subtly comments on decorum and the breaking of rules that normally govern society. A two-part projection into the corner of the room, it also has an ambient sound component that pulses throughout the gallery or museum space. On one screen we see a woman whose brilliant aquamarine dress and ruby-red slippers contrast with the drab backdrop of an urban street. On the other screen, the brilliant

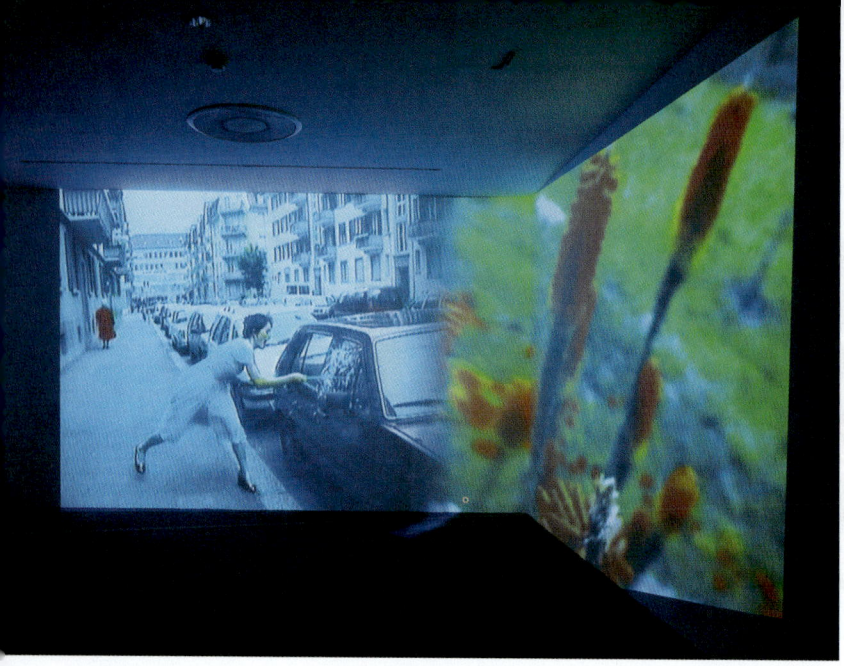

3.10.15 Pipilotti Rist, *Ever Is Over All*, 1997. Video installation with two monitors, dimensions variable. MoMA, New York

oranges, yellows, and greens of a luminous field of torch lilies, also called red-hot pokers, directly illuminate the room.

In her princess attire, the woman carries a torch lily like a staff. As she saunters down the street, she occasionally stops to smash out a car window with her flower. The violence of her vandalism does not have any effect on her happy-go-lucky demeanor. In fact, she does not even react when a police officer passes her on the sidewalk. The police officer does not react to her apparent vandalism either. They just exchange a pleasant greeting. Because the artist herself plays the part of the window-smasher, this piece could be seen as a self-portrait. Ultimately Rist has created for the contemporary viewer an enigmatic fairy tale in which we feel a release as the character's aggressions are acted out in unlikely ways, while the story that this piece tells empowers her (and us) to maintain or restore a sense of beauty in the world.

From 1994 to 2002 American artist Matthew Barney (b. 1967) produced, created, and starred in five full-length films called the *Cremaster* cycle. "Cremaster" literally refers to the set of muscles that control the height of male testicles. Barney adopted the cremaster as a metaphor because it expresses the sense that identity changes over time: from prenatal sexual differentiation (in *Cremaster 1*) to a fully formed, or "descended," being (in *Cremaster 5*). The films do not use narrative or dialogue in the conventional sense, but visually and conceptually incorporate the history of the place where the films are set, episodes of invented mythology, Barney's personal interests, and a symbol system that he has developed.

In the still shown here from *Cremaster 5* (**3.10.16**), Barney plays a fictional character known as the Queen's Giant, who is undergoing the final stages of his transformation to a fully formed man. In an interview in 2004, Barney explained that he was not searching for coherence in the *Cremaster* cycle, but that the films' ambiguity mimics his own wandering interests and the way he absorbs things on a day-to-day basis. The intricate symbolism that Barney invests in the people, places, and things in the films recalls all the simultaneous meanings that these elements can have (whether we are aware of them or not), and suggests that we can access them at the touch of a button or the whim of an artist.

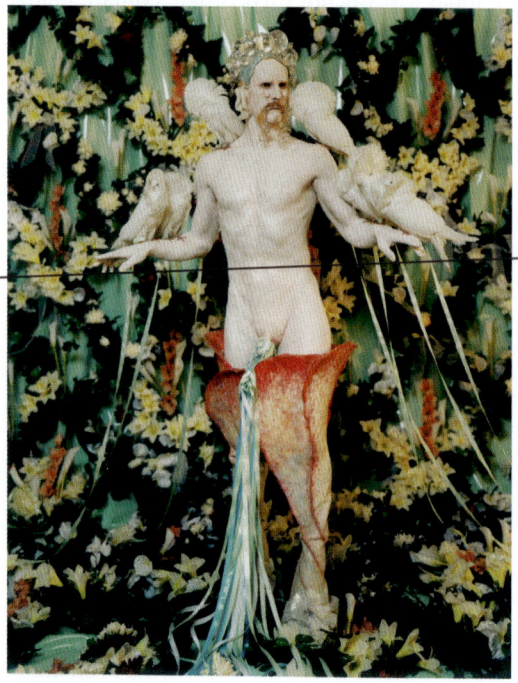

3.10.16 Matthew Barney, *Cremaster 5*, 1997. Production still

A joyous splash of vibrant color is the first sensation upon seeing the installation and narrative claymation work of Swedish artist Nathalie Djurberg (b. 1978). Claymation is a form of **stop-motion animation** using figures and objects made of plasticine clay. Each frame of the video involves slight adjustments to the objects and figures, such that when they are played in sequence, they appear to change and move. The ambient and dramatic music

Stop-motion animation: figures, puppets, or dolls are photographed in a pose, moved very slightly, and then photographed again; the process is repeated until the desired sequence of movements has been acted out

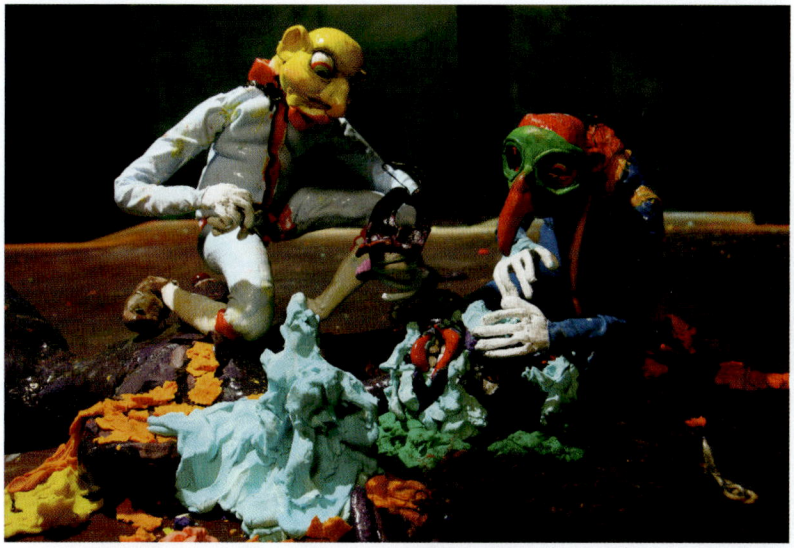

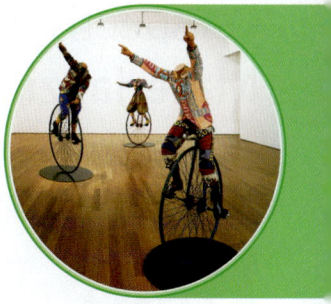

The installation *Mobility* by Yinka Shonibare consists of three headless sculptural figures on unicycles occupying the space of a gallery: see **2.10.10, p. 358**

contributed by Djurberg's collaborator, Hans Berg (who is also Swedish; b. 1978), enhances the feeling of whimsy and intrigue that infuses the carnivalesque atmosphere. Just like carnival, though, there is a darker side as the work takes sinister turns to include mutilation, destruction, and death.

I Wasn't Made to Play the Son (**3.10.17**), one of five videos in Djurberg's installation called *The Parade*, is no exception. After meandering through the gallery space filled with more than eighty brilliant hand-made birds of all sizes, shapes, and colors, one begins to take in the narratives of the videos. Many of the artist's characters are in fact caricatures, identifiable by their excessive traits. The physical violence of the pieces—often sexual in nature, perpetrated against women, or occurring between humans and animals—is so blatant that it becomes almost ludicrous. The contrast of brutality (albeit in clay) in the context of jubilant entertainment, with bright colors and whimsical music, creates distinct and conflicting feelings of attraction/repulsion. A cynical viewer might leave thinking that art has, once again, imitated the tragedies of life and made them palatable. For a politically minded observer, the installation might raise questions about the treatment of women, or inspire activism against domestic violence. Though the intentions and message are far from clear, Djurberg's work might be seen as similar to fairy tales, offering a release from the challenges and stresses of daily life.

3.10.17 Nathalie Djurberg, *I Wasn't Made to Play the Son* (video still), 2011. Clay animation, digital video, 6 min. 27 sec., music by Hans Berg, at Zach Feuer Gallery

Installation

Many contemporary artists continue practices established from previous artistic styles, movements, or individual approaches. Minimalism comes to mind when viewing the work of American Tara Donovan (b. 1969), both in materials and aesthetic effect. Donovan's *Untitled* (**3.10.18**) fills the entire room. From far away, it takes up the panorama of the space and the viewer is uncertain whether he or she is seeing fabric or a giant lamp in the contours of cloud-like shapes across the ceiling. Upon closer inspection, the details of the medium become clear: Styrofoam cups—lots of cups. The artist

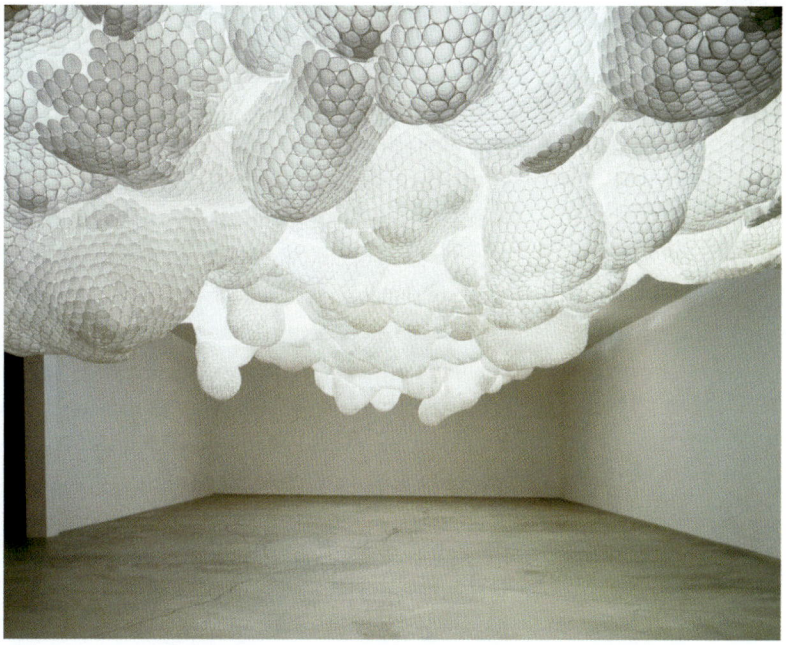

3.10.18 Tara Donovan, *Untitled*, 2003. Styrofoam cups and hot glue, 16 × 16'. Installation at Ace Gallery, Los Angeles, 2005

Perspectives on Art: Gabriel Dawe
Materializing Light, Inverting Constructs

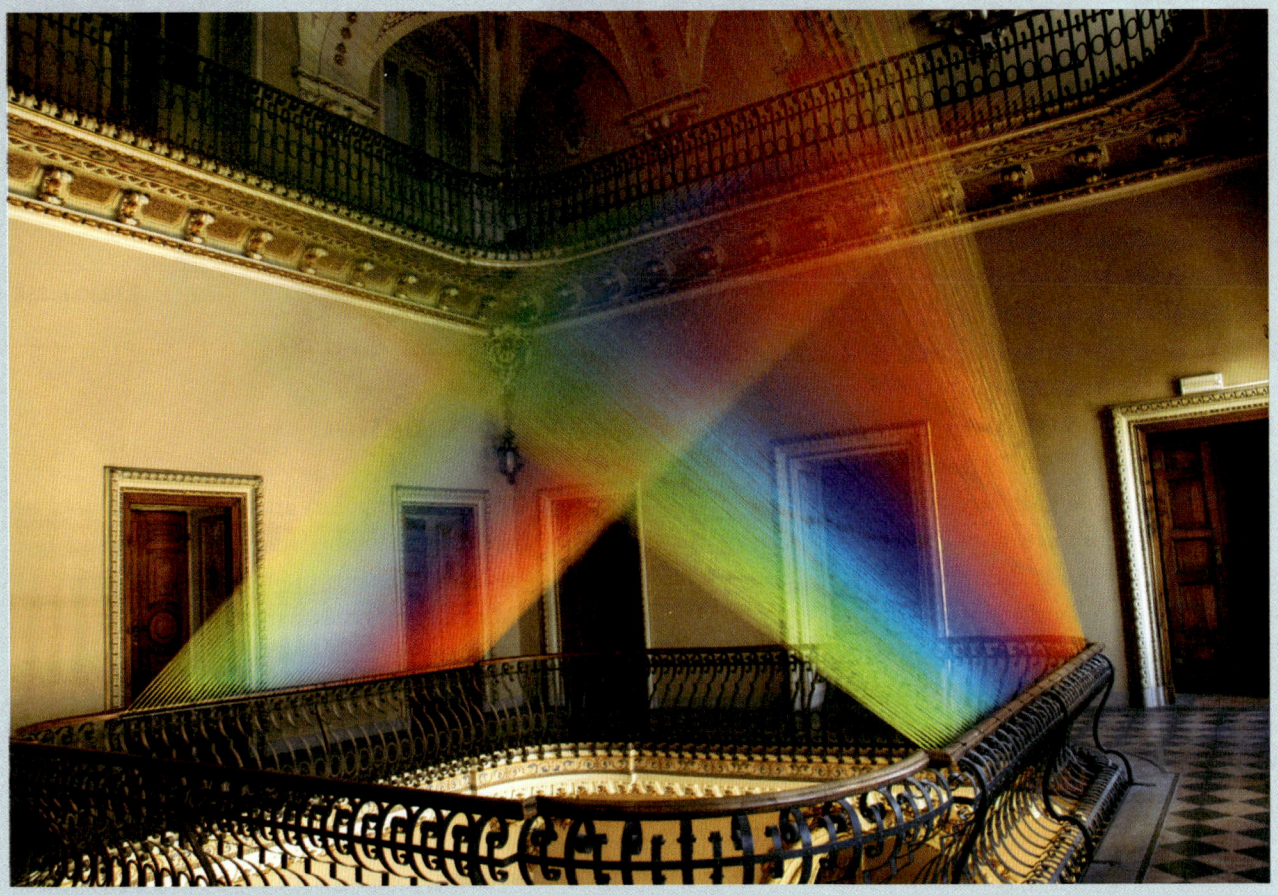

3.10.19 Gabriel Dawe, *Plexus no. 19*, site-specific installation at Villa Olmo, Como, Italy for *Miniartextil: Agora*, 2012. Gütermann thread, painted wood, and hooks, 23 × 23 × 23'

Gabriel Dawe was born in Mexico City (b. 1973) where he grew up surrounded by the intensity and color of Mexican culture. Here the artist describes what his colorful thread installations mean to him.

One of the first ideas I began developing...is related to the human need for shelter. I decided to create an architectural structure by using the core material of clothing. I realized that among the many intricacies of the raison d'être of both fashion and architecture is the capacity to offer shelter to the body. When we get cold, we wear a sweater. When it's raining we can go inside a building. By reversing scale and material to create an actual structure made of thread, the sheltering quality goes through a transformation, from protecting the body on a physical level, to soothing the human spirit in a subtle, yet powerful way.

Immediately, I had the desire to use gradations of color. It just made sense to subtly blend colors into a fine progression, and it was only later that I realized this was connected to the way light blends in the sky. The fineness of the thread makes these installations ethereal, almost immaterial, yet not, almost disappearing to the eye and leaving a color haze behind. This color mist alludes to a symbolic quest to materialize light, to give it density, so that I can offer the viewer an approximation of things otherwise inaccessible to us—a glimmer of hope that brings us closer to the transcendent, to show that there can be beauty in this messed-up world we live in.

The choice to use thread is a natural extension of my attempt to explore and subvert social constructs of gender. My growing up in Mexico, where machismo is ingrained in the very structure of society, led to many frustrations as a boy, one that looked up to his older sister—a sister who was privy to certain activities that were a definite no-no for boys. One particular activity was embroidery. Eventually, I grew out of that frustration, but the memory of it led me to explore this technique as an adult, and in doing so, to question the many social constructs that we sometimes presume to be permanent, rigid and inflexible. Eventually, I came to see the structures I was making with thread as symbolic representations of these social constructs, the viewer navigating and negotiating the installation in a dance that is analogous to what we all do in real life, without any particular thought, on a daily basis.

"Plexus" literally means the network of nerves or vessels informing and sustaining the body. It was the perfect name [for this series] because it not only refers to the connection of the body with its environment, but it also relates directly to the intricate network of threads forming the installation itself, and to the tension inherent in the thread, vibrating with an almost tangible luminosity. Plexus evokes the intrinsic order within the apparent chaos that exists in nature.

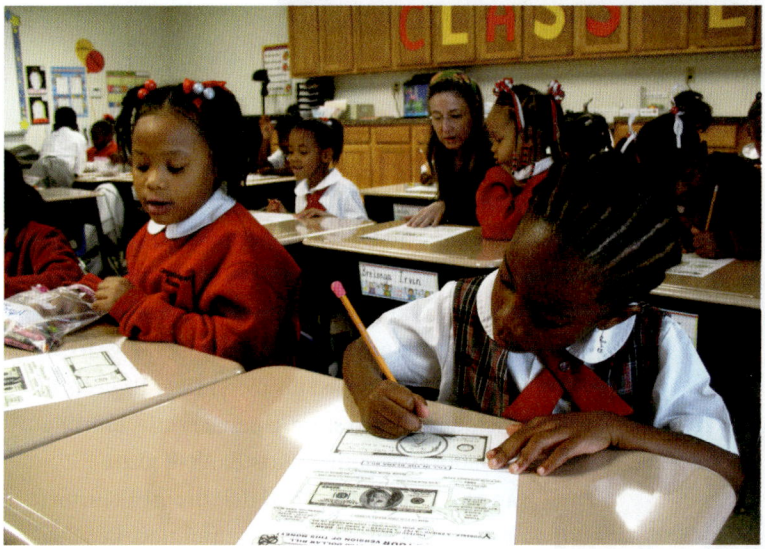

3.10.20a Mel Chin, *Operation Paydirt/Fundred Dollar Bill* project. Children making Fundreds at Langston Hughes Charter, New Orleans, 2008

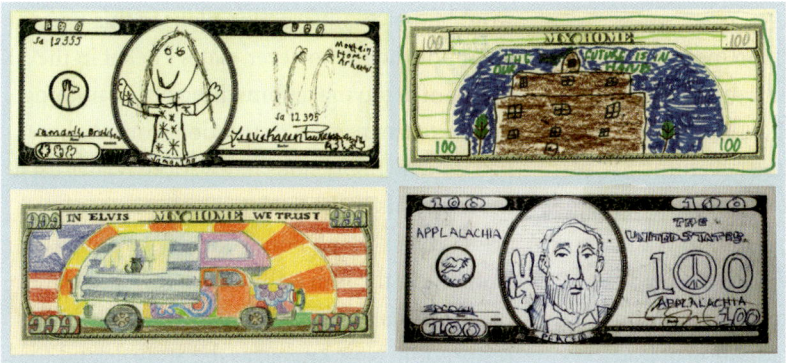

3.10.20b Mel Chin, *Operation Paydirt/Fundred Dollar Bill* project. Examples of the fundreds drawn by students in New Orleans, Louisiana (top left and right); Marfa, Texas (bottom left); and Collowhee, Tennessee (bottom right)

has also made sculptures out of toothpicks, pencils, tar paper, paper plates, short pieces of wire, buttons, and plastic straws (more than two million of them in another piece called *Haze*). Donovan states that the value of mass-produced objects in an art context is now widely accepted; the excitement comes from what happens to them. Donovan calls her work "site-responsive" because she selects her materials for their unique properties—here, the soft white color and curves of the cups—and the way in which these interact with aspects of a given space—for example, the ceiling, lighting, and shape of the room—to produce a very specific effect on the viewer.

Socially Engaged Art

The American conceptual artist Mel Chin (b. 1951) challenges the traditional role of the artist and the expected outcomes of artworks by engaging specialists and the community to generate solutions for an important environmental issue in his *Operation Paydirt/ Fundred Dollar Bill* projects (**3.10.20a** and **b**). After the devastation caused by Hurricane Katrina, Chin learned about the presence and severity of lead-toxic soil in and around New Orleans and its effects, especially on children. The creative capital, "Fundred Dollar Bills," are made by hundreds of thousands of contributors and the Fundred organization plans to request the equivalent of the drawings' value in exchange for the goods

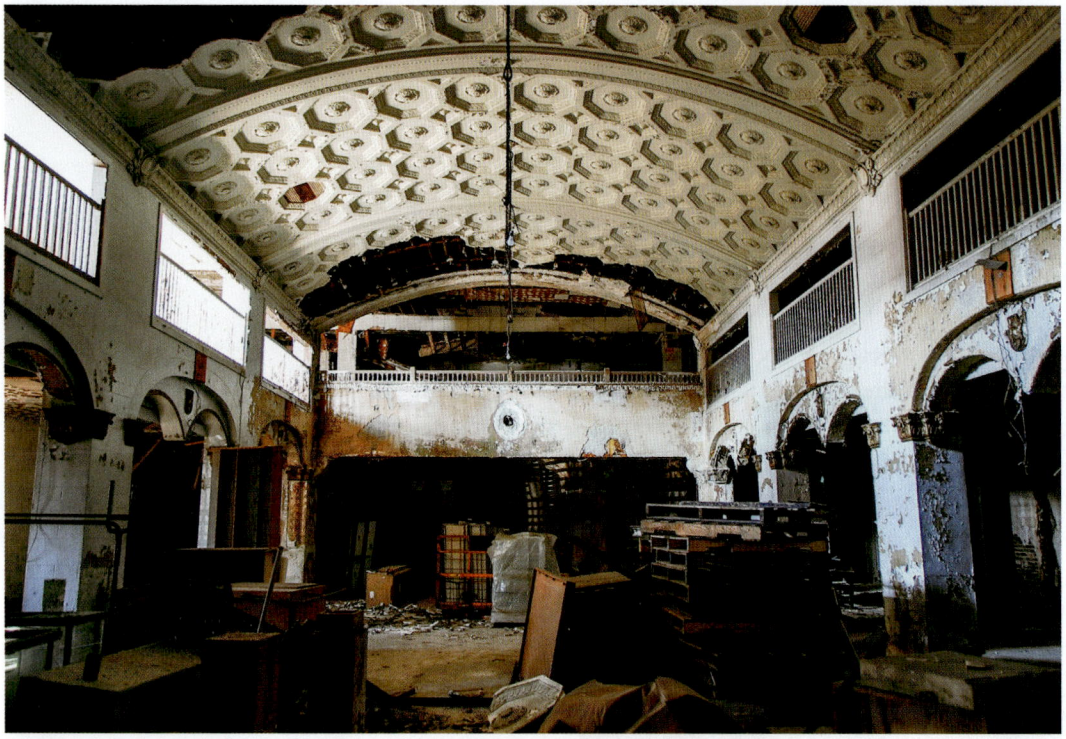

3.10.21a (left) Theaster Gates, Stony Island Arts Bank, Chicago, 2015, photo by Eric Allix Rogers

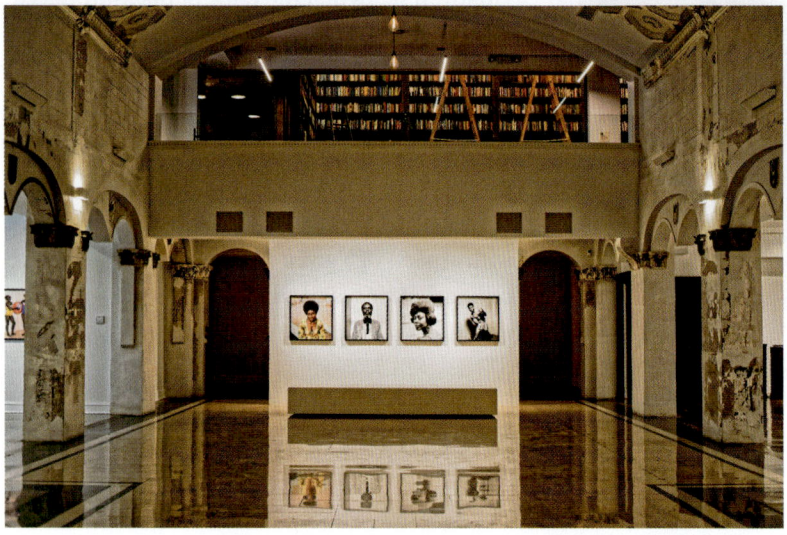

3.10.21b (above) Theaster Gates, Stony Island Arts Bank after restoration (photo by Cecil MacDonald)

and services needed for the bioremediation of the lead-toxic soil. The organization continues to raise awareness through Fundreds and to work toward municipal and government implementation of Operation Paydirt. In 2016 they moved Fundred headquarters to Washington D.C. and participated in the National Lead Summit to create a Blueprint for Action and ignite a national movement for eradication of lead poisoning in the US.

The American artist Theaster Gates (b. 1973) has similarly expanded the realm of art into life by focusing his art practice on community restoration. In 2006 he bought his first building (a house) on Dorchester Avenue. Located in a rough region of Southside Chicago, this block was known for violence, urban decay, and abandonment. Over a number of years, Gates has expanded his Dorchester Projects to include a record store, cinema house, housing collaborative, and an Arts Bank (**3.10.21a** and **b**). When he learned that the area's historic bank building was set for demolition, he was determined to save it. The city effectively gave him the building because it was in such a bad state, including being flooded with about 6 ft. of water. At the time, ironically, no banks would finance construction plans in this neighbourhood; however, Gates's belief in the power of art to make something out of nothing helped to finance the restoration work. As he had done with previous renovations, Gates used the materials in the bank to create pieces of art—such as "Bank Bonds" made out of marble from the bathroom walls—to in turn generate the proceeds needed to fund the million-dollar restoration. Now known as the Stony Island Arts Bank, the site serves as a repository for black historical experience, with archives and collections that would otherwise be lost to either demolition or renovation and gentrification.

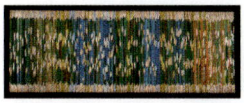

2.6.19 Sheila Hicks, *The Silk Rainforest*, c. 1975, p. 296

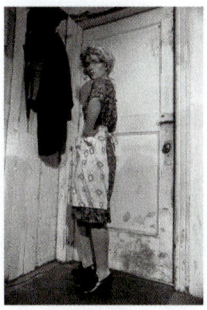

4.10.5 Cindy Sherman, "Untitled Film Still #35," 1979, p. 683

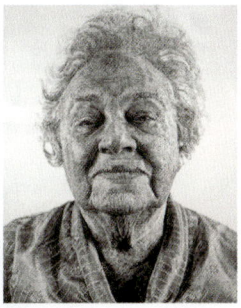

4.5.10 Chuck Close, *Fanny/Fingerpainting*, 1985, p. 622

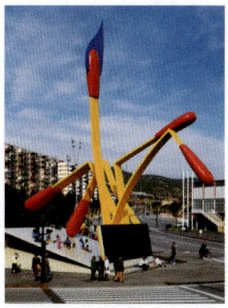

1.7.1 Claes Oldenburg and Coosje van Bruggen, *Mistos (Match Cover)*, 1992, p. 141

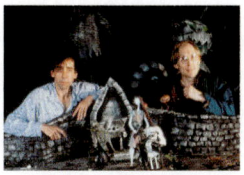

2.9.10 Tim Burton, set of *The Nightmare Before Christmas*, 1993, p. 339

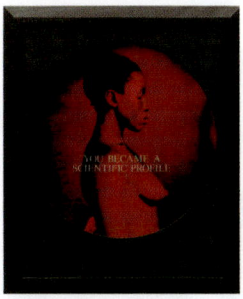

2.8.24 Carrie Mae Weems, "You Became a Scientific Profile," 1995, p. 329

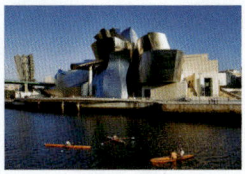

1.2.15 Frank Gehry, Guggenheim Museum, Bilbao, Spain, 1997, p. 70

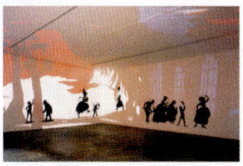

2.10.11 Kara Walker, *Insurrection!...*, 2000, p. 359

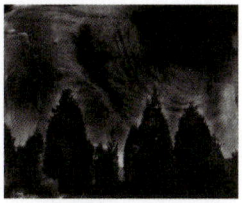

2.8.22 Sally Mann, *Untitled #7, Fredericksburg*, 2000, p. 328

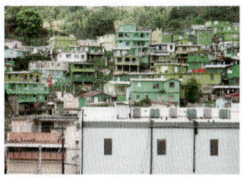

1.4.30 Chemi Rosado-Seijo, *El Cerro*, 2003, p. 109

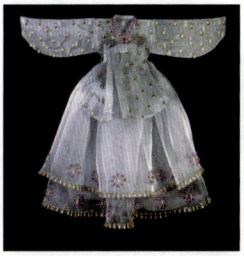

2.6.1 Hyo-In Kim, *To Be Modern #2*, 2004, p. 286

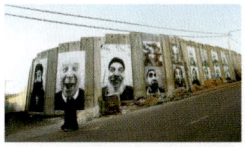

4.8. 11 JR and Marco, *28 Millimeters, Face2Face*, 2007, p. 660

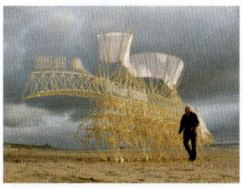

1.5.11 Theo Jansen, *Animaris Umeris (Strandbeest #48)*, 2009, p. 119

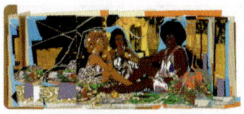

1.10.10 Mickalene Thomas, *Le Déjeuner sur l'herbe...*, 2009, p. 181

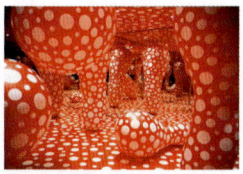

4.4.14 Yayoi Kusama, *Dots Obsession*, 2009, p. 611

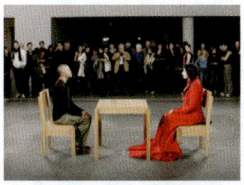

2.10.7 Marina Abramović, *The Artist Is Present*, 2010, p. 355

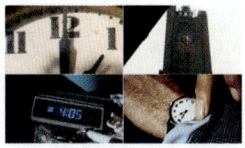

4.3.7 Christian Marclay, stills from *The Clock*, 2010, p. 596

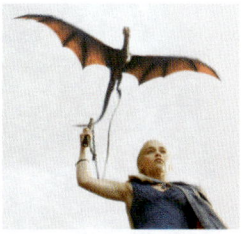

2.9.21 David Benioff and D.B. Weiss, still from *Game of Thrones*, 2011–present, p. 348

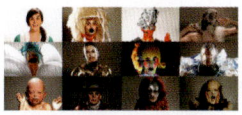

4.3.10 Jillian Mayer, *I Am Your Grandma* (selected video stills), 2011, p. 598

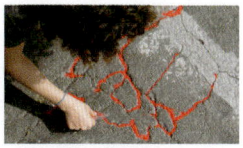

2.10.13 A *Red Sand Project* participant, p. 360

Artworks reveal the concerns of humanity. Throughout the world, similar issues, or themes, are explored by artists. By comparing artworks in terms of their meaning, we come closer to understanding the uniqueness of different cultures and artists. Exploring topics commonly addressed by artists throughout space and time, and through a variety of methods and materials, also makes us more aware of shared concerns. Artworks deal with belief systems, survival, the natural world, and technology; and with issues related to status, power, and identity. By studying art in this way we can better understand various cultures and ourselves.

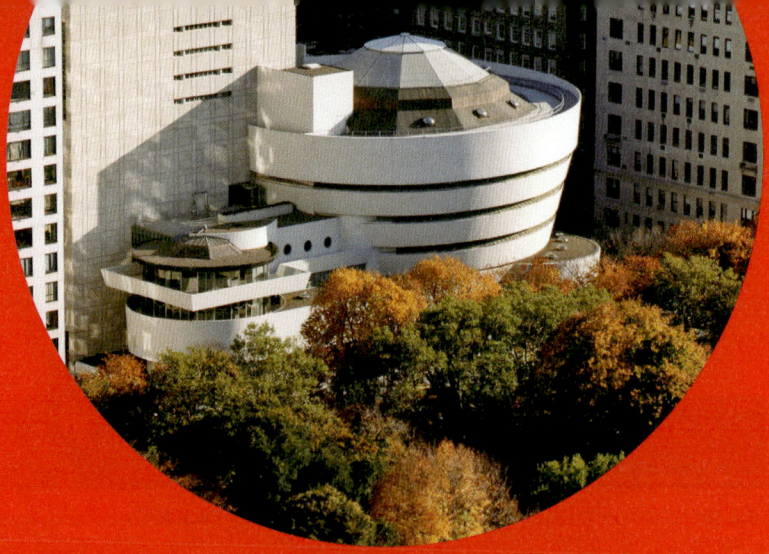

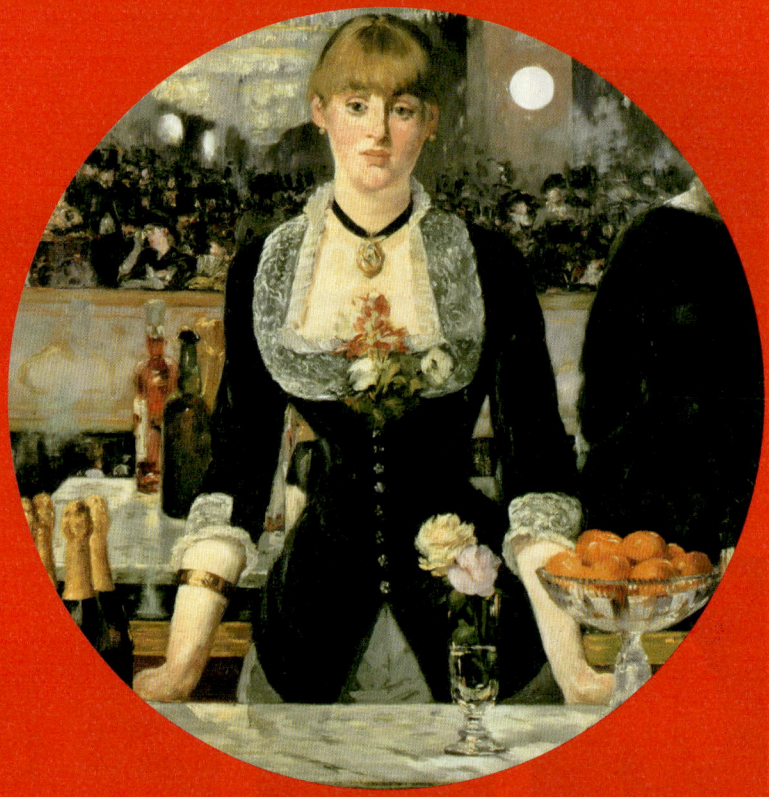

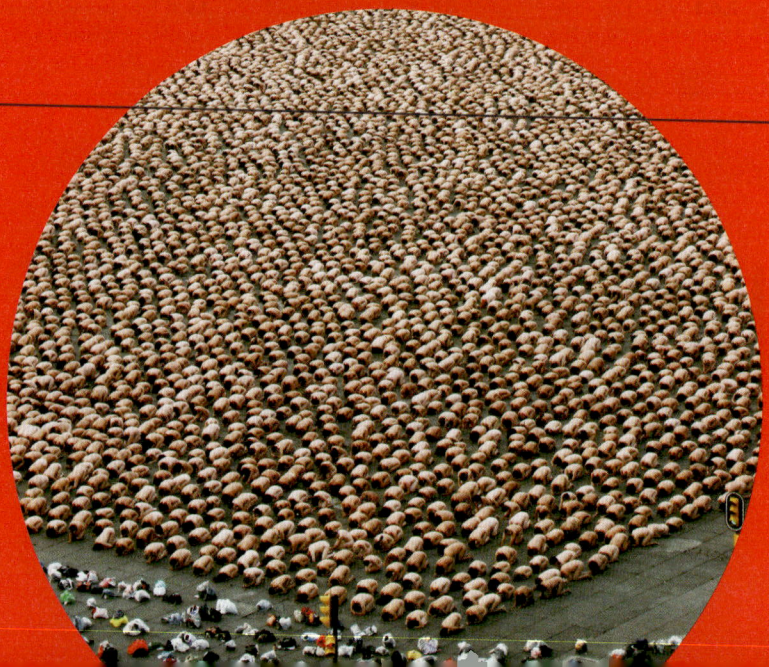

Part 4

Themes

In this part you will study:

Art and Community

Spirituality and Art

Art and the Cycle of Life

Art and Science

Art, Illusion, and Transformation

Art of Political Leaders and Rulers

Art, War, and Revolution

Art of Protest and Social Conscience

The Body in Art

Identity, Race, and Gender in Art

4.1 Art and Community

> The community mural process makes art more accessible; it brings art into the lives of people who didn't have it.
>
> (Susan Cervantes, San Francisco muralist)

> This is a way of getting your art on the street. Lots of people stop to look at it. It's not like being famous, but it's a way of getting your art looked at. You have an audience.
>
> (Aliseo Purpura-Pontoniere, urban youth arts student)

We tend to think of art as the work of a single individual. Art, however, often involves large numbers of people, even whole communities. As the statements above by professional artist Susan Cervantes and a student who worked with her demonstrate, artists can create art not just for the enjoyment and benefit of a single **patron**, or for a larger audience in an art gallery, but also for an entire community. Community art may require numerous people to become involved in its construction. Other times, artworks play important roles for performers in ceremonies and group events. Still other community artworks, situated in public places, are there to be contemplated by countless viewers. A community—whether a small rural town, an apartment complex, a college campus, or an Internet discussion group—shares a common interest, if not a physical space. Studying the art made by and for communities throughout history tells us a great deal about the interaction between artists and their environments.

In this chapter we will examine the many ways in which art has been used to pursue community objectives. Because buildings have such a direct impact on shaping a community, often becoming symbols of a particular place, we will look at several examples of architecture as well as at paintings and ritual performances. We will look first at an example of architecture built to unite communities through religion. We will then turn our attention to other types of community art, including artworks made by, for, and about the community; those that reflect shared beliefs or experiences; and art made to exist in public places.

Places to Gather

Structures designed to house ceremonies, civic events, and entertainments often draw crowds of people, whether they were originally intended to or not (see Box: Art, Super-Sized, pp. 570–71). Throughout history and in places as varied as ancient Rome, medieval France, and present-day New York City, communities have come together to build, visit, or acknowledge important locations. Whether because of their distinctive features, or because they reflect the concerns and practices of the communities that use them, buildings often become iconic destinations that people want to see when they travel.

The magnificent interior spaces found in **Gothic** cathedrals, which were built in many European countries between the twelfth and sixteenth centuries, were intended to inspire masses of worshipers to religious devotion. Today, Christians still visit cathedrals for

Patron: an organization or individual who sponsors the creation of works of art
Gothic: Western European architectural style of the twelfth to the sixteenth century, characterized by the use of pointed arches and ornate decoration
Passion: the arrest, trial, and execution of Jesus Christ, and his sufferings during them
Arches: structures, usually curved, that span an opening
Stained glass: colored glass used for windows or decorative applications
Vaulted: covered with an arch-shaped ceiling or roof
Nave: the central space of a cathedral or basilica

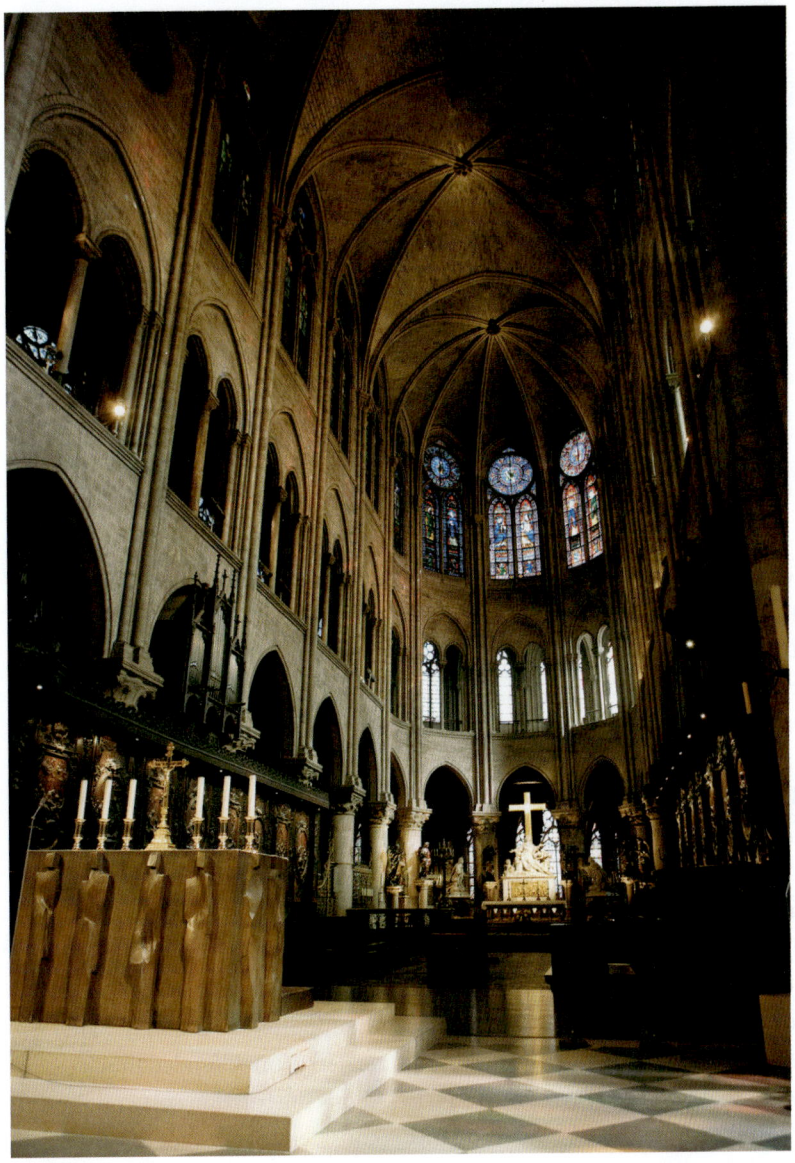

4.1.1 Notre Dame Cathedral, interior, 1163–1250, Île de la Cité, Paris, France

worship and prayer, but the beauty and religious significance of these buildings also attract visitors who do not share the Christian faith. These spectacular churches, built using the resources of the entire community, were and remain a source of great civic pride. Pilgrims traveled to Notre Dame Cathedral (**4.1.1**) in Paris, France, to worship and to experience a sense of religious community, both because the building was so impressive and because it held relics that Christians considered sacred, such as a piece of the True Cross on which Jesus Christ was crucified, a fragment of the Holy Lance used to pierce his side, and the Crown of Thorns that the Romans made to mock Christ as King of the Jews. Pilgrims curious to see these items from Christ's **Passion** also hoped to benefit from their mystical power. Notre Dame's grand interior combines all of the characteristic elements of Gothic architecture, including pointed **arches** and **stained-glass** windows. The **vaulted** ceiling is 102 ft. above the floor and the **nave** is more than 39 ft. wide, surrounding receptive visitors with soaring height and spiritual light to transport them beyond the cares and concerns of the ordinary world.

While cathedrals, churches, and other places of worship have become noteworthy as centers of community activity, buildings designed to gather together and entertain whole communities have existed since antiquity. Amongst the most famous arenas of the ancient world was the Colosseum, one of imperial Rome's largest public buildings

4.1.2 Colosseum, 72–80 CE, Rome, Italy

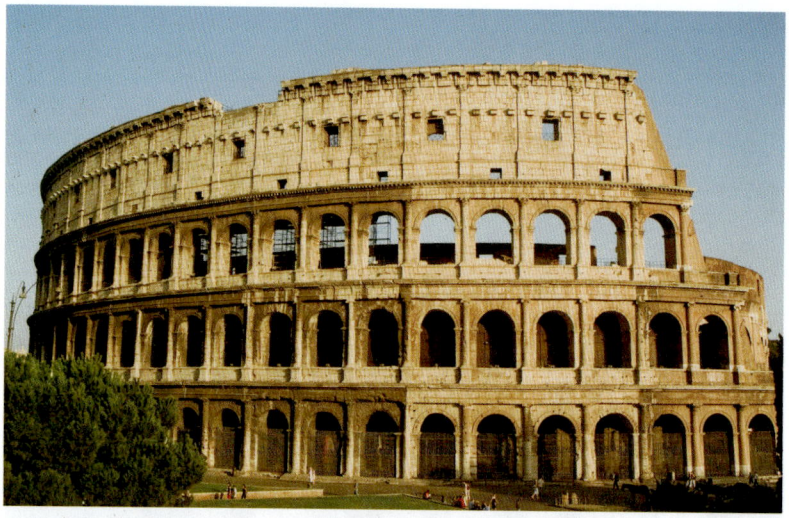

Concrete: a hard, strong, and versatile construction material made up of powdered lime, sand, and rubble
Travertine: light-colored limestone deposited in mineral springs and used as a building material
Pilaster: a vertical element, rectangular in shape, that provides architectural support for crossing horizontal elements in post-and-lintel construction; also used for decoration

and an extraordinary feat of architecture and engineering (**4.1.2**). Measuring 615 ft. long by 510 ft. across and standing 159 ft. tall, the Colosseum could hold between 45,000 and 55,000 people. The Romans were the first to exploit fully the structural possibilities of **concrete**, which they used to construct the Colosseum's massive foundations and parts of its vaulted ceilings. The exterior was covered with marble and **travertine** limestone (a light-colored form of limestone deposited in mineral springs) and decorated with columns and with **pilasters** made of another type of local limestone. There were seventy-six entrance doors, called *vomitoria*, a word that offers a vivid mental image of the crowds spilling from the doors after an event. Roman citizens flocked to the Colosseum to see mock sea battles and gladiatorial fights with both man and beast.

The Colosseum was designed almost 2,000 years ago for the entertainment of enormous crowds, but today's stadiums are built to hold far more people. The AT&T Stadium (**4.1.3**) was built in Arlington, Texas in 2009 to be the home of the Dallas Cowboys. It has the fourth largest seating capacity in the NFL, 80,000, with a maximum capacity of 105,000 including standing room. A true community venue, this stadium is city-owned and supported by taxpayers. The Cowboys owner, Jerry Jones, funded much of the $1.15 billion construction cost and the NFL loaned a considerable amount toward the

4.1.3 AT&T Stadium, Arlington, Texas, 2009

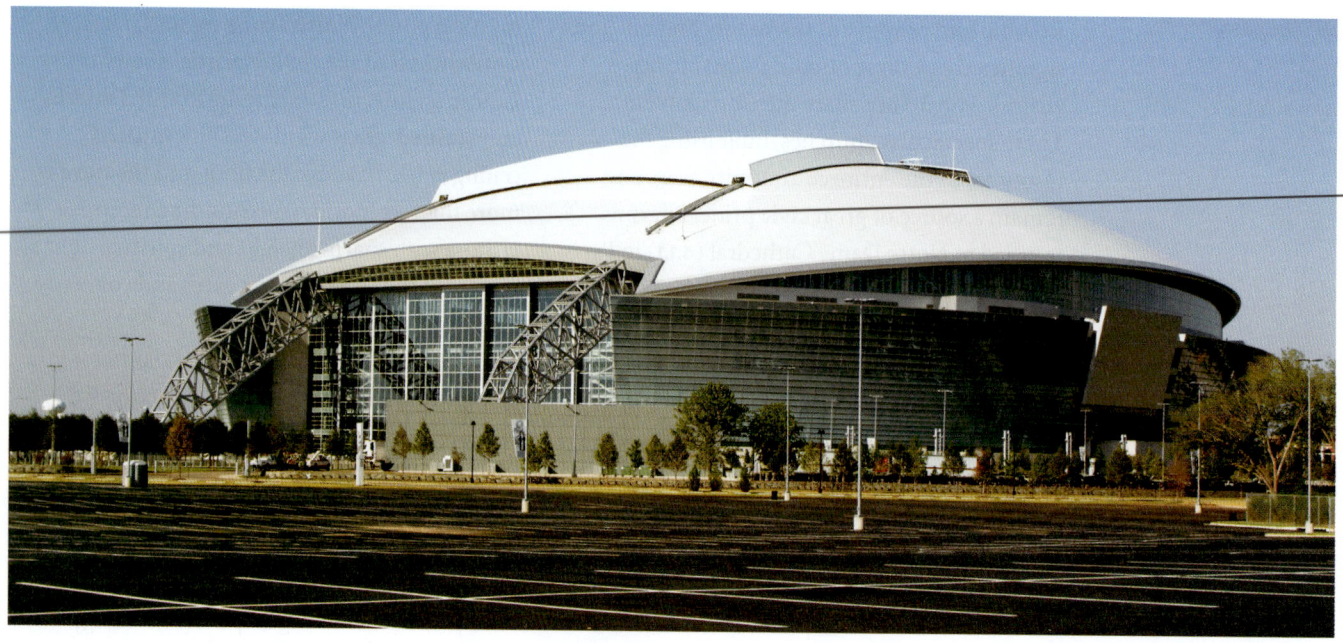

project. With a 3-million-square-foot interior, AT&T Stadium is the world's largest domed structure and column-free interior. The roof retracts and glass doors at the end zones can be opened. A true feat of twenty-first-century engineering, the building boasts LCD screens throughout and had the world's largest HDTV at the time of its construction. To attract an even wider audience, the building also houses an art museum with site-specific works commissioned from eighteen contemporary artists.

Art by and for the Community

In addition to attracting members of the public seeking entertainment, cultural instruction, and reflection, museums also serve as centers of local distinction, in much the same way as cathedrals and sports arenas do. In a bid to keep pace with the expanding attractions of other destination sites, many art museums, such as the Solomon R. Guggenheim Museum in New York City (**4.1.4**), have broadened their own appeal by hosting community programming, including festivals, concerts, and film screenings. For many visitors, however, the design of a museum can be as much of an attraction as the art collected inside. The design of the Guggenheim Museum employs strong geometric shapes, which is characteristic of many modern buildings, but this white, circular building is distinctive amongst the city's rectangular blocks and glass skyscrapers. The architect Frank Lloyd Wright (1867–1959) sought to provide what the director of the museum had asked for, "a temple of spirit, a monument." The interior is open, with a continuous spiral ramp around the central **atrium** connecting each successive floor. The space is filled with light from the domed skylight above.

Art can also form a center of community activity in its own right. The American artist

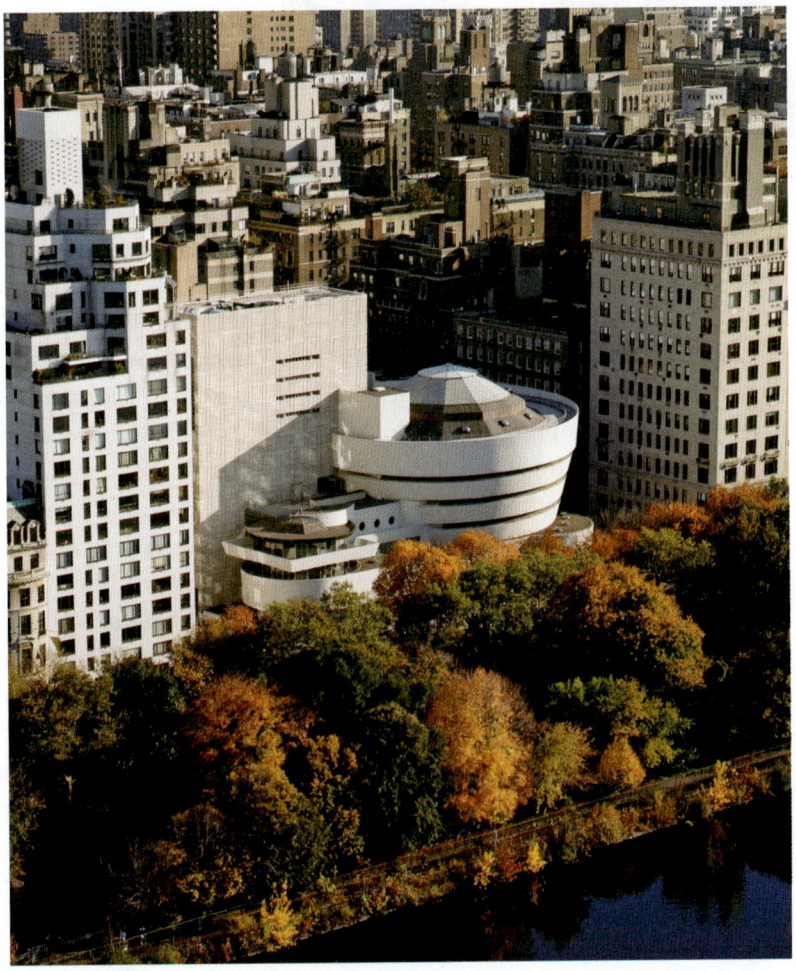

4.1.4 Frank Lloyd Wright, Solomon R. Guggenheim Museum, 1956–59, New York

Atrium: a central, normally public, interior space, first used in Roman houses

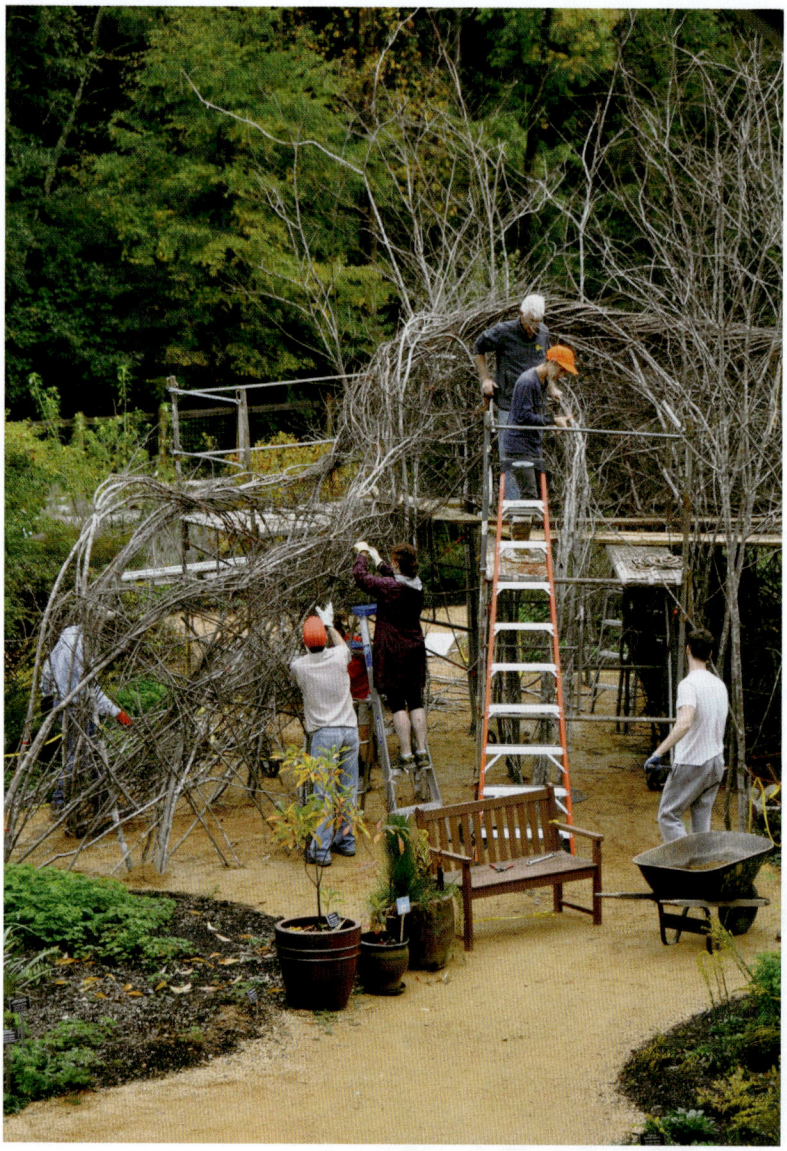

4.1.5 Patrick Dougherty, *Homegrown*, 2014. North Carolina Botanical Garden, Chapel Hill, North Carolina

Patrick Dougherty (b. 1945) makes site-specific stickworks throughout the United States and all over the world. The process of making a stickwork takes about two weeks and the lifespan of Dougherty's temporary sculptures is usually two years. A key part of the construction is the involvement of hundreds of community members. They collect saplings from the location in which the work is to be installed and together build the sculpture using a technique similar to weaving. *Homegrown* (**4.1.5**) was made by Dougherty and more than 100 volunteers using red maple and sweet gum to transform twigs and branches into a sculptural spectacle in the botanical gardens in Chapel Hill, North Carolina. Visitors are encouraged to enter and explore the sculpture's winding pathways and portals.

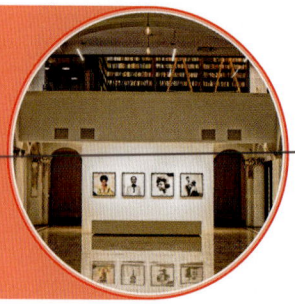

Theaster Gates has been regenerating neighborhoods in Chicago through art since 2006 by renovating buildings and creating cultural centers for the community: see **3.10.21b, p. 560**

Man-Made Mountains

Buildings and other constructions intended to shape and dominate the environment—as Wright surely intended with his design for the Guggenheim (**4.1.4**)—have been made since ancient times. Earthen mounds and **pyramids** are amongst the most intriguing kinds of architecture. Mysteries surround their creation, function, and symbolic significance. Why were such substantial human and material resources devoted to these man-made mountains? Whether they were built as memorials for the dead, for administrative purposes, or for religious worship and rituals, these structures had a dramatic and lasting impact on the geography of their locations.

While they resemble the Egyptian pyramids in form, the **ziggurats** of the ancient Near East, such as the one in the city-state of Ur in Sumer (now part of Iraq), were built for the benefit of the living community rather than to bury the dead (**4.1.6**). The ziggurat was part of a temple complex with civic and ceremonial purposes. The mud-brick structures are made up of at least three stepped levels, accessed by stairways or ramps. The lowest level is about 50 ft. high and about 210 by 150 ft. in area, with the others decreasing in size as they get closer to the heavens. The topmost platform, more than 100 ft. high, served as an elevated stage for the priest, who was one of the few people allowed access to that part of the ziggurat, and who served both as the principal human intermediary to the god who protected the city, and the chief administrator of the ziggurat. The city of Ur and its ziggurat were dedicated to the moon god Nanna, one of the three important sky deities in Sumerian religion. Festivals were organized around the phases of the moon, especially when

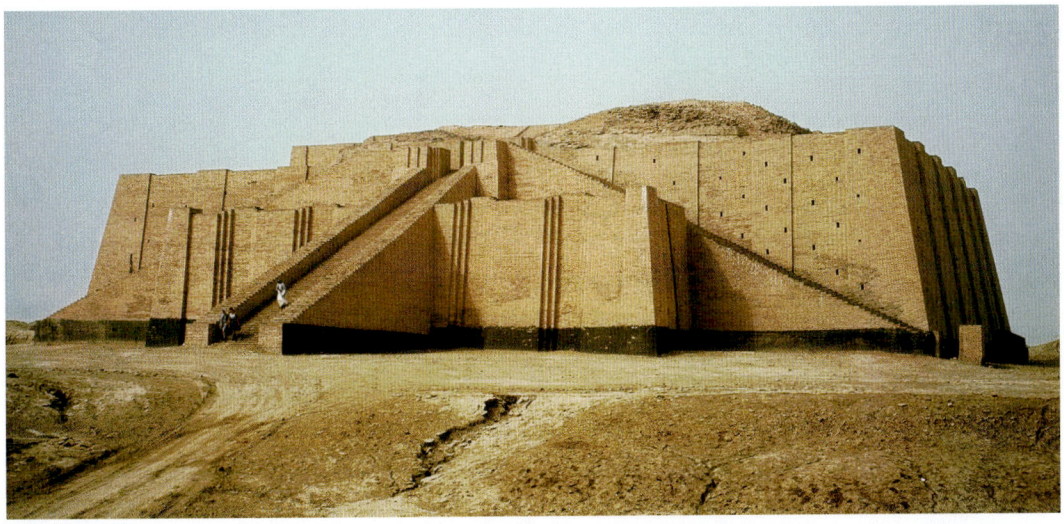

4.1.6 Ziggurat, Ur (near Nasiriyah, Iraq), originally built *c.* 2100 BCE and heavily restored

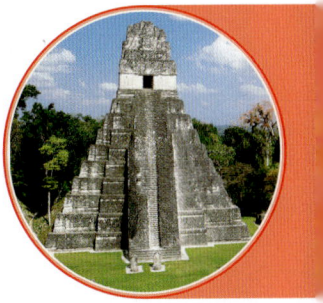

Such cultures as the ancient Egyptians and Maya created pyramid structures that resembled "mountains," which became icons of their communities over time: see **1.2.2, p. 62** and **2.5.5, p. 262**

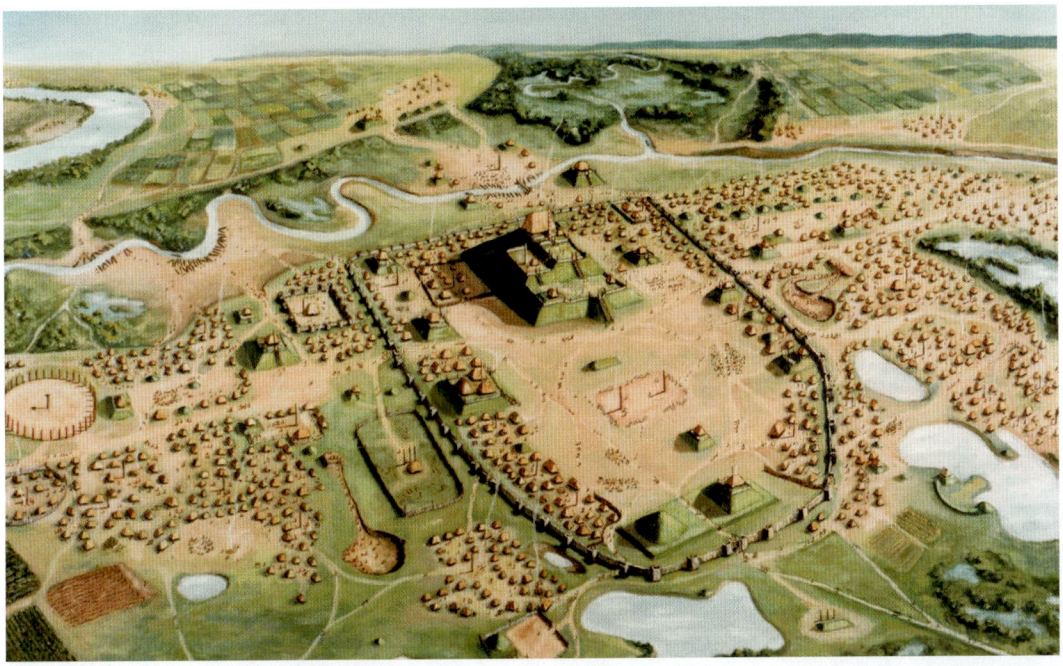

4.1.7 Monks Mound, Cahokia, Illinois, *c.* 1150 (reconstruction drawing)

Pyramid: ancient structure, usually massive in scale, consisting of a square base with four sides that meet at a point or apex with each side forming a triangular shape
Ziggurat: Mesopotamian stepped tower, roughly pyramid-shaped, that diminishes in size toward a platform summit

it appeared as a crescent, and offerings were left on the high platform to please Nanna and ensure the abundance of such sacred liquids as water, milk, and blood.

More than 3,000 years after the construction of the ziggurat at Ur, builders made the largest earthen mound ever discovered in North America (**4.1.7**). Cahokia, located in what is now southern Illinois, near St. Louis, covered 6 square miles and had an estimated population of 10,000–20,000. As with other communities that built such impressive structures, there is evidence of a highly organized society, advanced engineering knowledge, and a productive work force at this site.

The focal point of the settlement at Cahokia was Monks Mound, which was originally surrounded by about 120 smaller mounds. The base of Monks Mound measures 1,080 by 710 ft. and is topped by two smaller platforms. Though its exact purpose is uncertain, Monks Mound likely served as an elite residence, a temple, a burial structure, or perhaps all three. Monks Mound is aligned with the sun at the equinoxes, the two times of the year (in spring and fall) when day and night are exactly the same length. These alignments suggest that it may have functioned as a calendar and also served a ceremonial purpose. The site was abandoned around 600 years ago due to climate changes

Art, Super-Sized

Two famous works of art, made more than 4,000 years apart, occupied public spaces used by large numbers of people. Both structures were created by the efforts of masses of laborers. Considering these enormous works together can help us understand how a work of art can change a public place and how people interact with such works.

Very little is known about the makers of Stonehenge (**4.1.8**), but the creators of *The Gates* (**4.1.9**), Christo (b.1935) and Jeanne-Claude (1935–2009), explained themselves in countless statements and interviews. We know about the construction methods of Christo and Jeanne-Claude from descriptions and from video documentation, but the techniques used to erect Stonehenge, and the intentions of its builders, remain shrouded in mystery. Stonehenge is still standing after thousands of years, while *The Gates* was designed to be in place only temporarily. Despite their differences, both works share a common aim: to focus the attention and movements of crowds of people in directions calculated by the artists who designed them.

The oldest parts of Stonehenge, on Salisbury Plain in England, are the circular embankment and ditch that surround the monument. This site was used for hundreds of years before the stones were imported from as far as 23 miles away. The massive stones in the **sarsen** circle weigh up to 50 tons apiece, each one equaling the weight of 500 people or 5 buses. We will probably never know how the builders moved those stones. Most scholars believe that Stonehenge, 106 ft. in diameter and up to 20 ft. tall in places, served as a giant observatory or calendar. People who gathered at Stonehenge on the longest day of the year, the summer solstice, would have seen the sun rise precisely over the great stone known as the Heelstone, which stands outside the circle.

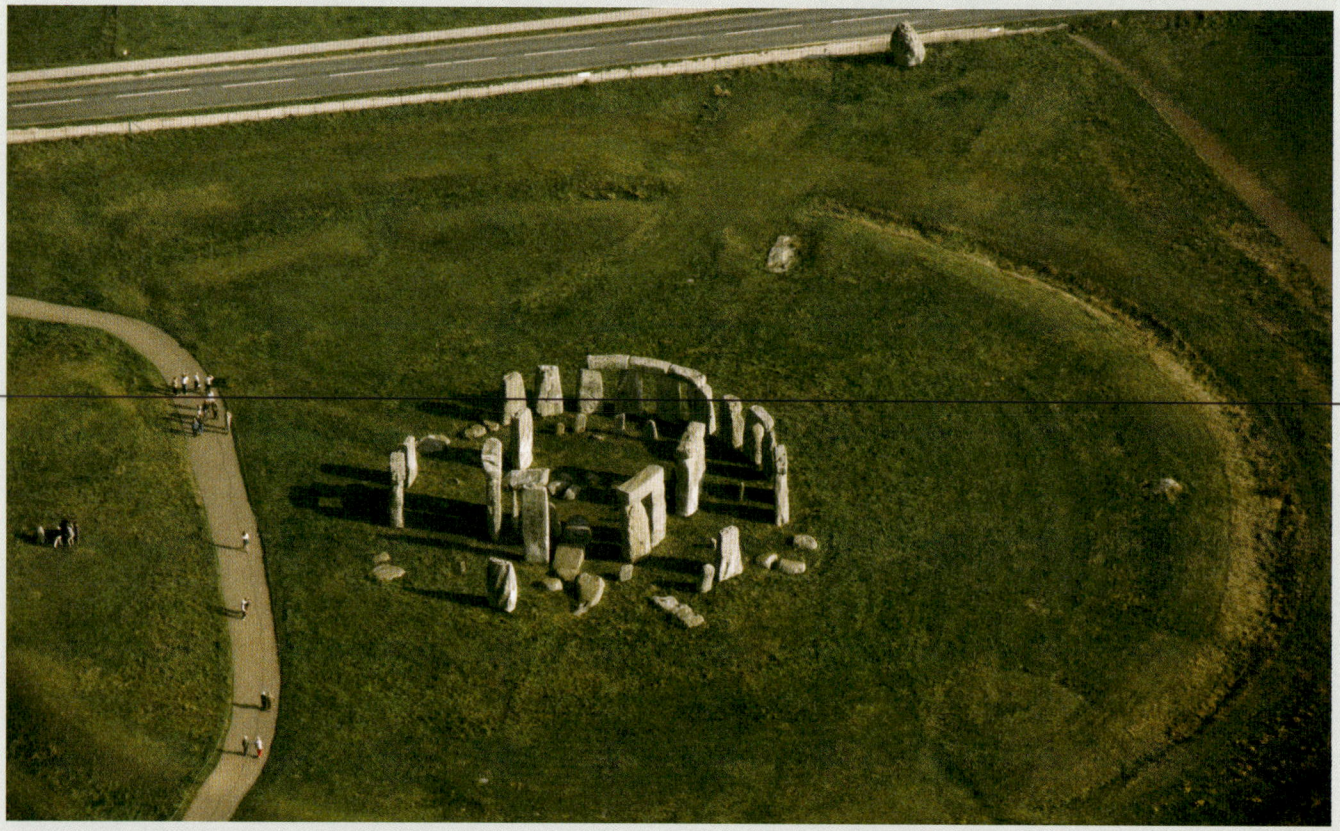

4.1.8 Stonehenge, *c.* 3200–1500 BCE, Salisbury Plain, Wiltshire, England

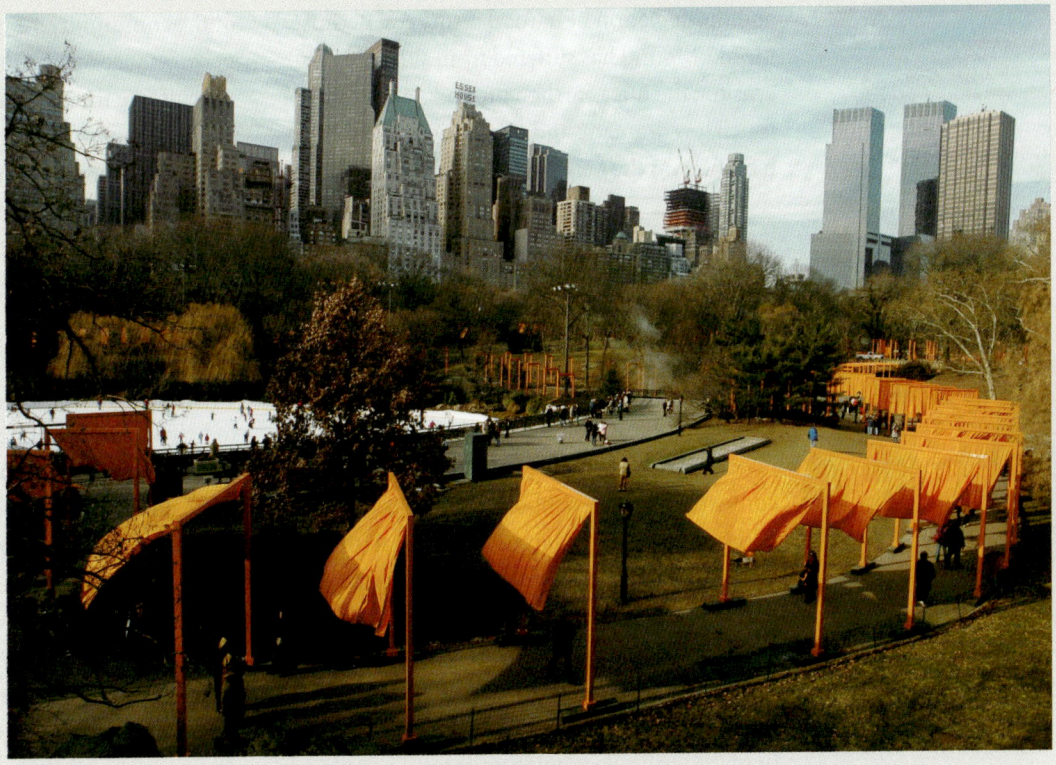

4.1.9 Christo and Jeanne-Claude, *The Gates*, Central Park, New York City, 1979–2005. Steel, vinyl tubing, and nylon fabric, height *c.* 16"

For a farming community, such as the one that built Stonehenge, the precise date of the summer solstice was important: it signaled the time to prepare for the fall harvest.

The Gates, installed in 2005, meandered through the 23 miles of walkways in New York's Central Park for just sixteen days. The installation was intended for public enjoyment, and an estimated four million people visited Central Park during the exhibition. The piece required community support garnered through petitions and meetings between the artists and New York City officials. Discussions about *The Gates* began in 1979 and the project was finally approved in 2003. The negotiation process was integral to the production of Christo's and Jeanne-Claude's installation, emphasizing the important role that the community plays in the conception and creation of their artworks.

Facts and figures provided on the artists' website indicate the mind-boggling amounts of material and labor involved in the making of *The Gates*. A total of 60 miles of saffron-colored nylon fabric hung from 7,503 gates. Each gate was 16 ft. tall, with fabric coming down to approximately 7 ft. above the ground. The gates ranged from about 5 ft. to 18 ft. across, depending on the width of the walkway. The artists employed engineers; project directors; fabricators for the materials in the United States and Germany; 600 paid workers to install, monitor, and remove the pieces; and security guards to protect the work at night. After *The Gates* was taken down the materials were recycled, reflecting the artists' environmentally sustainable practices.

Although these two works were made at different times on different continents, they have in common the fact that their construction required the efforts of significant numbers of people and that they were used or viewed by an entire community. While it is uncertain how or why Stonehenge was built, it is clear that a highly organized social structure must have been in place to see such a venture through. *The Gates* similarly required teams of experts and construction crews to carry out the artists' vision. Keen on involving the community and having their work enliven public spaces, but interested in maintaining creative freedom, Christo and Jeanne-Claude did not accept any government or public funding and themselves paid for the creation, installation, and maintenance of the work.

Sarsen: a type of hard, gray sandstone

Masquerade: performance in which participants wear masks and costumes for a ritual or cultural purpose
Gèlèdé ritual: ritual performed in Nigeria's Yoruba society to celebrate and honor women

and the depletion of natural resources. Because Monks Mound has suffered from slumping and erosion, the huge earthen mound's appearance is much less dramatic and impressive than it must have been at the height of Cahokia's occupation.

Rituals and Art of Healing and Community Solidarity

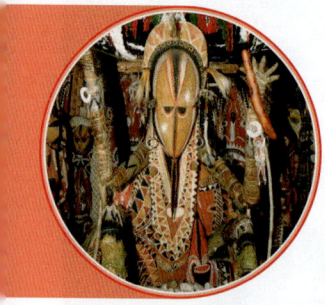

For coming-of-age rituals, the Abelam of Papua New Guinea carefully construct and decorate ceremonial houses; after the rituals take place, they no longer need them: see **3.5.18, p. 458**

The production of art is often deeply connected to philosophical, religious, and ideological beliefs. Artworks made to be used in a ritual context often have symbolic meanings in addition to their appearance and visual impact. With such artifacts as temporary constructions and masks, it is important to keep in mind that the way they were experienced in their original context would have been very different from the way we now see them in the pages of a book or inside glass museum cases. The objects themselves are suggestive of sights, sounds, and even smells to which we no longer have access.

Masks and **masquerades** serve the important communal function of mediating between the human and spiritual realms. Masquerades enable humans to communicate with the spirit world, as the masker's personality is temporarily replaced with that of the spirit being evoked. The spirit's message will then have a direct impact upon the functions and behavior of the community. At the same time, the ritual performance of masquerades is often designed to reinforce the cultural beliefs of a community. While the mask is generally the focal point of the performance, it must be combined with costumes, music, and dance in order to invoke a particular spirit. **Gèlèdé rituals** performed by the Yoruba in Nigeria, Africa celebrate female strength, honor women as mothers, and commemorate their life-giving powers in the hope that they will continue to use them to help sustain and improve the community (**4.1.10**). These ceremonies also acknowledge the important part played by female ancestors in Yoruba society and promote general spiritual well-being and social harmony.

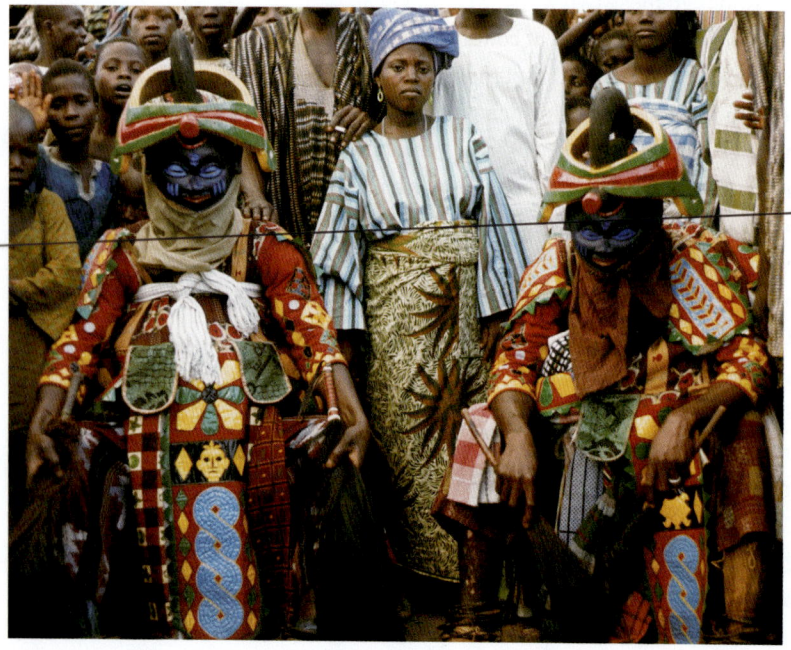

4.1.10 Pair of Gèlèdé masqueraders wearing appliquéd cloth panels, Ketu area, town of Idahin, Benin. Photo by Henry John Drewal, 1971

The Chinese artist Wenda Gu (b. 1956) says that he makes his so-called "hair monuments" in an effort to unite the people of the world through a chain of artworks. The monuments are made of walls or screens woven from human hair donated by people from countries around the globe. Gu then paints what appear to be ideograms (symbols that convey the meaning of words, such as numerals or Chinese characters) with a brush that is itself made from strands of human hair. The signs he paints are suggestive of particular cultures rather than literal transcriptions. "China Monument: Temple of Heaven" (**4.1.11**) is reminiscent of a Buddhist temple in which one partakes of a tea ceremony, and includes ancient-looking Chinese tables and chairs. Video monitors in the seats of the chairs show clouds and poetic text by the artist, so that the people experiencing this artwork are given the sense that they have entered a spiritual realm.

The space also unites a variety of cultures by including symbols that imitate Arabic, Hindi, and Chinese, as well as the Latin alphabet used by Western languages. Gu's *United Nations* series of hair monuments has been made in more than twenty countries on five continents. More than a million people have contributed their hair to it. Gu has therefore been able to unite humans from all over the world in his work, through their common biology. The artist hopes someday to create monuments in every country in the world, linking all the different human cultures.

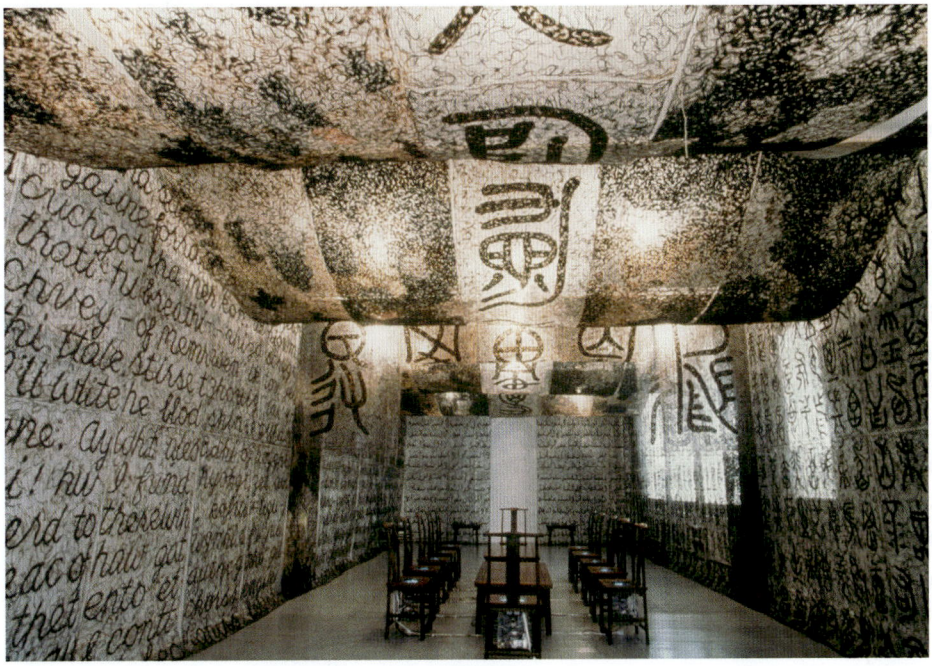

4.1.11 Wenda Gu, "China Monument: Temple of Heaven" (*United Nations* series), 1998. Mixed media, 52' × 20' × 13'. Hong Kong Museum of Art, China

Cor-ten steel: a type of steel that forms a coating of rust that protects it from the weather and further corrosion

Art in the Public Sphere

Not all art exists in galleries and museums. Public art generally appears in plazas and parks, or on the exterior walls of buildings. Public artworks are therefore accessible to a wide audience, as we have seen on pp. 570–71, and they are often much beloved by the community. But they can also cause problems. Sometimes public art can be taken out of context or misunderstood. Sometimes people can have different views about what should be seen in public or is appropriate in a particular environment. Public artworks can provoke strong reactions, both favorable and disapproving, and can sometimes spark fierce controversies.

Tilted Arc, by the American Minimalist sculptor Richard Serra (b. 1939), was commissioned by the federal General Services Administration (GSA) and installed on Federal Plaza in downtown New York City in 1981 (**4.1.12**, p. 575). It became the subject of controversy shortly after it was installed. The 12 by 120 ft. sculpture, a curving wall of **Cor-ten steel**, cut across the plaza. Some of the people who worked in the GSA building complained that it interfered with their use of the plaza and caused a safety hazard as well, attracting graffiti artists, rats, criminals, and potentially even terrorists. Although the majority of testimonies at a public hearing to decide whether or not to leave the sculpture in place were in favor of keeping the work, it was ordered to be removed. The artist's lawsuit against the GSA failed to reverse the decision and the sculpture was dismantled in 1989. Serra had argued that *Tilted Arc* was designed specifically for Federal Plaza and that relocating it was the equivalent of destroying it, so the metal was sent to a scrap yard (see Perspectives on Art Box: Richard Serra: A Sculptor Defends His Work, pp. 574–75). Even though the sculpture was demolished, the artist's hope of making people aware of their environment, pay attention to the path they follow on the way to work, and think about their surroundings was in some ways achieved by the attention generated by the controversy.

The dispute over Serra's *Tilted Arc* raises many questions that have a bearing on the form and functions of all public art. What is the desired impact of public art? Does it need to please its audience, or can it be used as a tool to challenge their beliefs and experiences? How much weight should be given to the artist's freedom of expression? Should consideration be given to whether the artwork is in keeping with the kind of work an artist is known to produce? How much power should public voices be given, whether they belong to specialists in the art world or members of the general community? What bearing does the issue of funding—which may come from the government through special programs aimed at promoting public art or from individual patrons—have on how one answers such questions?

The subject matter of public art, especially when it has political implications, has also been a source of debate. One of the most infamous scandals surrounding a public art project occurred in 1932 when the Mexican artist Diego Rivera (1886–1957) was commissioned by American businessman and millionaire Nelson Rockefeller to paint a **mural** in the Radio Corporation Arts (RCA) Building at Rockefeller Center in Manhattan. Rivera was inspired by Mexico's tradition of adorning walls with paintings and sculptures, which originated long before European contact. Such murals create an environment rich with stories related to all aspects of life. Rivera's written plan for *Man at the Crossroads Looking with Hope and High Vision to the Choosing of a New and Better Future*, which Rockefeller approved, included depictions of forces of nature as well as technology, and looked forward to "the liquidation of Tyranny" and a more perfect society. In the course of painting, however, Rivera made some changes inspired by his Communist inclinations. The most notable was on the right side of the mural, where he included a portrait of the Russian revolutionary Vladimir Lenin leading a demonstration of workers in a May Day parade.

When he was asked to remove Lenin's portrait, Rivera refused, and offered instead to balance it with a depiction of Abraham Lincoln. Rockefeller rejected this proposal, paid Rivera his full fee, and banned him from the building. Rockefeller then made plans to remove the mural. An outpouring of public support for the project followed: picket lines were formed, newspaper editorials were published, and Rivera made a speech at a rally outside City Hall. Despite suggestions that the mural be moved a few blocks away to the Museum of Modern Art, it was ultimately demolished with pickaxes in February 1934. That same year Rivera re-created the mural, with the new title *Man, Controller of the Universe*, in Mexico City (**4.1.13**, p. 576).

Mural: a painting executed directly onto a wall

Perspectives on Art: Richard Serra
A Sculptor Defends His Work

In 1979 the General Services Administration (GSA) contracted the American sculptor Richard Serra to install a work on Federal Plaza in New York City. The sculpture, Tilted Arc, *was erected in 1981. The work proved controversial and in 1985 Serra had to defend his sculpture at a public hearing.*

My name is Richard Serra and I am an American sculptor.

I don't make portable objects. I don't make works that can be relocated or site adjusted. I make works that deal with the environmental components of given places. The scale, size, and location of my site-specific works are determined by the topography of the site, whether it be urban, landscape, or an architectural enclosure. My works become part of and are built into the structure of the site, and they often restructure, both conceptually and perceptually, the organization of the site.

My sculptures are not objects for the viewer to stop and stare at. The historical purpose of placing sculpture on a pedestal was to establish a separation between the sculpture and the viewer. I am interested in creating a behavioral space in which the viewer interacts with the sculpture in its context.

One's identity as a person is closely connected with one's experience of space and place. When a known space is changed through the inclusion of a site-specific sculpture, one is called on to relate to the space differently. This is a condition that can be engendered only by sculpture. This experience of space may startle some people.

When the government invited me to propose a sculpture for the plaza it asked for a permanent, site-specific sculpture. As the

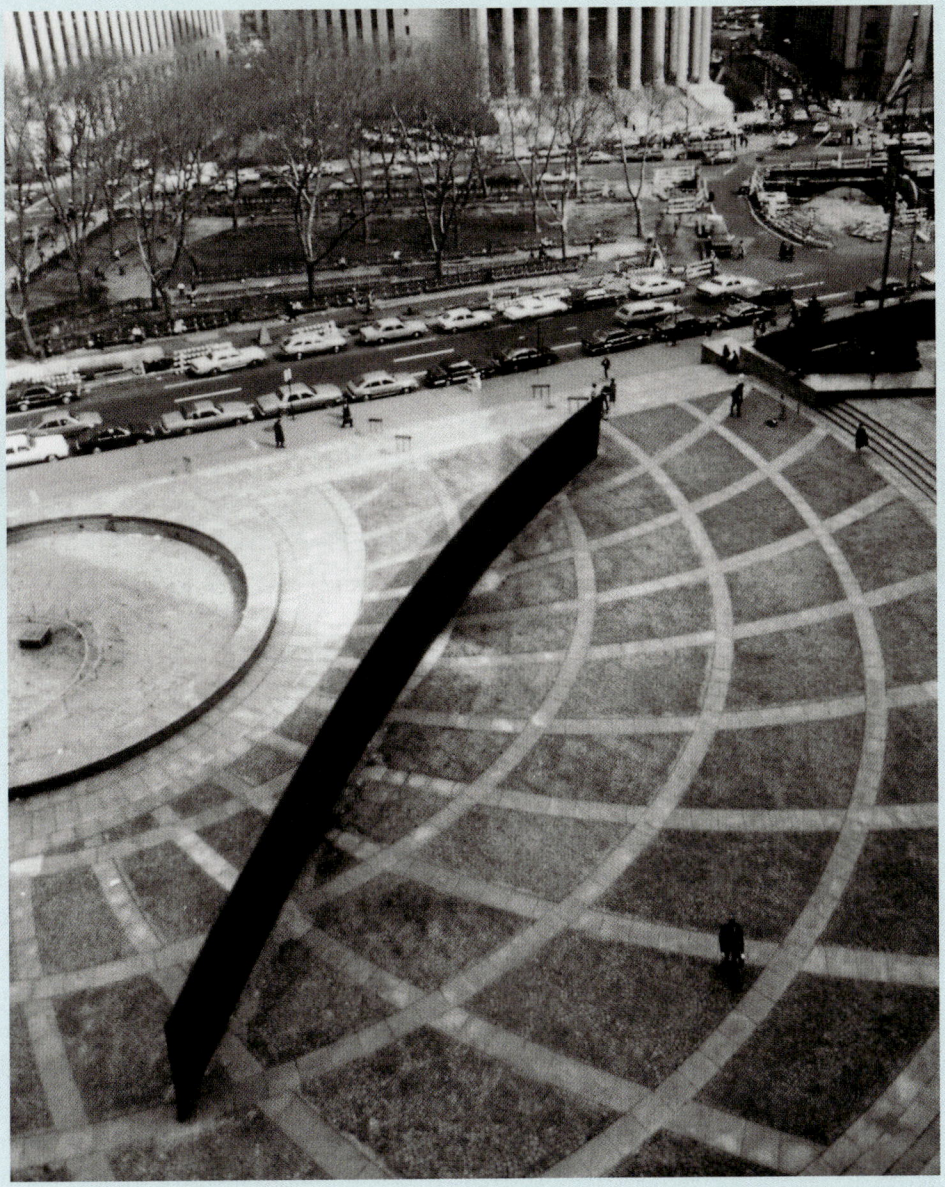

4.1.12 Richard Serra, *Tilted Arc*, 1981 (destroyed March 15, 1989). Weatherproof steel, 12' × 120' × 2½". Collection General Services Administration, Washington, D.C. Installed at Federal Plaza, New York

phrase implies, a site-specific sculpture is one that is conceived and created in relation to the particular conditions of a specific site, and only to those conditions.

To remove *Tilted Arc*, therefore, would be to destroy it...

It has been suggested that the public did not choose to install the work in the first place. In fact, the choice of the artist and the decision to install the sculpture permanently in the plaza were made by a public entity: the GSA. Its determination was made on the basis of national standards and carefully formulated procedures, and a jury system ensured impartiality and the selection of art of lasting value.

The selection of this sculpture was, therefore, made by, and on behalf of, the public.

The agency made its commitments and signed a contract. If its decision is reversed in response to pressure from outside sources, the integrity of governmental programs related to the arts will be compromised, and artists of integrity will not participate. If the government can destroy works of art when confronted with such pressure, its capacity to foster artistic diversity and its power to safeguard freedom of creative expression will be in jeopardy.

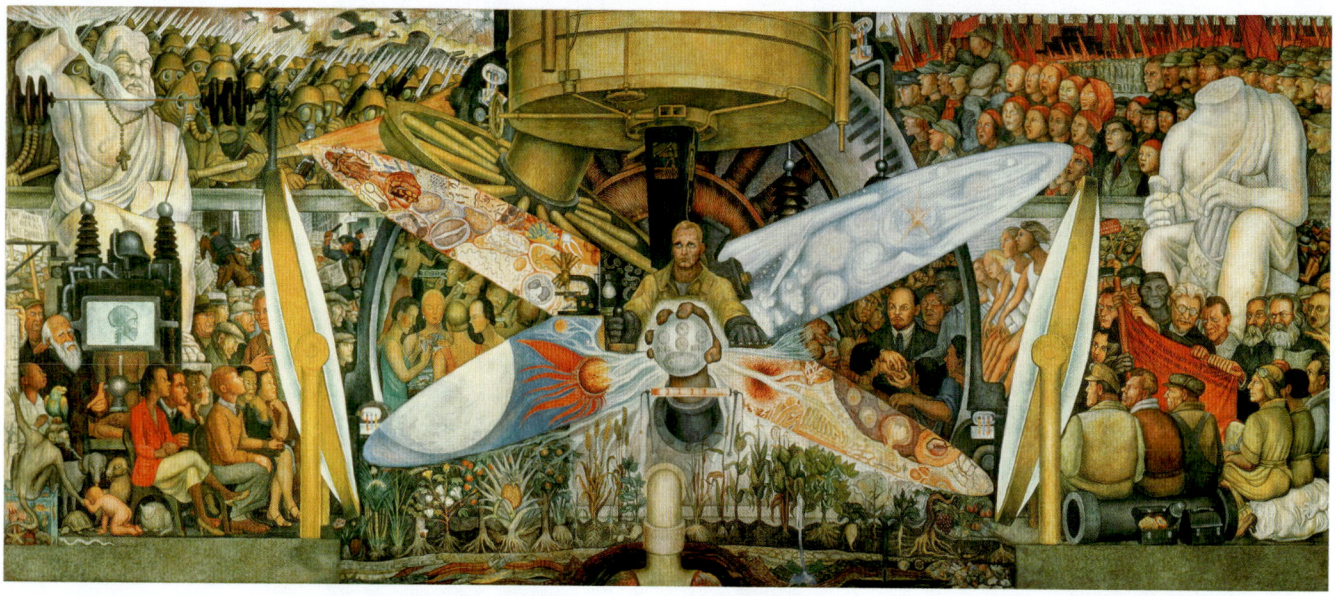

4.1.13 Diego Rivera, *Man, Controller of the Universe*, or *Man in the Time Machine*, 1934. Fresco, 15' × 37'6⅞". Full composite view of the fresco. Palacio de Bellas Artes, Mexico City, Mexico

Rivera rather bluntly described the conflict that can arise between the vision of artists with strong opinions and their audiences: "[The artist] must try to raise the level of taste of the masses, not debase himself to the level of unformed and impoverished taste."

Over the course of his career, the Polish-born artist Krzysztof Wodiczko (b. 1943) has created more than eighty video projection pieces intended to draw attention to situations of social injustice around the world. Images and text telling the stories of individuals who have been overlooked or mistreated are projected onto architectural facades and monuments, which were made by or for powerful figures in the community. The projections of socially conscious messages about human rights and democracy onto public buildings associated with collective memory and history reclaim these spaces for the people and build community solidarity. *Tijuana Projection* (**4.1.14**) gave voice to women in the maquiladora industry, which consists of assembly plants and factories close to the border between Mexico and the United States, where cheap labor can be hired, and is notorious for substandard working conditions. The women were recorded recalling a traumatic event and their testimonies were projected live for two consecutive nights on the spherical Centro Cultural Tijuana to a public plaza filled with more than 1,500 people. They told of terrible home and working conditions, instances of including rape, incest, poisoning in the factories due to exposure to toxic chemicals, and police abuse. Wodiczko commented, "Their situation is incomparably worse than anything I have tried to understand before." His hope, though, was that this project would be a catalyst for them to move out of this situation and toward a better life.

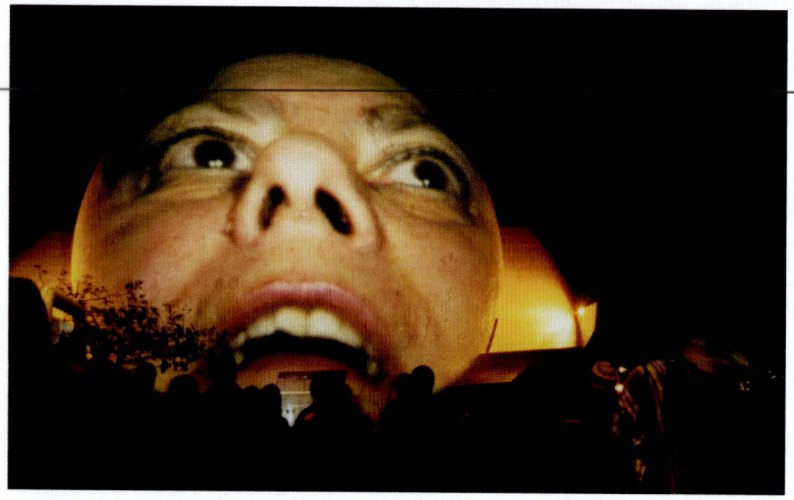

4.1.14 Krzysztof Wodiczko, *Tijuana Projection*, 2001. Public video projection at the Centro Cultural Tijuana, Mexico. Organized as part of the event InSite 2000

We can see from the work of Serra, Rivera, and Wodiczko that art displayed in public places often raises our awareness, either by drawing our attention to existing spaces and specific ideas, or by reflecting issues that resonate for the community and need to be addressed.

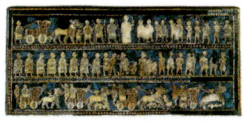

3.1.8a Standard of Ur, *c.* 2600–2400 BCE, p. 370

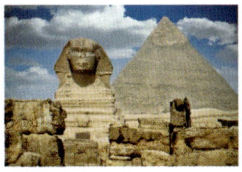

1.2.2 Great Sphinx of Giza, Egypt, *c.* 2500 BCE, p. 62

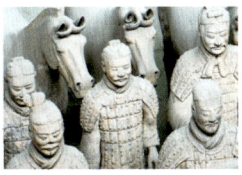

3.3.13b Soldiers, mausoleum of Qin Shi Huangdi, China, *c.* 210 BCE, p. 417

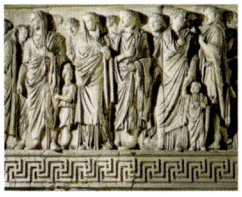

1.2.6 Imperial Procession from the Ara Pacis Augustae, 13 BCE, p. 65

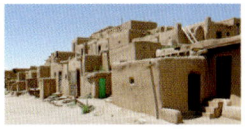

2.5.3 Taos Pueblo, New Mexico, pre-1500, p. 261

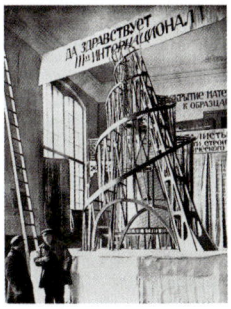

1.2.11 Vladimir Tatlin, Model for *Monument to the Third International*, 1919, p. 68

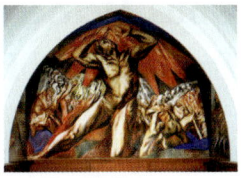

2.2.7 José Clemente Orozco, *Prometheus*, 1930, p. 213

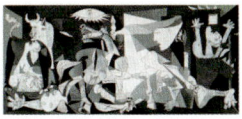

4.7.10 Pablo Picasso, *Guernica*, 1937, p. 646

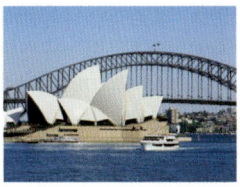

2.5.34 Jørn Utzon, Sydney Opera House, Australia, 1973, p. 280

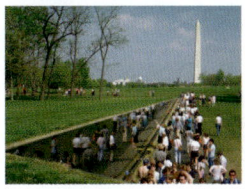

4.7.14a Maya Lin, Vietnam Veterans Memorial, 1981–83, p. 649

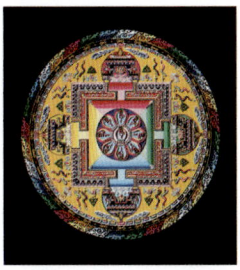

1.6.17 Amitayus Mandala, Drepung Loseling Monastery, Tibet, p. 138

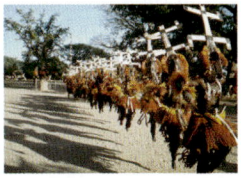

3.5.6b Dogon Kanaga mask ceremony, Mali, p. 450

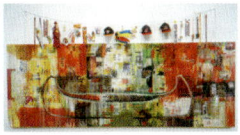

1.9.14 Jaune Quick-to-See Smith, *Trade...*, 1992. p. 168

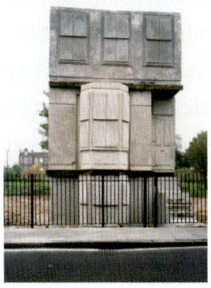

1.2.13 Rachel Whiteread, *House*, London, 1993, p. 69

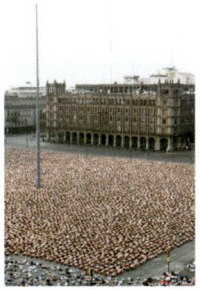

4.9.13a Spencer Tunick, Installation at Zócalo, Mexico City, 2007, p. 672

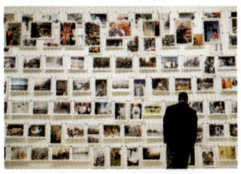

2.8.17 *Here Is New York: A Democracy of Photographs*, 2007, p. 325

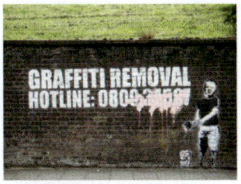

2.2.28 Banksy, *Graffiti Removal Hotline*, London, 2008, p. 224

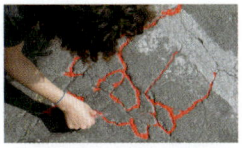

2.10.13 A *Red Sand Project* participant, p. 360

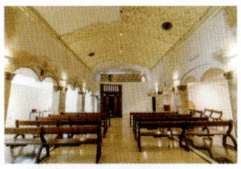

3.10.21b Theaster Gates, Stony Island Arts Bank, after restoration, p. 560

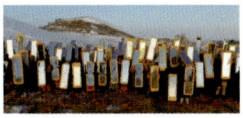

3.4.26 Cannupa Hanska Luger, mirror shields, Standing Rock, North Dakota, p. 444

4.2 Spirituality and Art

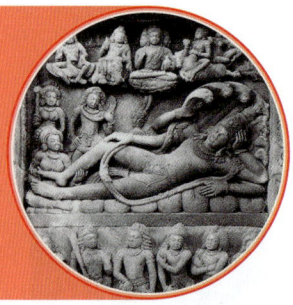

Vishnu, one of the three main gods of Hinduism, is the preserver and protector of creation, bringing order to a world that is threatened by chaos and destruction. Vishnu is often depicted (as in this example) sustaining the universe by dreaming about it: see **1.6.9, p. 131**

For as long as art has been made, there have been artworks inspired by beliefs in ancient deities, spirit beings, and the sacred figures of the world's religions. Through these works artists have sought to express things that cannot be seen and are little understood. In this chapter we use the term spirituality to examine the ways in which beliefs, including both narrative stories and their interpretations, have inspired artists for thousands of years. Spirituality encompasses our sense of being connected to others, our awareness of both mind and body, and our wish to understand life's meaning in the world and beyond. Spirituality serves as a source of inspiration and a way for us to share our beliefs. This chapter investigates six broad categories of artworks with a spiritual context: those that incorporate specific gods, deities, or central figures; those that refer to the spirits of the natural world or ancestors; suggestions of communication with the spirit world; reactions to places that have a sacred resonance; personal paths to spirituality; and depictions of judgment at the end of an earthly life.

Gods, Deities, and Enlightened Beings

Artists communicate the stories of specific religious figures or deities to help explain their importance. Depictions of individuals considered divine or singly important in Greek mythology, the Christian Bible, and Buddhist scripture can make those individuals more accessible and memorable.

The ancient Greeks often made artworks to honor their gods and deities. The sculptures in **4.2.1** are from the west **pediment** of the temple dedicated to the god Zeus at Olympia, Greece, where the Olympic games were born. The scene depicts the legendary battle between the Lapiths

Pediment: on the facade of a building in the Classical style, the triangular space situated above the row of columns

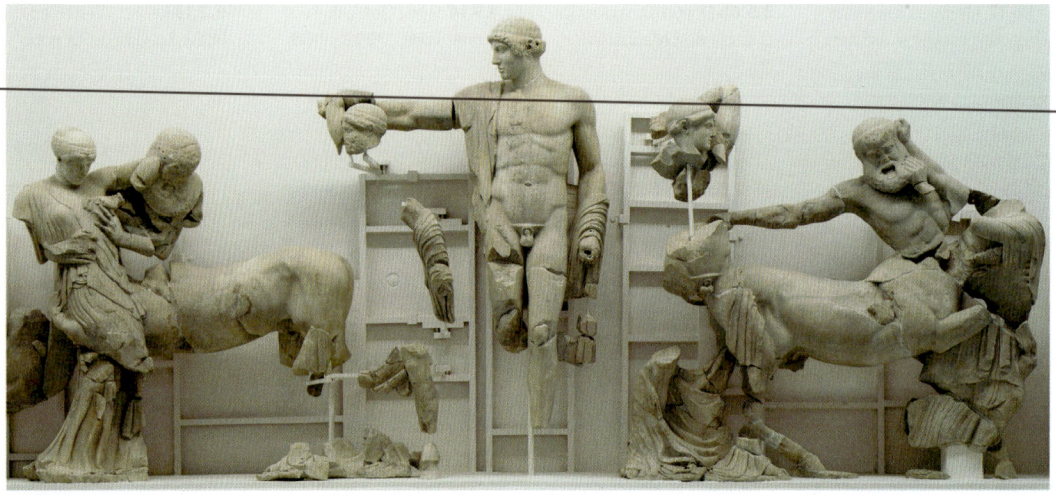

4.2.1 Apollo, centaur, and Lapith, fragments of relief sculptures from west pediment of Temple of Zeus, Olympia, Greece, c. 460 BCE. Marble, 8'8" × 10'10". Archaeological Museum, Olympia, Greece

Idealized: represented as perfect in form or character, corresponding to an ideal

of Thessaly and the centaurs—half-human and half-horse creatures, which, according to Greek mythology, lived in the nearby mountains. During the wedding feast of the Lapith king, the centaurs, who were amongst the guests, drank too much wine and tried to abduct the bride and the other women. The civilized Lapiths are depicted as **idealized**, rigid, and without emotion. The barbarian centaurs, on the other hand, are shown with more dramatic gestures and ferocious expressions. Apollo, the god of the sun, who was also associated with the poetic arts and medicine, stands at the center of the event and brings order to the violent struggle. He is the appropriate deity for this scene because he represents reason, order, and male beauty. The centaurs represent the opposite attributes: change, chaos, and even madness. Their drinking associates them with Dionysus, the god of wine.

Similarly, visual artists have often interpreted stories from the Bible in order to illustrate important Christian themes and events. In the eleventh century, Bishop Bernward was directing the building of the Abbey Church of St. Michael's at Hildesheim, Germany. He commissioned a set of doors that show scenes from the book of Genesis on the left side and scenes from the life of Christ on the right. In chronological order, the doors are read counterclockwise, beginning at the top of the left door. But the panels are also arranged so that events from the Old Testament are paired with related episodes from the New Testament (**4.2.2a–c**).

For example, the third panel from the top matches the Tree of Knowledge on the left with the Tree of Life on the right. In the left scene Eve accepts the forbidden fruit from the Tree of Knowledge, therefore committing the first, or original, sin; as a consequence, she and Adam were expelled from the Garden of Eden into the world of suffering and death. On the right, the cross on which Jesus was crucified—

4.2.2a (below) Detail of Hildesheim Doors: Temptation in the Garden of Eden

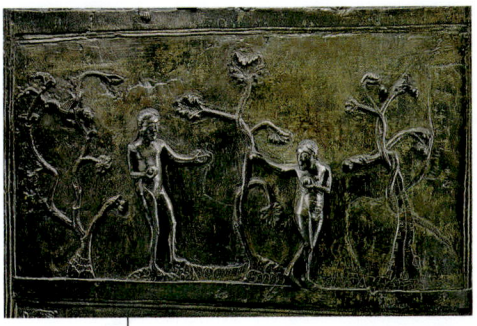

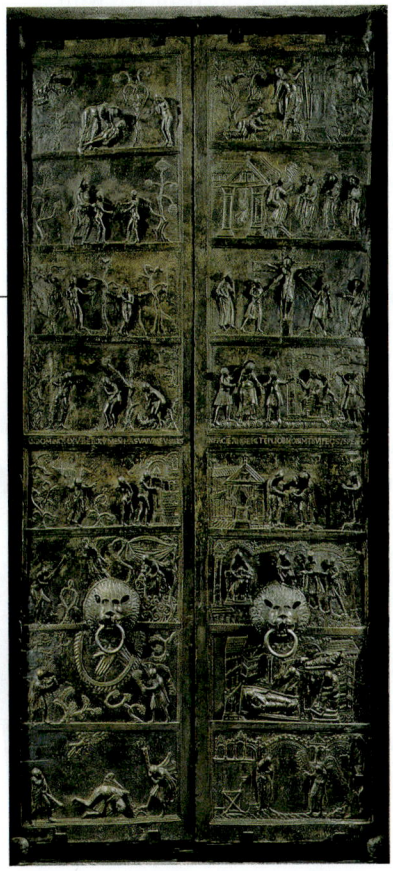

4.2.2b (right) Doors depicting scenes from Genesis and the life of Christ, commissioned by Bishop Bernward for the Abbey Church of St. Michael's, Hildesheim, 1015. Bronze, height 16'6". Dom-Museum, Hildesheim, Germany

4.2.2c (far right) Diagram with identification of panels on Hildesheim Doors

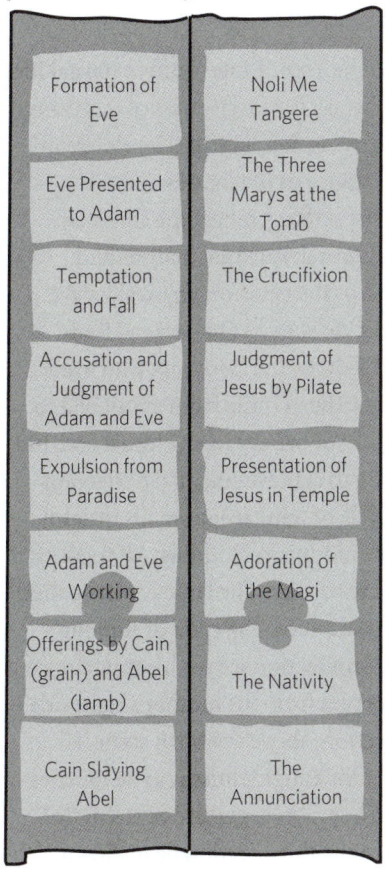

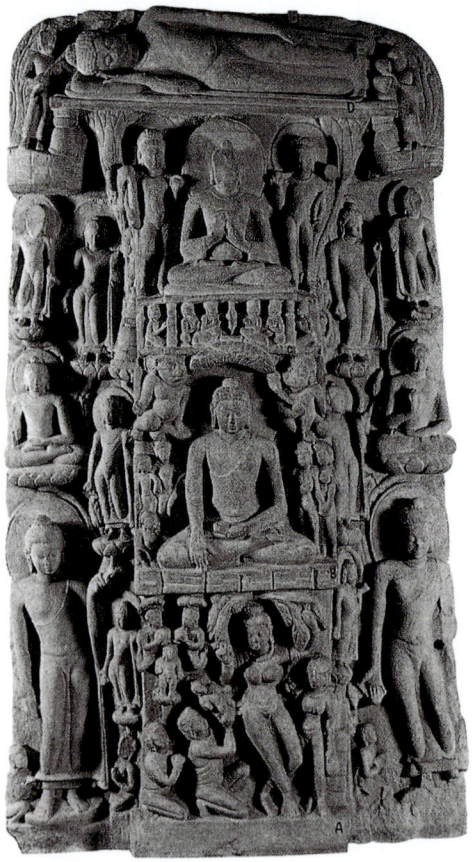

4.2.3 Life of Buddha, stela, Gupta period, c. 475 CE. Sandstone, height 41". India Museum, Calcutta, India

understood as the Tree of Life—offers eternal life to believers who ask for forgiveness of their sins and accept Christ as their savior. The elongated and frail appearance of the figures and the non-naturalistic settings reflect the Christian emphasis on internal, spiritual matters and themes instead of the exterior, physical world.

Buddha, the Awakened One, was a Hindu prince named Siddhartha Gautama who lived in Nepal and northern India from about 563 to 483 BCE. He did not believe in an eternal god, but focused on how to achieve spiritual perfection to break the cycle of reincarnation: his insights are the core of Buddhism. Buddhist art focuses on his life and teachings. The large central panels of the **stela** in **4.2.3** show the cycle of Buddha's life. In the bottom section we see his miraculous birth as he emerges from his mother's right side. The second section, above the birth scene, is the moment of his enlightenment as he touches the Earth with a symbolic gesture of strength and renewal. In the third section he is shown giving his first sermon, seated with his legs crossed and his hands posed in prayer, with the wheel of law behind him. At the top of the sculpture he is shown reclining as he achieves eternal tranquility, a state called nirvana. The smaller carvings along the sides of the stela show noteworthy moments after he decided to leave his princely life at the age of thirty to become a holy man.

Stela: upright stone slab decorated with inscriptions or pictorial relief carvings
Sand painting: also known as dry painting, a labor-intensive method of painting using colored grains of sand or other natural materials as the medium

Spirits and Ancestors

In African and Native American cultures, artworks often reflect the spiritual importance of gods and ancestors. According to some customary belief systems, objects can be infused with a spiritual presence. Through ritual, these objects help to continue and preserve cultural practices, ideas, and family ties; to establish or restore balance; and to enhance, or even transform, mundane life.

Creator deities, nature spirits, and ancestors feature prominently in the religion of the Senufo people of West Africa. Whether these spirits are beneficial or harmful, they are depicted with distortions in their anatomy to reveal that they are not humans. The head, legs, and detailed features of the Senufo sculpture in **4.2.4** are relatively small while the arms and breasts are notably exaggerated. The inclusion of a nursing baby suggests that this is one of the female ancestral spirits called "ancient mother" or "ancient woman." Such an "ancient woman" would serve as a guiding spirit for adult males of the Poro society, who were responsible for male initiation and maintaining religious practices, historical traditions, social customs, and political control.

Ancient rituals passed from generation to generation often reflect ideas that are central to that community's belief system, for example the sand-painting ritual of the Navajo of New Mexico. Navajo **sand paintings** are temporary works of art that are constructed as part of a prayer or ceremony (**4.2.5**). The paintings are closely connected to nature, both in materials used (such as corn, pollen, charcoal,

4.2.4 Senufo mother-and-child figure, late 19th–mid-20th century. Wood, height 25". Cleveland Museum of Art, Ohio

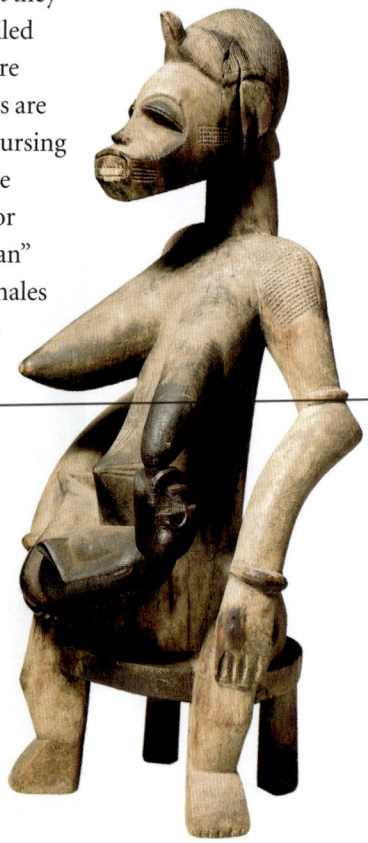

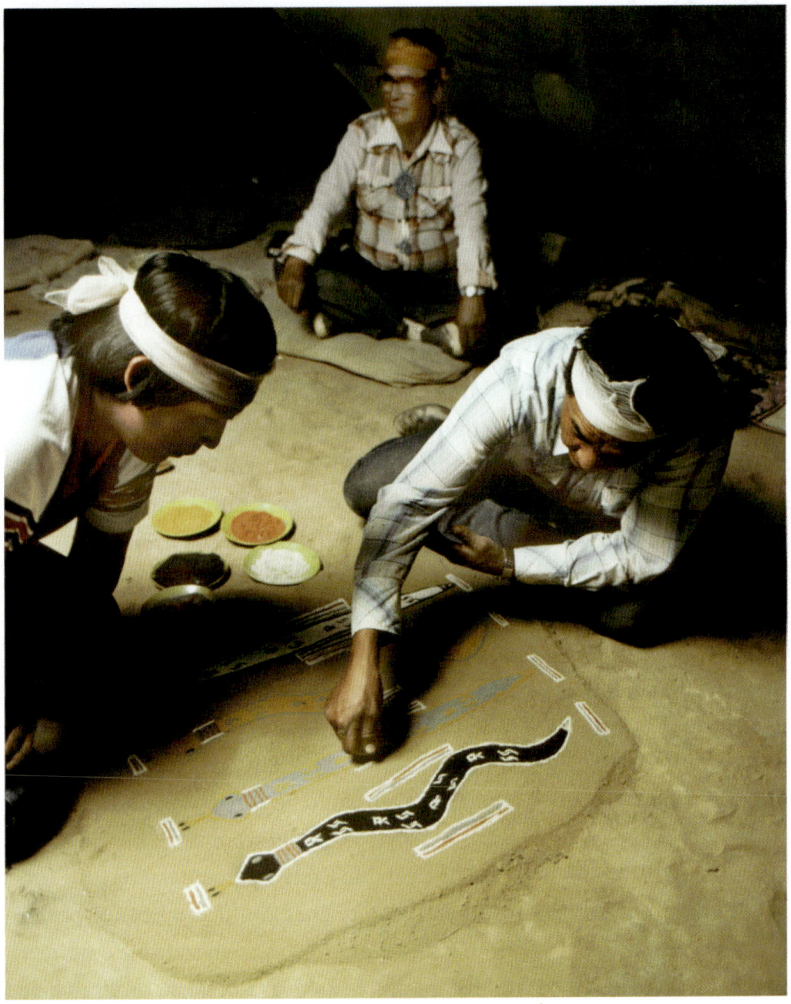

4.2.5 Navajo medicine man in healing ceremony. Photo 20th century

sand, and powdered stones) and imagery. The subject matter, from Navajo creation mythology, includes logs, holy plants, animals, and deities. After an image has been meticulously created over the course of days or weeks, a healing ceremony takes place, overseen by a shaman (a priest with the ability to communicate directly with the spirit world) or medicine man (rarely a woman). Seated in the painting's center, the person to be healed absorbs power from Navajo ancestors and from the gods depicted in the painting. The careful production of sand paintings and the choice of an impermanent medium channel powerful forces of nature and ancestry, forces that are ultimately out of human control but which can be tapped to benefit the community in the physical realm by promoting food, health, harmony, and well-being.

For the Hopi of the southwestern United States, rituals highlight the cycles of nature that are central to their daily activities. *Kachinas*, or supernatural spirits, personify events and such natural elements as the solstices (the longest and the shortest days of the year, which mark the beginning of a new stage in the seasonal ritual cycle), patterns of stars (constellations), plants, and animals. During the planting season, masked dancers assume the likeness of the kachinas in annual festivals dedicated to rain, fertility, and good hunting. Along with the masqueraders, dolls give a physical form to these spirits. The kachina doll shown in **4.2.6** represents the Jemez kachina, which appears near the end of the season when the kachinas are about to leave the mesas (steep-sided, elevated plateaus where the Hopi live) for six months. The elaborate headdress on the Jemez kachina contains cloud symbols, denoting its effectiveness in bringing rain. The doll carries a rattle in one hand and a sprig of Douglas fir (here represented by a feather) in the other. As the first kachina to bring mature corn to the Hopi, this figure helps ensure a successful corn crop.

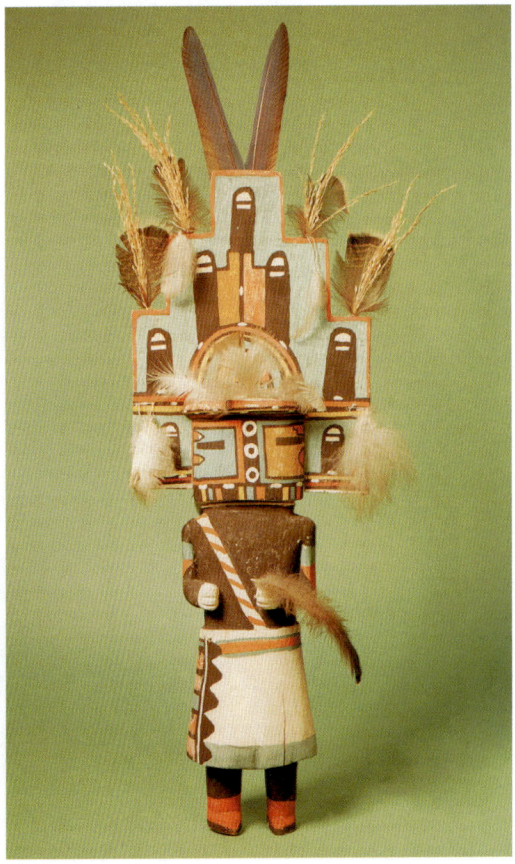

4.2.6 Hopi kachina doll, c. 1925. Wood, feathers, and pigment, height 25¼". Gustav Heye Center, New York (National Museum of the American Indian)

Icon: a religious image venerated by believers

Connecting with the Gods

Communication with the gods has been an important subject for art in many cultures, whether in the worship of multiple gods or just one. Sometimes special individuals serve as intermediaries between people and a deity. Rulers have been depicted interacting directly with divine beings or traveling into supernatural realms. Artworks showing such interactions reinforce the power of rulers by convincing their people that they are blessed, aided by the gods, and worthy of their exalted position.

The interaction between a ruler and a deity is the focal point of the Stela of Naram-Sin (**4.2.7**). Naram-Sin, an Akkadian king who ruled central Mesopotamia (part of modern-day Iraq) around 2254–2218 BCE, was head of both church and state. His stela commemorates the Akkadian military victory over the Lullubi people. The lower portions of the scene show signs of the battle that has taken place on a mountain. Above, Naram-Sin stands victorious near the summit, his horned helmet and larger size emphasizing his importance. The sun god is not depicted in human form but appears symbolically as a sunburst. Naram-Sin's location as close as possible to the sun god illustrates his own supreme, divine status in society and suggests that he was looked upon with approval by the many gods the Akkadians worshiped. As the godlike representative of his community, a ruler such as Naram-Sin needed to maintain a favorable connection with the supernatural realm in order to ensure continued prosperity for his kingdom.

In much Christian art, saints and mythological figures interact with God to provide role models or to help educate viewers about religious practices. During the Middle Ages, Christians in the Eastern Orthodox Church used **icons** (small portable religious images that depicted holy figures) as a focus of devotion and a source of inspiration. Icons were believed to have the power to communicate with God and sometimes even to have other miraculous powers. Many were painted on wood panels so they could be carried around, but some were attached to chapel screens in churches.

The portable icons were more accessible for ordinary people. They could also be transported from Constantinople in the Byzantine empire to distant places, such as Russia, in order to help spread and support Christian beliefs. The icons themselves were not worshiped as divine, but they became the subjects of intense reverence because they depicted individuals whose

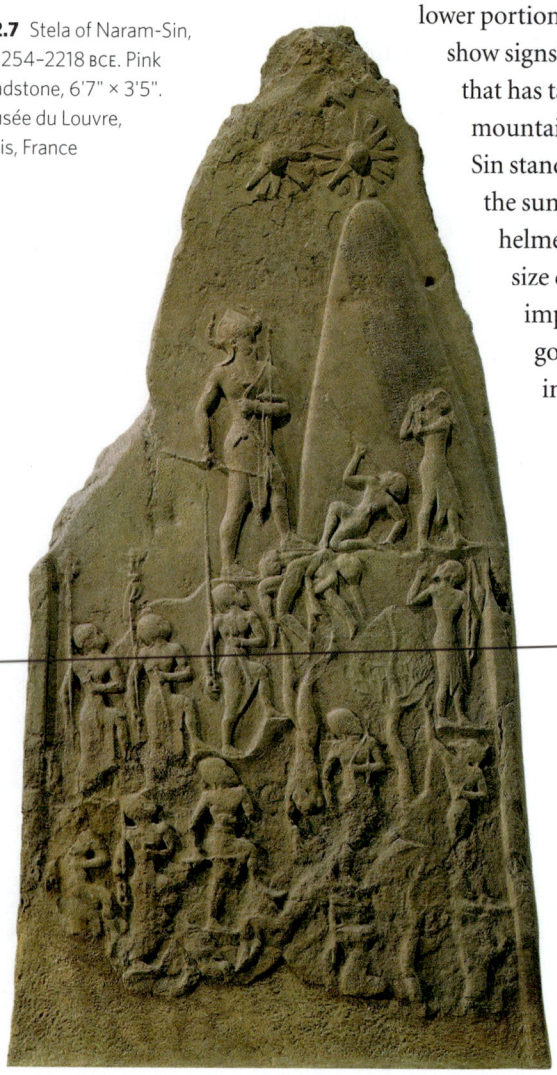

4.2.7 Stela of Naram-Sin, *c.* 2254–2218 BCE. Pink sandstone, 6'7" × 3'5". Musée du Louvre, Paris, France

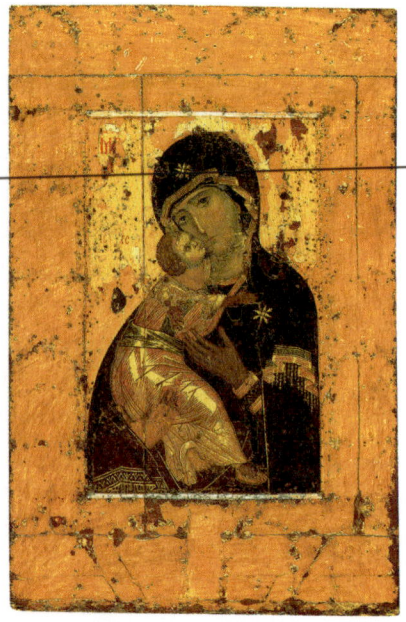

4.2.8 (right) *Virgin of Vladimir*, 12th century (before 1132). Tempera on panel, 30¾ × 21½". Tretyakov Gallery, Moscow, Russia

Linear outline: a line that clearly separates a figure from its surroundings
Stylized: art that represents objects in an exaggerated way to emphasize certain aspects of the object
Passion: the arrest, trial, and execution of Jesus Christ, and his sufferings during them

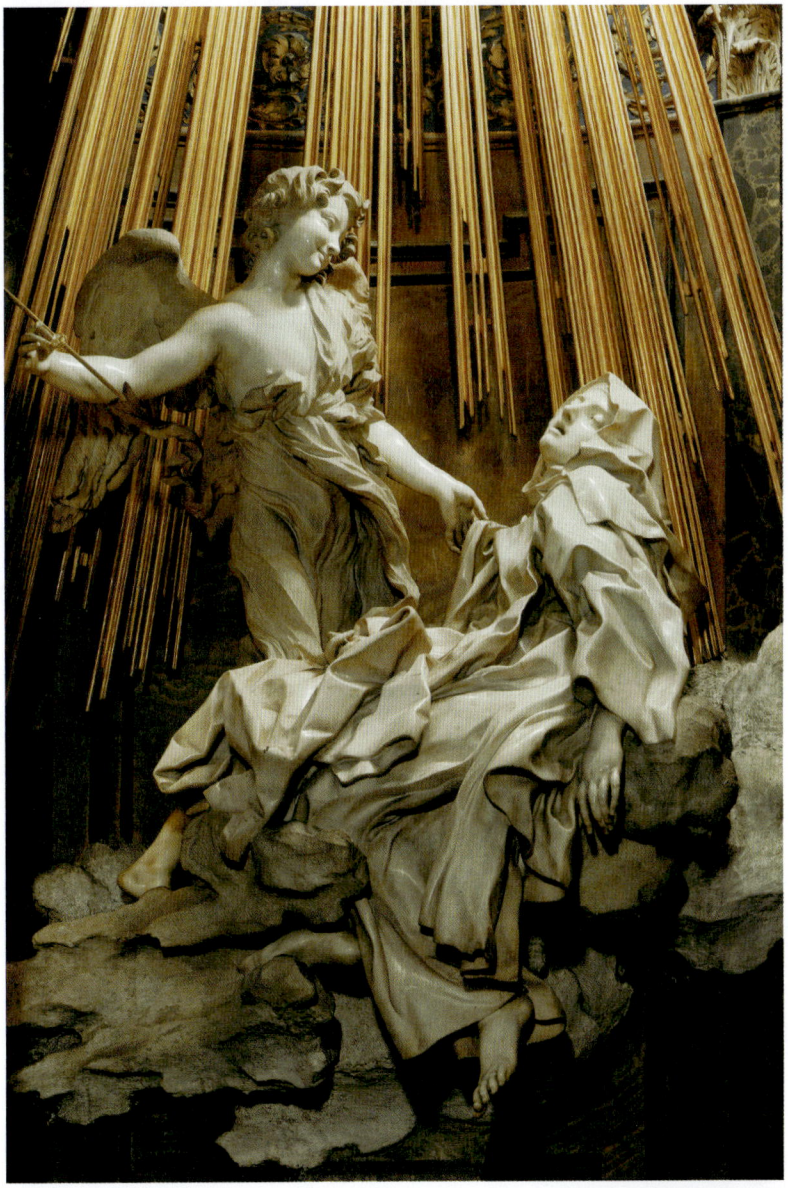

4.2.9 Gianlorenzo Bernini, *The Ecstasy of St. Teresa*, 1647–52. Polychromed marble, gilt, bronze, yellow glass, fresco, and stucco, height 4'11" (figures only). Cornaro Chapel, Santa Maria della Vittoria, Rome, Italy

saintliness meant that they were close to God, and therefore able to spread goodness.

The Orthodox Church required the form and content of icons to follow traditional rules. As a result, although each painting is unique, it has a family resemblance to other icons: gold backgrounds, **linear outlines**, and **stylized** but believable poses. It was important that the figures in the icons could be recognized by anyone who saw them. Thus the Madonna and Child were always shown with haloes to represent their holiness. The *Virgin of Vladimir* portrays Mary with her face touching Jesus to emphasize her virtue as the "Virgin of Loving Kindness" (**4.2.8**). This icon, probably made in the city of Constantinople (modern-day Istanbul), was intended to bless and protect the city in which it was housed (it has been in Moscow almost continuously since 1395). Only the faces are original; the rest of the panel, probably damaged by people touching it, has been repainted.

The Ecstasy of St. Teresa by Gianlorenzo Bernini (1598–1680) is another Christian artwork that is meant to inspire devotion and reverence (**4.2.9**). It was made between 1647 and 1652 to decorate a funerary chapel for the Cornaro family in the Church of Santa Maria della Vittoria in Rome, Italy. This massive sculpture (more than 11 ft. tall) depicts one of St. Teresa of Ávila's mystical visions: she is about to be pierced by an angel's arrow that will infuse her with divine love. The theatrical staging and the emphasis on dramatic light—created by the use of gilt bronze rays behind the figures and by the light falling from a hidden window above the sculpture—are typical of the Baroque style. Bernini's sculpture is executed with great attention to detail. The whole scene seems to take place in the clouds and the angel almost hovers above St. Teresa. Marble is made to suggest several different textures including smooth skin, gauzy fabric, clinging draperies, and the heavy wool of the nun's habit worn by the saint. The combination of accurate and believable details with an exaggerated picture of devotion reflects the Catholic Church's new emphasis at that time on believers establishing a strongly personal relationship with Christ. In Bernini's sculpture Christ's **Passion** is relived in the intensity of St. Teresa's piety, which serves as an example to be followed by the devout.

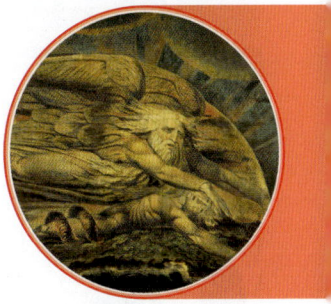

Because he was very religious but opposed to organized religion, William Blake interpreted the creation of man as anguished and full of suffering. Many of his artworks were inspired by his visions of angels, spirits, demons, and devils: see **3.7.14, p. 498**

Judgment and the Afterlife

Lintel: the horizontal beam over the doorway of a portal
Tympanum: an arched recess above a doorway, often decorated with carvings

As we live our lives, our choices determine the impact we will have and how we will be perceived. In many belief systems, the moral implications of our decisions have lasting consequences. As a result, the act of judging a life before the deceased is allowed to pass into the afterlife has been the theme of numerous artworks. In many judgment scenes, including those discussed here, scales are featured as a symbol of justice in which a life is "held in the balance" before the soul is allowed to pass on.

In ancient Egypt, the deceased were buried with a set of belongings that reflected their position in life. One of the most important of these possessions was a Book of the Dead, a scroll with spells and incantations designed to help the deceased navigate the passage into the afterlife. As we can see in the Book of the Dead that belonged to a scribe named Hunefer, who lived more than 3,000 years ago, a successful journey required proof that one had lived an honorable life and that proper respect had been paid to the gods (**4.2.10**).

At the top of the scroll, Hunefer pleads his case to the forty-two judges of the dead, represented here by just fourteen mummified deities because the artist did not have room to show them all.

In the bottom panel, Hunefer is escorted by Anubis (the jackal-headed god associated with mummification and the afterlife) to the scales where his soul will be weighed. As Ammit ("Eater of the Dead," with the head of a crocodile, mane and forequarters of a lion, and hindquarters of a hippopotamus) anxiously looks on, Anubis determines that Hunefer's soul, in the form of his heart in a canopic jar, is lighter than the ostrich feather it is weighed against. Having been proven worthy, Hunefer is presented by Horus (the falcon-headed god of the sun, sky, and war) to Osiris (god of goodness, vegetation, and death), who is seated on his throne. This Book of the Dead was placed in Hunefer's coffin in the hope that its script would be followed and he would successfully gain immortality in the afterlife.

In twelfth-century Europe, depictions of the Last Judgment took on an ominous tone in scenes showing the fate of the blessed and the damned side by side. In Gislebertus's version of *The Last Judgment* (**4.2.11**), the **lintel** underneath the main panel contains a row of figures awaiting judgment. The Romanesque characteristic of elongated and somewhat angular figures on the sculpture throughout the whole portal creates a visually dynamic tension.

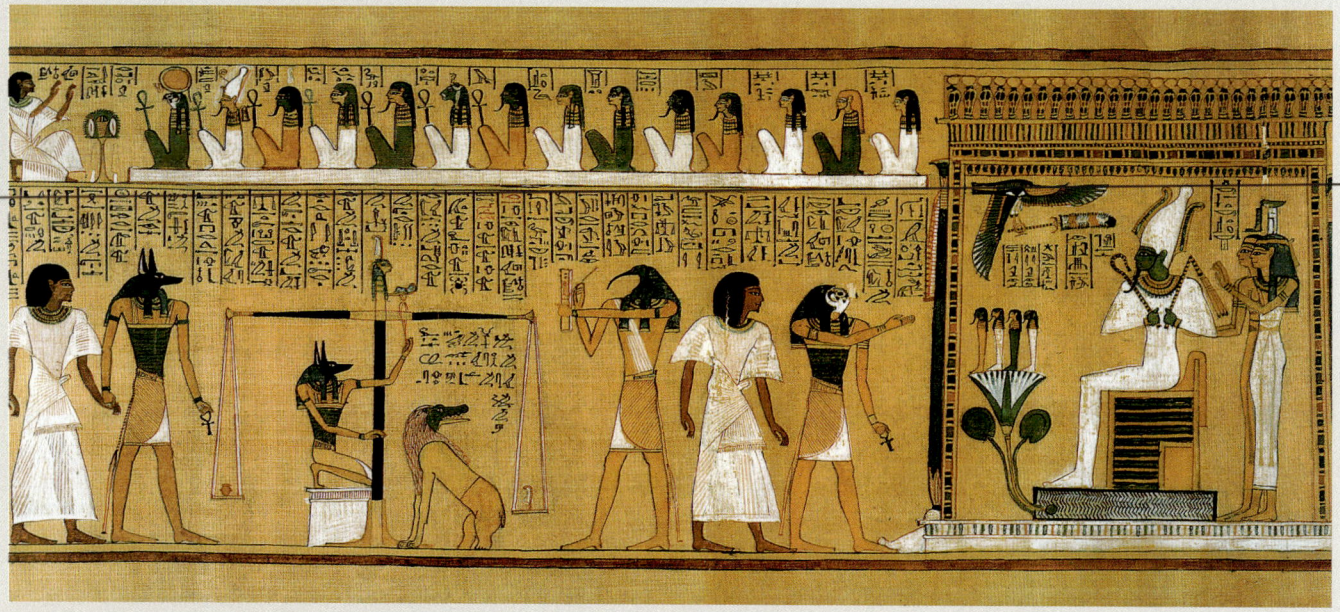

4.2.10 Book of the Dead of Hunefer: Last Judgment before Osiris, c. 1275 BCE. Painted papyrus, height 15⅜". British Museum, London, England

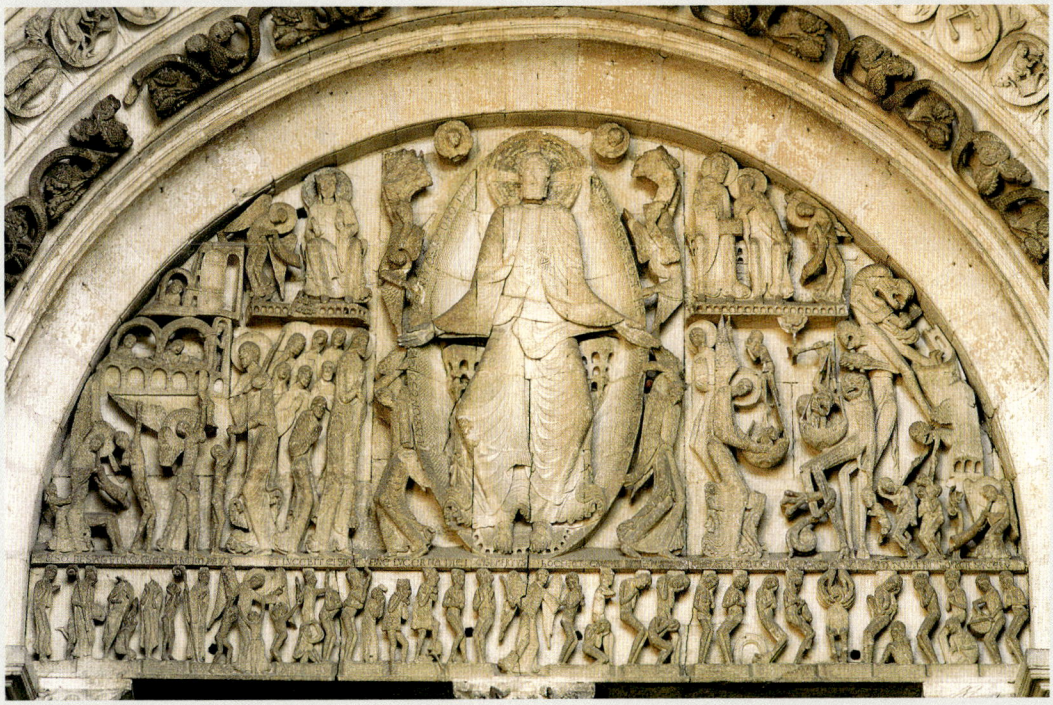

4.2.11 (left) Gislebertus, *The Last Judgment*, c. 1120–35. Tympanum from west Portal, Cathedral of Saint-Lazare, Autun, France

A pair of hands comes down from above to gather the eighth figure from the right for his weighing. In the center of the carved **tympanum** Christ is shown as larger than all the rest of the figures, indicating his key role in the judgment of humankind. On his right (our left) are the angels and the souls of the blessed, who will go on to live out eternity in heaven. Their bodies are smooth, elegant, and peaceful. On Christ's left are the scales in which souls are weighed, and the ravaged bodies of the damned. Their horrid, grotesque appearance was meant to send a strong message to churchgoers about the consequences of living a sinful life and give them a glimpse of the misery of spending the afterlife in hell.

The Dutch painter Johannes Vermeer (1632–1675) subtly includes religion in a scene from everyday life in his *Woman Holding a Balance* (**4.2.12**). Following a style that was popular at the time, Vermeer focuses on an ordinary moment, in which the woman is standing at a table by a window near her open jewelry boxes. The painting on the wall behind her provides a symbolic backdrop for her actions. It shows the Last Judgment, with Christ in the sky above and the souls to be judged below, and serves as a reminder that life is short and that it is important to be honest and decent. The scales the woman holds are empty, but perfectly balanced, suggesting that one's actions rather than one's possessions are the true indication of a person's worth.

4.2.12 (below) Johannes Vermeer, *Woman Holding a Balance*, c. 1664. Oil on canvas, 16¾ × 16". National Gallery of Art, Washington, D.C.

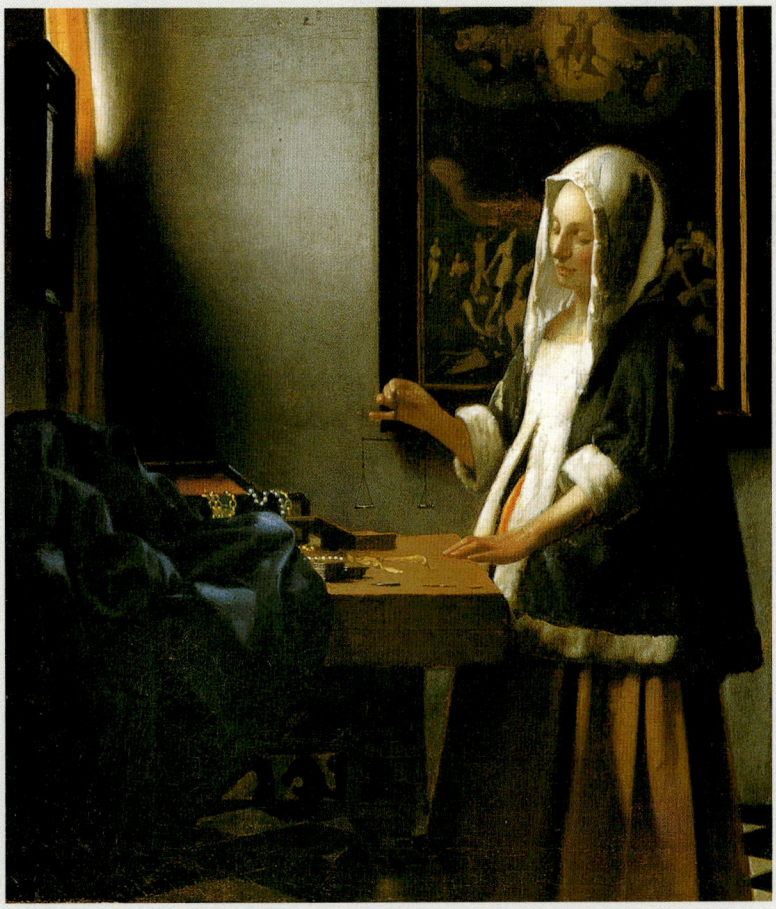

Sacred Places

We all have places that restore our souls. Whether it is the mountains, the beach, or the family dinner table, there are places that allow us to feel connected and at peace. In addition to the places themselves, certain artworks represent personal retreat or communal worship as sites of reverence, renewal, and contemplation. By marking these sites and communicating these experiences, artists and architects give us a sense of their connectedness to nature, religion, or community.

Places that people returned to again and again, such as the **prehistoric** caves of Lascaux and the **catacombs** of Rome, were clearly important for their users. Whether for memorial or religious purposes, such places were adorned with artworks giving their sacred nature a new dimension.

The walls of the Lascaux Caves in southern France (**4.2.13a**) were painted sometime between around 17,000 and 15,000 BCE. One section is densely packed with paintings of animals (**4.2.13b**). The effort required to paint the walls of the caves with so many images suggests that these animals, encountered on a daily basis, were extremely important. Some of the most magnificent paintings are found in the Hall of the Bulls in the main cave, which is 66 ft. wide and 16 ft. high. The hall is near the entrance to the system of caves and, as its name suggests, it is decorated with outlines and realistic details of numerous bulls—one of them more than 15 ft. long. The paintings in this area overlap, indicating that the site was visited repeatedly, that it was decorated over a period of time, and that making these paintings in this particular place was significant. They mark it as a location that was sacred in some way to the people who used it.

Because the makers of the paintings at Lascaux had no system of writing, we must interpret the stories of these images from the

4.2.13a (below, top) Plan of Lascaux Caves, Dordogne, France

4.2.13b (below, bottom) Hall of the Bulls. Pigment on limestone rock, Lascaux Caves

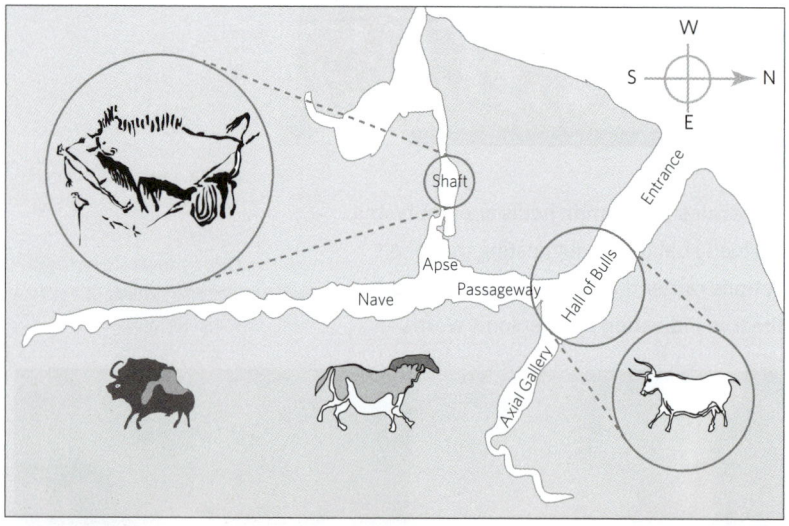

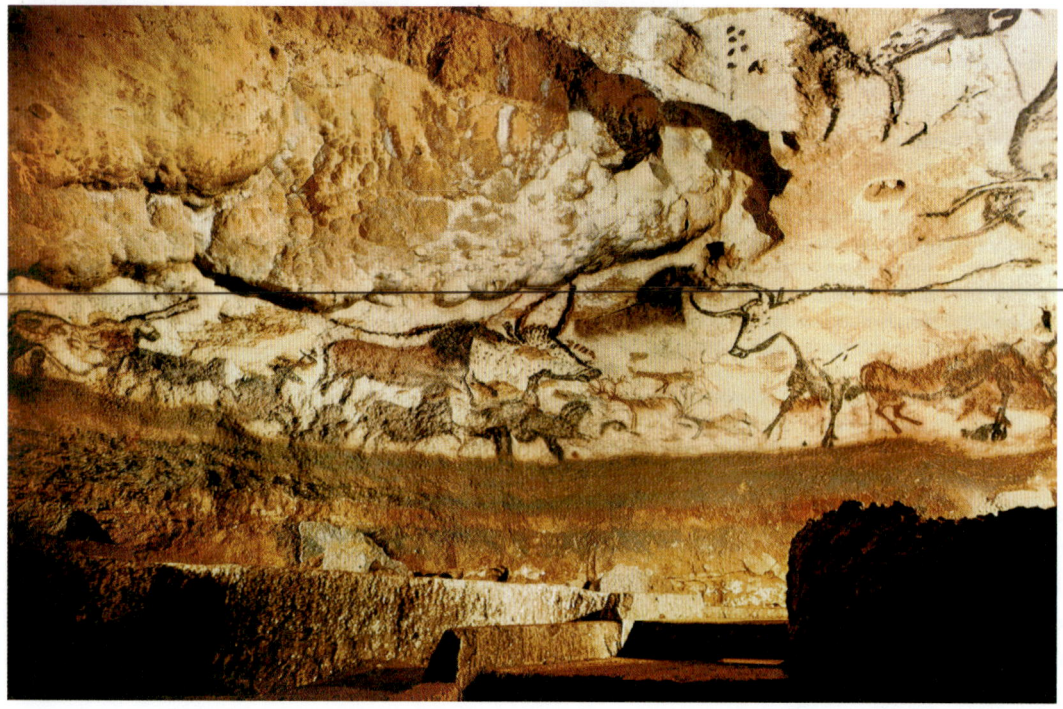

Prehistoric: dating from the period of human existence before the invention of writing
Catacombs: an underground system of tunnels used for burying and commemorating the dead
Fresco: a technique where the artist paints onto freshly applied plaster. From the Italian *fresco*, "fresh"

pictures themselves. In addition to telling stories, prehistoric cave paintings may also have been used to teach hunting and to represent shamanic or ritual practices. Paintings similar to those at Lascaux have been found in other places in France and also in Spain, indicating that these paintings were part of a wider cultural practice for people who either moved from place to place or shared ideas with others.

The human desire to paint important or sacred places can also be seen in the catacombs constructed outside the city of Rome, Italy, between the second and fourth centuries CE (**4.2.14a** and **b**). An underground system of tunnels measuring between 60 and 90 miles in length and containing the ancient remains of 4 million people, the catacombs were sacred spaces for Romans, who held a variety of religious beliefs and went there to visit their ancestors' burial places. While pagan Romans practiced both cremation and burial of the dead, burial was especially important for Jews and Christians. The catacombs were also used as temples for religious observances, a space where Christians could gather, and hiding places for fugitives.

As with Lascaux, the catacombs contain paintings in areas used for different purposes. In the catacombs, **frescoes** ornament both the burial areas and the rooms in which people could gather. The paintings include pagan, Jewish, and Christian scenes. Banquet scenes or images of shepherds, for example, could be seen by Romans of all three faiths and interpreted differently according to the viewer's religion. The central figure in the Christian fresco from the catacombs of Priscilla stands in a praying position (**4.2.14b**). Such a pose appears in pagan art, but it has a distinct meaning for Christians, who understand the figure to be praying to their God. Using familiar imagery, such as this prayerful person, probably made it easier for people to convert from other religions to

4.2.14a (below, top) Plan and section showing part of the catacomb of Priscilla, 2nd and 3rd centuries CE. Via Salaria, Rome, Italy

4.2.14b (below, bottom) Fresco from the Cubicle of the Velata, catacomb of Priscilla, 2nd and 3rd centuries CE. Via Salaria, Rome, Italy

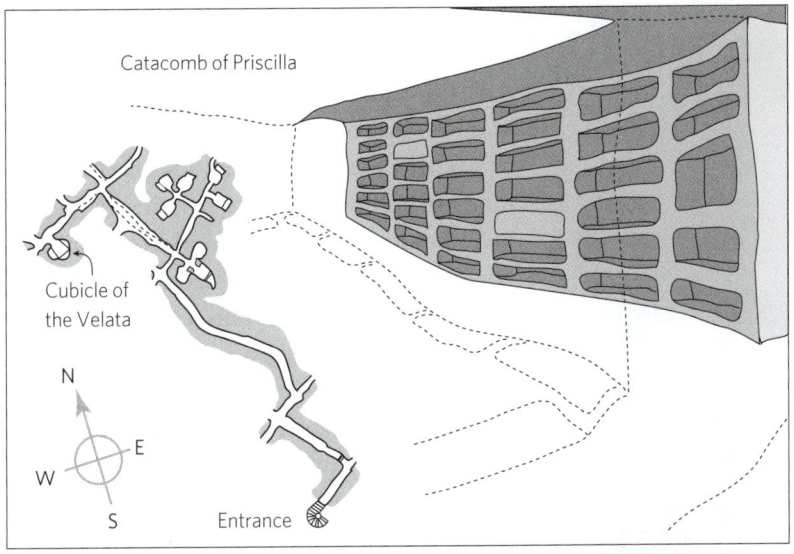

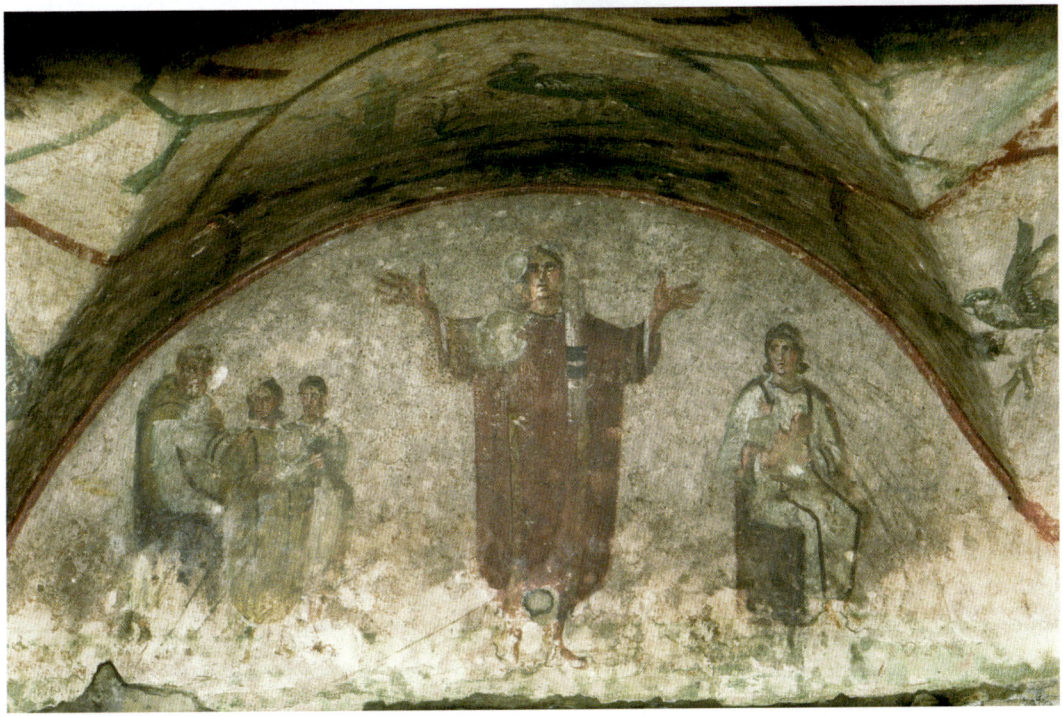

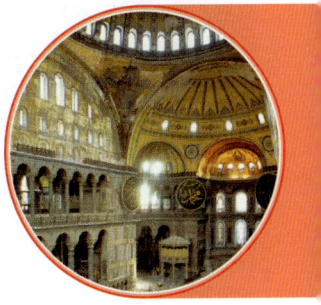

The structure of the Hagia Sophia is so impressive that it has transcended religious affiliations. It was built in Constantinople as a Byzantine basilica for the Eastern Orthodox Christian Church. It later became a mosque and it is now a museum: see **2.5.19, p. 270**

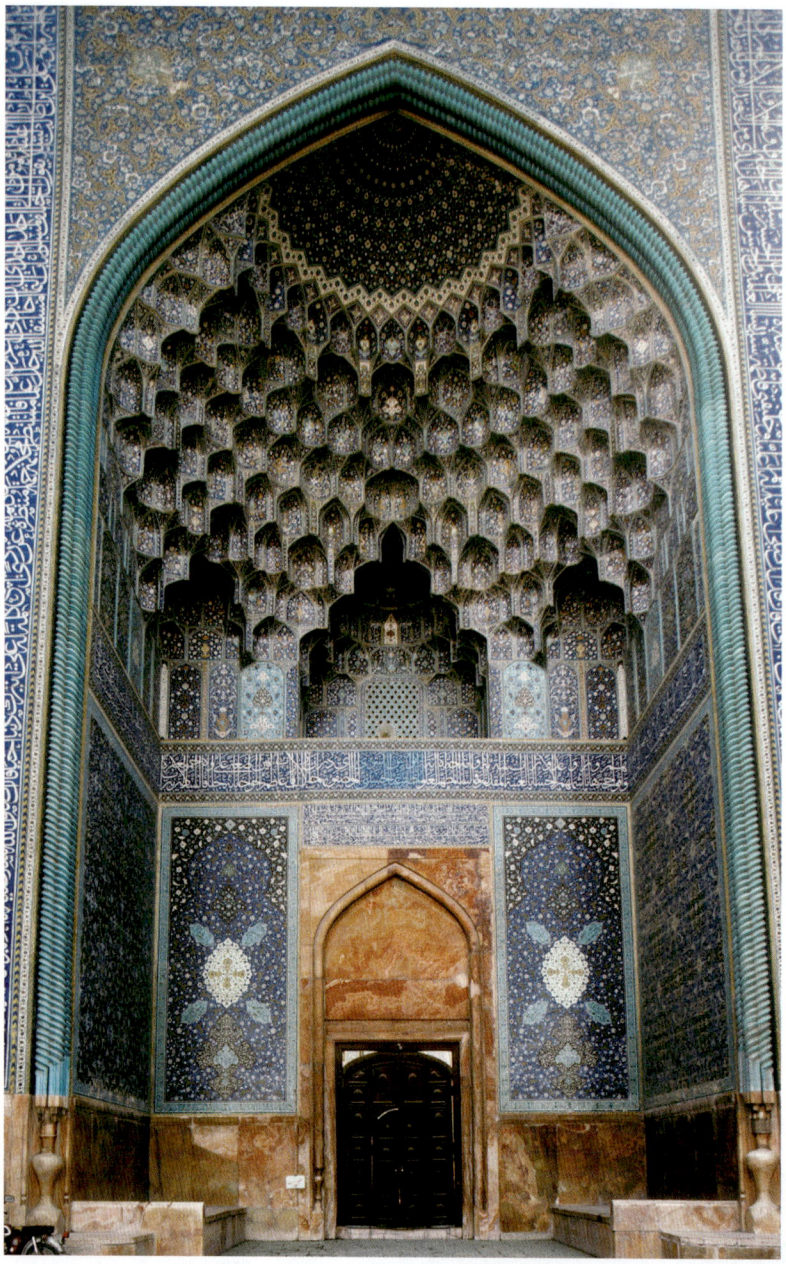

4.2.15 Main entrance portal (*iwan*) with *muqarnas* vaulting. Masjid-i-Shah, early 17th century, Isfahan, Iran

Christianity while also conveying a clear message to existing believers.

Muslims gather to pray to Allah in a building called a mosque. Because mosques are often the largest structures in a city, they have also played a significant role in community activities when used as schools or hospitals. In addition to the Taj Mahal (see Images Related to 4.2, p. 590), Shah Jahan was responsible for the building of Masjid-i-Shah, also known as The Mosque of the Imam in Isfahan, Iran. This mosque has four *iwans*, or vaulted entrances, between the courtyard and the mosque's interior. Other defining features of mosques include large towers (minarets) that rise above the city to call citizens to prayer, pointed arches, large pools for cleansing before prayer, and a *mihrab* (a special prayer niche). Muslims must pray five times a day facing the direction of the city of Mecca. The mihrab, placed on the wall oriented toward Mecca (*qibla* wall), indicates the correct direction for worshipers' prayers.

The walls of mosques are often decorated with elaborate designs. Small glazed tiles take the form of geometric shapes and blocks, organic floral designs, and different forms of calligraphic script that convey core concepts of the Muslim faith. A fine example of complex Islamic geometric patterning can be seen in the honeycomb design of the *muqarnas* (or stalactite vaults) in one iwan entrance to the Masjid-i-Shah (**4.2.15**). The muqarnas are decorative elements originally used to cover the tombs of holy men. The shape of the muqarnas in the pointed vault resembles a series of small domes lined up in rows and stacked on top of one another. One description suggests that the muqarnas sanctify the space by symbolizing "the rotating dome of heaven."

Unlike Christianity and Islam, the Shinto religion in Japan focuses on the here and now and reveres nature itself as a deity. For example, Shinto recognizes a mountain as a sacred object because it is the source of water for rice cultivation. Such a mountain was once worshiped directly, but over time shrines were built as places to worship a god, known as a *kami*, that was important to a particular area or community. Marking a site as sacred is a common practice in Shinto, which emphasizes the ways in which such natural elements as the sun, mountains, water, and trees are connected to well-being. These sites, such as the Grand Shrine of Ise, or Ise Jingu, started with small piles of stones in an area surrounded by stone enclosures, which have gradually evolved to include buildings, fences, and gates.

Ise Jingu is one of thousands of shrines throughout Japan dedicated to the sun goddess Amataerasu Omikami. Local residents visit the shrine to revere the goddess and seek her assistance. The site is now marked by a stately **A-framed** wooden building that is simple in

A-frame: an ancient form of structural support, made out of beams arranged so that the shape of the building resembles a capital letter A

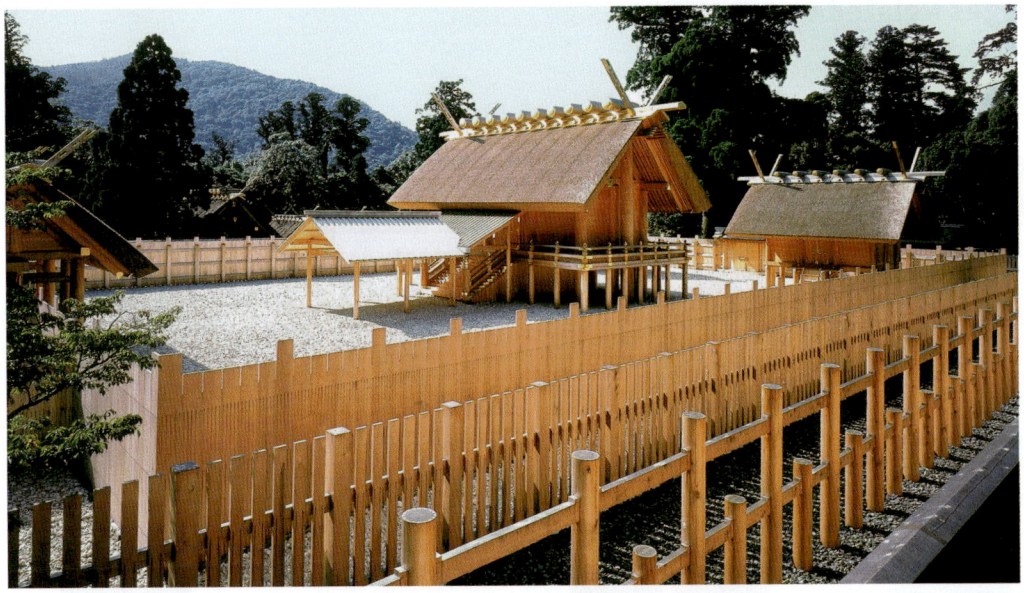

4.2.16 Ise Jingu, site dates from 4th century CE, rebuilt 1993. Mie Prefecture, Japan

design and made with natural materials (**4.2.16**). Because nature is cyclical, the shrine must also be renewed and refreshed. Since 690 CE, Ise Jingu has been rebuilt every twenty years with a special ceremony in which meals are shared with the kami, infusing the everyday act of eating with ritual significance.

Personal Paths to Spirituality

As we have seen in this chapter, many people develop their own approaches to spirituality, whether within an organized religion or independently. For some people, art works as an effective channel for not only expressing those beliefs, but also exploring them. The possible methods of expression and exploration are endless but include abstraction, visionary constructions, focus on personal journeys, and the search for one's inner light.

Unlike some of the structures affiliated with specific religions that we have looked at in this chapter, the Rothko Chapel in Houston, Texas, is a place of worship open to people of all beliefs (**4.2.17**). The chapel's octagonal interior walls hold fourteen paintings by the Russian-born American **Abstract Expressionist** painter Mark Rothko (1903–1970). Rothko worked closely with the architects on the designs for the chapel. He wanted his paintings to be hung a certain distance from the floor, presented in low lighting, and shown together in a group in order to create an environment that enveloped and transported viewers beyond their everyday experience.

The canvases at the Rothko Chapel employ a restricted, dark palette of colors ranging from maroon and plum to black. The fields of color are intense and powerful, creating a tranquil and contemplative atmosphere. The chapel marks a culmination in the artist's search for the simplest means to express universal truths that are spiritual in nature but unconnected to any particular religious experience or doctrine. The Rothko Chapel has become a sacred place for worship, a site for performances and scholarly lectures, and a space for visitors to contemplate while immersed in an experience that integrates Rothko's paintings with architecture.

Abstract Expressionism: a mid-twentieth-century artistic style characterized by its capacity to convey intense emotions using non-representational images

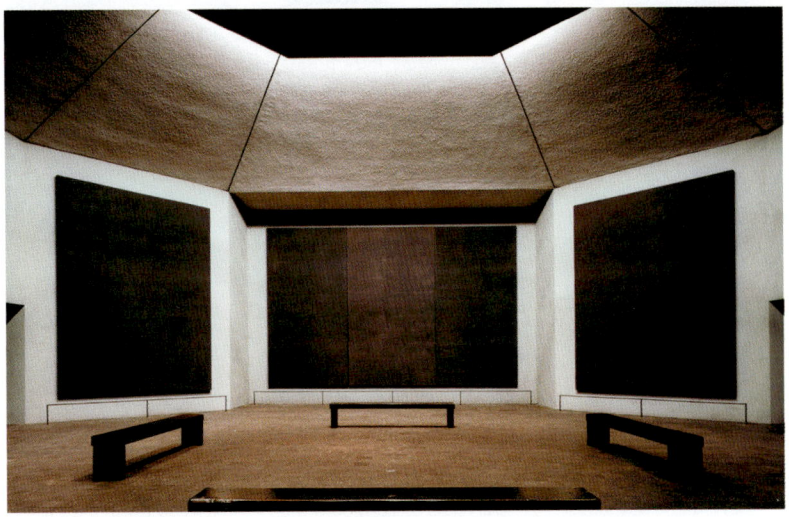

4.2.17 Rothko Chapel, 1966–71. Menil Collection, Houston, Texas

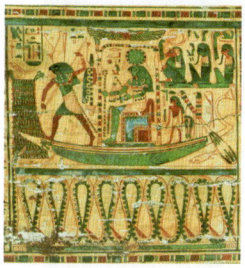

0.0.1 *The Journey of the Sun God Re*, detail from coffin, Egypt, 990–969 BCE, p. 20

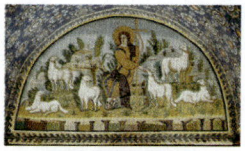

3.2.5 Good Shepherd, mosaic, Ravenna, Italy, 425–46 CE, p. 393

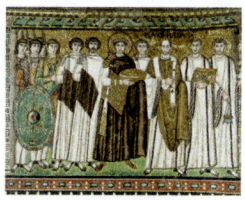

3.2.10 Emperor Justinian, glass mosaic, Ravenna, Italy, c. 547 CE, p. 397

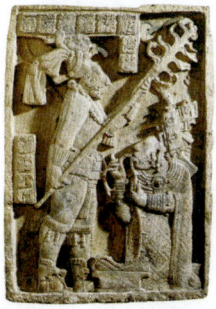

4.6.5 Maya lintel showing Shield Jaguar and Lady Xoc, c. 725 CE, p. 632

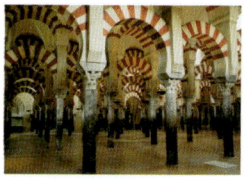

1.9.9 Great Mosque of Córdoba, Spain, 784–86 CE, p. 165

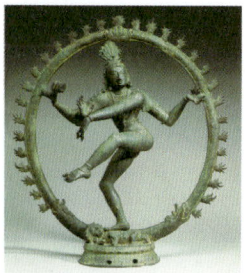

4.3.12 *Shiva Nataraja (Lord of the Dance)*, Chola period, India, 11th century, p. 599

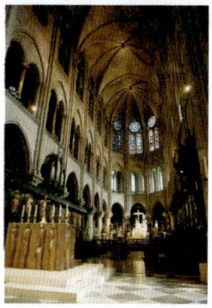

4.1.1 Notre Dame Cathedral, Paris, France, 1163–1250, p. 565

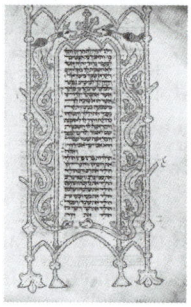

1.1.6a Franco-German hand, *Pentateuch*, 13th–14th century, p. 47

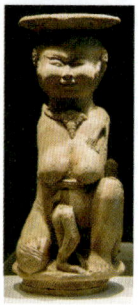

2.6.3 *The Mother Goddess Men Brajut*, Indonesian, c. 14th–15th century, p. 287

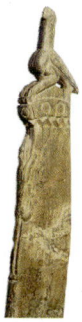

3.5.10 Bird on top of stone monolith, Great Zimbabwe, 15th century, p. 452

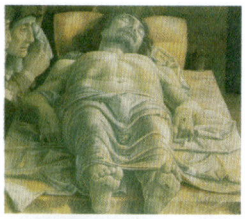

4.3.3 Andrea Mantegna, *Dead Christ*, c. 1480, p. 593

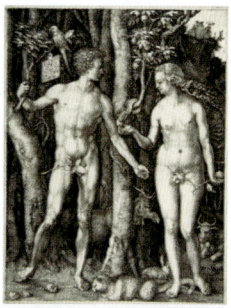

2.3.8 Albrecht Dürer, *Adam and Eve*, 1504, p. 231

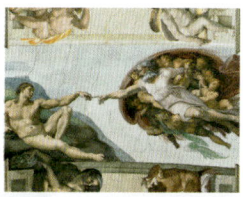

3.6.9b Michelangelo, detail of *Creation of Adam*, 1508–12, p. 468

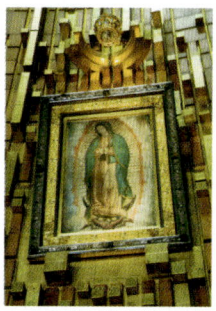

0.0.8 *The Virgin of Guadalupe*, Mexico City, 1531, p. 25

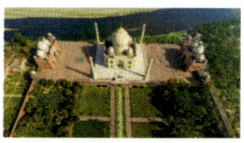

1.6.15a Taj Mahal, Agra, India, 1632–43, p. 136

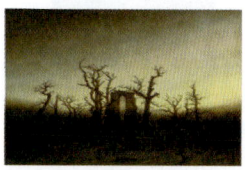

0.0.22 Caspar David Friedrich, *Abbey Among Oak Trees*, 1809–10, p. 37

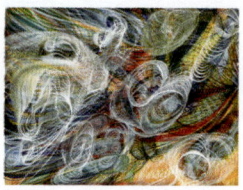

1.1.17 Georgiana Houghton, *Glory Be to God*, c. 1868, p. 53

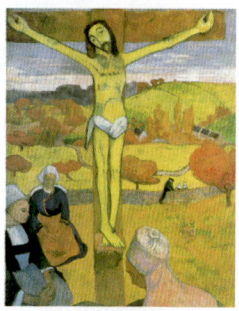

1.4.32 Paul Gauguin, *The Yellow Christ*, 1889, p. 111

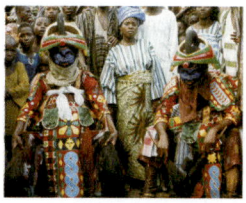

4.1.10 Pair of Gèlèdé masqueraders, Idahin, Benin, 1971, p. 572

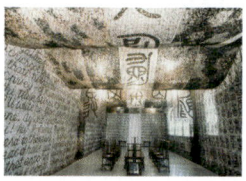

4.1.11 Wenda Gu, "China Monument: Temple of Heaven," 1998, p. 573

4.3 Art and the Cycle of Life

> How strange is the lot of us mortals! Each of us is here for a brief sojourn; for what purpose he knows not, though he senses it. But without deeper reflection one knows from daily life that one exists for other people.
>
> (Albert Einstein, physicist and Nobel Prize winner)

Human cultures from the earliest times to the twenty-first century have been deeply concerned with fundamental questions of existence: where do we come from? What happens when we die? What lies beyond death? These persistent concerns, not surprisingly, have also been a frequent subject of works of art.

In this chapter, we look at the ways in which artists have examined the cycle of life. Visual artists have dealt with topics as unfathomable as the beginning of human existence, as miraculous as the birth of a child, as enduring as natural forces or the passage of time, and as overwhelming as the finality of death. The examination of life's mysteries takes the form of mythical visions, narrative accounts, and direct portrayals of life's beginnings, its endings, and what happens in between.

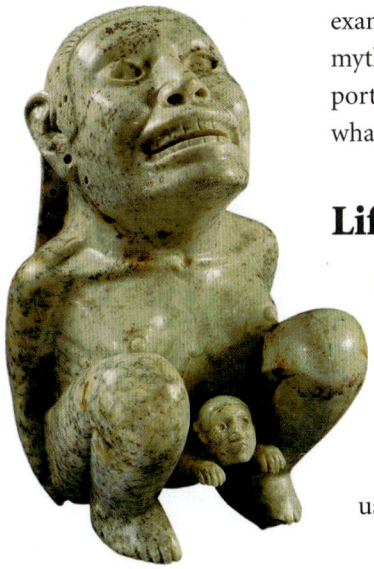

4.3.1 Tlazolteotl giving birth to the maize god, c. 1500. Aztec granite carving, 8 × 4¾ × 5⅞". Dumbarton Oaks Museum, Washington, D.C.

Life's Beginnings and Endings

Stories about the beginning of civilization and the creation of humankind are found throughout history in cultures across the globe. Creation myths use nature and natural occurrences, such as the movements of the stars or the actions of animals, to help us come to grips with concepts that we may not understand intellectually, such as the fact of life itself. Equally important are stories that tell about the process of childbirth and emphasize how we are connected to our family members. Artworks with such subjects often reflect the beliefs of an entire community.

For some cultures, such as the Aztecs of central Mexico, it was important to mark the physical, if still mystical, beginnings of human life. For the Aztecs, a woman giving birth was seen as a female warrior going to battle on behalf of the state. Women who died in childbirth were afforded the same respect as men who died on the battlefield; they resided in the same final resting place as heroes, accompanying the sun on its daily journey through the sky. The goddess Tlazolteotl, an Earth Mother and patron of childbirth, was known as the "filth eater" because she visited people at the end of their lives and absolved or ate their sins. A stone sculpture of Tlazolteotl shows her in the act of giving birth (**4.3.1**). The grimace on her face resembles that of a skull, and a tiny figure, a miniature adult, emerges from her body. Female deities worshiped by the Aztecs, such as Tlazolteotl, often had dual personalities; Tlazolteotl was responsible for bringing disease as well as curing it. Not only were these deities acknowledged as life-givers, but they were also feared as powerful and terrifying.

While the Tlazolteotl sculpture shows a semi-symbolic representation of childbirth, the Dutch artist Rineke Dijkstra (b. 1959) highlights some of the stark realities of birth in her *Mothers* series. "Julie" (**4.3.2**) captures a mother and her newborn baby just one hour after delivery, at a time and in a way that defies most expectations of mother-and-child imagery. They are standing against a cold, anonymous wall. Their position starkly exposes the vulnerability, even shock, that both mother and baby probably feel. Dijkstra makes public a time in a woman's life that is now generally considered private and personal. Inspired by watching the birth of a friend's baby, Dijkstra's photographs capture the awkwardness and enduring strength of the early moments of a new life.

In addition to life's beginnings, artists have also pondered physical death and created images of the deceased. Christian artists during the **Renaissance** often depicted the damaged body of Christ after his crucifixion. Such images were important because they emphasized the miraculous nature of Christ's later resurrection, and also the concept of eternal life after death, which is at the core of Christianity. The Italian artist Andrea Mantegna (*c.* 1431–1506) created a direct and intimate view of the body in *Dead Christ* (**4.3.3**). Because Mantegna has dramatically **foreshortened** the scene, we are first confronted by the stigmata (the wounds Christ suffered while hanging on the cross) in his feet and, further into the picture, in his hands. His body, covered in carefully depicted drapery, extends away from us on a marble slab. Beyond the muscular torso, we see his lifeless face. By Christ's side are the Virgin Mother and Mary Magdalene, who are mostly cropped out of the picture. While their grief adds to the atmosphere of the scene, the artist focuses our attention on the immediacy of Christ's body and the fact that he is no longer alive.

Perhaps because we are somewhat detached from death, or perhaps out of a sense of propriety, contemporary images of the deceased are not as common as they were during the Renaissance. Photographs of the dead can be especially shocking because today we no longer have such a direct relationship with the dead as people did in the past. Then, loved ones died at home, not in hospitals; bodies were laid out for burial by family members,

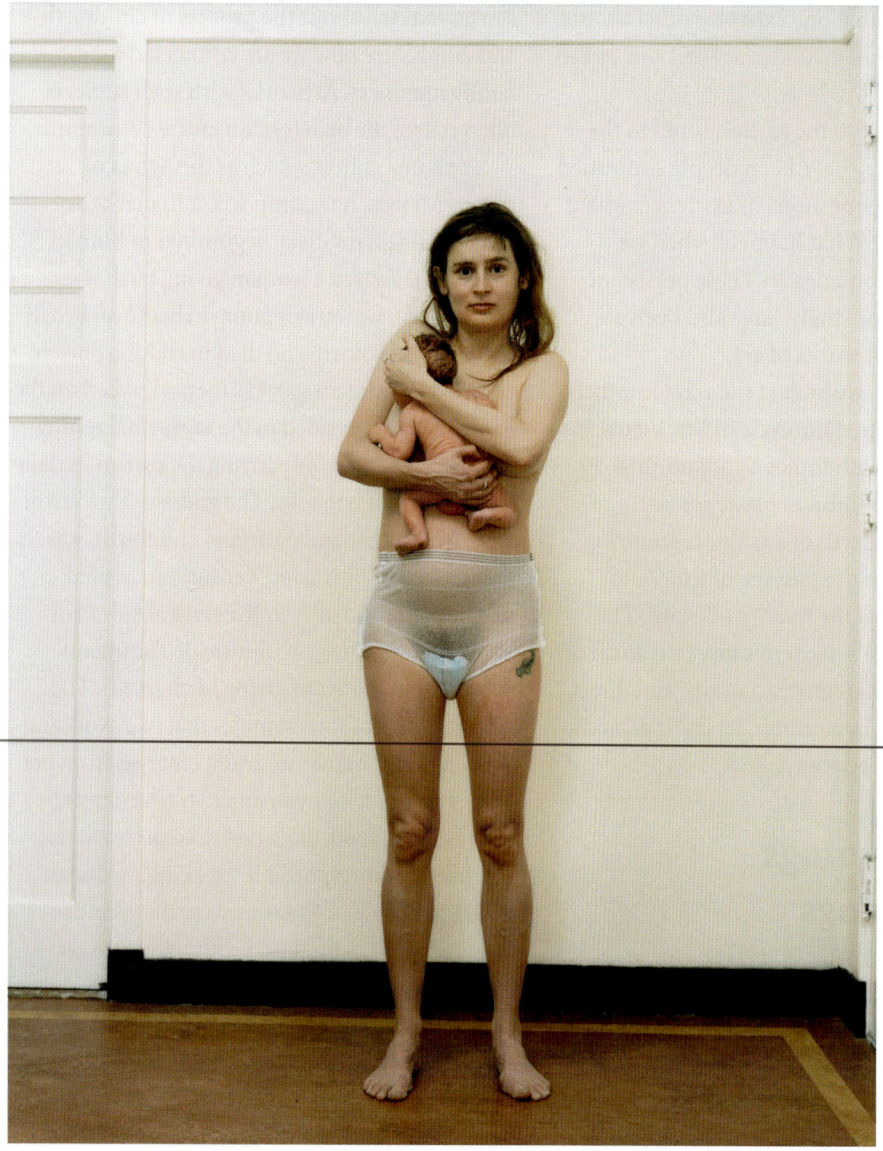

4.3.2 Rineke Dijkstra, "Julie, Den Haag, The Netherlands, February 29, 1994," from the *Mothers* series. C-print, 60¼ × 50¾"

Renaissance: a period of cultural and artistic change in Europe from the fourteenth to the seventeenth century

Foreshortened: a perspective technique that depicts a form at a very oblique (often dramatic) angle to the viewer in order to show depth in space

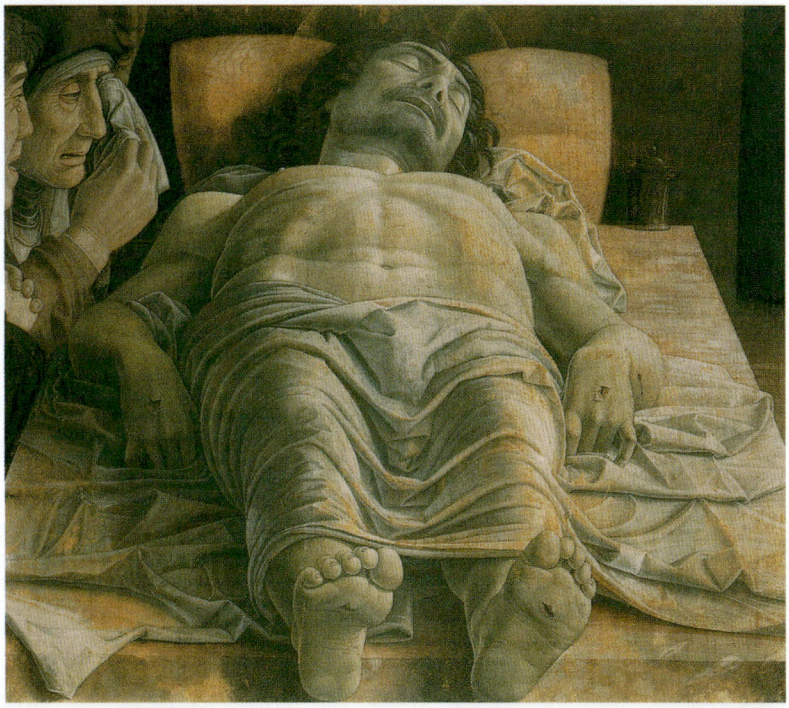

4.3.3 Andrea Mantegna, *Dead Christ*, c. 1480. Tempera on canvas, 26¾ × 31⅞". Pinoteca di Brera, Milan, Italy

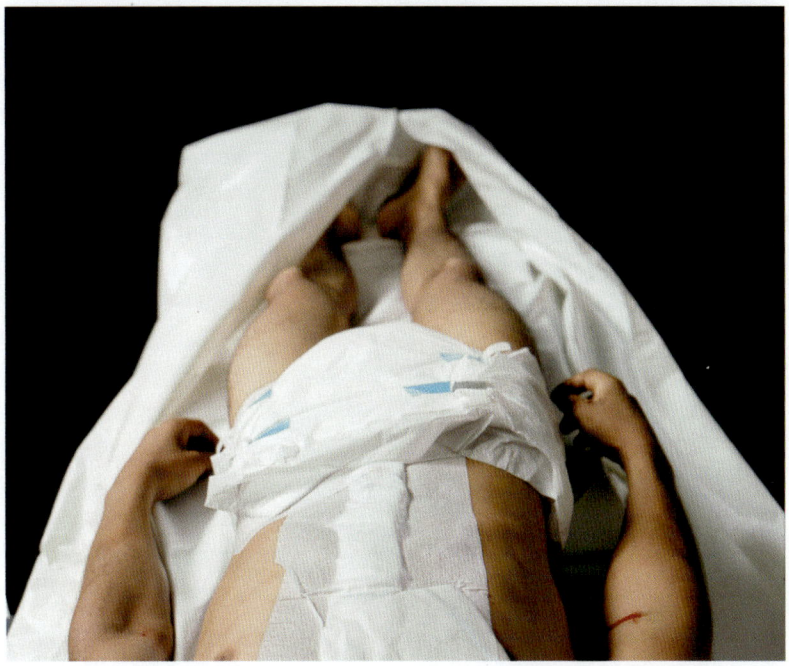

4.3.4 Andres Serrano, *The Morgue (Gun Murder)*, 1992. Cibachrome print, 50 × 60"

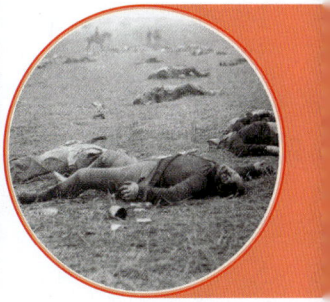

One of the most common subjects for photographers during the Civil War was dead bodies on the battlefield. The technology at the time required long exposure times, making it hard to photograph people in motion or action: see **4.7.1, p. 638**

not by funeral homes. The American artist Andres Serrano (b. 1950) made a series of photographs in a morgue in which the subjects are identified only by the manner of their deaths. The composition of *The Morgue (Gun Murder)* (**4.3.4**), with the feet pointing away from the viewer, is the opposite of Mantegna's *Dead Christ*. The dark background, the white bandages and body bag, and the strong lighting create a sense of drama and contrast. The formal beauty of the image itself contradicts the shocking reality that this person, whose identity we will never know, was murdered. As Serrano's photograph demonstrates, the visceral quality of art can often challenge us intellectually. Even if we do not find the imagery pleasant, it can convey a powerful message and provide us with a deeper understanding of difficult subjects.

Gateway to Art: The Taj Mahal
Mumtaz Mahal: A Life Remembered

For the other Taj Mahal Gateway boxes, see p. 136, p. 272, and p. 412

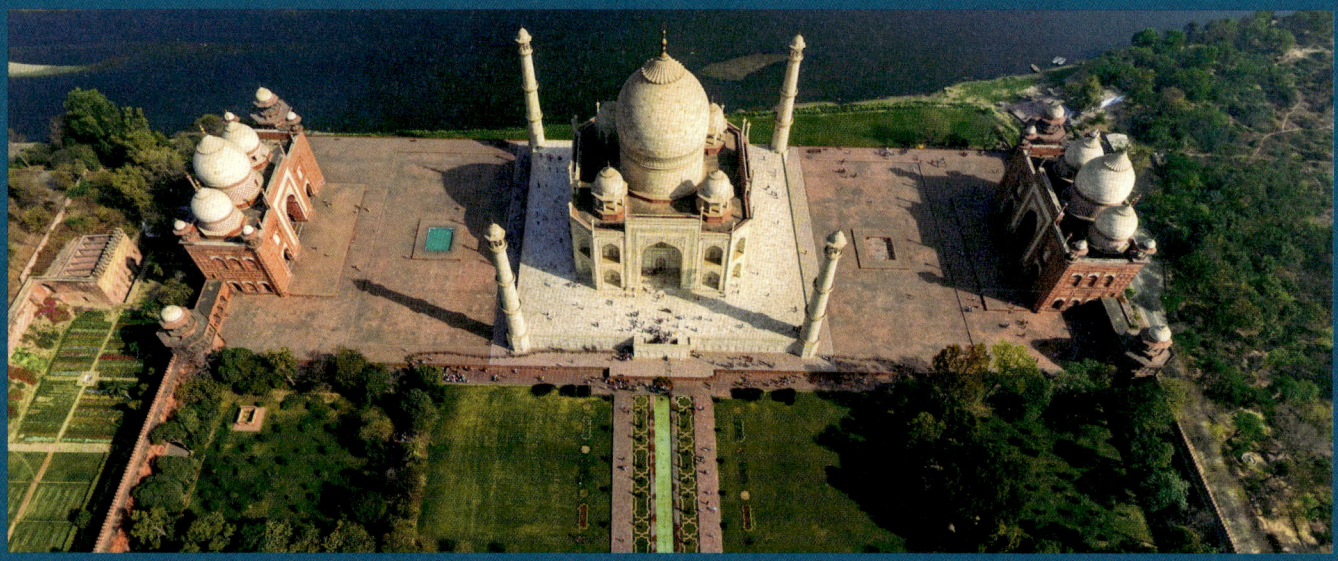

4.3.5a The Taj Mahal, designed by Ustad Ahmad Lahauri, Abd al-Karim Ma'mur Khan, and Makramat Khan; commissioned by Shah Jahan, 1632–43. Marble archtecture. Agra, India

When Shah Jahan commissioned the Taj Mahal (**4.3.5a**) he was grieving the loss of his wife Mumtaz Mahal, the love of his life. She was a princess of Persian nobility, born Arjumand Banu Begum in 1593. Most of what is known about her relates to her life as a Mughal empress, but she became legendary for her beauty, grace, and compassion as well as for the love she and Shah Jahan shared. Arjumand was Shah Jahan's third wife and by all accounts his favorite. They became engaged when she was fourteen and married five years later on May 10, 1612, a date the court astrologers calculated as auspicious and most likely to ensure a happy marriage. Shah Jahan bestowed on her the name Mumtaz Mahal meaning "Chosen One of the Palace" and he also gave her the royal seal Muhr Uzah, which was a great honor. She traveled with him on military campaigns but was said to have no political aspirations of her own.

Mumtaz died in 1631 at the age of thirty-nine giving birth to their fourteenth child. (Maternal death and infant mortality were common in India at the time: seven of Mumtaz and Shah Jahan's children died at birth or when they were very young.) The entire kingdom was ordered into mourning for two years. Perhaps responding to a deathbed wish, Shah Jahan set about building the world's richest mausoleum in history, which took twenty-two years in total. In keeping with the symmetry of the grounds, he planned to have a matching black marble mausoleum made for himself on the other side of the river. His successor, Aurangzeb, abandoned that scheme, and Shah Jahan's sarcophagus (the larger of the two in **4.3.5b**) now rests beside Mumtaz Mahal's in the crypts of the Taj Mahal. The surfaces of the crypt and sarcophagi are covered with calligraphy and floral motifs. The Arabic script on Mumtaz's sacred tomb includes the ninety names of God and a Koranic prayer recited by angels asking for the faithful to be allowed into paradise.

4.3.5b The crypt of the Taj Mahal

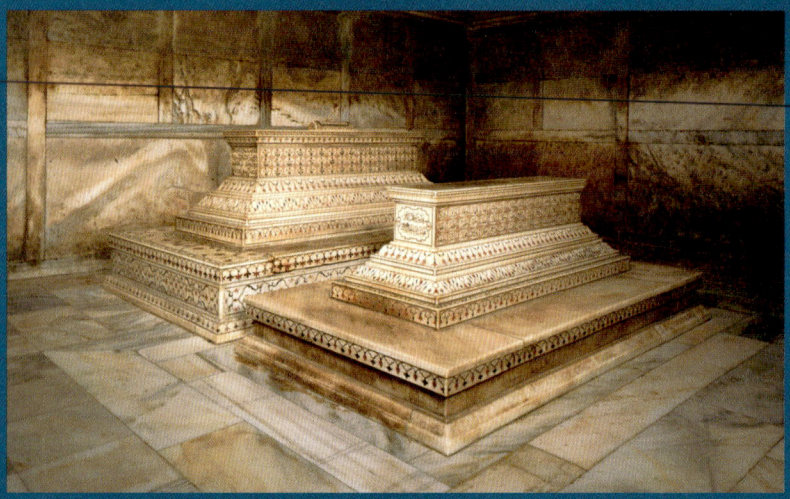

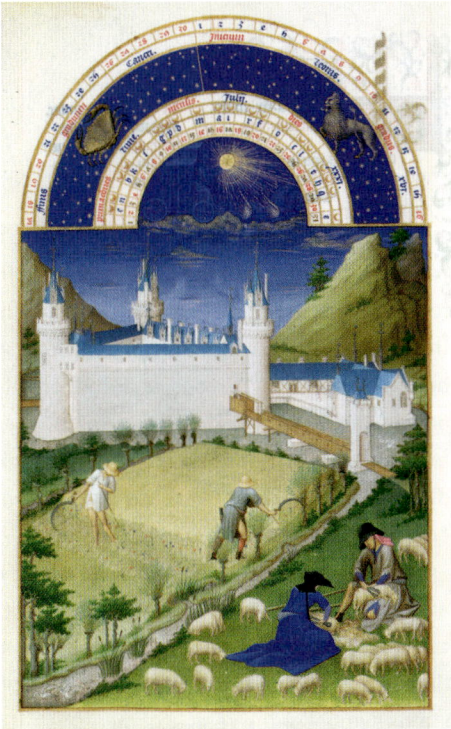

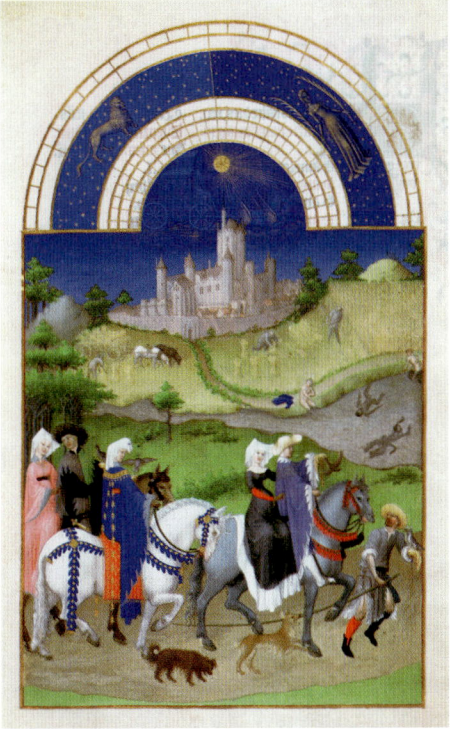

4.3.6 (left and below) Limbourg Brothers, July, August, and September from *Très Riches Heures du Duc de Berry*, 1412. Ink/colors on vellum, 11¼ × 8½" each page. Musée Condé, Chantilly, France

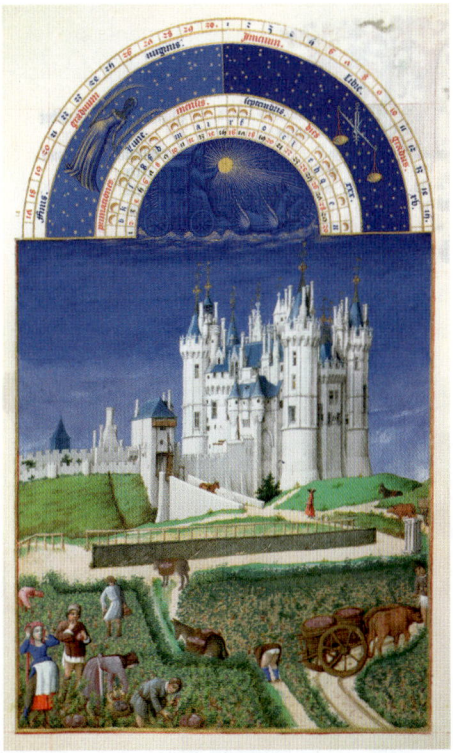

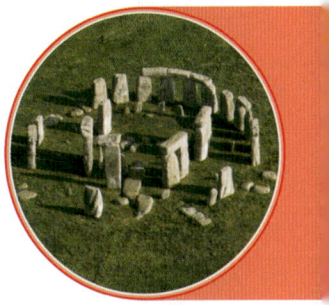

While many mysteries surround Stonehenge, the way that certain stones align with the sunrise on the summer solstice indicate that it was used as a giant calendar: see **4.1.8, p. 570**

Marking Time

The invention of time is one way that humanity has marked the cycles experienced in nature, the most obvious being the rotation of the Earth around the sun. Although we have a standard understanding of time today, throughout history different cultures have devised diverse systems, some of which were linear while others have emphasized recurring or simultaneous moments.

Much like a calendar today, a medieval book of hours tracked months of the year and times of the day. A now-famous French illuminated manuscript, *Très Riches Heures*, made during the Middle Ages by the Limbourg Brothers for the Duke of Berry (**4.3.6**) includes church feasts, saint days, prayers, and devotional texts. Each of the months includes timely narrative scenes with the Duke, his court, and peasants under his rule, and each setting is one of his castles and the surrounding land. July (above left) includes the Château de Poitiers with its drawbridge, harvesters reaping wheat with sickles in the middle ground, and shepherds shearing sheep in the foreground. August (above right) features the Château D'Étampes, peasants harvesting and bathing, and aristocrats about to go hawking. September (above) shows grapes being harvested at the Château de Saumur to make the region's celebrated wine. The hemisphere at the top of each panel shows the solar chariot with Phoebus the sun god at its appropriate spot and relevant signs and degrees of the zodiac: Cancer, Leo, Virgo, and Libra.

Perspectives on Art: Christian Marclay, *The Clock*
"Glue" by Darian Leader

In addition to tracking planting seasons, months, and days, technology helps us mark time to the hour, minute, and second. This kind of time-keeping became the subject of The Clock *(**4.3.7**), made by Swiss-American visual artist and composer Christian Marclay (b. 1955) and discussed here in an excerpt from an essay called "Glue" by Lacanian psychoanalyst and author Darian Leader (British, b. 1965).*

Christian Marclay's *The Clock* (2010) is just that: a mechanism that allows us to tell the time. Unlike other clocks, however, this one is made up of the representation of clocks. Thousands of brief film extracts in which the face of a clock or watch appears, or a time is referred to in the dialogue, mark out a 24-hour cycle. The fragments are taken from films of every genre and period: black-and-white comedies from the 1940s, 1950s sci-fi movies, continental art-house films, 1970s heist movies and modern horror. Spliced together with grace and invention, they form both a history of film and, as the title makes clear, a timepiece.

Marclay's clock is synchronized to the time zone in which it is being exhibited, so that it does exactly what a timepiece is meant to do: we can consult it to learn the time. One glance is enough to give us our temporal bearings. We'll just look at the screen and know how much time we've got left before our next rendezvous, or before our plane or train departs. If works of art are often deemed artificial or illusory, this one can't be: the time displayed or spoken is the real thing—the one that controls and regulates our lives.

Although Marclay's work is quite literally a clock, it is also much more than that, and it complicates the transparency that we ascribe to timepieces. Although a watch or a clock can be a status symbol or the vehicle of memories, it offers immediate access to its referent. We hardly ever have to decipher or interpret clock faces.... Clocks simply tell us—albeit in different ways—what the time is. Yet Marclay's clock not only marks the passing of minutes and hours, but invites us to reflect on our relation to time, as well as offering a rich and sometimes painful questioning of the nature of images, narrative...and indeed, the glue that holds all these together.

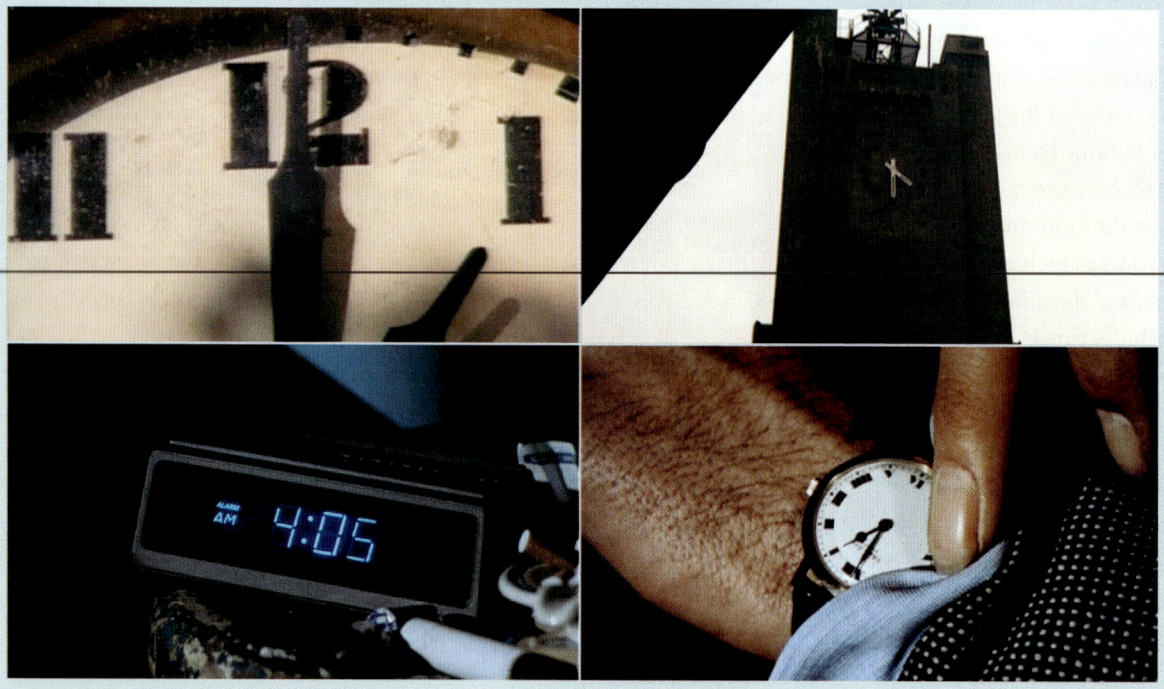

4.3.7 Christian Marclay, stills from *The Clock*, 2010. Single-channel video installation, duration 24-hours

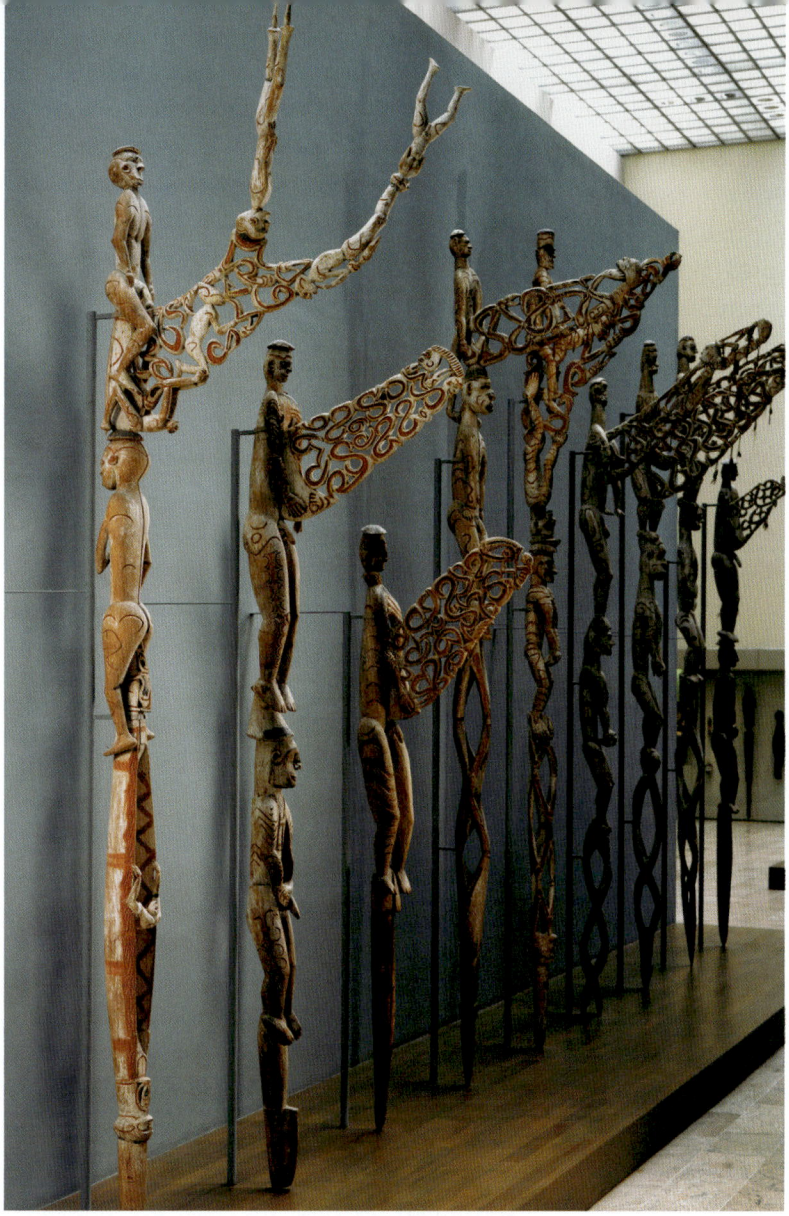

4.3.8 *Bis* poles, late 1950s. Wood, paint, and fiber, 18' × 3'6" × 5'3". Metropolitan Museum of Art, New York

Lineage and Ancestors

One way to make sense of one's place in the world is to explore connections with the past. Some people use family albums to chronicle their own life stories and consult pictures to find out about what their ancestors looked like and what events and details occurred during their lifetimes. Artists have explored similar connections, sometimes factual and sometimes fabricated. In addition to telling stories and satisfying curiosity, artworks related to family lineage can serve to legitimize a person's status and rank in society.

The Asmat people live on the island of New Guinea in the southern Pacific Ocean. They trace their origins to the mythical figure called Fumeripits, who carved the first humans from wood and brought them to life by playing a drum. Woodcarving is thus an esteemed tradition amongst the Asmat, and sculptures are often made to represent and honor people who have recently died and the ancestors they are joining in the afterlife.

Ancestor poles known as *bis* (**4.3.8**) represent both stories about the cyclical nature of human life and the social and family ties that connect the community. The bis is carved with imagery associated with power, virility, and fertility, including strong bodies, horns used in headhunting (a practice in which the head of a victim is removed, then preserved, after he or she has been killed), and trees where the spirits dwell. At the top, a root from the sago palm tree has been retained, creating a wing-like projection. In the main section of the sculpture, there are representations both of the dead individual for whom the bis was made and also of other ancestors. The lower part of the sculpture, called the "canoe," is believed to carry the deceased into the afterlife.

Ancestor poles such as these were once made in connection with headhunting and warfare, and continue to serve a ritual function for male initiation and memorial feasts. A profound bond exists between the figures the Asmat carve and the trees they come from, which are as important as the relationships between generations of ancestors. Once a sculpture has served its ritual function it is returned to the palm groves to decay and strengthen future harvests of the trees.

In many African cultures an important connection between past and present exists in the reverence people show for their ancestors and the nature spirits that influence their lives. The rituals they perform are as crucial to their livelihood as the chores and tasks of daily life. A painted wooden maternity sculpture (called a *pfemba*) from the Yombe (possibly Kongo) people shows a woman kneeling as she holds a bowl in one hand and supports a child with the other (**4.3.9**, p. 598). This sculpture could be a simple representation of a routine daily event—a woman goes to collect water and takes her child with her—but the artist has given us clues that it has further significance. This

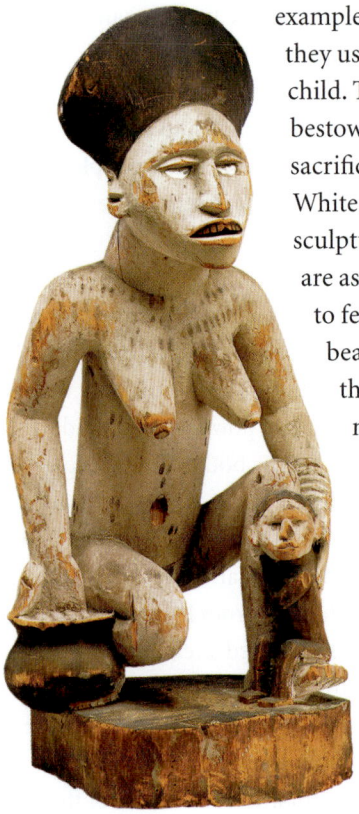

4.3.9 Kneeling female figure with bowl and child, late 19th/early 20th century. Wood, pigment, and glass. 21½ × 10 × 9½". Dallas Museum of Art, Texas

example is unlike other pfemba figures, because they usually show the woman nursing the child. The bowl and the child may be gifts bestowed by the god, or they may represent sacrifices the woman is prepared to make. White paint (as has been used on this sculpture) often identifies nature spirits, who are associated with the ancestors. Connected to female fertility, such sculptures convey beauty, strength, and dignity. This woman thus provides a role model for the living members of the community: they are to honor their ancestors with gifts of sustenance and with children who will continue the traditions they have worked so hard to establish.

Genealogy (an obsession of a family member) inspired contemporary American artist Jillian Mayer (b. 1984) to wonder what her descendants would know about her in the future. As she said, "we only know our grandparents as old." Her musings resulted in *I Am Your Grandma* (**4.3.10**), a minute-long video that went viral on YouTube (more than 3.8 million views at the time of writing). Like a self-portrait in the future tense, the video mixes fast-paced shots of Mayer wearing thirteen different masks and costumes and rapping a catchy tune:

> One day, I'm gonna have a baby, and you will call her mom. That baby will have a baby and you will have this song to know that I am your grandma....This is a gift I give to you, like I already said, that there was a time I was aware that one day I'd be dead. I wish we could have met. I would have loved you so, but you are in the future. You get love by video. I am your grandma...

Funny but somewhat unnerving, this "message to [her] future unborn grandchild" shows the artist to be anything but old. Mayer is interested in what she calls "legacy leaving," and she acknowledges the importance of "using technology to deal with identity." In the video, an informed viewer can find visual references to characters from art history—such as Pablo Picasso's images of the harlequin, a comic figure from European theater tradition—as well as from popular culture—for example, the singer Lady Gaga's Mother Monster—based on the experience and imagination of the artist. Whether we recognize the specific references or not, *I Am Your Grandma* embraces play, ambiguity, and uncertainty as ways to connect with the real world, a world in which attachments are sometimes made to people we have never met: including distant or long-dead relatives, characters in theater or art, or favorite singers.

4.3.10 Jillian Mayer, *I Am Your Grandma* (selected video stills), 2011. Duration 1 min. 3 secs. Music by Jillian Mayer and Michael-John Hancock

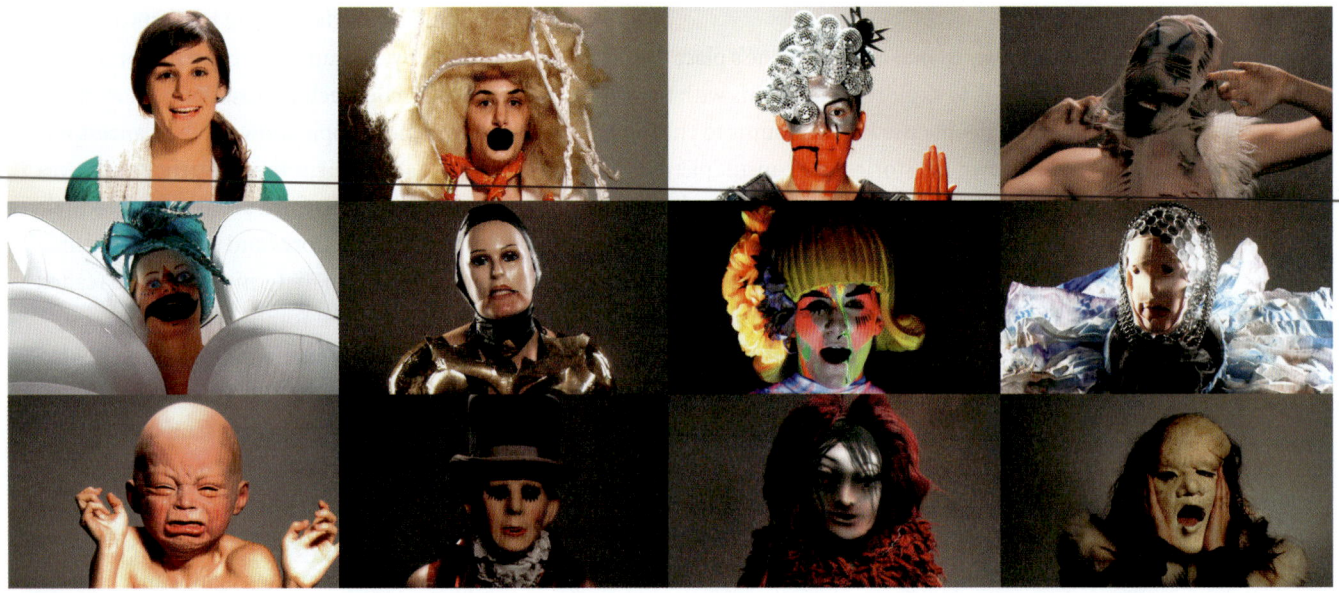

Low relief: carving in which the design stands out only slightly from the background surface

Mortality and Immortality

Artists have recorded images of birth and death as ways to consider the fleeting existence of the life force that ultimately defies comprehension. There are many questions, often unanswerable, that artists confront. After we die, do we leave the world of the living? Is it important for the body to stay intact? Is there a place to which the soul is believed to go? These concerns about life, death, and the afterlife have inspired artists for millennia.

Death and the afterlife are inseparably connected with life in many religions and belief systems. A sarcophagus lid made for Pacal, the seventh-century ruler of the Maya city-state of Palenque in southern Mexico, illustrates the king's integral role in the cycle of life (**4.3.11**). The elaborate scene, carved in **low relief**, shows Pacal reclining on a slab that marks the intersection of the earthly realm and the underworld. Just beneath Pacal is the face of the setting sun, representing death. From Pacal's navel sprouts the world tree, which connects the three cosmic realms: its roots are in the underworld, its trunk is in the earthly world, and its branches are in the sky. The ruler himself serves a similar purpose. By carrying on the lineage of his ancestors, he ensures sustenance and productivity for his people and provides a connection with the gods.

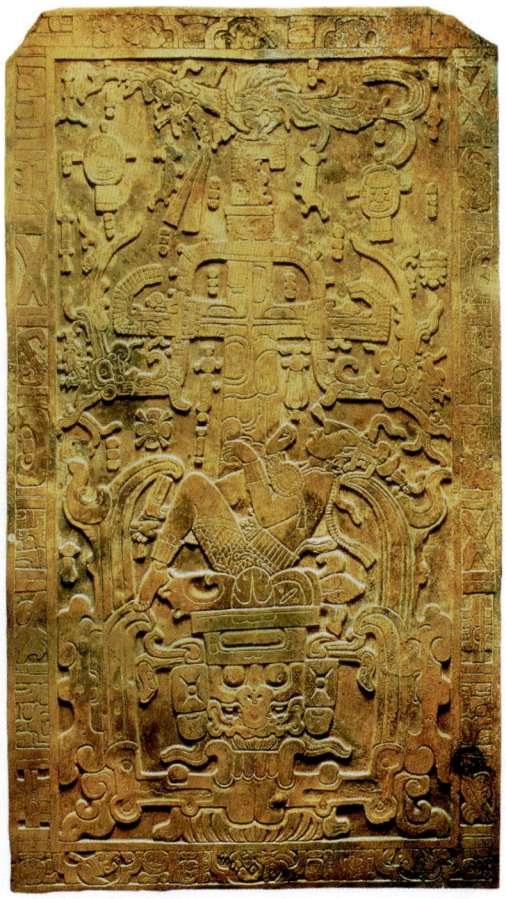

4.3.11 Sarcophagus lid, tomb of the Maya ruler Lord Pacal (Shield 2), c. 680. Limestone. Temple of the Inscriptions, Palenque, Mexico

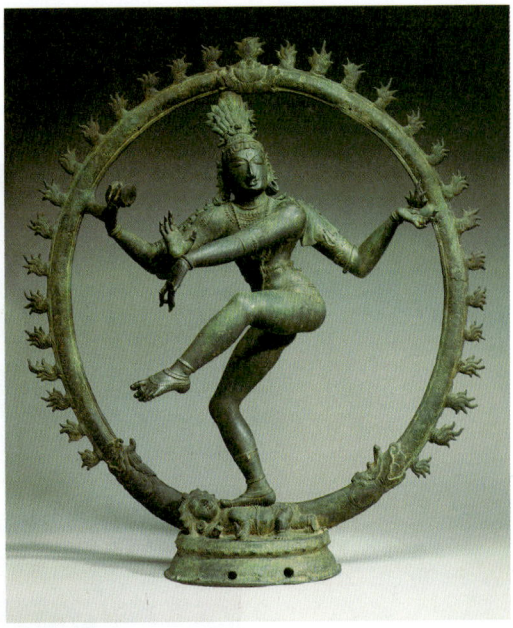

4.3.12 *Shiva Nataraja (Lord of the Dance)*, Chola Period, India, 11th century. Bronze, height 43⅞". Cleveland Museum of Art, Ohio

In India, connections between the present life and those before and after it are central to the Hindu belief system. One of the principal Hindu deities, Shiva, embodies a balancing of contradictory qualities: half-male and half-female, benevolent and fearsome, giver and taker of life. As Nataraja, or "Lord of the Dance" (**4.3.12**), Shiva is responsible for dancing the world into existence and generating *samsara*, the endless cycle of death and rebirth in which Hindus believe. The flames surrounding Shiva's agile form represent the periodic chaos and destruction that happen when the dance ceases. During these periods of inactivity, the fire cleanses the physical world while providing a release from samsara. Shiva dances while poised on top of a dwarf who represents the evil and ignorance that are stamped out during the dances. Shiva's dance creates a balance between creation and destruction that, over the course of time, manifests itself in the cycle of life.

Vanitas: Reminders of Transience

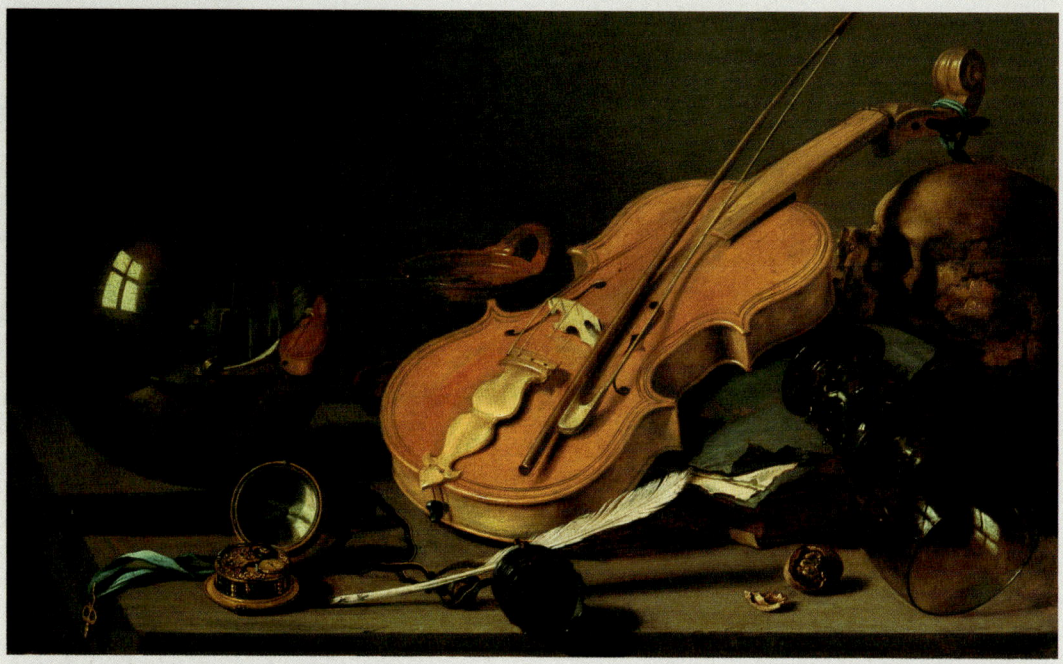

4.3.13 Pieter Claesz (attr.), *Vanitas (Still Life with Glass Globe)*, c. 1628. Oil on panel, 14⅛ × 23¼". Germanisches Nationalmuseum, Nürnberg, Germany

***Vanitas*:** a genre of painting that emphasizes the transient nature of earthly materials and beauty; often seen in still-life painting

Still life: a scene of inanimate objects, such as fruits, flowers, or dead animals

***Trompe l'oeil*:** an extreme kind of illusion meant to deceive the viewer that the objects included are real

***Memento mori*:** Latin phrase that means "remember you must die." In artworks, such symbols as skulls, flowers, and clocks are used to represent the transient nature of life on Earth

In the European tradition, "***vanitas***" artworks are based on the theme of the fleeting nature of life. They first became popular in seventeenth-century Dutch **still-life** paintings, for example *Vanitas (Still Life with Glass Globe)* (**4.3.13**) attributed to Pieter Claesz (1597–1660). The word vanitas refers to vanity (excessive pride in or admiration of one's own appearance or achievements), materialism (both physical limitations and the desire to own possessions), and inevitable mortality.

Still-life images, because they depict inanimate objects, give the artist the chance to display a great degree of technical ability using ***trompe-l'oeil*** techniques to trick the viewer into thinking that he or she is seeing a real scene. The passing of time is suggested in *Vanitas (Still Life with Glass Globe)* by the timepiece, and the skull is an obvious ***memento mori*** (literally meaning "remember that you must die"). The tipped glass and cracked walnut tell us that a person was here enjoying wine and food, but is now gone. The instrument reminds us that music, too, is only transient; it is not fixed in time and will at some point end. Claesz shows his own presence by including his reflection in the glass ball on the left side of the table. The tiny self-portrait displays the artist's virtuosity and presents a challenge to death as the painter lives on through his work.

Spanish artist Pablo Picasso's (1881–1973) keen awareness of the history of art allowed him to pick and choose influences from the past. In addition to the tradition of vanitas still life, Picasso would have known about Renaissance and

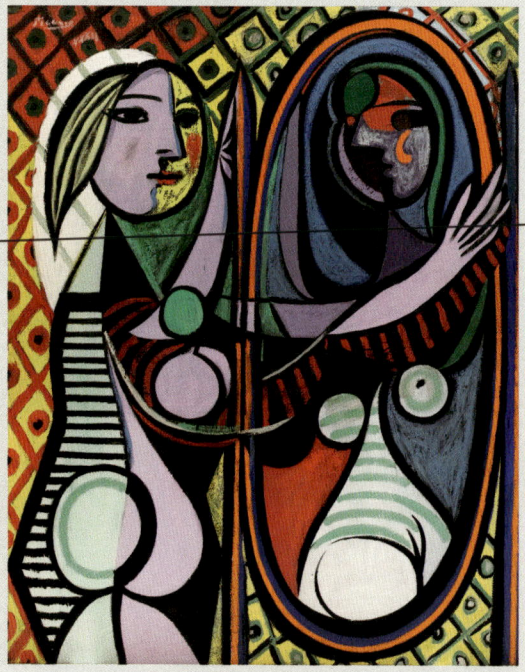

4.3.14 Pablo Picasso, *Girl before a Mirror*, Boisgeloup, March 1932. Oil on canvas, 64 × 51¼". MoMA, New York

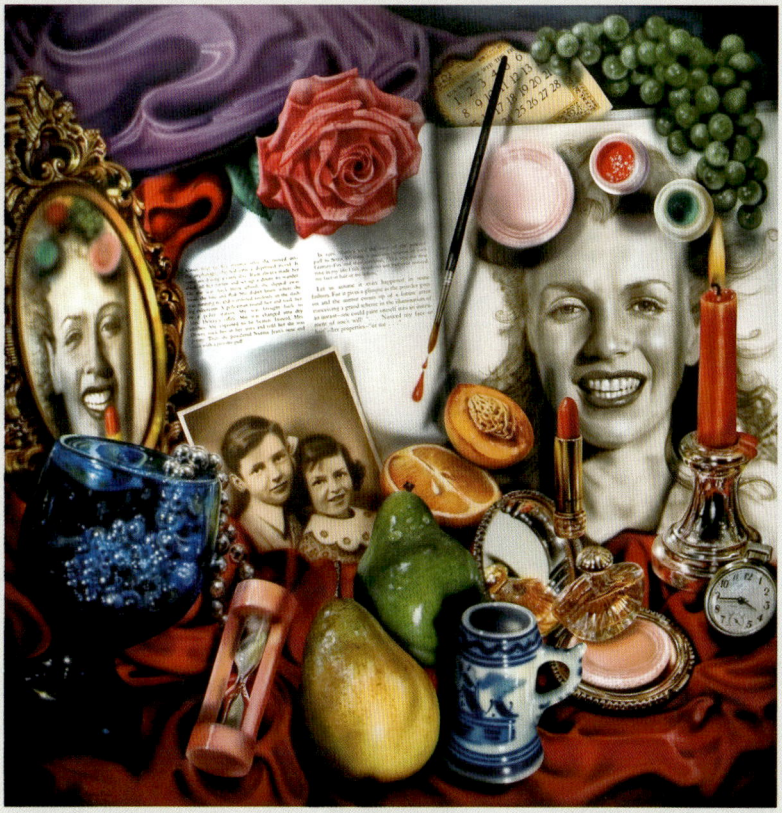

4.3.15 Audrey Flack, *Marilyn (Vanitas)*, 1977. Oil over acrylic on canvas, 8 × 8'. Collection of the University of Arizona Museum of Art, Tucson

Baroque figure studies depicting the goddess Venus looking at herself in a mirror. This subject connects in a direct way with the concept of vanitas, because beauty is ephemeral and destined to fade over time. Traditionally, the inclusion of a mirror in a painting symbolizes the artist's desire to compete with nature and produce as lifelike an image as possible. While Picasso is more interested in **Cubist** abstraction than *trompe-l'oeil* illusion, the vanitas theme plays a large part in his *Girl before a Mirror* (**4.3.14**). As the woman gazes on herself in the mirror she sees a dark, chaotic reflection. Perhaps the deathly head reflecting back at her is a prediction of her inevitable future, a *memento mori* restating the age-old message that life is short.

Photorealist Audrey Flack (b. 1931) also built on the Dutch-inspired tradition. In addition to commenting on human mortality, *Marilyn (Vanitas)* (**4.3.15**) is a homage to the American film actress Marilyn Monroe. The photograph on the right is reflected in the mirror on the left, showing Monroe's public persona as a blonde beauty. As we saw in Picasso's *Girl before a Mirror*, mirrors in art are understood to symbolize the transience of youth, beauty, and life. As with similar objects in Claez's work, the calendar, clock, and hourglass further represent the passing of time. They, too, are reminders of the brevity of life—as are the burning candle and the flower and fruit, all of which last only a short time.

The hyper-realistic colors and floating objects within Flack's painting give it an otherworldly quality—a dramatic contrast to the objects that symbolize time. By including a childhood portrait of herself with her brother, the artist further wishes to remind herself (and us) that the pleasures of her life are as fleeting as those of the movie idol. The mirrored compact, makeup, and pearls refer to Marilyn Monroe's mask to the world. Made fifteen years after the celebrity died of a drug overdose in 1962, this painting helps to preserve the past in the face of earthly beauty, to reflect on the glamorization of famous figures, and to promote art as a response to the inevitability of time's passing.

Baroque: European artistic and architectural style of the late sixteenth to the early eighteenth century, characterized by extravagance, movement, and emotional intensity

Cubism: twentieth-century movement and style in art, especially painting, in which perspective with a single viewpoint was abandoned and use was made of simple geometric shapes, interlocking planes, and, later, collage

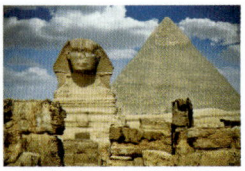

1.2.2 Great Sphinx of Giza, Egypt c. 2500 BCE, p. 62

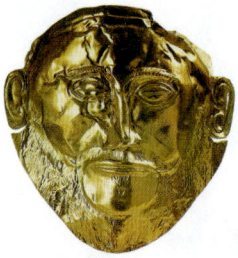

2.6.13 Gold death mask, Mycenae, Greece, c. 1550–1500 BCE, p. 293

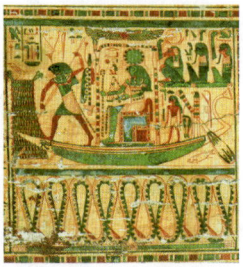

0.0.1 *The Journey of the Sun God Re*, detail from coffin, Egypt, 990–969 BCE, p. 20

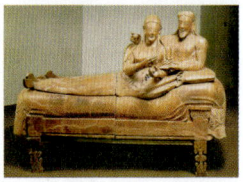

2.4.11 Sarcophagus from Cerveteri, Italy, c. 520 BCE, p. 249

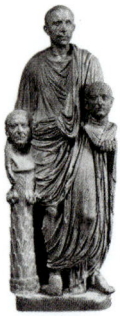

3.1.32 Roman carrying death masks of his ancestors, Italy, c. 80 BCE, p. 386

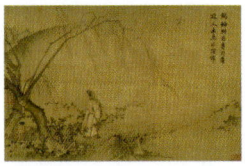

1.6.14 Ma Yuan, *Walking on a Mountain Path in Spring*, Song Dynasty (960–1279), p. 135

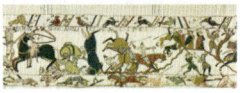

4.7.5 Detail of the Battle of Hastings, *Bayeux Tapestry*, c. 1066–82, p. 642

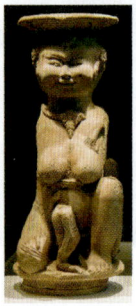

2.6.3 *The Mother Goddess Men Brajut*, Indonesian, c. 14th–15th century, p. 287

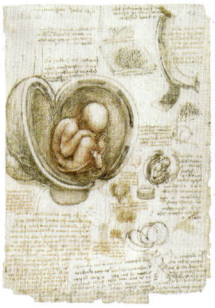

2.1.2 Leonardo da Vinci, *Studies of the fetus in the womb*, c. 1510–13, p. 193

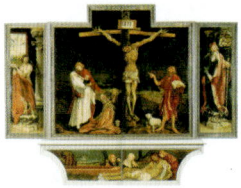

3.6.7 Matthias Grünewald, *Isenheim Altarpiece*, c. 1510–15, p. 465

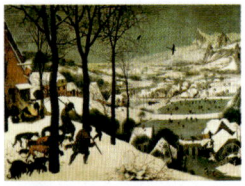

1.9.8 Pieter Bruegel, *Hunters in the Snow*, 1565, p. 164

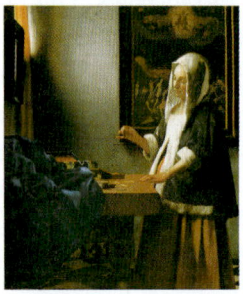

4.2.12 Johannes Vermeer, *Woman Holding a Balance*, c. 1664, p. 585

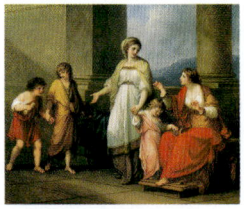

3.7.9 Angelica Kauffmann, *Cornelia Pointing to Her Children...*, c. 1785, p. 495

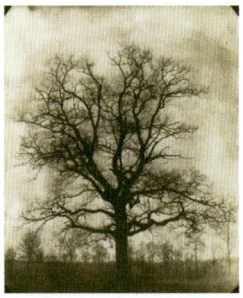

2.8.6 William Henry Fox Talbot, *Oak Tree in Winter*, c. 1842, p. 318

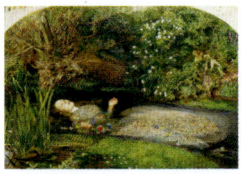

3.8.4 John Everett Millais, *Ophelia*, 1851–52, p. 505

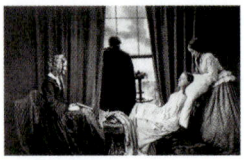

1.7.13a Henry Peach Robinson, *Fading Away*, 1858, p. 147

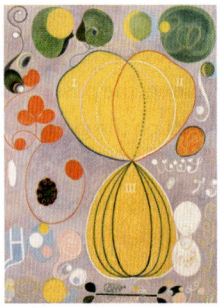

1.4.33 Hilma af Klint, *Group IV, No. 7, Adulthood*, 1907, p. 111

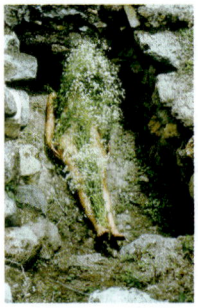

3.10.4 Ana Mendieta, "Untitled" (*Silueta* series, Mexico), 1973–80, p. 548

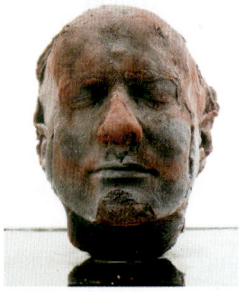

0.0.16 Marc Quinn, *Self*, 1991, p. 32

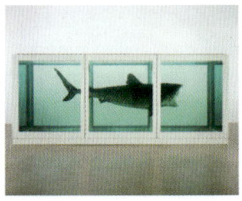

2.4.18 Damien Hirst, *The Physical Impossibility of Death in the Mind of Someone Living*, 1991, p. 253

4.4 Art and Science

Some consider science and art to be separate disciplines, even complete opposites. We tend to think of art as intuitive and emotional, and science as rational and objective. Both fields, however, are exploratory in nature and involve extensive trial and error; art and science interact more often than we might suppose. As with scientists, artists are keen observers of phenomena and events. In fact, many medical schools require students to take a course in art observation to hone their skills of diagnosis and empathy.

Some artworks openly celebrate scientific achievements, while some artists have even used scientific methods to make art. The appreciation of art relies, of course, on the human senses, and artists have always been particularly keen on manipulating the perception of those viewing an artwork. Due to advancements in science and technology, today we are able to study artworks using such techniques as X-radiography to better understand the practices of past artists, and to restore and conserve artworks for the future.

Art Celebrating Science

Renaissance: a period of cultural and artistic change in Europe from the fourteenth to the seventeenth century

Mirror writing: writing that reads correctly only when reflected in a mirror, as in the case of the journals and other writings of Leonardo da Vinci

The great **Renaissance** artist Leonardo da Vinci (1452–1519) was not only a painter, but also an engineer, anatomist, botanist, and mapmaker. The drawing *Vitruvian Man* (**4.4.1**) shows Leonardo's interest in the proportions of the human body. The **mirror writing** above and below the drawing—readable when reflected—consists of Leonardo's notes based on the ideas of the first-century BCE Roman architect Vitruvius. Vitruvius was an architect, engineer, and the author of *Ten Books on Architecture*, the only surviving treatise on architecture from the ancient world.

In this treatise Vitruvius outlined the ideal proportions of a man, and argued that architecture should imitate these proportions. Thus, in Leonardo's drawing, the length of both arms combined is equal to the height of a man, the distance from an elbow to the tip

4.4.1 Leonardo da Vinci, *Vitruvian Man: Study of the Human Body*, c. 1490. Pen and ink with wash over metalpoint, 13½ × 10". Gallerie dell'Accademia, Venice, Italy

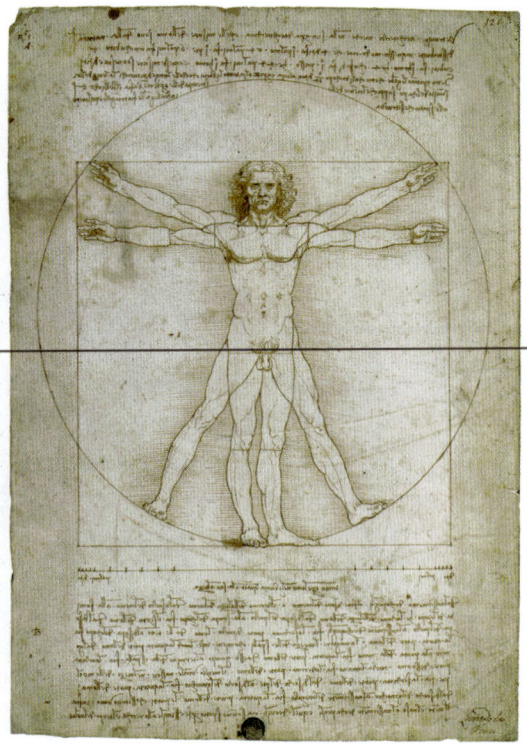

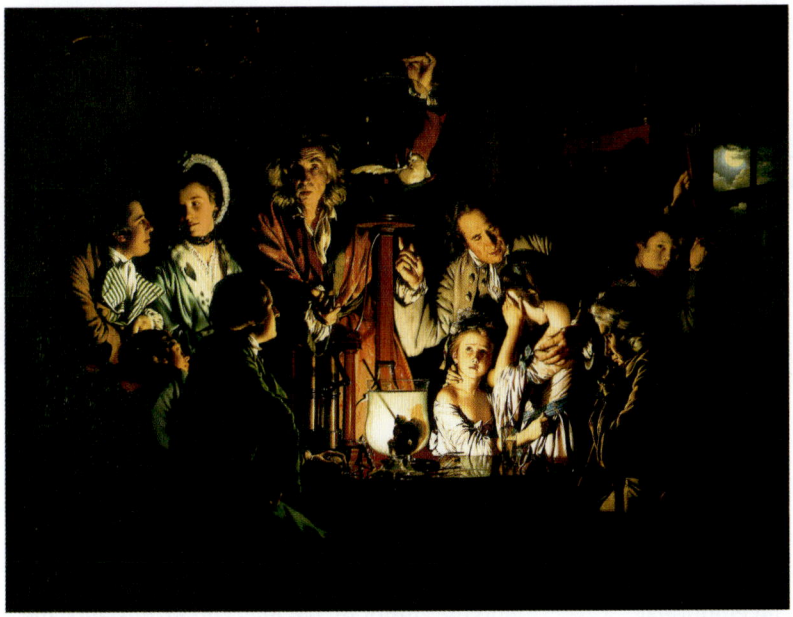

4.4.2 Joseph Wright of Derby, *An Experiment on a Bird in the Air Pump*, 1768. Oil on canvas, 6 × 8'. National Gallery, London, England

of a finger is one-quarter the height, and a man's foot is one-seventh his height. Leonardo also made his own observations of the human body, frequently studying corpses to determine whether the writings of Vitruvius were accurate. Rather than a drawing that simply illustrates the ideas of Vitruvius, Leonardo's work also shows his own exploration of the science of the human body.

The English painter Joseph Wright of Derby (1734–1797) was a member of the Lunar Society, an informal club of scientists, intellectuals, and manufacturers who met monthly to discuss developments in science and technology. Wright lived during the period known as the **Enlightenment**, a time of intense interest in science and reason. He often painted scientific and industrial subjects, employing a notably dramatic use of light and dark, called **tenebrism**.

Wright's work *An Experiment on a Bird in the Air Pump* shows a traveling scientist lecturing on pneumatics, or the study of air and other gases (**4.4.2**). He is using an air pump that adds and removes oxygen from the prominently placed glass container, inside of which a white bird lies on the bottom. The artist has chosen to depict the climactic moment when the bird is running out of air due to the vacuum that the scientist is creating in the vessel. Wright has also increased the drama by using a cockatoo—in reality a more common bird would have been used—and through his use of shadows and light, which highlights reactions of concern and indifference, contempt and resignation, or pity and fear. Light was also a symbol of knowledge during the Enlightenment, so the bright light shining on the children's faces represents the knowledge they are gaining from the experiment. The luminous moon visible through the window is a symbol of the Lunar Society.

Artists study anatomy to learn how to depict figures, and many artists have become interested in dissection and medical procedures. The American painter Thomas Eakins (1844–1916) depicted a demonstration he witnessed by a famous surgeon, Dr. Samuel Gross, in Philadelphia, in which the doctor removed dead tissue from a bone infection in the patient's thigh (a procedure developed by Dr. Gross) (**4.4.3**). In Eakins's painting, assistants surround the body while the white-haired doctor lectures to medical students, who are dimly lit in the seating in the background. Eakins himself can just be glimpsed, seated on the right, taking copious notes. The artist's detailed observation

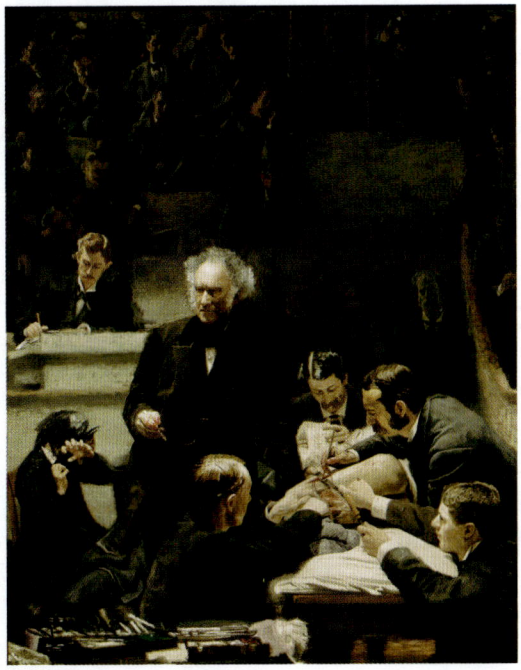

4.4.3 Thomas Eakins, *Portrait of Dr. Samuel D. Gross (The Gross Clinic)*, 1875. Oil on canvas, 8' × 6'6". Philadelphia Museum of Art and Pennsylvania Academy of the Fine Arts

Enlightenment: an intellectual movement in eighteenth-century Europe that argued for science, reason, and individualism. Challenging received ideas passed down by tradition, the Enlightenment also promoted the notion of equal rights for all men

Tenebrism: dramatic use of intense darkness and light to heighten the impact of a painting

of the procedure created such a brutally **realistic** depiction that a critic for the *New York Daily Tribune* commented,

> It is a picture that even strong men find difficult to look at long, if they can look at it at all.

Eakins's meticulous attention to detail makes his painting a useful historical document of early surgical procedure. For instance, he shows us the use of anesthesia (the anesthetist holds a white cloth over the patient's face), without which this procedure would not have been possible. Although the center of the auditorium would have been lit in a similar way from a skylight, the artist also uses theatrical lighting to heighten the emotional impact of the painting. Eakins also includes the patient's distraught mother, seen on the left, who in actuality was probably not present at the surgery.

Astronomy and Space Exploration in Art

For millennia, the regular yet ever-changing night sky was a source of endless fascination and study. In ancient Mexico, amongst the Maya and Aztecs, the planets were regarded as gods, and their movements were closely monitored. Some of the most fascinating artworks of the Maya and Aztecs reflect this interest in astronomy. This fascination with space continues in modern times as many artists have depicted space exploration and astronomical discoveries.

The **flint** in **4.4.4** incorporates elements of the cosmology (beliefs about the origin of the world) and astronomical knowledge of the Maya. The delicate carving of this very hard stone reveals a high level of craftsmanship. Light enough to be held in one hand, the flint depicts the story of creation, said by the Maya to have occurred precisely on August 13, 3114 BCE, when the First Father was sacrificed after losing a ball game against the Lords of Death. The First Father's soul is seen riding a crocodile to the Maya underworld (called the Place of Creation, ruled by a water-monster god) accompanied by other Maya lords. The **profiles** of the First Father and two of the lords appear on top of the crocodile, leaning back to suggest the speed of the journey. Two additional figures are shown facing downward toward the underside of the crocodile. The serrated edge on the bottom of the flint represents the forceful waves encountered on the journey. The moment shown here is the transformation of the crocodile into a sacred canoe just before it dives into the rough waters, signifying the death of the First Father. Soon thereafter, the First Father will rise from the waters, transform into the maize god, and become the creator of humans.

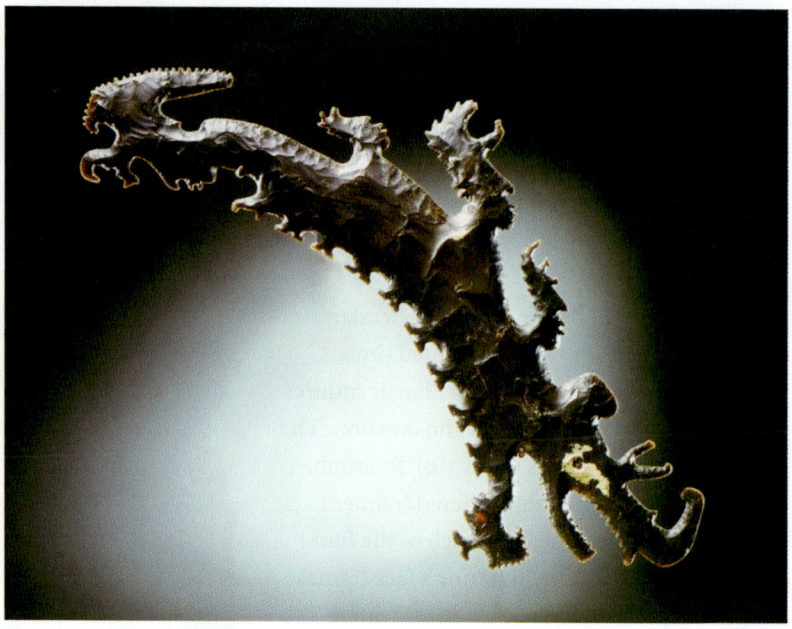

4.4.4 Maya flint depicting a crocodile canoe with passengers, 600–900 CE. 9¾ × 16¼ × ¾". Dallas Museum of Art, Texas

The flint, however, is more than a depiction of a Maya story; it is also an instrument for astronomical observations. When held up to the sky on August 13 each year, the five heads on this flint align with the brightest stars of the Milky Way galaxy. For the Maya, the stars re-enact the story of man's creation when, at midnight, the stars of the Milky Way align horizontally east to west. In the next several hours, the galaxy appears to pivot and fall out of the sky, resembling a canoe diving into water. Then, immediately before the sunrise, the three stars of Orion's belt appear, symbolizing for the Maya the three hearthstones at the site of the First Father's rebirth.

Similar to the Maya, the Aztecs were skillful observers of the skies. The Aztec Sun Stone

Realistic: artistic style that aims to represent appearances as accurately as possible
Flint: an object or tool made from the very hard, sharp-edged stone of the same name
Profile: the outline of an object, especially a face or head, represented from the side

is a store of astronomical and mathematical knowledge (**4.4.5**). Originally painted in shades of brown, red, white, blue, and green, the heavy Sun Stone (weighing 24 tons) stood atop the main temple at Tenochtitlan, the capital of the Aztec empire. Later it was buried, to be uncovered again only in 1790 in what is now downtown Mexico City.

The Sun Stone, also known as a calendar stone, reveals how the Aztecs counted time, and illustrates their belief that the Earth endures recurring cycles of destruction and creation. The center of the stone shows the face of Tonatiuh, the sun god to whom Aztecs offered frequent human and animal sacrifices. Each of the four squares emanating from Tonatiuh's face frames a symbol representing the ways in which the Earth previously came to an end: by wind, by fire, by floods, and by wild beasts. The Aztecs believed that the Earth would be destroyed again by an earthquake. In the ring surrounding these symbols are twenty animals, each framed by a rectangle. These represent the days of the Aztec month. Priests used the calendar stone to determine sacrificial periods.

In 1969, the American artist Robert Rauschenberg (1925–2008) was invited to witness the launch of *Apollo 11*, the spacecraft that put the first man on the moon. At the time, NASA gave Rauschenberg scientific maps and photographs of the launch from which he created a series called *Stoned*, containing thirty-three **lithographs**. Later, Rauschenberg was commissioned by NASA/ART (a program designed for artists to record the history of space exploration) to respond artistically to the first launch of the space shuttle *Columbia* on April 12, 1981. This was a significant moment because *Columbia* was the first shuttle to reach space and return (unfortunately, after decades of service, it disintegrated upon re-entry after a launch in 2003). In his lithograph *Hotshot* (**4.4.6**), Rauschenberg combined photographs related to the first space shuttle launch and the "shuttlemania" that surrounded it. When

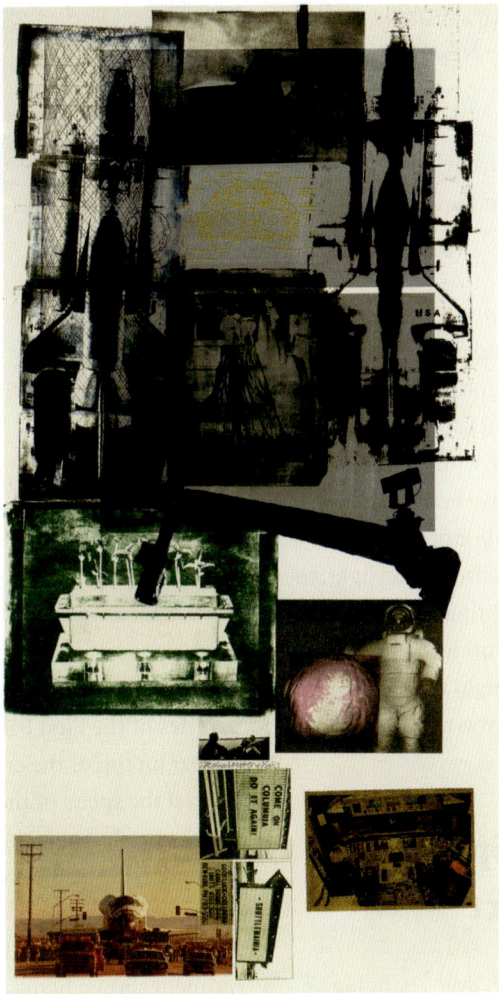

4.4.6 Robert Rauschenberg, *Hotshot*, 1983. Lithograph with stencil and paper and gold-leaf collage, 6'8¾" × 3'4⅜". MoMA, New York

4.4.5 Calendar stone (Sun Stone), c. 1502–1521. Basalt, 12' diameter. National Museum of Anthropology, Mexico City, Mexico

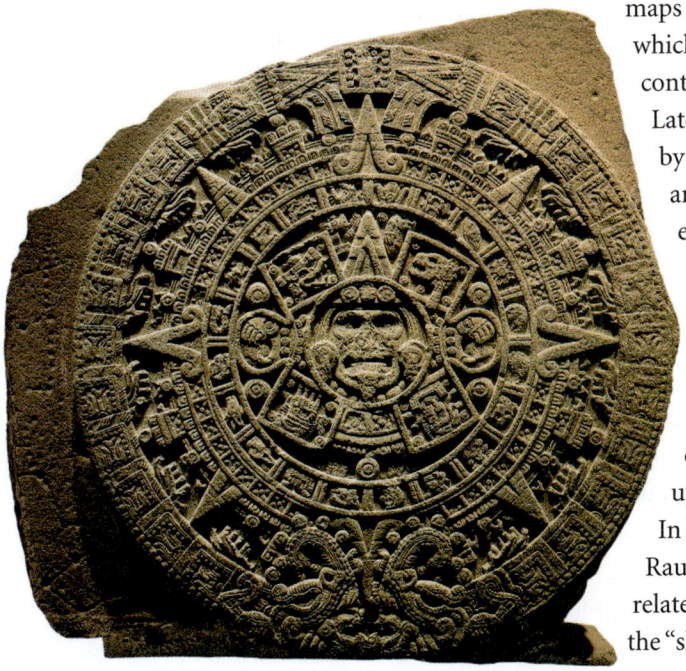

Lithography: a print process done on a flat, unmarred surface, such as a stone, in which the image is created using oil-based ink with resistance to water

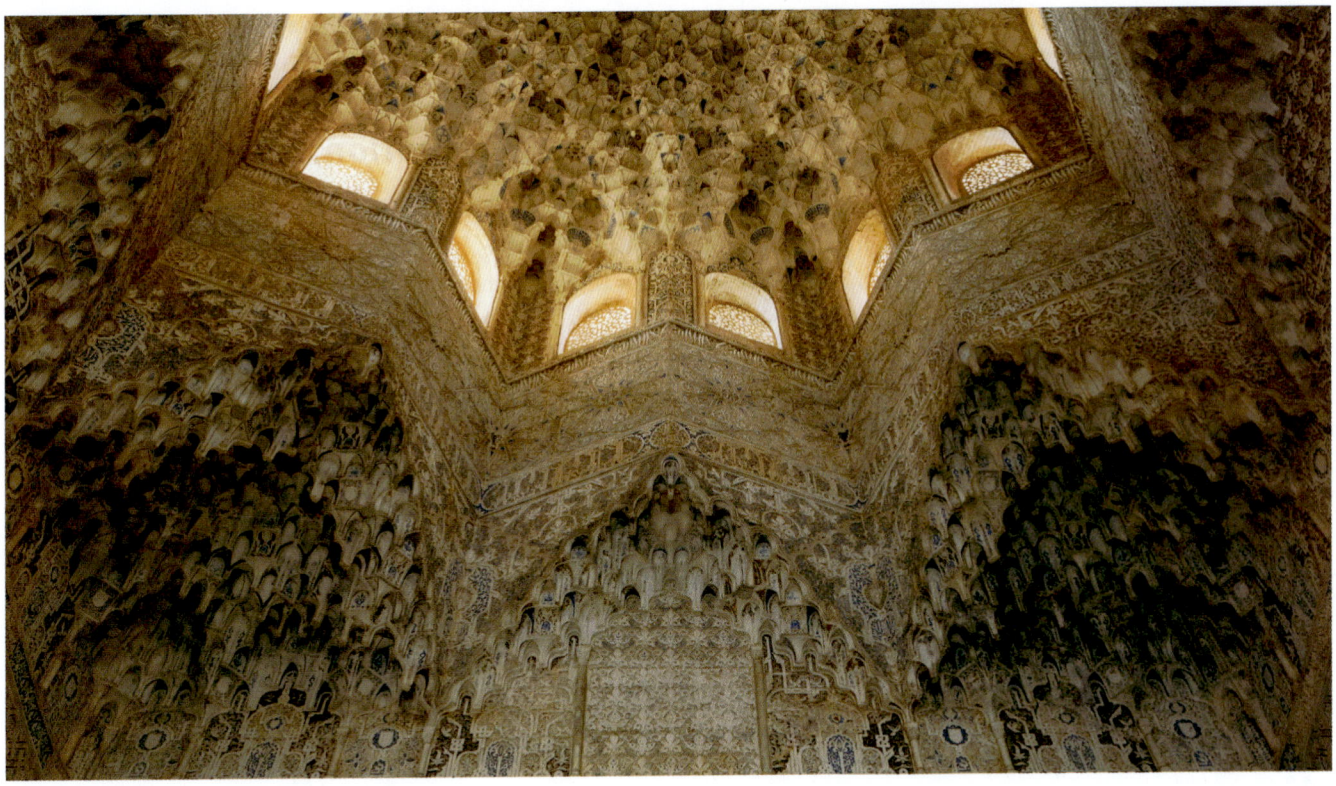

4.4.7 Ceiling in the Hall of the Abencerrages, Alhambra, Granada, Spain

developing this print, Rauschenberg wrote, "*Hotshot* was…to share and express my belief in the spiritual and physical improvement of life and mind through space curiosity."

Using Science and Mathematics to Create Art

Advancements in science and mathematics enable artists to create new kinds of art. In the examples shown here, Islamic artists used geometry and mathematics to mimic complex forms found in nature; the advent of the microscope enabled one artist to create minuscule artworks; and a sculptor uses DNA from discarded objects to determine the genetic profiles of humans.

The Arabic term *muqarnas* means "stalactite vaults," or the drips of calcium salt found within caves. Muqarnas are decorative elements in Islamic architecture made by combining individual cells (*bayt*) in various combinations to create a structure resembling a honeycomb. The earliest muqarnas have been found in structures from tenth-century Iran, but the design has spread throughout the Islamic world. A particularly stunning muqarnas dome covers a room called the Hall of the Abencerrages in the Alhambra in Granada, Spain (**4.4.7**). The seemingly inexplicable complexity of the design helps visitors to the holy space feel as if they are entering an otherworldly gateway. The ceiling contains 5,000 stucco muqarnas mathematically constructed to rise toward a central star motif.

The British artist Willard Wigan (b. 1957) has created artworks that are possible only because he uses a microscope—his creations can barely be seen by the naked eye. He carves his artworks on individual pieces of sand or grains of rice and places them on equally tiny bases, such as the head of a pin or a strand of human hair; the Statue of Liberty in **4.4.8** was re-created inside the eye of a needle. Wigan then paints his artworks using an eyelash for a brush. To create one of these microscopic works, Wigan puts himself into a very calm state of mind, which slows his heartbeat and decreases hand tremors: "I need to work between heartbeats, or else the pulse in my finger will cause a mistake," he says. He works through the night so that daylight activity, such as cars frequently driving by, will not disturb his steady hand. Wigan found that the intense concentration required for this

4.4.8 Willard Wigan, *Statue of Liberty*

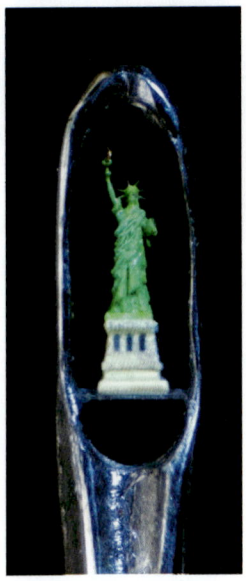

Bioart: art that is created with living, changing organisms
Pointillism: a late nineteenth-century painting style using short strokes or points of differing colors that optically combine to form new perceived colors
Color theory: the understanding of how colors relate to each other, especially when mixed or placed near one another
Optical mixture: when the eye blends two colors that are placed near each other, creating a new color
Afterimage effect: when the eye sees the complementary color of something that the viewer has spent an extended time viewing (also known as successive contrasts)

sculpting helped him come to terms with his difficulties as a dyslexic child. As he recalled:

> I became obsessed with making more and more tiny things. I think I was trying to find a way of compensating for my embarrassment at having learning difficulties: people had made me feel small so I wanted to show them how significant small could be.

Continual advancements in the medical sciences have led to the field of **bioart**. For the project *Stranger Visions* (**4.4.9**), the American artist Heather Dewey-Hagborg (b. 1982) gathered objects from the streets of New York City that had been touched by humans (such as gum and cigarettes) or discarded material from the human body itself (such as hair), and analysed the DNA found on these samples. From the DNA, she was able to determine genetic characteristics (such as eye color, hair color, gender, and race) of the people connected with these items and to print 3-D models of their faces. Dewey-Hagborg explains, "I was really struck by this idea that the very things that make us human—hair, skin, saliva, and fingernails—become a real liability for us as we constantly shed them in public." Although Dewey-Hagborg was able only to gather and reproduce general qualities from the DNA left on the found objects, her work highlights concerns about privacy and DNA profiling as genetic research continues to grow.

Perception, Senses, and Psychology

Since art is a visual medium, artists expect viewers to respond to the artwork through their sense of sight. It is not surprising, therefore, that artists have often been keenly aware of scientific studies of visual perception. Some artists have experimented with ways to use their images to trigger responses from the other senses, such as hearing or smell. Other artists have tried to express visually their personal experiences or portray their subconscious.

Sunday on La Grande Jatte (**4.4.10**) is a picture of people engaged in the activities of everyday life. But its artist, the Frenchman Georges Seurat (1859–1891), also applied to this artwork recent scientific studies on the way that the human eye perceives color. Seurat developed a process called **pointillism**, a meticulous way of applying **color theory** in his paintings. He relied on two optical effects (**optical mixture** and **afterimage effect**) to create scenes in which the figures are very distinct, almost like cutouts, because of the precise way in which he applied tiny dots of color to the canvas. The colors we see when we view *Sunday on La Grande Jatte* from several feet

4.4.9 (below right) Heather Dewey-Hagborg, *Stranger Visions*, 2012–13. Found genetic materials, custom software, 3D prints, documentation. Portrait dimensions 8 × 6 × 6", overall dimensions variable. Exhibition view from *Stranger Visions*, Saint-Gaudens National Historic Site, Cornish, New Hampshire, 2014

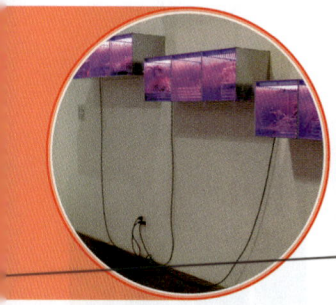

The bioartist Suzanne Anker examines the needs of plants in outer space: **1.5.17, p. 123**

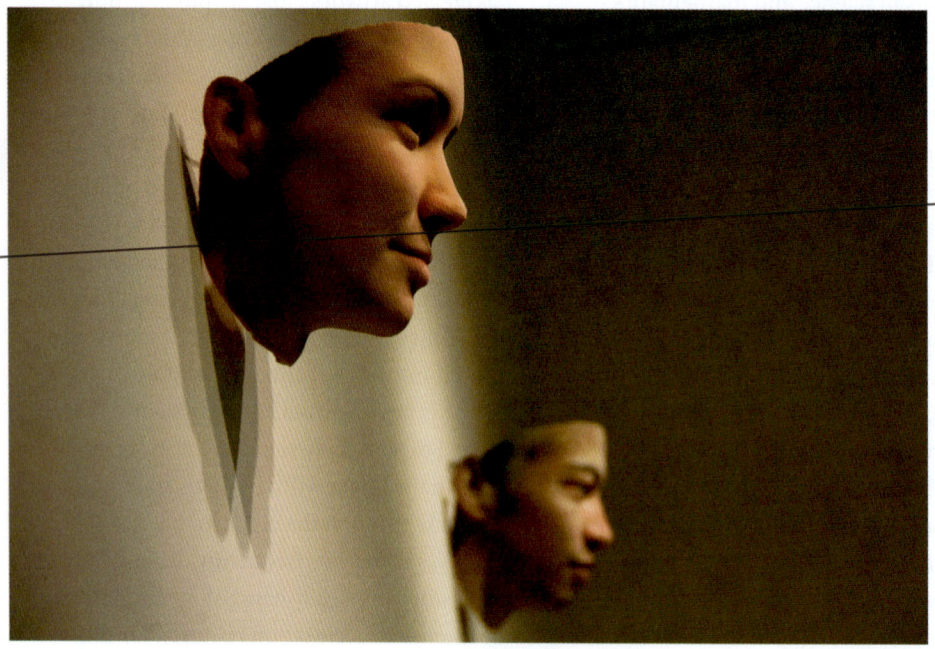

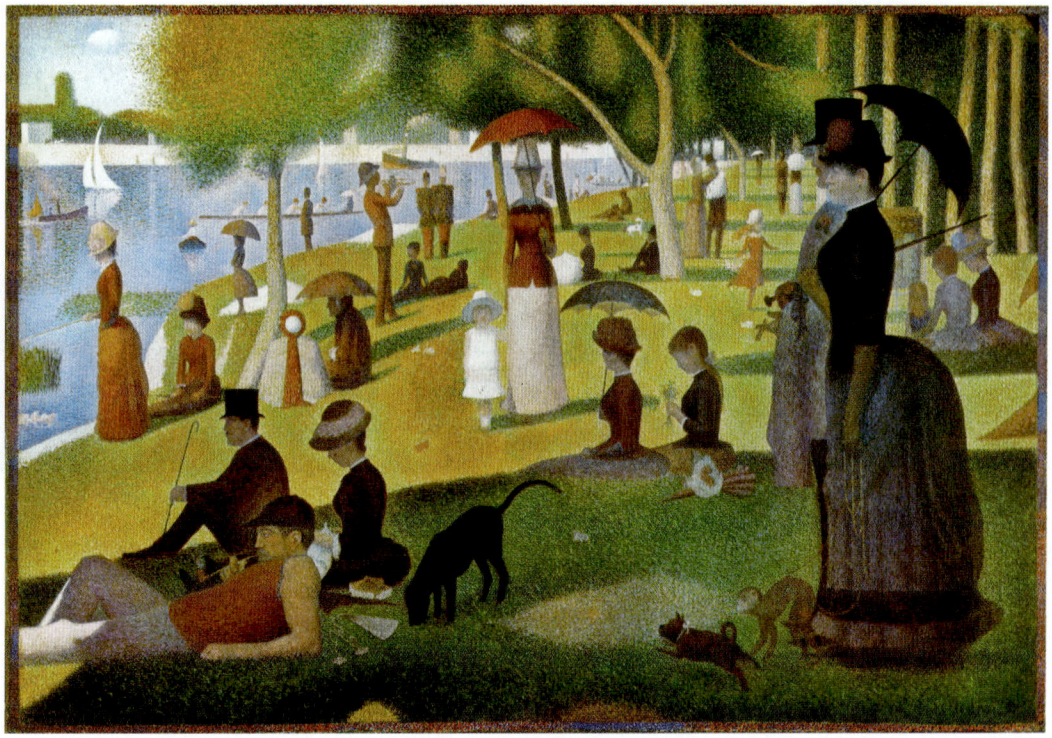

4.4.10 Georges Seurat, *Sunday on La Grande Jatte*, 1884–86. Oil on canvas, 6'9¾" × 10'¼". Art Institute of Chicago, Illinois

Palette: the range of colors used by an artist

away are quite different from the colors we see up close. For example, the green grass is made up of dots not only of various shades of green but also of oranges and purples. Seurat took three years to paint this work, meticulously applying dots while considering the effects of color theory on his **palette** choices. To ensure that the optical arrangement would not be disrupted when the painting was framed, Seurat also painted a border using the same pointillist technique.

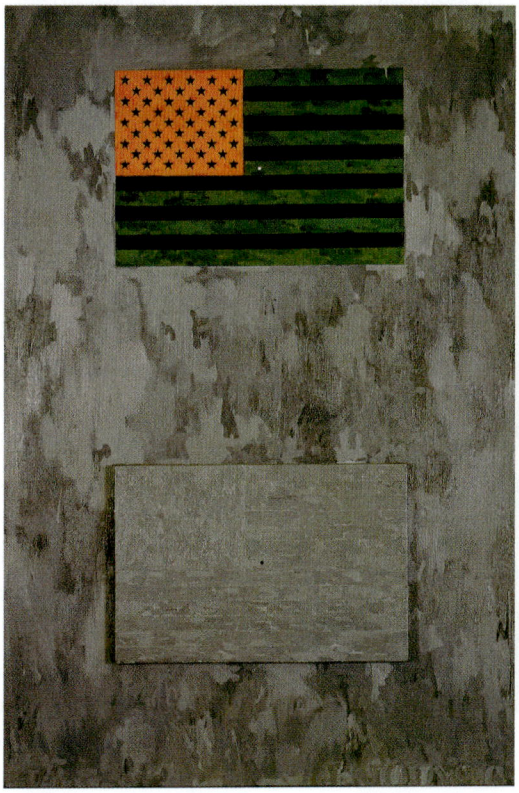

4.4.11 Jasper Johns, *Flag*, 1965. Private collection

The American artist Jasper Johns (b. 1930) makes us take a second look at familiar subjects, objects the artist says are "seen but not looked at." He uses such iconic images as numbers, letters, targets, and, perhaps most famously, the American flag, of which he painted several versions. In the version of *Flag* reproduced here, Johns uses his knowledge of color theory to create an optical illusion that forces a viewer to stare intently at an image of the flag (**4.4.11**). The top flag is made up of black and green stripes, while black stars are placed on a background of orange; these colors are complementary to the white, red, and blue colors of the American flag. (Johns's optical effect depends on the use of these complementary colors.) The rectangle in the bottom half of the painting is just a faded ghost of a flag. For the optical illusion to work, stare at the top flag for a full minute. Focus your attention on the white dot in the center. After a minute has passed, blink and look at the black dot in the center of the lower flag. The red, white, and blue of the American flag will appear. Johns is utilizing the science that lies

Synesthesia: when one of the five senses perceives something that was stimulated by a trigger from one of the other senses
Surrealism, Surrealist: an artistic movement in the 1920s and later; its works were inspired by dreams and the subconscious
Psychology: a science that studies the nature, development, and operation of the human mind
Psychoanalysis: a method of treating mental illness by making conscious the patient's subconscious fears or fantasies

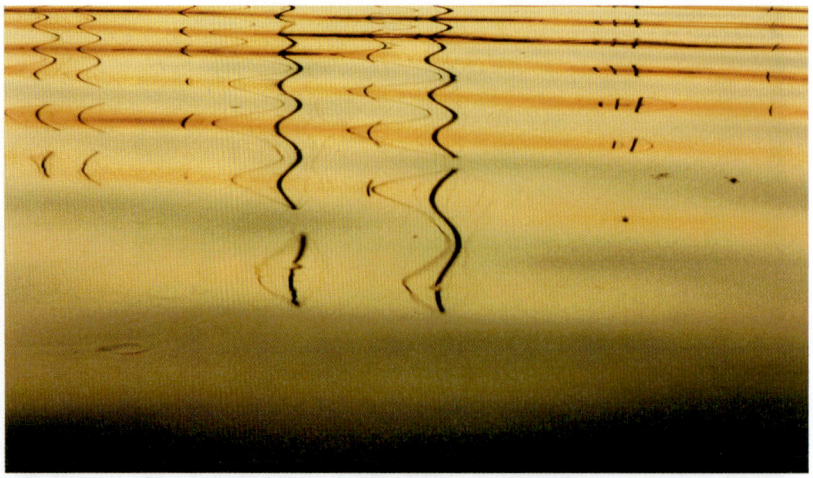

4.4.12 Marcia Smilack, *Cello Music*, 1992. Photograph, 12¾ × 24". Collection of the artist

behind afterimage effect. While looking at the top flag, your eyes became fatigued from the colors. Therefore, when you blinked your eyes and looked at the lower flag, your eyes produced the complementary colors of each aspect of the upper flag.

At times, artists have drawn upon other senses in addition to sight. The process whereby stimulation in one sense causes experiences in a different sense—such as visualizing color when we hear music—is called **synesthesia**. The American artist Marcia Smilack (b. 1949) experiences life as a synesthete, and creates artworks that reflect this correspondence between the senses. She describes her experience:

> The way I taught myself photography is to shoot when I hear a chord of color…I hear with my eyes and see with my ears.

Of the photograph *Cello Music* (**4.4.12**), Smilack says:

> I walked by the water and heard cello…
> I couldn't resist the sound so I gave in and aimed my camera at what had elicited it.
> As soon as I let go of my thoughts, the texture of the water washed over me in synch with the sound and turned to satin on my skin.
> When I felt myself climb into the shadows between the folds, I snapped the shutter.
> I hear cello every time I look at it today, though I discovered that if I turn it upside down, it becomes violin.

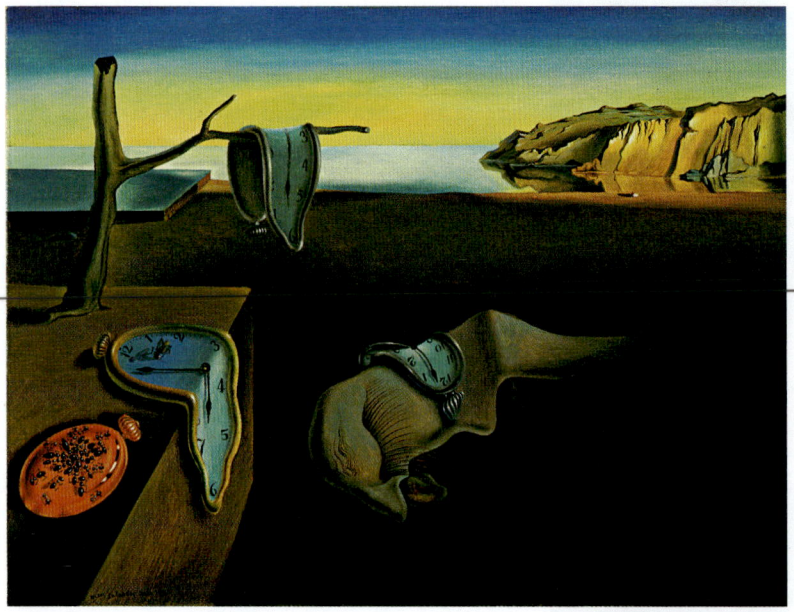

4.4.13 Salvador Dalí, *The Persistence of Memory*, 1931. Oil on canvas, 9½ × 13". MoMA, New York

While some artists have introduced the science of perception and color theory into their works, others have explored different aspects of the science of the mind. Salvador Dalí (1904–1989) was one of a group of artists known as the **Surrealists**, who were inspired by **psychology** and dream studies, and most particularly by the theories of the father of **psychoanalysis**, Sigmund Freud. Themes of sexual desire and fear are common in Dalí's paintings, which he associated with Freud's studies on sexual urges and behavior.

In *Persistence of Memory* (**4.4.13**), the stretched form in the center (a nose with long eyelashes and a tongue hanging out) is a self-portrait, and the cliffs in the background resemble the Catalan coast in Spain, where Dalí lived. After a late night, Dalí was inspired to paint the work while playing with some melted cheese from dinner. He said the painting was "nothing more than the soft, extravagant, solitary, paranoiac-critical Camembert cheese of space and time." Dalí invented the term paranoiac-critical, which he defined as the

> spontaneous method of irrational knowledge based on the critical and systematic objectivity of the associations and interpretations of delirious phenomena.

The consistency of the cheese inspired the three warped, dangling watch faces. The limp watches may be interpreted as symbols of both impotence and recent sexual satisfaction.

Scholars have remarked on a link between this work and the physicist Albert Einstein's theory of relativity, which addresses the complexities of time. In Dalí's painting, the clocks each read a different time, conveying a distorted sense of time and space. Dalí also painted a fly on the drooping watch on the ledge, a visual metaphor for the phrase "time flies."

Yayoi Kusama (b. 1929) is a Japanese artist who has used art to cope with her personal struggles and mental illness. Kusama compares the dots in her artworks to the cosmos; for her, the Earth, moon, stars, and each of us are dots. Like the cosmos, her paintings and **installations** have no boundaries. Upon entering a Kusama installation, the viewer will see dots of various sizes covering the floors, ceiling, and walls. The artist often uses mirrors, which multiply the number of dots experienced by the viewer and emphasize a sense of infinity (**4.4.14**).

Kusama has had hallucinatory episodes in which she sees the world around her covered in a net; for her, dots also symbolize the "holes" in this net pattern. She has said:

> When I was a child I experienced this state of self-obliteration, so I painted the same motif endlessly. When I was painting I found the same pattern on the ceiling, stairs, and windows, like they were all over. So I went closer and tried to touch them. Then they started to come up my arm as well. It was horrible but now it's over, almost.

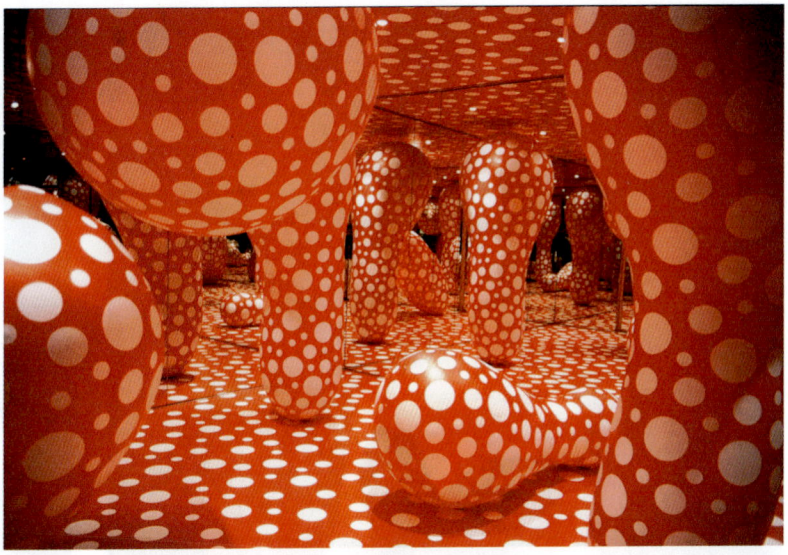

4.4.14 Yayoi Kusama, *Dots Obsession*, 2009. Vinyl balloons, dimensions variable, set of 8 pieces. Installation at Collection Les Abattoirs, Toulouse, France

Kusama frequently dresses in dots, and usually photographs herself within her installations wearing a coordinating dress or dot-shaped stickers on her clothes. The blending of the dots on her dress with those of the installation reflect Kusama's belief that by seeing oneself as part of the cosmos, in which the self exists as part of a larger system, the ego is lessened, even neutralized. Kusama has expanded her motif of dots to staging **happenings** around the world, in which she and others are covered in dots in public settings.

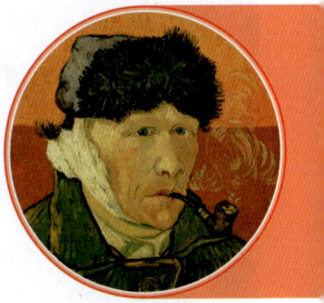

Vincent van Gogh's paintings are very expressive in terms of color and texture, often conveying the state of mind of the artist. See: **4.10.4, p. 682**

Science as a Tool to Understand and Care for Art

Scientific advancements have not only enabled the creation of artworks, but have also helped to improve the way experts can restore and understand them. Through the use of new technology, scientists have been able to study the layers of painting, both with X-rays and by analysing minute paint samples. The impetus for such studies is usually to determine how best to preserve or restore works. Scientists, however, often make discoveries that offer new information to art historians about an artist's creative process or the circumstances surrounding a commission.

Installation: originally referring to the hanging of pictures and arrangement of objects in an exhibition, installation may also refer to an intentional environment created as completed artwork
Happening: impromptu art action, initiated and planned by an artist, the outcome of which is not known in advance

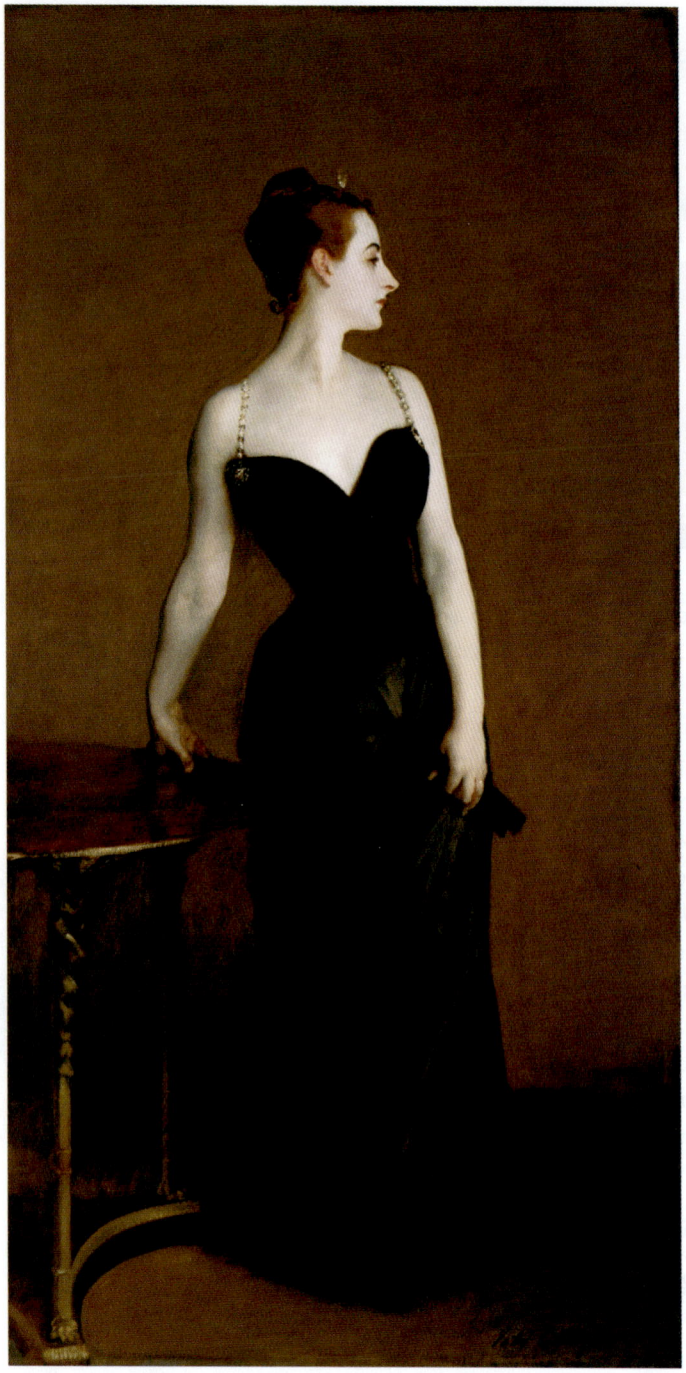

4.4.15a
John Singer Sargent, *Madame X (Madame Pierre Gautreau)*, 1883–84. Oil on canvas, 82⅛ × 43¼". Metropolitan Museum of Art, New York

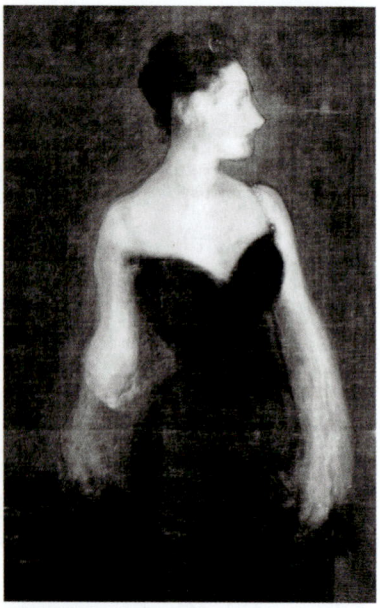

4.4.15b
John Singer Sargent, *Madame X (Madame Pierre Gautreau)*, 1883–84. Infrared reflectogram

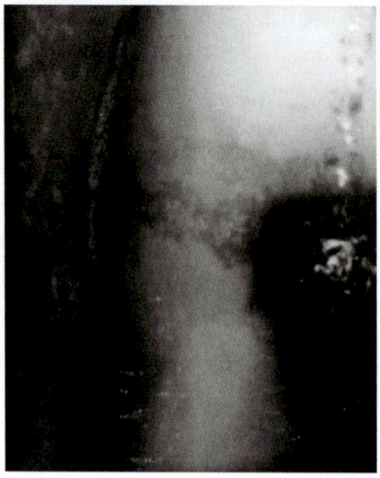

4.4.15c
John Singer Sargent, *Madame X (Madame Pierre Gautreau)*, 1883–84. Infrared reflectogram (detail)

John Singer Sargent (1856–1925) was a respected American portrait painter in the late nineteenth and early twentieth centuries, although at times his work caused a scandal. One of his most notorious works was of the socialite Madame Pierre Gautreau, the wife of a Parisian banker (**4.4.15a**). The portrait shows a young woman in a striking velvet-and-satin black dress, which markedly contrasts with her porcelain-colored skin. She leans on a table, which creates a line from her right hand up her arm to highlight the contour of her elegantly turned neck. To our modern eye, she looks wealthy, beautiful, and refined. From reviews of the Salon exhibition of 1884 in Paris, however, one finds that the work was highly criticized for being too erotic. Critics remarked that her plunging neckline, her pale skin against her dark clothing, and the fact that the gown looked as if it were about to fall off were all suggestive of a promiscuous woman. The artist argued that these aspects reflected how the **sitter** looked, but in an attempt to provide anonymity to the mortified socialite, he renamed the painting *Madame X*.

Sitter: person who poses, or "sits," for an artist to paint, sculpt, or photograph

Sargent kept the painting until he sold it to the Metropolitan Museum of New York in 1916. In 2005, conservators at the museum published an X-radiograph taken of *Madame X*, which revealed the changes Sargent had made to the painting since its initial creation (**4.4.15b**). The most striking change is that her right strap used to hang much lower down her arm, helping to explain some of the criticism of the figure's overt sensuality. (A photograph from the Salon in 1884 shows that Sargent made that change at some point during the exhibition.) The X-radiograph also shows other changes, such as Sargent's exploration of where to place each of the figure's arms, and slight adjustments to her face and neckline.

The most momentous restorations in recent times have been the cleaning of the **frescoes** at the Vatican in Rome, Italy. The restoration of Michelangelo's Sistine Chapel ceiling, which began in 1980, took nine years to complete, twice as long as it took Michelangelo to paint the ceiling originally (**4.4.16a** and **4.4.16b**). In order to decide how best to clean the frescoes, restorers first had to determine what was original and what was due to the effects of time, such as candle smoke, the interventions of previous restorers, rain damage, the settling of building foundations, and even bacteria introduced by the visits of millions of tourists. They analysed the chemical composition of minuscule samples of the paint, glue, wax, and varnish taken from the many layers they found on the ceiling. This analysis, plus their ability to examine the entire work at close range, led them to believe that Michelangelo had painted the ceiling almost entirely in *buon fresco* (when the plaster was still wet) with only slight corrections executed *a secco* (when the plaster had dried), and that all other layers were later additions.

The most shocking discovery, revealed after centuries of dirt were removed, was the bright colors that Michelangelo had used. Critics denounced the cleaning as a disaster, accusing the restorers of removing Michelangelo's original varnish. An international committee of the world's leading art conservators, however, reviewed the approach taken by the restoration team, and after a lengthy inspection of the restorers' research, methods, and handiwork, the panel declared that the team had been thorough and painstaking, and that their approach was accurate and correct: the original paintings had indeed been this bright.

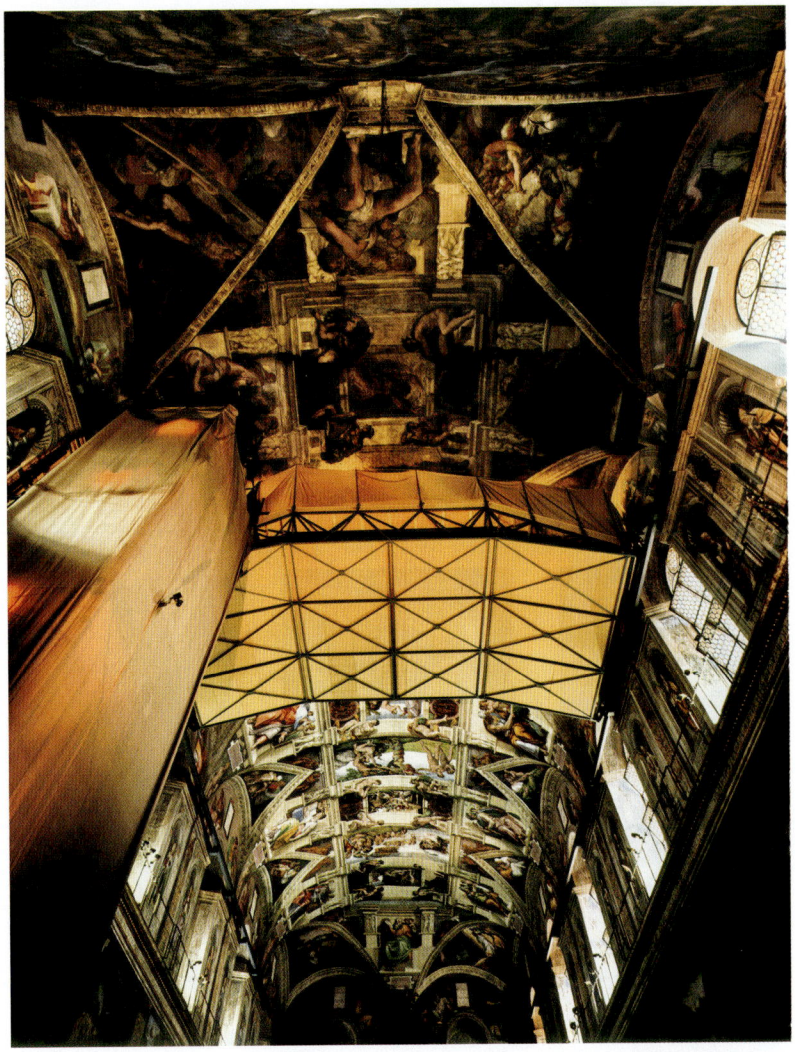

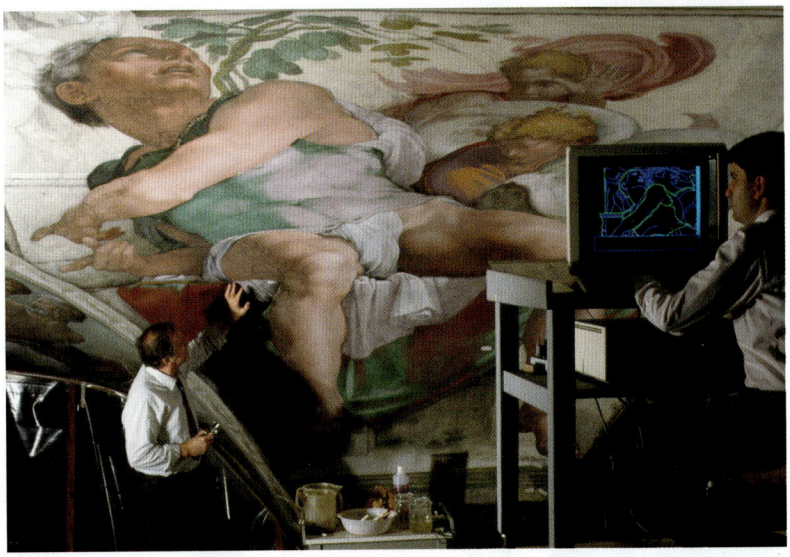

4.4.16a (top) and **4.4.16b** (bottom) Sistine Chapel ceiling during restoration, Vatican City, Italy, 1980–89

Fresco: a technique in which the artist paints onto freshly applied plaster. From the Italian *fresco*, "fresh"

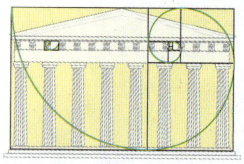

1.7.14b The use of the Golden Section in the design of the Parthenon, p. 148

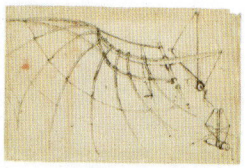

2.1.1 Leonardo da Vinci, *Drawing for a wing of a flying machine*, p. 192

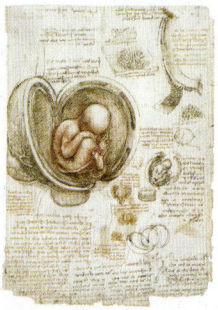

2.1.2 Leonardo da Vinci, *Studies of the fetus in the womb*, c. 1510–13, p. 193

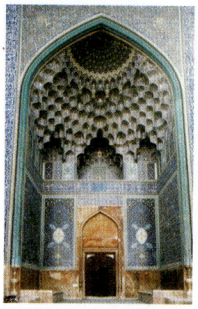

4.2.15 Main entrance portal, Masjid-i-Shah, Isfahan, Iran, early 17th century, p. 588

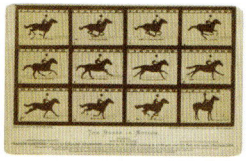

2.9.3 Eadweard Muybridge, *The Horse in Motion*, 1878, p. 336

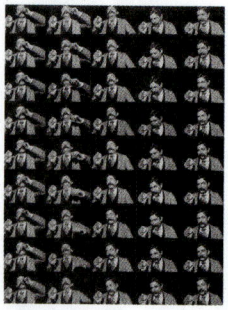

1.5.16 Thomas Edison and W. K. Dickson, *Fred Ott's Sneeze*, 1894, p. 122

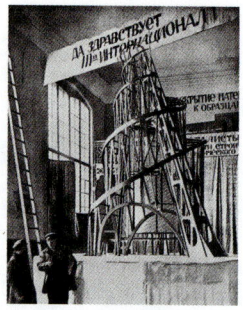

1.2.11 Vladimir Tatlin, Model for *Monument to the Third International*, 1919, p. 68

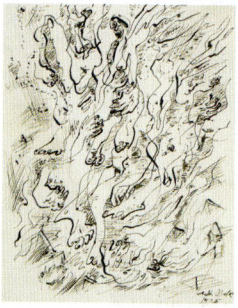

1.1.16 André Masson, *Automatic Drawing*, 1925–26, p. 53

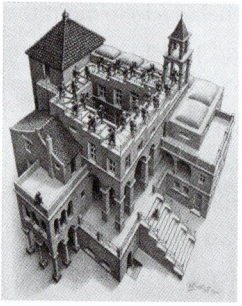

1.3.23 M. C. Escher, *Ascending and Descending*, 1960, p. 92

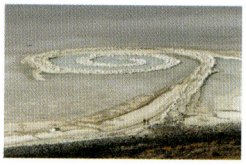

2.4.16 Robert Smithson, *Spiral Jetty*, 1969–70, p. 252

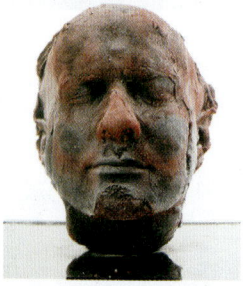

0.0.16 Marc Quinn, *Self*, 1991, p. 32

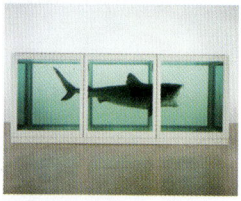

2.4.18 Damien Hirst, *The Physical Impossibility of Death in the Mind of Someone Living*, 1991, p. 253

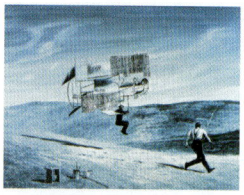

1.4.17 Mark Tansey, *Picasso and Braque*, 1992, p. 103

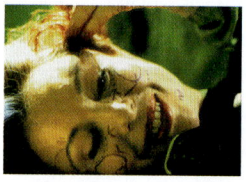

4.9.20b ORLAN, Seventh surgery-performance, entitled *Omnipresence*, 1993, p. 678

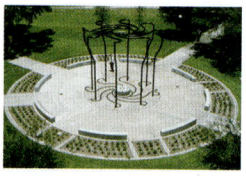

1.5.13 Nancy Holt, *Solar Rotary*, 1995, p. 120

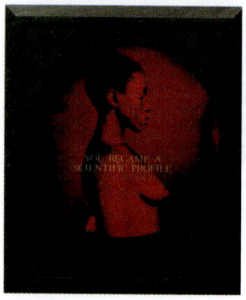

2.8.24 Carrie Mae Weems, "You Became a Scientific Profile," 1995, p. 329

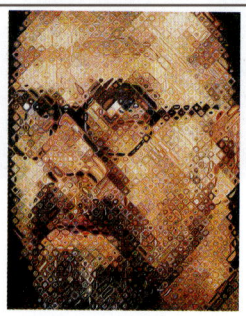

1.9.7a Chuck Close, *Self-Portrait*, 1997, p. 163

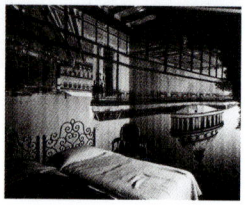

2.8.2 Abelardo Morell, *Camera Obscura Image...*, 1999, p. 316

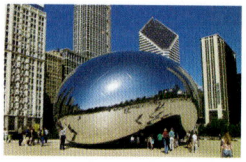

1.2.18 Anish Kapoor, *Cloud Gate*, 2004, p. 73

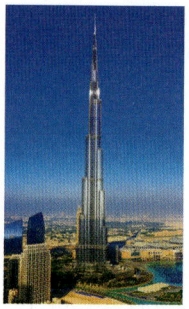

2.5.31 Adrian Smith and Bill Baker, Burj Khalifa, Dubai, 2010, p. 277

4.5 Art, Illusion, and Transformation

Illusionism: the artistic skill or trick of making something look real
***Trompe l'oeil*:** an extreme kind of illusion meant to deceive the viewer that the objects included are real
Two-dimensional: having height and width
Three-dimensional: having height, width, and depth
Renaissance: a period of cultural and artistic change in Europe from the fourteenth to the seventeenth century
Oculus: a round opening at the center of a dome
Putto (plural **putti**): a representation of a nude or scantily clad infant angel or boy, common in Renaissance and Baroque art
Balustrade: a railing supported by short pillars

Artists have utilized art to transform the way things appear and to direct the viewer's experience of the work. Beginning with the ancient Greeks, artists have often been judged by the degree to which they could re-create the real world. **Illusionism** is the use of mathematical and pictorical techniques to create works of art that appear to be replicas of real objects. ***Trompe l'oeil*** ("fool the eye") is the French term for **two-dimensional** artworks that convincingly appear to be **three-dimensional** objects or spaces. Artists have created art to impress, to trick, and to suggest a transformation of objects and ideas.

Art as an Illusionistic Window

The ancient Roman author Pliny the Elder tells a story that reveals the millennia-old efforts by artists to create convincing illusions. Pliny describes a contest between two great Greek painters, Zeuxis and Parrhasius, to see who could paint the most realistic picture. As Pliny tells it, Zeuxis's painting of grapes was so realistic that birds flew down to peck at them. Parrhasius in turn painted such a convincing curtain that Zeuxis reached for the drapery, hoping to see the painting on which his rival was working. After being fooled by the illusion of the curtain, Zeuxis conceded that Parrhasius had won the competition. Although the paintings of Zeuxis and Parrhasius have not survived, many artists since have striven to match and even surpass the achievements of these ancient painters, developing techniques that fool us into thinking we are looking at real spaces and objects rather than at artworks.

Artists of the Italian **Renaissance** revived the ideals of the ancient Greeks and Romans, including the desire to impress others with artworks that imitate the real world. The architect and thinker Leon Battista Alberti (1404–1472) wrote in his treatise *On Painting* that artists should design their paintings as illusionary windows through which viewers would be able to perceive a new reality (see Gateway Box: Raphael, p. 617). Since then, artists have been rigorously trained in illusionistic techniques in art academies throughout America and Europe (see Box: Satirizing Illusionism, p. 619).

During the Renaissance, the Italian artist Andrea Mantegna (*c.* 1431–1506) created *trompe l'oeil* paintings for an entire room of the palace of Ludovico Gonzaga, the Duke of Mantua. The chamber, known as the Camera degli Sposi (Room of the Newlyweds), was used both to greet government officials and as a bedroom for the duke and his wife (**4.5.1**, p. 616). Mantegna painted the walls with scenes of the royal family and of historical victories of the Gonzagas.

In the vaulted ceiling the artist painted the illusion of what seems to be an **oculus** opening onto a blue sky, and surrounded it with figures looking down at the people below. There are **putti** with their chubby baby bodies, some hanging onto the painted **balustrade**, others looking down through the painted oculus. Several young girls peer over the balustrade, as does an enigmatic turbaned figure. One

4.5.1 (right) Andrea Mantegna, detail of central oculus, ceiling of the Camera degli Sposi. Fresco, 8'9" diameter. Ducal Palace, Mantua, Italy

4.5.2 (below right) Parmigianino, *Self-Portrait in a Convex Mirror*, c. 1524. Oil on wood, 9½" diameter. Kunsthistorisches Museum, Vienna, Austria

Convex: curved outward, like the exterior of a sphere

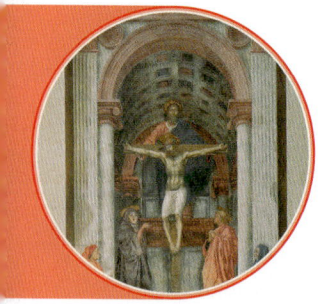

The Renaissance artist Masaccio utilized one-point perspective to create the illusion of a separate architectural niche in the painting *Trinity*: see **1.3.20, p. 89**

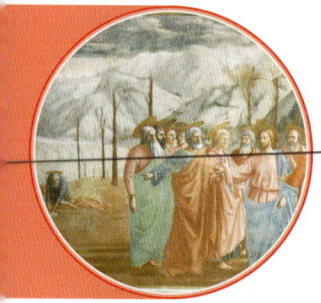

Masaccio utilized atmospheric perspective in *Tribute Money* by making the distance hazy, painted in cooler colors than the foreground, see **3.6.5, p. 463**

light-skinned girl wears a white veil, referring to the title of the room and to the duke's recent marriage. Similarly, the prominent peacock symbolizes Juno, the Roman goddess of marriage. All of this activity surprises the viewer below, who may feel particularly nervous about the potted plant precariously held in place with a pole by two smirking young girls.

The Italian artist Francesco Mazzola (1503–1540), known as Parmigianino ("the little one from Parma"), gave a self-portrait to Pope Clement VII in order to attract commissions (**4.5.2**). The painting is on a **convex** piece of wood; holding it, one seems to be looking into a convex mirror—except that one does not see one's own reflection in the artwork, but the portrait of Parmigianino, who studied himself in an actual convex mirror to create this painting. Parmigianino, however, made one change from what he saw when he studied his reflection. The artist accurately depicted himself as right-handed, but in order to do so he would presumably have had to study his left hand when he actually painted. Parmigianino also featured a portion of the frame of the painting he was

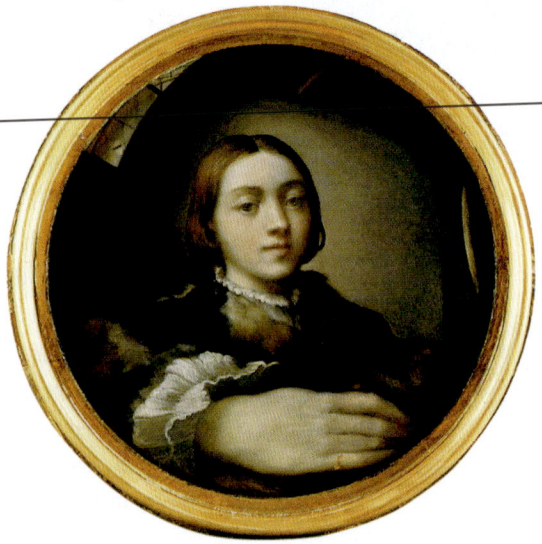

Gateway to Art: Raphael, *The School of Athens*
Architectural Illusion

For the other Raphael Gateway boxes, see p. 90, p. 146, p. 194, and p. 470

The Italian artist Raphael (1483–1520) painted *The School of Athens* on one of the walls of the library of Pope Julius II in the Vatican, in Rome, to create the illusion of an architectural space that was separate from the actual room and filled with lifesized figures who linked the Classical world with the **humanist** Renaissance (**4.5.3**). The arched frame and sculptural figures (painted by another artist) are all part of the illusion. This **frescoed** wall was designed as part of a larger program including three other paintings, an intricately tiled floor, and a painted ceiling, all choreographed thematically as a backdrop for Pope Julius II's library. The pope's hundreds of books were laid on shelves built directly under the paintings on each of the four walls (these shelves have since been removed).

The School of Athens highlights the development of learning in the ancient world, focusing on the great philosophers Plato and Aristotle, who are the central figures in the painting. The other large paintings, turning counterclockwise around the room, are: *Parnassus*, depicting the mountain sacred to the god Apollo and, in Classical mythology, the home of poetry (on the left wall in **4.5.3**); *Disputa*, a work that unites Classical ideas with Renaissance Christian theology; and *Jurisprudence*, which emphasizes law and justice. The thematic decorative scheme reflects the purpose of the room: Julius's books were arranged so their subjects corresponded with the Classical topic of the wall painting above them. Beneath *The School of Athens* were books on philosophy and mathematics; beneath *Parnassus*, poetry; and so on.

The ceiling further unites the themes of the walls through its depiction of four female figures, who personify Philosophy, Poetry, Theology, and Justice. If you stand in the room, the illusion of depth created in *The School of Athens* is even more successful because the paintings on all four walls appear to be separate rooms.

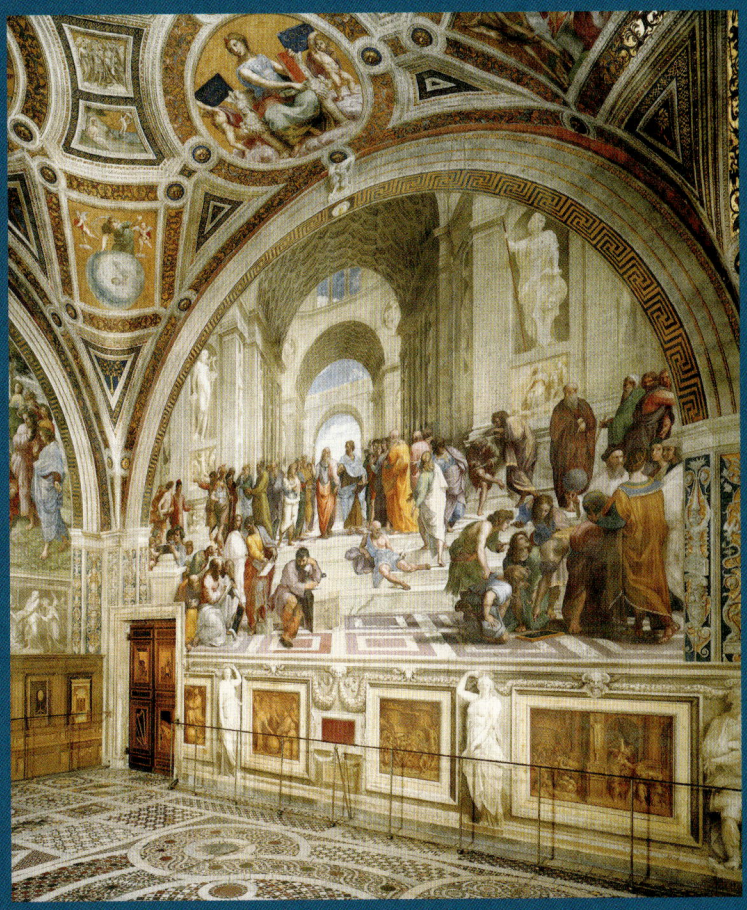

4.5.3 Raphael and assistants, Stanza della Segnatura, Vatican City, Italy, 1509–11

creating (visible on the right side of the artwork) in order to heighten the illusion of it being a hand-held mirror.

Renaissance painters utilized their skills to create illusions so lifelike that they appeared to be reality rather than art, and in so doing inspired artists in future generations to create increasingly convincing illusionistic works. In the nineteenth century, the American painter William M. Harnett (1848–1892) was so skillful at tricking his audiences with *trompe l'oeil* that, when he created a truly convincing dollar bill in one of his paintings, he was investigated for counterfeiting by the US Treasury Department. In *The Old Violin*, Harnett painted a violin and sheet music so that they appear to be hanging

Humanism, humanist: the study of such subjects as history, philosophy, languages, and literature, particularly in relation to those of ancient Greece and Rome

Fresco: a technique in which the artist paints onto freshly applied plaster. From the Italian *fresco*, "fresh"

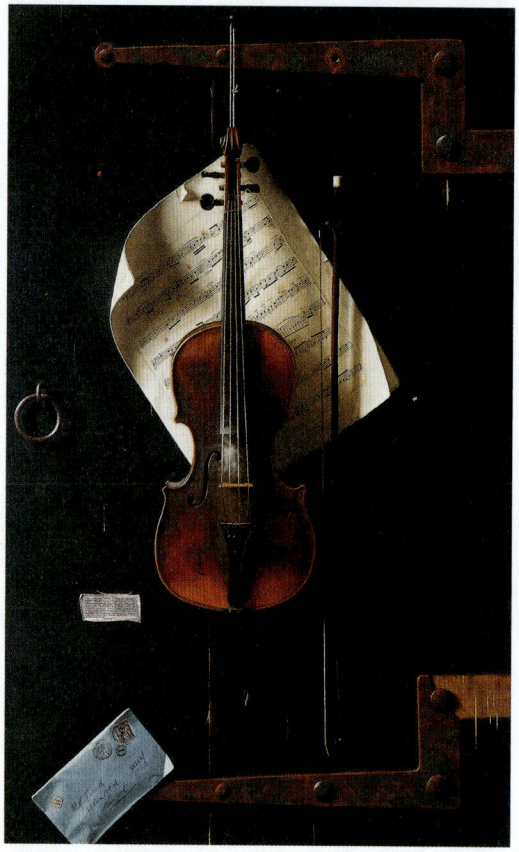

4.5.4 William M. Harnett, *The Old Violin*, 1886. Oil on canvas, 38 × 23⅝". National Gallery of Art, Washington, D.C

Anamorphosis: the distorted representation of an object so that it appears correctly proportioned only when viewed from one particular position

Foreshortening: a perspective technique that depicts a form at a very oblique (often dramatic) angle to the viewer in order to show depth in space

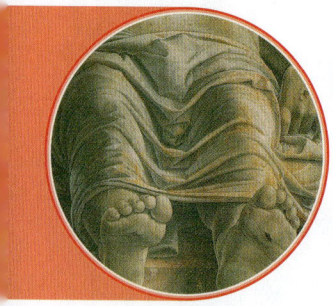

The Renaissance artist Mantegna utilized the perspective technique of foreshortening to emphasize the stigmata in Christ's feet: see **4.3.3, p. 593**

from a real wooden door (**4.5.4**). The artist teases viewers, leading us to question what is reality and what is illusion. If we were to read the small piece of torn newspaper so skillfully painted slightly to the left of the bottom of the violin, we would find that the text is gibberish: it is not a newspaper, but another superb illusion. The only part of the painting that is in fact real is a blue envelope signed by the artist, which he attached to the lower left corner of the painting. When this painting was first exhibited, guards had to be posted around the painting constantly to prevent viewers from reaching out to test if the objects were real. While some artists, such as Harnett, thrived working within the rules of illusionism, others found the obsession with illusion and perspective restrictive and somewhat absurd (see Box: Satirizing Illusionism).

The British artist Julian Beever (b. 1960) applies a special form of *trompe l'oeil* known as **anamorphosis** to his sidewalk art. An anamorphic image is one that is stretched and distorted, but becomes clear and realistic when viewed from a single, oblique angle. Beever's chalk drawings confront passersby with what appear to be convincing scenes taking place in three-dimensional space. When his *Woman in Pool* is viewed from the right vantage point, it appears that a woman is lying back in a swimming pool, drink in hand, kicking her leg in the air (**4.5.5a**). But when it is viewed from the opposite direction, the illusion is destroyed and one can see that Beever used extreme **foreshortening** to represent the woman's leg (**4.5.5b**). The only genuinely three-dimensional element in the photograph of the illusionistic drawing (**4.5.5a**) is the artist himself, who is holding a drink and has his foot placed flat on the pavement.

4.5.5a (below left) Julian Beever, *Woman in Pool*, drawn in Brussels, Belgium, 1992. Colored chalks, 14'9¼" × 13'1½" (correct viewing point)

4.5.5b (below) Julian Beever, *Woman in Pool*, drawn in Glasgow, Scotland, 1994. Colored chalks, 14'9¼" × 13'1½" (incorrect viewing point)

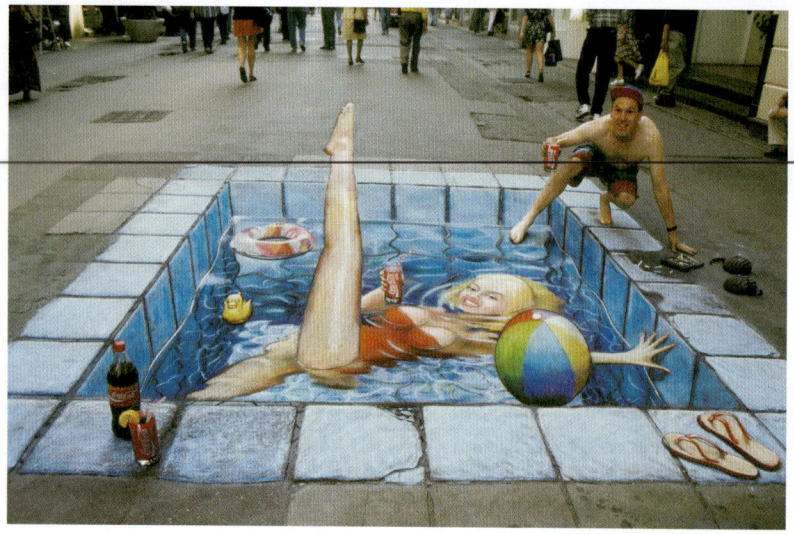

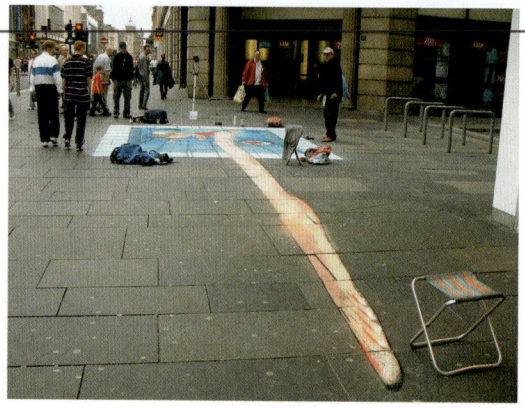

Satirizing Illusionism: Hogarth's *False Perspective*

In this work, William Hogarth (1697–1764), an eighteenth-century British artist, **satirizes** the traditional training of painters who were taught to use the rules of **perspective** to create believable spaces (**4.5.6**). In this **frontispiece**, Hogarth applies these rules in order to break them, creating the illusion of a space that is, in fact, impossible.

See if you can find these spatial impossibilities:

- The woman in the window of her building is lighting the pipe of the man standing outside the window but on top of a hill.
- The man in the right foreground must have quite an extraordinarily long fishing line in order to reach beyond the rod of the man in the distance.
- In the lower left, the sheep closest to us are smaller than those further away; in reality, objects of the same size would decrease in size as they recede into the distance.
- Similarly, the trees at the bottom of the hill get larger as they recede into the distance, suggesting that the bird on the furthest tree is improbably big.
- The church in the distance appears to be both grounded on land and floating on water.
- The man in the boat in the center of the scene wants to aim his gun at a swan, but instead shoots the underside of the bridge.
- The sign on the building in the foreground seems to be hanging behind the trees on the hill in the background.
- The barrels behind the large man in the foreground show both the top and bottom of the container, an impossibility from one viewpoint.
- The **vanishing point** of the grid upon which the man in the foreground stands is projecting into the viewer's space, rather than receding into the pictorial space, making it seem as if the man should be falling forward out of the picture.

Satire: work of art that exposes the weaknesses and mistakes of its subjects to ridicule
Perspective: the creation of the illusion of depth in a two-dimensional image by using mathematical principles
Frontispiece: an illustration facing the title-page in a book
Vanishing point: a point in a work of art at which imaginary sight lines appear to converge, suggesting depth

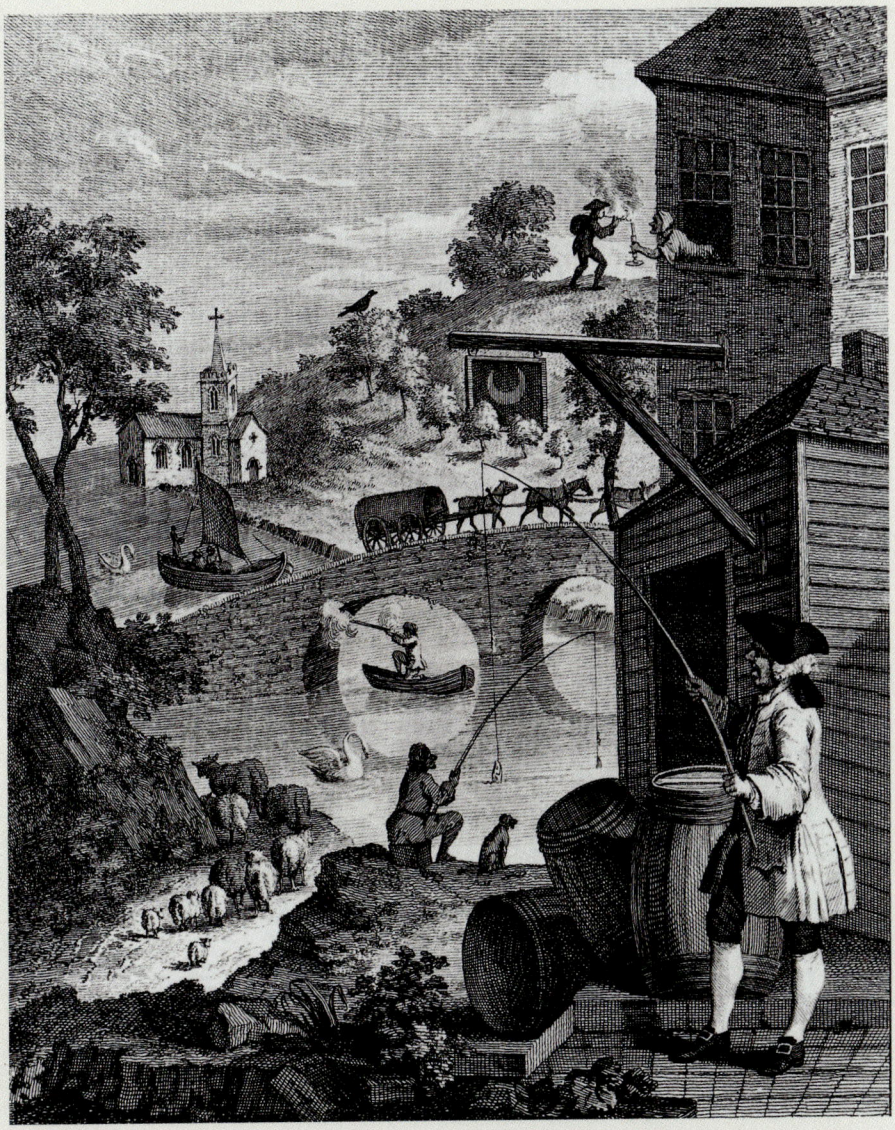

4.5.6 William Hogarth, *False Perspective*. Engraving from *Dr. Brook Taylor's Method of Perspective Made Easy, Both in Theory and in Practice*, 1754

Stylobate: the uppermost platform of a Classical temple, on which the columns stand
Entasis: the slight swelling or bulge at the midpoint of a column
Implied line: a line not actually drawn but suggested by elements in the work

Illusionism as Trickery

> With wonderful skill, he carved a figure, brilliantly, out of snow-white ivory…and fell in love with his own creation.
>
> (The ancient Roman poet Ovid on Pygmalion's carving of Galatea)

In Classical mythology, the sculptor Pygmalion created a statue of a woman so fine and beautiful that he fell in love with her. He dressed and pampered her, believing her more perfect than any human woman. He begged the gods to grant him a wife as perfect as his statue, and the goddess of love, Venus, granted his wish by bringing the statue to life. The myth suggests that an artist's love for his work, and his skill at re-creating the natural world, can create illusions even more divine than those made by nature.

As did Pygmalion, sculptors can use their skill to create works that appear to be convincingly real, and that share the physical and psychological space of those who observe them.

In ancient Greece, the designers of the Parthenon understood that the human eye could play tricks on the beholder. They used their knowledge of mathematics to ensure that the building would appear just as they wished it to (**4.5.7a**). Because of the great size of the temple, the base and columns would appear warped unless the architects could adjust their design to counteract these naturally occurring optical illusions. For example, the **stylobate**, or platform on which the columns stand, would appear to sag if it were constructed as a precisely straight horizontal structure. To counteract this, the architects created a slight upward swelling in the center of the stylobate, which makes the base of the temple seem perfectly horizontal when we look at it.

Several other visual manipulations were utilized in the design of the columns. For example, the columns of the Parthenon actually swell at about mid-height (**4.5.7b**). This optical trick prevents them from appearing, when looked at from a distance, to be hourglass-shaped, which would happen if the columns were flawlessly straight-sided. This swelling at the midpoint of such columns is called **entasis**. In addition, the columns are not perfectly vertical but actually tilted slightly inward. If they were extended into the air, the **implied lines** created by the four corner columns would eventually intersect at some point more than a mile into the sky. Finally, the columns are not all spaced equidistantly, as they appear to be; those closer to the corners have less space between them. This is another visual trick used to compensate for the optical illusion that makes columns near the end of a row appear further apart than ones near the middle.

4.5.7a (below) Kallikrates and Iktinos, Parthenon, 447–432 BCE, Acropolis, Athens, Greece

4.5.7b (below right) Diagram showing the optical illusions utilized in the Parthenon

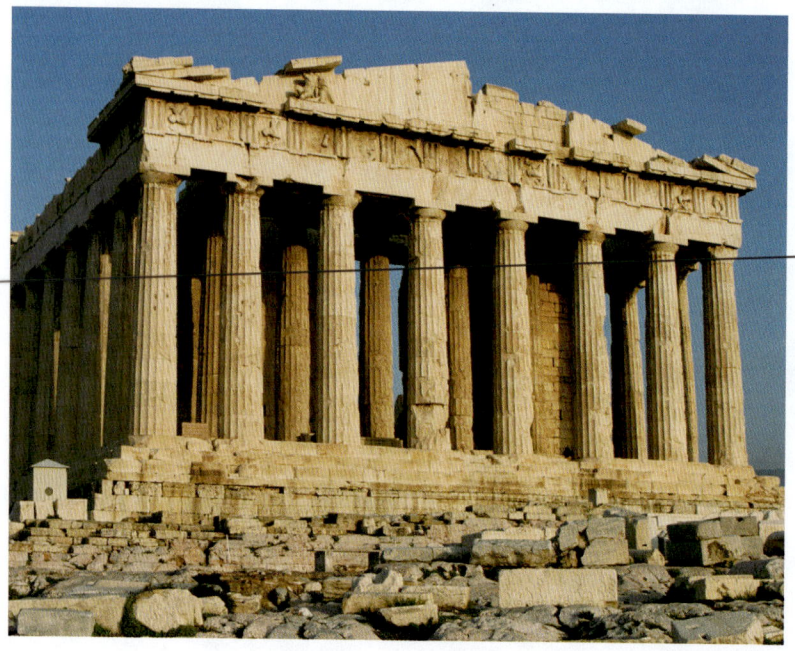

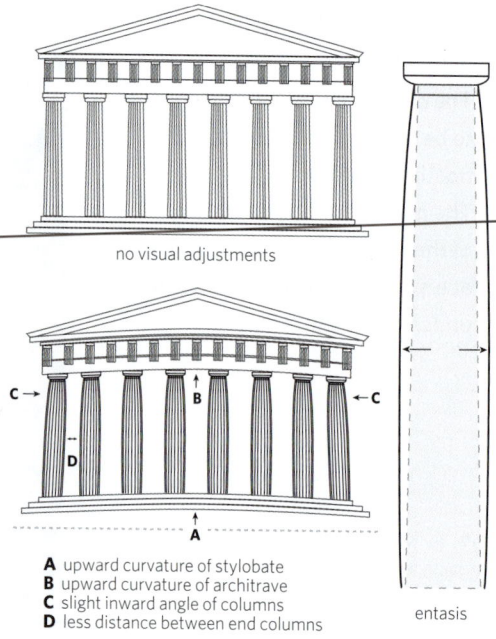

Architectural and two-dimensional illusory techniques were utilized by the Italian artist and architect Giulio Romano (*c.* 1499–1546), who designed a villa for the same Gonzaga family that had commissioned the decoration of the Camera degli Sposi from Mantegna (see **4.5.1**, p. 616). As both architect and interior painter for the Palazzo del Tè in Mantua (**4.5.8**), Giulio Romano designed a building that subtly broke many of the rules of Classical architecture, with the result that, when looked at closely, the villa appears to be unstable. Giulio Romano achieved this playful illusion by taking Classical architectural elements used in such buildings as the Parthenon, and arranging them to create the impression of instability rather than the solidity normally expected of architecture. The **architraves** that rest on the columns are narrower than would normally be the case; but, even stranger, they seem to break in the middle rather than reaching from one column to the next, as they should. As a result, some of the **triglyphs** in the **frieze** above the columns appear to be slipping down, as if they might even fall to the ground. The material of the structure itself is also an illusion; rather than marble or stone, which were normally used for luxurious buildings, the exterior is **stucco**-covered brick.

The explanation for the odd design of the Palazzo del Tè's exterior becomes apparent when one enters the building (**4.5.9**). A painted scene of the *Fall of the Giants* playfully suggests why the exterior appears to be falling apart. The painting depicts an episode from Greek mythology, when the gods defeated the giants in battle. Having been trained by Raphael, and having worked as his assistant on his paintings

Architrave: a beam that rests on the top of a row of columns
Triglyph: a projecting block carved with three raised bands, which alternates with figurative reliefs in a frieze
Frieze: the strip that goes around the top of a building, often filled with sculptural ornamentation
Stucco: a coarse plaster designed to give the appearance of stone

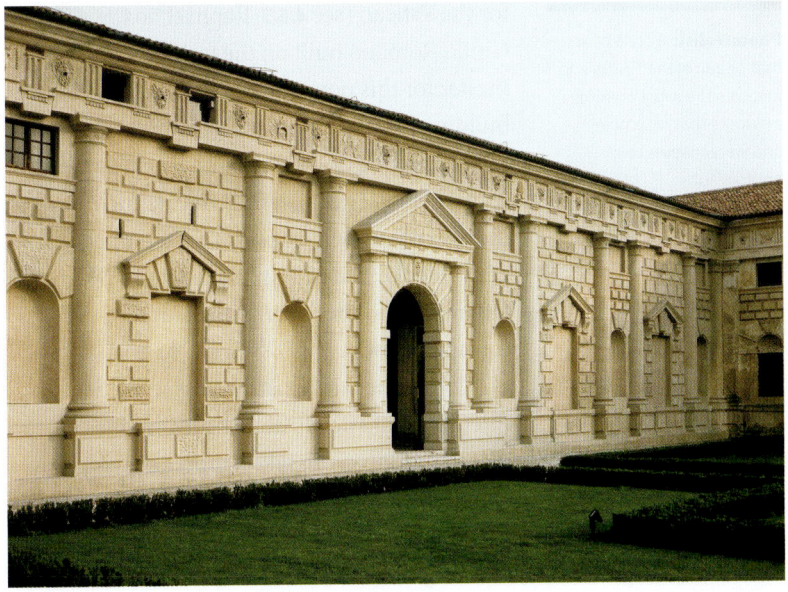

4.5.8 Giulio Romano, Palazzo del Tè, exterior, 1524–34, Mantua, Italy

4.5.9 Giulio Romano, *Fall of the Giants*, 1526–35. Fresco, Sale dei Giganti, Palazzo del Tè, Mantua, Italy

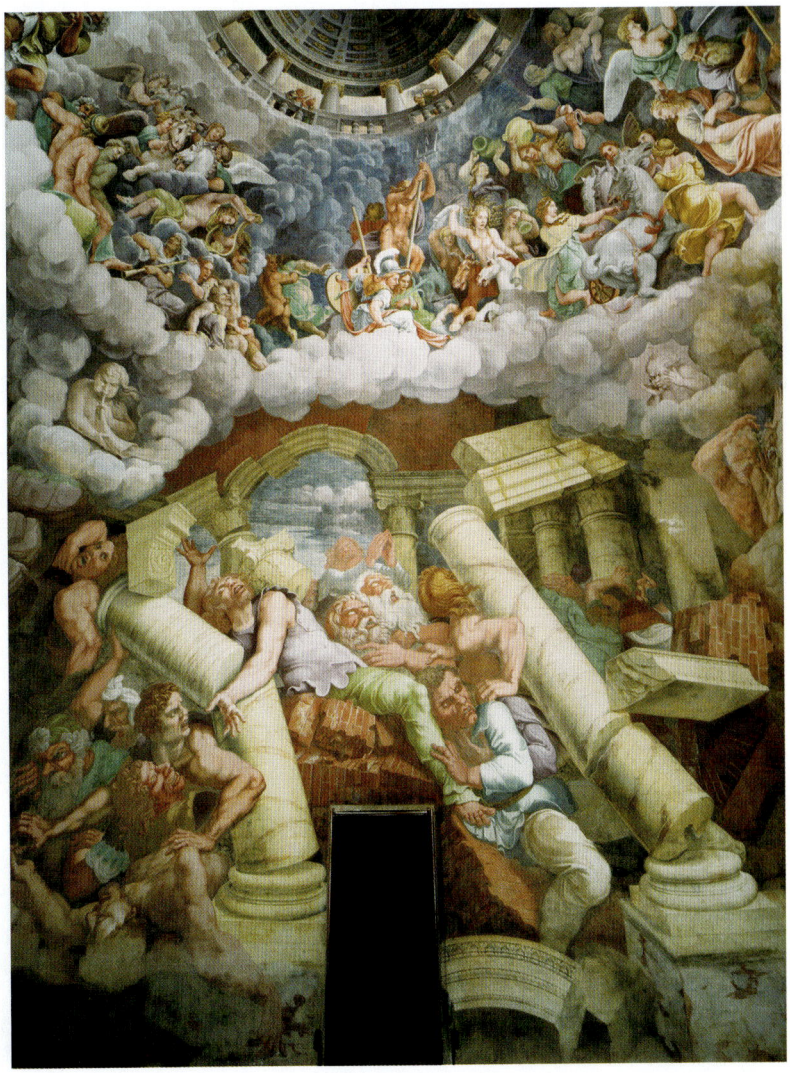

Photorealist: a style of art that began in the 1960s and involves the artist creating artworks that resemble, and were inspired by, photographs

Medium (plural **media**): the material on or from which an artist chooses to make a work of art

for the Vatican (see **4.5.3**, Raphael box, p. 617), Giulio Romano built on the techniques of his master for this powerful painted illusion. The building in Giulio Romano's painting appears to be tumbling down, crushing the struggling giants below. The powerful wind, shown at the viewer's upper left blowing a trumpet, is controlled by the gods in the clouds of Mount Olympus, and therefore protected from the turmoil below.

Contemporary artists have also used intensely realistic illusionistic techniques to inspire the viewer to take a more contemplative approach to looking at art. The **Photorealist** American artist Chuck Close (b. 1940) creates paintings that inspire us to question what we see. As a child, one of Close's favorite pastimes was to entertain neighbors and schoolmates by doing magic tricks. As an adult artist, he has become known for manipulating portraits of friends and family. He begins his creative process by taking photographs of them, which he then transforms into artworks in another **medium**. For example, although *Fanny/Fingerpainting* looks like a photograph, Close actually hand-painted an image of his wife's grandmother using only his thumb- and fingerprints (**4.5.10**). As with most of his artworks, Close laid a grid over the original photograph of the subject, and then carefully enlarged and copied each block so that the entire image fills an 8 ft. 6 in. by 7 ft. canvas. The original photograph is thus transformed into a much bigger image that appears to be a photographic enlargement produced by technology. Close's process, while still quite mechanical, remains personal because of the use of the artist's own hands in the act of creation.

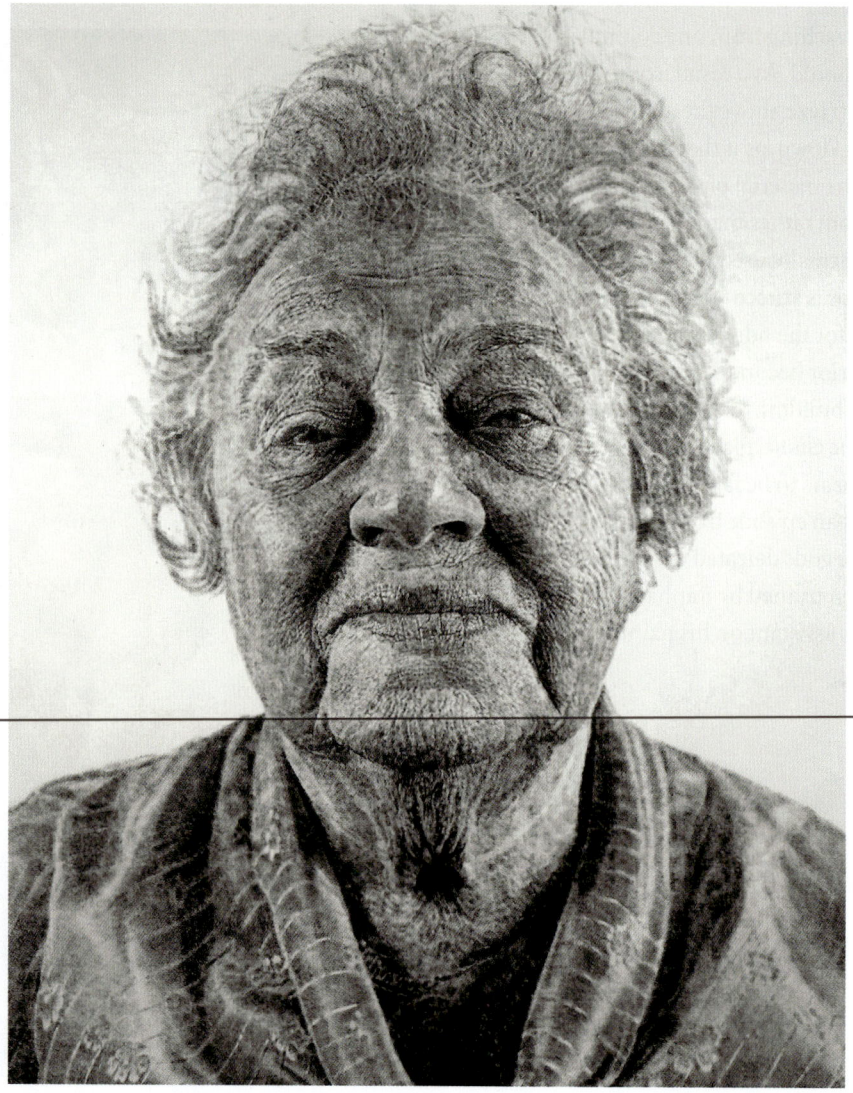

4.5.10 Chuck Close, *Fanny/Fingerpainting*, 1985. Oil on canvas, 8'6" × 7'. National Gallery of Art, Washington, D.C.

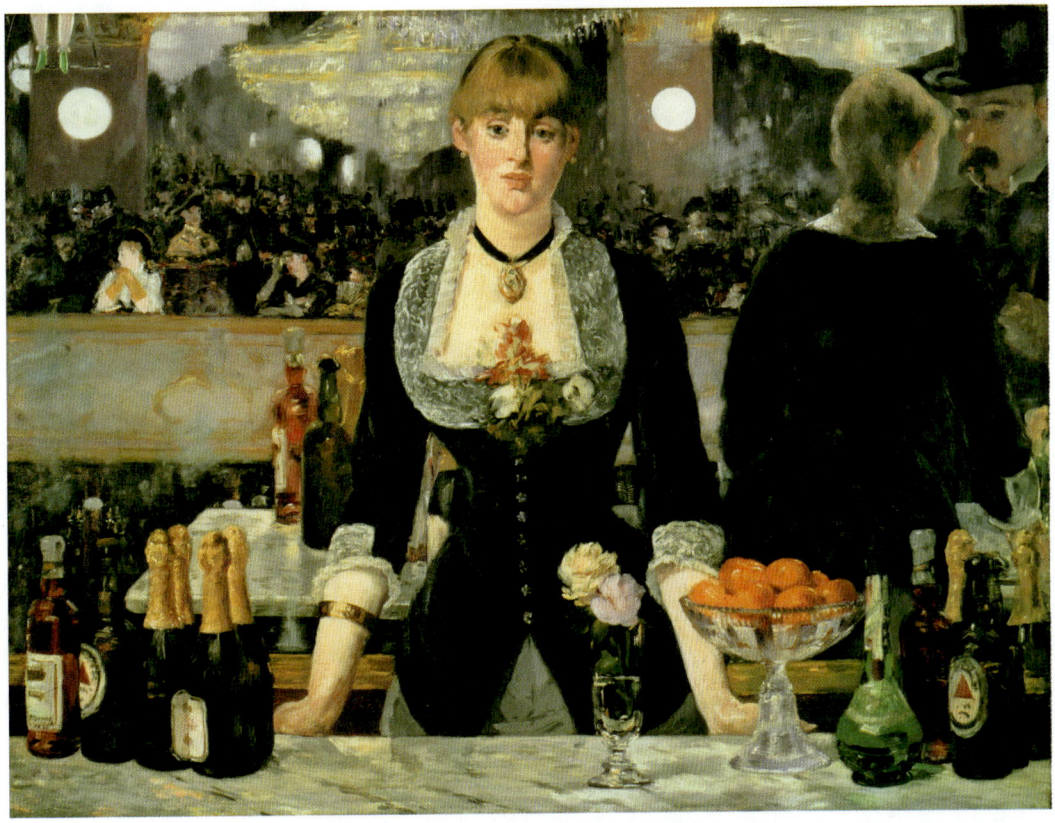

4.5.11 Édouard Manet, *A Bar at the Folies-Bergère*, 1882. Oil on canvas, 37⅞ × 51¼". Courtauld Gallery, London, England

Illusion and the Transformation of Ideas

Artists often create works that suggest or inspire physical, spiritual, or mental transformations. The painting *A Bar at the Folies-Bergère* (**4.5.11**), by French artist Édouard Manet (1832–1883), makes use of a mirror to transform the viewer's perception of the scene. The Folies-Bergère was one of the most popular bars and entertainment houses in Paris in the nineteenth century; the club offered entertainment by dancers, singers, and even trapeze artists (a pair of feet can be seen hanging in the upper left of Manet's painting), all dressed in revealing and provocative clothes. The blurry background behind the barmaid suggests she is standing in front of a mirror, which reflects the Parisian club scene she is facing. Discrepancies in the reflection, however, make one question the accuracy of what one sees. For example, the bottles next to the barmaid on the left of the canvas appear to be placed in a different order and in a different place in the reflection behind her. In addition, some viewers question whether the posture of the barmaid on the far right is an accurate reflection of the barmaid looking out at us. Manet certainly had the skill to depict perspective precisely, so one must consider why he chose to create such an ambiguous reflection.

Several interpretations of *A Bar at the Folies-Bergère* have been suggested. If we assume that the figure on the right is indeed a reflection of the barmaid, then we viewers are standing in the place of the man in the top hat to whom she is talking. He is presumably a client, as it was common for the female entertainers and barmaids at the Folies-Bergère to be hired by the clientele for sexual favors. Could that be what they are talking about? The ambiguities in the reflection may be a way for the artist to suggest different emotional states in the barmaid, contrasting her personal experience or feelings with her external appearance. Some have argued that she appears to be much more engaged in the reflected image than she is as she stands before us in the center of the painting. Her gaze leaves us questioning her state of mind: is she sad, distracted, or bored? Another interpretation suggests that the artist is depicting a fantasy.

Art and Spiritual Transformation

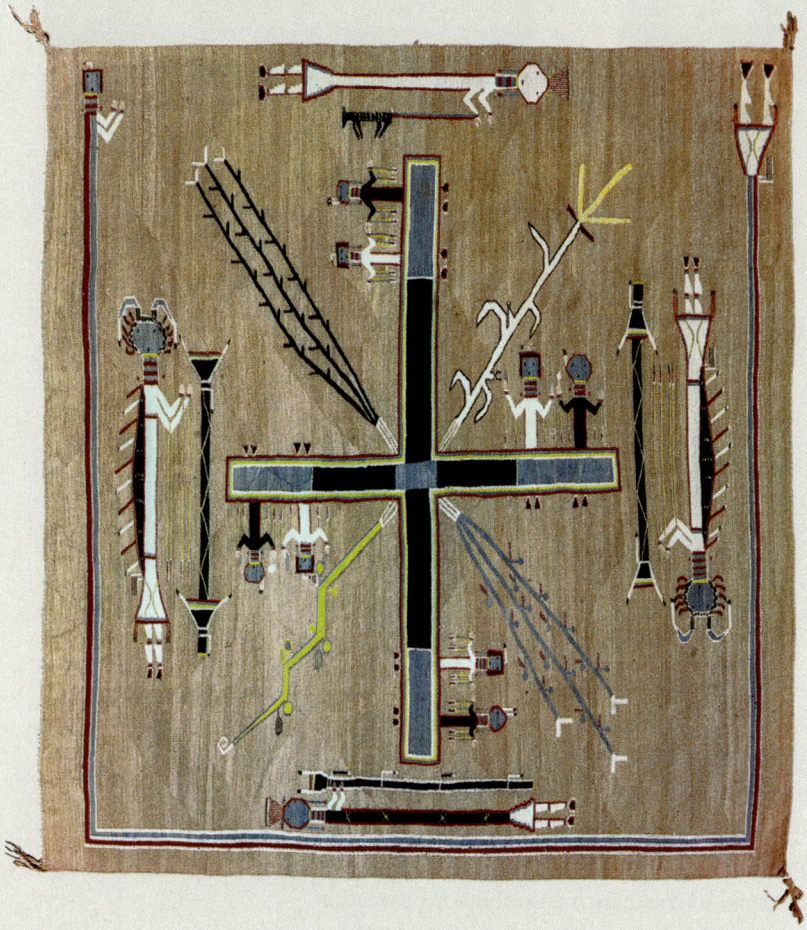

human, Tsil-ol-ne, partakes in a journey that is symbolic of the journey through life. His long journey will bring him to the Colorado River where he will be pulled ashore by the gods, shown one on each side holding a staff. Guides (male and female pairs placed in each quadrant standing on the edges of the crossed logs) will teach him everything he needs before he returns home. All the while Tsil-ol-ne is protected by the guardian god Rainbow Maiden, shown as a stretched figure that surrounds the scene. The Rainbow Maiden, however, does not border the East horizon (shown at the top of the picture) in order to allow for sunrise the next day, and symbolically a new beginning after the transformation of Tsil-ol-ne.

An Olmec transformation figure (**4.5.13**) is a representation of a shaman as he transforms

4.5.12 (left) *Whirling Log Ceremony*, c. 1925. Tapestry woven by Mrs Sam Manuelito, based on a sand painting by Hosteen Klah. Heard Museum, Phoenix, Arizona

4.5.13 (below) Crouching male transformation figurine, Olmec, Mexico, 900–300 BCE. Serpentine with traces of cinnabar, height 4¼". Los Angeles County Museum of Art (LACMA), California

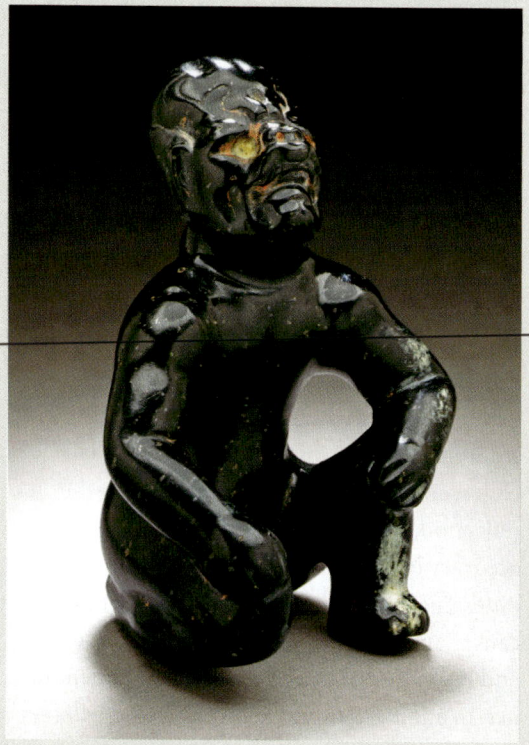

Artists often depict spiritual journeys experienced during religious ceremonies. Although an art object is static, artists have found ways to suggest the transformations of body and spirit that take place during sacred rituals.

Navajo American Indians have private ceremonies lasting several days during which men create intricate sand paintings. Through this ritual, the paintings are believed to transform into vehicles of power restoring harmony to the tribe or an individual. A shaman-singer, Hosteen Klah, started making weavings in 1919 that showed the kinds of designs made in sand paintings. While Klah was greatly respected, many Navajos attacked him for making outsiders aware of these private ceremonies. One tapestry, *Whirling Log Ceremony* (**4.5.12**)—in fact woven by someone else but based on a design by Klah—shows part of the Navajo creation myth in which an individual

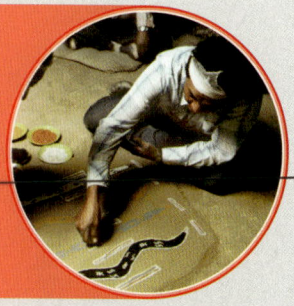

Navajo sand paintings, called *iikaah* (a "place where gods come and go"), are created in a ritualistic manner, with shaman figures singing chants and often dancing: see **4.2.5, p. 581**

into a jaguar, thus giving the human the strength to travel to other worlds through trance. Jaguars were considered powerful beasts in all Mesoamerican cultures and were believed to represent gods. This example is represented as a combat figure by virtue of its warrior stance and the holes in its hands that suggest it formerly held some kind of weapon. The green color of the material (either serpentine or jade) symbolizes rain and fertility. Traces of the red mineral cinnabar, painted ritualistically on the figure, symbolize the blood of life. Small enough to be held in one's hand, this object was used in rituals that transformed and gave power to shamans.

Perspective: the creation of the illusion of depth in a two-dimensional image by using mathematical principles
Cubism, Cubist: a twentieth-century art movement that favored a new perspective emphasizing geometric forms
Form: an object that can be defined in three dimensions (height, width, and depth)
Plane: a flat surface, often implied by the composition
Monochromatic: having one or more values of one color
Non-objective: art that does not depict a recognizable subject

By utilizing the tools of illusionism, Manet challenged our perceptions of reality and how we interpret what we believe to be true, and created a psychological mystery.

The French artist Georges Braque (1882–1963) worked alongside Pablo Picasso to develop a new style of art. Their objective was to move beyond the traditional depictions of previous centuries, in which paintings were illusionistic renderings drawn using conventional systems of **perspective**. This style became known as **Cubism**. Its first phase can be described as an analysis and fracturing of **form** and **planes** using only a **monochromatic** palette.

As Braque's *Man with a Guitar* (**4.5.14**) shows, Cubist art is not totally **non-objective**, or non-representational; some element of the artist's subject is always identifiable. Imagine that each object is a cube with a top, bottom, and sides. Cubist artists select portions (or sides) of each object to represent, and Cubist works, including Braque's painting, often show different faces of an object simultaneously. While it is difficult to find in the painting a clear representation of a man or a guitar, lines and shapes suggest the form of a human figure. At the edges of the figure are scrolls recalling parts of an instrument or sheets of music. Braque includes, in the upper left, a seemingly three-dimensional rendering of a rope, the tail of which hangs from a nail. By creating one clear element of illusionism, Braque was able to highlight the intentional breaking down of three dimensions elsewhere in the painting. Cubist artists were interested in emphasizing the two-dimensional painted surface rather than re-creating the illusion of three-dimensionality.

4.5.14 Georges Braque, *Man with a Guitar*, 1911–12. Oil on canvas, 45¾ × 31⅞". MoMA, New York

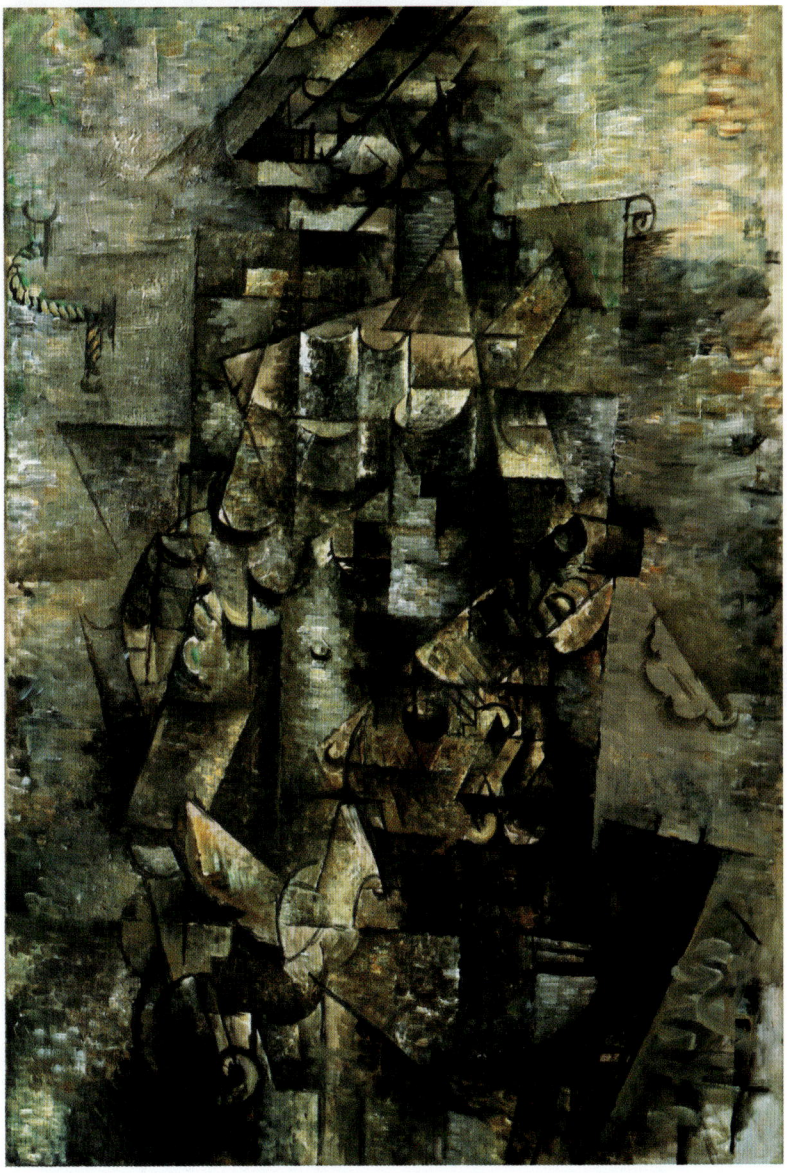

4.5.15 René Magritte, *The Human Condition*, 1933. Oil on canvas, 39⅜ × 31⅞ × ⅝". National Gallery of Art, Washington D.C.

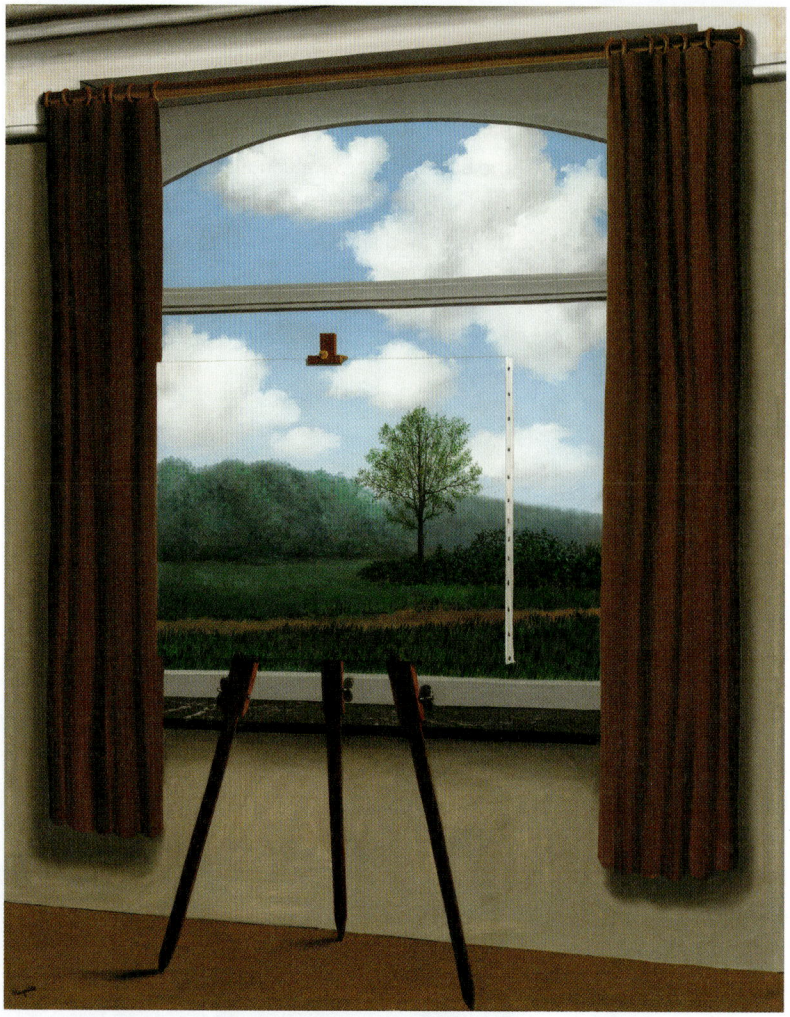

Linear perspective: a system using converging imaginary sight lines to create the illusion of depth

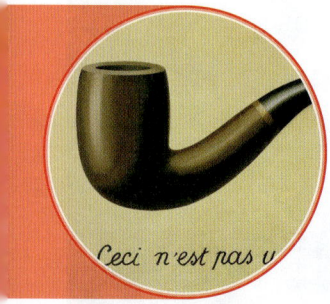

Magritte makes the viewer question the value of illusionism in his painting that states, "This is not a pipe." Instead, he argues that the image is just a symbol or idea of a pipe: see **1.3.1, p. 76**

Throughout his work, the Belgian artist René Magritte (1898–1967) asks the viewer to question Alberti's advice (introduced at the beginning of this chapter) that the goal of painting should be to create an illusionistic window.

Magritte's *The Human Condition* (1933) depicts a painting of a landscape that rests on an easel, which has been placed before a window that looks out onto the same landscape (**4.5.15**). The window, curtains, and easel, however, are also painted depictions, meaning that the first example of illusionism is viewed in the context of another example of illusionism. Objective reality appears tangible yet is in fact a construct. These layers of illusionism suggest that images are simply inventions that have symbolic meaning for the viewer. As the artist explains,

> [The tree] exists for the spectator, both inside the room in the painting, and outside in the real landscape, in thought. Which is how we see the world: we see it as being outside ourselves even though it is only a mental representation of it that we experience inside ourselves.

Magritte confronts us with issues of representation and truth and refers directly to the achievements in **linear perspective** made by the artists of the Renaissance. What at first seems an extension of the desire to create a convincing view through a window is shattered when Magritte forces us to consider what is real, and what is only of the mind. Magritte showed that the "illusionistic window" of the Renaissance is indeed only a scene on a canvas, and demonstrated that painting can be a powerful mode for expressing complex ideas, rather than solely re-creating what we see with our eyes.

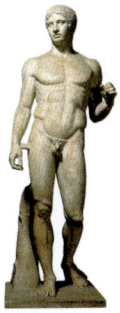

3.1.29 *Doryphoros* (Roman version), 120–50 BCE, p. 384

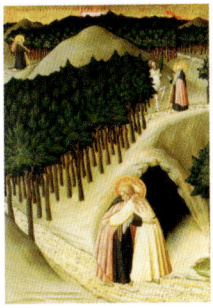

1.5.12 *The Meeting of Anthony and St. Paul*, c. 1430–35, p. 120

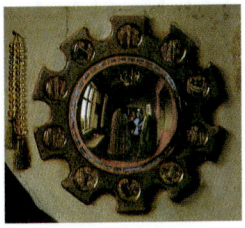

3.6.8b Jan van Eyck, *The Arnolfini Portrait* (detail), 1434, p. 467

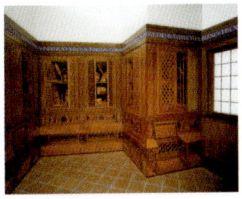

2.6.21 Francesco di Giorgio Martini, detail of *studiolo*, c. 1480, p. 298

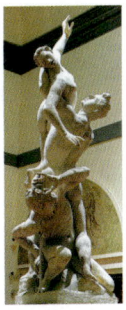

2.4.2a Giambologna, *Rape of a Sabine* (model), 1582, p. 243

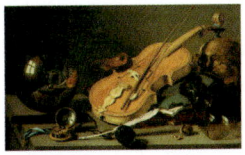

4.3.13 Pieter Claesz (attr.), *Vanitas (Still Life with Glass Globe)*, c. 1628, p. 600

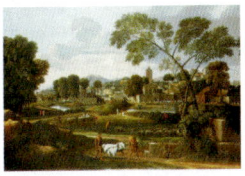

3.6.27 Nicolas Poussin, *The Funeral of Phocion*, 1648, p. 483

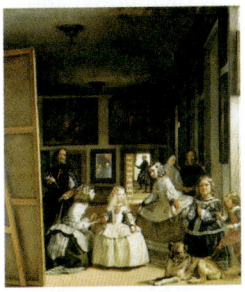

1.10.12a Diego de Silva y Velázquez, *Las Meninas*, c. 1656, p. 183

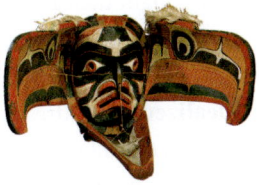

3.4.23 *Eagle Transformation Mask*, British Columbia, late 19th century, p. 442

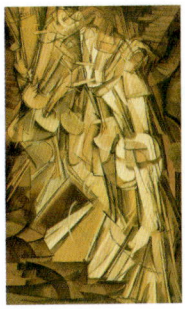

3.9.16 Marcel Duchamp, *Nude Descending a Staircase, No. 2*, 1912, p. 533

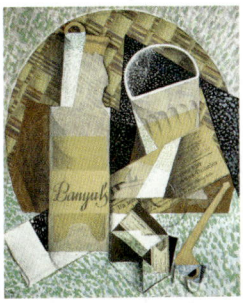

3.9.6 Juan Gris, *Bottle of Banyuls*, 1914, p. 528

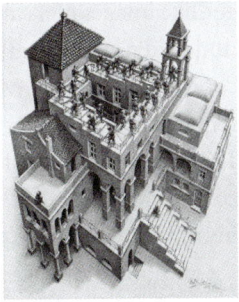

1.3.23 M. C. Escher, *Ascending and Descending*, 1960, p. 92

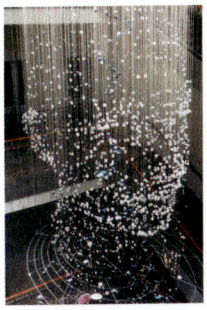

1.2.10a Ralph Helmick and Stuart Schechter, *Ghostwriter*, 1994, p. 67

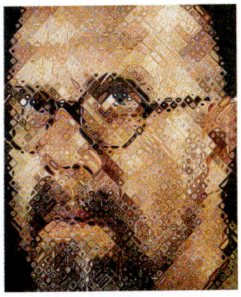

1.9.7a Chuck Close, *Self-Portrait*, 1997, p. 163

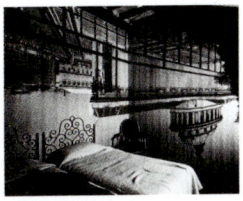

2.8.2 Abelardo Morell, *Camera Obscura Image...*, 1999, p. 316

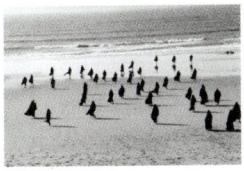

3.10.12b Shirin Neshat, *Rapture*, 1999, p. 553

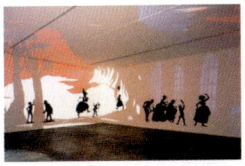

2.10.11 Kara Walker, *Insurrection!...*, 2000, p. 359

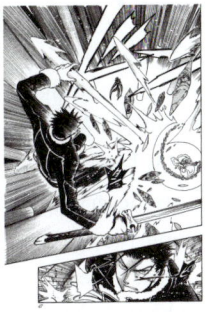

1.1.9 CLAMP, page from *Tsubasa RESERVoir CHRoNiCLE*, 2007, p. 49

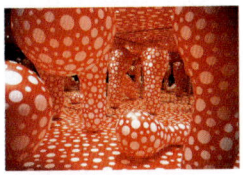

4.4.14 Yayoi Kusama, *Dots Obsession*, 2009, p. 611

1.3.16 Supergiant Games, screenshot from *Transistor*, 2014, p. 85

4.6 Art of Political Leaders and Rulers

Idealized: represented as perfect in form or character, corresponding to an ideal
Composition: the overall design or organization of a work
Portrait: image of a person or animal, usually focusing on the face
Propaganda: art that promotes an ideology or cause
Iconic: Possessing established and widely recognizable characteristics
Classical: art that conforms to Greek and Roman models
Contrapposto: a pose in sculpture in which the upper part of the body twists in one direction and the lower part in another
Romanticism: movement in nineteenth-century European culture, concerned with the power of the imagination and greatly valuing intense feeling

Political leaders have always made use of works of art to help define and assert their power and to influence their people. Seeking to demonstrate supreme control, leaders have used artworks to highlight their right to rule, sometimes even to claim that their authority has been granted by the gods. Leaders are often portrayed in an **idealized** way—dressed in elaborate clothing, placed centrally in the **composition**, depicted larger than other figures, and positioned so that the viewer looks up at them. National leaders have frequently commissioned artworks to reinforce their reputations as skillful commanders and to project an image of military strength. **Portraits** can be a potent **propaganda** tool for sustaining a leader's power. Such images are also potentially revealing of what a society might be looking for, or expecting, from its leader. This chapter explores how heads of state and other political leaders have seen themselves and how they wished to be viewed by both friend and foe, and also looks at how some artists have tried to challenge those portrayals.

Iconic Portraiture of Leaders

What image comes to mind when you think of a great leader? Artists have endeavored for centuries to develop ways to show leaders as figures with power and authority, deserving the respect and trust of the people they govern. Portraits vary in the degree to which they accurately depict the physical characteristics of the sitter, conveying instead the qualities a leader wants to be perceived to embody. The following portraits of George Washington (1732–1799) and Napoleon Bonaparte (1769–1821) have become **iconic**—recognizable worldwide for so strikingly depicting the historical impact of the leaders they represent.

It was a unique challenge to portray George Washington, the first president of the United States. Initially, attempts had been made to depict Washington in the manner of an ancient god, sculpted in white marble, wrapped in **Classical** drapery, and seated high atop a throne. Washington and many citizens argued that such godlike images of a ruler enthroned and partially nude did not represent the ideals of the young country of America. More fittingly, Washington requested that Jean-Antoine Houdon (1741–1828), one of the most respected sculptors of contemporary figures, carve a portrait of him in his military uniform (**4.6.1**).

Houdon did, however, maintain certain elements adopted from ancient sculpture: white marble was used, and Washington stood using a **contrapposto** stance adopted from ancient Greek figures. Washington's left hand is placed upon a *fasces* (a bundle of wooden rods), which was a symbol of power in ancient Rome. There are thirteen rods, which represent the number of US colonies; they are bound together in unity. Washington is shown with his sword set aside and his cape removed. He resigned from the position of Commander-in-Chief of the Continental Army after the Revolutionary War (1775–83) and returned to his farm (a plow is behind him in this sculpture), before being

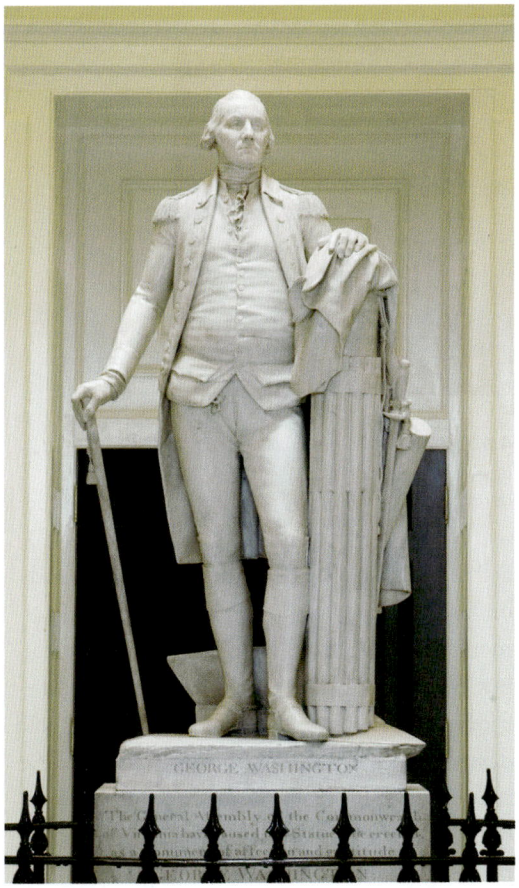

4.6.1 Jean-Antoine Houdon, *George Washington*, 1788–92. Marble, height 6'2". Virginia State Capitol, Richmond, Virginia

appointed America's first president in 1789. Washington's gaze—slightly to the left, upward, and into the distance—has become so iconic that it has often been repeated in other portraits, particularly of democratic leaders.

During his reign as emperor of France, from 1804 to 1815, Napoleon Bonaparte had painters create hundreds of portraits of him in an effort to persuade the French people of his leadership skills, military might, and humanitarian efforts. Many of these artworks were masterpieces of propaganda, fueling the French peoples' support of the emperor. Jacques-Louis David (1748–1825) became Napoleon's favorite painter, and his portrait *Napoleon Crossing the Alps* (**4.6.2**) became representative of Napoleon's leadership as he conquered much of the world.

In *Napoleon Crossing the Alps*, David displays the powerful force of nature, a characteristic of **Romanticism**, and the French leader's ability to withstand the wind and snow as he leads his troops. Here the painter memorializes an actual event, as Napoleon and his men victoriously crossed the dangerous Alpine pass of St. Bernard to enter and eventually conquer Italy. Although the journey was real, the artist deliberately glamorizes the moment, heightening its dramatic impact. In reality, Napoleon did not lead his army over the Alps but sent them ahead on foot while he followed on a mule.

In the painting, the horse struggles against the powerful wind, yet Napoleon fearlessly points toward the snow-covered mountains that his troops must cross: by implication, the artist suggests that the leader can master not only his horse but also nature. Napoleon's name is carved into the rock ("Bonaparte"), above the names of two earlier military leaders—the great Carthaginian general Hannibal and the Holy Roman Emperor Karolus Magnus, also known as Charlemagne—who had crossed the same treacherous path.

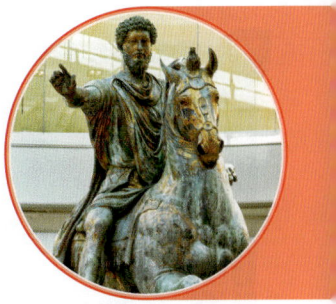

David borrowed the military pose of a ruler atop a horse from the equestrian monument tradition, popular in portraits of the emperors of ancient Rome: see **3.1.37, p. 388**

4.6.2 (below) Jacques-Louis David, *Napoleon Crossing the Alps* (or *Bonaparte Crossing the St. Bernard Pass, 20 May, 1800*), 1801. Oil on canvas, 8'9¼ × 7'3¾". Châteaux de Versailles et de Trianon, Versailles, France

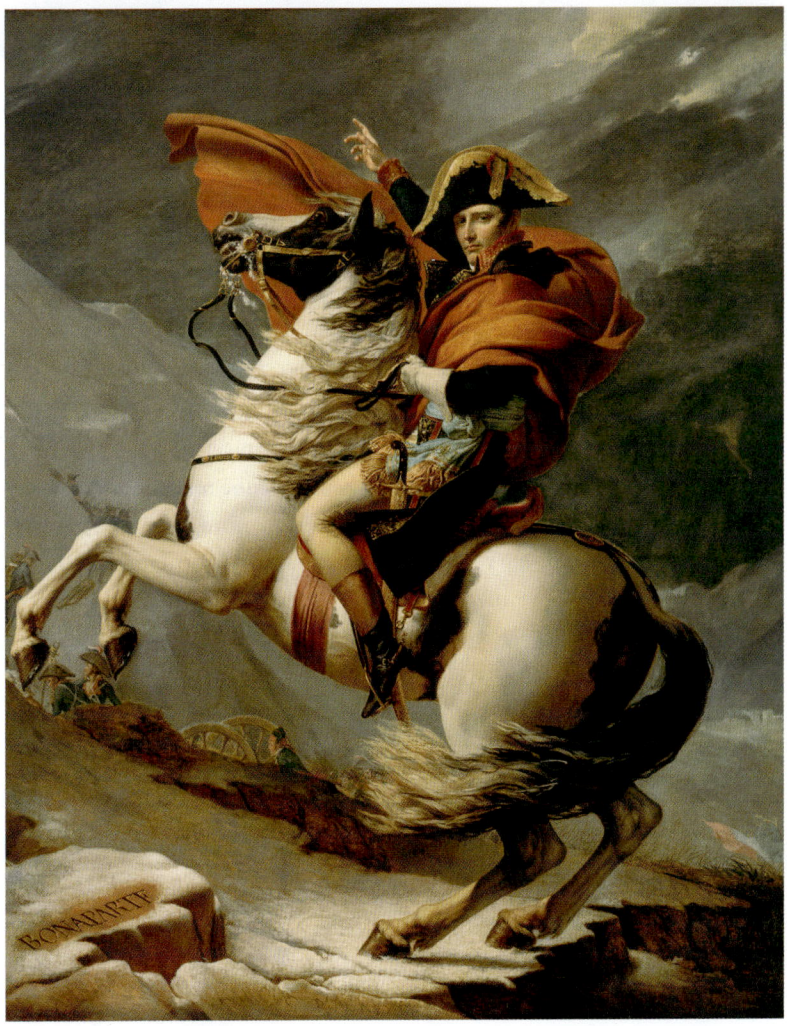

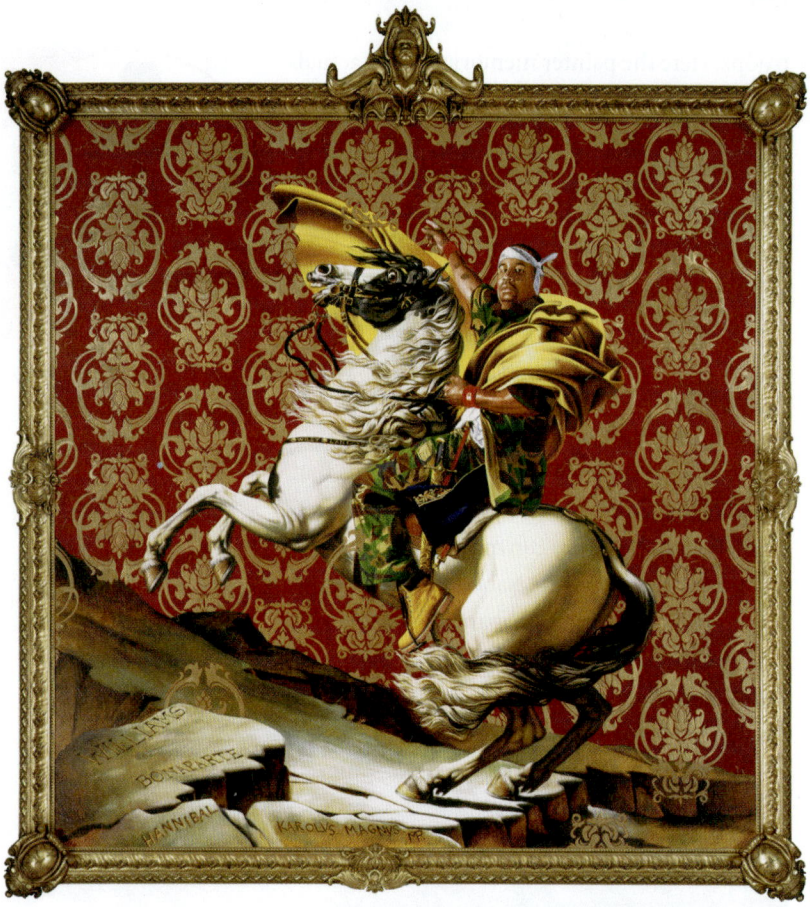

4.6.3a Kehinde Wiley, *Napoleon Leading the Army over the Alps*, 2005. Oil on canvas, 9 × 9'. Brooklyn Museum, New York

4.6.3b Kehinde Wiley, *Napoleon Leading the Army over the Alps*: detail of sperm in the background

> Painting is about the world that we live in. Black men live in the world. My choice is to include them. This is my way of saying yes to us.
>
> Kehinde Wiley

Kehinde Wiley (b. 1977) is an African American artist who noticed that the paintings in his local museum rarely showed dark-skinned figures. After studying many seminal portraits in the history of European art, he began to copy such artworks, replacing the main characters with people who looked more like him. He says, "When I watch television or participate in the media culture in America, sometimes the way that I've seen black people being portrayed in this country feels very strange and exotic because it has nothing to do with the life that I've lived or the people I've known." Wiley found strangers on the street to model for his portraits, asking them to wear their own clothing but mimic the poses of **sitters** in famous artworks.

In Wiley's *Napoleon Leading the Army over the Alps* (**4.6.3a**), the Caucasian leader Napoleon has been supplanted by an African American man wearing camouflage fatigues and fashionable work-wear boots, with sweat bands on his wrists and tattoos on his right arm. The men's poses and facial expressions are identical, but Wiley has replaced Jacques-Louis David's mountain background with a rich red-and-gold design, removing the specific location and time referenced in the original portrait. The ornate background also highlights the artificiality of painting: the way that some of the gold **motifs** overlap the figure and the rocky floor in the foreground makes clear to the viewer that this is an artistic imagining, not a real scene.

In many of Wiley's works, black men are shown in settings that historically were not available to them in Western society. By placing a figure of a different race within such an iconic scene, the artist forces the viewer to acknowledge the different cultural experiences of these two men. The tiny white sperm painted onto the luxurious background (**4.6.3b**) somewhat mockingly highlight how royal portraits have been designed to convey strength through masculinity. The artist pushes the viewer to confront racial and gender stereotypes and constructs a place for African American men to be viewed in traditional, preconceived realms of power. Adding to the names of earlier leaders on the rocks beneath the man and horse, Wiley has carved the name "Williams," a typical African American name, and, perhaps, the name of this sitter. By doing so, the artist attempts to conquer the restrictive past that limited black culture, and to challenge today's perceptions of culture, race, and masculinity.

Sitter: person who poses, or "sits," for an artist to paint, sculpt, or photograph
Motif: a design or color repeated as a unit in a pattern

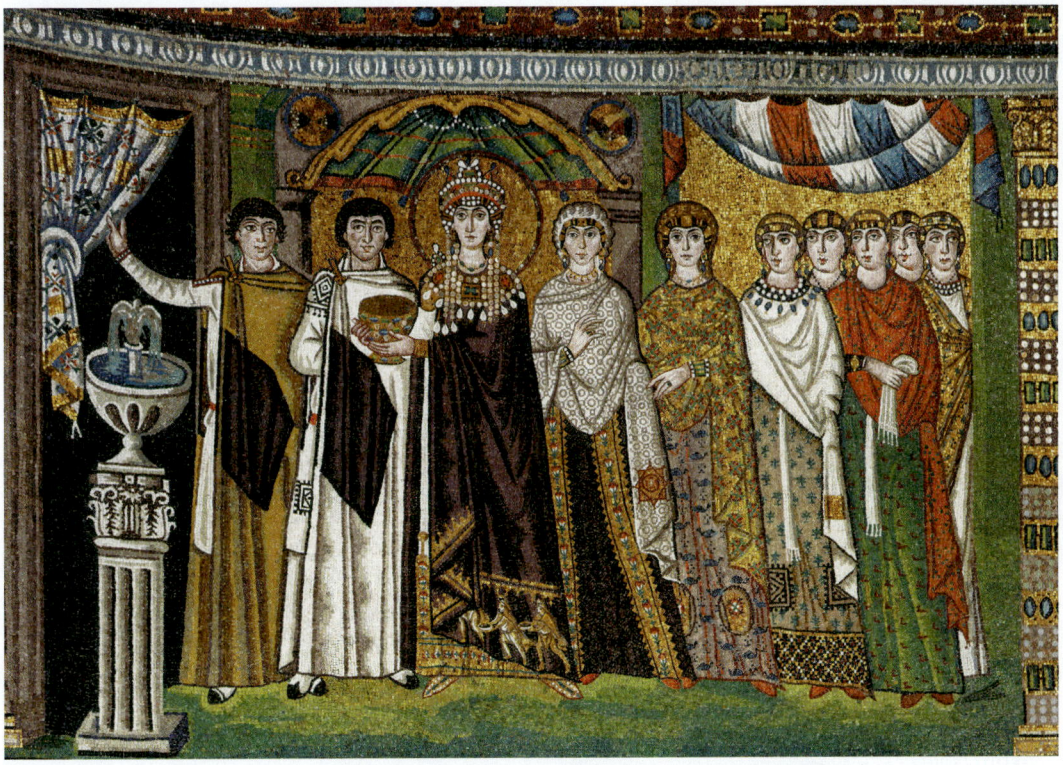

4.6.4 *Theodora and Attendants*, c. 547 CE. Mosaic. San Vitale, Ravenna, Italy

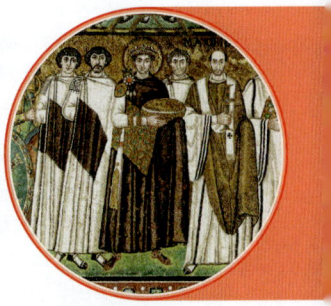

Compare the mosaic of Emperor Justinian, placed opposite Theodora's in the apse of the same church: see **3.2.10, p. 397**

Female Rulers

Female rulers commission portraits to convey power, just as male rulers do. Under pressure from patriarchal expectations of womanhood, however, female rulers have often felt the need to portray a kind of power that represents piety, sacrifice, motherhood, and support of their husbands. The following examples discuss how queens and empresses from Byzantium, England, Maya culture, Egypt, and France have used art to display and maintain their power.

The sixth-century depiction of the **Byzantine** empress Theodora (500–548 CE) and her attendants is filled with rich details, such as the Three Magi on the hem of the empress's stunning purple robe (**4.6.4**). The **mosaic** is positioned on the wall of the **apse**—a sacred part of a church, where the **altar** is placed—in the Church of San Vitale in Ravenna, Italy. Theodora, third from left, carries a jeweled chalice of wine that she raises up in the direction of the actual altar, which is located to the left of the mosaic. The figures in the image are layered so that their repetition creates a sense of movement toward the altar. It is significant, however, that in reality Theodora would not have been permitted to enter this space—not only because she was a woman, but also because she was from the lower classes, having been an actress and a prostitute when she met her husband, Emperor Justinian. As a woman, even a royal one, she was allowed only in the courtyard of the church, or on the second-story balcony surrounding the **nave**. The mosaic acknowledges these gender restrictions by situating Theodora outdoors, as shown by the green grass, canopies, and fountain.

Elizabeth I became queen of England in 1558 and maintained her rule until her death in 1603, despite the challenges of inheriting a religiously divided country and a poor economy, and being declared an illegitimate child of Henry VIII after her mother's execution. For all these obstacles, Elizabeth's reign was relatively peaceful, culturally rich, and saw England united under Protestantism. As an unmarried woman, she risked being seen as weak and unable to rule; however, Elizabeth used her status to her own advantage, and through art she was able to promote her chastity as evidence of her commitment first and foremost to her country. One of the great successes of her reign came in 1588 when the Spanish Armada, a fleet of more

Byzantine: relating to the East Roman empire, centered on Constantinople (modern-day Istanbul) from the fifth century CE to 1453
Mosaic: a picture or pattern created by fixing together small pieces of stone, glass, tile, etc.
Apse: semicircular vaulted space in a church
Altar: an area where sacrifices or offerings are made
Nave: the central space of a cathedral or basilica

Gateway to Art: Maya Lintel Showing Shield Jaguar and Lady Xoc
Queens in Support of Their Husbands

The Maya queen Lady Xoc and the Egyptian queen Nefertiti were both wives to powerful rulers; their authority was subordinate to that of their husbands, whose power was believed to have been granted by the gods. The two works discussed here have much in common: both are **reliefs** carved in limestone (the Egyptian work is a **sunken relief**), both feature **hieroglyphs**—or glyphs—that describe who the figures are and what is taking place, and both show how these queens were portrayed as supporters of their husbands and believers in their gods.

In ancient Maya culture, a ruler's power was reinforced through prayers and sacrifices to the gods. On one intricately carved **lintel** block Lady Xoc kneels before her husband Shield Jaguar as she performs a bloodletting ritual to pray for the health of her husband's son (**4.6.5**). The Maya rulers believed their power derived from the sun god, whose image is shown on ornaments on both of their chests. Although Lady Xoc is shown as clearly subordinate to Shield Jaguar, her elaborate costume, her role in the ritual, and the fact that this bloodletting scene was imitated in artworks of later generations, highlight that she too was a person of great importance. The fact that she is participating in a ritual to benefit the son of another of the king's wives perhaps shows the king's wish to display the high status of Lady Xoc, possibly to balance out the future in which another woman's child will become his heir.

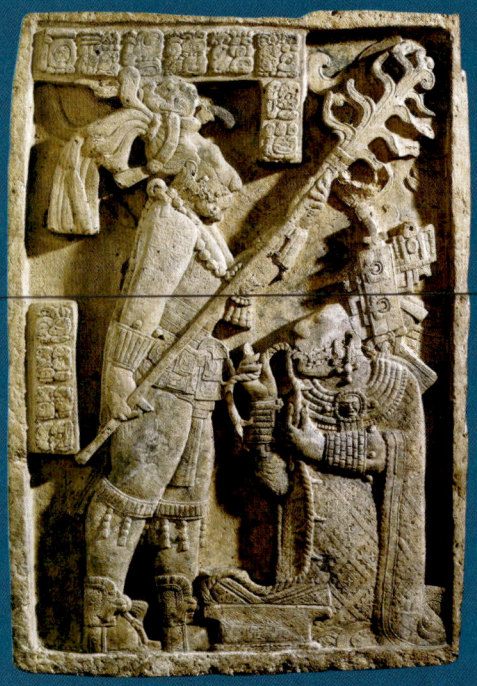

4.6.5 Maya lintel showing Shield Jaguar and Lady Xoc, *c.* 725 CE. Limestone, 43 × 30¾ × 2⅜". British Museum, London, England

For the other Maya lintel Gateway boxes, see p. 162, p. 245, and p. 436

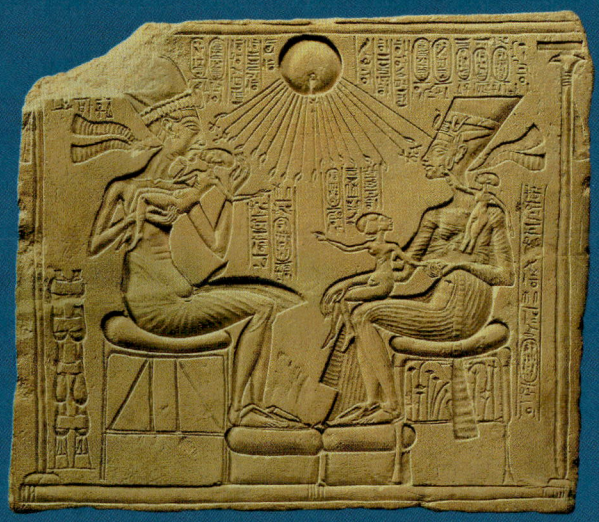

4.6.6 The Egyptian king Akhenaten, his queen Nefertiti, and three daughters, *c.* 1353–1335 BCE. Limestone, height 12¼". Aegyptisches Museum, Staatliche Museen, Berlin, Germany

The ancient Egyptians believed their kings, known as pharaohs, were descended from the gods. The pharaoh Akhenaten, like Shield Jaguar, ruled under the authority of a sun god. Although previous pharaohs had worshiped many gods, Akhenaten, who ruled in the fourteenth century BCE, used his supreme power to recognize only the sun god Aten. In one family portrait, Nefertiti (*c.* 1370–1330 BCE) is placed opposite her husband Akhenaten, holding one of her daughters while another climbs on her shoulder (**4.6.6**). The sun is carved deeper than anything else in the relief, which signifies visually its importance as a god, and its rays emanate toward the figures, suggesting the sun god's support of the royal family. The flames at the end of the rays are small hands, some holding an *ankh*, the character that symbolizes life in ancient Egyptian writing. Nefertiti is only slightly smaller in size than her husband, and light of the sun god shines equally on both the king and queen. Some historians believe that Nefertiti ruled the kingdom jointly with Akhenaten.

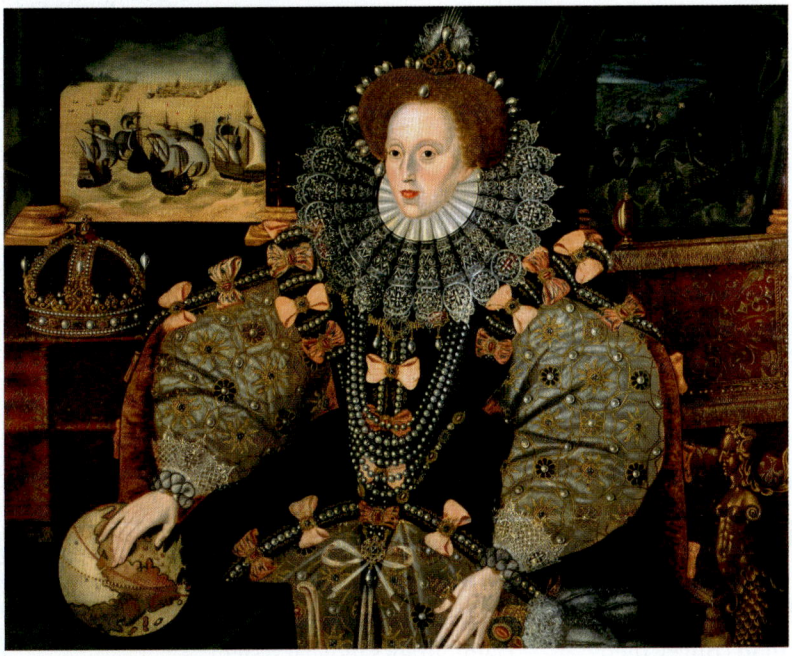

4.6.7 George Gower, *Elizabeth I (The Armada Portrait)*, 1588. Oil on panel, 41¼ × 52⅜". Woburn Abbey, Bedfordshire, England

Relief: a raised form on a largely flat background. For example, the design on a coin is "in relief"
Sunken relief: a carved panel where the figures are cut deeper into the stone than the background
Hieroglyphs: written language involving sacred characters that may be pictures as well as letters or signifiers of sounds
Lintel: the horizontal beam over the doorway of a portal

than a hundred ships—commanded by Philip II, whose one-time marriage proposal Elizabeth had rejected—tried to invade England only to be defeated by the waiting English navy.

In the *Armada Portrait* (**4.6.7**, painted to commemorate the English victory, the queen is shown in a rich gown covered with bows and pearls. The largest pearl hangs over her genital region, symbolizing the chastity she has maintained. She sits next to her royal crown, with her right hand on a globe, signifying English naval might throughout the world, and her desire to expand to the Americas. The scenes behind her depict events from the Armada. On the left, the English ships are stationed ready to attack the arriving Spanish fleet. On the right, in a now stormy sky, we see Spanish ships wrecking along a coastal shore, which in real life many of them did while trying to escape England's fire power. Although Elizabeth I's right to rule began quite tenuously, she became a famously powerful and independent queen, a status that she conveyed through portraits such as this one.

In late eighteenth-century France, Queen Marie Antoinette (1755–1793), the wife of King Louis XVI, had become a symbol of the royal family's extravagance. While the French state suffered financial strain and the people went hungry, Marie Antoinette wore expensive clothes and jewels and was given her own chateau, or palace, which she decorated lavishly.

This portrait (**4.6.8**) was painted in hopes of improving her dire reputation. Her location in the palace, within the painting, and her rich velvet dress show her status as Queen of France. Her wardrobe is purposely neither overly revealing nor lacking in French style and taste, which had been a criticism of previous portraits. In dramatic opposition to her growing reputation as promiscuous and unavailable to the king, she is shown as a loving mother, adored by her children, who cling to her. Her somber

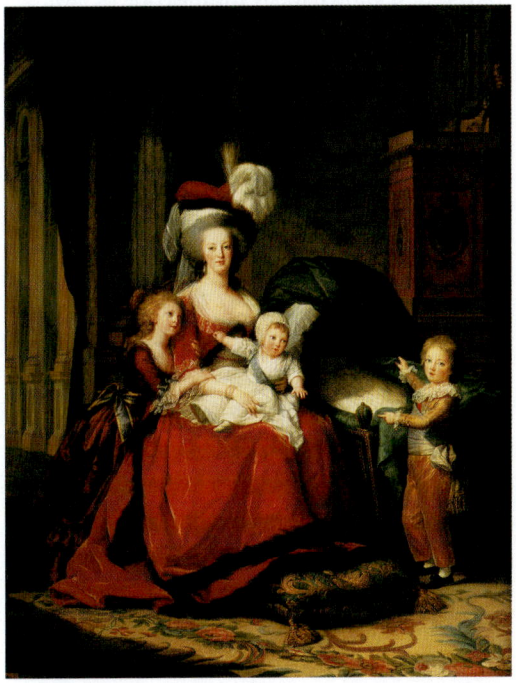

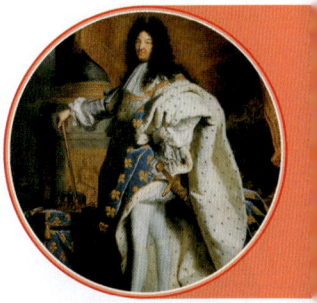

Louis XIV was Marie Antoinette's great-great grandfather through marriage. Here he stands before the Hall of Mirrors, Versailles, the same location in which Marie Antoinette posed in her portrait: see **3.6.28, p. 484**

4.6.8 (left) Elisabeth Louise Vigée Le Brun, *Marie Antoinette and Her Children*, 1787. Oil on canvas, 9'½ × 7'⅝". Musée National du Chateau de Versailles, France

4.6.9 Stela of Hammurabi, c. 1792–1750 BCE. Diorite, 88⅝ × 25⅝". Musée du Louvre, Paris, France

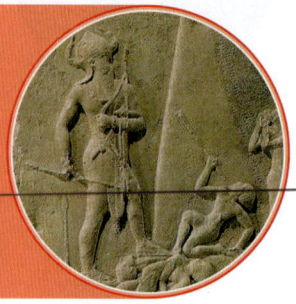

It was common in Near Eastern art for rulers to derive their power from the gods. As with Hammurabi of Babylon, the Akkadian ruler Naram-Sin was portrayed as having been given his power from a sun god: see **4.2.7, p. 582**

expression suggests sorrow over the recent loss of her youngest daughter, for whom the empty cradle was intended.

The portrait did not, however, assuage the growing anger of the French people. It was removed from public display shortly after being exhibited in 1788, for fear that it would be attacked. The following year, the French Revolution began. Three years later, in 1792, the monarchy was overthrown, and in 1793 Louis XVI and Marie Antoinette were beheaded.

Art Used by Rulers to Regulate Society

Strong leaders understand the power of art as a tool for propaganda, both to convey their messages and to influence people to obey their laws. The ancient Babylonian king Hammurabi used an image to emphasize his divine connection to the gods in order to persuade his people to follow his decrees. The Roman emperor Constantine utilized his own portraits to symbolize his political and military strength, and in the twentieth century, Chinese Communist leader Mao Zedong (1893–1976) commissioned art to promote his political ideology.

King Hammurabi of Babylon (now part of Iraq) is best known today for the code of law that he established around 1790 BCE. It was innovative for being a set of written statutes, as opposed to unwritten or arbitrary rules, which might vary by region or local authority. His code was carved in **cuneiform** writing into a **stela** for public viewing (**4.6.9**). King Hammurabi's code has often been summarized as "an eye for an eye," because it frequently called for a person to be punished for wrong doing by suffering in the same way as the person who had been wronged. Yet Hammurabi's laws tended to be more complex and less even-handed when they pertained to people with low status, such as slaves, freedmen, and women. For example, the law did not punish a husband for adultery, although it did consider the wife's financial well-being if her husband decided to leave her. In contrast, a woman caught in an adulterous affair was thrown into a river, with her hands tied, along with her lover. If her husband only suspected her of adultery, but had no proof, she was required to jump into the river. If she survived, she was deemed innocent.

The scene at the top of the stela shows that Hammurabi's power has been given to him by the gods. Shamash, the god of justice and the sun god, is enthroned and seen with flames radiating from his shoulders. The sun god reaches toward Hammurabi and hands him rings and a scepter, symbols of power, as he dictates to the king the laws he will implement. Written below this scene is a long description of the gods' support for Hammurabi and the king's law code. Monuments similar to this stela were placed throughout Mesopotamia to enforce Hammurabi's judicial system.

Constantine the Great ruled part of the Roman empire from 306 CE and was sole emperor from 324 until his death in 337. Constantine was successful in numerous military campaigns, and he is notable for having been the first Christian Roman emperor. A colossal marble-and-bronze statue of the emperor seated on a throne was made in 325 to be placed in a **basilica** in the center of Rome. Only parts of the statue survive (**4.6.10**), but the head alone, which is more than 8 ft. tall, gives an idea of the imposing force one must have felt when standing in the presence of this statue, which was made to enforce Constantine's power even when he was away.

In its youthful features and ideal athletic body, the statue was modeled after portraits of earlier emperors. The emperor was enthroned in a manner similar to seated statues of the Roman god Jupiter, but he held in his hand an orb on which a Christian cross was placed. This statue is one of the earliest examples of how pagan art was often reinterpreted to incorporate Christian symbolism and meaning. Constantine's far-off gaze toward the heavens is also distinct from earlier portraits of Roman emperors and signifies his close connection to God, and the power he therefore derived from the Almighty to rule over the Roman empire.

As we have seen, art is often used by leaders seeking to manipulate the people they govern.

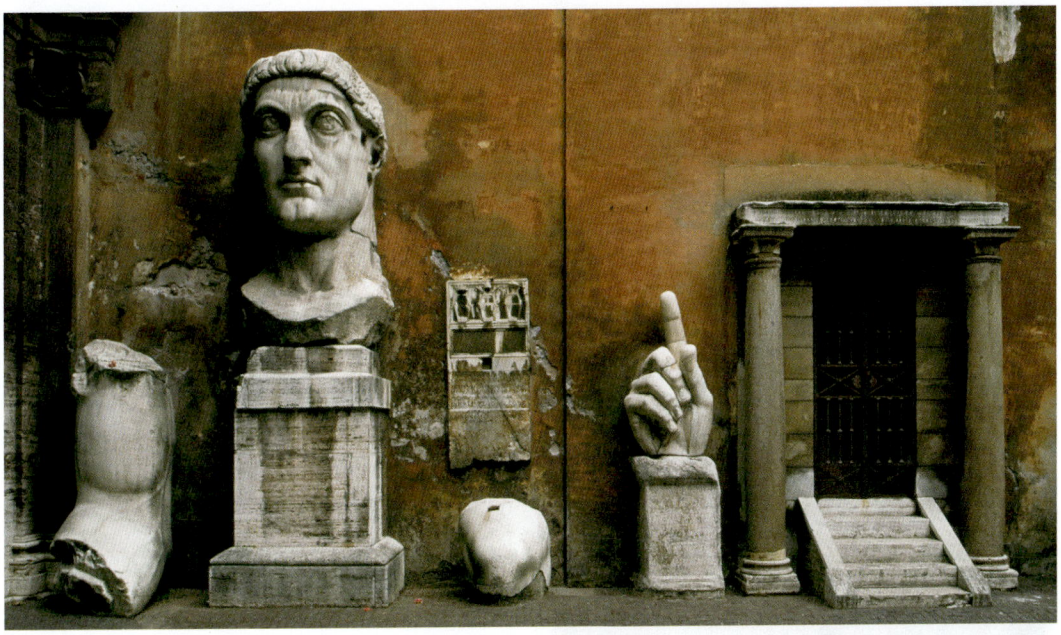

4.6.10 Remnants of colossal statue of Constantine the Great, 325–26 CE. Marble, height of head 8'6". Palazzo dei Conservatori, Rome, Italy

Cuneiform: a form of writing from ancient Mesopotamia that uses wedge shapes
Stela: upright stone slab decorated with inscriptions or pictorial relief carvings
Basilica: an early Christian church, either converted from or built to resemble a type of Roman civic building
Pop art: mid-twentieth-century artistic movement inspired by commercial art forms and popular culture
Silkscreen: method of printmaking using a stencil and paint pushed through a screen

Mao Zedong led the Communist Party to power in the Chinese civil war that ended in 1949. Mao, who ruled the most populous country in the world for twenty-seven years, understood the power of imagery and, like leaders for centuries before him, used artwork to promote his political and social agenda to his thousands of subjects. Mao installed a huge portrait of himself at Tiananmen in Beijing, the capital of China, when he declared the country to be the People's Republic of China (**4.6.11**). Tiananmen, the site of many important political and cultural events in China's history, was built in the fifteenth century as a gateway to the Forbidden City, the home of the Chinese emperors for centuries. As well as displaying Mao's portrait, Tiananmen Square has also been the site of bloody protests against China's Communist rule. The most famous example took place in 1989, when more than 100,000 people gathered in peaceful protest against government corruption and unfair wages. Sadly, the police responded with violence, and several thousand people were killed.

Mao's portrait is a powerful national symbol of China, even though his legacy remains very controversial. His "Great Leap Forward" campaign in 1958, an attempt to transform and industrialize China, resulted in widespread famine, and the Cultural Revolution that followed in 1966 led to the imprisonment and persecution of millions of people. Yet he maintained a hold on the Chinese people in part because of the image he projected as the benevolent leader of the Chinese Republic. Mao's face, typically similar in appearance to the portrait hanging in Tiananmen, decorated bank notes, stamps, statues, posters, and massive portraits in public spaces, conveying the idea that he was always watching over his citizens.

The American **Pop artist** Andy Warhol (1928–1987) created multiple series of **silkscreen** prints of Mao between 1972 and 1973, shortly after the US president Richard Nixon's historic trip to China, which opened up relations between China and the United States. Warhol's large-scale portraits highlight

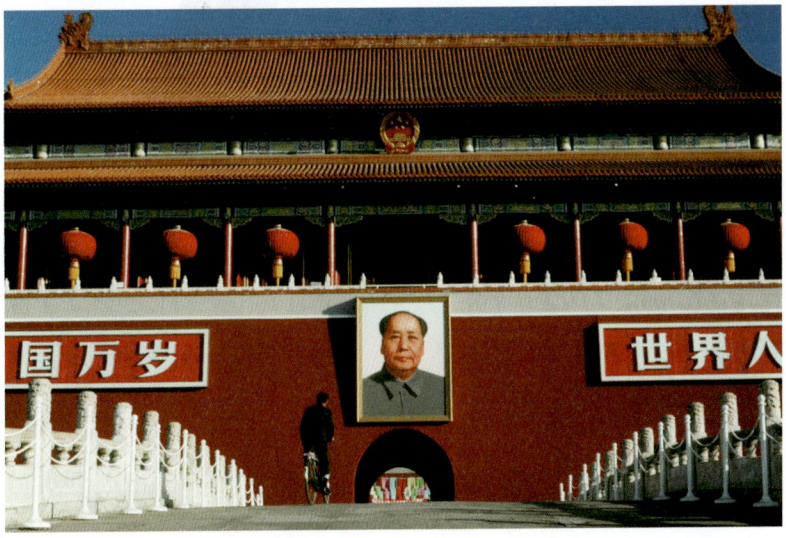

4.6.11 Mao Zedong's portrait. The Gate of Heavenly Peace, Tiananmen (south entrance to the old Forbidden City), Beijing, China

Icon: a religious image venerated by believers

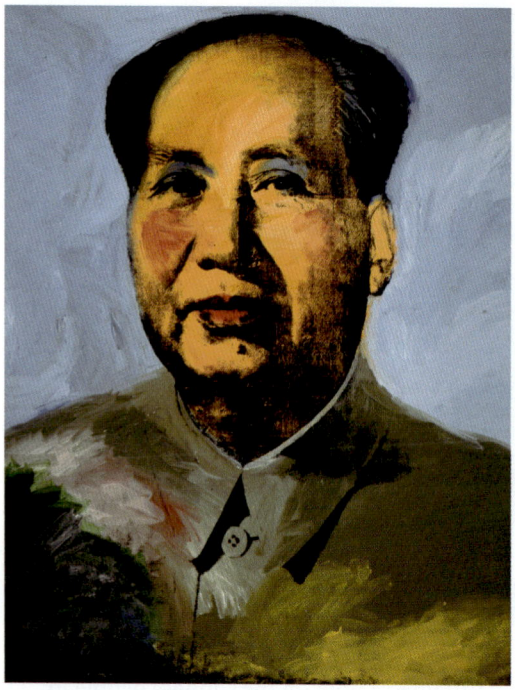

4.6.12 Andy Warhol, *Mao*, 1973. Synthetic polymer paint and silkscreen ink on canvas, 14' 8⅜" × 11' 4½". Art Institute of Chicago, Illinois

the perpetual replication of the ruler's image within China. The Mao portrait that hangs over Tiananmen is in fact not the same painting that was erected in 1949; it has been replaced with near-identical portraits almost yearly, or when the current portrait is damaged by acts of protest. In this way, Mao's image functions like an **icon**: while the original portrait is no longer on show, copies are believed by many to hold the same essence—or the essence of Mao himself.

In his series, Andy Warhol used the recognizable portrait of Mao—head turning slightly to the left from our point of view—and irreverently altered it with splatters of paint and bright colors, including eyeshadow and lipstick (**4.6.12**). The process of silkscreen printing and the large quantity of duplicates created by Warhol emphasize the manufacturing of Mao's image and its similarity to the commercialism of capitalist Western society. In one sense, Warhol continues to venerate the image; in another, he highlights its status as a reproduction, thereby lessening its power.

Like Mao Zedong and Emperor Constantine, Saddam Hussein (1937–2006), ruler of Iraq from 1979 to 2003, used public art to indicate his control over his people. Hussein became the president of Iraq in 1979, after a militaristic takeover. He was a brutal leader, and tens of thousands of citizens were killed under his regime. In 2003, controversially, the United States and its allies invaded Iraq and removed Hussein from power.

Prior to his overthrow, a colossal, 39-foot-tall, statue of Saddam (**4.6.13**) was placed in the central square of the capital city Baghdad in April 2002, to mark the ruler's sixty-fifth birthday. The potency of this symbol was validated when the statue was violently smashed one year later, after Hussein had been deposed. Unlike many other iconic portraits, it is the image of the destruction of the statue of Saddam Hussein that has become better known than the sculpture itself.

Video footage of the demolition shows crowds of local men surrounding the statue and cheering for it to be taken down. One Iraqi ties a rope around its neck, and another beats it with a sledgehammer. At one point, US soldiers cover its head with an American flag, and use a crane to help tear down the figure. Saddam Hussein was sentenced to death by an Iraqi court and executed in 2006. The violent destruction of his statue represents the immense anger felt toward the man seen as a cruel dictator by many of his people and by the wider international community.

4.6.13 Toppling of Saddam Hussein statue, April 9, 2003. Baghdad, Iraq

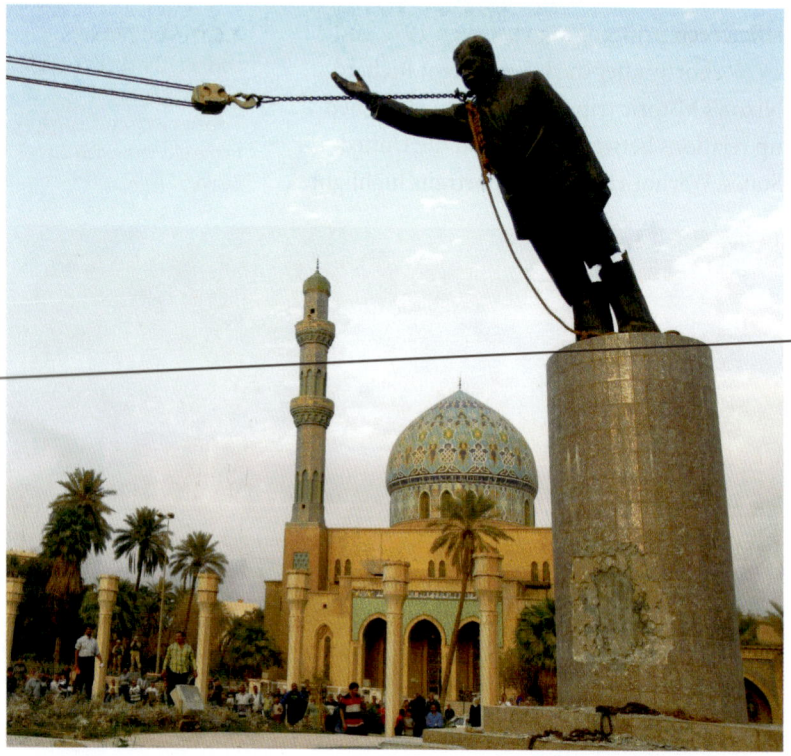

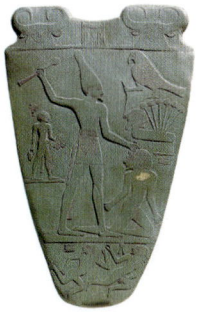

4.7.4b Palette of Narmer (back), Egypt, c. 2950–2775 BCE, p. 641

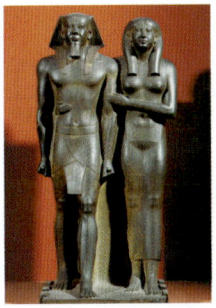

4.9.3b *Menkaure and His Wife, Queen Khamerernebty*, Egypt, c. 2520 BCE, p. 665

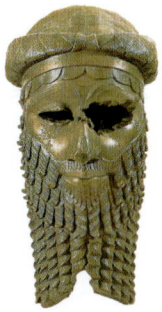

3.1.11 Head of an Akkadian ruler, c. 2300–2200 BCE, p. 372

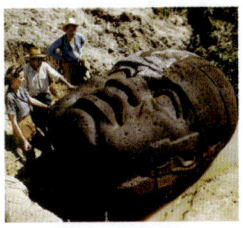

3.4.8 Colossal Olmec head, 1500–400 BCE, p. 434

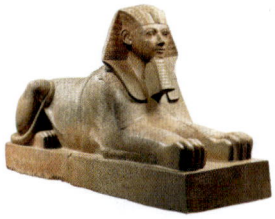

4.10.14 Sphinx of Hatshepsut, Egypt, 1479–1458 BCE, p. 689

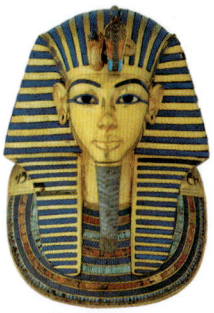

3.1.19 Funerary mask of Tutankhamun, 1333–1323 BCE, p. 378

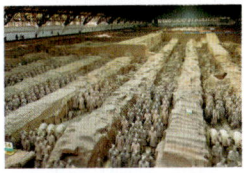

3.3.13a Terra-cotta army, mausoleum of Qin Shi Huangdi, China, c. 210 BCE, p. 417

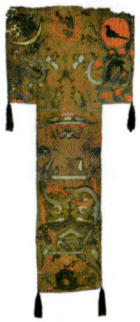

3.3.12 Painted banner from tomb of Lady Dai, China, c. 168 BCE, p. 417

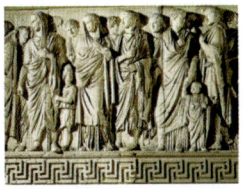

1.2.6 Imperial Procession from the Ara Pacis Augustae, 13 BCE, p. 65

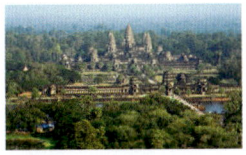

3.3.26 Angkor Wat, Siem Reap, Cambodia, 12th century, p. 426

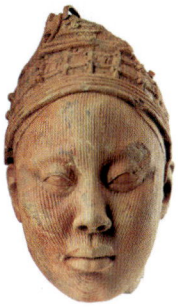

4.9.6 Head, possibly an Ife king, West Africa, 12th–14th century, p. 667

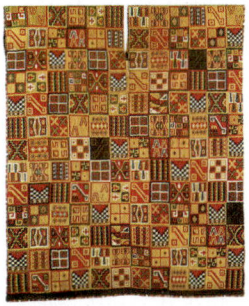

3.4.6 Inca tunic, Andes, c. 1500, p. 433

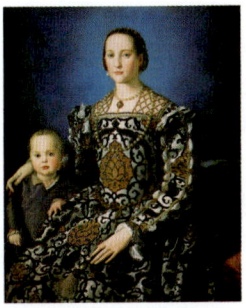

0.0.4 Bronzino, *Eleanora of Toledo and her Son Giovanni*, c. 1545, p. 23

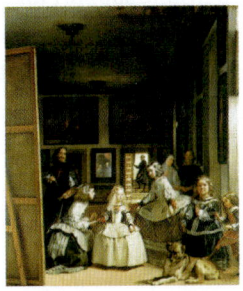

1.10.12a Diego de Silva y Velázquez, *Las Meninas*, c. 1656, p. 183

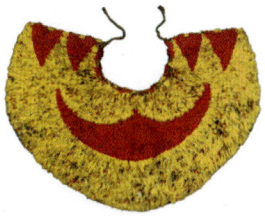

3.5.15a Feather cloak (*ahu'ula*), Hawaii, 18th century (?), p. 456

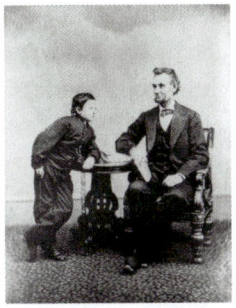

3.8.6 Alexander Gardner, *Abraham Lincoln and His Son Thomas (Tad)*, 1865, p. 506

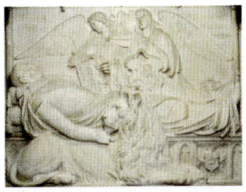

2.4.4 Susan Durant, *Memorial to King Leopold of the Belgians*, 1867, p. 244

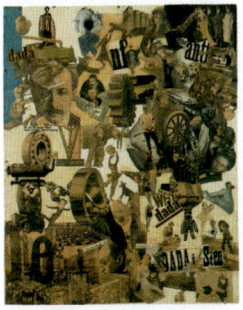

2.8.20 Hannah Höch, *Cut with the Kitchen Knife...*, 1919–20, p. 327

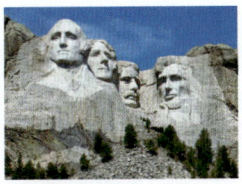

2.4.10 Mount Rushmore National Memorial, South Dakota, 1927–41, p. 248

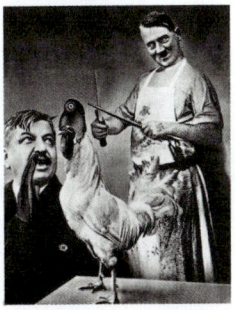

3.9.9 John Heartfield, *Have No Fear, He's a Vegetarian*, 1936, p. 530

4.7 Art, War, and Revolution

War has been a theme of artworks for millennia. Artists re-create the terror of battle, the tragedy of death, the joy of victory, and the sorrow of defeat. Artists choose the subjects of revolution or war for a variety of reasons: to educate us about the realities of conflict, to inspire us through the depiction of heroism, or to shock us into opposing violence. Artworks about historical events can be rich sources of information, skillfully documenting the kinds of weapons used in a particular battle or the uniforms the soldiers wore; but artists may also manipulate scenes in order, for example, to inspire support for one side over another. Art about war, revolutions, or uprisings should therefore be treated with caution, for just as we bring our own biases when we engage with an artwork, so artists may also be promoting a specific political point of view.

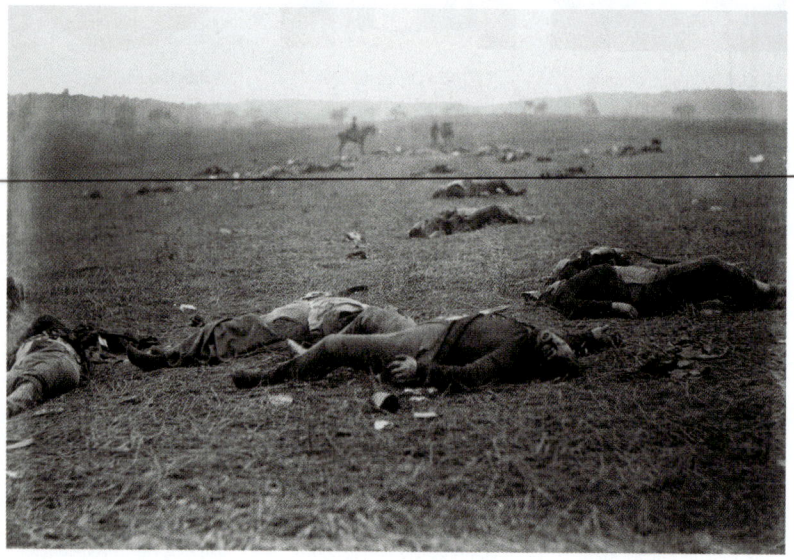

4.7.1 Timothy O'Sullivan, *Harvest of Death, Gettysburg, Pennsylvania*, July 1863. Photograph. Library of Congress, Washington, D.C.

Documenting the Tragedies of War

As a viewer, do you question certain visual documents of history more than others? Do you assume that visual images (such as photographs and video) that show current events are accurate, or do you sometimes think they might have been manipulated?

When artists document actual events, they may try to record exactly what they have seen. More frequently, however, artists tend to infuse their images with the emotions aroused by the sight of death, destruction, and tragedy. An image of battle, therefore, can have a profound impact on the people who see the artwork, even as the artist's emotions sometimes distort the facts of history. Art that seems to be documentary evidence may not be entirely factual. It is important to assess the art of war with great care and attention as to the context in which the work was created.

American Timothy O'Sullivan (1840–1882) took the famous Civil War photograph *Harvest of Death* after a day at Gettysburg, the battle that caused the most casualties of the entire conflict (**4.7.1**). His photograph shows a field covered with bodies, highlighting the tragic loss of life. The clothes of some of the soldiers have been partly removed, suggesting that thieves have been searching their bodies. O'Sullivan has focused the composition on the face of the soldier in the foreground, his arms flung out from his sides. By concentrating on this individual, whose features we can see, O'Sullivan

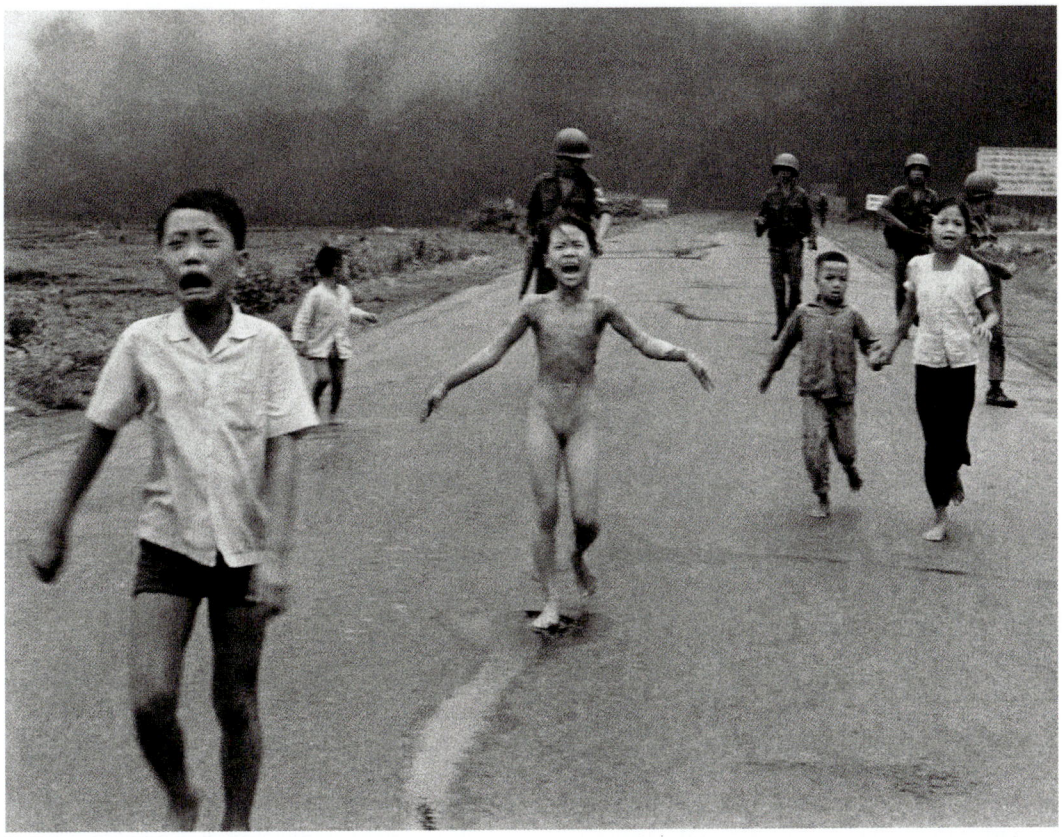

4.7.2 Nick Ut, *Vietnamese Girl Kim Phuc Running after Napalm Attack*, June 8, 1972. Photograph

brings home the human aspect of the great loss of life at Gettysburg.

One often assumes that a photograph can be trusted as an accurate documentation of an event. Yet photographers, like other artists, can manipulate their scenes through lighting and **composition**. O'Sullivan was known sometimes to rearrange bodies and otherwise alter the setting before taking his photographs. We do not know if he arranged the corpses or their clothing in order to heighten the emotional impact of this powerful image. If we knew he had staged the scene in some way, would we doubt the truth of the tragedy he represents?

The photograph by the Vietnamese Nick Ut (b. 1951) of children running from their village in Vietnam after a napalm attack was so shocking that some, including the US president Richard Nixon, questioned its authenticity when it appeared in newspapers on June 12, 1972 (**4.7.2**). The image also moved many Americans to question their nation's involvement in the Vietnam War. The photographer defended its authenticity for years:

> The picture for me and unquestionably for many others could not have been more real. The photo was as authentic as the Vietnam War itself. The horror of the Vietnam War recorded by me did not have to be fixed. That terrified little girl is still alive today and has become an eloquent testimony to the authenticity of that photo.

Although the photograph records an actual event, Ut's disapproval of the war and his concern for its victims influenced the way his shot was composed. He focused on the little girl, Kim Phuc, screaming in terror, running naked, her clothes having been burned off her body. Her two brothers are running on the left side of the image, while her two cousins hold hands behind her on the right. The soldiers in the background appear strangely calm, a dramatic contrast to the horrified expressions of the running children.

The story of the people in the photograph did not end with that moment. The nine-year-old girl kept screaming; the photographer gave her his water and rushed her to a hospital. Physicians predicted Phuc would die. But

Composition: the overall design or organization of a work

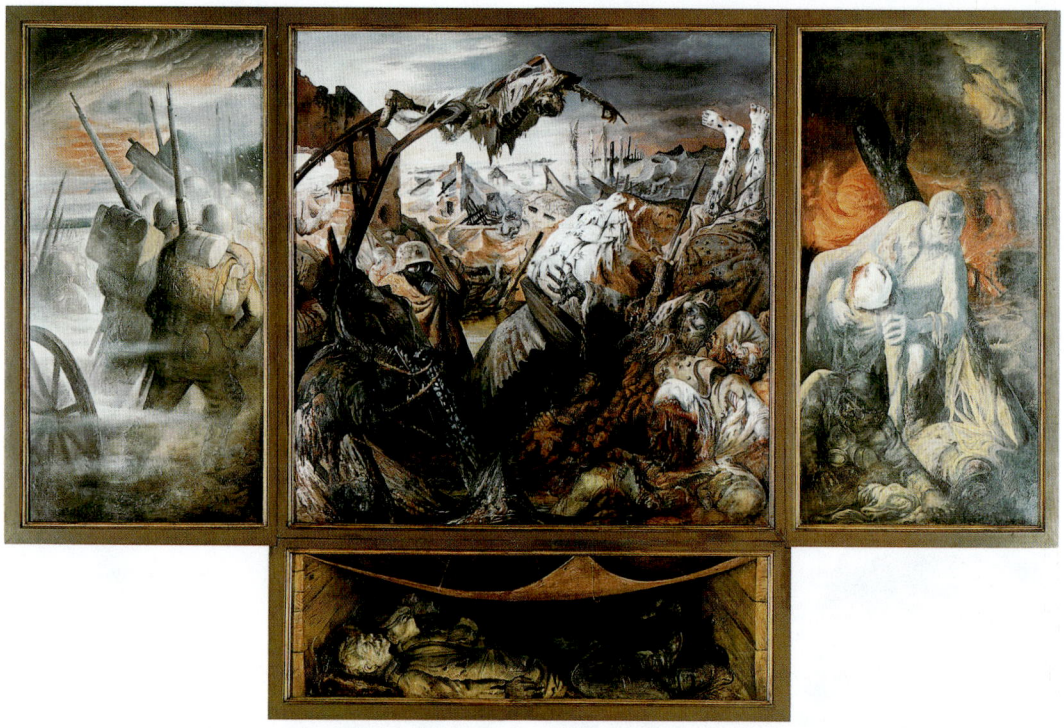

4.7.3 Otto Dix, *The War*, 1929–32. Oil and tempera on wood, central panel 80¼ × 80¼", side panels 80¼ × 40⅛", bottom panel (predella) 23⅝ x 80¼". Staatliche Kunstsammlungen, Gemäldegalerie Neue Meister, Dresden, Germany

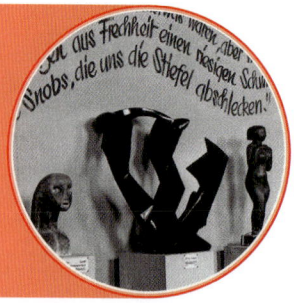

Otto Dix, along with other German Expressionists, would later be vilified by the Nazis for his criticism of WWI: see **4.8.7, p. 657**

because of the fame of the photograph, money poured in to save her. She underwent seventeen surgical operations and later emigrated to Canada. Nick Ut became "Uncle Nick" to the little girl and the two have remained in close contact throughout their lives. Although this photograph shows the suffering of a small group of people, it symbolizes for many the tragedy of the entire Vietnam War.

The German painter Otto Dix (1891–1969), who fought in World War I, also employed symbolism in his **triptych** *The War* (**4.7.3**) as he recorded the horrors he witnessed. The central panel shows death and destruction. A soldier wearing a gas mask, representing Dix himself, witnesses the devastation at first hand. Bloody bodies are piled on top of one another, one with legs in the air. Chaos fills the scene. Arched pieces of metal stretch out across the sky and support a skeletal figure, whose outstretched finger points toward the bullet-ridden body on the right. The arching forms enclose the scene, leaving us feeling smothered by the horror that is shown. Our anxiety is increased with nothing to calm us or to rest our eyes upon.

The left wing of the triptych shows heavily equipped soldiers, united in their duty and prepared for battle. The scene precedes the horror that will take place in the central panel. The right-hand wing shows a man, a self-portrait of Dix, carrying a wounded soldier. The sky in the triptych symbolizes the increasing danger of the situation, beginning on the left with pale sunlight, moving toward foreboding clouds, and ending with a stormy and destructive sky on the right. Underneath the central panel, in a section called the **predella**, Dix has painted a sleeping or dead soldier, lying in a trench.

The triptych format is traditionally used for religious scenes, with Christ's crucifixion portrayed in the center and his entombment in the predella below. By using this format, Dix elevates the importance of his subject matter. And in associating an ordinary soldier with the soon-to-be-resurrected Christ, he endows him with the status of a martyr.

Triptych: an artwork comprising three panels, normally joined together and sharing a common theme
Predella: the horizontal section on the bottom of a triptych altarpiece that often functions as a support or stand

Warriors and Battle Scenes

Artists have often recorded and celebrated the bravery of warriors, both their successes and defeats, in great detail. Although at times, as we have seen, an artist's interpretation of historical events is skewed and presented through an emotional lens, artworks can be valuable records of critical historical moments. They can teach us the significance of certain battles, and provide accurate studies of the weapons used and the uniforms worn by those who took part in them.

The Palette of Narmer, one of the earliest surviving ancient Egyptian artworks, records the unification of Egypt after a great war, and highlights the importance of the first pharaoh, Narmer, who was to rule over all of Egypt and keep the peace (**4.7.4a** and **4.7.4b**). Egyptian civilization survived along the north-flowing River Nile. Before the reign of Narmer, Egypt was divided into Upper Egypt (to the south) and Lower Egypt (in the more fertile north). **Palettes** were used to grind **pigment** that both men and women painted around their eyes to protect them from the sun. The round area on the front of the Palette of Narmer, in which the necks of two creatures intertwine, would have been used for the mixing of the paint.

The front of the palette is divided into four **registers**. The top register shows a pair of horned bull heads, which represent the aggressive strength of the king. In the next register the king is shown larger than the other figures in order to indicate his importance, a convention known as **hierarchical scale**. On the far right of this register are ten bodies with severed heads between their legs, indicating the scores of enemies Narmer has killed. The intertwining of the fantastical long-necked creatures in the next register embodies the unification of Upper and Lower Egypt. In the bottom register, Narmer is again represented as a bull, who bows his head toward a fortified city and tramples on an enemy.

The back of the palette features a large scene in which the pharaoh, wearing the White Crown that symbolizes Upper Egypt, prepares to club an enemy who kneels before him. The falcon represents the god Horus, suggesting that Narmer was supported by the gods. At the very bottom of the reverse side of the palette is a scene showing two fallen enemies, viewed as if from above. Much of the picture writing on the palette has not yet been interpreted, but it seems to record the names of places conquered by Narmer. Taken as a whole, the palette shows this pharaoh's military might as he unifies all of Egypt under his rule.

Some artists have focused on the heat of battle, and conveyed the sounds and sensations of war using completely different **media**. Both the *Bayeux Tapestry* and the *Tale of the Heiji Rebellion* (*Heiji Monogatari*) portray rousing battle scenes (**4.7.5** and **4.7.6** p. 642 and p. 643). We can almost hear the clanking of weapons and smell the odor of burning flesh. And while a few figures illustrate the courage of the enemy,

Palette: a smooth slab or board used for mixing paints or cosmetics
Pigment: the colorant in art materials. Often made from finely ground minerals
Register: one of two or more horizontal sections into which a space is divided in order to depict different episodes of a story
Hierarchical scale: the use of size to denote the relative importance of subjects in an artwork
Medium (plural **media**): the material on or from which an artist chooses to make a work of art

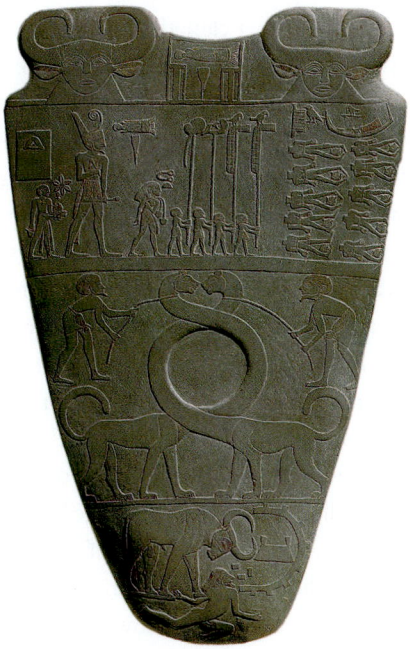

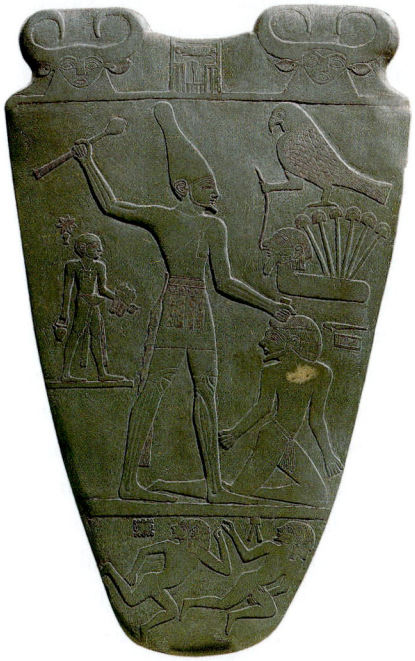

4.7.4a (far left) Palette of Narmer (front), Early Dynastic Period, Egypt, c. 2950–2775 BCE. Green schist, 25¼ × 16⅝". Egyptian Museum, Cairo, Egypt

4.7.4b (left) Palette of Narmer (back), Early Dynastic Period, Egypt, c. 2950–2775 BCE. Green schist, 25¼ × 16⅝". Egyptian Museum, Cairo, Egypt

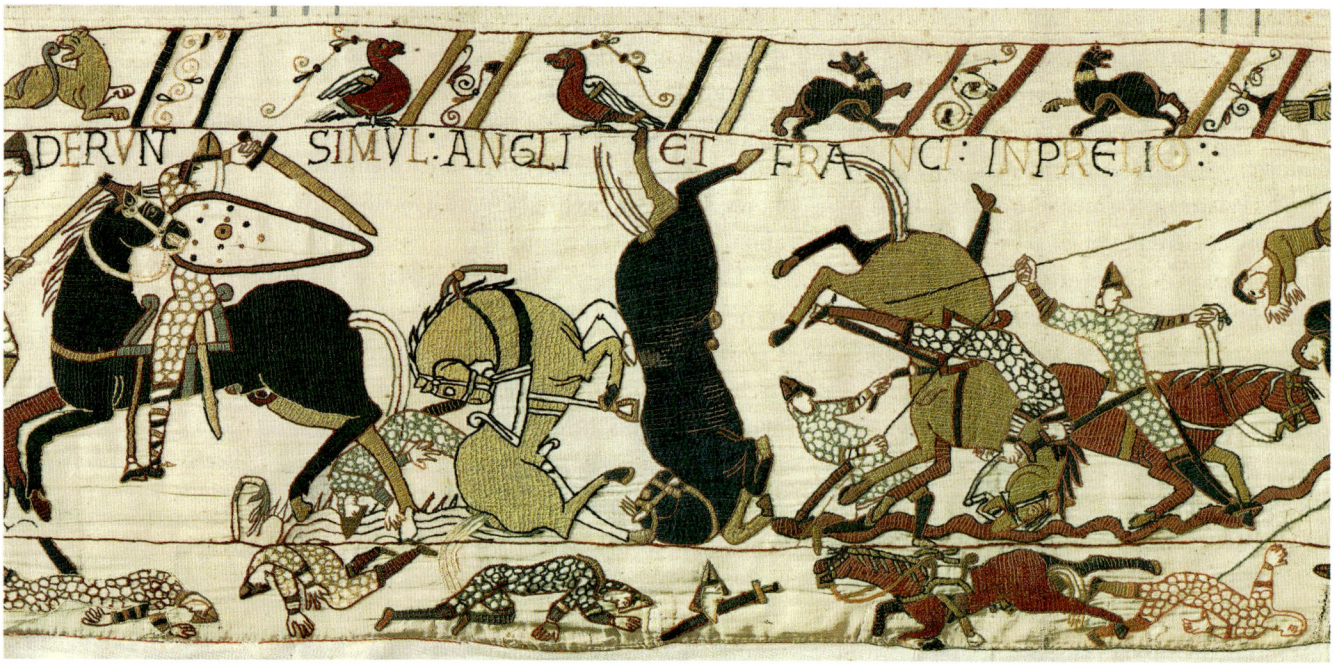

4.7.5 Detail of the Battle of Hastings, *Bayeux Tapestry*, c. 1066–82. Linen with wool, 275' long. Bayeux Tapestry Museum, Bayeux, France

both artworks are skewed toward celebrating the overwhelming prowess of the victors. Both artworks, too, consist of multiple scenes and are meant to be viewed slowly, unravelling their historical stories one incident at a time. Their very long horizontal formats take the viewer on a visual journey through history.

The 275-foot-long *Bayeux Tapestry* records the events surrounding the Battle of Hastings (1066), in which the Normans, led by William the Conqueror, seized control of England from the Anglo-Saxons. It was probably commissioned by William's brother Odo, the Bishop of Bayeux in France, shortly after the Norman victory. The so-called **tapestry** was embroidered by women (legend says William's wife was one of the embroiderers), and took more than ten years to complete. It shows the events that led to the battle, the preparations of the Norman fleet, the Battle of Hastings itself, and finally the coronation of William the Conqueror as King of England. More than six hundred men, but only three women, are shown in the fifty scenes on the tapestry. The embroiderers were highly skilled. To establish a sense of depth, each figure is given a border, which is filled in with stitches running in the opposite direction to the rest of the embroidery, and then outlined in boldly contrasting colors. The process creates clearly delineated figures, a flat sense of space (to guide the viewer in a horizontal direction), and, through repeated patterns, a sense of overall **rhythm**.

The *Night Attack on the Sanjo Palace* (**4.7.6**) is a single scene from one of five long painted scrolls that depict battles from the *Tale of the Heiji Rebellion*, a Japanese war epic about the short-lived Heiji era (1159–60). In this period several clans fought for control of Kyoto, the historical capital of Japan. This scene shows the burning of the palace by samurai warriors of the Fujiwara and Minamoto clans during the raid in which they captured the emperor Nijo. Soon afterward, another clan, the Taira, rescued the emperor and regained control of Kyoto.

Like the *Bayeux Tapestry*, the *Night Attack on the Sanjo Palace* is representative of the visual style of its period. The almost 23-foot-long Japanese scroll employs **isometric perspective** from a **bird's-eye view**. The horses and warriors are carefully delineated and detailed. The precise lines and limited use of blurry brushwork (as in the horses' tails and the billowing smoke) demonstrate the artist's skill. The story in the scroll is read from right to left, and the artist guides the viewer in that direction using the diagonal lines of the buildings, the layering of the figures, and the movement of the billowing smoke. In the section of the scroll shown here, the building on the right shows the palace under

Tapestry: hand-woven fabric—usually silk or wool—with a non-repeating, usually figurative, design woven into it
Rhythm: the regular or ordered repetition of elements in the work
Isometric perspective: a system using diagonal parallel lines to communicate depth
Bird's-eye view: an artistic technique in which a scene or subject is presented from some point above it

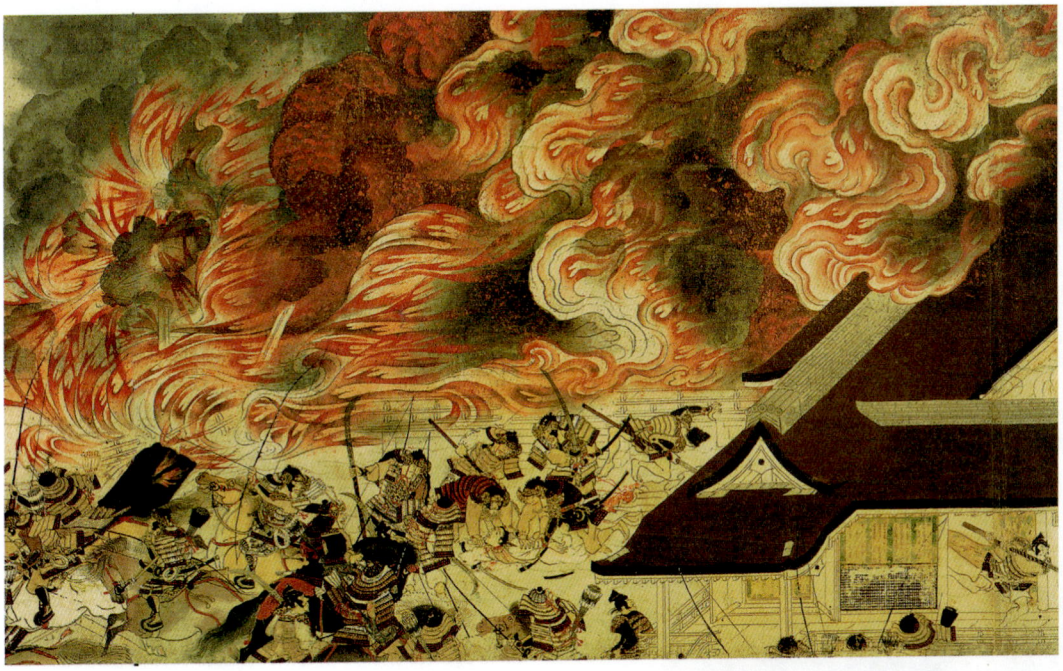

4.7.6 *Night Attack on the Sanjo Palace*, from *Heiji Monogatari*, Kamakura period, late 13th century. Hand scroll, ink and color on paper, 16⅛" × 22'11¼" (whole scroll). Museum of Fine Arts, Boston, Massachusetts

attack; then, moving left, prisoners are beheaded. The emperor is shown captured on a black cart in the lower left. Later in the scroll the emperor will be imprisoned and the decapitated heads will be displayed on pikes.

The attention to detail in both the Japanese scroll and the Norman tapestry gives us a strong sense of the equipment and weapons used by the warriors of these peoples. The Japanese samurai are shown covered in intricately detailed armor atop their fine and powerful horses. Lengthy bows and arching swords are their weapons of choice. The soldiers of the Bayeux tapestry wear patterned armor and conical helmets, and carry broadswords, kite-shaped shields, and spears.

Little is known about the militaristic society of the ancient Toltec people of Mexico except what can be learned from the legends of later cultures, such as the Aztecs, who often sought to demonstrate an ancestral link with the Toltec. These legends suggest that the Toltec ruled a substantial empire. It is believed that around 1000 CE the Toltec capital of Tula was the largest city in Mexico at that time, with a population of more than 50,000.

Four large warrior columns, standing between 15 and 20 ft. tall, are some of the few remaining artworks of the Toltec (**4.7.7**). The carved warriors stood high above the city, painted in bright colors. The imposing figures once supported the roof of a temple that stood on a pyramid and was reached by a steep stairway. The carving of the columns gives us some sense of how a Toltec warrior would have looked. The figures are identical, each wearing a feathered headdress, a butterfly-shaped chest ornament, sandals decorated with symbols of the gods, and a belt supporting a large mirror or shield on their lower back. Each warrior holds

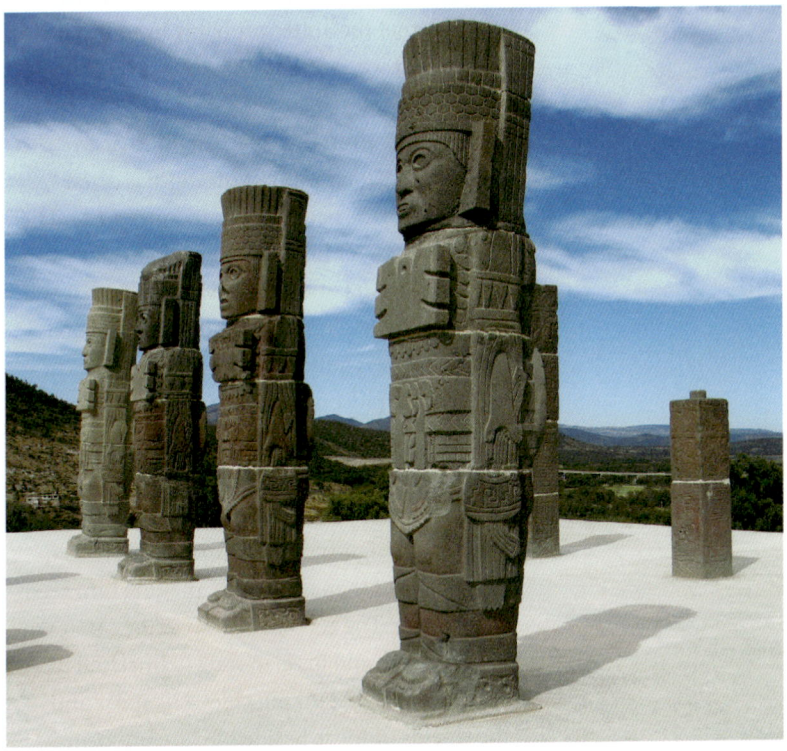

4.7.7 Tula warrior columns, 900–1000 CE. Basalt, height 15–20'. Tula, Hidalgo, Mexico

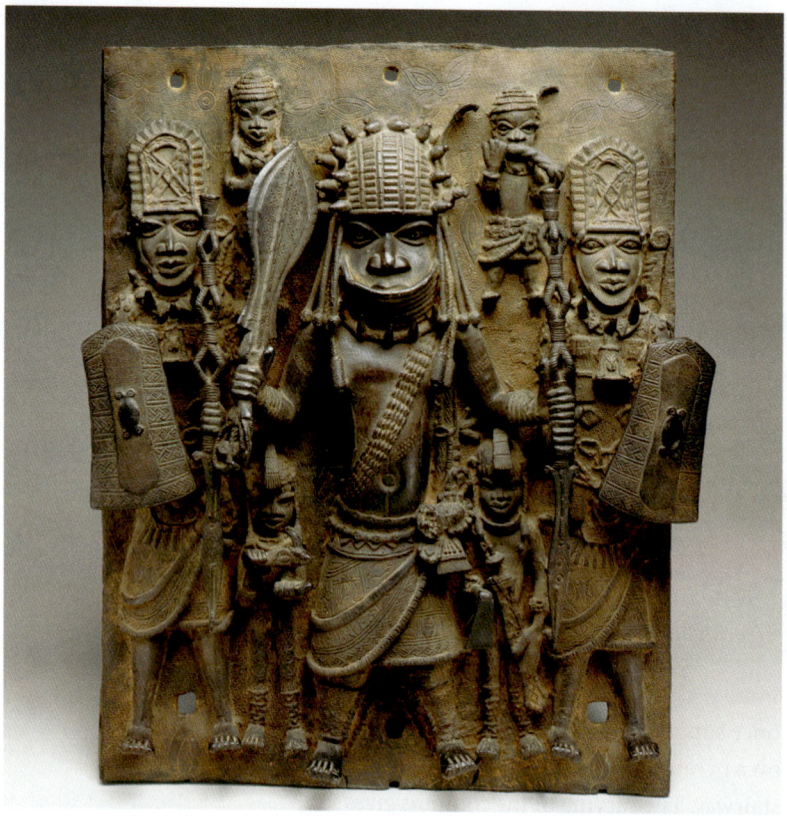

4.7.8 Benin plaque with warrior and attendants, 16th–17th century. Brass, height 18¾". Metropolitan Museum of Art, New York

spears or arrows in his left hand and a spear-throwing device in his right. Similar warriors—ranging from the small scale to the large, and occurring both as freestanding figures and as columns in temples—comprise the majority of the few Toltec sculptures that survive. This suggests that the Toltec probably lived in a time of frequent warfare, and that they revered their warrior rulers.

A plaque from the palace of an African king suggests that military strength is often needed to bring peace to a kingdom (**4.7.8**). The kings, or *obas*, of Benin, were both military and spiritual leaders of a West African state that was at its height between 1450 and 1700. The obas commissioned hundreds of brass artworks to reflect their power, including plaques to cover the royal palace, many of which depict warriors who followed the orders of the oba. The central warrior in this plaque is larger than the two beside him, signifying his importance; he is in **higher relief** than the others, making him seem closer to us. The ceremonial sword he carries in his left hand, and his elaborate helmet, tell us that he is a high-ranking chief. His spear and the shields of those beside him are imposing, emphasizing their physical power and that of their ruler, the oba. The chief wears a leopard-tooth necklace and has dotted markings on his stomach and arms resembling the spots of a leopard. Leopards, known for their power and speed, were a symbol of the oba.

High relief: a carved panel where the figures project with a great deal of depth from the background

The Artist's Response to War

Artists have often created artworks that attempt to convey their personal experience of war. This is sometimes a cathartic exercise, releasing emotion, and it is sometimes meant to inspire awareness of the realities of war. But by no means have all powerful responses to war been created by artists who actually witnessed the events they portray. Artists can produce powerful visual statements about the horrors of war from both their experiences and their own imagination. (See the Perspectives on Art Box: Wafaa Bilal, *Domestic Tension*: An Artist's Protest against War, p. 648.)

Francisco Goya's (1746–1828) painting *The Third of May, 1808* (**4.7.9**) is considered one of the most powerful portrayals of the horrors of war. The Spanish War of Independence (1808–14) was known for its guerrilla fighting and for the heroism of the civilian population. *The Third of May, 1808* documents the French emperor Napoleon's troops executing Spanish citizens during the French occupation of Madrid in 1808. The painting was commissioned in 1813 by the Spanish king Ferdinand VII to memorialize the event. Goya, a Spanish citizen who lived through the Napoleonic occupation, had complex views about the political situation as he watched it unfold, but in this work he made choices about how the image needed to be organized to evoke the horror of this event.

The figure given the most emphasis stands with his arms held high in a bright white shirt that glows from the light of a single lamp. He is about to be executed, which is suggested by the repeat of his pose in the dead figure lying bloodied on the ground. Terror is on the faces that surround this martyr, making him seem calm in comparison. Goya continually brings our attention back to this figure by using

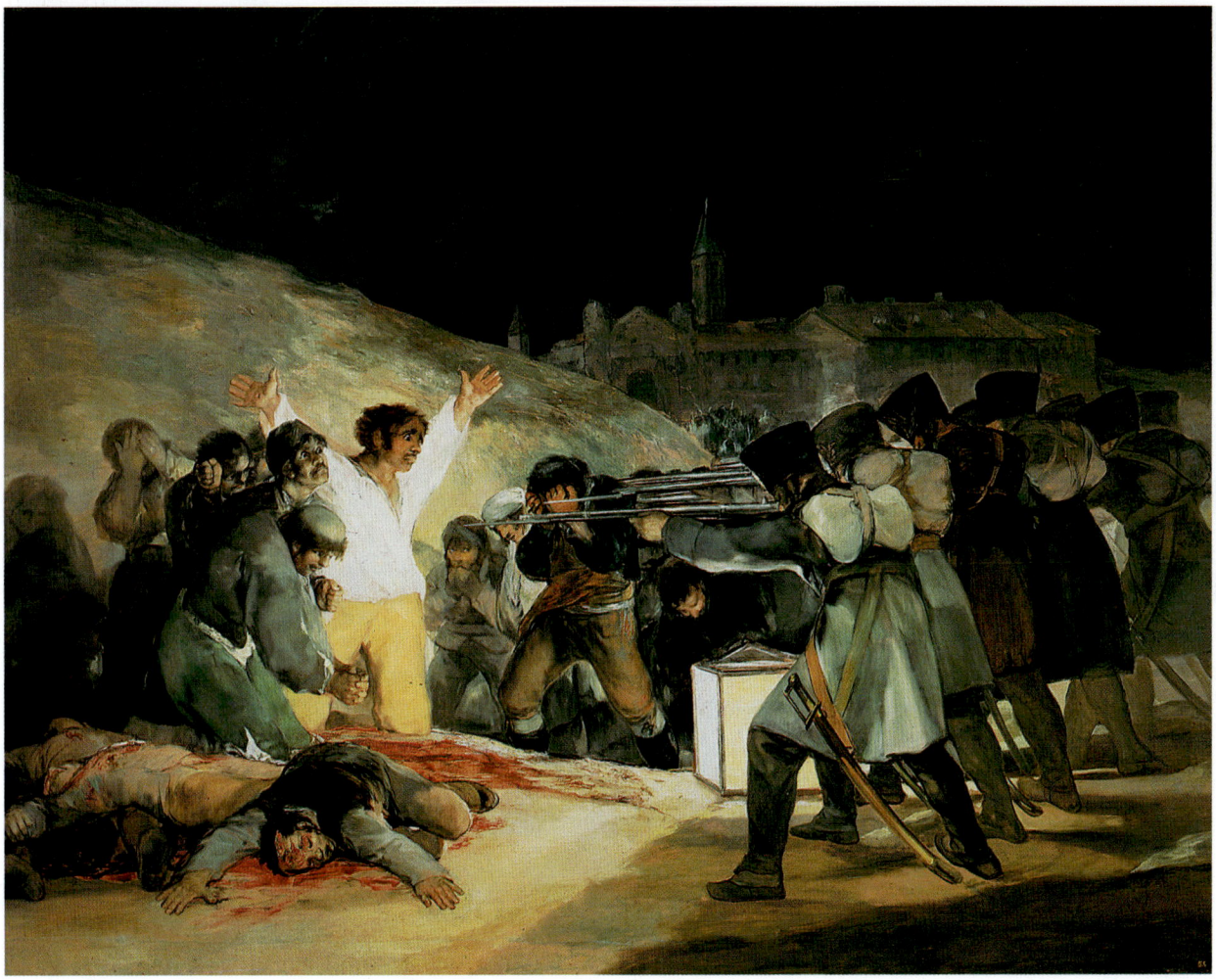

4.7.9 Francisco Goya, *The Third of May, 1808*, 1814. Oil on canvas, 8'4⅜ × 11'3⅞". Museo Nacional del Prado, Madrid, Spain

directional lines, such as the strong horizontals created by the rifles. The viewer identifies with the victims, not the line of faceless executioners.

Another great Spanish artist, Pablo Picasso (1881–1973), painted *Guernica* as a passionate response to the aerial attack carried out on April 26, 1937, on a small town of that name in northern Spain (**4.7.10**, p. 646). During the Spanish Civil War, the Nationalist general Francisco Franco, who would later become the country's ruler, allowed German and Italian planes to test their bombing tactics on Guernica and learn about the psychological effects of air warfare. Reports at the time stated more than 1,000 civilians were killed in three hours of bombing (though we now think the figure was closer to 240 people). News of the attack quickly spread to Paris, where Picasso read stories and saw photographs of the devastation.

While the general meaning of *Guernica* is clearly outrage against the violence directed at the citizens of the small Spanish town, Picasso never explained the specific symbolism of the figures in the painting, nor elaborated on his political motivations for the work. Picasso would have accepted multiple interpretations because he believed in viewers making their own reading of an artwork. He stated:

> A picture is not thought out and settled beforehand. While it is being done it changes as one's thoughts change. And when it is finished, it still goes on changing, according to the state of mind of whoever is looking at it.

The painting is black, gray, and white, perhaps because Picasso associated the attack with black-and-white newspaper photographs. The small dashes on the body of the horse also seem to recall the print from a newspaper.

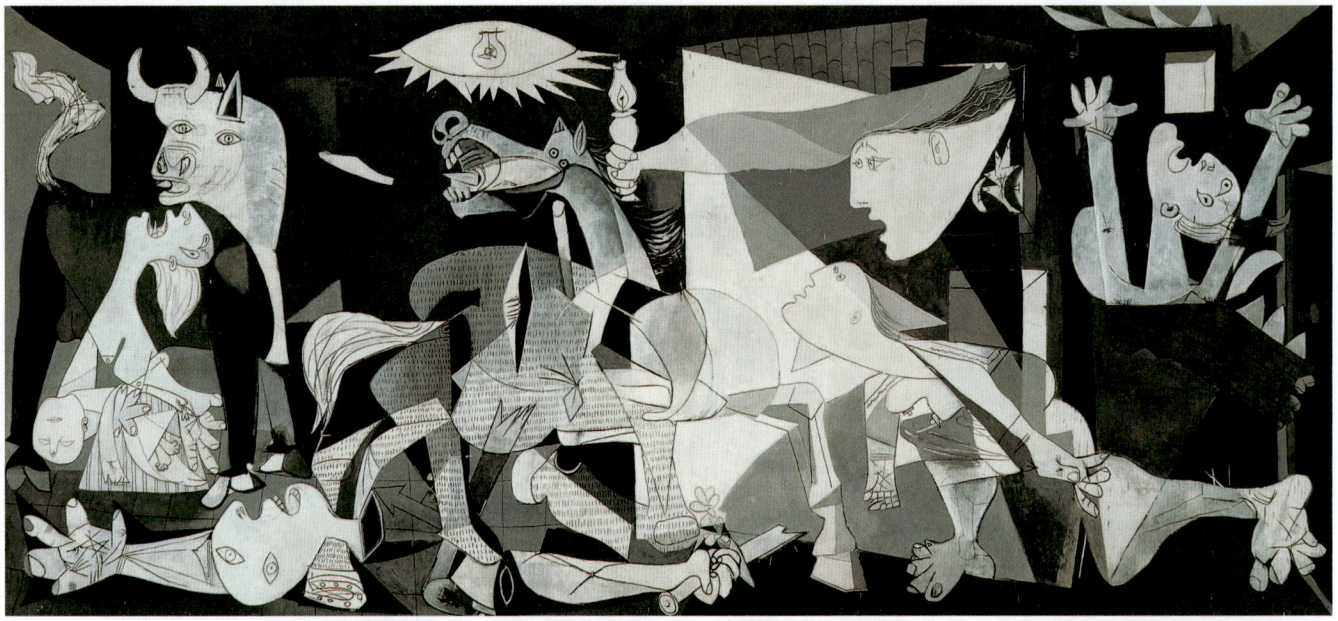

4.7.10 Pablo Picasso, *Guernica*, 1937. Oil on canvas, 11'5½" × 25'5¾". Museo Nacional Centro de Arte Reina Sofia, Madrid, Spain

Expressive faces with distorted necks scream and cry in despair. On the right, a figure reaches to the sky as it escapes from a burning building; flames appear like scales on the back of a dragon. The tortured figure on the left experiences the horror of her child's murder.

The bull, often associated with the violence of Spanish bullfighting, is seen by many as a symbol of Franco. The terrified horse, as it tramples upon a man lying on the ground, may represent the chaos inflicted upon the people by the attack. The lightbulb shining powerfully at the top of the canvas may symbolize awareness and knowledge, as if illuminating the situation.

Picasso exhibited this large protest statement at the Spanish Pavilion during the 1937 World's Fair in Paris, France, and declared that neither he nor the painting would go to Spain as long as Franco ruled. The artwork traveled the world before coming to rest in New York's Museum of Modern Art. Franco died in 1975, two years after Picasso. In 1981, *Guernica* was finally sent to Madrid, Spain, to be exhibited permanently.

The German artist Anselm Kiefer (b. 1945) was born in Germany just months before World War II ended. He grew up in a society ashamed of its past. His artworks force viewers to acknowledge the horrors of the Nazi regime that ruled Germany from 1933 until 1945. His attempts to confront this past have often shocked and angered Germans. For example, he photographed himself making the Nazi salute—a gesture that has been illegal in Germany since 1945.

Kiefer's *Breaking of the Vessels* conveys the loss of life and the destruction of knowledge caused by the extermination of millions of Jews during the Holocaust (**4.7.11**). The imposing 27-foot-tall artwork is made of lead and glass. The heavy lead books appear to be scorched, just as so many human beings (also holders of knowledge) were incinerated in concentration camps. The shattered glass also recalls *Kristallnacht* (Night of the Broken Glass), when the Nazis destroyed hundreds of Jewish stores and synagogues in 1938. The splintered glass on the ground makes any access to these books of knowledge a dangerous and frightening proposition. Symbolically, Kiefer has conveyed the fear and pain one must face to confront the past.

In *Breaking of the Vessels*, Kiefer draws upon the Jewish religion and more specifically the Kabbalah, a collection of Jewish mystical writings. The words "Ain-Sof," which mean the infinite presence of God, are written on the arched piece of glass above the bookshelf. Ten lead labels are placed around and on the bookshelf; these represent the ten vessels containing the essence of God as described in the Kabbalah. In this way, the books represent

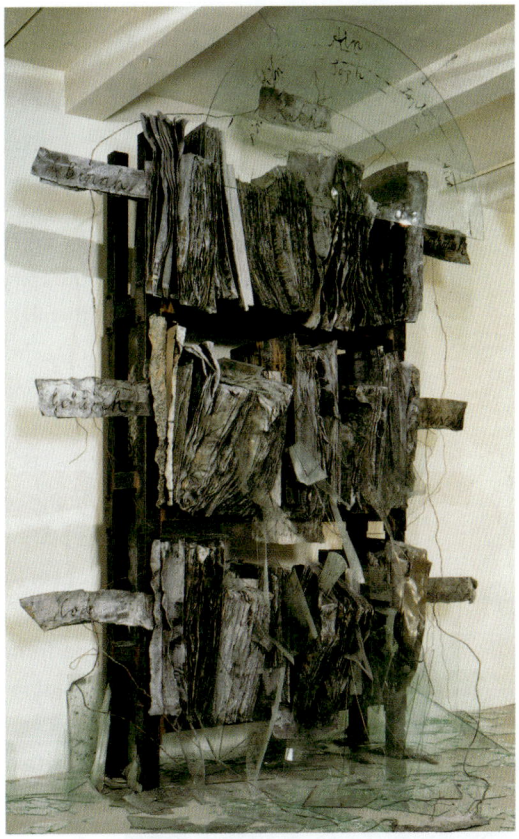

4.7.11 Anselm Kiefer, *Breaking of the Vessels*, 1990. Lead, iron, glass, copper wire, charcoal, and Aquatec, 12'5" × 27'5½" × 17'. St. Louis Art Museum, Missouri

the presence of God even in the midst of human destruction.

The Egyptian artist Mohamad Fahmy, known as Ganzeer, became internationally famous for his graffiti art criticizing the Supreme Council of the Armed Forces (SCAF), a council of military officials that ruled his country after the Egyptian Revolution in February 2011. Immediately following the revolution, Ganzeer began a series called the *Martyr Murals*, in which he created portraits of those killed during the revolution. Like much **street art**, this artwork was collaborative, the result of many artists who wished to raise their voices in protest against the massacre. During Mad Graffiti Weekend (May 20–21, 2011) Ganzeer produced his best-known work, *Tank vs. Bike*, in which an enormous tank points its gun at a young Egyptian boy on a pushbike, balancing a huge tray full of bread upon his head (**4.7.12**). Ganzeer was assisted by a team of volunteers to create the stencils for this work. Later, the artist known as Sad Panda added on his trademark figure behind the biker, and since then other artists have added to the image and it continues to evolve. For example, graffiti artist Khaled painted bodies being crushed under the tank. This recorded an actual event that took place in October 2011, when a group of peaceful civilians, protesting the demolition of a church, were attacked by security forces and the army. Graffiti and other street art has been a major form of protest throughout the uprisings against governments across the Middle East and North Africa, known as the Arab Spring.

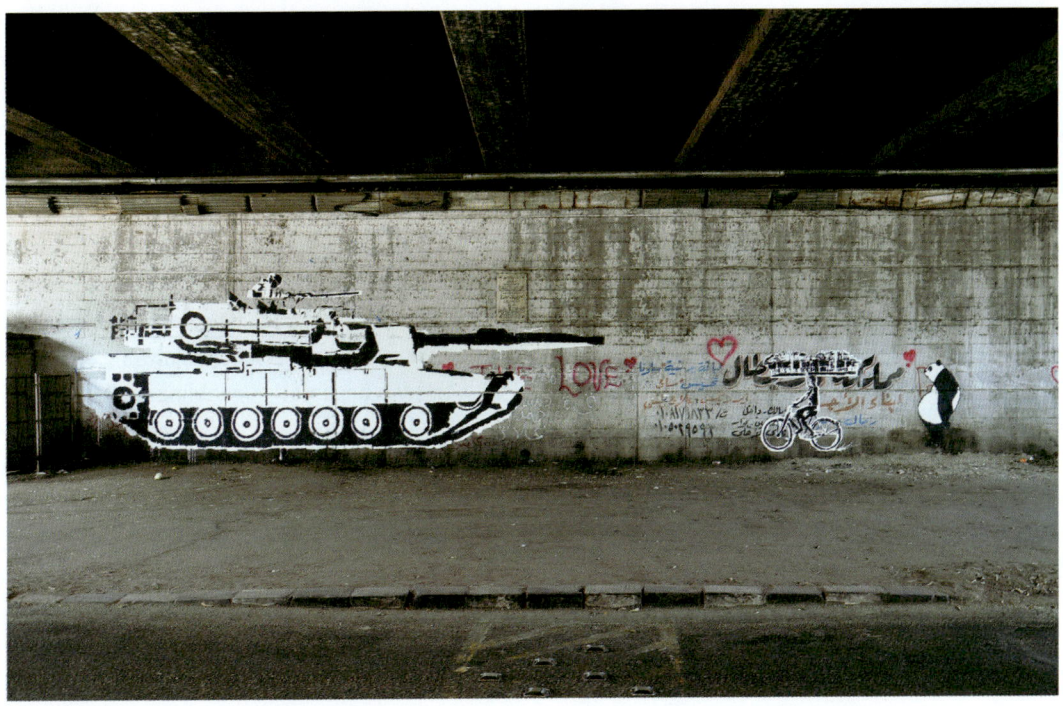

4.7.12 Ganzeer, *Tank vs. Bike*, with graffiti by Sad Panda, 2011. Cairo, Egypt

Street art: art created in public spaces (examples include graffiti, posters, and stickers)

Perspectives On Art: Wafaa Bilal
Domestic Tension: An Artist's Protest against War

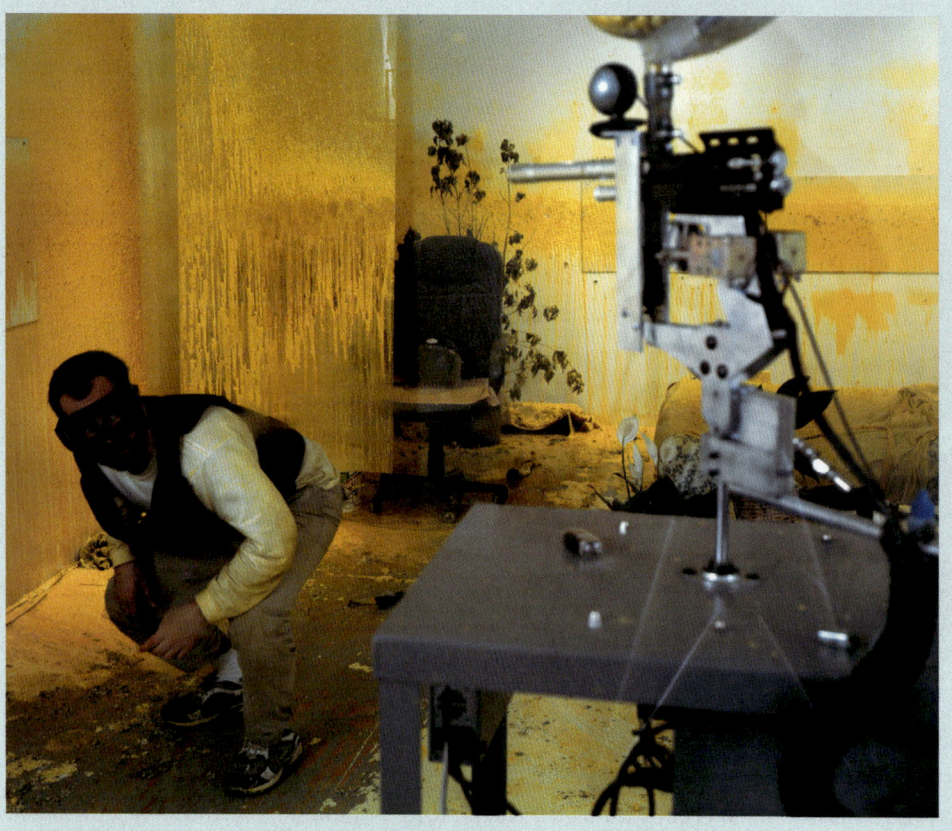

4.7.13 Wafaa Bilal, *Domestic Tension*, 2007. Flatfile Gallery, Chicago, Illinois

Iraqi-born Wafaa Bilal teaches in the Photography and Imaging department at the Tisch School of the Arts at NYU. His art reflects his concerns with the injustices committed in Iraq under the dictatorial regime of Saddam Hussein and, since then, during American military operations in the country.

As an Iraqi artist living in the US since 1992, I have created many provocative works to raise awareness and create dialogue about US–Iraq conflicts. But when my brother Haji was killed by an American bomb at a checkpoint in our hometown of Kufa, Iraq, in 2004, the war became deeply personal.

I had to find an unconventional new approach to translate this tragic event into a work of art that empowered its audience. Not something that lectured the audience, nor something dogmatic, but a dynamic encounter between me and my audience.

A TV news segment about a soldier in Colorado remotely dropping bombs on Iraq highlighted the anonymous and detached nature of this current war, and the complete disconnect between the comfort zone here in the US and the conflict zone in my home country. I needed to create a platform for people to be nudged out of their comfort zone.

The result was an interactive performance entitled *Domestic Tension* (**4.7.13**). I stayed in a Chicago gallery for a month with a paintball gun aimed at me. People could control the paintball gun, and command it to shoot at me, over the Internet.

I wanted to create a virtual and physical platform, turning the virtual to physical and vice versa, and, by putting my body on the line, create a physical impact in viewers by enabling them to identify with the physical effect on my body.

The project generated worldwide attention, with more than 60,000 shots taken and 80 million hits to the website from 137 countries.

I never anticipated how many people would be drawn to the project and how it would become a truly dynamic artwork in which the viewers had control over the **narrative**. It achieved an unexpected goal of democratizing the process of the viewing and the making of the artwork, by enabling the audience to participate.

As evidenced by dialogue on the website's chat room, the experience had a profound impact on many people from all sides of the political spectrum. At the conclusion of the project, I felt fulfilled in my mantra that "Today we silenced one gun; hopefully one day we will silence all guns."

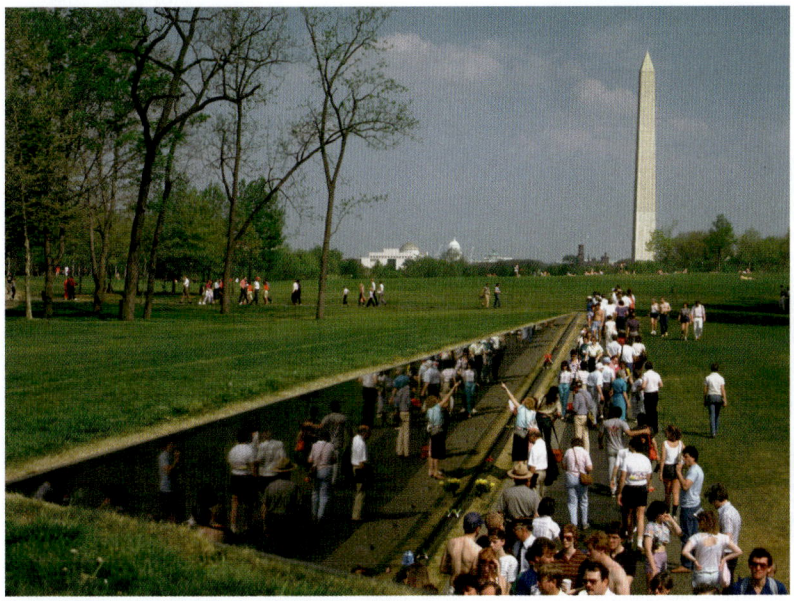

4.7.14a Maya Lin, Vietnam Veterans Memorial, Washington, D.C., 1981–83. Granite, each wing 246' long, height 10'1" at highest point

Remembrance and Memorials

Art can serve as a way to acknowledge a historical tragedy, mistreatment, or suffering, often in the hope that similar events will not be repeated. Memorials may address the history of a single individual or of many people. While memorials are often designed to promote healing and comfort the grieving, they can also be statements of tragedy, and can fuel uprisings. They can also express hope for a better world in the future.

Narrative: an artwork that tells a story

The Vietnam Veterans Memorial was built in Washington, D.C., to pay tribute to many fallen men and women and in the hope of laying to rest some of the lingering controversy over the war (**4.7.14a**). The design itself was immediately controversial, however. The competition to design the monument—which drew more than 1,400 submissions—was won by a twenty-one-year-old American of Chinese descent studying architecture at Yale University. Maya Lin (b. 1959) envisaged her monument as a place for mourning and healing. A black-granite, V-shaped wall descends into the earth, and then ascends, giving one a sense of coming into the light. The wall also becomes taller as one descends, creating a powerful visual expression for the enormous loss of life during the war. It symbolizes the eternal wound in America caused by the conflict, but also the healing that Lin hoped would take place as those who experienced the monument physically rose again.

The names of the dead are carved into the wall and organized by the date of death (**4.7.14b**). The surface is polished because, the artist explained, "the point is to see yourself reflected in the names." The walls are aligned toward two other monuments, the Washington Monument and the Lincoln Memorial. The integration of the Vietnam Veterans Memorial with these important structures acknowledges the significance of the Vietnam War to American history.

Lin intended the memorial as a tribute, and most visitors are moved upon experiencing it. Some veterans, however, saw it as part of a continued condemnation of the war. They said that rather than uplifting and instilling pride in the soldiers who fought, the monument's descent into the ground symbolized a moral criticism both of the war and its soldiers. The veterans also perceived the choice of black granite, as opposed to the more conventional use of pure white marble for memorials, as a criticism. In response to these protests, a bronze sculpture of three soldiers, more traditional in style, was later placed a short distance from the wall.

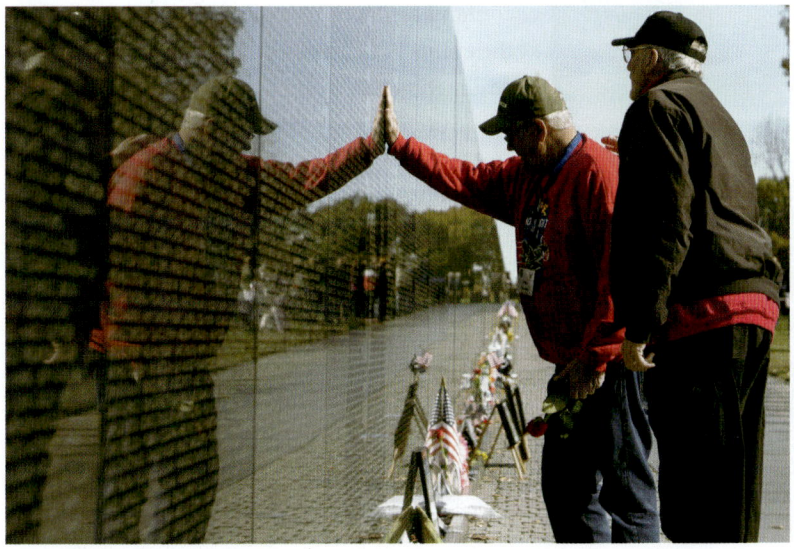

4.7.14b Maya Lin, detail of the Vietnam Veterans Memorial: visitors interacting with the wall

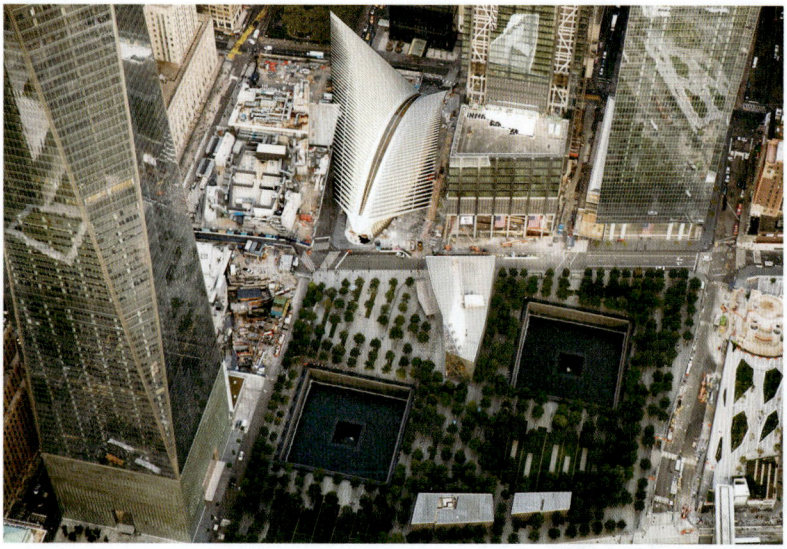

4.7.15a Michael Arad and Peter Walker, National September 11 Memorial & Museum, New York. Aerial view, September 8, 2016

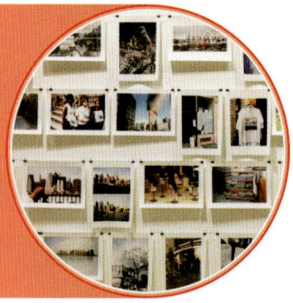

Here is New York... is an installation of photographs taken by people who recorded what they saw on 9/11: see **2.8.17, p. 325**

On September 11, 2001, the United States suffered the worst terrorist attack in its history. Two hijacked planes destroyed the Twin Towers of New York's World Trade Center, a third plane damaged the Pentagon in Washington, D.C., and a final plane crashed in a Pennsylvania field. The 9/11 attacks traumatized the nation and appalled the world. The perpetrators were members of Al Qaeda, an Islamic fundamentalist group that was born out of the Soviet War in Afghanistan (1979–89). The group's leader, Osama bin Laden, claimed the attacks were motivated by America's support of Israel and of the oppression of Muslims around the world. Hate crimes against Arab Americans rose dramatically in the United States in the aftermath of 9/11, and many felt as if they were being judged for their race or religion.

Ten years after the 9/11 attacks, a memorial and museum were created at the site of the World Trade Center towers (**4.7.15a** and **4.7.15b**). Although the memorial was designed with great awareness and respect for the survivors, those who lost loved ones, and those who had been persecuted, it has still been criticized by some. Perhaps most notably, the remains of many of the deceased are still buried underground, making the site sacred ground in the minds of some family members and therefore inappropriate as a site for a gift shop, admission prices, or gawkers.

Square footprints of the fallen towers, framed in steel, are now filled with waterfalls that represent the loss of so many lives. The edges of the squares are covered with bronze plaques inscribed with the names of the 2,977 who were killed, including those on the hijacked flights on 9/11, those at the Pentagon, and the rescuers who tried to help people escape, as well as victims of the World Trade Center bombing in 1993. Every effort was made to align the names most accurately to the location closest to where they perished in the buildings, and the victims of the other sites were placed together.

Located between and to the side of the tower waterfalls is the entrance to the 9/11 Memorial Museum, which is entirely underground. It contains artifacts from and information about the events of September 11. The entryway is designed so that visitors experience the sadness of the event as they descend underground and are introduced to the personal lives of the victims. When visitors rise above the earth again and visit the sites of the towers, the sound and sight of the rushing waters and trees are meant to invite contemplation and promote healing.

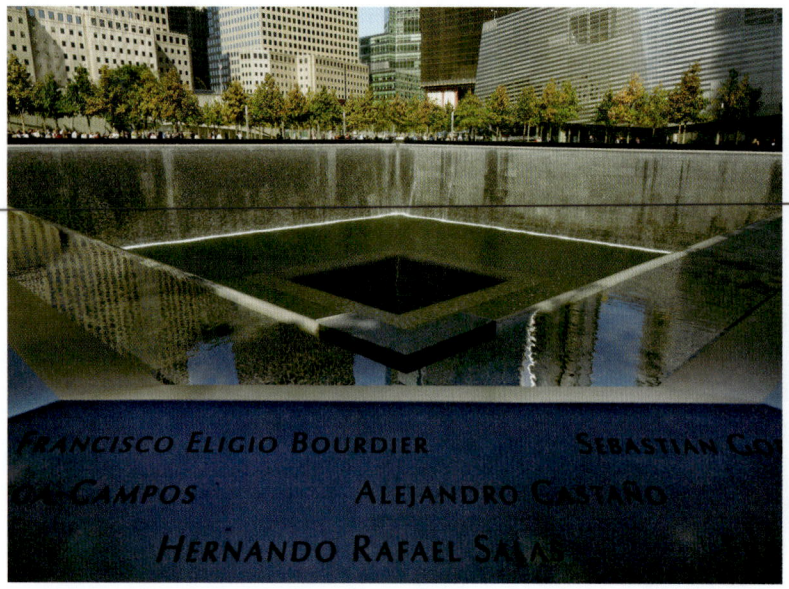

4.7.15b Michael Arad and Peter Walker, National September 11 Memorial & Museum, New York

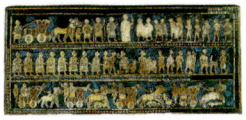

3.1.8a *Standard of Ur*, c. 2600–2400 BCE, p. 370

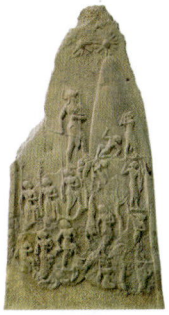

4.2.7 Stela of Naram-Sin, c. 2254–2218 BCE, p. 582

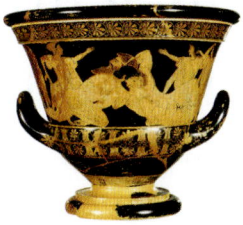

3.1.27 Krater showing Heracles and Antaios in battle, c. 515– 510 BCE, p. 383

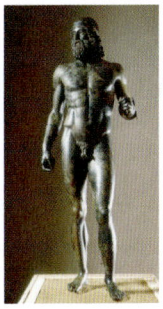

2.4.12 *Riace Warrior A*, c. 460 BCE, p. 250

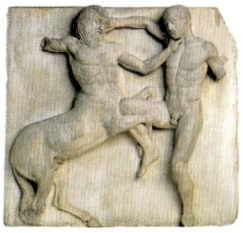

3.1.23 Metope of a Lapith and centaur, Parthenon, Greece, c. 445 BCE, p. 381

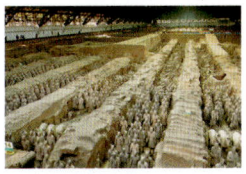

3.3.13a Terra-cotta army, mausoleum of Qin Shi Huangdi, c. 210 BCE, p.417

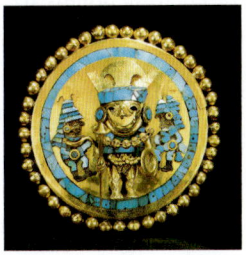

3.4.4 Moche earspool, Peru, c. 300 CE, p. 431

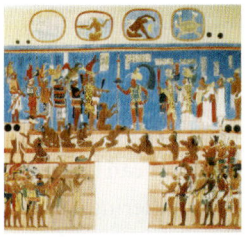

3.4.14 Bonampak mural, Mexico, 8th century, p. 438

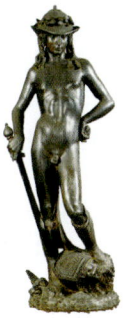

3.6.22 Donatello, *David*, c. 1430, p. 480

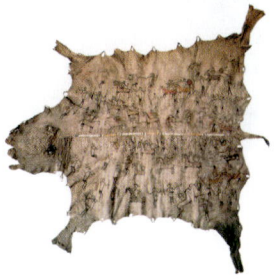

3.4.21b Hide robe with battle scene, US, 1797–1800, p. 441

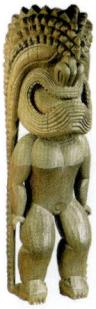

2.4.9 Figure of the war god Ku-ka'ili-moku, Hawaii, 18th or 19th century, p. 247

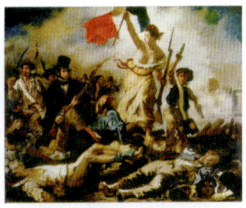

3.7.13 Eugène Delacroix, *Liberty Leading the People*, 1830, p. 497

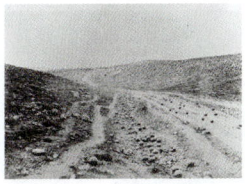

2.8.21 Roger Fenton, *Valley of the Shadow of Death*, 1855, p. 328

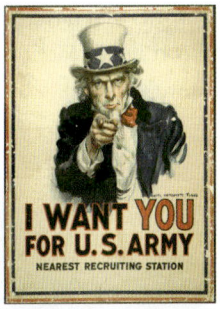

2.7.11 James Montgomery Flagg, recruitment poster, c. 1917, p. 305

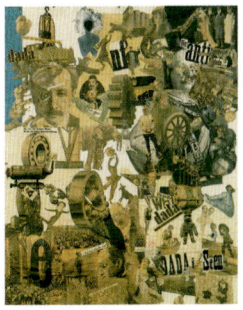

2.8.20 Hannah Höch, *Cut with the Kitchen Knife...*, 1919–20, p. 327

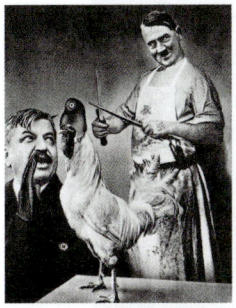

3.9.9 John Heartfield, *Have No Fear, He's a Vegetarian*, 1936, p. 530

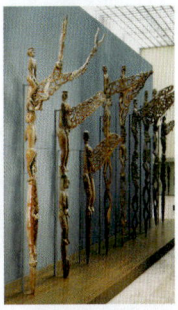

4.3.8 Asmat culture, *Bis* ancestor poles, late 1950s, p. 597

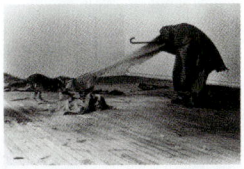

2.10.5 Joseph Beuys, *Coyote, I Like America and America Likes Me*, May 1974, p. 354

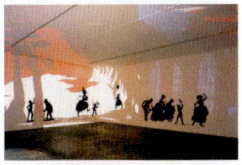

2.10.11 Kara Walker, *Insurrection!...*, 2009, p. 359

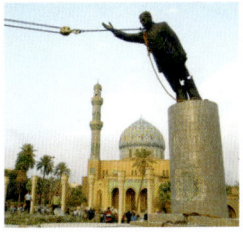

4.6.13 Toppling of Saddam Hussein statue, Baghdad, Iraq, 2003, p. 636

4.8 Art of Protest and Social Conscience

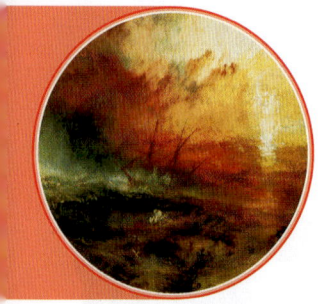

In a similar manner to Géricault, the British Romantic artist J. M. W. Turner used the sublime power of nature to convey the horror of human tragedy: see **3.7.15, p. 498**

The visual language of art can be an extremely effective means of communicating a point of view on social issues. While words can describe an event, art can demonstrate it visually with raw power. Art often reflects historical, social, and political concerns. It can even provoke change. Art is able to arouse such strong emotions that artworks themselves can become the focus of protest, sometimes suffering damage or destruction as a result. Art can also inspire us toward a better and more just world. This chapter is concerned with the ways that artists have expressed their convictions through artworks that have, at times, caused powerful, even violent, reactions (see Gateway Box: Ai Weiwei , p. 654).

Art as Protest and Activism

By creating potent artworks that activate emotional responses, artists can instigate social change. Here we examine artworks that have sought to combat cruelty, poverty, and inequality, for example the injustices of slavery and colonialism. While considering this section's protest artworks, think about your own response. Does the artist inspire you to agree with his or her point of view?

The painting *Raft of the Medusa* (**4.8.1**), by the French artist Théodore Géricault (1791–1824), memorializes on a grand scale a scandalous event in history. On July 2, 1816, the French naval vessel *Medusa* ran aground off

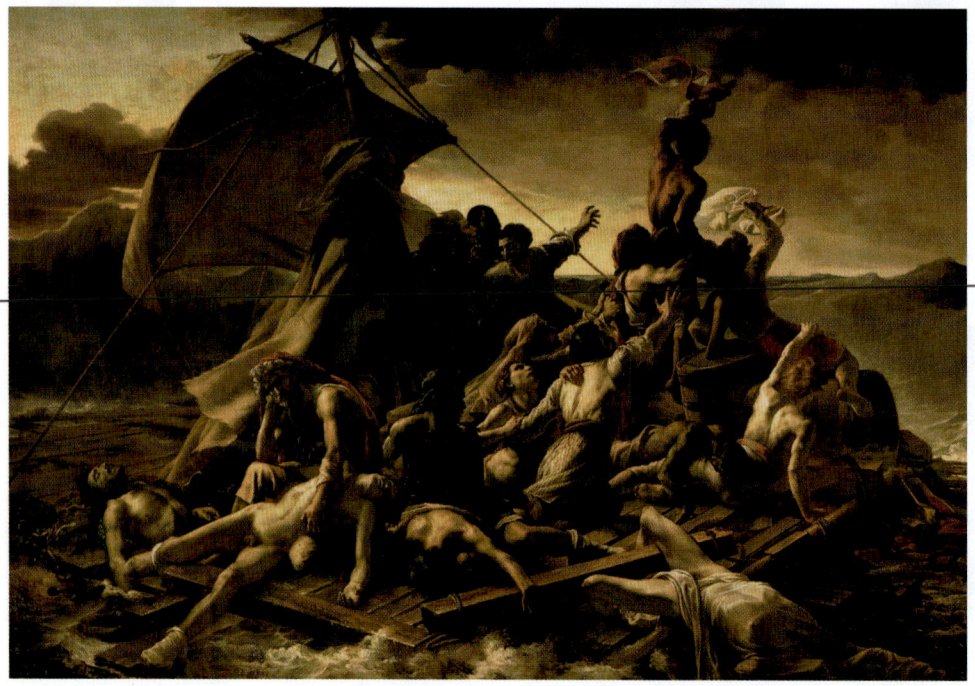

4.8.1 Théodore Géricault, *Raft of the Medusa*, 1819. Oil on canvas, 12'1⅜" × 17'9⅞". Musée du Louvre, Paris, France

the coast of West Africa. While the captain and approximately 250 crew boarded the lifeboats, the rest of the passengers—146 men and one woman, some of them slaves—got onto a makeshift raft that had been built from the wreckage. Although the raft was pulled by the lifeboats initially, the captain soon abandoned it. Left to battle starvation, sunburn, disease, and dehydration, only fifteen men survived the horrors of the sea; some cannibalized their shipmates. Géricault's painting shows with emotional intensity the moment when the raft's survivors are about to be rescued.

Géricault interviewed the survivors, studied corpses, and even had a replica of the raft built in his studio in preparation for this project. The survivors told him of their despair and madness when they saw a ship on the horizon on the thirteenth day. They had seen ships in the distance before but the ships' crews had not seen them, and many feared this ship, too, would disappear. But the survivors, all close to death, were rescued, and they told the world the story of their abandonment.

In *Raft of the Medusa*, Géricault depicts the emotions of the survivors. Several men, their arms reaching out toward the tiny ship in the distance, convey desperate hope. Another is shown still slouched in despair, and surrounded by corpses; he even holds one on his lap. The artist painted the skin of the men with a green pallor to indicate that they are near to death. Yet the musculature of their bodies gives them nobility. Standing at the painting's apex, atop a pyramid of bodies, a black man waves a piece of his clothing to get the attention of the ship in the distance. The dramatic intensity is heightened by the use of diagonal lines that compose the figures into a large X. From the bottom left corner of the **composition** the bodies of the men are arranged in a line that leads the viewer's eye to the black man in the upper right. An opposing diagonal is made from the mast in the upper left to the near-naked male body on the lower right, which appears to be falling from the raft.

Géricault's picture criticizes not only the *Medusa* disaster but also colonization and slavery. Only one African survived the tragic journey, and Géricault includes him as the powerful figure trying to attract the attention of the distant ship.

En el aire (In the Air) by Teresa Margolles is a seemingly peaceful, even playful, room filled with bubbles (**4.8.2**). Yet visitors to her **installation** are shocked when they discover that the bubbles are made from the water used to cleanse the bodies of corpses. Using her experience as a trained medical examiner who worked in a morgue in Mexico City, Margolles wishes to activate greater awareness of the large number of violent deaths in Mexico due to narco (drug-related) crimes. Margolles states that, "each bubble is a body," and she stuns us by creating a tactile experience in which the

Composition: the overall design or organization of a work

Installation: originally referring to the hanging of pictures and arrangement of objects in an exhibition, installation may also refer to an intentional environment created as a completed artwork

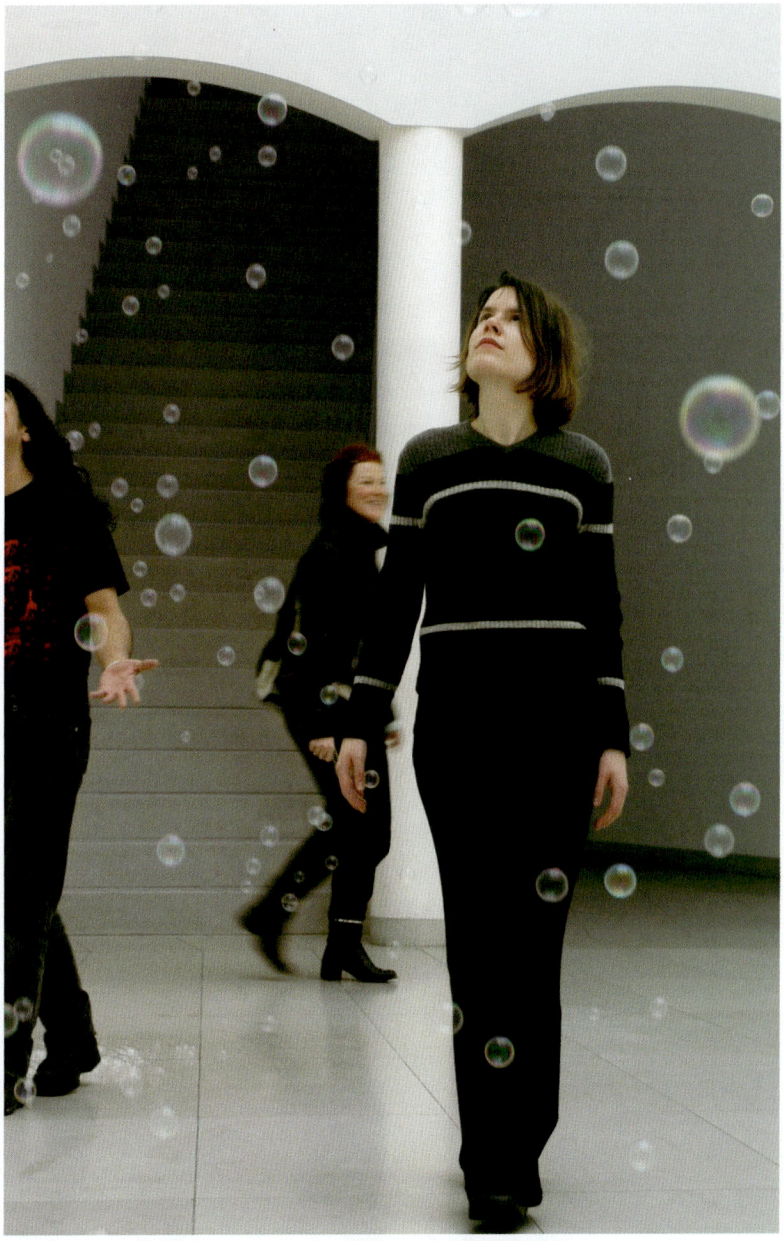

4.8.2 Teresa Margolles, *En el aire (In the Air)*, 2003. Installation view, "Muerte sin Fin," Museum für Moderne Kunst, Frankfurt, Germany, 2004

Gateway to Art: Ai Weiwei: *Dropping a Han Dynasty Urn* and *Colored Vases*

The Art of Activism: Speaking out at all Costs

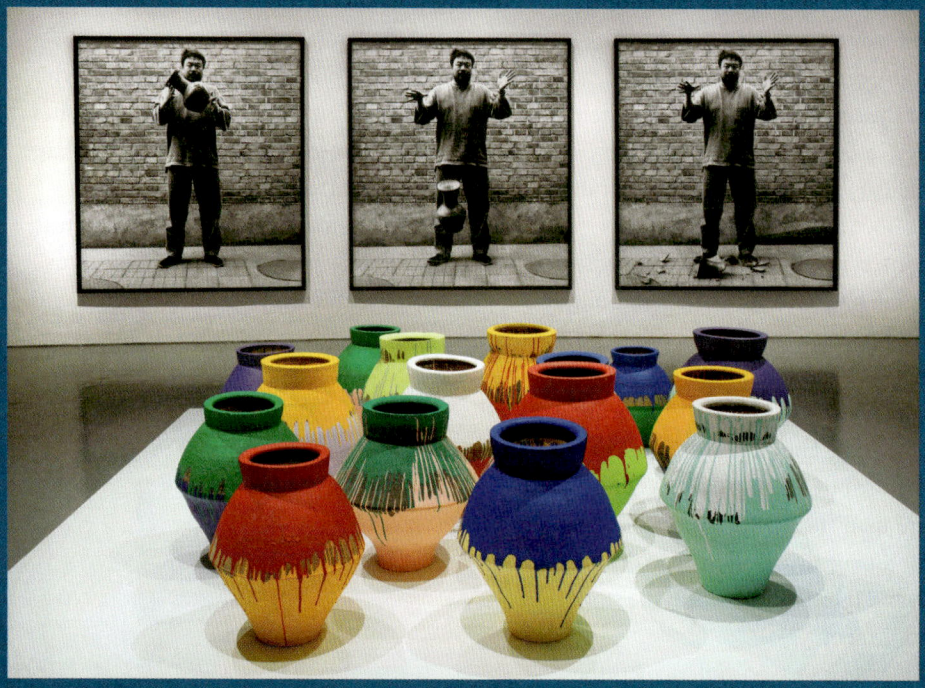

4.8.3 Installation view showing Ai Weiwei's *Colored Vases* in front of his *Dropping a Han Dynasty Urn*, displayed at the "According to What?" exhibition, held at the Hirshhorn Museum and Sculpture Garden, Washington, D.C.

Current news stories report on strict Chinese government controls over what the public has access to on the Internet, in the press, and in much of their daily lives. Similarly, artistic expression in China is forcefully restricted. The artist Ai Weiwei (b.1957) has become internationally famous for his works that question the Chinese government's conduct and for the price he has had to pay for such expression.

Ai Weiwei was raised in an activist family. His father, regarded as one of the finest modern Chinese poets, was imprisoned and exiled for opposing the Nationalist Party of China. After studying film and the arts in Beijing, Ai lived in the United States from 1981 to 1993, where he was particularly influenced by the ideas of Marcel Duchamp and Andy Warhol.

When he returned to Beijing, Ai created many works that have been censured by the Chinese government. The photographs *Dropping a Han Dynasty Urn* (**4.8.3**) were made the same year he photographed himself raising the middle figure toward Tiananmen Square, the symbol of Chinese government. In 2005, he began a blog in China that criticized government policies. His blog was shut down by the police in 2009 after he exposed poor construction standards as the cause of the high number of deaths from the 2008 Sichuan province earthquake (more than 69,000 people killed and at least 4.8 million left homeless). He also posted the names of all 5,385 children killed in the earthquake. Also in 2009, Ai was beaten by the police for his intention to testify about his observations of the earthquake aftermath. His injuries were so severe that brain surgery was required to treat them. In 2011, he filmed the government's destruction of his studio and, two months later, he, like his father had been, was imprisoned.

Ai Weiwei's work has been shown prolifically around the world, but only rarely in China. Shortly before the opening of a Shanghai exhibition of Chinese Contemporary art in 2014, Ai's works were forcibly removed and records of his previous awards were destroyed. Ai Weiwei continues to protest the Chinese government through his art.

For the other Ai Weiwei Gateway boxes, see p. 121, p. 357, and p. 419

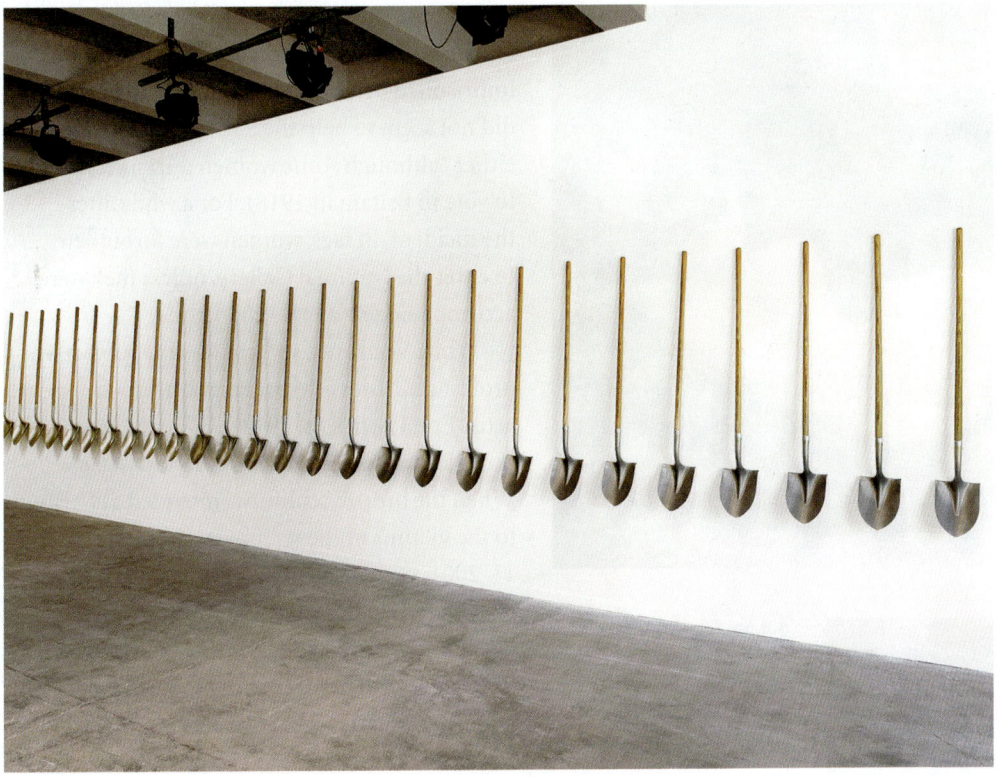

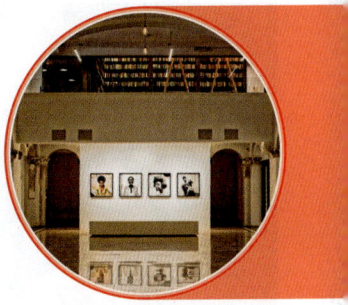

The artist Theaster Gates revitalizes buildings in downtown Chicago to create safe cultural and living spaces for the community: see **3.10.21b, p. 560**

4.8.4 Pedro Reyes, *Palas por Pistolas (Guns for Shovels)*, 2007–present. Installation view, Biennale de Lyon, France, 2009

visitor touches the remains of the deceased. The beauty of the bubbles and the cleanliness of the space create a setting in which the visitor's body can become traumatized by the knowledge of the material used to make the bubbles. Such trauma is necessary, Margolles argues, in order to trigger disgust and horror at the tragedy of the numerous violent deaths. Visitors to the exhibition are forced to acknowledge these deaths and asked to become involved in working to prevent more murders.

In an effort to create social participation in combating the many violent deaths in Mexico City, Pedro Reyes (b. 1972) produces art from weapons. Initially conceived in 2007, *Palas por Pistolas (Guns for Shovels)* is a public campaign in which the public donates firearms that are then melted down to make shovels (**4.8.4**). Equaling the number of guns initially donated, the 1,527 shovels Reyes created for this project were used to plant 1,527 trees around the world. Many of the shovels have since been exhibited in galleries to bring awareness to the scale of the Mexican weapons trade. Reyes utilizes art to promote peace and to physically transfigure such harmful objects. Since the conception of *Palas por Pistolas*, Reyes has continued to use donated guns as a medium and transform weapons, vehicles of violence, into objects that contribute to society, such as pieces of art, including musical instruments.

Art as the Victim of Protest: Censorship and Destruction

Art can inspire a forceful response. When the ideas an artwork represents are considered harmful or incompatible with a desired message or point of view, artworks might be censored or removed from public eyes. Sometimes the impact of a work of art is so powerful that viewers wish to destroy it, along with the message or attitude they see represented in it (see Box: Censorship of Art, p. 657).

The *Rokeby Venus* (or *The Toilet of Venus*) by the Spanish artist Diego de Silva y Velázquez (1599–1660) (**4.8.5a**, p. 656) may seem inoffensive to the modern viewer, but in 1914 it was the target of a violent protest. A woman called Mary Richardson, armed with a meat cleaver she had hidden inside her coat, slashed the *Rokeby Venus* seven times (**4.8.5b**, p. 656). Richardson was a member of the Suffragette movement, which

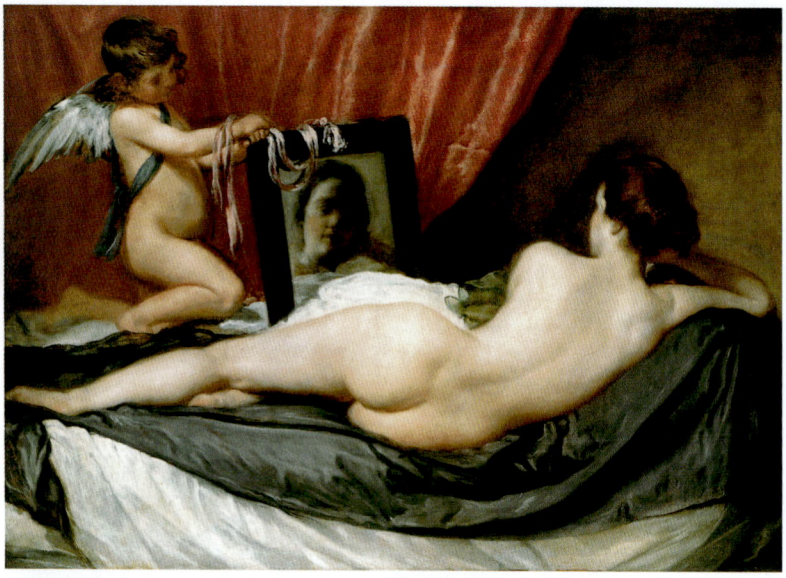

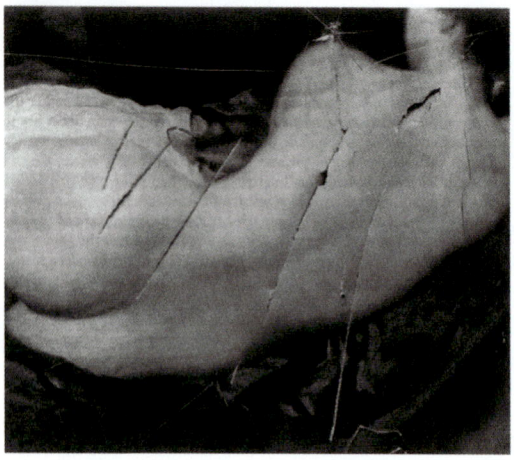

4.8.5a (above) Velázquez, *The Toilet of Venus (Rokeby Venus)*, 1647–51. Oil on canvas, 48½ × 69¾". National Gallery, London, England

4.8.5b (left) Photograph of damage to the *Rokeby Venus*, 1914

campaigned to give women the right to vote. For her, the painting represented a sexist definition of ideal beauty, showing a woman solely as an object of male desire. Richardson was motivated more specifically to protest against the imprisonment of the Suffragette leader Emmeline Pankhurst. Richardson later explained that she believed justice to be more valuable than art:

> I have tried to destroy the picture of the most beautiful woman in mythological history as a protest against the Government for destroying Mrs. Pankhurst, who is the most beautiful character in modern history.

Richardson's attack on the painting did not have its intended effect on perceptions of the *Rokeby Venus*. The seven slashes were soon completely repaired, and many still consider the painting to be a defining representation of female sensuality and beauty. Richardson was imprisoned briefly after the attack; the incident did not seem to help the Suffragette movement either (although some women did gain the right to vote in Britain in 1918). For a while after the incident, in fact, women were forbidden to enter the National Gallery, unless they were accompanied by a male chaperone.

While Velázquez's *Venus* was the subject of protest centuries after its creation, the American artist Eric Fischl's (b. 1948) *Falling Woman* provoked an instantaneous reaction (**4.8.6**). When the bronze sculpture, intended as a tribute to the victims of the terror attacks of September 11, 2001, was unveiled in New York City, it was considered so offensive that it was covered over almost immediately. It shows a woman in freefall, with her legs above her head and her arms flailing. Fischl placed a poem next to his artwork:

> We watched,
> Disbelieving and helpless,
> On that savage day.
> People we love
> Began falling,
> Helpless and in disbelief.

Many New Yorkers had witnessed firsthand the tragedy of desperate victims, trapped in the World Trade Center towers, jumping to their

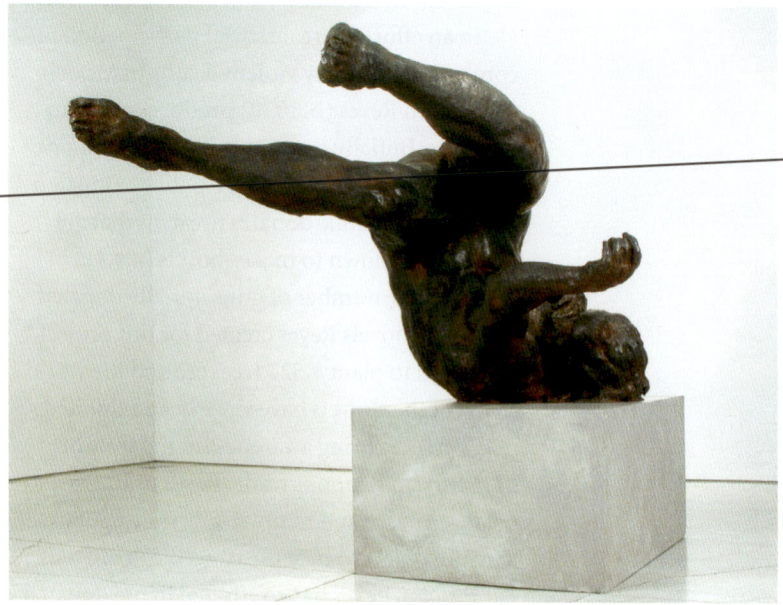

4.8.6 Eric Fischl, *Falling Woman*, 2001–2. Bronze, 38 × 72 × 48". Private collection

Censorship of Art: The Nazi Campaign against Modern Art

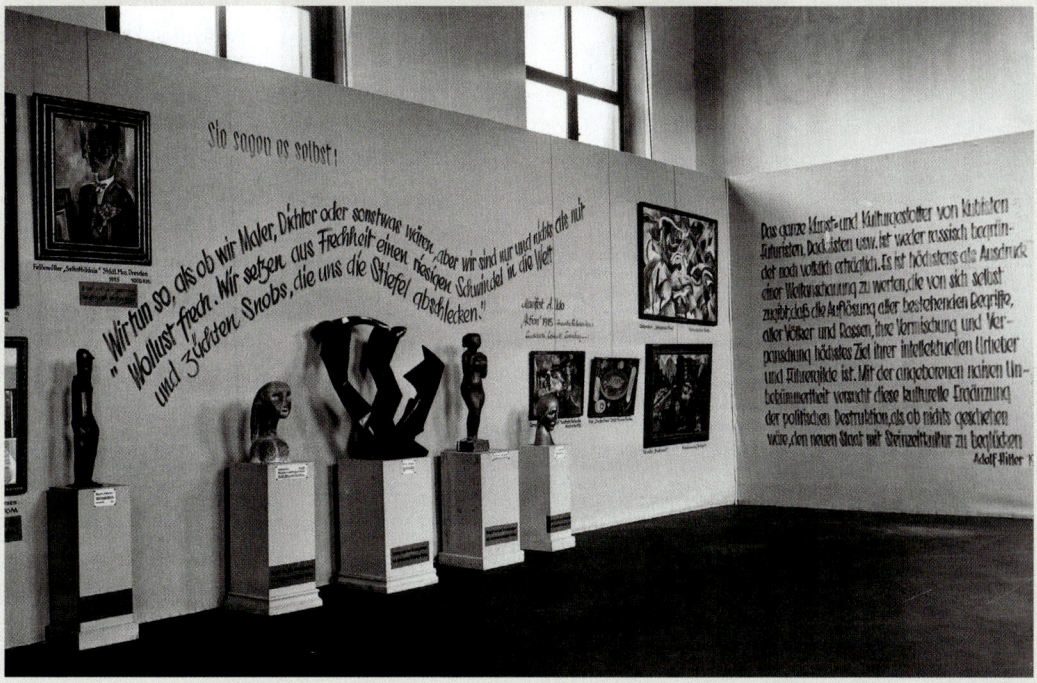

4.8.7 Photograph of the Nazi-curated traveling exhibition "Degenerate Art" ("*Enkartete Kunst*") at its first stop at the Hofgarten, Munich, Germany, 1937

Censorship has the ability to cause shifts in public opinion. For this reason, artworks and the artists who create them are often amongst the first to be targeted by dictatorial governments. They are also some of the first victims in times of war.

As a young man in his late teens, Adolf Hitler sold realistic watercolors and painted postcards on the streets of Vienna. He failed twice to be accepted into the Academy of Fine Arts Vienna, an institution that did accept several artists with more abstract styles, such as Egon Schiele. Hitler never got over the disappointment of being unable to become a successful artist, and he abhorred modern art, in particular, that of the German Expressionists.

In Germany in the 1930s, Hitler's National Socialist (Nazi) regime launched a systematic and large-scale attack on modern art that did not conform to Nazi party goals. The Nazis initially confiscated around 5,000 works of art from museums; they later took a further 16,500 from private collections. Some 4,000 of these were burned; others became the property of Nazi collectors, or were sold to foreign collectors for Nazi profit. The artists who made them were banned from working. The Nazis also dismissed museum directors, closed art schools, such as the famous **Bauhaus**, and burned books.

On July 18, 1937 the Nazis opened an exhibition of "Great German Art," which displayed the kind of art approved by the regime. The next day they opened another show of 730 works called "Degenerate Art," to suggest that these were the work of mentally deficient artists. Works were deliberately displayed awkwardly, and labels on the walls ridiculed the artworks (**4.8.7**). One read: "We act as if we were painters, poets, or whatever, but what we are is simply and ecstatically impudent. In our impudence we take the world for a ride and train snobs to lick our boots!" Artists vilified in the exhibition included Egon Schiele, Otto Dix (**4.7.3**, see p. 640), Paul Klee, Marc Chagall, Max Ernst, Pablo Picasso, Henri Matisse (**3.9.1**, see p. 525), and Vincent van Gogh.

One of the artists whose work was particularly ridiculed in the exhibition was Emil Nolde (1867–1956). His series of nine panels on the Life of Christ were hung together next to writing on the wall that said: "Mockery of the Divine." The *Crucifixion*, the largest of the series (**4.8.8**, p. 658) was placed in the center. Its unnaturally bright colors, the greenish pallor of Christ and other figures, and the blurry, →

Bauhaus: design school founded in Weimar, Germany, in 1919

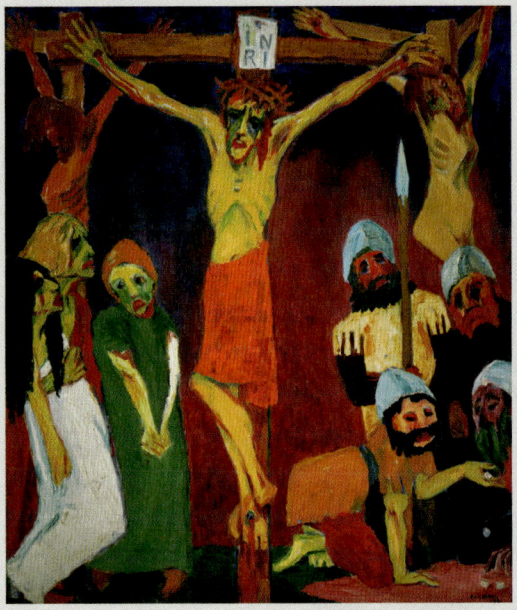

4.8.8 Emil Nolde, *The Crucifixion*, 1912, from a polyptych, *The Life of Christ*. Oil on canvas, 7'2⅝" × 6'3¼". Stiftung Seebüll A. & E. Nolde, Neukirchen, Germany

unfinished look of the paintings made them, in the eyes of the creators of the exhibition, anti-religious.

Yet unlike most of the artists mocked at the show, Nolde was himself a member of the Nazi party. He was so appalled to see his work in the exhibition that he wrote to Paul Joseph Goebbels, the Nazi Minister of Propaganda, demanding that the "defamation" against him cease. Nolde's paintings were returned to him but he was ordered to stop making art. He continued to create watercolors in secret, fearing that he would be discovered if he used strong-smelling oil paint. Yet despite the constraints he was under, Nolde was one of the lucky artists. Dozens of others whose work featured in the show fled Germany or committed suicide, and many were later sent to concentration camps.

Attendance at the Degenerate Art exhibition was unparalleled for its time, with more than two million visitors in Munich alone, and one million more when the show went on tour through the rest of Germany and Austria. Although there are records of people spitting on the artworks, there remains little other evidence of what visitors actually thought of the art in this propaganda spectacle.

When the exhibitions ended, the Nazis sold some artworks to raise money for their impending war effort, but most of the artworks were destroyed, along with thousands of others considered degenerate. The freedom to create art and to have opinions about it are emblems of a peaceful society; the Degenerate Art show and the book burnings perpetrated by the Nazis are two examples of how extreme censorship can result in the end of peace and freedom for many.

deaths to escape the fire. Perhaps because of this, Fischl's sculpture, displayed only a year after the terrorist attack, was seen as too potent and heart-wrenching. The artwork and the response to it reflect one of the challenges artists face when they address contemporary issues. Would Fischl's sculpture have been accepted if it had been unveiled many years later, when the event was no longer fresh in the minds of so many? Or was it simply too graphic, depicting a moment too shocking and too unbelievable for people ever to want to remember?

Some viewers, however, were upset that the sculpture was covered up, considering it a powerful reminder and a valid, even cathartic (emotionally releasing) response to what happened. "The sculpture was not meant to hurt anybody," said the artist:

> It was a sincere expression of the deepest sympathy for the vulnerability of the human condition. Both specifically towards the victims of Sept. 11 and towards humanity in general.

Art that Raises Social Awareness

Because of the power of visual language, artists can make people more aware of a social problem, spur people to become involved in a social issue, or even call for social change. These artists have used art to shine light on social, racial, and environmental issues (see Gateway Box: Hokusai, p. 661).

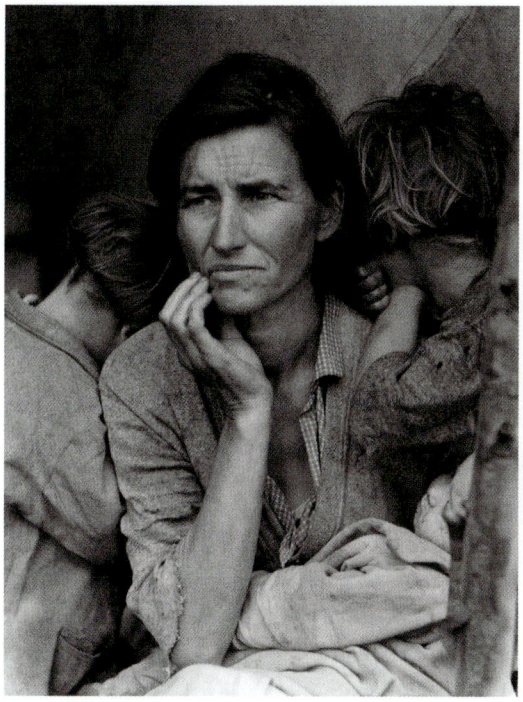

4.8.9 Dorothea Lange, *Migrant Mother*, 1936. Library of Congress, Washington, D.C.

Dorothea Lange's famous photograph of Florence Owens Thompson, known as *Migrant Mother*, was used to demonstrate the plight of the poor and remains a powerful symbol of the struggle against poverty (**4.8.9**). The picture was taken in 1936 when Florence and her children were living in the remains of a Californian pea-pickers' camp. Lange's image had an immediate impact. The photograph was published in several newspapers and *Time* magazine. The federal government sent 20,000 pounds of food to the camp. Unfortunately, the Thompson family had migrated elsewhere before the supplies arrived.

While the photograph had an incalculable effect on people's understanding of the devastation of the Great Depression, Thompson herself was always ashamed and irritated by the portrait. To her mind, it never had a positive effect on her life. When the photograph was taken she was recently widowed, had six children, and worked wherever she could to support her family. The identity of Thompson was not discovered until 1978, and she was quoted as saying, "I wish she hadn't taken my picture," and complained about never being compensated. Her experience raises questions about the role of an artist when depicting an actual event. To what extent should the subject's privacy be protected, and to what extent should he or she be compensated, if at all, when his or her image has demonstrable effects on the social conscience? More than eighty years after it was taken, Lange's photograph remains a memorable symbol of the plight of the poor, and since 1936 it has been published many times in books and newspapers and has twice featured on US postage stamps.

The series *Women of Allah* (1993–1997) by the Iranian-born artist Shirin Neshat's contains black-and-white photographs of armed and veiled Islamic women. These works explore Western stereotypes of Muslim women as well as the religious and personal convictions of these women. These beautiful images show women as powerful, and speak to the seemingly contradictory perception of Muslim women as both suppressed and soldiers of Islam. In "Speechless" (**4.8.10**), the muzzle of a gun is placed beside the woman's face, at first appearing to be an earring. Written on her face in Farsi calligraphy is text written by the female poet Tahereh Saffarzadeh, in which a woman addresses her brothers in the Iranian Revolution (1978–79) asking if she can participate as well. Neshat herself was exiled from Iran, but disagrees with Western interventions in

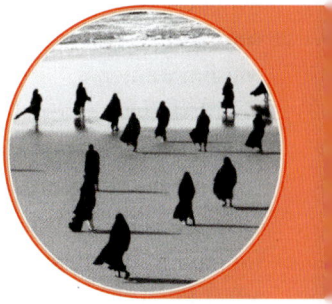

Shirin Neshat's *Rapture* series of films also considers gender roles in Iranian society: see **3.10.12b, p. 553**

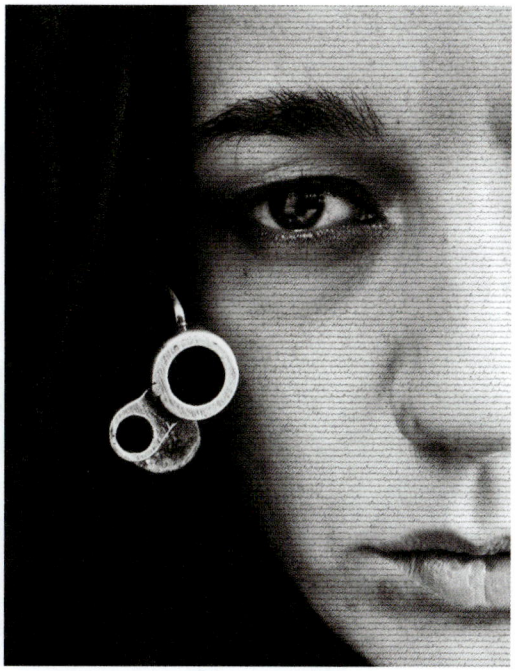

4.8.10 Shirin Neshat, "Speechless" (from *Women of Allah* series), 1996. RC print and ink, 3'10¾" × 2'9⅞"

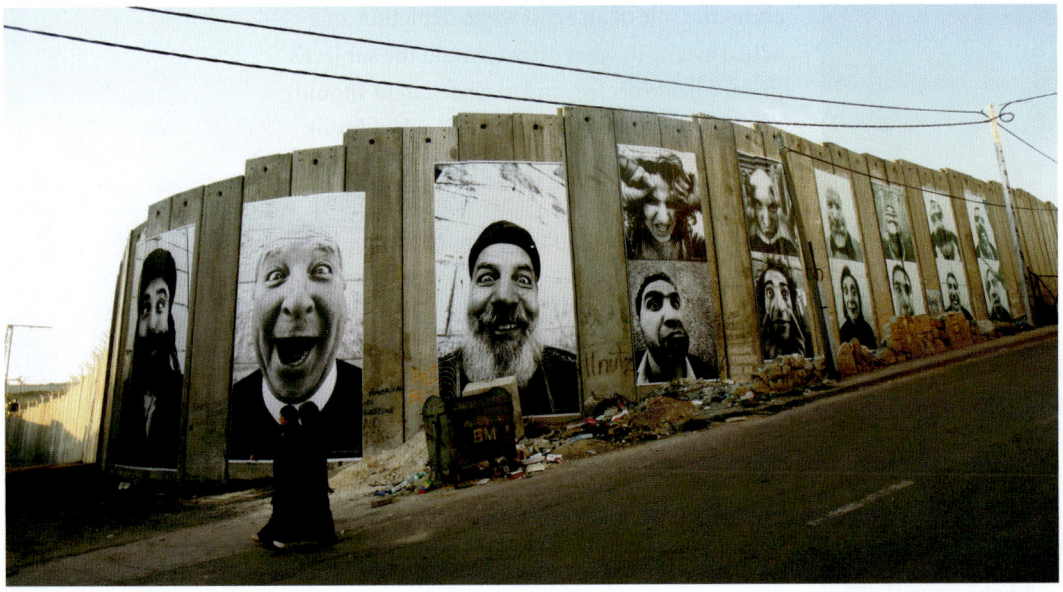

4.8.11 JR and Marco, *28 Millimeters, Face2Face*, Separation Wall, Palestinian Side In Bethlehem, March 2007

her home country. Her works address the complexities surrounding the identity of Muslim women.

28 Millimeters, Face2Face, by the French artist JR and the Swiss artist Marco, asks society to consider the differences and similarities between Israelis and Palestinians. JR, an artist known for mounting colossal photographs in order to affect social change, took corresponding (Israeli and Palestinian) portraits of people that have the same jobs or roles in society, such as doctors, teachers, and children. These images are often playful and show expressions of emotion that are universal. The artists hung large posters of these photographs throughout the Near East, but most noticeably on the West Bank wall that divides Palestine from Israel (**4.8.11**). Residents and visitors on either side of the wall were intrigued and entertained by the images, which highlighted how similar the two groups of people really are. In fact, in many cases, people could not tell which of the paired figures was the Israeli and which was the Palestinian. The three portraits shown together (on the left portion of the wall in image **4.8.11**) are all religious men who individually talked about how the face of all humans is a reflection of God. The *Face2Face* project enabled many Israelis and Palestinians to see one another not as stereotypes but as actual people.

The artist Sherrill Roland was a graduate student at the University of North Carolina in Greensboro in 2013 when he was wrongfully imprisoned for more than ten months. By the time he was exonerated, both he and the kind of art he wished to produce had radically changed. He returned to graduate school in 2016 and initiated *The Jumpsuit Project*, a performance piece in which he goes about his daily activities wearing an orange jumpsuit like the one he was forced to wear in prison (**4.8.12**). This act altered his interactions with others, just as being jailed had, and served to trigger conversations about the impact of the prevalence of false incarcerations, especially for African American males. Roland wants to raise awareness of the many lives affected by this social issue: "Incarceration happens every day. I could be anybody. It could be me today, it could be you tomorrow."

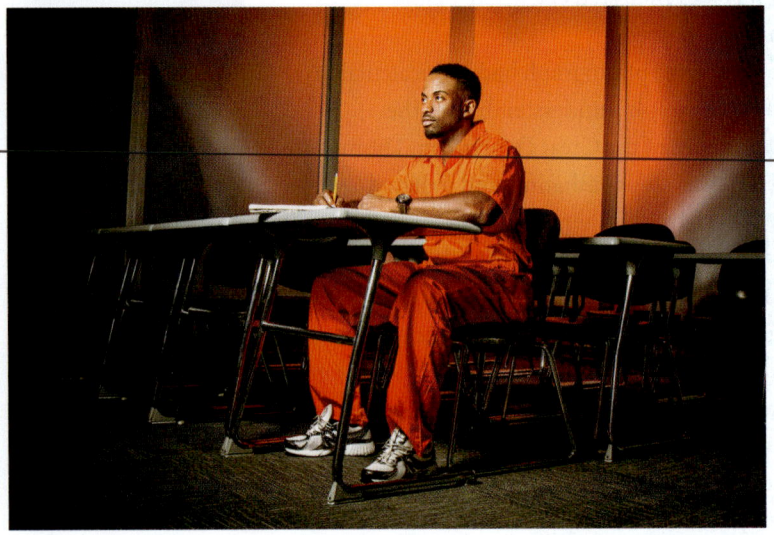

4.8.12 Sherrill Roland III, *The Jumpsuit Project*, 2016–2017, Socially Engaged Art, A Year-Long Performance

Gateway to Art: Hokusai, "The Great Wave off Shore at Kanagawa"

Using Famous Art to Make a Social Difference

In 2009, contemporary artist Chris Jordan created a likeness of "The Great Wave off Shore at Kanagawa" by Katsushika Hokusai (**4.8.13**) in a bid to highlight the environmental problem of consumer waste. Jordan assembled more than 2.4 million pieces of plastic to create his artwork, "Gyre" (**4.8.14a** and **4.8.14b**), to reflect the number of pounds of plastic that are estimated to enter the world's oceans every hour. Jordan's artwork attempts to show the inconceivability of that number. The plastic for the artwork was collected from the Pacific Ocean, and the artist named the work after the Pacific Gyre, a thousand-mile whirlpool where enormous quantities of trash collect. By gathering together all the junk we discard, Jordan draws attention to the huge volume of waste that humans create. By using such familiar objects as toothbrushes and combs, the artist hopes to show people how their individual trash contributes to the larger problem.

The artist has recycled trash to create several artworks, and explains the thinking behind these works, which are intended to address American mass consumption in particular:

> The pervasiveness of our consumerism holds a seductive kind of mob mentality. Collectively we are committing a vast and unsustainable act of taking, but we each are anonymous and no one is in charge or accountable for the consequences. I am appalled by these scenes, and yet also drawn into them with awe and fascination. I find evidence of a slow-motion apocalypse in progress.

Jordan's reference to Hokusai's famous scene, which emphasizes the beauty and power of nature, encourages the viewer to reflect on whether even the power of nature can survive this massive environmental problem and the threat it poses to the future of our planet.

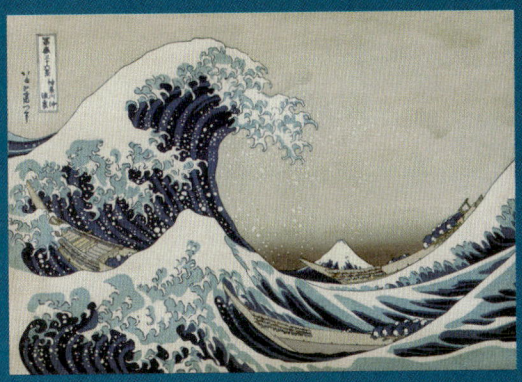

4.8.13 Katsushika Hokusai, "The Great Wave off Shore at Kanagawa", from *Thirty-Six Views of Mount Fuji*, 1826–33 (printed later). Print, color woodcut. Library of Congress, Washington, D.C.

For the other Hokusai Gateway boxes, see p. 126, p. 229, and p. 425

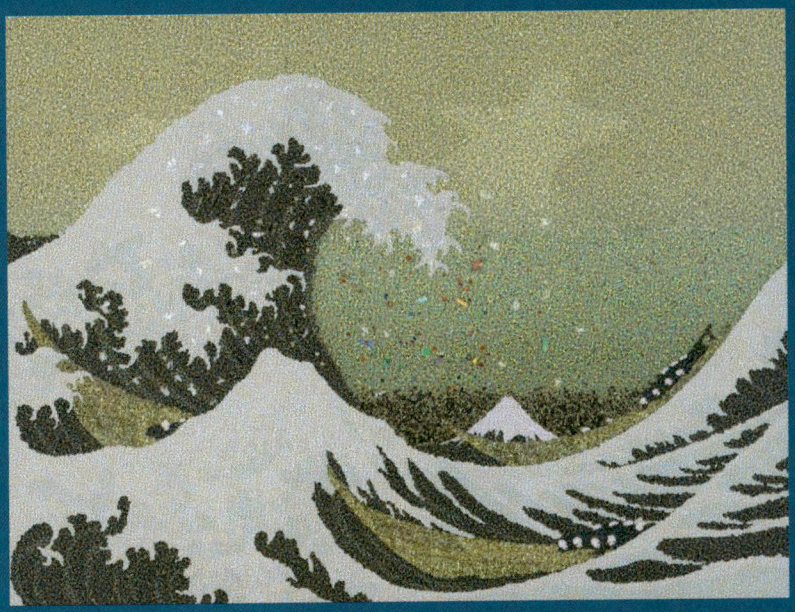

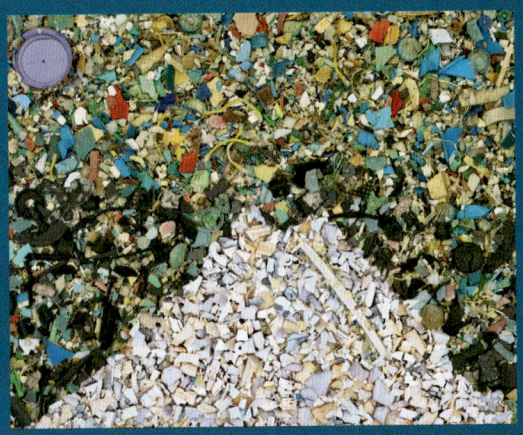

4.8.14a Chris Jordan, "Gyre," from the series *Running the Numbers II: Portraits of global mass culture*, 2009. 2.4 million plastic pieces, digitally assembled, 8 x 11'

4.8.14b Chris Jordan, "Gyre," 2009 (detail)

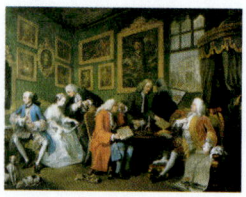

3.7.4 William Hogarth, *The Marriage Settlement*, c. 1743, p. 490

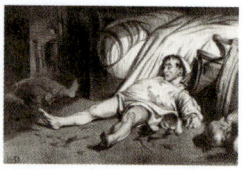

2.3.15 Honoré Daumier, *Rue Transnonain*, 1834, p. 234

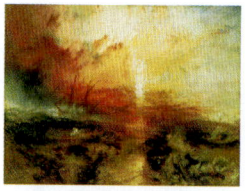

3.7.15 J. M. W. Turner, *Slave Ship...*, 1840, p. 498

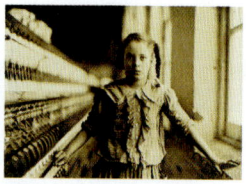

2.8.16 Lewis Wickes Hine, *Ten Year Old Spinner, Whitnel Cotton Mill*, 1908, p. 325

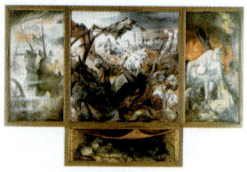

4.7.3 Otto Dix, *The War*, 1929–32, p. 640

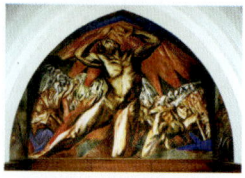

2.2.7 José Clemente Orozco, *Prometheus*, 1930, p. 213

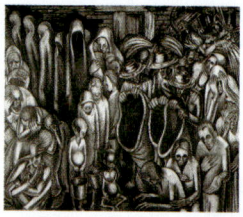

2.1.4 John Biggers, *Night of the Poor*, 1949, p. 195

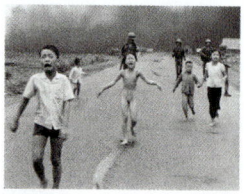

4.7.2 Nick Ut, *Vietnamese Girl Kim Phuc Running after Napalm Attack*, 1972, p. 639

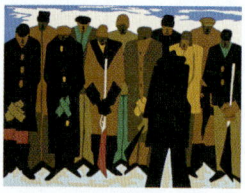

1.8.6 Jacob Lawrence, "John Brown Remained a Full Winter...," 1977, p. 154

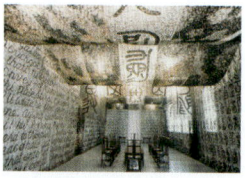

4.1.11 Wenda Gu, "China Monument: Temple of Heaven," 1998, p. 573

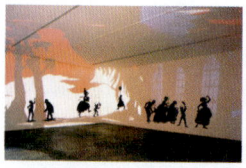

2.10.11 Kara Walker, *Insurrection!...*, 2000, p. 359

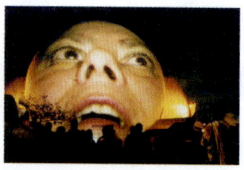

4.1.14 Krzysztof Wodiczko, *Tijuana Projection*, 2001, p. 576

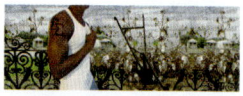

4.10.12 Stephen Marc, *Untitled—Passage on the Underground...*, 2002, p. 688

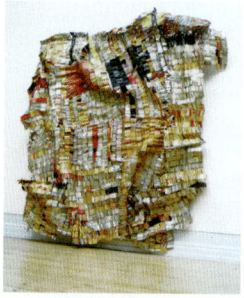

0.0.6 El Anatsui, *Old Man's Cloth*, 2002, p. 24

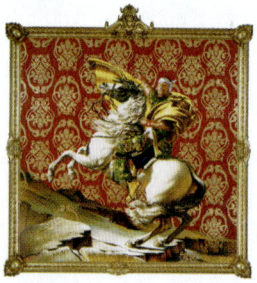

4.6.3a Kehinde Wiley, *Napoleon Leading the Army...*, 2005, p. 630

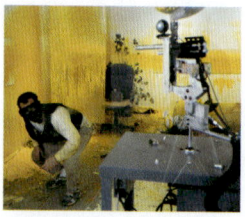

4.7.13 Wafaa Bilal, *Domestic Tension*, 2007, p. 648

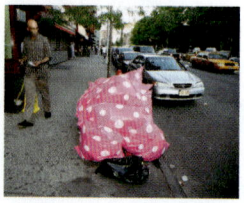

1.4.34 Adrian Kondratowicz, *TRASH project*, 2008–, p. 111

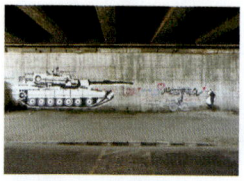

4.7.12 Ganzeer, *Tank vs. Bike*, with graffiti by Sad Panda, 2011, p. 647

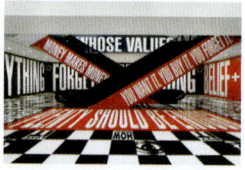

2.10.2 Barbara Kruger, *Belief + Doubt (=Sanity)*, 2012–present, p. 352

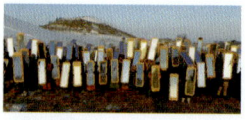

3.4.26 Cannupa Hanska Luger, mirror shields, Standing Rock, 2016, p. 444

4.9 The Body in Art

The human **form** is one of the most common **subjects** in art, perhaps because making art about the body allows us to reflect on, come to terms with, and literally express ourselves. Some of the earliest sculptures made during **prehistoric** times depict human figures. Since then, artists have continued to portray the body, both clothed and unclothed, in motion and in repose. The body is not always portrayed as it "actually looks," and it may even be altered so much that it does not resemble a human body at all. In art, the reality of the body can be distorted to suggest great beauty, or to emphasize such qualities as power, status, wisdom, or even godlike perfection. Personal and cultural preferences often determine the way an artist chooses to portray a body. Of course, the body itself can also participate in art: through performances, dances, rituals, and so on. As a subject, it offers endless expressive possibilities.

Form: an object that can be defined in three dimensions (height, width, and depth)
Subject: the person, object, or space depicted in a work of art
Prehistoric: dating from the period of human existence before the invention of writing
Iconic: possessing established and widely recognizable characteristics
Archaeology: the study of human history and prehistory by excavating sites of habitation to analyse artifacts and other cultural remains

Archetypal Images of the Body

Female figurines have been discovered all over the world, and are commonly amongst the oldest created objects in a number of societies. The *Woman from Willendorf* is one of the earliest known artworks, dating to about 26,000 years ago (**4.9.1**). The small size of this figurine, just over 4 in. tall, made it easily portable, a benefit for nomadic people. Because of the maker's emphasis on female anatomy (breasts, buttocks, and rotund belly), the *Woman from Willendorf* is believed to be a fertility figure. Perhaps it was used as a charm to encourage pregnancy, or as a teaching tool. It almost certainly celebrates the woman as a mother and bringer of life. These types of ancient figures have served as **iconic** artistic models for the idea and image of woman since their rediscovery through **archaeological** expeditions (the *Woman from Willendorf*, for example, was rediscovered in the early twentieth century).

The Dutch-born American artist Willem de Kooning (1904–1997) made a series of paintings of women that incorporate bold, apparently aggressive, even violent, marks and slashing

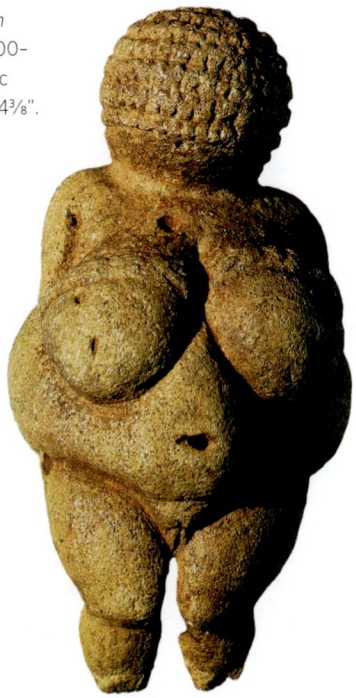

4.9.1 *Woman from Willendorf*, c. 24,000–22,000 BCE. Oolitic limestone, height 4⅜". Naturhistorisches Museum, Vienna, Austria

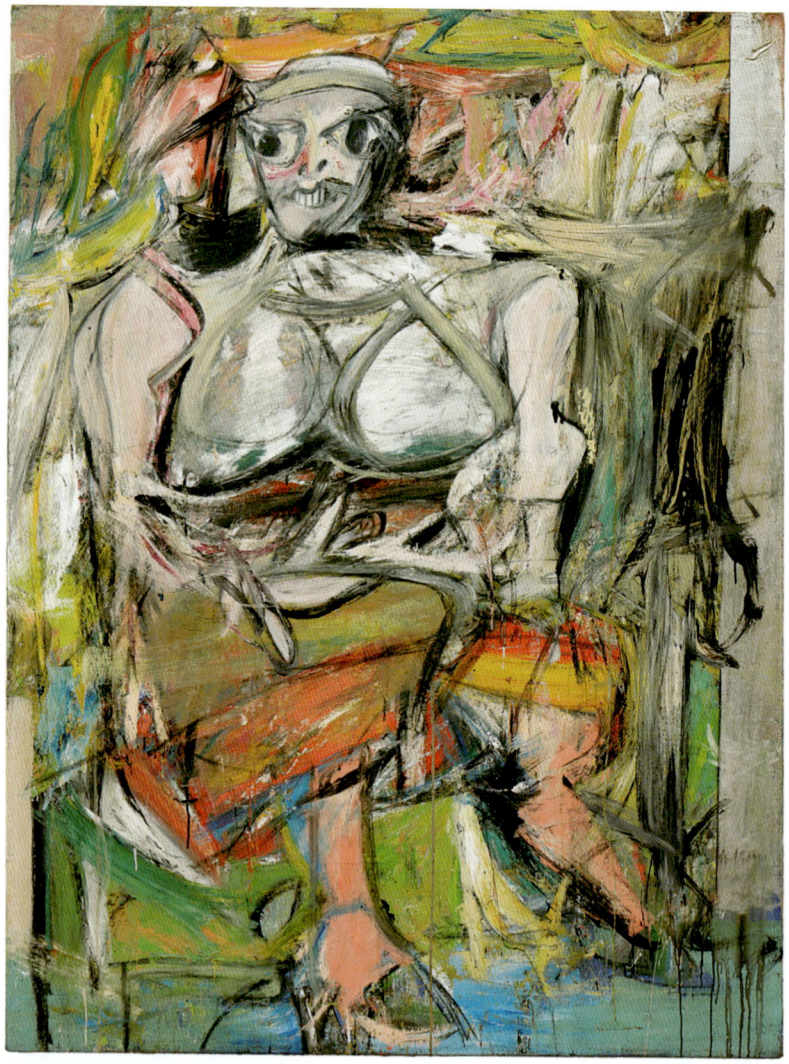

4.9.2 Willem de Kooning, *Woman I*, 1950–52. Oil on canvas, 6'3⅞" × 4'10". MoMA, New York

Abstract: art imagery that departs from recognizable images of the natural world
Canon of proportions: a set of ideal mathematical ratios in art, used to measure the various parts of the human body in relation to one another
Figurative: art that portrays items perceived in the visible world, especially human or animal forms
Renaissance: a period of cultural and artistic change in Europe from the fourteenth to the seventeenth century
Idealized: represented as perfect in form or character, corresponding to an ideal
Hierarchical scale: the use of size to denote the relative importance of subjects in an artwork

strokes. De Kooning said that his *Woman* series referred to "the female painted through all the ages, all those idols."

In de Kooning's *Woman I*, the exaggerated form and emphasis on characteristically female elements of human anatomy visually connect the modern artwork to the *Woman from Willendorf* (**4.9.2**). In this large painting, made thousands of years after the tiny sculpture was created, the most prominent parts of the body are the breasts, while the arms and legs are minimized in a manner similar to the *Woman from Willendorf*. Yet although both artworks convey the inherent power of women as givers and protectors of life, they do so very differently. De Kooning's woman seems strong to the point of being ferocious. The painting is physically big, over lifesized, making literal the larger-than-life feeling conveyed by the small sculpture, and features the glaring eyes and grinning mouth of a woman's face at the top of the composition. By contrast, the *Woman from Willendorf* does not include facial features at all.

Both figures, however, have an **abstracted** form, visible in the rough shapes of the *Woman from Willendorf* and the jagged brushstrokes of *Woman I*. Their appearance makes them less representations of individual people and more reflections of a universal idea of powerful women. As de Kooning's statement suggests, *Woman I* embodies "the female...through all the ages."

Ideal Proportion

Long after the Paleolithic sculptor and long before de Kooning searched to find something universal about the female figure, the ancient Egyptians applied formal mathematical systems in consistent ways to depict their ideal of the human form. They developed a standardized method for depicting men and women, known as the **canon of proportions**, and used it for thousands of years. A similar system of proportion was later adopted by the Greeks for their **figurative** sculpture and influenced European artists during the **Renaissance**. These **idealized** proportions, clearly visible in figurative paintings, reliefs, and three-dimensional sculpture, were applied to architectural construction as well.

Egyptians systematically depicted the human body to match their cultural notions of perfection. The Egyptian canon of proportions is calculated in the form of a grid that provides consistent measurements of the parts of the body (**4.9.3a**). Each square of the grid represents a standard small measurement, or a unit, based on the width of the pharaoh's clenched hand. Sometimes other ratios are used to make the grid, resulting in a slightly different but still standardized appearance. The pharaoh's body was used as the standard for measurement because all measure came from the king. In fact, the **hierarchical scale** used in Egyptian depictions of multiple figures shows the pharaoh and nobles as significantly larger than workers, members of lower classes, and animals, because they were viewed as being of greater importance.

Thus, in ancient Egyptian art, the portrayal of the body followed **conventions**, or prescribed methods, which produced consistent results. Egyptian depictions of the human body, as a result, look very similar even when they have been produced thousands of years apart. In sculpture, royal figures are shown either seated or standing, firmly connected to the stone from which they are carved, with their arms and hands close to their sides. In standing poses, the feet are firmly planted on the ground with the legs slightly apart and one foot in front of the other, as if the figure is about to take a step. Any suggestion of movement is potential, however, as if the figure is frozen; if it were in motion, its weight would shift to one side or the other. In the Egyptian figure, the feet are flat, the hips are even and immobile, and the shoulders are entirely square.

The use of the canon gives the sculpture of *Menkaure and His Wife, Queen Khamerernebty*, an austere strength (**4.9.3b**). Their poses make the figures look rigid, calm, and enduring. They stand close together, as a single unit, his hands close to his sides and hers embracing his arm and torso. Their bodies do not twist and the features are bilaterally symmetrical (meaning that the left side matches the right). The strong, frontal pose suggests that the power of the pharaoh is changeless, unwavering, and eternal. This representation is idealized: the couple's appearance is based on abstract concepts rather than direct observation.

Convention: a widely accepted way of doing something; using a particular style, following a certain method, or representing something in a specific way

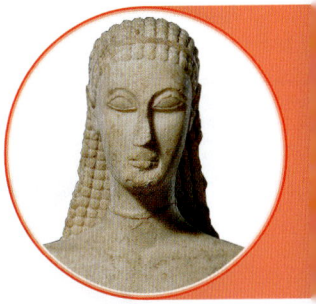

Archaic Greek artists closely copied the Egyptian canon and began developing their own lifelike and idealized sculptures: see **3.1.28, p. 384**

4.9.3a Canon of proportions: *Menkaure and His Wife, Queen Khamerernebty*

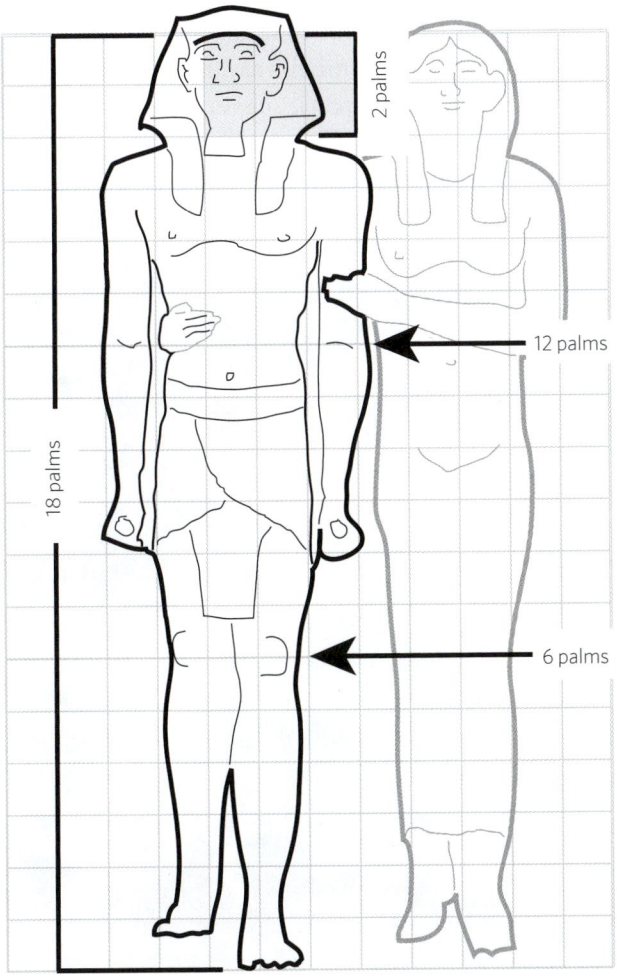

4.9.3b *Menkaure and His Wife, Queen Khamerernebty*, 4th Dynasty, c. 2520 BCE. Graywacke, 54¾ × 22½ × 21¼". Museum of Fine Arts, Boston, Massachusetts

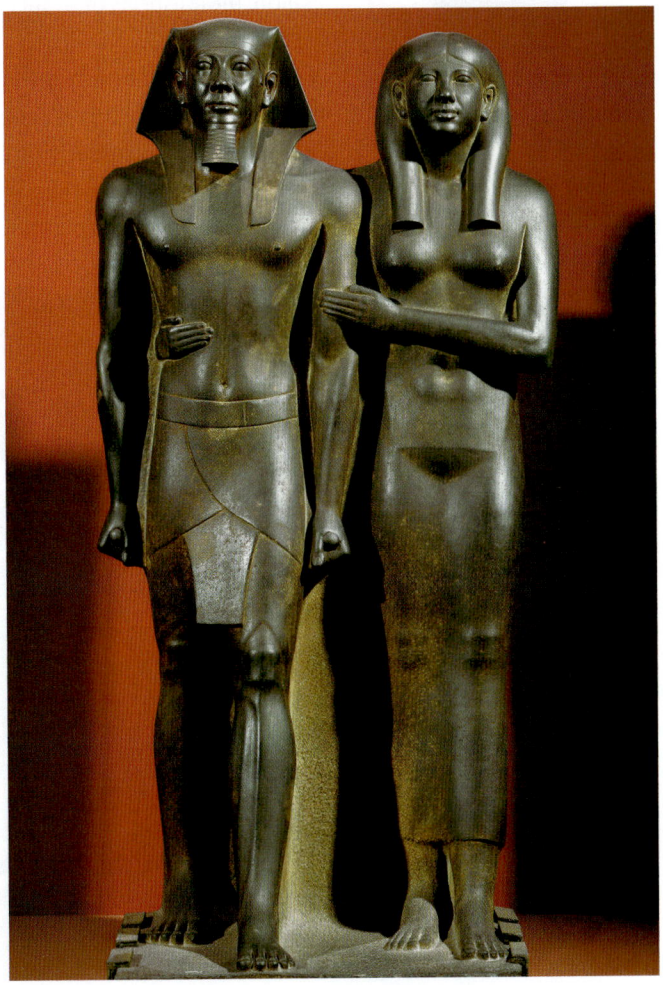

Nude: an artistic representation of an unclothed human figure, emphasizing the body's form rather than its exposure

Notions of Beauty

Ideal proportions inform many cultural notions of preferred body type. Our notions of beauty are formed by our personal experiences and by the society in which we live. If we look at the ways in which artists have depicted the human form, we soon realize that in different times and places beauty can mean very different things (see Box: Reclining Nudes, pp. 668–69). In some cultures small feet or long necks are admired. Some groups may favor plump, even voluptuous, bodies, while others prefer slender, very thin and angular physiques. Our bodies can also express many things about our personalities: we can appear calm or agitated, elegant or unkempt, smart or stupid, sensuous or intellectual. The complex relationship between internal characteristics and outward appearance has led artists to explore these aspects of beauty through the human form.

The notions of beauty held by the ancient Greeks were based upon the combination of an underlying canon of mathematical proportions with the finely honed physiques possessed by male athletes, who competed in the **nude**. (It was far more common to see a Greek male than a Greek female figure sculpted in the nude.) Depicting the body without clothes allowed artists to study musculature and to reflect observations and knowledge of the anatomy in a way that a clothed body does not. Because the Greeks hoped to model themselves after gods, they aimed for perfect balance between mind and body in both their lives and their art. Such sculptures as the *Discus Thrower* not only demonstrate the ideal musculature of the athletic body, celebrating the strength and virility inherent in the masculine form, but also show the competitor immersed in concentration, his mind in complete harmony with his physique (**4.9.4**).

In ancient Greece, although the male nude was certainly more common, the female nude eventually began to gain respectability in the late fourth century BCE. Years later, during the Renaissance, such Italian artists as Sandro Botticelli (*c.* 1445–1510) revived the appearance of the female nude as it had been depicted in antiquity. In Botticelli's day the female nude became an acceptable subject as long as it appeared in a historical or mythological context. According to Classical mythology, Venus, the goddess of love and beauty, first emerged from

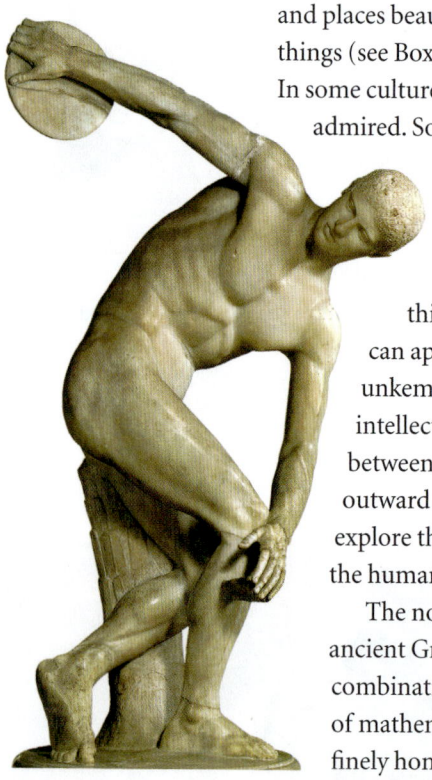

4.9.4 Myron, *Discus Thrower (Discobolos)*, Roman copy of Greek bronze original from *c.* 450 BCE. Marble, height 5'1". Museo delle Terme, Rome, Italy

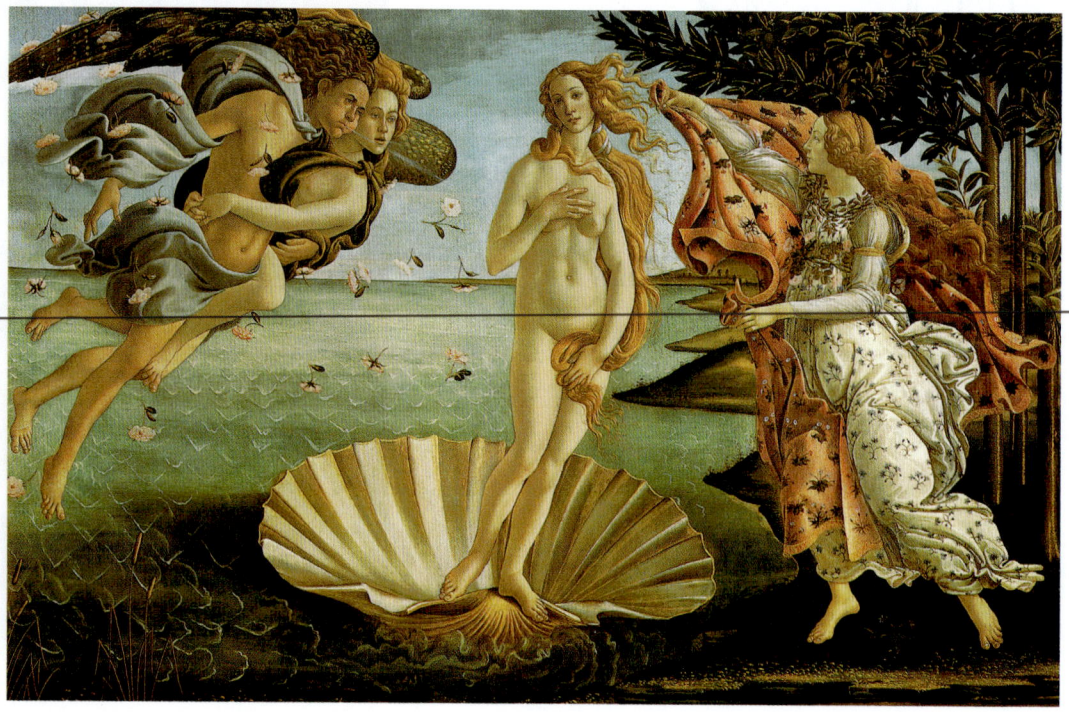

4.9.5 Sandro Botticelli, *The Birth of Venus*, *c.* 1482–86. Tempera on canvas, 5'8" × 9'1⅝". Uffizi Gallery, Florence, Italy

the sea as a fully formed adult on a shell. In his painting *The Birth of Venus* (**4.9.5**), Botticelli focuses on the moment when Venus has been blown to shore. She is wafted toward the land by Zephyr, the god of the west wind, who is accompanied by the earth nymph Chloris. Awaiting Venus is a goddess or nymph who will wrap her in a blanket of flowers. Venus has smooth ivory-colored skin, long flowing hair, and an elegant pose. She discreetly covers her nudity, indicating that chastity is part of her appeal. The graceful shape and the flawless quality of her body reflect the purity of the newborn goddess and create a harmonious and pleasing **composition**. Botticelli has modeled his figure on an ancient sculpture, thus basing his conception of beauty on Classical Greek standards.

In African societies, notions of beauty are often closely tied to the community's core values of composure and wisdom, believed to reflect, and even increase, a person's power. In other words, beauty is about more than external appearance. It is also about internal and societal principles. Being calm, wise, and composed were important attributes for the kings of Ife in West Africa. The elegant lines, delicate features, and elaborate headdress of the terra-cotta head in **4.9.6** indicate that it probably represents an Ife king, or *oni*. As the head was considered the seat of intelligence and the source of power, this sculpture's exquisite features draw our attention there. The lifelike details—the folds of the ears, the contours of the nose, and the plumpness of the lips—are extremely naturalistic, but also graceful and refined. The fine lines on the face resemble scarification patterns, or scars created by cutting or branding the skin. Beauty in this case is a balance of invisible internal characteristics and an idealized, visible, outward appearance.

Many cultures determine beauty by a person's ability to conform to expectations, whether through clothes, cosmetics, or body shape. In Japan, traditional female performers called *geisha* are known for their social skills and artistic talents, such as singing, dancing, and serving tea. Geisha, not to be confused with courtesans or prostitutes, have a professional relationship with their clients and are strongly discouraged from becoming too intimate with them. A geisha's appearance changes over the course of her career. Early on she wears dramatic hairstyles, heavy makeup, dark eyeliner, and red lip pencil applied to make her lips look small. As an apprentice, the source of her beauty lies in her appearance, but later it is seen to derive from her maturity and her *gei*, or art. After three years of apprenticeship, a geisha adopts less elaborate kimonos tied with simpler knots, lighter makeup, and a subdued hairstyle, such as the one seen in Kaigetsudo Dohan's *Beautiful Woman* (**4.9.7**). In common with other Japanese artists working at the time, Kaigetsudo Dohan (working 1710–16) celebrated beautiful women, here emphasizing the experienced geisha's impressive attire and relatively natural appearance. In addition to her musical skills and gift for intelligent conversation, this mature geisha would have been appreciated for her inner beauty.

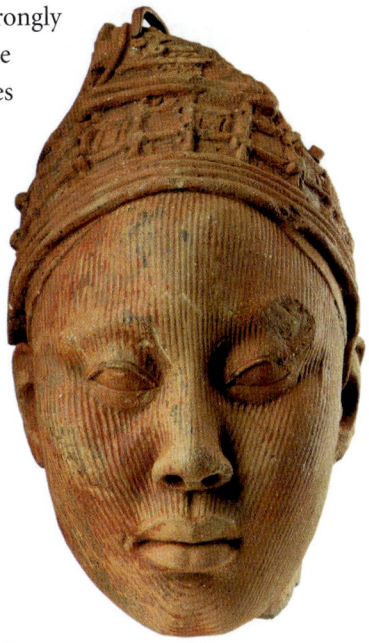

4.9.6 Head, possibly an Ife king from West Africa, 12th–14th century. Terra-cotta with residue of red pigment and traces of mica, 10½ × 5¾ × 7⅜". Kimbell Art Museum, Fort Worth, Texas

Composition: the overall design or organization of a work

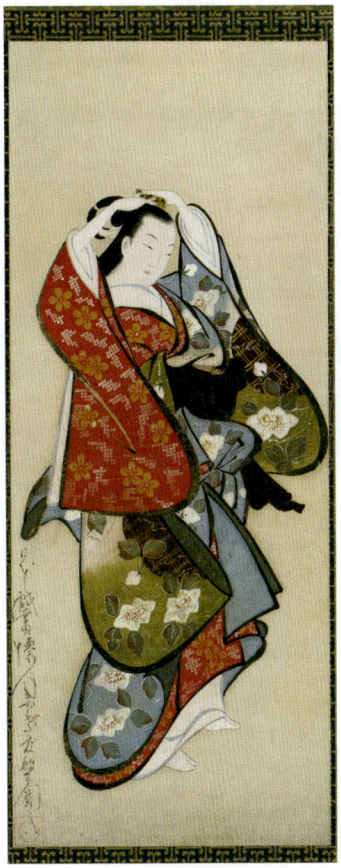

4.9.7 Kaigetsudō Dohan, *Beautiful Woman*, Edo Period, Japan, 18th century. Hanging scroll, ink and color on paper, 64⅜ × 20⅛". Metropolitan Museum of Art, New York

Reclining Nudes

While nudes have long been a subject in the history of art, the tradition of depicting the nude female figure lying down, or reclining, was established during the Renaissance. These types of picture recall the ancient Greek emphasis on the beauty and honesty conveyed by the nude human form. In some cases they also suggest the sensuality of the nude.

The Venetian painter known as Titian (*c.*1485/90–1576) was influenced by the Classical tradition when he painted a female nude for the duke of the Italian town of Urbino (**4.9.8**). The roses in the woman's right hand hint at her identity: they are a symbol of Venus, the Classical goddess of beauty (hence the name by which the painting is commonly known, the *Venus of Urbino*). She looks out from her couch with a coy expression and casually covers her pubic area, at once modest and inviting, as if she exists simply to be looked at. The presence of the maids in the background preparing her clothes, however, connects her to the concerns of a real woman. By suggesting that his painting depicted a mythological figure, Titian was able to explore in depth such secular themes as the nature of love and desire.

It is clear that the French artist Édouard Manet (1832–1883) was familiar with the *Venus of Urbino* when he painted his *Olympia* (**4.9.9**). The composition of the paintings and the posture of the women within them are almost identical. Manet, however, has replaced the sleeping dog at the foot of the bed with a hissing black cat. And instead of the maids in the background, there is a black servant who brings Olympia flowers. In this painting, as in others, Manet took a Classical subject and updated it for his own time. In modernizing the reclining nude, Manet considered the reality of the situation. Why would a woman be naked and on display? One obvious answer: because she is a prostitute. Not only was Olympia a common name for a prostitute, but Manet depicted her as a real woman, thin (at least by the standards of the time) and probably poor. Olympia's pose would have seemed confrontational because she stares out at the

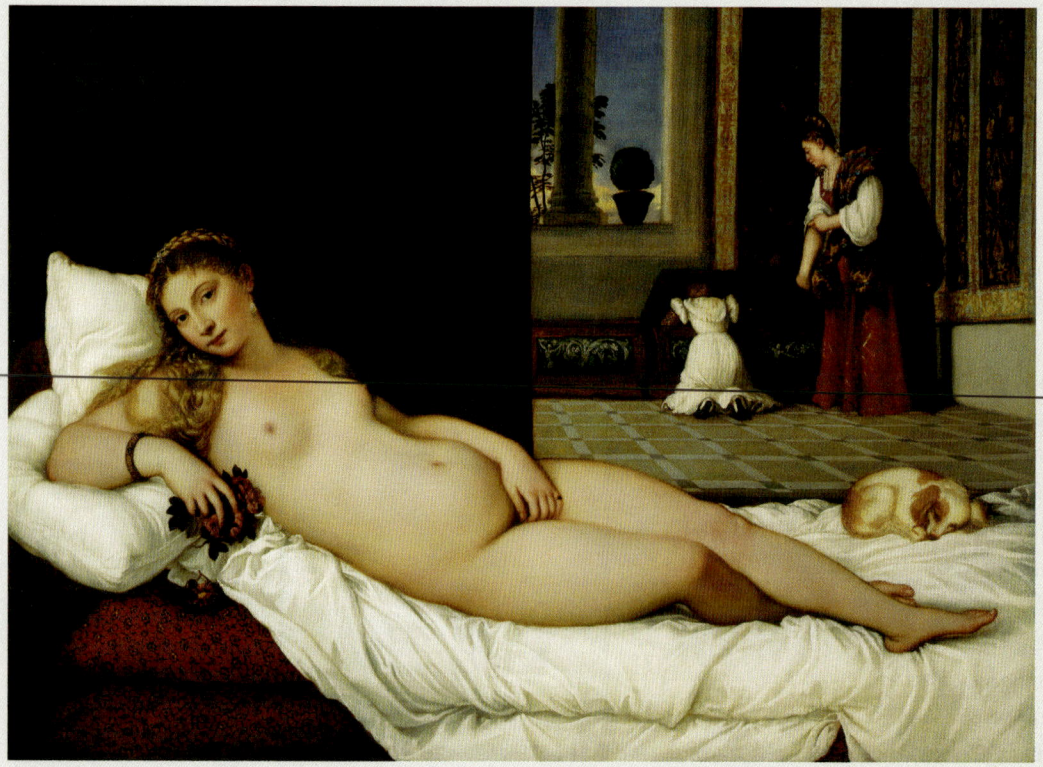

4.9.8 Titian, *Venus of Urbino*, 1538. Oil on canvas, 3'10⅞" × 5'5". Uffizi Gallery, Florence, Italy

viewer in an assertive way, while people at that time were used to seeing more passive women with voluptuous bodies and docile expressions similar to the figure depicted in the *Venus of Urbino*.

In the late twentieth century, the Japanese artist Yasumasa Morimura (b.1951) revisited the theme of the reclining nude (**4.9.10**). The meaning of this piece, like that of Manet's *Olympia*, gains depth if one knows about the earlier artworks to which it alludes. Morimura employs digital processes, which allow him to play the roles of both Olympia and the servant. The resulting photograph is part of a series that the artist made in which he impersonates famous female icons from Western culture, transcending race, gender, and ethnicity. Here, the act of covering the genitalia with the left hand takes on entirely new significance in disguising the truth of his masculinity. The robes of the earlier pieces are replaced with a kimono and the cat at the foot of the bed is a porcelain Lucky Cat, commonly found in Japanese restaurants and shops as a talisman of good fortune. Morimura's reclining nude updates the theme with current technology and raises pertinent questions about identity, suggesting that appearances can be deceptive, that race and gender are artificial constructions, that we should not make assumptions about identity, and that our understanding of who we are is influenced by the past.

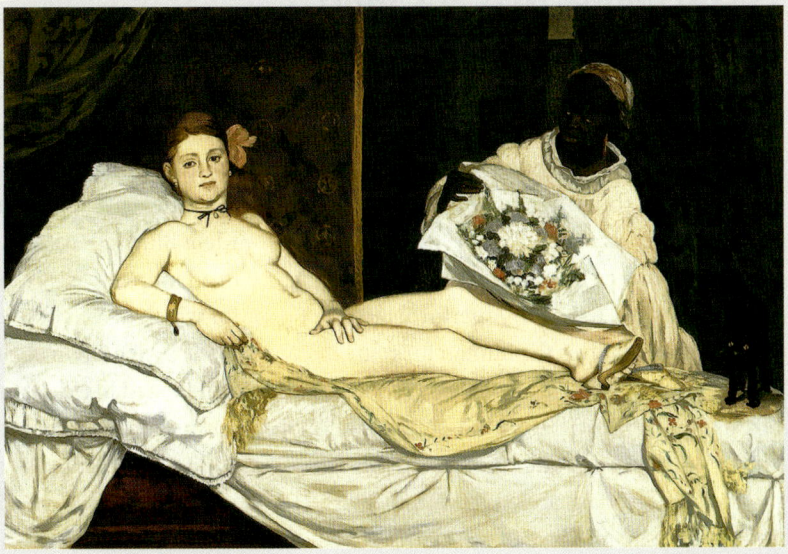

4.9.9 Édouard Manet, *Olympia*, 1863. Oil on canvas, 3'3⅜" × 6'2¾". Musée d'Orsay, Paris, France

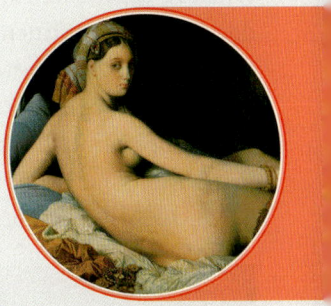

Some artists, such as Ingres, have used the reclining nude to express beauty and grace by exaggerating anatomy rather than rendering bodies in realistic proportion: see **1.10.8, p. 179**

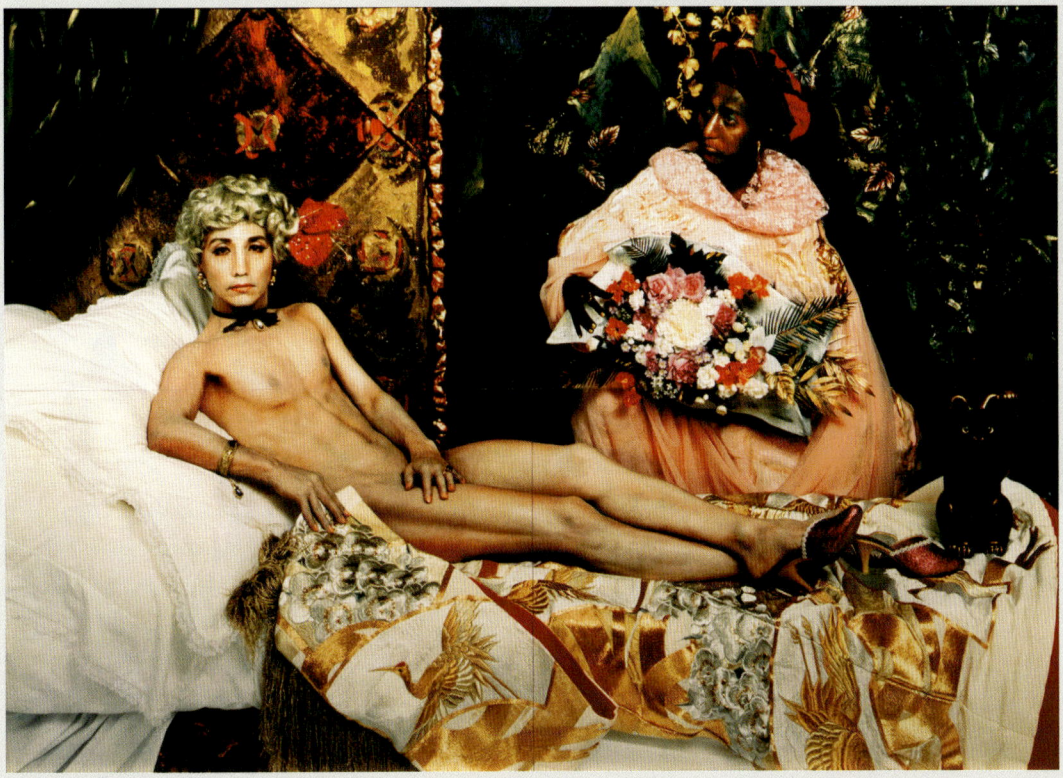

4.9.10 Yasumasa Morimura, *Portrait (Futago)*, 1988–90. Color photograph, printed in two editions at varying sizes

Performance Art: The Body Becomes the Artwork

Geisha are considered living works of art. Similarly, in **performance art**, and in some **installations**, the body and its actions become the artwork (see Perspectives on Art Box: Spencer Tunick: Human Bodies as Installations, pp. 672–73.) A performance by definition involves the human form in action, but by engaging all of a viewer's senses through movement, expression, sound, smell, and so on, it also activates the space itself. The performers share a space with the audience, and the art becomes part of the viewer's lived experience. Because performances are not permanent or static, once they are finished they can be re-experienced only indirectly, through documentation. Written accounts, photographs, and videos taken at the time remind us later of the performances themselves.

Perhaps inspired by his deep interest in the martial art of judo, the French artist Yves Klein (1928–1962) began experimenting with "living brushes," or women using their bodies as the vehicle for applying paint to canvas. In the late 1950s he became one of the first artists to make **monochromatic**, or one-color, paintings. He used a bright, dense, ultramarine blue, a color that he eventually patented as "International Klein Blue" (IKB). Klein integrated performance in an innovative way to make the blue paintings for which he was known. The first paintings made by the "living brushes" were monochromes that looked like the ones Klein himself had produced. Later, the women left imprints of their bodies on the canvas or paper (**4.9.11b**).

Klein devised the pieces, directed the women, and hired an orchestra for the first public performance of the "living brushes," called *Anthropométries de l'époque bleue* (or *Anthropometries of the Blue Period*) (**4.9.11a**). In order to create a musical accompaniment that was suitable for monochromatic paintings, Klein had the musicians play a single chord for twenty minutes and then sit in silence for twenty minutes. In an art gallery, works of art are usually inert, still objects and it is the viewers

Performance art: a work involving the human body, usually including the artist, in front of an audience
Installation: originally referring to the hanging of pictures and arrangement of objects in an exhibition, installation may also refer to an intentional environment created as a completed artwork
Monochromatic: having one or more values of one color

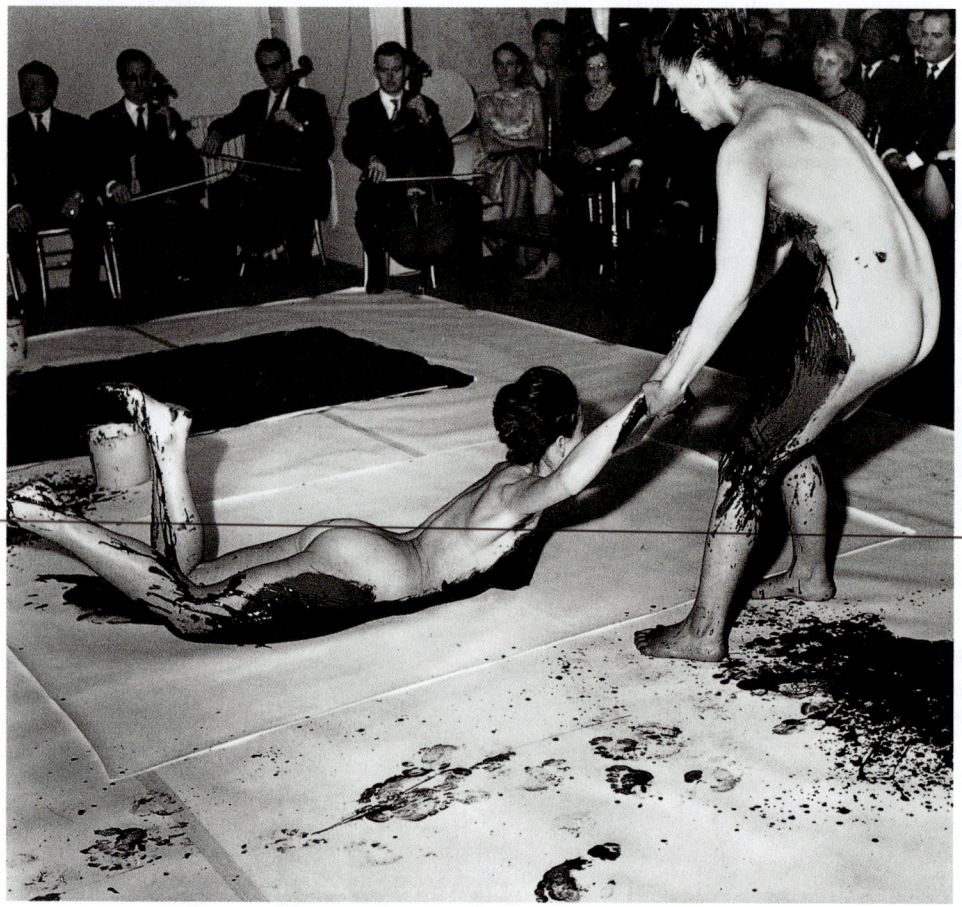

4.9.11a Yves Klein, *Anthropométries de l'époque bleue*, March 9, 1960. Galerie Internationale d'Art Contemporain, Paris, France

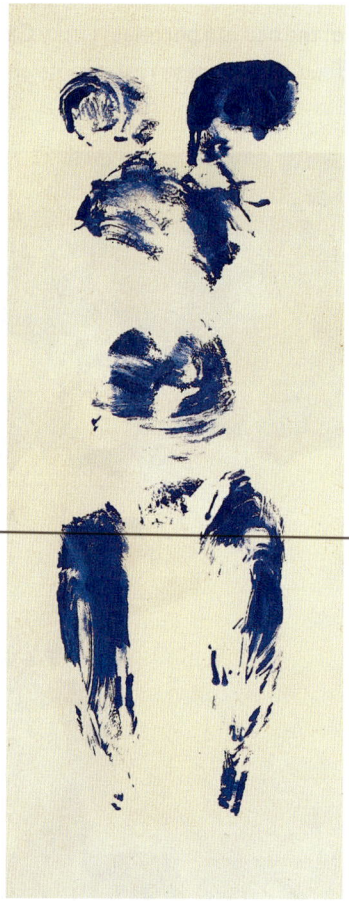

4.9.11b Yves Klein, *Anthropométrie sans titre*, 1960. Pure pigment and synthetic resin on paper mounted on canvas, 50⅞ × 14⅝". Private collection

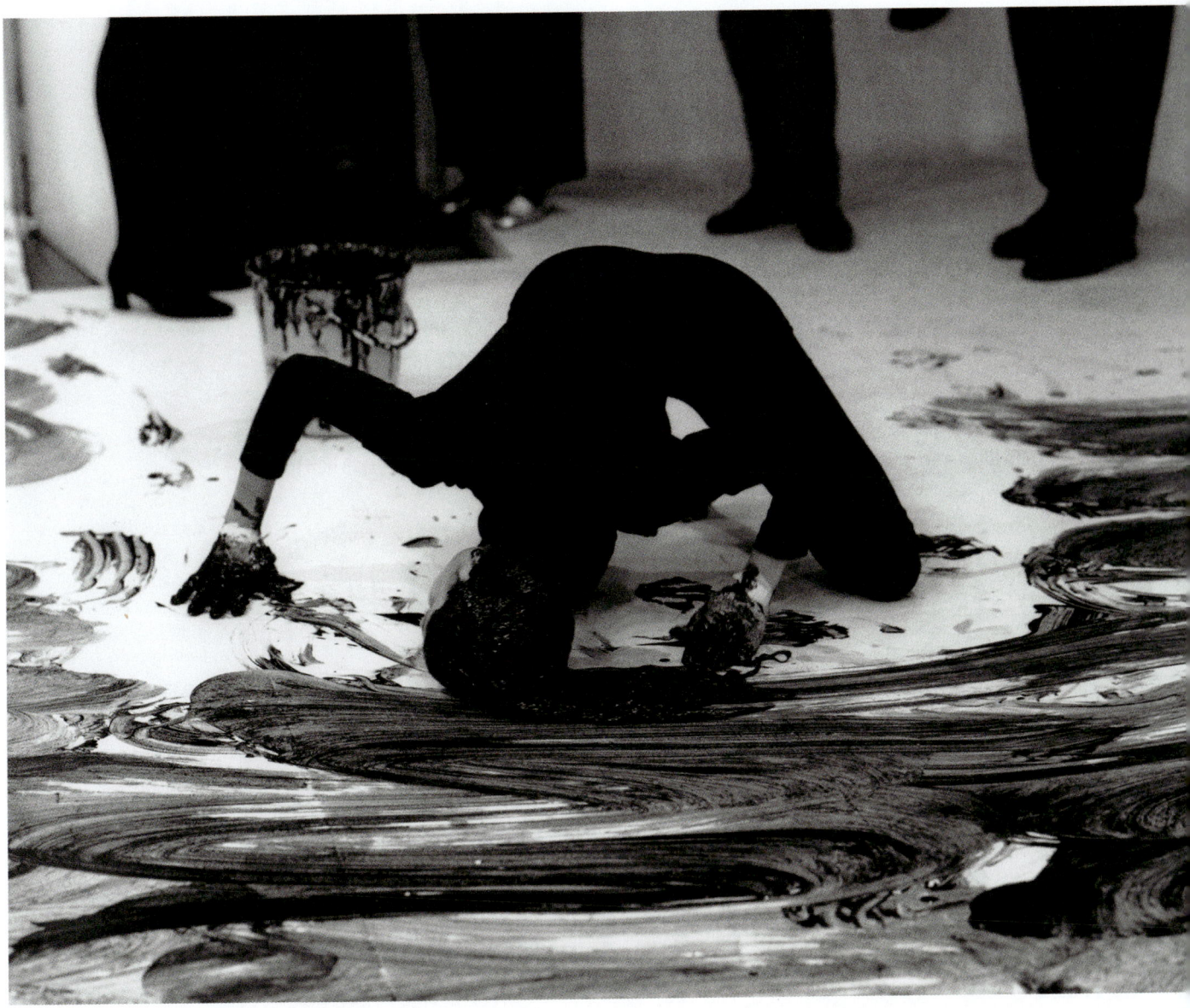

4.9.12 Janine Antoni, *Loving Care*, 1993. Performance with Loving Care hair dye Natural Black, dimensions variable. Photographed by Prudence Cuming Associates at Anthony d'Offay Gallery, London, England, 1993

who move around (often in silence). In the case of Klein's performances, the artwork itself moved and made sounds while the audience sat still, giving the work a very physical presence in the usually quiet and austere gallery. At the same time, attention was brought to the odd circumstance of living nude figures as "art," now active in the gallery space instead of represented in artworks, and surrounded by a fully clothed audience.

Unlike Klein, who directed rather than participated in his artworks, artist Janine Antoni (b. 1964 in the Bahamas) uses her own body and her own actions as the basis for most of her performances. In *Loving Care*, named for a brand of hair-care products, Antoni dipped her head in a bucket of hair color and proceeded to mop the floor with it, using her hair as a paintbrush (**4.9.12**). As more and more of the floor became covered with gestural marks, viewers were pushed out of the gallery space. The artwork comments on several typically "feminine" actions, including the domesticity of mopping and the messiness of using cosmetics for beautification. Antoni takes the dynamic creative role here, bringing attention to the actions she is performing as well as to the status of women in the art world and in society.

Perspectives on Art: Spencer Tunick
Human Bodies as Installations

*The American photographer Spencer Tunick (b. 1967) is famous for his installations involving crowds of nude people (**4.9.13a**). He explains how he came to make such work, and how complicated it can be to organize the people.*

I didn't start out photographing hundreds or thousands of nude people. From 1992 to 1994 I worked on individual portraits of nudes on the streets of New York. I gained confidence in my ability to work on a public street, to deal with traffic, traffic light intervals, and the police. I switched to multiples when I had so many people to work with. I would carry the photographs round in my wallet and show them to people. By 1994 I had phone numbers for twenty-eight people and I decided to photograph them all at once outside the UN building in New York. Then in 1997

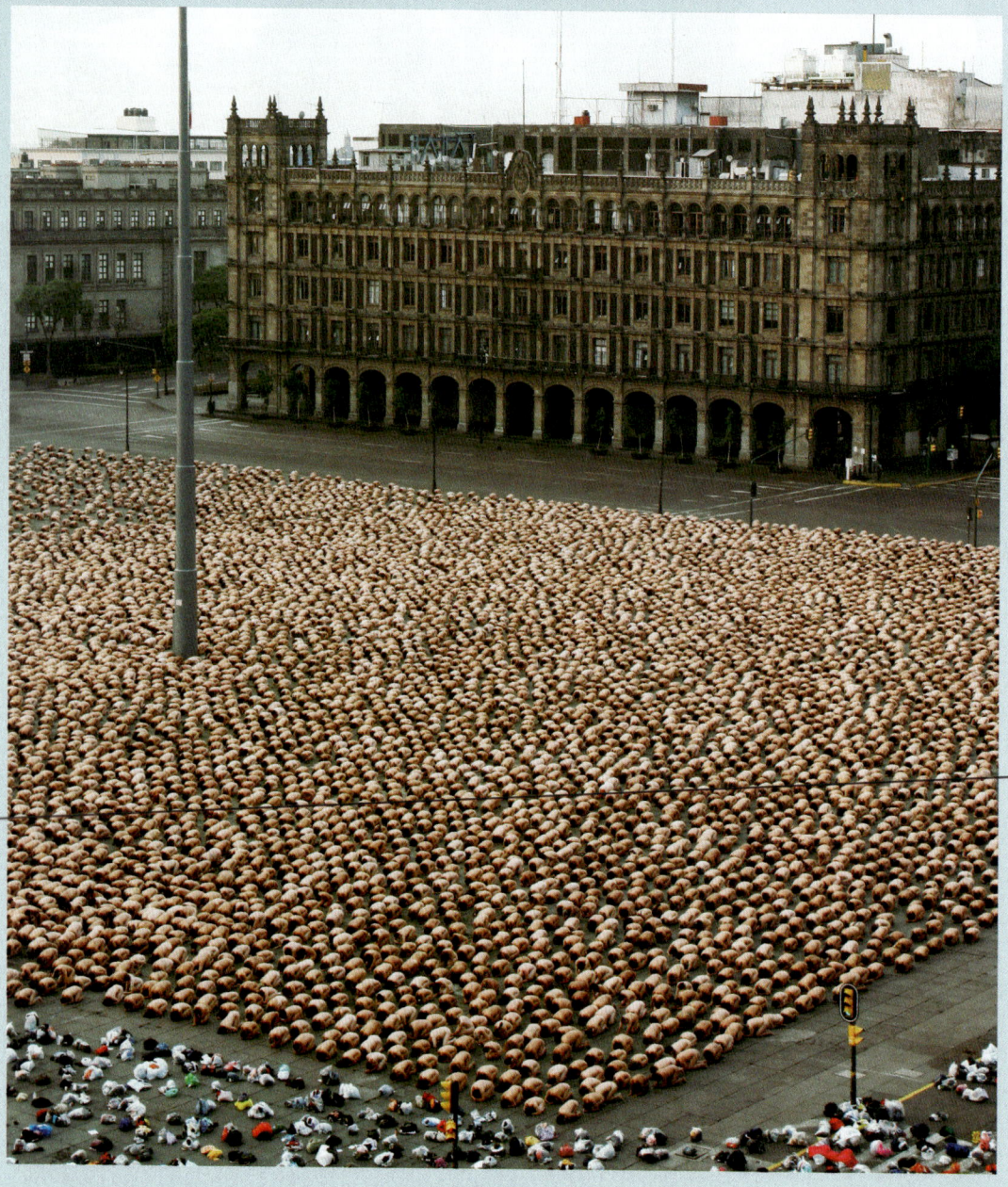

4.9.13a (left) Spencer Tunick, Installation at Zócalo, Mexico City, Mexico, May 6, 2007. More than 18,000 people participated

4.9.13b (opposite above) Spencer Tunick steps through 300 people whom he arranged as a living sculpture near City Hall, Fribourg, Switzerland, 2001

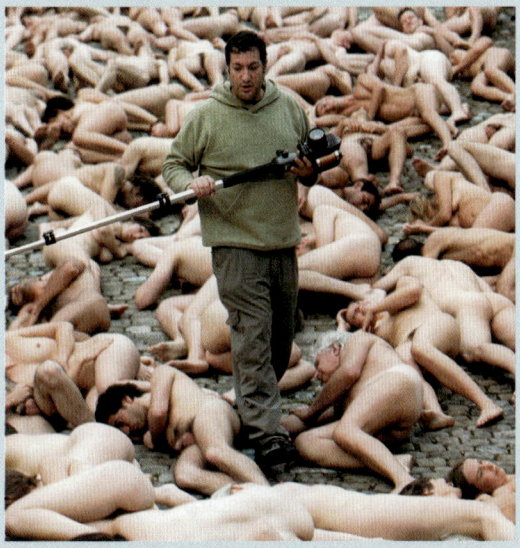

I gathered 1,000 people on an air-force base in Maine at a music concert.

I travel with a team of eight. In each city a contemporary art museum commissions my work and I can work wherever in the city I like. The museum provides team leaders and volunteers. Mexico City took three years to organize and one day to make the art. There were 250 team leaders and volunteers and 250 police officers. In Caracas, Venezuela, there were almost 1,000 police and military.

I know 75 percent of what I am going to do before we start but I like to keep an element of mystery. I have control of thousands of people, but in a way I don't like that control. I like to keep the event loose, personal, and intimate. Participants are not involving themselves in a spectacle but in a work of art. After ten minutes, once they get used to being nude, they get excited and start raising their hands in the air and so on, and then they calm down and we get organized.

I consider my works to be installations, not performances or photographs. I document the installations with photos and videos. I have two videographers and could have people take the photographs also, but I like to frame the photos and tweak them on location.

I still do individual portraits in streets. I am interested in the body and its relationship to the background. Instead of the body creating a meaning for the background, the background creates a new meaning for the body.

The Body in Pieces

Artists have used exaggeration, stylization, and innovation to create abstract representations of the human body. Approaches originating outside the Western European tradition, such as African masks and pre-Columbian sculptures from the Americas, have influenced some modern European artists to make works suggesting forms that are altered but recognizable. Others have taken certain elements of the anatomy out of their usual context by distorting or fragmenting the body. We do not have to see a whole body to read it as a human figure (see Perspectives on Art: "*The Blue Nude*: Cutouts and the Essence of Form," **4.9.17a** and **b**, p. 675). Recognizing this fact, artists have focused attention away from identifying a particular individual or illustrating a coherent story in order to emphasize ways in which the body can be broken down and presented as a product of the human imagination.

In his artworks, the French artist Auguste Rodin (1840–1917) altered the appearance of the human body, which is one of the reasons he is now known as a pioneer in the field of modern sculpture. His innovations influenced many twentieth-century sculptors, including Henry Moore and Alberto Giacometti (see **4.9.15** and **4.9.16**, p. 674). Although he had been formally trained, Rodin chose not to make his sculptures in the traditional, academic way. Instead of idealizing figures to look like perfected versions of actual people, Rodin intentionally left his surfaces rough, as seen in his sculpture *Walking Man* (**4.9.14**). The scrapes and gouges on the figure's chest, torso, and hips stand as evidence of the material the artist touched and manipulated to make the sculpture. Rodin also considered fragmentary representations, such as this one, which has no head or arms, to be completed sculptures rather than preparatory sketches. At the time, Rodin's pieces, which looked so different from the smooth, idealized figures people had come to expect, were

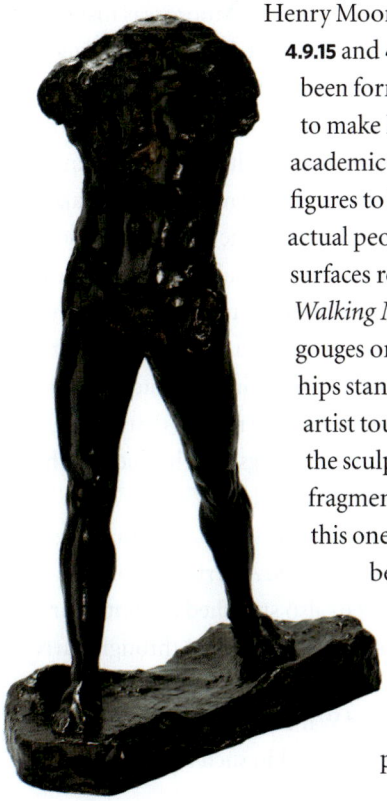

4.9.14 Auguste Rodin, *Walking Man*, c. 1890–95. Bronze, 33¾ × 22 × 11". MoMA, New York

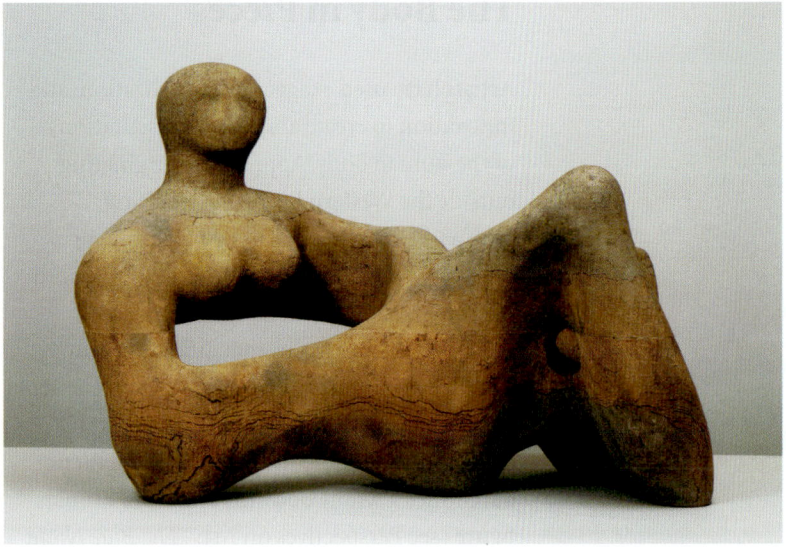

4.9.15 Henry Moore, *Recumbent Figure*, 1938. Green Hornton stone, 35 × 52¼ × 29". Tate, London, England

harshly criticized. Since then, his approach has been praised for allowing the figures to be more expressive, emotional, and individual.

Like Rodin, the British sculptor Henry Moore (1898–1986) created figures that did not match the way the human body actually looks. Instead Moore emphasized natural forms in the shapes of bodies and their parts, which in Moore's work often resemble mountains, hills, cliffs, and valleys. The organic lines in his sculptures mimic the organic **contours** of the materials he used, usually wood and stone. In addition to nature, Moore was inspired by other works of art. He studied a range of artistic traditions of Egypt, Africa, and Mexico, as well as Classical and **avant-garde** European approaches. As a result of these influences, he departed from visible reality for the sake of making a strong artistic statement. A consistent characteristic of his sculptures is his use of the void, an empty space that opens up the figure and creates visual interest. In *Recumbent Figure* the large hole in the center of the piece is surrounded by the masses that make up the body (**4.9.15**). The legs look like peaks while the abdomen is in the place of a valley. The breasts help to identify the shape as a female figure.

The Swiss artist Alberto Giacometti (1901–1966) also stretched the boundaries of the recognizable form: first through Surrealist examinations of the human body, and then, after World War II, through the existential views represented in such sculptures as *Man Pointing* (**4.9.16**). Giacometti's obsessive nature at times caused him to reduce figures to the point where they were almost nonexistent. Eventually he began to accept his own artistic vision, in which the bodies look as if they are being seen from an extreme distance. The figures seem to have stepped out of the artist's dreams and into reality, carrying with them an air of mystery. *Man Pointing* is an imposing figure, despite its apparent fragility. At 5 ft. 8 in. tall, it is hard to believe that it can support its own weight. Giacometti struck a delicate balance between the figure and its surroundings in this sculpture, which he first made in clay and then cast in bronze. Nothing indicates why the man is pointing, but the space around him seems almost heavy. The sculpture looks like a trace of the shadow the man casts rather than the man himself, emphasizing the figure's loneliness and isolation.

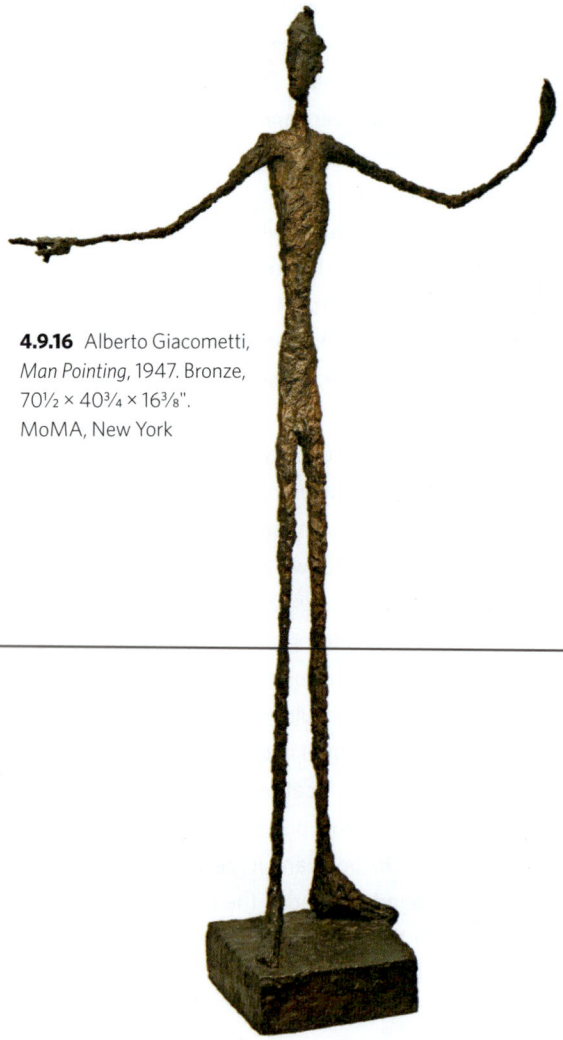

4.9.16 Alberto Giacometti, *Man Pointing*, 1947. Bronze, 70½ × 40¾ × 16⅜". MoMA, New York

Contour: the outline that defines a form
Avant-garde: early twentieth-century emphasis on artistic innovation, which challenged accepted values, traditions, and techniques
Palette: the range of colors used by an artist
Sketch: a rough preliminary version of a work or part of a work
Plane: a flat surface, often implied by the composition
Stencil: a perforated template allowing ink or paint to pass through to print a design
Artist's book: a book produced by an artist, usually an expensive limited edition, often using specialized printing processes
Silhouette: a portrait or figure represented in outline and solidly colored in

Perspectives on Art: Henri Matisse
The Blue Nude: Cutouts and the Essence of Form

Experimental artists, such as the Frenchman Henri Matisse (1869–1954), have consistently used the female nude as a subject for creative innovation. Throughout his career, Matisse was moving toward a more economical use of artistic elements. Early on, he made very detailed recordings of the world he observed around him. After the 1940s, he chose to isolate forms and reduce the range of his **palette**, emphasizing the elements he thought to be the most important for a particular subject, because, as he wrote, "exactitude is not truth." Even his **sketches** for individual artworks went from complex recordings of very detailed observations to pictures with selected details and limited colors. This approach suited the technique of making cutouts, as seen in both *Blue Nude II* (**4.9.17a**) and *Icarus* (**4.9.17b**).

In these works, Matisse gives us enough information to know that we are looking at a human body. Their shapes are rough, but energetic. The palette in *Blue Nude II* is restricted to blue only. The color blue is not used to shade the female figure or to make her look as if she is bathed in blue light. Instead, her form is made entirely of flat **planes** of color. Matisse started the cutout design for *Icarus* in the same way he made *Blue Nude II*, by shaping the figure with scissors. He then made a **stencil** print so he could produce multiple copies of *Icarus*, along with handwritten text about flight, for his **artist's book** called *Jazz*. Again, the work focuses on expressing the essence of the body's energy, which the artist also highlights by using the brilliant red dot to represent the heart, in a form otherwise shown as a simple black **silhouette**.

An essay of 1947 by Matisse, describing a series of self-portraits made using a mirror, helps explain how he arrived at this technique and what he hoped to communicate by making art the way he did:

> These drawings sum up, in my opinion, observations that I have made for many years about the character of drawing, a character that does not depend on forms being copied exactly as they are in nature, or on the patient assembling of exact details, but on the profound feeling of the artist before the objects that he has chosen, on which his attention is focused, and whose spirit he has penetrated.

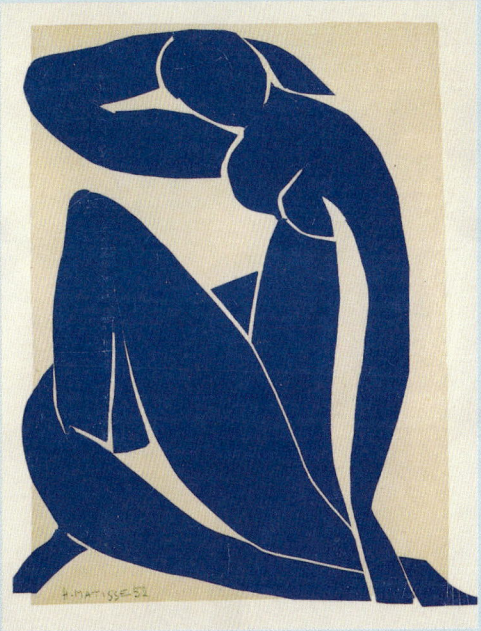

4.9.17 a (above) Henri Matisse, *Blue Nude II*, 1952. Gouache on paper, cut and pasted on white paper, 45¾ × 32¼". Musée National d'Art Moderne, Centre Georges Pompidou, Paris, France

4.9.17 b (below) Henri Matisse, *Icarus*, from *Jazz*, 1943–47. Page size 16⅞ × 12⅞". MoMA, New York

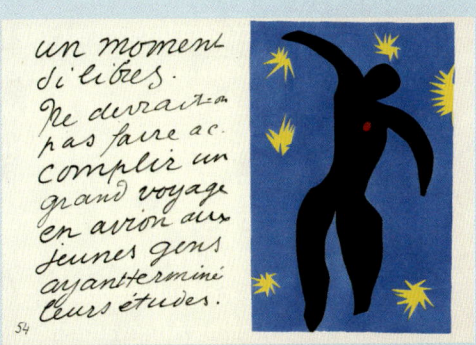

> My conviction about these things crystallized when I realized for example that in the leaves of a fig tree—of a fig tree particularly—the great difference of forms that exists among them does not keep them from sharing a common quality. Fig leaves, whatever their fantastic variations of form, always remain unmistakably fig leaves. I have made the same observation about other growing things: fruits, vegetables, etc.
>
> Thus there exists an essential truth that must be disengaged from the outward appearance of the objects to be represented. This is the only truth that matters...
>
> Exactitude is not truth.

Gateway to Art: Kahlo, *The Two Fridas*
A Body in Pain

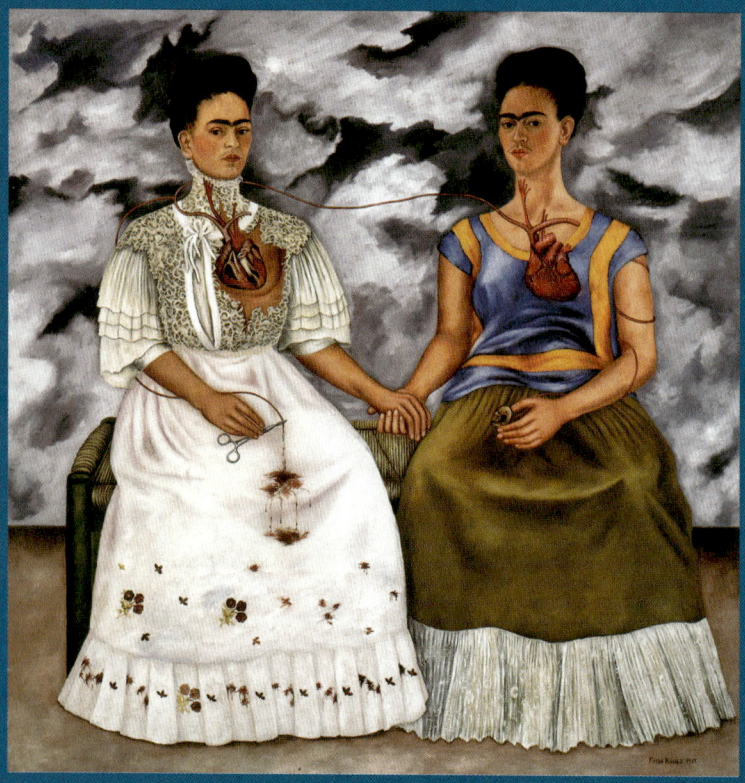

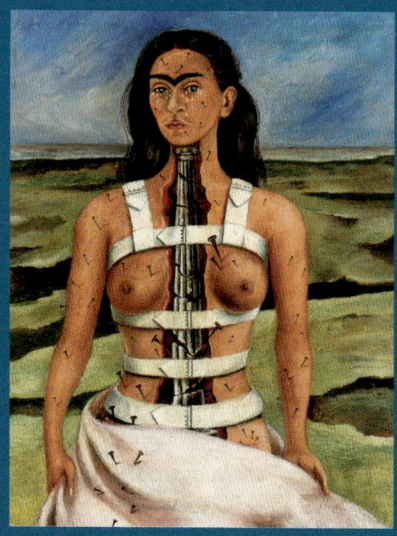

4.9.18a (above) Frida Kahlo, *The Two Fridas*, 1939. Oil on canvas, 5'8" × 5'8". Museo de Arte Moderno, Mexico City, Mexico

4.9.18b (above right) Frida Kahlo, *The Broken Column*, 1944. Oil on masonite, 13 × 17". Museo Dolores Olmedo Patino, Mexico City, Mexico

A terrible accident brought art into Frida Kahlo's life (1907–1954) in a new way. Around the age of eighteen she was riding in a bus with a friend when it collided with a trolley car. Her right leg and foot were crushed; her ribs, collarbone, and spine were broken; and her abdomen and uterus were pierced with an iron handrail. After the devastating accident she could not leave her bed for three months. Afterward, she endured as many as thirty-five surgeries and she experienced pain for the rest of her life.

While she was recuperating in a full body cast, her father brought her art supplies and she began painting. She created very personal portrayals of the psychological and physical suffering that plagued her throughout her life (even before the accident she had suffered polio as a child, compromising her right foot). Such paintings include *The Two Fridas* (**4.9.18a**) and *The Broken Column* (**4.9.18b**). Kahlo's self-portraits, which comprise up to a third of her artistic output, combine depictions of her outward appearance with metaphorical references to her feelings and graphic depictions of the physical agony she suffered.

In *The Two Fridas*, for example, the presentation of the hearts—one of which is radically torn open—on the outside of the bodies emphasizes the sensitive emotional content of the painting. A few years later, around the time she painted *The Broken Column*, Kahlo said, "I am disintegration." In this painting, nails pierce her skin all over, the front of her body is cracked open, and her spine is exposed. The nails recall depictions of the Catholic martyr St. Sebastian, and her spine takes the form of a Greek temple column. The Ionic column, considered the feminine architectural order, is ancient, ideal, and crumbling. No longer suited to support the body, the spinal column is reinforced by a metal corset.

We see subtle signs of Kahlo's constant anguish in the tears on her cheeks, but not in the expression on her face. It has the iconic, serene appearance seen in the numerous photographs taken of her and the many other self-portraits she made, including both faces in *The Two Fridas*. Like the column, Frida is fractured but whole, showing evidence of disintegration but still somehow surviving, even appearing almost ideal.

For the other Kahlo Gateway boxes, see p. 50, p. 204, and p. 532

The Body Reframed

In the late twentieth century a number of artists, many of them women, began to focus very deliberately on the female body with a view to challenging traditional preconceptions about women that they perceived as limiting. Some of the new artworks these artists created included the artist's own body, in more confrontational ways than had previously been attempted in art. Many of the works exposed a much more nuanced, often disturbing, view of the female "nude" than the frequently submissive images created by men in previous eras, and artists tried to express a whole new range of ways in which the female form could be presented. In so doing they rejected unrealistic notions of "ideal" body image: now, the female body could be seen as a source of power, action, and enquiry.

The British painter Jenny Saville (b. 1970) is an artist who has chosen an unconventional approach to depicting the female body. In such larger-than-lifesize self-portraits as *Branded*, which is 7 ft. tall, she appears as a **monumental** nude (**4.9.19**). From this vantage point Saville's breasts and stomach are far more prominent than her head, which is barely squeezed into the frame. She glances down with a look of disdain as she pinches a roll of flesh with her left hand, as if peering into a mirror. Not only does her nude figure appear fat, countering contemporary society's bias toward thin women (and noticeably exaggerating Saville's actual size), but her discolored skin is also far from ideal. To make her paintings, Saville refers to photographs and medical illustrations of flesh tones, bruises, dimples, and pockmarks. Such words as "delicate," "supportive," "irrational," "decorative," and "petite," inscribed on her body, comment on society's expectations of the kind of body a woman should have. Saville has said that she uses her body as a prop that she is willing to distort and manipulate. The results are direct, if harsh and critical. By confronting—even exaggerating—the imperfections of reality, Saville comments on the conflicted relationship women sometimes have with their own body image, and on society's unreasonable expectations of how they should appear in order to be perceived as "acceptable" or "attractive."

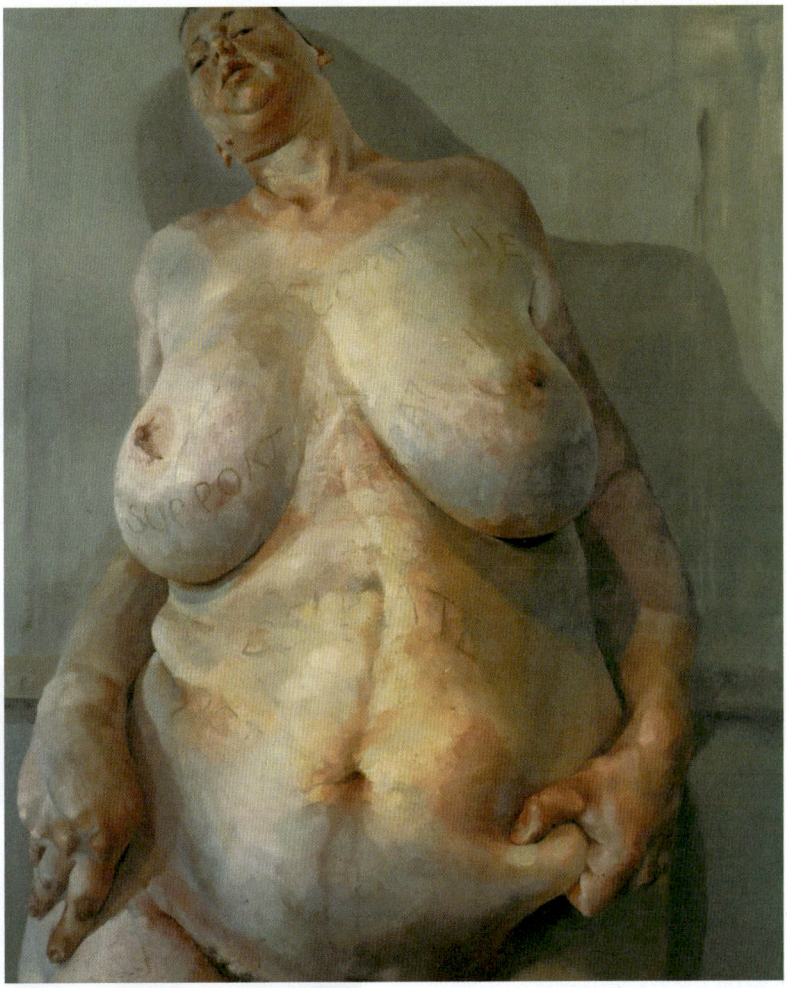

4.9.19 Jenny Saville, *Branded*, 1992. Oil on canvas, 7 × 6'

The French performance artist ORLAN (b. 1947) has adopted an even more extreme approach to constructing the female body. ORLAN's artistic medium is literally her own body: in order to create a new persona, she underwent plastic surgeries that transformed her appearance, and documented the entire process (**4.9.20a** and **b**, p. 678). An operating room became the stage for ORLAN's "performance." She was the star, the medical team the cast, with costumes created by famous fashion designers. Because she was given only a local anesthetic, ORLAN was able to remain conscious and read aloud from philosophical and poetic texts while the procedures were carried out. Video

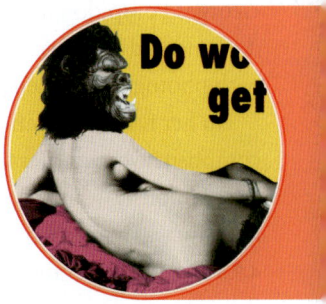

Feminist artists, such as the Guerrilla Girls, draw attention to the ways women have been overlooked and underappreciated in society and in the art world: see **4.10.7, p. 685**

Monumental: having massive or impressive scale

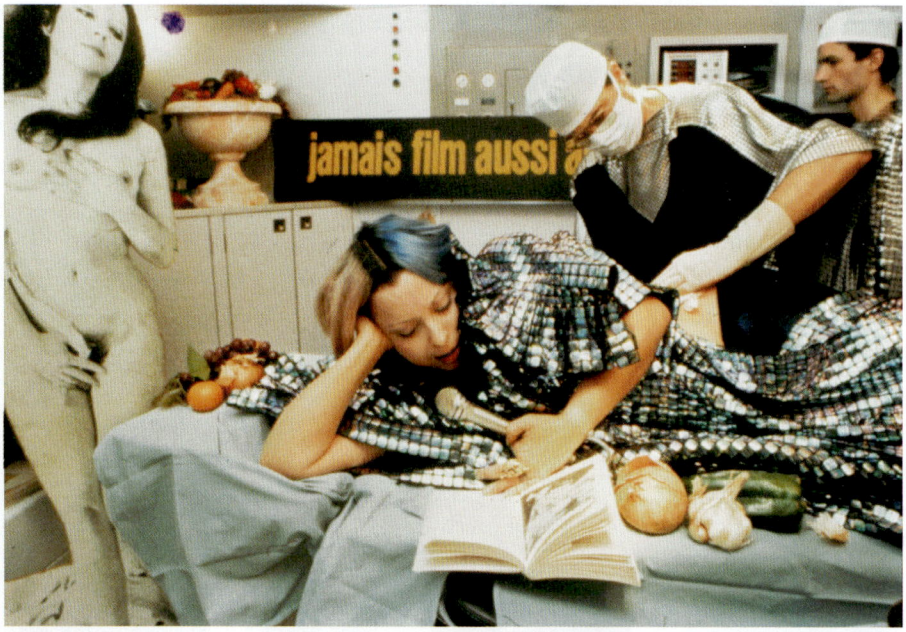

4.9.20a (above) ORLAN, Fourth surgery-performance, entitled *Successful Operation*, December 8, 1991, Paris

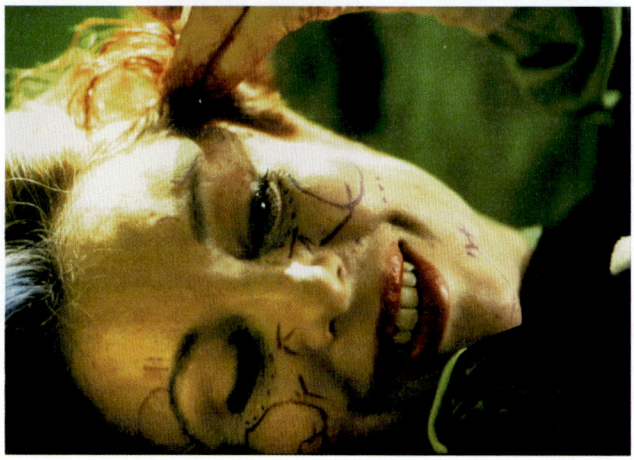

4.9.20b (right) ORLAN, Seventh surgery-performance, entitled *Omnipresence*, November 21, 1993. *Smile of Delight (Sourire de Plaisir)*. Cibachrome in diasec mount, 43¼ × 65"

cameras in the operating room transmitted a live feed of the surgery to CBS News, the Sandra Gering Gallery in New York, and the Centre Georges Pompidou in Paris. ORLAN also documented the stages of her transformation with photographs taken as she healed.

In her final incarnation, ORLAN became a composite woman. Her features were modeled after famously beautiful paintings of women: her chin was copied from Botticelli's Venus (see **4.9.5** on p. 666); her mouth from the Roman deity Diana in a renowned French Renaissance canvas; her nose from Psyche, the mythical lover of Cupid, in a French painting by François Gérard; and her brow from Leonardo da Vinci's *Mona Lisa*. ORLAN has said that her work aims to intervene in the historical representation of women in art by actively determining her own appearance; to comment on the ways technology empowers us to transcend our human limitations; to critique the cult of beauty that imposes unfair standards on women; and to make a statement about the impossibility of physical perfection even in an age when plastic surgery is performed routinely. The measures she takes expose the tyranny of societal preconceptions about physical appearance because, by having herself operated on, she shows how extreme the insistence on stereotypical notions of female beauty has been. Ultimately, she has used the platform of art to make a statement that she is taking possession of her own body and asserting the right to do with it as she sees fit. ORLAN's performances broach the subject of body image for a world of women, young and old, trying to live up to impossible standards.

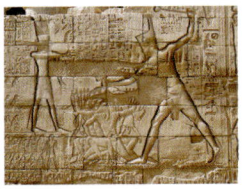

1.7.4a Relief from the temple of Amun, Egypt, c. 1295–1186 BCE, p. 143

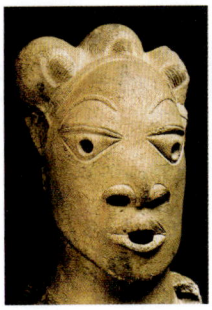

3.5.2 Head from Rafin Kura, Nok culture, Africa, c. 500 BCE–200 CE, p. 447

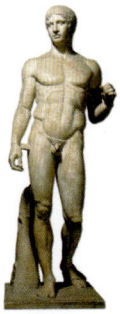

3.1.29 *Doryphoros* (Roman version), 120–50 BCE, p. 384

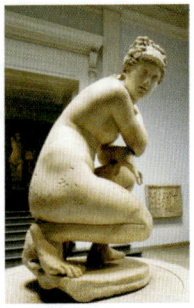

1.2.8b *Naked Aphrodite...* (*Lely's Venus*), Roman, 2nd century CE, p. 66

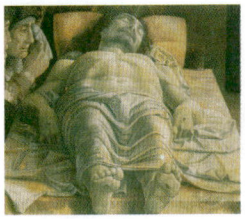

4.3.3 Andrea Mantegna, *Dead Christ*, c. 1480, p. 593

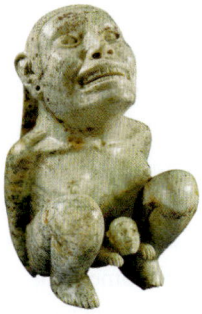

4.3.1 Tlazolteotl giving birth to the maize god, Aztec, c. 1500, p. 591

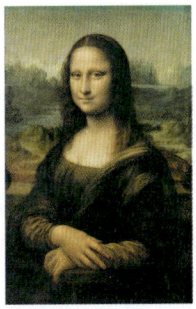

0.0.12 Leonardo da Vinci, *Mona Lisa*, c. 1503–6, p. 28

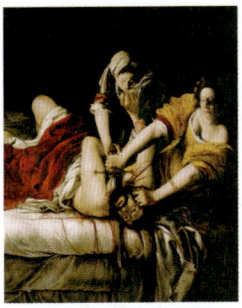

3.6.19 Artemisia Gentileschi, *Judith Decapitating Holofernes*, c. 1620, p. 478

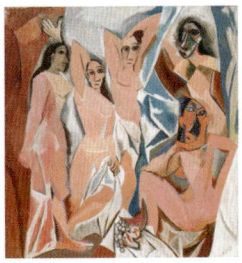

3.9.4 Pablo Picasso, *Les Demoiselles d'Avignon*, 1907, p. 527

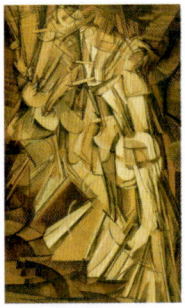

3.9.16 Marcel Duchamp, *Nude Descending a Staircase, No. 2*, 1912, p. 533

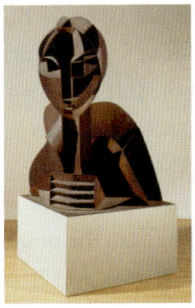

2.4.17 Naum Gabo, *Constructed Head No. 2*, 1916, p. 253

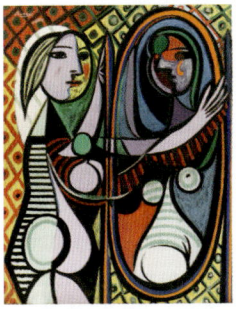

4.3.14 Pablo Picasso, *Girl before a Mirror*, 1932, p. 600

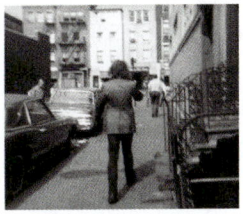

2.10.6 Vito Acconci, *Following Piece*, 1969, p. 354

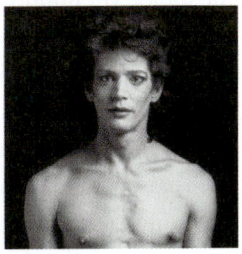

1.10.9 Robert Mapplethorpe, *Self-Portrait (#385)*, 1980, p. 180

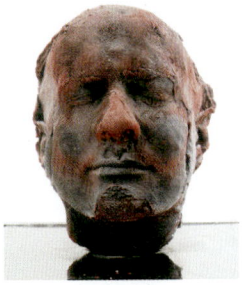

0.0.16 Marc Quinn, *Self*, 1991, p. 32

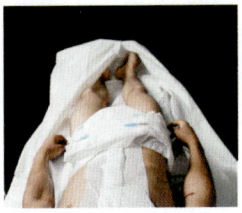

4.3.4 Andres Serrano, *The Morgue (Gun Murder)*, 1992, p. 593

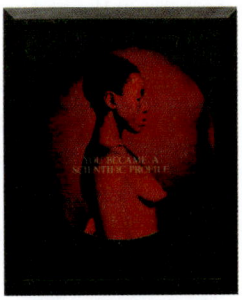

2.8.24 Carrie Mae Weems, "You Became a Scientific Profile," 1995, p. 329

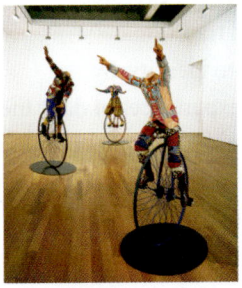

2.10.10 Yinka Shonibare, *Mobility*, 2005, installation view, p. 358

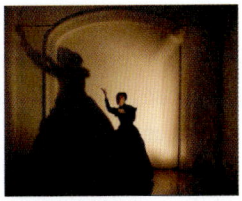

2.10.12 Yuki Kihara, *Taualuga: The Last Dance*, 2006, p. 359

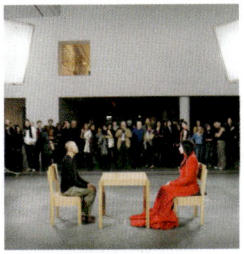

2.10.7 Marina Abramović, *The Artist Is Present*, 2010 p. 355

4.10 Identity, Race, and Gender in Art

While personal identity affects everyone on some level, it became a central issue for artists during the late twentieth century (see the discussion of Postmodernism in chapter 3.10). At that time groups that had been neglected by or indeed excluded from mainstream culture, which was male-dominated and Eurocentric, began to celebrate their differences, whether these lay in being part of a non-white ethnic minority, female, homosexual, or transgender. Earlier in the same century, social and cultural movements encouraged people to reconsider the status of women and communities of color in society by emphasizing their role as both the creators and the subjects of important artworks. The Harlem Renaissance (1920s and 1930s) and the Civil Rights movement (1955–68) in the US brought well-deserved attention to African American artists, while feminist and LGBT (lesbian, gay, bisexual, and transgender) movements have, since the 1960s and more recently, inspired a great deal of discussion and exploration of the effect gender has on our personalities, relationships, and preferences.

The artworks in this chapter illustrate some of the ways in which artists have explored, reinforced, and challenged traditional expectations with regards to identity. By presenting their personal experiences of daily life, their interpretations of historical events, and their response to particular social or political agendas, artists encourage us to question common assumptions about identity and to become aware of the possibilities of individual experience beyond simplistic labels and stereotypes.

Abstract: art imagery that departs from recognizable images of the natural world

Self-Portraits

One obvious way for an artist to explore his or her identity is to make a self-portrait. In a self-portrait, the maker and the subject are the same person, while in a portrait the artist depicts someone else. In addition to the more familiar practice of providing a physical likeness of the artist, self-portraits often tell us something about the artist's personality, experiences, or choices. The Italian artist Artemisia Gentileschi, for example, brought the characters of her paintings to life by using them to respond to intense personal experiences (see Gateway Box: Gentileschi). Another form of self-portraiture involves the artist assuming the role or persona of someone else, much as an actor portrays another person on the stage. Some artists, discussed later in this chapter, have become very inventive with their self-portraits to the point where the connection between work and artist is not always obvious: the work references the artist in indirect or **abstract** ways.

The Dutch artist Rembrandt Harmenszoon van Rijn (1606–1669), known as Rembrandt, was one of the first artists to dedicate a significant portion of his output to self-portraits, producing more than ninety of them over the course of forty years. Looking at them, we can observe the changes that occurred both in his appearance and in his artistic style during the course of his lifetime. In Rembrandt's self-portraits, he is shown in many guises, from a peasant to an aristocrat, which demonstrates his interest in exploring different facial expressions

Gateway to Art: Gentileschi, *Judith Decapitating Holofernes*

Self-Expression in the *Judith* paintings

The powerful heroines in the paintings of Artemisia Gentileschi (1593–c. 1656), such as Judith, who beheads Holofernes with steadfast determination, have a strong relationship with events in the artist's own life. Gentileschi was the victim of a sexual assault by Agostino Tassi, who was her painting teacher and a colleague of her father. During the public rape trial that followed, Tassi claimed that Gentileschi was not only a willing lover, but also quite promiscuous. Gentileschi and her father felt that, in addition to the physical violence she had suffered in the assault, their family name and reputation had been attacked. They feared that her prospects of marrying had been damaged both by the rape and the trial. Tassi was eventually found guilty and sentenced to exile. Gentileschi went on to marry another man, with whom she had five children.

Gentileschi is known to have painted seven works showing different events from the biblical story of Judith's encounter with Holofernes. The first, depicting Judith and her maidservant cutting off his head, was painted about a year after the Tassi trial (**4.10.1**). The painting of this violent assault by a brave and beautiful woman on the enemy commander who had conquered her city and tried to seduce her has been interpreted, using feminist analysis, both as an expression of the artist's anger at her own attacker, and as a way of healing the effects of her ordeal. In fact, Gentileschi's heroines in the Judith paintings resemble her own features. Another of the painter's depictions of the story, made about a decade later, shows Judith and her maidservant by candlelight while making their escape from the murder scene with the bloody head (**4.10.2**). While there may indeed be an element of autobiography at least in Gentileschi's earlier paintings, the numerous versions of the story that she made over a thirty-year period were probably created for a variety of other reasons, including the popularity of the theme at the time and the fact that her previous renditions of this subject had already attracted admiration.

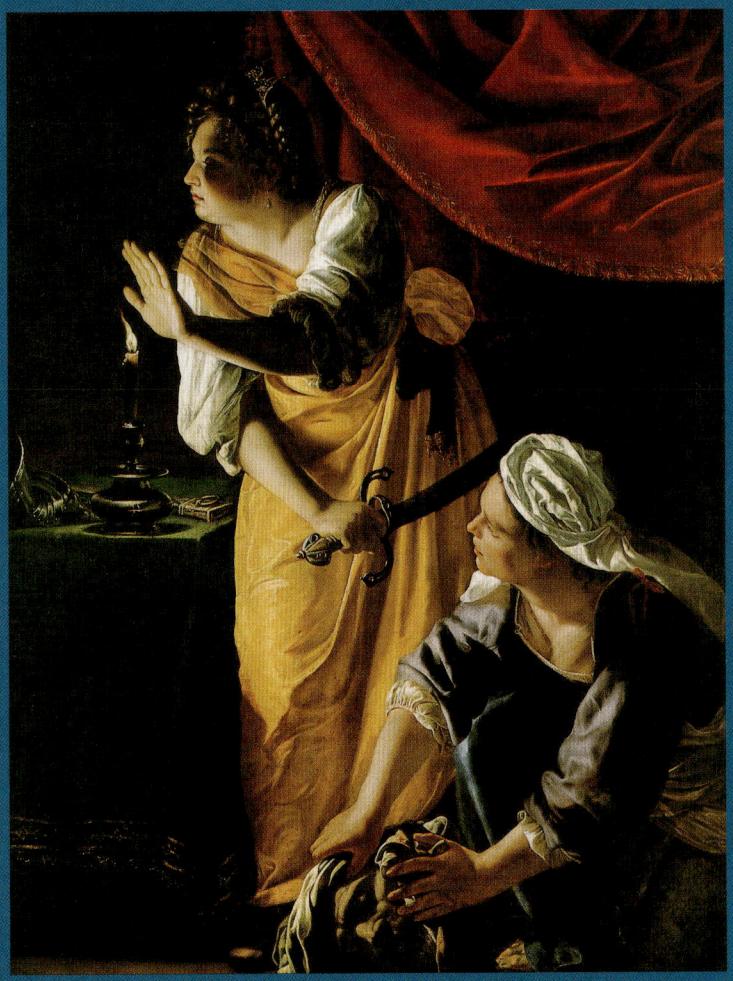

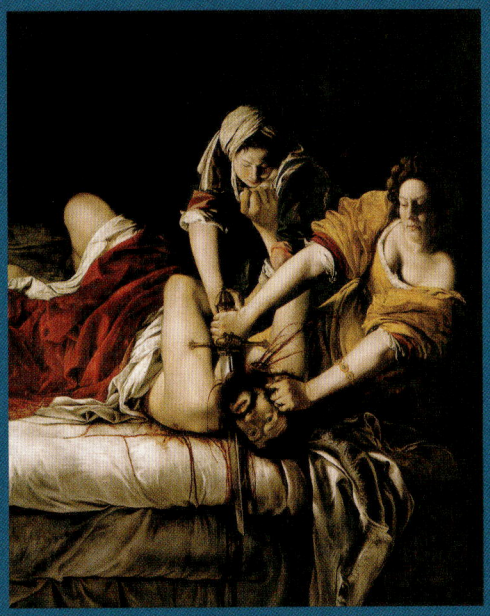

4.10.2 (above) Artemisia Gentileschi, *Judith and Her Maidservant with the Head of Holofernes*, 1623–25. Oil on canvas, 6'3⅜" × 4'7¾". Detroit Institute of Arts, Michigan

4.10.1 (left) Artemisia Gentileschi, *Judith Decapitating Holofernes*, c. 1620. Oil on canvas, 6'6⅜" × 5'3¾". Uffizi Gallery, Florence, Italy

For the other Gentileschi Gateway boxes, see p. 152, p. 219, p. 478, and p. 519

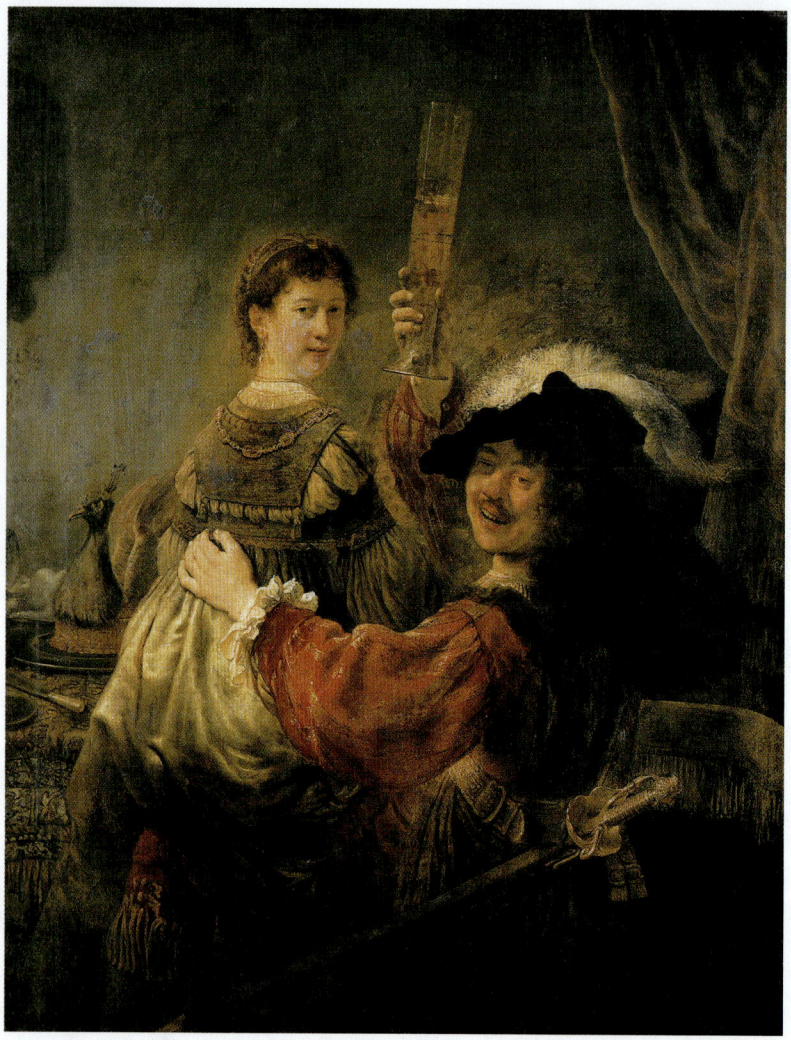

4.10.3 (above) Rembrandt van Rijn, *Self-Portrait with Saskia in the Scene of the Prodigal Son in the Tavern*, c. 1635. Oil on canvas, 5'3⅜" × 4'3⅝". Gemäldegalerie Alte Meister, Dresden, Germany

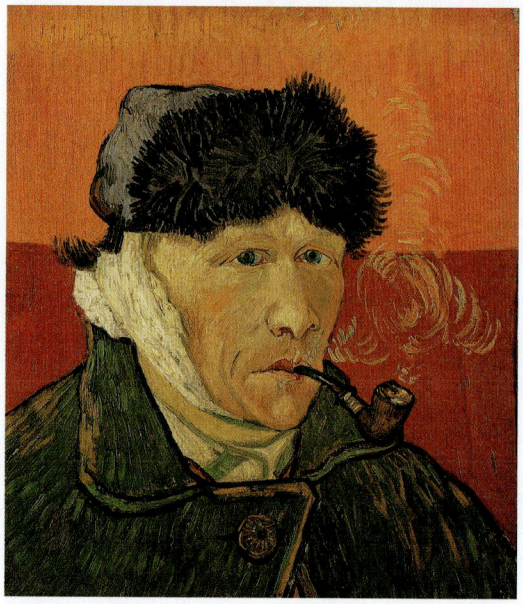

4.10.4 (above) Vincent van Gogh, *Self-Portrait with Bandaged Ear and Pipe*, 1889. Oil on canvas, 25¼ × 19¾". Private collection

and character types. In *Self-Portrait with Saskia in the Scene of the Prodigal Son in the Tavern*, Rembrandt appears as the prodigal son from the biblical story of the young man who rebels against his father's wishes by squandering his inheritance (**4.10.3**). Rembrandt creates a lively mood in the tavern: he raises his glass toward the viewer, while the barmaid, modeled on his wife Saskia, looks on.

More than two centuries after Rembrandt, another Dutch painter, Vincent van Gogh (1853–1890), specialized in self-portraits in which he emphasized the internal reality of what he felt rather than simply recording what he saw. His *Self-Portrait with Bandaged Ear and Pipe*, one of approximately thirty self-portraits that he made, refers to a famous incident in his life (**4.10.4**). At the time this painting was made Van Gogh lived in Arles, in the south of France, and was hoping to realize his dream of starting an artists' colony there. When he learned that his fellow artist and close friend Paul Gauguin was planning to return to Paris, they had an intense argument, during which Van Gogh threatened Gauguin's life. Afterward Van Gogh cut off a portion of his own ear. He then wrapped the severed lobe in newspaper and presented it to a prostitute in a brothel before he was hospitalized and treated for acute blood loss. In its restrained but nervous lines and bold, contrasting colors, the *Self-Portrait with Bandaged Ear and Pipe* displays some of the agitation that the artist experienced during the episode.

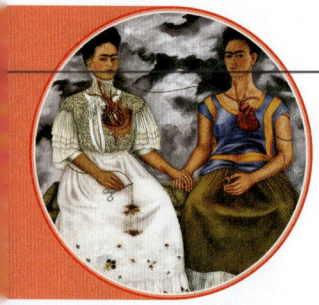

Frida Kahlo is perhaps best known for her self-portraits, which comprise up to a third of her artistic output: see **4.9.18a, p. 676**

The American photographer Cindy Sherman (b. 1954) plays the roles of all of the women portrayed in her acclaimed *Untitled Film Stills* series, creating an intriguing visual puzzle as we try to uncover the "real" Cindy Sherman. She makes images of herself that are not, however, intended conventionally to reflect her own identity: Sherman has explained that the images are not about her, but are about the representations of the women being shown and the ways that each viewer interprets them (see Perspectives on Art Box: Cindy Sherman: The Artist and Her Identitys).

For the *Untitled Film Stills*, Sherman fabricated backdrops and costumes for imagined characters from nonexistent 1950s B-movies. At that time, the film roles for women were limited to such stereotyped characters as housewife, starlet, country girl come to the city, and so on. In "Untitled Film Still #35" we see a woman—perhaps a housewife or a maid—with a distinctly bad attitude (**4.10.5**). The circumstances of the scene are far from clear, though. Is she sulking about something, planning to leave, or about to pull a wallet from the jacket hanging on the hook? Why are there so many scuff marks on the door? More questions are raised than answered in the scenarios Sherman invents. Her *Untitled Film Stills*, which were created between 1977 and 1980, revisit these 1950s-inspired women in order to make it clear how narrow the representations of and expectations for women had been only a few short years before. At the time Sherman made "Untitled Film Still #35," feminism was beginning to have a significant impact on artistic representations of women as well as on the possibilities for women in society.

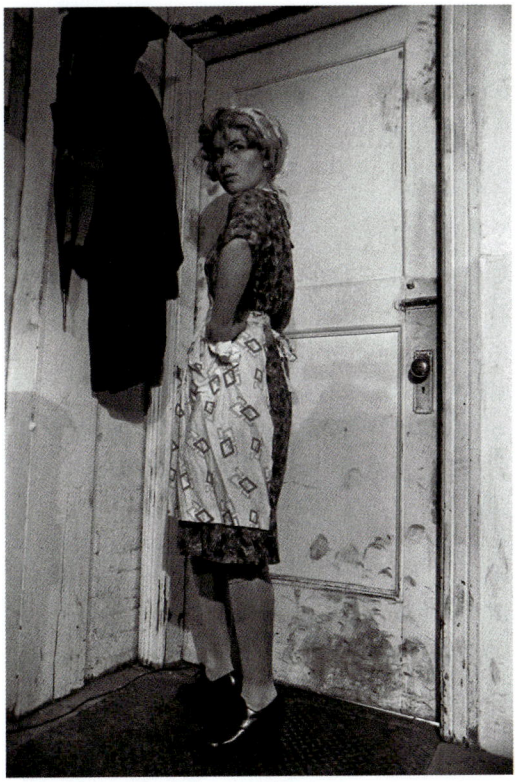

4.10.5 (left) Cindy Sherman, "Untitled Film Still #35," from the *Untitled Film Stills* series, 1979. Black-and-white photograph, 10 × 8". MoMA, New York

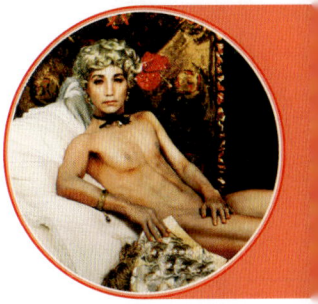

Yasumasa Morimura uses appropriation and digital technology to transform identity in such self-portraits as *Portrait (Futago)*: see **4.9.10, p. 669**

Perspectives on Art: Cindy Sherman
The Artist and Her Identity

*The American photographer and film director Cindy Sherman is best known for her photographs in which she is dressed in costumes as if she were another person (see above, **4.10.5**). Here she explains her general working process and one specific image, "Untitled Film Still #35," inspired by the Italian film actress Sophia Loren.*

There is a stereotype of a girl who dreams all her life of being a movie star. She tries to make it on the stage, in films, and either succeeds or fails. I was more interested in the types of characters that fail. Maybe I related to that. But why should I try to do it myself? I'd rather look at the reality of these kinds of fantasies, the fantasy of going away and becoming a star...

The black-and-white photographs were... fun to do. I think they were easy partly because throughout my childhood I had stored up so many images of role models. It was real easy to think of a different one in every scene. But they were so clichéd that after three years I couldn't do them anymore. I was really thinking about the movies, the characters are almost typecast from movies.

For the woman standing in front of my studio door, I was thinking of a film with Sophia Loren called *Two Women*. She plays this Italian peasant. Her husband is killed and she and her daughter are both raped. She is this tough strong woman, but all beaten-up and dirty. I liked that combination of Sophia Loren looking very dirty and very strong. So that's what I was thinking of...

I realized I had to become more specific in details, because that's what makes a person different from other people.

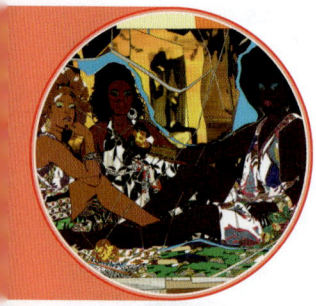

In many cases, successful women and people of color have not been given opportunities in the art world, while others have been simply written out of the history of art. Mickalene Thomas brings attention to these omissions by appropriating famous artworks: see **1.10.10, p. 181**

Sherman made sixty-nine photographs in the series. The women in them always seem as if they are being watched, the object of an unseen voyeur's gaze, so that these images call attention to and question the way we look at women.

Challenging the Status Quo

In Western countries, for many centuries marginalized individuals had far fewer opportunities to become artists, because they were discriminated against on grounds of their gender, race, and/or social class, and they were rarely given the recognition granted to their white male counterparts. For example, women were not allowed to draw from the nude in their art classes until the nineteenth century. It was also believed that "genius" was a trait exclusively available to men, and language with a gender bias—such as the word "masterpiece" to describe a great artwork—reinforced that belief. Before the 1970s few people even noticed that women and people of color had largely been excluded from the institutions and systems that produced serious artists.

The feminist movement of the 1960s and 1970s significantly impacted the production and understanding of artworks. Feminist artists and feminist critiques of art have expanded the subject matter and interpretation of art, making it more relevant to a wider set of issues and a wider range of experiences. As has been the case throughout history, artists give voice to experiences shared by many people. Acknowledging that women and artists of color had been left out of much of the history of art introduces the possibility that this situation can be rectified. By the late twentieth and early twenty-first centuries, an increased number of artworks made by diverse artists were being included in museums and galleries.

The American artist Judy Chicago (b. 1939) appreciated the achievement of such women as Gentileschi (who was well respected during her lifetime in the seventeenth century, only to be subsequently overlooked and then "rediscovered" in the early twentieth century). Chicago realized that many women had been forgotten over time and, likewise, that women who seem prominent today might in the future also be omitted from history. From 1974 to 1979, Chicago worked on an epic sculpture called *The Dinner Party* (**4.10.6**), which honors women from the past and present. Her huge triangular dinner table has thirteen place settings on each side. Every setting features a placemat, on which is embroidered the name of a famous historical or mythical woman, and an elaborate plate designed intentionally to resemble the shape of a butterfly or a vagina. The appearance of all the elements on each setting was inspired by the woman whose place it is. Layers of lace designate the place of the nineteenth-century poet Emily Dickinson, while the plate for the artist Georgia O'Keeffe resembles a sculpted version of one of her abstract flower paintings. Artemisia Gentileschi's place setting has a brightly colored plate surrounded by lush fabric similar to the kind shown in her paintings.

Chicago made the table an equilateral triangle not only because the shape was an ancient sign for both woman and goddess, but also because it could be used here to symbolize the world of fairness and equality that feminists sought. She chose to have thirteen guests to a side both because there were thirteen witches in a coven and because it was an important number for those ancient religions that worshiped a mother goddess. The number is also a reference

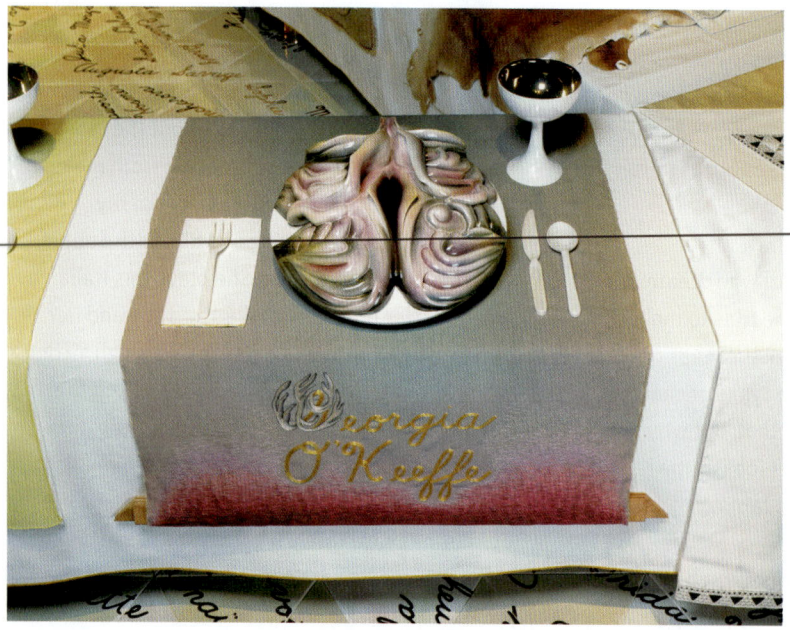

4.10.6 Judy Chicago, *The Dinner Party*, 1974–79. Installation view showing Georgia O'Keeffe place setting. Embroidery on linen and china paint on porcelain, entire work 48 × 48'. Brooklyn Museum, New York

Medium (plural **media**): the material on or from which an artist chooses to make a work of art
Ceramics: fire-hardened clay, often painted, and normally sealed with shiny protective coating
Nude: an artistic representation of an unclothed human figure, emphasizing the body's form rather than its exposure

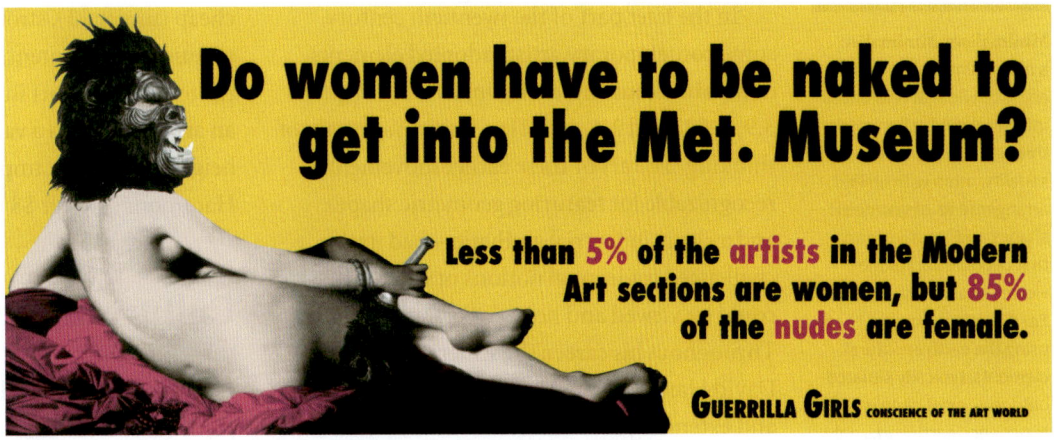

4.10.7 Guerrilla Girls, *Do Women Have to Be Naked to Get into the Met. Museum?*, 1989. Poster, dimensions variable

to the biblical Last Supper, here reconfigured with women as the guests instead of Jesus and his twelve disciples. The idea of a dinner party—as well as the **media**, such as needlework and **ceramics**, which are included in her piece—evokes the role of woman as homemaker, which Chicago and other feminists believed should be admired and praised.

In 1985, a group of women artists in New York City formed a collective organization called the Guerrilla Girls to protest at the unequal treatment of female artists in the art world. Their name indicates their willingness to engage in unconventional tactics in their fight for equality. The Guerrilla Girls, who are still active, are known for the gorilla masks the members wear to avoid being recognized by the art-world establishment and the institutions they might criticize. Their productions take the form of public protests and lectures as well as flyers and posters. One of their best-known posters, *Do Women Have to Be Naked to Get into the Met. Museum?* (**4.10.7**), includes statistics to highlight the disproportionate representation of women artists (5 percent) compared to female **nudes** (85 percent) in the collection of the Metropolitan Museum of Art in New York. As this poster shows, one of their principal goals is to oppose the lack of representation of women artists in major museum collections.

Also in the late twentieth century, nearly one hundred years after the Emancipation Proclamation, African Americans in Southern US states were still experiencing legalized discrimination and segregation that led directly to disenfranchisement, oppression, and violence. Using methods similar to those deployed by feminists, artists have brought attention to the experience of people of color and other marginalized groups.

The American artist and philosopher Adrian Piper (b. 1948) directly confronts racism and racial "passing" in her work of 1986, *My Calling (Card) #1 (for Dinners and Cocktail Parties)*. From 1986 to 1990, she performed this piece by handing out cards (see **4.10.8**) in such social situations as dinner- and cocktail parties. Although Piper is African American, many people assume, because of her light skin tone, that she is white. For that reason, she has frequently encountered racist remarks that would likely be considered in poor taste to make (and therefore avoided) in the company of a black person. After hearing a racist remark she would hand the card to the person, making them feel a similar discomfort to the way that remarks have made her feel.

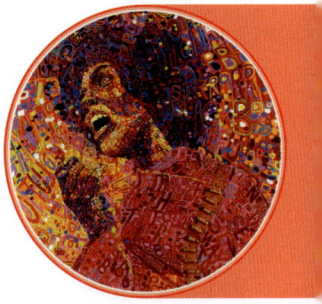

As seen in the work of Wadsworth Jarrell, art has often been used to draw attention to causes and inspire change, even revolution: see **3.10.6, p. 550**

4.10.8 Adrian Piper, *My Calling (Card) #1 (for Dinners and Cocktail Parties)*, 1986–present. Performance utensil: Business card with printed text on cardboard, 2 × 3½". Collection of the Adrian Piper Research Archive Foundation, Berlin, Germany

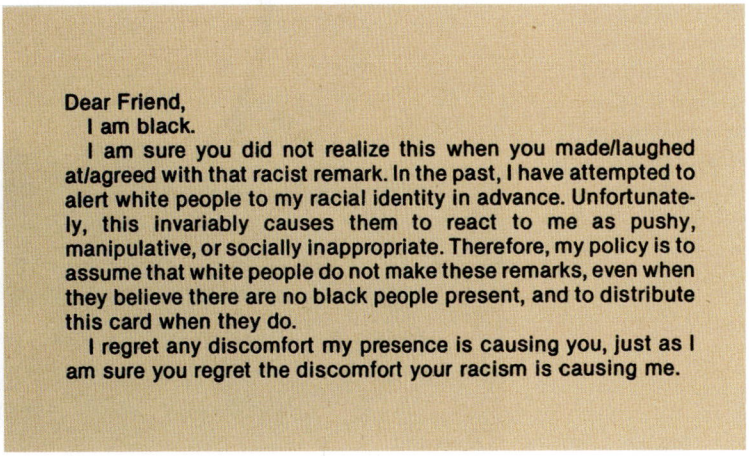

Dear Friend,
I am black.
I am sure you did not realize this when you made/laughed at/agreed with that racist remark. In the past, I have attempted to alert white people to my racial identity in advance. Unfortunately, this invariably causes them to react to me as pushy, manipulative, or socially inappropriate. Therefore, my policy is to assume that white people do not make these remarks, even when they believe there are no black people present, and to distribute this card when they do.
I regret any discomfort my presence is causing you, just as I am sure you regret the discomfort your racism is causing me.

Minimalism, Minimalist: a mid-twentieth-century artistic style that references industrial production modes through materials and seriality, often with unified arrangements of geometric shapes and massive forms that become part of the viewer's space also known

Earthworks: artworks made using the earth or natural elements; typically situated outdoors, most people experience earthworks only through photographs

In the later part of the twentieth century, some contemporary artists adopted elements of **Minimalism** and **earthworks** (see Chapter 3.9, p. 542 and 2.4, p. 252) to inspire new ways of thinking. The art of these earlier movements—recognizable for featuring geometric shapes and a clean, industrial aesthetic—had itself challenged traditional notions of where art could be viewed and how works were made. Throughout his career, the American artist David Hammons (b. 1943) has been disrupting and extending the confines of the art world and the definitions associated with that sphere. His work references cultural stereotypes of race and class and focuses on the power of symbols. Hammons often uses such found objects as discarded bottles from the streets of Harlem and Brooklyn. In *Untitled (Night Train)*, empty bottles of inexpensive "bum wine" take the shape of an elegant abstract spiral. In this new context, the bottles are transformed (**4.10.9**). While the historical remnants remain intact—cheap (under $3), strong (18 percent ABV), and, emptied of its content, trash—the bottles take the form of high art in the pristine setting of an art gallery with a value that is dramatically heightened (for example, another sculpture by Hammons sold for $8 million in 2013).

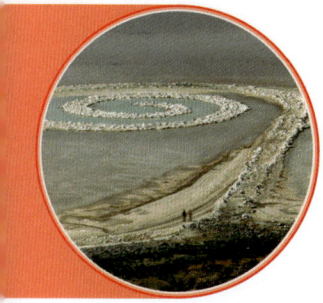

The work of Minimalist (see **3.9.33, p. 544**) and earthwork (see *Spiral Jetty*, above, and on **p. 252**) artists challenged expectations of fine art. They used unconventional media (industrial and natural materials instead of marble, bronze, etc.), fabrication methods (using machines rather than making by hand), and different expectations of the viewer's role (requiring direct experience as opposed to simply contemplation).

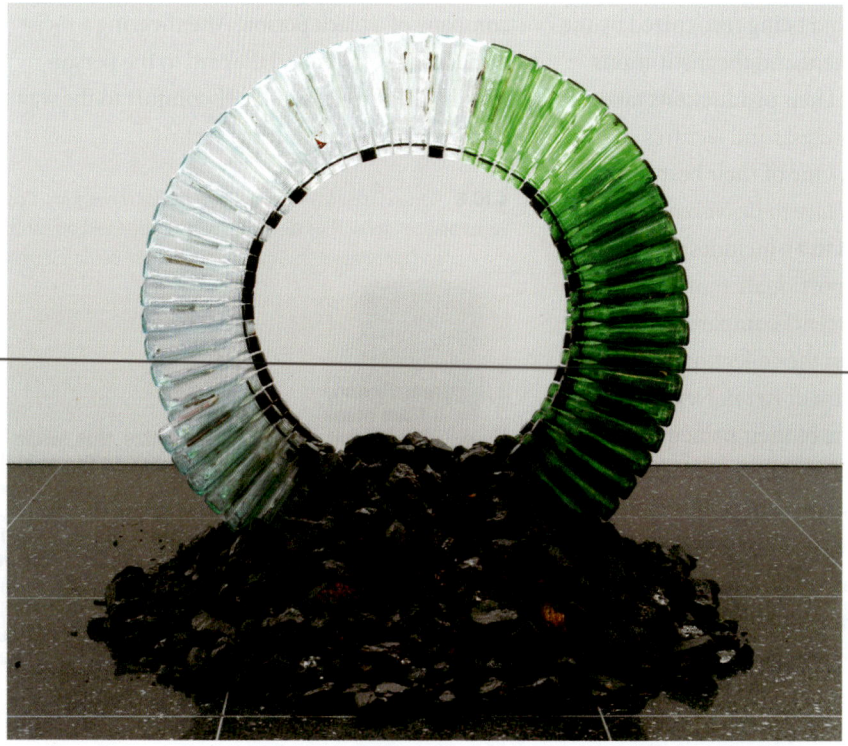

4.10.9 David Hammons, *Untitled (Night Train)*, 1989. Glass, silicon glue, and coal, 42 x 42 x 30". MoMA, New York

Culture on Display

Art is a powerful vehicle for telling stories about personal and cultural identity (see Gateway Box: Carrie Mae Weems, p. 687.) The work of American filmmaker, director, producer, writer, and actor, Shelton Jackson "Spike" Lee (b. 1957) is characterized by its strong commitment to social justice issues, and includes a film biography of Civil Rights leader Malcolm X (1992). Lee's landmark film *Do the Right Thing*, nominated for two academy awards, focuses on race relations between the Italian American owner of Sal's Famous Pizzeria and the African American residents of the neighborhood (**4.10.11**).

Modeled after Bedford-Stuyvesant, Lee's own Brooklyn neighborhood, and inspired by racial incidents in New York City in the 1980s, the movie also highlights the pervasiveness of

Gateway to Art: Weems, *Kitchen Table* Series
Cultural Diplomacy

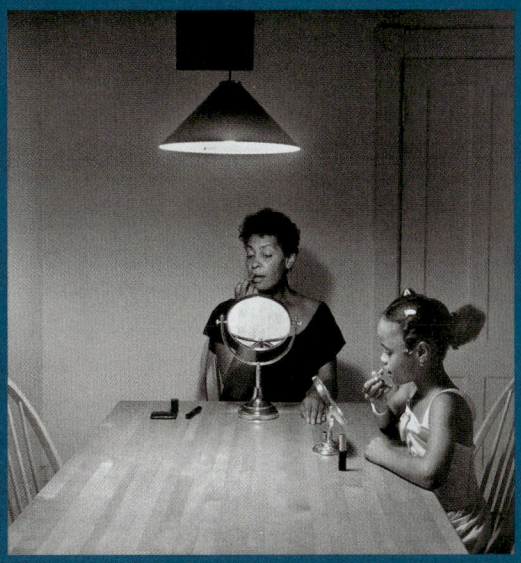

4.10.10 Carrie Mae Weems, "Untitled (Woman and Daughter with Makeup)," 1990, from *Kitchen Table* series, 1989–90. Inkjet print, 41¼ × 41¼ × 2¼" (framed)

Like all artists, Carrie Mae Weems interprets the world and chooses what to present in her art—in this case, photographs. Her work reflects her personal, artistic, and cultural experience. Some viewers have seen her vision as limited by race and gender, a subset of a more universal experience. That is not her intention, though. According to the artist's website, Weems wants "people of color to stand for the human multitudes." Her work has an important connection to black experience, but it is not about race.

The kitchen table itself is a part of most viewers' lives and is, in that way, universal. Family relationships are also something virtually everyone shares. Women teach children certain customs every day, everywhere. People all over celebrate rites of passage. Of course those widespread experiences have to take some kind of shape in order to be communicated and contemplated. Here, the specifics are a rectangular wooden table and Windsor-type chairs in a clean room with a woman and young girl applying makeup (**4.10.10**). This scene contains a set of circumstances that can intersect with the experience of most viewers, even if they have not lived a moment precisely identical to this one.

Weems's work contributes to efforts for equality and justice, moving forward what she calls a "cultural diplomacy," by focusing attention on a history, sharing intriguing insights into identity, and creating thoughtful work that speaks to all audiences.

For the other Weems Gateway boxes, seep. 56, p. 329, and p. 551

institutionalized racism in America decades after the advancements of the Civil Rights movement. This movie makes a frank statement about race relations as tension builds over the course of a hot summer's day, with tragic consequences. The heavy content of the film is combined with inventive visuals, strong storytelling, humor, and music. Effective character development, which is sympathetic to all parties, highlights the complexity of the characters' various viewpoints, prejudices, and relationships with each other in

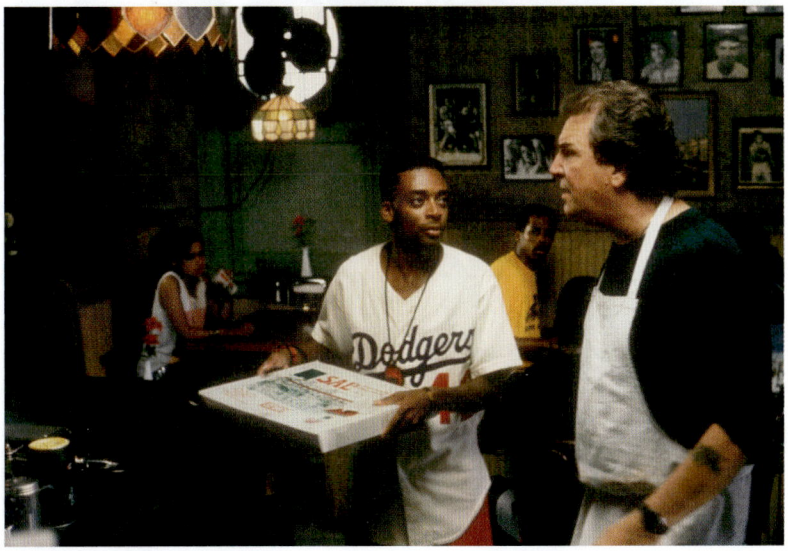

4.10.11 Spike Lee, *Do the Right Thing*, 1989. Duration 120 minutes. 40 Acres & A Mule Filmworks

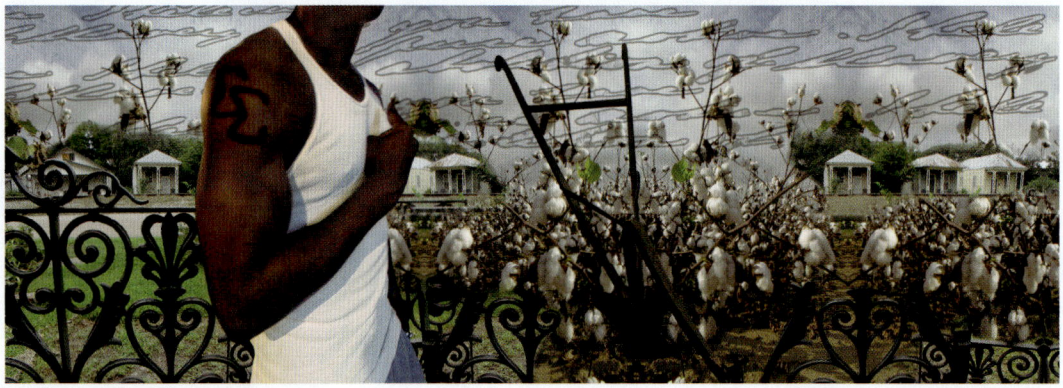

4.10.12 Stephen Marc, *Untitled—Passage on the Underground Railroad*, 2002. Digital photomontage, archival pigment inkjet print, 9 × 26". Arizona State University, Phoenix

a way that promotes understanding rather than perpetuating racial polarization.

American photographer Stephen Marc (b. 1954) manipulates and juxtaposes iconic images associated with the American South so that they take on new meanings. In *Untitled—Passage on the Underground Railroad*, the interwoven pictures from various sources create layers that are visually interesting (**4.10.12**). Marc photographed the slave quarters of the Cedar Grove Plantation in Vicksburg, Mississippi, highlighting its dark and powerful history. He includes an extract from a slave-owner's letter defending his decision not to emancipate his slaves. The rhythms of the fence, antique hoe, and cotton plants are punctuated by a young man who displays his Phi Beta Sigma fraternity brands, a voluntary celebration of fraternal commitment. The artist sees these markings as a contemporary crossover of African scarification and body marking, recalling the branding of livestock and slaves. The combination of elements communicates complex ideas about contemporary social dynamics and how the past informs the present.

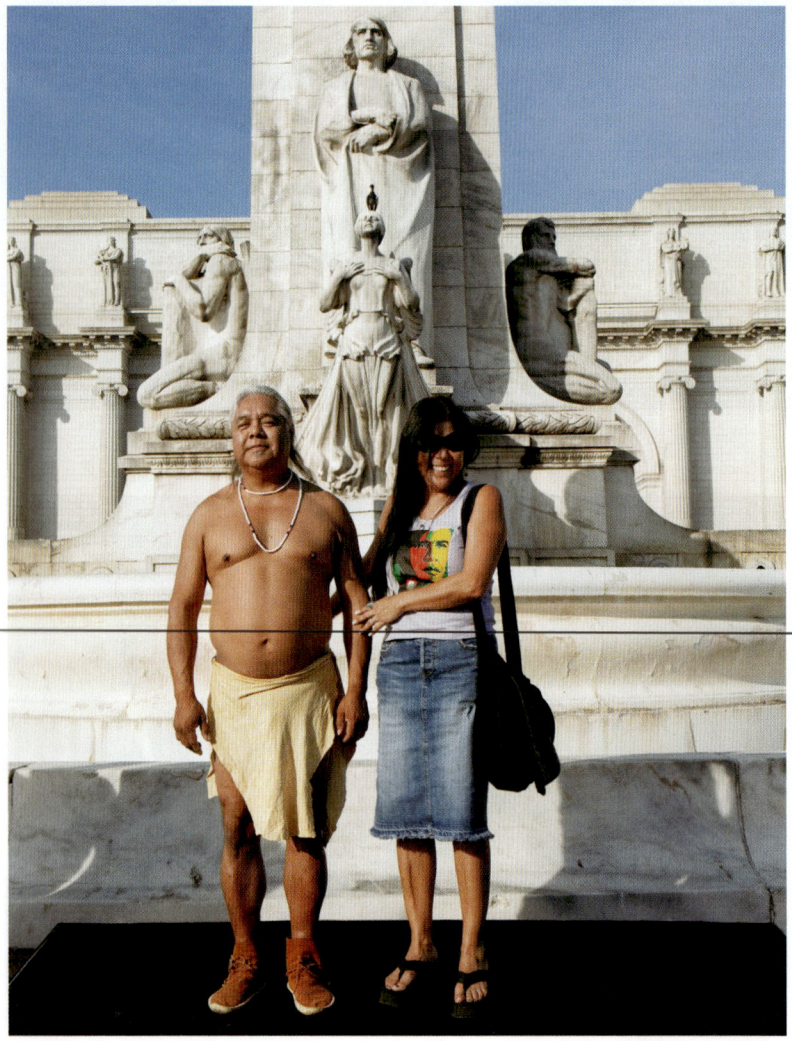

4.10.13 James Luna, *Take a Picture with a Real Indian*, Union Station, Washington, D.C., Columbus Day, October 11, 2010

Puyukitchum/Ipai and Mexican American artist James Luna (1950–2018) used performance as a way to bring cultural conceptions to light in simultaneously humorous and serious ways—seeing his role as similar to the American Indian Ceremonial Clown. Luna lived on the La Jolla Indian Reservation and built on his heritage and experience to comment on perceptions of Native Americans, which tend to be stereotypical and often offensive. In a performance of *Take a Picture with a Real Indian* (**4.10.13**), Luna wore an "outfit" and stood stoically for the snapshots. The performance lastd until he felt "mad enough or humiliated enough. It's a dual humiliation." Even as these interactions can be lively and fun, they contrast simplistic preconceptions with his embodied reality as a living person, hopefully leaving people with the idea that "This isn't a joke."

Identity and Ambiguity

Our expectations of people are often based on stereotypes and on our ideas of what is "normal" for their culture, gender, or race. These stereotypes are frequently challenged, of course: women have been primary breadwinners, worked in mines, and gone to war, men have been nurturers and raised children, and a black man can be elected as the President of the United States. In recent years, it has become more acceptable to address the ways in which people transcend the conventional boundaries of identity. Public awareness of such issues as transvestism and transgender surgery has been raised by increasingly open discussion. Investigations of the ways that bodies and identities can be transformed and racial identity can be transcended, however, are not entirely new to art. The question of identity is one that artists from many cultures and eras of history have sought to address. When the artworks are effective, they lead to a greater understanding of individuality.

Almost 3,500 years ago, ancient Egypt was governed by a woman called Hatshepsut, who abandoned the confines of gender that were customary during her lifetime. She was arguably the most powerful of the handful of female rulers in Egyptian history. Hatshepsut controlled the kingdom for about twenty years in the fifteenth century BCE, first as regent for her stepson and nephew Thutmose III, and then as pharaoh in her own right. To legitimize her reign, Hatshepsut emphasized that she was her father's choice as successor, ahead of her two brothers and half-brother. She also claimed direct lineage from Amun, the chief god who was worshiped at that time.

Like all Egyptian rulers, Hatshepsut commissioned many sculptures and relief carvings to replicate and immortalize her image. A few show her as a woman, but she is most often depicted in the conventional poses and clothing of a male king. The image in **4.10.14** is one of a group of sphinxes that all possess Hatshepsut's face. It was not uncommon for pharaohs to be represented in the form of a sphinx, a creature with the body of a lion and the head of a human. The artist has clearly followed the guidelines for depicting male pharaohs, including the traditional headcloth and royal beard. But, although the portrait is idealized, the sculptor has not attempted to disguise the delicate lines of Hatshepsut's features.

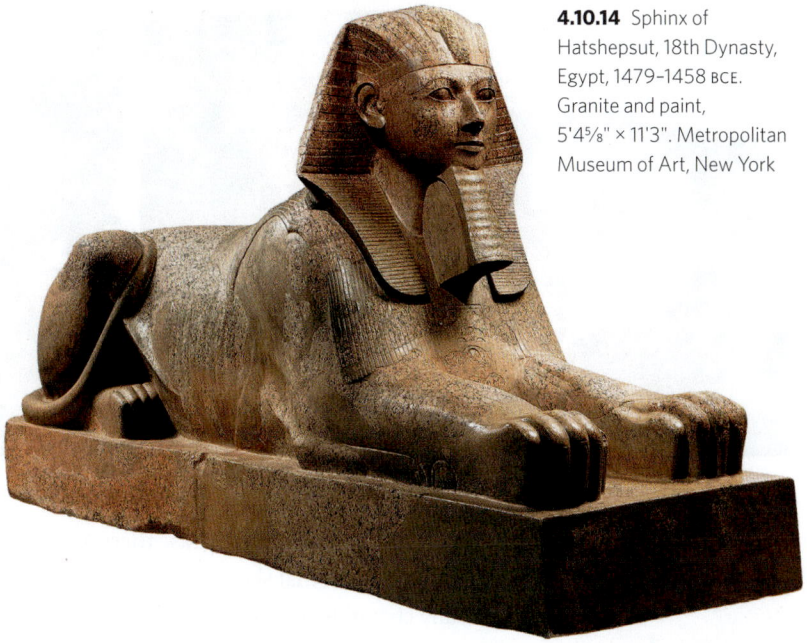

4.10.14 Sphinx of Hatshepsut, 18th Dynasty, Egypt, 1479–1458 BCE. Granite and paint, 5'4⅝" × 11'3". Metropolitan Museum of Art, New York

For her *Projects* series, the Korean artist Nikki S. Lee (b. 1970) joined a number of different communities, from yuppies and tourists to Hispanics and senior citizens, shopping in the stores they frequented and adopting their mannerisms. Lee said, "My goal is not to become black, white, or Hispanic. It's more like becoming an Asian person who really likes that culture." Once she felt she had become a genuine member of the group, she had a snapshot self-portrait of herself taken with her new peers. For her *Seniors Project* of 1999, Lee used a makeup artist and so thoroughly convinced her elderly acquaintances that they considered her story about being an artist to be a sign of her senility (**4.10.15**, p. 670). Similarly, for the *Hip Hop Project* in 2001, Lee went to a tanning salon three times a week to darken her skin, and then immersed herself in the subculture of the hip hop music scene (**4.10.16**, p. 670); although she told the people in the close-knit group depicted in this image that she was an artist, most of them did not believe her. It is surprising to learn that her interaction with

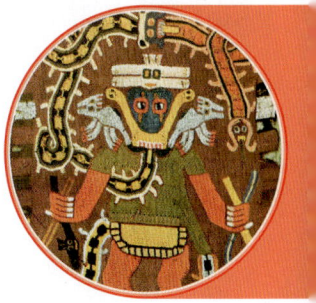

Traditional weavers in the Andes were able to create complex designs in their tapestries. In this example, the identity of the figure, probably a shaman in the process of transformation, is ambiguous because of its complexity and connections to both humans and animals: see **3.4.3, p. 431**

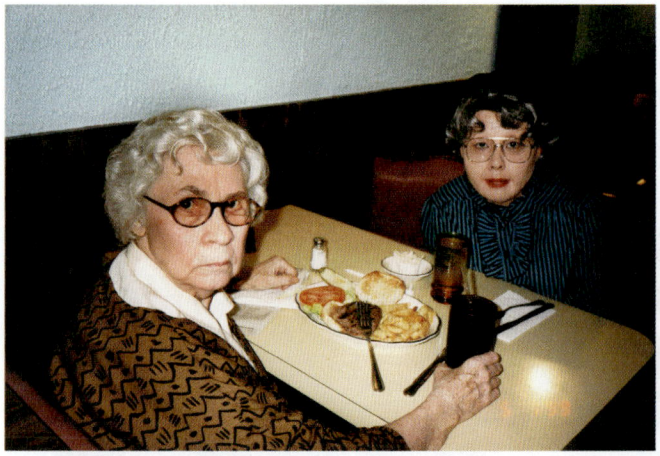

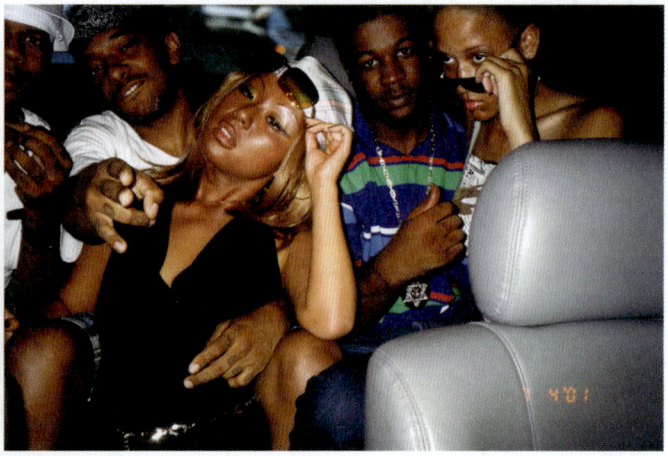

4.10.15 (above left) Nikki S. Lee, *Seniors Project*, 1999. Fujiflex print

4.10.16 (above right) Nikki S. Lee, *Hip Hop Project (25)*, 2001. Fujiflex print

these people is temporary, because there are no clues to suggest that she is not one of them. Radically changing her clothes and physical presentation allowed Lee to explore the variety of cultures she experienced in the US, which starkly contrasted with the homogeneity of South Korean culture. Such guises as the ones in *Projects* also become borrowed personalities for Lee, who considers her identity to be very fluid.

American artist Catherine Opie (b. 1961) uses photography to investigate the nuances of gender and identity. Her pictures include studio portraits of her lesbian friends dressed in leather or wearing false facial hair, staged depictions of radical performance artists, high school football games, and landscapes. Opie created her *Domestic* series while traveling across the US in order to photograph lesbian couples, such as Melissa and Lake, in their everyday settings (**4.10.17**). This photograph accentuates some of the similarities in the couple's appearance, such as their short haircuts with bangs. The point of the picture, however, is their bond, not their gender or sexual identity. Opie's portraits, by highlighting the lesbian community, introduce some viewers to new ways of life. They remind others that the familiar people, places, and things we see each day can be thought of in new ways. Such pictures are not about difference, they are celebrations of individuality.

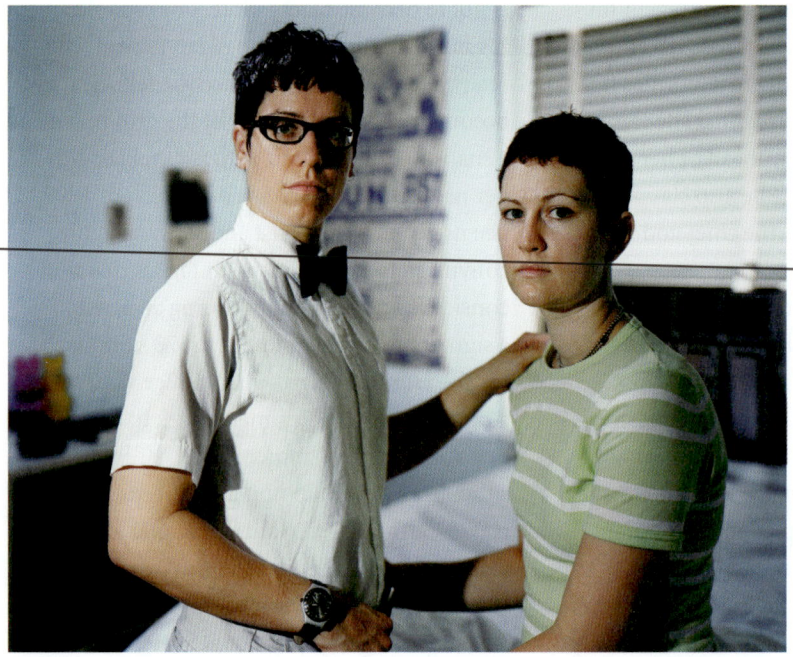

4.10.17 Catherine Opie, "Melissa & Lake, Durham, North Carolina," from *Domestic* series, 1998. Chromogenic print, 40 × 50"

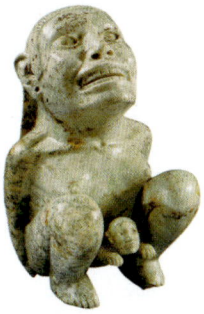

4.3.1 Tlazolteotl giving birth to the maize god, Aztec, c. 1500, p. 591

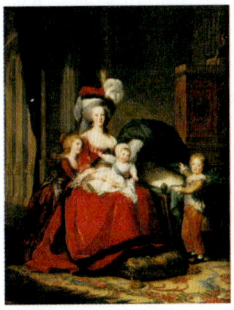

4.6.8 Elisabeth Louise Vigée Le Brun, *Marie Antoinette and Her Children*, 1787, p. 633

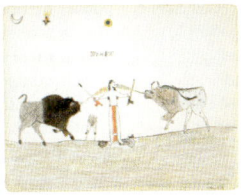

3.4.22 Wo-Haw, *Wo-Haw between Two Worlds*, c. 1875–77, p. 442

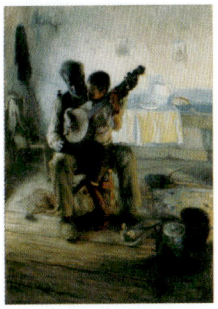

3.8.20 Henry Ossawa Tanner, *Banjo Lesson*, 1893, p. 517

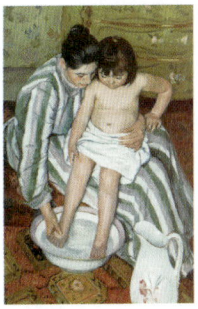

3.8.11 Mary Cassatt, *The Child's Bath*, 1893, p. 510

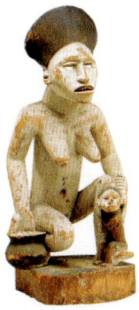

4.3.9 Kneeling female figure, Yombe, late 19th/ early 20th century, p. 598

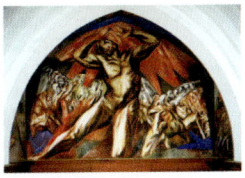

2.2.7 José Clemente Orozco, *Prometheus*, 1930, p. 213

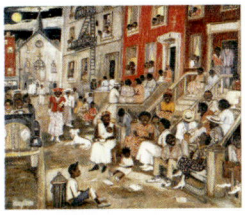

1.10.6 Palmer Hayden, *Midsummer Night in Harlem*, 1936, p. 177

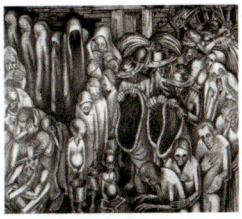

2.1.4 John Biggers, *Night of the Poor*, preparatory study, 1949, p. 195

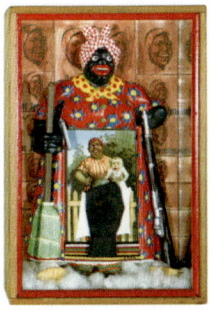

2.4.19 Betye Saar, *The Liberation of Aunt Jemima*, 1972, p. 254

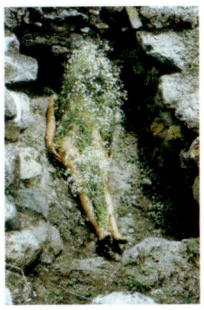

3.10.4 Ana Mendieta, "Untitled" (*Silueta* series, Mexico), 1973–80, p. 548

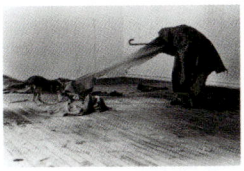

2.10.5 Joseph Beuys, *Coyote, I Like America and America Likes Me*, May 1974, p. 354

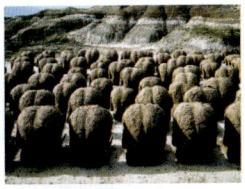

1.10.7 Magdalena Abakanowicz, *80 Backs*, 1976–80, p. 178

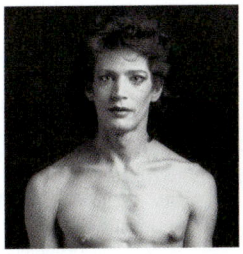

1.10.9 Robert Mapplethorpe, *Self-Portrait (#385)*, 1980, p. 180

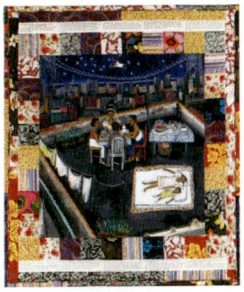

2.6.17 Faith Ringgold, *Tar Beach*, 1988, p. 295

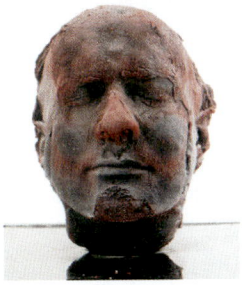

0.0.16 Marc Quinn, *Self*, 1991, p. 32

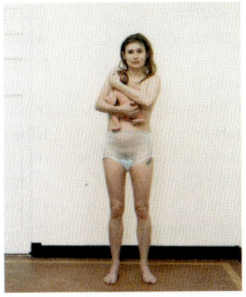

4.3.2 Rineke Dijkstra, "Julie, Den Haag...," from the *Mothers* series, 1994, p. 592

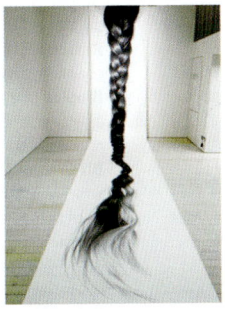

2.1.12 Zhang Chun Hong, *Life Strands*, 2004, p. 199

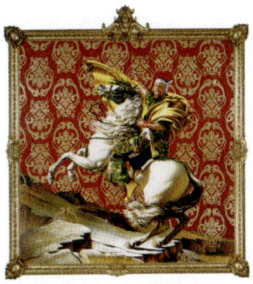

4.6.3a Kehinde Wiley, *Napoleon Leading the Army...*, 2005, p. 630

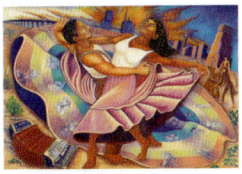

2.2.27 Judith F. Baca, *Danza de la Tierra*, 2008, p. 224

Glossary

NOTE: *A few terms have more than one definition, depending on the context in which they are used.*

2-D side-scrolling game: gameplay is seen from a side-view camera angle with onscreen characters generally moving left to right and backgrounds made up of scrolling graphics
3-D modeling: a computer-generated illusion that emulates an object in three dimensions; it can be modified to show visual movement

A-frame: an ancient form of structural support, made out of beams arranged so that the shape of the building resembles a capital letter A
Abstract: (1) art imagery that departs from recognizable images of the natural world; (2) an artwork the form of which is simplified, distorted, or exaggerated in appearance
Abstraction: the degree to which an image is altered from an easily recognizable subject
Abstract Expressionism: a mid-twentieth-century artistic style characterized by its capacity to convey intense emotions using non-representational images
Academies: institutions training artists in both the theory of art and practical techniques
Action painting: application of paint to canvas by dripping, splashing, or smearing that emphasizes the artist's gestures
Actual line: a continuous, uninterrupted line
Acrylic: a liquid polymer, or plastic, which is used as a binder for pigment in acrylic paint
Additive (sculpture): a sculpting process in which the artist builds a form by adding material
Additive color: the colors produced from light
Additive color process: creates colors by mixing RGB colors on a screen to create a direct positive print; same principle used in LED, LCD, plasma, and CRT video screens
Aesthetic: related to beauty, art, and taste
Afterimage effect: when the eye sees the complementary color of something that the viewer has spent an extended time viewing (also known as successive contrast)
Aisles: in a basilica or other church, the spaces between the columns of the nave and the side walls
Alloy: a mixture of a metal combined with at least one other element
Altar: an area where sacrifices or offerings are made
Altarpiece: an artwork that is placed behind an altar in a church
Ambulatory: a covered walkway, particularly around the apse of a church
American Scene: naturalistic style of painting in the US from the 1920s to 1950s that celebrated American themes, locations, and virtues
***Amphora*:** a type of pot used to carry and store such goods as wine or olive oil
Analog: photography or movie made using a film camera that chemically records images using a continuous gradation of value ranges from light to dark so that they directly match the actual appearance of the object or scene
Analogous colors: colors adjacent to each other on the color wheel
Anamorphosis: the distorted representation of an object so that it appears correctly proportioned only when viewed from one particular position
Animation: genre of film made using stop-motion, hand-drawn, or digitally produced still images set into motion by showing them in sequence
Appropriation: the deliberate incorporation in an artwork of material originally created by other artists
Apse: semicircular vaulted space in a church
Aquatint: an intaglio printmaking process that uses melted rosin or spray paint to create an acid-resistant ground
Aqueduct: a structure designed to carry water, often over long distances
Arabesque: an abstract pattern derived from geometric and vegetal lines and forms
Arcade: a series of connected arches
Archaeology: the study of human history and prehistory by excavating sites of habitation to analyse artifacts and other cultural remains
Archaic: Greek art of the period c. 620–480 BCE
Arches: structures, usually curved, that span an opening
Architectural order: a style of designing columns and related parts of a Greek or Roman building
Architrave: a beam that rests on the top of a row of columns
Armature: a framework or skeleton used to support a sculpture
Armory Show: exhibition in 1913 in New York City that introduced America to Modernist European abstraction; continues as an annual international exhibition
Art Nouveau: French for "new art," a visual style of the late nineteenth and early twentieth century, characterized by organic flowing lines, simulating forms in nature and involving decorative pattern
Artifact: an object made by a person
Artist's book: a book produced by an artist, usually an expensive limited edition, often using specialized printing processes
Ascetic: austerely simple; rigorously abstaining from pleasure or material satisfaction
Assemblage: artwork made of three-dimensional materials, including found objects
Asymmetry: a type of design in which balance is achieved by elements that contrast and complement one another without being the same on either side of an axis
Atmospheric perspective: use of shades of color and clarity to create the illusion of depth. Closer objects have warmer tones and clear outlines, while objects set further away are cooler and become hazy
Atrium: a central, normally public, interior space, first used in Roman houses
Auteur theory/auteur films: from the French word for "author," refers to films that notably reflect the director's creative vision above other criteria
Autochrome: early additive color photography process patented by the Lumière brothers in 1904 and primarily used from 1907 to the 1930s
Automatic: suppressing conscious control to access subconscious sources of creativity and truth
Avant-garde: early twentieth-century emphasis on artistic innovation, which challenged accepted values, traditions, and techniques
Axis: an imaginary line showing the center of a shape, volume, or composition

Background: the part of a work depicted furthest from the viewer's space, often behind the main subject matter
Balance: a principle of art in which elements are used to create a symmetrical or asymmetrical sense of visual weight in an artwork
Balustrade: a railing supported by short pillars
Baroque: European artistic and architectural style of the late sixteenth to early eighteenth century, characterized by extravagance and emotional intensity
Bas-relief (low relief): a sculpture carved with very little depth: the carved subjects rise only slightly above the surface of the work
Base: the projecting series of blocks between the shaft of a column and the surface where it rests
Basilica: an early Christian church, either converted from or built to resemble a type of Roman civic building
Bauhaus: design school founded in Weimar, Germany, in 1919
Ben-Day dots: technique used in printing to create gradations and suggest a range of tones; named for its inventor
Binder: a substance that makes pigments adhere to a surface
Bioart: art that is created with living, changing organisms
Biopic: movie that tells the story of a person's life, often filling in facts with narration and plotlines
Bird's-eye view: an artistic technique in which a scene or subject is presented from some point above it
Bisqueware: a ceramic form that has been fired but not glazed or that has not received other surface finishing
Bohemian: derived from the gypsies of the former Czech Kingdom of Bohemia who moved around; a wanderer; an artist or writer who functions outside the bounds of conventional rules and practices
Boldface: a darker and heavier typeface than its normal instance
Bust: a statue of a person depicting only his or her head and shoulders
Byzantine: relating to the East Roman empire, centered on Constantinople (modern-day Istanbul) from the fifth century CE to 1453

Calligraphy: the art of emotive or carefully descriptive hand lettering or handwriting
Canon of proportions: a set of ideal mathematical ratios in art, used to measure the various parts of the human body in relation to one another
Cantilever: a long support that projects out from a structure beyond a support
Capital: the architectural feature that crowns a column
Cardinal points: North, South, East, and West
Cartoon: full-scale drawing
Cast: a sculpture or artwork made by pouring a liquid (for example molten metal or plaster) into a mold
Catacombs: an underground system of tunnels used for burying and commemorating the dead
Celluloid: tough, transparent plastic used to make motion-picture film, photographic film, and X-rays; until relatively recently most movies were filmed on celluloid
Central-plan church: church design, often in the shape of a cross with all four arms of equal length
Ceramic: fire-hardened clay, often painted, and normally sealed with a shiny protective coating
Ceramist: a person who makes ceramics
CGI: computer-generated imagery
Chasing: a technique of hammering the front of a metal object to create a form or surface detail
Chiaroscuro: the use of light and dark in a painting to create the impression of volume
Chilkat: traditional form of weaving practiced by Tlingit and other Northwest Coast peoples of Alaska and British Columbia
Choir: part of a church traditionally reserved for singers and clergy, situated between the nave and the apse
Chroma (also known as **Saturation**): the degree of purity of a color
Chromogenic prints (c-prints): most widespread color process until digital prints; dyes couple with developers to create a negative image, reversed to make positive prints
Cibachrome: dye-destruction process for making direct positive photographic images available in the 1960s
Circumambulate: the act of walking around a sacred object
Classical: (1) Greek art of the period c. 480–323 BCE; (2) ancient Greek and Roman; art that conforms to Greek and Roman models, or is based on rational construction and emotional equilibrium

Classical period: a period in the history of Greek art, c. 480–323 BCE
Clerestory windows: a row of windows high up in a church to admit light into the nave
Cloud (or **the Cloud**)**:** can refer to any electronic network; generally refers to shared resources on the Internet rather than local servers or devices for storage and computer applications
CMYK: the primary colors used in inkjet printing: cyan, magenta, blue, and key (black)
Coffered: decorated with recessed paneling
Coiling: (1) the use of long coils of clay—rather than a wheel—to build the walls of a pottery vessel; (2) basket-weaving technique using a central foundation that is spiraled or coiled, and wrapped with another fiber that is stitched back into the previous row
Collage: a work of art assembled by gluing materials, often paper, onto a surface. From the French *coller*, to glue
Collagraphy, collagraphic, collagraph: a type of relief print that is created by building up or collaging material on or to a stiff surface, inking that surface, then printing
Collodion (wet plate) process: black-and-white darkroom photography process invented by Frederick Scott Archer in 1850–51 and popular until the 1880s
Color: the optical effect caused when reflected white light of the spectrum is divided into separate wavelengths
Color Field painting: branch of Abstract Expressionism focusing on non-objective abstractions
Color theory: the understanding of how colors relate to each other, especially when mixed or placed near one another
Column: freestanding pillar, usually circular in section
Complementary colors: colors opposite one another on the color wheel
Composite view: representation of a subject from multiple viewpoints at one time
Composition: the overall design or organization of a work
Conceptual art: a work in which the communication of an idea or group of ideas are most important to the work
Concrete: a hard, strong, and versatile construction material made up of powdered lime, sand, and rubble
Constructivism: an art movement in the Soviet Union in the 1920s, primarily concerned with making art that supports the working class
Content: the meaning, message, or feeling expressed in a work of art
Context: Circumstances surrounding the creation of a work of art, including historical events, social conditions, biographical facts about the artist, and his or her intentions
Continuous narrative: when different parts of a story are shown within the same visual space
Contour: the outline that defines a form
Contour rivalry: a design in which the lines can be read in more than one way at the same time, depending on the angle from which it is viewed
Contrapposto: a pose in sculpture in which the upper part of the body twists in one direction and the lower part in another
Contrast: a drastic difference between such elements as color or value (lightness/darkness) when they are presented together
Convention: a widely accepted way of doing something; using a particular style, following a certain method, or representing something in a specific way
Convex: curved outward, like the exterior of a sphere
Corbeled: with a series of corbels—architectural feature made of stone, brick, wood, etc.—each projecting beyond the one below
Cornice: horizontally projecting molding round the top of a building
Cor-ten steel: a type of steel that forms a coating of rust that protects it from the weather and further corrosion
Cropping: trimming the edges of an image, or composing it so that part of the subject matter is cut off
Cross-hatching: the use of overlapping parallel lines to convey darkness or lightness
Cubism, Cubist: twentieth-century movement and style in art, especially painting, in which perspective with a single viewpoint was abandoned and use was made of simple geometric shapes, interlocking planes, and, later, collage; the Cubists were artists who formed part of the movement. "Cubist" is also used to describe their style of painting
Cuneiform: a form of writing from ancient Mesopotamia that uses wedge shapes
Cyanotype: photographic process using light-sensitive iron salts that oxidize and produce a brilliant blue color where light penetrates and remain white where light is blocked; a variant of this process was used historically to copy architectural drawings

Dada: anarchic anti-art and anti-war movement, dating back to World War I, that reveled in absurdity and irrationality
Decorative: intentionally making an artwork pleasant or attractive
Deify: to worship and make into a god or goddess
Deposition: a scene showing the removal of Christ's body from the cross
Der Blaue Reiter: ("The Blue Rider") German Expressionist movement (1911–14) in Munich; used abstract forms to suggest spiritual content as a contrast to the corruption and materialism of the times
De Stijl: a group of artists originating in the Netherlands in the early twentieth century, associated with a utopian style of design that emphasized primary colors and straight lines
Developer: after an image has been recorded on light-sensitive film or photographic paper (usually in a camera), immersion in this liquid substance chemically transforms a latent (or invisible) image into a visible one
Diagonal: a line that runs obliquely, rather than horizontally or vertically
Didactic: with the aim of teaching or educating
Die Brücke: ("The Bridge") German Expressionist movement of painters and printmakers formed in Dresden (1905–13) with the aim of defying anything Classical and using art as a bridge between the past, present, and a utopian future
Dissonance: a lack of harmony
Documentary: non-fiction films based on actual people, settings, and events
Dome: an evenly curved vault forming the ceiling or roof of a building
Door jamb: vertical sections, often containing sculpture, that form the sides of a portal
Drypoint: an intaglio printmaking process where the artist raises a burr when gouging the printing plate
Dubbing: post-production addition or mixing of voices (or sounds) that do not belong to the original recording

Earthworks: artworks made using the earth or natural elements; typically situated outdoors, most people experience earthworks only through photographs
Edition: all the copies of a print made from a single printing
Elements of art: the basic vocabulary of art—line, shape, form, volume, mass, texture, value (lightness/darkness), space, color, and motion and time
Embroidery: decorative stitching generally made with colored thread applied to the surface of a fabric
Emphasis: the principle of drawing attention to particular content within a work
En plein air: French for "in the open air"; used to describe painting out of doors from start to finish rather than working in a studio for all or part of the process
Encaustic: a painting medium that primarily uses wax, usually beeswax, as the binding agent
Engraving: a printmaking technique where the artist gouges or scratches the image into the surface of the printing plate
Enlightenment: an intellectual movement in eighteenth-century Europe that argued for science, reason, and individualism. Challenging received ideas passed down by tradition, the Enlightenment also promoted the notion of equal rights for all men
Entablature: the part of a Greek or Roman building that rests on top of a column
Entasis: the slight swelling or bulge at the midpoint of a column
Epic: style or genre in film/television that focuses on grand-scale storytelling with dramatic music, elaborate costumes, and high production value; may use historical events or people but does not focus on historical accuracy
Etching: an intaglio printmaking process that uses acid to bite (or etch) the engraved design into the printing surface
Expressionism, Expressionist: an artistic style, at its height in 1920s Europe, devoted to representing subjective emotions and experiences instead of objective or external reality
Expressionistic: devoted to representing subjective emotions and experiences instead of objective or external reality
Expressive: capable of stirring the emotions of the viewer

Facade: any side of a building, usually the front or entrance
Faience: quartz or sand ground and heated to create a shiny, glasslike material
Fantasy: fiction genre set in an imaginary universe; often uses magical or supernatural elements in the plots, themes, or settings
Fauves, Fauvism: early twentieth-century art movement that emphasized bold, exaggerated colors and simplified forms to favor creative expression over accuracy. Fauves, "wild beast," were artists working in this style
Figurative: art that portrays items perceived in the visible world, especially human or animal forms
Figure–ground reversal: the reversal of the relationship between one shape (the figure) and its background (the ground), so that the figure becomes background and the ground becomes the figure
Firing: heating ceramic, glass, or enamel objects in a kiln, to harden them, fuse the components, or fuse a glaze to the surface
Fixing : the chemical process used to ensure a photographic image becomes permanent
Flashback: transition to an earlier time in a story that disrupts chronological order of events
Flint: an object or tool made from the very hard, sharp-edged stone of the same name
Flying buttress: an arch built on the exterior of a building that transfers some of the weight of the vault
Focal point: (1) the center of interest or activity in a work of art, often drawing the viewer's attention to the most important element; (2) the area in a composition to which the eye returns most naturally
Foreground: the part of a work depicted as nearest to the viewer
Foreshortening: a perspective technique that depicts a form—often distorting or reducing it—at an angle that is not parallel to the picture plane, in order to convey the illusion of depth
Form: an object that can be defined in three dimensions (height, width, and depth)
Formal: in art, refers to the visual elements and principles in a work
Format: the shape of the area an artist uses for making a two-dimensional artwork
Found image or **object:** an image or object found by an artist and presented, with little or no alteration, as part of a work or as a finished work of art
Frame: a single image from the sequence that makes up a motion picture; on average, a 90-minute film contains 129,600 separate frames
Freestanding: any sculpture that stands separate from walls or other surfaces so

that it can be viewed from a 360-degree range
Fresco: a technique in which the artist paints onto freshly applied plaster. From the Italian *fresco*, "fresh"
Frieze: the strip that goes around the top of a building, often filled with sculptural ornamentation
Frontispiece: an illustration facing the title-page of a book
Futurism, Futurist: an artistic movement originating in Italy in 1909 that violently rejected traditional forms in favor of celebrating and incorporating into art the energy and dynamism of modern technology; Futurists were artists working in this style

Gelatin silver print process (or **silver gelatin**): process for making glossy black-and- white photographic prints in the darkroom based on silver halide gelatin emulsions
Gèlèdé ritual: ritual performed in Nigeria's Yoruba society to celebrate and honor women
Genre: (1) category of artistic subject matter, often with a strongly influential history and tradition; (2) in painting, scenes that depict everyday life
Geometric: predictable and mathematical
Geometric form: three-dimensional form composed of predictable and mathematically derived planes and curves
Gestalt: complete order and indivisible unity of all aspects of an artwork's design
GIF (graphics interchange format): compressed image file type to reduce transfer time
Glazing: in oil painting, adding a transparent layer of paint to achieve a richness in texture, volume, and form
Golden Section: a unique ratio of a line divided into two segments so that the sum of both segments (a + b) is to the longer segment (a) as the longer segment (a) is to the shorter segment (b). The result is 1:1.618
Gothic: Western European architectural style of the twelfth to sixteenth century, characterized by the use of pointed arches and ornate decoration
Gouache: a type of paint medium in which pigments are bound with gum and a white filler added (for example, clay) to produce a paint that is used for opaque watercolor
Graffiti: markings that are scratched, scribbled, or sprayed on a wall without the consent of the owner
Grand Tour: a trip for the cultured and wealthy to study Classical and Renaissance artworks and culture found mostly in Italy
Graphic design: the use of images, typography, and technology to communicate ideas for a client or to a particular audience
Greenware: a clay form that has been shaped and dried, but not yet fired to become ceramic
Grid: a network of horizontal and vertical lines; in an artwork's composition, the lines are implied
Grisaille: painting in gray or grayish monochrome, either as a base or underpainting for the finished work, or as the final artwork itself
Groin vault: an architectural feature created by the intersection of two vaults
Ground: the surface or background onto which an artist paints or draws
Guilds: medieval associations of artists, craftsmen, or tradesmen

Hand-tint: early process for adding color to monochrome photographic products by adding pigment in a manner very much like painting
Happening: impromptu art actions, initiated and planned by an artist, the outcome of which is not known in advance
Harlem Renaissance: movement in literature, music, and the visual arts from the end of WWI into the 1930s celebrating black experience and culture
Hatching: the use of non-overlapping parallel lines to convey darkness or lightness
Hellenistic: Greek art of the period c. 323–100 BCE
Hemispherical: having half the form of a spherical shape divided into identical, symmetrical parts
Hierarchical scale: the use of size to denote the relative importance of subjects in an artwork
Hieroglyph: written language involving sacred characters that may be pictures as well as letters or signifiers of sounds
High relief: a carved panel where the figures project with a great deal of depth from the background
Highlight: an area of lightest value in a work
Historical drama: based on real-life events or time periods; can be factual or fictionalized
Hue: general classification of a color; the distinctive characteristics of a color as seen in the visible spectrum, such as green or red
Humanism, humanist: the study of such subjects as history, philosophy, languages, and literature, particularly in relation to those of ancient Greece and Rome

Icon: religious image venerated by believers
Iconic: Possessing established and widely recognizable characteristics
Iconoclasm: the destruction of images or artworks, often out of religious belief
Iconoclast: someone who destroys images, often out of religious belief
Iconographic analysis: the study of art by interpreting symbols, themes, and subject matter as sources of meaning
Ideal: more beautiful, harmonious, or perfect than reality; or exists as an idea
Idealism: elevating depictions of nature to achieve more beautiful, harmonious, and perfect depictions
Idealized: represented as perfect in form or character, corresponding to an ideal
Illuminated characters: highly decorated letters, usually found at the beginning of a page or paragraph
Illuminated manuscript: a hand-lettered text with hand-drawn pictures
Illuminations: illustrations and decorations in a manuscript
Illusionism, Illusionistic: the artistic skill or trick of making something look real
IMAX: "Image Maximum," a format for film presentation that allows presentation of films at ten times larger sizes than the conventional one
Impasto: paint applied in thick layers
Implied line: a line not actually drawn but suggested by elements in the work
Implied texture: a visual illusion expressing texture
Impression: an individual print, or pull, from a printing press
Impressionism: a late nineteenth-century painting style conveying the impression of the effects of light; Impressionists were painters working in this style
Incised: cut
***In situ*:** in the location for which it was originally made
In the round: a freestanding sculpted work that can be viewed from all sides
Installation: originally referring to the hanging of pictures and arrangement of objects in an exhibition, installation may also refer to an intentional environment created as a completed artwork
Intaglio: any print process where the inked image is lower than the surface of the printing plate; from the Italian for "cut into"
Intarsia: the art of setting pieces of wood into a surface to create a pattern
Intensity: the relative clarity of color in its purest raw form, demonstrated through luminous or muted variations
Intercessor: one who pleads with God on behalf of others.
Isometric perspective: a system using diagonal parallel lines to communicate depth

Ka: in Egyptian belief, the spirit of a person that leaves the body upon death and travels to the afterlife
***Kente* cloth:** well-known African textile made from silk and cotton fabric, consisting of interwoven strips of cloth; native to the Akan group in Ghana
Key-frame animation: technique in which an animator creates important frames in the sequence, and software fills in the gaps
Kinetic art/sculpture: three-dimensional art that moves, impelled by air currents, motors, or people
Kodachrome: Created by Kodak Research Laboratories, Kodachrome is a subtractive reversal process for making color photographic film slides
***Krater*:** a container for mixing wine with water, into which cups can then be dipped to ladle out the diluted wine for drinking

Lapis lazuli: bright-blue semiprecious stone containing sodium aluminum silicate and sulphur
Line: a mark, or implied mark, between two endpoints
Linear outline: a line that clearly separates a figure from its surroundings
Linear perspective: a system using converging imaginary sight lines to create the illusion of depth
Lintel: the horizontal beam over the doorway of a portal
Literati: Chinese scholar-painters who created expressive paintings rather than formal academic works
Lithography, lithographic: a print process done on a flat, unmarred surface, such as a stone, in which the image is created using oil-based ink with resistance to water
Logo: a graphic image used to identify an idea or entity
Low relief: carving in which the design stands out only slightly from the background surface
Luminosity: a bright, glowing quality

Mandala: a sacred diagram of the universe, often involving a square and a circle
Mandorla: an almond-shaped light that surrounds a holy person, somewhat like a halo
Mannerism: from Italian *di maniera*, meaning charm, grace, playfulness; mid- to late sixteenth-century style of painting, usually with elongated human figures elevating grace as an ideal
Manuscripts: handwritten texts
Mask: in spray painting or silkscreen printing, a barrier the shape of which blocks the paint or ink from passing through
Masquerade: performance in which participants wear masks and costumes for a ritual or cultural purpose
Mass: a volume that has, or gives the illusion of having, weight, density, and bulk
Matrix: an origination point, such as a woodblock, from which a print is derived
Medieval: relating to the Middle Ages; roughly, between the fall of the Roman empire and the start of the Renaissance
Medium (plural **media**): the material on or from which an artist chooses to make a work of art
Memento mori: Latin phrase that means "remember that you must die." In artworks, such symbols as skulls, flowers, and clocks are used to represent the transient nature of life on Earth
Mesoamerican: an archaeological term referring to people or objects from the area now occupied by Mexico and Central America
Metope: a square space between triglyphs, often decorated with sculpture
Mezzotint: an intaglio print-making process based on roughening the entire printing plate to accept ink; the artist smoothes non-image areas
Middle-ground: the part of a work between the foreground and the background
***Mihrab*:** a niche in a mosque that is in a wall oriented toward Mecca
Minaret: a tall slender tower, particularly on a mosque, from which the faithful are called to prayer
Minbar: a platform in a mosque, from which a leader delivers sermons
Minimalism, Minimalist: a mid-twentieth-century artistic style that references industrial production modes

through materials and seriality, often with unified arrangements of geometric shapes and massive forms that become part of the viewer's space
Mirror writing: writing that reads correctly only when reflected in a mirror, as in the case of the journals and other writings of Leonardo da Vinci
Mixed media: the use of a variety of materials to make a work of art
Mobile: suspended moving sculptures, usually impelled by natural air currents
Modeling: the representation of three-dimensional objects in two dimensions so that they appear solid
Modernist, Modernism: a radically new twentieth-century art and architectural movement that embraced modern industrial materials and a machine aesthetic
Monochromatic: having one or more values of one color
Monolith: a monument or sculpture made from a single piece of stone
Monumental: having massive or impressive scale
Mosaic: a picture or pattern created by fixing together small pieces of stone, glass, tile, etc.
Motif: (1) a design or color repeated as a unit in a pattern; (2) a distinctive visual element, the recurrence of which is often characteristic of an artist's work
Motion: the effect of changing placement in time
Motion capture ("mo-cap" or performance capture): technology developed to animate CGI characters by translating into a digital performance the live, exact motions of people or objects, using specially designed suits or equipment with sensors
Murals: performance in which participants wear masks and costumes for a ritual or cultural purpose
Musical: genre of film in which the story is told through song, usually combined with dialogue and dancing

Narrative: an artwork that tells a story
Naturalism: a very realistic or lifelike style of making images
Nave: the central space of a cathedral or basilica
Negative: a reversed image, in which light areas are dark and dark areas are light (opposite of a positive)
Negative space: an unoccupied or empty space that is created after positive shapes are positioned in a work of art
Neoclassicism: European style that flourished during the late eighteenth and early nineteenth centuries, characterized by an extreme interest in the Classical world, strictly ordered scenes, and heroic subjects
Neo-Expressionist : a broad term, first used in the late 1970s to early 1980s; describes figurative and allegorical, not totally abstract, art with materials used aggressively to give clear evidence of the artist's gestures
Neutral: colors (such as blacks, whites, grays, and dull gray-browns) made by mixing complementary hues
New Wave design: A design movement that exemplified the counter cultural currents of the 1980s
Nkisi nkondi (plural ***minkisi minkondi***)**:** combines the words for "sacred medicine" and "to hunt"; figurative sculpture(s) used in rituals by the Yombe of Nigeria
Non-objective, non-objectivity: art that does not depict a recognizable subject
Nude: an artistic representation of an unclothed human figure, emphasizing the body's form rather than its exposure

Ocher: a pigment found in nature containing hydrated iron oxide
Oculus: a round opening at the center of a dome
Oil paint: paint made of pigment suspended in oil
One-point perspective: a perspective system with a single vanishing point on the horizon
Op art: a style of art that exploits the physiology of seeing in order to create illusory optical effects
Opaque: not transparent
Optical mixture: when the eye blends two colors that are placed near one another, creating a new color
Organic: having irregular forms and shapes, as though derived from living organisms
Organic form: three-dimensional form made up of unpredictable, irregular planes that suggest the natural world
Orthogonals: in perspective systems, imaginary sightlines extending from forms to the vanishing point
Outline: the outermost line or implied line of an object or figure, by which it is defined or bounded

Pace: speed at which something moves; rhythmic flow of dialog or action related to an overall scene or sequence
Painterly: a loosely executed style in which paint and brushstrokes are evident
Palette (1) the range of colors used by an artist; (2) a smooth slab or board used for mixing paints or cosmetics
Passion: the arrest, trial, and execution of Jesus Christ, and his sufferings during them
Patina: surface color or texture on a metal caused by ageing
Patron: an organization or individual who sponsors the creation of works of art
Pattern: an arrangement of predictably repeated elements
Pedestal: a base upon which a statue or column rests
Pediment: the triangular space, situated above the row of columns, on the facade of a building in the Classical style
Pendentive: a curving triangular surface that links a dome to a square space below
Performance art: a work involving the human body, usually including the artist, for an audience
Personification: representation of a thing, an idea, or an abstract quality, such as "freedom," as a person or in human form
Perspective: the creation of the illusion of depth in a two-dimensional image by using mathematical principles
Photomontage: a single photographic image that combines (digitally or using multiple film exposures) several separate images
Photorealist: a style of art that began in the 1960s and involves the artist creating artworks that resemble, and were inspired by, photographs
Pictograph: picture used as a symbol in writing
Picture plane: (1) the surface of a painting or drawing; (2) the transparent division between the space depicted by the artist and the real space in which the viewer is placed
Piece-mold casting: a process for casting metal objects in which a mold is broken into several pieces that are then reassembled into a final sculpture
Pigment: the colorant in art materials. Often made from finely ground minerals
Pilaster: a vertical element, rectangular in shape, that provides architectural support for crossing horizontal elements in post-and-lintel construction; also used for decoration
Plane: a flat, two-dimensional surface on which an artist can create a drawing or painting. Planes can also be implied in a composition by areas that face toward, parallel to, or away from a light source
Planography: a print process—lithography and silkscreen printing—where the inked image area and non-inked areas are at the same height
Plastic, plasticity: referring to materials that are soft and can be manipulated, or to such properties in the materials
Pointed arches: arches with two curved sides that meet to form a point at the apex
Pointillism: a late nineteenth-century painting style using short strokes or points of differing colors that optically combine to form new perceived colors
Polymer: a chemical compound commonly referred to as plastic
Polytheism: the worship of more than one god or goddess
Pop art: mid-twentieth-century artistic movement inspired by commercial art forms and popular culture
Portal: an entrance. A royal portal (main entrance) is usually on the west front of a church and features sculpted forms of kings and queens
Portico: a roof supported by columns at the entrance to a building
Portrait: image of a person or animal, usually focusing on the face
Positive: an image in which light areas are light and dark areas are dark (opposite of a negative)
Positive–negative: the relationship between contrasting opposites
Post-and-lintel construction: a horizontal beam (the lintel) supported by a post at either end
Post-Impressionists: artists either from or living in France, c. 1885–1905, who moved away from the Impressionist style—notably Cézanne, Gauguin, Seurat, and Van Gogh
Postmodernism, Postmodernist: late twentieth-century movement in art, architecture, and criticism responding to Modernism (c. 1860–1960) with a distrust of grand narratives and questioning the very nature of art by acknowledging the constructed nature of reality and experience
Predella: the horizontal section on the bottom of a triptych altarpiece that often functions as a support or stand
Prehistoric: dating from the period of human existence before the invention of writing
Pre-Raphaelite Brotherhood: English art movement formed in 1848 by painters who rejected the academic rules of art, and often painted medieval subjects in a naïve style
Primary colors: three basic colors from which all others are derived
Principles: the principles, or "grammar" of art—contrast, unity, variety, balance, scale, proportion, focal point, emphasis, pattern, and rhythm—describe the ways the elements of art are arranged in an artwork
Print: a picture reproduced on paper, often in multiple copies
Prism: a transparent material with flat, polished surfaces—a form with at least three sides—that can be used to disperse light to reveal the range of color present in the visible spectrum
Profile: the outline of an object, especially a face or head, represented from the side
Propaganda: art that promotes an ideology or a cause
Proportion: the relationship in size between a work's individual parts and the whole
Psychology: a science that studies the nature, development, and operation of the human mind
Psychoanalysis: a method of treating mental illness by making conscious the patient's subconscious fears or fantasies
Puppet: figure in the form of an animal or person used for entertainment purposes that appears to move on its own but is actually controlled by a person's hand(s), strings, or another mechanism
Putto (plural **putti**)**:** a representation of a nude or scantily clad infant angel or boy, common in Renaissance and Baroque art
Pyramid: ancient structure, usually massive in scale, consisting of a square base with four sides that meet at a point or apex with each side forming a triangular shape

Quatrefoil: a symmetrical framework that has four lobes or leaves
Qibla: the direction to Mecca, toward which Muslims face when praying

Readymade: an everyday object presented as a work of art
Realism: nineteenth-century artistic style that aimed to depict nature and everyday subjects in an unidealized manner. "Realism" is also used to describe a historical movement from the same period, which tried to achieve social change and equality by highlighting, in art and literature, the predicament of the poor
Register: one of two or more horizontal sections into which a space is divided

in order to depict different episodes of a story

Regionalism: branch of American Scene painting that promoted rural, small-town virtues and values, especially related to the Deep South and Midwest US

Relative placement: the arrangement of shapes or lines to form a visual relationship to one another in a design

Relief: (1) a raised form on a largely flat background. For example, the design on a coin is "in relief"; (2) a print process where the inked image is higher than the non-printing areas

Renaissance: a period of cultural and artistic change in Europe from the fourteenth to the seventeenth century

Repatriation: return of cultural artifacts, often sacred remains, to their country of origin

Repoussé: a technique of hammering metal from the back to create a form or surface detail

Representation: the depiction of recognizable figures and objects

Representational: art that depicts figures and objects so that we recognize what is represented

RGB: additive system that mixes color based on the primary colors of light: red, green, and blue

Rhythm: the regular or ordered repetition of elements in the work

Rib vault: an arch-like structure supporting a ceiling or roof, with a web of protruding stonework

Rococo: an eighteenth-century style in France characterized by organic forms, ornate extravagance, and whimsy

Romanesque: an early medieval European style of architecture based on Roman-style rounded arches and heavy construction

Romantic/Romanticism: movement in nineteenth-century European culture, concerned with the power of the imagination and greatly valuing intense feeling

Rosin: a dry powdered resin that melts when heated, used in the aquatint process

Salon: an official exhibition of French painting, first held in 1667

Sand painting: also known as dry painting, a labor-intensive method of painting using colored grains of sand or other natural materials as the medium

Sarcophagus (plural **sarcophagi**): a coffin (usually made of stone or baked clay)

Sarsen: a type of hard, gray sandstone

Satire: work of art that exposes the weaknesses and mistakes of its subjects to ridicule

Saturation (also known as **Chroma**): the degree of purity of a color

Scale: the size of an object or artwork relative to another object or artwork, or to a system of measurement

Science-fiction (Sci-fi): genre of film in which fictional stories include advanced science and technology, often in futuristic settings

Secondary colors: colors mixed from two primary colors

Series: a group of related artworks that are created as a set

Serigraphy: printing that is achieved by creating a solid stencil in a porous screen and forcing ink through the screen onto the printing surface

Sfumato: in painting, the application of layers of translucent paint to create a hazy or smoky appearance and unify the composition

Shade: a color darker in value than its purest state

Shaft: the main vertical part of a column

Shaman: a priest or priestess regarded as having the ability to communicate directly with the spiritual world

Shape: a two-dimensional area, the boundaries of which are defined by lines or suggested by changes in color or value

Silhouette: a portrait or figure represented in outline and solidly colored in

Silkscreen: method of printmaking using a stencil and paint pushed through a screen

Sitter: person who poses, or "sits," for an artist to paint, sculpt, or photograph

Sketch: a rough preliminary version of a work or part of a work

SLR (single-lens reflex camera): hand-held digital or film camera that uses a mirror and prism system so the focus screen matches the image captured

Social Realism: branch of American Scene painting that focused on Depression-era social issues and hardships of daily life

Soft focus: deliberate blurring of the edges or lack of sharp focus in a photograph or movie

Space: the distance between identifiable points or planes

Span: the distance bridged between two supports, such as columns or walls

Stained glass: colored glass used for windows or decorative applications

Stela: upright stone slab decorated with inscriptions or pictorial relief carvings

Stencil: a perforated template allowing ink or paint to pass through to print a design

Stepped pyramid: a pyramid consisting of several rectangular structures placed one on top of another

Still life: a scene of inanimate objects, such as fruits, flowers, or dead animals

Stop-motion animation: figures, puppets, or dolls are photographed in a pose, moved very slightly, and then photographed again; the process is repeated until the desired sequence of movements has been acted out

Street art: art created in public spaces (examples include graffiti, posters, and stickers)

Stroboscopic motion: the effect created when we see two or more repeated images in quick succession in such a way that they visually to fuse together

Stucco: a coarse plaster designed to give the appearance of stone

Stupa: a burial mound containing Buddha's remains

Style: a characteristic way in which an artist or group of artists uses visual language to give a work an identifiable form of visual expression

Stylized: art that represents objects in an exaggerated way to emphasize certain aspects of the object

Stylobate: the uppermost platform of a Classical temple, on which the columns stand

Subject matter, subject: the person, object, or space depicted in a work of art

Sublime: feeling of awe or terror, provoked by the experience of limitless nature and the awareness of the smallness of an individual

Subordination: the opposite of emphasis; it draws our attention away from particular areas of a work

Subtractive (sculpture): the methodical removal of material to produce a sculptural form

Subtractive color: the colors produced from pigment

Subtractive color process: colors subtracted from white light by CMY dyes or pigments; in photography light-sensitive film or paper absorbs the opposite colors of cyan, magenta, and yellow dyes to create a negative image, reversed to make a positive print

Sunken relief: a carved panel where the figures are cut deeper into the stone than the background

Support: the material on which painting is done

Suprematism: Russian art movement of the early twentieth century focused on geometric shapes and limited colors that emphasized feeling over visual phenomena

Surreal: reminiscent of the Surrealist movement in the 1920s and later, whose art was inspired by dreams and the subconscious

Surrealism, Surrealist: an artistic movement in the 1920s and later; its works were inspired by dreams and the subconscious

Symbolism: using images or symbols in an artwork to convey meaning; often obvious when the work was made but requiring research for modern viewers to understand

Symbolist: artist or artistic style belonging to the movement in European art and literature, *c.* 1885–1910, that conveyed meaning by the use of powerful yet ambiguous symbols

Symmetrical balance: an image or shape that looks exactly (or nearly exactly) the same on both sides when cut in half

Symmetry: the correspondence in size, form, and arrangement of items on opposite sides of a plane, line, or point that creates direct visual balance

Syncretism: the blending of multiple religious or philosophical beliefs

Synesthesia: when one of the five senses perceives something that was stimulated by a trigger from one of the other senses

Tableau: a stationary scene arranged for artistic impact

Tapestry: hand-woven fabric—usually silk or wool—with a non-repeating, usually figurative, design woven into it

Tattoos: designs marked on the body by injecting dye under the skin

Tempera: fast-drying painting medium made from pigment mixed with water-soluble binder, such as egg yolk

Temperature: a description of color based on our associations with warmth or coolness

Temporal art: an artist's image or action that is transitory, existing in a passage of time

Tenebrism: dramatic use of intense darkness and light to heighten the impact of a painting

Terra-cotta: iron-rich clay, fired at a low temperature, which is traditionally brownish-orange in color

Tertiary colors: colors that can be mixed from a secondary and a primary color

Tesserae: small pieces of stone or glass or other materials used to make a mosaic

Texture: the surface quality of a work, for example fine/coarse, detailed/lacking in detail

Three-dimensional: having height, width, and depth

Three-point perspective: a perspective system with two vanishing points on the horizon and one not on the horizon

Throwing: the process of making a ceramic object on a potter's wheel

Tint: a color lighter in value than its purest state

Tone: a color that is weaker than its brightest, or most pure, state

Tooth: the textural quality of a paper surface for holding drawing media in place

Torana: a gateway used in Hindu and Buddhist architecture

Transept: structure crossing the main body of a Latin-cross-plan church

Translucent: semi-transparent

Transparency: in film and photography, a positive image on film that is visible when light is shone through it

Travertine: light-colored limestone deposited in mineral springs and used as a building material

Triglyph: a projecting block carved with three raised bands, which alternates with figurative reliefs in a frieze

Triptych: an artwork comprising three panels, normally joined together and sharing a common theme

Trompe l'oeil: an extreme kind of illusion meant to deceive the viewer that the objects included are real

Trumeau: within a portal, a central column that supports a tympanum

Twining: basket-weaving technique consisting of twisting two strands of material around a foundation of parallel sticks

Twisted perspective (also known as **composite view**): a representation of a figure, part in profile and part frontally

Two-dimensional: having height and width

Tympanum: an arched recess above a doorway, often decorated with carvings

Typefaces: The particular unified style of a family of typographical characters

Typography: the art of designing, arranging, and choosing type

Underpainting: in oil painting, the process of painting the canvas in a base, often monochrome color as a first step

in creating the areas of light and dark value
Unity: the appearance of oneness or harmony in a work of art: all of the elements appearing to be part of a cohesive whole

Value: the lightness or darkness of a plane or area
Vanishing point: the point or points in a work of art at which imaginary sight lines appear to converge, suggesting depth
Vanitas: a genre of painting that emphasizes the transient nature of earthly materials and beauty; often seen in still-life painting
Variety: the diversity of different ideas, media, and elements in a work
Vault: an arch-like structure supporting a ceiling or roof
Vaulted: covered with an arch-shaped ceiling or roof
Verdaccio: a mixture of black, white, and yellow pigments resulting in a grayish or yellowish soft greenish brown. It is used in oil painting, and sometimes in frescoes, as a base layer to refine the values in the work

Visionary art (also **Outsider Art**): art made by self-taught artists following a personal vision
Void: an area in an artwork that seems empty
Volume: the space filled or enclosed by a three-dimensional figure or object

Wavelength: a term from physics that measures light as the distance between two corresponding points on a wave of energy, e.g. between two high points of a wave
White space: in typography, the empty space around type or other features in a layout

Woodblock: a relief print process where the image is carved into a block of wood
Woodcut: a relief print made from a design cut into a block of wood

Ziggurat : Mesopotamian stepped tower, roughly pyramid-shaped, that diminishes in size toward a platform summit
Zoetrope: an antique, European toy; contains a rotating cylinder with a sequence of images on the inside that creates the impression of a single action in continuous motion when spun.

Further Reading

GATEWAY IMAGES

Bouquillard, Jocelyn, *Hokusai's Mount Fuji: The Complete Views in Color.* New York (Harry N. Abrams) 2007.
Brougher, Kerry, Mami Kataoka, and Charles Merewether, *Ai Weiwei: According to What?* (Prestel) 2012.
Burrus, Christina, *Frida Kahlo: "I Paint my Reality."* London (Thames & Hudson) 2008. Hall, Marcia, ed., *Raphael's School of Athens.* Cambridge, England (Cambridge University Press) 1997.
Garrard, Mary, *Artemisia Gentileschi.* New York (Princeton University Press) 1991.
Koch, Ebba, *The Complete Taj Mahal.* London (Thames & Hudson) 2006.
Lewis, Sarah and Adrienne Edwards, *Carrie Mae Weems: Kitchen Table Series* (Damiani) 2016.
Schele, Linda, in *The Blood of Kings: Dynasty and Ritual in Maya Art.* New York (G. Braziller) and Fort Worth, TX (Kimball Art Museum) 1992.

PART 1

Chapter 1.1 Line, Shape, and the Principle of Contrast

de Zegher, Catherine, and Cornelia Butler, *On Line: Drawing Through the Twentieth Century.* New York (The Museum of Modern Art) 2010.
Ocvirk, Otto, Robert Stinson, Philip Wigg, and Robert Bone, *Art Fundamentals: Theory and Practice,* 11th edn. New York (McGraw-Hill) 2008.

Chapter 1.2 Form, Volume, Mass, and Texture

Ching, Francis D. K., *Architecture: Form, Space, and Order,* 3rd edn. Hoboken, NJ (Wiley) 2007.
Wong, Wucius, *Principles of Three-Dimensional Design.* New York (Van Nostrand Reinhold) 1977.

Chapter 1.3 Implied Depth: Value and Space

Auvil, Kenneth W., *Perspective Drawing,* 2nd edn. New York (McGraw-Hill) 1996.
Curtis, Brian, *Drawing from Observation,* 2nd edn. New York (McGraw-Hill) 2009.

Chapter 1.4 Color

Albers, Josef, and Nicholas Fox Weber, *Interaction of Color: Revised and Expanded Edition.* New Haven, CT (Yale University Press) 2006.
Bleicher, Steven, *Contemporary Color: Theory and Use,* 2nd edn. Clifton Park, NY (Delmar Cengage Learning) 2011.
Finlay, Victoria, *Color: A Natural History of the Palette.* London/New York (Random House Trade Paperbacks) 2003.
Stewart, Jude, *ROY G. BIV: An Exceedingly Surprising Book about Color.* New York (Bloomsbury) 2013.

Chapter 1.5 Motion and Time

Krasner, Jon, *Motion Graphic Design: Applied History and Aesthetics,* 2nd edn. Burlington, MA (Focal Press [Elsevier]) 2008.
Stewart, Mary, *Launching the Imagination,* 3rd edn. New York (McGraw-Hill) 2007.

Chapter 1.6 Unity, Variety, and Balance

Bevlin, Marjorie Elliott, *Design Through Discovery: An Introduction,* 6th edn. Orlando, FL (Harcourt Brace & Co./ Wadsworth Publishing) 1993.
Lauer, David A., and Stephen Pentak, *Design Basics,* 8th edn. Boston, MA (Wadsworth Publishing) 2011.

Chapter 1.7 Scale and Proportion

Bridgman, George B., *Bridgman's Life Drawing.* Mineola, NY (Dover Publications) 1971.
Elam, Kimberly, *Geometry of Design: Studies in Proportion and Composition,* 1st edn. New York (Princeton Architectural Press) 2001.

Chapter 1.8 Focal Point and Emphasis

Lauer, David A., and Stephen Pentak, *Design Basics,* 8th edn. Boston, MA (Wadsworth Publishing) 2011.
Stewart, Mary, *Launching the Imagination,* 3rd edn. New York (McGraw-Hill) 2007.

Chapter 1.9 Pattern and Rhythm

Ocvirk, Otto, Robert Stinson, Philip Wigg, and Robert Bone, *Art Fundamentals: Theory and Practice,* 11th edn. New York (McGraw-Hill) 2008.
Wong, Wucius, *Principles of Two-Dimensional Design,* 1st edn. New York (Wiley) 1972.

Chapter 1.10 Engaging with Form and Content

Barnet, Sylvan, *Short Guide to Writing About Art.* Harlow, UK (Pearson Education) 2010.
Brown, Jonathan, *Velázquez: Painter and Courtier.* New Haven, CT (Yale University Press) 1988.
Hatt, Michael, and Charlotte Klonk, *Art History: A Critical Introduction to Its Methods.* New York (Manchester University Press; distributed exclusively in the USA by Palgrave) 2006.

PART 2

Chapter 2.1 Drawing

Faber, David L., and Daniel M. Mendelowitz, *A Guide to Drawing,* 8th edn. Boston, MA (Wadsworth Publishing) 2011.
Sale, Teel, and Claudia Betti, *Drawing: A Contemporary Approach,* 6th edn. Boston, MA (Wadsworth Publishing) 2007.

Chapter 2.2 Painting

Gottsegen, Mark David, *Painter's Handbook: Revised and Expanded.* New York (Watson-Guptill) 2006.
Robertson, Jean, and Craig McDaniel, *Painting as a Language: Material, Technique, Form, Content,* 1st edn. Boston, MA (Wadsworth Publishing) 1999.

Chapter 2.3 Printmaking

Hunter, Dard, *Papermaking.* Mineola, NY (Dover Publications) 2011.
Ross, John, *Complete Printmaker,* revised expanded edn. New York (Free Press) 1991.

Chapter 2.4 Sculpture

Rich, Jack C., *The Materials and Methods of Sculpture,* 10th edn. Mineola, NY (Dover Publications) 1988.
Tucker, William, *The Language of Sculpture.* London (Thames & Hudson) 1985.

Chapter 2.5 Architecture

Ching, Francis D. K., *Architecture: Form, Space, and Order,* 3rd edn. Hoboken, NJ (Wiley) 2007.
Glancey, Jonathan, *Story of Architecture.* New York (Dorling Kindersley/Prentice Hall) 2006.

Chapter 2.6 The Tradition of Craft

Speight, Charlotte, and John Toki, *Hands in Clay: An Introduction to Ceramics,* 5th edn. New York (McGraw-Hill) 2003.
Wight, Karol, *Molten Color: Glassmaking in Antiquity.* Los Angeles, CA (J. Paul Getty Museum) 2011.

Chapter 2.7 Visual Communication Design

Craig, James, William Bevington, and Irene Korol Scala, *Designing with Type, 5th Edition: The Essential Guide to Typography.* New York (Watson-Guptill) 2006.
Meggs, Philip B., and Alston W. Purvis, *Meggs' History of Graphic Design,* 4th edn. Hoboken, NJ (Wiley) 2005.

Chapter 2.8 Photography

Heiferman, Marvin, and Merry A. Foresta, *Photography Changes Everything.* New York (Aperture/co-published with the Smithsonian Institution) 2012.
Hirsch, Robert, *Light and Lens: Photography in the Digital Age.* London (Elsevier) 2007.
Jeffrey, Ian, *How to Read a Photograph.* New York (Abrams) 2010.
London, Barbara, John Upton, and Jim Stone, *Photography,* 10th edn. Upper Saddle River, NJ (Pearson) 2010.
Marien, Mary Warner, *Photography: A Cultural History,* 3rd edn. Upper Saddle River, NJ (Prentice Hall) 2010.
Rosenblum, Naomi, *A World History of Photography,* 4th edn. New York (Abbeville Press) 2008.
Trachtenberg, Alan, ed., *Classic Essays on Photography.* New York (Leete's Island Books) 1980.

Chapter 2.9 Film/Video and Digital Art

Cook, David A., *A History of Narrative Film,* 4th edn. New York (W. W. Norton) 2004.

Corrigan, Timothy, and Patricia White, *The Film Experience*, 2nd edn. New York (Bedford/St. Martin's) 2008.
Monaco, James, *How to Read a Film: Movies, Media, and Beyond.* New York (Oxford University Press) 2009.
Wands, Bruce, *Art of the Digital Age.* New York (Thames & Hudson) 2007.

Chapter 2.10 Alternative Media and Processes
Alberro, Alexander, and Blake Stimson, *Conceptual Art: A Critical Anthology.* Cambridge, MA (MIT Press) 2000.
Bishop, Claire, *Installation Art*, 2nd edn. London (Tate Publishing) 2010.
Goldberg, Rosalee, *Performance Art: From Futurism to the Present*, 2nd edn. New York (Thames & Hudson) 2001.
Helguda, Pablo, Education for Socially Engaged Art: A Materials and Techniques Handbook. New York (Jorge Pinto Books, Inc.) 2011.
Lippard, Lucy, *Six Years: The Dematerialization of the Art Object from 1966 to 1972.* Berkeley, CA (University of California Press) 1997.
Osborne, Peter, *Conceptual Art (Themes and Movements).* New York and London (Phaidon) 2011.
Rosenthal, Mark, *Understanding Installation Art: From Duchamp to Holzer.* New York (Prestel) 2003.

PART 3
Chapter 3.1 The Prehistoric and Ancient Mediterranean
Alfred, Cyril, *Egyptian Art.* New York (Oxford University Press) 1980.
Aruz, Joan, *Art of the First Cities: The Third Millennium B.C. from the Mediterranean to the Indus.* New York (The Metropolitan Museum of Art); New Haven, CT (Yale University Press) 2003.
Boardman, John, *The World of Ancient Art.* New York (Thames & Hudson) 2006.
Pedley, John Griffiths, *Greek Art and Archeology*, 5th edn. Upper Saddle River, NJ (Pearson/Prentice Hall) 2007.
Wheeler, Mortimer, *Roman Art and Architecture.* New York (Thames & Hudson) 1985.

Chapter 3.2 Art of the Middle Ages
Benton, Janetta, *Art of the Middle Ages.* New York (Thames & Hudson) 2002.
Bloom, Jonathan, and Sheila Blair, *Islamic Arts.* London (Phaidon) 1997.
Camille, Michael, *Gothic Art: Glorious Visions.* New York (Abrams) 1996.
Lowden, John, *Early Christian & Byzantine Art.* London (Phaidon) 1997.

Chapter 3.3 Art of India, China, Japan, Korea, and Southeast Asia
Craven, Roy, *Indian Art.* New York (Thames & Hudson) 1997.
Lee, Sherman, *History of Far Eastern Art.* New York (Abrams) 1994.
Stanley-Baker, Joan, *Japanese Art.* New York (Thames & Hudson) 2000.
Tregear, Mary, *Chinese Art.* New York (Thames & Hudson) 1997.

Chapter 3.4 Art of the Americas
Berlo, Janet Catherine, and Ruth B. Phillips, *Native North American Art.* New York (Oxford University Press) 1998.
Coe, Michael D., and Rex Koontz, *Mexico: From the Olmecs to the Aztecs*, 6th edn. New York (Thames & Hudson) 2008.
Deats, Suzanne and Kitty Leaken, *Contemporary Native American Artists.* Layton, OH (Gibbs Smith) 2012.
Miller, Mary Ellen, *The Art of Ancient Mesoamerica*, 4th edn. New York (Thames & Hudson) 2006.
Passalacqua, Veronica and Kate Morris, *Native Art Now!: Developments in Contemporary Native American Art Since 1992.* Indianapolis, IN (Eiteljorg Museum) 2017.
Rushing, Jackson III, *Native American Art in the Twentieth Century: Makers, Meanings, Histories.* New York (Taylor and Francis) 1999.
Stone, Rebecca, *Art of the Andes: From Chavin to Inca*, 3rd edn. New York (Thames & Hudson) 2002.

Chapter 3.5 Art of Africa and the Pacific Islands
Bacquart, Jean-Baptiste, *The Tribal Arts of Africa.* New York (Thames & Hudson) 2002.
Berlo, Janet Catherine, and Lee Anne Wilson, *Arts of Africa, Oceania, and the Americas.* Upper Saddle River, NJ (Prentice Hall) 1992.
D'Alleva, Anne, *Arts of the Pacific Islands.* New Haven, CT (Yale University Press) 2010.
Enwezor, Okuwui, *Contemporary African Art Since 1980.* Bologna, Italy (Damiani) 2009.
Kasfir, Sidney Littlefield, *Contemporary African Art.* New York (Thames & Hudson) 2000.
Willet, Frank, *African Art*, 3rd edn. New York (Thames & Hudson) 2003.

Chapter 3.6 Art of Renaissance and Baroque Europe (1400–1750)
Bazin, Germain, and Jonathan Griffin, *Baroque and Rococo.* New York (Thames & Hudson) 1985.
Garrard, Mary, *Artemisia Gentileschi.* Princeton, NJ (Princeton University Press) 1991.
Hartt, Frederick, *History of Italian Renaissance Art*, 7th edn. Upper Saddle River, NJ (Pearson) 2010.
Welch, Evelyn, *Art in Renaissance Italy: 1350–1500.* New York (Oxford University Press) 2001.

Chapter 3.7 Art of Europe and America (1700–1865): Rococo to Romanticism
Chu, Petra ten-Doesschate, *Nineteenth-Century European Art.* New York (Abrams) 2003.
Irwin, David, *Neoclassicism.* London (Phaidon) 1997.
Levey, Michael, *Rococo to Revolution: Major Trends in Eighteenth-Century Painting.* New York (Thames & Hudson) 1985.
Vaughan, William, *Romanticism and Art.* London (Thames & Hudson) 1994.

Chapter 3.8 The Modern Aesthetic: Realism to Expressionsim
Chipp, Herschel, *Theories of Modern Art: A Sourcebook by Artists and Critics* (University of California) 1984.
Chu, Petra ten-Doesschate, *Nineteenth-Century European Art.* New York (Abrams) 2003.
Denvir, Bernard, *Post-Impressionism.* New York (Thames & Hudson) 1992.
Thomson, Belinda, *Impressionism: Origins, Practice, Reception.* New York (Thames & Hudson) 2000.

Chapter 3.9 Late Modern and Early Contemporary Art in the Twentieth Century
Arnason, H. H., and Elizabeth C. Mansfield, *History of Modern Art*, 6th edn. Upper Saddle River, NJ (Pearson) 2009.
Dempsey, Amy, *Styles, Schools, and Movements*, 2nd edn. New York (Thames & Hudson) 2011.
Fineberg, Jonathan, *Art Since 1940: Strategies of Being*, 3rd edn. Upper Saddle River, NJ (Prentice Hall) 2010.
Jones, Amelia, *A Companion to Contemporary Art Since 1945.* Malden, MA (Blackwell Publishing) 2006.
Stiles, Kristine, and Peter Selz, *Theories and Documents of Contemporary Art: A Sourcebook of Artists' Writings*, 2nd edn, revised and expanded. Berkeley, CA (University of California Press) 2012.

Chapter 3.10 The Late Twentieth Century and Art of the Present Day
Barrett, Terry, *Why Is that Art?: Aesthetics and Criticism of Contemporary Art.* New York (Oxford University Press) 2007.
Evans, David, *Appropriation.* Cambridge, MA (MIT Press) and London (Whitechapel Gallery) 2009.
Thompson, Nato, *Living as Form: Socially Engaged Art from 1991–2011.* Cambridge, MA (MIT Press) 2012.

PART 4
Chapter 4.1 Art and Community
Art in Action: Nature, Creativity, and Our Collective Future. San Rafael, CA (Earth Aware Editions) 2007.
Iosifidis, Kiriakos, *Mural Art: Murals on Huge Public Surfaces Around the World from Graffiti to Trompe l'oeil.* Vancouver, BC (Adbusters) 2009.
Kwon, Miwon, *One Place after Another: Site-Specific Art and Location Identity.* Cambridge, MA (MIT Press) 2004.
Sholette, Gregory, Chloë Bass, and Social Practice Queens, eds., *Art As Social Action.* New York (Allworth Press) 2018.
Witley, David S., *Cave Paintings and the Human Spirit.* Amherst, NY (Prometheus Books) 2009.

Chapter 4.2 Spirituality and Art
Azara, Nancy J., *Spirit Taking Form: Making a Spiritual Practice of Making Art.* Boston, MA (Red Wheel) 2002.
Bloom, Jonathan, and Sheila S. Blair, *Islamic Arts.* London (Phaidon) 1997.
Fisher, Robert E., *Buddhist Art and Architecture.* New York (Thames & Hudson) 1993.
Guo, Xi, *Essay on Landscape Painting.* London (John Murray) 1959.
Lyle, Emily, *Sacred Architecture in the Traditions of India, China, Judaism, and Islam.* Edinburgh (Edinburgh University Press) 1992.
Williamson, Beth, *Christian Art: A Very Short Introduction.* New York (Oxford University Press) 2004.

Chapter 4.3 Art and the Cycle of Life
Dijkstra, Rineke, *Portraits.* Boston, MA (Institute of Contemporary Art) 2005.
Germer, Renate, Fiona Elliot, and Artwig Altenmuller, *Mummies: Life after Death in Ancient Egypt.* New York (Prestel) 1997.
Miller, Mary Ellen, and Karl Taube, *An Illustrated Dictionary of the Gods and Symbols of Ancient Mexico and the Maya.* New York (Thames & Hudson) 1997.
Ravenal, John B., *Vanitas: Meditations on Life and Death in Contemporary Art.* Richmond, VA (Virginia Museum of Fine Arts) 2000.
Steinberg, Leo, *The Sexuality of Christ in Renaissance Art and in Modern Oblivion.* Chicago, IL (University of Chicago Press) 1996.

Chapter 4.4 Art and Science
Bordin, Giorgio, *Medicine in Art.* Los Angeles (J. Paul Getty Museum) 2010.
Brouger, Kerry, et al., *Visual Music: Synaesthesia in Art and Music Since 1900.* London (Thames & Hudson); Washington, D.C. (Hirshhorn Museum); Los Angeles, CA (Museum of Contemporary Art) 2005.
Gamwell, Lynn, and Neil deGrasse Tyson, *Exploring the Invisible: Art, Science, and the Spiritual.* Princeton, NJ (Princeton University Press) 2004.
Milbrath, Susan, *Star Gods of the Maya: Astronomy in Art, Folklore, and Calendars.* Austin, TX (University of Texas Press) 2000.
Pietrangeli, Carlo, et al., *The Sistine Chapel: A Glorious Restoration.* New York (Abrams) 1999.
Rhodes, Colin, *Outsider Art: Spontaneous Alternatives.* New York (Thames & Hudson) 2000.

Chapter 4.5 Art, Illusion, and Transformation
Battistini, Matilde, *Astrology, Magic and Alchemy in Art.* Los Angeles, CA (J. Paul Getty Museum) 2007.
Ebert-Schifferer, Sybille, et al., *Deceptions and Illusions: Five Centuries of Trompe L'Oeil Painting.* Washington, D.C. (National Gallery of Art) 2003.
Gablik, Suzi, *Magritte.* New York (Thames & Hudson) 1985.
Kemp, Martin, *The Science of Art: Optical Themes in Western Art from Brunelleschi to Seurat.* New Haven, CT (Yale University Press) 1992.
Seckel, Al, and Douglas Hofstadter, *Masters of Deception: Escher, Dali, & The Artists of Optical Illusion.* New York (Sterling Publishing) 2007.

Chapter 4.6 Art of Political Leaders and Rulers

Cooper, Pia, *Art Mao: The Big Little Red Book of Maoist Art Since 1949.* (CN Times Books Inc.) 2015.

Freed, Rita, *Pharaohs of the Sun: Akhenaten, Nefertiti: Tutankhamen.* Boston, MA (Museum of Fine Arts in association with Bulfinch Press/Little, Brown and Co.) 1999.

Rapelli, Paola, *Symbols of Power in Art.* Los Angeles, CA (J. Paul Getty Museum, Getty Publications) 2011.

Spike, John T., *Europe in the Age of Monarchy.* New York (The Metropolitan Museum of Art) 1987.

Chapter 4.7 Art, War, and Revolution

Auping, Michael, *Anselm Kiefer Heaven and Earth.* Fort Worth, TX (Modern Art Museum of Fort Worth, in association with Prestel) 2005.

Blais, Allison, et al., *A Place of Remembrance: Official Book of the National September 11 Memorial.* Washington, D.C. (National Geographic) 2011.

Bourke, Joanna, ed., *War and Art: A Visual History of Modern Conflict.* London (Reaktion) 2017.

Hughes, Robert, *Goya.* New York (Alfred A. Knopf) 2003.

Steel, Andy, *The World's Top Photographers: Photojournalism: And the Stories Behind Their Greatest Images.* Mies, Switzerland, and Hove, UK (RotoVision) 2006.

Van Hensbergen, Gijs, *Guernica: The Biography of a Twentieth-Century Icon.* New York (Bloomsbury) 2005.

Wilson, David, *The Bayeux Tapestry.* London (Thames & Hudson) 2004.

Chapter 4.8 Art of Protest and Social Conscience

Alhadeff, Albert, *The Raft of the Medusa: Géricault, Art, and Race.* Munich and London (Prestel) 2002.

Barron, Stephanie, *Degenerate Art.* Los Angeles, CA (Los Angeles County Museum of Art) and New York (Abrams) 1991.

Kammen, Michael, *Visual Shock: A History of Art Controversies in American Culture.* New York (Alfred A. Knopf) 2007.

Chapter 4.9 The Body in Art

Clark, Kenneth, *The Nude: A Study in Ideal Form.* Princeton, NJ (Yale University Press) 1990/1956.

Dijkstra, Bram, *Naked: The Nude in America.* New York (Rizzoli) 2010.

Jones, Amelia, *Body Art/Performing the Self.* Minneapolis, MN (University of Minnesota Press) 1998.

Nairne, Sandy, and Sarah Howgate, *The Portrait Now.* New Haven, CT (Yale University Press) and London (National Portrait Gallery) 2006.

Chapter 4.10 Identity, Race, and Gender in Art

Broude, Norma, and Mary Garrard, *Feminism and Art History: Questioning the Litany.* New York (Harper & Row) 1982.

Doy, Gen, *Picturing the Self: Changing Views of the Subject in Visual Culture.* London (I. B. Tauris) 2004.

Hickey, Dave, *The Invisible Dragon: Essays on Beauty,* revised and expanded edition. Chicago, IL (University of Chicago Press) 2009.

Hooks, Bell, *Feminism is for Everybody: Passionate Politics.* Cambridge, MA (South End Press) 2000.

Jones, Amelia, *The Feminism and Visual Culture Reader.* New York (Routledge) 2010.

Patton, Sharon F., *African American Art* (Oxford University Press) 1998.

Perry, Gill, *Gender and Art.* New Haven, CT (Yale University Press) 1999.

Powell, Richard, *Black Art: A Cultural History,* 2nd edn. New York (Thames & Hudson) 2003.

Powell, Richard, Virginia Mecklenberg, and Theresa Slowik, *African American Art: Harlem Renaissance, Civil Rights Era, and Beyond.* New York (Skira Rizzoli) 2012.

Rebel, Ernst, *Self-Portraits.* Los Angeles, CA (Taschen) 2008.

Rugg, Linda Haverty, *Picturing Ourselves: Photography and Autobiography.* Chicago, IL (University of Chicago Press) 1997.

Valenti, Jessica, *Full Frontal Feminism: A Young Woman's Guide to Why Feminism Matters.* Emeryville, CA (Seal Press) 2007.

Sources of Quotations

Introduction

p. 21: Unspecified critic on Frederic Edwin Church from Pierre Berton, *Niagara: A History of the Falls* (New York: State University of New York, Albany, 1992), 119.

p. 35: Ai Weiwei from an article by Sylvia Poggioli, "Ai Weiwei Exhibit Shines Light on Time as Political Prisoner," August 19, 2013: http://www.opb.org/news/article/npr-ai-weiwei-exhibit-shines-light-on-time-as-political-prisoner/

PART I

Chapter 1.1

p. 52: Barbara Hepworth from Abraham Marie Hammacher, *The Sculpture of Barbara Hepworth* (New York: Harry N. Abrams, 1968), 98.

Chapter 1.2

p. 61: Vivant Denon from http://www.ancient-egypt-history.com/2011/04/napoleon-bonapartes-wise-men-at.html.

p. 64: Lino Tagliepietra from the artist's website at http://www.linotagliapietra.com/batman/index.htm.

Chapter 1.3

p. 76: Albert Einstein from Thomas Campbell, *My Big TOE: Inner Workings* (Huntsville, AL: Lightning Strike Books, 2003), 191.

Chapter 1.4

p. 95: Vasily Kandinsky from Robert L. Herbert, *Modern Artists on Art* (New York: Dover Publications, 1999), 19.

p. 109: Van Gogh quoted in Ian Chilvers, Harold Osborne, and Denis Farr (eds.), *The Oxford Dictionary of Art* (New York: Oxford University Press, 2009), 298.

p. 111: Kathleen Hall, *Hilma af Klint* (2014) from https://www.theosophyforward.com/theosophy-and-the-society-in-the-public-eye/1138-hilma-af-klint

Chapter 1.5

p. 113: William Faulkner from Philip Gourevitch (ed.), *The Paris Review: Interviews, Volume 2* (New York: Picador USA, 2007), 54.

p. 121: Gabrielle Cram and Daniela Zyman (eds.), "Interview with Ai Weiwei," in *Shooting Back* (Vienna: Thyssen-Bornemisza Art Contemporary, 2007), 36.

Chapter 1.7

p. 140: Baudelaire from Charles Baudelaire, *Flowers of Evil and Other Works,* ed. and trans. Wallace Fowlie (New York: Dover Publications, 1992), 201.

Chapter 1.9

p. 163: Elvis Presley from Dave Marsh and James Bernard, *The New Book of Rock Lists* (New York: Simon & Schuster [Fireside], 1994), 9.

Chapter 1.10

p. 172: Edward Hopper from Art Institute of Chicago website: www.artic.edu/aic/collections/artwork/111628.

p. 173: José de Sigüenza from Ian Chilvers, ed., "Bosch, Hieronymus," in *The Oxford Dictionary of Art and Artists* (Oxford University Press, 2009; and Oxford Reference Online, Oxford University Press).

p. 179: Magdalena Abakanowicz from Magdalena Abakanowicz, "Solitude," (1985) sent by the artist to the editors, Kristine Stiles and Peter Selz (eds.), *Theories and Documents of Contemporary Art: A Sourcebook of Artists' Writings* (Berkeley: University of California Press, 1996), 260.

PART 2

Chapter 2.1

p. 192: William Blake from *The Complete Poetry and Prose of William Blake* (Berkeley and Los Angeles, CA: Anchor/University of California Press, 1997), 574.

Chapter 2.2

p. 213: José Clemente Orozco from *The Artist in New York: Letters to Jean Charlot and Unpublished Writings, 1925–1929* (Austin, TX: University of Texas Press, 1974), 90–91.

p. 215: Andrew Wyeth from William Scheller, *America, a History in Art: The American Journey Told by Painters, Sculptors...* (New York: Black Dog & Leventhal Publishers, 2008), 22.

Chapter 2.4

p. 242: Michelangelo quoted by Henry Moore from Henry Moore and Alan G. Wilkinson, *Henry Moore–Writings and Conversations* (Berkeley, CA: University of California Press, 2002), 238.

Chapter 2.5

pp. 277, 278: Le Corbusier from Nicholas Fox Weber, *Le Corbusier: A Life* (New York: Alfred A. Knopf, 2008), 171.

pp. 277, 304: Mies van der Rohe from E. C. Relph, *The Modern Urban Landscape* (Baltimore, MD: The Johns Hopkins University Press, 1987), 191.

Chapter 2.6

p. 285: Geoffrey Chaucer from *The Works of Geoffrey Chaucer, Volume 5* (New York: Macmillan and Co., Limited, 1904), 341.

Chapter 2.8

pp. 324–25: Steve McCurry from "The Last Roll of Kodachrome," *Natgeo's Most Amazing Photos,* National Geographic Television (September 17, 2010), produced by Yvonne Russo and Hans Weise; editor Carol Slatkin: https://www.youtube.com/watch?v=DUL6MBVKVLI; and from "Exposed: The Last Roll of Kodachrome" (Brad Horn and Claire O'Neill), National Public Radio interview with Audie Cornish (July 24, 2010): http://www.npr.org/blogs/pictureshow/2010/07/23/128728114/kodachrome.

p. 328: "Sally Mann: Collodion Process" PBS.org, (November, 2011).

p. 332: Edward Burtynsky from *Manufactured Landscapes (U.S. Edition),* directed by Jennifer Baichwal (Zeitgeist Films, 2006).

p. 332: Daniela Edburg, Artist Statement: http://www.danielaedburg.com/statement

Chapter 2.9

p. 338: *The Artist* from Rick Groen, "The Artist: Mostly mute, it speaks volumes about silent film," *The Globe and Mail* (Toronto), December 9, 2011.

Chapter 2.10

p. 352: Cedar Pasori, "An Interview with Barbara Kruger Discussing Her New Installation and Art in the Digital Age," August 21, 2012 complex.com (accessed March 6, 2017): http://www.complex.com/style/2012/08/interview-barbara-kruger-talks-her-new-installation-and-art-in-the-digital-age

p. 352: Yoko Ono's text accompanying *Wish Tree* from Jessica Dawson, "Yoko Ono's Peaceful Message Takes Root," *Washington Post* (April 3, 2007): washingtonpost.com.

p. 354: Vito Acconci's description of *Following Piece* from documentation accompanying the photographs; reprinted in Lucy Lippard, *Six Years:*

The Dematerialization of the Art Object (Berkeley, CA: University of California Press, 1973/1997), 117.
p. 357: "Reconsidering Reality: An Interview with Ai Weiwei," by Kerry Brougher in Brougher, Kataoka, and Charles Merewether (eds.), *Ai Weiwei: According to What?*, Prestel (2012), 43.
p. 358: Kara Walker from "Interview: Projecting Fictions: 'Insurrection! Our Tools Were Rudimentary, Yet We Pressed On,'" *ART21* "Stories" Episode, Season 2 (PBS: 2003): http://www.pbs.org/art21/artists/walker/clip1.html.

PART 3

Chapter 3.1
p. 372: Inscription from Assyrian palace from Met Museum website and object file: http://www.metmuseum.org/works_of_art/collection_database/ancient_near_eastern_art/huzman_headed_winged_bull_and_winged_lion_lamassu/objectview.aspx?collID=3&OID=30009052.
p. 379: Protagoras from Kenneth Clark, *Protagoras* (New York: Harper and Row, 1969), 57.

Chapter 3.2
p. 400: Hildegard of Bingen from *Hildegard von Bingen's Mystical Visions*, trans. by Bruce Hozeski from *Scivias* (I,1), 8.

Chapter 3.3
p. 419: "Ai Weiwei in Conversation with Virginia Trioli," National Gallery of Victoria, (December 15, 2015).
p. 419: Gabrielle Cram and Daniela Zyman (eds.), "Interview with Ai Weiwei," in *Shooting Back* (Vienna: Thyssen-Bornemisza Art Contemporary, 2007), 36.

Chapter 3.4
p. 434: David Grove from David Grove, *In Search of the Olmec* (unpublished work), © David Grove.
p. 444: Carolina A. Miranda, "The artist who made protesters' mirrored shields says the 'struggle porn' media miss point of Standing Rock," *LA Times* (January 12, 2017).
p. 444: Cannupa Hanska Luger, Mirror Shield Community Workshop statement: http://www.allmyrelationsarts.com/mirror-shield-community-workshop/ (November 30, 2016).

Chapter 3.5
p. 453: Mphethi Morojele, "Architect Profile: MMA Design Studio," *African Design Magazine* (September, 2015), pp. 72–79.

Chapter 3.7
p. 491: Jacques-Louis David from the Revolutionary Convention, 1793, quoted in Robert Cumming, *Art Explained* (New York: DK Publishing, 2005), 70.

Chapter 3.8
p. 504: Gustave Courbet from Robert Williams, *Art Theory: An Historical Introduction* (Malden, MA: Blackwell Publishing, 2004), 127.
p. 507: Charles Baudelaire from *The Painter of Modern Life*, trans. and ed. Jonathan Mayne (London: Phaidon Press, 1995).
p. 514: Paul Gauguin from Charles Estienne, *Gauguin: Biographical and Critical Studies* (Geneva: Skira, 1953), 17.
p. 515: Van Gogh from Vincent Van Gogh, Letter to Emile Bernard, October 7, 1888 in Arles, France, in *The Complete Letters of Vincent Van Gogh*, vol. 3, no. B19 (New York: Bulfinch Press, 2000/1958).
p. 516: Unspecified critic on Claudel from Ruth Butler, *Rodin: The Shape of Genius* (New Haven, CT and London: Yale University Press, 1993), 271.

Chapter 3.9
p. 525: Henri Matisse from Jack Flam, *Matisse: The Man and His Art, 1869–1918* (Ithaca, NY: Cornell University Press, 1986), 196.
p. 529: Marcel Duchamp from Arturo Schwarz, *The Complete Works of Marcel Duchamp* (New York: Delano Greenidge Editions, 1997), II, 442.
p. 533: Filippo Marinetti from his "Manifesto for the Italo-Abyssinian War," (1936), quoted in Walter Benjamin, "The Work of Art in the Age of Mechanical Reproduction," in Walter Benjamin, *Illuminations: Essays and Reflections*, ed. Hannah Arendt (New York: Schocken Books, 1968), 241.
p. 540: Mark Rothko from Selden Rodman, *Conversations with Artists* (New York: Devin-Adair, Co., 1957).
p. 540: Henry Geldzahler, "Interview with Helen Frankenthaler" *Artforum* 4, no. 2 (October 1965), 36–38; reprinted in Kristine Stiles and Peter Selz (eds.), *Theories and Documents of Contemporary Art*, second edition (Berkeley: University of California Press, 2012), 32.

PART 4

Chapter 4.1
p. 559: Tara Donovan from Richard McCoy, "Prelude: A Discussion with Tara Donovan," *ART21* Magazine (April 8, 2010): http://blog.art21.org/2010/04/08/prelude-a-discussion-with-tara-donovan/#.VTAZECmp3dk.
p. 564: Susan Cervantes from Tyce Hendricks, "Celebrating Art that Draws People Together," *San Francisco Chronicle* (May 6, 2005), F1.
p. 564: Aliseo Purpura-Pontoniere from Tyce Hendricks, "Celebrating Art that Draws People Together," *San Francisco Chronicle* (May 6, 2005), F1.
p. 567: Hilla Rebay (the curator of the foundation and director of the Guggenheim Museum) from the Solomon R. Guggenheim website: http://www.guggenheim.org/guggenheim-foundation/architecture/new-york.
p. 571: Christo and Jeanne-Claude, "Selected Works: The Gates," *The Art of Christo and Jeanne-Claude* (© 2005; access date September 7, 2007) www.christojeanneclaude.net.
p. 576: Diego Rivera from Bertram D. Wolfe, *The Fabulous Life of Diego Rivera* (New York: Stein and Day, 1963), 423.
p. 576: Kryzstof Wodiczko, quoted in "Kryzstof Wodiczko, Tijuana Projection, 2001," *ART21* on pbs.org: http://www.art21.org/images/krzysztof-wodiczko/the-tijuana-projection-2001-0.

Chapter 4.2
p. 588: Description of the Mosque of the Imam, Isfahan, from The Metropolitan Museum of Art, "Works of Art: Islamic Highlights: Signatures, Inscriptions, and Markings," accessed September 13, 2010: www.metmuseum.org/works_of_art/collection_database/islamic?art/mihrab/objectview.aspx?collID=14OID=140006815.

Chapter 4.3
p. 591: Albert Einstein from "The World As I See It," *Forum and Century*, vol. 84 (October, 1930), 193–94; reprinted in *Living Philosophies*, vol. 13 (New York: Simon and Schuster, 1931), 3–7; also reprinted in Albert Einstein, *Ideas and Opinions, based on Mein Weltbild*, ed. Carl Seeling (New York: Bonanza Books, 1954), 8–11.
p. 596: Darian Leader, "Glue, " *The Clock* (London: White Cube, 2010)
p. 598: Jillian Mayer, *I Am Your Grandma*: https://www.youtube.com/watch?v=YfY1lfFu8j8.

Chapter 4.4
p. 607: Willard Wigan from *The Telegraph* article by Benjamin Secher on July 7, 2007: http://www.telegraph.co.uk/culture/art/3666352/The-tiny-world-of-Willard-Wigan-nano-sculptor.html.
p. 607: "The Artist and the Space Shuttle," *Discover*, December 1982, 74–81.
p. 608: Wang, Linda, "Guarding Our DNA: Art project exposes the vulnerability of the genetic material we unintentionally leave behind." *Chemical & Engineering News* 91 (25)
p. 609: Jasper Johns from Martin Friedman, *Visions of America: Landscape as Metaphor in the Late Twentieth Century* (Denver, CO: Denver Art Museum, 1994), 146.
p. 610: Marcia Smilack from Artist's Statement on her own website: http://www.marciasmilack.com/artist-statement.php
p. 611: Salvador Dalí from Dawn Ades et al., *Dalí* (Venice, Italy: Rizzoli, 2004), 559.
p. 611: Yayoi Kusama Courtesy KUSAMA Enterprise, Ota Fine Arts, Tokyo and Victoria Miro, London © Yayoi Kusama.

Chapter 4.5
p. 620: Ovid from *Metamorphoses*, trans. A. D. Melville and E. J. Kenney (New York and Oxford: Oxford World's Classics, 2009), 232.
p. 626: Magritte from Paul Crowther, *Language of 20th-Century Art* (New Haven, CT: Yale University Press, 1997), 116.

Chapter 4.6
p. 630: Dána-Ain Davis and Christa Craven, *Feminist Ethnography: Thinking Through Methodologies, Challenges & Possibilities* (Lanham, MD: Rowman & Littlefield, 2016), 4.

Chapter 4.7
p. 639: Nick Ut from William Kelly, *Art and Humanist Ideals: Contemporary Perspectives* (Australia: Palgrave Macmillan, 2003), 284.
p. 645: Picasso from Charles Harrison and Paul Wood, *Art in Theory, 1900–2000: An Anthology of Changing Ideas* (Oxford: Blackwell Publishing, 2003), 508.
p. 649: Maya Lin from Marilyn Stokstad, *Art History* (New York: Pearson Education, 2008), xliv.

Chapter 4.8
p. 653: Quote from Teresa Margolles in her lecture "Global Feminisms", Brooklyn Museum (2007): https://www.youtube.com/watch?v=HEO_iyYcFJ4.
p. 654: Interview by Zhuang Hui in *Ai Weiwei: Dropping the Urn* (Pennsylvania: Arcadia University Art Gallery, 2010), 23.
p. 656: Mary Richardson from June Purvis, *Emmeline Pankhurst: A Biography* (London and New York: Routledge, 2002), 255.
p. 656: Eric Fischl poem from Laura Brandon, *Art and War* (London: I. B. Tauris & Co. Ltd, 2007), 129; and Fischl's remarks from Daniel Sherman and Terry Nardin, *Terror, Culture, Politics: Rethinking 9/11* (Indiana: Indiana University Press, 2006), 60.
p. 657: Label from Nazi exhibition from Stephanie Barron, *Degenerate Art: The Fate of the Avant-Garde in Nazi Germany* (New York: Harry N. Abrams, 1991), 390.
p. 659: Florence Owens Thompson from Kiku Adatto, *Picture Perfect: Life in the Age of the Photo Op.* (Princeton, NJ: Princeton University Press, 2008), 247–48.
p. 660: John Newsom, "UNCG grad student sheds light on going to jail with jumpsuit", *The Washington Times* (December 3, 2016).
p. 661: Chris Jordan from http://www.bu.edu/sustainability/chris-jordan-photography/

Chapter 4.9
p. 664: Willem de Kooning from an interview with David Sylvester (BBC, 1960), "Content is a Glimpse…" in *Location I* (Spring, 1963) and reprinted in David Sylvester, "The Birth of 'Woman I,'" *Burlington Magazine* 137, no. 1105 (April, 1995), 223.
p. 675: Matisse from "Exactitude is not Truth," 1947, essay by Matisse written for an exhibition catalog (Liège: Association pour le progrès intellectuel et artistique de la Wallonie, with the participation of Galerie Maight, Paris); English translation (Philadelphia Museum of Art, 1948); reprinted in Jack Flam, *Matisse on Art* (Berkeley, CA: University of California Press, 1995/1973), 179–81.

Chapter 4.10
p. 683: Cindy Sherman from "Interview with Els Barents," in *Cindy Sherman* (Munich: Schirmer und Mosel, 1982); reprinted in Kristine Stiles and Peter Selz (eds.), *Theories and Documents of Contemporary Art: A Sourcebook of Artists' Writings* (Berkeley, CA: University of California Press, 1996), 792–93.
p. 688: Jess Righthand, "Q and A: James Luna," *Smithsonian Magazine* (January 2011).
p. 689: Nikki S. Lee from Erica Schlaikjer, "Woman's Art Requires Becoming a Chameleon," *The Daily Northwestern* (February 24, 2006), Campus Section.

Illustration Credits

0.0.1 Fitzwilliam Museum, University of Cambridge/Bridgeman Art Library; **0.0.2** White Images/Scala, Florence; **0.0.3** Solomon R. Guggenheim Museum, New York, Gift, Mr. and Mrs. James J. Shapiro, 85.3266. Photo David Heald © Solomon R. Guggenheim Foundation. © ARS, NY and DACS, London 2018; **0.0.4** Uffizi Gallery, Florence; **0.0.5** © 2015 FedEx Corporation. All Rights Reserved; **0.0.6** Image courtesy October Gallery, London; **0.0.7** © Sam74100/Dreamstime.com; **0.0.8** Robert Harding Picture Library/agefotostock.com; **0.0.9** © Nik Wheeler/Corbis; **0.0.10** Detroit Institute of Arts, Gift of Dexter M. Ferry, Jr., 46.309; **0.0.11** Sakai Collection, Tokyo; **0.0.12** Musée du Louvre, Paris; **0.0.13** Richard and Ellen Sandor Art Foundation. © Succession Picasso/DACS, London 2018. © Man Ray Trust/ADAGP, Paris and DACS, London 2018; **0.0.14** Collection of Yusaku Maezawa. Photograph courtesy Sotheby's, Inc., 2017. © The Estate of Jean-Michel Basquiat/ADAGP, Paris and DACS, London 2018; **0.0.15a** Collection of Diane and Dan Mossenson, Perth, Western Australia. © Mossenson Galleries and the artist; **0.0.15b** Photo Diane Mossenson. © Mossenson Galleries; **0.0.16** Photo Marc Quinn Studio. Courtesy White Cube. © the artist; **0.0.17** Mauritshuis, The Hague; **0.0.18a**, **0.0.18b** Photos © David Levene/eyevine. Courtesy Ai Weiwei Studio; **0.0.19** Howard University Art Gallery, Washington, D.C.; **0.0.20** Whitney Museum of American Art, New York; purchased with funds from Eli and Edythe L. Broad, the Mrs. Percy Uris Purchase Fund, and the Painting and Sculpture Committee, 88.17a-b. © The Estate of Eva Hesse. Courtesy Hauser & Wirth; **0.0.21** Allan Houser archives © Chiinde LLC; **0.0.22** Fine Art Images/Heritage Images/Scala, Florence; **0.0.23** Photo Art Gallery of New South Wales/Jenni Carter. © David Hockney; **p. 40** (above) Photo Andrew Hawthorne. Courtesy the artists; (center) © 2012 The M.C. Escher Company-Holland. All rights reserved. www.mcescher.com; (below) Museo Nacional del Prado, Madrid; **1.1.1** Photo Jarno Gonzalez Zarraonandia/iStockphoto.com; **1.1.2a** Photo Scala, Florence - courtesy the Ministero Beni e Att. Culturali; **1.1.2b** Photo Scala, Florence/Fondo Edifici di Culto - Min. dell'Interno; **1.1.3** Musée des Beaux-Arts de Lyon. © Succession H. Matisse/DACS 2018; **1.1.4** The Museum of Modern Art, New York, The Louis E. Stern Collection, 988.1964.6. Digital image, The Museum of Modern Art, New York/Scala, Florence. © Succession Picasso/DACS, London 2018; **1.1.5** Ralph Larmann; **1.1.6a**, **1.1.6b** British Library, London; **1.1.7** © Sauerkids; **1.1.8** British Museum, London; **1.1.9** © CLAMP/Kodansha Ltd; **1.1.10** Ralph Larmann; **1.1.11** Museo de Arte Moderno, Mexico City. © Banco de México Diego Rivera Frida Kahlo Museums Trust, Mexico, D.F./DACS 2018; **1.1.12** © Nike; **1.1.13** Art Institute of Chicago, Illinois/Helen Birch Bartlett Memorial Collection/Bridgeman Images; **1.1.14** Image courtesy Peter Freeman, Inc., New York; **1.1.15** © Bowness, Hepworth Estate; **1.1.16** © ADAGP, Paris and DACS, London 2018; **1.1.17** Courtesy the Victorian Spiritualists' Union, Melbourne; **1.1.18** National Gallery of Art, Washington, D.C., Collection of Mr. and Mrs. Paul Mellon, 1983.1.81; **1.1.19**, **1.1.20** Ralph Larmann; **1.1.21** Courtesy Flomenhaft Gallery, New York; **1.1.22** Ralph Larmann; **1.1.23** Courtesy AT&T Archives and History Center; **1.1.24** © Carrie Mae Weems. Courtesy the artist and Jack Shainman Gallery, New York; **1.1.25a** © 1996 Shepard Fairey/ObeyGiant.com; **1.1.25b** Photo © Elizabeth Daniels/www.elizabethdanielsphotography.com. © 1996 Shepard Fairey/ObeyGiant.com; **1.1.26** © Georgia O'Keeffe Museum/DACS 2018; **1.1.27** Noma Bar/Dutch Uncle; **1.1.28** © 2012 The M. C. Escher Company-Holland. All rights reserved. www.mcescher.com; **1.2.1** Ralph Larmann; **1.2.2** iStockphoto.com; **1.2.3** Photo courtesy the Marlborough Gallery Inc., New York. © Estate of David Smith/DACS, London/VAGA, New York 2018; **1.2.4** Rheinisches Landesmuseum, Bonn; **1.2.5** Photo Russell Johnson. Courtesy Lino Tagliapietra, Inc.; **1.2.6** Museo dell'Ara Pacis, Rome; **1.2.7** Fine Arts Museum of San Francisco, Museum Purchase, Gift of Mrs. Paul Wattis 1999, 42 a–k; **1.2.8a** Photo Mary Cameron-Sarani; **1.2.8b** Prisma/SuperStock; **1.2.9** Ralph Larmann; **1.2.10a**, **1.2.10b** Photo Clements/Howcroft, MA. Courtesy the artists; **1.2.11** Photo Nationalmuseum, Stockholm; **1.2.12** Photo Andrew Hawthorne. Courtesy the artists; **1.2.13** Photo Sue Ormerod. © Rachel Whiteread. Courtesy Gagosian Gallery, London; **1.2.14** © Marisol, DACS, London/VAGA, New York 2018; **1.2.15** © Romain Cintract/Hemis/Corbis; **1.2.16** Photo Carlos Sieiro Del Nido. © The Easton Foundation/VAGA, New York/DACS, London 2018; **1.2.17a** Philadelphia Museum of Art, The Louise and Walter Arensberg Collection, 1950-134-4. © Succession Brancusi - All rights reserved. ADAGP, Paris and DACS, London 2018; **1.2.17b** Photo Szilas; **1.2.18** Photononstop/SuperStock; **1.2.19a**, **1.2.19b** © Wangechi Mutu. Courtesy the artist and Victoria Miro, London; **1.2.20** Museum of Modern Art, New York, Purchase, 130.1946.a–c. Photo 2012, Museum of Modern Art, New York/Scala, Florence. © DACS 2018; **1.3.1** Los Angeles County Museum of Art (LACMA), California. Purchased with funds provided by the Mr. and Mrs. William Preston Harrison Collection, 78.7 (www.lacma.org). © ADAGP, Paris and DACS, London 2018; **1.3.2** Photo © Dzmitry Kliapitski/123RF.com; **1.3.3**, **1.3.4** Ralph Larmann; **1.3.5** Sterling & Francine Clark Art Institute, Williamstown, Massachusetts; **1.3.6** Contarelli Chapel, Church of San Luigi dei Francesci, Rome; **1.3.7** Ralph Larmann; **1.3.8** Musée du Louvre, Paris; **1.3.9** Courtesy K. H. Renlund Museum – Provincial Museum of Central Ostrobothnia, Kokkola, Finland; **1.3.10** The Nelson-Atkins Museum of Art, Kansas City, Missouri. Purchase William Rockhill Nelson Trust, 47-71. Photo John Lamberton; **1.3.11** © Benton Testamentary Trusts/UMB Bank Trustee/VAGA, NY/DACS, London 2018; **1.3.12** Ralph Larmann; **1.3.13** Crystal Bridges Museum of American Art, Bentonville, Arkansas; **1.3.14** Metropolitan Museum of Art, New York, Purchase, The Dillon Fund Gift, 1988; **1.3.15** Ralph Larmann; **1.3.16** © Supergiant Games, LLC 2014; **1.3.17a** JTB Photo/SuperStock; **1.3.17b** Ralph Larmann; **1.3.18** Private Collection; **1.3.19** Ralph Larmann; **1.3.20** Santa Maria Novella, Florence; **1.3.21a**, **1.3.21b** Stanza della Segnatura, Vatican Museums, Rome; **1.3.22** Ralph Larmann; **1.3.23** © 2012 The M. C. Escher Company-Holland. All rights reserved. www.mcescher.com; **1.3.24** Graphische Sammlung Albertina, Vienna; **1.3.25** From *Trinity: Volume 1*, TM and © DC Comics; **1.4.1**, **1.4.2** Ralph Larmann; **1.4.3** Courtesy Charles Csuri; **1.4.4** Ralph Larmann; **1.4.5** akg-images; **1.4.6**, **1.4.7** Ralph Larmann; **1.4.8** Photo Joshua White. Courtesy the artist and Thomas Solomon Gallery, Los Angeles. © Analia Saban 2008; **1.4.9**, **1.4.10**, **1.4.11**, **1.4.12** Ralph Larmann; **1.4.13** Cleveland Museum of Art, Mr. and Mrs. William H. Marlatt Fund, 1965.233; **1.4.14** National Gallery of Art, Washington, D.C., Chester Dale Collection, 1963.10.94; **1.4.15** Fine Arts Museum of San Francisco, Gift of Vivian Burns, Inc., 74.8; **1.4.16** Ralph Larmann; **1.4.17** © Mark Tansey. Courtesy Gagosian Gallery, New York; **1.4.18** The Art Institute of Chicago, Illinois/Helen Birch Bartlett Memorial Collection/Bridgeman Images. © Succession Picasso/DACS, London 2018; **1.4.19** Museum of Modern Art, New York, Gift of Mr. and Mrs. Ben Heller, 240.1969. Photo 2012, Museum of Modern Art, New York/Scala, Florence. © The Barnett Newman Foundation, New York/DACS, London 2018; **1.4.20** The Museum of Fine Arts, Houston, Gift of Audrey Jones Beck. © ADAGP, Paris and DACS, London 2018; **1.4.21** Ralph Larmann; **1.4.22** Kunstmuseum Basel, Switzerland; **1.4.23** British Museum, London; **1.4.24** Ralph Larmann; **1.4.25a**, **1.4.25b** Musée d'Orsay, Paris; **1.4.26a**, **1.4.26b** © Yale University Press; **1.4.27** Los Angeles County Museum of Art (LACMA), California. Gift of Dr. and Mrs. Sam K. Lee, M.86.330 (www.lacma.org); **1.4.29** Yale University Art Gallery, New Haven, Bequest of Stephen Carlton Clark, B.A. 1903, 1961.18.34; **1.4.30** Photo Edwin Medina. Courtesy the artist and Embajada Gallery; **1.4.31** National Gallery of Art, Washington, D.C. Collection of Mr. and Mrs. John Hay Whitney, 1998.74.7. © Succession H. Matisse/DACS 2018; **1.4.32** Albright-Knox Art Gallery, Buffalo, New York, General Purchase Funds, 1946; **1.4.33** Photo Albin Dahlström/Moderna Museet-Stockholm. Courtesy Hilma af Klint Foundation; **1.4.34** Courtesy the artist; **1.5.1** Galleria Borghese, Rome; **1.5.2** Albright-Knox Art Gallery, Buffalo, New York, Bequest of A. Conger Goodyear and Gift of George F. Goodyear, 1964. © DACS 2018; **1.5.3** Solomon R. Guggenheim Museum, New York, Partial gift of the artist, 1989, 89.3626. Photo David Heald © Solomon R. Guggenheim Foundation, New York. © Jenny Holzer. ARS, NY and DACS, London 2018; **1.5.4** © Bridget Riley, 2012. All rights reserved; **1.5.5** Courtesy The Bill Douglas Cinema Museum, University of Exeter, England; **1.5.6** © Gregory Barsamian 2013. Photo the artist; **1.5.7** Disney Enterprises/Album/akg-images; **1.5.8** Arte/Bavaria/WDR/Spauke, Bernd/The Kobal Collection; **1.5.9** Photo OSA Images; **1.5.10** © Board of Trustees, National Gallery of Art, Washington, D.C.; **1.5.11** Courtesy the artist; **1.5.12** National Gallery of Art, Washington, D.C., Samuel H. Kress Collection, 1939.1.293; **1.5.13** Photo University of South Florida. © Estate of Nancy Holt/DACS, London/VAGA, New York 2018; **1.5.14** Courtesy Ai Weiwei Studio; **1.5.15** Rotger/Iberfoto/photoaisa.com; **1.5.16** Library of Congress, Washington, D.C. Prints & Photographs Division, LC-USZ62-536; **1.5.17** © Suzanne Anker; **1.5.18** © the artist. Courtesy Catherine Person Gallery, Seattle, Washington; **1.6.1** Ralph Larmann; **1.6.2** Library of Congress, Washington, D.C. Prints & Photographs Division, H. Irving Olds collection, LC-DIG- jpd-02018; **1.6.3a** I. Michael Interior Design; **1.6.3b** Ralph Larmann; **1.6.4** Courtesy Galerie Berès, Paris. © ADAGP, Paris and DACS, London 2018; **1.6.5** © Kanayama Akira and Tanaka Atsuko Association; **1.6.6** Lito and Kim Camacho Collection, Manila. © Kanayama Akira and Tanaka Atsuko Association; **1.6.7** Museum of Modern Art, New York, Blanchette Hooker Rockefeller Fund, 377.1971. Photo 2012, Museum of Modern Art, New York/Scala, Florence. © Romare Bearden Foundation/DACS, London/VAGA, New York 2018; **1.6.8** © The Joseph and Robert Cornell Memorial Foundation/VAGA, NY/DACS, London 2018; **1.6.9** Photo John Freeman; **1.6.10** Ralph Larmann; **1.6.11** © Robert Rauschenberg Foundation/DACS, London/VAGA, New York 2018; **1.6.12** Private Collection; **1.6.13** Photo Mingli Yuan; **1.6.14** Collection National Palace Museum, Taipei, Taiwan; **1.6.15a** © Airpano (www.airpano.com); **1.6.15b** Ralph Larmann; **1.6.16a** © Tibor Bognar/Photononstop/Corbis; **1.6.16b** Ralph Larmann; **1.6.17** Courtesy Drepung Loseling Monastery, Inc.; **1.7.1** Photo Attilio Maranzano. Photo courtesy the Oldenburg Van Bruggen Foundation. Copyright 1992 Claes Oldenburg and Coosje van Bruggen; **1.7.2** Courtesy the artist; **1.7.3** Musée d'Orsay, Paris. Photo akg-images; **1.7.4a** Werner Forman Archive; **1.7.4b** Ralph Larmann; **1.7.5** Gemäldegalerie, Staatliche Museen, Berlin; **1.7.6** Purchased with assistance from the Art Fund and the American Fund for the Tate Gallery 1997. Photo Tate, London, 2012. © ADAGP, Paris and

DACS, London 2018; **1.7.7**, **1.7.8** Ralph Larmann; **1.7.9** National Museum, Ife, Nigeria; **1.7.10** Stanza della Segnatura, Vatican Museums, Rome. Line artwork Ralph Larmann; **1.7.11** Ralph Larmann; **1.7.12a** National Archaeological Museum, Athens; **1.7.12b** Ralph Larmann; **1.7.13a** George Eastman House, New York; **1.7.13b** Ralph Larmann; **1.7.14a** iStockphoto.com; **1.7.14b** Ralph Larmann; **1.8.1** Erich Lessing/akg-images; **1.8.2** Photo Scala, Florence. Chagall ®/© ADAGP, Paris and DACS, London 2018; **1.8.3** Galleria degli Uffizi, Florence; **1.8.4** San Francisco Museum of Modern Art, Bequest of Alfred M. Esberg. Photo Don Ross. © Vija Celmins. Courtesy Matthew Marks Gallery; **1.8.5** The Museum of Modern Art, New York, Gift of Sid Bass, Leon D. Black, Donald L. Bryant, Jr., Kathy and Richard S. Fuld, Jr., Agnes Gund, Mimi Haas, Marie-Josée and Henry R. Kravis, Jo Carole and Ronald S. Lauder, Donald B. Marron and Jerry Speyer on behalf of the Committee on Painting and Sculpture in honor of John Elderfield, 553.2008. Photo Jonathan Muzikar. Digital image, The Museum of Modern Art, New York/Scala, Florence. © Martin Puryear, Courtesy Matthew Marks Gallery; **1.8.6** Courtesy DC Moore Gallery, New York. © Estate of Jacob Lawrence. ARS, NY and DACS, London 2018; **1.8.7** Musées Royaux des Beaux-Arts de Belgique, Brussels; **1.8.8** Musée du Louvre, Paris; **1.8.9** Victoria & Albert Museum, London; **1.8.10** James A. Michener Collection, Honolulu Academy of Arts, Hawaii; **1.9.1** Ralph Larmann; **1.9.2** Musée National d'Art Moderne, Centre Georges Pompidou, Paris; **1.9.3** Metropolitan Museum of Art, Louis E. and Theresa S. Seley Purchase Fund for Islamic Art, and Rogers Fund, 1984, 1984.221; **1.9.4** Ralph Larmann; **1.9.5a, 1.9.5b** Heritage Center Museum: Lancaster Quilt and Textile Museum, Lancaster, Pennsylvania. Photo courtesy Hearts and Hands Media Arts from the book and film *Hearts and Hands: A Social History of 19th Century Women and Their Quilts*, distributed by New Day Films; **1.9.6** Photo Trustees of the British Museum, London; **1.9.7a, 1.9.7b**, **1.9.7c** Museum of Modern Art, New York, Gift of Agnes Gund, Jo Carole and Ronald S. Lauder, Donald L. Bryant, Jr., Leon Black, Michael and Judy Ovitz, Anna Marie and Robert F. Shapiro, Leila and Melville Straus, Doris and Donald Fisher, and purchase, 215.2000. Photo Ellen Page Wilson, courtesy The Pace Gallery © Chuck Close, The Pace Gallery; **1.9.8** Kunsthistorisches Museum, Vienna; **1.9.9** iStockphoto.com; **1.9.10** Collection Center for Creative Photography © 1981 Arizona Board of Regents; **1.9.11** © WaterFrame/Alamy; **1.9.12a** Musée d'Orsay, Paris; **1.9.12b** Musée d'Orsay, Paris. Line artwork by Ralph Larmann; **1.9.13** Metropolitan Museum of Art, New York. Gift of M. Knoedler & Co., 1918, 18.64 (43); **1.9.14** Courtesy the artist Jaune Quick-to-See Smith (Salish) and the Garth Greenan Gallery, NYC; **1.10.1a**, **1.10.1b** Photo Margarete Buesing. Photo Scala, Florence/BPK, Bildagentur für Kunst, Kultur und Geschichte, Berlin; **1.10.2** The Art Institute of Chicago, Friends of American Art Collection, 1942.51; **1.10.3** Museo Nacional del Prado, Madrid; **1.10.4a**, **1.10.4b**, **1.10.4c**, **1.10.4d** The National Gallery, London/Scala, Florence; **1.10.5** Erich Lessing/akg-images; **1.10.6** Museum of African American Art, Los Angeles, California, Gift of Mrs. Hayden; **1.10.7** Courtesy the artist; **1.10.8** Musée du Louvre, Paris; **1.10.9** © copyright The Robert Mapplethorpe Foundation. Courtesy Art + Commerce; **1.10.10** Private Collection. Photo Mickalene Thomas. © ARS, NY and DACS, London 2018; **1.10.11** Munch Museum, Oslo; **1.10.12a, 1.10.12b** Museo Nacional del Prado, Madrid; **1.10.12c** Museo Nacional del Prado, Madrid. Line artwork by Ralph Larmann; **1.10.13** © Succession Picasso/DACS, London 2018; **1.10.14** © Clive King; **p. 190** (above) Collection National Palace Museum, Taipei, Taiwan; (center) Library of Congress Prints, Washington, D.C., Prints & Photographs Division, LC-DIG-ppmsc-03521; (below) © Free Agents Limited/Corbis; **2.1.1** Biblioteca Ambrosiana, Milan; **2.1.2** The Royal Collection © Her Majesty The Queen; **2.1.3a** Biblioteca Ambrosiana, Milan; **2.1.3b** Stanza della Segnatura, Vatican Museums, Rome; **2.1.4** © John T. Biggers Estate/VAGA, NY/DACS, London Estate Represented by Michael Rosenfeld Gallery 2018; **2.1.5** British Museum, London; **2.1.6, 2.1.7** Ralph Larmann; **2.1.8** © DACS 2018; **2.1.9** Courtesy of D.J. Hall and Craig Krull Gallery, Santa Monica; **2.1.10** National Gallery of Art, Washington, D.C., Rosenwald Collection, 1943.3.5217; **2.1.11** National Gallery of Art, Washington, D.C., Gift of Mr. and Mrs. James T. Dyke, 1996.30.1; **2.1.12** Image courtesy the artist and White Rabbit Gallery, Sydney; **2.1.13** Metropolitan Museum of Art, Purchase, Joseph Pulitzer Bequest, 1924, 24.197.2; **2.1.14** Musée d'Orsay, Paris; **2.1.15** Photo RMN-Grand Palais (Musée d'Orsay)/Michèle Bellot; **2.1.16** San Francisco Museum of Modern Art, Purchased through a gift of Phyllis Wattis. © Robert Rauschenberg Foundation/DACS, London/VAGA, New York 2018; **2.1.17** Collection National Palace Museum, Taipei, Taiwan; **2.1.18** British Museum, London; **2.1.19a** © Banco de México Diego Rivera Frida Kahlo Museums Trust, Mexico, D.F./DACS 2018; **2.1.19b** Museo de Arte Moderno, Mexico City. © Banco de México Diego Rivera Frida Kahlo Museums Trust, Mexico, D.F./DACS 2018; **2.1.20** Van Gogh Museum (Vincent van Gogh Foundation), Amsterdam; **2.1.21** from *Wakoku Shoshoku Edzukushi*, 1681; **2.1.22** Ralph Larmann; **2.1.23** The Museum of Modern Art, New York, Gift of Alexander Liberman in honour of René d'Harnoncourt, 1365.1974. Digital image, The Museum of Modern Art, New York/Scala, Florence. © The Estate of Alberto Giacometti (Fondation Annette et Alberto Giacometti, Paris and ADAGP, Paris), licensed in the UK by ACS and DACS, London 2018; **2.1.24** Museum of Modern Art, New York, Purchase, 330.1949. Photo 2012, Museum of Modern Art, New York/Scala, Florence; **2.1.25** Christie's Images/Corbis; **2.2.1** Photo courtesy Dean Snow; **2.2.2**, **2.2.3** Ralph Larmann; **2.2.4** Metropolitan Museum of Art, Gift of Edward S. Harkness, 1918, 18.9.2; **2.2.5** Collection of the artist. © Mary Black; **2.2.6** Vatican Museums, Rome; **2.2.7** Photo Schenck & Schenk. © DACS 2018; **2.2.8** © Walter O'Neill; **2.2.9** Museo dell'Opera Metropolitana del Duomo, Siena; **2.2.10** Metropolitan Museum of Art, Purchase, Francis M. Weld Gift, 1950, Inv. 50.164; **2.2.11** Museum of Modern Art, New York, Purchase, 16.1949. Photo 2012, Museum of Modern Art, New York/Scala, Florence. © Andrew Wyeth; **2.2.12** Musée du Louvre, Paris; **2.2.13** Metropolitan Museum of Art, New York, Catharine Lorillard Wolfe Collection, Wolfe Fund, 1938, 38.65; **2.2.14** Metropolitan Museum of Art, New York, Gift of Cornelius Vanderbilt, 1887, 87.25; **2.2.15** Los Angeles County Museum of Art (LACMA), California. Gift of Mr. and Mrs. Robert H. Ginter, M.64.49 (www.lacma.org). Digital Image Museum Associates/LACMA/Art Resource NY/Scala, Florence. Courtesy Gallery Paule Anglim; **2.2.16** Kemper Museum of Contemporary Art, Kansas City. Bebe and Crosby Kemper Collection, Gift of the William T. Kemper Charitable Trust, UMB Bank, n.a., Trustee 2006.7. Photo Ben Blackwell. © the artist; **2.2.17** Galleria degli Uffizi, Florence; **2.2.18** The Royal Collection © Her Majesty The Queen; **2.2.19** Collection National Palace Museum, Taipei, Taiwan; **2.2.20** Metropolitan Museum of Art, New York, Purchase, Joseph Pulitzer Bequest, 1915, 15.142.2; **2.2.21** Photo Austrian Archives/Scala Florence; **2.2.22** Photo Tate, London 2012. © L&M Services B.V. The Hague 20110512. © Miriam Cendrars; **2.2.23** © Julie Mehretu. Courtesy the artist, Marian Goodman Gallery and White Cube; **2.2.24** © Ralph M. Larmann; **2.2.25** © Robert Rauschenberg Foundation/DACS, London/VAGA, New York 2018; **2.2.26** Smithsonian American Art Museum, Gift of Ruth M. Bernstein. Photo Smithsonian American Art Museum/Art Resource/Scala, Florence; **2.2.27** Photo courtesy of SPARC (sparcinla.org). Judith F. Baca © 2008; **2.2.28** Photo Kevin Flemen; **2.3.1** Ralph Larmann; **2.3.2** Metropolitan Museum of Art, New York, Gift of Junius Spencer Morgan, 1919, 19.73.209; **2.3.3** British Museum, London; **2.3.4** Museum of Modern Art, New York. Given anonymously (by exchange), 119.1956. Photo 2012, Museum of Modern Art, New York/Scala, Florence. © Nolde Stiftung Seebüll; **2.3.5** Library of Congress, Washington, D.C. Prints & Photographs Division, H. Irving Olds collection, LC-DIG-jpd-02018; **2.3.6** Courtesy Stanley Donwood/TAG Fine Arts; **2.3.7** Ralph Larmann; **2.3.8** Metropolitan Museum of Art, New York, Fletcher Fund, 1919, 19.73.1; **2.3.9** © DACS 2018; **2.3.10** Rijksmuseum, Amsterdam, Mr. and Mrs. De Bruijn-van der Leeuw Bequest, Muri, Switzerland; **2.3.11** Metropolitan Museum of Art, Harris Brisbane Dick Fund, 1935, 35.42; **2.3.12** Print and Picture Collection, Free Library of Philadelphia. Courtesy Fine Arts Program, Public Buildings Service, U.S. General Services Administration. Commissioned through the New Deal art projects; **2.3.13** Courtesy Martin-Zambito Fine Art, Seattle; **2.3.14** Ralph Larmann; **2.3.15** Metropolitan Museum of Art, New York, Rogers Fund, 1920, 20.23; **2.3.16** Photo Courtesy Phillips Auctioneers. © 2018 The Andy Warhol Foundation for the Visual Arts, Inc./Licensed by DACS, London; **2.3.17** Collection the artist, © Melanie Yazzie; **2.3.18** Fogg Art Museum, Harvard Art Museums, Margaret Fisher Fund, M25276. Photo Imaging Department © President & Fellows of Harvard College. © ARS, NY and DACS, London 2018; **2.3.19** © Kathy Strauss 2007; **2.3.20** Photo courtesy Skyline Printing LLC, Austin, Texas; **2.3.21** Photo courtesy Denis Bloch Fine Art, Los Angeles. © D.R. Rufino Tamayo/Herederos/México/Fundación Olga y Rufino Tamayo, A.C. 2018; **2.3.22** © Ilana Raviv (Oppenheim), www.ravivart.com. All rights reserved; **2.3.23** Museo de Arte Contemporano Costa da Morte, Corme. Courtesy Kurt Durhaug; **2.4.1** Museum of Fine Arts, Boston, Massachusetts/Harvard University – Museum of Fine Arts Expedition/Bridgeman Art Library; **2.4.2a, 2.4.2b** Ex S.S.P.S.A.E e per il Polo Museale della città di Firenze - Gabinetto Fotografico; **2.4.3** British Museum, London; **2.4.4** Photograph Jacqueline Banerjee, Associate Editor of the Victorian Web www.victorianweb.org; **2.4.5** Photo Trustees of the British Museum, London; **2.4.6** Photo Scala, Florence, courtesy Ministero Beni e Att. Culturali; **2.4.7** Photo 1998/Mondadori Portfolio/akg-images; **2.4.8** Photo Scala, Florence, courtesy Ministero Beni e Att. Culturali; **2.4.9** Photo Trustees of the British Museum, London; **2.4.10** Photo © Lynn Bystrom/123RF.com; **2.4.11** Museo Nazionale di Villa Giulia, Rome; **2.4.12** Nimatallah/akg-images; **2.4.13** Ralph Larmann; **2.4.14** top to bottom: © nagelestock.com/Alamy; Photo courtesy Andrew Early; The New York Historical Society, New York City; Museo del Templo Mayor, Mexico City, CONACULTA- INAH, 10-220302; Undercroft Museum, Westminster Abbey, London; © The Estate of Alberto Giacometti (Fondation Annette et Alberto Giacometti, Paris and ADAGP, Paris), licensed in the UK by ACS and DACS, London 2018; **2.4.15** © Richard A. Cooke/Corbis; **2.4.16** Photo Tom Smart; **2.4.17** Photo Tate, London 2012. The works of Naum Gabo © Nina Williams; **2.4.18** Photographed by Prudence Cuming Associates. © Damien Hirst and Science Ltd. All rights reserved, DACS 2018; **2.4.19** Collection University of California, Berkeley Art Museum; purchased with the aid of funds from the National Endowment for the Arts (selected by The Committee for the Acquisition of Afro-American Art). Photograph Joshua Nefsky. Courtesy Michael Rosenfeld Gallery LLC, New York; **2.4.20** © Succession Picasso/DACS, London 2018; **2.4.21** Photo Mark Pollock/Estate of George Rickey. © Estate of George Rickey/DACS, London/VAGA, New York 2018;

2.4.22 Harvard Art Museums, Busch-Reisinger Museum, Hildegard von Gontard Bequest Fund, 2007.105. Photo Junius Beebe, President & Fellows of Harvard College; **2.4.23** Commissioned by Parking Authority of River City, Louisville; glass fabrication by AGA of Louisville; fountain consulting by Waterline Fountains of Austin, TX; RGB animation by Color Kinetics of Boston. Photo Richard E. Spear. © Athena Tacha; **2.4.24a** Photograph by Zhang Haier; **2.4.24b** Photo Dai Wei, Shanghai © the artist; **2.5.1** © Jon Arnold Images Ltd/Alamy; **2.5.2** Maki and Associates. Courtesy Silverstein Properties; **2.5.3**, **2.5.4** iStockphoto.com; **2.5.5** DeAgostini Picture Library/Scala, Florence; **2.5.6**, **2.5.7** Ralph Larmann; **2.5.8** Bridgeman Art Library; **2.5.9** Index/Bridgeman Art Library; **2.5.10** top to bottom: A. Vergani/DeAgostini Picture Library/Diomedia.com; Marco Simoni/imagebroker RM/Diomedia; Photo © Spyros Arsenis/123RF.com; **2.5.11** Ralph Larmann; **2.5.12** © Natalia Pavlova/Dreamstime.com; **2.5.13** Ralph Larmann; **2.5.14** © Christophe Boisvieux/Corbis; **2.5.15** Ralph Larmann; **2.5.16** Photo Scala, Florence; **2.5.17a**, **2.5.17b** Ralph Larmann; **2.5.18** © John Kellerman/Alamy Stock Photo; **2.5.19** © Robert Harding Picture Library Ltd/Alamy; **2.5.20**, **2.5.21** Ralph Larmann; **2.5.22** © Photo Japan/Alamy; **2.5.23** © Martindata/Dreamstime.com; **2.5.24** Ralph Larmann; **2.5.25** SuperStock; **2.5.26** © Anthony Shaw/Dreamstime.com; **2.5.27** Photo Shannon Kyles, ontarioarchitecture.com; **2.5.29** Photo Sandak Inc, Stamford, CT; **2.5.30** © Interfoto/Alamy; **2.5.31** © Jose Fuste Raga/Corbis; **2.5.32** © Bildarchiv Monheim GmbH/Alamy; **2.5.33** © Richard A. Cooke/Corbis; **2.5.34** © Free Agents Limited/Corbis; **2.5.35** Photo courtesy Michael Graves & Associates; **2.5.36** © Chuck Eckert/Alamy; **2.5.37a** Courtesy Zaha Hadid Architects; **2.5.37b** © Roland Halbe/artur; **2.5.38** Photo © John Swain; **2.6.1** Courtesy Trudy Labell Fine Art, Florida. © the artist; **2.6.2** Photo Trudy Labell; **2.6.3** Metropolitan Museum of Art, New York, Gift of Jaap Polak, 2009, 2009.321; **2.6.4** Cleveland Museum of Art, Gift of the Hanna Fund, 1954.857; **2.6.5** Palace Museum, Beijing; **2.6.6** Photo Tyler Dingee. Courtesy Palace of the Governors Photo Archives (NMHM/DCA), Neg. No. 073453; **2.6.7** Photo T. Harmon Parkhurst. Courtesy Palace of the Governors Photo Archives (NMHM/DCA), Neg. No. 055204; **2.6.8** Newark Museum, Gift of Amelia Elizabeth White, 1937. 37.236 © 2014. Photo The Newark Museum/Art Resource/Scala, Florence; **2.6.9** Courtesy the Voulkos & Co. Catalogue Project, www.voulkos.com; **2.6.10** British Museum, London; **2.6.11** © Angelo Hornak/Corbis; **2.6.12** Photo Teresa Nouri Rishel © Dale Chihuly; **2.6.13** National Archaeological Museum, Athens; **2.6.14** The Walters Art Museum, Baltimore. Acquired by Henry Walters, 1929; **2.6.15** Kunsthistorisches Museum, Vienna; **2.6.16** Private Collection; **2.6.17** The Solomon R. Guggenheim Foundation, New York, 88.3620. Faith Ringgold © 1988; **2.6.18** © Christie's Images/Corbis; **2.6.19** Photo Smithsonian American Art Museum/Art Resource/Scala, Florence. © Sheila Hicks; **2.6.20** Collaborators: Charles MacAdam with Interplay Design & Manufacturing, Inc, Nova Scotia, Canada (design & production); Norihide Imagawa with T.I.S. & Partners., Co. Ltd, Tokyo (structural design). Photo Masaki Koizumi. Courtesy the artist; **2.6.21** Metropolitan Museum of Art, Rogers Fund, 1939, 39.153. Photo Metropolitan Museum of Art/Art Resource/Scala, Florence; **2.6.22** Seattle Art Museum, Gift of John H. Hauberg and John and Grace Putnam, 86.278. Photo Paul Macapia; **2.6.23** Photo courtesy Andrew Early; **2.7.1** British Museum, London; **2.7.2** Tokyo National Museum **2.7.3** V&A Images/Victoria & Albert Museum; **2.7.4** Ralph Larmann; **2.7.5** © Kok Cheow Yeoh (www.yeoh.com); **2.7.6** Koninklijke Bibliotheek, The Hague, folio 8r., shelf no. 69B 10; **2.7.7** General Motors Corp. Used with permission, GM Media Archives; **2.7.8a** © DACS 2018; **2.7.8b** © Lianem/Dreamstime.com; **2.7.9** © Annsunnyday/Dreamstime.com; **2.7.10** from *Works of Geoffrey Chaucer*, Kelmscott Press, 1896; **2.7.11** Library of Congress Prints, Washington, D.C., Prints & Photographs Division, LC-DIG-ppmsc-03521; **2.7.12** © Maxfield Parrish Family, LLC/VAGA, NY/DACS, London 2018; **2.7.13** Harry Potter characters, names and related indicia are © & TM Warner Bros. Entertainment Inc. Publishing Rights © J. K. Rowling. (s18); **2.7.14** © Jorge Colombo, courtesy *The New Yorker*; **2.7.15** Video-computer graphic © April Greiman; **2.7.16** The Art Institute of Chicago, Mr. and Mrs. Carter H. Harrison Collection, 1954.1193; **2.7.17** Shiseido Corporate Museum, Kakegawa-shi, Shizuoka-ken; **2.7.18** Courtesy Helen Musselwhite; **2.7.19a**, **2.7.19b** Courtesy Maple Leaf Sports & Entertainment Ltd. (MLSE); **2.7.20** Courtesy Spotify/spotify.com; **2.7.21a**, **2.7.21b** Website commissioned by The Museum of Modern Art, New York (www.moma.org/interactives/exhibitions/2013/magritte/). Artwork: The Museum of Modern Art, Kay Sage Tanguy Fund, 247.1966. The Museum of Modern Art, New York/Scala, Florence. © ADAGP, Paris and DACS, London 2018; **2.7.22** Ralph Larmann; **2.7.23** Private Collection; **2.7.24** Ralph Larmann; **2.7.25** Photo Helena Kristiansson, esportphoto.com; **2.8.1** Wellcome Library, London; **2.8.2** Image appears courtesy Abelardo Morell; **2.8.3** Gernsheim Collection, Harry Ransom Humanities Research Centre, University of Texas at Austin; **2.8.5** British Library, London; **2.8.6** British Library, London/British Library Board. All Rights Reserved/Bridgeman Images; **2.8.7** Ralph Larmann; **2.8.8** © Maia Dery; **2.8.9** Bibliothèque nationale, Paris; **2.8.10** J. Paul Getty Museum, Los Angeles (84.XM.443.3). Digital image courtesy the Getty's Open Content Program; **2.8.11** © Ansel Adams Publishing Rights Trust/Corbis; **2.8.12** Collection Center for Creative Photography © 1981 Arizona Board of Regents; **2.8.13** Photo Collection F. Van Hoof-Williame; **2.8.14** Sandy Skoglund, Radioactive Cats © 1980; **2.8.15** Copyright Steve McCurry/Magnum Photos; **2.8.16** Library of Congress, Washington, D.C., Prints & Photographs Division, LC-DIG-nclc-01555; **2.8.17** © Hiroko Masuike/New York Times/Eyevine; **2.8.18** Royal Photographic Society, Bath; **2.8.19** Courtesy Yossi Milo Gallery, New York. © DACS 2018; **2.8.20** Nationalgalerie, Staatliche Museen, Berlin. © DACS 2018; **2.8.21** Gernsheim Collection, Harry Ransom Humanities Research Centre, University of Texas at Austin; **2.8.22** © Sally Mann. Courtesy Gagosian; **2.8.23** © Carrie Mae Weems. Courtesy the artist and Jack Shainman Gallery, New York; **2.8.24** Museum of Modern Art, New York, Gift on behalf of The Friends of Education of The Museum of Modern Art, 70.1997.2. Photo 2012, Museum of Modern Art, New York/Scala, Florence. Courtesy the artist and Jack Shainman Gallery, New York; **2.8.25** J. Paul Getty Museum, Los Angeles (84.XM.695.19). Digital image courtesy of the Getty's Open Content Program; **2.8.26** © Estate of Garry Winogrand, courtesy Fraenkel Gallery, San Francisco; **2.8.27** Photo © Edward Burtynsky, courtesy Flowers, London & Nicholas Metivier, Toronto; **2.8.28** © Daniela Edburg; **2.9.1** Ralph Larmann; **2.9.2** Courtesy Laboratorio Paravicini; **2.9.3** Library of Congress, Washington, D.C., Prints & Photographs Division, LC-USZ62-45683; **2.9.4** Star Film Company; **2.9.5** akg-images; **2.9.6** RKO Radio Pictures/Ronald Grant Archive/Mary Evans; **2.9.7** British Film Institute (BFI); **2.9.8** M.G.M./Album/akg-images; **2.9.9** La Classe Americane/uFilm/France 3/The Kobal Collection; **2.9.10** Album/akg-images; **2.9.11** Disney Enterprises/Album/akg-images; **2.9.12** British Film Institute (BFI); **2.9.13a** New Line Cinema/The Kobal Collection; **2.9.13b** Album/akg-images; **2.9.14** Handprint Entertainment/Lions Gate Film/Miramax Films/Ronald Grant Archive/Mary Evans; **2.9.15** Fox 200 Pictures/Levantine Fils/Album/akg-images; **2.9.16** © AF Archive/Alamy; **2.9.17** British Film Institute (BFI); **2.9.18** Courtesy Electronic Arts Intermix (EAI), New York; **2.9.19a** Photo Mathias Schormann © Bill Viola; **2.9.19b**, **2.9.19c** Photo Kira Perov © Bill Viola; **2.9.20** © 2018 Playdead; **2.9.21** HBO/Kobal/REX/Shutterstock; **2.10.1** Photo © Estate of David Gahr. © ADAGP, Paris and DACS, London 2018; **2.10.2** Photo Cathy Carver. © Barbara Kruger, courtesy Mary Boone Gallery, New York; **2.10.3** Photo Karla Merrifield. © Yoko Ono; **2.10.4** Rowland Scherman/Hulton Archive/Getty Images; **2.10.5** © DACS 2018; **2.10.6** Photo Betsy Jackson. Courtesy the artist; **2.10.7** Photography by Marco Anelli. Courtesy the Marina Abramović Archives; **2.10.8a** Photo © Ed Jansen. Copyright Kienholz, courtesy L.A. Louver; **2.10.8b** Photo SuperStock. Copyright Kienholz, courtesy L. A. Louver; **2.10.9** Hirshhorn Museum and Sculpture Garden, Smithsonian Institution. Photo Cathy Carver. Courtesy Ai Weiwei Studio; **2.10.10** Photo courtesy James Cohan, New York. © Yinka Shonibare MBE. All Rights Reserved, DACS 2018; **2.10.11** Photo Sarina Basta. Artwork © Kara Walker, courtesy of Sikkema Jenkins & Co., New York; **2.10.12** Still courtesy of Milford Galleries, Dunedin and Yuki Kihara. © Yuki Kihara; **2.10.13** Photo Red Sand Project; **p. 362** (above) Egyptian Museum, Cairo; (center) iStockphoto.com; (below) Pushkin Museum, Moscow; **3.1.1** Drazen Tomic; **3.1.2** Photo © Pedro Saura; **3.1.3** Erich Lessing/akg-images; **3.1.4** J. Paul Getty Museum, Los Angeles (88.AA.80). Digital image courtesy of the Getty's Open Content Program; **3.1.5** Image courtesy the Mellaarts/Çatalhöyük Research Project; **3.1.6** Photo Jeff Morgan Travel/Alamy; **3.1.7** Archaeological Museum, Heraklion; **3.1.8a**, **3.1.8b** British Museum, London; **3.1.9** Erich Lessing/akg-images; **3.1.10** University of Pennsylvania Museum of Archaeology and Anthropology, Philadelphia, B17694; **3.1.11** Iraq Museum, Baghdad; **3.1.12** Metropolitan Museum of Art, New York, Gift of John D. Rockefeller Jr., 1932, 32.143.2; **3.1.13** Photo Scala, Florence/BPK, Bildagentur für Kunst, Kultur und Geschichte, Berlin; **3.1.14** National Geographic/SuperStock; **3.1.15** Gianni Dagli Orti/Egyptian Museum, Cairo/The Art Archive; **3.1.16** Photo Trustees of the British Museum, London; **3.1.17** Staatliche Museen, Berlin. Photo Sandra Steiss. Photo Scala, Florence/BPK, Bildagentur für Kunst, Kultur und Geschichte, Berlin; **3.1.18** British Museum, London; **3.1.19** Egyptian Museum, Cairo; **3.1.20** Peter Connolly/akg-images; **3.1.21** Ralph Larmann; **3.1.22** Nimatallah/akg-images; **3.1.23** British Museum, London; **3.1.24** © Grant Rooney/Alamy Stock Photo; **3.1.25**, **3.1.26**, **3.1.27** Photo Scala, Florence; **3.1.28** Metropolitan Museum of Art, New York, Fletcher Fund, 1932, 32.11.1; **3.1.29** Minneapolis Institute of Arts, Minnesota; **3.1.30** Vatican Museums, Rome; **3.1.31** Raimund Kutter/imagebroker.net; **3.1.32** Palazzo Torlonia, Rome; **3.1.33** Giovanni Caselli; **3.1.34** Image Source Pink/Alamy; **3.1.35** iStockphoto.com; **3.1.36** Photo iStockphoto.com; **3.1.37** Photo © Viacheslav Lopatin/123RF.com; **3.2.1** Drazen Tomic; **3.2.2**, **3.2.3** Zev Radovan/www.BibleLandPictures.com; **3.2.4** Canali Photobank, Milan, Italy; **3.2.5** Photo Scala, Florence; **3.2.6** © Alp S/Alamy Stock Photo; **3.2.7**, **3.2.8** Monastery of St. Catherine, Sinai, Egypt; **3.2.9** Photo Scala, Florence; **3.2.10** Scala, Florence; **3.2.11**, **3.2.12a**, **3.2.12b** British Library, London; **3.2.13** Biblioteca Governativa, Lucca; **3.2.14** British Library/akg-images; **3.2.15** Musées Royaux d'Art et d'Histoire, Brussels; **3.2.16** © Hanan Isachar/Corbis; **3.2.17** Mohamed Amin/Robert Harding; **3.2.18** Photo © Dilek Mermer/Anadolu Agency/Getty Images; **3.2.19** Nasser D. Khalili Collection of Islamic Art, MSS 745.2. © Nour Foundation, courtesy the Khalili Family Trust; **3.2.20** Drazen Tomic; **3.2.21** Photo © Gérard Labriet/Photononstop/Diomedia; **3.2.22**, **3.2.23** Ralph Larmann; **3.2.24** Photononstop/SuperStock; **3.2.25** Hervé Champollion/akg-images; **3.2.26** Sonia Halliday

Photographs; **3.2.27**, **3.2.28** Galleria degli Uffizi, Florence; **3.3.1** Drazen Tomic; **3.3.2** © Ebba Koch; **3.3.3** © Airpano (www.airpano.com); **3.3.4** iStockphoto.com; **3.3.5** © Dinodia Photos/Alamy Stock Photo; **3.3.6** Robert Harding Picture Library/SuperStock; **3.3.7** Photo © Zhang Peng/LightRocket/Getty Images; **3.3.8a** © Reuters/Corbis; **3.3.8b** © Ton Koene/ZUMA Press/Corbis; **3.3.9** Drazen Tomic; **3.3.10** © Frédéric Soltan/Sygma/Corbis; **3.3.11** © Pep Roig/Alamy; **3.3.12** Hunan Museum, Changsha, China; **3.3.13a** Melvyn Longhurst/SuperStock; **3.3.13b** Hemis.fr/SuperStock; **3.3.14** Palace Museum, Beijing, China; **3.3.15** Courtesy Ai Weiwei Studio; **3.3.16** Courtesy the artist; **3.3.17** Aflo Diversion/Diomedia; **3.3.19** Courtesy the artist; **3.3.20** Photo Shunji Ohkura; **3.3.21** Horyu-ji Treasure House, Ikaruga, Nara Prefecture, Japan; **3.3.22** The Tokugawa Art Museum, Nagoya, Japan; **3.3.23** Library of Congress, Washington, D.C., Prints & Photographs Division, H. Irving Olds collection, LC-DIG-jpd-02018; **3.3.24** iStockphoto.com; **3.3.25** © Do Ho Suh. Courtesy the artist and Lehmann Maupin, New York and Hong Kong; **3.3.26** © Shirley Hu/Dreamstime.com; **3.3.27** © Kevin R. Morris/Corbis; **3.3.28** Photo © acarapi/123RF.com; **3.4.1** Drazen Tomic; **3.4.2a** G. Dagli Orti/DeAgostini Picture Library/The Art Archive; **3.4.2b**, **3.4.2c** Anton, F., *Ancient Peruvian Textiles*, Thames & Hudson Ltd, London, 1987; **3.4.3** Museo Arqueología, Lima, Peru/Bridgeman Art Library; **3.4.4** Royal Tombs of Sipán Museum, Lambayeque; **3.4.5** iStockphoto.com; **3.4.6** Dumbarton Oaks Research Library and Collections, Washington, D.C.; **3.4.7** Drazen Tomic; **3.4.8** Richard Hewitt Stewart/National Geographic Stock; **3.4.9a** Drazen Tomic; **3.4.9b** © aerialarchives.com/Alamy; **3.4.10** © Ken Welsh/Alamy; **3.4.11a** Photo Trustees of the British Museum, London; **3.4.11b** British Museum, London/Werner Forman Archive; **3.4.11c** National Museum of Anthropology, Mexico City/Werner Forman Archive; **3.4.12** © Gianni Dagli Orti/Corbis; **3.4.13** Dallas Museum of Art, Gift of Patsy R. and Raymond D. Nasher, 1983.148; **3.4.14** Peabody Museum, Harvard University, Cambridge, Massachusetts, 48-63-20/17561; **3.4.15** Biblioteca Nazionale Centrale di Firenze; **3.4.16** Museo Nacional de Antropología, Mexico City; **3.4.17** Museo del Templo Mayor, Mexico City; **3.4.18** Museo de Aguascalientes – ICA, INBA; **3.4.19** Drazen Tomic; **3.4.20** © Chris Howes/Wild Places Photography/Alamy; **3.4.21a**, **3.4.21b** Peabody Museum, Harvard University, Cambridge, Massachusetts, 99-12-10/53121; **3.4.22** Missouri Historical Society, St. Louis, 1882.18.32; **3.4.23** American Museum of Natural History, New York; **3.4.24** Photo Jennifer Bresee; **3.4.25** Photo Keith Walklet. Courtesy Yosemite Conservancy; **3.4.26** Photo © Rory Wakemup. © Cannupa Hanska Luger; **3.5.1** Drazen Tomic; **3.5.2** National Museum, Lagos; **3.5.3** Linden Museum, Stuttgart; **3.5.4** Dallas Museum of Art, Foundation for the Arts Collection, Gift of the McDermott Foundation, 1996.184.FA; **3.5.5** National Museum of African Art, Smithsonian Institution, Washington, D.C.; **3.5.6a** Musée Barbier-Mueller, Geneva; **3.5.6b** © Michel Renaudeau; **3.5.7** © JTB Photo Communications, Inc./Alamy; **3.5.8** Photo © Alice Mutasa/placesandseasons.com; **3.5.9** Photo © Ed Kashi/National Geographic Creative; **3.5.10** Photo Barney Wayne; **3.5.11** Courtesy MMA Design Studio; **3.5.12** Drazen Tomic; **3.5.13** pl. XVI from Parkinson, S., *A Journal of a Voyage to the South Seas*, 1784; **3.5.14** Photo Paul S. C. Tacon; **3.5.15a** Photo Trustees of the British Museum, London; **3.5.15b** Chris Johns/National Geographic/Getty Images; **3.5.16** © Albertoloyo/Dreamstime.com; **3.5.17** Musée Barbier-Mueller, Geneva; **3.5.18** Collected by G. F. N. Gerrits, Vb 28418-28471 (1972). Photo Peter Horner 1981 Museum der Kulturen, Basel, Switzerland; **3.6.1** Drazen Tomic; **3.6.2a** G. Nimatallah/DeAgostini Picture Library/Diomedia; **3.6.2b** A. Dagli Orti/DeAgostini Picture Library/Diomedia; **3.6.3** © Michael S. Yamashita/Corbis; **3.6.4** Libreria dello Stato, Rome; **3.6.5** Brancacci Chapel, Church of Santa Maria del Carmine, Florence; **3.6.6** Photo RMN-Grand Palais (Musée du Louvre)/Tony Querrec; **3.6.7** Musée d'Unterlinden, Colmar; **3.6.8a**, **3.6.8b** National Gallery, London/Scala, Florence; **3.6.9a** Rabatti - Domingie/akg-images; **3.6.9b**, **3.6.9c** Vatican Museums, Rome; **3.6.9d** 1998/Mondadori Portfolio/akg-images; **3.6.9e** Mondadori Portfolio/akg-images; **3.6.10** Stanza della Segnatura, Vatican Museums, Rome; **3.6.11** Capponi Chapel, Church of Santa Felicità, Florence; **3.6.12** National Gallery of Art, Washington, D.C., Samuel H. Kress Collection, 1946.18.1; **3.6.13** Muzeum Narodowe, Poznan/Bridgeman Art Library; **3.6.14a** Cameraphoto/akg-images; **3.6.14b** pl. XIII, Book II from Wade, I. (ed.) *Palladio: Four Books of Architecture*, 1738; **3.6.15** Refectory of Santa Maria delle Grazie, Milan; **3.6.16** British Museum, London; **3.6.17** Cameraphoto/Scala, Florence; **3.6.18** National Gallery, London/Scala, Florence; **3.6.19** Galleria degli Uffizi, Florence; **3.6.20** Galleria Nazionale d'Arte Antica, Palazzo Barberini, Rome; **3.6.21a** Prisma/Album/akg-images; **3.6.21b** Ralph Larmann; **3.6.22** Photo Scala, Florence, courtesy Ministero Beni e Att. Culturali; **3.6.23** © nagelestock.com/Alamy; **3.6.24** Photo Scala, Florence, courtesy Ministero Beni e Att. Culturali; **3.6.25** Peter Willi/Bridgeman Images; **3.6.26** Rijksmuseum, Amsterdam; **3.6.27** The Earl of Plymouth. On loan to the National Museum of Wales, Cardiff; **3.6.28** Musée du Louvre, Paris; **3.6.29** © Bertrand Rieger/Hemis/Corbis; **3.7.1** The Wallace Collection, London; **3.7.2** © Florian Monheim/Arcaid/Corbis; **3.7.3** Photo Scala, Florence; **3.7.4** National Gallery, London/Scala, Florence; **3.7.5** Classic Image/Alamy; **3.7.6** Gianni Dagli Orti/Musée du Château de Versailles/The Art Archive; **3.7.7** Musée du Louvre, Paris; **3.7.8** DeAgostini Picture Library/The Art Archive; **3.7.9** Virginia Museum of Fine Arts, Richmond, The Adolf D. and Wilkins C. Williams Fund; **3.7.10** iStockphoto.com; **3.7.11** Wellcome Collection, London; **3.7.12** Photo RMN-Grand Palais (Château de Versailles)/Gérard Blot; **3.7.13** Musée du Louvre, Paris; **3.7.14** Photo Tate, London 2012; **3.7.15** Museum of Fine Arts, Boston, Henry Lillie Pierce Fund, BJ385; **3.7.16** Metropolitan Museum of Art, Gift of Mrs. Russell Sage, 1908, 08.228; **3.8.1**, **3.8.2** Musée d'Orsay, Paris; **3.8.4** Photo Tate, London 2012; **3.8.5** Photo Tate, London 2018; **3.8.6** Library of Congress Prints, Washington, D.C., Prints & Photographs Division, LC-USZ62-7990; **3.8.7** Museum purchase made possible by the Pauline Edwards Bequest. Photo Smithsonian American Art Museum/Art Resource/Scala, Florence; **3.8.8** Courtesy the Pennsylvania Academy of the Fine Arts, Philadelphia. Charles Bregler's Thomas Eakins Collection, purchased with the partial support of the Pew Memorial Trust, 1985.68.2.985; **3.8.9** Musée d'Orsay, Paris; **3.8.10** V&A Images/Alamy; **3.8.11** The Art Institute of Chicago, Robert A. Waller Fund, 1910.2; **3.8.12** Pushkin Museum, Moscow; **3.8.13** Photo courtesy Sotheby's, Inc. 2013; **3.8.14** Art Institute of Chicago, Charles H. and Mary F. S. Worcester Collection, 1964.336; **3.8.15** Martin Bache/Alamy Stock Photo; **3.8.16** Courtauld Gallery, London; **3.8.17** National Gallery of Scotland, Edinburgh; **3.8.18** Museum of Modern Art, New York. Acquired through the Lillie P. Bliss Bequest, 472.1941. Photo 2012, Museum of Modern Art, New York/Scala, Florence; **3.8.19** akg-images; **3.8.20** Hampton University Museum, Virginia; **3.8.21** Fogg Art Museum, Harvard Art Museums/Bequest of Grenville L. Winthrop/Bridgeman Images; **3.8.22** Erich Lessing/akg-images; **3.8.23** Galleria degli Uffizi, Florence; **3.8.24** Photo Austrian Archives/Scala, Florence; **3.8.25** Photo © Bastin & Evrard, Brussels; **3.8.26** Photo courtesy Sotheby's, Inc. 2013; **3.8.27** Museum Folkwang, Essen; **3.8.28** Art Institute of Chicago, Arthur Jerome Eddy Memorial Collection, 1931.511; **3.8.29** akg-images; **3.9.1** The Barnes Foundation, Merion, PA. © Succession H. Matisse/DACS 2018; **3.9.2** Museum of Modern Art, New York, Mrs. Simon Guggenheim Fund, 8.1949. Photo 2012, Museum of Modern Art, New York/Scala, Florence. © Succession H. Matisse/DACS 2018; **3.9.3** Photograph by Hélène Adant/RAPHO/GAMMA, Camera Press, London; **3.9.4** Museum of Modern Art, New York, acquired through the Lillie P. Bliss Bequest, 333.1939. Photo 2012, Museum of Modern Art, New York/Scala, Florence. © Succession Picasso/DACS, London 2018; **3.9.5** Kunstmuseum, Bern. © ADAGP, Paris and DACS, London 2018; **3.9.6** Kunstmuseum, Bern/SuperStock/The Art Archive; **3.9.8** Museum of Modern Art, New York, The Sidney and Harriet Janis Collection, 595.1967 a–b. Photo 2012, Museum of Modern Art, New York/Scala, Florence. © Association Marcel Duchamp/ADAGP, Paris and DACS, London 2018; **3.9.9** © The Heartfield Community of Heirs/DACS 2018; **3.9.10** © DACS 2018; **3.9.11** Photo Hickey-Robertson, Houston. The Menil Collection, Houston. © ADAGP, Paris and DACS, London 2018; **3.9.12** Museum of Modern Art, New York, Gift of Mr. and Mrs. Pierre Matisse, 940.1965.a-c. Photo 2012, Museum of Modern Art, New York/Scala, Florence. © Successió Miró/ADAGP, Paris and DACS London 2018; **3.9.13** Museo de Arte Moderno, Mexico City. © Banco de México Diego Rivera Frida Kahlo Museums Trust, Mexico, D.F./DACS 2018; **3.9.14** © Center for Creative Photography, The University of Arizona Foundation/DACS 2018; **3.9.15** Photo Francis Carr © Thames & Hudson Ltd, London; **3.9.16** Philadelphia Museum of Art, The Louise and Walter Arensberg Collection. © Association Marcel Duchamp/ADAGP, Paris and DACS, London 2018; **3.9.17** Fondation Beyeler, Riehen/Basel, Sammlung Beyeler; acquired with the contribution of Hartmann P. and Cécile Koechlin-Tanner, Riehen. Welsh/Joosten B 234, Photo Robert Bayer, Basel; **3.9.18** The Museum of Modern Art, New York. Acquisition confirmed in 1999 by agreement with the Estate of Kazimir Malevich and made possible with funds from the Mrs. John Hay Whitney Bequest (by exchange), 817.1935. Digital image, The Museum of Modern Art, New York/Scala, Florence; **3.9.19** The Museum of Modern Art, New York. Given anonymously, 153.1934. Digital image, The Museum of Modern Art, New York/Scala, Florence. © Succession Brancusi - All rights reserved. ADAGP, Paris and DACS, London 2018; **3.9.20** Christie's Images/Corbis. © Agnes Martin/DACS 2018; **3.9.21** Art Institute of Chicago, Friends of American Art Collection, 1930.934; **3.9.22** Photo The Newark Museum/Art Resource/Scala, Florence; **3.9.23** New York Public Library/Aaron Douglas/Science Photo Library. © Heirs of Aaron Douglas/VAGA, NY/DACS, London 2018; **3.9.24** New York World's Fair 1939–1940 records, Manuscripts and Archives Division, The New York Public Library, Astor, Lenox and Tilden Foundations; **3.9.25** Courtesy Center for Creative Photography, University of Arizona © 1991 Hans Namuth Estate; **3.9.26** The Museum of Modern Art, New York. Purchase, 77.1950. Digital image, The Museum of Modern Art, New York/Scala, Florence. © The Pollock-Krasner Foundation ARS, NY and DACS, London 2018; **3.9.27** The Museum of Modern Art, New York, Gift of the Artist, 1108.1969. Digital image, The Museum of Modern Art, New York/Scala, Florence. © 1998 Kate Rothko Prizel & Christopher Rothko ARS, NY and DACS, London; **3.9.28** Photo National Gallery of Art, Washington. © Helen Frankenthaler Foundation, Inc./ARS, NY and DACS, London 2018; **3.9.29** © 2018 The Andy Warhol Foundation for the Visual Arts, Inc./Licensed by DACS, London; **3.9.30** © Estate of Roy Lichtenstein/DACS 2018; **3.9.31** © EggImages/Alamy; **3.9.32** Photo courtesy Michael Graves & Associates; **3.9.33** Collection the Modern Art Museum of Fort Worth, Museum purchase, The Benjamin J. Tillar Memorial Trust. Acquired in 1970. © Judd Foundation/ARS, NY and DACS, London 2018; **3.9.34** Photo Hickey-Robertson, Houston. The

Menil Collection, Houston. © Stephen Flavin/Artists Rights Society (ARS), New York 2018; **3.10.1** Philadelphia Museum of Art, 125th Anniversary Acquisition. Gift (by exchange) of Mrs. Herbert Cameron Morris, 1998, 1998-74-1. © Association Marcel Duchamp/ADAGP, Paris and DACS, London 2018; **3.10.2** © Sherrie Levine. Courtesy Simon Lee Gallery, London; **3.10.3** Museum of Modern Art, New York, Larry Aldrich Foundation Fund, 393.1970.a-c. Photo 2012, Museum of Modern Art, New York/ Scala, Florence. © Joseph Kosuth. ARS, NY and DACS, London 2018; **3.10.4** © The Estate of Ana Mendieta. Courtesy Galerie Lelong, New York; **3.10.5** Copyright © Andy Goldsworthy; **3.10.6** Brooklyn Museum, Gift of R.M. Atwater, Anna Wolfrom Dove, Alice Fiebiger, Belle Campbell Harriss, and Emma L. Hyde, by exchange, Designated Purchase Fund. Mary Smith Dorward Fund, Dick S. Ramsey Fund, and Carl H. de Silver Fund, 2012.80. © Wadsworth Jarrell; **3.10.7** Photo courtesy John Michael Kohler Arts Center © the artist and Stefan Stux Gallery, NY; **3.10.8**, **3.10.9** © Carrie Mae Weems. Courtesy the artist and Jack Shainman Gallery, New York; **3.10.10** William Sr. and Dorothy Harmsen Collection, by exchange, 2007.47. Denver Art Museum. All Rights Reserved; **3.10.11** © the artist; **3.10.12a**, **3.10.12b** Courtesy Gladstone Gallery, New York. © Shirin Neshat; **3.10.13** Photo Smithsonian American Art Museum/Art Resource/ Scala, Florence; **3.10.14** Photo courtesy Galerie Enrico Navarra. © The Estate of Jean-Michel Basquiat/ADAGP, Paris and DACS, London 2018; **3.10.15** Museum of Modern Art, New York, Fractional gift offered by Donald L. Bryant, Jr., 241.2000.b. Photo 2012, Museum of Modern Art, New York/Scala, Florence. © 1997 Pipilotti Rist. Image courtesy the artist, Luhring Augustine, New York and Hauser & Wirth; **3.10.16** Courtesy Gladstone Gallery, New York. Photo Michael James O'Brien. © 1997 Matthew Barney; **3.10.17** Courtesy Giò Marconi, Milan and Lisson Gallery, London. © Nathalie Djurberg & Hans Berg; **3.10.18** Photo courtesy the artist and Pace Gallery. © Tara Donovan, courtesy Pace Gallery; **3.10.19** © Gabriel Dawe; **3.10.20a**, **3.10.20b** Courtesy The Fundred Dollar Bill Project; **3.10.21a** Photo © Eric Rogers; **3.10.21b** Photo © Kevin Nance; **p. 562** (above) Photo David Heald. The Solomon R. Guggenheim Foundation, New York. FLWW-10; (center) Courtauld Gallery, London; (below) Victor Chavez/ WireImage/Getty; **4.1.1** © guichaoua/ Alamy; **4.1.2** iStockphoto. com; **4.1.3** © Brad Calkins/Dreamstime.com; **4.1.4** Photo David Heald. The Solomon R. Guggenheim Foundation, New York. FLWW-10; **4.1.5** Photo John Randall. Courtesy the artist; **4.1.6** Silvio Fiore/ photolibrary.com; **4.1.7** Cahokia Mounds State Historic Site, painting by William R. Iseminger; **4.1.8** Martin Gray/National Geographic Stock; **4.1.9** Keith Bedford/ epa/Corbis; **4.1.10** Henry John Drewal and Margaret Thompson Drewal Collection, EEPA D00639. Eliot Elisofon Photographic Archives, National Museum of African Art, Smithsonian Institution, Washington, D.C., courtesy Henry John Drewal; **4.1.11** Courtesy the artist; **4.1.12** Photo Anne Chauvet; **4.1.13** Photo Art Resource/Bob Schalkwijk/Scala, Florence. © Banco de México Diego Rivera Frida Kahlo Museums Trust, Mexico, D.F./ DACS 2018; **4.1.14** Courtesy Galerie Lelong, New York. © Krzysztof Wodiczko; **4.2.1** John Hios/akg-images; **4.2.2a**, **4.2.2b** Dom-Museum Hildesheim; **4.2.2c** Ralph Larmann; **4.2.3** India Museum, Calcutta; **4.2.4** The Cleveland Museum of Art, James Albert and Mary Gardiner Ford Memorial Fund, 1961.198; **4.2.5** © Peter Arnold, Inc./Alamy; **4.2.6** Photo by Photo Services. Courtesy National Museum of the American Indian, Smithsonian Institution, Washington, D.C. (18/2023); **4.2.7** Musée du Louvre, Paris; **4.2.8** State Tretyakov Gallery, Moscow; **4.2.9** Photo Scala, Florence/ Fondo Edifici di Culto – Min. dell'Interno; **4.2.10** British Museum, London; **4.2.11** Hervé Champollion/ akg-images; **4.2.12** National Gallery of Art, Washington, D.C., Widener Collection, 1942.9.97; **4.2.13a** Ralph Larmann; **4.2.13b** Colorphoto Hans Hinz, Allschwil, Switzerland; **4.2.14a** Ralph Larmann; **4.2.14b** © Araldo de Luca/ Corbis; **4.2.15** © B. O'Kane/Alamy; **4.2.16** Courtesy Jingu Administration Office; **4.2.17** Photo Hickey-Robertson. © 1998 Kate Rothko Prizel & Christopher Rothko ARS, NY and DACS, London; **4.3.1** Dumbarton Oaks Museum, Washington, D.C.; **4.3.2** Courtesy the artist and Marian Goodman Gallery, New York/ Paris; **4.3.3** Pinoteca di Brera, Milan; **4.3.4** © Andres Serrano. Courtesy the artist and Yvon Lambert Paris, New York; **4.3.5a** © Airpano (www.airpano.com); **4.3.5b** Jean-Louis Nou/akg-image; **4.3.6** Musée Condé, Chantilly, France/ Bridgeman Images; **4.3.7** © the artist. Courtesy White Cube, London and Paula Cooper Gallery, New York; **4.3.8** Metropolitan Museum of Art, The Michael C. Rockefeller Memorial Collection, Bequest of Nelson A. Rockefeller, 1979, 1979.206.1611. Photo Metropolitan Museum of Art/Art Resource/Scala, Florence; **4.3.9** Dallas Museum of Art, The Clark and Frances Stillman Collection of Congo Sculpture, Gift of Eugene and Margaret McDermott, 1969.S.22; **4.3.10** Courtesy David Castillo Gallery and the artist; **4.3.11** Copyright Merle Greene Robertson, 1976; **4.3.12** The Cleveland Museum of Art, Purchase from the J. H. Wade Fund 1930.331; **4.3.13** akg-images; **4.3.14** The Museum of Modern Art, New York, Gift of Mrs. Simon Guggenheim, 2.1938. Digital image, The Museum of Modern Art, New York/Scala, Florence. © Succession Picasso/DACS, London 2018; **4.3.15** Collection University of Arizona Museum of Art, Tucson, Museum purchase with funds provided by the Edward J. Gallagher, Jr Memorial Fund 1982.35.1 © the artist; **4.4.1** Gallerie dell'Accademia, Venice; **4.4.2** National Gallery, London/ Scala, Florence; **4.4.3** Gift of the Alumni Association to Jefferson Medical College in 1878, purchased by the Pennsylvania Academy of the Fine Arts and the Philadelphia Museum of Art in 2007 with the generous support of more than 3,600 donors, 2007, 2007-1-1; **4.4.4** Photograph K2822 © Justin Kerr; **4.4.5** National Museum of Anthropology, Mexico City; **4.4.6** © Robert Rauschenberg Foundation/DACS, London/VAGA, New York 2018; **4.4.7** Photo © Thomas Dressler/imagebroker/ Alamy Stock Photo; **4.4.8** Courtesy the David Lloyd Gallery; **4.4.9** Courtesy Heather Dewey-Hagborg and Fridman Gallery, New York; **4.4.10** Art Institute of Chicago, Helen Birch Bartlett Memorial Collection, 1926.224; **4.4.11** © Jasper Johns/VAGA, New York/DACS, London 2018; **4.4.12** Courtesy Marcia Smilack; **4.4.13** Museum of Modern Art, New York. Given anonymously, 162.1934. Photo 2012, Museum of Modern Art, New York/Scala, Florence. © Salvador Dalí, Fundació Gala-Salvador Dalí, DACS 2018; **4.4.14** Courtesy KUSAMA Enterprise, Ota Fine Arts, Tokyo/ Singapore and Victoria Miro, London. © Yayoi Kusama; **4.4.15a** Metropolitan Museum of Art, New York, Arthur Hoppock Hearn Fund, 1916, 16.53; **4.4.15b**, **4.4.15c** Courtesy Department of Paintings Conservation, Metropolitan Museum of Art, New York; **4.4.16a** Victor R. Boswell, Jr./National Geographic Stock; **4.4.16b** Photo Vittoriano Rastelli/Corbis via Getty Images; **4.5.1** Photo Scala, Florence, courtesy Ministero Beni e Att. Culturali; **4.5.2** Kunsthistorisches Museum, Vienna; **4.5.3** Photo Scala, Florence; **4.5.4** National Gallery of Art, Washington, D.C. Gift of Mr. & Mrs. Richard Mellon Scaife in honour of Paul Mellon, 1993.15.1; **4.5.5a**, **4.5.5b** Courtesy the artist; **4.5.6** from Kirby, J., *Dr Brook Taylor's Method of Perspective Made Easy*, 1754; **4.5.7a** James Green/ Robert Harding; **4.5.7b** Ralph Larmann; **4.5.8** Gianni Dagli Orti/Palazzo del Tè Mantua/The Art Archive; **4.5.9** Pietro Baguzzi/akg-images; **4.5.10** National Gallery of Art, Washington, D.C., Gift of Lila Acheson Wallace, 1987.2.1. Photo Ellen Page Wilson, courtesy The Pace Gallery. © Chuck Close, The Pace Gallery; **4.5.11** Courtauld Gallery, London; **4.5.12** Heard Museum, Phoenix, Arizona; **4.5.13** Los Angeles County Museum of Art (LACMA), California. Gift of Constance McCormick Fearing, M.86.311.6 (www. lacma.org); **4.5.14** © ADAGP, Paris and DACS, London 2018; **4.5.15** National Gallery of Art, Washington, D.C., Gift of the Collectors Committee, 1987.55.1. © ADAGP, Paris and DACS, London 2018; **4.6.1** © Americanspirit/Dreamstime.com; **4.6.2** Photo RMN-Grand Palais (Château de Versailles)/Franck Raux; **4.6.3a**, **4.6.3b** Brooklyn Museum, Partial gift of Suzi and Andrew Booke Cohen in memory of Ilene R. Booke and in honor of Arnold L. Lehman, Mary Smith Dorward Fund, and William K. Jacobs, Jr. Fund , 2015.53. © 2005 Kehinde Wiley. Used by permission; **4.6.4** Cameraphoto/Scala, Florence; **4.6.5** Photo Trustees of the British Museum, London; **4.6.6** Ägyptisches Museum, Staatliche Museen, Berlin; **4.6.7** akg-images; **4.6.8** Musée National du Château de Versailles; **4.6.9** Musée du Louvre, Paris; **4.6.10** © Hubert Stadler/Corbis; **4.6.11** © Peter Guttman/ Corbis; **4.6.12** The Art Institute of Chicago, Illinois/ Mr. and Mrs. Frank G. Logan Purchase Prize and Wilson L. Mead funds/Bridgeman Images. © 2018 The Andy Warhol Foundation for the Visual Arts, Inc./Licensed by DACS, London; **4.6.13** Gilles Bassignac/Gamma-Rapho via Getty Images; **4.7.1** Library of Congress, Washington, D.C., Prints & Photographs Division, LC-B8184-7964-A; **4.7.2** Nick Ut/AP/Press Association Images; **4.7.3** © DACS 2018; **4.7.4a**, **4.7.4b** Egyptian Museum, Cairo; **4.7.5** Centre Guillaume le Conquérant, Bayeux; **4.7.6** Museum of Fine Arts, Boston, Fenollosa-Weld Collection; **4.7.7** Photograph Luidger; **4.7.8** Metropolitan Museum of Art, New York, Gift of Mr. and Mrs. Klaus G. Perls, 1990, 1990.332; **4.7.9** Museo Nacional del Prado, Madrid; **4.7.10** © Succession Picasso/DACS, London 2018; **4.7.11** © Anselm Kiefer; **4.7.12** Courtesy the artists. Photo JoAnne Pollonais; **4.7.13** Courtesy the artist; **4.7.14a** Stock Connection/SuperStock RM/Diomedia; **4.7.14b** Zuma Press/ Diomedia; **4.7.15a** Drew Angerer/Getty Images; **4.7.15b** Angelo Hornak/Alamy Stock Photo; **4.8.1** Musée du Louvre, Paris; **4.8.2** Photo Axel Schneider. Courtesy the artist and Galerie Peter Kilchmann, Zurich; **4.8.3** Hirshhorn Museum and Sculpture Garden, Smithsonian Institution, Washington, D.C. Photo Cathy Carver. Courtesy Ai Weiwei Studio; **4.8.4** Image courtesy Biennale de Lyon, France, and the artist; **4.8.5a** National Gallery, London/Scala, Florence; **4.8.6** Courtesy Mary Boone Gallery, New York; **4.8.7** Photo Heinrich Hoffmann, Presse-Illustrationen, 1937. © Ullsteinbild/Topfoto; **4.8.8** Erich Lessing/akg- images. © Nolde Stiftung Seebüll; **4.8.9** Library of Congress, Washington, D.C., Prints & Photographs Division, FSA/OWI Collection, LC-DIG-fsa-8b29516; **4.8.10** © Shirin Neshat. Courtesy the artist and Gladstone Gallery, New York and Brussels; **4.8.11** JR-art.net; **4.8.12** Photo Todd Turner. Courtesy the artist/www.JumpsuitProject.com; **4.8.13** Library of Congress, Washington, D.C., Prints & Photographs Division, H. Irving Olds collection, LC-DIG-jpd-02018; **4.8.14a**, **4.8.14b** Courtesy Chris Jordan; **4.9.1** Naturhistorisches Museum, Vienna; **4.9.2** Museum of Modern Art, New York. Purchase, 478.1953. Photo 2012, Museum of Modern Art, New York/Scala, Florence. © The Willem de Kooning Foundation/ Artists Rights Society (ARS), New York and DACS, London 2018; **4.9.3a** Ralph Larmann; **4.9.3b** Erich Lessing/ akg-images; **4.9.4** Museo delle Terme, Rome; **4.9.5** Uffizi Gallery, Florence; **4.9.6** Kimbell Art Museum, Fort Worth, Texas/Art Resource, NY/Scala, Florence; **4.9.7** Metropolitan Museum of Art, The Harry G. C. Packard Collection of Asian Art, Gift of Harry G. C. Packard, and Purchase, Fletcher, Rogers, Harris Brisbane Dick, and Louis V. Bell Funds, Joseph Pulitzer Bequest, and The Annenberg Fund Inc. gift, 1975, 1975.268.125; **4.9.8** Photo Scala, Florence, courtesy Ministero Beni e Att. Culturali;

4.9.9 Musée d'Orsay, Paris; **4.9.10** Courtesy the artist and Luhring Augustine, New York; **4.9.11a**, **4.9.11b** © The Estate of Yves Klein c/o DACS, London 2018; **4.9.12** Courtesy the artist and Luhring Augustine, New York; **4.9.13a** Victor Chavez/WireImage/Getty; **4.9.13b** Alessandro della Valle/epa/Corbis; **4.9.14** Museum of Modern Art, New York. Fractional and promised gift of Malcolm Wiener in memory of John Rewald, 183.1994. Photo 2012, Museum of Modern Art, New York/Scala, Florence; **4.9.15** Photo Tate, London, 2012. Reproduced by permission of The Henry Moore Foundation. © The Henry Moore Foundation. All Rights Reserved, DACS/ www.henry-moore.org 2018; **4.9.16** Museum of Modern Art, New York, Gift of Mrs. John D. Rockefeller III, 678.1954. Photo 2012, Museum of Modern Art, New York/Scala, Florence. © The Estate of Alberto Giacometti (Fondation Annette et Alberto Giacometti, Paris and ADAGP, Paris), licensed in the UK by ACS and DACS, London 2018; **4.9.17a** Musée National d'Art Moderne, Centre Georges Pompidou, Paris. © Succession H. Matisse/DACS 2018; **4.9.17b** Teriade Editeur, Paris, 1947. Printer Edmond Vairel, Paris. Edition 250. Museum of Modern Art, New York, The Louis E. Stern Collection, 930.1964.8. Photo 2012, Museum of Modern Art, New York/Scala, Florence. © Succession H. Matisse/DACS 2018; **4.9.18a** Museo de Arte Moderno, Mexico City. © Banco de México Diego Rivera Frida Kahlo Museums Trust, Mexico, D.F./DACS 2018; **4.9.18b** © Banco de México Diego Rivera Frida Kahlo Museums Trust, Mexico, D.F./ DACS 2018; **4.9.19** © Jenny Saville; **4.9.20a** Photo courtesy ORLAN. © ORLAN; **4.9.20b** Photo Vladimir Sichov, Sipa-Press. Courtesy the artist and Galerie Michel Rein, Paris. © ORLAN; **4.10.1** Galleria degli Uffizi, Florence; **4.10.2** Detroit Institute of Arts, Gift of Mr. Leslie H. Green; **4.10.3** Gemäldegalerie Alte Meister, Dresden; **4.10.4** Private Collection; **4.10.5** Courtesy the artist and Metro Pictures; **4.10.6** Brooklyn Museum, Gift of the Elizabeth A. Sackler Foundation, 2002.10. Photo © Donald Woodman. © Judy Chicago. ARS, NY and DACS, London 2018; **4.10.7** Copyright © by Guerrilla Girls, Inc. Courtesy www. guerrillagirls.com; **4.10.8** Collection the Adrian Piper Research Archive Foundation Berlin. © Adrian Piper Research Archive Foundation Berlin and Angry Art; **4.10.9** The Museum of Modern Art, New York, Gift of the Hudgins Family in memory of Lawrence D. "Butch" Morris, 53.2013. Photo 2017. Digital image, The Museum of Modern Art, New York/Scala, Florence. © David Hammons; **4.10.10** © Carrie Mae Weems. Courtesy the artist and Jack Shainman Gallery, New York; **4.10.11** Universal/The Kobal Collection; **4.10.12** © Stephen Marc; **4.10.13** National Museum of the American Indian, Smithsonian Institution, Washington, D.C. (20101011-1a-kjf-ps006). Courtesy the artist; **4.10.14** Metropolitan Museum of Art, New York, Rogers Fund, 1931, 31.3.166; **4.10.15**, **4.10.16** © Nikki S. Lee, courtesy Sikkema Jenkins & Co., New York; **4.10.17** Courtesy Regen Projects, Los Angeles.

Index

Figures in *italic* refer to pages on which illustrations appear. Figures followed by "gl." refer to a definition in the glossary.

28 Millimeters, Face2Face (JR and Marco) 660, *660*
2-D side scrolling games 348, 692gl.
3-D modeling 61, 116, 240, 608, 692gl.
9/11 attacks 325, 650, 656, 658
9/11 Memorial, New York (Arad and Walker) 650, *650*
14th Street School 536

A-frame 588, *589*, 692gl.
Abakanowicz, Magdalena 178–79; *80 Backs* 178, *178*, 179
Abbey Among Oak Trees (Friedrich) *37*, 37–38
Abelam culture 457–58; cult house 446, 458, *458*; yam mask *458*
Aberfan disaster 188
Abraham Lincoln and His Son Thomas (Tad) (Gardner) 506, *506*
Abramović, Marina 355–56; *The Artist Is Present* 355, *355*
Abstract Expressionism 538–40, 542, 589, 692gl.
abstraction/abstract art 36–37, 237, 499, 521–22, 524, 535–36, 692gl.; *see also* Abstract Expressionism; Cubism; Minimalism
academies 30, 492, 501, 615, 692gl.; Academy of Fine Arts Vienna 657; French 105, 484, 492–93, 494, 502, 503–4, 514; Pennsylvania Academy of the Fine Arts 25, 492, 507–8, 516; Royal Academy 88, 492, 494, 498, 505, 506
Acconci, Vito: *Following Piece* 350, *354*, 354–55
acrylic paints 210, 221–22, 692gl.
action painting 351, 539, 692gl.
actual line 47, 692gl.
Adam and Eve (Beckmann) 231, *231*
Adam and Eve (Dürer) 230–31, *231*
Adam and Eve (Rembrandt) 232, *232*
Adams, Ansel 321; *Sand Dunes, Sunrise—Death Valley...* 321, *321*
additive color/additive color process 97, 99, 322, 692gl.; *see also* RGB system
additive sculpture 247, 248–50, 692gl.
adobe 261, *261*, 441, *441*
advertising 236, 309–11, 541
aesthetic/aesthetics 692gl.; of collodion process 328; Modernist 277, 278, 543; snapshot 331; Suprematist 534; and value 34
African American art 536–38, 549–50, 680, 686–88; assemblage 254, *254*; drawing 195, *195*; film 686–88; mixed media *181*, 181–82, 295, *295*, 550, *550*; painting *154*, 154–55, *177*, 177–78, 516–17, *517*, 536–37, *537*, 630, *630*; performance 660, *660*; photography 688, *688* (*see also* Weems, Carrie Mae); screenprinting 550, *550*; sculpture 36, *36*, 37, 154, *154*, 538, *538*, 554, *554*, 686, *686*; *see also* Basquiat, Jean-Michel; Shetterly, Margot Lee; Walker, Kara
African cultures 22, 446–53, *447*, 580, 597, 667; architecture 450–53; contemporary art 24, 74, 102; Ghanaian coffins 102, *102*; masks 32, 154, 449–50, 572; sculpture 145, 447–49, 452–53, 580, 597–98, 644, 667; textiles 356, 449; wider influence 527, 537, 550, 555, 674; *see also* Egypt, ancient
afterimage effect 608, 609–10, 692gl.
ahu'ula cloaks 454, 456, *456*
Ai Weiwei 34–35, 121, 357, 419, 654; *Colored Vases* 357, *357*; *Dropping a Han Dynasty Urn* 121, *121*, 357, 419, *419*, 654, *654*; *S.A.C.R.E.D. 34*, 35, *35*
aisles 267, *268*, 692gl.
Akhenaten 377, 632; with Nefertiti and daughters (relief) 632, *632*
Akkadians 372, 582; head of a ruler 372, *372*; Stela of Naram-Sin 582, *582*
Albers, Josef 107; *Two Colors Look Like One* 107, *107*
Alberti, Leon Battista 615, 626
Alexander, Saint, reliquary head of 400, *400*
Alhambra, Granada 607, *607*
Allen, James: *The Connectors 48*, 48–49
alloys 292–93, 692gl.
Alps, Glen: *Roll-Up #2 233*, 233–34
altarpieces 214, *214*, 465, *465*, 467, 692gl.
altars 397, 631, 692gl.; Ara Pacis Augustae 65, *65*
Álvarez Bravo, Lola: *Frida Kahlo 532*
"Ambassadors, The" (Holbein) *174*, 174–75, *175*
ambulatory 405, *405*, 692gl.
Amélie (Jeunet) *340*, 341
American Gothic (Wood) 536, *536*
American Scene 524, 536, 692gl.
Americas, early and native peoples of 429–30; Mesoamerica 433–40; North America 440–44; South America 430–33; see also *names of individual peoples and cultures*
Amitayus Mandala 138, *138*
amphorae 383, *383*, 692gl.
analog technology 334, 692gl.
analogous colors 100, *100*, 692gl.
analysis and critique 176; combined analysis 183–88; contextual analysis 175, 176, 177–79; critical race theory 176; feminist 176; formal analysis 38–39, 170–72, 183–84, *185*; gender studies 176; iconographic analysis 174–75, 176; psychological analysis 176; scientific analysis 611–13; stylistic analysis 172–73, 176; *see also* interpretation
anamorphosis 175, 618, 692gl.
Anasazi 440–41
Anatsui, El: *Old Man's Cloth* 24, *24*
ancestors 597–98; Africa 447, 572, 580, 597–98; Asia 411, 416; Mesoamerica 437, 438, 599; Native American cultures 581; Pacific Islands 457, 597; Rome 386
Ancient Sound (Klee) *105*, 105–6
Andean cultures *see* South America
Angel of the Nativity (Cameron) *320*, 321
Angkor Wat, Cambodia *426*, 426–27, *427*
Anguissola, Sofonisba 472; *Portrait of the Artist's Sisters Playing Chess 472*, 472–73
animation 116, 117, 339–41, 556–57, 692gl.
Anker, Suzanne: *Astroculture (Shelf Life)* 123, *123*
Anthony, Saint *465*, 467
Antoni, Janine: *Loving Care* 671, *671*
Aphrodite Crouching at Her Bath 66, *66*
Aphrodite of Knidos (Praxiteles) 383, *383*
Apollo and Daphne (Bernini) *113*, 113–14
Apparition (Moreau) 518, *518*
appropriation 692gl.; of images 541, 542, 547, 630, 635–36, 661, 669; of physical objects 254–55, 419, 547; *see also* responses and reinterpretations
apse 397, *397*, 405, *405*, 631, 692gl.
aquatint 167, *167*, 232, *232*, 692gl.
aqueducts 266, *266*, 692gl.
Ara Pacis Augustae, Rome 65, *65*
Arab Spring 647
arabesque 398, 692gl.
Arad, Michael and Walker, Peter: 9/11 Memorial 650, *650*
arcades 692gl.
Arch of Constantine, Rome 388, *388*
archaeology 287, 292, 692gl.; Africa 27, 447; Americas 429, 432–33, 434; China 417, 418; Easter Island 457; Europe 367–70, 491, 663
Archaic Greece 384, 692gl.; *kouros* 384, *384*
Archer, Frederick Scott 320
arches 165, 265–66, 692gl.; pointed 269, 588; triumphal 388
architectural orders 264, *264*, 380, *380*, 692gl.
architecture (fundamental concepts) 259–61; balance 136–37; form 70, 259, 277, 281, 520, 567; proportion 148; rhythm 165, 166; scale 61; volume 67–68
architecture (styles and cultures): African 450–53; ancient Egyptian 263–64; Babylonian 265, 373; Baroque 264, 479, 484; Byzantine 270, 394, 395, 397, 401; cast-iron 275–76; Classical (Renaissance) 271, 273, 462–63, 473, 621; Classical Greek 148, 264, 380, 381; Gothic 268–69, 291–92, 391, 406–7, 565; Inca 432, 433; Islamic 165, 260, 402–4, 451–52, 588, 607; Japanese 270–71, 421, 423, 588–89; Mesoamerican 262, 434–35; Mesopotamian 370, 373, 568; Modernist 276–80, 276–81, 304, 453, 542–43; Mycenaean 265; Native American 440–41; Neoclassical 25, 273, 274, 494; Palauan 166; Postmodernist 281–83, 542, 543; Rococo 273–74, 488–89; Roman 264, 265–66, 271, 273, 380, 386, 387–88, 565–66; Romanesque 267, 269, 391, 404–6; Stick Style 274–75
architraves *380*, *620*, 692gl.
Armada Portrait (Gower) 633, *633*

armatures 248, 250, 692gl.
Armory Show 533–34, 536, 692gl.
Arnolfini Portrait (Van Eyck) *466*, 466–67, *467*
Arnolfo di Cambio and others: Florence Cathedral *462*, 462–63
"art for art's sake" 26
Art Nouveau 520–21, 692gl.
"art" *vs.* "craft" 22, 30, 285–86
Artichoke Halved (Weston) *165*, 165–66
artifacts 692gl.
Artist Is Present, The (Abramović) 355, *355*
Artist, The (Hazanavicius) 338–39, *339*
artist's books 692gl.; *Jazz* (Matisse) 675, *675*; *Prose of the Trans-Siberian Railway and of Little Jehanne of France* (Delaunay) 221, *221*
artist's proofs 236
Asante culture 449; *kente* cloth 449, *449*
Ascending and Descending (Escher) 92, *92*
Ascent of the Prophet Muhammed on His Steed..., The 400, *400*
ascetic 692gl.; Buddha as 413
Ashoka (Indian emperor) 413
Ashurbanipal 244; palace reliefs of 244, *244*
Ashurnasirpal II 372; palace reliefs of *372*, 372–73
Asian Field (Gormley) 256–57, *257*
Asmat culture 597; bis poles 597, *597*
Aspects of Negro Life: From Slavery Through Reconstruction (Douglas) 536–37, *537*
assemblage 254, 356, 529, 531, 692gl.; *see also* collage; mixed media
Assyrians 244, 372–73; *Dying Lioness* relief 244, *244*; *lamassu* reliefs *372*, 372–73
Astroculture (Shelf Life) (Anker) 123, *123*
asymmetry 67, 135, 692gl.
Athenian Acropolis 379, *379*, 381; Temple of Athena Nike 264, *264*; *see also* Parthenon
Atkins, Anna 318; *Halydrys siliquosa ß minor 318*
atmospheric perspective 38, 83–84, 514, 692gl.
atrium 67, 692gl.
AT&T logo (Bass) 55, *55*
AT&T Stadium, Arlington, Texas *566*, 566–67
Attributes of Painting, Sculpture, and Architecture (Vallayer-Coster) 494, *494*
Australian Aboriginal art 31, *31*, 455, *455*
auteur theory/auteur films 343–44, 692gl.
autochrome 322, 692gl.
automatic 53, 692gl.
Automatic Drawing (Masson) 53, *53*
avant-garde 521, 534, 535, 538, 692gl.
Awakening Slave (Michelangelo) 246, *246*
axis 692gl.
Aztecs 438–40, 591, 605–6; pictographs 434; stone carving 439, *439*, *591*, 606, *606*

Babur (Mughal emperor) 156, *157*
Baby Blocks (Schapiro) 54–55, *55*
Babylonians 265, 373, 634; Ishtar Gate 373, *373*; Stela of Hammurabi 634, *634*
Baca, Judith F. 223; *Danza de la Tierra* 223, *224*
background 692gl.; cel animation 340; to a pattern (*see* field); prepared surface (*see* ground)
Bai-ra-Irrai, Palau 166, *166*
Bailey, Xenobia 550; *(Re)Possessed* 550, *550*
Baker, Bill *see* Smith, Adrian
Bal du Moulin de la Galette (Renoir) 509, *509*
balance 125, 134–38, 692gl.
ball game, Mesoamerican *437*, 437–38, 605
Ball, Hugo 528–29; "Karawane" performance 528, *529*
Balla, Giacomo: *Dynamism of a Dog on a Leash* 114, *114*
balloon framing 274–75
Baltimore album quilts *133*, 133–34
balustrade 692gl.
bamboo drawing (Wu Zhen) 202, *203*
Bamiyan (Afghanistan), Buddhas of *414*, 414–15
Banksy: *Graffiti Removal Hotline* 224, *224*
Bar at the Folies-Bergère, A (Manet) 623, *623*
Bar, Noma: *Gun Crime* 58–59, *59*
Barney, Matthew: *Cremaster 5* 556, *556*
Barong dance masks 427, *427*
Baroque 461, 477, 692gl.; architecture 264, 479, 484; influence 281, 321, 601; painting 477–79, 481–84 (*see also* Caravaggio; Gentileschi, Artemisia; Rembrandt van Rijn); and Rococo 487; sculpture 480–81, 583 (see also *Apollo and Daphne*)
Barsamian, Gregory 116; *Drum 52* 116, *116*
bas-relief (low relief) 65, *65*, 244, *244*, 692gl.
base (column architecture) 264, *380*, 692gl.
basilicas 693gl.; St. Mary of Guadalupe 26; of Vierzehnheiligen (Neumann) *488*, 488–89; *see also* Hagia Sophia
basketwork 443, *443*, *458*
Basquiat, Jean-Michel 554–55; *The Nile* 554–55, *555*; *Untitled* 30, *30*
Bass, Saul: AT&T logo 55, *55*
Batman (Tagliapietra) 64, *64*
Baudelaire, Charles 140, 507
Bauhaus 107, 304, 657, 693gl.
Bauhaus building, Dessau (Gropius) 304, *304*
Bayer, Herbert: "Universal" typeface 304, *304*
Bayeux Tapestry 641–42, *642*
Beach at Nice, The (Morisot) 512, *512*
Beanery, The (Kienholz) 356, *356*
Bearden, Romare: *The Dove* 129, *129*
Beautiful Woman (Kaigetsudo Dohan) 667, *667*
Beckmann, Max: *Adam and Eve* 231, *231*
Bed (Rauschenberg) 222, *222*
Bedroom, The (Van Gogh) 51, *51*
Beever, Julian 618; *Woman in Pool* 618, *618*
Belief + Doubt (=Sanity) (Kruger) 352, *352*
Belley, Jean-Baptiste 496, *496*
Bellows, George: *Woodstock Road, Woodstock, New York, 1924* 54, *54*
Ben-Day dots *541*, 542, 693gl.
Benin 644; warrior plaque 644, *644*
Benioff, David and Weiss, D. B.: *Game of Thrones* 348, *348*
Benton, Thomas Hart: *The Wreck of the Ole '97* 83, *83*
Bernini, Gianlorenzo 113, 477; *Apollo and Daphne 113*, 113–14; *David 480*, 480–81; *The Ecstasy of St. Teresa* 583, *583*
Besten, Alfonse van 322; *Fragility* 322, *322*
Beuys, Joseph 118, 353–54; *Coyote, I Like America and America Likes Me* 354, *354*
Bicycle Wheel (Duchamp) 529, *529*
Biggers, John: *Night of the Poor* 195, *195*
Bilal, Wafaa 648; *Domestic Tension* 648, *648*
binders 200, 209, 210–11, 220, 693gl.
bioart 123, *123*, 608, *608*, 693gl.
biopics 342, 693gl.
Bird in Hand, A (Dougherty) 568, *568*
Bird in Space (Brancusi) 535, *535*
bird's-eye view 511, 642, 693gl.
Birren, Faber 108
Birth of a Nation (Griffith) 336–37; poster *337*
Birth of Venus (Cabanel) 502, *502*
Birth of Venus, The (Botticelli) *666*, 667
bis poles (Asmat) 597, *597*
Bishop, Isabel 536; *Waiting* 536, *537*
bisqueware 287, 693gl.
bister 202
Black Letter style 301, *302*
Black, Mary 211; *Natura 9* 211, *211*
Blake, William 192, 496, 498; *A negro hung alive by the ribs...* 496, *496*; *Elohim Creating Adam* 498, *498*
Blaue Reiter, Der *see* Der Blaue Reiter
Blizzard Entertainment: *Starcraft* 313
Blonde Woman in Profile (Picasso) 46, *46*
Blue Dancers (Degas) 511, *511*
Blue Nude III (Matisse) 675, *675*
Blue Room, The (Valadon) 159–60, *160*
Boating Party, The (Cassatt) 100, *101*
Boccioni, Umberto: *Muscular Dynamism* 207, *207*; *Unique Forms of Continuity in Space* 533, *533*
Bochner, Mel: *Vertigo* 52, *52*
body art 548, 670–73, 677–78; see also *Self*
Bohemian 693gl.
boldface 307, 693gl.
Bonampak: mural 438, *438*
Bonaparte Crossing the St. Bernard Pass... see *Napoleon Crossing the Alps*
Bonaparte, Napoleon *see* Napoleon I
Bonheur, Rosa 217–18; *The Horse Fair 217*, 217–18; *Plowing in the Nivernais: The Dressing of the Vines 166*, 166–67
Book of the Dead of Ani *301*
Book of the Dead of Hunefer 584, *584*
Borglum, John Gutzon de la Mothe: Mount Rushmore National Memorial 248, *248*
Borromini, Francesco: Church of San Carlo alle Quattro Fontane, Rome 479, *479*
Bosch, Hieronymus 173; *The Garden of Earthly Delights* 173, *173*
Botticelli, Sandro 666; *The Birth of Venus* 666, 667
Bottle of Banyuls (Gris) 528, *528*
Boulevard du Temple (Daguerre) *317*, 318
Bourgeois, Louise: *Maman* 71, *71*
Bouts, Dieric (the Elder): *The Coronation of the Virgin Mary* 150–51, *151*
Boyle, Richard, third Earl of Burlington: Chiswick House 274, *274*
Bramante, Donato 273; Tempietto of San Pietro in Montorio 273, *273*
Brancusi, Constantin 535; *Bird in Space* 535, *535*; *The Kiss* 72, *72*
Branded (Saville) 677, *677*
Braque, Georges 102, 526–28, 625; *Houses at L'Estaque 527*, 527–28; *Man with a Guitar* 625, *625*
Breaking Column (Rickey) 255, *255*
Breaking of the Vessels (Kiefer) 646–47, *647*
brightness 82–83, 97
Broken Column, The (Kahlo) 676, *676*
Bronzino, Agnolo: *Eleonora of Toledo and Her Son, Giovanni* 23, *23*
Brown, Joan 218; *Girl in Chair 218*
Brücke, Die *see* Die Brücke
Bruegel, Pieter, the Elder 164; *Hunters in the Snow* 164, *164*; *Landscape with the Fall of Icarus*, 153, *155*, 155–56
Bruggen, Coosje van: *Mistos (Match Cover)* (with Claes Oldenburg) 141, *141*
Brunelleschi, Filippo 87–88, 461–63; dome of Florence Cathedral *462*, 462–63; *Sacrifice of Isaac* 461, 462, *462*; Santo Spirito, Florence *44*
Buddha (Siddhartha Gautama) 108, 413, 414, *414*, 423, *423*, 580, *580*
Buddhism 411, 413–15, 425, 580; architecture 270–71, *271*, 413, *413*, 415, *421*, 423; color symbolism 108; Life of Buddha stela 580, *580*; mandalas 138, *138*, 415; painting 423, *423*, 424, *424*; *sutra* scrolls 227; Zen gardens 421, *421*
Bull-Leapers (Minoan fresco) 369, *369*
bull lyre, Sumerian *371*, 371–72
Bull's Head (Picasso) 254, *254*
buon fresco 212
Burj Khalifa, Dubai 277, *277*, 280
Burlington, Lord *see* Boyle, Richard
Burne-Jones, Edward *see* Morris, William
Burton, Tim *329*; *The Nightmare Before Christmas* 339–40
Burtynsky, Edward 331–32; *Manufacturing #17: Deda Chicken Processing Plant* 331–32, *332*
Bust of Queen Nefertiti 170–71, *171*
busts 693gl.; in paintings 494, 496; of Queen Nefertiti 170–71, *171*; Roman ancestral 386, *386*
Byzantine art 270, 390, 394–98, 631, 693gl.

c-prints *see* chromogenic prints
Cabanel, Alexandre: *Birth of Venus* 502, *502*
Caffenol process 319
Cage, John 353, *353*; *Theater Piece No. 1* 353
Cahokia, Illinois 569, *569*, 572
Caillebotte, Gustave 512; *Paris Street, Rainy Day 512*, 513
Calatrava, Santiago: Quadracci Pavilion, Milwaukee Art Museum 281, *281*, 283
Calder, Alexander 119; *Untitled* 119, *119*
California Indians 443
calligraphy 301, 693gl.; Chinese 22, 220, 301, *301*, 418, *418*, 420, *420*; Islamic 394, 398, *398*, 594, *594*, 659, *659*; *see also* micrography
Calling of St. Matthew, The (Caravaggio) 79, *79*
calotype 318, 320
Camera degli Sposi, Ducal Palace, Mantua (Mantegna) 615–16, *616*
camera obscura 86–87, 316
Camera Obscura Image of the Panthéon... (Morell) 316, *316*
Cameron, Julia Margaret 320–21; *Angel of the Nativity 320*, 321
Canada, native peoples: Kwakiutl masks *442*, 442–43; Tlingit textiles 296, *296*
canon of proportions 664–65, *665*, 693gl.
canopic jars 374, 376, *376*
cantilever 265, 693gl.

capitals (architecture) 264, *264*, 380, *380*, 543, *543*, 693gl.
Caprices, The (Goya) 167
car dashboard icons 303, 305, *305*
Caravaggio 477, 478; *The Calling of St. Matthew* 79, *79*; *Judith Decapitating Holofernes* 478, *478*
cardinal points 693gl.
Carpenter, Captain Richard: bent-corner chest 298, *298*
cartoons (comics/animation) 116, 140
cartoons (preparatory drawings) 194, *194*, 520, 693gl.
carving 246, 247–48
Cassatt, Mary: *The Boating Party* 100, *101*; *The Child's Bath 510*, 510–11
cast iron architecture 275–76
casting/casts 249–50, *250*, 693gl.; *see also* piece-mold casting
catacombs *392*, 392–93, *587*, 587–88, 693gl.
Çatalhöyük, Turkey 368–69; wall painting *368*, 368–69
Cataract 3 (Riley) 115, *115*
cathedrals 27–28, 407, 564–65; Chartres *291*, 291–92, 406, 407, *407*; Florence *462*, 462–64, *463*; Notre Dame, Paris 565, *565*; Saint-Lazare, Autun *585*; *see also* basilicas
caves: Mesoamerica 435; Mogao Caves, China 414; paintings 122, *122*, 209–10, *210*, 224, 367, *367*, *586*, 586–87 (*see also* rock paintings)
Cellini, Benvenuto: *Salt Cellar of Francis I* 293–94, *294*
celluloid 693gl.
Celmins, Vija 153; *Untitled (Ocean) 153*, 153–54
Cendrars, Blaise 221
censorship 34–35, 655–58
Central Park Zoo, New York City (Winogrand) 331, *331*
central-plan churches 273, 394, 395, 693gl.
ceramics 693gl.; ancient Greek 383, *383*, 385; Chinese 121, 288, *288*, 357, 419; Expressionist 290, *290*; Islamic 106, *106*; Japanese 28, *28*; Mesoamerican 288, *288*, *437*, 437–38; Native American 289, *289*; status 22, 285; techniques *251*, 287–90; *see also* terra-cotta
ceramists 285, 693gl.
Cézanne, Paul 514; influence 521, 527; *Mont Sainte-Victoire* 514, *514*
C.F.A.O (Puryear) 154, *154*
CGI 341, 693gl.
Chagall, Marc 657; *The Fall of Icarus* 151, *151*, 153
Chalice with Apostles Venerating the Cross (Byzantine silver) 293, *293*
chalk 200; as gouache additive 220
Champollion, Jean-François 376
"Chaos Machine" (King) *187*, 187–88
charcoal 198–99
Chartres Cathedral *291*, 291–92, 406, 407, *407*
chasing (metalwork) 293, 693gl.
Chaucer, Geoffrey 285; *Works of* (Morris and Burne-Jones) 305
Chavín culture 430–31; Raimondi Stela *430*, 430–31
Chevalier, Tracy 33
Chevrolet logo 303, *303*
chiaroscuro *78*, 78–79, 693gl.; *see also* tenebrism
Chicago, Judy 684; *The Dinner Party 684*, 684–85
Chihuly, Dale: *Fiori di Como* 292, *292*
childbirth 591–92
Child's Bath, The (Cassatt) *510*, 510–11
Chilkat weaving 296, *296*, 693gl.
Chin, Mel: *Operation Paydirt/Fundred Dollar Bill Project 559*, 559–60
China 410, 416–20; artistic training 30; bronze container, Shang Dynasty *134*, 134–35; Buddhist art 414, *414*; carved lacquer tray 108, *108*; ceramics 121, 288, *288*, 357, 419; ink drawing 202, *203*; invention of paper 205; Mao Zedong 635–36; painting *82*, 84–85, *85*, 135, *135*, 418, *418*, 420; silkscreen printing 235; Theory of Five Elements 108, *108*; writing and calligraphy 300, 301, *301*, 418, *418*, 420, *420*; *see also* Ai Weiwei; Gu, Wenda; Hung Liu; Zhang Chun Hong
"China Monument: Temple of Heaven" (Gu) 573, *573*
China series (Burtynsky) 331–32, *332*
Chirico, Giorgio de *see* De Chirico, Giorgio
Chiswick House, London (Lord Burlington) 274, *274*
choir (architecture) 405, *405*, 693gl.
Christian art 393, 394, 582–83; late antiquity *392*, 393, *393*, *587*, 587–88; Byzantine 293, *293*, 394–98, *395*, *396*, *397*, *582*, 582–83; medieval *63*, 63–64, 173, *173*, *399*, 399–400, *400*, *579*, 579–80, 595, *595* (*see also* Gothic; Romanesque); Italian Renaissance 120, *120*, 214, *214*, 460, 461–64, *462*, *463*, *474*, 474–75, *480*, 480–81, 592, *593* (*see also* Sistine Chapel); Northern Renaissance 143, *143*, 150–51, *151*, *216*, 231, *231*, 460, 465, *465*, 467, *475*, 475–76; Mannerist (Late Renaissance) *471*, 471–72, 476, *476*; Baroque 79, *79*, 156, *156*, *477*, 477–79, *478*, *480*, 480–81, 583, *583* (see also *Judith Decapitating Holofernes*); Northern Baroque 232, *232*, *481*, 481–82; Rococo *488*, 488–89; Romantic *37*, 37–38; modern 110, *111*, 231, *231*, 657–58, *658*; visionary 554, *554*; *see also* Virgin of Guadalupe
Christian symbolism and iconography 132–33, 393, 395, 397–98, 405, 554; color 108; Northern Renaissance 174–75, 464–65, 466–67; statue of Constantine 634; *The War* (Dix) 640; *Woman Holding a Balance* (Vermeer) 585
Christina's World (Wyeth) 215, *215*
Christo and Jeanne-Claude: *The Gates* 570, 571, *571*
chroma 104–5, 693gl.
chromogenic prints 322, 693gl.
Chungking Express (Wong) *343*, 343–44
church architecture: Baroque 479, *479*; central plan 273, 394, 395; Latin-cross plan 404–5, *405*; Rococo *488*, 488–89; *see also* Gothic; Romanesque
Church, Frederic Edwin: *Niagara* 21, *21*, 22; *Twilight in the Wilderness* 100, *101*
Church of Santo Spirito at Florence (Dosio) *44*, 45
Cibachrome 322, 693gl.
Cimabue: *Virgin and Child Enthroned* 408, *408*
circumambulation 415, 693gl.
Circus, The (Seurat) 106–7, *107*
Cirque du Soleil 118, *118*
Citizen Kane (Welles) 337, *337*
City Square, The (Giacometti) 206, *206*
Claesz, Pieter (attr.): *Vanitas (Still Life with Glass Globe)* 600, *600*
CLAMP: *Tsubasa RESERVoir CHRoNiCLE* 49, *49*
Classical art 461, 482–83, 491, 628–29, 666–67, 693gl.; architecture 271, 273–74, 462–63, 473, 621; *see also* Classical period (Greece); Neoclassicism; Roman art
Classical period (Greece) 145, 693gl.; architecture 148, *148*, 264, *264*, 380, *380*, 381, 620, *620*; freestanding sculpture 147, *147*, 250, *250*, 383, *383*, 384, *384*, 666, *666*; relief sculpture 381, *381*, *382*, *578*, 578–79
Claudel, Camille 516; *The Waltz* 516, *516*
clerestory windows 270, *270*, 693gl.
Clock, The (Marclay) 596, *596*
Close, Chuck 161, 622; *Fanny/Fingerpainting* 622, *622*; *Self Portrait* 161, 163, *163*
Cloud (electronics) 334, 693gl.
Cloud Gate (Kapoor) 73, *73*
Clovis points 429
CMYK *312*, 312–13, *313*, 693gl.
Coalopolis (Larmann) 222, *222*
Coates, Deborah: abolitionist quilts 161, *161*
Coatlicue Transformed (Herrán) 440, *440*
Codex Magliabechiano 439
coffered/coffering *387*, 693gl.
Coffin in the Shape of a Cocoa Pod (Coffin Orange) (Kwei) 102, *102*
coiling 693gl.; basketwork 443; ceramics 288, 448
Cole, Thomas 499; *View from Mount Holyoke, Massachusetts...The Oxbow* 499, *499*
collage *55*, *129*, *168*, *181*, 182, 222, 325–26, 528, *528*, 693gl.
collagraphy 233–34, 693gl.
collodion (wet plate) process 320, 328, 693gl.
Colombo, Jorge 307; *Finger Painting 307*
colonialism 24, 154, 356, 358, 496, 653
color 95–111, 693gl.; combining 97–99, 312–13; and depth effects 82–84, 514; in digital printing 239–40, *312*, 312–13, *313*; and emotion 95, 100, 103, 106, 108–11; and emphasis 151, 153; expressive 110–11, 514–15, 516, 525, 526; in films 337–39; in fresco 212, 613; Hockney and 38; and Impressionism 100, 508–9; and Mannerism 471; perception 95–97, 100, 106–7; in photography 322–23; *Plexus* series 558; properties 101–6; restricted palettes 534, 542, 675; symbolism 108, 109–10, 111, 224, 449, 456, 458; in tempera 214; in tsumugi-ori textiles 422–23; in typography 302; in woodblock printing 228, 229
Color Field painting *539*, 539–40, 693gl.
color pencil 197
color theory 107, 508–9, 693gl.
color wheels *97*, 97–100, *98*, *99*
Colored Vases (Ai) 357, *357*, *654*
Colosseum, Rome 565–66, *566*
columns 259, 263, *263*, 264, *264*, 380, *380*, 693gl.; Great Zimbabwe 452; of Parthenon 620, *620*; Postmodern interpretations 281, *281*, 543, *543*; Toltec warrior sculptures *643*, 643–44; triumphal 388
comic books 49, *49*, *93*
Communist regimes 178–79, 218, 253, 524, 635–36, 654
communities 564–76; architectural spaces for 560, 565–67; dispersed creative participation 360, 559–60; local creative participation 109–10, 111, 223, 256, 257, 352, 568; mass construction projects 253, 568–69; ritual performance 442–43, 450, 572; *see also* public spaces, art and
complementary colors 100, *100*, 693gl.
composite view 379, 527, 693gl.; and *japonisme* 511
composition 693gl.
Composition with Yellow and Blue (Mondrian) *534*
compositional unity 125, *125*, 127–29
computer art and design *96*, 97, 300, 307, 313; font style 302; *see also* 3-D modeling; video games
conceptual art 201, 255, 350, 351–52, 529, 546–48, 693gl.
conceptual unity 129–31
Concerning the Spiritual in Art (Kandinsky) 522
concrete 280, 387, 566, 693gl.
cone of vision 91, *91*
Confucianism 411
Connectors, The (Allen) *48*, 48–49
Conques, France: Church of Sainte-Foy *404*, 404–6, *405*, *406*
Constantine the Great 388, 390, 634; colossal statue of 634, *635*
Constructed Head No. 2 (Gabo) 253, *253*
Constructivism 253, 255, 693gl.
Conté crayon 200, 201
contemporary art 446, 524, 546–60; community engagement 109–10, 111, 223, 256–57, 559–60, 568; film and video 553, 555–57; outsider impact 554–55; and Postmodernism 549–53; *see also* installations; Minimalism; Op art; Pop art
Contemporary Arts Center, Cincinnati (Hadid) 282, *282*
content 35, 175, 693gl.
context 24, 37–38, 122, 175, 177–79, 693gl.
continuous narrative 392, *392*, 423, *423*, *463*, 464, 693gl.; see also *Bayeux Tapestry*; *Meeting of St. Anthony and St. Paul, The*; *Tale of the Heiji Rebellion*
contour rivalry 431, 693gl.
contours *45*, 45–46, *46*, 693gl.; contour drawing 207, *207*
contrapposto 250, 383, 384, 464, 480, 693gl.
contrast 55, 56, 57–59, *159*, 159–60, 693gl.; aquatint and 167; and emphasis 152, 153, 155, 156; of hues *see* complementary colors; in relief printmaking 228; in typography 302
controversies 121, 180–81, 382, 503–4, 612; art in public spaces 573–75, 649, 656, 658; Parthenon Marbles 382; *see also* censorship
convention 181, 501, 665, 693gl.
convex 693gl.; *see also under* mirrors
Cor-ten steel 573, 693gl.
corbeled arches 265, *265*, 693gl.
Córdoba: Great Mosque 165, *165*
Corn Blue Room (Rickard) *552*, 552–53
Cornelia Pointing to Her Children as Her Treasures (Kauffmann) 494, *495*
Cornell, Joseph 130; *Untitled (The Hotel Eden) 130*, 130–31
cornices 277, 693gl.
Coronation of the Virgin Mary, The (Bouts) 150–51, *151*
Council of Trent 474

Counter-Reformation 474, 476
Courbet, Gustave 504, 516; *Stonebreakers* 504, *504*
Course of the Art of Measurement with Compass and Ruler (Dürer) 301–2, *302*
Cova dels Cavalls, Valencia *122*
Coyote, I Like America and America Likes Me (Beuys) 354, *354*
craft traditions 285–98, 446; attitudes to 22, 285–86; ceramics 287–90; fiber crafts 294–97; glass working 290–92; metalwork 292–94; wood working 297–98
crayon 200, 201
Creation of Adam (Michelangelo) 468, *468*, 498
Cremaster 5 (Barney) 556, *556*
critique 176, 179–82
cropping 509, 510, 511, 694gl.
cross-hatching *80*, 80–81, 196, *196*, 694gl.
Crucifixion scenes 110, *111*, 405, 440, *440*, 465, *465*, 467, *579*, 579–80, 657–58, *658*
Crucifixion, The (Nolde) 657–58, *658*
Crystal Palace, London (Paxton) 275, *275*
Csuri, Charles 97; *Wondrous Spring 96*, 97
Cubi XIX (Smith) 63, *63*
Cubism 102, *127*, 127–28, 526–28, *527*, *528*, 625, 694gl.; influence 533–35
cuneiform 370, 694gl.
Cut with the Kitchen Knife... (Höch) 327, *327*
cyanotype 318, *318*, 694gl.
Cycladic sculpture 368, *368*
cylinder seals 227

Dada 327, 351, 524, 528–30, 694gl.; *see also* Duchamp, Marcel
Daguerre, Louis-Jacques-Mandé 317–18; *Boulevard du Temple 317*, 318
daguerrotypes *317*, 317–18, 329
Dakota Access Pipeline 444
Dalí, Salvador 610–11; *The Persistence of Memory 610*, 610–11
Danza de la Tierra (Baca) 223, *224*
Daoism 202, 411, 418, 420, 425, 535
Daumier, Honoré: *Rue Transnonain 234*, 235
David (Bernini) *480*, 480–81
David (Donatello) 480, *480*, 481
David (Michelangelo) 480, *480*, 481
David, Jacques-Louis 491; *Napoleon Crossing the Alps* 629, *629*; *The Oath of the Horatii* 491, *493*, 493–94
Davidson, Carolyn: Nike logo 51, *51*
Dawe, Gabriel 558–59; *Plexus no. 19 558*
Daybreak (Parrish) 306, *306*
De Chirico, Giorgio 530; *The Melancholy and Mystery of the Street* 530, *530*
de Kooning, Willem 201, 663–64; *Woman I* 664, *664*
De Stijl 534, 542, 694gl.
Dead Christ (Mantegna) 592, *593*
death 592–94, 599–601, 653, 655; Roman death masks 386, *386*; *see also* memorials; sarcophagi; tombs
"Death by Cotton Candy" (Edburg) 332, *332*
decorative 694gl.
Defense Worker (Thrash) 233, *233*
Degas, Edgar 511; *Blue Dancers* 511, *511*; *The Tub 200*, 201
"Degenerate Art" exhibition *657*, 657–58
deification 377, 456, 694gl.
Deir-el-Medina, Egypt 27
Déjeuner sur l'Herbe, Le (Manet) 181, 502–4, *503*
Déjeuner sur l'herbe, Le: les trois femmes noires (Thomas) 181, *181*, 182
Delacroix, Eugène: *Liberty Leading the People 497*, 497–98
Delaunay, Sonia 221; (with Blaise Cendrars): *Prose of the Trans-Siberian Railway and of Little Jehanne of France* 221, *221*
Demoiselles d'Avignon, Les (Picasso) 527, *527*
Denon, Vivant: *Travels in Upper and Lower Egypt* 61
deposition 694gl.
Deposition (Pontormo) *471*, 471–72
Der Blaue Reiter 521, 694gl.
Derain, André 105; *The Turning Road, L'Estaque 104*, 105
Deren, Maya: *Meshes of the Afternoon 344*, 344–45
Dery, Maia 319; *Storm Drain–Cape Fear River Basin 319*
Design Quarterly see *Does It Make Sense?*
destruction/loss of artworks: 1939 World's Fair 538; political 574, 636, 655–56, 657; religion and *414*, 415; ritual 597; site-specific 574–75; war and 372, 381, 636; see also *Dropping a Han Dynasty Urn*
developer 319, 694gl.
Deventer, Gherard Wessels van: *Dutch History Bible 303*
Devil Made Me Do It, The (Sauerkids) 48, *48*
Dewey-Hagborg, Heather: *Stranger Visions* 608, *608*
diagonals 156, 424, 694gl.; isometric perspective 84, *85*, 85–86; and motion 49, *49*, 51, 52, 63, 114
Dickson, W. K. *see* Edison, Thomas
didactic art 391, 399, 694gl.
Die Brücke 522, 694gl.
Diego, Juan 25
digital imagery: film and video 334–35, 341, 346–47; photography 315, 323, 325, 326; *see also* 3-D modeling; computer art and design; video games; web design
Dijkstra, Rineke: *Mothers* series 591–92, *592*
Dinner Party, The (Chicago) *684*, 684–85
directional line 48–49, 50, *50*, 152, 156, 645
Discus Thrower (*Discobolos*) (Myron) 666, *666*
Dismemberment of Coyolxauhqui, Goddess of the Moon, The (Aztec) 439, *439*
dissonance 471–72, 694gl.
Dix, Otto 657; *The War* 640, *640*
Djenné: Great Mosque *451*, 451–52
Djurberg, Nathalie 556; *I Wasn't Made to Play the Son* 557, *557*
Do Ho Suh: *Some/One* 424, 426, *426*
Do the Right Thing (Lee) 686–88, *687*
Do Women Have to Be Naked... (Guerrilla Girls) 685, *685*
documentaries 342, 694gl.
Does It Make Sense? (Greiman) 300, 308, *308*, 309
Dogon Kanaga masks 450, *450*
Dohan *see* Kaigetsudo Dohan
Doll with Toys (Raviv) *239*, 239–40
Dome of the Rock, Jerusalem 401, *401*
domes 270, 694gl.; Alhambra, Granada 607, *607*; AT&T Stadium, Arlington *566*, 567; Classical 273, 473, *473*; Dome of the Rock, Jerusalem 401, *401*; Florence Cathedral *462*, 462–63; Hagia Sofia, Istanbul 270, *270*, 394, *395*; Masjid al-Nabawi, Medina 403, *403*; Neoclassical 274, *274*, 494, *495*; Pantheon, Rome *387*, 387–88; Süleymaniye mosque, Istanbul 260, *260*; Taj Mahal *272*, 273
Domestic series (Opie) 690, *690*
Domestic Tension (Bilal) 648, *648*
Donatello: *David* 480, *480*, 481
Donen, Stanley and Kelly, Gene: *Singin' in the Rain* 338, *338*
Donovan, Tara 557, 559; *Haze* 559; *Untitled* 557, *557*, 559
Donwood, Stanley 230; "Hollywood Limousine" (*Lost Angeles*) 230, *230*
door jambs *405*, 694gl.
Doryphoros (Polykleitos) 384, *384*
Dosio, Giovanni Antonio: *Church of Santo Spirito at Florence 44*, 45
Dots Obsession (Kusama) 611, *611*
Dougherty, Patrick 568; *A Bird in Hand* 568, *568*
Douglas, Aaron: *Aspects of Negro Life: From Slavery Through Reconstruction* 536–37, *537*
Dove, The (Bearden) 129, *129*
Draftsman Drawing a Recumbent Woman (Dürer) 93, *93*
drawing 187, 193–207; layered with acrylic 221–22; life 206–7; preliminary 194, 195, 196, *260*, 261; *see also* line
Drawing for a wing of a flying machine (Leonardo) *192*, 193
Drawing for Sculpture (with color) (Hepworth) 52, *52*
Dreamhack conference 313, *313*
Driscoll, Clara 521; Tiffany "Wisteria" lamp *520*, 520–21
Drop Dead Gorgeous series (Edburg) 332, *332*
Dropping a Han Dynasty Urn (Ai) 121, *121*, 357, 419, *419*, 654, *654*
Drum 52 (Barsamian) 116, *116*
drypoint 231, *231*, 694gl.
dubbing 338, 694gl.
Duccio di Buoninsegna: *Maestà* altarpiece 214, *214*
Duchamp, Marcel 118–19, 254–55, 351, 529; *Bicycle Wheel* 118, 529, *529*; *Fountain* 351, 547, *547*; *Nude Descending a Staircase, No. 2 533*, 533–34
Dura Europos synagogue, Syria *391*, 391–92, *392*
Durand, Asher Brown: *Kindred Spirits* 84, *84*
Durant, Susan: *Memorial to King Leopold of the Belgians* 244, *244*
Dürer, Albrecht 221, 301, 475; *Adam and Eve* 230–31, *231*; *Course in the Art of Measurement with Compass and Ruler* 301–2, *302*; *Draftsman Drawing a Recumbent Woman* 93, *93*; "The Four Horsemen" (*Apocalypse* series) *227*, 227–28; *The Last Supper 475*, 475–76; *A Young Hare* 221, *221*
Dutch History Bible (copyist Van Deventer) *303*
Dying Lioness (Assyrian relief) 244, *244*
Dynamism of a Dog on a Leash (Balla) 114, *114*
Dyrhaug, Kurt 240; *Unterschieden Tonka* 240, *240*

Eagle Transformation Mask (Kwakiutl) *442*, 442–43
Eakins, Thomas 507–8, 516; *Motion Study: Male Nude, Standing Jump to Right* 508, *508*; *Portrait of Dr. Samuel D. Gross* (*The Gross Clinic*) *604*, 604–5
Early, Andrew 298; turned bowl 298, *298*
Early Spring (Guo Shi) 220, *220*
earthenware 287; *see also* terra-cotta
earthworks *252*, 252–53, 549, 686; *see also* Cahokia; Nazca Lines
Easter Island 456; *moai* 456–57, *457*
Ecstasy of St. Teresa, The (Bernini) 583, *583*
Edburg, Daniela 332; *Death By Cotton Candy* 332, *332*
Edison, Thomas and Dickson, W. K.: *Fred Ott's Sneeze* 122, *122*
editions 226, 236, 694gl.
Egypt, ancient 374–79; Book of the Dead *301*, 584, *584*; bust of Queen Nefertiti 170–71, *171*; canon of proportions 664–65; coffin of Nespawershefi *20*, 20–21; cylinder seals 227; glass 290; relief sculpture 142–43, *143*, 632, *632*, 641, *641*; sculpture of the Lady Sennuwy 243, *243*; sphinxes 62, *62*, 689, *689*; Temple of Amun-Re, Karnak *143*, *263*, 263–64; tomb paintings 212, 214, 377, *377*, 379; writing 300, *301*, 375, 376; see also *Nile, The* (Basquiat)
Egypt, Roman 211, 393
Egyptian Revolution 647
80 Backs (Abakanowicz) *178*, 178–79
Eine Kleine Nachtmusik (Tanning) 144, *144*
Einstein, Albert 76, 591, 611
El Castillo Cave, Spain 367, *367*
El Cerro (Rosado-Seijo) *109*, 109–10
Elderly Peasant Woman, An (Lhermitte) *198*, 199
Electric Dress (Tanaka) *128*, 129
elements of art 38, 41, 42, 170, 694gl.
Eleonora of Toledo and Her Son, Giovanni (Bronzino) 23, *23*
Elgin Marbles *see* Parthenon Marbles
Elizabeth I 631, 633, *633*; *Armada Portrait* (Gower) 633, *633*
Elohim Creating Adam (Blake) 498, *498*
embroidery 294, *294*, 295, 431, *431*, 694gl.; see also *Bayeux Tapestry*
Emperor Babur Overseeing His Gardeners, The (Mughal painting) 156, *157*
emphasis 38–39, 150, 153–55, 156–57, 302, 475, 694gl.; *see also* subordination
En el aire (Margolles) 653, *653*, 655
en plein air 694gl.; oil painting 216–17, 508; watercolor painting 220–21
encaustic 210–11, 694gl.
engraving *230*, 230–31, *231*, 694gl.; *see also* Nazca Lines
Enlightenment 486, 604, 694gl.
entablature 380, *380*, 694gl.
entasis 620, *620*, 694gl.
Entry into Jerusalem (Duccio) 214, *214*
epic 336–37, 348, 694gl.
Erased de Kooning Drawing (Rauschenberg) 201, *201*
erasing 201
Ernst, Max 530–31, 657; *Le Surréalisme et la Peinture* (*Surrealism and Painting*) 531, *531*
Escher, M. C.: *Ascending and Descending* 92, *92*; *Sky and Water I* 59, *59*
Escobar, Maria Sol *see* Marisol
etching *48*, *167*, 232, *232*, 694gl.
Etruscans 385–86; sarcophagus 249, *249*; Tomb of the Leopards 386, *386*
Euphronios and Euxitheos: red-figure calyx-krater 383, *383*, 385
Evans, Mary: album quilt *133*, 133–34
Ever Is Over All (Rist) 555–56, *556*

Excerpt (Suprematist Evasion) (Mehretu) 222, *222*
Exekias: black-figure amphora 383, *383*
Experiment on a Bird in the Air Pump, An (Wright) 604, *604*
Expressionism 182, 231, 501, 521–22, 554, 694gl.
expressionistic 694gl.; *see also* non-objectivity
expressive 694gl.
Eyck, Jan van 216, 464; *The Arnolfini Portrait* 466, 466–67, *467*; *Madonna in a Church* 143, *143*; *The Madonna of Chancellor Rolin* 216, *216*
"Eyesaurus" (Kahlo) 204, *204*

facade 694gl.
Fading Away (Robinson) *147*, 147–48
Fahmy, Mohamad *see* Ganzeer
faience 377, 378, 694gl.
Fairey, Shepard: *Obey* 57, *57*
Fall of Icarus, The (Chagall) 151, *151*, 153
Fall of the Giants (Romano) *621*, 621–22
Falling Woman (Fischl) 656, *656*, 658
Fallingwater, Pennsylvania (Wright) 279, *279*
False Perspective (Hogarth) 619, *619*
Family Pictures and Stories series (Weems) 551, *551*
Fanny/Fingerpainting (Close) 622, *622*
fantasy 337, 341, 342, 348, 694gl.
Father Damien (Marisol) 69, *69*, 73
Fauves 105, 110, 525, 694gl.
Fayum portraits 211, *211*
FedEx Express logo *23*, 23–24
feminism 680, 683, 684–85; feminist analysis 179–80, 681; protests 655–56
Fenton, Roger 327–28; *Valley of the Shadow of Death* 328, *328*
fiber art 294–97, 456, 550, *550*, 558–59; *see also* quilts; textiles
field 159
Fifth Vision of Hildegaard of Bingen, The 399, *399*
figurative 694gl.
figure-ground reversal 59, *59*, 694gl.
film 116–17, 122, *122*, 334–35, 336–45; auteur theory 343–44; clips 596, *596*; experimental 344–45, 556; genres 338, 342, 348; techniques 334, 336–41
fin de siècle 520
Finding Nemo (Walt Disney Pictures) 116, *117*
fine art 22–23
Finger Painting (Colombo) *307*
Fiori di Como (Chihuly) 292, *292*
firing 287, 383, 448, 694gl.
Fischl, Eric: *Falling Woman* 656, *656*, 658
fixatives (drawing) 202
fixing (photography) 316, 317, 319, 694gl.
Flack, Audrey: *Marilyn (Vanitas)* 601, *601*
Flag (Johns) *609*, 609–10
Flagg, James Montgomery: *I Want You for U.S. Army 305*, 305–6
flashback 337, 694gl.
Flavin, Dan: *Untitled* 544, *544*
Fleming, Victor: *The Wizard of Oz* 337–38, *338*
flint 694gl.; Maya carving *605*
floating perspective 220
Florence: Baptistry *87*, 461–62; Cathedral (Santa Maria del Fiore) *462*, 462–64, *463*; Medici rule 243–44, 480; Santa Maria del Carmine (*Tribute Money* fresco) *463*, 463–64; Santa Maria Novella 89, *89*; Santo Spirito *44*
flying buttresses 268, *268*, 406–7, *407*, 694gl.
focal point 150–53, 156–57, 694gl.
Following Piece (Acconci) 350, *354*, 354–55
fonts 302, *302*; *see also* typefaces
foreground 694gl.
foreshortening 92–93, 618, *618*, 694gl.
Forever Free (Lewis) 36, *36*
form 38, 61–66, 694gl.
formal 694gl.; formal analysis 38–39, 170–72, 183–84, *185*
format 144, 694gl.
found images/objects 223, 253, 529, 608, 661, 686, 694gl.
Fountain (After Marcel Duchamp: A. P.) (Levine) 547, *547*
Fountain (Duchamp) 351, 547, *547*
"Four Horsemen, The" (*Apocalypse* series) (Dürer) *227*, 227–28
Four Marilyns (Warhol) *235*, 235–36
Fragility (Van Besten) 322, *322*
Fragonard, Jean-Honoré: *The Swing 487*, 487–88
frames (film) 122, *122*, 334, 694gl.
Frank, Jane 223; *Frazer's Hog Cay #18* 223, *223*
Frankenthaler, Helen 540; *Mountains and Sea* 540, *540*
Frazer's Hog Cay #18 (Frank) 223, *223*
Fred Ott's Sneeze (Edison and Dickson) 122, *122*
freestanding sculpture 65–66, 242, 243–44, 694gl.
French Academy 105, 484, 492–93, 494, 502, 503–4, 514
frescoes 212–14, 695gl.; Dura Europos synagogue *391*, 391–92, *392*; Minoan 369, *369*; Renaissance *89*, *463*, 463–64 (see also *School of Athens*; Sistine Chapel frescoes); restoration of 613, *613*; Roman 386–87, *387*, *587*, 587–88; *see also* murals; wall and ceiling paintings
Freud, Sigmund 530
Frida (Taymor) 342, *342*
Frida Kahlo (Álvarez Bravo) *532*
Friedrich, Caspar David 37–38; *Abbey Among Oak Trees 37*, 37–38
friezes *380*, *387*, 695gl.
From Here I Saw What Happened and I Cried (Weems) 329, *329*
frontispiece *399*, *619*, 695gl.
Fundred Dollar Bill Project (Chin) *559*, 559–60
Funeral of Phocion, The (Poussin) 483, *483*
Funeral of St. Bonaventure, The (Zurbarán) 156, *156*
Futurism 114, 533–34, 695gl.

Gabo, Naum: *Constructed Head No. 2* 253, *253*
Gallas Rock (Voulkos) 290, *290*
galleries *see* museums and galleries
Game of Thrones (Benioff and Weiss) 348, *348*
Ganzeer: *Martyr Murals* 647; *Tank vs. Bike* 647, *647*
Garden of Earthly Delights, The (Bosch) 173, *173*
Gardner, Alexander: *Abraham Lincoln and His Son Thomas (Tad)* 506, *506*
Garner, Conrad: Toronto Maple Leafs Centennial Season Tickets *310*, 311, *311*
Gates, The (Christo and Jeanne-Claude) 570, 571, *571*
Gates, Theaster: Stony Island Arts Bank 560, *560*
Gauguin, Paul 514–15, 682; influence 518, 521; *The Vision after the Sermon (Jacob Wrestling with the Angel)* 514–15, *515*; *The Yellow Christ* 110, *111*
Ge Zhichuan Moving His Dwelling (Wang Meng) 418, *418*, 420
Gedö, Ilka 196–97; *Self-portrait* 196–97, *197*
Gehry, Frank: Guggenheim Museum, Bilbao *70*, 70–71
geisha 667
gelatin silver print process 321, 695gl.
Gèlèdé ritual 572, *572*, 695gl.
gender identity 359, 669, 689, 690
gender studies analysis 180–81
genre 342, 492, 493, 695gl.
Gentileschi, Artemisia 219, 680, 681, 684; *Judith and Her Maidservant with the Head of Holofernes* 681, *681*; *Judith Decapitating Holofernes* 152, *152*, *219*, 478, *478*, 519, *519*, 681, *681*; *Self-portrait as the Allegory of Painting (La Pittura)* 219, *219*
geometry/geometric 695gl.; forms 62–63, 70, 695gl.; shapes 54, *54*, 157; *see also* Cubism
George Washington (Houdon) 628–29, *629*
Géricault, Théodore: *Raft of the Medusa 652*, 652–53
Gertrude Stein with Portrait by Picasso (Man Ray) 29, *29*
gestalt 131, 695gl.
gesture drawing 206–7
Gettysburg, Battle of 638–39
Ghiberti, Lorenzo: *Sacrifice of Isaac* 461–62, *462*
Ghostwriter (Helmick and Schechter) 67, *67*
Giacometti, Alberto 206, 674; *The City Square* 206, *206*; *Man Pointing* 674, *674*
Giambologna: *Rape of a Sabine 243*, 243–44
Giant (Goya) 232, *232*
giclée 239–40
GIF (graphics interchange format) 347, 695gl.
Giotto di Bondone 461; *Virgin and Child Enthroned* 408, *408*
Girl before a Mirror (Picasso) *600*, 601
Girl in Chair (Brown) 218, *218*
Girl in Mirror (Lichtenstein) *541*, 541–42
Girl with a Pearl Earring (Vermeer) 33, *33*
Girodet, Anne-Louis: *Jean-Baptiste Belley* 496, *496*
Gislebertus: *The Last Judgment* 584–85, *585*
Giuliano da Maiano: studiolo in Ducal Palace, Gubbio 297–98, *298*
glass 290–92; architectural 275, 277, 282; sculpture 64, *64*, 256, *256*; *see also* stained glass
glazing (ceramics) 287, 288, 419
glazing (painting) 216, 219, 222, 464, 695gl.
Gleaners, The (Millet) 142, *142*
Glidehouse (Kaufmann) 283, *283*
Global Groove (Paik and Godfrey) 345, *345*
Glory Be to God (Houghton) 53, *53*
Gochman, Molly 360; *Red Sand Project* 360, *360*
Godfrey, John J., with Paik, Nam June: *Global Groove* 345, *345*
Gogh, Vincent van 30, 109, 515–16, 657, 682; *The Bedroom* 51, *51*; *The Night Café* 109, *109*; *Self-Portrait with Bandaged Ear and Pipe* 682, *682*; *Sower with Setting Sun* 205, *205*; *Starry Night 515*, 515–16
Going Forth by Day (Viola) *346*
Golden Section 147, *147*, 534, 695gl.; Golden Rectangles 147, *147*, 148, *148*
Goldsworthy, Andy 549; *Japanese maple...* 549, *549*
Good Shepherd (mosaic) 393, *393*
Gormley, Anthony 256–57; *Asian Field* 256–57, *257*
Gothic 268–69, 291–92, 391, 406–8, 695gl.
gouache 220, 695gl.
Goulue at the Moulin Rouge, La (Toulouse-Lautrec) 307, 309, *309*
Gower, George: *Elizabeth I (Armada Portrait)* 633, *633*
Goya, Francisco 167, 644; *The Caprices* 167; *Giant* 232, *232*; "The Sleep of Reason Produces Monsters" *167*, 167–68; *The Third of May, 1808* 644–45, *645*
graffiti 223–24, 554–55, 647, 695gl.
Graffiti Removal Hotline (Banksy) 224, *224*
Grand Tour 491, 695gl.
Grande Odalisque (Ingres) *179*, 179–80; see also *Odalisque in Grisaille*
Grandpré, Mary: *Harry Potter and the Sorcerer's Stone* cover art *306*, 306–7
graphic art 23
graphic design 23–24, *48*, 49, 51, 300, 308, 542, 695gl.; printed color 98–99, 312–13
Graves, Michael *281*, 543; Portland Public Services Building 543, *543*
Great Mosque of Córdoba 165, *165*
Great Mosque of Djenné *451*, 451–52
Great Plaza, Tikal *262*
Great Salt Lake, Utah *252*, 253
Great Serpent Mound, Ohio *252*, 252–53
Great Sphinx, Giza 62, *62*
Great Stupa, Sanchi 413, *413*, 415
"Great Wave off Shore at Kanagawa, The" (Hokusai) 126, *126*, 229, *229*, 425, *425*, 661, *661*
Great Zimbabwe *452*, 452–53
Greco, El (Domenikos Theotokopoulos): *Laocoön* 472, *472*
Greece, ancient 145, 379–85; ceramics 383, *383*, 385; ideals of beauty 666; painting 211, 383, 615; *see also* Classical period (Greece); Cycladic sculpture; Minoan Crete; Mycenae
greenware 287, 695gl.
Greiman, April 300, 308, 309; *Does It Make Sense?* 300, 308, *308*, 309
Greuze, Jean-Baptiste 489; *The Marriage Contract* 489, *489*
grid 125, 129, 131, 163, 695gl.; enlargement aid 622; perspective aid *92*, 92–93; proportion aid 664, *665*
Griffith, D. W.: *Birth of a Nation* 336–37; poster *337*
Gris, Juan: *Bottle of Banyuls* 528, *528*
grisaille 216, 695gl.
groin vaults 269, 695gl.
Gropius, Walter 304; Bauhaus building 304, *304*
Gross Clinic, The (Eakins) *604*, 604–5
ground 196, 695gl.
Grünewald, Matthias: *Isenheim Altarpiece* 465, *465*, 467

Gu, Wenda 572; "China Monument: Temple of Heaven" (*United Nations* series) 572, *573*
Guernica (Picasso) 645–46, *646*
Guerrilla Girls 685; *Do Women Have to Be Naked...* 685, *685*
Guggenheim Museum, Bilbao (Gehry) *70*, 70–71
Guggenheim Museum, New York (Wright) *115*, 567, *567*
guilds 30, 695gl.
Gun Crime (Bar) 58–59, *59*
Guns for Shovels (Reyes) 655, *655*
Guo Xi 220; *Early Spring* 220, *220*
Gutai group 128–29
Gutenberg, Johannes 301
"Gyre" (Jordan) 661, *661*

Hadid, Zaha 282; Contemporary Arts Center, Cincinnati 282, *282*
Hagia Sophia, Istanbul 270, *270*, 394, *395*
Hall, D. J.: *Piece of Cake* 197, *197*
Hall of Mirrors, Versailles 484, *484*
Hall of Two Sisters, Alhambra (Granada) 607, *607*
Halydrys siliquosa ß minor (Atkins) *318*
Hammons, David: *Untitled (Night Train)* 686, *686*
Hammurabi 634; stela of 634, *634*
Hampton, James 554; *The Throne of the Third Heaven of the Nations' Millennium General Assembly* 554, *554*
hand-tinting 322, 695gl.
Hanging Partridge (Linwood) *294*, 295
happenings 353, 611, 695gl.
Hardouin-Mansart, Jules: Hall of Mirrors, Versailles 484, *484*
Harlem Renaissance 177, 536–37, 680, 695gl.
harmony, visual 125, 126, 133, 136, 148
Harnett, William M. 617–18; *The Old Violin* 617–18, *618*
Harp, The (Savage) 538, *538*
Harry Potter and the Sorcerer's Stone cover art (Grandpré) *306*, 306–7
Harvest of Death (O'Sullivan) *638*, 638–39
hatching *80*, 80–81, 196, *196*, 695gl.
Hatshepsut 689; Sphinx of 689, *689*
Have No Fear, He's a Vegetarian (Heartfield) 530, *530*
Hawaii 454, 456; feather cloak 456, *456*; Ku-ka'ili-moku *247*, 247–48; NAGPRA 444
Hawass, Zahi 378
Hayden, Palmer: *Midsummer Night in Harlem 177*, 177–78
Hayllar, Edith 88; *A Summer Shower* 88, *88*
Hazanavicius, Michel: *The Artist* 338–39, *339*
Haze (Donovan) 559
Head of a Satyr (Michelangelo) *80*, 80–81
Heads of the Virgin and Child (Raphael) 196, *196*
Heartfield, John 529–30; *Have No Fear, He's a Vegetarian* 530, *530*
Hegemony (Yeoh) *302*, 302–3
Heiji Monogatari see *Tale of the Heiji Rebellion*
Hellenistic art 384–85, *385*, 695gl.
Hello Monday: "Magritte: The Mystery of the Ordinary, 1926–1938" 311–12, *312*
Helmick, Ralph and Schechter, Stuart: *Ghostwriter* 67, *67*
hemispherical 695gl.
Hepworth, Barbara 52; *Drawing for Sculpture (with color)* 52, *52*
Here Is New York: A Democracy of Photographs... 325, *325*
Herrán, Saturnino: *Coatlicue Transformed* 440, *440*
Herschel, John 318
Herzfeld, Helmut *see* Heartfield, John
Hesse, Eva 37; *Untitled (Rope Piece)* 36, *36*, 37
Hicks, Sheila 296–97; *The Silk Rainforest 296*, 297
Hidden Figures (book) (Shetterly) 342
Hidden Figures (film) (Melfi) 342, *343*
hierarchical scale 142–43, 371, 379, 405, 641, 695gl.
hieroglyphs 300, *301*, 375, 376, *377*, 379, 695gl.; *see also* Maya: writing system
high relief 65, 244, 695gl.
highlights 78, *78*, 79, 80, 201, 695gl.
Hildegard of Bingen *399*, 399–400
Hildesheim Doors *579*, 579–80
Hinduism 131, 410–11, 415, 599; Angkor Wat, Cambodia *426*, 426–27, *427*; Indian art 131, *131*, 413, 415–16, *416*, 599, *599*; Indonesian art *287*, 287–88
Hine, Lewis Wickes 323, 325; *Ten Year Old Spinner, Whitnel Cotton Mill* 325
Hip Hop Project (Lee) 689–90, *690*
Hiroshige, Ando: "Riverside Bamboo Market, Kyo-bashi" 156–57, *157*
Hirst, Damien 253–54; *The Physical Impossibility of Death in the Mind of Someone Living 253*, 253–54
Hishikawa Moronobu *see* Moronobu
historical drama 342, 695gl.
history paintings 492, 493
Hitler, Adolf 529–30, *530*, 657
Höch, Hannah 326–27; *Cut with the Kitchen Knife...* 327, *327*
Hockney, David 38; *Portrait of an Artist (Pool with two figures)* 38–39, *39*
Hodler, Ferdinand: *The Night* 518, *518*, 520
Hogarth, William 489–91; *False Perspective* 619, *619*; *Marriage a-la-Mode* series *490*, 490–91, *491*
Hokusai 20, 28; "The Great Wave off Shore at Kanagawa" 126, *126*, 229, *229*, 425, *425*, 661, *661*
Holbein, Hans, the Younger: *Jean de Dinteville and Georges de Selve ("The Ambassadors") 174*, 174–75, *175*
"Hollywood Limousine" (Donwood) 230, *230*
Holocaust 646–47
Holt, Nancy 120; *Solar Rotary* 120, *120*, 122
Holzer, Jenny 114–15; *Untitled (Selections from Truisms...)* 114–15, *115*
Homage to New York (Tinguely) *351*, 351–52
Hon'ami Koetsu *see* Koetsu
Hopi people 581; *kachina* doll 581, *581*
Hopper, Edward: *Nighthawks* 171–72, *172*
Horse Fair, The (Bonheur) *217*, 217–18
Horse in Motion, The (Muybridge) 335–36, *336*
Horta, Victor: Tassel House 520, *520*
Horyu-ji, Nara 270–71, *271*, 423
Hotshot (Rauschenberg) *606*, 606–7
Houdon, Jean-Antoine: *George Washington* 628–29, *629*
Houghton, Georgiana: *Glory Be to God* 53, *53*
House (Whiteread) 69, *69*
Houser, Allan: *Reverie* 36–37, *37*
Houses at L'Estaque (Braque) *527*, 527–28
Hudson River School 499
hue 97, 101–2, 695gl.
human body: abstract representations 673–75; anatomy 193, 508, 604; and beauty 666–67; in body and performance art 548, 670–73, 677–78; as organic form 63; proportions 145, *145*, 147, *147*, 384, 448, 603–4, 664–65, *665*
Human Condition, The (Magritte) 626, *626*
Humana Building, Louisville (Graves) 281, *281*
humanism 460, 470, 695gl.
Hummingbirds, The (Lostutter) 141, *141*
Hung Liu: *Interregnum* 218, *218*
Hungry Tigress, The (Japanese painting) 423, *423*
Hunters in the Snow (Bruegel) 164, *164*
Hunting Scene (cave painting) 122, *122*
huqqa base, Indian 160, *160*
Hurricane Katrina 559–60
Hussein, Saddam 636; statue of 636, *636*
Huysmans, Joris-Karl: *À rebours* (*About Nature*) 518

I Am Your Grandma (Mayer) 598, *598*
I Want You for U.S. Army (Flagg) *305*, 305–6
I Wasn't Made to Play the Son (Djurberg) 557, *557*
Icarus (Matisse) 675, *675*
iconic status 311, 609, 628, 629, 636, 663, 695gl.
iconoclasm/iconoclasts 396, 474, 695gl.
iconographic analysis 174–75, 182, 185, 466–67, 695gl.; *see also* symbolism
icons (religious art) 214, 394–95, *395*, 396, *396*, *582*, 582–83, 636, 695gl.
icons (symbolic graphics) 303, 305, *305*
idealized 695gl.
ideals/idealism 695gl.; Chinese calligraphy 301; and reality 218; depictions of leaders 628, 665; female beauty 170, 181, 656; Greek 145, 379, 381, 384, 579; Modernist 304, 543; moral 489; proportion 145, 603–4, 665; Renaissance 461, 480, 603–4
identity 669, 680–84; *see also* gender identity; racial identity
Ife dynasty (Nigeria) 145, 667; Oni figure 145, *145*; terra-cotta head 667, *667*
Iktinos: Parthenon 148, *148*, 381, *381*, 620, *620*
Ilfochrome 322
illuminated characters/illuminations 305, *305*, 399, *399*, 464, 695gl.
illuminated manuscripts 301, 303, *303*, 398–400, 695gl.
illusionism 465, 615–19, 626, 695gl.; in architecture 620–22; photorealism 153, 601, 622
illusions: color perception *106*, 106–7, *107*, 608–10; motion 114–17, *115*; perception of Parthenon 620, *620*
illustration 305–7
IMAX 335, 695gl.
impasto 218, 695gl.
implied line 39, *46*, *47*, 47–48, *48*, 695gl.
implied motion 113–14
implied texture 73, 196, 232, 695gl.
impression (printing) 226, 695gl.
Impression, Sunrise (Monet) 513
Impressionism 216–17, 501, 508–13, 514, 535, 695gl.
Improvisation #30 (Cannons) (Kandinsky) 522, *522*
in situ 695gl.
In the Air (*En el aire*) (Margolles) 653, *653*, 655
In the Blue (Crest) (Mickett and Stackhouse) 68, *68*
in the round (sculpture) 64, 481, 695gl.; *see also* freestanding sculpture
Inca 430, 432–33; checkerboard tunic 433, *433*; Machu Picchu *432*, 432–33
India 410, 411–16; Buddhism 413, 414, 415, 580; Hinduism 131, 415–16, 599; Islamic (Mughal) art 156, *157*, 160, *160*; McCurry photography of *324*, 324–25; *see also* Taj Mahal
India ink 202
Indonesia 287–88, 427
Ingres, Jean-Auguste Dominique: *Grande Odalisque 179*, 179–80; *Odalisque in Grisaille* 216, *217*
ink 202, 205; lithographic 235; painting 210, 220
installations 256, 350, 356–58, 695gl.; combinations of works 357; human bodies as *672*, 672–73; immersive 611, *611*; large-scale 256–57, *257*, 571, *571*, *672*, 672–73; light 256, *256*, 544, *544*; Minimalist 544, *544*, 557, *557*; naturally changing 123, *123*; projection, video, and images *346*, 346–47, 358, *359*, *552*, 552–53, 555–57, *556*, *557*, 596, *596*; sculptural 68, *68*, 256, *256*, 356, *356*, 358, *358*, 557, *557*, 559, *684*, 684–85; tactile 297, *297*, 653, *653*, 655; text display 114–15, *115*, 352, *352*; thread *558*, 558–59; *see also* Rothko Chapel; *Waterlilies*
Insurrection! (Our Tools Were Rudimentary ... (Walker) 358, *359*
intaglio 226, 230–33, 695gl.
intarsia 298–99, *299*, 695gl.
intensity 83, 106–7, 122, 695gl.
intercessors 396, 460, 695gl.
interior design 127, *127*, 259, 589
Interior with Portraits (Le Clear) 507, *507*
International Style 278–79, 543
interpretation 179, 180; ambiguity 33, 554, 556, 557, 598, 623, 645; *see also* analysis and critique
Interregnum (Hung) 218, *218*
Iraq War 372, 636, 648
Irascibles, the 237
iron gall ink 202
Ise Jingu, Japan 588–89, *589*
Isenheim Altarpiece (Grünewald) 465, *465*, 467
Ishtar Gate 373, *373*
Islam 160, 394, 401–4, 411; Alhambra 607, *607*; ceramics 106, *106*; Dome of the Rock 401, *401*; early prints 227; manuscripts 398, *398*, 400, *400*; metalwork huqqa base 160, *160*; mosques 165, *165*, 260, *260*, *402*, 402–4, *403*, *451*, 451–52, 588, *588*; painting 156, *157*, 215, *215*, 400, *400*; *see also* Neshat, Shirin; Taj Mahal
isometric perspective 83, 84–86, 642, 695gl.
Istanbul: Hagia Sophia 270, *270*; Süleymaniye mosque 260, *260*
Itten, Johannes 107

Jackson, Peter: *The Lord of the Rings: The Return of the King* 341, *341*
Jacob Wrestling with the Angel (Gauguin) 514–15, *515*

Jansen, Theodorus Gerardus Jozef ("Theo") 119; *Animaris Umeris (Strandbeest #48)* *119*
Japan 20, 410, 411, 421–24; architecture 270–71, *271*, 421, *421*, 423, 588–89, *589*; geisha 667; Gutai group *128*, 128–29; manga 49, *49*; tea ceremony 28, 421, 423; woodblock printing *228*, 228–29, *229*, *510*, 510–11 (*see also* Hokusai); *see also* MacAdam, Toshiko Horiuchi; Morimura, Yasumasa
Japanese maple... (Goldsworthy) 549, *549*
Japonisme 510–11
Jarrell, Wadsworth 549–50; *Revolutionary* 550, *550*
jars, canopic 376, *376*
Jazz (artist's book) (Matisse) 675, *675*
Jean-Baptiste Belley (Girodet) 496, *496*
Jean de Dinteville and Georges de Selve ("The Ambassadors") (Holbein) *174*, 174–75, *175*
Jeanne-Claude *see* Christo and Jeanne-Claude
Jefferson, Thomas: Monticello 494, *495*
Jeunet, Jean-Pierre: *Amélie 340*, 341
"John Brown Remained a Full Winter in Canada..." (Lawrence) *154*, 154–55
Johns, Jasper 540; *Flag 609*, 609–10
Jordan, Chris 661; "Gyre" 661, *661*
Journal of a Voyage to the South Seas, A (Parkinson) *454*
Journey of the Sun God Re, The (coffin painting) *20*, 20–21
Joy of Life (Matisse) 525, *525*
JR and Marco: *28 Millimeters, Face2Face* 660, *660*
Judaism 391, 394, 401, 587; color symbolism 108; Dura Europos synagogue *391*, 391–92, *392*; micrography 47, *47*; Nazi persecution 646–47
Judd, Donald 542, 544; *Untitled* 544, *544*
judgment scenes 405–6, *406*, 468–69, *469*, *584*, 584–85, *585*
Judith and Her Maidservant with the Head of Holofernes (Gentileschi) 681, *681*
Judith Decapitating Holofernes (Caravaggio) 478, *478*
Judith Decapitating Holofernes (Gentileschi) 152, *152*, 478, *478*, 519, *519*, 681, *681*
Judith I (Klimt) 519, *519*
"Julie, Den Haag..." (Dijkstra) 592, *592*
Julius II, Pope 468, 471; library of 617, *617*; tomb of 246, *247*
Jumpsuit Project, The (Roland) 660, *660*
Justinian I, Byzantine emperor 394, *397*, 397–98, 631

ka 374, 375, 695gl.
Kaaba, Mecca 402, *402*
kachinas (Hopi) 581, *581*
Kahlo, Frida 204, 342, 532, 676; *The Broken Column* 676, *676*; "Eyesaurus" 204, *204*; *The Two Fridas* 50, *50*, 204, *204*, 532, *532*, 676, *676*
Kaigetsudo Dohan: *Beautiful Woman* 667, *667*
Kallikrates: Parthenon 148, *148*, 381, *381*, 620, *620*; Temple of Athena Nike 264, *264*
Kanaga mask (Dogon) 450, *450*
Kandariya Mahadeva temple, Khajuraho 415–16, *416*
Kandinsky, Vasily 95, 521–22; *Concerning the Spiritual in Art* 522; *Improvisation #30 (Cannons)* 522, *522*; *Yellow-Red-Blue* 98, *98*
Kapoor, Anish: *Cloud Gate* 73, *73*
Karnak: Temple of Amun-Re 142–43, *143*, *263*, 263–64
Katsushika Hokusai *see* Hokusai
Kauffmann, Angelica 494; *Cornelia Pointing to Her Children as Her Treasures* 494, *495*
Kaufmann, Michelle: Glidehouse 283, *283*
Kelly, Gene *see* Donen, Stanley
kente cloth 449, *449*, 695gl.
Kepler Underneath 1 (Strauss) 237–38, *238*
key-frame animation 341, 695gl.
Khafre (pharaoh) 62; pyramid of 62, 374, *374*, 375; statue of 375, *375*
Khan, Abd al-Karim Ma'mur 137; *see also* Taj Mahal
Khan, Makramat 137; *see also* Taj Mahal
Kiefer, Anselm 646; *Breaking of the Vessels* 646–47, *647*
Kienholz, Edward: *The Beanery* 356, *356*
Kihara, Yuki: *Taualuga: The Last Dance* 358–59, *359*
Kim, Hyo-In *286*; *To Be Modern #2* 286, *286*
Kindred Spirits (Durand) 84, *84*
kinetic art/sculpture 116, *116*, 118–19, *119*, *255*, 255–56, 281, 283, 351–52, 529, 696gl.
King, Clive: "Chaos Machine" *187*, 187–88
Kirchner, Ernst Ludwig 522; *Potsdamer Platz* 522, *522*
Kiss, The (Brancusi) 72, *72*
Kiss, The (Rodin) 72, *72*
Kitagawa Utamaro *see* Utamaro
Kitchen Table series (Weems) 551, 687; "Untitled (Woman and daughter with makeup)" 56, *56*, 329, *329*, 551, *551*, 687, *687*
Klah, Hosteen: *Whirling Log Ceremony* 624, *624*
Klee, Paul 105, 657; *Ancient Sound 105*, 105–6
Klein, Yves: *Anthropométries de l'époque bleue 670*, 670–71
Klimt, Gustav: *Judith I* 519, *519*
Klint, Hilma af 110–11; *Group IV, No. 7, Adulthood* 111, *111*
knitting 297
Knossos, Palace of 369, *369*
Kodachrome 322, 324, 696gl.
Koetsu: tea bowl "Mount Fuji" 28, *28*
Kollwitz, Käthe: *Self-portrait in Profile to Left 198*, 199
Kondratowicz, Adrian: *TRASH maximalism NYC (Harlem)* 111, *111*
Kooning, Willem de *see* de Kooning
Koran 398, *398*
Korea 410, 424, 426; hanbok 286, *286*; *see also* Lee, Nikki S.; Moon, Jiha
Kosuth, Joseph 546, 548; *One and Three Chairs* 548, *548*
kouros statue 384, *384*
kraters 383, *383*, 385, 696gl.
Kruger, Barbara 352; *Belief + Doubt (=Sanity)* 352, *352*
Ku-ka'ili-moku, sculpture of (Hawaii) *247*, 247–48
Kusama, Yayoi: *Dots Obsession* 611, *611*
Kwakiutl 442–43; *Eagle Transformation Mask 442*, 442–43
Kwei, Kane: *Coffin in the Shape of a Cocoa Pod (Coffin Orange)* 102, *102*
La Source (Prud'hon) *78*, 78–79
Laboratorio Paravicini: "Play Plates" 335, *335*
"Lady's Death, The" (Hogarth) 490–91, *491*
Lahauri, Ustad Ahmad 137, 272; *see also* Taj Mahal
lamassu reliefs (Assyrian) *372*, 372–73
Lambert, Ron: *Sublimate (Cloud Cover)* 123, *123*
land art *see* earthworks; Nazca Lines
landscape art 492; acrylic 222, *222*; Çatalhöyük wall painting *368*, 368–69; crayon 54, *54*; ink painting 82, *82*, 84–85, *85*, 135, *135*, 202, *203*, 220, *220*, 418, *418*; oil painting 21, *21*, *37*, 37–38, 84, *84*, 100, *101*, 482–83, *483*, 499, *499*, 514, *514*; photography 321, *321*; watercolor *220*, 220–21
Landscape with the Fall of Icarus (Bruegel) *155*, 155–56
Lange, Dorothea: *Migrant Mother* 659, *659*
Laocoön (El Greco) 472, *472*
Laocoön and His Sons (sculpture) 384, *385*
lapis lazuli 209, 370, 371, 378, 696gl.
Lapiths and centaurs, battle of 381, *381*, *578*, 578–79
Larmann, Ralph M.: *Coalopolis* 222, *222*
Lascaux caves, France *586*, 586–87
Last Judgment (Sainte-Foy relief) 405–6, *406*
Last Judgment before Osiris (*from* Book of the Dead of Hunefer) 584, *584*
Last Judgment, The (Gislebertus) 584–85, *585*
Last Judgment, The (Michelangelo) 468–69, *469*
Last Measure series (Mann) 328, *328*
Last Supper, The (Dürer) *475*, 475–76
Last Supper, The (Leonardo) 468, *474*, 474–75
Last Supper, The (Tintoretto) 476, *476*
Lawrence, Jacob: "John Brown Remained a Full Winter in Canada..." *154*, 154–55
Layer Painting (CMY): Flowers (Saban) 99, *99*
layout design 307, 308, 309
Le Clear, Thomas: *Interior with Portraits* 507, *507*
Le Corbusier (Charles-Edouard Jeanneret) 278–79; Villa Savoye 278, *278*
Leader, Darian: "Glue" 596
Leader, Lindon: FedEx logo *23*, 23–24
leaders, depictions of 628–36; African 145, *145*, 667, *667*; Byzantine *397*, 397–98, 631, *631*; Egyptian (*see* Nefertiti; pharaohs; Tiye); Elizabeth I 633, *633*; Hitler 529–30, *530*; King Leopold of the Belgians 244, *244*; Louis XIV 483–84, *484*; Mao Zedong *635*, 635–36, *636*; Marie Antoinette *633*, 633–34; Maya 438, *438* (*see also* Shield Jaguar and Lady Xoc lintels); Mesopotamian *370*, 371, 372, *372*, 582, *582*, 634, *634*; Napoleon 629, *629*; Olmec heads 434, *434*; Roman 386, 388, *388*, 634, *635*; Saddam Hussein 636, *636*; US presidents 248, *248*, 506, *506*, 628–29, *629*
Lee, Nikki S.: *Hip Hop Project* 689–90, *690*; *Seniors Project* 689–90, *690*
Lee, Shelton Jackson ("Spike"): *Do the Right Thing* 686–88, *687*
Lely's Venus 66, *66*
Leo Burnett Company, Inc. 310; McDonald's Happy Meal campaign (with Helen Musselwhite) 310, *310*
Leonardo da Vinci 28–29, 192–93, 468; *Drawing for a wing of a flying machine 192*, 193; *The Last Supper* 468, *474*, 474–75; *Mona Lisa 28*, 29, 541; as Raphael's Plato 470, *470*; *Studies of the fetus in the womb 193*; *Vitruvian Man 603*, 603–4
Leopold of the Belgians: memorial to 244, *244*
Levine, Sherrie 547; *Fountain (After Marcel Duchamp: A. P.)* 547, *547*
Lewis, Edmonia: *Forever Free* 36, *36*, 37
Lhermitte, Léon Augustin: *An Elderly Peasant Woman 198*, 199
Li Cheng (attrib.): *A Solitary Temple Amid Clearing Peaks* 82, *82*
Liberation of Aunt Jemima, The (Saar) 254, *254*
Liberty Leading the People (Delacroix) *497*, 497–98
Libyan Sibyl, The (Michelangelo) 212, *212*; studies for *200*, 200–201
Lichtenstein, Roy 541–42; *Girl in Mirror 541*, 541–42
life drawing 206–7, 492–93, 508
Life of John Brown series (Lawrence) *154*, 154–55
Life Strands (Zhang) 199, *199*
"Lift Every Voice and Sing" (Savage) 538, *538*
light 77, 95–97, 99, 313; in architecture 260, 268–69, 291, 479; in Baroque art 477, 478, 481, 482; sculpture 255–56, 544, *544*; symbolism of 517, 604
Light Prop for an Electric Stage (Moholy-Nagy) *255*, 255–56
Limbo (Playdead) 347–48, *348*
Limbourg Brothers: *Très Riches Heures* 595, *595*
Lin, Maya: Vietnam Veterans Memorial, Washington, D.C. 649, *649*
Lin, Monika: *Ten Thousand* 420, *420*
Lincoln, Abraham 506, *506*
Lindisfarne Gospels 398–99, *399*
line 42–54, 696gl.; communicative 49, *49*, 51; contour 45–46, 207; directional 48–49, 50, *50*, 152, 156, 645; implied 39, *46*, *47*, 47–48, *48*; Nazca Lines 42–43, *43*; regularity 51–54
linear outline 696gl.; *see also* contours
linear perspective 86–92, 463, 696gl.
linocuts 227, 230, *230*
lintels *405*, 696gl.; *see also* post-and-lintel system; Shield Jaguar and Lady Xoc lintels
Linwood, Mary 295; *Hanging Partridge 294*, 295
literati (China) 420, 696gl.
lithography 226, *234*, 234–35, 696gl.; *see also* Mixografia®
Liu Ding (ritual container) *134*, 134–35
Locke, John 486
logos 49, 51, 303, 696gl.; AT&T 55, *55*; Chevrolet 303, *303*; FedEx Express *23*, 23–24; Nike 51, *51*
Loongkoonan 31, *31*; painting by *31*
Lord of the Rings trilogy (Jackson) 341, *341*
Lorrain, Claude: *The Tiber from Monte Mario Looking South* 202, *203*
Los Angeles: Watts Towers 26, *26*
Lost Angeles (Donwood) 230, *230*
lost-wax casting 250, *250*, 294
Lostutter, Robert 141; *The Hummingbirds 141*

Louis XIV of France 25, 483–84; portrait (Rigaud) 483–84, *484*
Louvre Museum, Paris 25, 221, 503
Lovers in an Upstairs Room (Utamaro) 228, *228*
Loving Care (Antoni) 671, *671*
low relief (bas-relief) 65, *65*, 244, *244*, 696gl.
Luger, Cannupa Hanska 444
luminosity 216, 696gl.
Luna, James: *Take a Picture with a Real Indian* 688, *688*
Luncheon on the Grass (Manet) 502–4, *503*
Lux, Loretta 326; *The Waiting Girl* 326, *327*

Ma Yuan: *Walking on a Mountain Path in Spring* 135, *135*
MacAdam, Toshiko Horiuchi 297; *Knitted Wonder Space II* 297, *297*
Machu Picchu *432*, 432–33
Madame X (Sargent) *612*, 612–13
Madonna in a Church (Van Eyck) 143, *143*
Madonna of Chancellor Rolin, The (Van Eyck) 216, *216*
Maestà altarpiece (Duccio) 214, *214*
Magritte, René 312, 626; *The Human Condition* 626, *626*; *The Menaced Assassin 312*; *The Treachery of Images 76*, 76–77
"Magritte: The Mystery of the Ordinary, 1926–1938" (Hello Monday) 312, *312*
Maki, Fumihiko: sketch of Four World Trade Center *260*, 261
Malevich, Kazimir 534; *Suprematist Composition: White on White* 534, *534*
Maman (Bourgeois) 71, *71*
Man at the Crossroads... (Rivera) 574
Man, Controller of the Universe (or *Man in the Time Machine*) (Rivera) 574, 576, *576*
Man Pointing (Giacometti) 674, *674*
Man Ray: *Gertrude Stein with Portrait by Picasso* 29, *29*
Man with a Guitar (Braque) 625, *625*
mandalas 138, *138*, 415, 696gl.
Mandan people 441–42; painted buffalo hide *441*, 441–42
mandorla 406, *406*, 696gl.
Manet, Édouard 512; *A Bar at the Folies-Bergère* 623, *623*, 625; *Le Déjeuner sur l'Herbe* (*Luncheon on the Grass*) 181, 502–4, *503*; *Olympia* 668–69, *669*
Mann, Sally: *Last Measure* series 328, *328*
Mannerism *471*, 471–72, *472*, 696gl.; *see also* Cellini, Benvenuto; Giambologna
Mantegna, Andrea: Camera degli Sposi 615–16, *616*; *Dead Christ* 592, *593*
Manufacturing #17: Deda Chicken Processing Plant (Burtynsky) 331–32, *332*
manuscripts 301, 303, 398–400, 696gl.
Mao (Warhol) 635–36, *636*
Mao Zedong 218, *635*, 635–36, *636*
Mapplethorpe, Robert 180–81; *Self-Portrait (#385) 180*, 181
Marc, Stephen: *Untitled—Passage on the Underground Railroad* 688, *688*
Marclay, Christian: *The Clock* 596, *596*
Marco *see* JR and Marco
Marcus Aurelius, equestrian statue 388, *388*
Marevna, Marie: *Nature morte à la bouteille 127*, 127–28
Margolles, Teresa: *En el Aire* (*In the Air*) 653, *653*, 655
Marie Antoinette *633*, 633–34
Marie Antoinette and Her Children (Vigée Le Brun) *633*, 633–34
Marilyn (Vanitas) (Flack) 601, *601*
Marinetti, Filippo 533
Marisol (Maria Sol Escobar): *Father Damien* 69, *69*, 73
Marriage à-la-Mode (Hogarth) *490*, 490–91, *491*
Marriage Contract, The (Greuze) 489, *489*
"Marriage Settlement, The" (Hogarth) 490, *490*
Martin, Agnes 535; *Starlight* 535, *535*
Martinez, Maria and Julian 289, *289*; bowl with plumed serpent 289, *289*
Martini, Francesco di Giorgio: *studiolo* in Ducal Palace, Gubbio 297–98, *298*
Martini, Pietro Antonio: *The Salon 492*, 493
Martyr Murals (Ganzeer) 647
Masaccio 463; *Tribute Money 463*, 463–64; *Trinity* 89, *89*, 91
Masjid al-Nabawi, Medina 402–4, *403*
Masjid-i-Shah, Isfahan 588, *588*
"Mask of Agamemnon" 293, *293*
masking (barrier) 224, 235, 696gl.
masks 572; Abelam 458, *458*; African 32, 154, 449–50, *450*, 572, *572*; funerary 293, *293*, 374, 378, *378*; Indonesian 427, *427*; Kwakiutl *442*, 442–43; see also *Demoiselles d'Avignon, Les*
masquerade 572, 696gl.
mass 62, 67, 69–73, 696gl.
mass production 236, 275, 276, 351, 357, 541, 559
Masson, André 52–53; *Automatic Drawing* 53, *53*
Master of Osservanza, Workshop of: *The Meeting of St. Anthony and St. Paul* 120, *120*
Matisse, Henri 29, 46, 110, 524–26, *526*, 535, 657, 675; *Blue Nude III* 675, *675*; *Icarus* 675, *675*; *Joy of Life* 525, *525*; *Open Window, Collioure* 110, *110*; *The Red Studio* 526, *526*; *Woman Seated in an Armchair 45*, 45–46
matrix: color 99; printmaking 226, 696gl.
mausoleums: of Galla Placida, Ravenna 393, *393*; of Mumtaz Mahal (*see* Taj Mahal); of Qin Shi Huangdi, Xi'an *417*, 417–18
Maya 437–38, 457; ball game *437*, 437–38, 605; flint carving 605, *605*; sarcophagus lid 599, *599*; lintels 162, *162*, 245, *245*, *436*, 436–37, 632, *632*; stela 65, *65*; writing system 162, *162*, 430
Mayer, Jillian: *I Am Your Grandma* 598, *598*
Mazzola, Francesco *see* Parmigianino
McCurry, Steve 324–25; *Rabari Tribal Elder 324*, 325
McDonald's Happy Meal campaign (Leo Burnett Company, Inc. and Musselwhite) 310, *310*
Mecca 401–2, 588
Medici, Cosimo de' 23
Medici, Francesco de' 243
Medici, Queen Marie de' 482
medieval art 173, *173*, 390–91, 595, *595*, 696gl.; *see also* Gothic; Romanesque
Medina 402; Masjid al-Nabawi 402–4, *403*
medium/media 696gl.; of drawing (dry) 195–202; of drawing (wet) 202–3, 205; fresco 212–14; of sculpture *251*; *see also* mixed media; paint; paper; support
Meeting of St. Anthony and St. Paul, The (Workshop of Master of Osservanza) 120, *120*
Mehretu, Julie 221–22; *Excerpt (Suprematist Evasion)* 222, *222*
Melancholy and Mystery of the Street, The (De Chirico) 530, *530*
Melfi, Theodore: *Hidden Figures* 342, *343*
Méliès, Georges 336; *A Trip to the Moon* (*Le Voyage dans la Lune*) 336, *336*
"Melissa & Lake..." (Opie) 690, *690*
memento mori 175, 600, 601, 696gl.
Memorial to King Leopold of the Belgians (Durant) 244, *244*
memorials 649–50
Menaced Assassin, The (Magritte) *312*
Mendieta, Ana: "Untitled" (*Silueta* series) 548, *548*
Meninas, Las (Picasso) *186*, 186–87
Meninas, Las (Velázquez) *183*, 183–86, *184*, *185*
Menkaure and His Wife, Queen Khamerernebty (Egyptian sculpture) 665, *665*
Mesa Verde, Colorado 441, *441*
Meshes of the Afternoon (Deren) *344*, 344–45
Mesoamerica 289, 429, 433–40, *434*, 625, 696gl.; *see also* Aztecs; Maya; Toltec; Zapotec
Mesopotamia 265, 290, 300, 370–73; *see also* Akkadians; Assyrians; Babylonians; Sumerians
metalwork 160, *160*, 292–94, *293*, *294*, 372, *372*, 378, *378*, 400, *400*; *see also* casting/casts
metopes 380, *380*
Metsys, Quentin: *The Moneylender and His Wife 464*, 464–65
Mexico 440, 558–59; contemporary art 653, 655; Mexican Mural Renaissance 213, 223; Toltec 643–44; Virgin of Guadalupe *25*, 25–26; Zapotec sculpture 288, *288*; *see also* Aztecs; Kahlo, Frida; Maya; Mesoamerica; Rivera, Diego
Mexico City: *Virgin of Guadalupe 25*, 25–26
mezzotint 233, *233*, 696gl.
Michelangelo Buonarroti 242, 246–47, 461, 462, 464, 468; *Awakening Slave* 246, *246*; *David* 480, *480*, 481; *Head of a Satyr 80*, 80–81; *Moses* 246, *247*; as Raphael's Heraclitus 470, *470*; *Studies for the Libyan Sibyl 200*, 200–201; *see also* Sistine Chapel frescoes
Mickett, Carol and Stackhouse, Robert: *In the Blue (Crest)* 68, *68*
micrography 47, *47*
middle-ground 696gl.
Mies van der Rohe, Ludwig 277, 304; Neue Nationalgalerie *277*
Migrant Mother (Lange) 659, *659*
mihrab 403, 588, 696gl.
Millais, John Everett: *Ophelia* 505, *505*
Millet, Jean-François: *The Gleaners* 142, *142*
minarets 273, 696gl.; *see also* Burj Khalifa
minbar 403, 404
Ming Dynasty porcelain 288, *288*, 419
Minimalism 542, 544, 557, 686, 696gl.; see also *Tilted Arc*
minkisi minkondi see nkisi nkondi
Minoan Crete 369–70; Knossos 369, *369*
Miró, Joan: *Object* 531, *531*
mirror writing 603, *603*, 696gl.
mirrors: *A Bar at the Folies-Bergère* 623, *623*; and Brunelleschi's proof 87; convex *464*, 465, 466, *467*, *616*, 616–17; Hall of Mirrors, Versailles 484, *484*; Kahlo and 532; in Kusama installations 611; *Las Meninas* 184, *184*; mirror shields 444, *444*; women with *541*, 542, *600*, 601, *601* (*see also* "Untitled (Woman and daughter with makeup)")
Mistos (Match Cover) (Oldenburg and Van Bruggen) 141, *141*
mixed media 182, 222–23, 696gl.
Mixografia® 238–39
Miyazaki, Hayao: *Spirited Away 340*, 340–41
moai, Easter Island 457, *457*
mobiles 119, *119*, 696gl.
Mobility (Shonibare) 356, 358, *358*
Moche culture 431–32; earspool *431*, 431–32
modeling (sculpture) 248–49, 256, 257, *257*
modeling (two-dimensional art) 696gl.
Modernism 446, 501, 524, 549, 696gl.; architecture 276–80, 281, 453, 542–43; *see also* Bauhaus
Modersohn-Becker, Paula 521; *Self-Portrait with Camellia 521*
Moget, Mark *see* Sauerkids
Moholy-Nagy, László 254–55; *Light Prop for an Electric Stage 255*, 255–56
Mona Lisa (Leonardo) *28*, 29, 541
Mondrian, Piet 534; *Composition with Yellow and Blue 534*
Monet, Claude 513, 514; *Impression, Sunrise* 513; *Waterlilies* 513, *513*
Moneylender and His Wife, The (Metsys) *464*, 464–65
Monks Mound, Cahokia 569, *569*, 572
monochromatic 56, 102, 670, 696gl.; *see also* grisaille
Monogram (Rauschenberg) *132*, 132–33
monoliths 452, 456, 696gl.; *see also* Great Sphinx
monoprints 237–38
monotypes 237
Monroe, Marilyn *235*, 235–36
Monticello (Jefferson) 494, *495*
Mont Sainte-Victoire (Cézanne) 514, *514*
Monument to the Third International (Tatlin) 67–68, *68*
monumental scale 140–41, 262, 696gl.
Moon, Jiha 553; *Mystery Myo... 552*, 553
Moore, Henry 674; *Recumbent Figure* 674, *674*
Moreau, Gustave: *Apparition* 518, *518*
Morell, Abelardo 316; *Camera Obscura Image of the Panthéon ...* 316, *316*
Morgue, The (Gun Murder) (Serrano) 593, *593*
Morimura, Yasumasa: *Portrait (Futago)* 669, *669*
Morisot, Berthe 512; *The Beach at Nice* 512, *512*
Morojele, Mphethi (MMA Architects) 453; South African Embassy, Berlin 453, *453*
Moronobu: *Papermaking in Japan* 205, *205*
Morris, William and Burne-Jones, Edward: *Works of Geoffrey Chaucer* 305, *305*
mosaics 393, *393*, 397, *397*, 520, *520*, 631, *631*, 696gl.
Moses (Michelangelo) 246, *247*

mosques 165, *165*, 260, *260*, *402*, 402–4, *403*, *451*, 451–52, 588, *588*; *see also* Dome of the Rock
Mother and Child (Schiele) 207, *207*
Mother Goddess, Coatlicue (Aztec) *439*
Mother Goddess Men Brajut (Hariti), The (Indonesian) *287*, 287–88
Mothers series (Dijkstra) 591–92, *592*
motifs 160–61, 163, 696gl.
motion 113–19, 335–36, 696gl.; *see also* film
motion capture 341, *341*, 696gl.
Motion Study: Male Nude, Standing Jump to Right (Eakins) 508, *508*
"Mount Fuji" tea bowl (Koetsu) 28, *28*
Mount Rushmore National Memorial (Borglum) 248, *248*
Mountain Stream (Sargent) *220*, 220–21
Mountains and Sea (Frankenthaler) 540, *540*
movies *see* film
Mughal empire 156; *see also* Taj Mahal
multiculturalism 546, 549, 550, 553
Mumtaz Mahal 136, 272, 594
Munch, Edvard: *The Scream* 182, *182*
muqarnas 588, *588*, 607, *607*
murals 213, *213*, 223, 438, *438*, 574, 696gl.; *see also* frescoes; wall and ceiling paintings
Murasaki Shikibu: *Tale of Genji* 424
Muscular Dynamism (Boccioni) 207, *207*
museums and galleries 25, 30, 32, 34; Contemporary Arts Center, Cincinnati 282, *282*; Guggenheim, Bilbao *70*, 70–71; Guggenheim, New York *115*, 567, *567*; Louvre, Paris 25, 221, 503; Milwaukee Art Museum 281, *281*, 283; Museum of Modern Art (MoMA), New York 312, 351–52, 355; National Gallery of Art, Washington, D.C. 119, *119*
musicals 338, 696gl.
Music—Pink and Blue II (O'Keeffe) 58, *58*
Musselwhite, Helen 310; McDonald's Happy Meal campaign 310, *310*
Mutu, Wangechi 74; *She's Got the Whole World in Her* 74, *74*
Muybridge, Eadweard: *The Horse in Motion* 335–36, *336*
My Calling (Card) #1... (Piper) 685, *685*
Mycenae: gold death mask 293, *293*; Treasury of Atreus 265, *265*
Myron: *Discus Thrower* 666, *666*
Mystery Myo... (Moon) *552*, 553

Nadar: *Sarah Bernhardt* 320, *320*
NAGPRA 444
Nameless and Friendless (Osborn) *505*, 505–6
Napoleon I, Emperor 376, 629, 629, 644
Napoleon III, Emperor 503, 513
Napoleon Crossing the Alps (David) 629, *629*
Napoleon Leading the Army over the Alps (Wiley) 630, *630*
Naram-Sin, stela of 582, *582*
narrative art 696gl.; ambiguity 530, 555–57; indigenous American 430, 442; interaction 648; medieval 269, 595; satirical 489–91; Sumerian 371; taualuga dance 359; *see also* continuous narrative; film; television
National Gallery of Art, Washington, D.C. 119, *119*
National September 11 Memorial 650, *650*
Native Americans *440*, 440–44; bent-corner chest 298, *298*; contemporary art 168, *168*, 236, *236*, 550, *552*, 552–53, 688, *688*; pottery 289, *289*; *see also* Navajo
Natura 9 (Black) 211, *211*
naturalism 460, 696gl.
Nature morte à la bouteille (Marevna) *127*, 127–28
Navajo 580–81, 624; sand painting 580–81, *581*, 624; screen print (Yazzie) 236, *236*; *Whirling Log Ceremony* (Klah) 624
nave *268*, 405, *405*, 696gl.; octagonal 395; oval 479, *479*
Nazca Lines 42–43, *43*
Nazism 304, 353–54, 529–30, 646, 657–58
Nebamun, tomb of 377, *377*, 379
Nefertiti 632; bust of 170–71, *171*; sunken relief 632, *632*
negative 315, 319, 696gl.; *see also* cyanotype
negative space 57, 59, 68, 71, 696gl.
Negro hung alive by the ribs... (Blake) 496, *496*
Neo-Expressionist 554, 696gl.
Neoclassicism 25, 273, 274, 491, 493–95, 496, 696gl.
Neshat, Shirin 553, 659–60; *Rapture* 553, *553*; "Speechless" 659, *659*
Netflix 348
Neue Nationalgalerie, Berlin (Mies van der Rohe) *277*
Neumann, Johann Balthasar: Basilica of Vierzehnheiligen *488*, 488–89
neutral colors 102, *103*, 696gl.
Nevelson, Louise: *White Vertical Water* 21, 22, *22*
New Wave design 308, 696gl.
New York City 261, 307; 9/11 Memorial 650, *650*; Armory Show 533–34, 536; Empire State Building 48, *48*; Federal Plaza 573, 574–75, *575*; *The Gates*, Central Park 570, 571, *571*; Guggenheim Museum *115*, 567, *567*; Harlem 177, *177*; Museum of Modern Art (MoMA) 312, 351–52, 355; New World Trade Center *260*, 261; RCA Building, Rockefeller Center 574; SoHo *261*; *TRASH* project 111, *111*
New Zealand 454
Newman, Barnett: *Vir Heroicus Sublimis* 104, *104*
Niagara (Church) 21, *21*, 22
Niépce, Joseph Nicéphore 317–18; *View from the Window at Le Gras* 317, *317*
Night Attack on the Sanjo Palace (from *Tale of the Heiji Rebellion*) 642–43, *643*
Night Café, The (Van Gogh) 109, *109*
Night of the Poor (Biggers) 195, *195*
Night, The (Hodler) 518, *518*, 520
Night Watch, The (Rembrandt) 482, *482*
Nighthawks (Hopper) 171–72, *172*
Nightmare Before Christmas, The (Burton) 339–40
Nike logo (Davidson) 51, *51*
Nile, The (Basquiat) 554–55, *555*
nkisi nkondi (pl. *minkisi minkondi*) 446, *448*, 448–49, 696gl.
No. 5/No. 22 (Rothko) *539*, 539–40
Nocturne in Black and Gold: The Falling Rocket (Whistler) 26–27, *27*
Nok sculpture *447*, 447–48
Nolde, Emil 657–58; *The Crucifixion* 657–58, *658*; *Prophet* 228, *228*
non-objectivity 36, 521–22, 534, 625, 696gl.
Northern Baroque 481–84; *see also* Rembrandt van Rijn
Northern Renaissance 460, 464–67; *see also* Dürer, Albrecht; Eyck, Jan van
Notre Dame Cathedral, Paris 565, *565*
Nude Descending a Staircase, No. 2 (Duchamp) *533*, 533–34
nudes 696gl.; *Blue Nude II* (Matisse) 675, *675*; feminist analysis 179–80; French academic art 492–93, 502–3; Greek 383, 384, 666; as installations 672–73; Manet 502–4, 668–69; Mapplethorpe 181; in performance art 670–71; Post-Impressionist 516; reclining 668–69; Renaissance 460, 461, 468, 480, 668; self-portraits 521, 669, *669*, 677, *677*
Nuestro Pueblo (Watts Towers) (Rodia) 26, *26*
Number 1A (Pollock) *539*

Oak Tree in Winter (Talbot) 318, *318*, 320
Oath of the Horatii, The (David) *493*, 493–94
Obey (Fairey) 57, *57*
Object (Miró) 531, *531*
Object (Oppenheim) 74, *74*
ocher 367, 696gl.
oculus 696gl.; illusionary 615–16, *616*; Neoclassicist 494; of Pantheon *387*, 388
Odalisque in Grisaille (Ingres) 216, *217*
oil paint 210, 216–18, 508, 540, 696gl.
O'Keeffe, Georgia 57–58; *Music—Pink and Blue II* 58, *58*
Old Guitarist, The (Picasso) 102–3, *103*
Old Man's Cloth (Anatsui) 24, *24*
Old Violin, The (Harnett) 617–18, *618*
Oldenburg, Claes 140–41; *Mistos (Match Cover)* (with Coosje van Bruggen) 141, *141*
Olmec 433–34; colossal heads 434, *434*; transformation figure *624*, 624–25
Olympia (Manet) 668–69, *669*
One and Three Chairs (Kosuth) 548, *548*
one-point perspective 88–89, *89*, 696gl.
O'Neill, Walter: *Untitled* (fresco) 214, *214*
Ono, Yoko 352; *Wish Tree* 350, 352, *353*
Op art 115, *115*, 696gl.
opaque 696gl.; gouache as 220
Open Window, Collioure (Matisse) 110, *110*
Operation Paydirt/Fundred Dollar Bill Project (Chin) *559*, 559–60
Ophelia (Millais) 505, *505*
Opie, Catherine 690; *Domestic* series 690, *690*
Oppenheim, Méret: *Object* 74, *74*
optical mixture *106*, 106–7, 509, 697gl.
Optics: the principle of the camera obscura (engraving) *316*
organic 697gl.; organic form 63–64, 70, 697gl.; organic shapes 54, *54*; organic texture 232
ORLAN: surgery-performances 677–78, *678*
Orozco, José Clemente 213; *Prometheus* *213*
orthogonals 88, *89*, 493, 697gl.
Osborn, Emily Mary 505–6; *Nameless and Friendless 505*, 505–6
O'Sullivan, Timothy: *Harvest of Death* *638*, 638–39
outline 207, 697gl.
outsider art 30, 554–55
Owens Thompson, Florence 659
pace 336, 697gl.
Pacific Islands 446, 453–58, *454*; Easter Island 457; Hawaii 247–48, 454, 456; influence on European artists 527; New Guinea 597; New Zealand 454; Palau 166; Papua New Guinea 457–58; Postcolonial 358–59
Paik, Nam June 345; *Global Groove* (with Godfrey, John J.) 345, *345*
paint 97, 209–10; acrylic 210, 221–22; encaustic 210–11; gouache 220; oil 210, 216–18, 464, 508, 540; spray paint 223–24; tempera 210, 214–15; watercolor 195, 210, 220–21; *see also* frescoes
painterly style 697gl.
painting *see* paint; painting tools; *and names of individual periods, movements, cultures and artists*
painting tools 209, *211*, 219, 539
Palas por Pistolas (Reyes) 655, *655*
Palazzo del Tè, Mantua (Romano) *621*, 621–22
palette (color range) 697gl.; harmonious 100; monochromatic 56, 102, 670, 675 (*see also* grisaille); neutral 184; restricted 103, 534, 542, 589, 675
palette (mixing surface) 219, 508, 641, 697gl.
palette knife 209, 211, *211*
Palette of Narmer (Egyptian) 641, *641*
Palladio, Andrea 473, 494; Villa Rotonda, Vicenza 473, *473*
Panofsky, Erwin 466–67
pantheism 131
Panthéon, Paris 316, *316*
Pantheon, Rome 270, *387*, 387–88
paper 195, 205–6, 220, 227, 313; tooth 199; colored 196
Papermaking in Japan (Moronobu) 205, *205*
Papua New Guinea 457–58
Paracas people 431; embroidery 431, *431*
Parade, The (Djurberg) 557
Paravicini, Costanza: "Play Plates" 335, *335*
Paris: Haussmanization 513; Louvre Museum 25; Notre Dame cathedral 565, *565*; Panthéon 316, *316*
Paris Street, Rainy Day (Caillebotte) *512*, 513
Parker Julia 443, *443*
Parkinson, Sydney: *A Journal of a Voyage to the South Seas 454*
Parmigianino: *Self-Portrait in a Convex Mirror 616*, 616–17
Parrish, Maxfield: *Daybreak* 306, *306*
Parthenon, Athens 148, *148*, 380, 381, *381*, 620, *620*
Parthenon Marbles *381*, 381–82, *382*
Passion 697gl.; *see also* Crucifixion scenes; *Dead Christ*; *Deposition*; *Last Supper*; *Roettgen Pietà*
pastel 195, 200, 201
Pastoral (Primavera) (Stjernschantz) 81, *81*
patina 250, 697gl.
patrons 29, 461, 479, 484, 487, 697gl.; Adele Bloch-Bauer 519, *519*
pattern 159–63, 697gl.
Paxton, Joseph: Crystal Palace 275, *275*
Pech Merle cave paintings 210, *210*, 224
pedestal 574, 697gl.
pediment *380*, 697gl.
pen-and-ink 205
pencil 196–97
pendentives 270, *270*, 697gl.

Pennsylvania Academy of the Fine Arts 25, 492, 507–8, 516
Pentateuch with Prophetical Readings and the Five Scrolls 47
Pepper No. 30 (Weston) 321, *321*
performance art 118, 350, 353–56, 548, 648, 670–71, 677–78, 697gl.
performance capture *see* motion capture
Perro de Luna (Tamayo) 239, *239*
Persistence of Memory, The (Dalí) *610*, 610–11
personification 497, 581, 697gl.
perspective 83–93, 220, 424, 461, 463, 697gl.; *see also* illusionism
Pevsner, Naum Neemia *see* Gabo, Naum
pfemba figures 597–98, *598*
pharaohs 374–75, 377; Akhenaten 377, 632, *632*; Hatshepsut 689, *689*; Khafre 375, *375*; Menkaure 665, *665*; Narmer 641, *641*; Seti I 142–43, *143*; Tutankhamun 377, 378, *378*
Pheidias: metope from the Parthenon *381*
phenakistoscope 116, *116*
Philadelphia Museum of Art 25, *25*
photocollage 325–26
photography 315–32; and anatomical study 508; art status 315, 330–31; color 322–23; cultural impact 315–16, 501, 506–7; darkroom processes 319; digital 315, 326; *Drop Dead Gorgeous* series (Edburg) 332, *332*; early techniques 316–18, 320–21, 327–28; gelatin silver prints 321; and Impressionism 511; McCurry Kodachrome project 324–25; portraits 321, *321*, 592, *592*; as record of time-limited artwork 549, 673; snapshot aesthetic 331; and social awareness 659–60; and synesthesia 610; and truth 315, 323, 331, 638–39; *see also* Weems, Carrie Mae
photojournalism 323–25, 639–40, 659
photomontage 326–27, 529, 697gl.
Photorealism 153, 601, 622
Physical Impossibility of Death in the Mind of Someone Living, The (Hirst) *253*, 253–54
Picasso and Braque (Tansey) 102, *103*
Picasso, Pablo 29, 46, 102–3, 186–87, 524–25, 526–27, 600–601, 645, 657; *Blonde Woman in Profile* 46, *46*; *Bull's Head* 254, *254*; *Girl before a Mirror 600*, 601; *Guernica* 645–46, *646*; *Las Meninas 186*, 186–87; *Les Demoiselles d'Avignon* 527, *527*; *The Old Guitarist* 102–3, *103*; *Portrait of Gertrude Stein* 29, *29*
pictographs 641, *641*, 697gl.; *see also* hieroglyphs
picture plane 697gl.; position in 81
piece-mold casting 419, 697gl.
Piece of Cake (Hall) 197, *197*
pigment 95, 96, 97, 209, 367, 641, 697gl.
pilaster 697gl.
pilgrimage 401–5, 414, 415
Piper, Adrian: *My Calling (Card) #1...* 685, *685*
Pittura, La (Gentileschi) 219, *219*
Plains Indians 441–42
planes 43, 45, 77, *196*, 697gl.; in Modernist painting 514, 522, 526 (*see also* Cubism)
planography 234–36, 697gl.
plasticity/plastic 287, 697gl.; three-dimensional prints 240
"Play Plates" (Paravicini) 335, *335*
Playdead: *Limbo* 347–48, *348*
Plexus no. 19 (Dawe) *558*
Pliny the Elder 615
Ploughing, The (Seurat) 201, *201*
Plowing in the Nivernais: The Dressing of the Vines (Bonheur) *166*, 166–67
pointed arches *268*, 269, 588, *588*, 697gl.
pointillism 106–7, *107*, 542, 608–9, 697gl.
Pollock, Jackson 351, *538*, 538–39; *Number 1A 539*
Polykleitos 145, 384; *Doryphoros* (*Spear Bearer*) 384, *384*
polymers 697gl.; casting 249; *see also* acrylic paints
polytheism 370, 377, 697gl.
Pompeii 386–87; Dionysiac frieze *387*
Pont du Gard, Nîmes 266, *266*
Pontormo, Jacopo da: *Deposition 471*, 471–72
Pop art 540–42, 635–36, 697gl.
porcelain 287, 288
portals 405, *405*, 588, *588*, 697gl.
porticoes 281, *281*, 697gl.
Portland Public Services Building (Graves) 543, *543*
Portland Vase *290*, 290–91
Portrait (Futago) (Morimura) 669, *669*
Portrait of an Artist (Pool with two figures) (Hockney) 38–39, *39*
Portrait of Dr. Samuel D. Gross (Eakins) *604*, 604–5
Portrait of Eleonora of Toledo... (Bronzino) 23, *23*
Portrait of Gertrude Stein (Picasso) 29, *29*
Portrait of the Artist's Sisters Playing Chess (Anguissola) *472*, 472–73
portraits 320, 492, 697gl. *(and see above)*; Biagio da Cesena as Minos (Sistine Chapel) 469, *469*; drawn 196–97, *197*, *198*, 199; of Eleonora of Toledo and her son 23, *23*; photographic 320, 501, 506–7, 592, 690; Roman sculpture 386, *386*, 634, *635*; in *The School of Athens* 470–71; silhouettes 358; statue of Saddam Hussein 636, *636*; see also *Arnolfini Portrait, The*; *Fanny/Fingerpainting*; *Jean de Dinteville and Georges de Selve ("The Ambassadors")*; leaders, depictions of; *Meninas, Las*; *Mona Lisa*; *Night Watch, The*; *Sennuwy*
Poseidon (Greek sculpture) 147, *147*
positive 315, 319, 320, 697gl.
positive-negative contrast 57–59, 115, 697gl.
post-and-beam construction 271–72, *272*
post-and-lintel construction 262–64, *263*, *264*, 697gl.
Post-Impressionists 501, 514–17, 535, 697gl.
postcolonialism 359, 524, 546
Postmodernism 281–83, 542, 543, 546, 549, 697gl.
Potsdamer Platz (Kirchner) 522, *522*
Poussin, Nicolas 482–83; *The Funeral of Phocion* 483, *483*
Praxiteles: *Aphrodite of Knidos* 383, *383*
Pre-Raphaelite Brotherhood 505, 697gl.
predella 640, *640*, 697gl.
Preface of the Lanting Gathering (Wang Xizhi), rubbing of *301*
prehistoric art *252*, 252–53, 366–70, 697gl.; *see also under* caves
Presley, Elvis 163
primary colors 98–99, 312–13, 697gl.
principles of art 38, 41, 42, 140, 170, 697gl.
printing presses 234, 301, 303
printmaking 226–40; collagraphy 233–34; contemporary 238–40; intaglio 230–33; lithography 234–35; multiple *vs.* unique works 236–38; print shops 238–40; relief 226, 227–30 (*see also* woodblock printing); rubbings 301; serigraphy (silkscreen) 235–36, 541
prints 697gl.; *see also* printmaking; woodcuts
prism 95, *95*, 697gl.
Prisoner (*Awakening Slave*) (Michelangelo) 246, *246*
profile 46, 171, 605, 697gl.
Prometheus (Orozco) *213*
propaganda 337, 628, 629, 634–36, 697gl.
Prophet (Nolde) 228, *228*
Prophet's Mosque *see* Masjid al-Nabawi
proportion 140, 144–48, 697gl.; distortion of 471, 472, 580
Prose of the Trans-Siberian Railway and of Little Jehanne of France (Delaunay) 221, *221*
protest: against artworks 636, 649, 655–56; through art 444, 499, 644–48, 652–55, 660, 685
Protestantism 174, 474, 475–76; Lutheran 37–38, 475
Prud'hon, Pierre-Paul: *Study for La Source 78*, 78–79
psychoanalysis 610, 697gl.
psychology 610–11, 697gl.; psychological analysis 182
public spaces, art and 70–71, 73, 256, 568, 570–71, 573–76, 672–73; *see also* street art
Puebloans, ancient 440–41
puppets 339, 697gl.
Puryear, Martin: *C.F.A.O* 154, *154*
putti (sing. putto) 502, *502*, 615, *616*, 697gl.
pyramids 61, *61*, 262, 697gl.; Giza 61, *62*, *374*, 374–75; Mesoamerican 262, *262*, 434–35, *435*, 437, *437*, 438; *see also* ziggurats

Qianlong Emperor's Southern Inspection Tour... (Xu Yang) 84–85, *85*
qibla 402–3, 697gl.
Qin Shi Huangdi, mausoleum of *417*, 417–18
Quadracci Pavilion, Milwaukee Art Museum (Calatrava) 281, *281*, 283
quatrefoil 461, *462*, 697gl.
Queen Tiye of Egypt portrait head 377, *377*
quilts *133*, 133–34, 160–61, *161*, 295
Quinn, Marc 32; *Self* 32, *32*

Rabari Tribal Elder (McCurry) *324*, 325
racial identity 181, 630, 684, 685, 686–88, 689–90
radial balance 135, 138
Radioactive Cats (Skoglund) 322, *323*
Raft of the Medusa (Géricault) *652*, 652–53
Raft, The (Viola) *346*, *347*
Raimondi Stela, Chavín de Huantar *430*, 430–31
Raising of the Cross, The (Rubens) *481*, 481–82
Rand, John G. 216
Rape of a Sabine (Giambologna) *243*, 243–44
Raphael 146, 468; *Heads of the Virgin and Child* 196, *196*; *The School of Athens 90*, 91, 146, *146*, 194, *194*, 468, *470*, 470–71, 617, *617*
Rapture (Neshat) 553, *553*
Rauschenberg, Robert 132, 222, 540; *Bed* 223, *223*; *Erased de Kooning Drawing* 201, *201*; *Hotshot 606*, 606–7; *Monogram 132*, 132–33; *Stoned* 606
Raviv, Ilana 239; *Doll with Toys 239*, 239–40
Razorfish 311; Taste Re-wind 311, *311*
readymades 254–55, 529, 697gl.
Realism 504–6, 697gl.; *see also* Manet, Édouard
Recumbent Figure (Moore) 674, *674*
Red Sand Project (Gochman) 360, *360*
Red Studio, The (Matisse) 526, *526*
Reformation 474, 475–76
Regionalism 536, 697–98gl.
registers 370, 406, 641, 697gl.
Rejlander, Oscar Gustav: *The Two Ways of Life* 326, *326*
relative placement 81, 156–57, 698gl.; in continuous narrative 120
relics 400, 404, 407, 565
relief printmaking 226, *227*, 227–30, 698gl.
relief sculpture 64–65, 242, 244–45, 698gl.; sunken 632, *632*
religion 394, 411; African 447, 450, 452–53, 580; Akkadian 582; Andean 430, 431; Assyrian 372–73; Egyptian 20–21, 374–75, 377, 379, 584; Indonesian 427; Mesoamerican 435–37, 438–40, 591, 605, 606; Native American 580–81; Pacific 247–48, 458; Sumerian 175, *175*; see also *Elohim Creating Adam*; spirituality; *and names of individual religions*
religious buildings *see* basilicas; cathedrals; church architecture; mosques; Rothko Chapel; shrines; temples
reliquary of the Head of St. Alexander 400, *400*
Rembrandt van Rijn 232, 482, 680, 682; *Adam and Eve* 232, *232*; *The Night Watch* 482, *482*; *Self-Portrait with Saskia...* 682, *682*
Renaissance 146, 460–76, 698gl.; architecture 271, 273, 462–63, 473, 621; chiaroscuro technique 78–79; Classical influence 460, 461, 470–71, 472, 473, 480, 615, 666–67; competition 461–62; Early 461–64; fresco technique 212; High 468–71 (*see also* Leonardo da Vinci; Michelangelo Buonarroti; Raphael; Sistine Chapel frescoes); idea of genius 28, 29; illusionism 615–17; Late 471–73, 476 (*see also* Giambologna); metalwork 293–94; Northern 460, 464–67 (*see also* Dürer, Albrecht; Eyck, Jan van); perspective techniques 86–91, 92–93, 463, 464, 465; reclining nudes 668; silverpoint 195–96; trends in thought and approach 460, 461, 666–67
Reni, Guido: *Susannah and the Elders* 477, *477*, 479
Renoir, Pierre-Auguste 514; *Bal du Moulin de la Galette* 509, *509*
repatriation 433, 444, 698gl.
repetition 126, 131, 236, 397; *see also* balance; pattern; rhythm
(Re)Possessed (Bailey) 550, *550*
repoussé 293, 400, 698gl.
representation/representational 35–36, 698gl.
responses and reinterpretations *181*, 181–82, *186*, 186–87; *see also* appropriation
Reverie (Houser) 36–37, *37*

Revolutionary (Jarrell) 550, *550*
Reyes, Pedro: *Palas por Pistolas* (*Guns for Shovels*) 655, *655*
RGB system 99, *99*, 313, *313*, 698gl.
rhythm 82, 156–57, 159, 163–68, 698gl.
Riace Warrior A (Greek sculpture) 250, *250*
rib vaults 269, *269*, 406, 698gl.
Richardson, Mary 655–56
Rickard, Jolene 550, 552; *Corn Blue Room 552*, 552–53
Rickey, George: *Breaking Column* 255, *255*
Rickwood, Dan *see* Donwood, Stanley
Rietveld, Gerrit 542–43; Schröder House 542–43, *543*
Rigaud, Hyacinthe: *Louis XIV* 483–84, *484*
Riley, Bridget: *Cataract 3* 115, *115*
Ringgold, Faith 295; *Tar Beach* 295, *295*
Risatti, Howard 286
Rist, Pipilotti: *Ever Is Over All* 555–56, *556*
Rivera, Diego 574; *Man at the Crossroads...* 574; *Man, Controller of the Universe* (or *Man in the Time Machine*) 574, 576, *576*
"Riverside Bamboo Market, Kyo-bashi" (Hiroshige) 156–57, *157*
Riza Abbasi 215; *Two Lovers* 215, *215*
Robinson, Henry Peach 147–48; *Fading Away 147*, 147–48
rock paintings 455, *455*
Rockefeller, Nelson 574
Rococo 273–74, 487–89, 698gl.
Rodia, Simon 26; *Nuestro Pueblo* (Watts Towers) 26, *26*
Rodin, Auguste 516, 673–74; *The Kiss* 72, *72*; *Walking Man* 673, *673*
Roettgen Pietà (*Vesperbild*) *63*, 63–64
Rokeby Venus (Velázquez) 655–56, *656*
Roland, Sherrill: *The Jumpsuit Project* 660, *660*
Roll-Up #2 (Alps) *233*, 233–34
Roman art 386–88; architecture 264, 265–66, *266*, 271, 273, 380, 386, *387*, 387–88, *388*, 565–66, *566*; encaustic painting 211, *211*; inscriptions 302; sculpture 66, *66*, 383, *383*, 386, *386*, 388, *388*, 634, *635*; wall and ceiling paintings 386–87, *387*, *392*, 393, *587*, 587–88
Roman empire 387–88, 390
Romanesque 267, 269, 391, 404–6, 584–85, 698gl.
Romano, Giulio: Palazzo del Tè, Mantua *621*, 621–22
Romanticism 37–38, 496, 497–99, 629, 698gl.
Rome (city of): Ara Pacis Augustae 65, *65*; Arch of Constantine 388, *388*; catacombs *392*, 392–93, *587*, 587–88; colossal statue of Constantine 634, *634*; Colosseum 565–66, *566*; Pantheon *387*, 387–88; sack of (1527) 471; Tempietto of San Pietro in Montorio 273, *273*; Vatican (see *School of Athens, The*; Sistine Chapel frescoes)
Rope Piece (Hesse) 36, *36*, 37
Rosado-Seijo, Chemi: *El Cerro 109*, 109–10
Rosetta Stone 376
rosin 232, 698gl.
Rothko Chapel, Houston 589, *589*
Rothko, Mark 539–40, 589; *No. 5/No. 22 539*, 539–40
Rousseau, Jean-Jacques 486
Royal Academy of Arts 88, 492, 494, 498, 505, 506
Rubens, Peter Paul 481; *The Raising of the Cross 481*, 481–82
Rue Transnonain (Daumier) *234*, 235
Rule of Thirds 146, *146*
Run Lola Run (Tykwer) 117, *117*
Running the Numbers II see "Gyre"
Ruskin, John 26–27

Saar, Betye 254; *The Liberation of Aunt Jemima* 254, *254*
Saban, Analia 99; *Layer Painting (CMY): Flowers* 99, *99*
S.A.C.R.E.D. (Ai) *34*, 35, *35*
Sacrifice of Isaac (Brunelleschi) 461, 462, *462*
Sacrifice of Isaac (Ghiberti) 461–62, *462*
Sad Panda: addition to *Tank vs. Bike* 647, *647*
Saddam Hussein 636; colossal statue of 636, *636*
St. Anthony, Abbey of, Isenheim 465, 467
St. Catherine, Monastery of, Mount Sinai 394, 396
Saint-Denis, Abbey Church of, nr. Paris 268–69, *269*
St. Michael, Abbey Church of, Hildesheim *579*, 579–80
Sainte-Foy, Conques *404*, 404–6, *405*, *406*
Sainte-Madeleine, Vézelay 267, *267*, 269
Salon 493, 503, 504, 612, 613, 698gl.
Salon des Refusés 503–4
Salon, The (Martini) *492*, 493
Salt Cellar of Francis I (Cellini) 293–94, *294*
Samoa: taualuga dance 359, *359*
San Carlo alle Quattro Fontane, Rome (Borromini) 479, *479*
San Ildefonso-style pottery 289, *289*
San Pietro in Montorio, Tempietto of, Rome (Bramante) 273, *273*
San Vitale, Ravenna 395, 397, *397*, 631
Sand Dunes, Sunrise—Death Valley... (Adams) 321, *321*
sand painting 138, *138*, 580–81, *581*, 624, 698gl.
Sano di Pietro *see* Master of Osservanza, Workshop of
Santiago de Compostela, pilgrimage to 404
Santo Spirito, Florence (Brunelleschi) *44*
Sarah Bernhardt (Nadar) 320, *320*
sarcophagi 249, *249*, 594, *594*, 599, *599*, 698gl.
Sargent, John Singer 220–21; *Madame X 612*, 612–13; *Mountain Stream 220*, 221
sarsen 570, 698gl.
Sasaki, Sonoko *422*, 422–23; *Sea in the Sky* 422, *422*
satire 489–91, 619, 698gl.
saturation 104–5, 698gl.
Sauerkids 47–48; *The Devil Made Me Do It* 48, *48*
Savage, Augusta: *The Harp ("Lift Every Voice and Sing")* 538, *538*
Saville, Jenny: *Branded* 677, *677*
scale 39, 61, 140–44, 146, 296–97, 698gl.
Schapiro, Miriam: *Baby Blocks* 54–55, *55*
Schechter, Stuart *see* Helmick, Ralph
Schiele, Egon 657; *Mother and Child* 207, *207*
School of Athens, The (Raphael) *90*, 91, 146, *146*, 194, *194*, 468, *470*, 470–71, 617, *617*
Schröder House (Rietveld) 542–43, *543*
science 603–13; astronomy and space 439, 477, 569, 570–71, 605–6; scientific drawing 192–93, 603–4; study of depicted 471, 604–5; use in artworks 607–10; use in study and care of art 611–13; of vision *see* visual perception
science-fiction (sci-fi) 342, 698gl.
Scream, The (Munch) 182, *182*
sculptural methods 247–56, *251*; assemblage 254; carving 246, 247–48, *251*, 481, 607–8; casting 32, 249–50, *251*, 480; construction 253–54; earthwork 252–53; installation 256; mass participation 256–57; modeling 248–49, *251*; movement and light 255–56; readymades 254–55
sculptural properties 62–74; abstraction 36–37, 535; form 63–66; mass 69–73; motion (*see* kinetic art/sculpture); texture 73; volume 67, 68, 71
sculpture 242–57; African 145, *145*, *447*, 447–49, *448*, *452*, 452–53, 580, *580*, 597–98, *598*, 644, *644*, 667, *667* (*see also* Anatsui, El; Kwei, Kane; Mutu, Wangechi); African American 36, *36*, 37, 154, *154*, 538, *538*, 554, *554*, 686, *686*; Baroque *480*, 480–81, 583, *583*; bioart 608, *608*; Buddhist *413*, 413–15, *414*, 580, *580*; Chinese *417*, 417–18; Constructivist 253, *253*; contemporary *178*, 178–79, 547, *547*, 646–47, *647*, 656, *656*, 658; Cycladic 368, *368*; Dada 529, *529*, 547, *547*; Egyptian (freestanding) 243, *243*, 375, *375*, 377, *377*, 665, *665*; Egyptian (relief) 142–43, *143*, 632, *632*, 641, *641*; Etruscan 249, *249*; Expressionist 290, *290*; Futurist 533, *533*; Greek 66, *66*, 384, *384*, 384–85, *385* (*see also under* Classical Period (Greece)); Hindu 131, *131*, *287*, 287–88, 415–16, *416*, 427, *427*, 599, *599*; Korean 424, 426, *426*; Mesoamerican (freestanding) 288, *288*, 434, *434*, 439, *439*, 591, *591*, 605, *605*, *624*, 624–25, *643*, 643–44; Mesoamerican (relief) 65, *65*, 435, 437, *437*, 439, *439*, 599, *599*, 606, *606* (*see also* Shield Jaguar and Lady Xoc lintels); Mesopotamian 175, *175*, *372*, 372–73, 582, *582*, 634, *634*; microscopic *607*, 607–8; Minimalist 542, 544, *544*, 573, 574–75, *575*; modern 516, *516*, 535, *535*, *673*, 673–74, *674*; Native American 581, *581*; outsider 26, *26*, 554, *554*; Pacific *247*, 247–48, 456–57, *457*, 597, *597*; prehistoric fertility figures 367–68, *368*, 663, *663*, 664; Renaissance *113*, 113–14, *243*, 243–44, *246*, 246–47, *247*, 294, *294*, 461–62, *462*, 480, *480*, 481; Roman 65, *65*, 66, *66*, 383, *383*, 386, *386*, 388, *388*, 634, *635*; Romanesque 405–6, *406*, *579*, 579–80, 584–85, *585*; of Saddam Hussein 636, *636*; South American *430*, 430–31; stickworks 568, *568*; Surrealist 74, *74*, 531, *531*; of US presidents 248, *248*, 628–29, *629*; *see also* installations; sculptural methods; sculptural properties
Sea in the Sky (Sasaki) 422, *422*
Seated Figure (Zapotec sculpture) 288, *288*
secondary colors 98, 99, 698gl.
Self (Quinn) 32, *32*
Self-Portrait (#385) (Mapplethorpe) *180*, 181
Self Portrait (Close) 161, 163, *163*
Self-portrait (Gedö) 196–97, *197*
Self-portrait as the Allegory of Painting (La Pittura) (Gentileschi) 219, *219*
Self-Portrait in a Convex Mirror (Parmigianino) *616*, 616–17
Self-portrait in Profile to Left (Kollwitz) *198*, 199
Self-Portrait with Bandaged Ear and Pipe (Van Gogh) 682, *682*
Self-Portrait with Camellia (Modersohn-Becker) *521*
Self-Portrait with Saskia... (Rembrandt) 682, *682*
self-portraits 521, 680, 682–84 *(and see above)*; Claesz 600, *600*; Eakins 604, *604*; Kahlo 676, *676* (see also *Two Fridas*); Michelangelo as St. Bartholomew 469, *469*; Quinn 32, *32*; Raphael as Apelles *470*, 471; Rist 556; Vallayer-Coster 494, *494*; Van Eyck in *Arnolfini Portrait* 466, *467*; see also *Kitchen Table* series; *Meninas, Las*
Sellick, Henry *339*
Sen no Rikyu 421, 423; Taian teahouse *421*, 423
Senefelder, Alois 234
Seniors Project (Lee) 689–90, *690*
Sennuwy, Lady, sculpture of 243, *243*
Senufo people 580; mother-and-child sculpture 580, *580*
Separation of Light and Darkness (Michelangelo) 246, *246*
sepia 202
series 698gl.
serigraphy (silkscreen) 226, 235–36, 541, 698gl.
Serkis, Andy 341, *341*
Serra, Richard 574–75; *Tilted Arc* 573, 574–75, *575*
Serrano, Andres: *The Morgue (Gun Murder)* 593, *593*
Seurat, Georges 608; *The Circus* 106–7, *107*; *The Ploughing* 201, *201*; *Sunday on La Grande Jatte* 608–9, *609*
sexual identity 690
sfumato 468, 698gl.
shade 102, *105*, 247, 698gl.
shafts 380, *380*, 698gl.
Shah Jahan 136, 137, 272–73, 594
shamans 368, 410, 431, *431*, 581, *624*, 624–25, 698gl.
shape *54*, 54–55, 56, 61, 698gl.; contour drawing and 207; implied 55, *55*, 129; positive and negative 57–59
Sherman, Cindy: "Untitled Film Still #35" 683, *683*; *Untitled Film Stills* 682–83
She's Got the Whole World in Her (Mutu) 74, *74*
Shetterly, Margot Lee: *Hidden Figures* 342
Shield Jaguar and Lady Xoc lintels (Maya) 162, *162*, 245, *245*, *436*, 436–37, 632, *632*
Shinto 411, 425, 588; Ise Jingu (shrine) 588–89, *589*
Shiseido advertisements *309*, 309–10
Shiva Nataraja (Lord of the Dance) 599, *599*
Shonibare, Yinka 356; *Mobility* 356, 358, *358*
shrines 391, *391*, 401, *401*, 413, 423, *423*, 588–89, *589*
silhouettes 358–59, *359*, 537, *537*, 698gl.
silk 294–95
Silk Rainforest, The (Hicks) *296*, 297
Silk Road 410, 414–15
silkscreen printing 226, 235–36, 541, 698gl.
Silueta series (Mendieta) 548, *548*
silver gelatin *see* gelatin silver print process
silverpoint 195–96
Sinan: Süleymaniye mosque 260, *260*

Singin' in the Rain (Donen and Kelly) 338, *338*
Sioux 441
Sipma, Taco *see* Sauerkids
Sistine Chapel frescoes (Michelangelo) 212, 246–47, *468*, 468–69; *Creation of Adam* 468, *468*, 498; *The Last Judgment* 468–69, *469*; *The Libyan Sibyl* 212, *212* (see also *Studies for the Libyan Sibyl*); restoration 613, *613*; *Separation of Light and Darkness* 246, *246*
site-specific art 350, 549; *see also* earthworks; installations; *Solar Rotary*; *Tilted Arc*
sitter 698gl.
sketches *192*, 192–93, *193*, 204, *204*, 206, *206*, 698gl.; cutouts 526
Skidmore, Owings & Merrill: Burj Khalifa 277, *277*, 280
Skoglund, Sandy: *Radioactive Cats* 322, *323*
Sky and Water I (Escher) 59, *59*
Skyline Art Editions 238, *238*
slab method (ceramics) 288, 290
Slave Ship, The (*Slavers Throwing Overboard the Dead...*) (Turner) *498*, 498–99
slavery 24, 37, 496, 499, 550, 555, 653, 688
"Sleep of Reason Produces Monsters, The" (Goya) *167*, 167–68
SLR (camera) 334, 698gl.
Smilack, Marcia 610; *Cello Music* 610, *610*
Smith, Adrian and Baker, Bill: Burj Khalifa 277, *277*, 280
Smith, David 63; *Cubi XIX* 63, *63*
Smith, Jaune Quick-to-See: *Trade (Gifts for Trading Land with White People)* 168, *168*
Smithson, Robert 549; *Spiral Jetty 252*, 253
Social Realism 536, 698gl.
soft-focus 321, 698gl.
Solar Rotary (Holt) 120, *120*, 122
Solitary Temple Amid Clearing Peaks, A (attrib. Li Cheng) 82, *82*
Solomon R. Guggenheim Museum (Wright) *115*, 567, *567*
Some/One (Do Ho Suh) 424, 426, *426*
sound: in film 338–39, 344; in installations 356, 555; in performance art 353, 528–29, 670–71; visual representation 105–6 (*see also* synesthesia)
South African Embassy, Berlin (Morojele) 453, *453*
South America 429, *429*, 430–33; Nazca Lines 42–43, *43*
Southeast Asia 410–11, 426–27; *see also* Indonesia
Sower with Setting Sun (Van Gogh) 205, *205*
space 38, 81–83, 408, 698gl.; *see also* perspective; volume
Spaceship Earth, Walt Disney World Resort 77, *77*
span 262–63, *263*, 265, 698gl.; of arches 266; of domes 270
Spear Bearer see *Doryphoros*
spectral light 96–97, 99, *99*, 698gl.; *see also* RGB system
"Speechless" (Neshat) 659, *659*
Sphinx of Hatshepsut 689, *689*
sphinxes 62, *62*, 689, *689*
Spider (Nazca Lines) 42–43, *43*
Spiral Jetty (Smithson) *252*, 253
Spirited Away (Miyazaki) *340*, 340–41
spirituality 447, 448, 457, 578, 589; prehistoric 586–87; and transformation 442–43, 624–25; *see also* religion; shamans
spray paint 223–24
Stackhouse, Robert *see* Mickett, Carol
stained glass 28, 269, *269*, *291*, 291–92, 399, 698gl.
Standard of Ur 370, 370–71
Standing Rock protests 444, *444*
Star Fountain (Tacha) 256, *256*
Starcraft (Blizzard Entertainment) 313
Starlight (Martin) 535, *535*
Starry Night (Van Gogh) *515*, 515–16
Statue of Liberty (Wigan) 607, *607*
Stedman, John Gabriel: *Narrative of a Five Years Expedition...* 496
steel-frame construction 276–77, 280
Steerage, The (Stieglitz) 330, *330*
Stein, Gertrude 29, *29*
Steiner Master (attrib.): reclining female figure *368*
stelae (sing. stela) 698gl.; Akkadian 582, *582*; Babylonian 634, *634*; Buddhist 580, *580*; Chavín *430*, 430–31; Chinese 301, *301*; Maya 65, *65*
stencils 224, 235, 367, 675, 698gl.
stepped pyramids 262, *262*, 435, *435*, 437, *437*, 698gl.
Sterne, Hedda 237; *Untitled (Machine Series)* 237, *237*
Stick Style *274*, 274–75
Stieglitz, Alfred 330; *The Steerage* 330, *330*
Stijl, De *see* De Stijl
still life *127*, 492, 494, *494*, 600, *600*, 698gl.
Stirling, Matthew and Marion 434
Stjernschantz, Beda 81–82; *Pastoral (Primavera)* 81, *81*
Stonebreakers (Courbet) 504, *504*
Stoned (Rauschenberg) 606
Stonehenge *570*, 570–71
stoneware 287, *290*
Stony Island Arts Bank 560, *560*
stop-motion animation 339–40, 556–57, 698gl.
Storm Drain–Cape Fear River Basin (Dery) *319*
Strandbeests (Jansen) 119; *Strandbeest #48 119*
Stranger Visions (Dewey-Hagborg) 608, *608*
Strauss, Kathy: *Kepler Underneath 1* 237–38, *238*
street art 57, *57*, 111, *111*, 618, *618*, 647, 698gl.
stroboscopic motion 115–17, 335, 698gl.
stucco 698gl.
Studies for the Libyan Sibyl (Michelangelo) *200*, 200–201
Studies of the fetus in the womb (Leonardo) *193*
stupas 413, 698gl.; Great Stupa, Sanchi 413, *413*, 415
style 172–73, 486, 698gl.
stylized 698gl.
stylobate 698gl.; curvature 620, *620*
subject/subject matter 21, 35–37, 659, 698gl.
Sublimate (Cloud Cover) (Lambert) 123, *123*
sublime 499, 698gl.
subordination 150, 155–56, 698gl.
subtractive color/subtractive color process 97–99, 322, 698gl.; *see also* CMYK
subtractive sculpture 247–48, 698gl.
Suger, Abbot 268–69, 270
Süleymaniye mosque, Istanbul (Sinan) 260, *260*
Sullivan, Louis 276–77; Wainwright Building *276*, 277
Sumerians 175, 370–72; bull lyre *371*, 371–72; *Standard of Ur 370*, 370–71; votive figures 175, *175*
Summer Shower, A (Hayllar) 88, *88*
Sun Stone (Aztec) 606, *606*
Sunday on La Grande Jatte (Seurat) 608–9, *609*
sunken relief 632, *632*, 698gl.
Supergiant Games: *Transistor 85*, 85–86
support (painting) 211, 216, 221, 698gl.
Suprematism 534, 698gl.
Suprematist Composition: White on White (Malevich) 534, *534*
surreal 698gl.
Surrealism 74, 130–31, 144, 524, 530–32, 539, 610–11, 698gl.
Surréalisme et la Peinture, Le (Ernst) 531, *531*
Susannah and the Elders (Reni) 477, *477*, 479
Swing, The (Fragonard) *487*, 487–88
Sydney Opera House (Utzon) *280*, 280–81
symbolism 130, 698gl.; Abelam 458; animals 132–33, 244, 375, 431, 625, 644; in *Armada Portrait* 633; Aztec 437, 439; Buddhist 138, 427; Classical 628, 668; color 108, 109–10, 111, 449, 456, 458, 625; in *Cremaster* cycle 556; Egyptian 376, 377, 632, 641; feminist 684–85; Hindu 426–27; Islamic 412; *lamassu* 372–73; logos and icons 303, 305; pyramids 375; shells 446, 448–49; *see also* Christian symbolism and iconography; *memento mori*; personification
Symbolists 81–82, 501, 517–20, 699gl.
symmetry 134–35, 699gl.; radial 135, 138; symmetrical balance 134–35, 473, *473*, 699gl.; of Taj Mahal *136*, 136–37, *137*, 273
syncretism 393, 411, 427, 440, 453, 699gl.
synesthesia 82, 610, 699gl.

tableau *323*, *356*, *554*, 699gl.
Tacha, Athena: *Star Fountain* 256, *256*
Tacon, Paul 455
Tagliapietra, Lino: *Batman* 64, *64*
Taian teahouse (Sen no Rikyu) *421*, 423
Taj Mahal, Agra *136*, 136–37, *137*, *272*, 272–73, 412, *412*, 594, *594*
Take a Picture with a Real Indian (Luna) 688, *688*
Talbot, William Henry Fox 316; *Oak Tree in Winter* 318, *318*, 320
Tale of Genji (Murasaki) 424; illustration of scene from 424, *424*
Tale of the Heiji Rebellion 641–42; *Night Attack on the Sanjo Palace* 642–43, *643*
Tamayo, Rufino 238; *Perro de Luna* 239, *239*
Tanaka, Atsuko 129; *Electric Dress 128*, 129; *Work 128*, 129
Tank vs. Bike (Ganzeer) 647, *647*
Tanner, Henry Ossawa 516; *Banjo Lesson* 517, *517*
Tanning, Dorothea: *Eine Kleine Nachtmusik* 144, *144*
Tansey, Mark 102; *Picasso and Braque* 102, *103*
t'ao t'ieh 134, 134–35
Taoism *see* Daoism
Taos Pueblo, New Mexico 261, *261*
tapestry 699gl.; Inca tunic 433, *433*; see also *Bayeux Tapestry*; *Whirling Log Ceremony*
Tar Beach (Ringgold) 295, *295*
Tassel House (Horta) 520, *520*
Taste Re-wind (Razorfish) 311, *311*
Tatlin, Vladimir: *Monument to the Third International* 67–68, *68*
tattoos 454, *454*, 699gl.
Taualuga: The Last Dance (Kihara) 358–59, *359*
Taymor, Julie: *Frida* 342, *342*
tea bowl ("Mount Fuji") (Koetsu) 28, *28*, 32
tea ceremony 28, 32, 421, 423
television 348
tempera 210, 214–15, 699gl.
temperature (color) 106, 699gl.
temples: of Amun-Re, Karnak 142–43, *143*, *263*, 263–64, 379; of Athena Nike, Athens 264, *264*; catacombs as 587; of the Feathered Serpent/of Quetzalcoatl, Teotihuacan 435, 437, *437*; Hindu 415–16, *416*, *426*, 426–27, *427*; Horyu-ji 270–71, *271*, 423; Maya 262, *262*; of Zeus, Olympia *578*, 578–79; *see also* Parthenon; ziggurats
temporal art 122, 699gl.
Ten Thousand (Lin) 420, *420*
tenebrism 79, 477, 478, 481, 604, 699gl.
Teotihuacan 434–35, *435*; Pyramid of the Sun 435, *435*; Temple of the Feathered Serpent/of Quetzalcoatl 435, 437, *437*
terra-cotta 699gl.; African sculpture *447*, 447–48, 667, *667*; army (mausoleum of Qin Shi Huangdi) *417*, 417–18; Etruscan sarcophagus 249, *249*; Indonesian pillar ornament 287–88, *288*
tertiary colors 98, 99, 699gl.
tesserae 393, 699gl.
Tewa people 289
textiles 285, 294–97; African 356, 358, *358*, 449, *449*; Andean 431, *431*, 433, *433*; Chinese 226, 417, *417*; Japanese 422–23; Navajo 624, *624*; *see also* fiber art; quilts
texture 62, 73, 74, 82, 699gl.; and oil painting 464; of paper 205, *206* (*see also* tooth); in prints 238–39
Theater Piece No. 1 (Cage) 353
Theodora and Attendants (mosaic) 631, *631*
Theodora, Empress 631, *631*
Third of May, 1808, The (Goya) 644–45, *645*
Thirty Are Better than One (Warhol) 541, *541*
Thirty-Six Views of Mount Fuji (Hokusai) 229; *see also* "Great Wave off Shore at Kanagawa, The"
"*This Is not a Pipe*" (Magritte) *76*, 76–77
Thomas, Mickalene: *Le Déjeuner sur l'herbe: les trois femmes noires* 181, *181*, 182
Thrash, Dox: *Defense Worker* 233, *233*
three-dimensional art 61, 699gl.
three-dimensional printing 240
three-point perspective 92, *92*, 699gl.
Throne of the Third Heaven of the Nations' Millennium General Assembly, The (Hampton) 554, *554*
throwing (ceramics) 287, 288, 370, 699gl.
Thutmosis, workshop of: *Bust of Queen Nefertiti* 170–71, *171*
Tiber from Monte Mario Looking South, The (Lorrain) 202, *203*
Tibet: sand paintings 138, *138*

Tiffany, Louis Comfort 520–21; "Wisteria lamp" *520*, 520–21
Tijuana Projection (Wodiczko) 576, *576*
Tikal, Guatemala: Temple I 262, *262*
Tilted Arc (Serra) 573, 574–75, *575*
time 120–23, 595–96, 600–601, 611; *see also* continuous narrative; motion
Tinguely, Jean 351; *Homage to New York* *351*, 351–52
tint 102, *105*, 699gl.
Tintoretto, Jacopo: *The Last Supper* 476, *476*
Titian: *Venus of Urbino* 668, *668*
Tiye, Queen 377; portrait head of *377*
Tlazolteotl (Aztec goddess) 591, *591*
Tlingit 296; Chilkat blanket 296, *296*
To Be Modern #2 (Kim) 286, *286*
Toilet of Venus, The (Velázquez) 655–56, *656*
Toltec 643; warrior columns *643*, 643–44
tombs: of Akbar, Sikandra 412, *412*; Chinese *417*, 417–18; Egyptian 374–75, 376, 377, 378; of Lady Dai Hou Fu-ren 416–17, *417*; mausoleum of Qin Shi Huangdi, Xi'an *417*, 417–18; Moche 431–32; of Muhammad 402, 403, *403*; of Mumtaz Mahal 136, *136*, *137*, 594, *594*; of Pacal (Maya ruler) 599, *599*; of Pope Julius II 246, *247*; Tomb of the Leopards (Etruscan) 385–86, *386*; *see also* sarcophagi
tone *105*, 105–6, 699gl.
tooth (paper) 199, 699gl.
toranas 413, *413*, 699gl.
Toronto Maple Leafs Centennial Season Tickets (Garner) *310*, 311, *311*
Toulouse-Lautrec, Henri de 307; *La Goulue at the Moulin Rouge* 307, 309, *309*
Trade (Gifts for Trading Land with White People) (Smith) 168, *168*
training 30; *see also* academies
transept 405, *405*, 699gl.
Transistor (Supergiant Games) *85*, 85–86
translucent 699gl.
transparency 699gl.; oil paint 216; watercolor *vs.* gouache 221
TRASH maximalism NYC (Harlem) (Kondratowicz) 111, *111*
travertine 566, 699gl.
Treachery of Images, The (Magritte) *76*, 76–77
Treasury of Atreus, Mycenae 265, *265*
Très Riches Heures (Limbourg Brothers) 595, *595*
Tribute Money (Masaccio) *463*, 463–64
triglyph 380, *380*, 699gl.
Trinity (Masaccio) 89, *89*
Trip to the Moon, A (Méliès) 336, *336*
triptychs 168, *168*, 173, *173*, *187*, 187–88, *555*, 640, *640*, 699gl.; *see also* altarpieces; *Dropping a Han Dynasty Urn*
trompe l'oeil 600, 615, 699gl.
trumeau *405*, 699gl.
Tsubasa RESERVoir CHRoNiCLE (CLAMP) 49, *49*
Tub, The (Degas) *200*, 201
Tunick, Spencer 672–73, *673*; living sculptures *672*, *673*
Turner, Joseph Mallord William: *Slave Ship, The* 498, 498–99
Turning Road, L'Estaque, The (Derain) *104*, 105
Tuscarora nation 552–53
Tutankhamun 377; funerary mask of 378, *378*
Twilight in the Wilderness (Church) 100, *101*
twining 443, 699gl.
twisted perspective 699gl.; *see also* composite view
Two Colors Look Like One (Albers) 107, *107*
Two Courtesans (Utamaro) *510*, 510–11
two-dimensional art 42, 43–44, 76–77, 699gl.; format 144
Two Fridas, The (Kahlo) 50, *50*, 204, *204*, 532, *532*, 676, *676*
Two Lovers (Riza Abbasi) 215, *215*
Two Ways of Life, The (Rejlander) 326, *326*
Tykwer, Tom: *Run Lola Run* 117, *117*
tympanum 699gl.; Saint-Lazare, Autun 585, *585*; Sainte-Foy, Conques *405*, 405–6, *406*
typefaces 304, 699gl.; *see also* fonts
typography 301–2, 699gl.

ukiyo-e 424
ultramarine 209
Uncle Sam *305*, 305–6
underpainting 216, 699gl.
Unique Forms of Continuity in Space (Boccioni) 533, *533*
United Nations series (Gu) 572, *573*
unity 125–31, 699gl.; *see also* proportion
"Universal" typeface (Bayer) 304, *304*
Unterschieden Tonka (Dyrhaug) 240, *240*
Untitled (Basquiat) 30, *30*
Untitled (Calder) 119, *119*
Untitled (Donovan) 557, *557*, 559
Untitled (Flavin) 544, *544*
Untitled (Judd) 544, *544*
Untitled (O'Neill) 214, *214*
Untitled (Yazzie) 236, *236*
Untitled (Machine Series) (Sterne) 237, *237*
Untitled (Night Train) (Hammons) 686, *686*
Untitled (Ocean) (Celmins) *153*, 153–54
Untitled (Rope Piece) (Hesse) 36, *36*, 37
Untitled (Selections from *Truisms...*) (Holzer) 114–15, *115*
Untitled (The Hotel Eden) (Cornell) *130*, 130–31
"Untitled (Woman and daughter with makeup)" (Weems) 56, *56*, 329, *329*, 551, *551*, 687, *687*
"Untitled" (*Family Pictures and Stories* series) (Weems) 551, *551*
"Untitled" (*Last Measure* series) (Mann) *328*
"Untitled" (*Silueta* series) (Mendieta) 548, *548*
Untitled Film Stills (Sherman) 682–83, *683*
Untitled—Passage on the Underground Railroad (Marc) 688, *688*
Ur 370; Standard of *370*, 370–71; ziggurat 568–69, *569*
Ut, Nick: *Vietnamese Girl Kim Phuc Running after Napalm Attack 639*, 639–40 (*see also* "Death by Cotton Candy")
Utamaro 228; *Lovers in an Upstairs Room* 228, *228*; *Two Courtesans 510*, 510–11
Utzon, Jørn: Sydney Opera House *280*, 280–81

Valadon, Suzanne: *The Blue Room* 159–60, *160*
Vallayer-Coster, Anne 494; *Attributes of Painting, Sculpture, and Architecture* 494, *494*
Valley of the Shadow of Death (Fenton) 328, *328*
value 77–81, 82, 102–3, *103*, *105*, 699gl.; Ben-Day dots 542; and emphasis 152, 156; in etching 232; in mezzotint 233; and space 38
vanishing points 88, *88*, *89*, 699gl.; multiple *90*, 91–92, *92*
vanitas 600–601, 699gl.
Vanitas (Still Life with Glass Globe) (attr. Claesz) 600, *600*
variety 125, 131–34, 699gl.
Vasari, Giorgio 216, 464; *Lives of the Great Artists* 461
vaults/vaulted *266*, 266–67, 269, 406, 565, 699gl.; *see also muqarnas*
Velázquez, Diego de Silva y 185; *Las Meninas 183*, 183–86, *184*, *185*; *The Toilet of Venus* (*Rokeby Venus*) 655–56, *656*
Venus of Laussel (rock carving) 367–68, *368*
Venus of Urbino (Titian) 668, *668*
verdaccio 216, 699gl.
Vermeer, Johannes: *Girl with a Pearl Earring* 33, *33*; *Woman Holding a Balance* 585, *585*
Versailles: Hall of Mirrors 484, *484*
Vertigo (Bochner) 52, *52*
video 334, 344–46, 555–56, 576, *576*, 596, *596*, 598, *598*
video games *85*, 85–86, 313, 347–48, *348*
Vierzehnheiligen, Basilica of (Neumann) *488*, 488–89
Vietnam Veterans Memorial (Lin) 649, *649*
Vietnam War 639–40, 649
Vietnamese Girl Kim Phuc Running after Napalm Attack (Ut) *639*, 639–40; *see also* "Death by Cotton Candy"
View from Mount Holyoke, Massachusetts...The Oxbow (Cole) 499, *499*
View from the Window at Le Gras (Niépce) 317, *317*
View of the Sanctuary at Medina 403, 403–4
Vigée Le Brun, Elisabeth Louise: *Marie Antoinette and Her Children 633*, 633–34
Villa Rotonda (Palladio) 473, *473*
Villa Savoye (Le Corbusier) 278, *278*
Viola, Bill 346–47, *347*; *Going Forth by Day 346*; *The Raft 346*, *347*
Vir Heroicus Sublimis (Newman) 104, *104*
Virgin and Child Enthroned (Cimabue) 408, *408*
Virgin and Child Enthroned (Giotto) 408, *408*
Virgin and Child Surrounded by Saints (icon) 396, *396*
Virgin of Guadalupe, The 25, 25–26
Virgin of Vladimir (icon) *582*, 583
Vishnu Churning the Ocean of Milk (relief) 427, *427*
Vishnu Dreaming the Universe (relief) 131, *131*
Vision after the Sermon, The (Gauguin) 514–15, *515*
visionary art 554, 699gl.
visual communication design 300–313; advertising 309–11; and color 312–13; illustration 305–7; layout 307–9; web design 311–12; written text 300–303, 304; *see also* logos
visual perception 83, *91*, 95–97, 100, 106–7, 608–10; focus 150; of motion 115–16, 335
Vitruvian Man (Leonardo) *603*, 603–4
Vitruvius: *On Architecture* 145, 473, 603
void 307, 699gl.
volume 62, 67–68, 699gl.
Vorobieff-Stebelska, Marie *see* Marevna, Marie
votive figures 175, *175*
Voulkos, Peter 290; *Gallas Rock* 290, *290*
Voyage dans la Lune see *Trip to the Moon*

Wainwright Building, St. Louis (Sullivan) *276*, 277
Waiting (Bishop) 536, *537*
Waiting Girl, The (Lux) 326, *327*
Walker, Kara 358, 359; *Insurrection! (Our Tools were Rudimentary ...* 358, *359*
Walker, Peter *see* Arad, Michael
Walking Man (Rodin) 673, *673*
Walking on a Mountain Path in Spring (Ma Yuan) 135, *135*
wall and ceiling paintings: Camera degli Sposi 615–16, *616*; Çatalhöyük *368*, 368–69; Egyptian *377*, 377–78; Roman *392*, 393; Tomb of the Leopards 386, *386*; *see also* frescoes; murals
Walt Disney Pictures: *Finding Nemo* 116, *117*
Walt Disney World Resort: Spaceship Earth 77, *77*
Waltz, The (Claudel) 516, *516*
Wang Meng: *Ge Zhichuan Moving His Dwelling* 418, *418*, 420
Wang Xizhi: *Preface of the Lanting Gathering 301*
War, The (Dix) 640, *640*
warfare and warriors *370*, 370–71, 438, *438*, 441, *441*, 497, *497*, 640–44; art as response and protest 644–48; documenting war 327–28, 638–40; memorials 649–50; terra-cotta army *417*, 417–18
Warhol, Andy 357; *Four Marilyns 235*, 235–36; *Mao* 635–36, *636*; *Thirty Are Better than One* 541, *541*
wash (ink) 202, *203*
Washington, D.C. 264, 380; National Gallery of Art 119, *119*; Vietnam Veterans Memorial 649, *649*
Washington, George 628–29, *629*
watercolor 195, 210, 220–21
Waterlilies (Monet) 513, *513*
Watts Towers (*Nuestro Pueblo*) (Rodia) 26, *26*
wavelength 95, 100, 699gl.
web design 311–12
Weems, Carrie Mae 56, 551; *Family Pictures and Stories* 551, *551*; *Kitchen Table* series 551; "Untitled (Woman and daughter with makeup)" 56, *56*, 329, *329*, 551, *551*, 687, *687*; "You Became a Scientific Profile" 329, *329*
Weiss, D. B. *see* Benioff, David
Welles, Orson: *Citizen Kane* 337, *337*
Weston, Edward 321; *Artichoke Halved 165*, 165–66; *Pepper No. 30* 321, *321*
wet plate (collodion) process 320, 328, 699gl.
Whirling Log Ceremony (Klah) 624, *624*
Whistler, James McNeil 26–27; *Nocturne in Black and Gold: The Falling Rocket* 26–27, *27*
white space 307, 699gl.
White Vertical Water (Nevelson) 21, 22, *22*

Whiteread, Rachel: *House* 69, *69*
Wigan, Willard 607–8; *Statue of Liberty* 607, *607*
Wiley, Kehinde 630; *Napoleon Leading the Army over the Alps* 630, *630*
Willendorf Venus see *Woman from Willendorf*
Williams, Scott A. 319
Winegrad, I. Michael: interior design 127, *127*
Winogrand, Garry 331; *Central Park Zoo, New York City* 331, *331*
Wise, Kirk and Miyazaki, Hayao: *Spirited Away 340*, 340–41
Wish Tree (Ono) 350, 352, *353*
Wisteria lamp (Tiffany Studios) *520*, 520–21
Wizard of Oz, The (Fleming) 337–38, *338*
Wo-Haw: *Wo-Haw between Two Worlds* 442, *442*
Wodiczko, Krzysztof 576; *Tijuana Projection* 576, *576*
Woman from Willendorf (limestone figurine) 663, *663*, 664
Woman Holding a Balance (Vermeer) 585, *585*
Woman I (de Kooning) 664, *664*
Woman in Pool (Beever) 618, *618*
Woman Seated in an Armchair (Matisse) *45*, 45–46
women artists, status of: Anguissola 472; Claudel 516; Delaunay 221; Driscoll 521; Durant 244; French Academy 492–93, 494; Gentileschi 219, 681, 684; life drawing 492–93, 508; prehistory 210; responses to historical exclusion 547, 684–85; Royal Academy 494, 506; social restrictions 506, 512
women as subjects: Archaic Greece 384; of Bishop 536; of Degas 511; Etruscan 386; Madame Pierre Gautreau (Madame X) 612–13; modern art 663–64; Muslims 553, 659–60; nudes 179–80, 383, 521, 656, 666–67, 668–69, 677; prehistoric sculpture 367–68, 663, 664; rulers 170–71, 377, 631–34, 689
Women of Allah (Neshat) 659, *659*
Wonder Woman, Superman, and Batman (comic art) *93*
Wondrous Spring (Csuri) *96*, 97
Wong Kar-wai: *Chungking Express 343*, 343–44
wood: in architecture 166, *166*, 260, 270–71, *271*, 274–75, *451*, 451–52, 588–89, *589*; in craft and sculpture 297–98, *298*, *370*, 370–72, *371*, 376, *376*, 377, *377*, 597, *597*, 597–98, *598*
Wood, Grant 536; *American Gothic* 536, *536*
woodblock printing 28, *205*, 227–29, 424, *475*, 475–76, 699gl.; *see also* woodcuts
woodcuts 59, *59*, *92*, *93*, 157, *157*, *227*, 699gl.; "The Great Wave off Shore at Kanagawa" 126, *126*, 229, *229*, 425, *425*, 661, *661*
Woodstock Road, Woodstock, New York, 1924 (Bellows) 54, *54*
Work (Tanaka) *128*, 129
Works of Geoffrey Chaucer (Morris and Burne-Jones) 305, *305*
Works Projects Administration 233
World Trade Center, New York *260*, 261; 9/11 attacks 325, 650, 656, 658
World War I 351, 501, 513, 522, 524, 528
World War II 233, 524, 646–47
Wreck of the Ole '97, The (Benton) 83, *83*
Wright, Frank Lloyd: Fallingwater 279, *279*; Solomon R. Guggenheim Museum, New York *115*, 567, *567*
Wright of Derby, Joseph 604; *An Experiment on a Bird in the Air Pump* 604, *604*
writing/text 300–304; conceptual art 352, 548; cuneiform 370; east Asian 202; Mesoamerican 162, *162*, 430, 434; printed 227; *see also* calligraphy; micrography
Wu Xing 108, *108*
Wu Zhen (Wu Chen): bamboo drawing 202, *203*
Wyeth, Andrew 215; *Christina's World* 215, *215*

Xu Yang: *The Qianlong Emperor's Southern Inspection Tour...* 84–85, *85*

yam masks, Abelam 458, *458*
Yazzie, Melanie: *Untitled* 236, *236*
Yellow Christ, The (Gauguin) 110, *111*
Yellow-Red-Blue (Kandinsky) 98, *98*
Yeoh, Kok Cheow 302; *Hegemony 302*, 302–3
yin and yang 425, *425*
Yombe sculpture *448*, 448–49, 597–98, *598*
Yoruba: Gèlèdé rituals 572, *572*; sculpture 145, *145*, 448, *448*; *see also* Ife dynasty
"You Became a Scientific Profile" (Weems) 329, *329*
Young Hare, A (Dürer) 221, *221*

Zapotec: *Seated Figure* 288, *288*
Zen gardens 421, *421*
Zeus (Greek sculpture) 147, *147*
Zhang Chun Hong: *Life Strands* 199, *199*
ziggurats 370, 373, 568–69, *569*, 699gl.
zoetropes 335, *335*, 336, 699gl.
Zurbarán, Francisco de: *The Funeral of St. Bonaventure* 156, *156*